HOLT
AMERICAN NATION

IN THE MODERN ERA

E PLURIBUS UNUM

INDIANA EDITION

correlated to

INDIANA
Academic Standards
for Social Studies

HOLT, RINEHART AND WINSTON

A Harcourt Education Company

Austin · New York · Orlando · Atlanta · San Francisco · Boston · Dallas · Toronto · London

Explanation of Correlation

The following document is a correlation of HOLT AMERICAN NATION IN THE MODERN ERA to the Indiana Academic Standards for Social Studies. The format for this correlation follows the same basic format established by the Standards modified to accommodate the addition of page references. The correlation provides a cross-reference between the skills in the Standards, and representative page numbers where those skills are taught or assessed. Those references marked with an asterisk represent pages which offer secondary support or where application of the required skill is implied.

The references contained in this correlation reflect Holt, Rinehart and Winston's interpretation of the Social Studies objectives outlined in the Indiana curriculum.

KEY TO REFERENCES

Prefix	Explanation
SE	*Student's Edition*
ATE	*Annotated Teacher's Edition*
OR	*online resources*

ISBN 0-03-069091-9

123 048 040302

Detailed Correlation of
Holt American Nation in the Modern Era to the
The Indiana Academic Standards for Social Studies

UNITED STATES HISTORY

STANDARD 1

Early National Development: 1775 to 1877

Students will trace and summarize key ideas, events, and developments from the Founding Era through the Civil War and Reconstruction, 1775 to 1877.

USH.1.1	Explain major ideas about government and key rights, rooted in the colonial and founding periods, which are embedded in key documents.	**SE** **ATE**	10, 19, 20, 24–27, 28, 29, 31–35, 39–43, 46 20, 24, 29–31, 34, 43, 46
USH.1.2	Explain major themes in the early national history of the United States.	**SE** **ATE**	70–74, 76–78 70–74, 76–78, 80
USH.1.3	Review and summarize key events and developments in the following periods of United States history: Founding the Republic (1775 to 1801), Expansion and Reform (1801 to 1861), Civil War and Reconstruction (1850 to 1877).	**SE** **ATE**	18, 20–23, 28–35, 36, 37, 70–74, 76–78, 79–81, 83–85, 86–91, 92, 93, 97–98, 101–102, 110–113, 113 114, 114–115, 116–117, 118–122, 123, 124, 131–134, 137–138, 142, 145–147, 150, 153, 154 19, 20, 21, 23, 28–31, 33, 70–74, 76–78, 80, 84, 86, 87, 89, 90, 91, 97, 101, 102, 111, 114, 115, 116, 119, 120, 121, 125, 127, 132, 133, 137, 139, 140, 145, 146, 150
USH.1.4	Investigate the impact of laws on the settlement and development of Indiana.	**SE***	30, 35
USH.1.5	Develop and explain time lines on different periods of United States history before 1900.	**SE** **ATE** **SE***	36, 92, 124, 154, 156, 188, 216, 240, 266, 324, 350 87, 95, 102, 117, 119, 123, 169, 328 3, 68, 69, 94, 95, 128, 129, 160, 161, 190, 191, 218, 219, 244, 245, 324
USH.1.6	Analyze statistical data to explain demographical changes in the United States during the nineteenth century.	**SE**	221, 222, 242, 243
USH.1.7	Interpret historical maps to explain the territorial expansion of the United States during the nineteenth century.	**SE** **SE*** **ATE***	77, 338, 341, 348, 352, 353 86, 327–329, 332 328, 329
USH.1.8	Identify issues pertaining to slavery, sectionalism and nationalism before the Civil War, and analyze the interests, perspectives, and points of view of those involved in the issue.	**SE** **ATE**	81–85, 89–91, 92, 93 81–83, 89, 91

INDIANA

STANDARD 2

Development of the Industrial United States: 1870 to 1900

Students will examine the political, economic, social, and cultural development of the United States during the period from 1870 to 1900.

USH.2.1	Identify and explain the importance of key events, persons, and groups associated with industrialization and its impact on urbanization, immigration, farmers, the labor movement, social reform, and government regulation.	**SE**	171, 173, 176, 188, 192–193, 194–200, 201–208, 209–215, 216, 217, 220–225, 226–232, 231–237, 238, 239, 240, 241, 274–279, 280–285, 286–293, 294, 295, 304–306, 309, 319–321, 322
		ATE	171, 172, 176, 189, 193, 194, 195, 196, 197, 198, 200, 202, 203, 204, 205, 207, 210, 212, 215, 217, 221, 222, 223, 225, 227, 229, 230, 231, 233, 237, 239, 271, 275, 276, 277, 281, 282, 283, 287, 289, 290, 291, 293, 295, 304–306, 319, 321
USH.2.2	Describe the economic development by which the United States became a major industrial power in the world and identify the factors necessary for industrialization.	**SE**	171, 176, 188, 192–195, 200, 201–208, 216, 216, 217
		ATE	171, 178, 189, 193, 202, 203, 204, 205, 207
USH.2.3	Explain the economic problems facing farmers during the late 19th century.	**SE**	259–265, 266
		ATE	259–264
USH.2.4	Explain how industrialization affected the environment and the emergence of a conservation movement.	**SE**	308–309, 323
		ATE	308, 309
USH.2.5	Analyze how new immigrant groups affected United States society and culture generally and Indiana particularly.	The following refer to the United States in general: **SE** 220–225, 240, 241 **ATE** 217, 221, 222, 223, 225	
USH.2.6	Explain various perspectives on federal government policy about Native American Indians and migration of settlers to western territories.	**SE**	162–163, 168–169, 170, 171, 176, 188, 189
		ATE	159, 163, 168
USH.2.7	Analyze and evaluate the majority and dissenting opinions of the following landmark decisions of the United States Supreme Court: *Civil Rights Cases* (1883), *Plessy v. Ferguson* (1896), and *United States v. Wong Kim Ark* (1898).	**SE**	150, 153, 155
		ATE	150, 151, 153
		OR	Go.hrw.com: The *Supreme Court Watch* website

USH.2.8	Construct and explain a time line of major technological inventions during the second half of the nineteenth century.	SE* ATE*	190, 191, 216 195, 198, 200
USH.2.9	Identify the main ideas from primary sources, such as nineteenth century political cartoons, about urban government, corruption, and social reform.	SE ATE SE* ATE*	241, 248, 250–255, 267, 278, 279 231, 232, 250, 278, 279 281 210, 211, 281
USH.2.10	Compare primary sources from different perspectives about immigrant experiences in the urban setting.	SE ATE	224, 225, 241 224
USH.2.11	Consider the different perspectives on industrial development and social problems expressed in primary documents.	SE ATE	204, 205, 231, 241, 277, 278, 280,281 203, 210, 211, 231, 278, 279, 281
USH.2.12	Investigate historical data from a variety of sources and perspectives about historical issues involving African Americans, Asian Americans, Hispanic Americans and American Indians.	SE ATE	162–163, 168–169, 188, 189, 220, 224, 225, 540–541, 556, 607–612, 615, 616, 650–655, 656–660, 661–666, 667–671, 672, 673, 682–688, 689–691, 693, 700, 701 159, 163, 168, 217, 221, 222, 223, 225, 525, 540, 589, 608, 609, 610, 611, 619, 647, 651, 655, 662, 663, 666, 670, 673, 682–688, 689, 690, 693

STANDARD 3

Emergence of the Modern United States: 1897 to 1920

Students will examine the political, economic, social, and cultural development of the United States during the period from 1897 to 1920.

USH.3.1	Identify and explain the importance of key events and persons in the emergence of the United States as a global power.	**SE** **ATE**	326–329, 332, 333–339, 340–344, 350, 351, 361–367, 377–378, 381, 382, 383 323, 328, 329, 334, 335, 336, 339, 341, 342, 343, 344, 353, 363, 364, 367, 378
USH.3.2	Identify and explain the importance of key events, persons, and groups associated with problems of industrial capitalism, urbanization, and political corruption.	**SE** **ATE**	201–205, 208, 211–215, 216, 230–232, 240, 241, 246–251, 252–255, 258, 266, 267, 274–279, 280–282, 285, 286–287, 294, 295 202, 203, 214, 217, 230, 246–251, 252–254, 271, 275, 276, 277, 281, 282, 283, 287, 289, 290, 291, 293, 295
USH.3.3	Explain the impact of Progressive ideas about political reform on the expansion of democracy in local and state governments, especially Indiana, and the federal government.		The following refer to local, state, and federal government, and the Midwest, in general: **SE** 298–302, 319–321, 322, 323 **ATE** 270, 299–302, 319–321 **SE*** 63, 85 **ATE*** 63
USH.3.4	Explain the impact of the following ideas on society and culture in the United States and Indiana: Progressivism, muckraking, women's suffrage, organized labor, temperance, prohibition, socialism, square deal, and new nationalism.	**SE** **ATE**	209–215, 216, 274–279, 280–283, 285, 286–289, 293, 294, 295, 303–309, 310–314, 315–321, 322, 323 189, 210, 212, 215, 271, 275, 276, 277, 281, 282, 283, 287, 289, 295, 305, 309, 311, 314, 316, 317

USH.3.5	Explain the constitutional significance of the following lankmark decisions of the United States Supreme Court: *Northern Securities Company v. United States* (1904), *Lochner v. United States* (1905), *Muller v. Oregon* (1908), *Schenck v. United States* (1919), and *Abrams v. United States* (1919).	SE 283, 285 ATE 283 OR Go.hrw.com: The *Supreme Court Watch* website
USH.3.6	Analyze "The Roosevelt Corollary to the Monroe Doctrine" (1904), and explain how it modified the Monroe Doctrine (1823) and justified a new direction in United States foreign policy.	SE 343, 344 ATE 343
USH.3.7	Analyze President Woodrow Wilson's "Fourteen Points" Address to Congress (1918), and explain how it differed from proposals by French and British leaders for a treaty to conclude World War I.	SE 377–379, 381 ATE 378, 379, 381
USH.3.8	Evaluate the positions of President Woodrow Wilson and his opponents, such as Senator Henry Cabot Lodge, in the debate over ratification of the Versailles Treaty and United States participation in the League of Nations.	SE 379–381, 382 ATE 378, 379
USH.3.9	Create and explain a time line of key events by which the United States became a world power.	SE 350, 382 ATE 328, 364 SE* 324, 325, 354, 355 ATE* 349, 358

INDIANA

STANDARD 4

The Modern United States in Prosperity and Depression: 1920 to 1940

Students will examine the political, economic, social, and cultural development of the United States during the period from 1920 to 1940.

USH.3.10	Locate on a world map territories acquired by the United States during its emergence as an imperial power in the world, and explain how these territories were acquired.	**SE** 326–329, 332, 338–339, 340–342, 344, 348, 350–353 **ATE** 323, 328, 329, 338, 340–342
USH.4.1	Identify and explain the importance of key events, persons, and groups in the period of prosperity before the Great Depression.	**SE** 414–421, 422–429, 430–437, 438, 439 **ATE** 411, 412, 413, 415, 416, 417, 418, 420, 424, 427–429, 431, 432, 433, 434, 435, 437, 441
USH.4.2	Identify and explain the importance of key events, persons, and groups in the period of the Great Depression.	**SE** 443–447, 452, 454, 455, 456–463, 464, 465, 468–474, 475–478, 480–481, 482–486, 487–491, 492, 493 **ATE** 165, 439, 443, 444, 447, 454, 457, 459, 465, 470, 471, 472, 477, 479, 481, 484, 485, 490, 491, 493, 497
USH.4.3	Compare and contrast the views of the Republican and Democratic parties during the 1920s and 1930s, and analyze continuity and change of views within each party from the 1920s through the 1930s.	**SE** 397–402, 410, 456–463, 464, 468–474, 475–481, 482, 483, 492, 497 **ATE** 397–401, 456–462, 468–474, 475–477, 479–481, 497
USH.4.4	Analyze the causes of economic prosperity in the 1920s and economic depression in the 1930s and describe the conflicts between business and labor.	**SE** 391–393, 406, 410, 414–421, 438, 442–447, 464, 465, 480 **ATE** 391–393, 396, 415–418, 420, 439, 443, 444, 447, 465
USH.4.5	Investigate the ways life was changing on the farm and in the city in the United States generally and in Indiana during the 1920s due to technological development, with particular emphasis on the impact of the automobile industry.	The following refer to the United States in general: **SE** 414–421, 424–426, 429, 438 **ATE** 411, 415, 416, 417, 418, 420

USH.4.6	Explain the differing and changing perspectives about the role of the government in American society during the 1920s and 1930s by explaining the views of Presidents Harding, Coolidge, Hoover, and Roosevelt.	**SE** 397–402, 456–463, 464, 465, 468–474, 476–478, 481, 492, 493 **ATE** 397–401, 439, 457, 459, 465, 466, 470, 471, 472, 477, 479, 481, 493, 497
USH.4.7	Explain and evaluate the role of values, morals, and ethics in a changing society by examining issues associated with the Red Scare, Prohibition, Scopes Trial, the changing role of women, the Ku Klux Klan (especially in Indiana), and restrictions on immigration.	**SE** 393–394, 396, 404–405, 407–409, 410, 422, 423, 428–429, 438 **ATE** 387, 393, 394, 404, 407, 409, 411, 412, 422–424, 428, 429 **SE*** 144–145, 147, 288–289 **ATE*** 144, 145
USH.4.8	Evaluate the constitutional significance of the following landmark decisions of the United States Supreme Court: *Gitlow v New York* (1925), *Stromberg v. California* (1931), *Near v. Minnesota* (1931), *Schechter v. United States* (1935), *West Coast Hotel v. Parrish* (1937).	**OR** Go.hrw.com: The *Supreme Court Watch* website
USH.4.9	Construct a time line to show the origin and development of key ideas and events in the 1920s and 1930s.	**SE** 410, 438, 464, 492, 524 **ATE** 508 **SE*** 388, 389, 412, 413, 440, 441, 466, 467, 500, 501

STANDARD 5

The United States and World War II: 1939 to 1945

Students will examine the causes and course of World War II, the effects of the war on the United States society and culture, and the consequences for United States involvement in world affairs.

USH.5.1	Analyze the causes of World War II in Europe and in the Pacific region and explain the involvement of the United States in World War II.	**SE** **ATE**	505–506, 512–517, 518–523, 524 499, 513, 514, 517, 519, 521, 522, 525
USH.5.2	Identify and explain the importance of key events and persons involved with the causes, course, and consequences of World War II.	**SE** **ATE**	505–506, 512–517, 518–519, 520–523, 524, 530–534, 536, 542–548, 549–552, 553–555, 556, 57, 560–562, 565, 586 499, 513, 514, 517, 519, 521, 522, 525, 527, 531, 532, 533, 544, 545, 546, 547, 548, 551, 552, 553, 554, 562, 565, 618
USH.5.3	Explain how the United States mobilized its economic and military resources to achieve victory in World War II.	**SE** **ATE**	528–531, 534, 553–555, 556 528–530, 552, 553
USH.5.4	Explain the constitutional significance of the following landmark decisions of the United States Supreme Court: *West Virginia State Board of Education v. Barnette* (1943), *Hirabayash v. United States* (1943), *Korematsu v. United States* (1944).	**SE*** **ATE*** **OR**	540–541, 556 525, 540 Go.hrw.com: The *Supreme Court Watch* website
USH.5.5	Analyze the economic and social changes in American life brought about by the United States' involvement in World War II, including the roles and status of women and African Americans.	**SE** **ATE**	530, 531, 535, 538–541, 593, 595, 597, 616 535, 538, 539, 595
USH.5.6	Analyze President Roosevelt's State of the Union Message to Congress (1941), which is called "The Four Freedoms" message, to contrast civic and political values of the United States with those of Nazi Germany.	**SE** **SE***	536 512, 523
USH.5.7	Create time lines of key events from the beginning to the end of World War II in Europe and in the Pacific region.	**SE** **ATE** **SE***	524, 556 547, 557 501, 526, 527
USH.5.8	Investigate Hitler's "final solution" policy and the Allies' responses to the Holocaust.	**SE** **ATE**	545–548, 556 545, 546, 618
USH.5.9	Use a variety of information sources, including primary documents and oral histories, to identify and analyze perspectives on issues related to World War II.	**SE** **ATE**	512, 516, 517, 521, 525, 528, 529, 535–538, 542, 544, 546, 552, 554, 557 519, 523, 525, 532, 537, 546, 547, 551

Students will examine the political, economic, social, and cultural development of the United States during the period from 1945 to 1960.

USH.6.1	Identify and explain the importance of key events, persons, and groups related to the causes, conditions, and consequences of the Cold War.	**SE**	566–571, 572–578, 579–585, 586, 627, 628, 629–630, 712, 713, 725, 647, 745, 746, 753, 759, 773–775, 792
		ATE	557, 559, 567, 568, 569, 570, 571, 576, 581, 583, 585, 588, 627, 628, 629–630, 713, 758, 766, 773, 774
USH.6.2	Identify and explain the importance of key events, persons, and groups connected to domestic problems and policies during the presidential administrations of Truman and Eisenhower.	**SE**	579, 580, 582, 583, 585, 586, 592–597, 598–600, 607–613, 615, 616, 617
		ATE	579, 580, 582, 583, 593–597, 598, 599, 607–614
USH.6.3	Analyze President Truman's proclamation of a new foreign policy, the Truman Doctrine, in his Address to Congress (March 12, 1947), and evaluate his decision to contain expansion of Soviet power in the world.	**SE**	567–569, 571, 586
		ATE	569
USH.6.4	Analyze President Truman's Announcement (June 27, 1950) that the United States would assist South Korea to oppose an invasion by North Korea, and evaluate his decision to involve United States armed forces in the Korean War.	**SE**	573
		SE*	574–575, 578, 586
		ATE*	574, 575
USH.6.5	Analyze the causes, conditions, and consequences of the struggle for civil rights by African-Americans.	**SE**	607–610, 615, 616, 617, 650–655, 656–660, 661–666, 667–671, 672, 673
		ATE	589, 608, 609, 610, 611, 619, 647, 651, 655, 662, 663, 666, 670, 673
USH.6.6	Analyze and interpret main ideas in President Eisenhower's Farewell Address (1961).	**SE***	599
USH.6.7	Explain the constitutional significance of the following landmark decisions of the United States Supreme Court: *Dennis v. United States* (1951), *Yates v. United States* (1957), and *Cooper v. Aaron* (1958).	**OR**	Go.hrw.com: The *Supreme Court Watch* website
USH.6.10	Construct a time line to show United States conflicts with other nations.	**SE**	586, 646, 732, 766, 792
		ATE	574, 626

STANDARD 7

The United States in Troubled Times: 1960 to 1980

Students will examine the political, economic, social, and cultural development of the United States during the period from 1960 to 1980.

USH.7.1	Identify and explain the importance of key events, persons, and groups associated with domestic problems and policies during the 1960s and 1970s.	**SE**	634–637, 639–645, 646, 647, 650–655, 656–660, 661–666, 667–671, 672, 673, 676–681, 682–688, 689–693, 700, 701, 740–744, 746–750, 753, 754–756, 759, 766, 767, 829
		ATE	620, 621, 634, 635, 639–641, 644, 647, 651, 655, 660, 662, 663, 666, 670, 673, 680, 681, 737, 743, 744, 748, 749, 750, 829
USH.7.2	Analyze and interpret main ideas of the "I Have a Dream" speech (1963) and the Letter from Birmingham City Jail (1963) by Reverend Martin Luther King, Jr.	**SE**	653–655
USH.7.3	Identify and explain the importance of key events and persons associated with foreign policy during the 1960s and 1970s.	**SE**	578, 626–630, 647, 710–711, 712–715, 717–719, 720–725, 726–731, 732, 733, 745, 746, 752, 753, 757–759, 766
		ATE	626–630, 710, 714–716, 721, 724, 727, 729, 731, 733, 737, 745, 752, 757–759
USH.7.4	Trace and explain the events that led the United States into and out of the Vietnam War.	**SE**	710, 711, 712–719, 720–725, 726–731, 732, 733
		ATE	710, 711, 714, 715, 718, 721, 724, 727, 729, 731, 733
USH.7.5	Recognize the changing relationship, as demonstrated in the Cuban Missile Crisis, the space race, the Vietnam War, and the SALT agreements, between the United States and the Soviet Union from 1960 to 1980.	**SE**	578, 585, 628–630, 647, 710–711, 712–719, 720–725, 726–731, 732, 733, 745, 746
		ATE	559, 585, 629–630, 710, 711, 714, 715, 718, 721, 724, 727, 729, 731, 733
USH.7.6	Analyze and explain the impact on American society and culture of the new immigration policies after 1965 that led to a new wave of immigration.	**SE**	760, 761
		ATE	761

USH.7.7	Trace and explain the gains made by women and minorities during the 1960s and 1970s.	SE	650–655, 656–660, 661–666, 667–671, 672, 673, 676–681, 682–688, 689–693, 700, 701
		ATE	647, 651, 655, 660, 662, 663, 666, 670, 673, 676–681, 682–688, 689–693
USH.7.8	Analyze Richard Nixon's decision to resign and explain the importance of this decision on constitutional grounds.	SE	749, 750, 766, 829
		ATE	736, 749, 750, 828, 829
USH.7.9	Explain the constitutional significance of the following landmark decisions of the United States Supreme Court: *Heart of Atlanta Motel v. United States* (1964), *Reynolds v. Simms* (1964), *New York Times Company v. United States* (1971), *Roe v. Wade* (1973), and *United States v. Nixon* (1974).	SE	680, R16
		ATE	680, 749
		OR	Go.hrw.com: The *Supreme Court Watch* website
USH.7.10	Construct time lines of major events and movements, such as the Civil Rights movement and the Vietnam War, in the 1960s and 1970s, and explain their causes and consequences.	SE	672, 673, 732
		ATE	673

Test-taking Tips For Students

Every school year, there are students who are asked to take one or more standardized tests to demonstrate the content and skills they have learned. You can share the following test-taking tips with your students to help them as they prepare for these assessments.

Remind students, though, that the best way to prepare for any standardized test is to pay close attention in class and to take every opportunity to improve their science, reading, writing, and mathematical skills.

Tips for Standardized Tests: Reading Sections

The main goal of the reading sections of standardized tests is to determine your understanding of different aspects of a reading passage. Basically, if you can grasp the main idea and the author's purpose, and then pay attention to the details and vocabulary so that you are able to draw inferences and conclusions, you will do well on a test.

Here are some suggestions for answering questions based on reading passages:

- First, **read the passage as if you were not even taking a test.** Do this to get a general overview of both the topic and the tone of a passage.

- **Look at the big picture.** In other words, examine the most obvious features of the passage. To do this, ask yourself the following questions as you read:

  What is the title?

  What do the illustrations or pictures tell me?

  What is the main idea?

  What is the author's purpose? To inform? To entertain? To show how to do something?

- Next, **read the questions.** This will help you to know what information to look for when you re-read.

- Re-read the passage. **Underline the information** that relates to the questions. This will help you when you begin answering the questions.

- **Go back to the questions.** Try to answer each one in your mind before looking at the answer choices.

- Finally, **read *all* the answer choices and eliminate those that are obviously incorrect.** After this process, mark the best answer.

Types of Multiple-Choice Questions Based on a Passage

Realize that many multiple-choice questions fall into categories. The following categories are the most common.

1. **Main idea:** The main idea of a reading passage is the most important point expressed in the passage. The main idea must relate to the entire passage, not just to a portion of a selection. After reading a passage, locate and underline the main idea.

2. **Significant details:** You will most probably be asked to recall specific details from a reading passage. You will know what details to look for if you read the questions before reading the passage. Underline these details as you read. *Remember that correct answers do not always use the precise phrases or words that appear in the passage.*

3. **Reading graphic information:** These kinds of items test your ability to interpret information presented in a visual form or a graphic, such as a map, schedule, time line, or chart. If the question involves a graphic, follow these steps:

   a) Look at the title and major labels to figure out the focus or purpose of the graphic;

   b) Read the other headings or labels to find out what data is given and how it is organized;

   c) If the item includes a map, look at the map's legend or key, which will explain symbols, lines, and shadings in the map;

   d) Analyze the data in the graphic to determine quantities, relationships, intervals of time, directions, sequences, or other patterns

4. **Vocabulary:** Standardized tests will often ask you to determine the meaning of a word within the context of the passage. In many instances, an answer choice will include an actual meaning of the word that does not fit the context in which the word appears. To avoid choosing such an incorrect answer, read the answer choices and then plug them into the sentence to determine which answer fits the context of the passage.

5. **Conclusion and inference:** Standardized tests often ask you to draw conclusions or make inferences. There is often some idea within a passage that the author is trying to convey but does not state directly. Consider various parts of the passage together in order to determine what the author is implying. *If an answer choice refers to only one or two sentences or details within the passage, this is probably not the correct answer.*

If you do not understand a passage at first, keep reading. Many times you will find that you know more answers than you first thought. Once you understand the main idea of a passage, you can go from there to figure out the specific information.

Strategies for Answering Short-Answer Questions

- **Read the passage in its entirety,** paying close attention to the main ideas and details. Jot down information you think is important.

- **If you can't answer a question, skip it and come back later.**

- Words such as *compare, contrast, interpret, discuss,* and *summarize* appear often in short answer questions. **Be sure you have a complete understanding of each of these words.**

- For answers based on a passage, **return to the passage and skim the parts you underlined to find support.**

- **Organize your thoughts on a separate sheet of paper.** Write a general statement with which to begin. This will be your topic sentence.

- When writing your answer, **be precise but brief.** Be sure to refer to details in the passage in your answer. Try to get to the point quickly and never pad your answer.

- **Remember that how you use your time** on these kinds of questions is usually critical. Therefore, look over the questions in the beginning and divide your time based on your knowledge, required time for each item, and the scoring weight of the question.

Strategies for Answering Math Questions

- **Decide the goal of the question.** Read or study the problem carefully and determine what information must be found.

- Locate the factual information. **Decide what information represents key facts—the ones you must have to solve the problem.** You may also find facts you do not need to reach your solution. In some cases, you may determine that more information is needed to solve the problem. If so, ask yourself, "What assumptions can I make about this problem?" or "Do I need a formula to help solve this problem?"

- **Decide what strategies you might use to solve the problem, how you might use them, and what form your solution will be in.** For example, will you need to create a graph or chart? Will you need to solve an equation? Will your answer be in words or numbers? By knowing what type of solution you should reach, you may be able to eliminate some of the choices.

- **Apply your strategy** to solve the problem and compare your answer to the choices.

- **If the answer is still not clear, read the problem again.** If you had to make calculations to reach your answer, use estimation to see if your answer makes sense.

HOLT
AMERICAN NATION

IN THE MODERN ERA

Paul Boyer
Sterling Stuckey

HOLT, RINEHART AND WINSTON

A Harcourt Education Company

Austin • New York • Orlando • Atlanta • San Francisco • Boston • Dallas • Toronto • London

Requests for permission to make copies of any part of the work should be mailed to the
following address: Permissions Department, Holt, Rinehart and Winston, 10801 N. MoPac
Expressway, Building 3, Austin, Texas 78759.

For acknowledgments, see page R63, which is an extension of the copyright page.

ONE-STOP PLANNER is a trademark licensed to Holt, Rinehart and Winston, registered in
the United States of America and/or other jurisdictions.

Copyright © 2000 CNN and CNNfyi.com are trademarks of Cable News Network LP, LLLP,
a Time Warner Company. All rights reserved. Copyright © 2000 Turner Learning logos are
trademarks of Turner Learning, Inc., a Time Warner Company. All rights reserved.

Printed in the United States of America

ISBN 0-03-065387-8

2 3 4 5 6 7 8 9 048 05 04 03 02

ABOUT THE AUTHORS

Dr. Paul Boyer

Paul Boyer is the Merle Curti Professor of History at the University of Wisconsin, Madison, and former director of the university's Institute for Research in the Humanities. He has served on the executive board of the Organization of American Historians and the national advisory board of the PBS *American Experience* series, and is Editor-In-Chief of the *Oxford Companion to United States History.* Awarded a Ph.D. from Harvard University in 1966, Dr. Boyer is the author of numerous articles and books. *Salem Possessed: The Social Origins of Witchcraft,* which he co-authored with Stephen Nissenbaum, won the John H. Dunning Prize of the American Historical Association.

Dr. Sterling Stuckey

Sterling Stuckey is Professor of History and holds the President's Chair at the University of California, Riverside, where he was presented the Distinguished Humanist Achievement Award. He is also a member of the editorial board of *The American Heritage Encyclopedia of American History.* Awarded a Ph.D. from Northwestern University in 1972, Dr. Stuckey is the author of numerous articles and the books *Slave Culture: Nationalist Theory and the Foundations of Black America* and *Going Through the Storm: The Influence of African American Art in History.* Dr. Stuckey is currently working on a biography of Paul Robeson and a volume on Herman Melville's *Benito Cereno.*

EDITORIAL REVIEW BOARD

DR. RONALD FOORE

Dr. Foore is the social studies department chair at Booker T. Washington Magnet High School in Tulsa, Oklahoma.

In addition to teaching American history, he also serves on the International Baccalaureate Faculty. He has served on the National Council for the Social Studies, was a vice president for the American Society for History Education, and is president-elect of the Oklahoma Council for the Social Studies. Dr. Foore is a recipient of the Tulsa Teacher of the Year award.

DR. YASUHIDE KAWASHIMA

Dr. Kawashima is a professor of history at the University of Texas at El Paso.

He received his Ph.D. from the University of California at Santa Barbara, as well as advanced legal degrees from Keio University in Japan. He specializes in American legal history. Dr. Kawashima is the author of numerous articles and three books, including *Puritan Justice and the American Indian.* He is a past winner of the Webb-Smith Essay Prize from the University of Texas at Arlington.

LUCINDA LUCERO SACHS

Ms. Sachs recently retired after teaching American history and other social studies courses for 29 years in the Albuquerque School District in New Mexico.

She holds Master's degrees in both Secondary Education and in History. She is a past recipient of the Crossing Boundaries writing contest from the *International Quarterly.* She has also been awarded numerous fellowships, including writing fellowships from the Provincetown Fine Arts Work Center in Massachusetts and from the Vermont Studio Center.

DR. NAN E. WOODRUFF

Dr. Woodruff is an associate professor of history at Penn State University.

She received her Ph.D. from the University of Tennessee. She specializes in 20th century southern history. Dr. Woodruff has published numerous articles as well as the book *Right as Rain: The Great Southern Drought, 1930–31.* She also served as an assistant editor for the *Booker T. Washington Papers.*

DR. ALFRED YOUNG

Dr. Young is a professor of history at Georgia Southern University.

He received his Ph.D. from Syracuse University. He specializes in African American history. Dr. Young has published numerous articles and is co-author of the book *Education and the Black Experience.* He is currently completing a biography of African American scholar John Hope Franklin. Dr. Young has served as an officer for the National Council for Black Studies and is a past recipient of the Black Student Union's Teaching Excellence Award.

HOLT SOCIAL STUDIES
HIGH SCHOOL

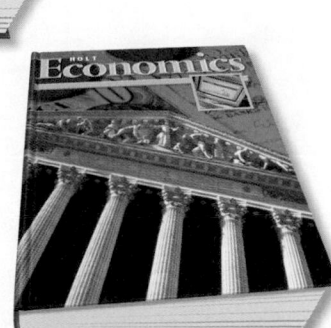

The Greater the Relevance, The Greater the Impact

The first step to success in the social studies classroom is capturing—and sustaining—the interest of your students. Holt Social Studies programs for high school nurture in your students an ability to be curious about and to make connections to other cultures, people, and places, and to see the impact of history on their lives.

BUILT-IN READING SUPPORT

Comprehensive, current content is the hallmark of Holt programs. But if students can't or won't read, this content is irrelevant. That's why Holt programs are designed to allow students to make *sense* of what they are reading by giving them the strategies they need to become successful readers.

STANDARDIZED TESTING AND SKILL BUILDING

In order for students to be successful, students must master skills that are measured by standardized testing. Holt programs are unique in providing teachers and students with the built-in tools needed to prepare them to perform well on standardized tests.

TECHNOLOGY WITH INSTRUCTIONAL VALUE

Our technology is designed to be an instructional tool that delivers excellent content. From online current events to **Homework Practice Online,** from drag-and-drop map activities to the ever-current **HRW Online Atlas,** from prescreened Internet links to our new **Online Textbooks** on the **go.hrw.com** Web site—you and your students will find valuable e-resources you'll use over and over again.

THE BEST TEACHER MANAGEMENT SYSTEM IN THE INDUSTRY

The *One-Stop Planner CD-ROM with Test Generator* is a unique planning tool that allows you to preview, customize, and edit program resources to make lesson management easy. Everything you need to plan is on one disc.

It's All About

TEEN LIFE uses engaging stories about young people's lives in history to get students involved with their text. They'll love learning about the traditions and cultures of our nation's past eras.

The first step to success in the social studies classroom is capturing and sustaining the interest of your students. *HOLT THE AMERICAN NATION* is designed to be open and friendly to all students, so that they develop an enthusiasm for learning and an appreciation for the past.

HOLT THE AMERICAN NATION offers
- **Built-in Reading Support**
- **Technology with Instructional Value**
- **Standardized Testing and Skill Building**
- **The Best Teacher Management System in the Industry**

RELEVANCE

CNNfyi.com™ is a site designed to give students in grades 6–12 access to people, places, and environments around the globe while offering "real-world" articles, career and college resources, and online activities.

CNNfyi.com > News

John Adams: A force for independence

July 3, 2001
Web posted at 5:45 PM EDT (2145 0MT)

RESOURCE:
Lesson plan for parents and educators — Click here

By Todd Leopold
CNN

(CNNfi) — On July 4, the United States celebrates its birthday — the anniversary of the Declaration of Independence. It's a celebration that wouldn't be possible without the actions of a frequently ignored Founding Father.

"Adams hasn't received the attention he deserves," says David McCullough, author of the recent biography "John Adams" And (Thomas)

An oil-on-wood portrait of John Adams, circa 1821, by Gilbert Stuart.

In-Text Features that Put History into Perspective

PRIMARY SOURCES
- **History Makers Speak**
- **Historical Documents**
- **Eyewitnesses to History**

INTERDISCIPLINARY CONNECTIONS
- **American Arts**
- **American Letters**
- **America's Geography**
- **The Religious Spirit**
- **Science & Technology**

PEOPLE AND HISTORY
- **Biographies**
- **Presidential Lives**

WHY HISTORY MATTERS
- **Visualizing Past and Present**
- **Then and Now**

HISTORICAL POINTS OF VIEW
- **Great Debates**
- **History in the Making**

Reading for

At Holt, we don't assume that students know how or have any desire to make sense of what they're reading, and we develop our programs based on that assumption. We don't just ask students questions about content, we give them strategies to get to that content. Through design, research, and the help of experts like Dr. Judith Irvin, we make sure students' reading needs are covered with our programs.

Helping Students Make Sense of What They're Reading

An Essay by Dr. Judith Irvin, Ph.D.

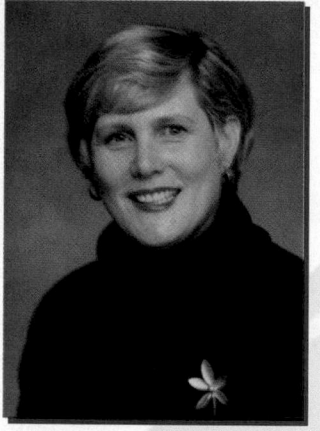

Who in middle and high schools helps students become more successful at reading and writing informational text? When I ask this question of a school faculty, the Language Arts/English teachers point to the social studies and science teachers because they are the ones with this type of textbook. The social studies and science teachers point to the Language Arts/English teachers because they are the ones that "do" words.

I advocate teachers taking an active role in helping students learn how to use text structure and context to understand what they read. Through consistent and systematic instruction that includes modeling of effective reading behavior, teachers can assist students in becoming better readers while at the same time helping them learn more content material.

The strategies in this book are designed to assist students with getting started, maintaining focus with reading, and organizing information for later retrieval. They engage students in learning material, provide the vehicle for them to organize and reorganize concepts, and extend their understanding through writing.

When teachers combine the teaching of reading and the teaching of content together into meaningful, systematic, and corrected instruction, students can apply what they have learned to understanding increasingly more difficult and complex texts as they progress through the school years.

READING STRATEGIES FOR THE SOCIAL STUDIES CLASSROOM

by Dr. Judith Irvin,
Ph.D. Reading Education

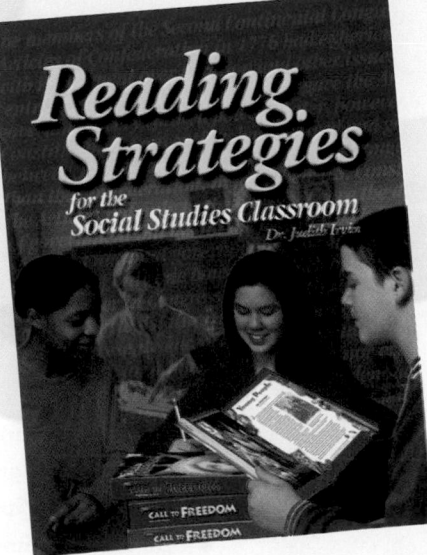

Reading Strategies for the Social Studies Classroom
Dr. Judith Irvin

Additional Reading Support

- **Main Idea Activities**
- **Graphic Organizer Activities**
- **Audio CD Program**
- **Guided Reading Strategies**
- **Vocabulary Activities**

MEANING

Successful Readers must have:

1 AN ENGAGING NARRATIVE

Great care is taken in selecting and presenting content in a way that students will find motivating and engaging. Features such as **Teen Life** help students connect their own lives to those who have played a role in the development of our nation.

2 A FORECAST OF WHAT THEY WILL LEARN

Read to Discover questions give students insight into the content they will cover in the chapter to come. In features such as **What's Your Opinion?** students are encouraged to give their opinions, thus helping them develop an ownership of the material.

3 OPPORTUNITIES TO ACTIVATE PRIOR KNOWLEDGE

In the pre-reading features **Build on What You Know** and **Chapter Timelines,** students are encouraged to connect content they have covered in previous chapters or other courses to the material they will learn about in the upcoming chapter.

4 VOCABULARY DEFINED IN CONTEXT

Important new terms are identified at the beginning of every section and are defined in context so students will develop an understanding of the contextual meaning of all terms.

5 STRATEGIES FOR UNDERSTANDING WHAT THEY READ

Through the design of the text, students are led through the content using built-in reading strategies. For example, **Reading Checks** in the text are used as a comprehension tool. The checks remind students to stop and engage with what they have read, functioning as a "Tutor in the Text."

Get Your Students

Your students love activities that get them involved with the content. That's why Holt offers active-learning resources that link directly to program content and provide a multitude of different lessons for large-group, small-group, and individual projects.

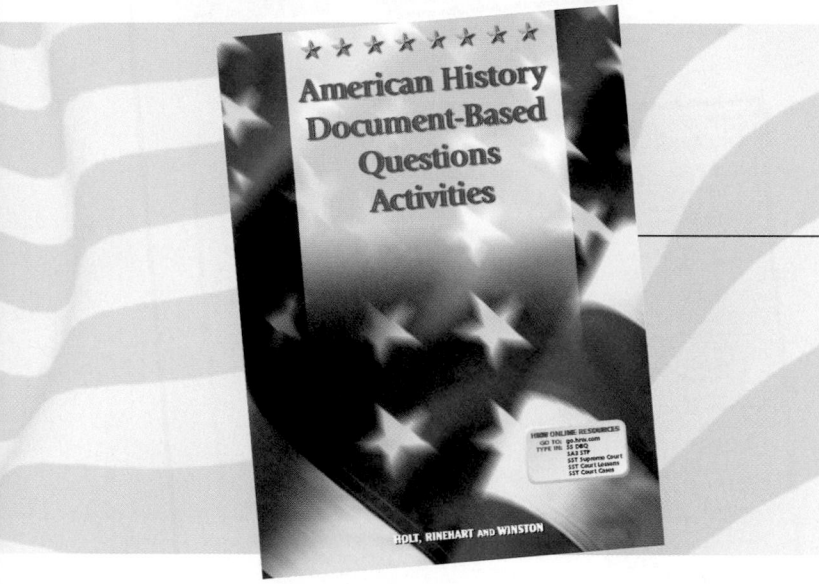

AMERICAN HISTORY DOCUMENT-BASED QUESTIONS ACTIVITIES

This resource includes a variety of primary sources with intriguing, thought-provoking questions. Important historical themes are grouped together to allow for scaffolded instruction.

PRIMARY SOURCES

Through readings, literature excerpts, political cartoons and more, students will gain insight into the nation's past by examining period accounts and first person voices. Not only will these resources provide excellent preparation for standardized assessment, but they will expose your students to the real people and events that helped shape our country.

CITIZENSHIP

Your students will explore issues about U.S. citizenship with these resources. These creative, hands-on activities encourage students to explore their rights and roles in their community by putting them in decision-making positions for Supreme Court cases, having them write a presidential magazine article, and more. These resources not only introduce politcal issues, but they also make citizenship a reality for your students.

Involved
in Learning

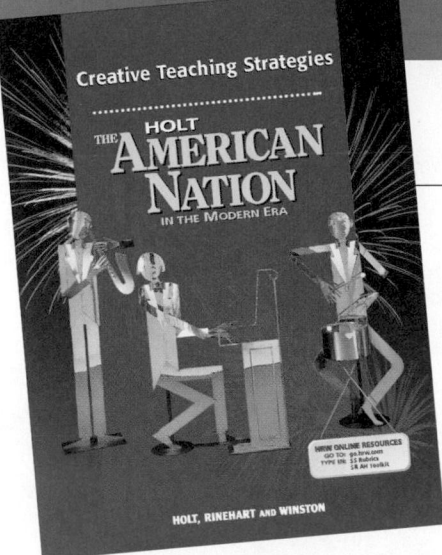

CREATIVE TEACHING STRATEGIES

These innovative teaching strategies can be utilized at various points in your lesson. The wide range of cooperative-learning activities, including learning stations and simulations, motivate your students and help them develop critical-thinking skills.

Other Skill-Based Ancillaries

- American History Visual Resources
- Art in American History Transparencies
- Geography Activities
- Guided Reading Strategies

Joining Forces

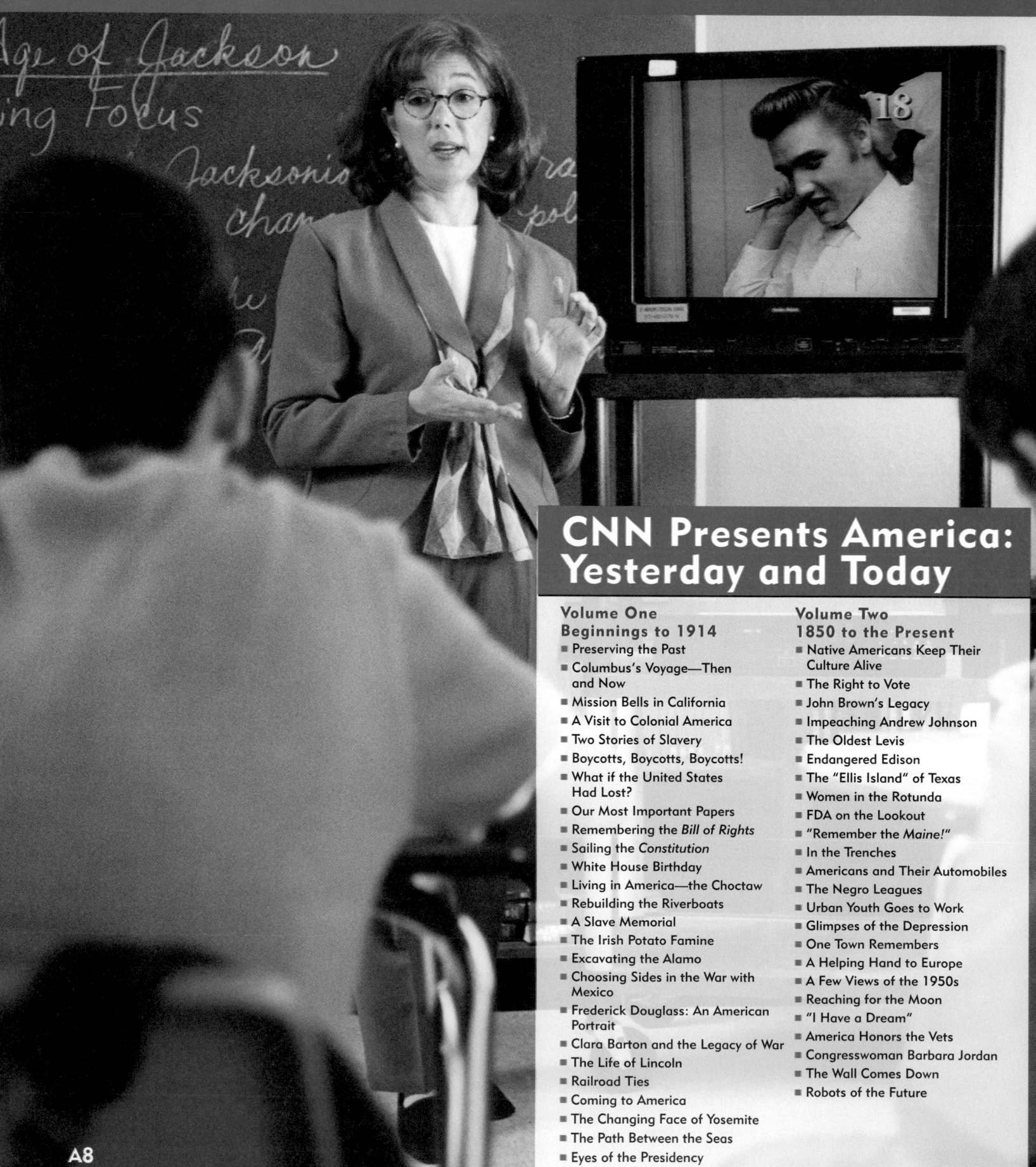

CNN Presents America: Yesterday and Today

to Enrich your Classroom

CNNfyi.com

At **CNNfyi.com**, students will love exploring news stories written by experienced journalists as well as student bureau reporters complete with links to homework help and lesson plans.

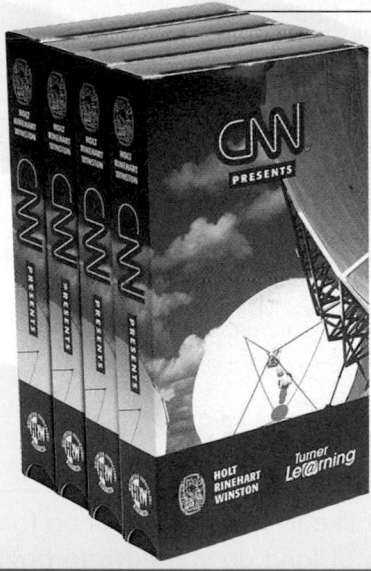

CNN PRESENTS VIDEO LIBRARY

The **CNN PRESENTS** video collection tackles the issue of making content relevant to students head on. Real-world news stories enable students to see the connections between classroom curriculum and today's issues and events around the nation and the world.

CNN PRESENTS...

- **America: Yesterday and Today, Beginnings to 1914**
- **America: Yesterday and Today, 1850 to the Present**
- **America: Yesterday and Today, Modern Times**
- **Geography: Yesterday and Today**
- **World Cultures: Yesterday and Today**
- **American Government**
- **Economics**

Holt is proud to team up with CNN/TURNER LEARNING to provide you and your students with exceptional current and historical news videos and online resources that add depth and relevance to your daily instruction. This information collection takes your classroom to the far corners of the globe without students ever leaving their desks!

Your Multi-talented Classroom

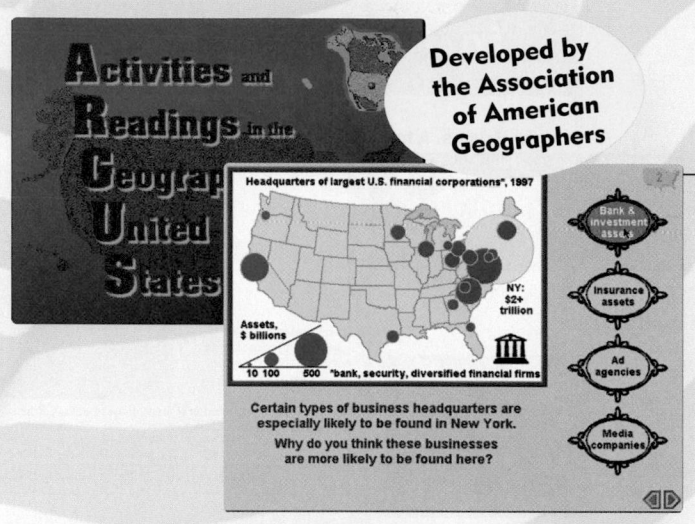

Developed by the Association of American Geographers

ACTIVITIES AND READINGS IN THE GEOGRAPHY OF THE UNITED STATES

Integrate real geography into the topic you're studying with *Activities and Readings in the Geography of the United States (ARGUS).* This CD-ROM features 26 American history case studies with a multitude of activities that focus around geographical themes, population geography, economic geography, political geography, and environmental issues. Case studies will help teachers address the National Geography Standards.

HOLT RESEARCHER CD-ROM: AMERICAN HISTORY

This CD-ROM contains a fully researchable database, including biographies, state and nation profiles, Supreme Court cases, statistics, and more. This outstanding research tool comes with an easy-to-use search engine, an Internet link to **www.hrw.com**, and powerful graphing capabilities.

AMERICAN HISTORY SIMULATIONS CD-ROM

What was it like to be a miner during the gold rush? How many acres of land do you have to buy to make a profit on cotton? All of these questions and more will be answered on this CD-ROM that allows your students to role-play as important decision-makers in our history.

needs Multimedia Tools

THE AMERICAN NATION VIDEO PROGRAM

This video captures your students' attentions and gives them a visual point of reference for the historical events they read about in their books. The accompanying **Teacher's Guide** includes lesson plans and worksheets. Available in English and in Spanish.

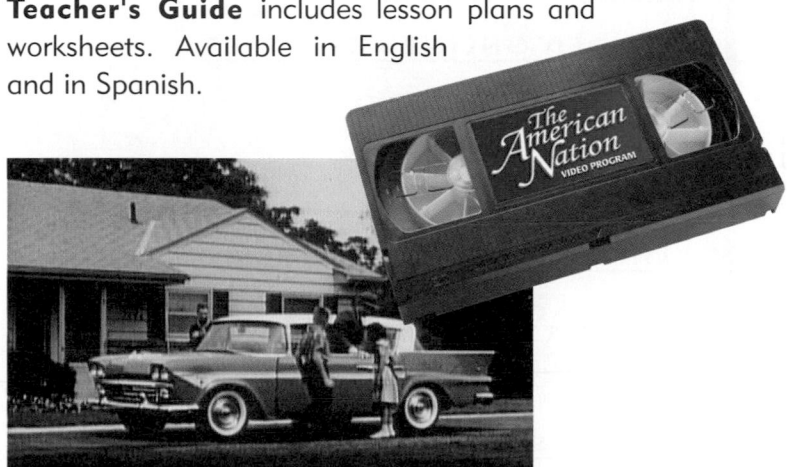

AMERICAN HISTORY INTERACTIVE MAPS CD-ROM

The maps, audio and video clips, text, and illustrations on this powerful tool provide hands-on activities for your students to examine geographic and economic issues. Interactive strategies ask students to collect and analyze data about the importance of the people, places, and events that affected our nation's past.

Other Multimedia Products

- **American Music Audio CD**
- **Global Skill Builder CD-ROM**
- **Chapter Summary Audio CD Program in English and Spanish**
- **Holt Researcher CD-ROM: American History**
- **Holt Researcher CD-ROM: Economy and Government**
- **Exploring America's Past Videodisc and Videocassette Program**

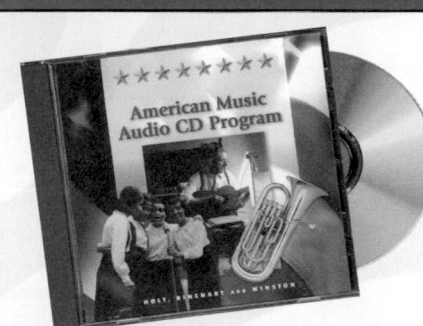

Technology with

go.hrw.com FOR TEACHERS

Throughout the *Annotated Teacher's Edition*, you'll find **Internet Connect** boxes that take you to specific chapter activities, links, current events, and more that correlate directly to the section you are teaching. Through **go.hrw.com** you'll find a wealth of teaching resources at your fingertips for fun, interactive lessons.

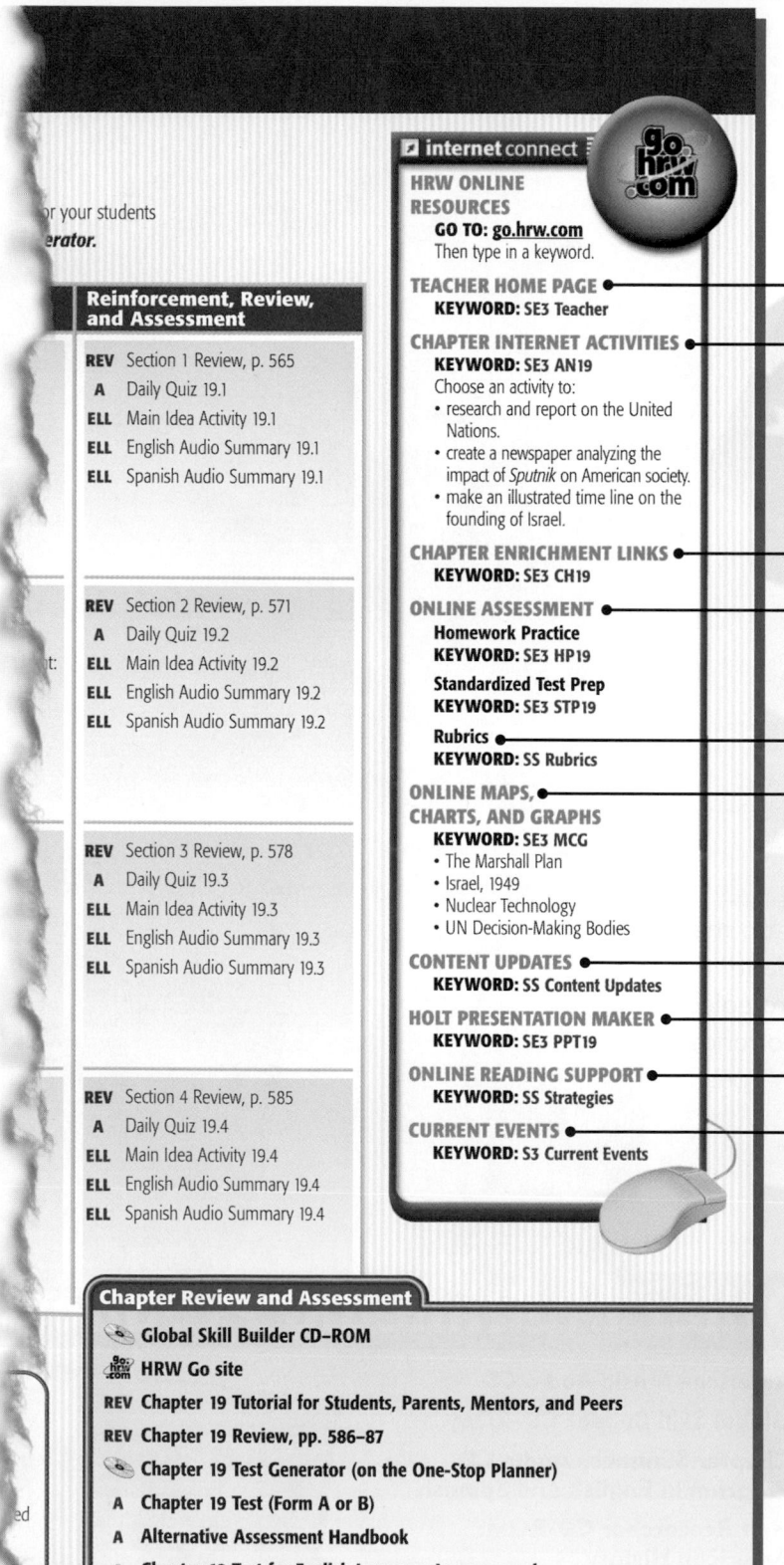

...or your students
...*erator.*

Reinforcement, Review, and Assessment

REV	Section 1 Review, p. 565	
A	Daily Quiz 19.1	
ELL	Main Idea Activity 19.1	
ELL	English Audio Summary 19.1	
ELL	Spanish Audio Summary 19.1	

REV	Section 2 Review, p. 571	
A	Daily Quiz 19.2	
ELL	Main Idea Activity 19.2	
ELL	English Audio Summary 19.2	
ELL	Spanish Audio Summary 19.2	

REV	Section 3 Review, p. 578	
A	Daily Quiz 19.3	
ELL	Main Idea Activity 19.3	
ELL	English Audio Summary 19.3	
ELL	Spanish Audio Summary 19.3	

REV	Section 4 Review, p. 585	
A	Daily Quiz 19.4	
ELL	Main Idea Activity 19.4	
ELL	English Audio Summary 19.4	
ELL	Spanish Audio Summary 19.4	

Chapter Review and Assessment

- Global Skill Builder CD-ROM
- HRW Go site
- **REV** Chapter 19 Tutorial for Students, Parents, Mentors, and Peers
- **REV** Chapter 19 Review, pp. 586–87
- Chapter 19 Test Generator (on the One-Stop Planner)
- **A** Chapter 19 Test (Form A or B)
- **A** Alternative Assessment Handbook
- **A** Chapter 19 Test for English Language Learners and Special-Needs Students

---

internet connect

HRW ONLINE RESOURCES
GO TO: go.hrw.com
Then type in a keyword.

TEACHER HOME PAGE
KEYWORD: SE3 Teacher

CHAPTER INTERNET ACTIVITIES
KEYWORD: SE3 AN19
Choose an activity to:
- research and report on the United Nations.
- create a newspaper analyzing the impact of *Sputnik* on American society.
- make an illustrated time line on the founding of Israel.

CHAPTER ENRICHMENT LINKS
KEYWORD: SE3 CH19

ONLINE ASSESSMENT
Homework Practice
KEYWORD: SE3 HP19

Standardized Test Prep
KEYWORD: SE3 STP19

Rubrics
KEYWORD: SS Rubrics

ONLINE MAPS, CHARTS, AND GRAPHS
KEYWORD: SE3 MCG
- The Marshall Plan
- Israel, 1949
- Nuclear Technology
- UN Decision-Making Bodies

CONTENT UPDATES
KEYWORD: SS Content Updates

HOLT PRESENTATION MAKER
KEYWORD: SE3 PPT19

ONLINE READING SUPPORT
KEYWORD: SS Strategies

CURRENT EVENTS
KEYWORD: S3 Current Events

DIRECT LAUNCH TO CHAPTER ACTIVITIES

GUIDED ONLINE ACTIVITIES

LINKS FOR EVERY SECTION

INTERACTIVE PRACTICE AND REVIEW

RUBRICS FOR SUBJECTIVE GRADING

MAPS AND CHARTS

UP-TO-DATE INFORMATION

PRESENTATION SUPPORT

PRACTICE FOR READING SUCCESS

WEB RESOURCES FOR CURRENT ISSUES

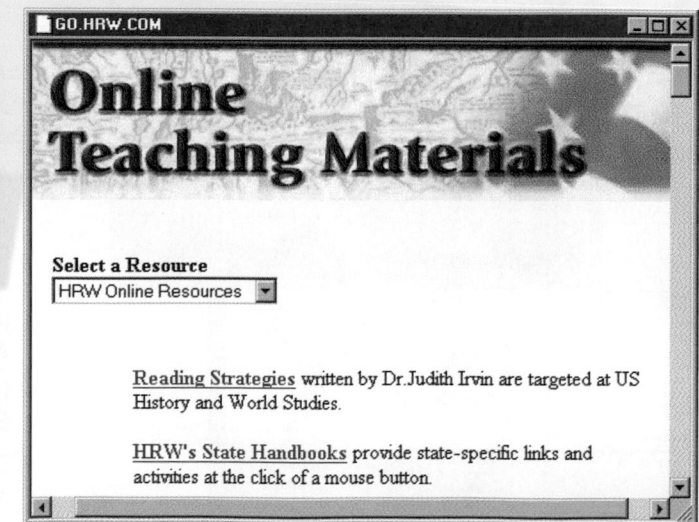

GO.HRW.COM

Online Teaching Materials

Select a Resource
HRW Online Resources ▼

Reading Strategies written by Dr. Judith Irvin are targeted at US History and World Studies.

HRW's State Handbooks provide state-specific links and activities at the click of a mouse button.

Instructional Value

ONLINE TEACHING SUPPORT

Teacher materials on **go.hrw.com** offer you multiple resources for keeping content current. From **American History Maps and Charts** to **State Handbooks,** we've got it all.

CLASSROOM PRESENTATION SUPPORT

Lecture notes and animated graphic organizers help add visual support to your classroom presentations.

Technology that

go.hrw.com FOR STUDENTS

Your students can access interactive activities, homework help, up-to-date maps, and more when they visit **go.hrw.com** and type in the keywords they find in their text.

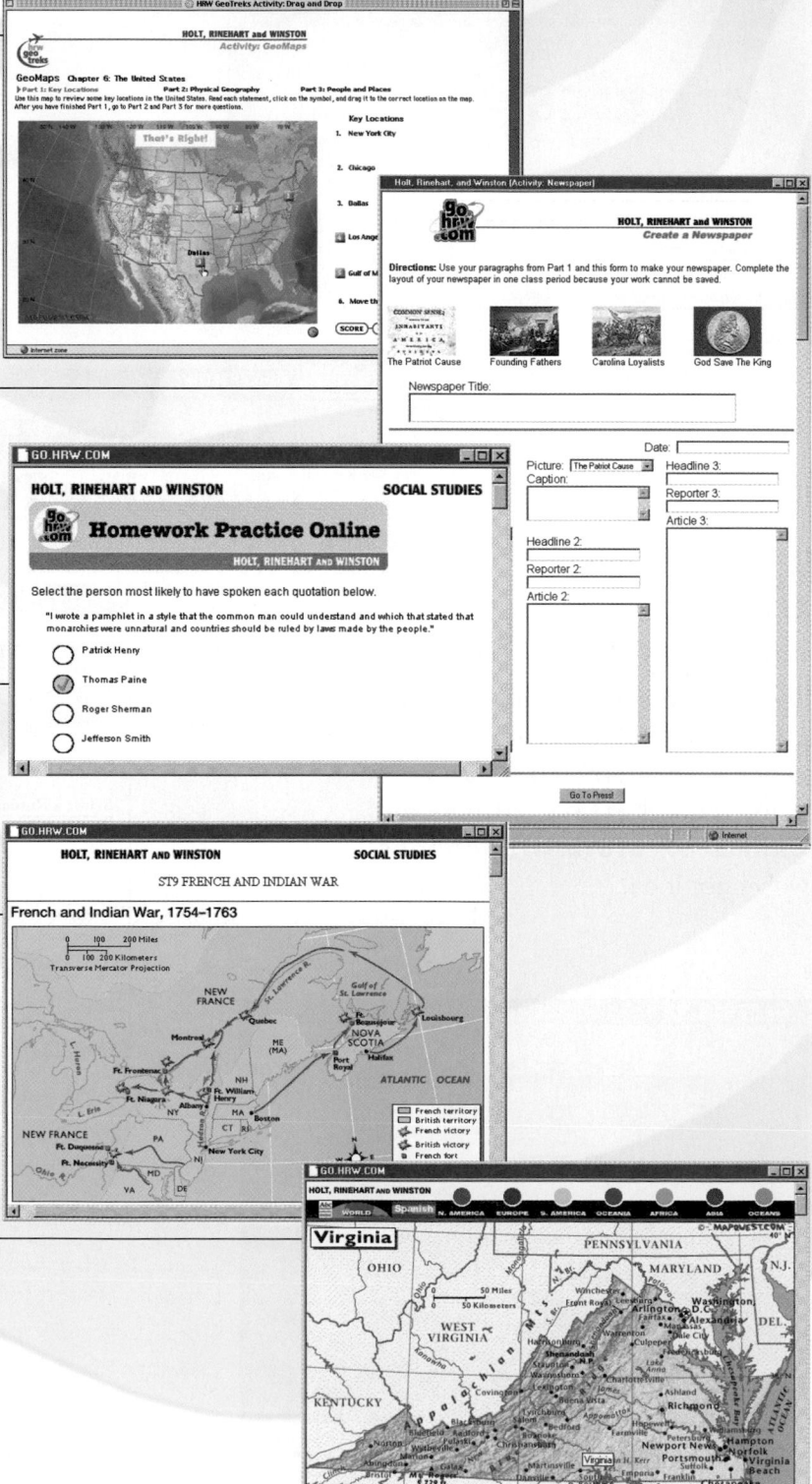

GEOMAPS

When you visit **go.hrw.com**, you can access **GeoMaps** which provides a unique opportunity to examine satellite maps that explore a region's land, water, places, and people.

ONLINE TEMPLATES

Your students can use these interactive templates to create newspapers, travel brochures, postcards, journals, creative works, and more. The instructional design of this tool allows students to do something with the content they have learned.

HOMEWORK PRACTICE

This helpful tool allows students to practice and review content by chapter anywhere there is a computer.

ONLINE HISTORICAL MAPS

These maps provide fascinating visual "snapshots" of the past. Students will relish the chance to explore medieval European trade routes, explorers' routes, ancient African kingdoms, and more.

HRW ONLINE ATLAS

This helpful online tool contains over 300 well-rendered and clearly labeled country and state maps. The clean design and easy-to-use navigational tools make accessing information simple. These maps are continually updated so you can rest assured that you and your students have the latest and most accurate geographical content available. Maps are available in English and Spanish.

Delivers Content

New Online Textbook

You'll know what to do when you see it!
Finally, an online textbook that takes full advantage of Web technology in a way that makes sense—*HOLT THE AMERICAN NATION ONLINE EDITION.*

- **Entire student edition online formatted to match printed text**
- **User-friendly navigation**
- **Hot links to interactive activities, practice, and assessment**
- **Student Notebook for online responses**

Unique Teacher's

In-Text Chapter Planning

Holt The American Nation Program Components

Reading Support
- Graphic Organizer Activities
- Guided Reading Strategies
- Main Idea Activities for English Language Learners and Special-Needs Students
- Reading Strategies for the Social Studies Classroom
- Writing About American History

Active-Learning Support
- Block Scheduling Handbook with Team-Teaching Strategies
- Citizenship Simulations and Case Studies
- Creative Teaching Strategies
- Hands-On History Activities: Classroom to Community

Primary Sources
- American History Document-Based Questions Activities
- American History Political Cartoons
- American History Visual Resources
- Art in American History Transparencies
- The Constitution: Past, Present, and Future
- Eyewitnesses and Others: Readings in American History
- Literature, Primary Source, and Biography Readings
- Transparency Directory for American History Visual Resources and Art in American History Transparencies

Geography Support
- American History Outline Maps
- The Complete School Atlas
- Geography Activities

Review and Assessment
- Alternative Assessment Handbook
- Chapter and Unit Tests
- Chapter and Unit Tests for English Language Learners and Special-Needs Students
- Chapter Tutorials for Students, Parents, Mentors, and Peers
- Daily Quizzes
- Reviewing Early American History Handbook
- Social Studies Skills Review
- Standardized Test Practice Handbook

Management System

Everything you need is on one disc!

One-Stop Planner
with Test Generator

ONE-STOP PLANNER CD-ROM WITH TEST GENERATOR

Holt brings you the most user-friendly management system in the industry with the *One-Stop Planner CD-ROM with Test Generator.* Plan and manage your lessons from this single disc containing all the teaching resources for *Holt The American Nation,* valuable planning and assessment tools, and more.

- **Editable lesson plans**
- **Classroom Presentations**
- **Easy-to-use test generator**
- **Previews of all teaching and video resources**
- **Easy printing feature**
- **Direct launch to go.hrw.com**

BLOCK SCHEDULING HANDBOOK WITH TEAM TEACHING STRATEGIES

This is more than a pacing guide—it provides daily lesson plans that suggest specific and practical ways to cover more than one textbook section in an extended class period and ways to make interdisciplinary connections.

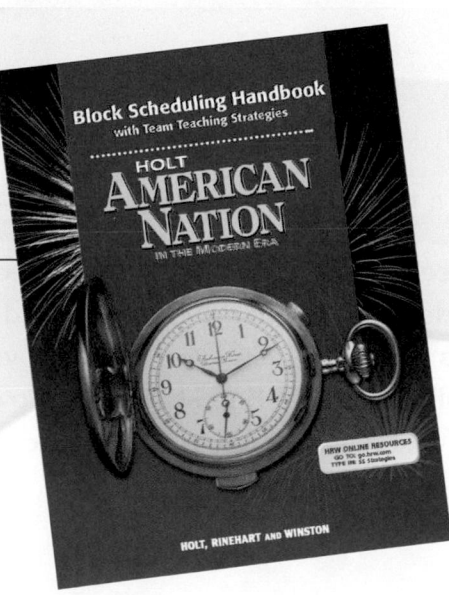

Block Scheduling Handbook
with Team Teaching Strategies

HOLT
AMERICAN
NATION
IN THE MODERN ERA

HOLT, RINEHART AND WINSTON

Energize

SECTION 3
The Cold War Turns Hot

The American Nation

CHINESE COMMUNISTS GAIN CONTROL OF CHINA

unstable republic established in 1911

↓

civil war between Nationalist and Communist forces

↓

nationalists and Communists cooperation to resist Japanese

↓

China under Mao's control by 1949; retreat of Chiang's forces to Taiwan

↓

establishment of People's Republic of China

↓

HOLT, RINEHART AND WINST

Presentations That Benefit Learning

Classroom presentations and lecture notes can be accessed with ease when you use Holt's **Presentation** tool found on the *One-Stop Planner CD-ROM*. This resource helps you spice up your presentations and gives you ideas to build on. You'll find Microsoft® PowerPoint® presentations that include lecture notes and animated graphic organizers for each chapter and section of your text.

Your Classroom Presentations

OBJECTIVE-BASED LESSON CYCLE IN THE ANNOTATED TEACHER'S EDITION

With lively activities and presentation strategies such as **Let's Get Started, Building Vocabulary,** and **Graphic Organizers,** your step-by-step lesson cycle makes planning your lessons easy and productive.

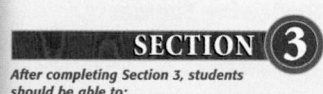

SECTION 3

After completing Section 3, students should be able to:

OBJECTIVE 1 *Explain how the Chinese Communists gained control of China.*

OBJECTIVE 2 *Analyze the factors that led to the escalation of the conflict in Korea.*

OBJECTIVE 3 *Describe the domestic and international effects of the Korean War.*

OBJECTIVE 4 *Discuss the methods that President Eisenhower used to promote U.S. interests abroad.*

LET'S GET STARTED!

As students enter the classroom, tell them to study the map of North and South Korea in this section and to consider the distance from those countries to the United States. Ask each student to list reasons for and against U.S. involvement in a war in such a distant place. Ask volunteers to share their answers, and compile a list of students' answers on the chalkboard. Tell students that in Section 3 they will learn how Americans fought communism overseas under the leadership of Presidents Truman and Eisenhower.

TEACH OBJECTIVE 1

ALL LEVELS: To help students understand how Chinese Communists gained control of China, copy the following graphic organizer on the chalkboard, omitting the italicized answers. Have each student complete it. Ask volunteers to share their answers with the class. Then ask students whether the Chinese Communists led a revolution that had popular support. *(Students might suggest that the Communists' resistance against the Japanese, coupled with land reforms, won them popular support.)* To conclude, lead a class discussion about whether the United States has the right to oppose a revolution that is supported by the majority of a country's residents. **English Language Learners**

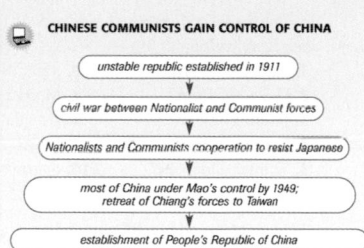

CHINESE COMMUNISTS GAIN CONTROL OF CHINA

unstable republic established in 1911
↓
civil war between Nationalist and Communist forces
↓
Nationalists and Communists cooperation to resist Japanese
↓
most of China under Mao's control by 1949; retreat of Chiang's forces to Taiwan
↓
establishment of People's Republic of China

TEACH OBJECTIVE 4

LEVEL 1: Pair students and have them draw political cartoons with written captions about the methods that President Eisenhower used to promote U.S. interests abroad. *(Students should depict Eisenhower using covert means—as he did in Guatemala and Iran—and diplomatic means—as he did when he issued the Eisenhower Doctrine and when he refused to support Hungarian rebels.)* Display students' cartoons around the classroom.
English Language Learners, Cooperative Learning

LEVEL 2: Tell students to imagine that they are writing books about U.S. foreign policy during the Eisenhower administration. Ask each student to write a detailed outline for a chapter about the various methods that Eisenhower used to promote U.S. interests abroad. *(See the Level 1 lesson for the correct methods.)* Ask volunteers to share their outlines with the class. ⭐19C, 25D

LEVEL 3: Have each student write a song about the methods that President Eisenhower used to promote U.S. interests abroad. *(See the Level 1 lesson for the correct methods.)* Ask volunteers to read or perform their songs for the class. Students may wish to include their songs in their portfolios. ⭐19C, 25C

 HOMEWORK *Distribute Cartoon 26, Brinkmanship, from* **American History Political Cartoons.** *Have each student study the cartoon and complete the accompanying lessons.*

REVIEW

Have students complete the **Section 3 Review** on p. 578.

ASSESS

Have students complete **Daily Quiz 19.3.** As **Alternative Assessment,** you may want to use the political cartoon or the television script in this section's lessons.

RETEACH

Have students complete **Main Idea Activity for English Language Learners and Special-Needs Students 19.3.** Then organize students into four groups. Have each group write sentences to identify each of the key terms, people, and places for Section 3. Collect groups' sentences and use them to quiz the class. **English Language Learners, Cooperative Learning**

EXTEND

Have students locate and use primary and secondary sources to conduct further research on the political and constitutional issues involved in the conflict between President Truman and General MacArthur over the escalation of the war in Korea. Have each student write an analytical essay based on his or her research. **Block Scheduling**

Teacher to Teacher

Jenifer Rowray of Runnells, Iowa, suggested the following activity: Write the following phrase on the chalkboard: the forgotten war. *Ask students how this phrase describes the Korean War. Write students' responses on the chalkboard and conduct a discussion on how Americans remember the Korean War.*

TEACHER TO TEACHER

These strategies are offered in the lesson cycle of your *Annotated Teacher's Edition* and provide you with valuable, classroom-tested ideas and activities that have been developed and successfully applied by your peers.

Classroom Activities and Anecdotes Found in Teacher's Edition Side Columns

- **American Arts**
- **American Letters**
- **America's Geography**
- **Biographies**
- **Eyewitnesses to History**
- **History in the Making**
- **History Makers Speak**
- **Presidential Lives**
- **The Religious Spirit**
- **Science & Technology**
- **Teen Life**
- **Then and Now**
- **Visualizing Past and Present**

Assessment for

INTERACTIVE PRACTICE ACTIVITIES

SECTION 3 REVIEW

1. **Define and explain:**
   brinkmanship

2. **Identify and explain:**
   Chiang Kai-shek
   Mao Zedong
   Kim Il Sung
   Syngman Rhee
   Douglas MacArthur
   Dwight D. Eisenhower
   Central Intelligence
   Nikita Khrushchev
   U-2 incident

3. **Categorizing** Copy the graphic organizer below. Use it to explain how the United States attempted to slow the spread of communism.

Communist Threat In:	U.S. Reaction
China	◯
Korea	◯
Guatemala	◯
Egypt	◯

   Homework Practice Online
   keyword: SE3 HP19

4. **Finding the Main Idea**
   a. How did a civil war between Nationalists and Communists in China lead to the creation of the People's Republic of China?
   b. How did conflicts in Asia affect politics in the United States?
   c. In what ways were President Eisenhower's covert operations and diplomatic strategies effective? What new problems did they present?

5. **Writing and Critical Thinking**
   Making Generalizations Imagine that you are a State Department official. Write a press release explaining how the fall of China to the Communists encouraged further U.S. military action in Korea.
   Consider:
   • how the fall of China related to U.S. containment policy
   • how the containment policy influenced U.S. actions in Korea
   • what role Communist China played in the Korean War

THIS SUPERIOR TEST GENERATOR REALLY WORKS!

CHAPTER 19 Review

Creating a Time Line

Copy the time line below onto a sheet of paper. Complete the time line by filling in the events and dates from the chapter that you think were most significant. Pick three events and explain why you think they were significant.

| 1945 | 1950 | 1955 | 1960 |

Writing a Summary

Using standard grammar, spelling, sentence structure, and punctuation, write an overview of events in the chapter.

Identifying People and Ideas

Identify the following terms or individuals and explain their significance.

1. Nuremberg Trials
2. United Nations
3. Eleanor Roosevelt
4. George Kennan
5. Truman Doctrine
6. Marshall Plan
7. Mao Zedong
8. Douglas MacArthur
9. Joseph McCarthy
10. *Sputnik*

Understanding Main Ideas

SECTION 1 (pp. 560–565)
1. How successful was the United Nations in stabilizing the conflict between Arabs and Jews in Palestine? Explain your answer.

SECTION 2 (pp. 566–571)
2. What were the main causes of the Cold War?

SECTION 3 (pp. 572–578)
3. What strategies did President Eisenhower use to slow the spread of communism?

SECTION 4 (pp. 579–585)
4. Why was Senator McCarthy able to generate so much attention with his accusations?
5. How did the U.S. government respond to the launch of *Sputnik*?

Reviewing Themes

1. **Global Relations** What other countries became involved in the conflict between the United States and the Soviet Union?
2. **Government** How did the U.S. government's response to Cold War tensions lead to limitations on civil liberties?
3. **Science, Technology, and Society** How did the development of atomic technology affect daily life in the United States?

Thinking Critically

1. **Problem Solving** Imagine that you are establishing an organization to maintain world peace. How would you organize it? Why?
2. **Sequencing** How did the United States respond to Soviet expansion after World War II?
3. **Evaluating** How did the fall of China to communism in 1949 affect the Korean War in 1950?
4. **Identifying Points of View** Why did many Palestinians, Iranians, and Guatemalans view the U.S. government with hostility during the 1950s?
5. **Analyzing Information** How did the Korean War affect the domestic and international affairs of the United States?

Writing About History

Summarizing Imagine that you are a senator in the mid-1950s who opposes communism. Using the graphic organizer below, write a speech describing the threat of Communist expansion around the world.

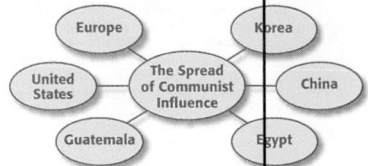

Europe — Korea — United States — The Spread of Communist Influence — China — Guatemala — Egypt

---

CRITICAL-THINKING REINFORCEMENT

OPPORTUNITIES FOR WRITING REINFORCEMENT

Every Student

STANDARDIZED TEST PRACTICE HANDBOOK

This resource helps your students gear up for future standardized tests. Content-specific practice exposes them to a variety of question types—like multiple choice and short answer—commonly found in today's standardized assessments.

Building Social Studies Skills

Interpreting the Visual Record
Study the image below. Then use it to help answer the questions that follow.

Anticommunist literature

1. How does this image portray communism in the United States?
   a. The United States under communism would benefit all Americans.
   b. Communism would have little to no effect on the United States.
   c. Communism would lead to destruction and violence.
   d. Communism would lead to massive fires in the United States.

2. What do you know about the 1950s that would lead this author to ask, "Is This Tomorrow"?

Analyzing Primary Sources
Read the following excerpt from an oral history provided by Steve McConnell, a U.S. citizen who grew up during the Cold War, and then answer the questions.

"We went through the bomb-shelter era in the late fifties. I remember it as kind of fun. You could go into a shopping center and at the corner of the parking lot was one of these bomb shelters. Gee, that was neat. . . . But there was that sense of nagging that maybe this was more than just fun. Nothing serious was imminent [soon to come] but . . . there was talk.

We had drills in school. The alarms would go off and you'd hit the floor and put your back to the windows and cover your head. You were mostly afraid of getting hit by glass. What most of us didn't realize was that that would be the least of our problems. (Laughs.)"

3. Which of the following statements best describes the author's point of view?
   a. Life during the Cold War was fun.
   b. Children growing up during the Cold War had no understanding of the seriousness of the situation.
   c. Bomb shelters and drills were adequate preparations for possible attack.
   d. Children had a sense that there was something more serious related to the bomb shelters and air raid drills.

4. In this excerpt McConnell is reflecting on his experiences. How might his point of view be different if he had recorded his thoughts as a child? Give specific examples.

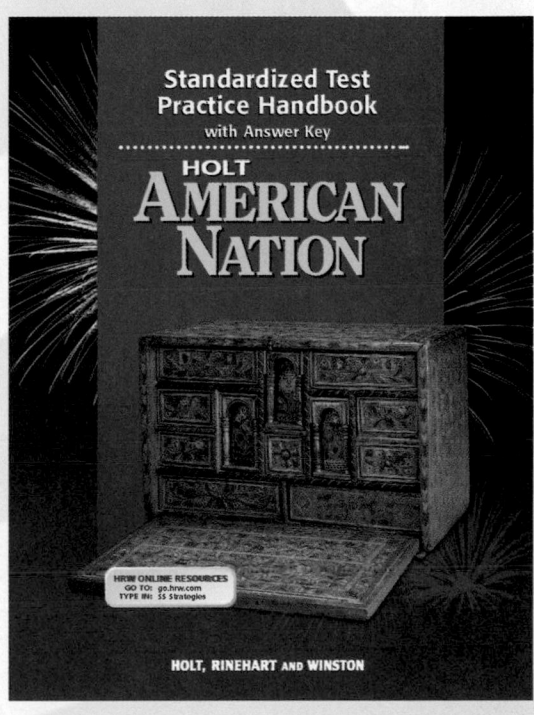

Standardized Test Practice Handbook with Answer Key

HOLT AMERICAN NATION

HRW ONLINE RESOURCES
GO TO: go.hrw.com
TYPE IN: SS Strategies

HOLT, RINEHART AND WINSTON

Alternative Assessment

Building Your Portfolio

U.S. HISTORY

Global Relations
Create an annotated world map. Your map should focus on the areas and events that led to the Cold War as well as events of the Cold War in the 1950s and early 1960s. Then write five questions for other students to answer using the map.

internet connect

Internet Activity: go.hrw.com
KEYWORD: SE3 AN19

Choose a topic on the Cold War to:
- research and report on the United Nations.
- create a newspaper analyzing the impact of *Sputnik* on American society.
- make an illustrated time line on the founding of Israel.

THE COLD WAR **587**

Additional Print and Technology Assessment Resources

- **Alternative Assessment Handbook**
- **Audio CD Program**
- **Chapter and Unit Tests**
- **Chapter and Unit Tests for English Language Learners and Special-Needs Students**
- **Chapter Tutorials for Students, Parents, Mentors, and Peers**
- **Daily Quizzes**
- **American History Document-Based Questions Activities**
- **Main Idea Activities**
- **Test Generator (located on the *One-Stop Planner CD-ROM with Test Generator*)**

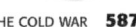

ACCESS ONLINE RUBRICS FOR GRADING PROJECTS AND PORTFOLIO ASSIGNMENTS

A21

Component Listing

TEXTS

- **Student Edition**
- **Annotated Teacher's Edition**
- **Online Textbook**

RESOURCES

Reading Support

- Graphic Organizer Activities
- Guided Reading Strategies
- Main Idea Activities for English Language Learners and Special-Needs Students
- Reading Strategies for the Social Studies Classroom
- Writing About American History

Primary Sources

- American History Document-Based Questions Activities
- American History Political Cartoons
- American History Visual Resources
- Art in American History Transparencies
- The Constitution: Past, Present, and Future
- Eyewitnesses and Others: Readings in American History (Vols. 1 and 2)
- Literature, Primary Source, and Biography Readings
- Transparency Directory for American History Visual Resources & Art in American History Transparencies

Geography Support

- American History Outline Maps
- The Complete School Atlas
- Geography Activities

Active-Learning Support

- Block Scheduling Handbook with Team Teaching Strategies
- Citizenship Simulations and Case Studies
- Creative Teaching Strategies
- Hand-On History Activities: Classroom to Community

Review and Assessment

- Alternative Assessment Handbook
- Chapter Tutorials for Students, Parents, Mentors, and Peers
- Chapter and Unit Tests
- Chapter and Unit Tests for English Language Learners and Special-Needs Students
- Daily Quizzes
- Reviewing Early American History Handbook
- Standardized Test Practice Handbook
- Social Studies Skills Review

TECHNOLOGY

CD and CD-ROM Resources

- American History Interactive Maps CD-ROM
- American History Simulations CD-ROM
- American Music Audio CD Program
- ARGUS—Activities and Readings in the Geography of the United States
- Chapter Summary Audio CD Programs (in English and Spanish)
- Global Skill Builder CD-ROM
- Holt Researcher CD-ROM: American History
- One-Stop Planner CD-ROM with Test Generator

Video Resources

- The American Nation Video Program (in English and Spanish)
- CNN Presents America: Yesterday and Today, Beginnings to 1914
- CNN Presents America: Yesterday and Today, 1850 to the Present
- CNN Presents America: Yesterday and Today, Modern Times

INTERNET

go.hrw.com FOR STUDENTS

- **Activities/Internet Connect**
- **Interactive templates** for creating newspapers, postcards, and travel brochures
- **Drag-and-drop exercises** to review chapter content with short, fun activities
- **Chapter Web links** for pre-screened, age-appropriate Web sites and current events
- **Holt Researcher Online: American History**
- **Homework Practice Online**
- **HRW World Atlas**
- **HRW State Handbooks**
- **Online Activities**
- **Online Historical Maps and Charts**
- **Online Textbook**
- **Fast Facts**

go.hrw.com FOR TEACHERS

- **American History Teaching Toolkit**
- **Chapter Home Page**
- **Current Events Connections**
- **Directory of Social Studies Web Sites**
- **Internet Connect Activities Homepage**
- **Portfolio and Performance Rubrics**
- **Sample Reading Strategies Exercises**
- **Supreme Court Watch**
- **Teaching Toolkit**
- **Writing Models**

Contents

An astrolabe

American Beginnings
Prehistory–1900

U·N·I·T 2

A Nation Transformed
1860–1910 158

THE GRANGER COLLECTION, NEW YORK

Thomas Edison's team at Menlo Park

A telegraph machine

Immigrant passport

The first transcontinental railroad, celebrated above, was completed in 1869 using tools such as these.

U·N·I·T 3

A World Power

U.S. forces in the Battle of Manila Bay

Prohibition items

A World War I German airplane

Herbert Hoover 1928 campaign button

President Roosevelt speaks to the American people.

A 1942 Packard

Rosie the Riveter

Berlin Airlift patch

TV Guide magazine from the 1950s

Button commemorating
the March on Washington

Primary Sources

The Homecoming
by Norman Rockwell

History Makers Speak

Sacagawea with Lewis and Clark

History Makers Speak **continued**

Ida Tarbell

★ PRIMARY SOURCE ★

***Huey Long's
Share-Our-Wealth Society***

★ HISTORICAL DOCUMENTS ★

The Emancipation Proclamation

★ INTERPRETING POLITICAL CARTOONS ★

History and Your World

Political cartoon depicting corruption in President Ulysses S. Grant's administration

▶ WHY IT MATTERS TODAY

Many important historical places in the United States have been protected and preserved. Use **CNNfyi.com** or other **current events** sources to find out about a historical site in the United States today. Record your findings in your journal.

CNNfyi.com

History and Your World

continued

Navajo Code Talkers Henry Bake and George Kirk operate a radio behind enemy lines in the Solomon Islands.

Then and Now

Basketball player Chamique Holdsclaw

Changing Ways

Technology then and now

Interdisciplinary Connections

AMERICA'S Geography

AMERICAN ARTS

AMERICAN Letters

Science & Technology

Early frigate

Historical Highlights

Traveling minister of the American West

Technology Activities

Research on the ROM

Juan Seguín

internet connect

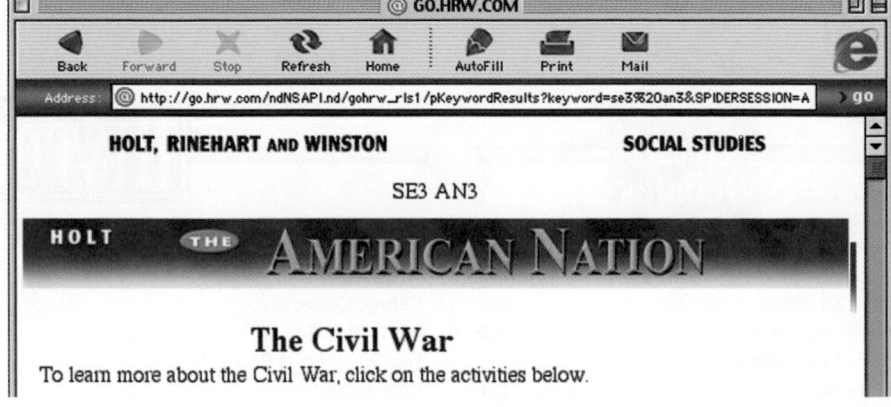

Skill-Building Activities

Skill-Building Strategies

Building Social Studies Skills

BUILDING YOUR PORTFOLIO

In this cartoon President Roosevelt is shown as a ventriloquist whose dummy refuses to cooperate.

Maps

Reconstruction in the South, 1868–1877

Learning from Maps The Reconstruction Acts established military districts in the South that would be removed when the southern states drafted new constitutions and adopted the Fourteenth Amendment.

? **REGION** During Reconstruction, which former Confederate state was not part of a military district?

Charts and Graphs

Causes and Effects of Vietnam War

Long-Term Causes
• Fear of communist expansion
• U.S. support of South Vietnam's government

Immediate Causes
• Gulf of Tonkin incident
• Communist attacks against South Vietnam

Vietnam War

Effects
• Many thousands of Americans and Vietnamese killed and injured
• Vietnam united as a communist nation
• Political divisions created in the United States
• Ailments suffered by U.S. veterans

Time Lines

*A pin celebrating
Earth Day 2000*

How to Use Your Textbook

Use the chapter opener to get an overview of the time period.

The Chapter Time Line shows you a comparison of U.S. and global events.

CHAPTER 19

1945–1960

The Cold War

UN medal

1945 World Events
Delegates from 50 nations meet in San Francisco to create the charter for the United Nations.

Poster of Mao Zedong after the Communist victory

1949 World Events
Mao Zedong's Communist forces gain control of most of China.

1952 Business and Finance
After 21 months of operation by federal troops, the U.S. government returns the country's railroads to private control.

1951 Daily Life
Americans organize a hero's welcome for General MacArthur upon his return from Korea.

Robert Rauschenberg's painting Bed

1955 The Arts
Robert Rauschenberg's *Bed* makes an important contribution to American art.

Sputnik

1957 Science and Technology
The Soviet Union launches *Sputnik*, the first artificial satellite, into orbit around Earth.

1958 Science and Technology
Congress establishes the National Aeronautics and Space Administration (NASA).

Francis Gary Powers holds a model of his U-2 spy plane.

1960 World Events
The Paris summit between Soviet premier Khrushchev and President Eisenhower is canceled after the Soviets shoot down a U.S. spy plane.

1945 — 1948 — 1951 — 1954 — 1957 — 1960

1947 Daily Life
Ten people working in the film industry refuse to testify before a House committee and are blacklisted.

A report on alleged Communists in the entertainment industry

1948 Politics
The U.S. Congress passes the European Recovery Act, establishing the Marshall Plan to help stabilize and rebuild Europe.

A cargo of sugar on its way to Europe as part of the Marshall Plan

1953 The Arts
Playwright Arthur Miller writes *The Crucible*, in which he compares McCarthyism to the Salem witch trials.

Arthur Miller's The Crucible

1956 World Events
Egypt seizes the Suez Canal after the United States withdraws support for an Egyptian dam project on the Nile River.

1959 Politics
Soviet premier Nikita Khrushchev visits the United States.

Soviet premier Khrushchev (second from left) visited an American supermarket in 1959.

Build on What You Know

Economic troubles during the 1930s contributed to the rise of dictatorships in Germany, Italy, and Japan. These countries' military expansion and acts of aggression led to World War II. The war destroyed parts of Europe and Asia. In this chapter you will learn that after the war many nations struggled to rebuild their war-torn economies. At the same time, tensions grew between the United States and the Soviet Union.

What's Your Opinion?

Themes Journal Do you agree or disagree with the following statements? Support your point of view in your journal.

Global Relations Rivalry between two powerful nations rarely affects the relationships between other countries.

Citizenship The fears of the majority of Americans often limit the rights of groups that hold unpopular views.

Science, Technology, and Society Americans' fear of technology affects their behavior and is often reflected in the literature and arts of the time.

558 — 559

Build on What You Know bridges the material you have studied in previous chapters with the material you are about to begin. As you read the Build on What You Know feature, take a few minutes to think about the topics that might apply to the chapter you are starting.

What's Your Opinion? puts you in the place of a historian looking at the past. In this feature, you will be asked to respond to three general statements about the chapter. Each statement is tied to one of the key themes of the program. You should respond based on your own knowledge and then record your responses in your journal. There are no right or wrong answers, just your informed opinion.

Use these built-in tools to read for understanding.

Eyewitnesses to History features an interesting episode from American history that shows you that history is not just a collection of facts but a blend of many individual stories and adventures.

Read to Discover questions begin each section of *The American Nation.* These questions serve as your guide as you read through the section. Keep them in mind as you explore the section content.

Define and Identify terms are introduced at the beginning of each section. The terms will be defined in context.

Why It Matters Today is an exciting way for you to make connections between what you are reading in your history book and the world around you. In each section, you will be invited to explore a topic that is relevant to our lives today by using **CNNfyi.com** connections.

The Hollywood Ten.

Interpreting the Visual Record features accompany many of the book's rich images. Pictures are one of the most important primary sources historians can use to help analyze the past. These features invite you to examine the images to interpret their content.

History Makers Speak quotations appear frequently throughout the book. These exciting primary source quotations give you a glimpse into the lives of actual people who made history. Many of these quotations are accompanied by an Analyzing Primary Sources question to help you better interpret the sources and draw inferences about their importance.

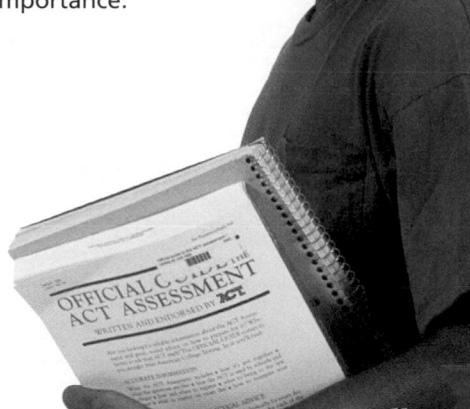

Reading Check questions appear throughout the book to allow you to check your comprehension while you are reading. As you read each section, pause for a moment to consider each Reading Check. If you have trouble answering the question, go back and examine the material you just read.

Use these review tools to pull together all the information you have learned.

Graphic Organizers will help you pull together important information from the section. You can complete the graphic organizer as a study tool to prepare for a test or writing assignment.

Homework Practice Online lets you log on to the go.hrw.com Web site to complete an interactive self-check.

Plus
The Chapter Review with:
- Creating a Time Line
- Writing a Summary
- Understanding Main Ideas
- Reviewing Themes
- Thinking Critically
- Building Social Studies Skills

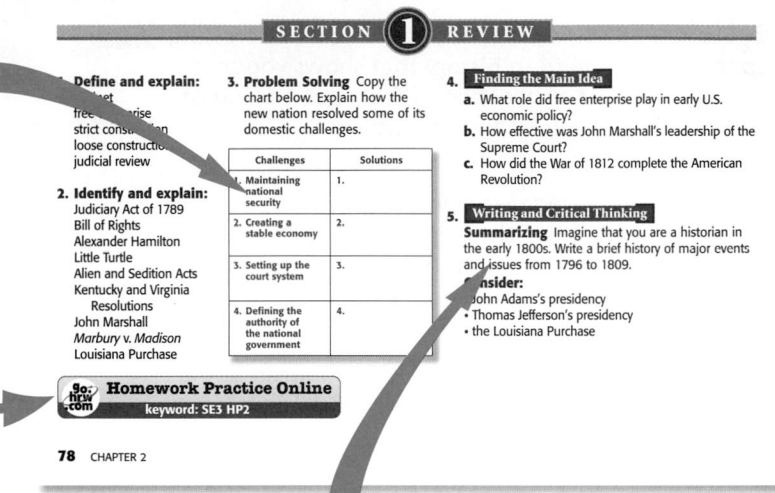

Writing and Critical Thinking activities allow you to explore a section topic in greater depth and to build your skills.

Use these online tools to review and complete online activities.

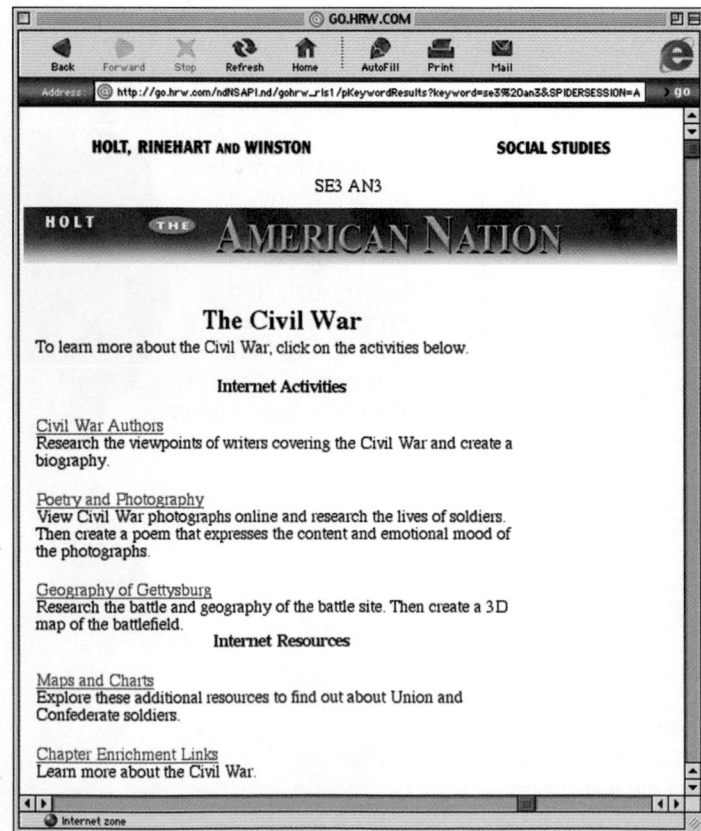

Internet Connect activities are just one part of the world of online learning experiences that awaits you on the **go.hrw.com** Web site. By exploring these online activities, you will take a journey through some of the richest American history materials available on the World Wide Web. You can then use these resources to create real-world projects, such as newspapers, brochures, reports, and even your own Web site!

internet connect

Internet Activity: go.hrw.com
KEYWORD: SE3 AN3

Access the Internet through the HRW Go site to research the geographic distribution of major battles during the Civil War. Then create a three-dimensional model of one of these battles. Your model should represent the terrain, any geographic features (such as rivers, woods or hills) that affected the battle, and any other important factors such as towns or railroads. As a review, pose and answer questions with a partner in which you analyze why the battle was fought at that location.

Themes in American History

The American Nation begins every chapter with a set of theme statements under the heading "What's your opinion?" These statements are drawn from several broad themes central to American history: Geography; Economics; Government; Citizenship; Culture; Science, Technology, and Society; Constitutional Heritage; and Global Relations. As you begin each chapter of *The American Nation,* you will be asked to respond to the theme statements in a general way, based on your own knowledge. At the end of the chapter, you will be asked to respond to more specific questions about the themes, based on the chapter content.

Geography

The Geography theme explores ways in which the nation's vast and diverse geography has played an important role in American history. The theme examines how the development of the nation's resources has helped shape its economy, society, and politics. In addition, the Geography theme traces how public and government attitudes about resources and the environment have changed over time.

Economics

President Calvin Coolidge said in 1925 that "the business of America is business." The Economics theme asks you to explore the relationship between history and economics in the United States. The theme traces the changing relationship between government, business, and labor in America. It examines how the growth of a strong national free-enterprise economic system has influenced the country's domestic and global politics as well as individual lives and American society.

Catalogs display hundreds of goods for consumers.

Government

Even before the nation had won its independence from Great Britain in the Revolution, the founders saw the need to establish a national government. The Government theme asks you to explore the workings of the American system of government—from the Articles of Confederation to the present. This theme also examines the relationships between federal, state, and local governments and how the system is designed to serve the people.

The American West

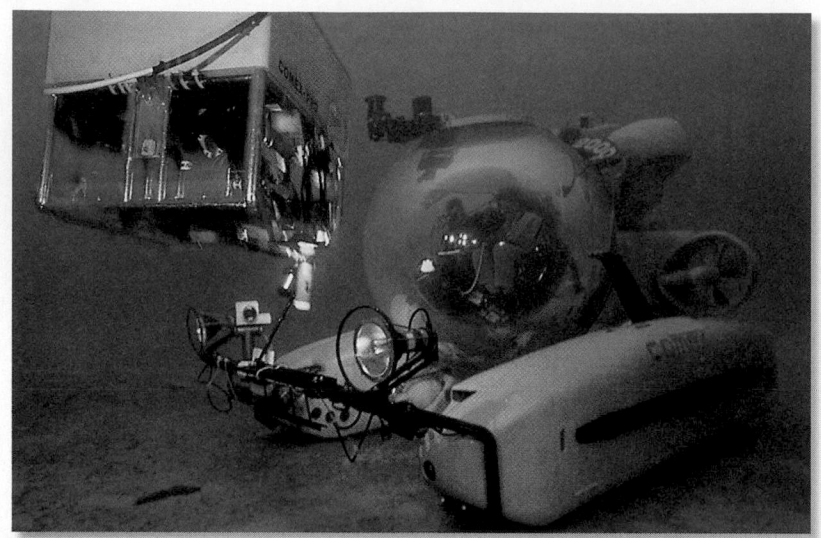

Underwater archaeologists search for sunken ships to learn more about U.S. history.

Citizenship

Throughout our history, Americans have struggled to define, possess, and protect individual rights and personal freedoms, such as the freedom of speech and of religion, the right to vote, and the right to privacy. Americans have also worked to uphold the responsibilities of citizenship that accompany participation in our democracy. The Citizenship theme explores how changing social, economic, and political conditions have influenced the theory and practices of these rights, freedoms, and responsibilities.

Culture

Our nation's rich and unique culture comes from its many ethnic, racial, and religious groups. The Culture theme examines the influences of diverse culture groups, from before the time of the European explorers to recent immigrants from around the world.

Science, Technology, and Society

From the building of the transcontinental railroad and the construction of skyscrapers during the Second Industrial Revolution, to the computers that help you with your school assignments and personal projects today, science and technology have influenced every aspect of our culture and society. The Science, Technology, and Society theme explores scientific and technological developments and their influence on the U.S. economy and life.

Constitutional Heritage

No study of American history would be complete without examining the U.S. Constitution, the document that provides the legal framework for our democratic government. The Constitutional Heritage theme will help you understand the Constitution's origins and how it has evolved through constitutional amendments, Supreme Court rulings, and congressional action. This theme also explores how individuals and different groups in the nations history have influenced the Constitution.

Global Relations

Since the first Asian nomads crossed a land bridge to this continent thousands of years ago, America has been involved in global events. The Global Relations theme invites you to trace ways in which our nation's political, social, and economic development has affected—and been affected by—other countries and their people.

Essential Elements of Geography

History and geography share many elements. History describes important events that have taken place from ancient times until the present day. Geography describes how physical environments affect human events. It also examines how people's actions influence the environment around them. One way to look at geography is to identify essential elements of its study. The following six essential elements, developed from the National Geography Standards, will be used throughout The American Nation:

▶ **The World in Spatial Terms** This essential element refers to the way geographers view the world. They look at where things are and how they are arranged on Earth's surface. For example, geographers might be interested to learn why certain cities developed where they did.

▶ **Places and Regions** Geographers often focus on the physical and human characteristics that make particular parts of Earth special. A region is an area with common characteristics that make it different from surrounding areas. People create regions as a convenient way to study the world. Regions can be large like North America, or small like a neighborhood.

▶ **Physical Systems** Geographers study the physical processes and interactions between four physical systems—Earth's atmosphere, land, water, and life. Physical processes shape and change Earth's physical features and environments.

▶ **Human Systems** As with physical systems, studying human systems can tell geographers much about the world around us. For example, studying population growth, distribution, and movement helps in understanding human events and their effects on the environment.

▶ **Environment and Society** One of the most important topics in geography is how people interact with the environment. People depend on the environment's natural resources for survival. However, human activities can have both positive and negative effects on Earth's environment.

▶ **The Uses of Geography** Historians use geography to understand the past. They look not only at when things happened but where and why they happened. Geography is important to the present as well as the past. People use geography every day to explore how to use Earth's limited resources, such as water and minerals, more effectively and in a way that ensures the success of future generations.

Anasazi homes were built of stone and sun-dried clay bricks. They were built in openings in high cliffs.

WHY HISTORY MATTERS TODAY

> **"H**istory and destiny have made America the leader of the world that would be free. And the world that would be free is looking to us for inspiration."
>
> **—Colin Powell**

Right now, at this very second, somewhere in the United States, someone is making history. It is impossible to know who, or in what way, but the actions of people today may become the history of tomorrow.

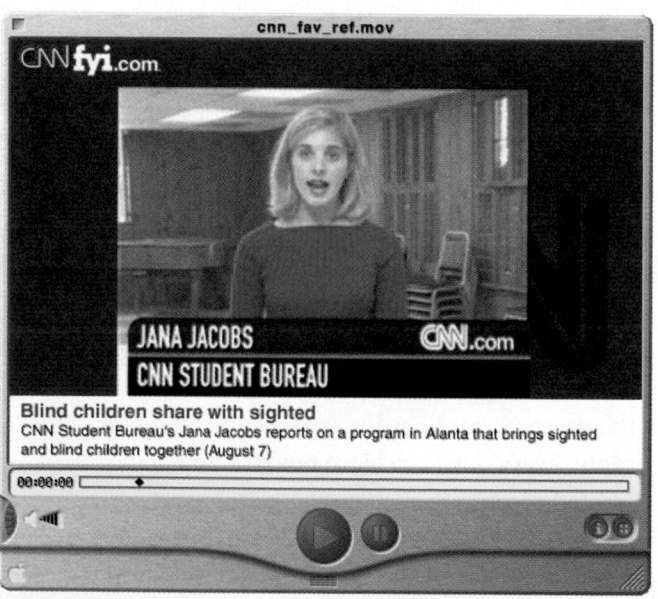

Blind children share with sighted
CNN Student Bureau's Jana Jacobs reports on a program in Alanta that brings sighted and blind children together (August 7)

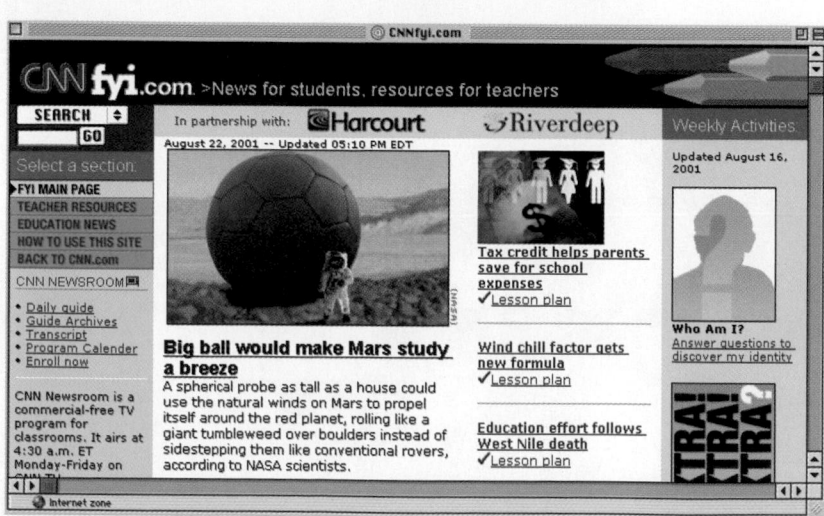

History and Your World

All you need to do is watch or read the news to see history unfolding. How many news stories do you see or hear about ordinary people doing extraordinary things? The Why It Matters Today feature beginning every section of *The American Nation* invites you to use the vast resources of **CNNfyi.com** or other current events sources to examine the links between past and present. Through this feature you will be able to draw connections between what you are studying in your history book and the events that are taking place today.

Anyone Can Be a History Maker

When you think of the word *history,* what comes to mind? Do you picture politicians sitting around a table deciding the future of the nation? Or do you see a long list of dates and boring facts to be memorized? Of course, politicians, dates, and facts are part of history, but there is actually much more to understanding and exploring our past. Our nation has developed through the efforts of many different people, from all backgrounds and walks of life. Many of them were teenagers like yourself. Did you know that teenagers helped settle the West? It's true. For example, teenager Nancy Kelsey was among the first pioneers to arrive in California in 1841.

Student reporters contribute to CNNfyi.com.

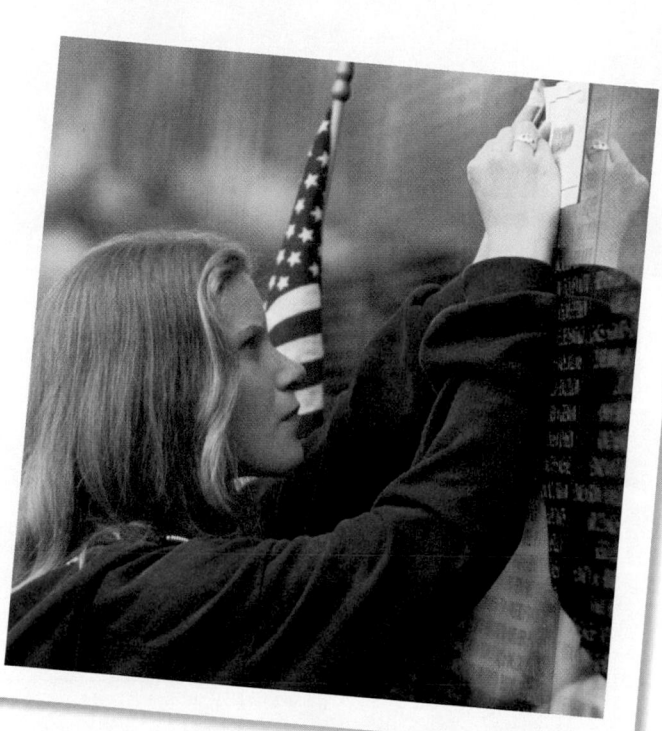

*Student visiting the
Vietnam Veterans Memorial*

History Makes Us
Who We Are

There is no one single "story" in history. Instead, the combined experiences of millions of people across time have come together to form the foundation of American society today.

Teenagers also played a role in the Civil War. Thousands of soldiers, like 15-year-old Thomas Galway, fought in this bloody conflict, which shaped the nation's future. You might also be interested to know that young Americans in the Civilian Conservation Corps played a key role in keeping the nation going during the darkest hours of the Great Depression. These are just a few of the many examples of how people about the same age as yourself have helped shape our nation's past. What contributions do you think your generation will make to our national history?

"So when someone asks you 'Why does history matter today?' you might answer, 'Because in our past, we see a reflection of ourselves.'"

These young people participate in a re-enactment to celebrate the unveiling of the African American Civil War Memorial at Arlington National Cemetery.

Skills Handbook

Critical Thinking

Throughout *The American Nation*, you will be asked to think critically about the events and issues that have shaped U.S. history. Critical thinking is the reasoned judgment of information and ideas. The development of critical thinking skills is essential to effective citizenship. Such skills empower you to exercise your civic rights and responsibilities. Helping you develop critical thinking skills is an important goal of *The American Nation*. The following critical thinking skills appear in the section reviews and chapter reviews of the book.

▶ **Analyzing Information** is the process of breaking something down and examining the relationships between its parts. Analyzing enables you to better understand the whole. For example, to analyze the outcome of the 1876 presidential election, you might study how—since the election results were disputed—both sides had to come to an agreement before Rutherford B. Hayes could become president.

▶ **Sequencing** is the process of placing events in correct chronological order to better understand the historical relationships between these events. You can sequence events in two basic ways: according to absolute or relative chronology. Absolute chronology means that you pay close attention to the actual dates on which events took place. Placing events on a time line would be an example of absolute chronology. Relative chronology refers to the way events relate to one another. To put events in relative order, you need to know which one happened first, which came next, and so forth.

Coat of arms granted to Christopher Columbus

▶ **Categorizing** is the process by which you group things together by the characteristics they have in common. By putting things or events into categories, it is easier to make comparisons and see differences among them.

▶ **Identifying Cause and Effect** is a part of interpreting the relationships between historical events. A *cause* is an action that leads to an event. The outcome of the action is an *effect*. To explain historical events, historians often point out multiple causes and effects. For example, economic and political differences between the North and South, as well as the issue of slavery, brought about the Civil War—which in turn had many far-reaching effects.

Emancipation Proclamation

▶ **Comparing and Contrasting** is examining events, situations, or points of view for their similarities and differences. *Comparing* focuses on both the similarities and the differences. *Contrasting* focuses only on the differences. For example, a comparison of early Irish and Chinese immigrants to the United States shows that both groups were recruited to help build railroads and that both groups faced discrimination. In contrast, language and racial barriers generally proved more of a problem for Chinese immigrants.

U.S. military railroad engine

Finding the Main Idea is combining and sifting through information to determine what is most important. Historical writing often uses many examples and details to support the author's main ideas. Throughout *The American Nation,* you will find numerous Reading Checks and questions in section reviews to help you focus on the main ideas in the text.

Summarizing is the process of taking a large amount of information and boiling it down into a short and clear statement. Summarizing is particularly useful when you need to give a brief account of a longer story or event. For example, the story of the Battle of Gettysburg during the Civil War is an exciting but detailed one. Many different events came together to make up this story. You could summarize these events by saying something like, "In 1863 General Lee led his army north into Pennsylvania where he met the Union forces under General Meade at Gettysburg. After several days of bloody fighting, Lee was forced to retreat. Lee's defeat at Gettysburg was a major turning point in the war."

Lee's surrender at Appomattox Courthouse

Making Generalizations and Predictions is the process of interpreting information to form more general statements and to guess about what will happen next. A *generalization* is a broad statement that holds true for a variety of historical events or situations. Making generalizations can help you see the "big picture" of historical events, rather than just focusing on details. It is very important, however, that when making generalizations you

try not to include situations that do not fit the statement. When this occurs, you run the risk of creating a stereotype, or overgeneralization. A *prediction* is an educated guess about an outcome. When you read history, you should always be asking yourself questions like, "What will happen next? If this person does this, what will that mean for . . . ?", and so on. These types of questions help you draw on information you already know to see patterns throughout history.

Drawing Inferences and Conclusions is forming possible explanations for an event, a situation, or a problem. When you make an *inference,* you take the information you know to be true and come up with an educated guess about what else you think is true about that situation. A *conclusion* is a prediction about the outcome of a situation based on what you already know. Often, you must be prepared to test your inferences and conclusions against new evidence or arguments. For example, a historian might conclude that women's leadership roles in the abolition movement led to the development of the early women's movement. The historian would then organize the evidence needed to support this conclusion and challenge other arguments.

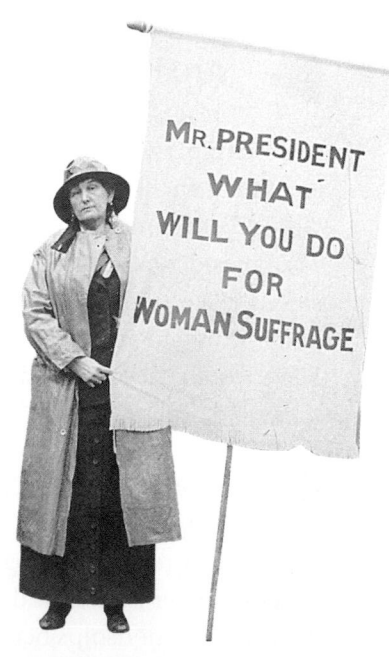

Women's suffrage supporter

Identifying Points of View is the process of identifying factors that influence the outlook of an individual or group. A person's point of view includes beliefs and attitudes that are shaped by factors such as age, gender, religion, race, and economic status. This critical thinking skill helps you examine why people see things as they do, and it reinforces the realization that people's views may change over time or with a change in circumstances.

Supporting a Point of View involves choosing a viewpoint on a particular event or issue and arguing persuasively for that position. Your argument should be well organized and based on specific evidence that supports the point of view you have chosen. Supporting a point of view often involves working with controversial or emotional issues. For example, you might consider the points of view involved in the struggles between labor unions and businesses in the late 1800s. Whether you choose a position in favor of unions or in favor of businesses, you should state your opinion clearly and give reasons to defend it.

Identifying Bias is the process of evaluating the opinions of others about events or situations. *Bias* is an opinion based on prejudice or strong emotions, rather than fact. It is important to identify bias when looking at historical sources, because biased sources often give you a false sense of what really happened. When looking at both primary and secondary sources, it is always important to keep the author's or speaker's point of view in mind and to adjust your interpretation of the source when you detect any bias.

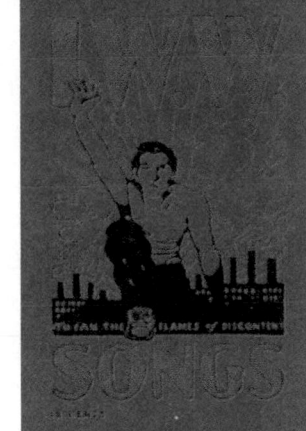

Labor union booklet

Evaluating is assessing the significance or overall importance of something, such as the success of a reform movement, the actions of a president, or the results of a major conflict. You should base your judgment on standards that others will understand and are likely to share. For example, you might consider the outcome of the Mexican War and evaluate its importance to U.S. politics and expansion. You could also evaluate the effect of the war on the peoples already living in the West.

Problem Solving is the process by which you pose workable solutions to difficult situations. The first step in the process is to identify a problem. Next you will need to gather information about the problem, such as its history and the various factors that contribute to the problem. Once you have gathered information, you should list and consider the options for solving the problem. For each of the possible solutions, weigh their advantages and disadvantages and, based on your evaluation, choose and implement a solution. Once the solution has been tried, go back and evaluate the effectiveness of the solution you selected.

Decision Making is the process of reviewing a situation and then making decisions or recommendations for the best possible outcome. To complete the process, first identify a situation that requires a solution. Next, gather information that will help you reach a decision. You may need to do some background research to study the history of the situation. Once you have done your research, identify options that might resolve the situation. For each option, predict what the possible consequences might be if that option were followed. Once you have identified the best option, take action by making a recommendation and following through on any tasks that option requires.

Becoming a Strategic Reader

by Dr. Judith Irvin

Everywhere you look, print is all around us. In fact, you would have a hard time stopping yourself from reading. In a normal day, you might read cereal boxes, movie posters, notes from friends, t-shirts, instructions for video games, song lyrics, catalogs, billboards, information on the Internet, magazines, the newspaper, and much, much more. Each form of print is read differently depending on your purpose for reading. You read a menu differently than the way you read poetry, and a motorcycle magazine is read differently than a letter from a friend. Good readers switch easily from one type of text to another. In fact, they probably do not even think about it, they just do it.

When you read, it is helpful to use a strategy to remember the most important ideas. You can use a strategy before you read to help connect information you already know to the new information you will encounter. Before you read, you can also predict what a text will be about by using a previewing strategy. During the reading you can use a strategy to help you focus on main ideas, and after reading you can use a strategy to help you organize what you learned so that you can remember it later. *The American Nation* was designed to help you more easily understand the ideas you read. Important reading strategies employed in *The American Nation* include the following:

1 Methods to help you **anticipate** what is to come

2 Tools to help you **preview and predict** what the text will be about

3 Ways to help you **use and analyze visual information**

4 Ideas to help you **organize the information** you have learned

1. Anticipate Information

How Can I Use Information I Already Know to Help Me Understand What a New Chapter Will Be About?

Anticipating what a new chapter will be about helps you connect the upcoming information to what you already know. By drawing on your background knowledge, you can build a bridge to the new material.

1 Each chapter of *The American Nation* asks you to explore the main themes of the chapter before you start reading by forming opinions based on your current knowledge.

What's Your Opinion?

Themes Journal *Do you agree or disagree with the following statements? Support your point of view in your journal.*

Geography Geography has a significant impact on the way wars are fought.

Economics Wars contribute to a nation's economic development.

Citizenship Americans choose to interpret the meaning of individual liberty in different ways.

Create a chart like this one to help you analyze the statements.

A Before Reading Agree/Disagree		B After Reading Agree/Disagree
2	Geography has a significant impact on the way wars are fought.	**4**
	Wars contribute to a nation's economic development	
	Americans choose to interpret the meaning of individual liberty in different ways.	

3 Read the text and discuss with classmates.

5 You can also refine your knowledge by answering the Reviewing Themes questions in the chapter review.

Anticipating Information

▶ **Step 1** Identify the major concepts of the chapter. In *The American Nation*, these are presented in the **What's Your Opinion?** feature at the beginning of each chapter.

▼

Step 2 Agree or disagree with each of the statements and record your opinions in your journal.

▼

Step 3 Read the text and discuss your responses with your classmates.

▼

Step 4 After reading the chapter, revisit the statements and respond to them again based on what you have learned.

▼

Step 5 Go back and check your knowledge by answering the **Reviewing Themes** questions in the chapter review.

Reviewing Themes

1. **Geography** What role did geography play in helping the North win the war?
2. **Economics** How did the economic resources of the North and the South affect the war?
3. **Citizenship** How did the draft challenge ideas about individual liberty in the North and in the South?

2. Preview and Predict

How Can I Figure out What the Text Is about before I Even Start Reading a Section?

Previewing and **predicting** are good methods to help you understand the text. If you take the time to preview and predict before you read, the text will make more sense to you during your reading.

1 Usually, your teacher will set the purpose for reading. After reading some new information, you may be asked to write a summary, take a test, or complete some other type of activity.

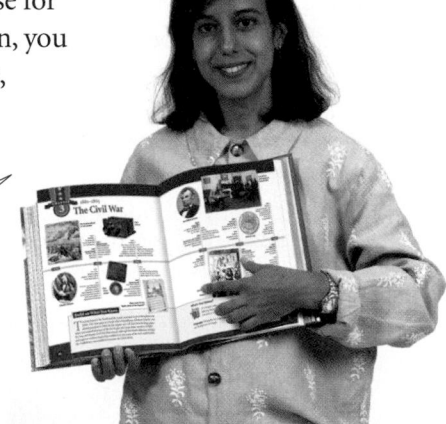

"After reading about the Civil War, you will work with a partner to create a historical museum exhibit describing…"

2 As you preview the text, use *graphic signals* such as headings, subheadings, and boldfaced type to help you determine what is important in the text. Each section of *The American Nation* opens by giving you important clues to help you preview the material.

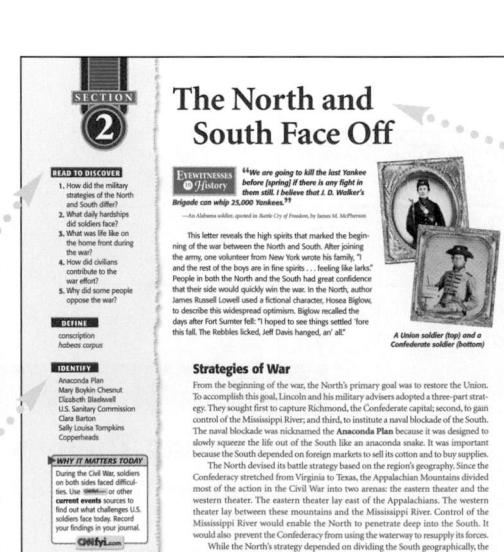

Read to Discover questions give you clues as to the section's main ideas.

Define and Identify terms let you know the key vocabulary you will encounter in the section.

Looking at the section's **main heading** and **subheadings** can give you an idea of what is to come.

3 Other tools that can help you in previewing are **signal words.** These words prepare you to think in a certain way. For example, when you see words such as *similar to, same as,* or *different from,* you know that the text will probably compare and contrast two or more ideas. Signal words indicate how the ideas in the text relate to each other. Look at the list below of some of the most common signal words grouped by the type of text structures they indicate.

Signal Words

Cause and Effect	Compare and Contrast	Description	Problem and Solution	Sequence or Chronological Order
• because	• different from	• for instance	• the question is	• not long after
• since	• same as	• for example	• a solution	• next
• consequently	• similar to	• such as	• one answer is	• then
• this led to . . . so	• as opposed to	• to illustrate		• initially
• if . . . then	• instead of	• in addition		• before
• nevertheless	• although	• most importantly		• after
• accordingly	• however	• another		• finally
• because of	• compared with	• furthermore		• preceding
• as a result of	• as well as	• first, second . . .		• following
• in order to	• either . . . or			• on (date)
• may be due to	• but			• over the years
• for this reason	• on the other hand			• today
• not only . . . but	• unless			• when

4 Learning something new requires that you connect it in some way with something you already know. This means you have to think before you read and while you read. You may want to use a chart like this one to remind yourself of the information already familiar to you and to come up with questions you want answered in your reading. The chart will also help you organize your ideas after you have finished reading.

What I know	What I want to know	What I learned

3. Use and Analyze Visual Information

How Can All the Pictures, Maps, Graphs, and Time Lines with the Text Help Me Be a Stronger Reader?

Analyzing Information

▶ **Step ❶** As you preview the text, ask yourself how the visual information relates to the text.

▼

Step ❷ Generate questions based on the visual information.

▼

Step ❸ After reading the text, go back and review the visual information again.

Step ❹ Make connections to what you already know.

Using visual information can help you understand and remember the information presented in *The American Nation*. Good readers form a picture in their mind when they read. The pictures, charts, graphs, cartoons, time lines, and diagrams that occur throughout *The American Nation* are placed strategically to increase your understanding.

❶ You might ask yourself questions like:

Why did the author include this information with text? What details about this visual are mentioned in the text?

After you have read the text, see if you can answer your own questions.

❷

1. Where are the people in this painting?

2. Why did the artist include them?

3. How might this painting encourage Americans to visit Yellowstone National Park?

❸ After reading, take another look at the visual information.

❹ Try to make connections to what you already know.

4. Organize Information

Once I Learn New Information, How Do I Keep It All Straight So That I Will Remember It?

To help you remember what you have read, you need to find a way of **organizing information.** Two good ways of doing this are by using graphic organizers and concept maps. **Graphic organizers** help you understand important relationships—such as cause-and-effect, compare/contrast, sequence of events, and problem/solution—within the text. **Concept maps** provide a useful tool to help you focus on the text's main ideas and organize supporting details.

Identifying Relationships

Using graphic organizers will help you recall important ideas from the section. They are also study tools you can use to prepare for a quiz or test or to help with a writing assignment. Some of the most common types of graphic organizers are shown below.

▶ Cause and Effect

Events in history cause people to react in certain ways. Cause-and-effect patterns show the relationship between results and the ideas or events that made the results occur. You may want to represent cause-and effect relationships as one cause leading to multiple effects,

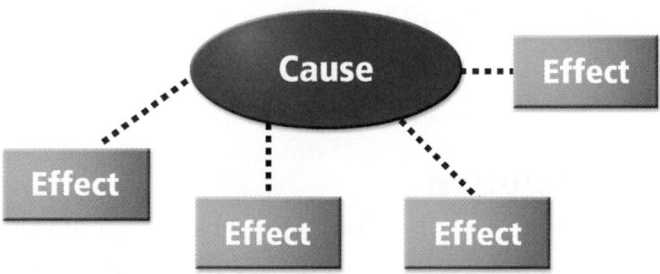

or as a chain of cause-and-effect relationships.

Constructing Graphic Organizers

▶ **Step 1** Preview the text, looking for signal words and the main idea.

▼

Step 2 Form a hypothesis as to which type of graphic organizer would work best to display the information presented.

▼

Step 3 Work individually or with your classmates to create a visual representation of what you read.

▶ Comparing and Contrasting

Graphic organizers are often useful when you are comparing or contrasting information. Compare-and-contrast diagrams point out similarities and differences between two concepts or ideas.

▶ Sequencing

Keeping track of dates and the order in which events took place is essential to understanding history. Sequence or chronological-order diagrams show events or ideas in the order in which they happened.

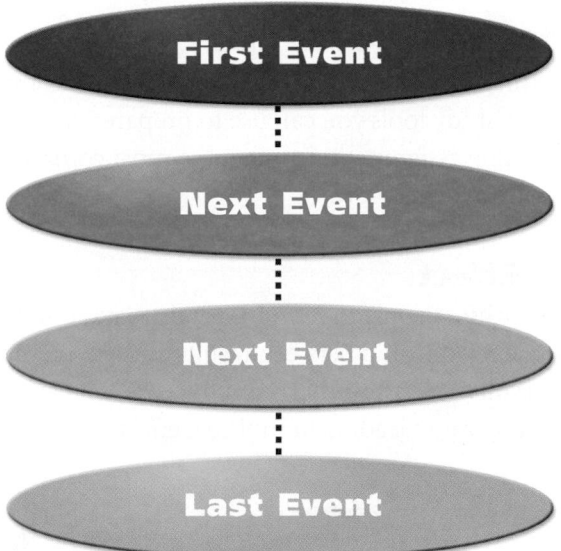

▶ Problem and Solution

Problem/solution patterns identify at least one problem, offer one or more solutions to the problem, and explain or predict outcomes of the solutions.

Identifying Main Ideas and Supporting Details

One special type of graphic organizer is the concept map. A concept map, sometimes called a semantic map, allows you to zero in on the most important points of the text. The map is made up of lines, boxes, circles, and/or arrows. It can be as simple or as complex as you need it to be to accurately represent the text.

Here are a few examples of concept maps you might use.

Constructing Concept Maps

▶ **Step ❶** Preview the text, looking for what type of structure might be appropriate to display a concept map.

▼

Step ❷ Taking note of the headings, boldfaced type, and text structure, sketch a concept map you think could best illustrate the text.

▼

Step ❸ Using boxes, lines, arrows, circles, or any shapes you like, display the ideas of the text in the concept map.

Standardized Test–Taking Strategies

A number of times throughout your school career, you may be asked to take standardized tests. These tests are designed to demonstrate the content and skills you have learned. It is important to keep in mind that in most cases the best way to prepare for these tests is to pay close attention in class and to take every opportunity to improve your general social studies, reading, writing, and mathematical skills.

Tips for Taking the Test

1. Be sure that you are well rested.
2. Be on time and be sure that you have the necessary materials.
3. Listen to the instructions of the teacher.
4. Read directions and questions carefully.
5. **DON'T STRESS!** Just remember what you have learned in class and you should do well.

► **Practice the Strategies at go.hrw.com**

go.hrw.com
Standardized Test–Prep Online
keyword: SE3 STP

Tackling Social Studies

The social studies portions of many standardized tests are designed to test your knowledge of the content and skills that you have been studying in one or more of your social studies classes. Specific objectives for the test vary, but some of the most common include:

1. Demonstrate an understanding of issues and events in history.
2. Demonstrate an understanding of geographic influences on historical issues and events.
3. Demonstrate an understanding of economic and social influences on historical issues and events.
4. Demonstrate an understanding of political influences on historical issues and events.
5. Use critical thinking skills to analyze social studies information.

Standardized tests usually contain multiple-choice and may also contain open-ended questions. The multiple-choice items will often be based on maps, tables, charts, graphs, pictures, cartoons, and/or reading passages and documents.

Tips for Answering Multiple-Choice Questions

1. If there is a written or visual piece accompanying the multiple-choice question, pay careful attention to the title, author, and date.
2. Then read through or glance over the content of the piece accompanying the question.
3. Next, read the multiple-choice question for its general intent. Then reread it carefully, looking for words that give clues. For example, words such as *most* or *best* tell you that there may be several correct answers, but you should look for the most appropriate answer.

4. Always read all of the possible answer choices even if the first one seems like the correct answer. There may be a better choice farther down in the list.

5. Reread the accompanying information (if any is included) carefully to determine the answer to the question. Again, note the title, author, and date of primary-source selections. The answer will rarely be stated exactly as it appears in the primary source, so you will need to use your critical thinking skills to read between the lines.

6. Use your knowledge of the time in history or person involved to help limit the answer choices.

7. Finally, re-read the question and selected answer to be sure that you made the best choice and that you marked it correctly on the answer sheet.

Strategies for Success

There are many strategies you can use to feel more confident about answering questions on social studies standardized tests. Here are a few suggestions:

1. Adopt an acronym—a word formed from the first letters of other words—that you will use for analyzing a document or visual that accompanies a question.

Helpful Acronyms

For a document, use **SOAPS**, which stands for

S Subject

O Occasion

A Audience

P Purpose

S Speaker/author

For a picture, cartoon, map, or other visual piece of information, use **OPTIC**, which stands for

O Overview

P Parts (labels or details of the visual)

T Title

I Interrelations (how the different parts of the visual work together)

C Conclusion (what the visual means)

2. Form visual images of maps and try to draw them from memory. The standardized test will most likely include important maps from the time period and subjects you have been studying. For example, in modern U.S. history, be able to see in your mind's eye such things as where the United States fought battles during the Spanish-American War, World War I, World War II, the Korean War, and the War in Vietnam; and what land the Great Plains covered. Know major physical features, such as the Mississippi River, the Appalachian and Rocky Mountains, the Great Plains, and the various regions of the United States and be able to place them on a map.

3. When you have finished studying any historical era, try to think of who or what might be important enough for the test. You may want to keep your ideas in a notebook to refer to when it is almost time for the test.

4. Pay particular attention to the Constitution and its development. Many standardized tests contain questions about this all-important document and the period during which it was written. Questions may include Magna Carta, the English Bill of Rights, the Declaration of Independence, and *Common Sense,* as well as many other important historical documents.

5. For the skills area of the tests, practice putting major events and personalities in order in your mind. Sequencing people and events by dates can become a game you play with a friend who also has to take the test. Always ask yourself "why" this event is important.

6. Follow the tips under Ready for Reading on the next page when you encounter a reading passage in social studies, but remember that what you have learned about history can help you answer reading-comprehension questions.

Ready for Reading

The main goal of the reading sections of most standardized tests is to determine your understanding of different aspects of a reading passage. Basically, if you can grasp the main idea and the author's purpose, then pay attention to the details and vocabulary so that you are able to draw inferences and conclusions, you will do well on the test.

Tips for Answering Multiple-Choice Questions

1. Read the passage as if you were not taking a test.
2. Look at the big picture. Ask yourself questions like, "What is the title?", "What do the illustrations or pictures tell me?", and "What is the author's purpose?"
3. Read the questions. This will help you know what information to look for.
4. Re-read the passage, underlining information related to the questions.
5. Go back to the questions and try to answer each one in your mind before looking at the answers.
6. Read all the answer choices and eliminate the ones that are obviously incorrect.

Types of Multiple Choice Questions

1. **Main Idea** This is the most important point of the passage. After reading the passage, locate and underline the main idea.
2. **Significant Details** You will often be asked to recall details from the passage. Read the question and underline the details as you read. But remember that the correct answers do not always match the wording of the passage precisely.
3. **Vocabulary** You will often need to define a word within the context of the passage. Read the answer choices and plug them into the sentence to see what fits best.
4. **Conclusion and Inference** There are often important ideas in the passage that the author does not state directly. Sometimes you must consider multiple parts of the passage to answer the question. If answers refer to only one or two sentences or details in the passage, they are probably incorrect.

Tips for Answering Short-Answer Questions

1. Read the passage in its entirety, paying close attention to the main events and characters. Jot down information you think is important.
2. If you cannot answer a question, skip it and come back later.
3. Words such as *compare, contrast, interpret, discuss,* and *summarize* appear often in short answer questions. Be sure you have a complete understanding of each of these words.
4. To help support your answer, return to the passage and skim the parts you underlined.
5. Organize your thoughts on a separate sheet of paper. Write a general statement with which to begin. This will be your topic statement.
6. When writing your answer, be precise but brief. Be sure to refer to details in the passage in your answer.

Targeting Writing

On many standardized tests, you will occasionally be asked to write an essay. In order to write a concise essay, you must learn to organize your thoughts before you begin writing the actual composition. This keeps you from straying too far from the essay's topic.

Tips for Answering Composition Questions

1. Read the question carefully.

2. Decide what kind of essay you are being asked to write. Essays usually fall into one of the following types: persuasive, classificatory, compare/contrast, or "how to." To determine the type of essay, ask yourself questions like, "Am I trying to persuade my audience?", "Am I comparing or contrasting ideas?", or "Am I trying to show the reader how to do something?"

3. Pay attention to key words, such as *compare, contrast, describe, advantages, disadvantages, classify,* or *speculate.* They will give you clues as to the structure that your essay should follow.

4. Organize your thoughts on a separate sheet of paper. You will want to come up with a general topic sentence that expresses your main idea. Make sure this sentence addresses the question. You should then create an outline or some type of graphic organizer to help you organize the points that support your topic sentence.

5. Write your composition using complete sentences. Also, be sure to use correct grammar, spelling, punctuation, and sentence structure.

6. Be sure to proofread your essay once you have finished writing.

Gearing up for Math

On most standardized tests you will be asked to solve a variety of mathematical problems that draw on the skills and information you have learned in class. If math problems sometimes give you difficulty, use the tips below to help you.

Tips for Solving Math Problems

1. Decide what the goal of the question is. Read or study the problem carefully and determine what information must be found.

2. Locate the factual information. Decide what information represents key facts—the ones you must use to solve the problem. You may also find facts you do not need to reach your solution. In some cases, you may determine that more information is needed to solve the problem. If so, ask yourself, "What assumptions can I make about this problem?" or "Do I need a formula to help solve this problem?"

3. Decide what strategies you might use to solve the problem, how you might use them, and what form your solution will be in. For example, will you need to create a graph or chart? Will you need to solve an equation? Will your answer be in words or numbers? By knowing what type of solution you should reach, you may be able to eliminate some of the choices.

4. Apply your strategy to solve the problem and compare your answer to the choices.

5. If the answer is still not clear, read the problem again. If you had to make calculations to reach your answer, use estimation to see if your answer makes sense.

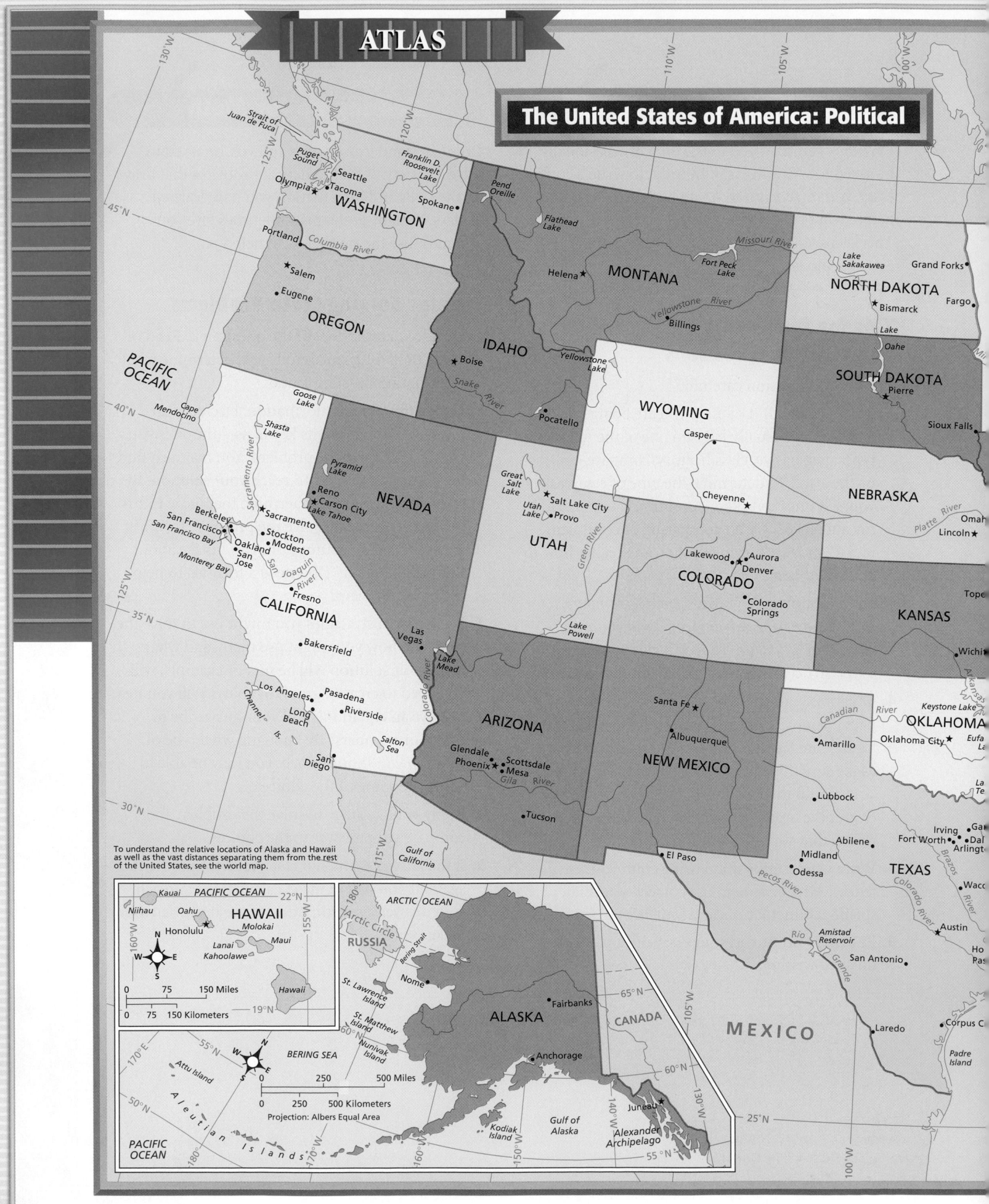

ATLAS

The United States of America: Political

To understand the relative locations of Alaska and Hawaii as well as the vast distances separating them from the rest of the United States, see the world map.

PACIFIC OCEAN

Strait of Juan de Fuca

Puget Sound

Seattle
Olympia ★ Tacoma
Spokane

WASHINGTON

Franklin D. Roosevelt Lake

Portland
Columbia River

Salem ★
Eugene

OREGON

Cape Mendocino

Goose Lake

Shasta Lake

Pyramid Lake

Reno
Carson City
Lake Tahoe

Sacramento River

Berkeley
San Francisco
San Francisco Bay
Oakland
San Jose
Stockton
Modesto
Sacramento

Monterey Bay

San Joaquin River

Fresno

CALIFORNIA

Bakersfield

NEVADA

Los Angeles
Pasadena
Long Beach
Riverside

Salton Sea

San Diego

"Channel" Is.

Las Vegas

Lake Mead

Colorado River

Gulf of California

ARIZONA

Glendale
Phoenix ★ Scottsdale
Mesa
Gila River

Tucson

Pend Oreille

Flathead Lake

Helena ★

MONTANA

Missouri River

Fort Peck Lake

IDAHO

Boise ★

Yellowstone River

Yellowstone Lake

Snake River

Billings

Pocatello

Great Salt Lake

Salt Lake City ★
Utah Lake Provo

UTAH

Green River

Lake Powell

WYOMING

Casper

Cheyenne ★

Lake Sakakawea

NORTH DAKOTA

Bismarck ★

Lake Oahe

SOUTH DAKOTA

Pierre ★

Sioux Falls

NEBRASKA

Platte River

Omaha
Lincoln ★

COLORADO

Lakewood
Aurora
Denver ★

Colorado Springs

KANSAS

Topeka

Wichita

Santa Fe ★

Albuquerque

NEW MEXICO

El Paso

Canadian River

Arkansas River

Keystone Lake

OKLAHOMA

Amarillo

Oklahoma City ★

Eufaula Lake

Lubbock

Abilene

Midland
Odessa

Pecos River

TEXAS

Irving
Fort Worth
Arlington
Dallas
Garland

Waco

Brazos River

Colorado River

Austin

San Antonio

Rio Grande

Amistad Reservoir

Laredo

MEXICO

Corpus Christi

Padre Island

Ho Pas

La Te

Kauai
Niihau
Oahu
Honolulu ★
Lanai
Kahoolawe
Molokai
Maui

HAWAII

PACIFIC OCEAN

22°N

19°N

0   75   150 Miles
0   75   150 Kilometers

ARCTIC OCEAN

Arctic Circle

RUSSIA

Bering Strait

Nome

St. Lawrence Island

St. Matthew Island

Nunivak Island

Fairbanks

ALASKA

CANADA

Anchorage

Kodiak Island

Gulf of Alaska

Juneau ★

Alexander Archipelago

Aleutian Islands

Attu Island

BERING SEA

0   250   500 Miles
0   250   500 Kilometers

Projection: Albers Equal Area

PACIFIC OCEAN

65°N

60°N

55°N

25°N

CANADA

MINNESOTA
Duluth

Lake Superior

MICHIGAN

Lake Huron

WISCONSIN
Minneapolis
St. Paul

Madison
Milwaukee

IOWA
Cedar Rapids
Davenport
Des Moines

Rockford
Chicago

Grand Rapids
Lansing
Jackson
Ann Arbor

Flint
Detroit

Lake Michigan

Lake Ontario
Buffalo   Rochester   Syracuse
Albany

MAINE
Augusta
Burlington   Montpelier   Portland
Lake Champlain
VT.   N.H.
Concord
Manchester

MASS.   Boston
Springfield   Worcester
Hartford   Providence   Cape Cod
CONN.   R.I.
New Haven   Long Island Sound

NEW YORK

Lake Erie

Cleveland   Youngstown   Akron

Peoria

ILLINOIS
Springfield

Gary   South Bend
Fort Wayne

INDIANA
Indianapolis

Toledo

OHIO
Columbus

Dayton
Cincinnati

PENNSYLVANIA   Allentown
Pittsburgh   Harrisburg
Philadelphia

Newark   New York City
Yonkers

Trenton
N.J.

Hudson R.
Susquehanna River

Missouri River

Independence   St. Louis
Lake of the Ozarks   Jefferson City

Kansas City

MISSOURI
Springfield

Fayetteville

ARKANSAS
Little Rock

Louisville   Frankfort
Evansville   Lexington
Ohio River

KENTUCKY

Lake Barkley

Kentucky Lake

Nashville   Knoxville

TENNESSEE
Chattanooga

Memphis

Mississippi River

WEST VIRGINIA
Charleston

VIRGINIA
Richmond

Roanoke   Newport News   Norfolk

Baltimore
MD.   Dover
Arlington   Annapolis   Delaware Bay
Alexandria   Washington, D.C.
DELAWARE

Chesapeake Bay

Cape Hatteras

ATLANTIC OCEAN

Winston-Salem   Greensboro   Durham
Raleigh

NORTH CAROLINA
Charlotte

SOUTH
Columbia
CAROLINA

Huntsville

Atlanta

Charleston

MISSISSIPPI

Birmingham

ALABAMA

Jackson
Meridian

Montgomery

GEORGIA
Macon
Columbus

Savannah River

Savannah
Sea Islands

Chattahoochee River

Shreveport

LOUISIANA   Baton Rouge
Beaumont
New Orleans

Mobile   Pensacola

Toledo Bend Reservoir

Chandeleur Islands

Tallahassee   Jacksonville

FLORIDA

Orlando   Cape Canaveral

Tampa
St. Petersburg
Lake Okeechobee

Fort Lauderdale
Hialeah   Miami

Cape Sable

Florida Keys   Straits of Florida

Gulf of Mexico

THE BAHAMAS

St. Lawrence River
Lake Erie

Connecticut R.

Long Island

	National capital
	State capitals
	Other cities

Projection: Albers Equal Area

0   250   500 Miles
0   250   500 Kilometers

90° W   85° W   80° W   75° W   70° W   65° W   60° W   50° W

45° N
40° N
35° N
30° N
25° N

65° W

The United States of America: Physical

To understand the relative locations of Alaska and Hawaii, as well as the vast distances separating them from the rest of the United States, see the world map.

PACIFIC OCEAN

Kauai
Niihau
Oahu
Molokai
Lanai
Kahoolawe
Maui
Mauna Kea
(13,796 ft.
4206 m)
Hawaii

22°N
155°W
160°W
19°N

N
W E
S

0   75   150 Miles
0   75   150 Kilometers

ARCTIC OCEAN

Arctic Circle
RUSSIA
Bering Strait
St. Lawrence Island
St. Matthew Island
Nunivak Island
Kuskokwim River
BROOKS RANGE
Yukon River
Tanana River
ALASKA RANGE
Mount McKinley
(20,320 ft.
6194 m)
CANADA

180°
65°N
60°N
55°N

N
W E
S

BERING SEA

Attu Island
170°E
55°N
50°N

0   250   500 Miles
0   250   500 Kilometers

Projection: Albers Equal Area

PACIFIC OCEAN

Aleutian Islands
Kodiak Island
Gulf of Alaska
Alexander Archipelago

170°W
180°
160°W
150°W
140°W
130°W

PACIFIC OCEAN

Strait of Juan de Fuca
Puget Sound
Mount Rainier (14,410 ft. 4392 m)
Columbia River
Cape Mendocino
Klamath River
Shasta Lake
Goose Lake
Sacramento River
San Francisco Bay
Monterey Bay
San Joaquin River
CENTRAL VALLEY
SIERRA NEVADA
Pyramid Lake
Lake Tahoe
Mount Whitney (14,494 ft. 4419 m)
DEATH VALLEY
MOJAVE DESERT
Channel Islands
Salton Sea
IMPERIAL VALLEY
Colorado River

COAST RANGES
CASCADE RANGE
COLUMBIA PLATEAU
COAST RANGES

Franklin D. Roosevelt Lake
Pend Oreille
Flathead Lake
Clark Fork
BITTERROOT RANGE
Salmon River
SALMON RIVER MTS.
SAWTOOTH MTS.
Snake River
LEWIS RANGE

GREAT BASIN
Great Salt Lake
Utah Lake
WASATCH RANGE
UINTA MTS.
Green River
Lake Powell
GRAND CANYON
Lake Mead
PAINTED DESERT
SONORAN DESERT
Gila River
CONTINENTAL DIVIDE

R O C K Y
M O U N T A I N S
Yellowstone Lake
GRAND TETONS
Gannett Peak (13,804 ft. 4207 m)
CONTINENTAL DIVIDE
WIND RIVER RANGE
FRONT RANGE
Mount Elbert (14,433 ft. 4400 m)
Pikes Peak (14,110 ft. 4301 m)
COLORADO PLATEAU
San Juan River
SAN LUIS VALLEY
SANGRE DE CRISTO MTS.

Milk River
Missouri River
Fort Peck Lake
Yellowstone River
BIGHORN MTS.
Bighorn River
Powder River
Lake Sakakawea
Lake Oahe
BLACK HILLS
Cheyenne River
White River
Niobrara River
North Platte River
South Platte River
Platte River
Republican River
Smoky Hill River
Keystone Lake
Canadian River
Arkansas River

G R E A T
I N T E R I O R
P L A I N S
G U

Red River
James River

MEXICO
Pecos River
Rio Grande
Amistad Reservoir
Nueces River
Brazos River
Colorado River
Falcon Lake
Padre Island
Gulf of California
Gulf of Mexico

Eufaula L.

130°W
125°W
120°W
115°W
110°W
105°W
100°W
45°N
40°N
35°N
30°N
25°N

CANADA

Isle Royale
MESABI RANGE
Lake Superior

Lake Huron

Lake Michigan

Wisconsin River

Mississippi River

Lake Erie

Lake Ontario

Finger Lakes

St. Lawrence River

St. Lawrence Seaway

Lake Champlain

ADIRONDACK MTS.

GREEN MTS.

LONGFELLOW MTS.

WHITE MTS.

Connecticut River

Penobscot River

St. John River

Cape Cod

Long Island Sound
Long Island

CATSKILL MTS.

Hudson R.

Delaware R.

Delaware Bay

Chesapeake Bay

ATLANTIC OCEAN

Allegheny River

Susquehanna River

PLATEAU

MOUNTAINS

ALLEGHENY

APPALACHIAN

Monongahela R.

Potomac River

Kanawha River

James River

Roanoke River

Scioto River

P L A I N S

Illinois River

Des Moines River

Lake of the Ozarks

Wabash River

Ohio River

Kentucky Lake

Lake Barkley

Cumberland River

White River

Mississippi River

Tennessee River

CUMBERLAND PLATEAU

BLUE RIDGE MOUNTAINS

GREAT SMOKY MTS.

PIEDMONT

ATLANTIC COASTAL PLAIN

Pamlico Sound

Cape Hatteras

Coosa River

Tombigbee River

Alabama R.

Chattahoochee River

Oconee River

Savannah River

Altamaha River

Sea Islands

Okefenokee Swamp

K PLATEAU

HITA. MTS.

Pearl River

COASTAL PLAIN

Chandeleur Islands

Mississippi Delta

Gulf of Mexico

FLORIDA PENINSULA

Cape Canaveral

Lake Okeechobee

The Everglades

Cape Sable

Florida Keys

Straits of Florida

THE BAHAMAS

CUBA

Elevation

Feet		Meters
13,120		4,000
6,560		2,000
1,640		500
656		200
(Sea level) 0		0 (Sea level)
Below sea level		Below sea level

Ice cap

SCALE
0   250   500 Miles
0   250   500 Kilometers
Projection: Albers Equal Area

N
W   E
S

The World: Political

ARCTIC OCEAN

GREENLAND (Denmark)

ALASKA (U.S.)

60°N

Aleutian Islands

Nuuk ⊛

Reykjavik ICELA

CANADA

Vancouver • Winnipeg

Ottawa ⊛ • Montreal

NORTH AMERICA Chicago • Toronto • New York City

40°N

UNITED STATES • Washington, D.C. ⊛

ATLANTIC OCEAN

Los Angeles •

Houston • BERMUDA (U.K.)

Rab
Casablanca
MORO

WESTERN SAHARA

Tropic of Cancer

MEXICO Havana ⊛ THE BAHAMAS
CUBA DOMINICAN REPUBLIC
PUERTO RICO (U.S.)

20°N

HAWAII (U.S.)

Mexico City ⊛ JAMAICA HAITI ST. KITTS AND NEVIS
ANTIGUA AND BARBUDA
VIRGIN ISLANDS (U.S., U.K.) DOMINICA
ST. LUCIA BARBADOS
ST. VINCENT AND THE GRENADINES
GRENADA
TRINIDAD AND TOBAGO

MAURITAN

Nouakchott

GUATEMALA BELIZE
Guatemala City ⊛ HONDURAS
EL SALVADOR NICARAGUA
Managua ⊛ PANAMA
COSTA RICA

CAPE VERDE SENEGAL
Dakar ⊛ Ba
GAMBIA
GUINEA-BISSAU GUINEA

PACIFIC

Caracas ⊛
VENEZUELA GUYANA
Georgetown ⊛ SURINAME
Bogotá ⊛ Paramaribo ⊛ FRENCH GUIANA (France)
COLOMBIA

SIERRA LEONE D
LIBERIA

N
W ⊛ E
S

KIRIBATI

0° Equator

OCEAN

Quito ⊛
Galápagos Islands (Ecuador) ECUADOR

SOUTH AMERICA

PERU

BRAZIL

SAMOA AMERICAN SAMOA

• Lima

• Brasília ⊛

BOLIVIA
La Paz ⊛
• Sucre

20°S TONGA

Rio de Janeiro •

Tropic of Capricorn

PARAGUAY

São Paulo •

CHILE

Asunción ⊛

ARGENTINA

URUGUAY

ATLANTIC

Santiago ⊛

Buenos Aires ⊛ • Montevideo ⊛

OCEAN

40°S

FALKLAND ISLANDS (U.K.)
SOUTH GEORGIA (U.K.)
SOUTH SANDW
ISLANDS (U.K.)

60°S
160°W 140°W 120°W 100°W 80°W 60°W 40°W 20°W

Antarctic Circle

⊛ National capital

• Other cities

SCALE: at Equator

0   500   1,000   1,500   2,000 Miles

0   1,000   2,000 Kilometers

Mollweide Projection

ARCTIC OCEAN

RUSSIA

Moscow

Astana

KAZAKHSTAN

60°N

EUROPE

GEORGIA

Ulaanbaatar

MONGOLIA

Harbin

Almaty

ASIA

UZBEKISTAN

Tashkent

KYRGYZSTAN

Istanbul

ARMENIA

Baku

Beijing

NORTH
KOREA

P'yŏngyang

JAPAN

Tokyo

40°N

Ankara

AZERBAIJAN

TURKMENISTAN

Ashgabat

TAJIKISTAN

Tianjin

Seoul

Nagoya

Yokohama

TURKEY

Tehran

Kabul

Islamabad

CHINA

SOUTH
KOREA

Pusan

Osaka

unis

MALTA

CYPRUS

SYRIA

Damascus

IRAN

AFGHANISTAN

Wuhan

Shanghai

rs

TUNISIA

Nicosia

Beirut

Baghdad

Chongqing

Tripoli

Jerusalem

IRAQ

LEBANON

PAKISTAN

Delhi

NEPAL

Kathmandu

Taipei

Alexandria

Amman

KUWAIT

New
Delhi

BHUTAN

TAIWAN

ERIA

Cairo

JORDAN

ISRAEL

BAHRAIN

QATAR

OMAN

Karachi

BANGLADESH

Guangzhou

Hong
Kong

Tropic of Cancer

LIBYA

EGYPT

SAUDI
ARABIA

UNITED ARAB
EMIRATES

Masqat

INDIA

Dhaka

MYANMAR
(BURMA)

Hanoi

20°N

AFRICA

Riyadh

OMAN

Mumbai
(Bombay)

Yangon
(Rangoon)

LAOS

NORTHERN
MARIANAS
(U.S.)

PACIFIC

NIGER

CHAD

Khartoum

ERITREA

YEMEN

THAILAND

VIETNAM

Manila

GUAM (U.S.)

OCEAN

amey

N'Djamena

Asmara

Sanaa

Chennai
(Madras)

Bangkok

CAMBODIA

Phnom Penh

PHILIPPINES

MARSHALL
ISLANDS

NIGERIA

SUDAN

DJIBOUTI

Ho Chi
Minh City

PALAU

Abuja

Addis Ababa

SRI
LANKA

BRUNEI

FEDERATED STATES
OF MICRONESIA

CENTRAL
AFRICAN
REPUBLIC

ETHIOPIA

Colombo

MALAYSIA

Kuala
Lumpur

CAMEROON

SOMALIA

MALDIVES

Singapore

SINGAPORE

Equator

NAURU

KIRIBATI

0°

GABON

REP.
OF
CONGO

UGANDA

RWANDA

KENYA

Nairobi

INDONESIA

PAPUA
NEW
GUINEA

ABINDA
(Angola)

DEMOCRATIC REP.
OF CONGO

BURUNDI

SEYCHELLES

Jakarta

Surabaya

Port Moresby

SOLOMON
ISLANDS

TUVALU

Kinshasa

TANZANIA

Dar es Salaam

Luanda

MALAWI

COMOROS

INDIAN OCEAN

ANGOLA

ZAMBIA

MOZAMBIQUE

FIJI

Lusaka

MADAGASCAR

Harare

VANUATU

20°S

NAMIBIA

ZIMBABWE

Antananarivo

MAURITIUS

NEW CALEDONIA
(Fr.)

Windhoek

BOTSWANA

RÉUNION
(Fr.)

AUSTRALIA

Tropic of Capricorn

Gaborone

Pretoria

Maputo

SWAZILAND

Johannesburg

LESOTHO

SOUTH
AFRICA

Sydney

Canberra

NEW
ZEALAND

Cape Town

Melbourne

Tasmania

Wellington

TARCTICA

20°E 40°E 60°E 80°E 100°E 120°E 140°E 160°E 60°S

Europe

0 250 500 750 Miles

0 250 500 750 Kilometers

Mollweide Projection

Arctic Circle

ICELAND

Reykjavik

SWEDEN

FINLAND

NORWAY

Helsinki

60°N

NORTH
SEA

Oslo

Stockholm

10

St. Petersburg

RUSSIA

DENMARK

9

UNITED
KINGDOM

Copenhagen

RUSSIA

Moscow

Dublin

NETHERLANDS

Amsterdam

8

Minsk

IRELAND

The Hague

Berlin

Warsaw

BELARUS

London

Brussels

GERMANY

POLAND

Kiev

50°N

BELGIUM

1

UKRAINE

Paris

LUXEMBOURG

Vienna

2

Budapest

MOLDOVA

ATLANTIC
OCEAN

Bern

AUSTRIA

Chişinău

SWITZERLAND

LIECHTENSTEIN

4

HUNGARY

ROMANIA

FRANCE

ITALY

5

MONACO

SAN
MARINO

3

Bucharest

ANDORRA

Corsica
(Fr.)

Rome

BULGARIA

BLACK SEA

40°N

Madrid

VATICAN
CITY

7

Tirane

Sofia

PORTUGAL

SPAIN

Balearic
Is. (Sp.)

Sardinia (It.)

ALBANIA

GREECE

Lisbon

MEDITERRANEAN

Sicily

SEA

Athens

Gibraltar (U.K.)

MALTA

Crete

COUNTRY	CAPITAL
1 Czech Republic	Prague
2 Slovakia	Bratislava
3 Slovenia	Ljubljana
4 Croatia	Zagreb
5 Bosnia and Herzegovina	Sarajevo
6 Macedonia	Skopje
7 Yugoslavia	Belgrade
(Serbia and Montenegro)	
8 Lithuania	Vilnius
9 Latvia	Riga
10 Estonia	Tallinn

American Beginnings

CHAPTER 1
The New Nation

As Paleo-Indians were populating North and South America, Asian and African kingdoms formed profitable trade networks. In the 1500s, competition for new trade routes led European countries to establish American colonies. In 1776 thirteen of Britain's North American colonies declared their independence. After winning the Revolutionary War, Americans created a new central government under the U.S. Constitution.

CHAPTER 2
The Expanding Nation

Under the new U.S. Constitution, George Washington became the nation's first president in 1789. During the following decades the nation experienced the rise of political parties and a second war with Britain. Differences between the North and South increased, when the North began to industrialize. As Americans moved westward, tensions—and eventually conflicts—increased over the spread of slavery.

American Beginnings
Prehistory–1900

Dennis Malone Carter's painting depicts Union patriot Barbara Frietschie opposing Confederate forces by flying the U.S. flag outside her home in Frederick, Maryland.

CHAPTER 3 — The Civil War

The Civil War began in April 1861, when Confederate forces attacked Fort Sumter in South Carolina. Southern forces were able to win the early battles of the war. Ultimately, however, the North's advantage in population and economic resources allowed Union forces to defeat the Confederacy. In April 1865 the Confederate Army surrendered to the Union Army. The Civil War devastated both sides. The Thirteenth Amendment, which was ratified in December 1865, formally abolished the institution of slavery.

CHAPTER 4 — Reconstruction and the New South

After the Civil War, the United States had to rebuild its society and political system to assimilate many freed slaves. The Republican-led Congress passed legislation to help former slaves and to protect the rights of African Americans. African Americans eagerly participated in Reconstruction. However, many white people in the United States objected to African American rights and Reconstruction. In the 1870s, Reconstruction gradually slowed as a depression overtook the country. Jim Crow laws and the Supreme Court's decision in *Plessy v. Ferguson* helped to create two societies—black and white, separate and unequal—in the South.

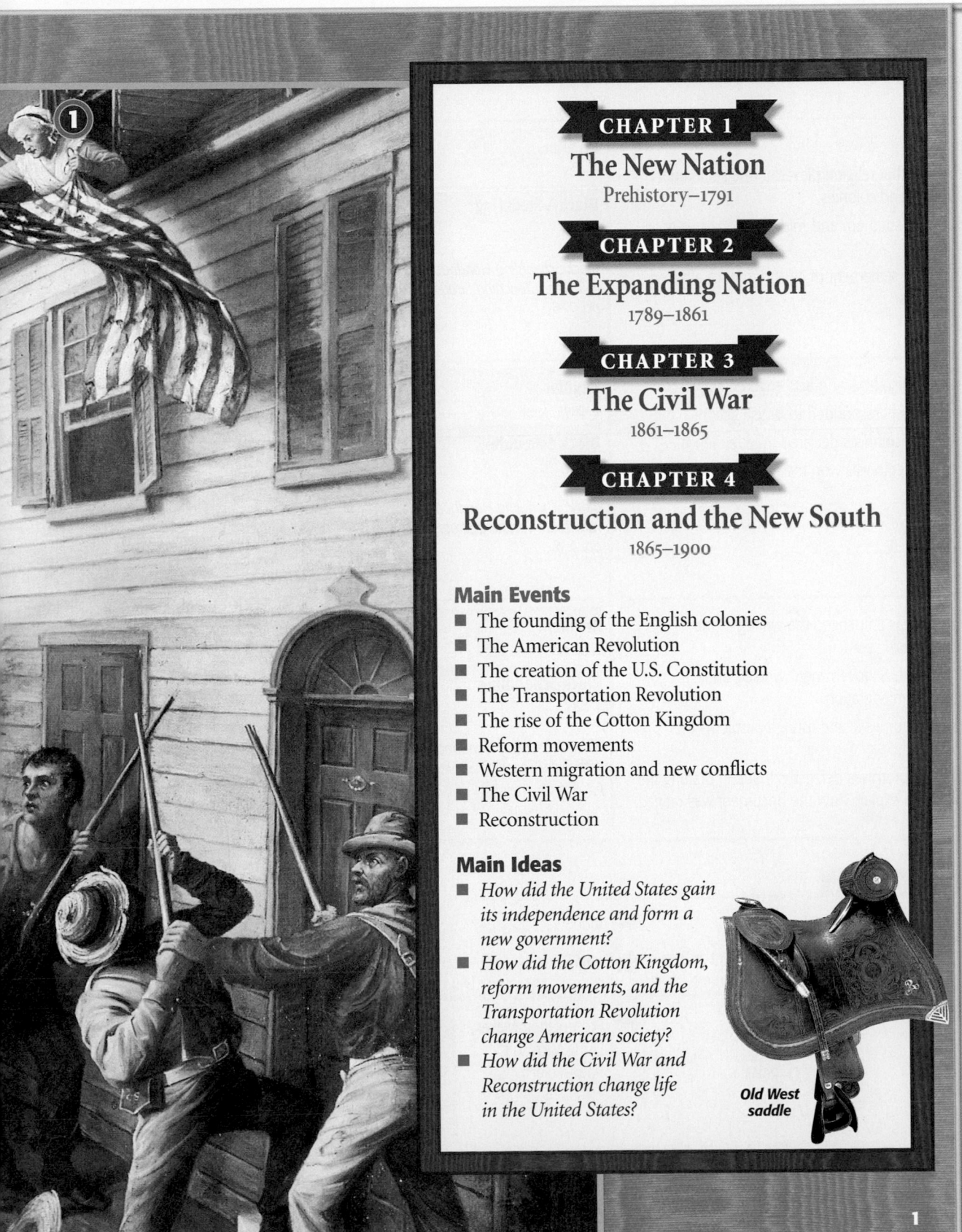

CHAPTER 1
The New Nation
Prehistory–1791

CHAPTER 2
The Expanding Nation
1789–1861

CHAPTER 3
The Civil War
1861–1865

CHAPTER 4
Reconstruction and the New South
1865–1900

Main Events
- The founding of the English colonies
- The American Revolution
- The creation of the U.S. Constitution
- The Transportation Revolution
- The rise of the Cotton Kingdom
- Reform movements
- Western migration and new conflicts
- The Civil War
- Reconstruction

Main Ideas
- *How did the United States gain its independence and form a new government?*
- *How did the Cotton Kingdom, reform movements, and the Transportation Revolution change American society?*
- *How did the Civil War and Reconstruction change life in the United States?*

Old West saddle

INTRODUCE UNIT 2

Main Events
List the Main Events on the chalkboard. Ask students to select two and briefly describe what they know about the topics. Have volunteers share their descriptions. Later, when you have finished Unit 1, ask students to return to their original descriptions and revise them using the information they learned in the unit. Students should also create new descriptions for the other Main Events.

Main Ideas
Ask each student to read the Main Ideas and briefly answer the questions in writing. Share the **Consider** points with students as necessary. Later, when you have finished Unit 1, ask students to return to their original answers and revise them using the information they learned in the unit.

Colonization of the Americas
Consider:
- why European nations colonized the Americas
- why thirteen North American colonies sought independence

Reconstruction Outcomes
Consider:
- the response of many white southerners to African Americans' attempts to exercise their civil rights
- the effect of Jim Crow laws and *Plessy v. Ferguson*

CHAPTER 1

The New Nation

CHAPTER RESOURCE MANAGER

	Objectives	Pacing Guide	Reproducible Resources
SECTION 1 **Early Exploration and Settlement** pp. 4–8	★ Explain how early Native American culture groups developed. ★ Describe how trade and exploration affected societies in Asia, Africa, and Europe. ★ Identify the ways that Spanish conquerors gained land in Central and South America. ★ Analyze how Spain developed a colonial empire in North America.	**Regular** 1 day **Block Scheduling** .5 day *Block Scheduling Handbook with Team Teaching Strategies, pp. 1–6*	**RS** Guided Reading Strategy 1.1 **PS** Primary Source Reading 1: Through the Eyes of a Spanish Missionary-Explorer **SM** American History Outline Map: Native American Culture Areas
SECTION 2 **The English Colonies** pp. 9–14	★ Describe how Virginia was settled. ★ Explain the role that religion played in the settlement of the New England colonies. ★ Discuss why the southern and middle colonies were established. ★ Analyze how the settlement of North America affected American Indians.	**Regular** 1 day **Block Scheduling** .5 day *Block Scheduling Handbook with Team Teaching Strategies, pp. 1–6*	**RS** Guided Reading Strategy 1.2 **PS** Biography Reading 1: Nathaniel Bacon **E** Creative Teaching Strategy: Continuum Lesson **E** Hands-On History Activity: Native Americans and Your Town
SECTION 3 **Independence!** pp. 15–23	★ Identify what British laws and acts angered colonists. ★ Trace how colonists responded to British actions. ★ Analyze why the colonists declared independence. ★ Explain how the colonists won the Revolutionary War.	**Regular** 2 days **Block Scheduling** 1 day *Block Scheduling Handbook with Team Teaching Strategies, pp. 1–6*	**RS** Guided Reading Strategy 1.3 **SM** Geography Activity 1: Boston at the Start of the Revolution **RS** Graphic Organizer Activity 1: The Battle for Independence **SM** American History Outline Map 5: The Treaty of Paris 1783
SECTION 4 **Founding the Nation** pp. 28–35	★ Analyze what ideas influenced the writing of the state constitutions. ★ Discuss how the U.S. government worked under the Articles of Confederation. ★ Summarize the domestic and foreign problems the new nation faced. ★ Identify the compromises delegates made in drafting the Constitution, and explain how the document was ratified.	**Regular** 2 days **Block Scheduling** 1 day *Block Scheduling Handbook with Team Teaching Strategies, pp. 1–6*	**RS** Guided Reading Strategy 1.4 **IC** Literature Reading 1: "On Mr. Paine's Rights of Man"

Chapter Resource Key

PS	Primary Sources	**REV**	Review		Video
RS	Reading Support	**ELL**	Reinforcement and English Language Learners	go.hrw.com	Internet
IC	Interdisciplinary Connections				Holt Presentation Maker Using Microsoft® PowerPoint®
E	Enrichment		Transparencies		
SM	Skills Mastery		CD–ROM		
A	Assessment		Music		

One-Stop Planner CD–ROM

See the *One-Stop Planner* for a complete list of additional resources for students and teachers.

One-Stop Planner CD-ROM

It's easy to plan lessons, select resources, and print out materials for your students when you use the **One-Stop Planner CD-ROM with Test Generator.**

Technology Resources	Reinforcement, Review, and Assessment

One-Stop Planner, Lesson 1.1
  CNN Presents America: Yesterday and Today, Beginnings to 1914 Segment: Columbus's Voyage: Then and Now
  Holt Researcher: American History CD–ROM
  Homework Practice Online
	REV Section 1 Review, p. 9
	 A Daily Quiz 1.1
	 ELL Main Idea Activity 1.1
	 ELL English Audio Summary 1.1
	 ELL Spanish Audio Summary 1.1

One-Stop Planner, Lesson 1.2
  Holt Researcher: American History CD–ROM
  The American Nation Video Program Segment: Designing a Nation: Teacher's Guide, pp. 27–32
  Homework Practice Online
  HRW Go site
	REV Section 2 Review, p. 14
	 A Daily Quiz 1.2
	 ELL Main Idea Activity 1.2
	 ELL English Audio Summary 1.2
	 ELL Spanish Audio Summary 1.2

One-Stop Planner, Lesson 1.3
  Holt Researcher: American History CD–ROM
  Homework Practice Online
	REV Section 3 Review, p. 23
	 A Daily Quiz 1.3
	 ELL Main Idea Activity 1.3
	 ELL English Audio Summary 1.3
	 ELL Spanish Audio Summary 1.3

One-Stop Planner, Lesson 1.4
  Holt Researcher: American History CD–ROM
  Homework Practice Online
	REV Section 4 Review, p. 33
	 A Daily Quiz 1.4
	 ELL Main Idea Activity 1.4
	 ELL English Audio Summary 1.4
	 ELL Spanish Audio Summary 1.4

Meeting Individual Needs

Ability Levels

Level 1 Basic-level activities designed for all students encountering new material

Level 2 Intermediate-level activities designed for average students

Level 3 Challenging activities designed for honors and gifted-and-talented students

English Language Learners Activities that address the needs of students with Limited English Proficiency

Chapter Review and Assessment

Global Skill Builder CD–ROM

HRW Go site

REV Chapter 1 Tutorial for Students, Parents, Mentors, and Peers

REV Chapter 1 Review, pp. 36–37

Chapter 1 Test Generator (on the One-Stop Planner)

A Chapter 1 Test (Form A or B)

A Alternative Assessment Handbook

A Chapter 1 Test for English Language Learners and Special-Needs Students

internet connect

HRW ONLINE RESOURCES
GO TO: go.hrw.com
Then type in a keyword.

TEACHER HOME PAGE
KEYWORD: SE3 Teacher

CHAPTER INTERNET ACTIVITIES
KEYWORD: SE3 AN1
Choose an activity to:
• create a brochure on the Great Wall of China.
• keep a journal on the *Mayflower.*
• research battles of the Revolutionary War and write a descriptive essay.

CHAPTER ENRICHMENT LINKS
KEYWORD: SE3 CH1

ONLINE ASSESSMENT
Homework Practice
KEYWORD: SE3 HP1

Standardized Test Prep
KEYWORD: SE3 STP1

Rubrics
KEYWORD: SS Rubrics

ONLINE MAPS, CHARTS, AND GRAPHS
KEYWORD: SE1 MCG
• Medieval Trade Routes
• Empires in the Americas
• Settling New England
• Federalist/Antifederalist
• The Federal System

CONTENT UPDATES
KEYWORD: SS Content Updates

HOLT PRESENTATION MAKER
KEYWORD: SE3 PPT1

ONLINE READING SUPPORT
KEYWORD: SS Strategies

CURRENT EVENTS
KEYWORD: S3 Current Events

Build on What You Know

Ask students to answer the following questions.

Why might the study of Asian, African, and European history be important to the study of American history?

Consider:

• the geographic origins of the first Americans

• the eventual connections between the different countries

What types of factors did the colonies have to consider when preparing to declare independence from Great Britain?

Consider:

• the difficulty of raising an army and getting supplies

• the consequences of losing the war

---

exploring the time line

AMERICAN EVENTS

GEOGRAPHY

5000 B.C. ■ The Spread of Crops. The crops that Native Americans cultivated in present-day Mexico gradually spread to other locations in North America. Corn arrived in the eastern United States about A.D. 200, although it did not flourish for another 700 years. Beans arrived a century or two later. After the arrival of corn and beans in North America, many Native American tribes abandoned their local crops.

ACTIVITY: Have students conduct research on when other agricultural crops reached North America.

CHAPTER 1

Prehistory–1791

The New Nation

Stone tools used to grind corn

A navigator's astrolabe

5000 B.C. Daily Life Communities in Mexico cultivate corn.

A.D. 850 Science and Technology Arabs develop an improved astrolabe.

1521 Politics Hernán Cortés captures the Aztec capital of Tenochtitlán.

| 5000 B.C. | | A.D. 1 | | 1500 | | 1550 |

2000–1500 B.C. Business and Finance Trade routes begin to spread from the eastern Mediterranean into Europe.

214 B.C. The Arts An intense period of construction begins on the Great Wall of China.

c. 1420 Science and Technology Prince Henry establishes a navigation school.

1565 World Events Europeans establish the first permanent settlement in what is now the United States at St. Augustine, Florida.

Caravels developed by Portuguese shipbuilders and navigators

THE GRANGER COLLECTION, NEW YORK

Build on What You Know

To understand America's diverse culture, it is necessary to know about the many different people and events that have contributed to the development of the United States. In this chapter you will learn about how America came to be settled first by Native Americans and later by European colonists. You will also learn how colonists won their independence from Great Britain and founded the United States of America.

What's Your Opinion?

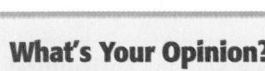

To help students create their Themes Journal entries, share the following examples of appropriate **agree**/**disagree** *statements.*

Economics

Agree The Spanish conquistadores became rich by exploring what is now South America.

Disagree Puritans explored and settled North America to escape religious persecution.

Geography

Agree Portugal is on the sea, so its people valued sailing and exploring via the water.

Disagree When the Spanish colonized South America, they lived just as they had in Spain.

Constitutional Heritage

Agree The U.S. Constitution says that all men are created equal.

Disagree Women and people of color were not considered in the drafting of the Constitution.

An early colonial tobacco plantation

George Washington

1627
Business and Finance
Virginia exports half a million pounds of tobacco.

1640
The Arts
The *Bay Psalm Book* is the first book published in the English colonies.

1775
World Events
George Washington leads American troops in the Revolutionary War.

1776
Politics
The Declaration of Independence is proclaimed.

| **1600** | **1650** | **1700** | **1750** | **1791** |

1607
World Events
Jamestown, the first permanent English settlement in America, is founded.

1721
Daily Life
Regular postal service is established between London and New England.

1754
Politics
American colonists adopt the Albany Plan of Union.

1784
Business and Finance
An economic depression begins in the United States.

Benjamin Franklin created this illustration of the Albany Plan of Union.

JOIN, or DIE.

Bills of credit called Continentals

exploring the time line

GLOBAL EVENTS

internet connect

TOPIC: The Great Wall of China
GO TO: go.hrw.com
KEYWORD: SE3 AN1

Have students access the Internet through the HRW Go site to conduct research on the Great Wall of China. Then ask students to create a brochure in which they outline the history of the wall, the myths and legends surrounding it, and the stages in which it was constructed.

What's Your Opinion?

Themes Journal

Do you **agree** *or* **disagree** *with the following statements? Support your point of view in your journal.*

Economics The promise of wealth lures people to settle and explore new and unknown territory.

Geography Communities develop different needs and values as a result of their climate, environment, and location.

Constitutional Heritage The desires of all people in a society must be met when making new laws and policies.

📀 *LET'S GET STARTED!*

Write the following topics on the chalkboard: *early Native American culture groups, trade and exploration during the Middle Ages, the Spanish colonies in America, effect of European settlement on American Indians.* As students enter the classroom, have them write as much as they can remember about one or more of these topics in two minutes. Set a timer and emphasize that students must write for the entire two minutes. Invite volunteers to summarize what they wrote for the class. Tell students that in Section 1 they will learn about early exploration and settlement in America.

SECTION ①

Early Exploration and Settlement

READ TO DISCOVER

1. How did early Native American culture groups develop?
2. What effects did trade and exploration have on societies in Asia, Africa, and Europe?
3. In what ways did Spanish conquerors gain land in Central and South America?
4. How did Spain develop a colonial empire in North America?

DEFINE
feudalism

IDENTIFY
Paleo-Indians
Agricultural Revolution
Maya
Aztec
Inca
Crusades
Renaissance
Christopher Columbus
Hernán Cortés

▶ **WHY IT MATTERS TODAY**

People continue to move to new places in search of better living conditions. Use CNNfyi.com or other **current events** sources to identify a group that is currently immigrating to the United States. Record your findings in your journal.

CNNfyi.com

EYEWITNESSES TO History *"[The islands were] full of trees of a thousand kinds, so lofty that they seem to reach the sky.... Some of them were in flower, some in fruit.... And the nightingale was singing, and other birds of a thousand sorts, in the month of November."*

—Christopher Columbus, quoted in *Original Narratives of Early American History,* edited by E. G. Bourne

On October 12, 1492, explorer Christopher Columbus landed on an island in the Bahamas. The landscape and vegetation were like nothing Columbus had seen before. He immediately decided to stake a claim for Spain. "[We] broke out the royal banner, and the captain's two flags with the green cross," Columbus recalled. The Spanish and later European explorers believed that these beautiful lands were theirs for the taking. This European contact brought profound changes to the Americas, as well as to Europe and Africa. Columbus's voyage introduced the Americas to the rest of the world, thus beginning a new era of trade, colonization, and cultural exchange. Columbus, however, was not the first person to arrive in the Americas.

Colored woodcut from 1572 showing fruit trees on the island of Hispaniola

Native Americans

Scientists have not been able to establish exactly when the first people arrived in the Americas. However, many believe that they came between 38,000 and 10,000 B.C. These people crossed over a land bridge that then connected Asia to what is now Alaska.

Early Americans. Called **Paleo-Indians**, the first Americans followed animal herds throughout North America. They hunted animals for food and clothing. Paleo-Indians also gathered edible plants. When the Ice Age ended about 8000 B.C., the climate in the Americas grew warmer. Scientists believe that during this period some Paleo-Indians moved south. Over thousands of years, different culture groups—each with its own language, laws, rituals, and ways of gathering food—came to populate the Americas.

The lifestyle of the Paleo-Indians changed dramatically with the **Agricultural Revolution**. This shift occurred when people first began domesticating, or adapting and controlling, animals and plants to meet specific human needs. Communities in Mexico had begun growing maize (corn) by 5000 B.C. By about 750 B.C. agricultural methods had spread north to what is now New Mexico. Farming increased the quantity and reliability of food supplies. As a result, human populations increased, and people began to settle permanently in one place. Eventually, villages and then cities formed.

LEVEL 1: Have students list some important advances in the development of early Native American culture groups. *(Students might mention the development of agriculture, the domestication of animals, and the creation of a number system, a written language, a canal system, and large cities.)* Write these on the chalkboard and tell students to select the one they feel was the most important development. Have students write a paragraph explaining why they feel their choice was the most important. Ask volunteers to read their paragraphs to the class. **English Language Learners**

LEVELS 2 AND 3: Have students make a collage of images that represent the development of early Native American culture groups. *(See the Level 1 lesson for important developments.)* Ask volunteers to present their collages to the class and explain the significance of various images. Display completed collages around the classroom.

Native American cultures. By the A.D. 1400s more than 650 distinct groups were living in the northern and central parts of the Americas. Some of the earliest large civilizations arose in Mesoamerica, or what is now southern Mexico and Central America.

The **Maya** civilization thrived from about A.D. 300 to A.D. 900, primarily in what is now southern Mexico and Guatemala. The Maya created a number system and wrote with glyphs—symbols and images that represent ideas. About A.D. 1200 the Aztec invaded central Mexico. At its height, the **Aztec** Empire ruled several million people. Aztec society was highly organized, with a strict class system. The Aztec built a capital city with a canal system.

Similar advances took place throughout the Americas. The **Inca**, a farming culture, rose to power in the Andes of South America. By the 1500s the Inca Empire had a population of 12 million, the largest in the Americas. In North America the various culture groups had smaller populations and were more spread out. As a result, Native Americans developed distinct, regional cultures in the Eastern Woodlands, the Southeast, and the Southwest.

Inca water ritual vessel

✔ **READING CHECK: Summarizing** What advances did early civilizations in the Americas make? *the rise of agriculture, number system, and glyphs*

Early World-Trading Kingdoms

While the cultures of North and South America developed in relative isolation from each other, trade networks already connected Africa, Asia, and Europe. These networks allowed for an exchange of cultural practices, goods, and ideas.

Asian and African trade. The Chinese Empire controlled much of ancient Asia. The Chinese made a variety of significant technological advances, including the invention of paper and a system of printing. In the A.D. 1200s Mongol invaders from Central Asia overran China. The Mongols transformed China into the world's largest empire and opened China to trade with the West. After the Chinese regained control in the 1300s, China's leaders adopted a policy of isolation.

Muslim merchants continued to carry Chinese and other Asian goods to Africa. Trade helped many East African city-states grow powerful and wealthy. Prosperous kingdoms also arose in West Africa. In the 770s Arab geographer al-Fazari described Ghana, the earliest of the West African kingdoms, as "the land of gold."

Europe during the Middle Ages. European trade with Africa and Asia had declined after the fall of the Roman Empire. From about A.D. 500 to about 1500—a period called the Middle Ages—European society gradually recovered from the collapse of Roman authority. During the Middle Ages Europeans developed a system that historians call **feudalism**. In return for land and protection from invasion, feudal nobles pledged their loyalty and military assistance to more-powerful leaders. Feudal society operated under a rigid class system, with nobles at the top and serfs at the bottom.

Copies of the Qur'an were carried by Muslim traders to introduce the Islamic faith to fellow travelers and merchants.

Muslim Achievements in Science. Between A.D. 800 and 875, many ancient Greek texts were translated into Arabic, allowing Muslim scholars to study the works of thinkers such as Euclid and Ptolemy. Muslim scholars used these texts to advance their own scientific inquiries, particularly in astronomy. In the 1200s and 1300s, three astronomers—'Urdi, Tusi, and Shirazi—completed studies that Copernicus, a European astronomer, technically duplicated some two centuries later. Modern-day astronomers call these Muslim thinkers the Maragha astronomers after an observatory in the Iranian city of the same name.

CRITICAL THINKING What role might the Greek texts have played in the development of Muslim science?

ANSWER: Students might suggest that the texts stimulated Muslim scholars and provided related knowledge from previous thinkers.

TEACH OBJECTIVE 2

ALL LEVELS: To help students understand how trade and exploration affected the societies in Africa, Asia, and Europe, copy the following graphic organizer on the chalkboard, omitting the italicized answers. Have each student complete it. **English Language Learners**

Society	Effects of Trade and Exploration
Asia	*China opened to West and became largest empire in the world; spread of Islam; spread of technology such as paper and printing*
Africa	*brought wealth and power to city-states and kingdoms; spread of Islam*
Europe	*Crusades opened new trade routes; trade contributed to Renaissance, which spread new ideas and knowledge*

TEACH OBJECTIVE 3

ALL LEVELS: Tell students to imagine that they are messengers from the Americas. They have been told to explain to Queen Isabella how the Spanish conquerors are gaining new lands for Spain. Have students write a short summary of the ways in which the Spanish conquerors are gaining land in Central and South America. *(Students should mention the encomienda system; introduction of diseases; establishing missions; using force to conquer native peoples.)* Have volunteers read their summaries to the class.
English Language Learners

GLOBAL RELATIONS

The Children's Crusades.
In 1212, thousands of children mounted their own crusade, hoping to win the Holy Land with love rather than force. In one children's crusade, a German boy named Nicholas traveled to Genoa, finally arriving with some 7,000 soldiers. Nicholas had told his troops that the waters of the Mediterranean Sea would part for them, but when the sea remained still, the crusade fell apart. Some participants returned home, while others traveled to Rome or Marseilles, where they were probably sold into slavery. Some historians argue that many of the soldiers on this children's crusade were not children at all, but rather people of all different ages. Other scholars argue that the story of children's crusades in general has been manipulated and misrepresented throughout history.

CRITICAL THINKING Why might the story of children's crusades have been misrepresented throughout history?

ANSWER: Students might suggest that the events have romantic and tragic elements that make for an appealing story, inviting others to put their own spin on it.

Sundial and compass used by explorers in the 1500s

Analyzing Primary Sources

Drawing Conclusions What hazards did sailors face?
rough living conditions, stormy seas, and death

Feudal society began to change about 1100, partly as a result of the **Crusades**. The Crusades were a series of religious wars that took place between 1096 and the late 1200s. Christian crusaders fought Muslims for control of Jerusalem in the eastern Mediterranean region. The Crusades opened new trading routes for European merchants. Crusaders and traders returned home with new ideas about art, philosophy, and science. These ideas contributed to a rebirth of European learning and artistic creativity later known as the **Renaissance**. The Renaissance began in Italy in the 1300s and soon spread to the rest of Europe. The development of an improved printing press in the mid-1400s greatly contributed to the spread of new ideas.

The Middle Ages faded with the rise of nation-states. National monarchies replaced feudal kingdoms throughout most of western Europe. England, France, Portugal, and Spain were among the first to achieve national unity during this period. Most often these changes came as a result of warfare, but sometimes they were the result of marriage between royal families.

✔ **READING CHECK: Analyzing Information** What factors led to the growth of trade before and during the Middle Ages? The Mongols helped Chinese trade grow; the Crusades opened new trading routes.

The Lure of Trade and Exploration

The new nations of western Europe wanted direct access to Asian goods. Italian and Muslim merchants controlled most trade routes so explorers looked for a new sea route to Asia. The astrolabe and compass as well as improved ship designs allowed Europeans to sail the often stormy Atlantic Ocean.

Despite these advances in technology, sea travel during the late Middle Ages remained extremely dangerous. In exchange for hazardous labor and difficult living conditions, most sailors earned wages, received clothing from their ship's owner, and were granted occasional bonuses. English writer Richard Braithwait described the life of a typical sailor.

History Makers Speak
❝He makes small or no choice of his pallet [bed]; he can sleep as well on a sack of pumice [rocks] as a pillow of down . . . . He has been so long acquainted with the surges of the sea, as too long a calm distempers [upsets] him. . . . He can spin up a rope like a Spider, and down again like lightning. . . . Death he has seen in so many shapes, as it cannot amaze him.❞

—Richard Braithwait, *Whimzies, or New Cast of Characters*

Portugal led the way in exploration. By the 1430s Portuguese adventurers had explored and colonized islands off the northwest coast of Africa. In 1497 Vasco da Gama sailed around Africa and reached Asia the following year. Portugal's control of this sea route and its trading posts in Africa and Asia gave the country a near monopoly of the East-West sea trade.

At first the Portuguese traded in spices and gold, but by the late 1500s they dominated the slave trade, which had long existed in Africa. The slave trade devastated African societies. Millions of Africans were taken from their homes and sold into slavery.

✔ **READING CHECK: Finding the Main Idea** Why did Europeans begin exploring other parts of the world? to gain direct access to Asian goods

TEACH OBJECTIVE 4

LEVEL 1: Have each student create a time line showing Spanish exploration of Central and South America. *(Important dates to include on the time line are—1492, Columbus lands in the Bahamas; 1519, Cortés conquers the Aztec; 1532, Pizarro attacks the Inca; 1780, Spanish colonial empire is the largest in the world.)* Pair students and have them discuss the spread of Spain's colonial empire from South to North America. Ask volunteers to outline their discussions on the chalkboard. **English Language Learners, Cooperative Learning**

LEVEL 2: Tell students to imagine that they are editors of an encyclopedia. Have each student write a short encyclopedia entry explaining how Spain developed a colonial empire in North America. *(See Level 1 lesson for sequence and methods.)* Ask volunteers to share their entries with the class.

LEVEL 3: Ask students to analyze the spread of the Spanish colonial empire from South to North America. *(See Level 1 lesson for sequence and methods.)* Tell students to brainstorm ways that American Indian nations might be able to slow the growth of Spanish colonies in North America. Then conduct a classroom discussion on the same issue.

The Explorers

Other European nations also desired a sea route to Asia. With Spain's financial support, explorer **Christopher Columbus** tried to reach Asia in 1492 by sailing west across the Atlantic Ocean.

Landing in the Americas. In October 1492 Christopher Columbus and his crew landed on an island in the Bahamas, which he named San Salvador. The people living there, whom Columbus called Indios, were farmers, fishers, and traders. Columbus did not realize that he had not reached Asia. In December he established a Spanish colony called La Navidad on the island of Hispaniola.

On a later voyage Columbus ordered the construction of settlements and introduced the *encomienda* system to the Americas. Under this system, Spanish colonists forced American Indians to work for them, often without pay. Some Spaniards, including Queen Isabella and Bartolomé de Las Casas, protested this treatment. Las Casas, a priest, urged Spaniards to respect the Indians.

History Makers Speak

❝Not only have [the Indians] shown themselves to be very wise peoples . . . but they have equaled many diverse nations of the . . . past and present . . . and exceed by no small measure the wisest of all these.❞

—Bartolomé de Las Casas, *Apologetic History of the Indies*

American Indians suffered from overwork and malnutrition under the *encomienda* system. Disease spread between Europe and the Americas. This was particularly deadly to American Indians, because they lacked resistance to these new sicknesses. In some areas the Indian population was nearly wiped out. To replace Indian laborers, the Spanish imported African slaves.

The conquest of the Americas. Spanish conquerors soon explored the Americas to claim land, gain riches, and spread Catholicism. **Hernán Cortés** arrived in Mexico in 1519 and soon conquered the wealthy Aztec Empire. Cortés built Mexico City

---

Sacred or Scientific Sites?

Over the years, researchers have unearthed and disturbed many Native American burial sites while removing bones and artifacts from graves. This practice has led to a bitter conflict between some American Indians and the anthropologists and archaeologists doing the digging. Researchers argue that studying skeletal remains and the objects buried with them reveals much about Native American cultures that might otherwise remain unknown. Skeletal remains also provide a physical record tracing the development and spread of many diseases. They show the effects of diet, pollution, and other factors on health that can be useful in preventing and treating diseases. "Indians living today," argues one anthropologist, "stand to benefit from our conclusions."

However, to many American Indians, the burial sites are sacred places that should not be disturbed. They believe that excavation of these sites shows a disregard for their cultural traditions. An attorney for a nation in New Mexico recently asked: "Why single out Indians? Why not dig up everybody's ancestors?" Through recent lawsuits, some American Indians have succeeded in obtaining the return of their ancestors' remains for reburial. American Indians have been assisted in their efforts by the Native American Grave Protection and Repatriation Act, which Congress passed in 1990.

Pot found at an American Indian burial site

PEOPLE IN HISTORY

Bartolomé de Las Casas. Although we often think of Bartolomé de Las Casas as a social reformer, he was also a historian, one of the first to write about the Americas. In his *History of the Indies*, Las Casas traced the history of the "New World" from exploration to *encomienda*. In addition to providing a conventional history of the Americas, he offered a harsh indictment of the way in which Spaniards treated American Indians. Many Spaniards objected to this aspect of Las Casas's work.

CRITICAL THINKING How might Las Casas's dual role as historian and reformer have affected his work? How might it affect modern readings of his work?

ANSWER: Students might suggest that in seeking both to inform and reform, Las Casas probably brought more passion—and less objectivity—to his writings. Modern readers should consider this factor when examining his work.

VISUAL RECORD ANSWER

(for p. 8)

Students might suggest that the settlers feared resistance from the American Indians.

Aztec drawing of the encomienda *system*

chalchicueyca

7

REVIEW

Have students complete the **Section 1 Review** on page 8.

ASSESS

Have students complete **Daily Quiz 1.1**. As **Alternative Assessment**, you may want to use student collages of early Native American culture groups or student maps of Spanish conquests in this section's lessons.

RETEACH

Have students complete **Main Idea Activity for English Language Learners and Special-Needs Students 1.1**. Then organize students into groups and assign each group a subsection of Section 1. Have each group develop at least five questions and answers about the main ideas in its assigned material. Then have each group quiz another group.
English Language Learners, Cooperative Learning

EXTEND

Have students write creative short stories set in one of the time periods and places covered in this section such as the ancient Americas, Europe in the Middle Ages, or the height of the Spanish Empire in the Americas. Have them make up believable characters and put them into interesting situations that reflect students' knowledge of the time period. Invite volunteers to read their stories to the class. **Block Scheduling**

SECTION 1 REVIEW ANSWERS

1. Define
- feudalism, p. 5

2. Identify
- Paleo-Indians, p. 4
- Agricultural Revolution, p. 4
- Maya, p. 5
- Aztec, p. 5
- Inca, p. 5
- Crusades, p. 6
- Renaissance, p. 6
- Christopher Columbus, p. 7
- Hernán Cortés, p. 7

3. Al-Fazari, to Ghana, to note its geography; Vasco da Gama, to Asia, to establish trading posts; Christopher Columbus, to find a western route to Asia, established first Spanish colonies in America; Hernán Cortés, to the Americas, conquered the Aztecs; Francisco Pizarro, South America, to conquer the Inca

4a. They developed number systems and glyphs, built canals and cities, and learned how to farm.

b. Trade created an exchange of cultural practices, goods, and ideas for European and Asian societies; for African and American societies, trade brought slavery, disease, and death.

c. The effects of disease and better weapons and organization allowed the Spanish to conquer large parts of the Americas.

5. Articles might suggest that the search for direct access to Asian goods led to the discovery, exploration, and colonization of the Americas by Europeans who enslaved the native population.

INTERPRETING THE VISUAL RECORD

Catholicism. Spanish settlers in North America wanted to convert American Indians to Catholicism. *In this image of the baptism of Indians, why do you think that Spanish settlers are carrying weapons during the ceremony?*

on top of the ruins of the Aztec capital of Tenochtitlán. He was soon appointed governor of the region and the Aztec were absorbed into the *encomienda* system. Another Spanish conquistador, Francisco Pizarro, attacked the Inca Empire in 1532. The Inca resisted for several years before their empire fell to the Spanish.

Spanish explorers traveled north from both Central and South America. They established settlements in what are now Arizona, California, Florida, New Mexico, and Texas. By 1780 Spanish America comprised one of the largest colonial empires the world had ever known. Spanish settlers divided the land into farming communities and large ranching estates.

Spanish America developed a social structure in which individuals of full or mixed European heritage held a higher social status than Africans and American Indians. The Catholic Church played a central role in the exploration and settlement of Spain's American colonies. Church-centered communities known as missions became a common form of Spanish settlement. Missionaries also attempted to convert American Indians to Catholicism. The Spanish influence on the Southwest is still visible today in the many Spanish place-names and in the culture of the region.

✔ **READING CHECK: Categorizing** What were the key characteristics of the Spanish Empire in the Americas? *encomienda* system, farming communities, ranching estates, and missions

---

SECTION 1 REVIEW

1. Define and explain:
feudalism

2. Identify and explain:
Paleo-Indians
Agricultural Revolution
Maya
Aztec
Inca
Crusades
Renaissance
Christopher Columbus
Hernán Cortés

3. Categorizing Copy the table below. Use it to list and describe the different voyages of exploration during the Middle Ages and in the 1400s and 1500s.

Explorer	Destination	Result

 Homework Practice Online
keyword: SE3 HP1

4. **Finding the Main Idea**

a. What were the key cultural and scientific accomplishments of early Mesoamerican cultural groups?
b. How did trade influence societies in Europe, Asia, Africa, and the Americas?
c. Why were the Spanish successful at colonizing and settling vast areas of North and South America?

5. **Writing and Critical Thinking**

Identifying Cause and Effect Write a short article explaining how European trading goals changed the history of the Americas.
Consider:
- how interest in trade led to the search for new trade routes
- how this search affected Christopher Columbus's journey
- how Columbus's landing in the Americas shaped its history

SECTION 2

After completing Section 2, students should be able to:

OBJECTIVE 1 Describe how Virginia was settled.

OBJECTIVE 2 Explain the role that religion played in the settlement of the New England colonies.

OBJECTIVE 3 Discuss why the southern and middle colonies were established.

OBJECTIVE 4 Analyze how the settlement of North America affected American Indians.

🔊 LET'S GET STARTED!

Write the following scenario on the chalkboard: *You want to start a new colony, and you need to come up with a system of government. What system would you use as a model?* As students enter the room, ask them to respond to the scenario in writing. Ask volunteers to share their responses. Tell students that in Section 2 they will learn how the English colonies were settled and governed.

SECTION 2

READ TO DISCOVER

1. How was Virginia settled?
2. What role did religion play in the settlement of the New England colonies?
3. Why were the southern and middle colonies established?
4. How did the settlement of North America affect American Indians?

IDENTIFY

Walter Raleigh
James I
House of Burgesses
Pilgrims
Mayflower Compact
John Winthrop
Fundamental Orders of Connecticut
Anne Hutchinson
Middle Passage
Olaudah Equiano

▶ WHY IT MATTERS TODAY

Many important historical places in the United States have been protected and preserved. Use **CNNfyi.com** or other **current events** sources to find out about a historical site in the United States today. Record your findings in your journal.

CNNfyi.com

The English Colonies

EYEWITNESSES TO History "*All our riches for the present do consist in Tobacco, wherein one man by his own labor hath in one year, raised to himself to the value of 200 £ sterling; and another by the means of six servants hath cleared [earned] at one crop a thousand pound english. These be true, yet indeed rare examples, yet possible to be done by others. Our principal wealth (I should have said) consisteth in servants.*"

—John Pory, letter to "The Right Honorable and My Singular Good Lord," September 30, 1619

Indentured servants often performed labor such as churning butter.

John Pory, the secretary of the Jamestown colony, wrote in 1619 about the beginning of the cultivation of tobacco and the role of servants in Virginia. Life as an early settler in an English colony proved extremely difficult for most people. However, individuals had significantly different experiences depending upon their social standing. Writing to his parents in 1623, servant Richard Frethorne described his life: "Since I came out of the ship, I never had any thing but peas, and loblollie (that is water gruell) as for deer or venison I never saw any since I came into this land, . . . [we] must work hard both early, and late for a mess of water gruel, and a mouthful of bread, and beef."

Settling Virginia

By the 1600s the Dutch, English, and French had begun settling land in eastern North America. England established thirteen North American colonies during the 1600s and early 1700s. These colonies provided raw materials for England and served as a market for English goods.

In 1584 English adventurer Sir **Walter Raleigh** sent an expedition to the Atlantic seaboard. He named the selected region Virginia, in honor of Elizabeth I, England's "Virgin Queen." The first attempts to settle there—on Roanoke Island, off the coast of what is now North Carolina—failed in the 1580s. About 20 years passed before the next English colonization effort.

King **James I** issued the Charter of 1606, which licensed two joint-stock companies to organize settlements in Virginia. In 1607 some 100 men recruited by the London Company reached Virginia and established what would become England's first permanent settlement. They settled near one of the rivers close to Chesapeake Bay and named the settlement Jamestown. The colonists survived with the help of local American Indians, but violence was common as the colonists' tobacco farms expanded onto Indian hunting grounds. To provide laborers for tobacco cultivation, Jamestown's backers introduced the headright system. Sponsors received 50 acres of land for each worker, or "head," they paid to bring to Jamestown. Other settlers arrived in the colony as indentured servants. They were required to work for a period of years for the person who had paid their way to America.

SECTION 2 RESOURCES

REPRODUCIBLE
▶ Guided Reading Strategy 1.2
▶ Biography Reading 1: Nathaniel Bacon

TECHNOLOGY
▶ One-Stop Planner, Lesson 1.2
▶ Holt Researcher: American History CD–ROM
▶ The American Nation Video Program Segment: Designing a Nation: Teacher's Guide, pp. 27–32
▶ Homework Practice Online
▶ HRW Go site

REINFORCEMENT, REVIEW, AND ASSESSMENT
▶ Section 2 Review, p. 14
▶ Daily Quiz 1.2
▶ Main Idea Activity 1.2
▶ English Audio Summary 1.2
▶ Spanish Audio Summary 1.2

TEACH OBJECTIVE 1

 LEVEL 1: Have students write a few sentences or paragraphs explaining how the English settled Virginia. *(Students should mention that King James I left colonization to private joint-stock companies; the London Company settled Jamestown by growing tobacco; use of indentured servants for cheap labor; House of Burgesses for government of colony.)*
English Language Learners

LEVEL 2: Tell students to imagine that they are indentured servants. They are part of the headright system and have been brought to Jamestown to farm tobacco. Have students write a letter to their families in England describing how the colonists have settled Virginia. *(See Level 1 lesson for methods of settlement.)* Student letters should describe the methods of settlement from the point of view of an indentured servant. Ask volunteers to read their letters to the class.

LEVEL 3: Tell students to imagine that they are modern-day museum curators preparing an exhibit on English settlement of Virginia. Have each student prepare a three-fold brochure advertising the exhibit. *(See Level 1 lesson for methods of settlement.)* As a way of attracting visitors, the brochure should provide general information about English settlement and material about the exhibit itself. Students might want to illustrate their brochures with paintings or artifacts from the Jamestown colony.

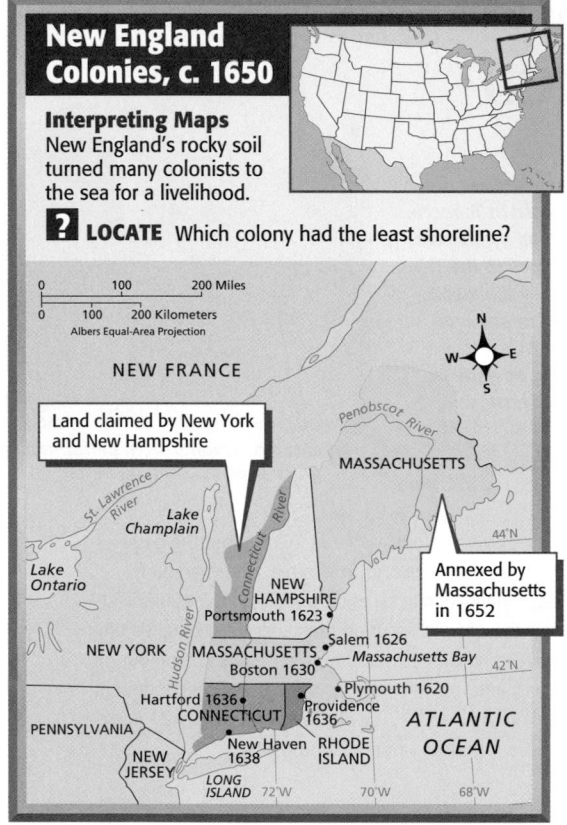

New England Colonies, c. 1650

Interpreting Maps
New England's rocky soil turned many colonists to the sea for a livelihood.

❓ LOCATE Which colony had the least shoreline?

Land claimed by New York and New Hampshire

NEW FRANCE

MASSACHUSETTS

Lake Champlain

Lake Ontario

Annexed by Massachusetts in 1652

NEW HAMPSHIRE
Portsmouth 1623

Salem 1626
Massachusetts Bay

NEW YORK   MASSACHUSETTS
Boston 1630

Plymouth 1620

Hartford 1636   Providence 1636
CONNECTICUT

PENNSYLVANIA

New Haven 1638   RHODE ISLAND

ATLANTIC OCEAN

NEW JERSEY

LONG ISLAND

Puritan boy's shoes

In 1619 a representative assembly of 22 burgesses, or delegates, chosen by the colonists met for the first time in Virginia. This assembly became known as the **House of Burgesses**. It was the first colonial legislature in England's overseas possessions. In 1624—after years of unprofitable business—the crown revoked the company's charter. Virginia became a royal colony, with a governor appointed by the king.

✔ **READING CHECK: Making Predictions** How might the settlement of Virginia affect future English settlements in North America? Future settlements might adopt Virginia's headright system or representative assembly.

The New England Colonies

In the early 1600s a group of Protestants known as Puritans emerged in England. The Puritans wished to reform, or "purify," the Church of England by eliminating all Catholic rituals and traditions.

The Puritan community. Many Puritans were persecuted for their religious beliefs. In the early 1600s some sought religious freedom in the Netherlands. In 1620 a group of these Puritans known as the **Pilgrims** decided to move to North America. More than 100 passengers and crew members set sail aboard the *Mayflower*. They reached Cape Cod Bay, near what is now Provincetown, Massachusetts, and founded the colony of Plymouth. Pilgrim leaders had drawn up an agreement for the men to sign. This document, the **Mayflower Compact**, established a self-governing colony based on the majority rule of male church members.

Beginning in 1630, in what is known as the Great Migration, some 60,000 Puritans left England for the Americas. While most went to the West Indies, 10,000 to 20,000 settled in New England. In 1629 another group of English Puritans obtained a charter for the Massachusetts Bay Colony. The company's fleet of 11 ships carried some 1,000 settlers to Massachusetts one year later. These Puritans hoped to provide other Christians with an example of a model community. Their leader **John Winthrop** expressed their vision: "We must consider that we shall be as a city upon a hill. The eyes of all people are upon us."

The Puritan community was based on cooperation between church and state—a relationship the colonists referred to as the New England Way. The Puritans stressed education, order, and moral living. In contrast to the Jamestown colonists, Puritan men brought along their wives and children. These families worked on farms. Some colonists set up fishing and trading businesses.

Conflicts in the colony. As time passed, some Puritans left Massachusetts for various reasons. Minister Thomas Hooker left partly because of religious differences with other Puritan leaders and partly because the "towns of the commonwealth

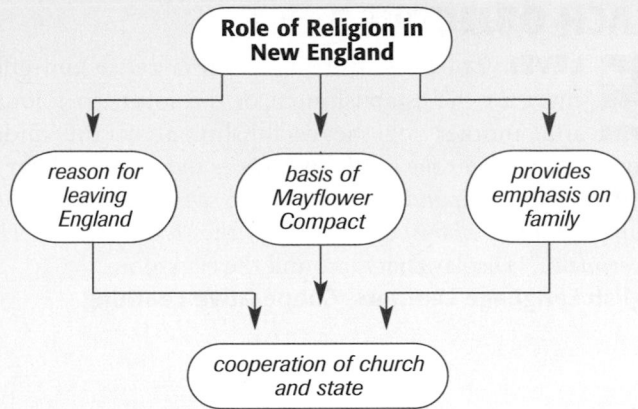

Role of Religion in New England

- *reason for leaving England*
- *basis of Mayflower Compact*
- *provides emphasis on family*

cooperation of church and state

AMERICAN Letters

Benjamin Franklin on Colonial Life

Well known throughout his lifetime as a statesman, printer, scientist, and inventor, Benjamin Franklin is equally remembered for his writings about colonial life in the 1700s. Poor Richard's Almanack, *which Franklin began publishing annually in 1732, contained advice for colonists on a variety of topics. In the following passage Franklin advises thrift rather than spending and debt. In his* Autobiography, *written over a period of 18 years, Franklin looked back on the lessons he had learned as the colonies grew. In the following excerpt he offers his summary of the ideal human values.*

from *Poor Richard Improved*

Now to save . . . observe these few Directions.

1. When you incline to have new Cloaths, look first well over the old Ones, and see if you cannot shift with them another Year, either by Scouring, Mending or even Patching if necessary.

Benjamin Franklin
THE GRANGER COLLECTION, NEW YORK

Remember a Patch on your Coat, and Money in your Pocket, is better and more creditable than a Writ on your Back [debt], and no money to take it off [pay it].

2. When you incline to buy China Ware, Chinces [fabric], *India* Silks, or any other of their flimsey slight Manufactures; I would not be so hard with you, as to insist on your absolutely *resolving against it*; all I advise is, to *put it off* (as you do your Repentance) *till another Year*; and this, in some Respects, may prevent an Occasion of Repentance. . . .

Thus at the Year's End, there will be *An Hundred Thousand Pounds* more Money in your country.

If Paper Money in ever so great a Quantity could be made, no Man could get any of it without giving something for it. But all he saves in this Way, will be *his own for nothing*; and his Country actually so much richer.

from *The Autobiography*

1. TEMPERANCE. Eat not to Dulness. Drink not to Elevation.
2. SILENCE. Speak not but what may benefit others or yourself. Avoid trifling Conversation.
3. ORDER. Let all Things have their Places. Let each Part of your Business have its Time.
4. RESOLUTION. Resolve to perform what you ought. Perform without fail what you resolve.
5. FRUGALITY. Make no Expense but to do good to others or yourself: i.e. Waste nothing.
6. INDUSTRY. Lose no Time. Be always emply'd in something useful. Cut off all Unnecessary Actions.
7. SINCERITY. Use no hurtful Deceit. Think innocently and justly; and, if you speak, speak accordingly.
8. JUSTICE. Wrong none, by doing Injuries or omitting the Benefits that are your Duty.
9. MODERATION. Avoid Extremes. Forbear resenting Injuries so much as you think they deserve.
10. CLEANLINESS. Tolerate no Uncleanliness in Body, Clothes or Habitation.

UNDERSTANDING LITERATURE

1. What advice does Benjamin Franklin give to colonists on saving money?
2. What do Franklin's virtues emphasize?
3. Based on Franklin's writings, what do you think were the main concerns of many colonists?

HISTORY MAKERS SPEAK

William Bradford in *Of Plymouth Plantation*

Bradford on Providence. William Bradford was a highly respected colonial author. Between 1630 and 1647, Bradford wrote *Of Plymouth Plantation*, a record of the Pilgrim colony. *Of Plymouth Plantation* reflected Bradford's belief in the idea of providence, or God's will. Bradford wrote, "May not and ought not the children of these fathers rightly say: 'Our fathers were Englishmen which came over this great ocean, and were ready to perish in this wilderness; but they cried unto the Lord, and He heard their voice and looked on their adversity.'"

CRITICAL THINKING What might the excerpt indicate about the Pilgrims' desire to build a society in a largely unsettled country?

ANSWER: Students might respond that the excerpt suggests that the Pilgrims felt that God would protect and guide them.

AMERICAN LETTERS ANSWERS

1. to avoid or postpone expenditures when possible
2. frugality, moderation, cleanliness, and industry
3. saving money and living in a simple, productive manner

LEVEL 1: Have students create a cause-and-effect chart for the establishment of the southern colonies, and another for the establishment of the middle colonies. *(Charts for the southern colonies should show desire for profit, need for land, and place for debtors; charts for the northern colonies should show conquest of the Dutch and "Holy Experiment.")* Display charts around the classroom.
English Language Learners, Cooperative Learning

LEVELS 2 AND 3: Have students create a proposal to obtain a charter for the establishment of a new southern colony and a new middle colony. Their proposals should give reasons why they want to establish their colonies. (See Level 1 lesson for appropriate reasons.) Students will address this proposal to the royal court of King Charles II. Their proposals should address some advantage Charles will receive from granting these charters. Have volunteers read their proposals to the class.

NOTE: For an additional teaching idea, see the Chapter 1 continuum lesson in the **Creative Teaching Strategies** handbook.

VISUAL RECORD ANSWER

Students might suggest that the building looks like a combination of a town hall and a church.

The American Nation VIDEO PROGRAM

Designing a Nation; Teacher's Guide, pp. 27–32

Search 06322, Play to 14238
Videodisc 1, Side A

Play   Pause

See *Teacher's Guide* for Spanish barcode.

COURTESY OF THE PILGRIM SOCIETY, PLYMOUTH, MASSACHUSETTS

INTERPRETING THE VISUAL RECORD

The meetinghouse. In 1683 the Puritans built a new meetinghouse in which they held town meetings and church services. **How does the building's design reflect the Puritans' beliefs?**

were set so near to each other." To get more farmland, he and his followers moved southwest, establishing the colony of Connecticut. Hooker's settlers adopted the **Fundamental Orders of Connecticut**, considered to be the first written constitution in the world.

Other colonists were forced to leave Massachusetts Bay Colony because they questioned Puritan ways. Unlike most other Puritans, minister Roger Williams believed in strict separation of church and state. His beliefs so angered Puritan leaders that they banished him. In 1636 Williams bought land from the Narranganset Indians and founded a settlement known as Providence, in what later became Rhode Island. He obtained a royal charter in 1644 that granted religious freedom to the colony's inhabitants.

Puritan **Anne Hutchinson** also found refuge in Rhode Island. She claimed to receive religious insights directly from God. The leaders of the Massachusetts Bay Colony found this claim threatening and banished Hutchinson in 1637.

✔ **READING CHECK: Finding the Main Idea** Why did Puritans settle in Massachusetts?
They were seeking religious freedom and wanted to create a model community.

Southern and Middle Colonies

By 1640 Virginia was a thriving colony with a population of some 10,000. Agriculture fueled its economy. The promise of huge profits led Cecilius Calvert to establish the colony of Maryland in the land surrounding Chesapeake Bay in 1632.

Tobacco and labor. The economies of Virginia and Maryland relied heavily on the cultivation of tobacco. At first, indentured servants performed much of the labor. During the mid-1600s, many colonists grew unhappy with conditions in Virginia. They were angered by the governor's tight control over the colony and his refusal to call elections. Poor colonists also believed that members of Virginia's assembly were ignoring their concerns. They complained about higher taxes and the lack of available farmland. Many of them began farming on land belonging to American Indians, ignoring treaties between the government and local Indians.

Colonial farmers used handmade tools such as these.

In 1678 a group of former indentured servants attacked some peaceful Indians. These colonists were led by Nathaniel Bacon, a wealthy frontier planter and a relative of the governor. When the governor tried to stop Bacon, he and his followers attacked and burned Jamestown. The uprising was known as Bacon's Rebellion. At one point Bacon controlled much of the colony. After he died of fever, however, the rebellion soon ended, and 23 of the remaining rebels were eventually hanged. Following the rebellion, the colonists found it difficult to make peace with American Indians. In addition, fears of future uprisings by former indentured servants led some planters in Virginia to depend more on slavery.

The experience of slavery. Surviving court records suggest that the institution of slavery developed gradually in the Chesapeake. The first Africans arrived there in 1619 and were probably treated as indentured servants. However, Virginia court records for 1640 include a reference to lifelong servitude.

TEACH OBJECTIVE 4

LEVEL 1: Have each student draw a series of pictures showing how European settlement of North America affected American Indians. (*Students might draw scenes of Indians fighting each other for hunting grounds, Europeans clearing land, war between the two groups, or the devastation of disease.*) Display students' pictures on the classroom walls.
English Language Learners

LEVEL 2: Tell students to imagine that they are American Indians during the first big wave of European settlement. Have them write and perform short monologues describing the effects European settlement of North America has had on their tribe. (*See Level 1 lesson for correct effects.*)

LEVEL 3: Organize students into groups of four or more. Have half of each group represent European settlers and the other half represent American Indians. Tell students to imagine that they are representatives at a peace conference between a European settlement and the American Indian tribe that once held the same land. Have them discuss their problems and brainstorm possible solutions before drafting a simple treaty that satisfies both groups. (*See Level 1 lesson for correct effects.*)
Cooperative Learning

NOTE: To help students make meaningful connections between events in U.S. history and those in their own hometown, use the Chapter 1 **Hands-On History Activity**, Native Americans and Your Town.

Traders brought enslaved Africans across the Atlantic Ocean to the Americas on a horrible voyage known as the **Middle Passage**. Slave traders packed their ships so tightly that, wrote one captain, the captives "had not so much room *as a man in his coffin.*" African **Olaudah Equiano** (oh-LOW-duh ek-wee-AHN-oh) described the ordeal of the Middle Passage. After being captured, he was put below deck.

History Makers Speak

"There I received such a salutation in my nostrils as I had never experienced in my life: so that with the loathsomeness [disgust] of the stench, and crying together, I became so sick and low that I was not able to eat, nor had I the least desire to taste any thing. I now wished for the last friend, death, to relieve me."

—Olaudah Equiano, *The Interesting Narrative of the Life of Olaudah Equiano or Gustavus Vassa, the African*

Olaudah Equiano

Although some people in the English colonies opposed slavery, it was practiced in all of the colonies.

The Carolinas and Georgia.
In the 1660s more colonization began. English colonists founded Carolina in 1663. They later divided the colony into North and South Carolina. Many settlers from the Chesapeake established small farms in North Carolina. South Carolina's first colonists came primarily from Barbados in the West Indies. They raised cattle, cut timber, and traded with American Indians. Settlers used enslaved West Africans' knowledge of rice-cultivation techniques to transform the swampy coastal region into profitable rice plantations.

The Carolinas and the port of Charles Town—present-day Charleston—attracted Scots, Scots-Irish, Germans, European Jews, and French Huguenots, or Protestants. In South Carolina, the demand for plantation workers was so great that slaves made up nearly two thirds of the population.

In 1732 James Oglethorpe and a group of trustees planned the colony of Georgia as a refuge for English debtors. Georgia also served as a buffer between South Carolina's plantations and Spanish Florida. Because of strict rules, the colony attracted few settlers in its first decades.

The middle colonies.
The Dutch West India Company established a trading post in North America in 1613. New Netherland extended along the Hudson River valley and included New Amsterdam, on Manhattan Island. In 1664 the English conquered the colony and split it into New Jersey and New York. New York City, formerly New Amsterdam, became an important trading center.

Research on the ROM

Free Find:
Olaudah Equiano
After reading about Olaudah Equiano on the **Holt Researcher CD–ROM**, create a museum exhibition that shows the different stages of his life.

This painting shows a view of colonial Charles Town, South Carolina, as seen from the harbor.

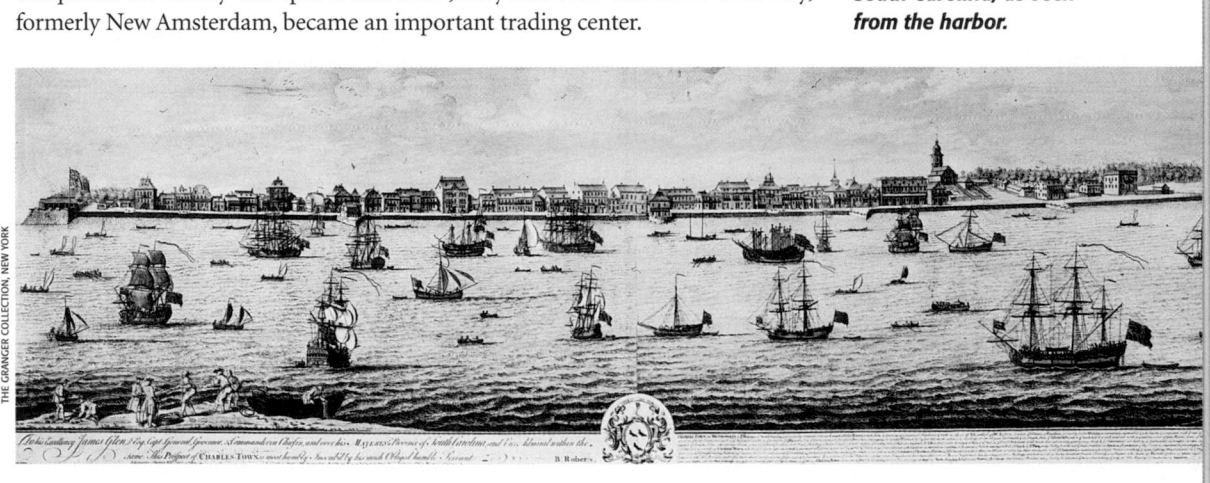

▶GOVERNMENT◀

Governing the Georgia Colony. The trustees of the Georgia colony ran their new settlement with a firm hand. They even dictated the amount of spices each colonist could possess—precisely eight ounces. They also constantly reminded the settlers that they were charity cases. One storekeeper announced in public that the colonists "had neither lands, rights or possessions; that the trustees gave and that the trustees could freely take away." Like the trustees, the colonists did not acquit themselves well in Georgia. They constantly complained about their food, supplies, and houses. The failure of the Georgia experiment led one trustee to say that people "who had been useless in England, were inclined to be useless in Georgia likewise."

ACTIVITY: Ask each student to think of four ways that the trustees and the colonists might have avoided the failure of the Georgia settlement. Have students explain and justify their ideas.

REVIEW

Have students complete the **Section 2 Review** on page 14.

ASSESS

Have students complete **Daily Quiz 1.2**. As **Alternative Assessment**, you may want to use the museum brochures or charter proposals in this section's lessons.

RETEACH

Have students complete **Main Idea Activity for English Language Learners and Special-Needs Students 1.2**. Then have each student create a detailed outline of the section. Pair students and have them exchange outlines. Tell them to use a different color ink to note any important information that is missing from each others' outlines.
English Language Learners, Cooperative Learning

EXTEND

Organize students into three groups. Ask student groups to conduct research on a particular American Indian tribe encountered by the English colonists. Assign the New England colonies to one group, the middle colonies to another group, and the southern colonies to the third group. Have each group write a report on their chosen tribe. Student reports should focus on how English colonists in their area have affected their way of life. **Block Scheduling, Cooperative Learning**

King Charles II of England granted land to William Penn, who founded the colony of Pennsylvania.

In 1681 King Charles II granted William Penn a large tract of land near New York. Penn named his colony Pennsylvania. He wanted to make it a safe home for fellow Quakers—members of a peaceful Protestant sect also known as the Society of Friends. Penn saw the colony as a "Holy Experiment" where people of different nationalities and religious beliefs could live together in harmony.

In 1682 the Duke of York granted Penn a region south of Pennsylvania called Delaware. Penn wanted the region so that Pennsylvania would have access to the Atlantic Ocean. Delaware gained the right to have a separate assembly in 1704 but did not adopt its own constitution until 1776.

✔ **READING CHECK: Categorizing** In what different ways were the southern and middle colonies settled? southern—search for financial gains, forced settlement, refuge for debtors; middle colonies—conquest and royal grants

Colonists and American Indians

The arrival of European settlers greatly altered the American Indian way of life. Europeans traded with American Indians, exchanging manufactured goods for animal pelts. The resulting fur trade contributed to the existing competition among American Indian nations for hunting grounds and furs.

Europeans' desire for land had other effects. Colonists cleared and settled what they considered wild or unused land. Such development threatened the American Indian way of life by destroying their food sources and damaging sites that were sacred to them. Diseases and warfare with colonists and other Indian groups also devastated American Indian nations throughout eastern North America. By the 1680s a Frenchman observed that American Indian nations in New England had been greatly weakened. "The last Wars . . . have reduced them to a small Number," he reported.

✔ **READING CHECK: Summarizing** What effect did colonial settlement have on American Indians? It threatened their hunting grounds, and diseases killed many of them.

SECTION ② REVIEW

1. Identify and explain:
- Walter Raleigh
- James I
- House of Burgesses
- Pilgrims
- Mayflower Compact
- John Winthrop
- Fundamental Orders of Connecticut
- Anne Hutchinson
- Middle Passage
- Olaudah Equiano

2. Comparing Copy the table below. Use it to list the key characteristics of the New England, middle, and southern colonies.

	Reasons for Settlement	Date Settled	How Settled
New England Colonies			
Middle Colonies			
Southern Colonies			

3. **Finding the Main Idea**
a. How did religion influence the founding of the New England colonies?
b. Why did Virginians and other southern colonists turn to slavery as a source of labor?
c. How might the establishment of a representative government in Virginia affect future relations between the colony and the king?

4. **Writing and Critical Thinking**
Identifying Points of View Imagine that you are an immigrant on your way to North America. Write a diary entry describing where you will settle.
Consider:
- location of the settlement
- possible occupations
- how your settlement might affect American Indians

Homework Practice Online
keyword: SE3 HP1

After completing Section 3, students should be able to:

OBJECTIVE 1 Identify what British laws and acts angered colonists.

OBJECTIVE 2 Trace how colonists responded to British actions.

OBJECTIVE 3 Analyze why the colonists declared independence.

OBJECTIVE 4 Explain how the colonists won the Revolutionary War.

🎙️ LET'S GET STARTED!

Write the following scenario on the chalkboard: *You were born in Country X, but you have lived in Colony Y since the age of 10. When Country X begins to place harsh demands on Colony Y and some colonists begin to call for independence, what do you do? Retain your allegiance to Country X, or fight for the freedom of Colony Y?* As students enter the classroom, ask them to respond to the scenario in writing. Have volunteers share their responses. Then tell students that in Section 3 they will learn why most colonists declared independence from England.

SECTION 3

READ TO DISCOVER

1. What British laws and acts angered colonists?
2. How did the colonists respond to British actions?
3. Why did the colonists declare independence?
4. How did the colonists win the Revolutionary War?

IDENTIFY

Stamp Act
Samuel Adams
George III
Intolerable Acts
George Washington
Battle of Bunker Hill
Thomas Paine
Common Sense
Declaration of
    Independence
Thomas Jefferson
Abigail Adams
John Adams
Battle of Yorktown
Treaty of Paris

▶ WHY IT MATTERS TODAY

At times Americans still have to defend their liberties. Sometimes the United States also helps protect the freedoms of people in other countries. Use CNNfyi.com or other **current events** sources to find a country in which the United States is protecting basic human rights. Record your findings in your journal.

CNNfyi.com

Independence!

 EYEWITNESSES TO *History*

COLONIAL WILLIAMSBURG FOUNDATION

Teapot bearing an anti-British slogan

"*It seems we have troublesome times a coming, for there is great disturbance abroad in the earth and they say it is tea that caused it. So then if they will quarrel about such a trifling thing as that, what must we expect but war. I think or at least fear it will be so.*"

—Jemima Condict Harrison, quoted in *Weathering the Storm*, by Elizabeth Evans

Jemima Condict Harrison was a young woman from New Jersey. She described the tension between Great Britain and the colonies in her diary in October 1774. During the early 1770s relations between Britain and the colonies worsened. Despite the growing crisis, some colonists still hoped for a peaceful resolution. Many, however, became convinced that war was inevitable.

Trouble in the Colonies

In the 1700s conflict between Great Britain and France spilled over into their North American colonies. The French had established colonies along the St. Lawrence River in what is now eastern Canada. British soldiers and colonial militia fought the French and their American Indian allies in what became known as the French and Indian War. With victory in 1763, the British gained Canada, Spanish Florida, and most French land east of the Mississippi River.

As large numbers of British settlers arrived in these areas, the American Indians already living there became alarmed. Ottawa chief Pontiac called upon Indian nations to unite and attack British forts on the frontier in what was known as Pontiac's Rebellion. Fear that conflict with American Indians would disrupt trade convinced British authorities to issue the Proclamation of 1763, which banned settlement west of the Appalachian Mountains. Many colonists ignored this proclamation.

Violations of colonists' rights. The British government passed a series of new colonial laws, which created new taxes to recover the costs of the war with France. These laws also violated a number of colonists' rights. British officials first passed a tax on sugar, molasses, and other items entering the American colonies. Because the colonists had no official representation in the British parliament, they objected to what they called "taxation without representation." In addition, the act violated colonists' right to a speedy trial by jury.

In 1765 Parliament passed the **Stamp Act**. It levied a tax on printed matter of all kinds—including legal documents, newspapers, and even playing cards. Angry colonial merchants vowed to boycott, or not to buy or import, British goods. Committees of artisans, lawyers, merchants, and politicians formed to protest the Stamp Act. They came to be called the Sons of Liberty.

SECTION 3 RESOURCES

REPRODUCIBLE

▶ Guided Reading Strategy 1.3
▶ Geography Activity 1: Boston at the Start of the Revolution
▶ Graphic Organizer Activity 1: The Battle for Independence
▶ American History Outline Map 5: The Treaty of Paris 1783

TECHNOLOGY

▶ One-Stop Planner, Lesson 1.3
▶ Holt Researcher: American History CD-ROM
▶ Homework Practice Online

REINFORCEMENT, REVIEW, AND ASSESSMENT

▶ Section 3 Review, p. 23
▶ Daily Quiz 1.3
▶ Main Idea Activity 1.3
▶ English Audio Summary 1.3
▶ Spanish Audio Summary 1.3

LEVELS 1 AND 2: Copy the following graphic organizer on the chalkboard, omitting the italicized answers, and have each student complete it by explaining what British laws and acts angered the colonists.
English Language Learners

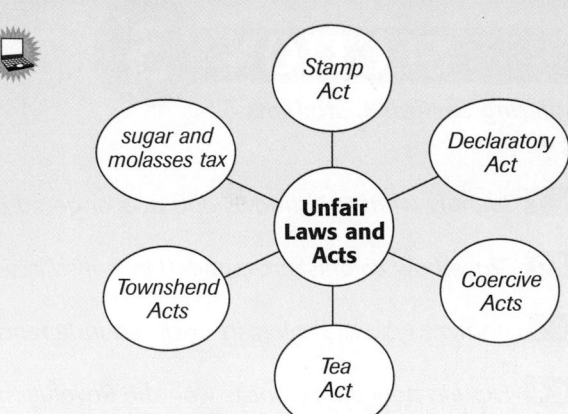

Boycotts. Colonists angered by the Stamp Act often signed nonimportation agreements, pledging not to buy or import British goods. By refusing to buy British goods, colonists were using a method of protest that is still widespread today— the boycott. Americans have boycotted goods for a wide variety of reasons. People have boycotted certain companies to protest high prices, disagreeable labor practices, or objectionable products. In recent years, many consumers boycotted food companies that caught and killed dolphins in the process of harvesting tuna. As a result, some companies changed their policies, and many tuna cans now bear the "dolphin-safe" label.

CRITICAL THINKING What might consumers hope to gain by boycotting a company's goods?

ANSWER: Students might suggest that if a company stands to lose a significant amount of business due to a boycott, the company might be persuaded to change the practices that upset consumers.

VISUAL RECORD ANSWER

Students might suggest tea was thrown in the water to prevent English tea from being sold in the colonies.

INTERPRETING THE VISUAL RECORD

Boston Tea Party. On December 16, 1773, a group of Boston colonists snuck onto British ships in the harbor. *Why did the colonists throw the tea in the water?*

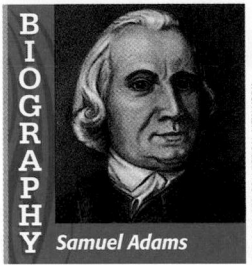

BIOGRAPHY

Samuel Adams

THE GRANGER COLLECTION, NEW YORK

Samuel Adams was a leader of the Boston Sons of Liberty. The son of a local merchant and brewer, Adams was born in 1722. He graduated from Harvard College and then worked for his family's brewing business. He also became involved in Boston politics and served in a series of local offices, including tax collector. In 1765 Adams was elected to the legislative assembly of Massachusetts. The Stamp Act crisis turned him into a key political leader.

Adams proved particularly skillful at staging demonstrations and writing articles that influenced the public's perception of events. His eloquent writings both expressed and heightened the colonists' anger at the British government.

History Makers Speak

"When the people are oppressed, when their Rights are infringed [violated], when their property is invaded, when taskmasters are set over them . . . in such circumstances the people will be discontented, and they are not to be blamed."

—Samuel Adams, *Boston Gazette,* August 8, 1768

The colonists respond. Led by Samuel Adams and others, the colonists decided to inform King **George III** of their dissatisfaction. In October 1765, delegates met in New York City for the Stamp Act Congress. They voiced their objections to the Stamp Act and declared that Parliament did not have the right to tax the colonies. The Stamp Act Congress marked an important step toward more unified resistance in the colonies.

Britain repealed this act in 1766 but passed the Declaratory Act at the same time. It stated that Parliament had the "full power and authority to make laws . . . to bind the colonies and people of *America*" in "all cases whatsoever." The following year Parliament passed the Townshend Acts, which placed import duties on common items such as glass, lead, and tea. These payments were used for military costs, which violated the colonists' right to not have a standing army without their consent. To enforce these acts, British custom officials revived the use of special search warrants called writs of assistance.

Once again the colonists opposed the tax. The British government sent troops—known as Redcoats because of their bright red uniforms—to Boston to enforce the law. In 1770 a confrontation between colonists and Redcoats led the soldiers to open fire on the crowd, killing five people. Colonists called this incident the Boston Massacre.

The Tea Act. Parliament repealed some of the new duties but again angered colonists when it passed the Tea Act in 1773. Colonists believed that the act gave Britain a monopoly on the tea trade. After the governor of Massachusetts allowed three shiploads of tea to enter Boston Harbor, colonists boarded the ships at night. They threw 342 chests of tea into the water. News of the so-called Boston Tea Party spread rapidly.

British officials were furious. Parliament passed the Coercive Acts, which colonists referred to as the **Intolerable Acts**. These laws closed the port of Boston, revoked the colony's charter, and ordered local

LEVEL 3: Organize students into small groups and tell them to organize a protest against one of the British laws or acts they feel is unfair (except the Stamp Act). Remind students what the colonists did to protest the Stamp Act, and then tell students to make signs, design pamphlets, or construct a model to demonstrate their protest. Have each group write a speech describing what it is about the law or act that is unfair. Have each student group organize the other students in the class into the form of protest the group has designed. After each protest, conduct a class discussion evaluating the effectiveness of the protest.
Cooperative Learning

SPOTLIGHT
on the Stamp Act Congress
Pair students and ask them to imagine they are delegates to the Stamp Act Congress. Have each pair write brief announcements on the following subjects: the reasons colonists formed the Stamp Act Congress, leading figures of the Congress, and the main actions of the Congress. Have volunteers read their announcements to the class.
Cooperative Learning, Block Scheduling

officials to provide food and housing for British soldiers. The acts went against many traditional rights of British citizens, such as freedom of travel in peacetime and no quartering of troops in private homes.

✔ **READING CHECK: Finding the Main Idea** What laws and actions contributed to the colonists' resentment toward the British government? Stamp Act, Boston Massacre, Tea Act, and Intolerable Acts

The Revolution Begins

In the fall of 1774, representatives met in Philadelphia at the First Continental Congress to discuss how to respond to British actions. The colonists resolved to remain loyal to the Crown but also claimed their rights as British subjects. King George considered the delegates and colonists who agreed with them to be rebels. Parliament ordered General Thomas Gage to stop the rebellion.

Early battles. General Gage tried to seize rebel military supplies stored in Concord, Massachusetts. On April 18, 1775, under cover of night, some 700 British troops left Boston and rowed across the Charles River. Patriots—colonists who supported independence—had stationed watchmen on the far shore. They spotted the British troops as they emerged from the darkness. Paul Revere and two other men rode horses through the countryside sounding the alarm that the British were coming. Patriots hurriedly gathered to confront the British.

The next day, Redcoats and Patriots clashed in Lexington near Concord. At the battle someone fired what was later called "the shot heard round the world." Eight colonists were killed, and 10 others were wounded. The Redcoats continued on to Concord but found few Patriot weapons. The colonists had hidden them elsewhere. Minutemen—members of the militia who promised to be ready at a minute's notice—fired on the British troops as they marched back to Boston. The Patriots killed or wounded 273 British soldiers while suffering fewer than 100 casualties in the day's fighting.

News of these events had spread through the colonies by the time the Second Continental Congress opened in May. The congressional delegates agreed to establish the Continental Army "for the defense of American liberty." The delegates unanimously chose **George Washington** of Virginia to command this new army. Washington had acquired military experience and a reputation for bravery while fighting for the British in the French and Indian War.

The Battle for Boston. On June 17, 1775, Patriot forces were again put to the test. Atop two hills overlooking Boston Harbor—Bunker Hill and Breed's Hill— New England militiamen waited for an attack by British troops. To save ammunition,

THE GRANGER COLLECTION, NEW YORK

Patriots and Redcoats battled at Concord bridge.

HISTORY MAKERS SPEAK

Ralph Waldo Emerson in *The Norton Anthology of American Literature*

The Shot Heard Round the World. In 1836 a monument was dedicated at Concord to those who had fought there. American poet Ralph Waldo Emerson wrote a hymn for the occasion. The first stanza of his hymn provided the famous description of the first gunshot at Concord in 1775:

> By the rude bridge
>   that arched the flood,
> Their flag to April's
>   breeze unfurled,
> Here once the embattled
>   farmers stood,
> And fired the shot heard
>   round the world.

CRITICAL THINKING What aspects of the Revolution might Emerson have wanted to emphasize by calling the soldiers "embattled farmers"?

ANSWER: Students might suggest that Emerson wanted to emphasize the idea of the Revolution as a war fought by and for common people. His words depict simple farmers fighting for basic rights, rather than wealthy statesmen protecting their import businesses.

Research on the ROM

Free Find:
George Washington
After reading about George Washington on the **Holt Researcher CD–ROM**, create a resumé for him that lists the information you think led the Second Continental Congress to select him to command the Continental Army.

LEVEL 1: Tell students to imagine they are colonists living in Boston during the passage of the British laws and acts they consider to be unfair. Have each student design a handbill with text and images, illustrating the colonial response to the British laws and acts. *(Handbills should refer to boycotts, the Sons of Liberty, the Stamp Act Congress, the Boston Tea Party, and the First Continental Congress.)* Display completed handbills in the classroom.
English Language Learners

LEVEL 2: Organize students into groups of six. Tell student groups to imagine they are newspaper editors living in Boston during the passage of the British laws and acts they consider to be unfair. Have each student in each group write one headline for each response colonists had to the unfair British laws. *(See Level 1 lesson for the correct colonists' responses.)* Have each group write each of its headlines on the board and discuss whether the headline accurately reflects the feelings of the colonists at the time. **Cooperative Learning**

LEVEL 3: Ask students to write a story from the point of view of a Boston colonist during the passage of the British laws and acts they consider to be unfair. Student stories should contain descriptions of the colonists' responses to these British laws and acts. *(See Level 1 lesson for the correct colonists' responses.)* Have volunteers present their stories to the class.

Thomas Paine. After the American Revolution, Thomas Paine traveled to Europe and attempted to incite revolution in his native Britain as well as in France. After the publication of Paine's *Rights of Man*, which supported the demise of Britain's monarchy, the British found him guilty of treason. Paine fled to France, where revolutionaries declared him a French citizen. Paine became deeply involved in the French Revolution, which caused some prominent Americans to turn against him. In 1802 Paine returned to America, no longer the hero of the American Revolution. John Adams, among others, called him "the filthy Tom Paine," and some London men actually wore "TP" nails in the heels of their boots to signify their belief that he had trampled on their principles. Paine spent his final years in poverty and poor health.

ACTIVITY: Have students imagine that they are Revolutionary War soldiers who have just heard of Paine's death. Have each student write a one-paragraph reaction to the news.

VISUAL RECORD ANSWER

Students might suggest that the hills gave the colonists good position to fire down on the British, while also providing cover from British fire.

an American commander ordered his soldiers: "Don't one of you fire until you see the whites of their eyes." British troops commanded by General William Howe advanced in three bold assaults. Corporal Amos Farnsworth of the Massachusetts militia described the battle.

"We . . . sustained the enemy's attacks with great bravery . . . and after bearing, for about 2 hours, as severe and heavy a fire as perhaps ever was known, and many having fired away all their ammunition . . . we were overpowered by numbers and obliged to leave."

—Amos Farnsworth, diary entry, June 17, 1775

INTERPRETING THE VISUAL RECORD

Battle of Bunker Hill. Flames erupt on Bunker Hill in this British engraving. *What obstacles did the hills pose for the British soldiers?*

During the **Battle of Bunker Hill**, the British took both hills but suffered more than 1,000 casualties. Fewer than 450 colonists were killed or injured. Even after the battle, some colonists worked to avoid a permanent break with Britain. They persuaded the Continental Congress to send a final plea to King George. Known as the Olive Branch Petition, this plea affirmed the colonists' loyalty to the king and asked for his help in ending the conflict. The king rejected the petition and ordered the Royal Navy to blockade all shipping to the colonies.

Meanwhile, Washington planned new military maneuvers. In a surprise move on March 4, 1776, he positioned troops and cannons on Dorchester Heights, which overlooked Boston. From there, the Patriots could fire on British forces in the city. On March 26 the British, joined by some 1,000 colonists loyal to the Crown, sailed for Nova Scotia. They left, according to Washington, "in so much . . . confusion as ever troops did."

Declaring Independence

Many colonists believed that the British government had violated their rights as British subjects. Patrick Henry and **Thomas Paine** emerged as powerful supporters of independence. Henry expressed these views in a speech he made in Virginia. He declared, "Give me liberty, or give me death!"

Paine promoted the Patriot cause in his January 1776 pamphlet *Common Sense*. It roused public support for the Revolution and called for the end of British rule. Paine argued, "Government, even in its best state, is but a necessary evil; in its worst state, an intolerable one." *Common Sense* eventually sold some 500,000 copies and helped transform a disorganized colonial rebellion into a focused movement for independence.

On June 7, 1776, Richard Henry Lee of Virginia introduced a resolution in the Second Continental Congress declaring the colonies "to be free and independent States." The resolution called for a plan of confederation, or an alliance,

TEACH OBJECTIVE 3

LEVEL 1: Organize students into small groups and have them read and discuss the Declaration of Independence on pp. 24–27. Ask each group to make a list of the reasons why the colonists declared their independence from Great Britain, as explained in the document. (*Lists should include the following: King George III's misdeeds, establishment of the doctrine of inalienable rights, and explanation that people have the right to abolish a government that deprives them of those rights.*) Discuss students' lists as a class.
Cooperative Learning

LEVEL 2: Organize students into small groups and have them read and discuss the Declaration of Independence on pp. 24–27. Ask each group to make a list of the reasons why the colonists declared their independence from Great Britain. (*See the Level 1 lesson for the correct reasons.*) ask students to select the three most significant reasons and explain why they believe these are the most significant. **Cooperative Learning**

The Fight for Independence, 1776–1781

Interpreting Maps The Revolutionary War was fought over a vast and varied landscape. Both sides faced the challenges of moving men and supplies across rivers and mountains and through dense forests and swamps.

? THE USES OF GEOGRAPHY George Rogers Clark moved his men and supplies from Fort Pitt to the western frontier by way of the Ohio River. Why do you think he chose this route? How much shorter or longer would his trip have been if he had taken a direct overland route from Fort Pitt to Kaskaskia?

Bernardo de Gálvez, the Spanish governor of Louisiana, defeated the British at Baton Rouge and Natchez in September 1779, Mobile in March 1780, and Pensacola in May 1781.

Maj. Gen. Benedict Arnold heroically fought at Saratoga, but he later turned traitor.

Battle of Saratoga

Lafayette, U.S.A. The French played an important role in the American Revolution, providing money and troops when the colonists needed them most. Americans honored important Revolutionary War officers such as the Marquis de Lafayette by naming towns and counties after them. Six states have towns named Lafayette, 12 have towns named Fayette, and four have towns named Fayetteville. The United States also includes 11 Fayette counties, six Lafayette counties, and one Lafayette Parish.

CRITICAL THINKING What other U.S. cities are named after historical figures?

ANSWER: Answers will vary. Students might mention Washington, D.C., named after George Washington, or Austin, Texas, named after Stephen F. Austin.

MAP ANSWER

Students might answer that it was easier to move supplies and troops by boat than on foot. The direct route would have been fewer miles but would have taken longer because of the difficulty of the land and crossing rivers.

LEVEL 3: Organize students into small groups and have them read and discuss the Declaration of Independence on pp. 24–27. Ask each group to make a list of the reasons why the colonists declared their independence from Great Britain. *(See the Level 1 lesson for the correct reasons.)* Ask each group to select one of the reasons listed and to write a one- to two-page brief explaining the background of the grievance, its significance, and how the Declaration proposes to solve it. **Cooperative Learning**

INTERDISCIPLINARY CONNECTIONS

▶LANGUAGE ARTS◀

The Words of the Declaration. The authors of the Declaration of Independence were not merely issuing a proclamation; they were trying to persuade colonists that King George had become a *despot.* In its original Greek form, despot meant "master" or "lord." Later, however, the word came to mean "absolute ruler" and referred to those who governed in a tyrannical, oppressive way.

ACTIVITY: Ask students to scan magazines and newspapers to find different uses of the word *despot*. Have each student select one example, bring it to class, and present it to the other students. Conduct a brief discussion on students' examples and the ways in which the term despot might have affected colonists who read it in the Declaration of Independence.

Before becoming a member of Virginia's Committee of Correspondence, Patrick Henry worked as a storekeeper and an attorney.

between the states. Before voting on Lee's proposal, the Congress appointed a five-person committee to draft a formal **Declaration of Independence**. **Thomas Jefferson**, a Virginia lawyer, planter, and slaveholder, became chairman of the committee and did most of the actual writing.

On June 28, congressmembers quickly accepted Lee's resolution. On July 2 the Congress officially declared the new United States of America to be independent from Britain. Two days later, on July 4, the Congress formally adopted the Declaration of Independence.

The Declaration's immediate purpose was to win support for independence, both at home and abroad. To weaken the public's lingering loyalty to King George, the Declaration described his misdeeds. It also outlined basic principles of representative government and listed "self-evident" truths.

Primary Source

❝We hold these truths to be self-evident, that all men are created equal, that they are endowed by their Creator with certain unalienable Rights, that among these are Life, Liberty, and the pursuit of Happiness.❞

—Declaration of Independence

The document also proclaimed the right of people "to alter or abolish" a government that deprived them of these "unalienable Rights."

✔ **READING CHECK: Evaluating** Why did the colonists declare their independence?
because they believed the British government had violated their rights as citizens

Reactions to Independence

The Declaration of Independence inspired mixed reactions throughout the colonies. Patriots rejoiced wildly—ringing "liberty bells," singing and dancing around bonfires, and celebrating at banquets. On July 13, Patriot Ezra Stiles noted in his diary, "The *thirteen united Colonies* now rise into an *Independent Republic* among the kingdoms, states and empires on earth."

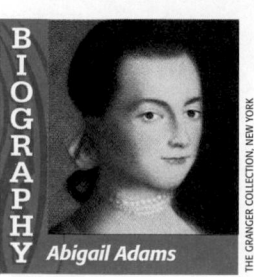

Some people, such as **Abigail Adams**, had a different reaction. The daughter of a Congregational minister, Adams was born in 1744 and grew up in rural Massachusetts. With little formal education, Adams was nevertheless a constant reader and developed remarkable letter-writing skills. In 1764 she married **John Adams**, with whom she raised four children, one of whom later became president.

During the Revolutionary War, John Adams spent much of his time attending to government matters in Philadelphia. Back in Massachusetts, Abigail Adams cared for their family and business interests. She also wrote a series of letters to her husband that frequently commented on important political issues. Abigail Adams strongly supported independence and women's rights and opposed slavery. A few months before her husband was chosen to serve on the committee that would draft the Declaration of Independence, she wrote to him:

TEACH OBJECTIVE 4

LEVEL 1: Write the following phrases on the chalkboard: *surprise attacks, British military mistakes, guerrilla warfare, French alliance.* Lead students in discussing each of these phrases and what they meant to the colonists. Then ask each student to write a one-paragraph summary of how these factors helped the colonists win the Revolutionary War. (*Paragraphs should indicate that surprise attacks made up fro troop shortages, British mistakes led to victories at Saratoga and Yorktown, guerrilla warfare used the terrain to the colonists' advantage, and the French alliance supplied the colonists with arms and troops.*) Students may wish to include their summaries in their portfolios. **English Language Learners**

LEVEL 2: Write the following phrases on the chalkboard: surprise attacks, British military mistakes, guerrilla warfare, French alliance. Lead students in discussing each of these phrases and what they meant to the colonists. Pair students and ask them to think about why the colonists won the Revolutionary War. (*See Level 1 lesson for correct reasons.*) Have each pair choose which of the factors on the chalkboard was the most significant. Then, ask students to write a one-page encyclopedia article describing the most significant factor and what made it so significant. **Cooperative Learning**

History Makers Speak

"By the way in the new Code of Laws which I suppose it will be necessary for you to make I desire you would Remember the Ladies, and be more generous and favorable to them than your ancestors. Do not put such unlimited power into the hands of the Husbands. Remember all Men would be tyrants if they could."

—Abigail Adams, letter to John Adams, March 31, 1776

Her ideas did not make it into the Declaration. Abigail Adams continued to remark on political affairs until her death in 1818.

Other Americans opposed or ignored the Declaration of Independence. A minority of colonists were Loyalists, also known as Tories. They remained loyal to Britain. Some Loyalists believed that resisting the king was the same as rebelling against God. Others feared losing power and wealth if royal authority ended.

✔ **READING CHECK: Categorizing** What were the different reactions to the Declaration of Independence? Some supported it; others wanted women's rights addressed; and Loyalists opposed or ignored it.

War!

To declare independence was one thing; to fight for it and win was another. The lack of a strong central government made the American war effort difficult. The Second Continental Congress could ask the states for help and supplies, but it had no formal authority to force them to comply. Some colonial merchants charged high prices for shoddy goods. Many farmers sold their produce to the highest bidder, whether American or British.

Without adequate supplies, George Washington's troops suffered. They endured bitter weather at Morristown, New Jersey, in January 1777 and at Valley Forge, Pennsylvania, the next winter. Washington also faced constant troop shortages. He had about 20,000 Continentals, or Patriot soldiers, available nationwide at any one time.

With General Howe's evacuation of Boston in March 1776, Washington knew that the British would soon strike elsewhere. The Redcoats attacked and captured New York City in September. They were close to winning the war until Washington's troops launched a Christmas-night attack on soldiers based in Trenton, New Jersey. This victory marked the Patriots' first major offensive attack, and it greatly raised American morale.

After setbacks in New Jersey, the British redoubled their efforts. In control of Canada and New York City, they decided to cut New England off from the other British colonies. British general "Gentleman Johnny" Burgoyne devised a plan to take New York and thus divide New England from the colonies to the south. His strategy failed miserably. Burgoyne's troops were badly outnumbered when they clashed with Patriot soldiers at Saratoga, New York, in October 1777. The Patriots achieved their greatest victory in the war up to that point.

Scots-Irish in the Backcountry

Some of the strongest opposition to the acts of the British government came from young Scots-Irish colonists. In the 50 years before the Revolutionary War, as many as 250,000 people of Scottish descent immigrated to North America. They came from Ulster, a province in northern Ireland. Their ancestors

An anvil used by Scots-Irish in Tennessee

had come to Ulster in the early 1600s. In the early 1700s, facing economic depression, drought, and religious discrimination, the Scots-Irish began crossing the Atlantic to start a new life in America.

Many of the Scots-Irish moved to the western backcountry, where they worked small farms and faced the danger of conflict with local American Indians. Despite the hardships of frontier life, they highly valued the institutions of church and school. Presbyterian ministers who doubled as schoolmasters taught Scots-Irish youngsters.

A strong distaste for the British government caused many Scots-Irish teens to enthusiastically support American independence. Andrew Jackson, for example, participated in a battle against the British when he was 13 years old. He and his brother Robert were captured and thrown in prison, where Andrew contracted smallpox. Robert died on the difficult journey home, but Andrew survived and went on to become the seventh president of the United States.

The Loyalists After Defeat. Loyalists represented a significant portion of the colonial population—about 15 to 20 percent of the adult white male population. White males were not the only Loyalists, however. American Indians from a number of tribes fought for the British, as did some African Americans, both enslaved and free. During and after the Revolution, many Loyalists fled to Canada, the West Indies, or Britain itself. Approximately 1,000 black Loyalists eventually relocated to Sierra Leone. Just as the victorious Patriots began to create new governments, these Loyalists began to build new communities.

CRITICAL THINKING How do you think the victorious Patriots should have treated the Loyalists after the war?

ANSWER: Answers will vary. Some students might suggest that the Patriots should have punished the Loyalists as traitors to the Revolution, while others might suggest that the Patriots should have attempted to absorb the Loyalists and benefit from their skills and knowledge.

Tell students to imagine that they are General Cornwallis. King George III has just received word that General Cornwallis has surrendered at Yorktown. Ask students to write a letter of apology to King George III. In the letter, students should explain, in the words of General Cornwallis, what went wrong for the British and what led to the colonists' victory in the Revolutionary War.

SPOTLIGHT
on European Allies in the American Revolution

Ask students to conduct research on Marquis de Lafayette, or another French sympathizer during the American Revolution. Then have each student create a design for a postage stamp commemorating the person. Ask volunteers to present their designs to the class and to provide some background information on the historical figures that they selected.
Block Scheduling

ECONOMICS

Funding the Revolution.
When the Second Continental Congress raised the Continental Army, it was reluctant to impose a new tax on the already tax-weary colonists. The Second Continental Congress thus printed and issued a new national currency with the expectation that individual states would eventually collect an equivalent amount in taxes. Because the Congress had no authority to force the states to tax their residents, its demands went largely unheeded, creating a significant national debt. To raise money, Congress borrowed from France, sold government bonds, and issued soldiers IOUs in lieu of pay. The financial debacle led some future leaders to believe that the new United States would need a national government as well as a national currency.

CRITICAL THINKING What advantages might a national government have over a state-centered government?

ANSWER: Answers will vary. Students might suggest that a national government is better able to collect taxes and regulate an economy.

VISUAL RECORD ANSWER

[for p. 23]

Students might suggest that the drum beat kept the soldiers marching in step.

Great Debates

Independence

The meaning of the American Revolution has provoked heated and ongoing debates among historians. While independence was one obvious consequence of the Revolution, Thomas Jefferson's words "all men are created equal" have been a source of controversy from the time they were written.

Some historians have chosen to focus on the limitations of revolutionary ideas. Clearly, the Declaration of Independence did not create political liberty for everyone. American women were excluded from political life until 1920. Some slaves fought for and gained their freedom during the Revolution, but slavery as a system did not end until after the Civil War. Many American Indians lost their lands and homes as a result of the war.

Other historians have viewed the Revolution as an event of great social consequence. While America in the 1700s was full of inequalities, these scholars argue that the Revolution began to change Americans' ideas about how power should be distributed in society. No longer did people assume that a few "well-born" individuals should rule over everyone else. This fundamental change in attitude would eventually lead to the expansion of democratic rights to include all Americans, whatever their gender, race, or economic condition.

This victory persuaded France to ally itself with the United States and to provide military and economic support. Individual French citizens, like the Marquis de Lafayette, were already fighting for the Patriots. Lafayette believed that "the welfare of America is intimately connected with the happiness of all mankind." The alliance with France came just in time. During the severe winter of 1777–78, Washington's army had been reduced to a handful of soldiers. The news of the alliance gave the Patriots new hope.

✔ **READING CHECK: Sequencing** What event led the French to support the Patriots? the Patriot victory at Saratoga

Fighting in the West and South

The Patriots also had success in the West. In 1778 George Rogers Clark led an expedition to secure the Illinois country. In February 1779 Clark's troops surprised the British at the Battle of Vincennes (vin-SENZ). Clark's army scored an easy victory and went on to neutralize British forces in the West.

Late in 1778 the British focused their attacks on the southern colonies. Backed by their navy, they occupied the seaport towns of Savannah, Georgia, and Charleston, South Carolina. From Charleston, General Charles Cornwallis attacked inland. After crushing the Americans in the Battle of Camden in 1780, British forces marched toward North Carolina.

Cornwallis did not find the Loyalist support he had expected. Some Loyalist militia patrolled the countryside, but so did small groups of Patriot soldiers. Continental officer Francis Marion led one of the most aggressive outfits. Marion and his South Carolina militia disrupted British communications and discouraged many Loyalists from fighting. Patriot commander Nathanael Greene ultimately stopped the British in the South. Greene was a master of guerrilla warfare—wearing down the enemy in hit-and-run battles. Even in defeat, Greene bragged, "We fight, get beat, rise, and fight again." Greene, Marion, and the Patriots eventually forced Cornwallis to retreat.

✔ **READING CHECK: Summarizing** How did Patriot forces fight the British in the West and the South? surprise attacks in the West; guerrilla warfare in the South

Victory

During the summer of 1781, General Cornwallis moved his army to Yorktown, Virginia, located on the peninsula between the York and James Rivers. There

REVIEW

Have students complete the **Section 3 Review** on page 23.

ASSESS

Have students complete **Daily Quiz 1.3**. As Alternative Assessment, you may want to use the protest handbills or the Declaration of Independence lists in this section's lessons.

RETEACH

Have students complete **Main Idea Activity for English Language Learners and Special-Needs Students 1.3**. Then ask students to define and identify the key terms and people from the section as you write each of them on the chalkboard. Have each student develop one question and answer for each of the terms and people. Collect the questions and use them to quiz students on section content. **English Language Learners**

EXTEND

Briefly review the goals of the American Revolution with students and list them on the chalkboard. Then organize students into two groups and conduct a debate on the following question: *Did the Revolution achieve its goals?* One group should argue that the Revolution achieved its ultimate goals, while the other group should argue that it did not.
Block Scheduling, Cooperative Learning

he had access to the British fleet and supplies.

On August 14 General Washington received news that a French naval commander was moving his fleet north to block Chesapeake Bay. Washington's army, along with a French force, rushed south to complete the trap. Boxed in by the French fleet, the British troops at Yorktown soon found themselves vastly outnumbered by American and French forces. Cornwallis soon admitted defeat.

On October 19, 1781, the British surrendered at the **Battle of Yorktown**. Cornwallis's surrender effectively marked the end of the war. The **Treaty of Paris**, signed on September 3, 1783, granted the United States independence. The nation also gained land from the Atlantic coast westward to the Mississippi River and from the Great Lakes south to Florida. The treaty also declared that Americans should repay any debts owed to the British. A new nation was born.

✔ **READING CHECK: Drawing Conclusions** How did the Treaty of Paris affect the growth of the United States? It granted independence and gave the new nation land.

INTERPRETING THE VISUAL RECORD

American troops. Minutemen march to the front lines. *What purpose did the drummer serve?*

SECTION 3 REVIEW

1. Identify and explain:
Stamp Act
Samuel Adams
George III
Intolerable Acts
George Washington
Battle of Bunker Hill
Thomas Paine
Common Sense
Declaration of Independence
Thomas Jefferson
Abigail Adams
John Adams
Battle of Yorktown
Treaty of Paris

2. Sequencing Copy the graphic organizer below. Use it to identify the colonists' responses to the British government's actions.

Revolutionary War

3. **Finding the Main Idea**
a. Why did the colonists object to taxes the British government imposed on them?
b. Why might rulers in Europe have viewed the Declaration of Independence as a dangerous document?
c. How were the colonists able to defeat the British forces?

4. **Writing and Critical Thinking**
Supporting a Point of View Imagine that you are an American colonist in the late 1700s. Write an editorial expressing your reaction to British taxation.
Consider:
• the right of the British Parliament to tax the colonies
• specific laws and acts that angered colonists
• other ways colonists could have responded

Homework Practice Online
keyword: SE3 HP1

THE DECLARATION OF INDEPENDENCE

INTERDISCIPLINARY CONNECTIONS

▶LANGUAGE ARTS◀

The Words of the Declaration. The authors of the Declaration of Independence were not merely issuing a proclamation; they were trying to persuade colonists that George III had become a *despot.* In its original Greek form, despot meant "master" or "lord." Later, however, the word came to mean "absolute ruler" and referred to those who governed in a tyrannical, oppressive way.

ACTIVITY: Ask students to scan magazines and newspapers to find different uses of the word *despot.* Have each student select one example, bring it to class, and present it to the other students. Conduct a brief discussion on students' examples and the ways in which the term *despot* might have affected colonists who read it in the Declaration of Independence.

GOVERNMENT ANSWER

Students might note that the Declaration insists that "a decent respect to the opinions of mankind requires that they should declare the causes which impel them to the separation"—in other words, consideration for both the colonial country and world observers mandated the justification of the break.

24

Thomas Jefferson wrote the first draft of the Declaration in a little more than two weeks. He drew upon the Virginia Declaration of Rights, written by George Mason, for the opening paragraphs.

 Government

According to the first paragraph, why is it important for the signers to justify their political break with Great Britain?

impel: force
endowed: provided

"Laws of Nature" and "Nature's God" refer to the belief common in the Scientific Revolution that certain patterns are constant and predictable and that they come from a supreme being. Natural or "unalienable" rights (the rights to life, liberty, and the pursuit of happiness) cannot be taken away. English philosopher John Locke had argued that people create governments to protect their natural rights. If a government abuses its powers, it is the right as well as the duty of the people to do away with that government.

usurpations: wrongful seizures of power
evinces: clearly displays
despotism: unlimited power

THE GRANGER COLLECTION, NEW YORK

The Declaration of Independence

*In Congress, July 4, 1776
The unanimous Declaration of the thirteen
united States of America,*

Whotel when in the Course of human events, it becomes necessary for one people to dissolve the political bands which have connected them with another, and to assume among the Powers of the earth, the separate and equal station to which the Laws of Nature and of Nature's God entitle them, a decent respect to the opinions of mankind requires that they should declare the causes which impel them to the separation.

We hold these truths to be self-evident, that all men are created equal, that they are endowed by their Creator with certain unalienable Rights, that among these are Life, Liberty, and the pursuit of Happiness. That to secure these rights, Governments are instituted among Men, deriving their just powers from the consent of the governed, That whenever any Form of Government becomes destructive of these ends, it is the Right of the People to alter or to abolish it, and to institute new Government, laying its foundation on such principles and organizing its powers in such form, as to them shall seem most likely to effect their Safety and Happiness. Prudence, indeed, will dictate that Governments long established should not be changed for light and transient causes; and accordingly all experience hath shown, that mankind are more disposed to suffer, while evils are sufferable, than to right themselves by abolishing the forms to which they are accustomed. But when a long train of abuses and usurpations, pursuing invariably the same Object evinces a design to reduce them under absolute Despotism, it is their right, it is their duty, to throw off such Government, and to provide new Guards for their future security.— Such has been the patient sufferance of these Colonies; and such is now the necessity which constrains them to alter their former Systems of Government. The history

The Declaration of Independence

of the present King of Great Britain is a history of repeated injuries and usurpations, all having in direct object the establishment of an absolute Tyranny over these States. To prove this, let Facts be submitted to a candid world.

He has refused his Assent to Laws, the most wholesome and necessary for the public good.

He has forbidden his Governors to pass Laws of immediate and pressing importance, unless suspended in their operation till his Assent should be obtained; and when so suspended, he has utterly neglected to attend to them.

He has refused to pass other Laws for the accommodation of large districts of people, unless those people would relinquish the right of Representation in the Legislature, a right inestimable to them and formidable to tyrants only.

He has called together legislative bodies at places unusual, uncomfortable, and distant from the depository of their Public Records, for the sole purpose of fatiguing them into compliance with his measures.

He has dissolved Representative Houses repeatedly, for opposing with manly firmness his invasions on the rights of the people.

He has refused for a long time, after such dissolutions, to cause others to be elected; whereby the Legislative Powers, incapable of Annihilation, have returned to the People at large for their exercise; the State remaining in the mean time exposed to all the dangers of invasion from without, and convulsions within.

He has endeavored to prevent the population of these States; for that purpose obstructing the Laws of Naturalization of Foreigners; refusing to pass others to encourage their migration hither, and raising the conditions of new Appropriations of Lands.

He has obstructed the Administration of Justice, by refusing his Assent to Laws for establishing Judiciary Powers.

He has made Judges dependent on his Will alone, for the tenure of their offices, and the amount and payment of their salaries.

He has erected a multitude of New Offices, and sent hither swarms of Officers to harass our people, and eat out their substance.

He has kept among us, in times of peace, Standing Armies without the Consent of our legislature.

He has affected to render the Military independent of and superior to the Civil Power.

He has combined with others to subject us to a jurisdiction foreign to our constitution, and unacknowledged by our laws; giving his Assent to their Acts of pretended legislation:

For quartering large bodies of armed troops among us:

For protecting them, by a mock Trial, from Punishment for any Murders which they should commit on the Inhabitants of these States:

For cutting off our Trade with all parts of the world:

tyranny: oppressive power exerted by a government or ruler
candid: fair
Beginning here the Declaration lists the colonists' charges against King George III.

relinquish: release, yield
inestimable: priceless
formidable: causing dread

annihilation: destruction

convulsions: violent disturbances

naturalization of foreigners: the process by which foreign-born persons become citizens
appropriations of land: setting aside land for settlement

tenure: term

a multitude of: many

 Government

What wrongful acts stated in the Declaration have been committed by the king and the British Parliament?

quartering: lodging, housing

CITIZENSHIP

The Signers of the Declaration. The men who eventually signed the Declaration came from diverse backgrounds. Many, such as Arthur Middleton and Lewis Morris, grew up in wealthy families and received good educations. Others, such as Samuel Huntington and Roger Sherman, were from humble beginnings. One signer, George Taylor, had come to the colonies as an indentured servant. Taylor eventually received his freedom. He served the Continental Army during the Revolutionary War by producing munitions.

CRITICAL THINKING How might George Taylor's life have reflected the ideals of the Declaration and the Revolution?

ANSWER: Students might suggest that Taylor's life reflected the importance of equal opportunity for all.

GOVERNMENT ANSWER

Students should note that the colonists protested the king's taxes because they were imposed without due consent.

GOVERNMENT ANSWER
(for p. 27)

Students should note that the colonists received their authority to declare independence from the colonial people themselves.

★ Government

Why were the colonists protesting British tax policies?

The "neighboring Province" referred to here is Quebec.
arbitrary: not based on law
render: make

abdicated: given up

foreign mercenaries: soldiers hired to fight for a country not their own
perfidy: violation of trust

insurrections: rebellions

petitioned for redress: asked formally for a correction of wrongs

---

For imposing taxes on us without our Consent:

For depriving us in many cases, of the benefits of Trial by Jury:

For transporting us beyond Seas to be tried for pretended offences:

For abolishing the free System of English Laws in a neighboring Province, establishing therein an Arbitrary government, and enlarging its Boundaries so as to render it at once an example and fit instrument for introducing the same absolute rule into these Colonies:

For taking away our Charters, abolishing our most valuable Laws, and altering fundamentally the Forms of our Governments:

For suspending our own Legislature, and declaring themselves invested with Power to legislate for us in all cases whatsoever.

He has abdicated Government here, by declaring us out of his Protection and waging War against us.

He has plundered our seas, ravaged our Coasts, burnt our towns, and destroyed the lives of our people.

He is at this time transporting large armies of foreign mercenaries to complete the works of death, desolation and tyranny, already begun with circumstances of Cruelty & perfidy scarcely paralleled in the most barbarous ages, and totally unworthy the Head of a civilized nation.

He has constrained our fellow Citizens taken Captive on the high Seas to bear Arms against their Country, to become the executioners of their friends and Brethren, or to fall themselves by their Hands.

He has excited domestic insurrections amongst us, and has endeavored to bring on the inhabitants of our frontiers, the merciless Indian Savages, whose known rule of warfare, is an undistinguished destruction of all ages, sexes and conditions.

In every stage of these Oppressions We have Petitioned for Redress in the most humble terms: Our repeated Petitions have been answered only by repeated injury. A Prince, whose character is thus marked by every act which may define a Tyrant, is unfit to be the ruler of a free People.

This painting by Robert Pine and Edward Savage depicts the Continental Congress voting for independence.

Nor have We been wanting in attention to our British brethren. We have warned them from time to time of attempts by their legislature to extend an unwarrantable jurisdiction over us. We have reminded them of the circumstances of our emigration and settlement here. We have appealed to their native justice and magnanimity, and we have conjured them by the ties of our common kindred to disavow these usurpations, which, would inevitably interrupt our connections and correspondence. They too have been deaf to the voice of justice and of consanguinity. We must, therefore, acquiesce in the necessity, which denounces our Separation, and hold them, as we hold the rest of mankind, Enemies in War, in Peace Friends.

We, therefore, the Representatives of the united States of America, in General Congress, Assembled, appealing to the Supreme Judge of the world for the rectitude of our intentions, do, in the Name, and by Authority of the good People of these Colonies, solemnly publish and declare, That these United Colonies are, and of Right ought to be Free and Independent States; that they are Absolved from all Allegiance to the British Crown, and that all political connection between them and the State of Great Britain, is and ought to be totally dissolved; and that as Free and Independent States, they have full Power to levy War, conclude Peace, contract Alliances, establish Commerce, and to do all other Acts and Things which Independent States may of right do. And for the support of this Declaration, with a firm reliance on the Protection of Divine Providence, we mutually pledge to each other our Lives, our Fortunes and our sacred Honor.

John Hancock	Benjamin Harrison	Lewis Morris
Button Gwinnett	Thomas Nelson Jr.	Richard Stockton
Lyman Hall	Francis Lightfoot Lee	John Witherspoon
George Walton	Carter Braxton	Francis Hopkinson
William Hooper	Robert Morris	John Hart
Joseph Hewes	Benjamin Rush	Abraham Clark
John Penn	Benjamin Franklin	Josiah Bartlett
Edward Rutledge	John Morton	William Whipple
Thomas Heyward Jr.	George Clymer	Samuel Adams
Thomas Lynch Jr.	James Smith	John Adams
Arthur Middleton	George Taylor	Robert Treat Paine
Samuel Chase	James Wilson	Elbridge Gerry
William Paca	George Ross	Stephen Hopkins
Thomas Stone	Caesar Rodney	William Ellery
Charles Carroll of Carrollton	George Read	Roger Sherman
	Thomas McKean	Samuel Huntington
George Wythe	William Floyd	William Williams
Richard Henry Lee	Phillip Livingston	Oliver Wolcott
Thomas Jefferson	Francis Lewis	Matthew Thornton

unwarrantable jurisdiction: unjustified authority

magnanimity: generous spirit

conjured: urgently called upon

consanguinity: common ancestry

acquiesce: consent to

rectitude: rightness

Congress adopted the final draft of the Declaration of Independence on July 4, 1776. A formal copy, written on parchment paper, was signed on August 2, 1776.

⭐ Government

From whom did the signers of the Declaration receive their authority to declare independence?

The following is part of a passage that the Congress took out of Jefferson's original draft: "He has waged cruel war against human nature itself, violating its most sacred rights of life and liberty in the persons of a distant people who never offended him, captivating and carrying them into slavery in another hemisphere, or to incur miserable death in their transportation thither." *Why do you think the Congress deleted this passage?*

SECTION 4

After completing Section 4, students should be able to:

OBJECTIVE 1 Analyze what ideas influenced the writing of the state constitutions.

OBJECTIVE 2 Discuss how the U.S. government worked under the Articles of Confederation.

OBJECTIVE 3 Summarize the domestic and foreign problems the new nation faced.

OBJECTIVE 4 Identify the compromises delegates made in drafting the Constitution, and explain how the document was ratified.

SECTION 4 RESOURCES

REPRODUCIBLE
▶ Guided Reading Strategy 1.4
▶ Literature Reading 1: "On Mr. Paine's Rights of Man"

TECHNOLOGY
▶ One-Stop Planner, Lesson 1.4
▶ Holt Researcher: American History CD–ROM
▶ Homework Practice Online

REINFORCEMENT, REVIEW, AND ASSESSMENT
▶ Section 4 Review, p. 35
▶ Daily Quiz 1.4
▶ Main Idea Activity 1.4
▶ English Audio Summary 1.4
▶ Spanish Audio Summary 1.4

READ TO DISCOVER
1. What ideas influenced the writing of the state constitutions?
2. How did the U.S. government work under the Articles of Confederation?
3. What domestic and foreign problems did the new nation face?
4. What compromises did delegates make in drafting the Constitution, and how was the document ratified?

DEFINE
republicanism
depression
electors
federalism
supremacy clause
elastic clause

IDENTIFY
Virginia Statute for Religious Freedom
Articles of Confederation
Northwest Ordinance
Constitutional Convention
Benjamin Franklin
Federalists
Antifederalists

▶ WHY IT MATTERS TODAY
The cabinet advises the president on important issues. Use CNNfyi.com or other **current events** sources to identify a member of the presidential cabinet and learn about that person's duties. Record your findings in your journal.

CNNfyi.com

LET'S GET STARTED!

Write the following statement on the chalkboard: *The Revolutionary War was only the first act of the drama of revolution.* What might this statement mean? Tell students to respond to the statement in writing. Ask volunteers to share their responses. Then tell students that in Section 4, they will learn about Americans' attempts to found a new nation.

Founding the Nation

The Continental Congress

EYEWITNESSES TO History

"You and I, my dear friend, have been sent into life at a time when the greatest lawgivers of antiquity would have wished to live. How few of the human race have ever enjoyed an opportunity of making . . . government . . . for themselves or their children!"

—John Adams, letter to George Wythe, 1776

John Adams expressed to a friend the optimism many early American leaders felt as they faced the challenge of designing a new nation. The American Revolution brought an end to the rule of the British monarchy in America and forced the royal governors from office. To fill this void, the Second Continental Congress advised the former colonies to form new governments "under the authority of the people."

Forming a New Government

American leaders drew upon a wide range of political ideas as they planned these new state governments. English legal tradition inspired many revolutionary leaders.

English political ideas. English nobles had drawn up Magna Carta, or "Great Charter," in 1215 during the reign of King John. Magna Carta limited the power of the monarchy. In addition to guaranteeing basic civil liberties for nobles, the charter protected their trading rights. The English Bill of Rights, which Parliament passed in 1689, also influenced the colonists. This document guaranteed English citizens rights such as freedom of speech. It also forbade raising an army during peacetime without the consent of Parliament.

The works of Enlightenment thinkers such as John Locke also influenced Americans. The English philosopher who developed the theory of "natural rights," Locke believed that all people were born with the rights to life, liberty, and property—rights outlined in English constitutional tradition. He thought that the role of government was to protect these rights.

State constitutions. Before declaring independence, the Second Continental Congress had urged the colonies to draft new constitutions to replace their British royal charters. Between 1776 and 1780 all of the states except Connecticut and Rhode Island drafted and ratified, or approved, new constitutions. Connecticut and Rhode Island revised their royal charters by deleting references to British authority.

Several state legislatures formed new governments based on **republicanism**. According to this theory, citizens hold the ultimate authority. They select representatives and give them the authority to make and enforce laws. The Mayflower Compact had incorporated this idea.

TEACH OBJECTIVE 1

LEVEL 1: Pair students and have them write an explanation for each of these terms: *Magna Carta, English Bill of Rights, republicanism, natural rights.* Have volunteers read their explanations and discuss these terms with students. Then have each pair write a short mock constitution that contains the ideas that were reflected in the first state constitutions. *(Constitutions should contain basic property rights, inalienable rights such as free speech, restrictions on governors, controls on the political power of the church, and statement that all people are born with the rights of life, liberty, and property.)* Display the mock constitutions around the classroom.
English Language Learners, Cooperative Learning

LEVEL 2: Tell students to imagine they are high-level state officials preparing to write a new state constitution in the days after the defeat of the British. Have each student write a new constitution that embodies the principles of the Magna Carta, the English Bill of Rights, republicanism, and natural rights. *(See Level 1 lesson for correct principles.)* Reflect on these constitutions in a classroom discussion.

The role of religion. Many state constitutions reduced the influence of the church on government. Before the Revolution, several colonies had used tax money to support a particular church. Colonists were required to pay these taxes even if they did not belong to the church. Some colonists, including Thomas Jefferson, opposed this relationship between the government and one religious affiliation.

In the late 1770s Jefferson drafted the **Virginia Statute for Religious Freedom**. It stated that the human mind was created free and that government control over religious beliefs or worship was tyrannical. In his argument for the adoption of the statute in 1785, James Madison declared, "Religion . . . must be left to the conviction and conscience of every man." Virginia adopted the statute in 1786. By 1833 every state had forbidden the establishment of official state churches supported by tax dollars.

✔ **READING CHECK: Finding the Main Idea** What political and social ideas were reflected in the state constitutions? English political tradition, republicanism, and separation of church and state

Thomas Jefferson drafted the Virginia Statute for Religious Freedom in 1777, but it was not enacted until 1786.

A Plan for Confederation

Facing the challenge of forming an entirely new government, political leaders decided to join the states in a loose union. A committee headed by John Dickinson presented its plan for a national government—the **Articles of Confederation**—to congressional delegates. The Articles—the first written constitution of the United States—went into effect in 1781.

The Articles of Confederation. The Articles of Confederation granted the new government the right to borrow and coin money, conduct foreign affairs, set policy toward American Indians, and settle disputes between the states. However, each state kept its "sovereignty, freedom, and independence." The Articles created a one-house legislature as the Confederation's main institution.

For the Articles to take effect, all 13 states had to ratify them. One major issue blocked ratification—control of the Allegheny Mountains and the land beyond them, just east of the Mississippi River. Based on their old royal charters, several states claimed vast tracts of western land. States without land claims wanted the other states to surrender these lands to the new national government.

This conflict centered around the need for money. The new Congress expected each state to help pay for Revolutionary War expenses. States with western lands had additional sources of revenue because they had more land to sell. States without surplus land faced the prospect of raising taxes. Leaders from some states without western lands refused to ratify the Articles unless the bigger states gave up some of their landholdings.

To promote national unity, New York and Virginia—the states with the largest landholdings—gave the disputed land to Congress. Other states followed suit. By 1781 all of the states had agreed to enter the Confederation. The thirteen former British colonies then officially became "The United States of America."

The Northwest Territory. Members of Congress knew that the issue of western land remained a problem. In 1787 Congress passed a land ordinance, commonly

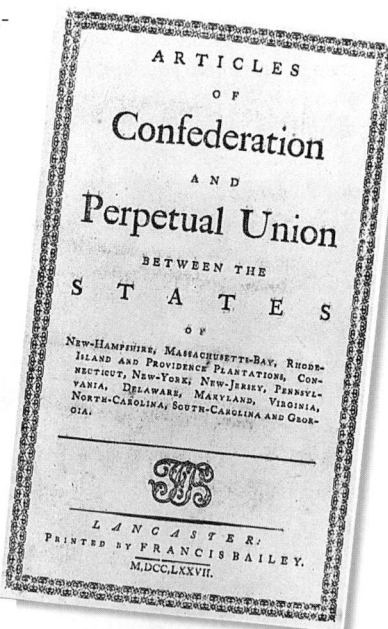

INTERPRETING THE VISUAL RECORD

Confederation. The Articles of Confederation established a national government. *Why might this cover refer to "Perpetual Union"?*

LEVEL 3: Tell students to imagine they are high-level state officials preparing to write a new state constitution in the days after the defeat of the British. Have each student write a new constitution that embodies the principles of Magna Carta, the English Bill of Rights, republicanism, and natural rights. *(See Level 1 lesson for correct principles.)* Then have each student conduct research on his or her state constitution and write a comparison/contrast essay between his or her constitution and the actual state constitution of his or her state. How do they differ? Which document offers the most advantages? Why?

Teacher to Teacher

Melissa Thomas of El Paso, Texas, suggested the following activity: Have students create an In the News *report. Write the following topics on index cards: Forming a New Government, A Plan for Confederation, Weaknesses in the Confederation, The Constitutional Convention, Federalists and Antifederalists, and The Living Constitution. Have students pick one topic and write an* In the News *report illustrating the key points of their topic. Students may want to use the Holt Presentation Maker to create their report.*

HISTORY MAKERS SPEAK

Melvin I. Urofsky in *A March of Liberty: A Constitutional History of the United States*

The Articles of Confederation—A Dangerous Weakness?
Historian Melvin I. Urofsky explains the inherent weaknesses of the Articles by writing: "Congress under the Confederation, to put it bluntly, lacked the minimal powers needed to govern. Congress could ask for money but not levy taxes; it could negotiate treaties but not enforce them; it could borrow money but not provide for repayment."

CRITICAL THINKING Why might the Articles have denied Congress the power to levy taxes?

ANSWER: Students might suggest that given the recent war against Great Britain—a war that was fought, in part, against unfair taxation—the authors of the Articles were wary of taxation. They wanted to protect state sovereignty.

VISUAL RECORD ANSWER

Answers will vary. Students should suggest that Shays's followers dress more like farmers and less like statesmen.

INTERPRETING THE VISUAL RECORD

Shays's Rebellion. Daniel Shays's rebels occupy a western Massachusetts courthouse in this illustration. ***How does their style of dress help you identify Shays's followers in the illustration?***

THE GRANGER COLLECTION, NEW YORK

---

referred to as the **Northwest Ordinance**. This measure established a system for governing the Northwest Territory—a vast area extending north of the Ohio River to the Great Lakes and west of Pennsylvania to the Mississippi River. Congress also outlined the steps to statehood for this territory. Each new state would be admitted with the same political powers as the original thirteen colonies. The present-day states of Illinois, Indiana, Michigan, Ohio, and Wisconsin eventually were carved out of the territory. This policy established a precedent that would be used for settling territories farther west. The Northwest Ordinance also guaranteed settlers' civil rights and banned slavery in the territory. This ban reflected a growing anti-slavery sentiment in the northern states.

✔ **READING CHECK: Summarizing** How did Congress resolve the conflict over states' claims to western land? New York and Virginia agreed to give up their lands, and Congress passed the Northwest Ordinance.

Weaknesses in the Confederation

On paper the Confederation government enjoyed broad powers, but in reality it was weak. Proposed changes to the Articles required the consent of all 13 states. Major new legislation needed the approval of at least nine states.

After the war, the nation faced serious financial problems. Congress desperately needed cash to pay its war debts. Because it could not tax the people directly, Congress had to appeal to the states for funds. Claiming their independent status as sovereign states, some state legislatures avoided paying their share of the debts.

Congress responded by printing paper money. The financial consequences proved disastrous. These bills of credit, called Continentals, were not backed by gold or silver. Thus, merchants and lenders refused to accept them at face value.

In 1784 the nation began to experience a **depression**, or a sharp drop in business activity accompanied by rising unemployment. One cause of this depression was the loss of British markets. Before the war, American merchants had traded with Britain and with other colonies within the British Empire. After the war, Britain kept some of its colonial markets closed to American commerce.

Britain worsened the economic crisis by flooding the United States with inexpensive goods. Struggling American merchants and artisans could not match the prices of British-made goods and survive. Congress was powerless to help, since the Articles did not give it the authority to draft international trade policies.

As the nation's economic problems grew, indebted farmers rebelled in western Massachusetts. In what became known as Shays's Rebellion, farmers shut down debtor courts and stopped property auctions. This rebellion caused many people to believe that the United States needed a more powerful government.

✔ **READING CHECK: Identifying Cause and Effect** How did weaknesses in the Articles of Confederation contribute to Shays's Rebellion? Congress's inability to raise funds contributed to economic problems that hurt indebted farmers.

LEVEL 1: Pair students and ask each pair to list the powers that the Articles of Confederation granted to the national government. *(Lists should mention the power to coin and borrow money, conduct foreign affairs, set policy toward American Indians, and settle disputes between the states.)* Then have each pair annotate its list, noting how the U.S. government actually operated under each of the powers granted by the Articles of Confederation.
English Language Learners, Cooperative Learning

LEVEL 2: Tell students to imagine that they helped draft the Articles of Confederation. Have each student write a one-page letter to a friend or relative in Britain describing how the national government will operate under the Articles of Confederation. *(Letters should mention that the national government will handle foreign affairs and settle state disputes, but in all matters involving individual states, will defer power to the states.)* Have volunteers read their letters to the class.

The Constitutional Convention

In 1786 Henry Knox explained in a letter to George Washington, "The powers of Congress are totally inadequate." Concerns about the Articles of Confederation led to the **Constitutional Convention**, held in Philadelphia in May 1787. George Washington, **Benjamin Franklin**, and 53 other state delegates debated how much power the central government should have.

The delegates. The delegates were a remarkable collection of politicians. Many had helped write their state constitutions; almost all had held public office. Most had served as delegates to the Continental Congress, including James Madison of Virginia and Alexander Hamilton of New York. At 81, Benjamin Franklin of Pennsylvania was the elder statesman of the convention. The delegates were generally wealthy and well educated. Many were bankers, merchants, and planters; more than half had studied law.

Compromise on representation. The Confederation Congress had asked the delegates to revise the Articles of Confederation. Some delegates, however, believed that the Articles should be replaced with an entirely new plan of government.

Relations among the states and between the states and the central government were a prominent concern. Madison was the major author of the Virginia Plan, which called for a national government made up of three branches: legislative, executive, and judicial. This plan also gave Congress the right to overturn state laws, tax the states, and "bring the force of the Union against any [state] . . . failing to fulfill its duty."

Under the Virginia plan, the legislature would be bicameral—made up of two houses. Voters would elect representatives to the lower house, who would then choose members of the upper house. State populations would determine the number of representatives in each house.

A dispute quickly arose over the number of representatives each state would have. William Paterson of New Jersey offered an alternative. His New Jersey Plan called for a strong unicameral legislature in which each state would have one vote. It also proposed giving the federal government the power to tax and regulate commerce.

To balance the interests of large and small states, delegate Roger Sherman of Connecticut proposed a bicameral legislature that would allow for both equal representation and representation based on population. This Great Compromise granted each state, regardless of size, an equal voice in the upper house. In the lower house, representation would be according to population. The delegates narrowly approved this proposal, ending the most serious debate of the Convention.

Other compromises. The delegates next debated whether slaves should be counted as part of a state's population to determine representation in the lower house. Southern delegates insisted that the slave population be included. Northern delegates strongly objected to this demand. Northern and southern delegates accepted a compromise. The final agreement, known as the Three-Fifths Compromise, established that three fifths of the slave population would count in determining total state population.

James Madison helped draft Virginia's state constitution before he served as a member of the Continental Congress.

Roger Sherman. Roger Sherman was a central figure in U.S. politics throughout the revolutionary and constitutional eras. A former cobbler who had taught himself law, he served in the Connecticut legislature for almost 20 years before attending the First Continental Congress and helping write the Articles of Confederation. At the Constitutional Convention Sherman was one of the most active participants, speaking to the group more than 135 times. After the ratification of the document he helped to create, Sherman served as one of the authors of the Bill of Rights and as a member of both the House of Representatives and the Senate.

ACTIVITY: Ask students to imagine that they are delegates at the Constitutional Convention. Then have each student write a short statement supporting or opposing Roger Sherman's Great Compromise.

LEVEL 3: Tell students to imagine that they are newspaper editors during the time of the Articles of Confederation. Have each student write an editorial criticizing the weaknesses of the Articles and how those weaknesses affect the way the government worked under the Articles. *(Government could not tax the states and so went into debt, created inflation by coining money not backed by anything, could not pass legislation without ratification by states.)* Gather student articles together, and make a newspaper editorial page to put up in the classroom.

 HOMEWORK *Ask students to revise the Articles of Confederation in order to allow the national government to work more efficiently.*

★ HISTORICAL DOCUMENTS ★

JAMES MADISON
The *Federalist Papers*

Papers No. 10 and No. 51 were two of the most significant essays from the Federalist Papers *arguing for the ratification of the Constitution. James Madison wrote both. In essay No. 10, he argues that a strong national government is necessary to reduce conflict among opposing groups. In essay No. 51, Madison contends that the balance of power among different branches of government would prevent any one branch from gaining too much power.* **In Madison's view, how will the Constitution create a "well-constructed" Union?**

Federalist Paper "No. 10" (1787)

Among the numerous advantages promised by a well-constructed Union, none deserves to be more accurately developed than its tendency to break and control the violence of faction [splinter group]. . . . The influence of factious [rebellious] leaders may kindle a flame within their particular states but will be unable to spread a general conflagration [larger fire] through the other states.

Federalist Paper "No. 51" (1788)

The great security against a gradual concentration of the several powers in the same department consists in giving to those who administer each department the necessary constitutional means and personal motives to resist encroachments [advances] of the others. The provision for defense must . . . be made commensurate [equal] to the danger of attack.

The Federalist

The delegates also debated the control of commerce. They agreed that Congress could levy tariffs, or taxes, on imports but not on exports. Southern planters worried that Congress might use its power to tax imports to restrict or abolish the slave trade. Bowing to pressure from southern delegates, the convention voted to permit the slave trade to continue until at least the end of 1807.

In September 1787 delegates presented the final version of the Constitution. Of the 42 delegates remaining in Philadelphia, 39 signed it. The Constitution went to Congress and then to the states for ratification.

✔ **READING CHECK: Comparing and Contrasting** How did the compromises at the Constitutional Convention reflect the concerns of both northern and southern states? Some slaves were counted toward southern states' population, and Congress gained the power to levy import tariffs.

Federalists and Antifederalists

To win ratification, the Constitution required the approval of 9 of the 13 states. Although many convention delegates hoped for unanimous approval, citizens were soon divided over ratification.

Support for ratification. One group who called themselves **Federalists** favored ratification of the Constitution. Wealthy merchants, planters, and lawyers typically were Federalists. They supported a strong national government that would be able to ensure a sound currency and would protect property rights. Alexander Hamilton, John Jay, James Madison, and John Marshall were among the leading Federalists. Madison spoke of the need for the new government.

History Makers Speak

❝If men were angels, no government would be necessary. If angels were to govern men, neither external nor internal controls on government would be necessary. In framing a government which is to be administered by men over men, the great difficulty is this: You must first enable the government to control the governed; and in the next place, oblige it to control itself.❞

—James Madison, *Federalist Paper* "No. 51"

Many Americans who were not wealthy also supported the Constitution. They believed that a strong national government would provide stability and

TEACH OBJECTIVE 3

LEVEL 1: Have students label one side of a sheet of paper, "Domestic Challenges" and the other side, "Foreign Challenges." Then tell students to list the domestic and foreign challenges the new nation faced. *(Students should include as domestic challenges: federal debt, land disputes, economic depression, and farmers' protests; foreign challenges should include: closure of British markets and inability to pay back foreign debt.)* **English Language Learners**

LEVELS 2 AND 3: Have students complete the Level 1 activity, leaving a few lines blank between items in each column. Tell them to fill in the blank spaces with reasons why the Articles of Confederation was responsible for many of the domestic and foreign problems the United States faced. *(Since the Articles did not provide the power to tax the states, the national government could not pay its domestic or foreign debts, which led to the printing of money and the depression; farmers who could not make money in the depression protested; no power over the states led to compromises over land disputes; national government had no power to enforce any treaties it might make with Great Britain.)*

---

security against political unrest like Shays's Rebellion. Speaking before the Massachusetts ratifying convention, farmer Jonathan Smith saw the Constitution as "a cure for these disorders."

Opposition to ratification.

Antifederalists, as their opponents called them, feared a powerful national government. Samuel Adams, John Hancock, Patrick Henry, and George Mason were among the Antifederalist leaders. They offered several objections. Saying he "smelled a rat," Henry claimed that the delegates were plotting to take away states' rights. He feared that "the tyranny of Philadelphia may be like the tyranny of [King] George III." The Antifederalists demanded that a bill of rights, or a written document protecting individual liberties, be added to the Constitution.

The Antifederalists pointed to the election procedures outlined in the Constitution as proof that the new national government was undemocratic. Under the Constitution, voters did not directly elect the president, the vice president, or U.S. senators. **Electors**, delegates selected by state governments, chose them. Ordinary voters would directly elect only members of the lower house of Congress—the House of Representatives.

Governor George Clinton of New York wrote several letters under the name "Cato." He challenged citizens to consider the dangers of the proposed national government.

> 💬 *History Makers Speak* **"For what did you throw off the yoke of Britain and call yourselves independent? Was it from a disposition fond of change, or to procure [get] new masters? . . . This new form of national government . . . will be dangerous to your liberty and happiness."**
>
> —Cato, letter to the *New-York Journal*, October 11, 1787

The Federalists answered their critics in a series of 85 essays written by John Jay, Alexander Hamilton, and James Madison. Between the fall of 1787 and the spring of 1788, 77 of the essays appeared in New York newspapers. The essays were later published in a book, entitled *The Federalist*, which was also known as the *Federalist Papers*. In order to get the Constitution ratified the Federalists promised to support amending the Constitution to include a bill of rights. By June 21, 1788, the required 9 out of 13 states had ratified the U.S. Constitution. A new national government was born.

✔ **READING CHECK: Categorizing** What were the main Antifederalist arguments against the new Constitution? How did the Federalists respond? The Antifederalists objected to the strong central government and the nondemocratic election procedures; the Federalists responded by writing a series of essays.

THE GRANGER COLLECTION, NEW YORK

INTERPRETING THE VISUAL RECORD

Ratification. In 1788 the people of New York City celebrated the adoption of the Constitution with a parade. A team of horses pulled this ship on wheels that represent the "ship of state." **Why might the base read "HAMILTON"?**

INTERDISCIPLINARY CONNECTIONS

▶LITERATURE◀

Debating Ratification. Like the Federalists, the Antifederalists published hundreds of essays during the debate over ratification. Leading Antifederalist pamphlets included *Letters from the Federal Farmer to the Republican, Observations on the New Constitution . . . by a Columbian Patriot,* and *the Letters of Brutus.* Like Alexander Hamilton, James Madison, and John Jay, who together published under the name "Publius," many Antifederalist writers used pseudonyms derived from classical sources.

ACTIVITY: Have students write letters either for or against ratification, signed with a pseudonym. Ask students to explain their choice of pseudonym.

SKILL-BUILDING STRATEGIES ANSWERS
(for p. 34)

Practicing the Skill

1. *Natural rights* are rights a person is born with. An example was given directly after the use of the phrase.

2. *Supremacy* means "above all others." It was used in relation to the Constitution, which is the supreme law of the land.

TEACH OBJECTIVE 4

ALL LEVELS: Tell students that the Constitution reflects compromises between large and small states over the issue of legislative representation, between slaveholding and free states over the issue of whether slaves would be counted for the purposes of representation, between southern and northern states over the issue of tariffs, and between Federalists and Antifederalists over the issue of the strength of the national government versus the state governments. Lead a discussion about the compromises related to these issues. Copy the following graphic organizer on the chalkboard, omitting the italicized answers, and have each student complete it. **English Language Learners**

CONSTITUTIONAL COMPROMISES

The Great Compromise
- *granted each state an equal voice in the upper house*
- *accorded representation in the lower house based on population*

The Three-Fifths Compromise
- *established that three fifths of a state's slave population would count in determining its representation*

Commerce Compromises
- *established that Congress could levy tariffs on imports, but not exports*
- *allowed the importation of slaves until the end of 1807*

Amending the Constitution
- *Allow for amendments to the Constitution in the form of a Bill of Rights*
- *insertion of the elastic clause to increase flexibility*

REVIEW SECTION 4 ANSWERS

1. Define
- republicanism, p. 28
- depression, p. 30
- electors, p. 33
- federalism, p. 34
- supremacy clause, p. 34
- elastic clause, p. 35

2. Identify
- Virginia Statute for Religious Freedom, p. 29
- Articles of Confederation, p. 29
- Northwest Ordinance, p. 30
- Constitutional Convention, p. 31
- Benjamin Franklin, p. 31
- Federalists, p. 32
- Antifederalists, p. 33

3. Articles—borrow and coin money, conduct foreign affairs, settle disputes between states; Constitution—tax, coin money, conduct foreign affairs, enforce treaties, and establish courts

4a. They followed the ideas of Magna Carta and John Locke to limit the power of the central government.

b. representation, the three-fifths compromise, control of commerce and tariffs, abolition of slavery

c. for—national government would ensure sound currency, protect property rights, and provide security; against—lead to tyranny, undemocratic; ratification—came with the promise of Bill of Rights

5. Articles will vary but should point to the weaknesses of the Articles, the closeness of state and U.S. constitutions, and the checks and balances to prevent tyranny.

The Living Constitution

The framers of the Constitution created a government based on **federalism**, or the division of powers between a strong central government and the state governments. The framers identified specific powers each government would have.

State and federal power. The Constitution grants the federal government the authority to raise armed forces, coin money, and establish foreign policy. State and local governments retain the power to establish schools and conduct elections. The central and state governments share the right to levy taxes and establish courts. The states retain any and all powers not expressly granted to the federal government. In cases of conflicting state and national laws, the delegates added a clause in Article VI of the Constitution. The **supremacy clause** asserts: "This Constitution, and the Laws of the United States which shall be made in Pursuance thereof; and all Treaties . . . of the United States, shall be the supreme Law of the Land."

Separation of powers. The framers of the Constitution wanted to prevent the central government from abusing its powers. As a result, they divided it into three branches. The legislative branch makes the laws. The executive branch sees that the laws are carried out. The judicial branch interprets and applies the laws. Through

---

Skill-Building Strategies

Building Vocabulary

In your study of history, you will regularly come across new and unfamiliar words. Learning the meaning of these words will enlarge your vocabulary and help you understand new information and ideas.

4. Review new vocabulary words. Look for ways to use new words—in homework assignments, classroom discussions, or everyday conversation. The best way to master a new word is to use it.

How to Build Vocabulary

1. **Identify new words.** As you read your textbook or supplemental assignments, create a list of words that you cannot pronounce or define. When reading the textbook, also make sure to review the key terms at the beginning of each section.
2. **Study the context of new words.** Study the paragraph and the sentence where you find a new word. This context, or setting, may provide clues to the word's meaning through examples or a definition using more familiar words.
3. **Use a dictionary.** Use a dictionary to learn the pronunciation and the precise meaning of each word on your list.

Applying the Skill

As you read Section 4, create a list of the new words that you encounter in the text. Write down what you think each word means, then check your definitions against those in a dictionary.

Practicing the Skill

Answer the following questions.
1. What does the phrase *natural rights* mean? How did its use in this section help you arrive at this definition?
2. What does the word *supremacy* mean? How did its use in this section help you arrive at this definition?

REVIEW

Have students complete the **Section 4 Review** on page 35.

ASSESS

Have students complete **Daily Quiz 1.4**. As Alternative Assessment, you may want to use the annotated Articles of Confederation lists or the constitutional compromises graphic organizer in this section's lessons.

RETEACH

Have students complete **Main Idea Activity for English Language Learners and Special-Needs Students 1.4**. Then assign groups of students to each objective in the section. Tell each student to create graphic organizers or other visual representations of the information pertaining to his or her assigned objectives. Have students study each other's graphic organizers within their groups.
English Language Learners, Cooperative Learning

EXTEND

Tell students that the Constitution has been amended 27 times since its creation. Assign each student one of the amendments. Have students conduct research on their assigned amendments. Ask each student to share his or her findings in a three- or four-minute report to the class. Students' reports should describe the amendment, provide a historical context, and analyze its impact. **Block Scheduling**

---

a system of checks and balances, each branch can restrict the actions of the other branches. For example, Congress has the power to propose and pass bills into law, but the president has the power to veto, or reject, these bills. The judicial branch can check legislative power by judging laws unconstitutional.

Flexibility and change. In 1788 the Constitution was well suited for an agricultural nation of 13 states and fewer than 4 million inhabitants. It also works today for an industrialized nation of 50 states and a population of more than 280 million. To allow for change to the Constitution, the framers specified an amendment procedure. Only 27 amendments have been added to the Constitution since 1789, although many have been proposed.

The Constitution's "necessary and proper" clause, also known as the **elastic clause**, has increased the document's flexibility. To the specific powers granted to Congress, this clause adds the power "to make all Laws which shall be necessary and proper for carrying into Execution the foregoing Powers." The elastic clause allows Congress to exert its powers in ways not specifically outlined in the Constitution. For example, the framers of the Constitution could not have anticipated the development of computers and the Internet. Congress, however, has the power to pass laws relating to new technology that may affect other Constitutional issues, such as commerce. In this way, the government has adapted the Constitution to fit changing times.

This 1788 print shows George Washington encircled by the seals of the 13 states and the seal of the United States.

✔ **READING CHECK: Analyzing Information** What provisions in the Constitution allow for its flexibility? its amendment procedure and the elastic clause

---

SECTION 4 REVIEW

1. Define and explain:
republicanism
depression
electors
federalism
supremacy clause
elastic clause

2. Identify and explain:
Virginia Statute for
Religious Freedom
Articles of Confederation
Northwest Ordinance
Constitutional Convention
Benjamin Franklin
Federalists
Antifederalists

3. Comparing Copy the chart below. Use it to compare the powers of federal government under the Articles of Confederation with those in the Constitution.

Articles of Confederation	Constitution

4. Finding the Main Idea

a. How did English political tradition influence the writing of the state constitutions?

b. What were the major compromises at the Constitutional Convention?

c. What were the major arguments for and against ratification? How was the document finally ratified?

5. Writing and Critical Thinking

Analyzing Information Write an article persuading your fellow colonists to ratify the Constitution.
Consider:
• the problems the nation faced under the Articles of Confederation
• the relationship between the state governments' constitutions and the U.S Constitution
• the strengths of the Constitution

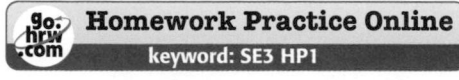

Homework Practice Online
keyword: SE3 HP1

CHAPTER 1

REVIEW AND ASSESSMENT RESOURCES

TECHNOLOGY

▶ Chapter 1 Test Generator (on the One-Stop Planner)
▶ Global Skill Builder CD–ROM
▶ HRW Go site

REINFORCEMENT, REVIEW, AND ASSESSMENT

▶ Chapter 1 Review, pp. 36–37
▶ Chapter 1 Tutorial for Students, Parents, Mentors, and Peers

▶ Chapter 1 Test (Form A or B)
▶ Portfolio Activities and Alternative Assessment Handbook, Chapter 1
▶ Chapter 1 Test for English Language Learners and Special-Needs Students

REVIEW

Have students complete the **Chapter 1 Review** on pp. 36–37.

ASSESS

Use one of the chapter tests to assess students' understanding of the content. For **Alternative Assessment**, see the **Portfolio Activities and Alternative Assessment Handbook**.

Understanding Main Ideas

1. They began as hunter-gatherers, learned agriculture, and later developed number systems and class structures.

2. New England colonies—by the Puritans; Middle colonies—by the Dutch and the Quakers; Southern colonies—by farmers and indentured servants

3. taxation without representation, the Stamp Act, the Boston Massacre, the Tea Act, the Intolerable Acts, battles of Lexington and Bunker Hill

4. They won the battle of Saratoga, then received help from the French and triumphed at the battle of Yorktown.

5. They saw the weakness of the Articles of Confederation and were able to compromise.

6. for—would ensure sound currency, property rights, and security; against—lead to tyranny, undemocratic, took away states' rights

Reviewing Themes

1. a trade route to Asia, the wealth of colonies, competition for land

2. The areas near the Atlantic Coast were settled first because the settlers came from Europe.

3. It created a strong national government which had been missing from the Articles of Confederation.

Review

Creating a Time Line

Copy the time line below onto a sheet of paper. Complete the time line by filling in the events and dates from the chapter that you think were most significant. Pick three events and explain why you think they were significant.

5000 B.C. — **1 A.D.** — **1500** — **1791**

Writing a Summary

Using standard grammar, spelling, sentence structure, and punctuation, write an overview of events in the chapter.

Identifying People and Ideas

Identify the following terms or individuals and explain their significance.

1. feudalism
2. Christopher Columbus
3. House of Burgesses
4. Pilgrims
5. Mayflower Compact
6. King George III
7. Declaration of Independence
8. Thomas Jefferson
9. Benjamin Franklin
10. federalism

Understanding Main Ideas

SECTION 1 *(pp. 4–8)*
1. How did early Native American cultures develop?

SECTION 2 *(pp. 9–14)*
2. How were the English colonies in North America settled?

SECTION 3 *(pp. 15–23)*
3. What events led British colonists to declare their independence from Great Britain?
4. How did the colonists achieve independence?

SECTION 4 *(pp. 28–35)*
5. How did the delegates at the Constitutional Convention create a new government?
6. What were the arguments for and against ratification of the Constitution?

Reviewing Themes

1. **Economics** What attracted explorers and traders to seek out distant lands?
2. **Geography** How did geography affect the settlement of North America?
3. **Constitutional Heritage** How did the Constitution reflect the colonists' desires for a new government?

Thinking Critically

1. **Comparing** What role did religion play in founding the New England colonies, the middle colonies, and the southern colonies?
2. **Making Generalizations** How did the colonists fill their demand for agricultural labor? Why did these methods change over time?
3. **Summarizing** Explain the significance of the following dates: 1607, 1776, and 1787.
4. **Analyzing Information** How did delegates address the weaknesses of the Articles of Confederation in the Constitution?
5. **Drawing Conclusions** Why can it be said that the U.S. Constitution is a "living document"?

Writing About History

Evaluating Copy the chart below. Use it to evaluate the importance of the Mayflower Compact, the Fundamental Orders of Connecticut, and the House of Burgesses to the growth of representative government in the colonies. Then write a paragraph suggesting how the delegates to the Constitutional Convention could incorporate these ideas into the Constitution.

The Mayflower Contract	Fundamental Orders of Connecticut	House of Burgesses

Organize the class into four groups and assign each group one of the sections of Chapter 1. Have each group create and present a lesson that covers the important points of its assigned section. Tell students to be sure to cover all of the sections' objectives when they teach the material to the class. Also encourage them to orally quiz the class after they present their lessons to confirm that their students understood the information.
English Language Learners, Cooperative Learning

Organize students into pairs or triads. Tell them to create a graphic novel—a long story told with pictures and dialogue, as in comic books—that covers all of the major objectives of the chapter. Students may create fictional characters to tell the story, or they may present the information as an illustrated history book. Help students to cover and bind their books, and display them in the classroom or elsewhere in the school.
Block Scheduling

Building Social Studies Skills

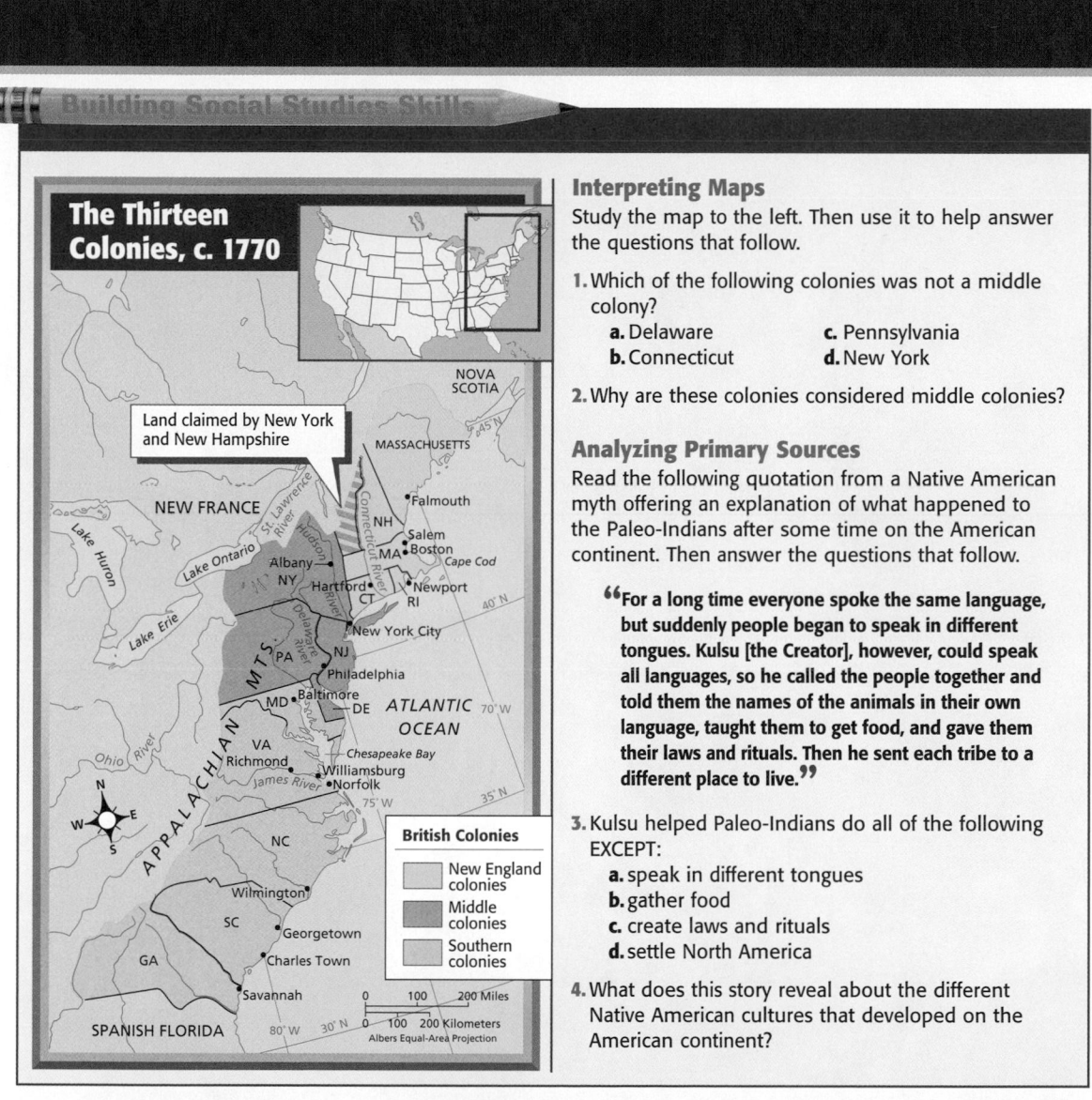

The Thirteen Colonies, c. 1770

British Colonies
- New England colonies
- Middle colonies
- Southern colonies

0   100   200 Miles
0   100   200 Kilometers
Albers Equal-Area Projection

Interpreting Maps

Study the map to the left. Then use it to help answer the questions that follow.

1. Which of the following colonies was not a middle colony?
   a. Delaware   **c.** Pennsylvania
   b. Connecticut   **d.** New York

2. Why are these colonies considered middle colonies?

Analyzing Primary Sources

Read the following quotation from a Native American myth offering an explanation of what happened to the Paleo-Indians after some time on the American continent. Then answer the questions that follow.

❝For a long time everyone spoke the same language, but suddenly people began to speak in different tongues. Kulsu [the Creator], however, could speak all languages, so he called the people together and told them the names of the animals in their own language, taught them to get food, and gave them their laws and rituals. Then he sent each tribe to a different place to live.❞

3. Kulsu helped Paleo-Indians do all of the following EXCEPT:
   a. speak in different tongues
   b. gather food
   c. create laws and rituals
   d. settle North America

4. What does this story reveal about the different Native American cultures that developed on the American continent?

Alternative Assessment

Building Your Portfolio

Government
Create a database that lists the economic, geographical, political, and social characteristics of the northern, southern, and middle colonies. Then write five questions on the database and have other students answer them.

U.S. HISTORY

internet connect

Internet Activity: go.hrw.com
KEYWORD: SE3 AN1

Choose a topic on the new nation to:
- trace the impact and development of the printing press.
- evaluate the effects of Columbus's journey to the Americas.
- research battles of the Revolutionary War and write a descriptive essay.

go. hrw. com

Thinking Critically

1. New England—colonies were founded on the basis of Puritan religion; Middle—Pennsylvania colony founded on Quaker basis; Southern—founded on basis of agriculture, not religion

2. Initially indentured servants performed agricultural labor, but they gained their freedom and rebellions led colonists to choose slave labor.

3. 1607—establishment of Jamestown settlement; 1776—Congress adopted the Declaration of Independence; 1787—drafting of the Constitution

4. They gave the federal government authority to levy taxes, enforce treaties, and control commerce.

5. Answers will vary. Students might suggest that the "elastic clause" gives the Constitution the ability to grow and change with the needs of the nation.

Writing

Paragraphs will vary but should mention the idea of self-government, through an assembly, based on a written Constitution.

Building Social Studies Skills

1. b

2. They are in the middle between the New England colonies in the far northeast, and the Southern colonies in the south.

3. a

4. They all once belonged to the same Native American group which came over from Asia.

THE CONSTITUTION

38

INTERDISCIPLINARY CONNECTIONS

▶ART◀

The Convention in Art.
Howard Chandler Christy, the artist who painted the work to the right, was best known as an illustrator. He began work for *Scribners' Magazine* in 1898, illustrating current-events articles and stories. He also traveled to Cuba and Puerto Rico to provide the magazine with firsthand illustrations of the Spanish-American War. His illustrations eventually appeared on World War I recruitment posters. Christy began creating large oil paintings, mostly of historical scenes, late in his life. The painting to the right is huge—20 feet by 30 feet. It now hangs above the grand staircase in the Capitol in Washington, D.C.

CRITICAL THINKING In this painting, how does Christy show the importance of the Constitution?

ANSWER: Answers will vary. Some students might mention the men's serious expressions, George Washington's noble stance, the light on the document, or the grandeur of the room.

Delegates to the Constitutional Convention in 1787 signed the document that established the democratic government of the United States.

CONSTITUTION HANDBOOK

> 66 We the People of the United States, in Order to form a more perfect Union, establish Justice, insure domestic Tranquility, provide for the common defense, promote the general Welfare, and secure the Blessings of Liberty to ourselves and our Posterity, do ordain and establish this Constitution for the United States of America. 99
>
> —Preamble to the Constitution

*T*he delegates who met in the spring of 1787 to revise the Articles of Confederation included many of the ablest leaders of the United States. Convinced that the Confederation was not strong enough to bring order and prosperity to the nation, they abandoned all thought of revising the Articles. Instead, they proceeded to draw up a completely new Constitution. Patrick Henry called this action "a revolution as radical as that which separated us from Great Britain." Drawing upon their long political experience, keen intelligence, and great learning, the framers of the Constitution fashioned a blueprint for a truly united nation—the United States of America.

Delegates met in Independence Hall in Philadelphia to draft the Constitution.

Charles Pinckney. Some historians argue that Charles Pinckney of South Carolina played an important but forgotten role in the creation of the Constitution. During the convention, Pinckney submitted a plan to the Constitutional Convention. The later document incorporated some of his ideas. James Madison, who kept the only detailed notes at the convention, never mentioned the Pinckney plan, however. It became public only in 1818, when Pinckney sent a copy to John Quincy Adams. Historians have debated Pinckney's role ever since. Some claim that Madison, who hated Pinckney, attempted to squash evidence of his role. Others maintain that Pinckney faked the document he sent to Adams in order to inflate his role. The mystery remains.

CRITICAL THINKING What additional evidence might resolve the debate on Pinckney's role?

ANSWER: Answers will vary. Some students might suggest that an authenticated copy of the Pinckney plan from the Convention would resolve the dispute.

The U.S. Constitution

*U.S. Constitution
commemorative stamps*

An unknown observer once referred to the U.S. Constitution as "the most wonderful work ever struck off at a given time by the brain and purpose of man." Revised, modified, and amended, the Constitution has served the American people for more than 200 years, becoming a model for representative government around the world. The Constitution has successfully survived the years for two reasons. First, it lays down rules of procedure and guarantees of rights and liberties that must be observed even in times of crisis. Second, it is a "living" document, capable of being amended to meet changing times and circumstances.

To Form a More Perfect Union

The framers of the Constitution wanted to establish a strong central government, one that could unite the country and help it meet the challenges of the future. At the same time, they feared a government that was too strong. The memories of the troubled years before the Revolution were still fresh. The framers knew that unchecked power in the hands of individuals, groups, or branches of government could lead to tyranny.

The framers' response was to devise a system of government in which power is divided between, in the words of James Madison, "two distinct governments"—the states and the federal government—and then within each government. In *Federalist Paper* "No. 51," Madison described the advantages of such a system.

> *History Makers Speak*
> **"In the compound republic of America, the power surrendered by the people is first divided between two distinct governments, and then the portion allotted to each subdivided among distinct and separate departments. Hence a double security arises to the rights of the people. The different governments will control each other, at the same time that each will be controlled by itself."**
>
> —James Madison, *Federalist Paper* "No. 51"

The seven Articles that make up the first part of the Constitution provide the blueprint for this system. To help guard against tyranny and to keep any one part of the federal government from becoming too strong, the framers divided the government into three branches—the legislative branch (Congress), the executive branch (the president and vice president), and the judicial branch (the federal courts)—each with specific powers. As a further safeguard, the framers wrote a system of checks and balances into the Constitution. Articles I, II, and III outline the powers of each branch of government and the checks and balances.

Article IV outlines the relations among the states and between the states and the federal government. Among the issues addressed are each state's recognition of other states' public records and citizens' rights, the admission of new states, and the rights and responsibilities of the federal government in relation to the states.

Article V specifies the process by which the Constitution can be amended. The framers purposely made the process slow and difficult. They feared that if the process was too easy, the Constitution—the fundamental law of the land—would soon carry no more weight than the most minor law passed by Congress.

Quill pen belonging to constitutional delegate James Madison

Article VI includes one provision that addressed the immediate concerns of the framers and two that have lasting significance. The short-term provision promises that the United States under the Constitution will honor all public debts entered into under the Confederation. The two long-term provisions declare the Constitution the supreme law of the land and prohibit religion being used as a qualification for holding public office.

Article VII is the framers' attempt to ensure ratification of the Constitution. The Constitutional Convention was summoned by the Congress to amend the Articles of Confederation. Under the Articles of Confederation, amendments had to be approved by all 13 states. Realizing that it would be difficult to get the approval of all the states—Rhode Island, for example, had not even sent delegates to Philadelphia—the framers specified that the Constitution would go into effect after ratification by only 9 states, not all 13. (This provision led some opponents of the Constitution to claim that it had been adopted by unfair means.)

Protecting Individual Liberty

Opposition to a strong central government was in part a concern over states' rights. It was also rooted in the desire to protect individual liberties. American colonists had always insisted on the protection of their civil liberties—their rights as individuals against the power of the government. The Constitution contains many important guarantees of civil liberties. On a broad level, the separation of powers and the system of checks and balances help safeguard citizens against the abuse of government power. The Constitution also contains provisions that speak directly to an individual's right to due process of law. For example, Section 9 of Article I prohibits both *ex post facto* laws and bills of attainder.

An *ex post facto* law is a law passed "after the deed." Such a law sets a penalty for an act that was not illegal when it was committed. A bill of attainder is a law that punishes a person by fine, imprisonment, or seizure of property without a court

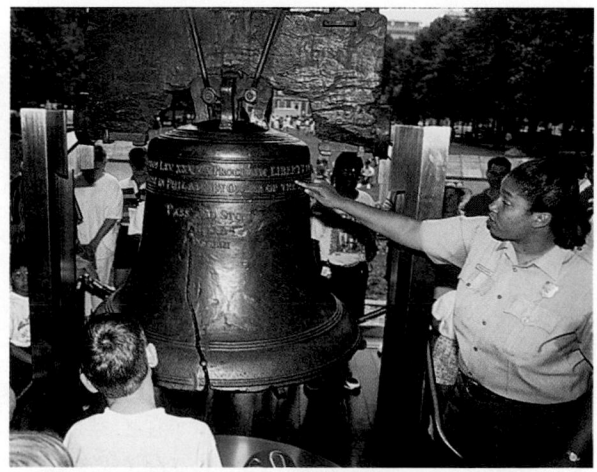

The Liberty Bell has become a symbol of the ideas of individual liberty protected in the Constitution.

CULTURE

Religion and the Oath of Office. Article VI requires that many government officers, including some at the state level, take an oath in support of the Constitution. Some people, such as Quakers, cannot take oaths because of their religious beliefs, however. To accommodate this, Article VI allows for the option of affirming, or agreeing, to support the Constitution.

CRITICAL THINKING Why might the authors of the Constitution have required state officials to take an oath or to affirm support for the Constitution?

ANSWER: Students might suggest that the authors wanted to re-emphasize the supremacy of the Constitution. They may also have wanted to ensure that state officials understood their dual responsibility: to enforce the Constitution as well as the state laws.

Treason and the Supreme Court. The U.S. Supreme Court has heard only one case involving charges of treason. During World War II, German saboteurs entered the United States by submarine with the intent of destroying the American war effort. Authorities accused Anthony Cramer, a U.S. citizen with German ties, of aiding these saboteurs. When Cramer was found guilty of treason, he appealed to the Supreme Court. In its 1945 decision in *Cramer* v. *United States*, the court overturned his conviction. The court determined that witnesses could testify only that Cramer had met with the saboteurs, not that he had provided them with any aid or assistance.

CRITICAL THINKING What provision in Article III led the Supreme Court to overturn Cramer's conviction for treason?

ANSWER: Students should indicate that his case did not meet the constitutional standard of providing "Aid and Comfort" to the enemy.

trial. If Congress had the power to adopt bills of attainder, lawmakers could punish any American at will, and that person could do nothing to appeal the sentence. Instead, the Constitution provides that only the courts can impose punishment for unlawful acts, and then only by following the duly established law.

Section 9 of Article I also protects citizens by guaranteeing the privilege of the writ of *habeas corpus*. The writ of *habeas corpus* is a legal document that forces a jailer to release a person from prison unless the person has been formally charged with, or convicted of, a crime. The Constitution states that "the privilege of the writ of *habeas corpus* shall not be suspended, unless when in cases of rebellion or invasion the public safety may require it."

The Constitution also gives special protection to people accused of treason. The framers of the Constitution knew that the charge of treason was an old device used by tyrants to get rid of persons they did not like. Such rulers might bring the charge of treason against persons who merely criticized the government. To prevent such use of this charge, Section 3 of Article III carefully defines treason.

"Treason against the United States, shall consist only in levying War against them, or in adhering to their Enemies, giving them Aid and Comfort. No Person shall be convicted of Treason unless on the Testimony of two Witnesses to the same overt Act, or on Confession in open Court."

—U.S. Constitution

Article III also protects the innocent relatives of a person accused of treason. Only the convicted person can be punished. No penalty can be imposed on the person's family.

The signing of the Constitution

Amending the Constitution

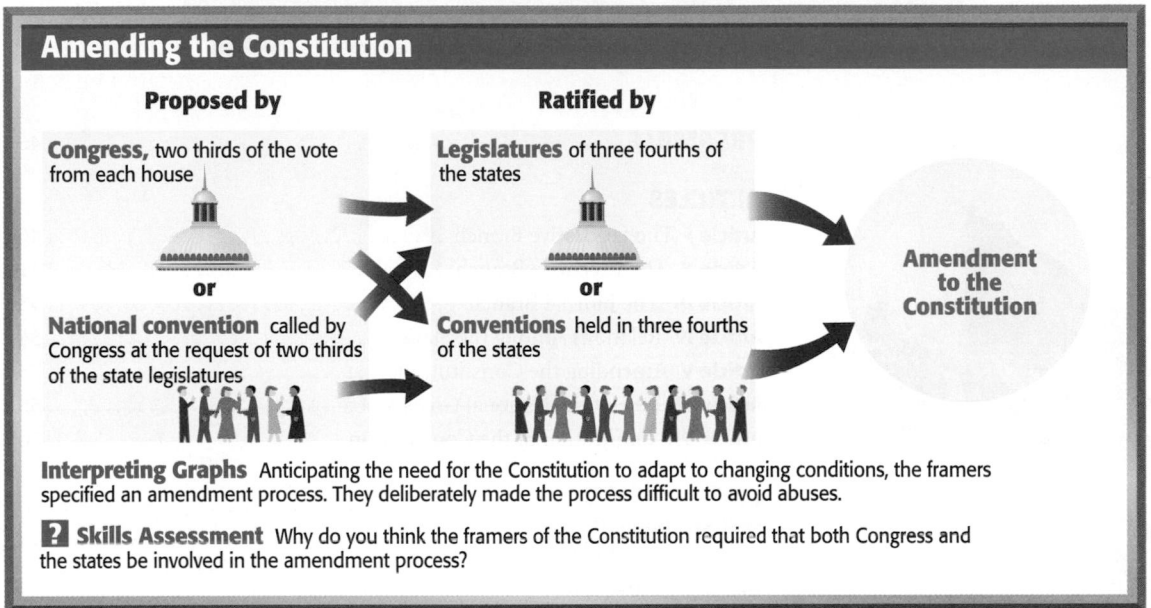

Proposed by	Ratified by
Congress, two thirds of the vote from each house	**Legislatures** of three fourths of the states
or	or
National convention called by Congress at the request of two thirds of the state legislatures	**Conventions** held in three fourths of the states

Amendment to the Constitution

Interpreting Graphs Anticipating the need for the Constitution to adapt to changing conditions, the framers specified an amendment process. They deliberately made the process difficult to avoid abuses.

? Skills Assessment Why do you think the framers of the Constitution required that both Congress and the states be involved in the amendment process?

The Bill of Rights

Despite the safeguards written into the Articles of the Constitution, some states at first refused to ratify the framework because it did not offer greater protection to the rights of individuals. They finally agreed to ratification after they had been promised that a bill of rights would be added to the Constitution by amendment when Congress was called into session following ratification.

In 1789 the first Congress of the United States wrote some of the ideals of the Declaration of Independence into the Bill of Rights, the first 10 amendments to the Constitution. The Bill of Rights includes a protection for individuals against any action by the federal government that may deprive them of life, liberty, or property without "due process of law."

Among the guarantees of liberty in the Bill of Rights, several are especially important. The First Amendment guarantees freedom of religion, speech, press, assembly, and petition. The Fourth Amendment forbids unreasonable searches and seizures of any person's home. The Fifth, Sixth, and Eighth Amendments protect individuals from arbitrary arrest and punishment by the federal government.

The Bill of Rights was ratified by the states in 1791. It has remained one of the best-known features of the Constitution. The American people have turned to it for support whenever their rights as individuals have seemed to be in danger. No document in U.S. history—except, perhaps, the Declaration of Independence—has been cherished more deeply.

HISTORY MAKERS SPEAK

Robert Whitehill in *The Bill of Rights: A Documentary History*

The Need for a Bill of Rights. Robert Whitehill, an Antifederalist who spoke at the Pennsylvania ratifying convention, explained the need for a Bill of Rights. "We know that it is the nature of power to seek its own augmentation [increase], and thus the loss of liberty is the necessary consequence of a loose or extravagant delegation of authority. . . . It is our duty to employ the present opportunity in stipulating [demanding] such restrictions as are best calculated to protect us from oppression and slavery."

CRITICAL THINKING

According to the excerpt, how did Whitehill view government entities?

ANSWER: Students should note that Whitehill believed that powerful bodies would always pose a threat to liberty, and that the people therefore needed protection against them.

GRAPH ANSWER

Students might suggest that the framers wanted to ensure that amendments would reflect the popular will instead of the desires of a small faction.

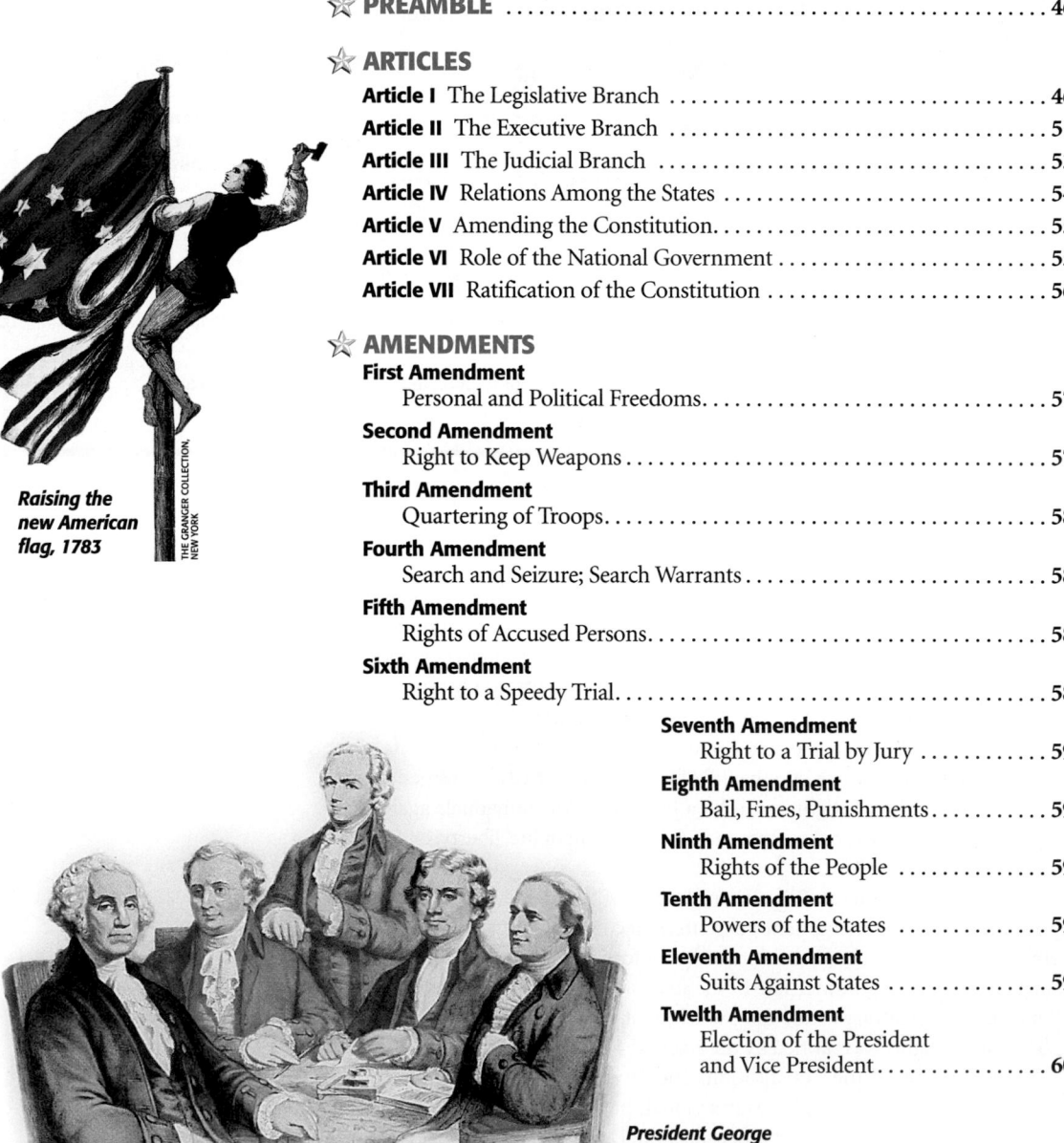

Raising the new American flag, 1783

THE GRANGER COLLECTION, NEW YORK

President George Washington (left) and his advisers

Contents of the Constitution

*State seals of
North Carolina,
Massachusetts,
and New York*

*The bald eagle, a symbol
of the United States*

PEOPLE IN HISTORY

George W. Norris, Constitutional Advocate. During his long congressional career, George W. Norris not only wrote the Twentieth Amendment and worked for its passage but also supported the introduction of presidential primaries and the direct election of senators. Although he was a Republican, Norris rarely voted along party lines. In defense of his independence, he claimed he "would rather be right than regular."

ACTIVITY: Ask students to find examples of recent political reforms. Then have each student draft a bill or constitutional amendment that could be used to enact one of the reforms.

THAT'S INTERESTING!

The passage of the Fourteenth and Fifteenth Amendments dramatically increased African American political participation. Almost every institution of black life, particularly the church, worked to mobilize the African American vote. So many African American workers attended the Republican state convention in Virginia that Richmond's tobacco factories had to close during the convention.

45

John Marshall in *The American Testament*

The Preamble. Chief Justice John Marshall cited the Preamble in his decision in the 1819 case of *McCulloch* v. *Maryland.* "The government proceeds directly from the people; is 'ordained and established' in the name of the people; and is declared to be ordained 'in order to form a more perfect union, establish justice, ensure domestic tranquility and secure the blessings of liberty' to themselves and to their posterity. . . . The government of the Union, then . . . is emphatically and truly, a government of the people. In form and substance it emanates from them. Its powers are granted by them and are to be exercised directly on them and for their benefit."

CRITICAL THINKING Why might Marshall have cited the Preamble?

ANSWER: Students might suggest that Marshall believed that the Preamble summarized the purpose of the U.S. Constitution and government.

CONSTITUTIONAL HERITAGE ANSWER

a better union, justice, domestic peace, and liberty

Preamble
The short and dignified Preamble explains the goals of the new government under the Constitution.

 Constitutional Heritage

According to the Preamble, what did the delegates hope the Constitution would provide for the nation?

Legislative Branch
Article I explains how the legislative branch, called Congress, is organized. The chief purpose of the legislative branch is to make the laws. Congress is made up of the Senate and the House of Representatives. The decision to have two bodies of government solved a difficult problem during the Constitutional Convention. The large states wanted membership in Congress to be based entirely on population. The small states wanted every state to have an equal vote. The solution to the problem of how the states were to be represented in Congress was known as the Great Compromise.

The number of members of the House is based on the population of the individual states. Each state has at least one representative. The current size of the House is 435 members, set by Congress in 1929.

The Constitution of the United States of America

PREAMBLE

*W*e the People of the United States, in Order to form a more perfect Union, establish Justice, insure domestic Tranquility, provide for the common defense, promote the general Welfare, and secure the Blessings of Liberty to ourselves and our Posterity, do ordain and establish this Constitution for the United States of America.*

ARTICLE I

Section 1. All legislative Powers herein granted shall be vested in a Congress of the United States, which shall consist of a Senate and House of Representatives.

Section 2. The House of Representatives shall be composed of Members chosen every second Year by the People of the several States, and the Electors in each State shall have the Qualifications requisite for Electors of the most numerous Branch of the State Legislature.

No Person shall be a Representative who shall not have attained to the Age of twenty-five Years, and been seven Years a Citizen of the United States, and who shall not, when elected, be an inhabitant of that State in which he shall be chosen.

Representatives and direct Taxes shall be apportioned among the several States which may be included within this Union, according to their respective Numbers, which shall be determined by adding to the whole Number of free Persons, including those bound to Service for a Term of Years, and excluding Indians not taxed, three fifths of all other Persons. The actual Enumeration shall be made within three Years after the first Meeting of the Congress of the United States, and within every subsequent Term of ten Years, in such Manner as they shall by Law direct. The Number of Representatives shall not exceed one for every thirty Thousand, but

* Parts of the Constitution that have been ruled through are no longer in force or no longer apply.

each State shall have at Least one Representative; ~~and until such enumeration shall be made, the State of New Hampshire shall be entitled to choose three; Massachusetts eight; Rhode Island and Providence Plantations one; Connecticut five; New York six; New Jersey four; Pennsylvania eight; Delaware one; Maryland six; Virginia ten; North Carolina five; South Carolina five; and Georgia three.~~

When vacancies happen in the Representation from any State, the Executive Authority thereof shall issue Writs of Election to fill such Vacancies.

The House of Representatives shall choose their Speaker and other Officers; and shall have the sole Power of Impeachment.

Section 3. The Senate of the United States shall be composed of two Senators from each State, ~~chosen by the Legislature thereof,~~ for six Years; and each Senator shall have one Vote.

Immediately after they shall be assembled in Consequence of the first Election, they shall be divided as equally as may be into three Classes. The Seats of the Senators of the first Class shall be vacated at the Expiration of the second Year, of the second Class at the Expiration of the fourth Year, and of the third Class at the Expiration of the sixth Year, so that one third may be chosen every second Year; ~~and if Vacancies happen by Resignation, or otherwise, during the Recess of the Legislature of any State, the Executive thereof may make temporary Appointments until the next Meeting of the Legislature, which shall then fill such Vacancies.~~

No Person shall be a Senator who shall not have attained to the Age of thirty Years, and been nine Years a Citizen of the United States, and who shall not, when elected, be an Inhabitant of that State for which he shall be chosen.

The Vice President of the United States shall be President of the Senate, but shall have no Vote, unless they be equally divided.

The Senate shall choose their other Officers, and also a President pro tempore, in the Absence of the Vice President, or when he shall exercise the Office of President of the United States.

The Senate shall have the sole Power to try all Impeachments. When sitting for that Purpose, they shall be on Oath or Affirmation. When the President of the United States is tried, the Chief Justice shall preside: And no Person shall be convicted without the Concurrence of two thirds of the Members present.

Judgment in Cases of Impeachment shall not extend further than to removal from Office, and disqualification to hold and enjoy any Office of honor, Trust or Profit under the United States: but the Party convicted shall nevertheless be liable and subject to Indictment, Trial, Judgment and Punishment, according to Law.

Section 4. The Times, Places and Manner of holding Elections for Senators and Representatives, shall be prescribed in each State by the Legislature thereof; but the Congress may at any time by Law make or alter such Regulations, except as to the Places of choosing Senators.

⭐ **Constitutional Heritage**

According to the Constitution, who has the authority to fill a vacancy in the House of Representatives?

Every state has two senators. Senators serve a six-year term, but only one third of the senators reach the end of their terms every two years. In any election, at least two thirds of the senators stay in office. This system ensures that there are experienced senators in office at all times.

The only duty that the Constitution assigns to the vice president is to preside over meetings of the Senate. Modern presidents have given their vice presidents more and varied responsibilities.

In an impeachment, the House charges a government official of wrongdoing, and the Senate acts as a court to decide if the official is guilty.

Congress has decided that elections will be held on the Tuesday following the first Monday in November of even-numbered years. The Twentieth Amendment states that Congress shall meet in regular session on January 3 of each year. The president may call a special session of Congress whenever necessary.

Impeachment. In December 1998 the House of Representatives impeached President Bill Clinton. The House brought two charges—perjury and obstruction of justice—against the president. In February 1999 the Senate voted on these charges. Forty-five senators voted to find him guilty on the perjury charge. Fifty-five voted not guilty. The senate vote was split 50-50 on the obstruction of justice charge. The votes did not reach the two-thirds majority required by the Constitution, and so the Senate acquitted Clinton of the impeachment charges.

CRITICAL THINKING Why might some observers have seen the Senate votes as a "humiliating defeat for the 13 House Republican 'managers' who had presented the case to the Senate"?

ANSWER: Students might suggest that neither charge garnered even a simple majority against Clinton, suggesting a weak initial case.

CONSTITUTIONAL HERITAGE ANSWER

the executive authority of the state

Tracking Congressional Votes. For many years, people learned about congressional proceedings in the *Congressional Record*, a bulky set of printed volumes. The Internet has allowed easier, faster access. The Library of Congress supports a Web site that covers every aspect of the government. In addition, independent organizations, such as Project Vote Smart, provide links to help track congressional votes.

CRITICAL THINKING Besides the *Congressional Record* and the Internet, how might citizens track votes or learn about congressional proceedings?

ANSWER: Answers will vary. Some students will suggest that citizens could call political offices, read newspapers, or watch television news programs.

CONSTITUTIONAL HERITAGE ANSWER

the House itself

Constitutional Heritage

According to the Constitution, who has the authority to judge elections, returns, and the behavior of congressmembers?

Congress makes most of its own rules of conduct. The Senate and the House each have a code of ethics that members must follow. It is the task of each house of Congress to discipline its own members. Each house keeps a journal, and a publication called the *Congressional Record* keeps records of what happens in congressional sessions. The general public can learn how their representatives voted on bills by reading the *Congressional Record*.

The framers of the Constitution wanted to protect members of Congress from being arrested on false charges by political enemies who did not want them to attend important meetings. The framers also wanted to protect members of Congress from being taken to court for something they said in a speech or in a debate.

The power to tax is the responsibility of the House of Representatives. Because members of the House are elected every two years, the framers felt that representatives would listen to the public and seek its approval before passing taxes.

The veto power of the president and the ability of Congress to override a presidential veto are two of the important checks and balances in the Constitution.

The Congress shall assemble at least once in every Year, and such Meeting shall be on the first Monday in December, unless they shall by Law appoint a different Day.

Section 5. Each House shall be the Judge of the Elections, Returns and Qualifications of its own Members, and a Majority of each shall constitute a Quorum to do Business; but a smaller Number may adjourn from day to day, and may be authorized to compel the Attendance of absent Members, in such Manner, and under such Penalties as each House may provide.

Each House may determine the Rules of its Proceedings, punish its Members for disorderly Behavior, and, with the Concurrence of two thirds, expel a Member.

Each House shall keep a Journal of its Proceedings, and from time to time publish the same, excepting such Parts as may in their Judgment require Secrecy; and the Yeas and Nays of the Members of either House on any question shall, at the Desire of one fifth of those Present, be entered on the Journal.

Neither House, during the Session of Congress, shall, without the Consent of the other, adjourn for more than three days, nor to any other Place than that in which the two Houses shall be sitting.

Section 6. The Senators and Representatives shall receive a Compensation for their Services, to be ascertained by Law, and paid out of the Treasury of the United States. They shall in all Cases, except Treason, Felony and Breach of the Peace, be privileged from Arrest during their Attendance at the Session of their respective Houses, and in going to and returning from the same; and for any Speech or Debate in either House, they shall not be questioned in any other Place.

No Senator or Representative shall, during the Time for which he was elected, be appointed to any civil Office under the Authority of the United States, which shall have been created, or the Emoluments whereof shall have been increased during such time; and no Person holding any Office under the United States, shall be a Member of either House during his Continuance in Office.

Section 7. All Bills for raising Revenue shall originate in the House of Representatives; but the Senate may propose or concur with Amendments as on other Bills.

Every Bill which shall have passed the House of Representatives and the Senate, shall, before it become a Law, be presented to the President of the United States; If he approve he shall sign it, but if not he shall return it, with his Objections to that House in which it shall have originated, who shall enter the Objections at large on their Journal, and proceed to reconsider it. If after such Reconsideration two thirds of that House shall agree to pass the Bill, it shall be sent, together with the Objections, to the other House, by which it shall likewise be reconsidered, and if approved by two thirds of that House, it shall become a Law. But in all such Cases the Votes of both Houses shall be determined by Yeas and Nays, and the Names of the Persons voting for and against the Bill shall be entered on the Journal of each House respectively. If any Bill shall not be returned by the President within ten Days (Sundays excepted) after it shall have been presented to him, the Same shall be a Law, in like Manner as if he had signed it, unless the Congress by their Adjournment prevent its Return, in which Case it shall not be a Law.

Every Order, Resolution, or Vote to which the Concurrence of the Senate and House of Representatives may be necessary (except on a question of Adjournment) shall be presented to the President of the United States; and before the Same shall take Effect, shall be approved by him, or being disapproved by him, shall be repassed by two thirds of the Senate and House of Representatives, according to the Rules and Limitations prescribed in the Case of a Bill.

Section 8. The Congress shall have Power To lay and collect Taxes, Duties, Imposts and Excises, to pay the Debts and provide for the common Defense and general Welfare of the United States; but all Duties, Imposts and Excises shall be uniform throughout the United States;

To borrow Money on the credit of the United States;

To regulate Commerce with foreign Nations, and among the several States, and with the Indian Tribes;

To establish an uniform Rule of Naturalization, and uniform Laws on the subject of Bankruptcies throughout the United States;

To coin Money, regulate the Value thereof, and of foreign Coin, and fix the Standard of Weights and Measures;

To provide for the Punishment of counterfeiting the Securities and current Coin of the United States;

To establish Post Offices and post Roads;

To promote the Progress of Science and useful Arts, by securing for limited Times to Authors and Inventors the exclusive Right to their respective Writings and Discoveries;

To constitute Tribunals inferior to the supreme Court;

To define and punish Piracies and Felonies committed on the high Seas, and Offenses against the Law of Nations;

To declare War, grant Letters of Marque and Reprisal, and make Rules concerning Captures on Land and Water;

To raise and support Armies, but no Appropriation of Money to that Use shall be for a longer Term than two Years;

To provide and maintain a Navy;

To make Rules for the Government and Regulation of the land and naval Forces;

To provide for calling forth the Militia to execute the Laws of the Union, suppress Insurrections and repel Invasions;

To provide for organizing, arming, and disciplining, the Militia, and for governing such Part of them as may be employed in the Service of the United States, reserving to the States respectively, the Appointment of the

 Constitutional Heritage

How does Section 8 of Article 1 address some of the weaknesses of the Articles of Confederation?

The framers of the Constitution wanted a national government that was strong enough to be effective. Section 8 lists the powers given to Congress. The last sentence in the section contains the so-called elastic clause, which has been stretched—like elastic—to fit many different circumstances. The clause was first disputed when Alexander Hamilton proposed a national bank. Thomas Jefferson said that the Constitution did not give Congress the power to establish a bank. Hamilton argued that the bank was "necessary and proper" in order to carry out other powers of Congress, such as borrowing money and regulating currency. This argument was tested in the court system in 1819 in the case of *McCulloch* v. *Maryland,* when Chief Justice John Marshall ruled in favor of the federal government. Powers exercised by the government using the elastic clause are called implied powers.

Suspending the Writ of Habeas Corpus. During the Civil War, President Abraham Lincoln suspended the writ of *habeas corpus*. Opposing his decision, Chief Justice Roger Taney argued that the authority to suspend the writ of *habeas corpus* belonged to Congress because that power was detailed in Article I, which is concerned with legislative matters. Lincoln, however, claimed that the Constitution was unclear on the matter. Congress resolved the dispute when it voted to approve the suspension. Presidents have suspended the writ of *habeas corpus* three times since the Civil War. Suspensions in 1871 and 1905 received congressional approval, but one instituted in 1941 did not. It was later ruled illegal by the Supreme Court.

CRITICAL THINKING Which branch of government has the authority to suspend the writ of *habeas corpus*?

ANSWER: Students might indicate that the history of suspensions indicates that presidents have the authority, with proper congressional approval.

CONSTITUTIONAL HERITAGE ANSWER

Students might answer that the colonists opposed many of these hereditary titles.

The delegates debated the articles of the Constitution in the Assembly Room of Independence Hall.

If Congress has implied powers, then there also must be limits to its powers. Section 9 lists powers that are denied to the federal government. Several of the clauses protect the people of the United States from unjust treatment. For instance, Section 9 guarantees the right of the writ of *habeas corpus* and prohibits bills of attainder and *ex post facto* laws.

⭐ **Constitutional Heritage**

How do these prohibitions against nobility and titles from monarchies address some of the colonists' grievances?

Officers, and the Authority of training the Militia according to the discipline prescribed by Congress.

To exercise exclusive Legislation in all Cases whatsoever, over such District (not exceeding ten Miles square) as may, by Cession of particular States, and the Acceptance of Congress, become the Seat of the Government of the United States, and to exercise like Authority over all Places purchased by the Consent of the Legislature of the State in which the Same shall be, for the Erection of Forts, Magazines, Arsenals, dock-Yards, and other needful Buildings;—And

To make all Laws which shall be necessary and proper for carrying into Execution the foregoing Powers, and all other Powers vested by this Constitution in the Government of the United States, or in any Department or Officer thereof.

Section 9. ~~The Migration or Importation of such Persons as any of the States now existing shall think proper to admit, shall not be prohibited by the Congress prior to the Year one thousand eight hundred and eight, but a Tax or duty may be imposed on such Importation, not exceeding ten dollars for each Person.~~

The Privilege of the Writ of Habeas Corpus shall not be suspended, unless when in Cases of Rebellion or Invasion the public Safety may require it.

No Bill of Attainder or ex post facto Law shall be passed.

No Capitation, or other direct, Tax shall be laid, unless in Proportion to the Census or Enumeration herein before directed to be taken.

No Tax or Duty shall be laid on Articles exported from any State.

No Preference shall be given by any Regulation of Commerce or Revenue to the Ports of one State over those of another: nor shall Vessels bound to, or from, one State, be obliged to enter, clear, or pay Duties in another.

No Money shall be drawn from the Treasury, but in Consequence of Appropriations made by Law; and a regular Statement and Account of the Receipts and Expenditures of all public Money shall be published from time to time.

No Title of Nobility shall be granted by the United States: And no Person holding any Office of Profit or Trust under them, shall, without the Consent of the Congress, accept of any present, Emolument, Office, or Title, of any kind whatever, from any King, Prince, or foreign State.

Section 10. No State shall enter into any Treaty, Alliance, or Confederation; grant Letters of Marque and Reprisal; coin Money; emit Bills of Credit; make any Thing but gold and silver Coin a Tender in Payment of Debts; pass any Bill of Attainder, ex post facto Law, or law impairing the Obligation of Contracts, or grant any Title of Nobility.

No State shall, without the Consent of the Congress, lay any Imposts or Duties on Imports or Exports, except what may be absolutely necessary for executing its inspection Laws: and the net Produce of all Duties and Imposts, laid by any State on Imports or Exports, shall be for the Use of the Treasury of the United States; and all such Laws shall be subject to the Revision and Control of the Congress.

No State shall, without the Consent of Congress, lay any Duty of Tonnage, keep Troops, or Ships of War in time of Peace, enter into any Agreement or Compact with another State, or with a foreign Power, or engage in War, unless actually invaded, or in such imminent Danger as will not admit of delay.

ARTICLE II

Section 1. The executive Power shall be vested in a President of the United States of America. He shall hold his Office during the Term of four Years, and, together with the Vice President, chosen for the same Term, be elected, as follows.

Each State shall appoint, in such Manner as the Legislature thereof may direct, a Number of Electors, equal to the whole Number of Senators and Representatives to which the State may be entitled in the Congress: but no Senator or Representative, or Person holding an Office of Trust or Profit under the United States, shall be appointed an Elector.

~~The Electors shall meet in their respective States, and vote by Ballot for two Persons, of whom one at least shall not be an Inhabitant of the same State with themselves. And they shall make a List of all the Persons voted for, and of the Number of Votes for each; which List they shall sign and certify, and transmit sealed to the Seat of the Government of the United States, directed to the President of the Senate. The President of the Senate shall, in the Presence of the Senate and House of Representatives, open all the Certificates, and the Votes shall then be counted. The Person having the greatest Number of Votes shall be the President, if such Number be a Majority of the whole Number of Electors appointed; and if there be more than one who have such majority, and have an equal Number of Votes, then the House of Representatives shall immediately choose by Ballot one of them for President; and if no Person have a Majority, then from the five highest on the List the said House shall in like Manner choose the President. But in choosing the President, the Votes shall be taken by States, the Representation from each State having one Vote; A quorum for this Purpose shall consist of a Member or Members from two thirds of the States, and a Majority of all the States shall be necessary to a Choice. In every Case, after~~

Section 10 lists the powers that are denied to the states. In our system of federalism, the state and federal governments have separate powers, share some powers, and are denied other powers. The states may not exercise any of the powers that belong solely to Congress.

 Constitutional Heritage

According to the Constitution, under what circumstances could a state engage in war?

Executive Branch
The president is the chief of the executive branch. It is the job of the president to enforce the laws. The framers wanted the president and vice president's terms of office and manner of selection to be different from those of members of Congress. They decided on four-year terms, but they had a difficult time agreeing on how to select the president and vice president. The framers finally set up an electoral system, which varies greatly from our electoral process today. The Twelfth Amendment changed the process by requiring that separate ballots be cast for president and vice president. The rise of political parties has since changed the process even more.

The Tyler Precedent.

After President William Henry Harrison died only one month after taking office in 1841, Vice President John Tyler took the presidential oath of office. Some observers—and Tyler himself—believed that this was unnecessary. The vice presidential oath had established him as the president's successor. At the same time, however, Tyler wanted to emphasize his claim on the presidency. He regarded himself as the rightful president, entitled to serve until the end of Harrison's term. Although some critics disagreed, Tyler established an important precedent—that when the president died, the vice president assumed the higher office with all its powers.

CRITICAL THINKING On what grounds might Tyler's critics have objected to his position?

ANSWER: Students might note that critics might have objected on constitutional grounds—Article II does not specify whether the vice president is an acting president or serves out the remaining term as president.

CONSTITUTIONAL HERITAGE ANSWER

It mentions the power that the president has to make treaties and appointments but also notes that Congress must approve them.

In 1845 Congress set the Tuesday following the first Monday in November of every fourth year as the general election date for selecting presidential electors.

Emolument means "salary, or payment." In 1999 Congress voted to set future presidents' salaries at $400,000 per year. The president also receives an annual expense account. The president must pay taxes only on the salary.

The oath of office is administered to the president by the chief justice of the United States. George Washington added "So help me, God." All succeeding presidents have followed this practice.

⭐ Constitutional Heritage

How does the description of the executive branch make clear the separation of powers established in the Constitution?

According to this section the president can form a cabinet of advisers. Every president, starting with George Washington, has appointed a cabinet.

Most of the president's appointments to office must be approved by the Senate.

the Choice of the President, the Person having the greatest Number of Votes of the Electors shall be the Vice President. But if there should remain two or more who have equal Votes, the Senate shall choose from them by Ballot the Vice President.

The Congress may determine the Time of choosing the Electors, and the Day on which they shall give their Votes; which Day shall be the same throughout the United States.

No Person except a natural born Citizen, or a Citizen of the United States, at the time of the Adoption of this Constitution, shall be eligible to the Office of President; neither shall any Person be eligible to that Office who shall not have attained to the Age of thirty-five Years, and been fourteen Years a Resident within the United States.

In Case of the Removal of the President from Office, or of his Death, Resignation, or Inability to discharge the Powers and Duties of the said Office, the Same shall devolve on the Vice President, and the Congress may by Law provide for the Case of Removal, Death, Resignation or Inability, both of the President and Vice President, declaring what Officer shall then act as President, and such Officer shall act accordingly, until the Disability be removed, or a President shall be elected.

The President shall, at stated Times, receive for his Services, a Compensation, which shall neither be increased nor diminished during the Period for which he shall have been elected, and he shall not receive within that Period any other Emolument from the United States, or any of them.

Before he enter on the Execution of his Office, he shall take the following Oath or Affirmation:—"I do solemnly swear (or affirm) that I will faithfully execute the Office of President of the United States, and will to the best of my Ability, preserve, protect and defend the Constitution of the United States."

Section 2. The President shall be Commander in Chief of the Army and Navy of the United States, and of the Militia of the several States, when called into the actual Service of the United States; he may require the Opinion, in writing, of the principal Officer in each of the executive Departments, upon any Subject relating to the Duties of their respective Offices, and he shall have Power to grant Reprieves and Pardons for Offenses against the United States, except in Cases of Impeachment.

He shall have Power, by and with the Advice and Consent of the Senate, to make Treaties, provided two thirds of the Senators present concur; and he shall nominate, and by and with the Advice and Consent of the Senate, shall appoint Ambassadors, other public Ministers and Consuls, Judges of the supreme Court, and all other Officers of the United States, whose Appointments are not herein otherwise provided for, and which shall be established by Law: but the Congress may by Law vest the Appointment of such inferior Officers, as they think proper, in the President alone, in the Courts of Law, or in the Heads of Departments.

The President shall have Power to fill up all Vacancies that may happen during the Recess of the Senate, by granting Commissions which shall expire at the End of their next Session.

Section 3. He shall from time to time give to the Congress Information of the State of the Union, and recommend to their Consideration such Measures as he shall judge necessary and expedient; he may, on extraordinary Occasions, convene both Houses, or either of them, and in Case of Disagreement between them, with Respect to the Time of Adjournment, he may adjourn them to such Time as he shall think proper; he shall receive Ambassadors and other public Ministers; he shall take Care that the Laws be faithfully executed, and shall Commission all the Officers of the United States.

Section 4. The President, Vice President and all civil Officers of the United States, shall be removed from Office on Impeachment for, and Conviction of, Treason, Bribery, or other high Crimes and Misdemeanors.

ARTICLE III

Section 1. The judicial Power of the United States, shall be vested in one supreme Court, and in such inferior Courts as the Congress may from time to time ordain and establish. The Judges, both of the supreme and inferior Courts, shall hold their Offices during good Behavior, and shall, at stated Times, receive for their Services, a Compensation, which shall not be diminished during their Continuance in Office.

Section 2. The judicial Power shall extend to all Cases, in Law and Equity, arising under this Constitution, the Laws of the United States, and

The members of the U.S. Supreme Court in 2001

Every year the president presents to Congress a State of the Union message. In this message, the president explains the executive branch's legislative plans for the coming year.

This clause states that one of the president's duties is to enforce the laws.

 Constitutional Heritage

What actions might lead to the impeachment of a president, vice president, or other civil officer?

Judicial Branch
The Articles of Confederation did not make any provisions for a federal court system. One of the first things that the framers of the Constitution agreed upon was to set up a national judiciary. With all the laws that Congress would be enacting, there would be a great need for a branch of government to interpret the laws. In the Judiciary Act of 1789, Congress provided for the establishment of lower courts, such as district courts, circuit courts of appeals, and various other federal courts. The judicial system provides a check on the legislative branch; it can declare a law unconstitutional.

Constitutional Heritage

What guidelines does the Constitution establish for criminal trials?

Congress has the power to decide the punishment for treason, but it can punish only the guilty person. Corruption of blood refers to punishing the family of a person who has committed treason. It is expressly forbidden by the Constitution.

The States
States must honor the laws, records, and court decisions of other states. A person cannot escape a legal obligation by moving from one state to another.

Treaties made, or which shall be made, under their Authority;—to all Cases affecting Ambassadors, other public Ministers and Consuls;—to all Cases of admiralty and maritime Jurisdiction;—to Controversies to which the United States shall be a Party;—to Controversies between two or more States;—between a State and Citizens of another State;—between Citizens of different States;—between Citizens of the same State claiming Lands under Grants of different States, and between a State, or the Citizens thereof, and foreign States, Citizens or Subjects.

In all Cases affecting Ambassadors, other public Ministers and Consuls, and those in which a State shall be Party, the supreme Court shall have original Jurisdiction. In all the other Cases before mentioned, the supreme Court shall have appellate Jurisdiction, both as to Law and fact, with such Exceptions, and under such Regulations as the Congress shall make.

The Trial of all Crimes, except in Cases of Impeachment, shall be by Jury; and such Trial shall be held in the State where the said Crimes shall have been committed; but when not committed within any State, the Trial shall be at such Place or Places as the Congress may by Law have directed.

Section 3. Treason against the United States, shall consist only in levying War against them, or in adhering to their Enemies, giving them Aid and Comfort. No Person shall be convicted of Treason unless on the Testimony of two Witnesses to the same overt Act, or on Confession in open Court.

The Congress shall have Power to declare the Punishment of Treason, but no Attainder of Treason shall work Corruption of Blood, or Forfeiture except during the Life of the Person attainted.

ARTICLE IV

Section 1. Full Faith and Credit shall be given in each State to the public Acts, Records, and judicial Proceedings of every other State. And the Congress may by general Laws prescribe the Manner in which such Acts, Records and Proceedings shall be proved, and the Effect thereof.

Section 2. The Citizens of each State shall be entitled to all Privileges and Immunities of Citizens in the several States.

A Person charged in any State with Treason, Felony, or other Crime, who shall flee from Justice, and be found in another State, shall on Demand of the executive Authority of the State from which he fled, be delivered up, to be removed to the State having Jurisdiction of the Crime.

No Person held to Service of Labor in one State, under the Laws thereof, escaping into another, shall, in Consequence of any Law or Regulation therein, be discharged from such Service or Labor, but shall be delivered up on Claim of the Party to whom such Service or Labor may be due.

Section 3. New States may be admitted by the Congress into this Union; but no new State shall be formed or erected within the Jurisdiction of any other State; nor any State be formed by the Junction of two or more States, or Parts of States, without the Consent of the Legislatures of the States concerned as well as of the Congress.

The Congress shall have Power to dispose of and make all needful Rules and Regulations respecting the Territory or other Property belonging to the United States; and nothing in this Constitution shall be so construed as to Prejudice any Claims of the United States, or of any particular State.

Section 4. The United States shall guarantee to every State in this Union a Republican Form of Government, and shall protect each of them against Invasion; and on Application of the Legislature, or of the Executive (when the Legislature cannot be convened) against domestic Violence.

ARTICLE V

The Congress, whenever two thirds of both Houses shall deem it necessary, shall propose Amendments to this Constitution, or, on the Application of the Legislatures of two thirds of the several States, shall call a Convention for proposing Amendments, which, in either Case, shall be valid to all Intents and Purposes, as Part of this Constitution, when ratified by the Legislatures of three fourths of the several States, or by Conventions in three fourths thereof, as the one or the other Mode of Ratification may be proposed by the Congress; Provided that no Amendment which may be made prior to the Year One thousand eight hundred and eight shall in any Manner affect the first and fourth Clauses in the Ninth Section of the first Article; and that no State, without its Consent, shall be deprived of its equal Suffrage in the Senate.

ARTICLE VI

All Debts contracted and Engagements entered into, before the Adoption of this Constitution, shall be as valid against the United States under this Constitution, as under the Confederation.

This Constitution, and the Laws of the United States which shall be made in Pursuance thereof; and all Treaties made, or which shall be made, under the Authority of the United States, shall be the supreme Law of the Land; and the Judges in every State shall be bound thereby, any Thing in the Constitution or Laws of any State to the Contrary notwithstanding.

The Senators and Representatives before mentioned, and the Members of the several State Legislatures, and all executive and judicial Officers, both of the United States and of the several States, shall be bound by Oath or Affirmation, to support this Constitution; but no religious Test shall ever be required as a Qualification to any Office or public Trust under the United States.

Section 3 permits Congress to admit new states to the Union. When a group of people living in an area that is not part of an existing state wishes to form a new state, it asks Congress for permission to do so. The people then write a state constitution and offer it to Congress for approval. The state constitution must set up a representative form of government and must not in any way contradict the federal Constitution. If a majority of Congress approves the state constitution, the state is admitted as a member of the United States of America.

The Amendment Process
America's founders may not have realized just how enduring the Constitution would be, but they did make provisions for changing or adding to the Constitution. They did not want to make it easy to change the Constitution. There are two different ways in which changes can be proposed to the states and two different ways in which states can approve the changes and make them part of the Constitution.

National Supremacy
One of the biggest problems facing the delegates to the Constitutional Convention was the question of what would happen if a state law and a national law conflicted. Which law would be followed? Who decided? The second clause of Article VI answers those questions. When a national and state law are in conflict, the national law overrides the state law. The Constitution is the supreme law of the land. This clause is often called the supremacy clause.

Safeguarding the Flag.
In June 1999 the House of Representatives approved a proposed constitutional amendment allowing Congress to pass laws against desecrating the American flag. For the third time in four years the House had passed the proposed amendment, which had always failed to pass in the Senate. Supporters maintain that the flag is a national symbol that deserves protection, while opponents argue that such an amendment violates the right to free speech.

CRITICAL THINKING Would you support an amendment protecting the flag? Explain your answer.

ANSWER: Answers will vary. Some students might argue that the flag merits protection, while others might argue that flag-burning is a protected form of political expression and protest.

THAT'S INTERESTING!

One scholar estimates that a total of 10,431 amendments were proposed between 1789 and 1990!

William Short in *The Founders' Constitution*

Ratifying the Constitution. Article VII required nine states to ratify the Constitution before it took effect. William Short expressed concerns over this figure in a 1787 letter to James Madison. "I think the adoption by nine & refusal by four of the States is the worst possible situation to which the new plan can give birth; & it seems probable that that will be the situation. Would it not have been better to have fixed on the number eleven or twelve instead of nine? In that case the plan would have been either refused altogether or adopted by such a commanding majority as would almost necessarily have brought in the others in the end."

ACTIVITY: Tell students to imagine that they are James Madison. Have each student write a half-page response to Short.

THAT'S INTERESTING!

Rhode Island initially refused to ratify the Constitution. In a popular vote just 237 people voted for it. 2,708 voted against ratification. The state finally ratified it in 1790, after the government created under the Constitution had already assumed control of the United States.

Ratification
The Articles of Confederation called for all 13 states to approve any revision to the Articles. The Constitution required that the vote of 9 out of the 13 states would be needed to ratify the Constitution. The first state to ratify was Delaware, on December 7, 1787. The last state to ratify the Constitution was Rhode Island, which finally did so on May 29, 1790, almost two and a half years later.

ARTICLE VII

The Ratification of the Conventions of nine States, shall be sufficient for the Establishment of this Constitution between the States so ratifying the Same.

Done in Convention by the Unanimous Consent of the States present the Seventeenth Day of September in the Year of our Lord one thousand seven hundred and Eighty seven and of the Independence of the United States of America the Twelfth. In witness whereof We have hereunto subscribed our Names.

George Washington—
President and deputy from Virginia

New Hampshire
John Langdon
Nicholas Gilman

Massachusetts
Nathaniel Gorham
Rufus King

Connecticut
William Samuel Johnson
Roger Sherman

New York
Alexander Hamilton

New Jersey
William Livingston
David Brearley
William Paterson
Jonathan Dayton

Pennsylvania
Benjamin Franklin
Thomas Mifflin
Robert Morris
George Clymer
Thomas FitzSimons
Jared Ingersoll
James Wilson
Gouverneur Morris

Delaware
George Read
Gunning Bedford Jr.
John Dickinson
Richard Bassett
Jacob Broom

Maryland
James McHenry
Daniel of St. Thomas Jenifer
Daniel Carroll

Virginia
John Blair
James Madison Jr.

North Carolina
William Blount
Richard Dobbs Spaight
Hugh Williamson

South Carolina
John Rutledge
Charles Cotesworth Pinckney
Charles Pinckney
Pierce Butler

Georgia
William Few
Abraham Baldwin

Attest: *William Jackson*, Secretary

THE AMENDMENTS

Articles in addition to, and Amendment of the Constitution of the United States of America, proposed by Congress, and ratified by the Legislatures of the several states, pursuant to the fifth Article of the original Constitution.

[The First through Tenth Amendments, now known as the Bill of Rights, were proposed on September 25, 1789, and declared in force on December 15, 1791.]

First Amendment

Congress shall make no law respecting an establishment of religion, or prohibiting the free exercise thereof; or abridging the freedom of speech, or of the press; or the right of the people peaceably to assemble, and to petition the Government for a redress of grievances.

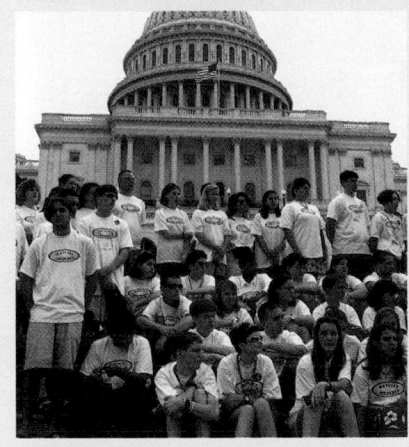

Members of the Students Against Drunk Driving exercise their First Amendment right to expression by gathering in Washington, D.C., to speak out against drinking and driving.

Second Amendment

A well regulated Militia, being necessary to the security of a free State, the right of the people to keep and bear Arms, shall not be infringed.

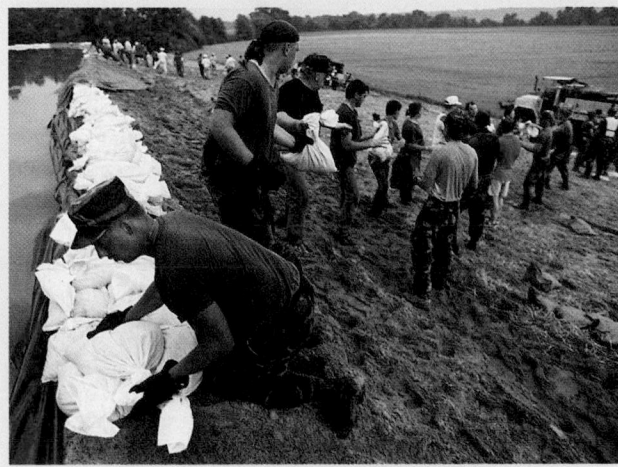

The National Guard, which has replaced state militias, helps local citizens prevent a river from flooding.

Bill of Rights

One of the conditions set by several states for ratifying the Constitution was the inclusion of a bill of rights. Many people feared that a stronger central government might take away basic rights of the people that had been guaranteed in state constitutions. If the three words that begin the Preamble—"We the people"—were truly meant, then the rights of the people needed to be protected.

The First Amendment protects freedom of speech and expression, and forbids Congress to make any law "respecting an establishment of religion" or restraining the freedom to practice religion as one chooses.

 Constitutional Heritage

How do the First and Second Amendments protect individual rights?

CITIZENSHIP

Children and Free Speech. Does the First Amendment protection of free speech extend to children in school? The Supreme Court responded to this question in its 1969 decision in *Tinker* v. *Des Moines Independent Community School District.* In December 1965 the school district had suspended five students for wearing black armbands as a symbol of protest against the Vietnam War. When lower courts upheld the suspension, attorneys asked the Supreme Court to consider the case. The Court determined that students in public schools had First Amendment rights. Schools could limit these expressions only if they could prove that such activities were disruptive to the educational process.

CRITICAL THINKING Do you agree with the Court's ruling? Explain your answer.

ANSWER: Answers will vary. Many students will probably agree with the ruling.

CONSTITUTIONAL HERITAGE ANSWER

by stating that Congress can not make laws limiting a free press, free speech, free exercise of religion, free assembly, and the right to bear arms

A police officer may enter a person's home with a search warrant, which allows the law officer to look for evidence that could convict someone of committing a crime.

The Fifth, Sixth, and Seventh Amendments describe the procedures that courts must follow when trying people accused of crimes. The Fifth Amendment guarantees that no one can be put on trial for a serious crime unless a grand jury agrees that the evidence justifies doing so. It also says that a person cannot be tried twice for the same crime.

The Sixth Amendment makes several promises, including a prompt trial and a trial by a jury chosen from the state and district in which the crime was committed. The Sixth Amendment also states that an accused person must be told why he or she is being tried and promises that an accused person has the right to be defended by a lawyer.

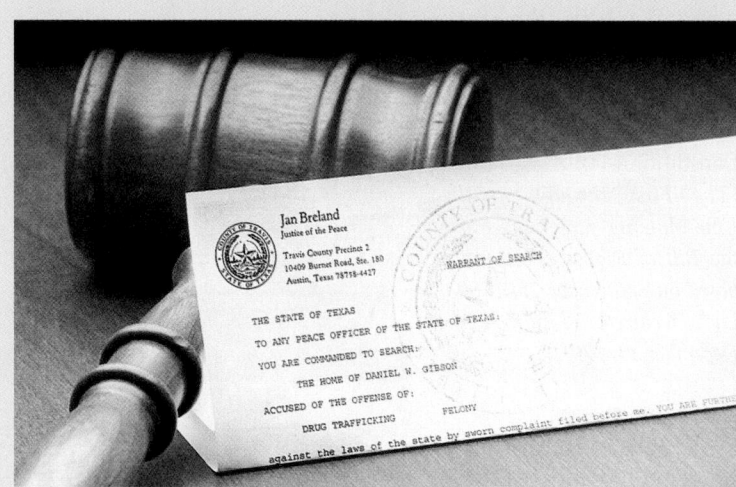

Judges issue search warrants like this one to allow law enforcement officials to legally search a suspected criminal's property.

Third Amendment

No Soldier shall, in time of peace, be quartered in any house, without the consent of the Owner, nor in time of war, but in a manner to be prescribed by law.

Fourth Amendment

The right of the people to be secure in their persons, houses, papers, and effects, against unreasonable searches and seizures, shall not be violated, and no Warrants shall issue, but upon probable cause, supported by Oath or affirmation, and particularly describing the place to be searched, and the persons or things to be seized.

Fifth Amendment

No person shall be held to answer for a capital, or otherwise infamous crime, unless on a presentment or indictment of a Grand Jury, except in cases arising in the land or naval forces, or in the Militia, when in actual service in time of War or public danger; nor shall any person be subject for the same offense to be twice put in jeopardy of life or limb; nor shall be compelled in any criminal case to be a witness against himself, nor be deprived of life, liberty, or property, without due process of law; nor shall private property be taken for public use, without just compensation.

Sixth Amendment

In all criminal prosecutions, the accused shall enjoy the right to a speedy and public trial, by an impartial jury of the State and district wherein the crime shall have been committed, which district shall have been previously ascertained by law, and to be informed of the nature and cause of the accusation; to be confronted with the witnesses against him; to have compulsory process for obtaining witnesses in his favor, and to have the Assistance of Counsel for his defense.

Seventh Amendment

In Suits at common law, where the value in controversy shall exceed twenty dollars, the right of trial by jury shall be preserved, and no fact tried by a jury shall be otherwise reexamined in any Court of the United States, than according to the rules of the common law.

Eighth Amendment

Excessive bail shall not be required, nor excessive fines imposed, nor cruel and unusual punishments inflicted.

Ninth Amendment

The enumeration in the Constitution, of certain rights, shall not be construed to deny or disparage others retained by the people.

Tenth Amendment

The powers not delegated to the United States by the Constitution, nor prohibited by it to the States, are reserved to the States respectively, or to the people.

Eleventh Amendment

[Proposed March 4, 1794; declared ratified January 8, 1798]

The Judicial power of the United States shall not be construed to extend to any suit in law or equity, commenced or prosecuted against one of the United States by Citizens of another State, or by Citizens or Subjects of any Foreign State.

The Seventh Amendment guarantees a trial by jury in cases that involve more than $20, but in modern times, usually much more money is at stake before a case is heard in federal court.

The Ninth and Tenth Amendments were added because not every right of the people or of the states could be listed in the Constitution.

 Constitutional Heritage

How does the Tenth Amendment limit the powers of the federal government?

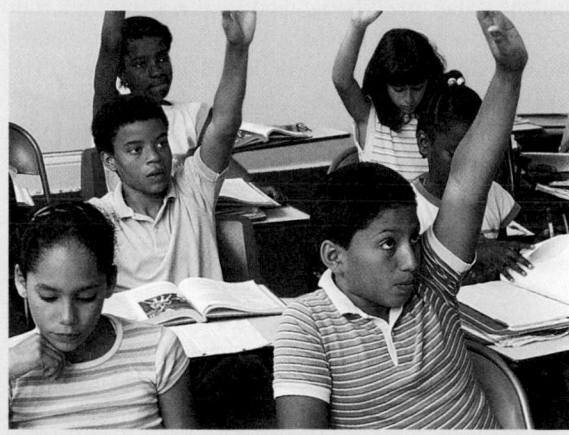

Many Americans consider attendance in free public schools a right of citizenship.

Ending Slavery. In 1863 President Abraham Lincoln freed slaves in certain areas—namely those in rebellion against the United States. Some observers questioned the president's power to end slavery, however, and many doubted that his proclamation would remain in effect after the Civil War. In order to ensure that slavery was forever banned in the United States, these people called for a constitutional amendment prohibiting slavery.

CRITICAL THINKING Why might a constitutional amendment banning slavery have been necessary?

ANSWER: Students should suggest that observers believed that an amendment was necessary due to the the legal questions surrounding Lincoln's actions. They might also have feared that white southerners would try to re-establish slavery after the war.

CONSTITUTIONAL HERITAGE ANSWER

the House of Representatives

The Twelfth Amendment changed the election procedure for president and vice president. Before this amendment, electors voted without distinguishing between president and vice president. Whoever received the most votes became president, and whoever received the next highest number of votes became vice president.

Constitutional Heritage

According to the Twelfth Amendment, who chooses the president if no candidate has received a majority of the electoral votes?

Poster commemorating President Abraham Lincoln's Emancipation Proclamation, which freed slaves in the Confederacy

---

Twelfth Amendment

[Proposed December 9, 1803; declared ratified September 25, 1804]

The Electors shall meet in their respective states and vote by ballot for President and Vice President, one of whom, at least, shall not be an inhabitant of the same state with themselves; they shall name in their ballots the person voted for as President, and in distinct ballots the person voted for as Vice President, and they shall make distinct lists of all persons voted for as President, and of all persons voted for as Vice President, and of the number of votes for each, which lists they shall sign and certify, and transmit sealed to the seat of the government of the United States, directed to the President of the Senate;—The President of the Senate shall, in the presence of the Senate and House of Representatives, open all the certificates and the votes shall then be counted;—The person having the greatest number of votes for President, shall be the President, if such number be a majority of the whole number of Electors appointed; and if no person have such majority, then from the persons having the highest numbers not exceeding three on the list of those voted for as President, the House of Representatives shall choose immediately, by ballot, the President. But in choosing the President, the votes shall be taken by states, the representation from each state having one vote; a quorum for this purpose shall consist of a member or members from two thirds of the states, and a majority of all the states shall be necessary to a choice. ~~And if the House of Representatives shall not choose a President whenever the right of choice shall devolve upon them, before the fourth day of March next following, then the Vice-President shall act as President, as in the case of the death or other constitutional disability of the President;~~—The person having the greatest number of votes as Vice President, shall be the Vice President, if such number be a majority of the whole number of Electors appointed, and if no person have a majority, then from the two highest numbers on the list, the Senate shall choose the Vice President; a quorum for the purpose shall consist of two thirds of the whole number of Senators, and a majority of the whole number shall be necessary to a choice. But no person constitutionally ineligible to the office of President shall be eligible to that of Vice President of the United States.

Thirteenth Amendment

[Proposed January 31, 1865; declared ratified December 18, 1865]

Section 1. Neither slavery nor involuntary servitude, except as a punishment for crime whereof the party shall have been duly convicted, shall exist within the United States, or any place subject to their jurisdiction.

Section 2. Congress shall have power to enforce this article by appropriate legislation.

Fourteenth Amendment

[Proposed June 13, 1866; declared ratified July 28, 1868]

Section 1. All persons born or naturalized in the United States and subject to the jurisdiction thereof, are citizens of the United States and of the State wherein they reside. No State shall make or enforce any law which shall abridge the privileges or immunities of citizens of the United States; nor shall any State deprive any person of life, liberty, or property, without due process of law; nor deny to any person within its jurisdiction the equal protection of the laws.

Section 2. Representatives shall be apportioned among the several States according to their respective numbers, counting the whole number of persons in each State, excluding Indians not taxed. But when the right to vote at any election for the choice of electors for President and Vice President of the United States, Representatives in Congress, the Executive and Judicial officers of a State, or the members of the Legislature thereof, is denied to any of the male inhabitants of such State, being twenty-one years of age, and citizens of the United States, or in any way abridged, except for participation in rebellion, or other crime, the basis of representation therein shall be reduced in the proportion which the number of such male citizens shall bear to the whole number of male citizens twenty-one years of age in such State.

Section 3. No person shall be a Senator or Representative in Congress, or elector of President and Vice President, or hold any office, civil or military, under the United States, or under any State, who, having previously taken an oath, as a member of Congress, or as an officer of the United States, or as a member of any State legislature, or as an executive or judicial officer of any State, to support the Constitution of the United States, shall have engaged in insurrection or rebellion against the same, or given aid or comfort to the enemies thereof. But Congress may by a vote of two thirds of each House, remove such disability.

Section 4. The validity of the public debt of the United States, authorized by law, including debts incurred for payment of pensions and bounties for services in suppressing insurrection or rebellion, shall not be questioned. But neither the United States nor any State shall assume or pay any debt or obligation incurred in aid of insurrection or rebellion against the United States, or any claim for the loss or emancipation of any slave; but all such debts, obligations and claims shall be held illegal and void.

Section 5. The Congress shall have power to enforce, by appropriate legislation, the provisions of this article.

Fifteenth Amendment

[Proposed February 26, 1869; declared ratified March 30, 1870]

Section 1. The right of citizens of the United States to vote shall not be denied or abridged by the United States or by any State on account of race, color, or previous condition of servitude.

Section 2. The Congress shall have power to enforce this article by appropriate legislation.

Constitutional Heritage

According to the Fourteenth Amendment, who is a citizen of the United States, and what rights do citizens have?

In 1833 Chief Justice John Marshall ruled that the Bill of Rights limited the national government but not the state governments. The later effect of this ruling was that states were able to keep African Americans from becoming state citizens. If African Americans were not citizens, they were not protected by the Bill of Rights. The Fourteenth Amendment defines citizenship and prevents states from interfering in the rights of citizens of the United States.

The Fifteenth Amendment extended the right to vote to African American men.

The Sixteenth Amendment.

On the whole, Democrats tended to favor an income tax, while conservative Republicans generally opposed it. Ironically, Senator Nelson Aldrich of Rhode Island, a conservative millionaire Republican, introduced the constitutional amendment permitting an income tax. Aldrich assumed that his amendment would fail to gain adoption. He introduced the measure as a political move to forestall some Democrats from adding another income tax provision to a piece of tariff legislation. The Senate passed the Aldrich measure 77 to 0, however, and the House passed it 318 to 14. The necessary number of states approved it as well, and the amendment became part of the Constitution.

CRITICAL THINKING In what way might the history of the constitutional amendment process have given Aldrich the confidence that the income tax amendment would never be ratified?

ANSWER: Students should note that by 1913 the Constitution had only been amended 5 times.

CONSTITUTIONAL HERITAGE ANSWER

by allowing the citizens of each state to directly elect their senators

Expanding on the federal government's right to levy taxes, outlined in Article I of the Constitution, the Sixteenth Amendment gave Congress the power to issue the income tax.

 Constitutional Heritage

How does the Seventeenth Amendment return authority to the people?

Although many people believed that prohibition was good for the health and welfare of the American people, the Eighteenth Amendment was repealed 14 years later.

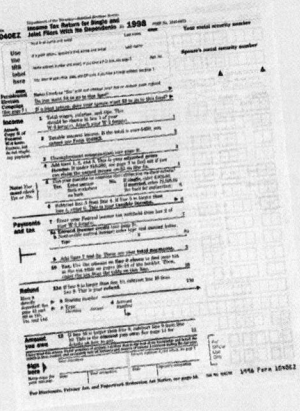

Federal income tax form

Federal agents dispose of alcohol after the passage of the Eighteenth Amendment.

Sixteenth Amendment
[Proposed July 12, 1909; declared ratified February 25, 1913]

The Congress shall have power to lay and collect taxes on incomes, from whatever source derived, without apportionment among the several States, and without regard to any census or enumeration.

Seventeenth Amendment
[Proposed May 13, 1912; declared ratified May 31, 1913]

The Senate of the United States shall be composed of two Senators from each State, elected by the people thereof, for six years; and each Senator shall have one vote. The electors in each State shall have the qualifications requisite for electors of the most numerous branch of the State legislatures.

When vacancies happen in the representation of any State in the Senate, the executive authority of such State shall issue writs of election to fill such vacancies: Provided, That the legislature of any State may empower the executive thereof to make temporary appointments until the people fill the vacancies by election as the legislature may direct.

This amendment shall not be so construed as to affect the election or term of any Senator chosen before it becomes valid as part of the Constitution.

Eighteenth Amendment
[Proposed December 18, 1917; declared ratified January 29, 1919; repealed by the Twenty-first Amendment December 5, 1933]

Section 1. After one year from the ratification of this article the manufacture, sale, or transportation of intoxicating liquors within, the importation thereof into, or the exportation thereof from the United States and all territory subject to the jurisdiction thereof for beverage purposes is hereby prohibited.

Section 2. The Congress and the several States shall have concurrent power to enforce this article by appropriate legislation.

Section 3. This article shall be inoperative unless it shall have been ratified as an amendment to the Constitution by the legislatures of the several States, as provided in the Constitution, within seven years from the date of the submission hereof to the States by the Congress.

Nineteenth Amendment

[Proposed June 4, 1919; declared ratified August 26, 1920]

The right of citizens of the United States to vote shall not be denied or abridged by the United States or by any State on account of sex.

Congress shall have power to enforce this article by appropriate legislation.

Twentieth Amendment

[Proposed March 2, 1932; declared ratified February 6, 1933]

Section 1. The terms of the President and Vice President shall end at noon on the 20th day of January, and the terms of Senators and Representatives at noon on the 3rd day of January, of the years in which such terms would have ended if this article had not been ratified; and the terms of their successors shall then begin.

Section 2. The Congress shall assemble at least once in every year, and such meeting shall begin at noon on the 3rd day of January, unless they shall by law appoint a different day.

Section 3. If, at the time fixed for the beginning of the term of the President, the President elect shall have died, the Vice President elect shall become President. If a President shall not have been chosen before the time fixed for the beginning of his term, or if the President elect shall have failed to qualify, then the Vice President elect shall act as President until a President shall have qualified; and the Congress may by law provide for the case wherein neither a President elect nor a Vice President elect shall have qualified, declaring who shall then act as President, or the manner in which one who is to act shall be selected, and such persons shall act accordingly until a President or Vice President shall have qualified.

Section 4. The Congress may by law provide for the case of the death of any of the persons from whom the House of Representatives may choose a President whenever the right of choice shall have devolved upon them, and for the case of the death of any of the persons from whom the Senate may choose a Vice President whenever the right of choice shall have devolved upon them.

~~**Section 5.** Sections 1 and 2 shall take effect on the 15th day of October following the ratification of this article.~~

~~**Section 6.** This article shall be inoperative unless it shall have been ratified as an amendment to the Constitution by the legislatures of three fourths of the several States within seven years from the date of its submission.~~

Women's suffrage button

Abigail Adams and others were disappointed that the Declaration of Independence and the Constitution did not specifically include women. It took almost 130 years and much campaigning before women's suffrage was added to the Constitution.

In the original Constitution, a newly elected president and Congress did not take office until March 4, which was four months after the November election. The officials who were leaving office were called "lame ducks" because they had little influence during those four months. The Twentieth Amendment changed the date that the new president and Congress take office. Members of Congress now take office in the first week of January, and the president takes office on January 20.

 Constitutional Heritage

According to the Twentieth Amendment, who becomes president if a president-elect dies before taking office?

The People and the Twenty-first Amendment.

Because state conventions rather than state legislatures ratified the Twenty-first Amendment, voters could express their opinion of the proposed document when they cast ballots for the delegates to the conventions. Some 73 percent of Americans voted for anti-prohibition delegates. Of the 38 states that held conventions on the amendment in a single year, 37 ratified it, and only one rejected it.

CRITICAL THINKING What might the reaction to the Twenty-first Amendment have indicated about reactions to the Eighteenth Amendment?

ANSWER: Students might indicate that the reaction to the Twenty-first Amendment indicated that the Eighteenth Amendment was highly unpopular.

THAT'S INTERESTING!

By rejecting the possibility of a third term in order to enjoy "the shade of retirement," President Washington set a two-term precedent that lasted until Franklin D. Roosevelt's presidency.

CONSTITUTIONAL HERITAGE ANSWER

indicates that no person can be elected to the office more than twice

The Twenty-first Amendment is the only amendment that has been ratified by state conventions rather than by state legislatures.

From the time of President Washington's administration, it was a custom for presidents to serve no more than two terms of office. Franklin D. Roosevelt, however, was elected to four consecutive terms. The Twenty-second Amendment made into law the custom of a two-term limit for each president.

 Constitutional Heritage

How does the Twenty-second Amendment limit the years a president can remain in office?

Until the Twenty-third Amendment, the residents of Washington, D.C., could not vote in presidential elections.

Aerial view of Washington, D.C.

Twenty-first Amendment
[Proposed February 20, 1933; declared ratified December 5, 1933]

Section 1. The eighteenth article of amendment to the Constitution of the United States is hereby repealed.

Section 2. The transportation or importation into any State, Territory, or possession of the United States for delivery or use therein of intoxicating liquors, in violation of the laws thereof, is hereby prohibited.

~~**Section 3.** This article shall be inoperative unless it shall have been ratified as an amendment to the Constitution by conventions in the several States, as provided in the Constitution, within seven years from the date of the submission hereof to the States by the Congress.~~

Twenty-second Amendment
[Proposed March 21, 1947; declared ratified March 1, 1951]

Section 1. No person shall be elected to the office of the President more than twice, and no person who has held the office of President, or acted as President, for more than two years of a term to which some other person was elected President shall be elected to the office of the President more than once. ~~But this Article shall not apply to any person holding the office of President when this Article was proposed by the Congress, and shall not prevent any person who may be holding the office of President, or acting as President, during the term within which this Article becomes operative from holding the office of President or acting as President during the remainder of such term.~~

~~**Section 2.** This Article shall be inoperative unless it shall have been ratified as an amendment to the Constitution by the legislatures of three fourths of the several States within seven years from the date of its submission to the States by the Congress.~~

Twenty-third Amendment
[Proposed June 16, 1960; ratified March 29, 1961]

Section 1. The District constituting the seat of Government of the United States shall appoint in such manner as the Congress may direct:

A number of electors of President and Vice President equal to the whole number of Senators and Representatives in Congress to which the District would be entitled if it were a State, but in no event more than the least populous State; they shall be in addition to those appointed by the States, but they shall be considered, for the purposes of the election of President and Vice President, to be electors appointed by a State; and they shall meet in the District and perform such duties as provided by the twelfth article of amendment.

Section 2. The Congress shall have power to enforce this article by appropriate legislation.

Twenty-fourth Amendment

[Proposed August 27, 1962; ratified January 23, 1964]

Section 1. The right of citizens of the United States to vote in any primary or other election for President or Vice President, for electors for President or Vice President, or for Senator or Representative in Congress, shall not be denied or abridged by the United States or any State by reason of failure to pay any poll tax or other tax.

Section 2. The Congress shall have power to enforce this article by appropriate legislation.

Twenty-fifth Amendment

[Proposed July 6, 1965; ratified February 10, 1967]

Section 1. In case of removal of the President from office or of his death or resignation, the Vice President shall become President.

Section 2. Whenever there is a vacancy in the office of the Vice President, the President shall nominate a Vice President who shall take office upon confirmation by a majority vote of both Houses of Congress.

Vice President Lyndon Johnson was sworn in as president after John F. Kennedy's assassination.

Section 3. Whenever the President transmits to the President pro tempore of the Senate and the Speaker of the House of Representatives his written declaration that he is unable to discharge the powers and duties of his office, and until he transmits to them a written declaration to the contrary, such powers and duties shall be discharged by the Vice President as Acting President.

Section 4. Whenever the Vice President and a majority of either the principal officers of the executive departments or of such other body as Congress may by law provide, transmit to the President pro tempore of the Senate and the Speaker of the House of Representatives their written declaration that the President is unable to discharge the powers and duties of his office, the Vice President shall immediately assume the powers and duties of the office as Acting President.

Thereafter, when the President transmits to the President pro tempore of the Senate and the Speaker of the House of Representatives his written declaration that no inability exists, he shall resume the powers and duties of his office unless the Vice President and a majority of either the principal officers of the executive department or of such other body as Congress may by law provide, transmit within four days to the President pro tempore of

---

⭐ **Constitutional Heritage**

What practices does the Twenty-fourth Amendment outlaw?

The illness of President Eisenhower in the 1950s and the assassination of President Kennedy in 1963 were the events behind the Twenty-fifth Amendment. The Constitution did not provide a clear-cut method for a vice president to take over for a disabled president or in the event of the death of a president. This amendment provides for filling the office of the vice president if a vacancy occurs. It also provides a way for the vice president to take over if the president is unable to perform the duties of that office.

Gregory Watson, Constitutional Advocate.

In 1982 Gregory Watson was a student at the University of Texas at Austin. In a paper for a political science class he argued that a proposed amendment regarding congressional pay, once part of the Bill of Rights, could still be ratified. Only six states had ratified the proposed amendment, which had then been ignored for more than 200 years. Watson received a "C" on his paper, but he was determined to prove that he was correct. He spent more than $5,000 of his own money in an effort to convince state legislatures throughout the nation to ratify the amendment. Watson was successful, and in 1992 the proposal became the Twenty-seventh Amendment.

CRITICAL THINKING Do you think that the proposed amendment should have become part of the Constitution? Explain your answer.

ANSWER: Some students might argue that it was not necessary, since the states had ignored it for more than 200 years. Others might argue that state legislatures ratified the amendment, and so it met all necessary qualifications.

CONSTITUTIONAL HERITAGE ANSWER

until an election of representatives had convened

The Voting Act of 1970 tried to set the voting age at 18 years old. However, the Supreme Court ruled that the act set the voting age for national elections only, not state or local elections. This ruling would make necessary several different ballots at elections. The Twenty-sixth Amendment gave 18-year-old citizens the right to vote in all elections.

 Constitutional Heritage

According to the Twenty-seventh Amendment, if senators or representatives were to vote for a pay raise for themselves, when would it take effect?

the Senate and the Speaker of the House of Representatives their written declaration that the President is unable to discharge the powers and duties of his office. Thereupon Congress shall decide the issue, assembling within forty-eight hours for that purpose if not in session. If the Congress, within twenty-one days after receipt of the latter written declaration, or, if Congress is not in session, within twenty-one days after Congress is required to assemble, determines by two-thirds vote of both Houses that the President is unable to discharge the powers and duties of his office, the Vice President shall continue to discharge the same as Acting President; otherwise, the President shall resume the powers and duties of his office.

Twenty-sixth Amendment
[Proposed March 23, 1971; ratified July 1, 1971]

Section 1. The right of citizens of the United States, who are eighteen years of age or older, to vote shall not be denied or abridged by the United States or by any State on account of age.

Section 2. The Congress shall have power to enforce this article by appropriate legislation.

Twenty-seventh Amendment
[Proposed September 25, 1789; declared ratified May 7, 1992]

No law, varying the compensation for the services of the Senators and Representatives, shall take effect, until an election of Representatives shall have intervened.

These students are helping a local candidate campaign for office.

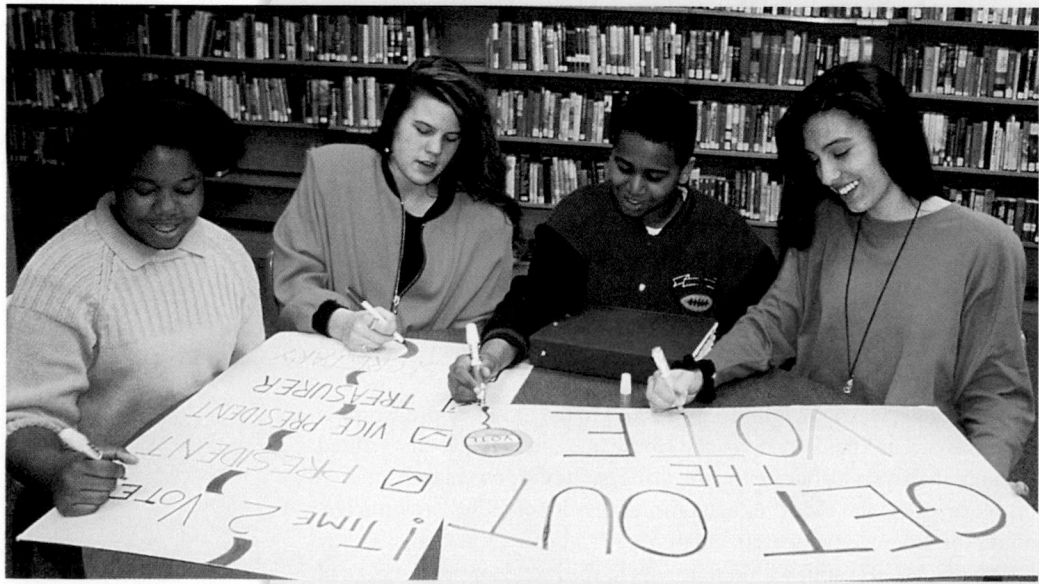

Amendments to the Constitution

Amendment	Year Enacted	Subject
1st	1791	Personal and political freedoms
2nd	1791	Right to keep weapons
3rd	1791	Quartering of troops
4th	1791	Search and seizure; search warrants
5th	1791	Rights of accused persons
6th	1791	Speedy trial
7th	1791	Jury trial
8th	1791	Bails, fines, punishments
9th	1791	Rights of the people
10th	1791	Powers of the states
11th	1798	Suits against the states
12th	1804	Election of president and vice president
13th	1865	Abolition of slavery
14th	1868	Rights of citizens; privileges and immunities, due process, and equal protection
15th	1870	Extension of suffrage to African American men
16th	1913	Income tax
17th	1913	Direct election of senators
18th	1919	Prohibition of liquor
19th	1920	Women's suffrage
20th	1933	Change in dates for presidential and congressional terms of office
21st	1933	Repeal of prohibition
22nd	1951	Two-term limit on presidential tenure
23rd	1961	Right to vote in presidential elections for residents of the District of Columbia
24th	1964	Poll tax banned in federal elections
25th	1967	Presidential disability and succession
26th	1971	Lowering of voting age to 18
27th	1992	Legislative salaries

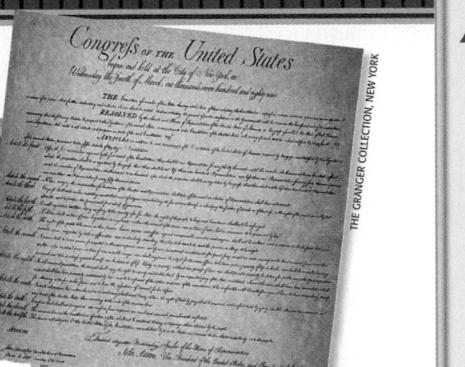

The Bill of Rights

THE GRANGER COLLECTION, NEW YORK

Slave chains

Women's suffrage button

Voter registration form

The Expanding Nation

CHAPTER RESOURCE MANAGER

Objectives	Pacing Guide	Reproducible Resources
SECTION 1 **The New Government Takes Shape** pp. 70–78 ★ Identify key decisions the first administration made. ★ Describe the domestic and international problems the nation faced in the 1790s. ★ Analyze major issues John Adams and Thomas Jefferson faced during their presidencies. ★ Explain the significance of the Louisiana Purchase. ★ Discuss the reasons for the United States's declaration of war on Great Britain in 1812.	**Regular** 2 days **Block Scheduling** 1 day *Block Scheduling Handbook with Team Teaching Strategies, pp. 7–12*	**RS** Guided Reading Strategy 2.1 **IC** Literature Reading: "A Visit to the Nation's Capital" **RS** Graphic Organizer 2: The New Government **SM** Geography Activity 2: The Louisiana Purchase **E** Hands-On History Activity: The Bill of Rights: A Survey **E** Creative Teaching Strategy: Quick Survey
SECTION 2 **Growth and Change** pp. 79–85 ★ Describe what changes took place in foreign and domestic policy in the early 1800s. ★ Identify how industrialization and immigration affected northern society. ★ Explain how southern society and the slave system were organized. ★ Relate what social issues reformers addressed in the early to mid-1800s.	**Regular** 1 day **Block Scheduling** .5 day *Block Scheduling Handbook with Team Teaching Strategies, pp. 7–12*	**RS** Guided Reading Strategy 2.2 **PS** Biography Reading 2: Denmark Vesey
SECTION 3 **Westward Expansion and Sectional Conflict** pp. 86–91 ★ Analyze what caused the Texas Revolution and the Mexican War. ★ Explain why Americans began to settle the West. ★ Discuss how politicians addressed the expansion of slavery. ★ Identify what events led to the secession of the southern states.	**Regular** 2 days **Block Scheduling** 1 day *Block Scheduling Handbook with Team Teaching Strategies, pp. 7–12*	**RS** Guided Reading Strategy 2.3 **PS** Primary Source Reading 2: Life on the Wagon Trail **SM** American History Outline Map 9: Conflict Over Slavery

Chapter Resource Key

PS Primary Sources	**REV** Review	Video	
RS Reading Support	**ELL** Reinforcement and English Language Learners	Internet	
IC Interdisciplinary Connections		🖥 Holt Presentation Maker Using Microsoft® PowerPoint®	
E Enrichment	🖴 Transparencies		
SM Skills Mastery	💿 CD-ROM		
A Assessment	🎵 Music		

One-Stop Planner CD-ROM

See the *One-Stop Planner* for a complete list of additional resources for students and teachers.

One-Stop Planner CD-ROM

It's easy to plan lessons, select resources, and print out materials for your students when you use the **One-Stop Planner CD–ROM with Test Generator.**

 One-Stop Planner, Lesson 2.1

 Holt Researcher: American History CD–ROM

 Homework Practice Online

REV Section 1 Review, p. 78

A Daily Quiz 2.1

ELL Main Idea Activity for 2.1

ELL English Audio Summary 2.1

ELL Spanish Audio Summary 2.1

 One-Stop Planner, Lesson 2.2

 The American Nation Video Program Segment: A Native American Confederacy; Teacher's Guide, pp. 33–38

 Holt Researcher: American History CD–ROM

 Homework Practice Online

 HRW Go site

REV Section 2 Review, p. 85

A Daily Quiz 2.2

ELL Main Idea Activity for 2.2

ELL English Audio Summary 2.2

ELL Spanish Audio Summary 2.2

 One-Stop Planner, Lesson 2.3

 CNN Presents America: Yesterday and Today, Beginnings to 1914 Segment: Excavating the Alamo

 Holt Researcher: American History CD–ROM

 Homework Practice Online

REV Section 3 Review, p. 91

A Daily Quiz 2.3

ELL Main Idea Activity for 2.3

ELL English Audio Summary 2.3

ELL Spanish Audio Summary 2.3

internet connect

HRW ONLINE RESOURCES
GO TO: go.hrw.com
Then type in a keyword.

TEACHER HOME PAGE
KEYWORD: SE3 Teacher

CHAPTER INTERNET ACTIVITIES
KEYWORD: SE3 AN2
Choose an activity to:
• research the Erie Canal and National Road and create a brochure.
• analyze the causes and effects of the Irish Potato Famine and its impact on immigration.
• create a newspaper on John Brown and resistance movements against slavery.

CHAPTER ENRICHMENT LINKS
KEYWORD: SE3 CH2

ONLINE ASSESSMENT
Homework Practice
KEYWORD: SE3 HP2

Standardized Test Prep
KEYWORD: SE3 STP2

Rubrics
KEYWORD: SS Rubrics

ONLINE MAPS, CHARTS, AND GRAPHS
KEYWORD: SE3 MCG
• The Louisiana Purchase
• Slave and Free Territory in 1850 and 1854

CONTENT UPDATES
KEYWORD: SS Content Updates

HOLT PRESENTATION MAKER
KEYWORD: SE3 PPT2

ONLINE READING SUPPORT
KEYWORD: SS Strategies

CURRENT EVENTS
KEYWORD: S3 Current Events

Meeting Individual Needs

Ability Levels

Level 1 Basic-level activities designed for all students encountering new material

Level 2 Intermediate-level activities designed for average students

Level 3 Challenging activities designed for honors and gifted-and-talented students

English Language Learners Activities that address the needs of students with Limited English Proficiency

Chapter Review and Assessment

 Global Skill Builder CD–ROM

 HRW Go site

REV **Chapter 2 Tutorial for Students, Parents, Mentors, and Peers**

REV **Chapter 2 Review, pp. 92–93**

 Chapter 2 Test Generator (on the One-Stop Planner)

A **Chapter 2 Test (Form A or B)**

A **Alternative Assessment Handbook**

A **Chapter 2 Test for English Language Learners and Special-Needs Students**

Build on What You Know

Ask students to answer the following questions.

What early signs showed that the United States might not be completely unified?

Consider:

• different interpretations of the Constitution

• conflicts over the justification of slavery

What types of conflicts might have arisen between Great Britain and the newly formed United States?

Consider:

• France's alliance with the colonies during the Revolution

• the question of land in the west and north

AMERICAN EVENTS

PEOPLE IN HISTORY

1842 ■ Kit Carson. Born in Kentucky in 1809, Kit Carson spent his childhood in Missouri. When he was 17 years old, he ran away to New Mexico. There he worked as a fur trapper, exploring the mountains and rivers of the Southwest. In 1842 explorer John C. Frémont hired Carson to guide him on his expeditions across the West. Carson spent the rest of his life serving in the U.S. Army as a guide, an Indian agent, and even as a lieutenant colonel for the Union during the Civil War.

ACTIVITY: Ask students to conduct research on a famous person of the Old West. Then have students write a short story about that person.

CHAPTER 2

1789–1861

The Expanding Nation

Journal from the Lewis and Clark exploration of the Louisiana Territory

1789
Politics
George Washington is elected president.

President Washington and his advisers

1803
World Events
The United States roughly doubles in size with the Louisiana Purchase.

1814
Science and Technology
Deborah Skinner tests the first power-driven spinning loom.

1816
Business and Finance
Representative John C. Calhoun calls for the creation of a Second Bank of the United States.

1789	1795	1800	1805	1810	1815	1820

1797
Science and Technology
The USS *Constitution* is launched.

1807
Science and Technology
Robert Fulton's steamboat, the *Clermont*, travels up the Hudson River in New York.

1810
World Events
Mexican priest Miguel Hidalgo y Costilla helps inspire Mexicans to fight for independence from Spain.

1820
Politics
Congress passes the Missouri Compromise, an attempt to settle the dispute over the western expansion of slavery.

USS Constitution

Slave nurses often tended to slaveholders' children.

Build on What You Know

By 1789 all 13 states except Rhode Island had ratified the new plan of government developed at the Constitutional Convention. Newly elected government officials—the president and the members of Congress—set out to put the Constitution into action. In this chapter you will learn how the new nation faced many challenges in its first 80 years. Finally, you will learn why the nation began to break apart.

What's Your Opinion?

To help students create their Themes Journal entries, share the following examples of appropriate agree/disagree statements.

Constitutional Heritage

Agree After declaring independence from Britain in 1776, some states included a bill of rights in their constitutions.

Disagree The states ratified the U.S. Constitution even though it did not contain a guarantee of individual rights.

Economics

Agree The federal government's inability under the Articles of Confederation to levy a direct tax or to set international trade policies led to an economic depression and chaos.

Disagree The Tea Act of 1773, passed by the British government, helped the British East India Company but hurt other merchants.

Geography

Agree The differing interests of the North and the South led to the Civil War.

Disagree The thirteen American colonies fought together for independence from Great Britain.

Sequoya

THE GRANGER COLLECTION NEW YORK

Fur trappers often wore coats like this one.

1821
Daily Life
Sequoya completes development of the Cherokee writing system.

1830
Science and Technology
The locomotive *Tom Thumb* is tested against a racehorse.

1842
Daily Life
Fur-trapper Kit Carson serves as a guide to U.S. government-financed explorations of the West.

1846
Business and Finance
Maine becomes the first state to prohibit the sale of alcohol.

1825	**1831**	**1837**	**1843**	**1849**	**1855**	**1861**

1828
Politics
Andrew Jackson is elected president.

1830
World Events
Simon Bolívar, the "Liberator" of South America, dies.

1837
Politics
Martin Van Buren, Andrew Jackson's vice president, is sworn in as president.

1860
Politics
Abraham Lincoln is elected president.

Painting of Simon Bolívar

Items from Lincoln's 1860 presidential campaign.

Lincoln and Hamlin

exploring the time line

GLOBAL EVENTS

internet connect
go.hrw.com

TOPIC: Mexican War of Independence
GO TO: go.hrw.com
KEYWORD: SE3 AN2

Have students access the Internet through the HRW Go site to conduct research on the Mexican War for Independence. Then have students create an illustrated and annotated time line detailing the major events of and the important people involved in this conflict.

What's Your Opinion?

Themes Journal *Do you agree or disagree with the following statements? Support your point of view in your journal.*

Constitutional Heritage Guaranteed protection of individual rights is needed even under a democratic government.

Economics The federal government should regulate economic development.

Geography Differences among people in various geographic regions can give rise to conflicting political interests.

After completing Section 1, students should be able to:

OBJECTIVE 1 Identify key decisions the first administration made.

OBJECTIVE 2 Describe the domestic and international problems the nation faced in the 1790s.

OBJECTIVE 3 Analyze major issues John Adams and Thomas Jefferson faced during their presidencies.

OBJECTIVE 4 Explain the significance of the Louisiana Purchase.

OBJECTIVE 5 Discuss the reasons for the United States's declaration of war on Great Britain in 1812.

 LET'S GET STARTED!

Write the following scenario on the chalkboard: *Your revolution has succeeded, but problems still remain. Your country's finances are in ruin. Debts are high; the currency is shaky. How would you solve the economic problems? How would you structure the country's finances?* As students enter the classroom, ask them to find a partner and to list three possible ways to solve the problems described in the scenario. Have volunteers share their solutions. Then tell students that in Section 1 they will learn about how U.S. officials dealt with the nation's economic problems.

SECTION 1 RESOURCES

REPRODUCIBLE
▶ Guided Reading Strategy 2.1
▶ Literature Reading 2: "A Visit to the Nation's Capital"
▶ Graphic Organizer 2: The New Government
▶ Geography Activity 2: The Louisiana Purchase

TECHNOLOGY
▶ One-Stop Planner, Lesson 2.1
▶ Holt Researcher: American History CD–ROM
▶ Homework Practice Online

REINFORCEMENT, REVIEW, AND ASSESSMENT
▶ Section 1 Review, p. 78
▶ Daily Quiz 2.1
▶ Main Idea Activity 2.1
▶ English Audio Summary 2.1
▶ Spanish Audio Summary 2.1

SECTION 1

READ TO DISCOVER
1. What key decisions did the first administration make?
2. What domestic and international problems did the nation face in the 1790s?
3. What major issues did John Adams and Thomas Jefferson face during their presidencies?
4. What was the significance of the Louisiana Purchase?
5. Why did the United States declare war on Great Britain in 1812?

DEFINE
cabinet
free enterprise
strict construction
loose construction
judicial review

IDENTIFY
Judiciary Act of 1789
Bill of Rights
Alexander Hamilton
Little Turtle
Alien and Sedition Acts
Kentucky and Virginia Resolutions
John Marshall
Marbury v. Madison
Louisiana Purchase

▶ WHY IT MATTERS TODAY
Today the United States has two main political parties. These are the Democratic Party and the Republican Party. Use **CNNfyi.com** or other **current events** sources to learn about an issue involving either of these parties. Record your findings in your journal.

CNNfyi.com

The New Government Takes Shape

 EYEWITNESSES TO History

"[For nearly] half a mile, you could see little else along the shore, in the street, and on board every vessel, but heads standing as thick as ears of corn before a harvest."

—Elias Boudinot, letter to his wife, 1789

Cup celebrating Washington's presidency

This observer described the scene on April 23, 1789. Crowds of people gathered to welcome President-elect George Washington to New York City, the nation's temporary capital. They came to witness the inauguration of the first president of the United States. Celebrations had been staged along the route that Washington followed from Mount Vernon, Virginia. As he neared his destination, the crowds gathered in the streets and along the shore to welcome the boat carrying him. A parade accompanied Washington to the presidential mansion. One week later, Washington took his oath of office on the balcony of Federal Hall. As his last words echoed in the air, the crowd burst into cheers.

The First President

When Congress opened the ballots from the states' electors on April 6, 1789, George Washington was the unanimous choice for president. Washington knew that each step he took would set a precedent, or serve as a guide, for future leaders. The task of molding the new government also belonged to the first Congress.

Congress first created a federal court system. The **Judiciary Act of 1789** established a federal district court for each state. This act specified that there would be five associate justices of the Supreme Court to be nominated by the president and approved by the Senate. The act also defined the federal courts' powers. Washington wrote to the first justices about the importance of their positions. He said, "The happiness of the people of the United States depend[s] in a considerable degree on the interpretation and execution of its laws."

Congress's next task was to add a protection of individual liberties to the Constitution. From the 210 proposed amendments, Congress recommended 12 for adoption. The states ratified 10 by late 1791. These amendments became known as the **Bill of Rights**. The Bill of Rights guarantees specific rights, such as freedom of speech, religion, and the press. It sets out some rules for criminal and trial procedures. It also recognizes that states or the people retain the powers not specifically delegated to the federal government or prohibited by the Constitution.

During its first session Congress also created three departments to assist the president. These were the State Department, to handle foreign affairs; the War Department, to manage military affairs; and the Treasury Department, to oversee the nation's finances. The president appointed the secretaries, or heads, of these departments to serve as his advisers. Over time, these advisers, along with the heads of departments created later, became known as the president's **cabinet**.

TEACH OBJECTIVE 1

ALL LEVELS: Tell students to imagine that they are rebel leaders who have just overthrown the ruling government and established their own nation. Ask students to describe their first major actions. To help students understand the key decisions of the first Congress, copy the following graphic organizer on the chalkboard, omitting the italicized answers, and have each student complete it. Then ask students to consider those decisions in light of the actions that they themselves wanted to take in their fictional nations. How do they differ? Would students change their actions, given the decisions that Congress made and the effects of those decisions?

English Language Learners

MAJOR ACTIONS OF THE FIRST CONGRESS

Bill of Rights	Judiciary Act of 1789	Executive Departments
• *guarantees freedom of speech* • *guarantees freedom of religion* • *guarantees freedom of the press* • *guarantees other freedoms as well*	• *established federal district courts* • *specified that five associate Supreme Court justices were to be nominated by the president* • *defined the Court's powers*	• *created the State Department to handle foreign affairs* • *created the War Department to manage military affairs* • *created the Treasury Department to oversee the nation's finances*

Bill of Rights

First Amendment
guarantees freedom of religion, speech, and the press and the right to assemble peacefully and to petition the government.

Second Amendment
recognizes the necessity of state militias and thus the right to bear arms.

Third Amendment
prohibits quartering of troops without consent as regulated by law.

Fourth Amendment
prohibits searches and seizures without warrants, which can be issued only upon probable cause.

Fifth Amendment
requires a grand jury indictment before persons can be tried for serious criminal charges; prohibits persons from being tried twice for the same offense; prohibits forcing the accused to testify against themselves; guarantees that no one may be deprived of life, liberty, or property without due process of law.

Sixth Amendment
guarantees the right to a speedy trial in criminal cases, the right to know all charges, the right to question and obtain witnesses, and the right to have counsel.

Seventh Amendment
guarantees a jury trial in most civil cases.

Eighth Amendment
prohibits excessive fines and bail; prohibits cruel and unusual punishment.

Ninth Amendment
protects individual rights not specifically mentioned in the Constitution.

Tenth Amendment
reserves for the states and the people those powers not delegated to the national government or prohibited by the Constitution.

Interpreting Charts James Madison helped narrow the list of proposed amendments for the Bill of Rights.

? Skills Assessment How do these amendments affect U.S. citizens today?

Restoring the Nation's Credit

After years of war and spending more money than it had, the U.S. government faced serious financial problems. The Treasury had neither funds to pay off war debts nor money to run the government.

The secretary of the Treasury. Lawmakers turned to Treasury Secretary **Alexander Hamilton**, Washington's most trusted adviser, for help. In doing so, they set an important precedent. Although Congress is responsible for passing laws, it has from the beginning sought direction from the executive branch.

B I O G R A P H Y

Alexander Hamilton

Hamilton was one of the most brilliant and controversial of the nation's founders. He was born in the British West Indies in 1757, the son of a failed Scottish merchant. At an early age Hamilton helped run a shipping company, where his business skills became evident. In 1773 Hamilton arrived in New York City, where he attended King's College (now Columbia University). During the Revolutionary War, Hamilton served as an aide to General Washington. Hamilton was also a delegate to the Constitutional Convention and helped write the *Federalist Papers*. Through his writings and public career, Hamilton exerted almost as great an influence on the young Republic as the early presidents did.

Research on the R●M

Free Find:
Alexander Hamilton

After reading about Alexander Hamilton on the **Holt Researcher CD-ROM**, write a short essay explaining his contributions to the new U.S. government.

Alexander Hamilton.
Despite Alexander Hamilton's political ambitions, he never ran for president. Although Hamilton wanted to be president, he recognized that several factors—his birth outside of colonial America, his arrogant manner, and his unpopularity in the South— would prevent him from winning the presidency. Determined not to lose a national election, the practical Hamilton gave up his presidential dreams.

CRITICAL THINKING Why might Hamilton's arrogant manner have prevented him from winning the presidency?

ANSWER: Students might suggest that many Americans viewed Hamilton's personal manner as an expression of his monarchist tendencies. These tendencies, which seemed to contradict the principles of the Revolution, irritated and concerned many.

CHART ANSWER
Answers will vary. Students might suggest that most personal freedoms people value today were first granted by the Bill of Rights.

Organize students into small groups. Ask groups to conduct research on Adam Smith and his theory of capitalism. Have each member of the group focus on a specific aspect of Smith's life, such as his childhood, his early adult years, his economic theories, and his influence on economic thought. Have each group compile its research into a detailed three- or four-page scrapbook on Smith. Have groups present their scrapbooks to the class.
Cooperative Learning, Block Scheduling

SPOTLIGHT
on the Physiocrats

Have students conduct research on the Physiocrats, a school of French economists and philosophers who influenced the thinking of Adam Smith and some of the framers of the Constitution. Have each student create a chart comparing the ideas of the Physiocrats, Adam Smith, and the framers of the Constitution. Have volunteers present their charts to the class.
Block Scheduling

NOTE: To help students make meaningful connections between events in U.S. history and those in their own hometown, use the Chapter 2 **Hands-On History Activity**, The Bill of Rights: A Survey.

HISTORY MAKERS SPEAK

Thomas Cooper in *The American Heritage History of the Making of the Nation*

Thomas Cooper on Government. Despite the controversy over debt repayment, some people admired the American economic system. Thomas Cooper, a chemist born in Britain, moved to the United States in 1793. In *Some Information Respecting America* he wrote: "There is little fault to find with the government of America, either in principle or in practice. We have very few taxes to pay, and those are out of acknowledged necessity, and moderate in amount. . . . There are no men of great rank, nor many of great riches. Nor have the rich there the power of oppressing the less rich, for poverty, such as in Great Britain, is almost unknown."

CRITICAL THINKING Do you think that Cooper's words are true today? Explain your answer.

ANSWER: Answers will vary. Some students might suggest that there is little class bias in the United States, while others might argue that the rich hold the most political and social power.

VISUAL RECORD ANSWER

Students might suggest that freedom and liberty are represented on the coins.

INTERPRETING THE VISUAL RECORD

U.S. currency. The U.S. Mint began to produce coins in 1792, providing a stable currency in the early years of the nation. *How do the decorative features on these coins represent the values on which the United States was founded?*

Hamilton argued that the nation's future depended on a strong federal government supported by the wealthy. He believed that economic policies that helped business and industry would strengthen the government. Scottish economists David Hume and Adam Smith influenced Hamilton's views. In his 1776 book *The Wealth of Nations,* Smith stated that industry and commerce—not just farming—were the most important sources of wealth. Smith advocated **free enterprise**—an economic system based on a free market, private ownership of property, voluntary exchange of goods and services, and the profit motive.

Hamilton's proposals. Hamilton advised Congress to strengthen the nation's credit by paying the national debt. This was the money that the federal government owed to its creditors. The total national and state debt was estimated to be $77 million, reflecting the heavy costs of the Revolutionary War. Congress moved quickly to pay the estimated $12 million it owed to foreign nations.

Hamilton proposed that the federal government repay about $21.5 million of the $25 million that states owed. This proposal faced strong opposition. Many of the southern states had already retired most of their debts. Hamilton negotiated a last-minute compromise. Some northerners agreed to support moving the national capital from Philadelphia southward to a site along the Potomac River, near northern Virginia. Virginians believed this new location, later named Washington, D.C. (District of Columbia), would give them more influence in the federal government. In return, some southerners voted for Hamilton's plan.

To provide economic stability, Hamilton asked Congress to create a national bank. The Bank of the United States would consist of a central bank with branches in major U.S. cities. The Bank would also issue a sound, uniform currency and would serve as a source for loans to assist the government.

Many Americans, particularly southern planters who depended on credit, did not share Hamilton's enthusiasm for a national bank. They feared that wealthy northeastern merchants would control it. Secretary of State Thomas Jefferson raised another objection. He believed that the proposed Bank was unconstitutional. The Constitution did not give the federal government the power to set up a bank.

Both Jefferson and Hamilton pointed to the clause in the Constitution that grants Congress the power "to make all laws . . . necessary and proper" for carrying out its delegated powers. They disagreed, however, on the clause's exact interpretation. Jefferson argued that the government could do only what was absolutely necessary to carry out its duties. This school of narrow constitutional interpretation is called **strict construction.** Hamilton supported the theory of constitutional interpretation called **loose construction.** He believed that within broad limits the government

PRESIDENTIAL *Lives*

George Washington

1732–1799
In Office 1789–1797

As president, George Washington refused to isolate himself from the general public, saying he did not want to be shut away "like an eastern Lama [holy man]." He set up a schedule for greeting citizens in his official residence. On Tuesday afternoons he met with men. On Friday evenings he and his wife, Martha, served refreshments to men and women.

Washington also had government officials to dinner every Thursday, rotating the invitations to avoid any appearance of playing favorites. The dinners were not formal functions as much as they were festive occasions. Washington loved social gatherings of all kinds, from intimate tea parties to fox hunts and lavish balls. He enjoyed playing games, attending the theater, and sharing good food and conversation.

LEVEL 1: Have students label one side of a sheet of paper "Domestic Challenges" and the other side "Foreign Challenges." Then tell students to list the domestic and foreign challenges the new nation faced. *(Students should include as domestic challenges: federal debt, farmers' protests, and conflicts with American Indians. Foreign challenges should include: inability to maintain neutrality in the face of British aggression, Britain's supplying arms to American Indians, and conflicts between Americans siding with the British versus those siding with the French.)* **English Language Learners**

LEVELS 2 AND 3: Have students complete the Level 1 activity, leaving a few lines blank between items in each column. Tell them to fill in the blank spaces with descriptions of how the federal government attempted to solve each problem. *(Students might answer that the government created a national bank and taxed whiskey to address the debt problem; called in state troops to deal with protest; signed a treaty with the Indians; signed a treaty on British aggression; did nothing to combat Britain's arming of Indians; and formed political parties to allow for British and French sympathies.)*

---

could take any reasonable action that the Constitution does not specifically forbid. The government's power to collect taxes and borrow money could only be properly exercised, Hamilton argued, with the aid of a national bank.

In the end, President Washington sided with Hamilton. Congress chartered the Bank of the United States in 1791. The charter granted the Bank the right to operate for 20 years.

✔ **READING CHECK: Analyzing Information** How did the actions of the first president and Congress strengthen the new nation? A Bill of Rights added to individual protections; a judiciary was created; and the nation resolved some of its financial problems.

New Challenges

As a new nation, the United States faced some old problems. These included debt, tensions with American Indians, and unresolved issues with Britain.

Domestic issues. To generate income, Congress passed a tax on the production of whiskey in 1791. Three years later, Pennsylvania farmers, who were hard hit by this measure, rebelled. An anonymous poet described their reaction: "Their liberty they will maintain, They fought for't, and they'll fight again." The farmers planned to march to the temporary capital of Philadelphia. However, they quickly disbanded when President Washington called out some 13,000 state militia.

Greater troubles brewed in the Northwest Territory. Settlers there continued to occupy American Indian land. Some members of American Indian nations joined together in a loose confederation to defend their homelands. Miami chief **Little Turtle** commanded this group. In 1791 Little Turtle's forces soundly defeated U.S. troops in a battle along the Wabash River in what is now Indiana. This defeat stunned the government. In response, President Washington ordered some 3,000 soldiers to protect the frontier. Little Turtle recognized that the Indians had little chance of defeating a well-trained force that outnumbered them. He gave his allies this advice.

U.S. forces overwhelmed American Indians in the Battle of Fallen Timbers.

History Makers Speak

"We have beaten the enemy twice under different commanders. We cannot expect the same good fortune to attend us always. The Americans are now led by a chief who never sleeps. Like the blacksnake, the day and the night are alike to him. . . . It would be prudent to listen to his offers of peace."

—Little Turtle, quoted in *Ark of Empire*, by Dale Van Every

In the summer of 1794, U.S. troops defeated the confederation in the Battle of Fallen Timbers, near what is now Toledo, Ohio. The following year American Indian leaders from more than 10 nations signed a treaty with the U.S. government in which they ceded much of their land in the Northwest.

Tensions with Great Britain. President Washington wanted the United States to remain neutral in foreign affairs. This goal proved difficult. Soon after France became a republic in 1792, France and Britain went to war. Both countries ignored

Analyzing Primary Sources

Drawing Conclusions Why did Little Turtle support listening to offers of peace?
because the Americans were too powerful

PEOPLE IN HISTORY

Little Turtle. Little Turtle demonstrated his impressive military-planning skills even before the American Indian victory at the battle along the Wabash River. In late September 1790 Brigadier General Josiah Harmar left present-day Cincinnati and marched north with 1,500 soldiers to attack the Indians. Hoping to convince Harmar that the American Indian coalition had broken down, Little Turtle ordered his soldiers to destroy the Miami Indian towns around Fort Wayne. In two battles that followed, Little Turtle's forces defeated Harmar's soldiers, killing more than 200 people. Harmar quickly retreated to the south.

ACTIVITY: Tell students to imagine that they are Josiah Harmar. Have each student write a half-page memo analyzing the reason's for Harmar's defeat and offering at least two strategies that might have prevented it.

LEVEL 1: Pair students and have each pair decide which student will be Adams and which will be Jefferson. Have each student write a letter to his or her family explaining the major issues he or she faced during the presidency. (*Letters from John Adams should include: sea battles with France, controversy over Alien and Sedition Acts, declining popularity and conflict with Democratic-Republicans. Letters from Jefferson should include: difficulties with Supreme Court, problems maintaining neutrality, Louisiana Purchase, Embargo Act.*) Have volunteers share their letters with the class. **English Language Learners, Cooperative Learning**

LEVEL 2: Divide students into two groups. Have one group make a list of the issues John Adams faced as president, and have the other group make a list of the issues Thomas Jefferson faced as president. Have volunteers from each group create a chart on the board of the issues each president faced. (*See the Level 1 lesson for the correct issues.*) Ask students to decide which president faced more difficult issues during his administration. Encourage debaters to provide evidence to support their opinions. Have each group write its evidence on the charts on the chalkboard. **Cooperative Learning**

ECONOMICS

Impressment. The rise in American trade during the late 1700s and early 1800s led to a growing need for sailors. Many American shippers hired British seamen to work on their vessels, contributing to a dangerous shortage in Britain's Royal Navy. To compensate, sailors from Royal Navy warships periodically boarded American vessels to reclaim British subjects. In the process they left American ships critically understaffed and sometimes seized U.S. citizens. Between 1803 and 1812 some 6,000 Americans were forced into service on British ships. Although the British government usually released Americans who could prove their citizenship, such appeals often took years.

CRITICAL THINKING What problems might impressment have created for sailors' families?

ANSWER: Students might suggest that impressment could have created emotional and financial problems for sailors' families.

SCIENCE & TECHNOLOGY ANSWERS

1. its careful construction
2. long-range fighting, close-range fighting, sleeping, and storage

---

the U.S. declaration of neutrality and seized American merchant vessels bound for enemy ports. Britain also angered U.S officials by kidnapping American sailors and forcing them to serve in the British navy—a practice called impressment. In 1794 the United States signed a treaty with Britain to resolve these disputed issues.

✔ **READING CHECK: Categorizing** How did the U.S. government respond to the challenges it faced in the late 1790s? Responses included calling out troops and signing peace treaties.

The Rise of Political Parties

The debate over foreign policy helped give rise to the first American political parties. Sectionalism, or loyalty to a particular part of the country, further contributed to the emergence of two opposing parties by the mid-1790s.

Federalists and Republicans. John Adams and Alexander Hamilton led the Federalist Party. Federalists favored a strong national government. They also wanted to promote the development of commerce, particularly with Britain.

★ ★ ★ ★ ★ ★ ★ **Science & Technology** ★ ★ ★ ★ ★ ★ ★

Building a Navy

As European nations violated U.S. neutrality, the United States expanded its military in the 1790s. This included increasing the enlistment of men to form the U.S. Navy.

Congress authorized the construction of six medium-sized ships known as frigates. The USS *Constitution*, designed by Joshua Humphreys and constructed by George Claghorn in a Boston shipyard, was part of the navy's first fleet. More than 1,500 trees were used in the ship's beams, masts, planking, frame, and almost three-foot-thick hull. Skilled carpenters fitted each piece individually, and Paul Revere formed the copper bolts, spikes, and fastenings. Crushed rock salt packed against the ship's frame helped preserve the wood. When it was finished, the *Constitution* carried 20 cannons, 32 long guns, more than 40 sails, and a crew of 450.

The newly launched *Constitution* fought pirates in the Caribbean in the late 1790s. The ship received its nickname, Old Ironsides, after a battle in the War of 1812. Despite severe bombardment, a British ship was unable to put even a dent in the *Constitution*'s oak sides. As the story goes, one of the sailors cried out, "Huzza! Her sides are made of iron!" After 85 years of service, the *Constitution* was retired from active duty in 1882.

❶ The gun deck held main guns used for long-range fighting.

❷ The spar deck held small cannons used for close-range fighting.

❸ The berth was used as sailors' sleeping quarters.

❹ The hold stored supplies and ammunition.

Understanding Science and History

1. What made the USS *Constitution* so strong?
2. What were the different levels of the ship used for?

LEVEL 3: Tell students that they are newspaper reporters in the early 1800s preparing an article on the presidencies of John Adams and Thomas Jefferson. Have each student write an editorial evaluating the methods each president employed to handle the issues facing his presidency. *(See the Level 1 lesson for the correct issues.)* Tell students to consider the relatively new idea of political parties and how that affected the work of presidents Adams and Jefferson. Ask volunteers to read their articles to the class.

NOTE: For an additional teaching idea, see the Chapter 2 quick survey lesson in the **Creative Teaching Strategies** handbook.

SPOTLIGHT
on Political Newspapers

Tell students that early newspapers were often closely connected to political parties. Then organize students into small groups. Tell them to imagine that they publish either a Federalist or a Republican newspaper. Have the members of each group work together to determine the following things about their newspaper: name, location, editorial philosophy, readers, and the titles of three possible articles. Ask the groups to present and explain their information.
Cooperative Learning, Block Scheduling

Church leaders, lawyers, manufacturers, and merchants from New England and the Atlantic seaboard tended to support the Federalist Party. Federalists expected the rich to provide national leadership, because, as one leading Federalist put it, "those who own the country ought to govern it."

Thomas Jefferson and James Madison led the Democratic-Republican Party, or the Republicans for short. The Republicans' main goal was to protect states' rights and individual liberties by limiting the power of the federal government. Because they distrusted the aristocratic British, Republicans tended to support the French. The party included artisans, planters, small farmers, tradespeople, wage earners, and workers. The party's influence was particularly strong on the frontier and in the South.

Adams's presidency. President Washington decided not to seek a third term in 1796. This decision led to the first real contest for the presidency. According to the Constitution, the candidate with the most electoral votes would become president, and the runner-up would become vice president. Federalist John Adams was elected president, and Thomas Jefferson—Adams's Republican opponent—became vice president.

President Adams faced challenges both at home and abroad. French warships had begun seizing American ships bound for British ports. Soon France and the United States were fighting an undeclared war at sea. In 1798 the Federalist majority in Congress passed the **Alien and Sedition Acts.** The Alien Act authorized the president to imprison or expel "all such aliens [foreigners] as he shall judge dangerous to the peace and safety of the United States." The Sedition Act targeted U.S. citizens—often Republicans—who printed, said, or wrote anything "false, scandalous, and malicious" about the government. Many Americans believed that the new laws violated the freedoms guaranteed by the Bill of Rights.

Critics of the Alien and Sedition Acts saw them as attempts to curb the rights of individuals. In response James Madison and Thomas Jefferson wrote the **Kentucky and Virginia Resolutions.** These resolutions denounced the acts as unconstitutional and asked Congress to repeal them. Both the Kentucky and Virginia legislatures approved the resolutions, but Congress refused to repeal the acts. Nevertheless, the resolutions revealed the declining popularity of President Adams and the Federalists.

Thomas Jefferson as President

After a heated election, the House of Representatives named Republican Thomas Jefferson president in 1801. The Republicans also won control of Congress. Although Jefferson later referred to the election as the "Revolution of 1800," the transition of power was relatively peaceful.

The defeated Federalists feared that their programs would be abandoned. Before Jefferson's inauguration in 1801, they pushed through a measure that created a number of new federal judgeships. President Adams worked late into the night of his last day in office, appointing Federalists to these posts. These last-minute appointees were nicknamed "midnight judges."

THE GRANGER COLLECTION, NEW YORK

INTERPRETING THE VISUAL RECORD

Conflict. During a heated congressional debate over the Alien and Sedition Acts, Federalist Roger Griswald attacked Republican Matthew Lyon. *How does this engraving reflect the political divisions in the United States?*

LEVEL 1: Have students list the reasons the United States wanted to buy the Louisiana Territory *(opportunity to expand the size of the United States and to obtain a port at the mouth of the Mississippi River, and the French offer).* Then lead a class discussion on the significance of the Louisiana Purchase *(added all or part of 13 states to the nation, ended French control, and opened the interior of the continent to settlement).* **English Language Learners**

LEVELS 2 AND 3: Tell students to imagine that they are members of the Lewis and Clark expedition. Have each student write a series of short journal entries explaining the significance of the Louisiana Purchase. *(See the Level 1 Activity for the significance.)* Ask volunteers to share their journal entries with the class.

 HOMEWORK *Distribute Geography Activity 2, The Louisiana Purchase, and ask each student to complete it.*

CITIZENSHIP

Thomas Jefferson and Slavery. Thomas Jefferson held some 200 slaves, a factor that created contradictions in both his personal and political life. In his original draft of the Declaration of Independence, Jefferson referred to the conduct of the slave trade as a "cruel war against human nature itself." He also sought to prohibit slavery in the western territories. Yet Jefferson depended on his many slaves to work his plantations and maintain his financial status. Jefferson never resolved the contradictions between his ideals and his practices. He died as a slaveholder.

CRITICAL THINKING When Jefferson called the slave trade a "cruel war against human nature," on what grounds might he have been objecting to slavery?

ANSWER: Students might suggest that he was probably objecting on moral grounds.

VISUAL RECORD ANSWER

Students might suggest that it led to conflicts between branches of government.

INTERPRETING THE VISUAL RECORD

John Marshall. Chief Justice John Marshall believed in the loose construction of the Constitution, a position that put him at odds with Thomas Jefferson. *How might this relationship affect the balance of powers?*

Adams's most significant appointment was his selection of **John Marshall** of Virginia as chief justice of the United States. During his more than 30 years on the bench, Marshall helped establish many basic principles of U.S. constitutional law. Among these was the principle of **judicial review**—the power of the courts to review acts of Congress and the laws passed by the states. The Court first exercised this power in 1803 with the case of *Marbury* v. *Madison*.

For political reasons, Jefferson and Secretary of State James Madison had refused to allow William Marbury, one of the "midnight judges," to take office in the District of Columbia. Marbury appealed to the Supreme Court. The Supreme Court ruled that it could hear the case only on appeal after the case had gone through the lower courts. By denying that the case could go straight to the Supreme Court, Marshall declared a part of the Judiciary Act of 1789 unconstitutional. With this decision, Marshall initiated the Court's most important role—that of final interpreter of the Constitution.

To fulfill a pledge of moderation, President Jefferson left some Federalist programs untouched. These included the National Bank and the debt payment plan, both of which he had once opposed. The Republican-led Congress repealed the whiskey tax and cut military funding. It also reduced the size of the army and the navy to save money to pay off the national debt.

✔ **READING CHECK: Summarizing** How did the rise of political parties affect the presidencies of John Adams and Thomas Jefferson? They led to conflicts in Congress and the Supreme Court.

The Louisiana Purchase

President Jefferson tried to maintain neutrality in foreign affairs. At the same time, he also seized an opportunity to expand the size of the United States. In 1803 Jefferson sent James Monroe to Paris to assist U.S. minister to France Robert Livingston. He was negotiating for a U.S. port at the mouth of the Mississippi River or for access to New Orleans. Jefferson had instructed Monroe to offer the French leader, Napoléon, as much as $10 million for New Orleans and West Florida. Napoléon's representative, however, offered to sell all of Louisiana. The astonished U.S. diplomats quickly agreed to pay about $15 million. Thus, for about four cents an acre, the United States completed the **Louisiana Purchase**. Some historians have called it the largest land deal in history.

Neither country knew the exact size of the Louisiana Territory. Jefferson selected Meriwether Lewis and William Clark, two skilled frontiersmen, to explore the area. With a crew of 45 explorers, the Lewis and Clark expedition left St. Louis in May 1804. Lewis and Clark kept detailed journals of their travels. Their attention to detail is shown in an entry from May 23, 1805.

 ❝The [Missouri] river has become more rapid, the country much the same as yesterday, except that there is rather more rocks on the face of the hills, and some small spruce pine appears among the pitch. The wild roses are very abundant and now in bloom; they differ from those of the United States only in having the leaves and the bush itself of a somewhat smaller size. We find the mosquitoes troublesome, notwithstanding the coolness of the morning. The buffalo is scarce to-day, but the elk, deer, and antelope, are very numerous.❞

—Meriwether Lewis and William Clark, *The Journals of Lewis and Clark*

TEACH OBJECTIVE 5

LEVEL 1: Have students design a recruiting poster for the War of 1812. The poster should explain why the United States is fighting in order to help inspire a sense of patriotism in possible recruits. *(Posters should include the practice of impressment, attacking an American ship, and the British aid of American Indians who were attacking American settlers as they pushed westward).* Ask volunteers to share their posters with the class. **English Language Learners**

LEVEL 2: Have students write an encyclopedia entry explaining why the United States fought the War of 1812. *(See the Level 1 lesson for the correct reasons.)* Entries should also discuss the outcome of the war. *(Entries might mention that the war strengthened U.S. control over Northwest Territory and somewhat improved relations with Great Britain).*

LEVEL 3: In a classroom discussion, have students list reasons why the United States fought the War of 1812. *(See the Level 1 lesson for the correct reasons.)* Then have students write an essay analyzing the outcome of the war and theorizing about the possible long-term impact if the United States had lost. Have volunteers read their paragraphs to the class and encourage the class to comment on each other's theories.

The Louisiana Purchase

Interpreting Maps The Louisiana Purchase added some 828,000 square miles of rich land to the United States, roughly doubling the nation's size.

? PHYSICAL SYSTEMS What rivers did Lewis and Clark follow from St. Louis on their way to the Pacific Ocean?

Legend:
- States in 1804
- U.S. territories in 1804
- Louisiana Purchase
- ■ Fort
- → Lewis and Clark, 1804–1806
- → Pike, 1805–1807

American Indians, particularly Mandan and Shoshone (shuh-SHOH-nee), helped the expedition. Lewis and Clark hired a French-Canadian fur trader and his Shoshone wife, Sacagawea (sak-uh-juh-WEE-uh), as guides and interpreters. Sacagawea showed the expedition the best places to fish, to hunt game, and to forage for wild vegetables. As an interpreter, she helped the expedition obtain supplies.

The Lewis and Clark expedition traveled up the Missouri River and crossed the Rocky Mountains. The explorers then canoed down the Snake and Columbia Rivers to the Pacific Ocean. After nearly two and a half years, the expedition returned. Its members brought plant and animal specimens, animal bones and pelts, and various soil and mineral samples.

The Louisiana Purchase added all or part of 13 future states to the nation. This vast increase in size stregthened the new United States. Robert Livingston noted at the time of the purchase, "From this day the United States take their place among the powers of the first rank." The purchase also ended French control of the region and opened the interior of the continent to settlement. As Americans devoted more energy to developing the frontier, they increasingly looked west, rather than east across the Atlantic. This shift promoted a greater sense of national identity.

✔ **READING CHECK: Finding the Main Idea** What was the international significance of the Louisiana Purchase? It doubled the nation's size and helped move the United States into a position of power.

As a guide and interpreter, Sacagawea greatly assisted Lewis and Clark during their exploration.

GEOGRAPHY

The Lewis and Clark Expedition. President Jefferson assigned Meriwether Lewis, who had been his private secretary, the task of observing and cataloguing the plants and animals of the West. With the help of other members of the expedition, Lewis recorded some 178 plants and 122 animals—all previously unknown in the United States. Among these were ponderosa pines, bighorn sheep, coyotes, prairie dogs, and grizzly bears. Lewis and Clark sent a prairie dog and a magpie back to the East. For a time the animals lived in the White House.

CRITICAL THINKING What might Lewis and Clark have had in common with present-day astronauts?

ANSWER: Students might suggest that astronauts explore the unknown, just as Lewis and Clark did.

MAP ANSWER
the Missouri River and the Columbia River

REVIEW

Have students complete the **Section 1 Review** on page 78.

ASSESS

Have students complete **Daily Quiz 2.1.** As **Alternative Assessment**, you may want to use the domestic and foreign challenges chart or the Louisiana Purchase graphic organizer in this section's lessons.

RETEACH

Have students complete **Main Idea Activity for English Language Learners and Special-Needs Students 2.1.** Then have each student create a detailed outline of the section. Pair students and have them exchange outlines. Tell them to use a different color ink to note any important information that is missing from each others' outlines.
English Language Learners, Cooperative Learning

EXTEND

Organize students into three groups and assign each group one of the following topics: issues facing Adams and Jefferson, the Louisiana Purchase, and the War of 1812. Then tell students to create a museum exhibit that focuses on their assigned topic. They may include "artifacts," models, drawings, maps, and graphic organizers. Have students set up their exhibits in the classroom. **Block Scheduling, Cooperative Learning**

SECTION 1 REVIEW ANSWERS

1. Define
- cabinet, p. 70
- free enterprise, p. 72
- strict construction, p. 72
- loose construction, p. 72
- judicial review, p. 76

2. Identify
- Judiciary Act of 1789, p. 70
- Bill of Rights, p. 70
- Alexander Hamilton, p. 71
- Little Turtle, p. 73
- Alien and Sedition Acts, p. 75
- Kentucky and Virginia Resolutions, p. 75
- John Marshall, p. 76
- *Marbury* v. *Madison*, p. 76
- Louisiana Purchase, p. 76

3. security—use of the militia, attempts to remain neutral in foreign affairs; economy—concepts of free enterprise and a national bank; court system—Judiciary Act of 1789; national government—loose construction and strict construction

4a. Hamilton thought it should serve as the basis of the national economy.

b. He established many basic principles of constitutional law, such as judicial review.

c. It demonstrated that the United States was its own country, and that its people were unified.

5. Answers will vary but should reflect a knowledge of the early presidencies, American Indian uprisings, the Louisiana Purchase, and the Lewis and Clark expedition.

Shawnee leader Tecumseh was both feared and respected by his opponents.

The War of 1812

By the early 1800s the United States was again drawn into a conflict. Britain continued its practice of impressment. In 1807 the British attacked an American ship, killing three American sailors. President Jefferson urged Congress to pass an embargo, which would stop shipments of American products to all foreign ports. The Embargo Act of 1807 backfired, hurting American merchants and farmers but having little effect on the warring nations.

Conflict also continued between American settlers pushing westward and American Indians living there. Tecumseh, a Shawnee leader, tried to build a confederation of Indian nations. He urged Indians not to sell land to the settlers. "Sell a country!" Tecumseh said. "Why not sell the air, the clouds, and the great sea?" As Tecumseh's army gained strength, settlers urged the U.S. government to act. In 1811 U.S. soldiers under the command of General William Henry Harrison defeated Tecumseh's army.

Many Americans believed that the British had helped Tecumseh's uprising. In 1812 Congress, at the urging of President James Madison, declared war on Britain. The U.S. Army failed to conquer Canada but did defeat the British and their Indian allies in the Northwest Territory. In 1814 the United States suffered a major blow when British troops burned much of Washington, the nation's capital.

Neither side could gain a clear advantage. U.S. forces under General Andrew Jackson finally won a decisive victory at New Orleans in January 1815. By that time, however, the war was officially over. The treaty that ended the war strengthened U.S. control in the Northwest Territory but did not solve some key disputes. Nevertheless British and U.S. relations improved in the years following the war.

✔ **READING CHECK: Summarizing** Why did the United States fight the War of 1812?
because of impressment and the British helping American Indians fight against Americans

SECTION 1 REVIEW

1. Define and explain:
cabinet
free enterprise
strict construction
loose construction
judicial review

2. Identify and explain:
Judiciary Act of 1789
Bill of Rights
Alexander Hamilton
Little Turtle
Alien and Sedition Acts
Kentucky and Virginia Resolutions
John Marshall
Marbury v. *Madison*
Louisiana Purchase

3. Problem Solving Copy the chart below. Explain how the new nation resolved some of its domestic challenges.

Challenges	Solutions
1. Maintaining national security	1.
2. Creating a stable economy	2.
3. Setting up the court system	3.
4. Defining the authority of the national government	4.

4. **Finding the Main Idea**

a. What role did free enterprise play in early U.S. economic policy?

b. How effective was John Marshall's leadership of the Supreme Court?

c. How did the War of 1812 complete the American Revolution?

5. **Writing and Critical Thinking**

Summarizing Imagine that you are a historian in the early 1800s. Write a brief history of major events and issues from 1796 to 1809.

Consider:
- John Adams's presidency
- Thomas Jefferson's presidency
- the Louisiana Purchase

 Homework Practice Online
keyword: SE3 HP2

After completing Section 2, students should be able to:

OBJECTIVE 1 Describe what changes took place in foreign and domestic policy in the early 1800s.

OBJECTIVE 2 Identify how industrialization and immigration affected northern society.

OBJECTIVE 3 Explain how southern society and the slave system were organized.

OBJECTIVE 4 Relate what social issues reformers addressed in the early to mid-1800s.

LET'S GET STARTED!

As students enter the room, play Selection 1, "The Erie Canal," from the **American Music Audio CD Program**. Pass out copies of the song's discussion guide and tell students to write a few sentences relating the song to what they can remember about the Transportation Revolution and westward expansion. Tell students that in Section 2 they will learn about changes in society, politics, and the economy during the 1800s.

SECTION 2

READ TO DISCOVER

1. What changes took place in foreign and domestic policy in the early 1800s?
2. How did industrialization and immigration affect northern society?
3. How were southern society and the slave system organized?
4. What social issues did reformers address in the early to mid-1800s?

DEFINE

nationalism
strike
nativism
cotton gin

IDENTIFY

Monroe Doctrine
Henry Clay
American System
Missouri Compromise
Andrew Jackson
Democratic Party
Trail of Tears
Underground Railroad
Harriet Tubman
Second Great Awakening
Dorothea Dix
Frederick Douglass
Sojourner Truth
Elizabeth Cady Stanton
Seneca Falls Convention
Susan B. Anthony

▶ WHY IT MATTERS TODAY

Industry in the United States continues to change. Use **CNNfyi.com** or other **current events** sources to find out more about industrialization and new technologies today. Record your findings in your journal.

CNNfyi.com

Growth and Change

EYEWITNESSES TO History

"[American pride] blazes out everywhere and on all occasions."

—Anonymous British observer

Americans' patriotism was particularly strong after the War of 1812. They displayed this pride in their Independence Day celebrations. Even some foreign citizens observed the holiday. In the 1820s Frances Wright of Scotland, a travel writer and sometime U.S. resident, gave a Fourth of July speech in New Harmony, Indiana. She praised the United States as the protector of "human liberty [and] the favored scene of human improvement." Soon, she predicted, "all mankind" would celebrate "the Jubilee of Independence."

Frances Wright

Building a Young Nation

The War of 1812 filled many Americans with a sense of **nationalism**, or national pride. As Americans celebrated their independence, the young nation began a period of prosperity. Manufacturing in the United States had expanded during the war. In 1816 Congress tried to aid the economy by chartering the Second Bank of the United States and passing a protective tariff on imported goods.

Foreign policy. To ensure continued prosperity, President James Monroe worked to avoid conflict with other nations. In 1817 the United States and Britain agreed to limit their naval presence on the Great Lakes. In 1818 the two nations set the U.S.-Canada border at the 49th parallel. One year later the United States settled a border dispute with Spain over Florida, gaining East Florida in the process.

By the early 1820s most of Spain's Latin American colonies had declared independence. The United States recognized these new republics. In 1823 President Monroe announced what came to be called the **Monroe Doctrine**. He vowed that the United States would oppose any European attempts to regain former Latin American colonies or to establish new ones in the Western Hemisphere.

The Transportation Revolution. In 1824 Representative **Henry Clay** of Kentucky proposed a plan known as the **American System**. This system would establish stronger protective tariffs to aid and encourage industrial development. The plan would also fund a national transportation system. Transportation was a major problem in the early 1800s. British actress Fanny Kemble described the experience of riding in a stagecoach in New York:

History Makers Speak

"[Traveling] through bog and marsh, and ruts, . . . with the roots of trees protruding across our path, . . . and, more than once, a half-demolished tree or stump lying in the middle of the road."

—Fanny Kemble, *Journal*

SECTION 2 RESOURCES

REPRODUCIBLE
▶ Guided Reading Strategy 2.2
▶ Biography Reading 2: Denmark Vesey

TECHNOLOGY
▶ One-Stop Planner, Lesson 2.2
▶ Holt Researcher: American History CD–ROM
▶ Homework Practice Online
▶ HRW Go site

REINFORCEMENT, REVIEW, AND ASSESSMENT
▶ Section 2 Review, p. 85
▶ Daily Quiz 2.2
▶ Main Idea Activity 2.2
▶ English Audio Summary 2.2
▶ Spanish Audio Summary 2.2

TEACH OBJECTIVE 1

ALL LEVELS: To help students understand what changes took place in foreign and domestic policy in the early 1800s, copy the following graphic organizer on the chalkboard, omitting the italicized answers. Have each student complete the graphic organizer.
English Language Learners

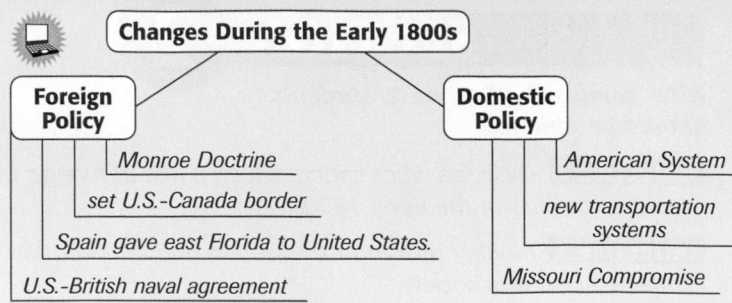

Changes During the Early 1800s

Foreign Policy
- *Monroe Doctrine*
- *set U.S.-Canada border*
- *Spain gave east Florida to United States.*
- *U.S.-British naval agreement*

Domestic Policy
- *American System*
- *new transportation systems*
- *Missouri Compromise*

HOMEWORK Tell students to use the information in the graphic organizer they just completed to design commemorative stamps to celebrate the "Revolution of 1800," as Thomas Jefferson called it. Display stamps on the classroom wall.

THAT'S INTERESTING!

In order to finance road construction without spending large sums of public money, some states permitted private companies to build turnpikes, or toll roads. Turnpikes were largely a northern phenomenon. New York had some 4,000 miles of turnpikes, and Pennsylvania had an estimated 2,400 miles of toll roads by 1832. By 1830 Maryland had only 300 miles of turnpikes.

PRESIDENTIAL Lives

James Monroe

1758–1831
In Office 1817–1825

James Monroe was the last president to have fought in the Revolutionary War. He was also the last of the Founding Fathers to occupy the White House. Indeed, Monroe looked very much the colonial statesman. He wore a powdered wig and dressed in the fashion of an earlier age. He wore a cutaway coat, waistcoat, knee britches, long stockings, and buckled shoes.

Monroe's generally quiet personality matched his elegant appearance. Thomas Jefferson was a longtime friend of Monroe. Jefferson remarked that Monroe was "a man whose soul might be turned wrong side outward, without discovering a blemish to the world."

The federal government enacted much of the American System. In addition, some states began building their own canals and major roads. Newly developed steamboats combined with canals to provide faster and cheaper ways of shipping goods. In the 1830s steam-powered locomotives were also carrying passengers and cargo. These new transportation systems made possible the creation of national markets.

In 1807 inventor Robert Fulton's steamboat *Clermont* traveled up the Hudson River. A case involving Aaron Ogden's purchase of Fulton's state monopoly to operate steamboats was brought to the Supreme Court in 1824. In *Gibbons* v. *Ogden*, the Court ruled that the Constitution gave control of interstate commerce to the U.S. Congress.

The Missouri Compromise. In 1819 the people of the Missouri Territory applied for statehood as a slave state. The nation was then equally divided between 11 free states and 11 slave states. To prevent the admission of Missouri from upsetting this balance, Congress approved the **Missouri Compromise** in 1820. The agreement admitted Missouri as a slave state and Maine as a free state. It also banned slavery in the rest of the Louisiana Purchase north of Missouri's southern boundary.

The Rise of Jacksonian Democracy

Westward expansion also affected the presidential elections of the 1820s. More adult white males, particularly those living in western states, gained suffrage. Such voters helped elect **Andrew Jackson** to the presidency in 1828. A hero of the War of 1812, Jackson portrayed himself as "a man of the people." His supporters began to refer to themselves as Democrats and became the **Democratic Party**.

Jackson changed the tone of politics in the United States. He replaced many existing government workers with his political supporters. Jackson also appointed officeholders without regard to their social or economic class. Jackson's victory reflected a shift in America from an aristocratic society to one based on individual effort and economic success.

Jackson's American Indian policy. During the 1820s American Indians living in the East found themselves pressured to leave their lands. President Jackson suggested that they be moved westward, "where their white brothers will not trouble them."

Guests at a party for President Andrew Jackson cut into a giant wheel of cheese.

THE GRANGER COLLECTION, NEW YORK

LEVEL 1: Organize students into groups of four or five. Tell each group to imagine that it is a family of either laborers or recent immigrants living in the northern United States during the early 1800s. Have group members work together to create a family scrapbook that explains how industrialization and immigration affected northern society. Students might include pictures, drawings, letters, newspaper clippings, and other items in their scrapbooks. *(Scrapbooks should include some of the following: increased use of machines in farming and manufacturing; increased poverty, worsening industrial conditions, more union and strike activity, new immigrant communities, and nativist protests.)* Call on a volunteer from each group to present his or her group's scrapbook to the class.
English Language Learners, Cooperative Learning

In 1830 Congress passed the Indian Removal Act. This act required American Indians living in the eastern United States to relocate to Indian Territory in what is now Oklahoma.

Most American Indians did not go willingly. Some wrote to Congress. Others chose to fight. In Florida, Seminole—aided by runaway slaves—fought the U.S. Army for seven years. Some Seminole managed to remain in Florida. The Cherokee used the court system to resist their removal. The Supreme Court ruled in their favor, limiting state power over them. However, Georgia officials—with the blessing of President Jackson—ignored the Court's order and continued their seizure of Cherokee lands. Without federal protection, the Cherokee were forced to move to Indian Territory. Some 4,000 Cherokee died on the march, which came to be known as the **Trail of Tears**. "Many fell . . . too faint with hunger or too weak to keep up with the rest," recalled one survivor.

States' rights and economic woes. Most Americans were more concerned with the issue of states' rights than with the rights of American Indians. In 1828 Congress had passed a new tariff that doubled the rates on certain import items. Southerners, who relied heavily on imported goods paid for with tobacco and cotton exports, argued that the laws unfairly favored the industrial North. South Carolina threatened to secede, and Congress agreed to lower the tariff rates.

Congress's proposed rechartering of the Second Bank of the United States also caused controversy. A few months before his re-election in 1832, Jackson vetoed the bank measure. By weakening federal control over the banking system, Jackson helped cause a financial crisis. Numerous banks were unable to meet people's demands to exchange their paper currency for gold and silver. As these banks failed, an economic panic began that lasted until 1843.

✔ **READING CHECK: Summarizing** What foreign and domestic challenges did the United States face in the early 1800s? independence of Latin American nations, the Transportation Revolution, compromises over slavery, conflicts with American Indians, secession threat, and economic crisis

Northern and Southern Society

The cultural and economic differences between the North and the South grew during the 1800s. The North became less dependent upon agriculture, and slavery expanded in the South.

The industrial North. Manufacturing changed dramatically in the early 1800s. Mill owner Francis Cabot Lowell and others shifted from hand-powered weaving to machine production, which allowed cloth to be made more quickly. Young, single women flocked to work in industrial towns like Lowell, Massachusetts.

While the power looms transformed the factories, new tools transformed northern farms. Improvements to the plow and the development of the mechanized reaper made farm work easier and faster. Englishman Joseph Whitworth noted in 1854 that Americans "call in the aid of machinery in almost every department of industry."

INTERPRETING THE VISUAL RECORD

American Indian removal. Thousands of Cherokee from the southeastern United States were forced to move west on a journey known as the Trail of Tears. *What does this image suggest about the conditions the Cherokee faced on their journey?*

LEVELS 2 AND 3: Pair students and tell them to imagine that they are historical consultants hired to ensure historical accuracy for a movie set in the northern United States during the early 1800s. Have students write a paragraph describing how industrialization and immigration affected northern society. *(See the Level 1 lesson for the correct effects.)* Encourage students to include drawings of what people of that era might have looked like. Ask volunteers to read their descriptions to the class. **Cooperative Learning**

TEACH OBJECTIVE 3

LEVELS 1 AND 2: Have students draw a series of pictures showing how southern society and the slave system were organized. *(Pictures should include plantation owners—leaders in society and politics; small farmers—the majority of southern whites; poor whites and free African Americans—the smallest group; slaves—most of whom were workers on plantations and farms.)* Drawings might be diagrams of plantations and farms, or they might be pictures of people in varying numbers to reflect relative population and political power, or any other reasonable imagery.
English Language Learners

HISTORY MAKERS SPEAK

John Avery in *The Way We Lived: Essays and Documents in American Social History*, vol. 1

Mill Regulations. In 1848 John Avery, a mill agent, released rules regarding mill employees' conduct. "The [Hamilton Manufacturing] company will not employ any one who is habitually absent from public worship on the Sabbath, or known to be guilty of immorality. . . . These regulations are considered part of the contract, with which all persons entering into the employment of the Hamilton Manufacturing Company engage to comply."

CRITICAL THINKING How might the rules that Avery established differ from typical workplace rules today?

ANSWER: Students might suggest that employers today cannot require that employees attend religious services.

THAT'S INTERESTING!

Slaves often resorted to ingenious means to gain their freedom. Some traveled north in disguise. Henry Box Brown mailed himself to freedom. In a journey lasting 26 hours, Brown was shipped from Richmond, Virginia, to Philadelphia, Pennsylvania.

Lowell Girls

Although working conditions in mills worsened in the 1830s, young women—many of them teenagers—continued to seek work in the mills. Many of the so-called Lowell girls decided for themselves to come to work at the mills, hoping to improve their lives. Mary Paul, a teenager employed as a farm servant, wrote to her father, "I want you to consent to let me go to Lowell if you can. I think it would be much better for me than to stay about here."

Life for the Lowell girls was difficult, and mill work was hard. However, many of the girls welcomed their independence and the opportunity to earn money. They used their salaries to help support their families, to pay for weddings, to purchase clothes and other personal items, and to pay for an education. Most girls saw mill work as a stepping-stone in their lives. This was a way of "bettering the condition of themselves and those they loved," wrote Lucy Larcom. She had come to Lowell at the age of 11 and went on to become a well-known poet.

Although labor in the mills was demanding, some teenagers coming from rural farms found that factory work opened up new paths and opportunities for them. Larcom wrote years later about her time at the mills. "I was every day making discoveries about life, and about myself. . . . I know that I was glad to be alive, and to be just where I was." Some Lowell girls took evening classes, formed literary societies, listened to lectures, attended plays and concerts, and even published a magazine, the *Lowell Offering*.

Industrial machinery provided new work opportunities for young women.

Despite the general prosperity, many workers lived in poverty. Entire families, including children, often worked long hours just to survive. Worsening industrial conditions prompted labor leaders to organize workers into unions. They sought such reforms as shorter workdays and higher wages. Unions used many methods to try to achieve their goals. These included the **strike**—the refusal to work until employers meet union demands. Union activity forced politicians to respond to the workers' complaints. By the early 1850s several states had reduced the length of the workday.

The labor force grew larger in the 1830s as immigration to the United States soared. The largest group of immigrants came from Ireland. Irish immigrants faced prejudice and were often forced to settle in crowded city slums. The Irish were followed in the mid-1800s by a wave of German immigrants. Many settled in the rural Midwest. Smaller numbers of Dutch, Scandinavian, and Swiss immigrants also settled in the region. All of these immigrant groups formed tightly knit communities.

Some native-born Americans protested the immigrants' arrival. One wealthy New Yorker claimed that of the new immigrants "not one in twenty is competent [capable] to keep [provide for] himself." Such feelings gave rise to **nativism**—the favoring of native-born Americans over foreign-born residents.

✔ **READING CHECK: Making Generalizations** How did industrialization improve the lives of some northerners?
Some grew rich from the new factories.

The Cotton Kingdom. The South had long relied on agriculture and slave labor. Industrialization developed more slowly than in the North. Eli Whitney's invention of the **cotton gin**, a machine that made it easier to remove cotton seeds, led to the emergence of the South as the Cotton Kingdom. From 1815 to 1860, cotton represented more than half of all U.S. exports. Farmers in the Upper South grew mostly corn and tobacco.

Southern society reflected the importance of slavery to the region's economy. Just one in four southern white families owned slaves, but this group of slaveholders dominated society and politics. Most plantation owners held fewer than 20 slaves. Small farmers, who made up the majority of southern whites, were located beneath the planters on the social scale. They lived simply, grew their own food, and rarely held slaves. Poorer white farmers made up a small percentage of the population.

By 1860 some 260,000 free African Americans lived in the South. White southerners greatly restricted the rights of free African Americans. Laws prohibited them from voting, holding public meetings, and testifying in court against whites. An editorial in a newspaper for free African Americans stated, "Though we are not slaves, we are not free."

LEVEL 3: Tell students to create the table of contents and the book jacket summary for a book entitled *Southern Society and the Slave System. (See the Levels 1 and 2 lesson for the correct organization.)* Inform students that the book discusses the organization and power structure of the South as well as the institution of slavery and those who rebelled against it.

SPOTLIGHT
on the Underground Railroad

Pair students and ask them to create an informational brochure on the Underground Railroad. Brochures should include information on and quotations from conductor Harriet Tubman. Students should also include a map suggesting a possible route from the South to freedom.
Cooperative Learning , Block Scheduling

The Slave System

The increase in cotton cultivation resulted in an expansion of slavery. Some southerners criticized slavery, but planters argued that it was the only way to ensure an adequate supply of field workers. More than 75 percent of enslaved African Americans lived and worked on plantations and farms. Many worked from dawn to dusk. One former field hand explained, "The rule on the place was: Wake up the slaves at daylight, begin work when they can see, and quit work when they can't see." Slaveholders relied on various means, including physical punishment, to control their slaves. Rebellious slaves were sold away from their families and communities.

To endure these harsh circumstances, slaves devoted their rare free time to family and community. They developed a unique culture that drew on both African customs and their experiences in America. Slaves were forbidden to learn how to read. They told oral histories and folk tales to preserve and pass on their culture. They also expressed their spiritual beliefs through folk art, music, and religious services.

As individuals or as part of a group, slaves constantly protested their bondage. Some small uprisings took place in the early 1800s. Then, in 1831 Nat Turner organized a violent revolt in Virginia. Turner and his followers killed some 60 white people before being captured. These uprisings led southern states to pass stricter slave codes that further limited slaves' activities.

Other slaves protested by disrupting the plantation routine. They faked illness or worked slowly. Some slaves ran away and tried to gain their freedom in the North. Assistance came from the **Underground Railroad**, a network of white and African American people who helped escaped slaves reach the North. Escaped slave **Harriet Tubman** was the most famous and successful "conductor" on the Underground Railroad. She made at least 19 trips and escorted more than 300 slaves to freedom. "There was one of two things I had a right to," Tubman stated. "Liberty or death: if I could not have one, I would have the other; for no man would take me alive."

✔ **READING CHECK: Drawing Conclusions** How did cotton growing make southern society different from northern society? mainly by contributing to the growth of slavery

The Second Great Awakening and Social Reform

The social changes transforming American society led many people to turn to religion for direction. In the 1790s a renewed and powerful interest in religion—the **Second Great Awakening**—began spreading westward from New York. Huge crowds gathered to listen to sermons, sing hymns, and seek God's help in reforming their lives. Ministers expressed an optimistic belief that individuals could receive eternal salvation. Church membership soared, particularly among women and African Americans.

Many participants in the Second Great Awakening also worked to help solve social problems. Women took an active role in these efforts, particularly in the temperance movement. Many reformers believed that alcohol abuse led to criminal behavior, family violence, and poverty. Temperance groups succeeded in

THE GRANGER COLLECTION, NEW YORK

INTERPRETING THE VISUAL RECORD

Slave life. This 1860s image shows members of a slave family in front of their log cabin in the woods of Georgia. *What does the image suggest about the living conditions of slaves?*

Newspapers often published advertisements for the capture of runaway slaves.

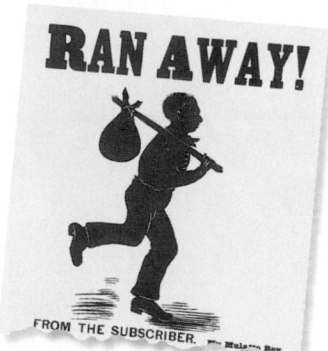

RAN AWAY!

FROM THE SUBSCRIBER.

INTERDISCIPLINARY CONNECTIONS

▶LITERATURE◀

Joel Chandler Harris and African American Folktales. Joel Chandler Harris, a white author, collected and presented African American folktales in his highly popular books. Harris grew up in Putnam County, Georgia, an area with a large African American population. As a boy, he worked on the *Countryman*, a weekly newspaper located on a local plantation. While there, he became acquainted with many slaves and spent much time listening to their stories. In the 1870s Harris began to work at the *Atlanta Constitution*, where he wrote articles about those tales. The articles were extremely successful, and Harris went on to write the books *Uncle Remus and his Friends, Mr. Rabbit at Home,* and *Uncle Remus and Brer Rabbit,* which were also quite popular.

CRITICAL THINKING What might the success of Harris's books indicate about the nature of American culture?

ANSWER: Students might suggest that the success indicates that aspects of slave culture have been absorbed into American culture.

VISUAL RECORD ANSWER

Students might suggest that it reveals poor conditions.

ALL LEVELS: Ask students to list the social issues reformers addressed in the early to mid-1800s. *(Students should mention temperance, education, poverty, care for people with mental illness, prison reform, abolition, and women's rights).* Record students' responses on the chalkboard. Then call on volunteers to tell the class how reformers set about addressing one or more of the social issues listed. Allow students to refer to their textbooks.
English Language Learners

Teacher to Teacher
Helen Bradley of Irving, Texas, suggested the following activity: Have students create a chart of the reform movements discussed in this section. The first column should have categories such as temperance, education, mental illness, and abolition. In the second, have students state the movement's goal. The next column should cite a success for the movement. The final column should include a current reform issue.

CULTURE

Dress Reform. Female reformers had to fight for what today most women consider an inalienable right: freedom to dress how one wants. During the mid-1800s, women were expected to wear long skirts that weighed about 20 pounds and corsets that put extreme pressure on the abdominal area. These corsets often broke ribs and damaged internal organs. When women tried to wear bloomers—baggy pantaloons under a short skirt—they were followed and jeered. Women's rights advocates had to forego their comfortable clothing because it distracted people from demands for suffrage.

CRITICAL THINKING Why might there have been resistance to a change in women's dress styles?

ANSWER: Students might suggest that some people feared that freedom of dress would encourage women to seek other freedoms.

VISUAL RECORD ANSWER

Students might mention a teacher, books, and desks.

SECTION
REVIEW ②ANSWERS

1. Define
• nationalism, p. 79
• strike, p. 82
• nativism, p. 82
• cotton gin, p. 82

Religious artwork illustrating the paths of good and evil

INTERPRETING THE VISUAL RECORD

Education. Some reformers argued that all children deserved an education. *What types of educational resources did this school have?*

THE METROPOLITAN MUSEUM OF ART

persuading many Americans to limit alcohol consumption. Some states even banned the sale of alcohol.

Reformers also worked to improve educational institutions. They wanted public tax-supported elementary schools. Reformers believed that schools were necessary to educate citizens about democratic values and to create a literate and disciplined workforce. Massachusetts established a model for free public elementary education. Other states soon followed. Public high schools also opened, and college opportunities for women and African Americans expanded.

Many reformers wanted to create and improve facilities for disadvantaged people, such as mentally ill or poor Americans. Reformers established poorhouses where able-bodied poor people could work. **Dorothea Dix** began her crusade to help people with mental illness after seeing how badly they were treated in a Massachusetts prison. Her efforts resulted in the establishment of more than 100 hospitals across the nation where the mentally ill could receive professional treatment. Some reformers believed that criminals could be rehabilitated and then returned to the community as productive citizens. They sought to improve living conditions in prisons.

Not all reformers supported every cause or agreed with the reasons for reform. Some reformers were motivated by their religious beliefs to seek fair treatment for all people. Others argued that social reforms helped create good citizens for the Republic. Regardless of their reasons, the reformers of the early 1800s helped improve the quality of life for many Americans.

The Fight to End Slavery

Most northern states had abolished slavery by the early 1800s. Reformers known as abolitionists believed that the institution of slavery should be outlawed in the entire United States. Some abolitionists established the African colony of Liberia for freed slaves. Many free African Americans rejected this plan, however. African American abolitionist Henry Highland Garnet initially opposed the idea. As his hopes for abolition faded in the early 1850s, he became a supporter of emigration to Africa.

In 1833 African American and white abolitionists formed the first national antislavery organization. The American Anti-Slavery Society called for abolition and racial justice. **Frederick Douglass**, an escaped slave, gave speeches about his life "suffered under the lash." He won the society many supporters.

The society excluded women from leadership positions. Nevertheless, women came to assume many important roles in its efforts. **Sojourner Truth**, also a former slave, traveled through New England supporting abolition. The Grimké sisters of South Carolina, Sarah and Angelina, gave many antislavery speeches. Angelina Grimké published a pamphlet in which she urged southern women to join her cause. "I know you do not make the laws," Grimké wrote, "but . . . if you really suppose you can do nothing to overthrow slavery, you are greatly mistaken."

Southerners felt increasingly threatened by the growing movement. Opposition to abolition also rose in the North. Some northerners held prejudices against African Americans and feared that abolition would cause increased job competition. Violence against abolitionists grew in the 1830s.

THE GRANGER COLLECTION, NEW YORK

A women's rights activist demands the right to vote.

The Fight for Women's Rights

In the late 1840s many female reformers began to struggle for their own rights. Sarah and Angelina Grimké and Sojourner Truth were among the first to combine the fight for abolition with the fight for women's rights. At a women's rights convention in Akron, Ohio, in 1851 Truth reportedly made the following remarks:

History Makers Speak

❝Look at my arm! I have ploughed and planted and gathered into barns ... and ain't I a woman? I could work as much and eat as much as a man— when I could get it—and bear the lash as well! And ain't I a woman? I have born thirteen children, and seen most of 'em sold into slavery, and when I cried out with my mother's grief, none but Jesus heard me—and ain't I a woman?❞

—Sojourner Truth, quoted in *Century of Struggle*, by Eleanor Flexner

Elizabeth Cady Stanton and Lucretia Mott organized the **Seneca Falls Convention** in New York in 1848. This gathering was the first national women's rights convention. Some 100 of the 300 participants signed a petition known as the Declaration of Sentiments. It called for legal reforms, particularly voting rights for women. Stanton argued, "the power to choose rulers and make laws was the right by which all others could be secured."

Stanton and **Susan B. Anthony** campaigned for property rights for women in New York State. Responding to petitions, New York began permitting married women to own property. Anthony also helped create a nationwide system of women's rights organizations. Achieving political and legal equality at the national level remained a struggle, however.

✔ **READING CHECK: Evaluating** What impact did reform movements of the early to mid-1800s have on American society? Educational facilities were reformed. Abolitionists applied pressure to southerners. Women's rights activists had some success.

Research on the ROM

Free Find: Sojourner Truth's Narrative
After reading the selection by Sojourner Truth on the **Holt Researcher CD-ROM**, write a short essay explaining how you think her speech might have helped the antislavery and women's rights causes.

SECTION ② REVIEW

1. Define and explain:
nationalism   nativism
strike   cotton gin

2. Identify and explain:
Monroe Doctrine   Second Great
Henry Clay   Awakening
American System   Dorothea Dix
Missouri   Frederick Douglass
   Compromise   Sojourner Truth
Andrew Jackson   Elizabeth Cady
Democratic Party   Stanton
Trail of Tears   Seneca Falls
Underground   Convention
   Railroad   Susan B. Anthony
Harriet Tubman

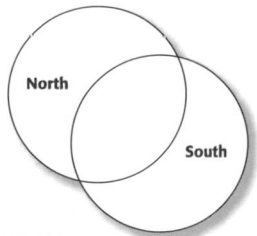

3. Comparing and Contrasting Copy the organizer below. Use it to show the similarities and differences between the societies of the North and the South.

North   South

4. Finding the Main Idea
a. How did nationalism affect the development of the U.S. foreign policy and economy?
b. How successful were the reform movements of the early to mid-1800s?
c. Imagine that you are a free African American living in the South. Write a brief letter comparing your experiences with those of the slaves on a nearby plantation in the mid-1800s.

5. Writing and Critical Thinking
Evaluating Some historians view the Jacksonian era as a period that contributed to the rise of American democracy. Write a paragraph expressing whether you agree with this assessment.
Consider:
• the process of American Indian removal
• the bank crisis and the tariff crisis
• how voting rights were expanded

Homework Practice Online
keyword: SE3 HP2

After completing Section 3, students should be able to:

OBJECTIVE 1 *Analyze what caused the Texas Revolution and the Mexican War.*

OBJECTIVE 2 *Explain why Americans began to settle the West.*

OBJECTIVE 3 *Discuss how politicians addressed the expansion of slavery.*

OBJECTIVE 4 *Identify what events led to the secession of the southern states.*

LET'S GET STARTED!

Write the following question on the chalkboard: *Should states be allowed to leave the Union if they disagree with the policies of the nation as a whole?* As students enter the room, ask them to respond briefly to the question, supporting their answer with solid reasons and examples. Then tell students that in Section 3 they will be learning about the events that led up to the secession of the southern states and the formation of the Confederacy.

SECTION 3

READ TO DISCOVER

1. What caused the Texas Revolution and the Mexican War?
2. Why did Americans begin to settle the West?
3. How did politicians address the expansion of slavery?
4. What events led to the secession of the southern states?

DEFINE

manifest destiny
popular sovereignty

IDENTIFY

Texas Revolution
Juan Seguín
Mexican Cession
Compromise of 1850
Harriet Beecher Stowe
Stephen Douglas
Kansas-Nebraska Act
John Brown
Republican Party
Dred Scott decision
Abraham Lincoln
Confederate States of America

WHY IT MATTERS TODAY

Congressional compromises are still an important part of the U.S. government. Use **CNNfyi.com** or other **current events** sources to learn about a recent issue that has led to compromise legislation in Congress. Record your findings in your journal.

CNNfyi.com

Westward Expansion and Sectional Conflict

 EYEWITNESSES TO History

"Some of the women I saw on the road went through a great deal of suffering and trial. I remember distinctly one girl in particular about my own age that died and was buried on the road. Her mother had a great deal of trouble and suffering. It strikes me as I think of it now that Mothers on the road had to undergo more trial and suffering than anybody else."

—Martha Ann Morrison

Conestoga wagon

Martha Ann Morrison traveled to Oregon Country at the age of 13. She recalled the extreme hardships many settlers endured during the westward journey. During the early 1800s American merchants and fur trappers had built trade links with residents of California, New Mexico, and Oregon Country. In the process, they established trails that brought a flood of new settlers like Morrison to the Far West in the 1840s and 1850s.

The Southwest

In 1845 magazine editor John L. O'Sullivan coined the term **manifest destiny**. This phrase expressed the belief held by many Americans that God intended the United States to expand westward to the Pacific Ocean. The idea of manifest destiny appealed to Americans who felt that access to lands in the West would lessen population pressures, create new markets, and expand farmland.

Texas. After Mexico won a long battle for independence from Spain in 1821, the Mexican government allowed people from the United States to settle in Texas. In 1830, however, Mexico greatly restricted U.S. immigration. In 1833 General Antonio López de Santa Anna became Mexico's president and established himself as a dictator. These events angered many Texans. They started a rebellion known as the **Texas Revolution** in December 1835. Mexican troops arrived in February 1836 to recapture the city of San Antonio from the rebels. After suffering heavy losses, the Mexican soldiers killed all the Texan troops occupying the Alamo, a Catholic mission. The revolution continued, and in April the Texans surprised Santa Anna's army near the San Jacinto River. Shouting "Remember the Alamo!" the Texans won a decisive victory. Mexico signed a treaty granting Texas its independence in the spring of 1836.

During the next few years, the government of the Republic of Texas encouraged European immigration in order to increase its population. European immigrants fared well in the new republic. However, Texans of Mexican descent—even those who had fought for Texas's independence—often found themselves the victims of violence and discrimination.

LEVEL 1: Have students work in pairs or triads to create illustrated time lines that show the sequence of events in the Texas Revolution and the Mexican War. *(Time lines should include: 1821—Americans begin settling in Texas; 1830—Mexico closes border to Americans; 1833—Santa Anna becomes Mexico's president; 1835—Texas Revolution begins; 1836—Texas independence; 1844—Polk elected president and wants to annex Texas; 1846—United States declares war on Mexico.)* Students should include illustrations to accompany important events. Ask volunteers to share their time lines with the class. **English Language Learners, Cooperative Learning**

LEVELS 2 AND 3: Tell students to imagine that they are military leaders who fought in both the Texas Revolution and the Mexican War. Have them write an official report on one of these conflicts—including the causes, major events, and outcome—to file with their commanding officers at the end of the war. *(See the Level 1 lesson for the correct events.)* Invite volunteers to read their reports to the class.

BIOGRAPHY
Juan Seguín

Juan Seguín (se-GEEN) faced such discrimination. Born into a prominent San Antonio family in 1806, Seguín developed a strong interest in politics. He harshly criticized Mexico's government during the 1830s and joined the rebels during the Texas Revolution. Seguín escaped the slaughter at the Alamo because he had left to find reinforcements for the besieged Texans. He later fought at San Jacinto. After the war Seguín served as the mayor of San Antonio.

Some U.S. settlers in San Antonio falsely accused Seguín of retaining his loyalties to Mexico, forcing him to resign in 1842. "The necessity to defend myself for the loyal patriotism with which I had always served Texas, wounded me deeply," he later recalled. Seguín fled to Mexico but returned to southern Texas to live out his final years. He died in 1890.

The Mexican War. Tensions between the United States and Mexico remained high. In 1844 James K. Polk was elected president. Polk wanted to annex Texas to the United States. Congress voted to admit Texas into the Union despite opposition from Mexico. A Mexican attack on U.S. troops along the disputed Texas-Mexico border led the United States to declare war on Mexico in May 1846.

During the Mexican War, U.S. forces marched into central Mexico and seized control of New Mexico and California. U.S. troops were sometimes aided by American settlers in these regions. Despite these early successes, fierce fighting raged in Mexico. In September 1847 Mexico City finally fell to U.S. forces.

In February 1848 a treaty ended the war. Mexico gave up all its claims to Texas and surrendered a vast territory known as the **Mexican Cession**. This area included what is now California, Nevada, and Utah, and parts of Arizona, Colorado, New Mexico, and Wyoming. The United States agreed to pay Mexico $15 million for this land, which was occupied by some 80,000 Spanish-speaking citizens. Despite the treaty's guarantees, many of these people lost their lands.

✔ **READING CHECK: Identifying Cause and Effect** What events led to the Mexican War? Texas revolted; the United States decided to annex it; Mexicans attacked U.S. troops along the disputed border.

The Lure of the West

When the United States took control of California, the area was lightly settled by Europeans. California changed dramatically with the discovery of gold in 1848, however. Thousands of people rushed to seek their fortune. By the end of 1849, the population of California had soared to more than 100,000.

Mining camps soon sprang up to accommodate the migrants. These camps were often dirty, disorderly, and dangerous. Most of the miners did not find the great wealth they had hoped for. José Fernandez lived in northern California. He later recalled that "just as every day many [gold diggers] set out full of hope and confidence in the future, so every day many returned, disgusted with the mines."

Research on the ROM
Free Find: Juan Seguín
After reading about Juan Seguín on the **Holt Researcher CD–ROM**, create a short story, song, or poem about Seguín's experiences in Texas.

INTERPRETING THE VISUAL RECORD
Miners. Miners at Auburn Ravine posed for this photograph in 1852. *What does this image reveal about the variety of people who came to California in search of gold?*

LEVELS 1 AND 2: Tell students to imagine that they are pioneers settling the West. Have them write a letter to a family member or friend who stayed in the East, telling him or her about why they moved to the West. *(Letters might include as reasons hunting and trapping, farm land, religious freedom, gold rush, adventure, and so on).*
English Language Learners

LEVEL 3: Have students write short stories set on a wagon train headed for the West. Students should mention in their stories why their characters are settling in the West. *(See the Levels 1 and 2 lesson for the correct reasons.)* Call on volunteers to read all or part of their stories to the class.

SPOTLIGHT
on American Indians in the West

Tell students to imagine that they are American Indians living in California or Oregon in the mid-1800s. Have them create an oral history describing what is happening to their lives and population as American settlers arrive in the area. Students should conduct additional research as necessary to complete their oral histories. Ask volunteers to share their work with the class. **Block Scheduling**

CITIZENSHIP

Governing the Wagon Trains. Some pioneers created their own rules and regulations to keep order in the wagon trains. One group formed a "Council of Ten" to settle disputes and try offenders. The settlers allowed all men over the age of 16 to vote for the members of this council.

ACTIVITY: Organize students into groups of eight or ten. Tell students to imagine that they are the members of a wagon train that will depart for Oregon Country tomorrow. Have each group create a list of at least five rules that will govern its group. Toward the end of class, have volunteers share their lists, justifying each rule.

SKILL-BUILDING STRATEGIES ANSWERS
Practicing the Skill
1. how slavery expanded westward, and the reactions to and consequences of its expansion

2. Students might mention Henry Clay, Franklin Pierce, Harriet Beecher Stowe, and John Brown.

3. Answers will vary. Questions should relate to the expansion of slavery and the conflict it caused.

By 1852 California's non–American Indian population had leaped from some 14,000 in 1848 to about 250,000. These new immigrants were often intolerant. They frequently prevented original Spanish settlers, Chinese immigrants, and African Americans from mining for gold. Additionally, the gold rush led to disaster for many American Indians. Miners drove them off their gold-rich lands and even forced some of them to work in the mines. Between 1845 and 1855 California's American Indian population decreased from some 150,000 to about 50,000.

The population of the Pacific Northwest also expanded in the mid-1800s. Thousands of families set out for Oregon Country along the Oregon Trail in the 1840s and 1850s, often in large groups of wagon trains. The settlement of Oregon Country led the United States and Britain to finalize the U.S.-Canada border.

American Indians often helped pioneers along the trail by serving as guides and selling them wild game for food. Yet eastern newspapers emphasized only the attacks and reported massacres of pioneers. To ease settlers' fears, the U.S. government negotiated with various American Indian nations. In return for their not attacking pioneers, the United States promised to pay those American Indians and honor territorial boundaries. However, pioneers often introduced diseases that killed many Indians. Settlers also wiped out wildlife by clearing land and hunting. As a result, some Indians tried to drive out the settlers.

✔ **READING CHECK: Categorizing** How did increasing migration affect the West?
Its non–American Indian population increased while its Indian population decreased; some violence occurred.

Skill-Building Strategies
Reading Effectively

Reading historical literature can be quite demanding. Textbook and supplemental reading assignments often cover large amounts of complex information. A well-planned reading strategy can help you organize and learn this information efficiently. It can also help you take note of questions and ideas that you should study further when preparing for a test.

How to Read Effectively

1. **Preview the assignment.** Before you begin reading the text of an assignment, carefully read the title, introduction, and any conclusions or summaries. Then look over any headings, subheadings, illustrations, and study questions. This process of previewing should give you a general idea of what you are about to learn.
2. **Read actively.** Divide the assignment into small, manageable sections. As you read each section, keep an active lookout for key people, events, ideas, and relationships. If you have time, create notes summarizing important information.

3. **Review regularly.** When you reach the end of a small section, pause and recall the highlights of what you have just read. Then answer any study questions that are addressed in the section. When you finish reading the assignment, make sure that you can formulate answers to any review questions.

Applying the Skill

Before you read the "Slavery's Expansion" segment of Section 3, spend a minute previewing it. Then write a short paragraph that explains what you expect to learn from the section. Read the section.

Practicing the Skill

Answer the following questions.
1. What is the general topic of this section?
2. Who took part in the events described in this section?
3. What are three questions that you expect this section to answer?

ALL LEVELS: To help students understand how politicians addressed the expansion of slavery, copy the following graphic organizer on the chalkboard, omitting the italicized answers. Have each student complete the graphic organizer. **English Language Learners**

CONFLICT OVER EXPANSION OF SLAVERY

Expansion	Congress's Efforts	Compromises and Acts
Texas and maintaining balance in Congress	admitted Texas as slave state; extended Missouri Compromise line west	
popular sovereignty versus prohibition of territories	Compromise of 1850	California admitted as free state; New Mexico divided and given popular sovereignty
continued pressure from southern slave holders	Fugitive Slave Act	made it a crime to assist runaway slaves and authorized arrest of escapees in free states
revived debate over slavery in new territories	Kansas-Nebraska Act	granted popular sovereignty to new territories

Slavery's Expansion

U.S. expansion westward reopened the debate over the spread of slavery. When the Republic of Texas petitioned for annexation to the United States in the 1840s, Congress had to decide whether Texas would be admitted as a slave or free state. In 1845 Congress settled on terms favorable to the South. It admitted Texas as a slave state and extended westward the dividing line that had been set by the Missouri Compromise.

The slavery debate in Congress. The addition of the Mexican Cession territories in 1848 caused further complications. Some senators proposed that any new territories rely on **popular sovereignty**. This practice would allow the citizens of each new territory to vote whether to permit slavery.

The presidential election of 1848 put Mexican War hero General Zachary Taylor in office. The recently formed Free-Soil Party also fared well. Its members demanded that Congress prohibit the expansion of slavery into the territories. When Congress assembled in December 1849, there was fierce debate over whether slavery would be allowed in California and New Mexico.

Representative Henry Clay presented a plan known as the **Compromise of 1850.** The plan tried to satisfy both northern and southern interests. California would be admitted as a free state. The New Mexico Territory would be divided into two territories, with the residents of each territory allowed to vote on whether to allow slavery. The plan also called for the abolition of the slave trade—but not slavery itself—in the District of Columbia. In addition, the plan proposed a new, stricter fugitive slave law, the Fugitive Slave Act. Congress passed Clay's compromise in September 1850 after a heated debate.

Reactions to the compromise. Although the Compromise of 1850 did not satisfy all Americans, most hoped that it had settled the slavery question. Some politicians vowed to avoid further debate over slavery. Democrat Franklin Pierce won the presidency in 1852 after persuading both pro-slavery and anti-slavery supporters that he shared their views. Pierce's efforts to satisfy both groups contributed to his weakness as a leader, however. Abolitionists soon labeled him "a northern man with southern principles."

Abolitionists made appeals through antislavery literature that showed the inhumanity of slavery. **Harriet Beecher Stowe**'s 1852 novel, *Uncle Tom's Cabin,* convinced many northern readers that slavery was morally wrong and should be abolished. In one year the book sold some 300,000 copies in the United States alone.

Henry Clay urged Congress to compromise on the slavery issue.

INTERPRETING THE VISUAL RECORD

Fugitive Slave Act. Many antislavery northerners opposed the Compromise of 1850, which authorized the forcible capture of runaway slaves in free states. *Does this engraving reflect a northern or southern perspective? Explain your answer.*

OPERATIONS OF THE FUGITIVE-SLAVE LAW.

HISTORY MAKERS SPEAK

Abraham Lincoln in *Battle Cry of Freedom: The Civil War Era*

During the 1858 Illinois senatorial campaign debates, candidate Stephen Douglas insisted that his opponent, Abraham Lincoln, supported full political and social equality for African Americans. Hoping to counteract Douglas's contentions—which were politically damaging at the time—Lincoln assured listeners, "I am not, nor ever have been in favor of bringing about in any way the social and political equality of the white and black races."

CRITICAL THINKING How might modern-day historians characterize Lincoln's position on the social and political equality of the races?

ANSWER: Students might suggest that historians might characterize his position according to the social and political context of the time.

VISUAL RECORD ANSWER
Answers will vary. Students might suggest a northern perspective because the slave is going unwillingly.

MAP ANSWER
(for p. 90)

allowed Kansas and Nebraska territories to vote whether to allow slavery

TEACH OBJECTIVE 4

ALL LEVELS: Ask students to list events that led to the secession of the southern states. *(Students should list the growth of the Republican Party, the* Dred Scott *decision, and Lincoln's victory in the 1860 presidential election.)* Then have students write a paragraph explaining the action of the southern states immediately following Lincoln's election. *(Students should mention that days after the election several southern states seceded and that by early 1861 they had formed the Confederate States of America.)* Ask volunteers to share their paragraphs with the class. **English Language Learners**

Slave and Free Territory in 1850 and 1854

Interpreting Maps The Compromise of 1850 and the Kansas-Nebraska Act of 1854 gave new states and territories the right to vote on whether to allow slavery.

? HUMAN SYSTEMS How did the Kansas-Nebraska Act extend slavery?

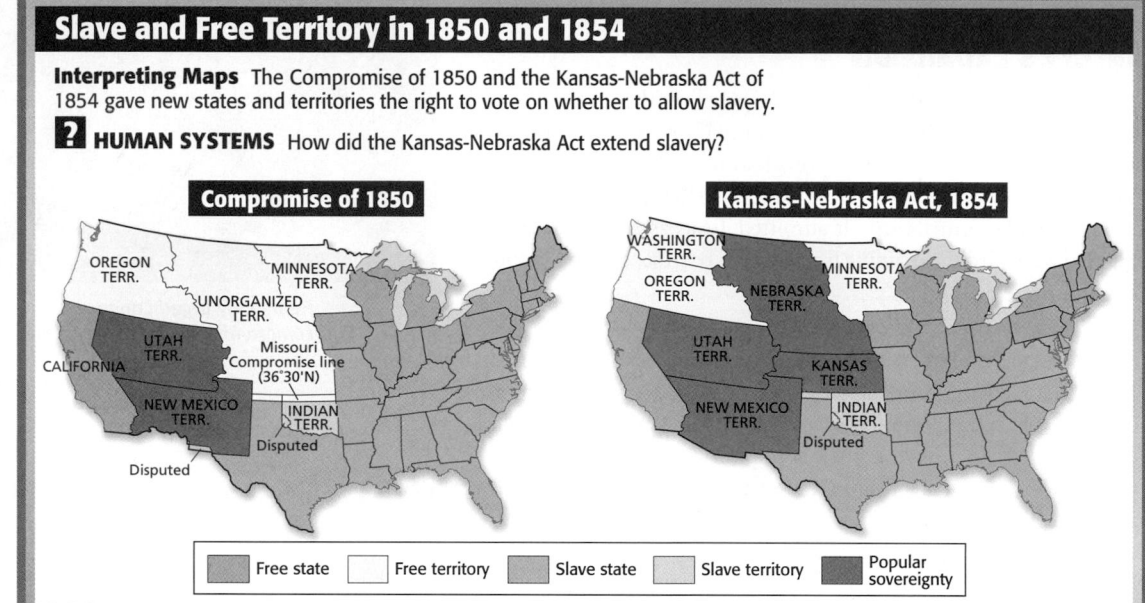

Free state | Free territory | Slave state | Slave territory | Popular sovereignty

Pro-slavery representative Preston Brooks attacks antislavery senator Charles Sumner on the floor of the Senate.

Trouble in Kansas. The slavery debate was revived in 1854. That year Illinois senator **Stephen Douglas** introduced the **Kansas-Nebraska Act**, which organized these new territories on the basis of popular sovereignty. By effectively repealing the Missouri Compromise, the act renewed southern hopes of expanding slavery. The Kansas-Nebraska Act also pitted antislavery and pro-slavery forces against one another for control of the new territories. As Kansas settlers prepared to elect their first territorial legislature in March 1855, some 5,000 pro-slavery Missouri residents crossed into the territory to cast ballots. These illegal votes helped elect a pro-slavery legislature that immediately passed laws supporting slavery. Antislavery settlers protested by electing their own legislature.

Soon violence erupted in Kansas. One well-known event was the Pottawatomie Massacre, ordered by abolitionist **John Brown**. He and his followers murdered five pro-slavery men. This action enraged southerners, shocked northerners, and sparked additional violence in Kansas. The escalating slavery debate also led to violence in the halls of Congress, where a southern congressman attacked a northern senator.

✔ **READING CHECK: Evaluating** How effective were Congress's efforts to address the expansion of slavery? They were ultimately not very effective because they led to violence.

On the Brink of War

Antislavery voters flocked to a new political party gaining power in the North. The **Republican Party** included antislavery Democrats, Free-Soilers, and Whigs. However, Democratic candidate James Buchanan of Pennsylvania won the presidential election in 1856.

By the time Buchanan took office, another debate had begun over slavery. Slave Dred Scott had sued in court for his freedom. Scott argued that since he had lived with his owner in the free state of Illinois, he should be free. The case eventually reached the U.S.

REVIEW

Have students complete the **Section 3 Review** on page 91.

ASSESS

Have students complete **Daily Quiz 2.3**. As **Alternative Assessment**, you may want to use the illustrated time lines or the pioneer letters activity in this section's lessons.

RETEACH

Have students complete **Main Idea Activity for English Language Learners and Special-Needs Students 2.3**. Then assign groups of students to each objective in the section. Tell each student to create graphic organizers or other visual representations of the information pertaining to his or her assigned objectives. Have students study each other's graphic organizers within their groups.
English Language Learners, Cooperative Learning

EXTEND

Organize students into four groups and assign each group one of the following topics: the Mexican War, settling the West, conflict over the expansion of slavery, or secession of the southern states. Have groups create and present a short multimedia presentation about their topic. Encourage students to assign roles within their groups to help them accomplish the assignment (i.e. writer, artist, researcher, media expert, and so on).
Cooperative Learning, Block Scheduling

Supreme Court. In the *Dred Scott* decision, the Court ruled that Scott was not a citizen and therefore could not bring suit in U.S. courts. The Court also declared the Missouri Compromise unconstitutional, stating that the federal government could not deprive slaveholders of their slaves.

The decision outraged abolitionists. African American leader Robert Purvis expressed the angry sentiments of the free African American community.

History Makers Speak

❝This atrocious [horrible] decision furnishes final confirmation of the already well-known fact that, under the Constitution and government of the United States, the colored people are nothing and can be nothing but an alien, disenfranchised [deprived of rights] and degraded class.❞

—Robert Purvis

Republican **Abraham Lincoln** won the presidential election of 1860 with just some 40 percent of the popular vote. Despite his moderate stance on slavery, many southerners viewed his election as a victory for abolition. Within days of the election, several southern states voted to secede. South Carolina was the first, followed by Mississippi, Florida, Alabama, Georgia, Louisiana, and Texas. Early in 1861, delegates from six of these states met to draft a constitution for the **Confederate States of America**. Jefferson Davis of Mississippi became the president of the Confederacy. Southerners justified their actions by asserting that because individual states had joined the Union voluntarily, they also had the right to withdraw from it. In a special session of Congress, President Lincoln said that the South must accept the election results. "When ballots have [been] fairly, and constitutionally decided," he said, "there can be no successful appeal back to bullets." Many southerners felt otherwise.

✔ **READING CHECK: Analyzing Information** Why did the southern states secede?
because they believed that Lincoln's election as president would threaten slavery

INTERPRETING THE VISUAL RECORD

Secession. Delegates from South Carolina were the first to vote to secede from the Union. *Why do you think a publication like* **Harper's Weekly** *would put the delegates' portraits on its cover?*

CHAPTER
REVIEW 2 ANSWERS

Creating a Time Line
Each event should have an explanation and the correct date.

Writing a Summary
See Reading Checks in each section for main ideas.

Identifying People and Ideas
1. first ten amendments to the U.S. Constitution

2. U.S. Treasury Secretary under President Washington

3. Supreme Court Chief Justice responsible for judicial review and other reforms

4. first Supreme Court case to test the idea of judicial review

5. western territory bought from France in 1803

6. banned slavery in Louisiana Purchase north of Missouri

7. women's rights activist

8. belief that God intended U.S. westward expansion

9. idea that each new territory would vote on slavery issue

10. six southern states that seceded from the Union in 1861

SECTION 3 REVIEW

1. Define and explain:
manifest destiny
popular sovereignty

2. Identify and explain:
Texas Revolution
Juan Seguín
Mexican Cession
Compromise of 1850
Harriet Beecher Stowe
Stephen Douglas
Kansas-Nebraska Act
John Brown
Republican Party
Dred Scott decision
Abraham Lincoln
Confederate States of America

3. Sequencing Create a flow-chart, using the boxes below as the first and last boxes of the chart. Fill in the events that led to the secession of the southern states.

The Republic of Texas petitions for annexation to the United States.

↓

Six southern states draft a constitution for the Confederate States of America.

4. Finding the Main Idea
a. What were the causes of the Texas Revolution and the Mexican War?
b. How might the history of the Far West have been different if gold had not been discovered in California?
c. What were the main reasons Americans began to settle the West Coast?

5. Writing and Critical Thinking
Categorizing Write a brief newspaper editorial explaining why attempts to resolve the slavery issue were ineffective.
Consider:
• northerners' reactions to the Fugitive Slave Act
• why the popular sovereignty proposal failed
• abolitionists' reactions to the *Dred Scott* decision

Homework Practice Online
keyword: SE3 HP2

TECHNOLOGY

▶ Chapter 2 Test Generator (on the One-Stop Planner)
▶ Global Skill Builder CD–ROM
▶ HRW Go site

REINFORCEMENT, REVIEW, AND ASSESSMENT

▶ Chapter 2 Review, pp. 92–93
▶ Chapter 2 Tutorial for Students, Parents, Mentors, and Peers

▶ Chapter 2 Test (Form A or B)
▶ Portfolio Activities and Alternative Assessment Handbook, Chapter 2
▶ Spanish Glossary
▶ Chapter 2 Test for English Language Learners and Special-Needs Students

REVIEW

Have students complete the **Chapter 2 Review** on pp. 92–93.

ASSESS

Use one of the chapter tests to assess students' understanding of the content. For **Alternative Assessment**, see the **Portfolio Activities and Alternative Assessment Handbook**.

Understanding Main Ideas

1. It created a national court system, the Bill of Rights, the presidential cabinet, and it went about restoring the nation's credit.

2. He completed the Louisiana Purchase, worked to pay off the national debt, and passed the Embargo Act.

3. alcohol consumption, education, treatment of the disadvantaged and mentally ill, prison conditions

4. annexation of Texas, the Mexican Cession, gold in California

5. It passed the Missouri Compromise, then the Compromise of 1850, then the Kansas-Nebraska Act, and then the Supreme Court issued the *Dred Scott* decision.

Reviewing Themes

1. Many states would not have ratified the Constitution without protections of individual liberty.

2. It protected American goods with tariffs and funded a national transportation system.

3. Politicians in the South wanted to expand slavery, and those in the North wanted to abolish it.

Thinking Critically

1. Answers will vary. Students might suggest that without them, a society tends to ignore the rights of its individual citizens.

Creating a Time Line

Copy the time line below onto a sheet of paper. Complete the time line by filling in the events and dates from the chapter that you think were most significant. Pick three events and explain why you think they were significant.

1789   1825   1861

Writing a Summary

Using standard grammar, spelling, sentence structure, and punctuation, write an overview of events in the chapter.

Identifying People and Ideas

Identify the following terms or individuals and explain their significance.

1. Bill of Rights
2. Alexander Hamilton
3. John Marshall
4. *Marbury v. Madison*
5. Louisiana Purchase
6. Missouri Compromise
7. Susan B. Anthony
8. manifest destiny
9. popular sovereignty
10. Confederate States of America

Understanding Main Ideas

SECTION 1 *(pp. 70–78)*

1. How did the first Congress help shape the national government?

SECTION 2 *(pp. 79–85)*

2. In what ways did Thomas Jefferson's presidency change the United States?
3. What social problems did reformers hope to correct?

SECTION 3 *(pp. 86–91)*

4. What events led to the expansion of the United States in the mid-1800s?
5. How did the U.S. government deal with the expansion of slavery?

Reviewing Themes

1. **Constitutional Heritage** Why was a Bill of Rights added to the Constitution?
2. **Economics** In what ways did Henry Clay's American Plan help economic development?
3. **Geography** How did conflicting political interests between regions lead to secession?

Thinking Critically

1. **Making Generalizations** How important are the protections in the Bill of Rights to a democratic society?
2. **Evaluating** What impact did Supreme Court decisions, in particular those made under John Marshall, have on life in the United States?
3. **Analyzing Information** How did the reform movements of the 1800s change American society?
4. **Summarizing** How did European colonization and the policies of the U.S. government affect American Indians?
5. **Sequencing** What events led to the secession of the southern states?

Writing About History

Summarizing Copy the chart below. Use it to list the major influences on life in the United States in the 1800s. Then choose one of these influences and write a poem about it.

The Economy	Key People/ Events	Foreign Policy	Domestic Changes/ Issues

RETEACH

Organize the class into four groups and assign each group one of the sections of Chapter 2. Have each group create and present a lesson that covers the important points of its assigned section. Tell students to be sure to cover all of the sections' objectives when they teach the material to the class. Also encourage them to orally quiz the class after they present their lessons to confirm that their students understood the information.

English Language Learners, Cooperative Learning

EXTEND

Organize students into pairs or triads. Tell them to create a graphic novel—a long story told with pictures and dialogue, as in comic books—that covers all of the major objectives of the chapter. Students may create fictional characters to tell the story, or they may present the information as an illustrated history book. Help students to cover and bind their books, and display them in the classroom or elsewhere in the school.

Block Scheduling

Building Social Studies Skills

Interpreting Maps

Study the map below. Then use it to help answer the questions that follow.

Latin American Nations in 1830

UNITED STATES

Mississippi River

30° N

MEXICO 1821 · Mexico City ⊕

BAHAMAS (British)
CUBA (Spanish)
HAITI 1804
Gulf of Mexico

ATLANTIC OCEAN

BRITISH HONDURAS
Guatemala City ⊕
CARIBBEAN SEA
JAMAICA (British)
PUERTO RICO (Spanish)
TRINIDAD (British)

UNITED PROVINCES OF CENTRAL AMERICA 1823
MOSQUITO COAST (British)

Caracas ⊕
VENEZUELA 1821
GUIANA (British) (Netherlands) (French)

COLOMBIA 1819 ⊕ Bogotá

0° Equator
Quito ⊕
ECUADOR 1822

Amazon River

PACIFIC OCEAN

Lima ⊕
PERU 1824
BOLIVIA 1825
Sucre ⊕

EMPIRE OF BRAZIL 1822

European colony
1821 Date of independence

PARAGUAY 1811
Asunción ⊕
Rio de Janeiro

ARGENTINA 1816
Santiago ⊕
CHILE 1818
Buenos Aires
URUGUAY 1828
Montevideo
Rio de la Plata

0   800   1,600 Miles
0   800   1,600 Kilometers
Miller Cylindrical Projection

An 1881 treaty divided Patagonia between Chile and Argentina.

PATAGONIA
Strait of Magellan
FALKLAND ISLANDS (Disputed)

120° W   90° W   Cape Horn   60° W

30° S

N W E S

1. Which Latin American colony was still under European control in 1830?
  a. Colombia
  b. Cuba
  c. Empire of Brazil
  d. Venezuela

2. How might independence movements in Latin America have affected the United States?

Analyzing Primary Sources

Read the following comments by U.S. senator Salmon P. Chase, opposing the Kansas-Nebraska Act. Then answer the questions that follow.

"We appeal to the people. We warn you that the dearest interests of freedom and the Union are in imminent peril. Demagogues [leaders who gain power by deceptive means] may tell you that the Union can be maintained only by submitting to the demands of slavery. We can tell you that the safety of the Union can only be insured by the full recognition of the just claims of freedom and man. The Union was formed to establish justice and secure the blessings of liberty. When it fails to accomplish these ends, it will be worthless; and when it becomes worthless, it cannot long endure."

3. What does Chase predict might happen if slavery is maintained?
  a. The safety of the Union will be assured.
  b. The Union will not endure.
  c. Justice and liberty will endure.
  d. Demagogues will rule the Union.

4. Based on this passage, to which political party do you think Chase belonged? Explain your answer.

Alternative Assessment

Building Your Portfolio

U.S. HISTORY

Citizenship

Imagine that you are a western farmer who supports Andrew Jackson for re-election in 1832. Create a political poster that illustrates why Jackson is a "man of the people." The poster should draw on events from Jackson's first term in office. It should also highlight the qualities that made Jackson an effective leader.

internet connect

go.hrw.com

Internet Activity: go.hrw.com
KEYWORD: SE3 AN2

Choose a topic on the expanding nation to:

- research transportation on the Erie Canal and National Road and create a brochure.
- analyze the causes and effects of the Irish Potato Famine and its impact on immigration.
- create a newspaper on John Brown and resistance movements against slavery.

---

2. *Marbury* v. *Madison* gave citizens a final court of appeal to preserve their constitutional rights.

3. They led to a reduced workday, more schools, reduced alcohol consumption, and better care for the mentally ill.

4. The Indians were forced off their lands, pushed out of the way of U.S. progress.

5. conflict over popular sovereignty, Compromise of 1850, Kansas-Nebraska Act, Pottawatomie Massacre, election of Abraham Lincoln

Writing
Students' poems will vary but should include some of the major people, events, and issues covered in the chapter.

Building Social Studies Skills
1. b.

2. Answers will vary. Students might suggest that Europeans fleeing Latin America would immigrate to the United States.

3. b

4. Students might suggest the Republican Party because it was the party of Lincoln and many abolitionists.

The Civil War

CHAPTER RESOURCE MANAGER

Objectives	Pacing Guide	Reproducible Resources
SECTION 1 **The Union Dissolves** pp. 96–102 ★ Discuss the attempts made to compromise with the secessionists. ★ Analyze how the fall of Fort Sumter affected the relationship between the Union and the Confederacy. ★ Identify the advantages each side possessed at the beginning of the war. ★ Summarize the consequences of the First Battle of Bull Run.	**Regular** 1.5 days **Block Scheduling** 1 day *Block Scheduling Handbook with Team Teaching Strategies, pp. 13–18*	**RS** Guided Reading Strategy 3.1 **SM** American History Outline Map 13: Union and Confederacy **E** Hand-On History Activity, Photography: Seeing Your Local History
SECTION 2 **The North and South Face Off** pp. 103–09 ★ Contrast the military strategies of the North and South. ★ Describe the daily hardships soldiers faced. ★ Report on what life was like on the home front during the war. ★ Explain how civilians contributed to the war effort. ★ Discuss why some people opposed the war.	**Regular** 1.5 days **Block Scheduling** 1 day *Block Scheduling Handbook with Team Teaching Strategies, pp. 13–18*	**RS** Guided Reading Strategy 3.2 **IC** Literature Reading 3: The Reality of War **PS** Biography Reading 3: Clara Barton
SECTION 3 **Fighting the War** pp. 110–17 ★ Explain how Union forces gained control of the Mississippi River. ★ Evaluate how the northern and southern forces fared in the eastern campaigns. ★ Analyze how the Union's victory at Antietam changed its war goals. ★ Recognize how African American soldiers aided the Union. ★ Assess the significance of the battles at Fredericksburg and Chancellorsville.	**Regular** 1 day **Block Scheduling** .5 day *Block Scheduling Handbook with Team Teaching Strategies, pp. 13–18*	**RS** Guided Reading Strategy 3.3 **PS** American History Political Cartoon 11: Changing Union Leadership
SECTION 4 **The Final Phase** pp. 118–23 ★ Explain the outcomes of the Battle of Gettysburg. ★ Assess the significance of the Union victory at Vicksburg. ★ Describe General Grant's strategy in the summer of 1864. ★ Describe General Sherman's strategies. ★ List the terms of surrender at Appomattox.	**Regular** 1.5 days **Block Scheduling** 1 day *Block Scheduling Handbook with Team Teaching Strategies, pp. 13–18*	**RS** Guided Reading Strategy 3.4 **PS** Primary Source Reading 3: The Gettysburg Address **SM** Geography Activity 3: The Siege of Vicksburg **RS** Graphic Organizer Activity 3: The Gettysburg Address **E** Creative Teaching Strategy: Resource Speaker

Chapter Resource Key

PS	Primary Sources	**REV**	Review		Video
RS	Reading Support	**ELL**	Reinforcement and English Language Learners		Internet
IC	Interdisciplinary Connections				Holt Presentation Maker Using Microsoft® PowerPoint®
E	Enrichment		Transparencies		
SM	Skills Mastery		CD–ROM		
A	Assessment		Music		

One-Stop Planner CD-ROM

See the *One-Stop Planner* for a complete list of additional resources for students and teachers.

One-Stop Planner CD–ROM

It's easy to plan lessons, select resources, and print out materials for your students when you use the **One-Stop Planner CD–ROM with Test Generator.**

HRW ONLINE RESOURCES
GO TO: go.hrw.com
Then type in a keyword.

TEACHER HOME PAGE
KEYWORD: SE3 Teacher

CHAPTER INTERNET ACTIVITIES
KEYWORD: SE3 AN3
Choose an activity to:
• write a report describing the life of a soldier in the war.
• create an annotated time line of the history of the International Red Cross.
• create a three-dimensional model of the battlefield at Gettysburg

CHAPTER ENRICHMENT LINKS
KEYWORD: SE3 CH3

ONLINE ASSESSMENT
Homework Practice
KEYWORD: SE3 HP3

Standardized Test Prep
KEYWORD: SE3 STP3

Rubrics
KEYWORD: SS Rubrics

ONLINE MAPS, CHARTS, AND GRAPHS
KEYWORD: SE3 MCG
• Theaters of War, 1861–1865
• Southern Railroads, 1862–1865
• Battle of Gettysburg
• Soldiers' Occupations

CONTENT UPDATES
KEYWORD: SS Content Updates

HOLT PRESENTATION MAKER
KEYWORD: SE3 PPT3

ONLINE READING SUPPORT
KEYWORD: SS Strategies

CURRENT EVENTS
KEYWORD: S3 Current Events

Technology Resources

 One-Stop Planner, Lesson 3.1
 American Music Selection 13: "All Quiet Along the Potomac"
 The American Nation Video Program Segment: Building an Army; Teacher's Guide, pp. 57–62
 Holt Researcher: American History CD–ROM
 Homework Practice Online

 One-Stop Planner, Lesson 3.2
 Everyday Life in America Transparency 12: Photograph of Civil War Casualties
 Holt Researcher: American History CD–ROM
 CNN Presents America: Yesterday and Today, Beginnings to 1914 Segment: Clara Barton and the Legacy of War
 Homework Practice Online

 One-Stop Planner, Lesson 3.3
 Linking Geography and History Transparency 14: The War in the East and the West, 1861–1863
 Holt Researcher: American History CD–ROM
 Homework Practice Online

 One-Stop Planner, Lesson 3.4
 Holt Researcher: American History CD–ROM
 Homework Practice Online
 HRW Go site

Reinforcement, Review, and Assessment

REV Section 1 Review, p. 102
A Daily Quiz 3.1
ELL Main Idea Activity 3.1
ELL English Audio Summary 3.1
ELL Spanish Audio Summary 3.1

REV Section 1 Review, p. 109
A Daily Quiz 3.2
ELL Main Idea Activity 3.2
ELL English Audio Summary 3.2
ELL Spanish Audio Summary 3.2

REV Section 1 Review, p. 117
A Daily Quiz 3.3
ELL Main Idea Activity 3.3
ELL English Audio Summary 3.3
ELL Spanish Audio Summary 3.3

REV Section 1 Review, p. 123
A Daily Quiz 3.4
ELL Main Idea Activity 3.4
ELL English Audio Summary 3.4
ELL Spanish Audio Summary 3.4

Meeting Individual Needs

Ability Levels
Level 1 Basic-level activities designed for all students encountering new material
Level 2 Intermediate-level activities designed for average students
Level 3 Challenging activities designed for honors and gifted-and-talented students
English Language Learners Activities that address the needs of students with Limited English Proficiency

Chapter Review and Assessment

 Global Skill Builder CD–ROM
HRW Go site
REV Chapter 3 Tutorial for Students, Parents, Mentors, and Peers
REV Chapter 3 Review, pp. 118–23
Chapter 3 Test Generator (on the One-Stop Planner)
A Chapter 3 Test (Form A or B)
A Alternative Assessment Handbook
A Chapter 3 Test for English Language Learners and Special-Needs Students

Build on What You Know

Ask students to answer the following questions.

What tensions between the North and South might have led to the Civil War?

Consider:

- the issue of slavery
- the secession of southern states

What advantages might the North have used to win the Civil War?

Consider:

- the North's industrial resources
- the North's larger population

AMERICAN EVENTS

INTERDISCIPLINARY CONNECTIONS

►MUSIC◄

The "Battle Hymn of the Republic." Poet and abolitionist Julia Ward Howe wished to contribute to the Union cause. While visiting a Union encampment during the autumn of 1861, she was inspired by the tune to "John Brown's Body." She decided to provide the tune with a better set of lyrics. Inspired in the middle of the night, she transformed, "John Brown's body lies a mouldering in the grave. . . ." into "Mine eyes have seen the glory of the coming of the Lord. . . ." Her poem, the "Battle Hymn of the Republic," was published in February 1862.

ACTIVITY: Ask students to provide examples of songs or works of art that are associated with a particular war.

CHAPTER 3

1861–1865
The Civil War

The bombardment of Fort Sumter

1864 camera

COURTESY GEORGE EASTMAN HOUSE

1861 Politics
Confederate forces open fire on Fort Sumter.

1861 World Events
Russian serfs gain their freedom.

1861 World Events
Great Britain and France purchase cotton from Egypt and India instead of from southern states.

1862 Politics
The Union captures New Orleans and wins the Battle of Antietam, while the Confederacy wins the Battle of Fredericksburg.

1862 The Arts
Mathew Brady presents "The Dead at Antietam," his first photographic exhibit of the Civil War.

1860

THE GRANGER COLLECTION, NEW YORK

Charles Dickens

1861

1861 The Arts
British author Charles Dickens writes *Great Expectations.*

1861 Science and Technology
Archaeopteryx—a prehistoric skeleton that suggests a possible evolutionary link between birds and reptiles—is discovered in Europe.

Red Cross medal

1862

1862 The Arts
Julia Ward Howe publishes a poem that becomes the "Battle Hymn of the Republic."

1862 World Events
Jean-Henri Dunant of Switzerland proposes the founding of a voluntary relief organization—the International Red Cross.

Sheet music for the "Battle Hymn of the Republic"

Build on What You Know

Tensions between the North and the South continued to grow throughout the 1850s. The crisis came to a head when a Republican, Abraham Lincoln, was elected president in 1860. In this chapter you will learn how the large population and industrial power of the North gave the Union better resources to fight the long and bloody Civil War that ensued. Although the South's defensive strategy and superior military leadership enabled it to win many of the war's early battles, the Confederacy was unable to overcome the Union forces.

What's Your Opinion?

To help students create their Themes Journal entries, provide the following examples of appropriate **agree**/**disagree** *statements.*

Geography

Agree During the Revolutionary War the Patriots successfully used guerrilla war tactics in forest regions.

Disagree During the Revolutionary War the Patriots lost their strategic advantage atop Bunker Hill.

Economics

Agree U.S. domestic manufacturing increased as a result of the War of 1812.

Disagree During the War of 1812, the British naval blockade hurt U.S. commerce.

Citizenship

Agree Abolitionists and slaveholders disagreed sharply over the moral and political ramifications of slavery.

Disagree The vast majority of U.S. citizens agree with the principles expressed in the Bill of Rights.

President Lincoln

General Lee surrendering to General Grant

1863
Daily Life
Congress establishes free mail delivery to U.S. cities.

1863
Business and Finance
Tailor Ebenezer Butterick markets the first paper dress pattern.

1863
Politics
The Confederacy wins a victory at Chancellorsville; the Union wins at Gettysburg and Vicksburg.

1864
Business and Finance
"In God We Trust" first appears on U.S. coins.

1864
Politics
President Lincoln is re-elected.

1864 U.S. coin

1865
Politics
General Robert E. Lee formally surrenders his Confederate army to General Grant's Union forces at Appomattox.

1865
Science and Technology
Thaddeus Lowe invents a machine that makes ice.

1863 | **1864** | **1865**

1863
Daily Life
Food riots break out in several southern states.

THE MUSEUM OF THE CONFEDERACY–RICHMOND, VIRGINIA

1864
World Events
The French capture Mexico City and proclaim Archduke Maximilian of Austria emperor of Mexico.

1864
Politics
General Ulysses S. Grant becomes commander of all Union armies.

1865
Daily Life
John MacGregor pioneers canoeing as a sport.

1865
Science and Technology
The federal armory at Springfield, Massachusetts, has produced 1.6 million rifled muskets since 1861.

Southern women rioting for bread in 1863

What's Your Opinion?

Themes Journal *Do you* **agree** *or* **disagree** *with the following statements? Support your point of view in your journal.*

Geography Geography has a significant impact on the way wars are fought.

Economics Wars contribute to a nation's economic development.

Citizenship Americans choose to interpret the meaning of individual liberty in different ways.

exploring the time line

GLOBAL EVENTS

internet connect

go.hrw.com

TOPIC: Red Cross
GO TO: go.hrw.com
KEYWORD: SE3 AN3

Have students access the Internet through the HRW Go site to conduct research on the history of the International Red Cross. Then have students create an annotated time line that presents the history of the Red Cross, including information about the work performed by the Red Cross, notable achievements of the organization, and how the Red Cross is funded.

After completing Section 1, students should be able to:

OBJECTIVE 1 Discuss the attempts made to compromise with the secessionists.

OBJECTIVE 2 Analyze how the fall of Fort Sumter affected the relationship between the Union and the Confederacy.

OBJECTIVE 3 Identify the advantages each side possessed at the beginning of the war.

OBJECTIVE 4 Summarize the consequences of the First Battle of Bull Run.

LET'S GET STARTED!

Play Selection 13, "All Quiet Along the Potomac," from the **American Music Audio CD Program** as students enter the class-room. Ask students to respond to "All Quiet Along the Potomac" in writing. After the song has ended, tell students that the song was written during the early part of the Civil War by a Confederate soldier. Tell students that in Section 1 they will learn about the beginning of the Civil War.

SECTION ①

READ TO DISCOVER
1. What attempts were made to compromise with the secessionists?
2. How did the fall of Fort Sumter affect the relationship between the Union and the Confederacy?
3. What advantages did each side possess at the beginning of the war?
4. What were the consequences of the First Battle of Bull Run?

IDENTIFY
Crittenden Compromise
Robert E. Lee
Joseph E. Johnston
First Battle of Bull Run
Thomas "Stonewall" Jackson

WHY IT MATTERS TODAY
Some countries around the world are currently experiencing civil wars. Use **CNNfyi.com** or other **current events** sources to find out about some of these places. Record your findings in your journal.

CNNfyi.com

The Union Dissolves

Mary Ashton Livermore

EYEWITNESSES TO History

❝*This proclamation was like the first peal of a surcharged thunder-cloud, clearing the murky air. The . . . whole North arose as one man. . . .*
Hastily formed companies marched to camps of rendezvous. . . . Merchants and clerks rushed out from stores, bareheaded, saluting them as they passed. Windows were flung up; and women leaned out into the rain, waving flags and handkerchiefs.
I had never dreamed that New England . . . could be fired with so warlike a spirit.❞

—Mary Ashton Livermore, quoted in *Voices of the Civil War*, by Richard Wheeler

Mary Ashton Livermore wrote about the northern response to President Abraham Lincoln's April 1861 call for volunteers to put down the southern rebellion. Such spirited enthusiasm swept the nation in early 1861. As war became inevitable, both sides prepared for what they believed would be a short conflict.

Last Attempts at Compromise

When President Abraham Lincoln took office in 1861, the nation stood on the brink of collapse. Seven southern states had already seceded from the Union—South Carolina, Mississippi, Florida, Alabama, Georgia, Louisiana, and Texas. Furthermore, the debate over secession continued to rage in the Upper South.

To preserve the Union, Senator John J. Crittenden of Kentucky had proposed the **Crittenden Compromise** in December 1860. Crittenden's plan called for the old Missouri Compromise line to be drawn west through the remaining territories. North of the line, slavery would be illegal; south of the line, slavery could expand. President-elect Lincoln quickly rejected the plan. Opposition to the spread of slavery united the Republican Party. Many Republicans might have turned against Lincoln if he had allowed slavery to expand. Lincoln did, however, support the part of Crittenden's plan that would protect slavery where it already existed.

Meanwhile, the secessionists were caught up in the excitement of creating a new nation. "It is a revolution . . . of the most intense character," wrote one southern senator. "It can no more be checked by human effort, for the time, than a prairie fire by a gardener's watering pot."

The new president was determined to preserve the Union. In his inaugural address, Lincoln insisted to southerners that secession was unconstitutional: "No State upon its own mere motion can lawfully get out of the Union." As president, he was bound to enforce the Constitution in every state.

✔ **READING CHECK: Finding the Main Idea** What was Lincoln's position on preserving the Union? Lincoln wanted to preserve the Union but would not allow for the expansion of slavery.

TEACH OBJECTIVE 1

ALL LEVELS: Copy the following graphic organizer onto the chalkboard. Tell students that it lists the positions of President Lincoln and secessionists as well as Senator Crittenden's attempts to find common ground with both sides. Discuss the organizer with students. Then organize them into groups of three and have each student in the triad play the role of either Abraham Lincoln, John J. Crittenden, or a secessionist leader. *(Students should use their completed organizers to assist in stating their positions in their roles.)* Have members of each group stage a discussion in which the secessionist describes the government policy he or she would like to see in place; Crittenden describes and offers his compromise; and Lincoln summarizes his beliefs and positions.

English Language Learners, Cooperative Learning

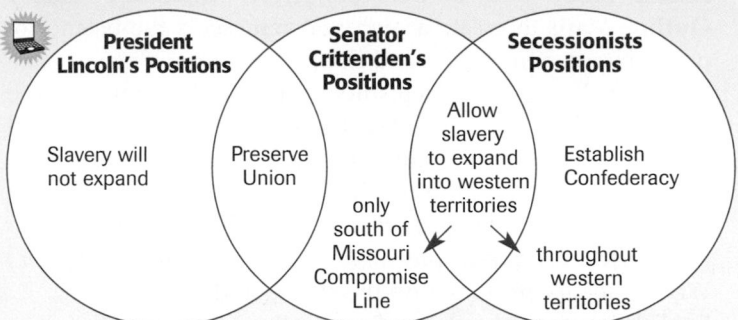

The Fall of Fort Sumter

Meeting little resistance, the Confederacy took over many federal forts, mints, and arsenals within its borders during the secession crisis. After Abraham Lincoln became president, one fort that was very important to the South—Fort Sumter—remained under federal control.

Fort Sumter lay in a strategic location in the harbor of Charleston, South Carolina. The South needed the fort in order to control access to this major port city. In early March 1861 the fort's commander, Major Robert Anderson, sent word to Washington that he was nearly out of supplies. Without reinforcements, Sumter would soon fall to the Confederates.

The North did not want to lose the fort. It would be a sign that Lincoln could not protect federal property in the seceded states. The president hesitated because most of the eight slave states that remained in the Union had threatened to secede if he used force against the Confederacy. Lincoln decided to resupply Fort Sumter, reasoning that if the Confederates fired on unarmed supply ships, then they, not the Union, would be the aggressors.

On April 6, 1861, Lincoln sent a messenger to alert South Carolina governor F. W. Pickens that supply ships were on their way, but that the ships carried only supplies, not troops or arms. Governor Pickens relayed the message to General P. G. T. Beauregard, the local Confederate military commander. Beauregard then ordered the federal troops to evacuate the fort. Major Anderson refused.

At 4:30 A.M. on April 12 the Confederate forces opened fire on Fort Sumter. Abner Doubleday, Anderson's second in command, described the scene within the fort.

INTERPRETING THE VISUAL RECORD

Fortifications. The Confederate attack on Fort Sumter marked the beginning of the Civil War. *What does the fort's location suggest about its importance?*

History Makers Speak

"Showers of balls . . . and shells . . . poured into the fort. . . . When the immense mortar shells, after sailing high in the air, came down in a vertical direction and buried themselves in the parade ground, their explosion shook the fort like an earthquake."

—Abner Doubleday, quoted in *Voices of the Civil War,* by Richard Wheeler

For 34 hours the Confederates bombarded Sumter. Finally, with much of the fort ablaze and their ammunition running low, Anderson and his men formally surrendered on April 13.

On April 15 Lincoln publicly announced the existence of a rebellion "too powerful to be suppressed by the ordinary

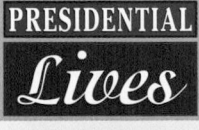 **PRESIDENTIAL Lives**

Abraham Lincoln

1809–1865
In Office 1861–1865

Superior leadership skills made Abraham Lincoln one of the nation's greatest presidents. The personal hardship of losing two children and the stresses of the Civil War took a toll, however. Lincoln endured periodic bouts of severe depression. He often used laughter to combat his depression. He believed laughter could "whistle down sadness," as a friend put it.

Throughout his life, Lincoln filled his everyday conversations with humor and homespun stories. "The Lord prefers common-looking people," he once said. "That is why he makes so many of them." On another occasion he commented about a book: "People who like this sort of thing will find this the sort of thing they like."

Even in personal defeat Lincoln put his famous dry wit to use. "I feel like the boy who stumped his toe," he said on losing the 1858 U.S. Senate race to Stephen Douglas. "I am too big to cry and too badly hurt to laugh."

CONSTITUTIONAL HERITAGE

Fort Sumter and the Civil War's First Casualties.
While no one on either side was killed or seriously wounded during the fighting at Fort Sumter, the conflict between the North and the South did not remain bloodless for long. Under the terms of his surrender, Major Anderson—who had been an instructor and friend of General Beauregard years earlier at West Point—was allowed to direct a 100-gun salute to the U.S. flag at Fort Sumter before evacuating the fort and returning to the North on a nearby steamship. During the salute, Private Daniel Hough's gun exploded, killing him instantly and wounding five other soldiers. Hough and his companions are now recognized as the first casualties of the Civil War.

ACTIVITY: Ask students to imagine that they are editors for a major northern newspaper in 1862. Then have them write a short editorial that discusses the importance of Fort Sumter's recent surrender.

VISUAL RECORD ANSWER
Students might mention that the fort is located in a harbor, which provides easy access to the city.

Technology Resources
American Music Selection 13: "All Quiet Along the Potomac"

LEVEL 1: Have students study the map on this page. Pair students and have each pair use Outline Map 13, Union and Confederacy, from **American History Outline Maps** to create a map that represents the balance of power between the Union and Confederacy immediately before the fall of Fort Sumter. Tell students to use different colors to shade in Union states, Confederate states, and territories. Call on volunteers to pose questions to the class on how Fort Sumter's fall affected the relationship between the Union and the Confederacy. (*Students should mention that after the fort's fall, Lincoln considered the South to be in a state of rebellion.*) Write students' responses on the chalkboard.

English Language Learners, Cooperative Learning

Teacher to Teacher

Doug Odom of El Dorado, Kansas, suggested the following activity: Tell students to imagine that Confederate forces have just captured Fort Sumter. Organize students into small groups. Have each group write a lead news story with a headline on the fall of Fort Sumter. Groups may assume the perspective of either a southern newspaper or a northern newspaper. Display students' articles around the classroom.

CITIZENSHIP

The Response to Lincoln's Call to Arms.
President Lincoln's call for 75,000 three-month recruits on April 15, 1862, was met with considerable enthusiasm. More than 90,000 quickly volunteered, creating temporary food and housing shortages at many army recruitment centers. Such problems, however, did little to discourage most of the new soldiers. One observer described the prevailing attitude as "one . . . of patriotic exultation, when everyone seems willing to sacrifice everything for a common cause."

CRITICAL THINKING Why might Lincoln's call to arms have been met with enthusiasm?

ANSWER: Students might say that young men volunteered for the Union army because they believed in preserving the Union, disapproved of slavery, or craved adventure.

The American Nation
VIDEO PROGRAM

Building an Army; Teacher's Guide, pp. 57–62

Search 00600, Play to 08592
Videodisc 1, Side B

Play   Pause

See Teacher's Guide for Spanish barcode.

The women featured on this magazine cover are filling cartridges at a federal arsenal in Watertown, Massachusetts.

course of judicial proceedings." He called for the states to provide 75,000 soldiers to put down the uprising. The recruits were to serve for just three months.

Choosing Sides

President Lincoln's fear of losing more states to the Confederacy quickly became a reality. Four more southern states—Arkansas, North Carolina, Tennessee, and Virginia—responded to the president's call for troops by seceding. The Confederates named Richmond, Virginia, as their capital.

Four other slave states—Delaware, Kentucky, Maryland, and Missouri—remained within the Union. Secession was never a serious threat in Delaware, where there were few slaves and most of the population sympathized more with the North than with the South. Kentucky, Maryland, and Missouri, on the other hand, were sharply divided over the issue of secession. The governors of both Missouri and Kentucky sympathized with the Confederacy, but neither state voted to secede. Lincoln kept Maryland in the Union by securing the state with federal troops. Maryland's secession would have meant losing the Union capital. Maryland surrounded Washington on three sides with already-seceded Virginia on the other side.

The mountainous counties of northwestern Virginia remained loyal to the Union as well. People living there held few slaves and had long resented the rich planter elite of the lowlands. They set up their own state government, and in 1863 the state was admitted to the Union as West Virginia. Although West Virginia had few slaves, slavery initially remained legal there.

The Upper South's white population remained divided over the issue of secession. Sections of several of these states raised Union regiments to fight the Confederacy. Some families were torn apart as members fought for opposing sides in the war.

One son of Kentucky senator John Crittenden became a Union general, and another became a Confederate general. President Lincoln's wife, Mary Todd, a southerner by birth, had four brothers and three brothers-in-law fighting in the Confederate army.

✔ **READING CHECK:**
Evaluating What was the significance of the fall of Fort Sumter? led Lincoln to call for troops and led four more southern states to secede

---

The Union and Confederacy in 1861

Interpreting Maps Southerners argued that the Constitution, as a compact among sovereign states, did not prohibit the states from seceding.

❓ PLACES AND REGIONS What did the seceding southern states have in common with Missouri, Kentucky, Maryland, and Delaware?

| Union states | Confederate states | West Virginia (separated from Virginia in 1861 and joined the Union in 1863) |
| Border states (part of the Union) | Territories | |

LEVELS 2 AND 3: Tell students to imagine that they are the captains of merchant ships that make frequent stops at Charleston, South Carolina, near Fort Sumter. In their roles as politically neutral traders, have them write three short letters to their ships' owners updating them on events and changes in South Carolina from 1860 to 1861. The first letter should cover rising tensions over Fort Sumter and its strategic importance; the second letter should describe the fall of Fort Sumter; and the third letter should evaluate the implications of its fall for the relationship between the Union and the Confederacy. *(See the Level 1 lesson for the correct strategic importance of Fort Sumter and the effect of the fort's fall on the relationship between the Union and the Confederacy.)* Students may wish to include their letters in their portfolios.

TEACH OBJECTIVE 3

LEVEL 1: Have students work in pairs to create a list of the Union's strengths. *(Students should mention larger population, greater industrial resources, more railroad lines, and retained U.S. Navy.)* Have each pair also compile a list of the Confederacy's strengths. *(Students should mention that Confederates had to fight a defensive war and had excellent military leaders.)* After pairs have completed their lists, ask volunteers to write their list on the chalkboard. Have other students supply any missing information. Conclude by leading a classroom discussion of the advantages of each side.
English Language Learners, Cooperative Learning

Comparing North and South

The war that loomed after the fall of Fort Sumter appeared to be a mismatch. In many respects the North enjoyed military superiority over the South. The advantages held by the South were so important, however, that many objective observers expected a quick southern victory.

Northern advantages. With more than 22 million residents, the North had a huge population advantage. The South's population totaled slightly more than 9 million, some 3.5 million of whom were slaves. As a result, the South had a much smaller pool of available soldiers.

The North also enjoyed an economic advantage. When the Civil War began, the North controlled more than 85 percent of the nation's industry and significant material resources. These advantages enabled the North to produce military supplies and replace lost or damaged equipment more rapidly than the Confederacy. Most southern wealth was in land and slaves.

In addition, since most of the nation's railroad lines were located in the Northeast and the Midwest, the Union could move troops and supplies with ease. Southern routes, in contrast, were short, with few connecting lines between major cities. Furthermore, because the North manufactured most of the nation's railroad equipment, the Confederacy found itself ill-prepared to replace broken or worn-out parts and equipment during the war.

Most of the U.S. Navy remained loyal to the Union, including southern naval officers David Farragut and Percival Drayton. With no ships and little naval expertise to draw upon, the South was forced to build its navy from scratch.

Southern advantages. The South had two important advantages over the North. The Confederacy had only to fight a defensive war, protecting its territory until the Union tired of the struggle. In contrast, the Union needed to conquer an area of about 750,000 square miles. This was twice the size of the original thirteen colonies. The South also had excellent military leadership. In fact, most southern victories would result from the battle strategies of skillful Confederate officers.

Among the ablest of southern military leaders was **Robert E. Lee**, who was born into a prominent Virginia family in 1807. His father was Henry "Light-Horse Harry" Lee, a Revolutionary War hero. Robert excelled as a student at the U.S. Military Academy at West Point. After graduating in 1829, he served first in the Army Corps of Engineers and then in the cavalry. In 1831 Lee married Mary Custis, great-granddaughter of Martha Washington and the heir to extensive landholdings in northern Virginia.

Robert E. Lee

Lee first tested his military abilities during the Mexican War of 1846. He took part in the capture of Veracruz, serving as a captain under General Winfield Scott.

Resources of the North and South in 1861

Resources	North 🇺🇸	South
Total population	22,000,000	9,000,000*
Bank deposits	$189,000,000	$47,000,000
Railroad mileage	20,000 miles	9,000 miles
Number of factories	100,500	20,600

*Southern population includes 3,500,000 slaves
Sources: *American Heritage Picture History of the Civil War; Encyclopedia of American History*

Interpreting Charts At the beginning of the Civil War, the North's abundant resources gave it a military advantage over the South.

❓ **Skills Assessment** Which resource do you think had the greatest influence on the outcome of the Civil War?

Research on the R⊙M

Free Find:
Robert E. Lee
After reading about Robert E. Lee on the **Holt Researcher CD–ROM**, write an obituary describing his accomplishments and his reasons for fighting for the Confederacy.

LEVELS 2 AND 3: Organize students into groups of four. Instruct half of the groups to act as Union military strategists and the other half as Confederate military strategists. Have each group draw up a list of its own strengths and weaknesses. (See the Level 1 answers for each side's strengths.) Then have each group speculate on how it can (1) best utilize its strengths and compensate for its weaknesses and (2) how it can defend against its opponent's strengths and take advantage of any weaknesses. Have each group put its recommendations in a strategy position paper and choose a spokesperson to read it to the class. **Cooperative Learning**

HOMEWORK *Have each student write a song, poem, or journal entry about the beginning of the Civil War from the point of view of a person who has family members fighting on both sides of the conflict.*

NOTE: To help students make meaningful connections between events in U.S. history and those in their own hometown, use the Chapter 3 **Hands-On History Activity**, Photography: Seeing Your Local History.

HISTORY MAKERS SPEAK

A writer for the London *Times* in *Battle Cry of Freedom*

A Daunting Military Challenge for the North.
During the opening stages of the Civil War, many observers thought that the Union army would be unable to conquer the entire Confederacy. The remarks of a writer for the London *Times* typified this opinion: "It is one thing to drive the rebels from the south bank of the Potomac, or even to occupy Richmond, but another to reduce and hold in permanent subjection a tract of country nearly as large as Russia in Europe. . . . No war of independence was ever terminated unsuccessfully except where the disparity of force was far greater than it is in this case."

CRITICAL THINKING How might the characterization of the Civil War as a "war of independence" have differed from Abraham Lincoln's view of the Civil War?

ANSWER: Students might suggest that Abraham Lincoln viewed the Civil War as a war to preserve the Union or a war to put down a rebellion.

PRIMARY SOURCE ANSWER

Answers will vary. Students might suggest that he will fight for the South because of his relatives there.

This sword belonged to General Robert E. Lee.

Analyzing Primary Sources

Identifying Points of View
Why did Lee resign from the U.S. Army? because he could not fight against his own relatives and state

Lee's skill and bravery impressed his commander and earned him a promotion. After working as superintendent of West Point from 1852 to 1855, Lee served briefly in Texas and eventually moved to Arlington, Virginia. In 1859 he led the federal troops that captured abolitionist John Brown at Harpers Ferry.

As southern states began to secede from the Union, General Scott advised President Lincoln to ask Lee to command the Union forces. Faced with a difficult choice between country and state, Lee regretfully declined and resigned his commission. Scott told him sadly, "You have made the greatest mistake of your life, but I feared it would be so." Lee opposed slavery and secession, but he refused to fight against Virginia. Lee wrote a letter to his sister.

History Makers Speak **❝With all my devotion to the Union and the feeling of loyalty and duty of an American citizen, I have not been able to make up my mind to raise my hand against my relatives, my children, my home. I have therefore resigned my commission in the Army, and save [except] in defense of my native State—with the sincere hope that my poor services may never be needed—I hope I may never be called on to draw my sword.❞**

—Robert E. Lee, letter to his sister, April 20, 1861

The armies. Lee eventually led the South's army. Both sides quickly built up their military strength. By the end of 1861 the Union had more than 527,000 soldiers and the Confederacy slightly more than 258,000. Most of these soldiers were between the ages of 18 and 29, with drummer boys as young as 9 years old.

Estimates of how many men fought in the war vary because many men re-enlisted after their initial commissions expired. The U.S. government placed the official wartime enlistment in the Union army at 2,672,341, with another 105,963 men enlisted in the navy or marines. According to U.S. government statistics, some 3,530 American Indians and some 180,000 African Americans served in the Union army. Noncommissioned African American officers numbered nearly 7,000. About 100 African Americans were commissioned officers.

Historians estimate that some 750,000 men enlisted in the Confederate army. This figure included about 5,500 Cherokee, Creek, Chickasaw, and Choctaw. These American Indians included many slaveholders lured by the promise of an all-Indian state following the war. Some Mexican Americans from New Mexico and Texas fought during the war. Most supported the Union.

PRIMARY SOURCE

Views of the Civil War

When the Civil War began, many Americans felt caught in the middle. Many had relatives in the North and the South. The family of Theodore Upson, an Indiana farm boy, faced this situation. **On which side do you think Upson would fight?**

❝Father and I were husking out some corn. . . . When William Cory came across the field (he had been down after the mail), he was excited and said, 'Jonathan, the Rebs have fired upon and taken Fort Sumter.' Father got white and couldn't say a word. . . .

I went in to dinner. Mother said, 'What is the matter with Father?' He had gone right upstairs. I told her what we had heard. She went to him. After a while, they came down. Father looked ten years older.

We sat down to the table. Grandma wanted to know what was the trouble. Father told her, and she began to cry. 'Oh my poor children in the South! Now they will suffer! . . .'

'They can come here and stay,' said Father.

'No, they will not do that. There is their home. There they will stay. Oh, to think I should have lived to see the day when brother should rise against brother.'❞

✔ **READING CHECK: Comparing** What advantages did the North and the South possess in 1861? The North had more people and money, and better transportation. The South had the easier strategy and superior military leadership.

TEACH OBJECTIVE 4

LEVEL 1: Pair students and have each pair create flash cards that identify significant people and events associated with the First Battle of Bull Run. *(Suggestions for side 1 and side 2 of the flash cards include: Union general—Irvin McDowell; Confederate general—Joseph E. Johnston; Confederate general—Thomas "Stonewall" Jackson; location of the battle—Manassas Junction (Virginia); result of the battle—Confederate victory; psychological consequences of battle—Union shock, Confederate overconfidence.)* When students have completed their flash cards, have them quiz each other using the flash cards. **English Language Learners, Cooperative Learning**

LEVELS 2 AND 3: Have students explain why the First Battle of Bull Run represented a psychological victory as well as a military victory for the Confederacy. *(Students should mention that it gave the Confederacy great confidence while it shocked and demoralized the Union forces.)* Then ask each student to write a one-page scenario describing whether he or she thinks the course of the war might have been different if the Union had won the First Battle of Bull Run. Tell students to explain and justify their thoughts with examples and logical arguments. Ask volunteers to share their scenarios with the class.

Skill-Building Strategies

Recognizing Fallacies in Reasoning

In order to evaluate historical arguments and ideas, students must be able to recognize fallacies in reasoning. A *fallacy* is a false or mistaken idea. When included in a sequence of reasoning, a fallacy may result in an unsound argument or unsupported conclusion.

Most fallacies in reasoning fall into several basic categories. *Single cause* means identifying one cause for an event while ignoring other causes. History is complex, and very few historical events resulted from just one cause. *Coincidence as cause* means attributing the cause of one event to another event simply because they occurred at or near the same time. *Irrelevant evidence* means an argument is based on information to which it is not logically related.

How to Recognize Fallacies in Reasoning

1. **Identify the main ideas.** As you read a historical source, identify its main ideas and supporting details. Each time you identify a main idea, make a preliminary judgment of its soundness.
2. **Identify cause and effect.** Take note of cause-and-effect relationships that are mentioned explicitly and that you can infer from the source. Make sure to check for complex connections such as multiple causes and long-term effects.
3. **Evaluate the reasoning.** After you finish reading the source, assess the quality of its historical reasoning. Ask yourself the following questions: Are the arguments in this source logical? Are the cause-and-effect relationships fully proven? Do the conclusions follow from the information provided?

Applying the Skill

Examine the following statement and identify the fallacy in its reasoning.

> "The Civil War was fought over the issue of a state's right to make its own laws. If northerners had not wanted to make slavery illegal in the South, the war would not have occurred."

Practicing the Skill

Answer the following questions.
1. What type of fallacy in reasoning does the statement contain?
2. How might providing more historical context of the Civil War help correct this reasoning error?

The First Battle of Bull Run

General Winfield Scott believed the new Union troops needed several months of training. Likewise, a Confederate officer reported his men to be so lacking in "discipline and instruction" that it would be "difficult to use them in the field." Despite these reservations, President Lincoln ordered General Irvin McDowell and some 35,000 barely trained troops to Richmond, Virginia, in mid-July 1861.

Fighting at Manassas. General McDowell's forces never reached Richmond. On July 21, 1861, some 35,000 Confederates met the Union troops near Manassas (muh-NAS-uhs) Junction, a railroad crossing about 30 miles outside Washington. Led by General **Joseph E. Johnston,** the Confederates dug in on high ground behind a creek called Bull Run. Northerners would call the fighting that followed the **First Battle of Bull Run.** Southerners called it the Battle of Manassas.

At first the battle went in the Union's favor. The left flank of the Confederate line came close to cracking. Confederate general **Thomas "Stonewall" Jackson** and his men stopped the Union assault, however. Jackson's troops raced toward the Union line, filling the air with a terrifying scream: "Woh—who—ey! Who—ey!"

INTERPRETING THE VISUAL RECORD

Union drums. Union troops carried drums like this one. *Why do you think it bears the eagle symbol of the federal government?*

SKILL-BUILDING STRATEGIES ANSWERS
Practicing the Skill
1. single cause

2. Students might suggest that information about the controversy over the expansion of slavery, the secession process, and proposed compromises would help correct the reasoning error.

VISUAL RECORD ANSWER

to show that the Union was fighting for the preservation of the Union

---

VISUAL RECORD ANSWER

(for p. 102)

Students might suggest that it depicts how close the troops were as they fought.

SECTION
REVIEW 1 ANSWERS

1. **Identify**
   - Crittenden Compromise, p. 96
   - Robert E. Lee, p. 99
   - Joseph E. Johnston, p. 101
   - First Battle of Bull Run, p. 101
   - Thomas "Stonewall" Jackson, p. 101

REVIEW

Have students complete the **Section 1 Review** on p. 102.

ASSESS

Have students complete **Daily Quiz 3.1**. As **Alternative Assessment**, you may want to use the flash cards or one-page scenarios for the Battle of Bull Run in this section's lessons.

RETEACH

Have students complete **Main Idea Activity for English Language Learners and Special-Needs Students 3.1**. Have students work in pairs to write short summaries of each of the subsections of Section 1. Then group each pair with another

pair and ask the foursome to review each other's summaries, looking for key points that may have been missed.
English Language Learners, Cooperative Learning

EXTEND

Have each student create an illustrated time line of the events leading up to the first battle of the Civil War. Tell students to start their time lines in January 1861 with the inauguration of President Lincoln and end in July 1861 with the First Battle of Bull Run. Tell students to include 6 to 10 entries with an appropriate illustration for each one—they do not need exact dates for every entry. When students have finished their time lines, display them in the classroom. **Block Scheduling**

---

2. northern advantages—larger population, more industry and material resources, extensive railroad lines, retention of U.S. Navy; southern advantages—defensive strategy, vast territory, excellent military leadership

3a. It controlled access to the harbor of Charleston, South Carolina, and was a symbol of Union property in the seceded states. Its fall led Lincoln to declare the existence of a rebellion in the South and to call for soldiers to put down the rebellion; in turn, four more southern states seceded from the Union and joined the Confederacy.

b. Before—Lincoln agreed to part of the Crittendon Compromise; in his inaugural address in 1861, he insisted that secession was unconstitutional; after—he called for volunteer soldiers.

c. It contributed to the hasty and disorganized nature of the Union retreat.

4. Northerners who thought the Union would win the war quickly were frustrated by the defeat and the prospects of a longer war; southerners who hoped to defend their territory until the Union tired of the struggle were encouraged by the victory.

THE GRANGER COLLECTION, NEW YORK

INTERPRETING THE VISUAL RECORD

Bull Run. The fierce fighting and number of casualties at Bull Run surprised many Americans. *What realities of war does this painting depict?*

The eerie sound, which came to be known as the rebel yell, sent chills through the northern troops.

The Union soldiers fell back and headed for Washington. Union colonel Andrew Porter wrote about the retreat.

 History Makers Speak
❝Soon the slopes . . . were swarming with our retreating and disorganized forces, while riderless horses and artillery teams ran furiously through the flying crowd. All further efforts were futile. The words, gestures, and threats of our officers were thrown away upon men who had lost all presence of mind, and only longed for absence of body.❞

—Andrew Porter, quoted in *Voices of the Civil War*, by Richard Wheeler

The aftermath of southern victory. The events at Bull Run caused most people to realize that the war would last longer than a few months. As a result, each side began to seriously train its forces for battle and to plan strategy. Confederate president Jefferson Davis named Joseph E. Johnston to command the Army of Northern Virginia and chose Robert E. Lee as his military adviser. President Lincoln named General George B. McClellan to head the Union forces.

The most important consequences of the First Battle of Bull Run may have been psychological. The defeat shamed and shocked the North. Southern newspaper editorials proclaimed the Confederacy's superiority. Meanwhile, the Union army was becoming more determined.

✔ **READING CHECK: Drawing Conclusions** How did the First Battle of Bull Run affect the nation? The battle caused most people to realize that the war would not be short.

SECTION 1 REVIEW

1. Identify and explain:
Crittenden Compromise
Robert E. Lee
Joseph E. Johnston
First Battle of Bull Run
Thomas "Stonewall" Jackson

2. Comparing Copy the graphic organizer below. Use it to list the military advantages of the North and the South at the beginning of the war.

Northern Advantages	Southern Advantages

3. **Finding the Main Idea**
a. Why was Sumter an important fort, and how did its fall affect both the Union and the Confederacy?
b. What steps did Lincoln take to preserve the Union before and after the fighting at Fort Sumter?
c. How did soldiers' lack of training affect the First Battle of Bull Run?

4. **Writing and Critical Thinking**
Identifying Points of View Imagine that you are a parent of two sons fighting in the First Battle of Bull Run. One son is in the Union army, and the other in the Confederate army. Write a diary entry expressing your feelings about the situation.
Consider:
• northern and southern attitudes toward the war before the battle
• northern and southern reactions after the battle

go. hrw .com Homework Practice Online
keyword: SE3 HP3

SECTION ②

After completing Section 2, students should be able to:

OBJECTIVE 1 Contrast the military strategies of the North and South.

OBJECTIVE 2 Describe the daily hardships soldiers faced.

OBJECTIVE 3 Report on what life was like on the home front during the war.

OBJECTIVE 4 Explain how civilians contributed to the war effort.

OBJECTIVE 5 Discuss why some people opposed the war.

🔊 LET'S GET STARTED!

Write the following scenario on the chalkboard and ask students to respond to it in writing as they enter the classroom. *You are a soldier in the Union army. The war has been going on now for more than three years, with no end in sight. How do you get through each day?* After students have completed their responses, tell them that in Section 2 they will learn about life during the Civil War.

SECTION ②

READ TO DISCOVER

1. How did the military strategies of the North and South differ?
2. What daily hardships did soldiers face?
3. What was life like on the home front during the war?
4. How did civilians contribute to the war effort?
5. Why did some people oppose the war?

DEFINE

conscription
habeas corpus

IDENTIFY

Anaconda Plan
Mary Boykin Chesnut
Elizabeth Blackwell
U.S. Sanitary Commission
Clara Barton
Sally Louisa Tompkins
Copperheads

WHY IT MATTERS TODAY

During the Civil War, soldiers on both sides faced difficulties. Use **CNNfyi.com** or other **current events** sources to find out what challenges U.S. soldiers face today. Record your findings in your journal.

CNNfyi.com

The North and South Face Off

EYEWITNESSES TO History *"We are going to kill the last Yankee before [spring] if there is any fight in them still. I believe that J. D. Walker's Brigade can whip 25,000 Yankees."*

—An Alabama soldier, quoted in *Battle Cry of Freedom*, by James M. McPherson

This letter reveals the high spirits that marked the beginning of the war between the North and South. After joining the army, one volunteer from New York wrote his family, "I and the rest of the boys are in fine spirits . . . feeling like larks." People in both the North and the South had great confidence that their side would quickly win the war. In the North, author James Russell Lowell used a fictional character, Hosea Biglow, to describe this widespread optimism. Biglow recalled the days after Fort Sumter fell: "I hoped to see things settled 'fore this fall. The Rebbles licked, Jeff Davis hanged, an' all."

A Union soldier (top) and a Confederate soldier (bottom)

Strategies of War

From the beginning of the war, the North's primary goal was to restore the Union. To accomplish this goal, Lincoln and his military advisers adopted a three-part strategy. They sought first to capture Richmond, the Confederate capital; second, to gain control of the Mississippi River; and third, to institute a naval blockade of the South. The naval blockade was nicknamed the **Anaconda Plan** because it was designed to slowly squeeze the life out of the South like an anaconda snake. It was important because the South depended on foreign markets to sell its cotton and to buy supplies.

The North devised its battle strategy based on the region's geography. Since the Confederacy stretched from Virginia to Texas, the Appalachian Mountains divided most of the action in the Civil War into two arenas: the eastern theater and the western theater. The eastern theater lay east of the Appalachians. The western theater lay between these mountains and the Mississippi River. Control of the Mississippi River would enable the North to penetrate deep into the South. It would also prevent the Confederacy from using the waterway to resupply its forces.

While the North's strategy depended on dividing the South geographically, the South planned to capture Washington and invade the North. Southern leaders hoped for a successful offensive strike northward through the Shenandoah Valley into Maryland and Pennsylvania. They hoped this would shatter northern morale, disrupt Union communications, win European support, and bring the war to a speedy end.

Confederate leaders knew that winning the support of France or Great Britain was crucial to a victory for the South. Because the French and British economies depended heavily on cotton, the Confederacy had confidence that one of the nations would respond to the naval blockade by coming to the South's aid.

SECTION ② RESOURCES

REPRODUCIBLE

▶ Guided Reading Strategy 3.2
▶ Literature Reading 3: The Reality of War
▶ Biography Reading 3: Clara Barton

TECHNOLOGY

▶ One-Stop Planner, Lesson 3.2
▶ Everyday Life in America Transparency 12: Photograph of Civil War Casualties
▶ **CNN** Presents America: Beginnings to 1914 Segment: Clara Barton and the Legacy of War
▶ Holt Researcher: American History CD–ROM
▶ Homework Practice Online

REINFORCEMENT, REVIEW, AND ASSESSMENT

▶ Section 2 Review, p. 109
▶ Daily Quiz 3.2
▶ Main Idea Activity 3.2
▶ English Audio Summary 3.2
▶ Spanish Audio Summary 3.2

TEACH OBJECTIVE 1

LEVEL 1: Pair students and tell them to imagine that they are high-level military advisers for the Union and the Confederacy. In each pair, one student should summarize one side's general battle strategies as a bulleted list of statements beginning with, "We will. . . ." The other student should summarize the other side's general battle strategies. (*Example: "We will capture Richmond, the Confederate capital.")* (*Students should mention that Union strategies included: capturing Richmond, gaining control of the Mississippi River, naval blockade of the South; Confederate strategies: capturing Washington, invading the North, and winning a foreign ally.)* Ask volunteers to share their list of statements with the class.
English Language Learners, Cooperative Learning

LEVELS 2 AND 3: Have students complete the Level 1 activity. Then have each student write a two-to-three-paragraph evaluation of each side's strategy. Tell students to ask themselves the following questions to help in writing their evaluations: *How strong is the strategy overall? Does it have any obvious weaknesses? How might leaders on each side work to ensure their plan's success? What could they use as a backup plan if their initial strategies fail?* Ask volunteers to read their evaluations to the class.

The South's strategy failed, however. Neither France nor Britain proved dependent on Confederate cotton. French and British mill owners had stockpiled cotton before Fort Sumter's fall. Once these reserves ran out, the mill owners turned to Egypt and India for new supplies. Additionally, French emperor Napoléon III's preoccupation with events in Mexico distracted him from the conflict between the Union and the Confederacy. With Napoléon's blessing, Mexico's ruling elite made the archduke of Austria, Maximilian, emperor in 1864. When widespread opposition to Maximilian broke out, Napoléon ordered French troops in Mexico to put down the resistance. In part because he did not want to fight two wars at the same time, Napoléon decided not to aid the Confederacy. The South's failure to secure French help meant that southerners had limited resources at their disposal.

✔ **READING CHECK: Making Predictions** What mistake did the South make in assessing its war resources? The South assumed that it would receive foreign aid from nations such as Britain and France.

The Military Experience

While high-level leaders planned battle strategies, the officers under their command attempted to train troops to carry out these strategies. Young recruits in both the Union and Confederate ranks were generally enthusiastic when they first enlisted. Most of these newly recruited soldiers had little experience with military life, however.

Both sides faced shortages of clothing, food, and even rifles. At the beginning of the war, most troops did not even have standard uniforms. Some simply wore their own clothes from home. Eventually, each side adopted a distinguishing uniform. The Union chose blue, and the Confederacy gray. However, many troops, particularly Confederates, lacked good shoes and warm coats throughout the war.

This persistent lack of provisions, coupled with unsanitary conditions in most field camps, led to deadly problems of disease. What little food existed in the camps often was spoiled. Describing the old meat served to his company, one Confederate soldier wrote, "A decent dog would have turned up his nose at it, but a hungry man will eat almost anything."

Thousands of soldiers died from illnesses such as influenza, pneumonia, and typhoid. Doctors and nurses could do little to help, since most hospitals had little in the way of medical provisions. As a result, some soldiers had to endure surgery without pain-killing anesthetics. Many with seemingly minor injuries died from infected wounds. In fact, disease, infection, and malnutrition took the lives of more than 65 percent of the soldiers who died during the war.

Nowhere were conditions worse than in the filthy, overcrowded prisoner-of-war camps in the North and South. One nun who worked as a nurse during the war commented, "It is hard to be sick, but to be a sick prisoner of war is indeed a heavy cross [burden]."

INTERPRETING THE VISUAL RECORD

Camp life. Union soldiers line up outside their tents at a camp in Virginia. *Based on this image, how would you describe camp life?*

LEVEL 1: Pair students and tell them to imagine that it is 1870—five years after the end of the Civil War. Have one student in each pair play the role of a veteran Union soldier describing his experiences during the war, and have the other student interview the soldier to record an oral history by taking notes. Then have students switch roles, but this time the veteran will be a former Confederate soldier. *(Students should mention that common experiences included unsanitary conditions, disease, and shortages of food, clothing, and rifles. Confederate soldiers often lacked good shoes and warm coats.)* Have students take turns sharing their interviews by summarizing their partners' oral histories for the class.
English Language Learners, Cooperative Learning

LEVELS 2 AND 3: Tell students to imagine that they have been hired as consultants by a modern film production company making a movie about the Civil War. They need to supply the filmmakers with detailed information about Union and Confederate soldiers' daily lives. Have each student prepare a short report covering clothing, food, sanitation, shelter, morale, pastimes, and so on. *(See the Level 1 lesson for the correct information.)* Ask volunteers to share their reports with the class.

Union prisoners held at Andersonville, a Confederate camp located in southwestern Georgia, endured the worst conditions, with no shelter and little food. At times, prisoners at Andersonville died at a rate of about 100 per day. In some camps more than 25 percent of the prisoners died before the end of the war.

In addition to their difficult living conditions, many soldiers suffered from extreme boredom, homesickness, and loneliness. Some men deserted, but most attempted to cope with their situation. Soldiers played cards, attended prayer meetings, sang, wrote letters home, or engaged in other recreational activities.

✔ **READING CHECK: Categorizing** What hardships did soldiers experience? They seldom had enough food or good clothing. They suffered from disease, malnutrition, boredom, and homesickness.

AMERICAN ARTS

Mathew Brady's Photographs

The carving on Mathew Brady's tombstone reads "renowned photographer of the Civil War." Before the Civil War began, Brady was already well known for his photographic portraits of wealthy and famous Americans. When the war broke out in 1861, he set a goal of recording all the "prominent incidents of the conflict."

Because he had lost much of his eyesight, Brady himself took very few of the war photographs that were displayed in his galleries. Nonetheless, he was one of the first photographers to understand the dramatic impact that the art form could have on society. With this in mind, Brady financed, supervised, and organized groups of photographers to accompany Union troops. They created a pictorial history of the people and events of the war. Brady's photographers traveled to the battlefields in horse-drawn wagons that doubled as portable darkrooms, allowing photographs to be developed on location.

The long exposures required for these early photographs prevented photographers from recording any scenes involving movement. While many photographers made portraits of soldiers and took pictures of equipment, fortifications, prisons, and hospitals, the most dramatic photographs are those of soldiers lying dead on battlefields. These images had a powerful effect on their audience. "If he has not brought bodies and laid them in our dooryards and along our streets, he has done something very like it," wrote the *New York Times* of one Brady exhibit.

Mathew Brady's Civil War photographs often shocked civilians by showing the horrors of the battlefield.

Understanding the Arts

1. What prevented Civil War photographers from recording movement in their photographs?
2. What is unusual about the bodies in the photograph above?

HISTORY MAKERS SPEAK

Sergeant James T. Wells in *Soldiers Blue and Gray*

Rations in a Union Prisoner-of-War Camp.
Confederate soldier James T. Wells described the rations at the prisoner-of-war camp where he was held: "For breakfast, half-pint coffee, or, rather, slop water; for dinner; half-pint greasy water (called soup for etiquette), also a small piece of meat, perhaps three or four ounces. For bread . . . per day; this you could press together in your hand and take at a mouthful. . . . The writer has known large, stout men to lay in their tents at night and cry like little babies from hunger."

CRITICAL THINKING How might Wells's opinion of the conditions at prisoner-of-war camps have been biased?

ANSWER: Answers will vary. Students might suggest that Wells is exaggerating how bad the conditions were because he hated the Union.

AMERICAN ARTS ANSWERS

1. the long exposures required
2. They are lined up in a neat row.

TEACH OBJECTIVES 3 AND 4

LEVEL 1: Pair students and ask each pair to create two illustrations that show the roles and responsibilities of civilians on the home front or battlefield during the Civil War. *(Students might draw pictures of women working in factories, teaching former slaves, making uniforms for soldiers, nursing wounded soldiers, or of women and boys cultivating crops, civilians organizing patriotic events, and so on.)* After students have finished their illustrations, ask each pair to write captions for them. Display students' work in the classroom.
English Language Learners, Cooperative Learning

LEVEL 2: Tell students to imagine that they are civilians on the Union or Confederate home front or battlefield during the Civil War. Have each student write a series of five diary entries over the course of two or three years in which he or she talks about changing living conditions, activities in support of the war, and his or her emotions. *(Tell students to concentrate on their daily life, their contributions to the war effort, and their attitudes about the war itself.)* Ask volunteers to share one or two of their entries with the class.

The Home Front

Mobilization for the war also had a profound effect on the Americans who stayed home during the conflict. Women and those men who were too young, too old, or physically unable to fight fulfilled important responsibilities on the home front.

The North. In the North, women replaced the male factory workers and farmers who left for the battlefields. The Union's need for military supplies opened up more than 100,000 jobs for women in arsenals, factories, and sewing rooms. The nearly 450 women working as clerks in the Treasury Department served as the government's first female office workers. Other women worked as bankers, morticians, saloon keepers, and steamboat captains during the war. Women and boys took responsibility for growing food during the war. They produced bumper crops with the help of new farm equipment such as the McCormick reaper. The *Detroit Free Press* reported in 1864 that women had grown much of the corn produced in Michigan that year.

Countless civilians also participated in volunteer groups that raised money for the Union cause or provided relief services for soldiers and their families. Ladies Aid Societies made bandages, bedclothes, and shirts for soldiers. The American Freedman's Aid Commission provided hundreds of female schoolteachers to educate former slaves. State and local governments established homes for injured soldiers and for children of soldiers who died in the war.

Research on the ROM

Free Find:
Mary Boykin Chesnut

After reading about Mary Boykin Chesnut on the **Holt Researcher CD–ROM**, create several fictional journal entries describing some of the events of the Civil War.

The South. The diary of southerner **Mary Boykin Chesnut** provides a glimpse of life on the home front during the war. The daughter of Mary and Stephen Miller, Mary Boykin was born in 1823 near Columbia, South Carolina. She grew up in a large and wealthy extended family that had lived in South Carolina since the 1750s. Mary followed her grandmother around like "her shadow." She learned how to manage the many different components of a plantation.

BIOGRAPHY

Mary Boykin Chesnut

At the age of 17, after receiving a private education, Mary wed James Chesnut, heir to a nearby plantation. James Chesnut became an active politician. He served as a U.S. senator and later held several different positions in the Confederate and South Carolina governments. Mary Chesnut grew somewhat bored by plantation life. She found an outlet for her energetic personality in her passionate support of the Confederacy after war broke out. Living in Richmond, Virginia, during part of the war, she played an important role in political and military circles. She often wrote of her frustration, however, with what she saw as the incompetence of southern leaders. "Oh if I could put some of my reckless spirit into these . . . cautious lazy men!"

As the war progressed, Chesnut experienced pain and grief at the death of friends and family, as well as fear for the South's prospects. "With horror and amazement" she watched her world, "the only world we cared for, literally kicked to pieces." Chesnut eased the difficulty of her postwar life by preparing her diary for publication. Between 1881 and 1884 she rewrote her diary from the notes and entries she made in the journal she kept during the war. Before the work was published, however, she died of heart failure in 1886 at the age of 63. Her diary was finally published in 1905.

This writing desk belonged to Mary Chesnut.

Have each student write a fictional short story about life on the home front and civilian contributions to the war effort during the Civil War. *(See the Level 1 lesson for the correct contributions.)* Encourage students to come up with creative and interesting stories, but remind them to stay within the historical context. When students have completed rough drafts of their stories, have them exchange papers with a classmate to peer-edit each other's work. Give students time to write their final drafts and then ask volunteers to summarize their stories for the class. **Cooperative Learning**

 HOMEWORK *Have each student make a broadside or sign protesting the continuation of the Civil War from a southern point of view.*

TEACH OBJECTIVE 5

 LEVEL 1: Copy the organizer located on the next page onto the chalkboard. Tell students it relates to general and specific reasons why northerners and southerners opposed the Civil War. Have students copy the organizer into their notes. Discuss the graphic organizer with students. Then have each student use information from the completed graphic organizers to write six newspaper headlines—three about southern opposition and three about northern opposition to the war. Have volunteers share their headlines with the class. **English Language Learners**

Southerners like Chesnut supported the war effort with a series of patriotic events. At parades and barbecues, public figures urged young men to join the army, and wealthy members of society pledged money to buy arms and uniforms. Raffles and auctions raised much-needed funds for the Confederacy.

By 1862 the harsh effects of the blockade and providing for the war effort set in. The short supply of basic necessities such as shoes, clothing, and farm equipment caused prices to rise. The inability to obtain medicines caused untold suffering. City residents were hardest hit by the war. Many families were forced to live in single rooms, using one fireplace for both heat and cooking. Food shortages forced people to live on beans, boiled potatoes, and corn fritters. Their social occasions became "starvation parties," with only water served for refreshment.

✔ **READING CHECK: Contrasting** What was life like on the northern and southern home fronts? Northern women worked in factories and on farms. They also raised money. Southern women raised money but later concentrated on survival.

Civilian Aid on the Battlefield

In addition to their roles on the home front, many civilians—women in particular—actively aided the military. Some women even dressed like men so that they could fight. Cuban-born Loreta Janeta Velázquez (vay-LAHS-kays) disguised herself as a man and enlisted in the Confederate army. When she was found out and discharged, she became a spy for the South. Other women also served as spies. Rose O'Neal Greenhow was imprisoned for supplying information to the Confederacy. Mary Elizabeth Bowser, a maid who worked in Confederate president Jefferson Davis's home, and abolitionist Harriet Tubman supplied information to the Union from behind enemy lines.

Many other women served the war effort in medical roles. Catholic nuns were among the most important female volunteers for medical duty. They sometimes transformed their convents into emergency hospitals. Many of these "nuns of the battlefield" were Irish or German immigrants. They remained neutral and treated all victims of the war, becoming the only group allowed to move freely between Union and Confederate lines.

In the North, **Elizabeth Blackwell**—the first woman to become a professionally licensed doctor in the United States—helped run the **U.S. Sanitary Commission**. The commission battled the diseases and infections that killed twice as many soldiers as bullets alone. About 3,000 women served as nurses in the Union army. Some, like **Clara Barton**, cared for the wounded on the battlefield. After the war, Barton founded the American Red Cross, which today serves disaster victims and others in need of assistance.

Growing Up During the Civil War
teen Life

Children experienced the impact of the Civil War both at home and on the battlefield. Many older boys and girls took on increased responsibilities in their households and on their farms when their fathers and older brothers left to fight in the war. Younger children also suffered from hardships such as malnutrition and a lack of clothing, particularly in the South.

Somewhere between 250,000 and 500,000 boys fought in the Civil War. Elisha Stockwell Jr., a 15-year-old living in Wisconsin, explained how he joined. "I told the recruiting officer I didn't know just how old I was but thought I was eighteen." Many boys served as company musicians, such as drummers or buglers.

Like the other soldiers, boys quickly learned that most of their time would be spent not in battle, but marching mile after mile and performing boring tasks in camp. When the time for combat did arrive, many boys, including Elisha Stockwell Jr., regretted their decision to leave home. "As we lay there and the shells were flying over us," Stockwell recalled, "my thoughts went back to my home, and I thought what a foolish boy I was to run away and get into such a mess as I was in. I would have been glad to have seen my father coming after me."

The young boys in this Mathew Brady photograph are members of a Union drum corps.

CITIZENSHIP

African American Women and the Union Army. While such instances were rare, a few African American women played active roles in the Union army. Maria Lewis served as a soldier in a cavalry regiment from New York. Mary Dyson, a former slave, took part in several battles on the Union side while masquerading as a man. Susie King Taylor, whose husband volunteered for the Union army, accompanied his all-black regiment as it traveled through South Carolina, Georgia, and Florida. Taylor served as a nurse, did laundry, helped clean and maintain guns, and taught many of the men in the regiment to read.

ACTIVITY: Ask students how the military roles of women in the Civil War contrast with the roles of women who serve in the U.S. military today. Then call on volunteers for answers. Discuss students' responses.

Opposition to the Civil War in the North and South

Northern Opposition to the Civil War
- sympathy for South
- war too costly
- draft
  - White working-class men fear that African Americans will take their jobs.

Southern Opposition to the Civil War
- draft
  - "a rich man's war and a poor man's fight"
  - violates states' rights
- impressment
  - burdened farmers

LEVELS 2 AND 3: Have each student create two political cartoons reflecting feelings of opposition toward the Civil War. One cartoon should express a southern point of view, and the other a northern point of view. *(See the graphic organizer above for the correct feelings.)* Display students' cartoons around the classroom.

INTERPRETING THE VISUAL RECORD

Hospitals. Wartime conditions led to the need for battlefield hospitals like this one. *How might the hospital's facilities have contributed to the spread of disease?*

Confederate soldiers carried this flag into battle.

Women in the South also provided medical aid to soldiers. **Sally Louisa Tompkins** was among the Confederate women who founded small hospitals and clinics. She was eventually commissioned as a captain in the Confederate army so that her Richmond, Virginia, hospital could qualify as a military hospital. This made Tompkins the only recognized female officer in the Confederate forces. Nurses experienced the horrors of war firsthand. A Confederate nurse from Alabama wrote in her diary about her experiences at a makeshift hospital.

History Makers Speak

❝The men are lying all over the house on their blankets, just as they were brought from the battlefield. . . . The foul air from this mass of human beings at first made me giddy and sick, but I soon got over it. We have to walk and, when we give the men anything, kneel in blood and water; but we think nothing of it at all.❞

—Kate Cumming, diary entry, April 12, 1862

✔ **READING CHECK: Analyzing Information** How did women contribute to the war effort? Women provided financial support, some served as military spies, and others helped minister to the sick and wounded in battlefield hospitals.

Opposition to the War

Although many people on the home front worked to keep the war effort going and morale high, others voiced their displeasure with the war. Opposition grew as the bloody conflict dragged on longer than anyone had envisioned.

Southern opposition. Southern discontent intensified in the spring of 1862, when the Confederacy passed the first **conscription**, or draft, act in U.S. history. Harsh living conditions in army camps as well as the difficulty of leaving families at home had resulted in a decrease in the number of southern volunteers. Southern military losses in the spring of 1862 convinced Jefferson Davis and Confederate generals of the draft's necessity.

The draft placed the major burden for fighting the war on poor farmers and working people. Draft exemptions for large plantation owners—who had led the Confederacy into war—created tension between wealthy southerners and non-slaveholding whites. Some southerners claimed that the policy proved that the conflict was a "rich man's war and a poor man's fight," as Confederate private Sam Watkins wrote in his memoirs. In response, plantation owners argued that some slaveholders had to remain at home to keep their slaves from running off. The Confederacy needed food and clothing, and few southerners believed that slaves would work without constant supervision.

Other southerners opposed the draft because they believed that it violated states' rights and freedom—the principles that had led southern states to secede. Georgia governor Joseph E. Brown argued that "no act of the Government of the United States prior to the secession struck a blow at constitutional liberty so [fatal] as has been stricken by this conscription act."

As the war intensified, the Confederacy began to allow soldiers to pay farmers prices far below the market value for food, animals, and other property. This policy placed a heavy burden on food-producing families and contributed to serious food shortages. Many farmers called it robbery. Fear of starvation led to food riots in cities from Richmond, Virginia, to Mobile, Alabama.

REVIEW

Have students complete the **Section 2 Review** on p. 109.

ASSESS

Have students complete **Daily Quiz 3.2**. As **Alternative Assessment**, you may want to use the oral history activity or the film company report on the daily life of soldiers in this section's lessons.

RETEACH

Have students complete **Main Idea Activity for English Language Learners and Special-Needs Students 3.2**. Then organize students into groups of three. Have each group make

an annotated outline of the section with brief summaries of each subsection.

English Language Learners, Cooperative Learning

EXTEND

Tell students that the Civil War was the first major American conflict to be well documented by photographers. Organize students into groups of four or five and have them put together a visual presentation of 10 or more photographs from the Civil War. They may use an opaque projector or scan images into a computer for their presentations. If such equipment is not available, have students create a standing display of photocopied images with captions.

Block Scheduling, Cooperative Learning

Northern opposition. Discontent also surfaced in the North. Some northerners sympathized with the South and urged peace. Others believed that the war was proving too costly in terms of money and human life.

Republican sponsorship of a Union draft law in 1863 caused violence to break out in New York City. Democratic newspapers stirred the fears and passions of their readers. They claimed that the draft was designed to force white working-class men to fight for the freedom of African Americans who would then come north and steal their jobs. Angry whites raged through African American neighborhoods. They attacked and killed people and looted and burned buildings. They also destroyed the property of wealthy Republicans. By the time Union troops brought the rioting under control, more than 100 people had been killed.

Most northern Democrats who sympathized with the South did not actively interfere with the war effort. Known as **Copperheads**—a type of poisonous snake—most of these southern sympathizers limited their antiwar activities to speeches and newspaper articles. In an attempt to quiet the Copperheads, President Lincoln suspended some civil liberties, including the constitutional right of *habeas corpus*—a protection against unlawful imprisonment. Thousands of Copperheads and other opponents of the war were arrested and held without trial.

THE GRANGER COLLECTION, NEW YORK

THE COPPERHEAD PARTY.—IN FAVOR OF A VIGOROUS PROSECUTION OF PEACE!

INTERPRETING POLITICAL CARTOONS

Copperheads. This cartoon shows the United States fighting the threat of the Copperheads. *Do you think the cartoonist had a favorable opinion of the Copperheads? Explain your answer.*

✔ **READING CHECK: Summarizing** How did some people express their opposition to the war? Some southerners protested the draft. Some northerners also protested the draft and started riots, while some northern Democrats called Copperheads wrote articles and made speeches against the war.

SECTION 2 REVIEW

1. **Define and explain:**
   conscription
   habeas corpus

2. **Identify and explain:**
   Anaconda Plan
   Mary Boykin Chesnut
   Elizabeth Blackwell
   U.S. Sanitary Commission
   Clara Barton
   Sally Louisa Tompkins
   Copperheads

3. **Categorizing** Copy the graphic organizer below. Use it to explain how civilians responded to the war effort. Include positive and negative responses.

War Condition	Civilian Response	Outcome

4. **Finding the Main Idea**
   a. At the war's beginning which side seemed to have the better military strategy and why?
   b. Why did some Americans on both sides, especially northern Democrats, oppose the war?
   c. Describe the war experiences of a young male soldier or a female civilian in the North or the South.

5. **Writing and Critical Thinking**
   Supporting a Point of View Write a letter to the draft board persuading its members that Sam Watkins was correct in saying that the Civil War was "a rich man's war and a poor man's fight."
   Consider:
   • what Watkins meant
   • who fought in the war
   • how the war affected the rich and the poor differently

Homework Practice Online
keyword: SE3 HP3

3. condition—supplies needed; response—in North, women work in factories and make supplies; in South, women organize fundraisers; outcome—North is well supplied; South has limited supplies. condition—draft; response—protests and riots; outcome—Many people die in riots; many more are drafted

4a. Answer will vary. Students might suggest that the North's military strategy was better because the naval blockade could halt supplies to the South, forcing the South to stop fighting. Students might suggest that the South had the better military strategy because foreign countries relied on its cotton.

b. Some northern Democrats sympathized with the South or believed that the war was proving too costly. Others claimed that the Republican Party was forcing white working-class men to fight for the freedom of African Americans who would later take their jobs. Many southerners resented draft exemptions for the rich.

c. Diary entries will vary but should describe clearly the responsibilities and hardships that the war placed on people.

5. Answers will vary. Students who agree might point out that poor people bore the majority of fighting responsibilities and wartime hardships. Those who disagree might contend that both the Union and Confederate causes were supported by people in all socioeconomic classes.

After completing Section 3, students should be able to:

OBJECTIVE 1 Explain how Union forces gained control of the Mississippi River.

OBJECTIVE 2 Evaluate how the northern and southern forces fared in the eastern campaigns.

OBJECTIVE 3 Analyze how the Union's victory at Antietam changed its war goals.

OBJECTIVE 4 Recognize how African American soldiers aided the Union.

OBJECTIVE 5 Assess the significance of the battles at Fredericksburg and Chancellorsville.

 LET'S GET STARTED!

Write this excerpt from the Emancipation Proclamation on the chalkboard: *"On the first day of January, A.D. 1863, all persons held as slaves within any state or designated part of a state, the people whereof shall then be in rebellion against the United States, shall be then, thenceforward, and forever free. . . ."* Tell students to respond to the excerpt. Tell students that in Section 3 they will learn about the Emancipation Proclamation.

SECTION 3 RESOURCES

REPRODUCIBLE

- ▶ Guided Reading Strategy 3.3
- ▶ American History Political Cartoon 11: Changing Union Leadership
- ▶ Section 3 Review, p. 117
- ▶ Daily Quiz 3.3

TECHNOLOGY

- ▶ One-Stop Planner, Lesson 3.3
- ▶ Linking Geography and History Transparency 14: The War in the East and the West, 1861–1863
- ▶ Holt Researcher: American History CD–ROM
- ▶ Homework Practice Online

REINFORCEMENT, REVIEW, AND ASSESSMENT

- ▶ Section 3 Review, p. 117
- ▶ Daily Quiz 3.3
- ▶ Main Idea Activity 3.3
- ▶ English Audio Summary 3.3
- ▶ Spanish Audio Summary 3.3

SECTION 3

READ TO DISCOVER

1. How did Union forces gain control of the Mississippi River?
2. How did the northern and southern forces fare in the eastern campaigns?
3. How did the Union victory at Antietam change the Union's war goals?
4. How did African American soldiers help the Union?
5. What was the significance of the battles at Fredericksburg and Chancellorsville?

IDENTIFY

Ulysses S. Grant
Battle of Shiloh
David Farragut
George B. McClellan
James E. B. "Jeb" Stuart
Emancipation Proclamation
Battle of Antietam
54th Massachusetts Infantry
Martin Delany
Ambrose E. Burnside

WHY IT MATTERS TODAY

Many people participate in re-enactments of Civil War battles or visit national parks located on Civil War battle sites. Use **CNNfyi.com** or other **current events** sources to find out about a historical re-enactment taking place today or a historical national park. Record your findings in your journal.

CNNfyi.com

Fighting the War

Ulysses S. Grant

EYEWITNESSES TO History *"My heart kept getting higher and higher until it felt to me as though it were in my throat. I would have given anything then to have been back in Illinois, but I had not the moral courage to know what to do; I kept right on."*

—Ulysses S. Grant, quoted in *Battle Cry of Freedom*, by James M. McPherson

Ulysses S. Grant began his service in the Union army as a colonel of the 21st Illinois Regiment. Leading an attack on a Confederate camp in Missouri, he pressed forward despite his fear. When he learned that the Confederates had fled, Grant realized that the enemy colonel "had been as much afraid of me as I had been of him. This was a view of the question I had never taken before; but it was one I never forgot. . . . The lesson was valuable." Many other Union military leaders never grasped this important lesson.

The War in the West

During 1862 the Confederacy won most of the major battles in the East. President Lincoln had little luck finding a general able to defeat Confederate generals Stonewall Jackson, Joseph E. Johnston, and Robert E. Lee in the eastern theater. As a result, the Union's eastern forces had four different commanders in just one year. In the West, however, the Union forces led by **Ulysses S. Grant** achieved great success.

General Grant had won a reputation as a determined military leader. President Lincoln found him invaluable, exclaiming *"I can't spare this man. He fights."* In February 1862 Grant captured Fort Henry and Fort Donelson in Tennessee. Command of these two forts plus the city of Nashville—captured by other Union forces—gave the North control over Kentucky and much of Tennessee.

Shiloh. Marching toward Mississippi in the spring of 1862, Grant rested his troops near a small log church named Shiloh and waited for reinforcements. Grant knew that Confederate generals Albert Johnston and P. G. T. Beauregard were nearby in Corinth, Mississippi. He did not expect them to attack. On April 6, 1862, thousands of Confederate troops surprised Grant's soldiers, beginning the **Battle of Shiloh**. By day's end the Confederate forces had pushed Grant's men back to the Tennessee River.

Confederate commanders believed that they could finish off Grant's army the next morning. The long day of fighting had reached a level of intensity not yet seen in the war. Some of Grant's officers advised him to retreat before the Confederates could renew their attack in the morning. "Retreat?" Grant replied. "No. I propose to attack at daylight and whip them." Grant's plan received more support after fresh Union troops arrived during the night.

TEACH OBJECTIVE 1

LEVEL 1: Copy the graphic organizer on the following page on the chalkboard, omitting the italicized answers. Ask volunteers to provide the results of the Union victories at Shiloh and New Orleans and write their responses on the chalkboard graphic organizer. Then have each student convert the information on the map on this page into a time line. Ask students to annotate the time line with information about critical battles in the fight for control of the Mississippi River.
English Language Learners

LEVELS 2 AND 3: Have students complete the graphic organizer activity from the Level 1 lesson. Then ask each student to write one or two paragraphs to summarize the significance of the Union victories at Shiloh and New Orleans in the Union's quest to control the Mississippi River. Have volunteers read their paragraphs to the class.

HOMEWORK *Have students act as Union army communications officers to compose telegrams to Washington after the Battles of Shiloh and New Orleans reporting the outcome of each battle. Remind students that telegrams must be brief, descriptive, and to the point.*

Grant's April 7 surprise counterattack led to another day of fierce battle. By the middle of the afternoon, Union forces had subdued the Confederates. Southern general Beauregard gave the order to retreat. Both sides had paid dearly. The Union suffered more than 13,000 casualties, and the Confederacy about 10,000—including General Albert Johnston. Grant's forces were too badly hurt to pursue the Confederates, but their victory at Shiloh gave the North a great advantage in the fight to control the Mississippi River valley.

New Orleans. Union control of the Mississippi River depended on the taking of New Orleans. It was the largest city in the South and a central port for supplying troops along and west of the river. Capturing New Orleans would allow the Union to cut off supplies to western Confederate forces and to move troops up the Mississippi River to join Grant's forces. In late April 1862, Union ships commanded by **David Farragut** attacked the two forts guarding the approach to New Orleans from the Gulf of Mexico. After six days of unsuccessfully shelling the forts, Farragut decided to try to sail past them.

Seventeen Union warships advanced during the dark morning hours of April 24. The ensuing battle created a spectacular fireworks display. Confederate forces opened fire from gunboats, launched bombs, and pushed rafts set ablaze with pine and pitch into enemy ships. Despite the heavy fighting and nearly 200 casualties, all but four Union warships arrived in New Orleans. On April 29 the city was forced to surrender. Seventeen-year-old George Washington Cable witnessed the Union's capture of the city as "the crowds on the levee howled and screamed with rage."

By May 1862 the Union had achieved "a Deluge of Victories" in the West, as the *New York Tribune* reported. After the South's loss of 50,000 square miles of territory, 1,000 miles of navigable rivers, two state capitals, and its largest city, Confederate morale began to weaken. Mary Boykin Chesnut wrote after the capture of New Orleans, "Are we not cut in two? . . . I have nothing to chronicle but disasters. . . . The reality is hideous."

✔ READING CHECK: Drawing Conclusions
Why were the Union victories at Shiloh and New Orleans important?
With those victories, the Union gained control of the Mississippi River.

Confederate forces fought desperately to stop the Union from controlling the Mississippi River.

The War in the West, 1862–1863

Interpreting Maps The Union army and navy cooperated in gaining control of the Mississippi River.

❓ HUMAN SYSTEMS Union victories at Fort Henry and Fort Donelson prevented the Confederates from moving into which Union state?

Union Strategy
Control of the Mississippi would split the Confederacy and enable northern forces to reach the Lower South.

- Union state
- Confederate state
- Union occupied
- Union forces
- Confederate forces
- Union victory
- Confederate victory

0   75   150 Miles
0   75   150 Kilometers
Albers Equal-Area Projection

After the Union victories at Murfreesboro and Chattanooga, the Union's western armies were in position to divide the Upper and Lower South.

Gulf of Mexico

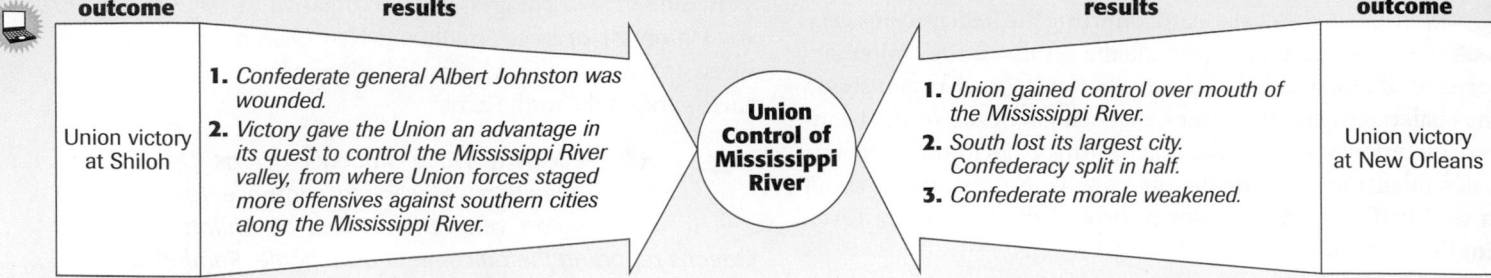

outcome	results		results	outcome
Union victory at Shiloh	1. Confederate general Albert Johnston was wounded. 2. Victory gave the Union an advantage in its quest to control the Mississippi River valley, from where Union forces staged more offensives against southern cities along the Mississippi River.	**Union Control of Mississippi River**	1. Union gained control over mouth of the Mississippi River. 2. South lost its largest city. Confederacy split in half. 3. Confederate morale weakened.	Union victory at New Orleans

INTERDISCIPLINARY CONNECTIONS

▶MILITARY SCIENCE◀

Officer Casualties During the Civil War. The severe wounds that General Joseph E. Johnston sustained at the Battle of Seven Pines were not unusual for a military officer during the Civil War. Because officers on both sides usually led their troops into battle, they were killed at a rate that was about 15 percent higher than that for enlisted men. Of all ranks, generals had the highest casualty rate—they were 50 percent more likely to be killed in battle than the soldiers they commanded.

CRITICAL THINKING Why might generals have had an even higher casualty rate than other officers during the Civil War?

ANSWER: Answers will vary. Students might suggest that both sides made a particular effort to kill opposing field generals in order to confuse and demoralize the enemy.

MAP ANSWER
Antietam and Gettysburg

Eastern Campaigns

While the Union racked up important victories in the West, President Lincoln remained committed to capturing Richmond. He ordered General **George B. McClellan** to return to Virginia in the spring of 1862.

The Peninsula Campaign. General McClellan trained his men well, teaching them both pride and discipline. His effectiveness as a military leader, however, suffered from his cautious nature. He often hesitated to commit his men to battle—much to the president's displeasure.

Lincoln reluctantly agreed to McClellan's strategy to take Richmond in what became known as the Peninsula Campaign. Rather than marching directly on the city, McClellan transported more than 100,000 men, 300 cannons, and 25,000 animals by water to the peninsula between the York and James Rivers. He planned to hit Richmond from the southeast, where the roads were better. This would put his army between Richmond and Confederate general Joseph E. Johnston's forces near Manassas, forcing the Confederates to move southward to defend Richmond. Once again, however, McClellan hesitated.

Yorktown and Seven Pines. In the first week of April 1862, General McClellan's forces met the Confederates at Yorktown, Virginia. Lincoln urged McClellan to attack, but the general refused. He claimed that there were too many enemy troops. Actually, at first he faced only some 13,000 Confederates, led by General John B. Magruder. Lincoln sent a message warning that McClellan's "present hesitation . . . is but the story of Manassas repeated." He ordered, "*You must act.*" Instead, McClellan decided to lay siege to Yorktown. He wrote to his wife that if Lincoln wanted to defeat the rebels "he had better come & do it himself." Meanwhile, General Johnston moved his Confederate troops to the peninsula.

Johnston's and Magruder's forces held Yorktown until the beginning of May. Just as McClellan was about to overrun the Confederate defenses, Johnston began a month-long retreat toward Richmond. McClellan followed, and on May 31, 1862, the two sides clashed just east of Richmond in the Battle of Seven Pines. The South fared badly. A Confederate colonel remembered the fighting:

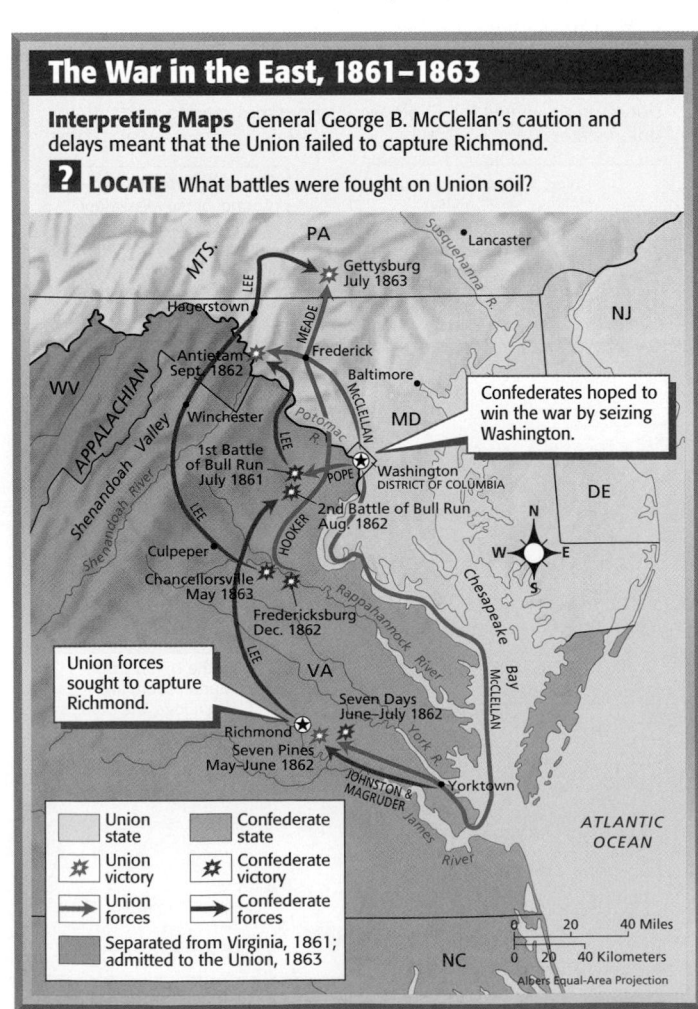

The War in the East, 1861–1863

Interpreting Maps General George B. McClellan's caution and delays meant that the Union failed to capture Richmond.

? LOCATE What battles were fought on Union soil?

Confederates hoped to win the war by seizing Washington.

Union forces sought to capture Richmond.

TEACH OBJECTIVE 2

LEVEL 1: Pair students and have each pair write thumbnail summaries of each of the battles in the eastern campaigns. *(Pairs should mention that during the Peninsula Campaign, McClellan hesitated to attack Richmond. At Yorktown, McClellan refused to engage Confederate forces and instead laid siege to the city, which Confederate forces held. Confederate forces retreated toward Richmond, and Union and Confederate forces fought the Battle of Seven Pines, in which the South fared badly. The Seven Days' Campaign was considered a victory for the South, even though McClellan's retreat resulted in more casualties.)* Ask volunteers to read their summaries to the class. **English Language Learners, Cooperative Learning**

LEVELS 2 AND 3: Tell students to imagine that they are military historians writing an article for a historical journal. Have each student write an article that discusses the outcomes of each of the eastern campaigns as well as the strategies employed by both sides. *(See the Level 1 lesson for the outcomes; students should analyze the strategies of McClellan and the Confederate generals.)* Ask students to title their essays. Then ask volunteers to read their articles to the class.

History Makers Speak

> ❝I was left alone on horseback, with my men dropping rapidly around me. . . . My field officers . . . were all dead. Every horse ridden into the fight, my own among them, was dead. Fully one half of my line officers and half my men were dead or wounded.❞
>
> —John B. Gordon, *Reminiscences of the Civil War*

General Johnston was among the seriously wounded. When Jefferson Davis placed Robert E. Lee in command of the Confederate forces in Johnston's place, Lee promptly halted the fighting.

Seven Days' Campaign. Even though the Confederates were badly weakened, McClellan again sat and waited. Lee did not. In a daring maneuver, Lee sent a cavalry unit commanded by 29-year-old **James E. B. "Jeb" Stuart** to gather information on enemy positions. Using Stuart's information, the combined forces of Lee and Stonewall Jackson attacked the Union army in the Seven Days' Battles. These fierce battles lasted from June 25 to July 1. Union casualties numbered nearly 16,000. Confederate casualties were even higher—more than 20,000—but the battles were considered a victory for the South because McClellan retreated.

President Lincoln soon removed McClellan and gave General John Pope command of the army in the field. In late August, while marching to Richmond, Pope and his men were defeated by Lee's forces at the Second Battle of Bull Run. Soon after, McClellan was back in command of the eastern forces.

✔ **READING CHECK: Finding the Main Idea** How did McClellan's hesitation affect the eastern campaigns? It cost the Union army a victory at Richmond and led to many more Union casualties in the Seven Days' Battles.

INTERPRETING THE VISUAL RECORD

Battles. Fighting in the Civil War was often fierce. *Whose perspective is the artist trying to portray? Explain your answer.*

A Shift in War Goals

As the war dragged on, many northerners began to question whether saving the Union without ending slavery was worth the price. "To fight against slaveholders, without fighting against slavery," charged abolitionist Frederick Douglass, "is but a half-hearted business."

Beginning to move against slavery. After fierce debate, Republicans pushed legislation through Congress in July 1862 that authorized African Americans to serve in the military. The legislation also freed slaves held by Confederate soldiers or by Confederate allies. President Lincoln signed the legislation. However, Horace Greeley, abolitionist editor of the *New York Tribune*, soon criticized Lincoln for not making slavery the central war issue. Lincoln replied by simply restating his original goal: "My paramount object in the struggle *is* to save the Union, and is *not* either to save or to destroy slavery."

Privately, however, the president had already concluded that slavery was too important to the southern war effort to be left alone. More slaves at work meant that more soldiers were available to fight against the Union. Lincoln hoped that if slaves learned that the North was fighting to free them, they would desert their masters, thereby weakening the South's economy.

This poster was made to commemorate Lincoln's decision to free southern slaves.

TEACH OBJECTIVE 3

LEVEL 1: Have students read the excerpted text of the Emancipation Proclamation on this page. Ask students how this Proclamation represented a change in the Union's war goals. *(Students should mention that Lincoln originally set out simply to save the Union without undue regard for the issue of slavery.)* With the class, develop on the chalkboard a flowchart that begins with the Union's victory at Antietam and develops the change in the Union's war goals and the participation of African Americans in the Union cause. *(The Union victory gave Lincoln the political support to issue the Proclamation. African American soldiers enlisted on behalf of the Union side.)* Tell students to copy the flowchart into their notes. **English Language Learners**

LEVELS 2 AND 3: Have students read the excerpted text of the Emancipation Proclamation on this page. Then organize students into triads and have each triad create a collage of images that represents the issuing and impact of the Emancipation Proclamation. Images might be symbolic or concrete reflections of events and emotions surrounding the Proclamation. Tell students that they should indicate the importance of Antietam to the change in Union war goals and characterize the Proclamation's reception in both the North and the South. *(See the Level 1 lesson for the correct importance of Antietam to the timing of the Emancipation Proclamation and the impact of the Proclamation.)* Display triads' collages around the classroom. **Cooperative Learning**

CITIZENSHIP

"Contrabands." In May 1861 three slaves escaped from a Confederate work camp in Virginia and fled to the Union outpost at Fortress Monroe. Similar to the strategy President Lincoln would use some two years later in characterizing the Emancipation Proclamation as part of the war effort, General Benjamin Butler, the commanding officer at Monroe, declared the slaves to be "contraband of war" and granted them sanctuary. Word of the incident spread quickly among local slaves, and by July almost 1,000 "contrabands" had escaped to the place they called Freedom Fort.

ACTIVITY: Tell students to locate and use other primary and secondary sources to learn more about how slaves were treated during the war. Have students write a brief report on what they find.

HISTORICAL DOCUMENTS ANSWER

Students might suggest that he did not want to upset slaveholders in border states.

VISUAL RECORD ANSWER

(for p. 115)

Students might suggest that the flag symbolizes freedom and opportunity; the slaves symbolize oppression; the soldier symbolizes the mighty power of the Union.

★ HISTORICAL DOCUMENTS ★

PRESIDENT ABRAHAM LINCOLN
The Emancipation Proclamation

After the Union victory at Antietam, President Lincoln believed he could take action toward freeing slaves in the South. The excerpts below are from the final Emancipation Proclamation. **Why did Lincoln choose not to free all slaves?**

On the first day of January, A.D. 1863, all persons held as slaves within any state or designated part of a state, the people whereof shall then be in rebellion against the United States, shall be then, thenceforward, and forever free....

Now, therefore, I, Abraham Lincoln, President of the United States . . . do order and declare that all persons held as slaves within said designated states . . . are, and henceforward shall be, free....

And I further declare and make known that such persons of suitable condition will be received into the armed service of the United States to garrison [defend] forts, positions, stations, and other places, and to man vessels of all sorts in said service.

And upon this act, sincerely believed to be an act of justice, warranted by the Constitution upon military necessity, I invoke [call upon] the considerate judgment of mankind and the gracious favor of Almighty God.

These soldiers are but a few of the thousands who died at Antietam.

The Emancipation Proclamation.

President Lincoln lacked the constitutional authority to abolish slavery. As commander in chief of the armed forces, however, he did have the authority to institute military measures. Thus, in July 1862, Lincoln informed his cabinet that he planned to issue a new military order. As of a certain date, all slaves living in areas still rebelling against the United States would be free.

To quiet constitutional concerns about this order, Lincoln assured his cabinet that this **Emancipation Proclamation** would apply only to the Confederate states. This assurance also relieved concerns about the status of slaves in the border states.

President Lincoln decided to keep his plan secret until the Union won a major military victory. To issue the Proclamation when the war was going badly for the Union would look like an act of desperation. The needed victory came in September 1862.

Antietam

General Robert E. Lee went on the offensive in September 1862. Confederate diplomats still believed that Britain might offer support to the Confederacy. Most British government officials were ready to formally recognize the Confederacy as an independent nation. They were waiting, though, to see if Lee could win a major victory on Union soil. On September 4, 1862, Lee began crossing the Potomac River into Maryland with about 40,000 men. Over the next few days, however, Lee lost about 5,000 soldiers as exhausted, hungry, and sick troops fell by the wayside. Union forces lost track of the Confederate troops for four days. Then, surprisingly, two Union soldiers happened upon a copy of Lee's battle plans wrapped around a discarded pack of cigars.

Armed with this information, General McClellan planned a counterattack. With some 75,000 troops, McClellan met Lee at Antietam (an-TEET-uhm) Creek in Maryland. The **Battle of Antietam** raged all day, becoming the bloodiest single-day battle in all of U.S. military history. The Confederates suffered more than 13,000 casualties; the Union more than 12,000.

Despite the Union army's good showing at Antietam, President Lincoln fired McClellan again after he allowed the Confederate troops to escape into Virginia. Although the Battle of Antietam was not a resounding Union victory, it raised confidence in the North. A major Confederate offensive had failed. This proved that General Lee could be defeated. Lee's loss also cost the South any hope of support from European countries.

LEVEL 1: Pair students and have each pair gather five or more interesting quotations by and about African American soldiers who served during the Civil War, and then put them together with appropriate images and symbols in a small collage. In addition, have students write a one- or two-paragraph caption that summarizes the contributions of African American soldiers. (*Students' captions should mention the following: African American soldiers participated in the attack on Fort Wagner; nearly 180,000 African American men served in the Union army; 33,000 lost their lives; some African Americans served in the navy; more than 20 African American soldiers and sailors won the Congressional Medal of Honor.*)

Display students' collages on the classroom wall.
English Language Learners, Cooperative Learning

LEVELS 2 AND 3: Organize students into groups of five and have each group create a visual display that highlights African American soldiers' contributions to the Union's war efforts. (*See the Level 1 lesson for the correct contributions.*) Students' displays might include drawings, paintings, and photographs of African American soldiers; biographical information about African American heroes and leaders of the Civil War; and graphic organizers to compare African Americans' wages to white soldiers' pay. Place students' displays around the classroom. **Cooperative Learning**

The Union victory at Antietam gave Lincoln the necessary political support to move forward with his plans to free the slaves in the South. On September 22, the president issued a preliminary draft of the Emancipation Proclamation that would go into effect the first of the year. When January 1, 1863, found the Confederacy still in rebellion, Lincoln's Proclamation brought a decisive change in the war.

✔ **READING CHECK: Analyzing Information** Why did Lincoln issue the Emancipation Proclamation when he did? The Union victory at Antietam gave Lincoln the necessary political support to issue the proclamation.

African Americans Take Up Arms

Both the July 1862 act allowing African Americans to serve in the military and the Emancipation Proclamation encouraged African Americans to enlist in the Union army. The first official black regiments were organized in August 1862 in the Union-controlled areas of South Carolina. Frederick Douglass viewed military service as a step toward citizenship for African Americans.

❝Let the black man get upon his person the brass letters, U.S.; let him get an eagle on his button, and a musket on his shoulder and bullets in his pocket, and there is no power on earth which can deny that he has earned the right to citizenship.**❞**

—Frederick Douglass, quoted in *Douglass' Monthly*, August 1863

African American troops faced a danger that white Union soldiers did not. Black soldiers captured by the Confederates were treated as outlaws. They could face execution or be sold into slavery.

Many of the first African American soldiers recruited by the Union served in the **54th Massachusetts Infantry**. This regiment earned an honored place in U.S. military history. In July 1863, Union forces began attacking Confederate-held forts near Charleston, South Carolina. The Union could not break the Confederates' hold. As a result, Brigadier General Truman Seymour decided to send some 6,000 Union troops in a desperate attack against Fort Wagner, which guarded the entrance to Charleston Harbor. The 54th Infantry would lead the charge.

The attack on Fort Wagner was the first time that African American troops had been assigned a key role in a military campaign. The Union commander knew that the 54th would suffer great losses in their frontal assault on the fort. On the night of July 18, in a storm of gunfire, commanding officer Colonel Robert Gould Shaw and the 54th made it to the top of Fort Wagner's walls. Union forces suffered staggering losses in a prolonged fight. The siege ended September 6, when Confederate forces decided to evacuate the fort.

Despite the courageous performance of African American troops, the Union army did not offer them full equality. For much of the war, black soldiers earned about half the pay of white soldiers. After much criticism by black soldiers and their commanding officers, Congress equalized the pay scale in June 1864. In addition, white officers commanded each black regiment. Only about 100 African Americans were commissioned as junior officers. In 1865 **Martin Delany** became the first African American promoted to the rank of major.

INTERPRETING THE VISUAL RECORD

Emancipation. This engraving celebrating the Emancipation Proclamation first appeared in 1863. *What do you think the various elements in the image symbolize?*

THE LIBRARY COMPANY OF PHILADELPHIA

FREEDOM TO THE SLAVE

PUBLIC SCHOOL

HISTORY MAKERS SPEAK

Union soldiers in *Battle Cry of Freedom* and *Brother Against Brother*

Describing the Battle of Antietam. By many accounts, the fighting at the Battle of Antietam was the fiercest and most horrifying of the war. "In a second the air was full of the hiss of bullets and the hurtle of grape-shot," one Union soldier described. "The mental strain was so great that . . . the whole landscape for an instant turned slightly red." "No matter in what direction we turned," wrote another of the scene after the battle, "it was all the same shocking picture, awakening awe rather than pity, benumbing the senses rather than touching the heart, glazing the eye with horror rather than filling it with tears."

ACTIVITY: Have each student find a short description of another battle from the Civil War. Ask volunteers to read their descriptions to the class. Then ask students to evaluate the validity of these sources based on the description of the other battle.

SCIENCE & TECHNOLOGY ANSWERS
(for p. 116)

1. They caused bullets to spin as they left the gun.

2. Soldiers needed faster-loading and less-expensive bullets.

LEVEL 1: Tell students to imagine that they are newspaper reporters during the Civil War. Pair students and have each pair create a headline and topic sentence to assess the significance of the Battles of Fredericksburg and Chancellorsville. *(Pairs' headlines and topics sentences should mention that Confederate forces defeated Union forces, led by General Ambrose Burnside, at Fredericksburg; the Union army suffered more than 12,000 casualties. At Chancellorsville, Union forces, led by Joseph Hooker, were defeated by Confederate forces* led by Robert E. Lee and Stonewall Jackson; however, the Confederates lost Stonewall Jackson, who was mistakenly shot by his own troops.) Ask volunteers to read their headlines and topic sentences to the class.

English Language Learners, Cooperative Learning

LEVELS 2 AND 3: Have each student write a poem to assess the significance of the Battles of Fredericksburg and Chancellorsville. *(See the Level 1 lesson for the significance of the battles.)* Ask volunteers to recite their poems to the class.

SECTION 3 REVIEW ANSWERS

1. Identify

- Ulysses S. Grant, p. 110
- Battle of Shiloh, p. 110
- David Farragut, p. 111
- George B. McClellan, p. 112
- James E. B. "Jeb" Stuart, p. 113
- Emancipation Proclamation, p. 114
- Battle of Antietam, p. 114
- 54th Massachusetts Infantry, p. 115
- Martin Delany, p. 115
- Ambrose E. Burnside, p. 116

2. Shiloh—April 1862, Tennessee, surprise attacks staged by Confederate and then Union forces on two consecutive days, Union victory; New Orleans, April 1862, Louisiana, naval combat surrounding Union attempt to land warships in New Orleans, Union victory; Yorktown—April 1862, Virginia, Confederate retreat, Seven Pines—May–June 1862, Virginia, clash near Richmond following Union victory; Seven Days'—June–July 1862, Virginia, daring Confederate offensive after recent defeat at Seven Pines, Confederate victory; Antietam—September 1862, Maryland, Union counterattack following Confederate offensive into Maryland, Union victory;

The Congressional Medal of Honor

Nearly 180,000 African American men served in the Union army, and more than 32,000 lost their lives. Some also served in the navy. More than 20 African American soldiers and sailors won the Congressional Medal of Honor.

✔ **READING CHECK: Summarizing** How did African Americans support the Union cause?
They participated in the attack on Fort Wagner. About 180,000 served in the Union army.

New Union Commanders

The addition of African American soldiers came at a key time for the Union, which suffered important defeats in the winter of 1862 and the spring of 1863. After Antietam, President Lincoln chose **Ambrose E. Burnside** to replace General McClellan.

Fredericksburg. On December 11 and 12, 1862, General Burnside sent some 114,000 Union soldiers across the Rappahannock (rap-uh-HAN-uhk) River near Fredericksburg, Virginia. General Lee and some 75,000 Confederate soldiers controlled the hills above the town. Reasoning that Lee would not expect a frontal attack, Burnside ordered his men across an open plain on the morning of December 13.

Lee took advantage of Burnside's positioning. From their high ground, the Confederates could easily fire on the Union soldiers as they crossed the open fields. The Union army suffered more than 12,000 casualties at Fredericksburg, and the

★ ★ ★ ★ ★ ★ ★ Science & Technology ★ ★ ★ ★ ★ ★ ★

Weapons and War

Technological developments changed the nature of warfare during the Civil War. Despite their great accuracy, rifles were seldom carried by the infantry before the 1850s. Rifles from this period had grooves carved inside the barrel that allowed a cone-shaped bullet to spin as it left the gun and travel four times farther than a bullet shot from a smoothbore barrel. Bullets large enough to spin, however, had to be rammed down the

barrel with a mallet—which was awkward and time-consuming.

In 1848 a French army captain named Claude E. Minié developed a smaller bullet that could be easily rammed down a rifle's barrel. These bullets were extremely expensive. James H. Burton,

an armorer at the Harpers Ferry Armory, created a less-expensive version of Minié's bullets. These "minié balls"—pronounced "minnie" by members of both armies—were used extensively during the Civil War.

By 1863 most soldiers on both sides of the conflict carried rifles. The primary effect of the change from smoothbores to rifles was an increase in the number of casualties.

rifling grooves

Understanding Science and History

1. What effect did the grooves in a rifle's barrel have?
2. How did the development of the rifle result from a specific military need?

REVIEW

Have students complete the **Section 3 Review** on p. 117.

ASSESS

Have students complete **Daily Quiz 3.3.** As **Alternative Assessment**, you may want to use the collage and caption activity or the visual display activity in this section's lessons.

RETEACH

Have students complete **Main Idea Activity for English Language Learners and Special-Needs Students 3.3.** Pair students and have each pair create a detailed, annotated time line for the years 1862 and 1863. Pairs should include a title for their time line as well as a one- or two-paragraph caption that summarizes the years' events and their significance for both sides.
English Language Learners, Cooperative Learning

EXTEND

Have students conduct research on recent civil war anywhere in the world and compare the causes, aims, tactics, and outcome of that conflict with the American Civil War. Tell students to present their conclusions in a three-to-five-page report.
Block Scheduling

Confederates some 5,000. One northerner bitterly referred to the battle as a "great slaughter pen."

Chancellorsville. President Lincoln transferred Burnside and gave command of the eastern forces to General Joseph "Fighting Joe" Hooker. The new commander offered a daring plan to crush Lee's forces. He proposed dividing his large army into three parts in order to cut off supply lines and attack them from both flanks. The strategy seemed workable, particularly since Hooker's 134,000 troops were more than double the Confederate troops.

By April 30, 1863, Hooker had positioned his men in a deep forest known as the Wilderness, near Chancellorsville, Virginia. Lee divided his troops, sending Stonewall Jackson and some 30,000 men through the Wilderness to outflank Hooker. When Hooker discovered the troop movements, he assumed that the Confederates were retreating. Instead, Lee and Jackson attacked the Union forces from two sides. After several days of fighting, Hooker withdrew in defeat.

The South paid dearly for its victory at Chancellorsville, however. Riding back to Confederate lines after dark, Jackson was mistaken for a Union cavalryman and shot by his own troops. The two bullets that hit his left arm required it to be amputated. As with countless other soldiers, Jackson's battle wounds led to serious infection. Eight days later, Lee's most valued general died.

General Stonewall Jackson was shot during the Battle of Chancellorsville in 1863.

✔ **READING CHECK: Comparing** Compare the losses at the Battles of Fredericksburg and Chancellorsville. At Fredericksburg both sides suffered heavy casualties; at Chancellorsville the Confederates lost an important leader.

SECTION REVIEW

1. Identify and explain:
Ulysses S. Grant
Battle of Shiloh
David Farragut
George B. McClellan
James E. B. "Jeb" Stuart
Emancipation
 Proclamation
Battle of Antietam
54th Massachusetts
 Infantry
Martin Delany
Ambrose E. Burnside

2. Summarizing Copy the graphic organizer below. Use it to list each major battle of 1862 and early 1863, including its date and location, a brief description of each battle, and the battle's outcome.

	Date	Location	Outcome
Shiloh			
New Orleans			
Yorktown			
Seven Pines			
Seven Days'			
Antietam			
Fredericksburg			
Chancellorsville			

3. **Finding the Main Idea**

a. What qualities made General Grant an effective leader?

b. Some white leaders argued that African Americans would not make good soldiers. What evidence from the Civil War would contradict this claim?

c. What role did the Emancipation Proclamation play in the war?

4. **Writing and Critical Thinking**

Supporting a Point of View Write a newspaper editorial supporting the shift in the Union's war goals. Give reasons why it would increase northerners' support of the war.
Consider:
• what the shift in war goals was
• why some northerners had wanted a shift
• how Lincoln's stated goals in 1863 satisfied some previous critics of the war

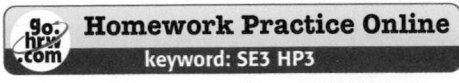
Homework Practice Online
keyword: SE3 HP3

Fredericksburg—December 1862, Virginia, Union advance across an open plain toward Confederate forces stationed in nearby hills, Confederate victory; Chancellorsville—April-May 1863, Virginia, multiple-flank fighting following complex troop movements through a dense forest, Confederate victory

3a. Grant was determined and decisive. He also refused to surrender.

b. the performance of African American soldiers in the 54th Massachusetts Infantry during the Union assault on Fort Wagner in July 1863

c. It signaled a shift in war goals by abolishing slavery in areas in rebellion and thus allowing African American soldiers to fight for the Union army.

4. Answers will vary. Most students will reason that including the end of slavery as a Union war goal brought greater support for the war from antislavery northerners.

After completing Section 4, students should be able to:

OBJECTIVE 1 Explain the outcomes of the Battle of Gettysburg.

OBJECTIVE 2 Assess the significance of the Union victory at Vicksburg.

OBJECTIVE 3 Describe General Grant's strategy in the summer of 1864.

OBJECTIVE 4 Describe General Sherman's strategies.

OBJECTIVE 5 List the terms of surrender at Appomattox.

🔊 LET'S GET STARTED!

Write the following quotation on the chalkboard: "*Should I fall in the next fight killed or wounded I hope to fall with my face to the foe [enemy]. . . .*" Tell students that this quotation is from a letter by Lewis Douglass, an African American soldier. As students enter the classroom, have them respond in writing to it. What does Douglass mean by his comment? Tell students that they will learn about the final phase of the war in Section 4.

SECTION 4

READ TO DISCOVER

1. What were the results of the Battle of Gettysburg?
2. Why was the Union victory at Vicksburg significant?
3. What was General Grant's strategy in the summer of 1864?
4. What were the strategy and tactics of General Sherman?
5. What were the terms of the surrender at Appomattox?

DEFINE

war of attrition
total war

IDENTIFY

George Meade
Battle of Gettysburg
Pickett's Charge
Gettysburg Address
Siege of Vicksburg
William Tecumseh Sherman

WHY IT MATTERS TODAY

The brave actions of the soldiers and civilians who participated in the Civil War are remembered today. Use CNNfyi.com or other **current events** sources to find out about different ways that the soldiers are honored. Record your findings in your journal.

CNN**fyi**.com

The Final Phase

"*There never were such men in an army before. They will go anywhere and do anything if properly led.*"

—Robert E. Lee, quoted in *Battle Cry of Freedom*, by James M. McPherson

General Robert E. Lee praised his troops following their victory at Chancellorsville. The South received an enormous boost in confidence from the victory, while northern morale plunged. When President Lincoln heard the news from the War Department on May 6, his face turned "ashen," a newspaper reporter recalled. "My God! my God! What will the country say?" Lincoln exclaimed. Republican Charles Sumner agreed. "Lost, lost, all is lost," he cried when he learned of the defeat. After achieving such an astounding victory with nearly half as many men as his enemy, Lee began to believe his men were invincible. Lee's confidence led him to devise his most ambitious plan to date—one that amazed and impressed other Confederate leaders.

General Robert E. Lee

Gettysburg

Following the victory at Chancellorsville, General Lee decided to invade the North again. This action would spare war-weary Virginia from further fighting. It also would allow Lee to resupply and feed his hungry troops by seizing provisions from the enemy.

In June 1863 Lee crossed into Pennsylvania. President Lincoln urged General Hooker to attack the Confederates before they could consolidate their troops. Hooker worried, however, that Lee's troops outnumbered his and hesitated to move. Fearing he had another General McClellan leading the army, Lincoln quickly replaced Hooker with General **George Meade**.

By the end of June, some 75,000 Confederate troops had begun to assemble near the town of Gettysburg, Pennsylvania. When scouts reported a supply of shoes in the town, the Confederates organized a raiding party. The troops were unaware that two Union brigades had positioned themselves on high ground northwest of Gettysburg. As the Confederate raiding party approached the small town on July 1, it met a blaze of Union fire.

On the first day of the **Battle of Gettysburg**, the Confederates pushed the Union line back to Cemetery Hill and Cemetery Ridge. The Confederates held Seminary Ridge, a lower line of hills about a half mile away. Nevertheless, Lee knew that the danger to his forces would remain as long as the North held the higher ground. Expecting that Union reinforcements would soon be arriving, he decided to attack quickly. On July 2 General Lee charged the Union's left flank, trying without success to capture a dome-shaped hill called Little Round Top. The next day he ordered some 15,000 men commanded by George Pickett to rush

TEACH OBJECTIVE 1

LEVEL 1: Pair students and have each pair create an annotated time line from June 1863 to November 1863 which includes the Battle of Gettysburg and related events. *(Time lines should include events beginning with Lee's move into Pennsylvania, gathering of Confederate troops near Gettysburg, first day of the Battle of Gettysburg, Pickett's Charge, Lee's retreat to Virginia, and ending with the Gettysburg Address.)* Have volunteers share their time lines with the class. Ask students to supply any information that may have been omitted from the time lines. Conclude by leading a class discussion about the outcomes of the battle.
English Language Learners, Cooperative Learning

LEVELS 2 AND 3: Have each student complete the time line activity from the Level 1 lesson. Students should incorporate a three-sentence summary of the outcome of the Battle of Gettysburg into their time lines. Then ask students to read the Gettysburg Address on this page. Have students paraphrase it using language more familiar to them. Encourage any student having trouble with the assignment to use a dictionary and a thesaurus to help them with difficult words. When students have finished paraphrasing Lincoln's speech, ask volunteers to read their summaries to the class.

NOTE: For an additional teaching idea, see the Chapter 3 resource speaker lesson in the **Creative Teaching Strategies** handbook.

---

the Union center on Cemetery Ridge. Less than half of the Confederate soldiers reached the top of the ridge during **Pickett's Charge**. Many of those were killed. Confederate lieutenant G. W. Finley later wrote, "Men were falling all around us, and cannon and muskets were raining death upon us." Bad weather prevented Meade from pursuing the Confederates, however, and Lee retreated to Virginia.

A staggering number of young men lost their lives at Gettysburg. After three days of fighting, Union casualties numbered more than 23,000, and Confederate casualties more than 28,000. In November 1863 President Lincoln helped dedicate a cemetery at the Gettysburg battlefield. Lincoln spoke for only a few minutes, but his **Gettysburg Address** remains a classic statement of democratic ideals.

Although the Union army emerged victorious at Gettysburg, it once again narrowly failed to end the war. A disappointed President Lincoln complained, "Our Army held the war in the hollow of their hand and they would not close it." The battle, however, marked a critical turning point. The Union army had proved that the Confederacy could be beaten.

★ HISTORICAL DOCUMENTS ★

PRESIDENT ABRAHAM LINCOLN
The Gettysburg Address

On November, 19, 1863, Abraham Lincoln dedicated a national cemetery at the Gettysburg battlefield. His speech reminded Americans of the nation's democratic ideals. **What is the "unfinished work" Lincoln mentions?**

Four score and seven years ago our fathers brought forth on this continent, a new nation, conceived [created] in Liberty, and dedicated to the proposition that all men are created equal.

Now we are engaged in a great civil war, testing whether that nation, or any nation so conceived and so dedicated, can long endure. We are met on a great battlefield of that war. We have come to dedicate a portion of that field, as a final resting place for those who here gave their lives that that nation might live. . . .

But, in a larger sense, we can not dedicate—we can not consecrate [make holy]—we cannot hallow—this ground. The brave men, living and dead, who struggled here, have consecrated it, far above our poor power to add or detract. The world will little note nor long remember what we say here, but it can never forget what they did here. It is for us the living, rather, to be dedicated here to the unfinished work which they who fought here have thus far so nobly advanced. It is rather for us to . . . highly resolve that these dead shall not have died in vain—that this nation, under God, shall have a new birth of freedom—and that government of the people, by the people, for the people, shall not perish from the earth.

📶 **internet** connect

TOPIC: War Photography
GO TO: go.hrw.com
KEYWORD: SE3 AN3

Have students access the Internet through the HRW Web site to conduct research on Civil War photography, including that of Mathew Brady. After viewing photographs and reading letters by soldiers and civilians, have students write a report describing the life of a soldier in the war. Students reports' should reflect the content of images in the photographs, the emotional mood of the photographs, and the context in which the photographs were taken.

HISTORICAL DOCUMENTS ANSWER
Students might answer restoring the Union.

✔ **READING CHECK: Summarizing** What gains did the Union army make at the Battle of Gettysburg? The Union army gained confidence that the Confederate army could be beaten.

Lincoln Finds His General

The war continued in the West in 1863, with the Union attempting to control the Mississippi River valley. General Ulysses S. Grant won several significant victories for the North. President Lincoln soon recognized Grant's invaluable leadership.

Vicksburg. Grant knew that gaining full control of the Mississippi River required taking Vicksburg, Mississippi. The city's high river bluffs allowed the Confederate artillery to command an extensive area. In May 1863 Grant hatched a risky plan to take Vicksburg. Marching deep into enemy territory, he bottled up one Confederate force in nearby Jackson. Then he raced west to trap the other enemy force inside Vicksburg.

For six weeks General Grant and his men laid siege to the city, preventing any Confederate reinforcements from arriving. During the long **Siege of Vicksburg**, the city's defenders began eating mules and rats to keep from starving. One woman

LEVEL 1: Discuss with students why the Siege of Vicksburg represented a turning point in the Civil War. *(Students should mention that along with the fall of Port Hudson, Louisiana, Vicksburg gave the Union complete control of the Mississippi River and cut off Arkansas, Louisiana, and Texas from the rest of the Confederacy.)* Then ask students what probably would have happened if the Confederates had not surrendered at Vicksburg. *(Students might suggest that the people of Vicksburg would have starved to death because of the siege, or the city's Confederate defenders would have deserted out of hunger.)* Have volunteers compile on the chalkboard a list of reasons for Vicksburg's significance and alternative outcomes if the Confederates had not surrendered. **English Language Learners**

LEVELS 2 AND 3: Have each student complete the Level 1 activity and write a one-to-two-paragraph analysis of Grant's strategy at Vicksburg and the significance of the Union victory there. Why was Grant's strategy considered so brilliant and daring? What was the consequence of the Union victory? *(Students should mention that it was a risky maneuver to press so deeply into Confederate territory, but it was clever because it eliminated potential Confederate reinforcements from Jackson before the siege of Vicksburg began; see the Level 1 lesson for the battle's significance.)* When students have finished writing, have volunteers share their analysis with the class.

GEOGRAPHY

Surviving the Siege of Vicksburg. During the Siege of Vicksburg, Union artillery hurled as many as 2,800 shells into the city every day. The constant threat of death by explosion prompted many civilians to abandon their homes and move into caves that were dug into area hillsides. Some families even divided the caves into separate rooms and furnished them with carpets, chairs, and other household objects.

ACTIVITY: Ask students to imagine that they are elderly residents of Vicksburg during the Siege of Vicksburg. Then have them compose a short diary entry that explains how they are trying to survive the attack.

MAP ANSWER
(for p. 121)

almost 7 miles a day

VISUAL RECORD ANSWER
(for p. 122)

Students might note that the railroad tracks and railcars have been destroyed, as has the railroad station.

GRAPH ANSWER
(for p. 122)

abut 250,000 Union deaths; about 170,000 Confederate deaths

Confederate cannons at Vicksburg fire at Union gunboats along the Mississippi River.

Research on the R⊙M

Free Find:
Southern Railroads
After reading about southern railroads on the **Holt Researcher CD–ROM**, create a map that shows how the railroads were vital to the Confederacy's war effort.

Ulysses S. Grant and his staff posed for this photograph at their headquarters in Cold Harbor, Virginia, in June 1864.

in the city wrote, "We are utterly cut off from the world, surrounded by a circle of fire." Finally, in late June the desperate Confederate soldiers sent a letter to their commander, urging him to surrender.

On July 3, 1863, General Grant and Confederate general John Pemberton met under an oak tree to discuss terms of surrender. The Confederates surrendered to Grant the next day. On July 8 the Confederate forces at Port Hudson, Louisiana, also fell. These victories gave the Union total control over the Mississippi River, thereby cutting off Arkansas, Louisiana, and Texas from the rest of the Confederacy.

Summer of 1864. President Lincoln promoted General Grant to general in chief, commander of all Union forces, in the spring of 1864. Grant understood better than previous commanders how to take advantage of the North's soldiers and supplies. His strategy was to use these advantages against an enemy that was reeling from shortages. Grant informed Lincoln that he would march on Richmond, take his losses, and press on. He planned a **war of attrition**—that is, to continue fighting until the South ran out of men, supplies, and the will to fight.

In May 1864 Grant moved some 122,000 troops into the Wilderness near Chancellorsville, Virginia. For two days the northerners hurled themselves at some 66,000 Confederates, but the rebels held their ground. Grant's forces suffered nearly 18,000 casualties; the Confederates lost nearly 10,000.

Rather than rest, Grant pushed on, mile by bloody mile, just as he had promised Lincoln he would do. "I propose to fight it out on this line if it takes all summer," he wrote. Moving his forces a few miles to the south, Grant forced Lee to keep his weary men in the field. At Spotsylvania Court House, Virginia, Union and Confederate forces clashed several times between May 10 and May 19. Again, the Union forces suffered horrible losses. Shocked by the number of casualties, a southern soldier remarked of Grant, "We have met a man this time, who either does not know when he is whipped, or who cares not if he loses his whole army."

In mid-June Grant traveled south once more to attack Petersburg, Virginia. He hoped that capturing this railroad center would cut off Richmond's supplies. Lee held on, however. After three days even Grant was discouraged. Since May 12 his army had suffered some 60,000 casualties. He called off the direct assault and settled down to lay siege to Petersburg. Nevertheless, Grant's strategy was slowly succeeding. Lee's army steadily dwindled, and few reserves remained.

✔ **READING CHECK: Finding the Main Idea** What was General Grant's strategy for winning the war in the summer of 1864?

to keep fighting until the Confederacy ran out of soldiers and supplies and would be forced to give up

WORKSHEET

HOMEWORK *Have students write a two-to-three-paragraph eulogy praising the Union soldiers who died while taking Vicksburg.*

TEACH OBJECTIVES 3 AND 4

LEVELS 1 AND 2: Copy the following chart onto the chalkboard, omitting the italicized answers. Have students copy the organizer into their notebooks and complete it. Then have volunteers complete the organizer on the chalkboard. Conclude by leading a class discussion about the tactics employed by Grant and Sherman and ask students if there are any recent or current wars to which they can apply one or both of these strategies. If yes, have them explain why the strategy applies; if no, have them contrast the tactics in recent wars to war of attrition and/or total war.

English Language Learners

Grant's Strategy in 1864	*Sherman's* Strategy in 1864
war of attrition	total war
Reasoning:	**Reasoning:**
Use North's advantages in number of soldiers and industrial resources to fight until South runs out of men, supplies, and will	*Win war by destroying South's economic resources and demoralizing the populace*
Key Battles in Campaign:	**Key Battles in Campaign:**
Wilderness, Spotsylvania Court House, siege of Petersburg	*burning of Atlanta, capture of Savannah*

The Final Campaigns, 1864–1865

Interpreting Maps When Grant failed to take Petersburg, he laid siege to the city for nine months. Defeated at Five Forks, Lee abandoned Petersburg and Richmond on April 2. A week later Lee surrendered to Grant.

2 THE WORLD IN SPATIAL TERMS Sherman's army marched from Savannah to Columbia in 17 days. How many miles did his army need to cover each day?

	Union state		Confederate state
	Union occupied	▼▼▼	Union blockade
→	Union forces	→	Confederate forces
☀	Union victory	☀	Confederate victory
☼	No victor		

Union forces shatter the Confederacy's major western army.

Johnston fails to stop Sherman at Bentonville and accepts final surrender terms on April 26, 1865.

Lee surrenders to Grant on April 9, 1865.

Nashville Dec. 1864
Chattanooga
Durham
Bentonville March 1865
JOHNSTON
Columbia Feb. 1865
Charleston
Atlanta Sept. 1864
Savannah Dec. 1864
HOOD
SHERMAN
BLOCKADE
UNION BLOCKADE

Washington, D.C.
Culpeper
Richmond
Appomattox Courthouse
See map at right

ATLANTIC OCEAN

Gulf of Mexico

Sherman's Campaign

0 100 200 Miles
0 100 200 Kilometers
Albers Equal-Area Projection

Washington, D.C.
APPALACHIAN MTS. WV
VA
Culpeper
Wilderness May 1864
Fredericksburg
Spotsylvania May 1864
Charlottesville
GRANT
James River
LEE
Richmond
Cold Harbor June 1864
Appomattox Courthouse
LEE
GRANT
Five Forks April 1865
Petersburg June 1864–April 1865
Chesapeake Bay

Grant's Campaign

0 25 50 Miles
0 25 50 Kilometers
Albers Equal-Area Projection

Sherman's March to the Sea

Union general **William Tecumseh Sherman** matched General Grant's determination. Moody, ambitious, and brilliant, Sherman had performed ably at Vicksburg. Grant rewarded Sherman by making him commander of the Tennessee army.

While Grant slowly pushed his way toward Richmond, Sherman undertook a campaign to destroy southern railroads and industries. In early May, he moved some 100,000 troops out of Tennessee toward Atlanta, Georgia. On his way, General Sherman repeatedly outmaneuvered Confederate general Johnston's forces. He then defeated General John Hood's attacks and pushed the Confederate forces back.

When Atlanta fell on September 2, 1864, the Confederates lost their last railroad link across the Appalachian Mountains. After ordering residents to evacuate, Sherman's men set fire to large portions of the city. Sherman defended his tactics.

History Makers Speak

"If [southerners] raise a howl against my barbarity and cruelty, I will answer that war is war, and not popularity-seeking. If they want peace, they and their relatives must stop the war."

—William T. Sherman, letter to General Halleck, September 4, 1864

General Sherman's troops burned much of Atlanta.

1. Define
- war of attrition, p. 120
- total war, p. 122

2. Identify
- George Meade, p. 118
- Battle of Gettysburg, p. 118
- Pickett's Charge, p. 119
- Gettysburg Address, p. 119
- Siege of Vicksburg, p. 119
- William Tecumseh Sherman, p. 121

3. 1. Grant is promoted to lead the Union Army.

2. Union forces under Grant and Confederate forces under Lee clash in the Wilderness and at Spotsylvania Court House in Virginia.

3. Union forces under Grant besiege Petersburg and then push their way toward Richmond, Virginia.

4. Union forces under Sherman capture Atlanta and march toward Savannah, Georgia.

5. President Lincoln wins re-election in 1864.

6. Union forces under Sherman capture Savannah.

7. Union forces under Grant capture Richmond.

8. Lee surrenders at Appomattox Courthouse.

4a. It proved that the Confederacy could ultimately be beaten.

b. Answers may vary. Students might suggest that preserving the Union was worth any number of lost lives. Others might suggest

LEVEL 3: Pair students to role-play Grant and Sherman. Have one student write a letter as Grant and the other student write a letter as Sherman explaining and justifying their military strategies. Then have each student exchange letters with his or her partner. When students have finished reading their partner's letter, ask volunteers to read their own letters to the class. Then lead the class in a discussion about how Grant's and Sherman's strategies differed from those of previous Union commanders. Ask students if they think the war would have ended any sooner or any differently if Grant and Sherman had been in charge from the beginning of the war.
Cooperative Learning

TEACH OBJECTIVE 5

ALL LEVELS: Have students list the terms of the Confederate surrender at Appomattox. *(Students should mention that Confederate officers could keep their side arms; all soldiers would be fed; they would be allowed to keep their horses and mules; and they would not be tried for treason.)* Ask students if they think these terms were fair and reasonable. *(Answers will vary. Encourage students to justify their opinions.)* Then have students design postage stamps commemorating the surrender at Appomattox and the end of the Civil War. Have students make oversized, full-color mock-ups of their stamps to display in the classroom. **English Language Learners**

that the southern states may have returned to the Union without the war.

c. Grant planned a war of attrition, or one in which he would continue fighting until the South ran out of men, supplies, and will. Sherman waged a total war, or one in which he destroyed the South's economic resources. Answers about alternatives will vary but should address the idea of using less-destructive tactics.

5. Answers will vary but should include an explanation of the surrender terms, Grant's reaction, and other conditions that Grant might have requested.

REVIEW 3 ANSWERS

Creating a Time Line
Each event should have an explanation and the correct date.

Writing a Summary
See the Reading Checks in each section for main ideas.

Identifying People and Ideas
1. commanded the Confederate army

2. Confederate general accidentally shot after Chancellorsville

3. commanded Union forces; fired by Lincoln

4. first U.S. professionally licensed female doctor; helped run the U.S. Sanitary Commission

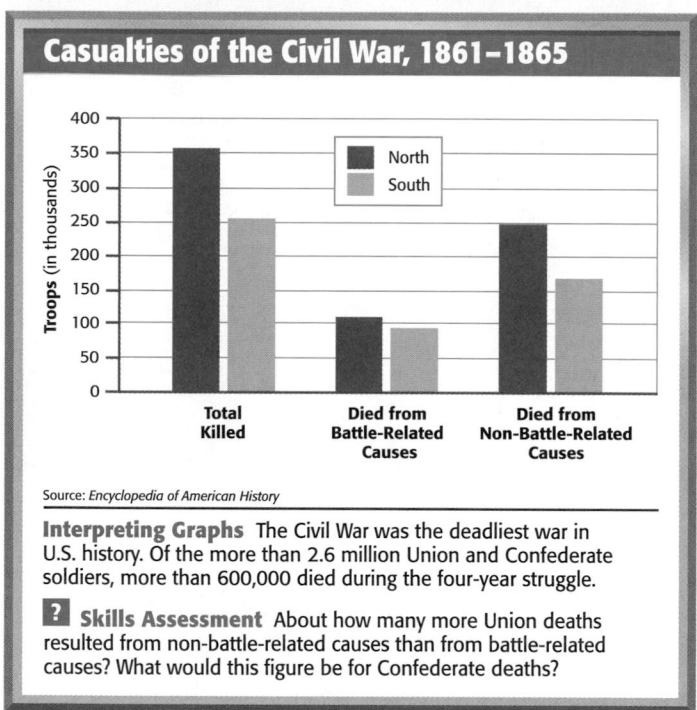

Casualties of the Civil War, 1861–1865

Troops (in thousands) — North, South

Source: *Encyclopedia of American History*

Interpreting Graphs The Civil War was the deadliest war in U.S. history. Of the more than 2.6 million Union and Confederate soldiers, more than 600,000 died during the four-year struggle.

? Skills Assessment About how many more Union deaths resulted from non-battle-related causes than from battle-related causes? What would this figure be for Confederate deaths?

INTERPRETING THE VISUAL RECORD

Total war. General William Tecumseh Sherman led his troops on a destructive march to the sea. *What evidence of Sherman's total-war strategy can you identify in the photograph?*

The fall of Atlanta boosted President Lincoln's re-election campaign. The Union victory came at a critical moment when Lincoln appeared in danger of not even receiving his party's nomination. Many Republicans were upset that the war had dragged on for so long. Sherman's success renewed hope that the conflict would soon end. Lincoln won the election of 1864 against the Democratic candidate, General George McClellan.

After the burning of Atlanta, General Sherman's army raced rapidly toward the port city of Savannah, Georgia. Sherman's men took what supplies they could use and destroyed anything that might be helpful to the Confederates. They uprooted crops, burned farmhouses, slaughtered livestock, and tore up railroad tracks. In South Carolina, Mary Boykin Chesnut wrote in her diary, "Since Atlanta I have felt as if all were dead within me, forever. We are going to be wiped off the earth."

Although much of the destruction went beyond Sherman's orders, it stemmed from the general's strategy of fighting a **total war.** He believed that it was not enough to wage war against enemy troops. Rather, to win the war, the Union must strike at the enemy's economic resources. Sherman believed they "must make old and young, rich and poor, feel the hard hand of war. . . . We cannot change the hearts of those people of the South," he said, "but we can make war so terrible . . . that generations would pass away before they would again appeal to it." Although Sherman's tactics brought the Union's goals within reach, his actions left deep and bitter scars across the South.

In early December 1864, Sherman and his men reached Savannah, where they were resupplied by the Union navy. On December 22, the general sent President Lincoln a message: "I beg to present you, as a Christmas gift, the city of Savannah." One month later Sherman and his troops turned north in an effort to link up with General Grant's troops.

✔ **READING CHECK: Drawing Conclusions** How did General Sherman change the tactics of war? employed strategy of total war, which meant that he tried to destroy everything that would allow the Confederacy to keep fighting

Surrender at Appomattox

As General Sherman's army pushed northward through the Carolinas, General Grant's troops battered Richmond. On April 2, 1865, with Grant close on his heels, General Lee withdrew from Richmond. Within hours Union troops poured into the Confederate capital.

REVIEW

Have students complete the **Section 4 Review** on p. 123.

ASSESS

Have students complete **Daily Quiz 3.4.** As **Alternative Assessment**, you may want to use the role-playing exercise or Appomattox activity in this section's lessons.

RETEACH

Have students complete **Main Idea Activity for English Language Learners and Special-Needs Students 3.4.** Then organize students into groups of five and have each group write

10 questions based on the information in the section (two questions per group member). Tell students to write the answers on a separate sheet of paper before exchanging questions with another group to answer. If time permits, have groups exchange questions again with different groups.
English Language Learners, Cooperative Learning

EXTEND

Have students study the time line at the beginning of this chapter. Tell students to choose what they believe to be the two most important turning points in the Civil War. Have students identify and justify their choices in a two-to-three-paragraph essay.
Block Scheduling

Lee's army was now only half the size of Grant's. Knowing his troops could not survive another summer like the one of 1864, Lee attempted to flee westward, hoping to join up with more troops. Grant cut off Lee's escape, however. With his once-proud army reduced to less than 30,000 men, many without food, Lee asked for terms of surrender.

On April 9, 1865, Grant and Lee met in a house in the tiny Virginia village of Appomattox Courthouse. Lee stood in full dress uniform with a jewel-studded sword at his side. Grant wore a private's shirt, unbuttoned at the neck. For a time the two men talked about their Mexican War days. Then they turned to the business at hand.

The terms of surrender were simple. Confederate officers could keep their side arms. All soldiers would be fed and allowed to keep their horses and mules. None would be tried for treason. "Let all the men who claim to own a horse or mule take the animals home with them to work their little farms," said Grant. "This will do much toward conciliating [uniting] our people," replied Lee.

As Lee rode off, Union troops started to celebrate the Union victory, but Grant silenced them. "The war is over," he said. "The rebels are our countrymen again." After the surrender, Lee returned to his men and quietly told them:

History Makers Speak

❝I have done for you all that it was in my power to do. You have done all your duty. Leave the result to God. Go to your homes and resume your occupations. Obey the laws and become as good citizens as you were soldiers.❞

—Robert E. Lee, quoted in *The Civil War Day by Day*, by E. B. Long

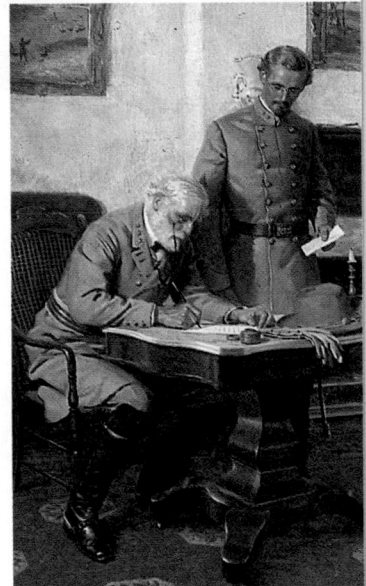

General Robert E. Lee signs the papers of surrender, ending the Civil War.

The weary Confederates were then fed and allowed to depart for home. On April 26, 1865, General Joseph E. Johnston surrendered to General Sherman under similar terms at Durham Station, North Carolina. The war was over.

✔ **READING CHECK: Making Predictions** Why were the terms of the surrender at Appomattox kept so simple? because both General Grant and General Lee wanted to emphasize that the two sides were once again joined together as one nation

SECTION 4 REVIEW

1. Define and explain:
war of attrition
total war

2. Identify and explain:
George Meade
Battle of Gettysburg
Pickett's Charge
Gettysburg Address
Siege of Vicksburg
William Tecumseh Sherman

3. Sequencing Copy the graphic organizer below. Use it to list the major events that occurred between General Grant's promotion and General Lee's surrender at Appomattox Courthouse.

1. Grant is promoted to lead the Union army
2. _____
3. _____
4. _____
5. _____
6. _____
7. _____
8. Lee surrenders at Appomattox Courthouse

4. ▌ **Finding the Main Idea** ▐

a. How did the battles of Gettysburg and Vicksburg affect the course of the Civil War?
b. Was preserving the Union worth its costs in terms of lives lost? Explain your answer.
c. What were the strategies of Ulysses S. Grant and William Tecumseh Sherman? Was there another strategy that could have succeeded and led to less destruction in the South?

5. ▌ **Writing and Critical Thinking** ▐

Summarizing Imagine that you are General Grant. Write a report for President Lincoln on the surrender of General Lee.
Consider:
• what the terms of the surrender were
• how both sides reacted to the terms
• what conditions Grant could have demanded

go.hrw.com Homework Practice Online
keyword: SE3 HP3

---

5. became commander of the Union army in 1864; accepted Lee's surrender in 1865

6. northerners who sympathized with the South

7. Lincoln's military order freeing slaves in areas held by the Confederacy

8. the destruction of enemy troops and economic resources

9. Grant's plan to continue fighting until the South ran out of men, supplies, and will

10. commanded the Union forces that captured Atlanta and Savannah

Understanding Main Ideas

1. Its fall led President Lincoln to declare the existence of a rebellion in the South and to call for soldiers to put down the rebellion.

2. They filled vacated jobs and aided the war efforts by producing food and supplies, participating in volunteer groups, and raising money.

3. The Union victory at Antietam provided Lincoln with the necessary political power to issue the Emancipation Proclamation.

4. Confederate officers could keep their side arms, and Confederate soldiers were fed, protected from trial for treason, and allowed to keep their animals and return home.

CHAPTER 3
REVIEW AND ASSESSMENT RESOURCES

TECHNOLOGY
- ▶ Chapter 3 Test Generator (on the One-Stop Planner)
- ▶ Global Skill Builder CD–ROM
- ▶ HRW Go site

REINFORCEMENT, REVIEW, AND ASSESSMENT
- ▶ Chapter 3 Review, pp. 124–25
- ▶ Chapter 3 Tutorial for Students, Parents, Mentors, and Peers

- ▶ Chapter 3 Test (Form A or B)
- ▶ Portfolio Activities and Alternative Assessment Handbook, Chapter 3
- ▶ Chapter 3 Test for English Language Learners and Special-Needs Students

REVIEW
Have students complete the **Chapter 3 Review** on pp. 124–25.

ASSESS
Use one of the chapter tests to assess students' understanding of the content. For **Alternative Assessment**, see the **Portfolio Activities and Alternative Assessment Handbook.**

Reviewing Themes

1. Capture of the Mississippi River enabled the Union to divide the Confederacy geographically and thus weaken it considerably.

2. The North's industry, material resources, and railroads gave it a significant advantage over the South, which had an increasingly hard time supplying its army over the course of the war because most of its wealth was in land and slaves.

3. It prompted some people to question whether it was a violation of an individual's liberty to force that individual to participate in the war.

Thinking Critically

1. Answers will vary. Some students might hypothesize that European aid to the South would have prompted the North to give up the struggle.

2. Some African Americans fought for the Union and helped win several battles; women raised money, cared for the sick, and in some cases spied for the army.

3. It enjoyed superior military leadership and employed defensive tactics for much of the war; it also constituted a huge geographical area for Union forces to subdue.

4. Students who agree with draft opponents might argue that it placed the burden of fighting on the poor. Those who disagree might contend that the draft was necessary to sustain the war efforts of both sides.

CHAPTER 3 Review

Creating a Time Line

Copy the time line below onto a sheet of paper. Complete the time line by filling in the events and dates from the chapter that you think were most significant. Pick three events and explain why you think they were significant.

| 1861 | 1863 | 1865 |

Writing a Summary

Using standard grammar, spelling, sentence structure, and punctuation, write an overview of events in the chapter.

Identifying People and Ideas

Identify the following terms or individuals and explain their significance.

1. Robert E. Lee
2. Thomas "Stonewall" Jackson
3. George B. McClellan
4. Elizabeth Blackwell
5. Ulysses S. Grant
6. Copperheads
7. Emancipation Proclamation
8. total war
9. war of attrition
10. William Tecumseh Sherman

Understanding Main Ideas

SECTION 1 *(pp. 96–102)*
1. What role did the attack on Fort Sumter play in the outbreak of the war?

SECTION 2 *(pp. 103–109)*
2. What contributions did civilians make during the war?

SECTION 3 *(pp. 110–117)*
3. What role did the Battle of Antietam play in the Emancipation Proclamation?

SECTION 4 *(pp. 118–123)*
4. What were the terms of Robert E. Lee's surrender at Appomattox Courthouse?

Reviewing Themes

1. **Geography** What role did geography play in helping the North win the war?
2. **Economics** How did the economic resources of the North and the South affect the war?
3. **Citizenship** How did the draft challenge ideas about individual liberty in the North and in the South?

Thinking Critically

1. **Making Predictions** How might the outcome of the Civil War have been different if European powers had aided the South?
2. **Summarizing** How did African Americans and women contribute to the war effort?
3. **Analyzing Information** How did the South, with fewer supplies and resources, manage to stall a northern victory for four years?
4. **Supporting a Point of View** Were those who opposed the draft correct in their assessment of its effects? Explain your answer.
5. **Contrasting** How did people in the North and in the South experience the war in different ways?

Writing About History

Evaluating Write an essay evaluating whether a total-war strategy was necessary for the Union to win the Civil War. Use the following chart to organize your thoughts.

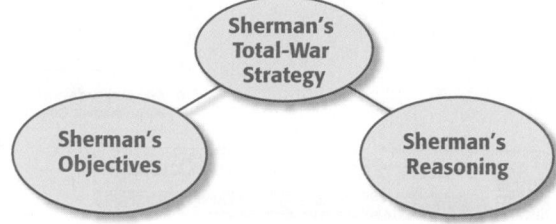

Sherman's Total-War Strategy

Sherman's Objectives

Sherman's Reasoning

RETEACH

Organize students into five groups and assign each group one of the following topics pertaining to the Civil War: the dissolution of the Union and the beginning of the war; daily life on the home front and on the battlefield; the early battles (through Antietam); the later battles; or the war's end and impact. Have each group prepare a magazine spread on its topic for a modern newsmagazine doing a special commemorative edition on the Civil War. They should focus on the events, people, and issues that most strongly affected their topic area. Tell groups to write a minimum of three articles and to include three or more images for their section of the magazine. Also tell them to use standard, grammar, spelling, sentence structure, and punctuation. When all the groups have finished their sections, have volunteers make a cover, a title page, and a table of contents for the completed magazine.
English Language Learners, Cooperative Learning

EXTEND

Have students use the library to find examples of correspondence written during the Civil War. They might look for soldiers' letters home, generals' letters to their presidents, or citizens' letters to editors of local newspapers. Have each student evaluate the validity of each source based on language, corroboration with other sources, and information about the author. **Block Scheduling**

Building Social Studies Skills

Interpreting Maps
Study the map below. Then use it to help answer the questions that follow.

The United States in 1860

Free states Slave states Territories

Analyzing Primary Sources
Analyze the following quotation from President Lincoln's first inaugural address in 1861 and then answer the questions that follow.

"We are not enemies, but friends. We must not be enemies. Though passion may have strained, it must not break our bonds of affection. The mystic chords of memory, stretching from every battlefield and patriot grave to every living heart and hearthstone all over this broad land, will yet swell the chorus of the Union when again touched, as surely they will be, by the better angels of our nature."

1. What was the ratio of slave states to free states in 1860?
   a. 8 slave states/16 free states
   b. 15 slave states/18 free states
   c. 16 slave states/15 free states
   d. 16 slave states/18 free states

2. Which slave states remained in the Union, and why did they do so?

3. Which of these statements best summarizes Lincoln's main idea?
   a. The memory of our history, particularly of the sacrifices made by soldiers in the past, will eventually draw us to restore the Union.
   b. The music of the army band, as it plays here at Gettysburg, reminds us of the unity we wish to restore.
   c. Although we have survived a cruel war that split families and strained our nation, the angels will restore our affection.
   d. The wickedness of our enemies is stretched from the bloody battlefields, so that we can never restore the Union.

4. In what ways does Lincoln demonstrate his optimism at the beginning of his first term?

Alternative Assessment

Building Your Portfolio

U.S. HISTORY

Government
Imagine that you are a member of a congressional committee attempting to formulate a compromise between the North and South to prevent a civil war. Create a chart listing the economic, political, and social differences between the two sides that might make an agreement difficult. Your chart should also include peaceful ways to resolve obstacles. Then write five questions for other students to answer using the chart.

internet connect

Internet Activity: go.hrw.com
KEYWORD: SE3 AN3

Access the Internet through the HRW Go site to research the geographic distribution of major battles during the Civil War. Then create a three-dimensional model of one of these battles. Your model should represent the terrain, any geographic features (such as rivers, woods or hills) that affected the battle, and any other important factors such as towns or railroads. As a review, pose and answer questions with a partner in which you analyze why the battle was fought at that location.

LET'S GET STARTED!

Direct students' attention to the maps of the North before the Civil War and the South before the Civil War. Tell students to imagine that they are British journalists who traveled by rail through both regions. Have each student write a few sentences or paragraphs describing both regions. Ask volunteers to share their sentences or paragraphs with the class. Tell students that they will learn more about regionalism in the United States in the Unit 1 America's Geography.

TEACH AMERICA'S GEOGRAPHY— REGIONALISM

Tell students that maps and graphs can complement each other to provide a complete picture of a particular historical subject. Have students study the maps and the graph in the America's Geography feature. Then ask each student to write a few sentences or paragraphs summarizing the information presented there. **English Language Learners**

THEN AND NOW

The Expansion of Education. Although the South and the West had relatively few colleges and universities before the Civil War, both regions greatly expanded their educational institutions after the war. In 1850, for example, there were no colleges and universities in California. By 1995 the state had 348 such institutions.

ACTIVITY: Ask students to conduct research on the founding dates of local colleges and universities. Have each student create a detailed time line on the subject and present it to the class. Alternately, ask each student to write a short report tracing the growth of local colleges and universities.

THAT'S INTERESTING!

Willamette University in Salem, Oregon, was founded in 1842, making it one of the oldest universities in the West. Even so, Willamette University is some 200 years younger than Harvard, the first American university.

AMERICA'S Geography

Regionalism

By the mid-1800s the United States consisted of three distinct geographic regions—the North, the West, and the South. Each had its own unique character and culture. Some people felt more loyalty to their region than to the nation as a whole. This concept of regionalism was particularly evident in the South. Unlike sectionalism, regionalism focuses more on cultural identity than political differences. If a state's cultural identification changes, so can its regional identity. For example, many residents of Missouri identified with the South before the Civil War. In the late 1800s, however, industrialization, trade, and transportation increased in the state. Its culture then became closely identified with that of the Midwest.

The North Before the Civil War

Colleges and universities in 1850 · | Canals to 1850 | Major railroads to 1861

Evergreen forest | Tallgrass prairie | Shrub
Deciduous forest | Shortgrass prairie | Desert
Mixed forest

The North. The smallest region—the North—was the center of industrialization in the United States. It was also the center of higher education. In 1850 most of the country's colleges and universities—63 percent—were located in the North.

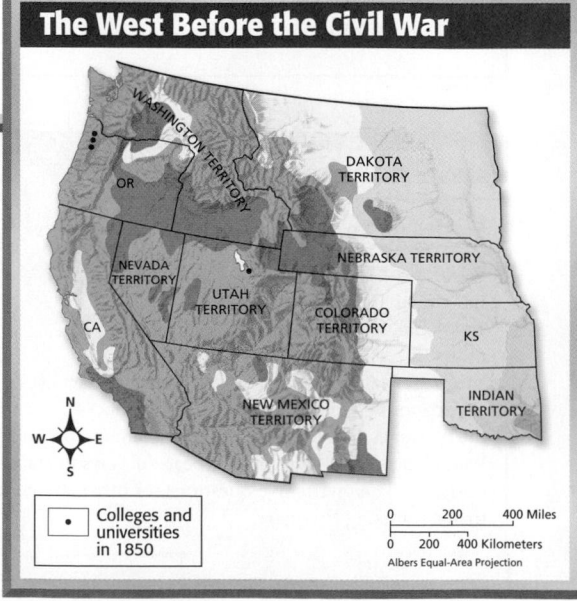

The West Before the Civil War

Colleges and universities in 1850

The West. Although the West was the largest region of the country in 1850, it had the smallest population. The first centers of education in the West were located on the frontier. The Mormons of Utah and followers of the Oregon Trail established the region's first universities.

SPOTLIGHT
on Oberlin College

Ask students to locate and use a variety of primary and secondary sources to learn more about Oberlin College, a leading northern college that played an important role in the abolition movement. Then tell students to imagine that they are modern-day historians. Have each student write a short paper explaining how Oberlin College typified the North and northern concerns in the era before the Civil War.
Block Scheduling

SPOTLIGHT
on the Look of the West

Pair students and ask them to study the map on the West before the Civil War, paying close attention to the map legend. Have each pair consult a dictionary, science textbook, or encyclopedia in order to write definitions for the terms on the legend. Then ask each pair to use its definitions to write a few sentences describing a particular territory in the West.
Block Scheduling, Cooperative Learning

AMERICA'S Geography

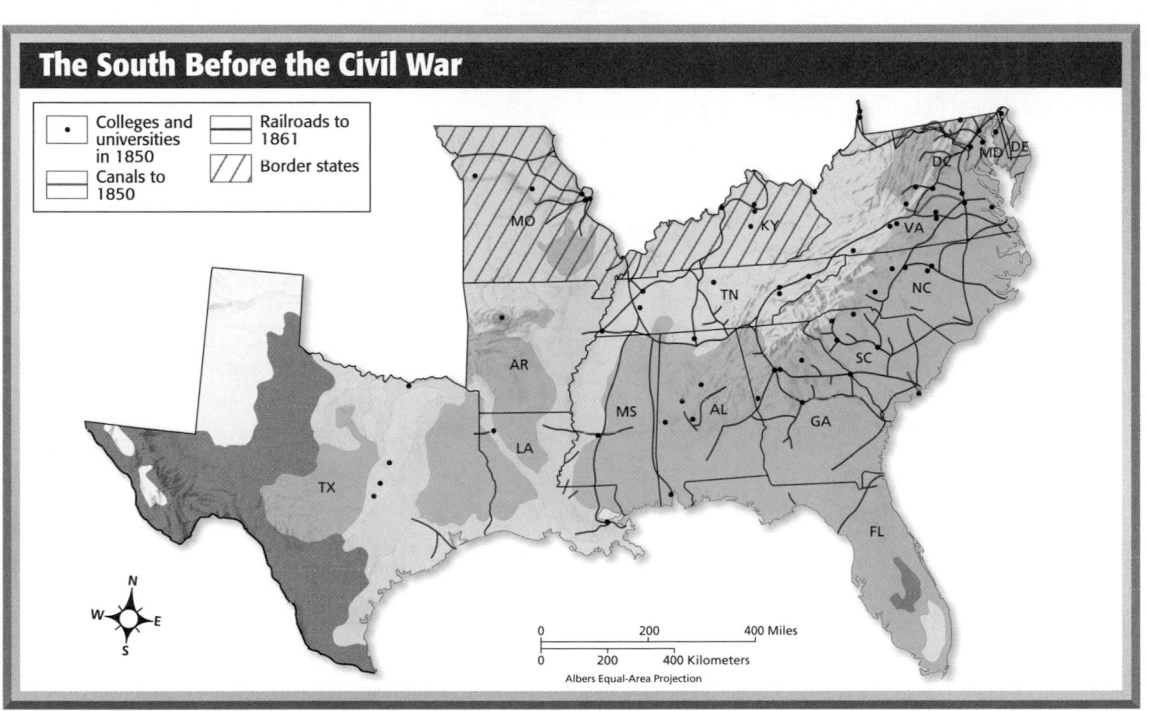

The South Before the Civil War

Legend:
- Colleges and universities in 1850
- Canals to 1850
- Railroads to 1861
- Border states

MO, KY, VA, DC, MD, DE, TN, NC, AR, SC, MS, AL, GA, LA, TX, FL

0 200 400 Miles
0 200 400 Kilometers
Albers Equal-Area Projection

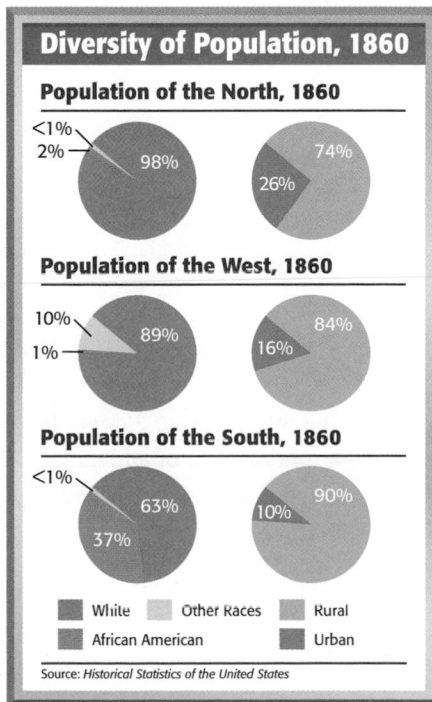

Diversity of Population, 1860

Population of the North, 1860
<1%
2%
98%
74%
26%

Population of the West, 1860
10%
89%
84%
1%
16%

Population of the South, 1860
<1%
63%
90%
37%
10%

Legend:
- White
- African American
- Other Races
- Rural
- Urban

Source: Historical Statistics of the United States

The South. The South had a larger population than the West, but a smaller percentage of its population lived in urban areas. Many western settlers tended to move to booming cities such as San Francisco. The South had more colleges than the West. Overall, however, it lagged far behind the North in education. A majority of the country's residents who could not read lived in the South. Most were slaves who were not allowed to learn to read.

GEOGRAPHY AND HISTORY Skills

PLACES AND REGIONS

1. How did the populations of the North, the South, and the West differ?
2. What might be the relationship between different physical environments and railroad construction?

SCIENCE, TECHNOLOGY, AND SOCIETY

The Transportation Revolution and Regionalism. The Transportation Revolution helped reduce the regional and sectional differences between the North and the South, even though the South had far fewer railroads than the North. Railroads and canals linked the nation, allowing the exchange of ideas and goods.

CRITICAL THINKING Ask students to consider the issue of regionalism today. What factors or developments have helped reduce regionalism in the modern-day United States?

ANSWER: Answers will vary. Students might suggest that the Internet helps people overcome both regional and national differences.

AMERICA'S GEOGRAPHY ANSWERS

1. The North had the largest percentage of white residents and was the most urbanized region. The West had the largest percentage of non-white, non-African American residents. The South had the largest percentage of African American residents and was the most rural region.

2. Answers will vary. Students might note the lack of railroads in the mountainous West, as well as the proximity of major railroad hubs to major harbors or waterways.

Reconstruction and the New South

CHAPTER RESOURCE MANAGER

Objectives	Pacing Guide	Reproducible Resources
SECTION 1 **Presidential Reconstruction** pp. 130–34 ★ Describe the hopes and expectations that African Americans in the South had for their lives as freedpeople. ★ Relate how President Lincoln and Congress differed over plans for Reconstruction. ★ Explain how President Johnson's programs benefited former Confederates. ★ Evaluate how the Black Codes affected freedpeople.	**Regular** 1 day **Block Scheduling** .5 day *Block Scheduling Handbook with Team Teaching Strategies, pp. 19–24*	**RS** Guided Reading Strategy 4.1 **PS** Primary Source Reading 4: The Emancipation Proclamation
SECTION 2 **Congressional Reconstruction** pp. 135–42 ★ Describe the issues that divided Republicans during the early Reconstruction era. ★ Explain why moderates and Radical Republicans joined forces and their actions. ★ Relate why President Johnson was impeached, and explain why the Senate acquitted him. ★ Explain why African Americans were crucial to the election of 1868 and how Republicans responded to their support.	**Regular** 2 days **Block Scheduling** 1 day *Block Scheduling Handbook with Team Teaching Strategies, pp. 19–24*	**RS** Guided Reading Strategy 4.2 **PS** American History Political Cartoon 3: Radical Reconstruction **E** Hands-On History Activity: People Helping People
SECTION 3 **Reconstruction in the South** pp. 143–47 ★ Explain how African Americans attempted to improve their lives during the Reconstruction era. ★ Identify Republican reforms. ★ Relate how some African Americans responded to harassment by the Ku Klux Klan. ★ Describe why Reconstruction ended.	**Regular** 1 day **Block Scheduling** .5 day *Block Scheduling Handbook with Team Teaching Strategies, pp. 19–24*	**RS** Guided Reading Strategy 4.3 **RS** Graphic Organizer Activity 4: Evaluating Reconstruction
SECTION 4 **The New South** pp. 148–53 ★ Analyze the drawbacks to the sharecropping system. ★ Assess how Jim Crow laws and the *Plessy* v. *Ferguson* decision changed life for southern African Americans. ★ Explain how African Americans attempted to improve their economic situation after Reconstruction. ★ Compare the views of Booker T. Washington and Ida B. Wells.	**Regular** 1 days **Block Scheduling** .5 days *Block Scheduling Handbook with Team Teaching Strategies, pp. 19–24*	**RS** Guided Reading Strategy 4.4 **SM** Geography Activity 4: Tenant Farming and Sharecropping **IC** Literature Reading 4: The Cruelty of Jim Crow Laws **PS** Biography Reading 4: Ida B. Wells **E** Creative Teaching Strategies: Open Interviewing

Chapter Resource Key

PS Primary Sources	**REV** Review	Video
RS Reading Support	**ELL** Reinforcement and English Language Learners	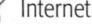 Internet
IC Interdisciplinary Connections		Holt Presentation Maker Using Microsoft® PowerPoint®
E Enrichment	Transparencies	
SM Skills Mastery	CD–ROM	
A Assessment	Music	

 One-Stop Planner CD–ROM

See the *One-Stop Planner* for a complete list of additional resources for students and teachers.

One-Stop Planner CD-ROM

It's easy to plan lessons, select resources, and print out materials for your students when you use the **One-Stop Planner CD-ROM with Test Generator.**

Technology Resources	Reinforcement, Review, and Assessment

One-Stop Planner, Lesson 4.1
American Music Selection 15: "When Johnny Comes Marching Home Again"
Holt Researcher: American History CD–ROM
CNN. Presents America: Yesterday and Today, Beginnings to 1914 Segment: The Life of Lincoln
Homework Practice Online

REV Section 1 Review, p. 134
A Daily Quiz 4.1
ELL Main Idea Activity 4.1
ELL English Audio Summary 4.1
ELL Spanish Audio Summary 4.1

One-Stop Planner, Lesson 4.2
Holt Researcher: American History CD–ROM
Homework Practice Online

REV Section 2 Review, p. 142
A Daily Quiz 4.2
ELL Main Idea Activity 4.2
ELL English Audio Summary 4.2
ELL Spanish Audio Summary 4.2

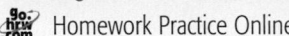
One-Stop Planner, Lesson 4.3
Holt Researcher: American History CD–ROM
Homework Practice Online
HRW Go site

REV Section 3 Review, p. 147
A Daily Quiz 4.3
ELL Main Idea Activity 4.3
ELL English Audio Summary 4.3
ELL Spanish Audio Summary 4.3

One-Stop Planner, Lesson 4.4
The American Nation Video Program Segment: The Tuskegee Institute; Teacher's Guide, pp. 63–68
Holt Researcher: American History CD–ROM
Homework Practice Online

REV Section 4 Review, p. 153
A Daily Quiz 4.4
ELL Main Idea Activity 4.4
ELL English Audio Summary 4.4
ELL Spanish Audio Summary 4.4

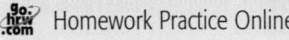

Meeting Individual Needs

Ability Levels

Level 1 Basic-level activities designed for all students encountering new material

Level 2 Intermediate-level activities designed for average students

Level 3 Challenging activities designed for honors and gifted-and-talented students

English Language Learners Activities that address the needs of students with Limited English Proficiency

Chapter Review and Assessment

 Global Skill Builder CD–ROM
 HRW Go site
REV **Chapter 4 Tutorial for Students, Parents, Mentors, and Peers**
REV **Chapter 4 Review, pp. 154–55**
Chapter 4 Test Generator (on the One-Stop Planner)
A **Chapter 4 Test (Form A or B)**
A **Alternative Assessment Handbook**
A **Chapter 4 Test for English Language Learners and Special-Needs Students**

Build on What You Know

Ask students to answer the following questions.

How might a society incorporate newly freed slaves?

Consider:
- the racial beliefs that contributed to the existence of slavery
- the economic and social needs of a disenfranchised population

How might a nation reunify after a bloody civil war?

Consider:
- the ideas and arguments that justified war
- the issue of lingering resentment

---

exploring the time line

AMERICAN EVENTS

internet connect

TOPIC: Fisk University
GO TO: go.hrw.com
KEYWORD: SE3 AN4

Have students access the Internet through the HRW Go site to conduct research on Fisk University and the Fisk Jubilee Singers. Then tell students to write a report in which they outline the role of Fisk University and the Jubilee Singers in the education of freedpeople and in African American community and culture. Use standard grammar, punctuation, sentence structure, and spelling.

CHAPTER 4

1865–1900

Reconstruction and the New South

Items President Lincoln had with him when he was shot

Harvesting cotton

THE GRANGER COLLECTION, NEW YORK

1865
Politics
President Lincoln is assassinated.

1868
Politics
President Andrew Johnson is impeached.

1878
Business and Finance
Good land for growing cotton can be purchased in North Carolina for as low as $5 an acre.

1881
The Arts
The Southern Art Union is organized.

1881
World Events
Alexander II, czar of Russia, is assassinated.

| 1865 | 1870 | 1875 | 1880 |

1865
Daily Life
Slavery is abolished by the Thirteenth Amendment.

1867
Business and Finance
Southern crops bring in just half their expected price, ruining many planters.

1867
Daily Life
Howard University is established for African American students.

1867
Politics
Congress passes the first Reconstruction Act.

1871
The Arts
The Fisk Jubilee Singers tour in the United States.

1881
Politics
The first Jim Crow law requires African Americans to ride in separate railway cars from whites.

The Fisk Jubilee Singers

Build on What You Know

Beginning with the framing of the Constitution and continuing through the Civil War, slavery caused political tension in the United States. Although many Americans agreed that slavery was incompatible with democratic ideals, it took a bloody civil war to finally bring an end to slavery. The war's end, however, raised a new challenge: how to bring emancipated slaves into a free society. In this chapter you will learn how the nation struggled to define the rights of freed African Americans, while also seeking to restore the southern states to the Union.

What's Your Opinion?

To help students create their Themes Journal entries, provide the following examples of appropriate agree/disagree statements.

Constitutional Heritage

Agree Colonists rebelled against Great Britain after officials failed to accommodate political and economic demands.

Disagree The framers of the Constitution made it fairly difficult to amend the document.

Government

Agree The Federalists passed the Alien and Sedition Acts to protect the United States against treason.

Disagree The Constitution and the Bill of Rights established permanent and unalienable freedoms.

Economics

Agree In the antebellum South, planters' dependence on cotton limited the development of industry in the region.

Disagree The Market Revolution allowed different regions to specialize in different products, fostering economic growth.

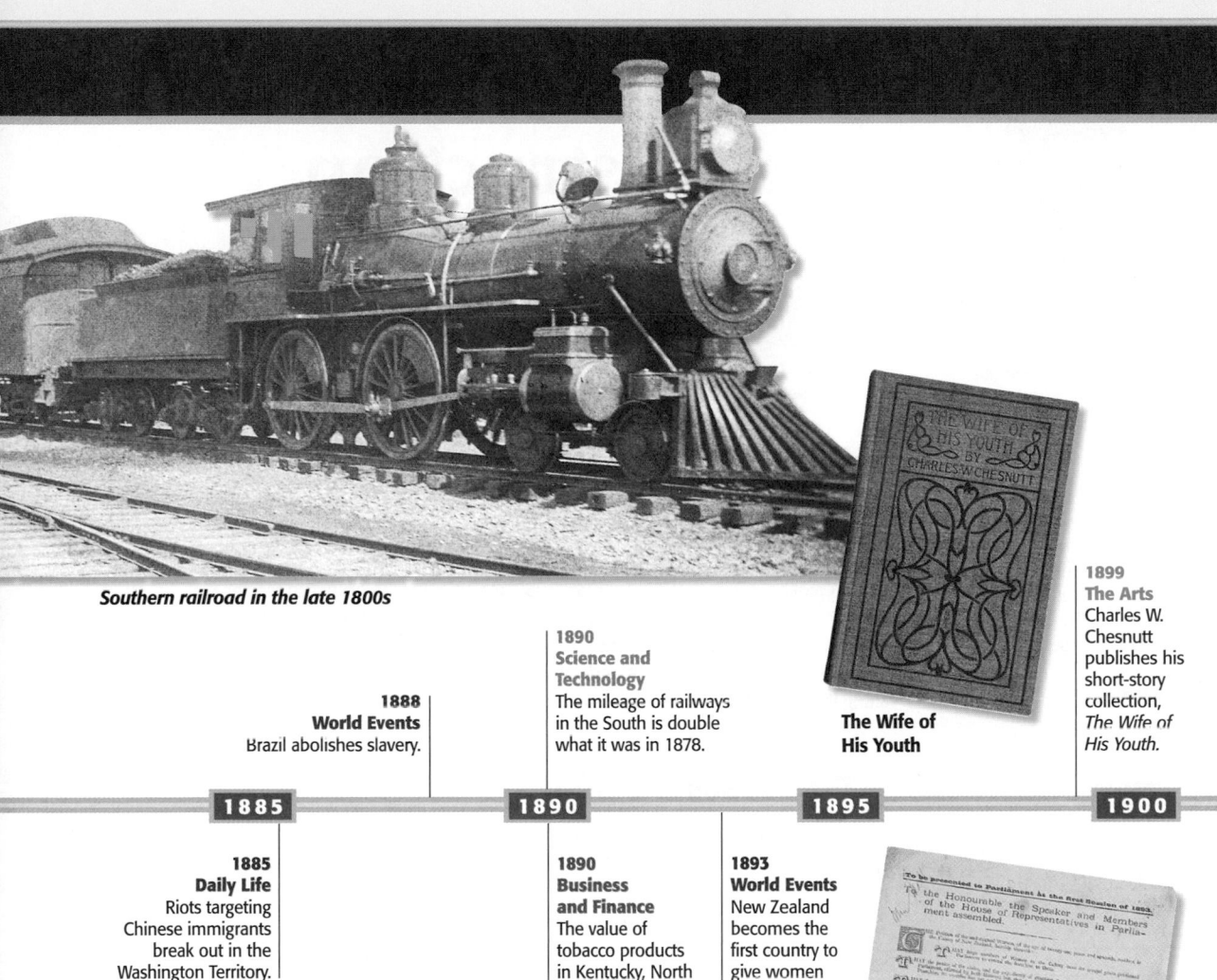

Southern railroad in the late 1800s

1885
Daily Life
Riots targeting Chinese immigrants break out in the Washington Territory.

1885 teapot brought by a Chinese immigrant to the United States

1888
World Events
Brazil abolishes slavery.

1890
Science and Technology
The mileage of railways in the South is double what it was in 1878.

1890
Business and Finance
The value of tobacco products in Kentucky, North Carolina, and Virginia is almost $31 million.

1893
World Events
New Zealand becomes the first country to give women the vote.

The Wife of His Youth

1899
The Arts
Charles W. Chesnutt publishes his short-story collection, *The Wife of His Youth.*

Petition for voting rights by New Zealand women

1885   **1890**   **1895**   **1900**

What's Your Opinion?

Themes Journal *Do you agree or disagree with the following statements? Support your point of view in your journal.*

Constitutional Heritage A government that cannot adapt to change poses a threat to the very society it has been created to govern.

Government A nation's definition of a democratic society changes over time in response to war and other significant events.

Economics A region's dependence on the sale of a single product ultimately serves to limit the region's economic development.

exploring the time line
GLOBAL EVENTS

GLOBAL RELATIONS

1888 ■ Brazil Abolishes Slavery. Slavery in Latin America was abolished gradually between 1823 and 1888. Many Latin American revolutionary leaders had realized the irony of using slaves to fight for freedom. Chile abolished slavery in 1823, and other nations soon followed until Brazil remained the only slaveholding country in Latin America. Many Brazilian slaves worked on *engenhos,* or sugar plantations; others worked on cattle ranches or in gold mines. The abolition of slavery in Brazil began with the 1871 Law of Free Birth, which stated that children born of slave mothers after that date were free. By the time Princess Isabel, daughter of Brazil's emperor, signed the "Golden Law" abolishing all slavery in 1888, only about 5 percent of Brazil's labor force was made up of slaves.

CRITICAL THINKING Why might Brazilians have called the law abolishing slavery the "Golden Law"?

ANSWER: Students might suggest that they might have wished to emphasize the law's goodness, beauty, and value to those whom it freed.

After completing Section 1, students should be able to:

OBJECTIVE 1 Describe the hopes and expectations that African Americans in the South had for their lives as freedpeople.

OBJECTIVE 2 Relate how President Lincoln and Congress differed over plans for Reconstruction.

OBJECTIVE 3 Explain how President Johnson's programs benefited former Confederates.

OBJECTIVE 4 Evaluate how the Black Codes affected freedpeople.

LET'S GET STARTED!

As students enter the classroom, play Selection 15, "When Johnny Comes Marching Home Again," from the **American Music Audio CD Program**. Ask students to respond to the song in writing. Have volunteers share their responses. Tell students that composer Patrick Sarsfield Gilmore wrote "When Johnny Comes Marching Home Again" to celebrate peace. Then tell students that in Section 1 they will learn about the challenges of peace in the Reconstruction era.

SECTION 1

READ TO DISCOVER
1. What hopes and expectations did African Americans in the South have for their lives as freedpeople?
2. How did President Lincoln and Congress differ over plans for Reconstruction?
3. How did President Johnson's programs benefit former Confederates?
4. How did the Black Codes affect freedpeople?

DEFINE
amnesty

IDENTIFY
Reconstruction
John Wilkes Booth
Andrew Johnson
Thirteenth Amendment
Black Codes

WHY IT MATTERS TODAY
Nations today continue to rebuild after wars or natural disasters. Use CNNfyi.com or other **current events** sources to find a modern country or region that is rebuilding after a destructive event or period. Record your findings in your journal.

Presidential Reconstruction

 EYEWITNESSES TO History

Let a great earthquake swallow us up first! Let us leave our land and emigrate to any desert spot of the earth, rather than return to the Union.

—Sarah Morgan, quoted in *Trial by Fire*, by Page Smith

Such feelings expressed by a white southern woman were common among many former Confederates after the Civil War. African Americans in the South reacted very differently. After Charleston, South Carolina, surrendered in February 1865, the city's African American residents hosted a parade they called a "jubilee of freedom." In April, after Union forces captured Richmond, Virginia, President Abraham Lincoln visited the city. African American T. Chester Morris wrote in the *Philadelphia Press*, "There is no describing the scene along the route. The colored population was wild with enthusiasm."

Emancipation parade

The Old South Destroyed

The Civil War inflicted mass devastation on the South, leaving many cities in ruins. A visitor to Columbia, South Carolina, described "a wilderness of crumbling walls, naked chimneys, and trees killed by flames." Illness swept the region, resulting in thousands of deaths in the South in the year after the war.

The Civil War also shattered the South's economy. Tens of thousands of Confederate veterans were left without jobs. Similarly, most of the approximately 4 million emancipated slaves found themselves homeless and penniless. "It came so sudden on 'em," recalled former slave Parke Johnston.

History Makers Speak

Just think of whole droves of people, that had always been kept so close, and hardly ever left the plantation before, turned loose all at once, with nothing in the world, but what they had on their backs.

—Parke Johnston, quoted in *Slave Testimony*, edited by John W. Blassingame

Despite the obstacles, most freedpeople looked eagerly to the future. Like former slave Henry Turner, they yearned to enjoy their "rights in common with other men." They hoped to establish their own churches and schools and to legalize their marriages. Many freedpeople expected to choose their own livelihood. With freedom anything seemed possible, even finding family members who had been sold away. Former slave Hawkins Wilson sent a letter to his sister, address unknown, believing that it would somehow find its way to her. "Your little brother Hawkins is trying to find out where you are and where his poor old mother is," he wrote. "Let me know and I will come to see you."

Above all, African Americans hoped, like Garrison Frazier, "to have land . . . and till it by our own labor." Most wanted land to support themselves and to protect

LEVEL 1: Ask each student to create a graphic organizer displaying African Americans' hopes and expectations for their lives as freedpeople. *(Students' organizers should include the desire to establish churches and schools, legalize marriages, find family members who had been sold away, own land, and enjoy basic human rights.)* Ask volunteers to sketch their graphic organizers on the chalkboard.
English Language Learners

LEVEL 2: Pair students and tell them to imagine that they are freedpeople living in Georgia. Have the members of each pair develop a short dialogue expressing their hopes and expectations

for their lives as freedpeople *(See the Level 1 lesson for the correct responses.)* Ask volunteers to perform their dialogues for the class. Then have each student write two or three paragraphs summarizing the material presented in the dialogues.
Cooperative Learning

LEVEL 3: Tell students to imagine that they are freedpeople living in Georgia. Have each student write a short speech expressing his or her hopes and expectations for life as a freedperson to be delivered at a gathering of former slaves. *(See the Level 1 lesson for the correct responses.)* Ask volunteers to deliver their speeches to the class.

---

their independence. Many believed that it was their due. "Our wives, our children, our husbands, has been sold over and over again to purchase the lands we now locates upon," argued former slave Bayley Wyat. "We have a divine right to the land." General William T. Sherman had encouraged such hopes in January 1865, when he ordered part of South Carolina to be divided into 40-acre parcels and given to freedpeople. Rumors spread that the federal government would give each freedman "40 acres and a mule."

✔ **READING CHECK: Categorizing** How did African Americans in the South want their lives to be different as freedpeople?
They wanted their own churches, schools, legalized marriages, land, and independence.

President Lincoln and Reconstruction

President Abraham Lincoln wanted to bring the rebel states back into the Union quickly. He had not gone to war to destroy the South, but to preserve the Union. Even before the war's end, he had begun planning for **Reconstruction**—rebuilding the former Confederate states and reuniting the nation.

The beginning of Reconstruction. To encourage southerners to abandon the Confederacy, Lincoln had issued the Proclamation of Amnesty and Reconstruction on December 8, 1863. The proclamation offered **amnesty**. This would give a full pardon to all southerners—except high-ranking Confederate leaders and a few others—who would swear allegiance to the U.S. Constitution and accept federal laws ending slavery. The proclamation also permitted a state to rejoin the Union when 10 percent of its residents who had voted in 1860 swore their loyalty to the nation.

Many members of Congress objected to this so-called Ten Percent Plan. They did not trust the Confederates to become loyal U.S. citizens or to protect the rights of former slaves. Congress laid out its own Reconstruction plan in the Wade-Davis Bill, passed in July 1864. The bill called for the Confederate states to abolish slavery and to delay Reconstruction until a majority of each state's white males took a loyalty oath. Lincoln said he vetoed the bill because he was not ready to "be inflexibly committed to any single plan of restoration." In his second inaugural address, delivered on March 4, 1865, Lincoln clarified his goal for Reconstruction.

 "With malice toward none, with charity for all, with firmness in the right as God gives us to see the right, let us strive on . . . to bind up the nation's wounds . . . to do all which may achieve . . . a just and lasting peace."

—Abraham Lincoln, "Second Inaugural Address"

✔ **READING CHECK: Contrasting** How did President Lincoln's and Congress's plans for Reconstruction differ? Lincoln proposed the Ten Percent Plan, and Congress presented the Wade-Davis Bill.

⭐ Then and Now

Juneteenth

O n June 19, 1865, Union soldiers arriving in Galveston, Texas, shared with the city's African Americans the contents of an important general order: "The people of Texas are informed that in accordance with a Proclamation from the Executive of the United States, all slaves are free." Since then, June 19 has been celebrated by African Americans in many areas of the South as Emancipation Day, or Juneteenth.

A recent Juneteenth parade in Texas

Complete with parades and marching bands, the earliest Juneteenth celebrations were usually held in rural areas. They often included rereadings of the proclamation, speeches, and songs. African Americans dressed up, cooked special food, danced, played baseball, and rejoiced in their freedom.

The celebration of Juneteenth declined in the early 1900s but regained its popularity in the 1960s. In 1980 Texas named Juneteenth an official state holiday. Today communities throughout the country still enthusiastically celebrate the holiday. Modern Juneteenth festivities include traditional elements, such as guest speakers, prayer services, and barbecues. Official Juneteenth festivals also offer a wide array of activities, such as pageants, lectures, art shows, and even a blues festival in Houston, Texas. Juneteenth celebrates African American freedom in addition to bringing people of all cultures together in harmony.

CITIZENSHIP

Wade-Davis Manifesto. After Lincoln vetoed the Wade-Davis Bill, Benjamin Franklin Wade and Henry Winter Davis, sponsors of the bill, attacked him in an editorial in the New York *Tribune*. Their attack, called the Wade-Davis Manifesto, accused Lincoln of "holding for naught the will of Congress" and declared that Lincoln's responsibility was "to obey and execute, not make the laws." The Manifesto was so bitter that it served to make Lincoln more popular and damaged the reputations of Wade and Davis.

ACTIVITY: Organize students into teams representing Congress and President Lincoln. Have teams debate the terms of the bill and Lincoln's right to override the popular congressional bill.

THAT'S INTERESTING!

During the Civil War, some freed slaves had formed their own towns. These towns were often established in areas where the Union Army had taken on the responsibility of supporting former slaves who had deserted the plantations.

LEVEL 1: Pair students and ask them to list the provisions of both President Lincoln's and Congress's Reconstruction plans. *(Pairs should list the following: Lincoln—wanted to abolish slavery, give amnesty to most southerners, and allow rebel states to rejoin the Union when 10 percent of the residents who had voted in 1860 pledged their loyalty to the Union. Congress—wanted to abolish slavery and delay Reconstruction until a majority of each state's white males took a loyalty oath.)* Create comprehensive lists on the chalkboard and ask students to evaluate the two plans.

English Language Learners, Cooperative Learning

LEVELS 2 AND 3: Organize students into two groups: President Lincoln and aides, and congresspeople and aides. Tell each group to prepare for a debate on the Reconstruction plans. Ask a spokesperson from each group to open the debate by summarizing the group's assigned Reconstruction plan. *(See the Level 1 lesson for the correct features of each plan.)* Then have students evaluate the advantages and disadvantages of each plan.

Cooperative Learning

HOMEWORK *Ask each student to write a one-page Reconstruction plan. Have students present their plans to the class. Then have students select the best plan. Ask students to justify their choices.*

THAT'S INTERESTING!

After news of Lincoln's assassination spread, many people worried that Confederates had plotted the crime. Mobs threatened imprisoned Confederate officers. Anyone resembling John Wilkes Booth was arrested, and even people who had once expressed antipathy to the North or toward Lincoln were thrown in jail by zealous law officers. Booth's brothers, also well-known actors, were threatened by a mob and arrested. In San Francisco, mobs destroyed newspaper offices that had shown Confederate sympathies.

SKILL-BUILDING STRATEGIES ANSWERS

Practicing the Skill

1. As a northerner, Greeley may have viewed the South with suspicion. As a southerner, Lee may have believed that the South was ready to rejoin the Union and obey its laws.

2. Greeley—the North should continue to control the South; based partly on his opinion that southerners were only waiting for a new chance to defeat the North; Lee—that it is time to restore harmony to the nation; based on the fact that the war had been won by the North

3. Answers will vary. Students may answer that Greeley is more reliable because he bases his argument on the South's previous actions.

Skill-Building Strategies

Comparing Points of View

Historians often encounter conflicting accounts of events because of differing points of view. Every person has a point of view, or personal frame of reference, from which he or she experiences and thinks about things. Factors such as age, sex, education, and family background, as well as social and historical circumstances, help to shape this point of view. Comparing points of view can lead to historical insights and a better understanding of the causes of historical conflicts.

How to Compare Points of View

1. **Identify the sources.** When you encounter conflicting historical accounts, verify the identity of each author or speaker. If possible, find out about the personal, social, and historical background of each source.
2. **Identify and compare the main ideas.** Identify the main idea expressed by each source. Then note the similarities and differences between these ideas.
3. **Examine the supporting details.** Determine whether each source supports its main idea with relevant facts, opinions, or a combination of both.
4. **Evaluate the points of view.** Use your analysis of the sources, main ideas, and supporting details, along with your knowledge of the historical period, to assess the reliability of each account and its accompanying point of view.

Applying the Skill

Read and compare the following statements about how the Union should treat the South.

> These gentlemen of the South mean to win. They meant it in 1861 when they opened fire on Sumter. . . . They mean it now. The moment we remove the iron hand from the Rebels' throats they will rise and attempt the mastery.
>
> —New York Tribune *editor Horace Greeley*

> The war being at an end, the Southern states having laid down their arms and the questions at issue between them and the Northern states having been decided, I believe it to be the duty of everyone to unite in the restoration of the country and the reestablishment of peace and harmony.
>
> —*Confederate general Robert E. Lee*

Practicing the Skill

Answer the following questions.

1. How do you think the background of each author affected his statement?
2. Analyze the main idea of each statement. What facts or opinions support this idea?
3. Whose point of view seems most reliable? Why?

After President Lincoln's assassination, the War Department offered a reward for the capture of John Wilkes Booth.

Lincoln's assassination. How Reconstruction might have developed under Lincoln's direction will never be known. On April 14, 1865, just days after General Robert E. Lee's surrender, Confederate sympathizer **John Wilkes Booth** shot the president as he and his wife watched a play at the Ford's Theatre in Washington. Lincoln died early the following morning.

Across the country, Americans remembered Lincoln by displaying bits of black cloth outside their homes. Thousands filed through the rotunda of the nation's Capitol to pay their respects before he was laid to rest. Hundreds of thousands more stood beside railroad tracks as the funeral train made its way from Washington to Lincoln's burial site in Illinois.

Many ordinary Americans feared the impact that Lincoln's death might have on the country. Sidney George Fisher believed that his death might be harder on the South than the North. He noted, "Mr. Lincoln's humanity & kindness of heart stood between them [southerners] and the party of the North who urge measures of vengeance & severity." The assassination also increased the distrust between the North and the South. Many northerners believed that Booth was part of a conspiracy organized or encouraged by Confederate leaders.

TEACH OBJECTIVES 3 AND 4

ALL LEVELS: Discuss with students the effects of President Johnson's Reconstruction plan on former Confederates and the effects of the Black Codes on freedpeople. To help students fully understand the issues, copy the following graphic organizer on the chalkboard, omitting the italicized answers. Have each student complete it.

English Language Learners

President Johnson's Reconstruction Plan

↓

Benefits to Former Confederates
- *Blanket pardon for most rebels*
- *Easy terms of readmission to the Union: states had to nullify their acts of secession, abolish slavery, and refuse to pay war debts*

↓

Former Confederates Enact Black Codes

↓

Effects of Codes on African Americans
- *Tried to deprive freedpeople of equality*
- *Re-established white control over African American labor*

President Johnson and Reconstruction

After President Lincoln's death, Vice President **Andrew Johnson** assumed the presidency. Johnson was a Democrat, a onetime slaveholder, and a former U.S. senator from Tennessee. He had been chosen as Lincoln's running mate in 1864 because of his pro-Union sympathies. Republican leaders had hoped he would appeal to northern Democrats and southern Unionists.

Despite his support for the Union and his wartime experience as Tennessee's military governor, Johnson proved ill-suited to the challenges of Reconstruction. He favored a government controlled by white citizens. He suffered, as one contemporary observer noted, from "almost unconquerable prejudices against the African race." Johnson also lacked Lincoln's political skill, often refusing to compromise.

In May 1865 Johnson issued a complete pardon to all rebels except former Confederate officeholders and the richest planters. He pardoned these people on an individual basis. Johnson's forgiveness extended to the rebel states as well. For readmission to the Union, his plan required only that they nullify their acts of secession, abolish slavery, and refuse to pay Confederate government debts. The last provision was intended to punish southerners who had financed the Confederacy.

Southerners, including General Robert E. Lee, enthusiastically supported President Johnson's plan. They liked it because it allowed Confederate leaders to take charge of Reconstruction. These men—some of whom continued to wear their army uniforms—dominated the new state legislatures. Even former Confederate vice president Alexander H. Stephens, who had been charged with treason, took office in the nation's capital as a representative.

As lawmakers, these former Confederates made sure that the new state constitutions did not grant voting rights to freedmen. When the lawmakers complained about the continued presence of Union troops—African American soldiers in particular—President Johnson supported their removal. By recognizing Mississippi's new government, Johnson even overlooked the state's refusal to ratify the **Thirteenth Amendment**—which Congress had passed in January 1865 to abolish slavery.

✔ **READING CHECK: Drawing Conclusions** Why was President Johnson lenient toward former Confederates? Johnson was a former slaveholder from Tennessee, a Confederate state. He wanted a government controlled by white citizens.

The Black Codes

President Johnson's actions encouraged former Confederates to adopt laws limiting the freedom of former slaves. These **Black Codes** closely resembled pre–Civil War slave codes. Mississippi, for example, simply recycled its old code, substituting the word *freedman* for *slave*.

The Black Codes varied from state to state. However, they all aimed to prevent African Americans from achieving social, political, and economic equality with southern whites. African Americans could not hold meetings unless whites were present. The code also forbade them to travel without permits, own guns, attend schools with whites, or serve on juries. Most importantly the codes re-established white control over African American labor.

Research on the ROM

Free Find:
Andrew Johnson

After reading about Andrew Johnson on the **Holt Researcher CD–ROM**, imagine that you are in Washington, D.C., at the time of Lincoln's assassination. Write a report on what plans for Reconstruction you expect Johnson to propose.

INTERPRETING THE VISUAL RECORD

Former Confederates. Many southern legislators like these continued to wear their Confederate uniforms when conducting political business. *What message would the wearing of such uniforms convey?*

INTERDISCIPLINARY CONNECTIONS

▶GOVERNMENT◀

A Nation Still Divided. Southern newspapers praised Johnson, calling him "a statesman of God's creation." At the same time, many northerners could not overcome their distrust of the South. One Ohioan who traveled in the South after the war observed, "Since the war ended I've been a conservative; I've considered [Radical Republicans] dangerous men, who didn't understand the South, wanted to humble it . . . and were standing in the way of peace. . . . I came [to the South] with the kindest feelings for the people down here. . . . I thought the South wanted [peace]. But I was tremendously mistaken. They hate us and despise us and all belonging to us. They call us cut-throats, liars, thieves, vandals, cowards, and the very scum of the earth. . . . I tell you I'm going home to be a radical."

CRITICAL THINKING Why might southerners have had such distrust for northerners?

ANSWER: Students might suggest that southerners were still angry about losing the Civil War and their way of life.

VISUAL RECORD ANSWER

Some students might suggest that the former Confederates retained their power or that the wearing of such uniforms signified defiance of Reconstruction measures.

REVIEW

Have students complete the **Section 1 Review** on p. 134.

ASSESS

Have students complete **Daily Quiz 4.1**. As **Alternative Assessment**, you may want to use the dialogue or the Reconstruction plan debate in this section's lessons.

RETEACH

Have students complete **Main Idea Activity for English Language Learners and Special-Needs Students 4.1**. Then organize the class into small groups and assign each group one of the section objectives. Have each group prepare two or three newspaper headlines capturing the main ideas of its assigned section. Ask each group to share its headlines with the class. Invite students to comment on the accuracy and insight of the headlines.
English Language Learners, Cooperative Learning

EXTEND

Ask students to conduct research on the Black Codes. Then organize students into triads and tell them to imagine that they are meeting to discuss the codes. Have each triad develop a plan responding to the Black Codes. Triads should fully determine the costs of the chosen action. Have each triad present its response plans to the class and ask students to evaluate the efficacy and applicability of each.
Cooperative Learning, Block Scheduling

Many laws in the South were passed to maintain an African American labor force to work the fields of white-owned plantations.

Without slaves to do the work, "our fields everywhere lie untilled," one white southerner said. To force former slaves to return to the fields, some local codes prohibited African Americans from living in towns unless they were servants and from renting land outside of towns or cities. Several states required freedpeople to sign long-term labor contracts. Those who refused could be arrested and have their labor put up for auction. Other codes required African Americans to obtain a special license to work in a skilled profession.

The codes also allowed judges to decide whether African American parents could support their children. Children without "adequate" support could be bound, or hired, out against their will. The former owner usually was given the first opportunity to bid. Judges' decisions were often arbitrary. In North Carolina an African American man who worked and supported a wife and child was still considered an "orphan" to be bound out. Some courts bound out children without even informing their parents.

Many African Americans realized that emancipation had not greatly improved their daily lives. Of the Black Codes, one African American veteran demanded, "If you call this Freedom, what do you call Slavery?" Although African Americans immediately denounced these laws as "a disgrace to civilization," they had little political power. Many felt they had to accept the codes in order to survive.

Northerners criticized the Black Codes as an attempt to re-establish slavery. The *Chicago Tribune* responded to the Mississippi code.

 History Makers Speak

❝The men of the North will convert the State of Mississippi into a frog pond before they will allow such laws to disgrace one foot of soil in which the bones of our soldiers sleep and over which the flag of freedom waves.❞

—*Chicago Tribune*, December 1, 1865

Analyzing Primary Sources

Identifying Bias How does the writer reveal his opinion of the Black Codes?

by writing that northern men will turn Mississippi into a frog pond before allowing the state to impose the Black Codes

✔ **READING CHECK: Comparing** Compare the lives of freedpeople under the Black Codes with their former lives as slaves. Black Codes made daily life for African Americans almost as restricted as it was under slavery.

SECTION 1 REVIEW

1. Define and explain:
amnesty

2. Identify and explain:
Reconstruction
John Wilkes Booth
Andrew Johnson
Thirteenth Amendment
Black Codes

3. Comparing Copy the chart below. Use it to compare the Reconstruction plans of President Lincoln, Congress, and President Johnson.

Lincoln's Plan	Congress's Plan	Johnson's Plan

4. Finding the Main Idea

a. What was life like for southern African Americans immediately after the Civil War?

b. Why might President Johnson's plan for Reconstruction have been considered unfair?

c. How did the Black Codes attempt to limit opportunities for African Americans?

5. Writing and Critical Thinking

Identifying Points of View Write a paragraph explaining how disagreements over Reconstruction policy reflected different views about what the lasting effects of the Civil War should be.

Consider:
• Congress's views
• President Lincoln's views
• President Johnson's views

 Homework Practice Online
keyword: SE3 HP4

SECTION 2

After completing Section 2, students should be able to:

OBJECTIVE 1 Describe the issues that divided Republicans during the early Reconstruction era.

OBJECTIVE 2 Explain why moderates and Radical Republicans joined forces and their actions on behalf of African Americans.

OBJECTIVE 3 Relate why President Johnson was impeached, and explain why the Senate acquitted him.

OBJECTIVE 4 Explain why African Americans were crucial to the election of 1868 and how Republicans responded to their support.

🎧 LET'S GET STARTED!

Write the following statement on the chalkboard: *It is 1867. In what circumstances—and for what offenses—is it right and proper to remove a president from office?* As students enter the classroom, ask them to answer the question. Have volunteers share their responses. Then tell students that in Section 2 they will learn more about the impeachment of President Johnson.

SECTION 2

Congressional Reconstruction

EYEWITNESSES TO History

"Reformation must be effected; the foundation of [southern] institutions, both political, municipal, and social must be broken up and relaid, or all our blood and treasure have been spent in vain. This can only be done by treating and holding them as a conquered people. . . . The whole fabric of southern society must be changed, and never can it be done if this opportunity is lost. Without this, this Government can never be, as it has never been, a true republic."

—Thaddeus Stevens, "Proposal Advocating the Redistribution of Land," 1865

Thaddeus Stevens

Pennsylvania representative Thaddeus Stevens issued this challenge to Congress in 1865. Many southerners argued that such a harsh approach to Reconstruction would only lead to another civil war. "The day of reckoning cometh, and it will be terrible," warned one southern newspaper.

READ TO DISCOVER

1. What issues divided Republicans during the early Reconstruction era?
2. Why did moderates and Radical Republicans join forces, and what actions did they take on behalf of African Americans?
3. Why was President Johnson impeached, and why did the Senate not remove him from office?
4. Why were African Americans crucial to the election of 1868, and how did Republicans respond to their support?

IDENTIFY

Thaddeus Stevens
Frederick Douglass
Freedmen's Bureau
Civil Rights Act of 1866
Fourteenth Amendment
Reconstruction Acts
Ulysses S. Grant
Fifteenth Amendment

▶ WHY IT MATTERS TODAY

In the 1860s the Radical Republicans used their control of Congress to pass major laws. Use CNNfyi.com or other **current events** sources to identify which political party controls each house of Congress today and one piece of legislation that party is trying to pass. Record your findings in your journal.

CNNfyi.com

The Moderates Versus the Radicals

Even Republicans disagreed over the course Reconstruction should take. The issue of African American voting rights proved particularly divisive. Most Republicans were moderates who viewed Reconstruction as a practical matter of restoring the southern states to the Union. Their main concern was keeping former Confederates out of government. They favored giving African Americans some civil equality but not the vote.

Supporters of African American suffrage. In contrast, Radical Republicans like **Thaddeus Stevens** insisted that African Americans be given the right to vote. These Republicans believed that the proper aim of Reconstruction was to create a new South where all men would enjoy equal rights.

Few northerners, even abolitionists, supported giving African Americans in the South the right to vote. Some Republicans even supported giving the vote only to northern African American men. Although few Americans publicly supported voting rights for African Americans, **Frederick Douglass** did. Douglass demanded "the immediate, unconditional, and universal 'enfranchisement [right to vote] of the black man, in every State in the Union.'"

BIOGRAPHY

Frederick Douglass

Frederick Douglass was born into slavery in 1817 on a tobacco plantation in eastern Maryland. His mother was hired out when he was still an infant. He later recalled that he did not see his mother "more than four or five times in my life." When Douglass was about six years old, he was sent to a nearby plantation where he ran errands and performed simple chores. Douglass learned in 1825 that he was to be sent away from the plantation to Baltimore. He received this news with

SECTION 2 RESOURCES

REPRODUCIBLE
▶ Guided Reading Strategy 4.2
▶ American History Political Cartoon 3: Radical Reconstruction

TECHNOLOGY
▶ One-Stop Planner, Lesson 4.2
▶ Holt Researcher: American History CD–ROM
▶ Homework Practice Online

REINFORCEMENT, REVIEW, AND ASSESSMENT
▶ Section 2 Review, p. 142
▶ Daily Quiz 4.2
▶ Main Idea Activity 4.2
▶ English Audio Summary 4.2
▶ Spanish Audio Summary 4.2

TEACH OBJECTIVE 1

LEVELS 1 AND 2: Write the following statements on the chalkboard: *1) The main goal of Reconstruction is to create an entirely new South and give African Americans the right to vote. 2) The main goal of Reconstruction is to restore the southern states to the Union, keep former Confederates out of government, and give African Americans some civil equality.* Have students label the statements as representing the views of either moderate Republicans or Radical Republicans. *(The first statement represents the views of Radical Republicans, while the second represents the views of moderate Republicans.)* Then have each student write one or two paragraphs explaining how these political issues affected the Republican Party during the early Reconstruction era. **English Language Learners**

LEVEL 3: Tell students to imagine that they are either a moderate Republican or a Radical Republican. Have each student write a one-page position statement describing his or her position on Reconstruction and analyzing how it differs from that of other Republicans. *(See the Level 1 lesson for the correct issues and divisions.)* Ask volunteers to read their position papers to the class.

HISTORY MAKERS SPEAK

Reverend E. J. Adams in
Lift Every Voice

A Stirring Public Speaker.
African American reverend E. J. Adams spoke to a gathering of people celebrating the passage of the Reconstruction Acts: "A perfect Union, justice, domestic tranquillity, the common defense, the general welfare, and the blessings of liberty cannot be secured without universal suffrage. It is the only means of defense for the illiterate and the poor. . . . I do not, however, wish to be understood that I advocate or wish for social equality. God forbid that. For some of my mean white drunken enemies may sneak into my house and marry my daughter."

CRITICAL THINKING To what historical document does Adams refer in his speech?

ANSWER: Students should mention the U.S. Constitution.

VISUAL RECORD ANSWER
Students might suggest that freedpeople dreamed of prosperity and a secure family life.

PRIMARY SOURCE ANSWER
Students might answer that he sells pegs to African Americans when there is no land for them.

INTERPRETING THE VISUAL RECORD

Family records. After the Civil War, many former slaves tried to find lost relatives. *What ideals does this family record registry suggest about life for African Americans after the Civil War?*

"joy" and "ecstasy." Douglass spent most of the next seven years in the household of Hugh and Sophia Auld, looking after their young son. Sophia Auld also taught him to read and write.

Douglass was sent to a farm some 40 miles from Baltimore when he was about 15 years old. Longing for freedom, Douglass began planning his escape. One of the other slaves involved, however, betrayed the plan. Douglass was spared the common punishment of being sold. Instead, his captors returned him to Baltimore, where he worked in the shipyards for the next two years. In 1838 he again decided to run away. Using borrowed papers that stated he was a free African American sailor, Douglass traveled north. Douglass arrived in New York on September 4, 1838. He became a leader in the antislavery cause and wrote his life story, the *Narrative of the Life of Frederick Douglass,* which was published in 1845.

After the war, Douglass embraced the policies of Reconstruction and Radical Republicanism. He remained active, editing a newspaper in Washington and serving as president of the Freedmen's Bank. Along with several other African Americans, Douglass attempted to advise President Johnson on how to keep "peace between races," hoping to bring an end to the ongoing violence in the South. He served as a U.S. marshal, a recorder of deeds, and as the U.S. minister to Haiti. Douglass died of heart failure on February 20, 1895.

Land reform. Some political leaders emphasized African American suffrage and civil equality. Others saw land reform as the key to changing southern society. Representative Thaddeus Stevens agreed with Senator Charles Sumner of Massachusetts, who insisted that "the great plantations . . . must be broken up, and the freedmen must have the pieces." According to Stevens, economic independence for the former slaves would ensure their freedom. Such independence would also destroy the political power of the "proud, bloated, and defiant rebels."

Despite the efforts of Stevens and Sumner, land reform—particularly government seizure of land—never won wide support. The *New York Times* accused land reformers of starting "a war on property . . . to succeed the war on Slavery." Even many Radical Republicans were skeptical of land reform. They believed that African Americans could achieve social and economic independence if they were granted civil equality, the right to vote, and the right to labor freely.

✔ **READING CHECK: Identifying Points of View** Describe the different views political leaders held about southern society in the Reconstruction era. *Some wanted African Americans to have suffrage and civil equality, while others supported land reform.*

PRIMARY SOURCE

Reconstruction and Land Reform

While land reform did not become part of Reconstruction, many freed slaves believed rumors that they would receive land. John G. Pierce reported to Congress on how these rumors led some people to try to take advantage of African Americans. **How does the man described in this quotation exploit African Americans' desire for land?**

"I can tell you from what I know and have seen myself, and also from what Negroes have told me, that they have been promised land and mules—forty acres and a mule—on diverse occasions. . . . I can illustrate it by one little thing that I saw on a visit once to [Alabama]. . . . I saw a man who was making a speech to the Negroes, telling them what good he had done for them, that he had been to Washington City and procured [got] from one of the departments here certain pegs. . . . He said that those pegs he had obtained from here at great expense to himself, that they had been made by the government for the purpose of staking out the Negroes' forty acres. He told the Negroes that all he wanted to have the expenses paid to him, which was about a dollar a peg."

TEACH OBJECTIVE 2

LEVEL 1: Working as a class, create a flowchart displaying why moderate and Radical Republicans joined forces and what actions they took on behalf of African Americans. *(Flowcharts should indicate that Republicans joined forces to protect African Americans from postwar violence. They overrode presidential vetoes to pass the Civil Rights Act of 1866 and extend the Freedmen's Bureau. They also passed the Fourteenth Amendment.)* Ask students to select the congressional action that they believe most helped southern African Americans. Conduct a debate on the issue.
English Language Learners

LEVEL 2: Tell students to imagine that it is 1866 and that they are editorial writers for a Washington newspaper. Have each student write two editorials: one urging moderate and Radical Republicans to join forces to protect African Americans against postwar violence, and one urging Republican congressmembers to pass the Civil Rights Act, extend the Freedmen's Bureau, or pass the Fourteenth Amendment. Ask volunteers to read their editorials to the class. Students may wish to include their editorials in their portfolios.

Congress Versus Johnson

The split between moderate Republicans and Radical Republicans did not last long. In early 1866 Congress held hearings on conditions in the South. Witnesses before the Joint Committee on Reconstruction presented evidence of postwar violence. African Americans recounted stories of murder and of homes, schools, and churches reduced to "ashes and cinders." Southern Unionists told of death threats. These reports and others like them convinced moderate Republicans to join forces with the Radical Republicans.

The Freedmen's Bureau. One move made by the Republicans was to extend the life of the **Freedmen's Bureau.** Congress had created the bureau in March 1865 to aid the millions of southerners left homeless and hungry by the war. The bureau distributed food and clothing, served as an employment agency, set up hospitals, and operated schools.

The Freedmen's Bureau played a major role in providing education for African Americans, who had been denied this opportunity under slavery. By 1869 thousands of schools for African Americans had been established in the South. Many of the teachers were women from the North. Northerners also helped establish colleges for black southerners, including Atlanta University in Georgia, Howard University in Washington, and Fisk University in Nashville, Tennessee. Union general Samuel Chapman Armstrong, who had led African American troops in the Civil War, founded the Hampton Institute in Virginia in 1868.

The Freedmen's Bureau also helped settle contract disputes between African American laborers and white planters. In most cases the bureau encouraged laborers to continue working on plantations, even under unfavorable conditions. Two freedmen who believed that their contracts were unfair sued Mary Jones, a plantation owner. The bureau agent forced the men to go back to work. Once they returned to the plantation, Jones expressed her feelings.

> "In . . . doubting my word they [the African American men] had offered me the greatest insult I ever received in my life; . . . I had considered them friends and treated them as such . . . ; but . . . now they were only laborers under contract, and only the law would rule between us."
>
> —Mary Jones, quoted in *Trial by Fire*, by Page Smith

Congress had originally intended for the Freedmen's Bureau to remain in operation for one year. In light of the congressional hearings on postwar violence, however, most members of Congress supported legislation to extend the life of the agency. African Americans largely agreed. Many thought that the Freedmen's Bureau too often encouraged former slaves to remain on plantations and to sign labor contracts. However, they acknowledged that the bureau's presence forced white southerners to recognize the emancipation of slaves. One African American told a government official that "if the Freedman Bureau was removed, a colored man would have better sense than to speak a word in behalf of the colored man's rights, for fear of his life."

INTERPRETING THE VISUAL RECORD

Freedmen's Bureau. Established by Congress, the Freedmen's Bureau provided southerners with food, clothing, and other services. *What does this drawing reveal about the role of the Freedmen's Bureau?*

Southern African Americans struggled to improve their lives after the Civil War.

LEVEL 3: Tell students to imagine that it is 1867 and that they are Radical Republican senators preparing to retire from Congress. Have each student write a résumé of the actions that he or she took on behalf of African Americans during the previous year. Students should preface their résumés with a brief statement explaining that they joined forces with moderate Republicans to pursue these actions. *(See the Level 1 lesson for the correct factors and actions.)* Post students' résumés and statements around the classroom.

HOMEWORK *Have each student write a summary of the subsection entitled Congress Versus Johnson. Tell each student to use standard grammar, spelling, sentence structure, and punctuation.*

SPOTLIGHT
on the Civil Rights Act of 1866
Have students closely examine the poster on this page. Then pair students and ask each pair to create a political cartoon, with caption, commenting on the Civil Rights Act of 1866. Then ask students to present their cartoons to the class. To conclude, conduct a brief discussion on the Civil Rights Act of 1866.
Block Scheduling, Cooperative Learning

NOTE: To help students make meaningful connections between events in U.S. history and those in their own hometown, use the Chapter 4 **Hands-On History Activity**, People Helping People.

THAT'S INTERESTING!

Philanthropists Anson M. Sperry and John W. Alford decided that a bank for freed slaves would help teach them thrift. African Americans were to set up societies to collect and deposit money in one of the Freedmen's Savings Banks. Unfortunately, when the bank was passed into the hands of a new board of directors, the money deposited there was no longer safe, and the bank eventually closed. More than 61,000 depositors lost nearly $3 million in savings.

VISUAL RECORD ANSWER

(for p. 137)

Students might suggest that the drawing reveals that the group helped maintain peace between white and black southerners.

VISUAL RECORD ANSWER

Students might mention that the poster shows a blind Liberty and a white man whipping a black man at her feet.

VISUAL RECORD ANSWER

(for p. 139)

Students might mention that the illustration shows the violence and the dead.

INTERPRETING THE VISUAL RECORD

Civil Rights Act of 1866.
Despite the passage of the Civil Rights Act of 1866, many African Americans continued to suffer, much as they did under slavery. *How does this poster mock the effectiveness of the civil rights legislation?*

In an attempt to weaken the bureau, President Johnson sent two generals to tour the South in 1866. Johnson hoped that the generals would uncover complaints about the organization. Instead, they encountered widespread support among African Americans for the agency. In February 1866 Congress passed the Freedmen's Bureau Bill to extend the life of the agency. To the surprise of many, Johnson vetoed the bill, citing constitutional and financial reasons. "It was never intended that the Freedmen should be fed, clothed, educated and sheltered by the United States," he said.

The Civil Rights Act of 1866. Furious with the president, Congress promptly passed the **Civil Rights Act of 1866**, the first civil rights law in the nation's history. Although the act declared that everyone born in the United States was a citizen with full civil rights, it did not guarantee voting rights. Legislators designed the act to overturn discriminatory laws and the Supreme Court's 1857 *Dred Scott* ruling that African Americans were not citizens. "If the President vetoes the Civil Rights Bill," wrote one Ohio senator, "we shall be obliged to draw our swords."

Johnson did not heed the warning, however. He vetoed the bill, arguing that it would centralize power in the federal government. Johnson's veto eroded his support in Congress and united both moderate and Radical Republicans against him. Congress overrode Johnson's veto of the Civil Rights Act. Returning to the matter of the Freedmen's Bureau, Congress passed a new bill to extend it and then overrode yet another presidential veto.

The Fourteenth Amendment. Congressional Republicans feared that a future Congress controlled by Democrats might repeal the Civil Rights Act. They therefore wrote the act's provisions into the **Fourteenth Amendment**, passed in June 1866. The amendment required states to extend equal citizenship to African Americans and all people "born or naturalized in the United States." It also denied states the right to deprive anyone of "life, liberty, or property without due process of law." Further, it promised all citizens the "equal protection of the laws." The amendment's ratification in July 1868 granted the nation's citizens rights—enjoyed equally by all—that could be enforced by the federal government.

The Fourteenth Amendment did not guarantee African American voting rights. It did, however, reduce the number of representatives a state could send to Congress based on how many of the state's male citizens were denied the right to vote. The more African American men who were not allowed to vote, the fewer representatives that state could send to Congress. Republicans hoped that southern states would give African Americans the right to vote rather than lose their representation in Congress.

✔ **READING CHECK: Analyzing Information** What actions did moderate and Radical Republican lawmakers take on behalf of African Americans?
established the Freedmen's Bureau and passed the Civil Rights Act of 1866 and the Fourteenth Amendment

SPOTLIGHT
on Andrew Johnson

Ask students to conduct research on Andrew Johnson and his Reconstruction policies. Then tell students to imagine that they are modern-day historians. Have each student evaluate Johnson's contributions as president and write a one-page essay justifying that evaluation. Ask students to share their evaluations with the class. Conduct a debate on students' different assessments of Johnson's presidency. **Block Scheduling**

SPOTLIGHT
on Race Riots

Ask students to create an annotated map of the race riots of 1866. Tell students to be sure to display information regarding the causes and effects of each riot. Then have students write five questions to be answered based on their maps. Ask students to trade maps and answer questions with a partner.

The Radicals Come to Power

President Johnson tried to make the Fourteenth Amendment an issue in the 1866 congressional elections. Calling the Radical Republicans traitors, he campaigned throughout the Midwest in support of candidates who opposed the amendment. Most voters were not receptive, however. Many people felt deeply troubled by the ongoing violence against African Americans in the South.

Race riots. Race riots were becoming increasingly common in the South. On May 1, 1866, two carriages collided on the streets of Memphis. When police officers arrested the African American driver but not the white one, a group of African American veterans protested. A white mob soon gathered. The resulting conflict led to a three-day spree of violence in which white rioters—consisting mainly of police officers and firefighters—killed 46 African Americans and burned 12 schools and four churches. "If anything could reveal . . . the demoniac spirit . . . toward the freedmen," one reporter noted, this violence would.

In July 1866 the Louisiana legislature called for new elections, which placed a Confederate mayor in power in New Orleans. In response, Louisiana governor James Madison Wells, a planter and former slaveholder, supported the Radical Republicans. He attempted to give African Americans the vote, to bar former Confederates from voting, and to form a new state government. His actions led to a white uprising. More than 30 African Americans and three white Republicans were killed in the resulting riot. General Philip H. Sheridan, President Johnson's military commander in Texas and Louisiana, referred to the event as "an absolute massacre."

The elections of 1866 and the Reconstruction Acts. Such violence made President Johnson's call for leniency toward the southern rebels seem particularly absurd. Johnson's campaign called for a stronger union between the North and the South. However, voters were displeased by his speeches filled with angry protest. While speaking in St. Louis, he even blamed Congress for the New Orleans riot. Wisconsin senator James R. Doolittle estimated that the president's campaign tour cost his candidates about 1 million votes. Fearing they might lose the fruits of their Civil War victory, northerners overwhelmingly voted Republican in 1866. Firmly in command of Congress, the Republicans, with the Radicals at the helm, seized control of the Reconstruction process.

Although the issue had previously divided their party, Republicans quickly decided that African Americans must have the vote. In January 1867 a bill granting African Americans the vote in the District of Columbia passed, despite Johnson's veto. Congress next extended this right to the country's territories. Although Johnson

PRESIDENTIAL
Lives
Andrew Johnson

1808–1875
In Office 1865–1869

Born in North Carolina, Andrew Johnson was a self-made man who never attended school. Johnson was very young when his father died, and his mother apprenticed him to a tailor when he was 14. One person commented that the young Johnson "was very industrious and quiet, talked but little, and always had a book by his side." Later, Johnson's wife helped him learn to write and to do simple arithmetic.

After moving to Tennessee in 1826, Johnson did well as a tailor. Although he bought property, Johnson never identified with the planter class. His loyalties were to farmers and artisans, and he always saw himself as a political outsider. Johnson never forgot his early poverty. He continued to make all his own clothes until he went to Washington. Even after he became president, Johnson often stopped by tailor shops to chat.

UNITED STATES POSTAGE

ANDREW JOHNSON 1808–1869

17 CENTS 17

INTERPRETING THE VISUAL RECORD

Race riots. In 1866, southern whites in Louisiana attacked African Americans and white Republicans. *How does this illustration reflect the event as "an absolute massacre"?*

INTERDISCIPLINARY CONNECTIONS

▶SOCIOLOGY◀

Race Riots and Lynchings. For decades after the Civil War, race riots continued to occur in areas of high racial tension. Ida B. Wells, an antilynching activist, chronicled the New Orleans riot of 1892. It began when African American Robert Charles shot at police officers who had—for no apparent reason—drawn guns on him. One police officer was killed and one was wounded. Charles then fled through the city while hundreds of white men flooded the streets in search of him. Rioters beat, shot, and killed many African Americans who crossed their paths, finally finding Charles and shooting him to death. In addition to riots, some white southerners participated in lynch mobs. Some lynchings were secret actions in the middle of the night, while others were well-publicized affairs attended by thousands.

CRITICAL THINKING How might race riots and lynchings have shown that the treatment of minorities represented one of the unmet challenges of Reconstruction?

ANSWER: Students might suggest that although Reconstruction granted legal equality to African Americans, many white southerners were determined to prevent African Americans from achieving social equality.

ALL LEVELS: To help students understand why President Johnson was impeached and why the Senate acquitted him, copy the following graphic organizer on the chalkboard, omitting the italicized answers. Ask each student to complete it. After students have completed their graphic organizers, discuss President Johnson's impeachment with the class. **English Language Learners**

The Impeachment of President Johnson

Reasons Why the House Voted to Impeach
- *General dislike of Johnson's lenient Reconstruction policies*
- *Johnson's violation of the Tenure of Office Act*
- *Johnson's "scandalous" speeches and "disgraceful" acts*

Reasons Why the Senate Voted to Acquit
- *Weak case against Johnson*
- *Hypercritical attacks on Johnson*
- *Fear that impeachment would weaken future presidents and threaten checks and balances*

HISTORY MAKERS SPEAK

Shelby M. Cullom and John Sherman in *In Their Own Words*

Impeachment Trial.
Shelby M. Cullom was a moderate Republican congressman. Cullom believed that President Johnson's public behavior contributed to the House's case against him: "[Johnson] denounced Congress. He threatened to 'kick people out of office,' in violation of the Tenure of Office Act. He was undignified in his actions and language." In the end, Cullom voted for the impeachment articles, "feeling at the same time a little doubtful of our course."

CRITICAL THINKING Why might Cullom have been doubtful about his decision, even when he knew that Johnson had declared his intention to violate the Tenure of Office Act?

ANSWER: Students might suggest that Cullom may have questioned the motives behind the impeachment proceedings or the constitutionality of the act.

VISUAL RECORD ANSWER

Students might suggest that the images' solemnity reflects the importance of the event.

INTERPRETING THE VISUAL RECORD

Impeachment. Admittance to President Johnson's impeachment trial was limited. Visitors and reporters were required to present a ticket to gain entry to the Senate gallery. *How do these images reflect the importance and drama of the event?*

declared, "Old southern leaders . . . must rule the South," Republicans passed the **Reconstruction Acts** of 1867. These acts divided the former Confederacy—with the exception of already-reconstructed Tennessee—into five military districts. Union army troops were stationed in each district to enforce order. To gain readmission to the Union, states were required to ratify the Fourteenth Amendment as well as submit to Congress new constitutions guaranteeing all men the vote. The act further required that African Americans be allowed to vote for delegates to the state constitutional conventions as well as to serve as delegates.

Presidential Impeachment

The Radical Republicans knew that the success of the Reconstruction Acts depended on strong enforcement. They were equally sure that President Johnson would not cooperate. To protect Reconstruction policies and Republican officeholders, Congress passed the Tenure of Office Act in 1867. This act required Senate approval of a replacement before the president could remove an appointed official who had been confirmed by the Senate.

Believing the law unconstitutional, Johnson put it to the test. In February 1868 he removed Secretary of War Edwin Stanton, an ally of the Radical Republicans. The House of Representatives responded by voting to impeach the president. The House charged Johnson with violating the Tenure of Office Act, making "scandalous" speeches, and bringing Congress "into disgrace."

Some senators argued that such flaws were not impeachable offenses. Senator Lyman Trumbull of Illinois, a Johnson critic, predicted, "No future President will be safe who happens to differ with a majority of the House and two-thirds of the Senate." Trumbull worried that an aggressive Congress threatened the checks and balances of the Constitution. Other senators shared his fear.

The case against Johnson was weak from the start. The impeachment articles did not really address the Radical Republicans' underlying grievances against Johnson: that he was unfair, governed poorly, and tried to halt Congress's plan for Reconstruction. Many members of Congress even feared that Johnson might lead the country into another civil war.

Johnson's Senate trial began in March 1868. Seven members of the House of Representatives stated the case for impeachment. These representatives were so critical in their attack, however, that public opinion began to turn against them. One representative even waved a blood-stained nightshirt that he asserted came from a white northerner who had been beaten by southerners. Within a month, some prominent people were calling for Johnson's acquittal. A writer for the *Nation* claimed that the House had made Johnson a villain without proving any charges.

The trial lasted eight weeks, unfolding in front of a gallery of eager spectators. On May 16, 1868, the Senate voted to acquit the president. The final tally fell one vote short of the two-thirds majority needed to convict Johnson and remove him from

LEVEL 1: Pair students and tell them to imagine that they are magazine editors preparing a special issue on the history of U.S. elections. Have each pair create an outline on the election of 1868 and its aftereffects. Students' outlines should explain why African Americans were crucial to this election and how Republicans responded to their support. *(African American votes helped Ulysses S. Grant win the presidency. The Republicans responded by passing the Fifteenth Amendment to extend the vote to African American men.)* Students may wish to include their outlines in their portfolios.
English Language Learners, Cooperative Learning

LEVELS 2 AND 3: Ask students to reread the quotation on this page. Then tell students to imagine that it is the week before the election of 1868 and that they are Republicans. Have each student write a half-page speech persuading African Americans to vote for Republicans despite intimidation in the South. Then tell students to imagine that it is the week after the election. Have each student write a half-page speech informing African Americans of how the Republican Party intends to respond to their support. *(See the Level 1 lesson for the correct responses.)* Ask volunteers to read their speeches to the class.

---

office. Risking the disapproval of their party and their constituents, seven Republican senators had joined 12 Democratic senators to vote for acquittal. The entire proceedings, concluded Republican senator Joseph Smith Fowler of Tennessee, had become "mere politics." The ordeal, however, took a toll on many of the legislators. Iowa senator James W. Grimes suffered a stroke after his constituents denounced him as a traitor for supporting the president. More importantly, with 35 senators from his own party against him, Johnson's power was broken.

✔ **READING CHECK: Sequencing** What events led to President Johnson's impeachment? Congress passed Tenure of Office Act; Johnson removed Stanton; House charged Johnson

Further Political Difficulties

The Radical Republicans' attempt to force President Johnson from office as well as their emphasis on African American suffrage cost them some popular support. Some northern legislatures even rejected proposals for African American voting rights.

The election of 1868. As the 1868 election neared, the Radical Republicans sensed trouble. To retain voters, they nominated General **Ulysses S. Grant** for president. General Grant lacked political experience but was a popular war hero.

The Democrats chose former New York governor Horatio Seymour to run against Grant. Seymour had sharply criticized the Lincoln administration during the Civil War. Secretary of State William Henry Seward noted that the Democrats "could have nominated no candidate who would have taken away fewer Republican votes." Seymour's running mate, Francis Preston Blair, further diminished Seymour's chances when he pursued a campaign strategy based on white supremacy.

Southern Democrats relied on economic threats against African Americans to keep them from voting for Republicans. One white Democrat addressed African Americans.

> "We have the capital and give employment. We own the lands and require labor to make them productive.... You desire to be employed.... We know we can do without you. We think you will find it very difficult to do without us.... We have the wealth."
>
> —A white Democrat

Despite such tactics, new African American voters supported the Republican ticket. Grant defeated Seymour in a very close race, and Republicans realized that African American voters had given them their narrow win.

Ulysses S. Grant

1822–1885
In Office 1869–1877

Born in Ohio, Ulysses S. Grant graduated from the U.S. Military Academy at West Point in 1843 but had no intentions of making a career of military service. "A military life had no charms for me, and I had not the faintest idea of staying in the army even if I should be graduated, which I did not expect." Contrary to his expectations, Grant stayed in the army until 1854.

Grant was plagued by failure after resigning his commission. He drifted through a series of jobs, including peddling firewood and collecting rents. He tried his hand at farming without much success. His financial problems were such that in 1857 Grant was forced to pawn his gold watch for $22. When the Civil War broke out in 1861, Grant was almost 39 years old and clerking at his family's leather-goods store in Galena, Illinois. He returned to the army as a colonel and at last found success. His presidency followed in 1869.

After leaving office, Grant and his wife toured the world for more than two years. Back in New York, he unsuccessfully tried to make his fortune in business. He had just finished writing his memoirs when he died in 1885.

Southern Democrat officials, such as the election judge shown in this engraving, often prevented African Americans from voting for Republican candidates.

INTERDISCIPLINARY CONNECTIONS

▶**POLITICAL SCIENCE**◀

Thomas Nast's Political Cartoons. For more than 20 years Thomas Nast sketched political cartoons for a popular magazine called *Harper's Weekly.* Nast's cutting cartoons showed his support for Radical Republicans and often made fun of Andrew Johnson and the Democrats. To make his points in the briefest way possible, Nast often created symbols to represent groups or ideas. For example, Nast invented the animal symbols that the major political parties still use today: the Republican elephant and the Democratic donkey.

ACTIVITY: Have each student draw an editorial cartoon depicting a Reconstruction-era issue.

VISUAL RECORD ANSWER

(for p. 142)
Students might suggest that they conveyed a sense of patriotism and signaled wider political inclusion.

REVIEW ② ANSWERS

1. Identify
- Thaddeus Stevens, p. 135
- Frederick Douglass, p. 135
- Freedmen's Bureau, p. 137
- Civil Rights Act of 1866, p. 138
- Fourteenth Amendment, p. 138

REVIEW

Have students complete the **Section 2 Review** on p. 142.

ASSESS

Have students complete **Daily Quiz 4.2**. As **Alternative Assessment,** you may want to use the Republican Party resumé or the election of 1868 outline in this section's lessons.

RETEACH

Have students complete **Main Idea Activity for English Language Learners and Special-Needs Students 4.2.** Then assign each student one of the subsections in Section 2. Have students write four questions about the material in their subsections. Then distribute the questions to students, making sure that no one receives his or her own, and ask them to answer the questions. Have students return their questions to the author, who should check them and correct them, if necessary.
English Language Learners

EXTEND

Have students conduct research on President Johnson's response to his impeachment trial. Then tell students to imagine that they are Johnson on the day after their vindication. Have each student write a speech responding to the trial and expressing his or her feelings about the acquittal. Have volunteers deliver their speeches to the class. **Block Scheduling**

- Reconstruction Acts, p. 140
- Ulysses S. Grant, p. 141
- Fifteenth Amendment, p. 142

2. Freedman's Bureau Bill—supported operation of the Freedman's Bureau; Civil Rights Act of 1866—declared everyone born in the U.S. a citizen with full rights; Fourteenth Amendment—gave all citizens equal citizenship and equal protection; Reconstruction Acts—divided South into military districts and required states to give black men the right to vote; Tenure of Office Act of 1867—required president to obtain Senate approval before removing an official confirmed by the Senate; Fifteenth Amendment—gave African American men the right to vote

3a. African American voting rights; Johnson's veto of the Freedman's Bureau Bill and the Civil Rights Act of 1866

b. Fourteenth Amendment—required states to extend equal citizenship to all people and promised equal protection under law; Fifteenth Amendment—gave African American men the vote

c. Answers will vary. Some students might suggest that white men could more easily accept giving the vote to men than to all women.

4. Some students might say yes because Johnson was limiting attempts to improve conditions in the South.

INTERPRETING THE VISUAL RECORD

Celebration. This poster was created to celebrate the passage of the Fifteenth Amendment. *What might be the significance of the images used on the poster?*

The Fifteenth Amendment. Eager to protect their power in the North as well as in the South, the Republicans drafted the **Fifteenth Amendment.** It stated, "The right of citizens of the United States to vote shall not be denied or abridged by the United States or by any state on account of race, color, or previous condition of servitude."

The passage of the Fifteenth Amendment in February 1869 and its subsequent ratification in 1870 brought triumph to African Americans and Radical Republicans. Abolitionist William Lloyd Garrison rejoiced in "this wonderful, quiet, sudden transformation of four millions of human beings from . . . the auction-block to the ballot-box." The amendment failed to guarantee African Americans the right to hold office, however. It also did not prevent states from limiting the voting rights of African Americans through discriminatory requirements.

Significantly, the Fifteenth Amendment failed to extend the vote to women. Women's rights leaders, most of them former abolitionists, had split over the amendment. Arguing that "this hour belongs to the negro," one group had urged women to postpone the more controversial women's suffrage issue so as not to endanger passage of the amendment. Elizabeth Cady Stanton replied: "My question is this: Do you believe the African race is composed entirely of males?" Stanton and others opposed ratification of the Fifteenth Amendment until all women were also given the vote. The bitter debate over the amendment alienated many African American women from the women's movement.

✔ **READING CHECK: Identifying Cause and Effect** How did African American voters affect the outcome of the presidential election of 1868? African American voters supported the Republicans and gave Grant a narrow victory.

SECTION REVIEW

1. Identify and explain:
Thaddeus Stevens
Frederick Douglass
Freedmen's Bureau
Civil Rights Act of 1866
Fourteenth Amendment
Reconstruction Acts
Ulysses S. Grant
Fifteenth Amendment

2. Summarizing Copy the graphic organizer below. Use it to describe the major legislation that Congress passed to implement its plan for Reconstruction.

Congressional Reconstruction

3. **Finding the Main Idea**
a. What issues divided the Republican Party in the 1860s? What actions of President Johnson served to unite the party?
b. What rights did the Fourteenth and Fifteenth Amendments guarantee African Americans?
c. How was the Fifteenth Amendment a reaction by the Republican Party to the 1868 election?

4. **Writing and Critical Thinking**
Supporting a Point of View Write a letter to Congress persuading members either to remove President Johnson from office or to stop their efforts to remove him.
Consider:
- why Congress impeached President Johnson
- what Johnson's defense was
- if the conflict could have been resolved any other way

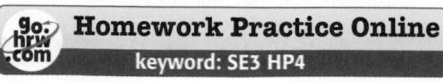

Homework Practice Online
keyword: SE3 HP4

After completing Section 3, students should be able to:

OBJECTIVE 1 Explain how African Americans attempted to improve their lives during the Reconstruction era.

OBJECTIVE 2 Identify Republican reforms.

OBJECTIVE 3 Relate how some African Americans responded to harassment by the Ku Klux Klan.

OBJECTIVE 4 Describe why Reconstruction ended.

LET'S GET STARTED!

Write the following question on the chalkboard: *Some historians have described the effects of Reconstruction as "revolutionary." What political, economic, and social changes would you expect from a "revolutionary" era?* As students enter the classroom, ask them to respond to the question in writing. Have volunteers share their responses. Then tell students that in Section 3 they will learn about the effects of Reconstruction in the South.

SECTION 3

READ TO DISCOVER

1. How did African Americans attempt to improve their lives during the Reconstruction era?
2. What reforms did Republican governments enact?
3. How did some African Americans respond to harassment by the Ku Klux Klan?
4. What caused Reconstruction to end?

DEFINE

carpetbaggers
scalawags

IDENTIFY

Ku Klux Klan
Enforcement Acts
Panic of 1873
Civil Rights Act of 1875
Redeemers
Samuel J. Tilden
Rutherford B. Hayes
Compromise of 1877

WHY IT MATTERS TODAY

During Reconstruction, there were many Republican governments in the South. As Reconstruction ended, Democrats returned to power. Use **CNNfyi.com** or other **current events** sources to learn which political party is leading a southern state today. Record your findings in your journal.

CNNfyi.com

Reconstruction in the South

EYEWITNESSES TO History ❝*The people of New Orleans witnessed last night one of the noblest scenes of which an American city can boast, . . . a phalanx [group] of freemen walking the streets with national colors flying and transparencies enunciating [spelling out] the principles of a free government.*❞

—*New Orleans Tribune*, May 1867

The African American newspaper the *New Orleans Tribune* described the festivities that took place in May 1867 after the passage of the Reconstruction Acts. The evening ended with skyrockets and dancing in the streets. "This marks a new and glorious era in our history," the newspaper proudly declared.

African Americans enjoying the right to vote

African American Activism

With the passage of the Reconstruction Acts by Congress, African Americans saw a new era begin. The rise of Congressional Reconstruction gave the former slaves further hope for equal citizenship. Many registered to vote and began lobbying for the equality promised by the Civil Rights Act and the Fourteenth Amendment. Even the churches found that "politics got in our midst" and overtook "our revival or religious work," according to one African American minister.

African Americans joined political groups such as the Union League. Begun in the North as a patriotic club, the league spread the views of the Republican Party to freed slaves as well as to poor whites. The Union League also built schools and churches for African Americans. African American education and literacy expanded greatly during Reconstruction. White northerners founded many schools, but African Americans launched educational institutions as well.

As African Americans became more involved in politics, they served as delegates to all the state constitutional conventions. In Louisiana and South Carolina, African American delegates outnumbered whites. In other states they made up 10 to 40 percent of the delegates. African Americans were the largest group of southern Republican voters. During Reconstruction, more than 600 African Americans were elected as representatives to state legislatures. Sixteen were elected to the U.S. Congress. African American Hiram Revels of Mississippi was elected to the U.S. Senate to fill the seat previously held by Jefferson Davis. Other African Americans held state and local offices.

✔ **READING CHECK: Identifying Cause and Effect** How did Reconstruction affect the lives of African Americans? African American men received the right to vote and many became involved in political groups.

RESOURCES

REPRODUCIBLE
▶ Guided Reading Strategy 4.3
▶ Graphic Organizer Activity 3: Evaluating Reconstruction

TECHNOLOGY
▶ One-Stop Planner, Lesson 4.3
▶ Holt Researcher: American History CD–ROM
▶ HRW Go site
▶ Homework Practice Online

REINFORCEMENT, REVIEW, AND ASSESSMENT
▶ Section 3 Review, p. 147
▶ Daily Quiz 4.3
▶ Main Idea Activity 4.3
▶ English Audio Summary 4.3
▶ Spanish Audio Summary 4.3

ALL LEVELS: Conduct a class discussion on the ways in which African Americans tried to improve their lives during Reconstruction and the ways in which some African Americans responded to harassment by the Ku Klux Klan. To help students understand these issues, copy the following graphic organizer on the chalkboard, omitting the italicized answers. Have each student complete it.
English Language Learners

Efforts to Improve Lives
- *registered to vote*
- *joined and formed political organizations*
- *lobbied for political equality*
- *built churches and schools*
- *served as delegates to state constitutional conventions*

African American Life During Reconstruction

Responses to Ku Klux Klan
- *retaliated by burning barns*
- *lobbied for congressional protection*

Blanche K. Bruce. Blanche K. Bruce was one of the first African American U.S. senators, serving for Mississippi from 1875 to 1881. Before his election to the Senate, Bruce was an educator and entrepreneur and was well respected among his colleagues. A fellow politician wrote that Bruce and other black congressmen "were as a rule studious, earnest, ambitious men, whose public conduct . . . would be honorable to any race." Bruce was not re-elected to the Senate in 1881 because Democrats had regained control of the South. He continued working in government, however, becoming the first African American register of the treasury under President Garfield and briefly under President McKinley.

CRITICAL THINKING Why might the Democrats' "redemption" of the South have affected Bruce's election to the Senate?

ANSWER: Students might suggest that in "redeeming" the South, the Democrats displaced many black voters and officials.

POLITICAL CARTOON ANSWER
Students might mention that the cartoon shows carpetbaggers riding to power on the back of a woman who represents the South.

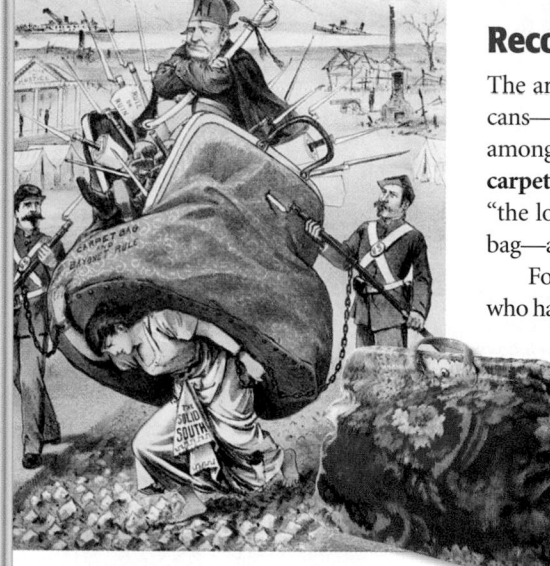

INTERPRETING POLITICAL CARTOONS
Carpetbaggers. Many southerners believed that northerners had come to impose their ideas and way of life on the South. *How is this belief expressed in this cartoon?*

Concealing their identity with hoods and robes, Klan members used threats and violence to prevent African Americans from voting.

Reconstruction Governments

The arrival of northern Republicans—both whites and African Americans—eager to participate in the state conventions increased resentment among many white southerners. They called these northern Republicans **carpetbaggers.** The newcomers, they joked, were "needy adventurers" of "the lowest class" who could carry everything they owned in a carpetbag—a type of cheap suitcase.

Former Confederates heaped even greater scorn on southern whites who had backed the Union cause and now supported Reconstruction. They called these whites **scalawags,** or scoundrels. They viewed them as "southern renegades, betrayers of their race and country."

Reconstruction supporters soon formed a Republican alliance. Although they disagreed on issues such as land reform, they saw themselves as the "party of progress, and civilization." They hoped to seize economic and political power from the planters and then rebuild the South, improving conditions for poor white farmers and African Americans alike.

The Republican alliance used its political leverage to draft new state constitutions. The Republican state governments abolished property qualifications for jurors and political candidates. They also guaranteed white and African American men the right to vote. Once Congress approved the new constitutions, state legislators raised taxes to finance new road, bridge, and railroad construction as well as to increase services, such as free public education.

✔ **READING CHECK: Categorizing** What groups formed a Republican alliance in the South during Reconstruction? white and African American northern Republicans, some southern whites, poor white farmers, and African Americans in the South

The Ku Klux Klan

The Reconstruction governments' reforms, the election of African Americans to office, and African Americans' growing political participation were soon met by a vicious response. Angry white southerners formed secret terrorist groups to prevent African Americans from voting. One such group, the **Ku Klux Klan,** was founded in 1866 by six former Confederates. The organization grew quickly, attracting planters, lawyers, and other professionals, as well as poor farmers and laborers.

Klan attacks. The head of the Klan—"Grand Wizard" Nathan Bedford Forrest, a former slave-trader and Confederate general—bluntly warned Republicans that he intended "to kill the radicals." This was no idle threat. The Klan and similar groups were determined to destroy the Republican Party, to keep African Americans from voting, and to frighten African American political leaders into submission. The Klan murdered or attacked many Republican legislators and leaders—both white and black. Klan members also attacked African Americans who voted for Republican candidates.

The Klan did not limit its attacks to politically active African American and white Republicans, however. Klansmen assaulted and killed thousands of African Americans whom they regarded as too successful. One North Carolina freedman recalled the words of the Klansmen who had beaten him:

LEVEL 1: Pair students and tell them to imagine that they are Republican officials in the South. Have each pair create two or three banners with slogans that describe reforms enacted by Republican governments. *(Pairs' banners should mention two or three of the following: the creation of new state constitutions, the abolition of property qualifications for jurors and candidates, the creation of new services, and the establishment of new roads and bridges.)* Ask volunteers to present and discuss their banners with the class.
English Language Learners, Cooperative Learning

LEVELS 2 AND 3: Tell students to imagine that they are Republican officials in the South. Have each student write a short political platform describing Republican reforms in the region. *(See the Level 1 lesson for the correct reforms.)* Ask volunteers to read their platforms to the class.

TEACH OBJECTIVE 4

LEVEL 1: Pair students and tell them to imagine that it is 1878 and that they are southern African Americans. Have each pair develop a short dialogue describing the factors that ended the Reconstruction era. *(Pairs' dialogues should discuss general economic and political issues, the Panic of 1873, the reaction to rising immigration, the actions of the southern Redeemers, and the Compromise of 1877.)* Ask volunteers to perform their dialogues for the class.
English Language Learners, Cooperative Learning

History Makers Speak

❝[They] told me the law—their law, that whenever I met a white person, no matter who he was, whether he was poor or rich, I was to take off my hat.❞

—North Carolina freedman, quoted in *Reconstruction*, by Eric Foner

Klansmen also burned homes, schools, and churches, and stole livestock in an effort to chase African Americans and pro-Reconstruction whites from the South.

Steps against the Klan. African Americans struck back at the Klan when possible. Often able to recognize their tormentors by voices and other physical characteristics—despite the members' hoods and long robes—some African Americans retaliated by burning barns of Klansmen. More often, African Americans gathered in defense of an intended victim. Residents of the African American town of Avery, Alabama, learned that Klan members planned to burn their schoolhouse. "Let them come," declared Miles Prior, who organized a group of armed men. "Fifty men couldn't burn that schoolhouse and let me live." The Klansmen backed down and left the schoolhouse intact.

As the violence mounted, African Americans demanded that Congress act to "enable us to exercise the rights of citizens." Congress responded to this call in 1870 and 1871 by passing legislation designed to stop violence against African Americans. Known as the **Enforcement Acts**, these three laws empowered the federal government to combat terrorism with military force and to prosecute guilty individuals. The Democrats called them the Force Acts and claimed that they threatened individual freedom.

✔ **READING CHECK: Summarizing** How did Congress respond to violence against African Americans? passed the Enforcement Acts

Changes in Reconstruction

For a time the federal government's intervention brought a dramatic decline in Ku Klux Klan violence. However, the attention of Republicans increasingly turned toward national economic issues and political corruption in the North. Gradually the interest of Republicans in Reconstruction faded.

Shifting Republican interests. A particularly severe economic depression, known as the **Panic of 1873**, hit the nation. Republican leaders came under pressure as workers threatened strikes and farmers demanded relief. The partnership between antilabor, northern businesspeople—who formed the core of the Republican Party—and the freed slaves had never been stable. Soon it dissolved.

Republicans also abandoned universal voting rights as thousands of immigrants joined the Democratic Party. Some Republicans claimed that universal suffrage "cheapened the ballot." Their calls to restrict the voting rights of immigrants and the urban poor weakened public support for African Americans' rights as well.

HISTORY IN THE MAKING

Interpretations of Reconstruction

By Otey Scruggs

For a century afterward, the standard interpretation of Reconstruction among historians was that northern "carpetbaggers," southern "scalawags," and uneducated African Americans combined to impose tyrannical rule over the defeated South. They forced southern whites to organize groups like the Ku Klux Klan in order to overturn corrupt Republican state governments. This view became permanently stamped on the popular mind through the 1915 film *Birth of a Nation*. African American historian W. E. B. Du Bois challenged this interpretation in his monumental 1935 study, *Black Reconstruction in America*. The civil rights movement of the 1950s and 1960s completely overturned the older historical view of Reconstruction.

More recent interpretations tend to analyze the intersection between economic forces—land, labor, and transportation—and the political process. Not only were the ex-slaves guaranteed political and civil rights, recent historians note, but some steps were also taken toward economic justice. Central in the new explanation is the assertive role played by African Americans themselves. Some historians argue that it was the fear that African Americans would leave their assigned place at the bottom of the sociopolitical structure that really ended Reconstruction.

Film and the Birth of a Myth. Southern Democrats, in their desire to return to the South's pre–Civil War social structure, helped to build myths about Reconstruction. These myths portrayed carpetbaggers as corrupt exploiters and freed slaves as either violent, lazy, or childlike. D. W. Griffith's 1915 film, *The Birth of a Nation*, contributed to this mythology and reinforced racist ideas of black inferiority and white supremacy. Based on Thomas Dixon's novel *The Clansman*, the movie portrayed black government officials as buffoons and most freedmen as lusting after white women. Griffith's heroes are members of the KKK who ride in on horses to restore the social order. *The Birth of a Nation* was the first movie to cost more than $100,000 to produce and the first ever to be shown at the White House.

CRITICAL THINKING How might *The Birth of a Nation* have reflected the characteristics and issues of the era of Reconstruction?

ANSWER: Students might suggest that the movie created myths regarding the issues of free slaves and northern carpet baggers, and widened the division between whites and blacks.

Reconstruction in the South, 1868–1877

Interpreting Maps The Reconstruction Acts established military districts in the South that would be removed when the southern states drafted new constitutions and adopted the Fourteenth Amendment.

? LOCATE During Reconstruction, which former Confederate state was not part of a military district? Why was that state not in a district?

As Republican attention shifted away from Reconstruction, southern African Americans faced increasing violence.

The southern Redeemers.

The discontent caused by the Panic of 1873 turned voters against the Republican-controlled Congress. In the 1874 congressional elections Democrats gained dozens of seats in the House, giving them a 60-seat majority. In the South the Democrats attracted white voters with promises of lower taxes and through appeals to white supremacy.

When Congress reconvened, Republicans made one final effort to enforce Reconstruction by enacting the **Civil Rights Act of 1875.** This bill prohibited businesses that served the public—such as hotels and transportation facilities—from discriminating against African Americans. However, white Republican supporters of the bill had begun to see Reconstruction as a political burden.

Many southern white Democrats reached the same conclusion. Convinced that the federal government would not stop them, Mississippi Democrats used terrorism to win the 1875 state elections. In Clay County, against a backdrop of Confederate flags, white Democrats shot and killed several African Americans who declared their intention of voting Republican. The next year Democrats in Louisiana and South Carolina adopted similar tactics to "redeem," or win back, their states from the Republicans. These supporters of white-controlled governments called themselves the **Redeemers.**

In 1876 the Redeemers focused on the presidential election, which pitted Democrat **Samuel J. Tilden** of New York against Republican **Rutherford B. Hayes**

REVIEW

Have students complete the **Section 3 Review** on p. 147.

ASSESS

Have students complete **Daily Quiz 4.3**. As **Alternative Assessment,** you may want to use the set of banners or the Reconstruction dialogue in this section's lessons.

RETEACH

Have students complete **Main Idea Activity for English Language Learners and Special-Needs Students 4.3**. Then ask each student to outline Section 3. Ask volunteers to share their

work and create a comprehensive outline on the chalkboard. Review the outline with students and ask them to determine likely short-answer and essay questions. **English Language Learners**

EXTEND

Have students conduct research on Reconstruction governments before "redemption." Ask students to pick one government. Then have each student write a two-to-three-page essay describing the actions of the selected government and evaluating its effectiveness. Students may wish to include their essays in their portfolios. **Block Scheduling**

---

of Ohio. Opponents of Reconstruction vowed to win the election even "if we have to wade in blood knee-deep." In the popular vote they succeeded: Tilden beat Hayes by some 250,000 votes. The electoral vote was another story.

The election results in four states were challenged by various parties. A commission set up to rule on the validity of the returns gave Hayes the presidency by one electoral vote. Democrats in the House protested. To defuse the crisis, leading Republicans and southern Democrats struck a deal—the **Compromise of 1877**. In return for the Democrats' acceptance of Hayes as president, the Republicans agreed to withdraw the remaining federal troops from the South.

Denied federal protection, the last of the Reconstruction governments fell. The individuals behind the Democratic Party's return to power were known as Redeemers. They rewrote state constitutions and overturned many of the Reconstruction governments' reforms. A former African American legislator from Alabama protested these changes.

❝We obey laws; others make them. We support state educational institutions, whose doors are virtually closed against us. . . . From these and many other oppressions . . . our people long to be free.❞

—Charles Harris, letter to William Coppinger, August 28, 1877

✔ **READING CHECK: Evaluating** What historical era came to an end in 1877? Reconstruction—federal troops withdrew after the Compromise of 1877 and Reconstruction governments fell

Great Debates

Reconstruction

The relative successes and failures of Reconstruction have long been debated by scholars. In many ways, Reconstruction did not accomplish its goals. The failure of land-reform efforts allowed white planters to maintain control over many southern institutions. Southern African Americans saw little economic improvement because the basic economic structure of the South remained intact. They also achieved few lasting civil and political rights.

The new state constitutions adopted in the South during the Reconstruction era, however, did help reform the states' judicial and legislative systems. African American leaders also created institutions—churches, schools, and strong family networks—that helped sustain black communities through the difficult post-Reconstruction years. The Reconstruction era also left a legal legacy. Although they were rarely enforced for almost a century, the Civil Rights Act of 1866 and the Fourteenth and Fifteenth Amendments provided an important legal framework that enabled later civil rights leaders to win back voting rights for African Americans and to end legal segregation.

SECTION 3 REVIEW

1. Define and explain:
carpetbaggers
scalawags

2. Identify and explain:
Ku Klux Klan
Enforcement Acts
Panic of 1873
Civil Rights Act of 1875
Redeemers
Samuel J. Tilden
Rutherford B. Hayes
Compromise of 1877

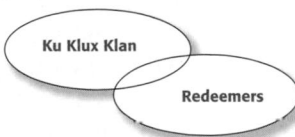

Homework Practice Online
keyword: SE3 HP4

3. Comparing and Contrasting
Copy the graphic organizer below. Use it to describe the similarities and differences between the tactics of the Ku Klux Klan and the Redeemers, and how African Americans responded to these groups.

Ku Klux Klan

Redeemers

4. Finding the Main Idea
a. What role did African Americans play in shaping Reconstruction?
b. How did the Republican governments change legislation in southern states?
c. What special abilities might African American legislators have been able to bring to the new southern governments?

5. Writing and Critical Thinking
Evaluating Write a paragraph explaining how and why Reconstruction failed to achieve its goals.
Consider:
• what the goals of Reconstruction were
• what events and issues ended Reconstruction
• what goals were left unmet

SECTION 3 REVIEW ANSWERS

1. Define
• carpetbaggers, p. 144
• scalawags, p. 144

2. Identify
• Ku Klux Klan, p. 144
• Enforcement Acts, p. 145
• Panic of 1873, p. 145
• Civil Rights Act of 1875, p. 146
• Redeemers, p. 146
• Samuel J. Tilden, p. 146
• Rutherford B. Hayes, p. 146
• Compromise of 1877, p. 147

3. similarities—terrorized and killed people to achieve their goals; differences—unlike the Klan, the Redeemers operated in the open, often as government officials. African Americans responded by burning barns of Klansmen or gathering in defense of an intended victim.

4a. joined political groups and tried to vote for candidates who supported their rights; opened churches and schools to educate black children

b. They helped extend voting rights, raised taxes for transportation and education, and abolished property qualifications for jurors and political candidates.

c. Answers will vary. Students might suggest that African Americans could pinpoint specific areas where their rights were violated to draft viable legislation.

5. Answers will vary. Students might indicate that the economic depression in 1873 refocused legislators' energy and allowed Democrats to gain control of Congress.

After completing Section 4, students should be able to:

OBJECTIVE 1 Analyze the drawbacks to the sharecropping system.

OBJECTIVE 2 Assess how Jim Crow laws and the *Plessy v. Ferguson* decision changed life for southern African Americans.

OBJECTIVE 3 Explain how African Americans attempted to improve their economic situation after Reconstruction.

OBJECTIVE 4 Compare the views of Booker T. Washington and Ida B. Wells.

LET'S GET STARTED!

Write the following question on the chalkboard: *Is freedom without equality really freedom?* As students enter the classroom, ask them to respond to the question in writing. Have volunteers share their responses. Then tell students that in Section 4 they will learn about conditions in the post-Reconstruction South and how African Americans responded to those conditions.

SECTION 4 RESOURCES

REPRODUCIBLE

▶ Guided Reading Strategy 4.4
▶ Geography Activity 4: Tenant Farming and Sharecropping
▶ Literature Reading 4: The Cruelty of Jim Crow Laws
▶ Biography Reading 3: Ida B. Wells

TECHNOLOGY

▶ One-Stop Planner, Lesson 4.4
▶ The American Nation Video Program Segment: The Tuskegee Institute; Teacher's Guide, pp. 63–68
▶ Holt Researcher: American History CD–ROM
▶ Homework Practice Online

REINFORCEMENT, REVIEW, AND ASSESSMENT

▶ Section 4 Review, p. 153
▶ Daily Quiz 4.4
▶ Main Idea Activity 4.4
▶ English Audio Summary 4.4
▶ Spanish Audio Summary 4.4

SECTION 4

READ TO DISCOVER

1. What were the drawbacks to the sharecropping system?
2. How did Jim Crow laws and the *Plessy* v. *Ferguson* decision change life for southern African Americans?
3. How did African Americans attempt to improve their economic situation after Reconstruction?
4. How did Booker T. Washington and Ida B. Wells think African Americans should respond to Jim Crow laws?

DEFINE

sharecropping
crop-lien system
poll taxes
literacy tests
segregation

IDENTIFY

Jim Crow laws
Plessy v. *Ferguson*
Madame C. J. Walker
Booker T. Washington
Ida B. Wells

WHY IT MATTERS TODAY

One of the many successful entrepreneurs of this period was Madame C. J. Walker. Use CNNfyi.com or other **current events** sources to find out what innovations entrepreneurs are making today. Record your findings in your journal.

CNNfyi.com

The New South

EYEWITNESSES TO History

"[Former slaves exhibit] a growing dislike to being controlled by or working for white men. They prefer to get a little patch where they can do as they choose."

—Anonymous white farmer, quoted in *Been in the Storm So Long,* by Leon F. Litwack

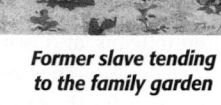

Former slave tending to the family garden

This Tennessee farmer noted the increasing desire among freedpeople to own their own land. Frances Leigh, another white farmer, remarked that as soon as her field hands were paid, many of them purchased small plots of land, usually in the pine woods "where the land was so poor they could not raise a peck of corn to the acre." Although Leigh thought the field hands had been cheated in these land deals, she could not help but notice the enthusiasm the African American farmers brought to their new lives under freedom.

Changing Economies in the South

Some southern planters lost their lands after the Civil War because they could not pay their debts or their taxes. Other planters or northern investors ended up with most of these lands.

Sharecropping. Whether planters were southerners or northerners, however, all faced labor shortages. Few whites or former slaves wanted to work for the low wages planters were willing—or, in many cases, able—to pay.

Some planters solved their labor problems with **sharecropping**. Under this system a farmer worked a parcel of land in return for a share of the crop, a cabin, seed, tools, and a mule. Sharecropping enabled planters to get their lands worked when they did not have enough cash to pay laborers. Laborers gained a place to live and lands to work without close supervision. By the end of the 1870s many poor white southerners and most African Americans in the South worked as sharecroppers.

The arrangement had a serious drawback, however. Sharecroppers had no income until harvest time. To obtain needed supplies each year, they had to promise their crops to local merchants who then sold them goods on credit. Any outstanding debts were added to their bills the following year. This arrangement was known as the **crop-lien system**. A lien is a creditor's legal claim on the debtor's property.

In effect, the system made it impossible for sharecroppers to work their way out of poverty or to gain independence. Former slave Thomas Hall judged the system to be "little better than slavery." The crop-lien system kept the southern economy tied primarily to one-crop agriculture. Merchants gave credit only to farmers who grew certain crops, most often cotton. As a result, cotton displaced other crops to such an extent that the South had to import food and animal feed from the North.

✔ **READING CHECK: Summarizing** What were the drawbacks of the sharecropping system? It forced many sharecroppers into debt and kept the South tied to a one-crop agriculture.

LEVEL 1: Pair students and tell them to imagine that they are African American sharecroppers who have decided to protest the system. Have each pair create two or three protest signs detailing the drawbacks to the sharecropping system. *(Pairs should note that sharecroppers had no income until harvest time, forcing them to participate in the crop-lien system. Pairs should also note that sharecropping required farmers to concentrate on one crop only, leaving them and the region dangerously dependent on outside suppliers for human and animal food.)* Have each pair present its protest signs to the class. Then display the signs around the classroom.
English Language Learners, Cooperative Learning

LEVEL 2: Tell students to imagine that they are African American sharecroppers talking with visiting northern relatives. Have each student write a brief monologue on the drawbacks to the sharecropping system. *(See the Level 1 lesson for the correct drawbacks.)* Ask volunteers to perform their monologues for the class.

★ Changing Ways   The South

■ **Understanding Change** Much has changed in the South since the late 1800s, yet much remains the same. Although the South's per capita income is almost as much as the national average, the region still lags behind in wealth. *How has the South's population changed? How has the average per capita income changed as compared to the rest of the country?*

THEN

Now

	THEN	Now
Population (Nonwhite / White)	36% / 64%	23% / 77%
(Rural / Urban)	12% / 88%	31% / 69%
Ratio of Per Capita Income Compared to the U.S. Average	32%	90%

Sources: *Historical Statistics of the United States; Statistical Abstract of the United States: 1999.* Data reflects 1870 and 1990.

Industrial growth. Henry W. Grady, the editor of the *Atlanta Constitution*, believed that one-crop agriculture kept the South in poverty and economically dependent on the North. The so-called New South, he argued, should manufacture its own goods. Supporters of this New South idea joined with northern and British investors to finance factories and ironworks, while southerners raised the money to build textile mills and other enterprises. Southern railroads were rebuilt and integrated into northern rail systems.

Not everyone benefited equally from industrialization in the South, however. Factory owners and investors profited at the expense of poorly paid workers. White industrial workers in the South earned far lower wages than their northern counterparts. Most African Americans could not find any factory work at all. Some industrial workers were forced to buy goods on credit from the company store and to live in ramshackle company houses. Like sharecroppers, they often found themselves locked in a cycle of debt.

The Rise of Jim Crow

For African Americans, the New South closely resembled the Old South. They were tied to the land through sharecropping and by their exclusion from most factory jobs. Moreover, Democrats had taken control of the southern state legislatures and stepped up their attempts to strip African Americans of their rights.

To deprive African Americans of the right to vote, southern legislatures instituted **poll taxes**—fixed taxes imposed on every voter—and **literacy tests**—tests that barred those who could not read from voting. Because most African American southerners were poor and had been denied an education, these legal barriers

THE GRANGER COLLECTION, NEW YORK

INTERPRETING THE VISUAL RECORD
The New South. Many southerners supported the building of new industries and railroad systems in the late 1800s. *How does this painting express the goals of the New South movement?*

LEVEL 3: Ask students to list the drawbacks of the sharecropping system. *(See the Level 1 lesson for the correct drawbacks.)* Then organize students into small groups. Have each group develop a post-Reconstruction agricultural plan that would provide planters with labor while also providing African Americans with land and supplies. Have students share their plans with the class. Then ask students to realistically evaluate the plans, given conditions in the post-Reconstruction South. Would they have worked there, given the existence of Redeemers and people who believed in African American inferiority? **Cooperative Learning**

NEGRO EXPULSION FROM RAILWAY CAR, PHILADELPHIA.

Jim Crow laws prohibited African Americans from riding on "whites only" railway cars.

INTERPRETING THE VISUAL RECORD

Segregation. African Americans established many institutions to serve their community. *How does this image of an African American church service reflect the importance of community during the Jim Crow era?*

effectively disfranchised African Americans. Even literate African Americans often "failed" the test, since white officials decided who passed. These rules, however, were often waived for poor or illiterate whites. Whites also used violence and intimidation to prevent African Americans from voting.

To further deprive African Americans of their rights, state legislatures initiated a series of laws designed to enforce **segregation**, or separation, of the races. These provisions were called **Jim Crow laws**, so-named after a minstrel song that contained the refrain "Jump—jump—jump Jim Crow." Passed in Tennessee in 1881, the first of these laws required separate railway cars for African Americans and whites. By the 1890s all southern states had legally segregated public transportation and schools. Segregation soon extended to cemeteries, parks, and other public places.

African Americans sued for equal treatment under the Civil Rights Act of 1875, but the Supreme Court refused to overturn the Jim Crow laws. In the Civil Rights Cases of 1883, the Court ruled that the Fourteenth Amendment prohibited only state governments, not individuals or businesses, from discriminating against African Americans. The Court upheld segregation in **Plessy v. Ferguson**, a lawsuit brought in 1896 after African American Homer Plessy was denied a seat in a first-class railway car. The Court ruled that "separate but equal" facilities did not violate the Fourteenth Amendment. Justice John Marshall Harlan disagreed, declaring, "Our Constitution is color-blind, and neither knows nor tolerates classes among citizens."

✔ **READING CHECK: Identifying Cause and Effect** How did Jim Crow laws and the *Plessy v. Ferguson* decision affect African Americans in the South?
Jim Crow laws segregated African Americans; *Plessy* v. *Ferguson* ruled that such segregation was legal.

African American Life

Despite segregation, in some southern cities a growing African American middle class began to emerge, made up of doctors, government workers, teachers, and lawyers. African Americans formed mutual aid societies, started businesses, supported churches, and built schools. The African Methodist Episcopal (AME) Church, the AME Zion Church, and the African American Baptist Church grew rapidly.

Farmers and planters. Most African Americans had little opportunity to improve their economic status. Despite numerous obstacles, however, some did purchase farmland and in a few cases large plantations. According to writer Charles Nordhoff, African Americans in Georgia owned "nearly 400,000 acres of farming real estate, besides city property."

Some African Americans also formed cooperatives to buy farmland. In addition to producing crops and providing jobs, the cooperatives often provided for the care of sick members "if unable to care for themselves." Cooperatives sometimes imposed taxes "to provide for the education of the young and the comfortable maintenance of the aged and helpless."

LEVEL 1: Have each student list the provisions of the Jim Crow laws and the *Plessy* v. *Ferguson* decision. *(Students should note that the Jim Crow laws introduced widespread segregation, and that the* Plessy v. Ferguson *decision codified that segregation.)* Then have students annotate their lists, describing how the laws and the decisions affected African Americans in the post-Reconstruction South. *(The laws limited African Americans' opportunities.)* Ask volunteers to share their annotations with the class. **English Language Learners**

LEVELS 2 AND 3: Tell students to imagine that it is 1896 and that they are southern African Americans. Have each student write a one-page letter to the editor of a northern African American newspaper describing how Jim Crow laws and the *Plessy* v. *Ferguson* decision has changed his or her lives. *(See the Level 1 lesson for the correct changes.)* Ask volunteers to read their letters to the class. Students may wish to include their letters in their portfolios.

NOTE: For an additional teaching idea, see the Chapter 4 open interviewing lesson in the **Creative Teaching Strategies** handbook.

AMERICAN Letters

Black Writers During the Late 1800s

Many African American writers of the post-Reconstruction period focused their attention on the difficulties faced by African Americans after their emancipation, as well as on the African American experience more generally. Charles W. Chesnutt's 1899 story "The Wife of His Youth" deals with the choice one man must make between the woman he married while still a slave and the young widow he is courting. Paul Laurence Dunbar's 1890s poem "Ode for Memorial Day" expresses the pain of the Civil War and its joyful outcome.

from "The Wife of His Youth"
by Charles W. Chesnutt

Suppose that this husband, soon after his escape, had learned that his wife had been sold away, and that such inquiries as he could make brought no information of her whereabouts. Suppose that he was young, and she much older than he;

Collection of fiction by Charles W. Chesnutt

that he was light, and she was black; that their marriage was a slave marriage, and legally binding only if they chose to make it so after the war. Suppose, too, that he made his way to the North, as some of us have done, and there, where he had larger opportunities, had improved them, and had in the course of all these years grown to be as different from the ignorant boy who ran away from fear of slavery as the day is from the night. Suppose, even, that he had qualified himself, by industry, by thrift, and by study, to win the friendship and be considered worthy. . . . And then suppose that accident should bring to his knowledge the fact that the wife of his youth, the wife he had left behind him, . . . was alive and seeking him, but that he was absolutely safe from recognition or discovery, unless he chose to reveal himself. My friends, what would the man do?"

from "Ode for Memorial Day"
by Paul Laurence Dunbar

Done are the toils and the
    wearisome marches. . . .
Out of the blood of a conflict
    fraternal,
Out of the dust and the
    dimness of death,
Burst into blossoms of glory
    eternal
Flowers that sweeten the world with their breath.
Flowers of charity, peace, and devotion
    Bloom in the hearts that are empty of strife;
Love that is boundless and broad as the ocean
    Leaps into beauty and fulness of life.
So, with the singing of paeans [praises] and chorals,
    And with the flag flashing high in the sun,
Place on the graves of our heroes the laurels
    Which their unfaltering valor has won!

Paul Laurence Dunbar

UNDERSTANDING LITERATURE

1. How does Chesnutt describe slave marriage in "The Wife of His Youth"?
2. How does Dunbar refer to the ideals behind the fighting of the Civil War?
3. What sentiments about life after the Civil War do these authors express?

AMERICAN LETTERS ANSWERS

1. as an informal contract that was not legally binding

2. heroic and valorous

3. Chesnutt shows that African Americans cannot escape their slave past; Dunbar envisions a peaceful world.

***The American Nation* VIDEO PROGRAM**

The Tuskegee Institute;
Teacher's Guide, pp. 63–68

Search 33609, Play to 40728
Videodisc 1, Side B

Play   Pause

See *Teacher's Guide* for Spanish barcode.

VISUAL RECORD ANSWER

(for p. 152)

Students might mention that the ad describes the products' virtues in great detail.

SECTION REVIEW 4 ANSWERS

1. Define
- sharecropping, p. 148
- crop-lien system, p. 148
- poll taxes, p. 149
- literacy tests, p. 149
- segregation, p. 150

2. Identify
- Jim Crow laws, p. 150
- *Plessy* v. *Ferguson*, p. 150

ALL LEVELS: To help students understand the ways in which African Americans attempted to improve their economic situation after Reconstruction—and how Booker T. Washington and Ida B. Wells responded to Jim Crow laws— copy the following graphic organizer on the chalkboard, omitting the italicized answers. Ask each student to complete it. Discuss students' organizers as a class.
English Language Learners

> **The End of Reconstruction and Jim Crow Laws**
>
> **African Americans' Attempts to Improve Their Economic Situation**
> • *Formed aid societies and cooperatives*
> • *Supported churches and schools*
> • *Supported businesses*
>
> **Booker T. Washington's Response to Jim Crow Laws**
> • *Wanted African Americans to achieve economic independence*
> • *Discouraged African Americans from protesting discrimination*
>
> **Ida B. Wells's Response to Jim Crow Laws**
> • *Urged African Americans to protest discrimination*
> • *Wanted African Americans to leave the South*

- Madame C. J. Walker, p. 152
- Booker T. Washington, p. 153
- Ida B. Wells, p. 153

3. advantages—allowed a small degree of personal freedom for African Americans and poor whites, allowed planters to maintain a cheap labor force; disadvantages—kept sharecroppers in permanent debt to planters and merchants, kept southern economy tied mostly to cotton crops

4a. limited their access to public transportation, services, and education

b. Students' articles will vary. Students should mention mutual aid societies and cooperatives.

c. Students should note that all three demonstrated that no one in a democracy must accept injustice. There are ways to fight both politically and economically.

5. Students might note that the two Souths were virtually the same, with African Americans in positions of servitude and whites in power both economically and politically.

Creating a Time Line
Each event should have an explanation and the correct date.

Writing a Summary
See the Reading Checks in each section for main ideas.

INTERPRETING THE VISUAL RECORD

Entrepreneurship. Madame C. J. Walker built a factory for the production of beauty products in Indianapolis, Indiana, in 1910. *How do you think this advertisement might have helped Walker sell her merchandise?*

Industry and business. African Americans also formed nonagricultural cooperatives. In cities such as Baltimore, Charleston, and Richmond, cooperatives bought large parcels of land. They then sold that land to members for building homes. After being excluded from dock work, African Americans in Baltimore organized the Chesapeake, Marine, and Dry Dock Company. This cooperative raised and borrowed thousands of dollars to buy a shipyard and a marine railway. It hired several hundred African American caulkers and carpenters, won a government contract, and paid off its entire debt within five years.

Some African Americans also owned small businesses such as barber shops, blacksmith shops, general stores, and restaurants. African American women could be found in open-air markets throughout southern cities, selling candy and vegetables. **Madame C. J. Walker,** a leading African American entrepreneur, was one of the first women in the United States to become a millionaire.

BIOGRAPHY *Madame C. J. Walker*

Madame C. J. Walker was born Sarah Breedlove in 1867 in Louisiana. Her parents were poverty-stricken sharecroppers, and Walker worked in the cotton fields as a child. She married at age 14 and gave birth to her daughter, A'Lelia, four years later. By the time Walker was 20, her first husband had died. For the next 17 years she worked as a cook and laundress.

By 1905 Walker had developed a hair-conditioner treatment for African American women. With her life savings of $1.50, she opened a hair preparations company, which she operated out of the attic of her home. Six months later she married journalist C. J. Walker. The couple traveled for the next year and a half to promote Walker's products, leaving A'Lelia Walker behind to run the mail-order business.

Walker and her daughter moved in 1908 to Pittsburgh, Pennsylvania, where they founded Lelia College, a beauty school. Soon cosmetologists were practicing the Walker method for hair care. In 1910 Walker established production facilities and a laboratory in Indianapolis, Indiana. After divorcing her husband, she traveled to the Caribbean and Central America in 1913. That year the Walkers opened a beauty salon in Harlem. In another six years 20,000 African American women were Walker "agents," selling her products.

By 1914 Walker's company was earning about $100,000 per year. Until her death in 1919, Walker was a generous contributor to African American causes, particularly schools and equal rights organizations. She relentlessly promoted the belief that African Americans could better themselves economically. In one public speech, Walker said:

History Makers Speak

> 66 The girls and women of our race must not be afraid to take hold of business endeavor. . . . I want to say to every Negro woman present, don't sit down and wait for the opportunities to come. . . . Get up and make them! 99

—Madame C. J. Walker, quoted in *Facts on File*, edited by Darlene Clark Hine and Kathleen Thompson

✔ **READING CHECK: Summarizing** What actions did African Americans take after Reconstruction to expand their economic opportunities?
Some became middle-class professionals; others formed farm and nonagricultural cooperatives and small businesses.

REVIEW

Have students complete the **Section 4 Review** on p. 153.

ASSESS

Have students complete **Daily Quiz 4.4**. As **Alternative Assessment**, you may want to use the sharecropper monologue or the post-Reconstruction agricultural plan in this section's lessons.

RETEACH

Have students complete **Main Idea Activity for English Language Learners and Special-Needs Students 4.4**. Then have students define the key terms in the section and use them all in two or three summary paragraphs.
English Language Learners

EXTEND

Have students conduct research on *Plessy* v. *Ferguson*. Then tell students to imagine that they are modern-day television reporters preparing a segment on historic Supreme Court cases. Have each student prepare a three-to-five minute segment on this case. Students' segments should explain how the case wound up in the Court, analyze the majority ruling, and assess the impact of the decision on race relations, particularly in the South. Ask volunteers to perform their news segments for the class. **Block Scheduling**

Responses to the Jim Crow Era

Despite the success of some individuals, African Americans continued to encounter widespread discrimination in the late 1870s. Two influential African American leaders differed in their approaches to this discrimination.

Booker T. Washington believed that African Americans should concentrate on achieving economic independence, which he saw as the key to political and social equality. He urged African Americans to seek practical training in trades and professions. He discouraged them from protesting against discrimination, arguing that it merely increased whites' hostility. At the same time, however, Washington secretly provided support to groups fighting Jim Crow laws and racial violence.

Some African American leaders disagreed with Washington's public position calling for cooperation with southern whites. They argued instead that African Americans should protest unfair treatment. Civil rights activist, journalist, and teacher **Ida B. Wells**—later Wells-Barnett—focused her attention on stopping the lynching of African Americans. In fiery editorials she urged African Americans to leave the South. She herself was driven out of Memphis and moved to Chicago. Wells urged others to follow her example.

Booker T. Washington founded the Tuskegee Institute in 1881.

History Makers Speak

66 **There is therefore only one thing left that we can do; save our money and leave a town which will neither protect our lives [nor] property.** 99

—Ida B. Wells, quoted in *Notable Black American Women*, edited by Jessie Carney Smith

Although lynchings decreased only slightly in the early 1900s, Wells's tireless efforts kept the public's attention focused on the issue.

✔ **READING CHECK: Contrasting** How did the beliefs of Booker T. Washington and Ida B. Wells represent different approaches to how African Americans should have responded to Jim Crow laws? Washington wanted African Americans to achieve economic independence and called for cooperation with southern whites; Wells wanted to stop lynching.

Research on the R**O**M

Free Find: Ida B. Wells
After reading about Ida B. Wells on the **Holt Researcher CD–ROM**, write a short biography that describes her political activities and accomplishments.

SECTION 4 REVIEW

1. Define and explain:
sharecropping
crop-lien system
poll taxes
literacy tests
segregation

2. Identify and explain:
Jim Crow laws
Plessy v. *Ferguson*
Madame C. J. Walker
Booker T. Washington
Ida B. Wells

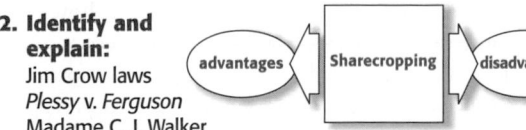
Homework Practice Online
keyword: SE3 HP4

3. Evaluating Copy the graphic organizer below. Use it to explain the advantages and disadvantages of the sharecropping system. Consider the effects of the sharecropping system on the landowner, the laborers, and the southern economy as a whole.

advantages ⟨ Sharecropping ⟩ disadvantages

4. ▎**Finding the Main Idea**
a. How did the Jim Crow laws affect African Americans?
b. Imagine that you are a reporter for a national magazine after Reconstruction. Write a brief article summarizing how African Americans are working together to improve their social and economic situations.
c. How did the contributions of Madame C. J. Walker, Booker T. Washington, and Ida B. Wells help shape the national identity?

5. ▎**Writing and Critical Thinking**
Comparing Write an article comparing the New South and the antebellum South.
Consider:
• how the economy changed or stayed the same
• how racial attitudes changed or stayed the same
• how political power changed or stayed the same

Identifying People and Ideas

1. full pardon, proposed for southerners after the Civil War

2. succeeded Lincoln as president and disagreed with Republicans about Reconstruction

3. laws limiting the freedom of African Americans in the South

4. divided the former Confederacy into five military districts and gave African American men the right to vote for delegates to the state constitutional convention as well as to serve as delegates

5. term used to describe northerners who moved to the South after the war

6. agreement in which Democrats accept Hayes as president and Republicans agree to withdraw remaining federal troops from the South

7. system under which poor farmers worked lands owned by others in exchange for a share of the crop

8. laws enacted to enforce segregation

9. African American female entrepreneur who made beauty products for African Americans

10. African American leader and educator who advocated economic independence and political neutrality

Understanding Main Ideas

1. Lincoln's plan offered amnesty to most southerners who would accept the new laws and permitted states to

TECHNOLOGY

▶ Chapter 4 Test Generator (on the One-Stop Planner)
▶ Global Skill Builder CD–ROM
▶ HRW Go site

REINFORCEMENT, REVIEW, AND ASSESSMENT

▶ Chapter 4 Review, pp. 154–55
▶ Chapter 4 Tutorial for Students, Parents, Mentors, and Peers

▶ Chapter 4 Test (Form A or B)
▶ Portfolio Activities and Alternative Assessment Handbook, Chapter 4
▶ Chapter 4 Test for English Language Learners and Special-Needs Students

REVIEW

Have students complete the **Chapter 4 Review** on pp. 154–55.

ASSESS

Use one of the chapter tests to assess students' understanding of the content. For **Alternative Assessment**, see the **Portfolio Activities and Alternative Assessment Handbook**.

---

rejoin the Union with a 10 percent vote. Johnson's plan pardoned most rebels and required states to abolish slavery and nullify acts of secession.

2. Johnson's plan pardoned most rebels and required states to abolish slavery and nullify acts of secession. The Radical Republicans' plan required Confederate states to abolish slavery and required white males of the states to take a loyalty oath.

3. Freedman's Bureau Bill, Civil Rights Acts of 1866 and 1875, Fourteenth and Fifteenth Amendments, Reconstruction Acts, Enforcement Acts

4. The Panic of 1873 forced legislators to change focus and helped Democrats win more seats in Congress. The withdrawal of federal troops from the South in 1877 allowed southerners to change social practices.

5. Most poor farmers had to become sharecroppers. Southern industry increased, but the workers were paid much less than workers in northern factories.

6. segregated blacks and whites in all facets of life

Reviewing Themes

1. acknowledged that African Americans were citizens and that the federal government had taken back control of the South

2. By recognizing that African Americans were citizens, the United States was expanding its definition of democracy.

3. The southern economy was dependent on cotton,

CHAPTER

4

Review

Creating a Time Line

Copy the time line below onto a sheet of paper. Complete the time line by filling in the events and dates from the chapter that you think were most significant. Pick three events and explain why you think they were significant.

| 1860 | 1875 | 1890 | 1905 |

Writing a Summary

Using standard grammar, spelling, sentence structure, and punctuation, write an overview of events in the chapter.

Identifying People and Ideas

Identify the following terms or individuals and explain their significance.

1. amnesty
2. Andrew Johnson
3. Black Codes
4. Reconstruction Acts
5. carpetbaggers
6. Compromise of 1877
7. sharecropping
8. Jim Crow laws
9. Madame C. J. Walker
10. Booker T. Washington

Understanding Main Ideas

SECTION 1 *(pp. 130–134)*

1. How did the Reconstruction plans of President Lincoln and President Johnson differ?

SECTION 2 *(pp. 135–142)*

2. How did President Johnson's plans for Reconstruction differ from Radical Republican plans?

3. What laws did Congress pass to protect the rights of African Americans?

SECTION 3 *(pp. 143–147)*

4. Why did Reconstruction come to an end?

SECTION 4 *(pp. 148–153)*

5. How did conditions for southern farmers and laborers change from 1865 to 1900?

6. How did Jim Crow laws affect African Americans?

Reviewing Themes

1. Constitutional Heritage How did the Reconstruction-era amendments alter the U.S. Constitution to reflect changing conditions after the Civil War?

2. Government How was the right to participate in the democratic process expanded during Reconstruction?

3. Economics What role did cotton play in the New South?

Thinking Critically

1. Making Generalizations and Predictions How might conditions in the New South have been different if land had been distributed to African Americans after the war?

2. Analyzing Information What were the defining characteristics of the Reconstruction era?

3. Identifying Cause and Effect What political gains did African Americans make during Reconstruction?

4. Identifying Points of View Imagine that you are a senator during the impeachment trial of President Johnson. How would you vote? Why?

5. Supporting a Point of View Do you agree or disagree with the Compromise of 1877? Why or why not?

Writing About History

Identifying Cause and Effect Imagine that you are an African American sharecropper in the postwar South. Write a letter to a local newspaper explaining how Reconstruction policies have affected your economic and social status and why you oppose the Compromise of 1877. Use the following graphic organizer to help organize your thoughts.

Reconstruction Policies → Effect on Economic Status → Reasons for Supporting Compromise

RETEACH

Write the following statement from the textbook (see Section 4 for full context) on the chalkboard: "*For African Americans, the so-called New South closely resembled the Old South.*" Organize the class into small groups. Have each group create a detailed outline of the events that created the reality of that statement. Compare groups' outlines and conduct a discussion on the failed promise of the Reconstruction era.

English Language Learners, Cooperative Learning

EXTEND

Ask students to conduct research on Booker T. Washington and Ida B. Wells. Then tell students to imagine that they are conducting a roundtable discussion with the two figures. Have each student write a transcript of the discussion. Students should include their questions and the figures' answers to those questions. Have students read portions of their transcripts to the class.

Block Scheduling

Building Social Studies Skills

Interpreting Maps

Study the map below. Then use it to help answer the questions that follow.

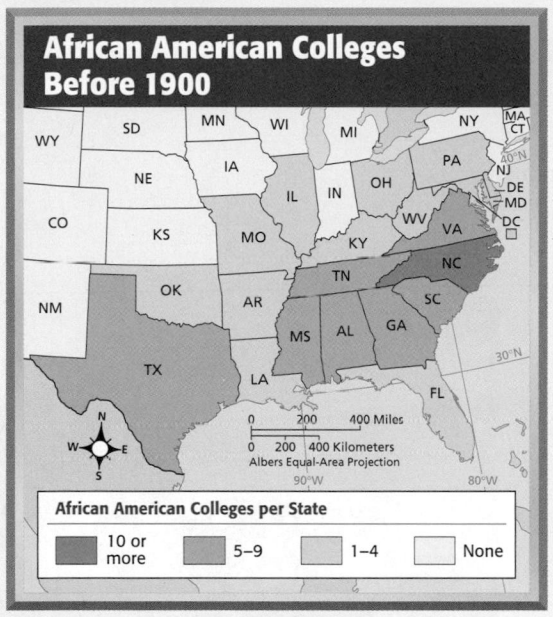

African American Colleges Before 1900

African American Colleges per State

10 or more	
5–9	
1–4	
None	

1. Where were most African American colleges that were founded before 1900 located?
   a. the West
   b. Texas
   c. the states of the former Confederacy
   d. the Northwest

2. What are some reasons for this geographic pattern?

Analyzing Primary Sources

Read the following excerpt from President Lincoln's second inaugural address, then answer the following questions.

"On the occasion corresponding to this four years ago, all thoughts were anxiously directed to an impending civil war. All dreaded it—all sought to avert it. While the inaugural address was being delivered from this place, devoted altogether to *saving* the Union without war, urgent agents were in the city seeking to *destroy* it without war—seeking to dissolve the Union and divide effects by negotiation. . . .

One-eighth of the whole population were colored slaves, not distributed generally over the Union, but localized in the Southern part of it. These slaves constituted a peculiar and powerful interest. All knew that this interest was, somehow, the cause of the war. To strengthen, perpetuate [continue], and extend this interest was the object for which the insurgents [rebels] would rend the Union, even by war; while the government claimed no right to do more than to restrict the territorial enlargement of it."

3. What does President Lincoln identify as the main cause of the Civil War?
   a. the existence of slavery
   b. abolition of slavery
   c. the desire to extend slavery
   d. states' rights

4. Based on this passage, how would you expect Lincoln to treat the former Confederate states as they tried to rejoin the Union?

Alternative Assessment

Building Your Portfolio

U.S. HISTORY

Constitutional Heritage

Imagine that you are an attorney representing Homer Plessy. Prepare a closing statement arguing that segregation, as practiced in separate-but-equal facilities for African Americans and whites, violates the equal protection guarantees of the Fourteenth Amendment. Your statement should include reasons why the amendment was passed.

internet connect

Internet Activity: go.hrw.com
KEYWORD: SE3 AN4

Choose a topic on Reconstruction to:
- analyze the circumstances resulting in Andrew Johnson's impeachment.
- explore gospel music and write a report on Fisk University.
- research the contributions of African Americans during Reconstruction.

---

which displaced other crops as a result of the crop-lien system.

Thinking Critically

1. Landownership would have given freedpeople more economic and political independence.

2. the end of slavery, political rights for African Americans, and Republican governments in the South

3. The Fourteenth and Fifteenth Amendments laid the groundwork for later enforcement of African American rights, and some African Americans served in state and national offices.

4. Answers will vary. Students should clearly identify the reasons for their positions.

5. Answers will vary. Students should clearly identify the reasons for their positions.

Writing

Answers will vary. Students should clearly identify the reasons for their positions.

Building Social Studies Skills

1. c

2. Because of their slave populations, the former Confederate states contained many African Americans; southern colleges would not allow African Americans to enroll.

3. c

4. Answers will vary. Students might suggest that Lincoln would be wary of the former Confederate states since he believed their rebellion had caused such a terrible war.

REVIEW AND ASSESSMENT RESOURCES

TECHNOLOGY

▶ Global Skill Builder CD–ROM

▶ Holt Researcher: American History CD–ROM

▶ HRW Go site

REINFORCEMENT, REVIEW, AND ASSESSMENT

▶ Unit 1 Review, pp. 156–57

▶ Unit 1 Test (Form A or B)

▶ Portfolio Activities and Alternative Assessment Handbook, Unit 1

▶ Unit 1 Test for English Language Learners and Special-Needs Students

To review elements of Unit 1 in a single class period, assign one of the following activities or graphic organizers, omitting the italicized answers, to individuals or groups.

1 Problem Solving

Ask students to imagine that they are delegates at the Constitutional Convention in 1787. They must create a new government that solves the problems of the Articles of Confederation, without creating a central government that is too powerful. Have students draft a document outlining a new form of government. Students should keep in mind particular issues their state wants addressed. In their document, students should first identify the problems of the Articles of

---

The Forty-Niners. In *The World Rushed In: The California Gold Rush Experience*, J. S. Holliday uses a variety of primary sources to create a composite portrait of miners. In the following excerpt, Holliday evaluates the motives of the forty-niners.

"Goldseekers were not settlers or pioneers in the tradition of America's westward migration. These people came as exploiters, transients, ready to take, not to build. Whether in the diggings or in San Francisco, Sacramento City, or Stockton, they found themselves surrounded by crowds of hurrying men concerned only with how to make the greatest amount of money in the shortest time. With that common motive, they also shared an indifference toward California and its future."

ANALYZING SOURCES

According to Holliday, what motivated the forty-niners?

ANSWER: Students might suggest that according to Holliday the miners were motivated by the prospect of making a quick profit without a long-term investment.

U·N·I·T 1

Review

BUILDING YOUR PORTFOLIO

Outlined below are three projects. Independently or cooperatively, complete one and use the products to demonstrate your mastery of the historical concepts involved.

1 Problem Solving

The year is 1890. The Thirteenth Amendment abolishing slavery was passed 15 years ago. Yet legal discrimination against African Americans remains. You and several other members of Congress are meeting to discuss other ways to reduce racial discrimination. Follow these steps to create a solution to the problem.

Use your textbook and other resources to *gather information* that might influence your plan. Remember that your plan must include a response to discrimination. You might need to gather information on various means to address discrimination including lobbying, passing laws, protesting, Supreme Court decisions, and amendments to the Constitution. You should also look at efforts taken by African Americans to expand their economic opportunities and political rights.

Once you have gathered information, *list and consider options*. These options might include new laws, additional amendments, or something not related to government action. Once you have identified these options, *consider the advantages and disadvantages* of each option. Which option do you think has the best chance for success?

Choose and implement a solution. Complete the plan for your solution. Have one student present a situation where legal discrimination exists and demonstrate how your plan would resolve the crisis. *Evaluate the effectiveness* of your solution. Was it the best option? Would one of your earlier options have been effective? How could you modify your plan to make it more effective?

Segregated classroom from the early 1900s

2 Culture

People from many different cultures exchanged technology, food, religion, and ideas in the Americas. Imagine that you are an anthropologist who studies the way people of different cultures meet and interact. *Create a journal entry* recording how two different groups interacted and chronicling their cultural differences. Describe what advantages and disadvantages each group experienced as a result of the contact. You may wish to use portfolio materials you designed in the unit chapters to help you.

Confederation. Their second section should focus on their new government, including the advantages and disadvantages of their plan. Students should conclude with a section on how to implement their new government. Ask volunteers to read their documents to the class. To conclude, ask students to evaluate the effectiveness of each group's plan.

2 Culture

Have each student write a poem expressing the ways in which people of different cultures interacted in the Americas. Students should describe the positive and negative aspects of these interactions. Ask volunteers to recite their poems to the class.

3 Geography

```
                    ┌─────────────────┐
                    │  RECONSTRUCTION │
                    └─────────────────┘
              ↙                              ↘
```

Benefits to the North
- *provided new economic opportunities to many northerners*
- *provided an opportunity to extend "northern" ideals into the South*

Benefits to the South
- *provided new economic and social opportunities to many African Americans in the region*
- *resulted in the creation of new roads and schools*

```
              ↘                              ↙
```

Which Region Reaped the Most Benefits? Why?

---

3 **Geography**
Differences between the North and the South created a rift that led to the Civil War and left deep scars that Reconstruction failed to erase. Locate and use primary and secondary sources to *create a database* on how the Civil War and Reconstruction affected the North and the South. Some statistics you might want to compare include: agricultural output, economic growth, industrial production, and population. Then write five questions for other students to answer based on the information provided in your database. Your questions should offer students the opportunity to evaluate the effects of the Civil War and Reconstruction. You may wish to use portfolio materials you designed in the unit chapters to help you.

Carpetbag carried by northerners traveling south during Reconstruction

The First Thanksgiving 1621 *by J. L. G. Ferris*

Further Reading

Ellis, Joseph J. *Founding Brothers: The Revolutionary Generation.* Knopf, 2000. An account of crucial moments in the life of the new nation.

Foner, Eric. *A Short History of Reconstruction, 1863–1877.* HarperCollins, 1990. An overview of Reconstruction.

Holliday, J. S. *The World Rushed In: The California Gold Rush Experience.* Simon and Schuster, 1983. Eyewitness accounts of the California Gold Rush.

Josephy, Alvin M. Jr., ed. *America in 1492: The World of the Indian Peoples Before the Arrival of Columbus.* Vintage, 1993. A panorama of North and South American life from prehistoric times to the early 1400s.

Mellon, James M. *Bullwhip Days: The Slaves Remember.* Avon Books, 1988. Interviews with former slaves.

Meltzer, Milton, ed. *Voices from the Civil War.* HarperCollins, 1989. Northern and southern views of the war and its effects from 1861 to 1865.

Rhodehamel, John, ed. *The American Revolution: Writings from the War of Independence.* Library of America, 2001. A collection of writings made by participants in the Revolution.

Internet Connect & Review on the R•M

In assigned groups, develop a multimedia presentation about the United States from prehistory to 1900. Choose information from the chapter Internet Connect activities and from the **Holt Researcher CD–ROM** that best reflect the major topics of the period. Write an outline and a script for your presentation.

A Selection from
Further Reading

African Americans in the South. In *A Short History of Reconstruction,* Eric Foner provides a survey of American society and politics during Reconstruction. In the following excerpt, Foner explains how Reconstruction affected African Americans in the South. "Although thwarted in their bid for land, blacks seized the opportunity created by the end of slavery to establish as much independence as possible in their working lives, consolidate their families and communities, and stake a claim to equal citizenship. Black participation in Southern public life after 1867 was the most radical development of the Reconstruction years."

ANALYZING SOURCES

According to Foner, how did the experience of African Americans in the South change during Reconstruction?

ANSWER: Students might note that during Reconstruction, southern African Americans were able to obtain some measure of economic independence, reinforce their families and communities, and begin to take part in politics.

A Nation Transformed

CHAPTER 5

The Western Crossroads

Beginning in the 1840s, large numbers of white settlers began to migrate to lands west of the Mississippi River. These settlers were drawn by the prospect of land, railroad construction work, the cattle boom, and gold and silver. Their migration and encroachment of American Indian land led to violent conflicts. Ultimately, the government forced the outnumbered Indians onto reservations.

CHAPTER 6

The Second Industrial Revolution

During the Second Industrial Revolution, innovations in the steel and oil industries led to new advances in transportation. The invention of the telegraph and the telephone made it easier for people to communicate. Entrepreneurs established profitable new corporations. Workers often labored in unsafe factories for low wages, joined labor unions, and went on strike.

EXAMINING THE VISUAL RECORD

Ask students the questions below. Then use the annotations to expand class discussion.

1 *Why might this building be the only one to include decorative elements?*
While it was cheaper and more efficient to leave industrial buildings undecorated, American business owners believed that it was important for some buildings—in this case, what seems to be the train station—to include decorative elements such as cupolas and fancy windows or lively paint colors.

2 *Why might this artist depict the factory in such a naturalistic scene?*
During the 1800s, many Americans hoped that machines and industry would coexist with the natural world. Some people worried that the machine would destroy pastoral scenes such as this one. Thus prints like this one often showed reassuring images of nature and industry peacefully coexisting.

ACTIVITY: Ask students to imagine that it is 1875 and that they are British journalists visiting this railcar works. Have each student write an article describing the factory, its setting, and American beliefs about industry and nature.

UNIT 2

A Nation Transformed

1860–1910

Wason Railcar Works used this facility to manufacture railroad cars during the 1870s.

1845. — WASON — 1872. CAR MANUFACTURING CO.

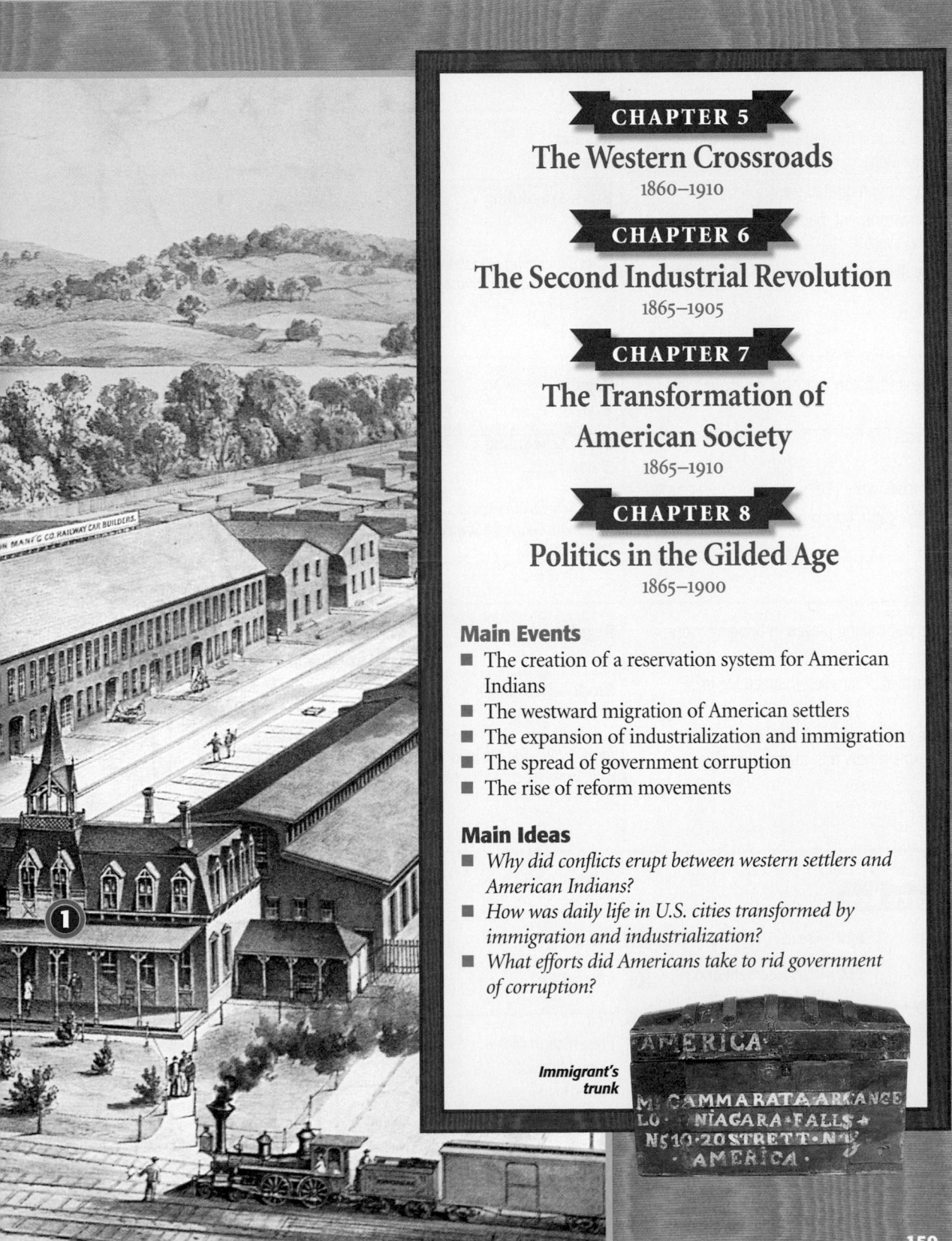

CHAPTER 7
The Transformation of American Society

In the late 1800s and early 1900s, the United States became a more urbanized, ethnically diverse society. Millions of immigrants came to the United States from southern and eastern Europe. The majority of these immigrants lived in cities, where they often worked and lived in difficult conditions. Technological advances also helped to reshape American life during the period.

CHAPTER 8
Politics in the Gilded Age

Political machines and political bosses dominated politics in some cities during the late 1800s. These machines and bosses supplied jobs and services in return for votes. Corruption in national politics led to calls for political reform, including the abolition of the patronage system. The desire for reform also motivated farmers, who formed cooperatives and lobbies. Farmers also joined the new Populist Party.

CHAPTER 5
The Western Crossroads
1860–1910

CHAPTER 6
The Second Industrial Revolution
1865–1905

CHAPTER 7
The Transformation of American Society
1865–1910

CHAPTER 8
Politics in the Gilded Age
1865–1900

Main Events
- The creation of a reservation system for American Indians
- The westward migration of American settlers
- The expansion of industrialization and immigration
- The spread of government corruption
- The rise of reform movements

Main Ideas
- *Why did conflicts erupt between western settlers and American Indians?*
- *How was daily life in U.S. cities transformed by immigration and industrialization?*
- *What efforts did Americans take to rid government of corruption?*

Immigrant's trunk

AMERICA
M: CAMMARATA·ARRANGE
LO   NIAGARA·FALLS·
N510·20STRETT·N·Y
AMERICA·

INTRODUCE UNIT 2

Main Events
List the Main Events on the chalkboard. Ask students to select two and briefly describe what they know about the topics. Have volunteers share their descriptions. Later, when you have finished Unit 2, ask students to return to their original descriptions and revise them using the information they learned in the unit. Students should also create new descriptions for the other Main Events.

Main Ideas
Ask each student to read the Main Ideas and briefly answer the questions in writing. Share the **Consider** points with students as necessary. Later, when you have finished Unit 2, ask students to return to their original answers and revise them using the information they learned in the unit.

Conflicts Between Western Settlers and American Indians
Consider:
- land ownership
- desire to expand vs. desire to maintain historic ties to land

Immigration and Industrialization
Consider:
- the social and cultural backgrounds of immigrants
- the effects of technological advances on workers and the workplace

The Western Crossroads

CHAPTER RESOURCE MANAGER

Objectives	Pacing Guide	Reproducible Resources
SECTION 1 **War in the West** pp. 162–69 ★ Explain why the U.S. government created the American Indian reservation system. ★ Identify the sources of conflict between the Plains Indians and the U.S. government. ★ Describe how Chief Joseph, Geronimo, and Sarah Winnemucca responded to white treatment of American Indians. ★ Discuss how the U.S. government tried to assimilate American Indians.	**Regular** 2 days **Block Scheduling** 1 day *Block Scheduling Handbook with Team Teaching Strategies,* *pp. 25–30*	**RS** Guided Reading Strategy 5.1 **SM** Geography Activity 5: American Indian Lands in the West **PS** Primary Source Reading 5: Massacre at Wounded Knee **PS** Biography Reading 5: Geronimo
SECTION 2 **Western Farmers** pp. 170–76 ★ Discuss how the U.S. government promoted economic development in the West. ★ Understand why people migrated west. ★ Explain how the environment influenced farming practices and daily life in the West. ★ Describe the difficulties that farm families faced on the Great Plains.	**Regular** 1 day **Block Scheduling** .5 day *Block Scheduling Handbook with Team Teaching Strategies,* *pp. 25–30*	**RS** Guided Reading Strategy 5.2 **IC** Literature Reading 5: Life on the Prairie **E** Hands-On History Activity: Agriculture and You
SECTION 3 **The Cattle Boom** pp. 177–82 ★ Discuss how cattle and sheep ranching developed in the West. ★ Explain what life was like for cowboys and residents of cattle towns. ★ Describe what ranches were like. ★ Understand why the cattle boom on the open range ended.	**Regular** 1 day **Block Scheduling** .5 day *Block Scheduling Handbook with Team Teaching Strategies,* *pp. 25–30*	**RS** Guided Reading Strategy 5.3 **SM** American History Outline Map 15: Western Railroads and Cattle Trails **E** Creative Teaching Strategy: Collage Lesson
SECTION 4 **The Mining Boom** pp. 183–87 ★ Describe the role that mining played in bringing more people west. ★ Explain how the arrival of families changed life in mining camps. ★ Discuss why large companies took over most mining operations, and explain how this changed the lives of miners.	**Regular** 1 days **Block Scheduling** .5 day *Block Scheduling Handbook with Team Teaching Strategies,* *pp. 25–30*	**RS** Guided Reading Strategy 5.4 **RS** Graphic Organizer Activity 5: American Indian Leaders

Chapter Resource Key

PS	Primary Sources	**REV**	Review	Video
RS	Reading Support	**ELL**	Reinforcement and English Language Learners	Internet
IC	Interdisciplinary Connections			Holt Presentation Maker Using Microsoft® PowerPoint®
E	Enrichment		Transparencies	
SM	Skills Mastery		CD-ROM	
A	Assessment		Music	

One-Stop Planner CD-ROM

See the *One-Stop Planner* for a complete list of additional resources for students and teachers.

One-Stop Planner CD-ROM

It's easy to plan lessons, select resources, and print out materials for your students when you use the **One-Stop Planner CD-ROM with Test Generator.**

Technology Resources

 One-Stop Planner, Lesson 5.1
 Art in American History Transparency 15: Navajo Eye Dazzler Blanket
 Holt Researcher: American History CD–ROM
Homework Practice Online
HRW Go site

 One-Stop Planner, Lesson 5.2
The American Nation Video Program Segment: Linking the Nation; Teacher's Guide, pp. 69–74
 CNN Presents America: Yesterday and Today, Beginnings to 1914 Segment: Railroad Ties
Holt Researcher: American History CD–ROM
Homework Practice Online

 One-Stop Planner, Lesson 5.3
 American Music Selection 16: "O Bury Me Not"
Art in American History Transparency 17: Prospecting for Cattle Range
Holt Researcher: American History CD–ROM
Homework Practice Online

 One-Stop Planner, Lesson 5.4
 Holt Researcher: American History CD–ROM
 Homework Practice Online

Reinforcement, Review, and Assessment

REV Section 1 Review, p. 169
A Daily Quiz 5.1
ELL Main Idea Activity 5.1
ELL English Audio Summary 5.1
ELL Spanish Audio Summary 5.1

REV Section 2 Review, p. 176
A Daily Quiz 5.2
ELL Main Idea Activity 5.2
ELL English Audio Summary 5.2
ELL Spanish Audio Summary 5.2

REV Section 3 Review, p. 182
A Daily Quiz 5.3
ELL Main Idea Activity 5.3
ELL English Audio Summary 5.3
ELL Spanish Audio Summary 5.3

REV Section 4 Review, p. 187
A Daily Quiz 5.4
ELL Main Idea Activity 5.4
ELL English Audio Summary 5.4
ELL Spanish Audio Summary 5.4

internet connect

HRW ONLINE RESOURCES
GO TO: go.hrw.com
Then type in a keyword.

TEACHER HOME PAGE
KEYWORD: SE3 Teacher

CHAPTER INTERNET ACTIVITIES
KEYWORD: SE3 AN5
Choose an activity to:
• learn about the writers who shaped the image of the American West.
• research the Pony Express.
• use pictographs to create a model of a Sioux story robe.

CHAPTER ENRICHMENT LINKS
KEYWORD: SE3 CH5

ONLINE ASSESSMENT
Homework Practice
KEYWORD: SE3 HP5

Standardized Test Prep
KEYWORD: SE3 STP5

Rubrics
KEYWORD: SS Rubrics

ONLINE MAPS, CHARTS, AND GRAPHS
KEYWORD: SE3 MCG
• The Oklahoma Land Rush
• The Great Plains
• Mining Centers
• The Bison Population
• The Cost of Establishing a Farm

CONTENT UPDATES
KEYWORD: SS Content Updates

HOLT PRESENTATION MAKER
KEYWORD: SE3 PPT5

ONLINE READING SUPPORT
KEYWORD: SS Strategies

CURRENT EVENTS
KEYWORD: S3 Current Events

Chapter Review and Assessment

 Global Skill Builder CD–ROM
HRW Go site
REV **Chapter 5 Tutorial for Students, Parents, Mentors, and Peers**
REV **Chapter 5 Review, pp. 188–89**
 Chapter 5 Test Generator (on the One-Stop Planner)
A **Chapter 5 Test (Form A or B)**
A **Alternative Assessment Handbook**
A **Chapter 5 Test for English Language Learners and Special-Needs Students**

Meeting Individual Needs

Ability Levels

Level 1 Basic-level activities designed for all students encountering new material

Level 2 Intermediate-level activities designed for average students

Level 3 Challenging activities designed for honors and gifted-and-talented students

English Language Learners Activities that address the needs of students with Limited English Proficiency

Build on What You Know

Ask students to answer the following questions.

Why might Americans have settled in the West?

Consider:

• "push" and "pull" factors, such as violence at home and better economic opportunities in another region

• political agreements that expanded U.S. territory in the West

How might American Indians have fared as a consequence of American settlement in the West?

Consider:

• the loss of American Indian lands to settlers

• violent conflict with settlers and the U.S. government

---

exploring the time line

AMERICAN EVENTS

internet connect

TOPIC: Pony Express
GO TO: go.hrw.com
KEYWORD: SE3 AN5

Have students access the Internet through the HRW Go site to conduct research on the history and mythology of the Pony Express. Then ask students to write an informative report that compares the actual history of the Pony Express with the myths that surround it. Remind students to use standard grammar, punctuation, spelling, and sentence structure.

CHAPTER 5

1860–1910
The Western Crossroads

Pony Express stamp

Signing of the Alaska treaty

Queen Victoria

1860
Daily Life
The Pony Express begins delivering mail between Missouri and California.

1867
Politics
Congress approves the purchase of Alaska from Russia.

1876
World Events
Queen Victoria of Great Britain becomes empress of India.

1876
Politics
Colorado becomes the 38th state admitted to the Union.

1860

1861
World Events
The Italian parliament declares Italy a kingdom.

1860
Science and Technology
Oliver Winchester introduces the repeating rifle.

1870

1870
The Arts
Bret Harte publishes *The Luck of Roaring Camp,* about life in California.

1873
Daily Life
Cable streetcars are introduced in San Francisco.

1873
Business and Finance
A severe economic depression slows the growth of railroad networks.

Bret Harte's **The Luck of Roaring Camp**

1880

1883
Business and Finance
Railroad companies create the time-zone system.

Late 1800s bull clock

Build on What You Know

The resolution of the Oregon boundary dispute in 1846 and the Treaty of Guadalupe Hidalgo in 1848 reshaped the United States. These treaties opened up more than 1 million square miles of western land for U.S. settlement. In this chapter you will learn that Americans who settled in the West came for many reasons. American Indians suffered the consequences of this settlement. They endured continued conflict and violence as non-Indians established farms and ranches in the lands of the American West.

What's Your Opinion?

 To help students create their Themes Journal entries, provide the following examples of appropriate **agree/disagree** statements.

Culture

Agree Cultural differences between the Cayuse and white settlers in Oregon Territory led to violence.

Disagree Despite substantial cultural differences, the Wampanoag helped the English settlers in the Plymouth colony.

Economics

Agree The environmental impact of the fishing trade in colonial New England was not readily apparent.

Disagree Americans' desire to expand trade between states led to the building of the Erie Canal, railroads, and the National Road.

Science, Technology, and Society

Agree The development of new manufacturing technologies led some factory owners to employ children, who often worked under harsh conditions.

Disagree Cyrus McCormick's mechanical reaper allowed farmers to harvest grain more easily.

A Sioux child's doll

U.S. troops posing with Hotchkiss guns

Russian Fabergé egg

1885
World Events
King Leopold II of Belgium assumes sovereignty over the African Congo.

1890
Politics
Troops of the U.S. 7th Cavalry attack Sioux camped at Wounded Knee Creek in South Dakota.

1890
Business and Finance
The Midwest is the center of the meatpacking industry.

1896
World Events
Italy recognizes Abyssinia—modern-day Ethiopia—as an independent nation.

1896
Daily Life
Americans living in rural areas receive mail delivery for free.

1905
World Events
Czar Nicholas II of Russia institutes reforms after a series of strikes paralyzes the nation.

1886–87
Daily Life
Devastating winter storms lash the Great Plains.

1889
Daily Life
President Harrison opens to settlers Oklahoma Territory lands that had been reserved for American Indians.

1898
The Arts
The Royal Italian Opera performs Puccini's *La Bohème* in San Francisco.

1906
Science and Technology
An astronomical observatory opens at Mount Wilson, California.

1890 **1900** **1910**

Settlers racing to claim land in Oklahoma

What's Your Opinion?

 Themes Journal *Do you* **agree** *or* **disagree** *with the following statements? Support your point of view in your journal.*

Culture Cultural differences between groups can lead to misunderstandings and even violence.

Economics The impact that some economic activities have upon the environment is not readily apparent.

Science, Technology, and Society Improvements in technology may actually worsen conditions for some laborers.

GLOBAL EVENTS

GLOBAL RELATIONS

1905 ■ Bloody Sunday in Russia. The series of strikes that prompted Czar Nicholas II to institute reforms in Russia were sparked by an event that occurred on January 9, 1905—a date that became known as Bloody Sunday. Early that morning, thousands of workers gathered in St. Petersburg to present the czar with a list of economic and political grievances. When the demonstrators ignored orders to disperse, Russian troops opened fire on them. By the end of the day more than 130 people lay dead. Bloody Sunday outraged people across Russia, inspiring many strikes.

CRITICAL THINKING Tell students that a priest led the Bloody Sunday march and that many participants viewed it as a religious procession. Why might some observers have viewed it as a primarily political function rather than a religious one?

ANSWER: Some students might point to the workers' grievances, which were economic and political rather than religious.

After completing Section 1, students should be able to:

OBJECTIVE 1 Explain why the U.S. government created the American Indian reservation system.

OBJECTIVE 2 Identify the sources of conflict between the Plains Indians and the U.S. government.

OBJECTIVE 3 Describe how Chief Joseph, Geronimo, and Sarah Winnemucca responded to white treatment of American Indians.

OBJECTIVE 4 Discuss how the U.S. government tried to assimilate American Indians.

LET'S GET STARTED!

Write the following quotation on the chalkboard: *"One of our hands holds the rifle and the other the peace-pipe, and we blaze away with both instruments at the same time. The chief consequence is a great smoke—and there it ends."* As students enter the classroom, ask them who might have made the statement and why. Students should respond in writing. Tell students that in Section 1 they will learn about American Indian resistance to U.S. government policies toward Indians.

SECTION ①

READ TO DISCOVER

1. Why did the U.S. government create the American Indian reservation system?
2. What were the sources of conflict between the Plains Indians and the U.S. government?
3. How did Chief Joseph, Geronimo, and Sarah Winnemucca respond to whites' treatment of American Indians?
4. How did the U.S. government try to assimilate American Indians?

IDENTIFY

Bureau of Indian Affairs
John M. Chivington
Sand Creek Massacre
Sitting Bull
George Armstrong Custer
Battle of the Little Bighorn
Wovoka
Massacre at Wounded Knee
Chief Joseph
Geronimo
Sarah Winnemucca
Dawes General Allotment Act

▶ WHY IT MATTERS TODAY

Many American Indians continue to live on reservations. Use **CNNfyi.com** or other **current events** sources to find out about American Indians living on reservations today. Record your findings in your journal.

CNNfyi.com

War in the West

A Cheyenne shield

THE GRANGER COLLECTION, NEW YORK

EYEWITNESSES TO History

"When I was young, I walked all over this country, east and west, and saw no other people than the Apaches. After many summers I walked again and found another race of people had come to take it."

—Cochise, quoted in *Bury My Heart at Wounded Knee*, by Dee Brown

Cochise, a Chiricahua (chir-uh-KAH-wuh) Apache leader, mourned over the crisis faced by American Indians as white settlers poured into their homelands. During the 1850s the Chiricahua had permitted settlers traveling to California to pass through Apache lands in what is now Arizona. In 1861, however, a rancher accused the Chiricahua of stealing a child and cattle from his ranch. U.S. Army officials attempted to hold Cochise and his relatives hostage until the child and cattle were returned. The incident led to years of deadly warfare between the Chiricahua and the U.S. government. It also reflected U.S. relations with many Indian nations in the late 1800s.

Indian Country

By 1850 most American Indians—some 360,000—lived west of the Mississippi River. Some were nomadic hunters and others established more permanent villages. Most American Indians did not own land. Instead they claimed a right to use land in a particular area. The 1851 Treaty of Fort Laramie had guaranteed American Indian land rights on the Great Plains. However, as non-Indians moved west, government officials tried to acquire additional Indian lands. They negotiated new treaties in which American Indians agreed to move to reservations. In return, Indians received some money and guarantees that the reservation lands would be theirs forever. These treaties also promised yearly supplies for 30 years.

Some government officials hoped that keeping American Indians on reservations would force them to become farmers and to abandon many of their traditional ways of life. The **Bureau of Indian Affairs** (BIA) was the government agency responsible for managing American Indian issues. BIA commissioner Luke Lea supported the reservation system. He declared in 1850 that American Indians should "be placed in positions where they can be controlled, and finally compelled by stern necessity to resort to agricultural labor or starve." Other officials recognized the harm this would do to American Indians. Thomas Fitzpatrick was an Indian agent who had helped to negotiate several treaties. In 1853 Fitzpatrick condemned the notion of a reservation system as "expensive, vicious, [and] inhumane."

American Indians who went willingly to the reservations discovered that the U.S. government often failed to honor its treaties. In addition, the government reduced the size of many reservations as settlers demanded more land. To make matters worse, in many cases the promised supplies never arrived. Government agents often diverted elsewhere the supplies intended for American Indians.

TEACH OBJECTIVE 1

LEVEL 1: Pair students and tell them to imagine that they are newspaper reporters who have been assigned to cover American Indian issues in the mid-1800s. Have each pair write four newspaper headlines that express the U.S. government's reasons for creating the American Indian reservation system. *(Pairs' headlines should include the desire for farmland and gold, the desire for control, and the desire for assimilation.)* Ask volunteers to share their headlines with the class.
English Language Learners, Cooperative Learning

LEVEL 2: Tell students to imagine that it is 1885 and that they live in New Jersey but plan to move to Arizona. Have each student write a short editorial explaining and commenting on why the U.S. government created the American Indian reservation system. *(See the Level 1 lesson for answers. Students' editorials should tend to support the reservation system out of consideration for their impending move.)* Have volunteers read their editorials to the class. Then ask students to consider the issue of historical self-interest. Would their responses to the reservation system have been different if they were American Indians in the West? If they were neutral French observers? How? Conduct a discussion on students' responses.

Anger over inadequate supplies and broken treaties exploded into violence on the Santee Sioux reservation in 1862. When a government agent refused to release food supplies even though people were starving, the Sioux attacked the Indian agency and nearby farms and towns. Army troops soon ended the uprising and executed 38 Sioux for their actions. The tribe was relocated, first to the Dakota Territory and then to Nebraska.

✔ **READING CHECK: Analyzing Information** What did the U.S. government give American Indians in exchange for their land? money and guarantees of other land

Years of Struggle

Many Plains Indians, including independent groups of Arapaho, Cheyenne, Comanche, and Sioux, refused to live on the reservations. The importance to their cultures of following the roaming buffalo herds caused them to reject the restrictions of settled life.

The Plains Indians faced strong opposition. Some 20,000 U.S. Army troops, many of them Civil War veterans, were assigned to confine the tribes to the reservations. The army also enlisted some American Indians as scouts or as soldiers. Struggling to perform their duties, U.S. troops occasionally became involved in violent conflicts with groups of Indians.

Sand Creek. One particularly violent confrontation occurred in Colorado Territory. Cheyenne and Arapaho forces clashed with the local militia throughout the summer of 1864. By fall, Cheyenne chief Black Kettle had tired of the fighting. On the way to make peace, his group camped along Sand Creek. While most of the Cheyenne men were away hunting, U.S. Army colonel **John M. Chivington** and some 700 Colorado volunteers arrived at the camp. Having raised a U.S. flag above his lodge as a sign of peace, Black Kettle reassured his people that they were safe. One eyewitness later recalled, "Suddenly the troops opened fire on this mass of men, women, and children, and all began to scatter and run." Some 200 of Black Kettle's group, most of them women and children, died in the **Sand Creek Massacre**.

Chivington defended his actions, declaring, "It is right and honorable to use any means under God's heaven to kill Indians." However, the slaughter horrified many Americans. A congressional committee investigating the incident called Sand Creek a "scene of murder and barbarity." Shock over the massacre led some members of Congress to call for reform of the government's Indian policy.

News of the Sand Creek Massacre swept across the Plains, prompting raids by the Arapaho and Cheyenne.

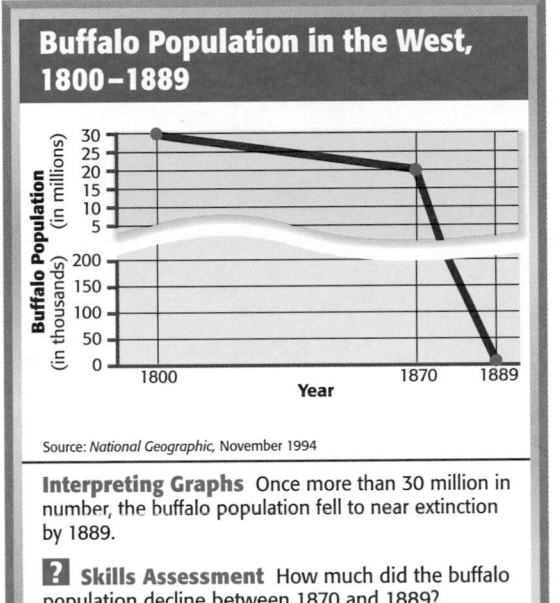

Buffalo Population in the West, 1800–1889

Source: *National Geographic*, November 1994

Interpreting Graphs Once more than 30 million in number, the buffalo population fell to near extinction by 1889.

❓ **Skills Assessment** How much did the buffalo population decline between 1870 and 1889?

INTERPRETING THE VISUAL RECORD

Buffalo. This painting by John Mix Stanley features a scene of the West. *What does the painting reveal about the techniques American Indians used to hunt buffalo?*

ECONOMICS

Private Property and American Indians. On the Great Plains some American Indians were nomadic hunters who traveled the area in search of buffalo. These groups usually traveled on horseback and carried portable housing. Other American Indians established permanent villages where they farmed or traded. Both groups of Indians saw themselves as a community. This spirit of community was reflected in their attitudes toward land. Individuals did not own land nor did groups. Communities claimed a right to use land in a particular area. If the resources in one area dwindled, Indians would move in search of additional resources. They would occasionally fight with other Indian groups over these lands.

CRITICAL THINKING How did American Indians' views on private property differ from those of Americans wanting to settle the Great Plains?

ANSWER: Students should note that American Indians viewed the land as communal while settlers wanted to purchase it.

VISUAL RECORD ANSWER

Students might suggest that Indian techniques required skill with the spear.

GRAPH ANSWER
by about 15 million

LEVEL 3: Tell students to imagine that they are high-level government officials preparing to unveil the American Indian reservation system. Have each student write a short speech explaining why the U.S. government created the system. (*See the Level 1 lesson for the correct answers.*) Ask volunteers to present their speeches to the class. Then ask students to consider the reasons presented in those speeches. Do any of those reasons seem justified today? If not, why? (*Press students to consider modern-day advances in civil rights.*) Conduct a discussion on students' responses.

TEACH OBJECTIVE 2

LEVEL 1: Pair students and have each pair list the sources of conflict between the Plains Indians and the U.S. government. (*Pairs should list the conflicts over land and reservations, the conflicts over broken promises and treaties, and the conflicts over the Ghost Dance.*) Then ask each pair to synthesize the material on its list into a written paragraph. Have volunteers read their paragraphs to the class.
English Language Learners, Cooperative Learning

The Sand Creek Massacre shocked many Americans.

The Sioux also stepped up their attacks. To end the fighting, the U.S. government created a peace commission. Meeting with some Indians in 1867, a U.S. senator told them that the buffalo would soon be gone, so "the Indian must change the road his father trod." One Comanche replied, "I love the open prairie, and I wish you would not insist on putting us on a reservation." Despite such feelings, tribal leaders signed the Treaty of Medicine Lodge. Southern Plains Indians agreed to give up much of their lands in exchange for reservations in Indian Territory. The following year, in a second Treaty of Fort Laramie, the Sioux agreed to move to a reservation in the Black Hills region of South Dakota.

✔ **READING CHECK: Identifying Cause and Effect** How did the Sand Creek Massacre lead to new treaties? Shock over the massacre led Congress to call for reform of government Indian policy.

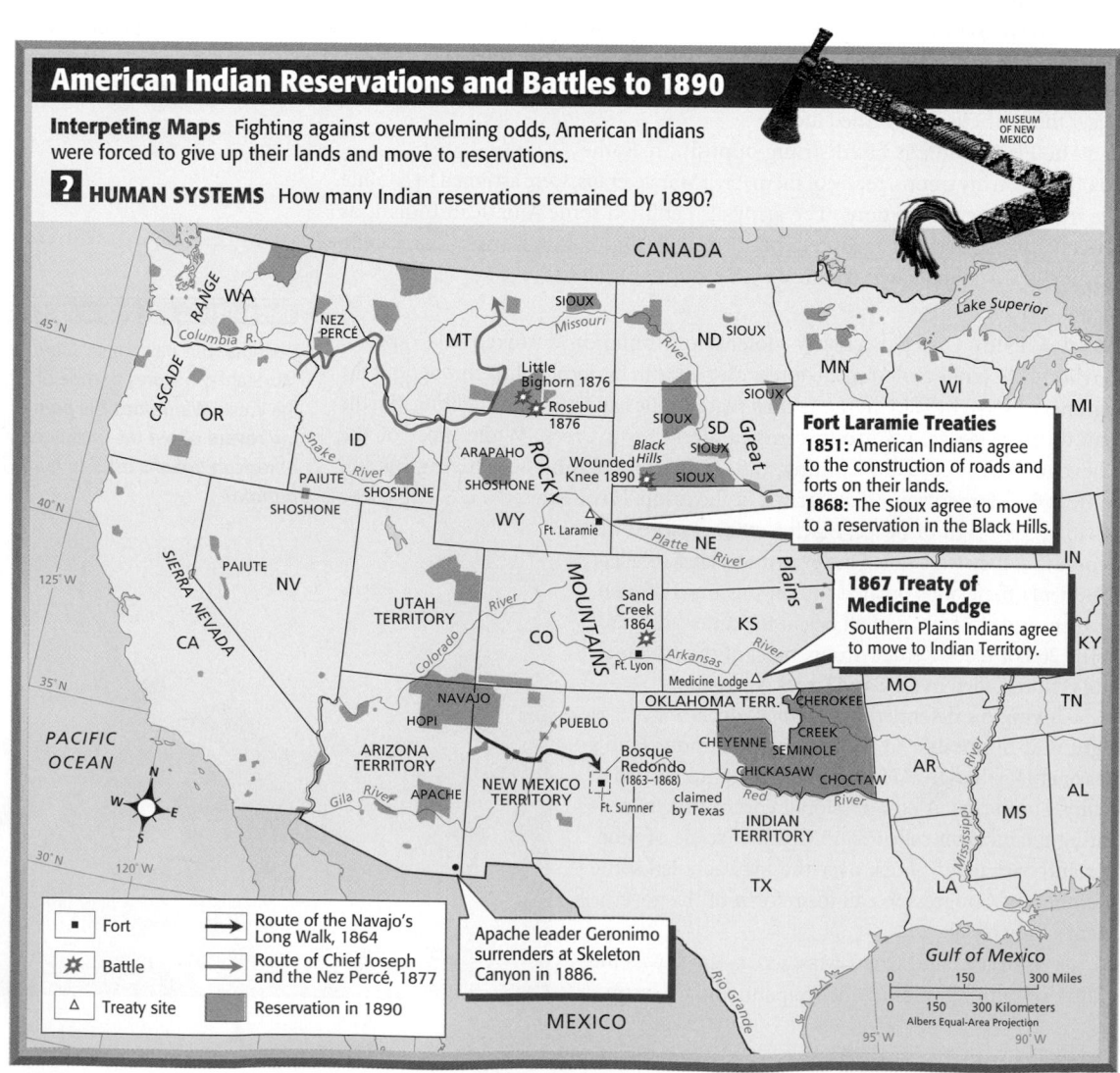

American Indian Reservations and Battles to 1890

Interpeting Maps Fighting against overwhelming odds, American Indians were forced to give up their lands and move to reservations.

? **HUMAN SYSTEMS** How many Indian reservations remained by 1890?

Fort Laramie Treaties
1851: American Indians agree to the construction of roads and forts on their lands.
1868: The Sioux agree to move to a reservation in the Black Hills.

1867 Treaty of Medicine Lodge
Southern Plains Indians agree to move to Indian Territory.

Apache leader Geronimo surrenders at Skeleton Canyon in 1886.

Fort
Battle
Treaty site
Route of the Navajo's Long Walk, 1864
Route of Chief Joseph and the Nez Percé, 1877
Reservation in 1890

LEVEL 2: Organize the class into groups of four, with two members of each group assuming the roles of U.S. government officials and two members assuming the roles of Plains Indians. Have the two sides within each group identify the sources of conflict between American Indians and the government. *(See the Level 1 lesson for the correct responses.)* Then ask groups to negotiate treaties with specific provisions to satisfy both sides. *(Groups' treaties should address the major sources of conflict identified in the Level 1 lesson.)* Ask a spokesperson from each group to share his or her group's treaty with the class, and have other students assess its recommendations, considering both fairness and practicality. **Cooperative Learning**

LEVEL 3: Tell students to imagine that they are investigative reporters for an 1890 edition of the *St. Louis Post-Dispatch*. Have each student write a short investigative report on the sources of conflict between American Indians and the U.S. government. *(See the Level 1 lesson for the correct responses.)* Have volunteers read their reports to the class.

HOMEWORK *Have each student create a crossword puzzle that utilizes all the key terms and key people in the subsection entitled Years of Struggle. Students should provide clues for the answers. Tell students to exchange their crossword puzzles and solve the puzzle they receive.*

Little Bighorn. The peace was short-lived. In 1874 the government violated the terms of the 1868 Treaty of Fort Laramie by sending an army expedition into the Black Hills to search for gold. Gold was discovered, and the government tried to negotiate a new treaty with the Sioux. The Sioux refused.

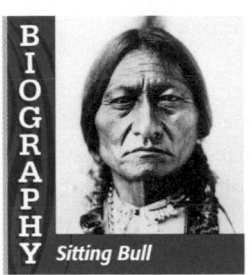

Sitting Bull

Tatanka Iyotake, a Lakota Sioux also called **Sitting Bull**, emerged as an important leader of Sioux resistance. He was born about 1831 along the banks of the Missouri River. At age 14 he fought in his first battle, a small skirmish with the Crow Indians. As a result, he earned the right to wear an eagle feather, a symbol of bravery, and was given the name Sitting Bull.

Sitting Bull gained the respect of his people for his courage, wisdom, and generosity. He became known as a spiritual leader and medicine chief. Committed to the traditional Sioux way of life, Sitting Bull strongly opposed the intrusion of non-Indians onto Sioux lands. He mocked American Indians who had willingly moved to reservations. "You are fools," he argued, "to make yourselves slaves to a piece of fat bacon, some hard-tack [biscuits], and a little sugar and coffee." Many agreed, and by the spring of 1876 thousands of Sioux and their Cheyenne allies were camped on Rosebud Creek in southern Montana.

During that summer, Sitting Bull had a vision in which he saw soldiers descending upon an American Indian village. The soldiers and their horses appeared upside down, which Sitting Bull understood to mean that they would all die. Inspired by this vision, several hundred American Indians rode off to fight U.S. troops advancing toward them. During the Battle of the Rosebud in June 1876, the Indians battled a larger army. Although they did not achieve an outright victory, their performance at Rosebud gave them confidence in their ability to fight U.S. soldiers.

After the battle, the Indians proceeded west to camp near a stream known by the army as Little Bighorn River. They were joined by hundreds of American Indians fleeing the BIA-sponsored encampments, where food was in short supply. By late June the camp contained some 2,500 men prepared to fight.

On the morning of June 25, 1876, General **George Armstrong Custer** and about 600 members of the U.S. Army 7th Cavalry reached the American Indian camp. Although his troops had ridden through most of the night, Custer ordered an immediate attack. After dividing his men so that they could attack from three sides, Custer led a battalion of more than 200 men into the camp. Cheyenne leader Two Moons described the battle: "We circled all round . . . swirling like water around a stone. We shoot, we ride fast, we shoot again. Soldiers drop, and horses fall on them." After the final attack, which lasted less than an hour, Custer and every soldier in his battalion lay dead.

The **Battle of the Little Bighorn** proved to be the last victory for the Sioux. The shock of Custer's defeat prompted the army to increase its efforts to move the

Research on the ROM

Free Find: Sitting Bull

After reading about Sitting Bull on the **Holt Researcher CD–ROM**, imagine that you are an author preparing a biography of him. Create an outline that shows the reasons why you think he was a good or bad leader for his people.

INTERPRETING THE VISUAL RECORD

The Little Bighorn. Kicking Bear created this painting of the Battle of the Little Bighorn. *What do you think Kicking Bear thought of the Battle of the Little Bighorn?*

CULTURE

Reservations and the Battle of the Little Bighorn. Like Sitting Bull, many American Indians despised reservations, a dislike that helped spark the Battle of the Little Bighorn. Several factors inspired this response. Many reservations were located on poor soil, unsuitable for farming. In addition, they rarely resembled traditional tribal grounds. Many American Indians regarded reservations as little more than concentration camps.

CRITICAL THINKING Why might many reservations have been located on poor soil?

ANSWER: Students might suggest that white settlers probably complained when reservations were located on good land.

THAT'S INTERESTING!

Although a popular general, George Armstrong Custer had a slightly checkered military record. He graduated at the bottom of his class at West Point, and in 1867 he was court-martialed and temporarily suspended from command for a number of offenses, including over-marching his troops and leaving his post without permission.

HISTORY IN THE MAKING

George Custer
BY PAUL F. HUTTON

Many Americans were shocked in 1876 to learn of George Armstrong Custer's death at the Battle of the Little Bighorn. A popular figure with the American people, Custer was the subject of magazine articles that celebrated his battles with Indians during the early 1870s. After his death, poets, novelists, and artists responded to the nation's sense of loss with works that portrayed Custer as a hero who gave his life to end the Indians' domination of the American West. The play *Custer's Last Charge* kept the image of the heroic Custer alive during the 1880s and 1890s. In the 1900s, filmmakers produced nearly 20 movies before 1941 that portrayed Custer as a defender of the settlers.

However, some people questioned Custer's reputation. Novels such as Frederic Van de Water's *Glory-Hunter* depicted Custer as a brutal man. Films such as *Sitting Bull* (1954) portrayed the American Indians as courageously defending their homelands against a cruel Custer. Histories that offered the Indian perspective of the wars on the Plains further eroded the Custer myth to such a degree that in 1991 Congress passed legislation removing Custer's name from the national monument at Little Bighorn.

Some Ghost Dancers believed that Ghost Shirts such as this one protected them from harm.

American Indians onto reservations. Over the next several months the American Indian forces broke into smaller groups to evade army troops. Group by group, they surrendered and settled near the Bureau of Indian Affairs encampments. Sitting Bull fled to Canada but eventually returned and settled on the Standing Rock Reservation in Dakota Territory.

The Ghost Dance. The final chapter of the Plains Indian–U.S. Army wars took place on the Pine Ridge Reservation in South Dakota. Unhappy with life on the reservation, many Sioux accepted the message of **Wovoka** (woh-VOH-kuh). A Paiute, Wovoka began a religious movement known as the Ghost Dance. It featured a dance ritual designed to bring Indian ancestors back to life. Wovoka also claimed that the Ghost Dance could bring about return of buffalo herds and traditional Indian ways of life.

Wovoka's message brought hope to discouraged American Indians throughout the West. Some Sioux living on reservations in the Dakotas wore "Ghost Shirts," believing that the shirts' special symbols could stop bullets.

James McLaughlin, BIA agent at Standing Rock Reservation, dismissed the Ghost Dance as an "absurd craze." However, some government officials feared that it would inspire rebellion. When the Ghost Dance spread to Standing Rock Reservation, the military ordered the arrest of Sitting Bull, who had joined the movement. When reservation police surrounded Sitting Bull's cabin on December 15, 1890, a skirmish broke out and 14 Indians—including Sitting Bull—were killed.

Wounded Knee. Frightened and angry after Sitting Bull's death, many Sioux joined the Ghost Dancers farther west. Some traveled with Big Foot, a Sioux leader who had initially supported the Ghost Dance but had gradually turned away from it. Government officials wanted to arrest Big Foot because they feared he might cause trouble. Hoping to avoid conflict with army troops, Big Foot decided to lead his group to the Pine Ridge Reservation. The Sioux made camp for the night along Wounded Knee Creek. On December 28, 1890, army troops found Big Foot and some 350 members of his group.

The next morning, Colonel James Forsyth of the 7th Cavalry ordered the seizure of Indian rifles. Reinforced by four Hotchkiss guns that fired exploding shells, some 500 mounted soldiers surrounded the camp. Dissatisfied with the number of guns the Sioux surrendered, soldiers began to search the tepees. Tensions ran high. The Sioux and U.S. soldiers began shooting. The Hotchkiss guns ripped into the camp. By day's end at least 150 Sioux and about 30 U.S. soldiers had been killed. Some people declared that Custer and the 7th Cavalry had been "avenged," but the **Massacre at Wounded Knee** shocked many

TEACH OBJECTIVE 3

ALL LEVELS: To help students understand how certain American Indians responded to white treatment, copy the graphic organizer on the chalkboard, omitting the italicized answers. Have each student complete it. Then pair students and ask each pair to write one or two paragraphs assessing the effectiveness of American Indian responses in the late 1800s. *(Pairs' paragraphs should indicate that many of the responses were ineffective, given the enormous power of the U.S. government.)* Have volunteers read their paragraphs to the class. **English Language Learners, Cooperative Learning**

AMERICAN INDIAN RESPONSES TO WHITE TREATMENT

Chief Joseph	Geronimo	Sarah Winnemucca
agreed to move tribe to a reservation; fled from the U.S Army; eventually surrendered	*fled a reservation with his tribe; raided settlements; eventually surrendered*	*called attention to problems; made speeches; participated in political activities*

HOMEWORK *Tell students to imagine that they are Chief Joseph, Geronimo, or Sarah Winnemucca. Have each student write a short speech responding to white treatment of American Indians.*

Americans. The incident marked the end of the bloody conflict between soldiers and American Indians on the Great Plains.

✔ **READING CHECK: Summarizing** What events led to the end of conflict between the Plains Indians and the U.S. government?
the death of Sitting Bull and the Massacre at Wounded Knee

The End of Resistance

American Indians west of the Great Plains were also forced to resettle. The Nez Percé tried to remain in their homelands in Idaho, northeastern Oregon, and parts of Washington. They surrendered much of their land in an 1855 treaty and agreed to remain on a reservation. When settlers moved onto reservation land, the Nez Percé did not turn to violence. When the government ordered the Nez Percé to relocate to a reservation in Idaho, their leader, **Chief Joseph**, reluctantly agreed. However, some young Nez Percé killed four white settlers. Fearing war, the Nez Percé fled, with the army in close pursuit.

The Nez Percé journeyed through Idaho, Wyoming, and Montana, picking up followers along the way. The group eventually numbered from 700 to 800. They hoped to escape to Canada, but winter weather made travel difficult. Chief Joseph surrendered to the U.S. Army less than 40 miles from the Canadian border. An interpreter wept as he relayed the leader's surrender statement.

❝I am tired of fighting. Our chiefs are killed. . . . It is cold and we have no blankets. The little children are freezing to death. . . . My heart is sick and sad. From where the sun now stands, I will fight no more forever.❞

—Chief Joseph, quoted at his surrender, 1877

The Nez Percé were first sent to prison in Kansas, then to a reservation in Indian Territory. In 1885 the U.S. government permitted some to return to the reservation in Idaho, but sent Chief Joseph and some 150 others to a reservation in Washington State.

In the mid-1870s, the government forced the seminomadic Apache in New Mexico and Arizona to settle on the San Carlos Reservation, along Arizona's Gila River. When army troops moved into the territory in 1881, Apache leader **Geronimo** fled the reservation with about 75 followers. Geronimo's group raided settlements throughout Arizona and Mexico. In 1884 Geronimo surrendered and briefly accepted reservation life. By 1885, however, Geronimo and more than 130 followers escaped from the reservation and resumed raids on settlements. On September 4, 1886, with his followers outnumbered, Geronimo gave up. "Once I moved about like the wind," he told his captors. "Now I surrender to you and that is all." After his final surrender, Geronimo and his followers were sent to Florida as prisoners of war. His surrender marked the end of armed resistance to the reservation system in the Southwest.

The Religious Spirit

THE GHOST DANCE

The Ghost Dance combined elements from American Indian religions and Christianity. The son of a medicine man, Wovoka lived for a time with a white family that regularly read Bible passages aloud. Kicking Bear, who brought Wovoka's message to the Sioux, told them they would be "led by the Messiah who came once to live on earth with the white man." This reference to Jesus Christ revealed Christianity's influence on Wovoka's thought.

A Ghost Dance

The Ghost Dance was similar to the Paiute round dance. Men and women formed a circle by holding hands and then stepped to the left. Dancers had their faces painted and wore Ghost Shirts—cotton garments decorated with pictures of animals and sacred symbols. The Sioux added features from their own Sun Dance, making the circle around a sacred pole and at times staring into the Sun as they performed the dance.

James Mooney was a social scientist who interviewed several Ghost Dancers in 1891. He interpreted the religion as the spiritual expression of a people whose societies had been devastated. "Hope becomes a faith and the faith becomes a creed [belief] of priests and prophets, until the hero is a god and the dream a religion, looking to some great miracle of nature for its culmination [climax] and accomplishment," he explained. The Ghost Dance movement faded away when the promised miracle never occurred. ■

PEOPLE IN HISTORY

Chief Joseph. Chief Joseph, whose Nez Percé name meant "thunder rolling down from the mountains," belonged to a family of prominent tribal leaders. His father, Joseph the Elder, was a respected buffalo hunter who helped negotiate the 1855 treaty that temporarily secured a reservation for the Nez Percé in their native homelands. His brother, Olikut, was a skilled warrior who helped plan the tribe's defense strategy during its unsuccessful flight to Canada. Chief Joseph himself had a reputation as both a brave fighter and a gifted diplomat, and by the time he was in his mid-30s he had been recognized by U.S. authorities as the most influential of the Nez Percé leaders.

CRITICAL THINKING What qualities made Chief Joseph an effective leader?

ANSWER: Students might suggest that Chief Joseph came from a family of leaders and was both a brave fighter and a gifted diplomat.

TEACH OBJECTIVE 4

ALL LEVELS: Ask volunteers to identify ways in which the federal government attempted to assimilate American Indians. Have volunteers list these ways on the chalkboard. (*Students should list the establishment of reservations, the creation of Indian schools, and the passage of the Dawes Act.*) Then ask students to assume the role of an army officer at Fort Sumner. Have each student write a short memo assessing the assimilation of the Navajo. Ask volunteers to read their memos to the class. Then lead a class discussion about how the government responded to the plan's failure and the resulting consequences for the Navajo.
English Language Learners

SPOTLIGHT
on the Carlisle Indian School

Have students conduct research on the Carlisle Indian School. Students should take note of the school's programs and operating period. Then have students consider the following questions: *Were American Indian students successfully assimilated into white culture? What was student life like at the school? Was the assimilation there designed to benefit American Indians?* Ask each student to respond to the questions in an essay. **Block Scheduling**

INTERDISCIPLINARY CONNECTIONS

▶LITERATURE◀

Helen Hunt Jackson.
Before she became an Indian rights activist, Helen Hunt Jackson was a successful poet and journalist. Under pseudonyms such as "No Name," "Rip Van Winkel," and "Sax Holm," she wrote hundreds of poems and articles that appeared in a variety of publications. Ralph Waldo Emerson once referred to her as the "greatest American woman poet."

ACTIVITY: Ask each student to consult a literary anthology and select a poem written by a woman in the late 1800s. Have students read their poems to the class. Then conduct a discussion on common themes and styles.

VISUAL RECORD ANSWER

(for p. 169)

Students might point to the boys' hair and clothing.

SECTION
REVIEW ①ANSWERS

1. Identify
- Bureau of Indian Affairs, p. 162
- John M. Chivington, p. 163
- Sand Creek Massacre, p. 163
- Sitting Bull, p. 165
- George Armstrong Custer, p. 165
- Battle of the Little Bighorn, p. 165

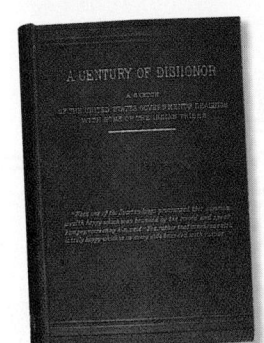

Helen Hunt Jackson's 1881 book chronicled the mistreatment of American Indians.

THE GRANGER COLLECTION, NEW YORK

Sarah Winnemucca demanded fair treatment for American Indians.

Voices of Protest

By the 1880s, the U.S. government had acquired more than half a billion acres of land formerly occupied by American Indians. Indians also suffered as settlers killed most of the buffalo herds. With the loss of the buffalo, American Indians had little hope of maintaining an independent existence on the Plains. "All our people now were settling down in square gray houses, scattered here and there across this hungry land," recalled Black Elk of the Teton Sioux.

Troubled by the treatment of American Indians, reformers organized groups such as the Indian Rights Association and the Women's National Indian Association. These groups urged the federal government to craft a more humane Indian policy. Helen Hunt Jackson of Massachusetts supported this cause. In 1881 she wrote an influential book, *A Century of Dishonor*, that criticized the government for its years of broken promises and mistreatment of American Indians.

Thoc-me-tony, a Paiute reformer also known as **Sarah Winnemucca**, called attention to the problems of American Indians. Winnemucca noted that although the government had authorized the building of two mills on the Paiute reservation, they were never constructed. She wondered what had happened.

 History Makers Speak ❝The [mills] were never seen or heard of by my people, though the printed report . . . says twenty-five thousand dollars was appropriated to build them. Where did [the money] go? . . . Is it that the government is cheated by its own agents who make these reports?❞

—Sarah Winnemucca, *Life Among the Piutes, Their Wrongs and Claims*, edited by Horace Mann

The forced removal of the Paiute to the Yakima Reservation in Washington Territory in 1878 so outraged Winnemucca that she began lecturing on the Paiute's behalf to non-Indian audiences. In 1880 she asked President Rutherford B. Hayes to allow the Paiute to return to their homelands. Hayes agreed, but the BIA's agents did not carry out the president's order.

✔ **READING CHECK: Categorizing** How did American Indians resist and protest white Americans' treatment of them in the late 1800s? Many Indians no longer resisted violently. Some formed reform groups such as the Indian Rights Association and the Women's National Indian Association.

Assimilating American Indians

Many government officials and most reformers viewed assimilation, or the cultural absorption of American Indians into "white America," as the only long-term way to ensure Indian survival. To speed this process, the U.S. government established American Indian schools. Some Indian children attended reservation schools, but others were forced to attend boarding schools. Students were forced to speak only English, to wear "proper" clothes, and to change their names to "American" ones. Luther Standing Bear later recalled, "How lonesome I felt for my father and mother!"

Government officials had hoped that life on reservations would force American Indians to become farmers and adopt the lifestyles of non-Indian settlers. In 1887 Congress passed the **Dawes General Allotment Act**, which required that Indian lands be surveyed and that American Indian families receive an allotment of 160 acres of reservation land for farming. Any land that remained

REVIEW

Have students complete the **Section 1 Review** on p. 169.

ASSESS

Have students complete **Daily Quiz 5.1**. As **Alternative Assessment**, you may want to use the headlines or the investigative reports in this section's lessons.

RETEACH

Have students complete **Main Idea Activity for English Language Learners and Special-Needs Students 5.1**. Then pair students and have each pair create an illustrated time line that covers the period from 1850 to 1890. For each entry on the time line, ask pairs to include a brief annotation describing its impact on American Indians. Have each pair work and discuss its time line with another pair.
English Language Learners, Cooperative Learning

EXTEND

Tell students to conduct research on the life of one of the American Indian leaders discussed in Section 1. Have each student present his or her research to the class in the form of a question-and-answer interview. **Block Scheduling**

would be sold. The Indian Rights Association claimed that private ownership of land would lead to "the gradual breaking up of the reservations." This assessment proved correct. In less than 50 years, they lost two thirds of their land. Some of the land was sold to settlers and developers as surplus when allotments were made. In other cases, Indians sold or were cheated out of their allotments.

Despite the government's hopes, many American Indians rejected individual family farming. Even before the Dawes Act, the government had tried to force the Navajo to abandon sheep raising and become settled farmers. The U.S. Army waged military campaigns against the Navajo in northwestern New Mexico and northeastern Arizona in 1863. Soldiers destroyed Navajo houses, herds of sheep, and corn crops. Without food or shelter, many Navajo surrendered in early 1864.

That same year, the U.S. Army led the Navajo on the Long Walk, a forced march to the Bosque Redondo Reservation in eastern New Mexico. Soldiers stationed at nearby Fort Sumner prevented the Navajo from leaving the reservation. The U.S. government gave the Navajo seeds and farming tools, but the land was not suitable for farming. Because the few trees were quickly cut down, the Navajo had to use roots for firewood. Many Navajo died from malnutrition and disease.

In 1868 the government admitted its failure and granted the Navajo a reservation in New Mexico and Arizona. They rebuilt their communities, concentrating on sheep raising, weaving, and silversmithing. By the 1880s their economy had improved and their population had begun to increase.

✔ READING CHECK: Drawing Conclusions Why did attempts to force the Plains Indians to become farmers fail? The Navajo rejected individual family farming, and the land was not suitable for farming.

INTERPRETING THE VISUAL RECORD

Assimilation. These photographs show three American Indian boys before and after they attended an American Indian school. *What evidence of their assimilation can you see?*

- Wovoka, p. 166
- Massacre at Wounded Knee, p. 166
- Chief Joseph, p. 167
- Geronimo, p. 167
- Sarah Winnemucca, p. 168
- Dawes General Allotment Act, p. 168

2. Cheyenne—Black Kettle; dispute over hunting grounds and move to reservations; Sand Creek Massacre and resettlement on a reservation. Sioux—Sitting Bull; government intrusion on Sioux lands; Battle of the Little Bighorn, Massacre at Wounded Knee. Nez Percé—Chief Joseph; settler intrusions on Nez Percé land; pursuit, by U.S. Army, surrender and imprisonment and eventual settlement of tribe on reservations. Apache—Geronimo; army intrusion on Apache territory; flight of Geronimo and followers, surrender of Geronimo

3a. to open new lands to settlement

b. BIA signed treaties with some Indians but many were broken; this led to many violent clashes.

c. Some organized protest groups; others rejected individual family farming.

4. Answers will vary. Stories should mention Sitting Bull's vision of victory and his plan to draw Custer in before surrounding his soldiers.

SECTION 1 REVIEW

1. Identify and explain:
Bureau of Indian Affairs
John M. Chivington
Sand Creek Massacre
Sitting Bull
George Armstrong Custer
Battle of the Little Bighorn
Wovoka
Massacre at Wounded Knee
Chief Joseph
Geronimo
Sarah Winnemucca
Dawes General Allotment Act

2. Categorizing Copy the chart below. Use it to describe the conflicts between the United States and various American Indian nations.

Nation & Leader	Conflict	Outcome
Cheyenne		
Sioux		
Nez Percé		
Apache		

3. **Finding the Main Idea**

a. Why did the U.S. government attempt to resettle American Indians on reservations?
b. Provide a brief history of the relations between the Bureau of Indian Affairs and the Plains Indians.
c. How did American Indians resist attempts to assimilate them into white culture?

4. **Writing and Critical Thinking**

Drawing Conclusions Imagine that you are a member of Sitting Bull's war party. Write a fictional short story about the Battle of the Little Bighorn.
Consider:
• what the root causes of the conflict were
• how each side viewed the other
• which mistakes each side made in dealing with the other side

Homework Practice Online
keyword: SE3 HP5

After completing Section 2, students should be able to:

OBJECTIVE 1 Discuss how the U.S. government promoted economic development in the West.

OBJECTIVE 2 Understand why people migrated west.

OBJECTIVE 3 Explain how the environment influenced farming practices and daily life in the West.

OBJECTIVE 4 Describe the difficulties that farm families faced on the Great Plains.

LET'S GET STARTED!

Write the following scenario on the chalkboard: *You are a farmer in the Mississippi Valley, where land has grown expensive. The government will give you 160 acres of land in Oklahoma, but you are unfamiliar with the land and climate there, and you will be separated from most of your family. Will you move to Oklahoma anyway?* Have students respond to the scenario in writing. Have volunteers share their responses with the class. Tell students that in Section 2 they will learn more about opportunities in the West.

SECTION 2

READ TO DISCOVER
1. How did the U.S. government promote economic development in the West?
2. Why did people migrate west?
3. How did the environment influence farming practices and daily life in the West?
4. What difficulties did farm families face on the Great Plains?

DEFINE
sod houses
bonanza farm

IDENTIFY
Homestead Act
Pacific Railway Act
Morrill Act
Exodusters
Benjamin Singleton
U.S. Department of Agriculture
Willa Cather

WHY IT MATTERS TODAY
Farming is still central to the economy of the Great Plains states, as well as much of the world. Use **CNNfyi**.com or other **current events** sources to learn about new farming methods being developed today. Record your findings in your journal.

CNNfyi.com

Western Farmers

EYEWITNESSES TO History

"To say that I was homesick, discouraged, and lonely, is but a faint [poor] description of my feelings. . . . Not a tree, plant nor shrub on which to rest my weary eye, to break the monotony of the sand beds and cactus of the Great American Desert."

—Annie Green, *Sixteen Days on the Great American Desert*

Annie Green moved to Colorado in 1870. She and her husband were among the thousands of American families who headed west to the Great Plains in the years following the Civil War. Green felt like "a stranger in a strange land" in her new home. In order to support her husband, she "resolved . . . to cultivate [develop] a cheerful disposition." Like many settlers, Green and her family discovered that hard work, determination, and a little luck were necessary to prosper.

COLLECTION OF THE NEW-YORK HISTORICAL SOCIETY

Posters like this one persuaded many people that a better life waited for them out west.

Economic Development of the West

During the Civil War, Republicans tried to manage western development so that new western states and territories would be free of slavery. They also wanted these areas to be populated by independent farmers who would improve the land. After the southern states seceded from the Union, Republicans passed a series of acts in 1862 to turn public lands into private property.

Land acts. Three government land acts increased non-Indian settlement of the Great Plains. The **Homestead Act** permitted "any citizen or intended citizen to select any surveyed land up to 160 acres and to gain title to it after five years' residence" if the person cultivated the land. The Civil War slowed the initial response to the act. Eventually, some 400,000 families took advantage of the offer. The **Pacific Railway Act** gave lands to railroad companies to develop a railroad line linking the East and West coasts. The **Morrill Act** granted a total of more than 17 million acres of federal land to the states. The act ordered the sale of this land to finance the construction of agricultural and engineering colleges. The Morrill Act led to the eventual founding of more than 70 state universities.

Competition for land was fierce. In March 1889, for example, President Benjamin Harrison announced that land would be available to the first takers beginning at noon on April 22. By the appointed day, about 50,000 people had gathered to race one another for the land. Some rode horses or bicycles. Others pushed wheelbarrows filled with supplies. Subsequent "runs" took place in other parts. In October 1889 a flood of prospective settlers responded to a government offer of inexpensive homesteads in Oklahoma. The acreage came from former Creek and Seminole lands. This occurred at the expense of American Indians, who lost more than 11 million acres in Oklahoma to non-Indian settlers.

TEACH OBJECTIVE 1

ALL LEVELS: To help students understand how the U.S. government promoted economic development in the West, copy the graphic organizer on the chalkboard, omitting the italicized answers. Have each student complete it. Then organize the class into triads and tell students to imagine that they are writers and artists hired to create full-page newspaper ads to publicize government programs designed to attract settlers and railroad companies to western lands. Tell students that their ads should combine appealing images with lists of incentives to attract settlers to the Great Plains. Have each triad present its advertisement to the class.

English Language Learners, Cooperative Learning

GOVERNMENT ACTIONS TO AID ECONOMIC DEVELOPMENT IN THE WEST

Homestead Act	Pacific Railway Act	Morrill Act
permitted "any citizen or intended citizen" to have 160 acres of land	*gave lands to railroad companies to develop a transcontinental railroad linking the East and West Coasts*	*granted more than 17 million acres of land to be sold to finance the construction of agricultural and engineering colleges*

The railroads. Railroad companies also lured settlers to the West. Between 1869 and 1883, four rail lines were built across the West. Within 10 years of the passage of the Pacific Railway Act, the U.S. government had given railroad companies more than 125 million acres of public land. State and local governments donated nearly 100 million acres of additional land. These grants limited the amount of land available to settlers under the Homestead Act. Government officials believed that railroad companies would promote western settlement and economic growth. Railroad companies sold any surplus land to homesteaders in an effort to offset the high cost of laying tracks. The homesteaders benefited from the nearby railroad lines, using them to ship their crops to distant markets.

Eager to encourage settlement along their rail routes, railroad companies advertised in the East and in Europe. They offered to pay the fares of potential land buyers and sell them land on credit. Some railroad companies gave free trips to newspaper reporters, who then wrote glowing reports. One Indiana editor wrote about his trip:

History Makers Speak
❝I never saw finer country in the world than that part of Kansas passed over by the Atchison, Topeka & Santa Fe [rail]road. Corn waist high, wheat in the shock [stacked], oats in fine condition, and vegetables in abundance.**❞**

—Indiana editor, quoted in *The Farmers' Frontier, 1865–1900,* by Gilbert C. Fite

✔ **READING CHECK: Drawing Conclusions** How did the U.S. government encourage the growth of private property ownership on the Great Plains? by passing the Homestead Act and granting 125 million acres of public land to railroad companies

Moving West

Three main groups traveled westward after the Civil War: white Americans from the East, African Americans from the South, and immigrants from foreign countries. Some sought economic opportunity. Others hoped to find racial tolerance.

The majority of white settlers moved from states in the Mississippi Valley, where land had grown expensive and difficult to obtain. Because of the high cost of transporting supplies, it was mainly middle-class farmers and businesspeople who could afford to move west. Some farmers came in search of more fertile soil. Civil War veterans, particularly those from the South, came to make a new start. A Nebraska newcomer explained, "I am well satisfied that I can do better here than I can in Illinois." Susan Lomax, who moved west with her family from Mississippi, offered a different reason: "We wanted to come to a new country so our children could grow up with the country."

For African Americans, moving west offered a chance to escape the violence and persecution they faced following the withdrawal of federal troops from the South in 1877. Kansas particularly appealed to African American settlers, as John Brown had fought against slavery there. The biggest exodus, or mass departure, of black settlers with so-called Kansas Fever occurred in 1879. Some 20,000 to 40,000 African Americans fled the South, where violence had broken out during

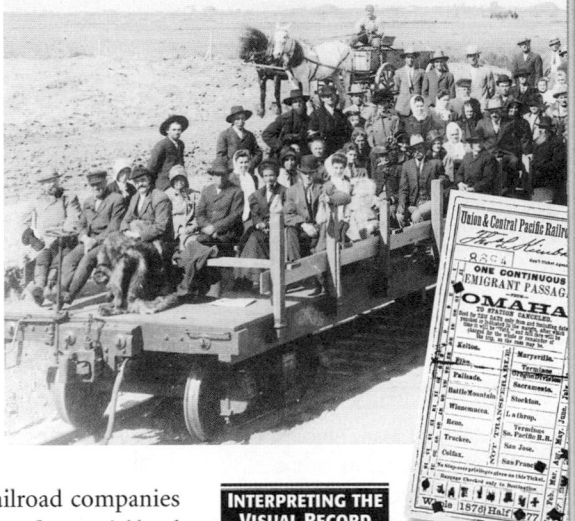

INTERPRETING THE VISUAL RECORD

The road west. With tickets like this one, many migrants rode the rails to their new homes in the West, sometimes riding on flatcars to get there. *What do you think travel conditions were like for the migrants in this photograph?*

This Schuttler Wagon Company advertisement depicts farmers migrating to the West in search of fertile soil.

GEOGRAPHY

Railroad Workers. Railroad workers for both companies, many of whom were immigrants from Ireland and China, braved severe weather and the threat of attack by American Indians as they laid more than 1,500 miles of track across rough terrain. Hundreds of these workers died in explosions and other industrial accidents along the way.

CRITICAL THINKING What other dangers might railroad workers have faced as they laid track?

ANSWER: Students might mention dangers such as animal attacks and snake bites.

The American Nation VIDEO PROGRAM
Linking the Nation; Teacher's Guide, pp. 69–74

Search 29399, Play to 33608
Videodisc 1, Side B

Play   Pause

See *Teacher's Guide* for Spanish barcode.

VISUAL RECORD ANSWER
Students might suggest that the travel conditions were uncomfortable and harsh.

TEACH OBJECTIVE 2

LEVEL 1: Pair students and assign each pair one of the following roles: white settlers from the East, African Americans from the South, Scandinavians, Irish, Germans, Russian Mennonites, or Chinese. Ask pairs to create advertising slogans urging people to move west. Remind students that their slogans should appeal to people like themselves. *(Pairs should indicate that white Americans sought cheaper lands or to make a new start, African Americans wanted to escape persecution in the South, Scandinavians had "America Fever," Irish moved to the Plains after building railroads, Germans moved from the Mississippi Valley, Russian Mennonites moved after they lost military service exemption, and many Chinese came during* the Gold Rush and turned to farming.) Have volunteers present their slogans to the class.
Cooperative Learning, English Language Learners

LEVELS 2 AND 3: Assign each student one of the roles mentioned in the Level 1 lesson. Have each student, in his or her assigned role, write a series of letters to a relative explaining his or her reasons for moving west. *(See the Level 1 lesson for the correct reasons.)* Students should describe what they think might surprise or disappoint their relative about life in the West, and how they are faring there. Have volunteers share their letters with the class.

INTERPRETING THE VISUAL RECORD

Exodusters. Many African Americans hoped to escape discrimination in the South by moving west. *What evidence can you see that this family is homesteading on the Great Plains?*

Some Chinese workers participated in a Fourth of July parade in Deadwood, South Dakota.

elections in 1878. Known as **Exodusters**, these African American settlers trekked west, following leaders such as **Benjamin Singleton**, a 70-year-old former slave.

European immigrants also flocked to the West. "America Fever" infected thousands of Danes, Norwegians, and Swedes. In 1882 alone, more than 100,000 Scandinavians moved to the American West. In addition, many Irish who had helped build the railroads and a great number of Germans who had settled in the Mississippi Valley decided to move to the Plains.

Russian Mennonites, members of a Protestant sect, also migrated to the Great Plains. After the Russian czar ended the Mennonites' special privileges, among them exemption from military service, American railroad companies urged them to move to the United States. The Mennonites brought with them experience in farming wheat on the Russian steppes, or grasslands, including a hardy wheat variety that thrived on the Great Plains. They may have also brought the Russian thistle, a plant that became well known throughout the West as the tumbleweed.

Many of the Chinese immigrants who had come to the United States during the California Gold Rush had also turned to farming by 1880. In California alone, some 3,200 Chinese farmers raised crops in 1880. Throughout the West, Chinese immigrants worked as farm laborers, produce vendors, or sharecroppers. Some owned large farms. In 1870 one Chinese farmer in Sacramento County, California, earned $9,500 from farming—an enormous amount for that period.

✔ **READING CHECK: Categorizing** Why did various groups of people migrate to the West? economic opportunity, escape from violence and persecution, and railroad construction work

Western Environments and Farming

Although settlers homesteaded some 80 million acres of public land in the Great Plains between 1862 and 1900, the region did not immediately prosper. Supplies were expensive, and the environment posed problems for farmers.

Scarce resources. Water was in short supply throughout much of the West. In parts of the Southwest, Hispanic and American Indian farmers had developed effective irrigation systems that used canals, dams, and sloping fields to control water flow. They established farms that fanned out in thin strips from water sources so that most community members had access to water. New settlers adopted these methods. The Great Plains also had few water sources. Many farmers had to travel several miles to a river or stream where they would fill large barrels and haul them back to the farm. Digging wells proved difficult and

TEACH OBJECTIVE 3

LEVEL 1: Pair students and have each pair create a graphic organizer that contains the problems western farmers faced and the solutions to those problems. *(Pairs should indicate: lack of water, lack of trees, strong winds, and harsh winters. Solutions should include: dry farming, buffalo manure for fuel and as a building material, irrigation, and new varieties of wheat suitable for the Great Plains weather.)* When students are finished, ask volunteers to draw their organizers on the chalkboard and explain them to the class.
English Language Learners, Cooperative Learning

LEVEL 2: Pair students and ask one to assume the role of a newspaper reporter and the other to assume the role of a Plains farmer. Have each pair develop a newspaper interview about how farmers adapted their farming practices and daily lives to the Great Plains environment. *(See the Level 1 lesson for the correct methods.)* Ask pairs to prepare transcripts of questions and answers. Have volunteers present their interviews to the class.
Cooperative Learning

NOTE: To help students make meaningful connections between events in U.S. history and those in their own hometown, use the Chapter 5 **Hands-On History Activity**, Agriculture and You.

time-consuming. One Nebraska farmer spent two years digging with a pick and shovel before reaching water 300 feet below the surface. Many settlers hired professional drillers who used drilling equipment developed by petroleum companies. Farmers also used new kinds of windmills to draw the water from their wells. These were wind-powered water pumps designed to withstand the region's strong winds.

Trees were another scarce resource on the Great Plains. Settlers developed clever solutions to cope with the lack of wood for fuel or building materials. Some burned dried buffalo manure, an excellent source of fuel. Settlers built **sod houses**, buildings made from chunks cut from the heavy topsoil that were stacked like bricks. A layer of soil covered the roof, which was made of a few scarce pieces of wood. Building with sod was difficult, however. A Kansas settler wrote, "The sod is heavy and when you take 3 or 4 bricks on a litter or hand barrow, and carry it 50 to 150 feet, I tell you it is no easy work."

Created in 1862, the **U.S. Department of Agriculture** (USDA) helped farmers adapt to their new environment. USDA experts sought out and publicized new varieties of wheat suitable for the Great Plains. These new wheat crops replaced the grasses that had once covered the Great Plains. USDA agents also began teaching dry farming—new planting and harvesting techniques that conserved moisture. For example, agents advised farmers to plow deep furrows to bring moisture to the surface and to break up the soil after a rainfall to prevent evaporation.

New farming equipment. The development of new farming equipment also helped the Plains farmers. James Oliver's plow factory in South Bend, Indiana, produced thousands of plows with sharp, durable blades that could slice through the tough sod of the Plains. "Self-binding" harvesters not only cut wheat but also tied it into bundles. The combine cut wheat, separated it from the plant, and cleaned the grain all in one operation. Many of the new farming devices used steam-powered engines. However, the new technology plunged many small farmers into debt when they bought the equipment necessary to compete with larger landholders.

Efficient new farm machinery and cheap, abundant land enabled some companies to create a new kind of large-scale operation, the **bonanza farm**. Most bonanza farms were owned by large companies and operated like factories, with machinery, professional managers, and specialized laborers for different tasks. These large farms required from 500 to 1,000 extra workers at planting and harvesting times. Most owners divided their vast enterprises into small units, with a foreman in charge of each. Migrant workers, who were often unemployed cowboys possessing "nothing but small bundles containing a clean shirt and a few socks," performed much of the seasonal labor.

The era of bonanza farming soon faded. When weather conditions were favorable, bonanza farms produced large profits because of lower production costs. Because owners of bonanza farms bought seed and equipment in bulk, suppliers often gave them special deals. However, in times of severe drought or low wheat prices, bonanza farm profits fell. With fewer workers to pay and less money invested in equipment, family farmers could better handle boom-and-bust cycles. By the 1890s most bonanza farms had been broken up into smaller farms.

✔ **READING CHECK: Finding the Main Idea** What technological innovations made farming profitable on the Great Plains? plows, "self-binding" harvesters, and devices with steam-powered engines

Windmills drew water from beneath the ground, allowing settlers to farm the Great Plains.

GLOBAL RELATIONS

The Global Grain Market. As well as plunging into debt to buy necessary equipment, farmers on the Great Plains confronted declining grain prices during most of the late 1800s. Much of this decline was because of the increased availability of grain on the world market. Along with the yield improvements brought about by mechanization, the opening of new farmland in Argentina, Canada, and Russia helped lead to large increases in global supplies of wheat and corn. As a result, the price of wheat fell from $1.45 a bushel in 1866 to 80 cents in the mid-1880s and less than 50 cents in the mid-1890s.

CRITICAL THINKING Besides supplies and equipment, what expenses might Great Plains farmers have had to meet in the course of raising and marketing their crops?

ANSWER: Students might suggest that farmers had to pay for the storage of their crops in grain elevators and the transport of their crops on railroads.

LEVEL 3: Tell students to assume the role of a member of a Plains farm family. Have each student write a short story that includes a description of the environmental hardships associated with living on the Great Plains and the ways in which farmers adapted to the environment. *(See the Level 1 lesson for the correct methods.)* Have volunteers read their stories to the class.

Teacher to Teacher

Jack Rousso of Seattle, Washington, suggested the following activity: Organize the class into two groups and write the following statement on the chalkboard: Government subsidies, not individual initiatives, were the main factor in the settlement of the American West. *Have one group support the statement and the other group oppose it. After each group has had time to prepare, conduct a debate on the statement.*

HISTORY MAKERS SPEAK

Washington Keller in *Far From Home: Families of the Westward Journey*

The Look of the West.
Washington Keller described the West in a letter to his son-in-law: "You have no idea how this country impresses itself on one who has never seen a treeless, fenceless & in many instances houseless country. . . . There is a lack of everything except land. There is plenty of fine land & if any person will get a lot of this land & then go to work & put all the labor that is necessary to make a home for a human being on it in the course of 9 or 10 years he will have one of the finest most productive farms in America."

CRITICAL THINKING How does Keller's description compare with others in the chapter?

ANSWER: Students might note that Keller's description was more enthusiastic.

AMERICAN LETTERS ANSWERS

1. Garland—"wide," and "sunny," "windy"; Foote—"high" and "great"

2. Garland describes the prairie, while Foote describes a wooded, hilly area with a river.

3. that it was wide, varied, and beautiful

AMERICAN Letters

The Western Novel

Several writers recognized the great beauty of the American West. Hamlin Garland, who as a boy hated farm life in Wisconsin, described the Great Plains in his 1899 novel, Boy Life on the Prairie. *Mary Hallock Foote, an artist and writer who lived in California, described the western landscape in her 1894 short story, "A Cloud on the Mountain."*

---

from *Boy Life on the Prairie*
by Hamlin Garland

Hamlin Garland

For a few days Lincoln and Owen had nothing to do but to keep the cattle from straying, and they seized the chance to become acquainted with the country round about. It burned deep into Lincoln's brain, this wide, sunny, windy country,—the sky was so big and the horizon line so low and so far away. The grasses and flowers were nearly all new to him. On the uplands the herbage [grasses] was short and dry and the plants stiff and woody, but in the swales the wild oat shook its quivers of barbed and twisted arrows, and the crow's-foot, tall and willowy, bowed softly under the feet of the wind, while everywhere in the lowlands, as well as on the sedges, the bleaching white antlers of monstrous elk lay scattered to testify of the swarming millions of wild cattle which once fed there.

To the south the settlement thickened, for in that direction lay the country town, but to the north and west the unclaimed prairie rolled, the feeding ground of the cattle, but the boys had little opportunity to explore that far. One day his father said:—

"Well, Lincoln, I guess you'll have to run the plough team this fall. I've got so much to do around the house, and we can't afford to hire."

This seemed a very fine and manly commission [task], and the boy drove his team out into the field one morning with vast pride.

---

from "A Cloud on the Mountain"
by Mary Hallock Foote

Ruth Mary . . . paused often in her work and looked towards the high pastures with the pale brown lights and purple shadows on them, rolling away and rising towards the great timbered ridges, and these lifting here and there along their profiles a treeless peak or bare divide into the regions above vegetation.

Mary Hallock Foote

She had no misgivings about her home. Fences would not have improved her father's vast lawn, to her mind, or white paint the low-browed front of his dwelling; nor did she feel the want of a stair-carpet and a parlor-organ. She was sure that they, the strangers, had never seen anything more lovely than her beloved river dancing down between the hills, tripping over rapids, wrinkling over sand-bars of its own spreading, and letting out its speed down the long reaches where the channel was deep.

UNDERSTANDING LITERATURE

1. Identify some of the words that each author uses to describe the landscape.

2. How did the geography described in the two excerpts differ?

3. Based on these passages, how did the two authors feel about the western landscape?

LEVEL 1: Have each pair create a list of the problems faced by farm families on the Plains. *(Pairs' lists should include poor housing, blizzards and bone-chilling cold weather, droughts, swarms of insects, prairie fires, and hard work.)* Then have pairs create graphic organizers that incorporate all of the problems mentioned above. Have volunteers draw their graphic organizers on the chalkboard and discuss them. **English Language Learners, Cooperative Learning**

LEVELS 2 AND 3: Tell students to imagine that they are travelers from New York stranded on the Nebraska plains. Have each student write a short memoir of the experience focusing on the problems that farm families faced in the region. *(See the Level 1 lesson for the correct problems.)* Have volunteers read their memoirs to the class. Students may wish to include their memoir in their portfolios.

HOMEWORK *Tell students to imagine that they are part of a Plains farm family. Have each student write a monologue describing his or her daily life. Encourage students to include their personal feelings about how the conditions are affecting their parents, siblings, neighbors, and themselves.*

Farm Life on the Plains

Farm families on the Plains faced many problems for which inventors, manufacturers, and agricultural experts had no ready answers. Sod houses were well insulated, windproof, and fireproof. However, they were also damp and dirty. The roofs leaked and sometimes even collapsed in rainy weather. Many families hung a canopy inside the house to prevent dirt falling from the ceiling from landing on the dinner table. One Kansas settler who lived in a sod house described his mother's efforts to keep the house clean.

History Makers Speak

❝[Sod houses] wet up when it rains, they dust off when it gets hot. Mama said she wasn't going to have neither, that she had brung a big roll of rag carpet . . . to cover the ceiling so's she could keep the dirt out of our victuals [food].❞

—Kansas settler, quoted in *The Expansion of Everyday Life*, by Daniel Sutherland

Great Plains resident Luna Kellie remembered, "I had thought a sod house would be kind of nice, but the sight of the first one sickened me."

Harsh weather and hard work. The climate of the Great Plains caused hardships for farming families. Winter on the Plains often brought blizzards and bone-chilling cold. The summer heat could be just as fierce. Settlers described droughts during which "the earth opened in great cracks several inches across and two feet deep." There was no relief as "the leaves on the trees shriveled and dried up, and every living thing was seeking shelter from the hot rays of the sun."

Insects also created problems on the Great Plains. In the 1870s farmers faced swarms of grasshoppers that devoured everything in their path, even the wooden handles of farming tools. Farmers killed thousands of the greedy insects to little effect. One homesteader moaned, "Two new grasshoppers arrived to attend each dead one's funeral."

Settlers dreaded the raging fires that sometimes swept across the prairies. Most families sent someone onto the roof at night to search the horizon for signs of fire in the distance. Farmers soon learned to plow firebreaks—cleared areas with nothing to burn—around their houses and fields.

Even in good times, Plains farming demanded hard work from everyone in the family. Men did most of the heavy labor of building houses, fencing the land, and farming. In addition to household and child-rearing tasks, women often spent hours in the field. In 1878 a Kansas newspaper praised a local woman who "does her own plowing. . . . This year she has one hundred acres of fine wheat and will cut and bind it herself." Another woman wrote home to her family in the East, explaining that she had been her husband's "sole help in getting up and stacking at least 25 tons of hay and oats." Many farm wives also tended garden plots, preserved fruits and vegetables, and cared for farm animals.

Children had to do their share, too. Their chores included fetching water, tending gardens, and churning butter. One farmer described his two-year-old son, Baz, who could "run all over, fetch up cows out of the stock fields, or oxen, carry in stove wood and climb in the corn crib and feed the hogs and go on errands down to his grandma's."

INTERPRETING THE VISUAL RECORD

Home on the plains. Ruben Beatty and his wife posed for this photograph outside their home in Milton, South Dakota, in the late 1800s. *What does this photograph reveal about the home's construction?*

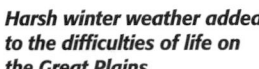

Harsh winter weather added to the difficulties of life on the Great Plains.

INTERDISCIPLINARY CONNECTIONS

▶BIOLOGY◀

Grasshopper Plagues on the Great Plains. The grasshopper plagues that swept through the Great Plains during the 1870s left a vivid impression on the people who lived through them. Years later, settlers recalled watching with horror as masses of the insects snapped off tree limbs and piled on the ground until they lay more than four inches deep. Homesteader Mary Lyon recalled: "When they came down they struck the ground so hard it sounded almost like hail. There was a watermelon patch in our garden and the melons were quite large. . . . By the evening of the second day they were all gone."

CRITICAL THINKING Why might the grasshopper plagues of the 1870s have persuaded some settlers to abandon farming on the Great Plains?

ANSWER: Students might suggest that the plagues persuaded some settlers that farming on the Great Plains would always be a risky enterprise.

VISUAL RECORD ANSWER

Students might suggest that it was made of sod.

REVIEW

Have students complete the **Section 2 Review** on p. 176.

ASSESS

Have students complete **Daily Quiz 5.2**. As **Alternative Assessment**, you may want to use the advertising slogans or short story in this section's lessons.

RETEACH

Have students complete **Main Idea Activity for English Language Learners and Special-Needs Students 5.2**. Then write the following statement on the chalkboard: *On the Great Plains, nature was sometimes the farmer's friend but more often the farmer's foe.* Have each student list evidence from the section to support the statement. Then have each student write a paragraph on the topic. **English Language Learners**

EXTEND

Have students conduct research on an invention or innovation that helped farmers on the Great Plains. Then have each student write a short report on his or her chosen invention or innovation. Have students present their work, including illustrations when possible, to the class. **Block Scheduling**

SECTION 2 REVIEW ANSWERS

1. Define
- sod houses, p. 173
- bonanza farm, p. 173

2. Identify
- Homestead Act, p. 170
- Pacific Railway Act, p. 170
- Morrill Act, p. 170
- Exodusters, p. 172
- Benjamin Singleton, p. 172
- U.S. Department of Agriculture, p. 173
- Willa Cather, p. 176

3. problem—scarce water; solution—irrigation systems, wells, windmills, and dry farming; problem—few trees; solution—buffalo chips for fuel and sod houses; problem—difficult growing conditions; solution—new varieties of wheat and new farming equipment

4a. The government passed the Homestead Act, Pacific Railway Act, the Morrill Act, and established the U.S. Department of Agriculture.

b. Immigrants from Europe and Asia as well as Civil War veterans and African Americans formed communities and settled much of the Great Plains.

c. Crops replaced grassland; irrigation methods were introduced; and cities and settlements were established.

5. Answers will vary. Song lyrics might include what travelers have left behind, the difficult journey, and what they hope to find in the West.

176

Research on the ROM

Free Find: Willa Cather
After reading about Willa Cather on the **Holt Researcher CD–ROM**, draw a picture of what you think her home on the Great Plains looked like. Include captions explaining the various elements in your drawing.

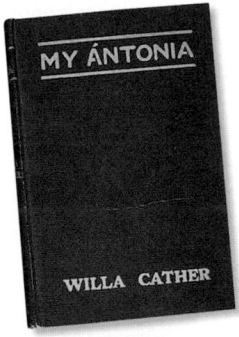

My Ántonia portrays prairie life.

Storytellers of the Plains. Western writers recorded stories about life on the Great Plains. **Willa Cather**, born in Virginia in 1873, was one such writer. As a young girl Cather traveled west with her family to a farm in Nebraska. Her grandparents had moved there several years earlier.

BIOGRAPHY

Willa Cather

Although she was homesick for Virginia, Cather soon found Nebraska fascinating. "I think the first thing that interested me after I got to the homestead was a heavy hickory cane . . . which my grandmother always carried with her when she went to the garden to kill rattlesnakes," Cather wrote. "She had killed a good many snakes with it, and that seemed to argue that life might not be so flat as it looked there."

The Cather family soon moved to the nearby town of Red Cloud, where Willa attended high school. After graduating from the University of Nebraska, she taught high school in Pittsburgh and then took an editorial job at *McClure's Magazine* in New York. She turned to writing full-time in 1912. Cather published her first novel about life on the Plains, *O Pioneers!*, in 1913. In a 1925 interview she explained, "I write only of the Mid-Western American life that I know thoroughly." Cather's other novels—including *My Ántonia*, published in 1918, and *Death Comes for the Archbishop*, published in 1927—also examined life in the American West.

Although some settlers such as Cather were inspired by the West, difficulties overwhelmed many Plains farmers. Many were forced to abandon their farms. However, thousands stayed. They formed communities with churches and schools, newspapers and clubs, and even theaters and concert halls. Although harvests might be poor one year, there was always hope for better luck to come.

✔ **READING CHECK: Summarizing** Provide examples of three hardships that farmers on the Great Plains faced. harsh weather, insects, prairie fires, and unending work

---

SECTION 2 REVIEW

1. Define and explain:
sod houses
bonanza farm

2. Identify and explain:
Homestead Act
Pacific Railway Act
Morrill Act
Exodusters
Benjamin Singleton
U.S. Department of Agriculture
Willa Cather

3. Summarizing Copy the flowchart below. Use it to describe environmental problems that western farmers faced and how they attempted to solve those problems.

Problems

↓

Solutions

4. **Finding the Main Idea**

a. How did the U.S. government promote economic development and assist farmers in the West?

b. How did migration and immigration change settlement patterns in the West?

c. How did the population growth in the West in the late 1800s affect its environment?

5. **Writing and Critical Thinking**

Identifying Points of View Imagine that you are on a wagon train migrating westward. Write a folk song that chronicles your experiences.
Consider:
• why most people moved west
• what their experiences were in the West
• what they gained and lost from the experience

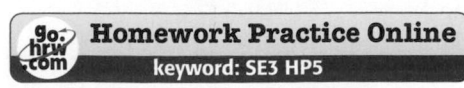

Homework Practice Online
keyword: SE3 HP5

SECTION 3

READ TO DISCOVER

1. How did cattle and sheep ranching develop in the West?
2. What was life like for cowboys and residents of cattle towns?
3. What were ranches like?
4. Why did the cattle boom on the open range end?

DEFINE

long drives
railhead
open range
barbed wire

IDENTIFY

Texas longhorn
Joseph Glidden

The Cattle Boom

 EYEWITNESSES TO History *"[Abilene was] a very small, dead place, consisting of about one dozen log huts, low, small, rude affairs, four-fifths of which were covered with dirt for roofing; indeed, but one shingle roof could be seen in the whole city."*

—Joseph McCoy, quoted in *Cowboy Culture*, by David Dary

Joseph McCoy

Joseph McCoy, a cattleman from Illinois, described the town of Abilene, Kansas, in 1867. Despite the town's appearance, McCoy saw opportunity there. Abilene had a railroad line. McCoy noted that the city was "the farthest point east at which a good depot for cattle business could be made." He purchased property and had stockyards constructed. Meanwhile, he instructed a friend to go to Texas to convince cattle owners to bring their herds to Abilene. From there the herds could be shipped east to packing plants. McCoy's vision transformed the West, sparking an economic boom that entered both American history and myth.

Ranching in the West

The earliest ranchers in the American West were Spaniards who imported cattle from Spain in the 1500s. By the 1850s, Texans had interbred English cattle with Spanish cattle to produce a new breed—the **Texas longhorn**. Although their meat was typically tough and stringy, longhorns were hardy, able to travel long distances on little water, and could live year-round on grass. Equally important, longhorns were immune to Texas fever, a cattle disease carried by ticks.

The growth of eastern cities ensured an increasing demand for beef. Texas cattle ranching grew rapidly after the Civil War, spreading across the Great Plains as the buffalo died out due to overhunting. In 1866 a steer that could bring about $4 in Texas could be sold for $40 or more in eastern markets.

The Spanish also introduced sheep ranching. American Indians, including the Pueblo and the Navajo, raised sheep in New Mexico and Arizona. During the California Gold Rush, sheep were herded to California to feed miners. Cowboys despised sheep, which they believed ate the roots of the grass and ruined it for cattle. Early environmentalist John Muir called them "hoofed locusts" for the damage they did to the prairie. Clashes between shepherds and cowboys at times became violent. Angry cowboys even drove herds of sheep off cliffs.

Despite such conflicts, sheep ranching remained a profitable enterprise. Basque shepherds, originally from Spain, emigrated from South America and ranged their sheep in California. By 1900 some 10,000 Basques were living in the West.

 ✔ **READING CHECK: Analyzing Information** What conflicts occurred between cattle and sheep ranchers? *Violent clashes occurred; cowboys sometimes drove sheep off cliffs because they believed that sheep ruined grass for cattle.*

ALL LEVELS: To help students understand how both cattle and sheep ranching developed in the West, copy the graphic organizer tot he right on the chalkboard, omitting the italicized answers. Have each student complete it. Then have students create fill-in-the-blank sentences using key terms from the subsection entitled Ranching in the West. Ask students to exchange sentences and complete them.

English Language Learners

 HOMEWORK *Write the following questions on the chalkboard:* How did cattle and sheep ranching develop in the West? What factors related to population

and the economy led to the growth of the cattle and sheep industry following the Civil War? *Have each student write several answers in response to the questions.*

The Development of Cattle Ranching
- the introduction of the Texas longhorn
- the expansion of the eastern beef market

Ranching in the West

The Development of Sheep Ranching
- the introduction of sheep ranching by the Spanish
- the participation of American Indian groups
- the market expansion sparked by the Gold Rush

A Famous African American Cowboy. A number of African American cowboys became well known for their extraordinary skills at the trade. Bill Pickett, a son of former slaves, achieved nationwide fame for inventing bulldogging, a rodeo event in which a contestant subdues a steer by grabbing its horns and wrestling it to the ground. Pickett toured the United States and abroad giving "bulldogging" demonstrations during the early 1900s, but discrimination often prevented him from competing on the rodeo circuit. In 1972—40 years after his death in a ranching accident—Pickett became the first black honoree at the National Rodeo Hall of Fame.

ACTIVITY: Ask students to conduct research on a famous cowboy. Then have each student prepare a short oral report on his or her subject to present to the class.

VISUAL RECORD ANSWER

Students might suggest that the men's clothing indicates that they are Mexican or Mexican American.

Technology Resources

 Art in American History Transparency 17: Prospecting for Cattle Range

The Cattle Industry

The workers who took care of a rancher's cattle were known as cowboys. Popular culture romanticized cowboy life, but it was difficult. Cowboys worked hard in all kinds of weather and made little money. Most worked the range for just seven years before settling down in towns or on farms.

The cowboys. Many of the cowboys were Confederate veterans of the Civil War. African American, Mexican, and Mexican American cowboys made up about one third of the some 35,000 cowboys in the West. African American cowboys escaped most of the discrimination of the postwar era. A few even became trail bosses. African American cowboys were, however, more likely to be assigned unpleasant tasks.

Mexican ranch hands known as vaqueros had worked with cattle and horses since long before the days of the cattle boom. In the 1880s most Mexican and Mexican American cowboys worked on ranches in Texas. Mostly sons of ranchers or farmers, vaqueros sometimes owned their own ranches. Although they were paid higher wages and treated better than those who handled menial ranch jobs, Mexican cowboys often encountered discrimination.

Life on the trail. Moving the cattle from Texas to the rail lines in Missouri and Kansas posed a major problem for cattle ranchers. To reach the railroads, cowboys herded as many as 3,000 cattle on **long drives**. These overland treks covered hundreds of miles and lasted several months. The trail usually ended in Kansas because the cattle in Missouri were not immune to Texas fever. Over the years, cowboys drove some 4 million cattle from Texas to Kansas.

On a typical long drive, a trail boss managed a crew of about 10 cowboys. The cook rode in front of the herds in a chuck wagon that carried food and the cowboys' bedrolls. Managing the herd was a tough job. River crossings, where swift currents might drown hundreds of animals, proved particularly hazardous. George Duffield headed a long drive in 1866. He described one river crossing: "We worked all day in the river & at dusk got the last beefe over. . . . There was one of our party drowned today . . . & several narrow escapes."

The worst danger was a stampede. Almost any unexpected sound—a coyote's wail, a thunderclap, a sneeze—could panic the cattle. Cowboys learned to prevent stampedes by "circling around and around the terrified herd, singing loudly and steadily, . . . [with other cowboys] separating a bunch here and there."

INTERPRETING THE VISUAL RECORD

Ranching. In 1877 James Walker painted this scene, called *Vaqueros of California Roping Horses in a Corral.* **From their clothing, what can you tell about the men in the painting?**

Cattle Towns

Every long drive ended at a **railhead**, a town located along a railroad, where brokers bought cattle to ship east on railroad cars. The Kansas towns of Abilene, Dodge City, and Wichita were among the best-known railhead stops. They came to be known as cattle towns. Farther north and west, long drives ended in Cheyenne, Wyoming, and Ogallala, Nebraska.

LEVEL 1: Pair students and have them write a series of sentences that describe what life was like for cowboys and residents of cattle towns. (*Pairs' sentences should mention demanding working conditions, isolation, and trail drives for cowboys. For residents of cattle towns, pairs' sentences should mention businesses, the end of drives, and the growth of towns.*) Ask volunteers to write their sentences on the chalkboard. **English Language Learners, Cooperative Learning**

LEVEL 2: Tell students to imagine that they are cowboys or residents of cattle towns. Have each student create a poem or song that describes his or her life. (*See the Level 1 lesson for the correct descriptions.*) Have volunteers recite or sing their compositions for the class.

Early cattle towns consisted of little more than a general store, a hotel or boardinghouse, a railroad depot, and a stockyard. Towns that attracted enough cattle business grew larger. They bustled with activity from spring to fall, when the long drives took place. Cowboys were paid at the end of the drive. After buying some new clothes and other goods, many cowboys visited gambling halls and saloons, freely spending their hard-earned money.

Prosperous cattle towns attracted businesspeople, doctors, lawyers, and their families. Once families arrived, the cattle towns built schools, hired teachers, and established police forces to maintain order. Reformers, many of them women, wanted to bring their middle-class Protestant values to the rough cowboy towns by organizing relief and temperance societies. However, their calls to limit alcohol consumption met with limited success since cattle town economies depended on saloons.

THE GRANGER COLLECTION, NEW YORK

This engraving of Dodge City shows the arrival of cowboys driving a herd of cattle to market.

✔ **READING CHECK: Identifying Cause and Effect** How did cattle drives affect the development of towns and cities in the West? Towns grew at railheads, where cattle drives ended.

AMERICAN ARTS

Frontier Artists

The American West captured the imagination of artists. They were eager to portray its natural beauty and the lives of its inhabitants. Perhaps the most influential artist was Frederic Remington. This New Yorker painted and sculpted a wide variety of subjects, including American Indians, cowboys, and mountain men. Remington's work celebrated western settlement, as did paintings by Charles (Carl) Wimar. Wimar saw the story of the West as an epic of heroic conquest. Not all artists glorified western settlement, however. Charles Russell lived in Montana for most of his life and worked for more than a decade as a cowboy. Russell was more sensitive to the settlers' impact on the land and on American Indians.

American Indians were often portrayed as either savages or noble people. In both cases, frontier art gave the general impression that they were doomed to vanish from the West. Art historians have also noted that frontier artists concentrated on images of men at work or play. They usually neglected the role that women played in the settlement of the West. Eliza Barchus became known for her depictions of life in Oregon. She was one of the few female artists in the West whose work received significant attention.

Frederic Remington's **Fight for the Waterhole**

Understanding the Arts

1. How did frontier art portray American Indians?
2. What elements of the West interested frontier artists the most?
3. What image of the West does the painting by Remington above suggest?

Charles Russell. Charles Russell was born in Missouri but moved to Montana as a teenager. Although he once considered traveling to Europe to study painting in "the noted art schools of the old world," he stayed in the United States and concentrated on western themes. Unlike many artists who portrayed the settlement of the West, Russell mourned the impact that this settlement had on American Indians. In a letter to a friend, he once wrote, "The Red Man was the true American. The history of how they fought for their country is written in blood, a stain that time cannot grind out."

CRITICAL THINKING What did Russell mean when he called Indians the "true Americans"?

ANSWER: Students might suggest that Russell was referring to the fact that American Indians populated North America before European Americans.

AMERICAN ARTS ANSWERS

1. as savages or noble people

2. its natural beauty and inhabitants

3. that it was an arid, threatening, dangerous region

TEACH OBJECTIVE 3

ALL LEVELS: Have students work in pairs to create a "business opportunity" ad for ranchers and their families and a "help wanted" ad for cowboys. Students' ads should describe ranch life. (*Ads should mention cattle, cowboys, drives, assorted ranch chores, and more. A business opportunity ad might read: Ranch with 5,000 acres, 400 head of cattle available in Texas to hardworking family. Men's duties include rounding up cattle and maintenance of fences and range. Women's duties include housework, cooking, fence-mending, and herding.*) Have volunteers share their ads with the class.
English Language Learners, Cooperative Learning

NOTE: For an additional teaching idea, see the Chapter 5 collage lesson in the **Creative Teaching Strategies** handbook.

Ranch Life

teen Life

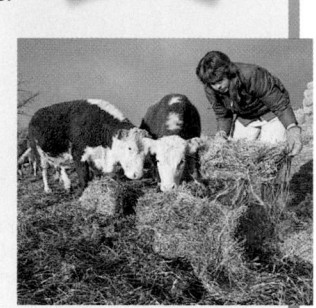

Raising cattle today

Teenagers in the late 1800s often shared the burden of the hard work of ranching. One of 14 children in a Colorado ranching family, Jake Goss started working with horses when he was 13. Two years later he found work on a neighboring ranch, cutting hay and branding cattle. By age 17, Goss owned 23 head of cattle. He knew the responsibilities that came with ownership. When he broke his arm so badly that "it was hangin' out my sleeve with splinters," he stayed with the calves until someone could take his place. A little more than a year later, he bought his own ranch, which he worked for most of the rest of his life.

Young women also did their share of work on the ranches. Agnes Morley Cleveland grew up on a family ranch in New Mexico. Later she recalled, "Cattle became the circumference of our universe and their behavior absorbed our entire waking hours." Cleveland rode the range in search of lost calves, checked fences for damage, and branded cattle. Once she discovered that a sheriff had mistreated one of her favorite horses. When the sheriff refused to return the horse, Cleveland stampeded a herd of 50 to 60 horses through his camp.

Ranching

As the U.S. government converted more American Indian territory into public land, cattle ranching spread west into Colorado and New Mexico and north into the Dakotas, Kansas, Montana, Nebraska, and Wyoming. The government allowed cattle ranchers to use public land as **open range**, or free grazing land. This access to free pastureland helped make cattle ranching profitable. The introduction of higher-grade cattle breeds from the East Coast and from Europe led to even bigger profits.

Ranch profits. Although many families established ranches, it was large investment companies for the most part that took advantage of the government's offer of land. Financed by eastern and European investors, these companies created huge ranches. Chicago investors owned the 3.5-million-acre XIT Ranch in the Texas Panhandle. A Scottish enterprise called the Prairie Cattle Company owned 5.5 million acres in Colorado, New Mexico, and Texas, with 139,000 head of cattle.

Most ranchers did not own this much land. Instead, they concentrated on buying range rights, or water rights to ponds and rivers. These rights gave ranchers access to scarce water as well as ownership of the land around it. With range rights, ranchers could stop farmers and ranchers from coming onto their private property and using the water. "Wherever there is any water, there is a ranch," noted one Colorado cattleman.

Ranch life. Both cattle and sheep ranches demanded hard labor from ranch families. On most ranches, women did housework, cooked for all the hired cowboys, and helped out with fence-mending, herding, and other chores. Because ranches were far apart, loneliness took its toll. A Texas ranch couple described the isolation of ranch life.

History Makers Speak

"A man that is cowhunting with a lively crowd has no idea how long and lonesome the time passes with his wife at home.... A man can see his friends, hear the news and pass the time ... while his wife is at home and sees and hears nothing until he returns."

—Susan and Samuel Newcomb, *Newcomb Diaries, 1865 and 1866*

During the spring and fall, ranch life centered on the roundup. With help from the cowboys, ranchers drove their cattle from the open range to a central location. Here cowboys from each ranch "cut out," or separated, the cattle, which were identified by each ranch's distinctive brand. The cattle would then be rounded up for the long drive to a railhead. When not working a roundup, cowboys rode the range to check water sources and search for lost or injured cattle.

✔ **READING CHECK: Summarizing** What was life on a ranch like? It was difficult, lonely, and centered on the roundup.

SPOTLIGHT
on Cattle Ranches

Have students conduct research on a well-known western cattle ranch in the late 1800s. Ask each student to write a report about the ranch. **Block Scheduling**

TEACH OBJECTIVE 4

LEVEL 1: Pair students and tell them to imagine that they are newspaper reporters. Have each pair write newspaper headlines announcing the decline of the cattle boom on the open range. Pairs' headlines should also explain this decline. *(Headlines should mention the cattle glut, barbed wire fencing, depletion of grass, and bad weather.)* Have volunteers read their headlines to the class.
English Language Learners, Cooperative Learning

LEVELS 2 AND 3: Ask students to complete the Level 1 lesson. Then have each student select a headline and write an article to accompany it. Students' headlines and articles should explain the end of the cattle boom. *(See the Level 1 lesson for the correct answers.)* Ask volunteers to read their articles to the class. Students may wish to include their articles in their portfolios.

The Cattle Boom and Western Railroads, late 1800s

Interpreting Maps The development of railroads and cattle trails allowed for the transportation of livestock and goods between eastern and western states.

? ENVIRONMENT AND SOCIETY What geographic features made travel from the East Coast to the West Coast particularly difficult?

Cattle trails
Railroads

The End of the Cattle Boom

The cattle boom lasted about 20 years. Several factors led to its early end. First, ranchers eager for large profits crowded the open range with too many cattle. Prices crashed in 1885 as supply far exceeded demand. In 1882 cattle had brought $35 a head in Chicago. They sold for only $8 in 1885. Second, ranchers faced increased competition for use of the open range. In 1874 Illinois farmer **Joseph Glidden** patented **barbed wire**, a cheap fencing material. Ranchers initially refused to use barbed wire, fearing that it would injure their cattle. However, by the 1880s cattle ranchers and farmers had erected miles of barbed wire across the open range to control access to land and water. Some farmers and small ranchers responded by cutting fences and moving onto the land or stealing cattle. This competition led to range wars among large ranchers, small ranchers, and farmers. Although the large ranchers often won these battles, few ranchers could continue to count on

A Colt revolver

CITIZENSHIP

Cattle Rustling in the West. In addition to searching for lost cattle, cowboys on the range watched for rustlers, or cattle thieves. After the Civil War, high beef prices and the enormity of the open range encouraged the formation of a few large "rustler gangs." Most rustlers were former cowboys who hoped to use the cattle to start their own ranches. The owners of large ranches hired special detectives to track down cattle thieves, but these efforts were usually fruitless. Juries rarely convicted accused rustlers, even with the presence of significant evidence against them.

CRITICAL THINKING Why might juries in the West have been reluctant to convict accused cattle rustlers?

ANSWER: Students might suggest that juries were often made up of cowboys or former cowboys who sympathized with the motives of the rustlers.

MAP ANSWER
the Mississippi River, the Rocky Mountains, the Sierra Nevada

THE WESTERN CROSSROADS **181**

181

REVIEW

Have students complete the **Section 3 Review** on p. 182.

ASSESS

Have students complete **Daily Quiz 5.3**. As **Alternative Assessment**, you may want to use the fill-in-the-blank sentences or the "business opportunity ad" in this section's lessons.

RETEACH

Have students complete **Main Idea Activity for English Language Learners and Special-Needs Students 5.3**. Have students draw a map of the different cattle trails cowboys used to transport cattle to the market. Then have students write questions based on their maps. Students should pair up and answer their partner's questions. **English Language Learners**

EXTEND

Ask students to conduct research on one of the prominent cattle towns of the West. Students should explore the town's economic and cultural activities. Then have each student write a report on the selected town. Students should provide illustrations and possibly maps to supplement their reports. **Block Scheduling**

REVIEW 3 ANSWERS

1. Define
- long drives, p. 178
- railhead, p. 178
- open range, p. 180
- barbed wire, p. 181

2. Identify
- Texas longhorn, p. 177
- Joseph Glidden, p. 181

3. rise—new cattle breeds, the growth of eastern cities, and access to free grazing land; fall—declining prices for beef, barbed wire, bad weather, and the blizzard of 1887

4a. stereotype—exciting and fun and all white men; reality—difficult work, little pay, and one third Mexican and African American

b. Cattle drives caused many towns at railheads to grow larger and prosper.

c. railroads—shipped cattle back east; barbed wire—limited rangeland and led to fighting

5. Answers will vary. Dialogues should compare the long hours, dangerous work, and isolated lifestyle with life in the East.

Barbed wire made fencing economical on the wide-open Great Plains.

letting their cattle roam free on public land. The end of the open range meant that ranchers had to buy their own rangeland. Some large ranching corporations went broke.

Bad weather dealt the final blow to the open range. On the southern Plains a severe winter in 1885–86 and a drought in 1886 diminished many herds. The following year, terrible blizzards hammered the northern Plains. On January 15, 1887, temperatures reached 46 degrees below zero in some areas. After the worst was over, thousands of starved and frozen cattle were discovered. The losses were incredible. Some ranchers lost up to 90 percent of their herds.

However, other ranchers learned from their experiences. They invested more money in ranching operations and raised hay to feed their cattle during harsh winters. Because sheep could survive on the weeds that replaced the native grasses destroyed by overgrazing, sheep ranching expanded during this period. A song of the time described the end of the cowboy era.

Primary Source

❝Good-by, old trail boss, I wish you no harm;
I'm quittin' this business to go on the farm.
I'll sell my old saddle and buy me a plow;
And never, no, never, will I rope another cow.❞

—"The Old Chisholm Trail"

✔ **READING CHECK: Identifying Cause and Effect** How did barbed wire hasten the end of the cattle boom? It limited access to land and water.

SECTION 3 REVIEW

1. Define and explain:
long drives
railhead
open range
barbed wire

2. Identify and explain:
Texas longhorn
Joseph Glidden

3. Identifying Cause and Effect
Copy the chart below. Use it to describe the factors that led to the growth of ranching and the factors that led to its decline.

Cattle Kingdom

Rise   Fall

Causes   Causes

4. **Finding the Main Idea**

a. Contrast the realities of an American cowboy's life to the popular stereotypes.
b. How did cattle drives affect the economy and growth of towns at railheads?
c. Give three examples of the impact of technological innovations on the cattle or sheep industry.

5. **Writing and Critical Thinking**

Comparing Imagine that you have traveled from the East to visit a relative on her ranch in the West. Write a humorous dialogue comparing your lives.
Consider:
- what the business goals of the ranches were
- how life was organized on the ranches
- who lived and worked on ranches

go. hrw .com **Homework Practice Online**
keyword: SE3 HP5

After completing Section 4, students should be able to:

OBJECTIVE 1 *Describe the role that mining played in bringing more people west.*

OBJECTIVE 2 *Explain how the arrival of families changed life in mining camps.*

OBJECTIVE 3 *Discuss why large companies took over most mining operations, and explain how this changed the lives of miners.*

🔊 LET'S GET STARTED!

As students enter the classroom, tell them to read the song on this page and respond to it in writing. Conduct a brief discussion on students' responses, focusing on how the song might have represented the sentiments of those who migrated west to seek their fortunes as miners. Tell students that in Section 4 they will learn more about mining and life in mining camps and towns.

SECTION 4

READ TO DISCOVER

1. What role did mining play in bringing more people west?
2. How did the arrival of families change life in mining camps?
3. Why did large companies take over most mining operations, and how did this change the lives of miners?

DEFINE

patio process
hydraulic mining
hard-rock mining

IDENTIFY

Comstock Lode
William H. Seward

▶ WHY IT MATTERS TODAY

Mining is no longer central to the economy in the West. Use **CNNfyi.com** or other **current events** sources to learn about mining today. Record your findings in your journal.

CNNfyi.com

The Mining Boom

 EYEWITNESSES TO History ❝*The men who worked in the mines . . . were [a] happy-go-easy set of fellows, fond of good living, and not particularly interested in religious affairs. . . .*

Men quarreled at times and firearms were discharged with but slight provocation. Nevertheless they all had an acute instinct of right and wrong . . . [and] a high sense of honor.❞

—J. N. Flint, quoted in *Mining Frontier*, edited by Marvin Lewis

This silver bar was minted in San Francisco.

Virginia City, Nevada, enjoyed an economic boom that began in 1859 when prospectors discovered silver in the region. Thirty years later, J. N. Flint recalled life in a prosperous mining town. While working in the mines he had longed for "the companionship of forest trees, green fields and running brooks," all of which were missing in the arid regions surrounding Virginia City. Flint's recollections capture the atmosphere of the towns where people hoped to make their fortunes by digging for gold and silver.

Western Mining

The economic impact of mining changed the face of the West. Farmers and ranchers slowly expanded across the Great Plains, establishing homesteads and ranches. Meanwhile, miners raced across the continent, hoping to be the first to strike it rich. Mining opened many new regions in the West to settlement.

Gold and silver. The first promising mining discoveries after the California Gold Rush took place in Colorado. Prospectors found gold near Pikes Peak in late 1858. By early 1859, thousands of people had flocked to Colorado. A popular tune captured their enthusiasm.

 Primary Source ❝The gold is there, 'most anywhere.
You can take it out rich, with an iron crowbar,
And where it is thick, with a shovel and pick,
You can pick it out in lumps as big as a brick.❞

—"Cherry Creek Emigrant's Song"

The song exaggerated the riches, however. Many prospectors left in disappointment by midsummer.

The Carson River valley in present-day Nevada was another center of frantic activity in 1859. In addition to gold, the area contained the famous **Comstock Lode**, one of the world's richest silver veins. Over a period of 20 years its mines yielded about $500 million worth of precious metals.

Some miners went south to Arizona, where Hispanics had been mining silver since the mid-1700s. Hispanic miners introduced mining methods that originated in Mexico and South America. These methods included a mill that separated gold

---

SECTION 4 RESOURCES

REPRODUCIBLE
▶ Guided Reading Strategy 5.4
▶ Graphic Organizer Activity 5: American Indian Leaders

TECHNOLOGY
▶ One-Stop Planner, Lesson 5.4
▶ Holt Researcher: American History CD–ROM
▶ Homework Practice Online

REINFORCEMENT, REVIEW, AND ASSESSMENT
▶ Section 4 Review, p. 187
▶ Daily Quiz 5.4
▶ Main Idea Activity 5.4
▶ English Audio Summary 5.4
▶ Spanish Audio Summary 5.4

TEACH OBJECTIVE 1

ALL LEVELS: Ask students what role mining played in bringing more people west. (*Students should indicate that mining lured people to the West by offering the possibility of enormous wealth.*) To help students understand where people migrated, copy the graphic organizer to the right on the chalkboard, omitting the italicized answers. Have each student complete it. **English Language Learners**

HOMEWORK *Write the following scenario on the chalkboard:* You have just heard about the enormous mineral deposits at the Comstock Lode in Nevada. Will you travel there and try to strike it rich despite the immense risks, or will you stay at home and try to get ahead in your regular job? *Have each student write a few paragraphs in response to the scenario.*

Nevada

Pike's Peak — **Where Prospective Miners Migrated** — *Arizona*

the Fraser River Valley

Alaska

the Klondike

GEOGRAPHY

Travel to the Gold Fields.
High boat fares forced most prospectors headed to the Klondike to travel through Alaska on foot. Once there, the extreme conditions forced many to give up their dreams of riches and return to the United States. Historians estimate that more than 50,000 people who embarked on the trip turned around and headed back before they reached the Klondike.

ACTIVITY: Tell students to imagine that they are prospectors traveling through Alaska to the Klondike. Have each student draw a map of the route they might travel.

Individual prospectors often made the first discovery of precious metals, but it took large companies to extract the valuable ore.

from quartz and the **patio process**—which used mercury to extract silver from ore. Some prospectors used these methods to mine the Comstock Lode and the region around Tucson, in what is now Arizona. Other miners headed north.

Northern ventures. During the late 1850s some miners pushed as far north as the Fraser River valley of British Columbia. This movement had important consequences for Russia and the United States. Russia, which at that time owned Alaska, offered to sell it to the United States. U.S. Secretary of State **William H. Seward** negotiated the purchase of Alaska in 1867. Seward believed the price, which came out to less than two cents an acre, was a good deal.

Many Americans, however, considered Alaska worthless, ridiculing the purchase as "Seward's Folly" or "Seward's Ice Box." Seward's confidence that Alaska "possesses treasures . . . equal to those of any other region of the continent" proved correct. In 1896, prospectors discovered gold in the Klondike district of Canada's Yukon Territory, which bordered Alaska. This discovery launched the Klondike Gold Rush. By the summer of 1897, Yukon miners had extracted gold worth more than $1 million. Gold discoveries in Alaska in 1898 and 1902 attracted even more settlers.

✔ **READING CHECK: Drawing Conclusions** How did mining bring more people to the West? The discovery of gold and silver attracted prospectors.

SKILL-BUILDING STRATEGIES ANSWERS

Practicing the Skill

1. for most cattle ranches and mining operations—well-financed investment companies; some ranches—private families

2. promoted both industries by acquiring land for ranches and mining companies

3. paid workers

4. promoted the rapid emergence of socially unstable communities

5. ranching—damaged the native grasses and resulted in overgrazing; mining—altered the physical landscape with mines and other operations

---

Skill-Building Strategies

Comparing and Contrasting

Comparing and contrasting are fundamental aspects of historical study. To *compare* is to examine the similarities and the differences between two or more events, ideas, people, situations, social groups, or things. To *contrast* is to explore only the differences between two or more subjects. Comparing and contrasting are particularly effective techniques for organizing historical information, tracking change over time, and understanding the origins of different points of view.

How to Compare and Contrast

1. **Identify the similarities.** When you encounter subjects that require comparison, observe the ways in which they are alike. Each time you identify a similarity, assess its importance. Record your findings.
2. **Identify the differences.** When you have noted as many similarities as possible, examine the ways in which your subjects are different. Each time you identify a difference, assess its importance. Record your findings.

3. **Put the comparison to use.** Use the results of your comparison, along with your knowledge of the historical period, to form generalizations and draw conclusions about your subjects.

Applying the Skill

Review the material on cattle ranches in Section 3 and mining companies in this section. Then create a list of similarities and differences between the two industries.

Practicing the Skill

Answer the following questions.
1. Who invested in cattle ranches and mining companies?
2. What role did the U.S. government play in the ranching and mining industries?
3. Who supplied the labor in each industry?
4. How did each industry affect community formation in the West?
5. How did each industry affect the western environment?

LEVEL 1: Pair students and have each pair create a before-and-after chart of the ways in which mining towns changed with the arrival of families. (*Pairs should indicate the following relationships: before—mining towns were unstable, temporary residences; after—families brought stability, transformed towns into permanent towns; before—mining towns were violent, vigilante communities; after—arrival of families brought law and order, establishment of churches, newspapers, schools, and cultural establishments.*) Then tell students to imagine that they are miners who witnessed a camp transform into a town. Have each student write a before-and-after paragraph expressing his or her impressions of that time.
English Language Learners, Cooperative Learning

LEVELS 2 AND 3: Ask students to create a chart noting the differences in mining towns upon the arrival of families. Charts should discuss the decrease in violence and lawlessness, an increase in law and order, and the establishment of churches and schools. Tell students their charts will act as visual summaries and can include photographs, maps, or illustrations.

Life in Mining Communities

Mining camps sprang up overnight wherever news of possible wealth brought prospectors together. Prospecting was typically not a family enterprise. Most camps consisted almost entirely of male residents. A visitor to one Colorado mining camp estimated the population to be about 4,000, with just 12 female inhabitants.

The settlers. Mining camps drew a wide range of settlers. One newspaper reporter wrote, "Here were congregated the most varied elements of humanity . . . belonging to almost every nationality and every status of life." In the mining regions of Southern California, many Californios, Chileans, Mexicans, and Peruvians maintained their own separate settlements. In other mining areas the mix of prospectors included U.S. citizens, miners from the Cornwall region of England, and Irish and Chinese immigrants.

At first, life in the mining camps was crude, and comforts were few. Moreover, the atmosphere in most camps was one of intense competition. Prospector William Parsons remembered,

Mining camps were often little more than a hastily constructed group of tents or shacks.

 History Makers Speak
"a mad, furious race for wealth, in which men lost their identity almost, and toiled and wrestled, and lived a fierce, riotous, wearing, fearfully excited life; forgetting home and kindred [family], abandoning old steady habits."
—William Parsons

Such competition led to discrimination. Miners in the Cripple Creek camp in Colorado forcibly excluded eastern and southern Europeans as well as Hispanics. In 1882 a mob of masked men drove the Chinese inhabitants of Rico, Colorado, out of town. The local newspaper called the incident "one of the most shameful affairs that ever disgraced any so-called civilized country and would have met the hearty approval of the most barbarous savage." Most Chinese miners left the Rocky Mountain camps because of such hostile treatment.

Instability. Western mining camps were some of the most violent places in the United States during the late 1800s. Tensions between ethnic groups often led to fighting. Gamblers and swindlers swarmed in, and conflicts over claims set off brawls. Deadwood, South Dakota, gained a reputation as a particularly rough town. An outlaw's haven, Deadwood became the final resting place of lawman Wild Bill Hickok, shot dead as he played cards. Legend has it that Hickok was holding a pair of aces and a pair of eights, which thereafter became known as the dead man's hand.

The absence of law enforcement sometimes led people in mining camps to form vigilante committees to combat theft and violence. Montana newspaper editor Thomas Dimsdale claimed that it was "an absolute necessity that good, law-loving, order-sustaining men should unite for mutual protection and salvation of the community." However, vigilante committees often used violence to resolve the community's problems, hanging the accused after a quick trial.

Analyzing Primary Sources

Supporting a Point of View
What evidence in this section supports Parsons's view?

all-male camps, ethnic tensions, and violent behavior

VISUAL RECORD ANSWER
(for p. 186)
Students might point to the permanent buildings in the background.

VISUAL RECORD ANSWER
(for p. 187)
Students might suggest that it degraded the landscape and environment.

REVIEW SECTION **4** ANSWERS

1. Define
- patio process, p. 184
- hydraulic mining, p. 187
- hard-rock mining, p. 187

2. Identify
- Comstock Lode, p. 183
- William H. Seward, p. 184

3. social effects—ethnic diversity, intense economic competition, violence, new growth of communities; political effects—formation of unions by miners; economic effects—establishment of prosperous businesses in mining towns, domination of large, well-financed companies in the mines; environmental effects—damage to rivers and flooding problems

4a. offered new economic opportunities

b. They established law and order, schools, churches, newspapers, and entertainment.

c. New technology was used; work became more dangerous; some miners formed unions.

TEACH OBJECTIVE 3

LEVELS 1 AND 2: Pair students and ask each pair to compile a list of the reasons why corporations took over mining operations and the changes that resulted for individual miners. *(Pairs should note the following causes and effects: causes—easily accessible ore deposits had been removed and expensive technologies were required to remove deep deposits; technological knowledge rather than luck was required to locate deep deposits of ore; effects—miners became laborers for corporations rather than self-employed individuals; working conditions in mines were dangerous; some miners formed unions to obtain better wages and working conditions.)* Then have pairs create picket signs that striking miners might have created to protest their working conditions.

English Language Learners, Cooperative Learning

LEVEL 3: Ask students to imagine that they are miners who were previously self-employed but have since started working for a mining company. Have each student write a short story that chronicles the changes that took place when mining companies took over mining operations, and how those changes affected individual miners. *(See the Levels 1 and 2 lesson for the correct causes and effects.)* Students should use the facts from their textbooks in writing their stories.

---

5. Answers will vary. Some students might claim that mining benefited the West because it promoted the establishment of multicultural communities, but harm came in the form of worker injuries.

CHAPTER REVIEW 5 ANSWERS

Creating a Time Line
Each event should have an explanation and the correct date.

Writing a Summary
See the Reading Checks in each section for main ideas.

Identifying People and Ideas
1. leader of Sioux resistance

2. encounter between the U.S. Army and the Sioux in 1890

3. congressional act requiring the allotment and sale of Indian lands

4. provided settlers with 160 acres of land in return for settling and cultivating it for five years

5. African Americans who migrated from the South to Kansas during the late 1870s

6. writer who wrote about life on the Great Plains

7. cattle breed suited for life on the Great Plains

8. obtained a patent for barbed wire in 1874

Great Debates

The Old West

Conflicting images of life in the West reflect the continuing debate over the meaning of western settlement. Books, movies, and television programs offer one side of the debate. Most Americans are familiar with images such as a solitary miner panning for gold in a remote mountain stream; a cowboy riding off alone into the sunset; and a farm or ranch family carving out a living on the empty Plains. These legendary western figures represent the American ideal of rugged individuals conquering a barren and uninhabited land. Seen this way, the history of western settlement is a powerful and deeply meaningful symbol of the American Dream.

However, many historians choose to focus on other aspects of western development. They argue that most westerners, including cowboys and miners, labored for others—often large companies—rather than for themselves. In addition, western settlers relied on the federal government to sell lands at low rates, subsidize railroad development, and use the military to remove American Indians. These historians view the West as a land shaped by technology, big business, and the federal government—a portrayal radically different from the "Wild West" of outlaws, lone cowboys, and isolated pioneers.

INTERPRETING THE VISUAL RECORD
A new town. Helena, Montana, is one mining camp that developed into a prosperous city. *What evidence indicates that Helena is no longer a temporary community?*

Stability came to the mining camps as they grew into towns. The camps attracted a host of businesses eager to feed and clothe the miners. James Morley of Montana noted, "I shouldn't have the patience to count the business places" in an area that "only eighteen months ago . . . was a 'howling desert.'" Owners of saloons and stores had a better chance of striking it rich than miners. Cooking, cleaning, and providing lodging were especially profitable. One industrious woman boasted that she earned "nine hundred dollars in nine weeks, clear of all expenses, by washing!" Later known as the Cattle Queen of Montana, Elizabeth Collins was offered a job as cook at a Montana mining camp. She recalled, "Prompted by kindness and a desire to see these hardworking men as comfortable as possible—also craving for the $75 per month—I promptly accepted the offer."

The few children living in the camps had unique opportunities to earn money. They hunted for gold dust under the raised sidewalks or panned and scavenged for gold dust after the miners had finished for the day. Selling fresh food to miners, who quickly grew tired of eating canned food, was much more profitable. One brother and sister made $800 one summer selling butter and bacon to the local miners.

With the arrival of more families, many camps turned into permanent communities. Prosperity brought law and order and the establishment of churches, newspapers, schools, and even theaters and music groups. Denver and Boulder, Colorado; Carson City, Nevada; and Helena, Montana, all began as mining camps before evolving into major urban centers.

✔ **READING CHECK: Analyzing Information** Besides mining, how did people in the West earn a living? They owned saloons, stores, and places for lodging.

Mining as Big Business

Individual prospectors roaming the West with their packhorses and hand tools made the earliest strikes, or mining discoveries. However, the era of the lone miner did not last long. Within a few years after a strike, most of the easily accessible mineral deposits were "worked out." Mining ore deposits deep below Earth's surface required resources and technology far beyond the means of the average prospector. As a result, mining became dominated by large, well-financed companies.

REVIEW

Have students complete the **Section 4 Review** on p. 187.

ASSESS

Have students complete **Daily Quiz 5.4.** As **Alternative Assessment**, you may want to use the picket signs or short stories in this section's lessons.

RETEACH

Have students complete **Main Idea Activity for English Language Learners and Special-Needs Students 5.4.** Organize students into small groups and assign each group a subsection.

Tell each group to develop questions about the main ideas in its subsection. Then have each group exchange its questions with another group and work to answer the questions.
English Language Learners, Cooperative Learning

EXTEND

Have students conduct research on the antiviolence movements that sprang up in many western towns. Then pair students and have each pair create a graphic organizer or a visual display comparing and contrasting antiviolence movements in the late 1800s with modern-day antiviolence movements. Ask volunteers to share their work with the class.
Cooperative Learning, Block Scheduling

Mining companies relied on technological know-how rather than on guesswork or luck. Corps of college-educated geologists and engineers located the ore and instructed the companies on how best to extract the minerals—copper, iron, lead, and zinc—in demand by factories in the East.

To reach the ore, companies used one of two methods. In **hydraulic mining**, water shot at high pressure ripped away gravel and dirt to expose the minerals beneath. This process devastated the environment. The displaced soil choked rivers and caused flooding. **Hard-rock mining** involved sinking deep shafts to obtain ore locked in veins of rocks.

New technology changed the working conditions in the mines. Laborers sank the shafts, built the tunnels, drilled, and processed the ore. The work was dirty and dangerous. Temperatures deep in the mines sometimes rose as high as 150°F. Poor ventilation contributed to respiratory illnesses. Cave-ins, rockfalls, and the use of explosives such as dynamite sometimes caused injury or death. Injured miners had little hope of receiving compensation for their suffering. After William Kelley was blinded in a mining accident, the Montana Supreme Court ruled that it was "an unforeseen and unavoidable accident incident to [part of] the risk of mining." The mining company did not have to pay Kelley any damages.

As the hope of sudden riches faded, miners grew dissatisfied with wages and working conditions. In some communities, miners formed unions. Union dues helped injured miners and the families of miners who had been killed on the job. Unions also negotiated with or battled against owners who tried to cut wages. Many unions opposed Chinese miners, who were willing to work for lower pay. During the early 1900s, mining increasingly became the task of large companies. Mining companies greatly affected the landscape and the environment of the West.

✔ **READING CHECK: Contrasting** How did the methods of early miners differ from those who worked in company-owned mines? *Early miners worked alone, and their ability to extract minerals was limited. Company miners used new technologies.*

INTERPRETING THE VISUAL RECORD

Hydraulic mining. These Colorado miners are using a water hose to sift through dirt in search of gold. *What impact did this type of mining have on the landscape and environment?*

SECTION 4 REVIEW

1. **Define and explain:**
   patio process
   hydraulic mining
   hard-rock mining

2. **Identify and explain:**
   Comstock Lode
   William H. Seward

3. **Evaluating** Copy the graphic organizer below. Use it to explain how mining affected the United States during the late 1800s.

   Mining
   → Social Effects
   → Political Effects
   → Economic Effects
   → Environmental Effects

4. **Finding the Main Idea**
   a. How did mining encourage the migration of people westward?
   b. How did the arrival of families in mining camps affect the growth of towns and cities?
   c. How did mining change as it became big business?

5. **Writing and Critical Thinking**
   Identifying Cause and Effect Imagine that you are a government official sent to investigate the effects of mining on the West. Prepare a report to Congress on your findings.
   Consider:
   • how the mining boom benefited the West
   • what harm the boom caused to the West
   • how the boom could have been handled differently

Homework Practice Online
keyword: SE3 HP5

9. rich silver vein that attracted miners to Nevada

10. mining method in which water ripped away gravel and dirt to expose minerals

Understanding Main Ideas

1. how—fled from and occasionally engaged in armed conflict with U.S. Army forces; why—did not want to give up their lands and traditional ways of life

2. By forcing American Indians to farm and assume private ownership of land, the government hoped to assimilate Indians into "white America." However, as a result of government actions, many American Indians lost their lands, and others rejected farming; many Navajo died from disease and malnutrition.

3. People came for large open areas of fertile land, climate favorable to farming, and mineral resources.

4. rise—the introduction of new cattle breeds, the growth of eastern cities, and access to free grazing land; fall—declining prices for beef, the impact of barbed wire on the open range, and severe weather during the mid-1880s

5. took over most of the mining business from individual prospectors and hired many miners to work under dangerous and unhealthy conditions

REVIEW AND ASSESSMENT RESOURCES

TECHNOLOGY

▶ Chapter 5 Test Generator (on the One-Stop Planner)
▶ Global Skill Builder CD-ROM
▶ HRW Go site

REINFORCEMENT, REVIEW, AND ASSESSMENT

▶ Chapter 5 Review, pp. 188–89
▶ Chapter 5 Tutorial for Students, Parents, Mentors, and Peers

▶ Chapter 5 Test (Form A or B)
▶ Portfolio Activities and Alternative Assessment Handbook, Chapter 5
▶ Chapter 5 Test for English Language Learners and Special-Needs Students

REVIEW

Have students complete the **Chapter 5 Review** on pp. 188–89.

ASSESS

Use one of the chapter tests to assess students' understanding of the content. For **Alternative Assessment**, see the **Portfolio Activities and Alternative Assessment Handbook.**

Reviewing Themes

1. Disagreements between the Sioux and the U.S. government over the dispensation of Sioux lands helped lead to the massacre.

2. farming—destroyed wildlife habitats and caused erosion; mining—choked rivers and caused flooding; ranching—depleted grass cover

3. The use of barbed wire helped create private property; windmills brought water; mining technology reached buried minerals; and railroads facilitated travel.

Thinking Critically

1. a series of broken treaties, unjust wars, and final removal of Indians to reservations

2. Answers will vary. Students might suggest that some settlers attained economic independence, but that others were disappointed by the hard work and living conditions.

3. African Americans were able to establish some small farms and towns, but they continued to experience discrimination and limited economic prospects. Some Mexican Americans were paid higher wages, but they experienced discrimination.

4. Ranchers—land should be open; farmers—land should be fenced; farmers' views won out and the Plains became a vast series of settled farms.

CHAPTER 5

Review

Creating a Time Line

Copy the time line below onto a sheet of paper. Complete the time line by filling in the events and dates from this chapter that you think were most significant. Pick three events and explain why you think they were significant.

1860 ———— **1885** ———— **1910**

Writing a Summary

Using standard grammar, spelling, sentence structure, and punctuation, write an overview of events in the chapter.

Identifying People and Ideas

Identify the following terms or individuals and explain their significance.

1. Sitting Bull
2. Massacre at Wounded Knee
3. Dawes General Allotment Act
4. Homestead Act
5. Exodusters
6. Willa Cather
7. Texas longhorn
8. Joseph Glidden
9. Comstock Lode
10. hydraulic mining

Understanding Main Ideas

SECTION 1 *(pp. 162–169)*
1. How and why did different American Indian nations resist relocation to reservations?
2. How did the government fail to achieve its goal of assimilation for American Indians?

SECTION 2 *(pp. 170–176)*
3. What role did the geography of the West play in shaping patterns of migration during the late 1800s?

SECTION 3 *(pp. 177–182)*
4. What led to the rise and fall of the cattle boom?

SECTION 4 *(pp. 183–187)*
5. How did mining companies change the daily lives of miners in the West?

Reviewing Themes

1. **Culture** How did differing views of white settlement in the West contribute to the Massacre at Wounded Knee?
2. **Economics** In what ways did farming, mining, and ranching alter the western landscape and environment?
3. **Science, Technology, and Society** Explain how technological innovations addressed specific needs during westward expansion.

Thinking Critically

1. **Sequencing** Describe the relationship between the U.S. government and the Plains Indians from 1850 to 1900.
2. **Evaluating** How did the growth of the railroads affect the West?
3. **Identifying Points of View** What opportunities and limitations did African Americans and Mexican Americans experience in the West?
4. **Analyzing Information** What views on private property did farmers and ranchers have, and how did these views affect the settlement of the Great Plains?
5. **Contrasting** How does the history of the Old West differ from many images of it presented in popular culture?

Writing About History

Comparing and Contrasting Copy the graphic organizer below. Use it to list the major aspects of life in Plains settlements, in cattle towns, and in mining towns. Then write an essay comparing and contrasting two of the types of communities.

Plains Settlements	Cattle Towns	Mining Towns

RETEACH

Pair students and tell them to imagine that they have been asked by a San Francisco newspaper to write a column discussing one of the four major issues discussed in the chapter—American Indian policy, Western farmers, the cattle boom, or the mining boom. In their articles, students should present background information as well as the positive and negative aspects of the topic. Students should include an original illustration related to the topic in their articles.
English Language Learners, Cooperative Learning

EXTEND

Have students use the process of historical inquiry to research a major discovery of gold or silver during the mining boom, such as Pikes Peak, Comstock Lode, Klondike Gold Rush, and the Alaskan gold discoveries. Ask students to concentrate on the pertinent facts associated with the find, such as the date and the value of the metals discovered there, and present those, along with any other interesting facts, in a paper. **Block Scheduling**

Building Social Studies Skills

Interpreting Charts
Study the chart below. Then use it to help answer the questions that follow.

Cost of Establishing a Farm in 1870

Item	Price
Land (per acre)	$3–$12
Team (horses or oxen)	$300
Wagon and yoke or harness	$150
Plow	$25
Cultivator and harrow	$45
Combination reaper and mower	$252
Other hand tools (ax, shovel, fork, rake, and scythe)	$50

Source: The Iowa Railroad Land Company, *Choice Iowa Farming Lands*, 1870

1. What was the most expensive piece of farm equipment in 1870?
   a. team of horses or oxen
   b. wagon and yoke or harness
   c. combination reaper and mower
   d. hand tools

2. By 1900 the total investment needed to start a farm had more than doubled. What might have contributed to the increase?

Analyzing Primary Sources
Analyze the following quotation from Kate Bighead, a Cheyenne woman who describes American Indian life before the Battle of the Little Bighorn. Then answer the questions that follow.

❝I was with the Southern Cheyennes during most of my childhood and young womanhood. . . . I came to the Northern Cheyennes when their reservation was in the Black Hills country (1868–1874). White people found gold there, so the Indians had to move out. The Cheyennes were told they must go to another reservation, but not many of them made the change. They said it was no use, as the white people might want that reservation too. . . . All who stayed on the reservations had their guns taken from them, so the hunters quit going there.❞

3. Which of these headlines would be the most accurate choice for this passage?
   a. Reservation System a Failure
   b. Gold Found, American Indians Stay
   c. American Indians Flock to Reservations
   d. Indian Women Are Hunters

4. How would you describe Bighead's view of white settlers? How might her opinion be biased?

5. What does this passage reveal about white settlers' views of American Indian land?

Building Your Portfolio

Global Relations

Imagine that you are a Sioux living on the Pine Ridge Reservation in South Dakota in 1895. Compose an oral account for your grandchildren that describes how conflict between the Sioux and non-Indian settlers has affected your life and the lives of other Sioux. Be sure to include details of the conflict.

U.S. HISTORY

☑ internet connect

Internet Activity: go.hrw.com
KEYWORD: SE3 AN5

Choose a topic on the western crossroads to:
• learn about the writers who shaped the image of the American West.
• research the facts and mythology surrounding the Pony Express.
• use pictographs to create a model of a Sioux story robe.

go.hrw.com

---

5. Answers will vary. Students might suggest that life in the West was more difficult and less romantic than typically portrayed.

Writing
plains settlements—farm work, environmental difficulties, harsh climate and living conditions; cattle towns—economic activity and growth, drinking and gambling, establishment of schools, police forces, and reform societies; mining towns: economic activity and growth, large male majority, ethnic diversity, competition and violence, civic institutions

Building Social Studies Skills

1. a

2. Students might mention the increasing cost of land and equipment.

3. a

4. Answers will vary. Students might suggest that Bighead viewed white people as greedy and wanting what the Indians had.

5. Answers will vary. Students might suggest that white settlers viewed American Indian land as property that could be taken.

CHAPTER 6

The Second Industrial Revolution

CHAPTER RESOURCE MANAGER

Objectives	Pacing Guide	Reproducible Resources
SECTION 1 **The Age of Invention** pp. 192–200 ★ Describe how the development of steel and oil refining affected U.S. industry. ★ Recount the innovations that were made in transportation. ★ Explain how innovations in communications technology changed business practices and daily life in the United States. ★ Discuss why Thomas Edison wanted to open a research laboratory, and describe how it changed American life.	**Regular** 2 days **Block Scheduling** 1 day *Block Scheduling Handbook with Team Teaching Strategies, pp. 31–36*	**RS** Guided Reading Strategy 6.1 **IC** Literature Reading 6: To a Locomotive in Winter **E** Hands-On History Activity: Technology and You
SECTION 2 **The Rise of Big Business** pp. 201–08 ★ Describe the arguments that business leaders and social critics made about government's role in business. ★ Recount how business strategies changed during the Second Industrial Revolution. ★ Discuss how entrepreneurs took advantage of changes in business organization. ★ Explain how new methods of marketing products changed American life.	**Regular** 2 days **Block Scheduling** 1 day *Block Scheduling Handbook with Team Teaching Strategies, pp. 31–36*	**RS** Guided Reading Strategy 6.2 **PS** American History Political Cartoon 17: The Power of Trusts **SM** Geography Activity 6: Pullman's Company Town **PS** Primary Source Reading 6: The First Department Store **PS** Biography Reading 6: Frank Woolworth
SECTION 3 **Labor Strives to Organize** pp. 209–15 ★ Understand why some Americans wanted trusts to be banned, and recount how the government responded. ★ Describe the working conditions that laborers faced in the new age of rapid industrialization. ★ Discuss how the Knights of Labor attempted to address the needs of many workers. ★ Explain how businesses reacted to strikes in the late 1800s, and describe how this affected unions.	**Regular** 2 days **Block Scheduling** 1 day *Block Scheduling Handbook with Team Teaching Strategies, pp. 31–36*	**RS** Guided Reading Strategy 6.3 **RS** Graphic Organizer Activity 6: Industrial Problems of the Late 1800s **E** Creative Teaching Strategy: Issue Strip Lesson

Chapter Resource Key

PS	Primary Sources	**REV**	Review		Video
RS	Reading Support	**ELL**	Reinforcement and English Language Learners		Internet
IC	Interdisciplinary Connections				Holt Presentation Maker Using Microsoft® PowerPoint®
E	Enrichment		Transparencies		
SM	Skills Mastery		CD-ROM		
A	Assessment		Music		

One-Stop Planner CD-ROM

See the *One-Stop Planner* for a complete list of additional resources for students and teachers.

One-Stop Planner CD–ROM

It's easy to plan lessons, select resources, and print out materials for your students when you use the **One-Stop Planner CD–ROM with Test Generator.**

Technology Resources	Reinforcement, Review, and Assessment

One-Stop Planner, Lesson 6.1
  CNN Presents America: Yesterday and Today, 1850 to the Present Segment: Endangered Edison
  Holt Researcher: American History CD–ROM
  Homework Practice Online
  HRW Go site
	REV Section 1 Review, p. 200
	 A Daily Quiz 6.1
	 ELL Main Idea Activity 6.1
	 ELL English Audio Summary 6.1
	 ELL Spanish Audio Summary 6.1

One-Stop Planner, Lesson 6.2
  The American Nation Video Program Segment: The Standard Oil Company; Teacher's Guide, pp. 81–86
  Holt Researcher: American History CD–ROM
  Homework Practice Online
	REV Section 2 Review, p. 208
	 A Daily Quiz 6.2
	 ELL Main Idea Activity 6.2
	 ELL English Audio Summary 6.2
	 ELL Spanish Audio Summary 6.2

One-Stop Planner, Lesson 6.3
  Holt Researcher: American History CD–ROM
  Homework Practice Online
	REV Section 3 Review, p. 215
	 A Daily Quiz 6.3
	 ELL Main Idea Activity 6.3
	 ELL English Audio Summary 6.3
	 ELL Spanish Audio Summary 6.3

internet connect

HRW ONLINE RESOURCES
GO TO: go.hrw.com
Then type in a keyword.

TEACHER HOME PAGE
KEYWORD: SE3 Teacher

CHAPTER INTERNET ACTIVITIES
KEYWORD: SE3 AN6
Choose an activity to:
- research the effects of selected inventions of Thomas Edison.
- understand the underlying causes and effects of strikes and union organizing.
- create a multimedia display that illustrates the science and technology of the Wright Brothers' airplane design.

CHAPTER ENRICHMENT LINKS
KEYWORD: SE3 CH6

ONLINE ASSESSMENT
Homework Practice
KEYWORD: SE3 HP6

Standardized Test Prep
KEYWORD: SE3 STP6

Rubrics
KEYWORD: SS Rubrics

ONLINE MAPS, CHARTS, AND GRAPHS
KEYWORD: SE3 MCG
- Labor Strikes, 1870–1900
- Inventions, 1850–1900

CONTENT UPDATES
KEYWORD: SS Content Updates

HOLT PRESENTATION MAKER
KEYWORD: SE3 PPT6

ONLINE READING SUPPORT
KEYWORD: SS Strategies

CURRENT EVENTS
KEYWORD: S3 Current Events

Chapter Review and Assessment

 Global Skill Builder CD–ROM

HRW Go site

REV Chapter 6 Tutorial for Students, Parents, Mentors, and Peers

REV Chapter 6 Review, pp. 216–17

Chapter 6 Test Generator (on the One-Stop Planner)

A Chapter 6 Test (Form A or B)

A Alternative Assessment Handbook

A Chapter 6 Test for English Language Learners and Special-Needs Students

Meeting Individual Needs

Ability Levels

Level 1 Basic-level activities designed for all students encountering new material

Level 2 Intermediate-level activities designed for average students

Level 3 Challenging activities designed for honors and gifted-and-talented students

English Language Learners Activities that address the needs of students with Limited English Proficiency

Build on What You Know

Ask students to answer the following questions.

How might inventions have begun to launch a new age of American industrialization?

Consider:

- the historical effects of single inventions such as the cotton gin
- the ways in which inventions can affect and transform the workplace and general productivity

Why might poor working conditions have led many American workers to organize unions?

Consider:

- the effects of dangerous working environments
- the effects of wide disparities in wealth

exploring the time line

AMERICAN EVENTS

PEOPLE IN HISTORY

1879 ■ Frank W. Woolworth. Frank W. Woolworth left his family farm to work as a sales clerk in Watertown, New York. After five years, Woolworth borrowed money to open his Great Five Cent Store, which closed because of its poor location. Woolworth then moved to Lancaster, Pennsylvania, where he opened the world's first five-and-ten cents store. Until his death in 1919, Woolworth continued to open more stores every year, building an international empire.

ACTIVITY: Have students research another business that began in the late 1800s. Then ask students to write a brief history of the company and its founders.

CHAPTER 6

1865–1905
The Second Industrial Revolution

Pullman Sleeping Car

1865 Business and Finance
George Pullman patents a railway sleeping car.

1869 Politics
Uriah Stephens establishes the Knights of Labor, the first major national union.

The first telephone

1876 Science and Technology
Alexander Graham Bell receives a patent for the telephone.

1879 Science and Technology
Thomas Edison uses bamboo fiber in his design for the first long-lasting incandescent lightbulb.

1879 Business and Finance
Frank W. Woolworth establishes the first of the Woolworth chain stores.

Edison's lightbulb

1865

1869 The Arts
Horatio Alger Jr. begins publishing the series *Luck and Pluck.*

1873

1874 Daily Life
Mary Ewing Outerbridge establishes the first American tennis courts, on Staten Island, New York.

1876 The Arts
American artist Winslow Homer paints *The Cotton Pickers.*

1881

Advertisement picturing a Staten Island sports club

The Cotton Pickers *by Winslow Homer*

Build on What You Know

During the first half of the 1800s, both the U.S. population and westward settlement expanded rapidly. This growth was fueled by immigration, industrialization, and the economic opportunities of the frontier. After the Civil War these trends accelerated even more. In this chapter you will learn about the many inventions that began a new age of industrialization in the United States. Poor working conditions in the new industries, however, led many American workers to organize unions to improve their daily lives.

What's Your Opinion?

 To help students create their Themes Journal entries, provide the following examples of appropriate agree/disagree statements.

Economics

Agree In the late 1700s, inventions such as the spinning jenny vastly increased American textile production, in turn leading to economic growth.

Disagree During the Spanish Golden Age, treasure from the Americas propelled Spain's economy.

Science, Technology, and Society

Agree Some women believed that their work in the Lowell mills gave them new economic and personal opportunities.

Disagree The invention of the cotton gin expanded slavery, leading to heightened misery for many African Americans.

Citizenship

Agree In furthering economic growth, business leaders helped widen the middle class, leading to greater equality. In protesting dangerous workplace conditions, labor leaders utilized the right to free speech.

Disagree Some business leaders broke unions, depriving laborers of the right to express themselves in the workplace.

The public humiliation of French army captain Alfred Dreyfus

A steelworker in Andrew Carnegie's largest mill in Pittsburgh, Pennsylvania

exploring the time line

GLOBAL EVENTS

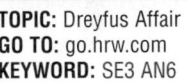

internet connect

TOPIC: Dreyfus Affair
GO TO: go.hrw.com
KEYWORD: SE3 AN6

Have students access the Internet through the HRW Go site to conduct research on the Dreyfus Affair. Then ask students to create one or two political cartoons about the incident. Have students write captions to accompany their political cartoons. Ask volunteers to present their cartoons and their captions to the class.

1884
The Arts
Mark Twain publishes *The Adventures of Huckleberry Finn.*

1890
Politics
The Sherman Antitrust Act is passed, outlawing monopolies and trusts that restrain trade.

1894
World Events
Alfred Dreyfus is convicted of questionable treason charges, leading to political upheaval in France.

1901
Business and Finance
Andrew Carnegie sells his steel company to J. P. Morgan for nearly $500 million.

1889 **1897** **1905**

1886
Politics
1,500 labor strikes erupt in the United States.

1894
Daily Life
The U.S. Congress establishes Labor Day as a national holiday.

1903
Science and Technology
The Wright brothers test their airplane near Kitty Hawk, North Carolina.

1893
Daily Life
The first motorcar to be built in the United States is completed by the Duryea brothers.

The Duryea brothers ride in their horseless carriage.

A strike turns violent in Chicago, Illinois.

What's Your Opinion?

Themes Journal *Do you agree or disagree with the following statements? Support your point of view in your journal.*

Economics The economic growth created by technological innovations is worth its costs.

Science, Technology, and Society New technologies bring social changes and improve people's daily lives.

Citizenship The actions of both American business leaders and labor organizers lead to greater equality and an expansion of democracy.

SECTION 1

After completing Section 1, students should be able to:

OBJECTIVE 1 Describe how the development of steel and oil refining affected U.S. industry.

OBJECTIVE 2 Recount the innovations that were made in transportation.

OBJECTIVE 3 Explain how innovations in communications technology changed business practices and daily life in the United States.

OBJECTIVE 4 Discuss why Thomas Edison wanted to open a research laboratory, and describe how it changed American life.

🔔 LET'S GET STARTED!

Write the names of the following inventions and innovations on the chalkboard: *computers, the Internet, airbags, cell phones,* and *video games.* As students enter the classroom, ask them to pick one or two and write a paragraph describing their importance in Americans' daily lives. Ask volunteers to read their paragraphs aloud. Then tell students that in Section 1 they will learn about the inventions and innovations that transformed Americans' daily lives in the late 1800s.

SECTION 1

READ TO DISCOVER
1. How did the development of steel and oil refining affect U.S. industry?
2. What innovations were made in transportation?
3. How did innovations in communications technology change business practices and daily life in the United States?
4. How did Thomas Edison's research laboratory change American life?

DEFINE
patent
transcontinental railroad
trunk lines
telegraph

IDENTIFY
Bessemer process
Edwin L. Drake
Elijah McCoy
George Westinghouse
Alexander Graham Bell
Thomas Alva Edison
Lewis Latimer

▶ WHY IT MATTERS TODAY
New inventions are still changing our world, and scientists are constantly seeking new sources of energy. Use CNNfyi.com or other **current events** sources to find out about new developments in technology or energy sources. Record your findings in your journal.

CNNfyi.com

The Age of Invention

EYEWITNESSES TO History

"The telephone is a curious device that might fairly find place in the magic of Arabian Tales. Of what use is such an invention? Well, there may be occasions of state when it is necessary for officials who are far apart to talk with each other."

—*New York Tribune* reporter, quoted in *America in 1876,* by Lally Weymouth

Demonstration of sound transmission in 1876

A reporter visiting the 1876 Centennial Exposition in Philadelphia discussed in the *New York Tribune* his amazement at the invention of the telephone. In the years following the Civil War, the United States experienced a wave of scientific discoveries and inventions. Americans celebrated this "age of invention" at the exposition in Philadelphia. Inventors presented new technologies such as the telephone to the public for the first time. The potential impact of these inventions on the future of American business and daily life was uncertain.

Industrial Innovations

From 1865 to 1905 the United States experienced a surge of industrial growth. These years marked the beginning of a Second Industrial Revolution. This new era of industrial transformation began with numerous discoveries and inventions that significantly altered manufacturing, transportation, and the everyday lives of Americans.

Coal and steam made possible the original Industrial Revolution in the United States. Coal-fed steam engines powered factories. These factories in turn produced the goods that generated economic growth. In the late 1800s an abundance of steel helped spur a second period of industrialization. Steel was used in the construction of heavy machinery that mass-produced goods. Steel was also used to build railroad tracks, bridges, and tall city buildings.

Steel. Before the mid-1800s, the process of converting iron ore into steel was too expensive to be used practically. In the 1850s Henry Bessemer in Great Britain and William Kelly in the United States both developed a method of steelmaking that burned off the impurities in molten iron with a blast of hot air. Known as the **Bessemer process,** this method could produce more steel in one day than the older techniques could turn out in one week. American engineer Alexander Holley adapted and improved the Bessemer process. Largely because of this process, American steel production skyrocketed from about 15,000 tons in 1865 to more than 28 million tons by 1910.

The production of steel required iron ore. Barges and steamers carried unprocessed iron ore from the Midwest through the Great Lakes to the southern shores of Lake Michigan and Lake Erie. Cities such as Gary, Indiana; Cleveland, Ohio; and Pittsburgh, Pennsylvania, became major centers for steel manufacturing.

ALL LEVELS: Ask students to define the words *refine* and *refinery*. (*Students might suggest that to refine something is to make it better.*) Ask students how improved refining processes might have affected industrial growth in the late 1800s. (*Students might suggest that improved processes would have fueled economic growth.*) To help students understand how the development of steel and oil refining affected U.S. industry, copy the following graphic organizer on the chalkboard, omitting the italicized answers. Have each student complete it.
English Language Learners

```
                    ┌─────────────────────┐
                    │  Refining Processes │
                    │  in the United States│
                    └─────────────────────┘
              ┌──────────────┴──────────────┐
        ┌─────────┐                    ┌─────────┐
        │  Steel  │                    │   Oil   │
        └─────────┘                    └─────────┘
```

Effects on Industry
- *provided a strong, inexpensive source of building material*
- *allowed the expansion of the railroad industry*
- *allowed the construction of sophisticated machinery, bridges, tall buildings, and so on*

Effects on Industry
- *resulted in the production of kerosene for fuel or light*
- *allowed the manufacturing of other important industrial petroleum products*
- *helped machinery operate*

Coal mined in Pennsylvania and West Virginia provided an inexpensive source of fuel for steel production.

The increased availability of steel in the late 1800s resulted in its widespread industrial use. The railroad industry began replacing iron rails with stronger, longer-lasting steel ones. Builders began to use steel in the construction of bridges and buildings. Using steel to create a skeletal frame in buildings allowed architects to design larger, multistory buildings. Steel's resistance to rust also made it an ideal material for everyday items such as nails and wire.

Oil. Like the advances in steel production, the development of a process to refine oil also affected industrial practices. American Indians and settlers had known of the existence of crude oil for hundreds of years. By the late 1850s, chemists and geologists had made significant progress in developing a process to refine crude oil. With this process, crude oil could be turned into kerosene, which could be burned in lamps to produce light or used as a fuel. Kerosene provided a cheap substitute for whale oil, which had become difficult to acquire.

Noting the growing demand for this inexpensive fuel, **Edwin L. Drake** used a steam engine to drill for oil near Titusville, Pennsylvania, in 1859. The venture seemed so impractical that curious onlookers questioned Drake's sanity, calling the project Drake's Folly. When the oil began to flow at a rate of some 20 barrels a day, however, other prospectors, or "wildcatters," hurried to dig their own wells. Like the California Gold Rush of 1849, the oil boom in western Pennsylvania encouraged prospecting. Prospectors even referred to oil as "black gold." By the 1880s oil wells dotted Ohio, Pennsylvania, and West Virginia. Production topped 25 million barrels of oil in 1880 alone.

Drake's success led others to search for oil. In 1901 a group led by engineer Anthony F. Lucas stuck oil at Spindletop, near Beaumont, Texas. This strike marked the beginning of the Texas oil boom. Oil production there peaked in 1902 at more than 17 million barrels. Nearly 20 percent of the oil produced in the United States that year came from Spindletop. By 1904 its reserves were drained, and it was producing only 10,000 barrels of oil a day.

Although kerosene remained a primary product of oil refining, by 1880 refiners had developed other petroleum products that increased the industrial uses of oil. Refiners developed waxes and lubricating oil for use in new industrial machines. **Elijah McCoy** made a significant contribution to the industrial use of oil. The son of runaway slaves, McCoy invented a lubricating cup that fed oil to parts of a machine while it was running.

Like other inventors, McCoy received a **patent**—a guarantee to protect an inventor's rights to make, use, or sell the invention. McCoy's innovative breakthrough helped many kinds of machines operate more smoothly and quickly.

✔ **READING CHECK: Identifying Cause and Effect** How did the advances in steel production and oil refining affect U.S. industry? Steel and oil production skyrocketed, and many uses were found for each.

INTERPRETING THE VISUAL RECORD

Black gold. Edwin L. Drake, wearing a top hat, visits his oil well drilled in 1859 near Titusville, Pennsylvania. *What materials did Drake use to construct his well?*

PEOPLE IN HISTORY

Elijah McCoy. Elijah McCoy's parents sent him to the University of Edinburgh in Scotland, where he studied to be an engineer. When he returned to the United States with his engineering certification, he could not find a job. Although many companies were looking for engineers, none would hire an African American. McCoy took a job shoveling coal and lubricating machines. Because the machines had to be stopped, lubricated by hand, and then restarted, companies lost production time. McCoy worked for two years, spending his own money and using scrap metal, to create an automatic lubricator. After patenting his invention, McCoy soon improved upon his creation and developed other lubricating devices. He also invented the ironing board, the rubber heel for shoes, and a lawn sprinkler. Others tried to sell their own versions of the automatic lubricator, but buyers knew that McCoy's was the most dependable. Before buying they would ask, "Is this the *real* McCoy?"

ACTIVITY: Have each student write a monologue about some aspect of McCoy's life.

VISUAL RECORD ANSWER

Students might mention wood and iron.

LEVEL 1: Pair students and assign pairs one of the following transportation innovations: the railroad, the automobile, or the airplane. Tell each pair to imagine that it is shortly after the introduction of its assigned innovation. Ask each pair to develop a two- to three-minute dialogue describing the effect of its innovation on Americans' daily lives. *(Pairs should indicate that all three innovations made travel more efficient and brought Americans into closer contact with each other. Railroads promoted western settlement, urban growth, and economic prosperity. Automobiles were largely limited to wealthy Americans. Airplanes offered new transportation possibilities.)*

Have at least three pairs—one representing each of the innovations—perform their dialogues for the class.
English Language Learners, Cooperative Learning

LEVEL 2: Assign students one of the following transportation innovations: the railroad, the automobile, or the airplane. Tell students to imagine that it is shortly after the introduction of their assigned innovation. Have each student write two or three half-page diary entries discussing the effects of his or her assigned innovation on Americans' daily lives. *(See the Level 1 lesson for the correct effects.)* Ask volunteers to read their entries to the class. Students may wish to include their diary entries in their portfolios.

INTERDISCIPLINARY CONNECTIONS

▶BUSINESS◀

Race of the Railroads.

The 1862 Railroad Act established that the transcontinental railroad would be built by two railroad companies: Union Pacific and Central Pacific. Union Pacific began building the railroad west from Omaha, Nebraska. It was to connect eventually with the Central Pacific, which was being constructed east from Sacramento, California. The two companies began a race to build the most rail, since they were paid and given land grants for each mile of track. In 1868, when completion was near, Charles Crocker of Central Pacific advised his partner, Leland Stanford, to "work on as though Heaven were before you and Hell behind you." Together, the two companies were granted more than 30 million acres of land.

CRITICAL THINKING How might the race to the last railroad spike be like other events in U.S. history?

ANSWER: Students might mention the Gold Rush, the settlers' competition for land grants after the Homestead Act, or any other instance of intense competition for economic gain.

Transportation

Innovations in the steel and oil industries led to a surge of advances in the transportation industry. Many of the discoveries during this "age of invention" contributed to the development of new, more technologically advanced forms of transportation.

New technology in the late 1800s resulted in a massive expansion of the American railroad network. Entirely new discoveries laid the groundwork for air flight and the automobile. These developments in transportation made travel much more efficient and brought Americans into closer contact with each other. Railroads linked isolated regions of the country to the rest of the United States.

INTERPRETING THE VISUAL RECORD

Transcontinental railroad. The completion of the first transcontinental railroad in 1869 allowed trains to transport goods and people from coast to coast in a matter of days. *How does this photograph reveal the importance of this moment to U.S. history?*

Railroads. The availability of cheap steel provided by the Bessemer process had a significant impact on railroad expansion. As steel production soared, prices dropped dramatically. Steel that had sold for $100 a ton in 1873 went for $12 a ton by the late 1890s. The availability of cheaper steel encouraged railroad companies to lay thousands of miles of new track.

The rapid increase of railroad lines led to a more efficient network of rail transportation. Prior to the Civil War, most railroads in the United States were short. They averaged some 100 miles in length and primarily served local transportation needs. In 1860, passengers and freight traveling between New York and Chicago, for example, had to change lines 17 times over a period of two days. By the next decade, however, the rapid expansion of rail lines allowed passengers and freight to make the same trip in less than 24 hours without changing trains.

The country's first **transcontinental railroad** was completed in 1869. The project was finished when the Central Pacific and Union Pacific Railroads were joined to create a single rail line from Omaha, Nebraska, to the Pacific Ocean. To celebrate its completion, railroad tycoon Leland Stanford hammered in the last spike at Promontory, Utah. By 1900 almost a half-dozen **trunk lines**, or major railroads, crossed the Great Plains to the Pacific coast. Feeder, or branch, lines connected the trunk lines to outlying areas. This huge railroad grid joined every state and linked remote towns to urban centers.

Additional innovations further improved rail transportation. Bigger, more efficient locomotives made it possible to pull larger loads at faster speeds. **George Westinghouse** developed a compressed-air brake. It increased railroad safety by enabling the locomotive and all its cars to stop at the same time. Granville T. Woods improved Westinghouse's air brake. He also developed a communications system that enabled trains and stations to send and receive messages.

Changes in track design also improved rail service. Double sets of tracks allowed trains traveling in opposite directions to pass each other. Equally important, the adoption in the 1870s of a standard gauge, or width between the rails, made rail transportation faster and cheaper. Passengers and freight no longer had to be transferred from train to train each time they reached a different line.

The growth of railroads had far-reaching consequences. Railroads increased western settlement by making travel affordable and easy. They also stimulated urban growth. Wherever railroads were built, new towns sprang up, and existing towns grew into major cities.

The economic impact of the railroads was immeasurable. For much of the late 1800s, railroad companies provided many of the country's jobs. They also spurred the growth of other industries. The railroad companies' demands for locomotives, rails, and railcars poured money into the steel and railroad-car construction industries. Innovations like refrigerated freight cars helped the development of the meatpacking industry. In addition, the network of railroad lines allowed companies to sell their products nationally. A Pennsylvania steel foundry could obtain iron ore from the Great Lakes region, and a Philadelphia furniture company could sell its products in small midwestern towns.

Railroads also shaped American popular culture and folk music. One ballad immortalized Casey Jones, the Illinois Central engineer killed in a crash with a freight train in 1900. Other songs celebrated famous trains like the Wabash Cannonball.

The horseless carriage.
The innovations in oil refining in the late 1800s led to advances in the development of motors and the creation of a new mode of transportation. The horseless carriage, a self-propelled vehicle and forerunner to the automobile, had originally been developed about 1770. A French artillery officer named Nicolas-Joseph Cugnot had mounted a steam engine to a three-wheeled carriage. The use of steam power for these early automobiles was expensive and inefficient for the small amount of power needed for these carriages.

Efforts to develop a gasoline-powered engine led to the creation of a more practical self-propelled vehicle. Innovations in oil refining led Nikolaus A. Otto to invent the first internal combustion engine powered by gasoline in 1876. In the 1880s ambitious designers in Europe and the United States attempted to use this gasoline engine to power horseless carriages. In 1893 Charles and J. Frank Duryea built the first practical motorcar in the United States.

The 1890s brought further innovations to the horseless carriage. By the turn of the century, more Americans had begun to use the carriages in their daily lives. The use of this new mode of transportation was limited, however, since only wealthy citizens could afford it. Nevertheless, automobile production rapidly became a substantial commercial industry.

Airplanes.
The internal combustion engine also led to advances in flight. Using small gasoline engines, Orville and Wilbur Wright of Dayton, Ohio, developed one of the first working airplanes.

The Wright brothers had experimented with glider designs. They also experimented with engines based on European designs in the mid-1890s. On

INTERPRETING THE VISUAL RECORD

Railroads. The Illinois Central Railroad connected rural Americans with the rest of the world. *What do the various images in this poster represent?*

VISUAL RECORD ANSWER

Students might suggest that the train represents the Illinois Central Railroad, the map represents the United States, and the inset images represent regions of the United States.

VISUAL RECORD ANSWER

(for p. 196)

Students might suggest that people tap it with their fingers.

CHANGING WAYS ANSWERS

(for p. 197)

Students should mention handwritten letters, live theater, hammer, fireplace, and livestock. Students might mention that it would take longer for people to get to their destinations, wash their clothes, or heat their food.

LEVEL 1: Write the names of the following innovations on the chalkboard: *the telegraph, the telephone,* and *the typewriter.* Then pair students and ask each pair to write before-and-after scenarios for the three innovations. Scenarios should describe how the innovations changed both business practices and daily lives. *(Pairs should indicate that the telegraph allowed businesses to place long-distance orders very quickly, as did the telephone. The telegraph allowed the quick production of legible documents. All three innovations brought Americans closer together.)* Have volunteers present their scenarios to the class. Students may wish to include their scenarios in their portfolios.

English Language Learners, Cooperative Learning

LEVEL 2: Tell students to imagine that it is 1884 and that they are businesspeople preparing to retire. Have each student write a one- to two-page memoir describing the impact of the telegraph, the telephone, and the typewriter on his or her business and personal lives. *(See the Level 1 lesson for the correct effects.)* Students may wish to illustrate their memoirs. Have volunteers read their memoirs to the class.

Telegraph Monopolies. In the early days of the telegraph, the six major companies agreed to divide the national market into six regions. By 1866, however, Western Union had consolidated all of the other companies, thereby creating a monopoly. The consolidation allowed Western Union to standardize its rates, equipment, and language, leading to a reduction in telegraph costs. The Associated Press (AP), a group of allied newspapers that used telegraphs to communicate news stories, formed an association with Western Union. This alliance gave the AP control of virtually all the news in the country—a situation that angered owners of smaller newspapers.

CRITICAL THINKING How did the invention of the telegraph affect the development of the United States?

ANSWER: Students might answer that the telegraph united people through shared information.

With experience gained from operating a bicycle shop and experimenting with small engines and gliders, the Wright brothers developed a plane and made the first piloted flight in December 1903.

December 17, 1903, near Kitty Hawk, North Carolina, Orville Wright made the first piloted flight—12 seconds and 120 feet—in a powered plane. He made a statement summing up the significance of the achievement.

History Makers Speak

❝This flight lasted only twelve seconds, but it was, nevertheless, the first in the history of the world in which a machine carrying a man had raised itself by its own power into the air in full flight, had sailed forward without reduction of speed, and had finally landed at a point as high as that from which it started.❞

—Orville Wright, quoted in *A History of Flying,* by C.H. Gibbs-Smith

The Wright brothers' first flight received little public attention or press coverage. However, as word of their achievement spread, a surge of related inventions and patents by other engineers dramatically demonstrated the importance of this new form of transportation.

✔ **READING CHECK: Finding the Main Idea** Describe the innovations that were made in transportation in the late 1800s. first transcontinental railroad completed, internal combustion engines for a motor vehicle and an airplane invented

Communications

Just as developments in transportation made traveling easier and brought people together, innovations in communications technology also brought Americans into closer contact. These advances also furthered the growth of American industry.

INTERPRETING THE VISUAL RECORD

Telegraph. Developed by Samuel F. B. Morse, this telegraph and receiver allowed for communication over long distances with electricity. *Based on these images, how do you think a telegraph would be operated?*

Telegraph. One of the most significant advances in communications in the 1800s was the **telegraph.** Samuel F. B. Morse developed the telegraph as a means of communicating over wires with electricity. The telegraph attracted little attention when Morse filed for a patent on his version in 1837. In time, however, people recognized its business potential. Using Morse's dot-and-dash code, a telegraph operator could send a business order to a distant location in minutes.

By 1866 Western Union, the leading telegraph company, had more than 2,000 telegraph offices. The telegraph grew along with the railroad. Telegraph companies established offices in train stations and strung telegraph wire on poles alongside the railroad lines. Telegraphs sent information for businesses, the government, newspapers, and private citizens.

LEVEL 3: Have students pick one of the following innovations: the telegraph, telephone, or typewriter. Tell students to imagine that they are businesspeople shortly after the widespread introduction of their chosen innovation. Have each student prepare a four-minute speech encouraging his or her manager to adopt the innovation and describing its possible effects. (*See the Level 1 lesson for the correct effects.*) Have at least three students—one for each innovation—deliver their speeches to the class. Students may wish to include the written version of their speeches in their portfolios.

 HOMEWORK *Have each student create a flowchart representing the effects of the telegraph, the telephone, and the typewriter on the development of the United States.*

SPOTLIGHT on Alexander Graham Bell

Pair students and tell them to imagine that it is 1876 and that they are preparing to interview Alexander Graham Bell. Have each student write five interview questions focusing on his contributions to American life. Then have each student exchange his or her list with their partner and answer the questions. Ask volunteers to enact their interviews for the class.
Cooperative Learning, Block Scheduling

NOTE: To help students make meaningful connections between events in U.S. history and those in their own hometown, use the Chapter 6 **Hands-On History Activity**, Technology and You.

Telephone. Patented by **Alexander Graham Bell** in March 1876, the "talking telegraph," or telephone, had an even greater impact. Bell demonstrated his invention at the Philadelphia Centennial Exposition in June 1876. Judges there pronounced it "perhaps the greatest marvel hitherto [thus far] achieved by the electric telegraph." Businesses quickly found the telephone indispensable. By the end of the 1800s more than a million telephones had been installed in American offices and homes. Bell Telephone Company eventually became American Telephone and Telegraph, one of the nation's largest and longest lasting monopolies.

Early telephones required operators to connect callers. Many women filled these new jobs. A former telephone operator described the fast-paced work.

THE GRANGER COLLECTION, NEW YORK

Alexander Graham Bell's invention of the telephone allowed Americans to stay in greater contact.

History Makers Speak
❝On the second floor where the switchboards were located there arose a dull roar like that of locusts on a sunburnt prairie, a sense of many voices without any one being distinguishable. . . . I could see their hands working swiftly, pulling cords out of the holes, jabbing others in. Serving the Thing that signaled them with little flashing lights, making them hurry, hurry.❞

— "Pilgrim's Progress in a Telephone Exchange," quoted in *Life and Labor*, 1921

Analyzing Primary Sources

Drawing Conclusions What is the "Thing" referred to in the quotation? the switchboards

Changing Ways   Technology in Daily Life

■ **Understanding Change** The "age of invention" transformed American life. Much of the technology developed in the late 1800s remains important today. Examine the chart, which compares items used in the mid-1800s and items used today. *What items used in the mid-1800s are still used by some people today? How have their uses changed? How would life today be different without the items in the right column?*

THE GRANGER COLLECTION, NEW YORK

Then

Now

Technology	Then	Now
Energy	firewood	oil, natural gas, nuclear power
Transportation	horse and carriage	automobile
Communication	handwritten letters	Internet
Popular Entertainment	live theater	television, films
Household Appliances	washboard hammer fireplace livestock underground icehouse	washing machine electric drill microwave oven lawnmower refrigerator

Data reflects mid-1800s and 2000.

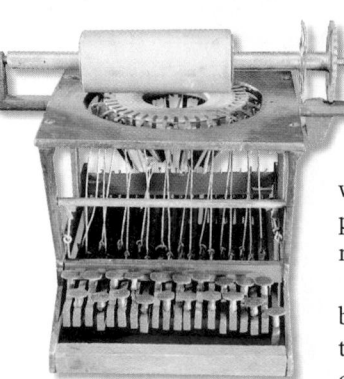

Christopher Sholes's typewriter revolutionized business communication.

Typewriter. Christopher Sholes developed the typewriter in 1867. By allowing users to quickly produce easily legible documents, the typewriter revolutionized communications. Sholes sold his typewriter patent in 1873 to E. Remington & Sons. Although other typewriter designs had preceded Sholes's design, his was the first to be marketed. Sholes's keyboard design, with only a few changes, is still used today in typewriters and computers. Carbon paper, also introduced during this period, allowed users of typewriters to produce multiple copies of a document at the same time.

The invention of the typewriter soon gave rise to the use of typing pools. These business departments were made up of many clerical workers whose main task was to type. Women made up the majority of workers in the typing pools. The pools offered many working-class women the opportunity to move into a skilled profession for the first time. Lillian Sholes, Christopher Sholes's daughter, was probably the first professional female typist. Christopher Sholes was aware of the impact of the typewriter on communications and on the expansion of job opportunities for women. He later wrote, "I feel that I have done something for the women who have always had to work so hard."

✔ **READING CHECK: Identifying Cause and Effect** How did innovations in communications technology affect American women? The invention of the telephone and typewriter created employment opportunities for women.

Science & Technology

Electricity

The late 1800s brought significant advances in the uses of electricity. One such advance was the lightbulb. In simple terms, the lightbulb produces light when electricity flows through a filament that resists that flow. This resistance gives off energy in the form of heat—so much heat that the filament glows, producing light. To prevent the filament from being consumed by the heat, inventors created a vacuum through the use of a glass bulb. This reduces the oxygen around the filament. The bulb was filled with inert gas.

While many inventors experimented with the incandescent lightbulb, Thomas Edison and his team at Menlo Park, New Jersey, made the most significant contributions by finding a filament that would light up without burning up. Edison and his associates discovered in 1880 that carbonized bamboo

fiber could last an average of 600 hours. Eventually filaments made of the element tungsten were used.

tungsten filament

inert gas

glass bulb

Power plants soon arose to supply electricity for lightbulbs in homes and industries. However, electricity could not be transmitted over long distances with direct current (DC) because too much energy was lost in transportation over power lines. Inventor Nikola Tesla patented an alternating current (AC) generator that could produce electricity for transmission over longer distance with less loss of energy. With this advance, the use of electricity spread rapidly.

Understanding Science and History

1. What purposes does the glass bulb serve?
2. How did advances made with electricity affect the development of the United States?

LEVEL 1: Tell students to imagine that it is 1876 and that Thomas Edison has just opened his research laboratory. Ask each student to write three headlines commemorating the event. Students' headlines should also explain why Edison wanted to open the laboratory. *(Headlines should note that Edison hoped to make important and profitable advances in science.)* Then tell students to imagine that it is 1880. Have each student write three headlines on Edison's various inventions and their effects on American life. *(Students should note that Edison's inventions included the lightbulb, the phonograph, and the early motion-picture camera. All transformed American life in various ways.)* Students may wish to include their headlines in their portfolios. **English Language Learners**

LEVELS 2 AND 3: Tell students to imagine that it is 1876 and that Thomas Edison has just opened his research laboratory. Ask each student to write a half-page newspaper article describing the event. Articles should also explain why Edison wanted to open the laboratory. *(See the Level 1 lesson for the correct reasons.)* Then tell students to imagine that it is 1880. Have each student write a half-page newspaper article on Edison's various inventions and their effects on American life. *(See the Level 1 lesson for the correct inventions and their effects.)* Students may wish to include their articles in their portfolios.

Edison and Menlo Park

Thomas Alva Edison was another pioneer of communications technology. His first major invention was a telegraph that could send up to four messages over the same wire simultaneously. Edison's early inventions had a significant impact on telegraphic communications. However, his influence on American life extends well beyond the history of the telegraph. An active innovator, Edison and his fellow researchers made significant discoveries and advances in electricity, lightbulbs, phonographs, and early motion-picture cameras.

BIOGRAPHY

Thomas Edison

Born in a small Ohio town in 1847, Edison received the majority of his schooling at home. He became a newsboy at age 12 and later worked as a telegraph operator. An eager amateur scientist, Edison conducted experiments and read widely in his spare time. In 1869 he patented an electric vote recorder. That year he also received his second patent, for a telegraphic stock ticker. Other inventions followed. In 1876 he went into the "invention business" full-time. He opened a workshop in Menlo Park, New Jersey, where he assembled a team of researchers.

Edison promised that he and his fellow researchers would deliver "a minor invention every ten days and a big thing every six months or so." He kept his word. His researchers invented the phonograph in 1877 and the lightbulb in 1879. Edison also improved Alexander Graham Bell's original design for a telephone transmitter. Edison's design made it possible to send stronger telephone signals, which greatly improved the sound quality. When he died in 1931, the "Wizard of Menlo Park" held more than 1,000 patents. Describing his process of invention to a colleague, Edison explained the secret to his success.

History Makers Speak

"I have the right principle and am on the right track, but time, hard work and some good luck are necessary too. It has been just so in all of my inventions. The first step is an intuition, and [it] comes with a burst, then difficulties arise. . . . Months of intense watching, study and labor are requisite [required] before commercial success or failure is certainly reached.**"**

—Thomas Edison, letter to colleague, November 13, 1878

Edison's work at Menlo Park was a team effort. Some of the most significant contributions to the development of the lightbulb were made not by Edison but by his assistant **Lewis Latimer.** Latimer was also a skilled draftsman. As an expert in patent law, Latimer testified in several court cases to support Edison's patents.

Research on the R⊙M

Free Find: Thomas Edison

After reading about Thomas Edison on the **Holt Researcher CD–ROM,** create a list of the most important of Edison's inventions and explain why each was significant.

INTERPRETING THE VISUAL RECORD

Menlo Park. Thomas Edison's team at Menlo Park developed more than 1,000 patented inventions. *What conclusions can be drawn from this image about the working environment at Menlo Park?*

THE GRANGER COLLECTION, NEW YORK

THAT'S INTERESTING!

Beginning in 1863, Thomas Edison worked at several different telegraph companies in Michigan, Ohio, Indiana, and Tennessee. The reason he worked at so many different companies was that he was repeatedly fired for experimenting with the office equipment without permission and for sometimes being careless in attending to his telegraph responsibilities.

VISUAL RECORD ANSWER

Students might conclude that the working environment was one of teamwork and experimentation.

REVIEW SECTION 1 ANSWERS

1. Define
- patent, p. 193
- transcontinental railroad, p. 194
- trunk lines, p. 194
- telegraph, p. 196

2. Identify
- Bessemer process, p. 192
- Edwin L. Drake, p. 193
- Elijah McCoy, p. 193
- George Westinghouse, p. 194
- Alexander Graham Bell, p. 197
- Thomas Alva Edison, p. 199
- Lewis Latimer, p. 199

3. industry—Bessemer process, Henry Bessemer and William Kelly, helped railroad expansion; transportation—compressed-air brake, George Westinghouse, increased railroad safety; internal-combustion engine, Nikolaus A. Otto, helped develop automobiles; airplane, Orville and Wilbur Wright, encouraged development of air travel; communication—telegraph, Samuel F. B. Morse, provided communication across wide distances; telephone, Alexander Graham Bell, provided communication across wide distances and jobs for women; typewriter, Christopher Sholes, increased print production

4a. More people worked in factories; electricity changed how people worked and played; transportation and communication over long distances brought people closer together.

b. There was no mass media or other method to make the accomplishments widely known.

c. Work became concentrated in urban areas. The railroad and communications industries increased number of jobs and led to greater industrial efficiency.

5. Student letters might explain that working as a team and in a laboratory provides opportunities for funding and for sharing ideas. They might also focus on the light bulb or the photograph.

J. TREGONING & L. H. LATIMER.
GLOBE SUPPORTER FOR ELECTRIC LAMPS.
No. 255,212.   Patented Mar. 21, 1882.

Lewis Latimer developed a globe supporter for the electric lightbulb in 1882.

In 1882 Edison opened one of the world's first electric power plants in New York City. Edison's New York plant used direct current (DC) electricity. This meant that the plant could only deliver electricity to the homes and offices in a very small area surrounding the plant. Despite the initial limitations, New Yorkers marveled at the new advances. One reporter from the *New York Times* explained that with electric lighting in the newspaper's offices, "it seemed almost like writing by daylight."

George Westinghouse and Nikola Tesla made additional advances beginning in the late 1880s. They developed a transformer that could transmit a high-voltage alternating current (AC) over long distances. The development of the alternating current allowed continued expansion of the use of electricity in urban households and industry.

At the 1893 World's Columbian Exposition in Chicago, Illinois, a Westinghouse-Tesla generator powered the twinkling lights outlining the major buildings at night. The electric lights enchanted visitors. They marveled at the "fairyland" and frequently referred to the illuminated exposition as the White City. To many witnesses, it symbolized a transformation of American life. Indeed, by the end of the century, electric lights had begun to replace gaslights. The availability of electrical power also made possible another major change. In many cities, horse-drawn vehicles gave way to electric streetcars.

✔ **READING CHECK: Evaluating** How did the inventions created by Thomas Edison's research laboratory affect daily life? Delivery of electricity to homes and offices was introduced.

SECTION 1 REVIEW

1. Define and explain:
patent
transcontinental railroad
trunk lines
telegraph

2. Identify and explain:
Bessemer process
Edwin L. Drake
Elijah McCoy
George Westinghouse
Alexander Graham Bell
Thomas Alva Edison
Lewis Latimer

3. Categorizing Copy the graphic organizer below. Use it to list and describe the various innovations that affected industry, transportation, and communications in the late 1800s.

Industry		
Inventions	Inventors	Effects

Transportation		
Inventions	Inventors	Effects

Communications		
Inventions	Inventors	Effects

4. **Finding the Main Idea**
a. How did American daily life change after the Second Industrial Revolution?
b. Why might important breakthroughs such as the telegraph or the Wright brothers' flight have attracted so little attention or recognition at the time they occurred?
c. How did innovations in industry, transportation, and communications affect the nature of work in American society?

5. **Writing and Critical Thinking**
Drawing Conclusions Imagine that you are an inventor working in Edison's Menlo Park laboratory. Write a letter to your family describing your job.
Consider:
• aspects of working on your own
• an invention you might have helped create
• how your work builds on earlier innovations

Homework Practice Online
keyword: SE3 HP6

After completing Section 2, students should be able to:

OBJECTIVE 1 Describe the arguments that business leaders and social critics made about government's role in business.

OBJECTIVE 2 Recount how business strategies changed during the Second Industrial Revolution.

OBJECTIVE 3 Discuss how entrepreneurs took advantage of changes in business organization.

OBJECTIVE 4 Explain how new methods of marketing products changed American life.

🔔 LET'S GET STARTED!

Write the following words on the chalkboard: *luck* and *pluck*. As students enter the classroom, ask them to define the terms. *(Students should define* luck *as good chance and* pluck *as being persistent.)* Have volunteers share their definitions. Then tell students that many business leaders of the late 1800s and early 1900s attributed their successes to a combination of luck and pluck. Tell students that in Section 2 they will learn more about these business leaders.

SECTION ②

READ TO DISCOVER

1. What arguments did business leaders and social critics make about the role of government in business?
2. How did business strategies change during the Second Industrial Revolution?
3. How did entrepreneurs take advantage of changes in business organization?
4. How did new methods of marketing products change American life?

DEFINE

capitalism
free enterprise
communism
social Darwinism
corporation
trust
monopoly
vertical integration
horizontal integration

IDENTIFY

Horatio Alger Jr.
Andrew Carnegie
John D. Rockefeller
Cornelius Vanderbilt
George Pullman

▶WHY IT MATTERS TODAY

The U.S. government still works to prevent unfair trusts, monopolies, and other illegal business practices that reduce healthy competition. Use CNNfyi.com or other **current events** sources to find out about recent investigations and court cases dealing with possible unfair business practices. Record your findings in your journal.

CNNfyi.com

The Rise of Big Business

EYEWITNESSES TO History

❝*Eureka! We have found it. Here was something new to all of us, for none of us had ever received anything but from toil.*❞

—Andrew Carnegie, quoted in *The Andrew Carnegie Reader*, edited by Joseph Frazier Wall

Certificate of business investment

Young Andrew Carnegie recalled his excitement after receiving his first payment of profits from investments. Carnegie was working as a private secretary to a railroad executive when he invested borrowed money in a company called Adams Express. Soon he began investing in the railroad and iron industries. Within a few years Carnegie's wise investments had made him a wealthy man.

A New Capitalist Spirit

The United States operated under an economic system known as **capitalism**, in which private business run most industries, and competition determines how much goods cost and workers are paid. In the late 1800s, entrepreneurs, or risk-taking businesspeople, set out to gain economic wealth by building industries that took advantage of the era's new technological advances. Many of these industries made enormous profits. With the rapid increase in business ventures and wealth, new ideas began to emerge that would transform traditional business practices.

Business leaders shared an American ideal of self-reliant individualism. During the Second Industrial Revolution, **Horatio Alger Jr.** published a popular series of novels that reflected the increasing importance placed on individualism. These novels, such as those in the 1869 *Luck and Pluck* series, were typically based on a rags-to-riches theme. Poor children improve their social and financial status through hard work and self-motivation. Like Alger's characters, many American business leaders attributed their success to their work ethic. A high regard for self-reliance led many leaders to support the ideal of laissez-faire capitalism. *Laissez-faire* means "to let people do as they choose." The theory of laissez-faire capitalism calls for no government intervention in the economy. Most business leaders believed that the economy would prosper if businesses were left free from government regulation and allowed to compete in a free market. This idea is sometimes called **free enterprise**. In a free-market economy, supply, demand, and profit margin determine what and how much businesses produce. These entrepreneurs argued that any government regulation would only serve to reduce individuals' prosperity and self reliance.

Critics respond. Some critics of this theory argued that the rapid industrialization of factory life was harmful and unjust to the working class. This view of capitalism

---

SECTION ② RESOURCES

REPRODUCIBLE
▶ Guided Reading Strategy 6.2
▶ American History Political Cartoon 17: The Power of Trusts
▶ Geography Activity 6: Pullman's Company Town
▶ Primary Source Reading 6: The First Department Store
▶ Biography Reading 6: Frank Woolworth

TECHNOLOGY
▶ One-Stop Planner, Lesson 6.2
▶ The American Nation Video Program Segment: The Standard Oil Company; Teacher's Guide, pp. 81–86
▶ Holt Researcher: American History CD–ROM
▶ Homework Practice Online

REINFORCEMENT, REVIEW, AND ASSESSMENT
▶ Section 2 Review, p. 208
▶ Daily Quiz 6.2
▶ Main Idea Activity 6.2
▶ English Audio Summary 6.2
▶ Spanish Audio Summary 6.2

ALL LEVELS: Ask students if, at present, the federal government has any role in business. (*Students should indicate that the federal government regulates businesses and, at times, assists them in various ways.*) Ask students if they approve of this involvement. (*Students' answers will vary.*) To help students understand how business leaders and social critics of the late 1800s and early 1900s regarded government involvement, copy the following graphic organizer on the chalkboard, omitting the italicized answers, and have each student complete it. After students have done so, ask them to re-evaluate their original answers based on information in their graphic organizers. **English Language Learners**

Business Leaders
- *argued that individuals should be self-reliant*
- *argued that businesses would prosper in the absence of government interference*
- *argued that government interference would reduce self-reliance*

ARGUMENTS REGARDING GOVERNMENT'S ROLE IN BUSINESS

Social Critics
- *argued that factory life and poor working conditions harmed worker*
- *argued that all citizens shou own all means of production*
- *argued that government assistance would prevent the best businesses from rising to the top*

HISTORY MAKERS SPEAK

Lester Ward in *Social Darwinism in American Thought*

Critique of Social Darwinism. Although some businessmen and philosophers subscribed to theories of social Darwinism, others were against it. Sociologist Lester Ward argued for a separation of natural law and social theory. Because Ward had grown up in poverty and observed the capabilities of those around him, he believed that poverty was not a clear indication of a person's inferiority. He argued that biological theories did not apply to the social world: "The fundamental principle of biology is natural selection, that of sociology is artificial selection. The survival of the fittest is simply the survival of the strong, which implies and would better be called the destruction of the weak. If nature progresses through the destruction of the weak, man progresses through protection of the weak."

CRITICAL THINKING In what two ways might Ward define "progresses" in the last sentence?

ANSWER: Students might indicate that for nature progress entails the survival of the strongest and most fit. For society, however, progress seems defined by humane actions rather than competitive success.

Charles Darwin never expected his scientific theories of biology to be applied to social issues.

Research on the R⊙M

Free Find:
Andrew Carnegie
After reading about Andrew Carnegie on the Holt Researcher CD–ROM, write a short essay about his values. Be sure to discuss Carnegie's work ethic and philanthropy.

was most forcefully argued in the mid-1800s by Karl Marx, a German philosopher. Marx proposed a political system that would remove the inequalities of wealth. He developed a political theory, later called Marxism, that called for the overthrow of the capitalist economic system.

Marx argued that capitalism allowed the bourgeoisie (boohzh-wah-ZEE)—the people who own the means of production—to take advantage of the proletariat, or the workers. He also suggested that a new society could be formed on principles of **communism**. This theory proposes that individual ownership of property should not be allowed. In a communist state, property and the means of production are owned by everyone in the community. The community in turn ideally provides for the needs of all the people equally without regard to social rank.

Social Darwinism. American businesspeople also responded to some of the same concerns Marx raised about the working class. These business leaders began to embrace the emerging theory of **social Darwinism**. Originally proposed by English social philosopher Herbert Spencer, social Darwinism adapted the ideas of Charles Darwin's biological theory of natural selection and evolution. Social Darwinists argued that society progressed through natural competition. The "fittest" people, businesses, or nations should and would rise to positions of wealth and power. The "unfit" would fail. Following the law of the "survival of the fittest," social Darwinists believed that any attempts to help the poor or less capable actually slowed social progress. "Nature's cure for most social and political diseases is better than man's," wrote American educator and philosopher Nicholas Murray Butler.

Some religious leaders offered religious support for social Darwinism by suggesting that great wealth was a sign of Christian virtue. Baptist minister Russell H. Conwell declared, "You ought to get rich, and it is your duty to get rich. . . . To make money honestly is to preach the gospel."

✔ **READING CHECK: Contrasting** What are the differences between the theories of free enterprise, communism, and social Darwinism? Free enterprise: no government regulation; communism: no individual ownership of property; and social Darwinism: society progresses through natural competition

The Corporation

In the late 1800s changes took place in the way businesses were organized. At the close of the Civil War, businesses typically consisted of small companies owned by individuals, families, or two or more people in a partnership. These traditional business organizations proved unable to manage some of the giant new industries such as oil, railroads, or steel. Nor could these organizations raise the money needed to fund such industries. Business leaders therefore turned to another form of business organization—the **corporation**. Corporations had existed in one form or another since colonial times. In a corporation, organizers raise money by selling shares of stock, or certificates of ownership, in the company. Stockholders—those who buy the shares—receive a percentage of the corporation's profits, known as dividends.

Giving advice to a group of young men, steel baron **Andrew Carnegie** urged them to invest in stocks as he had. He suggested, "If any of you have saved as much as $50 or $100 I do not know any branch of business into which you cannot plunge at once." Although stockholders could earn large profits from the companies, they played little or no part in the corporation's daily operations. One corporate

LEVEL 1: Pair students and ask pairs to list new forms of business strategies that emerged from the Second Industrial Revolution. (*Pairs should name the corporation, the trust, and the monopoly.*) Write responses on the chalkboard, along with the following entrepreneurs' names: *Andrew Carnegie, John D. Rockefeller, Cornelius Vanderbilt, George Westinghouse,* and *George Pullman.* Ask each pair to write topic sentences explaining how the entrepreneurs took advantage of changes in business organization. Pairs should write one

sentence for each entrepreneur. (*Pairs should indicate that Carnegie created corporations and used vertical integration to dominate the steel industry. Rockefeller also created corporations and used horizontal integration to dominate the oil industry. Vanderbilt bought and consolidated many railroad lines. Westinghouse introduced and controlled a crucial railroad innovation, and Pullman controlled the passenger-railroad-car industry.*) Ask volunteers to read their sentences to the class. Students may wish to include their sentences in their portfolios.
English Language Learners, Cooperative Learning

---

executive described owning shares of stock as simply representing "nothing more than good will and prospective [future] profits."

A corporation has several advantages over partnerships and family-owned businesses. First, a corporation's organizers can raise large sums of money by selling stock to many people. Second, unlike small-business owners, stockholders enjoy limited liability. In other words, they are not responsible for the corporation's debt. Finally, a corporation is a stable organization because it is not dependent on a specific owner or owners for its existence. A corporation continues to exist no matter who owns the stock. Moreover, the public ownership and trading of stock provides another source of income for entrepreneurs. For example, a former New York grocery clerk named Jay Gould later became a successful stock market manager. Gould earned an estimated $77 million just from trading railroad stock.

Corporations, however, needed more than organizational stability to deal with the economic climate of the late 1800s. Where competition was fierce, prices and profits tended to rise and fall wildly. Some corporations responded by forming trusts. In a **trust**, a group of companies turn control of their stock over to a common board of trustees. The trustees then run all of the companies as a single enterprise. This practice limits overproduction and other inefficient business practices by reducing competition in an industry. If a trust gains exclusive control of an industry, it holds a **monopoly**. With little or no competition, a company with a monopoly has almost complete control over the price and quality of a product.

✔ **READING CHECK: Analyzing Information** What are the advantages of a corporation? It can raise large sums of money by selling stock, its stockholders have limited liability, and it is not dependent on a specific owner or owners for its existence.

Carnegie and Steel

Steel leader Andrew Carnegie was a master at utilizing these new business strategies. Carnegie began life in humble surroundings. He was born in 1835 in the attic of a small one-story house in Dunfermline, Scotland. His father was a weaver in the textile industry. In 1848, at the age of 12, Carnegie immigrated to the United States. That same year, Carnegie began his first job, working at a cotton mill, winding thread onto bobbins, or spools, for $1.20 a week.

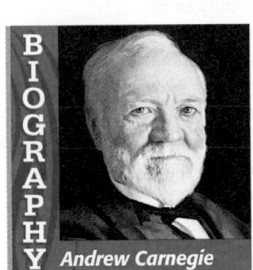
BIOGRAPHY *Andrew Carnegie*

At age 17, Carnegie took a job as a private secretary to a railroad company superintendent. He quickly advanced to a management position. Saving money from his earnings and borrowing from others, Carnegie began to invest in stock in numerous ventures such as bridges, iron, oil, railroads, and telegraph lines. These early investments further inspired Carnegie's entrepreneurial interest and provided the capital that allowed him to invest in the steel industry.

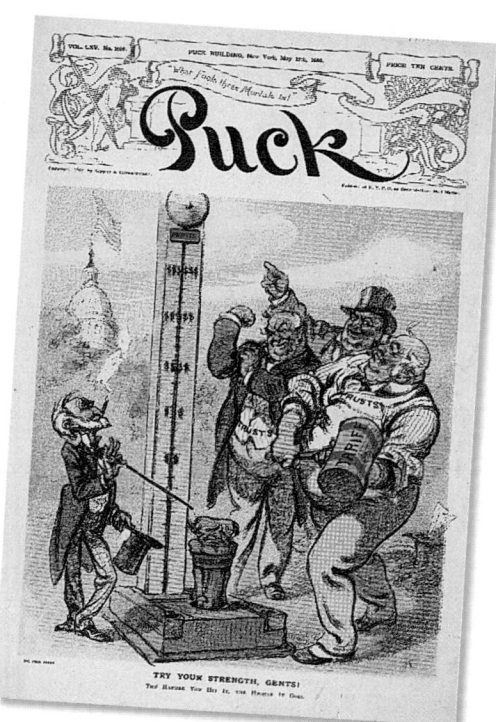

INTERPRETING THE VISUAL RECORD

Trusts. Many Americans grew tired of trusts and the control over the prices and quality of goods the companies could have. *How are trusts represented in this image? How does this reflect Americans' suspicions of trusts?*

LEVEL 2: Tell students to imagine that they are modern-day historians preparing to write entries for an encyclopedia on the Second Industrial Revolution. Have each student create a detailed outline describing how business strategies changed during the Second Industrial Revolution and the ways in which entrepreneurs took advantage of those new strategies. *(See the Level 1 lesson for the correct strategies and methods.)* Ask two or three volunteers to copy their outlines onto the chalkboard. Then conduct a debate on the material presented in the outlines. Do students regard vertical and horizontal integration and trusts and monopolies as fair?

LEVEL 3: Tell students to imagine that they are modern-day historians preparing to write entries for an encyclopedia on the Second Industrial Revolution. Have each student write a one to two page entry describing the business strategies that arose during this and the ways in which entrepreneurs took advantage of those new strategies. *(See the Level 1 lesson for the correct strategies and methods.)* Ask two or three volunteers to read their entries to the class. Then conduct a debate on the material presented in the entries. Do students regard vertical and horizontal integration and trusts and monopolies as fair?

 HOMEWORK *Distribute Cartoon 17, The Power of Trusts, from* **American History Political Cartoons**, *and have each student complete the attached questions and activity.*

Andrew Carnegie. After the sale of his company, Carnegie turned his attention to philanthropy. His first task was to establish free public libraries. He provided funds for almost 3,000 buildings for libraries in English-speaking countries, some 1,900 of them in the United States alone. Carnegie gave money to establish pension funds for his former steelworkers and for college professors. He also created four foundations as a way to help bring about world peace: the Carnegie Endowment for International Peace, the Carnegie Hero Fund, the Church Peace Union, and the Simplified Spelling Board. The latter foundation was established because Carnegie believed that if English spellings were more phonetic, English could become the universal language "for the promotion of international understanding."

CRITICAL THINKING What contributions to American society did Andrew Carnegie make?

ANSWER: Students might answer that public libraries he funded helped people learn; pension plans helped people save for their future; and his foundations worked for world peace.

The Religious Spirit

PHILANTHROPY AND THE GOSPEL OF WEALTH

During the late 1800s, many people began to see a relationship between religious values and earning great wealth. In fact, many supporters of free enterprise believed that accumulating great wealth was a sign of God's blessing, in spite of the sometimes ruthless business practices that might be used to gain that wealth. Nevertheless, these supporters were compelled by their religious values to believe that the power and wealth they accumulated must be used responsibly to better society. This philosophy became known as the Gospel of Wealth.

In his essay "The Gospel of Wealth," Andrew Carnegie insisted that the wealthy had a solemn obligation to use their riches for the advancement of society. In Carnegie's view the rich had been chosen to serve as "stewards of wealth."

"The man who dies . . . rich," Carnegie argued, "dies disgraced." He believed that the rich had a responsibility to give their wealth to society before their death. Like many social Darwinists, Carnegie believed that giving aid directly to the poor would increase the poor's dependency on others. The best way to help the poor, he said, was "to place within [their] reach the ladders upon which the aspiring can rise." Carnegie's "ladders" included universities and libraries. ■

Carnegie Library in Pittsburgh

Carnegie entered the iron and steel business in the early 1860s. He understood little about making steel, but he knew how to run an iron business. Carnegie hired the best people in the steel industry and fitted his plants with the most modern machinery.

Carnegie's real success, however, lay in reducing production costs. Carnegie realized that by buying supplies in bulk and producing goods in large quantities he could lower production costs and increase profits. This principle is known as economies of scale. To control costs, Carnegie also used **vertical integration**—that is, he acquired companies that provided the materials and services upon which his enterprises depended. For example, Carnegie purchased iron and coal mines, which provided the raw materials necessary to run his steel mills. He also bought steamship lines and railroads to transport these materials. An admirer explained the great advantages of this approach.

 "From the moment these crude stuffs were dug out of the earth until they flowed in a stream of liquid steel in the ladles, there was never a price, profit, or royalty paid to an outsider."

—Andrew Carnegie admirer, quoted in *Who Built America?*, edited by Joshua Freeman

Because Carnegie controlled businesses at each stage of production, he could sell steel at a much lower price than his competitors.

In 1899 Carnegie organized all of his companies into the Carnegie Steel Company. It dominated the steel industry. In 1901 Carnegie sold his company to banker J. P. Morgan for nearly $500 million. Carnegie retired as the world's richest man. Although he gained great wealth, money was not his only motivation. Through hard work, simple living, and large philanthropic, or charitable, donations, Carnegie also sought to be viewed as a virtuous citizen. Describing his philosophy as the "Gospel of Wealth," Carnegie insisted that the rich were morally obligated to manage their wealth in a way that benefited their fellow citizens. He explained this belief.

 "This, then, is held to be the duty of the man of wealth: To set an example of modest, unostentatious [simple] living, shunning display or extravagance . . . the man of wealth thus becoming the mere trustee and agent for his poorer brethren. . . . In bestowing [giving] charity, the main consideration should be to help those who will help themselves; . . . to give those who desire to rise the aids by which they may rise."

—Andrew Carnegie, quoted in *The Andrew Carnegie Reader*, edited by Joseph Frazier Wall

Carnegie donated more than $350 million to charity. Much of this money was used to establish public libraries and other institutions that allowed individuals to improve their lives.

Rockefeller and Oil

The business career of tycoon **John D. Rockefeller**, one founder of the Standard Oil Company, followed a course similar to Andrew Carnegie's. After earning a small fortune in the wholesale food business, Rockefeller entered the growing oil-refining industry in 1863. During its early years, the oil-refining industry was composed of numerous small, fiercely competitive companies. Arguing that such competition was inefficient, Rockefeller set out to gain control of the industry.

Like Carnegie, Rockefeller used vertical integration to make his company more competitive. He acquired barrel factories, oil fields, oil-storage facilities, pipelines, and railroad tanker cars. By owning companies that contributed to each stage of oil refining, Rockefeller was able to sell his oil for a cheaper price than his competitors. His main method of expansion was called **horizontal integration**—one company's control of other companies producing the same product. Standard Oil tried to control the oil refineries it could not buy, establishing one of the nation's first trusts in the early 1880s.

To drive his competitors out of business, Rockefeller made deals with suppliers and transporters to receive cheaper supplies and freight rates. George Rice, a small oil refiner driven out of business by Rockefeller's practices, complained to the U.S. Industrial Commission in 1899.

History Makers Speak

❝I have been driven from pillar to post, from one railway line to another, for twenty years, in the absolutely vain endeavor [wasted attempt] to get equal and just freight rates with the Standard Oil Trust, . . . but which I have been utterly unable to do. I have had to consequently shut down, with my business absolutely ruined.❞

—George Rice, U.S. Industrial Land Commission, 1899

INTERPRETING THE VISUAL RECORD

Standard Oil. Oil towns like this one in Pennsylvania became more common as Standard Oil grew. *How did the expansion of the oil industry alter the landscape in this photograph?*

Rockefeller forced most of his rivals to sell out. By 1880 the Standard Oil Company controlled some 90 percent of the country's petroleum-refining capacity. Despite his sometimes ruthless business practices, Rockefeller, like Carnegie, gave generously to various charities. He also supported the arts, created a medical institute, and gave more than $80 million to the University of Chicago. During his lifetime, Rockefeller donated approximately $550 million to philanthropic causes.

The Railroad Giants

Andrew Carnegie and John D. Rockefeller profited greatly from technological innovations in the steel and oil-refining industries, respectively. Other entrepreneurs built large fortunes by capitalizing on the booming railroad industry.

LEVEL 1: Write the following phrases on the chalkboard: *the creation of a consumer culture, department stores, catalogs,* and *chain stores.* Pair students and have each pair write a paragraph describing how these developments and items changed American life during the late 1800s and early 1900s. *(Paragraphs should indicate that the creation of a consumer culture strengthened economic growth during the period. Department stores and chain stores gave women a new place to work and shop, while catalogs gave rural residents access to a variety of goods.)* Ask volunteers to read their paragraphs to the class. **English Language Learners, Cooperative Learning**

LEVEL 2: Tell students to imagine that it is 1885 and that they work at a new advertising agency that has just landed a new industry account. Have each student create two or three advertisements that present new marketing methods and describe the ways in which the methods have changed American life. *(See the Level 1 lesson for the correct methods and changes.)* Students might create an advertisement for a national catalog, for example, or a national department store. Have volunteers present their advertisements to the class. Students may wish to include their advertisements in their portfolios. **English Language Learners**

THAT'S INTERESTING!

Wealthy families often showed off their riches at extravagant parties. At one Vanderbilt dinner party, guests found a trough filled with sand in the middle of the dining room table. Each guest received a sterling silver pail and shovel and were allowed to dig in the sand, where they found loose diamonds, emeralds, and rubies.

SKILL-BUILDING STRATEGIES ANSWERS

Practicing the Skill

1. Competition between various small companies was inefficient.

2. vertical and horizontal integration, deals for cheaper supplies

3. Carnegie Steel Company dominated the industry, and Carnegie sold the company for nearly $500 million.

4. It led to the establishment of many public libraries and other institutions. His business practices made him wealthy, which allowed him to contribute to charity.

5. Answers will vary. Students might answer that Carnegie's charitable contributions were beneficial. Others might argue that his business practices were unfair.

VISUAL RECORD ANSWER

(for p. 207)

Students might suggest that farm images appear wholesome and healthy.

Skill-Building Strategies

Evaluating Historical Actions

Students of history routinely evaluate the actions of individuals and groups. To *evaluate* is to make a judgment about the significance, worth, or desirability of something. An evaluation of a historical action should be based on the range of choices available to the historical actor as well as on the effects the action had on an individual or society.

How to Evaluate a Historical Action

1. **Establish the context.** When you encounter an action that requires evaluation, identify the historical setting and the specific steps through which the action was completed. Make sure that you understand the assumptions and the goals of the individual or group that took the action.

2. **Determine the outcome.** Once you have established the context of the action, determine its results. Make sure that you recognize any unintended consequences or long-term effects of the action.

3. **Consider alternative courses of action.** Identify other courses of action that the individual or group could have taken. Then assess the potential advantages and disadvantages of these alternatives.

4. **Evaluate the action.** Use your analysis of the action, along with your consideration of possible alternatives, to make a judgment about its value and significance.

Applying the Skill

Review the material in this section on Andrew Carnegie and the steel industry. As you do so, evaluate the business practices that Carnegie and his Carnegie Steel Company employed.

Practicing the Skill

Answer the following questions.

1. What were Carnegie's assumptions and goals concerning the steel industry?
2. What business practices did Carnegie employ at Carnegie Steel?
3. What were the results of Carnegie's business practices?
4. What impact did Carnegie's "Gospel of Wealth" philosophy have on American life? How did his business practices contribute to his philanthropy?
5. What is your evaluation of Carnegie's contributions to American society?

Cornelius Vanderbilt's railroad investments brought him power and wealth.

THE GRANGER COLLECTION, NEW YORK

Vanderbilt. **Cornelius Vanderbilt** was a pioneer of the railroad industry. Prior to the Civil War, Vanderbilt operated a profitable shipping business. When the war disrupted water traffic, he invested more in railroads. By 1869, just four years after the war's end, Vanderbilt had gained control over the New York Central Railroad and two other lines that connected the Central with New York City. He continued to add to his railroad holdings. Soon he controlled lines between Chicago, Cleveland, New York, and Toledo.

Vanderbilt extended his railroad system by purchasing smaller lines. He then combined them to make direct routes between urban centers. By providing more efficient service, Vanderbilt took advantage of the growing demand for rail transportation. At the time of his death in 1877, Vanderbilt controlled more than 4,500 miles of railroad track. His personal fortune was estimated at $100 million.

Westinghouse. George Westinghouse made a large fortune in the railroad industry. In 1869, at the age of 23, Westinghouse established the Westinghouse Air Brake Company. He hoped to capitalize on his invention, the compressed-air brake. The air brake was an important safety feature for the railroad industry. The brake made it possible for trains to haul more cars and to travel at greater speeds.

LEVEL 3: Tell students to imagine that they are modern-day historians studying the marketing methods and advertising used in the late 1800s and early 1900s. Have each student create a design for an artifact from that period. Students might draw a detailed illustration of a catalog, for example, or a department-store display window. Then have each student write three or four paragraphs describing how that artifact—and the method or form that it represented—changed American life. *(See the Level 1 lesson for the correct methods and changes.)* Students may wish to include their designs and their paragraphs in their portfolios.

SPOTLIGHT
on George Pullman and Company Towns

Ask students to conduct research on George Pullman and his company town. Then have each student complete one of the following activities: write a short biography of Pullman, create an annotated map of Pullman's community, or write a script for a tour of the town. Have volunteers present their work to the class. Then conduct a debate on the concept of company towns. Do such towns represent corporate paternalism or corporate generosity? Would students themselves want to live in a company town? Would they feel differently if they had been alive in the 1880s? **Block Scheduling**

Railroad investors were initially skeptical of the air brake. Vanderbilt ridiculed the invention as trying to "stop a train with wind." After several dramatic public demonstrations, Westinghouse's business grew. Within five years of his invention, more than 7,000 passenger cars were equipped with the compressed-air brake.

Pullman. One of the most successful railroad giants was **George Pullman**. He designed and manufactured railroad cars that made long-distance rail travel more comfortable. Pullman created a massive passenger-railroad-car industry. His factories built sleeping cars, dining cars, and luxurious cars for wealthy passengers. With an increasing demand for his sleeping cars, Pullman decided to build a new factory south of Chicago in 1880.

Disturbed by the poor conditions of city life, Pullman set out to create a company town. He hoped that it would encourage educated, healthy, peaceful, and virtuous workers. Pullman built a planned community next to his factory. The town offered Pullman's employees and their families clean, well-built homes, shops, a church, a library, a theater, medical and legal offices, and an athletic field. Pullman strictly controlled daily life in the company town, causing dissatisfaction to grow among many of the workers. Expressing a common feeling of the residents, economist Richard Ely proclaimed in 1884 that Pullman's town represented a "benevolent [kindly], well-wishing feudalism, which desires the happiness of the people, but in such a way as shall please the authorities."

The company town of Pullman, Illinois, contained or sold everything the company thought workers should need.

✔ READING CHECK: Comparing How did new corporate practices contribute to the rise of big business? Vertical integration, horizontal integration, and technological innovations in various industries helped big business grow.

Mass Marketing

Industrialists knew that using new inventions, cutting production costs, and reducing competition were not the only ways to increase profits. They also developed new methods of marketing to sell their products.

Marketing products. With the rapid growth of manufacturing, companies developed new ways of persuading consumers to purchase their products. Brand names and packaging played important roles in promoting goods. For example, the name "Standard Oil" conveyed the idea that the company's product set the industry standard. Other companies used brightly colored packages or unique logos to set their products apart.

Companies also used advertising to promote their products. Magazines, newspapers, and roadside billboards carried advertisements urging people to buy "the Purest" soap or telephones "warranted to work *one mile*, unaffected by changes in the weather."

INTERPRETING THE VISUAL RECORD

Advertising. During the late 1800s manufacturers began to use advertisements like this one to entice customers to buy their products. ***Why were these images chosen for this product?***

ECONOMICS

Collectibles and Contests. Advertisers in the late 1800s adopted methods still used today. To improve brand loyalty, manufacturers gave away trading cards with their product's name. To increase readership, magazines offered cash prizes to readers who created the best advertisement for a product featured in the magazine. The contest announcements also encouraged readers to try the product. One contest announcement urged, "*Try Ribbon Dental Cream, if you are not already using it. . . . Our advice is not to write [the ad] until you really believe every word that you write.*"

ACTIVITY: Have students create an advertisement to attract fans to the school's next sporting event.

VISUAL RECORD ANSWER
(for p. 208)
Students might mention activity and consumption.

SECTION
REVIEW ② ANSWERS

1. Define
- capitalism, p. 201
- free enterprise, p. 201
- communism, p. 202
- social Darwinism, p. 202
- corporation, p. 202
- trust, p. 203
- monopoly, p. 203

REVIEW

Have students complete the **Section 2 Review** on p. 208.

ASSESS

Have students complete **Daily Quiz 6.2.** As **Alternative Assessment**, you may want to use the Second Industrial Revolution outline or the marketing-method artifact in this section's lessons.

RETEACH

Have students complete **Main Idea Activity for English Language Learners and Special-Needs Students 6.2.** Then assign students subsections of Section 2. Ask each student to summarize the assigned subsection and to write five questions and answers on the material. Collect students' questions and use them to quiz the class. **English Language Learners**

EXTEND

Have students conduct research on Cornelius Vanderbilt. Then ask students to study the political cartoon on p. 206, which portrays Vanderbilt and his business activities. Have each student write a half-page analysis explaining whether their research supports Vanderbilt's depiction in the cartoon. Then have students create their own cartoons depicting Vanderbilt and based on their research. Ask students to present their cartoons to the class. Then, as a class, choose the most effective cartoon. Have students explain and justify their selections. **Block Scheduling**

- vertical integration, p. 204
- horizontal integration, p. 205

2. Identify
- Horatio Alger Jr., p. 201
- Andrew Carnegie, p. 202
- John D. Rockefeller, p. 205
- Cornelius Vanderbilt, p. 206
- George Pullman, p. 207

3. Carnegie—used vertical integration to revolutionize steel production; Rockefeller—used horizontal integration to expand his oil company; Vanderbilt—extended railroad system by buying small lines and making direct routes between cities; Westinghouse—revolutionized railroad industry with the air brake; Pullman—created comfortable passenger cars

4a. Business leaders opposed government intervention in the economy, as did social Darwinists. Other social critics believed that government should correct social inequalities.

b. Answers should mention that both used competitive and sometimes ruthless business practices. Both also gave much of their money to charitable institutions.

c. Rural residents were able to buy some products via catalog. Department stores provided a variety of goods at lower prices.

5. Brochures should explain how the company will make money and how it is positioned to take advantage of future conditions.

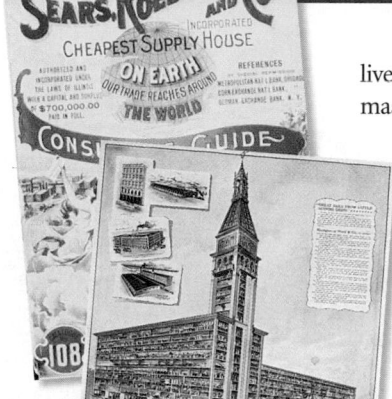

INTERPRETING THE VISUAL RECORD

Marketing. Mail-order companies offered goods such as clothing, farm equipment, furniture, and musical instruments. *What ideas do these catalog covers convey?*

This increase in the use of advertising and brand names helped create a new, lively consumer culture in the United States. The expansion of manufacturing and mass marketing transformed the daily lives of many Americans, even those outside the large urban centers who gained access to new products.

Products such as Ruthstein steel-soled shoes and the Scotch Knocker horse collar were advertised to farmers through local newspapers, mail-order publications, and special catalogs that catered to the rural market. Mail-order companies like Montgomery Ward and Sears, Roebuck, and Co. offered a seemingly endless variety of goods. Customers selected goods from a catalog, then ordered, paid for, and received the merchandise by mail.

The department store. In cities, new types of stores that sold a variety of goods were created to cater to the demands of the urban market. Department stores carried a wide variety of products under one roof. Pioneered by business leaders such as John Wanamaker in Philadelphia, Marshall Field in Chicago, and R. H. Macy in New York City, department stores bought products in bulk and could therefore offer low prices to consumers.

Department stores became the special domain of women, both as places to work and as places to shop. Wanting to create a homelike and welcoming atmosphere in their stores, department-store owners hired young women to work as clerks. Department-store advertisements also targeted women as customers.

Like department stores, chain stores—stores with branches in many cities—bought goods in large quantities. They then passed on their savings to customers. Perhaps the most famous chain store was founded by Frank W. Woolworth in 1879. By 1900 Woolworth had a network of 59 stores.

✔ **READING CHECK: Evaluating** How did mass marketing contribute to business growth?
It helped create a new consumer culture, which allowed department stores to thrive.

SECTION 2 REVIEW

1. Define and explain:
capitalism
free enterprise
communism
social Darwinism
corporation
trust
monopoly
vertical integration
horizontal integration

2. Identify and explain:
Horatio Alger Jr.
Andrew Carnegie
John D. Rockefeller
Cornelius Vanderbilt
George Pullman

3. Summarizing Copy the web below. Use it to describe the major entrepreneurs of the late 1800s, what business each pursued, and how they revolutionized their industries.

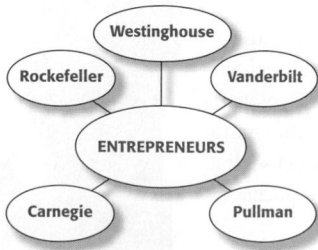

Westinghouse
Rockefeller
Vanderbilt
ENTREPRENEURS
Carnegie
Pullman

4. Finding the Main Idea

a. How did business leaders and social critics view government's role in business differently?

b. Evaluate the business and charitable contributions of Andrew Carnegie and John D. Rockefeller.

c. In what ways did new business and marketing practices change American life?

5. Writing and Critical Thinking

Supporting a Point of View Imagine that you are one of the entrepreneurs discussed in this section. Write a brochure persuading others to invest in your company.

Consider:
- what people would gain from investing in your company
- how they might react to your business practice
- what is the long-term potential of your company

 Homework Practice Online

keyword: SE3 HP6

SECTION 3

After completing Section 3, students should be able to:

OBJECTIVE 1 Understand why some Americans wanted trusts to be banned, and recount how the government responded.

OBJECTIVE 2 Describe the working conditions that laborers faced in the new age of rapid industrialization.

OBJECTIVE 3 Discuss how the Knights of Labor attempted to address the needs of many workers.

OBJECTIVE 4 Explain how businesses reacted to strikes in the late 1800s, and describe how this affected unions.

LET'S GET STARTED!

Write the following scenario on the chalkboard: *It is 1890. You work in a factory. Last month, your little brother was hurt in a workplace accident, but the company refuses to modify the machine that hurt him. Do you join a union to protest unsafe working conditions, even though the stakes may be high?* As students enter the classroom, ask them to respond to the scenario in writing. Have volunteers share their responses. Then tell students that in Section 3 they will learn more about efforts to form unions.

SECTION 3

READ TO DISCOVER

1. Why did some Americans want trusts to be banned, and how did the government respond?
2. What types of working conditions did laborers face in the new age of rapid industrialization?
3. How did the Knights of Labor attempt to address the needs of many workers?
4. How did businesses react to strikes in the late 1800s, and how did this affect unions?

DEFINE

anarchists

IDENTIFY

Sherman Antitrust Act
Knights of Labor
Terence V. Powderly
Mary Harris Jones
Great Upheaval
Haymarket Riot
American Federation of Labor
Eugene V. Debs

WHY IT MATTERS TODAY

Many workers still belong to unions. The AFL (now the AFL–CIO) remains a significant force in American industry. Use CNNfyi.com or other **current events** sources to find out about union activities in recent years. Record your findings in your journal.

CNNfyi.com

Labor Strives to Organize

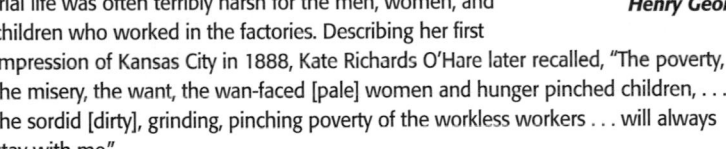

EYEWITNESSES TO History **"It is true that wealth has been greatly increased . . . but these gains are not general. In them the lowest class do not share. . . . This association of poverty with progress is the great enigma [mystery] of our times."**

—Henry George, *Progress and Poverty*

American economist Henry George

Henry George offered this critical look at American life during the 1870s in his book *Progress and Poverty*. Although a few entrepreneurs earned huge profits from rapid industrialization, many more Americans experienced severe poverty and poor working conditions. Indeed, industrial life was often terribly harsh for the men, women, and children who worked in the factories. Describing her first impression of Kansas City in 1888, Kate Richards O'Hare later recalled, "The poverty, the misery, the want, the wan-faced [pale] women and hunger pinched children, . . . the sordid [dirty], grinding, pinching poverty of the workless workers . . . will always stay with me."

Government and Business

The U.S. government's policies concerning business practices most often benefited the industrialists, not the workers. Supporters of laissez-faire capitalism claimed to oppose government interference in business activities. However, these same business leaders welcomed government assistance when it helped them. By placing high tariffs on imports, the U.S. government allowed American businesses to dominate the domestic market. In 1875, for example, Congress raised tariff rates to make imported steel considerably more expensive than domestic steel.

At the same time, the government did little to regulate business practices, despite growing pressure from the general public. As Carnegie Steel, Standard Oil, and other large corporations grew, many Americans demanded that trusts be outlawed. Critics reasoned that without competition, the large monopolies would have no incentive to maintain the quality of their goods or keep prices low. Congress responded in 1890 by passing the **Sherman Antitrust Act**, which outlawed all monopolies and trusts that restrained trade. The law failed to define what constituted a monopoly or trust and thus proved difficult to enforce. Corporations and trusts continued to grow in size and power.

While serving the interests of corporations, the U.S. government offered little assistance to American industrial workers. Government leaders were often distracted by issues of political corruption and paid little attention to the widening gulf between the wealthy and the poor. By 1890 just 10 percent of the population controlled close to 75 percent of the nation's wealth. At the same time, nearly

SECTION 3 RESOURCES

REPRODUCIBLE

▶ Guided Reading Strategy 6.3
▶ Graphic Organizer Activity 6: Industrial Problems of the Late 1800s

TECHNOLOGY

▶ One-Stop Planner, Lesson 6.3
▶ Holt Researcher: American History CD–ROM
▶ Homework Practice Online

REINFORCEMENT, REVIEW, AND ASSESSMENT

▶ Section 3 Review, p. 215
▶ Daily Quiz 6.3
▶ Main Idea Activity 6.3
▶ English Audio Summary 6.3
▶ Spanish Audio Summary 6.3

ALL LEVELS: Discuss the definition of *trusts* with the class. Then ask students to share their personal feelings about trusts. Do students think that trusts are fair? Do they think that trusts create quality or pricing issues? To help students understand why some Americans wanted trusts to be banned and how the government responded, copy the following graphic organizer on the chalkboard, omitting the italicized answers. Have each student complete it.
English Language Learners

Americans' Arguments Against Trusts
- argued that without competition, large monopolies would not maintain quality or keep prices low

Government Response
- *passed the Sherman Antitrust Act*

Problems with Act
- *failed to define a monopoly or trust*
- *presented serious enforcement problems*

HISTORY MAKERS SPEAK

Carroll D. Wright in *Working Girls of Boston*

Working Girls in Boston.
In the 1880s sociologist Carroll D. Wright sent investigators to interview working women in Boston. He recorded their observations in *Working Girls of Boston*. Wright wrote of one woman who often went "without her supper as well as other meals, because she did not have the money to pay for them." One woman had to support two children, working such long hours sewing that she damaged her eyesight. "Her eyes weep constantly, she cannot see across the room and 'the air seems always in a whirl' before her."

ACTIVITY: Have students interview a family member or neighbor about the kind of work he or she does. Then have each student write an oral history of that person's story.

VISUAL RECORD ANSWER

Students might mention the manufacturing industry.

VISUAL RECORD ANSWER

(for p. 211)

Students might mention the machinery's moving parts and the child's age and height.

---

50 percent of unskilled industrial workers in the United States earned less than $500 per year. By providing a cheap source of labor, these workers were essential to the nation's industrialization.

✔ **READING CHECK: Finding the Main Idea** How did the federal government support the rise of big business? Government did little to regulate business practices.

The New Working Class

The demand for labor soared under the new industrial order. These jobs were filled largely by the flood of immigrants who came to the United States during the late 1800s. *Workingman's Advocate*, a working-class newspaper, explained that immigrants "viewed a sojourn [temporary stay] in America as a means to acquire capital with which to purchase land, provide dowries for their daughters, and assist their sons to enter business." By 1900 about one third of the country's industrial workers were foreign-born.

African Americans. These immigrant workers were joined by hundreds of thousands of rural Americans who moved to the cities in search of jobs. Among this group were thousands of African Americans who moved from the South to find work. In Chicago, for example, by 1900 more than 80 percent of the city's African American workers had been born in states south of Illinois.

Some northern and midwestern industries offered working opportunities to African Americans. The vast majority of southern industries, however, barred African Americans from holding factory jobs. Nearly all southern textile workers were native-born whites. Cigar factories did employ some African Americans—women cleaned and sorted tobacco leaves, men made the cigars—but their numbers were few. In 1891 just 7,400 black southerners held industrial jobs.

Industrial employment remained out of reach for most African Americans. The best jobs still went to native-born white workers or to immigrants. Even skilled African American male laborers generally found themselves confined to the dirtiest or most dangerous work or to service-related jobs such as gardening.

Women and children. African American women in northern cities competed with poor immigrant women for domestic jobs and unskilled factory work. Most women worked because their families needed the income. As a state official in Massachusetts noted, "A family of workers can always live well, but the man with a family of small children to support, unless his wife works also, has a small chance of living properly." The number of female workers doubled between 1870 and 1890. By 1900 women accounted for about 18 percent of the labor force—with some 5 million workers.

The number of children in the workforce doubled during this period for the same reason. By 1890 close to 20 percent of American children between ages 10 and 15—some 1.5 million in all—worked for wages. In the textile mills of

INTERPRETING THE VISUAL RECORD

Workers. While southern industries often barred African Americans from holding factory jobs, African American workers occasionally found employment opportunities in northern and midwestern industries. *In what type of industry do you think these African American women might be employed?*

LEVEL 1: Pair students and tell them to imagine that they work in a factory in Michigan. Have each pair develop a two- to four-minute dialogue describing working conditions during the Second Industrial Revolution. (*Dialogues should reflect the following conditions: low pay, long hours, unsafe working environments, and the possibility of racial discrimination.*) Ask volunteers to perform their dialogues for the class. **English Language Learners, Cooperative Learning**

LEVEL 2: Tell students to imagine that they have just emigrated from Greece and that they work in a factory in Michigan. Have each student write a one-page letter to a friend back home describing working conditions in the United States. (*See the Level 1 lesson for the correct conditions.*) Have volunteers read their letters to the class. Students may wish to include their letters in their portfolios.

NOTE: For an additional teaching idea, see the Chapter 6 issue strip lesson in the **Creative Teaching Strategies handbook**.

North Carolina, one in every four workers was younger than 16 years old. The ratio was much lower in Massachusetts mills—1 in 20.

Across the nation, countless boys and girls worked in garment factories or at home, making clothing or other items by the piece. Others labored in the nation's canneries, mines, and shoe factories. Pauline Newman began working at a garment factory in New York in 1901 while still a child. Describing her experiences, she recalled, "It wasn't heavy work, but it was monotonous, because you did the same thing from seven-thirty in the morning till nine at night."

Working Conditions

Children in the labor force often faced terrible conditions. In some textile mills, for instance, children worked 12-hour shifts—often at night—for pennies a day. Low wages and long hours affected all industrial workers, however, regardless of their age, sex, or race. Conditions were particularly difficult for unskilled workers. Most unskilled white male laborers worked at least 10 hours a day, six days a week, for less than $10 a week. Many African American, Asian American, and Mexican American men worked the same number of hours for even lower wages. Furthermore, employers made few allowances for women and children, expecting them to work the same number of hours as men for sometimes as little as half the pay.

Such long hours left workers exhausted at the end of the day. This fatigue made already unsafe working conditions even more dangerous. In 1881 alone, some 30,000 railroad workers were killed or injured on the job. Most employers felt no responsibility for work-related deaths and injuries. They made little effort to improve workplace safety.

Many workers endured hardships that extended beyond the factory. Some employers sought to increase their control over their workers. They built company towns, where the company owned the workers' housing and the retail businesses they used. Residents of company towns usually received their wages in scrip. This paper money could be used only to pay rent to the company or to buy goods at company stores. Prices at these stores were usually much higher than at regular stores. Workers often spent entire paychecks on necessities like food and clothing.

✔ **READING CHECK: Categorizing** What hardships did industrial workers face?
low wages, long hours, and dangerous working conditions

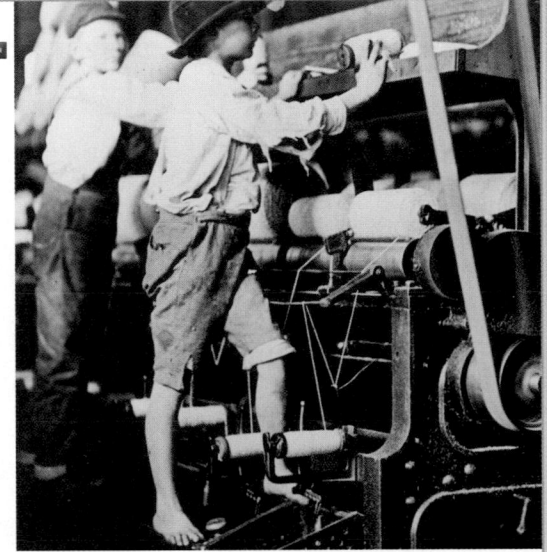

INTERPRETING THE VISUAL RECORD

Working conditions. Many child laborers worked long hours in factories with unsafe working conditions. *What aspects of this child's working conditions might be dangerous?*

PRIMARY SOURCE

A European View of U.S. Workers

In 1871 Austrian diplomat Joseph Alexander, Graf von Hübner, visited the United States. He was impressed by the opportunities Americans enjoyed in their increasingly industrialized society. He also noted that fierce competition took its toll on working people. **How does von Hübner describe the effects of industrialization on American workers?**

"In the New World man is born to conquer. Life is a perpetual struggle, . . . a race in the open field across terrible obstacles, with the prospect of enormous rewards for reaching the goal. The American cannot keep his arms folded. He must embark on something, and once embarked he must go on and on forever; for if he stops, those who follow him would crush him under their feet. His life is one long campaign, a succession of never-ending fights, marches, and countermarches.

In such a militant existence, what place is left for the sweetness, the repose [rest], the intimacy of home or its joys? Is he happy? Judging by his tired, sad, exhausted, anxious, and often delicate and unhealthy appearance, one would be inclined to doubt it. Such an excess of uninterrupted labor cannot be good for any man."

HISTORY MAKERS SPEAK

Henry George in *Progress and Poverty*

The Price of Industrialization. Henry George theorized why poverty increased despite great progress in production. He argued that "all advantages gained by the march of progress go to the owners of land, and wages do not increase. . . . The mere laborer has thus no more interest in the general advance of productive power than the Cuban slave has in advance in the price of sugar. . . . [Thus] labor is exposed to certain effects of advancing civilization which, . . . tend to reduce the free laborer to the helpless and degraded condition of the slave."

CRITICAL THINKING How might the basis of George's argument differ from Carnegie's or Rockefeller's beliefs about business practices?

ANSWER: Students might mention that George shares the perspective of poor workers, while Carnegie and Rockefeller share the perspective of rich business owners.

PRIMARY SOURCE ANSWER

Students might note that workers are tired, exhausted, and unhappy.

LEVEL 3: Tell students to imagine that they work in a factory in Michigan. Have each student develop a four- to five-minute monologue describing working conditions during the Second Industrial Revolution. *(See the Level 1 lesson for the correct conditions.)* Ask volunteers to present their monologues to the class.

HOMEWORK *Tell students to imagine that they work in a factory in Michigan. Have each student write a poem or short story describing working conditions during the Second Industrial Revolution.*

TEACH OBJECTIVE 3

LEVEL 1: Organize students into five groups. Assign each group one of the following roles: skilled workers, unskilled workers, female workers, African American workers, and Chinese workers. Ask each group to write a topic sentence explaining how or whether the Knights of Labor has met its needs as workers. *(The Knights of Labor welcomed skilled and unskilled workers along with women. Although the Knights admitted African American workers after a certain point, many members did not accept them. The Knights actively discriminated against Chinese workers.)* Have each group read its topic sentence to the class. Then, in a classroom discussion, ask students to evaluate the Knights' approach. Was it fair? Was it justifiable,

---

MAP ANSWER
(for p. 214)

Those areas were industrial, urban, and densely populated.

VISUAL RECORD ANSWER

(for p. 215)

Students might point out the fire and the weapons.

SECTION
REVIEW 3 ANSWERS

1. Define
anarchists, p. 213

2. Identify
• Sherman Antitrust Act, p. 209
• Knights of Labor, p. 212

Frank J. Ferrell, a member of the Knights of Labor, introduces the union leader Terence V. Powderly at a rally.

The Knights of Labor

As conditions grew worse, workers called for change. The National Labor Union, a nationwide federation of craft and industrial workers organized in 1866, had some limited success trying to establish an eight-hour workday. It fell apart in the 1870s.

In 1869, nine Philadelphia garment workers, led by Uriah Stephens, founded the **Knights of Labor**, a more successful early national union. It remained largely a white male organization until 1879, when **Terence V. Powderly**, an Irish Catholic machinist and the mayor of Scranton, Pennsylvania, became its leader. Under his leadership the Knights' membership expanded rapidly.

Powderly wanted the Knights of Labor to attract workers who were often excluded from other unions. He therefore opened the union to both skilled and unskilled laborers. Powderly also welcomed thousands of women into the union's ranks. A number of women, including **Mary Harris Jones**, played prominent roles in the union.

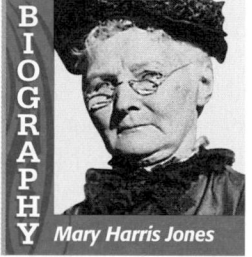

BIOGRAPHY

Mary Harris Jones

Born in Cork, Ireland, in 1830, Mary Harris came to the United States as a young child. She married George Jones, a union supporter, in 1861. Six years later, after her husband and four children died in a yellow fever epidemic, she began to devote herself to the labor movement. At the invitation of striking workers, Jones became an organizer for the Knights of Labor in the 1870s. Declaring that her place was "wherever there is a fight," she organized strikes, marches, and demonstrations. In 1912 Jones explained to a reporter the reasons behind her activism.

History Makers Speak

❝My life work has been to try to educate the worker to a sense of the wrongs he has had to suffer, and does suffer—and to stir up the oppressed to a point of getting off their knees and demanding that which I believe to be rightfully theirs.❞

—Mary Harris Jones, quoted in *Charleston (West Virginia) Gazette*, June 11, 1912

Jones's ambitious drive to educate and organize laborers was so effective that some opponents called her "the most dangerous woman in America." Because she viewed her actions as more motherly than radical, most people called her Mother Jones. Jones was sentenced to 20 years in jail for her part in a 1912 West Virginia strike, but a public outcry caused the governor of the state to free her. Mother Jones continued fighting for the rights of America's working people until her death in 1930. She was 100 years old.

Although the Knights of Labor offered membership to female workers, Powderly did not encourage African Americans to join the union until 1883. By the mid-1880s the Knights claimed some 60,000 black members. African American delegate Frank J. Ferrell spoke at the Knights' 1886 national convention in Richmond, Virginia. He told the crowd, "One of the objects of our Order is the abolition of these distinctions which are maintained by creed or color."

THE GRANGER COLLECTION, NEW YORK

given the prejudices of the time? If students had formed a union during the Second Industrial Revolution, which workers would they have admitted?

English Language Learners, Cooperative Learning

LEVEL 2: Tell students to imagine that they are members of the Knights of Labor who want to reform the organization. Have each student write a three- to four-minute speech describing the ways in which the Knights have succeeded and failed in their attempts to meet the needs of workers. *(See the Level 1 lesson for the correct successes and failures.)* Ask volunteers to deliver their speeches to the class.

LEVEL 3: Tell students to imagine that they are planning to start a new union, one that will rival the Knights of Labor. Have each student create a three-fold brochure advertising this new union. Remind students that in order to succeed, they will have to attract members from the Knights. In order to do so, their brochures should discuss the ways in which the Knights have both succeeded and failed in their attempts to meet workers' needs. Brochures should also outline the ways in which the new union will be better then the Knights. *(See the Level 1 lesson for the correct successes and failures.)* Ask students to present their brochures to the class. Have students select the best new union. Students should justify their choices.

Not all African American Knights agreed with this assessment. "The white Knights of Labor prevent me from getting employment because I am a colored man," complained a North Carolina mason, "although I belong to the same organization." Still, the Knights did more than other early unions to try to meet the needs of African American workers. The Knights were not equality-minded when it came to everyone, however. Powderly, like many working-class Americans, actively opposed Chinese workers, claiming they stole jobs from white Americans.

Powderly led the Knights of Labor for 15 years. Under his leadership, the union fought for temperance, the eight-hour workday, equal pay for equal work, and an end to child labor. By 1886 the Knights boasted a membership of more than 700,000.

✔ **READING CHECK: Summarizing** How did the Knights of Labor help workers? organized laborers and fought for the rights of working people

The Great Upheaval

The Knights of Labor owed its phenomenal growth partly to the great railroad strike of 1877, which helped revive the labor movement. In July 1877, railroad workers in Martinsburg, West Virginia, went on strike in reaction to a pay cut. President Rutherford B. Hayes ordered federal troops into the area to protect the railroad. The use of these troops angered workers, and the strike soon spread to 14 states. The Knights of Labor also grew after a successful strike against railroad tycoon Jay Gould in 1884. Workers became more willing to press for better working conditions. In 1886 the nation experienced a year of intense strikes and violent labor confrontations that became known as the **Great Upheaval**.

An economic depression in the early 1880s had led to massive wage cuts. Workers demanded relief. When negotiations with management failed, many workers took direct action. By the end of 1886 some 1,500 strikes involving more than 400,000 workers had swept the nation. Many of these strikes turned violent, as angry strikers clashed with aggressive employers and police officers. Perhaps the most notorious of these confrontations was the **Haymarket Riot**.

The Haymarket Riot. On May 1, 1886, some 40,000 Chicago workers joined a strike against the McCormick Harvesting Machine Company. They struck for an eight-hour workday. Although local craft unions launched the strike, it soon fell under the leadership of a group of political radicals and **anarchists**—people who oppose all forms of government. On May 3 a confrontation between police and strikers left two strikers dead.

In protest, strikers called a meeting for the next day in Chicago's Haymarket Square. Peaceful and small, the rally was about to break up when nearly 200 police

---

☆ Then and Now

Labor Unions

Labor unions' membership and organization have changed over the years. Their goals today, however, are not so different from earlier groups. Despite a gradual decline in membership, unions are still involved in American life.

Teamsters picketing during the UPS strike

They continue to have an impact on working conditions. Several strikes in recent years have attracted much media attention.

In 1997 about 185,000 members of the Teamsters' union struck against United Parcel Service (UPS) over pensions and the increasing use of part-time laborers. The 15-day strike caused delays in shipping for many businesses. However, during the strike, the union received a great deal of support. One Gallup poll reported that 55 percent of the public approved of the strike. Many Americans shared the concerns of the strikers. As one labor expert suggested, "What's on the bargaining table gets discussed at the dinner table, too." The strikers' efforts resulted in additional full-time jobs. In 1998 the United Auto Workers (UAW) union also received public support. That year it launched a strike against General Motors to protest both the loss of jobs to foreign factories and unsafe working conditions. However, the UAW strikers' gains were not as decisive as those of the Teamsters in the UPS strike.

- Terence V. Powderly, p. 212
- Mary Harris Jones, p. 212
- Great Upheaval, p. 213
- Haymarket Riot, p. 213
- American Federation of Labor, p. 214
- Eugene V. Debs, p. 215

3. Haymarket Riot—eight-hour workday; left people dead and allowed employers to tighten labor controls. Homestead—protest a wage cut; several deaths; Pullman—protest a wage cut; government troops, deaths, property damage, and end of ARU

4a. People feared that market-controlling trusts would raise prices or produce poor-quality goods; the government passed the Sherman Antitrust Act.

b. Students should mention long hours, low pay, and unsafe conditions.

c. Organizers encouraged women, African Americans, and unskilled workers to join unions

5. Answers will vary. Articles should mention that children under 16 worked to help support their families. The work was hard and dangerous, for half the wages adults were paid. Students might mention that women and children could not join many unions.

TEACH OBJECTIVE 4

 LEVEL 1: Ask students to list the ways in which businesses responded to strikes in the late 1800s. (*Students should list blacklists, yellow-dog contracts, lockouts, and violent attacks.*) Write students' responses on the chalkboard. Then ask students to list the effects of these strategies on unions. (*On the whole, these techniques hurt most unions. They also caused many skilled workers to break with unskilled workers and join the American Federation of Labor.*) Write students' responses on the chalkboard. Then ask each student to use the information on the chalkboard to write a paragraph explaining how businesses responded to strikes in the late 1800s and how those responses affected unions. **English Language Learners**

LEVELS 2 AND 3: Organize students into two groups—one representing business leaders and one representing union leaders. Ask the first group to discuss possible responses to strikes and the other group to discuss possible responses to business reprisals. Then have each group select several spokespeople. Have spokespeople make a three- to five-minute speech describing their possible responses. (*See the Level 1 lesson for the correct responses.*) Then conduct a debate between business leaders and union leaders on resolving conflicts. After the debate, ask students to consider the conflicts between the two groups. Was consensus possible, given the time and their different issues? What might have been a fair, acceptable agreement? **Cooperative Learning**

This poster encouraged workers to rally at Haymarket Square.

officers arrived. Suddenly, a bomb exploded in the midst of the police, who responded with gunfire. When the smoke cleared, some 60 officers lay wounded. Seven police officers and one civilian were dead. The police arrested eight well-known anarchists—only one of whom had been present—charging them with conspiracy. All eight were found guilty of incitement to murder. Four were hanged.

Worker activism declines. By the end of the year, worker activism had decreased. Encouraged by the Haymarket convictions, employers struck back at the unions. Employers drew up blacklists—lists of union supporters—that they shared with one another. Blacklisted workers found it almost impossible to get jobs. Many employers also forced job applicants to sign agreements—called yellow-dog contracts by the workers—promising not to join unions. When these measures failed and workers struck anyway, many companies instituted lockouts. They barred workers from their plants and brought in nonunion strikebreakers. Many of these strikebreakers were African Americans or others who felt abandoned by the unions. As labor suffered repeated defeats, the tide of public sentiment turned against workers. Union membership shrank.

Alarmed by the violence of the Great Upheaval and by the response of the employers, many skilled workers broke ranks with the unskilled laborers. They joined the **American Federation of Labor** (AFL), a new union founded by Samuel Gompers in 1886. The AFL organized independent craft unions into a group that worked to advance the interests of skilled workers.

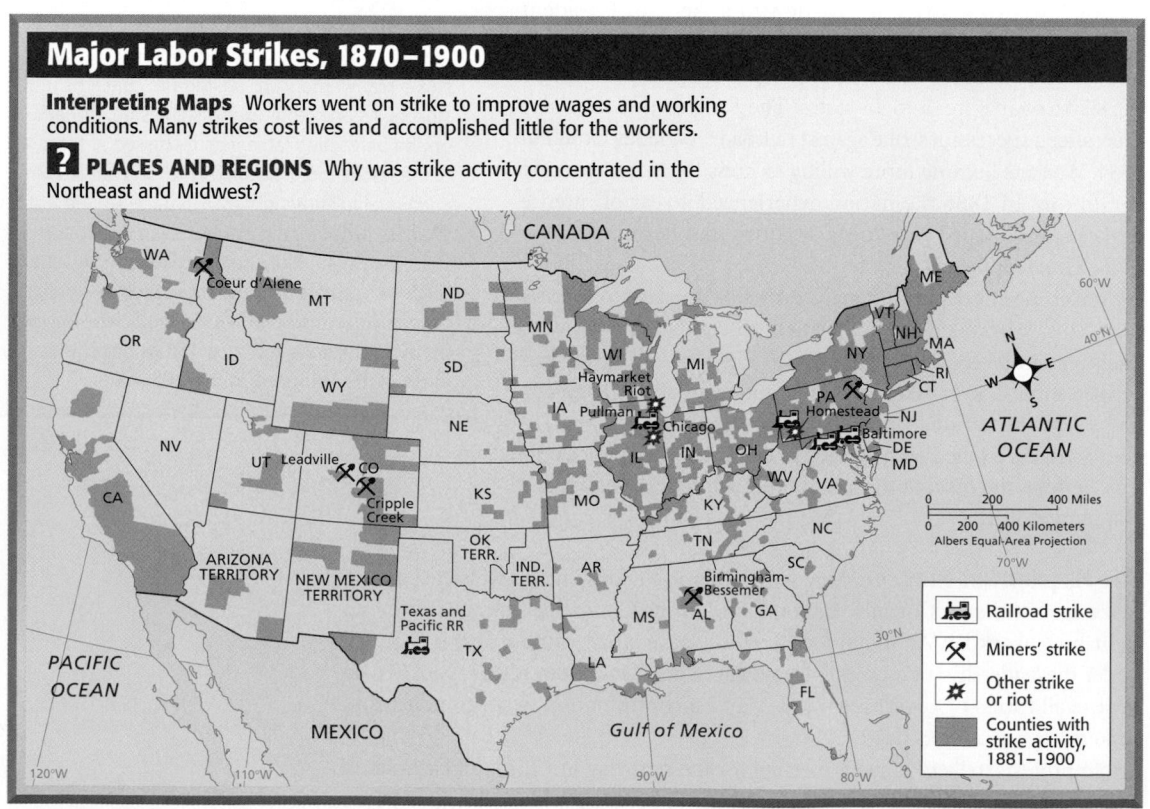

Major Labor Strikes, 1870–1900

Interpreting Maps Workers went on strike to improve wages and working conditions. Many strikes cost lives and accomplished little for the workers.

? PLACES AND REGIONS Why was strike activity concentrated in the Northeast and Midwest?

Legend:
- Railroad strike
- Miners' strike
- Other strike or riot
- Counties with strike activity, 1881–1900

REVIEW

Have students complete the **Section 3 Review** on p. 215.

ASSESS

Have students complete **Daily Quiz 6.3**. As **Alternative Assessment**, you may want to use the Knights of Labor brochure or the business leaders–union leaders presentation and debate in this section's lessons.

RETEACH

Have students complete **Main Idea Activity for English Language Learners and Special-Needs Students 6.3**. Then organize students into four groups. Assign each group one of the

Section 3 objectives. Have each group create an outline of the material relating to its assigned objective. Then ask each group to copy its outline onto the chalkboard, omitting some of the information in its original outlines. Have groups compete to fill in the most blanks.
English Language Learners, Cooperative Learning

EXTEND

Have students conduct research on labor songs. *(You might suggest that students start with Philip Sheldon Foner's* American Labor Songs of the Nineteenth Century.*)* Ask each pair to write lyrics for an original union song. Have students read their lyrics to the class. **Cooperative Learning, Block Scheduling**

The Homestead and Pullman Strikes

Industrial unrest broke out again in 1892 at Carnegie Steel Company in Homestead, Pennsylvania. In June, workers went on strike to protest a wage cut. Managers responded by instituting a lockout and hiring some 300 guards to protect the plant. A violent clash between strikers and the guards in early July resulted in 16 deaths.

In May 1894, workers at the Pullman sleeping-car factory in Pullman, Illinois, went on strike. George Pullman had cut wages but refused to lower rents or prices at the stores in his company town. As head of the American Railway Union (ARU), **Eugene V. Debs** supported the Pullman strikers. The strikers urged other ARU members to refuse to work or ride on trains that included Pullman cars. Debs proclaimed:

History Makers Speak

❝The struggle . . . has developed into a contest between the producing classes and the money power of the country. . . . Workingmen are entitled to a just proportion of the proceeds of their labor.❞

—Eugene V. Debs

In support of the strikers, railroad workers brought rail traffic to a halt throughout the Midwest. The railroad companies quickly turned to the federal government for help. The government ordered an end to the ARU strike, claiming that the strikers were committing a federal offense by preventing the delivery of U.S. mail. When ARU officials ignored the order, they were jailed.

Meanwhile, President Grover Cleveland ordered federal troops into Pullman in July. The troops helped restore normal factory operations. In the process, the Pullman strike had been broken and the ARU destroyed.

✔ **READING CHECK: Evaluating** How successful were labor strikes in the late 1800s?
Most were unsuccessful because of violence, federal troop intervention, and antiunion activities.

THE GRANGER COLLECTION, NEW YORK

INTERPRETING THE VISUAL RECORD

Homestead strike. After the violent confrontation between strikers and some 300 hired guards at Carnegie Steel Company, violence spread to other plants. *How does this image convey the tension caused by these strikes?*

Understanding Main Ideas

1. New technology increased steel production, which led to stronger railroad lines. Telegraph companies established offices in train stations and strung their lines alongside railroad lines.

2. Capitalists welcomed government intervention that allowed them to eliminate competition, but they did not want government to interfere in their operations. Marxists believed that government should regulate business operations to ensure that workers are treated fairly.

3. Workers faced low wages, long hours, and unsafe surroundings. Children worked the same long hours as adults. Some companies paid workers in scrip, forcing them to spend their pay in company stores.

Reviewing Themes

1. Railroads and communications aided the growth of many different kinds of businesses and created jobs for millions of people.

2. Students might mention increased ease of travel and communication as well as expanded job opportunities.

3. Unions organized workers to fight for better conditions and were sometimes successful, but businesses and government began limiting union activity and public sentiment turned against unions.

SECTION 3 REVIEW

1. Define and explain:
anarchists

2. Identify and explain:
Sherman Antitrust Act
Knights of Labor
Terence V. Powderly
Mary Harris Jones
Great Upheaval
Haymarket Riot
American Federation of Labor
Eugene V. Debs

3. Identifying Cause and Effect
Copy the graphic organizer below. Use it to explain what labor unions hoped to accomplish with strikes and what effects the strikes actually had.

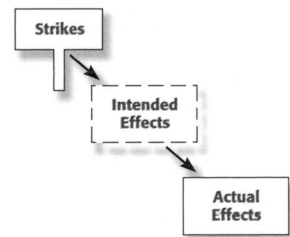

Strikes

Intended Effects

Actual Effects

4. [Finding the Main Idea]
a. Why did some Americans oppose trusts? How did the government respond to their concerns?
b. How did working conditions in the late 1800s contribute to the growth of labor unions?
c. How did union organizers such as Terence V. Powderly attempt to represent diverse groups of workers?

5. [Writing and Critical Thinking]
Analyzing Information Imagine that you are a reporter investigating child labor. Write an article about the working conditions for children in factories.
Consider:
• the age of the children and their reasons for working
• the type of work and the number of hours worked
• working conditions for adult factory laborers

go. hrw .com **Homework Practice Online**
keyword: SE3 HP6

REVIEW AND ASSESSMENT RESOURCES

TECHNOLOGY

▶ Chapter 6 Test Generator (on the One-Stop Planner)
▶ Global Skill Builder CD–ROM
▶ HRW Go site

REINFORCEMENT, REVIEW, AND ASSESSMENT

▶ Chapter 6 Review, pp. 216–17
▶ Chapter 6 Tutorial for Students, Parents, Mentors, and Peers

▶ Chapter 6 Test (Form A or B)
▶ Portfolio Activities and Alternative Assessment Handbook, Chapter 6
▶ Chapter 6 Test for English Language Learners and Special-Needs Students

REVIEW

Have students complete the **Chapter 6 Review** on pp. 216–17.

ASSESS

Use one of the chapter tests to assess students' understanding of the content. For **Alternative Assessment**, see the **Portfolio Activities and Alternative Assessment Handbook.**

Thinking Critically

1. The ability to produce more steel cheaply led to the rapid expansion of railroads. Cities like Philadelphia and Cleveland grew around the steel industry, and railroads connected these cities and allowed fast travel between cities all over the country. Telegraph companies followed railroads, stringing lines and setting up offices along with the railroad construction.

2. The U.S. economy grew rapidly and large industries replaced smaller businesses.

3. Technology changed the nature of work from primarily agricultural to industrial and made it more dangerous with longer hours. The demands of new technology also led to the growth of labor movements and business.

4. Although the claim that the corset always does good may pass for a fact with some supporting evidence, none of the words represent true facts and are only opinions about how the corset looks and how it can make women look. The adjectives "vigorous" and "graceful" are open to interpretation.

Review

Creating a Time Line

Copy the time line below onto a sheet of paper. Complete the time line by filling in the events and dates from the chapter that you think were most significant. Pick three events and explain why you think they were significant.

| 1865 | 1880 | 1895 | 1910 |

Writing a Summary

Using standard grammar, spelling, sentence structure, and punctuation, write an overview of events in the chapter.

Identifying People and Ideas

Identify the following terms or individuals and explain their significance.

1. Bessemer process
2. Elijah McCoy
3. telegraph
4. Thomas Edison
5. Andrew Carnegie
6. social Darwinism
7. trust
8. monopoly
9. Mary Harris Jones
10. Great Upheaval

Understanding Main Ideas

SECTION 1 *(pp. 192–200)*

1. How did innovations in transportation and steel production affect the growth of railroads?

SECTION 2 *(pp. 201–208)*

2. How did capitalism and Marxism interpret the role of government in business differently?

SECTION 3 *(pp. 209–215)*

3. Describe the working conditions laborers faced during the late 1800s.

Reviewing Themes

1. **Economics** What impact did new technology have on the rise of big business?

2. **Science, Technology, and Society** How did technological developments, such as electric power, change Americans' daily lives in the late 1800s?

3. **Citizenship** Why did unions only partially succeed in ensuring the rights of working people?

Thinking Critically

1. **Summarizing** Describe how the steel, railroad, and telegraph industries were interconnected.

2. **Analyzing Information** How did the industrialization of the late 1800s affect the U.S. economy?

3. **Comparing** What impact did technological innovations of the late 1800s have on businesses, the nature of work, and the American labor movement?

4. **Identifying Bias** Identify which words or phrases in the following statement from an 1882 advertisement for an "electric corset" represent opinions. "A wonderful invention for ladies who desire vigorous health and a graceful figure. They always do good, cannot harm."

5. **Making Generalizations and Predictions** What might have happened to unions if violence involving strikers had not occurred in the late 1800s?

Writing About History

Analyzing Information Using a business leader or an industrial factory worker as a main character, create an outline for a short story. Use the graphic organizer below to help you organize your story.

Setting:
Main Character:
Secondary Characters:
Conflict:
Plot:
Resolution:

RETEACH

Pair students and have each pair use at least three quarters of the key terms and key people in Chapter 5 to create a "hidden words" puzzle or a crossword puzzle. Ask each pair to exchange its puzzle with another pair and to solve them. Then conduct an overview discussion on the Second Industrial Revolution and ask students to fill in the gaps.

English Language Learners, Cooperative Learning

EXTEND

Organize students into groups of six and assign each member one of the following roles: factory owner, factory supervisor, union leader, worker from Ireland, worker from Russia, and child worker from Italy. Tell students to imagine that it is 1895 and that the factory owner is touring the plant. During the tour, however, a large machine topples over and blocks an exit, leaving the six people above trapped in a small room for hours. Have each group create a 10-to-15-minute play on the events and conversations that follow in the small room. Plays should focus on events related to the Second Industrial Revolution, such as working conditions, social beliefs, immigration, unions, and so on. Have each group perform its play for the class.

Block Scheduling, Cooperative Learning

Building Social Studies Skills

Interpreting Maps

Study the map below. Then use it to help answer the questions that follow.

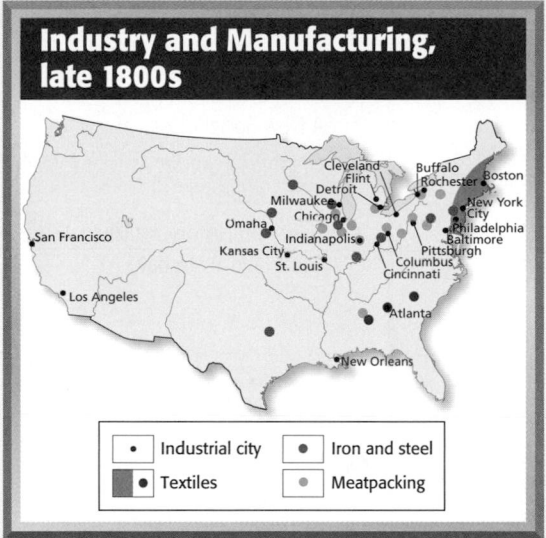

Industry and Manufacturing, late 1800s

San Francisco • Los Angeles • Omaha • Kansas City • St. Louis • Chicago • Milwaukee • Indianapolis • Cleveland • Flint • Detroit • Cincinnati • Columbus • Pittsburgh • Buffalo • Rochester • Boston • New York City • Philadelphia • Baltimore • Atlanta • New Orleans

Legend:
- • Industrial city
- ■ Textiles
- • Iron and steel
- • Meatpacking

1. Based on the map and information in the chapter, which generalization about geography and industrialization is most accurate?
   a. The North's climate was more conducive to growth of industry than the South's climate.
   b. Industrial growth occurred mostly in areas where there was easy access to water transportation.
   c. The farms and ranches that supplied the meatpacking industry were mostly in the North.
   d. Iron and steel factories are not found along the Atlantic coastline.

2. Explain why the textile industry continued to dominate the South's economy after the Civil War.

Analyzing Primary Sources

Analyze the following quotation from Thomas Edison's secretary, Alfred O. Tate. Then answer the questions that follow.

> "'I'm not a scientist,' exclaimed Edison. 'I'm an inventor. . . . I measure everything I do by the size of a silver dollar. If it don't come up to that standard then I know it's no good.'
>
> His meaning was clear. If his work would sell, if the public would buy and pay their silver dollars for it, then he would know that it was useful. And that was his vocation—the production of new and useful inventions. He was a utilitarian [practical] inventor, and money was the only barometer [gauge] that could be employed to indicate success. [But I believe Edison] was a Scientist most highly esteemed and admired by his contemporaries throughout the world."

3. Which of these interpretations of the passage is most accurate?
   a. Edison believed that inventors must focus on practical developments that people want to buy.
   b. Edison wanted to make money so he could live an extravagant lifestyle.
   c. Edison proved there was no connection between pure science and invention.
   d. Edison believed that inventors are more important than scientists.

4. Which three of Edison's inventions have had the greatest impact on your life? Why?

Alternative Assessment

Building Your Portfolio

U.S. HISTORY

Science, Technology, and Society
Imagine that you are a land speculator attempting to develop a rural area. Outline a plan to use new technologies such as the telephone, electric lighting, and the horseless carriage to attract residents and businesses. Use this information in a visual display of the new area.

⚡ internet connect

Internet Activity: go.hrw.com
KEYWORD: SE3 AN6

Access the Internet through the HRW Go site to research the effects of Thomas Edison's scientific discoveries and technological innovations on the development of the United States. Then create a quiz and answer key based upon your research. Have another student check your answers before you turn in the quiz.

go.hrw.com

---

5. Answers will vary. Some students might argue that union organization would have been more popular because some people were discouraged from joining unions by the violence associated with them. Other students might argue that unions would have been even less effective if companies and governments did not demonstrate their willingness to resort to violence against workers. This willingness may have encouraged some people to believe that workers really did need improvements.

Writing
Outlines should include the information presented in the graphic organizer.

Building Social Studies Skills
1. b

2. The land was developed for agriculture; workers were trained for field work; the main asset in the South was land for producing cotton, which was used in the textile industry to make garments.

3. a

4. Answers will vary. Students might suggest the light bulb, the phonograph (as evolved into the compact disc), the movie camera, or the battery.

The Transformation of American Society

CHAPTER RESOURCE MANAGER

	Objectives	Pacing Guide	Reproducible Resources
SECTION 1 **The New Immigrants** pp. 220–25	★ Explain how immigration changed during the late 1800s. ★ Describe the challenges immigrants faced as they settled in the United States. ★ Discuss where new immigrants found assistance. ★ Relate why nativists opposed new immigration.	**Regular** 2 days **Block Scheduling** 1 day *Block Scheduling Handbook with Team Teaching Strategies, pp. 37–42*	**RS** Guided Reading Strategy 7.1 **PS** American History Political Cartoon 14: Attitudes Toward Immigration **SM** Geography Activity 7: Immigrant Groups in New York City
SECTION 2 **The Urban World** pp. 226–32	★ Analyze how technological innovations altered the urban landscape. ★ Discuss the social values that the new class of wealthy city-dwellers expressed. ★ Explain how life changed for middle-class Americans during the late 1800s. ★ Describe what urban life was like for the poorest city-dwellers. ★ Identify how social reformers used settlement houses and churches to improve the lives of the poor.	**Regular** 2 days **Block Scheduling** 1 day *Block Scheduling Handbook with Team Teaching Strategies, pp. 37–42*	**RS** Guided Reading Strategy 7.2 **PS** American History Political Cartoon 15: Urban Life **IC** Literature Reading 7: A New Social Class **RS** Graphic Organizer Activity 7: Daily LIfe in the Cities **E** Hand-On History Activity: Leisure Time– Today and Yesterday
SECTION 3 **Daily Life in the Cities** pp. 233–39	★ Understand how public education and colleges changed in the late 1800s. ★ Explain how publishers appealed to readers. ★ Discuss how outdoor activities and sports provided a source of leisure for Americans. ★ Describe the new forms of popular theater and music that developed in the late 1800s.	**Regular** 1 day **Block Scheduling** .5 day *Block Scheduling Handbook with Team Teaching Strategies, pp. 37–42*	**RS** Guided Reading Strategy 7.3 **PS** Primary Source Reading 7: An Immigrant's Story **PS** Biography Reading 7: Frederick Law Olmsted **E** Creative Teaching Strategy: Brainstorming Lesson

Chapter Resource Key

PS	Primary Sources	**REV**	Review		Video
RS	Reading Support	**ELL**	Reinforcement and English Language Learners	Internet	
IC	Interdisciplinary Connections			Holt Presentation Maker Using Microsoft® PowerPoint®	
E	Enrichment		Transparencies		
SM	Skills Mastery		CD–ROM		
A	Assessment		Music		

One-Stop Planner CD–ROM

See the *One-Stop Planner* for a complete list of additional resources for students and teachers.

One-Stop Planner CD-ROM

It's easy to plan lessons, select resources, and print out materials for your students when you use the **One-Stop Planner CD–ROM with Test Generator.**

Technology Resources	Reinforcement, Review, and Assessment
One-Stop Planner, Lesson 7.1	**REV** Section 1 Review, p. 225
The American Nation Video Program Segment: Community Ties: San Francisco's Chinatown; Teacher's Guide, pp. 75–80	**A** Daily Quiz 7.1
CNN. Presents America: Yesterday and Today, Beginnings to 1914 Segment: Coming to America	**ELL** Main Idea Activity 7.1
Holt Researcher: American History CD–ROM	**ELL** English Audio Summary 7.1
Homework Practice Online	**ELL** Spanish Audio Summary 7.1
One-Stop Planner, Lesson 7.2	**REV** Section 2 Review, p. 232
Holt Researcher: American History CD–ROM	**A** Daily Quiz 7.2
Homework Practice Online	**ELL** Main Idea Activity 7.2
HRW Go site	**ELL** English Audio Summary 7.2
	ELL Spanish Audio Summary 7.2
One-Stop Planner, Lesson 7.2	**REV** Section 3 Review, p. 239
American Music Selection 18: "Twilight Rag"	**A** Daily Quiz 7.3
Holt Researcher: American History CD–ROM	**ELL** Main Idea Activity 7.3
Homework Practice Online	**ELL** English Audio Summary 7.3
	ELL Spanish Audio Summary 7.3

internet connect

HRW ONLINE RESOURCES
GO TO: go.hrw.com
Then type in a keyword.

TEACHER HOME PAGE
KEYWORD: SE3 Teacher

CHAPTER INTERNET ACTIVITIES
KEYWORD: SE3 AN7
Choose an activity to:
- compare and contrast immigration patterns and experiences of immigrants in the 1800s and 1900s.
- research the history of baseball and write a biography of an important player.
- create an architectural model based on the principles of Louis Sullivan.

CHAPTER ENRICHMENT LINKS
KEYWORD: SE3 CH7

ONLINE ASSESSMENT
Homework Practice
KEYWORD: SE3 HP7

Standardized Test Prep
KEYWORD: SE3 STP7

Rubrics
KEYWORD: SS Rubrics

ONLINE MAPS, CHARTS, AND GRAPHS
KEYWORD: SE3 MCG
- The Largest Cities, 1900

CONTENT UPDATES
KEYWORD: SS Content Updates

HOLT PRESENTATION MAKER
KEYWORD: SE3 PPT7

ONLINE READING SUPPORT
KEYWORD: SS Strategies

CURRENT EVENTS
KEYWORD: S3 Current Events

Meeting Individual Needs

Ability Levels

Level 1 Basic-level activities designed for all students encountering new material

Level 2 Intermediate-level activities designed for average students

Level 3 Challenging activities designed for honors and gifted-and-talented students

English Language Learners Activities that address the needs of students with Limited English Proficiency

Chapter Review and Assessment

- Global Skill Builder CD–ROM
- HRW Go site
- **REV** Chapter 7 Tutorial for Students, Parents, Mentors, and Peers
- **REV** Chapter 7 Review, pp. 240–41
- Chapter 7 Test Generator (on the One-Stop Planner)
- **A** Chapter 7 Test (Form A or B)
- **A** Alternative Assessment Handbook
- **A** Chapter 7 Test for English Language Learners and Special-Needs Students

Build on What You Know

Ask students to answer the following questions.

How might new technologies lead to economic development?

Consider:

• how technology changes the ways in which goods are produced

• how demand for new goods generates economic growth

Why might many immigrants choose to live in urban areas?

Consider:

• the point of entry for most new immigrants

• the existence of immigrant communities

---

exploring the time line

AMERICAN EVENTS

◢ internet connect

TOPIC: Baseball
GO TO: go.hrw.com
KEYWORD: SE3 AN7

Have students access the Internet through the HRW Go site to conduct research on the history of baseball and notable players of the game. Then ask students to write a biography of a notable player. Remind students to use standard grammar, punctuation, spelling, and sentence structure.

CHAPTER 7

1865–1910

The Transformation of American Society

Edwin Booth

New York's the World

1868
Business and Finance
The first university schools for pharmacy and architecture are established.

1869
The Arts
Romeo and Juliet opens in New York, starring the popular actor Edwin Booth.

1876
The Arts
Mark Twain publishes *The Adventures of Tom Sawyer.*

1883
Business and Finance
Joseph Pulitzer purchases the *World,* a New York City daily newspaper.

1865 | **1870** | **1875** | **1880** | **1885**

1865
World Events
The Salvation Army is founded in London by religious revivalist William Booth.

1869
Daily Life
Aaron Champion organizes the first professional baseball team, the Cincinnati Red Stockings.

1876
Science and Technology
British inventors introduce the first bicycle to the United States at the Centennial Exposition in Philadelphia.

1885
Science and Technology
William Le Baron Jenney constructs the Home Insurance Co. Building in Chicago.

Cincinnati Red Stockings professional baseball team in 1869

Bicycle advertisement from the 1800s

Build on What You Know

During the late 1800s many innovative thinkers made significant scientific discoveries, inventions, and advances in technology. These breakthroughs, along with developments in American business practices, launched a new age of industrialization. In this chapter you will learn about the impact of new immigrants on these industries and on American life. Immigration and industrialization led to rapid growth in U.S. cities. This growth generated a series of broad transformations in the daily lives of nearly all Americans.

What's Your Opinion?

 To help students create their Themes Journal entries, provide the following examples of appropriate **agree**/**disagree** *statements.*

Culture

Agree Beginning in the 1840s, Irish immigrants brought many new traditions to the United States.

Disagree Many German immigrants learned English and abandoned their native language.

Science, Technology, and Society

Agree Innovations in steel production resulted in increased railroad production to bring people together.

Disagree The development of the cotton gin expanded slavery, thus worsening life for enslaved African Americans.

Citizenship

Agree The expansion of democracy during Andrew Jackson's presidency allowed more Americans to participate.

Disagree Many public institutions denied equal access or services to African Americans in the 1800s.

Ellis Island immigration station

Phoebus Theodore Levene

1892
Politics
The U.S. Bureau of Immigration opens a processing station on Ellis Island.

1903
Daily Life
The first World Series is played between the Pittsburgh Pirates and the Boston Pilgrims.

1909
Science and Technology
Discoveries by Russian American chemist Phoebus Theodore Levene lead to the identification of RNA and eventually DNA.

| 1890 | 1895 | 1900 | 1905 | 1910 |

1891
Daily Life
James Naismith invents the game of basketball.

1896
The Arts
Charles M. Sheldon's best-selling novel, *In His Steps,* is published.

1897
Daily Life
Steeplechase, an amusement park on Coney Island, New York, opens.

1899
The Arts
Scott Joplin's "Maple Leaf Rag" becomes an instant commercial success and a ragtime classic.

1905
The Arts
Edith Wharton's *The House of Mirth* is published.

1905
Daily Life
In one season of intercollegiate football, 18 student athletes die and 154 are seriously injured.

"Maple Leaf Rag" sheet music

What's Your Opinion?

Do you **agree** *or* **disagree** *with the following statements? Support your point of view in your journal.*

Culture Mass immigration introduces new cultural values and ways of life to society.

Science, Technology, and Society New technological developments in construction and transportation improve life for Americans of all social and economic backgrounds.

Citizenship Public institutions such as schools improve the opportunities of all Americans.

GLOBAL EVENTS

THEN AND NOW

1865 ■ The Salvation Army. Apprenticed to a pawnbroker as a young boy, William Booth experienced a religious conversion as a teenager. This conversion led him to become a Methodist preacher and a revivalist. In 1865 Booth founded the religious and charitable organization that would eventually become the Salvation Army. Booth patterned his organization after the British Army, creating corps led by officers. He established himself as general for life. In the 1880s and beyond, the Salvation Army spread to the United States, Australia, and modern-day Sri Lanka. Today the organization works in more than 80 countries, using some 112 languages to teach the gospel.

CRITICAL THINKING Why might Booth have established himself as general for life? How might this have affected his organization?

ANSWER: Students might suggest that Booth wanted to retain absolute control over the Salvation Army. Students might suggest that this absolute control could have led to dissension within the ranks.

SECTION 1

After completing Section 1, students should be able to

OBJECTIVE 1 *Explain how immigration changed during the late 1800s.*

OBJECTIVE 2 *Describe the challenges immigrants faced as they settled in the United States.*

OBJECTIVE 3 *Discuss where new immigrants found assistance.*

OBJECTIVE 4 *Relate why nativists opposed new immigration.*

 LET'S GET STARTED!

Write the sentence from the following page on the chalkboard: *"Despite these harsh conditions, many immigrants clung to the hope for a better life."* Have students respond to the sentence in writing by creating a list of the "harsh conditions" to which the passage might refer. Then have students create a list of some characteristics of the "better life" that immigrants might have hoped to create for themselves. Tell students that in Section 1 they will learn more about the lives of immigrants who came to the United States in the late 1800s and early 1900s.

SECTION 1

READ TO DISCOVER
1. How did immigration change during the late 1800s?
2. What challenges did immigrants face as they settled in the United States?
3. Where did new immigrants find assistance?
4. Why did nativists oppose new immigration?

DEFINE
old immigrants
new immigrants
steerage
benevolent societies

IDENTIFY
Denis Kearney
Chinese Exclusion Act
Immigration Restriction League
Grover Cleveland

▶ **WHY IT MATTERS TODAY**

Immigration remains an issue in the United States today. Use **CNNfyi.com** or other **current events** sources to research current immigration trends in the United States. Record your findings in your journal.

CNNfyi.com

The New Immigrants

 EYEWITNESSES TO History

"All of a sudden, we heard a big commotion and we came to America and everybody started yelling—they see the Statue of Liberty.... I remember my father putting his arms around my mother and the two of them standing and crying and my father said to my mother, 'You're in America now. You have nothing to be afraid of.'"

—Esther Gidiwicz, quoted in *Ellis Island Interviews*, by Peter Morton Coan

Immigrant passport

Esther Gidiwicz and her mother immigrated to New York from Romania in 1905. Like many immigrants, Esther already had family members and friends in the United States, including her father. These friends provided a network of support for her. While urban life in New York for immigrants was frighteningly new and hectic, many immigrants settled in neighborhoods where residents often spoke their native language and provided a village-like community. Esther described her mother's first experience shopping in the United States. "The butcher was very nice to her, and she was so happy that they spoke to her. They spoke in her language."

The Lure of America

Esther Gidiwicz was just one of the millions of immigrants who came to the United States in search of opportunity and a better life. These hopes brought a new wave of immigrants to the United States during the late 1800s.

A new wave of immigrants. From 1800 to 1880, more than 10 million immigrants came to the United States. Often called the **old immigrants**, most of them were Protestants from northwestern Europe. Then a new wave of immigration swept over the United States. Between 1891 and 1910, some 12 million immigrants arrived on U.S. shores. The increase was so great that by the early 1900s about 60 percent of the people living in the nation's 12 largest cities either were foreign-born or had foreign-born parents.

About 70 percent of these **new immigrants** were from southern or eastern Europe. Czech, Greek, Hungarian, Italian, Polish, Russian, and Slovak were among the nationalities represented. Most of these new immigrants were Catholic, Greek Orthodox, or Jewish. Arabs, Armenians, Chinese, French Canadians, and Japanese also arrived by the thousands.

Like the old immigrants, many new immigrants came to the United States to escape poverty or persecution. Most of the Armenian and Jewish families fled their homelands to escape religious or political persecution. Most of the Italian and Slavic immigrants were men seeking economic opportunities in the United States that were scarce in their home countries. Many made enough money in the

LEVEL 1: Discuss changes in immigration to the United States during the late 1800s. Compare the national origins, religious backgrounds, and reasons for immigration of new immigrants to those of old immigrant groups coming to the United States. Pair students and have each pair create a graphic organizer to list and characterize these changes in immigration. (*Pairs should indicate that the majority of new immigrants came from southern and eastern Europe—old immigrants were primarily from northwestern Europe; new immigrants tended to be Roman Catholic, Greek Orthodox, or Jewish—old immigrants were mostly Protestant; new immigrants and old immigrants alike came to seek economic opportunity and* religious freedom.) Ask volunteers to display their organizers and present them to the class.
English Language Learners, Cooperative Learning

LEVELS 2 AND 3: Tell students to imagine that they work for a U.S. government agency that compiles immigration data in the year 1910. Pair students and have each pair create an informational pamphlet about how immigration to the United States in the late 1800s differed from immigration in previous eras. Encourage members of each group to illustrate their pamphlets and to include pertinent facts and statistics. (*See the Level 1 lesson for answers.*) Call on volunteers to present their pamphlets to the class. **Cooperative Learning**

United States to return home and buy land. Others, however, put down roots and stayed. Carla Martinelli's father left a poor village in southern Italy for the United States. "My *papà mia* was a barber. He went to America twice, back and forth," she recalled. "I was young. He went to get work. Make money." As Carla explained, her reasons for immigrating were more complicated.

History Makers Speak

❝When I was sixteen, I was supposed to marry a man in Italy, but I didn't want him. My mama tell me, 'Either you marry this guy or you go to America.' But I told her, 'I don't like him.' She say, 'Then you go to America.' That's why I came to America. There was nothing in Italy, nothing in Italy. That's why we came. To find work, because Italy didn't have no work. Mama used to say, 'America is rich, America is rich.'❞

—Carla Martinelli, quoted in *Ellis Island Interviews*, by Peter Morton Coan

The journey. Many immigrants learned of available opportunities from railroad and steamship company promoters. These companies painted a tempting—and often false—picture of the United States as a land of unlimited opportunity. Some railroad companies exaggerated the availability of employment. Steamship lines also charged low fares to attract passengers.

Most of the millions who answered these appeals found the ocean journey difficult. Most traveled in the poorest accommodations, called **steerage**. These accommodations were below deck on the ship's lower levels near the steering mechanisms. The quarters were cramped, with no privacy and little ventilation. Despite these conditions, many immigrants clung to their hope for a better life in the United States.

✔ **READING CHECK: Contrasting** How were immigrants who arrived between 1891 and 1910 different from earlier immigrants? They were much more likely to be from southern or eastern Europe and to be Catholic, Greek Orthodox, or Jewish.

Arriving in America

Millions of newcomers in the late 1800s first set foot on U.S. soil on Ellis Island in New York Harbor or on Angel Island in San Francisco Bay. Both islands served as immigration stations during this period.

Ellis Island opened in 1892. Upon arrival, many European immigrants caught their first glimpse of the Statue of Liberty, a symbol of hope for many. As one immigrant explained, "All of us [immigrants] . . . clustered on the foredeck . . . and looked with wonder on this miraculous land of our dreams."

All newcomers who passed through Ellis Island were subjected to a physical exam. Those with mental disorders, contagious diseases like tuberculosis, or other serious health problems were deported. Those who passed the physicals entered a maze of crowded aisles where inspectors questioned them about their background, job skills, and relatives. Those with criminal records or without the means to support themselves were sent back. The vast majority were allowed to stay.

Research on the R●M

Free Find:
Immigrant Voices
After reading the selection of immigrant stories on the **Holt Researcher CD–ROM**, write your own story about what you might have experienced as an immigrant coming to the United States.

Total Immigration to the United States, 1860–1900

Immigrants (in thousands) — y-axis: 0, 50, 100, 150, 200, 250, 300, 350, 400, 450, 500; x-axis (Year): 1860, 1870, 1880, 1890, 1900

Source: *Historical Statistics of the United States*

Interpreting Graphs Immigration generally increased between 1860 and 1900, mainly due to an arrival of people from southern and eastern Europe.

❓ **Skills Assessment** Approximately how many more immigrants arrived in the United States in 1900 than in 1860?

GRAPH ANSWER
about 290,000

LEVEL 1: Discuss what challenges immigrants faced as they settled in the United States in the late 1800s. Then pair students and provide them with the following list of answers: **1.** railroad and steamship companies, **2.** steerage, **3.** Ellis Island or Angel Island, **4.** physical exams, **5.** immigration inspectors, **6.** deportation, **7.** Chinese applicants. Ask pairs to create a crossword puzzle with clues for the answers provided. (*Pairs should provide the following clues:* **1.** *often advertised U.S. opportunities to immigrants;* **2.** *a ship's poorest accommodations;* **3.** *points of entry for European and Asian immigrants;* **4.** *immigrants had to undergo these to prove that they were healthy;* **5.** *questioned immigrants about their backgrounds, job skills, and relatives;* **6.** *fate for immigrants with serious diseases;* **7.** *faced strict immigration laws.*) Have pairs exchange and solve each other's puzzles.
English Language Learners, Cooperative Learning

LEVELS 2 AND 3: Tell students to imagine that they are new European or Asian immigrants to the United States in the late 1800s. Have each student write a letter to a family member or friend back home describing the challenges of his or her journey to the United States and the experience of passing through Ellis Island or Angel Island. (*See the Level 1 lesson for the correct challenges.*) Ask volunteers to read their letters to the class.

THEN AND NOW

Angel Island. In order to circumvent strict immigration laws, many Asian immigrants used false papers that claimed they were related to current residents. Immigration officials ruthlessly interrogated these "paper sons and daughters." The panel asked one 11-year-old boy 83 pages of questions, a process that took days. Immigrants who failed the Angel Island interrogations faced detainment and deportation. While detained, many carved poems in the walls of their cells. In the late 1970s, Victor "Trader Vic" Bergerson, a restaurant owner, donated a black granite monument to commemorate the immigrant experience on Angel Island. The inscription on the monument reads, "Leaving their homes and villages, they crossed the ocean/Only to endure confinement in these barracks/Conquering frontier and barriers, they pioneered/A new life by the Golden Gate."

ACTIVITY: Tell students to imagine that they are Asian immigrants detained at Angel Island. Have each student write a poem commemorating his or her experience.

CHANGING WAYS ANSWERS

other European countries; North and South America

Changing Ways — Immigration

■ **Understanding Change** In the late 1800s, immigration patterns changed dramatically as more immigrants came to the United States from eastern Europe. In recent years, immigration patterns have shifted again, as more immigrants come from other parts of North and South America and from Asia. *Where did the most immigrants come from then? now?*

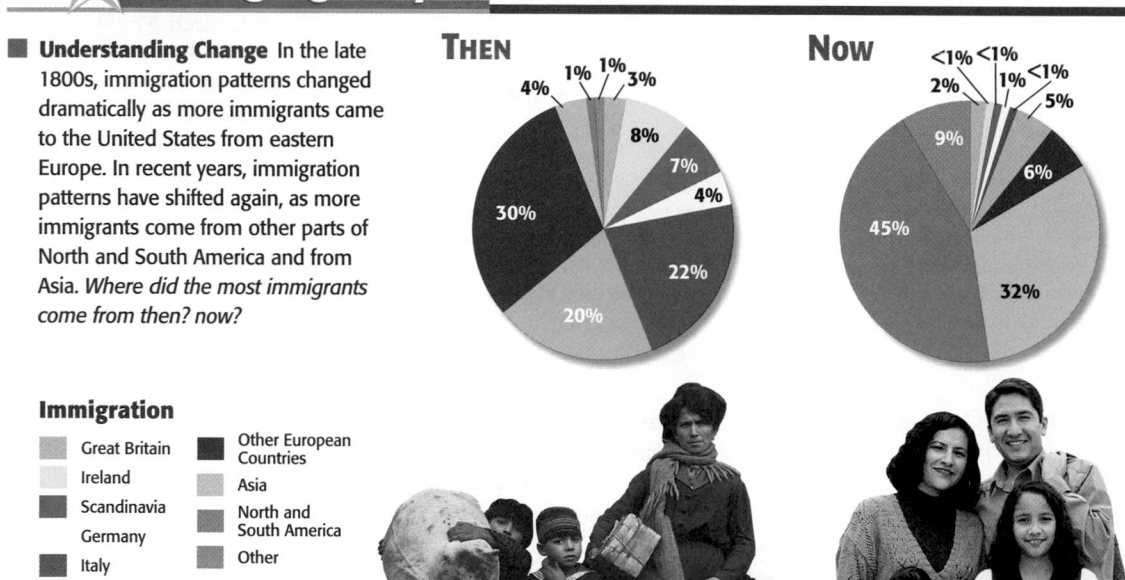

THEN 4%, 1%, 1%, 3%, 8%, 7%, 4%, 22%, 20%, 30%

NOW <1%, <1%, 2%, 1%, <1%, 5%, 9%, 6%, 45%, 32%

Immigration

- Great Britain
- Ireland
- Scandinavia
- Germany
- Italy
- Russia and the Baltic States
- Other European Countries
- Asia
- North and South America
- Other

Sources: *Historical Statistics of the United States; INS Statistical Yearbook: 1998.* Data reflect 1900 and 1998. Due to rounding, numbers may not add up to 100 percent.

Imprisoned and waiting for rulings in their cases, Chinese immigrants often carved poems such as this one on their cell walls.

詩莫各從　只可所木
成道位今　聽惜因屋
玉其鄉遠　音莫拘
勁聞君別　東雄例智
要皆眾此、策無致錢
如西歡樓　祖用牢十
籠武同中　鞭武運天

On Angel Island, thousands of Asian newcomers, who were mostly from China, underwent similar processing. Chinese applicants faced strict immigration laws. These laws limited entrance to certain skilled groups or to individuals who could show that their parents were born in the United States.

Some applicants who could not meet the restrictions were deported. Others were detained on the island as they awaited a ruling on their cases. For most immigrants, the anxiety they experienced during processing gave way to a renewed sense of hope once they finally set foot on their adopted homeland.

✔ **READING CHECK: Evaluating** What purpose did centers on Ellis Island and Angel Island serve?
to evaluate newcomers and to deport those who could not meet minimum eligibility standards

A New Life

Many immigrants found life in the United States an improvement on the conditions of their homeland. Nevertheless, the newcomers frequently endured hardships in their new home. Most immigrants settled in crowded cities where they could find only low-paying, unskilled jobs. As a result, they were generally forced into poor housing located in crowded neighborhoods and slums.

TEACH OBJECTIVE 3

ALL LEVELS: To help students understand where new immigrants found assistance, copy the following graphic organizer on the chalkboard, omitting the italicized answers. Have each student complete it.

English Language Learners, Cooperative Learning

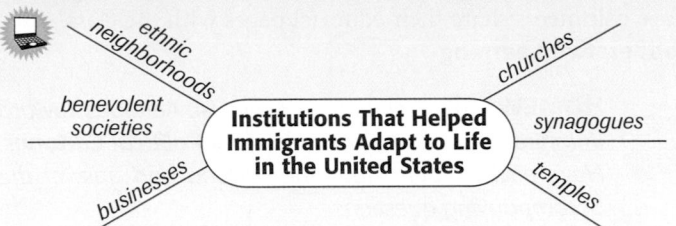

ethnic neighborhoods

benevolent societies

businesses

Institutions That Helped Immigrants Adapt to Life in the United States

churches

synagogues

temples

Teacher to Teacher

Ronald Foore of Tulsa, Oklahoma, suggested the following activity: Conduct a class discussion about the resources and institutions that help new immigrants adjust to life in the United States. Then organize students into triads. Have each triad create an immigration handbook that contains information for new immigrants. Ask volunteers to present their handbooks to the class.

Immigrant communities. Many industrial cities of the Northeast and Midwest became a patchwork of ethnic neighborhoods with numerous pockets of diverse immigrant communities. Social reformer Jacob Riis was himself a Danish immigrant. He noted that an 1890s map of New York City colored according to nationality "would show . . . more colors than any rainbow." Settling in close-knit immigrant communities, newcomers found institutions and neighbors that made their transition more bearable both financially and culturally. In these neighborhoods, for example, residents often spoke the same languages and followed the customs of the old country.

Religious institutions. Neighborhood churches, synagogues, and temples provided community centers that helped immigrants maintain a sense of identity and belonging. In Chicago religious organizations such as the United Hebrew Relief Association, which served Jews, and the St. Vincent de Paul Society, which served mainly Irish Catholics, provided economic assistance to needy immigrants in their communities. Moreover, some churches, such as St. George's Episcopal Church in New York City and Russell H. Conwell's Baptist Temple in Philadelphia, provided many services. They offered day care for children, gymnasiums, reading rooms, sewing classes, social clubs, and training courses for new immigrants.

Residents in many cities formed religious and nonreligious aid organizations, known as **benevolent societies**, to help immigrants in cases of sickness, unemployment, and death. The size and number of charitable organizations grew rapidly along with the boom in immigration. They attempted to provide an important function by helping immigrants obtain education, health care, and jobs. Some benevolent societies offered loans to new immigrants to start businesses. Others set up insurance plans that provided money for families whose breadwinners were sick or had died. "We visit our sick and bury our dead" was one society's slogan.

Cultural practices. Immigrants were often urged by employers, public institutions, and sometimes even family members to join the American mainstream. Many older immigrants cherished

The Religious Spirit

ORTHODOX RELIGIONS

Greek Orthodox icon

Many new immigrants were members of orthodox religious communities. Orthodox religions generally follow traditional practices that strictly conform to the faith's religious doctrines. For example, Orthodox Judaism is based on the Torah, the Jewish holy book, and applies its principles to daily life. The Greek and Russian Orthodox faiths strictly follow ancient rites and teachings of the early Christian Church.

The Greek and Russian Orthodox Churches grew out of a split between the Roman Catholic Church and the Christian Church of the Byzantine Empire in 1054. The split resulted from the breakup of the Roman Empire and controversies including the use of icons, or sacred images, and the role of the pope. The Greek Orthodox Church is particularly known for its intricate mosaics and decorative icons. The Russian Orthodox Church has a long tradition of missionary work. Russian missionaries established Orthodox churches in Alaska during the late 1700s when Russians were settling in the region. In 1864 the first Greek Orthodox church was established in the United States, in New Orleans. Orthodox churches, particularly in large cities, provided a community center and important services for immigrants. ■

INTERPRETING THE VISUAL RECORD

American culture. Some immigrant children embraced American culture as soon as they arrived in the United States. *How do the activities portrayed in this photo of immigrant children support this argument?*

CULTURE

Americanization. Americans conducted both public and private efforts to promote the Americanization of immigrants. The state of New Jersey provided civics and English language classes to newcomers. The North American Civic League conducted similar programs in many cities. The Immigrants Protective League offered such classes in Chicago. Some businesses also provided English classes to immigrant workers.

CRITICAL THINKING Why might so many businesses and organizations have attempted to Americanize immigrants?

ANSWER: Some students might argue that businesses and organizations intended to assist immigrants. Others might claim that Americans feared or disliked the immigrants' native cultures.

VISUAL RECORD ANSWER

Students might mention that many of the children are holding American flags.

VISUAL RECORD ANSWER

(for p. 224)

Students might mention that he sells food and other grocery items.

TEACH OBJECTIVE 4

 LEVEL 1: Have students work in pairs to identify and list the various cultural and economic reasons that nativists used to justify their opposition to immigration. *(Pairs should cite the following cultural reasons: immigrants had different religions, different languages, were held responsible for crime, poverty, violence, and radical politics; economic reasons: immigrants work cheaply to rob Americans of jobs and cause wages to be lowered.)* Ask students to share their lists with the class. Then lead a class discussion about the nativist response to immigration to the United States during the late 1800s.
English Language Learners, Cooperative Learning.

LEVELS 2 AND 3: Tell students to imagine that they must create an editorial page for an urban newspaper during the late 1800s or early 1900s. Pair students and have each pair write an editorial that summarizes and points out potential problems with the nativist view of immigration. *(See the Level 1 lesson for the correct nativist views.)* Tell students to also draw a political cartoon that is critical of the nativist response to immigration. Have volunteers share their editorial pages with the class.
Cooperative Learning

 HOMEWORK *Distribute Cartoon 14, Attitudes Toward Immigration, from* **American History Political Cartoons.** *Have each student study the cartoon and answer the accompanying questions.*

PEOPLE IN HISTORY

Denis Kearney. Denis Kearney was born in Ireland in 1847. In 1872 he moved to San Francisco, became a U.S. citizen, and opened a trucking business. Although he lacked a formal education, Kearney enjoyed reading and publicly debating social issues. He initially supported Chinese immigration, but later led the call for legislation excluding the Chinese from the United States. In his speeches, Kearney bitterly condemned journalists, businessmen, and lawyers as the enemies of the working class and demanded an end to Chinese immigration.

CRITICAL THINKING Why might Kearney, himself an immigrant, have opposed Chinese immigration?

ANSWER: Students might point to his fear of economic competition from the Chinese.

The American Nation
VIDEO PROGRAM

Community Ties: San Francisco's Chinatown; Teacher's Guide, pp. 75–80

Search 40729, Play to 48257
Videodisc 1, Side B

| Play | Pause |

See *Teacher's Guide* for Spanish barcode.

Analyzing Primary Sources

Drawing Conclusions In what ways is Frowne's work dangerous? The machines run fast, the needles might stick her, and she is so tired that she might make more mistakes.

INTERPRETING THE VISUAL RECORD

Chinese immigrants. Barred from many occupations, Chinese immigrants often opened their own businesses. *What services does this Chinese American merchant provide to his community?* ✱ 21A, 24A

their ties to the old country. By contrast, their children often adopted American cultural practices and tended to view their parents' old-world language and customs as old-fashioned. A second-generation Polish immigrant expressed bittersweet feelings about his parents' way of life. He noted, "One day it would pass and then there would remain only Americans whose forebears had once been Poles."

The immigrant worker. Whether they adopted American habits or remained tied to the traditions of their homeland, most new immigrants shared a common work experience. Many did the country's "dirty work."

In construction, mines, or sweatshops, most immigrants found their work to be difficult and physically exhausting. Hours were long, and wages were low. At the age of 15, Sadie Frowne began working in a garment factory in Brooklyn, New York. In 1902, Frowne recalled her experience there.

 History Makers Speak
❝The machines go like mad all day, because the faster you work the more money you get. Sometimes in my haste I get my finger caught and the needle goes right through it. . . . At the end of the day one feels so weak that there is a great temptation to lie right down and sleep.❞

—Sadie Frowne, quoted in *The Independent*, 1902

Some immigrants worked as many as 15 hours a day to earn a living wage. Even the best-paid workers made little more than the minimum necessary to support themselves and their families.

✔ **READING CHECK: Categorizing** Provide three examples of how new immigrants coped with problems in the United States. They relied on help from neighbors, community centers, and benevolent societies.

The Nativist Response

Immigrant workers played an important role in operating the factories that contributed to a strong U.S. economy. Nevertheless, many native-born Americans saw immigration as a threat. They agreed with poet Thomas Bailey Aldrich, who warned against a "wild motley [mixed] throng [crowd]." Many saw these newcomers as too different to fit into American society. Others went further, blaming immigrants for social problems such as crime, poverty, and violence as well as for spreading radical political ideas.

Nativists also opposed immigration for economic reasons. Many charged that the immigrants' willingness to work cheaply robbed native-born Americans of jobs and lowered wages for all. Supported by nativist workers, labor unions began demanding restrictions on immigration. Nativists achieved the greatest success in the West.

Chinese exclusion. For years Chinese laborers had been tolerated—and taken advantage of—on the West Coast, particularly in California. However, as unemployment mounted following the Panic of 1873, workers grew less tolerant. The new Workingmen's Party of California angrily cried, "The Chinese must go." **Denis Kearney**, the party's leader, was himself an Irish immigrant. He addressed crowds across the state, exciting them with his vicious speeches. Mobs attacked the Chinese, killing some and burning the property of others.

REVIEW

Have students complete the **Section 1 Review** on p. 225.

ASSESS

Have students complete **Daily Quiz 7.1.** As **Alternative Assessment**, you may want to use the crossword puzzle or letter to a friend or relative in this section's lessons.

RETEACH

Have students complete **Main Idea Activity for English Language Learners and Special-Needs Students 7.1.** Then organize students into triads. Have each triad create an

illustrated outline of Section 1. Display triads' outlines around the classroom.
English Language Learners, Cooperative Learning

EXTEND

Have students conduct research on nativist activities in the late 1800s and early 1900s. In addition to examining the Immigration Restriction League, students might analyze the American Protective Association, the Chinese Exclusion Act, or conflicts between native-born and immigrant workers in industries such as coal mining. Have each student share his or her findings in a report or narrative. **Block Scheduling**

Leaders of California's Chinese community appealed to the authorities for protection. Help, however, was not forthcoming. In fact, the state's political leaders responded by amending the state constitution to forbid Chinese residents to own property or to work at certain jobs.

In 1882 Congress passed the **Chinese Exclusion Act**, which denied citizenship to people born in China and prohibited the immigration of Chinese laborers. The act made conditions worse for Chinese Americans. In 1885 a mob in Rock Springs, Wyoming Territory, murdered 28 Chinese and drove out hundreds more. Neither the Chinese Exclusion Act nor the violence completely stopped Chinese immigrants from coming to the United States. Many Chinese immigrants still came to the United States only to be held for months at immigration stations.

Immigration Restriction League. Immigrants endured additional discrimination as new organizations took up the anti-immigration cause. Founded in 1894 by wealthy Bostonians, the **Immigration Restriction League** sought to impose a literacy test on all immigrants. Congress passed such a measure, but President **Grover Cleveland** vetoed it, calling it "illiberal, narrow, and un-American." Over the next several years Congress tried several times—without success—to pass a similar measure. Despite efforts to impose restrictions, immigration continued. Contrary to nativists' arguments, the new immigrants made positive contributions to American society. The rapid industrialization of the United States in the late 1800s would have been impossible without immigrant workers. Their varied cultures added new dimensions to American life.

✔ **READING CHECK: Drawing Conclusions** What problems did nativists create for new immigrants? Nativists threatened immigrants' personal safety and restricted their ability to own property.

INTERPRETING THE VISUAL RECORD

Nativist response. Nativists believed that immigration robbed native-born workers of jobs. *What does this 1886 soap ad reveal about the nativist reaction to Chinese immigration?*

REVIEW ① ANSWERS

1. Define
• old immigrants, p. 220
• new immigrants, p. 220
• steerage, p. 221
• benevolent societies, p. 223

2. Identify
• Denis Kearney, p. 224
• Chinese Exclusion Act, p. 225
• Immigration Restriction League, p. 225
• Grover Cleveland, p. 225

3. differences—countries of origin, religion; similarities—reasons for immigrating to the United States

4a. Answers will vary. Students might mention the experience of steerage, poor living conditions, or nativist attacks.

b. from religious institutions and benevolent societies

c. They brought cultural practices from their native countries.

5. Answers will vary. Speeches should include a discussion of the economic and cultural benefits that the Chinese contributed to the United States and should discuss racism aimed at the Chinese.

SECTION ① REVIEW

1. Define and explain:
old immigrants
new immigrants
steerage
benevolent societies

2. Identify and explain:
Denis Kearney
Chinese Exclusion Act
Immigration Restriction League
Grover Cleveland

3. Comparing and Contrasting
Copy the graphic organizer below. Use it to describe the differences and similarities of the old immigrants and the new immigrants.

Old Immigrants

New Immigrants

4. **Finding the Main Idea**

a. Imagine that you are a recent immigrant to the United States in 1900. What aspects of the journey to the United States and the adjustment to American life do you think were most difficult?
b. Where did immigrants find assistance in adjusting to American life?
c. How did new immigrants contribute to the diversity of American society?

5. **Writing and Critical Thinking**

Supporting a Point of View Imagine that you are a member of Congress arguing against nativist legislation like the Chinese Exclusion Act. Prepare a speech to support your cause.
Consider:
• how immigrants have contributed to U.S. history
• why nativists opposed immigration
• how the Chinese contributed to American life

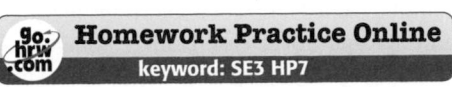
Homework Practice Online
keyword: SE3 HP7

OBJECTIVE 1 Analyze how technological innovations altered the urban landscape.

OBJECTIVE 2 Discuss the social values that the new class of wealthy city-dwellers expressed.

OBJECTIVE 3 Explain how life changed for middle-class Americans during the late 1800s.

OBJECTIVE 4 Describe what urban life was like for the poorest city-dwellers.

OBJECTIVE 5 Identify how social reformers used settlement houses and churches to improve the lives of the poor.

🎙 LET'S GET STARTED!

Write the following phrase on the chalkboard: *urban life*. As students enter the classroom, ask them to respond to the phrase in writing, identifying the images and ideas that it evokes on a personal level. Ask volunteers to share their responses. Tell students that in Section 2 they will learn more about how urban developments in the late 1800s have affected modern-day cities.

SECTION 2 RESOURCES

REPRODUCIBLE
▶ Guided Reading Strategy 7.2
▶ American History Political Cartoon 15: Urban Life
▶ Literature Reading 7: A New Social Class
▶ Graphic Organizer Activity 7: Daily Life in the Cities

TECHNOLOGY
▶ One-Stop Planner, Lesson 7.2
▶ Holt Researcher: American History CD–ROM
▶ HRW Go site
▶ Homework Practice Online

REINFORCEMENT, REVIEW, AND ASSESSMENT
▶ Section 2 Review, p. 232
▶ Daily Quiz 7.2
▶ Main Idea Activity 7.2
▶ English Audio Summary 7.2
▶ Spanish Audio Summary 7.2

SECTION 2

READ TO DISCOVER

1. How did technological innovations alter the urban landscape?
2. What social values did the new class of wealthy city-dwellers express?
3. How did life change for middle-class Americans during the late 1800s?
4. What was urban life like for the poorest city-dwellers?
5. How did social reformers use settlement houses and churches to improve the lives of the poor?

DEFINE

skyscrapers
mass transit
suburbs
nouveau riche
conspicuous consumption
tenements
settlement houses

IDENTIFY

Elisha Otis
Jane Addams
Janie Porter Barrett
Social Gospel
Caroline Bartlett

▶ WHY IT MATTERS TODAY

Many U.S. cities continue to grow rapidly. Use CNNfyi.com or other **current events** sources to learn more about how people are dealing with urban growth today. Record your findings in your journal.

CNNfyi.com

The Urban World

EYEWITNESSES TO History **"The rushing streams of commerce have worn many a deep and rugged chasm. Each of these canyons is closed in by a long frontage of towering cliffs, and these soaring walls of brick and limestone and granite rise higher and higher with each succeeding year."**

—Henry Blake Fuller, *The Cliff-Dwellers*

Henry Blake Fuller of Chicago described the emergence of multistory buildings in his 1893 novel *The Cliff-Dwellers*. During the late 1800s U.S. cities experienced "growing pains" as a result of a massive increase in population. Horace Greeley summed up the problem when he wrote, "We cannot all live in cities, yet nearly all seem determined to do so." New technological developments, such as multistory buildings, changed life for many residents in America's growing cities. The construction of tall buildings also greatly altered the urban landscape.

New York City in 1901

The Changing City

Before the Second Industrial Revolution, cities were compact. Even in the largest cities, most people lived less than a 45-minute walk from the city center. Few buildings were taller than three or four stories. By the late 1800s new technological innovations and a flood of immigrants began to transform the urban landscape. Between 1865 and 1900 the percentage of Americans living in cities doubled, from 20 percent to 40 percent. This population growth had a wide-ranging impact on urban life in the United States.

In order for urban centers to accommodate the growing number of residents, architects needed to build **skyscrapers**, or large, multistory buildings. The height of buildings had previously been limited to some five stories—in part because that was the number of flights of stairs that most people could comfortably climb. In 1853 **Elisha Otis** developed a mechanized elevator, which allowed people and materials to be transported more easily. Architects could then construct buildings well above the five-story limit.

Masonry walls used to support the structures had also limited building height. Architects solved this problem by developing steel frames. The steel frame relieved the walls from the burden of carrying the weight of the building. It allowed buildings to be built to new heights and with more windows and less wall space devoted to supporting the building. The introduction of the skyscraper transformed city life by concentrating more workers in the central business districts.

While skyscrapers extended cities upward, the development of **mass transit** extended U.S. cities outward. Mass transit included forms of public transportation such as electric commuter trains, subways, and trolley cars. Frank J. Sprague, an electrical engineer who had worked with Thomas Edison, designed one of the first

TEACH OBJECTIVE 1

LEVEL 1: Pair students and tell them to imagine that they are newspaper reporters. Ask each pair to create three headlines to describe how technological innovations altered the urban landscape. *(Pairs' headlines should note that steel frames and the elevator allowed architects to construct taller buildings, and mass transit enabled cities to expand outward.)* Ask volunteers to read their headlines to the class.
English Language Learners, Cooperative Learning

LEVEL 2: Have students study the photographs of cities on this page and the previous page. Then have each student create a detailed sketch of a fictional city block in 1899. Ask students to annotate their drawings with captions explaining how technological innovations changed the urban landscape. *(See the Level 1 lesson for the correct innovations and their effects.)* Students may wish to include their annotated sketches in their portfolios.

LEVEL 3: Tell students to imagine that they are living in a busy city during the late 1800s. Have each student write a letter to a family member living in a rural area to describe technological innovations and their impact on the urban landscape. *(See the Level 1 lesson for the correct innovations and their effects.)* Ask volunteers to read their letters to the class.

---

mass transit systems. Sprague's electric trolley, or streetcar, began serving Richmond, Virginia, in 1888. Other cities quickly adopted the invention. By 1895 the nation boasted more than 10,000 miles of electric railways.

Prior to the development of mass transit, a typical city covered about three square miles. A person could generally cross the city on foot in about two hours. With the development of mass transit, workers no longer had to live within walking distance of jobs or markets. As a result, some urban areas expanded to cover as much as 20 square miles.

The expansion of transportation to areas beyond the urban center led to the growth of **suburbs**—residential neighborhoods on the outskirts of a city. Commuter railroads offered the first chance for wealthy residents to settle outside the built-up city core. Daily fares of 15 to 25 cents for horse-drawn transportation had effectively excluded the working classes and poor from suburban life. The expansion of streetcar transportation made commuting and, in turn, suburban life more affordable. The five-cent flat-rate fares charged by some transit companies allowed middle-class office workers and some skilled laborers to leave the city. One Philadelphia resident noted that the streetcar encouraged the "spread of the city over a vast space, with all the advantages of compactness and also the advantages of pure air, gardens, and rural pleasure."

✔ **READING CHECK: Identifying Cause and Effect** How did the development of mass transit lead to the growth of suburbs? Workers no longer had to live within walking distance of jobs and markets.

INTERPRETING THE VISUAL RECORD

Electric streetcars. Streetcars such as this one in New York City provided transportation to areas previously outside the city limits. *What is the social background of these streetcar passengers?*

THAT'S INTERESTING!

Between August and December 1906 the Minneapolis city engineer conducted traffic surveys. These surveys revealed that on an average day, 786 bicycles, 183 cars, and 2,722 horse-drawn vehicles traveled the city's streets.

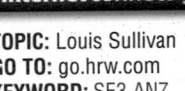

internet connect

TOPIC: Louis Sullivan
GO TO: go.hrw.com
KEYWORD: SE3 AN7

Have students access the Internet through the HRW Go site to conduct research on Louis Sullivan and his architecture. Then have each student create a model of the front of a hypothetical building based on Sullivan's architectural style. Ask students to write a short essay explaining how their buildings illustrate Sullivan's work principles.

VISUAL RECORD ANSWER

Students might suggest that based on clothing, the passengers are probably from the middle or upper-middle class.

MAP ANSWER
the East

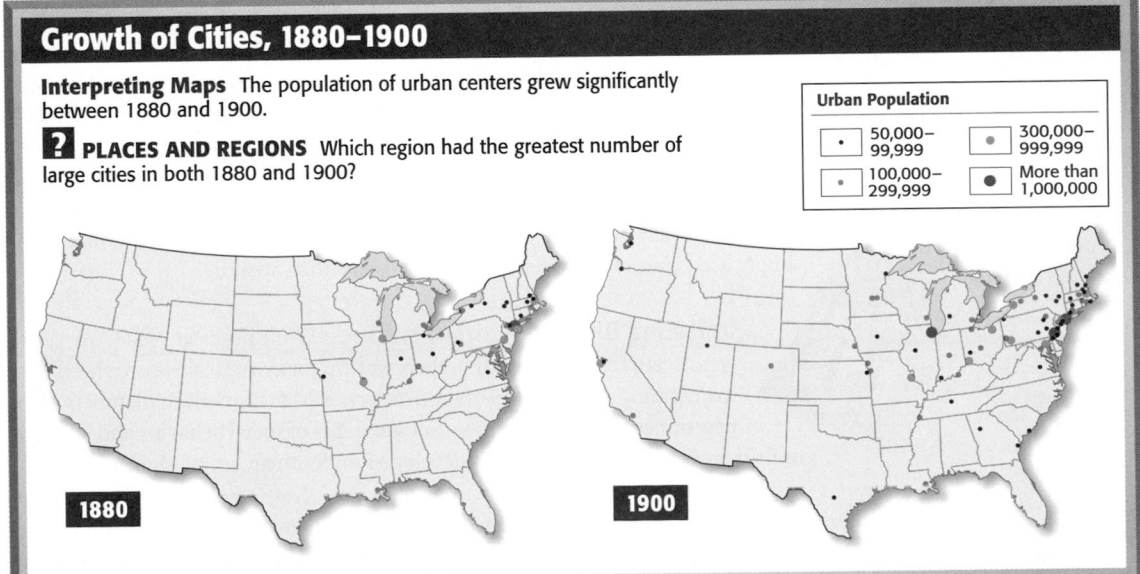

Growth of Cities, 1880–1900

Interpreting Maps The population of urban centers grew significantly between 1880 and 1900.

? PLACES AND REGIONS Which region had the greatest number of large cities in both 1880 and 1900?

Urban Population

· 50,000–99,999	● 300,000–999,999
100,000–299,999	● More than 1,000,000

1880

1900

TEACH OBJECTIVE 2

LEVEL 1: Tell students to imagine that they are editors of a school textbook. Pair students and have each pair create an outline for a section on the social values of the upper classes in the early 1900s. *(Outlines should show conspicuous consumption and imitation of British Victorian culture to be main topics; subtopics for conspicuous consumption include ostentatious homes, extravagant balls, and philanthropy; subtopics for British Victorian culture include the role of women as homemakers and obsession with maintaining proper decorum.)* Have volunteers read their outlines to the class.
English Language Learners, Cooperative Learning

LEVELS 2 AND 3: Have students work in groups of three or four to prepare an issue of a magazine designed to express the social values of wealthy city-dwellers during the early 1900s. *(See the Level 1 lesson for the correct values).* Have each group select images and prepare interviews and news stories on social events such as a debutante ball and present etiquette advice. Have each group assemble its magazine, create a title for it, and prepare a cover. Have students display their magazines and present them to the class. **Cooperative Learning**

Upper-Class Life

As the landscape of U.S. cities evolved, the social habits of city-dwellers were also changing. During the late 1800s a new class of wealthy city-dwellers emerged. Distinguished by their social values, these Americans became known as the **nouveau riche** (noo-voh REESH), a French term meaning "newly rich." There had been wealthy people in America since colonial times. However, the urban upper class of the late 1800s was a new breed. The nouveau riche—individuals like Andrew Carnegie, John D. Rockefeller, and Cornelius Vanderbilt—made their money in new industries, such as steel, mining, or railroads. Their quickly earned fortunes usually dwarfed those of the old upper-class bankers, landowners, and merchants.

INTERPRETING THE VISUAL RECORD

Nouveau riche. Many newly wealthy urban residents built large, elaborately decorated homes. *How does this photograph of Cornelius Vanderbilt's New York City home reflect his enormous wealth?*

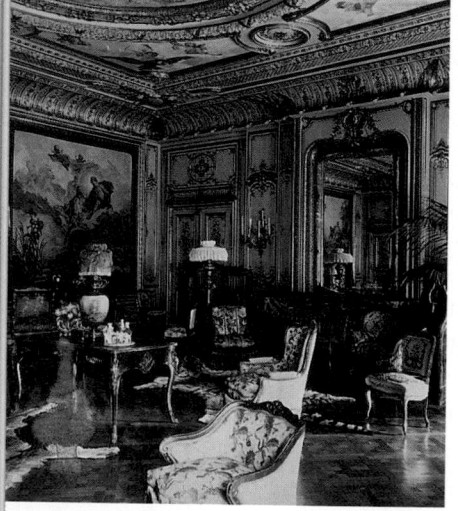

Conspicuous consumption. Many members of this nouveau riche class of city-dwellers made an effort to publicly display their wealth. Author William Dean Howells noted that for the nouveau riche, "The dollar is the measure of every value, the stamp of every success." Many of the nouveau riche spent their great wealth freely so that everyone would know how successful they were. Social scientist Thorstein Veblen labeled this behavior **conspicuous consumption**.

Elegant residential streets such as New York City's Fifth Avenue served as showcases for the wealth of the nouveau riche. They built large houses whose designs imitated Gothic castles or Italian Renaissance palaces. Andrew Carnegie even purchased an actual Scottish castle. In the summer the urban upper class left their city homes for equally magnificent country estates. The nouveau riche thought nothing of paying thousands of dollars to stage one night's amusement. Mr. and Mrs. Bradley Martin of New York, for example, hosted a fancy ball at the Waldorf-Astoria Hotel in 1897 that was estimated to cost $370,000.

Many Americans criticized such extravagances. Ward McAllister, a lawyer and member of the "Four Hundred"—the wealthiest group of New York's upper class—came to the defense of the nouveau riche. "The mistake made by the world at large is [in thinking] that fashionable people are selfish, frivolous, and indifferent to [do not care about] the welfare of their fellow creatures." Indeed, some wealthy people did support social causes. They gave money to art galleries, libraries, and museums; endowed universities; and established new opera companies, symphony orchestras, and theater groups. As critics quickly pointed out, however, not all rich men and women saw philanthropy as a way to do good. Some simply used it as another opportunity to display their wealth.

Imitating British Victorian culture. While nouveau riche Americans were occupied with parading their wealth, many were also concerned with maintaining a proper level of social behavior. Many American members of the new upper class imitated the strict standards of social behavior and etiquette of British Victorian culture, which developed under the reign of Queen Victoria.

During the late 1800s magazines like *Godey's Lady's Book, The Ladies' Home Journal,* and *The Modern Housewife* instructed upper-class Americans on how to behave properly while visiting social peers and dining. These publications governed marriage and home life in addition to setting standards for social interaction.

Some upper-class city-dwellers carried accessories such as this fan and pair of opera glasses when in public.

ALL LEVELS: Conduct a brief discussion on changes in middle-class life during the late 1800s. To help students understand these changes, copy the following chart on the chalkboard, omitting the italicized answers. Have each student complete it. **English Language Learners**

HOMEWORK *Have each student create an outline of the subsection entitled Middle-Class Life. Then have students write a brief paper comparing and contrasting middle-class life in the late 1800s and the late 1900s.*

MIDDLE-CLASS LIFE DURING THE LATE 1800s	
Change: Professionalization	**Change: Women's Lives**
created a demand for workers in specialized fields	*received more opportunities to work outside the home*
led to the establishment of professional schools and organizations	*lightened their domestic chores with sewing machines, servants, and so on*
expanded the middle class	*increased participation in cultural and social activities*

Victorian literature and instructive guides held up an ideal of domestic life. This ideal glorified the role of the woman as a homemaker. According to this vision, the home was the sole domain of the Victorian woman. Her responsibilities included organizing and decorating the home as well as offering moral and social guidance to her family. Although the Victorian woman had a certain moral authority within the home, her influence was typically limited to private life.

✔ **READING CHECK: Categorizing** What were the major characteristics of the nouveau riche? rich; made their money in new industries; conspicuous consumption; and Victorian standards of social behavior

Middle-Class Life

During the late 1800s the growth of new industries brought about an increase in the number of middle-class city-dwellers. As with the upper class, a middle class of doctors, lawyers, small-business owners, and teachers had existed since colonial times. However, by the late 1800s the rise of modern corporations had swelled the ranks of the middle class with accountants, clerks, engineers, managers, and salespeople.

Professionalization. New industries and a growing urban population created a huge demand for educated workers with a mastery of specialized fields. These fields included education, engineering, law, and medicine. Prior to the late 1800s, however, few standards or organizations existed to certify the professional standing of doctors, lawyers, teachers, or technicians. City-dwellers had few means for choosing truly skilled professionals.

During the 1870s and 1880s professional schools and organizations were formed to set standards, issue licenses, and review practices within specialized occupations. The creation of these schools and professional organizations brought more respect to these professions and their middle-class practitioners.

Middle-class women. Despite the demand for middle-class professionals, few women were permitted in professional occupations. Nevertheless, rapid urban growth did provide greater opportunities for women to work outside the home. The Victorian-era upper class and earlier generations of middle-class Americans had viewed work outside the home as a male activity. The rise of big business, however, created a variety of new jobs, such as salesclerks, secretaries, and stenographers. Business owners increasingly hired young, single women to fill these positions, paying them lower wages than men. By 1910 some 35 percent of the nearly 2 million clerical workers were women.

Most married middle-class women worked in the home. Smaller families, increased reliance on purchased goods, and new household technologies such as running water changed middle-class women's domestic work. For example, the

teen Life

The Debutante Ball

Prior to the age of 17 or 18, teenagers from wealthy families were not usually included in social functions in the late 1800s, although they were trained in proper etiquette. Some upper-class schools required students to take classes in "ballroom deportment," to prepare them to partici-

Debutante ball

pate in formal dances as adults. Debutante balls, also called coming-out parties, marked the time when young women of upper-class Victorian social circles were formally presented and accepted as members of high society.

Before a young woman's debut into society, she would spend weeks in training. She would practice gracefully climbing in and out of a carriage, walking elegantly, and acting according to proper etiquette when dining, greeting guests, and being courted. "There were so many of these little rules to remember," explained Katherine Chorley, reflecting upon her Victorian childhood, "but we were drilled (by Nanny) so that it was no effort to remember them."

One of the main functions of the debutante ball was for young women to meet prospective husbands. Most Victorian socialites viewed marriage as the most important event in a woman's life. Young women involved in high society during the Victorian Age usually married within two or three years after their coming-out parties.

ECONOMICS

Women and Work. In the early 1900s the entry of women into a given profession usually signaled the departure of men from that profession. Men did not want to compete with women because women usually received lower wages. In addition, the entry of women into a profession sometimes meant a decline in a job's status. Salesclerks, who were usually men, often had the authority to bargain with customers and purchase goods for the store. When department stores hired women to serve as clerks, however, the responsibilities of the position narrowed. Salesclerks were expected to do little more than display the merchandise and accept the customers' money.

CRITICAL THINKING What might the circumstances faced by women in the workplace have revealed about the status of women in American society during the early 1900s?

ANSWER: Students might suggest that many people still regarded women as second-class citizens who were not as capable as men.

LEVEL 1: Have students work in pairs to list the conditions associated with the lives of the urban poor. *(Pairs' lists should include housing shortages, high rent, crowded tenements, raw sewage, garbage, pollution from factories, spread of diseases, and discrimination against African Americans.)* Then have each pair use its lists to create three or four protest signs that demand an improvement in the living conditions of the poor. Have volunteers present their protest signs to the class. **English Language Learners, Cooperative Learning**

LEVELS 2 AND 3: Tell students to imagine that they live among the urban poor in the early 1900s. Have each student write a letter to his or her city alderman describing the conditions of life for the poor. *(See the Level 1 lesson for answers.)* The letter should conclude with a request that the alderman sponsor a program to improve the living conditions of the poor. Ask volunteers to read their letters to the class. Students may wish to include their letters in their portfolios.

NOTE: To help students make meaningful connections between events in U.S. history and those in their own hometown, use the Chapter 7 **Hands-On History Activity**, Leisure Time, Today and Yesterday.

In the late 1800s many middle-class women began to purchase machine-made clothing.

INTERPRETING THE VISUAL RECORD

Tenements. In his study of the urban working class, Jacob Riis explained that an entire immigrant family would frequently live in a single room that served as the bedroom, parlor, and dining room. **How does this photograph support Riis's description?**

availability of ready-made clothing lightened the sewing loads of many middle-class women. The use of hot and cold running water meant that doing laundry no longer required pumping, hauling, and heating the water. Some middle-class families could afford to hire servants to handle many household chores. In such families, women had more free time to focus on their children and to take part in the growing number of cultural events in cities. Many women joined reading and social clubs. Others participated in and led reform movements.

✔ **READING CHECK: Finding the Main Idea** What economic contributions did middle-class women make in the late 1800s? Single, middle-class women began to work outside the home, often in clerical positions.

How the Poor Lived

Most city-dwellers lived worlds away from the comfort of the middle class or the luxury of the wealthy. Although industries and factories offered new opportunities to working-class men and women, the ever-growing population of laborers eager to work kept wages low. Living conditions for the working-class city-dwellers during the late 1800s were made worse by housing shortages and the rising cost of rent. To make ends meet, working-class families often had to rent out parts of their homes or apartments to boarders.

New York City served as a magnet for hundreds of thousands of immigrants and other migrants. Some 43,000 **tenements**—poorly built apartment buildings—housed more than 1.6 million poor New Yorkers in 1900—nearly half the city's population. These rundown buildings were usually clustered in poor neighborhoods. These neighborhoods were typically within walking distance of the factories, ports, and stockyards where many poor city-dwellers worked. The dark, airless tenements sometimes housed as many as 12 families per floor. Outside the crowded tenements, raw sewage and piles of garbage littered unpaved streets and alleys. Worse still, the slums usually adjoined industrial areas where factories belched pollution. "The stink is enough to knock you down," one New York resident complained. In such an environment, sickness and death were common.

Although all residents of poor neighborhoods faced grim conditions, African Americans typically experienced the greatest difficulties. Because of widespread discrimination, most could get only low-paying jobs. African Americans also had to pay outrageous rents for the most appalling apartments and faced frequent police harassment. Yet many preferred life in the North to that in the South. As one African American journalist explained, "They sleep in peace at night; what they earn is paid them, if not they can appeal to the courts. They vote without fear of the shot-gun, and their children go to school."

✔ **READING CHECK: Summarizing** What was tenement life like? crowded conditions, raw sewage and piles of garbage outdoors, exposure to pollution, and widespread sickness

TEACH OBJECTIVE 5

LEVEL 1: Have students work in pairs to create a graphic organizer that shows the similarities and differences between settlement houses and churches of the Social Gospel movement. *(Organizers should note the following: similarities—both offered various educational and cultural opportunities for adults and children, both were committed to improving living conditions of the poor; differences—churches of the Social Gospel movement based their activities on Christian principles, while settlement houses were nonreligious/secular.)* Ask volunteers to present their organizers to the class. Then lead a class discussion about the work of social reformers in settlement houses and in churches during the Social Gospel movement.
English Language Learners, Cooperative Learning

LEVELS 2 AND 3: Have students work in pairs to create separate pamphlets that describe and promote the activities and programs sponsored by settlement houses and churches of the Social Gospel movement. *(See the Level 1 lesson for answers.)* Have volunteers share their pamphlets with the class.
Cooperative Learning

HOMEWORK *Tell students to imagine that they are settlement-house leaders or church officials who are preparing to retire after a long career that stretched from the late 1800s to the early 1900s. Have each student write a short memoir assessing his or her efforts to improve the lives of the poor.*

The Drive for Reform

In the late 1800s few government programs existed to help the poor. Some poor city-dwellers received charitable handouts of food and clothing. However, a group of idealistic young Americans was certain that more must be done.

The settlement houses. To confront the problem of urban poverty, some reformers established and lived in **settlement houses**—community service centers—in poor neighborhoods. Settlement houses offered neighborhood residents educational opportunities, skills training, and cultural events. **Jane Addams** was at the forefront of the American settlement-house movement.

BIOGRAPHY
Jane Addams

Jane Addams was born in 1860 to a wealthy family in Cedarville, Illinois. She grew up in an atmosphere of politics and philanthropy. Her Quaker father was a strong abolitionist. The young Addams set out to be a doctor. A back problem, however, ended her studies. She eventually decided to dedicate her life to helping the urban poor.

Addams began her settlement-house work in 1889. She and Ellen Gates Starr established Hull House, located in a run-down mansion in one of Chicago's immigrant neighborhoods. The early days of Hull House were busy. "Memory of the first years at Hull-House is more or less blurred with fatigue," Addams recalled.

Addams founded the settlement house with the ambition of providing social and cultural services to needy Americans. She elaborated in her memoir, *Twenty Years at Hull-House.*

History Makers Speak

> "The Settlement casts aside none of those things which cultivated men have come to consider reasonable and goodly, but it insists that those belong as well to that great body of people who, because of toilsome [hard-working] and underpaid labor, are unable to procure [obtain] them for themselves."
>
> —Jane Addams, *Twenty Years at Hull-House*

Addams's central goals were to provide educational and cultural opportunities to the poor and to improve living conditions in the neighborhoods. She also hoped that Hull House would provide fulfilling careers for settlement-house volunteers, who were mostly young women. She expected that for "young women who had been given over too exclusively to study," Hull House "might restore a balance of activity" and help them "learn of life from life itself."

The volunteers who joined Addams were mostly young, college-educated women. They set up a day nursery and kindergarten for the children of working mothers and gave adult-education classes. The experience gained at settlement houses provided the women with the skills and knowledge to make important contributions to social reform and politics.

In time, Addams's work expanded to include other important causes. She tirelessly promoted women's suffrage and

Research on the ROM

Free Find: Jane Addams
After reading about Jane Addams on the **Holt Researcher CD–ROM**, create a list of community services that you would provide if you worked in a settlement house.

INTERPRETING THE VISUAL RECORD

Hull House. Jane Addams recorded in her memoir how she and other volunteers at Hull House provided important services such as day care and education for immigrants. *How do you think these immigrant children benefited from the settlement house?*

HISTORY MAKERS SPEAK

Dorothea Moore in *Eighty Years at Hull-House*

Life at Hull House.
Social worker Dorothea Moore described Hull House in an 1897 article. "Hull-House stands not so much for a solution as a place of exchange. . . . This is the heart of the movement. This is the reason for the settlement. . . . It must help that direct human touch of richer with poorer, wise with simple, learned with untaught, dynamic with static which has for its aim the realization by all the children of their kinship with the great family."

CRITICAL THINKING What did Moore regard as the true importance of Hull House?

ANSWER: Students might suggest that Moore regarded "exchange," or interaction, as the true significance of Hull House. It brings people of diverse backgrounds together in a positive environment.

VISUAL RECORD ANSWER
Students might suggest that they benefited by receiving the opportunity to interact with other children.

VISUAL RECORD ANSWER
(for p. 232)
Students might answer that it offers education.

INTERPRETING THE VISUAL RECORD

Kindergarten. Caroline Bartlett organized kindergarten classes and other public services out of her People's Church in Kalamazoo, Michigan. *What public services does this kindergarten class provide to the community?*

served as president of the Women's International League for Peace and Freedom from 1919 until her death in 1935. Worldwide recognition for her efforts came in 1931, when she was awarded the Nobel Peace Prize.

Hull House served as a model for others hoping to aid the poor. In 1890 African American teacher **Janie Porter Barrett** founded one of the first African American settlement houses—the Locust Street Social Settlement—in Hampton, Virginia. Three years later, Lillian Wald started the Henry Street Settlement on New York's Lower East Side. By the end of the century, nearly 100 settlement houses had opened across the country.

The Social Gospel movement. At the same time that the settlement houses began their work, a number of Protestant ministers joined the battle against poverty. They developed the idea of the **Social Gospel**, which called for people to apply Christian principles to address social problems. Washington Gladden, a Congregational minister in Columbus, Ohio, was an early leader of the Social Gospel movement. Arguing that the church had a moral duty to confront social injustice, Gladden led crusades to improve conditions for industrial workers.

Many churches attempted to act according to the Social Gospel by providing classes, counseling, job training, libraries, and other social services. **Caroline Bartlett** organized People's Church in Kalamazoo, Michigan, according to the Social Gospel. Bartlett became a Unitarian minister in 1889, the same year she began her work at what became the People's Church. Bartlett opened the doors of her church seven days a week. She established a free public kindergarten and a gymnasium and offered classes in domestic and industrial skills. Bartlett also set up a meals program for workers and sponsored creative activities.

✔ **READING CHECK: Comparing** Compare the work of Jane Addams, Janie Porter Barrett, and Caroline Bartlett. Each attempted to help the needy. Addams and Barrett established settlement houses, and Bartlett established a free public kindergarten.

SECTION 2 REVIEW

1. Define and explain:
skyscrapers
mass transit
suburbs
nouveau riche
conspicuous consumption
tenements
settlement houses

2. Identify and explain:
Elisha Otis
Jane Addams
Janie Porter Barrett
Social Gospel
Caroline Bartlett

3. Categorizing Copy the graphic organizer below. Use it to describe the class divisions that developed in the cities and the characteristics that distinguished the different social groups.

4. [Finding the Main Idea]

a. Why did the physical landscape of U.S. cities change in the late 1800s?

b. In what ways did new technological developments affect daily life?

c. How was the work of Jane Addams at Hull House and Caroline Bartlett at the People's Church similar? How was it different?

5. [Writing and Critical Thinking]

Evaluating Imagine that you are a city resident in the late 1800s. Write a letter to a friend living in the country describing the opportunities and limitations of city life.
Consider:
- what opportunities the city offered
- what limitations the city imposed
- whether most city residents experienced more limits or more opportunities

Homework Practice Online
keyword: SE3 HP7

SECTION 3

Daily Life in the Cities

 EYEWITNESSES TO History

"It must be admitted unhesitatingly that we are only just learning how to play. We steal away for our holidays . . . determined to rest and take life at its easiest. We promise ourselves to forswear all thoughts of business and the outer world."

—Caspar W. Whitney, *Harper's New Monthly Magazine*, December 1894

Relaxing in a city park

Caspar W. Whitney described Americans' changing views of leisure in the late 1800s. The incredible pace of industrialization and urban growth greatly affected daily life in U.S. cities. The daily struggles of work and crowded living conditions prompted many city-dwellers to seek leisure activities. Many urban residents relaxed in new city parks. They enjoyed watching and playing sports, attended new musical and theater shows, and found leisure through reading daily newspapers and literature.

READ TO DISCOVER

1. How did public education and colleges change in the late 1800s?
2. How did publishers appeal to readers?
3. How did outdoor activities and sports provide a source of leisure for Americans?
4. What new forms of popular theater and music developed in the late 1800s?

DEFINE

compulsory education laws
yellow journalism
vaudeville
ragtime

IDENTIFY

John Dewey
Frederick Law Olmsted
City Beautiful movement
Walter Camp
James Naismith
Edwin Booth
Scott Joplin

WHY IT MATTERS TODAY

Today, modern technology has greatly changed the publishing industry. Use **CNNfyi.com** or other **current events** sources to learn more about how these changes affect what you read. Record your findings in your journal.

CNNfyi.com

Education

U.S. cities grew rapidly during the late 1800s. Urban life became increasingly difficult for workers and those with little education. To aid the urban working class, social reformers tried to expand educational opportunities.

Few children had access to public education during the early 1800s. Noting the steady growth of U.S. cities, reformers urged the expansion of public schools to educate this new population of urban children. The movement gained momentum after 1860, as more and more states began to pass **compulsory education laws**—laws requiring parents to send children to school. From 1870 to 1900, the number of students in public schools grew from some 7 million to more than 15 million—from 57 percent of the school-age population to 72 percent. Expenditures for these schools rose from about $63 million in 1870 to some $215 million in 1900.

As enrollments grew, educational reformers proposed that schools do more than teach reading, writing, and arithmetic by rote memorization. One of the main reformers was philosopher **John Dewey**. His "Laboratory School" at the University of Chicago stressed cooperative "learning by doing." He also emphasized art, history, and science. Ella Flagg Young, superintendent of schools in Chicago, worked with Dewey to fulfill his ideas. Most urban schools, however, were slow to adopt the new teaching methods.

Other reformers like William Torrey Harris and Elwood Cubberley stressed different issues. They believed that one essential function of public education was to instruct students in matters beyond reading and writing. They hoped to instruct students—particularly immigrant children—in proper behavior, civic loyalty, and American cultural values. Reformers like Harris and Cubberley feared the effects of mass immigration. They hoped that public education would help cities avoid social unrest by instilling a sense of order and discipline in the immigrant and working-class students.

LEVEL 1: Have students work in pairs to identify the major changes in public education and colleges after 1860. Then have pairs write topic sentences that summarize the changes in the educational system and their benefits. *(Sentences should mention the passage of compulsory education laws, new methods of teaching, an expanded curriculum and a greater number of colleges. Benefits included more students attending school, new subjects, and new opportunities for higher education.)* Ask volunteers to read their topic sentences to the class.
English Language Learners, Cooperative Learning

LEVELS 2 AND 3: Ask students to identify the changes in public education and colleges in the late 1800s. Then tell students to imagine that they are educational reformers in 1860. Have each student write a letter to the state board of education that advocates the changes that he or she has identified and explains how those changes will benefit students. *(See the Level 1 lesson for the correct changes and benefits.)* Ask students to read their letters to the class.

HOMEWORK *Have each student write a poem about how the public education system changed in the late 1800s.*

HISTORY MAKERS SPEAK

John Dewey in *Schools of Tomorrow*

Dewey on Education.
Philosopher John Dewey changed the way people thought about education. "We exaggerate school learning compared with what is learned in the ordinary course of living. We are, however, to correct this exaggeration, not by despising school learning, but by looking into that extensive and more efficient training given by the ordinary course of events."

CRITICAL THINKING Why might Dewey have praised "training given by the ordinary course of events"?

ANSWER: Students might suggest that Dewey appreciated the educational benefits of everyday life.

SKILL-BUILDING STRATEGIES ANSWERS
Practicing the Skill

1. compulsory school laws

2. increased from some 7 million to some 15 million

3. founded schools and developed new educational theories

4. enrolled and taught in schools

5. became more available and included some reforms

6. strengths—tried to improve learning and offered more access for women; weaknesses—discriminated against minorities

This teacher instructs her students in a Washington, D.C., public school classroom in the early 1900s.

Even with this drive to teach American values, children of many different cultures in most public schools during this era remained segregated by race. Most schools for African American, Asian American, and Hispanic students were poorly equipped. State and local governments spent little money on them. The expansion of public schools, however, did create more opportunities for young women. In 1900 about 60 percent of high school graduates were female.

The number of American colleges and their enrollments also rose during this period. At the end of the Civil War, the United States had approximately 500 colleges. By 1900 that number had grown to 1,000 institutions. Meanwhile, the enrollment in American colleges had expanded from 50,000 to 350,000 students. Although more students began to seek higher levels of education, colleges remained primarily accessible to wealthy and upper-middle-class students.

✔ **READING CHECK: Making Generalizations** How did changes in education affect students in the United States? *Compulsory education laws prompted a large increase in the number of children attending school.*

Skill-Building Strategies

Analyzing Information

Much like comparing and contrasting, analyzing is a basic skill used in historical study. To *analyze* is to break a topic or issue down into its essential parts and examine the relationships between those parts. Analyzing enables one to gain a more complete understanding of a subject, particularly when the subject can be interpreted in varying ways. As a result, analyzing helps one to draw conclusions about the subject.

How to Analyze Information

1. **Identify the subject.** Identify the topic or issue that you wish to analyze. You may want to rephrase the topic or issue as a question to be answered.
2. **Examine the facts.** Examine each piece of information that your source material provides about the subject. Make sure to study any statistics or graphic information carefully.
3. **Examine different points of view.** If the subject can be interpreted in varying ways, identify the main idea expressed by each side. Then determine whether each idea is supported by facts, opinions, or a combination of both.
4. **Draw conclusions.** Use your examination of facts and ideas to draw conclusions and evaluate any different

points of view. If you rephrased the subject for analysis as a question, answer it.

Applying the Skill

Formulate a question about U.S. public education during the late 1800s. Then analyze the material in the subsection entitled Education and answer your question.

Practicing the Skill

Answer the following questions.
1. What new education laws did some states begin to pass after 1860?
2. How did school attendance figures change between 1870 and 1900?
3. What activities did educational reformers engage in during the late 1800s?
4. How did women participate in the public education system during the late 1800s?
Use your responses to answer the following questions.
5. How did U.S. public education change during the late 1800s?
6. What were the strengths and weaknesses of the public education system during the late 1800s?

LEVEL 1: Pair students and have each pair compile a list of the ways in which newspaper and book publishers appealed to readers in the late 1800s and early 1900s. *(Lists should mention that newspaper publishers printed sensational news stories/"yellow journalism"; lavish illustrations and photographs; comic strips, including "The Yellow Kid"; advice columns; women's sections; and sports sections. Book publishers printed adventure stories, "Elsie Dinsmore" stories, realistic books about city life, and novels that focused on Christian principles.)* Ask volunteers to present their lists to the class. Conclude by leading a class discussion about the newspapers and books that appealed to readers during the late 1800s and why these newspapers and books held such appeal.
English Language Learners, Cooperative Learning

LEVELS 2 AND 3: Tell students to imagine that they are market analysts for the publishing industry during the late 1800s. Have each student prepare a market analysis report for his or her industry that describes how newspaper and book publishers appealed to readers and analyzes the popularity of certain newspaper features and novels. *(See the Level 1 lesson for the correct methods.)* Have volunteers present their reports to the class.

Publishing

The expansion of public education made newspapers and literature more important in the daily lives of many Americans. The growing number of students meant that by 1900 some 90 percent of Americans could read. This rise in literacy launched an age of publishing. Print media became the primary source of information for urban populations.

Popular journalism. Along with an increase in literacy, new developments in printing technology spurred a dramatic rise in the number of newspapers published during the late 1800s. During the 1870s and 1880s printers developed an inexpensive new type of paper that was durable enough to withstand high-speed printing. Using this paper allowed publishers to print a huge volume of newspapers. Between 1865 and 1910 the number of daily newspaper publications in the United States increased from about 500 to approximately 2,600. Circulation grew as these papers sold for just pennies each.

Daily newspapers in the same city often battled each other for a larger number of readers. The wildest circulation wars took place in New York City between Joseph Pulitzer's *World* and William Randolph Hearst's *New York Journal.* To attract readers, publishers developed new journalistic practices. The *World* tried to win readers by running sensational news stories. It also used fancy illustrations and photographs. The *Journal* competed with even more sensational stories. Both papers attempted to appeal to a broad readership by including comic strips, advice columns, special women's sections, and separate sports sections.

The newspapers also competed for readers by publishing the popular comic series "The Yellow Kid," one of the first cartoons published in color. The lead character was a young tenement-dweller who was dressed in a yellow gown and reflected stereotypes many Americans had about immigrants. The hugely popular cartoon inspired many critics to refer to the *World*'s and the *Journal*'s style of sensational reporting as **yellow journalism**.

Literature. The publication of popular literature also experienced significant growth as a result of Americans' increased literacy. Dime and nickel novels promoted by publishers like Erastus Beadle attempted to entice readers with adventure stories. Beadle wrote frontier novels such as *Deadly Eye* and *Spitfire Saul, the King of the Rustlers.* Martha Finley's stories about virtuous character Elsie Dinsmore gained a huge following among young girls.

Older readers favored realistic books about city life. For example, Edith Wharton's 1905 novel, *The House of Mirth,* describes the conflicts between New York City's nouveau riche and old upper class. Published in 1885, William Dean Howells's *Rise of Silas Lapham* weaves a tale of greed and social ambition.

INTERPRETING THE VISUAL RECORD

Yellow journalism. Newspapers such as the *World* published sensational stories and color cartoons, like this one featuring "The Yellow Kid" to attract readers. **What aspects of this cartoon might attract readers to the newspaper?**

CULTURE

Public Libraries. Public libraries expanded access to newspapers and books in the late 1800s. Early libraries tended to be organized as private reading rooms. In the mid-1800s, however, cities began to establish tax-supported public libraries. Historians regard the founding of the Boston Public Library in 1852 as the beginning of a large-scale trend. Although open to the public, many of the early public libraries served the interests of middle- and upper-class citizens. Librarians regarded it as their responsibility to provide readers with quality literature, often refusing to order dime novels and other pulp books that were popular with the working classes.

CRITICAL THINKING Why might librarians of early public libraries have wanted to order and stock only "good" novels?

ANSWER: Students might suggest that the librarians wanted to "improve" their patrons with "good" books.

VISUAL RECORD ANSWER

Students might point to its color, its vibrancy, and possibly its prejudicial portrait of Asian Americans.

TEACH OBJECTIVE 3

LEVEL 1: Pair students and have them create charts that list the different outdoor activities and spectator sports that engaged city-dwelling Americans in the late 1800s and explain how these activities provided sources of leisure for urban residents. *(Lists should mention that park excursions offered refuge from crowded city life, that bicycling and croquet provided activities for people who visited city parks, and that baseball and football attracted participants and spectators.)* Ask volunteers to present their charts to the class. Conclude by leading a class discussion about the outdoor activities and spectator sports that Americans enjoyed in the 1890s.
English Language Learners, Cooperative Learning

LEVELS 2 AND 3: Tell students to imagine that they work for a large city's chamber of commerce or tourist bureau in the 1890s. Pair students and have them create brochures that list the leisure activities popular with the city's residents as well as reasons why city residents find these activities to be appealing. *(See the Level 1 lesson for the correct reasons.)* Ask students to present their brochures to the class. **Cooperative Learning**

NOTE: For an additional teaching idea, see the Chapter 7 brainstorming lesson in the **Creative Teaching Strategies** handbook.

Central Park. Frederick Law Olmsted envisioned Central Park as a place where urban-dwellers could enjoy nature. In accordance with this vision, he opposed most recreational activities in the park. Park officials allowed only those recreational activities that did not affect the park environment, such as boating.

CRITICAL THINKING How might Olmsted's vision of the park as a place to enjoy nature have benefited visitors even while limiting them?

ANSWER: Students might suggest that Olmsted's vision allowed visitors to enjoy the natural world but deprived them of certain recreational activities, such as baseball.

THAT'S INTERESTING!

In many cities, park development benefited only middle- and upper-class citizens. In Chicago's suburbs, for example, there were 1,500 acres of world-renowned parks. In three of the city's largest and poorest urban neighborhoods, however, there were no parks at all.

Then and Now

Amusement Parks

Advertisement for an amusement park on Coney Island

The original amusement parks of the late 1800s provided places for middle- and working-class families to find inexpensive leisure activities just outside the city. Borrowing ideas from the hugely popular world fairs like the 1893 Chicago Exposition, parks like Dreamland, Luna, and Steeplechase on Coney Island offered grand architecture, mechanical rides, small replicas of exotic places and foreign villages, daily theatrical shows, and re-enactments of current events. One journalist described the amusement parks of Coney Island as an "enchanted, story book land of . . . domes, minarets [towers], lagoons, and lofty aerial flights. . . . It was a world removed—shut away from the sordid clatter and turmoil of the streets."

Today's theme parks offer a similarly fantastic escape. While the price has risen from the 10-cent admission to Coney Island to more than $35 for one day's admission to many amusement parks, parks continue to provide a way for many Americans to retreat from everyday life into a world of fantasy. Disneyland founder Walt Disney once explained, "I don't want the public to see the world they live in while they're in Disneyland, I want them to feel they're in another world."

Frederick Law Olmsted's design for Central Park created a rural setting in the heart of New York City.

THE GRANGER COLLECTION, NEW YORK

The most commercially successful novels during the late 1800s were ones that focused on Christian principles. Charles M. Sheldon's 1896 novel, *In His Steps,* was the era's most popular book, selling millions of copies. Sheldon depicted characters who addressed their personal problems by asking the question, "What would Jesus do?"

✔ **READING CHECK: Analyzing Information** What developments led to an increase in the number of newspapers and novels?
development of an inexpensive new type of paper and growth in the number of literate Americans

Leisure Time in Urban Parks

During the late 1800s Americans increasingly counted on leisure activities to provide relief from busy city life. City planners developed large urban parks to offer a natural refuge from the crowded, built-up city. Urban residents eagerly used these parks as a space for relaxation where they could participate in a variety of new leisure activities.

In 1857 landscape architect **Frederick Law Olmsted** designed Central Park in New York City. He sought to create a rural setting within New York's urban environment. The park included pedestrian paths, ponds, and trees. Olmsted designed the 2.5-mile-long park for people of all social classes to gather and enjoy the natural landscape. In 1871 more than 10 million people visited the park—roughly 30,000 visitors each day.

Olmsted's success helped spur an American planning movement known as the **City Beautiful movement**. The movement adopted a number of ideas from a British planning movement called Garden City. Supporters of the City Beautiful movement stressed the importance of including public parks and attractive boulevards in the design of cities. These city planners claimed that such designs could be a civilizing influence for city-dwellers.

Americans took advantage of these new city parks to pursue a variety of outdoor activities. Bicycling became immensely popular with both men and women during the late 1800s. By the turn of the century about 4 million Americans were riding bicycles. Playing croquet in city parks was also popular with Americans. In this simple game, a player uses a mallet to drive a ball through a series of wire wickets, or small arches. Played on lawns and park grounds, croquet was a sociable sport that became a fashionable pastime for many middle-class women.

Leisure and Sports

During the late 1800s many Americans spent their leisure time playing the era's new organized sports. Many urban residents found sports like baseball and football exciting to play as well as to watch. Afternoon games and matches became a regular activity

SPOTLIGHT
on Baseball, Football, and Basketball

Have students select either baseball, football, or basketball. Ask students to conduct research on the history of their chosen sport. Then have each student develop a project on the topic. Students might write a short story, essay, or report; create a visual display of some kind; develop a multimedia presentation; and so on. Ask students to complete their projects and then present their work to the class. **Block Scheduling**

TEACH OBJECTIVE 4

LEVELS 1 AND 2: Conduct a brief discussion on new forms of popular music and entertainment that developed in the late 1800s. Then copy the graphic organizer on the next page on the chalkboard, omitting the italicized answers. Have each student complete it. To conclude, pair students and ask each pair to write paragraphs comparing and contrasting popular entertainment in the late 1800s and the late 1900s. **English Language Learners, Cooperative Learning**

for many urban residents. During the late 1800s a number of spectator sports in the United States began to standardize their rules.

Baseball. Popular myth holds that Abner Doubleday invented the game of baseball. However, the basic organization and rules of the game actually evolved in the early and mid-1800s from the British game called rounders. Prior to the Civil War, young middle- and working-class city-dwellers organized neighborhood baseball teams. These teams, such as the New York Knickerbockers, played teams in surrounding neighborhoods and cities. While the outbreak of the Civil War interrupted the development of these clubs, it also greatly expanded baseball's popularity. During the war, troops from all over the United States became familiar with the game.

In 1869 Aaron Champion organized the first professional baseball team, the Cincinnati Red Stockings. Playing baseball became a full-time paid position for talented players such as Harry Wright. The Red Stockings were a success, beating every team they played that year. Soon other clubs also began to pay their ballplayers as professionals.

Concerned about issues of gambling, players' contracts, and standardized rules, William Hulbert organized the National League in 1876. He created a governing body for the sport. Hulbert also established rules for play, strict guidelines for players' contracts, and rules limiting players' association with gamblers.

Baseball's popularity continued to rise. By 1890 professional teams were drawing an estimated 60,000 fans daily. Another professional league was founded in 1900. Three years later the first World Series was held between the Pittsburgh Pirates and the Boston Pilgrims, later known as the Red Sox.

Baseball had become, in one sportswriter's words, "the national game of the United States." Not all Americans were allowed to play in the professional leagues, however. In 1887 team manager Adrian "Cap" Anson refused to let his team play against teams with African American players. Anson's action and the widespread discrimination in the baseball leagues resulted in African Americans being excluded from major league teams for 60 years. However, African Americans formed their own league, which produced many outstanding players.

Football. As with baseball, many Americans enjoyed watching football during their leisure time. Similar to soccer and the British game of rugby, football developed during the late 1800s on the college campuses of upper-class New England schools. **Walter Camp** played football for Yale during the late 1870s. He made considerable contributions to the structure of the sport, establishing many of its rules and principles. Discussing the spirit of football, Camp stated, "There is no substitute for hard work and effort beyond the call of mere duty. That is what strengthens the soul and ennobles one's character."

As football became popular with college students in the late 1800s, many people objected to its violent nature. The *Chicago Tribune* documented the deaths of 18 college players and 46 high school players in the 1905 season. The sport's brutality led to discussions in Congress about outlawing it. Rule changes reduced the sport's danger. Football's popularity continued to grow.

INTERPRETING THE VISUAL RECORD

Baseball. Fans used scorecards such as this one to keep track of their favorite teams' records and statistics. *How is the late-1800s baseball gear pictured here similar to the equipment used today?*

Walter Camp poses in his Yale football uniform.

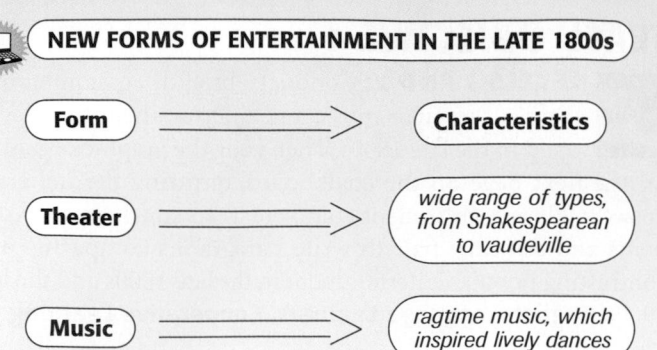
LEVEL 3: Have students complete the Levels 1 and 2 activity. *(See the graphic organizer on this page for the correct forms and characteristics.)* Pair students and tell them to imagine that they work for a musical theater in the 1890s. Have each pair create theater handbills that advertise the new forms of musical entertainment that appeared in the late 1800s. In their handbills, students should describe the unique characteristics of these forms of entertainment and explain why they appealed to the public. Have volunteers present their handbills to the class.
English Language Learners, Cooperative Learning

SECTION 3 REVIEW ANSWERS

1. Define
- compulsory education laws, p. 233
- yellow journalism, p. 235
- vaudeville, p. 238
- ragtime, p. 238

2. Identify
- John Dewey, p. 233
- Frederick Law Olmsted, p. 236
- City Beautiful movement, p. 236
- Walter Camp, p. 237
- James Naismith, p. 238
- Edwin Booth, p. 238
- Scott Joplin, p. 239

3. reading—popular journalism, novels; sports—baseball, football, basketball; entertainment—theater, vaudeville, ragtime music

4a. States passed compulsory education laws and enrollment increased; the number of colleges increased.

b. yellow journalism—attempted to a broader readership; popular literature—also grew as a result of increased literacy; some focused on Christian principles.

c. These groups had different access to events based on money and location.

5. Answers will vary. Letters might point to the benefits of having places to enjoy nature and to play games. Without such places, life in urban areas would be more stressful.

Basketball. Like football, basketball was first played by students. **James Naismith**, a physical educator in Springfield, Massachusetts, invented the game of basketball in 1891. He was attempting to find a sport that could entertain a group of unruly students during the long, cold months of winter. Naismith claimed that basketball "demanded and fostered alert minds and supple [flexible] bodies. Decisions had to be made quickly. Play had to be neat and nimble [quick]." By the mid-1890s colleges in the East and Midwest had created both male and female teams. Basketball was one of the few sports during the late 1800s in which women's participation was encouraged.

INTERPRETING THE VISUAL RECORD

Basketball. Basketball was a popular recreational activity for college students during the winter months. *How do these female basketball players differ from players today?*

✔ **READING CHECK: Drawing Conclusions** How did the growth of sports affect the daily lives of Americans? More Americans, including women, participated in sports and attended sporting events.

Entertainment

While sports like baseball provided entertainment for many city-dwellers, others sought different sources of amusement. During the late 1800s people of every income level spent leisure time enjoying the theater and music.

Theater. Rapid urban growth brought many new entertainment seekers into U.S. cities. Many of these city-dwellers turned to the stage for entertainment. Portraying William Shakespeare's tragic heroes, **Edwin Booth** proved to be one of the most popular attractions of the 1860s and 1870s. He was considered one of the premier actors of his day. Due to public demand one season, Booth acted in 100 consecutive performances of *Hamlet*. Tickets for his opening performance in *Romeo and Juliet* in 1869 sold for as much as $125 each.

While the classic Shakespearean plays attracted a sophisticated audience, many Americans preferred more melodramatic shows. Because of their easily identifiable character types, these shows attracted a broad working-class audience. Often the villain was cast as a wealthy aristocrat, while the hero and heroine represented working-class people.

Attracting a similar audience, **vaudeville**—the French word for "light play"—was a type of variety show that featured a wide selection of short performances. Vaudeville shows often included animal acts, comics, famous impersonations, jugglers, magicians, singers, and skits. Some promoters of vaudeville became highly successful and went on to open chains of theaters.

Ragtime. Performed in vaudeville shows at the turn of the century, a new form of music known as **ragtime** proved popular with audiences. Created by African American musicians, ragtime emerged during the 1890s. It varied radically from the traditional Victorian waltzes and marches popular earlier that century. Copying the customary foot stomping of audiences listening to folk songs, ragtime pianists played a stomping or driving rhythm with the left hand and a syncopated or improvised melody with the right hand.

REVIEW

Have students complete the **Section 3 Review** on p. 239.

ASSESS

Have students complete **Daily Quiz 7.3**. As **Alternative Assessment**, you may want to use the charts or handbills in this section's lessons.

RETEACH

Have students complete **Main Idea Activity for English Language Learners and Special-Needs Students 7.3**. Organize the class into small groups. Assign each group one of the following topics: education, publishing, leisure time in urban parks, leisure and sports, and entertainment. Have each group prepare a visual display illustrating the major events, trends, people, and ideas associated with the assigned topic. Have groups show and explain their posters to the class.
English Language Learners, Cooperative Learning

EXTEND

Have students conduct research on the history of vaudeville in the United States, including the types of acts included in vaudeville shows and popular vaudeville performers. Then have each student present his or her findings in an essay. Alternately, ask each student to create posters for a vaudeville show that would have been popular during the late 1800s. Ask volunteers to present their essays or show descriptions to the class.
Block Scheduling

Scott Joplin

Known as the King of Ragtime, **Scott Joplin** was born into a family of musicians from East Texas in 1868. Joplin learned to play the piano before the age of seven. In his early teens, he began playing in bars and saloons throughout the Mississippi Valley. After playing briefly at the Chicago Exposition in 1893, Joplin settled in the St. Louis area and concentrated on composing new musical arrangements and experimenting with syncopated melodies.

As the ragtime craze spread across the United States, Joplin further refined his style. He found a growing audience for his music. Hearing Joplin play at the Maple Leaf Club in 1899, John Stillwell Stark immediately offered to publish Joplin's tune, the "Maple Leaf Rag." The tune became an instant hit. It sold hundreds of thousands of copies in the first decade of publication and made Joplin's name a household word.

After the success of the "Maple Leaf Rag" and several vaudeville tours, Joplin gave up playing for audiences. He began to concentrate on teaching music and composing. He spent much of the rest of his life working on an opera that had little success. Nevertheless, Joplin's ragtime songs remained popular among young city-dwellers even after his death in 1917.

Known as rags, ragtime songs inspired a host of new dances whose liveliness and self-expression contrasted sharply with the restraint of Victorian culture. Dances like the Cakewalk, the Grizzly Bear, and the Turkey Trot became popular in dance halls. Young middle- and working-class city-dwellers eagerly pursued these new forms of entertainment and leisure.

✔ **READING CHECK: Making Predictions** How did the growth of cities contribute to the development of new forms of popular theater and music? Rapid urban growth brought many entertainment seekers into U.S. cities.

INTERPRETING THE VISUAL RECORD

Ragtime. The popularity of ragtime music grew with the emergence of lively dances. *How did the publisher of this ragtime tune incorporate the dance craze into the marketing of the sheet music?*

SECTION 3 REVIEW

1. Define and explain:
compulsory education laws
yellow journalism
vaudeville
ragtime

2. Identify and explain:
John Dewey
Frederick Law Olmsted
City Beautiful movement
Walter Camp
James Naismith
Edwin Booth
Scott Joplin

3. Summarizing Copy the graphic organizer below. Use it to describe the different leisure activities that were popular in the late 1800s.

Reading — LEISURE — Entertainment — Sports

4. Finding the Main Idea
a. How did education change in the late 1800s?
b. How did the development of yellow journalism and popular literature reflect the issues of the late 1800s?
c. What reasons can you give to explain why lower- and middle-class urban residents took up different leisure practices than wealthy Americans?

5. Writing and Critical Thinking
Making Generalizations Write a letter to the editor explaining why you think the city needs to set aside more public "green space," such as parks.
Consider:
• what benefits green space offers to city-dwellers
• what might happen if green space were not set aside

Homework Practice Online
keyword: SE3 HP7

REVIEW AND ASSESSMENT RESOURCES

TECHNOLOGY

► Chapter 7 Test Generator
  (on the One-Stop Planner)
► Global Skill Builder
  CD–ROM
► HRW Go site

REINFORCEMENT, REVIEW, AND ASSESSMENT

► Chapter 7 Review,
  pp. 240–41
► Chapter 7 Tutorial for
  Students, Parents, Mentors,
  and Peers

► Chapter 7 Test (Form A or B)
► Portfolio Activities and
  Alternative Assessment
  Handbook, Chapter 7
► Chapter 7 Test for English
  Language Learners and
  Special-Needs Students

REVIEW

Have students complete
the **Chapter 7 Review**
on pp. 240–41.

ASSESS

Use one of the chapter tests to
assess students' understanding
of the content. For **Alternative
Assessment**, see the **Portfolio
Activities and Alternative
Assessment Handbook**.

---

3. population—immigrants
and other Americans came
to cities in search of opportunities; size—mass transit
allowed cities to grow
outward

4. They organized settlement houses and provided
educational and cultural
opportunities to poor
Americans and immigrants.
Others provided relief from
poverty.

5. by offering popular,
appealing entertainment
to a wide variety of people

Reviewing Themes
1. native languages, cultures,
and religious beliefs

2. Mass transit changed
the size of cities; elevators
made skyscrapers feasible;
bicycles provided a new
leisure activity.

3. They offered education
and information to almost
all Americans.

Thinking Critically
1. It required children to
attend school, removing them
from the workforce and it led
to increased literacy, which
led to greater interest in
publications.

2. They took classes in
English and in American
cultural values.

3. It stressed the importance
of public parks and attractively
designed boulevards.

CHAPTER 7 Review

Creating a Time Line

*Copy the time line below onto a sheet of paper. Complete
the time line by filling in the events and dates from the
chapter that you think were most significant. Pick three
events and explain why you think they were significant.*

1865	1880	1895	1910

Writing a Summary

*Using standard grammar, spelling, sentence structure, and
punctuation, write an overview of events in the chapter.*

Identifying People and Ideas

*Identify the following terms or individuals and explain
their significance.*

1. new immigrants
2. benevolent societies
3. Elisha Otis
4. mass transit
5. conspicuous consumption
6. Caroline Bartlett
7. compulsory education laws
8. Frederick Law Olmsted
9. yellow journalism
10. Scott Joplin

Understanding Main Ideas

SECTION 1 *(pp. 220–225)*
1. What changes occurred in the pattern of immigration during the late 1800s?
2. Why did nativists argue against immigration?

SECTION 2 *(pp. 226–232)*
3. Why did cities grow in terms of population and
   size during the late 1800s?
4. What contributions did social leaders such as
   Jane Addams make?

SECTION 3 *(pp. 233–239)*
5. How did popular literature, journalism, and
   other types of entertainment cater to a broad
   audience?

Reviewing Themes

1. **Culture** What cultural practices did immigrants
   bring to the United States in the late 1800s?
2. **Science, Technology, and Society** How did
   technological developments alter U.S. cities and
   change the daily lives of city-dwellers?
3. **Citizenship** In what ways did settlement
   houses, public schools, and newspapers assist
   all Americans?

Thinking Critically

1. **Evaluating** How did the growth of the public
   school system change daily life for Americans?
2. **Summarizing** In what ways were new immigrants
   made "more American"?
3. **Drawing Conclusions** In what ways did the City
   Beautiful movement want to change the appearance of cities?
4. **Identifying Cause and Effect** How did the growth
   of the middle class and the nouveau riche affect
   culture?
5. **Analyzing Information** What was the relationship
   between the problems of immigrants and the
   growth of cities?

Writing About History

Supporting a Point of View Imagine that you run a
settlement house. Write a letter to a wealthy family
persuading them to donate money to your settlement
house. Be sure to explain the purpose of the settlement house, the specific programs it offers, and its
effects on the city. Use the following chart to help
organize your thoughts.

Settlement House		
Purpose	Programs and Services	Benefits

RETEACH

Organize the class into three groups. Assign each group one of the sections in this chapter. Have groups create outlines of the major topics and subtopics in their assigned sections. Then rotate the outlines to the next group and have that group add specific information. Rotate the detailed outlines to the next group to evaluate thoroughness and accuracy.

English Language Learners, Cooperative Learning

EXTEND

Have students locate and read excerpts of *Looking Backward* by Edward Bellamy. Have each student write an essay comparing the late 1800s with two other time periods: the late 1900s as described by Bellamy and the late 1900s as they actually were. You may wish to have each student concentrate on one theme in order to make the analysis more manageable.

Block Scheduling

Building Social Studies Skills

Interpreting Political Cartoons

Study the political cartoon below. Then use it to help answer the questions that follow.

THE GRANGER COLLECTION, NEW YORK

1. What is the most accurate inference from this cartoon?
   a. Lady Liberty is preparing to strike the U.S. Treasury Department with her torch.
   b. Lady Liberty is unhappy about the arrival of European immigrants.
   c. The U.S. Treasury Department is angrily preparing to close the port to further immigration.
   d. The U.S. Treasury Department is preparing to grab the torch from Lady Liberty.

2. What were the main causes of nativist attitudes?

Analyzing Primary Sources

Analyze the following quotation from Jacob Riis, a journalist and social reformer, describing some New York teenagers in the 1880s. Then answer the questions that follow.

> ❝The gang is an institution in New York. . . . [It] is the ripe fruit of the tenement-house growth. . . . Of the 82,200 persons arrested by the police in 1889, 10,505 were under twenty years old. The last report of the society for the prevention of Cruelty to Children enumerates [lists], as 'a few typical cases,' eighteen 'professional cracksmen,' between nine and fifteen years old, who had been caught with burglars' tools, or in the act of robbery. Four of them hardly yet in long trousers, had 'held up' a wayfarer in the public street and robbed him of $73. . . Four of the eighteen were girls and were quite as bad as the worst.❞

3. Which of these characteristics is NOT part of Riis's description of gang members?
   a. under twenty years old
   b. burglars
   c. tenement-house residents
   d. all male

4. How might the growth of tenement houses have contributed to an increase in gangs?

Alternative Assessment

Building Your Portfolio

U.S. HISTORY

Culture

Imagine that you are a new immigrant in the United States during the late 1800s and that you have a family member who is thinking about immigrating as well. Create a chart listing the positive and negative aspects of your life in the United States so that your relative can make an informed decision.

✐ **internet** connect

go.hrw.com

Internet Activity: go.hrw.com
KEYWORD: SE3 AN7

Choose a topic on the transformation of American society to:

- compare and contrast immigration patterns and experiences of immigrants in the 1800s and 1900s.
- research the history of baseball and write a biography of an important player.
- create an architectural model based on the principles of Louis Sullivan.

---

4. The nouveau riche and the middle class had more money and more time for leisure activities, which contributed to the growth of sporting events, theater, and music.

5. Increased immigrant population led to overcrowding in housing and led some people to move to the suburbs.

Writing
purpose—to aid the impoverished in American society; programs and services—education, skills training, cultural events; benefits—helped immigrants become productive laborers and improved the quality of urban life

Building Social Studies Skills
1. b

2. Some Americans feared that immigrants would take jobs from them; others did not approve of cultural differences.

3. d

4. Answers will vary. Students might suggest that the conditions in tenement houses were horrible, and that young people lived very close together and could be influenced more easily.

LET'S GET STARTED!

Write the following statement on the chalkboard: *The West has always been a land of immigrants and migrants—those who emigrated from another country, and those who migrated from another region.* Ask each student to respond to the statement in writing. Have volunteers share their responses. Tell students that they will learn more about immigration and shrinking distances in the United States in the Unit 2 America's Geography.

TEACH AMERICA'S GEOGRAPHY— CONQUERING DISTANCE

Pair students and tell them to imagine that they are modern-day historians studying the theme of conquering distance in the mid- to late 1800s. Have each student write a paragraph summarizing the information presented in the America's Geography feature. Remind students they will need to choose their wording very carefully to create a full, useful summary.
English Language Learners

GLOBAL RELATIONS

Immigration Rights. The U.S. government originally encouraged the increase in Chinese immigration in part to provide cheap labor for the transcontinental railroad companies. An 1869 U.S. treaty granted Chinese visitors and residents most-favored-nation treatment. Many Americans began to resent the growing Chinese population, however. In 1870 Congress banned Asian immigrants from naturalization. In 1882, under pressure from western states, Congress passed the Chinese Exclusion Act to completely bar the immigration of Chinese workers. Congress later expanded and extended the act.

CRITICAL THINKING How might Chinese officials have responded to the exclusion of their emigrants to the United States?

ANSWER: Students might suggest that Chinese officials disliked the ban and attempted to ban American visitors or emigrants to China.

AMERICA'S GEOGRAPHY ANSWERS

1. In 1900 a smaller percentage of Chinese Americans lived in California than in 1870. By 1900 some had settled in the North Atlantic region.

2. Germany

Conquering Distance

Massive population shifts occurred in the United States in the late 1800s. Between 1860 and 1910, some 23 million immigrants crossed the Atlantic and Pacific Oceans to reach the United States (see map at right). Many of these immigrants joined the millions of people making the cross-country trek to settle the American West. Railroad lines and improved systems of communication aided this westward migration. They linked numerous western cities together, forming the basis of a modern transcontinental economy.

Asian immigration. Immigrants from Asia had to travel twice as far as European immigrants to reach the United States. Although most Chinese immigrants initially settled along the West Coast, some eventually journeyed across the United States. In 1870 a Massachusetts factory owner began recruiting Chinese laborers from California to take the place of striking workers. As this practice caught on, more Chinese laborers made the trip to the East Coast. This migration led to the development of thriving Chinatowns in Boston and New York.

Conquering Distance Overseas

JAPAN 158,000
CHINA 290,000
NORTH AMERICA
UNITED STATES
CA
NY
SCANDINAVIA 1.9 MILLION
RUSSIA & THE BALTICS 2.36 MILLION
IRELAND 2.3 MILLION
GREAT BRITAIN 2.79 MILLION
GERMANY 3.86 MILLION
ITALY 3.07 MILLION
EUROPE
ASIA

Chinese American Areas of Residence

1870	1900
77% California, 23% All other areas	51% California, 33% All other areas, 16% North Atlantic

California   All other areas   North Atlantic

Sources: *World Book Encyclopedia*; Ronald Takaki, *Strangers from a Different Shore*

Percentage of California's Chinese Population Living in San Francisco

1870	1900
76% San Francisco, 24% Rest of California	55% San Francisco, 45% Rest of California

San Francisco   Rest of California

Sources: *World Book Encyclopedia*; Ronald Takaki, *Strangers from a Different Shore*

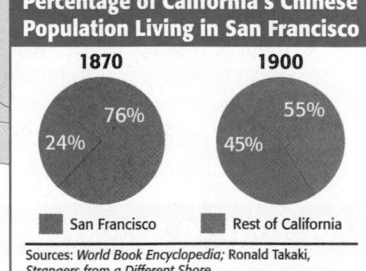

GEOGRAPHY AND HISTORY   Skills

HUMAN SYSTEMS

1. How did the locations of Chinese American settlement shift between 1870 and 1900?

2. What country contributed the most immigrants to the United States between 1860 and 1910?

Tell students to imagine that they are immigrants who just settled in the West. Students may choose to be Chinese immigrants in San Francisco, for example, or Finnish immigrants in Minneapolis. Have each student write a few sentences or paragraphs describing his or her experiences in the West. Remind students that they should discuss the theme of conquering distance in their sentences or paragraphs. **Block Scheduling**

Ask students to study the map on conquering distance across the West. Have students pick a western railroad line or company and locate and use a variety of primary and secondary sources to learn more about on its founding and influence in the West. Have each student write a short presentation on his or her topic. Ask volunteers to deliver their presentations to the class. **Block Scheduling**

AMERICA'S Geography

Conquering Distance Across the West

Major railroad
- - - - Cattle trail
Other trail
Area settled by 1890
DUTCH Ethnic settlement area
SIOUX American Indian reservation

0   200   400 Miles
0   200   400 Kilometers
Albers Equal Area Projection

Western Population Growth, 1860–1910

Population (in millions)

Year	Population	% Native born	% Foreign born
1860	619,000	71%	29%
1870	991,000	68%	32%
1880	1,801,000	72%	28%
1890	3,134,000	75%	25%
1900	4,309,000	80%	20%
1910	7,082,000	80%	20%

■ % Foreign born
■ % Native born

Source: *Historical Statistics of the United States*

Immigrant migration. As the network of railroads and western population increased, many immigrants began settling inland, rather than staying in cities on the East or West coast. This migration resulted in the presence of distinct ethnic traditions and cultures in many western cities.

GEOGRAPHY AND HISTORY Skills

HUMAN SYSTEMS

1. What reasons can you give for the West's population growth between 1900 and 1910?
2. Identify the ethnic groups that established western settlements.

San Francisco. In the late 1700s the Spanish built a fort and a mission on the site of present-day San Francisco. In 1835, traders built a small village in the region. By 1848 San Francisco was a town of some 800 people. The California Gold Rush brought massive changes to the area. Miners and merchants arrived in droves. The population reached 50,000 in 1860.

CRITICAL THINKING What might San Francisco have been like in the absence of the California Gold Rush?

ANSWER: Some students might suggest that San Francisco would have remained a small town or that San Francisco would have boomed at a later date.

AMERICA'S GEOGRAPHY ANSWERS

1. Answers will vary. Students might mention increased immigration, as well as the growth of railroads and other technologies.

2. Chinese, Czech, Danish, Dutch, Finnish, German, Irish, Mexican, Norwegian, Polish, and Swedish

Politics in the Gilded Age

CHAPTER RESOURCE MANAGER

Objectives	Pacing Guide	Reproducible Resources
SECTION 1 **Political Machines** pp. 246–51 ★ Explain how political machines emerged in U.S. cities. ★ Analyze why immigrants were important to political machines. ★ Describe how corruption and illegal activities developed in many political machines. ★ Identify the events that led to the collapse of public support for the Tweed Ring.	**Regular** 2 days **Block Scheduling** 1 day *Block Scheduling Handbook with Team Teaching Strategies, pp. 43–48*	**RS** Guided Reading Strategy 8.1 **PS** American History Political Cartoon 16: Tammany Hall **PS** Biography Reading 8: Thomas Nast **E** Hands-On History Activity: The Local Political Scene
SECTION 2 **Restoring Honest Government** pp. 252–58 ★ Identify the scandals that plagued the Grant administration. ★ Explain why Americans wanted political reform, and analyze how this desire affected the Republican Party. ★ Describe President Arthur's changing positions on civil service reform, and analyze how this affected his political party. ★ Describe how President Harrison dealt with President Cleveland's reforms.	**Regular** 2 days **Block Scheduling** 1 day *Block Scheduling Handbook with Team Teaching Strategies, pp. 43–48*	**RS** Guided Reading Strategy 8.2 **RS** Graphic Organizer Activity 8: An Expanding Population **IC** Literature Reading 8: A New Kind of Politician **E** Creative Teaching Strategy: Interrupted Film Lesson
SECTION 3 **The Populist Movement** pp. 259–65 ★ Describe the factors that led to economic hardships for farmers. ★ Explain what the farmers' movements hoped to achieve, and what weakened their efforts. ★ Discuss why farmers supported money backed by silver. ★ Identify the issues that the Populist Party supported. ★ Explain how silver affected the economy and the 1896 presidential election.	**Regular** 2 days **Block Scheduling** 1 day *Block Scheduling Handbook with Team Teaching Strategies, pp. 43–48*	**RS** Guided Reading Strategy 8.3 **PS** Primary Source Reading 8: A Call for Reform **SM** Geography Activity 8: The Growth of Urban Areas

Chapter Resource Key

PS Primary Sources	**REV** Review	Video	
RS Reading Support	**ELL** Reinforcement and English Language Learners	Internet	
IC Interdisciplinary Connections		Holt Presentation Maker Using Microsoft® PowerPoint®	
E Enrichment	Transparencies		
SM Skills Mastery	CD–ROM		
A Assessment	Music		

One-Stop Planner CD–ROM

See the *One-Stop Planner* for a complete list of additional resources for students and teachers.

One-Stop Planner CD-ROM

It's easy to plan lessons, select resources, and print out materials for your students when you use the **One-Stop Planner CD–ROM with Test Generator.**

Technology Resources

 One-Stop Planner, Lesson 8.1

 CNN Presents America: Modern Times Segment: George Washington Plunkitt and Tammany Hall

 Holt Researcher: American History CD–ROM

 Homework Practice Online

 HRW Go site

 One-Stop Planner, Lesson 8.2

 The American Nation Video Program Segment: The American Red Cross; Teacher's Guide, pp. 201–02

 Holt Researcher: American History CD–ROM

 Homework Practice Online

 One-Stop Planner, Lesson 8.3

 Everyday Life in America Transparency 16: Farming Technology, Late 1800s

 Holt Researcher: American History CD–ROM

 Homework Practice Online

Reinforcement, Review, and Assessment

REV Section 1 Review, p. 251
A Daily Quiz 8.1
ELL Main Idea Activity 8.1
ELL English Audio Summary 8.1
ELL Spanish Audio Summary 8.1

REV Section 2 Review, p. 258
A Daily Quiz 8.2
ELL Main Idea Activity 8.2
ELL English Audio Summary 8.2
ELL Spanish Audio Summary 8.2

REV Section 3 Review, p. 265
A Daily Quiz 8.3
ELL Main Idea Activity 8.3
ELL English Audio Summary 8.3
ELL Spanish Audio Summary 8.3

internet connect

HRW ONLINE RESOURCES
GO TO: go.hrw.com
Then type in a keyword.

TEACHER HOME PAGE
KEYWORD: SE3 Teacher

CHAPTER INTERNET ACTIVITIES
KEYWORD: SE3 AN8
Choose an activity to:
• analyze the work of Thomas Nast.
• learn about resistance to British rule in Africa.
• understand the complex role of the Tammany Hall political machine in the lives of citizens of New York City.

CHAPTER ENRICHMENT LINKS
KEYWORD: SE3 CH8

ONLINE ASSESSMENT
Homework Practice
KEYWORD: SE3 HP8

Standardized Test Prep
KEYWORD: SE3 STP8

Rubrics
KEYWORD: SS Rubrics

ONLINE MAPS, CHARTS, AND GRAPHS
KEYWORD: SE3 MCG
• Agricultural Regions, 1900

CONTENT UPDATES
KEYWORD: SS Content Updates

HOLT PRESENTATION MAKER
KEYWORD: SE3 PPT8

ONLINE READING SUPPORT
KEYWORD: SS Strategies

CURRENT EVENTS
KEYWORD: S3 Current Events

Meeting Individual Needs

Ability Levels

Level 1 Basic-level activities designed for all students encountering new material

Level 2 Intermediate-level activities designed for average students

Level 3 Challenging activities designed for honors and gifted-and-talented students

English Language Learners Activities that address the needs of students with Limited English Proficiency

Chapter Review and Assessment

 Global Skill Builder CD–ROM

 HRW Go site

REV **Chapter 8 Tutorial for Students, Parents, Mentors, and Peers**

REV **Chapter 8 Review, pp. 266–67**

Chapter 8 Test Generator (on the One-Stop Planner)

A **Chapter 8 Test (Form A or B)**

A **Alternative Assessment Handbook**

A **Chapter 8 Test for English Language Learners and Special-Needs Students**

Section 1 *Political Machines,
pp. 246–51*

Section 2 *Restoring Honest
Government,
pp. 252–58*

Section 3 *The Populist Movement,
pp. 259–65*

Chapter Review *pp. 266–67*

Build on What You Know

Ask students to answer the following questions.

**How might Americans attempt
to restore honest government?**
Consider:

• the existence of bribes and
"sweetheart" deals

• the issue of patronage versus
merit in hiring civil servants

**How might rural Americans
attempt to become more politically active?**
Consider:

• the importance of forming
mutual-interest associations

• the possible power of unified
economic actions

---

exploring the time line

AMERICAN EVENTS

PEOPLE IN HISTORY

1871 ■ Thomas Nast.
Born in Germany, Thomas
Nast moved to New York City
with his family as a boy. In 1855
Nast began drawing cartoons
for *Frank Leslie's Illustrated
Newspaper.* A fervid Unionist,
Nast made many sketches of
the Civil War, often concentrating on soldiers and their
daily routines. Ulysses S. Grant
commented, "He did as much
as any man to preserve the
Union and bring the war to an
end." Nast's Boss Tweed cartoons also had an enormous
impact, helping to bring down
the notorious political machine.

CRITICAL THINKING How
might Nast's drawings have
helped end the Civil War?

ANSWER: Students might indicate that Nast's drawings
focused on soldiers, and thus
showed the devastation of war.

CHAPTER
8

1865–1900

Politics in the Gilded Age

*U.S. gold
dollar*

*Young
Mother
Sewing
by
Mary
Cassatt*

**1869
Business
and Finance**
Jay Gould
and James Fisk's
attempt to corner
the gold market
fails, causing a
massive drop in
the price of gold.

**1870
World Events**
The kingdom
of Italy is
unified under
the leadership of
Victor Emmanuel II.

**1873
Business and Finance**
The U.S. Congress votes to
stop coining silver and to
convert money to the gold
standard.

**1877
Daily Life**
Puck, a weekly
periodical featuring
double-page
cartoons, is
published.

**1880
The Arts**
American
impressionist artist
Mary Cassatt paints
Young Mother Sewing.

1865   **1870**   **1875**   **1880**

**1866
Politics**
Political boss William Marcy
Tweed takes over the Tammany
Hall political machine.

**1871
The Arts**
Thomas Nast's series of
cartoons attacking the
Tweed Ring continues.

**1877
Politics**
The Farmers'
Alliance move-
ment begins
in Texas.

**1879
World Events**
The Zulu nation,
founded in 1816, is
dissolved by British
forces after a violent
military campaign.

*A Thomas Nast
cartoon depicts
the Tweed Ring.*

THE GRANGER COLLECTION, NEW YORK

*A leader of
the Zulu nation*

Build on What You Know

L ife for many Americans changed dramatically during the late 1800s.
Rapid industrialization and new opportunities drew increasing numbers
of people to U.S. cities. In this chapter you will learn that politics in the
United States during the late 1800s was frequently corrupt. These episodes of
corruption inspired new efforts to restore honest government. Meanwhile, rural
Americans grew more politically active, attempting to improve the conditions of
their daily lives.

What's Your Opinion?

*To help students create their Themes Journal entries, provide the following examples of appropriate **agree**/**disagree** statements.*

Culture

Agree The Republican Party stayed in power during Reconstruction because it had the support of Radical Republicans.

Disagree The Federalists rose to power despite their fairly limited group of supporters.

Government

Agree Hiring on the basis of test scores ensures the placement of qualified officials.

Disagree Elected officials have the right to fill posts with party supporters.

Geography

Agree On the whole, the densely populated Northeast has not supported agricultural parties and has thus limited their national effectiveness and popularity.

Disagree Abraham Lincoln won the presidency in the election of 1860 despite his views on slavery, an issue of crucial concern to the South.

The first gasoline-powered tractor

William Jennings Bryan 1896 election poster

W.J.BRYAN

NO CROWN OF THORNS   NO CROSS OF GOLD

Eastman Kodak's Brownie box camera

BROWNIE CAMERA

EASTMAN KODAK

BROWNIE CAMERA $1.

COURTESY GEORGE EASTMAN HOUSE

1883 Politics
The U.S. Congress establishes the Civil Service Commission.

1889 The Arts
Mark Twain publishes the novel *A Connecticut Yankee in King Arthur's Court.*

1892 Science and Technology
The first gasoline-powered tractor is built in Iowa.

1892 Politics
The Populist Party is founded.

1896 Politics
William Jennings Bryan delivers his "Cross of Gold" speech.

1900 Daily Life
Eastman Kodak introduces a Brownie box camera that sells for $1, making photography accessible to nearly everyone.

1885   **1890**   **1895**   **1900**

1885 World Events
The Indian National Congress is formed in British-controlled India.

1888 Science and Technology
William S. Burroughs patents a machine that adds, subtracts, and prints.

1895 Daily Life
The Kellogg brothers patent the process of making peanut butter.

1897 Science and Technology
The world's largest refracting telescope, with a 40-inch lens, is in use at the Yerkes Observatory in Wisconsin.

An adding machine

Sanitas Nuttolene VEGETABLE BUTTER. MADE BY SANITAS NUT FOOD CO. LTD. SOLD BY BATTLE CREEK SANITARIUM CO. LTD. BATTLE CREEK, MICH. U.S.A.

Peanut butter advertisement

What's Your Opinion?

Themes Journal *Do you **agree** or **disagree** with the following statements? Support your point of view in your journal.*

Culture In order to gain power, political parties in large U.S. cities must attract supporters from diverse groups of residents.

Government Testing is the best way to determine who should be hired to fill government jobs.

Geography New political parties cannot win national power if they focus only on issues of concern to one geographic region.

After completing Section 1, students should be able to:

OBJECTIVE 1 Explain how political machines emerged in U.S. cities.

OBJECTIVE 2 Analyze why immigrants were important to political machines.

OBJECTIVE 3 Describe how corruption and illegal activities developed in many political machines.

OBJECTIVE 4 Identify the events that led to the collapse of public support for the Tweed Ring.

🔔 LET'S GET STARTED!

Write the following term on the chalkboard: *Political Machine.* As students enter the classroom, ask them to list words or phrases that they associate with the term. Have volunteers share their words or phrases with the class. (*Answers will vary. Some students might list words such as corruption, boss, or immigrant.*) Discuss the term with students, providing a definition and examples of its use in this section. Then tell students that in Section 1 they will learn about political machines in the late 1800s.

SECTION ① RESOURCES

REPRODUCIBLE

▶ Guided Reading Strategy 8.1

▶ American History Political Cartoon 16: Tammany Hall

▶ Biography Reading 8: Thomas Nast

TECHNOLOGY

▶ One-Stop Planner, Lesson 8.1

▶ **CNN** Presents America: Modern Times Segment: George Washington Plunkitt and Tammany Hall

▶ Holt Researcher: American History CD–ROM

▶ HRW Go site

▶ Homework Practice Online

REINFORCEMENT, REVIEW, AND ASSESSMENT

▶ Section 1 Review, p. 251

▶ Daily Quiz 8.1

▶ Main Idea Activity 8.1

▶ English Audio Summary 8.1

▶ Spanish Audio Summary 8.1

SECTION ①

READ TO DISCOVER

1. How did political machines emerge in U.S. cities?
2. Why were immigrants important to political machines?
3. How did corruption and illegal activities develop in many political machines?
4. What events led to the collapse of public support for the Tweed Ring?

DEFINE

political machines
political bosses
graft
kickbacks

IDENTIFY

Alexander Shepherd
James Pendergast
George Washington Plunkitt
William Marcy Tweed
Thomas Nast

▶ WHY IT MATTERS TODAY

Political corruption still affects governments around the world. Use **CNNfyi.com** or other **current events** sources to find out about how some governments have responded to incidents of political corruption. Record your findings in your journal.

Political Machines

EYEWITNESSES TO History

❝I know what Parks is doing, but what do I care. He has raised my wages. Let him have his [illegal gains]!❞

—Anonymous city worker, quoted in *The Shame of the Cities,* by Lincoln Steffens

A New York City official voting in the early 1900s

This city worker was responding to the charges of corruption made against a New York City politician named Parks. Despite the public awareness of corruption, local political leaders managed to gain broad support from their voters by offering favors and jobs. Many of these jobs came from public-works projects. The growth of urban centers during the late 1800s meant that cities required new streets, new sewer systems, and larger police and fire departments. Unfortunately, the need for these services also created an opportunity for political leaders to gain power and personal wealth.

The Rise of the Political Machine

The overwhelming growth of urban populations in the United States during the late 1800s created new challenges for city governments. New demands were placed on public services such as fire, police, and sanitation departments. Growing urban populations also required the expansion or new construction of bridges, parks, schools, streets, sewer systems, and utility systems. With the support of very well-organized political parties, city council members and district representatives took charge of city governments. They oversaw new public services and, in many cases, pocketed money meant for the public good.

Political bosses. During the late 1800s well-organized political parties dominated city governments in the United States. Because of their success in getting their members elected to local political offices, these parties were called **political machines**. Powerful **political bosses** managed these machines. Bosses dictated party positions on city ordinances and made deals with business leaders. They also controlled the district leaders, city officials, and council members who kept the machine running smoothly.

The relationship between district leaders known as precinct captains and potential voters living in urban neighborhoods was the real strength of political machines. By offering jobs, political favors, and services to local residents, precinct captains won support for the political machine. At election time, bosses and precinct captains instructed local residents to vote for selected candidates. This practice ensured the continued power of the political machine.

ALL LEVELS: Pair students and tell them to imagine that they live in a large U.S. city in the late 1800s. Have each pair develop a list of urban problems and needs. *(Students should list the need for fire, police, and sanitation services as well as the need for stable jobs.)* Briefly discuss the lists and ask pairs to write paragraphs explaining how these urban problems and needs led to the emergence of political machines in cities. *(Students should note that by providing services and jobs to loyal supporters political machines continued to be supported by* *voters.)* Then ask students to consider their lists and paragraphs. Would they have supported political machines, even if those machines were corrupt? Did the pressing need for services justify any political machine that supplied them successfully?
English Language Learners, Cooperative Learning

NOTE: To help students make meaningful connections between events in U.S. history and those in their own hometown, use the Chapter 8 **Hands-On History Activity**, The Local Political Scene.

Public services. During the late 1800s political machines attempted to provide the public services required by growing U.S. cities. Political bosses such as **Alexander Shepherd** of Washington, D.C., financed expanded sewer and water systems, paved streets, and provided other public services. Between 1871 and 1873 Shepherd's board of public works spent $20 million, creating significant civic improvements and new jobs in the nation's capital. This boom of public-works projects meant that bosses could distribute many jobs among loyal supporters.

By providing jobs, political favors, and services to local residents, political machines were able to win support from many poor and working-class city-dwellers. Political bosses and local precinct representatives often formed close relationships with local voters.

✔ **READING CHECK: Analyzing Information** What role did political machines play in the growth of U.S. cities? They provided public services growing cities needed.

Immigrants and Political Machines

Because political machines helped the urban poor, new immigrants often became particularly loyal supporters of political machines. Machine politicians often met immigrants as soon as they arrived in the United States. They helped newcomers get settled in their new homeland. Tammany Hall, a political club that had gained considerable power in the 1860s and early 1870s, became a powerful Democratic political machine in New York City during the 1890s. It sent numerous party workers to Ellis Island to meet new immigrants. Party workers assisted immigrants by finding them temporary housing and jobs. Tammany Hall workers also helped immigrants become naturalized citizens and thus eligible to vote for Tammany Hall candidates. However, Tammany officials failed to offer any extensive programs to address poverty and poor housing conditions.

Political bosses ensured voter loyalty among immigrant groups by providing jobs in exchange for votes. **James Pendergast** was a particularly well-liked boss in Kansas City, Missouri. He began his political career while running a saloon in the industrial river-bottom district where many immigrants lived and worked. Pendergast gained considerable political support by providing jobs and special services to his African American, Irish American, and Italian American constituents. "There is no kinder hearted or more sympathetic man in Kansas City than Jim Pendergast," said one Kansas City resident. "He will go down in his pockets after his last cent to help a friend. No man is more easily moved to sympathy or good sense than Jim Pendergast." Another immigrant described the efforts of a local political boss.

History Makers Speak ❝To this one he lends a dollar; for another he obtains a railroad ticket without payment; he has coal distributed in the depth of winter; . . . he sometimes sends poultry at Christmas time; he buys medicine for a sick person; he helps bury the dead.❞

— Anonymous immigrant

INTERPRETING THE VISUAL RECORD

"Tammany Bank." Place a coin in the Tammany politician's hand and he deposits it in his pocket. *How does this bank reflect the political corruption of the 1870s?*

James Pendergast ran a political machine in Kansas City, Missouri.

VISUAL RECORD ANSWER
Students might mention putting the coin in the politician's pocket.

🔲 internet connect
TOPIC: Tammany Hall
GO TO: go.hrw.com
KEYWORD: SE3 AN8

Have students access the Internet through the HRW Go site to conduct research on the Tammany Hall political machine in New York City. Then ask students to imagine that they work for a newspaper in New York City. Have each student create a newspaper article about an issue related to Tammany Hall politics.

ALL LEVELS: Tell students to imagine that it is 1880 and that they are recent immigrants. Ask students to describe the ways in which political machines might help them survive and prosper in the United States. *(Answers will vary. Some students might note that the machines provided services and jobs.)* To help students understand why immigrants were important to political machines, copy the following graphic organizer on the chalkboard, omitting the italicized answers. Have each student complete it.

English Language Learners

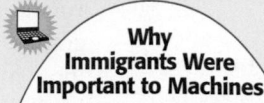

Why Immigrants Were Important to Machines

- *represented a huge supply of supporters and voters*
- *tended to be particularly loyal to machines*

Political Machines and Immigrants

Ways in Which Machines Recruited and Rewarded Immigrants

- *welcomed immigrants upon arrival*
- *found immigrants temporary housing and jobs*
- *helped immigrants become naturalized citizens*
- *helped immigrants with finances, funerals, and so on*

HISTORY MAKERS SPEAK

George Washington Plunkitt in *Eyewitnesses and Others*

The Secret of a Successful Boss. Political bosses provided far more than jobs and services to new immigrants. They also provided a sense of human contact and concern—a fact that endeared them to many people adjusting to a new country and a new society. One political boss said: "To learn real human nature you have to go among the people, see them and be seen. I know every man, woman, and child in the Fifteenth District. . . . I know what they like and what they don't like, what they are strong at and what they are weak in, and I reach them by approachin' at the right side. Here's how I gather in the young men. I hear a young feller that's proud of his voice, thinks that he can sing fine. I ask him to come around to Washington Hall and join our Glee Club. He comes and sings, and he's a follower of Plunkitt for life."

ACTIVITY: Have students suggest how modern-day politicians use similar strategies to reach their constituents.

VISUAL RECORD ANSWER

Students might point out that they were paid with things they could use like new shoes and socks.

248

Most political machines maintained their political power with the support of immigrant voters. In some cities, however, immigrants became active members of political machines, serving as officeholders, organizers, and representatives. In Boston, for example, the Irish American population was highly influential in the local Democratic machine. During the mid-1800s Irish Americans in Boston accounted for more than one third of the city's voters.

Because Irish Americans spoke English as a first language, they had slightly easier access to U.S. political processes than many other immigrant groups. Many Irish Americans who were loyal to the political machine in Boston were rewarded with jobs in the local police and fire departments. Ambitious Irish American politicians rose quickly through the ranks of the city's political machine. Second-generation immigrants John F. Fitzgerald—President John F. Kennedy's grandfather—and James Michael Curley both rose from the ranks of local boss to become mayor of the city during the late 1800s.

✔ **READING CHECK: Summarizing** Describe the relationship between immigrants and political machines. It was a mutually cooperative relationship. The immigrants needed jobs; the political machines needed votes.

Graft and Corruption

Political machines often resorted to corruption in their attempt to take control of city governments. Although political machines successfully got party members re-elected, machine corruption often interfered with the important functions of city government.

INTERPRETING THE VISUAL RECORD

Corruption. Working for the Tammany Hall political machine, these men are voting illegally. **What does this photograph reveal about the way the men were paid for their votes?**

Election fraud. For political machines to maintain their power, their candidates had to win elections. When jobs and political favors were not enough to build popular support during elections, some political machines turned to fraud. A New York resident testified before the U.S. House of Representatives on election fraud.

 "Gangs or bodies of men hired for the purpose, assembled at these headquarters where they were furnished with names and numbers, and under a leader or captain, they went out . . . in nearly every part of the city, registering many times each, and when the day of election came these repeaters, supplied abundantly with intoxicating drinks, and changing coats, hats, or caps, as occasion required to avoid recognition or detection, commenced the work of 'voting early and often.'"

—New York resident, U.S. House of Representatives Report No. 41 on Election Fraud in New York, 1868

Voting fraud was widespread in many U.S. cities. For example, during one election in Philadelphia, a voting district with fewer than 100 registered voters somehow returned 252 votes!

Graft. Once inside city government, political bosses often became even more corrupt. They looked for ways to increase their own political power and personal wealth. One way to get rich was to take advantage of the massive amounts of public funds involved in providing essential city services. Many city officials practiced

TEACH OBJECTIVE 3

LEVEL 1: Pair students and tell them to imagine that they are city officials attempting to end corruption in political machines. Have each pair create a dialogue describing how corruption and illegal activities developed in political machines. *(Students should note that machines hired men to "vote early and often" and that bosses took bribes, payoffs, and kickbacks.)* Ask volunteers to perform their dialogues for the class. **English Language Learners, Cooperative Learning**

LEVELS 2 AND 3: Briefly discuss political machines and corruption with students. Then organize students into small groups and tell them to imagine that they are investigative reporters. Have each group prepare an article describing how corruption developed in political machines. *(See the Level 1 lesson for the correct factors.)* Students should include examples of corruption, analyze its impact on city residents, and offer solutions. Ask volunteers to read their articles to the class. **Cooperative Learning**

HOMEWORK *Distribute Cartoon 16, Tammany Hall, from* **American History Political Cartoons,** *and have each student complete it.*

---

graft—the acquisition of money or political power through illegal or dishonest methods. Graft was a common problem in almost every U.S. city with a powerful political machine.

Politicians often received bribes, payoffs, or **kickbacks**—payments of part of the earnings from a job or contract. Business leaders often paid kickbacks when lobbying for an opportunity to provide public services for a city. During the late 1890s a railway corporation paid Chicago aldermen as much as $25,000 to vote for local ordinances that would grant it special privileges. Also in Chicago, business leader Charles Tyson Yerkes built an empire of street railway lines by paying Alderman John Powers to support city ordinances favorable to his company. Yerkes was granted a virtual monopoly over Chicago's mass transit system. Explaining his loyalty to Yerkes, Powers once confessed, "You can't get elected to the [city] council unless Mr. Yerkes says so."

NEW-YORK HISTORICAL SOCIETY

This painting shows Tammany Hall.

Graft in Action. Graft helped political machines make enormous profits. In order to claim these profits, machine-associated service providers padded their bills, charging cities up to 85 percent extra. This graft had an enormous impact on municipal funds. The New York City courthouse, for example, should have cost $3 million to construct. After widespread graft, however, it cost $11 million.

ACTIVITY: Tell students to imagine that they are investigative reporters who have found evidence of graft. Have them write the first few paragraphs of a newspaper article announcing the discovery.

Skill-Building Strategies

Synthesizing

Synthesizing is a key part of interpreting the past. To *synthesize* is to combine information and ideas from several different sources or points of view to obtain a new understanding of a topic or event. Most of the narrative writing in this textbook is a synthesis. It pulls together data from a variety of sources to form an original account of our nation's history.

How to Synthesize

1. **Identify the subject and sources.** Identify the general topic or issue addressed by your sources. Then, if possible, find out about the personal, social, and historical background of the author of each source.
2. **Analyze the sources.** Examine carefully the information that each source provides about the subject. If your sources present different points of view, identify the main idea expressed by each source and determine whether it is supported by facts, opinions, or a combination of both.
3. **Compare and contrast the sources.** Examine the similarities and the differences between the information and ideas in your sources. As you do so, look for ways to link the sources together. Try to account for any different points of view.
4. **Form your own interpretation of the subject.** Use your analysis and comparison of the sources, along with your knowledge of the historical period, to form your own interpretation of the subject.

Applying the Skill

Read George Washington Plunkitt's description of "honest graft" on the next page. Then synthesize his description with the following account of "honest graft" from a recent historical text.

> **George Washington Plunkitt, a Tammany ward 'heeler' or boss, liked to call [the practice of profiting from one's office] 'honest graft,' a fair exchange of cash, influence, liquor, and above all jobs for working-class votes. Plunkitt and his fellow Tammany bosses lined their own pockets, stealing millions of dollars from the public treasury while allowing important decisions on issues such as public transportation to be made by those private entrepreneurs willing to pay large bribes.**

Practicing the Skill

Answer the following questions.

1. Are the ideas expressed in each of these sources based on facts, opinions, or a combination of both?
2. How are these two accounts of "honest graft" similar? How are they different?
3. Based on these two sources and the knowledge you have gained from the text, what is your interpretation of "honest graft"?

SKILL-BUILDING STRATEGIES ANSWERS

Applying the Skill
Students should compare and contrast the sources and present their own interpretations of the material.

Practicing the Skill
1. combination of both

2. Both acknowledge that honest graft resulted in some improvements for urban residents. Plunkitt sees honest graft as acceptable, however, while the historian views it as inherently corrupt.

3. Students should offer evidence to support their interpretations.

TEACH OBJECTIVE 4

LEVEL 1: Ask students to name the events that led to the collapse of public support for the Tweed Ring. *(Students should name the Thomas Nast cartoons and the New York Times articles.)* Then tell students to imagine that it is 1880 and that they are newspaper headline writers. Have each student write three headlines for editorials denouncing the Tweed Ring. Post the headlines around the classroom.
English Language Learners

LEVEL 2: Ask students to name the events that led to the collapse of public support for the Tweed Ring. *(See the Level 1 lesson for the correct events.)* Then tell students to imagine that it is

1880 and that they are editorial writers. Have each student write a brief newspaper editorial denouncing the Tweed Ring. Have volunteers read their editorials to the class.

LEVEL 3: Ask students to name the events that led to the collapse of public support for the Tweed Ring. *(See the Level 1 lesson for the correct events.)* Then tell students to imagine that it is 1880 and that they are novelists. Have each student write a fable, or a story intended to prove a truth, denouncing the Tweed Ring. Remind students that fables often use animals to represent humans and human weaknesses. Ask volunteers to read their fables to the class. Students may wish to include their fables in their portfolios.

HISTORY MAKERS SPEAK

An unidentified writer in *The Nation*

Choosing a Candidate.
When George Washington Plunkitt, a Tammany Hall boss, died in 1924, *The Nation,* one of the leading reform journals of the time, eulogized him as "one of the wisest men in American politics." According to *The Nation,* Plunkitt understood that to voters "honesty doesn't matter; efficiency doesn't matter; progressive vision doesn't matter. What matters is the chance of a better job, a better price for wheat, better business conditions."

CRITICAL THINKING Is *The Nation's* view of politics idealistic or pragmatic? Explain.

ANSWER: Students might answer pragmatic because the writer suggests that the help Plunkitt provides makes his corruption irrelevant.

AMERICAN ARTS ANSWERS

1. donkey—the Democratic Party; elephant—the Republican Party

2. caricature, analogy, use of recognizable images, literary allusion

---

POLITICAL CARTOON ANSWER

(for p. 251)
Students might suggest that the striped clothes look like prison garb.

250

Some bosses attempted to defend their practices. Political boss **George Washington Plunkitt** of Tammany Hall explained what he called "honest graft."

Analyzing Primary Sources
Identifying Bias Why might people believe that Plunkitt's activities are honest? because they benefit from his activities

History Makers Speak
❝My party's in power in the city, and it's goin' to undertake a lot of public improvements. Well, I'm tipped off, say, that they're going to lay out a new park at a certain place. . . . I go to that place and I buy up all the land I can in the neighborhood. Then the board of this or that makes its plan public, and there is a rush to get my land. . . . Ain't it perfectly honest to charge a good price and make a profit on my investment and foresight? . . . Well, that's honest graft.❞

—George Washington Plunkitt

✔ **READING CHECK: Drawing Conclusions** How was graft a factor in the growth of political machines? Graft sometimes helped political machines gain and keep their power.

AMERICAN ARTS
Thomas Nast's Cartoons

One of the most influential political cartoonists of the late 1800s was Thomas Nast. His cartoons helped make political cartoons an important feature in the American press. Nast drew cartoons with recognizable images and made creative use of standard cartoonist techniques such as caricatures—the portrayal of figures with comically exaggerated features. Many of the common characters used in modern-day political cartoons, such as Uncle Sam, the Republican elephant, and the Democratic donkey, were first popularized by Nast. Editors for *Harper's Weekly* claimed that Nast's bold and witty cartoons increased the magazine's subscriptions by some 200,000.

The popularity of Nast's cartoons for *Harper's Weekly* inspired other journals to hire political cartoonists to boost circulation. Throughout the late 1800s publications such as *Puck*, *Judge*, and *Life* hired political cartoonists to offer witty and sharp commentary on political events. In doing so, these cartoonists perfected their use of analogies and literary allusions to refer to political events and characters. For example, many cartoonists portrayed politicians as Shakespearean characters such as Hamlet and Caesar, who engaged in political intrigue, to depict particular events of U.S. political life. As in modern-day political cartoons, the cartoons of the late 1800s offered critical political commentary as well as humor.

Thomas Nast cartoon depicting U.S. political parties in the 1880s

Understanding the Arts
1. What do the donkey and the elephant represent in this cartoon?
2. What techniques do cartoonists use to depict political events?

REVIEW

Have students complete the **Section 1 Review** on p. 251.

ASSESS

Have students complete **Daily Quiz 8.1**. As **Alternative Assessment**, you may want to use the political boss monologue or the corruption dialogue in this section's lessons.

RETEACH

Have students complete **Main Idea Activity for English Language Learners and Special-Needs Students 8.1**. Then assign students subsections of Section 1. Have each student create a crossword puzzle using important names and terms from the assigned subsection. Have students exchange puzzles, complete them, and then return them to their creators for grading.
English Language Learners

EXTEND

Write the names of the following political bosses on the chalkboard: *Alexander Shepherd, James Pendergast, John Powers, George Washington Plunkitt,* and *William Marcy Tweed.* Have students research one of these bosses. Tell students to present their research in the form of a report. Students' reports should include basic biographical information about the boss, detail his rise in the given political machine, and describe his fall, if appropriate. Ask volunteers to present their reports to the class.
Block Scheduling

The Tweed Ring. Plunkitt's bold admission of his own graft offers a clue to the extent of corruption in Tammany Hall. Tammany Hall had a long history as a social and political organization dating back to 1789. However, it is best known for the period during the 1860s when **William Marcy Tweed** reigned as its boss.

Tweed had considerable control over the issuing of contracts for public projects and government jobs. Tweed and his ring of political supporters used this position of power to gain bribes and kickbacks. Historians have estimated that the Tweed Ring collected $200 million in graft between 1865 and 1871.

Tweed's political power and control over the Tammany machine collapsed abruptly when public opinion turned against him. The corruption of Tammany Hall and the Tweed Ring was mercilessly revealed in a series of political cartoons drawn by **Thomas Nast**. In 1871 Nast published some 50 cartoons in *Harper's Weekly* that sharply criticized Tweed and Tammany Hall. Aware of the power of Nast's cartoons to influence public opinion, Tweed demanded, "Stop them . . . pictures. I don't care so much what the papers write about me. My constituents can't read. But . . . they can see pictures."

Along with a series of articles published in the *New York Times*, Nast's cartoons exposed the corruption of Tammany Hall and contributed to Tweed's conviction for fraud and extortion in 1873. In jail for another conviction, Tweed later escaped but was arrested in Spain. Officials there recognized him from one of Nast's drawings. Tweed died in jail in New York City.

✔ **READING CHECK: Identifying Cause and Effect** What effect did Thomas Nast's cartoons have on corruption at Tammany Hall? They exposed the corruption and contributed to Tweed's conviction.

INTERPRETING POLITICAL CARTOONS

Tweed Ring. Thomas Nast's cartoons helped expose Boss Tweed. *What characteristics of this cartoon suggest corruption?*

SECTION 1 REVIEW

1. Define and explain:
political machines
political bosses
graft
kickbacks

2. Identify and explain:
Alexander Shepherd
James Pendergast
George Washington Plunkitt
William Marcy Tweed
Thomas Nast

3. Analyzing Information
Copy the graphic organizer below. Use it to explain how political machines built support for their candidates.

```
Political Machine
Activities
      ↓
Building
Support
      ↓
Response of
Loyal Supporters
```

4. Finding the Main Idea
a. How did political bosses justify their graft?
b. What was the relationship between the need for greater city services and the growth of political machines?
c. Despite evidence of corruption, political machines retained strong public support. Why did people continue to support the machines?

5. Writing and Critical Thinking
Evaluating Review the Thomas Nast cartoon at the top of this page. Write a newspaper article on the effect Nast's political cartoons had on public support for the Tweed Ring.
Consider:
• how Tweed is portrayed in the cartoon
• what political statement a newspaper reader might be able to interpret from the drawing
• what the cartoon does that newspaper articles cannot do

Homework Practice Online
keyword: SE3 HP8

SECTION
REVIEW 1 ANSWERS

1. Define
• political machines, p. 246
• political bosses, p. 246
• graft, p. 249
• kickbacks, p. 249

2. Identify
• Alexander Shepherd, p. 247
• James Pendergast, p. 247
• George Washington Plunkitt, p. 250
• William Marcy Tweed, p. 251
• Thomas Nast, p. 251

3. political machine activities—created hierarchical political organizations, provided public services, favors, and jobs for voters, helped immigrants get settled and naturalized; response of supporters—voted for machine candidates, sometimes assisted in election fraud, ignored graft by leaders

4a. Bosses felt graft was honest because they profited only by doing useful public works.

b. As cities grew, greater city services were needed, providing political machines with more opportunities to provide these services.

c. Students might mention that political machines often rewarded citizens by improving their living situations and giving them government jobs.

5. Answers will vary. Articles might suggest that the cartoons turned public opinion against the Tweed Ring and that the cartoon portrays Tweed as a bully.

OBJECTIVE 1 Identify the scandals that plagued the Grant administration.

OBJECTIVE 2 Explain why Americans wanted political reform, and analyze how this desire affected the Republican Party.

OBJECTIVE 3 Describe President Arthur's changing positions on civil service reform, and analyze how this affected his political party.

OBJECTIVE 4 Describe how President Harrison dealt with President Cleveland's reforms.

📻 LET'S GET STARTED!

Write the following scenario on the chalkboard: *You are a leading member of Political Party X. You are extremely concerned about corruption in government. How do you attempt to reform the system? Do you make such attempts even though they might split your party and cause your own political demise?* As students enter the classroom, ask them to respond to the scenario in writing. Tell students that in Section 2 they will learn how Gilded Age officials attempted to reform politics—and how those reforms affected political parties.

SECTION 2 RESOURCES

REPRODUCIBLE

▶ Guided Reading Strategy 8.2
▶ Graphic Organizer Activity 8: An Expanding Population
▶ Literature Reading 8: A New Kind of Politician

TECHNOLOGY

▶ One-Stop Planner, Lesson 8.2
▶ The American Nation Video Program Segment: The American Red Cross; Teacher's Guide, pp. 201–02
▶ Holt Researcher: American History CD–ROM
▶ Homework Practice Online

REINFORCEMENT, REVIEW, AND ASSESSMENT

▶ Section 2 Review, p. 258
▶ Daily Quiz 8.2
▶ Main Idea Activity 8.2
▶ English Audio Summary 8.2
▶ Spanish Audio Summary 8.2

SECTION 2

READ TO DISCOVER

1. What scandals plagued the Grant administration?
2. Why did Americans want political reform, and how did this desire affect the Republican Party?
3. Why did President Arthur's positions on civil service reform change, and how did this affect his political party?
4. How did President Harrison deal with President Cleveland's reforms?

DEFINE

mugwumps

IDENTIFY

Gilded Age
Stalwarts
James A. Garfield
Chester A. Arthur
Pendleton Civil Service Act
Grover Cleveland
Benjamin Harrison

WHY IT MATTERS TODAY

Many applicants for federal and state government jobs are still required to take civil service examinations. Use CNNfyi.com or other **current events** sources to find out about how most federal and state government jobs are filled today. Record your findings in your journal.

CNNfyi.com

Restoring Honest Government

EYEWITNESSES TO History

"Mr. Lincoln . . . held that ours is a government of the people, by the people, for the people. I maintain, on the contrary, that it is a government of politicians, by politicians, for politicians."

—William McElroy, "An Old War Horse to a Young Politician," *Atlantic Monthly*, June 1880

Political cartoon depicting corruption

In this fictional letter of advice to a young politician that was printed in the *Atlantic Monthly* in 1880, William McElroy expressed a sentiment held by many Americans. Corruption and fraud affected politics at the national level as well as locally. During the late 1800s national scandals exposed illegal financial practices by high-ranking politicians. Many Americans began to question the character of some elected officials. Most observers of the time offered similar condemnations of national political life. "One might search the whole list of Congress, Judiciary, and Executive [branches] during the 25 years 1870 to 1895, and find little but damaged reputation," claimed historian Henry Adams. "The period was poor in purpose and barren in results."

Scandal in the White House

In 1869 political boss William Tweed and his gang looted the New York City treasury. That same year, Ulysses S. Grant began his service as president of the United States. Republican Party leaders seeking a moderate candidate had selected Grant to run for the presidency. His fame as a Union army general made him a popular candidate. With the slogan "Let us have peace," Grant won the election.

Grant's first term. Grant's first term in office was marred by several scandals. During the summer of 1869, financiers Jay Gould and James Fisk tried to corner, or gain a monopoly on, the gold market. They wanted to drive up the price of gold. In order to keep the supply of gold low and the price high, Gould and gold broker Abel Rathbone Corbin—President Grant's brother-in-law—tried to convince the president not to sell gold from the U.S. treasury. The president refused to go along with the plan, but Gold and Corbin spread rumors that he had. These rumors led to widespread speculation, or buying and selling, in the gold market. When Grant learned of the rumors, he ordered his secretary of treasury to sell $4 million of the government's gold. On Black Friday—September 24, 1869—the price of gold fell sharply. Many Wall Street investors and speculators were ruined financially. There was some evidence that the president's wife, Julia Grant, had invested $500,000 in the gold market.

In 1872 an even greater scandal surfaced. This time Grant's vice president, Schuyler Colfax, was involved. Five years earlier, directors of the Union Pacific

Railroad had formed a construction company called Crédit Mobilier of America. They then gave the company contracts to build a section of the transcontinental railroad. The owners of Union Pacific Railroad gave or sold shares of stock in Crédit Mobilier to congressmembers responsible for awarding federal land grants to the railroads.

The Crédit Mobilier stock proved to be a profitable deal for the members of Congress. Congress issued federal subsidies for the cost of the railroad construction. The U.S. government paid little attention to Crédit Mobilier's operations and was unaware of the costs of the construction it had subsidized. Crédit Mobilier was able to overcharge Union Pacific by more than $20 million. These excess profits went straight into the pockets of Crédit Mobilier's stockholders. These stockholders included members of Congress such as Schuyler Colfax, who was then Speaker of the House. Although the schemes took place before Grant became president, the subsequent scandal tarnished his administration's image because of Colfax's position as vice president.

The election of 1872. The multiplying scandals encouraged political opponents to challenge Grant in the presidential election of 1872. Many critics saw the corruption in Grant's administration as a by-product of the spoils system. Rather than award civil service jobs as rewards, they wanted ability to be the deciding factor. Reformers proposed that applicants who earned the highest grades on competitive examinations should receive the jobs.

Civil service reform was the battle cry of *New York Tribune* editor Horace Greeley, Grant's Liberal Republican opponent in 1872. The Liberal Republican Party was formed by Republicans shocked by the Grant scandals and tired of Reconstruction. Hoping to benefit from the split in the Republican Party, Democrats also threw their support behind Greeley.

Liberal Republicans saw the Crédit Mobilier scandal as a nail in Grant's political coffin. However, Grant played on his image as a war hero and easily won re-election. Disheartened and exhausted, Greeley died just 24 days after the election. His party did not last much longer. It seemed that civil service reform was finished too.

Grant's second term. The episodes of corruption continued during Grant's second term in office. In 1874 a new scandal erupted over the taxation of whiskey. Some officials at the Treasury Department who had received their positions as a result of the spoils system were charged with accepting bribes from distillers and distributors of whiskey. In return, treasury officials reduced the amount of taxes that the whiskey distributors had to pay. Public exposure of the so-called Whiskey Ring further encouraged reformers. Hoping to end the fraud under the spoils system, reformers pushed to end the practice of granting jobs as political rewards. The scandals also increased many Americans' distrust of politicians.

✔ **READING CHECK: Categorizing** What different types of scandals plagued the Grant administration? 1869 gold market scandal, 1872 Crédit Mobilier railroad scandal, and the 1874 Whiskey Ring scandal

Newspaper editor Horace Greeley ran against President Grant in the 1872 election.

INTERPRETING POLITICAL CARTOONS

Grant's administration. Public exposure of corruption in Grant's administration led to increasing opposition to the spoils system. **What does this cartoon suggest about Grant's administration?**

THE GRANGER COLLECTION, NEW YORK

LEVELS 2 AND 3: Ask students to name and describe the scandals that plagued the Grant administration. *(See the Level 1 lesson for the correct scandals.)* Briefly discuss those scandals. Then tell students to imagine that it is 1875 and that they have just read a magazine article devoted to the scandals. Have each student write a letter to the editor describing how the scandals have affected his or her view of politics. *(See the Level 1 lesson for the correct effects.)* Students' letters should also express their conception of "good government." Students may wish to include their letters in their portfolios.

HOMEWORK *Write the following quotation by Mark Twain (see this page for full context) on the chalkboard:* "In a free country like ours, where any man can run for Congress and anybody can vote for him, you can't expect immortal purity all the time—it ain't in nature." *Have each student write several paragraphs evaluating the quotation in light of what he or she has learned about politics in the Gilded Age.*

NOTE: For an additional teaching idea, see the Chapter 8 interrupted film lesson in the **Creative Teaching Strategies** handbook.

AMERICAN *Letters*

Mark Twain's Political Writings

Throughout his literary career, Mark Twain had a rare ability to present compelling and often humorous stories that dealt with important issues in American society. Twain used satire, a form of writing that uses humor to point out human faults. In the 1873 novel The Gilded Age, *Twain and coauthor Charles Dudley Warner present a satirical conversation about Congress's inability to weed out corrupt politicians. Twain's 1889 novel,* A Connecticut Yankee in King Arthur's Court, *offers a commentary on American political ambition. In the tale a Connecticut man finds himself transported back in time to medieval England. The excerpt describes the man's thoughts as he begins to discover that he is in the 500s, not the 1800s.*

from *The Gilded Age*

"I think Congress always tries to do as near right as it can, according to its lights. A man can't ask any fairer than that. The first preliminary it always starts out on, is to clean itself, so to speak. It will arraign [put on trial] two or three dozen of its members, or maybe four or five dozen, for taking bribes to vote for this and that and the other bill last winter."

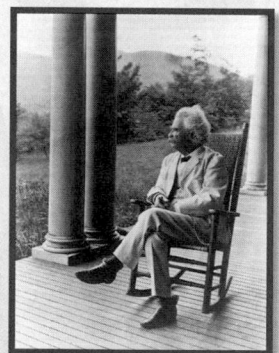

Mark Twain

"It goes up into the dozens, does it?"

"Well, yes; in a free country like ours, where any man can run for Congress and anybody can vote for him, you can't expect immortal purity all the time—it ain't in nature. . . ."

"So Congress always lies helpless in quarantine ten weeks of a session. That's encouraging. Colonel, poor Laura will never get any benefit from our bill. Her trial will be over before Congress has half purified itself.—And doesn't it occur to you that by the time it has expelled all its impure members there may not be enough members left to do business legally?"

"Why I did not say Congress would expel anybody. . . . But good God we *try* them, don't we!"

from *A Connecticut Yankee in King Arthur's Court*

Wherefore, being a practical Connecticut man, . . . I made up my mind to two things: if it was still the nineteenth century and I was among lunatics and couldn't get away, I would presently boss that asylum or know the reason why; and if, on the other hand, it was really the sixth century, all right, I didn't want any softer thing: I would boss the whole country inside of three months; for I judged I would have the start of the best-educated man in the kingdom by a matter of thirteen hundred years and upward.

Cover of A Connecticut Yankee in King Arthur's Court

UNDERSTANDING LITERATURE

1. Why would Congress try its members for corruption but not expel them?
2. How does the Connecticut man resemble many politicians in the late 1800s?
3. How does Twain use humor and exaggeration in these selections to portray American political life?

LEVEL 1: Tell students to imagine that they are pro-reform Americans. Have each student design a poster in support of reform. Posters should clearly explain why Americans wanted reform during the Gilded Age. (*Posters should somehow note the existence of widespread corruption and the desire for honest officials.*) Have students present their posters to the class. Then have students write a topic sentence explaining how the desire for reform affected the Republicans. (*Different views on reform split the party into the Stalwarts and the Half-Breeds.*) Students may wish to include their posters and sentences in their portfolios. **English Language Learners**

LEVEL 2: Tell students to imagine that they are pro-reform Americans preparing to speak at a congressional meeting on political corruption. Have each student write a brief speech explaining why he or she wants political reform. (*See the Level 1 lesson for the correct reasons.*) Ask volunteers to deliver their speeches to the class. Then ask students how different attitudes toward reform affected the Republicans. (*See the Level 1 lesson for the correct effect.*) Ask students if this split was inevitable. Was there any way, given the realities of the time, that the Republicans could have maintained party unity?

Politics of the Gilded Age. The politics of scandal and corruption shocked and troubled many voters. Citizens began to cast a more skeptical eye on the behavior and ethical standards of their political leaders. In 1873 Mark Twain and Charles Dudley Warner published a satirical novel. The book examined the values of wealthy Americans and the nature of national politics after the Civil War. Twain and Warner titled their novel *The Gilded Age*. They believed that politics was like the base material that hides beneath the glittering gold surface of a gilded object. In politics, corruption and greed lurked below the polite and prosperous luster of American society during the late 1800s. The image struck a chord, and the era became known as the **Gilded Age**.

The authors had ample evidence to support their view—particularly in the area of politics. Despite the upper and middle classes' adoption of British Victorian culture, Twain argued that Americans were actually driven by "money lust." Twain accused Americans of living by the motto "Get rich; dishonestly if we can, honestly if we must." Politicians of both parties—and at every level of government—made speeches about the great honor of holding public office. However, they often showed more interest in taking advantage of their positions to steal from the public treasury than in serving the public good. "Unless you can get . . . a Senator, or a Congressman, . . . to use his 'influence' in your behalf, you cannot get an employment of the most trivial nature in Washington," wrote Twain. "Mere merit, fitness and capability, arc useless baggage to you without 'influence.'" Motivated by a distrust of political leaders, many Americans began to push for political reforms during the Gilded Age.

The Struggle for Reform

Reforming the spoils system became a major issue in the 1876 presidential campaign. Democrats nominated New York governor Samuel J. Tilden as their candidate. Tilden had won national attention by helping break up the Tweed Ring. The Republicans nominated Ohio governor Rutherford B. Hayes, a well-known supporter of civil service reform. Hayes narrowly won the election.

A Republican split. In June 1877 President Hayes issued an executive order prohibiting federal employees from participating in political campaigns. When two associates of New York senator Roscoe Conkling defied this order, Hayes demanded their removal. This demand provoked a bitter struggle between Hayes and Conkling and led to a split within the Republican Party. Patronage, or rewarding political supporters with government jobs, was at issue.

Led by Conkling, the **Stalwarts** strongly opposed civil service reform. Hayes further angered the group when he proposed awarding federal jobs based on examinations rather than patronage. Conkling referred to Hayes's proposed merit system for government jobs as "snivel service."

James G. Blaine of Maine led the Half-Breeds, the other faction within the Republican Party. The Half-Breeds included members who strongly supported civil service reforms and others who did not completely oppose patronage jobs.

Mark Twain and Charles Dudley Warner's novel **The Gilded Age** *described American political life as a gilded surface with corruption and greed lying underneath.*

INTERPRETING THE VISUAL RECORD

Civil Service Reform. Examinations like this one, for railway mail clerks, helped ensure that government workers were qualified for the jobs they held. *What categories were railway mail clerks tested in?*

HISTORY MAKERS SPEAK

James Bryce in *Voices of America: Readings in American History*

The Trouble with Politics. One English observer blamed the political chaos of the Gilded Age on the politicians themselves. Historian James Bryce wrote: "The hard commercial spirit which pervades the meetings of a joint-stock company is the spirit in which most politicians speak of public business, and are not blamed for speaking. . . . In no country is the ideal side of public life . . . so ignored by the mass and repudiated by the leaders. This affects not only the elevation but the independence and courage of public men; and the country suffers from the lack of what we call distinction in its conspicuous figures."

CRITICAL THINKING

According to Bryce, what caused "the lack of distinction" in American politicians?

ANSWER: Students might point out Bryce's comments about politicians' desire for profit and the public's casual attitude toward corruption.

VISUAL RECORD ANSWER

Students might cite spelling, arithmetic, letter-writing, penmanship, copying from plain copy, geography, reading addresses, and systems of railway transportation.

LEVEL 3: Tell students to imagine that they are modern-day historians working on a history of the Gilded Age. Have each student write a one-page essay explaining why Americans wanted political reform and how that desire affected the Republicans. *(See the Level 1 lesson for the correct reasons and effect.)* Ask volunteers to read their essays to the class. Students may wish to include their essays in their portfolios.

SPOTLIGHT
on the Pendleton Civil Service Act

After students have read the entire section, ask them to conduct research on the Pendleton Civil Service Act. Then tell students to imagine that the following people attended a press conference on the act: Roscoe Conkling, Julius Bing, Chester A. Arthur, James Blaine, Grover Cleveland, Samuel Tilden, and Benjamin Harrison. Assign students to play these roles and ask other students to act as reporters, politicians, and interested citizens. Have each main participant present a short statement on his reaction to the Pendleton Civil Service Act. Then act as a moderator and conduct the press conference. Remind the reporters and citizens to question each participant about his position and his record.
Cooperative Learning, Block Scheduling

PEOPLE IN HISTORY

Chester A. Arthur. When Charles Guiteau shot President Garfield, many Americans were horrified at the thought of Chester A. Arthur becoming president. Many viewed Arthur as a corrupt spoilsman in thrall to Stalwart leader Senator Roscoe Conkling. Garfield lived for 80 days after the assassination attempt, however, and during that time Arthur rose in public opinion. Many people believed that he acted with dignity during the crisis and showed great concern for Garfield and his family. After Garfield died, Arthur participated in a national outpouring of grief.

CRITICAL THINKING Would Arthur's actions after the assassination attempt have convinced you to support him? Why or why not?

ANSWER: Some students might argue that the assassination attempt changed Arthur and made him a better person.

***The American Nation* VIDEO PROGRAM**

The American Red Cross; Teacher's Guide, pp. 201–02

Search 49210, Play to 50586
Videodisc 1, Side B

Play   Pause

See *Teacher's Guide* for Spanish barcode.

★ Then and Now

Civil Service

Although the Pendleton Civil Service Act transferred just 10 percent of federal jobs to a merit-based system of hiring, the act did create the Civil Service Commission (CSC). The CSC established policies for examination and hiring based on merit rather than political patronage. At the time, many officials were concerned that geographical biases of the testing would cause most jobs to go to well-educated New Englanders. To avoid this bias in testing, the CSC specified that the examinations should be "practical in character." The exam should test applicants on skills and knowledge closely related to the actual tasks of the job.

Modern Americans taking a civil service exam

The use of civil service examinations has greatly expanded since 1883. The variety of government jobs requiring exams has also grown. The federal government disbanded the CSC in 1978 and assigned its tasks to other federal agencies. Many state and city civil service commissions still exist to oversee nonfederal government jobs. Today, examinations are given to applicants for positions in fields such as air-traffic control, foreign service, law enforcement, and postal service. Once employed, civil service employees have special protection against politically motivated dismissals. To ensure the strength of the merit system, civil service commissions review dismissals to verify that employees are dismissed only for reasons directly related to job performance.

Civil service reform remained a controversial topic. For example, Congressional aide Julius Bing argued in favor of the use of civil service exams to grant jobs on merit rather than by patronage.

History Makers Speak

❝Argument against the reform of the present chaos is the fear of a permanent bureaucracy, and of the anti-republican tendencies of such permanent institutions. We entertain no such apprehensions [fears]. A permanent bureaucracy is only dangerous when it is incompetent and practically irresponsible.❞

—Julius Bing, "Civil Service of the United States," *The North American Review,* October 1867

Hayes chose not to run for re-election in 1880, noting the political conflict between the Stalwarts and the Half-Breeds. He explained to his wife, "I am heartily tired of this life of bondage, responsibility, and toil." At the Republican convention, the Half-Breeds won the battle to control the party ticket. They named relatively unknown senator **James A. Garfield** as the Republican Party's presidential candidate. To satisfy the Stalwarts, they named Conkling's political ally **Chester A. Arthur** the vice presidential nominee.

✔ **READING CHECK: Summarizing** How did calls for reform affect the Republican Party? led to a split in the party, which led Hayes to not run for re-election; Garfield became the Republican nominee

Garfield's assassination. Garfield edged out his Democratic rival, Civil War veteran General Winfield Scott Hancock, by fewer than 10,000 votes. His presidency was short-lived. On July 2, 1881—less than four months after his inauguration—Garfield was shot. His assassin was Charles Guiteau (guh-TOH), a mentally unstable man who had unsuccessfully sought a government job. In the days before the incident Garfield had refused to increase the security around the White House. He even commented, "Assassination can no more be guarded against than death by lightning; and it is not best to worry about either."

Charles Guiteau (left) is detained after shooting President Garfield in a Washington train station.

THE GRANGER COLLECTION, NEW YORK

256

ALL LEVELS: Write the following names on the chalkboard: *James A. Garfield, Chester A. Arthur, Grover Cleveland,* and *Benjamin Harrison.* Ask students to list what they know about these presidents. Have volunteers share their responses. *(Most students will probably not know much about the listed presidents.)* Tell students that this period can be confusing because of the quick shifts in political power. To help students understand how these presidents viewed political reform during the Gilded Age, copy the following graphic organizer on the chalkboard, omitting the italicized answers. Have each student complete it. **English Language Learners**

President Arthur and Reforms
- *supported reform after the assassination of President Garfield*
- *helped pass Pendleton Civil Service Act*

Effect on the Republicans and the Election of 1884
- *split the Republicans*
- *Stalwarts voted for James Blaine, the Half-Breed candidate; reform Republicans voted for Grover Cleveland, the Democratic candidate*

President Cleveland's Reforms
- *doubled the number of federal jobs requiring civil service exams*
- *promoted reform in general*

President Harrison's Response
- *returned to political patronage*
- *spent money on Republican pet projects*

Guiteau had believed that killing Garfield would further the Stalwart cause. The shooting had the opposite effect, however. After Garfield died in September, Arthur, his successor, responded sympathetically to the calls for reform and abandoned his opposition to it.

Reforms and reactions. In 1883 President Arthur helped secure passage of the **Pendleton Civil Service Act.** The bill established the Civil Service Commission to administer competitive examinations to those people seeking government jobs. The act proved to be an important step toward reform. It established as law the idea that federal jobs below the policy-making level should be filled based on merit. Critics charged, however, that the act was of limited value. They noted that it applied to only about 10 percent of all federal jobs.

Angered by Arthur's reform efforts, many Stalwarts refused to support his bid for the 1884 Republican presidential nomination. Instead, they cast their votes for James Blaine, the leader of the Half-Breeds. Blaine's nomination upset Republican reformers. They charged that the candidate "wallowed in spoils like a rhinoceros in an African pool." Called **mugwumps**—the Algonquian word for "big chiefs"—these reformers supported the Democratic candidate, **Grover Cleveland.** Like Samuel Tilden, Cleveland had gained national attention when he opposed Tammany Hall while governor of New York.

Instead of a discussion of the issues, mudslinging dominated the campaign. A bachelor, Cleveland was accused of fathering a child out of wedlock. He refused to participate in the mudslinging. He replied, "The other side can have a monopoly of all the dirt in this campaign." The New York *World* defended Cleveland, listing four reasons for supporting the candidate. "1. He is an honest man; 2. He is an honest man; 3. He is an honest man; 4. He is an honest man." Despite the charges against Cleveland's character and private life, he won the election.

✔ **READING CHECK: Sequencing** How did Garfield's assassination lead to civil service reform and a setback for the Republican Party? Garfield was assassinated by an unsuccessful government job seeker. Arthur responded with calls for reform. Many Republicans did not support Arthur's bid for re-election. Cleveland won in 1884.

Advances and Setbacks

Proclaiming that "a public office is a public trust," President Cleveland entered the White House determined to promote political reform. Cleveland hoped to end the days when government jobs were handed out in reward for political favors. Toward this end, he doubled the number of federal jobs requiring civil service exams.

PRESIDENTIAL Lives

Grover Cleveland

1837–1908
In Office 1885–1889
and 1893–1897

Grover Cleveland is the only U.S. president to serve two nonconsecutive terms. After completing his first term, Cleveland did not miss the busy life of the presidency. He wrote in 1889, "You cannot imagine the relief which has come to me with the termination of my official term." Enjoying his free time, Cleveland described his new interests, "I started the fishing branch of the firm business today. . . . I caught twenty-five fish with my own rod and line."

In 1892 the Democratic Party began searching for a candidate to run against Benjamin Harrison. They again called upon Cleveland. He was not eager to run again after his defeat four years earlier. "The office of President has not, to me personally, a single allurement [attraction]." Nevertheless, Cleveland felt compelled by a sense of duty to his party to run for the presidency.

James Blaine (left), leader of the Half-Breeds, won the Republican Party nomination for president in 1884. Grover Cleveland (right) received the Democratic nomination.

"Rum, Romanism, and Rebellion." New York governor Grover Cleveland should have been able to expect strong support from Democratic voters in New York City in the 1884 presidential election. Tammany Hall bosses were feuding with Cleveland, however, and it appeared that many of the organization's Democratic members would not vote in the upcoming election. Shortly before the election, a supporter of Blaine, the Republican candidate, commented that the Democrats were the party of "Rum, Romanism, and Rebellion." Newspapers widely reported the comment, and many of Tammany's Irish American voters interpreted it as a nativist insult to their heritage and religion. They voted for Cleveland in large numbers. This support helped Cleveland win the close election.

CRITICAL THINKING Why might Irish Americans have objected to the term "Romanism"?

ANSWER: Students might suggest that "Romanism" implied that they came from Italy rather than Ireland.

REVIEW

Have students complete the **Section 2 Review** on p. 258.

ASSESS

Have students complete **Daily Quiz 8.2**. As **Alternative Assessment**, you may want to use the political reform poster or the political reform speech in this section's lessons.

RETEACH

Have students complete **Main Idea Activity for English Language Learners and Special-Needs Students 8.2**. Then organize students into small groups. Ask groups to reread the objectives at the beginning of the section. Have each group discuss the objectives in round-robin style, with one student in each group recording the answers. Then have recorders read their groups' answers to the entire class.
English Language Learners, Cooperative Learning

EXTEND

Ask students to conduct research on various historical interpretations of the Gilded Age. Ask each student to select one historian and to find one sentence from his or her work that comments on the age in an interesting, enlightening way. Have students present their sentences in class, offering relevant background information and explaining why the sentence accurately reflects the Gilded Age. **Block Scheduling**

SECTION
REVIEW 2 ANSWERS

1. Define
- mugwumps, p. 257

2. Identify
- Gilded Age, p. 255
- Stalwarts, p. 255
- James A. Garfield, p. 256
- Chester A. Arthur, p. 256
- Pendleton Civil Service Act, p. 257
- Grover Cleveland, p. 257
- Benjamin Harrison, p. 258

3. reaction to the Grant administration—citizens become more skeptical about the behavior and ethical standards of their leaders; types of reform desired—civil service reform; impact on Republican Party—split into Stalwarts and Half-Breeds

4a. Black Friday—gold market speculation; Crédit Mobilier—excessive profits from Union Pacific Railroad deals; whiskey taxation—Treasury Department officials received bribes

b. because Garfield was assassinated; his efforts split the party and the mugwumps threw their support to the Democrat, Cleveland, who won.

c. Cleveland—supported civil service reform; Harrison—believed in the spoils system

5. Letters might mention that corruption led to mistrust of the government and that the Pendleton Civil Service Act would restore that trust.

Research on the R·O·M

Free Find:
Grover Cleveland
After reading about Grover Cleveland on the **Holt Researcher CD–ROM**, write a short essay summarizing the role of Cleveland in the history of civil service reform in the United States.

Cleveland's support of reform efforts outraged many Stalwarts and Democratic legislators. One Democratic member of Congress defended the spoils system by arguing that civil service reform was inconsistent with the U.S. republican electoral process.

History Makers Speak
❝Take the President. On this theory, Cleveland should have said to Arthur on March 4th [inauguration day], 'Mr. Arthur, it's true the people have chosen me to fill your place. But I believe that when a man is in office and is doing well, he should not be disturbed. Everyone says you are a good President, so I'll just go back to my law practice in Buffalo and leave you in the White House.'❞

—Democratic Congressmember, quoted in *The Gilded Age*, by Ari and Olive Hoogenboom

Although Cleveland's stand on reform annoyed some party leaders, he won the Democratic presidential nomination in 1888. To oppose him, the Republicans chose **Benjamin Harrison** of Indiana, a grandson of the ninth president, William Henry Harrison. Cleveland won the popular election by some 100,000 votes. However, Harrison came out on top in electoral votes and won the race.

The new president and Congress quickly set out to reward their supporters, thereby weakening Cleveland's reform efforts. The Republicans filled practically every job not on the civil service list with members of their own party. During 1890, Republican politicians controlled Congress and the presidency. They passed laws, including the Sherman Antitrust Act. They also spent considerable amounts of money on Civil War pensions for Union veterans—who mostly voted Republican—and other pet projects. Congress spent money so freely that it became known as the Billion Dollar Congress.

✔ **READING CHECK: Analyzing Information** What made the election of Benjamin Harrison unusual? *He won the electoral vote but lost the popular vote.*

SECTION 2 REVIEW

1. Define and explain:
mugwumps

2. Identify and explain:
Gilded Age
Stalwarts
James A. Garfield
Chester A. Arthur
Pendleton Civil Service Act
Grover Cleveland
Benjamin Harrison

3. Drawing Conclusions Copy the graphic organizer below. Use it to explain how the desire of voters for political reform influenced Republican Party politics.

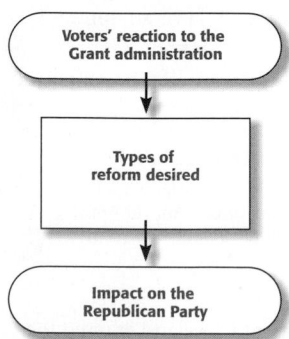

Voters' reaction to the Grant administration

Types of reform desired

Impact on the Republican Party

4. **Finding the Main Idea**
a. Identify and explain three of the scandals that tarnished the Grant administration.
b. Why did President Arthur change his position on civil service reform? What effect did this have on his party?
c. How did President Harrison's position on civil service reform differ from that of his predecessor?

5. **Writing and Critical Thinking**
Supporting a Point of View Imagine that you are a voter in 1888. Write a letter to a member of Congress supporting civil service reform.
Consider:
- the public's opinion of politics and politicians
- the efforts made by national politicians to rid government of corruption, including the Pendleton Civil Service Act

Homework Practice Online
keyword: SE3 HP8

SECTION 3

The Populist Movement

EYEWITNESSES TO History

"The farmers of the United States are up in arms. . . . The American farmer is steadily losing ground. His burdens are heavier every year and his gains are more meager [small]."

—Washington Gladden, quoted in the *Forum*, November 1890

Farmers' economic woes included paying for equipment, such as this tractor.

Washington Gladden, a Congregational minister in Columbus, Ohio, described the plight of the farmer during the late 1800s. Farmers had endured severe hardships and received little political support. Falling crop prices, rising railroad rates, and mounting expenses forced many farmers to default on their mortgages and loans. Foreclosures by banks forced many farmers off their land. Desperately attempting to preserve their way of life, many farmers began organizing, pressing for political solutions to their problems.

The Farmers' Plight

In addition to transforming urban life, the surge in industrialization during the late 1800s changed farmers' lives significantly. The rapidly growing population in the urban centers had to be fed. Farmers responded by planting more crops and raising more animals each year. Unfortunately for Americans, farmers in other nations did the same. Prices soon tumbled as supply exceeded demand. At the same time, expenses, such as railroad freight charges and the price of new machinery, continued to rise. As farm profits plunged, many farmers bought more land and increased production. This greater production pushed prices even lower.

To make matters worse, most farm families had borrowed money to pay for their land or to buy new equipment. They often put their farms up as security for loans. Those who could not repay the loans lost their farms. Many ended up as tenant farmers. Others were forced to become farm laborers. One Minnesota farmer expressed the bitterness felt by many farmers.

History Makers Speak

"I settled on this land in good faith; built house and barn, broken up part of the land. Spent years of hard labor grubbing [digging], fencing, and improving. Are they going to drive us out like trespassers?"

—Minnesota farmer

To farmers, the situation seemed terribly unfair. Merchants who sold farm equipment were making money. Bankers who lent farmers money and the railroads that hauled the farmers' grain and livestock to market were also prospering. All farmers had to show for their long days of backbreaking labor were rising debts. One farmer wrote, "The railroads have never been so prosperous. . . . The banks have never done a better . . . business. . . . And yet agriculture languishes [declines]."

✔ **READING CHECK: Categorizing** What economic hardships did farmers face?
oversupply, low prices, loans that could not be repaid, and lost farms

LEVEL 1: Tell students to imagine that it is 1875 and that they are farmers in the Midwest. Have each student create a flier or handbill describing the factors that led to economic hardships for farmers. *(Students' fliers should include the following: heavy debts, high freight and machinery costs, and falling crop prices.)* Ask volunteers to present their work to the class. Students may wish to include their fliers or handbills in their portfolios. **English Language Learners**

LEVELS 2 AND 3: Tell students to imagine that it is 1875 and that they are farmers in the Midwest. Have each student write a letter to a friend describing the factors that led to economic hardships for farmers. *(See the Level 1 lesson for the correct factors.)* Students might also want to discuss the formation of a farmers' organization to combat some of those factors. Have volunteers read their letters to the class. Students may wish to include their letters in their portfolios.

ECONOMICS

Farmers' Woes. The drop in crop prices during the late 1800s hurt many farm families. In 1870 wheat averaged $1.04 per bushel, corn $0.52 per bushel, and cotton about $15 per pound. By 1895 wheat averaged $0.51 per bushel, corn $0.25 per bushel, and cotton $7.62 per pound. As crop prices fell, western farmers faced higher prices for shipping their crops than eastern shippers did. In 1897 the price per ton per mile to ship goods on the Pennsylvania Railroad east of Chicago was $0.56; on the Burlington Railroad from Chicago to the Missouri River $0.78; and on the Burlington Railroad west of the Missouri River $1.28.

CRITICAL THINKING Why might railroads have charged western farmers higher rates for shipping their goods?

ANSWER: Answers will vary. Some students might mention that the western railroads ran through sparsely settled land where fewer goods were shipped.

VISUAL RECORD ANSWER

Students might answer that the poster shows farmers enjoying healthy, happy lives and depicts prosperous farms and communities.

INTERPRETING THE VISUAL RECORD

The National Grange. The National Grange established cooperatives and pushed for legislation that would assist farmers. *How does this poster portray the lives of American farmers?*

THE GRANGER COLLECTION, NEW YORK

Farmers Organize

Farmers began organizing in an attempt to improve their situation. Many farmers joined local organizations committed to assisting them in their day-to-day struggles. These organizations soon merged to form a nationwide movement. Hoping to improve their lives by forcing reforms in railroad and banking practices, many farmers supported these rapidly growing national organizations.

The Grange movement. The first major farmers' organization, the National Grange of the Patrons of Husbandry, or the **National Grange**, was founded by Oliver Hudson Kelley in 1867. Kelley created the Grange primarily as a social organization. As membership increased and farmers' financial problems grew, the Grange began tackling economic and political issues.

To lower costs, some Grange members formed **cooperatives**, or organizations in which groups of farmers pool their resources to buy and sell goods. Cooperative members sold their products directly to big-city markets. They bought farm equipment and other goods in large quantities at wholesale prices—thereby cutting costs. The Grange's main focus, however, was on forcing states to regulate railroad freight and grain-storage rates. In the early 1870s state legislatures began to respond to pressure from farmers. Illinois, Iowa, Minnesota, and Wisconsin passed "Granger laws" that created state commissions to standardize such rates.

Many railroad companies challenged the Granger laws in the courts. In a victory for farmers in 1877, the Supreme Court declared in the case of *Munn* v. *Illinois* that state legislatures had the right to regulate businesses such as railroads that involved the public interest. However, the Court modified its decision nine years later, in *Wabash* v. *Illinois*, ruling that state governments had no power to regulate traffic that moved across state boundaries. Only the federal government had that right, the justices ruled.

The Court's decision led directly to the passage of the **Interstate Commerce Act** in 1887. The act prohibited railroads from giving secret rebates, or refunds, to large shippers or charging more for short hauls than for long hauls over the same line. It also stated that railroad rates had to be "reasonable and just." To monitor railroad activities, the act created the Interstate Commerce Commission (ICC). However, the ICC was given little power to enforce its rulings. When it charged railroads with violating the law, the courts almost always ruled in the railroads' favor.

The Alliance movement. While the National Grange lobbied on behalf of railroad regulation, a more powerful farm organization—the Farmers' Alliance—took shape. Beginning in Texas in the 1870s, the Alliance movement spread quickly. Debt-ridden farm families eagerly embraced the Alliance message of unity and hope. Like the Grange, the Alliance organized cooperatives to buy equipment and to market farm products. The Alliance offered farmers low-cost insurance. It also lobbied for tougher bank regulations, government ownership of the railroads, and a **graduated income tax** that taxed higher incomes at a higher rate.

TEACH OBJECTIVE 2

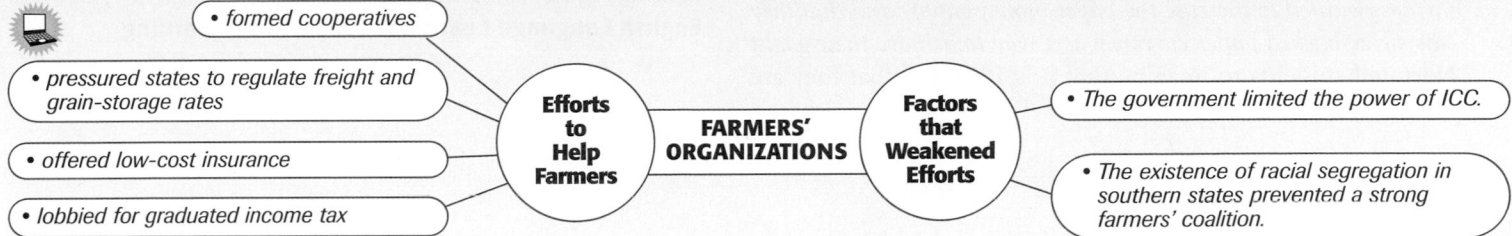

ALL LEVELS: To help students understand more about farmers' movements, copy the following graphic organizer on the chalkboard, omitting the italicized answers. Have each student complete it. Then ask students to consider the efforts that farmers' movements undertook to help farmers. Which effort would have been most helpful to farmers? Why? Make sure that students fully justify their selections.
English Language Learners

- *formed cooperatives*
- *pressured states to regulate freight and grain-storage rates*
- *offered low-cost insurance*
- *lobbied for graduated income tax*

Efforts to Help Farmers — **FARMERS' ORGANIZATIONS** — **Factors that Weakened Efforts**

- *The government limited the power of ICC.*
- *The existence of racial segregation in southern states prevented a strong farmers' coalition.*

Agricultural Regions in 1900

Interpreting Maps The diverse climates and soils of the United States allowed farmers to grow a wide variety of crops.

? ENVIRONMENT AND SOCIETY What environmental factors might contribute to the types of agricultural products grown in different regions of the United States in 1900?

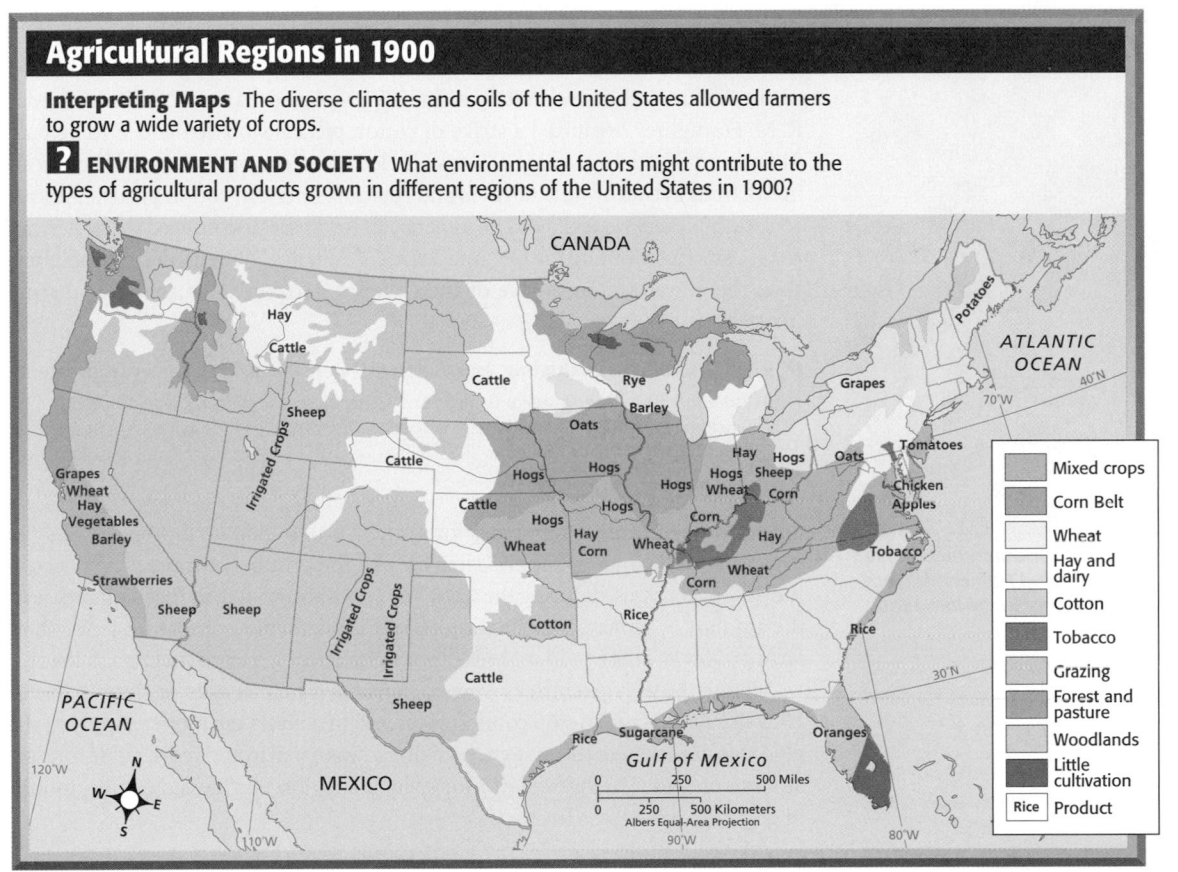

By 1890 the Alliance movement claimed more than 1 million members. Alliance leader **Mary Elizabeth Lease** from Kansas traveled the country urging people to take action.

> *History Makers Speak*
>
> **"The great common people of this country are slaves, and monopoly is the master. . . . The politicians said we suffered from overproduction. Overproduction, when 10,000 little children, so statistics tell us, starve to death every year in the United States. . . . We will stand by our homes and stay by our fireside by force if necessary, and we will not pay our debts to the loan-shark companies until the government pays its debts to us."**
>
> —Mary Elizabeth Lease

The Alliance movement consisted of three organizations: the National Farmers' Alliance, the all-white Southern Alliance, and the Colored Farmers' Alliance. Each organization pushed for the same legislative goals and helped their members in times of hardship. Nevertheless, a variety of reasons kept the Alliance organizations from consolidating their leadership into one single organization.

African American farmers.
Despite common goals, the Southern and Colored Farmers' Alliances remained separate, segregated institutions. Racial divisions in southern society prevented farmers from forming a tight coalition that crossed color lines.

THE GRANGER COLLECTION, NEW YORK

Alliance movement supporter Mary Elizabeth Lease spoke out against monopolies.

Populist farmers. Have each pair develop a brief dialogue on how the silver issue affected the 1896 presidential election. *(Students should note that silver was a central issue, that the Populists supported Bryan because of his stand on silver, and that William McKinley won the presidency with the support of business leaders who opposed free silver.)* Ask volunteers to perform their dialogues for the class.
English Language Learners, Cooperative Learning

African American farmers looked to the Colored Farmers' Alliance for assistance in the late 1880s.

The racial divisions within the Alliance movement brought about the end of the Colored Farmers' Alliance. In 1891 Colored Farmers' Alliance leader R. M. Humphrey organized a strike of cotton pickers who demanded to be paid $1 for every 100 pounds picked. The strike led to a series of violent confrontations in Arkansas between white farmers and African American cotton pickers. At least 15 cotton pickers were killed. The violence in Arkansas discouraged many African Americans from joining the Colored Farmers' Alliance. With dwindling membership, the power and influence of the Colored Farmers' Alliance faded during the 1890s.

✔ **READING CHECK: Evaluating** How successful were the national farmers' movements in the late 1800s? The National Grange had some success in railroad regulation; the Alliance movement had more success with its cooperatives and lobbying efforts; and the Colored Farmers' Alliance faded in the 1890s.

The Money Question

One of the most important issues for farmers in the Alliance movement was the expansion of the money supply. They favored the printing of more greenbacks—the paper money used during the Civil War. The farmers hoped that an increase in the amount of money in circulation would allow them to charge more for their farm products. This would make it easier for farmers to pay off their bank loans.

Before the war, greenbacks were redeemable for either gold or silver coins. In 1873 Congress voted to stop coining silver and to convert the money supply to the **gold standard**. Under this system, each dollar was equal to and redeemable for a set amount of gold. The amount of money in circulation was limited by the amount of gold held in the U.S. Treasury.

★ Changing Ways — The American Farmer

■ **Understanding Change** Farming was once the primary occupation of most Americans. *By how much has the percentage of workers engaged in farming changed? Calculate the average farm size then and now. How has it changed over time?*

	THEN	NOW
Population Employed in Farming ■ Farming ■ Nonfarming	38% / 62%	3% / 97%
Number of farms	5.7 million	2.2 million
Total farmland	841 million acres	954 million acres

Sources: *Historical Statistics of the United States; Statistical Abstract of the United States: 1999.* Data reflect 1900 and 1998.

THEN

NOW

LEVEL 3: Tell students to imagine that is 1902 and that they are midwestern farmers preparing to retire. Have each student write at least four short memoir pieces about his or her career: two entries discussing why he or she supported paper currency backed by silver, and two entries on how silver affected the election of 1896. *(See the Level 1 lesson for the correct reasons and effects.)* Have volunteers read their memoir pieces to the class.

HOMEWORK *Have each student write summaries of the following subsections: The Money Question and The Election of 1896. Ask two volunteers—one representing each subsection—to read their summaries to the class. Have these volunteers field questions from the other students about the content of their given subsection.*

TEACH OBJECTIVE 4

LEVEL 1: Tell students to imagine that they are Populist Party workers. Have each student design several pieces of political paraphernalia identifying the Populist position on various issues. *(Students' items should note that the Populists supported a graduated income tax, bank regulation, government ownership of railroad and telegraph companies, the free coinage of silver, immigration restrictions, a shorter workday, and voting reforms.)* Students might design campaign buttons, pens, shirts, and so on. Have students present their items to the class. Then have students select the most effective item, clearly justifying their choices. **English Language Learners**

The conversion to the gold standard resulted in a decrease in the amount of money in circulation and a lowering of prices. Many farmers demanded that the government back the money supply with silver. Silver was plentiful in the West. Bowing to pressure, Congress passed the **Bland-Allison Act** in 1878 and the **Sherman Silver Purchase Act** in 1890. Both acts required the government to buy silver each month and mint it into coins. Because the government bought so little silver, however, the money supply did not increase enough to satisfy silver supporters.

Disappointed Alliance members threw themselves into the 1890 elections, supporting any candidate who backed their pro-farmer platform. The results of their efforts were remarkable. Alliance-backed candidates won more than 40 seats in Congress, four southern governorships, and numerous other political offices.

✔ **READING CHECK: Analyzing Information** How did the conversion to the gold standard hurt farmers? It resulted in a decrease in the amount of money in supply and a lowering of prices.

A Decade of Populist Politics

Pleased by their successes in the 1890 election, Alliance movement leaders sought to build on their popular support by forming a new political party. Throughout the 1890s Alliance leaders began a large grassroots campaign, gaining a considerable amount of influence on national politics.

The Populist Party. Between 1891 and 1892 Alliance members met with labor leaders and other reformers to draw up plans for a national political party. The People's Party was founded at a convention in St. Louis in February 1892. This coalition of Alliance members, farmers, labor leaders, and reformers became more commonly known as the **Populist Party**.

The party platform echoed National Grange and Alliance demands. It called for a graduated income tax, bank regulation, government ownership of railroad and telegraph companies, and the free, or unlimited, coinage of silver. The platform also called for restrictions on immigration, a shorter workday, and voting reforms.

The Populists nominated **James B. Weaver** to run in the 1892 presidential election against Republican incumbent Benjamin Harrison and Democrat Grover Cleveland. Cleveland was a former president who had lost to Harrison in the 1888 election. Although Cleveland won the 1892 election, the Populist Party elected more than 10 party members to Congress as well as numerous state leaders. Weaver pulled in a respectable 1 million popular votes, carrying Kansas and three western states. He received 22 electoral votes.

✔ **READING CHECK: Finding the Main Idea** What was the platform of the Populist Party? graduated income tax, bank regulation, government ownership of railroad and telegraph companies, and the free coinage of silver

Economic depression. In May 1893 one of the nation's leading railroad companies failed. This failure triggered the Panic of 1893, a financial panic that sent stock prices plunging. The country quickly slid into an economic depression. By the end of 1893, some 3 million people were unemployed—100,000 in Chicago alone. In

INTERPRETING THE VISUAL RECORD

The silver issue. Many American farmers supported the printing of paper money backed by silver. *Which form of currency do you think most farmers would have preferred Americans to use? Why?*

This ticket entitled its holder to attend the Populist Party convention in 1892.

LEVEL 2: Tell students to imagine that they are high-level Populist Party officials preparing to speak at the organization's annual conference. Have each student write a speech identifying the issues supported by the Populist Party. *(See the Level 1 lesson for the correct issues.)* Ask volunteers to deliver their speeches to the class. Then conduct a discussion about the Populist Party. If students had been farmers in the 1890s, would they have joined the party? If students had been industrialists, would they have opposed it? Students may wish to include the text of their speeches in their portfolios.

LEVEL 3: Pair students and tell them to imagine that they are high-level Populist Party officials preparing to open an office in rural Iowa. Have each pair write a party platform identifying the issues supported by the Populist Party. *(See the Level 1 lesson for the correct issues.)* Have volunteers read their platforms to the class. Then conduct a discussion about the Populist Party. If students had been farmers in the 1890s, would they have joined the party? If students had been industrialists, would they have opposed it? **Cooperative Learning**

---

c. Business leaders who were terrified of Bryan's populism contributed millions of dollars to the Republican campaign.

5. Answers will vary. Debates should note that the silver standard would increase the money supply and make money less valuable. The gold supply would decrease supply and make money more valuable. The silver standard helped the farmers but hurt the economy during the Panic of 1893.

CHAPTER 8 REVIEW ANSWERS

Creating a Time Line
Each event should have an explanation and the correct date.

Writing a Summary
See the Reading Checks in each section for main ideas.

Identifying People and Ideas
1. well-organized political groups that dominated city governments in the United States in the late 1800s

2. the acquisition of money or political power through illegal or dishonest practices

3. Tammany Hall political boss in the 1860s who was indicted for fraud and extortion in 1871

4. Republican group that strongly opposed civil service reform

5. stated that railroad rates had to be "reasonable and just"

Research on the ROM

Free Find:
William Jennings Bryan

After reading about William Jennings Bryan on the **Holt Researcher CD–ROM**, explain how his political views were influenced by his family and his experiences growing up in the midwestern United States.

Judge magazine published this cartoon on its cover after William Jennings Bryan gave his "Cross of Gold" speech.

New York City some 20,000 homeless people desperately sought shelter in jails. Strikes and protests swept the country.

The depression had many causes, including a worldwide financial panic. However, President Cleveland chose to focus only on one cause—the Sherman Silver Purchase Act. This law required the government to pay for silver purchases with Treasury notes redeemable in either gold or silver. New discoveries of silver decreased the metal's value, and people rushed to exchange their notes for gold. The situation put a terrible strain on the Treasury's gold reserves. To protect the gold standard and to restore confidence in the economy, Cleveland called for Congress to repeal the Sherman Silver Purchase Act. Congress did so in October 1893.

The Election of 1896

President Cleveland's actions saved the gold standard, but this did not end the debate on the money supply. Silver became a central issue in the 1896 election. The Republicans chose Ohio governor **William McKinley** as their presidential candidate and adopted a conservative platform upholding the gold standard. A deeply split Democratic Party rejected President Cleveland. Instead, they nominated free-silver supporter **William Jennings Bryan**, a two-term representative from Nebraska. Because its free-silver platform had been adopted by the Democratic Party, the Populist Party threw its support behind Bryan. It soon faded as a national party.

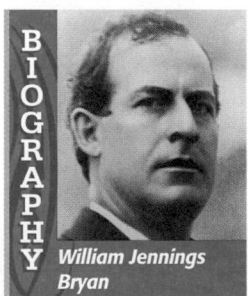

Bryan. William Jennings Bryan was born in 1860 into a very religious and Democratic family. His father served in the Illinois state senate and on the Illinois circuit court. He was guided by his religious beliefs and his Democratic ideals.

At the age of 21 Bryan left his childhood home in Salem, Illinois, to attend law school in Chicago. After receiving his law degree, he eventually moved to Lincoln, Nebraska. He established a law firm and ran for political office as a Democratic candidate in Nebraska, a predominantly Republican state. At the age of 31, Bryan was elected to the U.S. House of Representatives.

William Jennings Bryan

Bryan's youth, charisma, and strong support of silver-backed currency gained him broad support among populists within the Democratic Party in the 1890s. During the Democratic convention where he received the nomination to run for president, Bryan gave his now famous "Cross of Gold" speech. He stressed the importance of the silver issue to farmers and less-fortunate people all over the United States.

History Makers Speak

"If they [the Republicans] dare to come out in the open field and defend the gold standard as a good thing, we will fight them to the uttermost. Having behind us the producing masses of this nation and the world, supported by the commercial interests, the laboring interests, and the toilers everywhere, we will answer their demand for a gold standard by saying to them: You shall not press down upon the brow of labor this crown of thorns, you shall not crucify mankind upon a cross of gold."

—William Jennings Bryan

REVIEW

Have students complete the **Section 3 Review** on p. 265.

ASSESS

Have students complete **Daily Quiz 8.3**. As **Alternative Assessment**, you may want to use the silver graphic or the Populist Party political paraphernalia in this section's lessons.

RETEACH

Have students complete **Main Idea Activity for English Language Learners and Special-Needs Students 8.3**. Then pair students and have each pair create a detailed outline of Section 3. Ask volunteers to share their outlines and create a master outline on the chalkboard. Have students consult the outline and suggest five true-false questions, five matching questions, three short-answer questions, and one essay question. Ask students to provide brief answers to their questions.
English Language Learners, Cooperative Learning

EXTEND

Have students conduct research on farmers' problems in the 1890s and 1990s. Then have each student create a Venn diagram displaying the similarities and differences in farmers' problems in the two decades. Ask volunteers to present their diagrams to the class. Students may wish to include their diagrams in their portfolios. **Block Scheduling**

Bryan remained politically active throughout his life. He published several papers on populism and ran for political office repeatedly during the early 1900s. He died in 1925.

The end of populism. Terrified of Bryan's populism, many business leaders contributed millions of dollars to the Republican campaign. When the popular votes were counted, McKinley had edged out Bryan by some 500,000 votes. The Populists were in shock. Free silver had proven too weak an issue for a national campaign, and urban workers and immigrants had found little that appealed to them in the Populists' agenda.

The election defeat and improvements in farmers' economic conditions brought an end to the power of the Populist Party. However, the party's platform laid the groundwork for future reform. As Populist leader Mary Elizabeth Lease noted in 1914, "The seeds we sowed out in Kansas did not fall on barren ground."

PRESIDENTIAL Lives

1843–1901
In Office 1897–1901

William McKinley

William McKinley used presidential power so effectively that a Republican newspaper concluded: "No executive in the history of the country . . . has given a greater exhibition of his influence over Congress." Even his political enemies respected his tact and persuasiveness. Speaker of the House Tom Reed said of him with envy, "My opponents in Congress go at me tooth and nail, but they always apologize to William when they are going to call him names."

A courteous manner characterized McKinley in private life as well. He was devoted to protecting and caring for his wife, Ida. She suffered headaches and seizures that often kept her from fulfilling her role as first lady. He stayed close to her during state dinners and receptions. If she fainted, he would tend to her, continuing with conversation so as not to embarrass her.

✔ **READING CHECK: Drawing Conclusions** Why were business leaders worried about the growth of the Populist Party? because they did not want free silver

SECTION ❸ REVIEW

1. Define and explain:
cooperatives
graduated income tax
gold standard

2. Identify and explain:
National Grange
Interstate Commerce Act
Mary Elizabeth Lease
Bland-Allison Act
Sherman Silver Purchase Act
Populist Party
James B. Weaver
William McKinley
William Jennings Bryan

3. Categorizing Copy the chart below. List the political concerns and typical supporters of the National Grange, the Farmers' Alliance, and the Populist Party.

	Grange	Alliance	Populist
Political Issues			
Supporters			

4. Finding the Main Idea
a. What was the purpose of the Interstate Commerce Commission?
b. What impact did the Populist Party have as a third party in the election of 1896?
c. Why did William Jennings Bryan lose the 1896 presidential election?

5. Writing and Critical Thinking
Identifying Points of View Write a dialogue between two senators, one representing business interests and one representing western farmers, debating the shift from the silver to the gold standard.
Consider:
• who wanted a gold standard and who wanted silver-backed money
• what reasons each group had
• how silver influenced the economy

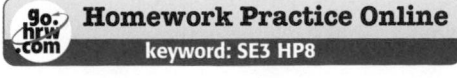
Homework Practice Online
keyword: SE3 HP8

---

6. elected president in 1884 and supported civil service reform

7. organization founded by Oliver Hudson Kelley in 1867 that tackled farmers' economic and political issues

8. speaker on behalf of the Alliance movement

9. system in which each dollar is equal to and redeemable for a set amount of gold, and the amount of money in circulation is limited by the amount of gold held in the U.S. Treasury

10. free-silver advocate who was the Democratic Party's candidate in the 1896 presidential campaign and who also received support from the Populist Party; lost the election to Republican William McKinley

Understanding Main Ideas
1. offered jobs, political favors, and services to local voters

2. Thomas Nast's political cartoons in *Harper's Weekly* and a series of articles in the *New York Times*

3. Stalwarts—strongly opposed civil service reform; Half-Breeds—favored the use of civil service exams to grant jobs on merit rather than by patronage

4. prompted reformers to call for the end of the spoils system

5. a graduated income tax, bank regulation, government ownership of railroad and telegraph companies, the free coinage of silver, immigration restrictions, a shorter workday, and voting reforms

TECHNOLOGY

▶ Chapter 8 Test Generator (on the One-Stop Planner)
▶ Global Skill Builder CD–ROM
▶ HRW Go site

REINFORCEMENT, REVIEW, AND ASSESSMENT

▶ Chapter 8 Review, pp. 266–67
▶ Chapter 8 Tutorial for Students, Parents, Mentors, and Peers

▶ Chapter 8 Test (Form A or B)
▶ Portfolio Activities and Alternative Assessment Handbook, Chapter 8
▶ Chapter 8 Test for English Language Learners and Special-Needs Students

REVIEW

Have students complete the **Chapter 8 Review** on pp. 266–67.

ASSESS

Use one of the chapter tests to assess students' understanding of the content. For **Alternative Assessment**, see the **Portfolio Activities and Alternative Assessment Handbook**.

---

6. Business leaders who were terrified of Bryan's populism contributed millions of dollars to McKinley's campaign.

Reviewing Themes
1. Political bosses provided jobs, political favors, and services to local residents in exchange for their vote.

2. Answers will vary. Students might suggest that Stalwarts felt that civil service reform would create a permanent bureaucracy with anti-republican tendencies.

3. Although farmers in the Midwest, West, and South supported Bryan's pro-farmer policies, urban workers and immigrants had found little that appealed to them in the Populists' agenda.

Thinking Critically
1. They received jobs or gained valuable city services in exchange for voting for particular candidates.

2. believed that killing Garfield would further the Stalwart cause; no, Arthur responded to the calls for civil service reform

3. Answers will vary. Students might mention that the Grange established cooperatives that allowed farmers to cut costs and were successful in getting Illinois, Iowa, Minnesota, and Wisconsin to pass "Granger laws."

Review

Creating a Time Line

Copy the time line below onto a sheet of paper. Complete the time line by filling in the events and dates from the chapter that you think were most significant. Pick three events and explain why you think they were significant.

| 1865 | 1875 | 1890 | 1900 |

Writing a Summary

Using standard grammar, spelling, sentence structure, and punctuation, write an overview of events in the chapter.

Identifying People and Ideas

Identify the following terms or individuals and explain their significance.

1. political machines
2. graft
3. William Marcy Tweed
4. Stalwarts
5. Interstate Commerce Act
6. Grover Cleveland
7. National Grange
8. Mary Elizabeth Lease
9. gold standard
10. William Jennings Bryan

Understanding Main Ideas

SECTION 1 *(pp. 246–251)*
1. What did political machines do to build and maintain support for their party?
2. What caused the decline in public support for the Tweed Ring?

SECTION 2 *(pp. 252–258)*
3. What did the Stalwarts want? What reforms did the Half-Breeds want?
4. What role did President Grant's administration play in the civil service reform movement?

SECTION 3 *(pp. 259–265)*
5. What issues did the Populist Party support?
6. Why did the Populists lose the 1896 election?

Reviewing Themes

1. **Culture** How were political machines able to unite immigrant groups to support their candidates?
2. **Government** Why might many Stalwarts have considered civil service reform a violation of the democratic heritage of the United States?
3. **Geography** Why did William Jennings Bryan win such strong support in some parts of the country but so little in other regions?

Thinking Critically

1. **Drawing Conclusions** Why do you think voters supported corrupt political machines?
2. **Identifying Cause and Effect** What motivated Charles Guiteau to assassinate President Garfield? Did he accomplish his political goal?
3. **Evaluating** Overall, were the National Grange and Farmers' Alliance movements a success or a failure? Explain your answer.
4. **Analyzing Information** In what ways was "the Gilded Age" an appropriate nickname for the late 1800s?
5. **Making Predictions** What contributions did William Jennings Bryan make to American society? How could he have done more to help farmers and poor Americans?

Writing About History

Summarizing Copy the following graphic organizer and use it to explain the give-and-take relationship between political machines and voters. Then write a letter to the editor of a newspaper to persuade the public to support civil service reform. Be sure to explain how civil service reform would change the relationship between political machines and voters.

| Political Machines | give and take | Voters |

Pair students and assign them one of the sections in Chapter 7. Have each pair write three questions about the material. Then have students present their questions to the entire class in the form of a "quiz game." The pair that answers the most questions correctly, excluding their own, will win the "quiz game." **English Language Learners, Cooperative Learning**

EXTEND

Have students conduct research on the Populist Party. Ask students to focus on a specific candidate—either national, regional, or local. Have each student write a brief biography on his or her chosen figure. Students' biographies should include basic biographical and political information. Students should also illustrate their biographies if possible. Have volunteers present their biographies to the class. Then compile the biographies into a Populist Party yearbook. **Block Scheduling**

Building Social Studies Skills

Interpreting Maps
Study the map below. Then use it to help answer the questions that follow.

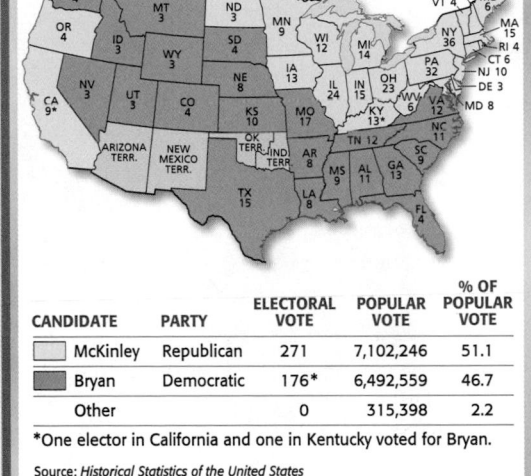

The Election of 1896

CANDIDATE	PARTY	ELECTORAL VOTE	POPULAR VOTE	% OF POPULAR VOTE
McKinley	Republican	271	7,102,246	51.1
Bryan	Democratic	176*	6,492,559	46.7
Other		0	315,398	2.2

*One elector in California and one in Kentucky voted for Bryan.

Source: *Historical Statistics of the United States*

1. Which comparison shows the number of states won by McKinley with the number of states won by Bryan?
   a. 271 for McKinley, 176 for Bryan
   b. 46.7% for McKinley, 51% for Bryan
   c. 23 for McKinley; 22 for Bryan
   d. 22 for McKinley; 23 for Bryan

2. Which regions gave the most support to William Jennings Bryan? to William McKinley? Why did each candidate gain support in those areas?

Analyzing Primary Sources
Refer to the Eyewitnesses to History at the beginning of Section 3 and to this statement by historian Lawrence Goodwyn. Then answer the questions that follow.

❝[The Alliance movement] was, first and most centrally, a movement that imparted [passed on] a sense of self-worth to individuals and provided them with the instruments of self-education about the world they lived in. The movement taught them to believe that they could perform specific political acts of self-determination.❞

3. Based on these two sources, which of these terms best describes the Alliance movement?
   a. an effort toward unity and hope
   b. an effort toward violent revolution
   c. an effort to silence political opponents
   d. an effort to convince farmers to wait passively for better times

4. What constitutional principles supported the Alliance movement's methods of gaining political influence?

Alternative Assessment

Building Your Portfolio

U.S. HISTORY

Citizenship
Imagine that you are a political boss greeting immigrants as they arrive in New York City. Perform a dialogue in which you explain how a political machine can help these new arrivals. Your dialogue should include information on some of the political, economic, and social changes in the United States in the late 1800s.

▣ **internet** connect

Internet Activity: go.hrw.com
KEYWORD: SE3 AN8

Choose a topic on politics in the Gilded Age to:
- analyze the work of Thomas Nast.
- learn about resistance to British rule in Africa.
- understand the complex role of the Tammany Hall political machine in the lives of citizens of New York City.

go. hrw .com

---

4. Answers will vary. Students might note that the name is appropriate for the late 1800s, since the prevalence of political machines showed that many politicians were interested in taking advantage of their positions.

5. Answers will vary. Students might mention his political activism, particularly his support of farmers, populism, and silver-backed currency. He might have done more if he had been elected president.

Writing
Letters should include the information presented in the graphic organizer.

Building Social Studies Skills
1. c

2. The West and the South supported Bryan; the Midwest and the East supported McKinley. The West and the South consisted mostly of farmers who supported Bryan's stand on silver; the Midwest and the East consisted of industrial business leaders and workers who supported the gold standard.

3. a

4. Answers will vary. Students might suggest that the right to vote, the right to assemble, and the right of government for the people by the people supported the Alliance Movement's methods.

TECHNOLOGY
▶ Global Skill Builder CD–ROM
▶ Holt Researcher: American History CD–ROM
▶ HRW Go site

REINFORCEMENT, REVIEW, AND ASSESSMENT
▶ Unit 2 Review, pp. 268–69
▶ Unit 2 Test (Form A or B)
▶ Portfolio Activities and Alternative Assessment Handbook, Unit 2
▶ Unit 2 Test for English Language Learners and Special-Needs Students

To review elements of Unit 2 in a single class period, assign one of the following activities or graphic organizers, omitting the italicized answers, to individuals or groups.

3 Geography

Write the following phrases on the chalkboard: population, size, new forms of transportation, the growth of the suburbs, and new immigrant neighborhoods. Have each student write one or two sentences describing how each item affected American cities during the late 1800s. Ask volunteers to read their sentences to the class.

A Selection from Further Reading

War on the Great Plains.
In *The Long Death: The Last Days of the Plains Indians*, Ralph K. Andrist provides a vivid account of the struggles between the U.S. Army and American Indians on the Great Plains. In the following excerpt, he describes the harsh reality of these conflicts: "Let there be no mistake: the wars of the plains were not clean, crisp little tableaux [scenes] of cavalry . . . meeting thundering charges of Sioux and Cheyenne warriors. . . . They were not that kind of conflict at all. As in all wars, men died unpleasantly, and often in extreme agony. Women and children suffered along with the warrior and soldier, and the Army made it a part of strategy to destroy the enemy's food and possessions in order to leave him cold, hungry, and without the will to resist."

ANALYZING SOURCES
According to Andrist, how did the reality of war on the Great Plains differ from popular myth?

ANSWER: Students might suggest that war on the Great Plains was not made up of picturesque clashes between fearless combatants but rather involved widespread suffering and deprivation.

U·N·I·T
2

Review

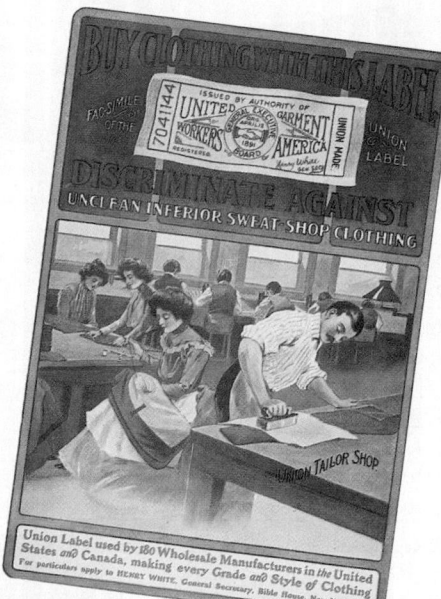

Advertisement for union labels

BUILDING YOUR PORTFOLIO

Outlined below are three projects. Independently or cooperatively, complete one and use the products to demonstrate your mastery of the historical concepts involved.

1 Decision Making
You are an artisan in 1886. Samuel Gompers has just announced that he is forming a union for skilled workers only. You need to decide whether to join the union. Follow these steps to make your decision.

Use your textbook and other resources to *gather information* that might influence your decision whether to join. Be sure to use what you have learned about the Second Industrial Revolution and the labor movement to help you make an effective decision.

Once you have gathered information, *identify options*. Based on the information you have gathered, consider your options. Are your only options to join or not to join? Do you have other options? Be sure to record your possible options for your presentation.

Once you have identified these options, *predict the consequences* for each option. For example, will the union become involved in violent strikes? How will joining a union affect you financially? Once you have predicted the consequences, record them as notes for your presentation.

Take action to implement your decision. Once you have considered your options, you should create a presentation about your decision. You will need to support your decision by including information you gathered and by explaining why you rejected other options. You may want to create a map or a chart to help explain your decision.

2 Science, Technology, and Society
In the late 1800s technological advances and the growth of industry dramatically changed the lifestyles and work habits of many Americans. Imagine that you own a factory. *Prepare a model of your factory* highlighting the technological developments being used in it. Be sure to describe how the changes in the factory affect the lives of workers and what problems you have encountered as workers have unionized. You may wish to use portfolio materials you designed in the unit chapters to help you.

1 Decision Making

Political Problems of the Late 1800s

Problem	Proposed Change	How to Accomplish
corruption and graft	the destruction of political machines and reform	use city officials and planners and jail corrupt politicians
lack of democracy	constitutional amendments and new voting procedures	institute the secret ballot, the referendum, and the recall
farm issues	government action, cooperatives, and unified organizations	form cooperatives and Progressive Party

2 Science, Technology, and Society

Positive and Negative Effects of the Second Industrial Revolution

Innovations of the Second Industrial Revolution
- railroads
- electricity
- factories
- new farming and mining techniques

Positive Effects
- economic growth
- social opportunity
- economic opportunity

Negative Effects
- workplace disease and danger
- urban poverty
- political corruption

3 Geography

With the increasing industrialization in the late 1800s, cities across the United States expanded in population and in size. *Create an annotated map* of a major U.S. city in 1910 that illustrates the growth of the city. Be sure to include new forms of transportation, the growth of suburbs, and the development of immigrant neighborhoods. Write five questions for other students to answer based on your map. You might want to ask about geographic patterns and distributions and how population growth affected your city's physical environment. You may wish to use portfolio materials you designed in the unit chapters to help you.

THE GRANGER COLLECTION, NEW YORK

Washington, D.C., streetcar

Further Reading

Andrist, Ralph K. *The Long Death: The Last Days of the Plains Indians.* Macmillan, 1993. History of the struggle of the Plains Indians.

Burrows, Edwin G., and Mike Wallace. *Gotham: A History of New York City to 1898.* Oxford University Press, 2000. A detailed history of how New York became an international urban center.

Coan, Peter Morton. *Ellis Island Interviews: In Their Own Words.* Facts on File, 1997. A broad collection of accounts recalling immigration experiences.

Katz, William L. *The Black West.* Simon & Schuster, 1996. History of the African American pioneers who helped develop the West.

Luchetti, Cathy, and Carol Olwell. *Women of the West.* W. W. Norton & Company, 2001. Firsthand accounts of women's lives in the West taken from photographs and diaries.

Schlereth, Thomas J. *Victorian America: Transformations in Everyday Life, 1876–1915.* HarperCollins, 1991. Detailed historical overview of the effects of immigration, expansion, and industrialization on American society.

Internet Connect & Review on the R●M

In assigned groups, develop a multi-media presentation about the United States between 1860 and 1910. Choose information from the chapter Internet Connect activities and from the **Holt Researcher CD–ROM** that best reflect the major topics of the period. Write an outline and a script for your presentation, which may be shown to the class.

A Selection from Further Reading

The Second Industrial Revolution. In *Victorian America: Transformations in Everyday Life, 1876–1915,* Thomas J. Schlereth analyzes the changes Americans experienced during the Second Industrial Revolution. In the following excerpt, he summarizes the changes Americans experienced between 1876 and 1915:

"Within that time span, what had been a fundamentally agrarian nation of 46,107,000 had more than doubled into a largely urban and industrial society of 100,549,000. Urbanization and industrialization, in turn, added to such trends as the increased homogenization [making different things the same] and quantification [measuring an explicit amount] of daily activities and a marked increase in money-oriented values."

ANALYZING SOURCES

According to Schlereth, what types of changes characterized daily life during the Second Industrial Revolution?

ANSWER: Students might note that the population more than doubled, the country was industrialized, and different values were formed.

A World Power

CHAPTER 9 The Age of Reform

Enormous differences in wealth developed during the Gilded Age. Progressive reformers sought to focus attention on the social problems created by these differences. Activists also hoped to bring about reform in business and politics. Labor unions attempted to organize workers and to obtain better working conditions and wages for industrial workers.

CHAPTER 10 Progressive Politicians

Progressive politicians hoped to improve the United States by making voting processes more democratic. President Theodore Roosevelt worked to regulate the food-and-drug industry and to preserve the environment. Roosevelt helped William Howard Taft win the 1908 election, but the two clashed soon after. Roosevelt re-entered politics, creating a split in the Republican Party and helping Democrat Woodrow Wilson win the 1912 presidential election.

U·N·I·T 3

A World Power
1897–1920

This 1898 painting by Fred Pansing depicts the U.S. fleet entering into New York Harbor.

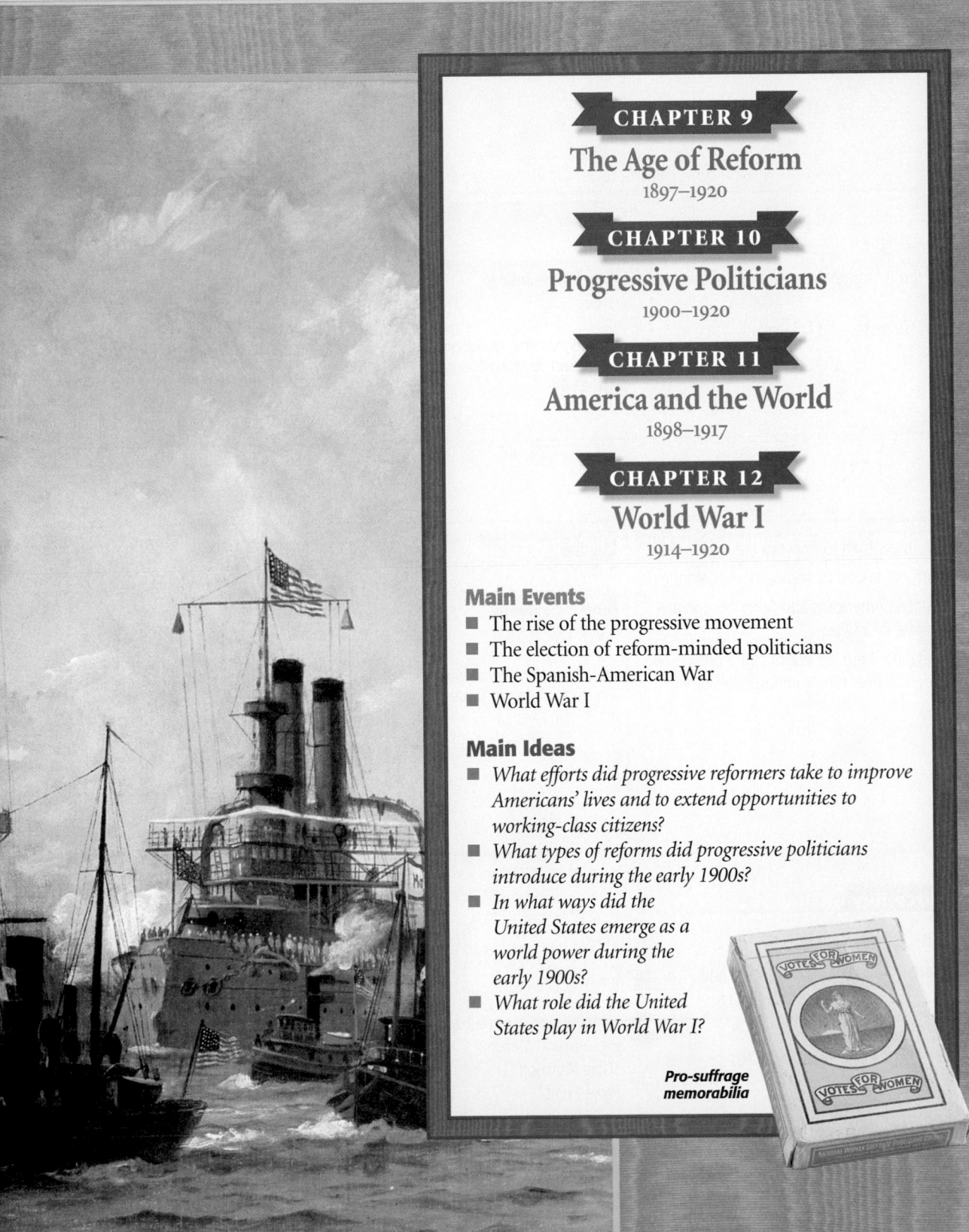

CHAPTER
11

America and the World

After the Second Industrial Revolution, the United States took a new interest in world affairs and imperialist expansion, partly out of the quest for new markets. The United States acquired Hawaii and seized control of Cuba, Puerto Rico, and the Philippines. Theodore Roosevelt used his Roosevelt Corollary to the Monroe Doctrine to justify interventions in several Latin American countries.

CHAPTER
12

World War I

In 1914 war engulfed Europe, with the Central Powers battling the Allied Powers. The war soon settled into a stalemate. The United States attempted to stay neutral in the conflict, but eventually declared war. The infusion of U.S. troops helped the Allies win the war. President Wilson encouraged the United States to accept the Treaty of Versailles, but a faction of Republican senators rejected the treaty.

CHAPTER 9
The Age of Reform
1897–1920

CHAPTER 10
Progressive Politicians
1900–1920

CHAPTER 11
America and the World
1898–1917

CHAPTER 12
World War I
1914–1920

Main Events
- The rise of the progressive movement
- The election of reform-minded politicians
- The Spanish-American War
- World War I

Main Ideas
- *What efforts did progressive reformers take to improve Americans' lives and to extend opportunities to working-class citizens?*
- *What types of reforms did progressive politicians introduce during the early 1900s?*
- *In what ways did the United States emerge as a world power during the early 1900s?*
- *What role did the United States play in World War I?*

Pro-suffrage memorabilia

INTRODUCE UNIT 3

Main Events
List the Main Events on the chalkboard. Ask students to select two and briefly describe what they know about the topics. Have volunteers share their descriptions. Later, when you have finished Unit 3, ask students to return to their original descriptions and revise them using the information they learned in the unit. Students should also create new descriptions for the other Main Events.

Main Ideas
Ask each student to read the Main Ideas and briefly answer the questions in writing. Share the *Consider* points with students as necessary. Later, when you have finished Unit 3, ask students to return to their original answers and revise them using the information they learned in the unit.

The Efforts of Progressive Reformers
Consider:
- the effects of high immigration, high population growth, and industrialization on cities
- issues such as workplace injuries and child labor

The American Role in World War I
Consider:
- the date that the United States entered the war
- the effect of a massive infusion of troops

CHAPTER 9

The Age of Reform

CHAPTER RESOURCE MANAGER

	Objectives	Pacing Guide	Reproducible Resources
SECTION 1 **The Progressive Movement** pp. 274–79	★ Discuss the backgrounds of the reformers. ★ Identify issues that concerned progressives, and explain how they tried to make changes. ★ Specify issues that muckrakers addressed. ★ Summarize how progressive writers and thinkers viewed American society.	**Regular** 2 days **Block Scheduling** 1 day *Block Scheduling Handbook with Team Teaching Strategies,* pp. 49–54	**RS** Guided Reading Strategy 9.1 **IC** Literature Reading 9: A Muckraker's Report **E** Creative Teaching Strategy: Structured Discussion Lesson
SECTION 2 **Reforming the New Industrial Order** pp. 280–85	★ Identify workplace problems that progressives targeted. ★ Explain what the results of the Triangle Shirtwaist Fire were. ★ List and describe the rulings that the Supreme Court made on labor laws. ★ Summarize union successes and failures.	**Regular** 2 days **Block Scheduling** 1 day *Block Scheduling Handbook with Team Teaching Strategies,* pp. 49–54	**RS** Guided Reading Strategy 9.2 **SM** Geography Activity 9: Limiting the Workday **RS** Graphic Organizer Activity 9: The Progressive Ideal **E** Hands-On History Activity: Workplace Reform in the Past and Present
SECTION 3 **Reforming Society** pp. 286–93	★ Describe how reformers tried to improve life in U.S. cities. ★ Discuss how reformers hoped to improve moral standards. ★ Report on how African Americans and American Indians organized to improve their lives. ★ Explain why immigrants were left out of some progressive reforms, and recognize how they contributed to other reforms.	**Regular** 2 days **Block Scheduling** 1 day *Block Scheduling Handbook with Team Teaching Strategies,* pp. 49–54	**RS** Guided Reading Strategy 9.3 **PS** Primary Source Reading 9: A Call for Urban Reform **PS** Biography Reading 9: Carry Nation

Chapter Resource Key

PS	Primary Sources	**REV**	Review		Video
RS	Reading Support	**ELL**	Reinforcement and English Language Learners		Internet
IC	Interdisciplinary Connections				Holt Presentation Maker Using Microsoft® PowerPoint®
E	Enrichment		Transparencies		
SM	Skills Mastery		CD-ROM		
A	Assessment	🎵	Music		

🖱 **One-Stop** Planner CD–ROM

See the *One-Stop Planner* for a complete list of additional resources for students and teachers.

One-Stop Planner CD–ROM

It's easy to plan lessons, select resources, and print out materials for your students when you use the *One-Stop Planner CD–ROM with Test Generator.*

Technology Resources

 One-Stop Planner, Lesson 9.1
 Everyday Life in America Transparency 18: Progressives and Children, Early 1900s
 Holt Researcher: American History CD–ROM
 Homework Practice Online

 One-Stop Planner, Lesson 9.2
 CNN. Presents America: Modern Times Segment: Triangle Fire Memories
 Holt Researcher: American History CD–ROM
 Homework Practice Online

 One-Stop Planner, Lesson 9.3
 Art in American History Transparency 20: Thompson and Bleecker Streets
 Holt Researcher: American History CD–ROM
 Homework Practice Online
 HRW Go site

Reinforcement, Review, and Assessment

REV Section 1 Review, p. 279
A Daily Quiz 9.1
ELL Main Idea Activity 9.1
ELL English Audio Summary 9.1
ELL Spanish Audio Summary 9.1

REV Section 2 Review, p. 285
A Daily Quiz 9.2
ELL Main Idea Activity 9.2
ELL English Audio Summary 9.2
ELL Spanish Audio Summary 9.2

REV Section 3 Review, p. 293
A Daily Quiz 9.3
ELL Main Idea Activity 9.3
ELL English Audio Summary 9.3
ELL Spanish Audio Summary 9.3

internet connect

HRW ONLINE RESOURCES
GO TO: go.hrw.com
Then type in a keyword.

TEACHER HOME PAGE
KEYWORD: SE3 Teacher

CHAPTER INTERNET ACTIVITIES
KEYWORD: SE3 AN9
Choose an activity to:
• locate and use databases on geographic distributions and patterns regarding immigration.
• write an informative essay on the NAACP.
• learn about silent films and the early days of the cinema.

CHAPTER ENRICHMENT LINKS
KEYWORD: SE3 CH9

ONLINE ASSESSMENT
Homework Practice
KEYWORD: SE3 HP9

Standardized Test Prep
KEYWORD: SE3 STP9

Rubrics
KEYWORD: SS Rubrics

ONLINE MAPS, CHARTS, AND GRAPHS
KEYWORD: SE3 MCG
• Dry States, 1890–1919
• Lynchings, 1890–1920
• Union Membership, 1864–1921

CONTENT UPDATES
KEYWORD: SS Content Updates

HOLT PRESENTATION MAKER
KEYWORD: SE3 PPT9

ONLINE READING SUPPORT
KEYWORD: SS Strategies

CURRENT EVENTS
KEYWORD: S3 Current Events

Chapter Review and Assessment

 Global Skill Builder CD–ROM
 HRW Go site
REV **Chapter 9 Tutorial for Students, Parents, Mentors, and Peers**
REV **Chapter 9 Review, pp. 294–95**
Chapter 9 Test Generator (on the One-Stop Planner)
A **Chapter 9 Test (Form A or B)**
A **Alternative Assessment Handbook**
A **Chapter 9 Test for English Language Learners and Special-Needs Students**

Meeting Individual Needs

Ability Levels

Level 1 Basic-level activities designed for all students encountering new material

Level 2 Intermediate-level activities designed for average students

Level 3 Challenging activities designed for honors and gifted-and-talented students

English Language Learners Activities that address the needs of students with Limited English Proficiency

CHAPTER 9

Section 1 *The Progressive Movement, pp. 274–79*

Section 2 *Reforming the New Industrial Order, pp. 280–85*

Section 3 *Reforming Society, pp. 286–93*

Chapter Review, *pp. 294–95*

CHAPTER 9

1897–1920
The Age of Reform

British troops in Africa

San Francisco view after the earthquake

1900
The Arts
Theodore Dreiser's novel *Sister Carrie* is published.

1902
World Events
The British defeat the Dutch Boers in Africa.

1904
Science and Technology
The first completed section of the New York City subway system opens to the public.

1906
Daily Life
Much of San Francisco is destroyed by an earthquake and the fire that follows it.

1898	1900	1902	1904	1906	1908

1900
Daily Life
The average laborer earns $1.50 a day for 10 hours of work.

No. 201
EDISON FILM
COPYRIGHTED 1903
THE GREAT TRAIN ROBBERY

Poster for The Great Train Robbery

1903
Daily Life
The Great Train Robbery, the first movie to tell a story, is produced.

1905
World Events
The Russian czar's troops fire on unarmed protesters, beginning the Russian Revolution of 1905.

1905
Business and Finance
Ty Cobb begins his professional baseball career with the Detroit Tigers.

1907
Science and Technology
Engineers develop suspension insulators, which soon allow power lines to carry up to 150,000 volts of electricity.

Ty Cobb baseball card

Build on What You Know

Although industrial development during the Gilded Age generated great profits for some Americans, it also created many problems. Moreover, politics became increasingly corrupt as leaders sought financial gains. Populists, ministers, and reformers such as Jane Addams tried to bring the nation's attention to those Americans left out of economic prosperity. In this chapter you will learn about the large-scale reform movements that swept the United States at the beginning of the 1900s and the effects that these movements had on American society.

What's Your Opinion?

To help students create their Themes Journal entries, provide the following examples of appropriate **agree/disagree** *statements.*

Economics

Agree The poor working conditions in the Lowell textile mills led the Massachusetts legislature to mandate a 10-hour limit on workdays.

Citizenship

Agree Abolitionists argued that the nation had a moral duty to put an end to the institution of slavery.

Disagree The constitutional guarantee of equal protection under the law does not provide for special assistance to the poor and weak.

Disagree In a capitalist economy, government regulation of business would interfere with the operation of the free market.

Constitutional Heritage

Agree The abolitionist movement provided the impetus behind the passage of the Thirteenth Amendment, which abolished slavery.

Disagree The Bill of Rights was passed without the backing of a reform movement.

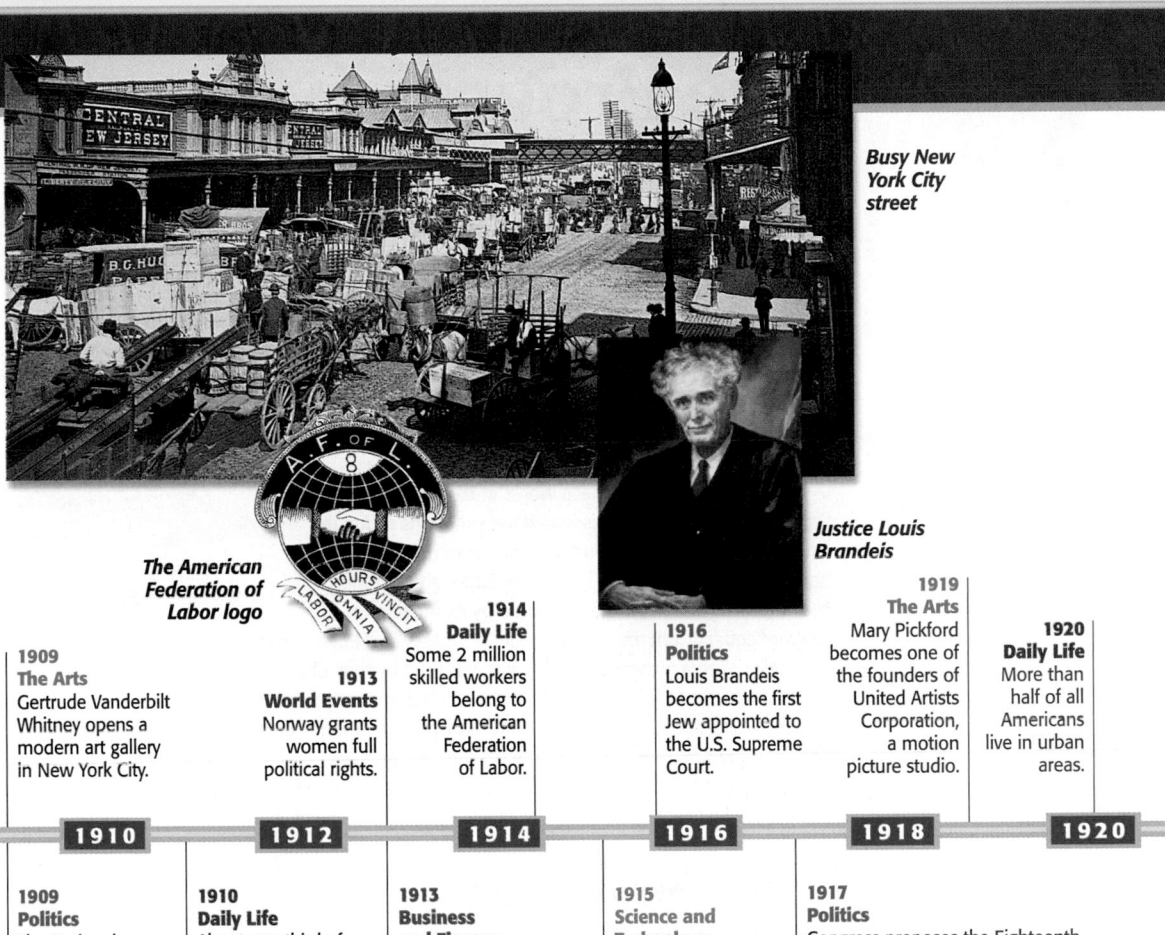

Busy New York City street

The American Federation of Labor logo

Justice Louis Brandeis

1909
The Arts
Gertrude Vanderbilt Whitney opens a modern art gallery in New York City.

1913
World Events
Norway grants women full political rights.

1914
Daily Life
Some 2 million skilled workers belong to the American Federation of Labor.

1916
Politics
Louis Brandeis becomes the first Jew appointed to the U.S. Supreme Court.

1919
The Arts
Mary Pickford becomes one of the founders of United Artists Corporation, a motion picture studio.

1920
Daily Life
More than half of all Americans live in urban areas.

| 1910 | 1912 | 1914 | 1916 | 1918 | 1920 |

1909
Politics
The National Association for the Advancement of Colored People is founded.

1910
Daily Life
About one third of American working men and women live in poverty.

1913
Business and Finance
The United States is the world's leading producer of coal.

1915
Science and Technology
Deaths from tuberculosis drop significantly, thanks to the efforts of the National Tuberculosis Association.

1917
Politics
Congress proposes the Eighteenth Amendment, which prohibits the manufacture, sale, and distribution of alcoholic beverages.

A young boy working in a coal mine

I'VE HAD MY CHEST X-RAY

Tuberculosis pin

Temperance leader Carry Nation

What's Your Opinion?

Themes Journal

Do you **agree** *or* **disagree** *with the following statements? Support your point of view in your journal.*

Economics State governments have a responsibility to regulate how businesses treat workers.

Citizenship A democracy has a duty to protect and assist the poorest and weakest of its citizens.

Constitutional Heritage Reform movements are necessary in order to lay the groundwork for constitutional change.

GLOBAL EVENTS

GLOBAL RELATIONS

1905 ■ The Russian Revolution. On Sunday, January 9, 1905, Father George Gapon led a group of workers, their wives, and their children toward the czar's Winter Palace in St. Petersburg, Russia. The marchers, singing hymns and bearing no weapons, intended to petition the czar to end an ongoing war, to grant civil rights, and to reduce the workday to eight hours. When the marchers ignored an order to stop marching, the czar's troops fired on them, killing hundreds. This incident, called Bloody Sunday, angered the nation and prompted hundreds of thousands of people to demand changes. The following strikes temporarily paralyzed Russia.

CRITICAL THINKING How might the 1905 revolution in Russia have compared to earlier events in the United States?

ANSWER: Answers will vary. Students might discuss the Boston Massacre or the Haymarket Riot.

The Progressive Movement

EYEWITNESSES TO History

"The 'tramp' comes with the locomotive, and almshouses [poorhouses] and prisons are as surely the marks of 'material progress' as are costly dwellings, rich warehouses, and magnificent churches."

—Henry George, *Progress and Poverty*

Henry George's Progress and Poverty

Henry George wrote these words in his 1879 book, *Progress and Poverty.* He discussed the problems facing the United States as both the number of poor people and the nation's wealth increased. George hoped for a time when the country's progress might be measured by its movement "toward equality, not toward inequality." *Progress and Poverty* soon became a best-seller. One economist noted that it was read by tens of thousands of members of the working and lower classes "who never before looked between the covers of an economics book." By the early 1900s a drive for economic and social reform had begun. Many Americans sought to make the country's laws and institutions more responsive to the conditions of the nation's poorest and most disadvantaged citizens.

The Progressive Spirit

By the early 1900s industrialization had transformed the United States. Economic growth led to a rise in the number of new goods and services as well as an expansion of the middle class. Growth also widened the gap between the rich and the poor, and industrialization led to unsafe working conditions and crowded cities.

Such problems aroused a spirit of reform known as **progressivism.** In the late 1800s members of the Populist Party had protested what they saw as unfair business practices and had pressed for government action to stop them. Populism was mainly a rural movement. Progressivism, however, focused on urban problems, such as the plight of workers, poor sanitation, and corrupt political machines.

The progressives. People from all walks of life participated in reform efforts during the Progressive Era. However, most progressives were native born, middle or upper class, and college educated. Their first exposure to social problems in the United States came at college. "My life began at Johns Hopkins University," progressive Frederic Howe recalled. "I came alive. I felt a sense of responsibility. I wanted to change things."

Men and women of the urban middle class—doctors, engineers, ministers, small-business owners, social workers, teachers, and writers—found progressivism particularly attractive. This urban middle class had grown from some 750,000 in 1870 to about 10 million by 1910. Kansas editor William Allen White described this change. He said that by the 1900s populism had "shaved its whiskers, washed its shirt, put on a derby [hat], and moved up into the middle class."

TEACH OBJECTIVE 1

LEVEL 1: Pair students and ask each pair to create a list of words that they associate with progressive reformers. *(Pairs might list words such as* urban *or* involved.*)* Have students share their lists with the class. To help students understand the backgrounds of reformers, copy the following graphic organizer on the chalkboard, omitting the italicized answers. Have pairs complete it.

English Language Learners, Cooperative Learning

REFORMERS' BACKGROUNDS

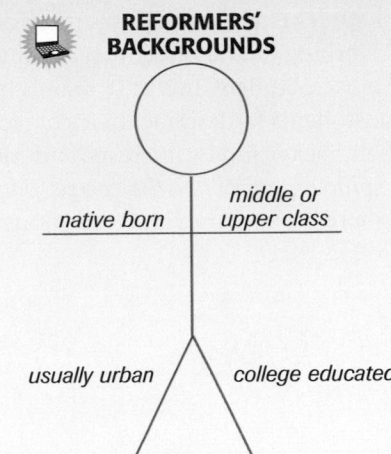

native born | *middle or upper class*

usually urban | *college educated*

Women and progressivism.

Women and progressivism. Previous generations of women had joined reform efforts because they were an acceptable way for women to influence politics and society. Many middle-class women were drawn to the progressive movement for the same reason. Women enrolled in colleges in increasing numbers during the early 1900s, but their career choices remained limited. Reform work offered college-educated women a way to use their knowledge of medicine, psychology, sociology, and other subjects.

In 1909 Ella Flagg Young became Chicago's superintendent of schools—the first woman to hold such a job in a major city. Young promoted public education by raising teachers' salaries. Journalist Rheta Childe Dorr wrote *What Eight Million Women Want* (1910). The widely read book noted the special role of women in the reform movement. "Women have ceased to exist as a subsidiary [lower] class in the community," she wrote. "The modern . . . educated woman came into a world which is losing faith in the commercial ideal and is endeavoring to substitute in its place a social ideal."

Some women made careers of reform work. Others volunteered their time through groups such as the General Federation of Women's Clubs and the National Association of Colored Women. Women also participated in the 1913 Progressive Party convention in Chicago. The party's platform supported women's suffrage and an end to child labor. Describing her experience as a delegate, Jane Addams wrote that it did not seem strange for women to take part. "It would have been much more unnatural if they had not been there, when such matters of social welfare were being considered."

✔ **READING CHECK: Finding the Main Idea** Who were progressives?

native-born, middle-or-upper class, college-educated reformers; many were women.

Progressive Issues

Progressives tried to reform American institutions while preserving ideals of the past, such as a sense of community. Progressive reformers took a leading role in promoting change in the United States.

A dangerous workplace. A major concern of the progressives was the way corporate America did business. Industrial workers often faced dangerous conditions and long hours. In 1910 some 70 percent of all American industrial laborers worked an average of 54 hours a week. As a result, American workers had higher accident rates than workers in other industrialized countries. In one Pittsburgh steel mill 25 percent of its workforce was injured or killed on the job each year between 1907 and 1910.

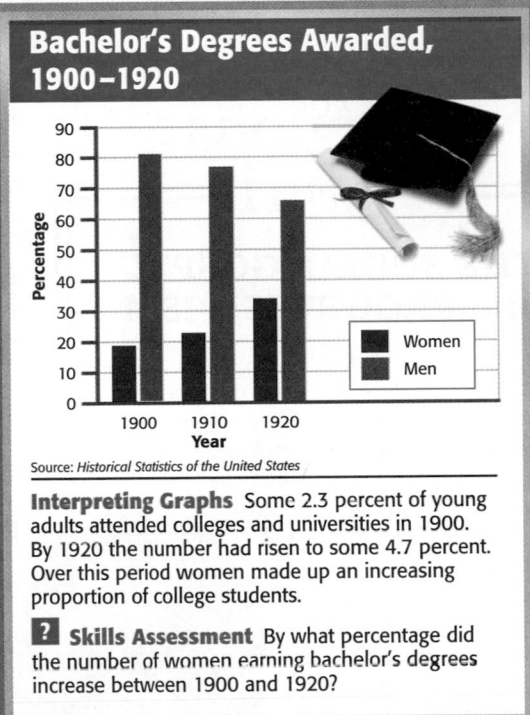

Bachelor's Degrees Awarded, 1900–1920

Source: *Historical Statistics of the United States*

Interpreting Graphs Some 2.3 percent of young adults attended colleges and universities in 1900. By 1920 the number had risen to some 4.7 percent. Over this period women made up an increasing proportion of college students.

? **Skills Assessment** By what percentage did the number of women earning bachelor's degrees increase between 1900 and 1920?

INTERPRETING THE VISUAL RECORD

Education for women. These women attended Vassar College in the 1920s. *What can you determine about their economic and social background?*

CITIZENSHIP

Women's Suffrage. Many female progressives worked for equal voting rights. Other female activists opposed women's suffrage. The National Association Opposed to Women's Suffrage (NAOWS), formed in 1911, was headed by Mrs. Arthur M. Dodge. The association distributed antisuffrage literature and coordinated state efforts. The women of NAOWS believed that suffrage and political involvement would cause women to lose their focus on being wives and mothers.

CRITICAL THINKING What arguments might pro-suffrage activists have advanced against antisuffragists?

ANSWER: Answers will vary. Students might suggest that pro-suffrage activists might have argued that female voters would be better able to care for their families if they had a voice in laws that affected them.

GRAPH ANSWER
just over 10 percent

VISUAL RECORD ANSWER
Students might suggest that the women appear to be from the middle or upper classes.

THE SOCIAL GOSPEL AND PROGRESSIVISM

Charles M. Sheldon's 1896 Social Gospel novel, *In His Steps,* focused on characters in a typical midwestern city who based their behavior on the question, "What would Jesus do?" The results were remarkable. Manufacturers ran their businesses for the benefit of employees, and wealthy business owners bought slum property and improved it for the benefit of the tenants. While such dramatic results were not often seen in real life, Social Gospel thought had a profound effect on the progressive movement. Many progressives, including Jane Addams, were greatly influenced by the Social Gospel writers. Progressivism promoted the same goals as Social Gospel thinkers, including the abolition of child labor as well as support for higher wages, industrial regulations, and shorter workweeks.

Walter Rauschenbusch

Walter Rauschenbusch, a professor at Rochester Theological Seminary in New York, was one of the leading writers and thinkers of both the Social Gospel movement and the progressive movement. In *Christianity and the Social Crisis* (1907), he called for "a new type of Christian." He wanted Christians to become involved in social issues as an extension of their love for God. Rauschenbusch wrote prayers for specific groups of workers, such as his "For Children Who Work," "For Workingmen," and "For Women Who Toil." He participated actively in the Social Gospel movement, helping to popularize it. He also moved it more concretely toward the progressive movement's goal of addressing the social consequences of industrialization and rapid urban growth. ▪

These conditions led progressives to demand limits on corporate power. They promoted laws to prohibit monopolies and to help smaller businesses compete in the economy. Progressives also called for an eight-hour workday, a minimum wage, safer working conditions, and an end to child labor. Not surprisingly, most business owners opposed such legislation.

Social problems. Like the Populists, progressives wanted the people to have greater control of the government. They called for new election reforms and proposed political measures to make government more responsive to the desires of the voters. Reformer Benjamin Parke De Witt wanted to give "the people direct and continuous control over all the branches of government." Like Populists and Social Gospel ministers, progressives were inspired by the spirit of social justice. Progressive Theodore Roosevelt wrote, "If we wish to do good work for our country, we must be unselfish."

Progressives firmly believed in the power of science and technology to solve social problems. Progressive philosopher John Dewey believed that public education should prepare students to function well and efficiently in society, not simply give them factual knowledge. To this end, Dewey promoted a curriculum closely tied to real-life activities.

With the help of universities, progressives began many social-research projects. Some progressives, however, worried that the university might become too involved. Jane Addams warned against turning settlement houses "into one more laboratory; another place in which to . . . observe and record."

✔ **READING CHECK: Analyzing Information** What were some of the methods used by progressives to expand the rights of others?
They lobbied for new laws, proposed new election reforms, and began social-research projects.

The "White City" at the 1893 World's Columbian Exposition in Chicago showed what many progressives thought cities should look like.

THE GRANGER COLLECTION, NEW YORK

TEACH OBJECTIVE 2

LEVEL 1: Conduct a brief discussion on the broad range of social issues that concerned progressive reformers, then tell students that progressives tried to reform business, government, and society. Pair students and have each pair create a graphic organizer that depicts progressive goals and the institutions that progressives tried to reform. *(Graphic organizers should note that progressives wanted to reform industrial practices, end child labor, reform the electoral system, and work for social justice. In order to do so, progressives demanded limits on corporate power, proposed new political measures, and tried to harness the power of science and technology to solve social problems.)* Have volunteers present their graphic organizers to the class.
English Language Learners, Cooperative Learning

LEVELS 2 AND 3: Ask students to identify the issues that were important to progressives. *(See the Level 1 lesson for the correct progressive issues.)* Then tell students to imagine that they are newspaper reporters during the Progressive Era. Have each student choose an issue that concerned progressive reformers and write an article that is sympathetic to progressive goals. Articles should assume a firsthand perspective, describe the problem or issue, and propose a solution to the problem. Ask volunteers to read their articles to the class.

Inspiration for Reform

Progressive journalists helped spread the reform message. Popular magazines such as *Munsey's* and *Everybody's* published stories exploring corruption in politics and business as well as social problems such as slums and child labor. *McClure's Magazine*, another national magazine, had been founded in 1893 by the reform-minded Scots-Irish immigrant S. S. McClure.

The muckraking press. In a 1906 speech Theodore Roosevelt described a man with a muckrake who "fixes his eyes . . . only on that which is vile and debasing [harmful and corrupt]." The vivid image stuck, and investigative journalists became known as **muckrakers**, because they "raked up" and exposed the muck, or filth, of society. Walter Lippmann, a young progressive, noted in 1914 that "muckraking was what the people wanted to hear."

McClure's publication in October 1902 of "Tweed Days in St. Louis," by journalists **Lincoln Steffens** and Claude Wetmore, marked the real beginning of this style of journalism. The article exposed the corrupt political machine in St. Louis, comparing it to Boss Tweed's control of New York City.

Articles in McClure's Magazine informed readers about how corruption in business and politics affected their lives.

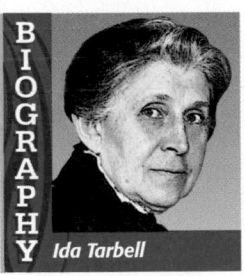
Ida Tarbell

Tarbell and Standard Oil. In November 1902 *McClure's* ran the first installment of "History of the Standard Oil Company" by **Ida Tarbell**. Born in western Pennsylvania in 1857, Tarbell was the daughter of an independent oil producer. She was deeply angered when John D. Rockefeller's Standard Oil Company began swallowing up independent oil companies. Her father's company went bankrupt.

In 1876 Tarbell entered Allegheny College as the only female student in a class of 40 "hostile or indifferent" males, as she recalled. After graduation she began her career as a writer. By the 1890s she was writing a popular series for *McClure's*. In 1900 *McClure's* assigned her to investigate Standard Oil. Tarbell published her findings in 19 articles on Standard Oil's business practices.

History Makers Speak

"One of the most depressing features . . . is that instead of such methods arousing contempt, they are more or less openly admired. . . . There is no gaming table in the world where loaded dice are tolerated, no athletic field where men must not start fair. Yet Mr. Rockefeller has systematically played with loaded dice. . . . Business played in this way loses all its sportsmanlike qualities. It is fit only for tricksters."

—Ida Tarbell, "History of the Standard Oil Company," *McClure's,* 1900

McClure's readers hailed Tarbell as "the Terror of the Trusts." Unlike many other reporters, Tarbell was dismayed to find that she had been labeled a muckraker. Many of her readers continued to expect such exposés and seemed uninterested in more positive findings. Later in life Tarbell participated in numerous government conferences and committees dealing with such issues as defense, industry, and unemployment. Five years before her death in 1944, she wrote her autobiography, *All in the Day's Work.*

Analyzing Primary Sources

Identifying Bias Is Tarbell's quotation fact or opinion? Explain your answer.
Opinion. There is no factual evidence cited.

Naturalism. Many of the novelists who focused on social problems during the Progressive Era wrote in a style called naturalism. Like literary realists, naturalists tried to portray "a direct impression of life," rather than a romantic, or unrealistic, impression. Naturalists went further, however, and chose to represent characters in situations completely beyond their control. Naturalist Jack London explained, "Man is not a free agent, and free will is a fallacy exploded by science long ago." Characters in naturalistic fiction usually have no chance to change their lives. They are controlled by their surroundings—such as the tenement and the factory. They are also controlled by inherited characteristics and unconscious, animalistic desires. Naturalistic fiction also often depicted scenes from impoverished and violent neighborhoods and followed characters as they descended into criminal activities.

CRITICAL THINKING Why might some reformers have found naturalistic fiction to be an impetus for reform?

ANSWER: Students might suggest that naturalistic fiction convinced some reformers that they could improve people's lives by improving their environments.

TEACH OBJECTIVES 3 AND 4

LEVEL 1: Pair students and ask each pair to list the issues explored by muckraking journalists and progressive writers. *(Pairs should note that muckrakers explored corruption in business and urban politics, social problems such as slums and child labor, and racism. Progressive writers explored exploitation of the weak by industrial society, the idea that government should use its powers to promote social welfare, and the social responsibility of private citizens.)* Then have pairs write topic sentences to describe how progressive writers and thinkers viewed American society. Have volunteers read their sentences to the class.
English Language Learners, Cooperative Learning

LEVELS 2 AND 3: Ask students to identify the issues explored by muckraking journalists and progressive writers. *(See the Level 1 lesson for the correct issues.)* Then have each student write a short essay on how progressive writers and thinkers viewed American society. *(See the Level 1 lesson for the correct perspective.)* Have students discuss their essays in small groups.
Cooperative Learning

HOMEWORK *Have each student write three slogans to generate public support for the progressive movement. Slogans should focus on one or more of the goals of the movement.*

The Railroad's Vast Influence. In *The Octopus,* Frank Norris depicts an epic struggle between California wheat farmers and the railroad. Norris based his novel on a real struggle between ranchers and a railroad corporation. The ranchers had leased land from the railroad and improved it with irrigation. The railroad had promised to sell them the land at a low price per acre, but at the time of the sale, the railroad raised the prices as much as eight times more than the original price. In his novel, Norris creates an image of the railroad as a tentacled beast that grabs up everything in its path—a "leviathan with tentacles of steel."

ACTIVITY: Have each student write a brief description of some aspect of industrialization using a metaphor from nature—such as an octopus—to enrich his or her description.

SKILL-BUILDING STRATEGIES ANSWERS
Practicing the Skill
1. the family's living conditions and the family itself

2. that the family is poor and struggling

3. Some students might point to evidence of poverty and suggest that the picture does accurately reflect conditions.

This cartoon depicts Standard Oil as a giant octopus that crushes all opposition in its tentacles.

Muckraking books. In 1904 Lincoln Steffens documented urban political corruption in *The Shame of the Cities.* That same year writer **Ray Stannard Baker** toured the nation examining the plight of African Americans. Published in 1908, his book described a lynching in Springfield, Ohio.

History Makers Speak

"The worst feature of all in this Springfield lynching was the apathy of the public. No one really seemed to care. . . . If ever there was an example of good citizenship lying flat on its back . . . Springfield furnished an example of that condition."

—Ray Stannard Baker, *Following the Color Line*

✔ **READING CHECK: Summarizing** How did muckrakers contribute to progressivism? **by exposing unfair business practices and political corruption**

Skill-Building Strategies

Interpreting the Visual Record: Photographs

The visual record of an event, period, or place can help one understand its history in ways the written word sometimes cannot. Like other primary sources, photographs must be interpreted carefully. If a photograph includes people, their knowledge of the photographer's presence is important. Spontaneous snapshots usually look much different than ones that are posed. Furthermore, every photograph has a frame, or set of borders, that includes some details and excludes others. The manner in which a photographer selects this frame is another crucial issue. Finally, a photographer's choice of camera equipment, lighting, and developing technique all affect the appearance of a photograph. It is therefore important to analyze the manner in which a photograph is produced along with its actual content.

How to Interpret a Photograph

1. **Identify the subject.** Look at the photograph as a whole and identify its basic subject.
2. **Study the details.** Examine the details in the photograph for information about its historical context.
3. **Determine the photographer's point of view.** Look for information that suggests the photographer's purpose. Note how the photograph was framed and if anyone in the photograph knew it was being taken.

Applying the Skill

The photograph below depicts an immigrant family in their New York City tenement. It was taken in 1910 by Jessie Tarbox Beals, a muckraking photographer who documented urban living conditions.

COURTESY GEORGE EASTMAN HOUSE

Practicing the Skill

Study the photograph above to answer the following questions.
1. What information is provided by the photograph?
2. What message is Beals trying to communicate about the family in the photograph?
3. Does the photograph seem to represent accurately the urban living conditions of immigrant workers during the early 1900s? Explain your answer.

REVIEW

Have students complete the **Section 1 Review** on p. 279.

ASSESS

Have students complete **Daily Quiz 9.1**. As **Alternative Assessment**, you may want to use the progressive reforms graphic organizer or the scene from the screenplay in this section's lessons.

RETEACH

Have students complete **Main Idea Activity for English Language Learners and Special-Needs Students 9.1**. Organize students into small groups. Assign one section objective to each group member. Direct students to write a few sentences or paragraphs describing their assigned objectives. Have students share their paragraphs with the rest of their group.
English Language Learners, Cooperative Learning

EXTEND

Have students read Upton Sinclair's *The Jungle,* Lincoln Steffens's *The Shame of the Cities,* Ray Stannard Baker's *Following the Color Line,* or another muckraking piece from the late 1800s or early 1900s. Have each student create a multimedia presentation on the muckraker's work and present it to the class.
Block Scheduling

Writers and Social Problems

Novelists and intellectuals also explored the darker side of the new industrial society's effect on people's behavior and values. In their works, these writers presented stories of the harsh effects of industrial society on the poor.

In novels such as *Sister Carrie* (1900) and *The Financier* (1912), **Theodore Dreiser** depicted workers brutalized by greedy business owners. In *The House of Mirth* (1905), **Edith Wharton** wrote about how the closed-mindedness of elite society leads a good-hearted heroine to social isolation and despair.

Progressive intellectuals proposed alternatives to the idea that fierce competition was the best formula for social progress. In *The Promise of American Life* (1909), political theorist **Herbert Croly** argued that the government should use its regulatory and taxation powers to promote the welfare of all its citizens. He opposed the government's support of the interests of business owners over other Americans.

In 1902, in *Democracy and Social Ethics,* Jane Addams urged private citizens to show more social responsibility as well. "We are bound to move forward or [slip backward] together. None of us can stand aside; our feet are mired [stuck] in the same soil, and our lungs breathe the same air." Although progressives such as Addams and Croly wanted to transform U.S. society and its values, they remained committed to democracy. Most progressives sought reforms of local government, businesses, and city life to ensure that the full promise of democracy could become available to all citizens.

These Progressive Era books explored the challenges of American life in the new industrial age.

✔ **READING CHECK: Categorizing** Provide three examples of books that furthered the progressive cause. *Sister Carrie, The Financier, The Promise of American Life,* and *Democracy and Social Ethics*

SECTION 1 REVIEW

1. Define and explain:
progressivism
muckrakers

2. Identify and explain:
McClure's Magazine
Lincoln Steffens
Ida Tarbell
Ray Stannard Baker
Theodore Dreiser
Edith Wharton
Herbert Croly

3. Summarizing Copy the graphic organizer below. Use it to explain what issues progressives addressed and how they hoped to bring about change.

Progressives		
Big Business	**Political Rights**	**Social Justice**

4. Finding the Main Idea
a. What role did women play in progressivism?
b. What issues did muckraking journalists concentrate on during the first decades of the 1900s? What effects did their articles have on politics and the lives of poor Americans?
c. How did books by progressive novelists and intellectuals reflect life in the United States?

5. Writing and Critical Thinking
Comparing and Contrasting Create a chart comparing and contrasting the goals and membership of the Populists and progressives. Imagine that you are trying to decide which of these reform movements to join. Create a list of reasons for joining either group.
Consider
• the goals and membership of the Populists
• the goals and membership of the progressives

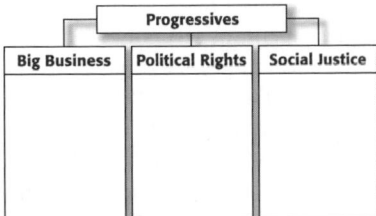
Homework Practice Online
keyword: SE3 HP9

SECTION 1 REVIEW ANSWERS

1. Define
• progressivism, p. 274
• muckrakers, p. 277

2. Identify
• *McClure's Magazine,* p. 277
• Lincoln Steffens, p. 277
• Ida Tarbell, p. 277
• Ray Stannard Baker, p. 278
• Theodore Dreiser, p. 279
• Edith Wharton, p. 279
• Herbert Croly, p. 279

3. big business—called for limiting monopolies, the eight-hour workday, a minimum wage, safer conditions, and child labor restrictions; political rights—election reforms; social justice—called for less poverty and the application of science and technology to solve social problems

4a. Some women made careers of reform; others were volunteers. Many saw progressivism as a way to influence politics and society.

b. corruption, urban living conditions, and child labor; captured public attention and helped create change

c. by exposing urban problems and corruption and discussing the effects of industrialization

5. Populists' goals—graduated income tax, bank regulation, government ownership of railroad and telegraph companies, and free silver; membership—Farmers' Alliance members, farmers, labor leaders, and reformers; progressives' goals—reform workplaces, tenements, and political machines; membership—urban middle class

After completing Section 2, students should be able to:

OBJECTIVE 1 Identify workplace problems that progressives targeted.

OBJECTIVE 2 Explain what the results of the Triangle Shirtwaist Fire were.

OBJECTIVE 3 List and describe the rulings that the Supreme Court made on labor laws.

OBJECTIVE 4 Summarize union successes and failures.

LET'S GET STARTED!

Write the following statements on the chalkboard: *Progressives were mostly native-born, college-educated individuals. (True.) Progressives wanted businesses to enact a 14-hour workday. (False.) Progressives wanted to limit or end child labor. (True.)* As students enter the classroom, ask them to determine if each statement is true or false. Tell students to rewrite false statements to make them true. Then tell students that in Section 2 they will learn more about progressives' efforts to reform the workplace.

SECTION 2 RESOURCES

REPRODUCIBLE
▶ Guided Reading Strategy 9.2
▶ Geography Activity 9: Limiting the Workday
▶ Graphic Organizer Activity 9: The Progressive Ideal

TECHNOLOGY
▶ One-Stop Planner, Lesson 9.2
▶ CNN Presents America: Modern Times Segment: Triangle Fire Memories
▶ Holt Researcher: American History CD–ROM
▶ Homework Practice Online

REINFORCEMENT, REVIEW, AND ASSESSMENT
▶ Section 2 Review, p. 285
▶ Daily Quiz 9.2
▶ Main Idea Activity 9.2
▶ English Audio Summary 9.2
▶ Spanish Audio Summary 9.2

SECTION 2

READ TO DISCOVER
1. What workplace problems did progressives target?
2. What were the results of the Triangle Shirtwaist Fire?
3. What rulings did the Supreme Court make on labor laws?
4. What were the successes and failures of unions in the early 1900s?

DEFINE
freedom of contract
closed shop
socialism
open shop

IDENTIFY
Florence Kelley
Triangle Shirtwaist Fire
Rose Schneiderman
Muller v. *Oregon*
Louis D. Brandeis
Samuel Gompers
International Ladies' Garment Workers Union
Industrial Workers of the World
William "Big Bill" Haywood

▶ WHY IT MATTERS TODAY
American workers still join unions in order to try to improve their economic conditions. Use CNNfyi.com or other **current events** sources to find out about one national labor union in the United States today. Record your findings in your journal.

CNNfyi.com

Reforming the New Industrial Order

EYEWITNESSES TO History

"*Miners' families . . . had to make their purchases of all the necessaries of life, meager [few] as they were, from the company stores at double the prices for which they could be had elsewhere. . . . It was a common saying that children were brought into the world by the company doctor, lived in a company house . . . were buried in a company coffin, and laid away in the company graveyard.*"

—Samuel Gompers, *Autobiography*

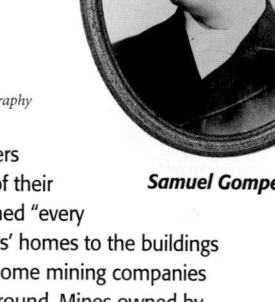

Samuel Gompers

In his *Autobiography*, union leader Samuel Gompers explained how mining companies controlled the lives of their workers. As one union official stated, the company owned "every single thing there is" in the entire town, from the miners' homes to the buildings in the community—even school and church buildings. Some mining companies paid little attention to providing safe conditions underground. Mines owned by John D. Rockefeller, for example, experienced cave-ins and serious explosions that took the lives of miners almost every year.

Reforming the Workplace

In 1900 the average laborer worked nearly 10 hours a day, six days a week, for about $1.50 a day. Women and children earned even less.

Female and child laborers. In the early 1910s almost half of the women who worked in such jobs as factory workers, store clerks, and laundresses earned less than $6 a week. The Commission on Industrial Relations reported in 1916 that this salary "means that every penny must be counted, every normal desire stifled, and each basic necessity of life barely satisfied."

Women often faced significant barriers when they tried to increase their income. For instance, pieceworkers could be penalized for working too fast. Rebecca August, a buttonhole maker in Chicago, recalled that she was paid 3.5 cents per buttonhole. When her supervisor realized how many buttonholes she was able to make—and thus how much money she could earn—he cut her pay. The supervisor said, "It was an *outrage* for a *girl* to make $25 a week." When August tried to organize a protest, her employer fired her.

The commission's report also attacked child labor practices. It declared, "The Nation is paying a heavy toll in ignorance, deformity of body or mind, and premature old age [among children]." In *The Bitter Cry of the Children* (1906), John Spargo charged the textile industries with the "enslavement of children." He reported that children were employed to do work that he "could not do . . . and live."

LEVEL 1: Conduct a discussion about the workplace reforms that progressives hoped to institute. Then have each student list progressives' goals for workplace reform in the early 1900s. *(Students should note that progressives wanted to limit or end child labor, increase women's wages, limit working hours, and establish minimum wages and workplace safety standards.)* Ask students to think about the jobs they might hold in a few years when they enter the working world. Write the following questions on the chalkboard: *What do you expect in terms of working conditions, wages, and hours? What conditions would you consider to be unacceptable? What would you do about unacceptable circumstances if you encountered them?* Have students take turns responding to these questions. Encourage students to make connections between their responses and the progressive agenda.

English Language Learners

LEVELS 2 AND 3: Tell students to imagine that it is 1904 and that they are progressive reformers. Have each student write a letter to a state legislator demanding laws to improve the workplace. *(See the Level 1 lesson for the correct reforms.)* Tell students to identify specific workplace problems, to suggest specific changes they would like to see made, and to provide evidence of poor workplace conditions to back up their demands. Ask volunteers to read their letters to the class.

Spargo found that few child laborers had ever attended school or could read. Many mothers explained that they put their children to work in the mills because it was either that or their entire family would starve. During an investigation of a miners' strike in 1903, a nine-year-old child reported that he was being forced to pay money that his father, who had died in the mine, owed the company for rent.

Labor laws. Progressives and labor union activists campaigned for new laws that would prohibit or limit child labor and improve conditions for female workers. Reformer **Florence Kelley** worked tirelessly for this cause. She helped persuade the Illinois legislature in 1893 to prohibit child labor and to limit the number of hours women could work.

Although most children worked in agriculture, children in the factories—more than 2 million by 1910—faced the worst conditions. Reformers heard stories of supervisors splashing cold water on children's faces to keep them awake and of girls working 16 or more hours a day in canning factories. Orphans also were sent to work in factories. "Capital has neither morals nor ideals," cried one critic.

In 1904 Kelley helped organize the National Child Labor Committee to persuade state legislatures to pass laws against employing young children. By 1912, child-labor laws had been passed in 39 states. Some states even limited older children's employment to 8 or 10 hours a day and barred them from working at night or in dangerous occupations. Other states required that children be able to read and write before they were sent to work.

Enforcement of such laws was lax, however. Claiming that their business success depended on cheap child labor, many employers simply refused to obey the laws and continued to hire child workers. George Creel was a journalist and the author of *Children in Bondage* (1913). He estimated that "at least two million children were being fed annually into the steel hoppers of the modern industrial machine . . . all mangled in mind, body, and soul."

Progressives also campaigned for laws to force factories to limit the hours employers demanded. In 1903 Florence Kelley helped lobby the Oregon legislature to pass a law limiting female laundry workers to 10-hour days. Earlier, Utah had enacted a law limiting workdays to eight hours in certain occupations.

Progressive reformers also fought for higher wages. Some 30 million men and 7.5 million women were employed in 1910, and about one third of them lived in poverty. That year Catholic Church official Monsignor John Ryan called for "the establishment by law of minimum rates of wages that will equal or approximate the normal standards of living for the different groups of workers." Two years later Massachusetts responded to progressive lobbying by passing the nation's first minimum-wage law. This law set base wages for women and children. Other states gradually followed suit. Not until 1938, however, did Congress pass a national minimum-wage law.

✔ **READING CHECK: Analyzing Information** Why did progressive reformers see a need for new labor laws in the early 1900s? **to prohibit or limit child labor and improve conditions for female workers**

INTERPRETING POLITICAL CARTOONS

Labor reform. This political cartoon shows child workers as the slaves of big business. *What does the overseer represent?*

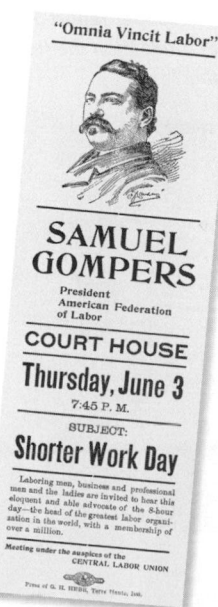

"Omnia Vincit Labor"

SAMUEL GOMPERS

President
American Federation
of Labor

COURT HOUSE

Thursday, June 3
7.45 P. M.

SUBJECT:

Shorter Work Day

Laboring men, business and professional men and the ladies are invited to hear this eloquent and able advocate of the 8-hour day—the head of the greatest labor organization in the world, with a membership of over a million.

Meeting under the auspices of the
CENTRAL LABOR UNION

This leaflet encouraged workers to attend a speech by labor leader Samuel Gompers.

John Spargo in *The Bitter Cry of the Children*

Children at Work. John Spargo's *The Bitter Cry of the Children* exposed the scandal of child labor. Spargo described the work of young boys in coal mines by writing: "Crouched over the chutes, the boys sit hour after hour. . . . From the cramped position they have to assume, most of them become more or less deformed and bent-backed like old men. . . . Sometimes . . . a boy is mangled and torn in the machinery, or disappears in the chute to be picked out later smothered and dead." Spargo concluded, "This great nation in its commercial madness devours its babes." Although Spargo's details alerted many reformers of the need for rapid change, the Supreme Court often overturned reform successes.

CRITICAL THINKING Why might the Supreme Court have ruled against child labor reforms?

ANSWER: Some students might argue that the Supreme Court may not have accepted the progressive philosophy of an expanded role for the government in business affairs.

VISUAL RECORD ANSWER

Students might mention big business.

TEACH OBJECTIVE 2

ALL LEVELS: Tell students about the workplace conditions that led to the deaths of so many women in the Triangle Shirtwaist Fire. Inform students that the New York legislature established the nation's strictest fire-safety code as a result of the fire. Then tell students to imagine that they are reporters for a New York City newspaper at the time of the fire. Have students work in pairs to create headlines about the fire and its aftermath. (*Headlines might mention that fire doors were kept locked; that the company's workers had demanded—and not obtained—safer working conditions during a strike; the number of deaths caused by the fire; the public's outrage; and the subsequent passage of the fire-safety code.*) Have volunteers read their headlines to the class.
English Language Learners, Cooperative Learning

NOTE: To help students make meaningful connections between events in U.S. history and those in their own hometown, use the Chapter 9 **Hands-On History Activity**, Workplace Reform in the Past and Present.

PRIMARY SOURCE

Urban Life in the early 1900s

Born in 1905, Charles Rohleder grew up in Pittsburgh, Pennsylvania. His experiences reflected many of the concerns of the Progressive Era. **Based on this quotation, what reforms might progressives in Pittsburgh try to achieve?**

❝Pittsburgh was very dirty back then. Everyone burned coal for heat. . . . It got so bad that on some days you couldn't see the sun at noontime because of the thick smoke from the factories. There were steamboats on the river, and they had these big smokestacks. When the boats went under low bridges, the smoke would come right up and cover the whole bridge. There were times when I walked across a bridge and went in clean on one side, but by the time I reached the other side, I needed a new shirt.❞

INTERPRETING THE VISUAL RECORD

Unsafe working conditions. The Triangle Shirtwaist Fire was a terrible tragedy that horrified many Americans. *Why might the newspaper report different death totals than the final number?*

The Triangle Shirtwaist Fire

Progressives also sought to improve workplace safety. A tragic event in 1911 highlighted the need for such reforms. On Saturday, March 25, some 500 employees—most of them young Jewish or Italian immigrant women—were completing their six-day workweek at New York City's Triangle Shirtwaist Company. As they rose from their crowded work tables and started to leave, a fire erupted in a rag bin.

Within moments the entire eighth floor of the 10-story building was ablaze. Escape was impossible. There were only two stairways, and because managers were afraid workers would steal fabric, most of the fire doors were kept locked. Some women tried to take a freight elevator to safety, but it jammed as women on higher floors jumped down the elevator shaft to flee the flames. Desperate for a way out, some 60 workers leaped from the windows to their death. "I looked upon the heap of dead bodies," wrote a journalist who witnessed the fire. "I remembered their great strike of last year in which these same girls demanded more sanitary conditions and more safety precautions in the shops. These dead bodies were the answer."

Through the night, weeping family members wandered among the crushed bodies on the sidewalk, looking for their loved ones. By the time firefighters gained control of the blaze, more than 140 workers had perished in the **Triangle Shirtwaist Fire. Rose Schneiderman**, a Women's Trade Union League organizer, argued that only a strong working-class movement could bring real change to the workplace.

❝This is not the first time girls have been burned alive in the city. Each week I must learn of the untimely death of one of my sister workers. Every year thousands of us are maimed. The life of men and women is so cheap and property is so sacred. There are so many of us for one job it matters little if 143 of us are burned to death.❞

—Rose Schneiderman, "Triangle Memorial Speech"

It did matter, however. Popular outrage was so great that lawmakers soon passed protective legislation to help workers. As a result of the fire, the New York legislature enacted the nation's strictest fire-safety code.

✔ **READING CHECK: Summarizing** What conditions made the Triangle Shirtwaist Fire so disastrous?
There were only two stairways in the 10-story building where the fire occurred, and fire-escape doors were locked.

TEACH OBJECTIVE 3

LEVEL 1: To help students understand the Supreme Court's rulings on labor laws copy the following graphic organizer on the chalkboard, omitting the italicized answers. Ask each student to complete it.

English Language Learners

LEVELS 2 AND 3: Have students complete the Level 1 lesson. Then tell students to imagine that they are editors of a labor law encyclopedia. Have each student write entries for the cases *Lochner* v. *New York* and *Muller* v. *Oregon*. Students should summarize each case, the Supreme Court's ruling, and the Court's reasoning in each case.

SUPREME COURT RULINGS ON LABOR LAWS	
Conflict or Case	**Ruling**
In response to social legislation, business owners claimed that laws regulating their businesses unfairly deprived them of property.	*The Court sided with business owners and overturned much early social legislation.*
Lochner v. *New York*—New York law limited bakers' workdays to 10 hours.	*The Court overturned the 10-hour workday, citing freedom of contract—workers should be free to accept any working conditions.*
Muller v. *Oregon*—Employer challenged the 10-hour workday.	*The Court upheld 10-hour workday law based on the "Brandeis Brief," which contained examples of the harm that long hours had on women's health.*

Progressivism and the Supreme Court

As more states passed protective legislation, business owners fought back through the courts. The Fourteenth Amendment to the Constitution prohibits states from depriving "any person of life, liberty, or property, without due process of law." Owners claimed that laws regulating their businesses unfairly deprived them of their property. The Supreme Court sided with business owners and declared much of the early social legislation unconstitutional.

The Court also ruled that some social legislation violated the Constitution by denying workers their **freedom of contract**, or the freedom to negotiate the terms of their employment. In the 1905 case *Lochner* v. *New York*, the Court overturned a New York law limiting bakers' workdays to 10 hours. Workers, the Court ruled, should be free to accept any conditions of employment that business owners required—even if that meant working 14 or 16 hours.

The Supreme Court did uphold some social legislation. In the 1908 case *Muller* v. *Oregon*, an employer challenged the 10-hour-workday law that Florence Kelley had helped push through the Oregon legislature. Kelley and Josephine Goldmark, another reformer, responded quickly. Goldmark gathered information for the brief, or legal argument, to defend the law. Kelley asked Goldmark's brother-in-law, a brilliant lawyer named **Louis D. Brandeis**, to argue the case.

The "Brandeis Brief" contained many examples of the harm that working long hours did to women's health and well-being. This research convinced the Court to uphold the Oregon law and became a model for the defense of other social legislation. Justice David Brewer noted that although the evidence presented by Brandeis might not be authoritative, "they are significant of a widespread belief that woman's physical structure . . . [justifies] special legislation restricting or qualifying the conditions under which she should be permitted to toil."

✔ **READING CHECK: Identifying Bias** Did the Supreme Court rulings on labor laws favor business or labor?
The rulings mostly favored business.

Labor Unions

Progressive reformers were not the only ones fighting for workers' rights. Labor unions continued to fight for better working conditions and for the **closed shop**—a workplace where all the employees must belong to a union. Most union members favored "working within the system." They wanted to change how workers were treated, but they did not want to threaten capitalism's very existence. Some, however, wanted to replace capitalism with an economic system controlled by workers. Many in this group favored **socialism**, or the system under which the government or worker cooperatives own most factories, utilities, and transportation and communications systems.

INTERPRETING THE VISUAL RECORD

Factory work. These women are canning olives in a California factory. *What does the picture reveal about the conditions of factory work?*

Labor Union Membership, 1900–1920

Membership (in millions) vs. Year

Source: *The Growth of American Trade Unions, 1880–1923*

Interpreting Graphs The spread of industrialization and the efforts of progressive reformers contributed to the growth of labor union membership in the early 1900s.

? **Skills Assessment** During which five-year period was the increase in union membership the smallest? During which period was it the largest?

TEACH OBJECTIVE 4

LEVEL 1: Write the following headers on the chalkboard: *Union Successes* and *Union Failures*. Then pair students and have each pair make a bulleted list of items that fit under each header. *(Pairs should note the following: successes—most unions increased membership; the ILGWU got wage increases and reduced working hours in some companies and got aid from progressive organizations; the IWW accepted women and minorities and won a major strike; failures—the AFL excluded many unskilled workers and promoted racist policies; the ILGWU did not get closed-shop status; the IWW failed in its goal to end capitalism and faded from power.)* After students have completed their lists, discuss unions' successes and failures as a class. **English Language Learners, Cooperative Learning**

LEVELS 2 AND 3: Have students complete the Level 1 lesson. Then have each student write two or three paragraphs comparing and contrasting the goals, strategies, and relative effectiveness of the AFL and the IWW. Ask volunteers to read their paragraphs to the class.

HOMEWORK *Write the following questions on the chalkboard:* What industrial reform accomplished by the progressives or labor unions do you consider to be the most important? Why? *Have each student write a one-to-two-paragraph response to the questions.*

CITIZENSHIP

The Boston Police Strike.
After World War I, when prices were increasing but wages were not, the Boston police union joined the American Federation of Labor (AFL). Boston's police commissioner, who argued that a police-union affiliation was illegal, suspended several officers. In response, the police union went on strike, and some of Boston's citizens engaged in rioting and looting. The governor of Massachusetts and future president, Calvin Coolidge, sent the State Guard to Boston to keep order. The police commissioner began hiring new police officers to replace the strikers. Samuel Gompers, head of the AFL, asked for Governor Coolidge's help in discussing settlement terms with the commissioner, but Coolidge refused, saying, "There is no right to strike against the public safety by anybody, anywhere, anytime."

CRITICAL THINKING Why might Coolidge have considered a police strike a threat to the public safety?

ANSWER: Students might argue that Coolidge considered police officers vital to upholding public safety.

SECTION 2 REVIEW ANSWERS

1. Define
- freedom of contract, p. 283
- closed shop, p. 283

This label identified clothes made by ILGWU members.

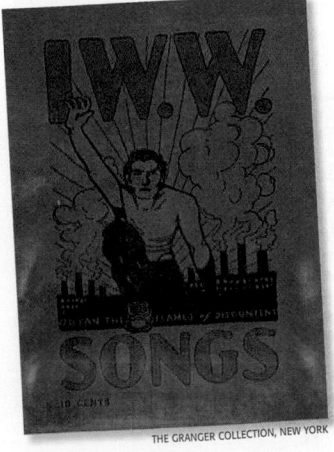

Songbooks, like this one for the IWW, helped strengthen support for the union cause.

THE GRANGER COLLECTION, NEW YORK

The AFL. The major labor organization in these years remained the American Federation of Labor (AFL). The AFL favored working within the system. Led by **Samuel Gompers**, the AFL grew fourfold from 1900 to 1914. Gompers used the same organizational structure as trusts. "We welcome their organization," he said. "When they assume a right for themselves, they cannot deny that same right to us."

The AFL excluded unskilled workers—most of whom were eastern European immigrants or African Americans. AFL leaders believed that skilled workers had the greatest potential to cause change. However, this approach left most urban workers without organized support. By 1902 only about 3 percent of African American workers were union members.

The ILGWU. One AFL union that tried to organize unskilled workers was the **International Ladies' Garment Workers Union** (ILGWU). Established in 1900 in New York City, it sought to unionize workers—mainly Jewish and Italian immigrant women—employed in sewing shops. In 1909, workers at three different New York factories walked off their jobs. The workers then turned to the ILGWU to call a general strike. Union leaders hesitated, but the speech of Clara Lemlich, a young Jewish immigrant, changed their minds. "I am a working girl, one of those striking against intolerable conditions," she addressed a crowd of garment workers. "I am tired of listening to speakers who talk in generalities. What we are here for is to decide whether or not to strike. I offer a resolution that a general strike be declared—now." The frenzied crowd agreed with her.

In November female garment workers staged the "Uprising of 20,000." Thousands of workers heeded the union's call and walked off their jobs to demand that their companies recognize the ILGWU as their union. The strike lasted through the bitter winter. Hard-pressed strikers received generous aid from progressive groups such as the Women's Trade Union League. This organization of wealthy women supported the efforts of working women to form unions. Many employers brought in African American women to take the place of strikers, but several hundred of these workers went on strike also. One young African American woman wrote, "It's a good thing, this strike is. It makes you feel like a real grown-up person."

The strike's results were mixed. Most employers agreed to many of the ILGWU's demands, including wage increases and reduced working hours. However, most employers were determined to run an **open shop**, or nonunion workplace. Thus, they refused to recognize the union—the ILGWU's most basic demand. After this strike, ILGWU membership rose from 400 to 65,000.

The IWW. While Gompers and the AFL unions negotiated with business owners for worker gains, a new union with a different agenda emerged. Founded in Chicago in 1905, the **Industrial Workers of the World** (IWW) opposed capitalism. Referring to the Continental Congress that had declared U.S. independence, IWW leader **William "Big Bill" Haywood** made claims for the working class.

History Makers Speak

❝Fellow workers, this is the Continental Congress of the working class. We are here to confederate the workers of this country into a working-class movement that shall have for its purpose the emancipation of the working class from the slave bondage of capitalism.❞

—William "Big Bill" Haywood, speech, June 1905

Haywood denounced the AFL's cooperation with business owners and its failure to include unskilled workers. He vowed to organize lumber workers, migrant farmworkers, miners, and textile workers to overthrow the capitalist system. The IWW enlisted African American, Asian American, and Hispanic American workers. An IWW-led union in Philadelphia succeeded in raising wages for its largely African American membership from $1.25 a day to $4 a day. The IWW also actively recruited female workers and the wives of male workers. An IWW newspaper expressed optimism that union women working "side by side with men in strikes will soon develop a fighting force that will end capitalism and its horrors in short order."

The Wobblies, as the members of the IWW came to be called, pursued their goals through boycotts, general strikes, and industrial sabotage. Their greatest hour came in 1912. That year, they led 10,000 workers in a strike against the textile mills of Lawrence, Massachusetts, to protest large cut in wages. After a bitter and much-publicized two-month strike, the mill owners gave in.

Success was short-lived, however. Several later IWW-led strikes failed miserably. Most Americans grew fearful of the IWW's revolutionary goals and methods. As member Frederick C. Mills put it, the IWW "is trying to teach them [poor or unemployed workers] how to get their share of the goods of this world." The government cracked down on the union with increasing force. Disagreements among IWW leaders also weakened the union's power. Within a few years the IWW collapsed and eventually faded from power.

INTERPRETING THE VISUAL RECORD

IWW strike. The local militia was called in to break the IWW-led strike in Lawrence, Massachusetts. *What does this picture reveal about the government's attitude toward strikers?*

✔ **READING CHECK: Comparing** Compare the goals of the AFL, ILGWA, and IWW in the early 1900s. Each provided organized support for American workers.

SECTION 2 REVIEW

1. Define and explain:
freedom of contract
closed shop
socialism
open shop

2. Identify and explain:
Florence Kelley
Triangle Shirtwaist Fire
Rose Schneiderman
Muller v. *Oregon*
Louis D. Brandeis
Samuel Gompers
International Ladies' Garment
   Workers Union
Industrial Workers of the World
William "Big Bill" Haywood

3. Categorizing Copy the chart below. Use it to describe the successes and failures unions experienced in the early 1900s.

Unions	
Successes	**Failures**

4. **Finding the Main Idea**

a. What solutions would you have proposed to improve working conditions for women and children?

b. How did the Triangle Shirtwaist Fire lead to improved workplace safety?

c. Contrast the Supreme Court rulings in *Lochner* v. *New York* and *Muller* v. *Oregon*.

5. **Writing and Critical Thinking**

Summarizing Imagine that you are a union organizer. Write a speech explaining why workers should join a union.
Consider:
• what the goals of employers were
• what the goals of employees were
• how meeting the goals of one group might affect the other group

Homework Practice Online
keyword: SE3 HP9

SECTION 3

After completing Section 3, students should be able to:

OBJECTIVE 1 Describe how reformers tried to improve life in U.S. cities.

OBJECTIVE 2 Discuss how reformers hoped to improve moral standards.

OBJECTIVE 3 Report on how African Americans and American Indians organized to improve their lives.

OBJECTIVE 4 Explain why immigrants were left out of some progressive reforms, and recognize how they contributed to other reforms.

LET'S GET STARTED!

Write the following categories on the chalkboard: *City Life, Morality, Racial Discrimination,* and *Immigrants' Lives.* As students enter the classroom, have them copy the list of headers, leaving a few lines between each. Tell students to write a sentence or two predicting how each topic will represent an issue for progressives in this section. Ask volunteers to read one or more of their predictions to the class. Tell students that in Section 3 they will learn more about progressive social reforms.

SECTION 3

READ TO DISCOVER

1. How did reformers try to improve life in U.S. cities?
2. How did reformers hope to improve moral standards?
3. How did African Americans and American Indians organize to improve their lives?
4. Why were immigrants left out of some progressive reforms, and how did they contribute to other reforms?

DEFINE

prohibition

IDENTIFY

Lawrence Veiller
Daniel Burnham
Woman's Christian Temperance Union
Billy Sunday
Frances Willard
Eighteenth Amendment
W. E. B. Du Bois
National Association for the Advancement of Colored People
National Urban League
Society of American Indians
Americanization

WHY IT MATTERS TODAY

Various groups around the world continue to seek full equality today. Use **CNNfyi.com** or other **current events** sources to find out about one group that faces inequality and what that group is doing to change the situation. Record your findings in your journal.

CNNfyi.com

Reforming Society

EYEWITNESSES TO History *"The home is very unattractive for children and they are glad to get out to meet their friends. They want to supply a social need, and they go out and meet other friends and the home has no tie upon them. . . . The tenement house is not the only thing, but a very strong influence. I believe the entire economic conditions in this country are another influence."*

—Henry Moscowitz, New York Tenement Housing Commission Investigation, 1900

A subway porter

Tenement resident Henry Moscowitz described the negative effects on a family that resulted from poverty and other urban ills. Reformers hoped that increasing wages would help bring many families out of poverty, but they knew that other factors affected the quality of people's lives. Progressives therefore set out to attack numerous social problems that they believed weakened American society.

Reforming City Life

By 1920, for the first time in U.S. history, more than 50 percent of Americans lived in urban areas. As urban populations soared, cities struggled to provide garbage collection, safe and affordable housing, health care, police and fire protection, and adequate public education. "The challenge of the city," declared one progressive, "has become one of decent human existence."

Cleaning up the city. Some reformers called for a campaign to make the cities a more healthful and livable home for all residents. "The community is one great family," explained Louise DeKoven Bowen, the president of Chicago's Woman's City Club. "Each member of it is bound to help the other." Various women's clubs, men's clubs, and reform organizations enlisted the aid of local governments to clean up the cities. Some groups took the cleanup campaign literally, working to rid the cities of garbage. Other organizations worked for better housing or to improve public education.

Lawrence Veiller (VYL-uhr), a settlement-house worker, attacked irresponsible tenement owners "who for the sake of a large profit on their investments sacrifice the health and welfare of countless thousands." As the secretary to the New York State Tenement House Commission, Veiller campaigned tirelessly for improved housing. In 1900 he questioned Henry Moscowitz, who in 17 years had lived in 14 different tenements on New York's Lower East Side. Moscowitz described the stench, dirt, noise, and the lack of light, fresh air, water, electricity, and bathing facilities.

The commission discovered that New York had "the most serious tenement house problem in the world." In 1901 Veiller succeeded in getting the New York

TEACH OBJECTIVE 1

LEVEL 1: Conduct a discussion about the steps that progressive reformers took to improve life in U.S. cities. Then pair students and tell them to imagine that they are progressive reformers who are going to lead a parade for urban reform. Ask each pair to create a series of parade banners that publicize the ways in which progressives tried to improve city life. *(Pairs should note that progressives tried to rid cities of garbage, provide better housing, improve public education and public health, build playgrounds, provide city planning, and redesign Chicago and other cities.)* Ask volunteers to display and describe their banners to the class.
English Language Learners, Cooperative Learning

LEVELS 2 AND 3: Tell students to imagine that they are muckraker journalists who have decided to target urban living conditions in their next exposé. Have each student write short articles describing urban life in any large city of the early 1900s. Tell them to conclude their articles with proposed solutions to the urban problems they have described. *(See the Level 1 lesson for the correct solutions.)* Students may wish to include their articles in their portfolios.

HOMEWORK *Have each student use the strategies of the 1900s progressives as a model to come up with a list of 10 ways to improve modern-day urban living conditions.*

State Tenement House Act passed. The law required that any new tenements be built around open courtyards to allow in light and air. New buildings also had to contain one bathroom for each apartment or for every three rooms. Previously, bathrooms in apartment buildings had been limited to one or two for an entire floor. Housing reformers in other states used the New York law as a model for their proposals.

To further improve urban living conditions, a group of physicians and reform-minded citizens formed the National Tuberculosis Association. The group focused on education and on lobbying the government to fund special hospitals to treat victims of tuberculosis. Thanks in part to this effort, by 1915 the death rate from "the white plague" had dropped significantly.

Other reformers campaigned for the creation of safe places for children to play. A 1908 Massachusetts law required all cities with a population greater than 10,000 to hold a referendum on whether that city should build at least one playground. Within the year, 41 out of 42 cities had shown their support for such actions. By 1920 cities had spent millions of dollars building playgrounds.

Some middle- and upper-class Americans objected to spending tax dollars on recreational facilities for the poor. One journalist in Lawrence, Massachusetts, reported that "pandemonium [disorder] reigned" when "bands of foreigners and trouble makers" used public space to celebrate the Fourth of July. Cleveland city council member Frederic Howe was shunned by his upper-class friends for supporting recreational facilities for the poor. However, Howe and his allies succeeded. "On Saturday and Sunday the whole population played baseball in the hundreds of parks laid out for that purpose," Howe reported.

City planning. The city-planning movement grew out of progressives' belief that cleaner cities would produce better citizens. The First National Conference on City Planning was held in 1909. Its participants hoped that wise planning could halt the spread of slums and beautify cities. Beautiful cities and impressive public architecture, they argued, would instill patriotism among the immigrant population.

In 1909 **Daniel Burnham**, a leading architect and city planner, produced a magnificent plan for redesigning Chicago. It was the first comprehensive plan to redesign a U.S. city. The centerpiece of Burnham's vision for Chicago was a soaring city hall that would inspire all residents to be good citizens. "Make no little plans," said Burnham. "They have no magic to stir men's blood."

City-planning commissions in Cleveland, San Francisco, and Washington, D.C., also hired Burnham. His plans were never fully built, but some, such as those for Washington, D.C., were a success. Above all, his efforts helped people realize that city planning—park construction, building codes, sanitation standards, and zoning—was a necessary function of municipal government.

✔ **READING CHECK: Making Generalizations** How did the growth of cities lead to urban reforms?
The growth of cities prompted a campaign to make cities more healthful and livable for residents.

INTERPRETING THE VISUAL RECORD
City planning. Daniel Burnham (left) created a plan to redesign Chicago. **What are the unique characteristics shown in the design?**

SPOTLIGHT
on Art

Tell students that the Ash Can School was a group of eight painters who painted realistic scenes of New York City during the Progressive Era. The term *ash can* refers to the often bleak nature of the painters' subjects, such as humble backyards, tenements, or garbage cans. Have students conduct research on one of the painters of the Ash Can School. Ask each student to write a report that includes biographical information about the artist as well as information about the artist's work, subjects, and methods. **Block Scheduling**

AMERICAN ARTS

Shaping Public Space

The City Beautiful movement in the early 1900s rose out of the success of several fairs that led architects and designers to create large open spaces in urban centers. For instance, Frederick Law Olmsted, a landscape architect for the World's Columbian Exposition of 1893, had created a series of lagoons surrounding Chicago's tall and shapely buildings. These pools of water, along with electric lights, reflected off the monumental buildings and led people to call Chicago the "Magic City."

Soon Daniel Burnham and other architects set to work to improve other U.S. cities. In Washington, D.C., the Senate Parks Commission assigned a team of architects, artists, and planners the task of completing Pierre Charles L'Enfant's original plans for the city. They looked to the colonial cities of the United States as well as the great capitals of Europe for inspiration.

One of Burnham's first actions was to move the railroad station from the Mall. He located it on Capitol Hill, where it served as a gateway to the city. The surrounding landscaping accented the station's monumental proportions. Although work halted during World War I, in the 1920s the lands around the Potomac River were transformed into level ground. Builders created the Lincoln Memorial and a decorative canal known as the Reflecting Pool, which

The design of Washington, D.C., incorporates many of the ideas of city planning.

connects the Lincoln Memorial to the Washington Monument. During the 1920s many public buildings made of white stone were built, and sculptures were erected, transforming Washington, D.C., into an impressive national capital.

Understanding the Arts

1. What gave rise to the City Beautiful movement of the early 1900s?
2. What did Daniel Burnham do to the railroad station in Washington, D.C.?

This poster encouraged support for prohibition.

Moral Reform

Progressives also wanted to "clean up" what they considered to be immoral behavior. They called for **prohibition**—a ban on the manufacture, sale, and transportation of alcoholic beverages—and the closing of the nation's saloons. Reformers believed that prohibition would reduce crime and the breakup of families.

Journalists described alcohol as "the archenemy of progress." Magazines published articles such as "The Story of an Alcohol Slave, as Told by Himself." Muckraker George Kibbe Turner wrote in *McClure's Magazine* in 1909 that to truly reform the rapidly growing U.S. cities, the saloons must be closed.

The drive for prohibition took many forms. During the Progressive Era, many colleges did not allow student athletes to drink. Some industrialists initiated programs intended to convince their workers not to drink alcohol. School textbooks included information on the dangers of alcohol.

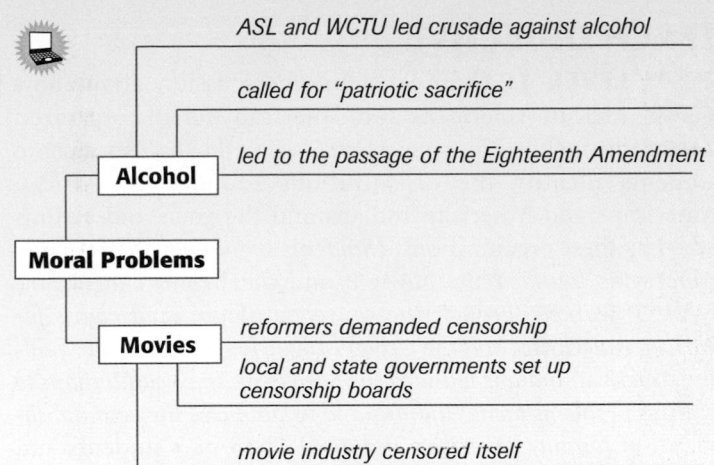
The passage of prohibition. The Anti-Saloon League (ASL) and the **Woman's Christian Temperance Union** (WCTU) led the crusade against alcohol. By 1902 the ASL had branches in 39 states with 200 paid staff members.

Thousands of volunteer speakers, many of them Protestant ministers, spread the antisaloon message in the nation's churches. **Billy Sunday**, a former ballplayer turned Presbyterian evangelist, preached that saloons were "the parent of crimes and the mother of sins." **Frances Willard** headed the WCTU from 1879 to 1898. Willard eventually made the WCTU a powerful national force for temperance, moral purity, and the rights of women.

During World War I, prohibitionists drew on Americans' spirit of patriotic sacrifice. The U.S. Navy banned the consumption of alcohol in 1914. During the vote on prohibition in Congress, Senator William Kenyon of Iowa mentioned this fact. He asked, "If liquor is a bad thing for the boys in the trenches, why is it a good thing for those at home?"

In 1917 Congress proposed the **Eighteenth Amendment**, which barred the manufacture, sale, and distribution of alcoholic beverages. The states ratified it in 1919. However, the amendment proved unpopular and difficult to enforce. It was repealed in 1933.

The coming of prohibition inspired this sheet music. This fan shows WCTU leader Frances Willard.

Moviegoing. The growing popularity of motion pictures worried some urban reformers who believed that movies were a threat to morality. The first movie to tell a story, *The Great Train Robbery*, was made in 1903. By 1910, millions of Americans were going to the movies each week. In 1916 the *New York Times* reported that films were the fifth-largest U.S. industry.

To the urban poor, a 5- or 10-cent movie ticket—bought at movie houses called nickelodeons—offered cheap, readily available entertainment. Many middle-class Americans, however, believed that movies—particularly the steamy romances—and movie houses were immoral and sources of temptation. Writer William Dean Howells described the situation.

History Makers Speak

"The pictures thrown upon the luminous [lighted] curtain of the stage have been declared extremely corrupting to the idle young people lurking in the darkness before it. The darkness itself has been held a condition of inexpressible depravity [immorality] and a means of allurement [attraction] to evil."

—William Dean Howells, "The Cinematographic Show," *Harper's Monthly,* September 1912

Declaring that moviegoing promoted immoral values, reformers demanded that movies be censored. Several states and cities set up censorship boards to ban movies they considered immoral. In 1909 the movie industry began to censor itself.

✔ **READING CHECK: Evaluating** How did the growing popularity of motion pictures affect the U.S. economy? The motion-picture industry became the fifth-largest U.S. industry.

Progressivism and Racial Discrimination

For nonwhites the progressive movement had mixed results. Most progressives were concerned about the plight of the poor. However, few white progressives devoted very much energy to the

INTERPRETING THE VISUAL RECORD

Movie theaters. The popularity of motion pictures led to the building of fancy theaters. *Why do you think the cost of admission varied by time of day?*

TEACH OBJECTIVE 3

LEVEL 1: Conduct a brief discussion about how African Americans and American Indians organized during the Progressive Era. During the discussion, have students identify the organizations founded by African Americans and American Indians and the goals and actions taken by these organizations. *(Students should note that African Americans founded the NAACP and the Urban League; the NAACP worked through the courts to obtain civil rights for African Americans, and the Urban League fought for racial equality; American Indians founded the Society of American Indians to address problems facing Indians and to publicize the accomplishments of famous American Indians.)* Then pair students and have each pair design a billboard publicizing the mission and activities of one of these organizations.
English Language Learners, Cooperative Learning

LEVELS 2 AND 3: Organize students into small groups and tell them to imagine that they are African Americans or American Indians working to obtain equal rights during the early 1900s. Have half of the groups draft an organizational platform for an African American civil rights group and have the other half of the groups draft a platform for an American Indian group. *(See the Level 1 activity for the correct goals.)* Both platforms should include specific wording related to improving the lives of African Americans and American Indians.
Cooperative Learning

CITIZENSHIP

The Niagara Movement.
In 1905, before the founding of the National Association for the Advancement of Colored People, W. E. B. Du Bois and others met at Niagara Falls, New York. The Niagara Movement, as this group was called, drafted a "Declaration of Principles," which protested discrimination against African Americans and asked for the support of others in ending that discrimination. "We believe that [African Americans] should protest emphatically and continually against the curtailment of their political rights. . . . We especially complain against the denial of equal opportunities to use in economic life. . . . We protest against the 'Jim Crow' car, since its effect is and must be, to make us pay first-class fare for third-class accommodations. . . . To ignore, overlook, or apologize for these wrongs is to prove ourselves unworthy of freedom." The Niagara Movement lasted only a few years before disbanding because of a lack of financial support.

CRITICAL THINKING Why might the declaration have argued that overlooking wrongs proved African Americans unworthy of freedom?

ANSWER: Students might suggest that the declaration implied that overlooking wrongs constituted a failure to assert constitutional rights.

Research on the ROM

Free Find: W. E. B. Du Bois
After learning about W. E. B. Du Bois on the **Holt Researcher CD–ROM**, write a poem that describes his life.

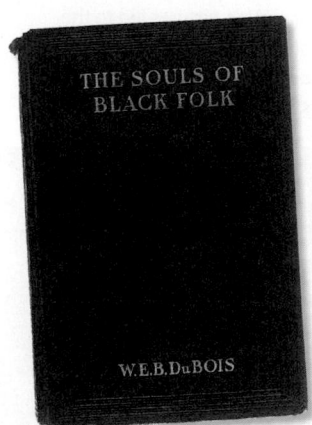

W. E. B. Du Bois's **The Souls of Black Folk**

problems of discrimination and prejudice against African Americans and American Indians. Some progressives expressed open prejudice against these groups. Many African Americans and American Indians, however, drew on progressive ideas to develop programs appropriate to their communities.

BIOGRAPHY

W. E. B. Du Bois

Views of Du Bois. One of the most influential African American leaders to emerge during this period was **W. E. B. Du Bois** (doo BOYS). He was born in 1868 in Great Barrington, Massachusetts. As a child Du Bois attended Sunday school with African American and white children. Not until high school did he realize that his skin color caused some people to not like him.

A bright student, Du Bois was encouraged by his school's principal to prepare for college. Local residents and churches raised money to send him to Fisk University, an African American school in Nashville, Tennessee. After graduating, he studied history in Germany and at Harvard University. In 1895 Du Bois became the first African American to earn a doctorate from Harvard. Two years later he was appointed professor of history and economics at Atlanta University, a leading African American college, where he taught until 1910.

By the early 1900s Du Bois was recognized as a strong supporter of civil rights. He believed that access to college education and vocational training offered the best chance of progress for African Americans. He also believed that African Americans should be politically active in the struggle for racial equality. Du Bois's view contrasted sharply with that of African American leader Booker T. Washington. Washington argued that African Americans should not spend their time fighting discrimination. He urged them to focus on improving their own education and economic prosperity. Du Bois, however, believed that this focus would unfairly make African Americans responsible for correcting racial injustice.

Throughout his life Du Bois maintained a passionate interest in Africa, which he regarded as the spiritual homeland of all black people. In his 1903 book, *The Souls of Black Folk*, Du Bois expressed his dual identity as both African and American.

History Makers Speak

"One ever feels his two-ness—an American, a Negro; two souls, two thoughts, two un-reconciled strivings. He [the African American] simply wishes to make it possible for a man to be both a Negro and an American, without being cursed and spit upon by his fellows, without having the doors of Opportunity closed roughly in his face."

—W. E. B. Du Bois, *The Souls of Black Folk*

In the 1920s Du Bois organized a series of Pan-African congresses that attracted black leaders from around the world. This was done to create greater unity among people of African descent. During the 1930s and 1940s Du Bois continued his career as a scholar and political activist. By the 1950s he, like many prominent American intellectuals, had embraced socialism for its promise of social justice. In 1961, at age 93, Du Bois joined the Communist Party and moved to Ghana. He died there two years later.

✔ **READING CHECK: Analyzing Information** How did W. E. B. Du Bois try to reform race relations? He urged African Americans to focus on improving their own education and economic prosperity.

TEACH OBJECTIVE 4

LEVEL 1: Pair students and have them list the reasons why immigrants were excluded from some progressive reforms. *(Pairs should mention racism and a lack of respect for immigrants' cultures.)* Then ask pairs to list how immigrants contributed to other reforms. *(Pairs should note that immigrants worked through political machines to establish worker-protection and public-health programs, playgrounds, public baths, and parks.)* Then have pairs create three political cartoons that comment on the situation of poor immigrants and the contributions that immigrant communities made to reform efforts. Display pairs' cartoons around the classroom.

Cooperative Learning, English Language Learners

LEVEL 2: Tell students to imagine that they are poor immigrant workers who are faced with the pressure to assimilate. Have each student write a series of diary entries describing the struggles of daily life and the reforms that he or she seeks to improve his or her life. *(See the Level 1 lesson for the correct struggles and contributions.)* Have volunteers read their diary entries to the class.

African Americans organize. In 1909 Du Bois and a group of African American and white progressives met in New York City. They discussed the lynching of two African American men in Springfield, Illinois, the previous year. Out of this meeting came the **National Association for the Advancement of Colored People** (NAACP), an organization dedicated to ending racial discrimination. Du Bois edited its monthly magazine, *The Crisis*, which publicized cases of racial inequality. The publication also called for social reforms that would ensure equal rights for African Americans. By 1918 the magazine's circulation had risen to 100,000.

The NAACP used the court system to fight civil rights restrictions. In 1915 the NAACP won its first major victory in *Guinn* v. *United States*. In this case the Supreme Court outlawed the "grandfather clause," which freed from other suffrage qualifications citizens whose fathers or grandfathers had voted. Southern states had used the clause to bar African Americans from voting but to keep whites eligible to vote. In 1917 NAACP lawyers won *Buchanan* v. *Warley*, which overturned a Louisville, Kentucky, law requiring racially segregated housing. As a result, similar laws were struck down across the country.

The **National Urban League** also fought for racial equality. Founded in 1911 by concerned African Americans and white reformers, the league worked to improve job opportunities and housing for urban African Americans. One of its goals was to help African American migrants from the South adjust to their new lives in northern cities. The NAACP and the National Urban League made some important gains for African American citizens. Nevertheless, most African Americans still faced discrimination.

W. E. B. Du Bois wanted The Crisis to address equal rights for African Americans.

Lynchings, 1889–1918

Interpreting Maps Some 75 percent of lynching victims were African American men. Most of the other victims were white men. However, women, American Indians, Hispanics, and Asian Americans were also victims of lynch mobs.

? **HUMAN SYSTEMS** In which region did most lynchings occur?

Lynchings of Whites and African Americans

Period	Whites	African Americans
1889–1893	261	571
1894–1898	223	549
1899–1903	77	465
1904–1908	25	342
1909–1913	32	308
1914–1918	27	253
TOTALS	645	2,488

Source: *Historical Statistics of the United States*

Number of Lynchings

None	51–100
1–5	101–200
6–20	201–300
21–50	301–386

(map legend states: 0 300 600 Miles / 0 300 600 Kilometers / Albers Equal-Area Projection)

LEVEL 3: Organize most of the students into two "face-off" panels. Ask one panel to assume the role of progressives in the early 1900s and the other panel to represent immigrants. Have the members of each panel discuss ways of helping the immigrant poor from that particular panel's point of view. *(See the Level 1 lesson for the correct struggles and contributions.)* Ask the rest of the class to question and challenge panel members on their positions. Close the discussion by asking the progressive panel to list on the chalkboard proposals for reforms to help immigrants, then have the immigrant panel support or reject each proposal and explain why. **Cooperative Learning**

SPOTLIGHT
on Immigrants and Political Machines

Have students conduct research on the relationship between immigrants and big-city political machines during the early 1900s. Then have each student write a report addressing the reasons why immigrants supported political machines despite the machines' reputation for corruption. Students' reports should also address the types of reforms that were supported by political machines. **Block Scheduling**

REVIEW SECTION 3 ANSWERS

1. Define
• prohibition, p. 288

2. Identify
• Lawrence Veiller, p. 286
• Daniel Burnham, p. 287
• Woman's Christian Temperance Union, p. 289
• Billy Sunday, p. 289
• Frances Willard, p. 289
• Eighteenth Amendment, p. 289
• W. E. B. Du Bois, p. 290
• National Association for the Advancement of Colored People, p. 291
• National Urban League, p. 291
• Americanization, p. 292
• Society of American Indians, p. 292

3. improving garbage collection, housing, and health education; making safe and healthy public spaces; prohibition

4a. Many believed alcohol caused crime and destroyed families.

b. They organized to call attention to discrimination, to emphasize the successes of their ethnic groups, and to work for governmental change. The NAACP changed some laws; the SAI suffered from internal dissension and lost influence.

c. He organized the NAACP to fight for equal rights and helped secure voting rights for African Americans.

American Indian Jim Thorpe was one of the greatest athletes in U.S. history.

American Indians organize. Demands for equal rights and greater opportunities for American Indians also surfaced during this period. The Dawes Act of 1887 had caused many Indians to lose their property to land speculators and fall deeper into poverty. Some progressives took up their cause. They wanted to slow down land allotment and maintain the reservation system for a time.

In 1911 a group of 50 American Indians, most of them middle-class professionals, formed the **Society of American Indians**. Members discussed ways to improve civil rights, education, health, and local government. The society publicized the accomplishments of American Indians such as Olympic gold medalist Jim Thorpe. It also lobbied against the use of insulting terms for Indians.

Some members supported strengthening native cultures, but most favored complete assimilation, or absorption, into white American culture. Society member and Seneca historian Arthur C. Parker urged American Indians "to strike out into the duties of modern life and . . . find every right that had escaped them before."

The organization's moderate positions on most issues led to disputes. Dr. Carlos Montezuma, a Yavapai Apache member of the society, criticized the Bureau of Indian Affairs for mismanaging reservations. Other members refused to take such a strong antigovernment stand, and the group's influence declined. Nevertheless, the organization provided a forum for American Indian leaders. It also laid the groundwork for later attempts to improve conditions for American Indians.

✔ **READING CHECK: Summarizing** What actions did African Americans and American Indians take to improve their economic and political positions during the Progressive Era?
African Americans organized the National Association for the Advancement of Colored People. American Indians established the Society of American Indians.

Immigrants and Assimilation

The progressive movement had mixed results for immigrants as well. Many reformers sympathized with the plight of the newcomers who labored in factories and were crowded into slum tenements. These reformers lobbied for laws to improve immigrants' lives, as well as conditions in the workplace and in city slums.

At the same time, progressives criticized immigrants. They accused them of immoral behavior such as drinking and gambling and denounced immigrant support for big-city political machines. Some native-born Americans with progressive ideals favored restricting immigration. In 1916 a prominent New Yorker named Madison Grant published *The Passing of the Great Race.* In this book he expressed racist opinions about African Americans, Jews, and immigrants from southern and eastern Europe. Yet Grant was also a progressive who supported environmental protection, urban planning, and other reforms.

Many progressives supported **Americanization**, a process of preparing foreign-born residents for full U.S. citizenship. These efforts to assimilate immigrants, or to make them more like native-born Americans, focused on education. In schools, voluntary associations, and public programs, immigrants were taught to read, write, and speak English. They also learned about U.S. history and government. Several cities and states passed Americanization measures. William Maxwell, a prominent New York educator, wanted to make the public school "a melting pot which converts the children of the immigrants of all races and languages into sturdy, independent American citizens." Russian immigrant Eugene Lyons described the effects of Americanization on immigrants:

REVIEW

Have students complete the **Section 3 Review** on p. 293.

ASSESS

Have students complete **Daily Quiz 9.3**. As **Alternative Assessment**, you may want to use the graphic organizer or the civil rights platform in this section's lessons.

RETEACH

Have students complete **Main Idea Activity for English Language Learners and Special-Needs Students 9.3**. Then ask students to write a question and answer that covers the main idea for each subsection in the section. Select students to read their questions to the class. Have the class try to answer each question. **English Language Learners**

EXTEND

Have students conduct research on reformers who are questioning the impact of television, movies, music, and video games on society today. Have each student write a short essay comparing and contrasting the present-day crusade with reformers' efforts in the Progressive Era. **Block Scheduling**

History Makers Speak

❝We sensed a disrespect for the alien traditions in our homes and came unconsciously to resent and despise those traditions . . . because they seemed [impossible] barriers between ourselves and the adopted land.❞

—Eugene Lyons, *Assignment in Utopia*

Chinese immigrant Victor Wong recalled that in school, teachers tried to "dissuade us . . . from everything Chinese. Their view of the Chinese ways was that they were evil, heathen, non-Christian." Some immigrants rejected the assistance of social reformers, because the reformers did not respect their cultural backgrounds.

Some progressives welcomed the diversity of immigrant groups. In his 1924 book, *Culture and Democracy in the United States*, philosopher Horace Kallen supported pluralism. He envisioned a nation that would be home to a number of distinctive cultures. Some immigrants also supported Americanization that could be achieved without giving up their own ethnic identities.

Poor immigrants and the political bosses who represented them supported middle-class progressives when they fought for practical reforms such as worker protection and public-health programs. For example, a New York state legislative committee that investigated factory conditions after the Triangle Shirtwaist Fire won strong backing from New York City's immigrant-based Democratic machine. In his autobiography, Frederic Howe asserted that New York City owed its playgrounds, public baths, and public parks, among other services, to Irish immigrants and their political machines. "Unconsciously aiming to shape the state to human ends," he declared, "the Irish have made New York what it is."

✔ **READING CHECK: Identifying Points of View** How did progressives view immigrants?
Some progressives wanted to help them but also accused many immigrants of behavior they considered immoral.

INTERPRETING THE VISUAL RECORD

Americanizing immigrants. This poster was created to encourage immigrants to learn English. *Do you think that the poster shows respect for immigrants' culture? Explain your answer.*

SECTION 3 REVIEW

1. Define and explain:
prohibition

2. Identify and explain:
Lawrence Veiller
Daniel Burnham
Woman's Christian
   Temperance Union
Billy Sunday
Frances Willard
Eighteenth Amendment
W. E. B. Du Bois
National Association for
   the Advancement of
   Colored People
National Urban League
Society of American Indians
Americanization

3. Evaluating Copy the organizational web below. Use it to explain the different approaches that progressives took in cleaning up cities.

Solutions for City Problems

4. **Finding the Main Idea**
a. Why did progressives support prohibition and the elimination of saloons?
b. What methods did African Americans and American Indians use to fight racism and discrimination, and how successful were they?
c. What impact did reform leader W. E. B. Du Bois have on American society?

5. **Writing and Critical Thinking**
Supporting a Point of View Imagine that you are an immigrant in 1910. Do you support the progressive movement? Explain your answer.
Consider:
• how some progressives treated immigrants
• Americanization efforts
• how some immigrants contributed to reform

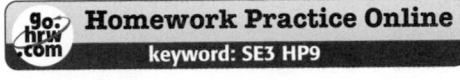
Homework Practice Online
keyword: SE3 HP9

---

5. Some students might argue against progressives because they want to limit immigrant rights. Others might argue for progressives because they want to improve the overall quality of life.

CHAPTER
REVIEW 9 ANSWERS

Creating a Time Line
Each event should have an explanation and a correct date.

Writing a Summary
See the Reading Checks in each section for main ideas.

Identifying People and Ideas
1. a reform movement focused on improving urban life

2. journalists who wrote about corruption in politics, business, and society

3. activist who worked for child labor restrictions

4. leader of the American Federation of Labor

5. system under which cooperatives own the means of production and services

6. settlement-house worker who campaigned for improved housing

7. scholar who formed NAACP and worked for political rights of African Americans

8. leader of the Woman's Christian Temperance Union

9. group formed to address injustices and problems faced by American Indians

CHAPTER 9

REVIEW AND ASSESSMENT RESOURCES

TECHNOLOGY

▶ Chapter 9 Test Generator (on the One-Stop Planner)
▶ Global Skill Builder CD–ROM
▶ HRW Go site

REINFORCEMENT, REVIEW, AND ASSESSMENT

▶ Chapter 9 Review, pp. 294–95
▶ Chapter 9 Tutorial for Students, Parents, Mentors, and Peers

▶ Chapter 9 Test (Form A or B)
▶ Portfolio Activities and Alternative Assessment Handbook, Chapter 9
▶ Chapter 9 Test for English Language Learners and Special-Needs Students

REVIEW

Have students complete the **Chapter 9 Review** on pp. 294–95.

ASSESS

Use one of the chapter tests to assess students' understanding of the content. For **Alternative Assessment**, see the **Portfolio Activities and Alternative Assessment Handbook**.

10. programs to teach immigrants American ways and English

Understanding Main Ideas

1. became activists for volunteer groups

2. publicized need for social reforms

3. the length of the workday, low wages, child labor, and wages for women and ethnic minorities

4. determined that laws could not limit employers' right to property or workers' freedom to contract; upheld laws limiting workday hours

5. improved garbage collection, housing, public education, and supported urban planning and prohibition

6. They organized to call attention to discrimination, to emphasize the successes of their ethnic groups, and to work for governmental change. The NAACP brought cases of discrimination to court.

Reviewing Themes

1. in response to pressures from progressive reformers

2. through education and child labor reforms; also worked to limit racial discrimination; efforts were partially successful, but government and businesses reversed some changes and blocked others

3. They formed organizations, published articles describing the evils of alcohol use, and advocated prohibition in churches.

294

CHAPTER 9 Review

Creating a Time Line

Copy the time line below onto a sheet of paper. Complete the time line by filling in the events and dates from the chapter that you think were most significant. Pick three events and explain why you think they were significant.

| 1900 | 1910 | 1920 |

Writing a Summary

Using standard grammar, spelling, sentence structure, and punctuation, write an overview of events in the chapter.

Identifying People and Ideas

Identify the following terms or individuals and explain their significance.

1. progressivism
2. muckrakers
3. Florence Kelley
4. Samuel Gompers
5. socialism
6. Lawrence Veiller
7. W. E. B. Du Bois
8. Frances Willard
9. Society of American Indians
10. Americanization

Understanding Main Ideas

SECTION 1 *(pp. 274–279)*
1. How did women work for progressive goals?
2. What roles did intellectuals, muckrakers, and writers play in the progressive movement?

SECTION 2 *(pp. 280–285)*
3. Which labor issues did reformers hope to remedy through legislation?
4. How did the Supreme Court rule on labor issues?

SECTION 3 *(pp. 286–293)*
5. What actions did progressive reformers take to improve conditions in cities?
6. How did African Americans and American Indians address the problems facing their communities?

Reviewing Themes

1. **Economics** Why did states pass laws to protect workers' rights?
2. **Citizenship** How did progressives propose to extend opportunities to all citizens? How successful were their efforts?
3. **Constitutional Heritage** How did progressives help win passage of the Eighteenth Amendment?

Thinking Critically

1. **Analyzing Information** How did industrialization influence progressive reform efforts?
2. **Making Predictions** How might the course of reform have been different if the Supreme Court had been more supportive of early social legislation?
3. **Contrasting** How did the American Federation of Labor and the Industrial Workers of the World differ in their views on the scope and nature of labor reform?
4. **Supporting a Point of View** Write a brief paragraph explaining your position on spending tax dollars on city improvements.
5. **Evaluating** What impact did Progressive Era reforms have?

Writing About History

Identifying Cause and Effect Imagine that you are a reformer in the Progressive Era. Write a pamphlet in support of legislation to help with some of the consequences of increased immigration to the United States. Use the following graph to organize your thoughts.

Increased Immigration → Effects → Reasons for Legislation

RETEACH

Organize students into groups of four or five. Assign each group one of the following topics: Reforming Big Business and the Workplace or Reforming Society. Have each group prepare a multimedia presentation on the assigned topic. Groups should focus on the people, events, and issues that were affected by the progressive movement during the late 1800s and early 1900s. Encourage groups to use a variety of audio and visual components in their presentations. Have members of each group make their presentations to the class. Tell students to take notes on each presentation.

English Language Learners, Cooperative Learning

EXTEND

Tell students that the progressives placed great emphasis on the value of education. They believed that a free and equal public education for all would ensure better involvement in the democratic process and help downtrodden groups to get attention for the issues that affected their communities. Have students conduct research to locate a sample curriculum for a typical public school of the early 1900s. Tell each student to write a short essay comparing this curriculum to his or her own.

Block Scheduling

Building Social Studies Skills

Interpreting Maps

Study the map below. Then use it to help answer the questions that follow.

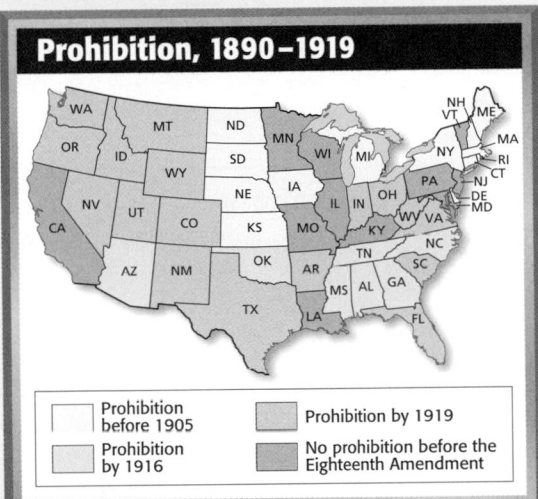

Prohibition, 1890–1919

Legend:
- Prohibition before 1905
- Prohibition by 1916
- Prohibition by 1919
- No prohibition before the Eighteenth Amendment

1. Approximately how much of the country had banned alcohol before the Eighteenth Amendment was ratified?
   a. about one-fourth of the states
   b. about one-half of the states
   c. about three-fourths of the states
   d. about 90% of the states

2. Describe the regional trends that characterized the prohibition movement at different times.

Interpreting The Visual Record

Study Arnold Genthe's photograph of a Chinese immigrant family. Then use it to help answer the questions that follow.

THE GRANGER COLLECTION, NEW YORK

3. Which of these titles would be most appropriate for this photograph?
   a. A Fully Assimilated Chinese Family
   b. A Candid View of a Chinese Family in Their Home
   c. A Proud Chinese Family
   d. A Family Waits to Board Ship to America

4. How does this photograph differ from the Jessie Tarbox Beals' photograph in the Skill-Building Strategies?

Alternative Assessment

Building Your Portfolio

U.S. HISTORY

Citizenship

Imagine that you are a reformer in the early 1900s. Create a training manual for new reformers. The manual should include information on various problems and issues, reform efforts to address them, and the qualities of effective leadership.

internet connect

Internet Activity: go.hrw.com
KEYWORD: SE3 AN9

Access the Internet through the HRW Go site to locate and use databases on geographic distributions and patterns regarding immigration. Before you go online, write five questions on geographic distributions or patterns related to immigration. Then answer your questions by finding data from the Web sites. Use the Holt Grapher to create your own database and to generate charts or graphs.

go.hrw.com

Thinking Critically

1. by contributing to poor working conditions and urban overcrowding

2. Students might suggest quicker changes in working conditions.

3. The AFL worked within the system for workers' rights and excluded unskilled workers. The IWW wanted to abolish capitalism and included workers of all skills and ethnicities.

4. Paragraphs will vary. Students should support their arguments with examples.

5. They led to some workplace reforms and the passage of the Eighteenth Amendment.

Writing

Pamphlets might include the following points: working conditions—safety hazards, low pay, and long work hours; social effects—death, injury, family disruption, and poverty; reasons for court protection—the need to protect workers.

Building Social Studies Skills

1. c

2. Some Great Plains and northeastern states banned alcohol first; then most of the southern states; many western states by 1919; some Midwest states and California not until the Eighteenth Amendment.

3. c

4. Answers will vary, but students might suggest that the Genthe photograph shows a family outside in proper dress, while the Beals photograph shows a family inside a dirty tenement.

Progressive Politicians

CHAPTER RESOURCE MANAGER

Objectives	Pacing Guide	Reproducible Resources
SECTION 1 **Reforming Government** pp. 298–302	⭐ Summarize the reforms that were enacted to make U.S. voting procedures more democratic. ⭐ Describe how reformers sought to improve city governments. ⭐ Discuss the goals of progressive state leaders.	**Regular** 1 day **Block Scheduling** .5 day *Block Scheduling Handbook with Team Teaching Strategies, pp. 55–60*	**RS** Guided Reading Strategy 10.1
SECTION 2 **Roosevelt and the Square Deal** pp. 303–09	⭐ Discuss how the response to the miners' strike and Square Deal reflected President Roosevelt's governing style. ⭐ Summarize why the government tried to regulate trusts and the food and drug industry. ⭐ Explain the stand that Gifford Pinchot and Theodore Roosevelt took on the environment.	**Regular** 2 days **Block Scheduling** 1 day *Block Scheduling Handbook with Team Teaching Strategies, pp. 55–60*	**RS** Guided Reading Strategy 10.2 **SM** Geography Activity 10: Theodore Roosevelt—A Biographical Map **E** Creative Teaching Strategy: Collage Lesson **E** Hands-On History Activity: Equal Rights for Women
SECTION 3 **Reform Under Taft** pp. 310–14	⭐ Relate what progressive reforms were enacted during President Taft's administration. ⭐ Explain what divisions in the Republican Party led to the formation of the Progressive Party. ⭐ Describe how Woodrow Wilson won the 1912 presidential election.	**Regular** 1 day **Block Scheduling** .5 day *Block Scheduling Handbook with Team Teaching Strategies, pp. 55–60*	**RS** Guided Reading Strategy 10.3 **PS** Biography Reading 10: Eugene Debs
SECTION 4 **Wilson's "New Freedom"** pp. 315–21	⭐ Describe how Woodrow Wilson's proposals affected big business and U.S. citizens. ⭐ Explain how President Wilson attempted to help farmers and laborers, and how successful his efforts were. ⭐ Discuss how American women gained the right to vote.	**Regular** 2 days **Block Scheduling** 1 day *Block Scheduling Handbook with Team Teaching Strategies, pp. 55–60*	**RS** Guided Reading Strategy 10.4 **IC** Literature Reading 10: Life as a Factory Worker **PS** Primary Source Reading 10: Child Labor Practices **RS** Graphic Organizer Activity 10: Women's Suffrage

Chapter Resource Key

PS	Primary Sources	**REV**	Review		Video
RS	Reading Support	**ELL**	Reinforcement and English Language Learners		Internet
IC	Interdisciplinary Connections				Holt Presentation Maker Using Microsoft® PowerPoint®
E	Enrichment		Transparencies		
SM	Skills Mastery		CD–ROM		
A	Assessment		Music		

One-Stop Planner CD-ROM

See the *One-Stop Planner* for a complete list of additional resources for students and teachers.

One-Stop Planner CD–ROM

It's easy to plan lessons, select resources, and print out materials for your students when you use the *One-Stop Planner CD–ROM with Test Generator.*

internet connect

HRW ONLINE RESOURCES
  GO TO: go.hrw.com
  Then type in a keyword.

TEACHER HOME PAGE
  KEYWORD: SE3 Teacher

CHAPTER INTERNET ACTIVITIES
  KEYWORD: SE3 AN10
  Choose an activity to:
- learn about Theodore Roosevelt and the national park system.
- use a database on oil and gasoline prices and create a graph that shows changes in price.
- research the conditions that resulted in the Meat Inspection Act and write a journal entry.

CHAPTER ENRICHMENT LINKS
  KEYWORD: SE3 CH10

ONLINE ASSESSMENT
  Homework Practice
  KEYWORD: SE3 HP10

  Standardized Test Prep
  KEYWORD: SE3 STP10

  Rubrics
  KEYWORD: SS Rubrics

ONLINE MAPS, CHARTS, AND GRAPHS
  KEYWORD: SE3 MCG
- National Parks
- Election of 1912

CONTENT UPDATES
  KEYWORD: SS Content Updates

HOLT PRESENTATION MAKER
  KEYWORD: SE3 PPT10

ONLINE READING SUPPORT
  KEYWORD: SS Strategies

CURRENT EVENTS
  KEYWORD: S3 Current Events

Technology Resources

 One-Stop Planner, Lesson 10.1
 Holt Researcher: American History CD–ROM
 Homework Practice Online

Reinforcement, Review, and Assessment

REV Section 1 Review, p. 302
A Daily Quiz 10.1
ELL Main Idea Activity 10.1
ELL English Audio Summary 10.1
ELL Spanish Audio Summary 10.1

 One-Stop Planner, Lesson 10.2
 The American Nation Video Program Segment: Yosemite National Park; Teacher's Guide, 87–92
CNN Presents America: Yesterday and Today, 1850 to the Present Segment: FDA on the Lookout
Holt Researcher: American History CD–ROM
Homework Practice Online
HRW Go site

REV Section 2 Review, p. 309
A Daily Quiz 10.2
ELL Main Idea Activity 10.2
ELL English Audio Summary 10.2
ELL Spanish Audio Summary 10.2

 One-Stop Planner, Lesson 10.3
 Holt Researcher: American History CD–ROM
 Homework Practice Online

REV Section 3 Review, p. 314
A Daily Quiz 10.3
ELL Main Idea Activity 10.3
ELL English Audio Summary 10.3
ELL Spanish Audio Summary 10.3

 One-Stop Planner, Lesson 10.4
 Holt Researcher: American History CD–ROM
 Homework Practice Online

REV Section 4 Review, p. 321
A Daily Quiz 10.4
ELL Main Idea Activity 10.4
ELL English Audio Summary 10.4
ELL Spanish Audio Summary 10.4

Chapter Review and Assessment

 Global Skill Builder CD–ROM
 HRW Go site
REV **Chapter 10 Tutorial for Students, Parents, Mentors, and Peers**
REV **Chapter 10 Review, pp. 322–23**
Chapter 10 Test Generator (on the One-Stop Planner)
A **Chapter 10 Test (Form A or B)**
A **Alternative Assessment Handbook**
A **Chapter 10 Test for English Language Learners and Special-Needs Students**

Meeting Individual Needs

Ability Levels

Level 1 Basic-level activities designed for all students encountering new material

Level 2 Intermediate-level activities designed for average students

Level 3 Challenging activities designed for honors and gifted-and-talented students

English Language Learners Activities that address the needs of students with Limited English Proficiency

Build on What You Know

Ask students to answer the following questions.

Why might many Americans have become interested in reforming society?
Consider:

• the many social problems created by rapid industrialization and urbanization

• the effects of a widening split between the rich and the poor

How might Americans have attempted to conquer the negative effects of industrialization and urbanization?
Consider:

• the causes of such problems

• the possible constitutional remedies to such problems

• the importance of protest

---

exploring the time line

AMERICAN EVENTS

☑ **internet** connect

TOPIC: Oil Production
GO TO: go.hrw.com
KEYWORD: SE3 AN10

Have students access the Internet through the HRW Go site to locate and use databases on oil and gas prices. Then have each student use the Holt Grapher to create two graphs: one that shows the increase in oil production and one that shows the price of gasoline. Have students write summary statements that compare and contrast the two graphs.

CHAPTER 10

1900–1920
Progressive Politicians

Oil gusher in Spindletop oil field

African American farmers in the early 1900s

1906
Politics
Congress passes the Meat Inspection Act.

1906
Science and Technology
Lee De Forest invents the three-element vacuum repeater for telephones, improving voice quality in long-distance calls.

1904
Business and Finance
The U.S. Supreme Court rules that the Northern Securities Company has violated antitrust laws and orders it dissolved.

1901
Science and Technology
Oil production increases with new drilling practices that yield an estimated 100,000 barrels a day in a nine-day period in one Texas well.

1908
Business and Finance
Thirty-five percent of American workers are employed in agriculture.

1900

1904

1908

1900
Daily Life
A hurricane strikes Galveston, Texas, killing at least 6,000 people.

1904
Daily Life
The winning vehicle in the Vanderbilt Challenge Cup automobile race averages 52.2 miles per hour.

1907
The Arts
Cartoonist Rube Goldberg creates a character who invents unusual contraptions for everyday problems.

1908
Politics
A White House conference on conservation leads to the creation of a commission to study natural resource issues.

Hurricane damage in Galveston, Texas, in 1900

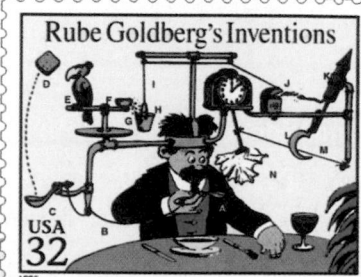

Rube Goldberg's Inventions

USA 32

Stamp honoring Rube Goldberg

Build on What You Know

During the early 1900s many Americans took a new interest in reforming society. Now known as the Progressive Era, this time period was marked by great optimism and faith in scientific efficiency. Progressive reformers set out to conquer such negative effects of industrialization and rapid urbanization as unsafe working conditions, long hours, low wages, and slum housing. In this chapter you will learn about the successes and failures of progressive politicians, including Presidents Theodore Roosevelt, William Howard Taft, and Woodrow Wilson.

To help students create their Themes Journal entries, provide the following examples of appropriate agree/disagree *statements.*

Government

Agree Some companies have developed sound, widely applicable management techniques.

Disagree Many leading entrepreneurs of the Second Industrial Revolution ran their companies as near dictatorships.

Economics

Agree Many entrepreneurs of the Second Industrial Revolution viewed laissez-faire economics as crucial to sound business operations.

Disagree Throughout American history, many reformers have argued that the federal government should regulate businesses in order to protect citizens and the environment.

Constitutional Heritage

Agree The Founding Fathers could not foresee the changes created by rapid industrialization and urbanization.

Disagree The Constitution contains timeless principles that are the foundation of American democracy.

THE GRANGER COLLECTION, NEW YORK

George Bellow's painting **Lone Tenement,** *completed in 1909*

1917
The Arts
The era of the American Renaissance in art draws to a close.

1917
Daily Life
Trolley-car ridership reaches 11 million in the United States.

1917
World Events
Mexico adopts a new constitution.

1919
Business and Finance
Per capita income among southerners is 40 percent lower than the national average.

1910
World Events
A Chinese army tries to take direct control of Tibet's government by force.

1913
Business and Finance
The Federal Reserve Act reorganizes the national banking system.

1914
Politics
The Clayton Antitrust Act is passed.

1912

1916

1920

1912
Politics
Theodore Roosevelt and his supporters form the Progressive Party.

1914
Science and Technology
The amount of electric power used in manufacturing industries reaches 3.8 million horsepower.

1920
Politics
The Nineteenth Amendment gives American women the right to vote.

PROGRESSIVE PARTY FOR PRESIDENT

THEODORE ROOSEVELT

Theodore Roosevelt campaign banner

MR. PRESIDENT WHAT WILL YOU DO FOR WOMAN SUFFRAGE

Suffrage supporter

What's Your Opinion?

Themes Journal *Do you* agree *or* disagree *with the following statements? Support your point of view in your journal.*

Government The management of a business corporation provides a good model for city government.

Economics Government regulation of business should never limit or restrict corporations' activities.

Constitutional Heritage Each generation should reinterpret the Constitution for itself, as social and economic realities change.

1910 ■ China and Tibet.
Conflict between China and Tibet continued throughout the 1900s. In 1951 China assumed control of Tibet, claiming that the region had always been a Chinese province. The Tibetans disagreed, arguing that they had long been an independent nation. The Tibetans later revolted, but the Chinese crushed the rebellion and the Dalai Lama, the spiritual leader of Tibet, went into exile. In November 1998 the Dalai Lama met with U.S. government officials, leading Chinese leaders to protest. Months later, Tibetans in India and Nepal held protests in remembrance of the rebellion. During the protests the Dalai Lama claimed that the Chinese continued to oppress the people of Tibet.

CRITICAL THINKING Why might Chinese leaders have protested the Dalai Lama's visit with top U.S. officials?

ANSWER: Students might suggest that the meeting gave support to the Tibetan contention that the Chinese occupation of Tibet was illegal.

After completing Section 1, students should be able to:

OBJECTIVE 1 *Summarize the reforms that were enacted to make U.S. voting procedures more democratic.*

OBJECTIVE 2 *Describe how reformers sought to improve city governments.*

OBJECTIVE 3 *Discuss the goals of progressive state leaders.*

🎙 LET'S GET STARTED!

As students enter the classroom, ask them to list two goals and two strategies of progressive reformers. *(Students might note that reformers wanted to improve cities, help immigrants, and end political corruption. They might also note that reformers attempted to lobby for new laws, pressure the federal government, and conduct protests.)* Have volunteers share their responses. Then tell students that in Section 1 they will learn how progressive reformers and politicians attempted to reform American politics in the early 1900s.

SECTION ① RESOURCES

REPRODUCIBLE
▶ Guided Reading Strategy 10.1

TECHNOLOGY
▶ One-Stop Planner, Lesson 10.1
▶ Holt Researcher: American History CD–ROM
▶ Homework Practice Online

REINFORCEMENT, REVIEW, AND ASSESSMENT
▶ Section 1 Review, p. 302
▶ Daily Quiz 10.1
▶ Main Idea Activity 10.1
▶ English Audio Summary 10.1
▶ Spanish Audio Summary 10.1

SECTION ①

▶ READ TO DISCOVER

1. What reforms were enacted to make U.S. voting procedures more democratic?
2. How did reformers seek to improve city governments?
3. What were the goals of progressive state leaders?

■ DEFINE

direct primary
initiative
referendum
recall

■ IDENTIFY

Seventeenth Amendment
Samuel M. Jones
Tom Johnson
Robert M. La Follette
Wisconsin Idea

▶ WHY IT MATTERS TODAY

The relationship between government and business is still changing. Use **CNNfyi.com** or other **current events** sources to find out one way in which government tries to regulate business today. Record your findings in your journal.

CNNfyi.com

Reforming Government

Author Lincoln Steffens

 EYEWITNESSES TO History

❝*The American reformer's story is a modern tragedy of defeat, humiliation, martyrdom. . . . [There is evidence] to show the regular, outrageous grafting . . . in all public business.*❞

—Oliver McClintock, quoted in *America Enters the World*, by Page Smith

Pittsburgh reformer Oliver McClintock "knew and could prove what was going on," progressive reformer Lincoln Steffens wrote. Steffens's book *The Shame of the Cities* vividly depicted the workings of turn-of-the-century urban politics. In many cities, he said, a political boss controlled municipal government. The boss had a strong opponent, however—the reformer.

Government Corruption

Progressive reformers such as Lincoln Steffens found corruption at all levels of government, from city hall to Washington, D.C. City political machines were often linked to the Democratic or Republican state machines. The state machines catered to special interests, making deals with railroads, lumber companies, or anyone else seeking tax breaks or other favors from state legislatures. In return, the machines expected generous gifts, often in the form of campaign contributions.

In the 1890s some people began referring to the U.S. Senate as the Millionaire's Club. Some said that Senator James McMillan of Michigan represented shipping and lumber interests instead of his constituents. Others argued that Senator Joseph Foraker of Ohio put Standard Oil's needs above all others. Often put into power by state machines, some U.S. senators accepted bribes to vote the way corporations wished. In 1906 progressive writer David Graham Phillips published a series of articles documenting how special interests influenced U.S. politics.

 History Makers Speak

❝*The greatest single hold of 'the interests' is the fact that they are the 'campaign contributors.' . . . Who pays the big election expenses of your congress man, of the men you send to the legislature to elect senators? Do you imagine those who foot those huge bills are fools? Don't you know that they make sure of getting their money back, with interest?*❞

—David Graham Phillips, "The Treason of the Senate," 1906

Election Reforms

Reformers seeking a return to honest government rallied to the slogan, "Give the government back to the people!" They believed that only when government listened to the public's voice could the urgent problems facing Americans be fixed.

Progressives sought to break the power of political bosses by reforming the election process. First, they wanted to take the power of choosing candidates away from political machines. Therefore, progressives pushed for the **direct primary**—a nominating election in which voters choose the candidates who later run in

ALL LEVELS: Ask students to characterize the state of voting practices in the United States before the advent of voting reforms in the early 1900s. (*Students should indicate that the practices were highly corrupt.*) Ask students how they would have attempted to reform such practices, had they been reformers or officials. (*Answers will vary. Some students will suggest measures to decrease corruption.*) To help students understand the actual reforms that took place during the period, copy the following graphic organizer on the chalkboard, omitting the italicized answers. Have each student complete it. **English Language Learners**

- **direct primary**—*voters pick the candidates to run in a general election*
- **Seventeenth Amendment**—*voters elect their senators directly*
- **secret ballot**—*candidates are selected from a single, uniform ballot*
- **initiative**—*gives voters the power to initiate legislation*
- **referendum**—*allows voters to approve or veto a recently passed law*
- **recall**—*enables voters to remove an elected official from office*

Election Reforms ↓

Greater Voter Rights

HOMEWORK *Ask each student to write two paragraphs explaining how the election reforms of the early 1900s made government more democratic and more responsive to the people.*

---

a general election. Previously, voters had elected delegates who then selected candidates. Mississippi adopted the direct primary in 1902. Wisconsin followed in 1903. By 1916 most others states had done the same.

Next, progressives proposed to change the method of electing U.S. senators. The U.S. Constitution gave state legislatures the power to elect senators. Progressives claimed that this procedure made it easy for political machines with influence over state officials to control government. By 1912 the progressive influence led Congress to propose the **Seventeenth Amendment**, which gave voters the power to elect their senators directly. The amendment was ratified the next year.

Progressives also sought to reform the voting-day process. At the time, each political party printed its own ballot in a distinctive color. At polling places, the colored ballots made it easy to see how people voted. Without secrecy, voters could be pressured to support certain candidates. To lessen this threat, progressives proposed using the secret ballot. Developed in Australia, the secret ballot lists all candidates on a single, uniform sheet of paper. By 1910 most states had switched to the secret ballot.

Finally, progressives urged states to adopt three additional election-reform measures: the initiative, the referendum, and the recall. The **initiative** gives voters the power to initiate, or introduce, legislation. If a certain percentage of voters in a state—usually 5 to 15 percent—signs a petition, a proposed policy must be put on the ballot for public approval. The **referendum** is a companion to the initiative. By securing a specified number of signatures on a petition, citizens can force the legislature to place a recently passed law on the ballot, allowing voters to approve or veto the measure. The **recall** enables voters to remove an elected official from office by calling for a special election.

William Allen White referred to voting reforms as "a big moral movement in democracy." In 1910 White claimed victory for reformers.

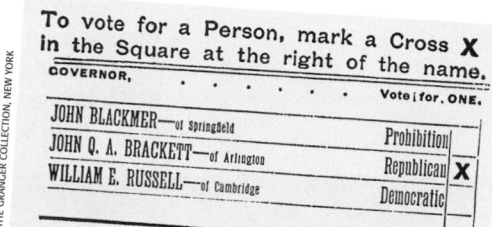

THE GRANGER COLLECTION, NEW YORK

To vote for a Person, mark a Cross **X** in the Square at the right of the name.

GOVERNOR,		Vote for ONE.
JOHN BLACKMER—*of Springfield*	Prohibition	
JOHN Q. A. BRACKETT—*of Arlington*	Republican	**X**
WILLIAM E. RUSSELL—*of Cambridge*	Democratic	

This Australian-style ballot lists all candidates on a single, uniform sheet of paper.

History Makers Speak

"Today in states having the primary under the state control the corporation [political machine] candidate for any public office is handicapped."

—William Allen White, "The Revival of Democracy," 1910

In practice, however, the effects of the voting reforms were mixed, and business continued to influence elections.

✔ **READING CHECK: Evaluating** How did progressive reforms make U.S. voting procedures more democratic? by allowing voters to directly nominate candidates, by giving voters the power to directly elect their senators, and by protecting voters' privacy

PRIMARY SOURCE

Another View of Government Reform

While most progressives supported election reforms as a way to return to honest government, some Americans offered other suggestions. In a 1915 magazine article, journalist Walker D. Hines argued that state governments needed to be restructured to improve their effectiveness and efficiency. **How does Hines' plan conflict with the idea of separation of powers?**

"Any change in the direction of providing a constitutional leadership in the legislature, responsible to the state as a whole, will be worthy of serious consideration. The plan of giving the governor himself this leadership is probably best, because thereby the serious disadvantages of separating the law-making function from the law-enforcing function will be seriously overcome. . . .

It is fair to inquire whether the blending of these two departments would not be in the direction of strengthening representative government, making it more responsive to the popular will and at the same time more efficient. . . . Popular government promises to be increasingly more complicated and difficult and to call for a higher order of training on their part of the public's representatives. It is a fair question whether the accomplishment of these important results would not be promoted by blending the Executive and Legislative Departments."

CITIZENSHIP

Third Parties and Secret Ballots. After the adoption of the secret ballot, states printed and issued the tickets, as opposed to political parties doing so. Even today, independent and third-party candidates sometimes face obstacles when they try to find a place on these ballots. In Florida, for example, independent party candidates must acquire signatures from 3 percent of the voters registered in the previous election before being placed on the ballot as a candidate for governor or U.S. senator. In 1992 third-party candidates needed 196,000 signatures.

CRITICAL THINKING Why might such requirements be imposed on third-party candidates?

ANSWER: Some students might argue that such requirements are used to prevent frivolous candidates from running, while others might argue that the two leading parties want to prevent challenges to their power.

PRIMARY SOURCE ANSWER

Students might suggest that it would blend the executive and legislative branches and give one branch the authority to make and enforce laws.

LEVEL 1: Pair students and tell them to imagine that it is 1905 and that they are reformist city officials in the Midwest. Have each pair develop a three- to four-minute dialogue describing how it will seek to improve its city government. (*Pairs should mention attempts to improve the police force, improve municipal services, enact labor reforms, and hire city managers.*) Ask volunteers to perform their dialogues for the class. **English Language Learners, Cooperative Learning**

LEVEL 2: Tell students to imagine that it is 1905 and that they are reformist city officials in the Midwest. Have each student write a half-page letter to the editor of the local newspaper describing how he or she will seek to improve city governments. (*See the Level 1 lesson for the correct plans.*) Ask volunteers to read their letters to the class. Students may wish to include their letters in their portfolios.

LEVEL 3: Organize students into triads and tell them to imagine that it is 1905 and that they are reformist city officials in the Midwest. Have each triad discuss the ways in which it will seek to improve city governments. (*See the Level 1 lesson for the correct plans.*) Then have each triad write short public notice statements describing the need for such reforms and explaining the benefits of such reforms. Ask volunteers to present their public notice statements to the class. **Cooperative Learning**

PEOPLE IN HISTORY

Samuel M. Jones. Samuel M. Jones was born in Wales and moved to the United States with his family soon after his birth. As a young man he worked in the Pennsylvania oil fields. He later became extremely wealthy manufacturing oil-field equipment. Concerned about the lives of his factory workers, Jones approved an eight-hour workday and gave his employees paid vacations. His efforts made him well known and immensely popular. Some 55,000 mourners attended his funeral in 1904.

CRITICAL THINKING How might Jones have differed from many other American businesspeople of the period?

ANSWER: Students might suggest that Jones adopted many labor reforms before they were required by law.

VISUAL RECORD ANSWER

Students might suggest that kindergartens provided education, socialization, and a sense of community.

INTERPRETING THE VISUAL RECORD

Reforming city government. Samuel M. Jones enacted many reforms as mayor of Toledo, Ohio. ***How do you think kindergartens like this one benefited the residents of Toledo?***

Reforming City Government

The drive to clean up city government typically owed its successes to enthusiastic local leaders and active reformers. Through such efforts, the "good-government" campaign put some reform mayors into office.

Two of the most successful reform mayors were elected in Ohio. Both **Samuel M. Jones** and **Tom Johnson** were self-made men who earned their fortunes early in life. Then in midlife they traded business for politics.

The mayors. Samuel M. "Golden Rule" Jones's nickname came from his belief in the biblical Golden Rule—"Do unto others as you would have them do unto you." Seeking to apply this principle to government, Jones successfully ran for mayor of Toledo in 1897. During the next seven years he overhauled the police force, improved municipal services, set a minimum wage for city workers, and opened kindergartens for children.

During this same period, Tom Johnson served as mayor of Cleveland. Johnson created new rules for Cleveland's police department and released debtors from prison. He also supported a new, fairer single tax system. Reformer Frederic Howe described Johnson's desire for such a system as "a passion for freedom, for a world of equal opportunity for all." Johnson's success led Lincoln Steffens to call him "the best mayor of the best governed city in the United States."

A mixed record. A few popular mayors alone, however, could not conquer established patterns of corruption in city government. The reformers' attempts to achieve basic governmental changes had mixed results. Lincoln Steffens concluded that voters did not necessarily prefer democratic governments because machine-run politics was more predictable. Reformers were also disappointed by some of the results of their direct government movement that encouraged voters' input in government decisions. For instance, voters rejected some measures favored by progressives such as municipal ownership of public utilities, tax reform, and pensions for city employees.

Electoral reform was further hindered by the fact that many middle-class progressives feared that the lower classes might gain too much power. They wanted to curb the power of big business, but feared that urban masses would gain too great a voice in political decision making. One reform leader, F. E. Chadwick of Newport, Rhode Island, maintained that a voter who paid higher taxes "should be assured a representation in the committee which . . . spends the money which he contributes." Chadwick believed that a "truly democratic" government would "give the property owner a fair show."

City commissions and managers. A devastating hurricane that struck Galveston, Texas, in 1900 produced an alternative to political machines. A tidal wave created by the storm killed at least 6,000 people and destroyed the city. Galveston's government was unable to cope with the emergency. The state legislature named a five-person city commission to rebuild the area. The commissioners were experts in their fields rather than party loyalists. Citizens praised the

TEACH OBJECTIVE 3

LEVEL 1: Conduct a discussion on progressive state leaders and their goals. *(On the whole, progressive state leaders wanted to enact the direct primary, increase taxes on railroads and public utilities, pass laws that curbed lobbying, establish stricter controls on certain industries, and so on.)* List the main points of this discussion on the chalkboard. Ask each student to use the chalkboard list to write a paragraph on the goals of progressive state leaders. Students may wish to include their paragraphs in their portfolios. **English Language Learners**

LEVELS 2 AND 3: Tell students to imagine that they are Robert M. La Follette, Charles Evans Hughes, James Vardaman, or another progressive state leader. Have each student write a three- to five-minute speech explaining and justifying his or her goals for progressive reforms. *(See the Level 1 lesson for the correct goals.)* Ask volunteers to deliver their speeches to the class. Students may wish to include their speeches in their portfolios.

HOMEWORK *Write the following statement on the chalkboard:* In cities, business was often the friend of government reform. At the state level, however, business was often its foe. *Have each student write two or three paragraphs assessing this statement, including evidence that supports his or her points.*

---

commission as being more honest and efficient than the city's previous government. Galveston kept the system, and other cities in the United States soon established similar commissions. The desire for increased efficiency also gave rise to the hiring of city managers. These individuals are expert administrators employed to run cities as they might run a business.

✔ **READING CHECK: Drawing Conclusions** How did city government reforms reflect the goals of progressivism? Establishing city commissions and employing city managers reflected the goal of ending corruption and increasing efficiency.

Skill-Building Strategies

Interpreting Political Cartoons

Much like photographs, political cartoons can serve as unique and valuable primary sources of historical information. A *political cartoon* is a humorous or satirical drawing that presents an opinion about a specific person, group, issue, idea, or event. Political cartoons usually appear in the editorial sections of newspapers and newsmagazines. While some express a positive outlook, the great majority are critical of their subjects.

Political cartoonists frequently use caricatures and symbolism to communicate their message. A *caricature* is a drawing that exaggerates or distorts a subject's physical features. *Symbolism* is the use of an image or thing to stand for something else. The image of "Uncle Sam," for instance, is often used to represent the United States in political cartoons. Along with caricatures and symbolism, many political cartoonists use labels, speech balloons, and other forms of text to clarify the meaning of their artistic works.

How to Interpret a Political Cartoon

1. **Identify the subject.** Look at the figures and objects in the cartoon and identify its basic subject. If the cartoon has a title, study it for clues about the cartoonist's point of view.
2. **Examine the caricatures and symbols.** If the cartoon uses caricatures, note how each figure is distorted or exaggerated and determine the meaning of the distortion or exaggeration. If the cartoon employs symbolism, determine what each symbol represents.
3. **Study the labels.** Read any labels, speech balloons, captions, or other text that may help clarify the meaning of the cartoon.

4. **Determine the cartoonist's message.** Use your examination of the figures, objects, and text in the cartoon to determine the cartoonist's message.
5. **Put the information to use.** Compare the cartoonist's message with information about the historical period that you have gained through other sources. In turn, use the results of this comparison to form generalizations and draw conclusions.

Applying the Skill

Study the political cartoon to the right, entitled "The Police Version of It." As you do so, note the cartoonist's use of symbolism and determine the cartoonist's message.

THE GRANGER COLLECTION, NEW YORK

THE POLICE VERSION OF IT.
"Let no guilty man (or woman) escape — widout dey put up de stuff!"

Practicing the Skill

Answer the following questions.

1. What does the vise in this cartoon symbolize?
2. How do the labels on the human figures help clarify the meaning of the cartoon?
3. What message is the cartoonist trying to communicate with this cartoon?
4. Why is the cartoon entitled "The Police Version of It"?

INTERDISCIPLINARY CONNECTIONS

▶GEOGRAPHY◀

The Galveston Hurricane. Many scholars regard the 1900 Galveston hurricane as one of the worst natural disasters in American history. At one point during the hurricane, the entire city was underwater—in some places by as much as 15 feet. The hurricane and flood destroyed some 2,600 houses. Aided by progressive managers and planners, however, the city was able to recover and flourish. To protect against future storms, officials built an enormous seawall. In 1961 this seawall lessened the damage from a potentially devastating hurricane and flood.

CRITICAL THINKING Besides seawalls, how else might city officials try to protect urban areas against natural disasters?

ANSWER: Some students might mention dikes or earthquake safeguards.

SKILL-BUILDING STRATEGIES ANSWERS
Practicing the Skill
1. the effort to squeeze out bribes or kickbacks
2. The labels indicate the identities of the figures.
3. that police officers tried to get bribes or kickbacks
4. The title refers to police graft.

REVIEW

Have students complete the **Section 1 Review** on p. 302.

ASSESS

Have students complete **Daily Quiz 10.1.** As **Alternative Assessment,** you may want to use the city official dialogue or progressive state leader speech in this section's lessons.

RETEACH

Have students complete **Main Idea Activity for English Language Learners and Special-Needs Students 10.1.** Then have each student write a summary sentence for each subsection in Section 1. Select students to read their statements to the class. Have the class choose the best summary sentence for each subsection, justifying its selections.
English Language Learners

EXTEND

Have students conduct research on Robert M. La Follette. Then pair students. Ask one member to act as a radio interviewer and the other to act as La Follette. Have both members prepare written material for the interview. Then ask volunteers to conduct their interviews in front of the class. To conclude, ask the students to discuss the accuracy of both the questions and the responses. Did they reflect the governor's personality? Did they reflect the political issues of the time?
Cooperative Learning, Block Scheduling

As one of the progressive movement's most energetic leaders, Robert M. La Follette supported a reform program in Wisconsin that became a model for other states.

Reforming State Government

The spirit of reform also stirred many politicians at the state level. In Wisconsin, **Robert M. La Follette** began his political career as a loyal Republican. However, he soon found himself at odds with Wisconsin's Republican political machine, which was dominated by railroad and lumber interests. La Follette served as a county district attorney and as a member of Congress in the late 1800s. He signaled his break with the party machine by refusing a bribe from a party boss.

Elected governor in 1900, La Follette vigorously backed a reform program—soon known as the **Wisconsin Idea**—that became a model for other states. First, La Follette called for a direct primary. Although the Republican machine opposed his efforts for two years, La Follette refused to accept a compromise. He declared that "in legislation *no bread* is often better than *half a loaf.*" He then urged the state legislature to increase taxes on railroads and public utilities—electric, gas, and streetcar companies—and to create commissions to regulate these companies in the public interest. La Follette helped pass laws that curbed excessive lobbying. He also backed labor reforms and worked to conserve Wisconsin's natural resources. In 1905 the Wisconsin legislature elected La Follette to the U.S. Senate. La Follette remained committed to "the struggle between labor and those who would control, through slavery in one form or another, the laborers."

La Follette influenced other state leaders. New York governor Charles Evans Hughes established stricter controls of insurance companies and utilities. Progressive Democrat James Vardaman of Mississippi and Hoke Smith of Georgia led white farmers in a fight against corporate power. As governor, Vardaman abolished the use of convict labor. He also regulated corporations and improved social services for poor whites. However, these southern progressives often supported racial segregation and tried to keep African Americans from voting.

✔ **READING CHECK: Contrasting** How did state government reforms differ from local government reforms? State reforms focused on regulation of statewide industries. Local reforms were focused on increasing the level of professionalism of municipal officials.

SECTION 1 REVIEW

1. Define and explain:
direct primary
initiative
referendum
recall

2. Identify and explain:
Seventeenth Amendment
Samuel M. Jones
Tom Johnson
Robert M. La Follette
Wisconsin Idea

3. Using Graphic Organizers
Copy the diagram below. Use it to explain what reforms progressives proposed at the city and state levels and where those reforms overlapped.

State Reforms — Shared — City Reforms

4. **Finding the Main Idea**
a. How did the growth of political machines contribute to corruption in government?
b. How did changes in voting procedures enable government leaders to be elected more democratically?
c. How did many U.S. cities try to increase government efficiency and lessen corruption?

5. **Writing and Critical Thinking**
Evaluating Write a brief biography of Robert M. La Follette focusing on his impact on American society.
Consider:
- the reforms that made up the Wisconsin Idea
- his leadership qualities
- the influence his ideas had on others

Homework Practice Online
keyword: SE3 HP10

SECTION 2

After completing Section 2, students should be able to:

OBJECTIVE 1 *Discuss how the response to the miners' strike and Square Deal reflected President Roosevelt's governing style.*

OBJECTIVE 2 *Summarize why the government tried to regulate trusts and the food and drug industry.*

OBJECTIVE 3 *Explain the stand that Gifford Pinchot and Theodore Roosevelt took on the environment.*

 LET'S GET STARTED

As students enter the classroom, have them examine the illustration of a drug advertisement in this section. Have them read the quotation by Samuel Hopkins Adams to the right of the illustration. Ask students to respond to the illustration and the quotation in writing, explaining what the pills were supposed to do and why Adams wrote what he did. Have volunteers share their responses. Tell students that in Section 2 they will learn about how reformers attempted to protect consumers against unsubstantiated claims.

SECTION 2

READ TO DISCOVER

1. What was President Roosevelt's governing style?
2. Why did the government attempt to regulate trusts and the food and drug industries?
3. How did the conservation movement develop during Theodore Roosevelt's presidency?

DEFINE

arbitration
reclamation

IDENTIFY

Theodore Roosevelt
Square Deal
Elkins Act
Hepburn Act
Upton Sinclair
Meat Inspection Act
Pure Food and Drug Act
Gifford Pinchot
National Park Service

WHY IT MATTERS TODAY

Environmental issues remain important in politics today. Use CNNfyi.com or other **current events** sources to learn about the opposing views on one or more environmental issues today. Record your findings in your journal.

CNNfyi.com

Roosevelt and the Square Deal

EYEWITNESSES TO History

❝*[The tower] assumes a magical aspect, as if it had been summoned forth by the genius of our united people.*❞

—Julian Hawthorne, *Cosmopolitan Magazine*, 1901

Pan-American Exposition button

A writer for *Cosmopolitan Magazine* described the Electric Tower at the Pan-American Exposition held in Buffalo, New York, in 1901. Standing 375 feet tall, the tower served as a powerful symbol of American success. Americans at the turn of the century saw this and the other exhibits at the Pan-American Exposition as commemorating their industrial progress, rising prosperity, and increasing world power. The visit of President William McKinley was intended to be the highlight of the exposition. He believed that such public festivities recorded American achievements and led to greater enthusiasm and energy for industrial pursuits. He also thought they brought joy to the American people.

Roosevelt Becomes President

In 1900 President McKinley ran for re-election with **Theodore Roosevelt** as his running mate. The Democrats again nominated William Jennings Bryan and made free silver and the economy the focus of their campaign. In 1900 most Americans felt prosperous, and McKinley and Roosevelt sailed to victory.

As governor of New York, Roosevelt had worked to reform government and regulate big business. New York's conservative Republican Party leaders were angered by this progressive activism. They had tried to ease Roosevelt out of state office by persuading him to run as vice president. Senator Mark Hanna, a conservative from Ohio, was alarmed by this move. He warned that there would be "only one life between this madman and the Presidency."

Roosevelt takes office. The nation was shocked when, on September 6, 1901, anarchist Leon Czolgosz (CHAWL-gawsh) shot McKinley at the Pan-American Exposition. An unemployed laborer, Czolgosz claimed to act on behalf of the poor and the forgotten. Eight days later McKinley died, and Roosevelt became president.

Roosevelt was just 42 years old when he took the presidential oath. He set about the task of reform with enthusiasm and energy. Roosevelt brought dynamic leadership to the progressive movement. He helped reshape the country as surely as he renamed the Executive Mansion the White House.

During the Gilded Age U.S. presidents generally took a hands-off approach to government. Roosevelt, however, believed that the president should use the office as a "bully pulpit" to speak out on vital issues. One of Roosevelt's goals as president was to fight class distinctions. "No republic can permanently exist when it becomes a republic of classes," he warned.

SECTION 2 RESOURCES

REPRODUCIBLE

▶ Guided Reading Strategy 10.2
▶ Geography Activity 10: Theodore Roosevelt— A Biographical Map

TECHNOLOGY

▶ One-Stop Planner, Lesson 10.2
▶ The American Nation Video Program Segment: Yosemite National Park; Teacher's Guide, 87–92
▶ CNN Presents America: Yesterday and Today Segment: FDA on the Lookout
▶ Holt Researcher: American History CD–ROM
▶ HRW Go site
▶ Homework Practice Online

REINFORCEMENT, REVIEW, AND ASSESSMENT

▶ Section 2 Review, p. 309
▶ Daily Quiz 10.2
▶ Main Idea Activity 10.2
▶ English Audio Summary 10.2
▶ Spanish Audio Summary 10.2

Teacher to Teacher

Lucinda Lucero Sachs of Albuquerque, New Mexico, suggested the following activity: Ask students to read the subsection entitled Roosevelt Becomes President. Ask them to consider his involvement in the United Mine Workers' Strike. Then write the following question on the chalkboard: Should government regulate business or keep its hands off? *Act as a moderator and conduct a debate on the topic.*

TEACH OBJECTIVE 1

LEVEL 1: Conduct a brief lecture on Theodore Roosevelt as a reform president. Then organize students into triads. Have each triad create four newspaper headlines on President Roosevelt's governing style—two on his handling of the miners' strike and two on his Square Deal. *(Students' headlines should indicate that Roosevelt encouraged both sides in the strike to accept arbitration, demonstrating his concern for both workers and businesses. This concern informed his Square Deal as well.)* Ask each triad to write topic sentences or lead-in sentences for each of its newspaper headlines. Have spokespeople read their triad's topic sentences to the class.
English Language Learners, Cooperative Learning

ECONOMICS

The Importance of Coal.
In the early 1900s, many Americans used coal to heat their homes. As the miners' strike continued into the cold autumn months, many Americans feared that they would be unable to heat their homes. The price of remaining coal supplies rose dramatically, from $5 to $20 per ton. Some people panicked at the prices and shortages. In one New York town residents chopped down telegraph poles to use as firewood.

CRITICAL THINKING Which energy supplies do Americans depend on today?

ANSWER: Students might suggest that many Americans now depend on electricity and gasoline.

THAT'S INTERESTING!

Coal miners purchased goods at mining company stores, which often took advantage of them. Andrew Chippie, a 12-year-old miner whose father had been killed in a mine accident, surrendered his wages—just 40 cents a day—to the Markle Coal Company in order to pay his dead father's store debt.

VISUAL RECORD ANSWER

Students might suggest that the handshake shows unity, and the badge says member.

PRESIDENTIAL Lives

Theodore Roosevelt

1858–1919
In Office 1901–1909

Theodore Roosevelt enjoyed the limelight. As one of his children remarked, Roosevelt always wanted to be "the bride at every wedding, the corpse at every funeral." This hero of the Rough Riders became a legend in his own time. Roosevelt always lived life to the fullest. "No President has ever enjoyed himself as much as I have enjoyed myself," he claimed. An old friend explained Roosevelt's great love of life: "You must always remember that the President is about six [years old]."

Roosevelt was an all-around athlete whose energy was legendary. For example, when the French ambassador once visited the White House, he and the president played tennis, jogged, and then worked out with weights. Roosevelt turned to his guest and asked, "What would you like to do now?" "If it's just the same with you, Mr. President," said the ambassador, "I'd like to lie down and die."

INTERPRETING THE VISUAL RECORD

Labor. President Theodore Roosevelt was sympathetic to coal miners during the 1902 United Mine Workers strike. *What does the badge reveal about the goals of the union?*

The United Mine Workers strike.
Soon after Roosevelt became president, a labor dispute helped define his approach to the office. In the spring of 1902 some 150,000 coal miners struck for higher wages and recognition of their United Mine Workers union. The mine owners refused to negotiate. As the strike dragged on, Washington Gladden, a reform minister, petitioned Roosevelt for help. Speaking on behalf of working-class laborers, Gladden wrote, "You can speak as no one else can speak for the plain people of this country. Every workingman knows you are his friend; no capitalist of common sense can imagine that you are his enemy." Thousands signed this petition, which was sent to the White House.

Conservatives urged Roosevelt to send in the U.S. Army to force the strikers to return to work, while some progressives wanted him to place the mines under federal control. Instead, Roosevelt encouraged the two sides to accept **arbitration**. Arbitration is the process by which two opposing sides allow a third party to settle a dispute. As winter approached, Roosevelt threatened to take over the mines. This convinced the mine owners to agree to his plan of appointing a commission of arbitrators.

After a five-week investigation, the arbitrators announced their decision. They gave both the miners and the mine owners part of what they had wanted. The workers won a shorter workday and higher pay, but the mining companies did not have to recognize the union or bargain with it. It was a landmark compromise. For the first time, the federal government had intervened in a strike to protect the interests of the workers and the public. Satisfied, Roosevelt pronounced the compromise a "square deal."

The Square Deal. The **Square Deal** became Roosevelt's 1904 campaign slogan. He promised to "see to it that every man has a square deal, no less and no more." This pledge summed up Roosevelt's belief in balancing the interests of business, consumers, and labor. Roosevelt's Square Deal called for limiting the power of trusts, promoting public health and safety, and improving working conditions.

The president was so popular with voters that no Republican dared challenge him for the 1904 nomination. Even the *New York Sun*, a pro-big business, antireform newspaper, supported Roosevelt. The paper preferred "the impulsive candidate of the party of conservatism to the conservative candidate of the party which the business interests regard as permanently and dangerously impulsive." Roosevelt won the election, easily defeating his Democratic opponent, Judge Alton Parker of New York.

✔ **READING CHECK: Contrasting** How did President Roosevelt's governing style differ from that of presidents during the Gilded Age? Most presidents during the Gilded Age took a hands-off approach; Roosevelt used his office as a "bully pulpit."

LEVELS 2 AND 3: Tell students to imagine that they are modern-day historians. Have each student write a one-page paper analyzing how the miners' strike and Square Deal reflected President Roosevelt's governing style. *(See the Level 1 lesson for the correct points.)* Ask volunteers to read their papers to the class. Then conduct a discussion on Roosevelt and his policies. Have students use information from their papers and their textbooks to assign Roosevelt a "grade" for his work as a reform president. Encourage students to fully explain and justify their ratings.

TEACH OBJECTIVE 2

LEVEL 1: Conduct a brief lecture on the practices of trusts and the food and drug industry in the early 1900s. *(Trusts often competed unfairly, forced companies to give* them rebates or discounts, sold inferior products, or corrupted public officials. Many companies sold inferior or dangerous products with little concern for consumers.) Pair students and tell them to imagine that it is 1906 and that they are reformers concerned about trusts and food and drug industry practices. Tell each pair to imagine that it has just discovered major corporate violations. Have each pair create two wanted posters for fictional violators. The posters should include text and illustrations that describe the violations. Ask volunteers to present their wanted posters to the class. Then ask students to explain how the government responded to such violations. *(Students should note that the government passed the Elkins Act, the Hepburn Act, and two consumer-protection laws in 1906.)*
English Language Learners, Cooperative Learning

Regulating Business

President Roosevelt sought to regulate large corporations during both of his terms in office. Although he considered big business essential to the nation's growth, he also believed companies should be forced to behave responsibly. "We don't wish to destroy corporations," he said, "but we do wish to make them subserve [serve] the public good." The public agreed with him. As journalist Walter Lippmann wrote, "The trusts made enemies right and left.... Labor was no match for them, state legislatures were impotent [powerless] before them."

Trustbusting. In 1902 the president took action, directing the U.S. attorney general to sue the Northern Securities Company. Controlled by J. P. Morgan and railroad barons James J. Hill and E. H. Harriman, the company monopolized railroad shipping from Chicago to the Northwest. In 1904 the Supreme Court ruled that the monopoly violated the Sherman Antitrust Act and ordered the corporation dissolved. Justice John Marshall Harlan wrote, "It is manifest [obvious] that if the Anti-Trust Act is held not to embrace a case such as is now before us, the plain intention of the legislative branch of the Government will be defeated."

Encouraged by this victory, the Roosevelt administration launched a "trustbusting" campaign. It filed 44 suits against business combinations believed not to be in the public interest. It was not size that mattered, Roosevelt declared, but whether a particular trust was good or bad for the public as a whole. "Bad" trusts did such things as forcing companies to give them discounts or rebates, selling inferior products, competing unfairly, and corrupting public officials. As Roosevelt put it, "We draw the line against misconduct, not against wealth."

The Roosevelt administration also promoted railroad regulation. At the president's urging, Congress passed two laws that turned the Interstate Commerce Commission (ICC) into a significant regulatory agency. The first, the 1903 **Elkins Act**, forbade shipping companies from accepting rebates, or money given back in return for business. Politicians as well as railroad owners supported this new law. The second, the 1906 **Hepburn Act**, authorized the ICC to set railroad rates and to regulate other companies engaged in interstate commerce, such as pipelines and ferries.

Practices of food and drug companies. Roosevelt also responded to growing public concern about practices of the food and drug industries. By the early 1900s clear evidence existed that some drug companies, food processors, and meat packers were selling dangerous products. Scientific developments had enabled industrial chemists to add substances to food to make it appear fresh. Chemists learned that churning spoiled butter with skim milk would make it look fresh. It was then sold as fresh butter. The chemical formaldehyde was added to old eggs to take away their odor. The eggs too were then sold as suitable for baking. North Dakota's food commissioner Edward F. Ladd found that most foods he analyzed had chemical additives. "There was but one brand of catsup which was pure," he reported at a meeting in 1904. The other brands contained pulp and skins, unripe and overripe tomatoes, and preservatives.

INTERPRETING POLITICAL CARTOONS

Trustbusting. Responding to public concerns, President Theodore Roosevelt made great efforts to break up trusts. *What roles are Roosevelt and the trust assigned in this 1904 cartoon entitled "Jack the Giant-Killer"? Why?*

HISTORY MAKERS SPEAK

Theodore Roosevelt in *For the Record: A Documentary History of America,* Vol. 2

Battling Trusts. In a 1901 message to Congress President Roosevelt explained his battle against trusts: "When the Constitution was adopted, at the end of the eighteenth century, no human wisdom could foretell the sweeping changes, alike in industrial and political conditions, which were to take place by the beginning of the twentieth century. . . . The conditions are now wholly different. . . . I believe that a law can be framed which will enable the National Government to exercise control along the line above indicated."

CRITICAL THINKING Did Roosevelt argue that the Constitution is flawed?

ANSWER: Students should suggest that he argued that contemporary circumstances required the government to expand its ability to regulate the trusts.

POLITICAL CARTOON ANSWER

Students might observe that President Roosevelt is portrayed as a small figure—the "Jack" of the title—against many large, imposing figures—the "Giants" of the title.

LEVEL 2: Tell students to imagine that it is 1904 and that they are reformers concerned about the practices of trusts or the food and drug industry. Have each student write a half-page letter to the editor describing such practices and calling for government action. (*See the Level 1 lesson for the correct practices.*) Ask volunteers to read their letters to the class. Then conduct a brief discussion on government responses to trusts and food and drug industry practices. Ask students to explain how the government attempted to curb violations. (*See the Level 1 lesson for the correct responses.*) Next, ask students to express their own opinions about these government actions. Were they enough, given the size of the problem? What more could the government have done?

LEVEL 3: Tell students to imagine that it is 1904 and that they are reformers concerned about the practices of trusts or the food and drug industry. Have each student prepare a two- to three-minute statement to the congressional committee investigating such practices. (*See the Level 1 lesson for the correct practices.*) Ask volunteers to read their letters to the class. Then ask students to explain how the government attempted to curb violations. (*See the Level 1 lesson for the correct responses.*) Next ask students to express their own opinions about these government actions. Were they enough, given the scope of the problem? What more could the government have done?

NOTE: For an additional teaching idea, see the Chapter 10 collage lesson in the **Creative Teaching Strategies** handbook.

INTERPRETING THE VISUAL RECORD

Protecting the consumer. The Pure Food and Drug Act established regulations to prevent drug companies from making false claims about their products. *What claims does this drug advertisement make?*

Stamps like this one from the early 1900s were used to label unsafe foods.

Some drug companies sold worthless medicines that contained dangerous drugs such as cocaine or morphine. Journalist Samuel Hopkins Adams wrote about drug industry abuses.

> *History Makers Speak*
>
> **"Gullible [easily fooled] America will spend this year some seventy-five millions of dollars in the purchase of patent [over-the-counter] medicines.... It will swallow huge quantities of alcohol, an appalling amount of opiates and narcotics."**
>
> —Samuel Hopkins Adams

Adams charged that the drug companies' claims that their "health tonics" could cure everything from baldness to cancer amounted to fraud. Edward Bok, another journalist, compared the label for Mrs. Winslow's Soothing Syrup, used to bring pain relief to teething babies, with a British label for the same medicine. The British label marked the tonic "Poison."

Protecting the consumer. Reformers worked to put pressure on the government to pass laws requiring manufacturers to use pure ingredients in their products. As the primary purchasers of foods and medicines, many women participated in this movement. For example, Alice Lakey gave lectures alerting Americans to the dangers of impure foods. At the St. Louis Exposition of 1904, groups working for food reform displayed artificially colored foods. They extracted the dyes from the foods, then demonstrated how that very dye could be used to color wool and silk fabric. The exhibit attracted attention from politicians, journalists, and consumers alike. In 1906 **Upton Sinclair** published *The Jungle*, an explosive novel that depicted the wretched and unsanitary conditions at a meatpacking plant.

Responding to public pressures, Roosevelt ordered Secretary of Agriculture James Wilson to investigate the conditions in the packing houses. "We saw meat shovelled from filthy wooden floors, piled on tables rarely washed, pushed from room to room in rotten box carts," Wilson stated in his final report. "In all of which processes it [the meat] was in the way of gathering dirt, splinters, floor filth, and the expectoration [saliva] of tuberculous and other diseased workers." The report was so shocking that the *New York Post* composed a jingle based on it.

> *Primary Source*
>
> **"Mary had a little lamb,
> And when she saw it sicken,
> She shipped it off to Packingtown,
> And now it's labelled chicken."**
>
> —*New York Post*

In 1906 the U.S. Congress enacted two new consumer-protection laws. The **Meat Inspection Act** required federal government inspection of meat shipped across state lines. The **Pure Food and Drug Act** forbade the manufacture, sale, or transportation of food and patent medicine containing harmful ingredients. The law also required that containers of food and medicines carry ingredient labels.

✔ **READING CHECK: Summarizing** How did Roosevelt and other government officials try to protect consumers? Roosevelt ordered an investigation of conditions in the meatpacking houses. Then in 1906 Congress enacted two new consumer-protection laws.

AMERICAN *Letters*

Progressive Literature

During the Progressive Era, literature reflected the characteristics and issues of the time. It also influenced political reform. Frank Norris's 1901 novel The Octopus *portrays railroad financiers as villains in a story involving railroads and wheat growers in California. In the excerpt below, wheat farmers have formed a committee to try to secure the election of a commissioner who will crack down on the railroads. Upton Sinclair's* The Jungle *(1906) revealed to a horrified American public the conditions of Chicago's meatpacking industry. The excerpt below describes a typical scene at a meatpacking plant.*

from *The Octopus*
by Frank Norris

The campaign for Railroad Commissioner had been very interesting. At the very outset [beginning] Magnus's committee found itself involved in corrupt politics. The primaries had to be captured at all costs and by any means, and when the convention assembled it was found necessary to buy outright the votes of certain delegates. The campaign fund raised by contributions from Magnus, Annixter, Broderson, and Osterman was drawn upon to the extent of five thousand dollars.

Only the committee knew of this corruption. The League, ignoring ways and means, supposed as a matter of course that the campaign was honourably conducted.

For a whole week after the consummation [completion] of this part of the deal, Magnus had kept to his house, refusing to be seen, alleging [complaining] that he was ill, which was not far from the truth. The shame of the business, the loathing [disgust] of what he had done, were to him things unspeakable. . . . He was hopelessly caught in the mesh. Wrong seemed indissolubly [permanently] knitted into the texture of Right. He was blinded, dizzied, overwhelmed, caught in the current of events, and hurried along he knew not where. He resigned himself.

Frank Norris's 1901 novel

from *The Jungle*
by Upton Sinclair

There were the wool-pluckers, whose hands went to pieces even sooner than the hands of the pickle-men; for the pelts of the sheep had to be painted with acid to loosen the wool, and then the pluckers had to pull out this wool with their bare hands, till the acid had eaten their fingers off. . . . Some worked at the stamping-machines, and it was very seldom that one could work long there at the pace that was set, and not give out and forget himself, and have a part of his hand chopped off. . . . Worst of any, however, were . . . those who served in the cooking-rooms. . . . Their peculiar trouble was that they fell into the vats; and when they were fished out, there was never enough of them left to be worth exhibiting,—sometimes they would be overlooked for days, till all but the bones of them had gone out to the world as Durham's Pure Leaf Lard!

Upton Sinclair's 1906 novel

UNDERSTANDING LITERATURE

1. How did Magnus win the election in *The Octopus?*
2. According to *The Jungle,* what were working conditions like in the meatpacking plant?
3. How do these excerpts reflect the issues of the Progressive Era?

ALL LEVELS: Ask students to identify three or four ways of protecting the environment. *(Students might mention creating national parks, creating sanctuaries, restoring damaged areas, and following other conservation policies.)* Ask students who it was that first instituted some of these environmental policies. *(Some students might identify Theodore Roosevelt or Gifford Pinchot, but more students will not know.)* To help students understand Roosevelt's and Pinchot's role in environmental protection, copy the following graphic organizer on the chalkboard, omitting the italicized answers. Have each student complete it. **English Language Learners**

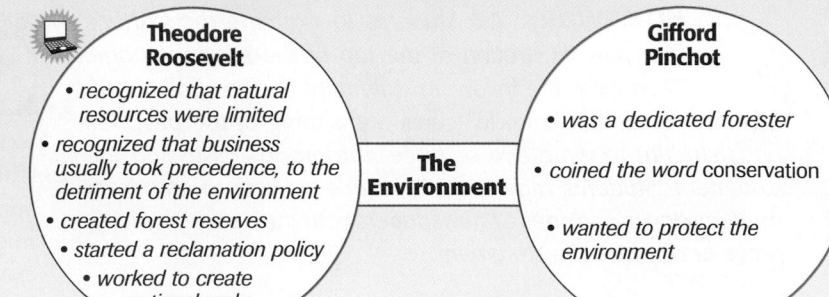

Theodore Roosevelt
- *recognized that natural resources were limited*
- *recognized that business usually took precedence, to the detriment of the environment*
- *created forest reserves*
- *started a reclamation policy*
- *worked to create national parks*

The Environment

Gifford Pinchot
- *was a dedicated forester*
- *coined the word* conservation
- *wanted to protect the environment*

HOMEWORK *Have each student create one or two editorial cartoons on Theodore Roosevelt and the environment.*

Conservation and Preservation. Advocates of conservation, such as Gifford Pinchot, viewed the environment as an important—although not inviolable—source of natural resources. Advocates of preservation, such as John Muir, opposed the commercial development of the environment. Pinchot and Muir had once been close friends, but their relationship ended when Pinchot promoted sheep grazing in forest areas. Ironically, magazine readers who lived in crowded urban areas proved to be the most ardent supporters of Muir and preservationist organizations such as the Sierra Club and the American Civil Association.

CRITICAL THINKING Why might urban residents have ardently supported preservation?

ANSWER: Students might mention that urban residents probably viewed natural areas as unsullied spaces.

The American Nation
VIDEO PROGRAM

Yosemite National Park; Teacher's Guide, pp. 87–92

Search 08593, Play to 15913
Videodisc 1, Side B

Play   Pause

See *Teacher's Guide* for Spanish barcode.

Thomas Moran attempted to convey the beauty and grandeur of Yellowstone National Park in his painting The Grand Canyon of the Yellowstone.

Protecting the Environment

President Roosevelt's most enduring legacy may be his work in the conservation movement. He recognized that the natural resources of the United States were limited and that the needs of business had always taken priority over the environment. "In the past, we have admitted the right of the individual to injure the future of the Republic for his own present profit," he charged. "The time has come for a change."

At the end of the 1800s the country's public land was being lost to greed and mismanagement. Lumber companies acquired the rights to forestland and proceeded to cut down every tree. Ranchers grazed cattle and sheep in government-owned forests. In 1891, fires destroyed 12 million acres of forests. Most had been started by cowhands, hunters, or sheepherders. When Roosevelt took office, only 46 million acres of land had been set aside as national reserves.

Gifford Pinchot (PIN-shoh) was a strong conservationist, forester, and a friend of Roosevelt. He first came up with the word *conservation* to describe the need to protect the country's natural environment. Pinchot wrote, "The conservation of

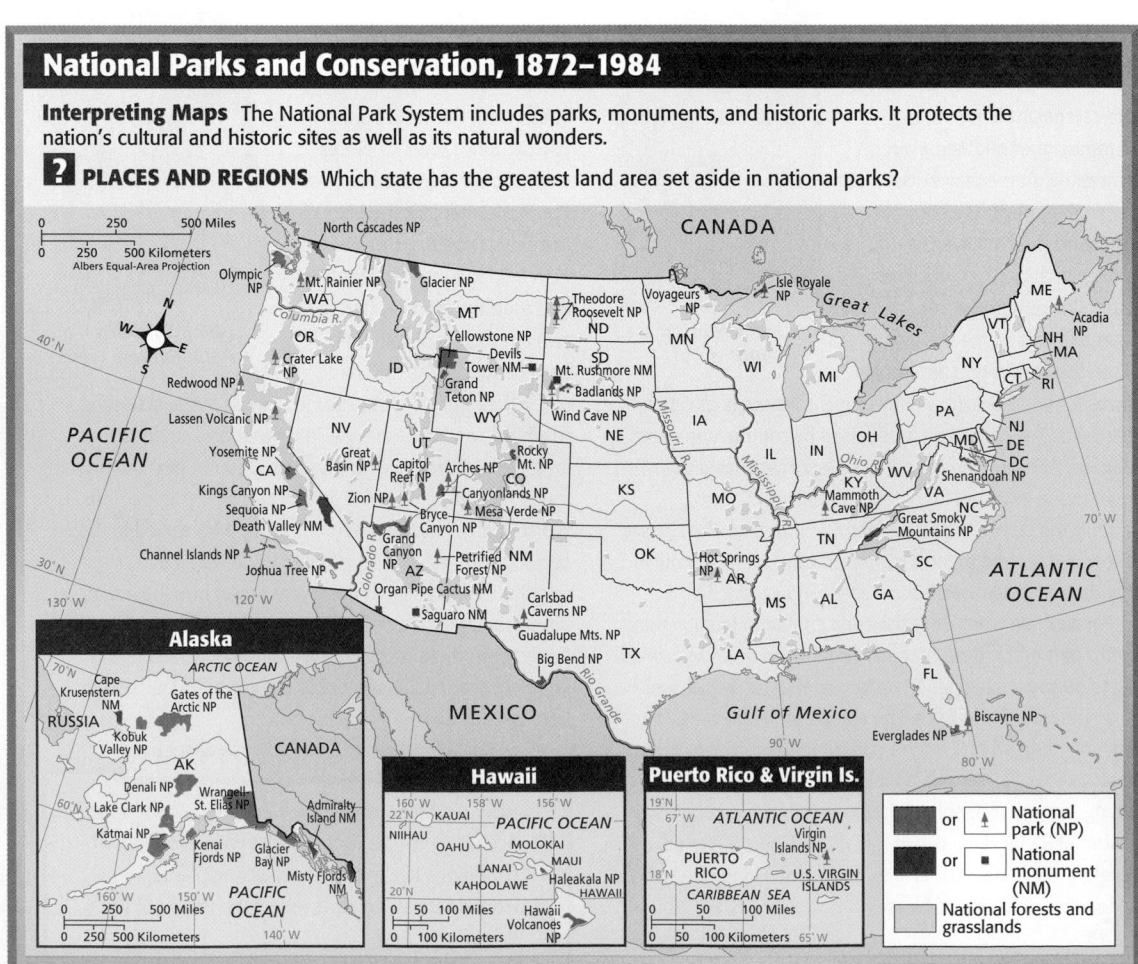

National Parks and Conservation, 1872–1984

Interpreting Maps The National Park System includes parks, monuments, and historic parks. It protects the nation's cultural and historic sites as well as its natural wonders.

? PLACES AND REGIONS Which state has the greatest land area set aside in national parks?

REVIEW

Have students complete the **Section 2 Review** on p. 309.

ASSESS

Have students complete **Daily Quiz 10.2**. As **Alternative Assessment**, you may want to use the President Roosevelt "grade" or the trust and food and drug industry wanted posters in this section's lessons.

RETEACH

Have students complete **Main Idea Activity for English Language Learners and Special-Needs Students 10.2**. Then tell each student to create an annotated time line of domestic affairs

during the Roosevelt presidency. Ask volunteers to present their time lines to the class. **English Language Learners**

EXTEND

Organize students into two groups, one focusing on Theodore Roosevelt and the other on Gifford Pinchot. Have students conduct research on the assigned figure. Then tell students to imagine that their figure has just died, and that they have been selected to deliver the eulogy at his funeral. Have each student write a three- to five-minute eulogy on either Roosevelt or Pinchot and his attempts to protect the environment. Have two students—one eulogizing Roosevelt and one eulogizing Pinchot—deliver their speeches to the class. **Block Scheduling**

---

natural resources is the key to the future. It is the key to the safety and prosperity of the American people." The president was receptive to Pinchot's ideas and made conservation a priority during his second term.

Roosevelt withdrew from sale millions of acres of public land and set aside nearly 150 million acres as forest reserves. In 1902 Congress passed the Newlands Reclamation Act. This law allowed money from the sale of public lands to be used for irrigation and **reclamation**—the process of making damaged land productive again. Roosevelt also doubled the number of national parks. He created 16 national monuments and founded 51 wildlife refuges. This newly protected territory included the Grand Canyon and the Petrified Forest in Arizona. To help supervise the parks and monuments, the **National Park Service** was created in 1916. The National Park system has continued to grow, adding new lands and services.

Although conservation plans limited the amount of land in private hands, some businesspeople supported this new trend. Minnesota railroad business leader James J. Hill, for instance, listened to Pinchot's predictions. Hill acknowledged that using up all of the nation's mineral resources would endanger future generations—and future business. At times, the needs of the industrialists and the reformers were not so far apart. One of Pinchot's associates pointed out that conservation "was only a means to an end and the end was economic justice."

✔ **READING CHECK: Analyzing Information** Why was the National Park Service established? to help supervise national parks and monuments

Then and Now

National Parks

National park guide

Today, the National Park Service manages some 380 sites on more than 80 million acres of land. As in previous years, the Park Service is caught between those who wish to preserve and expand park land and those who want to make use of the natural resources. Conservationists charge that businesses are destroying wildlife habitats and old-growth forests. Business leaders counter that the demand for wood and mineral products—not to mention the protection of thousands of jobs—requires the use of wilderness resources.

Lawmakers and Park Service officials also face the problem of maintaining the parks while containing costs. More than 280 million people visit the national parks annually. To counteract the strain on park resources, officials have proposed that visitation be limited.

SECTION 2 REVIEW

1. Define and explain:
arbitration
reclamation

2. Identify and explain:
Theodore Roosevelt
Square Deal
Elkins Act
Hepburn Act
Upton Sinclair
Meat Inspection Act
Pure Food and Drug Act
Gifford Pinchot
National Park Service

3. Analyzing Information
President Roosevelt's Square Deal promised to balance the interests of business, labor, and consumers. Copy the graphic organizer below. Use it to describe Roosevelt's actions toward these groups.

4. Finding the Main Idea
a. How were President Roosevelt's leadership skills reflected in the Square Deal and in his handling of the miners' strike?
b. Why did reformers support the Meat Inspection Act and the Pure Food and Drug Act? How did these acts help consumers?
c. Trace the development of the conservation movement in the early 1900s.

5. Writing and Critical Thinking
Classifying Imagine that you are an adviser to President Roosevelt. Write a report explaining how his actions against trusts and railroads reflect a break with the past.
Consider:
• Roosevelt's policies against trusts and railroads
• previous policies against trusts and railroads, such as the Sherman Antitrust Act

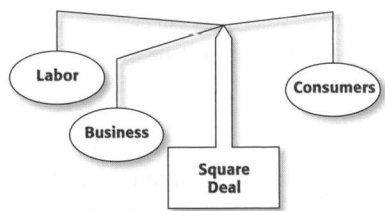

Homework Practice Online
keyword: SE3 HP10

REVIEW SECTION 2 ANSWERS

1. Define
• arbitration, p. 304
• reclamation, p. 309

2. Identify
• Theodore Roosevelt, p. 303
• Square Deal, p. 304
• Elkins Act, p. 305
• Hepburn Act, p. 305
• Upton Sinclair, p. 306
• Meat Inspection Act, p. 306
• Pure Food and Drug Act, p. 306
• Gifford Pinchot, p. 308
• National Park Service, p. 309

3. labor—allowed workers to bargain with business owners; business—regulated businesses, limited their power; consumers—protected them from dangerous products

4a. Both reflected his desire to offer opportunities to all Americans.

b. They saw the acts as a way to protect consumers and to force companies to act responsibly.

c. Pinchot supported conservation; his views influenced President Roosevelt, who withdrew lands from sale; Congress passed the Newlands Reclamation Act; the National Park Service was established.

5. Answers will vary. Reports might suggest that his efforts ended the era of unquestioned government support for business interests.

LET'S GET STARTED!

Write the following question on the chalkboard: *Is true unity ever possible within a political party, or are all parties bound to be split by dissension at some point?* As students enter the classroom, ask them to respond to the question in writing. Have volunteers share their responses. Then tell students that in Section 3 they will learn why the Republican Party split over the issue of reform and how that split affected the presidential election of 1912.

SECTION ③

READ TO DISCOVER
1. What progressive reforms were enacted during President Taft's administration?
2. What divisions in the Republican Party led to the formation of the Progressive Party?
3. How did Woodrow Wilson win the 1912 presidential election?

IDENTIFY
William Howard Taft
Mann-Elkins Act
Sixteenth Amendment
Payne-Aldrich Tariff
Richard Ballinger
Ballinger-Pinchot affair
Joseph Cannon
George Norris
Progressive Party
Woodrow Wilson
New Freedom
Eugene Debs

▶ WHY IT MATTERS TODAY
Divisions within a nationwide political party also frequently occur today in the United States. Use **CNNfyi.com** or other **current events** sources to learn about political issues currently causing divisions within the Republican and Democratic political parties. Record your findings in your journal.

Reform Under Taft

EYEWITNESSES TO History ❝*He is not an American, you know, he is America.*❞

—John Morley, quoted in *America Enters the World*, by Page Smith

Many people agreed with British diplomat John Morley's assessment of President Theodore Roosevelt. By the time Roosevelt neared the end of his second term in office, he was one of the most admired men in the world. Despite such international praise, Roosevelt decided not to run for president again. "The country needs a change," he declared. "We have had four years of uprooting and four years of crusading. The country has had enough of it and of me." To take himself out of the public eye, Roosevelt set out on a year-long safari to Africa as soon as the election of 1908 had ended.

Taft 1908 campaign plate

Taft Takes Office

At the 1908 Republican convention President Roosevelt threw his support behind **William Howard Taft**, his secretary of war. Taft won the nomination on the first ballot. At the time, Roosevelt fully believed that Taft had the same reform tendencies as he did. He even told a friend that rarely had "two public men . . . ever been so much at one in all the essentials of their beliefs and practices." The Democrats again nominated William Jennings Bryan, whose pro-labor platform won the backing of the American Federation of Labor. However, the Democratic platform and Taft's stances were actually quite similar. The Democrats lost the election by a wide margin in the electoral college, but by just 1.25 million popular votes.

It quickly became clear that Taft would be a different kind of president than Roosevelt. Roosevelt enjoyed being in the public eye. Taft did not. Although Taft had worked in government for years, most of his experience had come through appointed positions. He had avoided the often hostile realm of electoral politics. "I don't like politics," he once wrote. "I don't like the limelight."

An intelligent but cautious man, Taft was fearful of overstepping the bounds of his presidential authority. Nevertheless, he chalked up a long list of accomplishments. His administration filed 90 antitrust suits, more than twice the number begun under Roosevelt.

At Taft's urging, Congress passed the **Mann-Elkins Act** in 1910, extending the regulatory powers of the Interstate Commerce Commission to telephone and telegraph companies. Taft also promoted environmental conservation by adding vast areas to the nation's forest reserves. He supported reforms to help working people, particularly child laborers. With his approval, Congress created a separate Department of Labor to enforce labor laws. Congress also passed mine-safety laws

LEVEL 1: Organize students into triads. Draw a four-column chart on the chalkboard and label the columns with the following headings: *Business Regulations, Conservation Policies, Labor Policies, Economic Policies.* Have each triad note President Taft's progressive reforms in the correct areas. *(Triads should note that Taft urged Congress to extend the power of the Interstate Commerce Commission, added land to the forest reserves, helped create a Department of Labor and passed labor-safety laws, and worked for the adoption of the Sixteenth Amendment.)* Then have triads write paragraphs summarizing Taft's achievements as a reformer.

English Language Learners, Cooperative Learning

LEVEL 2: Tell students to imagine that they are progressive Republicans during William Howard Taft's presidency. Have each student write a short political memoir discussing Taft's progressive reforms and describing his or her own reactions to those reforms. *(See the Level 1 lesson for the correct reforms.)* Ask volunteers to read their memoirs to the class. Students may wish to include their memoirs in their portfolios.

---

and established an eight-hour workday for employees of companies holding contracts with the federal government.

The Taft administration was partly responsible for the adoption of the **Sixteenth Amendment.** Proposed in 1909 and ratified in 1913, the amendment permitted Congress to levy taxes based on an individual's income. Progressives had long supported such a graduated income tax as a way to fund needed government programs in a fair manner.

✔ **READING CHECK: Making Predictions** How might progressive reforms enacted during President Taft's administration affect Americans today? Whenever Americans today make a long-distance phone call or pay their income taxes, that activity reflects the legacy of the Taft administration.

Taft Angers the Progressives

Despite these reforms, President Taft lost the support of progressive Republicans. This split began in April 1909 with the passage of a bill on tariffs, or taxes charged on imports or exports.

The Payne-Aldrich Tariff. Both Taft and the progressives favored tariff reductions on imports to lower the prices of consumer goods. Some conservative members of Congress wanted high tariffs to protect American industries. They won out when the House sent a low-tariff bill to the Senate, and Senator Nelson Aldrich of Rhode Island turned it into a high-tariff measure.

Taft could have vetoed the bill or pressured Aldrich to change the tariff rates. However, Taft lacked the political skill to oppose conservative Republicans in Congress. Despite his misgivings, he signed the **Payne-Aldrich Tariff,** as the bill was called. To make matters worse, he called it "the best tariff bill that the Republican party ever passed." Outraged progressives accused Taft of betraying the reform cause.

The Ballinger-Pinchot affair. Progressives also attacked Taft for sabotaging former president Roosevelt's conservation program. The dispute revolved around **Richard Ballinger,** Taft's secretary of the interior. He believed that the Roosevelt administration had exceeded its authority when it stopped the sale of public land. Ballinger approved the sale of a vast tract of coal-rich Alaska timberland. As head of the U.S. Forest Service, Gifford Pinchot attacked Ballinger for favoring private interests over conservation. Taft warned Pinchot to stop criticizing Ballinger. When Pinchot ignored this warning, Taft fired him.

For progressives, the **Ballinger-Pinchot affair** signaled Taft's weakness on conservation. Taft also made one particularly dangerous enemy—Theodore Roosevelt. While Taft sent letters to Roosevelt, then on safari in Africa, defending the actions of his administration, Pinchot visited his old friend. After speaking with Pinchot, Roosevelt confided in Senator Henry Cabot Lodge, "I don't think that under the Taft . . . regime there has been a real appreciation of the needs of the

---

HISTORY
IN THE MAKING

Views of Taft
BY RAYMOND HYSER

Many historians have compared William Howard Taft with Theodore Roosevelt. While Roosevelt expanded the power of the presidency and supported social-welfare legislation, Taft was reluctant to use the full powers of the presidency. He believed that judicial interpretation of the law was paramount. In a time when the American people demanded progressive change and presidential leadership, Taft moved slowly and narrowed presidential power.

Historians have offered critical assessments of Taft's presidency. Making the inevitable comparison with the Roosevelt presidency, they have emphasized Taft's political blunders and indecisiveness to explain his failings as president. One early biographer, however, argued that he was successful because he supported important legislation through a hostile Congress. In recent years, historians have provided a more balanced, objective view of Taft. Donald Anderson argues that Taft believed in the constitutional limits on the presidency and he held an almost religious commitment to the rule of law. This philosophy helps explain the conflict between Roosevelt's and Taft's leadership styles. Paola Coletta argues that Taft ranks as an "average" president who had a solid legislative record. He was a "constitutional conservator," whose term was bracketed by two powerful progressive presidents—Roosevelt and Wilson.

The Sixteenth Amendment. The federal government enacted a personal income tax law in 1894. The next year, however, the Supreme Court determined that the tax was unconstitutional. In its ruling, the court noted that the Constitution bans direct taxes unless they are imposed equally upon the states according to their populations. Under the 1894 law, states with larger populations paid proportionally higher taxes. The Sixteenth Amendment eliminated this objection.

CRITICAL THINKING Why might some believe that the Sixteenth Amendment was necessary?

ANSWER: Students might respond that unless the Constitution was amended, all proposed income taxes would be declared unconstitutional.

THAT'S INTERESTING!

Theodore Roosevelt helped William Howard Taft devise a public relations strategy to win the presidency. Roosevelt advised his protégé to avoid being photographed while playing tennis or golf, both of which many Americans viewed as elitist sports.

LEVEL 3: Write the following statement on the chalkboard: *William Howard Taft was a true progressive.* Have each student write a one- to two-page essay responding to the statement. Students' essays should discuss Taft's reforms and evaluate those reforms in light of Theodore Roosevelt's performance as president. *(See the Level 1 lesson for the correct reforms.)* Have volunteers read their essays to the class. Students may wish to include their essays in their portfolios. After students have read their essays to the class, ask them to reread the feature on the previous page. Then conduct a discussion on Taft and his presidency. How was Taft's performance as a president? Have

historical views of Taft's presidency been irrevocably influenced by Theodore Roosevelt's strong personality and performance? Is it possible to have an "unbiased" view of Taft or any other president?

HOMEWORK *Tell students to imagine that they are progressive Republicans during William Howard Taft's presidency. Tell them to imagine that they are preparing to interview Taft. Have each student compile a list of five or more questions about his reforms. Tell students to answer their own questions as Taft might have answered them.*

PEOPLE IN HISTORY

Gifford Pinchot. After graduating from Yale University, Gifford Pinchot studied at forestry schools in Austria, France, Germany, and Switzerland. When he returned home, he practiced forest management and conservation at Biltmore, the lavish North Carolina estate of industrialist Cornelius Vanderbilt. In 1898 Pinchot became the head of the agency that eventually became the U.S. Forest Service. Under Pinchot's leadership, the organization expanded enormously. In 1898 it oversaw 19 national forests. By 1909 there were 149 national forests.

CRITICAL THINKING Why might Pinchot have reacted so strongly to Richard Ballinger's sale of the Alaskan timberland?

ANSWER: Students might respond that Pinchot had devoted his life to forestry preservation. He regarded Ballinger's act as extremely dangerous.

POLITICAL CARTOON ANSWER

Students might suggest that the cartoon shows the two taking totally different approaches to win the nomination.

MAP ANSWER
(for p. 313)

It split the Republican popular vote and gave the electoral vote to Wilson.

312

country." Roosevelt soon broke with Taft over the Pinchot controversy. Taft was not able to regain the support of progressives even though he transferred almost as much land into government reserves as Roosevelt had.

Roosevelt and the elections of 1910. In the congressional elections of 1910, Roosevelt campaigned on behalf of progressive Republicans who opposed Taft. Roosevelt proposed a program called New Nationalism—a series of tough laws to protect workers, ensure public health, and regulate business.

History Makers Speak

❝The true friend of property, the true conservative, is he who insists that property shall be the servant and not the master of the commonwealth. . . . The citizens of the United States must effectively control the mighty commercial forces which they have themselves called into being.❞

—Theodore Roosevelt, *The New Nationalism*

Government, Roosevelt said, must become the "steward [manager] of the public welfare." His call for a more activist federal government represented an even more progressive position than he had taken as president. Delighted, reformers hailed the New Nationalism as a revival of the progressive spirit.

Despite Roosevelt's help on the campaign trail, the Republicans lost control of the House of Representatives for the first time in 16 years. Nearly all the newly elected Democrats unseated conservative Republicans. Roosevelt and Taft both were deeply disappointed by the election.

The Republican Party Divides

Not long before Theodore Roosevelt proposed New Nationalism, a bitter dispute in Congress had further deepened the gulf between President Taft and the progressives. In the spring of 1910, progressive Republicans in Congress launched a major attack on Speaker of the House **Joseph Cannon** of Illinois, a conservative Republican. Seventy-three-year-old "Uncle Joe" Cannon was one of Washington's most powerful politicians. He ruled the House with an iron hand, appointing all its committees and naming their chairpersons. As head of the powerful Rules Committee, which determined the order of business in the House, Cannon prevented bills he opposed from even reaching the House floor for debate.

The Cannon debate. Progressives charged that Cannon used his power to block reform legislation. "Not one cent for scenery," he had growled in dismissing a call for environmental protection. In March 1910 Representative **George Norris**, a progressive from Nebraska, began an effort to break Cannon's power. Norris proposed that House members elect the Rules Committee and that the Speaker be excluded from membership on it.

After a heated debate, Norris's motion passed. A year later, the representatives also stripped the Speaker of the House of the power to appoint members to other committees—a major progressive victory. However, Taft's refusal to take their side throughout this bitter debate angered many progressives.

Analyzing Primary Sources

Identifying Points of View What does Roosevelt identify as the proper relationship between business and government? Citizens should be in control of business and commercial forces.

INTERPRETING POLITICAL CARTOONS

Political division. After the 1910 elections, President Taft and former president Theodore Roosevelt held increasingly opposing positions on progressive reforms. *How does this cartoon depict the opposition between Taft and Roosevelt?*

THE GRANGER COLLECTION, NEW YORK

ALL LEVELS: Ask students how and why Woodrow Wilson won the presidential election of 1912. *(Most students will not be able to answer the question.)* To help students understand how a split in the Republican Party and the creation of the Progressive Party helped ensure Wilson's election, copy the following graphic organizer on the chalkboard, omitting the italicized answers. Have each student complete it. After students have completed the graphic organizer, ask each student to write a half-page essay discussing the Republican Party and the election of 1912.
English Language Learners

Divisions in the Republican Party
• *members differed over William Howard Taft's performance–some saw him as eroding Theodore Roosevelt's policies*
• *the Ballinger-Pinchot affair*
• *the attack on Joseph Cannon*

The Formation of the Progressive Party

Effect on the Presidential Election of 1912
• *split the Republican Party*
• *siphoned votes from Taft and gave votes to Woodrow Wilson*
• *resulted in a Democratic victory and the election of Wilson*

Roosevelt returns to politics. Completely at odds with President Taft, Theodore Roosevelt decided to run again for the presidency. Borrowing a prizefighting term, he declared, "My hat is in the ring." Roosevelt won almost every Republican state primary, including the one in Taft's home state, Ohio.

Nevertheless, Taft's allies firmly held control of the party machinery. At the Republican Convention, they refused to seat many of Roosevelt's delegates. "Don't you realize you're wrecking the Republican Party?" shouted one progressive senator. When Taft won the nomination, Roosevelt's supporters walked out. Their leaders organized their own convention, asking those in the Roosevelt camp to oppose this "crime which represents treason to the people." They adopted a platform based on the New Nationalism and nominated Roosevelt as their presidential candidate. Thus was born the **Progressive Party**, also called the Bull Moose Party after Roosevelt declared that he felt "fit as a bull moose" to run.

✔ **READING CHECK: Analyzing Information** Why was the Progressive Party formed?
The party was formed because progressive Republicans charged that conservative Republicans blocked reform legislation.

A Democratic Victory

The division in the Republican Party practically assured a Democratic victory. The Democrats united behind one candidate, Governor **Woodrow Wilson** of New Jersey. He ran on a platform calling for tariff reduction, banking reform, laws benefiting wage earners and farmers, and stronger antitrust legislation.

The Wilson program. A native of Virginia and a political newcomer, Wilson had long nurtured dreams of high office. He became a professor of political science at Princeton University in New Jersey. Wilson later served as Princeton's president. He was elected governor of New Jersey in 1910. In his short time as governor, he fought the state's Democratic Party bosses and pushed through laws regulating business. Wilson's status as an outspoken reformer and eloquent speaker made him the presidential choice of progressives in the Democratic Party.

In the 1912 campaign, Wilson's **New Freedom** program made proposals to help small businesses. He also called for a return to an America where people were free from the heavy hand of big business and government. Wilson asserted:

While giving a speech in 1912, Theodore Roosevelt was wounded in an assassination attempt. He finished the speech with a bullet lodged in his body.

The Election of 1912

Interpreting Maps Although Wilson easily won the electoral vote and gained the highest percent of popular votes, he did not receive the vote of the majority of Americans.

❓ **THE USES OF GEOGRAPHY** How did Roosevelt's third-party candidacy affect the electoral and popular vote?

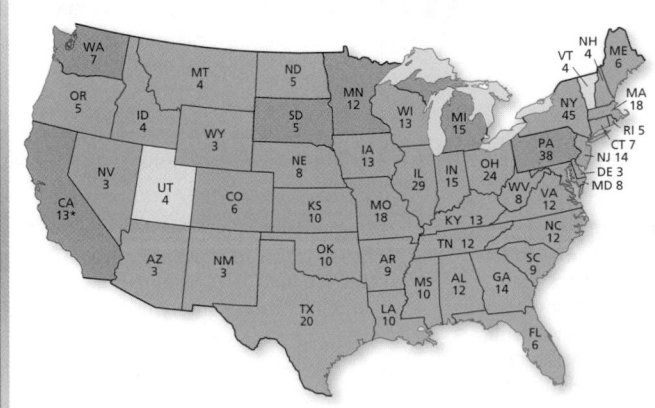

CANDIDATE	PARTY	ELECTORAL VOTE	POPULAR VOTE	% OF POPULAR VOTE
Wilson	Democratic	435*	6,296,547	41.9
T. Roosevelt	Progressive	88	4,118,571	27.4
Taft	Republican	8	3,486,720	23.2
Debs	Socialist		900,672	6.0
Other parties			235,025	1.6

*Two electors in California voted for Wilson.

Source: *Historical Statistics of the United States*

The Republican Nomination. On the whole, Republican voters favored Theodore Roosevelt over William Howard Taft. In the 13 states that held party primaries, Roosevelt received some 1.1 million votes, while Taft received only some 74,000. These results earned Roosevelt the votes of 278 delegates, while Taft earned the votes of only 48 delegates. However, Taft received most of the votes of the delegates from those states that used party conventions rather than primaries to select delegates, a fact that revealed his control of the party machinery.

CRITICAL THINKING Was the result of the nomination a democratic one?

ANSWER: Some students might argue that it did not represent the true preferences of the voters.

THAT'S INTERESTING!

Woodrow Wilson did not learn to read until he was nine years old, and for the rest of his life he read very slowly. Some historians believe that he may have suffered from a learning disability such as dyslexia. Nevertheless, Wilson graduated from Princeton and went on to teach at many prestigious universities.

REVIEW

Have students complete the **Section 3 Review** on p. 314.

ASSESS

Have students complete **Daily Quiz 10.3**. As **Alternative Assessment**, you may want to use the President Taft reforms graphic organizer or President Taft reforms essay in this section's lessons.

RETEACH

Have students complete **Main Idea Activity for English Language Learners and Special-Needs Students 10.3**. Then organize students into small groups. Have each group create a detailed outline of Section 3. Ask groups to exchange their outlines and to use them to write paragraphs summarizing the material in the section.
English Language Learners, Cooperative Learning

EXTEND

Write the following statement on the chalkboard: *President Taft identified the right problems, but offered the wrong solutions.* Have each student write a short essay evaluating the statement and responding to it. **Block Scheduling**

REVIEW SECTION 3 ANSWERS

1. Identify
- William Howard Taft, p. 310
- Mann-Elkins Act, p. 310
- Sixteenth Amendment, p. 311
- Payne-Aldrich Tariff, p. 311
- Richard Ballinger, p. 311
- Ballinger-Pinchot affair, p. 311
- Joseph Cannon, p. 312
- George Norris, p. 312
- Progressive Party, p. 313
- Woodrow Wilson, p. 313
- New Freedom, p. 313
- Eugene Debs, p. 314

2. Taft deviates from Roosevelt's programs; Roosevelt breaks with Taft; Taft defeats Roosevelt for the 1912 Republican nomination; Roosevelt runs as the Progressive Party candidate.

3a. It extended the regulatory powers of the Interstate Commerce Commission to telephone and telegraph companies.

b. The graduated income tax funded government programs in a fair manner.

c. It split the Republican vote and gave Wilson the election.

4. Answers will vary. Students' speeches should discuss reform and progressive goals.

Research on the ROM

Free Find:
Woodrow Wilson
After reading about Woodrow Wilson on the **Holt Researcher CD–ROM**, imagine that you are a political journalist. Write a short article on the outcome of the election.

History Makers Speak

"The only way that government is kept pure is by keeping ... channels open, so that ... there will constantly be coming new blood into the veins of the body politic."

—Woodrow Wilson

Although Wilson shared the progressive belief that government should be an agent of reform, he believed that if government became too strong it could limit individual freedom. He believed that reform efforts should seek to remove barriers to free competition but not significantly alter the free-enterprise system.

Wilson sweeps the election. Wilson's reform goals differed from those of Roosevelt, who accepted the new corporate and industrial order even as he proposed to regulate and control it. Wilson's ideas also differed from another candidate for president, **Eugene Debs** of the Socialist Party. The Socialist Party had done very well in the 1910 elections. It supported a radically different economic order, including public ownership of all major industries. In Debs, Wilson, and Roosevelt, American voters had a choice of three strong, reform-minded candidates. Even Taft supported some reform programs, although he appeared to represent a more conservative viewpoint.

As expected, Wilson won the election. Some Republicans even voted for him, seeing it as a vote against Roosevelt. Wilson received 435 electoral votes to Roosevelt's 88 and Taft's 8. Debs won more than 900,000 popular votes but no electoral votes. Of the more than 15 million votes cast, the three reform-minded challengers received some 8.5 million. Although Wilson won just 6 million popular votes, he took office with a strong call for reform.

Woodrow Wilson's moderate reform proposals attracted many voters during the 1912 election.

✔ **READING CHECK: Drawing Conclusions** How did the 1912 presidential election represent a call for moderate reform? Wilson opposed government reform that would limit individual freedom or alter the free-enterprise system.

SECTION 3 REVIEW

1. Identify and explain:
William Howard Taft
Mann-Elkins Act
Sixteenth Amendment
Payne-Aldrich Tariff
Richard Ballinger
Ballinger-Pinchot affair
Joseph Cannon
George Norris
Progressive Party
Woodrow Wilson
New Freedom
Eugene Debs

2. Sequencing Copy the diagram below. Use it to explain the steps that led from Taft's victory in 1908 to Wilson's victory in 1912.

1. Taft wins in 1908 with Roosevelt's support.

6. With the Republican Party divided, Wilson wins easily in 1912.

3. **Finding the Main Idea**
a. How did the Mann-Elkins Act alter the purpose of the Interstate Commerce Commission?
b. In what way was the Sixteenth Amendment a progressive reform?
c. What effect did the Bull Moose Party have on the 1912 presidential election?

4. **Writing and Critical Thinking**
Identifying Points of View Imagine that you are one of the candidates in the 1912 presidential election. Write a speech to persuade voters to elect you.
Consider:
• the candidates' positions on reform
• their past reform efforts
• how these positions and reforms reflect progressive goals

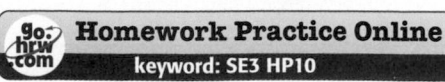
Homework Practice Online
keyword: SE3 HP10

SECTION ④

After completing Section 4, students should be able to:

OBJECTIVE 1 *Describe how Woodrow Wilson's proposals affected big business and U.S. citizens.*

OBJECTIVE 2 *Explain how President Wilson attempted to help farmers and laborers, and how successful his efforts were.*

OBJECTIVE 3 *Discuss how American women gained the right to vote.*

🎵 LET'S GET STARTED!

Write the following scenario on the chalkboard: *It is 1914. You are a woman. You do not have the right to vote. How do you go about winning that right? Do you work within the system for change, or do you stage protests? Do you use "any means necessary"—including illegal ones?* As students enter the classroom, ask them to respond to the scenario in writing. Have volunteers share their responses. Tell students that in Section 4 they will learn how American women gained the right to vote.

READ TO DISCOVER

1. How did President Wilson's proposals affect big business and U.S. citizens?
2. How did Wilson attempt to help farmers and laborers, and how successful were his efforts?
3. How did American women gain the right to vote?

IDENTIFY

Federal Reserve Act
Clayton Antitrust Act
Federal Trade Commission
Adamson Act
Keating-Owen Child Labor Act
National American Woman Suffrage Association
Alice Paul
Carrie Chapman Catt
Nineteenth Amendment

WHY IT MATTERS TODAY

The Federal Reserve plays an important role in today's national economy. Use **CNNfyi.com** or other **current events** sources to find out about a current policy of the Federal Reserve and how it affects the national economy. Record your findings in your journal.

CNNfyi.com

Wilson's "New Freedom"

EYEWITNESSES TO History

❝*We have been proud of our industrial achievements, but we have not . . . stopped . . . to count the . . . fearful physical and spiritual cost to the men and women and children upon whom the . . . weight and burden of it all has fallen. . . . This is not a day of triumph; it is a day of dedication. Here muster [gather], not the forces of party, but the forces of humanity.*❞

—Woodrow Wilson, "First Inaugural Address"

President Woodrow Wilson eloquently summed up the spirit of the progressive reform movement in his first inaugural address on March 4, 1913. In the months before his inauguration, Wilson prepared for the work ahead of him. He turned to his friend Edward M. House for help planning his cabinet and policies. Wilson considered House a man who "wants . . . to serve the common cause and to help me and others."

Wilson campaign item

Reform on Many Fronts

President Wilson and Edward M. House settled on a cabinet that included the first-ever secretary of labor, a position that went to a labor leader. Its creation was in itself a progressive act. Wilson's appointments attempted to reflect and satisfy the divisions within the Democratic Party.

After settling on a cabinet, Wilson presented his legislative agenda. It included tariff and banking reforms and stronger antitrust laws. The program was opposed by business groups and lobbyists, but Wilson skillfully rallied support in Congress and among the American people.

Tariffs. Wilson's first priority was to lower tariffs. This had long been a goal of the Democratic Party's southern pro-agriculture wing. Wilson knew that supporters of big business had blocked tariff reduction during Taft's presidency. To plead his case, Wilson addressed both houses of Congress in person—something that had not been done since President John Adams's administration. The opponents of a lower tariff did not easily give in to presidential pressure. Describing the strength of the business lobby, Secretary of Agriculture David Houston wrote, "It was impossible to move around without bumping into [lobbyists]—at hotels, clubs, and even private houses." Wilson criticized the "money without limit" spent by the lobbyists and began a public campaign to combat their influence.

His strategy worked. Despite initial Senate opposition Congress passed the Underwood Tariff Act in 1913. It reduced tariffs to their lowest levels in more than 50 years. To make up for lost revenue, the bill introduced a graduated income tax. This would tax people at different rates according to their incomes. The act levied a 1 percent annual tax on the income of single persons earning more than $3,000 and on married couples earning more than $4,000. The act included an additional graduated tax, which ranged from 1 percent for people earning $20,000

SECTION ④ RESOURCES

REPRODUCIBLE

▶ Guided Reading Strategy 10.4
▶ Literature Reading 10: Life as a Factory Worker
▶ Primary Source Reading 10: Child Labor Practices
▶ Graphic Organizer Activity 10: Women's Suffrage

TECHNOLOGY

▶ One-Stop Planner, Lesson 10.4
▶ Holt Researcher: American History CD–ROM
▶ Homework Practice Online

REINFORCEMENT, REVIEW, AND ASSESSMENT

▶ Section 4 Review, p. 321
▶ Daily Quiz 10.4
▶ Main Idea Activity 10.4
▶ English Audio Summary 10.4
▶ Spanish Audio Summary 10.4

ALL LEVELS: To help students understand how President Wilson's proposals affected big business and U.S. citizens, copy the graphic organizer at the right on the chalkboard, omitting the italicized answers. Ask each student to complete it. After students have finished their graphic organizers, ask them to write paragraphs evaluating the overall success of Wilson's reforms. **English Language Learners**

HOMEWORK *Tell students to imagine that they are advisers to President Wilson. Ask each student to develop a media campaign to "sell" Wilson's business reforms to the public. Remind students that their campaigns must explain the reforms and present supporting arguments.*

TARIFF REFORM
reform: *Underwood Tariff Act*
effects: *allowed the government to investigate corporations; allowed the government to issue "cease and desist" orders*

BANKING REFORM
reform: *Federal Reserve Act*
effects: *created "bankers' banks" stabilized the banking system; helped small farmers gain access to lower interest rates*

PRESIDENT WILSON AND BIG BUSINESS

GENERAL BUSINESS REFORM
reform: *Clayton Antitrust Act*
effects: *extended the 1890 Sherman Antitrust Act; helped the government regulate monopolies*

reform: *Federal Trade Commission*
effects: *allowed the government to investigate corporations; allowed the government to issue "cease and desist" orders*

HISTORY MAKERS SPEAK

Woodrow Wilson in *For the Record: A Documentary History of America,* Vol. 2

Wilson and the Trusts. Wilson explained his opposition to trusts in a campaign speech. "You know, of course, how the little man is crushed by the trusts. He gets a local market. The big concerns come in and undersell him in his local market, and that is the only market he has; if he cannot make a profit there, he is killed. They can make a profit through all the rest of the Union, while they are underselling him in his locality, and recouping themselves by what they can earn elsewhere. Thus their competitors can be put out of business, one by one, wherever they dare to show a head."

CRITICAL THINKING
According to Wilson, how did trusts eliminate competition?

ANSWER: Students should respond that Wilson indicated that trusts dropped their prices to drive local competitors out of markets. The trusts could do this because they made profits elsewhere.

VISUAL RECORD ANSWER
(for p. 317)
Students might answer children.

PRESIDENTIAL
Lives

1856–1924
In Office 1913–1921

Woodrow Wilson

Woodrow Wilson had a reputation for being overly serious and inflexible. He often found it difficult to compromise. At times he opposed legislation that he himself had originally proposed if it had been amended by someone else. He once told a political associate, "I am sorry for those who disagree with me. . . . Because I know they are wrong."

Yet, despite his seriousness, Wilson was superstitious when it came to the number 13, which he believed was his lucky number. He pointed out that there were 13 letters in his name and often referred to the fact that the United States originally had 13 states. When he sailed to Europe for the Paris Peace Conference following World War I, he even instructed the captain to delay docking for one day. He wanted to arrive on the 13th of December.

This 1913 cartoon depicts President Wilson's antitrust legislation as a fence protecting small businesses.

---

to 6 percent for those earning more than $500,000. Supporters argued that the income tax created a fairer tax system.

Banking. Next on Wilson's agenda was banking reform. At the time, no central fund existed from which banks could borrow to prevent collapse during financial panics. As a result, banks commonly failed when many people withdrew their deposits at the same time. Reform was clearly necessary, but Americans disagreed on how to change the banking system. Conservative business groups wanted to give the nation's large private banks more control. In contrast, many Democrats and progressive Republicans wanted the government to run the system.

Wilson helped draft the **Federal Reserve Act** of 1913, which combined these two views. It created a three-tiered banking system. At the top was the Federal Reserve Board, a group appointed by the president and charged with running the system. At the second level were 12 Federal Reserve banks, under mixed public and private control. These "bankers' banks" served other banks rather than individuals. At the third level were private banks, which could borrow from the Federal Reserve banks at interest rates set by the Board. The bill particularly helped farmers by giving them access to lower interest rates. "It puts them on a footing with other business men and masters of enterprise, as it should," Wilson pointed out. "They will find themselves quit [freed] of many of the difficulties which now hamper them in the field of credit."

Big business. Having achieved important tariff and banking reforms, Wilson turned to business regulation. He wanted to limit the power of monopolies, which he viewed as a threat to small businesses. Toward this end, Wilson backed passage of the **Clayton Antitrust Act** in October 1914. This act clarified and extended the 1890 Sherman Antitrust Act by clearly stating what corporations could not do. For example, companies could not sell goods below cost to drive competitors out of business. Nor could they buy competing companies' stock to create a monopoly. The bill did not outlaw these actions in all cases. It was only illegal when the government could prove that a company was doing these things to intentionally create a monopoly. One senator concluded that the original Clayton bill "was a raging lion with a mouth full of teeth." The act as passed, however, had "degenerated [been reduced] to a tabby cat with soft gums, a plaintive [sad] mew, and an anemic appearance." Despite its

LEVEL 1: Ask students to identify how President Wilson attempted to help farmers and laborers. *(Students should note that Wilson urged Congress to pass the Federal Farm Loan Act and the Federal Workmen's Compensation Act.)* Ask students to assess the success of these efforts. *(Students should note that Wilson prevented the 1916 railroad strike but failed to end child labor.)* Tell students to imagine that they are either farmers or workers. Have each student write a 25-word telegram to President Wilson urging him to support pro-farmer or pro-worker legislation. Ask volunteers to read their telegrams to the class. Students may wish to include their telegrams in their portfolios. **English Language Learners**

LEVELS 2 AND 3: Tell students to imagine that they are modern-day historians attending a conference. Tell students to imagine that the keynote speaker has just made the following statement: *President Wilson accomplished so much on behalf of farmers and laborers that he deserves to be known as "the friend of the people."* Have each student prepare a two- to three-minute response to the statement. *(See the Level 1 lesson for the correct points.)* Remind students that their responses must be grounded in fact and should draw on the material presented in the textbook. Ask volunteers to deliver their responses to the class.

shortcomings, the American Federation of Labor (AFL) enthusiastically praised Wilson's support of the Clayton Act. AFL leader Samuel Gompers called it "the Magna Charter of American labor."

As part of the New Freedom program, the Wilson administration backed the creation of the **Federal Trade Commission** (FTC) by Congress in September 1914. The FTC was authorized to investigate corporations. It could issue "cease and desist orders" to corporations engaged in unfair or fraudulent practices and use the courts to enforce its rulings. The FTC targeted abuses such as mislabeled products and false claims. Progressives were displeased, however, when Wilson appointed to the commission a number of people who were sympathetic to big business.

Advertisements like this one made unsupported claims about a product's benefits.

✔ **READING CHECK: Drawing Conclusions** How did Wilson's proposals represent "new freedom" for U.S. citizens? Lower tariffs and lower interest rates helped farmers. The Clayton Act protected smaller businesses from monopolies and the FTC protected people from unfair business practices.

Wilson and Workers

In 1914 Walter Lippmann assessed President Wilson's New Freedom program. He wrote, "The New Freedom means the effort of small business men and farmers to use the government against the larger collective organization of industry." Throughout his first term, Wilson supported legislation to aid working people.

Farm and labor acts. Congress passed the Federal Farm Loan Act in 1916. This act provided low-interest loans to farmers by setting up 12 federal farm-loan banks, each with $750,000 capital to distribute to needy farmers. The law won strong support in rural areas of the United States.

Also in 1916, a railroad strike threatened to paralyze the nation's rail lines. Wilson invited labor leaders and railroad managers to the White House to work out an agreement. He warned both sides about the disastrous effects such a strike could have on the nation's economy and citizens. When these efforts failed, he addressed Congress in support of a law that would reduce the workday for railroad workers from 10 hours to 8 hours without a cut in pay. The ensuing **Adamson Act** not only won applause from reformers but also prevented the strike.

With Wilson's support, Congress also passed the Federal Workmen's Compensation Act to provide benefits to federal workers injured on the job. Other Wilson labor initiatives included a provision in the Clayton Antitrust Act that affirmed labor's right to strike as long as property was not permanently damaged.

Child labor. The Wilson administration was less successful in its campaign against child labor. For years progressives had wanted to keep young children from working in factories, mills, and mines. Labor organizer Mary Harris Jones later recalled how such work affected the children.

 History Makers Speak

❝Every day little children came into Union Headquarters, some with their hands off, some with the thumb missing, some with their fingers off at the knuckle. They were stooped little things, round shouldered and skinny. Many were not over ten years of age.❞

—Mary Harris Jones, *The Autobiography of Mother Jones*

INTERPRETING THE VISUAL RECORD

Mother Jones. Mary Harris Jones fought for better working conditions and child labor laws throughout her life. At the age of 70, she marched in this 1910 protest march. *Who is marching with Mother Jones?*

The Federal Trade Commission. President Wilson viewed the Federal Trade Commission as an organization to foster cooperation between government and business. He therefore appointed businessmen, such as industrialist Edward Hurley, to head the FTC. Many progressives, however, saw the FTC as an agency to observe and regulate industries. Wilson's appointments confused and angered them.

CRITICAL THINKING What might Wilson's appointments to the FTC have revealed about his attitudes toward industry?

ANSWER: Students may suggest that Wilson's appointments revealed that he wanted to work with business leaders, not oppose them.

THAT'S INTERESTING!

Among the reform measures passed during Wilson's presidency was the Seaman's Act, which set labor standards for sailors on U.S. ships and those on foreign ships visiting U.S. ports. One provision of the act stipulated that at least 75 percent of a vessel's crew understand the language spoken by the ship's officers.

SPOTLIGHT
on the Armory Show

Ask students to conduct research on the Armory Show. Have students select one artist whose work appeared in the show, such as Vincent Van Gogh, Paul Cézanne, or Marcel Duchamp. Ask each student to create a five-minute multimedia presentation on his or her chosen artist. Students' presentations should offer general biographical information, discuss the person's entry into art, describe the artist's work, and possibly display selected pieces. Ask volunteers to display their multimedia presentations to the class. Students may wish to include tapes or scripts of their presentations in their portfolios.
Block Scheduling

SPOTLIGHT
on Child Labor

Ask students to conduct research on modern-day efforts to eradicate child labor, particularly those efforts led by teenagers. Have each student prepare a short oral presentation on the issue. Students should discuss specific efforts, describe their causes, and assess their effects. Ask volunteers to deliver their presentations to the class. Then have students select the most effective effort. To extend the lesson, ask students to somehow participate in the fight against child labor. Students might write letters to their representatives, for example, or collect signatures on petitions. **Block Scheduling**

ECONOMICS

Child Labor. Children played an important role in the nation's economy during the early 1900s. The 1900 census revealed that 1.75 million children between the ages of 10 and 15 held jobs. Ten years later, the number had risen to 1.99 million. Many parents forced their children to work. The average family needed $800 a year to survive, but the average unskilled job paid less than $500 a year, creating a dangerous shortfall.

ACTIVITY: Tell students to imagine that it is 1916 and that they are child workers. Have each student write a letter to President Wilson asking him to pass child labor laws.

THAT'S INTERESTING!

Children in Georgia's Columbus Manufacturing Mill worked from 5:30 A.M. to 5:30 P.M. without a lunch break. Mill owner Frederick Gordon opposed child labor laws because mill owners had made a "gentleman's agreement" to limit 10-year-olds to a 66-hour week.

AMERICAN ARTS ANSWERS

1. The artists fought back against control by big museums.

2. It made the show a huge success.

Rising protests against child labor from the National Consumers League and other groups prompted Congress to pass the **Keating-Owen Child Labor Act** in 1916. Backed by Wilson, the act outlawed the interstate sale of products produced by child labor. In 1918, however, the Supreme Court declared the law unconstitutional because it restricted commerce instead of directly outlawing child labor. Another law, passed in 1919, met the same fate.

✔ **READING CHECK: Evaluating** How successful were President Wilson's attempts to help farmers and laborers? The Federal Farm Loan Act of 1916 provided low-interest loans to farmers and won strong support in rural areas. The Keating-Owen Child Labor Act, however, was declared unconstitutional by the Supreme Court.

AMERICAN ARTS

The Armory Show

The progressive reform spirit influenced art as well as economic policies in the early 1900s. Just as reformers attacked business trusts, artists tackled the leading American museums' control over which paintings and sculptures the public saw. Determined to introduce the American public to modern art, a small group of artists formed the Association of American Painters and Sculptors (AAPS) in 1912. The group combed galleries and studios in Berlin, Munich, Paris, and The Hague in search of works to display. On February 17, 1913, the International Exhibition of Modern Art opened in the 69th Regiment Armory in New York City. The Armory Show, as it was called, presented some 1,600 works by both European and American artists.

Newspaper reporters raved about the show, calling it "an event not to be missed." Art critics were not so kind. They blasted Vincent Van Gogh as "unskilled" and Paul Cézanne as "absolutely without talent." As for Marcel Duchamp's *Nude Descending a Staircase, No. 2,* one critic described it as "an explosion in a shingle factory." Ironically, the critics' hostility boosted attendance, which exceeded the organizers' wildest dreams.

Even if it failed to win over some critics to modern art, the Armory Show was a huge success in terms of attendance and publicity. Before the show moved to Chicago, the AAPS honored its "friends and enemies" in the press with a steak dinner. Speeches were made; diners sang and danced. One hostile critic offered grudging praise. "It was a good show," he said, "but don't do it again."

Marcel Duchamp's Nude Descending a Staircase, No. 2

Understanding the Arts

1. How did the Armory Show reflect issues of the Progressive Era?
2. How did the public react to the show's artwork?

TEACH OBJECTIVE 3

LEVEL 1: Ask students to reread the subsection entitled Different approaches. Then organize students into two groups, one representing the National American Woman Suffrage Association's (NAWSA) approach to voting rights, and one representing the National Woman's Party's approach to voting rights. Act as the moderator and conduct a debate between the groups based on strategies. *(The NAWSA group should support a nonpartisan, local approach, while the National Woman's Party group should support a national, more radical approach.)* When the debate is finished, ask each student to write one or two paragraphs discussing the different strategies and explaining how American women gained the right to vote. *(Women pressed for a constitutional amendment, pressured appropriate senators, and finally gained the right to vote with the Nineteenth Amendment.)* Students may wish to include their paragraphs in their portfolios.
English Language Learners, Cooperative Learning

LEVEL 2: Tell students to imagine that it is 1930 and that they are suffragists preparing to speak at a 10th-anniversary celebration of the Nineteenth Amendment. Have each student write a three- to four-minute speech describing how women gained the right to vote. *(See the Level 1 lesson for the correct factors.)* Ask volunteers to deliver their speeches to the class. Students may wish to include their speeches in their portfolios.

The Struggle for Women's Suffrage

Another part of the progressive agenda—the campaign for women's suffrage—faced strong opposition. Liquor interests feared that women would vote for prohibition. Businesses feared that the vote would empower women to demand better wages and working conditions. When one state senator expressed the belief that the vote would rob women of their beauty and charm, a suffragist reacted angrily.

History Makers Speak

❝We have women working in the foundries.... Women in the laundries ... stand for 13 or 14 hours in the terrible steam and heat with their hands in hot starch. Surely these women won't lose any more of their beauty and charm by putting a ballot in a ballot box once a year than they are likely to lose standing in foundries or laundries all year.❞

—Rose Schneiderman, "Senators versus Working Women"

Different approaches. One leading force in the suffrage movement was the **National American Woman Suffrage Association** (NAWSA), founded in 1890. Its first two presidents, Elizabeth Cady Stanton and Susan B. Anthony, distrusted party politics because of Republican leaders' failure after the Civil War to press for voting rights for women. As a result, they took a nonpartisan, local approach, trying to get state legislatures to grant women the vote. They achieved few successes in their first few years of lobbying. By 1901 just four states, all located in the western region of the country, had given women full voting rights.

In 1914 **Alice Paul**, a militant young Quaker suffragist, broke away from NAWSA. She formed a second organization, the Congressional Union for Woman Suffrage, which in 1916 became the National Woman's Party. The party adopted a national, rather than a state-by-state, strategy. It focused on passing a constitutional amendment guaranteeing women the right to vote.

Paul had studied in Britain and adopted the attention-getting protest tactics used by British suffragists. For example, in January 1917, after Wilson's re-election, the National Woman's Party began round-the-clock picketing of the White House in an effort to pressure Wilson to support a suffrage amendment. They held banners asking, "Mr. President, What Will You Do for Woman Suffrage?" and "How Long Must Women Wait for Liberty?" Some women chained themselves to railings. Many were arrested. Some went on hunger strikes in prison. Paul's efforts convinced thousands of women of the importance of the suffragists' cause.

Meanwhile, the suffrage movement gained momentum. Massachusetts, New Jersey, New York, and Pennsylvania all held special referendums on women's suffrage in 1915. Although the motions were defeated in each state, support for women's suffrage ranged from 35 to 46 percent of the total votes. NAWSA saw its membership grow to nearly 2 million. Energized by the leadership of the highly skilled organizer **Carrie Chapman Catt**, NAWSA continued to use traditional political strategies to attain voting rights.

INTERPRETING THE VISUAL RECORD

Women's suffrage. Suffragists struggled to convince both men and women that politics was a proper activity for women. *In what ways do you think these demonstrators were able to further the suffragist cause?*

Alice Paul gives a speech to members of the National Woman's Party.

319

LEVEL 3: Tell students to imagine that they are suffragists who have been asked to supply political advice to women in a country without universal suffrage. Have each student write a one- to two-page paper summarizing how American women gained the right to vote. *(See the Level 1 lesson for the correct factors.)* Students may wish to conclude their papers with specific suggestions about how the women from the other country should go about winning the right to vote. Students may wish to include their papers in their portfolios.

HOMEWORK *Distribute Activity 10, Women's Suffrage, from* **Graphic Organizer Activities,** *and have each student complete it.*

Magazine covers from the 1920s celebrated the success of the suffrage movement.

Carrie Chapman Catt

A new NAWSA leader. Carrie Chapman Catt was born Carrie Clinton Lane in 1859 in Wisconsin. From childhood on, Catt was interested in women's rights. When she was 13, Catt was surprised that her mother was not going to vote in the presidential elections of 1872. "I think it's very unfair that women can't vote, don't you?" she asked a neighbor boy.

In 1877 Catt began attending Iowa State Agricultural College—now Iowa State University. While at school, Catt won for female students the right to speak at the school literary society. There she initiated a debate on women's suffrage. She argued: "How is it possible that a woman who is unfit to vote, should be the mother of, and bring up, a man who is?"

After graduating in 1880, Catt went to work as a teacher. She became superintendent of schools of Mason City, Iowa, in her second year. In 1885 she resigned her position after marrying Leo Chapman. Married women were not allowed to work in the schools. Catt began working as co-editor of the local newspaper. She also wrote a weekly feature called "Woman's World." After Chapman died of typhoid fever, Catt began a new career as a lecturer.

Catt soon became involved with the women's suffrage movement and served as a delegate at the NAWSA convention. About this time, she married George Catt. Over the next decade, Carrie Chapman Catt continued to travel and campaign on behalf of women's suffrage. In 1900 she became the president of NAWSA. She remained president until 1904, when she began serving as president of the International Woman Suffrage Alliance (IWSA). As president of IWSA, Catt traveled around the world, seeking to win women to the cause of feminism. After returning to the United States, Catt again threw herself into the task of achieving women's suffrage. She remained a political and social activist until her death in 1947.

Success. Launching what came to be called Catt's Winning Plan in 1916, NAWSA won a string of successes for suffrage at the state level. After the United States entered World War I in 1917, leaders of the movement—along with millions of American women—lent strong support to the war effort. Their patriotism helped weaken opposition to women's suffrage. Even President

Great Debates
The Progressive Legacy

Although progressivism led to reforms in many areas, some of its reforms failed to bring about the anticipated changes. The government's ability to regulate the economy and pay for new programs improved, but many business regulations fell short of remaking the capitalist system. Reforms such as the initiative, referendum, and recall were primarily used at the local level. Thus, they had little impact on broad questions of national public policy.

One of progressivism's greatest successes, the settlement-house movement, improved opportunities for women, brought urban reform, and focused attention on the plight of immigrants. However, few of the settlement-house programs addressed the needs of African Americans. The progressive presidents showed little interest in racial issues. Some critics argued that President Theodore Roosevelt set back the African American cause in 1906. White residents in Brownsville, Texas, had started violent protests against black soldiers at a nearby fort. Despite little evidence that the soldiers were involved in any violence, Roosevelt issued dishonorable discharges to the entire company to pacify the white community. Presidents Taft and Wilson both supported racial segregation.

Despite these shortcomings, some scholars note that progressives took real strides toward making the new industrial society more just, orderly, and humane. Their efforts to end child labor, protect workers and consumers, and promote conservation profoundly influenced the nation. Supporters argue that their greatest legacy was to demonstrate that the U.S. democratic system could respond and adapt to changes in American life.

REVIEW

Have students complete the **Section 4 Review** on p. 321.

ASSESS

Have students complete **Daily Quiz 10.4**. As **Alternative Assessment**, you may want to use the President Wilson telegram or the voting rights strategy debate in this section's lessons.

RETEACH

Have students complete **Main Idea Activity for English Language Learners and Special-Needs Students 10.4**. Then pair students and assign each pair a subsection. Ask each pair to write three true-or-false statements about the material in its assigned subsection. Collect these statements and use them to quiz the class as a whole. Have students recast false statements to make them true.
English Language Learners, Cooperative Learning

EXTEND

Have students conduct research on the women's rights movement during the 1910s and pick a significant figure. Have each student develop a three- to four-minute monologue about the figure, explaining his or her background, approach to women's rights, and overall success or failure. Ask volunteers to deliver their monologues to the class. **Block Scheduling**

Wilson came out in support of women's suffrage in a speech in 1918.

A 1918 Senate vote on a constitutional amendment to grant women the vote fell short by just two votes. Suffragists immediately targeted four senators who had voted against women's suffrage and who were running for re-election that November. Three of the four lost, sending other politicians a strong message. In 1919 Congress proposed the **Nineteenth Amendment**, granting women full voting rights. It was ratified in 1920.

Lawyer Crystal Eastman declared at the amendment's passage, "What we must do is to create conditions of outward freedom in which a free woman's soul can be born and grow." Catt commented, "Now that we have the vote let us remember we are . . . free and equal citizens. Let us do our part to keep it a true and triumphant democracy." She cautioned, however, that the vote was only an "entering wedge." Women still had to force their way through the "locked door" of political decision making.

Women's Suffrage, 1890–1920

Interpreting Maps Before 1920 women's suffrage rights in the United States varied widely according to where they lived.

2 PLACES AND REGIONS Which section of the United States took the lead in granting the vote to women? Why?

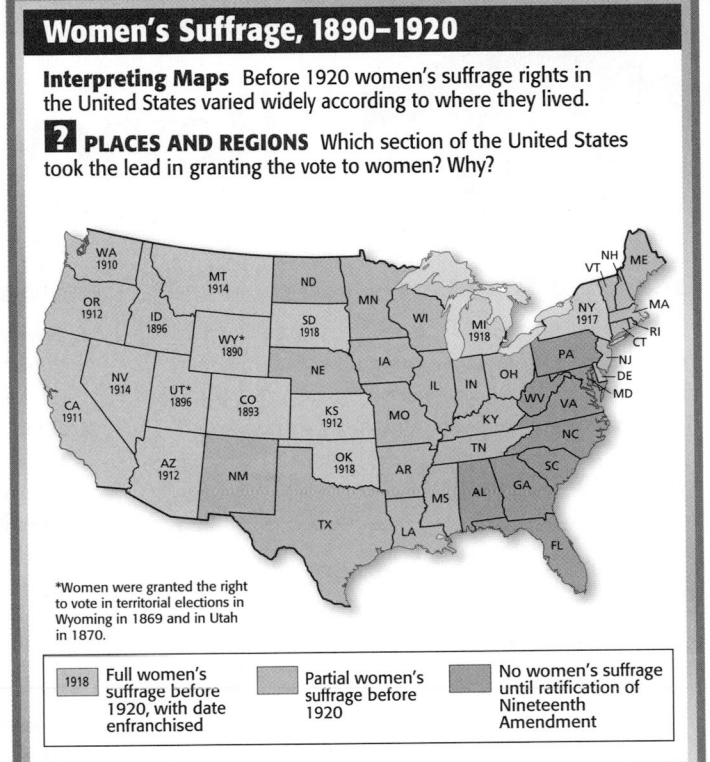

*Women were granted the right to vote in territorial elections in Wyoming in 1869 and in Utah in 1870.

| 1918 | Full women's suffrage before 1920, with date enfranchised | Partial women's suffrage before 1920 | No women's suffrage until ratification of Nineteenth Amendment |

✔ **READING CHECK: Sequencing** What steps did reformers take to achieve equality of political rights for women? **Suffrage supporters campaigned for the defeat of four U.S. senators who had voted against suffrage. In 1919 Congress proposed the Nineteenth Amendment granting women full voting rights.**

SECTION 4 REVIEW

1. Identify and explain:
Federal Reserve Act
Clayton Antitrust Act
Federal Trade Commission
Adamson Act
Keating-Owen Child Labor Act
National American Woman Suffrage Association
Alice Paul
Carrie Chapman Catt
Nineteenth Amendment

2. Categorizing Copy the web below. Use it to describe the reforms passed during Woodrow Wilson's administration.

- Big Business
- Child Labor
- Banking
- **WILSON'S ADMINISTRATION**
- Tariffs
- Women's Rights
- Farm & Labor

3. **Finding the Main Idea**
a. How did the Wilson administration build on the work of previous presidents?
b. How did the Nineteenth Amendment expand women's right to participate in the democratic process?
c. How well did the progressive politicians accomplish the goals of progressive reformers?

4. **Writing and Critical Thinking**
Evaluating Write a newspaper article evaluating Wilson's success in enlisting the "forces of humanity" to help child laborers, farmers, and railroad and federal workers.
Consider:
- what Wilson meant by "forces of humanity"
- Wilson's reforms for farmers, railroad and federal workers, and child laborers
- how these groups were helped by reforms

Homework Practice Online
keyword: SE3 HP10

CHAPTER 10 REVIEW ANSWERS

Creating a Time Line
Each event should have an explanation and the correct date.

Writing a Summary
See the Reading Checks in each section for main ideas.

Identifying People and Ideas
1. election reform that allowed voters to introduce legislation

2. progressive political leader who backed the Wisconsin Idea

3. permitted the federal government to set railroad rates and to regulate companies engaged in interstate commerce

4. Republican president who supported the conservation movement and later ran as the Progressive Party presidential candidate

5. process of making damaged land productive

6. Democrat elected to the presidency in 1912 and 1916

7. Wilson's reform platform

8. law that reorganized the banking system

9. suffragist who advocated militant strategies

10. granted woman the right to vote

CHAPTER 10

REVIEW AND ASSESSMENT RESOURCES

TECHNOLOGY RESOURCES

▶ Chapter 10 Test Generator (on the One-Stop Planner)
▶ Global Skill Builder CD-ROM
▶ HRW Go site

REINFORCEMENT, REVIEW, AND ASSESSMENT

▶ Chapter 10 Review, pp. 322–23
▶ Chapter 10 Tutorial for Students, Parents, Mentors, and Peers

▶ Chapter 10 Test (Form A or B)
▶ Portfolio Activities and Alternative Assessment Handbook, Chapter 10
▶ Chapter 10 Test for English Language Learners and Special-Needs Students

REVIEW

Have students complete the **Chapter 10 Review** on pp. 322–23.

ASSESS

Use one of the chapter tests to assess students' understanding of the content. For **Alternative Assessment**, see the **Portfolio Activities and Alternative Assessment Handbook.**

CHAPTER 10

Review

Creating a Time Line

Copy the time line below onto a sheet of paper. Complete the time line by filling in the events and dates from the chapter that you think were most significant. Pick three events and explain why you think they were significant.

1900   1910   1920

Writing a Summary

Using standard grammar, spelling, sentence structure, and punctuation, write an overview of events in the chapter.

Identifying People and Ideas

Identify the following terms or individuals and explain their significance.

1. initiative
2. Robert M. LaFollette
3. Hepburn Act
4. Theodore Roosevelt
5. reclamation
6. Woodrow Wilson
7. New Freedom
8. Federal Reserve Act
9. Alice Paul
10. Nineteenth Amendment

Understanding Main Ideas

SECTION 1 *(pp. 298–302)*

1. What were the strengths of the city-commission and city-manager forms of government?
2. How did the Wisconsin Idea lay the foundation for further reforms?

SECTION 2 *(pp. 303–309)*

3. How did the Square Deal reflect President Theodore Roosevelt's approach to government?

SECTION 3 *(pp. 310–314)*

4. What failures and successes did President Taft experience during his term in office?

SECTION 4 *(pp. 315–321)*

5. How did women's suffrage leaders achieve success?

Reviewing Themes

1. **Government** How did reformers seek to limit the power of big business and make government more democratic in the early 1900s?
2. **Economics** How did President Roosevelt attempt to regulate business without discouraging free enterprise?
3. **Constitutional Heritage** Why were the Sixteenth, Seventeenth, and Nineteenth Amendments adopted?

Thinking Critically

1. **Evaluating** Evaluate the impact of progressive reforms including initiative, referendum, and recall.
2. **Summarizing** What developments in the conservation of natural resources occurred in the early 1900s?
3. **Drawing Conclusions** How did the purpose of the Interstate Commerce Commission compare with its performance in the early 1900s?
4. **Comparing** Compare the successes of Presidents Roosevelt, Taft, and Wilson in enacting reform legislation.
5. **Analyzing Information** How did voting reforms in the Progressive Era expand the democratic process and the right to participate in that process?

Writing About History

Evaluating Write an essay evaluating the progressives' record. Use the following graphic to organize your thoughts.

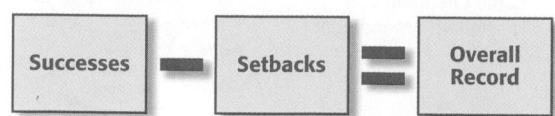

| Successes | ▬ | Setbacks | ▬ | Overall Record |

RETEACH

Pair students and randomly assign each pair one of the sections. Have each pair write three questions about the material, taking care to ensure the accuracy of the questions. Then have each pair present its questions to the entire class in the form of a quiz show. The pair that answers the most questions correctly, excluding its own, wins the quiz show.
English Language Learners, Cooperative Learning

EXTEND

Ask students to reconsider the basic problems caused by political machines. Then have students think about those problems in light of the local and state reforms initiated by the Progressive reformers. Ask students whether the reforms restored confidence or merely continued the status quo. To conclude, have students write a two- to three-page report on how other reforms might have improved American life in the early 1900s, conducting additional research as necessary.
Block Scheduling

Building Social Studies Skills

Interpreting Maps
Study the map below. Then use it to help answer the questions that follow.

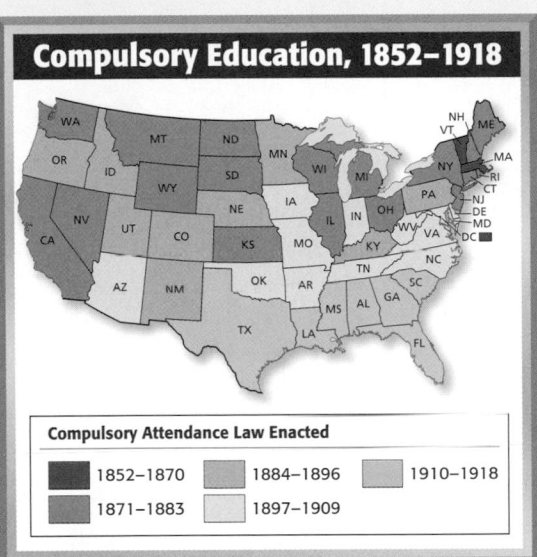

Compulsory Education, 1852–1918

Compulsory Attendance Law Enacted
- 1852–1870
- 1871–1883
- 1884–1896
- 1897–1909
- 1910–1918

1. Which section of the country was the last to adopt compulsory education laws?
   a. New England
   b. The Great Plains
   c. The South
   d. The Far West

2. What reasons might suggest the development of compulsory education laws according to this pattern?

Interpreting Political Cartoons
Study the political cartoon below. Then use it to help you answer the questions that follow.

THE LION-TAMER

3. Which of these progressive leaders is represented by the lion tamer?
   a. Theodore Roosevelt
   b. William Howard Taft
   c. Woodrow Wilson
   d. Eugene Debs

4. How might you represent in a political cartoon Theodore Roosevelt's run for the presidency in the election of 1912?

Alternative Assessment

Building Your Portfolio

Citizenship
Imagine that you are a delegate at the 1912 Progressive Party convention. Write a platform for the party that translates the problems of political machines, women's suffrage, business regulation, and worker protection into specific reforms your party hopes to institute. Be sure that your platform addresses the party's unique position as a third political party.

U.S. HISTORY

☑ **internet** connect

Internet Activity: go.hrw.com
KEYWORD: SE3 AN10

Choose a topic on progressive politicians to:
- learn about Theodore Roosevelt and the national park system and create a travel brochure.
- use a database on oil and gasoline prices and create a graph that shows changes in price.
- research the conditions that resulted in the Meat Inspection Act and write a journal entry from the point of view of a worker or legislator.

---

2. Roosevelt withdrew from sale millions of acres of public land; Congress passed the Newlands Reclamation Act and created the National Conservation Commission and the National park Service.

3. It became a very significant regulatory agency.

4. All three presidents approved reform legislation. Roosevelt's efforts protected consumers and the environment; Taft's efforts regulated or broke trusts; Wilson's efforts enacted some labor reform laws.

5. Answers will vary. Students should discuss the secret ballot, the recall, the referendum, the initiative as well as the Seventeenth and Nineteenth Amendments.

Writing
Students' essays should include information about business regulation, consumer protection, and voting reform. Essays should discuss specific progressives and should evaluate setbacks such as the failure of child labor laws.

Building Social Studies Skills
1. c

2. Answers will vary. Students might suggest Reconstruction; progressive reformers primarily in Northeast and Northwest; farming communities in South worked by entire families.

3. a

4. Answers will vary. Cartoons should represent the three-way race for the presidency.

America and the World

CHAPTER RESOURCE MANAGER

	Objectives	Pacing Guide	Reproducible Resources
SECTION 1 **Expansion in the Pacific** pp. 326–32	★ Identify the major factors that drove imperialism. ★ Explain how the United States acquired Hawaii. ★ Describe the U.S. role in China. ★ Discuss how Japan became a world power.	**Regular** 2 days **Block Scheduling** 1 day *Block Scheduling Handbook with Team Teaching Strategies, pp. 61–66*	**RS** Guided Reading Strategy 11.1 **SM** Geography Activity 11: Foreign Powers in China, 1911 **IC** Literature Reading 11: Protesting Military Action **E** Hands-On History Activity: Property Annexation in Your Community
SECTION 2 **War with Spain** pp. 333–39	★ Recount how Spain responded to the revolt in Cuba. ★ Discuss the major causes of the Spanish-American War. ★ Describe the major battles of the Spanish-American War. ★ Explain what happened to the Philippines after the Spanish-American War.	**Regular** 2 days **Block Scheduling** 1 day *Block Scheduling Handbook with Team Teaching Strategies, pp. 61–66*	**RS** Guided Reading Strategy 11.2 **PS** Primary Source Reading 11: Teddy Roosevelt's Cavalry
SECTION 3 **Expansion in Latin America** pp. 340–44	★ Describe how the United States governed Cuba and Puerto Rico. ★ Analyze the major obstacles to building the Panama Canal. ★ Summarize U.S. policy toward Latin America during the late 1800s and early 1900s.	**Regular** 1 day **Block Scheduling** .5 day *Block Scheduling Handbook with Team Teaching Strategies, pp. 61–66*	**RS** Guided Reading Strategy 11.3 **RS** Graphic Organizer Activity 11: Changes in Cuba **PS** Biography Reading 11: William Gorgas **E** Creative Teaching Strategy: Analyzing Political Cartoons
SECTION 4 **Conflict with Mexico** pp. 345–49	★ List the major events of the Mexican Revolution. ★ Explain why the United States intervened in Mexico. ★ Report on the outcomes of the Mexican Revolution.	**Regular** 1 day **Block Scheduling** .5 day *Block Scheduling Handbook with Team Teaching Strategies, pp. 61–66*	**RS** Guided Reading Strategy 11.4

Chapter Resource Key

PS	Primary Sources	**REV**	Review		Video
RS	Reading Support	**ELL**	Reinforcement and English Language Learners		Internet
IC	Interdisciplinary Connections				Holt Presentation Maker Using Microsoft® PowerPoint®
E	Enrichment		Transparencies		
SM	Skills Mastery		CD–ROM		
A	Assessment		Music		

One-Stop Planner CD-ROM

See the *One-Stop Planner* for a complete list of additional resources for students and teachers.

One-Stop Planner CD–ROM

It's easy to plan lessons, select resources, and print out materials for your students when you use the **One-Stop Planner CD–ROM with Test Generator.**

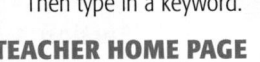

internet connect

HRW ONLINE RESOURCES
GO TO: go.hrw.com
Then type in a keyword.

Technology Resources	Reinforcement, Review, and Assessment
One-Stop Planner, Lesson 11.1 Holt Researcher: American History CD–ROM Homework Practice Online	**REV** Section 1 Review, p. 332 **A** Daily Quiz 11.1 **ELL** Main Idea Activity 11.1 **ELL** English Audio Summary 11.1 **ELL** Spanish Audio Summary 11.1
One-Stop Planner, Lesson 11.2 Everyday Life in America Transparency 19: Photojournalism in the Spanish-American War **CNN.** Presents America: Yesterday and Today, 1850 to the Present Segment: "Remember the *Maine!*" Holt Researcher: American History CD–ROM Homework Practice Online HRW Go site	**REV** Section 2 Review, p. 339 **A** Daily Quiz 11.2 **ELL** Main Idea Activity 11.2 **ELL** English Audio Summary 11.2 **ELL** Spanish Audio Summary 11.2
One-Stop Planner, Lesson 11.3 The American Nation Video Program Segment: The Panama Canal; Teacher's Guide, pp. 93–98 Holt Researcher: American History CD–ROM Homework Practice Online	**REV** Section 3 Review, p. 344 **A** Daily Quiz 11.3 **ELL** Main Idea Activity 11.3 **ELL** English Audio Summary 11.3 **ELL** Spanish Audio Summary 11.3
One-Stop Planner, Lesson 11.4 Holt Researcher: American History CD–ROM Homework Practice Online	**REV** Section 4 Review, p. 349 **A** Daily Quiz 11.4 **ELL** Main Idea Activity 11.4 **ELL** English Audio Summary 11.4 **ELL** Spanish Audio Summary 11.4

TEACHER HOME PAGE
KEYWORD: SE3 Teacher

CHAPTER INTERNET ACTIVITIES
KEYWORD: SE3 AN11
Choose an activity to:
• research the construction of the Panama Canal and create a poster.
• write a biography of an American Nobel Prize winner.
• research the causes of the Spanish-American War and create a radio script.

CHAPTER ENRICHMENT LINKS
KEYWORD: SE3 CH11

ONLINE ASSESSMENT
Homework Practice
KEYWORD: SE3 HP11

Standardized Test Prep
KEYWORD: SE3 STP11

Rubrics
KEYWORD: SS Rubrics

ONLINE MAPS, CHARTS, AND GRAPHS
KEYWORD: SE3 MCG
• Panama Canal Zone
• U.S. Interests in Latin America
• U.S. Foreign Trade, 1865–1915

CONTENT UPDATES
KEYWORD: SS Content Updates

HOLT PRESENTATION MAKER
KEYWORD: SE3 PPT11

ONLINE READING SUPPORT
KEYWORD: SS Strategies

CURRENT EVENTS
KEYWORD: S3 Current Events

Meeting Individual Needs

Ability Levels

Level 1 Basic-level activities designed for all students encountering new material

Level 2 Intermediate-level activities designed for average students

Level 3 Challenging activities designed for honors and gifted-and-talented students

English Language Learners Activities that address the needs of students with Limited English Proficiency

Chapter Review and Assessment

 Global Skill Builder CD–ROM

 HRW Go site

REV **Chapter 11 Tutorial for Students, Parents, Mentors, and Peers**

REV **Chapter 11 Review, pp. 350–51**

 Chapter 11 Test Generator (on the One-Stop Planner)

A **Chapter 11 Test (Form A or B)**

A **Alternative Assessment Handbook**

A **Chapter 11 Test for English Language Learners and Special-Needs Students**

11

Section 1 *Expansion in the Pacific, pp. 326–32*

Section 2 *War with Spain, pp. 333–39*

Section 3 *Expansion in Latin America, pp. 340–44*

Section 4 *Conflict with Mexico, pp. 345–49*

Chapter Review *pp. 350–51*

Build on What You Know

Ask students to answer the following questions.

Why might Americans have looked to expand abroad in the late 1800s?

Consider:

• the results of westward expansion

• the need for markets for American goods

Why might the United States have become involved in events in Cuba, Mexico, China, and Japan?

Consider:

• the proximity of Cuba and Mexico to the United States

• the economic interests of the United States on the global scale

exploring the time line

AMERICAN EVENTS

TOPIC: Nobel Prize Winners
GO TO: go.hrw.com
KEYWORD: SE3 AN11

Have students access the Internet through the HRW Go site to conduct research on one of the American Nobel Prize winners. Then have each student write a report that outlines the winner's achievements and contributions.

CHAPTER

11

1898–1917

America and the World

Items soldiers carried during the Spanish-American War

Theodore Roosevelt as an international police officer

THE GRANGER COLLECTION, NEW YORK

1900
Daily Life
The hamburger is introduced in New Haven, Connecticut.

1898
World Events
The Spanish-American War is fought.

1900
The Arts
The Wizard of Oz by L. Frank Baum is published.

1904
Politics
Theodore Roosevelt states his corollary to the Monroe Doctrine.

1898 **1900** **1902** **1904** **1906**

1898
The Arts
H. G. Wells's *War of the Worlds* is published.

1899
Politics
The U.S. Senate votes to annex the Philippines.

1901
Business and Finance
J. P. Morgan creates the United States Steel Company, the world's first billion-dollar corporation.

1904
World Events
American Edward Thompson begins excavation of a sacred well at Chichén Itzá in Mexico.

The Nobel Prize

1901
Science and Technology
The Nobel Prizes are awarded for the first time.

Chichén Itzá

Build on What You Know

After recovering from the Civil War, the United States resumed its economic growth and westward expansion. Creating tremendous wealth for some and jobs for many, the Industrial Revolution transformed the nation. In this chapter you will learn how the United States established itself as a world power. After more than a century of following George Washington's advice and avoiding foreign entanglements, the United States became deeply involved in events abroad, from nearby Cuba and Mexico to distant China and Japan.

Great White Fleet commemorative flag

Peso from a Mexican provisional government

Albert Einstein

1907
World Events
President Roosevelt sends a "Great White Fleet" of U.S. warships on a world cruise.

1910
World Events
The Mexican Revolution begins.

1916
Science and Technology
Albert Einstein publishes his general theory of relativity.

| 1908 | 1910 | 1912 | 1914 | 1916 |

1908
Science and Technology
The Geiger counter, which detects radioactivity, is invented.

1911
The Arts
W. C. Handy's song "Memphis Blues" gains great popularity.

1914
Politics
The United States occupies the city of Veracruz, Mexico.

An early Geiger counter

Sheet music of W. C. Handy's "Memphis Blues"

exploring the time line

GLOBAL EVENTS

GLOBAL RELATIONS

1907 ■ The Great White Fleet. After defeating Russia in the Russo-Japanese War of 1904, western nations began to fear the growing power of Japan. A stronger Japan threatened U.S. economic interests in the Far East. President Theodore Roosevelt wanted to send the U.S. Navy—nicknamed the Great White Fleet—on a worldwide tour as a display of strength. Congress refused to approve funding for the voyage. Roosevelt ordered the fleet to set sail nevertheless. He reasoned that once the fleet was at sea, Congress would have to approve funding. Congress did release funding after the fleet set sail in December 1907.

CRITICAL THINKING What might the Great White Fleet incident have revealed about the relations between the executive and legislative branches?

ANSWER: Students might suggest that the incident reveals the growing power of the presidency in relation to congress during the early 1900s.

SECTION 1

READ TO DISCOVER

1. What major factors drove imperialism?
2. How did the United States acquire Hawaii?
3. What was the U.S. role in China?
4. How did Japan become a world power?

DEFINE

imperialism
subsidy
spheres of influence

IDENTIFY

Henry Cabot Lodge
Alfred Thayer Mahan
Kalakaua
Liliuokalani
John Hay
Open Door Policy
Boxer Rebellion
Matthew Perry

WHY IT MATTERS TODAY

Relations between the United States and China continue to change. Use CNNfyi.com or other **current events** sources to find out about current economic, political, or social issues involving these two countries today. Record your findings in your journal.

Expansion in the Pacific

EYEWITNESSES TO History

"A new consciousness seems to have come upon us—the consciousness of strength—and with it a new appetite, the yearning to show our strength. . . . Ambition, interest, land hunger, pride, the mere joy of fighting, whatever it may be, we are animated by a new sensation. We are face to face with a strange destiny. The taste of Empire is in the mouth of the people even as the taste of blood in the jungle. It means an Imperial policy, the Republic, renascent [reawakened], taking her place with the armed nations."

—*Washington Post*, June 1896

This cartoon shows Uncle Sam harvesting the fruits of imperialism.

This editorial appeared in a June 1896 edition of the *Washington Post.* It reflected the growing strength of the United States and Americans' willingness to use this strength. The United States was ready to join the other great powers of the world and compete in a global economy.

The Impulse for Imperialism

In March 1889 in the South Pacific harbor of Apia, part of present-day Western Samoa, seven warships—one British, three German, and three U.S.—faced off. Before a shot could be fired, a typhoon struck, destroying all but the British ship and possibly preventing a war. **Imperialism**—the quest for colonial empires—had led these three nations to the brink of war. Between 1876 and 1915 a handful of industrialized nations seized control of vast areas of Africa, Asia, and Latin America.

Imperialism was driven by a need for markets and raw materials as well as the desire for power and prestige. Aided by efficient machines and abundant capital, workers in these industrial nations produced far more goods than could be consumed at home. In response, industrialists turned to Africa, Asia, and Latin America for new customers and new sources of raw materials. To protect these new markets from competition, industrialized nations tried to colonize these areas. Senator **Henry Cabot Lodge** of Massachusetts explained that the United States needed to join this competition to maintain its economic and military strength.

History Makers Speak

"Small states are of the past and have no future. . . . The great nations are rapidly absorbing for their future expansion and their present defense all the waste places of the earth. It is a movement which makes for civilization and the advancement of the race. As one of the great nations of the world, the United States must not fall out of the line of march."

—Henry Cabot Lodge, "Our Blundering Foreign Policy," March 1895

American enthusiasm for overseas expansion grew as industrial production surged in the late 1800s. **Alfred Thayer Mahan** of the U.S. Naval War College was

ALL LEVELS: To help students understand the forces that motivated imperialism between 1876 and 1915, copy the graphic organizer at right on the chalkboard, omitting the italicized answers. Have each student complete it. Ask volunteers to read their answers to the class. Conclude by discussing with students the implications of the factors listed in the graphic organizer. **English Language Learners**

HOMEWORK *Tell students to imagine that they are editors who need to prepare jacket copy for a book on imperialism. Have each student write a paragraph*

on the major factors that drove imperialism. (See the graphic organizer for the correct factors.) Ask volunteers to read their book jacket summaries to the class.

Factors That Drove Imperialism
1. *the need for markets*
2. *the need for raw materials*
3. *the desire for power*
4. *the desire for prestige*

→ **Imperialism**

---

one particularly influential supporter. In his widely read book *The Influence of Sea Power upon History*, Mahan argued that the United States needed a strong navy to protect its economic interests in foreign markets. He wrote that such a navy required overseas bases.

> **History Makers Speak**
>
> **"Having . . . no foreign establishments, either colonial or military, the ships of war of the United States, in war, will be like land birds, unable to fly far from their own shores. To provide resting-places for them, where they can coal and repair, would be one of the first duties of a government proposing to itself the development of the power of the nation at sea."**
>
> —Alfred Thayer Mahan, *The Influence of Sea Power upon History*

Other supporters of expansion claimed that the United States had a duty to spread its political system and the Christian religion throughout the world. Whatever the reason, many Americans supported expansion. The competition for territory and markets across the globe led the United States, Great Britain, and Germany to clash in Samoa in 1889. Ten years later, the United States won control over Eastern Samoa, and Germany gained control over Western Samoa.

✔ **READING CHECK: Identifying Points of View** Why did Henry Cabot Lodge and Alfred Thayer Mahan support U.S. expansion?

Both believed that the United States needed to protect its economic interests in foreign markets.

Acquiring Hawaii

Hawaii also interested imperial powers. The Hawaiian Islands had a tropical climate and fertile, lava-enriched soil. In 1778 British explorer Captain James Cook visited the islands and renamed them the Sandwich Islands. Hawaiian chief Kamehameha united the eight major islands during his reign, which lasted from 1795 to 1819. This monarchy held power until 1893.

The Hawaiian Islands lie in the Pacific Ocean some 2,000 miles west of California. They were a good place to build naval bases and coaling stations for ships traveling to and from Asia. Some viewed Hawaiians as an uncivilized people who needed to be introduced to modern industrial society and Christianity. One early visitor described Hawaiian culture.

> **History Makers Speak**
>
> **"The ease with which the Hawaiians on their own land can secure their food supply has undoubtably interfered with their social and industrial advancement. . . . [It] relieves the native from any struggle and unfits him for sustained competition with men from other lands. The fact that food is supplied by nature takes from the native all desire for the acquisition of more land. Today's food can be had for the picking, and tomorrow's as well. Instead of grasping all he can get, he divides with his neighbor, and confidently expects his neighbor to divide with him."**
>
> —Anonymous visitor

The Religious Spirit

THE AMERICAN MISSIONARY MOVEMENT

During the early 1800s Christian missionary societies in the United States began sending missionaries to other parts of the world. The missionary movement grew steadily over the years and then expanded rapidly toward the end of the century. It grew from 16 American missionary societies in the 1860s to 90 in 1900. Tens of thousands of American

Missionary Grace Roberts in Manchuria in 1903

Christians traveled abroad to spread their religious faith. Women played a major role in the missionary movement and made up many of the missionary groups in foreign countries.

Lottie Moon was one such woman. After teaching school in Kentucky and Georgia, she entered missionary service in 1873. For the next 40 years she worked at Southern Baptist stations in northeastern China. The missionary experience not only brought change to nations such as China, but also changed the missionaries themselves. As Lottie Moon wrote, her time in China changed her from "a timid self-distrustful girl into a brave self-reliant woman." In addition to teaching their religious beliefs, missionaries offered classes in mathematics, science, and English. ■

Alfred Thayer Mahan. Born in 1840, Alfred Thayer Mahan was the son of a professor at the U.S. Military Academy at West Point, New York. As a teenager, Mahan entered the U.S. Naval Academy. He served in the U.S. Navy during the Civil War, carrying out blockade duty and other jobs that did not require meritorious service. In 1884 he was invited to join the faculty of the U.S. Naval War College. His lecture notes from the classes he taught at the academy were published as *The Influence of Sea Power upon History.* Surprisingly, Mahan suffered from seasickness and an intense fear of the ocean. He hated to be on board ships at sea.

CRITICAL THINKING How might Mahan have gained his insights regarding the importance of sea power?

ANSWER: Students might suggest that he formulated these insights by studying history rather than by serving extensively on ocean-bound ships, which he hated.

TEACH OBJECTIVE 2

LEVEL 1: Pair students and have each pair create an annotated time line from the 1820s to the 1890s that chronicles the events leading to the U.S. acquisition of Hawaii. *(Time lines should include the following events: the 1820s—American missionaries arrive in Hawaii; the 1870s—Americans control most of the land and trade; 1875—a treaty exempts Hawaiian sugar from U.S. tariffs; 1876—U.S. officials demand Pearl Harbor in exchange for tax-free status for Hawaiian sugar; 1887—the Hawaiian League forces King Kalakaua to sign the Bayonet Constitution; 1891—Liliuokalani becomes queen of Hawaii; 1893—in response to Liliuokalani's* plan to publish a new constitution, supporters of annexation overthrow the monarchy, set up a provisional government, and proclaim Hawaii a U.S. protectorate; 1898—United States annexes Hawaii.) Ask volunteers to present their time lines to the class. **English Language Learners, Cooperative Learning**

LEVEL 2: Tell students to imagine that they are editors for an encyclopedia of Pacific history. Have each student write an entry tracing the factors that led to the acquisition of Hawaii. *(See the Level 1 lesson for the correct events.)* Have volunteers read their entries to the class. Students may wish to include their entries in their portfolios.

SCIENCE, TECHNOLOGY, AND SOCIETY

Henry Cabot Lodge. Born in 1850, Henry Cabot Lodge was the son of a wealthy Boston merchant. He received a law degree and a Ph.D.—one of the first granted in the United States—from Harvard. As a U.S. senator, Lodge helped draft the Sherman Antitrust Act and the Pure Food and Drug Act. In foreign affairs he supported building a strong navy. He adopted the ideas of Alfred Thayer Mahan and was a strong influence on President Theodore Roosevelt. Lodge later led the fight against the ratification of the Treaty of Versailles after World War I.

ACTIVITY: Tell students to locate and use brief biographies of Henry Cabot Lodge to write a report on how different sources describe Lodge's views on U.S. expansionism.

VISUAL RECORD ANSWER

Students might note that the harvesting appears extremely difficult and unpleasant.

INTERPRETING THE VISUAL RECORD

Sugar. These workers are harvesting sugarcane. American settlers built a profitable sugar industry in Hawaii. ***Does harvesting sugarcane appear to be difficult work? Explain your answer.***

Research on the ROM

Free Find: Liliuokalani
After reading about Liliuokalani on the **Holt Researcher CD–ROM**, write a song that honors her work on behalf of the Hawaiian people.

During the 1800s ships began arriving in Hawaii more often. The ships brought missionaries, settlers, and traders. They also brought diseases that reduced the Hawaiian population from about 300,000 in 1778 to fewer than 150,000 by 1819.

American influence. Pacific trading and whaling ships that stopped at the islands for supplies made the first U.S. contact with the Hawaiian Islands. In the 1820s Protestant missionaries from New England traveled to the islands to convert Hawaiians to Christianity. Missionaries and their families settled on the islands and began raising crops, particularly sugar.

American investors in the sugar industry gradually increased their control over the islands. As Hawaii's economy boomed, sugar planters grew rich. Hawaiian sugar production rose, and the influence of Americans increased. Expansion of the sugar industry meant that more laborers were needed. Since Hawaiians were dying off at a high rate, planters brought in thousands of Japanese and Chinese workers, who soon outnumbered Hawaiians. By the 1870s Americans controlled most of Hawaii's land and trade. They exercised growing influence over Hawaiian king **Kalakaua** (kah-LAH-KAH-ooh-ah), who took the throne in 1874.

An 1875 treaty exempted Hawaiian sugar from U.S. tariffs. In exchange, Hawaii promised not to grant territory or special privileges in the islands to any other country. In 1886 U.S. officials demanded control of Pearl Harbor in exchange for renewing tax-free status for Hawaiian sugar. Kalakaua refused. Some 400 American businesspeople, planters, and traders in Hawaii then formed the secret Hawaiian League. Their goal was to overthrow the monarchy and persuade the United States to annex Hawaii.

In July 1887 the League forced Kalakaua at gunpoint to sign a new constitution that limited his role to that of a figurehead. It also limited native Hawaiians' right to hold office in their own country. Hawaiians resented what they called the Bayonet Constitution. Kalakaua had no choice but to renew the treaty and grant the United States exclusive rights to build a fortified naval base at Pearl Harbor.

In 1890 Congress enacted the McKinley Tariff, which created a crisis by ending Hawaii's favored position in the sugar trade. The law permitted all countries to ship sugar duty-free to the United States. It also gave sugar producers in the United States a **subsidy**—a government bonus payment—of two cents per pound. This caused sugar prices to drop, and the Hawaiian economy suffered.

BIOGRAPHY
Liliuokalani

A nationalist queen. In 1891 Kalakaua died, and his sister **Liliuokalani** (li-lee-uh-woh-kuh-LAHN-ee) succeeded him. Liliuokalani was a champion of Hawaiian nationalism and pledged to regain "Hawaii for the Hawaiians." Liliuokalani was born into a Hawaiian ruling family in 1838. As a young girl she saw the monarchy reclaim Hawaiian independence after a brief British takeover. She never forgot the pride she felt as the Hawaiian flag was again raised over her native land.

Early in her reign, Queen Liliuokalani began working to overturn the Bayonet Constitution and replace it with one that would return power to native Hawaiians. In 1893 she announced her plan to publish a new constitution. In response, the supporters of annexation forcibly occupied government buildings, declared the end of the monarchy, and set up a provisional government of their own. Without authorization, the U.S. minister to Hawaii, John L. Stevens, ordered marines ashore from the cruiser *Boston*, supposedly to protect American lives and property. With Gatling guns and cannons in place, the marines took up positions facing Iolani Palace and Liliuokalani.

No shots were fired, and the revolutionaries established a new government with Sanford B. Dole as president. Again acting without authority, Stevens recognized the new government and proclaimed Hawaii to be under U.S. protection on February 1, 1893. "The Hawaiian pear is now fully ripe," proclaimed Stevens, "and this is the golden hour for the United States to pluck it." Not wanting to see Hawaiians killed, a deeply saddened Queen Liliuokalani reluctantly surrendered her throne.

SURRENDER!

Liliuokalani Relinquishes All Her Claims Connected With the Monarchy.

SAID TO FAVOR ANNEXATION.

Document Signed Yesterday After-noon in Executive Building.

The overthrow of the Hawaiian monarchy raised few criticisms in the American press.

> **History Makers Speak**
>
> **"I, Liliuokalani, . . . protest against any and all acts done against myself and the constitutional government of the Hawaiian kingdom. . . . Now, to avoid any collision of armed forces and perhaps the loss of life, I do, under this protest, and impelled by said forces, yield my authority until such time as the government of the United States shall . . . undo the action of its representatives and reinstate me."**
>
> —Queen Liliuokalani, quoted in *How Hawaii Lost its Queen*, by Shelly Hoose Quincey

The new government petitioned the United States for annexation, but anti-imperialists and Democratic senators blocked the proposed treaty. Newly elected president Grover Cleveland withdrew the treaty and ordered an investigation. The investigator's report condemned the revolt and the U.S. role in it. The report also proposed putting Liliuokalani back on the throne. Cleveland supported the report and asked the provisional government to resign. Dole, however, refused to step down.

Unwilling to use military force to restore Liliuokalani, Cleveland reluctantly recognized the Dole government but refused to approve annexation. From 1894 to 1898, the independent Republic of Hawaii waited for a friendly Washington administration. It came with the election of President William McKinley. The United States annexed Hawaii on July 7, 1898, despite the opposition of most of Hawaii's population.

Liliuokalani lived out the rest of her life in Honolulu, serving as a proud reminder of Hawaii's past. She died in 1917 and was buried in the Royal Mausoleum. Hawaii became a U.S. territory in 1900 and the 50th state in 1959. In 1993 Congress apologized for the U.S. role in Liliuokalani's overthrow.

Diamond Head from Kapiolani Park, Honolulu.

This postcard shows the tropical beauty of Hawaii.

✔ **READING CHECK: Sequencing** What events led to the U.S. annexation of Hawaii?
formation of secret Hawaiian League in 1886; McKinley Tariff in 1890; 1893 rebellion; election of President McKinley in 1898

LEVEL 1: Ask students to describe the U.S. role in China. *(Students should indicate that the U.S. called for an Open Door Policy, which was designed to give all nations equal access to trade and investment in China and to maintain Chinese sovereignty.)* Tell students to imagine that they are newspaper reporters covering U.S.-China relations in the 1890s and early 1900s. Pair students and have each pair write three or four headlines that delineate the principles of the U.S. Open Door Policy in China. *(Headlines should include the following principles: all ports in foreign spheres of influence should be open to all nations; Chinese officials should be allowed to collect all tariffs and duties; foreign nations should guarantee*

equal harbor, railroad, and tariff rates to all nations trading in China; and China should retain its sovereignty.) Ask volunteers to read their headlines to the class.
English Language Learners, Cooperative Learning

LEVELS 2 AND 3: Pair students and tell them to imagine that they are State Department advisers to Secretary of State John Hay. Have each pair write a summary and justification of the U.S. role in China and the Open Door Policy for President McKinley. *(See the Level 1 lesson for the correct U.S. role and the correct points of the Open Door Policy.)* Have spokespeople read the summaries to the class. **Cooperative Learning**

INTERPRETING THE VISUAL RECORD

China trade. Merchant ships unloaded their goods at Whampoa Anchorage near Canton, China. *How many flags of different nations can you identify?*

This Chinese print shows the Boxers attacking westerners.

U.S. Involvement in China

Hawaii was valuable to the United States in part because it was a convenient stopping point for American trading ships sailing to China. Trade between China and the United States began in 1784 when the American ship *Empress of China* sailed for the port of Guangzhou.

Spheres of influence. In 1843 China officially opened five ports to trade with the United States and Europe. For the next 50 years China's rulers struggled to keep foreign interests from overrunning the country. In 1895, however, the Chinese government faced a threat from another direction. Japan attacked and defeated China, seizing China's Liaotung Peninsula, the large island of Taiwan, and Korea. European powers quickly took advantage of China's weakened position. Britain, France, Germany, and Russia carved out **spheres of influence**—regions where a particular country has exclusive rights over mines, railroads, and trade.

The Open Door Policy. The United States was in danger of being forced out of the China trade. Senator Henry Cabot Lodge declared, "We ask no favors; we only ask that we shall be admitted to that great market upon the same terms with the rest of the world." In 1899 Secretary of State **John Hay** called for an **Open Door Policy**, which would give all nations equal access to trade and investment in China.

That September, Hay sent a series of Open Door notes to the European powers and Japan that asked them to agree to three principles. First, he asked that they keep all ports in their spheres open to all nations. Second, he asked that Chinese officials be allowed to collect all tariffs and duties. Finally, he requested that they guarantee equal harbor, railroad, and tariff rates in their spheres to all nations trading in China. Since the European nations and Japan neither rejected nor accepted the principles, Hay announced that the Open Door Policy had been approved.

The Boxer Rebellion. Chinese resentment of foreigners continued to grow. A secret society called the Fists of Righteous Harmony—known by westerners as the Boxers—circulated handbills blaming foreigners and missionaries for China's troubles. One handbill claimed that because "the Catholic and Protestant religions are insolent [disrespectful] to the gods, . . . the rain clouds no longer visit us. But 8 million Spirit Soldiers will descend from Heaven and sweep the Empire clean of all foreigners!"

In the spring of 1900 the Boxers attacked Western missionaries and traders in northern China, killing more than 200 people. Known as the **Boxer Rebellion**, this uprising was supported by some Chinese government officials. The Boxers laid siege to the large, walled-in foreign settlement in Beijing, China's capital. Foreign countries responded by sending troops to China. In August, after an eight-week siege, the international force rescued the foreigners.

John Hay feared that Japan and other nations would use the Boxer Rebellion as an excuse to seize control of additional Chinese

LEVEL 1: Pair students and ask pairs to list the steps that Japan took after 1854 to become a world power. *(Pairs should indicate the following steps: 1—Japan agreed to Western demands for trade; 2—Japan industrialized rapidly; 3—Japan built up its army and navy; 4—Japanese troops attacked Russian forces in 1904, starting the Russo-Japanese War; 5—Japan negotiated a peace treaty with Russia.)* Ask volunteers to read their lists to the class. Have other students fill in any gaps in the lists.

English Language Learners, Cooperative Learning

LEVELS 2 AND 3: Tell students to imagine that they are advisers to the leaders of a developing country who are seeking historical examples of countries that developed rapidly. Have each student write a short analysis of the steps Japan took to become a world power. *(See the Level 1 lesson for the correct steps.)* Ask volunteers to read their analyses to the class.

HOMEWORK Tell students to review George Washington's position on expansion and U.S. involvement in foreign countries. Then have each student write a one-page speculative essay to assess what Washington's reactions might have been to the expansion of U.S. territory and influence discussed in this section. Essays should specify three actions taken by the United States, speculate on Washington's response to each action, and give the reasons why Washington would react in a particular way.

---

territory. In a second series of Open Door notes, Hay pressured foreign powers to observe open trade throughout China and to preserve China's right to rule its own territory. China retained its sovereignty as a nation but was forced to pay the European powers $333 million for damages.

✔ **READING CHECK: Identifying Cause and Effect** How did the Open Door Policy affect U.S. trade with China? It allowed the United States to trade with China on the same basis as European nations.

Skill-Building Strategies

Interpreting Economic Data

The use of economic data can broaden one's understanding of many historical topics. Information about exports, imports, incomes, prices, and production rates, for instance, can provide one with valuable clues about everyday life in a nation or region or the interactions between different nations or regions.

Like other historical statistics, however, economic data must be interpreted carefully. The information in a given chart or graph serves as a snapshot that shows one specific part of an economy from one specific angle. When interpreting this information, it is important to consider what you already know about the historical period.

How to Interpret Economic Data

1. **Determine the nature of the data.** Read the title of the chart or graph to identify the type of economic data it presents. Then read all of its headings, subheadings, and labels to determine the categories, amounts, and time intervals in which it presents the data.
2. **Analyze the details.** Study the information in the chart or graph carefully and systematically. Take note of increases or decreases in quantities, and look for trends, relationships, and conflicts in the data.
3. **Put the data to use.** Use your analysis of the data, along with your knowledge of the historical period, to form generalizations and draw conclusions.

Applying the Skill

Study the graph below, which shows the value of U.S. exports to China between 1898 and 1908.

Practicing the Skill

Use the graph below to answer the following questions.
1. In which year was the value of U.S. exports to China at its lowest? In which year was it at its highest?
2. Why do you think the value of U.S. exports to China rose and fell several times between 1898 and 1908?

U.S. Exports to China, 1898–1908

Value of Exports (in millions of dollars) vs *Year* (1898–1908), ranging 0 to 60.

Sources: *Historical Statistics of the United States*

GLOBAL RELATIONS

Protecting China. The Open Door Policy guaranteed Chinese sovereignty by preventing European nations from carving the country up into smaller colonies. However, Chinese sovereignty was the result and not the goal of the Open Door Policy. Officials in the U.S. government never conducted any negotiations or consultations with Chinese leaders. Nonetheless, the Chinese were pleased by the policy, which remained an important part of U.S.-Sino relations for the first half of the 1900s.

CRITICAL THINKING Why might the United States have wanted China to remain an independent nation?

ANSWER: Students might suggest that an independent China provided the United States with important economic opportunities, such as trade.

SKILL-BUILDING STRATEGIES ANSWERS

Practicing the Skill
1. 1901; 1905

2. Students might suggest that events such as the Boxer Rebellion and Russo-Japanese War probably affected the volume of trade.

REVIEW

Have students complete the **Section 1 Review** on p. 332.

ASSESS

Have students complete **Daily Quiz 11.1**. As **Alternative Assessment**, you may want to use the annotated time line or the Japan list in this section's lessons.

RETEACH

Have students complete **Main Idea Activity for English Language Learners and Special-Needs Students 11.1**. Organize the class into four groups and assign each group one of this section's objectives. Have groups rewrite their objectives into question form. Finally, tell groups to formulate answers to their questions using relevant items such as key terms, key people, and key places, and other information from the textbook. Call on each group to read its question and answer to the class. Invite other students to correct errors or to add missing information.
English Language Learners, Cooperative Learning

EXTEND

Have students conduct research on the views of Alfred Thayer Mahan, Henry Cabot Lodge, or Theodore Roosevelt on the expansion of U.S. territory and influence at the beginning of the 1900s. Have each student report his or her findings in an essay. **Block Scheduling**

SECTION 1 REVIEW ANSWERS

1. Define
- imperialism, p. 326
- subsidy, p. 328
- spheres of influence, p. 330

2. Identify
- Henry Cabot Lodge, p. 326
- Alfred Thayer Mahan, p. 326
- Kalakaua, p. 328
- Liliuokalani, p. 328
- John Hay, p. 330
- Open Door Policy, p. 330
- Boxer Rebellion, p. 330
- Matthew Perry, p. 332

3. The Hawaiian League forces Kalakaua to sign the Bayonet Constitution; the McKinley Tariff creates a crisis in the sugar industry; Liliuokalani announces her intent to write a new constitution; annexationists carry out a revolt.

4a. They desired foreign resources and markets to help their domestic economies.

b. It invaded China in 1894, transformed itself into a military and industrial power, and attacked Russian forces in Manchuria.

c. They resulted in a second series of Open Door notes.

5. Answers will vary. Students might note that the Open Door policy would allow the United States greater trade opportunities with China but it would do the same for European countries.

During his 1854 trip to Japan, Matthew Perry received many gifts, including this lantern.

An Emerging Japan

Japan's 1894 invasion of China marked its emergence as an imperial power. Just 41 years earlier Japan had ended its almost complete isolation from the rest of the world. President Millard Fillmore had sent Commodore **Matthew Perry** to persuade Japan to open its doors to trade with the West. In 1854 Perry's fleet of seven warships sailed into Edo—present-day Tokyo—and presented Japan's rulers with gifts that included a telegraph transmitter and a model train.

The Japanese leaders agreed to the Western demands for trade. They reasoned that if they did not, foreigners might seize control of their nation. Japan rapidly transformed itself into an industrial power and built up its army and navy. Japan and Russia had long been rivals for Chinese territories. In February 1904, Japanese troops attacked Russian forces in Manchuria, starting the Russo-Japanese War.

The war worried President Theodore Roosevelt. He feared that if Russia won, it might cut off U.S. trade with Manchuria, and if Japan won, it might threaten free trade in Asia. By May 1905, after winning a series of crucial battles, the Japanese asked Roosevelt to negotiate peace with Russia. In Portsmouth, New Hampshire, Roosevelt and representatives of the two countries hammered out a treaty that granted neither side all it wanted. Roosevelt was awarded the Nobel Peace Prize for his efforts.

Japan had become a modern world power and a rival to the United States for influence in China and the Pacific. Concerned by Japan's growing power, Roosevelt decided to remind the Japanese of U.S. military might. In late 1907 he sent a fleet of four destroyers and 16 battleships, painted a dazzling white, on a 46,000-mile world cruise that included a stop in the Japanese port of Yokohama.

✔ **READING CHECK: Analyzing Information** How did the United States help Japan become a world power? Roosevelt negotiated Japan's peace with Russia, which upheld Japan's influence in China.

SECTION 1 REVIEW

1. Define and explain:
imperialism
subsidy
spheres of influence

2. Identify and explain:
Henry Cabot Lodge
Alfred Thayer Mahan
Kalakaua
Liliuokalani
John Hay
Open Door Policy
Boxer Rebellion
Matthew Perry

3. Sequencing Copy the chart below. Use it to list the events that led to the U.S. annexation of Hawaii.

1. Kalakaua becomes king of Hawaii in 1874.
2.
3.
4.
5.
6. The United States annexes Hawaii on July 7, 1898.

4. Finding the Main Idea
a. Why did the United States and European nations begin to follow a policy of imperialism in the 1800s?
b. How did Japan become a world power in the late 1800s and early 1900s?
c. How did foreign expansion in Asia and the Boxer Rebellion affect U.S. policy toward China?

5. Writing and Critical Thinking
Evaluating Imagine that you are economic adviser to President Roosevelt. Write a paper evaluating the economic effects of the Open Door Policy.
Consider:
- the reasons why Hay pursued the policy
- the other nations involved
- the policy's principles

 Homework Practice Online
keyword: SE3 HP11

SECTION ②

After completing Section 2, students should be able to:

OBJECTIVE 1 Recount how Spain responded to the revolt in Cuba.

OBJECTIVE 2 Explain the significance of the Spanish-American War.

OBJECTIVE 3 Describe the economic effects of the major battles of the Spanish-American War.

OBJECTIVE 4 Explain what happened to the Philippines after the Spanish-American War.

🔊 LET'S GET STARTED!

As students enter the classroom, tell them to imagine that they are the president of the United States. Ask each student to speculate, in writing, which circumstances justify U.S. intervention in the internal affairs of other countries. List students' responses on the chalkboard. Tell students that in Section 2 they will learn about U.S. involvement in disputes between Spain and its colonies in the Caribbean and in the Pacific during the 1890s.

SECTION ②

READ TO DISCOVER

1. How did Spain respond to the revolt in Cuba?
2. What were the major causes of the Spanish-American War?
3. What were the major battles of the Spanish-American War?
4. What happened to the Philippines after the Spanish-American War?

IDENTIFY

José Martí
Valeriano Weyler
William Randolph Hearst
William McKinley
USS *Maine*
Teller Amendment
George Dewey
Emilio Aguinaldo
Rough Riders
Philippine Government Act
Jones Act of 1916

WHY IT MATTERS TODAY

The United States still has military bases overseas today. Use CNNfyi.com or other **current events** sources to find out about one U.S. military base located overseas. Record your findings in your journal.

CNNfyi.com

War with Spain

EYEWITNESSES TO History **❝***We know that they have formed a government; that they have held two elections.... They have risen against oppression, compared to which the oppression which led us to rebel against England is as dust in the balance.... No useful end is being served by the bloody struggle that is now in progress in Cuba, and in the name of humanity it should be stopped.... The responsibility is on us; we cannot escape it. We should ... put a stop to that war which is now raging in Cuba and give to that island once more peace, liberty, and independence.***❞**

—Henry Cabot Lodge, "For Intervention in Cuba," February 20, 1896

THE GRANGER COLLECTION, NEW YORK

This cartoon shows the United States protecting Cuba from Spain.

In a speech delivered to the Senate on February 20, 1896, Senator Henry Cabot Lodge called for the United States to intervene in a rebellion in Cuba. Many Americans were eager to flex the nation's military muscle and put an end to a war so near its shores. Other people also wanted the United States to assert more authority and to drive Spain out of the Western Hemisphere.

Conflict in Cuba

Supporters of U.S. expansion had long been interested in the Caribbean island of Cuba, located just 90 miles from the Florida Keys. In the late 1800s Cuba simmered with unrest. Cuba and its Caribbean neighbor Puerto Rico were the last of the Spanish colonies in the Americas. Since 1868, Cubans had launched a series of unsuccessful revolts against Spanish rule. To put down the rebellion, the Spanish government exiled many leaders of the independence movement.

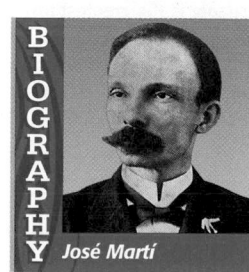
BIOGRAPHY *José Martí*

Foremost among these Cuban exiles was poet **José Martí**. Born in Havana, Cuba, on January 28, 1853, Martí joined in a revolt against Cuba's Spanish rulers when he was just 15 years old. For his actions, Martí was banished to Spain, where he earned a university degree. He later worked in Mexico and in Guatemala. Martí returned to Cuba in 1878 but was banished again for his activism. He moved to New York City, where he worked for Cuban independence.

While in New York, Martí wrote poems and newspaper articles promoting Cuban independence. He also urged Cuban exiles to mount an invasion of Cuba. "Let us rise up at once with a final burst of heartfelt energy ... for the true republic, those of us who, with our passion for right and our habit of hard work, will know how to preserve it." When Cubans launched another revolt in February 1895, Martí and other exiles joined them. Martí became a martyr for Cuban independence when he was killed months later in a battle.

SECTION ② RESOURCES

REPRODUCIBLE
▶ Guided Reading Strategy 11.2
▶ Primary Source Reading 11: Teddy Roosevelt's Cavalry

TECHNOLOGY
▶ One-Stop Planner, Lesson 11.2
▶ Everyday Life in America Transparency 19: Photojournalism in the Spanish-American War
▶ CNN Presents America: Yesterday and Today Segment: "Remember the *Maine!*"
▶ Holt Researcher: American History CD–ROM
▶ HRW Go site
▶ Homework Practice Online

REINFORCEMENT, REVIEW, AND ASSESSMENT
▶ Section 2 Review, p. 339
▶ Daily Quiz 11.2
▶ Main Idea Activity 11.2
▶ English Audio Summary 11.2
▶ Spanish Audio Summary 11.2

LEVEL 1: Tell students that the revolt in Cuba against Spanish rule provided supporters of U.S. expansion with an opportunity to intervene in Spanish-Cuban affairs. Copy the graphic organizer at right on the chalkboard, omitting the italicized answers. Then pair students and have each pair fill in the answers. Ask volunteers to share their answers with the class. Conclude by leading a discussion about the Spanish response to events in Cuba and the causes of the Spanish-American War.

English Language Learners, Cooperative Learning

Spanish Response to the Revolt in Cuba
- *exiled many leaders of the independence movement*
- *sent soldiers to fight rebels*
- *sent General Valeriano Weyler to put down the revolt*

U.S. Intervention in Spanish-Cuban Affairs

Major Causes of the Spanish-American War
- *imperialist ambition*
- *humanitarian sympathy for the rebels*
- *yellow journalism*
- *the destruction of the USS* Maine

General Weyler and the War. General Weyler ordered all *pacificos,* or farmers who took no part in the conflict between Cuba and Spain, to move to fortified towns. They were allowed only eight days to leave their farms, which Spanish troops then destroyed. However, no preparations were made to feed and house the *pacificos,* who were forced to live in abandoned buildings and to beg for food.

ACTIVITY: Have students discuss Weyler's concentration camp policy and the issue of human rights in wartime. Then ask each student to write a statement from a U.S. government official protesting Weyler's policy.

THAT'S INTERESTING!

Spain attempted to defend General Weyler's concentration camp policy by comparing it to General William Sherman's March to the Sea during the Civil War. This comparison did not impress Secretary of State John Sherman, who by coincidence was the brother of the Civil War general.

VISUAL RECORD ANSWER

Answers will vary. Some students might suggest that the artist tried to rally public opinion against Spain.

Research on the ROM

Free Find: William Randolph Hearst
After reading about William Randolph Hearst on the **Holt Researcher CD–ROM**, create a newspaper front page with current news stories that reflect Hearst's style of journalism.

INTERPRETING THE VISUAL RECORD

Remember the *Maine!* The explosion of the battleship *Maine* led to the Spanish-American War. *What do you think the artist's purpose was in painting this scene?*

In 1896 Spain sent General **Valeriano Weyler** to put down the revolt. He forced thousands of farmers into concentration camps to prevent them from aiding the rebels. Some 200,000 Cubans died from starvation and disease in the camps.

✔ **READING CHECK: Making Predictions** How did Spain's response to the revolt in Cuba increase pressure on the United States to intervene? The poor treatment of Cubans made it more likely that the United States would help Cuba.

The United States Reacts

Many Americans saw similarities between the Cubans' struggle and the American Revolution and were therefore sympathetic to the Cuban rebels. The American press encouraged war with Spain and branded Weyler "the Butcher." Two New York City newspapers, William Randolph Hearst's *New York Journal* and Joseph Pulitzer's *New York World*, used sensational tales of Spanish atrocities to attract readers and sell more papers.

BIOGRAPHY

William Randolph Hearst

The influence of the media. Perhaps no American journalist was more interested in the Cuban situation than **William Randolph Hearst**. His father had made a fortune in the California gold fields and was a rich man when his only son was born in 1863.

Hearst was an undisciplined student prone to mischief. He was expelled from high school and finished his studies at home with tutors. He then attended Harvard University, where he displayed little interest in academics but great enthusiasm for business and publishing. Hearst left Harvard in his junior year and got a job in New York as a reporter for Pulitzer's *World*.

Hearst's father owned the *San Francisco Examiner*. In 1887 Hearst persuaded his father to let him run the newspaper. Using sensational reporting or yellow journalism, Hearst soon turned the failing *Examiner* around. After reviving that newspaper, he returned to New York in 1895 to run the *Journal* and challenge Pulitzer. Hearst explained his view of the role of newspapers.

History Makers Speak

66 The newspaper is the greatest force in civilization. . . . Newspapers form and express public opinion. They suggest and control legislation. They declare wars. They punish criminals, especially the powerful. They reward with approving publicity the good deeds of citizens everywhere. The newspapers control the nation because they REPRESENT THE PEOPLE. 99

—William Randolph Hearst, quoted in *Popular Culture in the 20th Century,* edited by Richard Maltby

Hearst's growing newspaper empire made him a wealthy man. He built a mansion in San Simeon, California, and filled it with art and rare artifacts from around the globe. His lavish lifestyle continued until his death in 1951.

The *Maine* incident. Believing that newspapers should shape public opinion and policy, Hearst pressed for U.S. intervention in Cuba. In 1897 he sent artist Frederic Remington to Cuba to create drawings showing Spanish cruelty, which Hearst could use to increase U.S. support for war with Spain. President **William McKinley**, however, was a veteran of the Civil War and

LEVEL 2: Have each student write two or three paragraphs to summarize the Spanish response to the revolt in Cuba and the major causes of the Spanish-American War. *(See the Level 1 graphic organizer for the correct responses and causes.)* Ask volunteers to read their paragraphs to the class.

LEVEL 3: Tell students to imagine that they are historians who must write an article entitled "The Expansionist Moment: Spain's Response to the Revolt in Cuba and the Causes of the Spanish-American War" for a journal of history. Have each student write a one-page article on the topic. *(See the Level 1 graphic organizer for the correct responses and causes.)* Ask volunteers to read their articles to the class.

TEACH OBJECTIVE 3

LEVEL 1: Tell students that the battles of the Spanish-American War were fought in Cuba, the Philippines, and Puerto Rico. Pair students and have each pair write a multiple-choice test about the major battles of the Spanish-American War. *(Pairs should indicate that the major battles of the Spanish-American War were the U.S. naval bombardment of Manila Bay in the Philippines, the battle for Manila, the battle for El Caney, the battle for San Juan Hill in Cuba, the battle between the U.S. and Spanish navies off the coast of Cuba, and the battle between U.S. and Spanish forces in Puerto Rico.)* Ask students in each pair to exchange their tests with another pair and then complete them. **English Language Learners, Cooperative Learning**

resisted the calls for war. "I have been through one war. I have seen the dead piled up, and I do not want to see another," he explained.

Events soon changed McKinley's stance. On February 9, 1898, the *Journal* published a letter written by Spain's minister to the United States, Enrique Dupuy de Lôme, that had been intercepted by a Cuban spy and sold to Hearst. In this letter de Lôme ridiculed McKinley as "weak, and a bidder for the admiration of the crowd." Americans were outraged at the remarks, which the *Journal* called "the worst insult to the United States in its history."

The nation teetered on the brink of war until a tragedy in Cuba pushed it over the edge. The battleship **USS Maine** had been sent to Havana to protect U.S. lives and property. On February 15 the *Maine* blew up, killing 260 sailors. "DESTRUCTION OF THE WAR SHIP MAINE WAS THE WORK OF AN ENEMY!" screamed the *Journal's* headline, although there was no proof of this. Some historians believe that a fire in a coal bin caused the explosion. At the time, however, many Americans blamed Spain. "Remember the *Maine!*" became the rallying cry of war supporters.

Spanish officials agreed to a U.S.-proposed peace plan, but it was too late. On April 11 McKinley asked Congress to intervene in Cuba "in the name of humanity, in the name of civilization, and in behalf of endangered American interests." On April 25 Congress declared war on Spain. The Spanish-American War had begun.

✔ **READING CHECK: Identifying Cause and Effect** How did the USS *Maine* explosion spark the Spanish-American War in 1898? The United States was on the brink, and people believed Spain had blown up the USS *Maine*.

War with Spain

On April 20, 1898, Congress recognized Cuba's independence and voted to use U.S. military force to help Cuba attain it. Congress also adopted the **Teller Amendment**. This stated that once Cuba won its independence from Spain, the United States would "leave the government and control of the Island to its people."

Fighting in the Philippines. The war's first battle was fought in the Spanish-held Philippine Islands. Before war was declared, Assistant Secretary of the Navy Theodore Roosevelt had cabled secret orders to Commodore **George Dewey** in Hong Kong. In the event of war between the United States and Spain, Dewey was to attack the Philippines.

As dawn broke on May 1, 1898, Dewey's fleet steamed across Manila Bay, in the Philippines. Commodore Dewey stood on the bridge of his flagship, *Olympia*. He trained his eyes on the Spanish guns on the shore and the small Spanish fleet anchored in the harbor. The Spanish sighted the Americans and opened fire, but Dewey's ships were out of range. The U.S. ships slowly moved closer to shore. Shortly after 5:30 A.M., Dewey told the *Olympia's* captain: "You may fire when you are ready, Gridley." The bay echoed with the roar of naval guns. As shells crashed into several Spanish vessels, they erupted into flames.

INTERPRETING THE VISUAL RECORD

The media. The destruction of the *Maine* was front-page news throughout the United States. *How does the* **New York Journal** *explain the sinking?*

Led by George Dewey, U.S. forces destroyed the Spanish fleet in the Battle of Manila Bay.

THEN AND NOW

USS Maine. Shortly after the *Maine* exploded, a U.S. court of inquiry declared that a mine had caused the damage to the ship. In the 1970s, however, an investigatory team studied photographs of the ship and announced that an internal explosion had caused the damage. The debate continued when a later group examined the photographs and said that the evidence was inconclusive—the *Maine* might have been sunk by a mine or by an internal explosion.

CRITICAL THINKING What might the differing interpretations indicate?

ANSWER: Students might suggest that the interpretations indicate that the photographic evidence currently available is not sufficient to solve the mystery.

🖥 **internet** connect

TOPIC: Spanish-American War
GO TO: go.hrw.com
KEYWORD: SE3 AN11

Have students access the Internet through the HRW Go site to conduct research on the Spanish-American War, including the sinking of the *Maine*. Then have each student create a radio script describing the sinking of the *Maine* and reporting on the war.

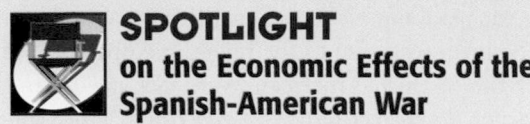

SPOTLIGHT
on the Economic Effects of the Spanish-American War

Have students use the process of historical inquiry to conduct research on the economic effects of the Spanish-American War. Students should research the cost of the war for Spain, the cost for the United States, and the war's effects on other countries or territories. Students should determine what effect the war had on trade relations for these countries. Ask students to present their findings in a short essay. Have volunteers present their essays to the class. **Block Scheduling**

U.S. troops in Cuba were poorly prepared for the tropical conditions they faced.

INTERPRETING THE VISUAL RECORD

San Juan Hill. Theodore Roosevelt led a cavalry unit known as the Rough Riders in the Spanish-American War. ***What is unusual about the cavalry soldiers shown in the painting?***

Dewey's fleet easily defeated the small Spanish fleet guarding the Philippine city of Manila. To capture the city, Dewey obtained the support of a rebel army of Filipino patriots led by **Emilio Aguinaldo** (ahg-ee-NAHL-doh). Filipinos had been fighting for independence from Spain for two years. Cut off by Dewey's warships and surrounded by Aguinaldo's rebels, Spanish forces in the Philippines surrendered on August 14, 1898.

Fighting in Cuba. Victory in Cuba proved more difficult. With a regular army of just some 28,000 soldiers, the U.S. War Department was unprepared for land battles. U.S. troops had received little training and were outfitted in heavy wool uniforms—the only ones available—when they sailed for tropical Cuba in mid-June 1898. A soldier later recalled life in Cuba.

History Makers Speak
"Heavy rains pouring down, no tents for cover, . . . standing in trenches in a foot of water and mud, day and night. . . . Ration issue consisting of a slice of sow belly, hardtack, and some grains of coffee. . . . Then came the issue of fleece-lined underwear in a 132 [degree] climate. . . . Then came on malaria."

—Captain Jacob Judson, Illinois National Guard, letter, April 15, 1956

On July 1, U.S. troops attacked the Spanish fort at Santiago. Their aim was to capture territory above Santiago, including El Caney and San Juan Hill. This would let them aim their guns down on Spanish troops. One U.S. division overcame Spanish forces at El Caney.

Lieutenant Colonel Theodore Roosevelt had resigned his naval post. In the war's most famous battle, he led a cavalry unit of about 1,000 soldiers toward the garrison on San Juan Hill. Composed largely of college athletes, cowboys, American Indians, and ranchers, the unit was known as the **Rough Riders**.

Because their horses had not been shipped to Cuba, the Rough Riders had to charge on foot under intense Spanish fire. The African American 9th and 10th Cavalries cleared the way for the final surge. By nightfall, U.S. troops controlled the ridge above Santiago. Then, on July 3, the U.S. Navy sank the Spanish fleet off the coast of Cuba. The battle resulted in 474 Spanish casualties. Two weeks later, Spanish troops in Cuba surrendered. Meanwhile, U.S. troops defeated Spanish forces in Puerto Rico.

The war proved costly for Spain. By the terms of the peace treaty, Spain gave up all claim to Cuba and ceded Puerto Rico and the Pacific island of Guam to the United States. Spain also gave up control of the Philippines in return for a U.S. payment of $20 million. By gaining control of overseas territories, the United States moved into the ranks of the imperialist world powers. The new trading bases also increased U.S. economic power. Expansionists expressed delight, but the quest for empire troubled many Americans. Furthermore, the United States paid a heavy human toll for the war. Some 5,400 soldiers died.

✔ **READING CHECK: Finding the Main Idea** Why did the United States fight in the Philippines? because it was Spanish-held

TEACH OBJECTIVE 4

LEVEL 1: Tell students to imagine that they are foreign correspondents who have been assigned to cover the Philippines for a newspaper. Pair students and have each pair write four headlines to describe events in the Philippines after the Spanish-American War. *(Headlines should note that Emilio Aguinaldo set up a provisional government in the Philippines, that the United States annexed the Philippines, Filipino independence fighters battled U.S. troops for control of the Philippines, that U.S. forces put down the rebellion in 1902, that the United States passed the Philippine Government Act* to establish a government for the Philippines, and that the Philippines gained its independence on July 4, 1946.) Ask volunteers to read their headlines to the class.
English Language Learners, Cooperative Learning

LEVEL 2: Pair students and ask them to write a two-paragraph summary of the fate of the Philippines after the Spanish-American War. *(See the Level 1 lesson for the correct events.)* Then ask pairs to draw a series of political cartoons with captions to illustrate the events in the Philippines. Display the cartoons around the classroom. **Cooperative Learning**

AMERICAN Letters

Literature of the Spanish-American War

At the time of the Spanish-American War, the United States was still deeply divided by sectional tensions. Some of the literature that was inspired by the war tried to encourage a sense of unity among all Americans. Other writers, particularly journalists, tried to portray an accurate picture of the fighting. The two excerpts below illustrate these themes. In the first, Stephen Crane reports for the New York World *on the real-life experiences of soldiers. In the second excerpt, from John Fox Jr.'s novel* Crittenden, *a former Confederate soldier is rewarded for his services in the Spanish-American War.*

from "Night Attacks on the Marines and a Brave Rescue"
by Stephen Crane

THE GRANGER COLLECTION, NEW YORK

Stephen Crane

GUANTANAMO, July 4.—The night attacks were heart-breaking affairs, from which the men emerged in the morning exhausted to a final degree, like people who had been swimming for miles. From colonel to smallest trumpeter went a great thrill when the dawn broke slowly in the eastern sky, and the weary band quite cheerfully ate breakfast. . . . Afterward the men slept, sunk upon the ground in an abandon [physical exhaustion] that was almost a stupor [daze].

Lieut. Neville, with his picket [forward group] of about twenty men, was entirely cut off from camp one night, and another night Neville's picket and the picket of Lieut. Shaw were cut off, fighting hard in the thickets [forests] for their lives. At the break of day the beleaguered [surrounded] camp could hear still the rifles of their lost pickets.

The guerrillas were still lurking [hiding] in the near woods, and it was unsafe enough in camp without venturing into the bush.

Volunteers from Company C . . . went out under Lieut. Lucas. They arrived in Neville's vicinity just as he and his men, together with Shaw and his men, were being finally surrounded at close range. Lucas and his seventeen men broke through the guerrillas and saved the pickets, and the whole body then fell back to Crest Hill. That is all there is to it.

from Crittenden: A Kentucky Story of Love and War
by John Fox Jr.

"You're a Sergeant, Crittenden," said the Captain.

He, Crittenden, in blood and sympathy the spirit of secession—bearer now of the Stars and Stripes! How his heart thumped, and how his head reeled when he caught the staff and looked dumbly up to the folds; and in spite of all his self-control, the tears came.

Right at that moment there was a great bustle in camp . . . and the victorious Stars and Stripes rose up. . . . On the very stroke of twelve, there came thunder—the thunder of two-score and one salutes. And the cheers—the cheers! . . . And on a little knoll not far away stood Sergeant Crittenden, swaying on his feet—colour-sergeant to the folds of the ever-victorious, ever-beloved Old Glory waving over him, with a strange new wave of feeling surging through him. For then and there, Crittenden, Southerner, died straightaway and through a travail of wounds, suffering, sickness, devotion, and love for that flag—Crittenden, American, was born.

UNDERSTANDING LITERATURE

1. What adjectives does Stephen Crane use to describe the soldiers' experiences?
2. How does the excerpt from *Crittenden* reflect the divisions in American society at the time?
3. What similarities and differences do you notice in the two excerpts?

LEVEL 3: Tell students to imagine that they are Filipinos after the Spanish-American War. Have each student write a series of diary entries that chronicle major events in the history of the Philippines from the end of the Spanish-American War through the Philippines' independence. *(See the Level 1 lesson for the correct events.)* Ask students, in their roles as Filipinos, to include their emotions during these major events. Ask volunteers to read their entries to the class.

HOMEWORK *Have each student write a position paper on the question of whether the United States should have annexed the Philippines. To help students form a position, tell students to ask themselves when and under what circumstances, if any, annexation is proper or justified? Encourage students to examine the issue of annexation of the Philippines in its historical context.*

CULTURE

Race and Annexation. Issues of race played a role on both sides of the debate regarding the annexation of the Philippines. Those who favored expansion declared that Americans had a responsibility to care for the nonwhite population of the islands. This group quoted the recently published poem, "The White Man's Burden," by British author Rudyard Kipling, in support of their claim. Opponents of annexation argued that Filipinos would demand entry into the United States. In order to calm these and other fears, the Senate approved a resolution that made it clear that Filipinos would not become U.S. citizens and the islands would never become a state.

ACTIVITY: Help students obtain a copy of Kipling's poem "The White Man's Burden." Conduct a discussion of the meaning of the poem and Kipling's justification of imperialism.

MAP ANSWER
Manila Bay

POLITICAL CARTOON ANSWER
(for p. 339)

Students might suggest that the cartoon seems to justify U.S. actions by portraying Emilio Aguinaldo as a dictator.

U.S. control brought modern developments like electricity, telephones, and streetcar service to the Philippines.

Uproar over the Philippines

In 1898 few Americans knew where the Philippines were located. President McKinley confessed that initially, he could not locate the islands "within two thousand miles." Americans wondered if Filipinos should be forced to accept U.S. rule.

The debate. Some Americans questioned whether it was proper to annex a foreign territory and rule its government and its people. Expansionists argued in favor of annexation. Businesspeople wanted the islands to serve as a trading post for goods from Asia as well as a place for merchant ships to refuel. Charles Denby, a former U.S. minister to China, warned opponents of annexation that times had changed. "We have a great commerce to take care of. We have to compete with the commercial nations of the world in far-distant markets. Commerce, not politics, is king." Some other supporters believed that the United States would bring democracy to the Philippines. Others held that U.S. rule of the islands was necessary to keep out European powers.

Opponents of annexation responded that by denying the Philippines independence, the United States would violate its own ideals expressed in the Declaration

Spanish-American War, 1898

Interpreting Maps The Spanish-American War was primarily decided at sea. The U.S. Navy easily conquered the Spanish fleets protecting Cuba and the Philippines. Both Spanish fleets were destroyed, while the Americans suffered few casualties.

❓ **PLACES AND REGIONS** Where did Commodore George Dewey destroy the Spanish fleet?

REVIEW

Have students complete the **Section 2 Review** on p. 339.

ASSESS

Have students complete **Daily Quiz 11.2**. As **Alternative Assessment**, you may want to use the war test or the Philippines headlines in this section's lessons.

RETEACH

Have students complete **Main Idea Activity for English Language Learners and Special-Needs Students 11.2**. Then write each term in the Section Review on an index card. Give one to each student. On the back of the card, have the student write a brief paragraph explaining the term and its importance for the causes, the course, or the consequences of the Spanish-American War. Then pair students. Have one student read the "clue" on the back of the card and have his or her partner guess the term that it describes. Have students then form different pairs and repeat the process.
English Language Learners, Cooperative Learning

EXTEND

Have students conduct research on the Anti-Imperialist League. Then pair students and have each pair compose a dialogue based on its research to explain the reasons why members of the league opposed annexation.
Cooperative Learning, Block Scheduling

---

of Independence. In June 1898, opponents of U.S. imperialism formed the Anti-Imperialist League and announced their beliefs.

History Makers Speak

❝We regret that it has become necessary . . . to reaffirm that all men, of whatever race or color, are entitled to life, liberty, and the pursuit of happiness. . . . The subjugation of any people is 'criminal aggression' and open disloyalty to the . . . principles of our Government.❞

—Anti-Imperialist League, quoted in *Speeches, Correspondence and Political Speeches*, by Carl Schurz

After a fierce debate, the Senate narrowly approved the treaty, annexing the Philippines on February 6, 1899.

Conquest and early rule. Emilio Aguinaldo had already set up a provisional government and proclaimed himself president of the new Philippine Republic. He warned that Filipinos would go to war if "American troops attempt to take forcible possession. Upon their heads will be all the blood which may be shed." For the next three years, Filipino independence fighters battled U.S. soldiers for control of the Philippines. By the time U.S. forces crushed the rebellion in 1902, hundreds of thousands of Filipinos and more than 4,000 U.S. soldiers had lost their lives.

In 1902 the U.S. Congress passed the **Philippine Government Act**, also known as the Organic Act, which established a governor and a two-house legislature to rule the Philippines. The United States would appoint the governor and the legislature's upper house, but Filipino voters would elect the lower house. The **Jones Act of 1916** granted Filipinos the right to elect both houses of their legislature. On July 4, 1946, the United States finally granted independence to the Philippines.

✔ **READING CHECK: Identifying Cause and Effect** How did the Spanish-American War affect the Philippines? The Philippines gained a brief independence and then was annexed by the United States after three years of fighting.

INTERPRETING POLITICAL CARTOONS

Filipino opposition. This cartoon shows U.S. military power crushing Emilio Aguinaldo's government. *How does the cartoon seem to justify U.S. actions in the Philippines?*

SECTION 2 REVIEW

1. Identify and explain:
José Martí
Valeriano Weyler
William Randolph Hearst
William McKinley
USS *Maine*
Teller Amendment
George Dewey
Emilio Aguinaldo
Rough Riders
Philippine Government Act
Jones Act of 1916

2. Identifying Cause and Effect Copy the chart below. Use it to list the actions taken by the United States and Spain leading up to and during the Spanish-American War.

United States	Spain

3. **Finding the Main Idea**
a. How did Spain's reaction to the revolt in Cuba lead the United States to declare war against Spain in 1898?
b. How did publisher William Randolph Hearst influence the U.S. government to declare war on Spain?
c. How did the United States emerge as a world power after the Spanish-American War?

4. **Writing and Critical Thinking**
Summarizing Write a newspaper account of events in the Philippines after the Spanish-American War.
Consider:
• the reasons the United States became involved in the Philippines
• the role of Filipino rebels in the war against Spain
• why the United States did not initially grant independence to the Philippines

Homework Practice Online
keyword: SE3 HP11

REVIEW SECTION 2 ANSWERS

1. Identify
• José Martí, p. 333
• Valeriano Weyler, p. 334
• William Randolph Hearst, p. 334
• William McKinley, p. 334
• USS *Maine*, p. 335
• Teller Amendment, p. 335
• George Dewey, p. 335
• Emilio Aguinaldo, p. 336
• Rough Riders, p. 336
• Philippine Government Act, p. 339
• Jones Act of 1916, p. 339

2. United States—bombarded Spanish fleet at Manila Bay, captured heights above Santiago, destroyed Spanish fleet in Cuba, defeated Spanish troops in Puerto Rico; Spain—defended Manila Bay, Santiago, and Puerto Rico

3a. The United States was sympathetic to the Cuban rebels.

b. He built public support for the war in his newspapers.

c. It gained new territories and increased its economic power.

4. Answers will vary. Students might suggest that Filipinos helped U.S. forces defeat Spain and expected independence in return. Filipinos turned against the United States when it annexed the Philippines instead of supporting independence.

After completing Section 3, students should be able to:

OBJECTIVE 1 Describe how the United States governed Cuba and Puerto Rico.

OBJECTIVE 2 Analyze the major obstacles to building the Panama Canal.

OBJECTIVE 3 Summarize U.S. policy toward Latin America during the late 1800s and early 1900s.

📻 LET'S GET STARTED!

As students enter the classroom, tell them to read the quotation from Charles Elliot Norton on this page. Ask students to respond to the quotation in writing, recalling the information presented in Sections 1 and 2 of this chapter. Students should explain what Norton might have meant when he referred to the United States's "unique position as a potential leader in the progress of civilization." Tell students that in Section 3 they will learn about the expansionist activities of the United States in Latin America.

SECTION ③

READ TO DISCOVER

1. How did the United States govern Cuba and Puerto Rico?
2. What were the major obstacles to building the Panama Canal?
3. What was U.S. policy toward Latin America during the late 1800s and early 1900s?

DEFINE

protectorate
dollar diplomacy

IDENTIFY

Leonard Wood
Platt Amendment
Foraker Act
Philippe Bunau-Varilla
Hay–Bunau-Varilla Treaty
Roosevelt Corollary

▶ WHY IT MATTERS TODAY

U.S. relations with Cuba have changed since the Spanish-American War. Use CNNfyi.com or other **current events** sources to find out about one aspect of the relationship between the United States and Cuba today. Record your findings in your journal.

CNN fyi.com

Expansion in Latin America

EYEWITNESSES TO History

"We believe that America had something better to offer to mankind than those aims she is now pursuing.... She has lost her unique position as a potential leader in the progress of civilization and has taken up her place simply as one of the grasping and selfish nations of the present day."

—Charles Elliot Norton, letter to Charles Waldstein, November 18, 1899

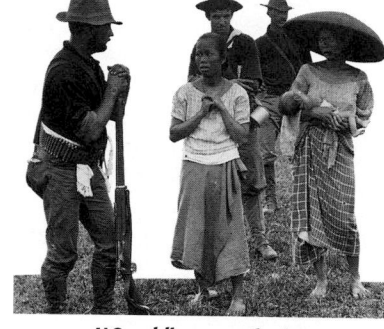

U.S. soldiers questioning Filipino women

In this 1899 letter, Harvard University professor Charles Elliot Norton expressed his disappointment with the United States for seizing an empire by force and for annexing the Philippines. Many Americans shared Norton's concerns. Supporters of U.S. actions, however, argued that the territories would benefit from U.S. rule and protection.

Governing Cuba and Puerto Rico

As the United States gained power in the Pacific region, it also expanded its role in Latin America. President McKinley set up military governments to restore order in Cuba and Puerto Rico quickly and protect U.S. investments. He appointed General **Leonard Wood** as governor of Cuba in 1899. Wood authorized the construction of schools and a sanitation system. U.S. Army doctors Walter Reed and William C. Gorgas led efforts to reduce the mosquito population. Cuban doctor Carlos Finlay (feen-LY) had theorized that mosquitoes spread yellow fever. He was right. The sanitation system drained pools of standing water where mosquitoes bred. This effort all but eliminated yellow fever.

Wood also oversaw the drafting of a new constitution that limited Cuba's independence. Congress agreed to remove U.S. troops from the island only if Cuba made the **Platt Amendment** part of its constitution. The amendment limited Cuba's freedom to make treaties with other countries and authorized the United States to intervene in Cuban affairs as it saw necessary. It also required Cuba to sell or lease land to the United States for naval and fueling stations. This last clause led to the establishment of a U.S. naval base at Guantánamo Bay. In effect, the Platt Amendment made Cuba a U.S. **protectorate**. This meant that the United States promised to protect Cuba from other nations but reserved the right to intervene in Cuba's affairs. In 1902, after Cuba reluctantly accepted the Platt Amendment, U.S. troops withdrew. The following year the United States and Cuba signed a trade agreement that brought Cuban sugar and minerals to the United States and sent American industrial products to Cuba. U.S.-Cuban trade jumped from $27 million in 1897 to more than $300 million in 1917.

U.S. policy in Puerto Rico followed a different course. The United States ruled the island as a territory, like Samoa or the Philippines in the Pacific. The **Foraker Act** of 1900 established that Puerto Rico's governor and upper house of the legislature would be appointed by the United States. According to the act, Puerto

TEACH OBJECTIVE 1

ALL LEVELS: Conduct a brief discussion of how the United States governed Cuba and Puerto Rico. Then copy the following graphic organizer on the chalkboard, omitting the italicized answers. Have students complete it. Ask volunteers to share their answers with the class.
English Language Learners

HOMEWORK *Have each student outline the provisions of the Platt Amendment and draw a political cartoon that illustrates his or her position on the question of whether the Platt Amendment violated the Teller Amendment passed by Congress in 1898.*

GOVERNING . . .

Puerto Rico

The Foraker Act
established a territorial government in Puerto Rico

The Jones Act
granted Puerto Ricans U.S. citizenship and the right to elect both houses of the legislature

1952—Puerto Rico became a self-governing commonwealth

Cuba

The Platt Amendment
made Cuba a protectorate

1934—the United States renounced the right to interfere in Cuban affairs

---

Ricans would elect a lower house. The Jones Act of 1917 granted Puerto Ricans U.S. citizenship and gave them the right to elect both houses of their legislature. In 1952 Puerto Rico became a self-governing commonwealth of the United States, with continuing ties of citizenship and trade with the mainland.

✔ **READING CHECK: Drawing Conclusions** What specific problems led to the sanitation system in Cuba? It was developed to combat yellow fever.

The Panama Canal

Having interests in both the Caribbean and the Pacific, the United States wanted to cut the travel time between the seas. Traveling around South America took several weeks. The United States proposed digging a canal across Central America.

Early steps toward a canal. In the 1880s, a French company began building a canal across the 50-mile-wide Isthmus of Panama. Ferdinand de Lesseps, who had built the Suez Canal in Egypt, led the project. After less than 10 years and the loss of some 20,000 lives and more than $280 million, the French abandoned the effort.

In 1901 Secretary of State John Hay began negotiations with the Republic of Colombia, which then included Panama. A treaty was drafted in 1903. In return for a 99-year lease on a six-mile strip of land across the isthmus, the United States agreed to pay Colombia $10 million and a yearly rental of $250,000. Colombia's senate held out for better terms and adjourned without ratifying the treaty. President Roosevelt was furious. He vowed that the Colombians would not be allowed "to bar one of the future highways of civilization."

Revolution in Panama. Events in Panama soon turned in Roosevelt's favor. Key Panamanian leaders who wanted the canal built began plotting revolution against the Colombian government. Helping them was **Philippe Bunau-Varilla** (boo-noh-vah-ree-yah), the former chief engineer for the French canal-building attempt.

Bunau-Varilla traveled to Washington, D.C., to get U.S. support for the revolution. On October 9, 1903, he met privately with President Roosevelt. On November 2 the U.S. gunboat *Nashville* arrived in Panama. The following day, Panamanians began their rebellion. U.S. Marines prevented Colombian forces from reaching the rebels.

The victorious rebels quickly set up a new government and declared Panama an independent nation. The United States recognized the Republic of Panama two days later, and Hay began negotiating a new canal treaty with Panama's special envoy, Bunau-Varilla. The **Hay–Bunau-Varilla Treaty** gave the United States complete and unending sovereignty over a 10-mile-wide Canal Zone. President Roosevelt later boasted, "I took the Canal Zone and let Congress debate."

Research on the ROM

Free Find: Foraker Act

After learning about the Foraker Act on the **Holt Researcher CD–ROM**, write an encyclopedia entry describing the act's historical importance.

Panama Canal Zone

Interpreting Maps After the Spanish-American War, pressure increased to build a U.S.-controlled canal through Central America.

❓ **HUMAN SYSTEMS** If you enter the Panama Canal from the Caribbean Sea, which direction will you travel to exit the canal?

80° W
CARIBBEAN SEA
Colón
Cristóbal
Gatún Locks
Gatún Lake
Río Chagres
CANAL ZONE
Panama Canal
Gaillard Cut
Pedro Miguel Locks
Miraflores Locks
Balboa
Panama
Fort Amador
Continental Divide
PANAMA
9° N
PACIFIC OCEAN
79°30′ W
0   5   10 Miles
0   5   10 Kilometers
Lambert Conformal Conic Projection

INTERDISCIPLINARY CONNECTIONS

▶GEOGRAPHY◀

A Home for the Canal. Panama was not the only location considered for the construction of a canal between the Atlantic and Pacific Oceans. During the 1800s, most Americans assumed that it would be built in Nicaragua, while others hoped that it would be built across southern Mexico.

CRITICAL THINKING Why might many Americans have favored the construction of a canal in Mexico?

ANSWER: Answers will vary. Some students might suggest that Mexico's proximity to the United States made it a favored site.

MAP ANSWER
southeast

***The American Nation*
VIDEO PROGRAM**

The Panama Canal;
Teacher's Guide, pp. 93–98

Search 00598, Play to 07996
Videodisc 2, Side A

Play

Pause

See *Teacher's Guide* for Spanish barcode.

LEVEL 1: Pair students and tell them to imagine that it is 1905 and that they are American artists living in Panama. Have each pair create four or five postcards depicting the construction of the canal. On the back of each postcard, students should write a brief description of the obstacles that workers encountered. (*Postcards should note the harsh working conditions, shortages of labor and materials, and an outbreak of yellow fever.*) Have volunteers present and display their postcards around the classroom.
English Language Learners, Cooperative Learning

LEVEL 2: Pair students and have them write a short poem describing the major obstacles to building the Panama Canal.

(*See the Level 1 lesson for the correct obstacles.*) Have volunteers read their poems to the class. **Cooperative Learning**

LEVEL 3: Organize the class into groups of four. Have each group write a brief play about the major obstacles to building the Panama Canal. (*See the Level 1 lesson for the correct obstacles.*) Have volunteers perform their plays for the class.
Cooperative Learning

HOMEWORK *Have each student write a one-page letter to a newspaper to support or oppose President Theodore Roosevelt's actions in securing for the United States the right to build a canal in Central America. Tell students to explain their positions.*

The Colombian Government. Colombians faced many problems as they considered the canal treaty with the United States. Colombia had just gone through a civil war, and the country's leader did not have firm control over the government. Colombia was very poor, and the legislature, which saw the proposed canal as a source of revenue, delayed ratification of the treaty, hoping to obtain more favorable terms from the United States. Theodore Roosevelt, however, called Colombia's actions "blackmail."

CRITICAL THINKING How might Roosevelt's perceptions and his eagerness to build the canal have affected his response to Colombia's delay in ratifying the treaty?

ANSWER: Students might suggest he ignored the concerns and needs of the Colombian people as expressed by the legislature.

SCIENCE & TECHNOLOGY ANSWERS

1. the Continental Divide, heavy rains, frequent avalanches

2. It gave the United States a "Path Between the Seas."

This cartoon pokes fun at the many schemes that led to the building of the Panama Canal.

THE GRANGER COLLECTION, NEW YORK

Building the canal. Work on the canal began in 1904. Harsh working conditions and shortages of labor and materials hampered U.S. efforts. The situation grew worse when a serious outbreak of yellow fever hit.

To put the project back on track, Roosevelt appointed John F. Stevens as chief engineer and architect. Stevens tackled the technical problems while army colonel Dr. William C. Gorgas worked on improving living conditions. Gorgas applied to Panama the lessons he had learned in Cuba. By 1906 yellow fever had almost been eliminated. Malaria was under control by 1913.

Canal construction soon resumed. More than 60 giant steam shovels bit into the land, digging out nearly 160 trainloads of earth each day. More than 43,000 workers, many recruited from the British West Indies, built the canal. On August 15, 1914, the SS *Ancon* completed the first passage through the Panama Canal.

✔ **READING CHECK: Evaluating** How did changing international boundaries affect the building of the Panama Canal? When Panama was no longer part of Colombia, Roosevelt negotiated a new canal treaty.

Science & Technology

The Panama Canal

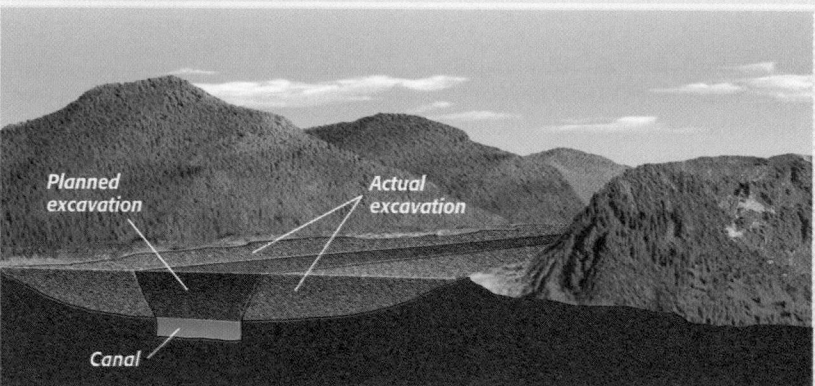

Planned excavation

Actual excavation

Canal

The Panama Canal was originally designed to be built at sea level. The difficulty of moving millions of tons of dirt and rock prompted a different design—an elevated waterway using locks. One group of workers dredged an approach channel and built a dam and locks on the Atlantic side. Another group dredged a passage from the Pacific Ocean through the Bay of Panama and constructed two smaller sets of locks.

The hardest task fell to another group, which had to blast an eight-mile-long channel through the mountainous Continental Divide. Geologic faults, heavy rains, and shifting earth caused frequent and often fatal avalanches. Finally, on October 10, 1913, President Woodrow Wilson signaled crews to dynamite the protective dike at the south end of the channel. In a dramatic

finale, water from the two sides rushed together—85 feet above sea level.

The human and economic costs of building the canal were staggering: some 6,000 workers died, and about $375 million was spent. However, the seemingly impossible had become a reality. The United States—and the rest of the world—now had a "Path Between the Seas."

Understanding Science and History

1. What physical geographic factors made building the Panama Canal difficult?

2. How did this technological innovation affect the United States?

TEACH OBJECTIVE 3

LEVELS 1 AND 2: Organize students into triads. Have each triad develop a graphic organizer that outlines U.S. policy toward Latin America during the Roosevelt, Taft, and Wilson administrations. *(Triads should note that Roosevelt's policy was shaped by the Roosevelt Corollary, which claimed police powers for the United States in the Western Hemisphere; Taft favored dollar diplomacy, or the investment of U.S. capital in Latin America to supplant European investments; and Wilson wanted to establish constitutional democracies in Latin America.)* Ask volunteers to present their graphic organizers to the class. **English Language Learners, Cooperative Learning**

LEVEL 3: Have each student compose an imaginary conversation among Roosevelt, Taft, and Wilson on U.S. policy toward Latin America. *(See the Levels 1 and 2 lesson for the correct policies.)* In the conversation, students should have each president argue in favor of his interpretation of the Monroe Doctrine and justify the application of U.S. power in support of his policy. Students may wish to include the text of their conversations in their portfolios.

NOTE: For an additional teaching idea, see the Chapter 11 analyzing political cartoons lesson in the **Creative Teaching Strategies** handbook.

Relations with Latin America

The United States has a long history of involvement in Latin America. Since the early 1800s it has sought to limit the influence of foreign nations there.

Applying the Monroe Doctrine. Beginning in 1823 the Monroe Doctrine cast the United States as protector of the Western Hemisphere. For much of the 1800s the doctrine served as little more than an idle threat. This changed following the Spanish-American War. Presidents Theodore Roosevelt, William H. Taft, and Woodrow Wilson actively enforced the Monroe Doctrine as a way to protect U.S. interests in Latin America.

Latin America's wealth of raw materials and its many potential laborers and consumers attracted a flood of European and American capital during the late 1800s. Much of this capital was in the form of high-interest bank loans. Many Latin American countries welcomed the loans, but the high interest rates made them difficult to repay. Foreign powers often intervened to collect the loans.

The Roosevelt Corollary. In 1904 President Roosevelt made it clear that he intended to enforce the Monroe Doctrine. The Dominican Republic was unable to repay its European lenders. Fearing that the Europeans would use force to collect the loans, he issued the **Roosevelt Corollary** to the Monroe Doctrine.

History Makers Speak

❝If a nation . . . keeps order and pays its obligations, it need fear no interference from the United States. Chronic wrongdoing . . . in the Western Hemisphere . . . may force the United States, however reluctantly, . . . to the exercise of an international police power.❞

—Theodore Roosevelt, "The Roosevelt Corollary"

Without seeking approval from any Latin American nation, Roosevelt had put into practice a West African proverb that he was fond of quoting: "Speak softly and carry a big stick; you will go far." The United States pledged to use armed forces to prevent any European country from seizing Dominican territory. To satisfy the Europeans' demand for repayment, the United States took control of collecting all Dominican customs duties. In 1916 civil unrest shook the Dominican Republic, and the U.S. government sent in marines. They remained until 1924. Despite protests, U.S. intervention in Latin America continued.

★ HISTORICAL DOCUMENTS ★

PRESIDENT THEODORE ROOSEVELT
The Roosevelt Corollary

The Monroe Doctrine warned European powers to stay out of Latin America. Events in the early 1900s led President Theodore Roosevelt to issue the Roosevelt Corollary. **How does the Roosevelt Corollary modify the Monroe Doctrine?**

It must be understood that under no circumstances will the United States use the Monroe Doctrine as a cloak for territorial aggression. We desire peace with all the world, but perhaps most of all with the other peoples of the American Continent. There are, of course, limits to the wrongs which any self-respecting nation can endure. It is always possible that wrong actions toward this Nation, or toward citizens of this Nation, in some State unable to keep order among its own people, unable to secure justice from outsiders, and unwilling to do justice to those outsiders who treat it well, may result in our having to take action to protect our rights; but such action will not be taken with a view to territorial aggression, and it will be taken at all only with extreme reluctance and when it has become evident that every other resource has been exhausted.

REVIEW

Have students complete the **Section 3 Review** on p. 344.

ASSESS

Have students complete **Daily Quiz 11.3**. As **Alternative Assessment**, you may want to use the Panama Canal postcards or the Latin America graphic organizer in this section's lessons.

RETEACH

Have students complete **Main Idea Activity for English Language Learners and Special-Needs Students 11.3**. Then organize students into pairs. Have each pair create a one-page outline of Section 3. Remind students that they will need to choose events and material very carefully to produce an inclusive outline in just one page. Have volunteers present their outlines to the class.
English Language Learners, Cooperative Learning

EXTEND

Write the following question on the chalkboard: *Did dollar diplomacy hurt U.S. diplomatic relations with European countries?* Have students investigate situations when the United States used dollar diplomacy to protect its interests in Latin America. Students should then identify the reaction of European countries. Have each student report his or her findings in an essay. **Block Scheduling**

INTERPRETING THE VISUAL RECORD

Intervention. These U.S. Marines were part of the force sent to Nicaragua by President Taft in 1912. *What does the photograph suggest about the type of fighting the marines did in Nicaragua?*

Dollar diplomacy. William H. Taft, Roosevelt's successor, expanded U.S. influence in Latin America. Taft favored "substituting dollars for bullets"—economic influence for military force—as a means of protecting U.S. interests in Latin America and Asia. This policy came to be called **dollar diplomacy**. Taft suggested replacing European loans with American ones. He argued that increasing U.S. economic power would reduce the chances of European intervention. By 1914 American capital in Latin America had grown to over $1.6 billion, invested mainly in mines, railroads, and banana and sugar plantations.

Taft tested dollar diplomacy in Nicaragua. In June 1911 the U.S. government agreed to help Nicaragua obtain private loans from American banks. In return, Nicaraguan leaders gave the United States the right to send troops into their country when U.S. leaders thought it necessary to protect American investments.

President Woodrow Wilson, Taft's successor, believed that democratic governments, not U.S. dollars, would keep European powers out of Latin America. To keep Germany from taking control of strategic Caribbean territory, Wilson sent marines to several countries to put down rebellions and establish constitutional governments. In 1915, when revolution shook Haiti, Wilson sent in marines. Haiti was forced to accept a treaty that gave the United States power to run its government. U.S. marines stayed until 1934. Some 1,500 Haitians died resisting U.S. control.

✔ **READING CHECK: Drawing Conclusions** How did dollar diplomacy change U.S. relations with Latin America? It expanded U.S. influence in Latin America because the United States wanted to protect the economic interests of American companies.

SECTION ③ REVIEW

1. Define and explain:
protectorate
dollar diplomacy

2. Identify and explain:
Leonard Wood
Platt Amendment
Foraker Act
Philippe Bunau-Varilla
Hay–Bunau-Varilla Treaty
Roosevelt Corollary

3. Analyzing Information
Copy the chart below. Use it to describe how Presidents Roosevelt, Taft, and Wilson interpreted the Monroe Doctrine. Then give an example of how each president applied the Monroe Doctrine in Latin America.

	Description	Example
Roosevelt		
Taft		
Wilson		

 Homework Practice Online
keyword: SE3 HP11

4. **Finding the Main Idea**
- **a.** How did the U.S. relationship with Cuba and Puerto Rico change after the Spanish-American War?
- **b.** How did the growth in trade with Asia affect American public support for building a canal in Panama?
- **c.** What obstacles did the physical and human environment of Panama present to building a canal, and how were they overcome?

5. **Writing and Critical Thinking**
Evaluating Write an evaluation of President Roosevelt's effectiveness as a leader.
Consider:
- U.S. interest in building a canal
- the negotiations between the United States and Colombia
- the Roosevelt Corollary

SECTION ④

Conflict with Mexico

EYEWITNESSES TO History

❝*A force of tyranny . . . oppresses us in such a manner that it has become intolerable. . . . The Mexican people . . . are thirsty for liberty, and . . . they reject with energy the Government of General Díaz. . . . Therefore, and in echo of the national will, I declare the late election illegal. . . . The people . . . anxiously call me from all parts of the country, to compel General Díaz by force of arms, to respect the national will.*❞

—Francisco Madero, "The Plan of San Luis Potosi," November 20, 1910

Francisco Madero was a leader of the Mexican Revolution.

Francisco Madero ran for president of Mexico in 1910. Porfirio Díaz—Mexico's longtime dictator—ordered Madero arrested and imprisoned. Madero fled to San Antonio, Texas, where on November 20, 1910, he issued the Plan of San Luis Potosi. He called upon Mexicans to take up arms against the government. The war he began would last 10 years.

Mexico Under Díaz

Mexican president **Porfirio Díaz** had come to power in 1877 after Mexico had suffered almost 66 years of war and unrest. When Díaz took over, Mexico was in sad shape. The mines that had once been sources of great wealth were neglected or abandoned. Crime and violence were widespread. Díaz's first goal was to impose order, which he did by crushing or controlling his opponents.

Díaz's success in bringing order to Mexico attracted foreign investors. Confident that Díaz's government would protect their investments, foreigners poured millions of dollars into building Mexico's industries. When Díaz took office, Mexico had less than 500 miles of railroads. By 1910 the country had 15,000 miles of railroads. Petroleum production began about the turn of the century and expanded rapidly. The mining industry, which had been largely inactive since colonial times, boomed again due to foreign capital. By 1908, American companies controlled three quarters of all Mexican mining operations.

Total foreign investments in Mexico amounted to some $2 billion by 1913. More than half came from the United States. Although Díaz did improve Mexico's economy, foreign investors and Díaz's friends were the primary beneficiaries of this economic growth. Little trickled down to workers and peasants, and most Mexicans lived in poverty.

The Mexican Revolution

In 1910 Porfirio Díaz ran for re-election. Using force and fraud, he won his eighth term as president. Meanwhile, opposition to Díaz's dictatorship had been growing. In the south, **Emiliano Zapata** led a rebel army that demanded land for the mostly American Indian peasant population. An American Indian himself, Zapata had

LEVEL 1: Have volunteers assume the role of one of the following people: Porfirio Díaz, Emiliano Zapata, Francisco Madero, or Victoriano Huerta. Then have volunteers line up in any order and explain why and how "he" participated in the Mexican Revolution. *(Volunteers should indicate the following: Porfirio Díaz—used force and fraud to win an eighth term as president of Mexico; Emiliano Zapata—led a rebel army demanding land for the mostly American Indian peasant population; Francisco Madero—unified the various opposition forces and won the presidency after Díaz's overthrow; Victoriano Huerta—seized control of the government and restored calm.)* As volunteers present their statements, have students guess the speaker's identity and write it on a sheet of paper with notes from his statement for review purposes. After all four speakers have made their statements, have students discuss who each speaker represented. **English Language Learners**

LEVELS 2 AND 3: Write the following statement on the chalkboard: *The Mexican Revolution was not really a revolution at all. Instead, it was a contest for power among military and political factions whose objective was control of government rather than implementation of a revolutionary program.* Have each student write an essay that supports or refutes the statement. Students should use the major events of the Mexican Revolution as evidence for their positions. *(See the Level 1 lesson for the correct events.)* Have volunteers read their essays to the class.

Mexico and Texas. Texas served as a refuge for many Mexican revolutionaries and rebels. However, individuals such as Francisco Madero had to be certain that they did not violate U.S. neutrality laws. While in San Antonio, Texas, he composed his Plan de San Luis Potosi. However, he backdated it by a month so that he could claim that he wrote it in Mexico rather than in the United States, thereby remaining in compliance with U.S. neutrality laws.

CRITICAL THINKING Why might Mexican rebels have fled to Texas?

ANSWER: Students might mention its geographic proximity to Mexico.

VISUAL RECORD ANSWER

Students might suggest that the revolutionaries look poor.

CHANGING WAYS ANSWER

Today the value of Mexican exports to the United States is greater than the value of U.S. exports to Mexico.

INTERPRETING THE VISUAL RECORD

The revolutionaries. Followers of Emiliano Zapata, known as *zapatistas,* march in August 1914. *What does the photograph reveal about the forces that fought the Mexican Revolution?*

been a tenant farmer on a sugar plantation. He is said to have been inspired to revolt because his master's horses lived in tiled stables while he and his family lived in dirt-floored shacks. Mexican intellectuals also organized against the Díaz government. In a book published in 1909, Andrés Molina Enríquez called for land redistribution. He predicted that "it will come, whether in peace . . . or by revolution."

A wealthy landowner from northern Mexico, **Francisco Madero** was an unlikely candidate to unify the various opposition forces. He was considered a dreamer and an idealist, but his ideas sparked the **Mexican Revolution** that toppled the Díaz dictatorship. Rebel forces defeated Díaz's troops in key cities in northern and central Mexico. In May 1911, with mobs roaming the streets of Mexico City, Díaz resigned. He went into exile in Paris, where he died in 1915.

In Mexico's first democratic elections in 30 years, Madero easily won the presidency. The United States recognized Madero's government and placed an embargo on arms sales to his opponents. Madero tried to establish a democratic government but was soon overwhelmed by the very forces that he had unleashed in toppling Díaz.

Led by Díaz's nephew, supporters of the former dictator rebelled against Madero. For 10 days in February 1913 the roar of cannons echoed through the streets of Mexico City as rebels fought for control of the country. Many people died in the violence before Madero's commanding general, **Victoriano Huerta** (WER-tah), seized control of the government and restored calm. Huerta imprisoned Madero, who was murdered when he allegedly attempted to escape. Four major revolutionary armies continued to fight Huerta. However, their leaders—

★ Changing Ways   Mexico and the United States

■ **Understanding Change** The economies of the United States and Mexico have been linked for many years. The United States used to ship more goods to Mexico than it received in return. In recent years that has changed. Fewer trade restrictions have boosted trade between the two countries. Mexico now produces many items for export to the United States. *Based on the information provided, how do you think the economic relationship between the United States and Mexico has changed?*

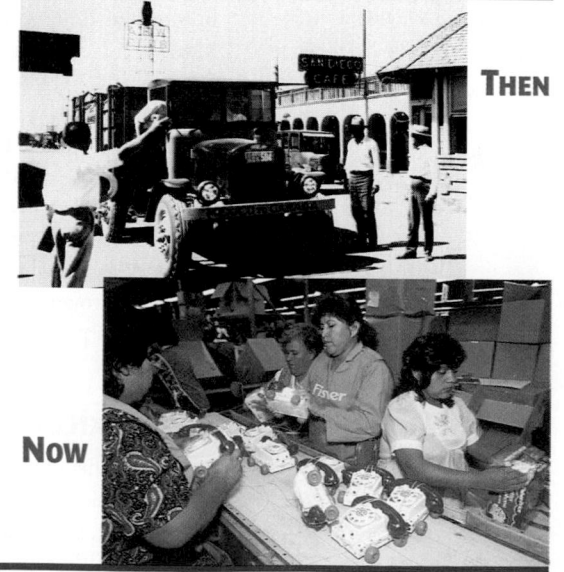

THEN

NOW

	THEN	**NOW**
Value of U.S. Exports to Mexico	$208 million	$79 billion
Value of Mexican Exports to the United States	$179 million	$94.7 billion

Sources: *Historical Statistics of the United States; Statistical Abstract of the United States: 1999.* Data reflect 1920 and 1998.

TEACH OBJECTIVE 2

 LEVEL 1: Tell students to imagine that they are President Wilson. Have each student write a few sentences explaining why he intervened in Mexico in 1914. *(Students' responses might suggest that the outrage over Francisco Madero's murder and the arrest of crew members from the USS Dolphin by soldiers loyal to Huerta contributed to Wilson's decision to intervene.)* Have volunteers read their sentences to the class. **English Language Learners**

LEVELS 2 AND 3: Tell students to imagine that they are exchange students living in Mexico during the Mexican Revolution. Have each student write a one-page letter to a friend at home that explains why the United States intervened in Mexico. *(See the Level 1 lesson for the correct reasons.)* Call on volunteers to read their letters to the class.

TEACH OBJECTIVE 3

 ALL LEVELS: To help students understand how the United States, Pancho Villa, and Venustiano Carranza contributed to the outcome of the Mexican Revolution, copy the graphic organizer on the following page on the chalkboard, omitting the italicized answers. Have each student complete it. Discuss the completed graphic organizer with students. **English Language Learners**

Venustiano Carranza (bay-noos-TYAHN-oh kahr-RAHN-sah), **Francisco "Pancho" Villa**, Emiliano Zapata, and Álvaro Obregón (oh-bray-GAWN)—were not united.

✔ **READING CHECK: Sequencing** What events led to the Mexican Revolution?
Porfirio Díaz tolerated conditions that kept people poor, arrested Francisco Madero, and conducted a dishonest election in 1910.

U.S. Intervention

Victoriano Huerta soon gained recognition from most European countries. Outraged by Francisco Madero's murder, Woodrow Wilson, the new U.S. president, refused to recognize Huerta. Wilson called Huerta's government a "government of butchers." In February 1914 Wilson lifted the embargo on arms sales to the revolutionary armies and adopted a policy of "watchful waiting." He was looking for an opportunity to drive Huerta from power.

Tampico. On April 9, 1914, an incident occurred that gave Wilson his opportunity. The USS *Dolphin* had been stationed in Mexican waters near the port of Tampico, which was under Huerta's control. Several crew members from the *Dolphin* went ashore for supplies and were arrested by soldiers loyal to Huerta. The Americans were quickly released unharmed, and the Mexicans' superior officer apologized for the incident. However, the U.S. admiral demanded a

 "formal . . . apology for the act, together with your assurance that the officer responsible for it will receive severe punishment. Also that you publicly hoist the American flag in a prominent position on shore and salute it with twenty-one guns.**"**

—Admiral Mayo, quoted in *Foreign Relations*, 1914

Wilson supported this unusual demand, which placed the United States in the ironic position of requesting an official apology from a government it did not recognize. On April 20 the president appeared before Congress asking to approve the use of armed forces against Mexico. Congress approved the use of force on April 22, but events in Mexico moved faster.

The occupation of Veracruz. Before Congress could act, Wilson learned that a German ship transporting arms to Huerta was heading for Veracruz. He ordered the U.S. Navy to seize the port of Veracruz. On April 21, U.S. forces stopped the German ship. Under the cover of a naval bombardment, marines then landed at Veracruz. Huerta's forces had already withdrawn from the city, and only civilians and local authorities remained. During the brief struggle for control of the city, 19 marines were killed. Some 300 Mexicans died during the bombardment.

At this critical stage, Argentina, Brazil, and Chile—sometimes called the ABC powers—organized a conference to resolve the crisis. In June the conference called for Huerta's resignation and for the creation of a provisional government. Huerta refused, but his enemies were closing in. That July Huerta resigned and fled to Spain.

✔ **READING CHECK: Identifying Cause and Effect** Why did the United States intervene in Mexico? because President Wilson was outraged by Madero's murder and further angered by the arrests of U.S. Navy members

---

Analyzing Primary Sources

Drawing Inferences Why might some Mexicans have objected to the terms of the apology? because of its unusual nature

INTERPRETING THE VISUAL RECORD

Veracruz. U.S. sailors help secure the customhouse in Veracruz. *What appears to be happening in the photograph?*

OUTCOMES OF THE MEXICAN REVOLUTION

United States	Pancho Villa	Venustiano Carranza
• President Wilson orders a military expedition into Mexico to capture Villa dead or alive • Gen. Pershing leads forces into Chihuahua • The United States stations National Guardsmen along the Mexican border	• controls nearly two thirds of Mexico with Emiliano Zapata • suffers defeat in 1915 by Álvaro Obregón, after which Villa disbands his army • raids Columbus, New Mexico • goes into hiding	• calls constitutional convention in December 1916 • puts new constitution into effect on February 5, 1917 • new constitution declares that Mexico owns all mineral, oil, and water rights

Teacher to Teacher

Richard G. Cheplick of Houston, Texas, suggested the following activity: Have students define yellow journalism. Then have them compare and contrast the yellow journalism of the Spanish American War period with current media descriptions of international events. Ask students to identify possible bias in the stories they find. Conduct a classroom debate on the issue of yellow journalism today.

SECTION REVIEW 4 ANSWERS

1. Identify
• Porfirio Díaz, p. 345
• Emiliano Zapata, p. 345
• Francisco Madero, p. 346
• Mexican Revolution, p. 346
• Victoriano Huerta, p. 346
• Venustiano Carranza, p. 347
• Francisco "Pancho" Villa, p. 347
• John J. Pershing, p. 349

2. Diaz—resigned and went into exile; Madero—overthrown and assassinated; Huerta—resigned and fled to Spain; Carranza—oversaw new constitution

3a. Many Americans regarded Mexico as unstable and a danger to U.S. security.

b. Answers will vary. Some students might argue that U.S. actions constituted a violation of Mexico's sovereignty.

c. U.S. intervention caused death and destruction but led to Huerta's removal from office.

4. Answers will vary. Some students might oppose the Veracruz occupation and U.S. demands in Tampico but support operations against Villa.

Pancho Villa (second from right) inspects his troops' rifles.

The Revolution Winds Down

By early 1915 Mexico was in chaos. Pancho Villa and Emiliano Zapata controlled nearly two thirds of the country. In March Venustiano Carranza re-entered Mexico City and became provisional president. He promised to protect American lives and property. The United States recognized his government in October 1915.

Pancho Villa's raid. In April 1915 Carranza's general, Álvaro Obregón, defeated Villa's troops in the central state of Guanajuato. After another major defeat, Villa disbanded his army. The U.S. recognition of Carranza had upset Villa. He decided to take revenge on Americans. Villa explained his reasoning.

History Makers Speak

❝We have decided not to fire a bullet more against Mexicans, our brothers, and to prepare and organize ourselves to attack the Americans in their own dens and make them know that Mexico is a land for the free and a tomb for thrones, crowns, and traitors.❞

—Pancho Villa, letter to Emiliano Zapata, 1916

In March 1916 Villa and his troops crossed the border into New Mexico to raid Columbus, a small, isolated town. Striking at dawn, these men burned and looted the town. In the battle 17 Americans—nine civilians and eight soldiers—and more than 100 of Villa's troops were killed.

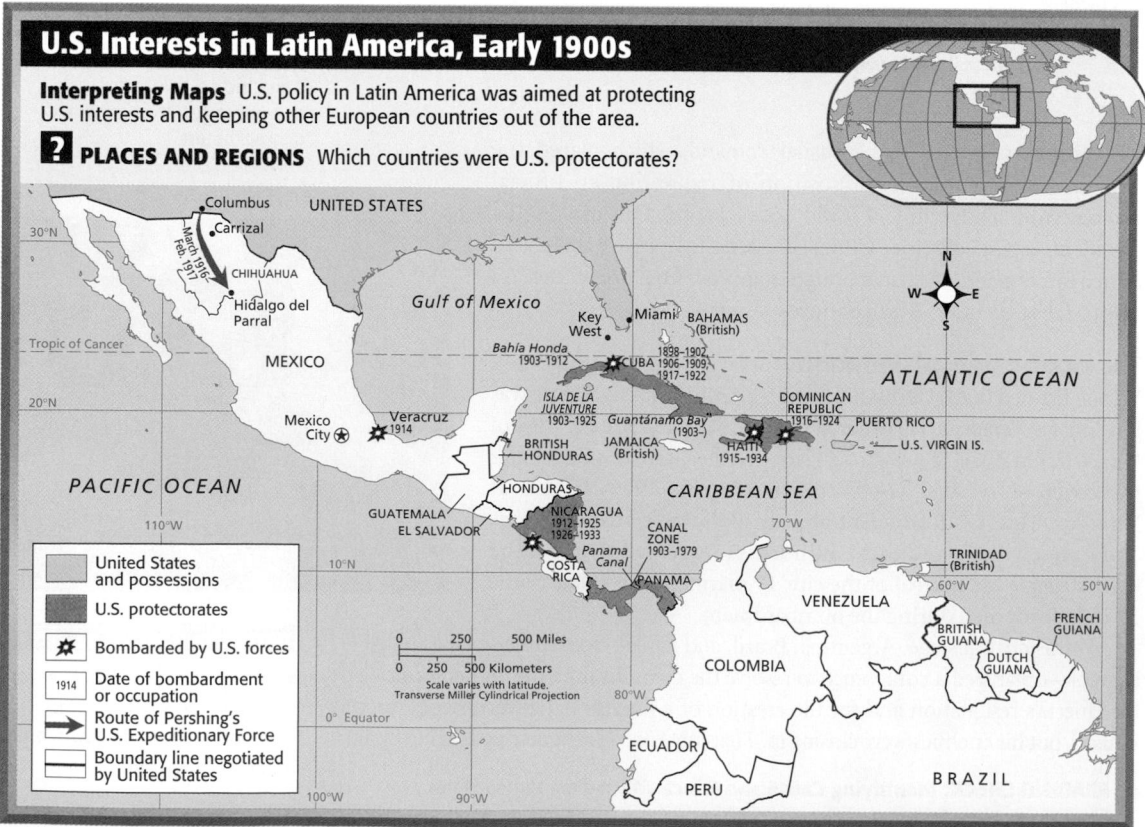

U.S. Interests in Latin America, Early 1900s

Interpreting Maps U.S. policy in Latin America was aimed at protecting U.S. interests and keeping other European countries out of the area.

? PLACES AND REGIONS Which countries were U.S. protectorates?

Legend:
- United States and possessions
- U.S. protectorates
- ✹ Bombarded by U.S. forces
- 1914 Date of bombardment or occupation
- → Route of Pershing's U.S. Expeditionary Force
- Boundary line negotiated by United States

REVIEW

Have students complete the **Section 4 Review** on p. 349.

ASSESS

Have students complete **Daily Quiz 11.4**. As **Alternative Assessment**, you may want to use the intervention sentences or the Mexican Revolution letter in this section's lessons.

RETEACH

Have students complete **Main Idea Activity for English Language Learners and Special-Needs Students 11.4**. Then organize students into triads. Have each triad create an annotated time line of the Mexican Revolution and its aftermath. Ask volunteers to present their time lines to the class. Then display the time lines around the classroom to help students review the material.
English Language Learners, Cooperative Learning

EXTEND

Ask students to conduct research on modern-day relations between the United States and Mexico. Have each student present his or her research in a short essay. Ask volunteers to read their essays to the class. Then conduct a discussion on the information presented in the essays. **Block Scheduling**

Pursuing Pancho Villa. Without requesting approval from the Carranza government, President Wilson ordered a military expedition into Mexico to capture Villa "dead or alive." A week after Villa's raid on Columbus, General **John J. Pershing** led his forces into Chihuahua, Villa's home state. Although Pershing later increased his troop size to 15,000 men, Villa still eluded capture. The farther Pershing went into Mexican territory, the more the Mexicans resented the Americans.

When one of Pershing's cavalry units attempted to pass through the town of Carrizal, the commander of the Mexican garrison refused passage. Pershing chose to enter Carrizal rather than bypass the town, and a battle followed.

By early September 1916 nearly 150,000 U.S. National Guardsmen were stationed along the Mexican border. Wilson realized that the threat of war increased each day that U.S. troops remained in Mexico. The president finally ordered U.S. troops withdrawn in January 1917.

THE GRANGER COLLECTION, NEW YORK

General John J. Pershing (front) led the unsuccessful expedition to capture Pancho Villa.

Carranza in power. With Villa in hiding and Zapata contained in the south, Carranza called a constitutional convention in December 1916. After two months of negotiations, a new constitution was put into effect on February 5, 1917. It contained several revolutionary ideas. The constitution placed the interests of common welfare above individual rights and provided protection for workers. This protection included an eight-hour workday, an end to child labor, and the right to form unions and bargain collectively.

The constitution also declared national ownership of all of Mexico's mineral, oil, and water rights. This part of the constitution would have important effects on American oil companies operating in Mexico in the 1930s.

✔ **READING CHECK: Making Predictions** How might Mexico's new constitution have affected Mexico's relations with the United States? Its labor laws and claim to ownership of oil and mineral rights might make it more difficult for American businesses in Mexico.

SECTION 4 REVIEW

1. Identify and explain:
Porfirio Díaz
Emiliano Zapata
Francisco Madero
Mexican Revolution
Victoriano Huerta
Venustiano Carranza
Francisco "Pancho" Villa
John J. Pershing

2. Categorizing Copy the chart below. Use it to list various leaders who fought for control of Mexico and what happened to them.

Leader		What Happened?
	→	
	→	
	→	
	→	
	→	

3. Finding the Main Idea
a. How did the Mexican Revolution affect American views of Mexico?
b. Did the United States have the right to stop a German ship from delivering its cargo to Mexico? Explain your answer.
c. How did U.S. intervention both help and hurt Mexico?

4. Writing and Critical Thinking
Drawing Conclusions Do you think the Mexican Revolution resulted in a positive outcome for Mexico? Write a paragraph to explain your answer.
Consider:
• the conditions under Porfirio Díaz
• the goals of the revolutionary leaders
• the government established by Venustiano Carranza

Homework Practice Online
keyword: SE3 HP11

CHAPTER 11
REVIEW ANSWERS

Creating a Time Line
Each event should have an explanation and the correct date.

Writing a Summary
See the Reading Checks in each section for main ideas.

Identifying People and Ideas
1. the quest for colonial empires that marked the late 1800s and early 1900s

2. Massachusetts senator who supported U.S. expansionism

3. Hawaiian queen overthrown in a revolt led by Americans

4. called for all nations to receive equal trade access with China

5. Cuban poet and exile who died in the 1895 revolt against Spain

6. Filipino rebel leader who initially allied with the United States to defeat the Spanish but later fought against U.S. troops

7. modified the Monroe Doctrine to allow United States to protect interests in Latin America more easily

8. Taft's policy of using economic power to limit European influence in Latin America

9. Mexican dictator driven from office by rebels

10. Mexican leader whose government received U.S. recognition in 1915

TECHNOLOGY
▶ Chapter 11 Test Generator (on the One-Stop Planner)
▶ Global Skill Builder CD–ROM
▶ HRW Go site

REINFORCEMENT, REVIEW, AND ASSESSMENT
▶ Chapter 11 Review, pp. 350–51
▶ Chapter 11 Tutorial for Students, Parents, Mentors, and Peers

▶ Chapter 11 Test (Form A or B)
▶ Portfolio Activities and Alternative Assessment Handbook, Chapter 11
▶ Chapter 11 Test for English Language Learners and Special-Needs Students

REVIEW
Have students complete the **Chapter 11 Review** on pp. 350–51.

ASSESS
Use one of the chapter tests to assess students' understanding of the content. For **Alternative Assessment**, see the **Portfolio Activities and Alternative Assessment Handbook**.

Understanding Main Ideas

1. the desire for markets, raw materials, power, and prestige as well as the desire to spread democracy and Christianity

2. imperialist ambition, yellow journalism, humanitarian concerns, and the *Maine* incident

3. The United States became more of a world power, increased its trade, and gained more territory.

4. tried to negotiate a treaty with Colombia, supported Panamanian rebels, negotiated the Hay–Bunau-Varilla Treaty to gain control over Canal Zone, and started to build the canal

5. President Wilson wanted Huerta, whom he regarded as a murderer, removed from office and ordered intervention.

Reviewing Themes

1. Americans wanted to protect their investments there.

2. They fostered economic growth, but failed to distribute profits to the impoverished Mexican people.

3. The United States imposed a government on the Filipinos against their will.

Thinking Critically

1. Lodge—the United States needs to join the competition for territory; Mahan—the United States needs a strong navy to protect its economic interests in foreign markets; Roosevelt—the United States has a right to intervene in Latin America to protects its economic interests

CHAPTER 11 Review

Creating a Time Line

Copy the time line below onto a sheet of paper. Complete the time line by filling in the events and dates from the chapter that you think were most significant. Pick three events and explain why you think they were significant.

1898   1907   1916

Writing a Summary

Using standard grammar, spelling, sentence structure, and punctuation, write an overview of events in the chapter.

Identifying People and Ideas

Identify the following terms or individuals and explain their significance.

1. imperialism
2. Henry Cabot Lodge
3. Liliuokalani
4. Open Door Policy
5. José Martí

6. Emilio Aguinaldo
7. Roosevelt Corollary
8. dollar diplomacy
9. Porfirio Díaz
10. Venustiano Carranza

Understanding Main Ideas

SECTION 1 (pp. 326–332)
1. What led industrialized nations to seek overseas colonies in the late 1800s and early 1900s?

SECTION 2 (pp. 333–339)
2. What were the major causes of the Spanish-American War?
3. What economic effects did the war have on the United States?

SECTION 3 (pp. 340–344)
4. What steps did the United States overcome to build the Panama Canal?

SECTION 4 (pp. 345–349)
5. How and why did the United States intervene in Mexico?

Reviewing Themes

1. **Global Relations** Why was the United States interested in controlling Cuba?
2. **Economics** How did foreign investors affect Mexico's economy?
3. **Citizenship** Why might some people argue that U.S. actions in the Philippines conflicted with democratic principles?

Thinking Critically

1. **Identifying Points of View** What arguments did Henry Cabot Lodge, Alfred Thayer Mahan, and Theodore Roosevelt make in support of U.S. expansionism?
2. **Analyzing Information** How did events in the late 1800s and early 1900s lead the United States into a position of world power?
3. **Drawing Conclusions** What effects did the Open Door Policy, dollar diplomacy, and the Roosevelt Corollary have on U.S. diplomacy?
4. **Evaluating** Why did the U.S. government oppose the revolution in the Philippines but support the Mexican Revolution?
5. **Making Predictions** What might have been the effect on U.S. relations with Cuba, Puerto Rico, and the Philippines, if the United States had adopted an Open Door Policy toward each of those countries?

Writing About History

Sequencing Write an essay that traces the geographic factors, negotiations, and events involved in the building of the Panama Canal. Use the following graphic organizer to help you prepare your essay.

1. A canal across Panama is proposed.
2.
3.
4.
5. United States builds Panama Canal.

RETEACH

Organize students into small groups. Ask half of the members in each group to write headlines reflecting the events discussed in Sections 1, 2, 3, and 4. Then have the other members in each group write two- or three-paragraph news stories that explain one of the headlines. Have a representative from each group read the headline and news story to the class.
English Language Learners, Cooperative Learning

EXTEND

Have each student use the textbook, the library, and other sources to create a biographical dictionary of the Mexican Revolution. Entries should include biographical data on key figures of the revolution who were discussed in this chapter, including Woodrow Wilson and John J. Pershing. Have students arrange their entries in alphabetical order and include pictures, maps, or other visuals where appropriate. **Block Scheduling**

Building Social Studies Skills

Interpreting Graphs

Study the graph below. Then use it to help answer the questions that follow.

U.S. Trade, 1885–1915

Source: *Historical Statistics of the United States*

1. Which statement accurately summarizes the trends shown in the graph?
   a. Both exports and imports declined in the years shown.
   b. Exports increased at a faster rate than exports.
   c. Imports increased at a faster rate than exports.
   d. Exports and imports grew at the same pace.

2. In 1913 the Underwood Tariff Act reduced tariffs to their lowest levels in more than 50 years. How did this act affect U.S. exports?

Analyzing Primary Sources

Read the following excerpt from a campaign speech by Senator Albert J. Beveridge in 1898. Then answer the questions that follow.

❝Today we are raising more than we can consume. Today we are making more than we can use. Today our industrial society is congested; there are more workers than there is work; there is more capital than there is investment. We do not need more money—we need more circulation, more employment. Therefore we must find new markets for our produce, new occupation for our capital, new work for our labor. And so, while we did not need the territory taken during the past century at the time it was required, we do need what we have taken in 1898, and we need it now.❞

3. According to Beveridge, what is the main reason the United States should annex the Philippines?
   a. The United States has a moral obligation to help the Filipinos.
   b. The Filipinos have asked to be annexed.
   c. The United States needs to recruit workers from the Philippines.
   d. The United States needs the Philippines as a new market.

4. How do Beveridge's views on imperialism compare with those of Henry Cabot Lodge?

Alternative Assessment

Building Your Portfolio

Global Relations

Imagine that you are a member of the State Department in the early 1900s. Write a memorandum to the president that addresses concerns about U.S. relations with China, Japan, Mexico, Spain, or South America. Your memorandum should mention specific issues dealing with your chosen country or region.

U.S. HISTORY

internet connect

Internet Activity: go.hrw.com
KEYWORD: SE3 AN11

Access the Internet through the HRW Go site to create a poster that analyzes the effects of both physical and geographic factors on the construction of the Panama Canal. Physical factors include landforms (such as mountains or jungle), climate, and weather. Human factors should focus on the use of technology, and the techniques and reasons humans modified the environment. As a review, pose and answer questions regarding the construction of the canal.

2. The United States won many conflicts with foreign countries and gained territory as a result. Other world powers saw U.S. strength and gained respect.

3. These policies led to a shift from diplomacy by military force to diplomacy by economic force.

4. Americans wanted to control the Philippines but only wanted a stable government of some kind in Mexico.

5. Each nation would have remained independent and had its own form of government, although each would probably have been economically exploited.

Writing
Essays will vary. However, students might refer to the following events: the French fail in their efforts to build a canal; Colombia refuses to ratify a treaty allowing the United States to build a canal; the United States supports the Panamanian revolution.

Building Social Studies Skills
1. b

2. It caused U.S. exports to increase.

3. d

4. Answers will vary. Students might suggest that both men supported U.S. expansionism to encourage its economic growth.

🔊 LET'S GET STARTED!

Write the following question on the chalkboard: *Is it ever right for one country to become deeply involved in the affairs of another nation, whether due to economic or political interests?* As students enter the classroom, ask them to answer the question in writing. Have volunteers share their responses. Then tell students that they will learn more about how and why the United States took a larger role in the world in the Unit 3 America's Geography.

TEACH AMERICA'S GEOGRAPHY—THE UNITED STATES AND THE WORLD

Ask students to study the America's Geography feature, paying careful attention to the graphs on foreign investment and the map legend on exported products. Then write the following question on the chalkboard: What factors motivated imperialism in the early 1900s? Have each student answer the question in a few sentences. (*Students should note that the graphs and the legend indicates that economic interests helped fuel imperialism.*) Then ask students to create political cartoons and captions commenting on imperialism. **English Language Learners**

Foreign Trade. The desire for foreign trade guided much of U.S. foreign policy in the early 1900s. Events such as the annexation of Hawaii, the construction of the Panama Canal, and even the Spanish-American War were all economically linked. Alfred Thayer Mahan, a well-known naval officer and author, argued that foreign trade was necessary for national growth. Mahan also advocated a strong merchant marine and overseas commercial outposts to help achieve this goal.

CRITICAL THINKING What else might Mahan have suggested to achieve national growth?

ANSWER: Students might suggest that Mahan probably would have supported a strong navy and possible overseas colonies.

THAT'S INTERESTING!

Henry Cabot Lodge expressed a common expansionist sentiment when he declared that "from the Rio Grande to the Arctic Ocean there should be but one flag and one country."

★ AMERICA'S ★ Geography

The United States and the World

By 1914, on the eve of World War I, many nations were connected to one another in a complex web of economic trade and investment. European nations, particularly Great Britain, controlled the vast majority of this economic activity. Compared to European empires, the United States had relatively little financial investment in other countries. Yet even the United States expanded its economic and political involvement in foreign nations during this period.

The United States and the World, 1900–1914

U.S. Foreign Investment, 1900–1910
Legend: 1900, 1910

German Foreign Investment in 1910*
* All investment data for Germany in 1900 either not available or negligible

British Foreign Investment, 1900–1910
Legend: 1900, 1910

Source: *Rand McNally Atlas of World History*

South America. South America had many valuable resources. These included tin from Brazil, copper from Argentina and Peru, and nitrates—used to make fertilizer and explosives—from Chile. European empires did not attempt to create new colonies in South America, as they did in Africa. However, they did invest heavily in the economies of self-governing South American countries. The United States also increased investment in South America, but many of its investments were concentrated in Central America and the Panama Canal region.

SPOTLIGHT
on the Imperialism Debate

Organize students into two large groups—one that supports U.S. imperialism and one that opposes it. Then ask students to locate and use a variety of primary and secondary sources to learn more about the imperialism debate in the United States during the late 1800s and early 1900s. Remind students that their research should cover both their own position and that of their opponents. Give groups time to prepare their arguments. Then conduct a debate on American imperialism. **Block Scheduling, Cooperative Learning**

SPOTLIGHT
on China

Pair students and ask each pair to locate and use a variety of primary and secondary sources to learn more about the overthrow of the Chinese emperor in 1911, focusing on how the event affected the country's domestic and international affairs. Tell students to create an annotated outline showing the rise and fall of Chinese imperialism.
Block Scheduling, Cooperative Learning

AMERICA'S Geography

Asia. Asian empires experienced dramatic changes around 1900. China, which had been the largest empire in the world, suffered a series of political crises. These led to the loss of many of its territories and eventually to the overthrow of its emperor in 1911. Meanwhile, the tiny nation of Japan was becoming the leading Asian power. Its empire expanded with military victories over China and Russia.

Exported Products

Co	Cocoa	M	Manufactured goods
Cf	Coffee	Me	Meat
Cp	Copper	O	Oil
C	Cotton	P	Palm products
D	Dairy products	Ri	Rice
Di	Diamonds	R	Rubber
F	Fish	S	Silk
Fr	Fruit	Sp	Spices
G	Gold	Su	Sugar
Gr	Grain	Te	Tea
I	Iron	T	Tobacco
J	Jute	W	Wool

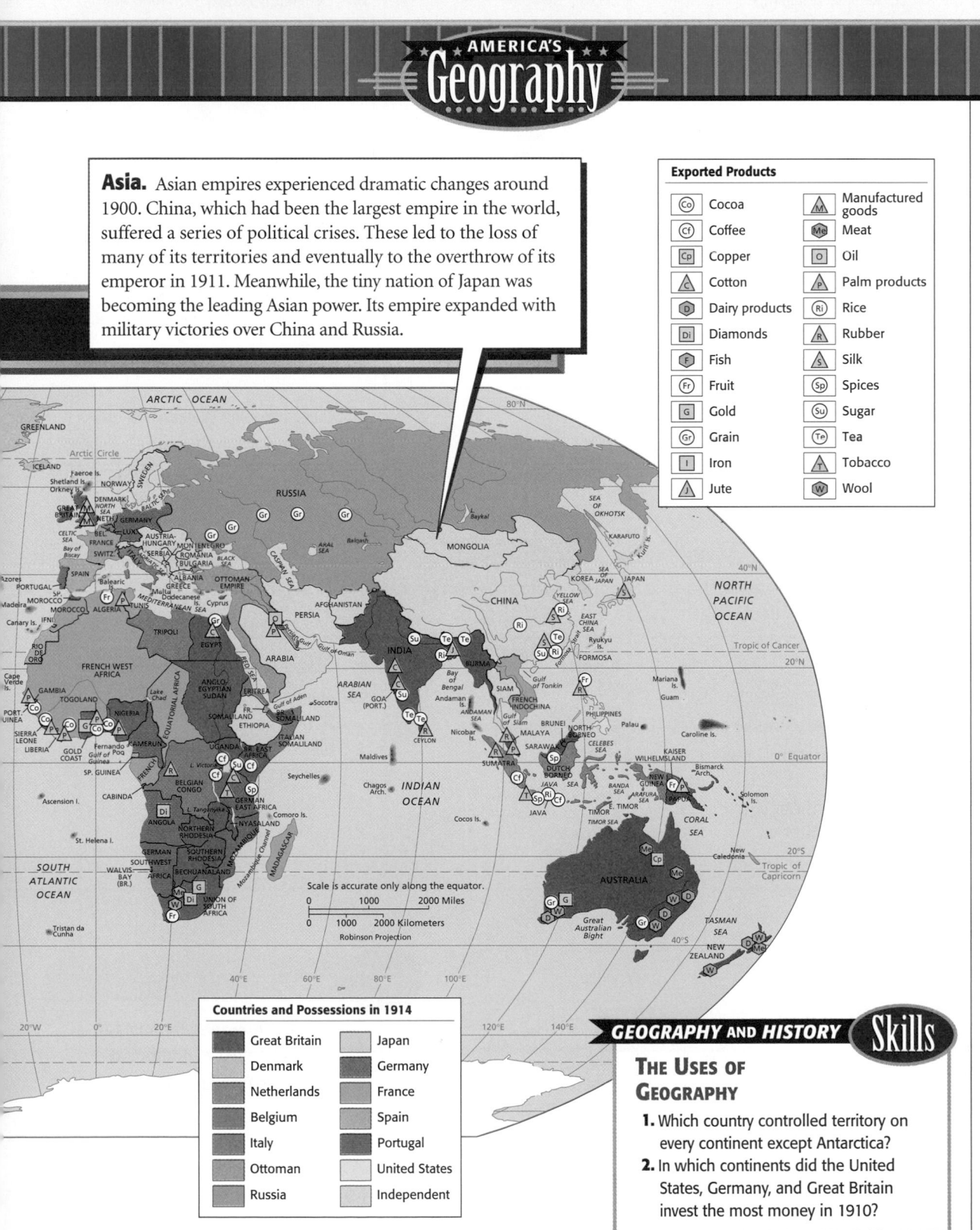

Countries and Possessions in 1914

Great Britain	Japan
Denmark	Germany
Netherlands	France
Belgium	Spain
Italy	Portugal
Ottoman	United States
Russia	Independent

Scale is accurate only along the equator.
0   1000   2000 Miles
0   1000   2000 Kilometers
Robinson Projection

GEOGRAPHY AND HISTORY Skills

THE USES OF GEOGRAPHY

1. Which country controlled territory on every continent except Antarctica?
2. In which continents did the United States, Germany, and Great Britain invest the most money in 1910?

353

World War I

CHAPTER RESOURCE MANAGER

Objectives	Pacing Guide	Reproducible Resources
SECTION 1 **World War I Breaks Out** pp. 356–60 ★ Identify the major causes of unrest in Europe. ★ Discuss the results of the strategy that was used during the early fighting in the war. ★ Explain why the war settled into a stalemate.	**Regular** 1 day **Block Scheduling** .5 day *Block Scheduling Handbook with Team Teaching Strategies, pp. 67–72*	**RS** Guided Reading Strategy 12.1 **PS** American History Political Cartoon 20: Conflict in the Balkans **SM** Geography Activity 12: World War I
SECTION 2 **The United States Goes to War** pp. 361–67 ★ Relate the challenges the United States faced while trying to remain neutral. ★ Identify the events that led to U.S. entry into the war. ★ Explain how the United States prepared its military for World War I. ★ Describe the types of experiences Americans had while serving in Europe.	**Regular** 2 days **Block Scheduling** 1 day *Block Scheduling Handbook with Team Teaching Strategies, pp. 67–72*	**RS** Guided Reading Strategy 12.2 **PS** Primary Source Reading 12: A Dark Moment in History **RS** Graphic Organizer Activity 12: Americans in World War I **IC** Literature Reading 12: Inside World War I **PS** Biography Reading 12: Jeannette Rankin
SECTION 3 **The War at Home** pp. 368–74 ★ Describe how the U.S. government prepared the nation for war. ★ Discuss how organized labor and volunteers contributed to the war effort. ★ Explain why African Americans moved north. ★ Relate how the government created support for, and limited opposition to, the war.	**Regular** 2 days **Block Scheduling** 1 day *Block Scheduling Handbook with Team Teaching Strategies, pp. 67–72*	**RS** Guided Reading Strategy 12.3 **E** Creative Teaching Strategy: Continuum Lesson
SECTION 4 **The War's End and Aftermath** pp. 375–81 ★ List the final events of World War I. ★ Identify the goals of President Wilson's Fourteen Points. ★ Summarize the terms of the Treaty of Versailles. ★ Explain why the U.S. Senate rejected the Treaty of Versailles. ★ Discuss the global impact of World War I.	**Regular** 2 days **Block Scheduling** 1 day *Block Scheduling Handbook with Team Teaching Strategies, pp. 67–72*	**RS** Guided Reading Strategy 12.4 **SM** American History Outline Map 17: World War I in Europe **E** Hands-On History Activity: Your Town's Volunteer

Chapter Resource Key

PS Primary Sources	**REV** Review	Video
RS Reading Support	**ELL** Reinforcement and English Language Learners	Internet
IC Interdisciplinary Connections		Holt Presentation Maker Using Microsoft® PowerPoint®
	Transparencies	
E Enrichment		
SM Skills Mastery	CD-ROM	
A Assessment	Music	

One-Stop Planner CD–ROM

See the *One-Stop Planner* for a complete list of additional resources for students and teachers.

One-Stop Planner CD-ROM

It's easy to plan lessons, select resources, and print out materials for your students when you use the **One-Stop Planner CD-ROM with Test Generator.**

Technology Resources	Reinforcement, Review, and Assessment

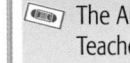 One-Stop Planner, Lesson 12.1
  The American Nation Video Program Segment: Weaponry and Warfare; Teacher's Guide, pp. 99–104
  Holt Researcher: American History CD–ROM
 Homework Practice Online
	REV Section 1 Review, p. 360
	 A Daily Quiz 12.1
	 ELL Main Idea Activity 12.1
	 ELL English Audio Summary 12.1
	 ELL Spanish Audio Summary 12.1

One-Stop Planner, Lesson 12.2
  Holt Researcher: American History CD–ROM
  Homework Practice Online
  HRW Go site
	REV Section 2 Review, p. 367
	 A Daily Quiz 12.2
	 ELL Main Idea Activity 12.2
	 ELL English Audio Summary 12.2
	 ELL Spanish Audio Summary 12.2

One-Stop Planner, Lesson 12.3
  Holt Researcher: American History CD–ROM
  Homework Practice Online
	REV Section 3 Review, p. 374
	 A Daily Quiz 12.3
	 ELL Main Idea Activity 12.3
	 ELL English Audio Summary 12.3
	 ELL Spanish Audio Summary 12.3

One-Stop Planner, Lesson 12.4
  CNN Presents America: Yesterday and Today, 1850 to the Present Segment: In the Trenches
  Holt Researcher: American History CD–ROM
  Homework Practice Online
	REV Section 4 Review, p. 381
	 A Daily Quiz 12.4
	 ELL Main Idea Activity 12.4
	 ELL English Audio Summary 12.4
	 ELL Spanish Audio Summary 12.4

internet connect

HRW ONLINE RESOURCES
GO TO: go.hrw.com
Then type in a keyword.

TEACHER HOME PAGE
KEYWORD: SE3 Teacher

CHAPTER INTERNET ACTIVITIES
KEYWORD: SE3 AN12
Choose an activity to:
• learn about new World War I weaponry.
• research the Battle of the Somme.
• create a propaganda poster that reflects bias for or against the Triple Alliance.

CHAPTER ENRICHMENT LINKS
KEYWORD: SE3 CH12

ONLINE ASSESSMENT
Homework Practice
KEYWORD: SE3 HP12

Standardized Test Prep
KEYWORD: SE3 STP12

Rubrics
KEYWORD: SS Rubrics

ONLINE MAPS, CHARTS, AND GRAPHS
KEYWORD: SE3 MCG
• Trench Warfare
• World War I Troop Strengths and Casualties
• The Weapons of World War I
• The Events of World War I

CONTENT UPDATES
KEYWORD: SS Content Updates

HOLT PRESENTATION MAKER
KEYWORD: SE3 PPT12

ONLINE READING SUPPORT
KEYWORD: SS Strategies

CURRENT EVENTS
KEYWORD: S3 Current Events

Chapter Review and Assessment

 Global Skill Builder CD–ROM

 HRW Go site

REV Chapter 12 Tutorial for Students, Parents, Mentors, and Peers

REV Chapter 12 Review, pp. 382–83

Chapter 12 Test Generator (on the One-Stop Planner)

A Chapter 12 Test (Form A or B)

A Alternative Assessment Handbook

A Chapter 12 Test for English Language Learners and Special-Needs Students

Meeting Individual Needs

Ability Levels

Level 1 Basic-level activities designed for all students encountering new material

Level 2 Intermediate-level activities designed for average students

Level 3 Challenging activities designed for honors and gifted-and-talented students

English Language Learners Activities that address the needs of students with Limited English Proficiency

Build on What You Know

Ask students to answer the following questions.

Why might the United States have wanted to remain neutral when war enveloped Europe?

Consider:

• the causes of the war
• the possible human and economic costs of entering a European war

Why might the United States have finally decided to enter the war in Europe?

Consider:

• incidents that might have provoked the United States to declare war
• the desire to protect European allies

---

exploring the time line

AMERICAN EVENTS

PEOPLE IN HISTORY

1916 ■ Jeannette Rankin. As a member of the House of Representatives, Jeannette Rankin worked for national women's suffrage. After she voted against U.S. involvement in World War I, however, she lost a senatorial bid and spent years working for pacifism and the rights of women and children. In 1940 Rankin again won a seat in the House. She soon voted against U.S. involvement in World War II, a stance that cost her the next election. Rankin continued her opposition to war and took an active role in anti–Vietnam War protests.

ACTIVITY: Have students imagine they are Jeannette Rankin. Ask them to write a letter to their constituents explaining why they voted against U.S. involvement in World War I.

CHAPTER 12

1914–1920

World War I

Panama Canal brochure

World War I gas mask

World War I tanks

**1914
Science and Technology**
The Panama Canal opens to traffic.

**1914
Daily Life**
President Wilson declares the first national Mother's Day.

**1915
Science and Technology**
Germany becomes the first nation to use poison gas in warfare, at the Second Battle of Ypres.

**1916
Science and Technology**
Tanks are used in battle for the first time, at the Battle of the Somme.

1914

1915

1916

German troops traveling to war

**1914
World Events**
World War I begins.

**1915
Business and Finance**
Driven by high prices and wartime demand, the U.S. wheat harvest tops 1 million bushels for the first time.

**1915
The Arts**
Carl Sandburg's *Chicago Poems* is published.

THE GRANGER COLLECTION, NEW YORK

Jeannette Rankin

**1916
Politics**
Montana representative Jeannette Rankin is the first woman elected to Congress.

**1916
Daily Life**
The Boston Red Sox win their second straight World Series.

Build on What You Know

During the 1800s several empires dominated Europe and much of the world. Nations scrambled to gain control of colonies and their natural resources to fuel the Industrial Revolution. European nations built up strong rivalries, which ultimately helped lead to war. In this chapter you will learn how the United States tried to remain neutral when war swept Europe. Once the United States joined the Allied cause in 1917, the government quickly mobilized the economy and built public support for the war.

What's Your Opinion?

To help students create their Themes Journal entries, provide the following examples of appropriate **agree**/**disagree** statements.

Global Relations

Agree Many of the early presidents followed an isolationist approach to global affairs, placing national self-interest at the top of their agendas.

Disagree Before deciding to join the Patriots in the Revolution, France considered its own rivalry with Great Britain but also the cause of independence in the colonies.

Economics

Agree Involvement in an overseas conflict can sometimes stimulate a nation's domestic economy by requiring additional production and spending to supply the country's military.

Disagree British involvement in the French and Indian War weakened the country's economy, leading it to tax the colonies.

Citizenship

Agree During wartime, citizens should forego their own liberties in consideration of national interests.

Disagree In democratic societies, individual liberties should never be sacrificed, not even temporarily.

exploring the time line

GLOBAL EVENTS

1917
Business and Finance
U.S. income tax revenue exceeds revenue from customs duties for the first time.

1917
Daily Life
The Selective Service Act is passed.

1917
Business and Finance
U.S. automakers produce 1,745,792 automobiles, more than three times as many as were made in 1914.

The U.S. secretary of war draws numbers for the draft lottery.

The Grand Canyon

1918
World Events
U.S. troops join the fighting in Europe.

1919
Daily Life
The Grand Canyon National Park is established.

1917 **1918** **1919** **1920**

1917
Business and Finance
Millionaires in the United States number about 40,000—up from 4,000 in 1892.

1917
Politics
The U.S. Congress declares war on Germany.

1919
World Events
World leaders sign the Treaty of Versailles.

1919
Politics
The U.S. Senate rejects the Treaty of Versailles.

The Paris Peace Conference meeting in the Hall of Mirrors at Versailles

☑ **internet** connect

TOPIC: Battle of the Somme
GO TO: go.hrw.com
KEYWORD: SE3 AN12

Have students access the Internet through the HRW Go site to conduct research on the Battle of the Somme. Then ask students to assume one of the following roles: a British general planning the attack, a German machine gunner defending the trenches, or a British soldier who survived the battle. Have each student write a series of journal entries describing the Battle of the Somme.

What's Your Opinion?

Themes Journal *Do you* **agree** *or* **disagree** *with the following statements? Support your point of view in your journal.*

Global Relations A country should consider only its own interests in deciding whether to go to war.

Economics Fighting in an overseas military conflict can help improve a nation's economy at home.

Citizenship During wartime, a government has the right to limit the individual liberties of citizens.

World War I Breaks Out

EYEWITNESSES TO History

"As I write, Germany is reported to have declared war against Russia and France, and the participation of England on the one side and of Italy on the other seems imminent [close at hand]. Nothing like it has occurred since the great Napoleonic wars, and with modern armaments and larger populations nothing has occurred like it since the world began. . . . All of Europe is to be a battleground. . . . The future looks dark indeed."

—William Howard Taft, *A Message to the People of the United States*

Former president William Howard Taft published "A Message to the People of the United States" in August 1914. He expressed the surprise and fear that many Americans felt at the news that Europe was at war. Few Americans had seen the war coming. Europe had appeared peaceful for more than 40 years. While the Wilson administration wrestled with problems created by the Mexican Revolution, tensions in Europe exploded into global war.

THE BOILING POINT.

This 1912 British cartoon shows European leaders trying to keep a lid on trouble in the Balkans.

The Causes of the War

One longterm cause of the war lay in the growth of nationalism throughout Europe. In the 1860s a spirit of nationalism united Italians in their fight to free themselves from Austrian rule. Nationalism also helped Otto von Bismarck join the German states into a single nation in the 1870s.

Nationalism and territorial rivalries. Nationalism was particularly strong in the central European region of the Balkans. This region was so unstable that it was called the powder keg of Europe. The Ottoman Empire (later known as Turkey) gained control of the Balkans in the 1400s and ruled the area until the 1800s. By then the region's four main ethnic groups—Albanians, Greeks, Romanians, and Slavs— were each struggling for independence. Greece began a successful revolt in the 1820s, and Romania followed in 1859. Following a war between Russia and the Ottoman Empire in 1878, Bulgarians, Montenegrins, and Serbs each staked their claims to nationhood. Soon after, Austria-Hungary occupied the small Balkan kingdoms of Bosnia and Herzegovina (often just called Bosnia).

The newly independent Serbia saw Bosnia as part of its rightful territory. Austria-Hungary's 1908 annexation of the territories produced open hostility. Serbia's growing strength threatened Austria-Hungary's control of its territories in the Balkans. This encouraged the Slavs to push for independence. Austro-Hungarian chief of staff Baron Conrad von Hötzendorf foresaw a major conflict:

LEVEL 1: Ask students to identify the causes of unrest in Europe. List students' responses on the chalkboard. *(Students should identify nationalism, militarism, and military alliances.)* Have students define these terms, then write these definitions on the chalkboard as well. *(Students should note that nationalism is loyalty to a nation, even one not in existence; that militarism is the glorification of military strength; and that military alliances are agreements among nations.)* Then ask each student to write a paragraph on the causes of unrest in Europe, incorporating all of the terms in the chalkboard list. Have volunteers read their paragraphs to the class.
English Language Learners

LEVEL 2: Pair students and ask them to complete the Level 1 activity. Then distribute Cartoon 20, Conflict in the Balkans, from **American History Political Cartoons**. Have each pair study the cartoon and answer the questions. To conclude, have each pair create its own political cartoon about the causes of unrest in Europe. Display pairs' cartoons around the classroom.
Cooperative Learning

LEVEL 3: Tell students to imagine that they are political analysts for President Wilson. Have each student write a memo to the president briefing him on the causes of unrest in Europe. *(See the Level 1 lesson for the correct causes.)* Students should conclude their memos by making predictions about the possible consequences of these factors.

History Makers Speak

❝The unification of the South Slav[s] . . . is one of the powerful national movements which can neither be ignored nor kept down. The question can only be, whether that unification will take place within the boundaries of the Monarchy [the Austro-Hungarian Empire]—that is, at the expense of Serbia's independence—or under Serbia's leadership at the expense of the Monarchy.❞

—Baron Conrad von Hötzendorf, quoted in *The First World War*, by Martin Gilbert

Militarism and alliances. Because large European countries frequently overpowered smaller ones, relations between nations were characterized by a strong spirit of **militarism**, or the glorification of military strength. Leaders of the major European powers believed that disputes would ultimately be settled on the battlefield. As a result, they engaged in an arms race in which they tried to develop larger armies and more powerful weapons than their rivals. In this dangerous atmosphere, leaders formed alliances with other nations, each promising to aid the other in case of attack by a third power.

Germany had a longtime ally in Austria. France's 1892 alliance with Russia threatened to surround Germany with enemies. Eventually, Italy joined Austria-Hungary and Germany in one alliance, and Great Britain joined France and Russia in another. The alliances avoided war for a time but created the risk that a single incident could trigger a major war.

✔ **READING CHECK: Making Generalizations** What role did nationalism and militarism play in the build-up to war?
They fueled an arms race among nations of Europe.

The Great War Begins

In June 1914 Archduke **Franz Ferdinand**, the heir to the Austro-Hungarian throne, visited Sarajevo (sahr-uh-YAY-voh), the Bosnian capital. As the archduke rode through the city streets, Serbian nationalist **Gavrilo Princip** (PREENT-seep) stepped out of the crowd. He fired two shots, killing the archduke and his wife, Sophie.

Austria-Hungary quickly declared war on Serbia. Germany immediately offered its support. Russia, with a large Slav population of its own, was compelled to honor its alliance with Serbia. The alliance system soon turned a local conflict into a global war. The **Allied Powers** of Britain, France, and Russia were pitted against the **Central Powers** of Germany, Austria-Hungary, the Ottoman Empire, and Bulgaria. Italy remained neutral until 1915, when it joined the Allies. Eventually, some 30 nations took sides in what became known as the Great War.

Germany's military strategy called for a massive strike against France to defeat it quickly, leaving British forces stranded on the other side of the English Channel. With France and Britain out of

---

⭐ **Then and Now**

Conflicts in Bosnia

Bosnia and Herzegovina—a nation about the size of West Virginia—has been a place of unrest for many years. After being controlled by various kingdoms for several centuries, Bosnia gained its independence in about 1200. It remained independent until 1463, when it was conquered by the Ottoman Turks. Bosnia remained under Ottoman rule for the next 400 years. In 1878 Austria-Hungary took control of Bosnia from the Turks.

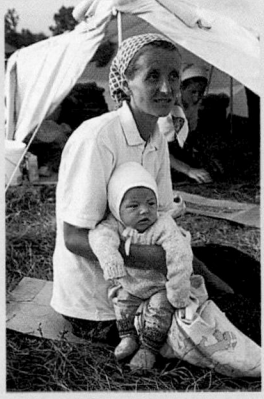
Bosnian refugee camp

At the end of World War I, Serbia's ruler was crowned king of the newly created nation of Yugoslavia, which included Bosnia. After World War II, Yugoslavia was reorganized into six republics—Bosnia and Herzegovina, Croatia, Macedonia, Montenegro, Serbia, and Slovenia.

In the late 1980s Yugoslavia's government began to disintegrate. Serbian president Slobodan Milosevic sought to create a Greater Serbia, uniting all Serbs in a single state under his leadership. At that time Bosnia's population of about 4 million included three main ethnic groups: Croats, Serbs, and Slavic Muslims. Early in 1992 some 70 percent of the country's voters—including many Bosnian Serbs—voted for independence from the rest of Yugoslavia. That March, Serbian forces began seizing territory in northern and eastern Bosnia. They drove out much of the non-Serbian population. The United States and most of the international community recognized Bosnia's independence in April 1992. Fighting continued, however, until a 1995 treaty ended the civil war. The United Nations sent in a peacekeeping force to help the country maintain peace.

INTERDISCIPLINARY CONNECTIONS

▶GEOGRAPHY◀

The Short-War Illusion. Historian L. L. Farrar Jr. argued that most European nations chose to enter the war because they saw it as a way to achieve their objectives after diplomacy had failed. Most European leaders believed that the war would be brief. Their military strategies depended on the accuracy of that assumption. Germany, for example, was surrounded by powerful enemies. German military leaders knew that they would have to quickly push through Belgium and conquer France to win the war. Belgian troops and Allied reinforcements soon quashed that plan, however, and the war became a long affair.

CRITICAL THINKING Why might the European nations have been eager to begin any war?

ANSWER: Some students might suggest that European leaders saw war as their only option. Other students might argue that the leaders thought war would boost their national economy and morale.

GRAPH ANSWER
(for p. 358)
about 10,000

ALL LEVELS: Have each student create a rudimentary time line of the early battles of World War I. To help students understand the results of the strategy that was used during the early fighting, copy the graphic organizer to the right on the chalkboard, omitting the italicized answers. Have each student complete it. **English Language Learners**

HOMEWORK *Ask each student to write two paragraphs on events in Belgium during the early days of World War I. One paragraph should explain the nation's role in foiling Germany's initial strategy and the other should speculate on the course the war might have taken had Belgium crumpled in the face of the German invasion.*

EARLY WORLD WAR I STRATEGY AND RESPONSE

Allied Power Nations
Britain, France, and Russia

Central Power Nations
Germany, Austria-Hungary, the Ottoman Empire, and Bulgaria

Allied Response
sent troops to support Belgium and fought the Battle of the Marne; began a war of attrition

Early Strategy
invade neutral Belgium and attack France, defeating France quickly and isolating Great Britain, then attack Russia

The Schlieffen Plan. German military officials formulated the Schlieffen Plan between 1891 and 1906 in response to an earlier alliance between France and Russia. The plan relied on the presumed weakness of the Belgian army and the presumed cooperation of Leopold, the Belgian king. Leopold died in 1909, however, after the plan had been formulated but well before the war had begun.

CRITICAL THINKING In addition to the unexpected Belgian resistance, what other factors might have contributed to the failure of the Schlieffen Plan?

ANSWER: Students might suggest that new forms of technology or weaponry—nonexistent at the time of the plan's creation—might have contributed to its failure.

THAT'S INTERESTING!

During the First Battle of the Marne, French officers experienced a shortage of automobiles and train cars. They ordered Paris taxi drivers to transport soldiers to the front. The taxis, along with various other kinds of vehicles, carried thousands of soldiers to the battle.

MAP ANSWER
(for p. 359)
on the eastern front

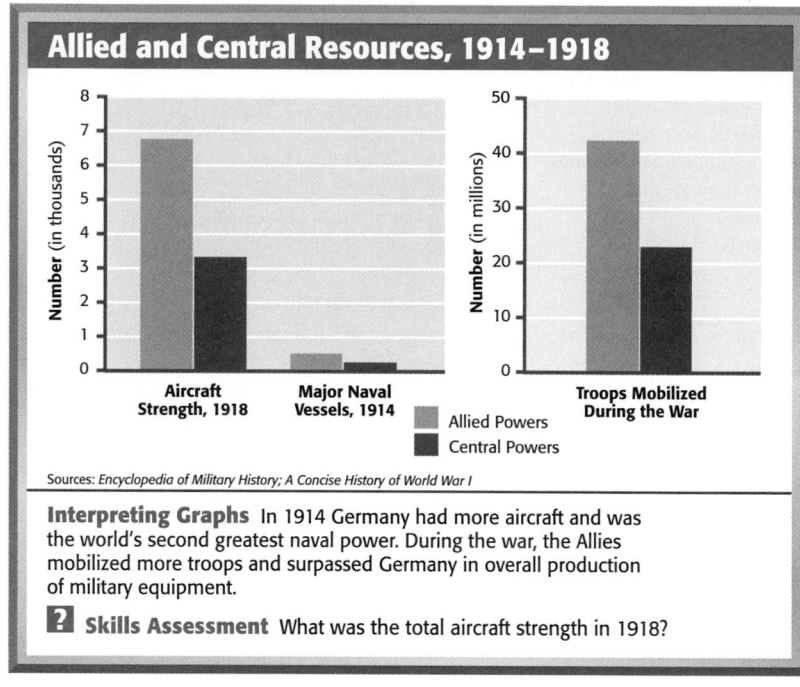

Allied and Central Resources, 1914–1918

Aircraft Strength, 1918 — Number (in thousands)
Major Naval Vessels, 1914 — Number (in thousands)
Troops Mobilized During the War — Number (in millions)

Allied Powers
Central Powers

Sources: *Encyclopedia of Military History; A Concise History of World War I*

Interpreting Graphs In 1914 Germany had more aircraft and was the world's second greatest naval power. During the war, the Allies mobilized more troops and surpassed Germany in overall production of military equipment.

? **Skills Assessment** What was the total aircraft strength in 1918?

Soldiers faced horrible conditions in World War I trenches.

the war, Germany would then focus its attention on defeating Russia in the east. Known as the Schlieffen Plan, this strategy called for German forces to avoid the heavily defended French-German border by invading France through the neutral country of Belgium.

German troops poured into Belgium on the night of August 3–4, 1914. The small Belgian army put up unexpectedly strong resistance, giving the French and British time to rush troops into the battle. The German invasion forced the Allies back to the Marne River in northeastern France. That September, during the **First Battle of the Marne**, the Allies pushed the German lines back some 40 miles. As 1914 drew to a close, leaders of both sides realized that there would be no quick victory.

✔ **READING CHECK: Identifying Cause and Effect** Why did the Great War begin?
The assassination of Archduke Ferdinand triggered war declarations by nations from opposing sides.

The War Reaches a Stalemate

Leaders had thought that this war would resemble earlier conflicts—with cavalry charges, decisive battles, and a quick victory. German kaiser Wilhelm II told troops they would be home "before the leaves have fallen from the trees." Both sides threw troops and arms into battle, expecting to achieve a clear victory. Instead, each side battered and bloodied the other in a brutal stalemate.

Trench warfare. By early 1915 both armies occupied trenches along a front running for hundreds of miles from the North Sea to the border of Switzerland. Separating the two sides was a thin strip of bombed-out territory—strewn with barbed wire and land mines—called **no-man's-land**. A new type of fighting, known as **trench warfare**, emerged on the western front. Battles began with massive artillery barrages. Then soldiers went "over the top" of the trenches and charged across the no-man's-land toward the enemy trenches. As they ran, thousands of soldiers were cut down by a hail of machine-gun fire.

The war remained locked in a stalemate throughout 1915. Determined to break out, each side prepared massive offensives for 1916. In February 1916 the Germans launched a huge offensive designed to "bleed the French army white" by causing unsustainable casualties. The Germans targeted the fortified French city of Verdun because they knew the French would feel compelled to defend it. The

LEVEL 1: Write the following terms on the chalkboard: *trench warfare, cavalry charges, artillery barrages, decisive battles.* Have pairs of students identify the terms that did and did not play an important role in the early years of World War I. *(Students' responses might indicate that unlike earlier conflicts, which featured cavalry charges and decisive battles, World War I was characterized by trench warfare and artillery barrages.)* Ask students to write several sentences explaining how trench warfare and artillery barrages led to a stalemate in World War I and how cavalry charges and decisive battles had prevented stalemates in earlier conflicts.

English Language Learners, Cooperative Learning

LEVEL 2: Tell students to imagine that they are American news reporters stationed in France during the early years of World War I. Have each student write a short article describing and explaining the stalemate in Europe. *(See the Level 1 lesson for the correct factors.)* Ask volunteers to read their articles to the class.

LEVEL 3: Write the following question on the chalkboard: *Why did World War I settle into a stalemate?* Have each student write a short essay in response to the question. *(See the Level 1 lesson for the correct factors.)* Have volunteers read their essays to the class.

---

battle began with a staggering 21-hour artillery barrage in which more than 1 million shells were fired. Then 1 million soldiers of the German Fifth Army advanced on some 200,000 French defenders. For months the battle raged back and forth.

In July the Allied Powers launched an offensive near the Somme River in northern France. They had the same goal as the German attack on Verdun—to exhaust the enemy's reserves. In the **Battle of the Somme**, British forces suffered some 60,000 casualties in a single day. This four-month-long battle left more than 1 million dead

World War I, 1914–1917

Interpreting Maps The warring powers fought on several battlefronts, with the most intense fighting occurring on the western front.

❓ LOCATE Where did the Central Powers gain the most territory?

The British blockade disrupts German supply lines. As a result, food riots break out in dozens of German cities.

The British withdraw from Gallipoli, ending any hope of sending supplies to Russia.

Legend	
Allied Powers, 1916	Farthest Russian advance (1914)
Central Powers, 1916	Farthest advance of Central Powers
Neutral countries	Trench line, western front
Allied forces	�ֹ Battle
Central Powers forces	▼ Food riots
British naval blockade	German submarine activity

INTERDISCIPLINARY CONNECTIONS

▶ART◀

Sculpting Faces. Anna Coleman Ladd, a well-known American sculptor, put her skills to use during World War I. Many soldiers incurred disfiguring facial injuries during battle. After plastic surgeons attempted to reshape soldiers' faces, Ladd sculpted "portrait masks" for the men. She took casts of their faces and then made thin copper masks lined with silver and covered with hard enamel paint.

ACTIVITY: Have each student write a poem or short story commenting on the violence of the war and the need for "portrait masks."

The American Nation
VIDEO PROGRAM

Weaponry and Warfare; Teacher's Guide, pp. 99–104

Search 14847, Play to 20155
Videodisc 2, Side A

Play   Pause

See *Teacher's Guide* for Spanish barcode.

REVIEW

Have students complete the **Section 1 Review** on p. 360.

ASSESS

Have students complete **Daily Quiz 12.1.** As **Alternative Assessment,** you may want to use the paragraph on unrest or the stalemate article in this section's lessons.

RETEACH

Have students complete **Main Idea Activity for English Language Learners and Special-Needs Students 12.1.** Then organize students into triads. Assign one section objective to each member of the triad. Have students create outlines of the material that relates to their assigned objectives. Have students share their outlines within their triads. **English Language Learners, Cooperative Learning**

EXTEND

Ask students to conduct research on the Schlieffen Plan. Students should focus on who devised the plan, the reasoning behind the plan, and when the plan was implemented. Students should also evaluate the success of the plan. Have each student present his or her findings in a detailed report. Students might also include diagrams or illustrations to supplement their reports. **Block Scheduling**

SECTION 1 REVIEW ANSWERS

1. Define
- militarism, p. 357
- no-man's-land, p. 358
- trench warfare, p. 358

2. Identify
- Franz Ferdinand, p. 357
- Gavrilo Princip, p. 357
- Allied Powers, p. 357
- Central Powers, p. 357
- First Battle of the Marne, p. 358
- Battle of the Somme, p. 359
- Manfred von Richthofen, p. 360
- Edward Rickenbacker, p. 360

3. nationalism, militarism, territorial rivalries, military alliances

4a. Serbia saw Bosnia and Herzegovina as part of its territory; Austria-Hungary's annexation of the territory led to hostilities, which eventually led to war.

b. Nationalism led smaller countries to fight for independence, and militarism led larger countries to settle disputes on the battlefield.

c. Deadly new weapons, such as tanks and poison gas, added to the horrors of trench warfare and helped turned the war into a stalemate.

5. Articles should describe the horrible conditions in the trenches, the stalemate, and new weapons such as machine guns, tanks, airplanes, submarines, and poison gas.

---

and wounded. At Verdun, the longest battle of the war, the two sides suffered nearly 1 million more casualties, half of them deaths.

For soldiers who avoided death, the trenches were a living nightmare. Rats and lice plagued the troops. Rain flooded the trenches, drenching soldiers in mud. Dead soldiers often lay unburied for days. Unsanitary conditions bred disease and sickness that claimed nearly as many lives as the fighting did.

New weapons. Deadly new weapons added to the horror of trench warfare. Machine guns fired hundreds of rounds per minute. Partly to counter the machine gun's deadly impact, the Allies introduced tanks at the Battle of the Somme. One British soldier reported that tanks scared the Germans "out of their wits" and made them "scuttle like frightened rabbits."

A World War I German airplane

Perhaps the most feared new weapon introduced during World War I was poison gas. It could be released as a cloud of mist that silently drifted over the trenches. It could also be launched inside an exploding shell. Either way, soldiers had only seconds to slip on their gas masks or else suffer a slow, suffocating death.

Modern machines such as submarines and airplanes brought terror to the seas and the skies. Submarines slipped silently beneath the waves to sink commercial and military ships with little or no warning. Some airplane pilots engaged enemy planes in aerobatic dogfights. Although these skirmishes did little to influence the course of the war, they made celebrities out of those who survived. Skilled pilots were known as aces. The most successful was the German Baron **Manfred von Richthofen,** known as the Red Baron. He had a reported 80 kills, or enemy aircraft shot down. The top American ace was **Edward Rickenbacker,** with 26 kills.

✔ **READING CHECK: Drawing Inferences** How did trench warfare affect the fighting?
It made the fighting more brutal and deadly.

SECTION 1 REVIEW

1. Define and explain:
militarism
no-man's-land
trench warfare

2. Identify and explain:
Franz Ferdinand
Gavrilo Princip
Allied Powers
Central Powers
First Battle of the Marne
Battle of the Somme
Manfred von Richthofen
Edward Rickenbacker

3. Identifying Cause and Effect
Copy the diagram below. Use it to list the factors that contributed to the outbreak of World War I.

World War I begins

4. **Finding the Main Idea**

a. What was the relationship between Serbia and Bosnia and Herzegovina?

b. How did nationalism and militarism contribute to conflicts among nations in Europe?

c. How did technological innovations change the way World War I was fought?

5. **Writing and Critical Thinking**

Analyzing Information Imagine you are a British reporter at the front during 1916. Write a newspaper article describing conditions at the front and encouraging the British people to continue fighting.

Consider:
- new weapons used during the war
- the tactics of trench warfare
- the transportation available to the opposing sides

go. hrw .com Homework Practice Online
keyword: SE3 HP12

SECTION ②

After completing Section 2, students should be able to:

OBJECTIVE 1 Relate the challenges the United States faced while trying to remain neutral.

OBJECTIVE 2 Identify the events that led to U.S. entry into the war.

OBJECTIVE 3 Explain how the United States prepared its military for World War I.

OBJECTIVE 4 Describe the types of experiences Americans had while serving in Europe.

🔊 LET'S GET STARTED!

Write the following question on the chalkboard: *If you had been living in the United States when war broke out in Europe, would you have supported U.S. neutrality, or would you have wanted the United States to immediately enter the war on the side of the Allies?* As students enter the classroom, have them respond to the question in writing. Have volunteers share their answers with the class. Then tell students that in Section 2 they will learn about the challenges of neutrality and U.S. entry into World War I.

SECTION ②

READ TO DISCOVER

1. What challenges did the United States face while trying to remain neutral?
2. What events led to U.S. entry into World War I?
3. How did the United States prepare its military for war?
4. What types of experiences did Americans have while serving in Europe?

DEFINE

convoy system

IDENTIFY

Sussex pledge
Robert Lansing
National Defense Act
Zimmermann Note
Jeannette Rankin
Selective Service Act
John J. Pershing

▶ WHY IT MATTERS TODAY

The United States continues to question whether to become involved in conflicts elsewhere in the world. Use **CNNfyi.com** or other **current events** sources to study a recent U.S. decision to play a role in an international conflict. Record your findings in your journal.

CNNfyi.com

The United States Goes to War

EYEWITNESSES TO History

"*In August, 1914, I was a cowboy on a ranch in the interior of British Columbia. . . . An early Saturday morning in August found me jogging slowly along the trail to Dog Creek . . . our post office and trading center. . . . We had heard rumors of a war in Europe. We all talked it over in the evening and decided it was another one of those fights that were always starting in the Balkans. One had just been finished a few months before and we thought it was about time another was underway so we gave the matter no particular thought. But when I got within sight of Dog Creek I knew something was up. The first thing I heard was that . . . the Germans were fighting. . . . Then a big Indian came up to me . . . and told me England's . . . going to war, or had gone. He wasn't certain which, but he was going too. Would I? I laughed at him. 'What do you mean, go to war?' I asked him. I wasn't English; I wasn't Canadian. I was from the good old U. S. A. And from all we could understand the States were neutral. So, I reasoned, I ought to be neutral too.*"

—Joseph Smith, *Over There and Back in Three Uniforms*

World War I soldiers carried all the equipment they needed on their backs.

After some thought, Joseph Smith decided to join his Canadian friends and volunteered to fight. Like many people, Smith and his friends first "regarded the whole war . . . as more or less of a lark." Enthusiasm for the glory of war faded quickly when soldiers actually witnessed the horrors of the battlefields.

U.S. Neutrality

The outbreak of war surprised most Americans. They tended to view the war as a strictly European matter. President Woodrow Wilson received strong support when he announced a policy of neutrality. He urged all Americans to be "neutral in fact as well as in name . . . impartial in thought as well as action." Wilson hoped that the United States would be able to negotiate a settlement to the conflict. He pursued this goal during 1915 and 1916 without success.

While the United States remained neutral in action, few of its citizens were impartial in thought. Some 28 million Americans—nearly 30 percent of the population—were either immigrants or the children of immigrants. Some Americans of Austrian, German, Hungarian, or Turkish background sympathized with the Central Powers. Some Irish Americans hoped the war would help free Ireland from the rule of Great Britain.

A greater number of Americans backed the Allies. A common language and culture bound many Americans to Great Britain. The British propaganda campaign, which painted the Germans as brutal killers, also increased American support for the Allied cause.

SECTION ② RESOURCES

REPRODUCIBLE

▶ Guided Reading Strategy 12.2
▶ Primary Source Reading 12: A Dark Moment in History
▶ Graphic Organizer Activity 12: Americans in World War I
▶ Literature Reading 12: Inside World War I
▶ Biography Reading 12: Jeannette Rankin

TECHNOLOGY

▶ One-Stop Planner, Lesson 12.2
▶ Holt Researcher: American History CD–ROM
▶ HRW Go site
▶ Homework Practice Online

REINFORCEMENT, REVIEW, AND ASSESSMENT

▶ Section 2 Review, p. 367
▶ Daily Quiz 12.2
▶ Main Idea Activity 12.2
▶ English Audio Summary 12.2
▶ Spanish Audio Summary 12.2

LEVEL 1: Conduct a brief discussion on the challenges the United States faced while trying to remain neutral in World War I. *(Students might suggest that Americans found neutrality difficult for a number of reasons—conflicting sympathies and opinions, the British propaganda campaign, the British navy blockade, and German submarine attacks on the* Lusitania *and other civilian ships.)* Then pair students and tell them to imagine that it is 1915. Have each pair develop a short dialogue on the challenges of neutrality. Ask volunteers to perform their dialogues for the class.
English Language Learners, Cooperative Learning

LEVEL 2: Conduct a brief discussion on the challenges the United States faced while trying to remain neutral in World War I. *(See the Level 1 lesson for the correct challenges.)* Then tell students to imagine that they are President Wilson. Have each student write a brief public address on the challenges of neutrality and the need to remain neutral. Ask volunteers to deliver their public addresses to the class. Students may wish to include their addresses in their portfolios.

LEVEL 3: Conduct a brief discussion on the challenges the United States faced while trying to remain neutral in World War I. *(See the Level 1 lesson for the correct challenges.)* Then organize students into two groups—one that supports neutrality

The sinking of the Lusitania, shown in this illustration, caused strong anti-German feelings in the United States.

Despite its policy of neutrality, the United States did not remain untouched by the war. When the war began, the British navy blockaded Germany and laid mines in the North Sea. The navy also stopped U.S. ships bound for neutral countries and searched their cargoes—including the mail. The British were looking for goods that might ultimately be destined for Germany. Wilson protested this violation of U.S. neutrality.

In 1915 the German navy responded to the blockade by establishing a "war zone" around Britain. Any ships entering this zone—even those from neutral nations—were subject to attack by U-boats, or German submarines. Wilson warned that, in accordance with international laws of neutrality, the United States would hold Germany accountable for any injury to American lives or property on the high seas.

On March 28, 1915, a U-boat sank a British passenger liner in the Irish Sea. More than 100 people, including one American, died. While the White House considered its response, a far more serious incident occurred. On May 7, 1915, a U-boat patrolling off the Irish coast torpedoed the *Lusitania*, another British passenger liner. The dead included 128 Americans. The *New York Times* called the Germans "savages drunk with blood." Outraged Americans agreed. German leaders pointed out that they had placed advertisements in American newspapers warning Americans against sailing into the war zone. They also charged that the *Lusitania* was transporting armaments for Britain—an accusation that later proved true.

Nevertheless, Wilson protested angrily to the German government. He demanded specific pledges to halt unrestricted submarine warfare against civilian ships. Secretary of State William Jennings Bryan charged that the president's protest amounted to an ultimatum and resigned. Bryan argued that the United States could not issue ultimatums to other nations and remain neutral.

PRIMARY SOURCE

The Sinking of the *Lusitania*

Germany's Baron von Schwarzenstein offered the following response to the *Lusitania* sinking.

What justification does the baron offer for the sinking of the *Lusitania*?

❝It was only after England declared the whole North Sea a war zone . . . that Germany with precisely the same right declared the waters around England a war zone and announced her purpose of sinking all hostile commercial vessels found therein. . . . In the case of the *Lusitania* the German Ambassador even further warned Americans through the great American newspapers against taking passage thereon. Does a pirate act thus? Does he take pains to save human lives? . . . Nobody regrets more sincerely than we Germans the hard necessity of sending to their deaths hundreds of men. Yet the sinking was a justifiable act of war. . . . We have sympathy with the victims and their relatives, of course, but did we hear anything about sympathy . . . when England adopted her diabolical [evil] plan of starving a great nation?❞

✔ **READING CHECK: Making Predictions**
How might unrestricted submarine warfare have led to U.S. entry into World War I?
Americans were outraged that their neutrality was violated.

and one that supports entry into the war. Give each group time to prepare supporting arguments for its position. Then conduct a classroom debate on neutrality in World War I.
Cooperative Learning

 HOMEWORK *Tell students to imagine that they are advisers to President Wilson. Have them write a speech on U.S. neutrality for Wilson to present to Congress. Remind students that they need to define neutrality and explain how their definition differs from that of other politicians such as William Jennings Bryan. Finally, have students explain how they can stress neutrality in their presidential campaign while at the same time prepare the military for war.*

The Road to War

For many Americans the sinking of the *Lusitania* brought the conflict in Europe closer to home. Even so, most still hoped the United States could stay out of the war. Further challenges to U.S. neutrality, however, appeared quickly.

Wilson's actions criticized. In August 1915 a German submarine sank the *Arabic,* another British liner, killing two Americans. Then, in March 1916, the French passenger vessel *Sussex* was attacked, injuring several Americans. In a sternly worded message to the German government, President Wilson threatened to cut diplomatic ties if Germany did not abandon its unrestricted submarine warfare. The German government responded with the *Sussex* **pledge,** a renewal of an earlier promise not to sink liners without warning or without ensuring the passengers' safety.

Most Americans supported the president's approach. However, a number of prominent politicians criticized Wilson for not responding more strongly to German aggression. Former president Theodore Roosevelt accused Wilson of "cowardice and weakness."

Others accused Wilson of abandoning neutrality. Former secretary of state William Jennings Bryan argued that Wilson's commercial and trade policies helped the Allies and therefore the United States was no longer impartial in action. As secretary of state, Bryan had discouraged American bankers from making loans to either side, but this policy was soon abandoned. Large American banks lent millions of dollars to Britain and France. Bryan's successor, **Robert Lansing,** encouraged the trade of war materials with the Allies. By 1916, U.S. arms sales to the Allies had reached some $500 million, about 80 times the amount sold in 1914.

Preparedness and peace. In 1916 President Wilson launched a military "preparedness" program. Banks and war industries that had a large economic interest in an Allied victory strongly supported this program. Passed by Congress in June 1916, the **National Defense Act** increased the number of soldiers in the regular army from some 90,000 to about 175,000, with an ultimate goal of 223,000. Wilson established the National Guard's size at some 450,000 troops. Two months later, Congress passed a bill appropriating $313 million to build up the navy.

With the presidential election nearing, President Wilson assured Americans that he had not abandoned neutrality. Running on the slogan "He Kept Us Out of War," Wilson narrowly defeated Republican Charles Evans Hughes to win re-election.

After the election, Wilson still hoped to negotiate a settlement to the war. In a January 1917 speech, he called for "peace without victory." A lasting peace, he said, had to be one between equals, not between the victor and the defeated. Once again, the warring nations rejected Wilson's effort to mediate.

Diplomatic relations broken. On February 1, 1917, Germany resumed full-scale U-boat warfare. The Germans hoped that their U-boat fleet would be able to defeat the Allies before the United States could join the war. Wilson followed through on his threat to break off diplomatic relations. He also ordered the arming of American merchant ships sailing into the war zone. Nonetheless, German torpedoes sank five American ships.

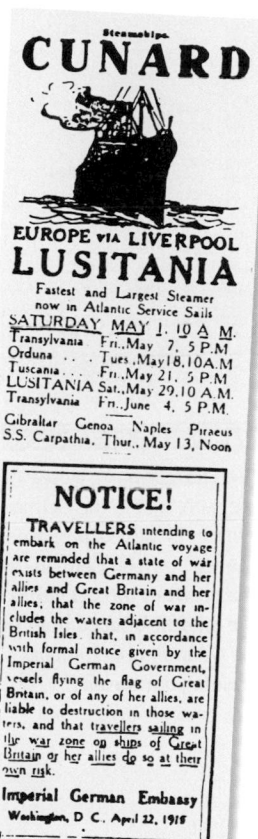

INTERPRETING THE VISUAL RECORD

The *Lusitania.* The German government ran this warning in the announcement of the *Lusitania*'s 1915 voyage. *Does this notice provide enough warning to Americans traveling on the Lusitania? Explain your answer.*

TEACH OBJECTIVE 2

ALL LEVELS: To help students identify the events that led to U.S. entry into the war, copy the time line to the right on the chalkboard, omitting the italicized events. Have each student complete it. After students have finished their time lines, ask students to rank the events in order of importance. Then ask students to name modern-day events that might encourage them to support a war. **English Language Learners**

HOMEWORK *Have each student write a newspaper headline for each of the events that led to U.S. entry into the war. Students' newspaper headlines should both announce the event and give some indication of its importance.*

U.S. ENTRY INTO WORLD WAR I

March 1916
Event: *The Germans attack the Sussex.*
Significance: *President Wilson threatens to cut diplomatic ties; Germany makes the Sussex pledge.*

February 1917
Event: *Germany resumes full-scale U-boat warfare.*
Significance: *Wilson breaks diplomatic ties; orders the arming of American merchant ships.*

March 1917
Event: American newspapers publish the Zimmermann Note.
Significance: This note proves German hostility.

April 1917
Event: The Senate declares war.
Significance: United States joins the war on the Allied side.

Military Service. As hostilities in Europe began to suggest the horrible possibility of a war, many U.S. leaders began thinking about how to prepare the military for a large-scale conflict. Some, such as Theodore Roosevelt and General Leonard Wood, advocated compulsory military training for all American men. Wood argued, "The volunteer system is not dependable because of the uncertainty as to returns, and in any case because of lack of time for training and organization." Others argued against compulsory service. Max Eastman, editor of *The Masses,* wrote, "For my part I do not recognize the right of a government to draft me to a war whose purposes I do not believe in. But to draft me to a war whose purposes it will not so much as communicate to my ear, seems an act of tyranny."

ACTIVITY: Have each student write an editorial either supporting compulsory military service or arguing against it.

VISUAL RECORD ANSWER

Some students might suggest that the German government would not send an official government document through Western Union. Other students might note that the telegram appears to be written in a secret code, suggesting an official origin.

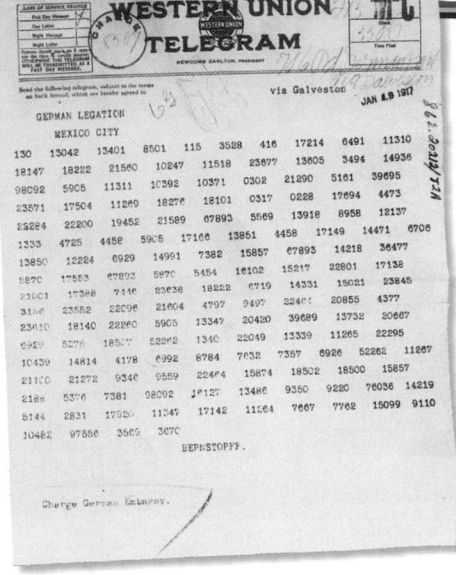

INTERPRETING THE VISUAL RECORD

The Zimmermann Note. This telegram, sent to the German minister in Mexico, proposed an alliance between Germany and Mexico. *Does this telegram look like an official document from the German government? Explain your answer.*

On March 1, 1917, American newspapers published an intercepted cable from German foreign secretary Arthur Zimmermann to the German minister in Mexico. Dubbed the **Zimmermann Note,** the cable proposed a Mexican alliance with Germany. The cable offered German support to help Mexico "reconquer the lost territory in New Mexico, Texas, and Arizona." The note infuriated many Americans.

As weeks passed, Wilson reluctantly concluded that the United States could no longer stay out of the conflict. On April 2, 1917, the president addressed Congress and asked for a declaration of war.

Congress declares war. In his speech Wilson condemned Germany's submarine warfare for its "wanton [vicious] and wholesale destruction." He also summoned Americans to crusade for a better world.

History Makers Speak

❝We are glad . . . to fight thus for the ultimate peace of the world and for the liberation of its peoples, . . . for the rights of nations—great and small—and the privilege of men everywhere to choose their way of life. . . . The world must be made safe for democracy.❞

—Woodrow Wilson, "For Declaration of War Against Germany," April 2, 1917

At these words, cheers and applause rang through the Capitol. Later, Wilson told an aide, "My message today was a message of death for our young men. How strange it seems to applaud that."

The Senate declared war on April 4, 1917. The House followed two days later. The vote was not unanimous—six senators and 50 representatives opposed the declaration. Representative **Jeannette Rankin** of Montana was among the opposition. "I want to stand by my country," she explained, "but I cannot vote for war."

✔ **READING CHECK: Sequencing** Create a time line of events that led to U.S. entry into the war. 1916—Sussex pledge from Germany; Congress approves the National Defense Act; 1917—the Zimmermann Note angers Wilson. He asks Congress to declare war on Germany.

Mobilizing U.S. Military Power

In his war message on April 2, President Wilson pledged all the nation's material resources to the Allied war effort. What the Allies most urgently needed were fresh troops. Few Americans, however, rushed to volunteer for military service.

Recruiting an army. Congress passed the **Selective Service Act** on May 18, 1917. It required men between the ages of 21 and 30 to register with local draft boards. This was later changed to men between the ages of 18 and 45. By the end of the war, some 24 million men had registered, and 2.8 million of them had been drafted. More than half of the almost 4.8 million Americans who served in the armed forces during World War I were draftees.

Supporters of the draft argued that it would help build a more democratic United States by bringing together soldiers from different backgrounds. In reality, African Americans, American Indians, Mexican Americans, and many foreign-born soldiers faced segregation and often discrimination. Most foreign-born

LEVEL 1: Pair students and have each pair write several sentences explaining how the United States prepared its military for the war. *(Sentences should indicate that Congress passed the Selective Service Act, recruited troops in other ways, and instituted a massive soldier-training program.)* Ask students to share their sentences. Using these responses, compile a comprehensive list on the chalkboard. Then have pairs create recruitment or training posters. Ask volunteers to present their posters to the class and identify the factors that would have made them effective recruitment or training tools.
English Language Learners, Cooperative Learning

LEVELS 2 AND 3: Tell students to imagine that it is 1917 and that they are new army recruits. Have each student write a series of short journal entries describing the ways in which the United States prepared its military for the war. *(See the Level 1 lesson for the correct methods.)* Have volunteers read their entries to the class. To conclude, ask students to consider how the United States prepared its military for the war. Do students think that those methods were adequate? How else might military officials have recruited and trained troops?

---

soldiers, for example, were assigned to separate units where they were taught civics and English. Some of the 10,000 American Indians who served during the war were not U.S. citizens. Their service contributed to Congress's decision in 1924 to grant citizenship to all American Indians.

More than 370,000 African American recruits served. They were blocked from service in the marines and limited to kitchen duties in the navy. Most African Americans in the army served in all-black support units commanded by white officers. African American draftees who were sent to army training camps in the South often faced harassment from the local population.

Pressure from the National Association for the Advancement of Colored People (NAACP) and other African American organizations convinced the army to open up more opportunities for black soldiers. A school was established to train African American officers, and more African American soldiers were assigned combat duty. However, the army made no effort to integrate black and white soldiers in the same units.

Training the troops. Massive training camps had to be hastily constructed to house and train the new soldiers. In the summer of 1917, workers began building barracks at 16 separate locations. Completing the task in the planned 60 days seemed impossible. However, by using simple designs, a huge workforce, and mass-production techniques, thousands of buildings were ready by September. There were not enough uniforms and equipment for all the troops yet, but at least they had a place to live while training.

The military hoped to use a similar accelerated process for the troops' training. Private Harry R. Richmond wrote about his training camp in New Mexico.

❝The burden of creating an army at short notice, falls most heavily upon the recruit. The rookie is expected to learn now in three weeks, what his fellow soldiers acquired a year ago in three months. We are drilled nearly 7 or 8 hours per day.❞

—Private Harry R. Richmond, letter, August 1, 1917

Upon arrival at a training camp, recruits underwent a series of medical examinations. They spent most of their days learning military rules, drilling with their equipment, exercising, and preparing for inspections. "Every man is supposed to be slicked up, shoes shined, clothes clean, and he must be shaved," recalled one recruit. "This is one thing they insist on in the army—everything must be clean."

Soldiers also spent a lot of time learning how to fight. Recruits spent many hours on the rifle range and practiced hand-to-hand combat using bayonets. Frank Sweeney wrote that recruits faced dummies "hanging from large cross beams" and were "taught the best method of approach and the proper jabs to get him before he gets us." Sweeney noted that "sometimes the

A doughboy's pack contained the essentials for survival.

HISTORY
IN THE MAKING

The Doughboy's Pack
BY PAUL BOYER

History is much more than a study of dates, documents, or facts about famous people. Ordinary objects also leave a historical record about an event or an era. For example, common items provided to soldiers during a war tell a story about how that war was fought.

During World War I, U.S. infantry troops, nicknamed doughboys, carried all their necessary equipment inside a canvas "field kit" strapped to their backs. The around-the-waist design with pockets was adopted during World War I because of automatic weapons. Rifles could now fire as many as five bullets per minute, and a soldier needed easy access to large amounts of ammunition during the heat of battle.

The gas mask filtered out poisonous fumes that could suffocate or blind a soldier. The steel helmet extended to the top of the ear line to help prevent head wounds. Soldiers also carried a tent, tent poles, a rain poncho, a bayonet, a blanket, a sewing kit, socks, identification tags, a compass, and a flashlight. Sturdy metal containers protected two days' worth of rations—hard biscuits called hardtack and dried meat—from rain, rats, and insects. On a long march, soldiers might have cursed their heavy packs, but they also knew that burden could mean the difference between life and death.

African Americans in the War. African American soldiers faced officially sanctioned discrimination. In a 1918 memorandum, Colonel E. D. Anderson suggested that most African American soldiers work solely as laborers, thereby freeing up white soldiers to train for battle. Despite this discrimination, many African Americans supported the war effort and welcomed the opportunities for travel, education, and honor that sometimes accompanied the experience. Addie W. Hunton and Kathryn M. Johnson, African American women who accompanied the American Expeditionary Force to France, wrote that some African American soldiers "received the rudiments of an education through direct instruction; a thing that would not have come to them in all the years of a lifetime at home. . . . In addition to this they had an opportunity of making a record for themselves that will be in no wise [ways] hidden from the generations of the future."

ACTIVITY: Tell students to imagine that they are African American soldiers in France. Have each student write a letter to a friend in Alabama describing his duties and expressing his feelings about World War I.

TEACH OBJECTIVE 4

LEVEL 1: Organize students in the class into two groups, one representing U.S. soldiers or nurses who have recently arrived in Europe and one representing American journalists who have also recently arrived in Europe. Give students time to prepare lists of possible interview questions and answers. Then pair students from the two groups. Ask each pair to conduct an interview on the types of experiences that Americans had while serving in Europe. *(Pairs should discuss John J. Pershing's general military strategy, marching through Paris upon arrival, encountering the battlefields for the first time, and so on.)* Have volunteers perform their interviews for the class. **English Language Learners, Cooperative Learning**

LEVELS 2 AND 3: Tell students to imagine that they are U.S. soldiers or nurses who have recently arrived in Europe with the U.S. Army. Have each student write a letter home describing his or her experiences serving in Europe. *(See the Level 1 lesson for the correct experiences.)* Encourage students to express their emotions upon reaching battlefields and the front lines regarding high casualty rates and the trenches. Have volunteers read their letters to the class. Students may wish to include their letters in their portfolios.

Research on the ROM

Free Find:
General Pershing
After reading about General John J. Pershing on the **Holt Researcher CD–ROM**, imagine that you are introducing him at a banquet being held in his honor. Write a short speech describing Pershing's accomplishments.

INTERPRETING THE VISUAL RECORD

Medical care. Many women served as ambulance drivers during World War I. *Do these ambulances look equipped to provide medical care at the scene of a battle? Explain your answer.*

men enter into this game so heartily that they break their bayonets." The training put most soldiers in excellent physical health. At the end of his training one soldier felt that "if I am here another year I could outwalk a horse and carry a hundred pounds besides." This strength would be severely tested in France.

✔ **READING CHECK: Summarizing** Who fought in the U.S. Army, and how did they prepare for war? American men between ages 18 and 45, more than half of them draftees; Training camps in the United States prepared them.

Over There

With mobilization well under way, U.S. troops began sailing to France as part of the American Expeditionary Force (AEF). The AEF included the regular army, the National Guard, and the new draftees and volunteers. Under the command of General **John J. Pershing**, the first U.S. troops reached France in late June 1917.

BIOGRAPHY
John J. Pershing
THE GRANGER COLLECTION, NEW YORK

Born in Missouri in 1860, General Pershing was the U.S. Army's most experienced combat officer. He graduated from the U.S. Military Academy at West Point in 1886. Pershing then spent four years fighting with the cavalry against American Indians in the Southwest and in South Dakota. In 1891 Pershing became a military instructor at the University of Nebraska. He later moved on to teach military tactics at the U.S. Military Academy in 1897.

Pershing fought in the Spanish-American War and served in the Philippines from 1899 to 1903. As brigadier general he returned to the Philippines for a second tour of duty in 1906 before being named commander of the 8th Cavalry Brigade.

In 1916 President Wilson ordered Pershing to lead the expedition into Mexico that pursued Pancho Villa. Despite the failure to capture Villa, Pershing's appointment to head the AEF came as no surprise. A determined leader, Pershing refused to allow the Allies to dictate how his troops would be used. He insisted that U.S. forces fight as a separate unit, rather than be added to the Allied forces bit by bit.

On July 4, 1917, thousands of "Yanks," or U.S. soldiers, marched through Paris, France. Huge crowds cheered them on. The troops stopped at the tomb of the Marquis de Lafayette, the French hero of the American Revolution. "Lafayette, we are here!" proclaimed one of Pershing's aides. By fighting for France's freedom, the United States was repaying the French for their help during the Revolutionary War.

U.S. Army lieutenant Edward F. Graham wrote home about the sense of purpose that he and many other soldiers felt. "The desperate contest between justice and empire . . . is

REVIEW

Have students complete the **Section 2 Review** on p. 367.

ASSESS

Have students complete **Daily Quiz 12.2.** As **Alternative Assessment**, you may want to use the neutrality dialogue or the European experiences interview in this section's lessons.

RETEACH

Have students complete **Main Idea Activity for English Language Learners and Special-Needs Students 12.2.** Then organize students into small groups and assign each group one subsection from Section 2. Have each group create an outline of its assigned subsection. Display the outlines around the class-room and ask students to study them. Have each student use the material on the outlines to write one or two questions about the content of Section 2. Collect students' questions and use them to quiz the class.
English Language Learners, Cooperative Learning

EXTEND

Have students obtain a copy of the Zimmermann Note and read it in its entirety. Ask each student to write a short essay discussing the document and explaining why it proved so inflammatory to Americans. Alternately, students could rewrite the telegram in modern-day, easy-to-understand language. Have students discuss their work with the class. **Block Scheduling**

now on. You should be proud to have me . . . participate in the struggle as a part of the human wall against a second Dark Ages." As the weeks went by, U.S. troops arrived in France in greater numbers. Army engineers built docks and railroads and strung up networks of telephone and telegraph lines. The engineers also constructed ammunition depots, camps, hospitals, and storage sheds. The troops did not participate in the fighting until 1918.

Some 10,000 American women worked in army hospitals. Emily Vuagniaux, an Army Medical Corps nurse, described life in a battlefield hospital.

"We . . . have worked . . . sometimes 18 hours straight. I have the operating room and they run four tables day and night and have between 200 and 300 patients right off the field, so you . . . know we are quite close in."

—Emily Vuagniaux, letter, June 20, 1918

Thousands more American women went to Europe as volunteers for the Red Cross, the YMCA, and other agencies.

Escorted by U.S. warships, merchant vessels transported troops, supplies, and volunteers through the submarine-infested North Atlantic. This **convoy system** proved quite effective. Of the more than 2 million U.S. soldiers who crossed the Atlantic Ocean, not one died as the result of an enemy attack on the high seas. U.S. warships also patrolled the waters of the western Atlantic, protecting the U.S. coastline. To contain U-boats, U.S. ships laid more than 60,000 mines in a lethal 240-mile necklace across the North Sea from Norway to the Orkney Islands off Britain. This barrier created hazards for German U-boats trying to return to their bases.

✔ **READING CHECK: Evaluating** What experiences made John J. Pershing a good choice for AEF commander? **Pershing was the U.S. Army's most experienced combat officer. He had fought in the Spanish-American War and commanded troops in the Philippines and in Mexico.**

World War I soldiers faced both brutal hand-to-hand combat and deadly new weapons.

SECTION 2 REVIEW

1. **Define and explain:**
   convoy system

2. **Identify and explain:**
   Sussex pledge
   Robert Lansing
   National Defense Act
   Zimmermann Note
   Jeannette Rankin
   Selective Service Act
   John J. Pershing

3. **Summarizing** Copy the graphic organizer below. Use it to list the steps the U.S. government took to prepare the military for war.

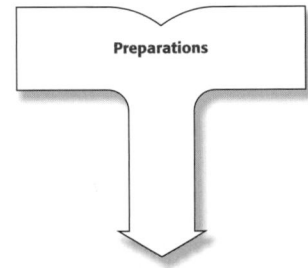

Preparations

World War I

4. **Finding the Main Idea**
   a. How might the United States have responded differently to the events that challenged its neutrality?
   b. How did the United States recruit and train its troops in a short period of time?
   c. What were the experiences of the AEF troops serving under General Pershing?

5. **Writing and Critical Thinking**
   Identifying Cause and Effect Write a short paragraph explaining why the United States joined the fighting in World War I.
   Consider:
   • the war's economic impact on the United States
   • unrestricted submarine warfare
   • the effect a German victory might have on the United States

Homework Practice Online
keyword: SE3 HP12

SECTION 2 REVIEW ANSWERS

1. **Define**
   • convoy system, p. 367

2. **Identify**
   • *Sussex* pledge, p. 363
   • Robert Lansing, p. 363
   • National Defense Act, p. 363
   • Zimmermann Note, p. 364
   • Jeannette Rankin, p. 364
   • Selective Service Act, p. 364
   • John J. Pershing, p. 366

3. The government recruited soldiers, constructed new barracks and training centers, and trained soldiers.

4a. Answers will vary. Some students might suggest that the United States should have adopted a "turn the other cheek" policy in response to U-boat attacks.

b. The Selective Service Act and the draft provided the quick recruitment of soldiers. Recruits were trained in an accelerated process for hours every day.

c. They reached France in late June 1917 and were greeted with cheers. They did not participate in the fighting until 1918.

5. Paragraphs should mention that the war and unrestricted submarine warfare disrupted shipping and commerce and that many Americans were swayed by anti-German propaganda from Great Britain.

SECTION 3

After completing Section 3, students should be able to:

OBJECTIVE 1 *Describe how the U.S. government prepared the nation for war.*

OBJECTIVE 2 *Discuss how organized labor and volunteers contributed to the war effort.*

OBJECTIVE 3 *Explain why African Americans moved to the North.*

OBJECTIVE 4 *Relate how the government created support for, and limited opposition to, the war.*

📡 *LET'S GET STARTED!*

As students enter the classroom, ask them to list three or four ways in which citizens might support a war effort. Have volunteers share their answers with the class. *(Students might suggest that citizens could fly the country's flag, buy war bonds, or go without certain items in order to save them for soldiers.)* Tell students that in Section 3 they will learn how Americans supported the war effort during World War I.

SECTION 3 RESOURCES

REPRODUCIBLE
▶ Guided Reading Strategy 12.3

TECHNOLOGY
▶ One-Stop Planner, Lesson 12.3
▶ Holt Researcher: American History CD–ROM
▶ Homework Practice Online

REINFORCEMENT, REVIEW, AND ASSESSMENT
▶ Section 3 Review, p. 374
▶ Daily Quiz 12.3
▶ Main Idea Activity 12.3
▶ English Audio Summary 12.3
▶ Spanish Audio Summary 12.3

SECTION 3

READ TO DISCOVER
1. How did the U.S. government prepare the nation for war?
2. How did organized labor and volunteers contribute to the war effort?
3. Why did African Americans move north?
4. How did the government create support for, and limit opposition to, the war?

IDENTIFY
William McAdoo
Food Administration
Herbert Hoover
War Industries Board
Bernard Baruch
National War Labor Board
Harriot Stanton Blatch
Juliette Gordon Low
Great Migration
Committee on Public Information
Espionage Act
Sedition Act

▶ WHY IT MATTERS TODAY
Today's U.S. military must still maintain its preparedness for war. Use CNNfyi.com or other **current events** sources to find out how the military recruits and keeps members. Record your findings in your journal.

CNNfyi.com

The War at Home

> 🔲 EYEWITNESSES TO *History*
>
> "*Billy, my nephew, is twelve years old. . . . They call the suburb in which Billy lives one hundred per cent patriotic. Everybody is in war work. Even the children under five years have an organization known as the Khaki Babes. . . . Billy's crowd is indefatigable [tireless] in its labors. . . . The boys usher at meetings, assist in parades, deliver bundles and run errands. They are tireless collectors of nutshells, peach pits and tinsel paper. . . . One bit of voluntary war work was carried on through the periods of the gasoline-less Sundays when the four boys took positions on Commonwealth Avenue in such a way as to obstruct passing vehicles. If a car did not carry a doctor's or military sign, they threw pebbles and yelled 'O you Slacker!' It was exciting work because guilty drivers put on full speed ahead and Billy admitted that he was almost run over, but he added that the cause was worth it.*"
>
> —Florence Woolston, "Billy and the World War," *New Republic*, January 1919

The U.S. government encouraged all Americans to support the war.

Florence Woolston described her nephew's contribution to the war effort in the *New Republic* magazine. The efforts of Billy and millions of other Americans helped win the war.

Mobilizing the Nation

Once the United States entered the war, President Wilson quickly moved to mobilize the nation. The government set up programs to finance the war, conserve scarce resources, and redirect industry and labor toward wartime production. The president also launched a huge propaganda campaign to mobilize support for the war effort. As the government whipped up enthusiasm for the war, intolerance of antiwar opinions also spread across the land.

Directing the economy. At the outset of the war, Wilson had noted that "there are no armies in this struggle; there are entire nations armed." Wilson realized that the U.S. economy had to be reorganized. The first step in this process was raising money to pay for the war, which eventually cost the United States about $35 billion, including loans to the Allies.

The government raised money through four issues of Liberty bonds during the war and one of Victory bonds after the end of the fighting. Posters, parades, and rallies promoted each bond issue. **William McAdoo** was secretary of the treasury and Wilson's son-in-law. He declared that "Every person who refuses to subscribe . . . is a friend of Germany," and "is not entitled to be an American citizen." These promotions were a huge success.

LEVEL 1: Conduct a brief discussion on how the U.S. government prepared the nation for war. *(Students' responses should include that the government established programs to finance the war, to conserve scarce resources, and to redirect industry and labor toward wartime production. President Wilson also launched a propaganda campaign.)* Then pair students and have them rank the efforts in order of significance. Ask students to share their rankings. Conduct a classroom debate between students with different rankings.
English Language Learners, Cooperative Learning

LEVEL 2: Conduct a brief discussion on how the U.S. government prepared the nation for war. *(See the Level 1 lesson for the correct steps.)* Then tell students to imagine that they are government information officers. Have each student write a short radio announcement describing the government's efforts. Tell students that they will need to carefully consider the wording of their announcements in order to describe all of the government's efforts in the time allotted. Remind students that their announcements should be both informative and entertaining. Have volunteers deliver their announcements to the class. Students may wish to include the text of their announcements in their portfolios.

The government also increased taxes. Congress debated a new tax program for months before reaching an agreement in October 1917. The new taxes on business incomes and large personal incomes produced about $10 billion for the war.

Mobilizing the economy for war entailed more than raising money, however. It also involved coordinating the actions of government, business, and industry. This was done through a number of federal war boards. Although the federal government never took complete control of the economy, it exercised sweeping economic power through these various agencies. It set the prices and production levels of commodities and regulated businesses crucial to the war effort.

Conserving resources. Among the most successful of the federal war boards were the **Food Administration** and the Fuel Administration. They were charged with regulating the production and supply of these essential resources. To direct the Food Administration, Wilson chose **Herbert Hoover**, a prosperous mining engineer who had managed a food-relief campaign for war-stricken Belgium. Hoover saw his task as twofold: to encourage increased agricultural production and to conserve existing food supplies.

To stimulate wartime production, Hoover guaranteed farmers high prices. Farm production soared. For example, farmers increased their production of wheat, harvesting some 921 million bushels in 1919—a dramatic increase over the 1917 figure of some 637 million bushels.

Announcing that "food will win the war," Hoover called on Americans to reduce their food consumption by observing wheatless and meatless days. To supplement their diets, he suggested that they plant "victory gardens" filled with vegetables. The campaign proved very effective—without, as Hoover proudly noted, resorting to forced rationing.

Fuel Administration director Harry Garfield, son of former president James A. Garfield, took a similar course of action, encouraging people to observe heatless Mondays. Garfield was not unwilling to use force, however. When the nation ran short of coal in early 1918, he closed all factories east of the Mississippi River for several days.

Organizing industry. Hundreds of other federal boards and agencies were created to regulate industrial production and distribution. Led by William McAdoo, the Railroad Administration reorganized the railroad system by setting limits on transportation rates and workers' wages.

The work of all these boards was coordinated by the government's central war agency, the **War Industries Board** (WIB). Its director, Wall Street investor **Bernard Baruch**, had overall responsibility for allocating scarce materials, establishing production priorities, and setting prices. Baruch preferred to persuade business leaders to comply with his wishes. However, when steel owners refused to cut prices, the government threatened to take over their foundries and mills.

At first some business leaders were critical of Wilson's economic mobilization programs. They argued that government intervention would permanently damage the U.S. system of free enterprise. When profits soared, however, these business leaders stopped complaining.

✔ **READING CHECK: Categorizing** What steps did the U.S. government take to finance the war? issuance of Liberty bonds and a new tax program approved by Congress

INTERPRETING THE VISUAL RECORD

Victory gardens. Many Americans supported the war effort by growing food at home to make more available for troops overseas. *Why does this poster use children to promote the war effort?*

GLOBAL RELATIONS

Herbert Hoover in Belgium. Many of Belgium's villages and crops were destroyed during Germany's attack on the country. With their nation on the brink of starvation, Belgian officials asked Britain for help. Through a series of misunderstandings and coincidences, Herbert Hoover, an American engineer working in Britain, found himself involved in supplying emergency food relief to Belgium. Hoover served on the Commission for Relief in Belgium and began a publicity campaign to urge American organizations to donate food and money. He wrote, "This is not a question of charity or relief to the chronic poor, it is a question of feeding an entire population. . . . There never was a famine emergency so great."

CRITICAL THINKING What role might Hoover's publicity campaign have served in persuading Americans not just to donate but to support U.S. involvement in the war?

ANSWER: Students might suggest that by reminding U.S. citizens of the devastation in Europe, Hoover might have convinced some people that it was necessary for the United States to intervene.

VISUAL RECORD ANSWER

Students might suggest that it shows that if young children can aid the war effort, everyone can.

LEVEL 3: Conduct a brief discussion on how the U.S. government prepared the nation for war. *(See the Level 1 lesson for the correct steps.)* Then have students select one particular administration or program involved in the war effort, such as the Food Administration, the War Industries Board, the victory garden program, and so on. Have each student write a few paragraphs describing how the chosen administration or program bolstered the war effort. Alternately, have each student develop an advertising campaign designed to promote his or her chosen agency or program. Ask volunteers to read their paragraphs or present their campaigns to the class.

SPOTLIGHT
on Female Workers During the War

Ask students to locate and use primary sources written by women who joined the labor force during World War I. [If students have difficulty finding such sources, ask them to reread the quotation from Norma B. Kastl on this page.] Then have students develop their own projects on the topic. Students might write war diaries from the perspective of female workers, design a postage stamp in commemoration of women's efforts, and so on. Ask each student to complete his or her project and present it to the class. **Block Scheduling**

INTERPRETING THE VISUAL RECORD

Working women. These women helped the war effort by working in a Detroit munitions factory. *What dangers do these women face in their workplace?*

EVERY GIRL PULLING FOR VICTORY

VICTORY GIRLS
UNITED WAR WORK CAMPAIGN

The U.S. government encouraged all Americans to contribute to the war effort.

Mobilizing Workers

Meeting the demands of the war required a massive, cooperative effort. Millions of people, paid employees and volunteers alike, pitched in as the nation mobilized for the military campaign.

Organized labor. Because of the war, hundreds of thousands of men were drafted into the army, and European immigration slowed to a trickle. American industries found themselves desperately short of labor as they geared up for the war effort. Taking advantage of this situation, unionized workers across the country went on strike. They demanded higher wages and other benefits. Nearly 4,500 strikes involving more than 1 million workers erupted in 1917 alone. The tactic worked. Working conditions substantially improved throughout the war.

To ensure that the voice of labor was heard, President Wilson established the **National War Labor Board** (NWLB) in April 1918. Composed of representatives from business and labor, the NWLB arbitrated disputes between workers and employers. The board heard more than 1,200 cases, ruling in favor of labor more often than not. In this climate of official support, union membership grew rapidly. Membership in the American Federation of Labor (AFL) rose from some 2 million in 1916 to roughly 3.2 million by 1919. By the end of the decade, some 15 percent of the nation's nonagricultural workforce was unionized.

The labor shortage strengthened unions and brought about changes in the workforce. The number of women working outside the home grew by about 6 percent during the war. Many of these women took traditionally male jobs. They worked as automobile mechanics, bricklayers, metalworkers, railroad engineers, or truck drivers. In all, some 1.5 million American women worked in industry during the war. Norma B. Kastl was an interviewer with a women's service bureau during World War I. She explained that many women considered it their patriotic duty to work.

 History Makers Speak **"The navy is taking on women as yeomen [clerks] to do shore duty. . . . Every girl that becomes a yeoman can have the satisfaction of knowing that she is releasing, as from prison, some sailor who had been fuming . . . because he had to spend his days in an office instead of on the deck of a destroyer."**

—Norma B. Kastl

Women also helped plan wartime mobilization. Carrie Chapman Catt, a women's suffrage leader, sat on the Women's Committee of the Council of National Defense. This was a civilian agency organized to support the war effort. **Harriot Stanton Blatch**, the daughter of suffragist Elizabeth Cady Stanton, headed the Food Administration's Speakers' Bureau.

Women's war efforts helped produce one very important political change—the passage of the Nineteenth Amendment. Wilson, who had previously wavered on women's suffrage, threw his support behind the amendment in recognition of women's wartime contributions. "The greatest thing that came out of the war," Catt later noted, "was the emancipation of women, for which no man fought."

ALL LEVELS: To help students understand how organized labor and volunteers contributed to the war effort, copy the graphic organizer to the right on the chalkboard, omitting the italicized answers. Have each student complete it. To conclude, have each student write a short essay assessing the contributions of both organized labor and volunteers to the war effort. **English Language Learners**

HOMEWORK *Have each student create a collage to represent the actions of organized labor during World War I.*

THE WAR EFFORT

Organized Labor—Contributions and Effects
- *filled posts to replace workers who left to fight in the war*
- *went on strike to demand higher wages and benefits*
- *improved working conditions during the war*

Volunteers—Contributions and Effects
- *conserved energy and recycled essential materials*
- *grew vegetables in victory gardens*
- *purchased liberty bonds*
- *founded support organizations*

Volunteerism. Intense patriotism swept the country. Many Americans, from young children to senior citizens, contributed to the war effort. Americans voluntarily conserved energy, recycled essential materials, and planted victory gardens. All these efforts were to make more items available for the soldiers overseas. Americans also purchased Liberty bonds, which provided the government with funds to pay for equipment and supplies.

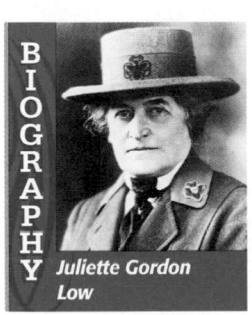

Juliette Gordon Low

Juliette Gordon Low was an active American volunteer. Born in 1860 to a wealthy family in Savannah, Georgia, Juliette Gordon received the finest private-school education. She was a serious student who was particularly gifted in the arts. After completing her education, she traveled extensively. On one trip to England she met wealthy William Low, whom she married in 1886.

The Lows divided their time between homes in the United States and Britain, living the leisurely life of the idle rich. Juliette's life was not a happy one, however. Marital troubles and the challenge of her increasing deafness, caused by two separate ear injuries, led her to suffer from frequent bouts of depression.

After her husband died in 1905, the financially independent widow traveled the world looking for a purpose in her life. She found this purpose in 1911, when she met British war hero Sir Robert Baden-Powell, the founder of the Boy Scouts. Low became actively involved in the Scouts' sister organization, the Girl Guides. She poured her energies into the movement, forming several troops in Britain before bringing the Girl Guides to the United States in 1912.

The organization grew quickly, and by 1915 the American Girl Guides were known as the Girl Scouts of America. Using mostly her own money and refusing to surrender to any obstacle, Low soon spread the Girl Scouts nationwide. The organization grew quickly during the war, and Low encouraged Girl Scouts to throw all their energies into helping the war effort. Many worked directly for the Food Administration. "A girl cannot die for her country, but she can live for it," Low declared. The Girl Scouts' role in the war effort helped boost membership from some 500 girls in 1915 to 50,000 by 1920. By the time of Juliette Low's death in 1927, total membership had reached almost 168,000.

✔ **READING CHECK: Analyzing Information** How did organized labor and some women benefit economically and politically from the war effort? new career opportunities for women in traditionally male jobs and passage of the Nineteenth Amendment

---

Mobilizing for the War Effort

teen Life

Wartime mobilization efforts targeted American children and teenagers as well as adults. Young people across the United States volunteered both money and labor to help win the war. Young Americans also contributed money from their own pockets, which they earned working at odd jobs such as painting barns, waiting tables, gathering nuts, and polishing shoes.

These Girl Scouts are collecting peach pits to be used in gas mask filters.

Helping to feed the soldiers overseas was a main task of American youth. "Do not permit your child to take a bite or two from an apple and throw the rest away," advised the February 21, 1918, edition of *Life* magazine. "Nowadays even children must be taught to be patriotic to the core." Many young people grew their own vegetable gardens. Some 2 million boys and girls eventually joined the U.S. Garden Army and grew $48 million worth of produce.

New York passed laws so that 12-year-old children could miss up to seven months of school in order to work on farms. In 1918, boys older than 16 were let out of high schools in the Northwest to help plant the spring wheat crop. They were rewarded with credit for the full school term. The U.S. Boy's Working Reserve, founded in 1917, formed a virtual army of agricultural labor. Some 200,000 young men between the ages of 16 and 20 were recruited to help harvest crops across the United States. In a time of desperate need, American youth performed the work of adults and helped win the war.

ECONOMICS

Children and the War Effort. Under Herbert Hoover's direction, the United States pushed to bring children into the war effort, particularly the food conservation effort. Hoover's officials went door-to-door asking people to sign a pledge to conserve food. Hoover also urged schools to teach food conservation. The Food Administration devised poems, slogans, and songs to interest children in the issue, even reworking popular nursery rhymes. The revised "Little Boy Blue" went as follows:

"Little Boy Blue, come blow your horn!
The cook's using wheat where she ought to use corn!
And terrible famine our country will sweep,
If the cooks and the housewives remain fast asleep!
Go wake them! Go wake them! It's now up to you!
Be a loyal American, Little Boy Blue!"

CRITICAL THINKING Why might the United States have attempted to encourage children to conserve food?

ANSWER: Students might suggest that children probably encouraged their parents to join the effort. Other students might argue that bringing children into the war effort showed the seriousness of the issue.

TEACH OBJECTIVE 3

LEVEL 1: Pair students and have each pair create a cause-and-effect diagram on the migration of African Americans north. *(Diagrams should note that job opportunities, the prospect of higher wages, and recruitment efforts encouraged African Americans to move to the North. Diagrams should note that the move brought better living conditions but also some racial violence.)* To conclude, tell students to imagine that they are African Americans who recently moved from Alabama to Illinois. Have pairs write short poems commenting on the move and on life in the North and in the South.
English Language Learners, Cooperative Learning

LEVELS 2 AND 3: Tell students to imagine that they are African Americans who have recently moved from Alabama to Illinois. Have each student write an editorial for a southern African American newspaper describing the causes and effects of the migration and offering advice to other African Americans thinking about moving north. *(See the Level 1 lesson for the correct causes and effects.)* Ask volunteers to read their editorials to the class. Students may wish to include their editorials in their portfolios.

NOTE: For an additional teaching idea, see the Chapter 12 continuum lesson in the **Creative Teaching Strategies** handbook.

The Great Migration.
African Americans left the South for many reasons. The boll weevil had ruined more than 85 percent of the South's cotton crop by 1922. Floods in the summer of 1915 worsened the situation for African American sharecroppers, most of whom were deeply in debt. An earlier depression had reduced workers' wages. In addition, racism and the fear of lynching led many African Americans to flee to the North. As an editorial in the *Chicago Defender* stated, "To die from the bite of frost is far more glorious than at the hands of a mob."

CRITICAL THINKING Tell students that in recent years many African Americans have moved from the North to the South. Why might this reverse migration be taking place?

ANSWER: Students might suggest that the civil rights movement improved life for African Americans in the South, that job opportunities exist in the South, or that some African Americans might want to escape the harsh northern winters.

SCIENCE & TECHNOLOGY ANSWERS

1. a virus
2. Asia, Africa

Science & Technology

Deadly Influenza

In 1918 World War I was raging in Europe, claiming thousands of lives. Meanwhile, a silent killer was sweeping the globe—influenza, commonly known as the flu. Initially, people believed that the illness was nothing serious and that doctors would find a cure. "Everybody had a preconception of what the flu was: it's a miserable cold and, after a few days, you're up and around," explains historian Alfred Crosby. "This was a flu that put people into bed as if they'd been hit with a 2 x 4. That turned into pneumonia, that turned people blue and black and killed them."

Decades of major discoveries and advances had given Americans great faith in science and medicine. However, scientists knew almost nothing about viruses at the time. They thought that a type of bacteria caused the flu. Wild rumors regarding the origin of the pandemic, or worldwide epidemic, spread quickly. One common rumor was that German agents had planted the virus in the United States.

The flu claimed some 12,000 lives in September, but the worst was still to come. In October more than 11,000 people died in the city of Philadelphia. Nearly 200,000 died nationwide that month. Then, like a fire burning itself out, the flu vanished.

The influenza epidemic left almost 600,000 dead in the United States alone, nearly as many Americans as were killed in the Civil War. At least 20 million people died worldwide.

Influenza Pandemic of 1918: The Second Wave

INDIAN OCEAN

ASIA
19.5–33.5 million

EUROPE
1.9 million

AFRICA
1.9–2.3 million

ARCTIC OCEAN

NORTH AMERICA
903,000–1.1 million

PACIFIC OCEAN

ATLANTIC OCEAN

AUSTRALIA
less than 100,000

SOUTH AMERICA
466,000–666,000

Extent of epidemic by:
August
September
October
November
Migration of epidemic

Azimuthal Equidistant Projection

19.5–33.5 million | Total estimated influenza deaths per continent (from all three waves)

Understanding Science and History

1. What causes influenza?
2. Which continents experienced the greatest number of deaths from influenza?

Many African Americans moved to northern cities in search of wartime jobs.

The Great Trek North

The labor shortage that drew women into the workforce also spurred immigration from Mexico. Some were fleeing the Mexican Revolution. Others were lured by southwestern employers who depended on Mexican labor. Some 150,000 men and women migrated from Mexico to the United States during the war.

Job opportunities and the chance of higher wages brought about one of the most important population shifts in U.S. history. This was the **Great Migration** of African Americans from the South to northern cities between 1915 and 1930. Hundreds of thousands of African Americans moved northward to escape discrimination and difficult living and working conditions. African American newspapers strongly encouraged the migration: "Get out of the South," declared an editorial in the *Chicago Defender*. "The *Defender* says come."

LEVEL 1: Ask students to identify the ways in which the government created support for, and limited opposition to, the war. *(Responses should mention that President Wilson created the Committee on Public Information, which issued propaganda. The government also suppressed dissent on war issues.)* Write students' responses on the chalkboard. Then organize students into triads. Have each triad develop at least two statements that might have merited punishment under the Espionage Act or the Sedition Act. *(Example: "The president is sending our young people to fight and die just to protect the rich bankers' overseas investments.")* Have volunteers read their statements to the class. Then conduct a discussion on those statements and wartime security.
English Language Learners, Cooperative Learning

LEVELS 2 AND 3: Ask students to identify the ways in which the government created support for, and limited opposition to, the war. *(See the Level 1 lesson for the correct methods.)* Then tell students to imagine that it is 1917. Have each student write a letter to the editor of a local magazine commenting on the government's efforts to limit opposition to the war. Remind students that they must discuss those efforts and comment on them in their letters. Have volunteers read their letters to the class. Students may wish to include their letters to the editor in their portfolios.

African Americans went north with great hope. They typically enjoyed a better standard of living than they had in the South, but racial violence remained a serious problem. The most brutal wartime racial incident occurred in East St. Louis, Illinois, on July 2, 1917. White rioters rampaged through African American neighborhoods, leaving at least 39 dead. Shocked and angered, many African Americans asked themselves why they should fight for freedom in Europe when they enjoyed so little of it at home.

✔ **READING CHECK: Making Generalizations** How did the Great Migration change American society? African Americans who migrated north enjoyed a better standard of living.

Influencing Attitudes

Whether for religious, political, or personal reasons, many Americans believed that the United States should have stayed out of the war. President Wilson wanted all Americans to support the war effort. Therefore, he established the **Committee on Public Information** (CPI) in the spring of 1917. Headed by George Creel, the CPI led a propaganda campaign to encourage the American people to support the war.

The CPI initially put out fact-based material that presented an upbeat picture of the war. Soon, however, the CPI began creating propaganda that pictured the Germans as evil monsters. Hollywood joined in, producing movies such as *The Claws of the Hun* and *The Kaiser, the Beast of Berlin*. CPI pamphlets warned citizens to be on the lookout for German spies. Dozens of "patriotic organizations" sprang up, with names like the American Protective League and the American Defense Society. These groups spied, tapped telephones, and opened other people's mail in an effort to identify "spies and traitors."

These groups were particularly hard on German Americans, many of whom lost their jobs. Sometimes this anti-German sentiment took absurd turns. German books vanished from library shelves, schools stopped teaching German language courses, and German music disappeared from concert programs. People even renamed German-sounding items: sauerkraut became liberty cabbage, dachshunds became liberty pups, and hamburger became Salisbury steak.

Other groups focused on Americanization efforts to prepare foreign-born residents for full U.S. citizenship. Education, in schools and by voluntary associations and public programs, was the main goal. Many Americans viewed teaching the English language and U.S. history and government to immigrants as a patriotic duty. Several cities and states passed Americanization measures. More than 150 cities celebrated Americanization Day on July 4, 1915.

Suppressing Opposition

Despite the atmosphere, some Americans continued to oppose the war. Quakers and Mennonites were particularly outspoken. They were committed by their faith to pacifism—the refusal to use violence to settle disputes. Considered traitors by many Americans, they experienced violence and abuse. Other opponents of the war included Representative Jeannette Rankin, Senator Robert La Follette, and settlement-house leader Jane Addams.

INTERPRETING THE VISUAL RECORD

Propaganda. The U.S. government directed most of its propaganda at Americans, encouraging them to work hard and make sacrifices to help win the war. *What elements in these posters reflect the behavior they are trying to inspire?*

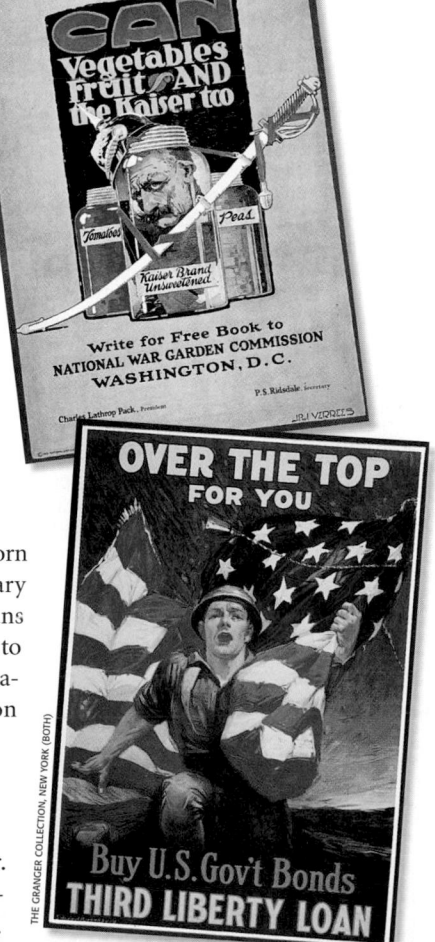

THE GRANGER COLLECTION, NEW YORK (BOTH)

George Creel. During President Wilson's re-election campaign, George Creel—once a muckraking journalist—supported Wilson by writing favorable political tracts. President Wilson repaid the favor by appointing Creel head of the Committee on Public Information (CPI). In this role, Creel blanketed the country with pro-war propaganda, distributing some 75 million pamphlets and 14,000 drawings. Creel also encouraged the exportation of films that depicted the "wholesome life of America." He even placed ads in magazines asking people to report anyone who "spreads pessimistic stories, cries for peace, or belittles our efforts to win this war."

ACTIVITY: Have students create pamphlets or drawings that might have been used as pro-war propaganda.

VISUAL RECORD ANSWER

Students might mention the canning jar containing the image of the kaiser with the dagger through it and the flag-waving soldier.

VISUAL RECORD ANSWER

(for p. 374)

Students might suggest that the party focused on uniting workers around the world.

REVIEW

Have students complete the **Section 3 Review** on p. 374.

ASSESS

Have students complete **Daily Quiz 12.3**. As **Alternative Assessment**, you may want to use the African American migration cause-and-effect diagram or the African American migration letter in this section's lessons.

RETEACH

Have students complete **Main Idea Activity for English Language Learners and Special-Needs Students 12.3**. Then write the following names on the chalkboard: *Bernard Baruch,* *Harriot Stanton Blatch, George Creel, Eugene V. Debs, Herbert Hoover, Juliette Gordon Low, William McAdoo,* and *Jeannette Rankin.* Assign each student two names. Ask students to write sentences identifying and describing the importance of their assigned people. Have volunteers—at least one for each assigned person—read their sentences to the class.
English Language Learners

EXTEND

Have students select examples of paintings or drawings that comment on the home front during World War I. Have each student pick one piece and write an analysis of it. Remind students to think about how the war affected the artist and thus the piece. **Block Scheduling**

INTERPRETING THE VISUAL RECORD

Socialists. Many Socialists questioned the reasons for fighting World War I. **What does this button suggest about the goals of the Socialist Party?**

Analyzing Primary Sources

Evaluating What effect did World War I have on the Court's ruling?

It made the Court uphold laws that it would not have upheld during peacetime.

The Socialist Party also proclaimed its opposition to the war. To most party members, the warring nations were simply using working people as tools in a capitalist struggle for control of world markets. The Industrial Workers of the World (IWW) had a similar view and led strikes in a number of war-related industries.

To silence opponents of the war, Congress passed the **Espionage Act** in June 1917 and the **Sedition Act** a year later. These measures outlawed acts of treason and made it a crime to "utter, print, write, or publish any disloyal . . . or abusive language" criticizing the government, the flag, or the military. Opposition to the draft, to war-bond drives, or to the arms industry also became a crime.

The CPI rallied support for the war, while the Espionage and Sedition Acts crushed opposition to the war. More than 1,000 people—including some 200 members of the IWW—were convicted of violating these laws. Socialist Party leader Eugene V. Debs was sentenced to 10 years in prison for making a speech against the war.

Many Americans, even some who supported the war, believed that the Espionage and Sedition Acts violated the First Amendment. The Supreme Court, however, disagreed. Justice Oliver Wendell Holmes wrote the opinion in the 1919 landmark case *Schenck* v. *United States.*

 History Makers Speak
❝The question . . . is whether the words used are used in such circumstances and are of such a nature as to create a clear and present danger. . . . When a nation is at war many things that might be said in time of peace . . . will not be endured [and] no Court could regard them as protected by any constitutional right.❞

—Justice Oliver Wendell Holmes, *Schenck* v. *United States*

✔ **READING CHECK: Evaluating** How effective were the Espionage Act and the Sedition Act? They were very effective. They crushed opposition to the war.

SECTION 3 REVIEW

1. Identify and explain:
William McAdoo
Food Administration
Herbert Hoover
War Industries Board
Bernard Baruch
National War Labor Board
Harriot Stanton Blatch
Juliette Gordon Low
Great Migration
Committee on Public Information
Espionage Act
Sedition Act

2. Sequencing Copy the diagram below. Use it to list the steps the U.S. government took to mobilize the economy for war.

 Neutrality

War

3. Finding the Main Idea
a. In what ways did World War I change the role of the federal government in American life?
b. How did women's war efforts help expand their political rights?
c. What social and economic forces contributed to Mexican immigration to the United States and African American migration northward?

4. Writing and Critical Thinking
Supporting a Point of View Write a newspaper editorial supporting or opposing the steps the government took to shape and control public opinion during the war.
Consider:
• the constitutional right to free speech
• the danger of spying and sabotage
• Americanization efforts

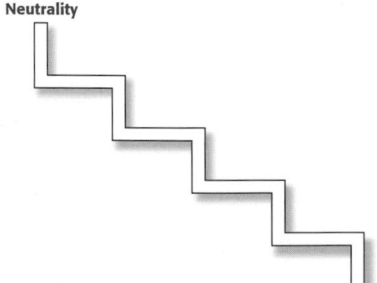
Homework Practice Online
keyword: SE3 HP12

SECTION 4

The War's End and Aftermath

EYEWITNESSES TO History

"*Along all the roads of France, in all the trenches, in every gunpit you can hear one song being sung. They sing it while they load their guns, they whistle it as they march up the line, they hum it while they munch their bully-beef [canned beef] and hardtack [biscuits]. You hear it on the regimental bands and grinding out from gramophones in hidden dugouts.*

Over there. Over there.
Send the word, send the word over there,
That the Yanks are coming—

Men repeat that ragtime promise as tho' it were a prayer. . . . We could have won without the Yanks—we're sure of that. Still, we're glad they're coming and we walk jauntily. We may die before the promise is sufficiently fulfilled to tell. What does that matter? The Yanks are coming."

—Coningsby Dawson, letter, 1918

George M. Cohan's "Over There" celebrated the arrival of U.S. forces in Europe.

Anticipating the arrival of U.S. forces, Coningsby Dawson wrote this letter home from his trench on the western front. His mixed emotions reflected the fact that no victory could erase the horrible costs of World War I. U.S. help was welcomed by the Allied Powers, but it could not undo the damage that had already been done.

The End of the War

The entry of the United States into the war came none too soon for the Allies. In the summer of 1917 the Allies launched an offensive to break the deadlock on the western front. It failed, shattering the Allied troops' already shaky morale. That fall, mutinies broke out in French units all along the front.

Revolution in Russia. More bad news arrived from Russia, which had been hit hard by the war. In March 1917, workers in Petrograd who were unable to buy bread marched out of the factories and protested in the streets. Demanding a change in government and an end to the war, the Russian people overthrew the czar.

Political turmoil continued until November, when the **Bolsheviks**, a group of radical Russian socialists, seized power. The Bolshevik leader, Vladimir Lenin, opposed the war and moved quickly to withdraw Russia from it. The Bolsheviks signed a treaty with the Central Powers in March 1918 that left the Central Powers free to concentrate their forces on the western front.

Germany's last bid for victory. On March 21, 1918, some 1 million German soldiers launched a tremendous offensive against the Allies. The Germans were backed by some 6,000 artillery pieces, including "Big Bertha," heavy guns capable

LEVELS 1 AND 2: Distribute Map 17, World War I in Europe, from the **American History Outline Maps**. Have each student label the locations of the final battles of World War I. *(Students should label Paris, Château-Thierry, Saint-Mihiel, and the Argonne Forest.)* Ask students to annotate their maps with statements explaining the effects of the Bolshevik Revolution and the German mutinies. *(Students' statements should mention that the Russian withdrawal allowed the Central Powers to mass their forces on the western front. The German mutinies weakened the Central Powers.)* Display students' annotated maps and statements around the classroom.
English Language Learners

LEVEL 3: Tell students to imagine that they are modern-day historians contributing to an encyclopedia on World War I. Have each student write a short entry on the final events of World War I. *(See the Levels 1 and 2 lesson for the correct events.)* Students' entries should mention important people, places, battles, and other events. Students might want to include maps and illustrations to help clarify their entries. Students may wish to include their entries in their portfolios.

INTERDISCIPLINARY CONNECTIONS

▶PSYCHOLOGY◀

The Wounds of War.
The intense, bloody fighting of World War I left some soldiers with a nervous disorder called shell shock. The term described a range of symptoms—from headaches to comas to suicidal depression. Shell shock was widespread during the war. One American doctor wrote that "the present war is the first in which . . . the functional nervous diseases [shell shock] have constituted a major medico-military problem. As every nation and race engaged is suffering from the symptoms, it is apparent that new conditions of warfare are chiefly responsible for their prevalence." In many cases, some doctors argued, the symptoms were brought on by horrible experiences that were "beyond [soldiers'] capacity to assimilate."

CRITICAL THINKING What modern-day psychological disorder might be akin to shell shock?

ANSWER: Students might name post-traumatic stress disorder.

SKILL-BUILDING STRATEGIES ANSWERS

Practicing the Skill
1. that trench warfare makes soldiers lose all sense of humanity
2. Viewpoints will vary.

Some soldiers turned cannon shells into art.

of firing a 2,100-pound shell almost nine miles. By late May the Germans had pushed the Allies back to the Marne River, just 50 miles from Paris.

In light of the desperate situation, General Pershing agreed to place U.S. troops under the command of Marshal Ferdinand Foch of France. The introduction of U.S. forces made the difference. In a last-ditch defense of Paris, U.S. troops helped the French stop the Germans at Château-Thierry on June 3–4. Nearby, a division of U.S. Marines attacked the Germans and recaptured Belleau Wood and two other villages. After fierce fighting, the German advance was halted. Paris was saved.

On July 15 the Germans threw everything into a final assault around Reims. The Allied lines held, however, and Foch ordered a counterattack three days later. Led by U.S. troops, the charge pushed the Germans back. The tide had turned in favor of the Allies.

Skill-Building Strategies

Interpreting Literature as Historical Evidence

Literature—imaginative or creative writing in its various forms—can serve as an extraordinary source of historical knowledge. Poetry and prose contain a wealth of information about the beliefs, customs, ideas, and values that were important to people of different cultures during different historical periods. Because most literature is meant to be subjective, it is particularly important to interpret it carefully.

How to Interpret Literature as Historical Evidence

1. **Become familiar with the source.** Before you begin to read a literary work, look over its title, publication information, and table of contents, if it has one. If possible, find out about the personal, social, and historical background of the author.
2. **Read the material carefully.** Read the work carefully and thoroughly. As you do so, take note of any references to real historical settings or events.
3. **Identify the work's themes.** Once you have finished reading the work, identify and think about its central themes. Consider how these themes may reflect the point of view of the author.
4. **Put the information to use.** Compare the themes to information about the historical period that you have gained through other sources. Then determine how the work can help you broaden your understanding of the historical period.

Applying the Skill

Erich Maria Remarque's novel *All Quiet on the Western Front* portrays fighting in World War I through the eyes of a German soldier. The following excerpt describes an encounter between German and French soldiers.

❝The moment we are about to retreat three faces rise up from the ground in front of us. Under one of the helmets [I see] a dark pointed beard and two eyes that are fastened on me. I raise my hand, but I cannot throw into those strange eyes; for one mad moment the whole slaughter whirls like a circus round me . . . then the head rises up . . . and my hand-grenade flies through the air and into him.

We make for the rear, pull wire cradles into the trench and leave bombs behind us with the strings pulled, which ensures us a fiery retreat. The machine-guns are already firing from the next position.

We have become wild beasts. We do not fight, we defend ourselves against annihilation. . . . No longer do we lie helpless, . . . we can destroy and kill, to save ourselves . . . and to be revenged.❞

Practicing the Skill

Use the passage above to answer the following questions.
1. What point is made about trench warfare?
2. How does the passage affect your view of war?

LEVEL 1: Ask students to summarize the main goals of President Wilson's Fourteen Points. (*Students should note that Wilson was concerned with self-determination, territorial disputes, secret diplomacy, the arms race, and trade barriers. He also wanted to establish a League of Nations.*) Then pair students and tell them to imagine that they are President Wilson. Ask each pair to write a short rationale of the Fourteen Points. Have volunteers read their rationales to the class.
English Language Learners, Cooperative Learning

LEVEL 2: Tell students to imagine that they are newspaper reporters. Have each student write a short, informative article explaining the goals of President Wilson's Fourteen Points. (*See the Level 1 lesson for the correct goals.*) Ask volunteers to read their articles to the class. Then ask students why the German government objected to the Fourteen Points. (*Students should indicate that the German government saw the Fourteen Points as evidence of Wilson's interference.*) Conduct a discussion on Wilson's desire to be involved in the postwar peace process.

Allied victory. In the late summer of 1918, Foch seized the initiative and ordered a major offensive along the entire western front. For three months the Allies pushed deep into German-held territory. Americans led the attack that pushed the Germans back at Saint-Mihiel, France, that September. The Americans next drove toward Sedan, a French rail center that the Germans had held since 1914. For more than a month the Americans pushed northward along the Meuse River and through the rugged Argonne Forest, facing artillery and machine-gun fire all the way. The Americans suffered some 120,000 casualties in the **Battle of the Argonne Forest**. By November, however, they had reached and occupied the hills around Sedan.

African American troops played a major role in the Argonne offensive. Members of the 369th Infantry, an African American regiment whose men hailed from New York, so distinguished themselves that the French awarded them the Croix de Guerre (krwah-di-GER), or "Cross of War," a French military honor.

Repeatedly hammered during the Allied offensive, the Central Powers' forces began to disintegrate. Morale in the German military sagged. One soldier expressed his hunger for peace in a letter home.

“In what way have we sinned, that we should be treated worse than animals? Hunted from place to place, cold, filthy . . . we are destroyed like vermin. Will they never make peace?”

—German soldier, quoted in *German Student's War Letters*, by A. F. Wedd

The French government rewarded these African American soldiers with the Croix de Guerre (left) for their bravery during the war.

In the fall of 1918, mutinies broke out in the German army and navy. German civilians rioted and demanded food. In October the German chancellor formally asked President Wilson for an armistice, or cease-fire. On November 9 Kaiser Wilhelm gave up the throne. The next day German government representatives arrived at Allied headquarters in Compiègne (kohmp-yehn) to hear the armistice terms. The Allies demanded that the Germans evacuate Alsace-Lorraine, Belgium, France, and Luxembourg and surrender an enormous amount of military equipment.

Early on the morning of November 11, the warring parties signed the armistice. At 11 A.M. the cease-fire went into effect. The constant crashing of guns was replaced, according to one American, by a "silence [that] was nearly unbearable." At long last, the war had ended. A peace conference was set for January 1919 in Paris.

✔ **READING CHECK: Identifying Cause and Effect** How did U.S. entry into World War I affect the war's outcome? U.S. entry into the war turned the tide in favor of the Allies.

Wilson's Fourteen Points

News of the November 11 armistice set off a joyful celebration in the United States. President Wilson shared the people's great happiness at the Allied victory, but he knew that the difficult task of forging a just peace lay ahead.

HISTORY MAKERS SPEAK

F. A. Voigt in *The Last Magnificent War: Rare Journalistic and Eyewitness Accounts of World War I*

War's End. British soldier F. A. Voigt described the moment of the armistice. While he and his group were in their tents, they heard a strange noise: "There it was again, a low, hollow sound like that of a distant sea. It grew louder and then ceased. Then it became audible once more and grew louder and still louder. Suddenly we realized what it was—it was the sound of cheering. It came nearer and nearer, gathering speed. It flooded the whole town with a great rush, paused a moment, and then burst over our camp." But in the midst of the soldiers' celebrations, they remembered the dead. Voigt wrote that he "saw innumerable rotting dead that lay unburied in all postures on the bare, shell-tossed earth. . . . I knew . . . that the world's misery had been too great ever to be shaken off."

ACTIVITY: Tell students to imagine that they are soldiers on the front who have just learned of the armistice. Have each student write a poem, a short story, or a letter describing his or her emotions.

Americans in Washington, D.C., celebrate the news that the war is over.

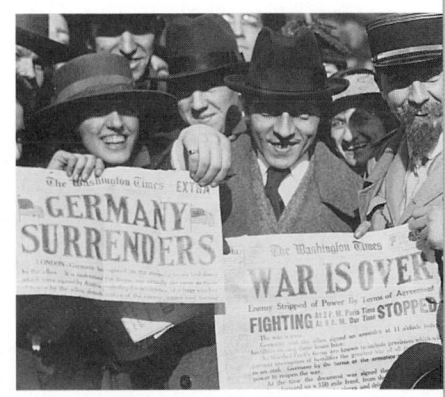

LEVEL 3: Ask students to reread the excerpt from President Wilson's Fourteen Points on this page. Then organize students into small groups. Have each group write an international Bill of Rights and Responsibilities based on the goals of Wilson's Fourteen Points. *(See the Level 1 lesson for the correct goals.)* Ask volunteers to present their bills to the class. Post these bills around the classroom. **Cooperative Learning**

NOTE: To help students make meaningful connections between events in U.S. history and those in their own hometown, use the Chapter 12 **Hands-On History Activity**, Your Town's Volunteer.

SPOTLIGHT on the Big Four

Organize students into four groups. Have each group represent one of the Big Four: Georges Clemenceau, David Lloyd George, Vittorio Orlando, or Woodrow Wilson. Ask each group to prepare for the Allied peace conference, conducting additional research as necessary to learn more about its figure's stance at the meeting. Then act as a moderator and re-enact the peace conference. Finally, ask students to comment on the conference after the re-enactment.
Cooperative Learning, Block Scheduling

ECONOMICS

John Maynard Keynes and Reparations. Shortly after the conference at Versailles, John Maynard Keynes, a British economist, published *The Economic Consequences of the Peace,* a book that condemned reparations. Keynes argued that the reparations were unreasonable, particularly in light of Allied confiscation of German land and Germany's merchant fleet. He also insisted that reparations would destroy the German economy and create future uprisings. In chilling words that foreshadowed the rise of Nazi Germany, Keynes wrote, "Who can say in what direction men will seek at last to escape from their misfortunes?"

CRITICAL THINKING How might the Allied nations have punished Germany without using reparations?

ANSWER: Answers will vary. Some students might suggest that the Allies could have required Germans to work on rebuilding projects in France or Belgium.

HISTORICAL DOCUMENTS ANSWER
Answers will vary. Students might mention that a lack of political independence and autonomy contributed to World War I.

★ HISTORICAL DOCUMENTS ★

PRESIDENT WOODROW WILSON

The Fourteen Points

On January 8, 1918, President Woodrow Wilson presented to Congress his plan for building peace in the postwar world. **Why does Wilson emphasize political independence and autonomy?**

The program of the world's peace . . . is this:
. . . no private international understandings of any kind. . . . Absolute freedom of navigation upon the seas. . . . The removal . . . of all economic barriers and . . . equality of trade conditions among all the nations . . . guarantees . . . that national armaments will be reduced. . . . A free, open-minded, and absolutely impartial adjustment of all colonial claims, . . . the evacuation of all Russian territory. . . . Belgium . . . must be evacuated and restored. . . . All French territory should be freed and the invaded portions restored. . . . A readjustment of the frontiers of Italy . . . along clearly recognizable lines of nationality. . . . The peoples of Austria-Hungary . . . should be accorded the freest opportunity of autonomous development. . . . Rumania, Serbia, and Montenegro should be evacuated, occupied territories restored. . . . The Turkish portions of the present Ottoman Empire should be assured a secure sovereignty, but the other nationalities . . . under Turkish rule should be assured an . . . opportunity of autonomous development. . . . An independent Polish state should be erected. . . . A general association of nations must be formed . . . for the purpose of affording mutual guarantees of political independence and territorial integrity to great and small states alike.

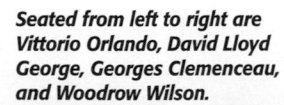

Seated from left to right are Vittorio Orlando, David Lloyd George, Georges Clemenceau, and Woodrow Wilson.

THE GRANGER COLLECTION, NEW YORK

This challenge had long been on Wilson's mind. Late in 1917 he had invited a group of scholars to advise him on peace terms. Drawing from their work, Wilson had developed the **Fourteen Points**, a program for world peace. He presented a summary of his principles and the Allied war aims to Congress on January 8, 1918.

Nine of the points dealt with the issue of self-determination—the right of people to govern themselves—and with the various territorial disputes created by the war. Other points focused on what Wilson considered the causes of modern war: secret diplomacy, the arms race, violations of freedom of the seas, and trade barriers. The final point—the establishment of the **League of Nations**—was the heart of the program. The League would be an international body designed to prevent offensive wars.

Congress and the American public warmly received the Fourteen Points. The Allies were not as enthusiastic, and the German government rejected the program. The Germans argued that Wilson was interfering in European affairs.

✔ **READING CHECK: Summarizing** What major issues did the Fourteen Points raise? self-determination, territorial disputes, secret diplomacy, the arms race, violations of freedom of the seas, and trade barriers

The Paris Peace Conference

On December 4, 1918, Woodrow Wilson boarded the USS *George Washington* for Europe—becoming the first president to cross the Atlantic Ocean while in office. A huge crowd gave Wilson a rousing send-off as the ship steamed out of New York Harbor. His reception at the French port of Brest was no less enthusiastic. Many Europeans welcomed him as a conquering hero.

The peace conference opened on January 18, 1919. It was dominated by the **Big Four**—Wilson, British prime minister **David Lloyd George**, French premier **Georges Clemenceau**, and Italian prime minister **Vittorio Orlando**.

Orlando, Lloyd George, and Clemenceau insisted that Germany bear the financial cost of the war by making huge **reparations**, or payments, to the Allies. They also wanted several secret spoils-of-war treaties honored. Such demands violated many of the principles included in President Wilson's peace plan.

ALL LEVELS: To help students understand the terms of the Treaty of Versailles and why the U.S. Senate rejected the treaty, copy the graphic organizer to the right on the chalkboard, omitting the italicized answers. Have each student complete it. To conclude, ask each student to write short press releases summarizing the Treaty of Versailles and announcing the Senate's rejection of the treaty.

English Language Learners

HOMEWORK *Tell each student to write one or two paragraphs expressing his or her personal opinions of the Treaty of Versailles and the Senate's rejection of the treaty.*

The Terms of the Treaty
- *divided Germany's colonies and the Ottoman Empire among Allied nations*
- *established a mandate system*
- *created new nations*

THE TREATY OF VERSAILLES

The Senate's Objections
- *irreconcilables completely rejected the League of Nations*
- *reservationists objected to Article 10 in the League Covenant, believing that it would force the United States into war in certain circumstances*

After six months of debate, the delegates agreed to a peace treaty. The official signing of the **Treaty of Versailles** took place in the palace of Versailles, just outside Paris, on June 28, 1919. Secretary of State Robert Lansing felt that "the terms of peace appear immeasurably harsh and humiliating."

Germany's colonies and the Ottoman Empire were divided among the Allied nations. At Wilson's insistence, however, the treaty required the new colonial rulers to report on their administration to the League of Nations. The peace treaty created the new nations of Czechoslovakia and Yugoslavia. It also re-established Estonia, Finland, Latvia, Lithuania, and Poland as independent nations. France reclaimed the Alsace-Lorraine region. France also won control of the Saarland, an industrial region of Germany rich in coal and iron, for 15 years. Germany was disarmed, forced to admit full responsibility for the war, and charged billions of dollars in reparations.

Wilson had strongly opposed some of the Allies' more extreme demands. Above all, the president made sure that the treaty included an agreement creating the League of Nations. He believed this would remedy any injustices the treaty might contain. The agreement required member nations to try to resolve disputes peacefully. If negotiations failed, the nations were to observe a waiting period before going to war. If any member nation failed to follow this procedure, the executive council could apply economic pressure and even recommend the use of force against the offending nation. Article 10, the heart of the agreement, required each member nation to "respect and preserve" the independence and territorial integrity of all other member nations.

✔ **READING CHECK: Contrasting** How did the European Allied leaders and President Wilson differ in their views on punishing Germany? Lloyd George, Clemenceau, and Orlando insisted that Germany make huge reparations. They also wanted several secret spoils-of-war treaties honored. Those demands conflicted with Wilson's peace plan.

Europe and the Middle East After World War I

Interpreting Maps Four empires—the Austro-Hungarian, German, Ottoman, and Russian—had collapsed by the end of the First World War.

❓ THE USES OF GEOGRAPHY What countries were created from or received land that had belonged to Russia before the war?

Legend:
- Lost by Germany
- Lost by Bulgaria
- Lost by Austria-Hungary
- Lost by Russia
- Lost by Ottoman Empire
- British mandate
- French mandate
- Occupied by Allies

In 1922 the Bolsheviks were firmly in control of Russia, and they organized the Union of Soviet Socialist Republics.

MAP ANSWER
Estonia, Finland, Latvia, Lithuania, Poland, Romania

GRAPH ANSWER
(for p. 380)
Russia; Bulgaria

VISUAL RECORD ANSWER
(for p. 381)
Students might suggest a church.

REVIEW SECTION 4 ANSWERS

1. Define
- reparations, p. 378

2. Identify
- Bolsheviks, p. 375
- Battle of the Argonne Forest, p. 377
- Fourteen Points, p. 378
- League of Nations, p. 378
- Big Four, p. 378
- David Lloyd George, p. 378
- Georges Clemenceau, p. 378
- Vittorio Orlando, p. 378
- Treaty of Versailles, p. 379
- Henry Cabot Lodge, p. 380

3. goal—impartial adjustment of colonial claims; compromise—Allies divided German colonies and Ottoman Empire among themselves; goal—no secret diplomacy; compromise—Allies worked for spoils-of-war treaties; goal—League of Nations; compromise—U.S. Senate refused to ratify

LEVELS 1 AND 2: Tell students to assume one of the following roles: an American woman on the home front, a U.S. soldier who fought in France, a German soldier who fought in France, or a French civilian. Have each student develop a detailed monologue about the global impact of World War I. (*Monologues should mention the incredible human and economic toll created by the war. Students should also mention the growing chaos in Germany and growing territorial disputes in Europe and the Middle East.*) Ask volunteers to perform their monologues for the class. Students may wish to include the scripts for their monologues in their portfolios.
English Language Learners

LEVEL 3: Conduct a discussion on the global impact of World War I. (*See the Levels 1 and 2 lesson for the correct impacts.*) Ask students to select, in their opinions, the most devastating human or economic cost of World War I. (*Answers will vary. Students should support their choices.*) Then ask each student to write a proposal outlining a plan for the recovery of Europe. Have volunteers present their plans to the class. Conclude by conducting a discussion on different approaches to recovery.

4a. It allowed the Americans to gain control of Sedan. German morale sagged, and the war soon ended.

b. the creation of new nations, the imposition of reparations, and the destruction of human life and property, among others

c. Answers will vary. Students might suggest that Wilson should have compromised on Article 10.

5. Answers will vary but should include the following terms: division of Germany's colonies and the Ottoman Empire among Allied nations, establishment of a mandate system; creation of Czechoslovakia and Yugoslavia; re-establishment of Estonia, Finland, Latvia, Lithuania, and Poland as independent nations; return of Alsace-Lorraine to France; and disarmament of and reparations to be paid by Germany.

CHAPTER
REVIEW (12) ANSWERS

Creating a Time Line
Each event should have an explanation and the correct date.

Writing a Summary
See the Reading Checks in each section for main ideas.

Publication No. 12

President Wilson's Address
TO THE
League to Enforce Peace

PUBLISHED BY THE
LEAGUE TO ENFORCE PEACE
70 FIFTH AVENUE, NEW YORK

This is a printed copy of one of the many speeches that President Wilson gave to win support for the Treaty of Versailles.

The treaty in the Senate. Wilson returned to the United States in July 1919. He immediately began working to win the Senate's approval of the Treaty of Versailles. Wilson expected to receive the votes of most Democratic senators, but he needed support from Republicans to gain the necessary two-thirds majority. Most Republican senators had doubts about the treaty. Fourteen of them—called the irreconcilables—wanted nothing to do with the League of Nations and flatly rejected the treaty. The other 35 Republican senators—the reservationists—said that they could support the treaty if the League Covenant was changed. They particularly objected to Article 10, which seemed to commit the United States to go to war in defense of any League member that came under attack. Wilson's only hope was to gain the support of close to 20 reservationists by compromising on the League. Wilson refused.

Henry Cabot Lodge of Massachusetts, head of the Senate Committee on Foreign Relations and Wilson's longtime enemy, led the reservationists. Lodge kept the treaty stalled in the Foreign Relations Committee through the summer of 1919. Angry and frustrated, on September 4 Wilson began a grueling 9,500-mile speaking tour by train to defend the treaty. The crowds grew more enthusiastic as the tour went on, but Lodge remained unmoved. He said, "The only people who have votes on the treaty are here in the Senate."

On the night of September 25, after a speech in Pueblo, Colorado, Wilson complained of a splitting headache. His doctor ordered him back to Washington, D.C. A few days later, Wilson collapsed from a near-fatal stroke. He lived out the rest of his term in seclusion in the White House, cut off from everyone except his wife and his closest aides. Increasingly out of touch with reality, Wilson still refused to compromise.

In November, Lodge presented the treaty, with a list of 14 reservations, to the Senate. On Wilson's orders, all of the Democrats rejected the modified treaty. Without the list of reservations, the treaty met the same fate at the hands of the Republicans. In March 1920 another vote on Lodge's version of the treaty failed. By the time Wilson left office, the League of Nations had been established in Geneva, Switzerland, but without U.S. participation.

Military Losses in World War I

Allied Powers

Central Powers

Casualties (in millions)

Legend:
Wounded
Dead

Allied Powers: Russia, British Empire, France, Italy, United States, Romania, Serbia, Belgium, Others

Central Powers: Germany, Austria-Hungary, Turkey, Bulgaria

Source: *Encyclopedia of Military History*

Interpreting Graphs It is estimated that more than 8.5 million soldiers died during World War I. An even higher number suffered from battle-inflicted wounds.

? Skills Assessment Which of the Allied Powers had the highest number of total casualties? Which of the Central Powers had the highest casualties?

✔ **READING CHECK: Analyzing Information** What reservations did some senators have about the Treaty of Versailles? Many Republican senators expressed concern about the proposed role of the League of Nations.

REVIEW

Have students complete the **Section 4 Review** on p. 381.

ASSESS

Have students complete **Daily Quiz 12.4**. As **Alternative Assessment**, you may want to use the final events map or the Fourteen Points rationale in this section's lessons.

RETEACH

Have students complete **Main Idea Activity for English Language Learners and Special-Needs Students 12.4**. Then pair students and have each pair devise a crossword puzzle or a hidden-word puzzle utilizing the key terms and key people in Section 4. Have each pair exchange its puzzle with another pair and then solve it.
English Language Learners, Cooperative Learning

EXTEND

Have students conduct research on the Treaty of Versailles and its role in helping to cause World War II. Ask students to discuss their research in a short essay. **Block Scheduling**

The Global Impact of the War

While U.S. leaders debated the Treaty of Versailles, Europeans struggled to recover. The war's destruction and human suffering had been almost incomprehensible. More than 8.5 million people had died in battle, and another 21 million were wounded.

The war had left the industry and agriculture of much of continental Europe in ruins. Northern France was completely destroyed. British economist John Maynard Keynes observed the landscape.

History Makers Speak

❝For mile after mile nothing was left. No building was habitable and no field fit for the plow. . . . One devastated area was exactly like another—a heap of rubble, a morass [jumble] of shell-holes, and tangle of wire.❞

—John Maynard Keynes, quoted in *America Enters the World,* by Page Smith

Those businesses still operating could not produce enough to meet demand. This resulted in rapid inflation. In Germany, food shortages were so extreme that it proved almost impossible to keep track of prices.

Throughout Europe, nations competed with one another over territories that they thought the treaty ought to have granted them. Arab nations in the Middle East had sided with the Allies in hopes of winning their independence from the Ottoman Turks. Instead, they found themselves living under French and British authority. Tensions in the region grew after Britain issued the Balfour Declaration in 1917, which declared British support for a Jewish homeland in Palestine.

✔ **READING CHECK: Making Predictions** How might World War I have affected future international relations? The Treaty of Versailles left Germany bitter and may have led to future conflict.

INTERPRETING THE VISUAL RECORD

The cost of war. At the end of the war, many towns and cities, like Houplines, France (above), lay in ruins. *What might the tall ruins in the middle of the photograph have been?*

SECTION 4 REVIEW

1. **Define and explain:**
   reparations

2. **Identify and explain:**
   Bolsheviks
   Battle of the Argonne Forest
   Fourteen Points
   League of Nations
   Big Four
   David Lloyd George
   Georges Clemenceau
   Vittorio Orlando
   Treaty of Versailles
   Henry Cabot Lodge

3. **Categorizing** Copy the chart below. Use it to list the goals of President Wilson's Fourteen Points and the compromises that Allied demands forced him to make.

Wilson's Goals	Compromises

4. **Finding the Main Idea**
   a. How did the Battle of the Argonne Forest contribute to the Allied victory?
   b. What were some of the effects of the war on Europe and the Middle East?
   c. How might Wilson have won Senate support for the League of Nations?

5. **Writing and Critical Thinking**
   Supporting a Point of View Imagine you are a U.S. Senator. Prepare a chart listing the terms of the Treaty of Versailles and your reasons for supporting or opposing each term.
   Consider:
   • concerns of Republicans who opposed the League
   • the mood of the American public at the end of the war
   • the possible benefits League membership offered the United States

go. hrw .com **Homework Practice Online**
keyword: SE3 HP12

Identifying People and Ideas

1. the glorification of military strength

2. Commander of the American Expeditionary Force during World War I.

3. the countries that fought against the Central Powers

4. cable from German foreign secretary proposing alliance with Mexico

5. groups of warships that accompanied merchant vessels transporting troops and supplies

6. director of the War Industries Board

7. activist and volunteer who helped expand the Girl Scouts

8. the movement of many African Americans from the rural South to the urban North

9. an international organization designed to prevent offensive wars

10. reservationist senator who opposed the Treaty of Versailles

Understanding Main Ideas

1. militarism, nationalism, and military alliances

2. German troops tried to overwhelm France by invading through Belgium, but Belgian troops delayed them, which gave Britain and France time to send soldiers to meet the offensive.

TECHNOLOGY RESOURCES

▶ Chapter 12 Test Generator (on the One-Stop Planner)
▶ Global Skill Builder CD–ROM
▶ HRW Go site

REINFORCEMENT, REVIEW, AND ASSESSMENT

▶ Chapter 12 Review, pp. 382–83
▶ Chapter 12 Tutorial for Students, Parents, Mentors, and Peers

▶ Chapter 12 Test (Form A or B)
▶ Portfolio Activities and Alternative Assessment Handbook, Chapter 12
▶ Chapter 12 Test for English Language Learners and Special-Needs Students

REVIEW

Have students complete the **Chapter 12 Review** on pp. 382–83.

ASSESS

Use one of the chapter tests to assess students' understanding of the content. For **Alternative Assessment**, see the **Portfolio Activities and Alternative Assessment Handbook**.

3. sold weapons to the Allies, offered moral support, and tried to force Germany to restrict submarine warfare

4. filled vacant jobs, served as nurses, and supported the war effort in the United States

5. formed the Committee for Public Information and passed antitreason laws

6. Château-Thierry and the Argonne Forest

Reviewing Themes
1. U-boat attacks and the Zimmermann Note led the United States to declare war. Some students might suggest that continued naval violations made U.S. involvement unavoidable, while other students might suggest that the United States could have worked harder to avoid entering the conflict.

2. The government raised money with war bonds and taxes, conserved resources, stimulated production, and regulated businesses and industries.

3. The government issued sanctions for verbal or written objections to the war; some argued that these violated the right to free speech.

Thinking Critically
1. positive—supplied many new soldiers, gave some soldiers new opportunities, and eventually helped some American Indians gain citizenship; negative—forced some people to fight against their will

---

Review

Creating a Time Line

Copy the time line below onto a sheet of paper. Complete the time line by filling in the events and dates from the chapter that you think were most significant. Pick three events and explain why you think they were significant.

| 1914 | 1916 | 1918 | 1920 |

Writing a Summary

Using standard grammar, spelling, sentence structure, and punctuation, write an overview of events in the chapter.

Identifying People and Ideas

Identify the following terms or individuals and explain their significance.

1. militarism
2. John J. Pershing
3. Allied Powers
4. Zimmermann Note
5. convoy system
6. Bernard Baruch
7. Juliette Gordon Low
8. Great Migration
9. League of Nations
10. Henry Cabot Lodge

Understanding Main Ideas

SECTION 1 *(pp. 356–360)*
1. What tensions contributed to the outbreak of war in Europe?
2. What happened during the early weeks of the war?

SECTION 2 *(pp. 361–367)*
3. What contributions did the United States make to the Allied war effort before entering the war?

SECTION 3 *(pp. 368–374)*
4. What role did women play in the war effort?
5. How did the U.S. government ensure the public's cooperation with the war effort?

SECTION 4 *(pp. 375–381)*
6. What were the decisive battles at the end of World War I?

Reviewing Themes

1. **Global Relations** What led to the U.S. declaration of war in 1917? Was U.S. involvement in the conflict unavoidable? Explain your answer.
2. **Economics** How was the U.S. economy mobilized for war?
3. **Citizenship** Did the U.S. government's attempts to rally support for the war interfere with citizens' First Amendment rights? Why or why not?

Thinking Critically

1. **Analyzing Information** What were the positive and the negative effects of the draft in the United States?
2. **Evaluating** What effect did the wartime labor shortage have on unions, women, African Americans, and Mexican Americans?
3. **Drawing Conclusions** How did U.S. participation in World War I further establish it as a world power?
4. **Making Predictions** What effect might issues raised by the Treaty of Versailles have on future international relations?
5. **Making Generalizations** In what ways did American society and daily life change between 1914 and 1920?

Writing About History

Supporting a Point of View Imagine that you are an African American soldier during the war. Write your commanding officer a letter to convince the army to open up more opportunities for African American soldiers. Use the following graphic to organize your thoughts.

Increased Opportunities for African American Soldiers			
Current Opportunities	Other Possible Opportunities	Benefit for Soldiers	Benefit for Army

RETEACH

Organize students into small groups. Have each group create a short children's book about World War I. Groups' books should be nonfiction and should use images, graphic organizers, and simple explanations to help young readers grasp the content. Encourage students to delegate tasks within their groups, assigning jobs such as researcher, illustrator, and writer. Display students' books in the classroom or in the school library.
English Language Learners, Cooperative Learning

EXTEND

Tell students that the German U-boat, or submarine, played an important role in World War I. Have each student conduct research on U-boats in World War I. Students should select their own topics, such as U-boat construction and strategy, life aboard a U-boat, Allied responses to the U-boat, and so on. Have students create written or oral reports on their topics.
Block Scheduling

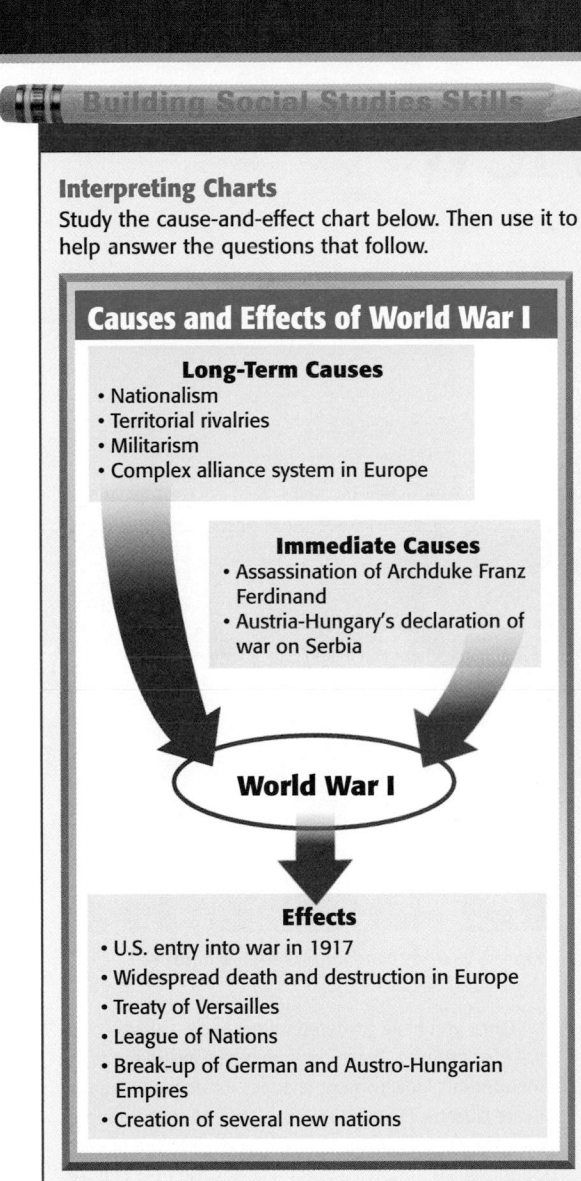

Building Social Studies Skills

Interpreting Charts
Study the cause-and-effect chart below. Then use it to help answer the questions that follow.

Causes and Effects of World War I

Long-Term Causes
• Nationalism
• Territorial rivalries
• Militarism
• Complex alliance system in Europe

Immediate Causes
• Assassination of Archduke Franz Ferdinand
• Austria-Hungary's declaration of war on Serbia

World War I

Effects
• U.S. entry into war in 1917
• Widespread death and destruction in Europe
• Treaty of Versailles
• League of Nations
• Break-up of German and Austro-Hungarian Empires
• Creation of several new nations

1. All of the following were causes of World War I EXCEPT:
   a. Archduke Franz Ferdinand's assassination
   b. militarism
   c. European alliances
   d. U.S. entry into the war

2. Which of the effects of World War I do you think has had the most lasting impact on the United States?

Analyzing Primary Sources
Read the excerpt from "The Ward At Night," a poem written anonymously by a member of the American Expeditionary Force. Then answer the questions that follow.

> ❝The blanket lying dark against the sheet,
> The heavy breathing of the sick,
> The fevered voices
> Telling of the battle
> At the front,
> Of Home and Mother.❞

3. What are the setting and subject of the poem?
   a. the sights and sounds of the battle
   b. the sights and sounds of the surrender
   c. the sights and sounds of the homecoming
   d. the sights and sounds of the hospital

4. Based on this poem, what conclusions can you draw about the fighting in World War I?

Alternative Assessment

Building Your Portfolio

Culture
Imagine that it is 1915 and you are a recent U.S. immigrant from one of the Allied Powers. Write a speech encouraging your fellow immigrants to support U.S. entry into World War I. Deliver the speech.

U.S. HISTORY

🔌 internet connect

Internet Activity: go.hrw.com
KEYWORD: SE3 AN12

Choose a topic on World War I to:
• learn about new World War I weaponry.
• research the Battle of the Somme.
• create a poster on the Central Powers.

go.hrw.com

---

2. allowed them to move into the workforce and earn better wages

3. The entry of the United States into the war turned the tide for the Allies. This made the United States seem powerful.

4. Answers will vary. Students might suggest that Germany might resent the treaty and future relations with Allied countries might be strained.

5. Students might suggest that the government became more involved in daily life, more women worked outside the home, immigrants and migrants changed the country, and the economy boomed.

Writing
Letters should note that African American soldiers face widespread discrimination and in the absence of discrimination, soldiers might make important military contributions.

Building Social Studies Skills
1. d

2. Answers will vary. Students might suggest creation of new nations or government influence on society.

3. d

4. Students might suggest that the fighting was deadly.

UNIT 3

REVIEW AND ASSESSMENT RESOURCES

TECHNOLOGY

▶ Global Skill Builder CD–ROM
▶ Holt Researcher: American History CD–ROM
▶ HRW Go site

REINFORCEMENT, REVIEW, AND ASSESSMENT

▶ Unit 3 Review, pp. 384–85
▶ Unit 3 Test (Form A or B)
▶ Portfolio Activities and Alternative Assessment Handbook, Unit 3
▶ Unit 3 Test for English Language Learners and Special-Needs Students

To review elements of Unit 3 in a single class period, assign one of the following activities or graphic organizers, omitting the italicized answers, to individuals or groups.

3 Global Relations

AMERICA'S INTERNATIONAL ROLE

Costs
• *heavy economic costs*
• *public opposition from some sectors*
• *conflicts and warfare*

Benefits
• *substantial economic rewards*
• *public support from some sectors*
• *the ability to expand American ideals and culture*

UNIT 3 Review

BUILDING YOUR PORTFOLIO

Outlined below are three projects. Independently or cooperatively, complete one and use the products to demonstrate your mastery of the historical concepts involved.

1 Problem Solving

You are a progressive reformer in the late 1800s. The transformation of the United States from a rural economy to an industrialized, urban society has created numerous social problems. Your assignment is to identify one such problem and create a solution.

Use your textbook and other resources to **gather information** that might influence your solution. Remember that your solution must include a plan of action. The information you might need to solve the problem includes the historical background of the Second Industrial Revolution and the Progressive Era, charts, graphs, and photographs.

Progressive Party candidate Theodore Roosevelt

Once you have gathered information, *list and consider options*. These options might include laws, amendments, government changes, or actions taken by private citizens. Once you have identified these options, *consider the advantages and disadvantages* of each option. Which option do you think has the best chance for success?

Choose and implement a solution. Complete the plan of action. *Evaluate the effectiveness* of your solution. Was it the best option? Would one of your earlier options have been effective? How could you modify your plan to make it more effective?

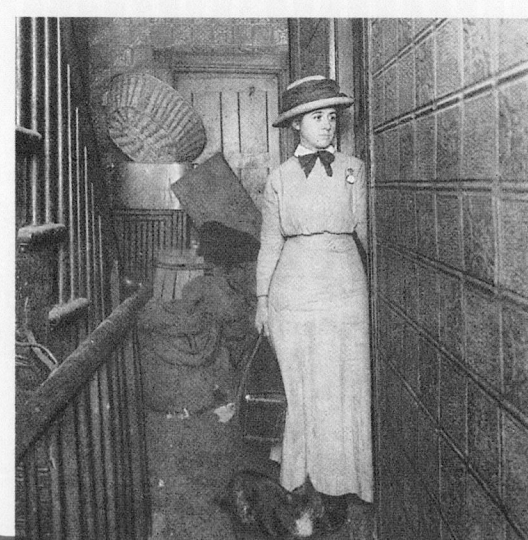

Nurse visiting a tenement house

1 Problem Solving

THE PROGRESSIVE PARTY

Goals	Actions	Effectiveness
to help immigrants	established settlement houses and provided kindergartens and schools	ran many successful settlement houses and schools
to reform big business	pursued court cases regarding labor laws and worked for health and safety standards	lost many labor cases but managed to pass certain laws and codes
to improve cities and city life	organized urban planning commissions and urged better services and standards	managed to provide better city services and facilities

2 Citizenship

Tell students to imagine that they are newspaper reporters in 1920 covering the ratification of the Nineteenth Amendment. Have each student create both questions and answers for an interview with either a suffrage activist or opponent. Students should emphasize the reactions of the interviewee to the Nineteenth Amendment, paying special attention to the tactics this person used to pass or prevent the amendment. Finally, ask students to include in their articles ideas about the impact the Nineteenth Amendment has had on American society. Ask volunteers to read their articles to the class.

2 Citizenship

The women's suffrage movement was an effort to expand participation in the democratic process. However, historians note that the primarily middle-class movement did not address the concerns of working-class women. *Create a script for a dialogue* between a middle-class suffragist and a working-class woman on how the movement could best serve the needs of all women. Your dialogue might also include a discussion of how participation in the democratic process reflects our national identity. You may wish to use portfolio materials you designed in the unit chapters to help you.

3 Global Relations

The Spanish-American War and World War I moved the United States into a position of world power. *Create a chart* for delivery to Congress outlining some of the economic and political costs and benefits of the U.S. role in international affairs. You may wish to use portfolio materials you designed in the unit chapters to help you.

U.S. troops in France at the close of World War I

Further Reading

DeSantis, Vincent P. *The Shaping of Modern America: 1877–1920.* Forum Press, 1989. A broad survey of reform movements at the turn of the century.

Diner, Steven J. *A Very Different Age: Americans of the Progressive Era.* Hill and Wang, 1998. An account of the effects of industrialization and reform movements on Americans.

Hall, Linda B., and Don M. Coerver. *Tangled Destinies: Latin America and the United States.* University of New Mexico Press, 1999. An examination of U.S.–Latin American relations from 1823 to the present.

Liliuokalani. *Hawaii's Story by Hawaii's Queen.* Charles E. Tuttle, 1991. First-hand account of Hawaii in the 1800s.

Mead, Gary. *The Doughboys: America and the First World War.* The Overlook Press, 2000. A history of the American Expeditionary Force based on firsthand accounts by U.S soldiers in World War I.

Schneider, Dorothy, and Carl J. Schneider. *Into the Breach.* Viking, 1991. An examination of the participation of American women in World War I.

Internet Connect & Review on the ROM

In assigned groups, develop a multimedia presentation about the United States between 1897 and 1920. Choose information from the chapter Internet Connect activities and the **Holt Researcher CD–ROM** that best reflect the major topics of the period. Write an outline and a script for your presentation, which may be shown to the class.

A Selection from Further Reading

American Women and World War I. In *Into the Breach: American Women Overseas in World War One*, Dorothy and Carl J. Schneider examine the roles that American women played in World War I. In the following excerpt, they provide firsthand testimony from two African American women who went overseas to open recreation rooms for black soldiers: "Above all . . . American women went overseas in the 'Great War' to serve. . . . They idealized the 'cause,' and wanted to serve it. . . . Triumphing over the harsh prejudice directed at them, the black women Addie Hunton and Kathryn Johnson wrote: 'We had the greatest opportunity for service that we have ever known; service that was constructive, and prolific with wonderful and satisfying result. For the privilege of serving in this capacity we will always be grateful.'"

ANALYZING SOURCES

According to Schneider and Schneider, what motivated American women to go overseas during World War I?

ANSWER: Students might note that a desire to serve the Allied cause motivated American women to go overseas during World War I.

Prosperity and Crisis

A Turbulent Decade
CHAPTER 13

The end of World War I did not bring calm to the United States. After undergoing a serious recession, the nation experienced protests and strikes. Many people began to fear the possibility of a Bolshevik infiltration and called for sanctions against Communists and other radicals. Over time, however, the Red Scare eased. A series of Republican presidents instituted economic policies that encouraged financial growth.

The Jazz Age
CHAPTER 14

Aided in part by growing prosperity, Americans in the 1920s experienced both the creation of a mass culture and a resurgence in all forms of art. Social attitudes, particularly those concerning women and young people, changed drastically during the decade. These changes worried many Americans. Such worries, in part, led to the rise of new religious movements.

EXAMINING THE VISUAL RECORD

Ask students the questions below. Then use the annotations to expand class discussion.

1 What might you infer about the economic class of the people depicted in the painting?

Some people, such as the middle- and upper-class people shown in the painting, prospered during the economic boom of the 1920s. Social divisions also deepened during this era, however, as many people did not share in the wealth created by big business and Wall Street.

2 What features of this scene represent innovations of the early 1900s?

Many corporations commissioned architects to design skyscrapers in the 1920s. Theaters were built to show movies, a popular form of entertainment. Also, corporations relied increasingly on advertising and marketing to influence the growing class of consumers with disposable income.

ACTIVITY: Have each student write a poem or a song about urban life during the 1920s. Students might concentrate on the more positive aspects of urban life, such as the excitement and the wide variety of things to do, or students might concentrate on the more negative aspects of urban life, such as crime and poverty.

U·N·I·T
4

Prosperity and Crisis

1919–1939

② ①

Howard Thain's painting The Great White Way *from 1928 portrays the vibrancy of urban life during the 1920s.*

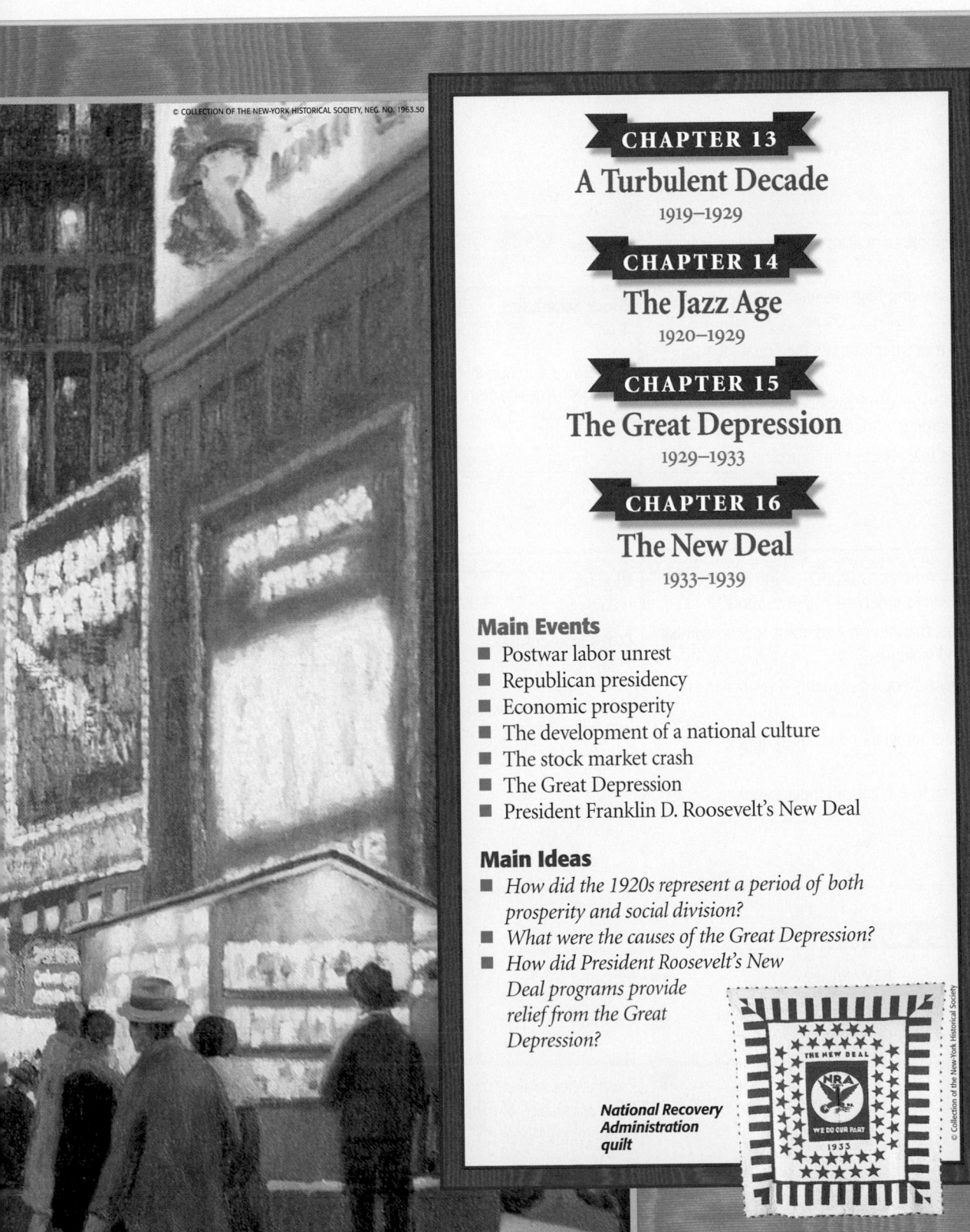

The Great Depression

CHAPTER 15

In 1929 the stock market crashed and the prosperity of the 1920s gave way to the Great Depression of the 1930s. The Great Depression had a number of causes, including the global economic crisis, the national income gap, and consumer debt. It devastated many Americans, who expressed anger at President Hoover's support of "rugged individualism." In 1932 Democrat Franklin D. Roosevelt won the presidency.

The New Deal

CHAPTER 16

After Franklin D. Roosevelt took office, he instituted a New Deal to rescue the economy and assist Americans. President Roosevelt believed that heavy government spending could help the nation recover from the Great Depression. Roosevelt's New Deal programs allocated government funds to create jobs, provide direct relief, and fund small and large-scale public-works projects. Over time, it led many Americans to believe that the federal government had a duty to help and assist its citizens.

© COLLECTION OF THE NEW-YORK HISTORICAL SOCIETY, NEG. NO. 1963.50

CHAPTER 13

A Turbulent Decade
1919–1929

CHAPTER 14

The Jazz Age
1920–1929

CHAPTER 15

The Great Depression
1929–1933

CHAPTER 16

The New Deal
1933–1939

Main Events
- Postwar labor unrest
- Republican presidency
- Economic prosperity
- The development of a national culture
- The stock market crash
- The Great Depression
- President Franklin D. Roosevelt's New Deal

Main Ideas
- *How did the 1920s represent a period of both prosperity and social division?*
- *What were the causes of the Great Depression?*
- *How did President Roosevelt's New Deal programs provide relief from the Great Depression?*

National Recovery Administration quilt

THE NEW DEAL
NRA
WE DO OUR PART
1933

© Collection of the New-York Historical Society

CHAPTER 13

A Turbulent Decade

CHAPTER RESOURCE MANAGER

Objectives	Pacing Guide	Reproducible Resources
SECTION 1 **Postwar Troubles** pp. 390–96	★ Discuss some of the economic outcomes of demobilization. ★ Analyze the main causes of the strikes of 1919 and how most Americans reacted to the strikes. ★ Explain what caused the public hysteria of the Red Scare. ★ Recount why the Sacco and Vanzetti trial aroused public interest.	**Regular** 2 days **Block Scheduling** 1 day *Block Scheduling Handbook with Team Teaching Strategies, pp. 73–78*	**RS** Guided Reading Strategy 13.1 **RS** Graphic Organizer Activity 13: Postwar Conflicts **IC** Literature Reading 13: Justice or Political and Ethnic Bias? **E** Hands-On History Activity: Labor Unions in Your Region **E** Creative Teaching Strategy: Interrupted Film Lesson
SECTION 2 **The Republicans in Power** pp. 397–402	★ Describe how Republican policies encouraged economic growth. ★ Evaluate the positive and negative effects of the Harding administration's pro-business policies. ★ Analyze why the movement to pass the Equal Rights Amendment failed. ★ Explain how the Republican Party overcame the political scandals of the Harding administration. ★ Discuss the issues that affected the outcome of the 1928 presidential election.	**Regular** 2 days **Block Scheduling** 1 day *Block Scheduling Handbook with Team Teaching Strategies, pp. 73–78*	**RS** Guided Reading Strategy 13.2 **SM** Geography Activity 13: The Republican Decade **PS** Primary Source Reading 13: A Scandalous Administration
SECTION 3 **A Nation Divided** pp. 403–09	★ Explain why many Americans supported the Ku Klux Klan and what factors led to a decline in that support. ★ Identify the actions that African Americans took to combat discrimination and violence. ★ Discuss why many Americans demanded restrictions on immigration. ★ State why Mexican immigration increased during the 1920s. ★ Recount the actions that American Indians took to protect their land.	**Regular** 2 days **Block Scheduling** 1 day *Block Scheduling Handbook with Team Teaching Strategies, pp. 73–78*	**RS** Guided Reading Strategy 13.3 **PS** Biography Reading 13: A. Philip Randolph

Chapter Resource Key

PS Primary Sources	**REV** Review	Video
RS Reading Support	**ELL** Reinforcement and English Language Learners	Internet
IC Interdisciplinary Connections		Holt Presentation Maker Using Microsoft® PowerPoint®
E Enrichment	Transparencies	
SM Skills Mastery	CD-ROM	
A Assessment	Music	

One-Stop Planner CD-ROM

See the *One-Stop Planner* for a complete list of additional resources for students and teachers.

One-Stop Planner CD-ROM

It's easy to plan lessons, select resources, and print out materials for your students when you use the *One-Stop Planner CD-ROM with Test Generator.*

Technology Resources

 One-Stop Planner, Lesson 13.1

 Holt Researcher: American History CD-ROM

 Homework Practice Online

 One-Stop Planner, Lesson 13.2

 CNN Presents America: Modern Times Segment: Harding's Inauguration

Holt Researcher: American History CD-ROM

Homework Practice Online

 One-Stop Planner, Lesson 13.3

 The American Nation Video Program Segment: A Nation of Immigrants; Teacher's Guide, pp. 153–57

 Holt Researcher: American History CD-ROM

 Homework Practice Online

 HRW Go site

Reinforcement, Review, and Assessment

REV Section 1 Review, p. 396
A Daily Quiz 13.1
ELL Main Idea Activity 13.1
ELL English Audio Summary 13.1
ELL Spanish Audio Summary 13.1

REV Section 2 Review, p. 402
A Daily Quiz 13.2
ELL Main Idea Activity 13.2
ELL English Audio Summary 13.2
ELL Spanish Audio Summary 13.2

REV Section 3 Review, p. 409
A Daily Quiz 13.3
ELL Main Idea Activity 13.3
ELL English Audio Summary 13.3
ELL Spanish Audio Summary 13.3

⊡ internet connect

HRW ONLINE RESOURCES
GO TO: go.hrw.com
Then type in a keyword.

TEACHER HOME PAGE
KEYWORD: SE3 Teacher

CHAPTER INTERNET ACTIVITIES
KEYWORD: SE3 AN13
Choose an activity to:
- research the Bolshevik revolution and write a radio broadcast.
- write a report on the Sacco and Vanzetti case.
- learn about the life and thought of Marcus Garvey and W. E. B. Du Bois and write a biography.

CHAPTER ENRICHMENT LINKS
KEYWORD: SE3 CH13

ONLINE ASSESSMENT
Homework Practice
KEYWORD: SE3 HP13

Standardized Test Prep
KEYWORD: SE3 STP13

Rubrics
KEYWORD: SS Rubrics

ONLINE MAPS, CHARTS, AND GRAPHS
KEYWORD: SE3 MCG
- The African American Population, 1900–1950

CONTENT UPDATES
KEYWORD: SS Content Updates

HOLT PRESENTATION MAKER
KEYWORD: SE3 PPT13

ONLINE READING SUPPORT
KEYWORD: SS Strategies

CURRENT EVENTS
KEYWORD: S3 Current Events

Meeting Individual Needs

Ability Levels

Level 1 Basic-level activities designed for all students encountering new material

Level 2 Intermediate-level activities designed for average students

Level 3 Challenging activities designed for honors and gifted-and-talented students

English Language Learners Activities that address the needs of students with Limited English Proficiency

Chapter Review and Assessment

 Global Skill Builder CD-ROM

HRW Go site

REV **Chapter 13 Tutorial for Students, Parents, Mentors, and Peers**

REV **Chapter 13 Review, pp. 410–11**

Chapter 13 Test Generator (on the One-Stop Planner)

A **Chapter 13 Test (Form A or B)**

A **Alternative Assessment Handbook**

A **Chapter 13 Test for English Language Learners and Special-Needs Students**

Build on What You Know

Ask students to answer the following questions.

How might demobilization have affected the daily lives of many Americans?

Consider:

• the large numbers of women and African Americans who worked in factories during the war

• the impact of heavy postwar consumer spending

How might oppressed groups have reacted to discrimination or unfair working conditions?

Consider:

• the actions taken by workers in response to bad working conditions

• the organizations created by various minority groups

---

exploring the time line

AMERICAN EVENTS

internet connect
go.hrw.com

TOPIC: Sacco and Vanzetti
GO TO: go.hrw.com
KEYWORD: SE3 AN13

Have students access the Internet through the HRW Go site to conduct research on the Sacco and Vanzetti case. Ask each student to write a report summarizing the evidence and supporting the guilt or innocence of the men.

CHAPTER 13

1919–1929

A Turbulent Decade

Harding campaign button

1921
Business and Finance
An economic recession caused by demobilization leads to 20,000 business failures.

1920
Politics
Warren G. Harding is elected president of the United States by the largest popular majority in U.S. history to date.

1921
Daily Life
A race riot erupts in Tulsa, Oklahoma, resulting in the deaths of at least 30 people.

1922
Business and Finance
Charles Dawes, head of the Bureau of the Budget, turns the federal government's annual deficit into a surplus.

THE GRANGER COLLECTION, NEW YORK

Teapot Dome political cartoon

1924
Politics
The Teapot Dome scandal is exposed.

1919 — **1921** — **1923**

1919
Daily Life
Looting and mob violence erupt in Boston as the city's police force goes on strike.

A soldier guards a store during the Boston police strike.

1922
The Arts
Sinclair Lewis publishes *Babbit,* a novel that criticizes middle-class conservatism and conformity.

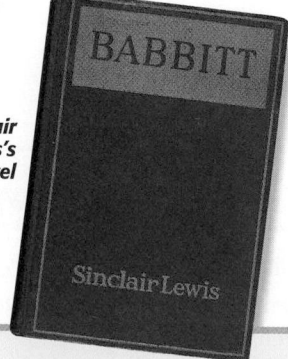

BABBITT

Sinclair Lewis

Sinclair Lewis's novel

Build on What You Know

World War I affected the daily lives of many Americans. The government mobilized industry to produce necessary goods for U.S. soldiers and their allies, who finally achieved victory against the Central Powers in 1918. During the war the U.S. government suppressed political protests. In this chapter you will learn about the changes in American life after the war. Although prosperity returned to the United States, economic benefits and political freedom were not enjoyed by everyone living there.

What's Your Opinion?

To help students create their Themes Journal entries, provide the following examples of appropriate agree/disagree statements.

Citizenship

Agree During World War I many Americans tried to suppress the opinions of those who voiced opposition to the war or criticized the government's actions.

Disagree Regardless of the threats to their personal safety, pacifists and socialists expressed their opposition to World War I.

Economics

Agree The U.S. government's pro-business policies during the Second Industrial Revolution created inequalities in wealth and led to worker dissatisfaction.

Disagree The implementation of Henry Clay's American System created prosperity in all regions of the country.

Culture

Agree Despite fighting in the Civil War, African Americans suffered from discrimination after the war ended.

Disagree Particularly since the Civil War, women and minorities have worked to obtain equal rights and to end discrimination.

Ku Klux Klan publication

Ben Shahn's painting of Sacco and Vanzetti on trial

SHAHN, BEN. *BARTOLOMEO VANZETTI AND NICOLA SACCO* (1931-1932). Estate of Ben Shahn/Licensed by VAGA, New York, NY

1925
Daily Life
More than 40,000 march in a Ku Klux Klan parade in Washington, D.C.

1925
The Arts
The *Grand Ole Opry* broadcasts its first performance over radio station WSM in Nashville, Tennessee.

1927
Politics
Italian immigrants Nicola Sacco and Bartolomeo Vanzetti are executed after being convicted of murder.

1927
Science and Technology
John Daniel Rust invents the mechanical cotton picker.

1928
World Events
Scottish doctor Alexander Fleming discovers penicillin, the first antibiotic.

1929
Daily Life
Eastman Kodak introduces 16 mm motion picture cameras and projectors for home use.

1929
The Arts
The Museum of Modern Art opens in New York City.

| 1925 | 1927 | 1929 |

1925
Business and Finance
The Pullman Company refuses to recognize the African American union founded by A. Philip Randolph.

1926
Science and Technology
Thomas Hunt Morgan proves a theory of heredity and locates genes in the chromosomes of fruit flies.

1926
Business and Finance
Congress passes the Revenue Act, reducing taxes for the wealthiest Americans.

1929
Science and Technology
Construction of the Empire State Building begins.

Members of A. Philip Randolph's union

The Empire State Building under construction

What's Your Opinion?

Themes Journal

Do you agree or disagree with the following statements? Support your point of view in your journal.

Citizenship The fear of radicalism in the United States causes many Americans to sacrifice personal liberties for a sense of security.

Economics Government policies that encourage economic growth can also lead to social instability.

Culture Restrictions on immigration hurt a country more than they help in the long run.

exploring the time line

GLOBAL EVENTS

SCIENCE, TECHNOLOGY, AND SOCIETY

1928 ■ Alexander Fleming Discovers Penicillin. The development of penicillin to treat infections illustrates the importance of scientific cooperation. In 1928 Alexander Fleming accidentally discovered that the penicillin mold inhibited the growth of certain bacteria. As he was untrained in clinical medicine, he published a few papers on his findings and then moved on to other work. In 1938 two other scientists, Ernst Boris Chain and Howard Walter Florey, used Fleming's early research and portions of the penicillin mold from Fleming's lab to produce penicillin in a form that could be used in medicines. In 1945 all three men were awarded the Nobel Prize in physiology.

CRITICAL THINKING How might Fleming's earlier experiments have helped Chain and Florey develop penicillin as a medicine?

ANSWER: Students might suggest that Fleming's reports established that the penicillin mold inhibited the growth of some kinds of bacteria and helped the other men narrow and concentrate their experiments.

After completing Section 1, students should be able to:

OBJECTIVE 1 Discuss some of the economic outcomes of demobilization.

OBJECTIVE 2 Analyze the main causes of the strikes of 1919 and how most Americans reacted to the strikes.

OBJECTIVE 3 Explain what caused the public hysteria of the Red Scare.

OBJECTIVE 4 Recount why the Sacco and Vanzetti trial aroused public interest.

LET'S GET STARTED!

Have students read the What's Your Opinion? feature on the previous page. Then have students list developments they expect to read about in this chapter, based on the themes themselves. Compile a master list on the chalkboard from the responses of volunteers. Tell students that in Section 1 they will learn about the troubles American society faced after World War I.

SECTION 1 RESOURCES

REPRODUCIBLE

- ▶ Guided Reading Strategy 13.1
- ▶ Graphic Organizer Activity 13: Postwar Conflicts
- ▶ Literature Reading 13: Justice or Political and Ethnic Bias?

TECHNOLOGY

- ▶ One-Stop Planner, Lesson 13.1
- ▶ Holt Researcher: American History CD–ROM
- ▶ Homework Practice Online

REINFORCEMENT, REVIEW, AND ASSESSMENT

- ▶ Section 1 Review, p. 396
- ▶ Daily Quiz 13.1
- ▶ Main Idea Activity 13.1
- ▶ English Audio Summary 13.1
- ▶ Spanish Audio Summary 13.1

SECTION 1

READ TO DISCOVER

1. What were some of the economic outcomes of demobilization?
2. What were the main causes of the strikes of 1919, and how did most Americans react to the strikes?
3. What caused the public hysteria of the Red Scare?
4. Why did the Sacco and Vanzetti trial arouse public interest?

DEFINE

demobilization

IDENTIFY

Seattle general strike
Boston police strike
United Mine Workers strike
John L. Lewis
Red Scare
A. Mitchell Palmer
Palmer raids
Nicola Sacco
Bartolomeo Vanzetti

▶ WHY IT MATTERS TODAY

How U.S. military involvement overseas affects American society remains an issue today. Use or other **current events** sources to find out more about that issue. Record your findings in your journal.

CNNfyi.com

Postwar Troubles

EYEWITNESSES TO History

"We danced in the streets, embraced old women and pretty girls, swore blood brotherhood with soldiers . . . [and] reeled through the streets."

—Malcolm Cowley, *Exile's Return*

Literary critic Malcolm Cowley recalled the spirit of celebration many Americans had after hearing news of the end of World War I. The carefree spirit was short-lived, however. For many Americans, postwar life did not appear promising.

Veteran searching for work

Demobilization

The abrupt ending of World War I caught American industries by surprise. Factories and war-related industries had been operating at full capacity when the demand for military supplies suddenly dried up. The process of **demobilization**, or the transition from wartime to peacetime production levels, caused social and economic strain. The return of some 4.5 million soldiers to the workforce caused unemployment to rise and wages to fall. Meanwhile, wartime shortages left prices high.

To make room for the returning veterans, women were urged to give up their jobs. "The same patriotism which induced women to enter industry during the war should induce them to vacate their positions," declared the New York Labor Federation. Many women were forced out of their jobs. As a result, the percentage of women in the workforce in 1920 fell slightly below what it had been in 1910.

Americans who were worried about the impact of demobilization on their jobs also faced a skyrocketing cost of living. With peace at hand, consumers went on a spending spree. They made purchases they had put off during the war. The demand for goods outpaced supply, and prices soared. The cost of goods and services roughly doubled from 1914 to 1920.

Soon, however, this trend reversed. Prices fell when a brief but deep recession struck in 1920–21. Demobilization was one of the factors behind the recession. During the war millions of Americans had worked in defense industries. At war's end, however, the government canceled more than $2 billion in military contracts. Factories responded by cutting back production and laying off workers. By 1921 some 5 million workers—nearly 12 percent of the labor force—were unemployed. Even Americans with jobs suffered. "Working conditions . . . seemed harder than ever," reported one steelworker. "We were only paid forty-two cents an hour, and we worked like a mule."

The impact of demobilization extended beyond factory life. A farm crisis added to the nation's economic problems. Farmers had benefited from wartime markets in Europe. As European farm production revived, these markets dried up, and farm prices fell. Cotton, for example, fell dramatically from 35 cents per pound

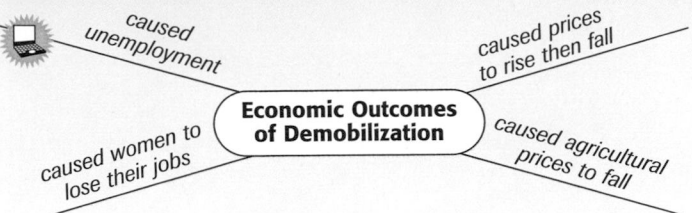
in 1919 to 16 cents a year later. Burdened with debt, hundreds of thousands of American farmers lost ownership of their land during the 1920s.

✔ **READING CHECK: Summarizing** How did demobilization affect male and female workers? Male workers had trouble finding work; female workers were forced to give their jobs up to men.

Labor Strife

Many workers protested in response to the difficulties of demobilization. They demanded higher wages and shorter work hours. When management ignored labor's pleas, many workers went on strike. More than 3,600 work stoppages—involving some 4 million workers—took place in 1919 alone.

The Seattle general strike. The first major strike of 1919 occurred when some 35,000 shipyard workers in Seattle walked off the job. They demanded higher wages and shorter hours. Some 110 local unions joined the workers. The **Seattle general strike** began on February 6 at 10:00 A.M. Some 60,000 workers left their jobs to participate in the strike, which was extremely well organized. "It was," declared one shipyard worker, "the most beautiful thing I [had] ever seen!" The General Strike Committee set up 21 community kitchens to feed strikers. The committee made arrangements for milk delivery to people caring for children.

The strike occurred without a single incident of violence. Nevertheless, city officials and business leaders expressed alarm. Newspapers blamed immigrants for the strike and called the strikers "muddle-headed foreigners." The strikers came under increased public pressure to go back to work. After five days they ended the strike without winning any of their demands.

The strike had been peaceful. However, antilabor forces tried to convince the public that Seattle had been on the brink of a revolution similar to Russia's Bolshevik Revolution. Seattle mayor Ole Hanson told the national press, "Revolution . . . doesn't need violence. The general strike . . . is of itself the weapon of revolution." Many people believed these charges. In the end, the strike helped turn public opinion against organized labor.

The Boston police strike. In September 1919 another strike, the **Boston police strike**, further inflamed antilabor sentiments. The Boston police officers had recently formed a union to seek better pay and working conditions. Officers in other cities had unionized without incident. However, Boston's police commissioner, Edwin Curtis, refused to recognize the union. Instead, he fired 19 officers for engaging in union activities. In response, some 75 percent of the Boston police force went on strike. Public order in the city quickly collapsed. Journalist William Allen White described the first night of the strike:

As the nation's economy suffered after World War I, American farmers experienced a severe crisis. Publications such as this one chronicled farmers' experiences.

INTERPRETING THE VISUAL RECORD

Seattle general strike. With many of the city services shut down during the Seattle general strike, organizers established community kitchens and provided some limited services. *What information does this photograph offer about the organization of the strikers?*

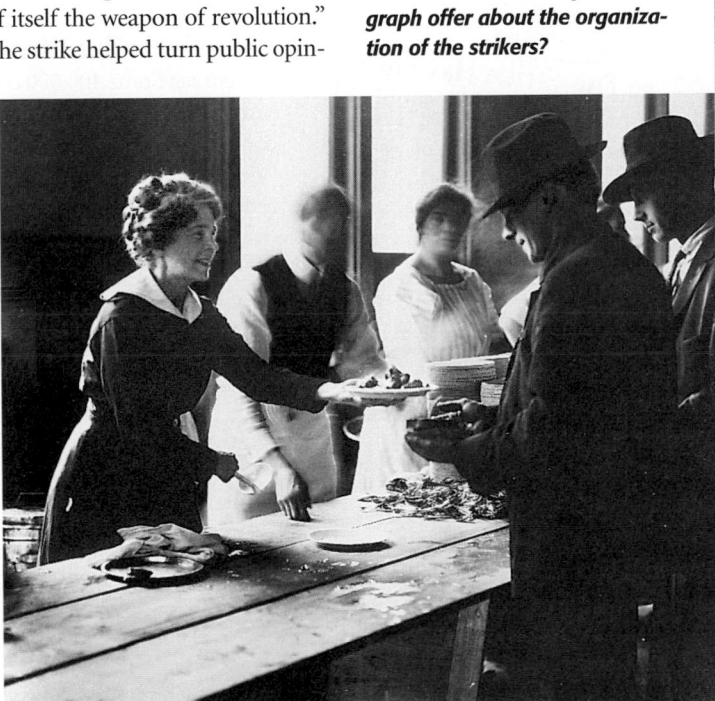

TEACH OBJECTIVE 2

LEVEL 1: Tell students to imagine that it is 1919 and that they are newspaper reporters. Pair students and have each pair write headlines reporting the main causes of the strikes of 1919 and the public response to the strikes. *(Pairs should mention the following: causes—inflation, low wages, and long work hours; reactions—violence, work loss, and accusations of radicalism and communism.)* Ask volunteers to present and explain their headlines to the class.
English Language Learners, Cooperative Learning

LEVEL 2: Tell students to imagine that it is 1919 and that they are newspaper reporters who have been assigned to cover the strikes. Have each student choose one of the strikes discussed in the textbook and write a short article analyzing the causes of the strike and public reaction to it. *(See the Level 1 lesson for the correct causes and reactions.)* Have volunteers read their articles to the class. Students may wish to include their articles in their portfolios.

HISTORY MAKERS SPEAK

Emma Goldman in *Red Emma Speaks*

An Anarchist Explains.
Emma Goldman wrote many essays expressing her views on life and society. Goldman championed the idea that people should be free to work for the love of the work itself, not simply for wages. A worker should be "one to whom the making of a table, the building of a house, or the tilling of the soil is . . . the result of inspiration, of intense longing, and deep interest in work as a creative force."

CRITICAL THINKING Given Goldman's emphasis on work as a personal creative endeavor, what might she have said about factory work?

ANSWER: Students might suggest that Goldman might have criticized factory work as repetitive and unfulfilling.

INTERPRETING THE VISUAL RECORD

Strikes. During the Boston police strike, civilians took over traffic control and other public-safety jobs. *How does this photograph suggest that this civilian is helping to preserve public safety during the strike?*

VISUAL RECORD ANSWER

Students might note that she is directing traffic.

During the Pittsburgh steel strike, newspapers such as the Pittsburgh Chronicle Telegraph urged strikers to go back to work.

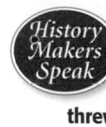

History Makers Speak

"The devil was loose in Boston. . . . Little knots of boys and young men began wandering through the streets. . . . By midnight, the . . . crowds had formed one raging mob, a drunken, noisy, irresponsible mob. . . . Someone threw a loose paving stone through a store window about one o'clock. The tension snapped. . . . By two o'clock, looting had begun."

—William Allen White, quoted in *1919: America's Loss of Innocence,* by Eliot Asinof

After two nights of violence, Governor Calvin Coolidge called in the state militia. Boston's newspapers denounced strikers as "agents of Lenin" and the strike as a "Bolshevist nightmare." Public opinion also came out firmly against the strike. Recognizing that their cause was doomed, the police voted unanimously to return to work. Commissioner Curtis refused to reinstate the officers. Instead, he hired a new force made up of unemployed veterans. Union sympathizers protested. Unmoved, Coolidge backed the commissioner. He proclaimed that "there is no right to strike against the public safety by anybody, anywhere, any time."

The steel strike. Two weeks after the Boston strike, some 365,000 steelworkers in western Pennsylvania—many of them immigrants—walked off the job. This action began the steel strike of 1919. The strikers demanded recognition of their union and protested low wages and long working hours. The massive walkout threatened to shut down the steel industry.

Having fought efforts to unionize steelworkers for years, the major steel companies did everything in their power to break the strike. To divide labor along ethnic lines, they portrayed foreign workers as radicals and called on "loyal" Americans to return to work. The steel companies also brought in thousands of workers—including African Americans and Mexicans—to replace the strikers.

The steel companies enlisted the aid of police officers to pressure the strikers and even hired armed thugs to intimidate them. Strikers were jailed, beaten, or shot. Faced with such tactics, union leaders called off the strike on January 9, 1920.

The United Mine Workers strike. The last major strike of 1919 erupted in November. Some 400,000 coal miners walked out of the mines in the **United Mine Workers strike.** Miners were protesting the continued enforcement of wartime contracts that kept workers' pay fixed at 1917 rates despite increases in consumer prices. Some members of the United Mine Workers (UMW) demanded a 50 percent pay increase, a five-day workweek, and a six-hour workday.

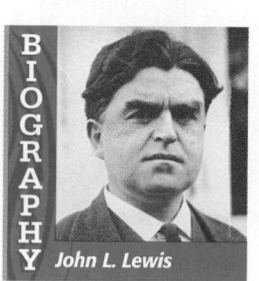

BIOGRAPHY

John L. Lewis

The strike was organized by **John L. Lewis**, the newly elected president of the UMW. Born in 1880, Lewis was 39 years old and had just gained control of the UMW when the strike was called on November 1, 1919. It was the first strike he organized.

Lewis was well acquainted with the life and concerns of miners and unionists. He was raised in an Iowa mining family. His father spent his days working in the coal pits and his nights organizing miners in the Knights of Labor union. Lewis briefly attended school, then followed in his father's footsteps. He was working in the mines by the age of 15. Lewis soon began to urge fellow workers to demand better and safer working

LEVEL 3: Have each student write a short imaginary dialogue between a striking worker and a member of the public or an official who opposes the strike. The dialogue should include the main reasons for the strike as well as the reaction of the person opposing the strike. *(See the Level 1 lesson for the correct causes and reactions.)* Students may wish to include the script for their dialogues in their portfolios.

TEACH OBJECTIVE 3

LEVEL 1: Have students study the political cartoon on this page. Then lead a discussion about the images depicted in the cartoon. Pair students and have each pair create two political cartoons that depict the causes of the public fears over the Red Scare. *(Cartoons should somehow reflect the fear of a Bolshevik revolution in the United States, the strikes of 1919, bomb scares in 1919, and the Palmer raids.)* Call on volunteers to display and explain their cartoons to the class. **English Language Learners, Cooperative Learning**

LEVEL 2: Organize students into small groups. Have each group write a short play summarizing the events of the Red Scare and capturing the public fears that resulted from those events. *(See the Level 1 lesson for the correct causes.)* Have volunteers perform their plays for the class. **Cooperative Learning**

---

conditions. By 1906 he had been elected a representative to the UMW national convention. In 1911 American Federation of Labor founder Samuel Gompers recruited Lewis to become a field representative who would organize mine workers.

Lewis's experience as a miner and union organizer served him well during the 1919 strike. President Woodrow Wilson condemned the strike, which violated the union's wartime agreement not to strike, as a "grave moral and legal wrong." After Wilson ordered an injunction to halt the strike, Lewis declared the strike over. However, he quietly urged miners not to return to work. The strategy worked. On December 6, President Wilson designed a compromise package in which miners would receive a 14 percent wage increase. Lewis called off the strike, stating, "I will not fight my Government, the greatest government on earth." The UMW victory ensured Lewis's position as a national labor leader. Lewis continued to push for miners' concerns until his death in 1969.

As with most of the strikes of 1919, public opinion did not side with labor during the UMW strike. Despite his many patriotic appeals, Lewis was accused of having ties to Bolsheviks in Russia and of urging revolution within the United States.

✔ **READING CHECK: Categorizing** What tactics did antilabor forces and business leaders use to influence public opinion about the strikes of 1919?
They called the strikers unpatriotic and communists.

The Red Scare

The wave of strikes during 1919 scared many Americans. Although laborers primarily desired a fair deal, many Americans saw the labor unrest as proof of a coming workers' revolution. Fear that a Bolshevik revolution would erupt in the United States reached its height during the **Red Scare**. This was a period of anticommunist hysteria during 1919 and 1920.

The Red Scare in the United States was a response to the 1917 revolution in Russia. This revolution resulted in the establishment of a communist government based on Marxist teachings. Under communism, the Russian government owned and controlled all private property, including every industry and factory. In 1919 Russia's Bolshevik leader Vladimir Lenin established an organization called the Communist International. It was designed to encourage a worldwide communist revolution by overthrowing capitalism and free enterprise. The idea that communism might take hold in the United States was frightening to many Americans during 1919.

Marxists in America. Karl Marx's message of an unavoidable working-class revolution has been interpreted in many ways over time. It even won some support in the United States. Labor leader Eugene V. Debs and others formed the Marxist-inspired Socialist Party in 1901. In contrast to the revolutionary Marxism of the Communist Party, Debs's Socialist Party foresaw a peaceful transition to socialism by democratic means. Debs ran for president five times between 1900 and 1920. His

Research on the ROM

Free Find: John L. Lewis

After reading about John L. Lewis on the **Holt Researcher CD–ROM**, write a short essay explaining how his experiences helped him lead the United Mine Workers union.

THE GRANGER COLLECTION, NEW YORK

INTERPRETING POLITICAL CARTOONS

Red Scare. This cartoon entitled "Put Them Out & Keep Them Out" appeared in the *Philadelphia Inquirer* in 1919. ***What fears does this cartoon express?***

CITIZENSHIP

The Aftermath of the Red Scare. As the Red Scare died down in the mid-1920s, the battle against radicalism continued in quieter but sometimes more widespread ways. Some groups insisted that teachers take loyalty oaths and that textbooks "preach on every page a vivid love of America." In addition, corporations adopted the "American Plan," which was a pledge to maintain open shops. One business owner said, "You can hardly conceive of a more un-American, a more anti-American institution than the closed shop." Some businesses even used union spies and blacklists—lists of people who were union members—to maintain a nonunionized workforce.

ACTIVITY: Have each student choose a short passage from this chapter and rewrite it to represent "a vivid love of America."

POLITICAL CARTOON ANSWER
Students might suggest that the cartoon expresses fears of Bolshevism and anarchism infiltrating the United States.

LEVEL 3: Organize students into two groups and tell them to imagine that they are modern-day participants in a roundtable discussion entitled Public Fears over the Red Scare of 1919–20. Have one group act as historians and the other group act as facilitators and questioners. Have members of each group prepare notes to assist them in their specific roles, and then conduct the roundtable discussion. *(See the Level 1 lesson for the correct causes.)* **Cooperative Learning**

NOTE: To help students make meaningful connections between events in U.S. history and those in their own hometown, use the Chapter 13 **Hands-On History Activity**, Labor Unions in Your Region.

TEACH OBJECTIVE 4

LEVEL 1: Pair students and have each pair write a paragraph explaining why the trial of Sacco and Vanzetti aroused public interest. *(Pairs should note that American society was deeply divided over the trial. Some people believed that Sacco and Vanzetti deserved punishment for their views. Others believed that the pair had been condemned to death because they were immigrant radicals and not because of the evidence presented.)* Have volunteers read their paragraphs to the class. **English Language Learners, Cooperative Learning**

GOVERNMENT

The Palmer Raids. In the first months of his role as attorney general, A. Mitchell Palmer strongly defended individual rights. After he received a mail bomb, however, he became a leading figure in the war against radicals—a war that many felt abridged individual rights. The Palmer raids began in November 1919 and soon led many Americans to call for the deportation of the supposed radicals. Palmer himself indulged these calls. In December 1919 an army transport ship called the *Buford* ferried some 249 aliens to Finland, where officials loaded them on railroad cars and sent them to the Soviet Union.

CRITICAL THINKING Why might U.S. officials have ordered the supposed radicals to be sent to the Soviet Union?

ANSWER: Students might note that many radicals were suspected of Bolshevism. U.S. officials might have felt that the Soviet Union was an appropriate place for these radicals.

VISUAL RECORD ANSWER
(for p. 396)
Students might note that the signs call for boycotts and strikes and criticize the executioners.

Eugene V. Debs spread socialist political beliefs during his five bids for the presidency between 1900 and 1920.

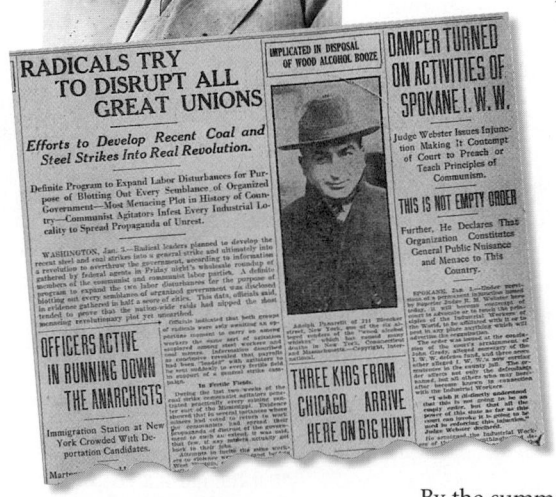

Attorney General A. Mitchell Palmer waged a public campaign against all perceived radicals.

Socialist Party platform called for the collective ownership of industry, which was to be achieved by nonviolent means. In the 1912 election Debs received about 900,000 votes.

When the Bolsheviks seized power in Russia in 1917, most American members of the Socialist Party joined Debs in refusing to support the violent overthrow of the government. A smaller number of American radicals did support the Bolsheviks. These Americans openly embraced Marx's revolutionary ideas. Some believed such a revolution should happen in the United States. Many Americans ignored differences between socialists and communists. After witnessing the massive strikes of 1919, many people believed that all radicals and labor activists were Bolshevik agents who wanted to overthrow the U.S. government. Some Americans believed that communists, or "Reds," were everywhere. Immigrants, particularly those involved in unions, came under great suspicion. Antiradical fears reached such heights that several elected members of the New York State Assembly were expelled because of their membership in the Socialist Party.

The Palmer raids. Many Americans interpreted a series of bomb scares in 1919 as justification for their antiradical fears. In April postal clerks discovered 36 bombs in the mail. These bombs were addressed to prominent citizens, including John D. Rockefeller, Justice Oliver Wendell Holmes of the Supreme Court, and Postmaster General Albert Burleson. Then, less than one month later, a bomb damaged the house of Attorney General **A. Mitchell Palmer.** The bomber, an Italian anarchist, died in the blast.

The bomb scares intensified the Red Scare hysteria. Newspapers began demanding harsh action against radicals. Hoping to further his presidential ambitions, Attorney General Palmer launched an anticommunist crusade. He created a special government office to gather information on radical activities. Palmer placed J. Edgar Hoover, future head of the Federal Bureau of Investigation, in charge.

Palmer's most dramatic action was a series of raids to capture alleged radicals. The **Palmer raids** began in November 1919. They peaked on January 2, 1920, when federal officials arrested thousands of suspected radicals in 33 cities nationwide. Although the government claimed that radicals were "armed to the teeth," just three pistols were seized during the raids.

Most of those arrested were poor immigrants who had recently arrived in the country. In most cases, there was no real evidence against them. Nevertheless, hundreds of foreigners suspected of radical activities were deported. Emma Goldman, a noted feminist, writer, and speaker, was among the deportees.

By the summer of 1920 public hysteria over radicalism died down. The predictions that a communist revolution was close at hand proved unfounded. Furthermore, many Americans had never supported the witch-hunting tactics employed by the anticommunist crusaders.

✔ **READING CHECK: Identifying Cause and Effect** What were the causes and effects of the Red Scare? causes—Bolshevik revolution, labor strikes, and mail bomb scares; effects—more racial hatred, mistrust of foreigners, Palmer raids on suspected radicals

LEVELS 2 AND 3: Tell students to imagine that it is 1927 and that they are newspaper editors after the execution of Sacco and Vanzetti. Have each student write a short editorial that explains the public interest in the trial of Sacco and Vanzetti. (*See the Level 1 lesson for the correct reasons.*) Based on the evidence presented in this chapter, students should explain to what extent or in what ways, if any, the Sacco and Vanzetti trial should be considered in the context of the Red Scare and hostility toward immigrants.

HOMEWORK *Tell students to read the quotation by John Dos Passos on the following page. Have each student create a collage to illustrate the meaning of his observation in the historical context discussed in this section.*

SPOTLIGHT
on Anarchists in Film

Have each student view a movie that portrays anarchist groups or individuals. Tell students to write a short analysis of the film's depiction of anarchists. **Block Scheduling**

NOTE: For an additional teaching idea, see the Chapter 13 interrupted film lesson in the **Creative Teaching Strategies** handbook.

Skill-Building Strategies

Evaluating News Stories

News stories are an extremely important resource for historians. Different types of news media contain an enormous amount of information that historians access regularly to help them create their accounts of the past. News stories, however, possess certain advantages and disadvantages as historical sources.

Although the print media frequently provide news coverage that is thorough and analytically sophisticated, this coverage lacks the sense of immediacy that is conveyed through the broadcast media. In contrast, radio and television reports often sacrifice detail and in-depth analysis of issues to provide news coverage that is as current as possible. In any case, all forms of news media must be examined carefully for fairness and accuracy in their presentation of events.

How to Evaluate a News Story

1. **Become familiar with the source.** First, determine whether the news story is presented through broadcast media or through print media. Then, if possible, find out about the historical background of the story's creator and the story's intended audience.

2. **Assess the story's coverage of events.** As you study the story, determine whether it covers its subject in sufficient depth. Check to see if it includes adequate background information and explores the possible consequences of events.

3. **Assess the fairness and accuracy of the reporting.** Examine the story carefully for fairness and accuracy in its presentation of events. Determine whether the reporting "sticks to the facts," explains any differing points of view in a balanced way, or displays any recognizable biases of its own.

4. **Put the information to use.** If possible, compare the story with other sources that address the same subject. Then use the results of your analysis, along with your knowledge of the historical period, to form generalizations and draw conclusions.

Applying the Skill

Examine the following excerpt from a news story that appeared in the *Atlanta Constitution* on August 23, 1927.

❝State Prison, Charlestown, Mass.—Nicola Sacco and Bartolomeo Vanzetti were put to death today.

They went to the embrace of the electric chair unswerving in the avowal of their innocence.

They paid with their lives for the murder of a paymaster and his guard at South Braintree [Massachusetts] seven years ago.

As the heavy voltage of electricity was shot through their bodies, bayoneted guards surrounded the ancient prison for blocks.

In cities on three continents millions awaited word of their death, many of them convinced that the two were executed for their political beliefs, not for the South Braintree murders.❞

Practicing the Skill

Use the excerpt above to answer the following questions.
1. Does this excerpt cover its subject in sufficient depth?
2. Is the reporting in the excerpt fair and accurate? What biases, if any, does it display?
3. How does the excerpt contribute to your understanding of the Red Scare?

An Urgent Appeal. People across the United States and in Europe protested the decision in the Sacco and Vanzetti case. Government officials from France, Germany, Great Britain, and Italy sent pleas for a new trial. Anatole France, a well-known French author, published an appeal to the "People of the United States." He wrote, "Save Sacco and Vanzetti. Save them for your honor, for the honor of your children, and for generations unborn."

CRITICAL THINKING Why might France have argued that saving Sacco and Vanzetti would save American honor?

ANSWER: Students might suggest that he meant that U.S. citizens would be dishonored by executing men who had not, in the opinion of many, been given a fair trial.

SKILL-BUILDING STRATEGIES ANSWERS
Practicing the Skill
1. The excerpt contains little background information about the crime or Sacco and Vanzetti's political beliefs.

2. It seems to stick to the facts of the execution, the prisoners' claims of innocence, and the public's opinions.

3. It expresses certain bare facts and also implies that officials expected some violent action during the execution, perhaps by the prisoners' radical supporters.

Sacco and Vanzetti

Although the Red Scare passed, hostility toward foreigners and radicals persisted. One of the most sensational trials of the 1920s involved two Italian immigrants who were convicted of murder and sentenced to death. Although both were anarchists, they lived fairly quiet lives. **Nicola Sacco** was a shoemaker, and **Bartolomeo Vanzetti** peddled fish from a pushcart. Sacco and Vanzetti were charged with the murders of a paymaster and a guard during a 1920 payroll robbery outside a shoe factory near Boston. Upon arrest, the police found the men armed with pistols. After an intense interrogation, the two were charged with murder.

REVIEW

Have students complete the **Section 1 Review** on p. 396.

ASSESS

Have students complete **Daily Quiz 13.1.** As **Alternative Assessment,** you may want to use the political cartoons or editorial in this section's lessons.

RETEACH

Have students complete **Main Idea Activity for English Language Learners and Special-Needs Students 13.1.** Then organize students into triads. Have each triad create a detailed outline of Section 1. Display triads' outlines around the classroom and ask students to examine them. Have each student note the topics or areas that are still confusing or unclear. Ask volunteers to share their topics or areas and conduct a brief discussion to correct the misunderstandings.
English Language Learners, Cooperative Learning

EXTEND

Organize the class into small groups. Have groups gather information about the Sacco and Vanzetti trial, the artifacts of the trial, and commentary on the trial during the 1920s. Have each group organize and present a multimedia presentation on the Sacco and Vanzetti case. Students may want to include the scripts of their presentations in their portfolios.
Cooperative Learning, Block Scheduling

INTERPRETING THE VISUAL RECORD

Sacco and Vanzetti. The trial and execution of Sacco and Vanzetti divided liberals and conservatives during the 1920s. *How do the picket signs reflect the views of the supporters of Sacco and Vanzetti?*

Sacco and Vanzetti were tried before Judge Webster Thayer, who was known for his strong dislike of radicals. The immigrants' radical political views and their avoidance of military service in 1917 helped turn the trial against them. Eyewitnesses who could offer alibis for Sacco and Vanzetti were dismissed. The jury returned a guilty verdict. Judge Thayer sentenced the two to death. He ended the trial with a bold statement.

History Makers Speak

❝This man [Vanzetti], although he may not actually have committed the crime attributed to him, is nevertheless morally culpable [guilty], because he is an enemy of our existing institutions. . . . The defendant's ideals are cognate [associated] with crime.❞

—Judge Thayer, quoted in *The Year the World Went Mad,* by Allen Churchill

The verdict outraged defenders of civil liberties. They argued that the two men had been convicted not because of the evidence presented but because they were immigrants and radicals. The verdict and subsequent appeals drew worldwide attention. In Paris, New York City, and elsewhere, thousands of people marched in protest. All pleas for a new trial failed. On August 23, 1927, Sacco and Vanzetti were executed. Many Americans believed that radicals like Sacco and Vanzetti deserved to be punished for their views. Others saw them as heroes. Some recently discovered evidence indicates that at least one of the men probably was involved in the crime. What remains clear, however, is that antiradical views severely tainted the trial. The case reflected the deep divisions tearing at American society in the postwar era. As American novelist John Dos Passos declared after the execution, "We are two nations."

✔ **READING CHECK: Contrasting** Who supported Sacco and Vanzetti and who did not?
Labor leaders and radical socialists supported them; people frightened by the Red Scare and antiradicalists opposed them.

SECTION 1 REVIEW

1. Define and explain:
demobilization

2. Identify and explain:
Seattle general strike
Boston police strike
United Mine Workers strike
John L. Lewis
Red Scare
A. Mitchell Palmer
Palmer raids
Nicola Sacco
Bartolomeo Vanzetti

3. Identifying Cause and Effect Copy the graphic organizer below. Use it to explain the causes of the 1919 strikes and public reaction to them.

Causes of 1919 Strikes

↓

Strikes

↓

Public Reaction

4. Finding the Main Idea

a. How did the process of demobilization alter the lives of many women, factory workers, and farmers?

b. What impact did Socialist Party candidate Eugene V. Debs have on American society?

c. How did the political climate of the Red Scare influence the results of the Sacco and Vanzetti case? What effect did the trial's verdict have on public opinion?

5. Writing and Critical Thinking

Analyzing Information Write a news article reporting on how international political events and postwar domestic life in the United States led to the mounting hysteria associated with the Red Scare.

Consider:
- the events in Russia between 1917 and 1919
- the role of socialists and communists in U.S. political life
- labor unrest of 1919

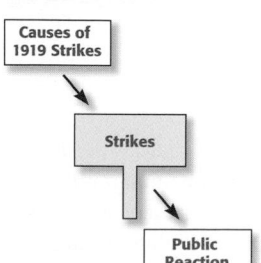
Homework Practice Online
keyword: SE3 HP13

SECTION 2

After completing Section 2, students should be able to:

OBJECTIVE 1 Describe how Republican policies encouraged economic growth.

OBJECTIVE 2 Evaluate the positive and negative effects of the Harding administration's pro-business policies.

OBJECTIVE 3 Analyze why the movement to pass the Equal Rights Amendment failed.

OBJECTIVE 4 Explain how the Republican Party overcame the political scandals of the Harding administration.

OBJECTIVE 5 Discuss the issues that affected the outcome of the 1928 presidential election.

LET'S GET STARTED!

Write the following question on the chalkboard: *If you had been running for president in 1920, what platform would you have adopted to win?* Have students respond to the question in writing, using the information from Section 1. Tell students that in Section 2 they will learn about Republican policies during the 1920s.

SECTION 2

READ TO DISCOVER

1. How did Republican policies encourage economic growth in the 1920s?
2. How did the Harding administration's pro-business policies affect the U.S. economy?
3. Why did the movement to pass the Equal Rights Amendment fail?
4. How did the Republican Party overcome the political scandals of the Harding administration?
5. What issues affected the outcome of the 1928 presidential election?

DEFINE

mergers
feminists

IDENTIFY

Warren G. Harding
Andrew Mellon
Charles Dawes
Fordney-McCumber Tariff Act
American Plan
Equal Rights Amendment
Mary Anderson
Teapot Dome scandal
Albert Fall
Calvin Coolidge
Alfred E. Smith

WHY IT MATTERS TODAY

U.S. presidential candidates continue to make pro-business campaign pledges. Use **CNNfyi.com** or other **current events** sources to study examples of those types of political pledges in recent U.S. presidential campaigns. Record your findings in your journal.

CNNfyi.com

The Republicans in Power

EYEWITNESSES TO History

"Keep Warren [G. Harding] at home. Don't let him make any speeches. If he goes out on a tour somebody's sure to ask him questions, and Warren's just the sort of . . . fool that will try to answer them."

—Boies Penrose, quoted in *The Perils of Prosperity, 1914-32*, by William E. Leuchtenburg

Harding campaign sign

Pennsylvania Republican political boss Boies (BOYZ) Penrose gave advice to party leaders after the relatively unknown Ohio senator Warren G. Harding was nominated as the Republican presidential candidate for the 1920 election. Penrose and the rest of the Republican Party were confident that their party would win the election. Strikes and the Democrats' preoccupation with the League of Nations had characterized the previous two years. The Republican Party leaders, therefore, believed they had a sure shot at the presidency no matter who ran.

The Election of 1920

Seeking a presidential candidate with broad appeal, Republican Party leaders nominated **Warren G. Harding**. While many party members thought Senator Harding was friendly and looked presidential, he lacked Woodrow Wilson's intelligence. Confident of their chances to win the election, the Republican leaders did not feel their candidate needed to be an intellectual genius.

Harding ran on a pro-business platform that promised tax revision, higher tariffs, limits on immigration, and some aid to farmers. What pleased war-weary voters the most, however, was Harding's call for a return to "normalcy." "America's present need is not heroics but healing, not nostrums [false cures] but normalcy, not revolution but restoration," he declared. In contrast, the Democratic candidate, Governor James M. Cox, also from Ohio, bowed to pressure from President Wilson and focused on the League of Nations during his campaign.

Suffering from falling crop prices, the nation's farmers rallied behind Harding. Many middle-class citizens, tired of labor strikes and high taxes, also voted Republican. Harding won the election of 1920 by a greater majority of the popular vote than any previous candidate. He received 16 million votes, about 60 percent of the popular vote, and 404 electoral votes to Cox's 127. "It wasn't a landslide," suggested Joseph Tumulty. "It was an earthquake."

Harding's Pro-Business Administration

President Harding's administration introduced many policy changes. Harding's primary goal was providing "less government in business and more business in government." His cabinet included such successful business leaders as Secretary of

SECTION 2 RESOURCES

REPRODUCIBLE

▶ Guided Reading Strategy 13.2
▶ Geography Activity 13: The Republican Decade
▶ Primary Source Reading 13: A Scandalous Administration

TECHNOLOGY

▶ One-Stop Planner, Lesson 13.2
▶ **CNN** Presents America: Modern Times Segment: Harding's Inauguration
▶ Holt Researcher: American History CD-ROM
▶ Homework Practice Online

REINFORCEMENT, REVIEW, AND ASSESSMENT

▶ Section 2 Review, p. 402
▶ Daily Quiz 13.2
▶ Main Idea Activity 13.2
▶ English Audio Summary 13.2
▶ Spanish Audio Summary 13.2

TEACH OBJECTIVES 1 AND 2

LEVEL 1: Pair students and copy the graphic organizer at right on the chalkboard, omitting the italicized answers. Have each pair complete the graphic organizer. Ask volunteers for their answers. To conclude, lead a discussion on Republican economic policies and the positive and negative consequences of those pro-business policies.

English Language Learners, Cooperative Learning

REPUBLICAN POLICIES TO ENCOURAGE ECONOMIC GROWTH

To reduce debt:
1. *cuts in government spending*
2. *the Fordney-McCumber Tariff*

To promote economic growth:
tax cut for the wealthy

POSITIVE AND NEGATIVE EFFECTS OF REPUBLICAN POLICIES

Positive effects:
1. *boom in industry*
2. *economic growth*

Negative effects:
1. *mergers*
2. *continuing struggles for workers who did not share in prosperity*
3. *continuing struggles for farmers*
4. *continuing struggles for organized labor as the government and courts tried to roll back labor gains*

HISTORY MAKERS SPEAK

Warren G. Harding in *His Speech of Acceptance Upon his Nomination for the Presidency*

Harding and Industry.
Warren G. Harding gave an acceptance speech when he was formally nominated as the Republican candidate for president. Harding called for cooperation between industry and laborers and referred to his prepolitical work experience, saying, "I want the employers in industry to understand the aspirations, the convictions, the yearnings of the millions of American wage-earners, and I want the wage-earners to understand the problems, the anxieties, the obligations of management and capital, and all of them must understand their relationship to the people and their obligation to the republic. . . . I am speaking as one who has counted the contents of the pay envelope from the view-point of the earner as well as the employer."

CRITICAL THINKING Do you think that Harding's policies met his call for workplace cooperation? Why or why not?

ANSWER: Answers will vary. Students might suggest that his policies did little to help workers and offered industrialists more opportunities for higher profits.

⭐ Then and Now

The Free Market

The United States has historically operated under a free-market economic system. Consumers and business leaders, not government officials, decide what, how, and for whom goods are produced. However, some political groups such as the Progressive Party have supported the regulation of some business practices.

The Republican administrations of the 1920s created several policies to reduce progressive controls over U.S. business practices. They hoped to encourage an even more open free-market system. "Business should be unhampered and free," President Coolidge argued.

Today the push for a free market has become an international issue. During the 1990s many countries began lowering trade barriers and removing restrictions on free-market practices. Governments have established trade agreements to allow an easier flow of goods between countries. These efforts have expanded the free market and increased economic prosperity. However, many modern Americans, like the progressives before them, are concerned that unregulated businesses fail to benefit everyone. Some companies have used free-trade agreements to get around U.S. labor laws preventing sweatshop labor. These corporations have moved production to underdeveloped countries where they can find workers willing to work long hours for little pay.

Trucks ship goods from American-owned factories in Mexico.

the Treasury **Andrew Mellon** and Secretary of Commerce Herbert Hoover. These men believed that government should not interfere with the economy except to aid business.

The administration set two main economic goals: to reduce the national debt and to promote economic growth. Wartime spending had raised the national debt from some $1 billion in 1914 to more than $25 billion in 1919. As head of the Bureau of the Budget, **Charles Dawes** set out to eliminate debt by slashing spending. In 1922 he turned the government's annual budget deficit into a surplus, which would help reduce the national debt.

The Republican-led Congress further supported businesses by passing the **Fordney-McCumber Tariff Act** in 1922. The law pushed tariff rates on manufactured goods to an all-time high. This helped U.S. manufacturers by enabling them to keep prices high and increase profits.

To achieve the second goal—economic growth—Mellon proposed eliminating the high wartime taxes imposed on wealthy Americans. If "government takes away an unreasonable share," he argued, "the incentive [encouragement] to work is no longer there and slackening of effort is the result." He claimed that if taxes were lower the rich would have more money to invest and the economy would grow. Mellon argued that benefits would then trickle down to the middle and lower classes in the form of jobs and higher wages. In accordance with Mellon's proposal, Congress cut taxes for wealthy Americans during the 1920s.

By 1923 Harding's economic policy appeared to be working. The postwar slump was over. Unemployment was low, and most economic sectors had entered a period of tremendous growth.

✔ **READING CHECK: Making Generalizations** How did Republican policies contribute to the economic growth and prosperity of the 1920s? The Fordney-McCumber Tariff Act helped manufacturers increase profits. Lower taxes made more money available for investment in the economy.

The Effects of Republican Policies

President Harding's pro-business policies significantly affected the economy and the lives of many Americans. The availability of surplus capital from tax cuts caused industry to boom. More than 1,000 **mergers**—the combining of two or more companies—took place in this era. Businesses favored mergers because they brought greater efficiency and higher profits. By 1930 some 200 corporations owned nearly half of the nation's corporate wealth. With its favorable attitude toward business, the federal government encouraged this process of consolidation. The government also made little effort to enforce antitrust laws.

For the most part, workers did not share in the business prosperity of the 1920s. From 1923 to 1929, business profits increased some 60 percent. Over the same period workers' incomes grew by about 10 percent. Many

LEVELS 2 AND 3: Tell students to imagine that they are producing an educational filmstrip about Republican economic policies during the Harding administration and the positive and negative impact of those policies. (*See the graphic organizer on page 398 for the correct policies and their effects.*) Then pair students and have each pair create a frame-by-frame presentation of the information it would include in its filmstrip. Have students present their storyboards to the class.
Cooperative Learning

 HOMEWORK *Distribute Activity 13, The Republican Decade, from* **Geography Activities** *and have each student complete it.*

 TEACH OBJECTIVE 3

LEVEL 1: Conduct a brief discussion on the Equal Rights Amendment and why the movement to pass the amendment failed. Then pair students and have each pair use the information from the discussion to write a paragraph explaining why the amendment failed. (*Paragraphs should indicate that political divisions and dissensions caused the amendment to falter. Women who opposed the ERA believed that protective legislation regulating the hours and working conditions of women would be declared illegal if the amendment were passed.*) Have volunteers read their paragraphs to the class.
English Language Learners, Cooperative Learning

workers in so-called sick industries such as the textile industry faced pay cuts and unemployment.

Farmers also struggled. Although the Fordney-McCumber Tariff was intended to help agriculture as well as business, it brought little relief to farmers. The act levied high duties on imported farm products in an effort to boost American crop prices. However, farmers continued to face shrinking markets, low prices, high interest rates, and crushing debt.

Organized labor also suffered during the 1920s. The government and courts sought to roll back the labor gains of the Progressive Era. Federal courts, for example, upheld "yellow-dog contracts," which prevented workers from joining unions. Business leaders promoted a policy known as the **American Plan**, which supported union-free open shops. As a result, union membership shrank from a high of more than 5 million in 1920 to some 3.6 million in 1923.

Some businesses in the 1920s used time clocks like this one to record workers' hours.

✔ **READING CHECK: Comparing** How did Harding's pro-business policies affect businesses, workers, and farmers? They increased business profits, but only marginally helped workers and farmers.

New Directions for Women

Working conditions also became a divisive issue among women's rights activists, often called **feminists**. The Nineteenth Amendment had granted women the right to vote. However, it did not revolutionize U.S. politics as many Americans had hoped—or feared. The suffrage issue had unified women with a wide variety of political interests, but after its passage, that unity dissolved.

Many women who had joined the suffrage campaign now moved in different directions. Jane Addams pursued the cause of world peace through the Women's International League for Peace and Freedom. Carrie Chapman Catt and other former suffrage leaders formed the League of Women Voters. Its aim was to inform women about public issues and about candidates for office.

Divisions in the women's movement emerged in the debate over the **Equal Rights Amendment** (ERA). This was a constitutional amendment proposed to Congress in 1923 by Alice Paul of the National Woman's Party. The proposed amendment stated: "Men and women shall have equal rights throughout the United States and every place subject to its jurisdiction."

Equal rights for women seemed a desirable goal. However, Paul's amendment met opposition from many reformers, including women. During the Progressive Era, reformers had battled for legislation regulating the hours and the working conditions of female workers. **Mary Anderson**, director of the U.S. Women's Bureau, was one of the opponents of the ERA who feared that the amendment would make such legislation unconstitutional:

Female Labor Force, 1890–1930

Legend: Single / Married / Widowed/Divorced

(Bar graph: Percentage of Working Women, years 1890 and 1930)

Total Labor Force

1890: 17% Women, 83% Men
1930: 22% Women, 78% Men

(Pie charts labeled Women / Men)

Source: *Historical Statistics of the United States*

Interpreting Graphs Not only did the size of the female labor force grow by 1930, its makeup also changed. By 1930 some 30 percent of working women were married, up from just over 10 percent in 1890.

❓ **Skills Assessment** Women made up what percentage of the total labor force in 1890? in 1930?

CITIZENSHIP

Female Voters. Despite the newfound right to vote, guaranteed in the Nineteenth Amendment, many women did not exercise their political liberties during the 1920s. Those who did vote often followed familial preferences in terms of candidates or parties rather than developing their own independent selections. In part to disseminate information to female voters and in part to replace the National Woman Suffrage Association, Carrie Chapman Catt founded the League of Women Voters in 1920.

CRITICAL THINKING Why might many women have chosen to abstain from voting during the 1920s?

ANSWER: Students might suggest that some women did not want the right to vote and so did not exercise it once granted.

VISUAL RECORD ANSWER
Students might identify hazards such as congestion and air pollution.

GRAPH ANSWERS
17 percent in 1890; 22 percent in 1930

LEVELS 2 AND 3: Tell students to imagine that they belong to the editorial board of a women's magazine of the 1920s. As members of the board, they have decided to include articles in their magazine that articulate both positions on the passage of the Equal Rights Amendment (ERA). Tell half of the students in the class to write an editorial supporting the ERA and have the other half write an editorial opposing the ERA. *(See the Level 1 lesson for the correct reasons.)* Have volunteers read their editorials to the class. To conclude, conduct a brief discussion on why the amendment failed.

TEACH OBJECTIVE 4

LEVEL 1: Pair students and tell them to imagine that they are members of the Republican Party's Platform Committee prior to the party's 1924 convention. Have each pair write an outline for a platform on which Calvin Coolidge will run for election. *(Platforms should indicate that Coolidge will work to limit the damage from the Harding scandals and will restore the reputation of the presidency. Coolidge will continue to promote pro-business policies.)* Have volunteers read their platforms to the class.

English Language Learners, Cooperative Learning

PEOPLE IN HISTORY

Alice Paul. Alice Paul's determination to ensure equal rights for women put her at the forefront of the women's suffrage movement and for the battle to pass the Equal Rights Amendment. Paul, a New Jersey native, studied at universities in the United States and Great Britain. While in Britain she became involved in the suffrage movement and was arrested three times during protests. After returning to the United States, Paul earned her Ph.D. and continued working for women's suffrage. As head of the National Woman's Party, Paul encouraged her organization to picket the White House and to go on hunger strikes. She was arrested three more times during such activities and was even force-fed while on a hunger strike during her imprisonment. Paul and her followers protested their arrests by claiming that they were political prisoners of their own government.

CRITICAL THINKING Why might Paul have considered herself a political prisoner?

ANSWER: Students might suggest that she felt that she was being held in jail for expressing her beliefs but not for breaking any laws.

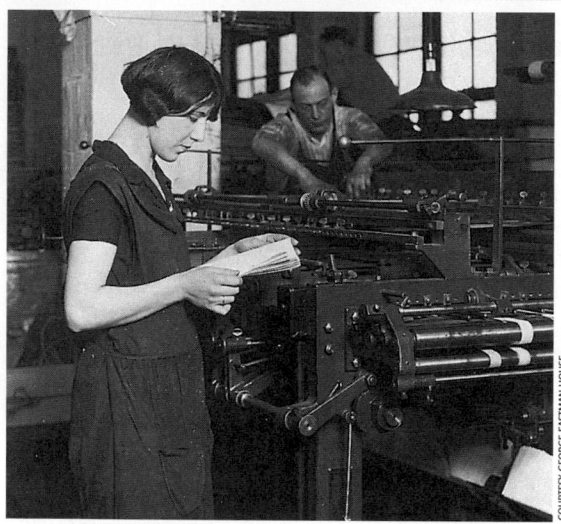

Many working-class women saw the Equal Rights Amendment as a middle-class issue that would remove the protective legislation passed during the reform era.

COURTESY GEORGE EASTMAN HOUSE

INTERPRETING POLITICAL CARTOONS

Teapot Dome scandal. Episodes of corruption like the Teapot Dome scandal threatened the Harding administration's public support. *How does this cartoon illustrate the danger of the scandal to the Republican administration?*

THE GRANGER COLLECTION, NEW YORK

History Makers Speak **"Women who are wage earners, with one job in the factory and another in the home, have little time and energy left to carry on the fight to better their economic status. They need the help of . . . labor laws."**

—Mary Anderson, "Should There Be Labor Laws For Women? Yes," *Good Housekeeping,* September 1925

ERA supporters argued that special legislation for women actually hurt female job-seekers, particularly in male-dominated occupations. They claimed that employers were discouraged from hiring or promoting women because of legal limitations on the hours women were allowed to work. In the end, the ERA movement failed to win political support.

✔ **READING CHECK: Categorizing** What were the arguments for and against the ERA?
for—legislation limiting work hours for women encouraged businesses to hire men; against—special legislation protecting women might become unconstitutional

The Enduring Republican Presidency

The proposal for the Equal Rights Amendment came as President Harding's administration was facing a storm of political scandals. Charges of political wrongdoing by members of the Harding administration began to surface in 1923.

The Harding scandals. The scandals came to light during the midpoint of Harding's term. A group of Harding's friends known as the Ohio Gang had followed him to Washington, D.C. They were using their connections to the president to enrich themselves at the public's expense.

The first scandal surfaced in the spring of 1923. Attorney General Harry Daugherty disclosed that Charles Forbes, Harding's close friend and director of the Veterans Bureau, had pocketed millions of dollars through corrupt schemes. The Forbes scandal and other evidence of wrongdoing in his administration deeply worried Harding. In June 1923 he confessed to journalist William Allen White, "I have no trouble with my enemies. I can take care of my enemies all right. [It's my] friends . . . that keep me walking the floor nights." Soon after talking to White, Harding set out on an extended tour of the West. On August 2 he died suddenly of an apparent heart attack in San Francisco.

After Harding's death other scandals were revealed. In 1924 Attorney General Daugherty came under suspicion himself. The Senate began to investigate Daugherty for his failure to end high-level corruption. The inquiry soon revealed that Daugherty was taking bribes. The attorney general was forced to resign.

The **Teapot Dome scandal**, the most notorious episode of corruption during the Harding administration, became news in 1924. Investigators discovered that in early 1921, Secretary of the Interior **Albert Fall** had persuaded Secretary of the Navy Edwin Denby to transfer control of naval oil reserves to his department. Fall granted private leases to the oil reserves in Elk Hills, California,

LEVELS 2 AND 3: Tell students to imagine that they are presidential historians who are writing a history of the Coolidge administration. Have each student write a short analysis describing the election of 1924 and explaining how Coolidge successfully overcame the political scandals of the Harding administration to win the election. *(See the Level 1 lesson for the correct details.)* Have students read their analyses to the class.

TEACH OBJECTIVE 5

LEVEL 1: Tell students to imagine that they are political analysts during the 1928 election. Then have each student write a few sentences on the issues that affected the outcome of the 1928 presidential election. *(Students should*

note that Herbert Hoover had a reputation for administrative skill and efficiency and enjoyed the legacy of prosperity during Republican rule. Al Smith was supported by urban immigrant voters. However, he was a Catholic, opposed prohibition, and had ties to Tammany Hall.)* Have volunteers read their sentences to the class. **English Language Learners**

LEVELS 2 AND 3: Tell students to imagine that it is December 1928 and that they are reporters preparing an election wrap-up. Have each student write a short article describing and assessing the presidential election of 1928. Remind students that their articles should focus on the issues that affected the outcome of the election. *(See the Level 1 lesson for the correct issues.)* Have volunteers read their articles to the class.

and the Teapot Dome reserves in Wyoming. In return, Fall received personal loans, cash, and cattle. Fall was convicted of accepting bribes and jailed.

Coolidge takes charge. After Harding's death, Vice President **Calvin Coolidge** was sworn in as president. He immediately began working to restore the reputation of the presidency by firing many of the people involved in the scandals. Coolidge's administration contrasted greatly with Harding's. Known as Silent Cal, Coolidge's stern, reserved nature contrasted with Harding's outgoing personality. However, Coolidge continued to promote Harding's popular pro-business policies because the national economy was booming.

Coolidge easily won the Republican presidential nomination in 1924. The Democrats were split over issues such as prohibition. They voted 103 times before finally choosing John W. Davis, a corporate lawyer, as their candidate. Both parties faced strong opposition from the Progressive Party's nominee, Robert La Follette. Backed by angry farmers and workers, the Progressive platform denounced federal policies favoring business and called for increased aid to working people.

Coolidge won by a landslide, receiving 15.7 million votes to Davis's 8.4 million. La Follette received some 4.8 million votes. The Progressive Party faded from the scene when La Follette died soon after the election. Nevertheless, the party's strength showed that not all Americans agreed with Republican pro-business policies.

Coolidge's pro-business position. A dedicated conservative, Coolidge was even more pro-business than Harding. "The business of America is business," he declared. Coolidge often invited prominent business leaders to social engagements at the White House. He favored legislation to aid business, and with his support, Congress passed the Revenue Act of 1926. This act repealed the gift tax, cut estate taxes in half, and reduced taxes on the wealthy. Coolidge expected these tax cuts to increase the economic prosperity of the country.

Coolidge also took a tightfisted approach to government spending. By keeping spending low, he made possible both a tax cut and further reductions in the national debt. Coolidge vetoed spending bills such as a bonus bill to provide aid to World War I veterans. He also vetoed the McNary-Haugen Bill, which was designed to boost farm prices by authorizing the government to buy surplus crops and sell them abroad. Coolidge generally opposed laws designed to help farmers or workers. He argued that such legislation limited private initiative and harmed the economy.

The president remained popular throughout his term and almost certainly could have won re-election in 1928. Instead, to almost everyone's surprise, he announced that he would not run. Speaking privately to his staff, Coolidge admitted that he found the work of the presidency burdensome. He looked forward to returning to a life of leisure at his home in Northampton, Massachusetts.

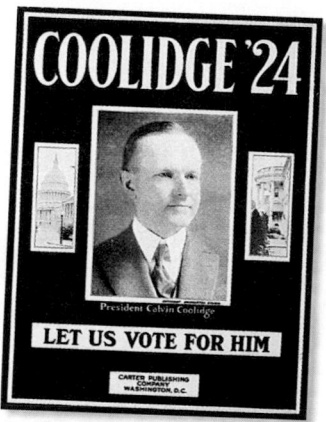

During the 1924 presidential election Coolidge supporters published songbooks such as this one to build support for his campaign.

Calvin Coolidge kept his campaign promise to support business. Here he meets with some of the country's most-prominent business leaders.

✔ **READING CHECK: Contrasting** How was Calvin Coolidge's approach to the presidency different than Harding's? Coolidge was more reserved and serious. He was more pro-business than Harding had been.

REVIEW

Have students complete the **Section 2 Review** on p. 402.

ASSESS

Have students complete **Daily Quiz 13.2**. As **Alternative Assessment,** you may want to use the Republican policies filmstrip or the party platform in this section's lessons.

RETEACH

Have students complete **Main Idea Activity for English Language Learners and Special-Needs Students 13.2.** Then prepare a set of index cards for each of the Section 2 objectives—each card should include a single key term or key person related

to the objective. Organize the class into small groups. Give each group the prepared cards for one objective. Have the students arrange the cards in an order that will enable them to discuss the objective. Call on each group to answer the question in front of the class, using the index cards as visual prompts to help the rest of the class follow the group's presentation. **English Language Learners, Cooperative Learning**

EXTEND

Tell students to imagine that they are journalists who are planning to interview either Alice Paul, Mary Anderson, or Carrie Chapman Catt. Have students conduct research on one of the women and prepare an imaginary interview with her. **Block Scheduling**

SECTION 2 REVIEW ANSWERS

1. Define
- mergers, p. 398
- feminists, p. 399

2. Identify
- Warren G. Harding, p. 397
- Andrew Mellon, p. 398
- Charles Dawes, p. 398
- Fordney-McCumber Tariff Act, p. 398
- American Plan, p. 399
- Equal Rights Amendment, p. 399
- Mary Anderson, p. 399
- Teapot Dome scandal, p. 400
- Albert Fall, p. 400
- Calvin Coolidge, p. 401
- Alfred E. Smith, p. 402

3. economic factors—prosperity encouraged Republican votes; Smith's weaknesses—his connections to Tammany Hall, his Catholicism, and his anti-prohibition stance; Hoover's strengths—reputation for skill and efficiency and connection to national prosperity

4a. Their trickle-down policies enabled wealthy business owners to save money and expand their businesses.

b. The ERA divided women, just as other women's rights issues did as women took on larger roles in public life.

c. The Progressive Party's strength led to a shift in the Democratic Party's strategy.

5. Answers will vary. Students might suggest that Coolidge had shown himself to be reserved and frugal and had offered economic prosperity.

INTERPRETING THE VISUAL RECORD

Herbert Hoover. During the 1928 election, Hoover ran on the same pro-business policies that Presidents Harding and Coolidge had supported. *How do you think these Hoover campaign items appealed to voters?*

The Election of 1928

In 1928 the Republican Party nominated Secretary of Commerce Herbert Hoover for president. Hoover had a reputation for administrative skill and efficiency. His strongest asset, however, was the nation's apparent prosperity. He referred to this prosperity in a campaign speech.

> **History Makers Speak**
> **"The poorhouse is vanishing from among us. We have not yet reached the goal, but, given a chance to go forward with the policies of the last eight years, we shall soon . . . be in sight of the day when poverty will be banished from this nation."**
>
> —Herbert Hoover, quoted in the *New York Times*, August 12, 1928

The Democrats nominated New York governor **Alfred E. Smith,** a moderate progressive. This choice signaled a shift in Democratic strategy—a response, in part, to the Progressive Party's strength in the 1924 election. By nominating Smith, the Democrats hoped to appear as "the party of progress and liberal thought," as vice presidential candidate Franklin D. Roosevelt put it. Smith's core support came from urban immigrant voters. However, many Americans opposed him because he was Catholic. They feared that a Catholic president would let the pope in Rome control the United States. Other voters worried about Smith's opposition to prohibition and his ties to New York City's Tammany Hall.

Hoover won the election, receiving 58 percent of the popular vote. For the first time since Reconstruction, several southern states voted Republican. Smith did well with urban voters, which offered Democrats hope for the future.

✔ **READING CHECK: Analyzing Information** Why did the Democrats nominate Governor Smith? Smith was more progressive and made the Democratic Party appear to be the party of progress.

SECTION 2 REVIEW

1. Define and explain:
mergers
feminists

2. Identify and explain:
Warren G. Harding
Andrew Mellon
Charles Dawes
Fordney-McCumber Tariff Act
American Plan
Equal Rights Amendment
Mary Anderson
Teapot Dome scandal
Albert Fall
Calvin Coolidge
Alfred E. Smith

3. Summarizing Copy the graphic organizer below. Use it to explain how each part of the pyramid helped lead to Herbert Hoover's victory in the 1928 election.

Hoover's Victory

Smith's Weaknesses | Hoover's Strengths

Economic Factors

4. **Finding the Main Idea**

a. How did Republican pro-business policies encourage economic growth?

b. How did the fight for an Equal Rights Amendment reflect the changing role of women in the 1920s?

c. What influence did the Progressive Party have on presidential elections in the 1920s?

5. **Writing and Critical Thinking**

Drawing Conclusions Write a paragraph explaining why Calvin Coolidge was able to win the 1924 election despite being vice president in Harding's scandal-ridden administration.
Consider:
- what Coolidge achieved in his term as president before the election
- the differences between Harding and Coolidge
- the significance of economic prosperity

go.hrw.com **Homework Practice Online**
keyword: SE3 HP13

SECTION ③

A Nation Divided

 EYEWITNESSES TO History

"Doubtless you have learned of the great exodus of our people to the north and west from this and other southern states. I wish to say that we are forced to go when . . . a grown man['s] wages is only fifty to seventy five cents per day for all grades of work. He is compelled to go where there is better wages and sociable conditions, believe me. . . . Many places here in this state . . . the black man . . . is treated as a slave. . . . As a minister of the Methodist Episcopal Church . . . I am on the verge of starvation simply because of the above conditions."

—Alabama minister, letter to *Chicago Defender*, April 7, 1917

Chicago Defender

In the spring of 1917 an African American minister from Alabama wrote this letter to the editors of the *Chicago Defender*. A weekly newspaper, the *Defender* covered the plight of African Americans in the South as well as the North. The *Defender* routinely encouraged African Americans from the South to migrate to northern cities. It contrasted the harsh conditions of the South with tales of freedom and jobs in the North. Although the North was not free of discrimination and racism, thousands of African Americans decided to try to better their lives by leaving the South to settle in northern cities.

African Americans Move Northward

During the 1920s some 800,000 African Americans joined the hundreds of thousands of African Americans who had moved north during World War I. By 1930 the African American population in the North and the Midwest had reached almost 2.5 million, more than double its size in 1910. Large African American communities sprang up in Chicago, Detroit, New York City, and other midwestern and northern cities.

Reasons for the move. African Americans who moved north searching for economic opportunities also longed for a new life free from discrimination. A migrant from Georgia who had left domestic work behind for a job in a Chicago box factory exclaimed, "I'll never work in nobody's kitchen but my own any more. No indeed! That's the one thing that makes me stick to this job. You do have some time to call your own." Yet as the demand for labor lessened during the recession of the early 1920s, African Americans were often the first to lose their jobs.

Violence erupts. Racial tension mounted with the move of African Americans from southern farms to cities. This tension sometimes erupted in violence. One of the worst incidents occurred in Chicago in July 1919. The trouble began when a white man threw rocks at an African American teenager swimming in Lake Michigan. The boy drowned. When the police refused to arrest anyone, fights broke out between whites and African Americans on shore and quickly spread to the rest

 **ALL LEVELS:** Conduct a brief discussion on why many Americans supported the Ku Klux Klan during the 1920s. To help students understand why the Klan declined, copy the graphic organizer at right on the chalkboard, omitting the italicized answers. Have each student complete it.
English Language Learners

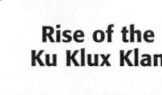

Rise of the Ku Klux Klan

- *racism toward African Americans in the South*
- *hostility toward African Americans, Catholics, immigrants, Jews, and suspected radicals in the North*
- *rising tensions and suspicions during the Red Scare*

- *decrease in Red Scare tensions*
- *publicity of the Klan's terrorism*
- *corruption and scandals at the Klan's national level*

Fall of the Ku Klux Klan

HISTORY MAKERS SPEAK

William Allen White and Oscar Ameringer in *Redeeming the Time*

Speaking Out Against the Klan. Political activists spoke out against the influence of the Ku Klux Klan. William Allen White wrote a tirade against Klan principles. White called the Klan "a self-constituted body of moral idiots" and "an organization of cowards." Oscar Ameringer mocked the Klan's beliefs by imagining their logical conclusion: "Unless these people are driven out of the country or are shown their proper places, the Reds will raise the . . . flag of socialism over the Capitol . . . (and) the unions wipe out what little business peace is left. . . . Just see what this latest lunacy is doing to your town."

CRITICAL THINKING Why might Ameringer's statement have been effective in revealing the absurdity of Klan beliefs?

ANSWER: Answers will vary. Students might suggest that Ameringer showed the unlikelihood of Klan beliefs and arguments.

MAP ANSWER
California, Michigan, Nevada, New York, and Wisconsin

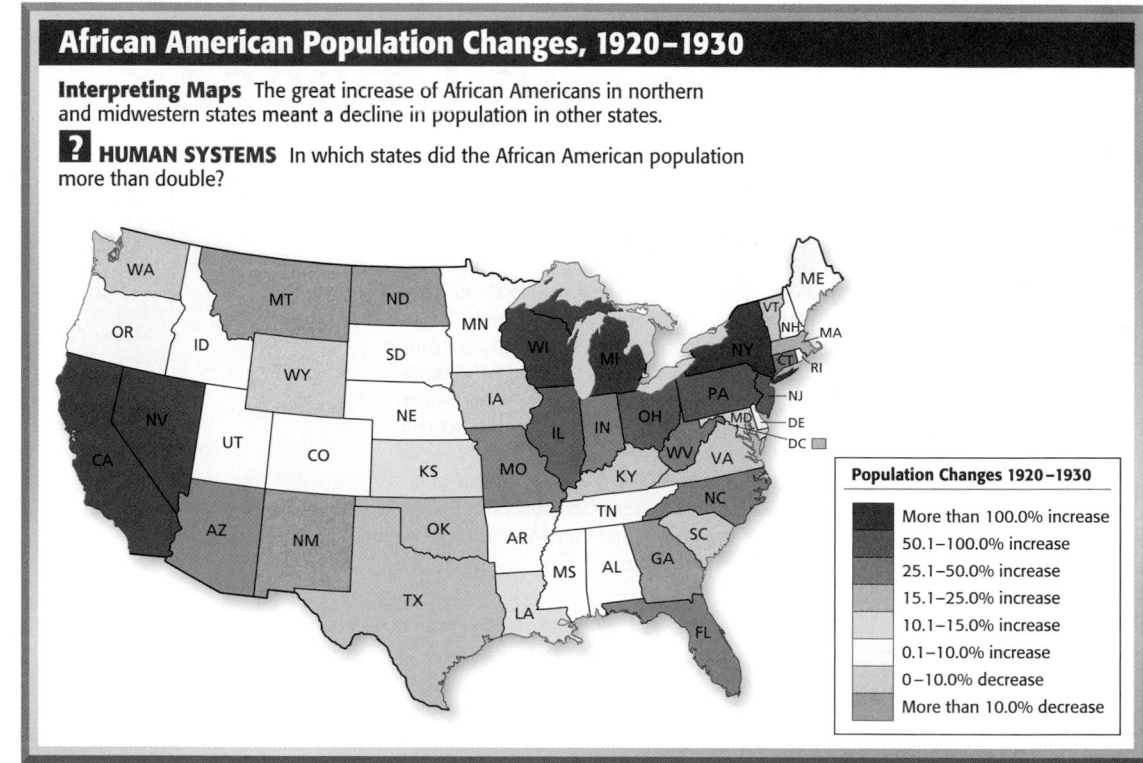

African American Population Changes, 1920–1930

Interpreting Maps The great increase of African Americans in northern and midwestern states meant a decline in population in other states.

? **HUMAN SYSTEMS** In which states did the African American population more than double?

Population Changes 1920–1930

- More than 100.0% increase
- 50.1–100.0% increase
- 25.1–50.0% increase
- 15.1–25.0% increase
- 10.1–15.0% increase
- 0.1–10.0% increase
- 0–10.0% decrease
- More than 10.0% decrease

During 1919, race riots erupted nationwide. Damage from fires left neighborhoods like this one in Chicago in ruins.

of the city. The rioting continued for more than a week. White gangs committed much of the violence, attacking African Americans and destroying property. By the time order was restored, 38 people had been killed, and 537 were injured.

By late 1919 some 25 race riots had erupted around the country. In June 1921 at least 30 people died during a race riot in Tulsa, Oklahoma. One resident described attacks on the African American section of town, "People were seen to flee from their burning homes, some with babes in their arms." The violence prompted African American soldiers with World War I combat experience to attempt to defend their communities. "The colored troops fought nobly," wrote one African American to a friend in Washington, D.C., after the riots in that city. "We have something to fight for now."

✔ **READING CHECK: Evaluating** How did African American migration affect urban areas in the North and Midwest? Racial tension and violence occurred.

The Return of the Ku Klux Klan

One sign of growing racism was the rebirth of the Ku Klux Klan (KKK), which had officially dissolved during Reconstruction. The new Klan was established in 1915 at Stone Mountain, Georgia, by a preacher named **William Joseph Simmons**. Like the Klan of post–Civil War days, the new Klan carried out kidnappings, beatings, and lynchings to terrorize African Americans in the South. The new KKK also grew rapidly outside of the South. In northern and midwestern towns and cities, the

RED SCARE

Fear that Communism would overthrow Capitalism

PALMER RAIDS. Att. General

Created special gov't office headed by J. Edgar Hoover

Sacco And Vanzetti - sentenced to Death

Republicans of The 20's
- Harding "Return to Normalcy"
- Boost economy
- Women and feminist
- Ohio Gang
- Teapot Dome Scandels
        Private leases of oilfields
- Coolidge
- Hoover

LEVEL 1: Pair students and tell each pair to create three political buttons that describe how the NAACP, A. Philip Randolph, and Marcus Garvey worked to end discrimination or violence against African Americans. *(Buttons should reflect that the NAACP organized an antilynching campaign, A. Philip Randolph established the Brotherhood of Sleeping Car Porters, and Marcus Garvey supported black nationalism and founded the UNIA.)* Have students display their buttons around the classroom and explain them to the class.
English Language Learners, Cooperative Learning

LEVELS 2 AND 3: Organize students into triads. Have each triad create scripts for radio commercials during the 1920s that publicize the campaigns of the NAACP, A. Philip Randolph, and Marcus Garvey to end discrimination against African Americans. *(See the Level 1 lesson for the correct actions.)* Have volunteers perform their radio commercials for the class.
Cooperative Learning

Klan targeted not only African Americans but also Catholics, immigrants, Jews, and suspected radicals.

The Klan grew slowly at first, but as the Red Scare took hold, membership soared. The group reached its peak in the mid-1920s. At one time it had perhaps as many as 5 million members. The Klan staged mass rallies where white-robed members burned crosses and spoke out against groups and ideas they considered undesirable. It also worked to help candidates win elections in such states as Louisiana, Ohio, Oklahoma, Oregon, and Texas. The group was particularly powerful in Indiana.

The Klan's rapid rise during the early 1920s was followed by an equally speedy fall in the late 1920s. By 1930 KKK membership had dropped to some 9,000. The decline resulted from several factors. Particularly significant was a decrease in the hysteria surrounding the Red Scare. With the economy booming in the late 1920s and anxiety about radicalism declining, the Klan's message of fear lost its appeal.

Publicity about the Klan's terrorism and violence also led to its decline. Newspapers throughout the country published investigative articles exposing the violence of local Klan chapters. With the national leadership of the Ku Klux Klan unable to control the actions of its local chapters, many people began to speak out against the group.

The Klan also suffered from corruption and scandals at the national level. Investigations revealed that Klan promoters were getting rich from membership fees and sales of various Klan products. In addition, Indiana Grand Dragon, or leader, **David Stephenson** was convicted of second-degree murder. In the face of such scandals, many local chapters broke away from the national organization. Nevertheless, the Klan did not completely die out.

✔ **READING CHECK: Sequencing** Chart the growth and decline of the Ku Klux Klan in the 1920s. started again in 1915; membership grew rapidly in early 1920s to peak in mid-1920s; then a speedy fall in the late 1920s

African Americans Defend Their Rights

Faced with continued violence and discrimination from the Ku Klux Klan and other groups, many African Americans took action to defend their rights. During the 1920s African Americans created several organizations dedicated to the prevention of discrimination and acts of violence.

Antilynching campaign. One early effort to stop the violence committed against African Americans came from the National Association for the Advancement of Colored People (NAACP). The NAACP formed the Antilynching Committee to generate support for antilynching legislation. It also put pressure on law enforcement officials to investigate acts of violence against African Americans. The NAACP published lynching statistics and detailed stories of atrocities in *The Crisis*,

INTERPRETING THE VISUAL RECORD

Ku Klux Klan. During the 1920s the Ku Klux Klan held rallies to build support for the organization. *What is the significance of the symbols used by Klan members in their rallies?*

Supporters of the NAACP campaign to end lynchings in the United States wore buttons such as this one to spread their message.

LEVEL 1: Pair students and have each pair create a chart to depict why many Americans demanded restrictions on immigration in the 1920s. (*Pairs should note the increase in immigration and the belief that immigrants were political radicals who took jobs from native-born Americans.*)
English Language Learners, Cooperative Learning

LEVELS 2 AND 3: Tell students to imagine that it is 1922 and that they are recent immigrants. Have each student write a letter to a relative back home describing and explaining the anti-immigrant sentiments of many Americans. (*See the Level 1 lesson for the correct reasons.*) Have volunteers read their letters to the class.

A. Philip Randolph established a union for sleeping-car porters and published a journal called **The Messenger** to help African American workers gain better wages and working conditions.

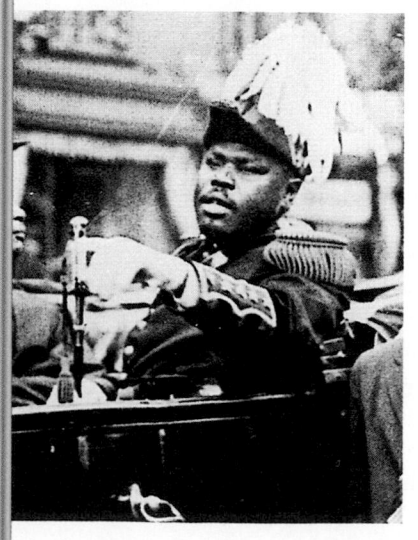

Marcus Garvey led the black nationalist movement.

its monthly magazine. In an article about a 17-year-old African American who was burned to death by a mob in Waco, Texas, W. E. B. Du Bois rallied support for the NAACP cause. He wrote, "This is an account of one lynching. It is horrible, but it is matched in horror by scores of others in the last thirty years. . . . What are we going to do about this record?"

The NAACP program generated considerable public support but achieved limited success. In 1921 Representative L. C. Dyer of Missouri sponsored a federal antilynching law that passed in the House but lost in the Senate. Nevertheless, the NAACP continued to fight for antilynching legislation and an end to discrimination against African Americans.

African American unionization. While some African Americans mobilized to put an end to lynching and racial violence, others attempted to fight discrimination in the workplace. In the early 1900s African American workers were rarely allowed to rise above unskilled, low-paying jobs. African Americans were also barred from joining local labor unions and the American Federation of Labor.

The unions' failure to help African American workers led black socialist **A. Philip Randolph** to found the **Brotherhood of Sleeping Car Porters** in 1925. Randolph started the union to improve working conditions for thousands of African Americans who worked for the Pullman Company. "[The worker's] object is not only to get more wages, better hours of work and improved working conditions," explained Randolph, "but to do his bit in order to raise and progressively improve the standard of Pullman service."

Randolph also sought to end union discrimination against African American workers. The Brotherhood of Sleeping Car Porters provided a union for African Americans. However, Randolph hoped to unite all workers, regardless of color, into a single force opposed to unjust working conditions.

Despite Randolph's efforts, the Pullman Company refused to recognize the Brotherhood of Sleeping Car Porters. The company even began to hire Filipino workers to replace African American porters. Supported by groups such as the NAACP, the union persisted in its efforts to organize. It eventually won recognition by the Pullman Company in the late 1930s.

Black nationalism. African Americans grew frustrated by the slow pace of change in the unions and the lack of results from NAACP's antilynching legislation. Some African Americans lost hope of ever achieving equality in the United States. They believed that African Americans needed a nation of their own.

The motivation for African Americans to form an independent nation grew out of an existing political movement. The movement known as **Pan-Africanism** aimed to unite people of African descent worldwide. Support for the movement had existed in the United States since the early 1800s. By the 1920s, a new leader within the Pan-African movement had emerged. **Marcus Garvey**, a native of Jamaica, supported the cause of **black nationalism**. This movement aimed to create a new political state for African Americans in Africa.

Marcus Garvey founded the **Universal Negro Improvement Association** (UNIA) in 1914. The UNIA had two main goals. Its members hoped to foster African

LEVEL 1: Tell students to imagine that they are writing a book about Mexican immigration to the United States during the 1920s. Pair students and have each pair write an outline for a chapter that explains why Mexican immigration to the United States increased in the 1920s. *(Pairs should note that limits on immigration during the 1920s did not affect Mexicans. Employers in the Southwest were eager for workers to fill low-wage jobs.)* Have volunteers present their outlines to the class.
English Language Learners, Cooperative Learning

LEVEL 2: Pair students and have each pair create a collage that illustrates the reasons why Mexican immigration to the United States increased in the 1920s. *(See the Level 1 lesson for the correct reasons.)* Students should write short descriptions of the different elements of their collages. Display pairs' collages around the classroom. **Cooperative Learning**

LEVEL 3: Organize the class into small groups. Have each group write a three-minute play about a Mexican immigrant family in the 1920s. Characters in the play should discuss why Mexican immigration to the United States increased in the 1920s. *(See the Level 1 lesson for reasons.)* Have volunteers perform their plays for the class. **Cooperative Learning**

Americans' economic independence through the establishment of black-owned businesses. They also worked to establish an independent black homeland in Africa. "We shall now organize," Garvey told the delegates to the UNIA's first international convention, "to plant the banner of freedom on the great continent of Africa."

In 1916 Garvey moved to New York, where he continued to try to organize an African American nation. A charismatic speaker, Garvey attracted considerable support from African American communities. Garvey organized attention-getting parades. He also urged African Americans to join him in forging a new homeland free from discrimination. Whereas W. E. B. Du Bois spoke to the well educated, Garvey's speeches and slogans attracted the African American masses. Many of his supporters were working-class African Americans living in urban areas.

To encourage economic independence, Garvey founded the Black Star Steamship Company in 1919. He urged African Americans to invest in his company so that they "may exert the same influence on the world as the white man does today." He promised investors huge returns. The company, however, never turned a profit. In 1925 he was jailed for mail fraud in connection with his fund-raising activities. President Coolidge pardoned Garvey in 1927 but ordered him deported.

The black nationalist movement declined after Garvey's imprisonment. Nevertheless, as a newspaper writer said in 1927, "He made black people proud.... He taught them that black is beautiful." Other African American leaders such as Du Bois shared Garvey's belief in racial pride and solidarity but opposed his back-to-Africa movement. They insisted that African Americans needed to fight for justice and equality in American society.

✔ **READING CHECK: Analyzing Information** How did African Americans try to improve their political and economic situation in the 1920s? They started their own unions, as well as political movements like Pan-Africanism and black nationalism.

Immigration Restrictions

The racism and discrimination that led to the resurgence of the Ku Klux Klan in the 1920s also encouraged nativist sentiments. Many Americans feared that the country was being overrun by immigrants. By 1920 nearly 25 percent of the nation's population was foreign born or nonwhite. Furthermore, after a decline during World War I, the number of immigrants was once again rising, increasing from some 140,000 in 1919 to some 805,000 in 1921. This dramatic growth—and the widespread belief that immigrants held radical views and took jobs from native-born Americans—led many citizens to demand federal limits on immigration.

PRIMARY SOURCE

The Back-to-Africa Movement

Marcus Garvey's back-to-Africa movement drew many followers both in the United States and in Africa. In 1922 a representative of the king of Abyssinia—present-day Ethiopia—read the following message to a UNIA convention. **How does the king see his goals for Abyssinia relating to UNIA goals?**

❝Assure them [Garvey's followers] of the cordiality with which I invite them back to the home land, particularly those qualified to help solve our big problems and to develop our vast resources. Teachers, artisans, mechanics, writers, musicians, professional men and women—all who are able to lend a hand in the constructive work which our country so deeply feels, and greatly needs.
　Here we have abundant room and great opportunities and here destiny is working to elevate and enthrone a race which has suffered slavery, poverty, persecution and martyrdom [death for a cause], but whose expanding soul and growing genius is now the hope of many millions of mankind.❞

Research on the R●M

Free Find: Marcus Garvey
After reading about Marcus Garvey and black nationalism on the **Holt Researcher CD–ROM**, create a script for a scene in a movie about Garvey's back-to-Africa movement.

THAT'S INTERESTING!

The first Mexican American U.S. senator took office during the 1920s, despite widespread anti-immigrant tensions. Octaviano Larrazolo was elected to complete the term of a New Mexico senator who had died. Larrazolo was re-elected for a second term in 1929.

The American Nation
VIDEO PROGRAM

A Nation of Immigrants; Teacher's Guide, pp. 153–57

Search 23298, Play to 28272
Videodisc 2, Side B

Play　　　　Pause

See *Teacher's Guide* for Spanish barcode.

PRIMARY SOURCE ANSWER

Students might answer that the king had positions for Africans Americans who wanted to move to Africa.

LEVELS 1 AND 2: Pair students and have each pair write a short poem describing the actions that American Indians took in the 1920s to protect their land. *(Pairs should note that American Indians organized to stop the Harding administration's attempt to buy back all tribal land. In 1922, Pueblo tribes organized to fight the Bursum Bill; during their fight the Pueblo appealed to and won the support of many Americans.)* Have volunteers read their poems to the class. Students may wish to include their poems in their portfolios.
English Language Learners, Cooperative Learning

LEVEL 3: Tell students to imagine that they are American Indian activists who fought government efforts to take Indian lands during the 1920s. Ask each student to write a series of diary entries describing American Indian actions. *(See the Levels 1 and 2 lesson for the correct actions.)* Have volunteers read their diary entries to the class. **Cooperative Learning**

HOMEWORK *Have each student create a detailed outline of the subsection entitled American Indian Life.*

SECTION 3 REVIEW ANSWERS

1. Define
- black nationalism, p. 406

2. Identify
- William Joseph Simmons, p. 404
- David Stephenson, p. 405
- A. Philip Randolph, p. 406
- Brotherhood of Sleeping Car Porters, p. 406
- Pan-Africanism, p. 406
- Marcus Garvey, p. 406
- Universal Negro Improvement Association, p. 406
- Immigration Act of 1924, p. 408
- Bursum Bill, p. 409

3. KKK–targeted African Americans as well as other ethnic and religious minority groups; African Americans—encountered discrimination and violence; immigration restriction—enacted because people feared the economic and political effects of immigration

4a. The Red Scare made people afraid, so they joined the Klan for power; the diminishing power of the scare lessened the appeal of the Klan's message of fear.

b. They feared economic competition and radical political ideas.

c. the desire for more workers and the lack of immigration restrictions

5. Some students might suggest that most groups, such as the Brotherhood of Sleeping Car Porters, made small gains in defending their rights.

"Ellis Island Blues" was one of the many songs written during the 1920s about immigrants.

Analyzing Primary Sources

Drawing Inferences Why might Mexicans immigrate to the United states if conditions were so harsh? job opportunities and the chance to get out of poverty

Mexican American Victor Villaseñor wrote about his family's experiences as immigrants in the 1920s. Shown here is the 1929 wedding of his parents.

In 1921 Congress passed a law limiting the number of immigrants from each country allowed into the United States. The law set a quota of 3 percent for each nationality already in the country by 1910, except for Asians, whose immigration was virtually barred. Three years later, the **Immigration Act of 1924** reduced this quota to 2 percent of the 1890 population figures for each nationality. This change limited southern and eastern European immigration because in 1890 most Americans traced their origins to Great Britain or northern and western Europe. The 1924 law excluded all Asian immigrants. In 1925 these restrictions reduced the total number of new immigrants from Africa, Asia, Australia, and Europe to some 153,000.

✔ **READING CHECK: Summarizing** Why was immigration restricted in the 1920s?
Some Americans believed that immigrants held radical views and were taking jobs from native-born Americans.

Mexican American Migration

The restrictive legislation of the 1920s did not affect Mexicans. Employers in the Southwest were eager to keep a steady flow of workers to fill low-wage jobs. As a result, during the 1920s some 500,000 immigrants arrived from Mexico, where poverty was widespread, jobs were scarce, and political upheaval from a revolution persisted.

Mexicans who took agricultural jobs in the Southwest worked for low wages and typically lived in ramshackle labor camps. An observer described one camp.

❝Shelters were made of almost every conceivable thing—burlap, canvas, palm branches. . . . We found one woman carrying water in large milk pails from the irrigation ditch. . . . This is evidently all the water which they have in camp.❞

—minister, quoted in *Who Built America?*, edited by Joshua Freeman

In the 1920s many Mexican immigrants also moved into urban areas. Some were drawn to well-paying factory jobs in cities such as Chicago and Detroit. Most, however, migrated to cities in the Southwest—such as Los Angeles, San Antonio, and El Paso, Texas. Usually men came alone. Once established, they sent for their wives and children. Many brought other relatives as well, establishing extended-family networks. These networks helped new arrivals find jobs and housing.

Economic hardship caused many families to allow their young, unmarried daughters to work outside the home. Many found employment in bakeries, hotels, and laundries. Their newfound independence, as one Mexican immigrant woman noted, brought young women "into conflict with their parents. They learn . . . about the outside world, learn how to speak English, and then they become ashamed of their parents who brought them up here." Despite such conflicts, these new immigrants contributed greatly to American life.

✔ **READING CHECK: Evaluating** Why did employers in the Southwest encourage Mexican immigration? Employers needed a steady flow of workers to fill low-wage jobs.

REVIEW

Have students complete the **Section 3 Review** on p. 409.

ASSESS

Have students complete **Daily Quiz 13.3**. As **Alternative Assessment**, you may want to use the play or the poem in this section's lessons.

RETEACH

Have students complete **Main Idea Activity for English Language Learners and Special-Needs Students 13.3**. Then have each student write a short summary of one of the objectives discussed in this section. Have students read their summaries to the class and ask the class to supply any missing information.
English Language Learners

EXTEND

Tell students to select a country with heavy immigration to the United States in the late 1800s or early 1900s. Have students conduct research on how the Immigration Act of 1924 affected the flow of immigrants from the selected nation. Have each student describe his or her findings in a short report.
Block Scheduling

American Indian Life

For American Indians the 1920s brought some acknowledgment of the difficulties they faced. The Dawes Act, which attempted to "Americanize" Indians by dividing tribal land into individual plots, had clearly failed. The Board of Indian Commissioners admitted that the act's allotment policies had often been "a short cut to the separation of . . . Indians from their land and cash."

In the 1920s American Indians successfully organized to fight new efforts to take tribal land. American Indian leaders stopped the Harding administration's attempt to buy back all tribal land. Then, in 1922, various Pueblo tribes of the Southwest organized to fight the **Bursum Bill**, which was designed to legalize non-Indian claims to Pueblo land. The Pueblo appealed to Americans to help defeat the bill.

 History Makers Speak ❝This bill will destroy our common life and will rob us of everything which we hold dear—our lands, our customs, our traditions. Are the American people willing to see this happen?❞

—member of the American Indian Defense Organization, quoted in *Native American Testimony*, edited by Peter Nabokov

The Pueblo won support from a variety of groups, including the General Federation of Women's Clubs and many anthropologists. As a result, the bill did not pass.

In 1924 Congress granted citizenship to all American Indians, partly in recognition of those who had fought in World War I. Citizenship, however, did not eliminate the poverty that many American Indians continued to experience.

✔ **READING CHECK: Summarizing** Why did the Bursum Bill fail? The Pueblo won support from groups like the General Federation of Women's Clubs.

Anthropologist James Schultz (left) supported the continuation of American Indian culture in the 1920s.

 SECTION 3 REVIEW

1. **Define and explain:**
   black nationalism

2. **Identify and explain:**
   William Joseph Simmons
   David Stephenson
   A. Philip Randolph
   Brotherhood of Sleeping Car Porters
   Pan-Africanism
   Marcus Garvey
   Universal Negro Improvement Association
   Immigration Act of 1924
   Bursum Bill

3. **Categorizing** Copy the web below. Use it to explain how each of the listed events reflected the intolerance and discrimination that existed in American society in the 1920s.

   - Experiences of African Americans Who Moved North
   - INTOLERANCE AND DISCRIMINATION
   - Immigration Restriction
   - Actions of the Ku Klux Klan

4. **Finding the Main Idea**
   a. How did the Red Scare contribute to the rise and fall of the Ku Klux Klan?
   b. Why did many Americans support more restrictive immigration laws in the 1920s?
   c. Why did the immigration of Mexicans to the United States increase during the 1920s?

5. **Writing and Critical Thinking**
   Evaluating In the face of intolerance, discrimination, and violence during the 1920s, many people took action to defend their rights. Write a paragraph evaluating their success.
   Consider:
   - how African Americans fought against lynching and discrimination
   - how Mexican Americans seeking economic opportunity formed communities
   - how American Indians defended their land

 Homework Practice Online
keyword: SE3 HP13

CHAPTER 13 REVIEW ANSWERS

Creating a Time Line
Each event should have an explanation and the correct date.

Writing a Summary
See the Reading Checks in each section for main ideas.

Identifying People and Ideas
1. transition from wartime to peacetime production

2. period of anticommunist hysteria

3. U.S. attorney general who authorized raids on suspected radicals

4. secretary of the Treasury who proposed cutting taxes on the wealthy to stimulate economic growth

5. proposed amendment to grant men and women equal rights

6. scandal in which some Harding administration officials accepted bribes

7. vice president and president who helped the nation recover from the Harding administration scandals

8. founder of the 1915 Ku Klux Klan

9. leader of the Pan-African movement

10. limited Asian immigration and encouraged western European immigration

Understanding Main Ideas
1. unemployment, falling agriculture prices, and the loss of farms

CHAPTER

13

REVIEW AND ASSESSMENT RESOURCES

TECHNOLOGY
▶ Chapter 13 Test Generator (on the One-Stop Planner)
▶ Global Skill Builder CD–ROM
▶ HRW Go site

REINFORCEMENT, REVIEW, AND ASSESSMENT
▶ Chapter 13 Review, pp. 410–11
▶ Chapter 13 Tutorial for Students, Parents, Mentors, and Peers

▶ Chapter 13 Test (Form A or B)
▶ Portfolio Activities and Alternative Assessment Handbook, Chapter 13
▶ Chapter 13 Test for English Language Learners and Special-Needs Students

REVIEW
Have students complete the **Chapter 13 Review** on pp. 410–11.

ASSESS
Use one of the chapter tests to assess students' understanding of the content. For **Alternative Assessment**, see the **Portfolio Activities and Alternative Assessment Handbook**.

2. Most strikes were undertaken by workers demanding higher wages and shorter workdays.

3. He offered a focus on domestic concerns and a promise of "normalcy."

4. They were the first workers fired when production decreased and they encountered violence and threats from some white people.

5. Mexican immigration was not restricted and southwestern employers needed many workers.

Reviewing Themes
1. The Red Scare made many people afraid to voice their opinions and led officials to ignore personal and legal rights when searching for and arresting suspected radicals.

2. Trickle-down policies enabled wealthy business owners to save money and expand their businesses; laborers did not benefit from these expansions because their pay did not grow along with the owners' profits.

3. Immigration increased during the decade, leading to calls for restriction.

Thinking Critically
1. fear and loathing; contributed to an atmosphere of distrust and intolerance

2. The end of the war brought high prices and fewer jobs, which contributed to increased labor agitation. The revolution in Russia contributed to American fears of supposed "radicals."

410

CHAPTER

13

Review

Creating a Time Line

Copy the time line below onto a sheet of paper. Complete the time line by filling in the events and dates from the chapter that you think were most significant. Pick three events and explain why you think they were significant.

`1919`   `1924`   `1929`

Writing a Summary

Using standard grammar, spelling, sentence structure, and punctuation, write an overview of events in the chapter.

Identifying People and Ideas

Identify the following terms or individuals and explain their significance.

1. demobilization
2. Red Scare
3. A. Mitchell Palmer
4. Andrew Mellon
5. Equal Rights Amendment
6. Teapot Dome scandal
7. Calvin Coolidge
8. William Joseph Simmons
9. Marcus Garvey
10. Immigration Act of 1924

Understanding Main Ideas

SECTION 1 *(pp. 390–396)*
1. What impact did demobilization after World War I have on women, factory workers, and farmers?
2. What were some of the causes of the strikes of 1919?

SECTION 2 *(pp. 397–402)*
3. How was Warren G. Harding able to win the election of 1920 by such a large majority?

SECTION 3 *(pp. 403–409)*
4. What types of discrimination did African Americans experience in northern cities?
5. Why did the immigration of Mexicans to the United States increase during the 1920s?

Reviewing Themes

1. **Citizenship** How did the hysteria of the Red Scare affect the lives of many Americans?
2. **Economics** How did the Republicans' pro-business policies affect economic growth?
3. **Culture** In what ways did immigration to the United States change in the 1920s?

Thinking Critically

1. **Identifying Cause and Effect** What was the public reaction to the wave of strikes in 1919? How did this reaction relate to the Red Scare?
2. **Summarizing** How did the ending of World War I and the communist revolution in Russia affect American life in the early 1920s?
3. **Evaluating** How did the Teapot Dome scandal and others during Harding's administration affect Americans' views of the federal government?
4. **Drawing Conclusions** How did the NAACP, the Brotherhood of Sleeping Car Porters, and black nationalists attempt to better the lives of African Americans? How successful were they?
5. **Making Generalizations** In what ways did immigration change in the 1920s, and what effects did it have?

Writing About History

Summarizing Copy the graphic organizer below. Use it to explain the fears and concerns felt by many Americans in 1920 and how the Republicans' pro-business policies proposed to address them. Then explain why Harding's speech on "normalcy," given on May 20, 1920, was a success.

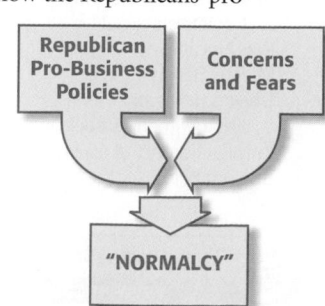

Republican Pro-Business Policies

Concerns and Fears

"NORMALCY"

RETEACH

Organize the class into groups of four. Have each group create a crossword puzzle using the key terms and key people from Chapter 12. Have each group exchange its puzzle with another group and then solve them.
English Language Learners, Cooperative Learning

EXTEND

Have each student locate several political cartoons from the 1920s that comment on one of the major events or developments of the decade. Have students write paragraphs explaining and analyzing their cartoons. Students should write one paragraph per cartoon. Ask students to present their cartoons and paragraphs to the class. Students should contextualize each cartoon. **Block Scheduling**

Building Social Studies Skills

Interpreting Maps
Study the map below. Then use it to help answer the questions that follow.

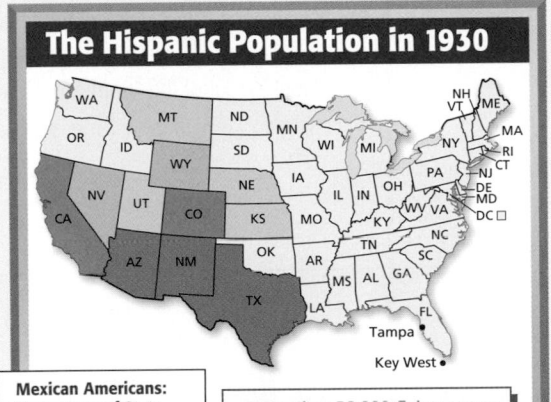

The Hispanic Population in 1930

Mexican Americans: Percentage of State Population, 1930

- More than 10.0%
- 5.1–10.0%
- 1.1–5.0%
- 0.5–1.0%
- Less than 0.5%

Total Mexican American population: 1,422,533

- Fewer than 20,000 Cubans came to the United States before 1930, and most settled in Key West or Tampa.
- Many of the some 37,000 Puerto Ricans who immigrated before World War II became agricultural laborers in Arizona, the Midwest, or the East.

1. Which states had the highest percentage of Hispanic residents by 1930?
   a. Arizona, New Mexico, Texas
   b. California, Colorado, Florida
   c. Nebraska, Kansas, Utah
   d. All states had about the same percentage.

2. What does the geographic distribution on the map reveal about the Hispanic population?

Analyzing Primary Sources
Read the excerpt from a story in the *Atlanta Constitution* about the Sacco and Vanzetti case. Then answer the questions that follow.

"Charlestown State Prison, Mass., Tuesday, August 23—Nicola Sacco and Bartolomeo Vanzetti died in the electric chair early this morning . . .
To the last they protested their innocence, and the efforts of many who believed them guiltless proved futile, although they fought a legal and extra legal battle unprecedented in the history of American jurisprudence [court system]."

3. Which of these phrases best describes the tone of the news story?
   a. complete objectivity
   b. slight bias showing sympathy for Sacco and Vanzetti
   c. slight bias against Sacco and Vanzetti
   d. strong bias against Sacco and Vanzetti

4. How was the trial and execution of Sacco and Vanzetti related to the Red Scare of the 1920s?

Alternative Assessment

Building Your Portfolio

Government
Imagine that you are interviewing presidential candidates to write an article for a popular magazine. Create an illustrated chart to compare and contrast the personalities of Presidents Harding and Coolidge. Then explain how Harding appealed to the voters of 1920 and how Coolidge appealed to voters in 1924.

U.S. HISTORY

☑ internet connect

Internet Activity: go.hrw.com
KEYWORD: SE3 AN13
Choose a topic on the 1920s to:
- research the Bolshevik revolution and write a radio broadcast.
- write a legal brief to prosecute or defend Sacco and Vanzetti.
- learn about Marcus Garvey and W. E. B. Du Bois and write a biography of either leader.

go. hrw. com

3. The scandals had very little effect because when Coolidge took over, he fired the people responsible and kept the economy booming.

4. The Brotherhood organized to improve working conditions for African Americans. The NAACP worked to decrease discrimination and violence against African Americans. Black nationalists encouraged African Americans to be proud of their heritage and supported the development of African American-owned businesses. All three had some success in reducing discrimination.

5. The number of immigrants rose and this rise resulted in federal limits on the number of immigrants allowed into the United States.

Writing
Students' explanations might cite the following: policies—tax revision, immigration limits, and some farm aid; concerns—economic troubles and political upheavals.

Building Social Studies Skills
1. a

2. Since the majority settled in the Southwest, the majority of Hispanic immigrants before 1930 probably came from Mexico.

3. b

4. Students might suggest that as immigrants and labor radicals, Sacco and Vanzetti represented everything that Americans at the time feared would result in a revolution similar to that in Russia.

The Jazz Age

CHAPTER RESOURCE MANAGER

Objectives	Pacing Guide	Reproducible Resources
SECTION 1 **Boom Times** pp. 414–21 ★ Evaluate how the economic boom affected consumers and American businesses. ★ Examine how the assembly line spurred the growth of the automobile industry. ★ Describe how Henry Ford changed working conditions during the 1920s. ★ Explain how widespread automobile use affected the daily lives of many Americans. ★ Discuss how American industries encouraged changes in consumer practices.	**Regular** 2 days **Block Scheduling** 1 day *Block Scheduling Handbook with Team Teaching Strategies, pp. 79–84*	**RS** Guided Reading Strategy 14.1 **E** Creative Teaching Strategy: Daily Journal Writing Lesson
SECTION 2 **Life in the Twenties** pp. 422–29 ★ Analyze the impact prohibition had on crime. ★ Describe the characteristics of the new youth culture. ★ Explain how celebrities and new forms of popular entertainment helped create a mass culture. ★ Examine what the Scopes trial and the religious movements of the 1920s revealed about American society.	**Regular** 2 days **Block Scheduling** 1 day *Block Scheduling Handbook with Team Teaching Strategies, pp. 79–84*	**RS** Guided Reading Strategy 14.2 **SM** Geography Activity 14: The Prohibition Era **PS** Primary Source Reading 14: Making a Monkey Out of the "Common Man" **PS** Biography Reading 14: Amelia Earhart
SECTION 3 **A Creative Era** pp. 430–37 ★ Explain how jazz and blues became popular nationwide. ★ Analyze how artists and writers of the Harlem Renaissance used their work to express pride in their cultural heritage. ★ Describe how writers of the Lost Generation portrayed American life. ★ Identify some of the major inspirations behind the new movements in visual arts and architecture.	**Regular** 2 days **Block Scheduling** 1 day *Block Scheduling Handbook with Team Teaching Strategies, pp. 79–84*	**RS** Guided Reading Strategy 14.3 **RS** Graphic Organizer Activity 14: Artists of the 1920s and 1930s **IC** Literature Reading 14: The Jazz Age **E** Hands-On History Activity: Guide to Local Arts and Artists

Chapter Resource Key

PS	Primary Sources	**REV**	Review		Video
RS	Reading Support	**ELL**	Reinforcement and English Language Learners		Internet
IC	Interdisciplinary Connections				Holt Presentation Maker Using Microsoft® PowerPoint®
E	Enrichment		Transparencies		
SM	Skills Mastery		CD-ROM		
A	Assessment		Music		

 One-Stop Planner CD-ROM

See the *One-Stop Planner* for a complete list of additional resources for students and teachers.

One-Stop Planner CD–ROM

It's easy to plan lessons, select resources, and print out materials for your students when you use the **One-Stop Planner CD–ROM with Test Generator.**

Technology Resources

 One-Stop Planner, Lesson 14.1

 The American Nation Video Program Segment: Automobile Assembly Line; Teacher's Guide, pp. 171–72

CNN. Presents America: Yesterday and Today, 1850 to the Present Segment: The Negro Leagues

 Holt Researcher: American History CD–ROM

 Homework Practice Online

 HRW Go site

 One-Stop Planner, Lesson 14.2

 The American Nation Video Program Segment: Prohibition; Teacher's Guide, pp. 211–12

 Holt Researcher: American History CD–ROM

 Homework Practice Online

 One-Stop Planner, Lesson 14.3

 Everyday Life in America Transparency 22: Harlem Renaissance Art, 1920s

 American Music Selection 19: "Harmonica Blues"

 Holt Researcher: American History CD–ROM

 Homework Practice Online

Reinforcement, Review, and Assessment

REV Section 1 Review, p. 421
A Daily Quiz 14.1
ELL Main Idea Activity 14.1
ELL English Audio Summary 14.1
ELL Spanish Audio Summary 14.1

REV Section 2 Review, p. 429
A Daily Quiz 14.2
ELL Main Idea Activity 14.2
ELL English Audio Summary 14.2
ELL Spanish Audio Summary 14.2

REV Section 3 Review, p. 437
A Daily Quiz 14.3
ELL Main Idea Activity 14.3
ELL English Audio Summary 14.3
ELL Spanish Audio Summary 14.3

internet connect

HRW ONLINE RESOURCES
GO TO: go.hrw.com
Then type in a keyword.

TEACHER HOME PAGE
KEYWORD: SE3 Teacher

CHAPTER INTERNET ACTIVITIES
KEYWORD: SE3 AN14
Choose an activity to:
• research jazz and the poetry and literature of the Harlem Renaissance.
• understand the modernist movement in the arts, literature, and music.
• learn about the development of the automobile and create an advertisement for a 1920s dream car.

CHAPTER ENRICHMENT LINKS
KEYWORD: SE3 CH14

ONLINE ASSESSMENT
Homework Practice
KEYWORD: SE3 HP14

Standardized Test Prep
KEYWORD: SE3 STP14

Rubrics
KEYWORD: SS Rubrics

ONLINE MAPS, CHARTS, AND GRAPHS
KEYWORD: SE3 MCG
• Households with Radios, 1922–1930
• Workforce, 1910, 1920, 1930

CONTENT UPDATES
KEYWORD: SS Content Updates

HOLT PRESENTATION MAKER
KEYWORD: SE3 PPT14

ONLINE READING SUPPORT
KEYWORD: SS Strategies

CURRENT EVENTS
KEYWORD: S3 Current Events**

Meeting Individual Needs

Ability Levels

Level 1 Basic-level activities designed for all students encountering new material

Level 2 Intermediate-level activities designed for average students

Level 3 Challenging activities designed for honors and gifted-and-talented students

English Language Learners Activities that address the needs of students with Limited English Proficiency

Chapter Review and Assessment

 Global Skill Builder CD–ROM

HRW Go site

REV Chapter 14 Tutorial for Students, Parents, Mentors, and Peers

REV Chapter 14 Review, pp. 438–39

Chapter 14 Test Generator (on the One-Stop Planner)

A Chapter 14 Test (Form A or B)

A Alternative Assessment Handbook

A Chapter 14 Test for English Language Learners and Special-Needs Students

Build on What You Know

Ask students to answer the following questions.

How might new products and new forms of entertainment have changed American life during the 1920s?

Consider:

- the advances in science and technology
- the capabilities of postwar American industry

Why might some Americans have found these changes unsettling?

Consider:

- the specific changes that might have affected women, young people, and rural-dwellers
- the concerns of religious leaders

---

exploring the time line

AMERICAN EVENTS

PEOPLE IN HISTORY

1925 ■ Clarence Darrow. By the time Clarence Darrow agreed to defend John Scopes, Darrow was already one of the nation's leading attorneys. He had defended labor leader Eugene Debs against conspiracy charges resulting from the railroad strike of 1894. Darrow had also served as an attorney in many high-profile cases, including a murder trial in which he introduced psychiatric evidence, a novelty at the time.

CRITICAL THINKING Why might Darrow have wanted to defend Scopes?

ANSWER: Students might suggest that Darrow believed that the Tennessee law banning the teaching of evolution violated a person's right to free speech.

CHAPTER 14

1920–1929

The Jazz Age

Louis Armstrong

Alvin "Shipwreck" Kelly sitting on top of a flagpole

1922
The Arts
Jazz trumpeter Louis Armstrong moves to Chicago and joins King Oliver's Creole Jazz Band.

1922
Business and Finance
New York radio station WEAF airs the first paid radio commercials.

1923
World Events
An earthquake in Japan destroys Tokyo, killing some 143,000 people.

1924
Business and Finance
A Hollywood theater hires Alvin "Shipwreck" Kelly to sit on top of a flagpole to generate publicity.

1920	1921	1922	1923	1924

1920
Science and Technology
The first radio broadcasting station, KDKA in Pittsburgh, goes on the air.

1923
Politics
The first Equal Rights Amendment is proposed to Congress.

1924
The Arts
George Gershwin "translates" jazz into symphonic form in his musical composition *Rhapsody in Blue.*

1924
Politics
The first radio broadcast of a political convention is conducted from the Republican National Convention in Cleveland.

One of the first broadcasters on KDKA

Many flappers wanted a greater role in politics.

Build on What You Know

World War I's sudden conclusion forced many Americans to make major changes in their lives. Many Americans lost their jobs in a postwar economic recession. Economic prosperity returned in the mid-1920s. In this chapter you will learn about the impact of postwar industrial products on American life. You will also learn about the new forms of entertainment—such as radio programs, movies, and jazz music—that were popular with Americans in the 1920s.

What's Your Opinion?

To help students create their Themes Journal entries, provide the following examples of appropriate **agree**/**disagree** *statements.*

Economics

Agree The economy of British North America grew stronger as the colonists' demand for consumer goods increased.

Disagree Despite the huge sums that the Spanish Empire spent on art, architecture, and the maintenance of colonies, its economic health and international prestige gradually declined.

Science, Technology, and Society

Agree The invention of steam-powered riverboats and locomotives helped lead to the expansion of trade across the nation.

Disagree The technological advances of the Second Industrial Revolution did not significantly alter the social status of working-class women.

Culture

Agree American movies and magazines are shipped all over the world, but foreign films and magazines rarely come to America.

Disagree Many Americans are from other cultures, and they help shape American popular culture as well as spread it to the rest of the world.

Poster from the Paris Exposition

MUSEUM OF FINE ARTS, BOSTON

Babe Ruth

Automobile advertisement

THE GRANGER COLLECTION, NEW YORK

**1925
World Events**
The Paris Exposition opens, introducing the "Art Deco" style of industrial design.

**1925
The Arts**
F. Scott Fitzgerald publishes *The Great Gatsby*.

**1925
Politics**
Clarence Darrow defends a Tennessee schoolteacher in the Scopes trial.

**1927
Daily Life**
Babe Ruth sets a new baseball record, hitting 60 home runs in a single season.

**1929
Business and Finance**
American businesses spend more than $3 billion on advertisements in a single year.

| 1925 | 1926 | 1927 | 1928 | 1929 |

THE METROPOLITAN MUSEUM OF ART, ALFRED STIEGLITZ COLLECTION

Georgia O'Keeffe's Black Iris

**1926
The Arts**
Georgia O'Keeffe paints *Black Iris*.

**1927
Science and Technology**
Charles Lindbergh becomes the first pilot to fly solo nonstop from New York to Paris.

**1927
Business and Finance**
The Ford Motor Company introduces the Model A automobile with a $1.3 million advertising campaign.

**1928
Daily Life**
Marathon dancers compete for 482 hours in the "Dance Derby of the Century."

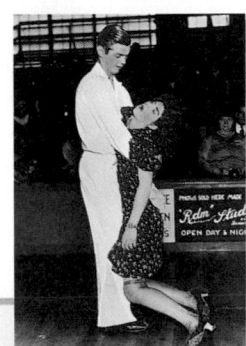

Dance marathon contestants

What's Your Opinion?

Themes Journal *Do you* **agree** *or* **disagree** *with the following statements? Support your point of view in your journal.*

Economics Increasing consumer spending will improve a nation's overall economic strength.

Science, Technology, and Society New technology transforms the way people interact with each other.

Culture American popular culture always spreads to the rest of the world but is not influenced by other cultures.

Boom Times

EYEWITNESSES TO History "*One hundred thousand people flocked into the showrooms of the Ford Company in Detroit; mounted police were called out to patrol the crowds in Cleveland; in Kansas City so great a mob stormed Convention Hall that platforms had to be built to lift the new car high enough for everyone to see it.*"

—Charles Merz, quoted in *Only Yesterday,* by Frederick Lewis Allen

A crowd gathers around a 1927 Model A.

In December 1927 the American public clamored to see the Ford Motor Company's new Model A automobile. Ford had kept the new design secret, and public excitement grew in the days before its unveiling. This interest was heightened by a massive advertising campaign that featured a five-day series of full-page newspaper ads costing $1.3 million. The prosperity of the 1920s increased the spending power of many families and allowed them to purchase the wide variety of new products being produced by American industries. These new products transformed Americans' daily lives, changing the way they worked, socialized, and ran their households.

Prosperity and Productivity

After recovering from the turbulent period of demobilization, the U.S. economy soared. The gross national product climbed from $70 billion in 1922 to $100 billion just seven years later. Republican pro-business policies and tax cuts, along with business leaders' confidence, encouraged investment and led to economic growth. Edward E. Purinton, a business leader during the 1920s, expressed the confidence of the era. "The finest game is business. The rewards are for everybody, and all can win."

Business expansion led to wage increases. The average employee's purchasing power increased by 32 percent between 1914 and 1928. With the rise in income, workers became interested in many new products, including electric appliances.

During the 1920s it became common for Americans to have electricity in their homes, particularly in cities. An abundant supply of energy as well as a large network of electrical power plants led to this expansion. Between 1920 and 1929 the annual electrical production rose from more than 56 billion to 117 billion kilowatt-hours. By 1930 more than two thirds of all American homes had electricity. The availability of electricity and the growing purchasing power of consumers provided a market for new products. American industries developed a variety of new electric appliances, such as mixers, food grinders, sewing machines, and washing machines. Radio and phonograph sales boomed.

As American industries attempted to keep pace with growing demand, many businesses began experimenting with new ways of increasing productivity. **Scientific management** was one of the new approaches. **Frederick W. Taylor**, an early supporter of the theory, explained that scientific management was based on

TEACH OBJECTIVE 1

LEVEL 1: List the following terms and phrases on the chalkboard: *economic prosperity, wage increases, new products, consumer demand, scientific management.* Pair students and have them write a short paragraph using all of the terms listed to analyze how the economic boom of the 1920s affected consumers and American businesses. *(Students' responses might include: Economic prosperity during the 1920s led to wage increases for workers. Workers, with their increased purchasing power, created a market for new products. To keep up with consumer demand, many businesses experimented with scientific management techniques to increase productivity.)* **English Language Learners, Cooperative Learning**

LEVELS 2 AND 3: Pair students and have each pair create a collage that depicts the impact of the economic boom of the 1920s on consumers and American businesses. Students should write a short explanation to accompany their collages. *(See the Level 1 lesson for the correct effects.)* Have students display their collages around the classroom. **Cooperative Learning**

the idea that every kind of work could be broken down into a series of smaller tasks. Trained observers conducted "time-and-motion" studies to identify these tasks. They then set rates of production that workers and machines had to meet. Soon "efficiency experts" were applying these methods to many types of business.

✔ **READING CHECK: Analyzing Information** What caused the economic boom of the 1920s? tax cuts, increased availability of electricity, and increased efficiency of factories

The Growth of the Automobile Industry

The innovations in productivity proved particularly important to the growing automobile industry. Automobile manufacturers such as **Henry Ford** lowered the cost of their cars by implementing scientific-management practices.

Ford had established an automobile company in 1903 that quickly emerged as the industry leader. By 1908 he had developed the **Model T**, a sturdy, low-cost automobile. The Model T was an instant success and sold more than 250,000 a year by 1914. Ford was eager to increase productivity and lower the price of the Model T. Adopting scientific-management techniques used in the slaughterhouses of Chicago, he developed a new production method—the **assembly line**—to help factories make goods faster. Workers stood in one place as partially assembled products such as automobiles moved past them on a conveyor belt.

Ford used the assembly line in his Detroit automobile plant. As the conveyor belt advanced at precisely six feet per minute, workers assembled the 5,000 parts of a Model T, or "Tin Lizzie." Machinery did much of the work by producing individual parts and carrying them to workers.

Ford's assembly line cut the engine assembly time for a Model T in half. Other large car manufacturers quickly followed Ford's lead and installed assembly lines. However, few small companies could afford the expense of building or maintaining the new technology. Unable to compete, many were driven out of business.

The assembly line allowed manufacturers to reduce the prices of cars, bringing them within reach of ordinary American families. The price of a Ford automobile dropped from $850 in 1909 to $290 in 1924. Automobile registrations during the 1920s rose from 8 million to 26 million—an average of one car to every five citizens.

In the 1920s the automobile industry was the nation's biggest business. This new industrial giant consumed huge quantities of glass, rubber, steel, and other materials. By 1929 more than 1 million people worked in the automobile industry or a related business.

✔ **READING CHECK: Finding the Main Idea** Describe the technological innovation that encouraged the growth of the automobile industry. The assembly line allowed workers to stay in one place as products moved past them on a conveyor belt.

Henry Ford achieved early success with his design for a streamlined racing car. In 1902 the Ford 999 set a world speed record of more than 90 miles per hour.

INTERPRETING THE VISUAL RECORD

The assembly line. Henry Ford developed an assembly-line system to manufacture his Model T efficiently. *How do you think the assembly line might have changed the nature of work for these Ford employees?*

415

TEACH OBJECTIVE 2

LEVEL 1: Pair students and have each pair draw a graphic organizer to depict how the assembly line spurred the growth of the automobile industry. *(Students might mention that the assembly line cut production time and costs. Manufacturers were able to reduce car prices, which allowed greater numbers of consumers to buy cars.)* Ask volunteers to present their graphic organizers to the class.
English Language Learners, Cooperative Learning

LEVELS 2 AND 3: Tell students to imagine that they are editors who must write a brief summary for the jacket of a book about the automobile industry. Have each student write a summary to describe how the development of the assembly line spurred the growth of the automobile industry. *(See the Level 1 lesson for the correct effects.)* Have volunteers read their summaries to the class. Students may wish to include their summaries in their portfolios.

TEACH OBJECTIVE 3

LEVEL 1: Pair students and have each pair draw a cartoon to show how Henry Ford changed working conditions during the 1920s. *(Students might indicate that Ford developed the assembly line, which increased productivity but made factory work repetitive. Ford also shortened the workday and raised wages.)* Have volunteers present and explain their cartoons to the class.
English Language Learners, Cooperative Learning

HISTORY MAKERS SPEAK

Henry Ford in *My Life and Work*

Ford's Assessment of Assembly-Line Work.

Henry Ford maintained an unapologetic attitude about the deadening nature of assembly-line work. In an autobiography published in 1922 Ford offered the following assessment of conditions in his factories: "Repetitive labour—the doing of one thing over and over again and always in the same way—is a terrifying prospect to a certain turn of mind. It is terrifying to me. I could not possibly do the same thing day in and day out, but to other minds, perhaps I might say to the majority of minds, repetitive operations hold no terrors. . . . The average worker, I am sorry to say, wants a job in which he does not have to put forth much physical exertion—above all, he wants a job in which he does not have to think."

ACTIVITY: Ask students to write a paragraph in response to Henry Ford's assessment of the "average worker."

SCIENCE & TECHNOLOGY ANSWERS

1. the simple design of its basic components and its high-strength steel chassis

2. The Model T was designed to be easily manufactured on an assembly line.

Science & Technology

The Model T

In addition to revolutionizing manufacturing, Henry Ford made important changes to the design of the automobile. During the early 1900s Ford began experimenting with new designs in an attempt to make cars more affordable.

Ford simplified the automobile's design to create a sturdy car that could be easily manufactured on an assembly line. The Model T contained four basic components: the frame, the front axle, the power plant, and the rear axle. The Model T had a 20-horsepower, four-cylinder engine that was built simply enough that almost anyone could maintain it. Ford's engineers designed a pedal-operated, two-speed transmission that was also easy to operate. To prevent the automobile from getting stuck in muddy roads, designers provided the Model T with a high ground clearance. The Model T's high-strength steel chassis, or frame, made it extremely durable.

Ford was able to sell the Model T at an affordable price, but his company offered few options. One Ford advertisement read, "We are making 40,000 cylinders, 10,000 engines, 40,000 wheels, 20,000 axles, 10,000 bodies, 10,000 of every part that goes into the car . . . all *exactly alike*." Even color options were limited. "The customer," Ford joked, "can have a Ford any color he wants—so long as it's black."

Engine

Drive shaft

Transmission

Starter

Understanding Science and History

1. What features made the Model T sturdy and reliable?
2. What impact did the assembly line have on the design of the Model T?

These assembly-line workers are leaving the Ford factory in Dearborn, Michigan, at the end of their shift.

Changes in Work

Assembly lines transformed the nature of work during the 1920s. They increased productivity. However, they also made factory work more repetitive and led to increased rates of employee turnover.

Unskilled factory workers had little chance for advancement beyond the assembly line. Greater productivity had increased the number of upper-level positions for clerical workers, managers, and salespeople. Most of these jobs required at least a high-school education, and few factory workers or recent immigrants qualified for them. Discriminatory hiring practices also closed most of these jobs to African Americans.

Ford and his workers. Henry Ford revolutionized automobile production by implementing the assembly line in his factories. He won fame for shortening the workday and raising the wages of his employees. Ford also tried to regulate the morality and personal behavior of his workers.

BIOGRAPHY

Henry Ford

Born in 1863 on a farm near Dearborn, Michigan, Ford was well acquainted with hard work. He began work as a machinist at the age of 16. During the 1890s Ford worked as an engineer for the Edison Illuminating Company in Detroit. In his free time he experimented with gasoline engines and automobiles. In the early 1900s he worked closely with talented engineers to design the assembly-line system.

Ford's highly automated system of production limited each worker to one or two specific tasks. The repetitive work was dull, and many workers quit within a few weeks. Concerned about the high turnover of employees, Ford shortened the workday to eight hours. He also doubled wages to $5 a day, significantly more than most unskilled workers were paid at the time.

Workers welcomed these bold steps. However, as the wife of one Ford worker noted, the pay increase did not change working conditions.

History Makers Speak

❝The chain system [assembly line] you have is a slave driver! My God! Mr. Ford. My husband has come home & thrown himself down & won't eat his supper—so done out! Can't it be remedied? . . . That $5 a day is a blessing—a bigger one than you know but oh they earn it.❞

—wife of Ford worker, quoted in "Personnel Complaints," cited by David Hounshell

The attractive wages paid to workers had strings attached. To earn the full $5 wage, workers were required to meet company standards at work and at home. Ford created a department within his company to analyze workers' home lives and offer plans to remedy any problems that Ford and his researchers believed existed.

Ford hoped to instruct his employees in the values and behaviors that he thought were proper. His personnel department kept a close watch over the private lives of employees. Ford strongly opposed tobacco and alcohol. His workers were warned, "It will cost a man his job to have the odor of beer, wine or liquor on his breath or have any of these intoxicants in his home."

During World War I, Ford stressed the importance of "American values" to his mostly foreign-born workforce. He instructed workers to move out of ethnic neighborhoods. Workers who did not speak English were required to attend the Ford English School, where they were taught the language and lectured on personal hygiene, manners, and proper work habits.

Ford managed his automobile company closely to ensure the efficiency of his workers and assembly-line system. When the company's profits declined in the 1930s, many people questioned his management skills. In 1945 Ford transferred control of his company to his grandson. He died two years later.

✔ **READING CHECK: Analyzing Information** How did Henry Ford change the nature of work during the 1920s? *He limited each worker to one or two specific tasks, shortened the workday, and increased wages.*

The impact of new products. The widespread use of the automobile and new products powered by electricity altered working conditions and decreased the availability of some jobs. Electric appliances made housework easier for those who could afford them. Many people hired fewer domestic servants. In the past, servants had done the laundry and heavy cleaning in most middle- and upper-class homes. With

Analyzing Primary Sources

Analyzing Information How does this speaker describe the assembly line? *as a tiring slave driver*

INTERPRETING THE VISUAL RECORD

Ford's workers. One of Henry Ford's goals was to instill American values in his workers. *How does this photograph reflect Ford's goal to Americanize his workers?*

INTERPRETING THE VISUAL RECORD

Automobiles. With the growing number of automobiles on the nation's roads, new businesses such as filling stations and drive-in restaurants opened. *How did this gas station from the 1920s serve the needs of automobile owners?*

Many Americans began driving cars as a leisure-time activity.

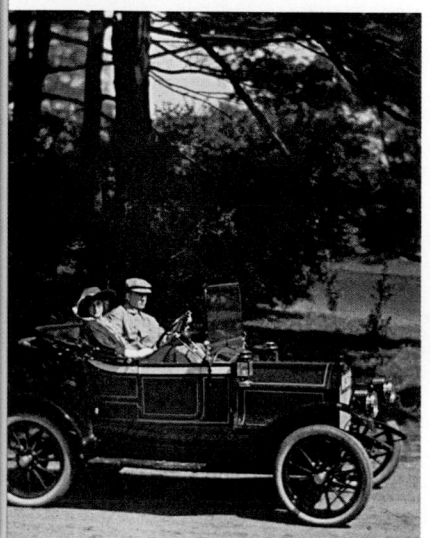

the introduction of electrical appliances, many middle-class housewives began doing this work themselves. The use of the automobile by middle-class families to run errands limited the need for delivery services and led to further unemployment.

A Land of Automobiles

Henry Ford's inexpensive Model T revolutionized the transportation industry. By 1930, cars, trucks, and buses had almost completely replaced horse-drawn vehicles. Trains and trolley cars also lost riders to automobiles.

To accommodate the increased traffic, more than 400,000 miles of new roads were built during the 1920s. A host of new structures—billboards, drive-in restaurants, filling stations, and tourist cabins—appeared along the nation's highways.

The automobile enabled rural residents to have greater contact with their neighbors and more access to shopping and leisure activities. Cars also made it easier for rural residents to relocate to cities and for city-dwellers to visit the country. At the same time, the automobile contributed to the depopulation of the nation's inner cities. Thousands of middle-class families moved to the suburbs, which were more accessible than ever.

Auto-tourism. Seeking the fresh air of the countryside, millions of Americans participated in a new craze—**auto-touring**. Taking part in this new pastime, Americans used their automobiles for camping and sightseeing vacations. Auto-touring allowed Americans to travel without the restrictions imposed by the schedules and routes of passenger trains. Guidebooks urged Americans to hit the road.

History Makers Speak **"Does father crave to fish for trout and bass and pike and musky? Take him auto-touring. Does sister want to dip in the surf . . . or see the world? Take her automobile vacationing. . . . Does mother sigh for a rest from daily routines? Take her touring."**

—Frank E. Brimmer, *Motor Campcraft*

Family life. Automobiles also transformed family life. The automobile created new social opportunities for teenagers. Sociologists Robert and Helen Lynd took note of this change in *Middletown*, their 1929 book chronicling life in Muncie, Indiana.

History Makers Speak **"The extensive use of this new tool [the automobile] by the young has enormously extended their mobility and the range of alternatives before them; joining a crowd motoring over to a dance . . . twenty miles away may be a matter of a moment's decision, with no one's permission asked."**

—Robert and Helen Lynd, *Middletown*

Before the use of automobiles became widespread, teenagers spent much of their leisure time at home with their families. With the arrival of the automobile, teenagers could spend their free time differently. "What on earth do you want me to do? Just sit around home all evening!" protested

TEACH OBJECTIVE 5

LEVELS 1 AND 2: To help students understand how American industries encouraged the transformation of consumer practices, copy the graphic organizer at right on the chalkboard, omitting the italicized answers. Have each student complete it. Ask volunteers to share their answers with the class. Conclude by leading a discussion with the class about how American industries transformed consumer practices.
English Language Learners

installment plan → **CHANGING CONSUMER PRACTICES** ← *new materials and designs*, *advertising*
planned obsolescence → **CHANGING CONSUMER PRACTICES** ← *retail chain stores*

---

one teenage girl when her father expressed his disapproval of her going riding in a car with a young man.

Critics claimed that cars reduced people's sense of community. The Lynds observed that "since the advent of the automobile and the movies," people in Muncie no longer spent "long summer evenings and Sunday afternoons on the porch or in the side yard." One mother explained, "in the nineties [1890s] we were all much more together. People brought chairs . . . and sat on the lawn evenings." By the 1920s cars had begun to cause pollution, traffic jams, and parking problems. Most serious was the rising accident rate.

✔ **READING CHECK: Contrasting** What were Americans' daily lives like after automobiles became more available? Cars, trucks, and buses replaced horse-drawn vehicles. Auto-touring became a national pastime. Teenagers gained greater social opportunities.

Skill-Building Strategies

Using Primary and Secondary Sources

Most of the wide variety of materials used by historians to form their accounts of the past can be classified into two basic categories: primary sources and secondary sources. Primary sources—materials made up of firsthand historical information—include artwork, diaries, and legal documents. In contrast, secondary sources are descriptions or interpretations of historical events that were written by nonparticipants after the events occurred. *The American Nation* is a secondary source. Primary and secondary sources are both essential tools for historians. Primary sources contain historical information that cannot be found anywhere else. Secondary sources can cover broad historical topics and evaluate the long-term consequences of events.

How to Use a Primary or Secondary Source

1. **Identify the type of source.** First, determine whether the source is a primary source or a secondary source. Then, if possible, find out about the historical background of the source's creator and the intended audience of the source.
2. **Examine the material carefully.** Study the source carefully, taking note of its main ideas and supporting details.
3. **Check for bias.** Check the source for any words, phrases, and ideas that express the point of view of its creator. Make sure to identify any instances in which a one-sided view of a event, person, or topic is presented.

4. **Put the information to use.** If possible, compare the source with other primary or secondary sources that address the same subject. Then use the results of your analysis to form generalizations and draw conclusions.

Applying the Skill

Study the magazine cover on the right, which was published in the November 1927 issue of the *Ladies' Home Journal.*

LADIES' HOME JOURNAL

Practicing the Skill

Using the cover, answer the following questions.
1. Is this image a primary source or a secondary source? Explain your answer.
2. Who created the image? Who do you think was the magazine's intended audience?
3. Does the magazine cover express any biases? If so, what are they?
4. How does the source contribute to your understanding of the United States during the 1920s?

INTERDISCIPLINARY CONNECTIONS

▶SOCIOLOGY◀

Robert and Helen Lynd's *Middletown.* To write *Middletown*, Robert Lynd and Helen Lynd applied cultural anthropology methods to the examination of a modern U.S. city. This sociological study examined everyday life in Muncie, Indiana, and showed how the consumer culture of the 1920s had influenced the values and behavior of the city's residents. Critic H. L. Mencken called the book "one of the richest and most valuable documents ever concocted by American sociologists." In 1937 Robert and Helen Lynd published *Middletown in Transition*, which described the social effects of the Great Depression on Muncie.

CRITICAL THINKING Why might the Lynds have entitled their book *Middletown*?

ANSWER: Students might suggest that the Lynds wanted to convey that Muncie was a "typical small American city."

SKILL-BUILDING STRATEGIES ANSWERS
Practicing the Skill
1. a primary source—it contains firsthand information

2. *Ladies' Home Journal;* middle-class women

3. middle-class tastes

4. reflects women's styles in hair and clothing during the 1920s

LEVEL 3: Tell students to imagine that they are participants in a panel discussion at a conference on the transformation of consumer practices during the 1920s. Organize the class into two groups. Have one group act as questioners and the other group act as cultural critics. Have both groups prepare for the discussion by taking notes on the techniques and strategies that businesses used to change consumer practices. (*See the Levels 1 and 2 lesson for the correct techniques and strategies.*) Then conduct the panel discussion. **Cooperative Learning**

The General Motors Corporation. Although General Motors Corporation (GM) eventually grew into the largest automobile manufacturer in the world, it began as a risky business venture. Organized in 1908 by William C. Durant, a wealthy carriage maker from Michigan, GM first acquired small car companies that were unable to compete on their own. By the end of 1909 it had acquired more than 20 such enterprises. Over the next decade, GM struggled to finance and coordinate these holdings. The company did not fully succeed until Alfred P. Sloan took control in 1920 and reorganized it into five basic manufacturing divisions: Buick, Cadillac, Chevrolet, Oldsmobile, and Pontiac.

CRITICAL THINKING How might Sloan's action have reflected a marketing strategy that differed from Ford's?

ANSWER: Students might suggest that each division was designed to produce cars in a specific price range.

VISUAL RECORD ANSWER

Students might mention the shining metal and the streamlined shape.

VISUAL RECORD ANSWER

(for p. 421)

Students might suggest soup or other canned goods.

INTERPRETING THE VISUAL RECORD

Design. In the 1920s, manufacturers began to pay attention to the way a product looked. *What elements of this iron do you think were designed to attract a customer's attention?*

Advertisements such as this one for mouthwash played on the social fears of many Americans.

She bags the *bouquets* but never a *Beau*

You never have it? — *what colossal conceit!*

End halitosis with LISTERINE

Creating Consumers

Henry Ford manufactured his affordable Model T throughout the 1920s. He made few changes to its design. However, other automobile companies, such as General Motors (GM), began designing more expensive cars that emphasized luxury. **Alfred P. Sloan**, head of GM, explained the effect of car owners buying a second car. They "created the demand, not for basic transportation, but for progress in new cars, for comfort, convenience, power, and style."

Marketing. To allow average consumers to buy his more expensive cars, Sloan offered an **installment plan**. These plans allowed consumers to pay for their cars over time. By 1926, buyers purchased about 75 percent of cars on credit. The practice soon spread to cover the purchase of many other items such as kitchen appliances, pianos, and sewing machines. As one car dealer noted, installment plans were a profitable venture.

History Makers Speak

"To keep America growing we must keep Americans working, and to keep Americans working we must keep them wanting; wanting more than the bare necessities; wanting the luxuries and frills that make life so much more worthwhile, and installment selling makes it easier to keep Americans wanting."

—car dealer, quoted in *Car Culture*, by Walter Engard

To make their goods more appealing, industrial designers began to create items that were pleasing to look at as well as functional. Industrial designers used new materials such as stainless steel and plastics to create a wide range of more modern-looking products. They developed streamlining—the shaping of surfaces to reduce wind resistance—for cars, planes, ships, and trains. Designers even applied streamlining to nonmoving objects such as clocks, radios, and appliances.

Manufacturers quickly learned that introducing new models of what was essentially the same product could boost sales. Manufacturers made products specifically designed to go out of style and then replaced them with an up-to-date model. They had discovered what came to be called **planned obsolescence**. Automobile manufacturers were among the first to adopt planned obsolescence. In the early 1920s General Motors introduced to the public the concept of the yearly model change and the trade-in. Thereafter, many families routinely traded in their "old" models and bought new cars every year.

The new consumer practice of purchasing goods on the installment plan only to turn around and purchase the latest style the next season caused problems for many Americans. A Department of Labor study in the 1920s reported that single working women were going into debt buying clothes to keep up with the latest styles.

Advertising. Advertising became big business in the 1920s. It fueled the demand for cars and other consumer goods. Before World War I, money spent on advertising totaled some $500 million yearly. By 1929 the total had soared to more than $3 billion. Ads were everywhere. Commercial messages appeared in magazines and newspapers, on billboards, and over the new medium of radio.

Most advertisements targeted women and used psychology to play on consumers' hopes and fears. Advertisements for Borden's milk, for example, warned mothers, "Hardly a family—well-to-do and poor alike—escapes the menace of malnutrition. Your own child may fall victim to this . . . evil."

Companies used slogans, jingles, and celebrity testimonials to fix product names in customers' minds. When her husband, Franklin D. Roosevelt, was governor of New York, Eleanor Roosevelt praised Cream of Wheat, a breakfast food that their son John had eaten since infancy. She claimed in advertisements that the cereal "has undoubtedly played its part in building his robust physique."

A growing retail industry. As the number of products increased to meet growing consumer demand, a new type of store spread across the country. Chain-style grocery stores slowly began to replace the traditional corner markets. The A&P grocery chain grew from some 3,000 stores in 1922 to about 14,000 by 1925. New technology allowed stores to stock a wider variety of products. The development of quick-freezing techniques and cellophane—a transparent wrapping material first produced in the United States in 1924—helped to preserve fresh foods longer. As a result, food could be shipped over greater distances.

INTERPRETING THE VISUAL RECORD

Retail. Chain stores like this A&P brought a wide variety of products to American shoppers. *What products are displayed in this window?*

✔ **READING CHECK: Identifying Cause and Effect** How did tactics such as planned obsolescence and advertising help increase consumer demand? They encouraged consumers to either buy a replacement for a product one year after purchasing it or to buy new products.

SECTION ① REVIEW

1. Define and explain:
scientific management
assembly line
auto-touring
installment plan
planned obsolescence

2. Identify and explain:
Frederick W. Taylor
Henry Ford
Model T
Alfred P. Sloan

3. Analyzing Information Copy the organizational web below. Use it to explain how the factors shown inspired the new consumer demands that emerged during the 1920s.

Electricity — Economic Prosperity — NEW CONSUMER DEMANDS — Scientific Management — New Products — Advertising

4. Finding the Main Idea
a. What impact did Henry Ford and his business practices have on life in the 1920s?
b. If you had been a factory worker during the 1920s, would you have taken a job with Ford? Why or why not?
c. How did the widespread use of the automobile affect family life, leisure activities, and working life for some Americans?

5. Writing and Critical Thinking
Comparing and Contrasting During the 1920s businesses used various tactics to encourage Americans to buy their products. Write a short essay on the positive and negative effects of these business practices.
Consider:
• how installment plans and planned obsolescence altered consumer practices
• what influence advertising had on American consumer habits
• how the growth of the retail industry contributed to the prosperity of the 1920s

go. hrw .com Homework Practice Online
keyword: SE3 HP14

SECTION 2

After completing Section 2, students should be able to:

OBJECTIVE 1 Analyze the impact prohibition had on crime.

OBJECTIVE 2 Describe the characteristics of the new youth culture.

OBJECTIVE 3 Explain how celebrities and new forms of popular entertainment helped create a mass culture.

OBJECTIVE 4 Examine what the Scopes trial and the religious movements of the 1920s revealed about American society.

LET'S GET STARTED!

Ask students to speculate on how new forms of culture and new trends in society might result in conflicts between traditional values and modern trends. Call on students to identify such conflicts apparent in American society today. List students' responses on the chalkboard. Tell students that in Section 2 they will learn about changes in American culture during the 1920s that led to conflicts between people who longed for traditional standards and people who embraced modern trends.

SECTION 2 RESOURCES

REPRODUCIBLE
▶ Guided Reading Strategy 14.2
▶ Geography Activity 14: The Prohibition Era
▶ Primary Source Reading 14: Making a Monkey Out of the "Common Man"
▶ Biography Reading 14: Amelia Earhart

TECHNOLOGY
▶ One-Stop Planner, Lesson 14.2
▶ The American Nation Video Program Segment: Prohibition; Teacher's Guide, p. 211–12
▶ Holt Researcher: American History CD–ROM
▶ Homework Practice Online

REINFORCEMENT, REVIEW, AND ASSESSMENT
▶ Section 2 Review, p. 429
▶ Daily Quiz 14.2
▶ Main Idea Activity 14.2
▶ English Audio Summary 14.2
▶ Spanish Audio Summary 14.2

SECTION 2

READ TO DISCOVER
1. What impact did prohibition have on crime?
2. What were the characteristics of the new youth culture?
3. How did celebrities and new forms of popular entertainment help create a mass culture?
4. What did the religious movements of the 1920s and the Scopes trial reveal about American society?

DEFINE
flappers

IDENTIFY
Volstead Act
Al Capone
Eliot Ness
Untouchables
Twenty-first Amendment
Cecil B. DeMille
Babe Ruth
Jim Thorpe
Charles Lindbergh
Amelia Earhart
Aimee Semple McPherson
Fundamentalism
Clarence Darrow
Scopes trial

WHY IT MATTERS TODAY
Fads and novelty events are still a feature of American life. Use **CNNfyi.com** or other **current events** sources to learn more about current fads. Record your findings in your journal.

CNNfyi.com

Life in the Twenties

EYEWITNESSES TO History
"About four or five days after I had gotten the vacuum tube hooked up, I started to hear music coming across the wires. Music! And then, between the music, I could hear somebody talking. . . . 'I am Dr. Conrad. I am experimenting with radio station 8XK.' . . . By January of 1921, I had decided to build my own broadcast station. I built a hundred-watter and then applied for an experimental broadcast license. In March I got a letter saying: 'One of my first official duties as Secretary of Commerce is to award you this license. Aren't you the young fellow I met . . . in Marion, Ohio? . . . What's a fourteen-year-old kid going to do with a broadcast station?"

—Albert Sindlinger, quoted in *The Century*, by Peter Jennings and Todd Brewster

1920s radio receiver

Albert Sindlinger began experimenting with radio broadcasts as a young teenager in the 1920s. The first licensed radio stations were just beginning to broadcast music, news reports, and sports events. Commercial radio linked Americans from coast to coast, leading some to call the decade of the 1920s the gateway to modern America. For the first time, a truly national mass culture took shape in the United States. This emerging mass culture led to conflicts between traditional values and modern trends.

Prohibition

One of the most disruptive issues of the 1920s was the prohibition of the sale and distribution of alcoholic beverages. Progressive reformers seeking to combat crime, family violence, and poverty had long called for a ban on alcohol. During World War I, many reformers had supported prohibition as a wartime measure. They pointed out that drinking reduced the efficiency of soldiers and workers. The Eighteenth Amendment—which prohibited the manufacture, sale, and transportation of alcoholic beverages—was ratified in January 1919. That October, Congress passed the **Volstead Act** to enforce the amendment.

In some regions prohibition was strictly enforced, and alcohol consumption declined. However, in many parts of the country, particularly in the cities, prohibition was extremely unpopular and widely ignored. Americans frequented speakeasies, clubs or bars where liquor was sold illegally. They also made their own liquor and bought bootleg alcohol or alcohol illegally smuggled in from Canada, Mexico, or the West Indies.

Bootlegging became one of the decade's most profitable businesses. In large cities, criminal gangs controlled liquor sales. **Al Capone** ruled Chicago's underworld with his small army of mobsters. To gain control over all liquor sales in Chicago, Capone's mob waged a violent war on rival gangs. Chicago's prohibition

![flag icon] **TEACH OBJECTIVE 1**

LEVEL 1: Tell students that many Americans ignored prohibition and made or sold liquor illegally. Pair students and ask them to list the impact that prohibition had on crime. *(Students might suggest that prohibition led to increased crime rates by creating an illegal market for alcohol. People frequented speakeasies, made their own liquor, or bought bootleg alcohol. In large cities, violent criminal gangs controlled this illegal market.)* Have volunteers read their lists to the class. Discuss students' responses as a class.
English Language Learners, Cooperative Learning

LEVELS 2 AND 3: Tell students to imagine that they are members of Congress during the 1920s. They are studying the impact of prohibition on crime in order to prepare a report for a committee meeting. Have each student prepare a brief report about the effects of prohibition on crime. *(See the Level 1 lesson for the correct effects.)* Ask volunteers to read their reports to the class.

gang wars reached a peak on Saint Valentine's Day in 1929. On that day, several members of Capone's gang massacred seven members of a rival gang.

Hoping to stem bootlegging, corruption, and violence, the federal Prohibition Bureau hired special agent **Eliot Ness**. He organized a top squad of young detectives to go after gangsters. Unlike corrupt city police officers who often ignored bootlegging, Ness's men strictly enforced prohibition laws. Because of their dedication and honesty, Ness and his detectives were nicknamed the **Untouchables**. Ness ended Capone's reign over the Chicago underworld in 1931. Capone was arrested for evading income tax payments. During his prison sentence Capone lost his control over organized crime in Chicago.

Despite the gang violence that plagued the era, prohibition had some positive consequences. Alcoholism and the number of alcohol-related deaths declined. Prohibition's negative results, however, drew more attention. Prohibition led to a widespread breakdown of law and order. It turned millions of otherwise law-abiding Americans into lawbreakers before it was repealed by the ratification of the **Twenty-first Amendment** in 1933.

Al Capone attracted public attention by dressing in expensive clothing and living a lavish lifestyle.

✔ **READING CHECK: Categorizing** What were the positive and negative effects of prohibition? positive—decline in alcoholism and the number of alcohol-related deaths; negative—widespread breakdown of law and order

Youth Culture

Many young Americans ignored prohibition laws. Some members of the younger generation openly rejected the values and conventions of previous generations. As a result, a new youth culture began to emerge in the 1920s.

The "new woman." Changes in women's behavior and dress represented many of these challenges to traditional ways. During the 1920s, magazines, movies, and literature began to discuss the life of the "new woman." This woman was stylish, adventurous, independent, and often career-minded.

Reacting against a strict pre–World War I code of behavior, some young women exercised new freedom in how they dressed. They stopped wearing heavy corsets and started wearing shorter skirts and transparent silk hose.

People began to refer to young women who adopted the new style as **flappers**. Flappers enjoyed defying traditional standards of female behavior. For example, many young women began to wear bobbed, or short, hair. Young women also drove cars and participated in sports. Although not all women adopted this new lifestyle, the image of the flapper caught the attention of the media.

The new woman also sought economic independence. Although the proportion of working women remained fairly constant throughout the 1920s, American women worked in a wider variety of occupations. Some drove taxis. Others ran telegraph lines, worked as stenographers, flew airplanes, and hauled freight. Most, however, continued to pursue traditionally female careers such as nursing, teaching, and domestic service.

INTERPRETING THE VISUAL RECORD

Youth culture. This 1920s magazine cover shows some of the characteristics of the new youth culture, such as the woman's bobbed hair and the man's baggy pants. *What other aspects of life in the 1920s does this magazine cover show?*

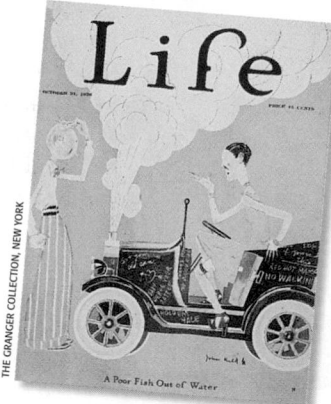

THE GRANGER COLLECTION, NEW YORK

***The American Nation* VIDEO PROGRAM**
Prohibition; Teacher's Guide, pp. 211–12

Search 37756, Play to 38875
Videodisc 2, Side A

Play   Pause

See *Teacher's Guide* for Spanish barcode.

VISUAL RECORD ANSWER
Students might suggest women's independence and changes in women's fashion.

LEVELS 1 AND 2: Tell students to imagine that they have been asked to create a series of trading cards featuring the characteristics of youth culture during the 1920s. Pair students and have them create trading cards depicting the characteristics of the "new woman," college life, and leisure activities. Have students illustrate the front of each card. On the back of each card, students should write a brief summary of the card's subject. (*Students might mention that the "new woman" sought social and economic independence. Young women often drove cars, wore bobbed hair and participated in sports. Many held jobs. College life also had its own fashions, including baggy flannel slacks and sport jackets. Leisure activities* included dance marathons and novelty events such as flagpole sitting.) Have students present their trading cards to the class. Conclude by leading a discussion comparing 1920s youth culture with today's youth culture.
English Language Learners, Cooperative Learning

LEVEL 3: Tell students to imagine that they are radio personalities during the 1920s. Pair students and have them write a script for a radio talk show in which they discuss the characteristics of youth culture. (*See the Levels 1 and 2 lesson for the correct characteristics.*) Ask each pair to perform its talk show for the class. **Cooperative Learning**

HISTORY MAKERS SPEAK

George Robinson in *Listening to Radio, 1920–1950*

The "Magical" Effect of Radio.
Radio broadcasts made many Americans feel "connected" to people in other parts of the United States in a way they had never experienced. George Robinson, who was a young boy in Mississippi when his family acquired a radio in 1926, later recalled this feeling: "The sounds which came from [the radio] were truly magic to a family in Greenville, Mississippi, who thought that Memphis was somewhere on the other side of the globe. We stared at the thing, and at each other, in wonderment as we realized that the voices were actually coming through the air from KMOX in St. Louis and WLW in Cincinnati and WJR in Detroit. I can't recall what was being broadcast, which is unimportant."

ACTIVITY: Ask students to create a list of other forms of technology that have "connected" Americans during the 1900s. Then call on volunteers for examples and discuss them with the class.

Collegiate clothing such as school sweaters became fashionable during the 1920s.

Hoping to better portray their characters, actors in 1920s radio programs such as Professor Ambrose Weems produced their programs in costume.

THE GRANGER COLLECTION, NEW YORK

College life. In the early 1900s, most Americans' formal education did not extend past high school. Between 1900 and 1930, however, college enrollment tripled. The greatest increase came during the 1920s. Most of these college students came from middle- and upper-class families.

The growing number of college students influenced popular culture. Advertising, magazines, and movies focused on collegiate fashions and lifestyles. According to a 1923 California university newspaper, "'College style' has a definite meaning. . . . Fall '23 can almost be called the young man's season with the style pace set by the collegian." The "collegiate" look included baggy flannel slacks and sports jackets.

Leisure fun and fads. New leisure activities and a variety of fads spread among American youth during the 1920s. Many young people participated in dance marathons. Couples danced for days, competing for prize money awarded to the last couple to collapse or drop out. To keep their partners awake, couples used smelling salts or ice packs. In 1928, couples danced for almost three weeks—482 hours—in the "Dance Derby of the Century."

Beauty contests were also introduced in the 1920s. Hotel operators and merchants in Atlantic City, New Jersey, founded the Miss America beauty pageant in 1921. Contestants were judged primarily on their hair, smile, and appearance in a bathing suit. Despite the emphasis on the competitive display of female beauty, managers of the first beauty contests also stressed traditional morals.

Novelty events such as flagpole sitting attracted media attention and drew crowds of Americans. Flagpole sitters climbed onto tiny platforms atop flagpoles and sat, with only stirrups for support. Taking short breaks every hour, flagpole sitters could last for days. Alvin "Shipwreck" Kelly was the most popular flagpole sitter. As the fad caught on, Kelly was routinely hired for publicity stunts by theaters and hotels. He claimed to have sat for a total of 145 days on flagpoles across the United States in 1929.

✔ **READING CHECK: Contrasting** How did the new youth culture of the 1920s represent change? Flappers adopted a new style of dress and emphasized independence. College enrollment jumped, and new fads developed among young people.

Mass Entertainment

Young people were not the only Americans enjoying new leisure activities. The economic boom of the 1920s meant that many—although not all—Americans had bigger paychecks and more free time than in years past. To help fill their leisure hours, many Americans turned to radio, movies, and professional sports for entertainment.

Radio. Commercial radio stations emerged during the early 1920s and grew in popularity as more Americans purchased radio receivers. The first stations, Detroit's WWJ and Pittsburgh's KDKA, went on the air in 1920. By 1929 more than 800 stations reached over 10 million homes.

The radio programming of the early 1920s was diverse. Stations broadcast church services, local news reports, music, and sporting events. Two early radio

HOMEWORK *Have each student create a mobile that displays symbols associated with the "new woman" of the 1920s. Students should write an explanation of the symbols they have chosen.*

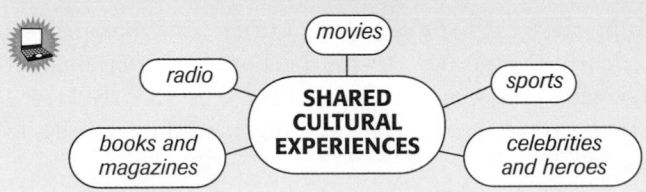

SHARED CULTURAL EXPERIENCES
- radio
- movies
- books and magazines
- sports
- celebrities and heroes

TEACH OBJECTIVE 3

LEVEL 1: To help students understand how celebrities and new forms of popular entertainment helped create a mass culture in the 1920s, copy the graphic organizer at right on the chalkboard, omitting the italicized answers. Have each student complete it. Ask volunteers to share their answers with the class. Conclude by leading a discussion about the mass culture that was created during the 1920s.
English Language Learners

LEVEL 2: Tell students to imagine that they are magazine editors during the 1920s and are responsible for creating a magazine cover on the emergence of a mass culture. Pair students and have them create a magazine cover that shows how celebrities and forms of popular entertainment helped create a mass culture. *(See the Level 1 lesson for the correct ways.)*
Cooperative Learning

---

events with the largest numbers of listeners were played in 1921. The Radio Corporation of America broadcast the Dempsey-Carpenter heavyweight title fight, and Westinghouse broadcast the World Series.

Radio stations soon discovered that they could make money by selling advertisement spots. Stations allowed businesses to sponsor programs and to thus advertise their products. Companies such as the A&P grocery store chain and the maker of Ipana toothpaste sponsored such music programs as the *A&P Gypsies* and the *Ipana Troubadours*.

During the late 1920s national radio networks such as the National Broadcasting Company (NBC) began offering local radio networks packages of programs to broadcast. These national radio programs provided Americans with a set of shared cultural experiences. Americans across the country laughed at the same jokes and listened to the same music and the same ads. One executive noted that by allowing companies to advertise nationwide, the radio served as "a latchkey to nearly every home in the United States."

Movies. In the 1920s Americans increasingly turned to movies for entertainment. The mass appeal of movie theaters impressed journalist Lloyd Lewis.

History Makers Speak

❝In the 'de luxe' [movie] house every man is a king and every woman a queen. Most of these cinema palaces sell all their seats at the same price,—and get it; the rich man stands in line with the poor. . . . In this suave atmosphere, the differences . . . that determine our lives outside are forgotten. All men enter these portals equal, and thus the movies are perhaps a symbol of democracy.❞

—Lloyd Lewis, *The New Republic*, March 27, 1929

New advances in the art of moviemaking attracted even larger audiences. Movie director **Cecil B. DeMille** introduced a new style of filmmaking marked by epic plots and complex characters. DeMille created biblical epics such as *The Ten Commandments* (1923). He also made films that focused on the changing morals of the 1920s, such as *Why Change Your Wife?* (1920) and *Forbidden Fruit* (1921). Many of these movies were made in Hollywood, California, which was quickly replacing New York and New Jersey as a filmmaking capital.

The performances of famous silent film actors such as Lon Chaney and Charlie Chaplin captivated moviegoers. Silent film star Tom Mix often played cowboys in popular westerns.

The era of silent films ended abruptly in 1927. That year, Warner Brothers released the first feature-length "talkie," *The Jazz Singer,* starring Al Jolson. The introduction of sound led to the creation of new types of films, such as musicals and newsreels—short films summing up the news of the day. In 1929 some 80 million Americans flocked to the theaters each week.

⭐ **Then and Now**

Censorship

The Roaring Twenties was a time of bathtub gin, gambling, jazz, short skirts, and the first talking movies. Old taboos were challenged one after the other. Alarmed and outraged by what they saw as the breakdown of the nation's moral standards, many community, government, and religious groups took action.

These activists pulled from library and store shelves books and magazines that used foul language, discussed sex frankly, or supported radical political ideas. U.S. Customs officials labeled many foreign books obscene. They even seized some books, including the acclaimed novel *Ulysses* by Irish author James Joyce. Groups like the American Civil Liberties Union (ACLU) opposed these restrictions on literature. They argued that censorship was a violation of the U.S. Constitution's First Amendment.

Today the battle between censorship and freedom of speech continues. The National Endowment for the Arts (NEA), for example, has come under attack for funding artists whose works some consider obscene. Although some critics judge the art as unsuitable for public funding, the artists defend their right to freedom of expression. The NEA and other agencies are caught in the middle of the battle.

Is such censorship a violation of free speech or a necessary form of protection? American society and U.S. courts continue to struggle with this question.

Protesting censorship

INTERPRETING THE VISUAL RECORD

The movies. Luxury movie houses such as this theater in New York attracted Americans of all income levels. *What features does this 1920s theater offer its customers?*

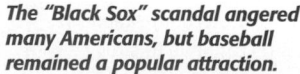

The "Black Sox" scandal angered many Americans, but baseball remained a popular attraction.

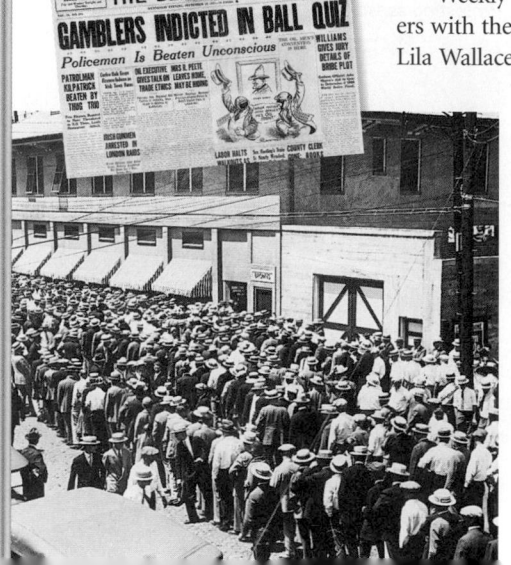

In the 1920s the rapidly changing standards of morality and sexuality portrayed in films troubled many Americans. Some popular films such as *The Sheik*, starring male sex symbol Rudolph Valentino, created controversy. Some Americans began to demand regulation. In 1922 Will Hays became the head of a newly created movie-industry group that set a code to limit offensive material in movies. By the early 1930s these regulations were rigorously enforced.

Sports. During the 1920s many Americans turned to sports for entertainment. Professional sports had emerged in the United States during the late 1800s. With the introduction of new technology in the 1920s, professional sports became a form of mass entertainment available to almost all Americans.

Professional and college-level football attracted many fans. Between 1921 and 1930 attendance at college football games doubled. College football stars like Red Grange joined professional football teams. Grange played his first game for the Chicago Bears on Thanksgiving Day 1925. The game attracted 35,000 fans, the largest crowd to attend a professional football game up to that time.

Baseball remained the nation's most popular sport despite charges of corruption. In the "Black Sox" scandal, "Shoeless" Joe Jackson and seven other Chicago White Sox players were accused of accepting money to lose the 1919 World Series. To restore order to the game, baseball team owners created a Commissioner of Baseball position and made Judge Kenesaw Mountain Landis the first commissioner. Landis expelled from professional baseball for life the suspected White Sox players. Legendary players such as **Babe Ruth**, Ty Cobb, and Lou Gehrig had outstanding seasons during the 1920s and attracted new fans. Millions of fans tuned in to radio broadcasts and attended games.

Books and magazines. In the 1920s new monthly and weekly publications provided Americans with sources of information and entertainment. For example, the Book-of-the-Month Club, founded in 1923, sold books directly to consumers. This enabled publishers to bypass bookstores.

Weekly magazines such as *Collier's* and *The Saturday Evening Post* drew readers with their cartoons, short stories, and many pages of advertising. DeWitt and Lila Wallace founded *Reader's Digest* in 1921. Designed for busy Americans with less time to read, *Reader's Digest* reprinted articles from other magazines in shortened form. It proved to be a big success.

✔ **READING CHECK: Drawing Conclusions** How did mass entertainment in the 1920s reflect the characteristics of the decade?
Movies reflected changing standards of morality. The Book-of-the-Month Club reflected the new consumerism.

Celebrities and Heroes

The mass appeal of movies, radio, and sports generated huge audiences who shared in celebrities' victories and accomplishments. Actors became instantly famous. Young Americans paid special attention to celebrities' personal habits. They often copied the

LEVEL 1: Have students design a "Coming Attractions" poster for a movie about the religious movements of the 1920s and the Scopes trial. Students' posters should reflect the characteristics of American society that the trial and the religious movements revealed. *(Posters might include Americans' differing opinions about social change, the influence of movies and radio on religion, or the deep division in American society between traditional religious values and new values based on scientific ways of thought.)*
English Language Learners

LEVEL 2: Tell students to imagine that they are visiting the United States in the 1920s and they attend both a religious revival and the Scopes trial. Have each student write a letter to a friend back home, describing these events and what they reveal about American society in the 1920s. *(See the Level 1 lesson for the correct characteristics.)* Ask volunteers to read their letters to the class.

HOMEWORK *Have students locate and bring to class an artifact that illustrates one form of mass culture during the 1920s. Students might obtain newspaper accounts of sporting events, radio scripts, sheet music, or silent films. Have students prepare an oral report or write a brief essay to explain the artifact.*

---

behavior of stars. For example, in the 1928 movie *A Woman of Affairs*, Greta Garbo wore a slouch hat. It instantly became the most popular women's hat style.

Athletes also received celebrity status during the 1920s. Babe Ruth was one sports favorite. Known as the Sultan of Swat, Ruth dominated baseball from 1920 to 1934. During this time he led the New York Yankees to four World Series championships. In 1927 Ruth astounded the sports world with a record 60 home runs. Ruth's flashy playing on the field and scandalous life off the field attracted much attention.

Few athletes of the 1920s had more talent than **Jim Thorpe**. As a student, Thorpe played every intercollegiate sport offered at his school. After leaving school, he began training for the Olympics. At the 1912 games, held in Stockholm, Sweden, Thorpe became the first competitor to win both the pentathlon and the decathlon. He then went on to a career in major-league baseball. Thorpe also played professional football for several years.

Pilot **Charles Lindbergh** was probably the biggest celebrity of the 1920s. Lindbergh was a young, clean-cut pilot from Minnesota who flew airmail cargo planes between St. Louis and Chicago. In May 1927 he took off in a small, single-engine plane named *Spirit of St. Louis*. He wanted to win a $25,000 prize that had been offered to the first pilot to fly nonstop from New York to Paris. Lindbergh overcame bad weather, hunger, and fatigue. He successfully completed his solo flight after 33.5 hours, landing on a Paris airfield.

Lindbergh's flight tapped into the American infatuation with contests and adventure. It became one of the most talked-about exploits of the 1920s. New Yorkers threw a ticker-tape parade for Lindbergh. President Coolidge received the modest young man at the White House. The next year, **Amelia Earhart** became the first woman to fly across the Atlantic Ocean.

✔ **READING CHECK: Making Generalizations** In what ways did celebrities help create a mass culture? People nationwide were able to learn about celebrities and copy their style.

Religion in the 1920s

Some Americans found the social changes of the 1920s more troubling than exciting. Many citizens' lives still centered on church, family, and neighborhood, and religion remained a vital part of American culture.

Revivalism. Many Americans were worried about declining moral standards. Religious leaders preached sermons and wrote books denouncing the evils of popular entertainment and alcohol. The message of these religious leaders inspired a new era of revivalism.

To compete with movies and radio for the public's attention, some religious leaders began using Hollywood-style entertainment to spread their message of morality. **Aimee Semple McPherson** was one of the most popular revivalists. She combined a strong Christian message with the glamour of Hollywood. Her signature outfit was a white dress,

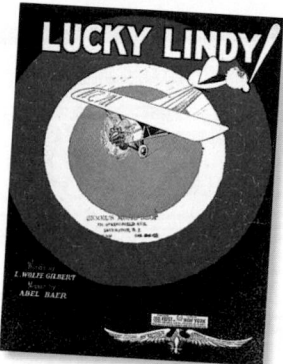

Charles Lindbergh's solo flight across the Atlantic Ocean captured the public's attention. This sheet music celebrates Lindbergh's flight.

INTERPRETING THE VISUAL RECORD

Religion. Aimee Semple McPherson was a popular revivalist preacher in the 1920s. *Does this image suggest that McPherson was influenced by the movie industry? Explain.*

Amelia Earhart. A Kansas native, Amelia Earhart took an interest in aviation while serving as a military nurse during World War I. She learned to fly while working in a Boston settlement house during the 1920s. In 1928 Earhart was a passenger on a transatlantic flight, which was organized by a New York publisher. It brought her instant fame. Four years later "Lady Lindy" became the first woman to fly solo across the Atlantic Ocean and in 1935 she completed the first solo flight from Hawaii to California. In 1937, after Purdue University presented her with a new, technologically advanced airplane, Earhart set out with navigator Fred Noonan to fly point-to-point around the world. After completing more than two thirds of the trip, they disappeared over the middle of the Pacific Ocean.

ACTIVITY: Ask students to conduct research on another celebrity from the 1920s. Then have them present brief oral reports on their research to the class.

VISUAL RECORD ANSWER

Students answering yes might cite her hair style and pose. Students answering no might mention her career choice.

LEVEL 3: Tell students to imagine that they are community leaders during the 1920s who must give a speech in the wake of the Scopes trial. Have each student prepare a brief speech that addresses the trial, and the religious movements of the 1920s, and what they reveal about American society. *(See the Level 1 lesson for the correct characteristics.)* Ask volunteers to deliver their speeches to the class.

PENTECOSTALISM

Pentecostalism grew rapidly during the 1920s. The movement, however, had begun decades earlier. Pentecostalism began as a series of multidenominational revivals held in the Midwest during the 1890s. Charles F. Parham led the first Pentecostal revival in Topeka, Kansas, in 1901. Parham started the movement because he was convinced that real spirituality lay in experiencing the "baptism of the Holy Spirit." With their emphasis on experiencing the Holy Spirit, Pentecostal worship services were lively and emotional. Services often included faith healing and people speaking in tongues, or unfamiliar languages. Parham and his followers believed that an individual possessed by the Holy Spirit would be able to speak in other languages, and therefore be able to spread the faith.

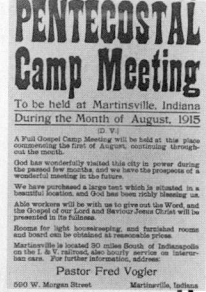

Revival meetings were popular in the 1920s.

The faith's focus on the direct experience of the Holy Spirit rather than on complex religious teachings attracted many Americans, particularly those with little formal education. In addition, the faith's emphasis on missionary work attracted a racially diverse following. In 1906 William Joseph Seymour, an African American preacher, brought the Pentecostal movement to California.

With the spread of Pentecostalism during the 1920s, hundreds of locally independent Pentecostal churches opened. The missionary movement of the Pentecostal faith proved remarkably successful. Today there are some 11.1 million Pentecostals in the United States and several hundred million worldwide. ▪

white shoes, and blue cape. Her church, the International Church of the Foursquare Gospel, was headquartered in Los Angeles, near Hollywood. McPherson's dramatic religious services combined an orchestra, chorus, and elaborate stage sets. Her church was closely tied to the rapidly expanding Protestant movement called Pentecostalism.

Fundamentalism. Responding to the rapidly changing society of the 1920s, many Americans turned to a more conservative approach to their religious faith. A Protestant movement called **Fundamentalism** gained popularity during the decade. Followers of Fundamentalist views resisted many of the new practices of other Protestant groups. The term *Fundamentalist* came from a series of booklets published between 1910 and 1915 called *The Fundamentals*. The booklets argued that traditional Christian doctrine should be accepted without question. Fundamentalists believed that every word of the Bible should be regarded as literally true. They attacked Christian "liberals" who had accepted modern scientific learning, such as the theory of evolution. Fundamentalists claimed that this "modernism" weakened Christianity and contributed to the moral decline of the nation.

Evangelical preachers who spread the Fundamentalist "old-time religion" found an eager audience in rural towns and in urban areas where traditional values remained strong. People were spellbound by preacher Billy Sunday's evangelical showmanship. He attracted people with his rousing attacks on card playing, dancing, and drinking.

The Scopes trial. Fundamentalism went on trial in a famous court case in July 1925. Earlier that year the Tennessee legislature had outlawed the teaching of Charles Darwin's theory of human evolution in the state's public schools. To test the law's constitutionality, the American Civil Liberties Union offered to defend any Tennessee schoolteacher who would challenge the statute. John Scopes, a science teacher from the town of Dayton, accepted the offer. Scopes's chief defense attorney was **Clarence Darrow**, a famous criminal lawyer from Chicago. The prosecution's star attorney was the elderly William Jennings Bryan. Bryan had been a three-time Democratic presidential candidate and secretary of state. A small group of journalists also traveled to Dayton for the trial.

The **Scopes trial** exposed a deep division in American society between traditional religious values and new values based on scientific ways of thought. Bryan spoke for many Americans who felt that the theory of evolution contradicted deeply held religious beliefs. Bryan spoke before the trial to an audience of local admirers:

REVIEW

Have students complete the **Section 2 Review** on p. 429.

ASSESS

Have students complete **Daily Quiz 14.2.** As **Alternative Assessment**, you may want to use the radio show script or the trading cards in this section's lessons.

RETEACH

Have students complete **Main Idea Activity for English Language Learners and Special-Needs Students 14.2.** Then prepare several sets of index cards. Write one of this section's key terms or key people on each card. Pair students and distribute a set of cards to each pair. Have each student in the pair take half of the cards. Have each student provide a series of clues about the terms on his or her cards to help his or her partner correctly identify the terms.
English Language Learners, Cooperative Learning

EXTEND

Using the library and other resources, have students conduct research on the famed exchange between Clarence Darrow and William Jennings Bryan during the Scopes trial. Have students write an essay based on their research in which they explain how Darrow's questioning of Bryan revealed the undercurrent of conflict in American life between traditional religious values and modern trends. **Block Scheduling**

History Makers Speak

❝Our purpose and our only purpose is to vindicate [uphold] the right of parents to guard the religion of their children against efforts made in the name of science to undermine faith in supernatural religion.❞

—William Jennings Bryan, quoted in *Bryan and Darrow at Dayton,* by Leslie Henri Allen

Clarence Darrow expressed a different yet also widely held view. He attacked the Tennessee law as a threat to free expression. In one courtroom speech, Darrow warned his listeners. "Today it is the public school teachers, tomorrow the private, the next day the preachers and the lecturers, the magazines, the books, the newspapers."

From the beginning, Darrow had little chance of winning the trial. Judge John T. Raulston opened the trial with a prayer and refused to allow testimony from scientific experts. Darrow responded by calling Bryan as an expert witness on the Bible. During his testimony, Bryan affirmed his belief in the literal truth of the Bible. Darrow forced Bryan to reveal inconsistencies in his interpretation of scripture. For example, Darrow asked Bryan if the world was literally created in six days, as stated in the Bible. Bryan responded that a "day" did not necessarily mean 24 hours.

Darrow's defense failed to convince the jury. Scopes was found guilty and fined $100. The verdict seemed a victory for Fundamentalists. However, some press accounts of the trial, which often portrayed Bryan and his cause as narrow-minded, lowered some people's opinions of Fundamentalism.

Clarence Darrow (left) and William Jennings Bryan (right) represented opposing sides in the Scopes trial.

✔ **READING CHECK: Evaluating** How did Fundamentalism help shape the national identity? Many Fundamentalists claimed that "modernism" weakened Christianity and contributed to the moral decline of the entire nation.

SECTION 2 REVIEW

1. Define and explain:
flappers

2. Identify and explain:
Volstead Act
Al Capone
Eliot Ness
Untouchables
Twenty-first Amendment
Cecil B. DeMille
Babe Ruth
Jim Thorpe
Charles Lindbergh
Amelia Earhart
Aimee Semple McPherson
Fundamentalism
Clarence Darrow
Scopes trial

3. Identifying Cause and Effect
Copy the graphic organizer below. Use it to explain how prohibition led to an increase in crime and how the government tried to combat this crime.

Prohibition
↓
Crime
↑
Government Efforts

4. Finding the Main Idea
a. What contributed to the changing role of women in the 1920s?
b. What was the relationship between mass entertainment and the U.S. economy in the 1920s?
c. What impact did Clarence Darrow and William Jennings Bryan have on life in the 1920s?

5. Writing and Critical Thinking
Analyzing Information Imagine that you are a reporter at the Scopes trial. Write an article describing the many changes in American society during the 1920s that led to revival of religious activity and the Scopes trial.
Consider:
• the impact of youth culture and popular entertainment on people's perception of American culture
• the message and activities of Aimee Semple McPherson and Billy Sunday
• the Fundamentalist movement

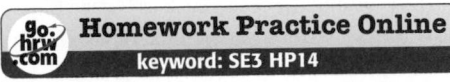
Homework Practice Online
keyword: SE3 HP14

---

3. prohibition—turned the sale of illegal liquor into a booming business and thus led to an increase in crime; government—tried to reduce the growth in crime by strictly enforcing prohibition laws and arresting gangsters such as Al Capone

4a. Magazines and movies discussed the idea of the "new woman," and they began to drive cars, play sports, and work in a wider variety of occupations.

b. The economy was booming and that meant many Americans had more free time for and bigger paychecks to spend on entertainment—radio, movies, and professional sports.

c. They represented the division in American society between traditional religious values and new values based on scientific ways of thought.

5. Answers will vary but students might suggest that the youth culture and popular entertainment prompted many Americans to believe that the United States was entering a period of moral decline and thus was in need of religious revitalization; McPherson and Sunday used new entertaining methods to encourage religious activism; the Scopes trial revealed a deep division in American society between traditional and modern values.

After completing Section 3, students should be able to:

OBJECTIVE 1 Explain how jazz and blues became popular nationwide.

OBJECTIVE 2 Analyze how artists and writers of the Harlem Renaissance used their work to express pride in their cultural heritage.

OBJECTIVE 3 Describe how writers of the Lost Generation portrayed American life.

OBJECTIVE 4 Identify some of the major inspirations behind the new movements in visual arts and architecture.

LET'S GET STARTED!

Write the term *Harlem Renaissance* on the chalkboard. As students enter the classroom, tell each student to make a list of artists and writers of the Harlem Renaissance. *(Students might name Countee Cullen, Langston Hughes, Rose McClendon, and Paul Robeson, among others.)* Ask volunteers to share their lists with the class. Tell students that in Section 3 they will learn about the Harlem Renaissance and other artistic movements in American society during the 1920s.

READ TO DISCOVER

1. How did jazz and blues become popular nationwide?
2. What impact did the Harlem Renaissance have on American society?
3. How did writers of the Lost Generation portray American life?
4. What were some of the major inspirations behind new movements in the visual arts and architecture?

DEFINE

jazz
blues

IDENTIFY

Bessie Smith
Louis Armstrong
Bix Beiderbecke
Duke Ellington
Langston Hughes
Harlem Renaissance
Paul Robeson
Rose McClendon
James Weldon Johnson
Ernest Hemingway
Lost Generation
F. Scott Fitzgerald
Alfred Stieglitz
Diego Rivera

WHY IT MATTERS TODAY

Jazz music remains popular in the United States and throughout the world. Use **CNNfyi.com** or other **current events** sources to find out more about jazz. Record your findings in your journal.

CNNfyi.com

A Creative Era

EYEWITNESSES TO History "*When I came back to New York in 1925 the Negro Renaissance was in full swing. Countee Cullen was publishing his early poems, Zora Neale Hurston, Rudolph Fisher, Jean Toomer, and Wallace Thurman were writing, Louis Armstrong was playing, Cora Le Redd was dancing, and the Savoy Ballroom was open with a specially built floor that rocked as the dancers swayed. . . . Art took heart from Harlem creativity. Jazz filled the night air . . . and people came from all around after dark to look upon our city within a city, Black Harlem.*"

—Langston Hughes, *Freedomways*

Scene outside the Renaissance Theater in Harlem

An explosion of creativity took place in Harlem, New York, during the 1920s. The 1920s was a period of great creative energy. African American musicians transformed popular music by introducing the nation to jazz. A new generation of writers explored the problems of postwar American life and the experience of being African American. New currents in art and architecture swept the nation.

Music

The 1920s is frequently referred to as the Jazz Age because **jazz** music first gained a wide following during that time. Jazz originated among African American musicians in the South. As a port city with residents of many different cultural traditions, New Orleans was an early center for the development of jazz. This innovative form of music is a hybrid of various musical styles that existed in New Orleans at the turn of the century. It incorporates West African rhythms, elements of African American spirituals, and ragtime as well as European harmonies.

The emergence of jazz. Jazz emerged during the early 1900s in the entertainment district of New Orleans known as Storyville. Big brass bands, which had been popular in New Orleans since the Civil War, began experimenting with the ragtime style of music popularized by Scott Joplin. Brass-band musicians such as Charles "Buddy" Bolden gained a wide audience with their new "ragged" or improvised tunes. Bolden and other early jazz musicians also experimented with another form of African American music known as the **blues**.

The blues grew out of a long history of slave music and religious spirituals. It gained popularity during the early 1900s. Blues songs featured heartfelt lyrics and altered or slurred notes that echoed the mood of the lyrics. In the early 1920s blues singers such as Mamie Smith, Gertrude "Ma" Rainey, and **Bessie Smith** brought blues music to a broader audience. Their recordings of songs such as "Crazy Blues," "Down Hearted Blues," and "St. Louis Blues" became classic hits. Bessie Smith's "Down Hearted Blues" sold more than 500,000 copies in 1923.

LEVEL 1: Pair students and have them create charts to explain how jazz and blues became popular nationwide. *(Students might mention that both jazz and blues originated in the South but became popular nationwide as musicians moved north. Some white musicians began to play jazz music, and jazz clubs opened. Big bands popularized jazz as dance music.)* Have volunteers present their charts to the class.
English Language Learners, Cooperative Learning

LEVEL 2: Pair students and have each pair write a jazz song that describes how jazz and blues became popular nationwide. *(See the Level 1 lesson for the correct reasons.)* Have volunteers sing or recite their songs to the class. **Cooperative Learning**

LEVEL 3: Have students write an essay discussing how jazz and blues became popular. *(See the Level 1 lesson for the correct reasons.)* Students should also address the question "Why might jazz be considered the ultimate American musical form?" *(Students might suggest that jazz is the ultimate American musical form because it is an indigenous yet hybrid form that draws on influences from around the world.)* Have volunteers read their essays to the class.

As blues music grew in popularity, New Orleans jazz musicians such as **Louis Armstrong** began to adopt some of its unique characteristics. Jazz musicians re-created the vocal traditions of blues music. They also used their instruments to imitate the expressive singing style of blues vocalists.

Jazz moves north. During the late 1910s thousands of African Americans moved northward. Many of New Orleans's most-noted jazz musicians relocated to Chicago and New York. Pianist and composer Ferdinand "Jelly Roll" Morton helped spread jazz when he moved from New Orleans to Chicago in 1922. Morton formed a band called the Red Hot Peppers and recorded his famous tune—the "Jelly Roll Blues."

Joseph "King" Oliver also moved from New Orleans to Chicago, where he founded the Creole Jazz Band. In 1922 the great jazz trumpeter Louis Armstrong joined Oliver's band in Chicago. Armstrong's brilliant solos were featured in the Creole Jazz Band's Chicago recordings of "Mabel's Dream" and "Froggie Moore." By 1924 Armstrong had begun a renowned solo career. He toured throughout the United States and Europe, performing such classics as "When the Saints Go Marching In," "Savoy Blues," and "Hotter Than That."

The popularization of jazz. As jazz became more popular, musicians of different backgrounds began incorporating jazz elements into their music. White musicians—among them the cornetist and pianist **Bix Beiderbecke**—wove jazz rhythms into their music. George Gershwin's *Rhapsody in Blue*, which premiered in 1924, "translated" jazz into symphonic form. Jazz also influenced classical musicians, including such noted composers as Igor Stravinsky and Aaron Copland.

The development of big-band music in the mid-1920s introduced jazz to a new audience. As dance music, big-band jazz swept the nation. Young men and their flapper partners shocked their elders by dancing cheek-to-cheek fox-trots.

Jazz clubs such as Harlem's Cotton Club catered to the growing audience. These clubs brought in the most famous jazz musicians of the era, including **Duke Ellington**, Ethel Waters, and Cab Calloway. Reflecting the racism of the era, many of these clubs admitted only white customers. This occurred even though the performers frequently were African Americans and the clubs were located in African American neighborhoods.

Jazz music expressed the sadness, pain, and joy of black America. African American poet **Langston Hughes** noted that jazz proclaimed, "Why should I want to be white? I am a Negro—and beautiful!"

After World War I, many Americans and African Americans traveled to France. Some were attracted by greater racial toleration while others came for the artistic spirit. Many of these Americans brought jazz with them. Musicians and singers such as Josephine Baker helped popularize the music, and Paris began experiencing its own Jazz Age.

✔ **READING CHECK: Analyzing Information** How did jazz music spread to the rest of the world? **In the late 1910s and early 1920s, many New Orleans jazz and blues musicians relocated to northern cities such as Chicago or New York. Some African Americans remained in Europe after World War I while others moved there, bringing jazz with them.**

INTERPRETING THE VISUAL RECORD

Jazz. Members of King Oliver's Creole Jazz Band joined thousands of other African Americans who migrated from the South to northern cities such as Chicago. *What types of instruments were used to make jazz music?*

This sheet music reflects the upbeat nature of the 1920s.

PEOPLE IN HISTORY

Louis Armstrong. Louis Armstrong became one of the world's most famous and influential jazz musicians. The son of a domestic servant, he grew up in one of the poorest neighborhoods in New Orleans. As a child, Armstrong earned pennies by singing in street-side barbershop quartets. At age 12 Armstrong was arrested for firing a pistol in public. He was sent to a reform school for African American boys, where he learned to play the trumpet. His immense talent at the instrument was obvious, and soon after his release in 1916 he began to play professionally. By 1918, when he was 18 years old, Armstrong was recognized as the best trumpet player in New Orleans.

CRITICAL THINKING How might Armstrong's life have been different if he had not gone to reform school?

ANSWER: Students might suggest that Armstrong would have never learned to play the trumpet.

VISUAL RECORD ANSWER

Answers might include banjos, clarinets, drums, trombones, trumpets, and pianos.

Technology Resources

American Music Selection 19: "Harmonica Blues"

SPOTLIGHT
on the Influence of Jazz

Have students conduct research on the popularity of jazz around the world. Each student should focus on a jazz musician or group native to a country other than the United States. Have students obtain recordings of the musician's or group's work and write a brief summary of the musician's or group's lives and the unique characteristics of his or her work. Have students present their summaries and play their recordings for the class. **Block Scheduling**

TEACH OBJECTIVE 2

LEVEL 1: Pair students and ask each pair to read the poems on the following page. Instruct students to use information from the textbook to prepare oral reports on the ways in which Harlem Renaissance artists and writers expressed pride in their cultural heritage. *(Students might answer that performers and playwrights brought new respect to black theater. Writers celebrated their ethnic identity and discussed the struggles faced by many African Americans.)* Have students deliver their reports to the class.
English Language Learners, Cooperative Learning

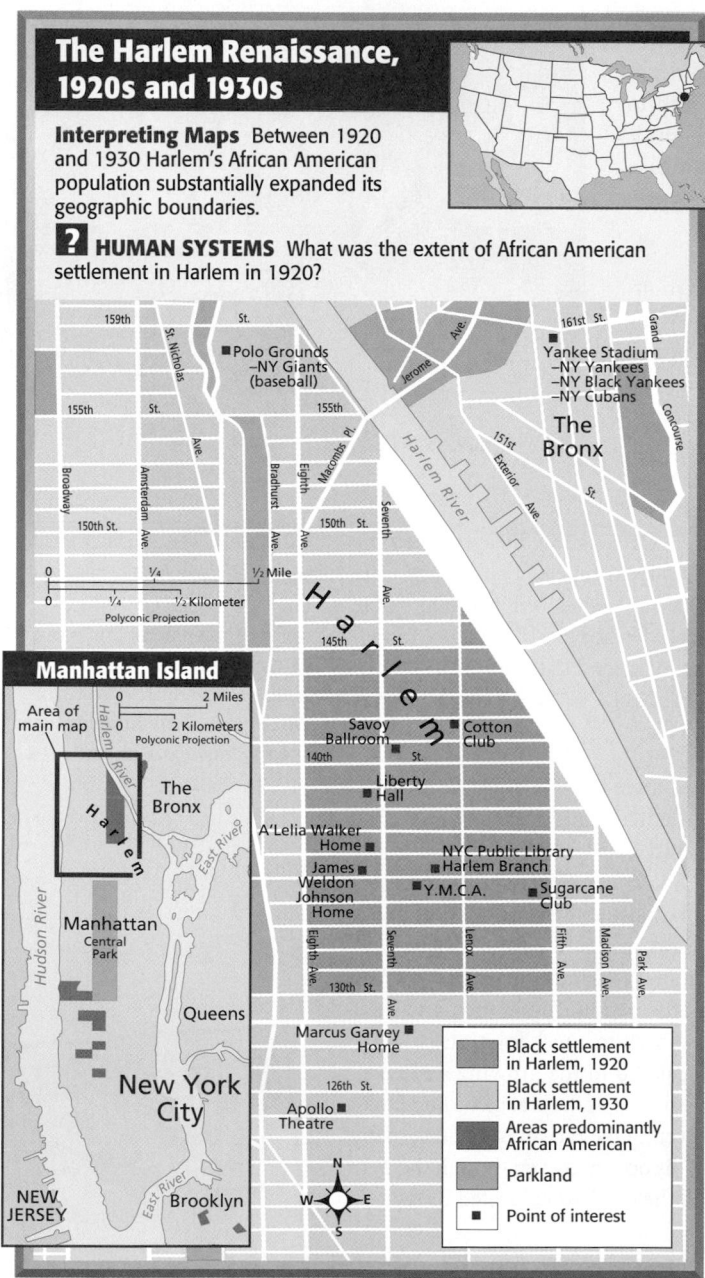

The Harlem Renaissance, 1920s and 1930s

Interpreting Maps Between 1920 and 1930 Harlem's African American population substantially expanded its geographic boundaries.

? **HUMAN SYSTEMS** What was the extent of African American settlement in Harlem in 1920?

The Harlem Renaissance

In the 1920s African Americans expressed a growing pride in their heritage. Nowhere was this pride more evident than in Harlem. This New York City neighborhood became the cultural center of African American life. So many creative black writers, musicians, and artists lived in Harlem that the flourishing of artistic development in the 1920s is known as the **Harlem Renaissance**.

Theater. During the 1920s African American theater experienced both critical acclaim and increasing popularity. The work of black performers and playwrights brought new respect to black theater. African American theater critic Alain Locke explained, "The black playwright and the black actor will interpret the soul of their people in a way to win the attention and admiration of the world."

The theatrical roles available to African Americans were restricted by the prejudices of the era. Nevertheless, African Americans produced and staged several enormously successful Broadway plays and musicals. One of the most critically successful actors of the 1920s was **Paul Robeson**, who received praise for his title role in Eugene O'Neill's drama *Emperor Jones*. The son of a former slave, Robeson turned to acting after graduating from Rutgers University and Columbia University Law School. His performances received high praise. "Robeson . . . is one of the most thoroughly eloquent, impressive and convincing actors that I have looked at and listened to in the past twenty years of theater going," offered one critic. Robeson was also an accomplished singer. He used his powerful baritone voice in such numbers as "Ol' Man River" from the musical *Showboat*. Robeson made history in 1924 as the first African American actor to play a leading role opposite a white actress.

Rose McClendon was another leading African American actor of the 1920s. McClendon first won fame in the 1926 production *Deep River*, a "native opera with jazz." That same year she performed in the Pulitzer Prize–winning tragedy *In Abraham's Bosom*. In 1927 she appeared in the first production of *Porgy*.

LEVEL 2: Ask each student to write a short poem that discusses the ways in which Harlem Renaissance artists and writers expressed pride in their cultural heritage. *(See the Level 1 lesson for the correct ways.)* Have volunteers recite their poems to the class. Students may wish to include their poems in their portfolios.

LEVEL 3: Pair students and have one student in each pair adopt the role of Countee Cullen and the other the role of Langston Hughes. Have each pair write a brief dialogue in which the poets analyze the poems "Yet Do I Marvel" and "I, Too" and discuss how their work expresses their pride in their cultural heritage. *(See the Level 1 lesson for the correct ways.)* Ask volunteers to perform their dialogues for the class.

Cooperative Learning

HOMEWORK *Ask students to consult the dictionary and one other source to define the word* renaissance. *Have students write a brief explanation of why this term might have been used to describe the artistic activity that occurred in Harlem during the 1920s and 1930s.*

Harlem Renaissance Writers

During the Harlem Renaissance, African American writers drew upon their personal experiences to create exciting and meaningful works. Poems such as Countee Cullen's "Yet Do I Marvel" and Langston Hughes's "I, Too" expressed the pride many Harlem writers had for their cultural heritage. Although the two poems explore a similar theme, the distinct style of each poem reflects the diversity of Harlem Renaissance literature.

"Yet Do I Marvel"
by Countee Cullen

I doubt not God is good,
  well-meaning, kind,
And did He stoop to
  quibble could tell why
The little buried mole
  continues blind,
Why flesh that mirrors
  Him must some day die,
Make plain the reason
  tortured Tantalus*
Is baited by the fickle fruit,
  declare
If merely brute caprice [whimsy] dooms Sisyphus**
To struggle up a never-ending stair.
Inscrutable [mysterious] His ways are, and immune
To catechism by a mind too strewn
With petty cares to slightly understand
What awful brain compels His awful hand.
Yet do I marvel at this curious thing:
To make a poet black, and bid him sing!

Countee Cullen's collection of poems

* Tantalus was a character in Greek mythology known for the punishment and torture he suffered in Hades (hell).

** According to Greek mythology, Sisyphus must endlessly push a heavy rock up a steep hill.

"I, Too"
by Langston Hughes

I, too, sing America.

I am the darker brother.
They send me to eat in the
  kitchen
When company comes,
But I laugh,
And eat well,
And grow strong.

Tomorrow,
I'll be at the table
When company comes.
Nobody'll dare
Say to me,
"Eat in the kitchen,"
Then.

Besides,
They'll see how beautiful I am
And be ashamed—

I, too, am America.

Langston Hughes

UNDERSTANDING LITERATURE

1. What point does Countee Cullen make in his poem?
2. How did Langston Hughes's experience as an African American influence his poem?
3. What universal themes do these poets address?

SPOTLIGHT
on Paul Robeson

Have each student conduct research on the life and career of Paul Robeson, focusing on his educational background, popularity as an artist in the United States and around the world, and political activities. Have students write brief reports on their findings. Ask volunteers to read their reports to the class. **Block Scheduling**

NOTE: To help students make meaningful connections between events in U.S. history and those in their own hometown, use the Chapter 14 **Hands-On History Activity**, Guide to Local Arts and Artists.

SPOTLIGHT
on Rose McClendon

Pair students and have them conduct research on the life and career of Rose McClendon. Students should focus on her career as an actor, director, and one of the founders of the Negro People's Theater in Harlem. Then have students write transcripts of an interview with McClendon. Ask volunteers to conduct their interviews for the class.
Cooperative Learning, Block Scheduling

CULTURE

Sponsorship of African American Writers.
Two magazines served as important forums for the Harlem Renaissance writers. *The Crisis,* the NAACP periodical, had a peak monthly circulation of more than 100,000. It published young talents such as Claude McKay and Countee Cullen. *Opportunity,* a magazine founded in 1923 by the National Urban League, sponsored literary contests. Zora Neale Hurston and Langston Hughes were among the winners.

CRITICAL THINKING What might have made *The Crisis* an excellent forum for new writers, other than its wide circulation?

ANSWER: Students might suggest that *The Crisis* was directed to an audience of activists interested in nurturing the talents of African Americans.

Technology Resources
Everyday Life in America Transparency 22: Harlem Renaissance Art, 1920s

VISUAL RECORD ANSWER
(for p. 435)
Students might suggest that Hemmingway's injuries led to his anger at the uselessness of war.

Claude McKay and many other writers made Harlem a center of American literature.

Literature. African American literature was central to the Harlem Renaissance. African American novelists and poets produced work marked by bitterness and defiance but also by joy and hope. Writer Nella Larsen described the quest for racial identity in her 1928 novel, *Quicksand.* Also published in 1928, Claude McKay's novel *Home to Harlem* explored the excitement and stresses of life in Harlem for an African American soldier returning from World War I.

Harlem poets celebrated their ethnic identity and acknowledged the struggles faced by many African Americans. McKay expressed his determination to fight racial injustices in his poem "If We Must Die."

"If we must die, let it not be like hogs
Hunted and penned in an inglorious spot,
While round us bark the mad and hungry dogs....
What though before us lies the open grave?
Like men we'll face the murderous, cowardly pack,
Pressed to the wall, dying, but fighting back!"

—"If We Must Die"

Poet Langston Hughes distinguished himself by addressing his poems to African American readers. He focused on the everyday experiences of African Americans, using language and themes familiar to his readers.

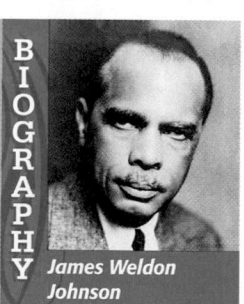

James Weldon Johnson

One of the most active Harlem Renaissance supporters was **James Weldon Johnson**. Born in 1871 in Jacksonville, Florida, Johnson was the son of the first African American woman to teach in Florida's public schools. Johnson excelled as a student and attended Atlanta University. There, he studied the classics and poetry. A man of many talents, Johnson's occupations included educator, lawyer, diplomat to Venezuela and Nicaragua, and official in the National Association for the Advancement of Colored People (NAACP).

As a writer Johnson published a wide variety of works. His 1900 poem "Lift Ev'ry Voice and Sing" became the basis for a song. His brother, J. Rosamond Johnson, provided the music. By the 1920s the song was commonly known as the African American national anthem. Johnson also wrote several novels, including *The Autobiography of an Ex-Colored Man,* published in 1912.

Johnson's main contribution to the Harlem Renaissance was his support of other authors. In 1922 he published *The Book of American Negro Poetry.* As executive secretary of the NAACP during the 1920s, Johnson raised money to support African American artists and art programs in Harlem.

Johnson supported the arts because he believed that the artistic advances of the Harlem Renaissance would help further the cause of equal rights. Johnson claimed that the "demonstration of intellectual parity [equality] by the Negro through the production of literature and art" could best eliminate racial prejudice. Johnson continued this work until his death in 1938.

✓ READING CHECK: Drawing Conclusions In what ways did the work of the artists and writers of the Harlem Renaissance help shape the national identity?
African Americans expressed a growing pride in their heritage and hoped to further the cause of equal rights.

LEVEL 1: To help students understand how writers of the Lost Generation portrayed American life, copy the following graphic organizer on the chalkboard, omitting the italicized answers. Have each student complete it.

English Language Learners

PORTRAYAL OF AMERICAN LIFE BY LOST GENERATION WRITERS

Ernest Hemingway	F. Scott Fitzgerald	Sinclair Lewis
showed the devastation and uselessness of war	*revealed superficiality of college life and the emptiness associated with the pursuit of status and wealth*	*discussed the emptiness and conformity of middle-class life*

LEVEL 2: Have each student write several proverbs that encapsulate the portrayal of American life by the writers of the Lost Generation. *(See the Level 1 lesson for the correct portrayals.)* Ask volunteers to recite their proverbs to the class.

LEVEL 3: Have each student write a brief summary of the portrayal of American life by writers of the Lost Generation. *(See the Level 1 lesson for the correct portrayals.)* Then have students write a short story that applies one or more of the Lost Generation's portrayals to contemporary life. Ask volunteers to read their stories to the class.

The Lost Generation

The Harlem Renaissance coincided with the rise of a new generation of American writers. Their work reflected their horror at the death and destruction of World War I. These writers scorned middle-class consumerism and the superficiality of the postwar years in their works. "You are all a lost generation," said poet Gertrude Stein to one such writer, **Ernest Hemingway**. The label stuck, and the writers of the era became known as the **Lost Generation**.

Stories of disillusionment. Ernest Hemingway spent much of his life in France, Spain, and Cuba. During World War I, he served as an ambulance driver as a way to experience war. Hemingway was seriously wounded while serving on the Italian front. He later expressed his anger at the uselessness of war. His 1929 novel, *A Farewell to Arms*, depicts the devastation of war. In a famous passage the soldier explains what the war means to him.

❝I was always embarrassed by the words sacred, glorious, and sacrifice and the expression in vain. We had heard them . . . and had read them . . . now for a long time, and I had seen nothing sacred, and the things that were glorious had no glory and the sacrifices were like the stockyards at Chicago if nothing was done with the meat except to bury it.❞

—Ernest Hemingway, *A Farewell to Arms*

F. Scott Fitzgerald was another Lost Generation writer. His novels chronicled the Jazz Age. In *This Side of Paradise* (1920), Fitzgerald wrote about wealthy college students bored by fast living. In *The Great Gatsby* (1925), Fitzgerald portrayed the emptiness of one man's pursuit of money and social status.

Fitzgerald defined the Jazz Age as a time when "a new generation [had] grown up to find . . . all wars fought, all faiths in man shaken." His life was filled with some of the same tragedies and the sense of disillusionment that plagued his characters. With the success of his first novel and his marriage to Zelda Sayre, Fitzgerald's future appeared bright. The couple's glamorous lifestyle was cut short, however, by Zelda Fitzgerald's incurable mental illness and Fitzgerald's own alcoholism and declining creativity.

Criticizing the middle class. Sinclair Lewis shared Fitzgerald's skeptical attitude toward American society during the 1920s. However, Lewis focused his criticism on the emptiness and conformity of middle-class life. In *Main Street* (1920), Lewis satirized the close-mindedness of a typical small midwestern town. In his 1922 novel, *Babbitt*, he told the story of a middle-aged realtor and city booster who is dissatisfied with his middle-class life but lacks the courage to change.

Journalist and critic H. L. Mencken served as a champion of these new writers. In his magazine, *The American Mercury*, Mencken promoted novelists who satirized middle-class Americans, whom he ridiculed as "the booboisie." Mencken made fun of Republican politicians, Fundamentalist Christians, rural southerners, residents of small towns, and many other Americans.

✔ **READING CHECK: Summarizing** Describe the writers of the Lost Generation and their views on the postwar years. **These writers' works reflected their horror over World War I and their scorn for middle-class consumerism in the 1920s.**

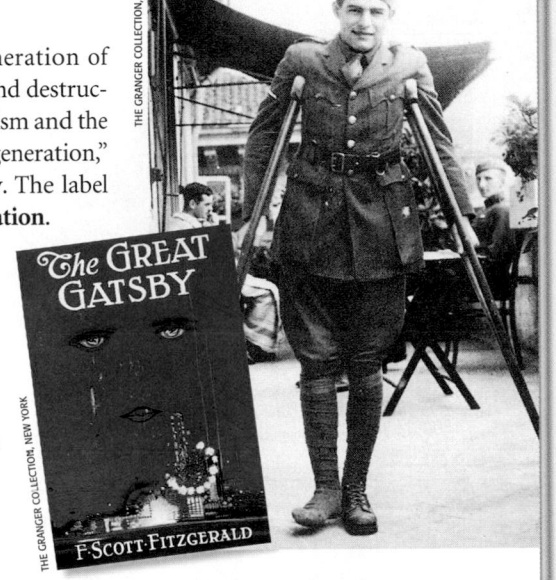

THE GRANGER COLLECTION, NEW YORK

THE GRANGER COLLECTION, NEW YORK

INTERPRETING THE VISUAL RECORD

Memories of war. World War I influenced the writers of the 1920s, such as F. Scott Fitzgerald and Ernest Hemingway. *How might Hemingway (above) have been affected by his wartime military service?*

Research on the R✺M

Free Find:
F. Scott Fitzgerald
After reading about F. Scott Fitzgerald on the **Holt Researcher CD–ROM**, create an outline for a story set in the 1920s about Fitzgerald.

HISTORY MAKERS SPEAK

Malcolm Cowley in *Exile's Return: A Literary Odyssey of the 1920s*

The Lost Generation.
In his memoir, writer Malcolm Cowley reflected on the appropriateness of the "Lost Generation" label: "The [lost] generation deserved for a long time the adjective that Gertrude Stein had applied to it. The reasons aren't hard to find. It was lost, first of all, because it was uprooted, schooled away and almost wrenched away from its attachment to any region or tradition. It was lost because its training had prepared it for another world than [that which] existed after the war. . . . It was lost because it accepted no older guides to conduct."

ACTIVITY: Ask students to read a short story by Ernest Hemingway, F. Scott Fitzgerald, or another Lost Generation writer. Then have students write an essay examining the story's major themes.

VISUAL RECORD ANSWER

(for p. 436)

Students might suggest that positive aspects include employment for many different ethnic groups and that negative aspects include the exhausting work.

TEACH OBJECTIVE 4

LEVEL 1: Pair students and have each pair compile a list of the major visual artists and architects of the 1920s and their sources of inspiration. *(Students might indicate that a number of painters and photographers were inspired by urban, industrial settings. Many Mexican muralists were inspired by the nobility of workers and the tyranny of the wealthy. Architects found inspiration in Louis Sullivan's ideas about form and function and in Frank Lloyd Wright's "prairie style.")* Conclude by discussing with students the contributions of these artists and architects.
English Language Learners, Cooperative Learning

LEVELS 2 AND 3: Tell students to imagine that they are participants in a panel discussion entitled Inspiration for the New Movements in Visual Arts and Architecture. Ask volunteers to play the roles of Edward Hopper, Georgia O'Keeffe, Diego Rivera, Charles Sheeler, Alfred Stieglitz, and Frank Lloyd Wright. Ask the other students to act as facilitators and questioners. Have the students who are role-playing the artists prepare for their roles by taking notes on what inspired the artists and architects. Have the other group prepare a list of questions to use during the panel discussion. *(See the Level 1 lesson for the correct sources of inspiration.)* Then conduct the panel discussion.

In this 1928 painting, Manhattan Bridge Loop, Edward Hopper conveys the isolation and industrialization that many associated with U.S. cities.

INTERPRETING THE VISUAL RECORD

Murals. Diego Rivera completed the mural *Detroit Industry* in 1932, after spending months in the city. He attempted to capture the positive and negative aspects of industrialization. *How do you think these themes are revealed in this work?*

The Visual Arts

As the writers of the Lost Generation confronted the boredom and frustration of life after the war, many visual artists concerned themselves with other changes occurring in the United States. Artists of the 1920s addressed the impact of growing cities and the increasing use of machinery on American life.

Painting and photography. Many American painters of the 1920s depicted urban, industrial settings. Edward Hopper's scenes of New York City convey a sense of loneliness and serene stillness. *Early Sunday Morning* (1930) shows a row of darkened stores and a street empty of people. Hopper believed that art should reflect the experiences of modern life. He explained, "The province [role] of art is to react to it [life] and not to shun it." Before moving to New Mexico, artist Georgia O'Keeffe depicted city life in her paintings of New York factories and tenements.

Photography came to be widely appreciated as an art form in the 1900s. **Alfred Stieglitz** (STEEG-luhts) helped popularize photography. In addition to operating an influential New York gallery, Stieglitz photographed people, airplanes, skyscrapers, and crowded city streets. Photographer and painter Charles Sheeler won fame for his portraits revealing the beauty of machinery. The Ford Motor Company hired him to photograph its plant near Detroit, Michigan, in 1927.

Murals. Another artistic renaissance of the 1920s took place in Mexico. Mexican muralists emphasized the nobility of ordinary people—peasants and other workers—and the tyranny of the wealthy class. Their favorite medium was the monumental public mural. In the words of artist José Clemente Orozco (oh-ROHS-koh), the public murals "cannot be hidden away for the benefit of a certain privileged few. It is for the people. It is for ALL."

The movement's three major artists—known in Mexico as *los tres grandes,* or "the big three"—were Orozco, David Alfaro Siqueiros (see-KAY-rohs), and **Diego Rivera.** Each artist visited the United States in the early 1930s to paint murals. Rivera, the most prominent muralist, focused on workers' problems and industrial development in his American murals. In 1932 Rivera painted a mural at the Detroit Institute of Art that featured assembly-line workers in automobile factories.

Rivera and his wife, Frida Kahlo—an accomplished painter—lived and traveled throughout the United States from 1930 to 1933. Some Americans found Rivera's radical politics offensive. In 1933, sponsors of a new Rivera mural commissioned by the Rockefeller Center destroyed the work they had funded. Titled *Man at the Crossroads,* the mural upset the sponsors because it featured an image of the Bolshevik leader Vladimir Lenin. After returning to Mexico, Rivera re-created the mural at the Palace of Fine Arts in Mexico City.

REVIEW

Have students complete the **Section 3 Review** on p. 437.

ASSESS

Have students complete **Daily Quiz 14.3.** As **Alternative Assessment,** you may want to use the short story or the proverbs in this section's lessons.

RETEACH

Have students complete **Main Idea Activity for English Language Learners and Special-Needs Students 14.3.** Then have each student write two or three sentences that summarize the main ideas of each subsection in this section. Have volunteers read their sentences to the class, then have the class supply any information missing from volunteers' sentences.
English Language Learners

EXTEND

Using the library and other resources, have students locate and read some of the works of one Harlem Renaissance writer mentioned in this section. Have students analyze the works' major themes and report their findings by writing an essay, poem, play, or short story. **Block Scheduling**

Architecture. The spirit of creativity that emerged in the United States in the 1920s also appeared in architecture. The works of Louis Sullivan and Frank Lloyd Wright inspired many architects. Sullivan designed buildings in which each part of the structure had a functional purpose. Wright studied under Sullivan during the 1890s. By the early 1910s Wright had gained a worldwide reputation for his innovative designs.

Wright developed the "prairie style" of domestic architecture. This new style used rectangular shapes and clean, horizontal lines that echoed the flatness of the prairies. Wright also incorporated Sullivan's philosophy that every aspect of a house's structure must have a functional purpose.

Many architects of the 1920s embraced the idea that a building's materials and form should reflect its purpose. The structure that most clearly illustrated this principle was the modern skyscraper. Clean-cut vertical lines and the lack of ornamentation emphasized the height of the skyscraper while the use of steel, concrete, and glass allowed it to rise so high.

New York City experienced a boom in skyscraper construction during the 1920s. Builders began construction of two landmarks—the Chrysler Building and the Empire State Building. Completed in 1930, the Chrysler Building was the tallest building in the world—at 1,048 feet—until the Empire State Building was completed in 1931. The 102-story Empire State Building cleared 1,250 feet and remained the world's tallest building until 1954.

✔ **READING CHECK: Categorizing** How did the new movements within the visual arts and architecture reflect the characteristics of the 1920s? Visual artists addressed the impact of growing cities and the increasing use of machinery. Architects emphasized function.

INTERPRETING THE VISUAL RECORD

The Robie House. Drawing attention to the horizontal lines of his design, Frank Lloyd Wright completed this prairie-style home for Chicago bicycle manufacturer Frederick C. Robie in 1909. *What aspects of this design help draw out the horizontal lines of this house?*

5. Students should note that writers and artists focused on the effects of urbanization, prejudice, disillusionment, and World War I on American life.

VISUAL RECORD ANSWER

Students might cite the lighter rows of stone and the various levels.

REVIEW (14) ANSWERS

Creating a Time Line
Each event should have an explanation and the correct date.

Writing a Summary
See the Reading Checks in each section for main ideas.

Identifying People and Ideas
1. inexpensive car designed by Henry Ford

2. production method developed by Ford for the Model T

3. provided for the enforcement of prohibition

4. young women who adopted new styles of dress and behavior

5. first pilot to fly nonstop across the Atlantic Ocean

6. defense attorney in 1925 Scopes trial

7. period of great artistic creativity among African Americans

8. blues singer who helped popularize the style

SECTION 3 REVIEW

1. Define and explain:
jazz   blues

2. Identify and explain:
Bessie Smith
Louis Armstrong
Bix Beiderbecke
Duke Ellington
Langston Hughes
Harlem Renaissance
Paul Robeson
Rose McClendon
James Weldon Johnson
Ernest Hemingway
Lost Generation
F. Scott Fitzgerald
Alfred Stieglitz
Diego Rivera

3. Sequencing Copy the graphic organizer below. List the original influences of jazz and the blues. Then explain how jazz and the blues expanded nationally and internationally.

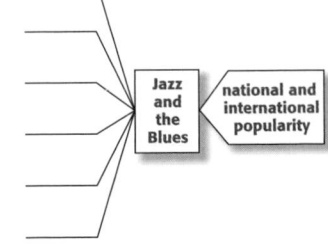

Jazz and the Blues → national and international popularity

4. **Finding the Main Idea**
a. How did the writers and musicians of the Harlem Renaissance contribute to American culture?
b. How did the major themes expressed in the novels of Lost Generation writers reflect the issues of the 1920s?
c. How did the growth of U.S. cities and the introduction of new technology influence the visual arts of the 1920s?

5. **Writing and Critical Thinking**
Categorizing Write a television news report depicting writers and artists of the 1920s as social critics.
Consider:
• how the African American writers of the Harlem Renaissance wrote about their lives
• what experiences the writers of the Lost Generation captured in their novels
• what the visual artists of the 1920s focused on in their works

go. Homework Practice Online
hrw .com keyword: SE3 HP14

TECHNOLOGY

▶ Chapter 14 Test Generator (on the One-Stop Planner)
▶ Global Skill Builder CD–ROM
▶ HRW Go site

REINFORCEMENT, REVIEW, AND ASSESSMENT

▶ Chapter 14 Review, pp. 438–39
▶ Chapter 14 Tutorial for Students, Parents, Mentors, and Peers

▶ Chapter 14 Test (Form A or B)
▶ Portfolio Activities and Alternative Assessment Handbook, Chapter 14
▶ Chapter 14 Test for English Language Learners and Special-Needs Students

REVIEW

Have students complete the **Chapter 14 Review** on pp. 438–39.

ASSESS

Use one of the chapter tests to assess students' understanding of the content. For **Alternative Assessment**, see the **Portfolio Activities and Alternative Assessment Handbook**.

---

9. writers who explored the disillusioning experience of World War I and the superficiality of middle- and upper-class life during the 1920s

10. Mexican muralist whose work focused on industrial development

Understanding Main Ideas

1. by making cars more affordable for consumers and thus encouraging the growth of the automobile industry

2. By dressing and behaving more independently and less strictly than they had in the past, young people rejected traditional American values.

3. by struggling with issues of ethnic identity and racial prejudice and serving as important examples of black artistic achievement

4. the superficiality of middle- and upper-class life during the 1920s

Reviewing Themes

1. Increasing desire for new goods, making them easier to acquire, and designing goods to "go out of style" helped promote consumer demand.

2. They provided millions of Americans with shared cultural experiences.

3. by incorporating elements of African American spirituals, blues, European harmonies, ragtime, and West African and Latin American rhythms; jazz musicians played around the world

---

CHAPTER 14 Review

Creating a Time Line

Copy the time line below onto a sheet of paper. Complete the time line by filling in the events and dates from the chapter that you think were most significant. Pick three events and explain why you think they were significant.

| 1920 | 1925 | 1930 |

Writing a Summary

Using standard grammar, spelling, sentence structure, and punctuation, write an overview of events in the chapter.

Identifying People and Ideas

Identify the following terms or individuals and explain their significance.

1. Model T
2. assembly line
3. Volstead Act
4. flappers
5. Charles Lindbergh
6. Clarence Darrow
7. Harlem Renaissance
8. Bessie Smith
9. Lost Generation
10. Diego Rivera

Understanding Main Ideas

SECTION 1 *(pp. 414–421)*

1. How did the development of the assembly line encourage the growth of the American automobile industry and affect American life?

SECTION 2 *(pp. 422–429)*

2. In what ways did the activities of many younger Americans during the 1920s represent a rejection of traditional American values?

SECTION 3 *(pp. 430–437)*

3. How did the work of writers and artists of the Harlem Renaissance affect American society?

4. What aspects of American life did writers of the Lost Generation criticize?

Reviewing Themes

1. **Economics** How did advertising, installment buying, and planned obsolescence boost the nation's economy in the 1920s?

2. **Science, Technology, and Society** How did the spread of inventions such as radio and movies affect Americans' daily life during the 1920s?

3. **Culture** In what ways did jazz both reflect and influence international culture?

Thinking Critically

1. **Comparing** How did the rise in productivity during the 1920s have both positive and negative effects for workers and industry?

2. **Drawing Conclusions** Why might Henry Ford be considered a symbol of the 1920s?

3. **Evaluating** How did the emergence of popular entertainment contribute to the economic prosperity of the 1920s?

4. **Identifying Cause and Effect** What were the causes and effects of prohibition and its repeal?

5. **Identifying Points of View** How did women's roles change in the 1920s and how did these changes affect others?

Writing About History

Summarizing Write an essay that describes the impact of nationwide broadcasting of radio programs on the lives of Americans. Use the following graphic to organize your thoughts.

| New Music | National News | Advertise-ments | Religious Services | Sports Events |

Radio in the home

RETEACH

Organize the class into three groups and assign each group one of the sections of this chapter. Have each group prepare an outline of its assigned section and either duplicate and distribute it to other members of the class or deliver an oral report to the class. The outline should include the main ideas of the section as well as examples to illustrate each main idea. Call on other class members to comment on the accuracy and thoroughness of each group's outline.

English Language Learners, Cooperative Learning

EXTEND

Direct the attention of students to the characterization of the 1920s as the "gateway to modern America" in this chapter. Based on this chapter and outside research, have each student write an essay on the extent to which that characterization is valid. Students should use one of the major figures, events, or developments associated with the material in the chapter as a case study or representative example to explain their point of view.

Block Scheduling

Building Social Studies Skills

Interpreting Maps

Study the map below. Then use it to help answer the questions that follow.

Arrests Under Prohibition in 1929

Number of Persons Arrested by or with the Aid of Federal Prohibition Officers

- 3,000 or more
- 2,000–2,999
- 1,000–1,999
- 500-999
- 499 or fewer
- WI — No state prohibition law, 1930

1. Approximately how many more arrests were made in Texas in 1929 than in Kansas?
   - **a.** 2 times as many
   - **b.** 3 times as many
   - **c.** 5 times as many
   - **d.** 6 times as many

2. What pattern might explain why the six states with the largest number of arrests had so many arrests?

Analyzing Primary Sources

Read the following excerpt from *Middletown* by Robert and Helen Lynd. Then answer the questions that follow.

> **"Advertising has grown rapidly since 1890. . . . Today all sorts of advertising devices are tried: . . . a shoe store conducting a sale offers one dollar each to the first twenty-five women appearing at the store on Monday morning; semi-annual 'dollar days' and 'suburban days' are conducted by the press. . . . The advertising carried in the leading daily paper is six times that in the leading daily of 1890."**

3. What is the main idea of the passage?
   - **a.** Advertising has grown rapidly since 1890.
   - **b.** A shoe store offers one dollar each to the first 25 women appearing at the store.
   - **c.** Today all sorts of advertising are tried.
   - **d.** The advertising carried in the leading daily paper is six times more than that in the leading daily of 1890.

4. How does this passage from *Middletown* support the statement in Section 1 that "Most advertisements targeted women"?

Alternative Assessment

Building Your Portfolio

U.S. HISTORY

Economics

Imagine that you are a prosperous business owner in the late 1920s. Create an advertising campaign for a new household product aimed at the expanding consumer market. Be sure to explain how the prosperity of the 1920s and installment plans will help the consumer buy this item. You might also want to include a model of the product in your material.

✔ internet connect

Internet Activity: go.hrw.com
KEYWORD: SE3 AN14

Choose a topic on the Jazz Age to:

- research jazz and the poetry and literature of the Harlem Renaissance.
- understand the modernist movement in the arts, literature, and music.
- learn about the development of the automobile and create an advertisement for a 1920s dream car.

Thinking Critically

1. positive—helped make a variety of consumer goods available and affordable; negative—made factory work more tedious and caused many skilled workers to lose their jobs

2. He used technological innovations to create his own economic boom.

3. provided an outlet for people with extra money to spend; gave people a reason to earn and spend money

4. Causes—people seeking to combat crime, family violence, and poverty; effects—increased crime, less alcoholism; repeal led to a decrease in lawlessness

5. Women became more independent, dressing differently and getting traditionally male jobs. This led some people to worry that traditional values were disappearing.

Writing

Essays will vary but should describe how radio provided new and shared cultural experiences, creating a mass culture.

Building Social Studies Skills

1. d

2. Students might suggest that the six states are surrounded by states with few arrests, so those violators were captured in other states.

3. a

4. Students might note that the passage mentions an advertisement directed at women.

The Great Depression

CHAPTER RESOURCE MANAGER

Objectives	Pacing Guide	Reproducible Resources
SECTION 1 **Prosperity Shattered** pp. 442–47	★ Recount why financial experts issued warnings about business practices during the 1920s. ★ Describe why the stock market crashed in 1929. ★ Understand how the banking crisis and subsequent business failures signaled the beginning of the Great Depression. ★ Analyze the main causes of the Great Depression.	**Regular** 2 days **Block Scheduling** 1 day *Block Scheduling Handbook with Team Teaching Strategies, pp. 85–90*	**RS** Guided Reading Strategy 15.1 **PS** Primary Source Reading 15: A Shattering of Spirit
SECTION 2 **Hard Times** pp. 448–55	★ Describe how unemployment during the Great Depression affected the lives of American workers. ★ Compare and contrast the hardships that urban and rural residents faced during the depression. ★ Analyze how the Great Depression affected family life and the attitudes of Americans. ★ Explain how popular culture provided an escape from the Great Depression.	**Regular** 2 days **Block Scheduling** 1 day *Block Scheduling Handbook with Team Teaching Strategies, pp. 85–90*	**RS** Guided Reading Strategy 15.2 **RS** Graphic Organizer Activity 15: Life During the Depression **IC** Literature Reading 15: The Depression Takes Its Toll **PS** Biography Reading 15: Walt Disney
SECTION 3 **Hoover's Policies** pp. 456–63	★ Explain why President Hoover opposed government-sponsored direct relief for needy individuals during the Great Depression. ★ Outline the Hoover administration's attempts to solve the economic problems of the depression, and analyze the success of these efforts. ★ Relate how radicals and veterans responded to President Hoover's policies. ★ Analyze why Franklin D. Roosevelt was such a popular candidate in the 1932 election.	**Regular** 1 day **Block Scheduling** .5 day *Block Scheduling Handbook with Team Teaching Strategies, pp. 85–90*	**RS** Guided Reading Strategy 15.3 **PS** American History Political Cartoon 23: Herbert Hoover and the Depression **SM** Geography Activity 15: Public Unrest During the Depression **E** Creative Teaching Strategy: Role Playing Lesson **E** Hands-On History Activity: The Economic State of Your State

Chapter Resource Key

PS	Primary Sources	**REV**	Review		Video
RS	Reading Support	**ELL**	Reinforcement and English Language Learners	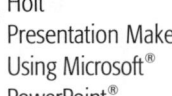	Internet
IC	Interdisciplinary Connections				Holt Presentation Maker Using Microsoft® PowerPoint®
E	Enrichment		Transparencies		
SM	Skills Mastery		CD–ROM		
A	Assessment		Music		

One-Stop Planner CD–ROM

See the *One-Stop Planner* for a complete list of additional resources for students and teachers.

One-Stop Planner CD–ROM

It's easy to plan lessons, select resources, and print out materials for your students when you use the *One-Stop Planner CD–ROM with Test Generator.*

 One-Stop Planner, Lesson 15.1

 The American Nation Video Program Segment: The Great Depression; Teacher's Guide, pp. 111–16

 Holt Researcher: American History CD–ROM

 Homework Practice Online

 HRW Go site

REV Section 1 Review, p. 447

A Daily Quiz 15.1

ELL Main Idea Activity 15.1

ELL English Audio Summary 15.1

ELL Spanish Audio Summary 15.1

 One-Stop Planner, Lesson 15.2

 Everyday Life in America Transparency 24: America's Darling: Shirley Temple, 1930s

 Holt Researcher: American History CD–ROM

 Homework Practice Online

REV Section 2 Review, p. 455

A Daily Quiz 15.2

ELL Main Idea Activity 15.2

ELL English Audio Summary 15.2

ELL Spanish Audio Summary 15.2

 One-Stop Planner, Lesson 15.3

  Presents America: Yesterday and Today, 1850 to the Present Segment: Glimpses of the Depression

 Holt Researcher: American History CD–ROM

 Homework Practice Online

REV Section 3 Review, p. 463

A Daily Quiz 15.3

ELL Main Idea Activity 15.3

ELL English Audio Summary 15.3

ELL Spanish Audio Summary 15.3

⬛ internet connect

HRW ONLINE RESOURCES
> **GO TO: go.hrw.com**
> Then type in a keyword.

TEACHER HOME PAGE
> **KEYWORD: SE3 Teacher**

CHAPTER INTERNET ACTIVITIES
> **KEYWORD: SE3 AN15**
> Choose an activity to:
> • research conditions during the depression and write a journal entry.
> • explore the construction of Hoover Dam.
> • create a model that illustrates the causes of the Great Depression.

CHAPTER ENRICHMENT LINKS
> **KEYWORD: SE3 CH15**

ONLINE ASSESSMENT
> **Homework Practice**
> **KEYWORD: SE3 HP15**
>
> **Standardized Test Prep**
> **KEYWORD: SE3 STP15**
>
> **Rubrics**
> **KEYWORD: SS Rubrics**

ONLINE MAPS, CHARTS, AND GRAPHS
> **KEYWORD: SE3 MCG**
> • Unemployment in Europe, 1932
> • Unemployment, 1929–1941
> • Personal Income, 1929–1941

CONTENT UPDATES
> **KEYWORD: SS Content Updates**

HOLT PRESENTATION MAKER
> **KEYWORD: SE3 PPT15**

ONLINE READING SUPPORT
> **KEYWORD: SS Strategies**

CURRENT EVENTS
> **KEYWORD: S3 Current Events**

Chapter Review and Assessment

 Global Skill Builder CD–ROM

 HRW Go site

REV **Chapter 15 Tutorial for Students, Parents, Mentors, and Peers**

REV **Chapter 15 Review, pp. 464–65**

Chapter 15 Test Generator (on the One-Stop Planner)

A **Chapter 15 Test (Form A or B)**

A **Alternative Assessment Handbook**

A **Chapter 15 Test for English Language Learners and Special-Needs Students**

Meeting Individual Needs

Ability Levels

Level 1 Basic-level activities designed for all students encountering new material

Level 2 Intermediate-level activities designed for average students

Level 3 Challenging activities designed for honors and gifted-and-talented students

English Language Learners Activities that address the needs of students with Limited English Proficiency

Section 1 *Prosperity Shattered,*
pp. 442–47

Section 2 *Hard Times,*
pp. 448–55

Section 3 *Hoover's Policies,*
pp. 456–63

Chapter Review *pp. 464–65*

Build on What You Know

Ask students to answer the following questions.

How might enormous debts have led to economic problems in the United States?

Consider:

• the need to make payments on debts and the widespread purchasing repercussions of those payments

• the financial instability of debt

How might the federal government have reversed the country's economic decline?

Consider:

• the limited role of the federal government during the 1920s

• the scope of the government's power

---

exploring the time line

AMERICAN EVENTS

CHAPTER
15

1929–1933

The Great Depression

Ticker tape stock machine

1929
Business and Finance
The U.S. stock market crashes.

1929
Science and Technology
The Cascade Tunnel, the longest railroad tunnel in North America, is completed.

1929
Politics
Congress establishes the Federal Farm Board to assist farmers.

1930
Business and Finance
Approximately $180 million of depositors' savings are lost with the financial collapse of one New York City bank.

1930
World Events
France establishes a workers' insurance law.

Bank closing

1929

1930

1929
Science and Technology
Harvard physician Samuel Albert Levine establishes a connection between high blood pressure and heart disease.

1929
The Arts
William Faulkner publishes *The Sound and the Fury.*

British election poster portraying the effects of the Great Depression

1930
Daily Life
In New York City more than 6,000 unemployed workers sell apples on the streets to earn money.

1930
World Events
An economic depression hits countries in Europe and South America.

Build on What You Know

The economic boom of the 1920s gave most Americans tremendous faith in the future. For many Americans, prosperity seemed limitless. The economic gains were unevenly distributed, however. The lifestyle of the Jazz Age led to enormous consumer debt. In this chapter you will learn how debt and many other factors led to the Great Depression. When President Hoover's efforts to revive the economy failed, Americans elected a Democratic president, Franklin D. Roosevelt, in hopes of reversing the country's economic decline.

Boulder Dam on the Colorado River

1932
Business and Finance
Industrial output falls to half its 1929 level.

1932
World Events
Chile's income from the export of copper and nitrates declines by more than 1.5 billion pesos in less than four years.

1932
Daily Life
Veterans form the Bonus Army and demonstrate in Washington, D.C., demanding early payment of their pensions.

Members of the Bonus Army

1931
Science and Technology
U.S. engineer Henry J. Kaiser designs Boulder Dam.

1931
Politics
President Hoover refuses to support a bill providing direct federal relief for unemployed workers.

1932
Business and Finance
Since 1930 more than 5,000 banks have closed.

1932
Politics
Congress establishes the Reconstruction Finance Corporation to stabilize the economy by assisting banks and other financial institutions.

1931 **1932** **1933**

1931
Daily Life
Cotton prices fall below 6 cents per pound, forcing many tenant farmers from their land.

1931
World Events
President Hoover announces a one-year halt on war reparations, hoping to promote European economic recovery.

Franklin D. Roosevelt campaigning

1932
Politics
Franklin D. Roosevelt is elected president.

1933
The Arts
The movie *King Kong* is released.

1933
Daily Life
The unemployment rate reaches 24.9 percent of the workforce, as 15 million Americans are out of work.

Fay Wray starred in King Kong.

GLOBAL EVENTS

ECONOMICS

1931 ■ A Halt on Reparations. Many European countries incurred heavy debts to the United States during World War I. After the war, several of these countries asked the United States for total debt amnesty, but were refused. As a result, these countries pressed Germany to pay its war reparations, virtually destroying the German economy and slowing economic recovery in Europe. At times, Germany even borrowed money from the United States to pay its debts to other countries, which then used the money to repay their own debts to the United States. Hoping to end this lunacy and encourage economic growth in Europe, Hoover announced a one-year halt on reparations in 1931. The following year, the reparations were abandoned.

CRITICAL THINKING Do you think the United States should have agreed to total debt amnesty? Why or why not?

ANSWER: Some students might suggest that as a wealthy nation, the United States had an obligation to accept debt amnesty. Other students might suggest that Germany had a duty to pay its war reparations.

SECTION 1

READ TO DISCOVER

1. Why did financial experts issue warnings about business practices during the 1920s?
2. Why did the stock market crash in 1929?
3. How did the banking crisis and subsequent business failures signal the beginning of the Great Depression?
4. What were the main causes of the Great Depression?

 DEFINE

bull market
bear market
margin buying
gross national product
business cycle

IDENTIFY

Herbert Hoover
Black Thursday
Black Tuesday
Great Depression
Smoot-Hawley Tariff

WHY IT MATTERS TODAY

Americans continue to invest heavily in the stock market. Use **CNNfyi.com** or other **current events** sources to find an important financial news story today. Record your findings in your journal.

CNNfyi.com

Prosperity Shattered

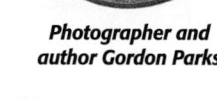

Photographer and author Gordon Parks

EYEWITNESSES TO History "'MARKET CRASHES—PANIC HITS NATION!' one headline blared.... I couldn't imagine such financial disaster touching my small world; it surely concerned only the rich. But by the first week of November I too knew differently; along with millions of others across the nation, I was without a job. All that next week I searched for any kind of work that would prevent my leaving school. Again it was, 'We're firing, not hiring.' ... Finally, on the seventh of November I went to school and cleaned out my locker, knowing it was impossible to stay on. A piercing chill was in the air as I walked back to the rooming house. The hawk had come. I could already feel his wings shadowing me."

—Gordon Parks, quoted in *Brother Can You Spare a Dime? The Great Depression*, by Milton Meltzer

Gordon Parks was 16 years old when the prosperity of the 1920s came to an abrupt halt. The booming stock market crashed on Thursday, October 24, 1929. In the first few hours of stock trading, share prices fell sharply. At first, investors remained calm. However, as prices continued to fall, panic struck. Frantic orders to sell stock came pouring in. The economic prosperity of the 1920s was over. The worst economic depression in U.S. history had begun. For many Americans, their daily lives became a constant struggle for survival.

Economic Troubles on the Horizon

Although the 1920s appeared to be a decade of unlimited economic prosperity, a few isolated voices warned of problems within the U.S. economy. Some economists identified the nation's agricultural crisis and "sick" industries as problems in need of attention. Despite these early warnings of economic troubles, few Americans worried about the nation's economic health. The widespread prosperity led many Americans to believe that the economy would continue to grow. President **Herbert Hoover** expressed this confidence and optimism in his inaugural address in March 1929.

 History Makers Speak "Ours is a land rich in resources; stimulating in its glorious beauty; filled with millions of happy homes; blessed with comfort and opportunity.... I have no fears for the future of our country. It is bright with hope."

—Herbert Hoover, "Inaugural Address," March 4, 1929

Credit. Assured by their faith in the nation's economic prosperity, many Americans purchased new consumer products on credit. By 1929 the total number of purchases made with credit was six times higher than in 1915. Purchases on credit in 1929 reached a total of $7 billion.

The federal government encouraged this borrowing by keeping interest rates low during the late 1920s. The Republican administrations of the time reasoned that

TEACH OBJECTIVE 1

LEVEL 1: Ask students to identify the warnings that financial experts issued during the 1920s. (*Experts warned that the economy was in potential danger and pointed to the farm crisis, "sick" industries, consumers' reliance on credit, and stock speculation as evidence to support their claims.*) Ask students why the public largely ignored such warnings. (*Students should mention that the economy was booming, and the public believed that it would continue to grow.*) Have each student write a paragraph summarizing these warnings and explaining the public's response. **English Language Learners**

LEVELS 2 AND 3: Ask students to identify the warnings that financial experts issued during the 1920s. (*See the Level 1 lesson for the correct warnings.*) Assign each student one of the warnings. Have students create diagrams displaying the economic rationales behind the warnings. (*The farm crisis and "sick" industries pointed to ingrained supply and production problems. Consumers' reliance on credit indicated their financial vulnerability. Stock speculation indicated an overheated market.*) Ask at least four students—one representing each of the specific warnings in the Level 1 lesson—to draw their diagrams on the chalkboard and explain them to the class.

---

an easy-credit policy would promote business. Easy access to credit enabled consumers to buy goods when they did not actually have the money to pay for them.

Industries' increasing reliance on customers who made purchases with credit concerned some economic experts. These experts noted that in an economic downturn, such debt could cripple consumers. Consumers ignored these warnings and continued to purchase automobiles, radios, and appliances on credit.

Playing the market. Americans' confidence in the economy of the 1920s was also reflected in the stock market. Investors poured millions of dollars into the market. Stock sales had increased steadily for several years. As demand rose, so did stock prices. Many experts saw no end to the **bull market**—one with an upward trend in stock prices. "There have been bull markets before," observed the *New York Times*, "but the present one surpasses them all." Investors and analysts claimed that the stock market was in no danger of becoming a **bear market**—one with a downward trend in stock prices.

By the late 1920s, stock speculation—"playing" the market by buying and selling to make a quick profit—was widespread. Although speculation fueled economic growth, it also created problems. Rapid buying and selling inflated the prices of stocks to the point that many stocks were selling for far more than they were actually worth. This speculative buying was fine as long as demand was high, but if investor confidence weakened, prices would tumble.

The situation was made shakier still by **margin buying**—the practice of purchasing stocks with borrowed money. Many speculators put up as little as 10 percent of the price of a stock and borrowed the rest. Buying on margin worked as long as the bull market continued. If prices were to ever fall steeply, however, investors would find themselves deep in debt.

Although consumer confidence in the market remained high throughout the summer of 1929, a few gloomy voices were heard. In early September stock analyst Roger Babson wrote, "Sooner or later a crash is coming, and it may be terrific [immense]." Some shrewd investors began to sell their stocks, but most people ignored the warnings.

✔ **READING CHECK: Summarizing** What business practices concerned economic experts during the 1920s? reliance on consumers who used credit for purchases, margin buying, and stock speculation

The Stock Market Crashes

The bubble burst on **Black Thursday**—October 24, 1929. A large number of investors, made nervous by factors such as rising interest rates, suddenly began to sell their shares. The dumping of so much stock on the market jolted investor

Ticker tape machines like this one were used to get up-to-date stock market prices during the 1920s.

The Crash, 1929

Company	High Price Sept. 3, 1929	Low Price Nov. 13, 1929
American Telephone and Telegraph	304	197 1/4
General Electric	396 1/4	168 1/8
General Motors	72 3/4	36
Montgomery Ward	137 7/8	49 1/4
United States Steel	261 3/4	150
Woolworth	100 3/8	52 1/4

Source: *Only Yesterday*

Interpreting Charts In the days following the stock market crash on October 29, 1929, stock prices continued to fall. Average stock prices reached their lowest point for the year on November 13, 1929, about two months after they had reached the high point for the year on September 3.

❓ **Skills Assessment** Which company's stock price fell the most between September 3 and November 13, 1929?

ALL LEVELS: Write the following question on the chalkboard: *Once the stock market starts to fall, can anything reverse that decline?* Have students answer the question in writing. Then ask volunteers to share their responses. *(Answers will vary. Some students will suggest that investors themselves might be able to reverse a decline by buying heavily.)* To help students understand why the stock market crashed in 1929, copy the graphic organizer at right on the chalkboard, omitting the italicized answers. Have each student complete it. **English Language Learners**

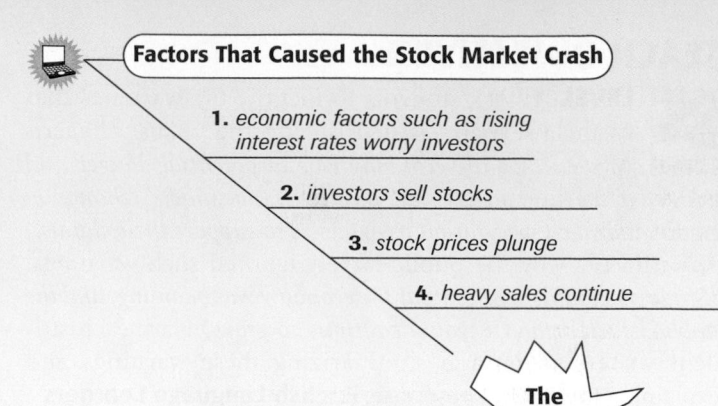

Factors That Caused the Stock Market Crash

1. *economic factors such as rising interest rates worry investors*

2. *investors sell stocks*

3. *stock prices plunge*

4. *heavy sales continue*

The Crash

HISTORY MAKERS SPEAK

John Hersch in *Hard Times*

Remembering the Crash.
John Hersch, an investment broker, described Black Thursday. "I had about $3,000 in the stock market, which was all the money I had. On Black Friday—Thursday, was it?—that margin account went out of the window. I may have had about $62 left. My wife had a colossal $125 a week job. . . . That night, she came home to our little apartment, and she said, 'Guess what happened today?' I said, 'What?' She said, 'I quit.' I was making about $60 a week and she was making $125. Two-thirds of our income and all of our savings disappeared that day."

CRITICAL THINKING How might the Hersches' financial troubles have affected their later spending? How might such behavior have deepened the Great Depression?

ANSWER: Answers will vary. Students might suggest that the Hersch family probably stopped making all but the most crucial purchases. Taken as a whole, this lack of consumer spending hurt businesses and deepened the depression.

INTERPRETING THE VISUAL RECORD

Stock market crash. The stock market crash of 1929 left many stockholders with huge losses. Some investors who had borrowed money during the prosperous days of the 1920s were unable to pay off their loans. *How do you think this photograph reflects the transition from a time of prosperity to one of depression for this investor?*

VISUAL RECORD ANSWER

Students might suggest that this man is trying to sell his luxury car for a small amount of cash.

---

confidence and caused prices to plunge. Panic gripped Wall Street. A *New York Times* reporter described the crash.

History Makers Speak

❝It came with a speed and ferocity [cruelty] that left men dazed. The bottom simply fell out of the market. . . . The streets were crammed with a mixed crowd—agonized little speculators, . . . sold-out traders, . . . inquisitive individuals and tourists seeking . . . a closer view of the national catastrophe. . . . Where was it going to end?❞

—*New York Times,* October 24, 1929

Black Thursday was just the beginning of a long downward spiral. Prices dropped still lower the following week, as more investors sold their stocks. On **Black Tuesday**—October 29—prices sank to a shocking new low when panicked investors dumped more than 16 million shares of stock on the market.

As prices fell, brokers contacted customers who owed them money for stocks purchased on margin. The brokers demanded cash to cover their loans. Unable to raise the funds, thousands of people were forced to sell their stocks at huge losses. Many investors were ruined. By mid-November the average value of leading stocks had been cut in half, and stockholders had lost some $30 billion. By year's end, stock losses exceeded the total cost of U.S. involvement in World War I.

✔ **READING CHECK: Drawing Conclusions** Why are October 24 and 29 referred to as black days? On October 24, stock prices plunged, and on October 29, they reached a new low. The days are black because bad things happened.

The Depression Begins

In the first months after the stock market crash, business leaders and public officials insisted that the setback was minor and temporary. President Hoover declared, "We have now passed the worst and . . . shall rapidly recover." Within the first months of 1930, however, it became clear that the nation was slipping into a severe economic depression.

Banking crisis. Just a small percentage of Americans had invested in the stock market in 1929. However, the impact of the crash was soon felt by the entire country. The crash provoked a major banking crisis. Like many other investors, large banks suffered significant losses. The worst crisis for banks came when borrowers began defaulting on their loans. Having lost their investments in the stock market, many investors could not repay their loans. Banks were left with depreciating assets and little income. With dwindling cash reserves, some banks were forced to close.

Fear of additional bank failures further aggravated the crisis. Customers could lose their entire life savings if their bank closed. Many depositors panicked and tried to withdraw their savings. This caused even more bank failures. Reporting on a banking panic in Akron, Ohio, one newspaper commented, "The bank was failing. Its cash reserve was dropping. Bank depositors waited in dread for a teller to say, 'We cannot give you ten percent of your account. We can't give you anything.'" Between 1930 and 1932 more than 5,000 banks failed. The 1930 collapse of one large New York City bank wiped out some 400,000 depositors.

TEACH OBJECTIVE 3

 LEVEL 1: Pair students and write the following phrase on the chalkboard: *The Banking Crisis and Subsequent Business Failures.* Have each pair create a flowchart displaying the effects of bank and business failures and noting how those events signaled the beginning of the Great Depression. *(Flowcharts should indicate that banks failed due to heavy defaults, margin calls, and depositor withdrawals. Bank failures deprived businesses of necessary resources and customers and forced layoffs and closings.)* Ask volunteers to present their flowcharts to the class.

English Language Learners, Cooperative Learning

LEVELS 2 AND 3: Conduct a brief discussion on the ways in which the banking crisis and subsequent business failures signaled the beginning of the Great Depression. *(See the Level 1 lesson for the correct details.)* Then organize students into small groups. Have each group create an outline for a skit depicting an event related to a bank or business failure. Skits might show depositors trying to withdraw their savings from an undercapitalized bank, for example. Have each group present its outline to the class. If time allows, ask each group to rehearse and perform its skit for the class. **Cooperative Learning**

Business failures. Many American businesses suffered from the banking crisis. Industries that had already lost money in the stock market crash faced additional hardships. Consumers were unable or unwilling to buy their products. Debt and the fear of bank failures brought an end to the consumer habit of purchasing new goods on credit. Many companies were forced to trim inventories, scale back production schedules, and lay off employees.

During the early 1930s businesses began to fail at an alarming rate as the economy's downward slide accelerated. More than 26,000 businesses went bankrupt in 1930. Another 28,285 went under the following year. In 1929 the U.S. **gross national product**—the total value of all goods and services produced in a given year—had reached $103 billion. At the height of the depression in 1933 it fell below $56 billion. Factories and mines stood idle. Railroad cars sat silent and empty.

As businesses failed, unemployment reached staggering levels. In 1932 the rate rose to 23.6 percent, up from 3.2 percent three years earlier. The crisis in the banking industry, business failures, and massive unemployment in the early 1930s marked the beginning of the **Great Depression**. This deep economic downturn gripped the United States from 1929 until the beginning of World War II.

Many Americans thought that their bank accounts would be safe during economic hard times.

✔ **READING CHECK: Sequencing** What events signaled the beginning of the Great Depression? The stock market crash provoked a banking crisis, and many businesses failed because of the banking crisis, leading to massive unemployment.

What Caused the Great Depression?

The stock market crash of 1929 provoked the banking crisis and business failures that jolted the U.S. economy and destroyed individual fortunes. It alone, however, did not cause the Great Depression.

Global depression. Economic trouble in Europe and other parts of the world was one of the many factors that brought down the U.S. economy. As the economy sank during the early 1930s, many observers, including President Hoover, blamed the U.S. depression on the state of global finances following World War I.

The global economy had suffered enormous setbacks. This was primarily because of the massive war debts built up by European countries. World trade rapidly declined during the late 1920s and early 1930s. The global depression further worsened the economic crisis in the United States. Foreign consumers were unable to purchase American goods. American industries, which relied on sales to consumers abroad, were stuck with large surpluses.

PRIMARY SOURCE

The Global Depression

The impact of the Great Depression was felt worldwide. In a 1931 radio broadcast, British economist John Maynard Keynes described the severe effects of the economic downturn. **According to Keynes, how widespread was the depression?**

❝The slump in trade and employment and the business losses . . . are as bad as the worst which have ever occurred in the modern history of the world. No country is exempt. The privation [hardship] and—what is sometimes worse—the anxiety which exist today in millions of homes all over the world is extreme. In the three chief industrial countries of the world, Great Britain, Germany, and the United States, I estimate that probably 12 million industrial workers stand idle. But I am not sure that there is not even more human misery today in the great agricultural countries of the world—Canada, Australia, and South America, where millions of small farmers see themselves ruined. ❞

LEVELS 1 AND 2: Ask each student to list the main causes of the Great Depression on a sheet of paper. *(Students should list the global economic crisis, the income gap, and consumer debt.)* Have students write a sentence for each factor explaining how it contributed to the depression. *(The global economic crisis deprived the United States of foreign consumers, and the income gap deprived businesses of national consumers. Consumer debt led to individual vulnerability and economic chaos.)* As a class, have students rank these causes from least important to most important. To conclude, describe a normal business cycle and discuss with the class how the Great Depression deviated from that cycle.

English Language Learners

LEVEL 3: Tell students to imagine that it is 1930 and that they are economists who have been asked to appear on a radio program and explain the causes of the Great Depression to listeners. Have each student write a script for a broadcast discussing those causes and contrasting the depression with a normal business cycle. *(See the Levels 1 and 2 lesson for the correct causes and explanations.)* Have volunteers perform their broadcasts for the class.

HOMEWORK *Have each student create a diagram representing a typical business cycle. Then ask students to write paragraphs describing how the Great Depression represented a significant deviation from that typical cycle.*

---

internet connect

TOPIC: Causes of the Great Depression
GO TO: go.hrw.com
KEYWORD: SE3 AN15

Have students access the Internet through the HRW Go site to conduct research on the causes of the Great Depression. Then have each student create a 3D model displaying those causes. Tell students to make sure that their models account for each of the major causes of the depression.

THAT'S INTERESTING!

In 1929 nearly 80 percent of the nation's families had no savings at all. These families had no financial cushion when the depression hit.

MAP ANSWER
Norway, Denmark, and Germany

VISUAL RECORD ANSWER

(for p. 447)

Students might note the claim that a person who purchases an automobile will provide three months of work to someone.

U.S. policies could have eased the global depression. Instead, the United States contributed to the worldwide economic downturn by placing high tariffs on imported goods. Even after the crash, Congress continued to pass high tariffs such as the **Smoot-Hawley Tariff** of 1930. It was the highest in U.S. history. The act protected American industries from inexpensive imports. However, it accelerated the global depression by eliminating the American market for foreign manufacturers and industries.

The income gap and consumer debt. Historians have argued that the unequal distribution of income was another central cause of the Great Depression.

The Beginnings of the Global Depression, 1928–1933

Interpreting Maps The worldwide depression created record levels of unemployment.

? HUMAN SYSTEMS In 1932 which countries had unemployment rates greater than 30 percent?

United States
The United States remains determined to collect war debts despite the European countries' inability to pay them.

Japan
Except from 1930 to 1932, Japan's rate of industrial production continues to climb. Military spending helps fuel this expansion.

USSR
The Communists organize agriculture and build up heavy industry in order to become economically self-sufficient.

France
Unemployment remains low because foreign workers are sent home, and many factory workers return to family farms.

Germany and Italy
Government economic policies and centralized control help bring these countries out of the depression.

South America
Dependent on selling raw materials, Chile, Bolivia, and Peru see exports fall by more than 69 percent from 1928–29 to 1932–33.

Percentage of Workforce Unemployed
1929 1932

*Figure for Italy is from 1931

REVIEW

Have students complete the **Section 1 Review** on p. 447.

ASSESS

Have students complete **Daily Quiz 15.1.** As **Alternative Assessment**, you may want to use the bank crisis skit outline or the depression broadcast in this section's lessons.

RETEACH

Have students complete **Main Idea Activity for English Language Learners and Special-Needs Students 15.1.** Then organize students into small groups. Have each group create an outline of Section 1. Ask each group to copy its outline on the

chalkboard. Conduct a brief discussion on the outlines and the material in the section.
English Language Learners, Cooperative Learning

EXTEND

Have students conduct introductory research on the workings of the stock market. Then have each student create a mock stock portfolio, starting with a fictional $5,000. Tell students to use the newspaper's financial section to track the performance of their stocks over a specified period of time. After that period, have students write a brief report analyzing the performance of their stocks—gains, losses, and so on. In their reports, students should compare and contrast their stock market experiences with those of Americans in the 1920s. **Block Scheduling**

Between 1923 and 1929 the disposable income of the wealthiest 1 percent of Americans increased by 63 percent. Meanwhile, the income of the poorest 93 percent of Americans decreased by 4 percent. Writer Upton Sinclair noted, "The . . . depression is one of abundance, not of scarcity. . . . The cause of the trouble is that a small class has the wealth, while the rest have the debts." This income gap meant that most people did not have the buying power needed to boost the economy. According to many economists, if workers had received higher wages for their labor and farmers better prices for their crops, the depression would have been less severe. Some even argue that it could have been avoided.

Some Americans bridged the income gap by using credit to purchase goods. The reliance on consumer credit also contributed to economic chaos. Once the economy began to slow and the government raised interest rates, many consumers could not pay their debts. After the crash many businesses stopped extending credit altogether.

The business cycle. Some economists argue that better fiscal planning in the 1920s would not have prevented the onset of the Great Depression. These economists view depressions as an inevitable part of the **business cycle**—the regular ups and downs of business in a free-enterprise economy. According to business-cycle theory, industries increase production and hire more workers during prosperous times, with the result that over time surpluses pile up. Industries then cut back on production and lay off workers, triggering a recession or a depression. According to this theory, once the surplus goods are sold, industries again gear up for production and the downturn comes to an end. However, the length and severity of the Great Depression went far beyond the normal rhythms of the business cycle.

✔ **READING CHECK: Analyzing Information** What caused the Great Depression?
The global economic crisis and the unequal distribution of wealth were two causes.

When You BUY an AUTOMOBILE You GIVE 3 Months' Work to Someone Which Allows Him to BUY OTHER PRODUCTS

BUY A CAR NOW—HELP BRING BACK PROSPERITY

INTERPRETING THE VISUAL RECORD

The depression. Some businesses encouraged Americans to spend money during the depression. They believed that it would lead to more demand for products, more jobs, and eventually an end to the depression. *How does this automobile advertisement reflect this viewpoint?*

SECTION 1 REVIEW

1. **Define and explain:**
   bull market
   bear market
   margin buying
   gross national product
   business cycle

2. **Identify and explain:**
   Herbert Hoover
   Black Thursday
   Black Tuesday
   Great Depression
   Smoot-Hawley Tariff

3. **Identifying Cause and Effect** Copy the web below. Use it to explain how each factor contributed to the Great Depression.

Income Gap — Consumer Debt — GREAT DEPRESSION — Business Cycles — Global Depression — Banking Crisis

4. **Finding the Main Idea**
   a. What events in 1929 were historically significant? Why?
   b. How did the stock market crash provoke a banking crisis, and how did the banking crisis lead to business failures?
   c. What effects did the Great Depression have on the U.S. economy?

5. **Writing and Critical Thinking**
   Drawing Conclusions Imagine that you are an economist during the late 1920s. Write an article explaining what problems point to a possible economic downturn.
   Consider:
   • the nation's agricultural crisis and sick industries
   • growth of consumer credit
   • the bull market in stocks

Homework Practice Online
keyword: SE3 HP15

SECTION 1 ANSWERS

1. Define
• bull market, p. 443
• bear market, p. 443
• margin buying, p. 443
• gross national product, p. 445
• business cycle, p. 447

2. Identify
• Herbert Hoover, p. 442
• Black Thursday, p. 443
• Black Tuesday, p. 444
• Great Depression, p. 445
• Smoot-Hawley Tariff, p. 446

3. banking crisis—destroyed personal savings, hurt businesses; business cycles—led to periodic economic downturns; income gap—decreased purchasing power of much of the population; consumer debt—increased instability, deprived debtors of money; global depression—decreased purchasing ability of foreign consumers

4a. Answers may vary but should suggest that the stock market crash and bank crisis were significant as the start of the Great Depression.

b. Investors who lost money in the stock market could not repay loans to banks, many of which then failed. The bank failures hurt businesses.

c. People withdrew their savings, banks folded, businesses shut down, and the GNP fell by half.

5. Articles will vary but should mention the agricultural crisis, consumer debt, the overvalued bull market and the income gap.

SECTION 2

Hard Times

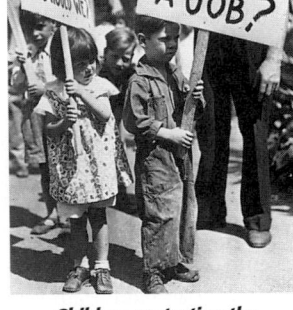

Children protesting the high rate of unemployment

 EYEWITNESSES TO History *"My father walked the streets everyday. . . . My mother went to work. I even worked, playing the piano for dancing class on Saturday mornings for fifty cents an hour. My mother would find a few pennies and we would go to the greengrocer and wait until he threw out the stuff that was beginning to rot. We would pick out the best rotted potato and greens and carrots that were already soft. Then we would go to the butcher and beg a marrow bone. And then with the few pennies we would buy a box of barley, and we'd have soup to last us for three or four days. I remember she would say to me sometimes, 'You go out and do it. I'm ashamed.'"*

—Clara Hancox, quoted in *The Century*, by Peter Jennings and Todd Brewster

Clara Hancox was 11 years old when the Great Depression began in 1929. She soon became acquainted with the unemployment, poverty, and homelessness that many city-dwellers of the era experienced. Rural Americans also suffered from poverty and despair. Eager to escape the grim reality of the depression, many Americans sought inexpensive forms of popular entertainment, such as movies, radio programs, and popular fiction.

American Workers Face Unemployment

After the stock market crash of 1929 and the subsequent banking crisis, the U.S. economy entered into a serious depression whose effects quickly became visible. Stores closed, factories stopped production, and millions of unemployed workers walked the streets looking for jobs. "These [unemployed] are dead men," wrote one observer, "They are ghosts that walk the streets."

Increasing joblessness. In 1929 some 1.5 million Americans were unemployed. By 1933 the figure had risen to about 15 million. In Chicago, approximately 50 percent of the city's workforce was unemployed, while 80 percent of the workers in Toledo, Ohio, were searching for jobs. As poet Langston Hughes observed, it seemed that "everybody in America was looking for work."

Even for those who managed to keep their jobs, wages fell dramatically—in some cases to as low as 10 cents an hour. Factory workers' average annual income fell by nearly one third between 1929 and 1933. Some of the country's largest employers tried to keep as many experienced employees as possible. Rather than laying employees off, companies reduced the number of hours they worked. One General Electric employee explained, "They'd just say, 'You come in Monday. Take the rest of the week off.'" This left employees with little income.

With the drop in wages and employment, the promise of economic prosperity that had attracted waves of immigrants to the United States quickly faded. Immigration to the United States greatly decreased.

TEACH OBJECTIVE 1

LEVEL 1: Pair students and tell them to imagine that it is 1933 and that they are autoworkers who have recently been fired, along with the rest of their coworkers. Have students in each pair develop a dialogue describing the effects of unemployment for themselves and other American workers. *(Pairs should indicate that unemployment rose sharply during the depression and created severe financial and emotional problems for workers.)* Have volunteers perform their dialogues for the class. **English Language Learners, Cooperative Learning**

LEVEL 2: Tell students to imagine that it is 1933 and that they are autoworkers who have recently been fired, along with the rest of their coworkers. Have students write a series of diary entries detailing the effects of unemployment for themselves and others during the Great Depression. *(See the Level 1 lesson for the correct effects.)* In their diary entries, students also might want to discuss the psychological implications of chronic unemployment. Have volunteers read their entries to the class. Students may wish to include their diary entries in their portfolios.

The American worker. Workers across the country were hard hit by the depression. African Americans faced particularly difficult times, as economic troubles added to the chronic problem of racial discrimination. When factories laid off employees, African American workers were often the first to go. According to one study, white workers in Chicago believed that African Americans "should not be hired as long as there are white men without work."

Many African American women, who made up the vast majority of domestic servants, lost their jobs. Those domestic servants without regular work often stood on street corners to try to obtain work for the day. Ella Baker and Marvel Cooke, two black women, saw this happen in New York City and referred to it as the "Bronx Slave Market." They described a typical scene in an article they wrote for *The Crisis.*

> **"**Rain or shine, cold or hot, you will find them there—Negro women, old and young—sometimes bedraggled [shabby looking], sometimes neatly dressed . . . waiting expectantly for Bronx housewives to buy their strength and energy.**"**
>
> —Ella Baker and Marvel Cooke, "The Bronx Slave Market," *The Crisis,* November 1935

Since many employers could hire women more cheaply than men, the percentage of women in the workforce actually increased in the 1930s. Most were employed as office workers or domestic servants. As the percentage of women in the workforce rose overall, however, competition in domestic and agricultural work increased. This caused the percentage of employed African American women to fall.

Trying to maintain a steady source of income and a sense of self-reliance, some unemployed workers took to selling apples on the street. Charging a nickel for each apple, a seller might earn $1.15 on a good day. In the fall of 1930 more than 6,000 unemployed workers sold apples in New York City. President Hoover claimed that "many people have left their jobs for the more profitable one of selling apples." However, during the depression few people had any choice in how or where they worked.

✔ **READING CHECK: Analyzing Information** How did unemployment during the Great Depression affect female workers? Since women could be hired more cheaply than men, the percentage of female workers increased.

Life in the City

Life in U.S. cities during the Great Depression was difficult. Many city-dwellers faced unemployment and poverty. "We saw the city at its worst. One vivid moment of those dark days we shall never forget," recalled Louise V. Armstrong. "We saw a crowd of some fifty men fighting over a barrel of garbage which had

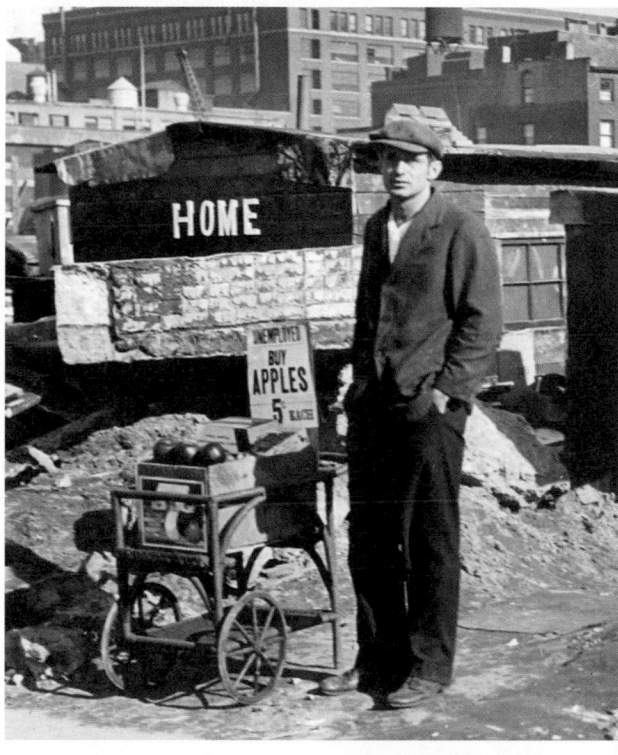

INTERPRETING THE VISUAL RECORD

Poverty. Unemployed workers sold apples for 5 cents apiece to earn money for survival. *What else do you think unemployed workers such as this young man did to acquire food and shelter?*

450

LEVEL 3: Conduct a brief discussion on unemployment during the Great Depression, concentrating on the economic and psychological effects of joblessness. *(See the Level 1 lesson for the correct effects.)* Then tell students to create a fictional depression-era character. This character should be unemployed and struggling to survive. Encourage students to fully detail their characters, creating fictional backgrounds, appearances, and so on. Then tell students to imagine that they are journalists during the Great Depression. Have each student write a profile of his or her fictional character, detailing the effects of unemployment on that figure. Ask volunteers to read their profiles to the class. Students may wish to include their profiles in their portfolios.

Teacher to Teacher

Janie Maldonado of Austin, Texas, suggested the following activity: Organize students into small groups. Have members of each group conduct research on the ways in which charitable organizations in the community assisted the needy during the Great Depression. If possible, have groups obtain a copy of an organization's budget to determine how it allocated its resources. Have each group prepare an oral report to present its findings.

ECONOMICS

Relief Efforts. Although city governments and charities tried to provide assistance to poor people, they simply could not meet the needs of the unemployed. New York City, for example, spent $79 million on relief in 1932—an amount that totaled one month's wages for the city's unemployed. In 1931 Chicago spent $100,000 a day on relief in an effort to replace lost wages that totaled some $2 million per day.

CRITICAL THINKING How might the relatively small aid amounts offered by some cities have affected public opinion toward city and state governments?

ANSWER: Students might suggest that the small amounts of aid probably convinced some people that city and state governments did not care about their problems.

THAT'S INTERESTING!

In 1932 some 250,000 Americans lost their homes because they could not pay their mortgages. In desperation, one New York City couple moved to a cave in Central Park, where they lived for the next year.

VISUAL RECORD ANSWER

Students might mention despair, fatigue, and hopelessness.

INTERPRETING THE VISUAL RECORD

The homeless. During the depression, many city-dwellers lost their homes. *In your opinion, what emotions does the artist portray in the characters of this depression-era painting?*

As homelessness increased, shantytowns of makeshift shelters spread into the vacant lots of American cities.

been set outside the back door of a restaurant. American citizens fighting for scraps of food like animals!"

During the early 1930s the federal government did little to assist struggling city-dwellers or their local communities. City governments, religious groups such as the Salvation Army, and charitable organizations including the Red Cross tried to provide direct relief to the needy. Neighbors also helped one another. One woman told a visitor, "My neighbors help me, by bringing me a little to eat, when they knows I ain't got nothing in the house to cook." Mexican American communities formed mutual-aid societies known as *mutualistas* to help each other. Some Chinese American communities set out open barrels of rice so that people could draw from them privately, without having to ask for handouts. Harlem residents organized "rent parties." These large social gatherings charged a small admission fee to help pay a neighbor's monthly rent.

Across the country, people engaged in a daily struggle to feed themselves and their children. Poverty-stricken men and women waited in **breadlines** for bowls of soup and pieces of bread given out by charitable organizations. Karl Monroe recalled standing in the breadline on 25th Street in New York City. "To my surprise, I found . . . all types of men—the majority being skilled craftsmen unable to find work." Hunger was so widespread that by 1932 one out of every five children in New York City suffered from malnutrition. When one hungry schoolchild was told to go home for lunch, she replied, "It won't do any good. . . . This is my sister's day to eat." Poor diets caused some Americans to suffer long-term health effects, such as problems with their teeth and eyes.

In addition to hunger, homelessness was a serious urban problem during the depression. Faced with unemployment and falling wages, many urban residents were unable to pay their rent and were evicted from their homes.

The homeless often gathered in **shantytowns**—collections of makeshift shelters built out of packing boxes, scrap lumber, corrugated iron, and other thrown-away items. Shantytowns rose up outside most cities. Blaming an unresponsive president for their plight, the homeless mockingly referred to these shantytowns as Hoovervilles.

Life on the Farm

The impact of the depression spread all across the United States. It affected not only city-dwellers but also people living on farms. Increasing poverty during the

The Great Depression in the City and the Country

Urban

- received some aid from charities
- formed mutual-aid organizations
- experienced hunger
- experienced homelessness

- *experienced poverty*
- *experienced diminished expectations*

Rural

- *faced lower prices for food products*
- *forced to let crops rot and kill animals*
- *faced farm foreclosures*
- *Mexican aliens and immigrants faced deportation*

depression made it harder and harder for urban residents to purchase farm products. Shrinking demand for farm products caused prices to drop. Farmers found themselves with more goods than they could sell. While people in the cities went hungry, farmers in some areas were forced to let crops rot in the fields and to slaughter excess livestock they could not afford to feed. One newspaper editor, Oscar Ameringer, noted the irony of this situation. "While Oregon sheep raisers fed mutton to the buzzards," Ameringer recalled, "I saw men picking for meat scraps in the garbage cans in the cities of New York and Chicago."

As their incomes fell, many farmers were unable to keep up their mortgage payments. Banks began foreclosing on farms. In some communities, residents banded together to fight the foreclosures. Often when a bank held a foreclosure auction to sell off a family's possessions, neighbors would arrive and bid absurdly low prices, such as 25 cents for a plow. In one example, a farm with an $800 mortgage was sold for $1.90. After the auction the neighbors would then give the goods back to the original owners. This tactic was so successful that several farm states, beginning with Iowa in 1933, passed laws that temporarily banned foreclosure sales.

Conditions were particularly bad for tenant farmers in the South, where most rural residents already faced crippling poverty. Cotton prices fell from 16 cents per pound in 1929 to less than 6 cents in 1931. Many tenant farmers—mostly African Americans—were ruined. Some were forced off the land they had lived on all their lives. While farmers in the Midwest faced an overabundance of food, southern cotton farmers faced poverty and devastating harvests. Gracie Turner, a sharecropper's wife, testified to the hardships of a tenant farmer's life in the 1930s.

INTERPRETING THE VISUAL RECORD

Farm life. During the depression, many farm families were evicted from their land. *What economic circumstances do you believe this African American family experienced during the depression?*

History Makers Speak

"That's all there is to expect—work hard and go hungry part time. . . . This year's been so hard we had to drop our burial insurance. . . . All it costs is twenty-five cents . . . but they don't come many twenty-five cents in this house.**"**

—Gracie Turner, quoted in *These Are Our Lives,* by the Federal Writers' Project

Migrant farmworkers in the Southwest, most of them recent immigrants from Mexico, also experienced difficulties. Government officials and many Americans wanted to remove illegal aliens and recent Mexican immigrants from the United States. They believed that this would ease the strain of the depression. To avoid paying the soaring cost of relief efforts for unemployed migrant farmworkers, local authorities provided funds to transport Mexican migrant farmworkers to Mexico. They pressured and even forced the farmworkers to return to their native land. During the 1930s approximately 500,000 people of Mexican descent—some of them U.S. citizens—were pressured into leaving the country. Those who remained often faced discrimination and harsh working conditions.

HISTORY MAKERS SPEAK

Harry Terrell in *Hard Times*

Trouble on the Farm.
Harry Terrell, an Iowa resident, described the sense of desperation that a group of farmers felt as they almost lost their farms to foreclosure: "They came very near hanging that judge. Because they caught this judge foreclosing farm mortgages, and they had no other way of stopping it. He had issued the whole bunch of foreclosures on his docket. . . . They took the judge out of his court and took him to the fairgrounds and they had a rope around his neck, and they had the rope over the limb of a tree. They were gonna string him up in the old horse thief fashion. But somebody had sense enough to stop the thing before it got too far."

CRITICAL THINKING What might the farmers' response to the judge have indicated about the severity of the Great Depression?

ANSWER: Students might mention that the farmers' response revealed the incredible financial and personal stresses many people experienced during the depression.

VISUAL RECORD ANSWER

Students might note that the loaded car and the rickety house suggest that the family experienced severe poverty.

LEVEL 1: Tell students to imagine that they are journalists preparing to write a series of articles about the effects of the Great Depression on family life and American attitudes. Have each student write three headlines for the series. *(Headlines should note that the depression fractured some families, although it forced others to band together for survival. Divorce rates went up, and birthrates went down. Many Americans suffered psychological problems during the era.)* Have volunteers write their headlines on the chalkboard. Discuss these headlines and the topic as a class. Students may wish to include the headlines in their portfolios.
English Language Learners

LEVELS 2 AND 3: Tell students to imagine that they are journalists preparing to write a series of articles about the effects of the Great Depression on family life and American attitudes. Have each student write the first article in the series. *(See the Level 1 lesson for the correct effects.)* Students might choose to focus their articles on a particular family, for example, or to provide a general analysis of the subject. Ask volunteers to read their articles to the class. Students may wish to include their articles in their portfolios.

HOMEWORK *Have students prepare collages that reflect how the Great Depression affected family life and the attitudes of Americans.*

GOVERNMENT

Discrimination Against Mexicans.
In May 1935 the governor of Colorado ordered sheriffs in the southern part of the state to prevent workers, almost all of whom were Mexican, from entering Colorado. The following year the governor declared martial law along the border. Officers prevented people from entering the state and took some in Colorado to the New Mexico border. This blockade and resettlement was illegal, but took place nonetheless.

CRITICAL THINKING Why might the governor have wanted to deport Mexican workers from the state?

ANSWER: Students might note that the governor wanted to protect jobs for Americans. Students might also suggest that the governor held anti-Mexican prejudices.

SKILL-BUILDING STRATEGIES ANSWERS
(for p. 453)

Practicing the Skill

1. to transport people's belongings

2. its rusted condition, the goods strapped to the sides; demonstrate the severity of the Great Depression

3. Answers will vary. Some students might suggest that the truck indicates that the depression left many Americans with virtually nothing.

Research on the R◉M

Free Find:
Josefina Fierro de Bright
After reading about Josefina Fierro de Bright on the **Holt Researcher CD–ROM**, write a short essay describing how growing up during the Great Depression affected her life.

Photographs such as this one by Dorothea Lange captured the struggles many American families experienced during the depression.

Josefina Fierro de Bright

Some of the Mexican American families that remained in the United States organized against discrimination in the Southwest. One such activist was **Josefina Fierro de Bright**, the daughter of migrants who had fled from revolution in Mexico to settle in California. The experience of growing up during the depression in the midst of poverty and ethnic discrimination had a profound effect on Fierro. As with many children of the depression, her life was unstable. Her family moved often, causing Fierro to change schools eight times. Throughout the hard times, however, her mother always encouraged her to strive for success. "Rely on yourself, be independent," Mrs. Fierro advised. She also emphasized the importance of getting an education.

In 1938, at age 18, Josefina Fierro entered the University of California at Los Angeles. She had planned to study medicine, but activism on behalf of the Mexican American community soon took up most of her time. Aided by her activist husband, Hollywood screenwriter John Bright, she led boycotts of companies that did business in Mexican American communities but did not hire Mexican American workers. Enlisting financial support from a few well-known movie stars, Fierro de Bright also started a radio program for Spanish-speaking audiences.

These activities brought her to the attention of a Mexican American group called El Congreso, which organized Hispanic migrants to resist oppressive conditions. In 1939 El Congreso leaders asked Fierro de Bright to help them establish a branch in Los Angeles. Over the next few years, she worked tirelessly, leading marches and hunger strikes, lobbying for expanded relief programs for Hispanic Americans, and encouraging bilingual education for migrant children. "I used to work so hard it used to kill me," she recalled. Throughout her life she never forgot the lessons her mother taught her during the depression. Those memories spurred her efforts to improve the lives of all working people.

✔ **READING CHECK: Summarizing** How did urban and rural residents cope during the depression? urban—fought for food, helped each other, waited in breadlines, and lived in shantytowns; rural—farmers let crops rot and killed animals they could not feed; many immigrant farmers were forced to return home

Family Life in the 1930s

The crisis of the Great Depression required that family members pull together to help one another cope with their difficulties. Farmers and city-dwellers alike shared food and money and provided the support and encouragement necessary to get through hard times. In many cases, relatives doubled up in small houses, and young adults moved back in with their parents. Frederick Lewis Allen reported on the changing roles of family members trying to survive the depression. He wrote, "Mrs. Jones, who went daily to her stenographic job, was now the economic mainstay of her family, for Mr. Jones was jobless and was doing the cooking and looking after the children."

Family strains. Economic hardship took its toll on families, and some eventually broke apart under the strain. The marriage rate fell dramatically during the depression. Because many young people put

SPOTLIGHT
on Family Life During the Great Depression

Ask students to closely examine the image in the lower left-hand corner of the previous page. Then have each student write a short story about the family pictured in the image. Students should create names, personalities, and situations for the people. Invite volunteers to read part or all of their short stories to the class. **Block Scheduling**

TEACH OBJECTIVE 4

LEVEL 1: Write the following scenario on the chalkboard: *It is 1933. There are no televisions, computers, or video games. What do you do to entertain yourself? You have five cents a week to spend on leisure activities.* Ask students to respond to the scenario in writing. Discuss students' responses. Then conduct a brief discussion on how popular culture provided an escape from the Great Depression. (*Americans went to movies, listened to the radio, and read new forms of popular literature, such as comic books and popular novels. These helped Americans temporarily escape the depression and their troubles.*) After the discussion, ask students to reflect back on their scenario answers. **English Language Learners**

---

off getting married and starting their own families, birthrates declined, particularly during the early years of the depression. A Chicago schoolteacher looked back on those years.

History Makers Speak

"Do you realize how many people in my generation are not married? . . . It wasn't that we didn't have a chance. I was going with someone when the Depression hit. We probably would have gotten married. . . . Suddenly he was laid off. It hit him like a ton of bricks. And he just disappeared."

—Elsa Ponselle, quoted in *America's History*, edited by James A. Henretta

Life was difficult for women during the depression. In the face of economic hardship, the mothers of hard-hit families often played roles of quiet heroism. Such daily challenges as putting food on the table and making clothes and shoes last for one more year brought constant worry. As one woman remarked, "I figured every which way I could to make ends meet . . . but some of [those] ends just wouldn't meet." In rural and small-town households, women made their own soap and baked their own bread.

Analyzing Primary Sources

Drawing Conclusions What connection does this speaker suggest between male unemployment and lower marriage rates in the 1930s?

Unemployed men were less likely than employed men to get married in the 1930s.

Skill-Building Strategies

Evaluating Artifacts as Historical Evidence

Artifacts are objects created or shaped by humans. They are a unique type of evidence that historians use to gain a more complete understanding of the past. Much like photographs, artifacts offer valuable clues about the customs, values, and details of daily life in the past that are difficult to find in written sources. Because they were handled by real individuals in history, artifacts also provide a sense of closeness to the past that is usually lacking in other types of evidence.

Artifacts must be analyzed with care. The insights they provide must be considered in the context of knowledge one has gained from other, more traditional sources.

How to Evaluate an Artifact as Historical Evidence

1. **Identify the artifact.** First, identify the artifact and determine its general purpose. Then find out when and where the artifact was created and used and, if possible, who created and used it.
2. **Examine the artifact carefully.** Study the artifact carefully, taking note of its construction and design. If it shows wear, try to determine what this wear says about how the artifact was used.
3. **Put the information to use.** Determine how your analysis of the artifact corresponds to information about the historical period that you have gained

through other sources. Then think about how the artifact contributes to your understanding of the historical period.

Applying the Skill

Examine the photograph below of a truck that was used by migrants during the Great Depression.

Practicing the Skill

Use the photograph above to answer the following questions.
1. What do you think this truck was used for?
2. What details about the truck do you think are significant? Why?
3. How does the truck contribute to your understanding of the Great Depression?

HISTORY MAKERS SPEAK

Meridel Le Sueur in *For the Record: A Documentary History of America*, Vol. 2

Women in the Depression. Meridel Le Sueur described in an article the effects of the depression. "I've lived in cites for many months broke, without help, too timid to get in bread lines. I've known many women to live like this until they simply faint on the street from privations, without saying a word to anyone. A woman will shut herself up in a room until it is taken away from her, and eat a cracker a day and be as quiet as a mouse so there are no social statistics concerning her. I don't know why it is, but a woman will do this unless she has dependents, will go for weeks, verging on starvation, crawling in some hole, going through the streets ashamed."

CRITICAL THINKING

According to the statement above, how might women have responded to aid offers? Do you think that this response was different from that of men?

ANSWER: Students might suggest that many women refused to take advantage of aid offers. Students might suggest that many men, too, refused to take handouts or charity.

LEVEL 2: Organize students into small groups and tell them to imagine that they are entertainment reporters during the depression. Have each group create an entertainment section for a newspaper. Groups' sections should describe entertainment offerings that were popular during the era, such as movies and radio shows. Ask each group to present its entertainment section to the class, explaining how popular culture provided an escape from the depression. *(See the Level 1 lesson for the correct forms of entertainment and the correct effects.)* Display groups' sections around the classroom. **Cooperative Learning**

LEVEL 3: Conduct a brief discussion on the forms and uses of popular culture during the 1930s. *(See the Level 1 lesson for the correct forms and effects.)* Then organize students into triads and tell them to imagine that they are movie producers during the early years of the Great Depression. Have each triad develop two written movie proposals. Triads' proposals should appeal to Americans who want to escape the depression for a while. Ask each triad to present its proposals to the class, and have students select the most promising movie idea. To extend the lesson, have each triad create storyboards for its favorite proposals. **Cooperative Learning**

Gangster Films. Gangster movies, such as the 1930 release *Little Caesar*, were popular with audiences during the early years of the Great Depression. Some historians have argued that people responded positively to these movies because they portrayed acquisitive individuals as selfish, evil, and ultimately self-destructive.

CRITICAL THINKING Ask students to name a popular modern-day film genre. What might the popularity of this genre indicate about the national mood?

ANSWER: Students might name the horror genre and suggest that it reveals Americans' desires to safely experience and express their fears of violence.

THAT'S INTERESTING!

In 1933 Walt Disney released the cartoon *Three Little Pigs.* A song from the cartoon, "Who's Afraid of the Big Bad Wolf?" became a huge hit, perhaps because it reflected an optimistic response to "the wolf at the door"—the Great Depression itself.

Then and Now

Baseball

In their search for inexpensive entertainment during the Great Depression, many Americans turned to baseball. Players such as Babe Ruth had made baseball popular. By the 1930s it had become the country's favorite sport. Radio broadcasts of baseball games provided cheap entertainment for fans in the depression era. Since fans could listen to the game for free on the radio, baseball teams had lower ticket sales. Team owners, however, made money from selling broadcasting privileges to radio stations.

Hoping to attract more fans to the ballparks, team owners began to consider new ideas. In 1933 owners organized the first all-star game. In 1935 Larry MacPhail of the Cincinnati Reds revolutionized the sport by introducing nighttime ball games to professional baseball. Owners also rented out their stadiums to African American baseball teams.

As white team owners maintained a so-called gentleman's agreement not to sign black players, African Americans played in clubs and leagues of their own. The Negro National League and the Negro American League attracted fans with future hall-of-fame players like Satchel Paige and William "Judy" Johnson.

Baseball is now racially integrated. Many of the game's 1930s innovations remain, however. For example, nighttime baseball and all-star games still attract eager fans to the ballpark today.

A nighttime baseball game

Psychological effects. The economic crisis of the 1930s affected the mental health and attitudes of many Americans. The term *depression* described the mood of the country as much as it did the economy. More than 20,000 Americans committed suicide in 1932, a 28 percent increase over 1929. For middle-class and wealthy Americans, many of whom had never known poverty, the depression was a cruel blow. Many would never forget the shame they felt at being unemployed, losing their businesses or homes, and being unable to provide for their families. The attitude of an unemployed teacher in New Orleans was typical. "If with all the advantages I've had, I can't make a living, I'm just no good, I guess. I've given up ever amounting to anything. It's no use."

Many men whose lives had been dominated by work did not know what to do without a job. They often spent their days dawdling around the house or roaming the streets. The depression proved equally difficult for working women who lost their jobs, particularly those who were single or whose families depended on two incomes to survive. Many parents who could not support their families were consumed by guilt.

Even after the depression, the memories of those lean years remained vivid. Habits of scrimping and saving and of making every penny count would stay with members of this generation for the rest of their lives. A strong desire for financial stability and material comforts shaped the outlook of many Americans who came of age during the depression.

✔ **READING CHECK: Finding the Main Idea** What were the psychological effects of the Great Depression? *Depression described both the economic collapse and the mood of the country.*

Popular Culture in the 1930s

As the psychological strain of the Great Depression increased, many Americans looked to popular culture and entertainment for escape. Many people took up inexpensive pastimes, such as reading and playing games at home. Movies and radio were particularly popular.

The sound explosion. With low ticket prices and double features, movie theaters offered inexpensive entertainment. Talking pictures, which had begun to replace silent films in the late 1920s, thrilled audiences. Among the most popular movies of the early 1930s were gangster films that portrayed tough guys fighting their way to the top against all odds. Similarly, strong women such as Bette Davis, Greta Garbo, Mae West, and Marlene Dietrich reinforced the theme of survival in a difficult world.

Movie cartoons also brightened the 1930s, thanks to Walt Disney's Mickey Mouse and Donald Duck. Disney cartoons were often as popular with movie audiences as feature films.

REVIEW

Have students complete the **Section 2 Review** on p. 455.

ASSESS

Have students complete **Daily Quiz 15.2**. As **Alternative Assessment**, you may want to use the unemployment dialogue or the depression entertainment section in this section's lessons.

RETEACH

Have students complete **Main Idea Activity for English Language Learners and Special-Needs Students 15.2**. Then organize students into four groups. Assign each group one objective. Have each group write paragraphs addressing its assigned

objective. Ask each group to read its paragraphs to the class.
English Language Learners, Cooperative Learning

EXTEND

Ask students to interview a person who lived through the Great Depression about the era. Alternately, have students read a primary source from an individual who experienced the period. *(You might direct students to Studs Terkel's* Hard Times, *a widely available book.)* Ask each student to prepare a short, casual presentation about his or her interview or primary source, focusing on the person's impressions of the depression. Have students make their presentations to the class. **Block Scheduling**

Radio, which experienced its golden age during the depression, offered free entertainment at home. During the 1930s the number of radios nationwide rose from about 12 million to 28 million. Popular programs allowed listeners to forget the hard times. Heroes such as the Lone Ranger, Little Orphan Annie, and the Shadow always triumphed over evil, offering a hopeful message.

Literature. The public's desire to escape the harsh reality of the depression was also reflected in popular literature. Inexpensive comic books presented heroes such as Flash Gordon and Tarzan. Many of the era's most popular novels offered tales that took readers' minds off their economic worries. In *Lost Horizon* (1933) by **James Hilton**, a weary traveler stumbles upon a peaceful, prosperous utopia hidden in the mountains of Tibet. The idea of discovering a perfect world appealed to many readers.

Not all fiction of the early depression offered an escape. **James T. Farrell** portrayed the grim life of Chicago's Irish immigrants in his *Studs Lonigan* trilogy (1932–1935). Nathanael West presented the American dream as a nightmare in *Miss Lonelyhearts* (1933). Novelist **William Faulkner** wrote *The Sound and the Fury* (1929) and *As I Lay Dying* (1930), which portrayed tragic events in small-town Mississippi.

INTERPRETING THE VISUAL RECORD

Entertainment. During the depression, Americans sought affordable ways to escape their troubles, such as books and radio programs. *What does this image suggest about the importance of radio to this family?*

✔ **READING CHECK: Categorizing** How did popular culture reflect Americans' desire to escape from the depression? Movies, radio, and literature portrayed survival in a difficult world.

SECTION 2 REVIEW

1. Define and explain:
mutualistas
breadlines
shantytowns

2. Identify and explain:
Josefina Fierro de Bright
James Hilton
James T. Farrell
William Faulkner

3. Identifying Cause and Effect Copy the graphic organizer below. Use it to explain how unemployment had a psychological impact on many Americans and how that psychological impact affected family life.

4. Finding the Main Idea
a. How did poverty in urban areas create such a drop in agricultural prices that farmers let their crops rot in the field?
b. How did the hardships of the Great Depression further inflame racial prejudices against African American workers and Mexican migrant farmworkers?
c. How did the burdens of the Great Depression create challenges to traditional beliefs in the importance of family?

5. Writing and Critical Thinking
Problem Solving Imagine that you are a 1930s newspaper reporter. Write an article explaining what steps Americans took to better their lives during the Great Depression.
Consider:
• how urban residents formed organizations to help their communities
• how migrant farmworkers took action to defend their rights
• how popular entertainment helped Americans deal with the depression

Homework Practice Online
keyword: SE3 HP15

SECTION
REVIEW 2 ANSWERS

1. Define
• *mutualistas*, p. 450
• breadlines, p. 450
• shantytowns, p. 450

2. Identify
• Josefina Fierro de Bright, p. 452
• James Hilton, p. 455
• James T. Farrell, p. 455
• William Faulkner, p. 455

3. Unemployment often led to psychological depression and shame, which placed stress on family relationships. Some families broke up under the pressure.

4a. Urban-dwellers could not afford to buy farm products, which meant that farmers could not sell their goods.

b. Many white Americans believed that jobs should go to white citizens rather than to African American or Mexican American.

c. Economic stresses led to rising divorce rates and lower birthrates.

5. Answers will vary. Student articles should include how people tried to help neighbors, sold apples in the street, formed aid organizations, and tried to distract themselves with popular culture.

SECTION 3

After completing Section 3, students should be able to:

OBJECTIVE 1 Explain why President Hoover opposed government-sponsored direct relief for needy individuals during the Great Depression.

OBJECTIVE 2 Outline the Hoover administration's attempts to solve the economic problems of the depression, and analyze the success of these efforts.

OBJECTIVE 3 Relate how radicals and veterans responded to President Hoover's policies.

OBJECTIVE 4 Analyze why Franklin D. Roosevelt was such a popular candidate in the 1932 election.

 LET'S GET STARTED!

As students enter the classroom, distribute Cartoon 23, Herbert Hoover and the Depression, from **American History Political Cartoons**. Ask students to study the cartoon. Discuss the cartoon and accompanying questions with students. Then tell students that in Section 3 they will learn how resentment toward President Hoover and the Republicans affected the 1932 election.

SECTION 3 RESOURCES

REPRODUCIBLE
- Guided Reading Strategy 15.3
- American History Political Cartoon 23: Herbert Hoover and the Depression
- Geography Activity 15: Public Unrest During the Depression

TECHNOLOGY
- One-Stop Planner, Lesson 15.3
- **CNN** Presents America: Yesterday and Today Segment: Glimpses of the Depression
- Holt Researcher: American History CD–ROM
- Homework Practice Online

REINFORCEMENT, REVIEW, AND ASSESSMENT
- Section 3 Review, p. 463
- Daily Quiz 15.3
- Main Idea Activity 15.3
- English Audio Summary 15.3
- Spanish Audio Summary 15.3

SECTION 3

READ TO DISCOVER
1. Why did President Hoover oppose government-sponsored direct relief for individuals during the Great Depression?
2. How did the Hoover administration attempt to solve the depression's economic problems, and how successful were these efforts?
3. How did radicals and veterans respond to Hoover's policies?
4. Why was Franklin D. Roosevelt such a popular candidate in the 1932 election?

DEFINE
rugged individualism

IDENTIFY
Andrew Mellon
Reconstruction Finance Corporation
Bonus Army
Franklin D. Roosevelt
Eleanor Roosevelt

WHY IT MATTERS TODAY

Support for voluntarism as a way of solving social or economic problems is also found in American society today. Use **CNNfyi.com** or other **current events** sources to find out about the types of volunteer activities currently being pursued. Record your findings in your journal.

CNNfyi.com

Hoover's Policies

SECTION 3

 EYEWITNESSES TO History

"What the country needs is a good big laugh. There seems to be a condition of hysteria. If someone could get off a good joke every ten days I think our troubles would be over."

—Herbert Hoover, quoted in *The Century*, by Peter Jennings and Todd Brewster

Many Americans blamed Hoover for the depression.

Businesses were failing at record levels, and unemployment soared. Yet President Herbert Hoover believed that if only Americans were more optimistic, the troubles of the Great Depression would soon pass. At the beginning of the depression, many Americans had great faith in Herbert Hoover. His skills as a businessman and as an administrator inspired confidence. Under his direction the government did undertake some important measures to fight the depression, but they were not enough to end the crisis.

Hoover's Philosophy

As the U.S. economy failed, many Americans looked to President Hoover for leadership. Despite the nation's problems, Hoover remained optimistic. He characterized the depression as "a temporary halt in the prosperity of a great people."

As the depression worsened, Hoover's most urgent task was to ease human suffering. Prior to the crash, most Americans believed that the government should not interfere in the free-enterprise system. Even after the crash, the *New York Times* advised that "the fundamental prescriptions for recovery [are] such homely [simple] things as savings . . . and hopeful waiting for the turn." Hoover agreed that the way to economic recovery was through individual effort and not from government assistance.

Opposing direct relief. As the depression wore on and the crisis worsened, many Americans began to demand that the federal government provide direct relief to the needy. This would include food, clothing, shelter, and money. Writing the president for assistance, one poverty-stricken American complained, "Why are we reduced to poverty and starving and anxiety and Sorrow So quickly under your administration as Chief Executor. Can you not find a quicker way of Executing us than to starve us to death." Despite these pleas, Hoover rejected the idea of direct government aid.

History Makers Speak

"I do not believe that the power and duty of the [federal] Government ought to be extended to the relief of individual suffering. . . . The lesson should be constantly enforced that though the people support the Government the Government should not support the people."

—Herbert Hoover

TEACH OBJECTIVE 1

LEVEL 1: Ask each student to write a few sentences explaining President Hoover's philosophy regarding government-sponsored relief for needy individuals during the Great Depression. *(President Hoover believed that individuals and businesses were responsible for themselves. He thought that government relief would create a bureaucracy.)* Have volunteers share their sentences. Then ask students if they agree or disagree with Hoover's philosophy. Conduct a debate between students with different opinions.
English Language Learners

LEVEL 2: Tell students to imagine that they are aides to President Hoover. Have each student write a short speech for the president to deliver that explains his opposition to government-sponsored relief programs. *(See the Level 1 lesson for the correct points.)* Ask volunteers to deliver their speeches to the class. To conclude, ask students if they agree or disagree with Hoover's philosophy. Conduct a debate between students with different opinions.

Hoover argued that direct federal relief would create a large bureaucracy. He feared that it would inflate the federal budget and reduce the self-respect of people receiving the aid. Instead, Hoover urged Americans to lift themselves up through hard work and strength of character.

With unemployment rising, some congressmembers responded to demands from constituents for direct relief and assistance. Senators Robert La Follette Jr. and Edward Costigan proposed a bill in 1931 to create a Federal Emergency Relief Board. The board would be authorized to give states $375 million for direct aid to the unemployed. Hoover refused to support the bill. Without the president's support, the proposal fell 14 votes shy of passing in February 1932.

Hoover's firm belief in individualism and the value of character-building experiences kept him from establishing a federal system that would directly aid Americans in need. Referring to Hoover's training as an engineer early in life, Rexford Tugwell remarked, "We all thought he [Hoover] was an engineer, but, in fact, he was a moral philosopher."

Hoover's idea of **rugged individualism** was that success comes through individual effort and private enterprise. He also believed that private charities and local communities, not the federal government, could best provide for those in need. "A voluntary deed," claimed Hoover, "is infinitely more precious to our national ideas and spirit than a thousandfold poured from the Treasury."

Encouraging voluntarism. Hoover was not alone in his beliefs. Many Americans agreed that voluntary efforts were preferable to government aid. It soon became clear, however, that voluntary efforts alone would not be enough. Communities and private charities lacked the resources to cope with the ever-rising tide of human misery. Local governments were forced to stretch already inadequate funds to cover growing numbers of needy families. For example, in February 1933 families on public welfare in New York City received $39 a month. By August 1933 they received just $23.

In 1930 Hoover created the President's Committee for Unemployment Relief (PCUR). It was designed to assist state and local relief efforts. He appointed experienced philanthropists and businesspersons to encourage donations to private relief organizations. The most prominent were the Community Chest, the Red Cross, the Salvation Army, and the YMCA. The PCUR collected information about local relief agencies and distributed it to Americans interested in aiding the unemployed.

The committee did little beyond urging Americans to contribute more to charity, however. Provided with little funding, the committee spent just $157,000 on its work during the years of the Hoover administration. The misery of the depression

THE SALVATION ARMY

The Salvation Army was founded in London during the mid-1800s. It was an evangelical organization dedicated to spreading the Protestant Christian faith to nonbelievers. The founders recognized that before a nonbeliever could be convinced of God's love, his or her practical needs for food, shelter, and clothing must be met. Throughout the late 1800s and early 1900s the organization extended its missionary efforts to the United States and throughout the world.

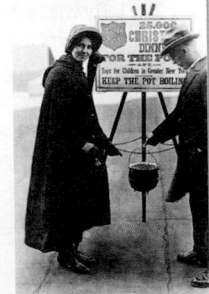
Salvation Army donation site

During the Great Depression divisions of the Salvation Army in the United States worked to provide for the basic needs of the poor. Since President Hoover opposed direct federal aid to the needy, religious institutions became important sources of aid for the unemployed. The Salvation Army was one of the foremost aid providers during the early years of the depression. It organized soup kitchens, shelters for the homeless, and rehabilitation programs for the unemployed.

As resources grew slim for many Americans during the depression, donations to the Salvation Army slowed. The organization faced the challenge of meeting the needs of a greater number of people with dwindling revenue. Some state and local government agencies gave funds directly to aid organizations such as the Salvation Army. These government-provided funds helped organizations offer needed relief to Americans during the Great Depression. ■

HISTORY MAKERS SPEAK

Herbert Hoover in *For the Record: A Documentary History of America*, Vol. 2

Hoover on Government Action. Herbert Hoover explained his reasons for opposing large-scale government intervention in American life in a 1928 campaign speech: "During the war [World War I] we necessarily turned to the government to solve every difficult economic problem. . . . However justified in time of war if continued in peace time it would destroy not only our American system but with it our progress and freedom as well. . . . We were challenged with a peace-time choice between the American system of rugged individualism and a European philosophy of . . . paternalism and state socialism. The acceptance of these ideas would have meant . . . the undermining of the individual initiative and enterprise through which our people have grown to unparalleled greatness."

ACTIVITY: Tell students to imagine that they heard Hoover deliver the campaign speech excerpted above. Have each student write a letter to the editor expressing his or her opinion of the speech and Hoover's ideas.

LEVEL 3: Tell students to imagine that they are shop clerks who have recently lost their jobs. Tell students that they are struggling to feed three children. Have each student write a letter to the editor criticizing President Hoover's opposition to government-sponsored relief for needy individuals. Students might want to describe their personal situations in their letters. Have volunteers read their letters to the class. Then ask students how Hoover himself might have responded to the arguments contained in the letters. (*See the Level 1 lesson for the correct points.*) Students may wish to include their letters in their portfolios.

HOMEWORK *Tell students that the current debate over federal assistance to needy individuals is a heated one. Have each student find an article on the issue from a reputable newspaper or newsmagazine. Ask each student to write a brief summary of the article. Have volunteers share their summaries with the class, then conduct a discussion on the issues.*

NOTE: For an additional teaching idea, see the Chapter 15 role playing lesson in the **Creative Teaching Strategies** handbook.

NOTE: To help students make meaningful connections between events in U.S. history and those in their own hometown, use the Chapter 15 **Hands-On History Activity**, The Economic State of Your State.

INTERPRETING THE VISUAL RECORD

Hoover. President Hoover (far left) met regularly with business leaders such as Henry Ford, Thomas Edison, and Harvey Firestone (left to right). *How does this photograph reflect the close relationship between big business and the White House?*

continued practically unchecked. Despite the worsening conditions, Hoover firmly held to his policies opposing direct relief for workers. His press secretary claimed that "the number of times he [Hoover] reversed himself or modified an important position could be counted on the fingers of one hand."

✔ **READING CHECK: Summarizing** What was President Hoover's philosophy on direct relief? Hoover believed in rugged individualism. He felt the people should support the government, not the other way around.

Boosting the Economy

Critics later charged that President Hoover's relief plans failed because of his refusal to get the government involved. However, Hoover was not totally opposed to government intervention in the economy. Despite its opposition to direct public relief, the Hoover administration played a more active role in attempting to shape the economy than any previous administration.

Stimulating the economy. As the nation sank into depression, Hoover's cabinet members proposed a laissez-faire approach to the economy. Secretary of the Treasury **Andrew Mellon** argued that the government should keep its hands off the economy. He wanted American businesses to deal with the crisis on their own. Aware that this hands-off policy would result in even greater unemployment and suffering, Hoover rejected Mellon's advice. The president believed that something should be done to stimulate the economy.

Within weeks of the stock market crash, Hoover called a White House conference of top business, labor, and political leaders to discuss solutions to the economic crisis. The *New York Times* hailed the meeting as a step in the right direction.

Primary Source

❝[It is] the largest gathering of noted heads of industrial and other corporations in Washington since the resources of the nation were marshalled for participation in the World War!❞

—*New York Times*, November 19, 1929

Hoover urged these leaders to voluntarily maintain predepression levels of production, employment, and wages. Hoover saw this as the first step toward reviving business activity and promoting recovery. The National Business Survey Conference and the U.S. Chamber of Commerce supported the president's plan.

Hoover issued cheerful public statements designed to boost confidence. On March 7, 1930, he declared, "The worst effects of the crash upon unemployment will have passed during the next sixty days." Many citizens grew increasingly doubtful about the administration. "Every time an administration official gives out an optimistic statement about business conditions, the market immediately drops," moaned the head of the Republican National Committee.

At Hoover's request, Congress and state governments funded several public-works programs. By providing contracts for construction and materials, Hoover hoped that these projects would stimulate business and reduce unemployment. One of the largest public-works programs was the construction of the giant Boulder

ALL LEVELS: Tell students to imagine that they are advisers to President Hoover. Have each student brainstorm and develop two or three measures to foster economic recovery. (*Answers will vary. Some students might suggest direct cash payments to the needy or massive government work programs.*) To help students understand how the Hoover administration attempted to solve the depression—and the success of those efforts—copy the chart at right on the chalkboard, omitting the italicized answers. Have each student complete it. After students have completed their charts, ask them to consider their own plans in light of Hoover's efforts.

English Language Learners

THE HOOVER ADMINISTRATION AND THE GREAT DEPRESSION

Effort	Description	Effectiveness
public-works programs	*poured money into public construction projects such as the Boulder Dam*	*failed to affect the entrenched depression*
agricultural efforts	*created the Federal Farm Board; made loans, established cooperatives, and bought surplus goods*	*helped some farmers take advantage of cooperatives and avoid foreclosure, but failed to end the farm crisis*
Reconstruction Finance Corporation (RFC)	*loaned taxpayer money to stabilize industries*	*helped some companies avoid bankruptcy; used money for businesses, not people*

Dam—later renamed Hoover Dam—on the Colorado River. The federal government also built more than 800 public buildings and assisted states in building approximately 37,000 miles of highway. Overall, Hoover approved some $800 million in funding for public-works projects. Yet this had little impact on the depression.

Coping with the farm crisis. Hoover also sought to ease the plight of farmers. In 1929 Congress passed the Agricultural Marketing Act, which established the Federal Farm Board (FFB), and granted it a budget of $500 million. In line with Hoover's notion of rugged individualism, the Federal Farm Board was instructed to find ways to help farmers help themselves. The FFB offered loans and also financed the creation of farmers' cooperatives. These organizations reduced farmers' expenses by allowing them to purchase necessary materials—such as equipment, fertilizer, and pesticides—in bulk. The cooperatives were also able to gain higher prices for the farmers' crops by providing crop storage facilities. Crops were stored until they could be sold during the periods between harvests when market prices were at their highest.

Crop prices continued to fall, however. Hoover instructed the Federal Farm Board to buy up surplus corn, cotton, wheat, and other farm products. Officials believed that a reduction in the volume of crops reaching the market would cause prices to rise. The government could store these goods and then sell them when prices were higher. The plan did not work. Farmers refused to limit production and reacted to low prices by planting even more crops. In 1931 the Farm Board stopped buying surplus crops, having already spent some $180 million.

Just as he opposed direct relief for jobless factory workers, Hoover resisted giving direct aid to desperate farmers. He did try to aid farmers indirectly, though. He recommended the passage of the Home Loan Bank Act in 1932. The act established the Home Loan Bank Board and provided money to savings banks,

INTERPRETING THE VISUAL RECORD

Public-works projects. Hoover began large public-works projects such as the construction of Boulder Dam. *What benefits of such projects does this mural portray?*

PRESIDENTIAL *Lives*

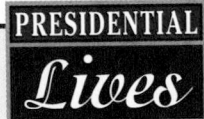

Herbert Hoover

1874–1964
In Office 1929–1933

As a young man Herbert Hoover was shy and awkward but very hardworking. Born into a Quaker family in Iowa, he became an orphan at age nine. Hoover had few friends in college and wandered around with his eyes glued to the ground as if to avoid people. One friend noted that he had an awkward habit of standing "with one foot thrust forward, jingling the keys in his trouser pocket," chuckling sometimes, but rarely laughing out loud. Even as president he remained self-conscious and shy.

After college, Hoover rapidly built a career as a successful mining engineer and business consultant. By the age of 40 he was a millionaire. His role as coordinator of food relief during World War I also won him a reputation as a kind and humanitarian leader. After his presidency he continued to work in public service and wrote many books and articles. "There is little importance to men's lives," he wrote, "except the accomplishments they leave to posterity."

SCIENCE, TECHNOLOGY, AND SOCIETY

Boulder Dam. The Boulder Dam project served several important purposes. In 1906 the Colorado River had flooded, causing extensive damage. Boulder Dam was designed to regulate the flow of the river and to prevent further floods. The dam also ensured that water would be available to Los Angeles, a rapidly growing city that previously would have been unable to meet its water needs after 1940. Finally, the dam created enough hydroelectric power to supply electricity to the entire Southwest.

CRITICAL THINKING How might Boulder Dam have benefited the long-term economic development of the Southwest?

ANSWER: Students might suggest that the dam controlled the Colorado River, ensured the future growth of Los Angeles, and provided power to businesses and industries in the region.

VISUAL RECORD ANSWER

Students' answers might include providing work for the unemployed.

Riding the Rails

The Great Depression transformed everyday life for many teenagers. Thousands of schools were forced to cut their schedules or to close altogether, and many families were evicted from their homes. Many teenagers left their hometowns in search of work, traveling from city to city by hopping railroad freight cars. Some began traveling at the age of 14.

Teen riding the rails

During the early 1930s sociologist Thomas Minehan studied the teenagers who rode the rails. He noted that most traveled in groups for security. "The boys and girls have friends to comfort and care for them," he reported.

Life for these teenagers was hard. One teenager whom Minehan met had lost an eye when a piece of burning coal blew into his face as he rode in an open freight car. In his diary, this teenager described a typical day.

❝Slept in paper box. Bummed swell breakfast three eggs and four pieces meat. Hit guy in big car in front of garage. Cop told me to scram. Rode freight to Roessville. Small burg, but got dinner. Walked [to] Bronson. . . . Rode to Sidell. . . . Hit homes for meals and turned down. Had to buy supper 20 cents. Raining.❞

building and loan associations, and insurance companies for low-interest mortgages.

Hoover believed that the act would reduce foreclosures on homes and farms. This would thus allow more farmers to keep their land. He also believed that the act would encourage home construction. This construction would boost employment and increase the flow of money through the entire economy.

The Reconstruction Finance Corporation. Hoover also tried to stimulate the economy with the **Reconstruction Finance Corporation** (RFC), created by Congress in February 1932. The RFC was authorized to lend up to $2 billion of taxpayer money to stabilize troubled banks, insurance companies, railroad companies, and other institutions. By strengthening key businesses, Hoover hoped to reduce business failures and create more jobs. By the end of Hoover's term, RFC loans had helped many large corporations avoid collapse. Yet the economy continued to decline, in part because the RFC was not created until the depression was already in full swing. The RFC also provided no direct aid to industries or to small businesses, which continued to fail at an alarming rate.

Critics attacked the RFC's trickle-down approach to economic recovery. "We have the dole [welfare] in America," explained economist Sumner H. Slichter. "But the real recipients . . . are not the men who stand for hours before the Salvation Army soup stations. . . . [They] are the great industries of America." Critics argued that money lent to big business would not filter down quickly enough to help ordinary citizens—the real victims of the depression. A more effective approach, said critics, would be to funnel money directly to those in need. This would increase consumers' buying power and consequently stimulate business. Newspaper columnist Walter Lippmann expressed the sentiments of most Americans.

History Makers Speak
❝It is hard for the country to realize that this era of easy finance is over. . . . In respect to government finance, as in respect to so many other things, Congress and the people of the country have radically to readjust their minds.❞

—Walter Lippmann, "Social Problems of the Depression," *Interpretations*, 1931–1932

Government activism. Hoover's policies failed to end the Great Depression. However, the RFC and other measures—such as the Home Loan Bank Act and funding for public works—represented a major shift in government policy. The president and Congress accepted the idea that the federal government can and should do something to boost the economy in times of crisis. The government became more active than ever before.

In the early 1930s Secretary of the Treasury Andrew Mellon advised the government to maintain its traditional laissez-faire approach to the economy. He even

TEACH OBJECTIVE 3

 LEVEL 1: Pair students and have each pair write topic sentences explaining how both radicals and veterans responded to President Hoover's ineffective policies. *(Radicals staged protests and became involved in at least one legal case; veterans gathered in Washington, D.C., to demand payment of their pension bonuses.)* Then ask pairs to consider these responses, considering the drastic conditions of the Great Depression. Do those responses seem overblown? desperate? possibly treasonous? Conduct a discussion on students' responses and the issue of historical hindsight.
English Language Learners, Cooperative Learning

LEVELS 2 AND 3: Organize students into two large groups, one representing radicals and one representing veterans. Have each student write a short memoir of the Great Depression from his or her assigned perspective. Students' memoirs, written in their notes, should both describe their reactions to Hoover's ineffective policies and explain those reactions in light of the conditions during the depression. *(See the Level 1 lesson for the correct reactions.)* Have volunteers read their memoirs to the class. Students may wish to include their memoirs in their portfolios. **Cooperative Learning**

argued that a short depression would be good for the country because "it will purge the rottenness out of the system." As the depression grew more severe, however, the government took dramatic steps to promote economic recovery. Unfortunately, these measures were not sufficient to halt the downward trend. Americans increasingly blamed their suffering on Herbert Hoover.

✔ **READING CHECK: Evaluating** How did the federal government change in response to the Great Depression? The government tried to stimulate the economy by establishing the Federal Farm Board and the Reconstruction Finance Corporation to provide loans to farmers and businesses, respectively.

Rumblings of Discontent

By 1932 President Hoover was perhaps the most hated man in America. His appearance in movie newsreels provoked boos and catcalls from audiences. Yet the president made no attempt to win public support by changing his manner. "This is not a showman's job," Hoover remarked. "I will not step out of character."

Radical protests. As public confidence in Hoover eroded, radical political parties grew more vocal. Both the Communist Party and the Socialist Party condemned capitalism, which they believed was to blame for the depression. The two parties helped organize several mass protests in the early 1930s. Socialist leader A. J. Muste gathered the jobless into Unemployed Leagues to demand work. The Communist Party encouraged labor-union activism and led strikes by migrant farmworkers.

The Communist Party also helped expose racial injustice. In 1931 an all-white jury in Scottsboro, Alabama, sentenced to death nine African American youths aged 13 to 21 on a highly questionable rape charge. The Communist Party helped supply legal defense for the defendants and organized mass demonstrations against the verdict. By 1950 all nine had been released from jail.

Many desperate Americans responded to Communist and Socialist calls for direct action. Thousands of unemployed men demanding work participated in a hunger march early in 1932 at the Ford auto plant near Detroit. Four were killed when police opened fire. In Seattle some 5,000 unemployed protesters seized a government building. After two days, local officials finally forced them out.

Some activism was spontaneous, reflecting the desperation of the times. In rural areas people armed with clubs, pitchforks, and shotguns confronted officials trying to foreclose on homes. Hoping that limiting food supplies would push prices up, farmers destroyed crops and blocked roads to prevent food from being shipped to market. "They say blockading the highway's illegal," an Iowa farmer said. "Seems to me there was a Tea Party in Boston that was illegal too."

The Bonus Army. The biggest protest was staged in May 1932 by more than 10,000 World War I veterans and their families. They came to Washington, D.C., to support a veterans' bonus bill then before Congress. The bill would have granted the veterans—many of whom were unemployed—early payment of the pension bonuses owed them for their service during the war. This group was soon labeled the **Bonus Army.**

Lawyer Samuel Leibowitz (left) meets with Heywood Patterson, one of the defendants in the Scottsboro case, to prepare for the trial.

INTERPRETING THE VISUAL RECORD

Bonus Army. In May 1932 more than 10,000 veterans marched in Washington, D.C., to petition Congress for payment of pension bonuses earned during World War I. *What do you think the organizers of the march did to generate support for their cause?*

TEACH OBJECTIVE 4

LEVEL 1: Conduct a brief discussion on why Franklin D. Roosevelt was such a popular candidate in the 1932 election. *(Roosevelt's optimism contrasted with Hoover's gloom. In addition, Roosevelt had designed imaginative relief programs as governor of New York.)* Then tell students to imagine that they are volunteers on Franklin D. Roosevelt's presidential campaign. Have each student create a poster, flyer, or button promoting Roosevelt's bid for the presidency. Encourage students to include a slogan or statement explaining Roosevelt's superiority over Hoover. Ask volunteers to present their items to the class. **English Language Learners**

LEVELS 2 AND 3: Organize students into two large groups—one representing President Hoover and one representing Franklin D. Roosevelt. Then pair students within the larger groups. Have each pair write a resumé for its assigned presidential candidate. You may want to supply students with real resumés or resumé-writing programs to use as models or templates. Have members of a Hoover pair and members of a Roosevelt pair present their resumés to the class. Then ask students to select a candidate to "hire" for the job of president. Call on volunteers to explain their choices. Regardless of students' choices, tell them that Roosevelt won the election and conduct a brief discussion on his appeal. *(See the Level 1 lesson for the correct points.)* **Cooperative Learning**

SECTION 3 REVIEW ANSWERS

1. Define
- rugged individualism, p. 457

2. Identify
- Andrew Mellon, p. 458
- Reconstruction Finance Corporation, p. 460
- Bonus Army, p. 461
- Franklin D. Roosevelt, p. 462
- Eleanor Roosevelt, p. 462

3. relief board—deviated from Hoover's belief in individualism; president's committee—coordinated voluntary relief efforts; met with business—encouraged voluntary economic planning; public-works programs—created jobs; Federal Farm Board—assisted farmers with individual initiatives; RFC—created jobs by helping businesses

4a. The federal government became more involved in the lives of its citizens in an effort to boost the economy.

b. radical workers—faulted capitalism itself; veterans—demanded war bonuses

c. Roosevelt's optimism contrasted with Hoover's gloom and Roosevelt pushed for a fairer distribution of wealth.

5. Entries will vary but should show that Hoover's philosophies reflected the belief in a limited role for the federal government as in the past; the depression created a desire for an expanded federal government, which Hoover tried to provide.

462

Violence erupts as military and law-enforcement officers attempt to remove the Bonus marchers from their camps.

INTERPRETING THE VISUAL RECORD

Roosevelt. As the Democratic presidential candidate in 1932, Franklin D. Roosevelt developed a platform based on relief programs he had initiated as governor of New York. *Based on this photograph, what other campaign strategies do you think Roosevelt used to gain public support?*

Officials initially allowed the Bonus Army demonstrators to live in empty government buildings and to camp in an open area across the Potomac River. When Congress rejected the bonus bill, most of the demonstrators returned home. Some 2,000 veterans remained, however, defying orders to leave. In a clash with authorities, two veterans and two police officers were killed. The police requested aid, and President Hoover ordered the army to disperse the squatters.

In late July the U.S. Army moved in with machine guns, tanks, and tear gas. One woman recalled her husband's experience that day.

History Makers Speak

66My husband went to Washington. To march with . . . the bonus boys. He was a machine gunner in the war. He'd say them . . . Germans gassed him in Germany. And [then] his own government . . . gassed him and run him off the country up there with a water hose, half drowned him.99

—Wife of Bonus Army member, quoted in *Hard Times*, by Studs Terkel

Commanded by General Douglas MacArthur, the troops drove the veterans from the buildings, broke up their encampment, and burned their shacks. Hundreds were injured and three died, including an 11-week-old baby. Many Americans found the government's treatment of the veterans shocking. Across the nation, anger against Hoover grew. As the 1932 presidential election approached, Americans joked bitterly, "In Hoover we trusted and now we are busted."

✔ **READING CHECK: Identifying Points of View** Why did radicals and veterans organize protests? Some radicals condemned capitalism, which they believed was responsible for the depression; veterans protested not receiving their bonus.

The Election of 1932

In the summer of 1932 the Republicans reluctantly renominated Herbert Hoover as their presidential candidate. With public sentiment running strongly against the Republicans, no other member of the party was eager for the nomination. The Democrats, sensing victory, chose New York governor **Franklin D. Roosevelt** as their candidate.

The Democratic challenger. Roosevelt—who was often called by his initials, FDR—was a determined and skillful politician. He was born into a wealthy and famous family. Roosevelt's background suggested that he would be more likely to identify with the wealthy than with working-class citizens. He could easily have become a Wall Street stockbroker but chose a career in public service instead.

Roosevelt was greatly influenced by the progressivism of his distant cousin, former president Theodore Roosevelt. His wife, **Eleanor Roosevelt**—who was Theodore Roosevelt's niece—also proved influential. With her earnest belief in social reform, Mrs. Roosevelt would become one of FDR's most important political assets.

Roosevelt ran as a vice presidential candidate in 1920. His political career, however, appeared to be over after polio left him paralyzed from the waist down in 1921. With the help of his wife, Roosevelt overcame his physical challenges and was elected governor of New York in 1928. As governor he earned high marks for his imaginative

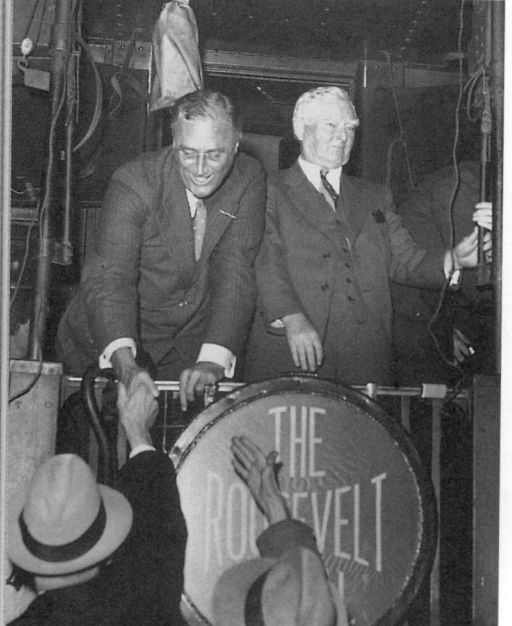

REVIEW

Have students complete the **Section 3 Review** on p. 463.

ASSESS

Have students complete **Daily Quiz 15.3**. As **Alternative Assessment**, you may want to use the President Hoover speech or the election paraphernalia in this section's lessons.

RETEACH

Have students complete **Main Idea Activity for English Language Learners and Special-Needs Students 15.3**. Then have each student write a summary sentence for each of the

subsections in Section 3. Have volunteers read their sentences to the class. **English Language Learners**

EXTEND

Tell students that Franklin D. Roosevelt's wife, Eleanor, was a powerful woman in her own right. Have students conduct research on Eleanor Roosevelt. Then have each student write a biography of Eleanor Roosevelt. Alternately, students might create a multimedia presentation on Eleanor Roosevelt. Encourage students to share some of their more interesting discoveries about this influential first lady. **Block Scheduling**

---

relief programs that had instituted unemployment benefits and supported failing industries. In 1932 Roosevelt accepted his party's nomination for president.

> **"Republican leaders not only have failed in material things, they have failed in national vision, because in disaster they have held out no hope. . . . I pledge you, I pledge myself, to a new deal for the American people."**
>
> —Franklin D. Roosevelt, "Democratic Nomination Acceptance Speech"

A change in leadership. The 1932 campaign revolved around the depression. Although Hoover tried to defend his policies, he realized he had little chance of victory. Roosevelt's campaign was short on specifics. Instead, he repeatedly attacked Hoover's record and promised that he would seek a fairer distribution of wealth. He promised to put the U.S. political and economic systems at "the service of the people." Most important, Roosevelt conveyed a genuine spirit of optimism and confidence that contrasted sharply with Hoover's seeming gloom.

On election day Roosevelt and his running mate, John Nance Garner of Texas, carried 42 states. Roosevelt captured 23 million popular votes and 472 electoral votes to Hoover's 16 million popular votes and 59 electoral votes. The Democrats won decisive majorities in both houses of Congress. As a result, Roosevelt knew that his programs would receive strong congressional support.

In the 1920s most Americans had credited the Republicans with the era's glowing prosperity. In 1932, voters made it clear that the Republicans must take the blame for the depression. Other Americans saw in Roosevelt the kind of dynamic personality they believed could lead the country out of its troubles. Roosevelt had promised a "new deal."

This Roosevelt campaign button was used during the 1932 presidential election.

✔ **READING CHECK: Making Predictions** What did Franklin D. Roosevelt mean by a "new deal"? Roosevelt meant that he would do things differently than Hoover had.

SECTION 3 REVIEW

1. Define and explain:
rugged individualism

2. Identify and explain:
Andrew Mellon
Reconstruction Finance Corporation
Bonus Army
Franklin D. Roosevelt
Eleanor Roosevelt

3. Categorizing Copy the chart below. Use it to explain how each action taken by President Hoover related to his philosophy of rugged individualism.

Hoover's actions	Relationship to rugged individualism
Opposed the creation of the Federal Emergency Relief Board	
Created the President's Committee for Unemployment Relief	
Met with business leaders	
Funded public-works programs	
Established the Federal Farm Board	
Created the Reconstruction Finance Corporation	

4. **Finding the Main Idea**
a. How did the Great Depression affect the role of the federal government?
b. Why did World War I veterans and unemployed workers resort to mass protest during the early years of the depression?
c. How did Herbert Hoover's and Franklin D. Roosevelt's personalities and philosophies differ?

5. **Writing and Critical Thinking**
Supporting a Point of View Imagine that you are Herbert Hoover. Write a journal entry explaining how your philosophy reflects the policies of previous presidents and how it reflects a new era of the presidency.
Consider:
• how rugged individualism related to the policies of previous presidencies
• how Hoover's programs corresponded to this philosophy, and how his programs also departed from Republican policies

Homework Practice Online
keyword: SE3 HP15

REVIEW CHAPTER 15 ANSWERS

Creating a Time Line
Each event should have an explanation and the correct date.

Writing a Summary
See the Reading Checks in each section for main ideas.

Identifying People and Ideas
1. practice of purchasing stocks with borrowed money

2. deep economic downturn that lasted from 1929 to the beginning of World War II

3. regular ups and downs of business in a free-enterprise economy

4. mutual-aid societies formed in Mexican American communities

5. Mexican American activist who fought racial discrimination

6. makeshift shelters built by the homeless

7. president who believed in rugged individualism

8. Hoover's belief that success comes through individual effort and private enterprise

9. veterans who demanded early payments of pension bonuses

10. Democrat elected president in 1932

TECHNOLOGY
▶ Chapter 15 Test Generator (on the One-Stop Planner)
▶ Global Skill Builder CD–ROM
▶ HRW Go site

REINFORCEMENT, REVIEW, AND ASSESSMENT
▶ Chapter 15 Review, pp. 464–65
▶ Chapter 15 Tutorial for Students, Parents, Mentors, and Peers

▶ Chapter 15 Test (Form A or B)
▶ Portfolio Activities and Alternative Assessment Handbook, Chapter 15
▶ Chapter 15 Test for English Language Learners and Special-Needs Students

REVIEW
Have students complete the **Chapter 15 Review** on pp. 464–65.

ASSESS
Use one of the chapter tests to assess students' understanding of the content. For **Alternative Assessment**, see the **Portfolio Activities and Alternative Assessment Handbook.**

Understanding Main Ideas

1. created a heavy surplus and encouraged consumers to use credit

2. The crash hurt individuals and banks; the banking crisis hurt individuals, banks, and businesses; the global depression hurt the United States.

3. urban: charitable organizations and mutual aid societies; rural: neighbors protected each other against foreclosure.

4. It provided an escape from daily pressures.

5. He believed that people had the responsibility to help themselves rather than rely on the government.

Reviewing Themes

1. The global economic crisis and the national income gap deprived American businesses of customers. Consumer debt lessened disposable income and increased financial instability.

2. rural residents—unable to sell their crops and faced homelessness; urban residents—experienced homelessness and hunger

3. Discrimination in the workplace meant that African Americans and Mexican Americans experienced lower wages and higher levels of unemployment.

Thinking Critically

1. He was overlooking the multiple factors of the depression, the farming crisis, and the income gap.

CHAPTER 15

Review

Creating a Time Line

Copy the time line below onto a sheet of paper. Complete the time line by filling in the events and dates from the chapter that you think were most significant. Pick three events and explain why you think they were significant.

| 1929 | 1931 | 1933 |

Writing a Summary

Using standard grammar, spelling, sentence structure, and punctuation, write an overview of events in the chapter.

Identifying People and Ideas

Identify the following terms or individuals and explain their significance.

1. margin buying
2. Great Depression
3. business cycle
4. *mutualistas*
5. Josefina Fierro de Bright

6. shantytowns
7. Herbert Hoover
8. rugged individualism
9. Bonus Army
10. Franklin D. Roosevelt

Understanding Main Ideas

SECTION 1 *(pp. 442–447)*
1. How did the business practices of the 1920s contribute to the stock market crash of 1929?
2. How did the crash, the banking crisis, and the global depression contribute to the Great Depression?

SECTION 2 *(pp. 448–455)*
3. How did urban and rural residents organize to survive?
4. How did popular culture provide an escape from the psychological burdens of the depression?

SECTION 3 *(pp. 456–463)*
5. Why did President Hoover oppose direct federal aid for the unemployed?

Reviewing Themes

1. **Economics** What were the multiple factors that contributed to the Great Depression?
2. **Geography** How did the hardships of the depression differ for rural and urban residents?
3. **Culture** How did racial prejudices magnify the effects of the depression for African Americans and Mexican Americans?

Thinking Critically

1. **Identifying Bias** When President Hoover announced in 1929 that America was "nearer to the final triumph over poverty than ever before," what facts was he overlooking?
2. **Drawing Conclusions** How did the depression affect men and women differently?
3. **Problem Solving** What type of program would you have developed to ease the burdens of urban residents and farmers during the depression?
4. **Identifying Points of View** How did Hoover's depression-era programs reflect his belief in rugged individualism and self-reliance?
5. **Contrasting** How was Franklin D. Roosevelt's mood and style during the 1932 presidential election a major change from Hoover?

Writing About History

Summarizing Write a dialogue between two unemployed factory workers in the 1930s discussing the factors that contributed to their joblessness. Use this organizer to help you.

1. Stock market crash or global depression
2. Bank failures or loss of foreign markets
3. Reduction of purchases on credit
4. Businesses left with surpluses
5. Businesses scale back production
6. Factory workers laid off

RETEACH

Organize students into three groups and assign each group one of the following topics: the causes of the Great Depression, American life during the Great Depression, or the politics of the Great Depression. Have each group develop a visual display covering its assigned topic. Post groups' displays around the classroom. Then assign each group to a topic that it did not work on and have each group study the appropriate display. Have groups write five to ten quiz questions on the material. Use groups' questions to quiz the class.

English Language Learners, Cooperative Learning

EXTEND

Ask students to find examples of depression art, particularly pieces that depict Americans' lives during the economic downturn. Have each student select one piece of art and write an analysis of it. Have volunteers present their pieces to the class and share the information in their analyses.

Block Scheduling

Building Social Studies Skills

Interpreting Maps

Study the map below. Then use it to help answer the questions that follow.

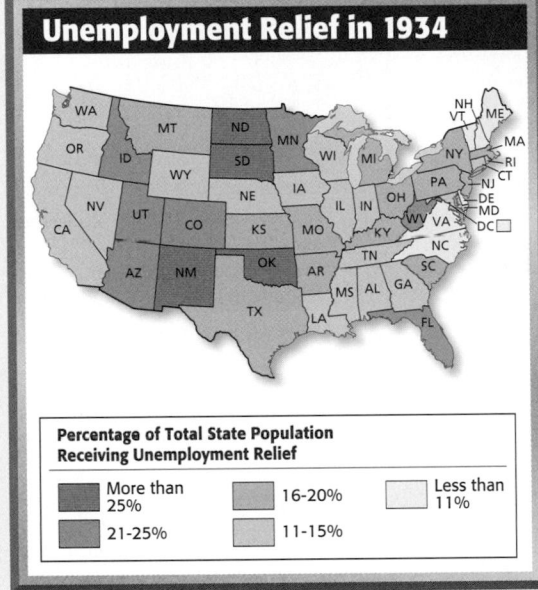

Unemployment Relief in 1934

Percentage of Total State Population Receiving Unemployment Relief

- More than 25%
- 21-25%
- 16-20%
- 11-15%
- Less than 11%

1. Based on this map, which of these states probably had the best economic situation?
   - **a.** Maine
   - **b.** Texas
   - **c.** North Dakota
   - **d.** Florida

2. What does this map suggest about the chances of unemployed migrant workers in New Mexico finding work by moving westward?

Analyzing Primary Sources

Read the following excerpt from *A Nation in Torment* by Edward Robb Ellis. Then answer the questions that follow.

> "Forty experienced secretaries found work after being unemployed a year, but the first few days on the job they were unable to take dictation from their bosses without weeping from sheer nervousness. After seeking employment for a long time, a man finally landed a job and became so overwrought with joy that he died of excitement. A corporation executive was given the nasty chore of firing several hundred men. A kind and compassionate person, he insisted on talking to each of them personally and asking what plans each had for the future. In a few months the executive's hair had turned gray."

3. What mood does the author convey in this passage?
   - **a.** confidence
   - **b.** uncertainty
   - **c.** sorrow
   - **d.** anger

4. What other quotations in the chapter convey each of the other moods listed above?

Alternative Assessment

Building Your Portfolio

U.S. HISTORY

Economics

Imagine that you are a journalist in the early 1930s during the Great Depression. Write an article on the worldwide economic crisis and create a cause-and-effect chart to accompany your article. Your chart should include the long-term causes of the global depression as well as the short-term causes of the crisis in the United States. The effects of the depression can be short-term or long-term. Write five questions based on your chart. Have other students answer them.

internet connect

Internet Activity: go.hrw.com
KEYWORD: SE3 AN15

Choose a topic on the Great Depression to:

- research conditions during the depression and then write a journal entry to illustrate the point of view of people affected by it.
- explore the construction of Boulder Dam and its impact on the environment.
- create a model that illustrates the causes of the Great Depression.

---

2. Men—moped around the house or walked the streets depressed; women—were forced to earn money and keep their families together.

3. Answers will vary. Students might suggest school lunch programs, mortgage payment programs, and rural food purchase programs to feed urban residents.

4. Hoover supported voluntary relief efforts and business aid while he opposed direct relief.

5. Roosevelt's optimism and vitality inspired hope, while Hoover's gloom inspired fear and loathing.

Writing

Dialogues will vary. Students should note that the stock market crash meant that investors could not repay their debts, which led to decreased purchases and bank failures. Decreased purchases and high business surpluses led to overall business instability.

Building Social Studies Skills

1. a

2. They have a better chance of finding work in far western states but not in Arizona.

3. b

4. Answers will vary. Students might suggest that Hoover's speech in the beginning of Section 1 suggests confidence; the quote from Gracie Turner in Section 2 suggests sorrow; the quote from the wife of a Bonus Army member in Section 3 suggests anger.

The New Deal

CHAPTER RESOURCE MANAGER

Objectives	Pacing Guide	Reproducible Resources
SECTION 1 **Restoring Hope** pp. 468–74	★ Describe how the New Deal provided relief for the unemployed. ★ Explain how the New Deal promoted industrial and agricultural recovery. ★ Discuss the New Deal goals for the Tennessee Valley region. ★ Recount how the Roosevelt administration addressed the concerns of African Americans and American Indians.	**Regular** 2 days **Block Scheduling** 1 day *Block Scheduling Handbook with Team Teaching Strategies, pp. 91–96*	**RS** Guided Reading Strategy 16.1 **PS** Biography Reading 16: Frances Perkins **SM** Geography Activity 16: The Public Works Administration **E** Creative Teaching Strategy: Ranking Lesson
SECTION 2 **New Challenges** pp. 475–81	★ Discuss the criticisms aimed at the New Deal. ★ Recount how the Second New Deal enabled President Roosevelt to win re-election easily in 1936. ★ Describe how Roosevelt tried to prevent the Supreme Court from overturning his programs. ★ Analyze how the Second New Deal benefited labor and agriculture. ★ Explain the Roosevelt recession, and describe the effect it had.	**Regular** 2 days **Block Scheduling** 1 day *Block Scheduling Handbook with Team Teaching Strategies, pp. 91–96*	**RS** Guided Reading Strategy 16.2 **PS** Primary Source Reading 16: "Every Man a King" **PS** American History Political Cartoon 24: FDR and the New Deal
SECTION 3 **Life in the New Deal Era** pp. 482–86	★ Discuss the effects of the Dust Bowl. ★ Explain how New Deal agencies used photography to promote their goals. ★ Describe how the New Deal improved the lives of ordinary Americans.	**Regular** 2 days **Block Scheduling** 1 day *Block Scheduling Handbook with Team Teaching Strategies, pp. 91–96*	**RS** Guided Reading Strategy 16.3 **SM** American History Outline Map 18: The Dust Bowl **E** Hands-On History Activity: A Project for Your Town
SECTION 4 **The New Deal and the Arts** pp. 487–91	★ Explain how Federal Project Number One aided writers and artists. ★ Identify the common themes that emerged in the novels, films, and plays of the New Deal Era. ★ Describe how music evolved in the 1930s. ★ Discuss the subject matter that influenced American painters in the 1930s.	**Regular** 1 day **Block Scheduling** .5 day *Block Scheduling Handbook with Team Teaching Strategies, pp. 91–96*	**RS** Guided Reading Strategy 16.4 **RS** Graphic Organizer Activity 16: Social Change in the 1930s **IC** Literature Reading 16: Thoughts of a Young African American

Chapter Resource Key

PS	Primary Sources	**REV** Review	Video
RS	Reading Support	**ELL** Reinforcement and English Language Learners	Internet
IC	Interdisciplinary Connections		Holt Presentation Maker Using Microsoft® PowerPoint®
E	Enrichment	Transparencies	
SM	Skills Mastery	CD-ROM	
A	Assessment	Music	

One-Stop Planner CD-ROM

See the *One-Stop Planner* for a complete list of additional resources for students and teachers.

One-Stop Planner CD–ROM

It's easy to plan lessons, select resources, and print out materials for your students when you use the *One-Stop Planner CD–ROM with Test Generator.*

Technology Resources	Reinforcement, Review, and Assessment
One-Stop Planner, Lesson 16.1 The American Nation Video Program Segment: Serving the Nation; Teacher's Guide, pp. 117–22 Holt Researcher: American History CD–ROM Homework Practice Online	**REV** Section 1 Review, p. 474 **A** Daily Quiz 16.1 **ELL** Main Idea Activity 16.1 **ELL** English Audio Summary 16.1 **ELL** Spanish Audio Summary 16.1
One-Stop Planner, Lesson 16.2 **CNN** Presents America: Yesterday and Today, 1850 to the Present Segment: Urban Youth Goes to Work Holt Researcher: American History CD–ROM Homework Practice Online	**REV** Section 2 Review, p. 481 **A** Daily Quiz 16.2 **ELL** Main Idea Activity 16.2 **ELL** English Audio Summary 16.2 **ELL** Spanish Audio Summary 16.2
One-Stop Planner, Lesson 16.3 American Music Selection 21: "Talkin' Dust Bowl" Holt Researcher: American History CD–ROM Homework Practice Online HRW Go site	**REV** Section 3 Review, p. 486 **A** Daily Quiz 16.3 **ELL** Main Idea Activity 16.3 **ELL** English Audio Summary 16.3 **ELL** Spanish Audio Summary 16.3
One-Stop Planner, Lesson 16.4 Holt Researcher: American History CD–ROM Homework Practice Online	**REV** Section 4 Review, p. 491 **A** Daily Quiz 16.4 **ELL** Main Idea Activity 16.4 **ELL** English Audio Summary 16.4 **ELL** Spanish Audio Summary 16.4

 internet connect

HRW ONLINE RESOURCES
GO TO: go.hrw.com
Then type in a keyword.

TEACHER HOME PAGE
KEYWORD: SE3 Teacher

CHAPTER INTERNET ACTIVITIES
KEYWORD: SE3 AN16
Choose an activity to:
- learn about WPA art projects.
- research the possible causes of the *Hindenburg* disaster.
- create a newspaper to dramatize the plight of families displaced by the Dust Bowl.

CHAPTER ENRICHMENT LINKS
KEYWORD: SE3 CH16

ONLINE ASSESSMENT
Homework Practice
KEYWORD: SE3 HP16

Standardized Test Prep
KEYWORD: SE3 STP16

Rubrics
KEYWORD: SS Rubrics

ONLINE MAPS, CHARTS, AND GRAPHS
KEYWORD: SE3 MCG
- Unemployment Relief
- Personal Income, 1929–1941
- Unemployment, 1929–1941

CONTENT UPDATES
KEYWORD: SS Content Updates

HOLT PRESENTATION MAKER
KEYWORD: SE3 PPT16

ONLINE READING SUPPORT
KEYWORD: SS Strategies

CURRENT EVENTS
KEYWORD: S3 Current Events

Meeting Individual Needs

Ability Levels
Level 1 Basic-level activities designed for all students encountering new material

Level 2 Intermediate-level activities designed for average students

Level 3 Challenging activities designed for honors and gifted-and-talented students

English Language Learners Activities that address the needs of students with Limited English Proficiency

Chapter Review and Assessment

 Global Skill Builder CD–ROM

 HRW Go site

REV Chapter 16 Tutorial for Students, Parents, Mentors, and Peers

REV Chapter 16 Review, pp. 492–93

 Chapter 16 Test Generator (on the One-Stop Planner)

A Chapter 16 Test (Form A or B)

A Alternative Assessment Handbook

A Chapter 16 Test for English Language Learners and Special-Needs Students

Build on What You Know

Ask students to answer the following questions.

What kinds of problems might occur during a nationwide economic crisis?

Consider:
- what happened during earlier recessions
- how businesses might react during an economic downturn

What might the federal government do to help the nation out of a crisis?

Consider:
- how the government responded during earlier recessions
- how the government might provide money or employment to those out of work

---

exploring the time line

AMERICAN EVENTS

ECONOMICS

1935 ■ The Social Security Act. Passed in 1935, the Social Security Act ensured an income for many Americans. President Franklin D. Roosevelt, however, had wanted the act to include all Americans. He said, "Everybody ought to be in on it—the farmer and his wife and family. . . . I don't see why not. Cradle to the grave—from the cradle to the grave they ought to be in a social insurance system."

CRITICAL THINKING Why might Congress have passed a Social Security Act that did not cover everyone?

ANSWER: Students might suggest that Congress thought that an act covering everyone would be too costly or would be seen as a government handout.

CHAPTER 16

1933–1939
The New Deal

A bank closure

United Automobile Workers union buttons

1935
The Arts
Federal Project Number One seeks to revive the arts in the United States.

1935
Science and Technology
The development of sulfa drugs marks a breakthrough in the treatment of bacterial diseases.

1933
Business and Finance
A federal bank holiday helps restore public trust in banks.

1934
Daily Life
The board game Monopoly premieres, using themes of the depression.

1936
Business and Finance
American industries begin to experience large-scale sit-down strikes.

| **1933** | **1934** | **1935** | **1936** |

1934
Daily Life
Drought hits the Great Plains, marking the beginning of the Dust Bowl.

A dust storm

1935
Politics
Congress passes the Social Security Act.

1936
Daily Life
Life magazine begins publication.

1936
World Events
British king Edward VIII abdicates the throne to marry American divorcée Wallis Simpson.

Social Security poster

Build on What You Know

The prosperous economic times of the 1920s came to a devastating end with the stock market crash in 1929 and the Great Depression that followed. President Hoover's administration dealt cautiously with the economic crisis. American voters elected Franklin D. Roosevelt as president in 1932 in the hope that the federal government would take a more active role in shaping the economy. In this chapter you will learn how Roosevelt's administration dealt with the economic crisis and changed the role of government in American life.

What's Your Opinion?

To help students create their Themes Journal entries, provide the following examples of appropriate agree/disagree statements.

Economics

Agree According to the Constitution, one purpose of government is to "promote the general welfare."

Disagree The Constitution does not guarantee the economic well-being of U.S. citizens.

Constitutional Heritage

Agree The Constitution does not explicitly give the federal government authority to regulate markets.

Disagree The government should abide by the spirit of the Constitution, which favors actions that benefit citizens.

Geography

Agree People migrated west because of the Dust Bowl, and they have migrated south because of harsh weather in the North.

Disagree During Reconstruction, a huge migration resulted from people wanting to take advantage of industrial jobs in the North.

The **Hindenburg** *explosion*

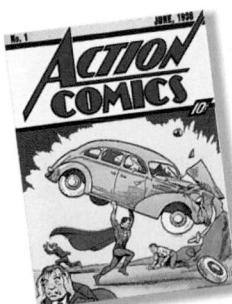

Action Comics'
first issue

Unemployed Americans

1937
World Events
The German airship *Hindenburg* explodes, killing 36 people.

1938
Daily Life
Superman makes his debut in *Action Comics*.

1939
Business and Finance
More than 17 percent of the American workforce is unemployed.

1939
The Arts
John Steinbeck's *The Grapes of Wrath* is published.

1937

1938

1939

1937
Politics
President Roosevelt tries to "pack" the Supreme Court.

1937
Business and Finance
A recession sets back recovery from the Great Depression.

Ballpoint pen ad

1938
Science and Technology
The Biro brothers invent the ballpoint pen.

Gone With the Wind

1939
The Arts
Gone With the Wind becomes the most popular film of the 1930s.

What's Your Opinion?

Do you agree or disagree with the following statements? Support your point of view in your journal.

Economics The federal government must take responsibility for the economic well-being of its citizens during a crisis.

Constitutional Heritage Government interference in a free-market economy may be unconstitutional.

Geography Migration within the United States is always the result of harsh environmental conditions.

LET'S GET STARTED!

Write the following passage from Franklin Roosevelt's inaugural address on the chalkboard: "*Let me assert my firm belief that the only thing we have to fear is fear itself. . . . The people of the United States have not failed.*" As students enter the classroom, ask them to respond to the passage in writing. Have volunteers share their responses with the class. Tell students that in Section 1 they will learn about New Deal measures intended to provide relief for the unemployed and promote economic recovery.

SECTION 1

READ TO DISCOVER
1. How did the New Deal provide relief for the unemployed?
2. How did the New Deal promote industrial and agricultural recovery?
3. What were the New Deal goals for the Tennessee Valley region?
4. How did the Roosevelt administration address the concerns of African Americans and American Indians?

DEFINE
bank holiday

IDENTIFY
New Deal
Federal Deposit Insurance Corporation
Frances Perkins
Harry L. Hopkins
Civilian Conservation Corps
Securities and Exchange Commission
John Maynard Keynes
National Industrial Recovery Act
Agricultural Adjustment Administration
Tennessee Valley Authority
Robert C. Weaver
Marian Anderson
John Collier

▶ WHY IT MATTERS TODAY
The U.S. government continues to give farmers economic aid. Use **CNNfyi.com** or other **current events** sources to find out about programs to help farmers today. Record your findings in your journal.

CNNfyi.com

Restoring Hope

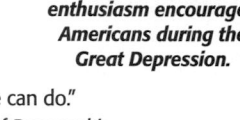

EYEWITNESSES TO History

"*The whole country is with him, just so he does something. If he burned down the Capitol, we would cheer and say, 'Well, we at least got a fire started anyhow.'*"

—Will Rogers, *The Autobiography of Will Rogers*

American humorist Will Rogers was not alone in his assessment of Franklin D. Roosevelt. The new president offered the American people much-needed hope. By 1933, Americans had endured three years of economic depression—each year more desperate than the last. On his last day in office, President Herbert Hoover was heard to sigh, "We are at the end of our string. There is nothing more we can do." Roosevelt did not share this despair. The optimistic words of Roosevelt's inaugural address rang out across the land, lifting Americans' spirits and stirring their hopes.

Franklin Roosevelt's (right) enthusiasm encouraged Americans during the Great Depression.

Roosevelt Confronts the Emergency

President Roosevelt did indeed get a fire started. In 1932, while campaigning for the presidency, Roosevelt had formed an advisory group known as the Brain Trust. With the help of this group, the energetic new president drew up his promised "new deal for the American people," a series of 15 relief and recovery measures. In his inaugural address, Roosevelt told the nation that a "temporary departure" from the "normal balance of executive and legislative authority" might be necessary. If fighting the depression required it, the president would ask Congress for "broad executive power to wage a war against the emergency." Immediately after taking office on March 5, 1933, Roosevelt called Congress into special session. During the next 100 days Congress approved all 15 measures that made up the heart of the president's **New Deal** program.

Roosevelt first focused on the banking system. On March 6 he issued a proclamation closing every bank in the nation for a few days. This so-called **bank holiday** was designed to stop massive withdrawals. On Thursday, March 9, Congress passed the Emergency Banking Act. This act authorized the federal government to examine all banks and allow those that were financially sound to reopen. Roosevelt hoped that the act would restore public confidence in the banking system.

Caught without cash during the bank holiday, Americans scrambled to find substitutes. Many used subway and bus tokens, postage stamps, and IOUs. On Sunday evening, March 12, some 60 million anxious Americans tuned in their radios to hear the president. He explained how the bank holiday would protect their money. In this first of many "fireside chats"—radio broadcasts from the White House—Roosevelt urged Americans to return their money to banks. "I can assure you that it is safer to keep your money in a reopened bank than under the mattress," he advised.

LEVEL 1: Tell students to imagine that it is 1933 and that they are artists who have been hired by the federal government to create informational posters about New Deal programs. Pair students and have each pair create posters describing New Deal unemployment relief programs. *(Posters might mention the FERA, which provided direct federal aid; the CWA, which created jobs such as raking leaves and picking up litter; and the CCC, which put young men to work in parks and forests.)* Display students' posters around the classroom.
English Language Learners, Cooperative Learning

LEVEL 2: Tell students to imagine that it is 1933 and that they work in the White House press office. Pair students and have each pair write a short press release informing the public about one of the federal programs that assists the unemployed. *(See the Level 1 lesson for the correct programs and their provisions.)* Ask volunteers to read their press releases to the class.
Cooperative Learning

LEVEL 3: Tell students to imagine that they are editing an encyclopedia of the New Deal. Have each student write entries about the New Deal programs that provided unemployment relief. *(See the Level 1 lesson for the correct programs and their provisions.)* Have volunteers read their entries to the class.

Banks began to reopen. By the end of the month about $1 billion in deposits had flowed into the system. Confidence in banks increased even more when Congress created the **Federal Deposit Insurance Corporation** (FDIC) in June 1933. This organization insured each bank deposit up to $5,000. It now insures some deposits up to $100,000.

In April 1933 Roosevelt urged Congress to create the Home Owners Loan Corporation (HOLC). Congress passed the measure to assist home owners who could not meet their mortgage payments. By June 1936 the HOLC had saved the homes of some 1 million American families by granting them low-interest, long-term mortgage loans. Roosevelt then issued an executive order to create the Farm Credit Administration (FCA) in 1933. The FCA provided low-interest, long-term loans to farmers. It allowed many farmers to pay off mortgages and back taxes, buy back lost farms, and purchase seed, fertilizer, and equipment.

Relief for the Needy

Other measures launched by the Roosevelt administration included large-scale programs of direct relief to aid the nation's 13 million unemployed workers. Helped by First Lady Eleanor Roosevelt and Democratic National Committee member Molly Dewson, the president brought in many veteran reformers to direct his programs, including **Frances Perkins** as secretary of labor.

In May 1933, Congress established the Federal Emergency Relief Administration (FERA). It was created to distribute $500 million in relief aid to state and local agencies. At least half of the FERA's relief money went to the states for direct distribution to families. For the other half, the federal government contributed $1 for every $3 state and local governments spent on relief. The FERA provided these governments direct grants—not loans as under Hoover's programs. The states and cities were then responsible for creating work-relief projects. **Harry L. Hopkins**, a former relief supervisor in New York, headed the FERA.

A Washington, D.C., newspaper reported the eagerness of the FERA director to get relief to the needy.

 Primary Source

"The half-billion dollars for direct relief of States won't last a month if Harry L. Hopkins, the new relief administrator, maintains the pace he set yesterday in disbursing [paying out] more than $5,000,000 during his first two hours in office."

—*Washington Post*

★ HISTORICAL DOCUMENTS ★

PRESIDENT FRANKLIN D. ROOSEVELT
First Inaugural Address

President Roosevelt set the tone for his administration with his first inaugural address. **What words or phrases does Roosevelt use to inspire confidence?**

First of all, let me assert my firm belief that the only thing we have to fear is fear itself—nameless, unreasoning, unjustified terror which paralyzes needed efforts to convert retreat into advance. In every dark hour of our national life a leadership of frankness and vigor has met with that understanding and support of the people themselves which is essential to victory. I am convinced that you will again give that support to leadership in these critical days. . . .

The people of the United States have not failed. In their need they have registered a mandate [command] that they want direct, vigorous action. They have asked for discipline and direction under leadership. They have made me the present instrument of their wishes. In the spirit of the gift I take it.

INTERPRETING POLITICAL CARTOONS

Government spending. Senator Harry Byrd of Virginia questions Harry L. Hopkins about the effectiveness of government spending. *What is Hopkins trying to fix by spending money?*

A DOUBTING DEMOCRAT

Frances Perkins. Before her appointment as Franklin Roosevelt's secretary of labor, Frances Perkins had been a social worker. She had worked with a variety of progressive reformers and groups, most of whom considered her a dynamic figure. However, some people misunderstood her desire to be taken seriously and called Perkins colorless. This assessment may have arisen from her habit of dressing in a plain black dress and small hat. Despite some of her conservative ideas, particularly her distrust of labor unions, Perkins was a symbol of the New Deal's liberal policies.

CRITICAL THINKING Why might Perkins have believed that dressing in black would invite confidence in her common sense?

ANSWER: Students might suggest that she believed that women who dressed fashionably were perceived as frivolous rather than serious.

POLITICAL CARTOON ANSWER
Students might suggest that Hopkins was trying to reduce unemployment.

HISTORICAL DOCUMENTS ANSWER
Answers will vary. Students might mention frankness, vigor, and "the only thing we have to fear is fear itself."

LEVEL 1: Tell students to imagine that it is 1933 and that they are newspaper reporters. Pair students and have each pair write a headline and topic sentences for articles on New Deal programs promoting industrial and agricultural recovery. *(Headlines and topic sentences should mention that the NIRA was passed in June 1933 to stimulate business activity and reduce unemployment. The NIRA created the PWA, which initiated public-works projects, and the NRA, which encouraged businesses to draw up codes to regulate hours, prices, production levels, and wages. The Agricultural Adjustment Act,* passed in May 1933, created the Agricultural Adjustment Administration, which paid farmers subsidies to reduce their output.) Ask volunteers to read their headlines and topic sentences to the class.

English Language Learners, Cooperative Learning

LEVEL 2: Have students write a brief essay about the New Deal programs that promoted agricultural and industrial recovery. Students' essays should describe how each program promoted recovery. *(See the Level 1 lesson for the correct programs and the major provisions of each program.)* Ask volunteers to read their essays to the class.

INTERDISCIPLINARY CONNECTIONS

▶ECONOMICS◀

The National Recovery Administration (NRA).

General Hugh S. Johnson, head of the NRA, tried to win support for his agency by associating compliance with the NRA codes with patriotism. When labor leaders, liberals, and progressives complained that the NRA catered to big business, Roosevelt created a review board to investigate complaints. Lawyer Clarence Darrow was appointed to head the inquiry. He soon agreed that the NRA was dominated by monopolies and was not solving any economic problems.

CRITICAL THINKING How might the NRA have boosted public morale?

ANSWER: Students might suggest that the belief that government was taking an active role to solve economic problems boosted morale.

The American Nation
VIDEO PROGRAM

Serving the Nation; Teacher's Guide, pp. 117–22

Search 21056, Play to 25391
Videodisc 2, Side A

| Play | Pause |

See *Teacher's Guide* for Spanish barcode.

INTERPRETING THE VISUAL RECORD

The CCC. Americans working for the CCC earned a living and helped improve the environment. *What do these workers appear to be doing?*

Research on the ROM

Free Find:
John Maynard Keynes

After reading about John Maynard Keynes on the **Holt Researcher CD–ROM**, imagine that you are Keynes. Write a letter to President Roosevelt explaining why you agree or disagree with his New Deal programs.

By 1935 some $3 billion in direct federal aid had been distributed. At one point nearly 8 million American families were receiving public assistance.

Most Americans disliked direct relief. They wanted jobs, not handouts. Hopkins created the Civil Works Administration (CWA) to address this problem. Most CWA jobs were federal, state, and local "make-work" projects such as raking leaves and picking up park litter. From 1933 to 1934, the CWA paid more than $740 million in wages to some 4 million men and women.

To provide relief for many unemployed young men between the ages of 18 and 25, Congress established the **Civilian Conservation Corps** (CCC) in 1933. Some 250,000 young men left their homes and went to army camps for CCC training. Once trained, they planted trees, cleared underbrush, created park trails, and developed campgrounds and beaches in the nation's parks and forests. They earned $30 a month. Most of their earnings were sent back home to help their families. During the nearly 10 years of its existence, the CCC employed more than 2.5 million young men. They planted millions of trees, mostly in the South and the Southwest.

✔ **READING CHECK: Analyzing Information** In what ways did the FERA, the CWA, and the CCC provide different types of relief? FERA provided direct federal aid; the CWA invented "make-work" jobs for people; and the CCC trained younger workers to develop the nation's parks and forests.

Helping the Nation Recover

In addition to the New Deal relief programs designed to help needy Americans, President Roosevelt pursued reform and recovery programs. The president saw relief as a short-term remedy. Recovery was his long-term goal.

Roosevelt saw reforming some business practices as vital to the economy's recovery. To protect investors and guard against stock fraud, Roosevelt supported the passage of the Federal Securities Act, which created the **Securities and Exchange Commission** (SEC). The SEC regulates companies that sell stocks and bonds.

To stimulate the recovery of businesses and industries, Roosevelt poured money into the economy through federal loans and government spending. This process is sometimes called "priming the pump." Many New Deal recovery programs were based on the theories of **John Maynard Keynes**, a noted British economist. Keynes argued that for a nation to recover fully from a depression, the government had to spend money to encourage investment and consumption.

In June 1933 Congress passed the **National Industrial Recovery Act** (NIRA) to stimulate industrial and business activity and reduce unemployment. It would do this by stabilizing prices, raising wages, limiting work hours, and providing jobs. To achieve these goals, the NIRA created two new federal agencies—the Public Works Administration (PWA) and the National Recovery Administration (NRA).

Secretary of the Interior Harold Ickes led the PWA. Using federal funds, the PWA contracted with private firms to build roads, public buildings, and other public-works projects. Between 1933 and 1939 the PWA spent more than $4 billion on some 34,000 projects. The NRA encouraged businesses to draw up "codes of fair competition." Under these codes, competing businesses agreed to work together to set

LEVEL 3: Tell students to imagine that they are representatives of one of the New Deal agencies created to promote industrial or agricultural recovery. Ask each student to write a brief speech about the goals of his or her agency and the steps his or her agency is taking to promote recovery. *(See the Level 1 lesson for the correct programs and the major provisions of each program.)* Ask volunteers to deliver their speeches to the class.

 HOMEWORK *Distribute Activity 16, The Public Works Administration, from* **Geography Activities,** *and have each student complete it.*

SPOTLIGHT
on the STFU

Have students conduct research on the Southern Tenant Farmers' Union (STFU), focusing on who joined the STFU, the goals of the organization, and its major victories. Then have each student write a short poem about the organization's goals and activities. Ask volunteers to recite their poems to the class. **Block Scheduling**

hours, prices, production levels, and wages. Businesses were able to do this because the NIRA had suspended antitrust laws. To help protect labor during this period, the NIRA guaranteed workers the "right to organize and bargain collectively through representatives of their own choosing."

Led by former army general Hugh S. Johnson, the NRA was initially popular. Parades of workers marched through cities displaying the NRA banner. The banner contained a blue eagle clutching lightning bolts in its claw, with the slogan "We Do Our Part." Johnson compared the NRA to an army.

 History Makers Speak 66This campaign is a frank dependence on the power and the willingness of the American people to act together as one person in an hour of great danger. . . . The Blue Eagle is a symbol of industrial solidarity and self-government.99

—Hugh S. Johnson, *The Blue Eagle from Egg to Earth*

The blue eagle of the NRA

Enthusiasm for the NRA soon faded. Businesses did not always obey the codes. Workers complained that the codes kept their wages down. Consumers complained that the codes pushed prices up. As people lost confidence, they joked that NRA stood for "National Run Around" and "No Recovery Allowed." In 1935 the Supreme Court declared the NIRA and its creation—the NRA—unconstitutional.

Agricultural Recovery

President Roosevelt included farmers in his attempts to encourage economic recovery. As part of his plan, Roosevelt called for farmers to cut production. The president believed that such a cut would cause the prices of agricultural goods—and therefore farmers' purchasing power—to rise. Passed by Congress in May 1933, the Agricultural Adjustment Act created the **Agricultural Adjustment Administration** (AAA). The AAA paid farmers to reduce their output of corn, cotton, dairy products, hogs, rice, tobacco, wheat, and other commodities. The money for these subsidies came from taxes levied on food processors, including canners, flour millers, and meat packers.

In one year the plan reduced the cotton crop by more than 3 million bales. This reduction helped to raise cotton prices. Increased income allowed cotton growers and large-scale farmers to spend more cash, thus stimulating overall economic recovery. New Deal supporters pointed to these favorable results as proof of the value of sound federal planning. However, critics pointed out that the taxes on food processors were passed along to consumers in the form of higher prices. They noted that the increase in farmers' incomes came at the expense of consumers.

Critics also claimed that farmers with large landholdings benefited far more from AAA assistance than did small farmers. When large landowners cut production, they forced sharecroppers off their land. They would then keep all of the government payments for themselves. The poorest farmers were forced into even deeper poverty. In response, a group of Arkansas sharecroppers formed the Southern Tenant Farmers' Union (STFU) in 1934. This racially integrated union lobbied the government to halt tenant evictions. They urged the government to force landowners to share federal payments with the farmers who rented land from them.

At meetings like this one, members of the Southern Tenant Farmers' Union worked to win government assistance for some of the poorest farmers in the United States.

CITIZENSHIP

STFU: Racial Integration and Labor Organizing. When the STFU was created in 1934, African Americans and white people joined the union in segregated local branches. Eventually the groups merged to form a racially integrated union. The STFU helped gather evidence against planters who denied their tenants a share of AAA subsidies. Members also protested discriminatory practices such as the poll tax, demonstrated in favor of labor reforms, and conducted strikes. Planters threatened members with violence. Some members disappeared or were found murdered. The STFU's work eventually led to the creation of the Farm Security Administration.

CRITICAL THINKING Why might a racially integrated union have been effective for sharecroppers?

ANSWER: Students might suggest that if only one group protested, owners could easily undermine the position of the protesters by hiring members of the other group to work the fields.

VISUAL RECORD ANSWER
(for p. 470)
Students might answer that they are clearing away fallen trees.

ALL LEVELS: Tell students that before the New Deal's program in the Tennessee River valley, the region's residents suffered from disease, floods, illiteracy, and poverty. To help students understand the New Deal's goals for the Tennessee River valley, copy the graphic organizer at right on the chalkboard, omitting the italicized answers. Have each student complete the organizer. Ask students why people might have criticized the TVA, despite its efforts to improve the quality of life in the region. (*Students might suggest that the government did not have the constitutional authority to undertake such a project or that private utility companies feared that they would lose money.*) To conclude, lead a class discussion. Ask students to consider whether government or the private sector is responsible for improving the quality of life in impoverished regions.

English Language Learners

provide electricity · provide flood control · provide recreational facilities · combat malaria · **TVA Goals for the Tennessee River Valley** · improve standard of living · combat illiteracy · combat soil erosion

Antilynching Bill Is Not Passed. For years, activists had been trying to get a federal antilynching bill passed. In 1922 a filibuster by southern congressmembers defeated an antilynching bill. In 1934 Senators Robert Wagner and Edward Costigan introduced an antilynching bill drafted by the NAACP. Despite support from several northern governors, the bill was defeated. Wagner and Costigan reintroduced it in 1935, but southern congressmembers again launched a filibuster. The bill was never brought up for a vote. Supporters abandoned the bill altogether in 1938.

CRITICAL THINKING At what other times might southern senators have claimed that a federal bill violated states' rights?

ANSWER: Students might suggest during the Civil War and Reconstruction.

MAP ANSWER
seven

VISUAL RECORD ANSWER
(for p. 473)
Students might suggest that the painting depicts racial harmony because white people and African Americans are shown enjoying the concert together.

Early in 1936 the Supreme Court struck down the AAA. The Court claimed that the tax on food processors was unconstitutional. Like the ruling against the NIRA and NRA, this decision reflected the Supreme Court's general opposition to New Deal legislation.

✔ **READING CHECK: Evaluating** How effective were New Deal programs designed to promote industrial and agricultural recovery? somewhat; the PWA created new jobs, but the Supreme Court struck down the NIRA and the AAA as unconstitutional

Revitalizing a Region

The largest of the early New Deal programs took place in the Tennessee River valley. This project sought to aid a rural seven-state region that was scarred by deforestation and frequent flooding. Disease, illiteracy, malnutrition, and poverty plagued its 2 million residents. The **Tennessee Valley Authority** (TVA), which was created in May 1933, transformed the economic and social life of the region. Headed by David E. Lilienthal, the TVA built a number of new dams. It also built several power stations that provided electricity, flood control, and recreational facilities for the region. Other TVA projects combated malaria, illiteracy, and soil erosion and tried to improve the region's low standard of living.

Some Americans criticized the TVA, saying it was an example of the federal government abusing its power. Shareholders in private utility companies worried that the TVA projects would cause them to lose money. Shareholders brought several court cases against the TVA, but the Supreme Court refused to strike it down.

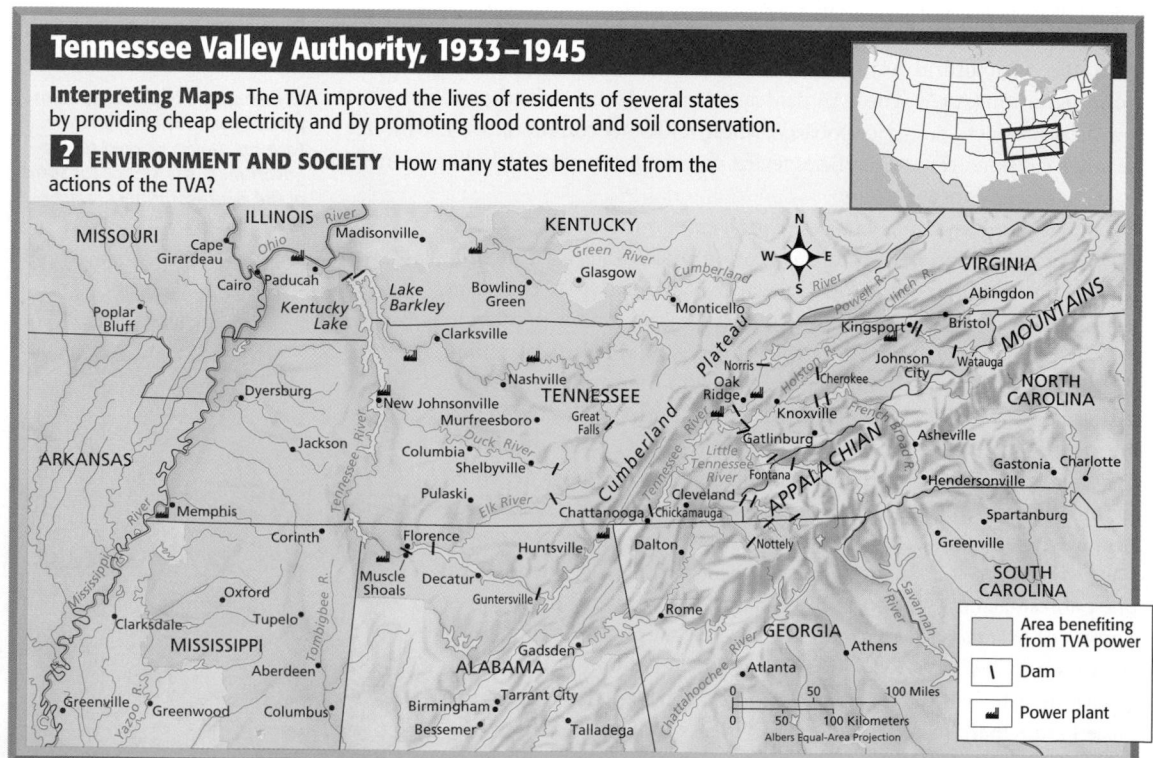

Tennessee Valley Authority, 1933–1945

Interpreting Maps The TVA improved the lives of residents of several states by providing cheap electricity and by promoting flood control and soil conservation.

❓ ENVIRONMENT AND SOCIETY How many states benefited from the actions of the TVA?

Legend: Area benefiting from TVA power · Dam · Power plant

TEACH OBJECTIVE 4

ALL LEVELS: Pair students and ask each pair to create a chart depicting how the Roosevelt administration addressed the concerns of African Americans and American Indians. *(Charts should mention the appointment of African Americans to government posts, establishment of the Federal Council on Negro Affairs, and Marian Anderson's concert at the Lincoln Memorial. American Indians concerns were addressed through the appointment of John Collier as commissioner of Indian Affairs and by the passage of the Indian Reorganization Act of 1934.)* Ask volunteers to present their charts to the class.

English Language Learners, Cooperative Learning

NOTE: For an additional teaching idea, see the Chapter 16 ranking lesson in the **Creative Teaching Strategies** handbook.

Equality Under the New Deal

Although New Deal programs provided aid to people of all races, some programs discriminated. Some 200,000 young African American men received work and training though the CCC. In most states, they were strictly segregated from white workers. The TVA employed African American workers. Yet they were not allowed to live in some of the model towns built by the organization. NRA codes often set lower wages for African Americans than for whites. This practice led some black leaders to call the NRA the "Negro Run Around" or "Negroes Ruined Again."

This discrimination reflected the social attitudes of many Americans at that time. The depression increased racial tensions in the country, particularly in the South. In 1933 alone, 24 African Americans were lynched. Roosevelt offered little support to legislation to help African Americans, such as a federal antilynching law sponsored by the National Association for the Advancement of Colored People (NAACP). Roosevelt feared a political backlash from southern Democrats.

Fighting discrimination. Despite the lack of progress on civil rights legislation, African Americans did make some advances under the Roosevelt administration. Former NAACP leader Harold Ickes brought in several prominent African Americans to advise the Department of the Interior on racial matters. These advisers included **Robert C. Weaver**, who held a Ph.D. in economics from Harvard.

Roosevelt named more than 100 African Americans to posts in the federal government during his terms in office. This was more than any other president since Ulysses S. Grant. These appointees included a wide variety of professionals, such as educators, legal scholars, newspaper editors, and social workers. One core group of these African American government officials evolved into the Federal Council on Negro Affairs. The council became known as the Black Cabinet or the Black Brain Trust. According to Weaver, their "common cause was to maximize the participation of blacks in all phases of the New Deal."

Many of these appointments came at the request of Eleanor Roosevelt, who was a champion of civil rights. African American leaders noted Mrs. Roosevelt's unusual ability to understand their struggles. "We [white people] are largely to blame" for poverty among the black community, she once said. It was her goal to open greater educational and economic opportunities for African Americans.

In 1939 the Daughters of the American Revolution (DAR) refused to allow **Marian Anderson**, a world-famous African American singer, to perform at their Washington, D.C., hall. Both Mrs. Roosevelt and Ickes reacted strongly. Roosevelt resigned her longtime membership in the DAR. She argued that "to remain as a member implies approval of that action." Roosevelt and Ickes then arranged for Anderson to give a free concert at the Lincoln Memorial. The concert was a success and attracted an audience of some 75,000 people.

INTERPRETING THE VISUAL RECORD

Race relations. This painting shows the enormous crowd that attended Marian Anderson's concert at the Lincoln Memorial. *Do you think the artist intended to show racial tension or racial harmony in this painting? Explain your answer.*

VISUAL RECORD ANSWER

(for p. 474)

Students might answer that it is very low because her home is made of canvas and tree branches and her shoes look worn.

REVIEW SECTION **1** **ANSWERS**

1. Define
- bank holiday, p. 468

2. Identify
- New Deal, p. 468
- Federal Deposit Insurance Corporation, p. 469
- Frances Perkins, p. 469
- Harry L. Hopkins, p. 469
- Civilian Conservation Corps, p. 470
- Securities and Exchange Commission, p. 470
- John Maynard Keynes, p. 470
- National Industrial Recovery Act, p. 470
- Agricultural Adjustment Administration, p. 471
- Tennessee Valley Authority, p. 472

ASSESS

Have students complete **Daily Quiz 16.1.** As **Alternative Assessment,** you may want to use the poster or the press release in this section's lessons.

RETEACH

Have students complete **Main Idea Activity for English Language Learners and Special-Needs Students 16.1.** Then organize the class into small groups. Have each group write some questions about New Deal initiatives that can be answered by naming a specific program or person. *(For example, students might ask, "What program insured the savings of bank depositors?" [FDIC])* Collect groups' questions and use them to quiz the class.
English Language Learners, Cooperative Learning

EXTEND

Organize the class into small groups. Assign each group one of the key people for Section 1. Have each group conduct research on its assigned individual. Each group should use the information it gathers to prepare a multimedia presentation on its subject. Have each group give its presentation to the class.
Block Scheduling, Cooperative Learning

- Robert C. Weaver, p. 473
- Marian Anderson, p. 473
- John Collier, p. 474

3. banking—examined banks for financial soundness, encouraged people to deposit money, created FDIC; industry—passed NIRA to stabilize prices and contract with business for public projects; agriculture—loans to farmers, passed AAA to limit production and raise prices

4a. Many Americans disliked direct aid, but the CWA and CCC were more successful because they created jobs that put Americans to work.

b. The TVA educated citizens, limited effects of disease, provided electricity and flood control, and raised standard of living.

c. Answers will vary. Eleanor Roosevelt was behind African American government appointments; John Collier helped pass the Indian Reorganization Act.

5. Answers will vary. Students might suggest that Roosevelt based many policies on Keynes's theories. Keynes supported government spending to stimulate the economy. The Roosevelt administration used government funds to stimulate agriculture, business, and industry and to provide jobs.

INTERPRETING THE VISUAL RECORD

American Indians. This woman and her child were photographed in 1936 at their home on the Mescalero Apache Reservation. *What can you tell about this woman's standard of living?*

Rights of American Indians. The Roosevelt administration also addressed the concerns of American Indians. At the beginning of the New Deal Era, life for many American Indians was bleak. A late-1920s report on American Indian life across the country listed numerous problems facing these communities. Inadequate housing, poor health care, and malnutrition left many of the nation's more than 300,000 American Indians vulnerable to disease. American Indians argued that their culture had been stripped away by measures like the Dawes Act of 1887. The act had ended tribal government and sold off tribal land.

In the 1920s a social worker named **John Collier** observed the poor living conditions in American Indian communities. Deeply moved by what he had seen, Collier founded the American Indian Defense Association. The organization fought to protect religious freedom and tribal property. For the next decade Collier championed American Indian reform efforts. Then, in 1933, President Roosevelt appointed Collier as the new commissioner of Indian Affairs. Collier worked to redirect government policy in an attempt to revitalize American Indian life and culture. "Anything less than to let Indian culture live on would be a crime against the earth itself," Collier declared.

Congress put these reforms into law with the Indian Reorganization Act of 1934. Reversing the Dawes Act policy, the new law tried to revive tribal rule. It provided funds to start tribal business ventures and to pay for the college education of young American Indians. The bill also ordered Congress "to promote the study of Indian civilization and preserve and develop . . . Indian arts, crafts, skills, and traditions."

✔ **READING CHECK: Summarizing** What efforts did the Roosevelt administration make to improve economic opportunities and political rights for African Americans and American Indians? *Roosevelt gave African Americans influential government posts and helped American Indians with the Indian Reorganization Act.*

SECTION 1 REVIEW

1. Define and explain:
bank holiday

2. Identify and explain:
New Deal
Federal Deposit Insurance Corporation
Frances Perkins
Harry L. Hopkins
Civilian Conservation Corps
Securities and Exchange Commission
John Maynard Keynes
National Industrial Recovery Act
Agricultural Adjustment Administration
Tennessee Valley Authority
Robert C. Weaver
Marian Anderson
John Collier

3. Categorizing Copy the graphic organizer below. Use it to describe the various measures that President Roosevelt took to help banking, industry, and agriculture.

[Graphic organizer: New Deal → Banking, Industry, Agriculture]

4. **Finding the Main Idea**

a. How effective were New Deal programs that granted direct relief to unemployed workers and created jobs? Explain your answer.

b. How did the programs of the Tennessee Valley Authority affect daily life and the standard of living in the area?

c. What contributions did Eleanor Roosevelt and John Collier make to reforms for African Americans and American Indians?

5. **Writing and Critical Thinking**

Drawing Conclusions Prepare a report for Congress discussing Roosevelt's economic policies.
Consider:
- how the economic theories of John Maynard Keynes are reflected in Roosevelt's approach
- what approach Keynes supported
- what approach the Roosevelt administration took toward the economy

Homework Practice Online
keyword: SE3 HP16

SECTION ②

After completing Section 2, students should be able to:

OBJECTIVE 1 *Discuss the criticisms aimed at the New Deal.*

OBJECTIVE 2 *Recount how the Second New Deal enabled President Roosevelt to win re-election easily in 1936.*

OBJECTIVE 3 *Describe how Roosevelt tried to prevent the Supreme Court from overturning his programs.*

OBJECTIVE 4 *Analyze how the Second New Deal benefited labor and agriculture.*

OBJECTIVE 5 *Explain the Roosevelt recession, and describe the effect it had.*

🎧 LET'S GET STARTED!

As students enter the classroom, distribute copies of Cartoon 24, FDR and the New Deal, from **American History Political Cartoons**. Ask students to study the cartoon and complete the questions on the worksheet. Have volunteers share their answers with the class. Tell students that in Section 2 they will learn about the programs of the Second New Deal.

SECTION ②

READ TO DISCOVER

1. What were the criticisms aimed at the New Deal?
2. How did the Second New Deal enable President Roosevelt to win re-election easily in 1936?
3. How did Roosevelt try to prevent the Supreme Court from overturning his programs?
4. How did the Second New Deal benefit labor and agriculture?
5. What was Roosevelt's recession, and what effect did it have?

DEFINE

sit-down strike

IDENTIFY

Francis E. Townsend
Charles E. Coughlin
Huey Long
Share-Our-Wealth
Works Progress
 Administration
National Youth
 Administration
Mary McLeod Bethune
Social Security Act
Wagner-Connery Act
Congress of Industrial
 Organizations

▶ WHY IT MATTERS TODAY

State and local governments continue to support programs for people in need. Use **CNNfyi.com** or other **current events** sources to investigate government programs designed to help families and children. Record your findings in your journal.

CNNfyi.com

New Challenges

EYEWITNESSES TO History

❝*President Roosevelt was elected on November 8, 1932. . . . This is January 1935. We are in our third year of the Roosevelt depression, with the conditions growing worse. . . . We must become awakened! We must know the truth and speak the truth. There is no use to wait three more years. It is not Roosevelt or ruin; it is Roosevelt's ruin.***❞**

—Huey Long, radio address, January 1935

Supporters of Huey Long's Share-Our-Wealth program wore badges such as this one.

U.S. senator Huey Long of Louisiana was one of several prominent critics who argued that the New Deal was too slow in easing the economic troubles of the nation. Critics like Long increased the administration's determination to enact another series of innovative programs that would provide more relief to the nation.

Critics of the New Deal

Both conservatives and liberals criticized the New Deal. Most conservative complaints came from the American Liberty League, an organization made up largely of Republican business leaders. Some dissatisfied Democrats led by Al Smith also joined. Smith accused New Deal supporters of "irresponsible ravings against millionaires and big business." The league complained that the New Deal measures were destroying both the Constitution and free enterprise.

Among the liberal reformers who opposed the New Deal was Dr. **Francis E. Townsend** of California. Townsend wanted the government to grant a pension of $200 a month to every American over 60 years old. All recipients were to spend the pensions within 30 days and thus pump money into the economy. Father **Charles E. Coughlin**, a radio priest from Michigan, urged the government to nationalize all banks and return to the silver standard.

Huey Long, a colorful but corrupt U.S. senator from Louisiana, had probably the most radical plan. Like Robin Hood, Long wanted to take from the rich and give to the poor. In 1934 Long proposed a new kind of relief program, which he called **Share-Our-Wealth**. The program would empower the government to seize wealth from the rich through taxes and then provide a guaranteed minimum income and a home to every American family. Long even had a theme song.

Primary Source

**❝Ev'ry man a king, ev'ry man a king,
For you can be a millionaire,
There's enough for all people to share.
When it's sunny June and December too,
Or in the wintertime or spring:
There'll be peace without end,
Ev'ry neighbor a friend,
With ev'ry man a king.❞**

—"Ev'ry Man a King"

SECTION ② RESOURCES

REPRODUCIBLE

▶ Guided Reading Strategy 16.2
▶ Primary Source Reading 16: "Every Man a King"
▶ American History Political Cartoon 24: FDR and the New Deal

TECHNOLOGY

▶ One-Stop Planner, Lesson 16.2
▶ **CNN** Presents America: Yesterday and Today Segment: Urban Youth Goes to Work
▶ Holt Researcher: American History CD–ROM
▶ Homework Practice Online

REINFORCEMENT, REVIEW, AND ASSESSMENT

▶ Section 2 Review, p. 481
▶ Daily Quiz 16.2
▶ Main Idea Activity 16.2
▶ English Audio Summary 16.2
▶ Spanish Audio Summary 16.2

ALL LEVELS: Tell students that New Deal measures received criticism from the right and left of the political spectrum. Ask students why criticism of the New Deal may have been so widespread. (*Students might suggest that some people believed that the administration was not doing enough to help poor or older Americans or that business interests felt threatened by government intervention in the economy.*) To help students understand the criticisms aimed at the New Deal, copy the chart at right on the chalkboard, omitting the italicized answers. Have each student complete the organizer. Ask volunteers to share their answers with the class.

English Language Learners

Criticism from the Left	Criticism from the Right
Francis Townsend—wanted the government to grant a pension of $200 a month to Americans over 60 years old	*American Liberty League/ Al Smith—claimed New Deal measures were destroying the Constitution and free enterprise; accused New Deal supporters of "irresponsible ravings against millionaires and big business"*
Father Coughlin—wanted the government to nationalize banks and return to the silver standard	
Huey Long—wanted the Share-Our-Wealth program	

HOMEWORK *Distribute copies of Reading 16, "Every Man a King," from* **Literature, Primary Source, and Biography Readings***. Have each student read the text and complete the questions and activity accompanying the text.*

Huey Long. Louisiana politician Huey Long held populist ideas from the beginning of his career, when he attacked Standard Oil and opposed the Ku Klux Klan. As governor, Long abolished his state's local governments and personally controlled the courts, the militia, police forces, schools, and the tax assessors. He was impeached by the state legislature but not convicted. A supporter of some New Deal programs, Long liked Roosevelt's proposal to regulate public utilities, but worried that "we might as well try to regulate a rattlesnake." He warned that rich people would rather let the nation "go slap down to hell" than give up their economic supremacy. Some 27,000 Share-Our-Wealth clubs had formed across the nation by the time Long was assassinated in 1935.

CRITICAL THINKING Why might Long's Share-Our-Wealth program have been particularly popular during the Great Depression?

ANSWER: Students might suggest that during a time of unemployment and extremely low wages, people would have been more aware of disparities in wealth and been more willing to change them.

PRESIDENTIAL Lives

Franklin D. Roosevelt

1882–1945
In Office 1933–1945

"Mr. Roosevelt is a unique figure in the modern world: the one statesman . . . who seems able to relax," wrote one journalist about the charming leader. Indeed, President Roosevelt always appeared to be warm, energetic, and easy-going, despite the enormous pressures he faced as president. His optimistic outlook may have helped in his recuperation from polio.

The president always hid his private thoughts behind a dazzling smile. One of his speechwriters noted that one could never tell what was going on in Roosevelt's "heavily forested interior." The president often relied on instinct and idealism in making

1882 1982 USA 20c
Franklin D. Roosevelt

decisions. Political theories held little value for him. His warm style and caring manner, expressed in his weekly "fireside chats," helped win support for many of his programs. Years after the depression, many Americans would remember Roosevelt almost as a beloved family member.

Posters like this one (below right) encouraged Americans to support WPA programs, such as the project shown below.

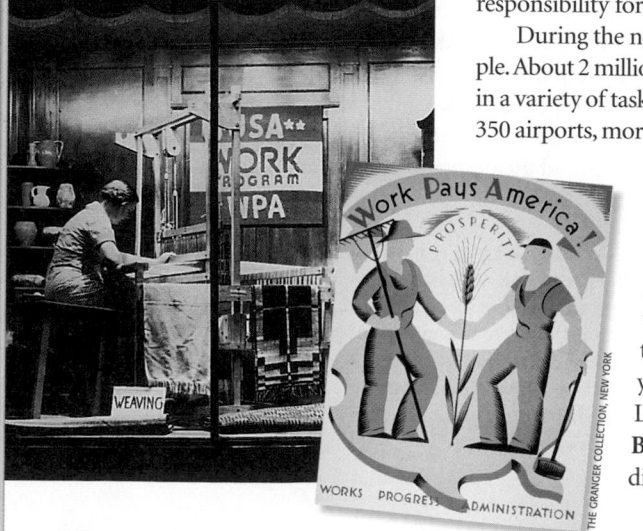

WEAVING

Work Pays America!
PROSPERITY

WORKS PROGRESS ADMINISTRATION

THE GRANGER COLLECTION, NEW YORK

The Share-Our-Wealth program received a great deal of popular support. Some critics, however, suspected that Long harbored dreams of becoming a dictator. The popular senator threatened to challenge Roosevelt as a third-party candidate in the 1936 election. Both this threat and the Share-Our-Wealth program died when an assassin killed Long in 1935.

✔ **READING CHECK: Summarizing** How did conservatives and liberals criticize the New Deal? Conservatives said it destroyed free enterprise, and some liberals believed it did not go far enough.

The Second New Deal

The Democrats gained additional congressional seats in the 1934 elections. The victory, coupled with pressure from liberals, encouraged New Deal planners to initiate more public-works programs, a social-security plan, and wage and hour improvements for laborers. This series of programs eventually came to be called the Second New Deal. Although it continued to promote social relief and economic recovery, the Second New Deal increasingly emphasized long-term reform.

The Works Progress Administration. After the Civil Works Administration (CWA) ended, President Roosevelt created the **Works Progress Administration** (WPA) in 1935. Led by Harry L. Hopkins, this program was designed to help Americans find work. Congress budgeted some $5 billion for the WPA's job-creation programs. In January 1935 the federal government returned responsibility for direct relief to state and local governments.

During the next eight years, the WPA employed some 8.5 million people. About 2 million were in the program at any given time. Workers engaged in a variety of tasks. Male blue-collar workers built or rebuilt a total of some 350 airports, more than 100,000 public buildings, some 78,000 bridges, and about 500,000 miles of roads. White-collar workers took on research projects and teaching jobs.

The WPA tried to help young people between the ages of 16 and 25 by establishing the **National Youth Administration** (NYA), a "junior WPA." The NYA provided high-school and college-age Americans with part-time jobs that allowed them to stay in school. Within a year the NYA was providing aid to 500,000 people. First Lady Eleanor Roosevelt insisted that **Mary McLeod Bethune**, a member of the Black Cabinet, be appointed director of the Division of Negro Affairs in the NYA.

LEVEL 1: Pair students and have each pair compile a list of major initiatives from the Second New Deal and write a paragraph explaining how those initiatives enabled President Roosevelt to win re-election easily in 1936. *(Pairs' lists should include the WPA, the NYA, the Social Security Act, the REA, and the Revenue Act of 1935. Students should explain that these initiatives enabled FDR to gain the support of a broad range of Americans, including African Americans, farmers, labor union members, many Republicans, and unemployed workers.)* Ask volunteers to read their paragraphs to the class.

English Language Learners, Cooperative Learning

LEVEL 2: Tell students to imagine that FDR has just been elected to a second term in office and that they are reporters covering his re-election. Have each student write a headline and a brief newspaper article recounting how the programs of the Second New Deal enabled Roosevelt to win re-election easily. *(See the Level 1 lesson for the correct programs and how those programs contributed to FDR's victory.)* Ask volunteers to read their headlines and articles to the class.

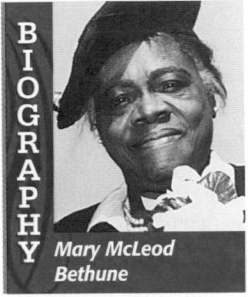

BIOGRAPHY

Mary McLeod Bethune

Mary McLeod Bethune was born in 1875 in Mayesville, South Carolina. Her parents were farmers who had once been slaves. The young girl's chances for an education seemed slim, since the Mayesville school was for whites only. With the aid of a Presbyterian mission school and a series of scholarships, however, she eventually attended the Moody Bible Institute in Chicago.

Bethune initially intended to become a missionary in Africa but soon found her mission to be educating African American children. She once said of her decision: "The drums of Africa still beat in my heart. They will not let me rest while there is a single Negro boy or girl without a chance to prove his [or her] worth." In 1904 she founded a primary school for African American girls in Florida. It evolved into Bethune-Cookman College, a four-year coeducational institution with a mostly African American student body.

Bethune became involved with numerous African American groups, including the NAACP and the Urban League. In 1935 she helped unite all national organizations working on behalf of African American women into the National Council of Negro Women. Through her work with this association, she became close friends with Eleanor Roosevelt. Bethune fought hard, although not always successfully, to rid the NYA of discrimination. Although Bethune left government service after the NYA ended, she continued to promote civil rights and educational opportunities for young African Americans until her death in 1955.

Social Security. Another important reform effort of the Second New Deal was the **Social Security Act**, which Congress passed in August 1935. The act contained three major provisions. First, it provided unemployment insurance to workers who lost their jobs. The funds for this insurance came from a payroll tax on businesses. Second, the act provided pensions to retired workers older than age 65. The money for these pensions came from two sources—a payroll tax on employers and a tax on employees' wages. Third, in a shared federal-state program, the act provided payments to people with disabilities, the elderly, and the wives and children of male workers who had died.

Other programs. In May 1935 Roosevelt created the Rural Electrification Administration (REA) as part of his program to help underprivileged Americans. The REA provided electricity to isolated rural areas. Congress also passed a law giving the government the right to regulate the interstate production, transmission, and sale of gas and electricity. This helped keep utility costs low.

Research on the ROM

Free Find:
Mary McLeod Bethune

After reading about Mary McLeod Bethune on the **Holt Researcher CD–ROM**, design a memorial plaque that illustrates her achievements.

★ Then and Now

Social Security

Referring to the Social Security Act, Frances Perkins recalled, "Nothing of the sort had ever come before the Congress of the United States." The act altered many Americans' ideas about the government's responsibility to ensure the welfare of citizens. Since its beginning in the 1930s, the program has expanded to cover children, people with disabilities, and many others. Social Security also manages numerous other welfare programs, including subsidized school lunches. Providing monthly pensions to retired people or their survivors is the best-known Social Security program. Ida May Fuller of Ludlow, Vermont, was the first person to receive a monthly Social Security pension. Her first check, for $22.54, arrived January 31, 1940.

Over time, the monthly payments have risen along with the cost of living. At the same time, more people are covered by Social Security. Although many people feared that this situation would eventually force the Social Security program into bankruptcy, legislators have long been reluctant to alter the system. Finally, in the late 1990s Congress enacted several measures to reform Social Security and guard it for future generations.

Ida May Fuller holds a Social Security check.

Food Programs for People in Poverty. The Second New Deal introduced a plan to provide surplus food to people who were eligible for federal work relief. This early food-stamp plan allowed participants to buy orange-colored food stamps. For each dollar of orange stamps purchased, the buyer would be given 50-cents worth of blue stamps. Orange stamps could be used to buy any kind of food, but blue stamps could be used only for surplus foods. Critics of the program noted that it helped only some people in need and that it required people to purchase the orange stamps in order to receive blue stamps. The program operated until World War II. The Food Stamp Act of 1964 initiated the program in use today. Under this program, financial assets and income determine participants' eligibility.

ACTIVITY: Have students conduct research on depression-era federal assistance programs that have survived in some form to the present day. Ask each student to write paragraphs about the history and goals of a few such programs.

TEACH OBJECTIVE 3

LEVEL 1: Pair students and ask each pair to write a short paragraph summarizing Roosevelt's plan to prevent the Supreme Court from overturning his New Deal programs and explaining the criticism of his plan. *(Paragraphs should mention that FDR asked Congress to give him the power to appoint one new justice for each justice over 70 years old. Critics of the court-packing plan believed that it would tamper with the balance of powers and that Roosevelt was trying to assume dictatorial powers.)* Ask volunteers to read their paragraphs to the class.
English Language Learners, Cooperative Learning

INTERPRETING POLITICAL CARTOONS

Dr. New Deal. Treating the United States like a sick patient, Franklin D. Roosevelt tried many cures to get the country healthy again. ***Do you think the cartoonist expected Roosevelt's remedies to work? Explain your answer.***

In this cartoon President Roosevelt is shown as a ventriloquist whose dummy refuses to cooperate.

Roosevelt then targeted the rich. He declared that the existing tax laws had not done enough "to prevent an unjust concentration of wealth and economic power." Congress passed the Revenue Act of 1935. Often called the Wealth Tax Act, the bill sharply raised taxes for the nation's richest people.

The election of 1936. In June 1936 the Democrats nominated Roosevelt for a second term. Labor unions, farmers, those on relief, and even many Republicans also endorsed him. For the first time since Reconstruction, most African Americans in the North supported the Democrats. The Republicans nominated the capable but unexciting governor of Kansas, Alfred M. Landon.

President Roosevelt pledged to continue the New Deal. He won easily, receiving some 28 million popular votes to Landon's 17 million. Roosevelt carried every state but Maine and Vermont—the most lopsided electoral victory in more than 100 years. The Democrats also increased their majorities in both houses of Congress.

✔ **READING CHECK: Analyzing Information** How did President Roosevelt win re-election easily in 1936? His Second New Deal programs earned him the support of labor, farmers, African Americans, and some Republicans.

Roosevelt and the Supreme Court

Fresh from his victory, President Roosevelt moved to "reform" the Supreme Court. Roosevelt was angered that the Court had declared several New Deal measures unconstitutional. He labeled the justices "Nine Old Men"—six were 70 or older.

In February 1937 Roosevelt asked Congress to grant him the power to appoint one new justice for each of those 70 or older, up to six new justices. Roosevelt's proposal triggered a storm of protests. Democrats as well as Republicans charged that this "court packing" tampered with the balance of powers. Dorothy Thompson, a popular political columnist, considered Roosevelt's scheme a move toward dictatorship.

> *History Makers Speak*
>
> **"If the American people accept this last audacity [boldness] of the President without letting out a yell to high heaven, they have ceased to be jealous of their liberties and are ripe for ruin. This is the beginning of a pure personal government."**
>
> —Dorothy Thompson, *Washington Star*, February 10, 1937

Congress rejected Roosevelt's request. The Court, however, soon upheld the Social Security Act and the National Labor Relations Act. Some Americans concluded that the justices had become more tolerant of New Deal programs in an attempt to prevent drastic reform. During the next four years, several justices died or retired. They were replaced by Roosevelt appointees. By 1945 eight of the nine justices were Roosevelt appointees.

✔ **READING CHECK: Making Generalizations** How did Roosevelt's court-packing plan affect the relationships among the executive, judicial, and legislative branches? It threatened to give the executive branch more power than the other two branches.

LEVELS 2 AND 3: Tell students to imagine that it is February 1937 and that they have just heard about FDR's court-packing plan. Have each student write a short letter to a newspaper either supporting or opposing Roosevelt's plan. Tell students to describe the provisions of Roosevelt's plan in their letters and to base their support or opposition on the possible results of the plan. *(See the Level 1 lesson for the provisions of the court-packing plan and reasons why people opposed it.)* Have volunteers read their letters to the class.

TEACH OBJECTIVE 4

LEVEL 1: Tell students to imagine that they are artists hired by the WPA to create advertisements for New Deal programs. Pair students and have each pair create three billboards advertising programs of the Second New Deal that benefited labor and agriculture. *(Billboards should mention the Wagner-Connery Act, which guaranteed labor's right to organize and bargain collectively; the FSA, which provided low-interest, long-term loans to help tenant farmers and sharecroppers buy land and also established camps providing shelter and medical care for migrant farmworkers; and the AAA of 1938, which authorized subsidies to farmers who practiced soil conservation and crop reduction.)* Display pairs' billboards around the classroom.

English Language Learners, Cooperative Learning

Selected New Deal Programs

Year	First New Deal	Provisions
1933	Emergency Banking Act	Gave the administration the right to regulate banks
1933	Farm Credit Administration (FCA)	Refinanced farm mortgages at lower interest and for longer terms
1933	Economy Act	Proposed to balance the budget through savings measures
1933	Civilian Conservation Corps (CCC)	Employed young men on public-works projects
1933	Federal Emergency Relief Administration (FERA)	Provided grants to states for relief efforts
1933	Agricultural Adjustment Administration (AAA)	Paid farmers to reduce crops; funded by a tax on food processors; later declared unconstitutional
1933	Tennessee Valley Authority (TVA)	Constructed dams and power plants to improve social and economic welfare in the region
1933	Home Owners Loan Corporation (HOLC)	Loaned money to home owners to refinance mortgages
1933	Banking Act of 1933	Created FDIC and authorized branch banking
1933	Federal Deposit Insurance Corporation (FDIC)	Insured individual bank deposits up to $5,000
1933	National Industrial Recovery Act (NIRA)	Established NRA and PWA; later declared unconstitutional
1933	National Recovery Administration (NRA)	Regulated industry through fair-trade codes for businesses
1933	Public Works Administration (PWA)	Constructed roads, public buildings, and other projects designed to increase employment and business activity
1933	Civil Works Administration (CWA)	Employed jobless people to work on federal, state, and local projects
1934	Securities and Exchange Commission (SEC)	Regulated the securities market
1934	Federal Housing Administration (FHA)	Insured bank loans for building and repairing houses

Year	Second New Deal	Provisions
1935	Works Progress Administration (WPA)	Employed people to do artistic, public-works, and research projects
1935	Soil Conservation Service (SCS)	Promoted control and prevention of soil erosion
1935	Rural Electrification Administration (REA)	Provided electricity to rural areas lacking public utilities
1935	National Youth Administration (NYA)	Provided job training and work for people ages 16–25; provided part-time jobs for needy students
1935	National Labor Relations Act (Wagner-Connery Act)	Recognized rights of labor to organize and bargain collectively; regulated labor practices
1935	Social Security Act	Provided unemployment benefits, pensions for the elderly, and survivor's insurance
1935	Revenue Act of 1935 (Wealth Tax Act)	Increased taxes on the wealthy
1937	Farm Security Administration (FSA)	Provided loans to help tenant farmers buy land
1938	Agricultural Adjustment Act of 1938 (AAA)	Increased government regulation of crop production and increased payments to farmers
1938	Revenue Act of 1938	Reduced taxes on large corporations and increased taxes on smaller businesses
1938	Fair Labor Standards Act (Wages and Hours Law)	Established minimum wage of 40 cents per hour and maximum workweek of 40 hours for businesses in interstate commerce

Source: *Encyclopedia of American History*

Interpreting Charts Franklin D. Roosevelt proposed a wide number of programs to aid in the nation's recovery after he assumed office in 1933. These programs became the first New Deal. Two years later he outlined a broader program of social reform in the Second New Deal.

? Skills Assessment Which New Deal programs continue to affect the lives of U.S. citizens?

ECONOMICS

Resettlement and Greenbelt Towns. One New Deal program involved resettling poor families in new communities. The government then built them small homes, gave them farm equipment, and trained them in farming techniques. The families would repay the government with low-interest mortgages. Rexford Tugwell, a member of FDR's Brain Trust, administered the program. One of Tugwell's plans that was only partially realized was the creation of "greenbelt towns." These were to be planned communities outside of cities, where families would live with the best features of both urban and rural environments. Only a few cities ever established greenbelt towns, and so few people were resettled under the program that it had little impact on the economy.

CRITICAL THINKING How might the creation of greenbelt towns be considered a utopian ideal?

ANSWER: Students might suggest that greenbelt towns seemed to promise a perfect combination of urban and rural living.

CHART ANSWER
FERA, TVA, FDIC, SEC, Social Security Act, and the Fair Labor Standards Act

LEVELS 2 AND 3: Tell students to imagine that they are historians assessing the effects of the Second New Deal on labor and agriculture. Have each student write a short essay examining how the programs of the Second New Deal affected workers and farmers. *(See the Level 1 lesson for the correct programs and their provisions.)* Ask volunteers to read their essays to the class.

TEACH OBJECTIVE 5

LEVEL 1: Organize students into triads. Have each triad create a cause-and-effect chart explaining the Roosevelt recession and why it occurred. *(Students might cite that an economic recession occurred in response to FDR's reductions on relief programs and public-works projects in response to criticism of excessive spending. Private industry could* not employ those dropped from government rolls, and the economy took a downturn as factories closed and unemployment rose. In response to the recession, FDR and Congress increased government spending, unemployment declined, and production increased.) Ask volunteers to present their charts to the class. **English Language Learners, Cooperative Learning**

LEVELS 2 AND 3: Pair students and have each pair complete the chart activity from the Level 1 lesson. Then have each pair prepare a brief lecture on the Roosevelt recession, why it occurred, and its effects. *(See the Level 1 lesson for the correct causes and effects.)* Ask volunteers to present their charts and deliver their lectures to the class. **Cooperative Learning**

THAT'S INTERESTING!

Observers remember great excitement among industrial workers in response to the founding of the CIO. The *CIO News* editor wrote, "The workers were waiting for the CIO, pounding on its doors long before the CIO was ready for them." An organizer recalled, "It is difficult to impart on ordinary paper the magic that surrounded the letters *C-I-O* in 1937." A song that soon became popular explained some of the CIO's popularity:

"A union for the masses
To include every craft,
Better wages for each worker,
In CIO there is no class."

VISUAL RECORD ANSWER

Students might suggest that by occupying the plant, the strikers prevented the company from resuming production with replacement workers.

SECTION
REVIEW ② ANSWERS

1. Define
• sit-down strike, p. 480

2. Identify
• Francis E. Townsend, p. 475
• Charles E. Coughlin, p. 475
• Huey Long, p. 475
• Share-Our-Wealth, p. 475
• Works Progress Administration, p. 476
• National Youth Administration, p. 476
• Mary McLeod Bethune, p. 476

Effects of the Second New Deal

The legislation of the Second New Deal responded to some of the Supreme Court's rulings. In May 1935 the Court had ruled that certain provisions of the National Industrial Recovery Act (NIRA) were unconstitutional. Several weeks later, Congress passed the National Labor Relations Act, or **Wagner-Connery Act**. The act guaranteed labor's right to organize unions and to bargain collectively for better wages and working conditions.

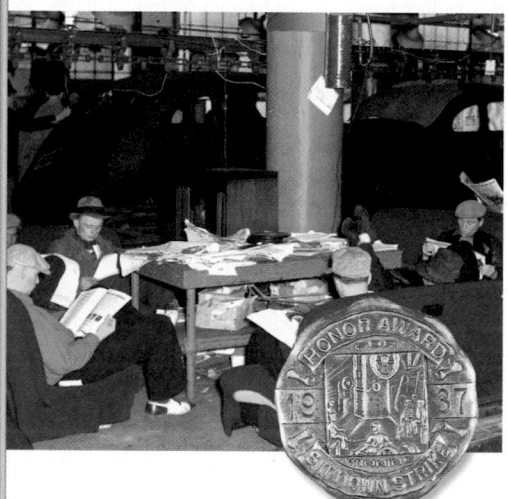

INTERPRETING THE VISUAL RECORD

Sit-down strike. These striking autoworkers, using car seats as couches, have settled in for a long fight. The medal shown was given to workers who took part in the strike against General Motors. *How are these workers affecting their employer?*

Labor. The American Federation of Labor (AFL) continued its efforts to organize skilled workers. However, the AFL did not move fast enough to please John L. Lewis, the leader of the United Mine Workers union. In 1935 Lewis and several other labor leaders organized what became the **Congress of Industrial Organizations** (CIO). The CIO tried to unite workers in various industries. The new CIO unions included all workers, skilled and unskilled, in a given industry.

The organizing efforts of both the AFL and the CIO resulted in a wave of strikes. One of the most bitter strikes was waged against General Motors (GM) in the winter of 1936–37. The United Automobile Workers (UAW) had tried to unionize GM factory workers but GM strongly opposed their efforts. Meanwhile, GM workers grew increasingly frustrated with factory conditions. On December 31, 1936, this frustration led to a **sit-down strike**. Instead of leaving the automobile plants, workers occupied them. They vowed to remain until management met their demands. Finally, after six weeks, General Motors gave in and granted the UAW the right to organize GM workers. Within eight months, the total UAW membership had grown to some 400,000. Owing in part to the Wagner-Connery Act, union membership nationwide rose from about 4 million in 1936 to some 9 million in 1939.

Farmers. The Second New Deal also helped farmers through reform measures. After the Supreme Court struck down the Agricultural Adjustment Act in January 1936, Congress created another program to replace it. Like the AAA, the new program sought to keep the prices of agricultural goods high by cutting crop production. To avoid opposition from the Supreme Court, however, Congress linked this crop reduction to a soil conservation plan—a legitimate governmental activity.

The Roosevelt administration claimed that the soil conservation program did not do enough to promote crop reduction. Congress responded by passing a second Agricultural Adjustment Act in 1938. The law authorized payments to farmers who withdrew land from production and practiced conservation. It also authorized the Department of Agriculture to limit the amount of specific crops that could be brought to market each year. When harvests surpassed these limits, the government stored the surpluses until prices rose. Farmers participating in the program could get government loans based on the value of their stored crops.

The Second New Deal also brought aid to migrant farmworkers, sharecroppers, and tenant farmers. In 1937 Congress created the Farm Security Administration (FSA). It provided low-interest, long-term loans to help tenant farmers and

REVIEW

Have students complete the **Section 2 Review** on p. 481.

ASSESS

Have students complete **Daily Quiz 16.2**. As **Alternative Assessment**, you may want to use the radio script or the newspaper article in this section's lessons.

RETEACH

Have students complete **Main Idea Activity for English Language Learners and Special-Needs Students 16.2.** Organize students into small groups. Assign each group a subsection of Section 2. Have each group create a poster summarizing the major points in its subsection. Have volunteers present their posters to the class. Ask the class to supply any information that might be missing from each poster.
English Language Learners, Cooperative Learning

EXTEND

Have students conduct research on New Deal programs that employed young people and current government programs that employ young people. Students might examine the scale and size of the employment programs or the types of work available. Have each student write an essay comparing a New Deal program and a current program. **Block Scheduling**

---

sharecroppers buy land. The FSA also established camps where migrant farmworkers could seek shelter and medical care.

✔ **READING CHECK: Analyzing Information** How did Congress react to the Supreme Court's rulings on New Deal programs? It passed new legislation that would be less likely to be struck down.

Roosevelt's Recession

In 1936 President Roosevelt began cutting back on relief and public-works programs. He was reacting to criticism of excessive government spending. Private industry, however, was not yet strong enough to give jobs to those dropped from government rolls. The economy worsened. By the fall of 1937, factories were closing, and unemployment was rising. Republicans called this economic downturn "Roosevelt's recession."

Roosevelt and Congress responded by approving more than $3 billion to expand the WPA, restart the PWA, and fund other agencies. The increase in federal spending reduced some unemployment and prevented the recession from worsening. The strain of the lengthy economic problem was beginning to show, however.

During the 1938 congressional elections, President Roosevelt opposed conservative Democrats in Congress who did not support the Second New Deal. His actions divided the party. All but one of the members of Congress Roosevelt opposed were re-elected. Several other Democratic critics of the New Deal were also elected. Republicans gained seven seats in the Senate and 75 in the House. Faced with increasing criticism, Roosevelt did not propose any new reforms in 1939. However, his leadership and popularity had already permanently shifted the balance of power in the federal government from the legislative branch to the executive branch.

✔ **READING CHECK: Summarizing** What caused Roosevelt's recession? Roosevelt cut back on New Deal relief and public-works programs.

During the depression many farms, like this one in Connecticut, were sold at auctions.

- Social Security Act, p. 477
- Wagner-Connery Act, p. 480
- Congress of Industrial Organizations, p. 480

3. critics—argued that more government programs were needed to eliminate unemployment and stimulate the economy; Roosevelt's response—initiated more public-works and employment programs, signed the Social Security Act, regulated utility companies, and imposed more taxes upon the wealthy; effect—African Americans in the North, farmers, and workers voted for him.

4a. Conservatives thought that the New Deal intervened too much in business; liberals believed that more government intervention was necessary.

b. Answers will vary. Members of Congress and other critics felt that Roosevelt was trying to shift the balance of power to the executive branch.

c. It allowed unions to strike for better wages and working conditions. They kept food prices high and provided low-interest loans to tenant farmers and sharecroppers.

5. Answers will vary. Students might answer that although both New Deals had similar programs, the Second New Deal's programs were more acceptable to the Supreme Court and more successful initially. The Roosevelt recession showed that these programs were necessary.

SECTION 2 REVIEW

1. Define and explain:
   sit-down strike

2. Identify and explain:
   Francis E. Townsend
   Charles E. Coughlin
   Huey Long
   Share-Our-Wealth
   Works Progress Administration
   National Youth Administration
   Mary McLeod Bethune
   Social Security Act
   Wagner-Connery Act
   Congress of Industrial
      Organizations

3. Identifying Cause and Effect Copy the graphic organizer below. Use it to explain how President Roosevelt won re-election in 1936.

Critics of Roosevelt

↓

Roosevelt's Response

↓

Effect on 1936 Election

4. Finding the Main Idea

a. How did criticisms of the New Deal reveal the different views that various leaders held about government?

b. What impact did President Roosevelt's efforts to add up to six new members to the Supreme Court have on the relationships between the three branches of government?

c. How did the Wagner-Connery Act benefit labor? How did other Second New Deal programs benefit agriculture?

5. Writing and Critical Thinking

Contrasting Write a brief essay explaining how the Second New Deal differed from the first New Deal.
Consider:
- the major programs of the first New Deal
- the major programs of the Second New Deal
- the effect of the Roosevelt recession

go. Homework Practice Online
keyword: SE3 HP16

🎵 *LET'S GET STARTED!*

As students enter the classroom, play Selection 21, "Talkin' Dust Bowl," from the **American Music Audio CD Program**. Have students respond to the song in writing. Ask volunteers to share their responses. Tell students that in Section 3 they will learn how the Dust Bowl affected Americans who lived on the Great Plains.

SECTION ③ RESOURCES

REPRODUCIBLE
▶ Guided Reading Strategy 16.3
▶ American History Outline Map 18: The Dust Bowl

TECHNOLOGY
▶ One-Stop Planner, Lesson 16.3
▶ American Music Selection 21: "Talkin' Dust Bowl"
▶ Holt Researcher: American History CD–ROM
▶ HRW Go site
▶ Homework Practice Online

REINFORCEMENT, REVIEW, AND ASSESSMENT
▶ Section 3 Review, p. 486
▶ Daily Quiz 16.3
▶ Main Idea Activity 16.3
▶ English Audio Summary 16.3
▶ Spanish Audio Summary 16.3

Technology Resources
 American Music Selection 21: "Talkin' Dust Bowl"

SECTION ③

READ TO DISCOVER
1. What were the effects of the Dust Bowl?
2. How did New Deal agencies use photography to promote their goals?
3. How effective was the New Deal in ending the Great Depression?

IDENTIFY
Dust Bowl
Roy E. Stryker
Walker Evans
Gordon Parks
Margaret Bourke-White
Dorothea Lange
Migrant Mother

WHY IT MATTERS TODAY
New Deal agencies and programs continue to affect the lives of Americans today Use CNNfyi.com or other **current events** sources to learn about how one such agency or program functions today. Record your findings in your journal.

Life in the New Deal Era

EYEWITNESSES TO History ❝*NO JOBS in California. IF YOU are looking for work— KEEP OUT!*❞
—Billboard message

This billboard message appeared on Route 66 just outside Tulsa, Oklahoma, toward the end of the 1930s. The message was clear. The job market for migrant workers on the West Coast was full. The sign was directed at the thousands of migrant farmers who traveled west to California in the mid-1930s. Driven off their land by the forces of nature, they sought a better life elsewhere.

This sign warned unemployed Americans to keep moving.

The Dust Bowl and Migration

The mass migration to California was spurred by a natural disaster. In the mid-1930s a severe drought struck the Great Plains. Winds picked up the topsoil that had loosened and dried, turning a 50-million-acre region into a wasteland.

The Dust Bowl. Throughout the **Dust Bowl**, as the affected region came to be called, clouds of dust darkened the skies at noon and buried fences and farm machinery. Dust crept into houses through tiny cracks. Ships reported great dust clouds hundreds of miles out to sea. One Texas farmer recalled the drought's effects.

History Makers Speak ❝If the wind blew one way, here came the dark dust from Oklahoma. Another way and it was the gray dust from Kansas. Still another way, the brown dust from Colorado and New Mexico. Little farms were buried. And the towns were blackened.❞
—Texas farmer, quoted in *This Fabulous Century,* edited by Maitland A. Edey

To prevent similar natural disasters from occurring in the future, the Department of Agriculture started extensive programs in soil-erosion control. The most dramatic was the planting of some 217 million trees by workers from the Civilian Conservation Corps (CCC). These trees created a windbreak that stretched through the Great Plains from Texas to Canada.

By 1939 the amount of dried-out farmland had decreased dramatically. However, many Dust Bowl farmers had already lost their land. They packed their few belongings into battered old cars or trucks and headed west on Route 66. These migrants saw California and other parts of the West Coast as a Promised Land where they could find work harvesting crops. Since many came from Oklahoma, they were nicknamed "Okies." Once they reached the West Coast they found themselves in fierce competition with other farm laborers looking for work.

LEVEL 1: Tell students that the Dust Bowl was the result of a severe drought that struck the Great Plains. Winds carried away the region's dry and loose topsoil. Pair students and ask each pair to create a cartoon depicting the effects of the Dust Bowl. *(Cartoons should show that many farmers lost their land, that Dust Bowl farmers migrated west to find work harvesting crops, and that migrants to the West Coast faced stiff competition for jobs.)* Ask volunteers to present their cartoons to the class.
English Language Learners, Cooperative Learning

LEVEL 2: Tell students to imagine that they left their homes during the Dust Bowl to migrate west to California. Ask each student to write a poem about the causes of the Dust Bowl and its effects on farmers' lives. *(See the Level 1 lesson for the correct causes and effects.)* Ask volunteers to recite their poems to the class.

LEVEL 3: Tell students to imagine that they have left their homes during the Dust Bowl and migrated west to California. Have each student write a series of short diary entries about the causes of the Dust Bowl and its effect on his or her life and the lives of other farmers. *(See the Level 1 lesson for the correct causes and effects.)* In their entries, students should reflect on the hardships that they have encountered. Ask volunteers to read their entries to the class.

AMERICAN ARTS

Woody Guthrie and American Folk Music

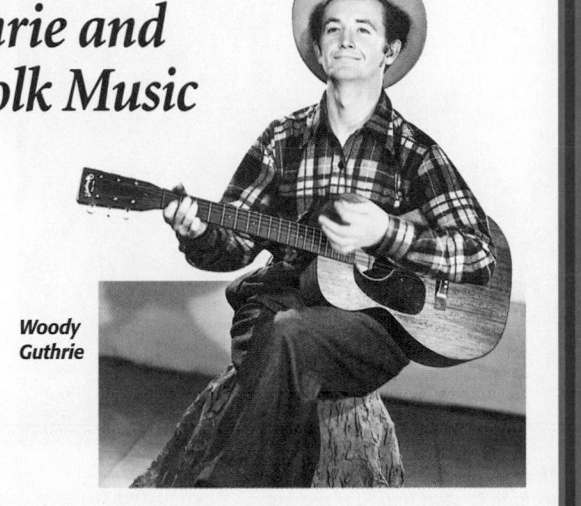

Woody Guthrie

A merican folk music experienced a revival during the 1930s. Perhaps the most popular folk-singer of the era was Woody Guthrie. Born in Oklahoma, Guthrie became one of many Americans displaced by the storms of the Dust Bowl. Although he had no formal training in music, he wrote dozens of songs that touched millions of listeners. "I don't know nothing about music. Never could read or write it," Guthrie admitted. Guthrie described the experiences of common people in his music, mostly through ballads. Among his numerous songs was the popular "Talking Dust Bowl."

> **"Back in nineteen twenty-seven
> I had a little farm and I called that heaven,
> Well, the price was up and the rain came down
> And I hauled my crops all in to town. . . .
> Rain quit and the wind got high,
> And a black old dust storm filled the sky,
> And I swapped my farm for a Ford machine
> And I poured it full of this gasoline. . . .
> We got out to the West Coast broke,
> So dad gum hungry I thought I'd croak,
> And I bummed up a spud or two,
> And my wife fixed up a 'tater stew."**
> *TRO—© 1960, 1963 by Ludlow Music, Inc.*

The federal government hired Guthrie to write songs that promoted projects designed to help rural Americans. While touring a federal dam project, he wrote 26 songs in just 26 days. Guthrie's lyrics praised the federal projects, but his songs reflected the sadness of the era. "It's always we ramble, that river and I," he wrote. "Along your green valley I'll work till I die."

Understanding the Arts

1. According to Guthrie's song, how did the Dust Bowl storms affect life in the United States?
2. Why might Guthrie's style of music have been popular?

Competition for migrant work. Even before the Dust Bowl refugees started arriving, Mexican Americans had a hard time finding work in the West. Like African Americans, Mexican Americans often found themselves the victims of discrimination in many New Deal programs.

Mexican Americans also faced increased job competition from Filipino laborers. During the 1920s California's Filipino population had grown to more than 30,000. Like Mexican American migrants, most Filipinos worked in agriculture. When the depression hit, both groups faced tough economic times. Filipino workers fought declining wages by organizing. Throughout the early 1930s the Filipino Labor Union launched a series of strikes to protest wage reductions. In 1936 the American Federation of Labor sponsored the Field Workers Union. The union was a combined organization for Mexican American and Filipino laborers.

📡 **internet** connect

TOPIC: The Dust Bowl
GO TO: go.hrw.com
KEYWORD: SE3 AN16

Have students access the Internet through the HRW Go site to conduct research on the causes of the Dust Bowl. Ask each student to create a newspaper summarizing the environmental and economic conditions that forced thousands of people to leave their homes and migrate westward.

THAT'S INTERESTING!

The state of California enacted a law making it illegal to bring anyone who was unemployed into the state. One California resident, Fred F. Edwards, was convicted under this law for bringing his unemployed brother-in-law from Texas into the state. The U.S. Supreme Court eventually heard Edwards's case and ruled that California's law was unconstitutional.

AMERICAN ARTS ANSWERS

1. Life was like heaven before the storms. After the storms, people were broke and hungry.

2. Guthrie's songs were simple and focused on problems that were common to millions of people affected by the depression and the Dust Bowl.

TEACH OBJECTIVE 2

LEVEL 1: Ask students why photographs might be a powerful way to convey ideas. (*Students might suggest that photographs provide an objective record of an event or that images of people carry an emotional weight that verbal descriptions might lack.*) Pair students and ask each pair to compile a list of ways that New Deal agencies used photography to promote their goals. (*Lists should mention that New Deal agencies hoped that opponents of relief programs would change their minds if they saw photographs of suffering Americans, that agencies used photographs in government pamphlets, and that photos were published in magazines to publicize the work of federal agencies.*) Ask volunteers to present their lists to the class.
English Language Learners, Cooperative Learning

LEVELS 2 AND 3: Tell students to imagine that they are advisers to President Roosevelt. Ask each student to write a memo persuading FDR to approve the use of photography to promote the New Deal. In their memos, students should suggest how New Deal agencies might use photography. (*See the Level 1 lesson for the correct uses.*) Ask volunteers to read their memos to the class.

NOTE: To help students make meaningful connections between events in U.S. history and those in their own hometown, use the Chapter 16 **Hands-On History Activity**, A Project for Your Town.

HISTORY MAKERS SPEAK

James Agee in *Let Us Now Praise Famous Men*

Sharecropping in Alabama.
In 1936 journalist James Agee and photographer Walker Evans spent eight weeks with three families who were sharecroppers in rural Alabama. Agee and Evans produced a book-length record of their experiences, *Let Us Now Praise Famous Men.* Most of these impoverished farmers received little help from New Deal programs. Agee wrote, "WPA work is available to very few tenants: they are, technically, employed, and thus have no right to it: and if by chance they manage to get it, landlords are more likely than not to intervene. They feel it spoils a tenant to be paid wages, even for a little while. A tenant who so much as tries to get such work is under disapproval."

CRITICAL THINKING Why might owners feel that tenants would be spoiled by wages?

ANSWER: Students might suggest that landlords feared that tenants might abandon sharecropping in favor of wage labor, which would provide a guaranteed income.

These migrant workers are waiting to start their day picking carrots in Santa Maria, Texas.

Research on the R⊙M

Free Find: Dorothea Lange
After reading about Dorothea Lange on the **Holt Researcher CD–ROM,** imagine that you are a photographer. Choose a topic for a photographic project and decide what photographs you would take. Write captions that explain the photographs.

The unions were able to slow the fall of wages. Yet, with the arrival of additional migrants from the Dust Bowl, competition for jobs increased. Thus, life for all migrants remained difficult.

✔ **READING CHECK: Analyzing Information** How did environmental changes in the Great Plains lead to changes in migration? A severe drought turned the area into a wasteland, which forced more people to migrate west.

Picturing Life in the Depression

The grim experiences of migrants and others in rural areas provided powerful subject matter for documentary filmmakers and photographers. These artists created a memorable record of the New Deal Era. Their images of the slumped shoulders of unemployed men, the staring faces of hungry children, and the worried expressions of exhausted women convey the human suffering of the era.

Most of these photographers were hired by the federal government. President Roosevelt believed that opponents of federal relief programs might change their minds if they could see the frightful living conditions of city-dwellers and migrant farmworkers. With Roosevelt's encouragement, numerous federal agencies and departments—including the Department of the Interior, the Works Progress Administration (WPA), the Department of Agriculture, and the Farm Security Administration (FSA)—hired photographers to travel across the country and document the lives of ordinary Americans.

No agency used photography more effectively than the FSA, whose staff gathered more than 250,000 images of American life during the depression. **Roy E. Stryker**, head of the FSA historical section, assembled a team of renowned photographers that included **Walker Evans**, who depicted life among sharecroppers in rural Alabama. Other photographers included African American **Gordon Parks**, who later became a filmmaker; international photojournalist **Margaret Bourke-White**; and **Dorothea Lange**, probably the best known of the FSA photographers.

BIOGRAPHY

Dorothea Lange

THE GRANGER COLLECTION, NEW YORK

Dorothea Lange was one of the most talented photographers of the depression era. Born in 1895 in Hoboken, New Jersey, she decided in her late teens to become a photographer. After studying the craft for several years, she set out to tour the world and record her impressions. Lange was out of money by the time she reached San Francisco. She stayed there and opened a portrait studio.

When the depression struck, Lange began taking pictures of the homeless men wandering the streets of San Francisco. Soon the federal government hired her to photograph migrant farmworkers in California. Lange often traveled for weeks at a time, working up to 14 hours a day. Her photographs reveal the migrants' poverty and suffering as well as their great dignity. Lange's most famous photograph, *Migrant Mother,* is considered a masterpiece. It shows an exhausted single mother whose children

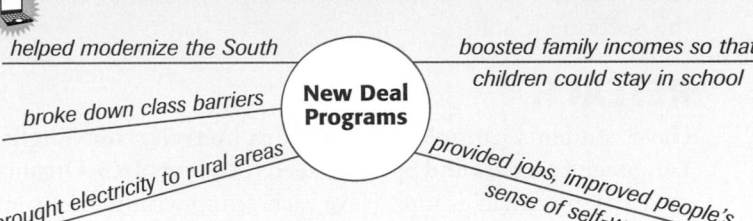

helped modernize the South   *boosted family incomes so that children could stay in school*

New Deal Programs

broke down class barriers

brought electricity to rural areas   *provided jobs, improved people's sense of self-worth*

survived by eating vegetables they scavenged from California fields. When it appeared in 1936, *Migrant Mother* inspired Californians to defy the state's powerful growers' associations and insist on decent, government-sponsored housing for seasonal harvesters.

During World War II, Lange continued her documentary work by taking photographs of the many Japanese Americans in California relocation camps. She later produced photo essays for *Life* magazine and traveled the world taking pictures. By the time of her death in 1965, Lange ranked as one of the world's foremost photographers.

Other FSA photographs helped achieve Roosevelt's goal of gaining support for government programs. From 1936 to 1941, FSA photographs were widely published in government pamphlets and in *Time, Life,* and other magazines. The photographs strengthened congressional and public support for federal relief.

✔ **READING CHECK: Summarizing** How did FSA photographers document the New Deal Era? FSA photographs conveyed the human suffering of the era and were published in pamphlets and magazines.

Evaluating the New Deal

By the late 1930s few American families were untouched by New Deal reforms. By supplying jobs, the New Deal programs improved many Americans' sense of self-worth. Government administrator Louise Armstrong recalled that most people preferred jobs to handouts. "I don't want charity," one person told her. "I want work—any kind of work."

Programs sponsored by the National Youth Administration (NYA) helped boost family incomes so that children could stay in school. Helen Farmer recalled working in an NYA program as a teenager.

History Makers Speak

"I lugged . . . drafts and reams of paper home, night after night. . . . Sometimes I typed all night. . . . This was a good program. It got necessary work done. It gave teenagers a chance to work for pay. . . . It gave my mother relief from my necessary demands for money.**"**

—Helen Farmer, quoted in *The Great Depression,* by T. H. Watkins

Critics charged that the New Deal created a welfare state—a system of government institutions that provides for the basic needs of citizens. These needs might include health care and unemployment benefits. Critics also argued that the New Deal promoted deficit spending—having the government spend more money than it receives in revenue. The New Deal Era represented the first time during a period of peace that the federal government had spent more than it brought in as revenue. Other critics argued that the federal government—the president, in particular—had become too involved in the economy, which threatened the free enterprise system.

INTERPRETING THE VISUAL RECORD

Migrant Mother. Photographs like this one by Dorothea Lange capture the suffering of rural Americans. *What emotions do you think this picture captures?*

Unemployment in the United States, 1925–1939

Source: *Historical Statistics of the United States*

Interpreting Graphs In the mid-1930s unemployment rose to its highest rate in U.S. history.

❓ Skills Assessment By how much did the unemployment rate change between 1925 and 1939?

THAT'S INTERESTING!

During the Great Depression, thousands of people wrote to Eleanor Roosevelt, telling her of their hardships and suggesting ways that she or the president could help. One pregnant housewife in Troy, New York, begged Mrs. Roosevelt for a small loan: "*Please* Mrs. Roosevelt, I do not want charity, only a chance from someone who will trust me until we can get enough to repay the amount spent for the things I need. As a proof that I am really sincere, I am sending you two of my dearest possessions to keep as security, a ring my husband gave me before we were married, and a ring my mother used to wear."

VISUAL RECORD ANSWER

Answers will vary. Students might suggest despair and apprehension.

REVIEW

Have students complete the **Section 3 Review** on p. 486.

ASSESS

Have students complete **Daily Quiz 16.3**. As **Alternative Assessment**, you may want to use the poem or the cartoon in this section's lessons.

RETEACH

Have students complete **Main Idea Activity for English Language Learners and Special-Needs Students 16.3**. Organize students into small groups. Have each group write a brief summary of the section incorporating all the key terms and key people listed at the beginning of the section. Have volunteers read their summaries to the class. Ask the class to supply any important information or themes that might be missing from each summary.
English Language Learners, Cooperative Learning

EXTEND

Ask students to conduct research on one of the Farm Security Administration photographers mentioned in the section. Tell each student to write a short biographical capsule for his or her subject, compile examples of the photographer's most famous or compelling images, and explain each image's significance. Have each student present his or her findings to the class in an oral presentation. **Block Scheduling**

SECTION 3 REVIEW ANSWERS

1. Identify
- Dust Bowl, p. 482
- Roy E. Stryker, p. 484
- Walker Evans, p. 484
- Gordon Parks, p. 484
- Margaret Bourke-White, p. 484
- Dorothea Lange, p. 484
- *Migrant Mother*, p. 484

2. causes—drought in the Great Plains made it impossible to grow crops; migration—farmers moved to the Southwest hoping to find work; effects—so many people looked for work in the Southwest that there was fierce competition among farmworkers, and many owners lowered wages

3a. They pictured people who were trying to survive the depression with dignity. The photographs persuaded people to take action to help end hunger and suffering.

b. Critics said the New Deal created a welfare state, but supporters argued that the programs were necessary to help Americans survive the Depression.

c. The programs provided money and food but also allowed people to work for these benefits, thus giving the recipients a sense of meaning and accomplishment.

4. Answers will vary. Students might suggest the woman is exhausted and hungry like most California farmworkers, and that others like her have nothing to lose by standing up for their rights.

INTERPRETING THE VISUAL RECORD

Jobs. With the economy struggling, the government stepped in to help Americans find work.
What types of jobs do you think this poster was advertising?

New Deal supporters argued that the federal government's expanded role was necessary. Home loans, farm subsidies, bank deposit insurance, relief payment and jobs, pension programs, and unemployment insurance helped Americans survive the Great Depression. The New Deal also established minimum standards for working conditions and the protection of workers' rights.

Most historians argue that the New Deal was not completely effective in its attempt to end the Great Depression. It did relieve the suffering of many Americans by providing direct relief and jobs. However, the economy did not fully recover until the United States began its preparations for World War II. Nonetheless, the New Deal has had lasting results, creating programs and agencies that still exist today. The Federal Deposit Insurance Corporation has increased the protection it offers to depositors. The Securities and Exchange Commission continues to regulate companies that sell stocks or bonds. The Social Security Act, which originally did not cover farmworkers or domestic workers, has been expanded to include 95 percent of the nation's workers.

Few New Deal programs had a greater long-term effect on people's lives than the efforts made to provide electricity to rural areas. Millions of American homes did not have electricity or indoor plumbing in the early 1930s. In 1935 only about 11 percent of American farms had electricity. By 1950 nearly 90 percent did. Improvements in electricity and plumbing made life easier and greatly improved people's health by providing better sanitation and safer water supplies. The availability of electricity and other government services also brought modern practices and industry to many parts of the country. During the New Deal Era the South finally began to diversify its economy and rely less on traditional cash crops like cotton. One southern historian has said, "Electrification must be considered one of the most significant stimulants for modernization of the rural South."

✔ **READING CHECK: Categorizing** In what ways did the New Deal improve the daily lives of Americans? It improved people's self-esteem; boosted family incomes; and improved people's health through better sanitation and water supplies.

SECTION 3 REVIEW

1. Identify and explain:
Dust Bowl
Roy E. Stryker
Walker Evans
Gordon Parks
Margaret Bourke-White
Dorothea Lange
Migrant Mother

2. Identifying Cause and Effect
Copy the graphic organizer below. Use it to explain why farmers migrated from the Dust Bowl region and what effects this migration had.

Causes of Migration → Migration → Effects of Migration

3. **Finding the Main Idea**
a. How were photographs used to build support for the New Deal?
b. How did critics and supporters evaluate the New Deal?
c. How did New Deal programs address both physical and psychological needs of Americans?

4. **Writing and Critical Thinking**
Supporting a Point of View Imagine that you are the subject of *Migrant Mother*. Write a diary entry describing how the photograph inspired protests against large agricultural growers in California.
Consider:
- the subject of the photograph
- the experiences of migrants in California
- how Californians might have felt upon seeing the image

go.hrw.com **Homework Practice Online**
keyword: SE3 HP16

SECTION 4

After completing Section 4, students should be able to:

OBJECTIVE 1 Explain how Federal Project Number One aided writers and artists.

OBJECTIVE 2 Identify the common themes that emerged in the novels, films, and plays of the New Deal Era.

OBJECTIVE 3 Describe how music evolved in the 1930s.

OBJECTIVE 4 Discuss the subject matter that influenced American painters in the 1930s.

LET'S GET STARTED!

Write the following statement on the chalkboard: *The federal government has a responsibility to support the arts and artists.* As students enter the classroom, ask them to respond to the statement in writing and to include specific reasons why government support for the arts is or is not vital to the cultural life of the United States. Have volunteers share their responses. Tell students that in Section 4 they will learn about the arts in the United States during the New Deal Era.

SECTION 4

READ TO DISCOVER

1. How did Federal Project Number One aid writers and artists?
2. What common themes emerged in the novels, films, and plays of the New Deal Era?
3. How did music evolve in the 1930s?
4. What subject matter influenced American painters in the 1930s?

DEFINE

regionalists

IDENTIFY

Federal Project Number One
John Steinbeck
The Grapes of Wrath
Zora Neale Hurston
Richard Wright
Gone With the Wind
Frank Capra
Aaron Copland
Thomas A. Dorsey
Mahalia Jackson
Benny Goodman
Jacob Lawrence
Georgia O'Keeffe
American Gothic
Anna "Grandma" Moses

▶ WHY IT MATTERS TODAY

The U.S. government has long regulated and supported communications media such as television and radio. Use **CNNfyi.com** or other **current events** sources to learn about the relationship between communications media and the federal government today. Record your findings in your journal.

CNNfyi.com

The New Deal and the Arts

EYEWITNESSES TO History

"*Two years ago I was living in comfort and apparent security. My husband had a good position in a well-known orchestra, and I was teaching a large and promising class of piano students. When the orchestra disbanded we started on a rapid downhill path. My husband was unable to secure another position. My class gradually dwindled away.*"

—Ann Rivington, quoted in "We Lived on Relief," *Scribner's Magazine*, 1934

Poster announcing a concert sponsored by the Federal Music Project

Ann Rivington and her husband were among many people trained in the arts who found no job opportunities during the depression. In its attempts to put Americans back to work, the Roosevelt administration did not forget about those who were skilled in the arts.

WPA Programs

All American workers, including artists, struggled with unemployment during the depression. Referring to unemployed artists, Harry Hopkins declared, "They've got to eat just like other people." The Roosevelt administration soon launched a new program to aid writers, musicians, actors, and other artists. In 1935 the Works Progress Administration (WPA) set aside $300 million to create **Federal Project Number One**. This program sought to encourage pride in American culture by providing work to artists in the fields of writing, theater, music, and visual arts.

The WPA's Federal Writers' Project (FWP) hired some 6,600 unemployed writers to produce a variety of works. The works included state travel guides and histories of various ethnic groups. Writers also conducted oral history interviews with hundreds of elderly former slaves. Project members also studied American folklore and wrote down folktales. These eventually became the basis for the best-selling *Treasury of American Folklore* (1944), one of the more than 1,000 books and pamphlets published by the FWP.

The WPA's Federal Theater Project hired unemployed actors, directors, designers, stagehands, and playwrights to encourage theatrical productions. The project entertained millions of Americans and brought productions to many small towns that had never experienced live theater. The Federal Music Project hired musicians to form orchestras and present some 4,000 musical productions each month to audiences nationwide. The Federal Arts Project hired unemployed artists and designers to produce posters for New Deal programs, teach art in public schools, and paint murals on public buildings.

✔ **READING CHECK: Finding the Main Idea** What was the purpose of Federal Project Number One? It sought to provide artists with jobs.

SECTION 4 RESOURCES

REPRODUCIBLE
▶ Guided Reading Strategy 16.4
▶ Graphic Organizer Activity 16: Social Change in the 1930s
▶ Literature Reading 16: Thoughts of a Young African American

TECHNOLOGY
▶ One-Stop Planner, Lesson 16.4
▶ Holt Researcher: American History CD–ROM
▶ Homework Practice Online

REINFORCEMENT, REVIEW, AND ASSESSMENT
▶ Section 4 Review, p. 491
▶ Daily Quiz 16.4
▶ Main Idea Activity 16.4
▶ English Audio Summary 16.4
▶ Spanish Audio Summary 16.4

ALL LEVELS: Tell students to imagine that they are artists hired through Federal Project Number One to publicize its activities. Pair students and have each pair create a pamphlet explaining how the Project helps unemployed writers and artists. *(Pamphlets should mention that the Federal Writers' Project hired writers to produce a variety of works, that the Federal Theater Project hired theater artists to produce plays, that the Federal Music Project hired musicians to present musical productions, and that the Federal Arts Project hired artists and designers to paint murals, produce posters, and teach art.)* **English Language Learners, Cooperative Learning**

Teacher to Teacher

Doug Odom of El Dorado, Kansas, suggested the following activity: Organize the class into two groups. Have one group prepare arguments supporting Federal Project Number One and have the other group prepare arguments opposing Federal Project Number One. When students have finished preparing, conduct a debate.

VISUAL RECORD ANSWER

Students might suggest that the extravagance of the dance number contrasted with the poverty and worries of the audience.

AMERICAN LETTERS ANSWERS
(for p. 489)

1. Both convey a mood of impatience. The people in their works are waiting for something to change their desperate situations.

2. Steinbeck uses images like streams and ants to demonstrate the people's ongoing search for food and work. Hurston compares her character Janie to a tree that is struggling to burst into bloom.

3. Both writers reveal both physical and emotional desperation.

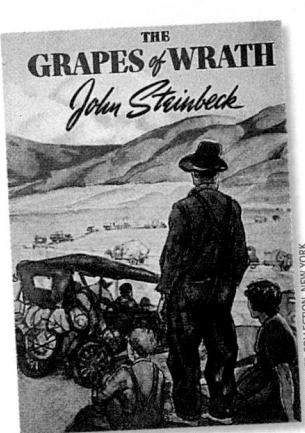

John Steinbeck's The Grapes of Wrath is a gritty tale of life in the United States during the Great Depression.

Portraying the Depression

The Federal Writers' Project helped launch the careers of numerous successful writers. Many of these writers incorporated themes of the depression into their works.

Novels. John Steinbeck produced a gripping picture of the depression years in *The Grapes of Wrath* (1939). The story follows the fortunes of a poor family as they travel from the Dust Bowl region to California.

Other novels described the depression-era experiences of ethnic minorities. **Zora Neale Hurston** wrote *Their Eyes Were Watching God* (1937). Her novel explores a black woman's search for fulfillment in rural Florida. **Richard Wright** offered a grim picture of black urban life in *Native Son* (1940). His work chronicles the journey of a young African American man lost in a racist world.

One of the best-selling novels of the decade was Margaret Mitchell's *Gone With the Wind* (1936), a sweeping story of the Old South set during the Civil War and Reconstruction. Many depression-era readers could relate to the turmoil faced by the novel's main character, Scarlett O'Hara, who survives war and economic chaos.

Films. Margaret Mitchell's book became the basis of the most popular film of the 1930s. To lift people's spirits, the major studios offered a number of "escapist" films to help viewers forget their troubles. These included the Marx Brothers' comedy *Duck Soup* (1933) and Ginger Rogers's upbeat musical *Gold-Diggers of 1933*. This musical contained "We're in the Money," one of the most optimistic tunes of the decade.

Soon some filmmakers began to tackle social issues. Director **Frank Capra** celebrated simple values and criticized the wealthy and politicians in films like *Mr. Deeds Goes to Town* (1936) and *Mr. Smith Goes to Washington* (1939). Jefferson Smith, appointed to fill a vacant U.S. Senate seat, comments on the corruption he finds in Washington, D.C.

 Primary Source

❝There's no place out there for graft, or greed, or lies, or compromise within human liberties.... Great principles don't get lost once they come to light. They're right here; you just have to see them again!❞

—*Jefferson Smith, Mr. Smith Goes to Washington*

INTERPRETING THE VISUAL RECORD

Film. Films such as the musical *Gold-Diggers of 1933* offered Americans optimism during the depression. *How do you think this dance number contrasted with the lives of the audience?*

By the late 1930s the major studios had recovered sufficiently from the depression to launch several big-budget spectacles. Two such films, the color epic *Gone With the Wind* and the special-effects fantasy *The Wizard of Oz*, were both released in 1939.

Theater. Some films of the 1930s were based on popular plays. On the theatrical stage, plays that dealt with the nation's labor and class struggles drew large audiences. Robert Sherwood's *The Petrified Forest* (1935) attacked the "petrified forest" of ideas destroying the country. Lillian Hellman's *The Little Foxes* (1939) attacked upper-class greed. By the end of the decade, popular plays, like popular films, focused increasingly on traditional American values. Two examples are Thornton Wilder's *Our Town* (1938) and William Saroyan's *The Time of Your Life* (1939).

✔ **READING CHECK: Making Generalizations** How were the issues of the New Deal Era reflected in novels, films, and plays of the 1930s? Novels focused on westward migration and racism; films and plays attacked upper-class greed and focused on American values.

ALL LEVELS: Ask students to identify common themes in present-day books, films, and music. *(Students might suggest teenagers' anxieties about growing up, conspiracy theories, theories of impending disease epidemics, and so on.)* Lead a class discussion about events or situations that might be generating the concerns they have identified. Tell students that common themes appeared in the films, novels, and plays of the New Deal Era. To help students understand these themes, copy the chart at right on the chalkboard, omitting the italicized answers. Have each student complete the organizer. Ask volunteers to share their answers with the class.

English Language Learners

COMMON THEMES OF NEW DEAL ERA NOVELS, FILMS, AND PLAYS

Novels	*themes of the depression, depression-era experiences of ethnic minorities, economic chaos*
Films	*"escapist" themes, exploration of social issues*
Plays	*labor and class struggles, upper-class greed, traditional American values*

HOMEWORK *Distribute Literature Reading 16, Thoughts of a Young African American, from* **Literature, Primary Source, and Biography Readings,** *and have each student complete it.*

AMERICAN Letters

Literature of the Great Depression

The late 1930s gave rise to a new era of realism in American literature as authors wrote stories that captured the struggles and mood of the country during the Great Depression. In The Grapes of Wrath, *John Steinbeck portrays the saga of migrants from the Dust Bowl who travel to California in search of work. In* Their Eyes Were Watching God, *Zora Neale Hurston presents the story of Janie, an African American woman struggling to find meaning and happiness.*

from *The Grapes of Wrath*
by John Steinbeck

John Steinbeck

Those families who had lived on a little piece of land, who had lived and died on forty acres, had eaten or starved on the produce of forty acres, had now the whole West to rove in. And they scampered about, looking for work; and the highways were streams of people, and the ditch banks were lines of people. . . . The great highways streamed with moving people. . . .

And this was good, for wages went down and prices stayed up. The great owners were glad. . . . And wages went down and prices stayed up. And pretty soon now we'll have serfs again. . . .

And the little farmers . . . lost their farms, and they were taken by the great owners, the banks, and the companies. . . . As time went on, there were fewer farms. The little farmers moved into town for a while and exhausted their credit, exhausted their friends, their relatives. And then they too were on the highways. And the roads were crowded with men ravenous for work, murderous for work.

And the companies, the banks worked at their own doom and they did not know it. The fields were fruitful, and starving men moved on the roads. . . .

The great companies did not know that the line between hunger and anger is a thin line. . . . On the highways the people moved like ants and searched for work, for food. And the anger began to ferment.

from *Their Eyes Were Watching God*
by Zora Neale Hurston

Janie saw her life like a great tree in leaf with the things suffered, things enjoyed, things done and undone. Dawn and doom was in the branches. . . .

Zora Neale Hurston

After awhile she got up from where she was and went over the little garden field entire. She was seeking confirmation of the voice and vision, and everywhere she found and acknowledged answers. . . . Oh to be a pear tree—*any* tree in bloom! With kissing bees singing of the beginning of the world! She was sixteen. She had glossy leaves and bursting buds and she wanted to struggle with life but it seemed to elude her. . . . She searched as much of the world as she could from the top of the front steps and then went on down to the front gate and leaned over to gaze up and down the road. Looking, waiting, breathing short with impatience. Waiting for the world to be made.

UNDERSTANDING LITERATURE

1. What mood do both Steinbeck and Hurston convey?
2. How do both writers use images from nature to describe their characters' feelings?
3. What do both writers reveal about the issues of the depression years?

SKILL-BUILDING STRATEGIES ANSWERS
(for p. 490)

Practicing the Skill

1. rural America

2. the setting, the subjects' occupation, emotions, and outlook

3. Wood was trying to convey the austere character of rural life in the 1930s. The title attempts to establish a link between Gothic architecture, which was monumental, and rural America.

4. The painting captures despair and uncertainty.

SECTION
REVIEW 4 ANSWERS

1. Define
• regionalists, p. 491

2. Identify
• Federal Project Number One, p. 487
• John Steinbeck, p. 488
• *The Grapes of Wrath,* p. 488
• Zora Neale Hurston, p. 488
• Richard Wright, p. 488
• *Gone With the Wind,* p. 488
• Frank Capra, p. 488
• Aaron Copland, p. 490
• Thomas A. Dorsey, p. 490
• Mahalia Jackson, p. 490
• Benny Goodman, p. 491
• Jacob Lawrence, p. 491

ALL LEVELS: Tell students to imagine that they are music editors working for a record company that is about to release a compilation of 1930s music. Have each student write liner notes for this release to discuss the evolution of musical forms in the 1930s. (*Liner notes should mention the use of folk songs and folktales, the popularization of country music, gospel music, jazz, and swing.*) Ask volunteers to read their liner notes to the class. **English Language Learners**

ALL LEVELS: Pair students and have each pair create a chart identifying painters of the New Deal Era and the subject matter that influenced them. (*Charts should mention Jacob Lawrence, who portrayed the daily lives of African American heroes; Georgia O'Keeffe, who was influenced by the southwestern landscape; the regionalists, including Thomas Hart Benton, John Steuart Curry, and Grant Wood, who were influenced by the rural United States; and Grandma Moses, a folk artist.*) Ask volunteers to present their charts to the class. Then tell each student to use his or her chart to write a paragraph about New Deal–era painters and the subject matter that influenced them. **English Language Learners, Cooperative Learning**

- Georgia O'Keeffe, p. 491
- *American Gothic*, p. 491
- Anna "Grandma" Moses, p. 491

3. writers—wrote travel guides and ethnic histories, conducted oral history interviews, collected folktales; theater workers—produced entertainment; musicians—formed orchestras and performed; visual artists—produced posters, taught art, and painted murals

4a. It incorporated American traditions and sounds; gospel also became popular.

b. *The Grapes of Wrath* focuses on a poor family's move west, and O'Keeffe's paintings show the natural difficulty of the rural landscape.

c. The Federal Writers' Project launched careers of artists that people read and study today. Also, the National Endowment for the Arts has roots in the New Deal.

5. Answers will vary, but students might mention that the project provided jobs, encouraged the production of art, and provided entertainment. Without the project, the New Deal Era would not have produced or encouraged art, and many artists would never have started their careers.

Skill-Building Strategies

Evaluating Art As Historical Evidence

Like photographs and artifacts, visual art can help one understand the past in a number of unique ways. Drawings, engravings, paintings, and sculptures can provide valuable clues about a given historical period. Because visual art often reflects the views of individuals who created it, it is important to interpret it carefully.

How to Evaluate Art As Historical Evidence

1. **Identify the subject.** Look at the work of art as a whole and identify its basic subject. If the work has a title, examine it for clues about the artist's intentions.
2. **Study the details.** Examine the details in the work for information about its subject and the historical context.
3. **Determine the artist's point of view.** Make sure to note if the subject of the work is depicted in a favorable or unfavorable manner. If possible, find out when the work was created and what may have helped to shape the artist's point of view.
4. **Put the information to use.** Compare the results of your analysis with information about the historical period that you have gained through other sources. Then determine how the work contributes to your understanding of the historical period.

Applying the Skill

Study the reproduction of Grant Wood's painting *American Gothic* to the right.

Practicing the Skill

After looking at the reproduction of the painting, answer the following questions.

1. What is the subject of this painting?
2. What information is provided by the details in the painting?
3. What message do you think Grant Wood was trying to convey in the painting? Why do you think he titled the painting *American Gothic*?
4. How does this painting transcend American culture and portray universal themes?

Grant Wood's American Gothic

Music in the New Deal Era

Popular music in the late 1930s incorporated American traditions and sounds. Some WPA researchers collected folk songs and folktales. Composer **Aaron Copland** used these as the basis for his most popular compositions, including his 1938 piece, *Billy the Kid*. Country music drew from southern folk music traditions to gain a national audience. Broadcast live from Nashville, Tennessee, the *Grand Ole Opry* radio show popularized country music.

Gospel music, a cross between traditional spirituals and jazz, also became popular. African American composer **Thomas A. Dorsey** wrote songs such as "Precious Lord, Take My Hand." Sister Rosetta Tharpe and **Mahalia Jackson** were popular gospel singers. Jackson later recalled that some ministers objected to this new style.

Analyzing Primary Sources

Identifying Bias Why might some preachers have objected to gospel music? Preachers who objected to gospel music might not have liked the behavior it inspired.

History Makers Speak

❝They didn't like the hand-clapping and the stomping and they said we were bringing jazz into the church and it wasn't dignified. Once at church one of the preachers got up in the pulpit and spoke out against me. I got right up, too. I told him I was born to sing gospel music.❞

—Mahalia Jackson, *Movin' on Up*

REVIEW

Have students complete the **Section 4 Review** on p. 491.

ASSESS

Have students complete **Daily Quiz 16.4**. As **Alternative Assessment**, you may want to use the dialogue or the liner notes in this section's lessons.

RETEACH

Have students complete **Main Idea Activity for English Language Learners and Special-Needs Students 16.4**. Organize the class into small groups. Have each group write two or three sentences about each of 10 Define/Identify terms in the section.

Collect groups' sentences and use them to conduct a quiz bowl in which each group will work as a team to answer the questions.
English Language Learners, Cooperative Learning

EXTEND

Organize the class into small groups and assign each group one of the following subjects: Frank Capra, Aaron Copland, Benny Goodman, Lillian Hellman, Zora Neale Hurston, Mahalia Jackson, Jacob Lawrence, Grandma Moses, Thornton Wilder, or Richard Wright. Have each group develop a multimedia presentation about its assigned subject, complete with musical or visual examples to illustrate its subject's work. Have each group give its multimedia presentation to the class.
Block Scheduling, Cooperative Learning

Jazz continued to rise in popularity, largely through swing, a smooth big-band style popular in dance halls. Swing received its name from Duke Ellington's 1932 hit "It Don't Mean a Thing If It Ain't Got That Swing." White conductor **Benny Goodman** helped popularize swing with his integrated band.

Painters Examine Local Culture

American depression-era painters captured a variety of images in their work. Harlem artist **Jacob Lawrence** portrayed the daily lives of African American heroes, such as Frederick Douglass and Harriet Tubman. New Mexico artist **Georgia O'Keeffe** painted haunting images of the southwestern desert landscape.

Many artists looked to rural America for their subject matter. A group of midwestern artists known as the **regionalists** stressed local folk themes and customs. The regionalists included Thomas Hart Benton of Missouri, John Steuart Curry of Kansas, and Grant Wood of Iowa. They reminded urban art lovers of America's rural traditions. Wood claimed that his best ideas "came while milking a cow." The most famous of the regionalist paintings is probably Wood's *American Gothic*.

As interest in regional culture grew, people began to rediscover American folk art, such as handmade quilts and woodcarvings. Some folk artists, including the elderly painter **Anna "Grandma" Moses**, became well known during this period.

THE METROPOLITAN MUSEUM OF ART

Georgia O'Keeffe's **Cow's Skull: Red, White, and Blue**

✔ **READING CHECK: Drawing Conclusions** How did music and painting styles change during the Great Depression? Both turned to American and rural traditions.

SECTION 4 REVIEW

1. **Define and explain:**
   regionalists

2. **Identify and explain:**
   Federal Project Number One
   John Steinbeck
   The Grapes of Wrath
   Zora Neale Hurston
   Richard Wright
   Gone With the Wind
   Frank Capra
   Aaron Copland
   Thomas A. Dorsey
   Mahalia Jackson
   Benny Goodman
   Jacob Lawrence
   Georgia O'Keeffe
   American Gothic
   Anna "Grandma" Moses

3. **Categorizing** Copy the chart below. Use it to describe the various ways that Federal Project Number One provided work for writers, theater workers, musicians, and visual artists.

	Federal Project Number One
Writers	
Theater Workers	
Musicians	
Visual Artists	

4. **Finding the Main Idea**
   a. How did music change in the 1930s?
   b. How did the works of artists such as John Steinbeck and Georgia O'Keeffe reflect the hard times of the depression?
   c. How might New Deal arts programs affect Americans' lives today?

5. **Writing and Critical Thinking**
   Supporting a Point of View Imagine that you are an artist hired by Federal Project Number One. Write a letter to President Roosevelt describing how your life has changed.
   Consider:
   • what problems artists were facing before the project
   • how the project promoted the arts
   • what might have happened to the arts without the project

Homework Practice Online
keyword: SE3 HP16

CHAPTER 16

REVIEW AND ASSESSMENT RESOURCES

REVIEW

Have students complete the **Chapter 16 Review** on pp. 492–93.

TECHNOLOGY

▶ Chapter 16 Test Generator (on the One-Stop Planner)
▶ Global Skill Builder CD–ROM
▶ HRW Go site

REINFORCEMENT, REVIEW, AND ASSESSMENT

▶ Chapter 16 Review, pp. 492–93
▶ Chapter 16 Tutorial for Students, Parents, Mentors, and Peers

▶ Chapter 16 Test (Form A or B)
▶ Portfolio Activities and Alternative Assessment Handbook, Chapter 16
▶ Chapter 16 Test for English Language Learners and Special-Needs Students

ASSESS

Use one of the chapter tests to assess students' understanding of the content. For **Alternative Assessment**, see the **Portfolio Activities and Alternative Assessment Handbook**.

CHAPTER 16

Review

Creating a Time Line

Copy the time line below onto a sheet of paper. Complete the time line by filling in the events and dates from the chapter that you think were most significant. Pick three events and explain why you think they were significant.

1933	1936	1939

Writing a Summary

Using standard grammar, spelling, sentence structure, and punctuation, write an overview of events in the chapter.

Identifying People and Ideas

Identify the following terms or individuals and explain their significance.

1. New Deal
2. Frances Perkins
3. bank holiday
4. Huey Long
5. Mary McLeod Bethune
6. Social Security Act
7. sit-down strike
8. Dust Bowl
9. Georgia O'Keeffe
10. *The Grapes of Wrath*

Understanding Main Ideas

SECTION 1 *(pp. 468–474)*

1. How did the Great Depression change the role of the U.S. government?

SECTION 2 *(pp. 475–481)*

2. What were some of the major criticisms of the New Deal?
3. What was President Roosevelt's "court-packing" plan, and how well did it succeed?

SECTION 3 *(pp. 482–486)*

4. How effective were New Deal measures in ending the Great Depression?

SECTION 4 *(pp. 487–491)*

5. How did novels, films, plays, and paintings reflect themes of the depression years?

Reviewing Themes

1. **Economics** How did the Roosevelt administration expand the role of the federal government in regulating the economy?
2. **Constitutional Heritage** Why might the Supreme Court have declared some New Deal measures unconstitutional?
3. **Geography** What effects did migration from the Dust Bowl have on the West Coast?

Thinking Critically

1. **Identifying Cause and Effect** How did criticism of the first New Deal shape the Second New Deal?
2. **Evaluating** Some people consider Franklin D. Roosevelt our greatest president. Use facts from the chapter to evaluate his contributions.
3. **Making Generalizations** How do New Deal programs affect the lives of U.S. citizens today?
4. **Analyzing Information** What impact did New Deal legislation have on the roles of state and federal government?
5. **Drawing Conclusions** What actions did people from various ethnic and racial groups take in the 1930s to expand their economic and political opportunities?

Writing About History

Summarizing Write a brief summary of 10 major New Deal programs. Note whether they were designed to help banks, farmers, labor, or business and evaluate their effectiveness. Use the following graphic to organize your thoughts.

New Deal			
Banks	Farmers	Labor	Business

RETEACH

Organize the class into small groups. Have each group use 25 terms from the Define/Identify sections of the chapter to create a crossword puzzle. Ask groups to trade crossword puzzles and then complete them.
English Language Learners, Cooperative Learning

EXTEND

Ask students to conduct research on historians' and economists' assessment of the effectiveness of New Deal programs in restoring the economic health of the United States. Ask each student to discuss his or her findings in an essay. **Block Scheduling**

Building Social Studies Skills

Interpreting Maps
Study the map below. Then use it to help answer the questions that follow.

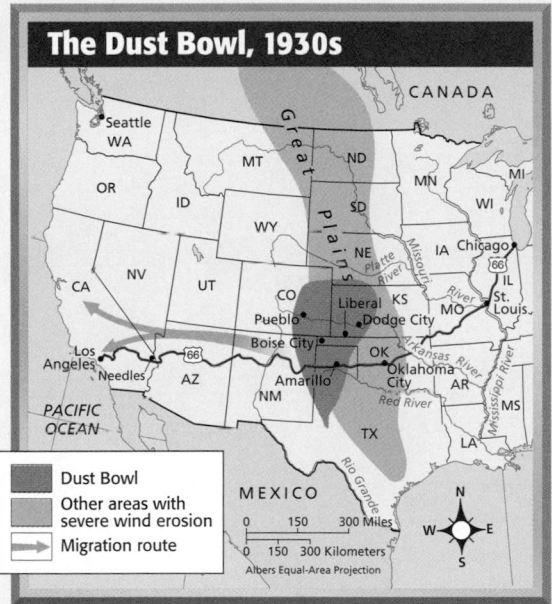

The Dust Bowl, 1930s

Legend:
- Dust Bowl
- Other areas with severe wind erosion
- Migration route

0   150   300 Miles
0 150 300 Kilometers
Albers Equal-Area Projection

1. Which of these states experienced the worst of the Dust Bowl?
a. Colorado
b. Nebraska
c. Arizona
d. South Dakota

2. Compare this map with the map "Unemployment Relief in 1934" in the last chapter. What similarities can be noted between the two maps?

Analyzing Primary Sources
Read the excerpt from Karl Monroe, a young journalist who was without a job in the 1930s, and then answer the questions that follow.

> "Sleeping in the parks, I found, was much less satisfactory than the comfort offered by the rapid-transit companies [subway cars]. Tired, hungry, and cold, I stretched out on the bench, and despite the lack of downy mattress and comforter eventually fell asleep. The soles of my feet were swollen with blisters, because my shoes had not been removed in at least seventy-two hours and I had tramped the sidewalks for three days. Suddenly I was awakened by a patrolman who had swung his night stick sharply against the soles of my feet."

3. What was the main reason that Monroe thought it was less satisfactory to sleep on a park bench than it was to sleep on a subway train?
a. In the park, he was cold, hungry, and tired.
b. In the park, he had a mattress and blanket.
c. In the park a patrolman rudely woke him up and forced him to move.
d. In the park his shoes were stolen.

4. How is this passage similar to and different from the earlier passage you read from John Steinbeck's *The Grapes of Wrath*?

Alternative Assessment

Building Your Portfolio
U.S. HISTORY

Constitutional Heritage
Imagine that you are a member of Congress when President Roosevelt proposes adding more justices to the Supreme Court. Write a script for a debate analyzing the constitutionality of his request. Be sure to discuss how the "court-packing" scheme would affect the relationships among the three branches of government. Conduct the debate with other students.

internet connect

Internet Activity: go.hrw.com
KEYWORD: SE3 AN16

Choose a topic on the New Deal to:
- learn about WPA-sponsored art projects and create a mural.
- research the possible causes of the *Hindenburg* disaster.
- create a newspaper to dramatize the plight of families displaced by the Dust Bowl.

---

2. Answers will vary. Students might argue that Roosevelt's success with many New Deal programs make him the best president. Others might argue that Roosevelt's programs often failed, and his court-packing attempt was unconstitutional.

3. by providing many national landmarks, public works, and art projects

4. State governments had to work more closely with the federal government in order to give out aid money provided by the federal government.

5. African Americans worked within the U.S. government; American Indians protested the Dawes Act; Filipino workers organized labor strikes.

Writing
Answers will vary. Students might mention: banks—FDIC; farmers—AAA, TVA, FSA; labor—FERA, CCC, NIRA, PWA; business—NIRA, NRA

Building Social Studies Skills
1. a

2. Answers will vary. Students might suggest that many of the states with the highest amount of unemployment relief were in the Dust Bowl.

3. c

4. Answers will vary. Students might suggest that the passages are similar because both discuss the effects of the depression.

LET'S GET STARTED!

Pair students and have each pair write a few sentences describing their local environment, classifying it according to the options offered in the map legends. Ask volunteers to read their sentences to the class. Tell students that they will learn more about land use in the United States in the Unit 4 America's Geography. **Cooperative Learning**

TEACH AMERICA'S GEOGRAPHY— LAND USE

Write the following question on the chalkboard: *How did land use change in the United States between 1620 and 1999?* Then pair students and tell them to study the America's Geography feature. Have each pair write a few sentences or paragraphs answering the question on the chalkboard. *(Pairs should note that the amount of grasslands and forests declined, that the area of buffalo range declined, that the number of cattle and hogs and pigs increased, and so on.)* Ask volunteers to read their statements to the class. **English Language Learners, Cooperative Learning**

Pesticides. The introduction of pesticides contributed to the agricultural boom of the 1900s. Pesticides are chemicals designed to destroy certain pests, usually insects, that harm crops. American farmers used pesticides in order to realize larger crop yields. One of the most widely used pesticides was an insecticide called DDT. The letters represent the chemical compound, dichloro-diphenyl-trichloroethane. Over time, scientists discovered that DDT kills beneficial species as well as harmful ones and possibly poses a danger to human food sources. In 1972 the U.S. government banned the widespread use of DDT to prevent health problems.

CRITICAL THINKING How might DDT continue to cause health problems in the United States and around the world?

ANSWER: Students might suggest that many foreign countries do not regulate or ban DDT, giving rise to the possibility of import contamination in the United States.

AMERICA'S GEOGRAPHY ANSWERS

1. forests

2. 2.3 billion bushels

3. Graphs should reflect the information in the Agricultural Production chart.

Land Use

For thousands of years, Americans have used the land to grow crops. Many Native American groups cultivated crops on small plots of land long before the arrival of Europeans. In the early days of the nation, most northern and midwestern farmers grew crops on small plots of land. In the South, agriculture was dominated by large plantations that grew great quantities of tobacco and cotton. By the late 1800s improved farm machinery and fertilizers allowed farmers to grow larger quantities of food on fewer acres of land. Today the amount of land devoted to crops and wild vegetation has dropped significantly.

Land Use in 1620

Grasslands
Forests
Buffalo range
Present-day boundaries

0   250   500 Miles
0   250   500 Kilometers
Albers Equal-Area Projection

Soybeans. The multipurpose, high-protein soybean became the agricultural wonder of the 1900s. By the 1990s it was one of the most common crops in the United States. Soybeans are used in the processing of cattle feed, fertilizer, insect sprays, and paint as well as in food products such as soy sauce, soy milk, baby food, processed meats, and tofu.

Agricultural Production, 1910–1999

	1910	1999
Corn (in bushels)	2.85 billion	9.44 billion
Wheat (in bushels)	625 million	2.3 billion
Cotton (in bales)	11.61 million	17 million
Tobacco (in pounds)	1.14 billion	1.28 billion
Soybeans (in bushels)	< 50,000	2.64 billion

Sources: *Historical Statistics of the United States; Statistical Abstract of the United States: 2000*

GEOGRAPHY AND HISTORY **Skills**

PLACES AND REGIONS

1. What type of vegetation covered the most land in North America in 1620?

2. How many bushels of soybeans were harvested in 1999?

3. Create a bar graph of agricultural production, 1910–99.

SPOTLIGHT
on Animals and the Environment

Write the following animals on the chalkboard: *buffalo*, *cattle*, and *hogs and pigs*. Have each student select one animal group. Then ask students to conduct research on how their chosen group affected land use and the environment in American history. Suggest that students consider such issues as desertification, overgrazing, and so on. Then have students create graphic organizers or other visual presentations to display their research. Have volunteers present their graphic organizers or presentations to the class. **Block Scheduling**

SPOTLIGHT
on Local Land Use

Pair students and ask them to locate and use a variety of primary and secondary sources to learn more about land use in their local community during the 1800s or 1900s. Remind students to compare and contrast this land use with modern-day land use. Then tell each pair to write a short report describing local land use over time. Have volunteers read their reports to the class. To conclude, conduct a brief discussion on the material presented in the reports.

Block Scheduling, Cooperative Learning

AMERICA'S Geography

Land Use in 1850

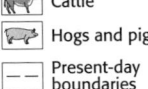

Grasslands
Forests
Wheat
Corn
Buffalo range
Cattle
Hogs and pigs
Present-day boundaries

Land Use in 1990

Land changes. Agricultural production in the United States had become increasingly diverse by the early 1900s. As the population of buffalo declined in the West, hogs and cattle grew in popularity elsewhere. The biggest change to affect agriculture in the late 1900s was the decline of the small family farm. Although the number of farmers decreased dramatically, the size of farms actually increased as large-scale mechanized farming became the norm.

GEOGRAPHY AND HISTORY Skills

ENVIRONMENT AND SOCIETY

1. How did the land used for cattle ranching change between 1850 and 1990?
2. In what way did grasslands and forests change between 1850 and 1990?

INTERDISCIPLINARY CONNECTIONS
▶GEOGRAPHY◀

Land Use in Iowa. Grasslands covered most of Iowa in 1850. Some 13 years later a young woman who moved there from Norway identified the factors that made it a farmer's paradise. "Our land is beautiful, though there are few trees. . . . We have good spring water near by. Best of all, the land is good meadowland and easily plowed and cultivated."

CRITICAL THINKING Why do you think that the young woman mentioned the lack of trees?

ANSWER: Some students might suggest that she was not used to life on the Great Plains and nostalgic for trees.

THAT'S INTERESTING!

In 1890 the average wage for a farm worker was just 90¢ per day. That amount was only 45¢ higher by 1910. Wages continued to increase slowly until the Great Depression of the 1930s, when wages fell. In 1945, pay averaged $4.35 a day.

AMERICA'S GEOGRAPHY ANSWERS

1. The land used for cattle ranching increased.

2. Both grasslands and forests decreased in size.

UNIT 4

REVIEW AND ASSESSMENT RESOURCES

TECHNOLOGY

▶ Global Skill Builder CD–ROM

▶ Holt Researcher: American History CD–ROM

▶ HRW Go site

REINFORCEMENT, REVIEW, AND ASSESSMENT

▶ Unit 4 Review, pp. 496–97

▶ Unit 4 Test (Form A or B)

▶ Portfolio Activities and Alternative Assessment Handbook, Unit 4

▶ Unit 4 Test for English Language Learners and Special-Needs Students

To review elements of Unit 4 in a single class period, assign one of the following activities or graphic organizers, omitting the italicized answers, to individuals or groups.

1 Decision Making

Tell students to create the first scene of a play about farming families during the Great Depression. The family must decide whether they will move from their home in Oklahoma to California. This first scene must center around the family's decision-making process. How will the family decide? What will they base their decision upon? What other options will they consider? The scene should conclude with a decision either to stay or to leave. After they finish the scene, ask students to write a

---

A Selection from Further Reading

The Stock Market Crash.

In *The Great Crash 1929*, John Kenneth Galbraith investigates the stock market crash and its influence on the Great Depression. In the following excerpt, he discusses the months before the crash, comparing what historians know now with what people knew then. "Purely in retrospect it is easy to see how 1929 was destined to be a year to remember. . . . [A] roaring boom was in progress in the stock market and, like all booms, it had to end. . . . Some of those in positions of authority wanted the boom to continue. . . . But there were also some who saw, however dimly, that a wild speculation was in progress and that something should be done. For these people, however, every proposal to act raised the same . . . problem. The consequences of successful action seemed almost as terrible as the consequences of inaction, and they could be more horrible for those who took the action."

ANALYZING SOURCES How might Galbraith's knowledge of what happened after the crash affect his interpretation?

ANSWER: Students might suggest that Galbraith can give meaning to actions that might not have seemed relevant.

UNIT 4 Review

BUILDING YOUR PORTFOLIO

Outlined below are three projects. Independently or cooperatively, complete one and use the products to demonstrate your mastery of the historical concepts involved.

1 Decision Making

The year is 1935. You and your family live in Oklahoma in the Dust Bowl. Your family farm has been ruined by the drought so you must decide either to stay where your family has lived for almost 30 years or move to California in search of greater opportunity. Follow these steps to make a decision.

Use your textbook and other resources to ***gather information*** that might influence your decision whether to move. Be sure to use what you have learned about the Dust Bowl, the Great Depression, and the New Deal to help you make an effective decision.

Once you have gathered information, ***identify options***. Based on the information you have gathered, consider the options to stay or to leave. Be sure to record your possible options for your presentation.

Once you have identified these options, ***predict the consequences*** for each one. For example, what will happen if you and your family stay in Oklahoma? If you leave, will you find work in California? Once you have predicted the consequences, record them as notes for your presentation.

Studio photograph of the St. Louis Cotton Club Jazz Band from 1926

Take action to implement your decision. Once you have considered your options, you should create a presentation about your decision. You will need to support your decision by including information you gathered and by explaining why you rejected other options. You may want to create maps or charts to help you explain your decision.

brief scene that would take place at the end of the play, showing the consequences for the family of the decision made in the first scene. Ask volunteers to perform the scenes for the class.

2 Culture

Tell students to imagine that it is 1925, that they live in Chicago, and that they are either new immigrants or African Americans who have recently migrated from the South. Have each student write a series of diary entries detailing his or her encounters with prejudice and racism and his or her efforts to overcome these factors.

3 Government

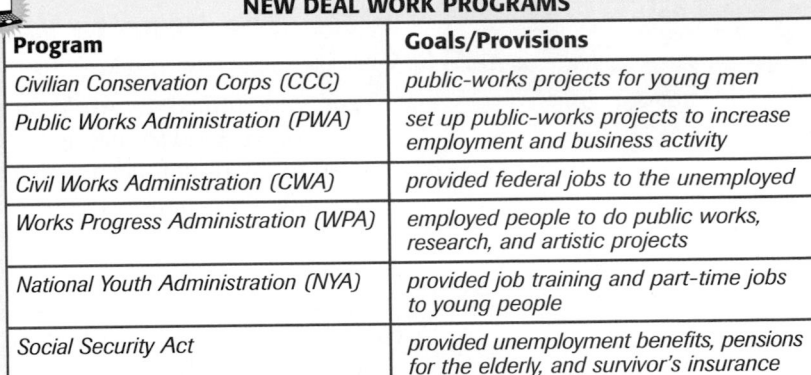

NEW DEAL WORK PROGRAMS

Program	Goals/Provisions
Civilian Conservation Corps (CCC)	public-works projects for young men
Public Works Administration (PWA)	set up public-works projects to increase employment and business activity
Civil Works Administration (CWA)	provided federal jobs to the unemployed
Works Progress Administration (WPA)	employed people to do public works, research, and artistic projects
National Youth Administration (NYA)	provided job training and part-time jobs to young people
Social Security Act	provided unemployment benefits, pensions for the elderly, and survivor's insurance

2 Culture

Technological developments in the areas of entertainment and communications helped create a national culture during the 1920s. *Create a script for a radio program* that highlights the issues of the era. Programs might include daily news, a jazz presentation, a book review, or an interview with a celebrity. Your script should include examples of American art, music, and literature that transcend American culture and convey universal themes. You may wish to use portfolio materials you designed in the unit chapters to help you.

Works Progress Administration project

3 Government

To provide relief from the economic troubles caused by the Great Depression, the federal government worked to implement programs from President Roosevelt's New Deal. *Create a diagram* that explains how the New Deal changed the role of the federal government as well as its effects on state governments. You may wish to use portfolio materials you designed in the unit chapters to help you.

Further Reading

Galbraith, John Kenneth. *The Great Crash 1929.* Houghton Mifflin Co., 1997. An economic interpretation of the stock market crash that was originally published in 1955.

Kennedy, David M. *Freedom from Fear: The American People in Depression and War, 1929–1945.* Oxford University Press, 2001. An account of how Americans coped with the Great Depression and World War II.

McElvaine, Robert S. *The Great Depression: America, 1929–1941.* Times Books, 1994. An overview of the Great Depression in the United States.

Streissguth, Thomas, and Tom Streissguth. *The Roaring Twenties.* Facts on File, 2001. Firsthand accounts of American life in the 1920s.

Terkel, Studs. *Hard Times: An Oral History of the Great Depression.* New Press, 2000. Personal accounts of the effects of the Great Depression on working-class Americans.

Watson, Steven. *The Harlem Renaissance: Hub of African-American Culture, 1920–1930.* Pantheon Books, 1996. An illustrated history of the art, music, and literature of the Harlem Renaissance.

Internet Connect & Review on the ROM

In assigned groups, develop a multi-media presentation about the United States between 1919 and 1939. Choose information from the chapter Internet Connect activities and from the **Holt Researcher CD–ROM** that best reflects the major topics of the period. Write an outline and a script for your presentation, which may be shown to the class.

A Selection from Further Reading

The Great Depression, Franklin D. Roosevelt, and the American People.

In *The Great Depression,* Robert S. McElvaine provides an informative survey of American society during the Great Depression. In the following excerpt, he discusses the relationship that President Franklin D. Roosevelt shared with many Americans during the Great Depression. "What Franklin D. Roosevelt sought, he said in a 1932 speech, was 'social justice through social action.' The key to understanding FDR's political success is that his positions so often coincided with the values of a people struggling for economic—and in many cases, physical—survival. Roosevelt stated the relationship perfectly in his first inaugural address: 'The people of the United States . . . have made me the present instrument of their wishes.' . . . It was an accurate forecast of the relationship between President and people during the next few years."

ANALYZING SOURCES

According to McElvaine, why was Roosevelt so successful during the 1930s?

ANSWER: Students might note that Roosevelt viewed himself as an instrument of the people, a stance that made him very popular.

World Conflicts

U·N·I·T 5

CHAPTER 17 — The Road to War

After World War I, many nations attempted to work for world peace. These efforts proved fruitless as the global depression led to the rise of dictators in Germany, Italy, Japan, and other countries. During the 1930s, for example, Adolf Hitler came to power in Germany and quickly launched an aggressive expansionist campaign. Other European leaders struggled to control Hitler, finally settling on a policy of appeasement.

CHAPTER 18 — Americans in World War II

After Japan bombed Pearl Harbor in December 1941, the United States entered World War II on the Allied side. While U.S. soldiers fought in Europe and Japan, Americans at home attempted to support the war effort and boost productivity. In May 1945 the Allies finally conquered Europe. Victory in Japan came in August, after the United States dropped atomic bombs on Hiroshima and Nagasaki.

EXAMINING THE VISUAL RECORD

Ask students the questions below. Then use the annotations to expand class discussion.

1 What is the U.S. military attempting to do in this scene?
U.S. forces are invading Fox Green Beach as part of the invasion of Normandy on D-Day, June 6, 1944. The invasion of Normandy was a key turning point in World War II. The invasion forced the German army to fight on two fronts—against the Soviet Union in the east and the United States and Great Britain in the west.

2 What does the physical geography indicate about the fighting at Fox Green Beach?
Fox Green Beach was a part of Omaha Beach, where the German defenses were the strongest. The cliffs were easy for the German army to defend and left the U.S. soldiers vulnerable below. The cliffs also made it difficult to aim naval weapons with much accuracy.

World Conflicts
1921–1960

U.S. forces fought at Fox Green Beach during the invasion of Normandy in World War II.

The Cold War

CHAPTER 19

After the Allies defeated the Axis Powers, many world nations searched for ways to guarantee peace in the future. As the Soviet Union established satellite states throughout Eastern Europe, however, a Cold War between the United States and Soviet Union developed. The Cold War and the massive nuclear arms buildup that accompanied it led to increased fears and tensions at home. Many Americans began to worry about Communists in the U.S. government and nuclear attacks.

Society After World War II

CHAPTER 20

After World War II ended, the United States feared an economic depression and labor problems. In part due to the GI Bill, which provided training, schooling, and housing loans to veterans, the depression never materialized. In fact, the United States entered an era of unprecedented prosperity. In the midst of this material wealth, however, racial discrimination and segregation existed. To expand their rights, African Americans began the modern civil rights movement.

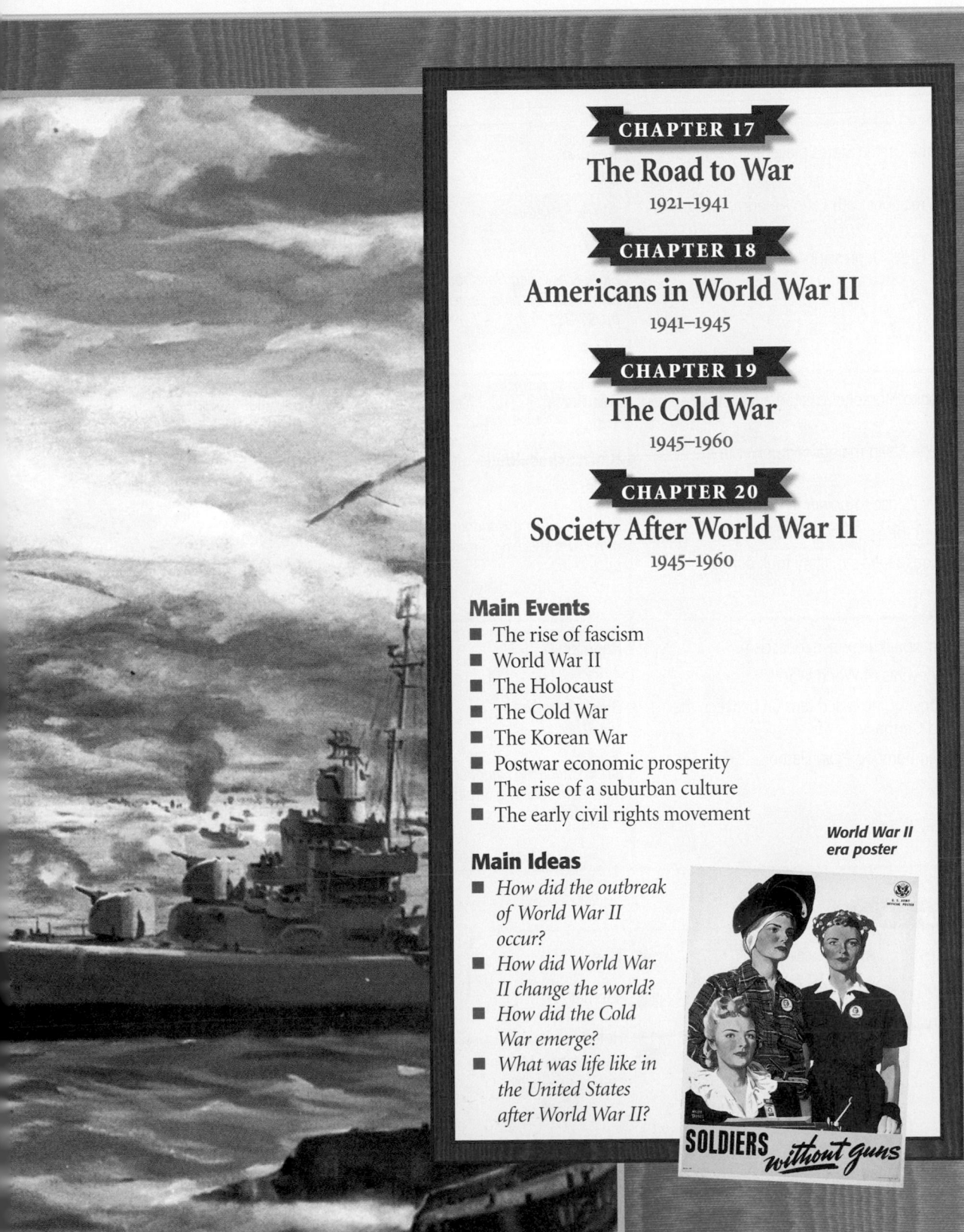

CHAPTER 17
The Road to War
1921–1941

CHAPTER 18
Americans in World War II
1941–1945

CHAPTER 19
The Cold War
1945–1960

CHAPTER 20
Society After World War II
1945–1960

Main Events
- The rise of fascism
- World War II
- The Holocaust
- The Cold War
- The Korean War
- Postwar economic prosperity
- The rise of a suburban culture
- The early civil rights movement

Main Ideas
- *How did the outbreak of World War II occur?*
- *How did World War II change the world?*
- *How did the Cold War emerge?*
- *What was life like in the United States after World War II?*

World War II era poster

SOLDIERS *without guns*

CHAPTER 17

The Road to War

CHAPTER RESOURCE MANAGER

Objectives	Pacing Guide	Reproducible Resources
SECTION 1 **The Search for Peace** pp. 502–06 ★ Outline the foreign policy the United States followed after World War I. ★ Identify the major postwar peace initiatives. ★ Discuss how war debts and reparations affected European nations after World War I.	**Regular** 1 day **Block Scheduling** .5 day *Block Scheduling Handbook with Team Teaching Strategies, pp. 97–102*	**RS** Guided Reading Strategy 17.1 **PS** Biography Reading 17: Emily Greene Balch **PS** Primary Source Reading 17: A Diplomatic Failure
SECTION 2 **Relations with Latin America** pp. 507–11 ★ Discuss the role the United States played in Nicaraguan politics. ★ Explain how U.S. relations with Latin America changed in the 1930s. ★ Analyze how the Great Depression affected Latin American countries.	**Regular** 2 days **Block Scheduling** 1 day *Block Scheduling Handbook with Team Teaching Strategies, pp. 97–102*	**RS** Guided Reading Strategy 17.2 **SM** Geography Activity 17: The Good Neighbor Policy
SECTION 3 **The Rise of Militarism** pp. 512–17 ★ Describe how Benito Mussolini created a fascist state in Italy. ★ Explain how Joseph Stalin maintained power in the Soviet Union. ★ Analyze Adolf Hitler's rise to power in Germany. ★ Relate what caused the Spanish Civil War. ★ Discuss what actions Japan's military took during the 1930s.	**Regular** 1 day **Block Scheduling** .5 day *Block Scheduling Handbook with Team Teaching Strategies, pp. 97–102*	**RS** Guided Reading Strategy 17.3 **RS** Graphic Organizer Activity 17: A Shift in International Relations **IC** Literature Reading 17: Wartime Poet **SM** American History Outline Map 32: East and Southeast Asia
SECTION 4 **War Breaks Out** pp. 518–23 ★ Explain the international response to fascism. ★ Analyze the early events of World War II. ★ Discuss the reasons for increased tension between the United States and Germany. ★ Analyze why Japan bombed Pearl Harbor.	**Regular** 2 days **Block Scheduling** 1 day *Block Scheduling Handbook with Team Teaching Strategies, pp. 97–102*	**RS** Guided Reading Strategy 17.4

Chapter Resource Key

PS Primary Sources
RS Reading Support
IC Interdisciplinary Connections
E Enrichment
SM Skills Mastery
A Assessment

REV Review
ELL Reinforcement and English Language Learners
 Transparencies
 CD-ROM
 Music

 Video
 Internet
 Holt Presentation Maker Using Microsoft® PowerPoint®

 One-Stop Planner CD-ROM

See the *One-Stop Planner* for a complete list of additional resources for students and teachers.

One-Stop Planner CD-ROM

It's easy to plan lessons, select resources, and print out materials for your students when you use the **One-Stop Planner CD–ROM with Test Generator.**

HRW ONLINE RESOURCES
GO TO: go.hrw.com
Then type in a keyword.

Technology Resources

 One-Stop Planner, Lesson 17.1
 Holt Researcher: American History CD–ROM
 Homework Practice Online

 One-Stop Planner, Lesson 17.2
The American Nation Video Program Segment: U.S. Warships in Havana Harbor; Teacher's Guide, pp. 191–92
Holt Researcher: American History CD–ROM
Homework Practice Online

 One-Stop Planner, Lesson 17.3
Everyday Life in America Transparency 25: The Rise of the Third Reich
Holt Researcher: American History CD–ROM
Homework Practice Online
HRW Go site

 One-Stop Planner, Lesson 17.4
CNN Presents America: Yesterday and Today, Modern Times Segment: Nuremberg Laws
Holt Researcher: American History CD–ROM
Homework Practice Online

Reinforcement, Review, and Assessment

REV Section 1 Review, p. 506
A Daily Quiz 17.1
ELL Main Idea Activity 17.1
ELL English Audio Summary 17.1
ELL Spanish Audio Summary 17.1

REV Section 2 Review, p. 511
A Daily Quiz 17.2
ELL Main Idea Activity 17.2
ELL English Audio Summary 17.2
ELL Spanish Audio Summary 17.2

REV Section 3 Review, p. 517
A Daily Quiz 17.3
ELL Main Idea Activity 17.3
ELL English Audio Summary 17.3
ELL Spanish Audio Summary 17.3

REV Section 4 Review, p. 523
A Daily Quiz 17.4
ELL Main Idea Activity 17.4
ELL English Audio Summary 17.4
ELL Spanish Audio Summary 17.4

TEACHER HOME PAGE
KEYWORD: SE3 Teacher

CHAPTER INTERNET ACTIVITIES
KEYWORD: SE3 AN17
Choose an activity to:
- research the Spanish Civil War.
- understand the developments that led to the atomic bomb.
- learn about fascist and antifascist activity in the United States.

CHAPTER ENRICHMENT LINKS
KEYWORD: SE3 CH17

ONLINE ASSESSMENT
Homework Practice
KEYWORD: SE3 HP17

Standardized Test Prep
KEYWORD: SE3 STP17

Rubrics
KEYWORD: SS Rubrics

ONLINE MAPS, CHARTS, AND GRAPHS
KEYWORD: SE3 MCG
- Attack on Pearl Harbor
- Prelude to War: Germany 1939
- Prelude to War: Italy 1939
- Prelude to War: Japan 1939
- U.S. Entry into World War II

CONTENT UPDATES
KEYWORD: SS Content Updates

HOLT PRESENTATION MAKER
KEYWORD: SE3 PPT17

ONLINE READING SUPPORT
KEYWORD: SS Strategies

CURRENT EVENTS
KEYWORD: S3 Current Events

Meeting Individual Needs

Ability Levels

Level 1 Basic-level activities designed for all students encountering new material

Level 2 Intermediate-level activities designed for average students

Level 3 Challenging activities designed for honors and gifted-and-talented students

English Language Learners Activities that address the needs of students with Limited English Proficiency

Chapter Review and Assessment

 Global Skill Builder CD–ROM
HRW Go site
REV Chapter 17 Tutorial for Students, Parents, Mentors, and Peers
REV Chapter 17 Review, pp. 524–25
Chapter 17 Test Generator (on the One-Stop Planner)
A Chapter 17 Test (Form A or B)
A Alternative Assessment Handbook
A Chapter 17 Test for English Language Learners and Special-Needs Students

Build on What You Know

Ask students to answer the following questions.

Why might World War I have left so many European countries in debt?

Consider:

- the cost of war weapons, machinery, and personnel
- the need to rebuild after the war
- the war's disruption of trade and other sources of revenue

Why might Americans have wanted to focus on matters at home after the war?

Consider:

- the experiences Americans had both in Europe and on the home front during the war
- the desire of the United States to avoid foreign entanglements

---

exploring the time line

AMERICAN EVENTS

GOVERNMENT

Roosevelt's Third Term.
Franklin D. Roosevelt's third term as president was unprecedented but not unconstitutional. George Washington's precedent of a two-term limit had been followed by all other presidents. In 1940 Roosevelt challenged this pattern. He won a third term and later a fourth. In 1951 the Twenty-second Amendment officially put a limit on presidential terms.

CRITICAL THINKING Why might Americans have placed an official limit on presidential terms?

ANSWER: Students may suggest that Americans were concerned that allowing presidents to serve an unlimited number of terms would give the executive branch too much power.

CHAPTER
17

1921–1941
The Road to War

Symbol of the Italian Fascist Party that appeared on its membership cards

Red Grange

1921
World Events
Benito Mussolini founds Italy's Fascist Party.

1924
Daily Life
University of Illinois player Red Grange and Notre Dame coach Knute Rockne boost the popularity of football.

1931
Business and Finance
President Herbert Hoover proposes a halt to war-debt and reparations payments.

1921 | **1925** | **1929**

1922
Science and Technology
British archaeologist Howard Carter discovers the tomb of Egypt's King Tutankhamen.

Pendant from Tutankhamen's tomb

1926
Politics
President Coolidge sends U.S. troops to Nicaragua to preserve order and protect American interests during a civil war.

1929
Daily Life
Some 71 percent of American families have incomes below $2,500, considered the minimum for a decent standard of living.

Unemployed man selling apples

Build on What You Know

World War I left Europe in a state of chaos. Germany was required to pay substantial war reparations, and other European countries owed the United States large war debts. In this chapter you will learn how after World War I many Americans hoped to focus on matters at home. However, the Great Depression touched off global economic problems. The rise of dictators in Europe set the stage for another war. Dictators also took power in several Latin American countries. Other Latin American countries tried to reduce U.S. influence in the region.

What's Your Opinion?

To help students create their Themes Journal entries, provide the following examples of appropriate agree/disagree statements.

Global Relations

Agree The desire for peace motivated many nations to give up some of their power and join the League of Nations after World War I.

Disagree Prior to World War I, leaders of the major European powers believed that war was a legitimate means to settle political disputes.

Economics

Agree The political and economic consequences of the Revolutionary War led to the War of 1812.

Disagree Despite the Civil War's political and economic consequences, the North and South did not fight another war.

Citizenship

Agree Americans accepted the government's crackdown on suspected Communists during the boom years of the 1920s.

Disagree Many Americans demanded a bill of rights even though the U.S. Constitution offered to bring about greater economic stability.

1933
Politics
The United States establishes diplomatic relations with the Soviet Union.

1933
World Events
Adolf Hitler becomes chancellor of Germany.

1932
Daily Life
The average American's weekly wage drops to $17 from $28, its 1929 level.

German leader Adolf Hitler (center)

Headline announcing "The War of the Worlds" broadcast

1938
The Arts
The Mercury Theater radio production of "The War of the Worlds" sets off a national panic.

1941
World Events
Japanese forces attack Pearl Harbor.

1933

1937

1941

1935
The Arts
Bette Davis wins an Oscar for her role in the film *Dangerous*.

1936
The Arts
American athlete Jesse Owens wins four gold medals at the 1936 Olympic Games in Berlin.

1939
World Events
World War II begins when German troops invade Poland.

1940
Politics
Franklin D. Roosevelt wins an unprecedented third term as president.

1939
Science and Technology
Swiss chemist Paul Müller develops the insecticide DDT.

Poster advertising Dangerous

Judge's badge from 1936 Olympics

exploring the time line

GLOBAL EVENTS

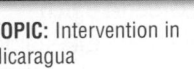

internet connect

TOPIC: Intervention in Nicaragua
GO TO: go.hrw.com
KEYWORD: SE3 AN17

Have students access the Internet through the HRW Go site to conduct research on the circumstances, events, and results of the intervention by U.S. Marines in Nicaragua beginning in 1926. Then ask students to create an illustrated chart with which to present their information.

What's Your Opinion?

Themes Journal *Do you agree or disagree with the following statements? Support your point of view in your journal.*

Global Relations Nations should be willing to give up some of their power in order to promote world peace.

Economics Wars always have economic and political consequences that inevitably lead to more wars.

Citizenship Citizens will give up certain liberties if their government provides economic stability.

After completing Section 1, students should be able to:

OBJECTIVE 1 Outline the foreign policy the United States followed after World War I.

OBJECTIVE 2 Identify the major postwar peace initiatives.

OBJECTIVE 3 Discuss how war debts and reparations affected European nations after World War I.

LET'S GET STARTED!

As students enter the classroom, ask them to read the quotation from Senator William E. Borah on this page. Have each student attempt to rewrite the quotation from Borah in his or her own words. *(Borah was expressing his fear that U.S. sovereignty would be undermined if the nation joined the League of Nations.)* Have volunteers share their rewritten quotations with the class. Tell students that in Section 1 they will learn about U.S. foreign policy after World War I.

SECTION 1

READ TO DISCOVER
1. What foreign policy did the United States follow after World War I?
2. What were the major postwar peace initiatives?
3. How did war debts and reparations affect European nations after World War I?

DEFINE
isolationism
disarmament

IDENTIFY
Emily Greene Balch
Washington Conference
Charles Evans Hughes
Kellogg-Briand Pact
Adolf Hitler

WHY IT MATTERS TODAY
Some American political leaders today support a foreign policy of isolationism. Use CNNfyi.com or other **current events** sources to identify some modern isolationists and their views. Record your findings in your journal.

The Search for Peace

 EYEWITNESSES TO History

Senator William E. Borah

❝The whole scheme [the League of Nations] has just one ultimate power and that is military force—the same power and the same principle which every despot [dictator] has relied upon in his efforts against the people when the people were seeking greater liberty and greater freedom, the same power which George III and Wilhelm II made the basis of their infamous designs [shameful plans]. . . . Let us leave these things—the lives of our people, the liberty of our whole nation—in the keeping and under the control of those people who have brought this Republic to its present place of prestige and power.❞

—William E. Borah, "Militarism in a League of Nations," *Forum,* 1919

Senator William E. Borah of Idaho argued against membership in the League of Nations shortly after the end of World War I. Like many Americans, Borah feared that involvement in European affairs might draw the United States into another war.

Legacies of World War I

More than 8 million people, including more than 112,000 Americans, died fighting in the Great War. The U.S. federal government increased in size and authority. Some Americans believed that the government had exceeded its authority with the Espionage and Sedition Acts. Few Americans believed that the war had made the world "safe for democracy." They noted the postwar chaos in government and the founding of a communist government in Russia. The Women's International League for Peace and Freedom summed up the nation's doubts: "War to end war has proved a failure. The war is won, yet nowhere is there peace, security or happiness."

Americans worried about being dragged into another foreign conflict. "We ask only to live our own life in our own way, in friendship and sympathy with all, in alliance with none," declared Senator Hiram W. Johnson in 1922. Such sentiments led the United States to follow a policy of partial **isolationism**, or withdrawal from world affairs, in the 1920s and 1930s.

Isolationists did not want to cut off the United States completely from the affairs of the rest of the world. They merely wanted to avoid what Thomas Jefferson had called "entangling alliances" that could drag the United States into another war. Isolationism led the United States to shun membership in international organizations that were set up after World War I. These included the League of Nations and the Permanent Court of International Justice, or World Court.

The World Court had been created to resolve international disputes. Presidents Coolidge, Hoover, and Roosevelt all proposed that the United States join the organization. Public opinion ran strongly against membership, however. The U.S. Senate set strict terms for joining in order to safeguard its right to make treaties.

ALL LEVELS: Ask students why the United States might have involved itself in faraway conflicts that did not directly threaten the security of the United States. *(Students might suggest that the United States intervened to prevent aggressive leaders from expanding their territorial influence.)* To help students understand the post–World War I U.S. foreign policy, copy the graphic organizer at right on the chalkboard, omitting the italicized answers. Have each student complete it. Ask volunteers to share their answers with the class. To conclude, tell students that many Americans were disillusioned by the death, destruction, and political turmoil that resulted from World War I. **English Language Learners**

Americans' Concerns After World War I

Many Americans are worried about entering another foreign conflict.

U.S. Foreign Policy After World War I

The United States follows a foreign policy of partial isolationism. The country declines membership in the League of Nations and the World Court.

HOMEWORK *Have each student draw a political cartoon that illustrates U.S. foreign policy after World War I. Display students' cartoons around the classroom.*

The nations that already belonged to the World Court rejected the Senate's terms, and the matter was dropped.

✔ **READING CHECK: Making Generalizations** How did World War I affect the role of the federal government? It increased in size and authority.

Promoting Peace

Rather than joining international peacekeeping organizations, the United States used diplomacy to promote world peace. American groups working for peace urged the U.S. government to bring world leaders together to negotiate **disarmament**, or reducing the size of a country's military. Jane Addams, **Emily Greene Balch**, Jeannette Rankin, and other leaders of the women's movement played important roles in these peace efforts. Balch and Addams were active members of the Women's International League for Peace and Freedom. For their organizing efforts in the United States and abroad, both Addams—in 1931—and Balch—in 1946—received the Nobel Peace Prize.

The Washington Conference. Beginning in November 1921 the United States hosted the **Washington Conference**, an international conference in Washington, D.C., that focused on naval disarmament and Pacific security. The meeting was organized by U.S. secretary of state **Charles Evans Hughes**.

BIOGRAPHY

Charles Evans Hughes

Charles Evans Hughes was born in New York in April 1862. He graduated from Brown University in 1881 and received a law degree from Columbia University Law School three years later. After teaching and practicing law for several years, Hughes began his career in public service. Hughes was so busy, it was reported, that he grew his beard in 1890 just to save the time it took to get a shave. Hughes served as legal adviser to Progressive Era legislators investigating corruption in the utilities industry. In 1906 he won his first public office when he defeated publishing tycoon William Randolph Hearst to become governor of New York.

Hughes served as a justice on the Supreme Court from 1910 to 1916, when he resigned his position to run for president. Hughes went to bed on election night believing himself the victor. The next morning he awoke to the news that he had lost to Woodrow Wilson by just 23 electoral votes.

After this crushing defeat, Hughes turned to the issue of world peace. Putting aside political rivalries, Hughes supported U.S. entry into the League of Nations, which was the creation of President Wilson. At the end of World War I, Hughes envisioned the United States taking an active role in future world affairs.

⭐ **Then and Now**

Peace Movements

The 1920s and 1930s saw a rise in the number of groups working for peace throughout the world. After experiencing the horrors of World War I, many people began to organize in an effort to abolish war. Some American opponents of war belonged to religious groups such as the Mennonites and Quakers. Others were members of political organizations such as the Committee on the Cause and Cure of War. All the groups urged U.S. leaders to reject war as a means of solving conflicts.

Although war has persisted, many groups continue to work to stop the use of violence as a political tool. Some, like the National Campaign for a Peace Tax Fund, have lobbied to allow citizens to redirect the portion of their tax payments that would go into military spending to a special fund to promote international peace. Many peace organizations are affiliated with religious groups, including the Jewish Peace Fellowship, the Muslim Peace Fellowship, and Pax Christi (Peace of Christ) U.S.A. These groups use modern means of communication such as the Internet to spread their message. Many also use film and television to publicize the horrors of war.

These protesters demonstrated in front of the U.S. Capitol.

Emily Greene Balch. Emily Greene Balch became interested in international peace efforts in 1914 when World War I began. She remained active in the peace movement for the rest of her life, helping to found the Women's International League for Peace and Freedom in 1919. She donated most of her Nobel Prize winnings to that organization in 1946. Despite her advocacy of peace, she supported the U.S. entry into World War II as necessary to stop the growth of Nazi Germany.

CRITICAL THINKING How might you reconcile Balch's call for peace with her support for U.S. entry into World War II?

ANSWER: Students might suggest that although Balch believed that wars should be avoided if possible, she believed that some wars must be fought to stop aggression.

THAT'S INTERESTING!

If just 1,711 California voters had cast their ballots for Charles Evans Hughes instead of Woodrow Wilson, Hughes would have won that state's 23 electoral votes and would have been elected president of the United States in 1916.

TEACH OBJECTIVE 2

LEVEL 1: Pair students and have each pair draw cartoons identifying the major peace initiatives after World War I. *(Cartoons should depict the agreements produced by the Washington Conference to limit nations' naval strength [the Five-Power Naval Treaty], guarantee respect for nations' territorial possessions in the Pacific [the Four-Power Treaty], and guarantee China's territorial integrity [the Nine-Power Treaty] and the Kellogg-Briand Pact, which outlawed war.)* Have students present their cartoons to the class.
English Language Learners, Cooperative Learning

LEVELS 2 AND 3: Ask each student to write a brief transcript for an imaginary news conference at which a U.S. diplomat of the 1920s and 1930s answers questions about the major peace initiatives after World War I. *(See the Level 1 lesson for the correct initiatives.)* Students' transcripts should include reporters' questions about the efforts of the United States and the diplomats' responses.

HOMEWORK *Tell students to imagine that they are Americans living in 1930. Have each student write a letter to his or her congressional representative either supporting or rejecting postwar peace initiatives. Students should give specific reasons why they agree or disagree with these peace efforts.*

Analyzing Primary Sources

Making Predictions How did the goal "destroy the . . . spirit of tyranny" set the stage for future U.S. involvement abroad?

It suggested that the United States must take an active role in world peace.

Research on the R·O·M

Free Find:
Charles Evans Hughes
After reading about Charles Evans Hughes on the **Holt Researcher CD-ROM**, write a proposal for an arms-reduction conference to be held this year.

History Makers Speak

❝We emerge from the war with a new national consciousness; with a consciousness of power stimulated by extraordinary effort; with a consciousness of the possibility and potency [power] of cooperation. . . . We are unworthy of our victory, if we look forward with timidity. This is the hour and power of light, not of darkness. . . . We have made the world safe for democracy, but democracy is not a phrase or a form, but a life, and what shall that life be? . . . We have fought this War to substitute reason for force. We love our Republic because it represents to us the promise of the rule of reason. . . . If we are to establish peace within our own borders, we must cooperate to destroy the . . . spirit of tyranny wherever we find it.❞

—Charles Evans Hughes, "Our After-War Dangers," *Forum*, 1919

In 1930 Charles Evans Hughes was appointed Chief Justice of the United States, a position he held until retiring in 1941. He died seven years later.

As President Harding's secretary of state, Hughes tried to make his goal of a peaceful world a reality at the Washington Conference. Hughes surprised the other delegates at the conference with a bold proposal. He suggested that the major powers destroy 66 large warships. He also called for a 10-year "naval holiday" during which no battleships or battle cruisers would be built.

Hughes proposed that the United States, Great Britain, and Japan destroy or retire some of their warships in order to limit their individual naval strength. Britain and the United States would have equal naval strength. The size of Japan's navy would be limited to 60 percent of that of the British and U.S. navies. Italy and France would both be limited to navies roughly half the size of Japan's. This disarmament plan became known as the Five-Power Naval Treaty. Marveled one observer, "[Secretary Hughes sank more] ships than all the admirals of the world had sunk in a cycle of centuries."

The Washington Conference produced other important agreements as well. In the Four-Power Treaty, Britain, France, Japan, and the United States pledged to respect one another's territory in the Pacific. The Nine-Power Treaty included the nations that had signed the Five-Power Naval Treaty as well as Belgium, China, the Netherlands, and Portugal. The treaty guaranteed China's territorial integrity and required its signers to uphold the Open Door Policy.

Japan's minister of the navy, Admiral Kato Tomosaburo, explained Japan's support for disarmament.

History Makers Speak

❝Japan is ready for the new order of thought—the spirit of international friendship and cooperation for the greater good of humanity—which the Conference has brought about.❞

—Admiral Kato Tomosaburo, quoted in *Literary Digest*, February 18, 1922

For a time the treaties produced at the Washington Conference eased tensions in Asia. Japan began withdrawing from China's Shandong Peninsula, which it had invaded in 1914. Japan also withdrew from parts of Siberia. Japan's 1930 agreement to extend the 10-year ban on warship construction marked the high point of postwar international cooperation efforts.

Unsuccessful efforts.
April 6, 1927, marked the 10th anniversary of the U.S. entry into World War I. On that day French foreign minister Aristide Briand (ah-ree-steed bree-ahn) proposed that France and the United States enter into an

LEVEL 1: Pair students and have each pair create a cause-and-effect chart showing how war debts and reparations affected European nations. *(Charts should show that Britain, France, and Italy were in debt to the United States. In order to pay their debt to the United States, these nations demanded harsh reparations from Germany. Germany was forced to borrow money from Britain and to print paper money, causing hyperinflation. This inflation led to a severe economic downturn; financial troubles made Germans increasingly bitter.)* Ask volunteers to present their charts to the class.
English Language Learners, Cooperative Learning

LEVEL 2: Tell students to imagine that they are living in Europe after World War I. Have each student write several diary entries describing the effect of war debts and reparations on European countries. Students should express their opinions and feelings about the situation in their entries. *(See the Level 1 lesson for the correct effects.)* Ask volunteers to read their diary entries to the class.

LEVEL 3: Tell students to imagine that they are newspaper reporters in the late 1920s who have been to Europe and seen firsthand the effects of war debts and reparations on European nations. Have each student write a newspaper editorial summarizing these effects. *(See the Level 1 lesson for the correct effects.)* Ask volunteers to read their editorials to the class.

---

agreement to outlaw war. U.S. secretary of state Frank Kellogg suggested that the pact include all nations. Eventually, 62 countries signed the **Kellogg-Briand Pact.** The treaty outlawed war "as an instrument of national policy" but allowed countries to go to war in self-defense. The treaty lacked provisions for enforcement, however. One U.S. senator remarked that the pact was "as effective to keep down war as a carpet would be to smother an earthquake."

The pact's weaknesses became clear in September 1931 when Japan invaded Manchuria, a territory in China. The invasion led to war between Japan and China. Many Americans called for an economic boycott of Japan, but U.S. leaders refused to support such sanctions. The failure of diplomacy to prevent Japanese aggression marked the end of attempts to reach international accords. Preoccupied by the Japanese invasion and the worldwide economic depression, delegates to the 1932 League of Nations World Disarmament Conference went home without agreeing to reduce weapons.

✔ **READING CHECK: Finding the Main Idea** Describe the attempts made by Charles Evans Hughes and others to prevent another war. Hughes organized a disarmament conference; treaties were signed to prevent war.

War Debts and Reparations

The issue of war debts also weakened efforts to maintain peace. In the late 1800s, European investors had loaned money to finance U.S. industrial growth. After 1914, however, the United States became a creditor nation. At the start of World War I, U.S. banks lent money to Britain and France so that they could buy armaments from the United States. The U.S. government granted billions more in credit to the Allies. By 1920 the Allies owed more than $10 billion to the United States.

The debtor nations argued that their debts to the United States should be canceled. David Lloyd George, the British prime minister when the United States entered the war, explained their reasoning.

History Makers Speak

> **"The United States did not from first to last make any sacrifice or contribution remotely comparable to those of her European Associates, in life, limb, money, material or trade, towards the victory which she shared with them."**

—David Lloyd George, *The Truth About Reparations and War-Debts*

U.S. officials rejected appeals from Britain, France, and Italy to cancel their war debts completely. However, the U.S. government did cancel part of the debts. It also reduced the interest rates on the balances. Still, the only way the Allies could pay their war debts to the United States was to collect reparations, or damages, from defeated Germany. In 1921 a reparations commission had set total German reparations at 132 billion gold marks, or $32 billion. The Germans bitterly condemned the reparations as too harsh. Chancellor Joseph Wirth paid part of the reparations by borrowing money from Britain. The German government also printed paper money, resulting in massive inflation and causing the value of the German mark to plunge.

In 1922 writer Ernest Hemingway traveled from Strasburg, France, to Kehl, Germany. He described the extreme difference in prices between France and Germany, an effect of severe inflation in Germany:

These Japanese troops are celebrating their victory in Manchuria, China.

British prime minister David Lloyd George urged U.S. leaders to cancel the debts Britain and other European nations owed the United States from World War I.

Henry Cabot Lodge in *The Meaning of the Kellogg Treaty*

Criticizing the Kellogg-Briand Pact. Henry Cabot Lodge criticized the Kellogg-Briand Pact in a 1928 article. Lodge wrote: "The conception of renouncing war by governmental fiat [declaration] seems inherently absurd. The great forces in modern society—and especially American society—are quite independent of the government. We are in great measure our own masters. The banks, the newspapers, the great organizations of business—that whole body of influences which affect our thoughts, our food, our clothes, and our incomes are forging along no matter what Washington says."

CRITICAL THINKING Why might Lodge have believed that the Kellogg-Briand Pact was absurd?

ANSWER: Students might suggest that Lodge believed that governments do not have the power to stop wars from occurring.

VISUAL RECORD ANSWER
(for p. 506)
Students might suggest that inflation was very high in Germany.

REVIEW

Have students complete the **Section 1 Review** on p. 506.

ASSESS

Have students complete **Daily Quiz 17.1.** As **Alternative Assessment**, you may want to use the cause-and-effect chart or the diary entries in this section's lessons.

RETEACH

Have students complete **Main Idea Activity for English Language Learners and Special-Needs Students 17.1.** Then organize the class into small groups. Have each group create a list of important results of World War I in the United States and Europe that are discussed in this chapter. Then have groups prepare some illustrations that will help other students study these effects. Display these illustrations around the classroom. **English Language Learners, Cooperative Learning**

EXTEND

Have each student interview a local economics expert, such as an economics professor or a banker, to learn more about inflation. Then have students interview family members or other community members about their memories of recent periods of inflation. To conclude, have students present the results of their interviews to the class. **Block Scheduling**

SECTION
REVIEW ❶ ANSWERS

1. Define
- isolationism, p. 502
- disarmament, p. 503

2. Identify
- Emily Greene Balch, p. 503
- Washington Conference, p. 503
- Charles Evans Hughes, p. 503
- Kellogg-Briand Pact, p. 505
- Adolf Hitler, p. 506

3. Five-Power Naval Treaty—limit size of navies; Four-Power Treaty—respect territories in the Pacific to avoid conflict; Nine-Power Treaty—guarantee China's territorial integrity

4a. They and other leaders of the women's movement helped try to negotiate disarmament.

b. Nations could not agree on a method of enforcing the pact.

c. The Allies could not repay their debts to the United States. They called in Germany's war debts, which Germany could not pay, leading to high inflation and economic depression.

5. Answers will vary. Students should mention that many Americans regretted the cost in lives and money of World War I and believed that the traditional practice of avoiding European conflicts should again be the U.S. foreign policy since it worked so well in the past.

INTERPRETING THE VISUAL RECORD

The depression abroad. These German children are using bundles of German marks as building blocks. *What do you think this photograph reveals about the German economy?*

History Makers Speak
"We changed some French money in the railway station at Kehl. For 10 francs I received 670 marks. Ten francs amounted to about 90 cents in Canadian money. That 90 cents lasted Mrs. Hemingway and me for a day of heavy spending and at the end of the day we had 120 marks left! . . . Kehl's best hotel, which is a very well turned-out place, served a five-course table d'hôte meal for 120 marks, which amounts to 15 cents in our money.**"**

—Ernest Hemingway, quoted in *By-Line*, edited by William White

With his country near financial collapse, one particularly embittered German World War I veteran sought someone to blame. **Adolf Hitler** had survived a poison gas attack during the war and remained convinced that politicians, not the German army, were responsible for Germany losing the war. Feeling betrayed, Hitler joined a radical political organization and hatched a plot to overthrow the German government in 1923. The plot failed, and Hitler was sent to jail. There he continued to plan revenge against those whom he believed had betrayed Germany.

In 1924 a plan proposed by Charles Dawes temporarily eased Germany's economic crisis. The Dawes Plan provided loans and gave Germany more time to make its reparations payments. In 1931, as the worldwide depression deepened, President Herbert Hoover declared a year's moratorium, or halt, on reparations and war-debt payments. The moratorium, however, only prolonged the crisis. Most of the war debts remained unpaid. By 1934 Finland was the only debtor nation that could make even a token payment on its debts.

✔ **READING CHECK: Drawing Inferences** How did the U.S. role as a creditor nation affect its foreign policy after World War I? U.S. foreign policy emphasized seeking debt payments from other nations.

SECTION ❶ REVIEW

1. Define and explain:
isolationism
disarmament

2. Identify and explain:
Emily Greene Balch
Washington Conference
Charles Evans Hughes
Kellogg-Briand Pact
Adolf Hitler

3. Summarizing Copy the graphic organizer below. Use it to list the treaties signed at the Washington Conference and their objectives.

Washington Conference

4. **Finding the Main Idea**
a. What contributions did Jane Addams and Emily Greene Balch make to postwar peace efforts?
b. Why was the Kellogg-Briand Pact unsuccessful in resolving the conflict in Manchuria?
c. How did war debts and reparations lead to economic crisis in Germany and other European countries?

5. **Writing and Critical Thinking**

Supporting a Point of View Write an editorial supporting an isolationist policy for the United States.
Consider:
- the effects of World War I
- traditional U.S. foreign policy
- public opinion toward Europe

Homework Practice Online
keyword: SE3 HP17

506

SECTION ②

After completing Section 2, students should be able to:

OBJECTIVE 1 Discuss the role the United States played in Nicaraguan politics.

OBJECTIVE 2 Explain how U.S. relations with Latin America changed in the 1930s.

OBJECTIVE 3 Analyze how the Great Depression affected Latin American countries.

LET'S GET STARTED!

Write the following terms on the chalkboard: *Monroe Doctrine* and *Roosevelt Corollary*. As students enter the classroom, have them write as much as they can about these two U.S. foreign-policy doctrines. Have volunteers share their responses with the class. *(Students might mention that the Monroe Doctrine stipulated that European intervention in the Western Hemisphere would be considered a threat to U.S. security and that the Americas were off-limits to European expansion. The Roosevelt Corollary extended the Monroe Doctrine to claim a greater U.S. role in maintaining order in Latin America.)* Tell students that in Section 2 they will learn about how U.S. policy toward Latin America changed in the 1920s and 1930s.

SECTION 2

Relations with Latin America

READ TO DISCOVER

1. What role did the United States play in Nicaraguan politics?
2. How did U.S. relations with Latin America change in the 1930s?
3. How did the Great Depression affect Latin American countries?

DEFINE

nationalize
caudillos

IDENTIFY

Emiliano Chamorro
Henry Stimson
Augusto César Sandino
Adolfo Díaz
Anastasio Somoza
Good Neighbor policy
Lázaro Cárdenas
Josephus Daniels

▶ **WHY IT MATTERS TODAY**

The U.S. relationship with Latin America remains important to both regions. Use CNNfyi.com or other **current events** sources to identify a recent political or economic agreement between the United States and one or more Latin American countries. Record your findings in your journal.

CNNfyi.com

EYEWITNESSES TO History "*Ever since the World War we have been manufacturing more goods than we can sell. We are looking for new markets. Latin America and South America afford [provide] these markets. And yet in order to allow a few bankers to exploit [take advantage of] Nicaragua, our oil interests to exploit Mexico, we are willing to ruin the legitimate commercial business of this country. We are willing to let thousands of men remain out of employment who could be working in the manufacturing plants of this country if we by peaceful means sought the friendship and trade of Central and South America.*"

—Burton K. Wheeler, "Condemns the Intervention in Nicaragua," 1927

Senator Burton K. Wheeler

In 1927 Senator Burton K. Wheeler of Montana condemned U.S. policy toward Latin America. For many years the United States had dominated Latin America both economically and militarily. This began to change during the 1930s as the United States tried to build a more equal relationship with its southern neighbors.

Intervention in Nicaragua

The United States played a large role in Nicaraguan politics throughout the 1920s and 1930s. In 1925 General **Emiliano Chamorro** (chah-MAWR-roh) overthrew the government, sparking a bitter civil war. The United States refused to recognize Chamorro's government. In May 1926 President Coolidge ordered in the U.S. Marine Corps to protect American commercial interests. He also sent **Henry Stimson**, a longtime public official, to negotiate an end to the civil war. Stimson brought the two sides together, and they negotiated a peace treaty in May 1927. In the treaty, Stimson called for the abolition of Nicaragua's armed forces. U.S. troops would then train a new Nicaraguan National Guard to maintain order after the U.S. withdrawal.

Augusto César Sandino (sahn-DEE-noh), a general who opposed Chamorro, refused to accept Stimson's proposal. During the 1920s Sandino had worked as a mechanic for U.S. companies in Honduras and Guatemala. In 1923 he began working for a U.S.-owned oil company in Tampico, Mexico. There Sandino read about Simon Bolívar, the great hero of the Latin American independence struggle.

In 1926, after his return to Nicaragua, Sandino organized a revolt against Chamorro and Chamorro's successor, **Adolfo Díaz**. Sandino hoped to rid Nicaragua of the Americans, whom he viewed as invaders. He also wanted to allow ordinary Nicaraguans to control their country's land and wealth. Sandino planned to help workers and peasants "exploit our own natural resources for the benefit of the Nicaraguan family in general."

SECTION 2 RESOURCES

REPRODUCIBLE
▶ Guided Reading Strategy 17.2
▶ Geography Activity 17: The Good Neighbor Policy

TECHNOLOGY
▶ One-Stop Planner, Lesson 17.2
▶ The American Nation Video Program Segment: U.S. Warships in Havana Harbor; Teacher's Guide, pp. 191–92
▶ Holt Researcher: American History CD–ROM
▶ Homework Practice Online

REINFORCEMENT, REVIEW, AND ASSESSMENT
▶ Section 2 Review, p. 511
▶ Daily Quiz 17.2
▶ Main Idea Activity 17.2
▶ English Audio Summary 17.2
▶ Spanish Audio Summary 17.2

TEACH OBJECTIVE 1

LEVEL 1: Pair students and have each pair create an annotated time line chronicling U.S. intervention in Nicaragua during the 1920s and 1930s. *(Time lines should include: 1926—U.S. Marines invade Nicaragua to protect American commercial interests; May 1927—Henry Stimson helps negotiate an end to civil war in Nicaragua; 1927—U.S. troops train the Nicaraguan National Guard; 1926–33—U.S. troops fight against Sandino's forces; 1933—U.S. Marines withdraw from Nicaragua; 1936 and beyond—the U.S. government backs the Somoza regime.)* Have students present their time lines to the class. **English Language Learners, Cooperative Learning**

LEVELS 2 AND 3: Tell students to imagine that they are reporters covering the U.S. role in Nicaraguan politics. It is 1936 and Somoza has just seized political power. Have each student write a newspaper article explaining the role that the United States has played in Nicaraguan politics up to that point. *(See the Level 1 lesson for the correct events related to the U.S. role in Nicaragua.)* Have volunteers read their articles to the class. Students may wish to include their articles in their portfolios.

GLOBAL RELATIONS

The Clark Memorandum. Written by State Department official J. Reuben Clark, the Clark Memorandum declared that the Monroe Doctrine could not be interpreted to mean that the United States had the right to intervene in the internal affairs of Latin American countries. Published in 1930, the Clark Memorandum differed from the Roosevelt Corollary, which had declared that the Monroe Doctrine included the right of intervention.

ACTIVITY: Have students conduct research on current foreign-policy statements about Latin America. Ask students to summarize these statements.

GRAPH ANSWER
from 1920 to 1925

The American Nation
VIDEO PROGRAM

U.S. Warships in Havana Harbor; Teacher's Guide, pp. 191–92

Search 41576, Play to 42493
Videodisc 2, Side A

Play   Pause

See *Teacher's Guide* for Spanish barcode.

508

Latin American Exports to the United States, 1920–1940

Value (in millions of dollars) vs **Year**

Source: *Historical Statistics of the United States*

Interpreting Graphs Latin American economies became more closely linked to the U.S. economy in the early 1900s.

? Skills Assessment During which five-year period did the value of Latin American exports to the United States decrease the most?

In 1936 Franklin Roosevelt proposed an inter-American conference for peace in Argentina.

Sandino's forces ranged from as few as 30 to as many as 3,000 soldiers. They relied on sympathetic farmers to feed and house them. Sandino's forces proved a tough opponent for the U.S. Marines. The marines never defeated Sandino.

The war became increasingly costly for the United States, which was in the midst of the Great Depression. In 1933 President Hoover withdrew the last of the U.S. troops. A year later, the commander of the U.S.-trained National Guard, General **Anastasio Somoza**, ordered Sandino's assassination. With Sandino dead, organized resistance to Somoza and his military evaporated. Somoza forced out the Nicaraguan president in 1936 and took over the presidency the next year. With U.S. backing, Somoza and other members of his family ruled Nicaragua almost without interruption until the Sandinista revolution—named for Sandino—overthrew the dynasty in 1979.

✔ **READING CHECK: Sequencing** Trace U.S.-Nicaraguan relations in the 1920s and 1930s. **Coolidge ordered the U.S. Marines into Nicaragua, Stimson demanded abolition of Nicaragua's armed forces, and U.S. troops withdrew.**

A Change in Policy

While the United States isolated itself from events in Europe and Asia, Presidents Coolidge, Hoover, and Roosevelt all tried to improve relations with Latin American countries. Before his inauguration, Hoover toured Latin America to promote goodwill, winning many new friends for the United States.

The Good Neighbor. President Franklin D. Roosevelt built upon the goodwill created by previous presidents. In his 1933 inaugural address Roosevelt spelled out his policy of mutual respect toward Latin America, which became known as the **Good Neighbor policy**.

> **History Makers Speak**
>
> **"In the field of world policy I would dedicate this nation to the policy of the good neighbor—the neighbor who resolutely respects himself and, because he does so, respects the rights of others."**
>
> —Franklin D. Roosevelt, "Inaugural Address," 1933

To back up his words, Roosevelt signed a treaty with Cuba that canceled the Platt Amendment. This amendment had given the United States the right to intervene in Cuban affairs. In 1936 he gave up the U.S. right to intervene in Panama. Roosevelt also withdrew marines from Haiti, where they had been stationed as an occupying force since 1915.

In economic matters the United States had often behaved more like a landlord than a good neighbor. After World War I, large U.S. companies increased their investments in banana, coffee, and sugar

TEACH OBJECTIVE 2

LEVEL 1: Pair students and ask each pair to write a paragraph describing how U.S. relations with Latin America changed in the 1930s. *(Students should explain that the United States established the Good Neighbor policy, a policy of mutual respect. As a result, the United States canceled the Platt Amendment, gave up its right to intervene unilaterally in Panama, withdrew marines from Haiti, and did not intervene when the Mexican government decided to nationalize the oil industry.)* Have volunteers read their paragraphs to the class.
English Language Learners, Cooperative Learning

LEVELS 2 AND 3: Pair students and tell them to imagine that they are news analysts for a radio station in the late 1930s. Have each pair create a transcript of a radio talk show discussion about how U.S. relations with Latin America changed during the1930s. Have one student prepare the reporter's transcript and the other student prepare the transcript for the interviewee. *(See the Level 1 lesson for how U.S. relations with Latin America changed.)* Have students perform their discussions for the class.
Cooperative Learning

---

plantations in Central America and the Caribbean. The governments of some countries existed mainly to serve the interests of these foreign companies and became known as banana republics.

The United Fruit Company was the largest U.S. company in Latin America. It owned millions of acres in Central America and the Caribbean, and was Guatemala's largest landowner, exporter, and employer. In addition to establishing plantations, United Fruit and other companies built roads and railroads. They also controlled the ports and shipping lines necessary to export their products.

U.S. companies played a central economic role in Latin America. They also had tremendous political power. The companies made alliances with Latin American landowners and politicians and often played a direct role in governing the countries in which they operated. Many Latin Americans resented the economic and political power of the large U.S. companies. Chilean poet Pablo Neruda (nay-ROO-dah) wrote:

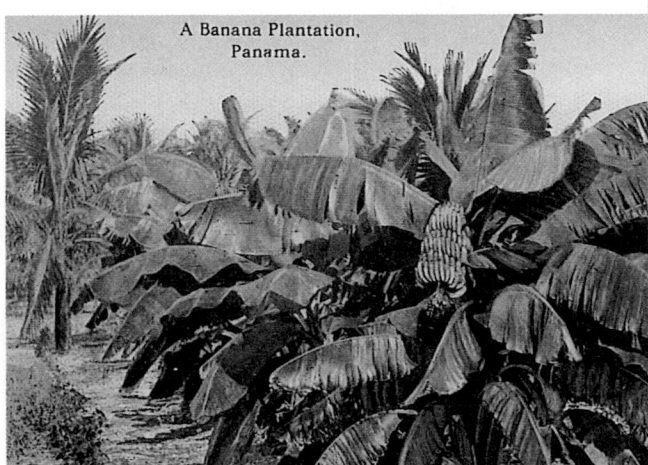

A Banana Plantation, Panama.

U.S. companies invested in banana plantations like this one in Panama.

> **❝The Fruit Company, Inc. reserved for itself the most succulent, the central coast of my own land, the delicate waist of America. It rechristened its territories as the 'Banana Republics.'❞**
>
> —"The United Fruit Co."

Relations with Mexico. A serious test of the Good Neighbor policy came in March 1938. Mexico's president, **Lázaro Cárdenas** (KAHR-day-nahs), began to **nationalize**, or assert government control over, the country's oil industry. Although the Mexican constitution of 1917 proclaimed that Mexico controlled all its underground resources, U.S. and British firms had continued to own and operate oil companies in Mexico. When the companies refused to meet the demands of Mexican oil workers for higher wages and better working conditions, President Cárdenas nationalized the oil fields.

U.S. oil companies hotly criticized Mexico's seizure of their property. They pressed President Roosevelt to intervene. Meanwhile, the U.S. ambassador to Mexico, **Josephus Daniels**, argued for a compromise between the Mexican government and the oil companies. He urged the

PRIMARY SOURCE

Latin American Views of Foreign Investment

The United States has historically dominated Latin America, both politically and economically. In 1933 a member of the Honduran congress described the effect of foreign investment on his country. **What points of view do these sources offer?**

> **❝The national farmers are condemned to disappear, for the fruit companies are becoming owners of the lands on the coast, including the alternate lots, which they now have almost entirely in their possession, through transfers made by the Hondurans themselves. The villages, the small riverside farms disappear, and the depopulation of the region follows.❞**

A 1929 report by the Sociedad Económica de Amigos del País described the power of foreign companies in Costa Rica.

> **❝It is evident . . . that the fruit company, besides having taken possession of a large portion of the Atlantic Zone, is exercising over it a predominance and control such as not even the government of the republic itself exercises; there it is the company which commands.❞**

HISTORY MAKERS SPEAK

Franklin D. Roosevelt in *Foreign Affairs*

International Relations.
In a 1928 article Franklin D. Roosevelt expressed his reasons for wanting to improve U.S. foreign relations: "The outside world views us with less goodwill today than at any previous period. This is serious unless we take the deliberate position that the people of the United States owe nothing to the rest of mankind and care nothing for the opinion of others so long as our seacoasts are impregnable and our pocketbooks are well filled."

CRITICAL THINKING What might Roosevelt's statement have revealed about his attitude toward isolationism?

ANSWER: Students might suggest that he believed isolationism to be a selfish policy.

VISUAL RECORD ANSWER
Students might suggest that the postcard inaccurately portrays plantation life because no workers are shown.

PRIMARY SOURCE ANSWER
Students might suggest that the first shows what large fruit companies are doing to small native farmers; the second compares the power of large fruit companies to governments.

TEACH OBJECTIVE 3

ALL LEVELS: Tell students that an economic depression can have political and social effects on a country, as well as economic ones. Ask students to identify the possible social and political effects. *(Students might suggest that a depression might affect some sectors of society more than others or that a country's political leaders may be held accountable for an economic downturn.)* To help students understand how the Great Depression affected Latin American countries, copy the following graphic organizer on the chalkboard, omitting the italicized answers. Have each student complete it. Ask volunteers to share their answers with the class.
English Language Learners

HOMEWORK *Tell students to imagine that they are editors for an encyclopedia. Have each student write a short entry on the rise of caudillos in Latin American countries during the Great Depression.*

Relations with Mexico.
Officials in the U.S. State Department sent a diplomatic note to the Mexican government demanding immediate payment for the properties seized when the Mexican government nationalized the country's oil fields. To give force to the message, U.S. purchases of Mexican silver were immediately suspended. Ambassador Josephus Daniels, however, advised the Mexican government to ignore the note. With President Franklin D. Roosevelt's approval, administration officials authorized additional silver purchases from Mexico above the world market price.

CRITICAL THINKING Why might Roosevelt have approved silver purchases from Mexico?

ANSWER: Students might suggest that he wanted to send a clear message to Mexico that conflict over the oil properties would not damage relations between the two nations.

CHANGING WAYS ANSWERS

greatly increased; the United States

VISUAL RECORD ANSWER

(for p. 511)
Students might cite the poor condition of the house and the cattle.

Mexican president Lázaro Cárdenas (center) and his secretary of foreign relations (right) meet with Britain's minister to Mexico (left).

United States to recognize Mexico's right to control its oil resources but added that U.S. companies should be compensated for the property they had lost.

Most Mexicans supported Cárdenas's bold action against the oil companies. Many worried, however, that the United States might invade their country to restore U.S. oil companies' property rights. Roosevelt decided to maintain good relations with Mexico. He acknowledged Mexico's right to control its own resources and urged the oil companies to reach an agreement with the Mexican government for fair compensation. Mexico agreed to the compromise and began payments in 1939.

✔ **READING CHECK: Making Generalizations** How did the economic interests of large companies affect U.S. relations with Latin America? The U.S. government sometimes defended the companies' economic interests.

★ Changing Ways Investments in Latin America

■ **Understanding Change** The economies of the United States and Latin American countries have long been connected. The industrialization of the United States during the late 1800s resulted in a rapid expansion of this connection. Today the United States and the countries of Latin America continue to strengthen the links between their economies. *How has the value of U.S. investments in Latin America changed over time? Has the changing balance of trade between the two regions been more beneficial for the United States or for Latin America?*

THEN

NOW

	THEN	**NOW**
Value of Direct U.S. Investments in Latin America	$3.52 billion	$196.66 billion
Value of U.S. Exports to Latin America	$698 million	$131.09 billion
Value of U.S. Imports from Latin America	$1.12 billion	$136.84 billion

Sources: *Historical Statistics of the United States* and *Statistical Abstract of the United States: 2000.* Data reflect 1929 and 1998.

REVIEW

Have students complete the **Section 2 Review** on p. 511.

ASSESS

Have students complete **Daily Quiz 17.2.** As **Alternative Assessment**, you may want to use the radio talk show or the newspaper article in this section's lessons.

RETEACH

Have students complete **Main Idea Activity for English Language Learners and Special-Needs Students 17.2.** Then organize students into three groups. Have each group create a graphic organizer for one of the objectives in this section. Then

have each group exchange its graphic organizer—with answers omitted—with another group and complete the graphic organizer that it receives.

English Language Learners, Cooperative Learning

EXTEND

Have students conduct research on the history of one of the Latin American countries discussed in this section. Students should focus their research on events that occurred during the 1920s and 1930s. Then have students write a series of diary entries that discuss the political, social, and economic changes that occurred in the country. **Block Scheduling**

New Latin American Leaders

The Wall Street crash of 1929 sent shock waves through Latin America. The worldwide economic depression meant lower prices for bananas, coffee, and other Latin American crops. Farm wages dropped to eight cents a day.

As workers lost their jobs, the gulf between Latin America's small class of wealthy landowners and the large class of poor landless people widened. One U.S. diplomat, Major A. R. Harris, commented on the inequality he saw between the classes in El Salvador in 1931.

History Makers Speak

❝The first thing one observes . . . is the number of expensive automobiles on the streets. . . . There seems to be nothing between these high-priced cars and the ox-cart with its barefooted attendant. . . . Roughly 90 percent of the wealth of the country is held by about one-half of one percent of the population.❞

—Major A. R. Harris, quoted in *The Good Neighbor*, by George Black

In the 1930s **caudillos** (kow-DEE-yohs) took power in many Latin American countries. Caudillos were military leaders who used force to maintain order. During the 1930s caudillos seized power in Cuba, the Dominican Republic, Guatemala, and Honduras. Some U.S. diplomats denounced the bans on opposition parties and restrictions on freedom of speech that the caudillos employed to maintain their power. However, the United States often supported the caudillos because they created favorable environments for American companies to do business.

INTERPRETING THE VISUAL RECORD

Poverty. The Great Depression devastated many Latin American nations and contributed to the rise of dictators. *What signs of economic hardship do you see in this picture of a Salvadoran family?*

✔ **READING CHECK: Identifying Cause and Effect** How did the Great Depression contribute to the rise to power of caudillos?
Caudillos seized power after widespread unemployment led to instability.

SECTION (2) REVIEW

1. **Define and explain:**
   nationalize
   caudillos

2. **Identify and explain:**
   Emiliano Chamorro
   Henry Stimson
   Augusto César Sandino
   Adolfo Díaz
   Anastasio Somoza
   Good Neighbor policy
   Lázaro Cárdenas
   Josephus Daniels

3. **Identifying Cause and Effect** Copy the graphic organizer below. Use it to list changes that the Good Neighbor policy brought to the U.S. relationship with Latin America.

   Good Neighbor policy
   Results

4. **Finding the Main Idea**
   a. Why did the United States intervene in Nicaraguan politics throughout the 1920s and into the 1930s? What was the effect of this intervention?
   b. What economic and political roles did U.S. companies have in Latin American countries?
   c. How did President Roosevelt respond to the nationalization of Mexican oil fields?

5. **Writing and Critical Thinking**
   Summarizing Imagine that you are a documentary filmmaker. Prepare a background report for your film, *A History of U.S. Relations in Latin America.*
   Consider:
   • U.S. policy toward Latin America in the 1920s
   • the goals of the Good Neighbor policy
   • the effects of the Great Depression on Latin America

go. hrw .com Homework Practice Online
keyword: SE3 HP17

SECTION 2 REVIEW ANSWERS

1. Define
• nationalize, p. 509
• caudillos, p. 511

2. Identify
• Emiliano Chamorro, p. 507
• Henry Stimson, p. 507
• Augusto César Sandino, p. 507
• Adolfo Díaz, p. 507
• Anastasio Somoza, p. 508
• Good Neighbor policy, p. 508
• Lázaro Cárdenas, p. 509
• Josephus Daniels, p. 509

3. The policy limited military intervention but did not end U.S. economic or political domination.

4a. to protect U.S. economic interests; but intervention was costly and led to Sandino's revolution

b. Some countries were run to serve the economic interests of U.S. companies, and many companies played a direct role in governing countries in which they operated.

c. He decided to maintain good relations by recognizing Mexico's right to control its own resources. He encouraged Mexico to fairly compensate U.S. oil companies for their losses.

5. Answers will vary. Reports should explain that the United States has always tried to protect U.S. commercial interests in Latin America. In 1933 Roosevelt's Good Neighbor Policy promoted mutual respect for Latin America, but U.S. companies still controlled many Latin American countries.

The Rise of Militarism

❝The peace, the freedom, and the security of 90 percent of the population of the world is being jeopardized by the remaining 10 percent who are threatening a breakdown of all international order and law. . . . War is a contagion [disease]. . . . It can engulf states and peoples remote from the original scene of hostilities. . . . If civilization is to survive, the principles of [peace] must be restored.❞

—Franklin D. Roosevelt, speech, October 5, 1937

President Roosevelt speaks to the American people.

In this 1937 speech, President Franklin D. Roosevelt warned Americans of the growing danger of war. A rise in military activity by a number of nations and leaders made peace seem increasingly fragile.

Mussolini in Italy

Although Italy had been on the winning side when World War I ended, many Italians felt they had not benefited from the Treaty of Versailles. Thousands of Italian veterans were unable to find jobs. Many joined the Italian Communist Party, which urged Italian peasants to take over land and called on workers to seize factories.

To destroy the Communist Party and promote his own rise to power, **Benito Mussolini** founded the **Fascist Party** in 1921. The Fascists believed that a military-dominated government should control all aspects of society. Beginning in 1921, bloody clashes between Communists and Fascists created a situation bordering on civil war. In October 1922 Mussolini led an army of his followers, named **Blackshirts** for the color of their uniforms, in a march on Rome. Supported by nationalists who wanted to strengthen Italy and businesspeople who opposed the Socialists and Communists, the Fascists occupied the city.

The Italian king appointed Mussolini prime minister and granted him dictatorial powers. Mussolini limited freedom of speech, arrested political opponents, and restricted voting rights. Acting on a pledge to make Italy an imperial power, Mussolini sent Italian forces into the African nation of Ethiopia in 1935. The small, poorly equipped Ethiopian army proved no match for Italy's airplanes and machine guns. The U.S. Congress, fearful of being drawn into the conflict, passed a neutrality act banning arms shipments to both sides. The embargo hurt Ethiopia more than it did Italy, which continued to receive weapons from Germany and oil from American companies.

African Americans raised money to send relief and medical aid to the Ethiopians. Thousands of African Americans volunteered to fight in Ethiopia, but pressure from the U.S. government forced Ethiopia to reject the offer. This lack of support convinced other fascist countries, such as Germany, that aggression would go unpunished.

✔ **READING CHECK: Identifying Cause and Effect** Why did Italy become a fascist state?
the high unemployment rate, leadership of Mussolini, and widespread opposition to Socialists and Communists

TEACH OBJECTIVES 1 AND 2

LEVEL 1: On the chalkboard create a two-column chart. In one column write the heading *Mussolini Creates a Fascist State* and in the other column write *Stalin Maintains Power in the Soviet Union.* Have students suggest events to include under each heading. *(Students might suggest that Mussolini's actions included: leading Fascists in a power struggle against Communists, occupying Rome with the Blackshirts and the support of nationalists and industrialists, being appointed prime minister and given dictatorial powers, limiting freedom of speech and voting rights, and arresting opponents. Students might suggest that Stalin maintained power by seizing private land and collectivizing agriculture, by sending opponents*

to forced labor camps, by using the police and army to suppress dissent, and by purging the party and army of opposition.) Conclude by leading a discussion about these two leaders.
English Language Learners

TEACH OBJECTIVE 1

LEVELS 2 AND 3: Tell students to imagine that they are foreign-exchange students in Italy witnessing Mussolini's rise to power. Have each student write a letter to a family member in the United States. Students' letters should describe the steps that Mussolini is taking to establish a fascist regime in Italy and their response to these actions. *(See the Level 1 lesson for the correct list of events.)* Have volunteers read their letters to the class.

Stalin in the Soviet Union

As Benito Mussolini seized power in Italy, a battle was being waged for power in the Soviet Union—the communist nation formed from Russia and several other surrounding states in 1922. By the early 1920s Vladimir Lenin, leader of the Bolshevik Revolution, was in poor health. His death in 1924 spurred a struggle for power among Communist Party leaders. Using underhanded tactics and even organizing the assassination of his enemies, **Joseph Stalin** eventually emerged as the nation's leader.

Driven by ambition, Stalin turned the Soviet Union into a **totalitarian state**—a country where the government has complete control. In 1927 the government began taking control of privately owned lands and reorganizing them into large state-run farms. Farmers who protested this policy were sent to forced labor camps. In all, some 15 million people were sent to Soviet labor camps by 1933. The reorganization policy resulted in decreased food production and widespread famine.

Stalin imposed his will through the Soviet Union's powerful Red Army. He used the army and other police forces to crush all opposition. In the late 1930s, fearing opponents were trying to weaken him, Stalin began a campaign to purge all perceived enemies from the Communist Party and the Red Army. Although the exact figure is not known, some historians estimate that eventually as many as 30 million people may have died as a result of Stalin's policies.

✔ **READING CHECK: Summarizing** In what ways was Soviet leader Joseph Stalin a dictator? Stalin took control of privately owned lands and used the Red Army to crush opposition.

Hitler in Germany

In 1932 Adolf Hitler's National Socialist Party, or **Nazi Party**, won nearly 40 percent of the vote in national elections. Hitler became chancellor of Germany the next year. While in prison, he had written *Mein Kampf [My Struggle]*, which laid out his plans to restore German power. Hitler blamed Jews, Communists, and intellectuals for Germany's decline. Hitler's views won him many supporters, particularly among those ruined by the depression.

The Third Reich. Hitler's government, called the Third Reich (the Third Empire), claimed dictatorial powers. Hitler prohibited Jews and non-Nazis from holding government positions, outlawed strikes, and made military service mandatory. Nazi storm troopers, known as **Brownshirts** because of the color of their uniforms, crushed all political opposition.

Hitler used his tight control over German industry to rearm the country, in violation of the Treaty of Versailles. He declared that this rearmament strengthened the economy and reduced unemployment. In a speech that Hitler gave in 1933, he declared, "The buildup of the armed forces is the most important precondition for . . . political power." He wanted to use this power for the "conquest of new Lebensraum [space for expansion] in the East."

These workers at the "Lenin's Way Collective Farm" in Russia are sharing a communal lunch.

The German press often portrayed Adolf Hitler as Germany's savior, as in this image from a 1934 German magazine.

GLOBAL RELATIONS

The United States and the Soviets. Soviet leaders such as Vladimir Lenin and Joseph Stalin believed that the U.S. capitalist economy would eventually fall to a communist revolution. Nonetheless, they admired the technological achievements and efficiency of the U.S. economy. For their part, many American business leaders were eager to work with the Soviets. These attitudes led to growing economic ties between the two nations during the turmoil of Stalin's reign.

CRITICAL THINKING Why might American businesses have wanted to develop ties to the Soviet Union?

ANSWER: Students might suggest that American business leaders viewed the Soviet Union as a large potential market for their products.

THAT'S INTERESTING!

Stalin was born Iosif Dzhugashvili in 1879. He took the name Stalin, which means "steel," in 1912 when he began writing articles for a communist newspaper.

Technology Resources
Everyday Life in America Transparency 25: The Rise of the Third Reich

TEACH OBJECTIVE 2

LEVELS 2 AND 3: Ask students to imagine that they are living in the Soviet Union under the Stalin regime. Have each student write a diary entry that discusses steps that Stalin has taken to maintain his power and his or her response to those steps. *(See the Level 1 lesson for the correct steps.)* Ask volunteers to read their diary entries to the class.

TEACH OBJECTIVE 3

ALL LEVELS: Review with students the events in Germany that led to Hitler's imprisonment. *(Tell students that Hitler's belief that politicians were responsible for Germany's defeat in World War I motivated him to attempt to overthrow the government.)* Ask students to recall why Germans were dissatisfied with the government. *(Students might suggest that Germans were bitter about war reparations and suffered from inflation and the falling value of the German mark.)* To help students understand Hitler's rise to power, copy the following graphic organizer on the chalkboard, omitting the italicized answers. Have each student complete it.

English Language Learners

Hitler's Rise to Power in Germany

Hitler's views win him many supporters. → *The Nazi Party wins 40 percent of the vote in national elections.* → *Hitler is appointed chancellor of Germany.* → *Hitler claims dictatorial powers; Hitler crushes political opposition.*

The Refugee Crisis. U.S. immigration laws permitted 23,370 German immigrants to enter the country annually. However, this quota was rarely met during the early and mid-1930s. As early as 1934, German laws kept Jews from leaving the country with any more than the equivalent of $4. Meanwhile, U.S. laws forbade the entry of impoverished immigrants. By the time the war began more emigrants from Germany, most of whom were Jews, arrived in the United States. However, the U.S. government refused to increase the quota for refugees.

CRITICAL THINKING Why did the U.S. government forbid impoverished immigrants from entering the country during the early and mid-1930s?

ANSWER: Students might suggest that the depression led government officials to tighten restrictions and to deny entry to immigrants who might need economic assistance.

The Nazis used posters like this one to appeal to Germans' desire to see their country reclaim its role as a world power.

THE GRANGER COLLECTION, NEW YORK

INTERPRETING THE VISUAL RECORD

The Spanish Civil War. These Spanish Loyalists are marching from Madrid to fight a rebel army heading toward the city. *In what ways do these troops appear to differ from a regular army?*

VISUAL RECORD ANSWER
Students might suggest that the women wearing civilian clothing do not look like typical soldiers.

In March 1936, German troops moved into the Rhineland. Two years later they overran Austria. Hitler then turned toward the Sudetenland (soo-DAYT-uhn-land) region of western Czechoslovakia, where more than 3 million German-speaking people lived. Hitler demanded that Czechoslovakia turn over the region to Germany. Czechoslovakia refused Hitler's demand.

Anti-Semitism. Meanwhile, Hitler's **anti-Semitism**, or hatred of Jews, became official government policy. In 1935 Hitler instituted the Nuremberg Laws, which deprived Jews of their German citizenship and authorized the destruction of Jewish property. Gradually the oppression of Jews increased. On November 9, 1938, Nazi thugs burned down synagogues and destroyed Jewish businesses. Known as *Kristallnacht*, or "the night of broken glass," the violence provided a chilling preview of the fate that awaited European Jews and others whom Hitler opposed.

Increased oppression caused many Jews to flee the country. Most wealthy or famous Jewish refugees were able to find safe haven abroad. Hundreds of writers, artists, and scientists came to the United States. The vast majority of Jewish refugees, however, had no place to turn. Many countries, including the United States, had strict immigration laws. Despite outrage at events like *Kristallnacht*, most Americans remained unwilling to encourage Jewish immigration.

✔ **READING CHECK: Sequencing** List in order the events that led to Adolf Hitler's rise to power in Germany. *Mein Kampf* won Hitler many supporters, and electoral success by the Nazi Party led to Hitler becoming chancellor in 1933.

Franco in Spain

Fascism also spread to Spain. In the 1930s Spain experienced bitter political conflicts. In 1931 a constitution that limited the power of the military and the Catholic Church went into effect. It called for reforms including universal suffrage, the nationalization of public utilities, and land for peasants. Conservative military men who felt threatened by the reforms united under the leadership of General **Francisco Franco**. In July 1936 the Fascist army officers tried to overthrow the government, starting the Spanish Civil War between Fascists and Loyalists.

After almost three years of fighting, Franco took over the government with German and Italian military aid. The Soviet Union aided the Loyalists, but President Roosevelt's fears of being drawn into a European war kept the United States from sending direct aid. Some 3,000 individual Americans, however, did join the fight against fascism. Ernest Hemingway covered the Spanish Civil War as a journalist. He expressed his support for the Loyalist cause in the powerful novel *For Whom the Bell Tolls* (1940).

These Americans were part of what was called the **Popular Front**—an international alliance of organizations united against fascism. Joseph Stalin had used the term Popular Front in a 1935 speech denouncing fascism. Fearful of Adolf Hitler's military motives, Stalin declared that communism and fascism were incompatible. Although he used many of the same totalitarian tactics as the fascist leaders, Stalin's efforts encouraged many noncommunists to oppose fascism.

TEACH OBJECTIVE 4

LEVEL 1: Organize students into small groups. Have each group create a cause-and-effect chart explaining the causes of the Spanish Civil War. *(Groups' charts should show that the populist reforms in Spain's new constitution threatened conservative military men. Led by General Franco, Fascist army officers attempted to overthrow the government, thus starting the civil war.)* Have each group present its chart to the class. **English Language Learners, Cooperative Learning**

LEVELS 2 AND 3: Tell students to imagine that it is July 1936 and that they are radio announcers describing the outbreak of the Spanish Civil War. Organize students into small groups.

Have each group prepare a radio broadcast describing the events that led to the conflict. *(See the Level 1 lesson for the correct events.)* Have students perform their broadcasts for the class. **Cooperative Learning**

HOMEWORK *Tell students to imagine that they are Americans who have decided to join the fighting in the Spanish Civil War. Have each student write a letter to a friend describing how the fighting started and why he or she has decided to join the Loyalist cause.*

NOTE: For an additional teaching idea, see the Chapter 17 open interviewing lesson in the **Creative Teaching Strategies** handbook.

After the Spanish Civil War, many Loyalists remained bitter over Western nations' failure to support their cause. In 1940 Julio Alvarez del Vayo, a wartime diplomat for the defeated Spanish republic, charged that this lack of support had cost the Loyalists the war.

> **"No, it was not Spanish democracy that failed. It was the other democracies who failed to save democratic Spain, as they will one day learn to their cost."**
>
> —Julio Alvarez del Vayo, *Freedom's Battle*

✔ **READING CHECK: Drawing Conclusions** How did the U.S. government and individual Americans respond to the Spanish Civil War? **President Roosevelt decided against sending direct aid, but some 3,000 Americans fought on the side of the Loyalists.**

Residents of Barcelona, Spain, often blocked the streets during the Spanish Civil War.

Skill-Building Strategies

Using Oral Histories

Oral histories—verbal accounts of historical events supplied by people who observed or participated in the events—are useful tools for learning about the past. They provide a close-up view of how specific people experienced the past. Oral histories also furnish valuable information about the opinions and feelings that people in history had about issues that affected them.

Oral histories are often taken down years or even decades after the events in question. It is therefore important to consider how the passage of time may have affected an interviewee's account of the past.

How to Use Oral Histories

1. **Become familiar with the source.** First, identify the person who was interviewed for the oral history and the general topic that he or she addressed. Then find out when the interview was conducted and, if possible, who conducted it.
2. **Study the account carefully.** Read the oral history thoroughly and carefully, taking note of any words or phrases that signal a statement of opinion.
3. **Assess the reliability of the account.** After you have read the oral history, evaluate its reliability as a piece of historical evidence. Be sure to consider how the interviewee's role in the events described, as well as the passage of time between the events and the interview, may have affected the account.
4. **Put the information to use.** Compare the oral history with other sources that address the same topic. Then use the results of your analysis and your knowledge of the historical period to draw conclusions.

Applying the Skill

Examine the following excerpt from an oral history from the 1980s provided by Hans Massaquoi, the son of a German mother and a Liberian father, who grew up in Germany during the 1930s.

> **"In '32, when I started school, I was six years old. In '33, my first teacher was fired for political reasons. I don't know what her involvements were. Gradually, the old teachers were replaced with younger ones, those with Nazi orientations. Then I began to notice a change in attitude. Teachers would make snide remarks about my race. One teacher would point me out as an example of the non-Aryan race. One time, I must have been ten, a teacher took me aside and said, 'When we're finished with the Jews, you're next.' He still had some inhibitions [reluctance]. He did not make that announcement before the class. (Laughs.) It was a private thing."**

Practicing the Skill

Use the excerpt above to answer the following questions.
1. What is the general topic of the excerpt?
2. How do you think the passage of time between the events described in the excerpt and the interview affected Massaquoi's account?
3. What is your opinion of the excerpt as a piece of historical evidence?
4. How does the excerpt contribute to your understanding of Nazi Germany during the 1930s?

CULTURE

Americans in Spain.

The Americans who fought in the Spanish Civil War were a diverse group, hailing from every part of the United States. However, most of them came from urban, industrial areas where they had been exposed to radical political ideas. The Americans, many of whom fought in a group called the Abraham Lincoln Battalion, were not well-trained soldiers. They suffered high casualty rates during the war. About one third of the American volunteers were killed.

CRITICAL THINKING Why might one American battalion have been named after Abraham Lincoln?

ANSWER: Students might suggest that Abraham Lincoln served as a symbol of the struggle for freedom.

SKILL-BUILDING STRATEGIES ANSWERS
Practicing the Skill
1. racial discrimination experienced by a young schoolboy
2. Massaquoi is able to laugh about discrimination he faced. He also knows that his teacher's inhibitions would later change.
3. Answers may vary. Massaquoi was a witness to the events preceding the war.
4. Answers will vary. Students might mention that they have a better understanding of the racial discrimination in Nazi Germany.

ALL LEVELS: Distribute Outline Map 32, East and Southeast Asia, from **American History Outline Maps.** Pair students and have each pair use the map on Japanese expansion in Section 4 to locate Beijing, Manchuria, Nanjing, and northern China on the blank map. Then have students label each of these places on their map with a short description of Japanese military actions at each location. *(Maps should include the following actions: 1931—Japanese troops invade Manchuria; July 1937—Japanese troops clash with Chinese troops near Beijing; Japanese troops occupy northern China and launch bombing raids against Chinese cities;*

November 1937—Japanese troops assault and occupy Nanjing.) In addition, tell students that Japan built up its naval forces in violation of Washington Conference pledges. Display students' maps around the classroom.
English Language Learners, Cooperative Learning

NOTE: To help students make meaningful connections between events in U.S. history and those in their own hometown, use the Chapter 17 **Hands-On History Activity**, The Military in Your Community.

⚡ internet connect

TOPIC: The Spanish Civil War
GO TO: go.hrw.com
KEYWORD: SE3 AN17

Have students access the Internet through the HRW Go site to conduct research on the causes, effects, and outcome of the Spanish Civil War. Then have students present their research in the form of a brochure in which veterans explain why they fought in the war and recount how they were viewed by Americans who did not participate in the war.

THAT'S INTERESTING!

Most Americans showed little interest in the events in Spain. Some two thirds of respondents to a 1937 opinion poll expressed no opinion about the Spanish Civil War.

UNDERSTANDING LITERATURE ANSWERS

1. Mike's lack of regard or respect for military medals reveals his disillusionment with the war.

2. Hemingway urges immediate action.

3. The first excerpt touches on the theme of the meaninglessness of war; the second conveys the theme of persistence and fighting for a belief.

AMERICAN Letters

Ernest Hemingway and War

Before the United States entered World War I, Ernest Hemingway served with the Italian infantry. He was seriously wounded. Hemingway's novels of the 1920s, including The Sun Also Rises *(1926), reflected many people's disillusionment with war. The story focuses on a group of World War I veterans trying to forget their experiences. In 1940, after working as a correspondent during the Spanish Civil War, Hemingway published* For Whom the Bell Tolls, *which depicted Loyalists battling nobly against Fascists.*

from *The Sun Also Rises*

"What medals have you got, Mike?"

"I haven't got any medals."

"You must have some."

"I suppose I've the usual medals. But I never sent in for them. One time there was this whopping big dinner . . . and the cards said medals will be worn. So naturally I had no medals, and I stopped at my tailor's . . . and I said to him: 'You've got to fix me up with some medals.' He said: 'What medals, sir?' And I said: 'Oh, any medals. Just give me a few medals.' So he said: 'What medals *have* you, sir?' And I said: 'How should I know?' . . . So he got me some medals, you know, miniature medals, and handed me the box, and I put it in my pocket and forgot it. . . .

Later on in the evening I found the box in my pocket. What's this? I said. Medals? Bloody military medals? So I cut them off their backing—you know, they put them on a strip—and gave them all around. Gave one to each girl. Form of souvenir. . . ."

"Tell the rest," Brett said.

"Don't you think that was funny?" Mike asked. We were all laughing. "It was. I swear it was. Any rate, my tailor wrote me and wanted the medals back. Sent a man around. Kept on writing for months. Seems some chap had left them to be cleaned. . . ." Mike paused. "Rotten luck for the tailor."

Ernest Hemingway

from *For Whom the Bell Tolls*

Why don't you ever think of how it is to win? You've been on the defensive for so long that you can't think of that. . . . But remember this that as long as we can hold them here we keep the fascists tied up. They can't attack any other country until they finish with us and

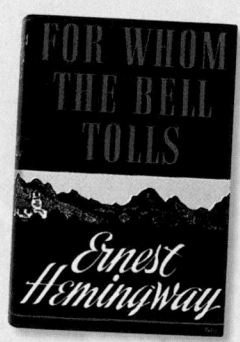

For Whom the Bell Tolls

they can never finish with us. If the French help at all, if only they leave the frontier open and if we get planes from America they can never finish with us. Never, if we get anything at all. These people will fight forever if they're well armed.

No you must not expect victory here, not for several years maybe. This is just a holding attack. . . .

Today is only one day in all the days that will ever be. But what will happen in all the other days that ever come can depend on what you do today.

UNDERSTANDING LITERATURE

1. In the first excerpt, what does Mike's attitude about military medals reveal about his attitude toward his service in World War I?

2. What is the meaning of the last two lines in the excerpt from *For Whom the Bell Tolls?*

3. How do these two excerpts convey universal themes?

REVIEW

Have students complete the **Section 3 Review** on p. 517.

ASSESS

Have students complete **Daily Quiz 17.3**. As **Alternative Assessment**, you may want to use the Soviet diary entries or the map activity in this section's lessons.

RETEACH

Have students complete **Main Idea Activity for English Language Learners and Special-Needs Students 17.3**. Then organize students into five groups and assign each group one of the following countries: Germany, Italy, Japan, Spain, and the

Soviet Union. Have each group answer these questions about its country: What actions were taken by the country's leader(s)? What were the leader's policies? How did these policies result in war (if applicable)? Have students discuss their answers with the class.

English Language Learners, Cooperative Learning

EXTEND

Have students conduct research on the Italian invasion of Ethiopia, Ethiopian monarch Haile Selassie's efforts to organize a defense for his country, or the impact of the U.S. neutrality act that banned arms shipments to the Italians and Ethiopians. Have each student write a report on his or her findings.

Block Scheduling

Militarists in Japan

As German aggression threatened Europe, Japanese expansion loomed in Asia. In the 1920s the leaders of Japan's military forces had gained increasing power. These military men wanted to lessen Japan's reliance on foreign imports. They also aimed to reduce the influence of Western countries in Asia and promote Japanese expansion throughout East Asia and the Pacific.

The creation of a Japanese empire would give Japan direct control over territories that produced iron, petroleum, rubber, and timber. Worsening economic conditions in Japan strengthened the popular appeal of the militarists' position. Japan's 1931 invasion of Manchuria signaled its imperialist ambitions. In 1934 and 1935, in violation of their Washington Conference pledges, the Japanese began a rapid naval buildup. Viscount Inoue, a member of the Japanese House of Peers, explained Japan's position during a 1937 visit to London.

Uchida Ryohei was president of the Black Dragon Society, which wanted to drive the Soviet Union out of East Asia.

 "Not only do we possess no oil supplies but this is true of very many other materials without which today a nation is helpless in wartime. To secure . . . raw materials has become a problem of greatly increased importance. The very life of Japan as a first-class power is dependent on this question."

—Viscount Inoue, quoted in *Tojo*, by Courtney Browne

On July 7, 1937, Japanese and Chinese troops clashed near Beijing. The incident soon developed into a full-scale war. Japan occupied northern China and launched devastating bombing raids against Chinese cities. In December 1937, Japanese troops brutally assaulted and occupied the Chinese city of Nanjing. Although the League of Nations and the United States condemned Japan's actions, they failed to halt Japanese expansion.

✔ **READING CHECK: Evaluating** Why did Japan's military promote expansion during the 1930s? Japan's military sought to lessen Japanese reliance on foreign imports and reduce the influence of Western nations in Asia.

SECTION 3 REVIEW

1. **Define and explain:**
   totalitarian state
   anti-Semitism

2. **Identify and explain:**
   Benito Mussolini
   Fascist Party
   Blackshirts
   Joseph Stalin
   Nazi Party
   Brownshirts
   Kristallnacht
   Francisco Franco
   Popular Front

3. **Comparing** Copy the chart below. Use it to describe how aggressive world leaders came to power and what their major policies were.

Leaders	Rise to Power	Policies
Mussolini		
Stalin		
Hitler		
Franco		
Japanese Militarists		

4. **Finding the Main Idea**
   a. How did dictators in the 1930s use military power against their own people?
   b. How did fascists gain power and influence in the 1920s and 1930s?
   c. Imagine that you are an American supporter of the Popular Front in the 1930s. Why are you fighting for the Spanish Loyalists?

5. **Writing and Critical Thinking**
   Making Generalizations Write a paragraph explaining why the United States, the League of Nations, and European nations did not stop Germany's or Japan's expansion in the 1930s.
   Consider:
   • Hitler's claims on the territory
   • the actions of other nations at the time
   • international cooperation that existed in the 1930s

go. Homework Practice Online
hrw .com   keyword: SE3 HP17

REVIEW SECTION 3 ANSWERS

1. **Define**
   • totalitarian state, p. 513
   • anti-Semitism, p. 514

2. **Identify**
   • Benito Mussolini, p. 512
   • Fascist Party, p. 512
   • Blackshirts, p. 512
   • Joseph Stalin, p. 513
   • Nazi Party, p. 513
   • Brownshirts, p. 513
   • *Kristallnacht*, p. 514
   • Francisco Franco, p. 514
   • Popular Front, p. 514

3. Mussolini—appointed prime minister by king; restrict political rights, make Italy an imperial power; Stalin—used assassination and terror; complete government control of country; Hitler—voted into power; oppression of political opposition and Jews, conquest of territory; Franco—through civil war; destruction of Loyalist reforms; Japanese militarists—gained power within the government; territorial expansion

4a. to suppress dissent and terrorize opponents

b. They were given power by people or kings and then they restricted or eliminated political and civil rights in order to keep power.

c. Answers will vary. Students might suggest they wanted to fight fascism.

5. Answers will vary. Students might mention that there was no way to enforce international military cooperation; German-speaking territories were easy for Hitler to claim; and many countries did not want to get involved in another country's affairs.

After completing Section 4, students should be able to:

OBJECTIVE 1 *Explain the international response to fascism.*

OBJECTIVE 2 *Analyze the early events of World War II.*

OBJECTIVE 3 *Discuss the reasons for increased tension between the United States and Germany.*

OBJECTIVE 4 *Analyze why Japan bombed Pearl Harbor.*

SECTION 4

READ TO DISCOVER
1. What was the international response to fascism?
2. What were the early events of World War II?
3. Why did tension between the United States and Germany increase?
4. Why did Japan bomb Pearl Harbor?

DEFINE
appeasement
nonaggression pact

IDENTIFY
Axis Powers
Munich Conference
Winston Churchill
Allied Powers
Lend-Lease Act
Blitzkrieg
Maginot Line
Atlantic Charter
Hideki Tōjō

▶ WHY IT MATTERS TODAY

U.S. naval ships today defend U.S. interests all around the world. Use CNNfyi.com or other **current events** sources for more information on recent U.S. naval activities. Record your findings in your journal.

CNNfyi.com

War Breaks Out

Orson Welles

EYEWITNESSES TO History
"Ladies and gentlemen, this is the most terrifying thing I have ever witnessed. . . .
A humped shape is rising out of the pit. I can make out a small beam of light against a mirror. What's that? There's a jet of flame springing from that mirror, and it leaps right at the advancing men. It strikes them head on! Good Lord, they're turning into flame!"

—Orson Welles, "The War of the Worlds," CBS Radio, October 30, 1938

Although this report of an attack on the United States by invaders from Mars was purely fictional, many Americans believed it. On October 30, 1938, the Mercury Theatre on the Air, led by Orson Welles, performed a live radio broadcast of H. G. Wells's science fiction novel *The War of the Worlds*. To enhance the dramatic effect, they staged it as a series of news reports. Many listeners thought the broadcast was real. Throughout the nation, widespread panic ensued, with many people fleeing their homes and preparing to battle the space creatures. The panic reflected very real fears many people had that dangerous invaders were lurking on the horizon.

The Response to Fascism

The spread of fascism in Europe and Asia caused a shake-up in international diplomatic relationships. The most surprising of these realignments was the shift in U.S.-Soviet relations. The Soviets were concerned about stopping the Japanese, who had massed troops in nearby Manchuria. Hoping "to avert the Japanese danger," Soviet foreign-affairs commissar Maksim Litvinov mended diplomatic ties with the United States. In November 1933, after years of hostility between the two countries, the United States formally recognized the Soviet Union.

The fascist powers also formalized their ties. In 1936 the rest of Europe trembled when Germany and Italy formed a military alliance known as the **Axis Powers**. Japan later joined the alliance.

President Roosevelt called for European leaders to meet and resolve their conflicts peacefully. Adolf Hitler and Benito Mussolini joined British prime minister Neville Chamberlain and French premier Édouard Daladier (dah-lahd-yay) in Munich, Germany, in September 1938. The four leaders at the **Munich Conference** signed a pact giving Germany control of the Sudetenland. The European leaders had adopted a policy of **appeasement**, or giving in to demands in an attempt to avoid a larger conflict.

Many politicians underestimated Hitler's expansionist goals. They believed that Hitler sought only to remedy what he considered wrongs created by the Treaty of Versailles. Other politicians, such as **Winston Churchill** of Great Britain, feared

ALL LEVELS: Ask students to speculate on how European countries might have responded to fascism, given the horrors of World War I and the U.S. foreign policy of partial isolationism. *(Students might suggest that countries would have been initially reluctant to enter into another conflict.)* To help students understand the international response to fascism, copy the graphic organizer at right on the chalkboard, omitting the italicized answers. Have each student complete it. Ask volunteers to share their answers. Conclude by leading a discussion about the motivation behind various nations' responses to fascism. **English Language Learners**

U.S. Congress passes neutrality laws.

European nations speed up rearmament.

The Response to Fascism

European leaders adopt a policy of appeasement.

Soviets and the United States mend fences.

HOMEWORK *Ask students to create a collage to represent the initial international response to fascism. Display students' collages around the classroom*

that appeasement would encourage Hitler to seize additional territory. Britain and other nations in Europe sped up their rearmament.

Congress passed a series of neutrality laws between 1935 and 1939 that reflected Americans' desire for peace. The neutrality laws prohibited the shipment of U.S. munitions to warring nations and required warring nations that bought goods from the United States to transport these goods in their own ships. The laws also forbade Americans to travel on the vessels of warring nations.

By 1937 Roosevelt had become convinced that the United States must assist in the quarantine, or isolation, of warring nations. However, most Americans did not yet support this expanded role. In December 1937, Japanese planes attacked the U.S. gunboat *Panay* and three American oil tankers on China's Chang River. Two U.S. citizens were killed, and many others were wounded. Even so, a public-opinion poll revealed that 54 percent of Americans thought the United States should reduce its role in China rather than risk becoming involved in a war.

Japan's sinking of the U.S. gunboat Panay *angered many Americans but not enough to push the country into war.*

✔ **READING CHECK: Analyzing Information** How did the United States respond to fascism? Congress passed a series of neutrality laws.

War!

American public opinion slowly changed, however, as Germany's aggression continued. In March 1939 Adolf Hitler's armies occupied all of Czechoslovakia. Hitler also proposed to annex the Polish port city of Danzig (DAHNT-sik)—modern-day Gdańsk—but the Poles refused. That same year, Italian troops invaded Albania on April 7.

Fighting begins. Recognizing the growing threat to European security, Britain and France announced that they would go to war if Germany attacked Poland. They called on the Soviet Union to join them in resisting further aggression. Instead, on August 23, 1939, Joseph Stalin—who had been trying to rally the world against fascism—signed a **nonaggression pact** with Hitler. In it Stalin and Hitler agreed not to attack each other. This shocking development came about in part because of a secret clause in the pact in which the two nations agreed to divide Poland between them.

On September 1, 1939, German bombers and armored divisions moved into Poland. Two days later, Britain and France—who became known as the **Allied Powers**—declared war on Germany. World War II had begun. Meanwhile, Soviet troops invaded Poland from the east, occupied Estonia, Latvia, and Lithuania, and demanded the right to establish military bases in Finland. When Finland refused, the Soviet Union attacked the small nation and soon annexed part of its territory.

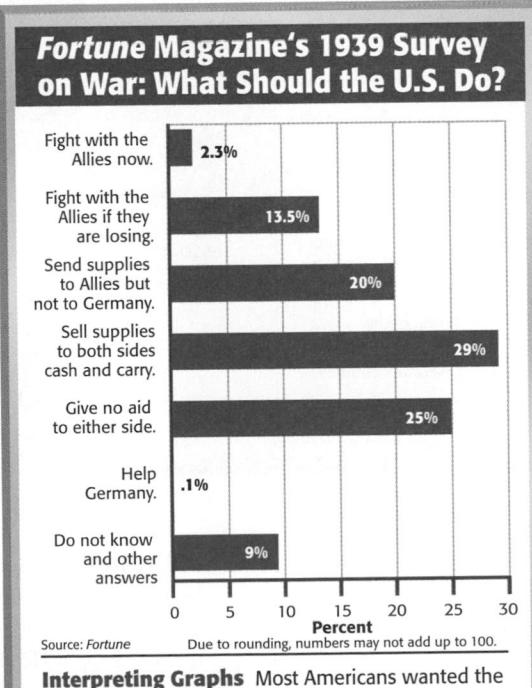

Fortune Magazine's 1939 Survey on War: What Should the U.S. Do?

Response	Percent
Fight with the Allies now.	2.3%
Fight with the Allies if they are losing.	13.5%
Send supplies to Allies but not to Germany.	20%
Sell supplies to both sides cash and carry.	29%
Give no aid to either side.	25%
Help Germany.	.1%
Do not know and other answers	9%

Source: *Fortune*   Due to rounding, numbers may not add up to 100.

Interpreting Graphs Most Americans wanted the Allies to win the war, but many were unsure what role the United States should play.

❓ **Skills Assessment** What percentage of Americans wanted the United States to remain totally neutral in the war, either by selling supplies to both sides or by refusing aid to either side?

HISTORY MAKERS SPEAK

Joseph Grew in *Turbulent Era*

Stopping Japanese Aggression. Joseph Grew, U.S. ambassador to Japan, recorded his thoughts about that nation's aggression in a 1937 diary entry: "If our branding of Japan as an aggressor and our appeal to the Nine Power Treaty and the Kellogg-Briand Pact and our support of the League of Nations . . . could serve to stop the fighting in China or limit its sphere or prevent similar aggression in the future, my accord with this step would be complete and wholehearted. But . . . with Manchuria, Ethiopia, and Spain written in big letters across the pages of history, how can we ignore the practical experience of those events and the hopelessness of deterring them *unless we are willing to fight?*"

CRITICAL THINKING What conclusion did Grew draw from the events of the mid-1930s?

ANSWER: Students might suggest that Grew believed that aggression could only be stopped by threats or the use of military force.

GRAPH ANSWER

54 percent

TEACH OBJECTIVE 2

LEVELS 1 AND 2: Organize students into groups and provide each group with a sheet of paper that has the dates *1939* and *1940* written on it. Each group should list and illustrate the events of World War II that took place during those years. *(Illustrations for 1939 should depict France and Britain declaring war on Germany, the signing of the non-aggression pact between the Soviet Union and Germany, and the Soviet invasions of Poland, the Baltic states, and Finland. Illustrations for 1940 should show Roosevelt's efforts to aid Europe with the Lend-Lease Act, the German Blitzkrieg against France and other European nations, the creation of the Vichy government,* and *Hitler's attack on Britain.)* Ask volunteers to explain their illustrations to the class.
English Language Learners, Cooperative Learning

LEVEL 3: Tell students to imagine that they are U.S. politicians who believe that the United States should enter the war. Have each student write a speech describing the early events of the war and explaining how these events justify U.S. entry into the conflict. *(See the Levels 1 and 2 lesson for the correct events.)* Ask volunteers to deliver their speeches to the class. Students may wish to include their speeches in their portfolios.

PEOPLE IN HISTORY

Charles Lindbergh. The congressional debate over revising the neutrality act that barred the export of military supplies prompted many prominent isolationists to speak out against any revisions. Famous aviator Charles Lindbergh made radio broadcasts calling upon the United States to maintain its isolationist stance. Lindbergh had visited Germany three times during the 1930s and tested new German aircraft before he spoke out against exporting military supplies. Once the United States joined the fighting, Lindbergh served his country, flying on several combat missions in the Pacific.

CRITICAL THINKING Why might Lindbergh's support for isolationism have hurt his historical reputation?

ANSWER: Students might suggest that critics have linked Lindbergh's isolationist views with support for the Nazis.

MAP ANSWER
bordered Germany on the east

German and Italian Expansion, 1935–1941

Interpreting Maps Hitler's and Mussolini's aggressions brought war to most of Europe for a second time in the 1900s.

? PLACES AND REGIONS Why was Poland a target for a German attack?

Legend:
- Germany, 1929
- German expansion, 1935–1939
- Italy and possessions, 1929
- Italian expansion, 1935–1939
- Vichy France
- Under Axis control by December 1941
- Under Allied control by December 1941
- Area of the Battle of Britain
- Neutral countries
- Farthest Russian advance, 1940

U.S. response. Some three weeks after the German invasion of Poland, President Roosevelt urged Congress to amend the neutrality act that barred the export of military supplies. Congress agreed on a compromise. It allowed any nation to buy military supplies from the United States but required that the goods be shipped on foreign vessels.

The fighting in Europe was a major issue in the 1940 presidential election. Both candidates—Roosevelt, who sought re-election to an unprecedented third term, and Republican Wendell Willkie—promised to keep the United States out of the conflict. On September 3, 1939, Roosevelt pledged, "As long as it remains in my power to prevent, there will be no blackout of peace in the United States." Roosevelt won. Despite his public promises, he viewed U.S. military involvement in Europe as unavoidable.

ALL LEVELS: Pair students and have pairs create a list of events that increased tensions between the United States and Germany. *(Lists should include: an increase in U.S. aid to the Allies, German submarine attacks, and Roosevelt's "shoot-on-sight" orders.)* Ask each pair to use its list to create a political cartoon depicting relations between the United States and Germany in 1941. Each cartoon should include a descriptive caption. Display cartoons around the classroom.
English Language Learners, Cooperative Learning

Teacher to Teacher

Karen Hoppes of Lake Oswego, Oregon, suggested the following activity: Tell students to imagine that they are participants in a discussion entitled Will We Go to War with Germany? Organize students into two groups. One group should play the following roles: Emily Greene Balch, Franklin D. Roosevelt, Ernest Hemingway, and Wendell Willkie. Have the other group act as questioners. Have each group prepare by taking notes, and then conduct the discussion.

Lend-Lease. By the end of 1940, a variety of needed war materials flowed from the United States to Britain. The British, however, had little cash to pay for them. Roosevelt proposed that the United States lend or lease arms and other supplies to the Allies. Congress passed the **Lend-Lease Act** in March 1941. It appropriated $7 billion for ships, planes, tanks, and other supplies to non-Axis countries.

While Hitler carried on his **Blitzkrieg** (BLITS-kreeg), or "lightning war," against Poland, the French mobilized. In May 1940, German troops began an attack around the **Maginot Line**, a line of defenses along the French border with Germany. The Germans occupied Belgium, Denmark, northern France, Luxembourg, the Netherlands, and Norway. Hundreds of thousands of British, French, and Belgian troops were trapped along the French coast near the town of Dunkirk. Only an evacuation across the English Channel to Britain prevented their capture.

Germany established a puppet government in southern France in the town of Vichy (VI-shee). A secret French organization known as the Resistance continued to oppose the Germans. In London, French general Charles de Gaulle headed a committee called Free France, which organized opposition against the Germans.

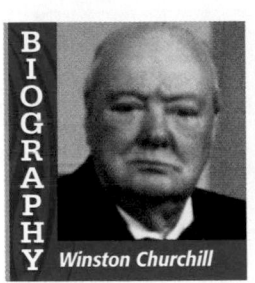

A new British leader. With the fall of France, Britain stood alone against the Axis Powers. On May 10, 1940, Winston Churchill became prime minister. Born in 1874, Churchill attended Royal Military College and then served in the British army for several years. He began his political career in 1900 as a member of Parliament. Ten years later, Churchill was appointed to lead the British navy. After receiving widespread criticism for Britain's failure in a World War I campaign, Churchill resigned his position and volunteered to fight on the front lines.

Winston Churchill

After the war Churchill resumed his rise in British politics. When many other British leaders were pushing for appeasement with Hitler, Churchill warned of the dangers he posed. Once appointed prime minister, Churchill rallied the British.

History Makers Speak

❝Hitler knows that he will have to break us in this island or lose the war. . . . Let us therefore brace ourselves to our duties, and so bear ourselves that, if the British Empire and its Commonwealth last for a thousand years, men will still say, 'This was their finest hour.'❞

—Winston Churchill, "Their Finest Hour," June 18, 1940

On June 10, 1940, Italy declared war on France and Britain. In August, Hitler unleashed his bombers against Britain. Although outnumbered, the British Royal Air Force (RAF) flew day and night to combat the German attack.

✔ **READING CHECK: Sequencing** How did World War II begin? **The German invasion of Poland prompted Great Britain and France to declare war on Germany.**

Tensions Mount in the Atlantic

As German attacks increased, so did U.S. aid to the Allies. By the spring of 1941, German submarines were turning the North Atlantic into a graveyard of ships. In September, President Roosevelt issued "shoot-on-sight" orders to U.S. warships operating in the North Atlantic.

Citizens of Warsaw, Poland, flee before the destructive power of the German Blitzkrieg as fire consumes a working-class neighborhood.

Research on the R⊙M

Free Find:
Winston Churchill
After reading about Winston Churchill on the **Holt Researcher CD–ROM**, create a sketch of a memorial that will honor Churchill's inspiring leadership during World War II.

SCIENCE, TECHNOLOGY, AND SOCIETY

The Blitzkrieg. The German method of attack that came to be known as the Blitzkrieg was made possible by technological advances. The development of tanks that could move rapidly, the use of airplanes, bombs, and paratroopers, and coordinated radio communication allowed the German army to make rapid offensive moves that overwhelmed the enemy. The Blitzkrieg was successful in the early years of the war but proved ineffective in later years.

CRITICAL THINKING Why might the Blitzkrieg have become less effective over time?

ANSWER: Students might suggest that the Allies learned ways to defend against the Blitzkrieg, often by using tanks and planes in a similar manner.

THAT'S INTERESTING!

Winston Churchill and Franklin D. Roosevelt met briefly in London in 1918. They began corresponding by letter and telegram in 1939, and by 1945 they had exchanged 1,949 messages.

MAP ANSWER
(for p. 522)

Beijing, Hangzhou, Nanjing, Shanghai, Shenyang, and Tianjin

LEVEL 1: Pair students and have each pair create a graphic organizer showing why the Japanese bombed Pearl Harbor. (*Organizers should note that Roosevelt froze all Japanese assets in the United States and instituted an embargo on American shipments of gasoline, machine tools, scrap iron, and steel to Japan.*) Have students present and explain their graphic organizers to the class.
English Language Learners, Cooperative Learning

LEVEL 2: Tell students to imagine that they are encyclopedia editors who must write an entry about the motivations behind the Japanese attack on Pearl Harbor. Have each student write an entry about the reasons for Japan's attack. (*See the Level 1 lesson for the correct reasons.*) Have volunteers read their entries to the class.

LEVEL 3: Ask students to imagine that it is December 8, 1941, and that they are advisers to President Roosevelt who have been asked to write a memo analyzing Japan's reasons for bombing Pearl Harbor. Have each student write a short memo analyzing the motivations behind the Japanese attack. (*See Level 1 lesson for the correct reasons.*) Ask volunteers to read their memos to the class.

VISUAL RECORD ANSWER

(for p. 523)

Students might suggest that the damage was extensive.

Convoys of ships bringing supplies to the Allies were escorted by U.S. warships to protect against attack by German submarines.

SECTION 4 REVIEW ANSWERS

1. Define
- appeasement, p. 518
- nonaggression pact, p. 519

2. Identify
- Axis Powers, p. 518
- Munich Conference, p. 518
- Winston Churchill, p. 518
- Allied Powers, p. 519
- Lend-Lease Act, p. 521
- Blitzkrieg, p. 521
- Maginot Line, p. 521
- Atlantic Charter, p. 522
- Hideki Tōjō, p. 523

3. 2. Germany invades Poland; 3. Germany defeats France; 4. Britain repels Germany's attacks; 5. Japan attacks Pearl Harbor

4a. The European policy of appeasement failed to stop Germany's aggression; then Germany invaded Poland, and France and England declared war on Germany; German submarines turned the Atlantic into a graveyard of ships; and finally Japan attacked Pearl Harbor.

b. He tried to compromise between isolationism and actively assisting the Allies by amending neutrality laws and using cash-and-carry and Lend-Lease; he also tried to prevent German U-boats from taking American lives.

In August 1941, with the United States moving rapidly toward undeclared war with Germany, Roosevelt and Winston Churchill met secretly off the coast of Newfoundland. The two leaders agreed to the **Atlantic Charter**, a joint pledge to not pursue territorial expansion. The two countries affirmed that every nation has the right to choose its own form of government. They also called for freedom of international trade and equal access for all countries to raw materials. Once the war was over, the charter declared, aggressor states should be disarmed, and all nations should work together to rid the world of fear and poverty.

Concern over Adolf Hitler's growing power increased when German troops invaded the Soviet Union in June 1941. Caught off guard by this violation of the German-Soviet nonaggression pact, Soviet troops fared badly in the initial fighting. By the fall of 1941, German troops had advanced deep into Soviet territory.

✔ **READING CHECK: Summarizing** Why did the United States and Britain draw up the Atlantic Charter? to pledge their shared opposition to Nazi Germany

Japanese Expansion, 1931–1941

Interpreting Maps Japan's military leaders believed that conquering neighboring lands would solve the country's economic problems.

? LOCATE What important Chinese cities had Japan captured by 1938?

Japanese-Soviet border clashes occur in 1938 and 1939.

Japanese invade Manchuria in 1931.

Japanese attack U.S. ships in Dec. 1937.

UNION OF SOVIET SOCIALIST REPUBLICS

MONGOLIA

MANCHURIA

Nomonham 1939

Shenyang

Vladivostok
Changkufeng 1938

Beijing

Tianjin

Lüshun (Port Arthur)

CHINA

Yan'an

TIBET

Yellow R. (Huang)

Shandong Peninsula

Qingdao

YELLOW SEA

KOREA

SEA OF JAPAN

JAPAN

Tokyo

SEA OF OKHOTSK

SAKHALIN

KURIL ISLANDS

Nanjing 1937
Capital, 1928–1937

Shanghai

Hangzhou

Hankou

Chongqing
Capital, 1937–1945

Yangtze R. (Chang)

INDIA (British)

EAST CHINA SEA

PACIFIC OCEAN

Xiamen

Shantou

Guangzhou

HONG KONG (British)

MACAO (Portuguese)

HAINAN

BURMA (British)

TAIWAN

RYUKYU ISLANDS

BONIN IS. (Japanese)

VOLCANO IS. (Japanese)

Bay of Bengal

THAILAND

SOUTH CHINA SEA

PHILIPPINE ISLANDS (U.S.)

CEYLON

FRENCH INDOCHINA

50°N

40°N

30°N

20°N

160°E

150°E

140°E

130°E

120°E

110°E

90°E

80°E

10°N

Japanese Empire in 1930

Extent of Japanese Empire by 1938

Extent of Japanese Empire, December 7, 1941

✿ Point of conflict

N W E S

0   500   1,000 Miles
0 500 1,000 Kilometers
Orthographic Projection

REVIEW

Have students complete the **Section 4 Review** on p. 523.

ASSESS

Have students complete **Daily Quiz 17.4**. As **Alternative Assessment**, you may want to use the speech about early events of World War II or the Pearl Harbor graphic organizer.

RETEACH

Have students complete **Main Idea Activity for English Language Learners and Special-Needs Students 17.4**. Then organize students into four groups. Assign each group one of the four objectives and ask each group to create a 10-question quiz about its objective, writing the answers on a separate page. Have groups trade quizzes and try to answer other groups' quizzes. Ask groups to grade each other's quizzes and discuss questions with which other groups had trouble.
English Language Learners, Cooperative Learning

EXTEND

Have students watch the film *Casablanca*. Tell them that this film was made in part to encourage the United States to enter the war. After they watch the film, tell students to imagine that they are Americans seeing the film in 1940. Have each student write a review of the film. **Block Scheduling**

Japan Attacks

As war raged in Europe, Japan continued its expansion in Asia. In July 1941, Japanese troops occupied French Indochina. President Roosevelt immediately froze all Japanese assets in the United States. He also approved an embargo on shipments of gasoline, machine tools, scrap iron, and steel to Japan. Japan responded by freezing all American assets in areas under its control.

In October minister of war **Hideki Tōjō** became prime minister of Japan. Tojo committed his nation to expansion as part of the Greater East Asia Co-prosperity Sphere. Japan's military leaders also secretly planned an attack on the United States. Even as the plan went forward, however, a Japanese peace mission visited Washington, D.C. On November 20, 1941, this mission demanded that the United States unfreeze Japanese assets, supply Japan's gasoline needs, and cease all aid to China. By this time the United States had broken the secret code used to send messages between Tokyo and the Japanese embassy in Washington. The Americans knew that the Japanese planned a strike, but they did not know where.

Shortly before 8:00 A.M. on December 7, 1941, the Japanese launched their attack on the U.S. naval base at Pearl Harbor in the Hawaiian Islands. The core of the U.S. Pacific Fleet was anchored there, and more than 100 U.S. planes lined nearby airfields. Almost 20 U.S. warships and nearly 200 aircraft were destroyed. Some 2,400 Americans were killed, including 1,103 sailors entombed on the USS *Arizona* when the battleship sank.

The bombing shocked and united Americans. The next day, a somber President Roosevelt described December 7, 1941, as "a date which will live in infamy." He called on Congress to pass a declaration of war against Japan. Congress quickly approved the call for war.

✔ **READING CHECK: Evaluating** Why did Japan's attack on Pearl Harbor lead the United States to declare war? because 2,400 Americans were killed

THE GRANGER COLLECTION, NEW YORK

INTERPRETING THE VISUAL RECORD

Pearl Harbor. The USS *Shaw* explodes after Japanese planes bombed Pearl Harbor. *What does this image tell you about the damage done by the Japanese attack?*

SECTION 4 REVIEW

1. **Define and explain:**
   appeasement
   nonaggression pact

2. **Identify and explain:**
   Axis Powers
   Munich Conference
   Winston Churchill
   Allied Powers
   Lend-Lease Act
   Blitzkrieg
   Maginot Line
   Atlantic Charter
   Hideki Tōjō

3. **Sequencing** Copy the chart below. Use it to list the early events of World War II.

1. The Munich Conference
2.
3.
4.
5.
6. The United States enters the war.

4. **Finding the Main Idea**
   a. What events led to U.S. involvement in World War II?
   b. What leadership qualities did President Roosevelt exhibit as he responded to events in Europe?
   c. Why did Japanese leaders respond to conflicts with the United States by bombing Pearl Harbor?

5. **Writing and Critical Thinking**
   Supporting a Point of View Write a paragraph discussing how the war in Europe affected the relationship between Congress and the president.
   Consider:
   • U.S. foreign policy at the start of the war
   • neutrality acts
   • Land-Lease Act

Homework Practice Online
keyword: SE3 HP17

CHAPTER REVIEW 17 ANSWERS

Creating a Time Line
Each event should have an explanation and the correct date.

Writing a Summary
See the Reading Checks in each section for main ideas.

Identifying People and Ideas
1. withdrawal from world affairs that characterized U.S. foreign policy in the 1920s and 1930s

2. U.S. secretary of state who engineered the Washington Conference

3. Nicaraguan general who opposed American forces

4. assert government control over industries

5. Italian Fascist who was appointed prime minister

6. November 9, 1938, the "night of broken glass," in which Nazis destroyed Jewish businesses and synagogues

7. military alliance consisting of Germany, Italy, and Japan

CHAPTER 17

REVIEW AND ASSESSMENT RESOURCES

TECHNOLOGY
▶ Chapter 17 Test Generator (on the One-Stop Planner)
▶ Global Skill Builder CD–ROM
▶ HRW Go site

REINFORCEMENT, REVIEW, AND ASSESSMENT
▶ Chapter 17 Review, pp. 524–25
▶ Chapter 17 Tutorial for Students, Parents, Mentors, and Peers

▶ Chapter 17 Test (Form A or B)
▶ Portfolio Activities and Alternative Assessment Handbook, Chapter 17
▶ Chapter 17 Test for English Language Learners and Special-Needs Students

REVIEW
Have students complete the **Chapter 17 Review** on pp. 524–25.

ASSESS
Use one of the chapter tests to assess students' understanding of the content. For **Alternative Assessment**, see the **Portfolio Activities and Alternative Assessment Handbook.**

CHAPTER 17

Review

Creating a Time Line

Copy the time line below onto a sheet of paper. Complete the time line by filling in the events and dates from the chapter that you think were most significant. Pick three events and explain why you think they were significant.

1921   1931   1941

Writing a Summary

Using standard grammar, spelling, sentence structure, and punctuation, write an overview of events in the chapter.

Identifying People and Ideas

Identify the following terms or individuals and explain their significance.

1. isolationism
2. Charles Evans Hughes
3. Augusto César Sandino
4. nationalize
5. Benito Mussolini
6. *Kristallnacht*
7. Axis Powers
8. appeasement
9. nonaggression pact
10. Winston Churchill

Understanding Main Ideas

SECTION 1 *(pp. 502–506)*
1. What factors encouraged the United States to follow a foreign policy of isolationism after World War I?

SECTION 2 *(pp. 507–511)*
2. What economic and political role did the United States play in Latin America?
3. Why did Mexican president Lázaro Cárdenas nationalize his country's oil fields in 1938?

SECTION 3 *(pp. 512–517)*
4. How did dictators come to power in Europe in the 1930s?
5. What aggressive actions did Japan take during the 1930s?

SECTION 4 *(pp. 518–523)*
6. Why did the United States enter World War II?

Reviewing Themes

1. **Global Relations** In what ways did countries promote world peace after World War I?
2. **Economics** How did economic problems contribute to political unrest after World War I?
3. **Citizenship** How did the fascist dictatorships in Europe restrict civil liberties?

Thinking Critically

1. **Identifying Points of View** Why do you think many people supported Benito Mussolini and Adolf Hitler?
2. **Analyzing Information** In what ways did the Treaty of Versailles and the Great Depression contribute to World War II?
3. **Summarizing** Why did Japan's militarists want to create an empire in East Asia and the Pacific?
4. **Identifying Cause and Effect** How did the U.S. policy of neutrality change between 1935 and 1941?
5. **Drawing Conclusions** How did the attack on Pearl Harbor change Americans' commitment to fight in World War II?

Writing About History

Supporting a Point of View Imagine that you are a Loyalist who fought during the Spanish Civil War. Write a letter to an American friend describing events during that period. Use this outline to organize your thoughts.

> I. Franco's Rise
> II. Loyalist Views
> III. The Spanish Civil War
>   A. Foreign Aid
>   1. Soviet Union
>   2. United States
>   B. Outcome
> IV. Views of the War

RETEACH

Organize students into six groups and assign each group one of the following countries: Germany, Italy, Japan, Mexico, Nicaragua, or the Soviet Union. Have each group create a graphic organizer that shows the key terms and events of this chapter that relate to its country. Have students present their organizers to the class and discuss their country's place in world events during the 1920s and 1930s.
English Language Learners, Cooperative Learning

EXTEND

Have students conduct research on newspaper or magazine coverage of U.S. foreign relations between 1920 and 1940. Have each student find several different articles that discuss U.S. relations with a particular country. Then ask students to write a report tracing how U.S. relations with this country changed over time. **Block Scheduling**

Building Social Studies Skills

Interpreting Maps
Study the map below. Then use it to help answer the questions that follow.

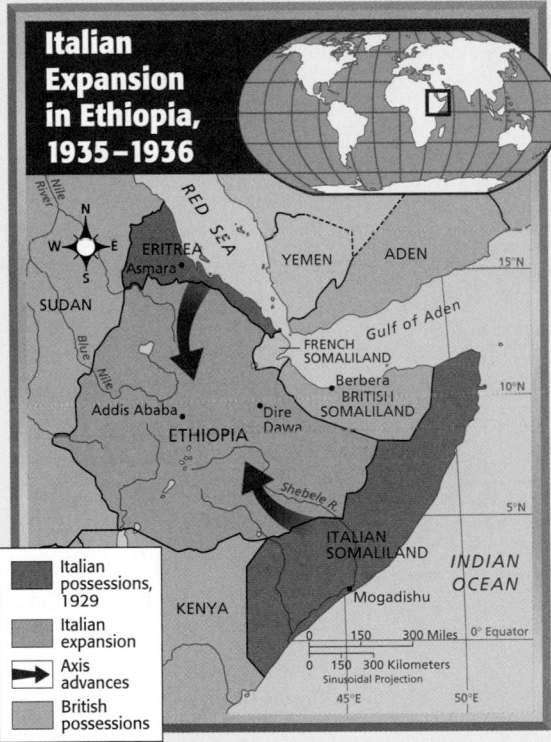

Italian Expansion in Ethiopia, 1935–1936

Key:
- Italian possessions, 1929
- Italian expansion
- Axis advances
- British possessions

1. How might Italy have expected to benefit from conquering Ethiopia?

2. Which of these pairs of countries was under Italian control before Italy's invasion of Ethiopia?
   a. Aden and Yemen
   b. British Somaliland and French Somaliland
   c. Kenya and Sudan
   d. Italian Somaliland and Eritrea

Analyzing Primary Sources
Read the excerpt from a 1941 interview with Thomas Page, a student at Harvard Law School. Then answer the questions that follow.

> "A guy named Tom Harris and his wife . . . would observe what people were eating, reading, and the way of advertisements to determine what people really were doing. . . . And I looked at the *New York Times Sunday Magazine*. . . . It was filled with semi-warlike copy and ads. And I thought, my God, this is really an illustration of this guy Harris's theory of mass observation—the country has almost accepted the inevitability of some kind of military action and is all geared up for it mentally."

3. Based on this excerpt, what is Harris's theory of mass observation?
   a. One can determine important facts about public opinion by analyzing popular advertisements.
   b. Harris supported the warlike attitude that was building by 1941.
   c. Thomas Page was a pacifist.
   d. People tend to watch what others are doing and thinking before they make up their own minds about an issue.

4. In order to support or reject Harris's theory, what additional sources might you consult?

Alternative Assessment

Building Your Portfolio

Citizenship

Imagine that you are a diplomat at the 1938 Munich Conference. Write a speech aimed at convincing the Allies to abandon their policy of appeasement toward Germany's Adolf Hitler. Your speech should include information on Hitler's rise to power and how his policies threaten democracy.

U.S. HISTORY

internet connect

Internet Activity: go.hrw.com
KEYWORD: SE3 AN17

Choose a topic on the road to war to:
- research the Spanish Civil War and create a pamphlet supporting the Loyalist cause.
- understand the developments in physics that led to the construction of an atomic bomb.
- learn about fascist and antifascist activity in the United States.

---

3. by limiting free speech and voting, banning strikes, and persecuting religious or ethnic groups

Thinking Critically
1. Answers will vary, but students should note that they promised economic growth and expansion.

2. Hitler felt the treaty had set unfair war reparations; Italians felt they had not benefited from the treaty.

3. to seize resources and reduce Japan's dependence on imports

4. Strict neutrality gave way to the Lend-Lease Act. In 1941 the United States entered the war.

5. The attack shocked and united Americans. It showed that the war involved the United States.

Writing
Letters will vary but should contrast the views of the Loyalists and the Fascists, the failure of the United States to provide aid, and the war's influence on the growing international crisis.

Building Social Studies Skills
1. Answers will vary. Students might suggest that it would allow Italy to push Britain out of Africa.

2. d

3. a

4. Answers will vary. Students might suggest back issues of the *New York Times Sunday Magazine*.

CHAPTER
18

Americans in World War II

CHAPTER RESOURCE MANAGER

Objectives	Pacing Guide	Reproducible Resources
SECTION 1 **Early Difficulties** pp. 528–34 ★ Analyze the strengths and weaknesses of the Allied and Axis Powers in 1941. ★ Outline the steps that the United States took to prepare for war. ★ Identify locations where the Japanese military attacked after Pearl Harbor. ★ Discuss the early turning points of the war in the Pacific. ★ Relate the major battles in Europe and North Africa in 1942.	**Regular** 2 days **Block Scheduling** 1 day *Block Scheduling Handbook with Team Teaching Strategies, pp. 103–08*	**RS** Guided Reading Strategy 18.1 **SM** Geography Activity 18: Hitler's War Machine **SM** American History Outline Map 19: World War II in Europe **SM** American History Outline Map 20: World War II in the Pacific
SECTION 2 **The Home Front** pp. 535–41 ★ Describe how the U.S. government tried to keep wartime morale high. ★ Describe what life was like in the United States during World War II. ★ Relate how women contributed to the war effort. ★ Analyze what actions the government took to protect the rights of minority groups. ★ Discuss the war's effect on Japanese Americans.	**Regular** 2 days **Block Scheduling** 1 day *Block Scheduling Handbook with Team Teaching Strategies, pp. 103–08*	**RS** Guided Reading Strategy 18.2 **PS** Primary Source Reading 18: A Mountain Woman's Tale **RS** Graphic Organizer Activity 18: The Effect of War on Life at Home
SECTION 3 **Victory in Europe** pp. 542–48 ★ Identify where the Allied offensive in Europe began. ★ Explain the impact of fighting in the Atlantic and in the air. ★ Analyze how the Allies successfully invaded Normandy. ★ Describe the Holocaust. ★ Analyze how the Allies finally defeated Germany.	**Regular** 2 days **Block Scheduling** 1 day *Block Scheduling Handbook with Team Teaching Strategies, pp. 103–08*	**RS** Guided Reading Strategy 18.3 **E** Creative Teaching Strategy: Predicting Consequences Lesson
SECTION 4 **Victory in Asia** pp. 549–55 ★ Describe the U.S. island-hopping plan. ★ Analyze the effect that the battles at Iwo Jima and Okinawa had on the war. ★ Explain why the United States used atomic weapons against Japan. ★ Discuss the costs of the war.	**Regular** 1 day **Block Scheduling** .5 day *Block Scheduling Handbook with Team Teaching Strategies, pp. 103–08*	**RS** Guided Reading Strategy 18.4 **PS** Biography Reading 18: Enrico Fermi **IC** Literature Reading 18: A City and Its People Destroyed **E** Hands-On History Activity: Your Town During World War II

Chapter Resource Key

PS	Primary Sources	**REV**	Review		Video
RS	Reading Support	**ELL**	Reinforcement and English Language Learners	Internet
IC	Interdisciplinary Connections				Holt Presentation Maker Using Microsoft® PowerPoint®
E	Enrichment		Transparencies		
SM	Skills Mastery		CD-ROM		
A	Assessment		Music		

 One-Stop Planner CD-ROM

See the *One-Stop Planner* for a complete list of additional resources for students and teachers.

One-Stop Planner CD-ROM

It's easy to plan lessons, select resources, and print out materials for your students when you use the **One-Stop Planner CD-ROM with Test Generator.**

Technology Resources

 One-Stop Planner, Lesson 18.1
 Holt Researcher: American History CD–ROM
 Homework Practice Online

 One-Stop Planner, Lesson 18.2
The American Nation Video Program Segment: Japanese Americans in Relocation Camps; Teacher's Guide, pp. 159–60
Holt Researcher: American History CD–ROM
Homework Practice Online
HRW Go site

One-Stop Planner, Lesson 18.3
Linking Geography and History Transparency 18: World War II in Europe, 1942–1945
Holt Researcher: American History CD–ROM
Homework Practice Online

One-Stop Planner, Lesson 18.4
CNN Presents America: Yesterday and Today, 1850 to the Present Segment: One Town Remembers
Holt Researcher: American History CD–ROM
Homework Practice Online

Reinforcement, Review, and Assessment

REV	Section 1 Review, p. 534
A	Daily Quiz 18.1
ELL	Main Idea Activity 18.1
ELL	English Audio Summary 18.1
ELL	Spanish Audio Summary 18.1

REV	Section 2 Review, p. 541
A	Daily Quiz 18.2
ELL	Main Idea Activity 18.2
ELL	English Audio Summary 18.2
ELL	Spanish Audio Summary 18.2

REV	Section 3 Review, p. 548
A	Daily Quiz 18.3
ELL	Main Idea Activity 18.3
ELL	English Audio Summary 18.3
ELL	Spanish Audio Summary 18.3

REV	Section 4 Review, p. 555
A	Daily Quiz 18.4
ELL	Main Idea Activity 18.4
ELL	English Audio Summary 18.4
ELL	Spanish Audio Summary 18.4

internet connect

HRW ONLINE RESOURCES
GO TO: go.hrw.com
Then type in a keyword.

TEACHER HOME PAGE
KEYWORD: SE3 Teacher

CHAPTER INTERNET ACTIVITIES
KEYWORD: SE3 AN18
Choose an activity to:
• research the role of journalism during the war.
• analyze how scientific discoveries and innovations in military technology resulted from specific needs.
• write a "biography" of Rosie the Riveter.

CHAPTER ENRICHMENT LINKS
KEYWORD: SE3 CH18

ONLINE ASSESSMENT
Homework Practice
KEYWORD: SE3 HP18

Standardized Test Prep
KEYWORD: SE3 STP18

Rubrics
KEYWORD: SS Rubrics

ONLINE MAPS, CHARTS, AND GRAPHS
KEYWORD: SE3 MCG
• Operation Barbarossa, 1941
• Relocating Japanese Americans
• U.S. Entry into World War II
• World War II Alliances
• Holocaust Camps

CONTENT UPDATES
KEYWORD: SS Content Updates

HOLT PRESENTATION MAKER
KEYWORD: SE3 PPT18

ONLINE READING SUPPORT
KEYWORD: SS Strategies

CURRENT EVENTS
KEYWORD: S3 Current Events

Meeting Individual Needs

Ability Levels

Level 1 Basic-level activities designed for all students encountering new material

Level 2 Intermediate-level activities designed for average students

Level 3 Challenging activities designed for honors and gifted-and-talented students

English Language Learners Activities that address the needs of students with Limited English Proficiency

Chapter Review and Assessment

 Global Skill Builder CD-ROM

HRW Go site

REV Chapter 18 Tutorial for Students, Parents, Mentors, and Peers

REV Chapter 18 Review, pp. 556–57

Chapter 18 Test Generator (on the One-Stop Planner)

A Chapter 18 Test (Form A or B)

A Alternative Assessment Handbook

A Chapter 18 Test for English Language Learners and Special-Needs Students

Build on What You Know

Ask students to answer the following questions.

How might the Allied Powers have battled the Axis Powers in different areas around the world?
Consider:

• the difficulties of fighting wars on multiple fronts

• the factors that would facilitate a multifront war—coordination, cooperation, and so on

How might the Allies have defeated the Axis Powers?
Consider:

• the importance of human and economic resources

• the military importance of new technologies

---

exploring the time line

AMERICAN EVENTS

internet connect go.hrw.com

TOPIC: World War II Journalism
GO TO: go.hrw.com
KEYWORD: SE3 AN18

Have students access the Internet through the HRW Go site to conduct research on World War II journalists, such as Ernie Pyle and Ernest Hemingway. Then have each student complete the interactive worksheet for the activity. After students have finished, ask them to discuss the ways in which coverage of another war, such as the Vietnam War or Persian Gulf War, would be different.

CHAPTER
18

1941–1945

Americans in World War II

A Glenn Miller album cover

**1941
The Arts**
Orson Welles's film *Citizen Kane,* inspired by the life of William Randolph Hearst, is released.

Poster advertising **Citizen Kane**

A zinc-coated penny

**1941
Science and Technology**
Physicists Glenn Seaborg and Edwin McMillan isolate the element plutonium.

**1941
World Events**
Japanese planes bomb Pearl Harbor.

**1942
Daily Life**
The U.S. Mint begins issuing pennies made of zinc-coated steel to conserve copper for weapons production.

**1942
The Arts**
Glenn Miller receives the first gold record for having sold more than 1 million copies of his hit song "Chattanooga Choo Choo."

1941

1942

A 1942 Packard

**1942
Business and Finance**
On February 10 the last automobile to be produced in the United States until the end of the war rolls off the Ford assembly line.

**1942
World Events**
U.S. forces in the Philippines surrender after an extended siege.

U.S. prisoners in the Philippines

Build on What You Know

The economic distress of the Great Depression contributed to the rise of dictatorships in some nations. Military aggression by Germany, Italy, and Japan plunged the world into war. In December 1941 the Japanese bombed Pearl Harbor, bringing the United States into World War II. In this chapter you will learn that the United States and the Allies battled the Axis Powers on land and at sea in Europe, North Africa, and Asia. By August 1945 the Allies had won a difficult war.

What's Your Opinion?

 To help students create their Themes Journal entries, provide the following examples of appropriate **agree**/**disagree** statements.

Global Relations

Agree The United States supplied crucial weapons and supplies to the Allies during World War I.

Disagree The Union won the Civil War without significant economic assistance from other countries.

Constitutional Heritage

Agree The arrest of Copperheads and other opponents of the Civil War helped restore peace in New York City during the draft riots of 1863.

Disagree American officials unfairly silenced and imprisoned critics of World War I under the Espionage Act of 1917 and the Sedition Act of 1918.

Science, Technology, and Society

Agree Given the destructive power of some technologies, governments must consider political and moral issues.

Disagree In some circumstances, such as wartime, deadly technologies must be developed and used without delay in order to secure victory.

Diego Rivera's mural La Gran Tenochtitlán

1943
Science and Technology
Chicago's first subway opens.

1943
Politics
President Roosevelt, British prime minister Winston Churchill, and Soviet premier Joseph Stalin meet at the Tehran Conference.

1944
World Events
On the morning of June 6, some 176,000 Allied troops storm the beaches of Normandy, France.

1944
Business and Finance
The International Bank for Reconstruction, or World Bank, is established in July.

1945
The Arts
Mexican artist Diego Rivera completes his mural *La Gran Tenochtitlán* in Mexico City's National Palace.

1945
World Events
The United States drops atomic bombs on Hiroshima and Nagasaki.

1943 | **1944** | **1945**

1943
The Arts
The musical *Oklahoma!* opens.

1943
Daily Life
The United States begins rationing shoes, allowing each person three pairs per year.

1943
World Events
Italy surrenders to the Allies, but German forces occupy the country to prevent the Allies from doing so.

1944
World Events
Allied forces liberate Paris, France.

1945
Daily Life
In November, rationing of all food items except sugar ends in the United States.

Allied forces arrive in Paris.

World War II ration stamps

What's Your Opinion?

Themes Journal *Do you* **agree** *or* **disagree** *with the following statements? Support your point of view in your journal.*

Global Relations Allied nations must pool their economic and military resources in order to win a global war.

Constitutional Heritage A government should be allowed to restrict the rights of citizens during a national emergency.

Science, Technology, and Society A government should consider more than just military concerns when developing new technology.

---

exploring the time line

GLOBAL EVENTS

GLOBAL RELATIONS

1944 ■ The Normandy Invasion. The Normandy invasion was incredibly deadly. The U.S. Navy launched its assault craft 12 miles from the shore. Many of the amphibious craft were sunk on the long journey to land, and many soldiers drowned. Once the troops actually reached land, they faced minefields and machine-gun fire. One general summarized the danger saying, "Two kinds of people are staying on this beach, the dead and those who are going to die—now let's get the hell out of here."

CRITICAL THINKING What might the symbolic importance of the Normandy invasion have been?

ANSWER: Students might suggest that the invasion of German-occupied France demonstrated the Allies' growing strength in the war.

THAT'S INTERESTING!

Hours before the landing on the Normandy beaches, U.S. and British parachutists began to drop into the French countryside. One scholar has called this dangerous mission "a lethal lottery."

SECTION ①

After completing Section 1, students should be able to:

OBJECTIVE 1 *Analyze the strengths and weaknesses of the Allied and Axis Powers in 1941.*

OBJECTIVE 2 *Outline the steps that the United States took to prepare for war.*

OBJECTIVE 3 *Identify locations where the Japanese military attacked after Pearl Harbor.*

OBJECTIVE 4 *Discuss the early turning points of the war in the Pacific.*

OBJECTIVE 5 *Relate the major battles in Europe and North Africa in 1942.*

LET'S GET STARTED!

Write the following term on the chalkboard: *Pearl Harbor.* As students enter the classroom, ask them to write down anything they know about the term. *(Most students will know something about the term from Chapter 16.)* Discuss students' responses. Tell students that in Section 1 they will learn about the war in the Pacific.

SECTION ① RESOURCES

REPRODUCIBLE

▶ Guided Reading Strategy 18.1
▶ Geography Activity 18: Hitler's War Machine
▶ American History Outline Map 19: World War II in Europe
▶ American History Outline Map 20: World War II in the Pacific

TECHNOLOGY

▶ One-Stop Planner, Lesson 18.1
▶ Holt Researcher: American History CD–ROM
▶ Homework Practice Online

REINFORCEMENT, REVIEW, AND ASSESSMENT

▶ Section 1 Review, p. 534
▶ Daily Quiz 18.1
▶ Main Idea Activity 18.1
▶ English Audio Summary 18.1
▶ Spanish Audio Summary 18.1

SECTION ①

READ TO DISCOVER

1. What were the strengths and weaknesses of the Allied Powers and Axis Powers in 1941?
2. What steps did the United States take to prepare for war?
3. Where did the Japanese military attack after Pearl Harbor?
4. What were the early turning points of the war in the Pacific?
5. What were the major battles in Europe and North Africa in 1942?

IDENTIFY

War Production Board
Office of War Mobilization
Selective Training and Service Act
Douglas MacArthur
Bataan Death March
Chester Nimitz
Battle of the Coral Sea
Battle of Midway
Erwin Rommel
Bernard Montgomery

WHY IT MATTERS TODAY

Although most nations try to solve their problems without going to war, disagreements between different countries still arise. Use **CNNfyi.com** or other **current events** sources to find out about one international conflict in the world today. Record your findings in your journal.

CNNfyi.com

Early Difficulties

EYEWITNESSES TO History

"I was sixteen years old, employed . . . at Pearl Harbor Navy Yard. On December 7, 1941, oh, around 8:00 A.M., my grandmother awoke me. She informed me that the Japanese were bombing Pearl Harbor. . . . I was asked . . . to go into the water and get sailors out that had been blown off the ships. Some were unconscious, some were dead. I brought out I don't know how many bodies. . . . I tried to get into the military, but they refused. . . . Finally, I wrote a letter to President Roosevelt. I told him I was angry at the Japanese bombing and had lost some friends. He okayed that I be accepted."

—U. S. sailor, quoted in *The Good War*, by Studs Terkel

This medal was made to commemorate the bombing of Pearl Harbor.

Like this young sailor, millions of Americans rushed to join the fight after Pearl Harbor. Neutrality was quickly forgotten. Their nation had been attacked. Friends, children, and parents had been killed. Americans were determined to bring an end to the madness of war.

Strengths and Weaknesses

When the United States entered World War II, the Axis Powers had two big advantages. First, Germany and Japan had already secured firm control of the areas they had invaded. As a result, the United States and the Allies faced a long, drawn-out fight on multiple fronts. Second, Germany and Japan were better prepared for war. In the 1930s both nations had rearmed and built airfields, barracks, and military training centers. By the mid-1930s the Nazis had converted most of the German economy to military production, as had Japan's military-led government.

The Allies did have some advantages, however. The Axis forces were spread over an enormous area stretching from the coast of France to deep into the Soviet Union and from Norway to North Africa. In the Pacific, Japan had occupied a similarly large area. The Germans had not defeated the British or the Soviets and therefore had to maintain troops on two active fronts. The Allies' hopes rested on two factors—the enormous size of the Soviet Union's military and the tremendous production capacity of the United States.

Axis leaders hoped that they could win the conflict before these two factors could combine and overwhelm their smaller but better-prepared forces. The Allies sought to continue to resist long enough to allow the United States to gather its strength.

✔ **READING CHECK: Comparing** Compare the advantages of the Allied Powers and Axis Powers in 1941. Allies advantages—Axis powers spread over enormous area, size of Soviet military, production capacity of the United States; Axis advantages—control of invaded areas, well prepared for war

ALL LEVELS: To help students understand the strengths and weaknesses of the Allied and Axis Powers in 1941, copy the graphic organizer at right on the chalkboard, omitting the italicized answers. Have each student complete it. **English Language Learners**

HOMEWORK *Have students list the strengths and weaknesses of the Allied and Axis Powers. Then ask students to develop three or four ways in which the United States might have countered Axis advantages. Have each student discuss these strategies in a memo to President Roosevelt.*

 THE ALLIED AND AXIS POWERS—STRENGTHS AND WEAKNESSES

The Allied Powers

advantage: *the United States had tremendous production capacity*

advantage: *the Soviet Union had vast manpower*

advantage: *Britain and the Soviet Union had not been defeated*

disadvantage: *faced a long, drawn-out fight on several fronts*

disadvantage: *enemy held firm control of conquered areas spread over an enormous area—both in Europe and the Pacific*

The Axis Powers

advantage: *better prepared for war*

advantage: *had firm control over invaded areas*

advantage: *had been rearmed since the 1930s*

advantage: *already had airfields, barracks, and military training centers*

advantage: *economies ready for war*

disadvantage: *had to defend multiple fronts*

Mobilizing for War

After the bombing of Pearl Harbor the United States switched from a peacetime to a wartime economy. Government and private industry cooperated to increase production, and union leaders agreed not to strike during the war.

A production boom. In 1940, government arsenals employed about 22,000 workers who produced ammunition, cannon shells, and rifles. Three years later some 486,000 workers were working in the arsenals. By war's end the United States had built some 300,000 aircraft. Car production was suspended for the duration of the war. Between 1940 and 1945, American factories produced huge numbers of planes, tanks, jeeps, and guns. American shipyards built 88,000 landing craft, 215 submarines, 147 aircraft carriers, 952 other warships, and 5,200 merchant ships.

This massive increase in production created an economic boom that ended the Great Depression. Unemployment dropped from 14.6 percent in 1940 to 1.2 percent in 1944. Earnings nearly doubled between 1939 and 1945. People who had stood in breadlines a decade earlier now brought home fat paychecks. The lure of high-paying jobs in war industries led to vast population shifts. More than 4 million workers left their homes to find work in factories in other states.

Sharecroppers, tenant farmers, and others struggling to make a living on farms flocked to the centers of wartime production. Many went to shipyards on the Gulf and Pacific coasts and to factories in the Midwest and West. The West experienced particularly strong growth during the war.

American farms also became marvels of productivity. During the war years, farmers produced enough food to supply both the American people and many of the Allied Powers overseas. Although many agricultural workers went off to fight in the war or to work in wartime factories, farm production increased. As part of its lend-lease aid, the United States exported 10 percent of the food it produced, mostly to Great Britain and the Soviet Union.

Government expansion. Mobilizing for war required a greatly expanded federal government. Between 1940 and 1945 the number of federal employees nearly tripled. To fight the Axis Powers, the United States needed to channel all of its resources into producing the maximum amount of military goods. In January 1942 President Roosevelt created the **War Production Board** (WPB) to increase military production. The WPB directed the conversion of existing factories to wartime production and

PRIMARY SOURCE

Japanese View of World War II

The day after Japan's attack on Pearl Harbor, Emperor Hirohito made a speech that provided Japan's reasons for declaring war on the United States and Great Britain. **How does Emperor Hirohito attempt to justify the attack on Pearl Harbor?**

❝Both America and Britain . . . have aggravated the disturbances in East Asia. . . . These two powers, inducing other countries to follow suit, increased military preparations on all sides of Our Empire. . . . They have obstructed by every means Our peaceful commerce, and finally resorted to a direct severance [cutting off] of economic relations. . . . Patiently have We waited and long have We endured, in hope that Our Government might retrieve the situation in peace. But Our adversaries [enemies], showing not the least spirit of conciliation [peacemaking], have unduly [excessively] delayed a settlement. . . . Our Empire for its existence and self defense has no other recourse [choice] but to appeal to arms and to crush every obstacle in its path.❞

INTERPRETING THE VISUAL RECORD

Preparing for war. This assembly line at North American Aviation's Inglewood, California, plant turned out B-25 bombers. *How does this image point to a U.S. advantage in the war?*

ECONOMICS

No-Strike Agreements. The federal government began to pressure union leaders to avoid strikes well before the United States declared war. In January 1941 President Roosevelt declared that "whatever stands in the way of speed and efficiency in defense preparations must give way to the national need." A short time later his administration established the National Defense Mediation Board to bring union leaders and business managers together to establish a series of wage agreements and a system for arbitrating industrial disputes.

CRITICAL THINKING How might no-strike agreements have affected unions?

ANSWER: Students might suggest that the agreements weakened unions or that they actually strengthened unions by presenting them as intensely patriotic.

VISUAL RECORD ANSWER

Students might suggest that assembly lines increased American productivity.

PRIMARY SOURCE ANSWER

Students might mention that the emperor blamed the United States and Britain for encouraging disturbances in East Asia and for failing to help Japan's commerce.

TEACH OBJECTIVE 2

LEVEL 1: Ask students to outline the steps that the United States took to prepare for war. *(Students should mention the efforts to increase production, expand the government, direct the economy, and raise the army.)* List students' responses on the chalkboard. Then ask each student to consult the chalkboard list to write a paragraph explaining how the United States prepared to fight in World War II.
English Language Learners

LEVEL 2: Pair students and ask students to outline the steps that the United States took to prepare for war. *(See the Level 1 lesson for the correct steps.)* Have each pair select one particular step and create a poster in support of that measure. Students' posters should include catchy phrases and illustrations to attract support for the war. Have each pair write two or three paragraphs explaining its poster.
English Language Learners, Cooperative Learning

LEVEL 3: Tell students to imagine that it is early 1942 and that they are aides to President Roosevelt. Have each student write a brief speech for Roosevelt to deliver to the nation outlining the steps that the United States has taken to prepare for war. *(See the Level 1 lesson for the correct steps.)* In their speeches, students should both describe and justify the steps. Have volunteers deliver their speeches to the class.

Rationing. The Office of Price Administration (OPA) was in charge of rationing. Local boards of the OPA distributed monthly ration books with an allotted number of coupons for individuals. Shoppers spent red coupons on animal products such as red meat, and green, brown, or blue coupons on processed items such as canned goods. Gasoline was also rationed. Price tags showed cost in both dollars and coupons.

CRITICAL THINKING Why might gasoline have been an important ration item?

ANSWER: Students might suggest that the government needed fuel. In addition, gasoline rationing decreased driving and thus helped conserve rubber.

THAT'S INTERESTING!

Approximately one half of the men who were called up during the first year of the draft were rejected for failing to meet the military's minimum physical standards. These standards included a height of at least five feet, a weight of at least 105 pounds, correctable vision, at least 16 natural teeth, and no flat feet.

GRAPH ANSWER
about $250 billion

Defense Expenditures, 1940–1945

Note: Percentages represent the portion of the total federal budget spent on defense.
Source: *Historical Statistics of the United States*

Interpreting Graphs The United States prepared itself for war by boosting the defense budget, increasing technological research, and organizing industry. By the end of the war, more than 80 percent of all government spending went toward defense.

② Skills Assessment How much did the U.S. government spend on national defense from 1942 to 1945?

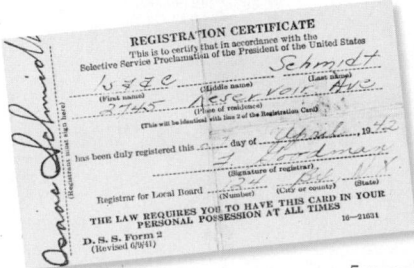

Registration certificates like this one proved that a man had made himself available to be drafted.

supervised the building of new plants. It assigned raw materials to industry, including scrap iron from factories and recyclable aluminum, paper, tin, and other items from homes. Created on May 27, 1943, the **Office of War Mobilization** (OWM) coordinated all government agencies involved in the war effort. OWM director James F. Byrnes wielded such power that he was often called the assistant president.

The OWM coordinated the production and distribution of consumer goods. For example, it diverted nylon to use for making parachutes and even regulated clothing styles to save fabric. Cuffs on men's trousers and pleats in women's skirts were canceled. Martha Wood of Raleigh, North Carolina, remembers that "rationing was hard to live with, particularly silk stockings.... If you had a run in your stocking, you took a needle and thread and worked it back up, because there was no chance of getting any [more]."

Directing the economy. The government also expanded its control over the economy. In order to pay for the war, the government increased by about nine times the number of Americans who had to pay income tax. The new taxes affected most middle- and lower-income groups. The rest of the money came from borrowing, mainly through war bonds.

The sale of war bonds also helped the government deal with another major concern—keeping inflation down. When incomes remain high but few consumer items are available for people to buy, prices go up and inflation results. Selling war bonds offered a way to channel excess income, thus keeping inflation down.

As a further anti-inflation measure, the government established the Office of Price Administration (OPA), which set maximum prices on consumer goods. The OPA also began rationing scarce items in December 1941. Rationed items included gasoline, tires, coffee, sugar, meat, butter, and canned goods. At its peak the OPA oversaw 13 rationing programs. The government also tried to keep wages and prices down by freezing wages. After the cost of living rose, the government allowed wages to rise by 15 percent.

Raising an army. Mobilizing for a war also meant recruiting soldiers. In the summer of 1940, the United States called the National Guard to active duty and passed the **Selective Training and Service Act.** This act provided for the first peacetime draft in U.S. history. The law required all men ages 21 to 35 (later 18 to 45) to register. Local draft boards determined fitness and deferred men for family, religious, or health reasons. At the time of the draft there were just 269,023 soldiers in the U.S. Army, 160,997 in the Navy, and 28,345 in the Marines. They made up less than 5 percent of the 12 million trained soldiers the military needed to fight the war.

About two thirds of the Americans who served during World War II were draftees and the rest volunteers, including more than 300,000 women. Women enrolled in the Women's Auxiliary Army Corps (WAAC), Women Airforce Service

TEACH OBJECTIVE 3

ALL LEVELS: Distribute Outline Map 20, World War II in the Pacific, from **American History Outline Maps**. Have each student use information from the textbook to label locations where the Japanese military attacked after Pearl Harbor. *(Students should label Clark Airforce Base in the Philippines, Burma, Borneo, the Netherlands East Indies, Wake Island, and Hong Kong.)* Have students annotate their maps with specific details about each military attack. Students may wish to include their maps in their portfolios.
English Language Learners

TEACH OBJECTIVE 4

LEVEL 1: Ask students to name the early turning points of the war in the Pacific. *(Students should name the Battle of the Coral Sea, the Battle of Midway, and Guadalcanal.)* List students' responses on the chalkboard. Then organize students into triads. Assign each triad one of the battles. Have triads develop an outline for a radio news report relaying the four "Ws" of the battle: What, When, Where, and Why it was significant. *(See pp. 532–33 for specific details about the three battles.)* Ask at least three volunteers—one for each battle—to present their outlines to the class.
English Language Learners, Cooperative Learning

Pilots (WASPs), and auxiliary branches of the navy, coast guard, and marines. They worked as nurses, drove vehicles, and ferried planes in order to free men for active duty. Eunice Hatchitt, a nurse in the Philippines, described the conditions.

 "Days and nights were an endless nightmare, until it seemed we couldn't stand it any longer. Patients came in by the hundreds, and the doctors and nurses worked continuously under the tents amid the flies and heat and dust. We had from eight to nine hundred victims a day."

—Eunice Hatchitt, *Bataan Nurse*

✔ **READING CHECK: Categorizing** What new powers or authority did the U.S. government assume in response to World War II? The WPB directed the conversion of factories to wartime production; the OPA started rationing; taxes were raised; the Selective Training and Service Act introduced a draft.

War in the Pacific

Japan's assault on Pearl Harbor was just one part of a giant offensive throughout the Pacific region. On December 8, 1941, Japanese planes bombed Clark Air Force Base in the Philippines. Over the following two weeks the Japanese attacked Burma, Borneo, the Netherlands East Indies, Wake Island, and Hong Kong.

On February 27, 1942, in what became known as the Battle of the Java Sea, the Japanese navy crushed a fleet of Australian, British, Dutch, and U.S. warships that had been trying to block a Japanese invasion of Java. The Japanese invaded Java the next day and soon after began their conquest of New Guinea.

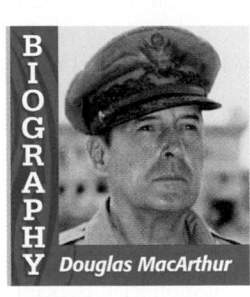
B I O G R A P H Y
Douglas MacArthur

Defending the Philippines were more than 30,000 U.S. and 110,000 Filipino troops under the overall command of General **Douglas MacArthur**. Born in 1880, he was the son of Arthur MacArthur, a distinguished general. Douglas MacArthur graduated from the U.S. Military Academy at West Point in 1903. MacArthur then served in the Philippines and was later wounded twice in World War I. From 1919 to 1922 he was superintendent of West Point. In 1937 he retired from the U.S. Army and served as a military adviser in the Philippines for several years. President Roosevelt recalled MacArthur to active duty in the summer of 1941. He eventually was given command of all U.S. Army units in the Pacific.

When Japanese bombers attacked Clark Air Force Base, they found the U.S. aircraft sitting on the runway. One Japanese pilot recalled, "They squatted there like sitting ducks." The planes that were needed to provide air support for the U.S. fleet in the Philippines were destroyed. Therefore, the fleet had to withdraw out of range of the Japanese planes based in Taiwan. With no air or naval opposition, Japanese forces advanced toward Manila. MacArthur recognized that his outnumbered forces would be unable to stop the Japanese advance. He ordered his troops to evacuate the city and retreat to the Bataan Peninsula.

The rapid pace of the evacuation prevented U.S. forces from stockpiling enough supplies, particularly food. The fighting soon settled into a war of attrition. The Japanese kept the pressure on the starving defenders, who were outnumbered, outgunned, and inexperienced. President Roosevelt ordered MacArthur to Australia. MacArthur vowed about the Philippines, "I shall return."

Nurses worked under battlefield conditions to save the lives of wounded soldiers.

Research on the R⊙M

Free Find:
Douglas MacArthur
After reading about Douglas MacArthur on the **Holt Researcher CD–ROM**, write a short speech to be given at the dedication of a memorial to MacArthur.

LEVEL 2: Ask students to name the early turning points of the war in the Pacific. (*See the Level 1 lesson for the correct battles.*) List students' responses on the chalkboard. Then tell students to imagine that they are radio news announcers. Assign each student one of the battles. Have students develop a short "You Are There" radio presentation about their assigned battles. (*See this two-page spread for specific details about the three battles.*) Have volunteers deliver their radio presentations to the class.

LEVEL 3: Ask students to name the early turning points of the war in the Pacific. (*See the Level 1 lesson for the correct battles.*)

List students' responses on the chalkboard. Then organize students into three groups and tell each group to imagine that it is a group of naval officers stationed in the Pacific. Assign each group one of the battles. Have each group write military briefings on its assigned battle. (*See this two-page spread for specific details about the three battles.*) Groups' briefings should review the war in the Pacific up to the time of the battle, identify the battle's location, describe the military action during the battle, note the battle's outcome, and explain how the battle furthered the Allied cause. Have each group present its briefings to the class. **Cooperative Learning**

HISTORY MAKERS SPEAK

Anton Bilek in *"The Good War": An Oral History of World War Two*

The Bataan Death March. The Bataan Death March permanently scarred many of those who lived through it. Anton Bilek, an American survivor, recalled the cruelty of his captors years later:

"The Japanese emptied out the hospitals. Anybody that could walk, they forced 'em into line. You found all kinda bodies along the road. Some of 'em bloated, some had just been killed. If you fell out to the side, you were either shot by the guards or you were bayoneted and left there. We lost somewhere between six hundred and seven hundred Americans in the four days of the march. The Filipinos lost close to ten thousand."

CRITICAL THINKING Why might the Japanese have treated the captured soldiers with such extraordinary cruelty?

ANSWER: Some students might suggest that the Japanese soldiers, like soldiers from many nations, regarded their enemies as inhuman.

The Navajo Code Talkers

teen Life

Young American Indians served in several branches of the U.S. armed forces during World War II. Their languages allowed them to play a unique role in the Signal Corps, the communication units responsible for coding and sending classified military information. In March 1942 the Marine Signal Corps organized a unit composed entirely of Navajo, some of whom were teenagers. They believed that because the Navajo language was unfamiliar to the Japanese it would provide an unbreakable code.

The new unit devised and memorized a special Navajo dictionary containing 413 military terms. For example, the Navajo word for "chicken hawk" meant dive-bomber in the code. "Hummingbird" meant fighter plane. "Iron fish" meant submarine. The Navajo Code Talkers first went into action in the fall of 1942 in the Pacific. U.S. field commanders soon reported that the Navajo methods reduced by half the time needed for decoding and encoding messages. As radio operators who tracked Japanese movements, the code talkers often had to work in dangerous conditions behind enemy lines.

By August 1943 nearly 200 Navajo were participating in the Code Talker program, and by the war's end more than 400 had served in the Marine Signal Corps. Their codes completely baffled the Japanese and were never broken.

Navajo Code Talkers Henry Bake and George Kirk operate a radio behind enemy lines in the Solomon Islands.

After fighting against overwhelming odds, the survivors who remained on Bataan surrendered in April 1942. Japanese soldiers forced the more than 70,000 survivors to march through the jungle on their way to prison camp. More than 10,000 died on what came to be called the **Bataan Death March**. The Japanese treated U.S. and Filipino soldiers brutally. Some prisoners were prevented from drinking water. Others were beaten or shot. Conditions did not improve when they reached the prison camps. Disease soon spread among the sick and poorly fed prisoners.

✔ **READING CHECK: Drawing Conclusions** How did Japan use its military advantages early in the war? It had a well-planned major offensive that allowed it to attack quickly and keep the pressure on U.S. troops.

Halting the Japanese Advance

By the summer of 1942, the Japanese were ready to strike Australia, India, and through Hawaii to the Pacific coast of the United States. The commander of the U.S. Pacific Fleet, Admiral **Chester Nimitz**, did not consider the attack on Pearl Harbor a complete disaster. "It was God's mercy that our fleet was in Pearl Harbor on 7 December 1941," Nimitz said. Much of the sunken battle fleet was salvageable because the ships sat in the shallow waters of the harbor. Furthermore, none of the aircraft carriers had been in port at the time of the attack. The U.S. fleet recovered quickly and was soon fighting again.

The Battle of the Coral Sea. Nimitz was an aggressive commander who preferred to attack, thereby pressuring his opponents into making mistakes. On May 7, 1942, a Japanese force on its way to attack Port Moresby, New Guinea, seized Tulagi (too-LAH-gee) Island, one of the Solomon Islands. Before the Japanese could reach New Guinea, however, a joint British-U.S. naval force intercepted them. Planes from U.S. aircraft carriers damaged one Japanese carrier and destroyed another and several aircraft. The **Battle of the Coral Sea** was an important Allied victory. Although the Allies lost a carrier, the battle stopped the Japanese advance on Australia.

The Battle of Midway. The second major naval battle in the Pacific, the **Battle of Midway**, took place early in June 1942. Seeking to crush the U.S. Pacific Fleet, Japan launched a two-pronged attack. One unit seized two of the Aleutian Islands, near Alaska. They hoped to lure part of the U.S. fleet away from Hawaii. Meanwhile, the Japanese carried out their main attack against Midway, two small islands northwest of Hawaii. U.S. experts had broken the Japanese fleet code so the United States had advance warning of the Japanese strategy. Nimitz later recalled, "Had we lacked early information of the Japanese

LEVEL 1: Distribute Outline Map 19, World War II in Europe, from **American History Outline Maps**. Have each student use information from the textbook to label the map with the major battles in Europe and North Africa in 1942. (*Students should label the Battle of El Alamein and the Battle of Stalingrad.*) Then pair students and have pairs develop four headlines—two for each battle—relating the significance of the conflicts. (*Headlines should note that both battles broke the Axis momentum and gave the Allies renewed confidence.*) Ask volunteers to read their headlines to the class.
English Language Learners, Cooperative Learning

LEVELS 2 AND 3: Distribute Outline Map 19, World War II in Europe, from **American History Outline Maps**. Have each student use information from the textbook to label the map with the major battles in Europe and North Africa in 1942. (*See the Level 1 lesson for the correct battles.*) Then tell students to imagine that they are newspaper reporters. Have students write two half-page newspaper articles—one for each battle—relating the significance of the conflicts. (*See the Level 1 lesson for the correct significance.*) Ask volunteers to read their articles to the class. Students may wish to include their articles in their portfolios.

movements, . . . the Battle of Midway would have ended differently." Instead, Nimitz was able to assemble U.S. aircraft carriers and destroyers north of Midway to ambush the Japanese attack.

Americans and Japanese clashed June 3–6. U.S. fighters, dive-bombers, and torpedo planes sank four Japanese aircraft carriers and shot down many enemy planes. The U.S. victory proved crucial. Japan lost ships, planes, and a number of skilled pilots.

Guadalcanal. After the Battle of Midway, the United States launched its first major offensive. In August 1942, American marines waded ashore at Guadalcanal, in the Solomon Islands. For six desperate months, they clung to a toehold around the airport.

Major General Alexander A. Vandegrift, commander of the U.S. Marines on Guadalcanal, described the ferocious fighting. "I have never heard or read of this kind of fighting. These people [the Japanese] refuse to surrender. The wounded will wait till men come up to examine them, and blow themselves and the other fellow to death with a hand grenade."

In November the Japanese sent a huge fleet to the Solomons. They hoped to recapture Guadalcanal, but the U.S. fleet defeated the Japanese in a bloody battle. The tide of battle in the Pacific had finally turned in the Allies' favor.

✔ **READING CHECK: Sequencing** Describe in order the events that led to the Allies' control of the Pacific. The United States stopped the Japanese advance on Australia, then defeated them at the Battle of Midway. The United States defeated the Japanese fleet at Guadalcanal.

Early Fighting in Europe and the Mediterranean

By the time of the attack on Pearl Harbor, the Axis Powers controlled much of Europe and the lands around the Mediterranean. Bulgaria, Hungary, and Romania had joined the Axis Powers. Yugoslavia and Greece had been occupied, and southern Europe was firmly under Axis control. Throughout most of 1942 the Axis Powers achieved one victory after another.

The Germans and their allies scored victories on many different fronts. German submarines, or U-boats, patrolled the Atlantic Ocean. They sank Allied military and merchant ships and nearly cut off British supply lines. In the first half of 1942, German U-boats sank more than 500 ships off the U.S. East Coast.

North Africa. Italian forces had launched an invasion of North Africa in 1940. When British troops later began to inflict heavy damage on the Italians, Adolf Hitler sent in the German Afrika Korps under commander **Erwin Rommel**. Known as the Desert Fox, Rommel had advanced as far as El Alamein, Egypt, by July 1942. His troops were ready to take the Suez Canal and the oil fields of the Middle East.

Rommel's skill as a military leader led even Winston Churchill to later admit that "[he was] a great general." However, Rommel suffered from shortages of men and supplies. The British, led by General **Bernard Montgomery**, turned this shortage to their advantage. In the fall of 1942 Montgomery pushed Rommel's troops steadily westward out of Egypt and into Libya. The British victory in the Battle of El Alamein helped turn the corner for the Allies in North Africa.

INTERPRETING THE VISUAL RECORD

Midway. The U.S. victory in the Battle of Midway crippled the Japanese navy. *From the painting, what can you determine about the type of fighting that took place during the Battle of Midway?*

Effective transportation was vital for troops battling in the wide-open spaces of North Africa.

VISUAL RECORD ANSWER

Students might suggest that the fighting included heavy artillery shelling and aerial bombing.

REVIEW SECTION **1** **ANSWERS**

1. Identify
- War Production Board, p. 529
- Office of War Mobilization, p. 530

REVIEW

Have students complete the **Section 1 Review** on p. 534.

ASSESS

Have students complete **Daily Quiz 18.1**. As **Alternative Assessment**, you may want to use the war preparation poster or the Pacific war radio broadcast in this section's lessons.

RETEACH

Have students complete **Main Idea Activity for English Language Learners and Special-Needs Students 18.1**. Then ask each student to outline Section 1. After students have completed

their outlines, organize students into triads. Have members of the triads quiz each other on the material in Section 1. **English Language Learners, Cooperative Learning**

EXTEND

Organize students into four groups, assigning each group one of the following military leaders: Douglas MacArthur, Chester Nimitz, Erwin Rommel, or Bernard Montgomery. Have each group conduct research on its assigned leader. Then ask each group to present oral reports on its leader's activities during World War II. Groups' presentations should include illustrations and graphics. **Cooperative Learning, Block Scheduling**

- Selective Training and Service Act, p. 530
- Douglas MacArthur, p. 531
- Bataan Death March, p. 532
- Chester Nimitz, p. 532
- Battle of the Coral Sea, p. 532
- Battle of Midway, p. 532
- Erwin Rommel, p. 533
- Bernard Montgomery, p. 533

2. Battle of Java Sea, MacArthur, Japanese victory; Battle of the Coral Sea, Nimitz, Allied victory; Battle of Midway, Nimitz, Allied victory; Battle of Guadalcanal, Vandegrift, Allied victory; Battle of El Alamein, Rommel-Axis and Montgomery-Allies, Allied victory; Battle of Stalingrad, Allied victory

3a. The massive increase in production for wartime created an economic boom. Wages and farm production increased.

b. Japan lost ships, planes, and pilots, and the United States gained experience and confidence

c. Both broke Axis momentum and gave Allies a sense of confidence.

4. Reports will vary but should include: strengths—Axis were prepared for war; Allies hoped to benefit from the size of the Soviet Union's army and U.S. production capacity; weaknesses—Axis had to fight on two fronts; Allies were ill-prepared for war, and the United States did not enter until Pearl Harbor.

These soldiers are scrambling across a trench that used to be a city street in Stalingrad.

Analyzing Primary Sources

Drawing Inferences What does this quotation suggest about the importance of the Battle of Stalingrad?

Each side regarded possession of Stalingrad as crucial to its success.

Stalingrad. In Europe, German troops had penetrated far into the Soviet Union after their initial attack in June 1941. As the Germans advanced, they captured many industrial centers as well as rich grainfields in the Ukraine. By winter German forces were closing in on Moscow. The Germans also laid siege to Leningrad. For months the men, women, and children defending the city endured a nightmare of shell fire and starvation.

In the summer of 1942, German troops that had been pushing toward the oil fields of southern Russia approached the key city of Stalingrad. By the fall of 1942, German troops were fighting for control of the city. A German officer described the fighting.

History Makers Speak

❝We have fought during fifteen days for a single house. The 'front' is a corridor between burned-out rooms; it is the thin ceiling between two floors. . . . From story to story, faces black with sweat, we bombard each other with grenades in the middle of explosions, clouds of dust and smoke, heaps of mortar, floods of blood, fragments of furniture and human beings.❞

—German officer, quoted in *The Century*, by Peter Jennings and Todd Brewster

The Soviet forces refused to surrender, however, and eventually surrounded the German soldiers in Stalingrad. Throughout a terrible winter the Germans hung on, forbidden by Hitler to surrender. Trapped in the ruined city with few supplies and little food, the Axis troops finally surrendered in late January 1943. The German force suffered about 200,000 casualties. The Allied victories at El Alamein and Stalingrad broke the momentum of the Axis advance. Said British prime minister Winston Churchill: "Before Alamein we never had a victory. After Alamein we never had a defeat."

✔ **READING CHECK: Summarizing** Why was the Axis defeat in Stalingrad important?
German troops had penetrated far into the Soviet Union, but the Soviet victory at Stalingrad broke the Axis momentum.

SECTION ① REVIEW

1. Identify and explain:
War Production Board
Office of War Mobilization
Selective Training and Service Act
Douglas MacArthur
Bataan Death March
Chester Nimitz
Battle of the Coral Sea
Battle of Midway
Erwin Rommel
Bernard Montgomery

2. Analyzing Information Copy the graphic organizer below. Use it to list battles, their leaders, and their outcomes.

Battle	Leader	Outcome

3. Finding the Main Idea
a. How did mobilization for World War II end the Great Depression in the United States?
b. What was the significance of the U.S. victories at the Battles of Midway and Guadalcanal?
c. Why were the Battles of El Alamein and Stalingrad turning points for the Allies?

4. Writing and Critical Thinking
Comparing Imagine that you are a military adviser to President Roosevelt. Write a brief report comparing the strengths and weaknesses of the Allied Powers and the Axis Powers in 1941.
Consider:
- the results of the attack on Pearl Harbor
- when the United States entered the war
- the multiple fronts of the war

Homework Practice Online
keyword: SE3 HP18

SECTION 2

After completing Section 2, students should be able to:

OBJECTIVE 1 *Describe how the U.S. government tried to keep wartime morale high.*

OBJECTIVE 2 *Describe what life was like in the United States during World War II.*

OBJECTIVE 3 *Relate how women contributed to the war effort.*

OBJECTIVE 4 *Analyze what actions the government took to protect the rights of minority groups.*

OBJECTIVE 5 *Discuss the war's effect on Japanese Americans.*

LET'S GET STARTED!

As students enter the classroom, ask them to describe, in writing, a popular culture depiction of life on the home front during World War II or historical artifact relating to life on the home front. Ask volunteers to share their responses. Then tell students that in Section 2 they will learn about life on the home front during World War II.

SECTION 2

The Home Front

 EYEWITNESSES TO History

"*When my son enlisted in the air force, he went to McDill Field in Florida. So I went there. . . . Then I came back to Westminster . . . [and] found that people who didn't have someone overseas were not too concerned. They were interested in bacon and sugar and gas, which I was not. . . . I did a lot of war work . . . when I was at McDill, I worked in the hospital. . . . I started to do some volunteer work in Westminster, like rolling bandages, but I couldn't make it. The people I was doing it with were not in my situation at all. They were more concerned with what they were having to give up than with what was happening in Europe. I had people call me up and ask, 'Do you have coupons? We can get butter tomorrow.' I never stood in a line for a thing. I thought that if the men could do without it, so could I.*"

—Mary Speir, quoted in
Americans Remember the Home Front, by Roy Hoopes

Americans eagerly planted victory gardens to support the war effort.

Mary Speir of Westminster, Maryland, understood all too well the sacrifices people made to support the war effort. Her husband and son fought in the war, and her son was killed in combat.

Promoting the War

Most Americans supported U.S. involvement in World War II. Many families proudly displayed window banners with a star. A blue star represented a loved one in the service. A gold star stood for a death in combat.

The U.S. government tried to keep morale high. This was particularly important in the early days of the war, when Allied troops faced many setbacks. The government encouraged the media to do their part. Moviemakers, songwriters, and radio-station programmers responded by urging all-out participation in the war effort.

Movie stars advertised war bonds and traveled overseas to entertain the troops. Hollywood studios produced hundreds of war movies. *So Proudly We Hail*—a story about army nurses in the Philippines—was just one of the patriotic films that built support for the war. Striking a lighter note were comedies like Bob Hope's *Caught in the Draft.* A few films, such as *Wake Island* and *Report from the Aleutians,* offered more realistic views of combat.

Radio stations broadcast both war news and entertainment. Foreign correspondents such as Edward R. Murrow and Eric Sevareid gave on-the-scene accounts of war-ravaged Europe. The government-run **Office of War Information** controlled the flow of war news at home.

READ TO DISCOVER

1. How did the U.S. government try to keep wartime morale high?
2. What was life like in the United States during World War II?
3. How did women contribute to the war effort?
4. What actions did the government take to protect the rights of minority groups?
5. How were Japanese Americans affected by the war?

DEFINE

braceros
zoot-suit riots
internment

IDENTIFY

Office of War Information
Rosie the Riveter
A. Philip Randolph
Fair Employment Practices Committee
Carlos E. Castañeda
Norman Mineta

WHY IT MATTERS TODAY

Fair treatment of workers continues to be a major concern in the United States. Use CNNfyi.com or other **current events** sources to find out one method or government agency that deals with issues of fairness in the workplace. Record your findings in your journal.

CNNfyi.com

SECTION 2 RESOURCES

REPRODUCIBLE

▶ Guided Reading Strategy 18.2
▶ Primary Source Reading 18: A Mountain Woman's Tale
▶ Graphic Organizer Activity 18: The Effect of War on Life at Home

TECHNOLOGY

▶ One-Stop Planner, Lesson 18.2
▶ The American Nation Video Program Segment: Japanese Americans in Relocation Camps; Teacher's Guide, pp. 159–60
▶ Holt Researcher: American History CD–ROM
▶ HRW Go site
▶ Homework Practice Online

REINFORCEMENT, REVIEW, AND ASSESSMENT

▶ Section 2 Review, p. 541
▶ Daily Quiz 18.2
▶ Main Idea Activity 18.2
▶ English Audio Summary 18.2
▶ Spanish Audio Summary 18.2

Teacher to Teacher

Ron Foore of Tulsa, Oklahoma, suggested the following activity: Pair students and have them conduct research on swing dancing in the 1940s and the 1990s. Then tell pairs to choose one of the two decades. Have each pair use its research to develop a short swing dance presentation. Each pair should demonstrate one popular dance and discuss the importance of swing dancing in its chosen decade.

TEACH OBJECTIVE 1

LEVELS 1 AND 2: Conduct a brief discussion on the ways in which the U.S. government tried to keep wartime morale high. *(The government created the Office of War Information. Radio programmers and filmmakers created programs and movies that supported the war effort.)* Then pair students and tell them to imagine that it is 1942. Ask each pair to create two or three slogans in support of the war effort. Provide the following slogans as examples: *Pay Your Taxes, Beat the Axis; Don't Let Them Catch Us with Our Plants Down.* Have each pair write a paragraph explaining how its slogan would benefit wartime morale and the war effort.
English Language Learners, Cooperative Learning

★ HISTORICAL DOCUMENTS ★

PRESIDENT FRANKLIN D. ROOSEVELT
The Four Freedoms

On January 6, 1941, President Roosevelt requested support for the Lend-Lease program. In what became known as the Four Freedoms speech, Roosevelt defined the freedoms that came to represent why Americans were fighting. **Do you think that Roosevelt selected the most significant freedoms? Explain your answer.**

*I*n the future days, which we seek to make secure, we look forward to a world founded upon four essential human freedoms.

The first is freedom of speech and expression everywhere in the world.

The second is freedom of every person to worship God in his own way everywhere in the world.

The third is freedom from want, which, translated into world terms, means economic understandings which will secure to every nation a healthy peacetime life for its inhabitants everywhere in the world.

The fourth is freedom from fear—which, translated into world terms, means a worldwide reduction of armaments to such a point and in such a thorough fashion that no nation will be in a position to commit an act of physical aggression against any neighbor—anywhere in the world.

That is no vision of a distant millennium. It is a definite basis for a kind of world attainable in our own time and generation. That kind of world is the very antithesis [opposite] of the so-called new order of tyranny which the dictators seek to create with the crash of a bomb.

AIR RAID PRECAUTIONS HAVE BEEN TAKEN HERE

CD

Auxiliary Defense Manual

Signed by ———

Civil-defense units helped prepare Americans in case of attack by Axis forces.

The war also affected popular radio serials. Radio stations abandoned spy and sabotage programs for the duration of the war. Some even banned certain sound effects, such as wailing sirens, to avoid alarming listeners.

✔ **READING CHECK: Summarizing** How did the U.S. government use the media to keep wartime morale high? It encouraged war movies and movie stars to advertise war bonds and controlled the flow of war news.

Life During Wartime

Americans cut back their consumption of both luxuries and necessities to help the war effort. Millions of people grew vegetables and other produce in their backyards. These so-called victory gardens helped make more food available to U.S. and Allied soldiers. Martha Wood recalled that she and her neighbors

History Makers Speak

❝[formed] a neighborhood Victory Garden, plowed up the backyards of three houses, and planted beans, corn, tomatoes, okra, squash, and all the things we could use. When the crop came in, . . . [we] used a pressure cooker and canned all day. I was canning until midnight and later, night after night, and I frequently said, 'I wish I had Hitler in that pressure cooker.'❞

—Martha Wood, quoted in
Americans Remember the Home Front, by Roy Hoopes

After the bombing of Pearl Harbor, U.S. authorities imposed restrictions in case of attack on the mainland. West Coast cities began practicing nighttime blackouts. Authorities feared that brightly lit U.S. cities would make easy targets for Japanese bombers. Civil-defense units searched for signs of enemy aircraft. Across the nation, practice air-raid drills sent Americans scrambling for cover.

People worked longer hours and made many sacrifices, but daily life in the United States did not change radically during the war. On Broadway stages, musicals such as Irving Berlin's *This Is the Army* (1942) and Leonard Bernstein and Jerome Robbins's *On the Town* (1944) provided laughs and avoided the painful side of wartime. Richard Rodgers and Oscar Hammerstein's production *Oklahoma!* (1943) was the biggest hit during the war.

Wartime music did not have the same innocence of World War I hits such as "Over There." Instead, big hits like "Remember Pearl Harbor" and "Praise the Lord and Pass the Ammunition!" captured the harsh reality of war. Irving Berlin's song

LEVEL 3: Ask students to identify the ways in which the U.S. government attempted to keep wartime morale high. (*See the Level 1 lesson for the correct methods.*) Then tell students to imagine that they are Hollywood screenwriters. Have each student write a proposal for a movie in support of the war effort and to boost wartime morale. Ask volunteers to share their proposals. Students may wish to include their proposals in their portfolios.

TEACH OBJECTIVE 2

LEVEL 1: Pair students and tell them to imagine that it is 1942 and that they are U.S. citizens involved in the home front war effort. Have each pair create a dialogue on life in the United States during World War II. (*Pairs might mention victory gardens, long work hours, restrictions, and so on.*) Ask volunteers to perform their dialogues for the class.
English Language Learners, Cooperative Learning

"God Bless America" became a sort of unofficial national anthem. Big-band swing music remained popular, and sentimental songs such as "White Christmas" expressed Americans' longing for a return to peace.

In part as a result of widespread interest in the war, nonfiction became more popular than fiction. The best-selling books of 1941 were William Shirer's *Berlin Diary*, a frightening look inside Nazi Germany, and Joseph Davies's *Mission to Moscow*, a positive portrayal of the Soviet Union. Wartime also brought a change to the publishing industry. Paperback books first appeared in 1939, and wartime rationing helped them quickly surpass hardcover as the format of choice. The lower cost, light weight, and smaller size of paperbacks made them very popular. The military boosted the growth of the paperback format with the Armed Services Editions, which provided paperback books free of charge to U.S. troops. Some 60 million books of all types were distributed during the war.

✔ **READING CHECK: Drawing Inferences** How did popular entertainment in the 1940s convey universal themes? **by expressing a longing for peace**

AMERICAN ARTS
Norman Rockwell

Norman Rockwell was born in New York City in 1894. For six decades, until his death in 1978, Rockwell showed the positive side of American life in his illustrations. He once said, "As I grew up . . . I unconsciously decided that, even if it wasn't an ideal world, it should be so, and so I painted the ideal aspects of it." He is best known for the covers he drew for the *Saturday Evening Post*. In 47 years Rockwell drew 322 covers for the *Post*, more than any other artist.

Rockwell lived in Vermont during World War II and often used his neighbors as models for his illustrations. Despite painting just one combat scene during the war, he managed to capture the mood of a nation at war. He did so by reminding people of the reasons behind the war without downplaying the difficulty of the struggle. Rockwell said that he tried to create an image that "makes the reader want to sigh and smile at the same time."

Rockwell's cover for the September 4, 1943, *Saturday Evening Post* celebrated the Labor Day holiday. *Liberty Girl* honored women's contributions to the war effort with its representations of the many different kinds of work that women were performing.

Norman Rockwell's Liberty Girl

Understanding the Arts

1. How many different occupations are represented in this image?
2. How does this image reflect the experiences of American women on the home front?

LEVELS 2 AND 3: Tell students to imagine that it is 1942 and that they are U.S. citizens involved in the home front war effort. Have each student write four or five brief diary entries describing life in the United States during World War II. *(See the Level 1 lesson for appropriate elements.)* Ask volunteers to read their diary entries to the class.

TEACH OBJECTIVE 3

ALL LEVELS: To help students understand how women contributed to the war effort, copy the graphic organizer at right on the chalkboard, omitting the italicized answers. Have each student complete it.
English Language Learners

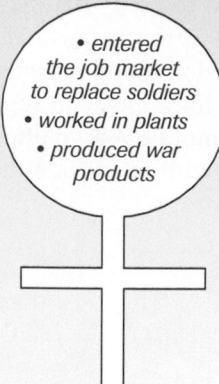

WOMEN AND THE WAR EFFORT

- *entered the job market to replace soldiers*
- *worked in plants*
- *produced war products*

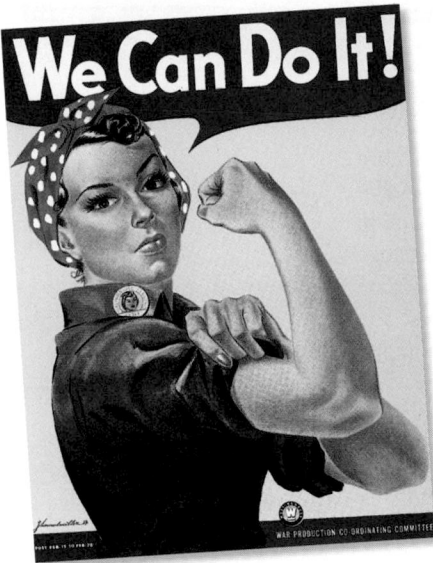

This image of Rosie the Riveter shows the importance of female workers to the war effort.

Female workers. Without the efforts of American women, the United States could not have produced the materials needed to win the war. *What are these female workers doing?*

Rosie the Riveter

For some Americans on the home front, particularly for women, daily life did change dramatically. During the depression, the government had discouraged women, particularly married women, from working. The government now urged them to enter the job market to replace departing soldiers. One government poster showed a female worker in bandanna and overalls. The caption read: "I'm Proud . . . my husband wants me to do my part." Advertisements and a popular song promoted **Rosie the Riveter**, the symbol of patriotic female defense workers.

From 1940 to 1944, the number of women in the workforce increased by about 6 million. Women worked in war plants and replaced men in a host of jobs ranging from newspaper reporting to truck driving. Many of these new workers were married women who were taking jobs outside the home for the first time. Many women already in the paid workforce left traditional "women's work" such as domestic service to work in factories.

Women's participation in the war effort gave many a new sense of pride and self-worth. One female aircraft worker finally felt a sense of achievement after feeling "average" at other jobs.

History Makers Speak
❝Foremen from other departments come to my machine to ask me to do some work for them if I have time because they say I'm the best countersinker in the vast building! At forty-nine I've at last become not better than average, but the best!❞

—Female aircraft worker, quoted in *Independent Women*, November 1943

Female workers continued to be paid less than men for the same work. African American women and women over 40 found few employers willing to hire them. Many women and men assumed that most of the jobs held by women during the war were temporary. However, some people expected more permanent change. A shipyard manager predicted that "these women who are willing . . . to lend a hand with the war will be the . . . office personnel of . . . the future."

✔ **READING CHECK: Making Predictions** How might increased female employment during the war change American society after the war?
Some women expected to work after the war was over.

Discrimination During the War

Racial tensions did not disappear during wartime. However, the cooperation the war effort required caused the government to try to reduce discrimination in war industries.

Demands for equal treatment. For African Americans, the war brought both continued discrimination and greater opportunities. Many black workers moved into better-paying industrial jobs and played a key role in the military effort. About 1 million African American soldiers served in the armed forces, including several thousand women in the Women's Auxiliary Army Corps. However, African Americans continued to serve in segregated units, and most were kept out of combat. Black soldiers were often assigned to low-level work.

LEVEL 1: Have each student create a graphic organizer displaying the ways in which the government attempted to protect the rights of minorities during World War II. *(The government created the Fair Employment Practices Committee and made attempts to end discrimination in businesses with federal contracts.)* Ask volunteers to copy their graphic organizers on the chalkboard. Then have students consult those organizers to write summary paragraphs explaining how the government attempted to protect minority rights during the war. Students may wish to include their paragraphs in their portfolios. **English Language Learners**

LEVELS 2 AND 3: Pair students and tell one member of each pair to act as a newspaper reporter and the other member to act as a government official. Have members prepare for an interview on governmental actions to protect the rights of minority groups during World War II. Newspaper reporters should develop at least five questions on the subject, while government officials should think of at least five possible questions they may be asked and answers to those questions. Have students conduct their interviews. *(See the Level 1 lesson for the correct government actions.)* Then hold a discussion on the material presented in the interviews. Conclude the lesson by having each student write a brief newspaper article that reflects the interview on governmental actions on behalf of minority groups during World War II. **Cooperative Learning**

Millions of African Americans in the workforce struggled to gain acceptance. Many war plants would not hire African Americans. Some would employ black workers only as janitors. Despite labor leaders' no-strike pledge, some white workers staged strikes—called hate strikes—designed to keep black workers out of high-paying factory jobs.

In 1941, before the United States entered the war, African American labor leader **A. Philip Randolph** planned a march on Washington, D.C., to protest discrimination against black workers. Fearing the unrest it might cause, President Roosevelt wanted to prevent the march. Randolph agreed to call off the march after Roosevelt issued an executive order forbidding racial discrimination in defense plants and government offices.

To enforce the order, on June 25, 1941, Roosevelt created the **Fair Employment Practices Committee** (FEPC). The FEPC investigated companies engaged in defense work to make sure that all qualified applicants, regardless of race, were considered for job openings. It was strengthened by a May 27, 1943, executive order requiring nondiscrimination clauses in all war contracts. The FEPC, however, lacked strong enforcement powers and was unable to prevent widespread abuses.

As during World War I, many African Americans moved northward to take advantage of the high wages being offered in war plants. In crowded cities where no new homes were being built, African Americans faced discrimination in housing. Competition for limited housing created tensions that sometimes led to outbursts of violence against African Americans. In Detroit in 1943 a fight between African American and white residents at Belle Isle, a popular Detroit park, spread to other parts of the city. Some 34 people died in several days of rioting before federal troops sent by President Roosevelt restored calm.

The zoot-suit riots.
World War II brought both opportunities and problems to Mexican Americans as well. More than 300,000 Mexican Americans served in the military, and 17 earned the Congressional Medal of Honor. The 88th Division, a top combat unit known as the Blue Devils, consisted mostly of Mexican American soldiers.

Mexican Americans also helped meet home-front labor needs. University of Texas history professor **Carlos E. Castañeda** served as assistant to the chair of the FEPC and worked to improve working conditions for Mexican Americans in Texas. In 1945 the FEPC ordered a major Texas oil company to discontinue hiring and promotion practices that discriminated against Hispanics.

Many Mexican Americans moved from the Southwest to industrial centers in the Midwest and on the West Coast. Under a 1942 agreement between the United States and Mexico, thousands of Mexican farm and railroad workers—known as **braceros**—came north to work in the Southwest during World War II.

During a rally at Madison Square Garden, A. Philip Randolph fights to save the Fair Employment Practices Committee.

These Mexican Americans were arrested during the zoot-suit riots. Many others served heroically during World War II, and 17 won the Congressional Medal of Honor (left).

The Tuskegee Airmen.
While most African American soldiers served in noncombat positions during the war, others took part in the fighting. The Tuskegee Airmen were an all-black unit of fighter pilots that served with distinction in the air war over Europe. Trained at Tuskegee Army Air Field in Tuskegee, Alabama, the Airmen engaged in their first combat mission in June 1943, when they launched an assault on a small Italian island. During the next two years they played a key role in the Allied air campaign, escorting bombing missions and attacking Axis air fields, supply centers, and communication lines. By the end of the war the Tuskegee Airmen were the only U.S. escort group that had not lost a single bomber to enemy planes.

CRITICAL THINKING How might the service of the Tuskegee Airmen have affected the racial attitudes of some white Americans?

ANSWER: Students may suggest that the Airmen's outstanding performance might have prompted some white Americans to support civil rights.

MAP ANSWER
(for p. 540)
Immigrants from Japan landed first in San Francisco rather than New York.

LEVEL 1: Pair students and tell them to imagine that they are Japanese Americans who lived in an internment camp during the war. Have each pair develop a dialogue discussing how the war affected Japanese Americans. *(Pairs should note that the government interned Japanese Americans in some states. Interned Japanese Americans often lost their property. Some Japanese Americans received limited military service opportunities.)* Ask volunteers to perform their dialogues for the class.

English Language Learners, Cooperative Learning

LEVELS 2 AND 3: Tell students to imagine that they are Japanese Americans who lived in an internment camp during the war. Have each student write a one-page memoir describing how Japanese Americans were affected by the war. *(See the Level 1 lesson for the correct effects.)* Ask volunteers to read their memoirs to the class. Students may wish to include their memoirs in their portfolios.

HOMEWORK *Have each student create an outline of the subsection titled Japanese American Relocation. Have students use their outlines to develop three possible essay questions on Japanese American life during the war.*

CITIZENSHIP

The Injustice of Internment. Many interned Japanese Americans were justifiably angry about the treatment they received. One man registered the following protest: "I was born in Hawaii. I worked most of my life on the west coast. I have never been to Japan. We would have done anything to show our loyalty. . . . That's not democracy. That's not the American way, taking everything away from people. . . . Where are the Germans? Where are the Italians? Do they ask them questions about loyalty?"

CRITICAL THINKING Why might the government have focused suspicion on Japanese Americans?

ANSWER: Some students might point to the existence of anti-Japanese prejudice.

The American Nation
VIDEO PROGRAM

Japanese Americans in Relocation Camps; Teacher's Guide, pp. 159–60

Search 43252, Play to 43455
Videodisc 2, Side A

Play   Pause

See *Teacher's Guide* for Spanish barcode.

The prejudice and discrimination endured by Hispanics in jobs, housing, and recreational facilities caused bitter resentment. Relations grew particularly hostile in Los Angeles. Mexican American youths had adopted the fad of wearing zoot suits—long, wide-shouldered jackets, trousers pegged at the ankle, and wide-brimmed hats. In June 1943, U.S. sailors roamed the city attacking zoot-suit-clad Mexican American youths in what became known as the **zoot-suit riots**. The government eventually clamped down on the sailors, but not before they had viciously beaten many Mexican Americans.

A citizens' committee later determined that the attacks were motivated by racial prejudice. The committee assigned partial responsibility to the Los Angeles police, who had responded to the riots by arresting Mexican Americans. The committee also blamed biased newspaper reports.

✔ **READING CHECK: Analyzing Information** How did World War II affect patterns of migration? **African Americans moved north in search of jobs; many Mexican Americans moved to industrial centers; braceros came to work in the Southwest.**

Japanese American Relocation

In general, World War II did not produce the same level of home-front intolerance as did World War I. A tragic exception was the **internment**, or forced relocation and imprisonment, of Japanese Americans living on the Pacific Coast. U.S. State Department adviser Eugene Rostow called relocation "a tragic and dangerous mistake." In 1941 about 119,000 people of Japanese ancestry lived in California, Oregon, and Washington. About one third of these people—the issei (ee-SAY)—had been born in Japan and were regarded by the U.S. government as aliens ineligible for U.S. citizenship. The rest—the nisei (nee-SAY)—had been born in the United States and thus were U.S. citizens.

No evidence of disloyalty on the part of any issei or nisei existed. Nevertheless, because of strong anti-Japanese feelings among some politicians and residents of western states, the federal government decided to remove people of Japanese descent from the West Coast. In February 1942, Japanese Americans were ordered to detention camps in Wyoming, Utah, and other states. Because Hawaii's Japanese population was too large to relocate, the islands were placed under martial law for the duration of the war.

Japanese American Relocation, 1942–1945

Interpreting Maps By September 1942 more than 110,000 Japanese Americans were interned in 10 camps located in relatively isolated, underdeveloped areas.

❓ **HUMAN SYSTEMS** Why was the Japanese American population located primarily on the West Coast?

Japanese American Population, 1940

- More than 10,000
- 1,000 to 10,000
- Less than 1,000
- ▲ Relocation center
- ■ Internment camp

U.S. Citizenship
About two thirds of the 127,000 people of Japanese ancestry living in the continental United States were American born and thus U.S. citizens.

REVIEW

Have students complete the **Section 2 Review** on p. 541.

ASSESS

Have students complete **Daily Quiz 18.2**. As **Alternative Assessment**, you may want to use the minority rights interview or the Japanese American dialogue in this section's lessons.

RETEACH

Have students complete **Main Idea Activity for English Language Learners and Special-Needs Students 18.2**. Then organize students into triads and assign each triad a subsection of Section 2. Ask each triad to develop a poster that summarizes the information in its assigned subsection. Have each triad present its poster to the class.
English Language Learners, Cooperative Learning

EXTEND

Have students conduct research on the United Service Organization (USO) during World War II. Ask each student to prepare some kind of oral presentation on a specific topic related to the USO. Students might focus on a particular performer, for example, or a particular show or tour. Have students present their work to the class. **Block Scheduling**

Norman Mineta

One imprisoned Japanese American was **Norman Mineta**, a nisei from San Jose, California. On the day of the Pearl Harbor bombing, the young Mineta fearfully watched his neighbors being taken away for questioning by the FBI. He recalled bitterly that "they had done nothing; the only thing that they had done was to be born of Japanese ancestry."

Just 10 years old when his family was uprooted, Mineta wore his Cub Scout uniform on the train. He hoped that it would show his loyalty to the United States. Mineta's family was interned with some 10,000 others at a camp at Heart Mountain, Wyoming. "These camps were all barbed wire, guard towers, searchlights," recalled Mineta.

After the war Mineta attended college and became an insurance agent. He later went into local politics in San Jose. In 1974 he was elected to the House of Representatives. Mineta introduced legislation seeking reparations for Japanese American internees. He retired from the House in 1995. He later served as Secretary of Commerce under President Bill Clinton and as Secretary of Transportation under President George W. Bush.

Patriotism and the desire to disprove accusations of disloyalty inspired many young men in the camps to volunteer for military duty, even though they served in segregated units. One nisei combat team, the 442nd, fought in Europe and became one of the most decorated units in the armed services. Several thousand Japanese Americans also served in the Military Intelligence Service as interpreters and translators in the Pacific. The U.S. Supreme Court upheld internment in 1944, and many Japanese Americans remained imprisoned until 1945.

Research on the ROM

Free Find:
Norman Mineta
After reading about Norman Mineta on the **Holt Researcher CD–ROM**, create a campaign poster that illustrates Mineta's service during the war.

✔ **READING CHECK: Identifying Points of View** Why were Japanese Americans interned and relocated during the war? because of strong anti-Japanese feelings among politicians and people in some western states

---

SECTION ② REVIEW

1. Define and explain:
braceros
zoot-suit riots
internment

2. Identify and explain:
Office of War Information
Rosie the Riveter
A. Philip Randolph
Fair Employment
    Practices Committee
Carlos E. Castañeda
Norman Mineta

3. Analyzing Information Copy the web below. Use it to describe how various groups experienced greater opportunities and/or discrimination as a result of the war.

4. Finding the Main Idea

a. How did the U.S. government seek to keep morale high and to control the flow of information during World War II?

b. What long-term effects do you think women's experiences in World War II had on their lives after the war?

c. What were the economic effects of World War II on the home front?

5. Writing and Critical Thinking

Summarizing Imagine that you are living on the home front during World War II. Write a journal entry describing your daily routine.
Consider:
• changes in popular culture
• changes in daily life, such as rationing
• the war's effects on job opportunities and racial issues

go.hrw.com Homework Practice Online
keyword: SE3 HP18

SECTION ③

Victory in Europe

EYEWITNESSES TO History   *"Buck Eversole is a platoon sergeant in an infantry company. His platoon has turned over many times as battle whittles down the old ones and the replacement system brings up the new ones. Only a handful now are veterans. 'It gets so it kinda gets you, seein' these new kids come up,' Buck told me one night. . . . 'Some of them have just got fuzz on their faces, and don't know what it's all about, and they're scared to death. No matter what, some of them are bound to get killed. . . . I know it ain't my fault that they get killed,' Buck finally said. 'And I do the best I can for them, but I've got so I feel like it's me killin' 'em instead of a German. I've got so I feel like a murderer. I hate to look at them when the new ones come in.'"*

Ernie Pyle often visited troops at the battlefront.

—Ernie Pyle, quoted in *Ernie's War*, edited by David Nichols

Reporter Ernie Pyle brought the reality of war home to Americans in numerous news stories, including this interview. Pyle himself was eventually killed while covering the war in the Pacific.

Allied Attacks in the Mediterranean

By late 1942 U.S. supplies and troops began to make a difference in the war. However, it would take another two years of hard fighting to defeat the Axis Powers. Soon after Pearl Harbor, the Allies agreed that they would open a second front against the Axis Powers in order to relieve pressure on the Soviet Union. However, Allied forces were not prepared to launch a direct assault on either German-occupied France or Vichy-controlled southern France. At British prime minister Winston Churchill's urging, the Allies decided to attack first in the Mediterranean region.

Axis surrender in North Africa. After France surrendered in 1940, Germany placed France's colonies in North Africa under the control of Vichy France. The following year British forces turned back the Axis attempt to capture the Suez Canal and drove the German and Italian forces into Libya. In November 1942 the Allies planned Operation Torch, an invasion of the French territory in northwest Africa. General **Dwight D. Eisenhower** commanded the invasion force of U.S. and British soldiers.

Allied leaders were unsure if the French forces in North Africa would oppose the invasion. Early on the morning of November 8, some 65,000 Allied troops landed at Casablanca in Morocco and Oran and Algiers in Algeria. Nearly twice that number of French forces awaited them. Troops landing at Casablanca faced the greatest difficulties, encountering both heavy surf and French resistance. Allied troops captured Algiers that day and Oran two days later.

LEVEL 1: Pair students and display Linking Geography and History Transparency 18, World War II in Europe, 1942–1945, from **American History Visual Resources**. Ask each pair to identify where the Allied offensive in Europe began. *(Pairs should identify Sicily and southern Europe.)* Then have each pair write a caption for its map explaining why the Allies chose to invade through Sicily and southern Italy. *(The Allies saw Sicily as a launching pad for the invasion of Italy, and Italy as a launching pad for the invasion of Europe.)* Ask each pair to read its caption to the class.
English Language Learners, Cooperative Learning

LEVEL 2: Tell students to imagine that they are military reporters in Washington, D.C. Have each student prepare a broadcast announcement explaining the Allied offensive in Europe with a focus on where it began. *(See the Level 1 lesson for specific details.)* Ask volunteers to read their broadcasts to the class.

LEVEL 3: Tell students to imagine that they are high-level military officials in the days before the Allied invasion of Europe. Have each student prepare a one-page military brief presenting Sicily and Italy as the starting point for the Allied offensive in Europe. Students' briefs should also discuss the advantages and disadvantages of that choice. *(See the Level 1 lesson for specific details.)* Have volunteers read their briefs to the class.

As the soldiers established beachheads in Morocco and Algeria, Allied planes and ships cut Axis supply lines from Italy. Then, during the winter of 1942–43, two Allied land forces—one from the west and the other from the east—began to force the Axis troops into a trap. Several fierce battles took place in Tunisia. Finally, in May 1943, the Axis force of some 250,000 soldiers surrendered.

The invasion of Italy. North Africa offered a gateway to the Italian island of Sicily. Allied leaders decided to invade Sicily next. They sought to clear the Axis forces out of the central Mediterranean and to acquire a launching point for an invasion of the Italian mainland. Battling high winds and rough seas, Allied troops landed in July 1943. They subdued Sicily in a little more than a month. General **George S. Patton**, who had emerged as a leader during the North Africa campaign, guided the U.S. forces.

The Italian king named a new prime minister to replace Benito Mussolini and ordered Mussolini's arrest. Determined not to surrender the Italian peninsula, the Germans took Mussolini to Germany and then set up a base for him in northern Italy. In September the Italian government signed an armistice with the Allies. Soon afterward the Allies invaded southern Italy to attack the Germans. Although the Allies took Naples on October 1, they soon bogged down.

Hoping to outflank the German forces, the Allies landed to the south of Rome at Anzio in January 1944. After the landing, however, the Allies were pinned down for months. U.S. and British forces then began driving slowly north. They were joined by small units of troops from more than 25 countries. After months of bitter mountain warfare, the Germans occupying Italy were finally defeated. Soon afterward Mussolini was captured and shot by Italian rebels. In June 1944 the Allies marched into Rome, making it the first Axis capital to fall.

✔ **READING CHECK: Drawing Conclusions** Why was victory in North Africa so important to the Allies?
It offered the Allies a gateway to Italy.

Sea and Air Assaults

During the fighting in the Mediterranean, the Allies waged campaigns on other fronts. In the Atlantic, German U-boats continued to take a staggering toll on Allied ships, lives, and supplies. Not until 1943 did this **Battle of the Atlantic** begin to turn in the Allies' favor. An important factor was the refinement of **sonar** equipment, which uses sound waves to detect underwater objects. The Allies also developed fast escort ships for convoys and air-bombed German U-boats and submarine yards. By 1944 the Allies had won the Battle of the Atlantic.

In 1943 the Allies intensified their air campaign of strategic bombing aimed at destroying German military production and undermining the morale of the German people. "It was sound strategy to prevent the *Wehrmacht* [German armed forces] from falling back to regroup and be lethal [deadly] again," Lieutenant John Morris explained. "We bombed . . . the railroad marshaling yards and road hubs along the *Wehrmacht*'s line of retreat, up and down Germany's eastern border." British Royal

INTERPRETING THE VISUAL RECORD

Anzio landing. U.S. forces made water landings on the Italian coast. *What does this photograph suggest about the difficulties of arriving by sea?*

PEOPLE IN HISTORY

George S. Patton. George S. Patton had a notoriously gruff demeanor and earned the nickname "Old Blood and Guts" for his aggressive tactics and matter-of-fact attitudes toward war. During the invasion of Sicily, Patton's hard-edged personality almost ended his military career. While visiting an army field hospital, he slapped a crying soldier who was suffering from shell shock. News of the incident spread quickly, and Dwight D. Eisenhower reprimanded Patton sharply before deciding not to relieve him of his duties.

ACTIVITY: Ask students to conduct research on an Allied military leader. Then have each student present two-to-four-minute oral reports on his or her chosen leader.

THAT'S INTERESTING!

German attacks trapped Allied forces on the Anzio beach for almost four months. During the siege German propaganda broadcasts attempted to discourage Allied soldiers by calling the area the largest self-supporting prisoner-of-war camp in the world.

VISUAL RECORD ANSWER

Students might suggest exploding mines in the water and attacks from covered places on shore.

TEACH OBJECTIVES 2 AND 3

ALL LEVELS: Display Linking Geography and History Transparency 18, World War II in Europe, 1942–1945, from **American History Visual Resources**. Have students label the location of the Battle of the Atlantic and the site of the Normandy invasion. To help students understand those conflicts, copy the graphic organizer at right on the chalkboard, omitting the italicized answers. Have each student complete it.
English Language Learners

THE WAR IN EUROPE	
Fighting in the Atlantic	• *Axis attacks took a huge Allied toll* • *with sonar, Allies turned the tide in 1943* • *sea dominance allowed the Allies to protect cargo ships and bomb Axis vessels*
Fighting in the Air	• *as with the Battle of the Atlantic, 1943 was an important year* • *Allies conducted strategic bombing to destroy important German cities*
The Normandy Invasion	• *took place on June 6, 1944* • *Allies needed to invade German-occupied France* • *created a dummy invasion as a decoy* • *stormed the beach with high casualties but ultimate success*

GLOBAL RELATIONS

Operation Fortitude.
Code-named Fortitude, the campaign of deception that preceded Operation Overlord was quite elaborate. Months before the invasion at Normandy, U.S. commanders created a "phantom" army, the First U.S. Army Group, which received false radio transmissions at its "base" in southeastern England. Allied planes also dropped tons of bombs on the northeastern coast of France, and on the eve of the invasion thousands of soldiers gathered near a "fleet" of unseaworthy landing craft in British ports across the English Channel from Calais. This dummy invasion force was equipped with cardboard tanks that were made by members of the American and British film industries.

CRITICAL THINKING Why might the northeastern coast of France have seemed like a logical area for the Allies to stage an invasion?

ANSWER: Students might suggest that the northeastern coast of France is near the narrowest part of the English Channel.

VISUAL RECORD ANSWER
Students might mention the open beach, the hills beyond and enemy gunfire.

Research on the ROM

Free Find: D-Day
After learning about the D-Day invasion on the **Holt Researcher CD–ROM**, create a drawing of the invasion site that shows the obstacles the Allied troops faced.

INTERPRETING THE VISUAL RECORD

D-Day. The invasion of France was a risky venture that paid off for the Allies. *What obstacles do these soldiers face as they prepare to land?*

Air Force (RAF) planes flew chiefly at night, dropping their bombs in the general area of a given target. U.S. aircraft concentrated on precision bombing in daylight raids. By 1944, bombers had dropped hundreds of thousands of tons of explosives on German factories, supply lines, and military centers.

✔ **READING CHECK: Analyzing Information** How did the Allies overcome difficulties of fighting in the Atlantic and in the air? They refined sonar and bombed German factories and military centers at night.

Operation Overlord

Victory in the Atlantic and air assaults on Germany paved the way for Operation Overlord—the long-awaited Allied invasion of German-occupied France. U.S. Army chief of staff and key Allied strategist **George C. Marshall** led the planning. Many believed that he would also lead the Allied forces, but he chose to remain in Washington to advise President Roosevelt. Instead, General Eisenhower commanded the invasion. The Allies put in place a system of dummy installations and false clues to convince the Germans that the invasion would take place near Calais on the English Channel.

Instead, the Allies landed farther south, in Normandy, on **D-Day**, June 6, 1944. Nearly 5,000 troop transports, landing craft, and warships carried some 150,000 U.S., British, and Canadian soldiers across the Channel. General **Omar Bradley** led the U.S. troops that landed at Normandy. Overhead, planes dropped close to 23,000 airborne troops and bombed roads, bridges, and German troop concentrations. Corporal Samuel Fuller recalled encountering fierce resistance with the U.S. 1st Infantry Division on Omaha Beach.

History Makers Speak

❝The only way to get off the beach was to blow a big tank trap that was blocking our way. Finally one of our guys took the trap out. . . . I stood up and tried to run. When you run over unconscious men, or men lying on their bellies, it's tough to keep your balance. You go into the water, but the water is washing bodies in and out. Bodies, heads, flesh, intestines; that's what Omaha Beach was.❞

—Corporal Samuel Fuller, quoted in "The Men Who Fought," *Time*, June 9, 1994

The Germans had fortified the Normandy beaches with concrete bunkers, tank traps, and mines. The beaches resembled a giant fortress, but the Allied campaign of disinformation and distraction had done its job. Adolf Hitler refused to send reinforcements to the area around Normandy. He still believed that the main invasion would occur elsewhere.

Although the Allies met determined opposition, they managed to penetrate 20 miles into France by early July. Aided by the French Resistance, the Allies drove steadily eastward. They liberated Paris on August 25, 1944. By early September more than 2 million Allied troops had landed in western Europe. Another Allied force drove northward through France from the Mediterranean. Meanwhile, Soviet troops pressed Germany from the east.

✔ **READING CHECK: Evaluating** What was the significance of D-Day? It was a decisive Allied victory, which led to the liberation of France.

TEACH OBJECTIVE 4

LEVEL 1: Pair students and ask each pair to create a flowchart that defines the Holocaust and displays the factors that allowed it to happen. *(Charts should note that the Holocaust was Nazi Germany's slaughter of European Jews. Factors such as Nazi propaganda, long-standing anti-Semitism, and Allied inaction allowed the Holocaust to happen.)* Have each pair present its flowchart to the class. Then conduct a discussion on the material presented in the flowcharts. **English Language Learners, Cooperative Learning**

LEVEL 2: Organize students into small groups. Ask each group to conduct a discussion in which students define the Holocaust and identify the factors that allowed it to happen. *(See the Level 1 lesson for the correct definition and factors.)* After students have completed their discussions, ask each student to write a one-page essay on the Holocaust. Students may wish to include their essays in their portfolios. **Cooperative Learning**

Skill-Building Strategies

Preparing questions is one of the most crucial steps in conducting a successful oral history interview. Most good interview questions are formulated with a specific purpose in mind. At the same time, they are broad enough to allow the subject of the interview to express himself or herself freely. *Who, what, when, where, why,* and *how* are words that often prove particularly useful in creating such questions.

How to Prepare Questions

1. **Do preliminary research.** Gather as much information as you can about the general topic the interview will address and the particular person you will be interviewing.
2. **Decide what you need to know.** Once you have completed your preliminary research, determine what you hope to learn from the interview. Keep in mind what you already know and the types of information that the subject of your interview is likely to possess.
3. **Formulate logical, open-ended questions.** Create questions that address what you hope to learn and

Preparing Questions

that follow one another in a logical fashion. Make sure that the questions are designed to allow your subject to speak freely and that they cannot be answered with a simple "yes" or "no."

Applying the Skill

Imagine that you have arranged to conduct an oral history interview with a U.S. Army veteran who took part in the D-Day invasion at Normandy on June 6, 1944. Prepare at least six questions that you plan to ask during the interview.

Practicing the Skill

Answer the following questions.
1. What background information did you use when formulating your questions?
2. What kind of information would you hope to gain from interviewing a veteran of the D-Day invasion at Normandy?
3. What answers do you expect to your questions?

The Holocaust

Not even the savage fighting of D-Day prepared the Allies for the horror of the **Holocaust**, Nazi Germany's systematic slaughter of European Jews. Germany's occupation of France and other countries in western Europe, as well as its attacks on Poland and the Soviet Union, put millions of additional Jews under German rule. In many regions, special squads of German soldiers rounded up Jews and shot them. Elsewhere, Jews were forced into cities and isolated in ghettos. In 1941 the Germans began constructing camps specifically for the purpose of **genocide**—the deliberate annihilation of an entire people. Hitler and senior Nazi officials called this extermination program the "final solution of the Jewish question."

Major death camps included Auschwitz (OWSH-vits), Treblinka, and Majdanek, all in Poland. Jewish men, women, and children were transported to camps in sealed railroad cars. They were then marched into rooms disguised as shower facilities and gassed. Their bodies were cremated. Some 6 million Jews—two thirds of Europe's Jewish population—perished. The Nazis also killed hundreds of thousands of Gypsies, Poles, mentally disabled people, and religious and political prisoners.

These ovens were used to cremate the bodies of the victims of the Holocaust.

LEVEL 3: Tell students to imagine that they are Holocaust survivors. Have each student write three diary entries from one of the assigned perspectives. One perspective should describe the factors that gave rise to the Holocaust, another should define and describe the Holocaust itself, and another should discuss the lingering psychological effects of the Holocaust. *(See the Level 1 lesson for the correct definition and factors.)* Have volunteers read their diary entries to the class. Students may wish to include their diary entries in their portfolios.

HOMEWORK *Write the following questions on the chalkboard:* How did the Holocaust happen? Could something like the Holocaust happen today? *Have each student write a short essay answering the questions.*

SPOTLIGHT on Holocaust Literature

Have students obtain works by authors who wrote about the Holocaust, such as Elie Wiesel, Anne Frank, or Primo Levi. Ask each student to select and read an entire work or a clearly definable portion of a work, such as a chapter. Then have each student prepare a written book report on the work. In their reports, students should summarize and discuss the work or the subsection. Ask volunteers to discuss their book reports with the class. **Block Scheduling**

HISTORY MAKERS SPEAK

Viktor Frankl in *Never to Forget*

Arriving at Auschwitz.

Most of the people arrested and transported to death camps by the Nazis knew the horrible fate that awaited them. Viktor Frankl, a physician from Austria who survived the Holocaust, described his terror upon arriving at Auschwitz. "The train shunted, obviously nearing a main station. Suddenly a cry broke from the ranks of the anxious passengers. 'There is a sign, Auschwitz!' Everyone's heart missed a beat at that moment. Auschwitz—the very name stood for all that was horrible: gas chambers, crematoriums, massacres. . . . There were isolated shouts and whistles of command. We did not know their meaning. My imagination led me to see gallows with people dangling on them. I was horrified."

ACTIVITY: Ask students if they have seen movies, television programs, or museum exhibits about the Holocaust. Call on volunteers to share their experiences. Have students bring in and discuss brochures from museum exhibits or other information about the Holocaust.

VISUAL RECORD ANSWER

Students might suggest that cities were reduced to rubble.

546

These survivors of the Buchenwald concentration camp were liberated by Allied soldiers in April 1945. Elie Wiesel is on the far right of the top row.

INTERPRETING THE VISUAL RECORD

Nearing the end. These members of the U.S. 325th Regiment put down German resistance in 1945. *What does this photograph reveal about the destruction caused by the war?*

When the Allies liberated the death camps, they found thousands of starving survivors. Romanian-born writer **Elie Wiesel** was one such survivor. He described the deep psychological scars left on concentration camp survivors.

 ❝One day I was able to get up, after gathering all my strength. I wanted to see myself in the mirror hanging on the opposite wall. I had not seen myself since the ghetto. From the depths of the mirror, a corpse gazed back at me. The look in his eyes, as they stared into mine, has never left me.❞

—Elie Wiesel, *Night*

To carry out this monstrous genocide, the Nazis took advantage of a long history of anti-Semitism in Europe that stretched back to the Middle Ages. A flood of Nazi propaganda against Jews stirred up this anti-Semitism. Some non-Jews in Nazi-occupied countries either assisted the Nazis or failed to prevent them from sending Jewish citizens off to the death camps. Others worked heroically to save the lives of Jews.

✔ **READING CHECK: Summarizing** How was the Holocaust carried out?
Germans constructed death camps, transported Jews and others in sealed railroad cars, marched them into rooms disguised as showers, and gassed them.

Defeating Germany

Although Germany's situation was grave, Adolf Hitler refused to give up. In September 1944 the Germans launched their first V-2s, or long-range rockets, at cities in England and Belgium. These bombs could not be shot down easily.

The Battle of the Bulge. By September 1944 the Allies had crossed the German border. As they paused to bring in supplies and to regroup, the Germans launched their final counterattack. In heavy snow, they drove against the Allies in the thickly wooded Ardennes region of Belgium and northern France. They pushed westward to create a dangerous bulge in the Allied lines. In the resulting **Battle of the Bulge** some 200,000 Germans attacked an initial U.S. force of about 80,000 troops.

The U.S. 101st Airborne Division defending the Belgian town of Bastogne was completely surrounded. When German officers demanded the 101st's surrender, General Anthony McAuliff offered a one-word reply: "Nuts." Allied generals rushed in reinforcements, and the Allies pushed the Germans back. Francis Tsuzuki, whose Japanese American battalion pursued the Germans, recalled, "the Germans were retreating so fast. At times we were moving . . . more than 100 miles a day." By January 1945 it was clear that the German offensive had failed.

The Yalta Conference. In February 1945 President Franklin D. Roosevelt, Winston Churchill, and Joseph Stalin met at the **Yalta Conference** to plan for the postwar peace. At the conference Stalin pledged to declare war on Japan three months after Germany's surrender. They agreed to divide and occupy Germany after the war and outlined plans for a new international peace organization.

TEACH OBJECTIVE 5

LEVEL 1: Ask each student to create a time line of the events that allowed the Allies to finally defeat Germany. *(Time lines should include the following events: September 1944—Battle of the Bulge; February 1945—Yalta Conference; early 1945—Allies bomb Germany; March 1945—Allies invade Germany; April 1945—Hitler commits suicide; May 7, 1945—Germany surrenders.)* Have students annotate their time lines by explaining how each event allowed the Allies to triumph over Germany. Display students' time lines around the classroom. Students may wish to include their time lines in their portfolios. **English Language Learners**

LEVELS 2 AND 3: Ask students to identify the factors that allowed the Allies to finally defeat Germany. *(See the Level 1 lesson for the correct factors.)* Then ask each student to invent a fictional Allied character who would have been involved in the defeat of Germany—a soldier, for example, or a pilot—and either write an eyewitness account or develop a monologue account of the defeat. Have volunteers share their work with the class.

NOTE: For an additional teaching idea, see the Chapter 18 predicting consequences lesson in the **Creative Teaching Strategies** handbook.

World War II in Europe, 1942–1945

Interpreting Maps After being battered at El Alamein, Rommel retreated some 1,250 miles to Tunisia in eight weeks. By 1943 Africa was cleared of Axis forces.

? LOCATE Where did the major battles in the European theater take place?

The German defeat at Stalingrad marked the turning point in the war in the East.

(Map labels:) 30°W, 10°W, 0°, 10°E, 30°E, 60°N, 50°N, 40°N, Arctic Circle, ICELAND, ATLANTIC OCEAN, NORWAY, SWEDEN, FINLAND, Leningrad, Moscow, NORTH SEA, DENMARK, BALTIC SEA, IRELAND, GREAT BRITAIN, London, English Channel, NETHERLANDS, BELGIUM, Berlin April–May 1945, Warsaw, Leipzig, Dresden, Elbe, Rhine, GERMANY, D-Day June 1944, Paris, FRANCE, Battle of the Bulge Dec. 1944, Vistula, UNION OF SOVIET SOCIALIST REPUBLICS, Stalingrad Nov. 1942–Jan. 1943, Volga, UKRAINE, Vichy, SWITZERLAND, SLOVAKIA, HUNGARY, VICHY FRANCE, Milan, ROMANIA, Yalta, CROATIA, SERBIA, Danube, BLACK SEA, PORTUGAL, SPAIN, ITALY, MONTENEGRO, BULGARIA, Rome, CORSICA, Anzio Jan. 1944, Naples, ALBANIA, Istanbul, GIBRALTAR (Br.), SARDINIA, GREECE, AEGEAN SEA, TURKEY, Oran, Algiers, SICILY, SYRIA (Vichy Fr.), Casablanca, Tunis, MALTA, CRETE, CYPRUS (Br.), LEBANON (Vichy Fr.), MOROCCO (Vichy Fr.), ALGERIA (Vichy Fr.), TUNISIA (Vichy Fr.), MEDITERRANEAN SEA, PALESTINE (Br.), Alexandria, Suez Canal, Cairo, TRANS-JORDAN (Br.), LIBYA (Italian), EGYPT, RED SEA, SAUDI ARABIA, El Alamein Oct.–Nov. 1942

Normandy Landings, June 6, 1944

(Inset map labels:) GREAT BRITAIN, London, Portsmouth, 50°N, English Channel, CHANNEL IS. (Br.), Cherbourg, Utah (U.S.), Omaha (U.S.), Gold (Br.), Juno (Br. & Canadian), Sword (Br. & Canadian), NORMANDY, Caen, Le Havre, Rouen, Seine River, FRANCE, Paris

0   50   100 Miles
0   50   100 Kilometers

Legend:
- Axis controlled, Jan. 1942
- Allied controlled, Jan. 1942
- Neutral country
- Farthest Axis advance, 1942
- Allied advance
- ☀ Major battle
- Invasion beach

0   200   400 Miles
0   200   400 Kilometers
Azimuthal Equal-Area Projection

CRITICAL THINKING Why might many of the German soldiers at the Battle of the Bulge have been teenagers?

ANSWER: Students might suggest that high casualty rates forced the German army to induct teenagers.

MAP ANSWER

the coast of France, the border of Belgium and Germany, Berlin, Stalingrad, Anzio, and El Alamein

REVIEW

Have students complete the **Section 3 Review** on p. 548.

ASSESS

Have students complete **Daily Quiz 18.3. As Alternative Assessment,** you may want to use the Holocaust flowchart or the final defeat time line in this section's lessons.

RETEACH

Have students complete **Main Idea Activity for English Language Learners and Special-Needs Students 18.3.** Then organize students into small groups and assign each group a subsection of Section 3. Have groups write three to five questions about the material in the assigned subsection. Collect the questions and use them to quiz the class.
English Language Learners, Cooperative Learning

EXTEND

Ask students to conduct research on the bombing of German cities, including Dresden and Leipzig. Have students focus some of their research on the moral questions and issues raised by those bombings. Then ask each student to list and discuss those questions in a short essay. Have volunteers read their essays to the class. Then conduct a discussion about the issues presented in the essays. **Block Scheduling**

REVIEW SECTION 3 ANSWERS

1. Define
- sonar, p. 543
- genocide, p. 545

2. Identify
- Dwight D. Eisenhower, p. 542
- George S. Patton, p. 543
- Battle of the Atlantic, p. 543
- George C. Marshall, p. 544
- D-Day, p. 544
- Omar Bradley, p. 544
- Holocaust, p. 545
- Elie Wiesel, p. 546
- Battle of the Bulge, p. 546
- Yalta Conference, p. 546

3. Allies liberate Paris; Soviets continue to push westward; Battle of the Bulge; Allies continue to bomb German cities; Allies occupy Berlin

4a. helped the Allies wear down the Axis Powers and eventually close in on Germany from multiple fronts

b. Eisenhower commanded the invasion; Marshall led the planning for it; and Bradley led the troops that landed at Normandy.

c. Roosevelt felt the urgency of the war effort when he decided to run again; the people shared his sense of urgency and remained unified and involved in the war effort.

5. grew out of earlier anti-Semitism in Europe, Nazi propaganda, and Allied inaction; resulted in the murder of millions of human beings and depleted the continent's Jewish population

These Soviet soldiers celebrate their capture of Berlin by planting the Soviet flag on top of the Reichstag, or German parliament, building.

The urgency of the war effort convinced President Roosevelt to run for an unprecedented fourth term. With Missouri senator Harry S Truman as his running mate, Roosevelt won his party's nomination with little opposition. The Republicans chose Thomas E. Dewey, governor of New York. Dewey lacked the charisma and experience of Roosevelt and was defeated by an electoral vote of 432 to 99.

The race to Berlin. During the early months of 1945, Allied bombers continued to blast German cities, including Leipzig and Berlin. One of the most devastating attacks hit Dresden in February. In one massive two-day attack, Allied bombers caused the worst firestorms of the European war. Total civilian deaths have been estimated at between 30,000 and 60,000.

In March, Allied troops crossed the Rhine River from the west and drove into the heart of Germany. By then, Soviet troops occupied much of eastern Europe. Churchill wanted General Eisenhower to push east as far and as fast as possible. Churchill worried that the Soviets might later lay claim to territories they seized. Eisenhower did not want military strategy to be determined by political considerations and therefore halted the Allied advance at the Elbe River in April.

On April 30, 1945, Hitler committed suicide in his bunker deep under the ruins of Berlin. U.S. sergeant Mack Morriss described the grim mood of the fallen city. "There is a feeling that here has ended not only a city but a nation, that here a titanic force has come to catastrophe." Germany surrendered unconditionally on May 7. The next day, known as V-E (Victory in Europe) Day, marked the formal end of a brutal war that had held Europe in its grip for more than five years.

✔ **READING CHECK: Drawing Inferences** How did the U.S. victory at the Battle of the Bulge contribute to the Allied defeat of Germany? **The Battle of the Bulge was the final German counterattack, which failed.**

SECTION 3 REVIEW

1. Define and explain:
sonar
genocide

2. Identify and explain:
Dwight D. Eisenhower
George S. Patton
Battle of the Atlantic
George C. Marshall
D-Day
Omar Bradley
Holocaust
Elie Wiesel
Battle of the Bulge
Yalta Conference

3. Sequencing Copy the chart below. Use it to list the military events that led to Germany's surrender in 1945.

| 1. D-Day |
| 2. |
| 3. |
| 4. |
| 5. |
| 6. |
| 7. Germany surrenders |

4. **Finding the Main Idea**

a. How did the campaigns in North Africa, Sicily, the Atlantic, and in the air help the Allies prepare to defeat Italy and Germany?

b. What role did U.S. military leaders such as Dwight D. Eisenhower, George C. Marshall, and Omar Bradley play in the invasion of Normandy?

c. How did President Roosevelt's decision to run for a fourth term affect the war effort?

5. **Writing and Critical Thinking**

Summarizing Write a brief history of the Holocaust. Explain how it occurred and how it affected Europe.
Consider:
- how the Holocaust developed
- why it was not stopped
- what its effects were

Homework Practice Online
keyword: SE3 HP18

SECTION 4

After completing Section 4, students should be able to:

OBJECTIVE 1 Describe the U.S. island-hopping plan.

OBJECTIVE 2 Analyze the effect that the battles at Iwo Jima and Okinawa had on the war.

OBJECTIVE 3 Explain why the United States used atomic weapons against Japan.

OBJECTIVE 4 Discuss the costs of the war.

LET'S GET STARTED!

Copy the following statements on the chalkboard: *The Japanese used the strategy of island-hopping in their conquest of the Pacific. The victory at Iwo Jima gave the Japanese a great psychological advantage. The Manhattan Project helped rebuild Japanese cities after the war.* As students enter the classroom, tell them to preview Section 4 by correcting these incorrect statements. (*The Allies used island-hopping; the Allies won the Iwo Jima conflict; the Manhattan Project was established to create and test nuclear bombs.*) Tell students that in Section 4 they will learn how the United States won the war in the Pacific.

SECTION 4

Victory in Asia

READ TO DISCOVER

1. How did the United States carry out its island-hopping plan?
2. How did the battles at Iwo Jima and Okinawa affect the war?
3. What led the United States to use atomic weapons against Japan?
4. What were the human and economic costs of World War II?

DEFINE

island-hopping
kamikaze

IDENTIFY

Battle of Leyte Gulf
Battle of Iwo Jima
Battle of Okinawa
Harry S Truman
Manhattan Project
Albert Einstein
Enola Gay

WHY IT MATTERS TODAY

Relations between the United States and Japan have changed greatly since the end of World War II. Use CNNfyi.com or other **current events** sources to find out about U.S.-Japan economic or political relations today. Record your findings in your journal.

CNNfyi.com

EYEWITNESSES TO History

"*The Japanese fought by a code they thought was right: bushido. The code of the warrior: no surrender. You don't really comprehend it until you get out there and fight people who are faced with an absolutely hopeless situation and will not give up. If you tried to help one of the Japanese, he'd usually detonate a grenade and kill himself as well as you. To be captured was a disgrace. . . . You developed an attitude of no mercy because they had no mercy on us. It was a no-quarter, savage kind of thing. . . . If you're reduced to savagery by a situation, anything's possible. When [Charles] Lindbergh made a trip to the Philippines, he was horrified at the way American GIs talked about the Japanese. It was so savage. We were savages.*"

—Eugene B. Sledge, quoted in *Ordinary Americans*, edited by Linda R. Monk

Japanese sword

As U.S. marine Eugene B. Sledge described, the fighting in the Pacific was fierce. The Japanese considered surrender disgraceful and often fought to the death. The U.S. advance across the Pacific was met with ferocious resistance as Japanese defenders dug in, committed to saving their empire or die trying.

Pacific Offensives

After their victory at Guadalcanal, in the Solomon Islands, the Allies had gone on the offensive in the Pacific. Their ultimate objective was to come within striking distance of Japan itself.

Island-hopping. Air and sea power were the keys to victory in the Pacific, unlike in Europe where land forces played a much larger role. As early as 1942 the U.S. high command had adopted a strategy of **island-hopping**. This meant that troops would attack and seize only certain strategic Japanese-held islands, rather than trying to recapture all of them. Japanese garrisons located on islands bypassed by the Allies would be cut off from supplies and troop reinforcements. Airstrips built on seized islands would help support the next Allied advance. In the central Pacific, an island-hopping offensive began in November 1943 in the Gilbert Islands. Army troops quickly took Makin Island.

Tarawa. The island of Tarawa proved much more difficult to capture than Makin. A coral reef encircled the island, which the Japanese had heavily fortified. According to Sergeant John Bushemi, the marines who landed there had to wade onto the beach "in the face of murderous Japanese fire, with no protection." Almost 1,000 marines lost their lives and some 2,000 others were wounded before the island was secured. The victory gave the United States control of a vital airstrip and put its forces in position to provide air support for the next landings.

SECTION 4 RESOURCES

REPRODUCIBLE

▶ Guided Reading Strategy 18.4
▶ Biography Reading 18: Enrico Fermi
▶ Literature Reading 18: A City and Its People Destroyed

TECHNOLOGY

▶ One-Stop Planner, Lesson 18.4
▶ CNN. Presents America: Modern Times Segment: One Town Remembers
▶ Holt Researcher: American History CD–ROM
▶ Homework Practice Online

REINFORCEMENT, REVIEW, AND ASSESSMENT

▶ Section 4 Review, p. 555
▶ Daily Quiz 18.4
▶ Main Idea Activity 18.4
▶ English Audio Summary 18.4
▶ Spanish Audio Summary 18.4

LEVELS 1 AND 2: Distribute Outline Map 20, World War II in the Pacific, from **American History Outline Maps.** Have each student label the Pacific islands that the United States conquered in the island-hopping offensive. *(Students should label the Gilbert Islands, Makin Island, Tarawa, Saipan, and the Philippines.)* Then ask students to write one or two paragraphs explaining the rationale behind island-hopping. *(The United States used island-hopping to conquer strategically important islands while cutting off other islands. With the conquered islands, the United States hoped to gain* *important launching pads for an invasion of Japan.)* Display students' maps and rationales around the classroom.
English Language Learners

LEVEL 3: Tell students to imagine that they are military commanders in the Pacific. Have each student write a one-page military brief explaining and justifying the island-hopping strategy. *(See the Level 1 lesson for the correct details.)* Ask volunteers to read their briefs to the class. Then ask students to consult the map on the following page. Ask students if they can think of any other effective strategy besides island-hopping to conquer the Pacific. Have students share their responses.

Australia's Contribution to the Allied War Effort.
The Australian soldiers who helped recapture the Philippines performed one vital part of their country's overall contribution to the Allied war effort. Australia joined Britain in declaring war against Germany in 1939, and after the fall of the Philippines served as an important base of operations for U.S. forces in the South Pacific. Australian tradition prohibited the drafting of citizens to serve overseas, but the all-volunteer Australian Imperial Force provided the Allies with troops that fought in North Africa, Greece, and the Middle East, as well as the Pacific. Ultimately, more than 550,000 Australian citizens left their homeland to take part in the war; of these, more than 23,000 were killed in action and 8,000 died in Japanese war camps.

ACTIVITY: Tell students to imagine that they are soldiers in the Australian Imperial Force. Then have each student write a short letter home explaining his or her service in the war.

MAP ANSWER
(for p. 551)
west

VISUAL RECORD ANSWER
Students might suggest liberty.

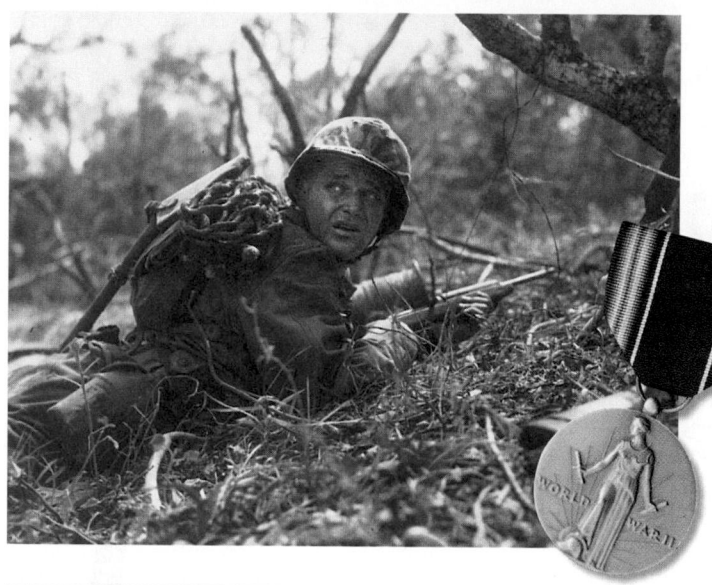

INTERPRETING THE VISUAL RECORD

Fighting in the Pacific. Foxholes like this one on Saipan were often the only protection U.S. soldiers had during battles on the islands in the Pacific. The medal at right celebrates the Allied victory in World War II. ***What might the figure on the medal represent?***

Saipan. The next important series of landings targeted the Marshall Islands, located north of the Gilbert Islands. In the Marshalls, U.S. forces captured several key bases from which they bombed the Truk Islands, where the headquarters of the Japanese fleet was located.

By the summer of 1944, Allied forces had advanced to the Mariana Islands. In June 535 ships carried 127,000 soldiers, two thirds of whom were marines, to the shores of Saipan. Under cover of intense air and naval bombardments from nearby aircraft carriers, landing craft loaded with troops swept onto the beaches. The Japanese gathered the bulk of their remaining fleet and sent it to stop the U.S. offensive.

Japan was already running low on aircraft, and in the battle that followed the United States won a decisive victory. U.S. pilots downed 350 Japanese planes while losing just 30 of their own planes. Running low on fuel and returning to their carriers at night, 80 U.S. pilots had to crash their planes in the ocean. Nearly all the pilots were rescued, and the Japanese aircraft carriers were no longer a threat.

Meanwhile, Saipan's 32,000 Japanese defenders were waging a fierce battle. U.S. forces suffered some 16,000 casualties, including more than 3,400 dead. U.S. troops fighting on Guam experienced equally tough resistance before the island fell in August. These U.S. victories were important because the islands provided airstrips from which U.S. bombers could begin launching missions against the main islands of Japan.

Recapturing the Philippines. Despite these setbacks, Japanese resistance stiffened when the Allies began their New Guinea–Philippines campaign in June 1943. General Douglas MacArthur led U.S. and Australian troops in a series of landings along the north coast of New Guinea. By late July 1944 they had reached the western end of this large island. Allied forces also took smaller islands nearby, such as the Admiralty Islands.

By the fall of 1944, the United States was ready to invade the Philippines. Allied forces poured onto the beaches of the island of Leyte in October. The Japanese navy's counterattack led to the **Battle of Leyte Gulf**—the last, largest, and most decisive naval engagement in the Pacific. The battle was a disaster for the Japanese, who lost four aircraft carriers, two battleships, and several cruisers. From this time on, the Japanese fleet no longer seriously threatened the Allies.

Aided by Filipino guerrillas, Allied troops fanned out over the islands of the Philippines. Overcoming bitter opposition, they entered Manila in February 1945 and subdued most Japanese defense forces within weeks. "I'm a little late," said MacArthur, "but we finally came."

✔ **READING CHECK: Sequencing** In what order did the United States island-hop?
Makin Island, Tarawa, the Marshall Islands, the Truk Islands, the Mariana Islands of Saipan and Guam, New Guinea, and the Philippines

TEACH OBJECTIVE 2

LEVEL 1: Pair students and write the following statements on the chalkboard: *The fighting on Iwo Jima and Okinawa displayed continued Japanese resistance. The two battles proved that the Japanese would not surrender.* Have each pair create a list of points that support the statements. *(Lists should note that the fighting on both islands was incredibly difficult and bloody, although the United States triumphed on both fronts. Pairs should note the existence of kamikaze attacks and high casualty rates.)* Then ask students how Japanese resistance on Iwo Jima and Okinawa affected the Pacific War. *(Students should mention that Japanese resistance forced Truman to decide whether to use atomic weapons.)*

English Language Learners, Cooperative Learning

LEVELS 2 AND 3: Tell students to imagine that they are U.S. soldiers or sailors who are fighting on Iwo Jima or Okinawa. Have each student write a letter home describing the fighting and explaining how that fighting demonstrated continued Japanese resistance. *(See the Level 1 lesson for correct points.)* Have volunteers read their letters to the class. Then ask students how Japanese resistance in Iwo Jima and Okinawa affected the Pacific War. *(See the Level 1 lesson for the correct effect.)* Students may wish to include their letters in their portfolios.

HOMEWORK *Have students write letters from the perspective of kamikaze pilots preparing for their final flights. Students' letters should be written to relatives indicating their feelings about this act.*

Victory in the Pacific

These Pacific victories gave the United States several strategic bases from which to launch B-29 bombers against the Japanese home islands. U.S. planes bombed most of the country's major cities in an effort to weaken the fighting spirit of the Japanese. The worst raid took place over Tokyo in March 1945 and created huge firestorms that destroyed much of the city. The massive destruction caused Japanese civilian morale to sag, but the country's military leaders refused to surrender.

World War II in the Pacific, 1941–1945

Interpreting Maps The Allies gained momentum in the Pacific war after the Battle of Midway, which cost Japan four aircraft carriers and many of its pilots.

? THE USES OF GEOGRAPHY In which direction did battles in the Pacific progress?

Japanese controlled, 1942
Farthest Japanese advance, May 1942
Allied advance
Major battle

HISTORY MAKERS SPEAK

John Ciardi in *"The Good War": An Oral History of World War Two*

The Bombing of Japan.
John Ciardi, a B-29 machine gunner who took part in many of the bombing raids on Japan, reflected on the incredible destruction caused by the raids. "We were in the terrible business of burning out Japanese towns. That meant women and old people, children. . . . I have some of my strike photos at home. Tokyo looked like one leveled bed of ash. The only things standing were some stone buildings. If you looked at the photos carefully, you'd see they were gutted. Some of the people jumped into rivers to get away from these fire storms. They were packed in so tight to get away from the fire, they suffocated. They were so close to one another, they couldn't fall over. It must have been horrible."

CRITICAL THINKING Why might the United States have conducted large-scale bombing raids over Japan during the final year of the war?

ANSWER: Students may respond that the bombing raids were meant to eliminate as much of Japan's infrastructure as possible and to lower civilian morale by killing people and destroying their homes.

LEVEL 1: Conduct a brief discussion on the factors that led the United States to use atomic weapons against Japan. *(Students should mention the enormous costs of an invasion, continued Japanese resistance, and the desire to demonstrate U.S. power to the Soviet Union.)* Then organize the class into two groups. Have students in one group develop headlines for a newspaper that support the use of atomic weapons against Japan. Have students in the second group develop headlines that oppose the use of atomic weapons against Japan. Have volunteers in each group share their headlines with the class.

English Language Learners, Cooperative Learning

LEVEL 2: Tell students to imagine that they are high-level military officials who support the use of atomic weapons against Japan. Have each student write a one-page military brief to President Truman explaining the factors that necessitate the use of atomic weapons. *(See the Level 1 lesson for the correct factors.)* Ask volunteers to read their briefs to the class. Students may wish to include their briefs in their portfolios.

HOMEWORK *Have students look in newspapers, magazines and so on for articles related to the development or use of atomic weapons. Have students bring their articles to class and discuss them.*

SCIENCE, TECHNOLOGY, AND SOCIETY

Kamikaze Attacks.
Kamikaze attacks were an important part of the Japanese military effort during the final months of the war. Introduced in the Battle of Leyte Gulf, they were usually undertaken by young, inexperienced pilots who considered it an honor to die in the line of duty. Before they embarked on their assignments, these pilots performed a solemn ritual that included a final toast to the emperor and the singing of the verse "Let us die close by the side of our sovereign." Approximately 1,300 kamikaze pilots completed their missions, sinking some 30 Allied combat ships and causing some 3,000 deaths.

CRITICAL THINKING Besides the physical and human destruction, how might kamikaze attacks have aided the Japanese war effort?

ANSWER: Students may mention that kamikaze attacks lowered morale on Allied ships.

THAT'S INTERESTING!

The temperature at Ground Zero of the Alamogordo atomic bomb test was 100,000,000 degrees Fahrenheit—approximately 10,000 times hotter than the surface of the sun. All life within a mile of the explosion point was destroyed almost instantly.

Iwo Jima. In February 1945, U.S. Marines attacked the island of Iwo Jima—just 750 miles from Tokyo—and met strong resistance. Despite a U.S. victory being nearly certain, Japanese forces fought as fiercely as ever. The **Battle of Iwo Jima** lasted six weeks. Several thousand marines and more than 20,000 Japanese soldiers were killed. One marine who fought on Iwo Jima described the fighting.

History Makers Speak

"**The casualty rate was enormous. It was ghastly. Iwo was a volcanic island with very little concealment. Cover is something you hide behind—a tree, a bush, a rock. Few trees. No grass. It was almost like a piece of the moon that had dropped down to earth.**"

—Ted Allenby, quoted in *Ordinary Americans,* edited by Linda R. Monk

U.S. Marines struggled to take Mount Suribachi, which the Japanese held with a strong system of tunnels and bunkers. When the marines finally reached the mountaintop, they planted the U.S. flag in the rocky soil to celebrate their hard-fought victory. Photographer Joe Rosenthal recorded the moment in a picture that would win him a Pulitzer Prize.

Okinawa. On April 1, 1945, the largest landing force in Pacific history invaded Okinawa, about 350 miles from Japan. The Japanese forces chose not to challenge the landing. To avoid putting themselves in range of the massive guns of U.S. battleships and other warships, the Japanese retreated to the southern tip of the island. Five hours after the landing began, the marines had captured one airfield and not a single shot had been fired.

Five days later, the Japanese attacked. Some 700 Japanese planes attacked the U.S. beachheads and naval task force. Three-hundred fifty of these planes were **kamikaze,** or suicide planes. *Kamikaze* is a Japanese word meaning "divine wind."

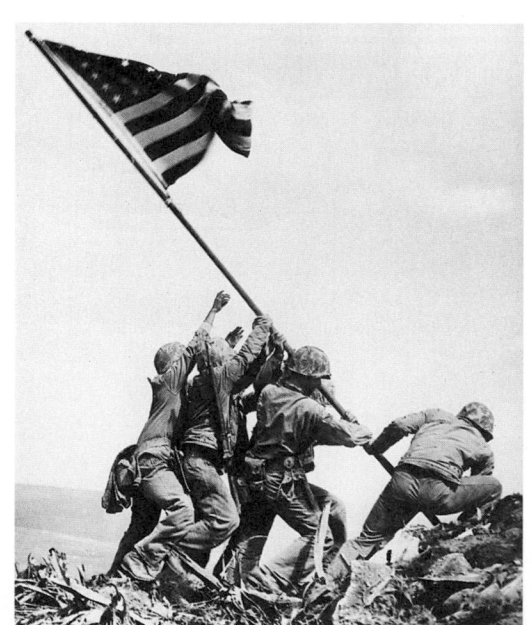

Joe Rosenthal's Pulitzer Prize–winning photograph of U.S. soldiers raising the flag over Mount Suribachi was the model for the U.S. Marine Corps Memorial.

Six U.S. ships were sunk, and 135 kamikaze pilots died. After the war, Admiral Nimitz recalled, "Nothing that happened in the war was a surprise, absolutely nothing except the kamikaze tactics toward the end; we had not visualized these."

This **Battle of Okinawa** was perhaps the bloodiest of the Pacific war. The Japanese troops dug in deeply and fought to the death. Japanese troops hid in caves that dotted the island. The U.S. troops had to attack and subdue each individual cave, often by filling the cave with fire from flamethrowers. About 49,000 U.S. troops were killed or wounded in the battle. More than 100,000 Japanese died in the fighting.

By early April, an Allied victory in the Pacific was near, but President Roosevelt did not live to see the end of hostilities with Japan. The world was stunned when he died suddenly on April 12. The new president, **Harry S Truman,** faced a grave decision. Germany's surrender had allowed Allied forces to concentrate their efforts on the war in the Pacific. Despite repeated Allied bombings, however, Japan remained a dangerous opponent, willing to fight to the very end. Truman had to decide whether the United States should use its fearsome new weapon, the atomic bomb.

✔ **READING CHECK: Making Generalizations** What made the Japanese forces such fierce opponents? their willingness to die for the cause

LEVEL 3: Tell students to imagine that they are President Truman preparing to tell the American people that the United States will use atomic weapons against Japan. Have each student write a speech explaining and justifying the decision. *(See the Level 1 lesson for the correct factors.)* Ask volunteers to deliver their speeches to the class. Students may wish to include their speeches in their portfolios.

HOMEWORK *Have each student list the consequences both of using atomic weapons against Japan and not using atomic weapons. Have students consult their lists and write two or three paragraphs presenting their personal opinions on President Truman's decision to use atomic weapons in the fight against Japan.*

SPOTLIGHT
on J. Robert Oppenheimer

Have students conduct research on the career of physicist J. Robert Oppenheimer. Students may wish to focus either on his scientific research or on the controversy surrounding his political views. Then have each student write a report on his or her findings. **Block Scheduling**

NOTE: To help students make meaningful connections between events in U.S. history and those in their own hometown, use the Chapter 18 **Hands-On History Activity**, Your Town During World War II.

The Atomic Bomb

The new U.S. weapon had been developed by the top-secret **Manhattan Project**, the effort of a group of scientists who had been working to create an atomic bomb since 1942. Many European scientists participated in the Manhattan Project. In 1933 physicist **Albert Einstein** moved from Germany to the United States. During the 1930s many European Jewish scientists followed Einstein's example. Enrico Fermi was an Italian physicist who had fled to the United States. He persuaded the world-famous Einstein to warn the U.S. government about research being done by German scientists. In August 1939 Einstein wrote to President Roosevelt. He warned that "a single bomb of this type, carried by boat and exploded in a port, might very well destroy the whole port, together with some of the surrounding territory." He was describing an atomic bomb. The race was on to be the first nation to build one.

In 1942 Brigadier General Leslie R. Groves took charge of the Manhattan Project. By year's end, scientists led by Enrico Fermi had created an atomic chain reaction, a major step in the development of a bomb. Huge research centers were established in Los Alamos, New Mexico; Oak Ridge, Tennessee; and Hanford, Washington. At the Los Alamos center, director J. Robert Oppenheimer's team worked on building the first atomic bomb.

The scientists successfully tested their bomb at Alamogordo, New Mexico, on July 16, 1945. The next day, President Truman met with Allied leaders at Potsdam, south of Berlin. On July 26 the Allies demanded Japan's unconditional surrender. Japan refused. Truman gave the order to use atomic weapons against Japan. As Iwo Jima and Okinawa had shown, the Japanese were still capable of inflicting heavy losses on U.S. forces. An invasion of Japan would be very costly. Estimates ran as high as 1 million U.S. casualties. Japanese losses could be even greater. Using the atomic bomb might end the war quickly and save many lives on both sides. The president may also have wanted to demonstrate the power of this new weapon to the Soviet Union.

At 8:15 A.M. on August 6, the U.S. B-29 bomber *Enola Gay*, commanded by Colonel Paul Tibbets, dropped an atomic bomb on the city of Hiroshima. A column of fire shot skyward, threatening to bring down the *Enola Gay*. It was followed by an enormous, mushroom-shaped cloud. The city looked like "lava or molasses," tail gunner Robert Caron recalled. As the B-29 passed over the ruined city, co-pilot Robert Lewis wrote in his journal, "My God, what have we done?"

The scene on the ground was even worse than the *Enola Gay*'s crew could imagine. The explosion flattened a huge area of the city and killed an

PRESIDENTIAL
Lives

1884–1972
In Office 1945–1953

Harry S Truman

Harry S Truman was born on May 8, 1884, in Missouri. As a boy he developed a strong appetite for reading. "I don't know anybody in the world ever read as much or as consistently as he did," a friend remembered. "He was what you call a 'book worm.'" Truman had no obligation to fight in World War I. Any one of several factors—his poor eyesight, his occupation as a farmer, and his status as his mother's sole support—would have allowed him to avoid service. Instead, saying it was "a job somebody had to do," Truman volunteered and commanded an artillery battery in France.

After the war, Truman returned to Missouri where his habit of studying people helped him begin his political career. "When I was growing up," Truman said, "it occurred to me to watch the people around me to find out what they thought and what pleased them the most."

Harry S. Truman
U.S. Postage 8 cents

On July 16, 1945, the first atomic bomb was exploded at Alamogordo, New Mexico.

J. Robert Oppenheimer. J. Robert Oppenheimer, who is often called the father of the atomic bomb, was a logical but nonetheless controversial pick for director of the Los Alamos Scientific Laboratory. Oppenheimer was a brilliant nuclear physicist. He was also an avowed political activist, however, and some critics claimed that his liberal political views made him a security risk. Convinced that "we were not going to find a better man," Brigadier General Leslie R. Groves ended the issue by signing a memo taking full responsibility for hiring Oppenheimer.

CRITICAL THINKING Why might some of Oppenheimer's critics have claimed that his liberal political views made him a "security risk" for the Manhattan Project?

ANSWER: Students may suggest that some of Oppenheimer's critics feared, groundlessly, that his liberal political views might incline him to share nuclear secrets with the Soviet Union.

GRAPH ANSWER
(for p. 555)
the Soviet Union; China and France

ALL LEVELS: Ask students to select, in their opinions, the most devastating human or economic cost of World War II. *(Answers will vary. Students should support their choices.)* Conduct a brief discussion on students' selections. To help students understand all the human and economic costs of World War II, copy the graphic organizer at right on the chalkboard, omitting the italicized answers. Have each student complete it. **English Language Learners**

WORLD WAR II—THE FINAL COSTS

Human Costs
- *killed millions of people*
- *resulted in the Holocaust*
- *wounded many soldiers and civilians*

- *the most devastating war in history*
- *enormous human and economic losses*

Economic Costs
- *destroyed many nations' economies*
- *ruined countless cities*
- *destroyed national infrastructures*

Great Debates

The Atomic Bomb

President Truman justified his decision to drop atomic bombs on two Japanese cities by noting Japan's refusal to surrender unconditionally. He claimed that the atomic bomb had prevented a costly U.S. invasion of Japan. He also linked the atomic bomb to Pearl Harbor. "The Japanese began the war," said Truman. "They have been repaid manyfold."

Some historians have questioned Truman's explanations. They point out that Tokyo was considering peace negotiations. They note that with the promised Soviet declaration of war by early August, victory would have been possible without either dropping the atomic bomb or launching a U.S. invasion. These scholars argue that Truman dropped the bomb not only to end the war but also to demonstrate the U.S. atomic might and thus strengthen its postwar position.

Other historians point to Japan's wartime atrocities and to the country's bitter-end defense of Okinawa. They note that top military leaders in Tokyo fiercely opposed the peace overtures and favored a desperate defense of the home islands. Although the debate over President Truman's decision continues, all historians agree that it has had long-range consequences that few anticipated at the time.

Nearly every building in the city of Hiroshima was flattened by the atomic bomb. The watch below was found in the rubble, stopped at the exact time of the explosion.

estimated 75,000 people. Junji Sarashina, a 16-year-old high school junior, later recalled his experiences after the blast.

History Makers Speak

66 The entire town of Hiroshima was ablaze. . . . A lot of people were floating in the river; some were swimming, but some of them were dead, drifting with the current downstream. Their skin was red and their clothes were nothing but strips of cloth hanging from them. 99

—Junji Sarashina, quoted in *The Century,* by Peter Jennings and Todd Brewster

Three days later, the United States dropped a second atomic bomb on Nagasaki. The explosion vaporized people, melted stones, and spontaneously ignited everything combustible within eight tenths of a mile. Japanese estimates put the total number of deaths caused by both bombs at around 200,000.

A day before the bombing of Nagasaki, the Soviet Union had declared war on Japan and begun an invasion of Manchuria. Stunned by the destruction of Hiroshima and Nagasaki, the Japanese soon offered to surrender. Despite their demand for unconditional surrender, the Allies allowed the Japanese emperor to remain on his throne. The formal surrender was signed on September 2, 1945, aboard the USS *Missouri* in Tokyo Bay.

✔ **READING CHECK: Analyzing Information** Why did President Truman decide to use atomic weapons against Japan? *Japan refused to surrender, and an invasion of Japan would have produced many casualties. Truman may also have wanted to demonstrate the power of the bomb to the Soviet Union.*

Costs of the War

After years of struggle and sacrifice, World War II had ended in victory for the Allies. The price of this victory was high, however. The toll in lives and property was without precedent. Most disturbing was the knowledge—fully revealed only after Germany's defeat—that Hitler had attempted to exterminate all the Jews of Europe. However, the Allies had achieved their war goals. Germany's Nazi government was destroyed, and Japan's military warlords were overthrown.

World War II was the most devastating war the world has ever known. It resulted in more deaths and destroyed more property than any other war in history. When it finally ended, hundreds of cities lay in ruins. Beautiful churches

REVIEW

Have students complete the **Section 4 Review** on p. 555.

ASSESS

Have students complete **Daily Quiz 18.4**. As **Alternative Assessment**, you may want to use the atomic bomb debate or the President Truman speech in this section's lessons.

RETEACH

Have students complete **Main Idea Activity for English Language Learners and Special-Needs Students 18.4**. Then

pair students and have each pair create a detailed outline of Section 4. Display students' outlines around the classroom.
English Language Learners, Cooperative Learning

EXTEND

Have each student create a replica or diorama of some aspect of the final war in the Pacific. Students might make a model of the *Enola Gay*, for example, or of the flag-raising on Iwo Jima. Have students write a one-page paper explaining the importance of the event represented by their work. Display students' replicas or dioramas around the classroom.
Block Scheduling

---

and palaces were reduced to rubble, and priceless works of art had gone up in smoke. Millions of people lacked heat, electricity, running water, adequate food, and the means to travel from one place to another. In some regions, mile upon mile of field and forest had been reduced to utter desolation.

Two examples indicate the extent of property lost in the war. In Düsseldorf, Germany, more than 90 percent of the homes were uninhabitable. The cities of Kiev and Minsk in the Soviet Union had to be completely rebuilt. The war brought untold suffering to civilians. According to one estimate, some 30 million civilians lost their lives from bombing, disease, shelling, or starvation. Millions more suffered from injuries or malnutrition. The Soviet Union and China were particularly hard hit. As in World War I, U.S. civilian losses were relatively light. In economic terms, armaments and other military costs probably totaled more than $1 trillion. Along with peace came many uncertainties about the future.

✔ **READING CHECK: Evaluating** What were the costs of World War II? more deaths and more property destroyed than in any war in history; some 30 million civilians lives lost; armaments and other military costs totaling more than $1 trillion

Deaths in World War II

Major Allied Powers / Major Axis Powers

Legend: Military, Civilian

Wartime deaths (in millions) — y-axis 0 to 10

Major Allied Powers: Soviet Union, China, Great Britain, United States, France
Major Axis Powers: Germany, Japan, Italy

Source: *The Oxford Companion to World War II*

Interpreting Graphs Some 50 million people died in World War II. Many were civilians.

? Skills Assessment Which country suffered the most in total losses? Which countries lost more civilians than military personnel?

SECTION 4 REVIEW

1. Define and explain:
island-hopping
kamikaze

2. Identify and explain:
Battle of Leyte Gulf
Battle of Iwo Jima
Battle of Okinawa
Harry S Truman
Manhattan Project
Albert Einstein
Enola Gay

3. Evaluating Copy the diagram below. Use it to explain the significance of the islands that U.S. forces captured after Guadalcanal as they advanced across the Pacific.

Guadalcanal — Islands / Significance

4. **Finding the Main Idea**
  a. How did U.S. military leaders adapt their strategy to suit the geography of the South Pacific?
  b. How did the Battles of Iwo Jima and Okinawa affect U.S. fighting in the Pacific?
  c. Summarize the international consequences of World War II for the Allied Powers and Axis Powers.

5. **Writing and Critical Thinking**
Supporting a Point of View Write an editorial discussing whether the United States was justified in using the atomic bomb against Japan.
Consider:
• what U.S. leaders knew about the bomb
• the casualties in the Battles of Iwo Jima and Okinawa
• the long-term effects of a nuclear blast and the risks of a future nuclear war

Homework Practice Online
keyword: SE3 HP18

CHAPTER 18

REVIEW AND ASSESSMENT RESOURCES

TECHNOLOGY

▶ Chapter 18 Test Generator (on the One-Stop Planner)
▶ Global Skill Builder CD–ROM
▶ HRW Go site

REINFORCEMENT, REVIEW, AND ASSESSMENT

▶ Chapter 18 Review, pp. 556–57
▶ Chapter 18 Tutorial for Students, Parents, Mentors, and Peers

▶ Chapter 18 Test (Form A or B)
▶ Portfolio Activities and Alternative Assessment Handbook, Chapter 18
▶ Chapter 18 Test for English Language Learners and Special-Needs Students

REVIEW

Have students complete the **Chapter 18 Review** on pp. 556–57.

ASSESS

Use one of the chapter tests to assess students' understanding of the content. **For Alternative Assessment**, see the **Portfolio Activities and Alternative Assessment Handbook.**

2. created the War Production Board and Office of War Mobilization, passed the Selective Service and Training Act, expanded the income tax, sold war bonds, and instituted rationing during its mobilization effort

3. The war changed the content of entertainment, the availability of consumer goods, and the wages people earned.

4. arrested millions of people and sent them to concentration and death camps

5. El Alamein and Stalingrad, the Axis surrender in North Africa, the Allied invasions of Italy and Normandy

6. island-hopping

Reviewing Themes
1. The United States provided the Allies with military supplies and food, and the Soviet Union provided the Allied war effort with millions of soldiers. Allied soldiers from different countries also served and fought together in a number of military campaigns.

2. Wartime conditions aggravated anti-Japanese prejudice in the United States, thereby prompting many Americans to question the loyalty of Japanese Americans. In turn, the government interned Japanese Americans living on the West Coast.

3. The dropping of atom bombs on Japan ended the war without a costly invasion of Japan.

CHAPTER 18

Review

Creating a Time Line

Copy the time line below onto a sheet of paper. Complete the time line by filling in the events and dates from the chapter that you think were most significant. Pick three events and explain why you think they were significant.

1941   1943   1945

Writing a Summary

Using standard grammar, spelling, sentence structure, and punctuation, write an overview of events in the chapter.

Identifying People and Ideas

Identify the following terms or individuals and explain their significance.

1. War Production Board
2. Douglas MacArthur
3. Battle of Midway
4. braceros
5. George S. Patton
6. D-Day
7. genocide
8. Elie Wiesel
9. island-hopping
10. Manhattan Project

Understanding Main Ideas

SECTION 1 *(pp. 528–534)*
1. What advantages did the Axis Powers have over the Allies at the beginning of the war?
2. What steps did the U.S. government take to mobilize for war?

SECTION 2 *(pp. 535–541)*
3. What changes did World War II bring to the American home front?

SECTION 3 *(pp. 542–548)*
4. How did the Nazis carry out the Holocaust?
5. What were the major turning points in the war with Germany?

SECTION 4 *(pp. 549–555)*
6. What was the Allied strategy in the Pacific?

Reviewing Themes

1. **Global Relations** How did the Allies pool their resources to win World War II?
2. **Constitutional Heritage** How did wartime conditions lead to the internment of Japanese Americans?
3. **Science, Technology, and Society** What role did nuclear weapons play in the Allied victory during World War II?

Thinking Critically

1. **Evaluating** How did the Japanese miscalculate the U.S. response to the attack on Pearl Harbor?
2. **Analyzing Information** How did fighting on multiple fronts affect the course of World War II?
3. **Supporting a Point of View** Imagine that you are President Truman. Would you have chosen to drop the atomic bomb or invade Japan? Explain your answer.
4. **Summarizing** What were the final costs and consequences of World War II?
5. **Making Predictions** How might the Yalta Conference and the Allied race to Berlin affect post–World War II U.S.-Soviet relations?

Writing About History

Categorizing Copy the organizational web below. Use it to list the important battles, strategic decisions, and weapons that led to the Allied victory in the Pacific. Then write an encyclopedia entry explaining how the Allies achieved victory.

RETEACH

Assign each student one of the key terms or people from Chapter 17. Tell students to keep their assignments secret. Have each student develop a set of clues about the identity of the assigned term or person. Then ask each student to deliver those clues to the class. Have students compete to guess the identities of the secret terms and people. **English Language Learners**

EXTEND

Organize students into seven groups and assign each group a year from 1939 to 1945. Have groups conduct research on events relating to World War II that took place during the assigned year. Ask groups to create an annotated time line of the assigned year. Have each group present its time line to the class. Then display the time lines in chronological order around the classroom. **Block Scheduling, Cooperative Learning**

Building Social Studies Skills

Interpreting Charts

Study the cause-and-effect chart below. Then use it to help answer the questions that follow.

Causes and Effects of World War II

Long-Term Causes
- Treaty of Versailles
- Debts from World War I
- Global and local economic depression
- Growth of dictatorships
- Rise of militarism

Immediate Causes
- Germany's invasion of Poland
- Japanese aggression in Asia
- Japanese attack on Pearl Harbor

World War II

Effects
- Millions of deaths and widespread destruction in Europe and Asia
- The Holocaust
- U.S. emergence as a superpower

1. Which of the long-term causes occurred first?
   a. Treaty of Versailles
   b. debts from World War I
   c. global and local economic depression
   d. growth of dictatorships

2. How did the Treaty of Versailles contribute to World War II?

Analyzing Primary Sources

Read the excerpt from the Civil Liberties Act of 1988, and then answer the questions that follow.

"The Congress recognizes that . . . a grave injustice was done to both citizens and permanent residents of Japanese ancestry by the evacuation, relocation, and internment of civilians during World War II. . . .

The excluded individuals of Japanese ancestry suffered enormous damages, . . . all of which resulted in significant human suffering for which appropriate compensation has not been made. . . .

For these fundamental violations of the basic civil liberties and constitutional rights of these individuals of Japanese ancestry, the Congress apologizes on behalf of the Nation."

3. To what actions does this act refer?
   a. the Holocaust
   b. Japanese internment in the United States during World War II
   c. Japanese internment in Japan during World War II
   d. the Bataan Death March

4. How does this act show an effect that World War II had on the United States?

Alternative Assessment

Building Your Portfolio

U.S. HISTORY

Science, Technology, and Society
Imagine that you are a military commander during World War II. Create a plan for defeating Japan. Be sure to include a map of the Pacific islands that need to be conquered, an analysis of the effects of technology on the war, and a suggestion for a final attack. Your plan should also discuss how to overcome any difficulties of fighting on islands.

internet connect

Internet Activity: go.hrw.com
KEYWORD: SE3 AN18

Access the Internet through the HRW Go site to analyze how scientific discoveries and technological innovations in the military resulted from specific needs. Choose one of the following examples of applied technology: the ENIAC, sonar, and radar. Then create an illustrated chart or model that explains who developed the technology, the specific need it was supposed to fulfill, how it was used in the war, and what technology has been developed as a result of it.

Thinking Critically

1. The Japanese might not have expected such a forceful response.

2. It hampered the Allies because the war in the Pacific kept the United States from immediately assisting the Allies in Europe.

3. Answers will vary. Students should compare the atomic bomb's destructive potential to the human cost of an invasion.

4. millions of deaths and incalculable property damage

5. Both events might suggest that the United States and the Soviet Union would not agree on many issues.

Writing

battles—Coral Sea, Midway, Guadalcanal, Saipan, Leyte Gulf, Iwo Jima, Okinawa; strategies—surprise interception of Japanese naval forces, island-hopping, use of atomic bomb; weapons—warships, fighter planes, atomic bombs

Building Social Studies Skills

1. a

2. Answers will vary. Students might note that the treaty's economic reparations angered and bankrupted Germany.

3. b

4. Answers will vary. Students might suggest that it shows the war's long-term effects as the act was passed more than 40 years after the war.

CHAPTER 19

The Cold War

CHAPTER RESOURCE MANAGER

Objectives	Pacing Guide	Reproducible Resources
SECTION 1 **Healing the Wounds of War** pp. 560–65 ★ Describe the actions Allied forces took to stabilize Germany and Japan after the war. ★ Discuss how the Allied Powers tried war criminals. ★ Explain why the United Nations was founded, and relate how it was organized. ★ Trace the events that led to the founding of the new country of Israel, and describe how Arab countries responded.	**Regular** 2 days **Block Scheduling** 1 day *Block Scheduling Handbook with Team Teaching Strategies, pp. 109–14*	**RS** Guided Reading Strategy 19.1 **SM** Geography Activity 19: Postwar Tensions in the Eastern Mediterranean **PS** Biography Reading 19: Ralph Bunche
SECTION 2 **The Cold War Begins** pp. 566–71 ★ Explain what caused the Cold War, and describe U.S. strategy during the Cold War. ★ Describe how the U.S. government tried to control the development of atomic weapons. ★ Analyze how the Marshall Plan helped block the spread of communism in Europe. ★ Trace how the Western Allies responded to Soviet expansion.	**Regular** 2 days **Block Scheduling** 1 day *Block Scheduling Handbook with Team Teaching Strategies, pp. 109–14*	**RS** Guided Reading Strategy 19.2 **PS** Primary Source Reading 19: New Foreign Policy
SECTION 3 **The Cold War Turns Hot** pp. 572–78 ★ Explain how the Chinese Communists gained control of China. ★ Analyze the factors that led to the escalation of the conflict in Korea. ★ Describe the domestic and international effects of the Korean War. ★ Discuss the methods that President Eisenhower used to promote U.S. interests abroad.	**Regular** 2 days **Block Scheduling** .5 day *Block Scheduling Handbook with Team Teaching Strategies, pp. 109–14*	**RS** Guided Reading Strategy 19.3 **PS** American History Political Cartoon 26: Brinkmanship
SECTION 4 **The Cold War at Home** pp. 579–85 ★ Discuss the actions the U.S. government took to limit communism at home, and describe how these actions affected Americans' everyday lives. ★ Explain how Senator Joseph McCarthy was able to play upon Americans' fears of communism. ★ Describe how Americans reacted to the prospect of nuclear war and the launch of *Sputnik*.	**Regular** 2 days **Block Scheduling** 1 day *Block Scheduling Handbook with Team Teaching Strategies, pp. 109–14*	**RS** Guided Reading Strategy 19.4 **PS** Graphic Organizer 19: U.S. Presence in Global Affairs **IC** Literature Reading 19: Fighting in Korea **E** Hands-On History Activity: Living with Nuclear Weapons **E** Creative Teaching Strategy: Quick Survey

Chapter Resource Key

PS	Primary Sources	**REV**	Review		Video
RS	Reading Support	**ELL**	Reinforcement and English Language Learners		Internet
IC	Interdisciplinary Connections				Holt Presentation Maker Using Microsoft® PowerPoint®
E	Enrichment		Transparencies		
SM	Skills Mastery		CD-ROM		
A	Assessment		Music		

One-Stop Planner CD-ROM

See the *One-Stop Planner* for a complete list of additional resources for students and teachers.

One-Stop Planner CD–ROM

It's easy to plan lessons, select resources, and print out materials for your students when you use the **One-Stop Planner CD–ROM with Test Generator.**

Technology Resources	Reinforcement, Review, and Assessment

 One-Stop Planner, Lesson 19.1
 Holt Researcher: American History CD–ROM
Homework Practice Online
HRW Go site

REV Section 1 Review, p. 565
A Daily Quiz 19.1
ELL Main Idea Activity 19.1
ELL English Audio Summary 19.1
ELL Spanish Audio Summary 19.1

 One-Stop Planner, Lesson 19.2
 Holt Researcher: American History CD–ROM
 CNN Presents America: Yesterday and Today, Modern Times Segment: A Helping Hand to Europe
Homework Practice Online

REV Section 2 Review, p. 571
A Daily Quiz 19.2
ELL Main Idea Activity 19.2
ELL English Audio Summary 19.2
ELL Spanish Audio Summary 19.2

 One-Stop Planner, Lesson 19.3
 The American Nation Video Program Segment: MacArthur in Korea; Teacher's Guide, pp. 193–94
Homework Practice Online

REV Section 3 Review, p. 578
A Daily Quiz 19.3
ELL Main Idea Activity 19.3
ELL English Audio Summary 19.3
ELL Spanish Audio Summary 19.3

 One Stop Planner, Lesson 19.4
 Holt Researcher: American History CD–ROM
 The American Nation Video Program Segment: Bomb Shelters; Teacher's Guide, pp. 175–76
Homework Practice Online

REV Section 4 Review, p. 585
A Daily Quiz 19.4
ELL Main Idea Activity 19.4
ELL English Audio Summary 19.4
ELL Spanish Audio Summary 19.4

Meeting Individual Needs

Ability Levels

Level 1 Basic-level activities designed for all students encountering new material

Level 2 Intermediate-level activities designed for average students

Level 3 Challenging activities designed for honors and gifted-and-talented students

English Language Learners Activities that address the needs of students with Limited English Proficiency

internet connect

HRW ONLINE RESOURCES
GO TO: go.hrw.com
Then type in a keyword.

TEACHER HOME PAGE
KEYWORD: SE3 Teacher

CHAPTER INTERNET ACTIVITIES
KEYWORD: SE3 AN19
Choose an activity to:
• research and report on the United Nations.
• create a newspaper analyzing the impact of *Sputnik* on American society.
• make an illustrated time line on the founding of Israel.

CHAPTER ENRICHMENT LINKS
KEYWORD: SE3 CH19

ONLINE ASSESSMENT
Homework Practice
KEYWORD: SE3 HP19

Standardized Test Prep
KEYWORD: SE3 STP19

Rubrics
KEYWORD: SS Rubrics

ONLINE MAPS, CHARTS, AND GRAPHS
KEYWORD: SE3 MCG
• The Marshall Plan
• Israel, 1949
• Nuclear Technology
• UN Decision-Making Bodies

CONTENT UPDATES
KEYWORD: SS Content Updates

HOLT PRESENTATION MAKER
KEYWORD: SE3 PPT19

ONLINE READING SUPPORT
KEYWORD: SS Strategies

CURRENT EVENTS
KEYWORD: S3 Current Events

Chapter Review and Assessment

 Global Skill Builder CD–ROM

HRW Go site

REV **Chapter 19 Tutorial for Students, Parents, Mentors, and Peers**

REV **Chapter 19 Review, pp. 586–87**

Chapter 19 Test Generator (on the One-Stop Planner)

A **Chapter 19 Test (Form A or B)**

A **Alternative Assessment Handbook**

A **Chapter 19 Test for English Language Learners and Special-Needs Students**

Build on What You Know

Ask students to answer the following questions.

Why might tensions have existed between the United States and the Soviet Union after World War II?

Consider:
- the U.S. military advantage gained from the atomic bomb
- the political tensions that existed before the war

What problems might countries have faced as they rebuilt after the war?

Consider:
- the devastation and loss of life that resulted from the war
- the need to establish new systems of government

---

exploring the time line

AMERICAN EVENTS

GLOBAL RELATIONS

1960 ■ The U-2 Incident.
After the Paris summit was cancelled, President Eisenhower discussed the U-2 incident. "Aerial photography has been one of many methods we have used to keep ourselves and the free world abreast of major Soviet developments. . . . The Soviets were well aware of it. Why all the furor concerning one particular flight? . . . It is apparent that the Soviets had decided even before the Soviet delegation left Moscow that . . . nothing constructive would come out of the summit conference."

CRITICAL THINKING What does Eisenhower's statement reveal about U.S.–Soviet relations in 1960?

ANSWER: Students might answer that it shows that neither country trusted the other.

1945–1960
The Cold War

UN medal

Poster of Mao Zedong after the Communist victory

1945 World Events Delegates from 50 nations meet in San Francisco to create the charter for the United Nations.

1949 World Events Mao Zedong's Communist forces gain control of most of China.

1951 Daily Life Americans organize a hero's welcome for General MacArthur upon his return from Korea.

1952 Business and Finance After 21 months of operation by federal troops, the U.S. government returns the country's railroads to private control.

`1945` `1948` `1951`

1947 Daily Life Ten people working in the film industry refuse to testify before a House committee and are blacklisted.

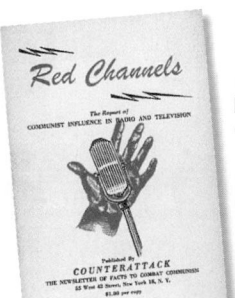

A report on alleged Communists in the entertainment industry

1948 Politics The U.S. Congress passes the European Recovery Act, establishing the Marshall Plan to help stabilize and rebuild Europe.

A cargo of sugar on its way to Europe as part of the Marshall Plan

Build on What You Know

Economic troubles during the 1930s contributed to the rise of dictatorships in Germany, Italy, and Japan. These countries' military expansion and acts of aggression led to World War II. The war destroyed parts of Europe and Asia. In this chapter you will learn that after the war many nations struggled to rebuild their war-torn economies. At the same time, tensions grew between the United States and the Soviet Union.

What's Your Opinion?

To help students create their Themes Journal entries, provide the following examples of appropriate **agree**/**disagree** statements.

Global Relations

Agree The rivalry between Russia and Japan during the early 1900s did not affect relationships between the United States and other countries.

Disagree The competitive rivalry between European nations resulted in World War I.

Citizenship

Agree During the Red Scare in 1919, the U.S. government violated the civil rights of suspected Communists.

Disagree Americans' fears about corruption in city government led to improvements in city election processes, improving civil rights.

Science, Technology, and Society

Agree During the early 1800s many authors in the transcendentalist movement expressed their anxiety about machines by retreating from industrial society.

Disagree Much of the literature in the science-fiction genre reflects Americans' fascination with technology and its possibilities.

Robert Rauschenberg's painting **Bed**

Sputnik

Francis Gary Powers holds a model of his U-2 spy plane.

exploring the time line

GLOBAL EVENTS

internet connect

TOPIC: *Sputnik:* The October Surprise
GO TO: go.hrw.com
KEYWORD: SE3 AN19

Have students access the Internet through the HRW Go site to conduct research on the launch of *Sputnik* and the beginning of the space race. Then ask students to create a newspaper in which to present their research. Remind students to use standard grammar, punctuation, spelling, and sentence structure.

1955
The Arts
Robert Rauschenberg's *Bed* makes an important contribution to American art.

1957
Science and Technology
The Soviet Union launches *Sputnik*, the first artificial satellite, into orbit around Earth.

1958
Science and Technology
Congress establishes the National Aeronautics and Space Administration (NASA).

1960
World Events
The Paris summit between Soviet premier Khrushchev and President Eisenhower is canceled after the Soviets shoot down a U.S. spy plane.

1954

1957

1960

1953
The Arts
Playwright Arthur Miller writes *The Crucible*, in which he compares McCarthyism to the Salem witch trials.

1956
World Events
Egypt seizes the Suez Canal after the United States withdraws support for an Egyptian dam project on the Nile River.

1959
Politics
Soviet premier Nikita Khrushchev visits the United States.

Arthur Miller's **The Crucible**

Soviet premier Khrushchev (second from left) visited an American supermarket in 1959.

What's Your Opinion?

Themes Journal

Do you **agree** *or* **disagree** *with the following statements? Support your point of view in your journal.*

Global Relations Rivalry between two powerful nations rarely affects the relationships between other countries.

Citizenship The fears of the majority of Americans often limit the rights of groups that hold unpopular views.

Science, Technology, and Society Americans' fear of technology affects their behavior and is often reflected in the literature and arts of the time.

OBJECTIVE 1 Describe the actions Allied forces took to stabilize Germany and Japan after the war.

OBJECTIVE 2 Discuss how the Allied Powers tried war criminals.

OBJECTIVE 3 Explain why the United Nations was founded, and relate how it was organized.

OBJECTIVE 4 Trace the events that led to the founding of the new country of Israel, and describe how Arab countries responded.

LET'S GET STARTED!

Write the following question on the chalkboard: *What are the steps that countries devastated by war must take to rebuild?* As students enter the classroom, tell them to answer the question in writing. Ask volunteers to share their responses with the class. Tell students that in Section 1 they will learn about the actions that countries took to rebuild after World War II.

SECTION 1 RESOURCES

REPRODUCIBLE

▶ Guided Reading Strategy 19.1
▶ Geography Activity 19: Postwar Tensions in the Eastern Mediterranean
▶ Biography Reading 19: Ralph Bunche

TECHNOLOGY

▶ One-Stop Planner, Lesson 19.1
▶ Holt Researcher: American History CD–ROM
▶ Homework Practice Online

REINFORCEMENT, REVIEW, AND ASSESSMENT

▶ Section 1 Review, p. 565
▶ Daily Quiz 19.1
▶ Main Idea Activity 19.1
▶ English Audio Summary 19.1
▶ Spanish Audio Summary 19.1

SECTION 1

▶ READ TO DISCOVER

1. What actions did Allied forces take to stabilize Germany and Japan after the war?
2. How did the Allied Powers try war criminals?
3. Why was the United Nations founded, and how was it organized?
4. What events led to the founding of the new country of Israel, and how did Arab countries respond?

▶ DEFINE

zaibatsu

▶ IDENTIFY

Potsdam Conference
Nuremberg Trials
Adolf Eichmann
Hideki Tōjō
United Nations
Trygve Lie
Eleanor Roosevelt
Zionism
David Ben-Gurion
Ralph Bunche

▶ WHY IT MATTERS TODAY

The United Nations continues to play an active role in world affairs. Use **CNNfyi.com** or other **current events** sources to find out about world conflicts in which the UN has recently been involved. Record your findings in your journal.

CNNfyi.com

Healing the Wounds of War

EYEWITNESSES TO History

"There are moments when the drama of our times seems to focus on a single scene. The meeting at Potsdam [Germany] is one of those moments. We can hardly take in the sense of what happened until it is spelled out in a picture like this. The picture of three men walking in a graveyard. They are the men who hold in their hands most of the power in the world."

—Anne O'Hare McCormick, quoted in *Truman*, by David McCullough

President Truman views the destruction in Germany.

Journalist Anne O'Hare McCormick imagined the scene at a conference where Winston Churchill, Joseph Stalin, and Harry S Truman met to determine the fate of postwar Germany. The most powerful nations of the world were left with the urgent task of easing the human suffering and political chaos resulting from the war. Many Americans believed that the United States should lead the way. "The war and the victory showed us what we could do in the world," said Melville Grosvenor, a magazine editor. The United States worked with the other Allies to restore peace by occupying Germany and Japan and by creating a new international organization called the United Nations.

Occupation Rule

After the war, Germany and Japan lay in ruins, their wartime governments shattered. German actress Hildegard Knef described a German town "without houses, without windowpanes, without roofs; holes in the asphalt, rubble, rubbish, rats." An American soldier noted that in the area around Tokyo, "there was practically nothing left; the rubble did not even look like much." A Japanese American soldier remarked of the devastation, "Tokyo was all flattened, and people were living in holes with corrugated roofs. They were desperate for food." With the fighting over, Germany and Japan faced the task of rebuilding their governments, economies, and cities under the watchful eye of the Allies.

The occupation of Germany. To decide how to handle postwar Germany, Allied leaders met in Potsdam, Germany, in July 1945. The **Potsdam Conference** marked the first time President Truman had met with Winston Churchill and Joseph Stalin since President Roosevelt's death. Churchill was replaced during the conference by Great Britain's new prime minister, Clement Attlee. The three leaders worked out an agreement over the details of their joint occupation of Germany. The leaders divided Germany into four occupation zones. The British, the French, and the Americans each took control of an area in the western, industrialized part of Germany. The Soviets agreed to control the poorer, more rural eastern part. The four powers also divided Austria into zones and agreed to jointly administer the city of Berlin, within the Soviet-controlled part of Germany.

LEVEL 1: Tell students to imagine that they are advisers to the U.S. government after World War II. Pair students and have them compile lists of actions that the Allies must take to stabilize Germany and Japan. *(Lists for Germany should include dividing the country into four occupation zones under Allied control, crushing the Nazi Party, re-establishing local governments, and returning refugees to their homes; lists for Japan should include ending militarism, creating a democratic government and constitution, and reforming the economy.)* Have volunteers read their lists to the class.

English Language Learners, Cooperative Learning

LEVELS 2 AND 3: Tell students to imagine that they are advisers to President Truman after World War II. Have each student write a brief memo to the president describing the actions the Allies must take to stabilize Germany and Japan. *(See the Level 1 lesson for the correct actions.)* Ask volunteers to read their memos to the class.

HOMEWORK *Have each student create an illustrated pamphlet that describes for the American public the actions the Allies must take to stabilize Germany and Japan.*

In order to stabilize Germany, the occupying powers pledged to crush the Nazi Party, re-establish local governments, and rebuild German industry. The Allies also agreed to return German refugees to their homes. The Potsdam Conference attendees recognized that the joint occupation of Germany would require cooperation. However, Soviet occupation of much of Eastern Europe caused tensions among the Allies. Stalin demanded that the other Allies recognize Soviet-backed Poland's claims to German territory it had occupied during the war. They reluctantly agreed but grew increasingly concerned about Soviet expansion in Eastern Europe. Another source of tension was the Soviet Union's demand for immediate reparations from Germany.

The occupation of Japan.
Postwar Japan also faced huge challenges in its efforts to rebuild. Its economy lay in shambles, and Hiroshima and Nagasaki had been devastated by atomic bombs. The United States occupied defeated Japan from 1945 to 1952.

In addition to helping rebuild the Japanese economy, the United States worked to end Japanese militarism and to establish a democratic government. During the occupation, Emperor Hirohito remained in the imperial palace, but he had no power. Allied Supreme Commander Douglas MacArthur, his staff, and a new Japanese congress ran the country.

Under MacArthur's direction, Japan demobilized several million troops and adopted a new constitution in 1947. The constitution set up a democratic system of government, which gave voting rights to women and granted freedom of religion. The constitution also abolished the army and navy and prohibited Japan from ever again becoming a military power. Although the constitution was clearly influenced by American ideals, it won wide support from the Japanese people.

The Japanese also made important economic reforms. One program gave land to Japanese farmers. The government allowed labor unions to organize. It also broke up the *zaibatsu*, huge corporations run by single families that had monopolized the Japanese economy. These political and economic reforms laid the foundation for Japan's tremendous postwar economic recovery.

✔ **READING CHECK: Making Predictions** How might actions the Allies took to stabilize Germany and Japan after the war have affected future relations?
led to increased tensions between the United States and the Soviet Union, may have improved Japan's relationship with Allies

Occupied Germany, 1945–1950

Interpreting Maps The United States and the Soviet Union occupied the largest portions of Germany.

❓ PLACES AND REGIONS Which country controlled the zone in which Munich was located?

Occupied Berlin

West Berlin · East Berlin

Azimuthal Equal-Area Projection

Zones:
- U.S.
- Soviet
- British
- French

1949 Date created

Azimuthal Equal-Area Projection

Figurine made in Japan during U.S. occupation

GLOBAL RELATIONS

The Potsdam Conference. The Potsdam Conference revealed that tensions between the United States and the Soviet Union were on the rise. Scholar David McCullough summed up the atmosphere that surrounded the meeting's end: "The Potsdam Conference should have been a time of celebration . . . marking the start of a new era of good feeling among the Allied powers now that the common foe, the detested Nazi, was destroyed. . . . But it wasn't that way, nor in practicality had there ever been much chance it would be. . . . The first day they met, Stalin had told Truman he wanted to cooperate with the United States in peace as in war, but in peace, he said, that would be more difficult. It was what they all knew, and the underlying tensions felt at the beginning remained to the end."

CRITICAL THINKING Why might it have been easier for the Allies to cooperate during the war than after it?

ANSWER: Students might suggest that the Allies had the common goal of defeating the Axis Powers but that after the war each country would act in its own self-interest.

MAP ANSWER
the United States

LEVEL 1: Tell students to imagine that they are American journalists who have been sent to postwar Germany and Japan to cover the punishment of war criminals. Have each student write two postcards to a friend or family member back home that discuss how the Allies punished war criminals and describe why some people were dissatisfied with the trials. (*Students should mention the war crimes trials in Germany and Japan, the verdicts in the trials, and that the war crimes were so shocking that many Americans felt that more German and Japanese officials should have been punished.*) Have volunteers read their postcards to the class.
English Language Learners

LEVELS 2 AND 3: Tell students to imagine that they are newspaper editors in the period following World War II. Have each student write an editorial about the punishment of war criminals and some people's dissatisfaction with the trials. (*See the Level 1 lesson for the correct Allied procedures, punishments.*) Students may wish to include their editorials in their portfolios.

HISTORICAL DOCUMENTS ANSWER

(for p. 563)

Answers will vary. Students might mention that the UN's aims are similar to those of life, liberty, and the pursuit of happiness in the U.S. Declaration of Independence.

VISUAL RECORD ANSWER

Students might note the presence of military police in the courtroom.

The War Crimes Trials

After the war, Allied leaders began to think about how to punish the military leaders who committed or ordered atrocities during the war. At the Potsdam Conference, the Allied leaders agreed that "stern justice shall be meted [given] out to all war criminals, including those who have visited cruelties upon our prisoners." The Allied leaders agreed that convicted German and Japanese war criminals must be punished for waging war and for the mistreatment of prisoners.

INTERPRETING THE VISUAL RECORD
Nuremberg Trials. Allied judges tried German officers in Nuremberg, Germany. Hermann Göring, the commander of the German air force, is shown on the witness stand. *What characteristics of this courtroom could lead you to assume that this is a military trial?*

Nuremberg Trials. The German war crimes trials were known as the **Nuremberg Trials** because they took place in Nuremberg, Germany, the former rallying place of Adolf Hitler's Nazi Party. The trials began in November 1945. Before an international military court, witnesses gave chilling accounts of Nazi atrocities, including the torture and murder of millions of Jews, Gypsies, and others. Marie Vaillant, a concentration camp survivor, testified.

> *History Makers Speak*
>
> "For months, for years we had one wish only: the wish that some of us would escape alive, in order to tell the world what the Nazi convict prisons were like.... There was the systematic ... urge to use human beings as slaves and to kill them when they could work no more."
>
> — Marie Vaillant, quoted in *Justice at Nuremberg*, by Robert E. Conot

In September 1946 the court made its first rulings. The court had tried a number of Nazi leaders on four charges. They were charged with planning the war, committing war crimes and other crimes against humanity, and conspiring to commit the crimes. Twelve Nazi leaders were sentenced to death. Seven others received jail sentences, and three were acquitted.

In other trials held in the U.S. occupation zone, thousands of former Nazi leaders were tried and jailed, fined, or barred from public office. However, many Nazis, including **Adolf Eichmann**, an architect of the Jewish extermination program, avoided immediate prosecution by hiding their identities and escaping to Latin America.

Trials in Tokyo. In Tokyo General MacArthur set up the International Military Tribunal for the Far East in early 1946. This court conducted trials against suspected war criminals from the war in the Pacific. The court prosecuted more than 20 leaders of Japan's military. The trials lasted from May 1946 to November 1948. Seven people were sentenced to death, including **Hideki Tōjō**, Japan's premier during the war. Others were sentenced to life in prison.

Shocked by the war crimes, many Americans argued that more German and Japanese officials should have been punished. Nevertheless, the judges followed legal procedures and tried not to act out of anger. The trials set important standards for international law and the conduct of war. The chief lesson was that countries and individuals can be held accountable for their actions during war. Many countries now accept the idea that war crimes cannot be excused on the grounds that those responsible were "just following orders."

✔ **READING CHECK: Summarizing** How did the Allies punish war criminals?
The Allies set up international military courts at Nuremberg and Tokyo.

TEACH OBJECTIVE 3

LEVEL 1: Pair students and have them create a collage that depicts why the United Nations was founded. *(Students should show that the United Nations was founded to promote world peace, human rights, equality between the sexes and between nations, respect for justice and treaty obligations, and social progress and better standards of living.)* Ask students to explain how the United Nations was organized. *(Students should mention that all member nations were included in a General Assembly, and the United States, Great Britain, France, China, the Soviet Union and 10 additional rotating members composed the Security Council.)*

English Language Learners, Cooperative Learning

LEVELS 2 AND 3: Tell students to imagine that it is 1945 and that they are U.S. diplomats working to gain Senate approval for U.S. membership in the United Nations. Have each student write a speech describing why the United Nations is being founded and how the United Nations will be organized. *(See the Level 1 lesson for the correct reasons and description.)* Have volunteers deliver their speeches to the class.

The United Nations

During the war, the Allies had met several times to map out military strategies. Delegates from the United States, Britain, the Soviet Union, and China met in 1944 at Dumbarton Oaks, an estate in Washington, D.C. They worked out a proposal for a postwar international organization called the **United Nations** (UN).

The founding of the UN. The Allies hoped to use the UN to work for world peace. In April 1945, delegates from 50 nations met in San Francisco to draw up the Charter of the United Nations. The charter provided for a General Assembly and a Security Council. The General Assembly includes all member nations. The 15-member Security Council includes 5 permanent members and 10 rotating members. The United States, the Soviet Union, Britain, France, and China are the permanent members. It addresses military and political problems and has the power to veto any action proposed by the General Assembly.

Soon after the creation of the UN Charter, the Senate overwhelmingly approved U.S. membership in the UN. On October 24, 1945, the UN officially came into existence. The UN established its headquarters in New York City. **Trygve Lie** (TRIG-vuh LEE) of Norway served as the UN's first secretary-general. Former first lady **Eleanor Roosevelt** served as one of the first U.S. delegates to the UN.

The Charter of the United Nations

In 1944 Britain, China, the Soviet Union, and the United States drew up a tentative charter to form "a general international organization, based on the sovereign equality of all peace-loving states." After another planning conference, the United Nations Charter was adopted by the United States on July 28, 1945. An excerpt from the introduction follows. **How do the aims of the United Nations compare to the goals listed in the U.S. Declaration of Independence?**

WE THE PEOPLES OF THE UNITED NATIONS DETERMINED to save succeeding generations from the scourge [destruction] of war, which twice in our lifetime has brought untold sorrow to mankind, and to reaffirm faith in fundamental human rights, in the dignity and worth of the human person, in the equal rights of men and women and of nations large and small, and to establish conditions under which justice and respect for the obligations arising from treaties . . . to promote social progress and better standards of life in larger freedom, AND FOR THESE ENDS to practice tolerance and live together in peace with one another as good neighbors . . . HAVE RESOLVED TO COMBINE OUR EFFORTS TO ACCOMPLISH THESE AIMS.

Accordingly, our respective Governments . . . have agreed to the present Charter of the United Nations and do hereby establish an international organization to be known as the United Nations.

Eleanor Roosevelt

Eleanor Roosevelt's contribution. Born to a distinguished New York City family on October 11, 1884, Eleanor Roosevelt lived a solemn and often lonely childhood. Both of her parents died when she was 10. "It was the grimmest childhood I had ever known. Who did she have? Nobody," sympathized one of Roosevelt's cousins.

At the age of 14, Roosevelt was enrolled in Allenswood, a girl's school outside of London. There Roosevelt found warmth and intellectual encouragement. Describing her years at Allenswood, Roosevelt later explained that "whatever I have become since had its seeds in those three years of contact with a liberal mind and strong personality."

After leaving the boarding school at age 17, Roosevelt returned to New York. She eagerly turned toward a life of social activism and settlement-house work. By

Research on the R◎M

Free Find:
Eleanor Roosevelt
After reading more about Eleanor Roosevelt on the **Holt Researcher CD–ROM**, write a short essay explaining how her concern for social issues influenced her political career.

The United Nations. Two major disputes arose between the United States and the Soviet Union at the Dumbarton Oaks conference. First, the Soviet Union wanted the five permanent members of the UN Security Council to have the power to veto discussion of any issue by the General Assembly. The United States wanted the veto power to apply only to proposed actions. Second, the Soviet Union demanded a vote in the General Assembly for each of its 15 constituent republics. The United States countered that it should receive a vote for each of its 48 states. At the Yalta Conference these issues were resolved. The Soviet Union yielded to the U.S. version of the Security Council veto. In return, the United States agreed that three Soviet republics—Russia, Byelorussia, and Ukraine—should receive seats in the General Assembly.

CRITICAL THINKING How might the Security Council's veto power over General Assembly actions be considered undemocratic?

ANSWER: Students might suggest that the fact that a minority vote can override the vote of an overwhelming majority goes against democratic principles.

![US flag icon] **ALL LEVELS:** To help students understand the events that led to the founding of Israel and Arab countries' response to Israel's founding, copy the following graphic organizer on the chalkboard, omitting the italicized answers. Have each student complete the graphic organizer. Ask volunteers to share their answers with the class. Lead the class in a discussion about the issues involved in the Arab-Israeli dispute.

English Language Learners

Founding of Israel		Arab countries' response
After World War II, European Jews settle in Palestine.		
↓		
UN creates partition plan for Palestine.	→	*reject UN plan*
↓		
British forces withdraw from Palestine.		
↓		
State of Israel proclaimed.	→	*refuse to recognize Israel; attack Israel*
↓		
1949 UN plan divides Jerusalem.		

☐ internet connect ≡

TOPIC: The Founding of Israel
GO TO: go.hrw.com
KEYWORD: SE3 AN19

Have students access the Internet through the HRW Go site to conduct research on the founding of Israel. Then have each student create an illustrated time line that traces the major events leading to the formation of the state of Israel. Students should include information on the reasons Israel was founded, international support for its founding, the national origins of immigrants to Israel, and the reactions of Palestinian Arabs.

SECTION
REVIEW ① ANSWERS

1. Define
- *zaibatsu*, p. 561

2. Identify
- Potsdam Conference, p. 560
- Nuremberg Trials, p. 560
- Adolf Eichmann, p. 562
- Hideki Tōjō, p. 562
- United Nations, p. 563
- Trygve Lie, p. 563
- Eleanor Roosevelt, p. 563
- Zionism, p. 564
- David Ben-Gurion, p. 564
- Ralph Bunche, p. 565

The Religious Spirit

AMERICAN JUDAISM

Thousands of Jewish refugees and Holocaust survivors from Europe resettled in what would become the nation of Israel. Many others headed for the United States. Between 1935 and 1941 some 150,000 European Jews immigrated to the United States. These new immigrants contributed to the already diverse Jewish American community in the United States.

The menorah is used to celebrate the Jewish holiday of Hanukkah.

During the 1950s American Judaism was dominated by three denominations—Orthodox, Conservative, and Reform. Some Jewish immigrants embraced Orthodox Judaism's emphasis on a unity of past and present faith and on the strict observance of religious laws. Conservative and Reform Judaism, however, proved much more popular.

Some immigrants liked the relaxed interpretation of religious observance offered by Reform Judaism. This denomination had been popular in the United States since the late 1800s. It presented a somewhat Americanized, modern Judaism—holding services primarily in English and experimenting with a Sunday Sabbath. Reform Judaism also presented the Jewish faith simply as an organized religion. Emphasizing both Jewish religious heritage and Jewish ethnic identity, Conservative Judaism attracted the majority of the Jewish immigrants. All three denominations attempted to spread awareness of anti-Semitism. Most Jews in the United States—Conservative Jews in particular—encouraged Jewish nationalism, primarily in terms of support for the nation of Israel. ■

her early twenties, Roosevelt had gained recognition in New York City's growing community of social reformers.

Roosevelt continued her social activism and political work throughout her marriage to Franklin D. Roosevelt, her distant cousin. Her political career continued well after his death. In 1945 she was selected as a U.S. delegate to the UN. In this role, Roosevelt helped create a declaration of human rights that would provide a universal set of inalienable rights. Roosevelt and other UN delegates realized that building world peace after World War II required cooperation among nations.

History Makers Speak

❝Security requires both control of the use of force and the elimination of want. No people are secure unless they have the things needed not only to preserve existence, but to make life worth living. . . . All peoples throughout the world must know that there is an organization where their interests can be considered and where justice and security will be sought for all.❞

— Eleanor Roosevelt, *My Day*, edited by David Emblidge. Copyright © 1990 by Pharos Books. Reprinted by permission of *United Feature Syndicate, Inc.*

Roosevelt remained politically active and worked for human rights until her death in 1962.

Early critics of the UN insisted that it was doomed to fail because it did not have the power to enforce its own decisions. Nevertheless, most Americans were as optimistic as President Truman, who noted in 1945, "This [UN] charter points down the only road to enduring peace. There is no other."

✔ **READING CHECK: Identifying Points of View** How did Eleanor Roosevelt's views reflect those of the UN founders? She believed that world peace depended on cooperation among nations and security.

The Founding of Israel

One of the first major conflicts the United Nations faced concerned Palestine, a small eastern Mediterranean region claimed by both Jews and Arabs. After World War II, many European Jews moved to Palestine—despite Arab protest—rather than return to Europe. Britain, which had ruled Palestine since World War I, could not resolve conflicting claims over the territory. In 1947 Britain turned the issue over to the United Nations. The UN came up with a plan to divide Palestine into two states—one for Jews, the other for Arabs—but Arabs rejected the proposal.

Zionism. The UN plan was a victory for **Zionism**, the movement seeking a Jewish homeland in Palestine. Zionist leader **David Ben-Gurion** (ben-goohr-YAWN) had supported the idea since the early 1900s. Born in what is now Poland, Ben-Gurion moved to Palestine in 1906. He was expelled in 1915 for Zionist activities. Exiled, he went to the United States to raise money and recruit volunteers among the American Jewish community.

REVIEW

Have students complete the **Section 1 Review** on p. 537.

ASSESS

Have students complete **Daily Quiz 19.1**. As **Alternative Assessment**, you may want to use the UN collage or the war crimes editorial in this section's lessons.

RETEACH

Have students complete **Main Idea Activity for English Language Learners and Special-Needs Students 19.1**. Then create a five-column chart on the chalkboard entitled *Healing the Wounds of War*. Label the columns Stabilizing Germany, Stabilizing Japan, War Crimes Trials and Responses to Them, Founding the UN, and Founding Israel and the Response of Arab Countries. Then organize students into five groups and assign one column to each group. Have each group present the information from its column to the class.
English Language Learners, Cooperative Learning

EXTEND

Ask each student to conduct research on the founding of the United Nations and the creation of the UN Charter. Students should focus their research on delegates' philosophical differences and important compromises. Have students present their research in the form of a booklet entitled "Creating the United Nations." **Block Scheduling**

When the British forces withdrew from Palestine in 1948, Ben-Gurion and other Jewish leaders promptly proclaimed the new state of Israel. Both the United States and the Soviet Union immediately recognized the new nation.

The Arab-Israeli War. The Arab states, however, reacted violently. They refused to recognize Israel and organized military forces to reclaim the state for Palestine. Armies from the Arab states of Egypt, Iraq, Lebanon, Syria, and Transjordan joined Palestinian forces to attack Israel. Although vastly outnumbered, Israeli forces under Ben-Gurion's overall command captured and held much of Palestine. Israeli soldiers used an arsenal bought in part with millions of dollars that poured in from the American Jewish community.

In an attempt to end the war, the UN sent a mediator, Count Folke Bernadotte of Sweden, to the Middle East. Bernadotte negotiated a shaky cease-fire, but he was assassinated by Israeli extremists. In 1949 a second UN mediator, U.S. diplomat **Ralph Bunche**, persuaded both sides to accept an armistice. Bunche won the Nobel Peace Prize in 1950. He was the first African American to receive that honor.

The 1949 agreement gave Israel more territory than the earlier UN partition plan had, but it divided Jerusalem into Arab and Israeli zones. The plan gave Egypt control of the Gaza Strip, and Jordan took over the West Bank of the Jordan River. The Arab countries, however, still refused to recognize the state of Israel. Also left unresolved was the fate of the Palestinian Arabs remaining in Israel.

INTERPRETING THE VISUAL RECORD

Zionism. After World War II, thousands of European Jews made their way to Palestine. These three Holocaust survivors traveled there in June 1945. *What emotions do you think these settlers felt as they arrived in their new homeland?*

✔ **READING CHECK: Identifying Cause and Effect** What events led to the founding of the new country of Israel? How did Arab countries respond? Palestine created by UN partition; UN forces withdraw; Jewish leaders proclaim the state of Israel; Arab countries react violently

---

SECTION 1 REVIEW

1. Define and explain:
zaibatsu

2. Identify and explain:
Potsdam Conference
Nuremberg Trials
Adolf Eichmann
Hideki Tōjō
United Nations
Trygve Lie
Eleanor Roosevelt
Zionism
David Ben-Gurion
Ralph Bunche

3. Comparing Copy the graphic organizer below. Use it to compare the ways Allied forces attempted to stabilize Germany and Japan after World War II.

Allied Efforts to Stabilize Germany	Allied Efforts to Stabilize Japan

4. Finding the Main Idea

a. Was justice served in the Nuremberg and Tokyo war crimes trials? Consider both the victims' and criminals' perspectives.
b. How do you think World War II influenced the creation and structure of the United Nations?
c. What events led the UN to try to resolve the conflict over Jewish and Arab claims to Palestine? How successful was this effort?

5. Writing and Critical Thinking

Analyzing Information Write a brief article explaining how nations acted in a spirit of cooperation after World War II and how these same nations competed.
Consider:
• what actions nations took during the occupation of Germany and Japan
• what the purpose and goals of the UN were
• how the conflict in Palestine developed and was resolved

Homework Practice Online
keyword: SE3 HP19

---

3. Germany—division into occupation zones, joint administration of Berlin, destruction of Nazi Party, re-establishment of local governments, reconstruction of industry, return of refugees; Japan—occupation by U.S. military, demobilization of Japanese military, establishment of a democratic constitution, encouragement of economic reforms

4a. Answers will vary. Some students might suggest that a greater number of German and Japanese officials should have been put on trial. Others might suggest that a prolonged period of trials would have been counterproductive to efforts to rebuild Germany and Japan.

b. Answers will vary. Some students might point out that World War II had a direct influence on the basic UN mission and that the membership of the UN Security Council included all the major Allies.

c. The Arab-Israeli war led to UN involvement, but the UN could not resolve conflicting claims over territory.

5. cooperation—joint occupation of Germany and establishment of the United Nations; competition—conflict between Arabs and Jews over creation of Israel

VISUAL RECORD ANSWER

Students might mention excitement, joy, and pride.

After completing Section 2, students should be able to:

OBJECTIVE 1 Explain what caused the Cold War, and describe U.S. strategy during the Cold War.

OBJECTIVE 2 Trace how the U.S. government tried to control the development of atomic weapons.

OBJECTIVE 3 Analyze how the Marshall Plan helped block the spread of communism in Europe.

OBJECTIVE 4 Describe how the Western Allies responded to Soviet expansion.

LET'S GET STARTED!

Write the following question on the chalkboard: *What do you know about the Cold War?* As students enter the classroom, tell them to respond to the question in writing. Ask volunteers to share their responses with the class. Tell students that in Section 2 they will learn about the origins of the Cold War.

SECTION 2 RESOURCES

REPRODUCIBLE
▶ Guided Reading Strategy 19.2
▶ Primary Source Reading 19: New Foreign Policy

TECHNOLOGY
▶ One-Stop Planner, Lesson 19.2
▶ Holt Researcher: American History CD–ROM
▶ Homework Practice Online

REINFORCEMENT, REVIEW, AND ASSESSMENT
▶ Section 2 Review, p. 571
▶ Daily Quiz 19.2
▶ Main Idea Activity 19.2
▶ English Audio Summary 19.2
▶ Spanish Audio Summary 19.2

SECTION 2

READ TO DISCOVER
1. What caused the Cold War, and what was the U.S. strategy during the Cold War?
2. How did the U.S. government try to control the development of atomic weapons?
3. How did the Marshall Plan help block the spread of communism in Europe?
4. How did the Western Allies respond to Soviet expansion?

DEFINE
satellite nations
containment

IDENTIFY
Cold War
George Kennan
Baruch Plan
Atomic Energy Act
Truman Doctrine
George C. Marshall
Marshall Plan
Berlin Airlift
NATO
Warsaw Pact

▶ WHY IT MATTERS TODAY
NATO has expanded its membership since the Cold War ended. Use **CNNfyi.com** or other **current events** sources to find out about new members in NATO and plans to include more nations. Record your findings in your journal.

CNNfyi.com

The Cold War Begins

EYEWITNESSES TO History

"Only two great powers remained in the world, the United States and the Soviet Union. . . . And it was clear that the Soviet Union was aggressive and expanding. For the United States to take steps to strengthen countries threatened with Soviet aggression . . . was to protect not only the security of the United States—it was to protect freedom itself."

—Anonymous, quoting Dean Acheson, in *The Marshall Plan,* by Charles L. Mee Jr.

One State Department official recalled Secretary of State Dean Acheson's reflections on the developing political stand-off between the United States and the Soviet Union after World War II. As the war ended, the wartime alliance between the United States and the Soviet Union collapsed. At odds over competing global objectives and different economic and political systems, the two countries fought for control of Europe and control of atomic weapons.

This poster reflects the fear of the spread of communism.

The Roots of the Cold War

An intense rivalry between the United States and the Soviet Union began after World War II. With once mighty Germany, Japan, and Great Britain weakened, only the United States and the Soviet Union were left to struggle for international dominance. The competition for global power and influence between these two superpowers came to be known as the **Cold War**. It was waged mostly on political and economic fronts. Nonetheless, the threat of all-out war was always present.

The origins of the Cold War lay in economic, political, and philosophical differences between the two nations. Committed to the principles of democratic government, individual freedom, and a capitalist economy, most Americans deeply opposed the Soviet system. Founded on communist theories, the Soviet system had evolved to include a state-run economy, one-party rule, suppression of religion, and the use of force to crush opposition.

Soviet expansionism after World War II fueled American mistrust. During World War II the Soviets had taken over the Baltic states of Estonia, Latvia, and Lithuania. Then they captured large areas of Poland and Romania. By war's end the Soviets also controlled Manchuria. After the war, Soviet leader Joseph Stalin made clear his determination to maintain Soviet influence in Eastern Europe. He claimed the need for a buffer zone of "friendly nations" on the Soviet Union's western border. He installed pro-Soviet governments in Poland and Romania and worked to establish communist rule throughout Eastern Europe. These countries under Soviet control became known as **satellite nations**.

Concerned by Stalin's actions, Britain, France, and the United States strengthened their control of western Germany and revived its industries. Winston Churchill, Britain's wartime prime minister, described this expansion of Soviet

TEACH OBJECTIVE 1

LEVEL 1: Organize students into triads and have them create political cartoons with captions to explain the causes of the Cold War and U.S. strategy during the Cold War. *(Students should depict the major economic, political, and philosophical differences between the United States and the Soviet Union and the U.S. strategy of containment.)* Have each group present and explain its cartoons to the class.
English Language Learners, Cooperative Learning

LEVEL 2: Tell students to imagine that they are editing an encyclopedia. Have each student write a brief entry that discusses the causes of the Cold War and the U.S. strategy during the Cold War. *(See the Level 1 lesson for the correct causes and the U.S. strategy.)* Ask volunteers to read their entries to the class.

LEVEL 3: Tell students to imagine that they are history professors who must deliver brief lectures about the Cold War to their classes. Have each student prepare a lecture about the origins of the Cold War and the U.S. strategy during the Cold War. *(See the Level 1 lesson for the correct causes and the U.S. strategy.)* Have volunteers deliver their lectures to the class.

---

influence. Churchill declared that a Soviet "Iron Curtain has descended across the Continent," isolating Western Europe from Soviet-dominated Eastern Europe. Churchill called for closer cooperation between Britain and the United States to control Soviet power. At the time, **George Kennan**, a State Department official and Soviet expert, advised similar action. Kennan suggested a policy of **containment**, or restricting the expansion of Soviet communism. Many Americans applauded this tough stand against communism. Kennan explained his philosophy:

“The Soviet pressure against the free institutions of the Western world is something that can be contained by the . . . vigilant [determined] application of counterforce at a series of constantly shifting geographical and political points. . . . The Russians look forward to a duel of infinite duration.”

—George Kennan, *The Source of Soviet Conduct*

Dictator Joseph Stalin ruled the Soviet Union with an iron fist.

✔ **READING CHECK: Analyzing Information** What were the origins of the Cold War?
economic, political, and philosophical differences between the Soviet Union and the United States; Soviet expansion into Eastern Europe; and Allied strengthening of Western Europe

SKILL-BUILDING STRATEGIES ANSWERS

Applying the Skill
Students should concentrate on the change in headquarters's priorities.

Practicing the Skill
1. a new anticommunist focus in the U.S. military after World War II

2. that the focus of military intelligence switched from dealing with former Nazis to gathering information about Communists

3. He reports the opinion of headquarters that focusing on Communists is more important than focusing on former Nazis.

Skill-Building Strategies

Taking Notes

Taking notes—writing down information in a concise and orderly manner—is a basic skill that is particularly important for conducting a successful oral history interview. Taking notes allows you to clarify and organize the content of an interview and provides a valuable key for remembering and working with this content later.

How to Take Notes

1. **Select specific information.** Select specific information to include in your notes, concentrating on the main ideas and any strong opinions that your subject communicates in the interview. Take note of any particularly interesting examples or stories mentioned by your subject.
2. **Paraphrase the information.** Put the information in your own words, rather than trying to copy what your subject says exactly. Feel free to use shorthand terms and symbols, but make sure to write legibly so that you will understand your notes when you review them.
3. **Review the notes thoroughly.** Shortly after the interview has been completed, review your notes and add any important supplementary information that you may remember. If the interview was recorded, listen to the recording and make sure that your notes accurately represent what was said.

Applying the Skill

Take notes on the following excerpt from an oral history provided by Erhard Dabringhaus, a former U.S. military intelligence officer who took part in the occupation of Germany after World War II. Dabringhaus was interviewed during the early 1980s.

“[In] 1948, a new directive came from [intelligence] headquarters. We're no longer interested as we used to be in former German Nazis. We're now interested in what's happening behind the East-West border. Communism becomes our most important interest. We're now looking for communists. We want to know about the newly organized government in France, after the war. How many communists are in it?”

Practicing the Skill

Use the excerpt above to answer the following questions.
1. What is the general topic of the excerpt?
2. What ideas does Dabringhaus communicate in the excerpt?
3. What opinions does Dabringhaus express in the excerpt?

LEVEL 1: Pair students and have each pair create a graphic organizer that summarizes the U.S. government's efforts to control the development of nuclear weapons. *(Students should describe the Baruch Plan and the Atomic Energy Act.)* Have students present their graphic organizers to the class. Students may wish to include their organizers in their portfolios.
English Language Learners, Cooperative Learning

LEVELS 2 AND 3: Have each student create a cause-and-effect chart that describes the efforts of the U.S. government to control the development of atomic weapons. *(See the Level 1 lesson for the correct efforts.)* Then instruct students to write essays in which they suggest alternatives that might have prevented the nuclear arms race. Students may wish to include their charts and essays in their portfolios.

HOMEWORK *Have students design a public relations campaign to inform Americans in the mid-1940s about the U.S. government's efforts to control the development of atomic weapons.*

HISTORY MAKERS SPEAK

Robert Frost in *By the Bomb's Early Light*

International Controls and the Atomic Bomb.

While many people were hopeful about U.S.-led attempts to place controls on atomic weapons, others—not just Soviets—suspected that such plans were designed to maintain a permanent U.S. monopoly on the bomb. In "U.S. 1946 King's X," American poet Robert Frost expressed his doubts about the motivation behind U.S. proposals:

Having invented a new Holocaust,
And been the first with it to win a war,
How they make haste to cry with their fingers crossed,
King's X—no fairs to use it any more!

CRITICAL THINKING How might the U.S. government have reassured Americans and Soviets that it wanted to limit nuclear weapons?

ANSWER: Students might suggest that the United States could have stopped building and testing nuclear weapons before proposing to limit weapons.

VISUAL RECORD ANSWER

Students might suggest that the size of the mushroom cloud shows how powerful they are.

Deadlock over Atomic Weapons

After World War II the Soviet Union began to develop atomic technology. The United States and the Soviet Union soon became locked in a dispute over the issue. This standoff terrified many Americans, who feared the outbreak of nuclear war. Most people shared lawyer David E. Lilienthal's opinion that "the awful strength of atomic power . . . directly affects every man, woman, and child in the world."

U.S. presidential adviser Bernard Baruch called for the creation of a special international agency with the authority to inspect any country's atomic-energy plants. This proposal, known as the **Baruch Plan**, would impose penalties on countries that did not follow international rules. Until such a plan was in place, Baruch said, the United States would not reveal any atomic-energy secrets or give up its atomic weapons. At the time, U.S. physicists were developing more-powerful nuclear weapons.

Working feverishly on its own bomb, the Soviet Union rejected all inspection and enforcement provisions. With neither country willing to compromise, hopes for international control of atomic energy died. When the Soviet Union tested its first atomic bomb in 1949, the feared nuclear arms race became a reality.

In response to fears of nuclear warfare, Congress passed the **Atomic Energy Act** in August 1946. The act created the civilian-controlled Atomic Energy Commission (AEC) to oversee nuclear weapons research and to promote peacetime uses of atomic energy.

✔ **READING CHECK: Summarizing** How did the U.S. government attempt to limit the development of atomic weapons? **by creating international and national commissions to oversee atomic energy plants and research**

INTERPRETING THE VISUAL RECORD

Atomic testing. In 1953, as part of Operation Upshot-Knothole, the U.S. Army exploded an artillery shell filled with uranium. *What do you think this photograph reveals about the power of atomic weapons?*

Containment Around the World

As the Cold War continued, the Truman administration followed a more aggressive foreign policy. The U.S. containment policy was adopted in reaction to events in Greece. A civil war had broken out there in 1946. Communist-led rebels fought against the Greek monarchy, which relied on military and financial aid from Britain. In early 1947, however, Britain announced that it could no longer help Greece. Without aid, Greece's pro-Western government could not defend itself from communist forces.

The Mediterranean. At the same time, the Soviet Union pressured Turkey to give up sole control of the Dardanelles. This narrow strait links the Black Sea and the Mediterranean. President Truman knew that control of this area would give the Soviets a dominant position in the eastern Mediterranean. In a speech to Congress, Truman stated, "It must be the policy of the United States to support free peoples who are resisting attempted subjugation [conquest] by armed minorities or by outside pressures."

LEVELS 1 AND 2: Lead a class discussion about the problems that Europe faced after World War II and why Americans feared that these problems would make European nations more vulnerable to communist influence. (*Students might suggest that people in countries experiencing economic difficulties would find communism more appealing.*) Then ask students to explain how the Marshall Plan helped contain the spread of communism in Europe. (*Students should explain that Marshall Plan aid stabilized European economies and led to European economic recovery.*) To conclude, ask students why economic welfare might be vital to the existence of democratic political institutions.

English Language Learners

LEVEL 3: Have each student write an essay analyzing why George C. Marshall believed that the United States should provide aid to European countries after World War II and how this aid was a response to Soviet expansion after the war. (*See the Levels 1 and 2 lesson for the correct reasons.*) Students may wish to include their essays in their portfolios.

His statement became known as the **Truman Doctrine**. It made no mention of the Soviet Union, although clearly Truman had the Soviets in mind. In support of Truman's plan, Congress soon approved $400 million to aid Greece and Turkey.

Europe. After World War II, European economies were in shambles. Horrible blizzards in the winter of 1946–47 worsened the situation. Some Americans believed that the United States should help Europe. They feared that economic problems would make Western Europe more vulnerable to Communists' influence.

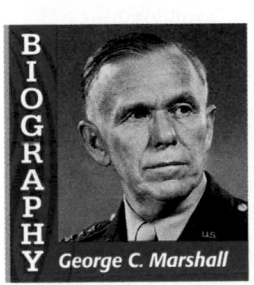

George C. Marshall

Secretary of State **George C. Marshall** shared this belief. Born in 1880 in Uniontown, Pennsylvania, Marshall was a very shy boy. In his first year at the Virginia Military Institute, he did poorly. Marshall developed his leadership skills and graduated near the top of his class.

Following his graduation in 1901, he pursued a career in the army. During World War I Marshall served under General John J. Pershing and helped develop military strategy. Franklin D. Roosevelt appointed Marshall army chief of staff in 1939.

After the war, Marshall served briefly as a U.S. representative to China before Truman appointed him secretary of state in 1947. Marshall gave a speech at Harvard University on June 5, 1947. He warned that if steps were not taken soon, Europe faced "economic, social, and political" collapse. He called for a major U.S. effort to promote European recovery. Its goal was "to permit the emergence of political and social conditions in which free institutions can exist." Marshall warned that any attempt to block recovery or to take advantage of Europe's difficulties for political ends would face strong U.S. opposition.

In response, Truman asked Congress for $17 billion in economic aid for Europe. Truman's request sparked heated debate. A turning point came in early 1948, when pro-Soviet Communists overthrew the government of Czechoslovakia. Congress funded the European Recovery Program, or **Marshall Plan**, in April 1948. Marshall won the Nobel Peace Prize in 1953.

Marshall resigned as secretary of state in 1949. The following year, Truman appointed him secretary of defense to prepare the U.S. armed forces for possible confrontations with Communist forces. After 1951 Marshall became an adviser on defense and military matters. He died in Washington, D.C., in 1959.

✔ **READING CHECK: Drawing Conclusions** What methods did the Marshall Plan use to contain the spread of communism?
economic support of European nations

★ Then and Now

Extending Economic Aid Abroad

With the Marshall Plan, the United States established a lasting standard. Through financial aid, the United States provided the resources for nations to rebuild industries and economic institutions after a crisis. The Marshall Plan supplied billions of dollars that were used to rebuild European factories, increase agricultural production, and restore roads and bridges. Many Americans believed that the aid would strengthen the postwar U.S. economy, as Europeans would eventually begin to buy American products.

Since the end of World War II, the United States has assisted many nations and maintained international influence by extending economic aid. In recent years, the U.S. government has helped several Latin American countries rebuild after devastating natural disasters. After Hurricane Mitch struck the coasts of Nicaragua and Honduras in 1998, the U.S. Congress passed the Emergency Supplemental Appropriations Bill. It provided some $950 million to aid countries affected by floods and mudslides. Congress also approved aid requests for Belize after Hurricane Keith struck in 2000 and for El Salvador after three earthquakes in five weeks struck the country in early 2001.

U.S. aid also extends to other countries, including some in Africa and Asia. For example, the U.S. government agreed to provide assistance to help victims of a major earthquake in India in January 2001. Giving economic aid helps the U.S. economy by strengthening its trading partners.

U.S. aid delivery in Liberia

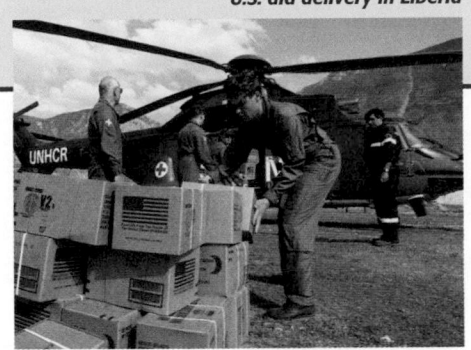

GLOBAL RELATIONS

The Marshall Plan. Although the Marshall Plan was originally intended to provide economic aid to almost all European countries, the Soviet Union refused to participate. At an economic conference held in Paris soon after George C. Marshall's speech, Soviet foreign minister Vyacheslav Molotov derided the secretary of state's proposal as "nothing but a vicious American scheme for using dollars to buy its way" into European affairs. Ultimately, Soviet pressure prevented Czechoslovakia, Poland, Romania, and other Eastern European nations from taking part in the Marshall Plan.

ACTIVITY: Ask each student to conduct research on the ways that economic aid from the United States has been used in a specific country during the past 20 years. Then have students present short oral reports on their research to the class.

THAT'S INTERESTING!

George C. Marshall was sworn in as chief of staff of the U.S. Army on September 1, 1939—the same day that Germany invaded Poland. Under his guidance, U.S. forces grew from about 200,000 to 8.5 million soldiers, a feat that prompted Winston Churchill to call Marshall "the true organizer of victory" for the Allies.

ALL LEVELS: Lead a class discussion about why the Western powers might have supported the creation of a West German government. (*Students might suggest that the Western powers wanted to create a cohesive political and economic unit that would support the Western Allies.*) To help students understand how the Western Allies tried to limit Soviet expansion, copy the following graphic organizer on the chalkboard, omitting the italicized answers. Have each student complete the organizer. Ask volunteers to share their answers with the class. **English Language Learners**

created NATO, a military alliance

Western Allies' responses to Soviet expansion

created Federal Republic of Germany

supplied West Berlin during Soviet blockade

HOMEWORK *Tell students to imagine that they are residents of West Berlin during the Soviet blockade. Have each student write a poem about his or her reaction to the Berlin Airlift, and how the airlift might help contain Soviet expansion.*

The Soviet blockade of West Berlin stranded about 2.5 million people with less than 45 days' worth of food, coal, and other supplies. During the airlift, American and British pilots made more than 270,000 flights into West Berlin. Each plane carried thousands of pounds of provisions. At peak times, a supply plane landed in the city every four minutes.

MAP ANSWER
five

VISUAL RECORD ANSWER

(for p. 571)

Students might mention that the need to guard the shared border signaled a rise in tensions in Berlin.

SECTION
REVIEW 2 ANSWERS

1. Define
• satellite nations, p. 566
• containment, p. 567

2. Identify
• Cold War, p. 566
• George Kennan, p. 567
• Baruch Plan, p. 568
• Atomic Energy Act, p. 568
• Truman Doctrine, p. 569

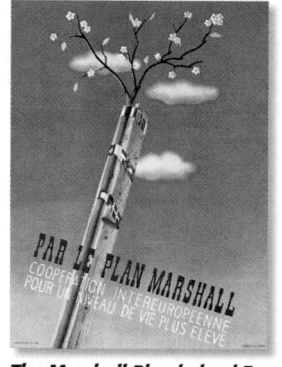

PAR LE PLAN MARSHALL
COOPERATION INTEREUROPEENNE
POUR UN NIVEAU DE VIE PLUS ELEVE

The Marshall Plan helped Europe gain a higher standard of living.

Crisis in Berlin

The non-Soviet zones of Germany grew stronger as a result of the Marshall Plan. In early June 1948 Britain, France, and the United States announced plans to combine their zones and support the formation of a West German government.

The Berlin Airlift. The Soviet Union opposed this action. On June 24, 1948, the Soviets suddenly blocked all roads, canals, and railways linking Berlin to western Germany. They cut off shipments of food, fuel, and other crucial supplies to the city. The Soviets hoped to drive the Western powers out of Berlin.

Western leaders responded to the Soviet move with the **Berlin Airlift.** Over the next 10 months, U.S. and British planes carried more than 2 million tons of food

Cold War Alliances in Europe, 1955

Interpreting Maps The Soviet Union dominated Eastern Europe after World War II. The Soviets and their allies united to form the Warsaw Pact in 1955.

? LOCATE How many more nations were members of NATO than of the Warsaw Pact?

The United States and Canada also were members of NATO in 1955.

NATO member, 1955
Warsaw Pact member, 1955
Nonaligned communist nation
Nonaligned nation
Territory USSR gained by 1945
National boundary, 1937

REVIEW

Have students complete the **Section 2 Review** on p. 571.

ASSESS

Have students complete **Daily Quiz 19.2**. As **Alternative Assessment**, you may want to use the political cartoon or the lecture in this section's lessons.

RETEACH

Have students complete **Main Idea Activity for English Language Learners and Special-Needs Students 19.2**. Then organize students into four groups and assign each group one of this section's objectives. Ask each group to create a fill-in-the-blank

exam by writing a paragraph and leaving blanks for key words and phrases. Make copies of each group's exam and distribute them to other groups. Have students complete the exams.
English Language Learners, Cooperative Learning

EXTEND

Pair students and tell one student in each pair to imagine that he or she is a journalist. Tell the other student to imagine that he or she is a general from the Warsaw Pact or NATO alliance. Have students use primary and secondary sources to conduct research on either the NATO or Warsaw Pact alliance. Then have each pair incorporate its findings into a brief mock interview. Ask students to conduct their interviews for the class.
Cooperative Learning, Block Scheduling

---

and supplies to the people of West Berlin. As one Berliner recalled, the airlift became the city's lifeline to the rest of the world.

History Makers Speak

"Early in the morning, when we woke up, the first thing we did was listen to see whether the noise of aircraft engines could be heard. That gave us the certainty that we were not alone, that the whole civilized world took part in the fight for Berlin's freedom."

—A Berlin resident, quoted in *Bridge in the Sky*, by Frank Donovan

The success of the Berlin Airlift embarrassed the Soviet Union. In May 1949 the Soviets lifted the blockade. Soon after, the Federal Republic of Germany, known as West Germany, was founded. In response, the Soviets set up the German Democratic Republic— East Germany—in the Soviet zone. The division of Germany would last for more than 40 years.

The Western alliance. After the Berlin crisis, the United States shifted its attention in Europe from economic recovery to military security. In April 1949 nine Western European nations joined the United States, Canada, and Iceland in a military alliance called the North Atlantic Treaty Organization, or **NATO**. Under the terms of the NATO treaty, each member nation pledged to defend the others in the event of an outside attack.

In 1951 General Dwight D. Eisenhower became the supreme commander of NATO forces. As its contribution to NATO, the United States stationed troops in Europe and gave massive military aid to its European allies. The Soviet Union responded in 1955 by forming its own military alliance with other communist countries in Eastern Europe. This alliance came to be called the **Warsaw Pact**.

✔ **READING CHECK: Identifying Cause and Effect** How did the Western Allies respond to the Soviet blockade of Berlin? *with the Berlin Airlift*

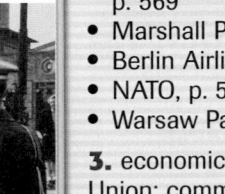

INTERPRETING THE VISUAL RECORD

Berlin crisis. U.S. military police in Berlin face their Soviet counterparts across the dividing line between the Allied and Soviet zones. *How do the soldiers and the sign in this photograph reflect the growing tension in Berlin?*

SECTION ② REVIEW

1. Define and explain:
satellite nations
containment

2. Identify and explain:
Cold War
George Kennan
Baruch Plan
Atomic Energy Act
Truman Doctrine
George C. Marshall
Marshall Plan
Berlin Airlift
NATO
Warsaw Pact

3. Contrasting Copy the chart below. Use it to explain how differences between the Soviet Union and the United States led to the Cold War.

Differences in:	Soviet Union	United States
Economic Structure		
Views of Democracy		
Personal Freedom		
Goals for Expansion		

4. ▓ **Finding the Main Idea**

a. Imagine that you are working for the U.S. government in 1946. What measures would you propose to help curb the development of atomic weapons?
b. What do you think might have happened if the United States had not implemented the Marshall Plan?
c. Why did the Soviet Union view the formation of a West German state and NATO as a threat?

5. ▓ **Writing and Critical Thinking**

Summarizing Write a paragraph describing how Kennan's containment policy was put into practice.
Consider:
• what the policy of containment was
• how the Marshall Plan and the Truman Doctrine fit into the containment strategy
• how NATO and the Berlin Airlift aided the containment strategy

Homework Practice Online
keyword: SE3 HP19

• George C. Marshall, p. 569
• Marshall Plan, p. 569
• Berlin Airlift, P. 570
• NATO, p. 571
• Warsaw Pact, p. 571

3. economic structure—Soviet Union: communist, state-run economy; United States: capitalist, free-market economy; views of democracy—Soviet Union: one-party rule, suppression of political opposition; United States: democratic government; personal freedom—Soviet Union: suppression of religion and other freedoms; United States: committed to principles of individual freedom; goals for expansion—Soviet Union: establishment of satellite nations in Eastern Europe as "buffer"; United States: exertion of influence in Western Europe

4a. Answers will vary. Students might suggest sharing of atomic knowledge between nations or the imposition of penalties.

b. Answers will vary. Students might suggest that it might have resulted in political chaos and the expansion of communism in Europe.

c. because they helped revive Germany, helped maintain a strong U.S. political presence in Europe, and posed obstacles to Soviet expansion

5. Answers will vary but should define containment and explain the Marshall Plan, the Truman Doctrine, NATO, and the Berlin Airlift.

SECTION 3

After completing Section 3, students should be able to:

OBJECTIVE 1 Explain how the Chinese Communists gained control of China.

OBJECTIVE 2 Analyze the factors that led to the escalation of the conflict in Korea.

OBJECTIVE 3 Describe the domestic and international effects of the Korean War.

OBJECTIVE 4 Discuss the methods that President Eisenhower used to promote U.S. interests abroad.

LET'S GET STARTED!

As students enter the classroom, tell them to study the map of North and South Korea in this section and to consider the distance from those countries to the United States. Ask each student to list reasons for and against U.S. involvement in a war in such a distant place. Ask volunteers to share their answers, and compile a list of students' answers on the chalkboard. Tell students that in Section 3 they will learn how Americans fought communism overseas under the leadership of Presidents Truman and Eisenhower.

SECTION 3 RESOURCES

REPRODUCIBLE
▶ Guided Reading Strategy 19.3
▶ American History Political Cartoon 26: Brinkmanship

TECHNOLOGY
▶ One-Stop Planner, Lesson 19.3
▶ The American Nation Video Program Segment: MacArthur in Korea; Teacher's Guide, pp. 193–94
▶ Holt Researcher: American History CD–ROM
▶ Homework Practice Online

REINFORCEMENT, REVIEW, AND ASSESSMENT
▶ Section 3 Review, p. 578
▶ Daily Quiz 19.3
▶ Main Idea Activity 19.3
▶ English Audio Summary 19.3
▶ Spanish Audio Summary 19.3

SECTION 3

READ TO DISCOVER
1. How did the Chinese Communists gain control of China?
2. What factors led to the escalation of the conflict in Korea?
3. What were the domestic and international effects of the Korean War?
4. What methods did President Eisenhower use to promote U.S. interests abroad?

DEFINE
brinkmanship

IDENTIFY
Chiang Kai-shek
Mao Zedong
Kim Il Sung
Syngman Rhee
Douglas MacArthur
Dwight D. Eisenhower
Central Intelligence Agency
Nikita Khrushchev
U-2 incident

▶ WHY IT MATTERS TODAY

North and South Korea remain divided but continue to look for ways to have a closer relationship. Use **CNNfyi.com** or other **current events** sources to find out about the current relationship between the two countries. Record your findings in your journal.

CNNfyi.com

The Cold War Turns Hot

 EYEWITNESSES TO History "The responsibility for the failure of our foreign policy in the Far East rests squarely with the White House and the Department of State. . . . Our diplomats and their advisers . . . lost sight of our tremendous stake in a non-Communist China. . . . This House must now assume the responsibility of preventing the onrushing tide of communism from engulfing all of Asia."

—John F. Kennedy, speech to the U.S. House of Representatives, 1949

U.S. representative John F. Kennedy of Massachusetts expressed his dismay that Communists in China had taken over the city of Beijing in 1949. Like most Americans, Kennedy feared that a Communist victory in China would allow communism to spread throughout Asia.

Chinese Communist troops enter Shanghai.

Communist Victory in China

Tensions over the spread of communism came to a head in China. In the early 1900s, revolutionary forces had attempted to overthrow the Qing imperial dynasty. The revolution of 1911 left China an unstable republic. Upset with how the republic was run and inspired by the Bolshevik Revolution, some Chinese students established the Chinese Communist Party. By the mid-1920s a civil war had erupted between Nationalist and Communist forces. **Chiang Kai-shek** (also known as Jiang Jieshi) led the Kuomintang (KWOH-min-TANG), or Nationalist Party, against the Chinese Communists. Chiang's war with the Communists kept him from devoting his full attention to Japanese aggression. During World War II, the Communists and the Nationalists cooperated to resist Japanese attacks.

At war's end, the conflict resumed. The Communists had prevented Japan from controlling all of northwest China. There Communist Party leader **Mao Zedong** made reforms that gave land to peasants. This and their fight against the Japanese won additional support for the Communists and increased army recruits.

The United States did not want China to become a communist country. During and after World War II, the United States sent economic and military aid, including troops, to China to unite the country under the Nationalists. President Truman sent General George C. Marshall to China in 1945 to arrange a truce between the warring parties, but neither Chiang nor Mao would compromise.

Opposition to Chiang mounted, and Mao's forces gained control of most of the country by 1949. Realizing defeat, Chiang and his army retreated to the island of Taiwan, off the coast of southeast China. The Chinese Communists established the People's Republic of China. The United States rejected this new government, however, and continued to recognize the Nationalists as China's legal government.

✔ **READING CHECK: Sequencing** Following what order of events did China become a communist country? **1911—revolution results in republic; mid-1920s—civil war between Nationalists and Communists; post–World War II—conflict resumes; 1949—Communists gain control**

TEACH OBJECTIVE 1

ALL LEVELS: To help students understand how Chinese Communists gained control of China, copy the following graphic organizer on the chalkboard, omitting the italicized answers. Have each student complete it. Ask volunteers to share their answers with the class. Then ask students whether the Chinese Communists led a revolution that had popular support. (*Students might suggest that the Communists' resistance against the Japanese, coupled with land reforms, won them popular support.*) To conclude, lead a class discussion about whether the United States has the right to oppose a revolution that is supported by the majority of a country's residents. **English Language Learners**

CHINESE COMMUNISTS GAIN CONTROL OF CHINA

unstable republic established in 1911
↓
civil war between Nationalist and Communist forces
↓
Nationalists and Communists cooperation to resist Japanese
↓
most of China under Mao's control by 1949; retreat of Chiang's forces to Taiwan
↓
establishment of People's Republic of China

The Korean War Begins

During the 1940s political tensions were also increasing in Korea, a peninsula jutting southward from the northeast corner of China. Japan had ruled Korea from 1910 to 1945 but had been driven out by Soviet and U.S. troops at the end of World War II. In 1945 the Allies divided Korea into two zones. Soviet forces occupied the northern zone, and U.S. troops held the southern zone.

A divided Korea. The division was meant to be temporary, but Cold War tensions cemented it. In 1948 North Korea and South Korea set up separate governments. Communist North Korea, led by **Kim Il Sung**, became known as the Democratic People's Republic of Korea. South Korea, under President **Syngman Rhee** (SING-muhn REE), called itself the Republic of Korea.

The United States did not want economically unstable South Korea to fall to the Communists. The U.S. government built up the South Korean army. By 1949 both the United States and the Soviet Union had pulled their troops out of Korea. The pullout left the two Korean armies facing each other tensely across the border at the 38th parallel.

After repeated clashes, North Korea invaded South Korea on June 25, 1950. The UN Security Council called for an immediate cease-fire. At the time the Soviet Union was boycotting the Security Council over its refusal to admit Communist China. Therefore, the Soviet delegate was not on hand to veto the UN resolution. On June 27, President Truman pledged U.S. support for South Korea. That same day, the Security Council adopted a U.S.-sponsored resolution branding North Korea an "aggressor" and calling on UN members to come to South Korea's defense. Truman later explained, "I felt certain that if South Korea was allowed to fall, Communist leaders would be emboldened [encouraged] to override nations closer to our own shores."

Bitter fighting. Truman ordered U.S. forces into action under the command of General **Douglas MacArthur**, who was the U.S. Army's Far East commander. Truman also ordered the U.S. Seventh Fleet to protect Taiwan. Although 15 other UN members contributed monetary and military support, the United States and South Korea played the major role in the Korean War. At first North Korean forces with their Soviet-made weapons were overwhelming. The U.S. and South Korean troops fell back. One soldier recalled his first encounter with the North Korean army.

 History Makers Speak

❝Someone fired a green flare, and [the enemy] saw us. . . . They were right on top of us . . . firing down on us. . . . Some colonel—don't know who—said, 'Get out the best way you can.' . . . All day and night we ran like antelopes. We didn't know our officers. They didn't know us. We lost everything we had.❞

—Sergeant Raymond Remp, quoted in *The Crucial Decade—And After*, by Eric F. Goldman

By September the North Koreans had overrun nearly all of South Korea. The U.S. and South Korean forces were backed into an area around the port city of Pusan.

INTERPRETING THE VISUAL RECORD

The Korean War. Composed primarily of U.S. troops, UN forces scaled Korea's mountainous landscape to advance against Communist forces. Many U.S. soldiers received the Korean service medal shown. ***Based on this photograph, what difficulties do you think U.S. soldiers faced during the conflict?***

Analyzing Primary Sources

Identifying Points of View
What emotions does Remp convey in this quotation?
fear, loss, and uncertainty

PEOPLE IN HISTORY

Syngman Rhee and Kim Il Sung. Syngman Rhee was in his seventies when he became president of South Korea. A strong anticommunist and advocate of Korean independence, Rhee had spent more than 30 years in the United States as a political exile. Kim Il Sung was in his mid-thirties when he became premier of communist North Korea. As a guerrilla fighter in the 1930s, he had opposed the Japanese occupation of Korea. Kim had received training in the Soviet Union and was the leader of a special Korean unit of the Soviet army in World War II.

CRITICAL THINKING How might the goals of Syngman and Kim have been similar?

ANSWER: Students might suggest that each wanted to reunite Korea.

VISUAL RECORD ANSWER

Students might suggest that soldiers had to carry bulky equipment over difficult terrain.

LEVEL 1: Pair students and have them create annotated time lines showing the events leading to the escalation of the conflict in Korea. (*Time lines should include: 1945—Allies divide Korea into two zones; 1948—North and South Korea set up separate governments; 1949—the United States and the Soviet Union pull their troops out of Korea; 1949–50—North and South Korean armies face off at the 38th parallel and engage in repeated clashes; June 1950—North Korea invades South Korea, the UN Security Council brands North Korea an "aggressor," and Truman pledges U.S. support for South Korea.*) To conclude, read aloud President Truman's quotation on the previous page and Jou En-lai's quotation on this page. Ask students what these statements reveal about why the United States and China increased their involvement in the Korean conflict. (*Students might suggest that the United States was motivated by a concern about the worldwide spread of communism, while the Chinese were concerned that anticommunist sentiments would lead the United States to invade China.*) **English Language Learners, Cooperative Learning**

HISTORY MAKERS SPEAK

Leonard Korgie in *The Korean War*

China's Entry into the Korean War. China's intervention in the Korean War came as an unpleasant surprise to many U.S. troops. Leonard Korgie was a U.S. Army private in North Korea in late 1950. He recalled the effect that China's entry had on his infantry unit: "We slept soundly that night in a dry, cozy, well-built schoolhouse. Next morning we received hot chow—pancakes and coffee. Heck, North Korea was all right. Things were definitely looking up. . . . [Then,] around 9:00 in the morning, we were ordered to saddle up, we were moving again. This time it would be south! . . . We'd have to move fast or we stood a chance of being cut off. The Chinese were in North Korea in force."

ACTIVITY: Ask students to locate other sources on the Korean War and use them to evaluate the validity of this quotation.

MAP ANSWER

into North Korea north of the 41st parallel

On September 15, 1950, MacArthur launched a counterattack. Coming ashore at Inch'ŏn, MacArthur's forces swept inland and recaptured Seoul (SOHL), South Korea's capital. At the same time, a well-equipped UN army attacked from the south. North Koreans surrendered by the thousands. Others fled north across the 38th parallel with UN forces in hot pursuit. By late October the UN army was approaching the Yalu River, the boundary between North Korea and China.

The tide soon turned again. Late in November, China entered the war on North Korea's side, sending some 300,000 troops across the Yalu. Chinese foreign minister Jou En-lai (JOH EN-LY) explained why China had intervened.

"The U.S. imperialists have adopted a hostile attitude towards us . . . while paying lip service to nonaggression and nonintervention. From the information we got, they wanted to calm China first and after occupying North Korea, they will come to attack China."

—Jou En-lai, *The Selected Works of Zhou Enlai*

Outnumbered and with their troops stretched dangerously thin, the UN forces fell back. After desperate fighting and heavy losses in the cold winter, MacArthur's troops finally established a defensive line near the 38th parallel.

✔ **READING CHECK: Analyzing Information** Why did the conflict in Korea escalate? North Korea invaded South Korea. The UN responded. The United States sent troops.

Ending the Korean War

With China involved, General MacArthur called for a major expansion of the war. He proposed to blockade China's coast, bomb its interior, and "unleash" Chiang's Nationalist forces to invade mainland China. The plan sparked fierce debate. Supporters said it would bring victory in Korea and overthrow the Chinese Communists. Opponents argued that an attack on China could bring the Soviet Union into the conflict.

The Korean War, 1950–1953

Interpreting Maps Fearing that UN forces would cross the Yalu River into Manchuria, the Chinese entered the war and invaded Korea.

? THE WORLD IN SPATIAL TERMS How far north of the 38th parallel did UN forces advance?

- ➡ UN forces
- ➡ Communist forces (Chinese, North Korean)

USSR
CHINA
42° N
Ch'ŏngjin
MANCHURIA
Ch'osan
Yalu River
Farthest UN advance, Nov. 1950
40° N
Hŭngnam
NORTH KOREA
SEA OF JAPAN
P'yŏngyang
Armistice line, July 1953
Kaesŏng
P'anmunjŏm
38th parallel—boundary set by Allies after World War II
Seoul
Inch'ŏn
UN landings, Sept. 1950
SOUTH KOREA
38° N
Farthest Chinese/North Korean advance, Jan. 1951
36° N
Taegu
YELLOW SEA
Pusan
Farthest North Korean advance, Sept. 1950
Korea Strait
34° N
0 50 100 Miles
0 50 100 Kilometers
Conic Projection
126° E 128° E 130° E

Conflict between Truman and MacArthur. President Truman strongly opposed MacArthur's plan. He did not want the war in Korea to lead to another world war. MacArthur, however, refused to accept the Korean War as a limited conflict. Publicly criticizing the president, MacArthur appealed to Republican leaders in Congress. He also delivered an ultimatum to the enemy in which he demanded unconditional surrender. The demand upset Truman's plans for peace negotiations. As commander in chief of the military, Truman removed the general from his post in April 1951. Many Americans opposed this move and gave MacArthur a hero's welcome upon his return to the United States. Americans spoke out against Truman's actions, booing the president during his public appearances.

By the summer of 1951 the war had settled into a stalemate. Bitter fighting continued, but little territory changed hands. Combat in Korea's mountainous terrain became frustrating as the American death toll mounted. The conflict became a major issue in the 1952 presidential election.

The election of 1952. As 1952 began, President Truman found himself confronted with a series of problems. The Korean War had come to a bloody stalemate, and peace talks were making little progress. Having served as president for almost two full terms, Truman decided not to run again. Republicans saw their chance to break the Democrats' 20-year hold on the White House. They chose popular World War II hero General **Dwight D. Eisenhower** as their presidential candidate. Conservative senator Richard M. Nixon of California served as his running mate.

The Democrats selected Governor Adlai Stevenson of Illinois as their candidate and John Sparkman as his running mate. Stevenson defended Truman's foreign and domestic policies. However, many voters saw him as an intellectual who was out of touch with the common people. Some jokingly referred to Stevenson as an "egghead"—"someone with more brains than hair."

Stevenson also could not match Eisenhower's patriotic appeal. Eisenhower's warmth, vitality, and self-confidence reassured voters that the United States would remain strong throughout the Cold War. The upbeat campaign slogan "I Like Ike" reflected his popularity. Eisenhower promised to resist communism and to end the Korean War. A triumphant Eisenhower received 55 percent of the popular vote and swept the electoral vote 442 to 89.

The war ends. The new president kept his promise to end the war. Eisenhower used military force to get peace negotiations moving. He stepped up bombing raids on North Korea in May 1953 and dropped hints that he would use nuclear weapons, if necessary, to end the conflict.

On July 27, 1953, negotiators agreed to an armistice. Korea was divided into two nations roughly at the 38th parallel—the same dividing line as before the war. Some Americans questioned whether this outcome justified U.S. losses—some 54,000 dead and 103,000 wounded. More than 1.5 million Koreans and Chinese had also died.

✔ **READING CHECK: Drawing Conclusions** How did the Korean War affect domestic U.S. politics? Truman became unpopular after removing MacArthur. Eisenhower won the 1952 election.

Research on the ROM

Free Find:
Douglas MacArthur

After reading more about Douglas MacArthur on the **Holt Researcher CD-ROM,** write a short essay that hypothesizes how MacArthur's military experiences might have led him to develop his strategy for the Korean conflict.

INTERPRETING THE VISUAL RECORD

Eisenhower. Presidential candidate Dwight D. Eisenhower campaigns in Manhasset, New York, in 1952. *What evidence of Eisenhower's popularity is there in this picture?*

TEACH OBJECTIVE 3

![flag icon] **LEVEL 1:** Lead students in a discussion about the domestic and international effects of the Korean War. *(Students should note that MacArthur's removal and the rising number of casualties in Korea made Truman and the Democrats unpopular, while Eisenhower's World War II war record, patriotic appeal, and promise to end the Korean War made him an extremely popular candidate. International effects included millions of deaths but the borders of North and South Korea remained almost unchanged.)* Then pair students and have them create campaign slogans—both for Stevenson and for Eisenhower—that focus on the Korean War.
English Language Learners, Cooperative Learning

LEVELS 2 AND 3: Tell students to imagine that they are television news commentators on the eve of the 1952 elections. Organize students into triads and have each triad create a script for a television news discussion about the potential international and domestic effects of the Korean War. *(See the Level 1 lesson for the correct effects.)* Have each triad conduct its discussion for the class. **Cooperative Learning**

GLOBAL RELATIONS

Nonalignment. Some political leaders resisted pressures to ally with either the Soviet Union or the United States. Jawaharlal Nehru, India's prime minister from 1947 to 1964, distanced his country from the Cold War as much as possible. Nehru initiated a foreign policy of nonalignment, or a refusal to take sides with either the United States or the Soviet Union. Many countries, particularly in Asia and Africa, declared their own nonalignment policies during the late 1950s and the 1960s.

CRITICAL THINKING How might a policy of nonalignment have benefited some nations during the Cold War?

ANSWER: Students might suggest that it enabled some nations to receive economic aid from both the United States and the Soviet Union during the Cold War.

The American Nation VIDEO PROGRAM

MacArthur in Korea;
Teacher's Guide, pp. 193–94

Search 46063, Play to 48003
Videodisc 2, Side A

Play   Pause

See *Teacher's Guide* for Spanish barcode.

PRESIDENTIAL *Lives*

1890–1969
In Office 1953–1961

Dwight D. Eisenhower

After graduating from the U.S. Military Academy at West Point in the lower half of his class, Dwight D. Eisenhower began his army career slowly. When the United States entered World War I, he hoped to be put in command of a tank battalion. Although he was scheduled to command a tank unit in the spring of 1919, the Germans surrendered before Eisenhower saw any action. Eisenhower went on to graduate from command and general staff school at the top of his class. He rose quickly in rank.

Eisenhower incorporated other people's expertise into the decisions he made. This contributed greatly to his many successes as a World War II general and as president. "No man can be a Napoleon in modern war," the president once said. "I don't believe this government was set up to be operated by anyone acting alone." Discussing the power of the presidency, Eisenhower told friends, "Some people think there is a lot of power and glory attached to the job. On the contrary, the very workings of a democratic system see to it that the job has very little power."

U.S. 6c POSTAGE

DWIGHT D. EISENHOWER

These Iranians are demonstrating to show their support for the return of the shah, Mohammad Reza Pahlavi.

Fighting Communism Abroad

The Eisenhower administration viewed nuclear arms and technology as crucial to ending the expansion of communism. Secretary of State John Foster Dulles called for the liberation of all nations that had fallen under Soviet control since 1945. To fulfill this goal, the United States would have to confront Communist aggression and not back down—even if that meant going all the way to the brink of war. "The ability to get to the verge [brink] without getting into war is the necessary art," Dulles said. This policy of **brinkmanship** rested on the threat of massive retaliation, including the use of nuclear weapons.

Eisenhower proved less confrontational than Dulles's policy might have suggested. Instead, he pursued U.S. goals with more covert, or secret, means and through diplomacy. He used the newly created **Central Intelligence Agency** (CIA) to gather strategic information and pursue his Cold War goals.

Covert war and the CIA. Eisenhower tested his covert approach to the Cold War in Iran. Shortly after coming to power in 1951, Iranian premier Mohammad Mosaddeq (MAWS-ad-dek) nationalized British-owned oil fields in Iran. After Eisenhower took office he suspended aid to Iran. Eisenhower also authorized a covert action by the CIA to organize a military coup against the Iranian leader. The plan succeeded. Mosaddeq was arrested and replaced with the young pro-American shah of Iran, Mohammad Reza Pahlavi (RAY-zah pah-HLAHV-ee). Eisenhower achieved his goal of removing Mosaddeq, but this interference in Iranian affairs provoked anti-American feelings in that country.

In 1954 Eisenhower ordered a covert action in Guatemala. That year the democratically elected Guatemalan president, Jacobo Arbenz Guzmán, took possession of uncultivated sections of Guatemala's largest plantations in order to redistribute land among the rural poor.

Suspecting Arbenz of being sympathetic to communism, Eisenhower called on the CIA to gather a small army to oust him. The CIA-led forces bombed the capital in June 1954 and installed a new pro-U.S. government, which quickly reversed Arbenz's reform program. U.S. intervention in Guatemala stirred up bitter resentment throughout Latin America.

TEACH OBJECTIVE 4

 LEVEL 1: Pair students and have them draw political cartoons with written captions about the methods that President Eisenhower used to promote U.S. interests abroad. *(Students should depict Eisenhower using covert means—as he did in Guatemala and Iran—and diplomatic means—as he did when he issued the Eisenhower Doctrine and when he refused to support Hungarian rebels.)* Display students' cartoons around the classroom.

English Language Learners, Cooperative Learning

LEVEL 2: Tell students to imagine that they are writing books about U.S. foreign policy during the Eisenhower administration. Ask each student to write a detailed outline for a chapter about the various methods that Eisenhower used to promote U.S. interests abroad. *(See the Level 1 lesson for the correct methods.)* Ask volunteers to share their outlines with the class.

LEVEL 3: Have each student write a song about the methods that President Eisenhower used to promote U.S. interests abroad. *(See the Level 1 lesson for the correct methods.)* Ask volunteers to read or perform their songs for the class. Students may wish to include their songs in their portfolios.

 HOMEWORK *Distribute Cartoon 26, Brinkmanship, from **American History Political Cartoons**. Have each student study the cartoon and complete the accompanying lessons.*

The Suez crisis. In some cases, Eisenhower used diplomacy rather than covert actions to influence foreign policy. In 1955, after the U.S. government withdrew an offer to finance a large dam in Egypt, Egyptian leader Gamal Abdel Nasser nationalized the Suez Canal. This presented many political problems, including a threat to the Western oil trade. Egypt also refused to allow ships bound for Israel to pass through the canal. Late in October 1956, Israel launched an attack into Egyptian territory toward the Suez Canal. Britain and France seized the Mediterranean end of the waterway a few days later. The Soviet Union threatened war if the three nations did not withdraw from Egypt at once.

Eisenhower supported a UN resolution that called for an immediate cease-fire and the withdrawal of the invading troops. Grudgingly, Britain, France, and Israel withdrew their forces, and the crisis eased. The Soviet Union's support of Egypt during the Suez crisis led to a friendlier relationship between the Soviet Union and Arab nations. Seeking to counter Soviet influence in the Middle East, the president issued the Eisenhower Doctrine in January 1957. Eisenhower offered military aid to any Middle Eastern nation seeking help in resisting Communist aggression.

Uprising in Eastern Europe. While the Suez crisis unfolded, an equally dangerous situation was developing in Eastern Europe. In February 1956 Soviet leader **Nikita Khrushchev** (KROOSH-chawf) stunned political observers by publicly accusing his predecessor, Joseph Stalin—who had died in 1953—of having committed many ruthless crimes. Observers hoped that this move signaled a new era of reform in the Soviet Union and Eastern Europe. Later in 1956, Polish reformers tested Khrushchev by calling for greater political freedom.

Inspired by Poland's boldness, thousands of Hungarians took to the streets in late October to demand reform. Moderates seized control of the government and called for a Western-style democracy and for Hungary's secession from the Warsaw Pact. Khrushchev responded with swift force. On November 4, heavily armed Soviet troops moved into Budapest, the Hungarian capital, and crushed the revolt within days. A new pro-Soviet government imposed martial law and executed or imprisoned the rebel leaders.

Throughout their struggle, the Hungarian rebels pleaded for help from the West. Eisenhower feared that U.S. intervention in Eastern Europe would lead to all-out nuclear war with the Soviet Union. He condemned the Soviets' actions but refused to aid the rebels. He did help ease immigration laws to allow more Eastern European refugees into the United States, however. As a result, some 40,000 Hungarians fled to the United States after the uprising.

To some observers, Eisenhower's lack of support for the Hungarian uprising indicated a retreat from Dulles's talk of liberating Soviet-dominated countries. However, most of the American public supported Eisenhower, whom they re-elected by a landslide against Adlai Stevenson in November 1956.

The Nuclear Threat, 1955–1960

Estimated Size of Nuclear-Weapon Stockpiles

Legend:
- United States
- Soviet Union

Years: 1955, 1956, 1957, 1958, 1959, 1960

Source: *Nuclear Weapons Databook*

Interpreting Graphs With the discovery of atomic power, the competition for superiority between the United States and the Soviet Union spilled over into a nuclear arms race.

? Skills Assessment In which year was the gap between the stockpiles of the United States and the Soviet Union the greatest?

GRAPH ANSWER
1960

SECTION REVIEW 3 ANSWERS

1. Define
- brinkmanship, p. 576

2. Identify
- Chiang Kai-shek, p. 572
- Mao Zedong, p. 572
- Kim Il Sung, p. 573
- Syngman Rhee, p. 573
- Douglas MacArthur, p. 573
- Dwight D. Eisenhower, p. 575
- Central Intelligence Agency, p. 576
- Nikita Khrushchev, p. 577
- U-2 incident, p. 578

REVIEW

Have students complete the **Section 3 Review** on p. 578.

ASSESS

Have students complete **Daily Quiz 19.3**. As **Alternative Assessment**, you may want to use the political cartoon or the television script in this section's lessons.

RETEACH

Have students complete **Main Idea Activity for English Language Learners and Special-Needs Students 19.3**. Then organize students into four groups. Have each group write sentences to identify each of the key terms, people, and places for Section 3. Collect groups' sentences and use them to quiz the class. **English Language Learners, Cooperative Learning**

EXTEND

Have students locate and use primary and secondary sources to conduct further research on the political and constitutional issues involved in the conflict between President Truman and General MacArthur over the escalation of the war in Korea. Have each student write an analytical essay based on his or her research. **Block Scheduling**

3. China—gave economic and military aid to Nationalists, recognized the Nationalist government in Taiwan; Korea—gave military aid to South Korea, participated in Korean War; Guatemala—sponsored forces that overthrew Guatemala's suspected pro-communist government; Egypt—issued Eisenhower Doctrine

4a. Nationalists retreated to the island of Taiwan and the Chinese Communists established the People's Republic of China.

b. Answers will vary. Students might suggest that the events in Asia helped Eisenhower win the 1952 presidential election.

c. effective—established pro-U.S. governments in Iran and Guatemala, helped end the Korean War and the Suez crisis; new problems—stirred up anti-American feelings in Iran and Latin America, ineffective strategy when Soviets invaded Hungary

5. Answers will vary but articles should explain that the fall of China caused many Americans to worry that communism would continue to spread throughout Asia, and thus encouraged U.S. participation in the Korean War.

Soviet leader Nikita Khrushchev (center) studies a turkey for photographers during his goodwill tour of the United States.

A Brief Thaw in the Cold War

In the late 1950s, the United States and the Soviet Union moved to improve their diplomatic relations. Vice President Richard M. Nixon visited the Soviet Union in 1959, and Premier Khrushchev then came to the United States. Touring Iowa farms, Pittsburgh steel plants, and Hollywood movie studios, the jovial Khrushchev charmed the American media. He and Eisenhower agreed to meet at a summit conference in Paris the following year to discuss arms reductions.

In May 1960, just before the summit was to begin, Khrushchev announced that an American U-2—a high-altitude spy plane—had been shot down over the Soviet Union. At first U.S. officials insisted that it was a weather-research plane that had strayed off course. However, Francis Gary Powers, the captured pilot, admitted he had been on a spying mission.

Khrushchev refused to proceed with the summit unless the United States halted such spying missions and apologized for past flights. Eisenhower promised that the U-2 flights would stop, but he did not apologize. Khrushchev refused to meet with Eisenhower again. The **U-2 incident** caused the brief thaw in the Cold War to come to an abrupt end.

✔ **READING CHECK: Finding the Main Idea** How did President Eisenhower fight communism abroad? He pursued the policy of brinkmanship and used the CIA in covert actions.

SECTION 3 REVIEW

1. Define and explain:
brinkmanship

2. Identify and explain:
Chiang Kai-shek
Mao Zedong
Kim Il Sung
Syngman Rhee
Douglas MacArthur
Dwight D. Eisenhower
Central Intelligence Agency
Nikita Khrushchev
U-2 incident

3. Categorizing Copy the graphic organizer below. Use it to explain how the United States attempted to slow the spread of communism.

Communist Threat In:	U.S. Reaction
China	
Korea	
Guatemala	
Egypt	

Homework Practice Online
keyword: SE3 HP19

4. **Finding the Main Idea**

a. How did a civil war between Nationalists and Communists in China lead to the creation of the People's Republic of China?

b. How did conflicts in Asia affect politics in the United States?

c. In what ways were President Eisenhower's covert operations and diplomatic strategies effective? What new problems did they present?

5. **Writing and Critical Thinking**

Making Generalizations Imagine that you are a State Department official. Write a press release explaining how the fall of China to the Communists encouraged further U.S. military action in Korea.
Consider:
• how the fall of China related to U.S. containment policy
• how the containment policy influenced U.S. actions in Korea
• what role Communist China played in the Korean War

SECTION 4

The Cold War at Home

"Beware, commies, spies, traitors, and foreign agents! Captain America, all loyal, free men behind him, is looking for you."

—Captain America, quoted in *The Twentieth Century*, by Howard Zinn

Captain America comic book

Comic book hero Captain America was enormously popular during the 1950s. He reassured Americans that he and other loyal citizens would rid the country of the communist threat within its borders. Concerned about the spread of communism abroad, many Americans also began to worry about Communists infiltrating the U.S. government, the media, and schools. Americans were afraid that leaving Communists unchecked both abroad and within the United States would threaten American values of democracy and freedom. This fear led to a string of public inquiries, loyalty oaths, and trials of suspected Communists and traitors. In addition to communism, Americans also feared nuclear war.

Cold War Fears

The Cold War had a major impact on the United States. As a result of Cold War pressures, the nation streamlined its military to allow for peacetime rearmament. In July 1947 Congress replaced the War Department with the Department of Defense, combining the leadership of the army, navy, and air force under the Joint Chiefs of Staff. In addition, Congress created the **National Security Council** (NSC) to advise the president on strategic matters. Congress also established the CIA to gather strategic military and political information overseas.

Another Red Scare. International Cold War tensions sparked new fears of communism at home. Although President Truman opposed communism abroad, some Republicans accused him of allowing Communists in the U.S. government. Truman responded to the charges by setting up the Loyalty Review Board in 1947 to investigate all federal employees. By the end of 1951, more than 20,000 federal workers had been investigated, some 2,000 had resigned, and more than 300 had been deemed "security risks" and fired.

Meanwhile, Congress cracked down on the Communist Party in the United States. Leading the fight was the **House Un-American Activities Committee** (HUAC), which had originally been established in 1938 to investigate fascist groups in the United States. HUAC questioned the political ties of members of peace organizations, liberal political groups, and labor unions. In 1947 HUAC responded to charges that Hollywood was full of Communists by holding hearings to investigate people in the movie industry. A group of California film directors and writers known as the **Hollywood Ten** went to jail rather than answer HUAC's questions. They were blacklisted—denied work—from the film industry and saw their careers destroyed. Author Bernard De Voto described the fear of blacklisting during this

ALL LEVELS: To help students understand the U.S. government's actions to limit communism and how these actions affected Americans' everyday lives during the Cold War, copy the following graphic organizer onto the chalkboard, omitting the italicized answers. Have each student complete the organizer. Ask students to share their answers with the class. Lead the class in a discussion about how the loss of these rights might affect Americans' everyday lives.

English Language Learners

GOVERNMENT ACTIONS TO LIMIT COMMUNISM AND THE RESULTS

Internal Security Act—required Communist Party members and organizations to register with the federal government and imposed controls on immigrants suspected of being Communist sympathizers

↓

created public hysteria about Communist infiltration and led to the infringement of many Americans' civil rights

Loyalty Review Board—investigation of more than 20,000 federal employees, resignation of some 2,000 federal employees, and firing of 300 others

HUAC—investigation of peace organizations, liberal political groups, labor unions, the movie industry, and individuals accused of spying; resulted in blacklisting, hysteria, and scaring people away from unions and progressive groups

---

THAT'S INTERESTING!

For decades following his release from prison, Alger Hiss continued to assert publicly that he had never been a Communist spy. In 1992 Russian historian D. A. Volkogonov announced that a search of the former Soviet government's military intelligence archives had revealed nothing to dispute Hiss's claim. Other scholars questioned the comprehensiveness of Volkogonov's investigation, however, and in 1996 the release of secret Soviet cables from World War II provided new evidence that suggested Hiss was indeed guilty. Hiss died that same year.

AMERICAN LETTERS ANSWERS

(for p. 581)

1. suburban life and anxiety about nuclear war

2. by discussing the distance of the travelers from Earth, and the "long and many" days of space travel

3. important but hopelessly doomed in *The Martian Chronicles*; remote and almost unrealistic in "The Martian Way"

VISUAL RECORD ANSWER

Students might point out that the protesters are holding picket signs with the names of the Hollywood Ten.

INTERPRETING THE VISUAL RECORD

The Hollywood Ten. Protesters demonstrate against HUAC's investigation of alleged communist activities of Americans in the film industry. *How are these activists protesting the actions of HUAC?*

The trial and conviction of Julius and Ethel Rosenberg for spying and giving away U.S. atomic secrets shocked many Americans.

---

era. He explained that "gossip, rumor, slander, backbiting, malice and drunken invention, . . . when it makes the head-lines, shatters the reputations of innocent and harmless people. . . . We are shocked. We are scared."

The hysteria generated by HUAC spread quickly. The Women's International League for Peace and Freedom, one group that spoke out against HUAC, argued in 1949 that the hearings violated democratic rights.

> **History Makers Speak**
>
> **"Fully recognizing the danger of fascist and communist totalitarianism, the League believes that such forces can be best opposed by open discussion and by the strengthening of our own democratic procedures, rather than by attempts at direct control."**
>
> —Women's International League for Peace and Freedom

Because of the League's support for progressive causes, the Federal Bureau of Investigation (FBI) investigated the national organization and several of its local chapters. The investigation scared many potential members away. HUAC investigations had a similar effect on labor unions and many liberal political groups.

The search for spies. HUAC also investigated individuals accused of spying for the Soviets. In 1948 Whittaker Chambers, a former member of the Communist Party, accused **Alger Hiss** of being a Communist spy. Chambers told HUAC that Hiss, a New Deal lawyer who had joined the State Department in 1936, had given him secret State Department documents to pass on to the Soviets.

Hiss denied the charges, but persistent questioning by HUAC member Richard M. Nixon, a young Republican member of Congress from California, revealed apparent inconsistencies in Hiss's testimony. When Hiss sued Chambers for slander, Chambers produced microfilmed copies of documents he had kept hidden in a pumpkin at his home. These so-called pumpkin papers revealed evidence that indicated Hiss had lied to HUAC. In 1950 Hiss was convicted of perjury, or lying under oath, and sentenced to five years in prison.

Another notorious spy case also helped fuel domestic fears of communism. In 1951 a U.S. court convicted two Americans, **Julius and Ethel Rosenberg**, of providing the Soviet Union with atomic-energy secrets during World War II. Defenders of the Rosenbergs claimed that the two were innocent victims of anti-communist hysteria. Despite worldwide protests, the Rosenbergs were executed in June 1953.

Other anticommunist measures included the **Internal Security Act**, passed in 1950. The act required Communist Party members and organizations to register with the federal government. It also imposed strict controls on immigrants suspected of being Communist sympathizers. The anticommunist hysteria of these years shattered many lives and careers. Writer Abe Burrows described his experiences after being blacklisted. "My Americanism being under suspicion is very painful to me, not just painful economically but painful as it is to a guy who loves his country."

✔ **READING CHECK: Analyzing Information** How did the U.S. government try to limit communism at home? **Congress created the National Security Council and HUAC and passed the Internal Security Act.**

AMERICAN Letters

Science Fiction

During the 1950s, science fiction became popular. Science-fiction literature often reflects Americans' fear of or interest in technology, space exploration, and nuclear warfare. Ray Bradbury's novel The Martian Chronicles *(1950) describes the colonization of Mars by Earthlings while Earth is destroyed by nuclear war. Isaac Asimov discusses the adventures and isolation of space travel in his 1952 short story "The Martian Way."*

from *The Martian Chronicles*
by Ray Bradbury

Ray Bradbury's novel

They all came out and looked at the sky that night. They left their suppers or their washing up or their dressing for the show and they came out upon their now-not-quite-as-new porches and watched the green star of Earth there. It was a move without conscious effort; they all did it, to help them understand the news they had heard on the radio a moment before. There was Earth and there the coming war, and there hundreds of thousands of mothers or grandmothers or fathers or brothers or aunts or uncles or cousins. They stood on the porches and tried to believe in the existence of Earth, much as they had once tried to believe in the existence of Mars; it was a problem reversed. To all intents and purposes, Earth was now dead; they had been away from it for three or four years. Space was an anesthetic; seventy million miles of space numbed you, put memory to sleep, depopulated Earth, erased the past, and allowed these people here to go on with their work. But now, tonight, the dead were risen, Earth was reinhabited, memory awoke, a million names were spoken: What was so-and-so doing tonight on Earth? What about this one and that one? The people on the porches glanced sideways at each other's faces.

At nine o'clock Earth seemed to explode, catch fire, and burn.

from "The Martian Way"
by Isaac Asimov

Isaac Asimov's collection of short stories

At first . . . the weeks flew past . . . except for the gnawing feeling that every minute meant an additional number of thousands of miles away from all humanity. That made it worse. . . .

The days were long and many, space was empty. . . .

"Mario?" The voice that broke upon his ear phones was questioning. . . .

"Speaking," he said. . . .

"You know, I've read Earth books—"

"Grounder books, you mean." Rioz yawned.

"—and sometimes I read descriptions of people lying on grass," continued Long. "You know that green stuff like thin, long pieces of paper they have all over the ground down there, and they look up at the blue sky with clouds in it. Did you ever see any films of that?"

"Sure. It didn't attract me. It looked cold."

UNDERSTANDING LITERATURE

1. What aspects of American life in the 1950s does *The Martian Chronicles* address?
2. How does "The Martian Way" describe the isolation of space travel?
3. How important is life on Earth in these two selections?

LEVEL 1: Ask students how Senator Joseph McCarthy was able to play upon Americans' fears of communism. *(Students might explain that McCarthy tapped into fears about communism infiltrating American society and the growing power of the Soviet Union by claiming to have evidence of Communists working in the federal government and using his Senate subcommittee to question the patriotism of hundreds of government workers.)* Pair students and have them create signs to protest McCarthy's tactics. Display protest signs around the classroom.
English Language Learners, Cooperative Learning

LEVEL 2: Tell students to imagine that they are newspaper editors during the era of McCarthyism. Have each student write an editorial in which he or she describes how Senator Joseph McCarthy was able to play upon Americans' fears of communism. *(See the Level 1 lesson for the correct tactics.)* Students' editorials should also suggest ways that such situations might be prevented in the future and describe how McCarthy's activities led to violations of people's constitutional rights. Students may wish to include their editorials in their portfolios.

NOTE: To help students make meaningful connections between events in U.S. history and those in their own hometown, use the Chapter 19 **Hands-On History Activity**, Living with Nuclear Weapons.

The American Nation
VIDEO PROGRAM

Bomb Shelters; Teacher's Guide, pp. 175–76

Search 48004, Play to 49285
Videodisc 2, Side A

Play   Pause

See *Teacher's Guide* for Spanish barcode.

McCarthyism

As the Korean conflict escalated during the early 1950s, Americans' fears of communism intensified. This anxiety continued even after the war ended. Many Americans became convinced that spies and Communist sympathizers were everywhere. **Joseph McCarthy**, a U.S. senator from Wisconsin, helped fuel these suspicions. He argued that "the Communists within our borders have been more responsible for the success of communism abroad than Soviet Russia."

McCarthy's rise. Senator McCarthy came to public attention in 1950 when he claimed to have a list of known Communists who worked at the State Department. Although he never produced the list, dozens of federal employees lost their jobs after being labeled "security risks." McCarthy used his position as chairman of the Senate Permanent Subcommittee on Investigations to wage war against alleged Communist sympathizers in the federal government. With almost no supporting evidence, McCarthy questioned the patriotism—and ruined the reputations—of hundreds of government workers. Frustrated by McCarthy's lack of hard evidence, one journalist claimed, "Joe [McCarthy] couldn't find a Communist in Red Square—he didn't know Karl Marx from Groucho[Marx]." Nevertheless, many Americans, consumed by their fear of communism and the power of the Soviet Union, supported his crusade.

McCarthy's popularity and ruthlessness made many politicians wary of challenging him. One who did challenge him was **Margaret Chase Smith**, a Republican senator from Maine.

INTERPRETING THE VISUAL RECORD

McCarthyism. Senator McCarthy claimed that Communist organizations throughout the United States were plotting to overthrow the government. *How does McCarthy's style of presentation for this hearing give support to his claims?*

"I think that it is high time that we remembered that the Constitution, as amended, speaks not only of the freedom of speech but also of trial by jury instead of trial by accusation."

—Margaret Chase Smith, Declaration of Conscience

In 1950 Smith and several other senators issued the Declaration of Conscience, which condemned those who had turned the Senate into "a forum of hate and character assassination." The report never mentioned McCarthy by name, but it was clearly directed at him.

McCarthy's downfall. Few others joined in the condemnation. Even the president refused to criticize McCarthy. Most of those who did speak out came from the arts or the media. In *The Crucible* (1953), playwright Arthur Miller drew parallels between McCarthyism and the Salem witch trials of 1692. On the television program *See It Now*, newscaster Edward R. Murrow questioned McCarthy's tactics. "We cannot defend freedom abroad," Murrow cautioned, "by deserting it at home." While some viewers praised Murrow, others bombarded him with hate mail.

LEVEL 3: Organize students into small groups and have each group write a skit about how Joseph McCarthy was able to play upon Americans' fears of communism. *(See the Level 1 lesson for the correct tactics.)* Have students perform their skits for the class. **Cooperative Learning**

TEACH OBJECTIVE 3

 LEVEL 1: Pair students and have them list ways that Americans reacted to the prospect of nuclear war and the launch of *Sputnik*. *(Students might include turning toward religion, building bomb shelters, conducting air-raid drills, Civil Defense educational campaigns, the organization of SANE,*

and continued support for the arms race and space exploration.) Then have each pair create a poster that reflects one of the ways that Americans responded to the prospect of nuclear war and the launch of *Sputnik*.
English Language Learners, Cooperative Learning

LEVEL 2: Have each student create a collage that depicts how Americans reacted to the prospect of nuclear war and the launch of *Sputnik*. *(See the Level 1 lesson for the correct reactions.)* Ask volunteers to present and explain their collages to the class.

In 1954 McCarthy's congressional committee investigated charges that there were Communists in the U.S. Army. Each day a vast television audience—sometimes as many as 20 million people—tuned in to the Army-McCarthy hearings. In the circuslike proceedings, McCarthy repeatedly interrupted and ridiculed witnesses. One victim of this treatment complained that McCarthy "acted like the gangster in a B movie rubbing out someone who had got in his way."

On television, McCarthy's bullying tactics contrasted with the dignified behavior of Joseph Welch, the army's chief counsel. Soon public opinion turned against the senator. At one point, Welch criticized McCarthy for his wild charges. "Let us not assassinate this lad further, Senator. You have done enough. Have you no sense of decency, sir, at long last? Have you left no sense of decency?" The 35 days of hearings failed to produce any evidence to support McCarthy's claims. A few months later, the Senate condemned McCarthy for conduct unbecoming a senator.

✔ **READING CHECK: Summarizing** How did Senator Joseph McCarthy play upon Americans' fears of communism?
He suggested that Communists were everywhere.

Nuclear Anxiety

Increased conflict between the United States and Communists abroad plunged the Soviet Union and the United States into a race to develop ever-more-powerful nuclear weapons. This arms race contributed to Americans' fears of nuclear war. In 1950, U.S. scientists began work on a **hydrogen bomb**, or H-bomb. They claimed it would be 1,000 times more powerful than the atomic bombs dropped on Hiroshima and Nagasaki in World War II. The first U.S. test of an H-bomb in 1952 completely vaporized a small island in the Pacific. Some nine months later, the Soviet Union tested its own H-bomb. J. Robert Oppenheimer, one of the creators of the U.S. atomic bomb, urged caution in the growing arms race.

 ❝[The United States and the Soviet Union] are like two scorpions in a bottle, each capable of killing the other but only at the risk of his own life. . . . The atomic clock ticks faster and faster.❞

—J. Robert Oppenheimer, quoted in *American Chronicle*, by Lois Gordon and Alan Gordon

Religion and nuclear war. Anxiety about nuclear war caused many Americans to seek comfort. Many turned to religion. Evangelists such as **Billy Graham** attracted large audiences during the 1950s. He warned of the danger of nuclear war and urged Americans to turn to God. Church membership grew rapidly. As a result, investment in the construction of religious institutions rose from $76 million in 1946 to $868 million in 1957.

"Duck and Cover"

The fear of nuclear war greatly affected American teenagers' lives during the 1950s. Daily news of the Communists' advances and nuclear tests threw children and teenagers into a quiet panic.

Many schools implemented civil defense plans and conducted "cover drills." Teachers

These schoolchildren are performing a duck-and-cover drill.

stopped in the middle of normal classroom activities and yelled "drop" or "duck and cover" to simulate what students should do during an attack. Some schools even distributed dog tags and identification necklaces to students to identify them in case of a nuclear blast. Although well-intentioned, these measures increased the youths' fears that nuclear war was soon to come. As an adult, Mary Mackey recalled the terror she experienced during the classroom drills.

❝Obediently we would fold our bodies into that attitude [position] of prayer and supplication [worship] known only to the children of the fifties: legs folded, head between the knees, hands raised to protect the fragile, invisible nerve that floated somewhere in the blackness behind our eyes.❞

One author explained the impact of such drills on many adults who grew up during the 1950s. They "never forgot the lesson that their world could someday end in a flash of light and heat while they were crouched helplessly in gyms and basements."

LEVEL 3: Tell students to imagine that they are conducting an oral history interview with an American who lived during the 1950s. Pair students and have each pair write a transcript for an interview that focuses on how Americans reacted to the prospect of nuclear war and the launch of *Sputnik*. *(See the Level 1 lesson for the correct reactions.)* Have one student assume the role of interviewer and the other assume the role of interviewee. Have volunteers conduct their interviews for the class.
Cooperative Learning

NOTE: For an additional teaching idea, see the Chapter 19 quick survey lesson in the **Creative Teaching Strategies** handbook.

SPOTLIGHT
on American Life during the Cold War

Ask students to interview Americans who lived during the Cold War. Each student should focus his or her interview on the activities that the interviewee participated in that were related to fears of nuclear war, any personal fears about the Cold War that the interviewee may have had, and the interviewee's reaction to various Cold War–related events. Have volunteers present their transcripts or recorded interviews to the class.
Block Scheduling

---

2. Identify
- National Security Council, p. 579
- House Un-American Activities Committee, p. 579
- Hollywood Ten, p. 579
- Alger Hiss, p. 580
- Julius and Ethel Rosenberg, p. 580
- Internal Security Act, p. 580
- Joseph McCarthy, p. 582
- Margaret Chase Smith, p. 582
- Billy Graham, p. 583
- *Sputnik*, p. 585
- National Aeronautics and Space Administration, p. 585
- National Defense Act, p. 585

3. fallout shelters—construction and sale; religion—increased church membership and popularity of evangelists; government programs—Federal Civil Defense Administration campaign; space exploration—NASA

4a. generated hysteria, infringed on civil rights, undermined membership of unions and liberal political groups

b. almost none

c. Communists—by the U.S.-Soviet relationship; threat of nuclear war—by the arms race, hydrogen bomb and the dangers of nuclear fallout

5. Answers will vary but articles should relate the goals of HUAC, the spy cases, and the launch of *Sputnik* to the Red Scare.

INTERPRETING THE VISUAL RECORD

Cold War fears. The threat of nuclear war led some Americans to build bomb shelters in their yards. This booklet offered Americans advice on how to survive a nuclear war. *Do you think this shelter would protect someone during a nuclear war? Explain your answer.*

Americans' religious devotion contrasted sharply with the official atheism of the Soviet Union. Reflecting this religious zeal, Congress added the phrase "One Nation Under God" to the Pledge of Allegiance and "In God We Trust" to U.S. coins.

Calming public fears. As concerns about nuclear war grew, the U.S government launched a campaign to calm public fears. In 1951 the Federal Civil Defense Administration began a campaign to educate the public on what to do in case of a nuclear attack. Pamphlets, films, television shows, magazines, and the "Duck and Cover" program for children encouraged citizens to protect themselves. For example, one booklet encouraged Americans to be prepared.

Primary Source
"You can live through an atom bomb raid and you won't have to have a Geiger counter, protective clothing, or special training in order to do it. The secrets of survival are: KNOW THE BOMB'S TRUE DANGERS. KNOW THE STEPS YOU CAN TAKE TO ESCAPE THEM."

—*Survival Under Atomic Attack*

Nuclear fallout. While a nuclear attack remained a grim possibility, radioactive fallout—a by-product of nuclear explosions—already posed a threat. U.S. and Soviet H-bomb tests spewed tons of radioactive material into the atmosphere. H-bomb tests in the Pacific Ocean revealed the far-reaching effects of nuclear fallout. The crew of a Japanese fishing boat 85 miles away from the test site developed radiation sickness. People realized that no one would be safe in a nuclear attack. "The alternatives," one civil defense official said, "are to dig, die, or get out." No one wanted to die, and evacuation would be almost impossible. So some Americans began to dig, constructing backyard fallout shelters.

Shelter manufacturers sprang up, selling their concrete-and-steel igloos at county fairs for about $1,500. A typical shelter contained flashlights, a first-aid kit, battery radio, portable toilet, two-week supply of food—mainly canned meats and vegetables—and water.

In 1957 Congress held a hearing on the dangers of radioactive fallout. Defense officials claimed that nuclear testing was safe. Many scientists disagreed. They argued that radiation released during the tests presented a serious danger to the environment and possibly increased the risk of cancer in humans. Soon the fear of radiation led to a campaign against nuclear testing. In 1957 a group of Americans, including well-known doctor Benjamin Spock, organized the Committee for a Sane Nuclear Policy (SANE). SANE urged the United States to begin negotiations with the Soviet Union to end nuclear tests. Within a year, SANE had grown to more than 25,000 members in some 130 chapters across the country.

ASSESS

Have students complete **Daily Quiz 19.4.** As **Alternative Assessment**, you may want to use the newspaper editorial or the skit from this section's lessons.

RETEACH

Have students complete **Main Idea Activity for English Language Learners and Special-Needs Students 19.4.** Then organize students into small groups. Assign each group one of two topics: "Fear of Communism" or "Fear of Nuclear War."

Have each group create an outline of the events discussed in Section 4 that pertain to its topic. Have volunteers present their outlines to the class. Ask the class to supply any information missing from outlines.
English Language Learners, Cooperative Learning

EXTEND

Have students conduct research on one of the early satellites, such as *Sputnik* or *Explorer I.* Then have each student create a model or a poster of one of these satellites and write a short report containing technical information about the satellite. Have volunteers present their reports to the class.
Block Scheduling

Space programs. The arms race sped on, however, particularly after the Soviet Union launched *Sputnik*, the first artificial satellite, into orbit in October 1957. Weighing close to 200 pounds, the satellite was much larger than the 3.5-pound device U.S. scientists were developing. Many Americans worried that this launch proved the United States was falling behind the Soviet Union in technological development. Governor G. Mennen Williams of Michigan wrote a poem expressing the opinion of many Americans after the launch.

**"Oh little Sputnik, flying high
With made-in-Moscow beep,
You tell the world it's a Commie sky
and Uncle Sam's asleep."**

—G. Mennen Williams, quoted in "Sputnik and the Origins of the Space Age," by Roger D. Launius

The Soviet Union shocked the world again one month later. In November it launched *Sputnik II*, which had a dog aboard. The spacecraft weighed more than 1,000 pounds and orbited Earth for almost 200 days. Its primitive life-support system kept the dog alive for a few days. In January 1958 the U.S. government sent its first satellite, *Explorer I*, into orbit. The space race had begun.

President Eisenhower urged Congress to promote U.S. space technology by establishing the **National Aeronautics and Space Administration** (NASA). In 1958 Congress approved the **National Defense Education Act.** This act appropriated millions of dollars to improve education in science, mathematics, and foreign languages.

✔ **READING CHECK: Evaluating** Why was 1957 a significant year in U.S. history? 1957 was the launch of *Sputnik*. It led to the creation of NASA and to the National Defense Education Act.

"Wonder Why We're Not Keeping Pace?"

The launch of Sputnik made Americans fear they were falling behind the Soviets.

SECTION 4 REVIEW

1. Define and explain:
hydrogen bomb

2. Identify and explain:
National Security Council
House Un-American
   Activities Committee
Hollywood Ten
Alger Hiss
Julius and Ethel
   Rosenberg
Internal Security Act
Joseph McCarthy
Margaret Chase Smith
Billy Graham
Sputnik
National Aeronautics and
   Space Administration
National Defense Education Act

3. Summarizing Copy the graphic organizer below. Use it to explain how the possibility of nuclear war affected Americans' lives during the 1950s.

4. Finding the Main Idea
a. What effect did HUAC's investigations have on American society?
b. What evidence did Joseph McCarthy present to prove that Communists inside the United States did more to spread communism around the world than Communists abroad?
c. How were Americans' fears of Communists and the threat of nuclear war justified?

5. Writing and Critical Thinking
Supporting a Point of View Imagine that you are a member of HUAC. Write a report identifying why a new Red Scare has developed and how events in the 1950s have contributed to Americans' fears of communism.
Consider:
• the goals of HUAC and McCarthy's committee
• the spy cases of Alger Hiss and Julius and Ethel Rosenberg
• the launch of *Sputnik*

Homework Practice Online
keyword: SE3 HP19

Creating a Time Line
Each event should have an explanation and the correct date.

Writing a Summary
See the Reading Checks in each section for main ideas.

Identifying People and Ideas
1. war crimes trials that took place in Germany after World War II

2. postwar international organization founded to promote world peace

3. former first lady and one of the U.S. representatives to the United Nations

4. State Department official who suggested the containment policy

5. U.S. policy to "support free peoples who are resisting attempted subjugation"

6. economic aid that the United States provided to European countries after World War II

7. leader of Chinese Communists who established the People's Republic of China

8. commander of U.S. forces in the Korean War

9. U.S. senator who made unsubstantiated allegations about Communists in the federal government

10. the first artificial satellite, launched by the Soviet Union

REVIEW AND ASSESSMENT RESOURCES

TECHNOLOGY

▶ Chapter 19 Test Generator (on the One-Stop Planner)
▶ Global Skill Builder CD–ROM
▶ HRW Go site

REINFORCEMENT, REVIEW, AND ASSESSMENT

▶ Chapter 19 Review, pp. 586–87
▶ Chapter 19 Tutorial for Students, Parents, Mentors, and Peers

▶ Chapter 19 Test (Form A or B)
▶ Portfolio Activities and Alternative Assessment Handbook, Chapter 19
▶ Chapter 19 Test for English Language Learners and Special-Needs Students

REVIEW

Have students complete the **Chapter 19 Review** on pp. 586–87.

ASSESS

Use one of the chapter tests to assess students' understanding of the content. For **Alternative Assessment**, see the **Portfolio Activities and Alternative Assessment Handbook**.

Understanding Main Ideas

1. The UN helped create Israel but failed to prevent the outbreak of the Arab-Israeli War or to end that region's tensions.

2. the economic, political, and philosophical differences between the United States and the Soviet Union

3. diplomacy and covert operations

4. because many Americans were extremely fearful of communism and the power of the Soviet Union

5. by creating NASA and passing the National Defense Education Act

Reviewing Themes

1. the nations in NATO and the Warsaw Pact, East and West Germany, Greece, Guatemala, Hungary, Iran, North and South Korea, Turkey

2. the search for Communists resulted in infringement on civil rights

3. put a new premium on science and math education, contributed to the popularity of science-fiction literature, and led to widespread fears about the possibility of a nuclear attack

Thinking Critically

1. Answers will vary, but students should outline standards for membership and identify committees and mechanisms to enforce the organization's decisions.

Review

Creating a Time Line

Copy the time line below onto a sheet of paper. Complete the time line by filling in the events and dates from the chapter that you think were most significant. Pick three events and explain why you think they were significant.

1945	1950	1955	1960

Writing a Summary

Using standard grammar, spelling, sentence structure, and punctuation, write an overview of events in the chapter.

Identifying People and Ideas

Identify the following terms or individuals and explain their significance.

1. Nuremberg Trials
2. United Nations
3. Eleanor Roosevelt
4. George Kennan
5. Truman Doctrine
6. Marshall Plan
7. Mao Zedong
8. Douglas MacArthur
9. Joseph McCarthy
10. *Sputnik*

Understanding Main Ideas

SECTION 1 *(pp. 560–565)*

1. How successful was the United Nations in stabilizing the conflict between Arabs and Jews in Palestine? Explain your answer.

SECTION 2 *(pp. 566–571)*

2. What were the main causes of the Cold War?

SECTION 3 *(pp. 572–578)*

3. What strategies did President Eisenhower use to slow the spread of communism?

SECTION 4 *(pp. 579–585)*

4. Why was Senator McCarthy able to generate so much attention with his accusations?

5. How did the U.S. government respond to the launch of *Sputnik*?

Reviewing Themes

1. **Global Relations** What other countries became involved in the conflict between the United States and the Soviet Union?

2. **Government** How did the U.S. government's response to Cold War tensions lead to limitations on civil liberties?

3. **Science, Technology, and Society** How did the development of atomic technology affect daily life in the United States?

Thinking Critically

1. **Problem Solving** Imagine that you are establishing an organization to maintain world peace. How would you organize it? Why?

2. **Sequencing** How did the United States respond to Soviet expansion after World War II?

3. **Evaluating** How did the fall of China to communism in 1949 affect the Korean War in 1950?

4. **Identifying Points of View** Why did many Palestinians, Iranians, and Guatemalans view the U.S. government with hostility during the 1950s?

5. **Analyzing Information** How did the Korean War affect the domestic and international affairs of the United States?

Writing About History

Summarizing Imagine that you are a senator in the mid-1950s who opposes communism. Using the graphic organizer below, write a speech describing the threat of Communist expansion around the world.

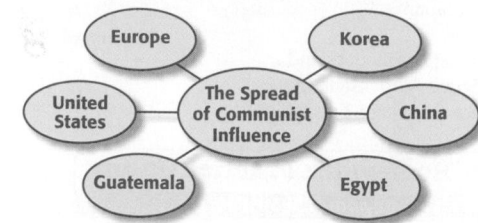

RETEACH

Organize students into small groups and have each group select one key person and one key term from each of the four sections. Then have each group create job descriptions for its key persons and newspaper headlines pertaining to its key terms. Have students read their job descriptions and headlines to the class, and have the class guess what or whom each describes.
English Language Learners, Cooperative Learning

EXTEND

Have students use the process of historical inquiry to explore recent actions taken by the United Nations. Students should locate and use a variety of primary and secondary sources in their research. Then have them write an essay describing how these actions reflect the initial mission and founding principles of the United Nations. **Block Scheduling**

Building Social Studies Skills

Interpreting the Visual Record

Study the image below. Then use it to help answer the questions that follow.

Anticommunist literature

1. How does this image portray communism in the United States?
   a. The United States under communism would benefit all Americans.
   b. Communism would have little to no effect on the United States.
   c. Communism would lead to destruction and violence.
   d. Communism would lead to massive fires in the United States.

2. What do you know about the 1950s that would lead this author to ask, "Is This Tomorrow"?

Analyzing Primary Sources

Read the following excerpt from an oral history provided by Steve McConnell, a U.S. citizen who grew up during the Cold War, and then answer the questions.

66 We went through the bomb-shelter era in the late fifties. I remember it as kind of fun. You could go into a shopping center and at the corner of the parking lot was one of these bomb shelters. Gee, that was neat. . . . But there was that sense of nagging that maybe this was more than just fun. Nothing serious was imminent [soon to come] but . . . there was talk.

We had drills in school. The alarms would go off and you'd hit the floor and put your back to the windows and cover your head. You were mostly afraid of getting hit by glass. What most of us didn't realize was that that would be the least of our problems. (Laughs.) 99

3. Which of the following statements best describes the author's point of view?
   a. Life during the Cold War was fun.
   b. Children growing up during the Cold War had no understanding of the seriousness of the situation.
   c. Bomb shelters and drills were adequate preparations for possible attack.
   d. Children had a sense that there was something more serious related to the bomb shelters and air raid drills.

4. In this excerpt McConnell is reflecting on his experiences. How might his point of view be different if he had recorded his thoughts as a child? Give specific examples.

Alternative Assessment

Building Your Portfolio

U.S. HISTORY

Global Relations

Create an annotated world map. Your map should focus on the areas and events that led to the Cold War as well as events of the Cold War in the 1950s and early 1960s. Then write five questions for other students to answer using the map.

☑ internet connect

go.hrw.com

Internet Activity: go.hrw.com
KEYWORD: SE3 AN19

Choose a topic on the Cold War to:
• research and report on the United Nations.
• create a newspaper analyzing the impact of *Sputnik* on American society.
• make an illustrated time line on the founding of Israel.

---

2. with the Truman Doctrine, the Marshall Plan, the Berlin Airlift, NATO membership, participation in the Korean War, and covert operations in Iran and Guatemala

3. by encouraging the U.S. government's fears that communism would continue to spread throughout Asia

4. Palestinians—U.S. support for Israel; Iranians and Guatemalans—U.S.-sponsored overthrows of their governments

5. led to election of first Republican president in 20 years and may have hurt the international reputation of the United States because it failed to achieve much in the war

Writing

Europe—establishment of satellite nations in Eastern Europe; Korea—establishment of communist government in North Korea, invasion of South Korea; China—Communist takeover; Egypt—support from the Soviet Union during the Suez crisis; Guatemala—seizure and redistribution of plantation land; United States—fears about communist influence

Building Social Studies Skills

1. c

2. Answers will vary but students should relate the image to the rise of Communism.

3. d

4. Answers will vary but students should mention that as a child McConnell would not have known about events to come.

🔊 LET'S GET STARTED!

Write the following term on the chalkboard: *Cold War.* Have students list everything they know about the term and the topic. *(Students might identify the Cold War as an ideological conflict between the United States and the Soviet Union and mention conflicts such as the Hungary uprising and the Suez Canal conflict.)* Ask volunteers to read their lists to the class. Then tell students that they will learn more about the defenses of the Cold War in the Unit 5 America's Geography.

TEACH AMERICA'S GEOGRAPHY— DEFENSES OF THE COLD WAR

Have each student write a few sentences about the graph and the maps in the America's Geography feature, explaining how the information presented relates to Cold War defenses. *(Students should note that the graph on federal spending reveals the high levels of defense spending during the Cold War, that the map on radar systems indicates the high number of squadrons and bombing bases and North American radar systems, and that the map on military bases displays the sheer number of bases and conflicts of the Cold War.)* **English Language Learners**

ECONOMICS

Cold War Defense.
National defense was a top priority in the 1950s. Between 1950 and 1955 the total number of military personnel doubled from some 1.4 million to almost 3 million. The amount of money spent on defense also increased.

CRITICAL THINKING How might the increase in military personnel have affected the national economy?

ANSWER: Students might suggest that the increase helped fuel economic growth.

THAT'S INTERESTING!

During the Cold War, some Americans suggested that the United States barrage the Soviet people with the products of American capitalism. One Montgomery Ward businessperson wanted to ship mail-order catalogs to the Soviet Union to display the enormous variety and availability of goods in the United States. A sociologist even suggested air-dropping pantyhose on the country.

AMERICA'S GEOGRAPHY ANSWERS

1. Most North American radar lines ran through Canada.

2. Defense spending increased dramatically during the Cold War.

Defenses of the Cold War

During the Cold War the U.S. government spent large sums of money to improve national defense. Much of this investment was in new types of technology, including the space program, which was initially run by the Defense Department. Some of the military technology developed changed Americans' daily lives. During the Cold War, for example, scientists experimented with radio waves. They improved existing radar systems—which relied on radio waves—and developed satellite technology. These experiments eventually led to the development of such everyday conveniences as the microwave oven and cable television.

▲	ICBM squadrons
⊙	Strategic Air Command bomber bases
■	Nuclear submarine shipyards
━━	ICBM early warning radar systems
▭	Ballistic missile early warning System

Radar Systems and Defenses in North America, 1959–1964

USSR · ARCTIC OCEAN · 180° · Distant Early Warning Line · 160°W · CANADA · Mid-Canada Line · PACIFIC OCEAN · Pinetree Line · UNITED STATES · ATLANTIC OCEAN · 140°W · 120°W · MEXICO · CUBA

0   500   1,000 Miles
0 500 1,000 Kilometers
Azimuthal Equal-Area Projection

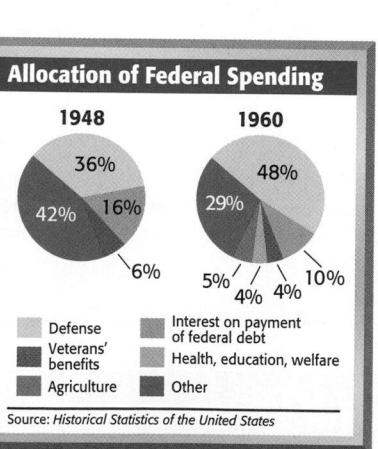

Allocation of Federal Spending

1948
36%
42%
16%
6%

1960
48%
29%
5% 4% 4% 10%

Defense
Veterans' benefits
Agriculture
Interest on payment of federal debt
Health, education, welfare
Other

Source: *Historical Statistics of the United States*

Radar. As the percentage of the federal budget allocated for defense increased, so did the amount of the defense budget spent on technology. Concern over the Soviet weapons buildup led the United States to create an intricate radar system to detect incoming enemy missiles. At the same time, the United States built up its own supply of intercontinental ballistic missiles (ICBMs).

GEOGRAPHY AND HISTORY Skills

PLACES AND REGIONS

1. Through which country did most North American radar lines run?
2. How did the Cold War affect defense spending?

Have each student pick a major military base during the 1960s, such as Okinawa in Japan or Holy Loch in the United Kingdom. Ask students to conduct research on their selected military base. Students should investigate the history of the base, its importance during the Cold War, and daily life there. Then write the following statement on the chalkboard: *U.S. military bases were crucial components of Cold War defenses.* Have students write essays on their chosen bases in response to the statement. **Block Scheduling**

SPOTLIGHT
on Forms of Technology

Have each student pick one of the forms of military technology listed in the map legend on the previous page. Ask students to locate and use a variety of primary and secondary sources to learn more about their chosen technology. Have students concentrate on its development, deployment, and significance during the Cold War and summarize the findings of their research in short papers. Ask volunteers to read their papers to the class. **Block Scheduling**

AMERICA'S Geography

Major U.S. Military Bases, c. 1965

MALAYSIA
CAMBODIA
EAST PAKISTAN
INDIA
INDIAN OCEAN
SOUTH VIETNAM
THAILAND
NORTH VIETNAM
LAOS
BURMA
WEST PAKISTAN
Subic Bay
Clark
PHILIPPINES
Peshawar
IRAN 1953
SAUDI ARABIA
CHINA
TAIWAN
Okinawa
SOUTH KOREA
MONGOLIA
EGYPT
Suez Canal 1956
Kimpo
TURKEY Incirlik
Ankara
Sasebo
NORTH KOREA
Korean War 1950–1953
U-2 Incident 1960
LIBYA
Yokosuka
JAPAN
UNION OF SOVIET SOCIALIST REPUBLICS
HUNGARY 1956
GREECE
YUGOSLAVIA
Wheelus
Naples
ITALY
Berlin 1958–1959
Wiesbaden
ALGERIA (French)
WEST GERMANY
FINLAND
SWEDEN
NORWAY
NATO HQ
FRANCE
Taranto
SPAIN
MOROCCO
ARCTIC OCEAN
North Pole
Holy Loch
UNITED KINGDOM
PORTUGAL
ICELAND
Keflavik
Adak
GREENLAND (Danish)
Thule
AZORES (Portuguese) Lajes
Midway
Unalaska
ALASKA
Sondrestrom
PACIFIC OCEAN
Goose
Pearl Harbor
HAWAII
CANADA
ATLANTIC OCEAN
BERMUDA (British)
NORAD HQ
SAC HQ
UNITED STATES
Roosevelt Roads
PUERTO RICO (U.S.)
MEXICO
CUBA
Guantánamo Bay
GUATEMALA 1954
Albrook
PANAMA
CANAL ZONE

Legend:
☐ United States and allies
☐ Soviet Union and allies
⊙ Major U.S. base
✹ Point of conflict
Political status as of 1960

0   1,000   2,000 Miles
0   1,000   2,000 Kilometers
Azimuthal Equidistant Projection

Military bases. During the Cold War the United States increased its commitment to help protect other nations from their enemies. In order to achieve this goal, the U.S. military established many new bases around the world. Some conflicts erupted between the U.S. backed countries and Soviet-backed countries, but most were short-lived skirmishes.

Dwindling Forces. Since an all-time high in the late 1960s, the size of U.S. armed forces has decreased. By 1993, there were fewer troops in the army and air force than had been in 1955. In 1993 the government awarded $138.3 billion in military contracts to businesses.

CRITICAL THINKING How might this trend affect the nation's workforce?

ANSWER: Answers may vary. Students might suggest that military personnel may compete for civilian jobs or private defense contractors may need more employees.

AMERICA'S GEOGRAPHY ANSWERS
1. 25
2. Berlin, Guatemala, Hungary, Iran, Korea, the Suez Canal, and the USSR

GEOGRAPHY AND HISTORY Skills

THE USES OF GEOGRAPHY

1. How many major U.S. military bases existed outside the United States?
2. Where did conflicts erupt during the 1950s?

Society After World War II

CHAPTER RESOURCE MANAGER

Objectives	Pacing Guide	Reproducible Resources
SECTION 1 **The Challenges of Peace** pp. 592–97 ★ Explain how the U.S. economy and American workers fared after World War II. ★ Identify the most important issues of the 1948 election. ★ Describe the major goals of President Truman's Fair Deal, and relate whether they were accomplished.	**Regular** 2 days **Block Scheduling** 1 days *Block Scheduling Handbook with Team Teaching Strategies, pp. 115–20*	**RS** Guided Reading Strategy 20.1 **PS** Biography Reading 20: Jackie Robinson **E** Creative Teaching Strategy: Listing and Coding Lesson
SECTION 2 **The Affluent Society** pp. 598–606 ★ Relate how President Eisenhower tried to manage the nation's problems. ★ Explain how the workforce changed in the 1950s. ★ Describe suburban life during the 1950s. ★ Discuss early television programming. ★ Analyze how the trends in popular culture reflected the larger social changes among teenagers in the 1950s.	**Regular** 2 days **Block Scheduling** 1 day *Block Scheduling Handbook with Team Teaching Strategies, pp. 115–20*	**RS** Guided Reading Strategy 20.2 **SM** Geography Activity 20: Shifting Populations **PS** Primary Source Reading 20: Rock 'n' Roll Era **E** Hands-On History Activity: What Things Do You Really Need
SECTION 3 **Voices of Dissent** pp. 607–15 ★ Relate how the *Brown* decision affected school segregation and exposed conflict over the segregation issue. ★ Explain how the Montgomery bus boycott was a major turning point in the civil rights movement. ★ Identify the challenges that Hispanics, Asian Americans, and American Indians faced in the 1950s. ★ Identify the criticisms that writers and scholars expressed about 1950s society. ★ Describe the problems that the poorest Americans faced in the 1950s.	**Regular** 2 days **Block Scheduling** 1 day *Block Scheduling Handbook with Team Teaching Strategies, pp. 115–20*	**RS** Guided Reading Strategy 20.3 **RS** Graphic Organizer Activity 20: Voices of Dissent **IC** Literature Reading 20: Lingering Racial Tension

Chapter Resource Key

PS	Primary Sources	**REV**	Review		Video
RS	Reading Support	**ELL**	Reinforcement and English Language Learners		Internet
IC	Interdisciplinary Connections				Holt Presentation Maker Using Microsoft® PowerPoint®
E	Enrichment		Transparencies		
SM	Skills Mastery		CD–ROM		
A	Assessment		Music		

One-Stop Planner CD–ROM

See the *One-Stop Planner* for a complete list of additional resources for students and teachers.

One-Stop Planner CD–ROM

It's easy to plan lessons, select resources, and print out materials for your students when you use the **One-Stop Planner CD–ROM with Test Generator.**

 One-Stop Planner, Lesson 20.1

 Holt Researcher: American History CD–ROM

 Homework Practice Online

REV Section 1 Review, p. 597

A Daily Quiz 20.1

ELL Main Idea Activity 20.1

ELL English Audio Summary 20.1

ELL Spanish Audio Summary 20.1

 One-Stop Planner, Lesson 20.2

Everyday Life in America Transparency 28: Queen of 1950s TV: Lucille Ball

The American Nation Video Program Segment: The Growth of Suburbia; Teacher's Guide, pp. 129–34

Holt Researcher: American History CD–ROM

Homework Practice Online

REV Section 2 Review, p. 606

A Daily Quiz 20.2

ELL Main Idea Activity 20.2

ELL English Audio Summary 20.2

ELL Spanish Audio Summary 20.2

One-Stop Planner, Lesson 20.3

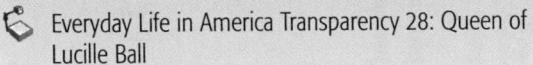 **CNN** Presents America: Yesterday and Today, 1850 to the Present Segment: A Few Views of the 1950s

Holt Researcher: American History CD–ROM

Homework Practice Online

HRW Go site

REV Section 3 Review, p. 615

A Daily Quiz 20.3

ELL Main Idea Activity 20.3

ELL English Audio Summary 20.3

ELL Spanish Audio Summary 20.3

internet connect

HRW ONLINE RESOURCES
 GO TO: go.hrw.com
 Then type in a keyword.

TEACHER HOME PAGE
 KEYWORD: SE3 Teacher

CHAPTER INTERNET ACTIVITIES
 KEYWORD: SE3 AN20
 Choose an activity to:
 • understand how popular culture reflected the social events and culture of the 1950s.
 • learn about passive resistance and write a biography of Mohandas K. Gandhi.
 • create a time line of Hispanic civil rights.

CHAPTER ENRICHMENT LINKS
 KEYWORD: SE3 CH20

ONLINE ASSESSMENT
 Homework Practice
 KEYWORD: SE3 HP20

 Standardized Test Prep
 KEYWORD: SE3 STP20

 Rubrics
 KEYWORD: SS Rubrics

ONLINE MAPS, CHARTS, AND GRAPHS
 KEYWORD: SE3 MCG
 • Election of 1948
 • Civil Rights in the Truman Era
 • Homes with Television Sets

CONTENT UPDATES
 KEYWORD: SS Content Updates

HOLT PRESENTATION MAKER
 KEYWORD: SE3 PPT20

ONLINE READING SUPPORT
 KEYWORD: SS Strategies

CURRENT EVENTS
 KEYWORD: S3 Current Events

Meeting Individual Needs

Ability Levels

Level 1 Basic-level activities designed for all students encountering new material

Level 2 Intermediate-level activities designed for average students

Level 3 Challenging activities designed for honors and gifted-and-talented students

English Language Learners Activities that address the needs of students with Limited English Proficiency

---

Chapter Review and Assessment

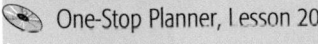 **Global Skill Builder CD–ROM**

HRW Go site

REV **Chapter 20 Tutorial for Students, Parents, Mentors, and Peers**

REV **Chapter 20 Review, pp. 616–17**

Chapter 20 Test Generator (on the One-Stop Planner)

A **Chapter 20 Test (Form A or B)**

A **Alternative Assessment Handbook**

A **Chapter 20 Test for English Language Learners and Special-Needs Students**

Build on What You Know

Ask students to answer the following questions.

How might Americans have adjusted to domestic life after the war?

Consider:
- the economic impact of peace—the return of soldiers and the return to a peacetime economy
- the response of labor freed from wartime "no strike" agreements

What kind of tensions might have been apparent by the end of the 1950s?

Consider:
- the experiences and expectations of returning veterans
- the hopes and feelings of Americans who wanted more than simple economic security

---

exploring the time line

AMERICAN EVENTS

CITIZENSHIP

1948 ■ Dewey Defeats Truman? As the election of 1948 approached, President Truman found himself in a difficult position. Liberal Democrats had defected to the Progressive Party, and conservative southern Democrats had defected to the Dixiecrats. The *Chicago Daily Tribune* was so certain that Truman would lose to Thomas Dewey that it actually printed election-day newspapers with the headline "Dewey Defeats Truman."

ACTIVITY: Have students create newspaper headlines for the day after the 2000 presidential election.

CHAPTER 20

1945–1960

Society After World War II

Mohandas K. Gandhi

Harry S Truman

1948 Politics
Harry S Truman narrowly wins re-election.

1949 The Arts
Frank Sinatra's song "New York, New York" is a smash hit.

1951 Daily Life
I Love Lucy premieres, quickly becoming the most popular television show in the United States.

1952 Politics
Dwight D. Eisenhower is elected president.

Eisenhower campaign sign

| 1945 | 1946 | 1947 | 1948 | 1949 | 1950 | 1951 | 1952 |

1945 The Arts
Mary Chase wins the Pulitzer Prize for her play *Harvey*.

1946 Daily Life
Dr. Benjamin Spock's *Common Sense Book of Baby and Child Care* becomes the leading guide for parents of the baby boom.

1947 Science and Technology
American pilot Chuck Yeager breaks the sound barrier, traveling at about 662 miles per hour.

1948 World Events
Mohandas K. Gandhi is assassinated.

1951 Science and Technology
UNIVAC, the first computer for commercial use, is developed.

1951 Business and Finance
Some 30 percent of the American workforce is employed in commerce and industry.

X-1 plane flown by Chuck Yeager

Build on What You Know

The end of World War II renewed Americans' optimism about the future. Soon, however, the country was caught up in a Cold War with the Soviet Union. President Truman's commitment to contain the spread of communism led to greater U.S. involvement in Korea and a growing suspicion that there were spies at home. The Cold War intensified as President Eisenhower stepped up the nuclear arms race. In this chapter you will learn how Americans adjusted to the domestic transition from war to peace.

What's Your Opinion?

To help students create their Themes Journal entries, provide the following examples of appropriate **agree/disagree** *statements.*

Economics

Agree Prosperity during the 1920s allowed many people to move to new suburbs.

Disagree The boom during the Second Industrial Revolution led to crowded, dirty cities.

Culture

Agree Many people in Nazi Germany went along with Adolf Hitler.

Disagree Abolitionists such as William Lloyd Garrison went against the crowd.

Citizenship

Agree In the Jim Crow era, African Americans could not end widespread governmental discrimination.

Disagree Women worked to pass the Nineteenth Amendment.

Queen Elizabeth II

Elvis Presley

1953
World Events
Queen Elizabeth II is crowned ruler of Great Britain.

1954
The Arts
Elvis Presley releases his first record.

1958
World Events
Guinea, the former French-African colony, gains independence.

1959
Politics
Alaska and Hawaii become the 49th and 50th states of the Union, respectively.

| 1953 | 1954 | 1955 | 1956 | 1957 | 1958 | 1959 | 1960 |

1953
Daily Life
Maureen "Little Mo" Connolly becomes the first woman to win tennis's Grand Slam.

1954
Politics
The Supreme Court outlaws school segregation with its *Brown v. Board of Education* ruling.

1955
Business and Finance
The number of American shopping centers increases to about 1,800.

1955
Business and Finance
Ray Kroc opens the first McDonald's franchise.

1957
The Arts
Jack Kerouac publishes *On the Road.*

1959
Daily Life
The average wholesale price of an American car is $1,880, or $580 more than it cost 10 years earlier.

A handheld adding machine helped American consumers.

Cars fill the Los Angeles highways.

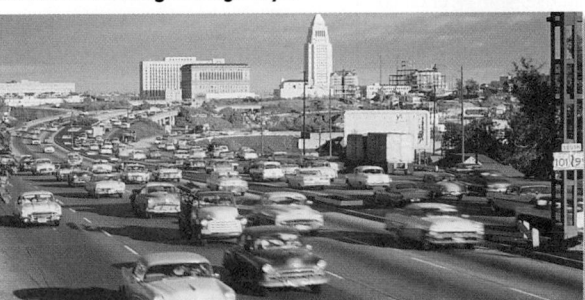

---

exploring the time line

GLOBAL EVENTS

internet connect

go. hrw .com

TOPIC: Mohandas K. Gandhi
GO TO: go.hrw.com
KEYWORD: SE3 AN20

Have students access the Internet through the HRW Go site to conduct research on Mohandas K. Gandhi. Then ask each student to create an illustrated biography that describes Gandhi's life, his philosophical outlook, and his influence today. Remind students that they should synthesize and summarize material in their biographies in order to present a full portrait of Gandhi.

What's Your Opinion?

Themes Journal

Do you **agree** *or* **disagree** *with the following statements? Support your point of view in your journal.*

Economics An economic boom will affect population growth and residential patterns.

Culture People generally prefer to "follow the crowd" rather than express their individuality.

Citizenship Citizens are powerless to change government policies that discriminate against them.

SECTION 1

OBJECTIVE 1 *Explain how the U.S. economy and American workers fared after World War II.*

OBJECTIVE 2 *Identify the most important issues of the 1948 election.*

OBJECTIVE 3 *Describe the major goals of President Truman's Fair Deal, and relate whether they were accomplished.*

LET'S GET STARTED!

Write the following questions on the chalkboard: *How might the transition to peace affect a nation's economy after years of war? Why?* As students enter the classroom, ask them to answer the questions in writing. Have volunteers share their responses. *(Students might suggest that the transition to peace reduces defense spending, which results in a loss of jobs, and the resulting unemployment can hurt the economy.)* Tell students that in Section 1 they will learn how the U.S. government attempted to bolster the economy after World War II.

SECTION 1 RESOURCES

REPRODUCIBLE
▶ Guided Reading Strategy 20.1
▶ Biography Reading 20: Jackie Robinson

TECHNOLOGY
▶ One-Stop Planner, Lesson 20.1
▶ Holt Researcher: American History CD–ROM
▶ Homework Practice Online

REINFORCEMENT, REVIEW, AND ASSESSMENT
▶ Section 1 Review, p. 597
▶ Daily Quiz 20.1
▶ Main Idea Activity 20.1
▶ English Audio Summary 20.1
▶ Spanish Audio Summary 20.1

SECTION 1

READ TO DISCOVER
1. How did the U.S. economy and American workers fare after World War II?
2. What were the most important issues of the 1948 election?
3. What were the major goals of President Truman's Fair Deal, and were they accomplished?

IDENTIFY
GI Bill of Rights
Employment Act
Council of Economic Advisers
Taft-Hartley Act
Committee on Civil Rights
Dixiecrats
J. Strom Thurmond
Henry Wallace
Thomas Dewey
Fair Deal

▶ WHY IT MATTERS TODAY
Democratic nations around the world continue to protect the civil rights of their citizens today. Use CNNfyi.com or other **current events** sources to learn about various countries' recent civil rights records. Record your findings in your journal.

CNNfyi.com

The Challenges of Peace

 EYEWITNESSES TO History

"When [the war] finally came to a conclusion, I think it set in motion [questions like] 'Here we are now. What are we going to do about life as we try to reestablish it in our community?'"

—Reverend Harold Toliver, quoted in *Americans Remember the Home Front*, edited by Roy Hoopes

The Homecoming by Norman Rockwell

Reverend Harold Toliver recalled how the end of World War II stirred both hopes and concerns for many Americans. Many New Deal supporters like Toliver looked to President Harry S Truman for guidance. They hoped that he would help the nation recover from World War II by continuing the reforms that President Roosevelt had initiated. "Franklin Roosevelt is not dead. His ideals live," declared New York mayor Fiorello La Guardia. President Truman tried to meet these expectations by promoting Roosevelt's ideals with his own reform programs.

The Problems of Demobilization

By mid-1946 more than 9 million men and women had been discharged from the military. The soldiers received a hero's welcome, but their return also sparked concern. How could the economy absorb all these new workers? Many Americans feared that the country would fall into an economic decline similar to the one that had followed World War I.

Postwar measures. Even before the war had ended, Congress began preparing for peace. Preventing an economic depression and helping war-weary veterans make the difficult transition to civilian life were top priorities. Congress passed the Servicemen's Readjustment Act of 1944, more commonly known as the **GI Bill of Rights**. The bill provided pensions and government loans to help veterans start businesses and buy homes or farms. Millions of veterans also received money through the GI Bill to attend college. Between 1944 and 1956 almost 8 million veterans attended college or technical schools on the GI Bill. This led to a dramatic increase in the number of American college graduates. Government worker Nelson Poynter described the impact of the GI Bill.

 History Makers Speak

"The GI Bill ... had more to do with thrusting us into a new era than anything else. Millions of people whose parents or grandparents had never dreamed of going to college saw that they could go.... Essentially I think it made us a far more democratic people."

—Nelson Poynter, quoted in *Americans Remember the Home Front*, edited by Roy Hoopes

To ensure postwar economic growth, Congress passed the **Employment Act** of 1946. The act committed the government to promoting full employment and production. It also established the **Council of Economic Advisers** to confer with the president on economic policy.

SPOTLIGHT on the GI Bill

Ask each student to interview a World War II veteran who received GI Bill benefits. *(If students cannot locate a veteran, ask them to read a primary source on the subject.)* Interviewers should focus on how receiving GI Bill benefits affected the veterans. Then organize students into groups and have each group write a script for a documentary film about the GI Bill.

Cooperative Learning, Block Scheduling

NOTE: For an additional teaching idea, see the Chapter 20 listing and coding lesson in the **Creative Teaching Strategies** handbook.

TEACH OBJECTIVE 1

LEVEL 1: Pair students and tell them to imagine that they are American workers in 1948. Have each pair develop a short dialogue about how the U.S. economy and American workers fared after World War II. *(Students should note that the economy remained fairly strong, despite fears of a depression. Workers suffered many problems, however, including antiunion legislation, high inflation, and job loss.)* Ask volunteers to perform their dialogues for the class.

English Language Learners, Cooperative Learning

Changing Ways — Higher Education

■ **Understanding Change** Before the GI Bill, a college education was often something only wealthy Americans could afford. Since then, obtaining a college education has become much more common. *What differences do you observe between the images of college students in the late 1940s and the late 1990s? What statistics in the chart surprise you the most? Why?*

	THEN	NOW
Number of Institutions of Higher Education	1,863	4,064
Annual Student Body Enrollment	2,281,000	14,350,000
Annual Number of Bachelor Degrees Conferred	496,874	1,172,000
Student Body	32% / 68%	43% / 57%

Female
Male

Sources: *Historical Statistics of the United States; Statistical Abstract of the United States: 2000.* Data reflect 1950 and 1997.

THEN

Now

Despite widespread fears, the postwar depression never came. For example, the government canceled some $23 billion in military contracts. Those plants that had been making tanks and bombers began producing consumer goods instead. Employment levels remained high. Many Americans also began to spend the money they had saved during the war. Furthermore, because agricultural output in other countries had been shattered by the war, U.S. food exports increased.

Problems for workers. Not all was rosy on the economic front, however. Government measures encouraged employers to give priority to veterans in hiring. As a result, many workers lost their jobs to returning veterans. Congress abolished the Fair Employment Practices Committee, which had helped protect African Americans from discrimination. The government also retired the character of Rosie the Riveter. Instead, the government started a campaign to encourage women to quit their jobs and become full-time homemakers. Some women wanted to keep their jobs. This was particularly true for working-class women whose families needed their incomes. "If [women] are capable, I don't see why they should give up their position," said one female steelworker. Despite these sentiments, most women who did not willingly give up their jobs were fired or pressured to quit their jobs after the war.

Workers were also concerned about the effect of postwar inflation. The cost of goods soared after most wartime price controls were lifted in 1946. Meat prices became so high that some markets began selling horse meat. Blaming President Truman, angry consumers called him "Horsemeat Harry."

MORE ON THE GRAPH

The Changing Ivy League. The GI Bill profoundly affected the social order at Ivy League universities. In the immediate postwar era, Harvard and other prestigious schools charged $400 per year for tuition. The GI Bill gave veterans up to $500 per year for tuition, making it possible for people some Harvard students disdainfully called "poor boys" to enroll in virtually any school in the country. A *Time* magazine article asked, "Why Go to Podunk College?, When the Government Will Send You to Yale?" Many veterans heeded the implicit advice and enrolled in Ivy League schools. In 1946 alone, Harvard's student population nearly doubled, from 2,750 in February to 5,000 in September.

CRITICAL THINKING Based on the preceding figures, by what percentage did Harvard's enrollment increase in 1946?

ANSWER: Students should indicate that enrollment increased by about 82 percent.

CHANGING WAYS ANSWERS

differences—the 1990s photograph shows a larger, more diverse, and more casually dressed classroom population; statistics—female students now outnumber male students; students' answers will vary.

LEVEL 2: Organize students into small groups and tell them to imagine that they are newsmagazine editors preparing an issue entitled The Postwar Economy. Ask each group to write brief summaries of articles that might appear in the magazine. Remind groups that their articles should describe how the U.S. economy and American workers fared after World War II. *(See the Level 1 lesson for the correct issues.)* After groups have completed their summaries, conduct a discussion on the economy and workers after World War II. **Cooperative Learning**

LEVEL 3: Conduct a brief discussion on how the U.S. economy and American workers fared after World War II. *(See the Level 1 lesson for the correct issues.)* Then have each student write a brief economic analysis of the period from 1945 to 1950. Students should explain why many Americans feared a postwar depression, why that depression failed to materialize, why many workers lost ground after the war, and why the government enacted antilabor policies. Have volunteers read their analyses to the class. Students may wish to include their analyses in their portfolios.

 HOMEWORK *Have each student create a detailed outline of the subsection entitled The Problems of Demobilization. Alternately, have each student interview a person who lived through the demobilization era. Ask students to present the results of their interviews in a short paper.*

<table><tr><td>

ECONOMICS

A Reason to Strike.
A month after World War II ended, the *CIO News* reported that between the five-year periods 1935 and 1939 and 1940 and 1944, after-tax profits in the steel industry had risen 113 percent, to more than $1 billion. A University of California study published in 1945 indicated that steel-workers earned just $45.60 per week—totaling far less than the $2,700 per year then needed to achieve a moderate standard of living. Workers in other industries earned even lower weekly wages.

CRITICAL THINKING How might the *CIO News* article, the University of California study, and other similar documents have affected labor?

ANSWER: Students might indicate that the article, the study, and other documents helped give rise to the many strikes launched after World War II.

VISUAL RECORD ANSWER
Students might suggest the importance of worldwide unity of workers.

</td><td>

Labor unrest. As inflation continued to rise, people took matters into their own hands. Freed from their wartime pledges not to strike, millions of workers walked off the job. They fought for wage increases and the preservation of some wartime price controls. In 1946 almost 5 million workers walked the picket lines.

President Truman generally supported labor unions. However, he opposed these strikes because he feared they would disrupt the economy. After some 400,000 coal miners went on strike in the spring of 1946, Truman ordered the army to take control of the mines. John L. Lewis, president of the United Mine Workers, responded, "You can't dig coal with bayonets." After the courts slapped heavy fines on the union, Lewis ordered the miners back to work. Later, Truman threatened to end a railway strike by drafting strikers into the army. Truman's threat spurred union leaders to negotiate an end to the strike.

In 1947 the Republican-controlled Congress passed a bill to reduce the strength of organized labor. The bill was known as the **Taft-Hartley Act**. It gave judges the power to end some strikes and outlawed closed-shop agreements. It also restricted unions' political contributions and required union officers to swear that they were not Communists. Truman vetoed the bill, but Congress overrode his veto.

The Taft-Hartley Act stirred angry debate. Conservative supporters of the bill argued that it corrected unfair advantages that had been given to labor by New Deal measures. Pro-labor supporters argued that it was a "slave labor law." Although the act limited the actions that unions could take, organized labor continued to make some gains in the postwar years. For example, in 1948 General Motors and the United Automobile Workers (UAW) signed a contract that linked wage increases to increases in the cost of living. Union contracts also began to include benefits such as retirement pensions and health insurance.

</td></tr></table>

INTERPRETING THE VISUAL RECORD

Labor unions. These workers marched in support of labor unions in 1946. *What message do you think is conveyed by the signs the marchers are using?*

✔ **READING CHECK: Contrasting** How did the post–World War II economy differ from the post–World War I economy? World War I—high unemployment, low wages; World War II—Employment Act and GI Bill of Rights put veterans to work.

The 1948 Election

By 1948 high inflation and labor unrest had decreased public support for President Truman. "To err is Truman," people joked. Despite his low standing in the polls, Truman continued to take a strong stand on controversial issues. His position on civil rights in particular became an important issue in the 1948 campaign.

The Committee on Civil Rights.
In 1946 civil rights groups had urged Truman to take action against racism. They noted that most African Americans throughout the nation faced segregation in schools and on buses and discrimination in housing and employment. Furthermore, in some areas lynchings of African Americans still occurred. Previous efforts to battle these conditions had met resistance.

ALL LEVELS: Ask students why so many Americans believed that Republican Thomas Dewey would win the presidential election of 1948. *(Students might suggest that Truman's stances on civil rights, labor, and foreign policy alienated many Democrats.)* To help students understand the most important issues of the election, copy the following graphic organizer on the chalkboard, omitting the italicized answers. Have each student complete it.

English Language Learners

THE 1948 ELECTION

President Truman's Platform
- *supported civil rights in general and issued executive orders banning racial discrimination in the military and in federal hiring*
- *supported the repeal of the Taft-Hartley Act*
- *supported increased federal aid for agriculture, education, and housing*

The Two-Way Split in the Democratic Party
Cause: *southern Democrats' dislike of Truman's stance on civil rights*
Cause: *liberal Democrats' dislike of Truman's stance on labor and foreign policy*
Effects: *split the party and created the possibility of a Republican win*

Election and Results
- *massive campaign effort mounted by Truman*
- *attacked Republicans' conservatism*
- *election won by Truman*

In December 1946 Truman created the **Committee on Civil Rights** to examine racial issues. The committee's report, *To Secure These Rights,* appeared in October 1947. The report documented widespread civil rights abuses. These abuses included discrimination against African American veterans and an increase in racial violence. The report also called for an end to racial segregation in interstate transportation. Based on the committee's findings, Truman urged Congress to pass an antilynching law and an anti–poll-tax measure. He also worked to end discrimination in federal agencies and in the military.

When Congress did not immediately act on the report's recommendations, African American leader A. Philip Randolph threatened to launch a campaign of civil disobedience. In July 1948 Truman issued executive orders banning racial discrimination in the military and in federal hiring. He also took steps to end employment discrimination by companies holding government contracts.

White southern Democrats were outraged both by African American demands for civil rights and by Truman's actions. Senator Olin Johnston of South Carolina warned angrily that the South's electoral votes "won't be for Truman. They'll be for somebody else. He ain't going to be re-elected."

To win the 1948 election, President Truman carried out a "whistle-stop" campaign aboard a train.

CITIZENSHIP

President Truman and Civil Rights. President Truman appointed both African American and white citizens to serve on the Committee on Civil Rights. In addition to decrying racial violence, the committee's report called for "the elimination of segregation, based on race, color, creed, or national origin, from American life." Although Truman's later executive orders did not achieve this goal, they did expand opportunities for African Americans.

CRITICAL THINKING How might Truman's executive order on the military have affected recruitment?

ANSWER: Students might suggest that it probably encouraged African American enlistment.

SKILL-BUILDING STRATEGIES ANSWERS

Applying the Skill
Students should research both the topic and the interviewee and prepare questions before conducting the interview.

Practicing the Skill
1. Answers will vary. Students should have gathered some preliminary information.

2. Answers will vary. Students' questions should be on the topic and open-ended.

3. Answers will vary. Students should have a better understanding of it.

Skill-Building Strategies

Conducting an Interview

Oral history interviews are one of the most important methods that historians use to gather information about the past. An effective oral history interview must be accompanied by preliminary research as well as follow-up analysis.

How to Conduct an Interview

1. **Identify and research the topic.** Identify the general topic you wish to investigate and a specific person with firsthand knowledge of the topic. Then gather as much information as you can about the topic and your potential interview subject.
2. **Set up the interview.** Contact your potential interview subject, identify yourself, and clearly state your purpose in requesting an interview. Schedule a convenient time and place for the interview.
3. **Prepare questions.** Prepare questions for the interview that address what you need to know and that follow one another in a logical fashion.
4. **Conduct the interview.** Be an active listener during the interview. Allow your interview subject to respond to your questions freely, but remain in charge of the general direction of the interview. Ask follow-up questions if you need additional information.

5. **Analyze the interview.** Shortly after the interview has been completed, review your notes and listen to a recording of the interview. Summarize the content of the interview and evaluate its reliability as historical evidence. Use the results to form generalizations and draw conclusions about your topic.

Applying the Skill

Prepare for and conduct an oral history interview with one of the following:

    a. a U.S. military veteran who received financial aid for college under the GI Bill
    b. a person who voted in the 1948 presidential election
    c. a person who was a teenager in the late 1940s

Practicing the Skill

Answer the following questions.

1. What information about your subject were you able to acquire before the interview?
2. What questions did you prepare for the interview?
3. How did the interview contribute to your understanding of the United States after World War II?

LEVEL 1: Pair students and have them write a series of newspaper headlines on President Truman's Fair Deal—several headlines on the major goals of the policy and several headlines on whether those goals were accomplished. *(Students should note that Truman's Fair Deal promised full employment, a higher minimum wage, a national health insurance program, affordable housing, increased aid to farmers, and expansion of welfare benefits. He did not achieve most of these goals, although Congress did extend Social Security benefits, raise the minimum wage, approve urban renewal programs, and* expand water programs.*)* Ask volunteers to share their headlines with the class. Post the headlines around the classroom.
English Language Learners, Cooperative Learning

LEVELS 2 AND 3: Tell students to imagine that it is 1952 and that they are Americans with strong views on President Truman's Fair Deal. Have each student write a letter to the editor of a local newspaper, commenting on the Fair Deal. In their editorials, students should briefly describe the goals of the Fair Deal, note whether President Truman accomplished those goals, and offer their own opinions of the Fair Deal. *(See the Level 1 lesson for the correct goals and achievements.)* Students may wish to include their editorials in their portfolios.

Henry Wallace and the Progressive Party.
As vice president during Franklin D. Roosevelt's third term, Henry Wallace traveled to China, Latin America, and Siberia. His journeys strongly influenced his political views. As the Progressive Party's presidential candidate in 1948, he ran on a platform largely devoted to international issues. Wallace, who had been replaced by Harry S Truman for Roosevelt's fourth term, believed that Truman's firm stand toward the Soviet Union had the potential to result in war. He also feared that it could lead to political persecution. Some commentators called Wallace a "communist dupe" and a "Stalinist stooge." However, his views appealed to many Americans. He won more than 1 million popular votes in the 1948 election.

CRITICAL THINKING Why might Wallace have believed that Truman's approach toward the Soviet Union could result in war?

ANSWER: Students might suggest that Wallace believed that Truman's approach was too confrontational.

MAP ANSWER
the Great Plains, the lower South, and the Northeast

This NAACP button was worn by some Truman supporters who rallied behind the Democratic Party platform committee's proposal of a strong civil rights plank.

The Democratic convention. Southern opposition did not prevent Truman from winning his party's nomination. His support, however, remained weak. Some delegates even wore buttons proclaiming, "We're just mild about Harry," a twist on his campaign slogan "We're just wild about Harry."

The Democratic platform called for the repeal of the Taft-Hartley Act. It also pushed for broader Social Security benefits and an increase in federal aid for housing, education, and agriculture. The platform committee's proposal of a strong civil rights plank divided the Democratic Party. The all-white southern delegation threatened to walk out of the convention. The National Association for the Advancement of Colored People (NAACP) declared, "LET 'EM WALK."

 Primary Source **“There is no room . . . for compromise. . . . Those Democrats who say the President's recommendation of such a program is a 'stab in the back' of the South are saying they do not choose to abide by the Constitution. They are also saying . . . that the whole section of our nation believes as they do. . . . We know it is not true!”**

—NAACP advertisement

After bitter debate, the delegates adopted the civil rights plank. Southern delegates then stormed out of the convention and formed the States' Rights Party. The party was nicknamed the **Dixiecrats**. The Dixiecrats called for continued racial segregation. The party nominated South Carolina governor **J. Strom Thurmond** as its presidential candidate.

The gulf widens. A different issue caused another break within the Democratic Party. Troubled by Truman's antilabor actions in 1946, former vice president **Henry Wallace** and other liberal New Dealers left the Democratic Party to found a new Progressive Party. This group called for an extension of the New Deal. They also called for efforts to improve relations with the Soviet Union.

With the Democratic vote split three ways, the Republicans smelled victory. They nominated Governor **Thomas Dewey** of New York as their presidential candidate. Earl Warren, the popular governor of California, was nominated as Dewey's running mate. Opinion polls and most newspapers predicted a Dewey victory.

The Truman campaign attacked the conservatism of the Republicans and the radicalism of the Progressives. Truman crisscrossed the country by train, criticizing the "do-nothing" Republican-led Congress.

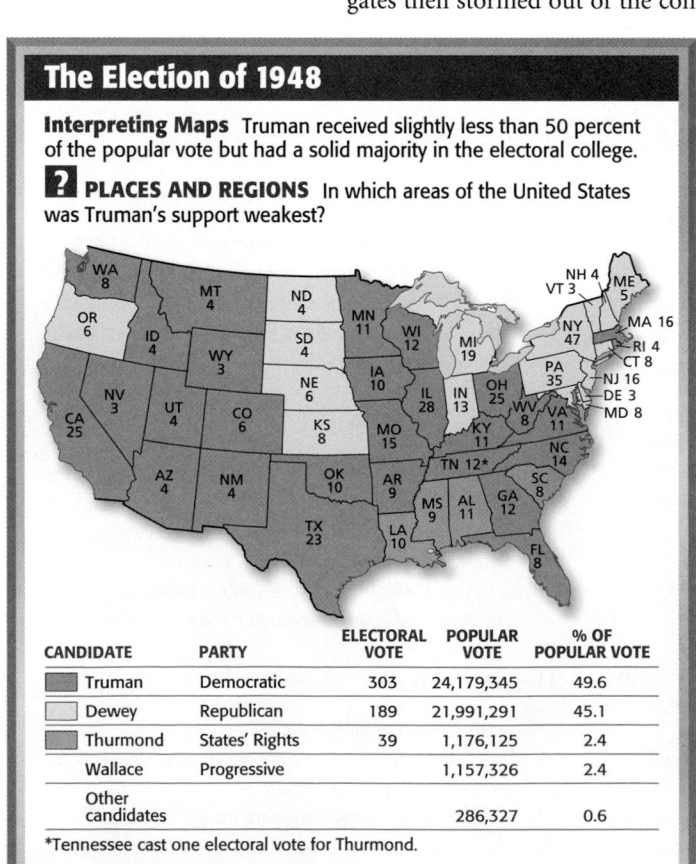

The Election of 1948

Interpreting Maps Truman received slightly less than 50 percent of the popular vote but had a solid majority in the electoral college.

❓ PLACES AND REGIONS In which areas of the United States was Truman's support weakest?

CANDIDATE	PARTY	ELECTORAL VOTE	POPULAR VOTE	% OF POPULAR VOTE
Truman	Democratic	303	24,179,345	49.6
Dewey	Republican	189	21,991,291	45.1
Thurmond	States' Rights	39	1,176,125	2.4
Wallace	Progressive		1,157,326	2.4
Other candidates			286,327	0.6

*Tennessee cast one electoral vote for Thurmond.

Source: *Historical Statistics of the United States*

REVIEW

Have students complete the **Section 1 Review** on p. 597.

ASSESS

Have students complete **Daily Quiz 20.1**. As **Alternative Assessment**, you may want to use the GI Bill documentary script or the Fair Deal headlines in this section's lessons.

RETEACH

Have students complete **Main Idea Activity for English Language Learners and Special-Needs Students 20.1**. Have students create charts or graphic organizers on one of the following issues: the postwar economy, the presidential election of 1948, or the Fair Deal. After students have finished their charts, organize students into triads and have them discuss the material in Section 1.
English Language Learners, Cooperative Learning

EXTEND

Have students conduct research on both the Wagner-Connery Act and the Taft-Hartley Act. Then have each student compare and contrast the acts in a brief paper. Ask volunteers to read their papers to the class. **Block Scheduling**

Crowds began to chant, "Give 'em hell, Harry." In one of the great upsets of U.S. political history, Truman won the election with 303 electoral votes to Dewey's 189 electoral votes.

✔ **READING CHECK: Summarizing** What were the causes of the three-way split in the Democratic Party? **Southern Democrats' opposition to civil rights legislation; other Democrats' opposition to antilabor actions.**

The Fair Deal

Encouraged by his victory, President Truman urged Congress to continue Franklin D. Roosevelt's New Deal reforms. Truman proclaimed that "every segment of our population . . . has a right to expect from our government a fair deal." He proposed a series of new reforms called the **Fair Deal**. Truman's Fair Deal promised full employment, a higher minimum wage, a national health insurance program, construction of affordable housing, increased aid to farmers, and the expansion of welfare benefits to more people.

Most Republicans and some Democrats opposed the president's program. Nevertheless, Truman managed to push through some of his reforms. Between 1949 and 1952 Congress extended Social Security benefits to some 10 million additional people, raised the minimum wage from 40 to 75 cents an hour, and approved programs to demolish or rebuild slums. Congress also expanded federal programs to promote flood control, hydroelectric power, and irrigation.

Overall, though, the Fair Deal had limited success in an increasingly conservative postwar political climate. Americans had become less enthusiastic about reform programs that would further expand the government. Most people, weary of the upheavals of recent years, just wanted peace, stability, and gradual prosperity.

✔ **READING CHECK: Drawing Conclusions** How did Truman's Fair Deal propose to extend the effects of the New Deal? **It promised full employment and a national health insurance plan, proposed extending Social Security benefits, and promoted hydroelectric power.**

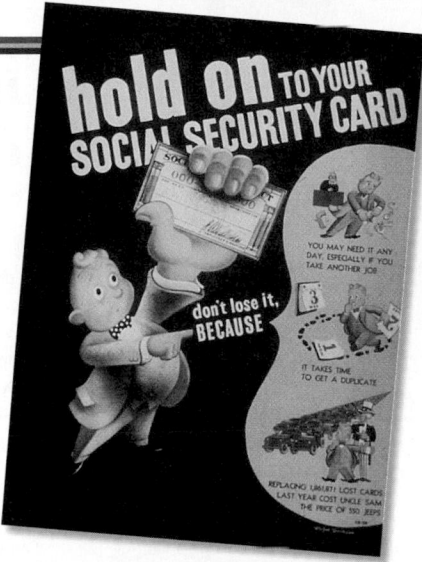

INTERPRETING THE VISUAL RECORD

Social Security. Although Congress expanded Social Security benefits, President Truman had trouble getting other Fair Deal legislation passed. *How does this poster reflect the importance of Social Security?*

VISUAL RECORD ANSWER

Students might cite the difficulty of getting a Social Security card replaced.

SECTION 1 REVIEW ANSWERS

1. Identify
- GI Bill of Rights, p. 592
- Employment Act, p. 592
- Council of Economic Advisers, p. 592
- Taft-Hartley Act, p. 594
- Committee on Civil Rights, p. 596
- Dixiecrats, p. 596
- J. Strom Thurmond, p. 596
- Henry Wallace, p. 596
- Thomas Dewey, p. 596
- Fair Deal, p. 597

2. successes—extended Social Security, raised minimum wage, began urban renewal, passed water policies; public opinion—more conservative; wary of reform; weary of upheavals; wanted prosperity

3a. forced some workers out of jobs; resulted in high inflation, strikes, and passage of the Taft-Hartley Act

b. It gave veterans money to start businesses, buy farms, and attend college.

c. They enraged southern Democrats who formed the Dixiecrats.

4. Answers will vary. Students might answer that politics reflected postwar economic difficulties, such as high inflation and labor unrest as well as the rights of veterans and the growing tension over civil rights issues.

SECTION 1 REVIEW

1. Identify and explain:
GI Bill of Rights
Employment Act
Council of Economic Advisers
Taft-Hartley Act
Committee on Civil Rights
Dixiecrats
J. Strom Thurmond
Henry Wallace
Thomas Dewey
Fair Deal

2. Evaluating Copy the chart below. Use it to list the major successes of President Truman's Fair Deal program and changing public opinion of reform.

Successes	Public opinion
1.	1.
2.	2.
3.	3.
4.	4.

3. Finding the Main Idea

a. How did the end of World War II affect American workers?

b. How did the GI Bill of Rights affect veterans and the U.S. economy?

c. How did Truman's efforts to expand civil rights for African Americans lead to division in the Democratic Party?

4. Writing and Critical Thinking

Drawing Conclusions Write a paragraph describing how politics in the late 1940s reflected the ways that World War II had changed the United States.
Consider:
- what political steps were taken to ensure economic stability
- what political actions were taken to help veterans
- how political actions reflected desires to expand democracy

Homework Practice Online
keyword: SE3 HP20

After completing Section 2, students should be able to:

OBJECTIVE 1 Relate how President Eisenhower tried to manage the nation's problems.

OBJECTIVE 2 Explain how the workforce changed in the 1950s.

OBJECTIVE 3 Describe suburban life during the 1950s.

OBJECTIVE 4 Discuss early television programming.

OBJECTIVE 5 Analyze how the trends in popular culture reflected the larger social changes among teenagers in the 1950s.

LET'S GET STARTED!

As students enter the classroom, display Everyday Life in America Transparency 28, Queen of 1950s TV: Lucille Ball, from **American History Visual Resources**. Distribute the accompanying worksheet and ask students to answer the questions. Have volunteers share their answers. Then tell students that in Section 2 they will learn more about American society and popular culture during the 1950s.

SECTION 2

READ TO DISCOVER

1. How did President Eisenhower try to manage the nation's problems?
2. How did the workforce change in the 1950s?
3. What was suburban life like during the 1950s?
4. What was early television programming like?
5. How did trends in popular culture reflect larger social changes among teenagers in the 1950s?

DEFINE

automation
baby boom
juvenile delinquency
rock 'n' roll

IDENTIFY

Oveta Culp Hobby
Modern Republicanism
George Meany
Highway Act
Elvis Presley

WHY IT MATTERS TODAY

People in suburbs and those in urban areas still face different challenges. Use **CNNfyi.com** or other **current events** sources to learn about the challenges faced by the people living in each of these areas today. Record your findings in your journal.

CNNfyi.com

The Affluent Society

Eisenhower, often referred to by his nickname, Ike, was a calming force for Americans.

❝Who decides whether you shall be happy or unhappy? You do! Happiness is achievable and the process for obtaining it is not complicated. Anyone who desires it, who wills it, and who learns and applies the right formula may become a happy person.❞

—Reverend Norman Vincent Peale,
The Power of Positive Thinking

During the 1950s millions of Americans listened to the advice of Reverend Norman Vincent Peale, a dynamic speaker and Protestant minister who wrote the 1952 book *The Power of Positive Thinking*. Peale's claim that all people could achieve success if they had the right attitude represented the optimism of the decade. In an era dominated by Cold War fears, Peale offered a formula to help people overcome their anxieties.

The Eisenhower Era

President Dwight D. Eisenhower also reflected the optimism of the 1950s. Rejecting the Democrats' reform proposals, Americans elected Eisenhower, a Republican, in 1952. He took office in 1953 determined to boost the economy and reform the federal government. He pledged to cut bureaucracy, to curb what he called the "creeping socialism" of the New Deal, to balance the budget, and to reduce government regulation of the economy.

In his first year as president, Eisenhower eliminated thousands of government jobs and cut billions of dollars from the federal budget. To reduce government influence over the economy, he cut farm subsidies. He also turned over federally owned coastal lands to the states, which could then allow those lands to be developed. Nevertheless, Social Security and unemployment benefits were expanded during his administration, and the minimum wage was increased. Eisenhower established the Department of Health, Education, and Welfare, under the supervision of Texan **Oveta Culp Hobby**. The president also supported the largest increase in educational spending up to that time. This approach to domestic affairs, which Eisenhower described as "conservative when it comes to money and liberal when it comes to human beings," became known as **Modern Republicanism**.

Providing funding for social programs, defense, and other government obligations weakened Eisenhower's pledge to balance the federal budget. Only three of the eight budgets he presided over were balanced. During his years in office the federal debt grew by about 9 percent, to $291 billion.

✔ **READING CHECK: Summarizing** Why did many Americans support Eisenhower in the 1950s? because he pledged to boost the economy and reform the government

TEACH OBJECTIVE 1

LEVEL 1: Pair students and ask them to write paragraphs describing how President Eisenhower tried to manage the nation's problems. *(Students should indicate that Eisenhower followed an approach known as Modern Republicanism. He cut some government programs while protecting and expanding others.)* Have volunteers read their paragraphs to the class.
English Language Learners, Cooperative Learning

LEVEL 2: Tell students to imagine that they are President Eisenhower and that they have just retired from politics. Ask each student to write a short memoir explaining how Eisenhower attempted to manage the nation's problems. *(See the Level 1 lesson for the correct approaches.)* Have volunteers read their memoirs to the class.

LEVEL 3: Conduct a brief discussion on how President Eisenhower attempted to manage the nation's problems. *(See the Level 1 lesson for the correct approaches.)* Then ask each student to create a detailed graphic organizer that compares and contrasts Eisenhower's approaches with those of previous presidents during the 1900s. Suggest that students consult their textbooks if they do not remember specific details about earlier presidents. Have volunteers present their graphic organizers to the class. Then ask students to "grade" Eisenhower as a president. Conduct a debate between students with different opinions.

The Economy

For many Americans the 1950s was a decade of economic prosperity. One man described the era as an escalator. "You just stood there and you moved up," he said. Unemployment and inflation remained very low. By the mid-1950s about 60 percent of Americans were earning a middle-class income, which at that time was considered to be $3,000 to $10,000 annually. According to the popular media, never before had so many people enjoyed such prosperity. "This is a new kind of capitalism," declared *Reader's Digest*, "capitalism for the many, not for the few."

Changes in the workplace. The economy received a boost from changes in the workplace. Large corporations prospered during the decade. Some 5,000 companies merged to form larger corporations. American factories were changing as well. Throughout the 1950s companies introduced machines that could perform industrial operations faster and more efficiently than human workers. This process of **automation** greatly increased productivity. However, it also reduced the number of manufacturing jobs. Many workers began to fear an automated future, as the song "Automation" noted.

> **❝**I walked, walked, walked into the foreman's office
> To find out what was what.
> I looked him in the eye and said, 'What goes?'
> And this is the answer I got:
> His eyes turned red, then green, then blue
> And it suddenly dawned on me—
> There was a robot sitting In the seat
> Where the foreman used to be.**❞**
>
> —"Automation," by Joe Glazer

As the number of blue-collar, or manufacturing, jobs decreased, professional and service jobs increased. Huge new corporations required a multitude of managers and clerical workers, positions referred to as white-collar jobs.

Many of the newly created service jobs were in occupations traditionally filled by women. Those jobs included nursing, teaching, retail sales, and low-level clerical work, sometimes called pink-collar jobs. By 1960, women made up about one third of the total workforce.

The new union style. Changes in the workforce also influenced organized labor. Boosted in part by the merger of the American Federation of Labor (AFL) and the Congress of Industrial Organizations (CIO) in 1955, union membership grew in the 1950s. It peaked at some 18.5 million in 1956.

INTERPRETING THE VISUAL RECORD

Automation. The use of machines allowed workers to make products faster. *What examples of automation can you identify in this picture?*

Technology Resources

Everyday Life in America Transparency 28: Queen of 1950s TV: Lucille Ball

ALL LEVELS: Ask students to share their preconceptions, if any, about the workforce in the 1950s. *(Answers will vary. Some students might suggest that many workers of the era were "men in gray flannel suits.")* Conduct a brief discussion of these preconceptions and stereotypes. To help students understand how the workforce changed in the 1950s, copy the graphic organizer on the chalkboard, omitting the italicized answers. Have each student complete it.
English Language Learners

automation increased productivity and decreased manufacturing jobs

expansion of service positions created new pink-collar jobs

Changes in the 1950s Workforce

corporate mergers created new white-collar jobs

corruption decreased support for unions

HOMEWORK *Write the following terms on the chalkboard:* automation, white collar, pink collar, *and* Landrum-Griffin Act. *Have each student write a sentence defining each term and explaining how it affected the workforce during the 1950s.*

ECONOMICS

Building the Suburbs.

Builder William Levitt led the great postwar surge in suburban housing construction. A longtime admirer of Henry Ford, Levitt used mass-production techniques to build communities of small, modestly priced, almost identical single-family homes. In a note to himself for a typical day he wrote, "Eighteen houses completed on the shift from 8 to noon, and 19 more houses finished on the shift from 12:20 to 4:30." By the end of the 1950s other contractors had built similar developments on the outskirts of every major U.S. city.

CRITICAL THINKING How might mass-production techniques have made Levittown homes more affordable?

ANSWER: Students might note that mass-production techniques lowered the cost of Levittown homes by increasing the builder's efficiency.

INTERPRETING THE VISUAL RECORD

Suburbs. The movement of Americans to new suburbs became common in the 1950s. *How does this photograph from the 1950s reflect this trend in American life?*

To help workers improve their economic position, union leaders sought to cooperate with management. **George Meany**, the AFL–CIO's first president, boasted that he had never led a strike. Meany claimed that he had no interest in reforming society. He stated that his only goal was to ensure "an ever rising standard of living" for his union's members. Many unions fought for and won guaranteed annual wages and cost-of-living adjustments—automatic pay raises linked to the rate of inflation. In return, unions made concessions to management. These included accepting automation plans or changes in work rules or production levels.

Union support weakened in the late 1950s when newspapers reported widespread corruption. They linked many unions to organized crime. As a result of these reports, Congress attempted to crack down on union corruption. In 1959 Congress passed the Landrum-Griffin Act, which banned ex-convicts from holding union offices, required frequent elections of officers, and regulated the investment of union funds. The negative publicity hurt union membership, which declined steadily after 1957.

✔ **READING CHECK: Making Generalizations** Why did union membership grow in the early 1950s? It was boosted by the AFL and CIO merger. Joining a union also helped workers achieve a higher standard of living.

Suburban Migration

Workforce and income changes also led to increased geographic mobility for Americans. Millions of newly prosperous middle-class workers, particularly young couples, moved to the suburbs surrounding the nation's cities. By 1960 close to 60 million Americans—one third of the total U.S. population—lived in the suburbs.

Many of these suburbs were "planned communities." Developers built entire neighborhoods to attract new homeowners. To save time and money, developers used the same floorplan to build most houses in the community. As a result, the houses in the neighborhoods looked almost exactly alike. The best known of these suburban developments were the two Levittowns, one in Pennsylvania and one in New York, built by the Levitt Company. These developments expanded so rapidly that they soon grew into small cities. As more companies followed the Levitt Company example, the number of suburbs grew. An average of 1 million new suburban homes were built each year between 1950 and 1960.

The explosion of suburban growth occurred in part because developers were able to keep housing costs low. Growth also occurred because more Americans could afford to purchase homes. Veterans could get low-interest mortgages from such government agencies as the Veterans Administration and the Federal Housing Administration. Private savings and loan associations offered mortgages with relatively easy terms. The **Highway Act** of 1956 also contributed to suburban growth. This bill greatly expanded the nation's highway system, making it easier for suburban residents to commute to jobs in the cities.

TEACH OBJECTIVE 3

LEVEL 1: Conduct a discussion on suburban life during the 1950s. *(Suburban residents lived in nearly identical communities. Suburban life centered around the family. Consumption and conformity played important roles.)* Then ask students to identify some words that they associate with suburbs. *(Answers will vary. Students might list words such as* boring, pretty, *or* safe.*)* List the most common words on the chalkboard. Have each student use these words in a sentence describing suburban life during the 1950s. To conclude, ask students to express some of their own views on suburban life during the 1950s. Would they have wanted to live in a 1950s suburb? Why or why not? **English Language Learners**

LEVEL 2: Tell students to imagine that they are architects for a suburban-development firm during the 1950s. Have each student design and map a fictional suburb. Remind students to include items such as churches, community centers, and schools. Then ask students to write short reports to accompany their suburb plans. Students' reports should describe suburban life during the 1950s as well as discuss their own fictional suburbs. *(See the Level 1 lesson for the correct description.)* Have volunteers present their suburbs to the class. Students may wish to include their suburban maps and reports in their portfolios.

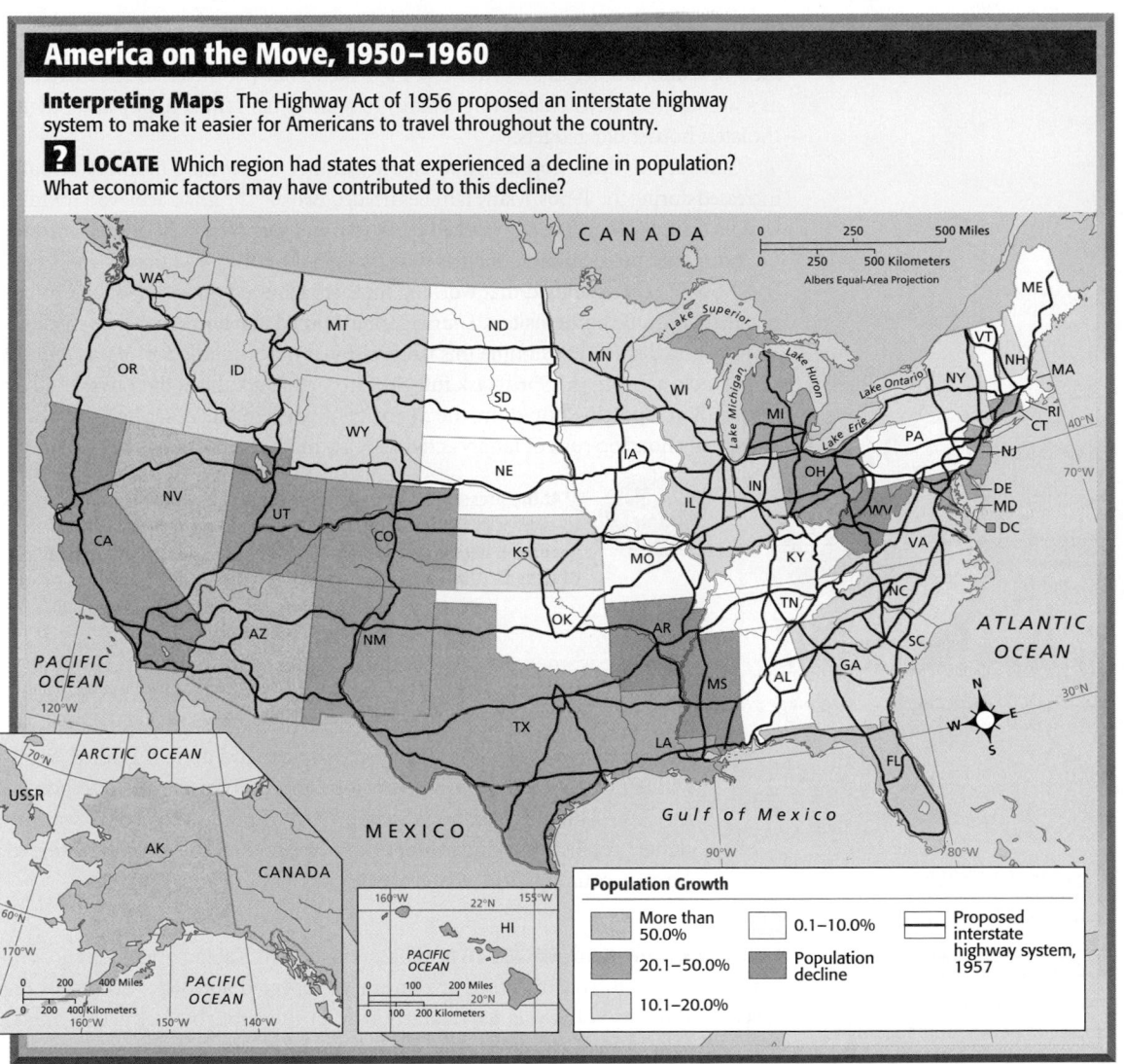

America on the Move, 1950–1960

Interpreting Maps The Highway Act of 1956 proposed an interstate highway system to make it easier for Americans to travel throughout the country.

? LOCATE Which region had states that experienced a decline in population? What economic factors may have contributed to this decline?

Population Growth

- More than 50.0%
- 20.1–50.0%
- 10.1–20.0%
- 0.1–10.0%
- Population decline
- Proposed interstate highway system, 1957

Suburban Life

An expanding population moved into the growing suburbs. During the Great Depression and World War II, many people had postponed getting married or starting a family. After the war, Americans got married at younger ages and in greater numbers than they had for generations. They also began having more children. The soaring birthrate accounted for more than 90 percent of the increase—some 30 million people—in the U.S. population during the 1950s. People began to refer to this increase as the **baby boom**.

Raising the family. An emphasis on child rearing, focusing on the role of mothers, accompanied the baby boom. Many mothers followed the advice of pediatrician Benjamin Spock, who wrote *The Common Sense Book of Baby and Child Care* in 1946. Advertisements, popular magazines, and self-help books depicted the

HISTORY MAKERS SPEAK

Harriet Osborn in *The Century*

Children in the Suburbs. Harriet Osborn, who moved into a suburb in 1953, described the role children played in the new communities: "The suburbs was the perfect place to raise children, and children were our primary focus. . . . There was much emphasis placed on babies and bringing them up during their first year of life. We used Dr. Spock's guide religiously, and we would compare notes all the time. . . . There were few worries. We could afford the house, and we could afford to clothe our child, and everybody else clothed their children. It was a good life. It was the American dream. . . ."

ACTIVITY: Tell students that Osborn's husband was a World War II veteran. Ask students to offer reasons why veterans and their families might have viewed suburban life as "the American dream."

VISUAL RECORD ANSWER

(for p. 600)

Students might point out that it shows newly built streets and buildings and newly planted trees.

MAP ANSWER

the South; cuts in farm subsidies, elimination of factory jobs due to automation

LEVEL 3: Ask a volunteer to read Lewis Mumford's statement on this page to the class. Then ask students to support or challenge Mumford's statement by describing suburban life during the 1950s. *(See the Level 1 lesson for the correct description.)* Note students' responses on the chalkboard. To extend the lesson, ask each student to outline or write a short story set in a suburb.

 HOMEWORK *Have students create cartoons that discuss suburban life during the 1950s. Have students write captions to accompany their cartoons.*

NOTE: To help students make meaningful connections between events in U.S. history and those in their own hometown, use the Chapter 20 **Hands-On History Activity**, What Things Do You Really Need.

CULTURE

A Religious Decade.
Religion was an important social force during the 1950s. Church membership had grown dramatically. Roman Catholic seminaries, monasteries, and convents had numerous applicants. Even popular culture reflected the decade's interest in religion. A variety of books with religious themes, such as Billy Graham's *Peace with God* and Dale Evans Rogers's *Angel Unaware*, became best-sellers. Westminster Press began publishing its 26-volume *Library of Christian Classics* in the early 1950s. Hollywood made religiously oriented movies, producing *Ben Hur*, *The Robe*, and *The Ten Commandments*.

CRITICAL THINKING What factors might have accounted for the increased interest in religion in the 1950s?

ANSWER: Answers will vary. Students might mention the influence of Cold War fears or the desire to give thanks for peace and prosperity.

VISUAL RECORD ANSWER
Students might suggest that the advertisement portrays the women as thrilled by achieving "white white" laundry.

INTERPRETING THE VISUAL RECORD

Consumerism. Advertisements directed at new suburban families maintained the image of women as happy homemakers who spent all of their time doing chores and buying household products. *How does this advertisement reinforce this image?*

ideal wife and mother as a full-time homemaker. They portrayed the homemaker as a woman who devoted all of her energy to making her family happy and buying the latest household gadgets.

Contrary to these popular images, the number of working mothers actually increased during the 1950s. Many families needed two paychecks to achieve a middle-class income. Mothers usually worked part-time and spent the bulk of their income on "extras" for their children, such as music lessons or family vacations.

Some experts argued that working mothers achieved more personal satisfaction than full-time homemakers. *Life* magazine claimed that homemakers were often "bored stiff." To examine this issue, popular magazine *Ladies' Home Journal* held a forum in 1956 to ask full-time homemakers about their lives. Rather than reporting boredom, the majority of participants described their lives as a nonstop rush of family activities. One mother reported on her situation.

 History Makers Speak

❝At the present time I don't think there is anything I would like to change in the household. We happen to be very close, and we are all happy. I will admit there are times when I am a little overtired . . . but actually it doesn't last too long.❞

—Mrs. Townsend, "Young Mother," *Ladies Home Journal*, 1956

Some women did say that they felt pressured to make their families fit the ideal image portrayed in popular books and magazines. In other studies, some working mothers, particularly those with young children, said that they felt pressured by other people to live up to this ideal. Many women considered quitting their jobs and becoming full-time homemakers. "The only person who approved of me in those days was my father," recalled working mother Gail Kaplan. "He had encouraged me to be an accountant and whatever I did was all right with him."

Consumerism and social life. The pressure that Kaplan and many forum participants felt to conform to a certain image reflected a broader emphasis on social conformity. This was particularly true in the suburbs. Suburban areas, reported writer Lewis Mumford, "[are] inhabited by people in the same class, the same income, the same age group."

Advertising played a large role in promoting conformity in the 1950s. It encouraged Americans to enjoy the general prosperity by buying consumer goods. In response, Americans went shopping. Each year they bought many household gadgets and a total of almost 8 million new automobiles. Some suburban families worked hard to "keep up with the Joneses"—that is, to make sure that they had as many modern conveniences as their neighbors.

In addition to buying the same consumer items, suburban families participated in many of the same social activities as their neighbors. These included Parent-Teacher Associations (PTAs), scouting, Little League sports, and religious activities. For uprooted Americans in the suburbs, membership in religious institutions provided not only spiritual guidance but also a sense of belonging. Churches and synagogues often tried to appeal to new members by sponsoring a variety of social and recreational activities.

✔ **READING CHECK: Categorizing** How did the baby boom change American life?
It led to an emphasis on child rearing and promoted the role of the woman as a homemaker.

LEVEL 1: Pair students and ask them to list characteristics of early television programming. *(Pairs should note that major corporations sponsored many early television programs. These programs included dramas, quiz shows, situation comedies, sporting events, and variety shows.)* Have each pair write sentences describing each of the elements on its list. Ask volunteers to share their sentences. To conclude, have students create typical television listings from a newspaper as they might have appeared in the 1950s.

English Language Learners, Cooperative Learning

LEVEL 2: Conduct a brief discussion on early television programming. *(See the Level 1 lesson for the correct description.)* Then tell students to imagine that it is 1957 and they have been asked to rate the quality of television programming. Have each student create a television-viewing log describing all of the programs that he or she watched on a given day, noting which programs they liked best. *(Students should consider what types of programs would have appealed to them and why.)* Ask volunteers to share their viewing logs with the class.

★ ★ ★ ★ ★ ★ ★ Science & Technology ★ ★ ★ ★ ★ ★ ★

Jonas Salk's Polio Vaccine

The United States emerged from World War II stronger both economically and militarily. However, many American families lived in fear of a new danger—a deadly polio epidemic that struck the country in the late 1940s. In 1952 alone the disease attacked some 60,000 Americans, many of whom were children. Hospitals were overwhelmed by the number of polio patients.

As the epidemic spread, scientists worked night and day to develop a cure or a way to prevent the disease. In 1952 Jonas Salk finally developed a successful vaccine against polio. "If it works," predicted one journalist of the vaccine, "Salk will have scored one of the greatest triumphs in the history of medicine." The vaccine did succeed in ending the epidemic. The number of polio cases continued to drop dramatically after an even better vaccine was developed in 1957.

Dead poliovirus

1 A small amount of dead poliovirus is injected into a healthy person.

2 The dead virus does not cause polio, but tricks cells into creating polio-killing antibodies.

Antibodies

Live poliovirus

4 Antibodies prevent the disease by attaching themselves to, and killing, any new, live polioviruses that invade the body.

3 Antibodies are released from cells.

Understanding Science and History

1. How does the polio vaccine prevent polio?
2. How did the vaccine affect Americans?

The Golden Age of Television

One of the most popular family activities was watching television together. Introduced commercially after World War II, television quickly became a favorite form of entertainment. By the end of the 1950s some 46 million households owned at least one television set.

Advertising played a major role in television programming. By reaching viewers daily in their homes, television advertising influenced consumer habits more than any previous medium had ever done. Particularly effective were ads in which television stars promoted their sponsors' products. By 1960, advertisers were spending $1.6 billion annually trying to convince viewers to buy their products. Often one business would sponsor an entire show, such as *General Electric Theatre* and *Kraft Television Theatre*. Their viewers would often connect the program with a company and its products. This advertising monopoly also gave many companies great control over program content.

Viewers could choose from several types of programming. Early television programs included sporting events such as the World Series, situation comedies like *The Honeymooners*, and variety programs like *Your Show of Shows*. Quiz shows like *The $64,000 Question* shared the airwaves with serious dramas like *Playhouse 90*. The most popular

Television became so popular in the 1950s that some companies began to market "TV dinners."

SCIENCE & TECHNOLOGY ANSWERS

1. by tricking cells into creating polio-fighting antibodies

2. It saved the lives of many Americans affected with polio.

LEVEL 3: Conduct a brief discussion on early television programming. *(See the Level 1 lesson for the correct description.)* Then tell students to imagine that it is 1957 and that a major television studio has just announced a contest entitled Create the Show of the Year! Have each student write a proposal for a new television show. Students should also write brief analyses to accompany their proposals. Students' analyses should explain why their proposed shows would be popular in the 1950s national market. Students may wish to include their proposals and analyses in their portfolios.

SPOTLIGHT
on the Game Show Scandal

Ask students to conduct research on the game-show scandal of the 1950s. Then tell students to imagine that they are modern-day historians. Have each student write a short article describing and analyzing the scandal, focusing on what it revealed about American culture during the 1950s. Alternately, tell students to imagine that they are Americans who watched game shows regularly and recently learned of the scandal. Have students write letters to the contestants or the networks describing their reactions to the charges of corruption. Ask volunteers to read their articles or letters to the class.
Block Scheduling

SCIENCE, TECHNOLOGY, AND SOCIETY

Early Television Sets. The television sets of the 1940s were nothing like today's sleek, clearly focused sets. Early sets displayed a fuzzy black-and-white picture. One observer likened the experience to "watching through venetian blinds"! In addition to their technological inferiority, television sets were extremely expensive—about $500 each at a time when many families earned less than $3,000 a year. In the early 1950s, however, the quality improved and the price dropped. By 1960, Americans owned some 45 million television sets.

CRITICAL THINKING Why might some families have spent so much money on television sets during the 1940s?

ANSWER: Students might suggest that these families wanted the latest technology.

VISUAL RECORD ANSWER

Answers will vary. Some students might name Lucille Ball and suggest that her image is familiar from television reruns.

INTERPRETING THE VISUAL RECORD

Television stars. Television stars like the cast of *I Love Lucy* (top) and *The Honeymooners* (bottom) were beloved by their millions of fans. *Can you name any of the actors in the images above? Why might they look familiar?*

program of the decade was the situation comedy *I Love Lucy,* starring real-life wife and husband Lucille Ball and Desi Arnaz. Thousands of fans tuned in every week to witness Lucy's crazy antics.

Television grew in popularity but remained a selective mirror, showing primarily white, middle-class, suburban experiences. Poverty, if shown at all, was treated as a minor problem. Working women, ethnic minorities, and inner-city life rarely appeared. When they were shown, it was usually in a way that reinforced stereotypes. One of the era's most controversial programs was *Amos 'n' Andy,* a comedy about African American urban life. The show was based on a popular radio program that had featured two white men providing the voices of African American characters. When the show moved to television, African American actors took over the roles. Still, for many viewers the characters represented white stereotypes of the African American community. The NAACP launched a protest against the program. Others joined in the protest, and *Amos 'n' Andy* was taken off the air. In 1966 it was banned from being shown in reruns.

Some critics also complained that television advertising reinforced materialism. Game shows in which contestants competed for prizes met with particular criticism. A congressional investigation revealed that some game shows were rigged. Popular contestants such as Columbia University professor Charles Van Doren were given the answers in advance. Producers hoped to keep popular contestants on the show and thus keep ratings up. Some critics argued that the game-show scandal revealed the dangers of television and its corrupting effect on American values.

✔ **READING CHECK: Analyzing Information** In what ways did early television affect American life? Families spent more time watching television, which may have reinforced stereotypes and materialism.

Teenagers and Popular Culture

Some parents expressed concern about the impact of popular culture on teenagers. With more free time and spending money than any previous generation, American teenagers in the 1950s sought new leisure-time activities. These activities often seemed to glamorize rebellion against suburban conformity.

Fictional rebels. Many young people found meaning in literature and films that featured discontented rebels. Some identified with Holden Caulfield, the main character of J. D. Salinger's 1951 novel, *The Catcher in the Rye.* Disgusted by the hypocrisy of the adult world, Caulfield declares it "crumby" and "phony." Although the book was very popular with young readers, some adults found its language and content offensive. Some groups demanded that it be banned from school libraries.

Many young people also enjoyed reading satirical comic books or magazines, such as *MAD.* The magazine dedicated itself to making fun of everything associated with "the American way of life." *MAD* soon rivaled *Life* as the most widely read magazine among young people. Many parents worried that reading such magazines would increase **juvenile delinquency**—antisocial behavior by the young.

Several of the decade's most popular films showed images of juvenile delinquency and young, angry rebels frustrated with life. Often their anger was directed not at any one particular thing, but at all of society in general. In the 1954 film *The Wild One*, a character asks the motorcycle-gang leader played by Marlon Brando what he is rebelling against. Brando snarls back, "Whadda ya got?"

This image of the rebel with no direction was reinforced in the 1955 movie *Rebel Without a Cause*. The film starred James Dean, Natalie Wood, and Sal Mineo as teenagers confused about the values of their suburban families. Many teenagers could identify with the characters' frustration. One teenager described his feelings when he saw the film. "I walked out of the movie house that day confirmed in my sense of isolation," he said, "but not without taking something precious with me: the feeling that others shared my pain." James Dean became an idol to many young people when the 24-year-old actor died in a car accident following the premiere of the film.

Rock 'n' roll. Teenagers also escaped from the conformity of suburbia through a new type of music called **rock 'n' roll**. This music reworked rhythm and blues, a style popular among African American performers and audiences that combined blues music with more energetic rhythms. Rhythm-and-blues music was particularly popular in dance halls. Rock 'n' roll took the music one step further and created a raw sound very different from other popular music of the time. Cleveland disc jockey Alan Freed made the term *rock 'n' roll* popular in 1951 when he started a rhythm-and-blues show aimed at young white audiences. Soon the sound caught on among teenagers across the country.

Elvis Presley emerged as rock's

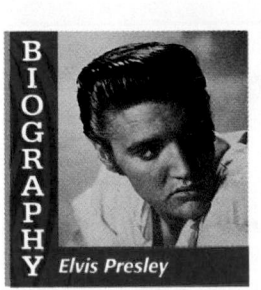

BIOGRAPHY
Elvis Presley

leading talent. Presley was born in 1935 to a poor family in Tupelo, Mississippi. He loved music, particularly gospel. When he was 13 years old, his family moved to Memphis, Tennessee, where he listened to and learned from numerous African American gospel and rhythm-and-blues musicians. After graduating from high school, Presley worked as a truck driver while occasionally singing professionally. In 1954 he made his first major record, "That's All Right, Mama." By 1955 he was one of the biggest music stars in the country.

Presley once said of his sudden popularity, "I just fell into it, really." Others recognized that this success came from his originality. His record producer noted that Presley sounded like no other singer he had ever heard. He also had a stage presence that electrified audiences. Shy in person, Presley came alive on stage. Journalist Jean Yothers was amazed by her own reaction when she reported on one of Presley's concerts in 1955. "I was awed," she said. "I got a tremendous boot out of this loud, uninhibited music that's sending the country crazy." Presley's many fans were

Teenagers as Consumers

teen Life

Some scholars have argued that the modern teenager was "invented" by advertising agencies in the 1950s. This was the first time that advertisers recognized teenagers as potentially powerful consumers. Many teenagers received allowances from their families or earned money from after-school jobs. Previously, teenagers' earnings usually went to help their families survive. In the 1950s most teenagers were allowed to

Advertisement from the 1950s

spend their earnings as they wanted. By 1956 teenagers' earnings represented some $7 billion in purchasing power.

Businesses quickly went after this market, launching dozens of new products geared toward teenage tastes and desires. Advertising also shaped teenagers' desires, presenting ideal images of what a popular teenager should own and wear. If teenagers would buy their products, the advertisers implied, they would enjoy social success.

Research on the R●M

Free Find: Elvis Presley
After reading about Elvis Presley on the **Holt Researcher CD–ROM**, write a fictional article for a teen music magazine describing how Elvis Presley's early life influenced his music.

During the 1950s teenagers listened to rock 'n' roll groups such as the Silhouettes on jukeboxes in local hangouts.

heartbroken when he was forced to take a break from his music career in the late 1950s after being drafted into the army. After completing his service he resumed his successful recording career and starred in 33 films before his death in 1977.

Despite its popularity, many adults disliked rock 'n' roll. They feared that it promoted antisocial behavior in teenagers. Some critics called it immoral. Others dismissed it as gibberish. They pointed out that the lyrics of many popular songs included made-up words or sounds that did not seem to make sense. The Coasters 1958 hit "Yakety Yak" made fun of how parents treated teenagers.

Primary Source

**Take out the papers and the trash
Or you don't get no spendin' cash
If you don't scrub that kitchen floor
You ain't gonna rock and roll no more
Yakety yak (don't talk back)**

—The Coasters, "Yakety Yak"

Rock 'n' roll also upset many people because it challenged racial segregation. African American musicians such as Little Richard, Chuck Berry, and Fats Domino, as well as Hispanic performers like Ritchie Valens, influenced early rock 'n' roll. White rockers such as Presley, Jerry Lee Lewis, and Buddy Holly shared the airwaves, and sometimes the stage, with noted black artists. This breaking down of racial barriers reflected larger social changes on the horizon.

✔ **READING CHECK: Analyzing Information** How did rock 'n' roll reflect the larger social issues in the 1950s? Popular culture featured rebellion and criticized racial segregation.

SECTION 2 REVIEW

1. Define and explain:
automation
baby boom
juvenile delinquency
rock 'n' roll

2. Identify and explain:
Oveta Culp Hobby
Modern Republicanism
George Meany
Highway Act
Elvis Presley

3. Identifying Cause and Effect
Copy the chart below. Use it to explain the growth of the suburbs and how that growth affected American middle-class culture.

Causes

Suburbs

Effects

4. Finding the Main Idea

a. How did President Eisenhower approach the nation's problems?

b. How did automation change the nature of work and affect unions?

c. In what ways did popular culture such as rock 'n' roll reflect changes in American life?

5. Writing and Critical Thinking

Making Generalizations Write a proposal for a 1950s television show that reflects and shapes American society.

Consider:
- how television shows portrayed American society
- the role of advertising on television
- how television encouraged certain ideals and consumer habits

Homework Practice Online
keyword: SE3 HP20

SECTION ③

After completing Section 3, students should be able to:

OBJECTIVE 1 *Relate how the* Brown *decision affected school segregation and exposed conflict over the segregation issue.*

OBJECTIVE 2 *Explain how the Montgomery bus boycott was a major turning point in the civil rights movement.*

OBJECTIVE 3 *Identify the challenges that Hispanics, Asian Americans, and American Indians faced in the 1950s.*

OBJECTIVE 4 *Identify the criticisms that writers and scholars expressed about 1950s society.*

OBJECTIVE 5 *Describe the problems that the poorest Americans faced in the 1950s.*

🔊 LET'S GET STARTED!

As students enter the classroom, ask them to imagine that they are returning war veterans facing discrimination at home. Have them respond to this scenario in writing and ask volunteers to share their responses. Tell students that in Section 3 they will learn about the civil rights movement in the 1940s and 1950s—and how veterans helped launch that movement.

SECTION ③

READ TO DISCOVER

1. How did the *Brown* decision affect school segregation and expose conflict over segregation?
2. How was the Montgomery bus boycott a major turning point in the civil rights movement?
3. What challenges did Hispanics, Asian Americans, and American Indians face in the 1950s?
4. How did writers and scholars criticize 1950s society?
5. What problems did poor Americans face in the 1950s?

DEFINE

beats
urban renewal

IDENTIFY

Brown v. *Board of Education*
Thurgood Marshall
Little Rock Nine
Rosa Parks
Montgomery Improvement Association
Martin Luther King Jr.
Civil Rights Act of 1957
Félix Longoria
League of United Latin American Citizens
Ralph Ellison
Jack Kerouac

WHY IT MATTERS TODAY

Contemporary literature continues to influence people's lives. Use **CNNfyi.com** or other **current events** sources to learn about a current influential author. Record your findings in your journal.

CNNfyi.com

Voices of Dissent

 EYEWITNESSES TO History

❝*I had grown up in a society where there were very clear lines. The civil rights movement gave me the power to challenge any line that limits me. . . . The movement said that if something puts you down, you have to fight against it.*❞

—Bernice Johnson, quoted in *Eyes on the Prize*, by Juan Williams

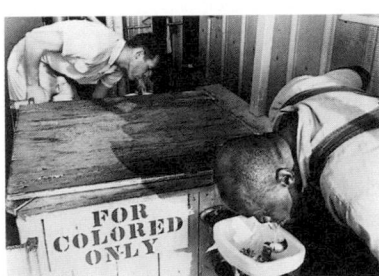

A segregated water fountain

Some people felt held back by society in the 1950s. Bernice Johnson of Albany, Georgia, recalled how society tried to limit opportunities for her and many other young African Americans. Johnson drew inspiration from the civil rights movement that emerged during the era. A gifted singer, Johnson was unable to afford musical instruments as a child. She later rose to become a musical scholar for the Smithsonian Institution, a college professor, a successful recording artist, and founder of the internationally known singing group Sweet Honey in the Rock.

Brown v. Board of Education

The 1896 Supreme Court decision *Plessy* v. *Ferguson* established the legality of "separate-but-equal" schools. The NAACP waged a long campaign against such segregation in educational facilities. It succeeded in opening some all-white universities and graduate schools to African American students. They did this by demonstrating that in most cases separate schools for black students were far inferior to the facilities reserved for white students. However, the Court continued to maintain that segregation in and of itself was legal.

In 1952 the NAACP supported a group of legal challenges to segregation in public schools that came before the Supreme Court. The main case was **Brown v. Board of Education**. It involved Linda Brown, an African American student from Topeka, Kansas. Segregation in Topeka's schools prevented her from attending an all-white elementary school a short walk from her home. Instead, she had to travel a long distance and cross dangerous railroad tracks to attend an African American school.

NAACP lawyer **Thurgood Marshall** argued on Brown's behalf. He introduced data suggesting that segregation psychologically damaged African American students by lowering their self-worth. Marshall's arguments greatly influenced the Court's unanimous ruling, which was issued on May 17, 1954. Written by Chief Justice Earl Warren, the opinion declared racial segregation illegal in public schools.

Many Americans praised the decision as a long-overdue step toward completely ending segregation. Some African Americans were skeptical that white leaders would really support desegregation. As one NAACP leader warned, history had shown African Americans that there was a "difference between the law in books and the law in action."

SECTION ③ RESOURCES

REPRODUCIBLE

▶ Guided Reading Strategy 20.3
▶ Graphic Organizer Activity 20: Voices of Dissent
▶ Literature Reading 20: LIngering Racial Tension

TECHNOLOGY

▶ One-Stop Planner, Lesson 20.3
▶ **CNN** Presents America: Yesterday and Today Segment: A Few Views of the 1950s
▶ Holt Researcher: American History CD–ROM
▶ HRW Go site
▶ Homework Practice Online

REINFORCEMENT, REVIEW, AND ASSESSMENT

▶ Section 3 Review, p. 615
▶ Daily Quiz 20.3
▶ Main Idea Activity 20.3
▶ English Audio Summary 20.3
▶ Spanish Audio Summary 20.3

TEACH OBJECTIVE 1

LEVEL 1: Pair students and have each pair define the *Brown* v. *Board of Education* decision in writing. *(Students should indicate that the decision banned racial segregation in public schools.)* Then ask pairs to write a paragraph describing how the decision exposed conflict over the segregation issue. *(Students should note that when the Little Rock Nine attempted to integrate Central High School in Little Rock, Arkansas, they experienced harassment and violence.)* Have volunteers read their paragraphs to the class.
English Language Learners, Cooperative Learning

LEVEL 2: Tell students to imagine that they are newspaper reporters who were present for the announcement of the *Brown* v. *Board of Education* decision and the subsequent desegregation struggle in Little Rock. Have each student write a short memoir describing how the decision affected school segregation and exposed conflict over the segregation issue. *(See the Level 1 lesson for the correct answers.)* Ask volunteers to read their memoirs to the class. Students may wish to include their memoirs in their portfolios.

Although some states moved quickly to end school segregation, many white southern leaders reacted to the decision with anger and defiance. South Carolina governor James F. Byrnes declared that desegregation "would mark the beginning of the end of civilization in the South as we have known it." Southern resistance caused the Supreme Court to issue a ruling in 1955 instructing federal district courts to end school segregation "with all deliberate speed."

Showdown in Little Rock

Despite the Supreme Court ruling, school desegregation in the South moved slowly. By the end of the 1956–57 school year, the vast majority of southern school systems remained segregated. In Arkansas, however, school desegregation was progressing with relatively little opposition. Two of the three southern school districts that began desegregating in 1954 were in Arkansas. The Little Rock school board was the first in the South to announce that it would comply with the *Brown* decision.

Little Rock's desegregation plan was set to begin in September 1957 with the admission of nine African American students to the all-white Central High School. However, Governor Orval Faubus spoke out against the plan. The night before school was to start, he ordered the Arkansas National Guard to surround Central High. He did so, he claimed, to protect the school from attacks by armed protesters. "It will not be possible to restore or to maintain order . . . if forcible integration is carried out tomorrow in the schools of this community," he warned.

Faubus exaggerated the danger, but his claims spread panic. One of the nine black students, Elizabeth Eckford, did not receive a message that instructed her not to go to school alone. When she attempted to enter the school, a mob of angry protesters and a line of armed National Guardsmen met her. She described the ordeal:

INTERPRETING THE VISUAL RECORD
Little Rock. Elizabeth Eckford faces a hostile crowd as she walks by herself to Central High School. ***How does Eckford's expression in this image contrast with those of the people behind her?***

History Makers Speak

❝When I got in front of the school . . . I didn't know what to do. . . . Just then the guards let some white students through. . . . I walked up to the guard who had let [them] in. . . . When I tried to squeeze past him, he raised his bayonet, and then the other guard moved in. . . . Somebody [in the crowd] started yelling, 'Lynch her! Lynch her!'❞

—Elizabeth Eckford

For nearly three weeks, members of the Arkansas National Guard prevented the African American students, now known as the **Little Rock Nine,** from entering the school. Then, under court order, Faubus removed the National Guard. When the nine attempted to enter the school on September 23, the white mob rioted. Angered by the "disgraceful occurrences" at the school, President Eisenhower ordered some 1,000 federal troops to Little Rock. On September 25, 1957, under the protection of the soldiers' fixed bayonets, the Little Rock Nine finally entered Central High.

The Little Rock Nine endured a difficult year that included frequent harassment. One of the group, Minniejean Brown, was suspended for dumping food on

LEVEL 3: Tell students to imagine that they are advisers to President Eisenhower in September 1957. Have each student write a detailed memo describing how the *Brown* decision affected school segregation and exposed conflict over the segregation issue. *(See the Level 1 lesson for the correct answers.)* In their memos, students should recommend a course of action on the Little Rock crisis. Have volunteers share their suggested actions. Then conduct a brief discussion on Eisenhower's response to the Little Rock crisis.

 HOMEWORK *Have each student create an annotated time line of the* Brown v. Board of Education *decision and the Little Rock crisis.*

TEACH OBJECTIVE 2

 LEVEL 1: Pair students and tell them to imagine that they participated in the Montgomery bus boycott. Have each pair develop a short dialogue discussing the boycott and explaining how it represented a major turning point in the civil rights movement. *(Students should indicate that the boycott struck an important blow against segregation, established Martin Luther King Jr. as a civil rights leader, and lessened the fear of standing up to people in positions of power.)* Ask volunteers to perform their dialogues for the class.
English Language Learners, Cooperative Learning

a white boy who had made a racist comment. In February, when another white student called her a racial and obscene name, Brown responded with much milder insults of her own. For this incident, Brown was permanently expelled from school. After that, white students distributed cards that read, "One Down . . . Eight to Go."

Despite such pressure, the other African American students stayed. In May 1958 Ernest Green became the first African American student ever to graduate from Central High School. "When they called my name . . . nobody clapped," Green recalled of his graduation ceremony. "But I figured they didn't have to . . . because after I got that diploma, that was it. I had accomplished what I had come there for."

Governor Faubus continued to look for ways to resist integration. He ordered the shutdown of the Little Rock public school system during the 1958–59 school year. He also helped establish a private school system to serve white students. Most African Americans, including the rest of the Little Rock Nine, as well as poor whites, had no school to attend. In 1959 the school district reopened under court order and slowly began to desegregate.

✔ **READING CHECK: Analyzing Information** How did the *Brown* decision affect school segregation, particularly in the South? Some states moved quickly. In the South, however, desegregation moved slowly.

The Montgomery Bus Boycott

In addition to fighting segregation in schools, the NAACP sought to end racial segregation on southern transportation systems. In Montgomery, Alabama, local NAACP leaders planned to challenge the practice of forcing African American citizens to ride in the back of city buses.

 A boycott begins. On December 1, 1955, **Rosa Parks**, an African American seamstress, provided the NAACP with its opportunity. Parks refused to give up her bus seat to a white passenger and was arrested. Born in 1913 in Tuskegee, Alabama, Parks moved to the Montgomery area at a young age. Her mother was determined that Parks would receive a good education. Montgomery did not have a high school for African American students, so her parents sent her to the laboratory school at Alabama State College. Discrimination prevented her from obtaining a job that matched her education, however. Parks found work as a seamstress. She also became involved in the civil rights movement and held an office in the Montgomery chapter of the NAACP.

In the late 1950s Parks moved to Detroit, where she began working for Representative John Conyers in 1967. She remains committed to civil rights and

INTERPRETING THE VISUAL RECORD

Segregation. In most southern cities, African Americans had to sit in the back of buses even if seats were available up front. After a court order, this Dallas Transit Company employee is removing a segregation sign. *How do you think African American bus riders would view the removal of this sign?*

Research on the ROM

Free Find: Rosa Parks
After reading about Rosa Parks on the **Holt Researcher CD–ROM**, write a short essay explaining the significance of her contribution to the civil rights movement.

VISUAL RECORD ANSWER

Students might answer that most African Americans would see it as a positive step.

CITIZENSHIP

The Montgomery Car Pools. Montgomery's African American residents formed car pools to support the bus boycott and provide transportation. Some people donated as much as 20 percent of their weekly salaries to fund the car pools. The NAACP, the United Auto Workers, and sympathetic white residents also lent support. Police officers often stopped the carpoolers for tiny violations. To avoid these encounters, carpool drivers proceeded at very slow speeds and signaled turns far in advance.

ACTIVITY: Tell students to imagine that they live in Montgomery, Alabama, and support the bus boycott. Have each student create a flier supporting the boycott and advertising a car pool service.

THAT'S INTERESTING!

Throughout the Montgomery bus boycott, Martin Luther King Jr. urged his followers to adhere to nonviolence. He said, "We want to love our enemies. . . . We must meet hate with love."

VISUAL RECORD ANSWER

Answers will vary. Some students might suggest that the photograph shows King as charismatic and stylish.

610

INTERPRETING THE VISUAL RECORD

Civil rights. During the Montgomery Bus Boycott Martin Luther King Jr.'s charisma and ability to motivate supporters made him an important leader in the movement. *How do you think this photograph captures King's personality and role as a leader?*

has won numerous awards, including the Congressional Gold Medal of Honor, the highest honor the United States can award a private citizen.

In the summer of 1955 Parks attended a workshop on social justice that deeply influenced her views. "I found out for the first time . . . that this could be a unified society," she said. "I gained there the strength to persevere in my work for freedom." Her actions in December of that year would put her training to the test. Parks's arrest for refusing to give up her seat led to her conviction for violating the city's segregation laws. In protest, many of Montgomery's 50,000 African Americans organized a boycott against the bus system. The **Montgomery Improvement Association** (MIA), a group of local civil rights leaders, persuaded the community to continue the boycott while the NAACP and Parks appealed her conviction.

The MIA chose as its spokesperson **Martin Luther King Jr.**, a 26-year-old Baptist minister. An energetic and moving speaker, King could inspire large audiences. His ability to move people helped hold the African American community together as the bus boycott dragged on for months. White protesters tried every method from intimidation to physical violence to break the boycott. The houses of King and other MIA leaders were bombed. Many boycotters—including Rosa Parks—lost their jobs. King, who had studied the nonviolent tactics of Indian nationalist Mohandas K. Gandhi, urged the African American community not to respond to violence with more violence.

The boycott succeeds. Finally, the nonviolent protest worked. In November 1956 the Supreme Court declared both the Montgomery and the Alabama segregation laws unconstitutional. By the end of the year, Montgomery had a desegregated bus system, and the civil rights movement had a new leader—Martin Luther King Jr. "We had won self-respect," declared boycott organizer Jo Ann Robinson. "It . . . makes you feel that America is a great country and we're going to do more to make it greater."

The Montgomery victory marked a blow to racial discrimination and to the fear of standing up to people in positions of power. Cold War hysteria had contributed to this fear of authority. Not surprisingly, Martin Luther King Jr. was accused of being a Communist by opponents of the civil rights movement. Some southern whites, however, accepted that change had to come. As one South Carolina newspaper declared, "Segregation is going—it's all but gone. . . . The South can't reverse the trend."

Congress aided this trend by passing the first new civil rights law since Reconstruction. This **Civil Rights Act of 1957** bill made it a federal crime to prevent qualified persons from voting. It also set up the federal Civil Rights Commission to investigate violations of the law. A follow-up law enacted in 1960 strengthened the courts' power to protect the voting rights of African Americans.

✔ **READING CHECK: Evaluating** How effective were Rosa Parks and Martin Luther King Jr. as leaders in the Montgomery bus boycott? **Both were very effective. Parks sparked the protest while King inspired unity and nonviolent protest.**

TEACH OBJECTIVE 3

ALL LEVELS: Write the following statement on the chalkboard: *During the 1950s many white Americans regarded Hispanics, Asian Americans, and American Indians as "the other," which led them to discriminate against these minority groups.* Have students respond to the statement in writing. Ask volunteers to share their responses. *(Answers will vary. Students might discuss the emphasis on conformity during the 1950s or mention the long-term history of discrimination in the United States.)* To help students understand the challenges certain minority groups faced in the 1950s, copy the graphic organizer on the chalkboard, omitting the italicized answers. Have each student complete it.
English Language Learners

MINORITY GROUPS IN THE 1950s

Group	Challenges
Hispanics	discrimination and segregation, particularly in public schools; continued nativism
Asian Americans	discrimination; belief that they did not fit the American "ideal"
American Indians	relocation and termination policies; government pressure to assimilate

HOMEWORK *Have each student create a detailed outline of the subsection entitled Beyond Black and White.*

Beyond Black and White

Segregation and discrimination affected others in the 1950s besides African Americans. Nonwhite Americans faced prejudice. The experience of fighting for democratic ideals overseas in World War II, however, motivated more people to stand up and defend those ideals at home.

The Hispanic experience. One particular incident revealed the extent of discrimination endured by Hispanics. **Félix Longoria** was a Mexican American soldier killed during World War II. In 1948 his body was recovered and returned to his hometown, Three Rivers, Texas. The town's only funeral home director refused to allow the use of the chapel for Longoria's burial because the soldier was Mexican American. When the media publicized this story, many Americans expressed outrage at this treatment of a veteran. Senator Lyndon B. Johnson of Texas arranged for Longoria to be buried with full military honors at Arlington National Cemetery near Washington, D.C.

The Longoria incident led to the formation of the American GI Forum, a group dedicated to protecting the rights of Hispanic veterans. Over time the organization expanded to become a powerful lobbying group on behalf of all Hispanics. The GI Forum received help in its efforts from the **League of United Latin American Citizens** (LULAC). Formed in 1929, LULAC adopted many of the same tactics to fight for Hispanic rights that the NAACP used to champion African American rights.

Like the NAACP, LULAC focused on ending segregation, particularly in schools. In 1945 LULAC won an important case in *Méndez et al. v. Westminster School District et al.* In this case a federal judge ruled that the segregation of Mexican American children in a California school district was illegal. An even bigger victory came in 1948 with *Delgado* v. *Bastrop Independent School District*. In the *Delgado* case a judge ruled that the segregation of Mexican American children in a Texas school district was illegal. Soon afterward, state officials ended the segregation of Hispanic children in all Texas public schools.

Asian immigration. Some of the prejudice against Hispanics was the result of continued nativism. Nevertheless, fear of immigration began to ease somewhat after World War II. Asian immigrants in particular experienced the effects of this change. In 1952 Congress repealed the Chinese Exclusion Act to allow more Chinese immigrants into the United States.

Many Asian Americans achieved great success in the United States. However, they still faced constant reminders that they did not fit the profile of an "ideal" American. In 1952, for example, Sing Sheng, a Chinese immigrant and Allied war hero, attempted to buy a house in a San Francisco suburb called Southwood. When the neighborhood's white residents discovered that an Asian family might move in, they began a drive to prevent the Sheng family from buying the house. Noting that his family had fled communism in China, Sheng appealed to the residents of Southwood to practice the values of democracy and equality. "Do not make us the victims of a false

After Félix Longoria was finally buried at Arlington National Cemetery, Hispanic veterans organized the American GI Forum to fight for other rights.

Asian immigration to the United States increased after Congress repealed the Chinese Exclusion Act.

CITIZENSHIP

Discrimination in the Southwest. During the 1960s, segregation affected Hispanics in many southwestern states. In southern and western Texas towns, for example, there were "Anglo schools" and "Mexican schools" in "white towns" and "little Mexicos." Churches and even cemeteries were also strictly segregated. In Texas legal segregation largely ended in 1969, when the legislature passed five laws banning various forms of segregation and discrimination. Despite the laws, however, segregation continued in a few towns. For example, in Ozona, the bowling alley, the cemeteries, and the swimming pools remained segregated through the early 1970s.

CRITICAL THINKING Why might cemeteries have been segregated in the South and Southwest? What might this segregation reveal about race relations there?

ANSWER: Students might suggest that cemeteries were segregated because churches were segregated. Students might argue that the segregation of cemeteries revealed the deep-seated nature of racial discrimination.

TEACH OBJECTIVE 4

LEVEL 1: Pair students and ask each pair to list some of the criticisms that writers and scholars expressed about 1950s society. *(Students should include conformity, poverty, racism, and a lack of creativity.)* Ask volunteers to share the contents of their lists and then note the most common criticisms on the chalkboard. Then ask pairs to write paragraphs evaluating the validity of the criticisms.
English Language Learners, Cooperative Learning

LEVEL 2: Conduct a brief discussion on the criticisms that writers and scholars expressed about 1950s society. *(See the Level 1 lesson for the correct criticisms.)* Then organize students into small groups and tell them to imagine that they are magazine editors preparing a special insert entitled The 1950s: An Age of Criticism. Have each group plan its insert, identifying potential articles, editorials, interviews, and so on. Then divide the elements among students and have each student create an item for the insert. Tell students to collect their items and compile them into inserts. Students may wish to include their individual items in their portfolios. **Cooperative Learning**

internet connect

TOPIC: LULAC
GO TO: go.hrw.com
KEYWORD: SE3 AN20

Have students access the Internet through the HRW Go site to conduct research on the history and political work of the League of United Latin American Citizens (LULAC) and the Mexican American Legal Defense Fund (MALDEF). Then have each student create an annotated and illustrated time line that outlines the activities of both organizations from 1929 to the present.

VISUAL RECORD ANSWER

Students might suggest that people would be more sympathetic toward a young child.

INTERPRETING THE VISUAL RECORD

Protesting. This young American Indian is protesting the government's takeover of reservation land to build a power plant. *Why might this protester be more effective than others?*

democracy," he pleaded. Despite this request, the neighborhood association voted overwhelmingly to fight the Shengs. When white residents of other communities heard about the Southwood incident, many sent the Shengs personal letters inviting them to move into their neighborhoods. The Shengs accepted one such offer, settling peacefully in the town of Sonoma, California.

Relocation of American Indians.
American Indians moved under pressure from the federal government. The government adopted a policy of termination in 1953. Termination involved ending the reservation system on a tribe-by-tribe basis. It also cut most federal funding for American Indians. Various tribal groups launched protests and lawsuits against the termination policy. They considered it an attempt to wipe out American Indian communities.

To promote the assimilation of American Indians into mainstream society, the Eisenhower administration supported the Relocation Act of 1956. The act set up procedures to encourage Indians to move to urban areas. It also established relocation offices in major cities to assist newcomers. Critics of the legislation feared that it would empty the reservations of future leaders and destroy tribal cultures. Oglala Lakota activist Gerald One Feather recalled the impact of the program.

 History Makers Speak

❝The relocation program had an impact on our . . . government at Pine Ridge [South Dakota]. Many people who could have provided leadership were lost because they had motivation to go off the reservation to find employment or obtain an education. Relocation drained off a lot of our potential leadership.❞

—Gerald One Feather, quoted in *Indian Self-Rule*, edited by Kenneth R. Philp

By 1958 the Eisenhower administration backed away from the termination policy. It stated that it would no longer support legislation "to terminate tribes without their consent."

✔ **READING CHECK: Summarizing** What kinds of discrimination did Hispanics, Asian Americans, and American Indians face in the 1950s? discrimination in funeral homes, schools, and in buying homes; American Indians were pressured into moving off their reservations

Questioning Conformity

For some scholars, discrimination against nonwhites was a symptom of broader societal trouble. They argued that beneath its surface of conformity, economic prosperity, and peace, the United States faced serious problems. These social critics sought to expose what they called the "crack in the picture window." This meant that the problems grew within a seemingly happy and peaceful society.

Some novelists depicted the experiences of those facing poverty and discrimination. African American writer **Ralph Ellison** published *Invisible Man* in 1952. In the novel an African American man searches for his place in a society that is at once both hostile and indifferent to him. Referring to his exclusion from mainstream society, the man states, "I am an invisible man. . . . I am invisible, understand, simply because people refuse to see me."

Several important scholars wrote nonfiction works that reinforced Ellison's message. Harvard economist John Kenneth Galbraith issued a warning to privileged Americans in *The Affluent Society* (1958). He wrote that they were ignoring pressing social issues in their pursuit of material possessions and comfort. Sociologists William Whyte, C. Wright Mills, and David Riesman criticized the new corporate system. Whyte's *The Organization Man* (1956) and Mills's *White Collar* (1951) argued that the pressure to conform in the new corporate order was wiping out workers' independence and individualism. Riesman warned in *The Lonely Crowd* (1950) that the United States faced "a silent revolution against work" because jobs no longer had meaning for people.

The **beats**, a small but influential group of writers and poets, challenged both the literary conventions of the day and the lifestyle of the middle class. Beat writer Allen Ginsberg's poem "Howl," for instance, raged against the threat of nuclear war and the conventions of corporate America. The beats wrote as they lived—on the spur of the moment, without any planning. One of the best-known beat works was written by **Jack Kerouac** in 1957. His novel *On the Road* was written in a continuous three-week-long session at the typewriter. Kerouac celebrated the search for individual identity and the rejection of security and stability. One sentence in the novel captures the beat philosophy. "We gotta go and never stop till we get there."

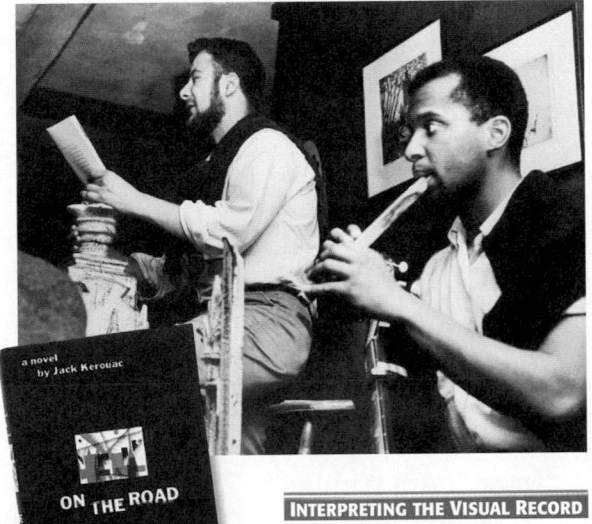

INTERPRETING THE VISUAL RECORD

The beats. Jack Kerouac was the most famous beat writer. His book *On the Road* inspired ordinary people like these students (above) to join the movement as well. *How do the styles and activities of the beats differ from those of other teenagers in the 1950s?*

✔ **READING CHECK: Categorizing** How did writers and scholars of the 1950s criticize conformity? They criticized discrimination against nonwhites, conformity, and the middle class.

The Nonaffluent Society

Some writers noted that despite the overall strength of the postwar economy, many people were left out of this prosperity. Studies in the late 1950s found that some 30–40 million Americans were living below a poverty level of $2,500–$3,000 in annual income for a household or family of four.

The rural poor. Rural residents, particularly farmers, represented the poorest segment of the American population. In some areas of the country, including parts of the Appalachian Mountains, many people still had no indoor plumbing or electricity. One study characterized the Appalachians as being filled with "a mood of apathy and despair."

Although farming productivity increased from 1950 to 1960, the income generated from farms actually shrank. As foreign countries recovered from World War II, they imported less food from the United States. The price of agricultural products fell dramatically. Large farms tended to do better than small farms. This was particularly true for those large farms whose owners could afford to invest in new, efficient farm equipment. Increased use of farm technology such as gasoline-powered tractors and other large equipment allowed farm owners to operate with fewer workers. As a result, many of the poorest farm laborers, particularly migrant field hands, found fewer opportunities for employment.

Tractors like this one replaced farmworkers during the 1950s.

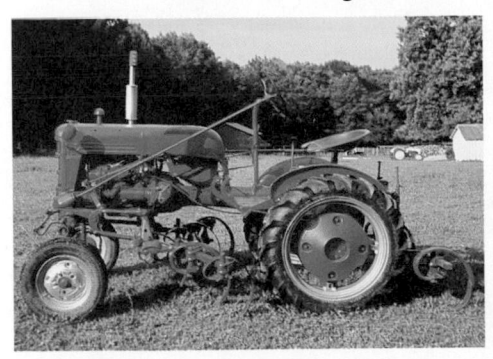

HISTORY MAKERS SPEAK

Jack Trachsel in *The Century*

Businesses and Conformity. During the 1950s large corporations often encouraged conformity in their employees. This affected all aspects of workers' lives, right down to their clothes. Some businesses issued "company neckties." Jack Trachsel, who worked for an Oregon gas company in the late 1950s and early 1960s, remembered: "There was a certain amount of conformity in the atmosphere at the office. Our dress code was pretty rigid, so we were always expected to wear conservative business suits, with conservative ties and white shirts, and polished shoes. Just about everybody in the office had a gray flannel suit—at least the younger crowd. I had two of them. It just didn't do your career any good at all to wear, say, a checkered sport coat."

CRITICAL THINKING Why might companies have encouraged conformity?

ANSWER: Students might suggest that corporations viewed conformity as a way to ensure cooperation and efficiency.

VISUAL RECORD ANSWER

Answers will vary. Students might mention the beats' clothes and hairstyles. In addition, they appear to be performing poetry and music.

LEVELS 1 AND 2: Ask each student to develop a short monologue describing the problems faced by either the rural or urban poor. *(Students' monologues should mention falling farm prices, high cost of farm equipment, fewer farm jobs, increasingly poor urban populations, discrimination, and poor housing, as appropriate.)* Ask volunteers to perform their monologues for the class. To conclude, conduct a discussion about poverty in the United States during the 1930s and 1950s. How might the experience of poverty have differed in those two decades? *(Students might suggest that there was less stigma attached to poverty during the depression, since so many people were affected by it.)* **English Language Learners**

LEVEL 3: Ask students to imagine that they are novelists preparing to write a chapter about poor people in the 1950s. Have each student create a set of research notes to use in his or her later work. Students' research notes should describe the problems that the poorest Americans faced in the 1950s. *(See the Levels 1 and 2 lesson for the correct problems.)* Have students share their notes with the class. To conclude, conduct a discussion about poverty in the United States during the 1930s and 1950s. How might the experience of poverty have differed in those two decades? *(See the Levels 1 and 2 lesson for the correct answer.)*

AMERICAN LETTERS ANSWERS

1. as a time of prosperity overshadowed by the threat of nuclear warfare

2. white society; African Americans

3. Both criticize American culture, but Madgett seems more optimistic about the possibility of positive change.

VISUAL RECORD ANSWER
(for p. 615)

Students might answer that the housing project is newer and taller and has a cleaner appearance.

REVIEW SECTION 3 ANSWERS

1. Define
- beats, p. 613
- urban renewal, p. 615

2. Identify
- *Brown* v. *Board of Education*, p. 607
- Thurgood Marshall, p. 607
- Little Rock Nine, p. 608
- Rosa Parks, p. 609
- Montgomery Improvement Association, p. 610
- Martin Luther King Jr., p. 610
- Civil Rights Act of 1957, p. 610
- Félix Longoria, p. 611
- League of United Latin American Citizens, p. 611
- Ralph Ellison, p. 612
- Jack Kerouac, p. 613

AMERICAN Letters

Voices of the Fifties

Many poets captured the spirit of the era in their verse. Beat poet Lawrence Ferlinghetti's "I Am Waiting" challenged the confidence of postwar society. African American poet Naomi Long Madgett captured the feelings of many participants in the early civil rights movement in her poem "Midway."

from "I Am Waiting"
by Lawrence Ferlinghetti

Lawrence Ferlinghetti

I am waiting for my number to
    be called
and I am waiting for the living
    end
and I am waiting
for dad to come home
his pockets full
of irradiated [radioactive] silver
    dollars
and I am waiting
for the atomic tests to end
and I am waiting happily
for things to get much worse
before they improve . . .
and I am waiting
for the human crowd
to wander off a cliff somewhere
clutching its atomic umbrella . . .
and I am waiting
for the meek to be blessed
and inherit the earth . . .
and I am waiting for forests and animals
to reclaim the earth as theirs
and I am waiting
for a way to be devised
to destroy all nationalisms
without killing anybody
and I am waiting
for linnets [birds] and planets to fall like rain
and I am waiting for lovers and weepers
to lie down together again
in a new rebirth of wonder.

"Midway"
by Naomi Long Madgett

Naomi Long Madgett

I've come this far to freedom
and I won't turn back.
I'm climbing to the highway
from my old dirt track.
    I'm coming and I'm going
    And I'm stretching and I'm
growing
And I'll reap what I've been
sowing or my skin's not black.

I've prayed and slaved and waited and I've sung my song.
You've bled me and you've starved me but I've still grown strong.
    You've lashed me and you've treed me
    And you've everything but freed me
But in time you'll know you need me and it won't be long.

I've seen the daylight breaking high above the bough.
I've found my destination and I've made my vow;
    So whether you abhor me
    Or deride me or ignore me,
Mighty mountains loom before me and I won't stop now.

UNDERSTANDING LITERATURE

1. What image does Ferlinghetti present of life in the 1950s?

2. Who is the "you" in Madgett's poem? Other than the poet, who does the "I" in the poem represent?

3. How are Madgett's and Ferlinghetti's views of the 1950s similar? How are they different?

REVIEW

Have students complete the **Section 3 Review** on p. 615.

ASSESS

Have students complete **Daily Quiz 20.3**. As **Alternative Assessment**, you may want to use the social criticism piece or the poverty monologue in this section's lessons.

RETEACH

Have students complete **Main Idea Activity for English Language Learners and Special-Needs Students 20.3**. Then list the major headings of Section 3 on the chalkboard. Tell students to imagine that these headings are newsmagazine headlines. Ask students to fill in the main points of each story. Note students' responses on the chalkboard. **English Language Learners**

EXTEND

Ask students to identify individuals or groups that criticize American society today. Encourage students to identify issues of concern and methods these critics use. Then have students compare the nature of current social criticism with the criticism produced in the 1950s. **Block Scheduling**

Urban communities. Many displaced workers from rural areas flocked to U.S. cities in search of a better life. In the Appalachian area alone, some 1.5 million young people left the mountains for cities. One Cincinnati newspaper referred to the city's Appalachian migrants as "our 50,000 refugees."

Many rural-to-urban migrants experienced little improvement in their economic status. By 1960 more than 20 million city-dwellers were living in poverty. As more middle-class white residents moved to the suburbs, poor inner-city communities increasingly consisted of nonwhite residents. In addition to the continuing African American migration to the cities, the Hispanic urban population increased. Poverty and discriminatory real estate practices prevented most nonwhite city-dwellers from getting decent housing. They were generally limited to crowded tenements and old housing in the poorest neighborhoods, which were usually segregated by ethnicity.

Despite their poverty, ethnic neighborhoods provided a sense of community for many of those who lived there. Local stores, churches, synagogues, temples, and social clubs gave structure to the lives of new migrants struggling to adjust to city life.

To improve inner-city housing, the federal government proposed **urban renewal** programs. These were created to replace old, run-down inner-city buildings with new ones. Throughout the country, federally financed urban renewal programs bulldozed older neighborhoods to make way for more than 400,000 low-income public housing units. These new high-rise buildings often had a cold, impersonal atmosphere. Most quickly became run-down themselves and were plagued by problems such as high crime rates.

✔ **READING CHECK: Summarizing** What caused poverty in the 1950s? a drop in agricultural prices, growing unemployment among farm laborers, and discrimination against minorities in the cities

INTERPRETING THE VISUAL RECORD

Urban renewal. High-rise housing projects were supposed to replace poor neighborhoods. *How does the housing project in the background of this image contrast with the building in front?*

SECTION **3** REVIEW

1. Define and explain:
  beats   urban renewal

2. Identify and explain:
  Brown v. *Board of Education*
  Thurgood Marshall
  Little Rock Nine
  Rosa Parks
  Montgomery Improvement
    Association
  Martin Luther King Jr.
  Civil Rights Act of 1957
  Félix Longoria
  League of United Latin
    American Citizens
  Ralph Ellison
  Jack Kerouac

3. Comparing Copy the graphic organizer below. Use it to list aspects of rural and urban life in the 1950s, noting shared traits of both.

4. **Finding the Main Idea**
  a. What effect did the *Brown* decision, the Little Rock crisis, and the Montgomery bus boycott have on the civil rights movement?
  b. What did the experiences of Hispanics, Asian Americans, and American Indians reveal about the United States in the 1950s?
  c. How did agricultural problems contribute to migration within the United States?

5. **Writing and Critical Thinking**
  Comparing and Contrasting Is it accurate to portray the 1950s as an era of good times for all Americans? Write a brief answer explaining why or why not.
  Consider:
  • how different people might define "good times"
  • what the experiences of minorities and the poor were
  • what criticisms were given of society in the 1950s

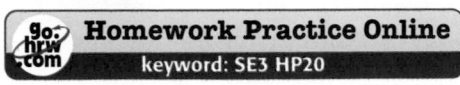
Homework Practice Online
keyword: SE3 HP20

---

3. rural—falling farm incomes, fewer farm jobs, young people migrate to cities; urban—white, middle class move to suburbs, discrimination, lack of decent housing; shared traits—poverty and struggle

4a. *Brown*—banned public school segregation; Little Rock—exposed conflict over segregation; boycott—King emerges as a leader, desegregates Montgomery buses

b. that many people held prejudices against minorities

c. Falling farm prices and competition from larger farms meant rural people migrated to cities to find jobs.

5. Answers will vary. Students might note how not all citizens shared in the good times.

CHAPTER
REVIEW **20** ANSWERS

Creating a Time Line
Each event should have an explanation and the correct date.

Writing a Summary
See the Reading Checks in each section for main ideas.

Identifying People and Ideas
1. bill that provided assistance to veterans

2. conservative party of white southern Democrats

3. Truman's reform program

4. the use of machines to perform manufacturing tasks

CHAPTER 20 Review

Creating a Time Line
Copy the time line below onto a sheet of paper. Complete the time line by filling in the events and dates from the chapter that you think were most significant. Pick three events and explain why you think they were significant.

1945   1950   1955   1960

Writing a Summary
Using standard grammar, spelling, sentence structure, and punctuation, write an overview of events in the chapter.

Identifying People and Ideas
Identify the following terms or individuals and explain their significance.

1. GI Bill of Rights
2. Dixiecrats
3. Fair Deal
4. automation
5. George Meany
6. baby boom
7. Elvis Presley
8. *Brown* v. *Board of Education*
9. Rosa Parks
10. beats

Understanding Main Ideas

SECTION 1 *(pp. 592–597)*
1. What impact did the GI Bill of Rights and other government actions have on the postwar economy?
2. How did civil rights issues affect the 1948 election?

SECTION 2 *(pp. 598–606)*
3. How did the economic prosperity of the 1950s affect the workforce?
4. What was suburban life like in the 1950s?

SECTION 3 *(pp. 607–615)*
5. What were some of the major successes and setbacks in ending segregation in the 1950s?
6. According to social critics, what were the weaknesses of American society in the 1950s?

Reviewing Themes
1. **Economics** How was the increase in population influenced by the economic boom of the 1950s?
2. **Culture** How did some Americans rebel against the conformity of the 1950s?
3. **Citizenship** How did some members of minority groups fight discrimination during this decade?

Thinking Critically
1. **Comparing and Contrasting** What was the popular image of a mother's role in society in the 1950s? How did this image conflict with reality?
2. **Categorizing** How did popular entertainment in the 1950s shape the economy?
3. **Summarizing** What actions did Thurgood Marshall, Rosa Parks, and Martin Luther King Jr. take to achieve equality for African Americans?
4. **Supporting a Point of View** Imagine that you are one of the Little Rock Nine. Are you willing to face harassment and violence to go to a better school? Explain your answer.
5. **Identifying Cause and Effect** What were the causes and effects of economic prosperity in the 1950s?

Writing About History
Identifying Cause and Effect Write a brief paragraph describing the major concerns of workers in the late 1940s and how the government reacted to union efforts to address these problems. Use the following graphic to organize your thoughts.

Concerns of Workers → Union Efforts → Government Reaction

RETEACH

Tell students to imagine that they are planning a museum exhibit on the 1950s. The exhibit will contain a number of different rooms, each of which should focus on a different aspect of the 1950s. Have each student pick and plan a room in the exhibit, using the following topics as a guide: Soldiers Return Home, Labor Issues, The 1948 Election and the Fair Deal, A Booming Economy, The Move to the Suburbs, Popular Culture, The Fight for School Desegregation, The Fight for Transportation Desegregation, and Social Critics. Ask students to present their room plans to the class.
English Language Learners

EXTEND

Ask students to select and watch a modern-day movie that is set in the 1950s. Then have each student write a movie review that both comments on the movie and discusses its portrayal of the decade. **Block Scheduling**

Building Social Studies Skills

Interpreting Maps
Study the map below. Then use it to help answer the questions that follow.

School Segregation in 1964

Percentage of African Americans Attending School with Whites

| 57.1–68% | 20.1–57% | 10.1–20% | 4.1–10% | 0–4% |

1. Which states had the highest rates of integration?
   a. Missouri and Oklahoma
   b. Maryland and Delaware
   c. Texas, Tennessee, and Virginia
   d. Kentucky and West Virginia

2. Write a statement describing the geographic pattern represented on this map.

Analyzing Primary Sources
Read this excerpt from President Eisenhower's radio message after he intervened in Little Rock. Then answer the questions that follow.

"Whenever normal agencies prove inadequate to the task and it becomes necessary for the Executive Branch of the Federal Government to use its powers and authority to uphold Federal Courts, the President's responsibility is inescapable.

In accordance with that responsibility, I have today issued an Executive Order directing the use of troops under Federal authority to aid in the execution of Federal law at Little Rock, Arkansas. . . .

The very basis of our individual rights and freedoms rests upon the certainty that the President and the Executive Branch of Government will support and insure the carrying out of the decisions of the Federal Courts."

3. Which characterization of the president's tone is most accurate?
   a. eagerness to intervene
   b. refusal to become involved
   c. reluctant but required by executive responsibility to take action
   d. reluctantly transferring the responsibility for enforcement to the state's governor

4. How does Eisenhower describe the relationship between the executive and judicial branches?

Alternative Assessment

Building Your Portfolio

Economics
Imagine that you are a staff member of the Department of Labor. Prepare an illustrated chart that shows how the U.S. government is assisting returning soldiers through various programs designed to help them find civilian jobs, attain college educations, or own their own homes. Your chart should include information on how these efforts contributed to the prosperity of the 1950s.

U.S. HISTORY

internet connect

Internet Activity: go.hrw.com
KEYWORD: SE3 AN20

Choose a topic on society after World War II to:
- understand how popular culture reflected the social events and culture of the 1950s.
- learn about passive resistance and write a biography of Mohandas K. Gandhi.
- create an illustrated time line of the efforts of LULAC on behalf of Hispanic civil rights.

---

2. Advertising supported the consumer culture.

3. Marshall—argued *Brown* v. *Board of Education*; Parks—helped start the Montgomery bus boycott; King—led Montgomery bus boycott and began nonviolent protest for civil rights

4. Answers will vary. Students should support their position.

5. The GI Bill of Rights and the Employment Act helped reduce unemployment. The Council of Economic Advisers was established. Businesses merged and created new jobs; union membership grew and created higher wages for workers; new white collar jobs led to more wealthy workers; migration to suburbia led to growing urban poor; and loss of farm subsidies led to growing rural poor.

Writing
concerns—automation, high inflation, low wages; responses—strikes and other protests; effects—led to antilabor legislation

Building Social Studies Skills
1. d

2. The states of the Lower South were slower to integrate.

3. c

4. Answers will vary. Students might suggest that Eisenhower believes the only way government will work is if the two branches support one another.

REVIEW AND ASSESSMENT RESOURCES

TECHNOLOGY

▶ Global Skill Builder CD–ROM

▶ Holt Researcher: American History CD–ROM

▶ HRW Go site

REINFORCEMENT, REVIEW, AND ASSESSMENT

▶ Unit 5 Review, pp. 590–91

▶ Unit 5 Test (Form A or B)

▶ Portfolio Activities and Alternative Assessment Handbook, Unit 5

▶ Unit 5 Test for English Language Learners and Special-Needs Students

To review elements of Unit 5 in a single class period, assign one of the following activities or graphic organizers, omitting the italicized answers, to individuals or groups.

1 Problem Solving

Ask students to imagine that they are representatives to the United Nations in 1946. In the past thirty years the world has experienced two world wars. Have students prepare a report on how the UN might work to prevent war. Each report should begin by addressing why conflict between countries often turns into war. In their reports, students should list specific ways in which the UN would resolve conflicts. Finally, students should conclude their reports with an evaluation of these options. Ask volunteers to present their reports to the class.

A Selection from

Further Reading

The United States and the Holocaust. In *The World Must Know*, Michael Berenbaum provides an overview of one of history's greatest tragedies. In the following excerpt, he laments the U.S. government's failure to provide a haven for large numbers of European Jews during the late 1930s. "The United States raised a formidable series of paper walls to keep refugees out. . . . There were financial tests to weed out refugees who were likely to become a public charge. One of the requirements was a certificate of good conduct attesting to the exemplary character of the immigrant. This was supposed to be obtained from one's local police authority, in this case the Gestapo. . . . The United States, a nation of immigrants, was reluctant to become a haven for Jewish refugees. Reflexive nationalism went hand in hand with widespread antisemitism."

COMPREHENSION According to Berenbaum, why did the United States fail to provide a haven for large numbers of European Jews during the late 1930s?

ANSWER: Students might identify factors such as nationalism and anti-Jewish prejudice.

U·N·I·T 5 Review

BUILDING YOUR PORTFOLIO

Outlined below are three projects. Independently or cooperatively, complete one and use the products to demonstrate your mastery of the historical concepts involved.

1 Problem Solving

The year is 1945. You and representatives from several nations are meeting to discuss global relations after World War II. The world experienced severe economic, political, and social unrest in the years leading up to World War II. Your assignment is to consider how the United States and other nations could resolve future problems without resorting to war. You need to create a plan of how best to respond. Follow these steps to create a solution to the problem.

Use your textbook and other resources to *gather information* that might influence your plan of action. Remember that your plan of action must include a way to respond to the rise of dictatorships. The information you need in order to come up with a solution might include historical background of the war, maps, and charts.

Once you have gathered information, *list and consider options*. These options might include an international organization, a worldwide antiwar pledge, or a strong military presence in certain countries. Once you have identified these options, *consider the advantages and disadvantages* of each option. Which option do you think has the best chance for success?

Choose and implement a solution. Complete the plan for your solution. Have one student present an international crisis and demonstrate how your plan would resolve the crisis. *Evaluate the effectiveness* of your solution. Was it the best option? Would one of your earlier options have been effective? How could you modify your plan to make it more effective?

Holocaust survivors being liberated

2 Global Relations

Between 1941 and 1950 the United States became involved in three very different wars: World War II, the Cold War, and the Korean War. *Write and perform a 15-minute documentary* on how these wars were similar and how they differed. Make sure to include how these wars were fought, who emerged victorious, and the domestic and international effects of the war. Your documentary should also discuss how changing relationships among nations today pose different types of challenges. You may wish to use portfolio materials you designed in the unit chapters to help you.

2 Global Relations

Tell students to imagine that it is 1940 and that they are newspaper editors. Have each student write an editorial describing the growth of dictatorships around the world and how the United States should respond to those dictators.

3 Government

- sets minimum wage
- regulates businesses and industry, both large and small
- provides aid to ailing industries, farmers, and certain companies

Business, Industry, and Labor

Government Involvement in the Economy

Banking and Finance
- allows the Federal Reserve Board to control interest rates
- allows the FDIC to guarantee deposits in individual accounts

Public Health and Welfare
- dispenses social security, welfare, unemployment benefits
- provides emergency and disaster relief
- offers Medicare and Medicaid and regulates health care and insurance

---

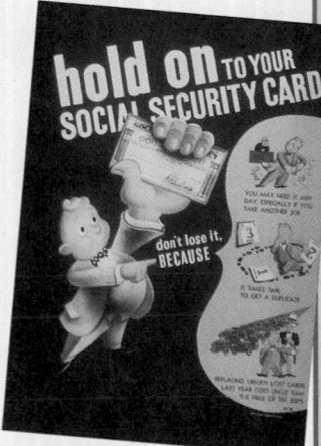

UN troops fighting against Communist forces in Korea

3 Government

During and after World War II, the federal government became increasingly involved in managing and influencing the U.S. economy. **Create a chart** of the different areas of the economy in which the government played a role in the 1940s and 1950s. Make sure your display shows how each type of government involvement affected the lives of average citizens. You may wish to use portfolio materials you designed in the unit chapters to help you.

Social Security Administration poster

Further Reading

Berenbaum, Michael. *The World Must Know: The History of the Holocaust as Told in the United States Holocaust Memorial Museum.* Little, Brown, 1993. A pictorial and eyewitness history of the Holocaust.

Cohen, Stan. *V for Victory: America's Home Front During World War II.* Motorbooks International, 1991. An overview of the effect of World War II on Americans on the home front.

Cook, Haruko Taya, and Theodore F. Cook. *Japan at War: An Oral History.* New Press, 1993. Accounts of war's effects on the Japanese.

Goodwin, Doris Kearns. *No Ordinary Time: Franklin & Eleanor Roosevelt: The Home Front in World War II.* Touchstone Books, 1995. A biography of the Roosevelts during World War II.

Halberstam, David. *The Fifties.* Villard Books, 1993. A broad account of American life in the 1950s.

King, Martin Luther Jr. *Stride Toward Freedom: The Montgomery Story.* Harper & Row, 1986. Martin Luther King Jr.'s own story of the Montgomery bus boycott.

Knox, Donald. *The Korean War: Uncertain Victory.* Harcourt Brace Jovanovich, 1991. An oral history of the war.

Internet Connect & Review on the ROM

In assigned groups, develop a multimedia presentation about the United States between 1921 and 1960. Choose information from the chapter Internet Connect activities and from the **Holt Researcher CD–ROM** that best reflects the major topics of the period. Write an outline and a script for your presentation, which may be shown to the class.

A Selection from
Further Reading

Nonviolent Resistance.

In *Stride Toward Freedom*, Martin Luther King Jr. presents his account of the Montgomery bus boycott. In the following excerpt, he discusses the philosophy of nonviolent resistance. "Nonviolent resistance is not a method for cowards; it does resist. . . . It is not a method of stagnant passivity. The phrase 'passive resistance' often gives the false impression that this is a sort of 'do-nothing' method in which the resister quietly and passively accepts evil. But nothing is farther than the truth. For while the nonviolent resister is passive in the sense that he is not physically aggressive toward his opponent, his mind and emotions are always active, constantly seeking to persuade his opponent that he is wrong. The method is passive physically, but strongly active spiritually."

ANALYZING SOURCES

According to King, how does a nonviolent resister actively resist injustice?

ANSWER: Students might note that the nonviolent resister behaves in a manner that is intended to persuade the perpetrators of injustice that they are wrong.

A Changing Home Front

CHAPTER 21
The New Frontier and the Great Society

After winning the presidential election of 1960 in an extremely close contest, John F. Kennedy attempted to manage numerous Cold War conflicts. The popular President Kennedy helped invigorate the nation. In November 1963 an assassin killed Kennedy, ending "Camelot." Lyndon B. Johnson, who succeeded Kennedy, soon launched a War on Poverty and announced social programs called the Great Society.

CHAPTER 22
The Civil Rights Movement

African Americans continued to work for equality during the 1960s, a decade dominated by the civil rights movement. Under the leadership of Martin Luther King Jr. the civil rights movement utilized nonviolent resistance to end segregation and work for equal rights. These efforts led to the passage of major legislation. Other civil rights leaders advocated separatism and violent resistance, however.

A Changing Home Front

1954–1978

Martin Luther King Jr. (front, waving) leads the Selma to Montgomery march for voting rights into Montgomery.

Struggles for Change

CHAPTER 23

Many minority groups worked for equality during the 1960s and 1970s, including women, American Indians, Hispanics, and disabled Americans. As they pushed for civil rights, many college students pushed for the creation of a new society, one that did not include racism or war. Some even "dropped out" to form a counterculture. Art, religion, and music reflected the upheavals of the time.

War in Vietnam

CHAPTER 24

After winning its independence in 1954, Vietnam was divided into two separate nations—communist North Vietnam and anticommunist South Vietnam. The United States, fearful of communism in Southeast Asia, aided the South Vietnamese in their fight against the North Vietnamese and became involved in the Vietnam War. The conflict was long and devastating. The United States agreed to a cease-fire in 1973.

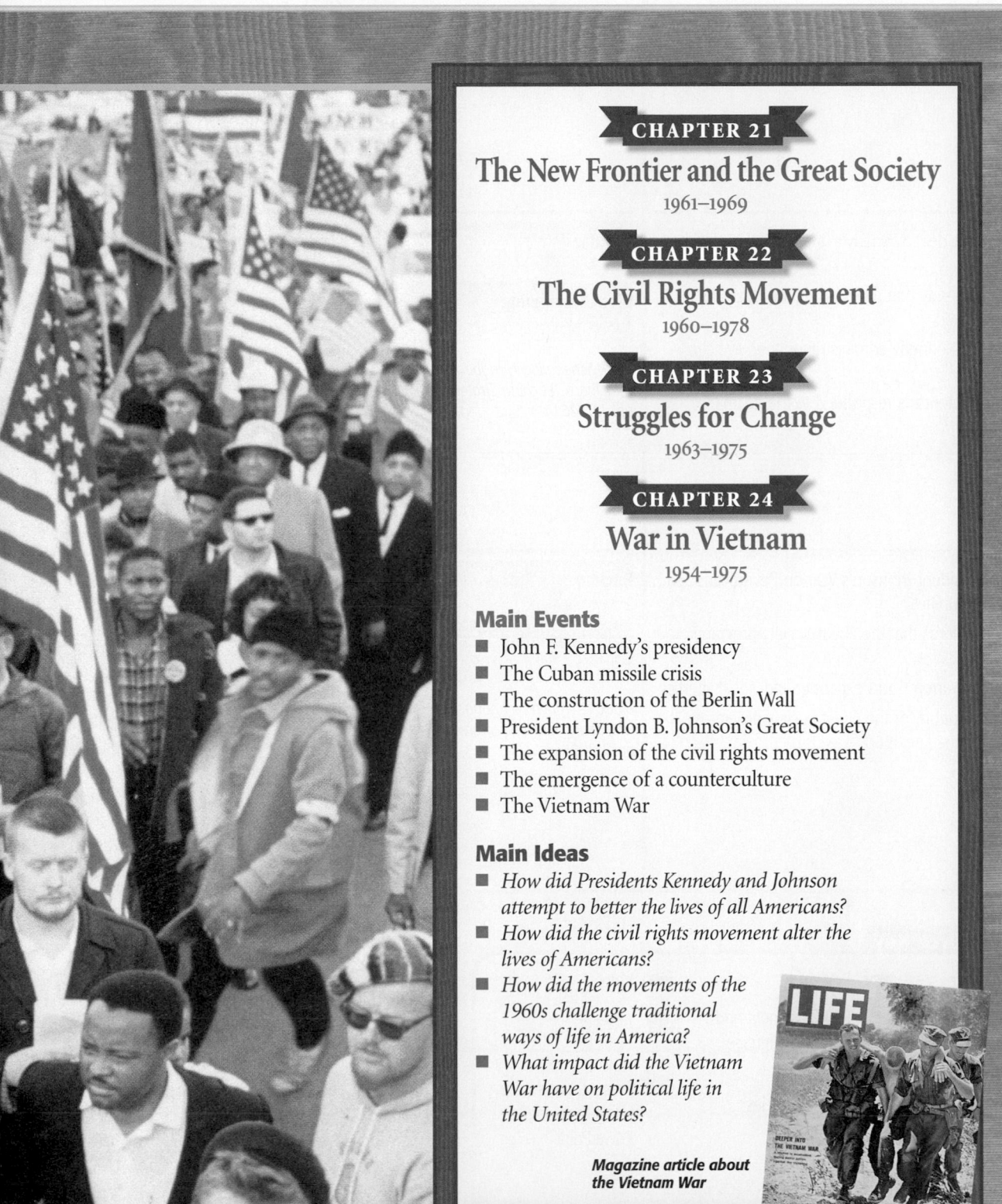

CHAPTER 21

The New Frontier and the Great Society

1961–1969

CHAPTER 22

The Civil Rights Movement

1960–1978

CHAPTER 23

Struggles for Change

1963–1975

CHAPTER 24

War in Vietnam

1954–1975

Main Events

- John F. Kennedy's presidency
- The Cuban missile crisis
- The construction of the Berlin Wall
- President Lyndon B. Johnson's Great Society
- The expansion of the civil rights movement
- The emergence of a counterculture
- The Vietnam War

Main Ideas

- *How did Presidents Kennedy and Johnson attempt to better the lives of all Americans?*
- *How did the civil rights movement alter the lives of Americans?*
- *How did the movements of the 1960s challenge traditional ways of life in America?*
- *What impact did the Vietnam War have on political life in the United States?*

LIFE

Magazine article about the Vietnam War

INTRODUCE UNIT 6

Main Events

List the Main Events on the chalkboard. Ask students to select two and briefly describe what they know about the topics. Have volunteers share their descriptions. Later, when you have finished Unit 6, ask students to return to their original descriptions and revise them using the information they learned in the unit. Students should also create new descriptions for the other Main Events.

Main Ideas

Ask each student to read the Main Ideas and briefly answer the questions in writing. Share the *Consider* points with students as necessary. Later, when you have finished Unit 6, ask students to return to their original answers and revise them using the information they learned in the unit.

The Civil Rights Movement
Consider:

- the opportunities provided by social and economic integration
- the social impact of a movement that redefined race relations

The Vietnam War
Consider:

- the political effects of a divisive war and conflict
- the political effects of mistrust in the government

The New Frontier and the Great Society

CHAPTER RESOURCE MANAGER

	Objectives	Pacing Guide	Reproducible Resources
SECTION 1 **Kennedy and the Cold War** pp. 624–30	★ Analyze how television coverage influenced the presidential election of 1960. ★ Summarize how President Kennedy planned to stop the spread of communism. ★ Explain why the Bay of Pigs invasion of Cuba failed. ★ Describe how the Cuban missile crisis almost led to war.	**Regular** 2 days **Block Scheduling** 1 day *Block Scheduling Handbook with Team Teaching Strategies, pp. 121–26*	**RS** Guided Reading Strategy 21.1 **SM** Geography Activity 21: The Cuban Missile Crisis **RS** Graphic Organizer Activity 21: The Cuban Missile Crisis **IC** Literature Reading 21: A View of Nikita Khrushchev **PS** Primary Source Reading 21: America's Fascination with the "Final Frontier"
SECTION 2 **The Kennedy White House** pp. 631–37	★ Discuss how President Kennedy's image conflicted with reality. ★ Identify why Kennedy had difficulty getting legislation passed. ★ Explain how the Kennedy administration tried to help poor Americans. ★ Describe how Americans responded to the death of the president.	**Regular** 2 days **Block Scheduling** 1 day *Block Scheduling Handbook with Team Teaching Strategies, pp. 121–26*	**RS** Guided Reading Strategy 21.2 **PS** Biography Reading 21: Robert F. Kennedy
SECTION 3 **Johnson's Great Society** pp. 638–45	★ Explain how President Johnson's War on Poverty affected American communities. ★ Identify the problems that the Great Society programs addressed. ★ Detail how the Warren Court expanded individual liberties. ★ Describe why support for the Great Society programs declined during the late 1960s.	**Regular** 2 days **Block Scheduling** 1 day *Block Scheduling Handbook with Team Teaching Strategies, pp. 121–26*	**RS** Guided Reading Strategy 21.3 **E** Hands-On History Activity: The Great Society **E** Creative Teaching Strategy: Interpreting Cartoons Lesson

Chapter Resource Key

PS	Primary Sources	**REV**	Review		Video
RS	Reading Support	**ELL**	Reinforcement and English Language Learners		Internet
IC	Interdisciplinary Connections				Holt Presentation Maker Using Microsoft® PowerPoint®
E	Enrichment		Transparencies		
SM	Skills Mastery		CD–ROM		
A	Assessment		Music		

One-Stop Planner CD-ROM

See the *One-Stop Planner* for a complete list of additional resources for students and teachers.

One-Stop Planner CD–ROM

It's easy to plan lessons, select resources, and print out materials for your students when you use the *One-Stop Planner CD–ROM with Test Generator.*

 One-Stop Planner, Lesson 21.1
One-Stop Planner, Lesson 21.1
 American History Simulations CD–ROM: Race to the Moon
 Holt Researcher: American History CD–ROM
 Homework Practice Online

REV Section 1 Review, p. 630
A Daily Quiz 21.1
ELL Main Idea Activity 21.1
ELL English Audio Summary 21.1
ELL Spanish Audio Summary 21.1

 One-Stop Planner, Lesson 21.2
 Holt Researcher: American History CD–ROM
 Homework Practice Online
 HRW Go site

REV Section 2 Review, p. 637
A Daily Quiz 21.2
ELL Main Idea Activity 21.2
ELL English Audio Summary 21.2
ELL Spanish Audio Summary 21.2

 One-Stop Planner, Lesson 21.3
 The American Nation Video Program Segment: VISTA Volunteers; Teacher's Guide, pp. 207–08
  Presents America: Yesterday and Today, 1850 to the Present Segment: Reaching for the Moon
 Holt Researcher: American History CD–ROM
 Homework Practice Online

REV Section 3 Review, p. 645
A Daily Quiz 21.3
ELL Main Idea Activity 21.3
ELL English Audio Summary 21.3
ELL Spanish Audio Summary 21.3

Meeting Individual Needs

Ability Levels

Level 1 Basic-level activities designed for all students encountering new material

Level 2 Intermediate-level activities designed for average students

Level 3 Challenging activities designed for honors and gifted-and-talented students

English Language Learners Activities that address the needs of students with Limited English Proficiency

  internet connect

HRW ONLINE RESOURCES
GO TO: go.hrw.com
Then type in a keyword.

TEACHER HOME PAGE
KEYWORD: SE3 Teacher

CHAPTER INTERNET ACTIVITIES
KEYWORD: SE3 AN21
Choose an activity to:
- create a historical poster on John Glenn and the early space race.
- research the life and accomplishments of President John F. Kennedy.
- explore the history and legacy of the Great Society.

CHAPTER ENRICHMENT LINKS
KEYWORD: SE3 CH21

ONLINE ASSESSMENT
Homework Practice
KEYWORD: SE3 HP3

Standardized Test Prep
KEYWORD: SE3 STP21

Rubrics
KEYWORD: SS Rubrics

ONLINE MAPS, CHARTS, AND GRAPHS
KEYWORD: SE3 MCG
- NASA
- Space Race

CONTENT UPDATES
KEYWORD: SS Content Updates

HOLT PRESENTATION MAKER
KEYWORD: SE3 PPT21

ONLINE READING SUPPORT
KEYWORD: SS Strategies

CURRENT EVENTS
KEYWORD: S3 Current Events

Chapter Review and Assessment

 Global Skill Builder CD–ROM
 HRW Go site
REV Chapter 21 Tutorial for Students, Parents, Mentors, and Peers
REV Chapter 21 Review, pp. 646–47
Chapter 21 Test Generator (on the One-Stop Planner)
A Chapter 21 Test (Form A or B)
A Alternative Assessment Handbook
A Chapter 21 Test for English Language Learners and Special-Needs Students

Section 1 *Kennedy and the Cold War, pp. 624–30*

Section 2 *The Kennedy White House, pp. 631–37*

Section 3 *Johnson's Great Society, pp. 638–45*

Chapter Review *pp. 646–47*

Build on What You Know

Ask students to answer the following questions.

What sorts of programs might Presidents Kennedy and Johnson have implemented to change American life?

Consider:
- social and economic problems during the late 1950s
- the domestic goals of both presidents

How might Kennedy and Johnson have dealt with foreign-policy crises that arose from Cold War tensions?

Consider:
- the seriousness of the communist threat
- the foreign-policy goals of both presidents

exploring the time line

AMERICAN EVENTS

internet connect

TOPIC: John Glenn
GO TO: go.hrw.com
KEYWORD: SE3 AN21

Have students access the Internet through the HRW Go site to conduct research on John Glenn and the early space program. Then ask each student to create a poster with which to present their findings.

CHAPTER 21

1961–1969

The New Frontier and the Great Society

Building the Berlin Wall

1961 World Events
The East German government builds a wall that divides East and West Berlin.

Abraham Zapruder filmed Kennedy's assassination with this camera.

1963 Politics
President Kennedy is assassinated.

1963 The Arts
Stanley Kubrick's film *Dr. Strangelove*, a black comedy about the Cold War, is released.

| 1961 | 1962 | 1963 | 1964 |

1961 Politics
President John F. Kennedy gives an inaugural address that calls for Americans to sacrifice in the struggle to defend liberty across the globe.

Pin honoring John F. Kennedy's military service

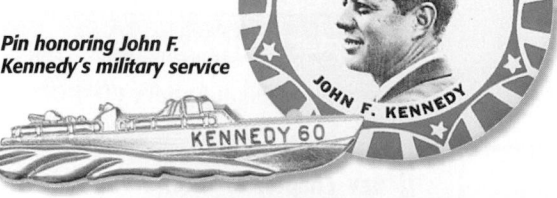
KENNEDY 60

Kennedy campaign button

OUR NEXT PRESIDENT
JOHN F. KENNEDY

1963 Science and Technology
A vaccine against measles becomes available.

A child receiving a measles vaccine

1964 Politics
Lyndon B. Johnson is elected president by a landslide.

1964 Science and Technology
The U.S. surgeon general reports that cigarette smoking is the leading cause of lung cancer.

Build on What You Know

During the late 1950s President Eisenhower opposed the expansion of communism. He used secret means to keep communism from spreading and threatened to use nuclear weapons. At home, Eisenhower shifted domestic policy from the New Deal and Fair Deal to Modern Republicanism. In this chapter you will learn how the Democratic administrations of John F. Kennedy and Lyndon B. Johnson implemented new policies and programs that changed American life. You will also learn how they dealt with foreign-policy crises caused by Cold War tensions.

What's Your Opinion?

To help students create their Themes Journal entries, provide the following examples of appropriate **agree**/**disagree** *statements.*

Global Relations

Agree The Marshall Plan helped solidify the alliance between the United States and Western European nations during the early stages of the Cold War.

Disagree The payment of reparations heightened political tensions between Germany and other Western European nations during the 1920s and 1930s.

Economics

Agree The New Deal included a variety of programs that provided economic assistance to poor Americans during the Great Depression.

Disagree The U.S. government provided relatively little economic aid to formerly enslaved African Americans during Reconstruction.

Government

Agree Certain circumstances, such as war or national security, require presidents to keep information from the public.

Disagree As national leaders, presidents have a responsibility to share information with the public.

The Apollo I space capsule

1965
Science and Technology
The *Pioneer 6* spacecraft, designed to orbit the Sun, is launched.

1965
Business and Finance
France redeems $200 million for U.S. gold, shaking the gold market and prompting President Johnson to ask Americans to take vacations in the United States rather than abroad.

India's prime minister, Indira Gandhi

1966
World Events
Indira Gandhi becomes prime minister of India.

1967
Science and Technology
Three *Apollo I* crewmembers are killed when fire breaks out in the space capsule on the launchpad.

1967
World Events
The Six-Day War between Israel and several Arab nations occurs.

1968
Politics
Congress rejects Abe Fortas, President Johnson's nominee for Chief Justice of the United States.

1968
World Events
North Korea seizes the USS *Pueblo*, a U.S. Navy ship, and releases the crew nearly a year later.

1965   **1966**   **1967**   **1968**

1965
Politics
Congress creates the Department of Housing and Urban Development.

James Hoffa testifying before Congress

1967
Politics
The Twenty-fifth Amendment, which details procedures for presidential succession, is ratified.

1967
Business and Finance
James Hoffa, president of the Teamsters Union, is jailed for jury tampering.

1968
Business and Finance
Corporate profits after taxes exceed $47 billion.

1968
The Arts
The musical play *You're a Good Man, Charlie Brown* premieres.

1968
Daily Life
Surveys reveal that 86 percent of elementary school teachers are women, while 78 percent of the principals are men.

What's Your Opinion?

Themes Journal *Do you* **agree** *or* **disagree** *with the following statements? Support your point of view in your journal.*

Global Relations Providing economic assistance to a foreign nation is an effective way to guarantee a political alliance.

Economics Governments have a responsibility to provide economic aid to citizens living in poverty.

Government Under certain circumstances, presidents should conceal facts from the public.

SECTION 1

After completing Section 1, students should be able to:

OBJECTIVE 1 Analyze how television coverage influenced the presidential election of 1960.

OBJECTIVE 2 Summarize how President Kennedy planned to stop the spread of communism.

OBJECTIVE 3 Explain why the Bay of Pigs invasion of Cuba failed.

OBJECTIVE 4 Describe how the Cuban missile crisis almost led to war.

LET'S GET STARTED!

Write the following question on the chalkboard: *Based on what you have learned about international relations in the 1950s, what do you think international relations in the 1960s were like?* As students enter the classroom, ask them to respond to the question. Have volunteers share their responses. Then tell students that in Section 1 they will learn how President Kennedy struggled to stop the advance of communism.

SECTION 1

READ TO DISCOVER
1. How did television coverage influence the presidential election of 1960?
2. How did President Kennedy plan to stop the spread of communism?
3. Why did the Bay of Pigs invasion of Cuba fail?
4. How did the Cuban missile crisis almost lead to war?

DEFINE
flexible response
hot line

IDENTIFY
John F. Kennedy
Lyndon B. Johnson
Peace Corps
Alliance for Progress
Fidel Castro
Berlin Wall
Cuban missile crisis
Limited Nuclear Test Ban Treaty

▶ WHY IT MATTERS TODAY
The United States continues to use compromise as a foreign-policy tool. Use **CNNfyi.com** or other **current events** sources to learn about ways that the United States is compromising with a foreign country today. Record your findings in your journal.

CNNfyi.com

Kennedy and the Cold War

EYEWITNESSES TO History

"For six days, time was deformed, everyday life suddenly dwarfed and illuminated, as if by the glare of an explosion that had not yet taken place."

—Todd Gitlin, *The Sixties*

Fear of communism played a key role in the 1960 presidential election.

Todd Gitlin reflected on the tense days of October 1962. At that time Gitlin was a student at Harvard University with a strong interest in politics. When President John F. Kennedy appeared on television on October 22 to announce a naval blockade against Cuba, Gitlin and many other Americans feared that a nuclear war between the United States and the Soviet Union might soon occur. He remembered that during the crisis "the country lived out the awe . . . and simmering near-panic always implicit in the thermonuclear age." The incident reflected the crises that President Kennedy faced during his brief presidency.

The 1960 Campaign

Most Americans were satisfied with President Eisenhower's performance in the White House. However, the Twenty-second Amendment, passed in 1951, limited a president's tenure in office to two elected terms. This meant that Eisenhower could not run for a third term in 1960.

As expected, the Republicans chose Richard Nixon as their presidential candidate for the upcoming election. His solid performance as Eisenhower's vice president had won him support from many Republican Party members. Trying to appeal to a wide variety of voters, Nixon downplayed his participation in such events as the investigations by the House Un-American Activities Committee.

Senator **John F. Kennedy** of Massachusetts eventually emerged as the Democratic candidate. His charm, wit, good looks, and record of service during World War II impressed many voters. However, as a Roman Catholic he faced the same religious prejudices that had hurt Al Smith's presidential bid in 1928. Kennedy assured voters that he believed firmly in the separation of church and state. Recalling his brother Joseph, who was killed in combat during World War II, Kennedy told voters, "Nobody asked my brother if he was a Catholic or Protestant before he climbed into an American bomber plane to fly his last mission." Kennedy's reassurances and the Republicans' refusal to exploit the issue convinced many voters that religion need not play a role in their voting decisions.

Nixon chose Henry Cabot Lodge of Massachusetts as his running mate. Kennedy selected Texas senator **Lyndon B. Johnson**, who had failed in his own attempt to obtain the Democratic nomination. Kennedy's decision shocked his supporters, many of whom intensely disliked the senator. One aide told Kennedy that choosing Johnson was the "worst mistake" he could possibly make. However,

TEACH OBJECTIVE 1

ALL LEVELS: Ask students how television coverage affects modern elections. (*Students might suggest that television coverage affects voters' perceptions and candidates' positions.*) To help students understand how television coverage affected the election of 1960, copy the following graphic organizer on the chalkboard, omitting the italicized answers. Have each student complete it. After students have finished their graphic organizers, conduct a brief discussion on television and politics. Do students think that television coverage affects politics positively or negatively? Does it help either the voters or the candidates? **English Language Learners**

> ### TELEVISION COVERAGE AND THE ELECTION OF 1960
>
> - **pre-debates**—*Nixon led in the polls*
> - **debates**—*showed a vibrant Kennedy and a weary Nixon; radio listeners thought Nixon won and television viewers thought Kennedy won*
> - **post debates**—*Kennedy won the election with a narrow victory*

Kennedy had made a strategic choice. Johnson could help the Democrats win votes in Texas and other southern states where Kennedy was not particularly popular. Moreover, Johnson could work closely with Congress where he was regarded as a master at getting legislation passed.

During the campaign, Kennedy told Americans they would have to make sacrifices in the coming years. In a speech to South Dakota farmers, he explained his vision of the future.

History Makers Speak

❝I promise you no sure solutions, no easy life. The years ahead for all of us will be as difficult as any in our history. There are new frontiers for America to conquer in education, in science, in national purpose—not frontiers on a map, but frontiers of the mind, the will, the spirit of man.❞

—John F. Kennedy, quoted in *A Question of Character*, by Thomas C. Reeves

Nixon argued that he had the maturity and experience to serve as president. He led in the polls until the first of four televised debates. Public reaction to the debates revealed the growing influence of television on American life. Nixon was weary from nonstop campaigning and was suffering from a painful injury to his knee. The tired candidate stood before the television cameras in a shirt that looked too large and with his make-up smeared by sweat. Kennedy, on the other hand, appeared fit, confident, and relaxed. Many Americans who listened to the first debate on the radio believed that Nixon had won. However, most of those who saw the television broadcast decided that Kennedy would make a better president than Nixon.

Kennedy aide Kenneth O'Donnell later recalled, "After the first debate, the 1960 campaign was an entirely different ball game." Kennedy later recognized the importance of television to his campaign. He confided, "We wouldn't have had a prayer without that gadget." Despite Kennedy's rapidly growing popularity, the election was very close. Kennedy defeated Nixon by fewer than 120,000 popular votes. His electoral victory was more clear-cut—303 votes to Nixon's 219. At age 43, John F. Kennedy became the youngest person ever elected to the White House.

✔ **READING CHECK: Analyzing Information** What factors helped John F. Kennedy win the 1960 presidential election? **Kennedy's appearance in the televised debates; selection of Johnson as running mate**

The Election of 1960

Interpreting Maps John F. Kennedy won an extremely close victory over Richard Nixon in 1960.

❓ THE WORLD IN SPATIAL TERMS By how many votes did Kennedy win the popular vote? By what percentage?

CANDIDATE	PARTY	ELECTORAL VOTE	POPULAR VOTE	% OF POPULAR VOTE
Kennedy	Democratic	303	34,226,731	49.7
Nixon	Republican	219	34,108,157	49.5
Byrd	Not an official candidate	15*		

*Six unpledged Democratic electors in Alabama, all eight unpledged Democratic electors in Mississippi, and one Republican elector in Oklahoma voted for Senator Henry Byrd of Virginia.

Source: *Historical Statistics of the United States*

Televised debates with Richard Nixon helped John F. Kennedy win the 1960 presidential election.

The 1960 Presidential Election. A number of factors contributed to John F. Kennedy's narrow victory in the election of 1960. First, Kennedy spent the majority of his efforts campaigning in industrial states with large numbers of electoral votes, while Nixon exhausted himself by visiting all 50 states. Second, the Nixon campaign received relatively little help from President Dwight D. Eisenhower, who had mixed feelings about his vice president. Finally, Kennedy won the late support of some African American voters in October 1960, when he called Coretta Scott King to comfort her after her husband, Martin Luther King Jr., was imprisoned in Georgia for a traffic violation.

CRITICAL THINKING Which of the three factors stated above do you think most helped Kennedy win the election?

ANSWER: Answers will vary. Students should explain and justify their choices.

MAP ANSWER

118,574 votes; 0.2 percent

TEACH OBJECTIVE 2

LEVELS 1 AND 2: Conduct a brief discussion on the ways in which President Kennedy hoped to stop the advance of communism. *(President Kennedy's foreign policy was based on a strategy called flexible response.)* Ask volunteers to offer examples of military and nonmilitary options within the flexible-response policy. *(For military options, students should mention the Bay of Pigs invasion. For nonmilitary options, students should mention the Peace Corps or economic aid programs.)* Then pair students and ask them to create an annotated time line of international events discussed in the section. Ask pairs to label the events as military or nonmilitary and to explain the role of the events in President Kennedy's anticommunism campaign.
English Language Learners, Cooperative Learning

LEVEL 3: Tell students to imagine that they are President Kennedy. Have each student write a speech explaining how he or she plans to halt the spread of communism. *(See the Level 1 lesson for the correct methods.)* Students may choose to organize their speeches around the "general/specific" rule of speaking and writing—providing a general explanation and then specific examples. Ask volunteers to present their speeches to the class. Students may wish to include their speeches in their portfolios.

ECONOMICS

Defense Spending.

During the early 1960s the U.S. defense budget rose approximately 13 percent, from $47.4 billion in 1961 to $53.6 billion in 1964. Much of the increase went to the construction of nuclear submarines and missiles. The monies also funded an increase in the number of U.S. military personnel—from 2.5 million in 1960 to 2.7 million in 1964.

CRITICAL THINKING How might increased defense spending have affected the national economy?

ANSWER: Students might suggest that the increase probably provided new job opportunities.

VISUAL RECORD ANSWER

Students might answer that the public saw them as powerful, admirable men.

INTERPRETING THE VISUAL RECORD

The Green Berets. Named for the hats they wore (above), the Green Berets had their own theme song. *What do these images suggest about the popularity of the Green Berets?*

Research on the ROM

Free Find: Peace Corps
After reading about the Peace Corps on the **Holt Researcher CD–ROM**, create a proposal for a similar program to help people living in the United States.

Kennedy's Foreign Policy

In foreign affairs, President Kennedy tended to follow the Cold War policies of his predecessors. He continued the nuclear arms buildup begun by President Eisenhower. However, unlike his predecessors, Kennedy did not want to rely solely on the threat of nuclear weapons to block communist expansion. He preferred to have a number of options in case of international crises. This strategy was called **flexible response**. Kennedy strengthened conventional military forces and established special units like the Green Berets to assist countries struggling to fight communism. He took great pride in this special fighting unit and kept one of the berets they wore on his desk in the Oval Office.

Foreign aid. Kennedy also introduced a number of aid programs designed to help countries in Africa, Asia, and Latin America. He realized that helping developing countries could strengthen their dependence on the United States and block Soviet influence. His first program was the **Peace Corps**, which sent American volunteers to work for two years in developing countries.

Africa was an area of concern for the Kennedy administration. In 1960 a total of 17 African countries gained their independence from colonial powers. To support African nationalism, Kennedy called for increased economic aid. This aid included sending Peace Corps volunteers and food. During the Kennedy years the United States nearly doubled the amount of loans offered to African countries.

Kennedy also introduced a program to expand economic aid to Latin America. This **Alliance for Progress** offered billions of dollars in aid to participating countries. In exchange for financial assistance, the countries were expected to begin democratic reforms and encourage capitalism. The Alliance proved a disappointment. The rapidly growing population of Latin American countries required far more money than the United States was willing to provide. Moreover, much of the money given to participating countries soon fell into the hands of corrupt politicians. Few Latin American leaders enacted significant reforms. Víctor Alba, a Latin American writer, blamed the program's failure on its inability to motivate the poor majority in Latin American countries.

The Peace Corps offered help to developing nations.

History Makers Speak

"We know who killed the Alliance: the oligarchic governments [governments ruled by a few] of Latin America.... We know who supplied the poison: the bureaucrats and technicians. And we know who would have defended it if anyone had bothered to let them know that it existed and needed defenders: the people."

—Víctor Alba, *Alliance Without Allies*

✔ **READING CHECK: Summarizing** Describe President Kennedy's successes and failures in his efforts to stop the spread of communism. Successes—flexible response, Peace Corps; failures—Alliance for Progress

TEACH OBJECTIVE 3

LEVEL 1: Write the following question on the chalkboard: *Why did the Bay of Pigs invasion fail?* Pair students and have each pair list at least three answers to the question. *(Students should note the existence of strong Cuban counterattacks, the absence of a popular revolt, the lack of air strikes, and the lack of naval and air support.)* Ask each pair to use its list to write a paragraph in response to the question. Then conduct a classroom discussion on the various ways President Kennedy might have handled the Cuban situation and the Bay of Pigs invasion.
English Language Learners, Cooperative Learning

LEVEL 2: Tell students to imagine that they are members of the CIA who trained the Bay of Pigs invasion force. Have each student write a letter to a friend stationed in Berlin explaining the causes behind the failed mission and expressing his or her feelings about that failure. *(See the Level 1 lesson for the correct causes.)* Have volunteers read their letters to the class. Students may wish to include their letters in their portfolios.

★ Changing Ways   The Peace Corps

■ **Understanding Change** The Peace Corps has continued to aid countries throughout the world. *How has the number of countries served and number of Peace Corps volunteers changed over the years? How has the type of work performed by Peace Corps workers changed?*

THEN

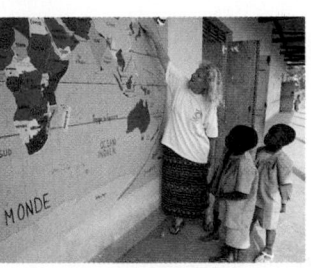

Now

	THEN	**NOW**
Number of Volunteers	7,000	6,700
Number of Countries Being Served	44	80

Areas of Service
- Education
- Environment
- Health
- Business
- Agriculture
- Community Development
- Agriculture, Health Care, and Public Works
- Other

24%
51%
25%

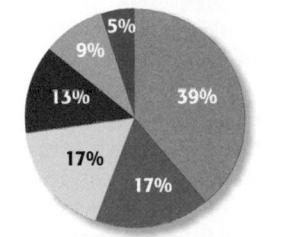

5%
9%
13%
39%
17%
17%

Source: The Peace Corps. Data reflect 1963 and 1999.

The Bay of Pigs. Latin America was a special target for aid from the United States because the Soviet Union had recently gained a foothold in the region. In 1959 rebel leader **Fidel Castro** led an uprising that succeeded in overthrowing the Cuban dictator, Fulgencio Batista. Castro quickly established a communist-style dictatorship with ties to the Soviet Union.

Castro boasted that his success was "the reason that President Kennedy can't sleep at night." Indeed, Kennedy was deeply troubled by the fact that a communist government flourished only 90 miles from the United States. He soon learned that during President Eisenhower's administration the Central Intelligence Agency (CIA) had developed a plan for overthrowing Castro. The CIA was training and financing a group of anti-Castro Cuban refugees who were to invade Cuba. After taking office, Kennedy gave his approval for the plan to proceed.

The invasion resulted in disaster. Cuban forces quickly pinned down the nearly 1,500 rebels who came ashore at Cuba's Bay of Pigs on April 17, 1961. The U.S. naval and air support that the rebels expected never materialized. At the last minute, Kennedy had decided not to send in air strikes. The invasion also failed to spark a popular uprising among the Cuban people. It took Cuban military forces less than 72 hours to crush the invasion and take prisoner some 1,200 surviving rebels.

One American journalist complained that the Bay of Pigs had made the United States look "like fools to our friends, rascals to our enemies, and incompetents to the rest." The invasion also brought Cuban leaders closer to the Soviets. Kennedy took full responsibility for the incident. After the Bay of Pigs, he resolved to take more control over foreign affairs. He told a close friend, "From now on it's John Kennedy that makes the decisions as to whether or not we're going to do these things."

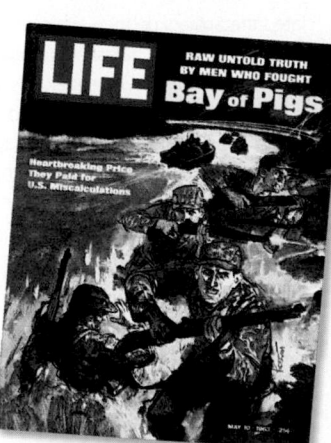

INTERPRETING THE VISUAL RECORD

The Bay of Pigs. The Bay of Pigs invasion was the cover story of this issue of *Life* magazine. *How do you think the magazine portrayed the event?*

✔ **READING CHECK: Sequencing** What events led up to the Bay of Pigs invasion?
Castro overthrew Batista and allied with the Soviet Union; Kennedy decided to pursue the Eisenhower administration's plan to overthrow Castro.

GEOGRAPHY

The Bay of Pigs. The Bay of Pigs was an extremely poor site for an invasion. Sharp coral reefs sank a number of landing craft before they reached the shore. The bay's swampy terrain made it difficult for invading soldiers to find cover from enemy fire. Furthermore, floodlights from a nearby apartment complex illuminated the beach where the rebels landed, ruining their expected nighttime advantage.

ACTIVITY: Tell students to imagine that they are soldiers who participated in the Bay of Pigs invasion. Have each student write a short military report explaining the geographic factors that contributed to the failure of the mission. Students may wish to include their military reports in their portfolios.

CHANGING WAYS ANSWERS

almost doubled; decreased; now includes environmental and business work.

VISUAL RECORD ANSWER

Students might answer that given the cover's portrayal of the soldiers, the magazine probably portrayed the event in a positive light.

LEVEL 3: Tell students to imagine that they are American newspaper reporters in the days following the failed Bay of Pigs invasion. Have each student write an article explaining the failure of the invasion. *(See the Level 1 lesson for the correct causes.)* Then tell students to imagine that they are Americans living in Florida who have just read that article. Have each student write a letter to the editor expressing his or her feelings about the failed invasion. Ask volunteers to read their articles and letters to the class.

 HOMEWORK *Have each student create an outline of the subsection entitled The Bay of Pigs.*

 SPOTLIGHT
on Fidel Castro and Nikita Khrushchev

Tell students that Fidel Castro and Nikita Khrushchev embodied communism to many Americans during the 1960s. Have each student select either Castro or Khrushchev and conduct research on his or her chosen leader. Students should also conduct research on Cuba or the Soviet Union as appropriate. Then tell students to write biographies of their selected figures, emphasizing political beliefs and career. Have volunteers share excerpts from their biographies with the class.
Block Scheduling

HISTORY MAKERS SPEAK

John F. Kennedy in *President Kennedy: Profile of Power*

In June 1961 President Kennedy traveled to West Berlin to see the newly erected Berlin Wall. Shortly after his arrival he delivered a rousing indictment of communism to a crowd of West German citizens. "Freedom has many difficulties and democracy is not perfect, but we have never had to put a wall up to keep our people in. . . . All free men, wherever they may live, are citizens of Berlin, and therefore, as a free man, I take pride in the words 'Ich bin ein Berliner [I am a Berliner].' "

CRITICAL THINKING Some of President Kennedy's advisers disapproved of his speech. Why might they have done so?

ANSWER: Students might suggest that these advisers felt that Kennedy's blunt speech could lead to conflict with the Soviet Union.

Technology Resources
 American History Simulations CD–ROM: Race to the Moon

SCIENCE & TECHNOLOGY ANSWERS

1. the fuel tanks

2. missile technology used in rockets; more money spent due to competition with the Soviets

---

Science & Technology

The Space Program

As the United States and the Soviet Union developed missiles to carry nuclear weapons, both nations also sought to use missile technology to begin the exploration of outer space. In 1958, a year after the Soviets successfully launched *Sputnik*, the United States initiated Project Mercury, a program to send a human being into space. However, the United States lost the race to be the first nation to send a human into orbit. On April 12, 1961, Soviet cosmonaut Yuri Gagarin became the first human to circle Earth.

President Kennedy publicly congratulated the Soviets on their achievement. Privately, however, he asked his advisers, "Is there any place where we can catch them [the Soviets]? What can we do? Are we working twenty-four hours a day? Can we go around the moon before them?" Less than a month later, the United States enjoyed its first success when Alan Shepard completed a suborbital flight. In February 1962 John Glenn left Earth in the Mercury spacecraft *Friendship 7*, lifted into space by an Atlas intercontinental ballistic missile. Glenn spent five hours in space and orbited Earth three times. This event restored American confidence in the space program and set the stage for the race to the Moon. The Apollo program achieved that goal in 1969, using space capsules like the one shown above.

Astronauts
Main rocket engine
Fuel tanks
Guidance rocket

Understanding Science and History

1. What takes up the most room in the spacecraft shown?
2. How did the Cold War contribute to the space program?

The Berlin Crisis

The Bay of Pigs convinced Soviet leader Nikita Khrushchev that President Kennedy was weak and could be intimidated. At a summit meeting in June 1961, Khrushchev issued an ultimatum: the West must recognize the sovereignty of communist East Germany and remove all troops from West Berlin. Khrushchev's demands shocked Kennedy. He had no desire to risk war over Berlin but worried that if he gave in to the Soviets he would lose the confidence of the American people.

In mid-August the East Germans erected a barbed-wire barrier that cut off traffic between East and West Berlin. Kennedy responded by sending additional U.S. troops to the city. For several days U.S. and Soviet soldiers eyed each other nervously across the barbed wire. Tensions gradually eased when it became clear that Khrushchev's real goal had been achieved. The barrier had halted the mass departure of East Germans to the West through Berlin. In time, the East Germans replaced the barbed wire with a wall of gray concrete and watchtowers. The **Berlin Wall** became the most widely recognized symbol of the Cold War.

TEACH OBJECTIVE 4

LEVEL 1: Pair students and have each pair write a series of newspaper headlines on the Cuban missile crisis. Students should explain how the Soviet Union and the United States reached the brink of war, present actual events in the crisis, and discuss Americans' reactions to the crisis. *(Students should note that the two nations nearly went to war when the Soviet Union provided offensive missiles to Cuba and that the United States instituted a blockade to prevent those missiles from reaching the island.)* Ask each pair to write topic sentences or introductory sentences for each of its headlines. Have volunteers read their headlines to the class.
English Language Learners, Cooperative Learning

LEVELS 2 AND 3: Have students reread the subsection entitled The Missiles of October. Then ask each student to create a political cartoon commenting on the Cuban missile crisis. Students' cartoons should depict how the United States and the Soviet Union reached the brink of war. *(See the Level 1 lesson for the correct reasons.)* Have students write captions for their cartoons. Display students' cartoons and captions around the classroom.

HOMEWORK *Have each student create a flowchart tracing the relationship between the Bay of Pigs invasion, the building of the Berlin Wall, and the Cuban missile crisis.*

The Missiles of October

Soviet leader Khrushchev's continued testing of the U.S. commitment to containment led to the Cold War's greatest crisis. To protect Cuba from other invasions, leader Fidel Castro asked the Soviet Union to provide him with defensive weapons. The Soviets complied and also offered offensive weapons—nuclear missiles that could reach the cities of the eastern United States.

CIA officials monitored the Soviet arms buildup in Cuba throughout the summer of 1962. Photographs taken by a U.S. U-2 spy plane on October 14 revealed the existence of ballistic-missile launching pads near the Cuban town of San Cristóbal. Additional U-2 flights over the island located more missiles capable of striking targets in the United States within minutes of launching.

On October 22 Kennedy appeared on national television to announce that any armed ships bound for Cuba would be forcibly turned back by the U.S. Navy. He also demanded that the Soviets remove the missiles.

Cuban leader Fidel Castro

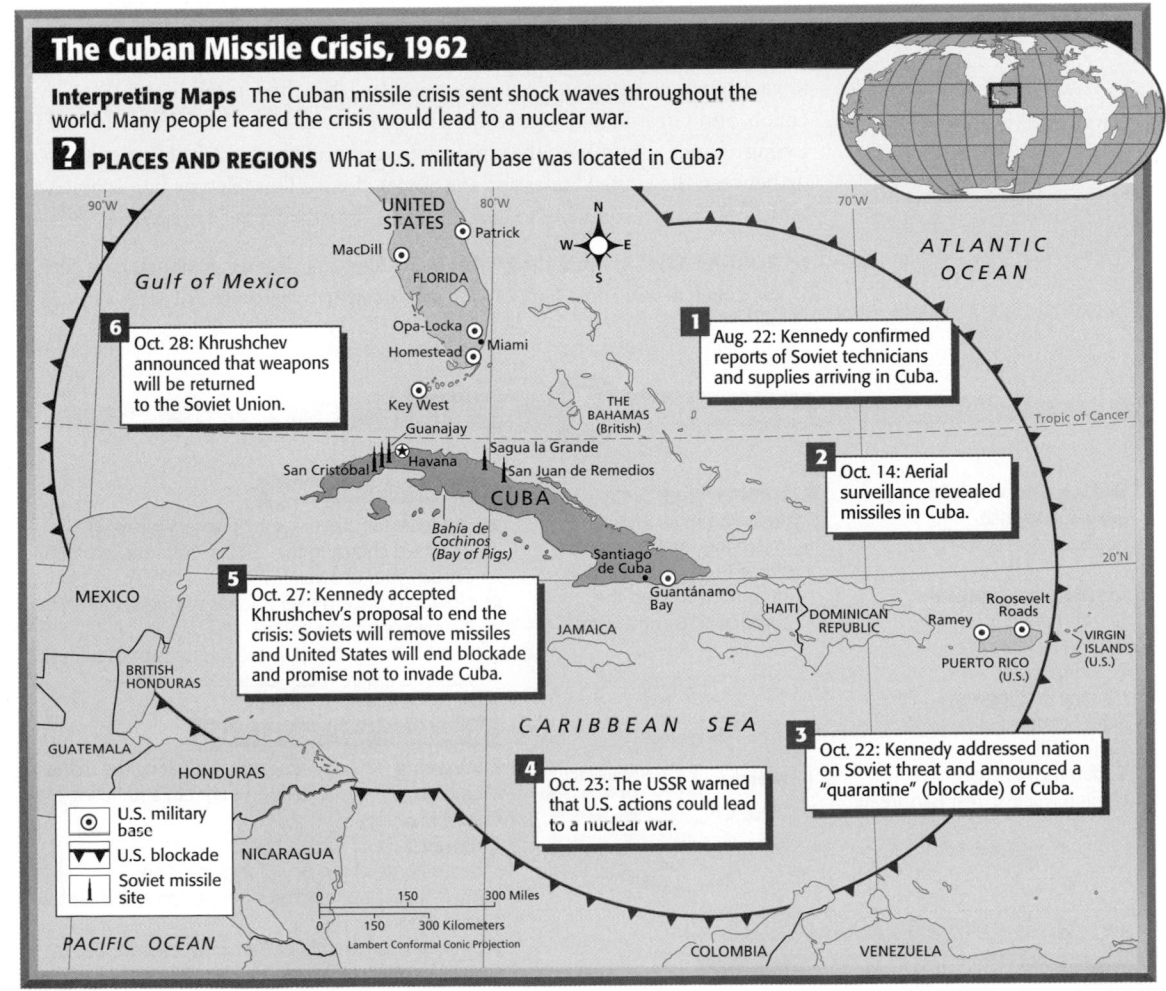

The Cuban Missile Crisis, 1962

Interpreting Maps The Cuban missile crisis sent shock waves throughout the world. Many people feared the crisis would lead to a nuclear war.

? PLACES AND REGIONS What U.S. military base was located in Cuba?

6 Oct. 28: Khrushchev announced that weapons will be returned to the Soviet Union.

1 Aug. 22: Kennedy confirmed reports of Soviet technicians and supplies arriving in Cuba.

2 Oct. 14: Aerial surveillance revealed missiles in Cuba.

5 Oct. 27: Kennedy accepted Khrushchev's proposal to end the crisis: Soviets will remove missiles and United States will end blockade and promise not to invade Cuba.

3 Oct. 22: Kennedy addressed nation on Soviet threat and announced a "quarantine" (blockade) of Cuba.

4 Oct. 23: The USSR warned that U.S. actions could lead to a nuclear war.

- ⊙ U.S. military base
- ▼▼ U.S. blockade
- ⌶ Soviet missile site

0   150   300 Miles
0 150 300 Kilometers
Lambert Conformal Conic Projection

PEOPLE IN HISTORY

Fidel Castro. By the time he displaced Cuban dictator Fulgencio Batista, Fidel Castro had a considerable history as a revolutionary. The son of a prosperous sugarcane farmer, Castro entered law school in 1945 at the University of Havana, where he became deeply involved in politics. Batista's refusal to hold elections convinced Castro that meaningful change in Cuba required violent rebellion. In late 1953 Castro led a group in an attack on a government military barracks. Officials arrested him and sentenced him to 15 years in prison. He was released after serving only 11 months and promptly organized another rebel group. This group soon began to wage guerrilla warfare against Batista's government. After years of bloody fighting, the dictator conceded defeat and fled the country.

ACTIVITY: Have students find recent articles about Cuba. Have volunteers share their articles with the class.

MAP ANSWER
Guantánamo Bay

PRIMARY SOURCE ANSWER
(for p. 630)
Students might suggest the "button" that would launch each country's nuclear weapons.

REVIEW

Have students complete the **Section 1 Review** on p. 630.

ASSESS

Have students complete **Daily Quiz 21.1.** As **Alternative Assessment,** you may want to use the Cuban missile crisis headline or the Cuban missile crisis political cartoon in this section's lessons.

RETEACH

Have students complete **Main Idea Activity for English Language Learners and Special-Needs Students 21.1.** Then organize students into groups of four. Assign one section

objective to each group member. Direct students to write paragraphs summarizing their assigned objectives. Have students share their paragraphs with the rest of their group.
English Language Learners, Cooperative Learning

EXTEND

Ask students to conduct research on the Alliance for Progress and to select a country that received aid under the program. Students should also conduct research on the dissemination of aid in the selected country. Ask each student to create a poster assessing the success of the program in the selected country. Conduct a discussion on why the program was more effective in some countries than in others. **Block Scheduling**

SECTION 1 REVIEW ANSWERS

1. Define
- flexible response, p. 626
- hot line, p. 630

2. Identify
- John F. Kennedy, p. 624
- Lyndon B. Johnson, p. 624
- Peace Corps, p. 626
- Alliance for Progress, p. 626
- Fidel Castro, p. 627
- Berlin Wall, p. 628
- Cuban missile crisis, p. 630
- Limited Nuclear Test Ban Treaty, p. 630

3. weapons—nuclear weapons buildup; military forces—strengthened conventional forces, established special military units, such as Green Berets; nonmilitary options—Peace Corps, Alliance for Progress, economic aid

4a. Some students might suggest that a president's appearance affects success in office and that television coverage in the 1960s allowed voters to select the most vital, attractive president.

b. It prompted him to continue a nuclear weapons buildup, but also to seek other options.

c. Answers will vary; support— the blockade ended the threat of nuclear weapons in Cuba; oppose—the blockade risked the threat of nuclear war

5. It led Khrushchev to see Kennedy as weak, and led Kennedy to pursue aggressive action against communism in Cuba and Berlin.

630

PRIMARY SOURCE

Soviet View of the Cuban Missile Crisis

During the Cuban missile crisis, the world teetered on the brink of nuclear war. In the end, the Soviets agreed to remove the missiles. Soviet leader Nikita Khrushchev related his memory of the crisis. **To what "button" is Khrushchev referring?**

❝It had been, to say the least, an interesting and challenging situation. The two most powerful nations of the world had squared off against each other, each with its finger on the button. You'd have thought that war was inevitable. But both sides showed that if the desire to avoid war is strong enough, even the most pressing dispute can be solved by compromise. . . . I'll always remember the late President Kennedy with deep respect because, in the final analysis, he showed himself to be sober-minded and determined to avoid war.❞

Over the next two days, nuclear war loomed. Soviet military advisers armed the missiles in Cuba. U.S. B-52 bombers armed with nuclear weapons prepared for battle. Meanwhile, armed Soviet ships sailed toward the blockade line.

Suddenly, on October 24, Kennedy was informed that most of the Soviet ships had "stopped dead in the water" before reaching the blockade line. The ships then turned and sailed home. "We're eyeball to eyeball," said Secretary of State Dean Rusk, "and I think the other fellow just blinked." On October 28 Khrushchev agreed to dismantle the missile bases in response to Kennedy's promise not to invade Cuba. Kennedy also secretly agreed to remove U.S. missiles from some foreign sites.

The **Cuban missile crisis** marked a historic turning point in U.S.-Soviet relations. Sobered by their brush with nuclear war, Kennedy and Khrushchev sought to ease tensions between their countries. In 1963 the United States, the Soviet Union, and Great Britain signed the **Limited Nuclear Test Ban Treaty** to end the testing of nuclear bombs in the atmosphere and underwater. A **hot line** was also set up between the United States and the Soviet Union. This teletype line enabled the leaders of the two countries to communicate directly during a crisis.

✔ **READING CHECK: Evaluating** What events kept a nuclear war from occurring during the Cuban missile crisis? **both nations' willingness to compromise and desire to avoid nuclear war**

SECTION 1 REVIEW

1. Define and explain:
flexible response
hot line

2. Identify and explain:
John F. Kennedy
Lyndon B. Johnson
Peace Corps
Alliance for Progress
Fidel Castro
Berlin Wall
Cuban missile crisis
Limited Nuclear Test Ban Treaty

3. Summarizing Copy the web below. Use it to explain the ways in which President Kennedy attempted to stop the advance of communism.

4. **Finding the Main Idea**

a. Did television coverage help voters make an informed choice in the 1960 presidential election? Explain your answer.

b. How did concern over nuclear weapons influence Kennedy's foreign policy?

c. Would you have supported Kennedy's naval blockade of Cuba in 1962? Explain your answer.

5. **Writing and Critical Thinking**

Evaluating Write a paragraph evaluating the influence of the Bay of Pigs incident on Kennedy's handling of Cold War events.
Consider:
- the outcome of the Bay of Pigs invasion
- Soviet leader Khrushchev's perception of Kennedy's leadership
- Kennedy's foreign-policy decisions after the Bay of Pigs invasion

 Homework Practice Online
keyword: SE3 HP21

After completing Section 2, students should be able to:

OBJECTIVE 1 Discuss how President Kennedy's image conflicted with reality.

OBJECTIVE 2 Identify why Kennedy had difficulty getting legislation passed.

OBJECTIVE 3 Explain how the Kennedy administration tried to help poor Americans.

OBJECTIVE 4 Describe how Americans responded to the death of the president.

LET'S GET STARTED!

Create a three-column chart on the chalkboard with the following headings: *What You Definitely Know About President Kennedy and His Administration; What You Probably Know About President Kennedy and His Administration; What You Want to Know About President Kennedy and His Administration.* As students enter the classroom, tell them to copy and complete the chart. Have volunteers share their entries with the class. Tell students that in Section 2 they will learn more about Kennedy myths and realities.

SECTION 2

READ TO DISCOVER

1. How did President Kennedy's image conflict with reality?
2. Why did Kennedy have difficulty getting legislation passed?
3. How did the Kennedy administration try to help poor Americans?
4. How did Americans respond to the death of the president?

IDENTIFY

Jacqueline Kennedy
Donna Shalala
Robert Kennedy
New Frontier
Area Redevelopment Act
Michael Harrington
Lee Harvey Oswald
Warren Commission

WHY IT MATTERS TODAY

In the 1960s young Americans wanted a stronger voice in political issues. Use **CNNfyi.com** or other **current events** sources to find out about how high-school or college students take part in politics today. Record your findings in your journal.

CNNfyi.com

The Kennedy White House

EYEWITNESSES TO History

"*[He] had a deep orange-brown suntan of a ski instructor, and when he smiled at the crowd his teeth were amazingly white and clearly visible at a distance of fifty yards.*"

—Norman Mailer, *The Presidential Papers*

Author Norman Mailer described presidential candidate John F. Kennedy in 1960. Mailer attended the Democratic National Convention and offered his observations of Kennedy in an article published later that year. Mailer compared Kennedy's arrival at the convention to "the scene where the hero, the matinee movie idol, comes to the palace to claim the princess." Explaining Kennedy's enormous appeal, Mailer argued, "It was a hero America needed . . . because only a hero can capture the secret imagination of a people, and so be good for the vitality of his nation."

President Kennedy sails off the coast of Maine.

The Kennedy Charisma

Youthful John F. Kennedy offered a marked contrast to the elderly outgoing president, Dwight D. Eisenhower. Kennedy captured the hearts of many Americans in a way that few politicians have. He became so popular that a few months after taking office he had to ask Americans to stop sending congratulatory telegrams to the White House.

Kennedy's appeal stemmed from his cool intellectual personality, athletic appearance, and handsome features. Americans could not doubt that their president had a keen mind. A graduate of Harvard University, he had published two books. His best-selling *Profiles in Courage* won a Pulitzer Prize for biography. Kennedy presented an image of youth and vitality throughout his career in politics. He was frequently photographed engaged in sporting activities such as football, sailing, and swimming.

The first family. The president's attractive young wife, **Jacqueline** "Jackie" **Kennedy**, contributed to the glamour and mystique that surrounded the Kennedy White House. The first lady quickly rose to the top of polls of women whom Americans most admired. Her popularity spread beyond U.S. borders. When the Kennedys met with Soviet leader Nikita Khrushchev, he said, "I'd like to shake her hand first." The first lady received so much attention on a trip to France that the president called himself "the man who accompanied Jacqueline Kennedy to Paris, and I have enjoyed it."

Jacqueline Kennedy brought an appreciation for the fine arts to the Kennedy administration. She invited prominent artists and musicians to social events.

ALL LEVELS: Tell students that the Kennedy mystique is still a powerful force today, almost 40 years after "Camelot." Call students' attention to the death of John F. Kennedy Jr. and the widespread public mourning that followed the event. Ask students why the public responded so strongly to his death and why national newsmagazines afforded him the title of "America's Prince." *(Some students might suggest that the "Kennedy myth" has led many Americans to view the family as elegant, attractive, and youthful—almost royal.)* To help students understand how President Kennedy's image conflicted with reality, copy the following graphic organizer on the chalkboard, omitting the italicized answers. Have each student complete it. **English Language Learners**

The Kennedy Image
- *took pains to control his image*
- *knew the immense power of the media*
- *promoted an image of health and vitality*

THE KENNEDY ADMINIS-TRATION

The Kennedy Reality
- *suffered from many physical ailments, including Addison's disease*
- *wore reading glasses*

Jacqueline Kennedy. Jacqueline Kennedy's status as the country's "unofficial Minister of Culture" was partially a result of her privileged upbringing. The daughter of a wealthy stockbroker, she attended exclusive private schools as a child and studied at the Sorbonne in Paris before receiving a degree from George Washington University. In 1951 she won a *Vogue* magazine talent contest. The publication offered her a job, but she chose instead to travel in Europe. She then worked as a society photographer in Washington, D.C. A short time later she met John F. Kennedy, who was serving as a congressmember. They were married in 1953.

ACTIVITY: Have students compare and contrast Jacqueline Kennedy's role as first lady to the role of another first lady.

THAT'S INTERESTING!

Just before the first televised debate, Richard M. Nixon applied a product called Lazy Shave to hide his five o'clock shadow. The Lazy Shave dulled his complexion, making Nixon look washed-out.

HISTORICAL DOCUMENTS ANSWER
(for p. 633)

Students might suggest the threat of communism.

PRESIDENTIAL Lives

1917–1963
In Office 1961–1963

John F. Kennedy

John F. Kennedy's heroism in World War II enhanced the mystique that surrounded him when he took office. During the war, he served as the commander of a U.S. Navy patrol torpedo boat in the Pacific theater. In the early morning hours of August 2, 1943, Kennedy's boat, the *PT-109,* was rammed by a Japanese destroyer. Two crewmen were killed. The next morning, as the boat slowly sank, Kennedy ordered his men to use a plank as a float and head for a small island about three miles away. Kennedy swam the entire distance, towing a wounded man by clenching the man's life jacket strap in his teeth. The men made it to the island, and they were rescued several days later.

Kennedy received some criticism for his role in the affair. Questions were raised as to why the Japanese destroyer had been able to ram the PT boat, a small, fast ship. Nevertheless, he received a medal for his heroic efforts to save his men. A national magazine printed the story of his actions, and the *PT-109* was mentioned frequently during Kennedy's political campaigns. Members of his crew were present during Kennedy's inauguration, and a model of the *PT-109* was displayed in the inaugural parade.

JOHN F KENNEDY

13¢ UNITED STATES

Research on the ROM

Free Find: Donna Shalala

After reading about Donna Shalala on the **Holt Researcher CD–ROM,** write a resumé for her to use in applying for a cabinet position in a future administration.

One newspaper referred to her as the "unofficial Minister of Culture." She also organized a major restoration of the White House, declaring, "I want to make the White House the first house in the land." Mrs. Kennedy later hosted a nationally televised tour of the White House.

Americans were also fascinated by the Kennedy children. Caroline, born in 1957, and John Jr., born a few weeks after his father's election to office, were the first young children to live in the White House since Theodore Roosevelt's presidency. One Kennedy aide later recalled that "Caroline Kennedy quickly became a national figure." The public enjoyed seeing photographs of her and her brother playing in the White House. Complaining about the president's popularity, one senator who opposed Kennedy's programs claimed, "The difference is Caroline, and there's nothing we can do about it."

Effects on youth. Although many Americans regarded the Kennedy family as attractive and interesting, young people found Kennedy particularly inspiring. During the presidential campaign, Kennedy's public appearances drew large numbers of young Americans. Many of them responded to Kennedy's call for service and sacrifice. Some of these Americans joined the Peace Corps. One volunteer recalled, "I'd never done anything political, patriotic, or unselfish because nobody ever asked me to. Kennedy asked."

One of the many Americans motivated to action by Kennedy's vision was **Donna Shalala.** During the 1990s Shalala served as secretary of health and human services in the administration of President Bill Clinton. In 1961, as a young college graduate, Shalala had responded to Kennedy's call and joined the Peace Corps. She later recalled, "Kennedy was the first president we had voted for. He represented a break with the past." Shalala spent two years in a tiny village called Molasani in Iran, living in a mud hut and teaching English.

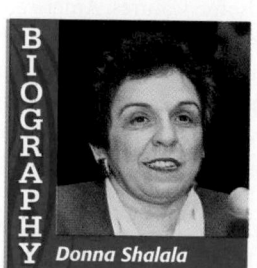

BIOGRAPHY

Donna Shalala

Shalala remembered that "everybody laughed" at Kennedy's idea of American volunteers fanning out across the globe, "but it worked." She claimed that her years of Peace Corps service "made me a world citizen. It just changed me at such a young age, giving me confidence in my ability to be dropped down anywhere on earth and be comfortable." Her experience also gave her confidence in young people. She declared, "Having faith in young Americans may be a simple idea, but it works."

TEACH OBJECTIVE 2

LEVEL 1: Pair students and have each pair create a graphic organizer depicting why Kennedy had difficulty getting legislation passed. *(Students should show that a coalition of southern Democrats and conservative Republicans in Congress opposed Kennedy's agenda.)* Then ask students to consider the impact of those difficulties on Kennedy's presidency. Did those difficulties reflect badly on Kennedy's abilities? Did those difficulties adversely affect the nation? How might they have been prevented?
English Language Learners, Cooperative Learning

LEVELS 2 AND 3: Organize students into two large groups. Tell one group to imagine that it represents President Kennedy or his top aides and the other group to imagine that it represents southern Democrats or conservative Republicans. Have each student write three or four short journal entries in his or her assigned role describing the difficulties President Kennedy had getting legislation passed. *(See the Level 1 lesson for the correct issues.)* Have volunteers from both groups read their journal entries to the class. Then conduct a discussion on how students' different—and opposing—roles affected their reactions, as represented in the journal entries, to the political issues at hand.
Cooperative Learning

Reality. The images of the first family masked a more complex reality. Kennedy took great pains to control his public appearance. He avoided being photographed while wearing his reading glasses, and later during his administration had television lights adjusted to hide a double chin.

Despite his interest in athletic pursuits, President Kennedy was not a healthy man. He struggled with illness throughout his life. His brother Robert once recalled that "at least one half of the days that he spent on this earth were days of intense physical pain." Kennedy suffered from a sometimes fatal condition called Addison's disease. His back had troubled him since childhood, and Kennedy had nearly died in 1954 during an operation on his spine.

✔ **READING CHECK: Summarizing** How did President Kennedy inspire young people to volunteer for public service?
Kennedy asked them, and they were attracted by his youth, charisma, and break from the past.

Kennedy's Advisers

President Kennedy hoped to use the government to offer solutions to national and global problems. To advance his programs, Kennedy surrounded himself with others who shared his vision. The average age of his cabinet members was 47, a decade younger than that of President Eisenhower's cabinet. Special Counsel Theodore Sorensen, the speechwriter who composed most of Kennedy's inaugural address, was just 32 years old at the time.

The president wanted only "the brightest and best," and his advisers were well educated. "There's nothing like brains. You can't beat brains," Kennedy claimed. Secretary of Defense Robert McNamara was a graduate of the Harvard Business School. Secretary of State Dean Rusk was a former Rhodes Scholar, and McGeorge Bundy, special assistant for national security affairs, had been a dean at Harvard. However, few of Kennedy's advisers had political experience, and not everyone was impressed by their credentials. Speaker of the House Sam Rayburn told Lyndon B. Johnson, "You may be right and they may be every bit as intelligent as you say, but I'd feel a whole lot better about them if just one of them had run for sheriff once."

For the position of attorney general, Kennedy selected his younger brother **Robert** "Bobby" **Kennedy**. Although Robert Kennedy had graduated from law school, he had never practiced law. Some members of Congress and presidential advisers opposed the president's decision to appoint his brother to high office. Even Robert expressed doubts. Nonetheless, the president told his brother, "I need you. . . . I need someone I know to talk to in this government." Robert proved to be the

---

★ HISTORICAL DOCUMENTS ★

PRESIDENT JOHN F. KENNEDY
Inaugural Address

John F. Kennedy delivered his inaugural address on January 20, 1961. It contained the themes of challenge and sacrifice that had filled his speeches during the presidential campaign. His address remains one of the most famous speeches in U.S. history. **What is the "maximum danger" to which Kennedy refers?**

*I*n the long history of the world, only a few generations have been granted the role of defending freedom in its hour of maximum danger. I do not shrink from this responsibility—I welcome it. I do not believe that any of us would exchange places with any other people or any other generation. The energy, the faith, the devotion which we bring to this endeavor will light our country and all who serve it—and the glow from that fire can truly light the world.

And so my fellow Americans: ask not what your country can do for you—ask what you can do for your country.

My fellow citizens of the world: ask not what America will do for you, but what together we can do for the freedom of man.

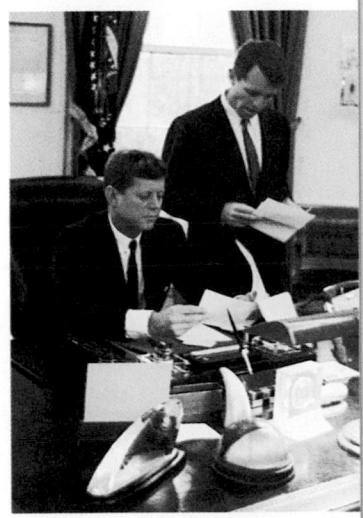

President Kennedy and his brother Robert work together in the Oval Office.

TEACH OBJECTIVE 3

 LEVEL 1: Organize students into triads and have each triad create a poster illustrating how the Kennedy administration tried to help poor Americans. *(Students should indicate that President Kennedy supported the Area Redevelopment Act and other antipoverty programs.)* Ask triads to write paragraphs explaining the rationale of those antipoverty programs. Have volunteers read their paragraphs to the class. Then conduct a brief discussion on how Kennedy might have tried to eradicate poverty in the United States if he had survived the assassination attempt.
English Language Learners, Cooperative Learning

LEVELS 2 AND 3: Ask students to name modern-day government programs designed to alleviate poverty. *(Students might mention foodstamps, Social Security, and so on.)* Tell students to identify President Kennedy's attempts to help poor Americans. *(See the Level 1 lesson for the correct attempts.)* Tell students to imagine that it is 1961 and that Congress is considering the Area Redevelopment Act. Have each student write a letter about the act to his or her congressperson. Students' letters should explain the rationale of the act as well as discuss poverty in general. Have volunteers read their letters to the class. Students may wish to include their letters in their portfolios.

POLITICAL CARTOON ANSWER

Students might suggest the steel industry's rising prices; the various steel companies.

president's closest adviser. Kennedy also valued advice from a small circle of White House staff members that included Sorensen, speechwriter Richard Goodwin, and Press Secretary Pierre Salinger. Goodwin later recalled that staff members did not "hesitate to approach Kennedy directly on matters we thought of presidential interest or concern."

The Domestic Frontier

Because John F. Kennedy had spoken of a "new frontier" during the presidential campaign, his agenda became known as the **New Frontier.** Managing the economy was one of Kennedy's first domestic challenges. He wanted to reassure business leaders that his policies would not be disruptive. To do so, he appointed C. Douglas Dillon, a Republican who had served in the Eisenhower administration, as secretary of the treasury. This selection also gave his administration a bipartisan appearance.

Economic matters. When he took office, Kennedy faced economic problems that included rising unemployment and inflation. To stimulate economic growth, Kennedy called for an increase in government spending. By the end of 1961, inflation had gone down, but unemployment remained high. Kennedy hoped to keep inflation down and to further the economic recovery by persuading labor and business to agree to informal wage and price controls. Businesses had been granting higher wages to employees and then passing the costs on to consumers in the form of higher prices. Kennedy called on businesses to limit prices in return for workers agreeing to fewer pay raises.

Administration officials worked particularly hard to reach an agreement with the steel industry. They feared that a rise in steel prices would lead manufacturers who used steel to raise the prices of their goods. This could lead to inflation throughout the economy. One adviser told the president that steel was "so large in the manufacturing sector of the economy that it can upset the price applecart all by itself." Thus, Kennedy was furious when Roger Blough, the president of U.S. Steel, announced higher prices. Just two weeks earlier, steelworkers had agreed to accept only small increases in their benefits packages. Kennedy told Blough, "I think you have made a terrible mistake."

The following day Kennedy lashed out at U.S. Steel and five other companies that had announced similar price hikes. The president blamed the crisis on "a tiny handful of steel executives whose pursuit of private power and profit exceeds their sense of public responsibility." He accused the steel executives of showing "utter contempt for the interests of one hundred eighty-five million Americans." Recalling his inaugural theme of sacrifice, Kennedy declared, "Some time ago I asked each American to consider what he would do for this country and I asked the steel companies. In the last twenty-four hours we had their answer."

The Kennedy administration proceeded to wage a nonstop campaign against the steel company executives that included canceling government contracts. Faced with such pressure, steel company executives announced that prices would not increase after all. Although Kennedy received criticism for his heavy-handed tactics, he had scored a significant victory in his efforts to manage the economy.

INTERPRETING POLITICAL CARTOONS

The New Frontier. President Kennedy faced many challenges while trying to create his New Frontier. **What does the cat in this cartoon represent? What do the cat's many tails represent?**

SPOTLIGHT
on *The Other America*

Have students conduct research on poverty in the 1960s and read sections of Michael Harrington's *The Other America*. Then ask each student to select and assume one of the following roles: President Kennedy, a Kennedy administration official, Michael Harrington, a news reporter, and so on. Have students prepare to speak on the issue of poverty in the 1960s in a roundtable discussion. Students should create a list of talking points for the discussion. After students have finished their lists of talking points, act as a moderator and conduct the roundtable discussion. **Block Scheduling**

TEACH OBJECTIVE 4

LEVEL 1: Tell students to imagine that it is November 22, 1963, and that they have just learned that President Kennedy has been assassinated. Ask each student to list at least five words that describe his or her emotions. *(Students might list words such as* shock, fear, vulnerability, anger, *or* sadness.*)* Have volunteers share their chosen words with the class. Then ask students to draw on their lists to write paragraphs describing how Americans responded to the death of the president. *(Most Americans felt shocked, saddened, and outraged. Many felt that they had grown older instantly.)* Have volunteers read their paragraphs to the class. Students may wish to include their paragraphs in their portfolios. **English Language Learners**

Kennedy and Congress. Kennedy received little cooperation for his legislative agenda from Congress. Although Democrats controlled both houses of Congress, Republicans had gained 21 seats in the House of Representatives and 2 seats in the Senate in the 1960 election. More important, a coalition of southern Democrats and conservative Republicans in Congress opposed Kennedy's agenda and successfully blocked most of the president's domestic programs.

Even before Kennedy took office, his advisers recommended a tax cut as a means of stimulating economic growth. Lower taxes would give consumers more money to spend and in turn would lead businesses to produce more goods and hire more workers. Kennedy initially rejected the idea. He argued that such a program conflicted with his calls for personal sacrifice on behalf of national good.

A sharp drop in the stock market in May 1962, however, convinced Kennedy to ask Congress to reduce taxes. In his 1963 State of the Union Address, he declared, "I am convinced that the enactment this year of tax reduction and tax reform overshadows all other domestic problems in this Congress." Several members of Congress balked, however, when Kennedy introduced legislation that reduced taxes by some $10 billion. Critics included former president Eisenhower. They charged that without a comparable cut in federal spending, the tax cut would lead to "a vast wasteland of debt and financial chaos." Despite Kennedy's urging, Congress failed to pass the measure in 1963. Other Kennedy initiatives rejected by Congress included legislation to assist older Americans in paying their medical bills and a bill to provide federal aid for education.

✔ **READING CHECK: Analyzing Information** How did Kennedy try to solve some of the nation's economic problems? **informal wage and price controls, a nonstop campaign against the steel companies, and a proposed tax reduction**

Helping the Disadvantaged

John F. Kennedy ranked high among the wealthiest presidents—in 1962 his personal fortune stood at about $2.5 million. He donated his annual salary of $100,000 to charities. During the presidential campaign, Kennedy was astonished when he saw the living conditions of poor West Virginians. Once he took office he sought ways to help poor Americans improve their standard of living. Kennedy supported passage of the **Area Redevelopment Act** (ARA)—a bill to provide financial assistance to economically distressed regions that former president Eisenhower had previously vetoed. Kennedy signed the ARA into law in May 1961, winning the first legislative victory of his presidency.

The president's interest in poverty was renewed in 1962 when social activist **Michael Harrington** published *The Other America*, a well-documented study of poverty in the United States. The book shattered the popular notion that all Americans had benefited from the prosperity of the 1950s. Harrington reported that more than 42 million Americans lived on less than $1,000 per year. He challenged the nation's leaders to face the reality of poverty:

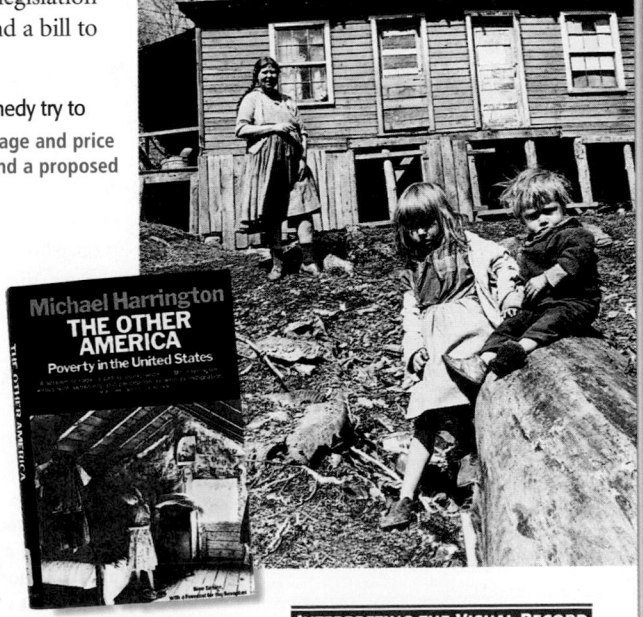

INTERPRETING THE VISUAL RECORD

Poverty. Inspired in part by Michael Harrington's *The Other America*, President Kennedy tried to help the poorest Americans. *What types of assistance could this family use?*

HISTORY MAKERS SPEAK

Michael Harrington in *The Other America*

The "Culture of Poverty." Michael Harrington's *The Other America* offered a vivid description of poverty in the United States. "Being poor is not one aspect of a person's life in this country; it is his life. Taken as a whole, poverty is a culture. . . . These are people who lack education and skill, who have bad health, poor housing, low levels of aspiration and high levels of mental distress. . . . Each disability is the more intense because it exists within a web of disabilities. And if one problem is solved, and the others are left constant, there is little gain."

CRITICAL THINKING What kinds of antipoverty programs might Harrington have endorsed?

ANSWER: Students might suggest programs that aimed at all of poverty's symptoms.

VISUAL RECORD ANSWER
Students might suggest housing, clothing, and sanitation.

LEVEL 2: Tell students to imagine that they are members of the Kennedy family or friends that knew John F. Kennedy before he became president. Then tell students to imagine that it is the week after Kennedy's assassination. Have each student write a eulogy for Kennedy. Eulogies should describe how much the president meant to his family and friends as well as to the public he served as president. *(See the Level 1 lesson for the public's responses.)* Ask volunteers to deliver their eulogies to the class. Students may wish to include their eulogies in their portfolios.

LEVEL 3: Pair students and tell them to imagine that they are artists who have been asked to design a memorial for President John F. Kennedy. Have each pair create a design for a memorial. Memorials should be dignified and respectful. Have each pair write a brief artists' statement to accompany its memorial. Artists' statements should describe Americans' feelings toward the president and his death and include the text that will appear on the memorial. *(See the Level 1 lesson for the correct responses.)* If time and resources permit, have students build or sculpt scale models of their proposed memorials.

Cooperative Learning

HOMEWORK *Have students ask people who were teenagers or adults in 1963 about their reactions to President Kennedy's assassination. Ask each student to write two or three paragraphs describing and analyzing these reactions. Conduct a class discussion on students' findings.*

PEOPLE IN HISTORY

The Kennedy Family.
President Kennedy was not the last member of his immediate family to die tragically. In 1968 an assassin killed his brother Robert. In 1999 President Kennedy's son, John Jr., died with his wife and her sister when his private plane crashed into the Atlantic Ocean. Commentator Garrison Keillor described the impact of his death. "[John F. Kennedy Jr. was] a hero sprung up from tragedy, the son of the murdered President bearing his name whose life was meant in our minds to redeem that evil day in Dallas. I doubt that there were many Americans who didn't want the best for John F. Kennedy Jr. And when his plane was reported missing on Saturday morning, although there was no precedent, no justification, for television to maintain the vigil that it did, there was a rightness about it. He was our boy."

CRITICAL THINKING What might the response to John F. Kennedy Jr.'s death reveal about Americans' lingering feelings toward his father?

ANSWER: Students might offer that, as Keillor indicates, Americans' strong emotional responses to John F. Kennedy Jr.'s death revealed their warm feelings toward his father and their sadness and anger over his father's death.

Analyzing Primary Sources

Drawing Inferences Why did "millions of human beings" seem "invisible" in the 1960s?

According to Harrington, the poor became "invisible" because the majority of the nation viewed itself as wealthy.

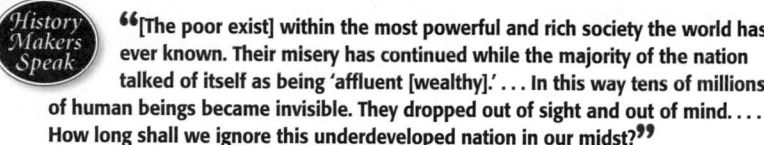

History Makers Speak

"[The poor exist] within the most powerful and rich society the world has ever known. Their misery has continued while the majority of the nation talked of itself as being 'affluent [wealthy].' . . . In this way tens of millions of human beings became invisible. They dropped out of sight and out of mind. . . . How long shall we ignore this underdeveloped nation in our midst?**"**

—Michael Harrington, *The Other America*

Harrington also noted that racism continued to keep many ethnic groups—particularly African Americans—in poverty. He warned that the end of legalized segregation would not change the economic condition of most poor African Americans. "The laws against [discrimination based on] color can be removed," he wrote, "but that will leave the poverty that is the historic consequence of color. As long as this is the case, being born a Negro will continue to be the most profound disability that the United States imposes upon a citizen."

Harrington's work impressed Kennedy and members of his administration. The president told one adviser, "I want to go beyond the things that have already been accomplished. . . . For example, what about the poverty problem in the United States?" Kennedy's staff began work on the antipoverty programs that the president wanted to present as part of a campaign planned for 1964.

✔ **READING CHECK: Identifying Points of View** What link did Harrington make between poverty and racism? He noted that racism kept many ethnic groups in poverty.

Newspapers across the country reported the shocking news of President Kennedy's death.

Tragedy in Dallas

To build support for his 1964 presidential campaign, President Kennedy traveled to Texas in November 1963. In Dallas on November 22, crowds lined the route of Kennedy's open-car motorcade from the airport. At about 12:30 P.M., as the motorcade moved through the downtown area, shots rang out. Kennedy slumped over, fatally wounded. Within hours, Vice President Lyndon B. Johnson was sworn in as president. Over the next few days Americans came together to mourn their dead president. Millions watched the funeral on television. Many felt that Kennedy's assassination had also killed something in them. "We'll never be young again," Kennedy staff member Daniel Patrick Moynihan observed. Donna Shalala later recalled hearing the news while serving in the Peace Corps in Iran.

History Makers Speak

"I remember staying up all night listening to the funeral on the radio. I also recall a beggar walking up to me in the street and I said, 'No, I don't have any money.' He said, 'I don't want any money. I just want to tell you how sorry I am that your young president died.' I remember how difficult it was to sleep and I remember turning cold, which is one of the first signs of shock. . . . His assassination forced us all to grow up.**"**

—Donna Shalala, quoted in *Ordinary Americans*, edited by Linda R. Monk

Within hours of the shooting, Dallas police arrested **Lee Harvey Oswald** as a suspect. Two days later, while being moved from one jail to another, Oswald was shot to death by nightclub owner Jack Ruby. This strange turn of events caused many people to question whether Oswald had acted alone in killing the president.

REVIEW

Have students complete the **Section 2 Review** on on p. 637.

ASSESS

Have students complete **Daily Quiz 21.2**. As **Alternative Assessment**, you may want to use the image and reality graphic organizer or the President Kennedy eulogy in this section's lessons.

RETEACH

Have students complete **Main Idea Activity for English Language Learners and Special-Needs Students 21.2**. Assign each student one subsection of Section 2. Have students write three or four questions about the material in their assigned subsections. Collect students' questions and use them to quiz the class. **English Language Learners**

EXTEND

Have students conduct research on the Kennedy administration and the myth of "Camelot." Ask each student to create a collage on the subject. Students should include images that represent President Kennedy's domestic and international policies as well as his public image. Have each student write a short paper analyzing the administration and the myth of Camelot to accompany his or her collage. **Block Scheduling**

To end speculation, President Johnson named a commission headed by Chief Justice Earl Warren to investigate the assassination. This **Warren Commission** spent 10 months reviewing the evidence. It concluded that there was no conspiracy and that both Oswald and Ruby had acted alone. Despite these findings, many Americans continued to believe that more than one person was involved in Kennedy's assassination.

After Kennedy's death, his family and friends worked diligently to shape the memory of the fallen president. Jacqueline Kennedy told reporter Theodore White that her husband's life "had more to do with myth, magic, legend, saga, and story than with political theory or political science." She asked White, who was writing a magazine article on the president, to compare his administration to Camelot, King Arthur's medieval court. White agreed, and the image of Camelot became another part of the Kennedy mystique.

Clark Clifford, an adviser to several presidents, offered a different assessment. He wrote, "In many ways the drama of [Kennedy's] presidency outweighed its achievements." Clifford argued that Kennedy nonetheless had an important influence on American life.

History Makers Speak

❝He offered a vast promise to a new generation of Americans. He inspired the nation with a heroic vision of the Presidency as the center of action in American life. No President during my lifetime, with the exception of Franklin Roosevelt, matched Kennedy in creating a sense that the Presidency was the center of our national life, the place from which we could solve our most pressing problems.❞

—Clark Clifford, *Counsel to the President*

✔ **READING CHECK: Drawing Inferences** What different views of President Kennedy were expressed after his death? *a man of "myth, magic, legend, saga, and story" or that "the drama of his presidency outweighed its achievements"*

First lighted on November 25, 1963, a flame burns continually at the grave of President John F. Kennedy.

SECTION 2 REVIEW

1. Identify and explain:
Jacqueline Kennedy
Donna Shalala
Robert Kennedy
New Frontier
Area Redevelopment Act
Michael Harrington
Lee Harvey Oswald
Warren Commission

2. Evaluating Copy the chart below. Use it to explain President Kennedy's economic policies and how well they succeeded.

Kennedy's Economic Policies

Labor	Taxes	Poverty
Outcome	Outcome	Outcome

3. Finding the Main Idea

a. How did the reality of the Kennedy administration differ from the popular image?
b. How did Kennedy try to assist the poor?
c. Did Kennedy's difficulty in getting legislation passed reduce his effectiveness as a leader? Explain your answer.

4. Writing and Critical Thinking

Making Predictions Imagine that you are a teenager in 1963 just after President Kennedy's assassination. Write a journal entry describing how his death has changed your expectations of the nation's future.
Consider:
• the impact of Kennedy's youthful image
• his influence on the nation's young people
• doubts that surrounded his death

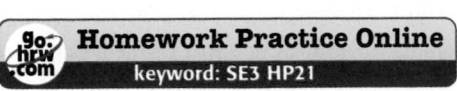
Homework Practice Online
keyword: SE3 HP21

SECTION 2 REVIEW ANSWERS

1. Identify
• Jacqueline Kennedy, p. 631
• Donna Shalala, p. 632
• Robert Kennedy, p. 633
• New Frontier, p. 634
• Area Redevelopment Act, p. 635
• Michael Harrington, p. 635
• Lee Harvey Oswald, p. 636
• Warren Commission, p. 637

2. Kennedy wanted to use informal wage and price controls to curb inflation and force steel companies to freeze their prices. He hoped to cut taxes to stimulate economic growth, but Congress rejected the proposal. He wanted to reduce poverty and passed the Area Redevelopment Act.

3a. President Kennedy was not as physically healthy as he led people to believe.

b. He supported the Area Redevelopment Act.

c. effective—the president's ability to inspire Americans and his antipoverty campaign; ineffective—the president's inability to influence Congress

4. Answers will vary. Journals might suggest that his death deeply saddened Americans and made many feel less hopeful about the nation's future.

After completing Section 3, students should be able to:

OBJECTIVE 1 Explain how President Johnson's War on Poverty affected American communities.

OBJECTIVE 2 Identify the problems that the Great Society programs addressed.

OBJECTIVE 3 Detail how the Warren Court expanded individual liberties.

OBJECTIVE 4 Describe why support for the Great Society programs declined during the late 1960s.

🔊 LET'S GET STARTED!

As students enter the classroom, ask them to list some of President Kennedy's unfulfilled goals. Then tell them to write a brief paragraph speculating about the ways in which President Johnson might have responded to those unfulfilled goals. Have volunteers read their paragraphs to the class. Tell students that in Section 3 they will learn about Johnson's policies, actions, and legacies.

SECTION ③ RESOURCES

REPRODUCIBLE
▶ Guided Reading Strategy 21.3

TECHNOLOGY
▶ One-Stop Planner, Lesson 21.3
▶ The American Nation Video Program Segment: VISTA Volunteers; Teacher's Guide, pp. 207–08
▶ CNN. Presents America: Yesterday and Today Segment: Reaching for the Moon
▶ Holt Researcher: American History CD–ROM
▶ Homework Practice Online

REINFORCEMENT, REVIEW, AND ASSESSMENT
▶ Section 3 Review, p. 645
▶ Daily Quiz 21.3
▶ Main Idea Activity 21.3
▶ English Audio Summary 21.3
▶ Spanish Audio Summary 21.3

SECTION ③

READ TO DISCOVER
1. How did President Johnson's War on Poverty affect American communities?
2. What problems did the Great Society programs address?
3. How did the Warren Court expand individual liberties?
4. Why did support for Great Society programs decline during the late 1960s?

IDENTIFY
War on Poverty
Office of Economic Opportunity
Volunteers in Service to America
Great Society
Barry Goldwater
Medicare
Medicaid
Elementary and Secondary Education Act
Robert C. Weaver
Corporation for Public Broadcasting
Rachel Carson
Earl Warren
Reynolds v. *Sims*

▶ WHY IT MATTERS TODAY

Many of the social programs created during the Johnson administration still help people today. Johnson's programs included Head Start, HUD, Medicaid, Medicare, and VISTA. Use CNNfyi.com or other **current events** sources to learn about one of these programs. Record your findings in your journal.

CNNfyi.com

Johnson's Great Society

EYEWITNESSES TO History ❝We have received official confirmation that President Kennedy is dead. I am saddened to have to tell you this grievous news.... We have a new President. May God bless our new president and our nation.❞

—Dean Rusk, quoted in *With Kennedy,* by Pierre Salinger

Secretary of State Dean Rusk broke the news to his fellow airplane passengers. Earlier that day, Rusk and several other members of President Kennedy's cabinet and staff had boarded an airplane bound for Tokyo to attend an economic conference in Japan. As the plane flew across the Pacific, those on board received garbled teletype messages indicating that something terrible had happened to the president. Secretary Rusk ordered the plane to return to the United States immediately. After Rusk discovered that Kennedy was dead, he shared the news with those on board the flight. His words reflected the anxiety that many Americans felt for the nation and their new president as they faced the tragedy that had unfolded in Dallas that day.

Lyndon B. Johnson takes the oath of office. His wife, Lady Bird Johnson, is on the left, and Jacqueline Kennedy is on the right.

Johnson Takes Over

President Lyndon B. Johnson was very different from the charismatic and engaging John F. Kennedy. Born in the Hill Country of central Texas, Johnson grew up in a household that had experienced both poverty and relative prosperity. Ambitious and hardworking, Johnson rose rapidly through the Democratic Party ranks. In 1948 he narrowly won a hard-fought race for a seat in the U.S. Senate. After he was re-elected in 1954, Johnson's colleagues made him the Senate majority leader. The position gave him a great deal of influence over legislation. A master of compromise, Johnson always seemed to find the middle course on which most people could agree.

Establishing continuity. Johnson's mastery of the political process, along with years of experience in Washington, enabled him to manage the transition to the presidency with considerable skill and tact. Johnson reassured the nation with promises of continuity between his administration and that of Kennedy. He later recalled, "I felt from the first day in office that I had to carry on for President Kennedy. I considered myself the caretaker of both his people and his policies." Johnson asked Kennedy's cabinet and advisers to continue serving under him. When he spoke to a joint session of Congress on November 27, 1963, Johnson detailed many of Kennedy's achievements. He then declared, "The ideas and ideals which he so nobly represented must and will be translated into effective action." Members of Congress, many of whom had vigorously opposed Kennedy's agenda, applauded enthusiastically to show their support for Johnson.

Ask students to identify ways in which President Johnson made the transition into the Oval Office. *(Students should indicate that Johnson comforted the nation in its sorrow and worked to continue President Kennedy's programs.)* Ask students to assess the effectiveness of this transition. *(Most students will indicate that Johnson handled the transition quite well.)* Then ask students to speculate about how Johnson's presidency might have proceeded had he not made an effort to maintain and implement President Kennedy's policies. Tell students to write several scenarios describing the effects and long-term consequences of this course. **Block Scheduling**

TEACH OBJECTIVE 1

LEVEL 1: Pair students and tell them to imagine that they are people living in a community that has greatly benefited from President Johnson's War on Poverty. Have each pair develop a dialogue discussing certain programs and describing the effects of the programs. *(Students should mention the Office of Economic Opportunity, the Head Start program, and the Volunteers in Service to America program. These initiatives provided antipoverty programs such as job training and preschool education.)* Ask volunteers to perform their dialogues for the class. **English Language Learners, Cooperative Learning**

Johnson later claimed, "During my first thirty days in office I believe I averaged no more than three or four hours' sleep a night." He focused his attention on securing passage of Kennedy's tax cut bill and civil rights legislation, both of which had stalled in the Congress. In order to gain support for the tax cut, Johnson had his aides craft a federal budget that held spending to $100 billion. Convinced that the budget offered proof that Johnson intended to curb government spending, Congress approved the tax cut bill in February 1964.

During his first year in office, Johnson kept his pledge to follow in Kennedy's footsteps. However, the ambitious Texan also had plans of his own. "If you look at my record, you would know that I am a Roosevelt New Dealer," he told a former Kennedy aide. "As a matter of fact, John F. Kennedy was a little too conservative to suit my taste."

At his first cabinet meeting in January 1964 he announced, "The day is over when top jobs are reserved for men." Johnson eventually appointed 27 women to upper-level government positions, including consumer activist Betty Furness, economists Alice Rivlin and Penelope Thunberg, and Texas legislator Barbara Jordan. He also appointed Mexican Americans to high positions, assigning Vicente T. Ximenes to chair a presidential committee on Mexican American affairs. Other top appointments went to Héctor P. García, a Texas spokesperson for Mexican American veterans, and to Raúl H. Castro. Castro later became the first Mexican American governor of Arizona.

The War on Poverty. Johnson learned of President Kennedy's antipoverty initiative on November 23, 1963, his first full day in office. Walter Heller, chair of the Council of Economic Advisers, gave Johnson an outline of the plan. Johnson responded, "I'm sympathetic. Go ahead. Give it the highest priority. Push ahead full tilt."

Advisers urged Johnson to implement the antipoverty program slowly, testing its effectiveness in a few cities before expanding its scope. Johnson, however, insisted that the program "be big and bold and hit the nation with real impact." In his first State of the Union Address, delivered on January 8, 1964, the president declared "unconditional war on poverty in America." To launch his **War on Poverty**, Johnson sent to Congress a bill calling for the creation of an **Office of Economic Opportunity** (OEO). With a budget of $1 billion, OEO coordinated a series of new antipoverty programs. These programs included the Job

PRESIDENTIAL *Lives*

Lyndon B. Johnson

1908–1973
In Office 1963–1969

Many observers saw Lyndon B. Johnson as a stereotypical Texas politician—loud and slightly crude. Johnson loved to shock people with his language, stories, and behavior. He was also a very physical politician. He would shake people's hands until his own bled and slap others on their backs in a friendly gesture. When Johnson visited Thailand in 1961, aides warned him that the Thai people regarded touching someone on the head as offensive. Johnson, however, could not restrain himself. He insisted upon patting the heads of the small children he met.

During his years in the Senate, fellow senators joked that Johnson had two techniques for getting another senator's attention. There was the Half-Johnson—"when he just put a hand on your shoulder"—and the Full-Johnson—"when he put his arm clear around you and thrust his face close to yours." Johnson's techniques got results, however.

Johnson was known as a workaholic who drove himself and his staff to exhaustion to complete multiple tasks. "What's the hurry?" one senator asked another about Johnson's busy schedule. "Rome wasn't built in a day." The other senator replied, "No, but Lyndon Johnson wasn't foreman on that job."

These children are part of a Head Start program.

Claudia "Lady Bird" Johnson. President Johnson's wife, Claudia "Lady Bird" Johnson, was very different from Jacqueline Kennedy, just as her husband was very different from John F. Kennedy. The daughter of a general store owner, Claudia Alta Taylor grew up in a remote Texas town. She graduated with a degree in journalism from the University of Texas at Austin. In 1934 she met and married Lyndon B. Johnson, a former schoolteacher. She later used money from her family inheritance to fund his successful campaign for the U.S. House of Representatives. While her husband served in the U.S. Navy during World War II, Lady Bird Johnson managed his congressional office. In the early 1940s she purchased a debt-ridden radio station in Austin, Texas, and turned it into a broadcasting empire worth millions of dollars. After the war Lady Bird Johnson played an active role in her husband's campaigns. In 1960 she traveled some 35,000 miles and gave many speeches supporting his candidacy for vice president.

CRITICAL THINKING How might Lady Bird Johnson's life belie the myth of the "backseat" political wife?

ANSWER: Students might suggest that Lady Bird Johnson was an educated, successful businessperson.

LEVEL 2: Ask students to describe President Johnson's War on Poverty. *(See the Level 1 lesson for the correct programs.)* Ask students how these programs affected American communities. *(See the Level 1 lesson for the correct effects.)* Then tell each student to invent a fictional community and to create "before" and "after" illustrated and annotated maps displaying the effects of Johnson's policies. In the "before" map, for example, students might draw a dilapidated downtown area. In the "after" map, students might depict a VISTA-refurbished downtown area with a bustling Head Start center. Students may wish to include their maps in their portfolios.

LEVEL 3: Tell students to imagine that they are people who have benefited from President Johnson's War on Poverty. Have each student write a series of journal entries over the course of several years, recording the changes in his or her life due to these programs. *(See the Level 1 lesson for the correct programs and effects.)* Ask volunteers to read portions of their journal entries to the class. Students may wish to include their journal entries in their portfolios.

NOTE: To help students make meaningful connections between events in U.S. history and those in their own hometown, use the Chapter 21 **Hands-On History Activity**, The Great Society.

ECONOMICS

Antipoverty Spending.
Federal spending on the poor more than doubled between 1962 and 1968, from almost $12 billion to approximately $27 billion. Government statistics show that an estimated 12 million Americans rose above the official poverty line during this period, reducing the incidence of poverty from 20 percent of the population to 12 percent.

CRITICAL THINKING
Antipoverty programs cost large amounts of money. In theory, how might antipoverty spending actually result in increased government revenues?

ANSWER: Students might mention that antipoverty programs can help people become more prosperous. In general, increasing incomes result in increasing tax revenues.

The American Nation
VIDEO PROGRAM
VISTA Volunteers; Teacher's Guide, pp. 207–08

Search 37160, Play to 37755
Videodisc 2, Side B

Play   Pause

See *Teacher's Guide* for Spanish barcode.

VISTA Volunteers

teen Life

John Hough became a VISTA volunteer in 1968. He joined with the support of his parents, who "thought the country could be saved by the determined, idealistic young." Hough was from a small Massachusetts town and had never seen a poverty-stricken inner city. Nevertheless, he still "felt equipped to invade the world

VISTA volunteer Rissa Schiff of Brooklyn, New York, plays with Navajo children in Rough Rock, Arizona.

of urban poverty, stark and menacing as that world seemed."

After a six-week training period in Chicago, Hough tutored students in English and mathematics at a school in Detroit, Michigan. Although he was dedicated to his work, Hough soon discovered that the problems he and his students faced were overwhelming. In addition to the constant threat of violence and the presence of drugs, overworked VISTA offices provided little support. Hough left VISTA after one year. In the end, however, he decided that making the effort to help people was in itself of great value.

Johnson campaign item

Corps, a work training program for young people between the ages of 16 and 21; Head Start, a preschool education program for low-income families; and **Volunteers in Service to America** (VISTA), a domestic version of the Peace Corps. Congress passed the antipoverty legislation in late August 1964.

The War on Poverty brought improvements to many communities, including American Indian reservations. It allowed American Indians to establish and operate their own antipoverty programs on the reservations. LaDonna Harris, a Comanche involved in OEO programs in Oklahoma, defended the program.

History Makers Speak

❝I will stand up and defend OEO as long as I live. Indian leadership developed out of that program. . . . OEO taught us to use our imagination and to look at the future as an exciting adventure. It taught us that there are other ways of doing things.❞

—LaDonna Harris, quoted in *Indian Self-Rule*, edited by Kenneth R. Philp

✔ **READING CHECK: Contrasting** How did President Johnson's first year in office differ from President Kennedy's term? Kennedy had dealt primarily with international issues. Johnson focused on a domestic agenda and got much of his legislation passed.

Johnson's Vision for America

Unlike President Kennedy, President Johnson had little trouble pushing legislation through Congress. He fulfilled the major legislative goals of his first term within eight months. Texas journalist Liz Carpenter noted, "Kennedy inspired. . . . Johnson delivered." Johnson was not content with fulfilling Kennedy's agenda. He hoped to be elected president in 1964 and to advance his own vision for the nation's future. Johnson called his domestic reform program the **Great Society**. He shared his vision in a May 1964 speech at the University of Michigan.

History Makers Speak

❝The Great Society rests on abundance and liberty for all. It demands an end to poverty and racial injustice. . . . The Great Society is a place where every child can find knowledge to enrich his mind and to enlarge his talents. . . . It is a place where the city of man serves not only the needs of the body and the demands of commerce but the desire for beauty and the hunger for community.❞

—Lyndon B. Johnson, remarks at the University of Michigan, May 22, 1964

Johnson wanted the United States to be a place where people would be "more concerned with the quality of their goals than the quantity of their goods."

In order to achieve these goals, Johnson worked hard to ensure victory in the upcoming presidential election. Opinion polls revealed that Americans were impressed with Johnson's achievements. Johnson easily won the Democratic presidential nomination in 1964. He selected Hubert Humphrey, a liberal senator from Minnesota, as his running mate. The Republicans chose Senator **Barry Goldwater**, a conservative from Arizona,

LEVEL 1: Organize students into triads. Tell each triad to create a poster depicting problems in American life and advertising Great Society programs designed to alleviate those problems. (*Students should indicate that the Great Society hoped to improve health care, education, housing, American culture, and the environment. Johnson supported Medicare and Medicaid, the Elementary and Secondary Education Act and the Omnibus Housing Act, cultural programs, and environmental protection acts.*) Display the posters around the classroom.

English Language Learners, Cooperative Learning

LEVEL 2: Tell students to imagine that it is 1965. Have each student write a letter to the editor of a local newspaper describing problems in American life and discussing Great Society efforts to alleviate those problems. (*See the Level 1 lesson for correct problems and Great Society solutions.*) Ask volunteers to read their letters to the class. Students may wish to include their letters in their portfolios.

HOMEWORK *Have students create collages with a center image representing a problem in American life. The images surrounding the center should represent Great Society solutions to the problem.*

---

as their presidential nominee. New York representative William E. Miller was his running mate. The Republican platform rejected former president Eisenhower's Modern Republicanism.

In his acceptance speech at the Republican National Convention, Goldwater declared, "Extremism in the defense of liberty is no vice! . . . Moderation in the pursuit of justice is no virtue!" However, many voters regarded Goldwater's conservatism as too extreme. When Goldwater supporters displayed bumper stickers that read "IN YOUR HEART YOU KNOW HE'S RIGHT," Democrats responded with "IN YOUR GUT YOU KNOW HE'S NUTS." The Johnson campaign also produced a commercial that showed a small girl counting to 10 as she pulled petals from a daisy. When she reached "10," an image of an atomic bomb exploding filled the screen. The commercial implied that Goldwater could not be trusted with the nation's nuclear arsenal. The White House was flooded with complaints about the advertisement. It aired only once.

Despite criticism of such campaign tactics, Johnson won the election by a landslide, taking 61 percent of the popular vote and 486 electoral votes to Goldwater's 52. The last president to receive such a mandate was Franklin D. Roosevelt in 1936.

✔ **READING CHECK: Drawing Conclusions** How did President Johnson plan to change the role of the federal government to create his Great Society? by directing the government's resources toward improving the lives of poor Americans and minorities

These Lyndon Johnson and Barry Goldwater dolls were made for the 1964 campaign.

Johnson and Congress

At an inaugural ball on January 20, 1965, Lyndon Johnson told partygoers, "Don't stay up late. There's work to be done. We're on our way to the Great Society." Johnson moved quickly to make his vision a reality. Civil rights legislation, health care, education, and urban renewal were all part of the Great Society program. Many members of the Democrat-dominated 89th Congress supported his call for a Great Society.

The programs. In 1965 Johnson persuaded Congress to establish **Medicare**—a national health insurance program for people over age 65. Congress also authorized funds for states to set up **Medicaid**—a government program that provides free health care to the needy. Johnson traveled to Independence, Missouri, to sign the bill in front of 81-year-old Harry Truman. Truman had first proposed federally funded health insurance in his Fair Deal.

Johnson also urged Congress to take action on funding for education. He gave a moving speech.

President Johnson returned to his childhood school and had his first-grade teacher join him as he signed education legislation.

History Makers Speak

❝My first job after college was a teacher in Cotulla, Texas, in a small Mexican American school. . . . Somehow you never forget what poverty and hatred can do when you see its scars on the hopeful face of a young child. . . . It never even occurred to me in my fondest dreams that I might have the chance to help the sons and daughters of those students and to help people like them all over the country. But now I do have that chance—and I'll let you in on a secret: *I mean to use it.*❞

—Lyndon B. Johnson, address to Congress, March 15, 1965

Barry Goldwater. Native Arizonan Barry Goldwater went to work in his family's department store chain at the age of 20. During World War II he served in the Army Air Force. After the war, he served as chief of staff of the Arizona Air National Guard, eventually attaining the rank of major general. Goldwater's first experience with politics occurred in 1949, when he successfully ran for a seat on the Phoenix city council. Three years later, in a major political upset, he won the U.S. Senate seat occupied by Majority Leader Ernest MacFarland. In the following years Goldwater established himself as one of the Republican Party's most conservative members. He voted against the censure of Joseph McCarthy and published a widely read book, *The Conscience of a Conservative*, that called for a limited federal government and the elimination of communism. Goldwater became the Republican presidential candidate after winning several key victories in the 1964 primary elections.

ACTIVITY: Have each student select the candidate for whom they might have voted in the 1964 election and write several paragraphs defending his or her choice. Ask volunteers to share their responses. Finally, conduct a mock election.

LEVEL 3: Organize the class into five groups. Assign each group one of the following topics related to Johnson's Great Society: health care, education, housing, culture, or the environment. Have each group develop an outline for a multimedia presentation on its assigned topic. Groups' outlines should include a general summary, possible images, an analysis of Johnson's programs in the given area, and a discussion of the programs' short- and long-term effectiveness. *(See the Level 1 lesson for the correct programs and effects.)* To extend the lesson, have each group create its multimedia presentation.
Cooperative Learning

Teacher to Teacher

Paul Horne of Columbia, South Carolina, suggested the following activity: Have students choose a problem that President Johnson's Great Society legislation attempted to correct and conduct research on how this legislation affected their city, county, and state. Students should look for specific data such as government grants. Have students report their findings to the class.

HISTORY MAKERS SPEAK

Lyndon B. Johnson in
*Remembering America:
A Voice from the Sixties*

The Fragile Environment.
Like Rachel Carson, President Johnson feared environmental destruction. During a speech to Congress he warned, "The storm of modern change is threatening to blight and diminish in a few decades what has been cherished and protected for generations. . . . Modern technology also has a darker side. Its uncontrolled waste products are menacing the world we live in, our enjoyment and our health. The air we breathe, our water, our soil and wildlife, are being blighted by the poisons and chemicals which are the by-product of technology and industry. The society which receives the benefits of technology must . . . take responsibility for control."

CRITICAL THINKING What might have been some ways for Americans to "take responsibility for control"?

ANSWER: Students might mention industrial controls, pollution controls, or public education.

President Johnson supported educational television shows like Sesame Street.

Research on the R⊙M

Free Find: Rachel Carson
After reading about Rachel Carson on the **Holt Researcher CD–ROM**, write a brief description of a book you might write about environmental problems today. Then create a cover for your book that illustrates the issues you would address.

Congress responded by passing the **Elementary and Secondary Education Act** of 1965, which provided $1.3 billion in aid to schools in poor areas.

Johnson also persuaded Congress to pass the Omnibus Housing Act in 1965. This act authorized billions of dollars to be spent on urban renewal and housing assistance for low-income families. Congress also established the Department of Housing and Urban Development (HUD) to oversee federal housing programs. **Robert C. Weaver** headed this new department, making him the first African American member of a presidential cabinet. Weaver declared that the new programs had made Americans aware that "our cities are filled with poorly housed, badly educated, underemployed, desperate, unhappy Americans."

Quality of life. Johnson saw the Great Society as a place that fulfilled "the desire for beauty." He supported such programs as the National Endowment for the Arts (NEA) and the National Endowment for the Humanities (NEH), which offered grants and fellowships to artists, writers, and scholars. The Johnson administration also created the **Corporation for Public Broadcasting**, a nonprofit organization dedicated to offering educational television programming.

The president's interest in the quality of life extended to environmental issues. Johnson later recalled, "The cost of our careless technology had caught up with us." Many other Americans also felt a growing concern for the environment.

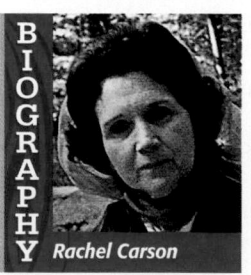

Rachel Carson

Marine biologist **Rachel Carson** contributed to this environmental movement. Born in Pennsylvania in 1907, Carson later recalled, "I can remember no time when I wasn't interested in the out-of-doors and the whole world of nature." After graduating with honors from Johns Hopkins University in 1929, she taught at the college level and then worked for the U.S. Bureau of Fisheries. She wrote several works on marine science before turning to writing full-time in 1952.

When a friend asked Carson to investigate the impact of the pesticide DDT on birds and other wildlife, she responded with enthusiasm. The resulting book, *Silent Spring*, was published in 1962. Warning Americans that "a grim specter [spirit] has crept upon us almost unnoticed," Carson condemned the uncontrolled use of chemical pesticides, which she called "elixirs [medication] of death." She wrote, "Although today's poisons are more dangerous than any known before, they have amazingly become something to be showered down indiscriminately [carelessly] from the skies [by airplanes]." In her book, Carson chronicled the health and safety risks that pesticide use posed for humans and wildlife.

"We should no longer accept the counsel of those who tell us that we must fill our world with poisonous chemicals," Carson argued in the final chapter of *Silent Spring*. "We should look about and see what other course is open to us." In an attempt to protect their industry, pesticide manufacturers attacked Carson and her conclusions. However, her claims prompted President John F. Kennedy to

ALL LEVELS: Ask students to identify individual liberties that they exercise every day. *(Students may mention freedom of speech, freedom of association, or freedom of religion.)* Ask students to identify the guarantee of those liberties. *(Students should note that the First Amendment protects those rights. If students do not identify the First Amendment, remind them and have them reread the amendment.)* Tell students that court decisions throughout U.S. history have expanded individual liberties. To help them understand how the Warren court expanded individual liberties, copy the following graphic organizer onto the chalkboard, omitting the italicized answers. Have each student complete it. **English Language Learners**

WARREN COURT DECISIONS

Case	Year	Decision
Baker v. Carr	1962	*led to ruling that electoral districts had to have the same number of voters*
Gideon v. Wainwright	1963	*declared that states had to provide lawyers for impoverished defendants charged with serious crimes*
Escobedo v. Illinois	1964	*declared that the accused had the right to have a lawyer present during police investigations*
Miranda v. Arizona	1966	*declared that accused persons had to be informed of their rights at the time of arrest*

create a panel to study the issue. A final report issued by the panel agreed with Carson's conclusions.

Rachel Carson died in 1964. She did not live to witness the environmental legislation passed during the Johnson years. During his presidency, Johnson signed the Water Quality Act of 1965, the Air Quality Act of 1967, the Water Pollution Act of 1968, and several other environmental bills. In addition, Johnson's administration created several new national parks and wilderness areas, making his record on environmental issues one of the most impressive of any U.S. president.

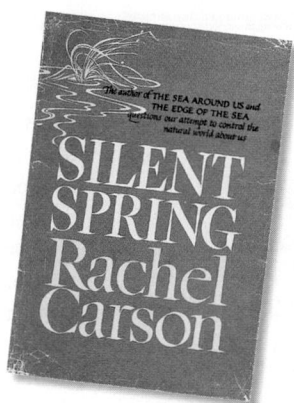

Rachel Carson's Silent Spring brought environmental issues to the attention of many Americans.

✔ **READING CHECK: Identifying Cause and Effect** What impact did *Silent Spring* have on American life? It brought attention to environmental issues, which contributed to the passage of environmental bills.

Skill-Building Strategies

Using the Library

When conducting historical research, one should try to consult as broad an array of sources as possible. Most of the time, these sources are best found in a library. Thus, knowing how to use the library is a crucial skill for students to develop.

Although almost all libraries use the same basic guidelines for organizing their materials, each one has a unique layout, staff, and set of specific holdings. Taking a tour and becoming familiar with one's school or local public library can help make one's subsequent research more efficient and productive.

How to Use the Library

1. **Identify the topic.** First, identify the general topic that you wish to research. Then make a short list of events, issues, or people related to the topic that you can look to for further information if necessary.
2. **Check the reference section.** In the library's reference section, you will find almanacs, atlases, encyclopedias, specialized dictionaries, and indexes to newspaper and magazine articles. Consult each of these sources, when appropriate, to find information about your topic.
3. **Consult the library catalog.** Look in the library's card catalog or electronic catalog to locate books about your topic. Most library catalogs list books by author, title, and subject and assign each book a call number based on the Library of Congress classification system or the Dewey decimal system. An index of subject headings can usually be found in or near the library catalog.

4. **Look for Internet and multimedia sources.** If possible, use the library's computer system to look for information about your topic on the Internet. Then check for CD–ROMS, databases, videotapes, or other multimedia sources that may aid your research.
5. **Consult a librarian.** Librarians can help you use reference sources and the library catalog and can help direct you to a book's location. They can also suggest additional resources that may aid your research.

Applying the Skill

Use your school or local public library to conduct research on one of the following topics:
a. the political career of Lyndon B. Johnson
b. a specific government program that was part of President Johnson's War on Poverty, such as the Job Corps, Head Start, or VISTA
c. the 1964 presidential campaign
d. the Housing and Urban Development Act of 1968

Practicing the Skill

Answer the following questions.
1. What reference sources did you use to find information about your topic?
2. What books about your topic were listed in the library catalog?
3. What other sources, if any, did you find during your research?

LEVEL 1: Pair students and ask each pair to list reasons why support for the Great Society programs declined during the late 1960s. *(Students should note that the Vietnam War diverted funds and attention, that the fast legislative pace worried legislators, that Republicans gained congressional seats in the 1966 midterm elections, that state and local politicians disliked some programs because they had no control, and that some Americans viewed some programs as worthless.)* Have pairs rank the reasons for the decline in support from most damaging to least damaging. Ask volunteers to share and explain their rankings.

English Language Learners, Cooperative Learning

LEVELS 2 AND 3: Have students complete the Level 1 lesson on an individual basis. Then tell students to imagine that it is 1966 and that they are political cartoonists. Have each student create two political cartoons explaining the declining support for the Great Society programs during the late 1960s. *(See the Level 1 lesson for the correct reasons.)* Ask students to write captions for their cartoons. Have volunteers present their captions and cartoons to the class. Students may wish to include their captions and cartoons in their portfolios.

NOTE: For an additional teaching idea, see the Chapter 21 interpreting cartoons lesson in the **Creative Teaching Strategies** handbook.

REVIEW SECTION 3 ANSWERS

1. Identify
- War on Poverty, p. 639
- Office of Economic Opportunity, p. 639
- Volunteers in Service to America, p. 640
- Great Society, p. 640
- Barry Goldwater, p. 641
- Medicare, p. 641
- Medicaid, p. 641
- Elementary and Secondary Education Act, p. 642
- Robert C. Weaver, p. 642
- Corporation for Public Broadcasting, p. 642
- Rachel Carson, p. 642
- Earl Warren, p. 644
- *Reynolds* v. *Sims*, p. 644

2. education—Head Start, Elementary and Secondary Education Act; housing—Omnibus Housing Act, establishment of the Department of Housing and Urban Development; health care—Medicare, Medicaid; environment—Water Quality Act of 1965 and other laws, creation of new national parks and wilderness areas

3a. by honoring President Kennedy's legacy and working to fulfill Kennedy's domestic agenda; elected Johnson in 1964

b. defined and extended individual liberties; many approved, others thought Court had overstepped its authority

c. Students might suggest that many state and local politicians felt that Great Society programs gave the federal government too much control.

INTERPRETING THE VISUAL RECORD

Warren Court. Some Americans disagreed with many Supreme Court decisions in the 1960s. *How do billboards like this one show Americans' dissatisfaction with Chief Justice Earl Warren?*

The Warren Court Decisions

Like the Johnson administration, the Supreme Court of the 1960s reflected a spirit of activism. Under the leadership of Chief Justice **Earl Warren**, the Court further defined and extended individual rights. In many congressional districts, sparsely populated rural areas were granted the same number of representatives as densely populated urban areas. In the 1962 case *Baker* v. *Carr,* voters in Tennessee argued that this apportionment, or division, of representatives violated the equal protection clause of the Fourteenth Amendment. The Court agreed. In ***Reynolds* v. *Sims*** (1964) and *Wesberry* v. *Sanders* (1964), the Court further extended equality in the voting booth by affirming the "one person, one vote" principle. It declared that electoral districts must contain approximately the same number of voters to ensure fair representation for all Americans. Within two years almost all states had redrawn their legislative districts.

The Warren Court also issued a series of decisions protecting the rights of persons accused of crimes. *Gideon* v. *Wainwright* (1963) declared that the states must provide lawyers, at public expense, for poor defendants charged with serious crimes. *Escobedo* v. *Illinois* (1964) granted the accused the right to have a lawyer present during police investigations. *Miranda* v. *Arizona* (1966) said that accused persons must be informed of their rights at the time of their arrest.

Many people saw these decisions as an attempt to ensure that the criminal justice system did not violate individual rights. Others charged that the Court had overstepped its authority by making law rather than interpreting it. One critic claimed, "Earl Warren . . . has defiled [corrupted] our jurisprudence [court system] and made war against the public order."

✔ **READING CHECK: Evaluating** How did the Warren Court expand individual liberties and participation in the democratic process? **by extending voting rights and protecting the rights of the accused**

The Decline of the Great Society

Like other postwar presidents, Lyndon B. Johnson was committed to fighting the Cold War. Although he was far more interested in domestic policy, foreign affairs demanded his attention.

Foreign policy. Johnson quickly became involved in the affairs of the Dominican Republic. In April 1965, factions within the country's military rebelled against the military-led government. The U.S. ambassador believed that the rebels were under communist influence and insisted that Johnson intervene.

Johnson promptly sent some 22,000 marines to the Dominican Republic. With U.S. support, troops loyal to the military government gained the upper hand, and the situation stabilized. Johnson withdrew the marines in 1966 when relatively free and fair elections put a pro-American government in power.

Many Latin Americans condemned the intervention. Even those who supported Johnson's action did so reluctantly. However, a majority of Americans backed Johnson and praised his aggressive stand against the threat of communist expansion.

By the spring of 1965, Johnson's focus had shifted to fighting in the southeast Asian country of Vietnam and away from the Great Society. In 1966 the government spent about 18 times more on the Vietnam War than it did on the War on

REVIEW

Have students complete the **Section 3 Review** on p. 645.

ASSESS

Have students complete **Daily Quiz 21.3**. As **Alternative Assessment,** you may want to use the War on Poverty map or the Great Society political cartoon in this section's lessons.

RETEACH

Have students complete **Main Idea Activity for English Language Learners and Special-Needs Students 21.3**. Then ask each student to list the titles of the subsections in Section 3 on a sheet of paper. Have students write summary sentences for each of the subsections. Ask volunteers to read their sentences to the class. Have students choose the best summary sentence for each subsection. **English Language Learners**

EXTEND

Tell students that Head Start was a cornerstone program of the War on Poverty. Have students conduct research on Head Start programs in the 1960s and today. Ask each student to write a paper discussing and evaluating the program. **Block Scheduling**

Poverty. Civil rights leader Martin Luther King Jr. complained that the Great Society had been "shot down on the battlefields of Vietnam."

Domestic opposition. Growing domestic opposition to the Great Society also contributed to its decline. Johnson's legislative success record was extraordinary—the 89th Congress passed 181 of the 200 major bills that the president requested in 1965 and 1966. However, many members of Congress urged the president to slow down.

The results of the 1966 midterm elections signaled an additional change in the relations between Congress and the White House. Although Democrats retained their majorities in Congress, Republicans gained 47 House seats and three Senate seats, significantly reducing Johnson's opportunities to press for more legislation.

Problems with specific Great Society programs also raised doubts about Johnson's plan. Many state and local politicians disliked the War on Poverty because they had no control over the selection and funding of community projects. Members of Congress complained that many programs did not merit funding. Representative Frank Bow of Ohio declared, "We cannot have guns and butter," meaning that the Vietnam War should take priority over social programs. Bow ridiculed funding the NEH as wanting "guns with strawberry shortcake covered with whipped cream and cherry on top."

Although support for his programs weakened, Johnson's influence on American life endured long after his presidency ended. Medicare, Medicaid, the NEH, Head Start, and other Great Society programs continued to bring benefits to Americans in the decades that followed.

✔ **READING CHECK: Summarizing** How did foreign-policy issues affect Great Society programs? **Great Society programs were neglected during Johnson's second term because of his focus on the war in Vietnam.**

"GIVE IT TO HIM!"

INTERPRETING POLITICAL CARTOONS

The Great Society. Many critics of President Johnson's programs argued that they cost too much. *What does this cartoon show about the artist's point of view?*

4. Answers will vary. Student pamphlets might mention that some Americans disliked specific antipoverty programs, while others wanted more funding for the Vietnam War.

POLITICAL CARTOON ANSWER
The artist takes the point of view of the taxpayer.

REVIEW 21 ANSWERS

Creating a Time Line
Each event should have an explanation and the correct date.

Writing a Summary
See the Reading Checks in each section for main ideas.

Identifying People and Ideas
1. Kennedy administration strategy of having a wide range of foreign-policy options

2. program that expanded U.S. economic aid to Latin America

3. leader of an uprising that established a communist dictatorship in Cuba

4. John F. Kennedy's presidential agenda

5. 35th president of the United States, 1961–63

6. investigated the assassination of President Kennedy

7. President Johnson's antipoverty legislation and programs

8. Johnson's social vision

SECTION 3 REVIEW

1. Identify and explain:
- War on Poverty
- Office of Economic Opportunity
- Volunteers in Service to America
- Great Society
- Barry Goldwater
- Medicare
- Medicaid
- Elementary and Secondary Education Act
- Robert C. Weaver
- Corporation for Public Broadcasting
- Rachel Carson
- Earl Warren
- *Reynolds* v. *Sims*

2. Categorizing Copy the chart below. Use it to explain the effects of the Great Society in education, housing, health care, and the environment.

GREAT SOCIETY	
Education	Housing
Health Care	Environment

3. **Finding the Main Idea**
a. How did President Johnson win the support of the American people during his first year in office? How did Americans show their support?
b. What were the effects of the decisions of the Warren Court, and how did Americans' reactions to them vary?
c. How did Johnson's Great Society programs affect the relationship between state and local governments and the federal government?

4. **Writing and Critical Thinking**
Analyzing Information Write a pamphlet detailing Johnson's efforts to help poor Americans and why they generated opposition.
Consider:
- the specific design of the poverty programs
- the reaction of local and state politicians
- concern over government spending during the Vietnam War

Homework Practice Online
keyword: SE3 HP21

TECHNOLOGY

▶ Chapter 21 Test Generator (on the One-Stop Planner)
▶ Global Skill Builder CD–ROM
▶ HRW Go site

REINFORCEMENT, REVIEW, AND ASSESSMENT

▶ Chapter 21 Review, pp. 646–47
▶ Chapter 21 Tutorial for Students, Parents, Mentors, and Peers

▶ Chapter 21 Test (Form A or B)
▶ Portfolio Activities and Alternative Assessment Handbook, Chapter 21
▶ Chapter 21 Test for English Language Learners and Special-Needs Students

REVIEW

Have students complete the **Chapter 21 Review** on pp. 646–47.

ASSESS

Use one of the chapter tests to assess students' understanding of the content. For **Alternative Assessment**, see the **Portfolio Activities and Alternative Assessment Handbook**.

9. 36th president of the United States, 1963–69

10. marine biologist who wrote *Silent Spring*

Understanding Main Ideas

1. helped John F. Kennedy win a close election over Richard Nixon

2. Cuba's promixity to the United States made the prospect of Soviet missiles on the island very threatening.

3. attempted to reduce unemployment, curb inflation, and stimulate economic growth

4. opposition from congressional coalition of southern Democrats and conservative Republicans

5. worked to fulfill Kennedy's domestic agenda

6. Medicare, Medicaid, education efforts, urban renewal and housing programs, support for the arts, environmental legislation

Reviewing Themes

1. continued to build nuclear weapons and oppose communism; expanded conventional weapons options and used economic aid

2. personal concerns, Michael Harrington's book *The Other America*, and the belief that the government had an obligation to help the poor

3. President Kennedy probably knew that his public image augmented his political popularity and authority.

Thinking Critically

1. fear of debt

Review

Creating a Time Line

Copy the time line below onto a sheet of paper. Complete the time line by filling in the events and dates from the chapter that you think were most significant. Pick three events and explain why you think they were significant.

1961　　1964　　1969

Writing a Summary

Using standard grammar, spelling, sentence structure, and punctuation, write an overview of events in the chapter.

Identifying People and Ideas

Identify the following terms or individuals and explain their significance.

1. flexible response
2. Alliance for Progress
3. Fidel Castro
4. New Frontier
5. John F. Kennedy
6. Warren Commission
7. War on Poverty
8. Great Society
9. Lyndon B. Johnson
10. Rachel Carson

Understanding Main Ideas

SECTION 1 *(pp. 624–630)*

1. What role did television play in the 1960 presidential election?
2. How did the establishment of a communist government in Cuba lead to increased Cold War tensions?

SECTION 2 *(pp. 631–637)*

3. How did Kennedy attempt to manage the economy?
4. Why did Kennedy fail to gain passage of most of his legislative initiatives?

SECTION 3 *(pp. 638–645)*

5. How did President Johnson establish continuity between his administration and that of John F. Kennedy?

6. What were some of the successes of the Great Society programs?

Reviewing Themes

1. **Global Relations** How did President Kennedy's Cold War foreign policy resemble that of his predecessors? How did it differ?
2. **Economics** Why did Presidents Kennedy and Johnson both develop programs to help poor Americans?
3. **Government** Why did Kennedy work so hard to control his public image?

Thinking Critically

1. **Identifying Points of View** Why did many members of Congress oppose President Kennedy's tax cut proposal?
2. **Categorizing** How did President Kennedy try to stop the spread of communism?
3. **Analyzing Information** What were Lyndon B. Johnson's achievements as president?
4. **Evaluating** How did the Warren Court's decisions in *Baker* v. *Carr*, *Reynolds* v. *Sims*, and *Wesberry* v. *Sanders* strengthen equal participation in government?
5. **Drawing Conclusions** In what ways was the Great Society an extension of the New Deal and the Fair Deal?

Writing about History

Comparing Copy the chart below and use it to write an essay that describes the different goals and achievements of Presidents Kennedy and Johnson.

KENNEDY		JOHNSON	
Goals	Achievements	Goals	Achievements

Organize students into three groups. Assign each group one of the sections in Chapter 21. Have each group work together to develop a lesson plan that covers its assigned section. Then have groups present a brief lesson to the class. Be prepared to round out information gaps or correct misinformation. Encourage students to use visual aids in their lessons. Tell students to take notes on each presentation.
English Language Learners, Cooperative Learning

EXTEND

Have each student list the presidents of the United States from Franklin D. Roosevelt to Lyndon B. Johnson. Have students pick one adjective to describe each president. Caution students to think carefully about their selections. Then ask volunteers to share their adjectives with the class. Conclude by conducting a discussion on the public's perceptions of the presidents of the mid-1900s. **Block Scheduling**

Building Social Studies Skills

Interpreting Maps
Study the map below. Then use it to help answer the questions that follow.

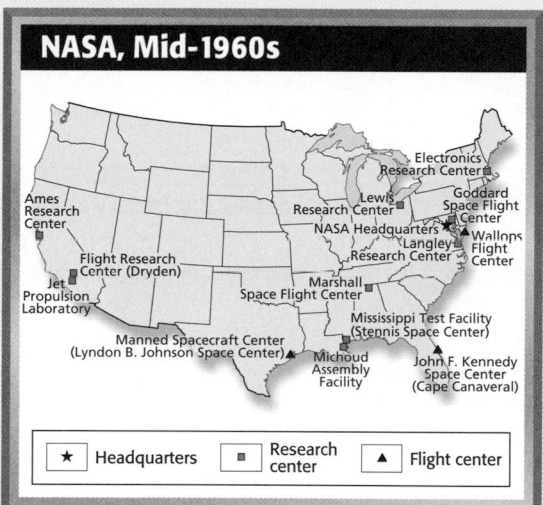

NASA, Mid-1960s

Electronics Research Center
Ames Research Center
Lewis Research Center
Goddard Space Flight Center
NASA Headquarters
Wallops Flight Center
Langley Research Center
Flight Research Center (Dryden)
Jet Propulsion Laboratory
Marshall Space Flight Center
Mississippi Test Facility (Stennis Space Center)
Manned Spacecraft Center (Lyndon B. Johnson Space Center)
Michoud Assembly Facility
John F. Kennedy Space Center (Cape Canaveral)

★ Headquarters   ■ Research center   ▲ Flight center

1. Which statement is true of the NASA sites?
   a. All sites are located in coastal regions.
   b. All flight centers are located in coastal regions.
   c. All research centers are located in coastal regions.
   d. All sites are located in areas known for their mild climate.

2. What geographic factors might have contributed to this selection of sites for the flight centers?

Interpreting Political Cartoons
Study the political cartoon below, and then use it to help answer the questions that follow.

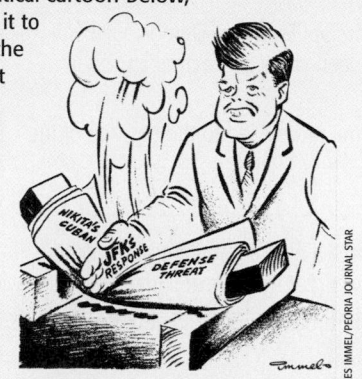

LES IMMEL/PEORIA JOURNAL STAR

3. Which is the most accurate explanation of the cartoon?
   a. President Kennedy attacked Fidel Castro's missiles in Cuba.
   b. President Kennedy attacked Nikita Khrushchev.
   c. President Kennedy frightened Khrushchev, resulting in his building defenses in Cuba.
   d. President Kennedy responded vigorously to missiles in Cuba, ending the Soviet threat.

4. Draw your own cartoon illustrating one or more of the following concepts:
   • "We're eyeball to eyeball, and I think the other fellow just blinked."
   • Khrushchev agreed to dismantle the missile sites; Kennedy secretly agreed to remove U.S. missiles from some foreign sites.
   • A hot line between U.S. and Soviet leaders is established.

Alternative Assessment

Building Your Portfolio

U.S. HISTORY

Global Relations
Imagine that you are a television news reporter. Prepare a news bulletin summarizing President Kennedy's announcement of the naval blockade of Cuba in 1962. Deliver your bulletin to the class. You might want to create a map of Cuba and the surrounding area for the presentation of your report.

🖅 internet connect

go hrw .com

Internet Activity: go.hrw.com
KEYWORD: SE3 AN21

Choose a topic on the New Frontier to:
• create a historical poster on John Glenn and the early space race.
• research the life and accomplishments of President John F. Kennedy.
• explore the history and legacy of the Great Society.

---

2. militarily with flexible response and economically with the Peace Corps and the Alliance for Progress

3. aided people in poverty; Medicare and Medicaid; advanced civil rights, individual rights, and education; and increased environmental protections

4. by declaring that electoral districts must contain approximately the same number of voters, affirming the "one person, one vote" principal

5. Federal programs addressed issues formerly administered by state and local governments. Medicaid was originally part of Truman's Fair Deal.

Writing
Kennedy: goals—containment of communism, reduction of unemployment and inflation, economic growth, antipoverty programs; achievements—defense of West Berlin, removal of Soviet missiles from Cuba, Area Redevelopment Act. Johnson: goals—expansion of Kennedy's domestic agenda, creation of a Great Society; achievements—War on Poverty and Great Society legislation

Building Social Studies Skills
1. b

2. Answers will vary. Students might note the mild climate for takeoffs and landings.

3. d

4. Cartoons will vary but should address one of the suggested topics.

The Civil Rights Movement

CHAPTER RESOURCE MANAGER

Objectives	Pacing Guide	Reproducible Resources
SECTION 1 **Freedom Now!** pp. 650–55 ★ Explain how civil rights demonstrators used nonviolence to achieve their goals, and note what the effect was. ★ Discuss why civil rights leaders used nonviolent tactics, and explain how protests in Albany, Georgia, and Birmingham, Alabama, differed. ★ Analyze why supporters pushed for a civil rights bill, and discuss what factors influenced the bill's passage.	**Regular** 2 days **Block Scheduling** 1 day *Block Scheduling Handbook with Team Teaching Strategies, pp. 126–32*	**RS** Guided Reading Strategy 22.1 **PS** Primary Source Reading 22: James Baldwin: Wordsmith and Social Critic **IC** Literature Reading 22: Harper Lee's Masterpiece **PS** Biography Reading 22: Ralph Abernathy
SECTION 2 **Voting Rights** pp. 656–60 ★ Explain why early efforts to register voters in Mississippi failed. ★ Relate why the Freedom Summer project met with limited success. ★ Discuss how the Mississippi Freedom Democratic Party affected relations between civil rights activists and the federal government. ★ Describe how the Selma protest led to the passage of the Voting Rights Act.	**Regular** 2 days **Block Scheduling** 1 day *Block Scheduling Handbook with Team Teaching Strategies, pp. 126–32*	**RS** Guided Reading Strategy 22.2 **SM** Geography Activity 22: The Civil Rights Movement **RS** Graphic Organizer Activity 22: In the Words of the Leaders **SM** American History Outline Map 21: Desegregation
SECTION 3 **Challenges for the Movement** pp. 661–66 ★ Describe how Malcolm X's message differed from that of other leaders of the civil rights movement in the early 1960s. ★ Explain why nonviolent protest and the goal of racial integration lost support. ★ Discuss how northern racial discrimination and urban riots changed the civil rights movement.	**Regular** 2 days **Block Scheduling** 1 day *Block Scheduling Handbook with Team Teaching Strategies, pp. 126–32*	**RS** Guided Reading Strategy 22.3 **E** Hands-On History Activity: Voters and Voting Rights in Your Community
SECTION 4 **The Movement Continues** pp. 667–71 ★ Describe the problems many leading African American organizations encountered in the early 1970s. ★ Explain the effects of Supreme Court decisions on busing and affirmative action programs. ★ Identify the gains African Americans made during the early 1970s.	**Regular** 1 day **Block Scheduling** .5 day *Block Scheduling Handbook with Team Teaching Strategies, pp. 126–32*	**RS** Guided Reading Strategy 22.4 **E** Creative Teaching Strategy: Ranking Lesson

Chapter Resource Key

PS Primary Sources	**REV** Review	Video
RS Reading Support	**ELL** Reinforcement and English Language Learners	Internet
IC Interdisciplinary Connections		Holt Presentation Maker Using Microsoft® PowerPoint®
E Enrichment	Transparencies	
SM Skills Mastery	CD-ROM	
A Assessment	Music	

One-Stop Planner CD-ROM

See the *One-Stop Planner* for a complete list of additional resources for students and teachers.

One-Stop Planner CD–ROM

It's easy to plan lessons, select resources, and print out materials for your students when you use the **One-Stop Planner CD–ROM with Test Generator.**

Technology Resources	**Reinforcement, Review, and Assessment**

 One-Stop Planner, Lesson 22.1
 American Music Selection 23: "He's Got the Whole World in His Hands"
Holt Researcher: American History CD–ROM
 Homework Practice Online
HRW Go site

REV	Section 1 Review, p. 655
A	Daily Quiz 22.1
ELL	Main Idea Activity 22.1
ELL	English Audio Summary 22.1
ELL	Spanish Audio Summary 22.1

 One-Stop Planner, Lesson 22.2
 Holt Researcher: American History CD–ROM
 Homework Practice Online

REV	Section 2 Review, p. 660
A	Daily Quiz 22.2
ELL	Main Idea Activity 22.2
ELL	English Audio Summary 22.2
ELL	Spanish Audio Summary 22.2

 One-Stop Planner, Lesson 22.3
 The American Nation Video Program Segment: Malcolm X; Teacher's Guide, pp. 135–40
CNN Presents America: Yesterday and Today, 1850 to the Present Segment: "I Have a Dream"
Holt Researcher: American History CD–ROM
Homework Practice Online

REV	Section 3 Review, p. 666
A	Daily Quiz 22.3
ELL	Main Idea Activity 22.3
ELL	English Audio Summary 22.3
ELL	Spanish Audio Summary 22.3

 One-Stop Planner, Lesson 22.4
 Holt Researcher: American History CD–ROM
 Homework Practice Online

REV	Section 4 Review, p. 671
A	Daily Quiz 22.4
ELL	Main Idea Activity 22.4
ELL	English Audio Summary 22.4
ELL	Spanish Audio Summary 22.4

internet connect

HRW ONLINE RESOURCES
GO TO: go.hrw.com
Then type in a keyword.

TEACHER HOME PAGE
KEYWORD: SE3 Teacher

CHAPTER INTERNET ACTIVITIES
KEYWORD: SE3 AN22
Choose an activity to:
• create a poster comparing Malcolm X and Martin Luther King Jr.
• learn about the movement to end apartheid in South Africa.
• create a newspaper reporting on the main events of the movement in 1963

CHAPTER ENRICHMENT LINKS
KEYWORD: SE3 CH22

ONLINE ASSESSMENT
Homework Practice
KEYWORD: SE3 HP22
Standardized Test Prep
KEYWORD: SE3 STP22
Rubrics
KEYWORD: SS Rubrics

ONLINE MAPS, CHARTS, AND GRAPHS
KEYWORD: SE3 MCG
• Black Voter Registration
• School Segregation, 1964
• Urban Unrest

CONTENT UPDATES
KEYWORD: SS Content Updates

HOLT PRESENTATION MAKER
KEYWORD: SE3 PPT22

ONLINE READING SUPPORT
KEYWORD: SS Strategies

CURRENT EVENTS
KEYWORD: S3 Current Events

Chapter Review and Assessment

 Global Skill Builder CD–ROM
 HRW Go site
REV Chapter 22 Tutorial for Students, Parents, Mentors, and Peers
REV Chapter 22 Review, pp. 672–73
Chapter 22 Test Generator (on the One-Stop Planner)
A Chapter 22 Test (Form A or B)
A Alternative Assessment Handbook
A Chapter 22 Test for English Language Learners and Special-Needs Students

Meeting Individual Needs

Ability Levels

Level 1 Basic-level activities designed for all students encountering new material

Level 2 Intermediate-level activities designed for average students

Level 3 Challenging activities designed for honors and gifted-and-talented students

English Language Learners Activities that address the needs of students with Limited English Proficiency

Build on What You Know

Ask students to answer the following questions.

How might some Americans have worked to expand civil rights?

Consider:

• the success of the Montgomery bus boycott

• the leadership of Martin Luther King Jr.

How might some people have resisted moves for African American civil rights?

Consider:

• the violence surrounding desegregation efforts in Little Rock

• the actions of state officials who opposed desegregation

---

exploring the time line

AMERICAN EVENTS

PEOPLE IN HISTORY

1974 ■ Hank Aaron. In 1972 it became clear that Atlanta Braves outfielder Hank Aaron had a chance to break Babe Ruth's home-run record. Aaron soon began receiving racist hate mail threatening to "punish" him for attempting to break a white man's record. In 1973 Aaron discussed the hate mail with a journalist and, as a result, began to receive tens of thousands of encouraging letters. By the end of the year, Aaron had received more mail than any non-politician in the United States.

ACTIVITY: Have students conduct research on Hank Aaron and his career after he retired from playing baseball. Then have them write a brief biography of Aaron.

CHAPTER 22

1960–1978

The Civil Rights Movement

March on Washington for civil rights

Martin Luther King Jr. receiving the Nobel Peace Prize

1963
Politics
The March on Washington takes place.

1964
World Events
Martin Luther King Jr. is awarded the Nobel Peace Prize.

| 1960 | 1962 | 1964 | 1966 | 1968 |

1960
World Events
Dahomey (later Benin) becomes an independent nation.

1962
Daily Life
James Meredith integrates the University of Mississippi.

Headdress made by Dahomeyan artist

1964
The Arts
Jazz pianist Thelonious Monk is featured on the cover of *Time* magazine.

Thelonious Monk

1966
Politics
The Black Panther Party is founded in Oakland, California.

1968
Science and Technology
Julian Earls heads NASA's Health Physics Section.

1968
Daily Life
Less than 21 percent of African American students in the former Confederate states attend integrated schools.

1968
Politics
The Kerner Commission releases its report on the urban riots that erupted in several major U.S. cities in 1967.

Build on What You Know

The civil rights movement gained momentum from the Supreme Court's 1954 ruling on school desegregation. The success of the Montgomery Bus Boycott showed the effectiveness of peaceful protest in ending racial discrimination. It also transformed Martin Luther King Jr. into a prominent figure in the struggle for civil rights. In this chapter you will learn how some Americans worked to expand civil rights and equality for all Americans. However, many Americans continued to oppose racial equality.

What's Your Opinion?

To help students create their Themes Journal entries, provide the following examples of appropriate **agree/disagree** *statements.*

Citizenship

Agree Certain methods of social protest, such as boycotts, have been used in many different regions of the country.

Disagree Support for slavery in the antebellum South rendered certain forms of social protest, such as abolitionist organizations, largely irrelevant.

Constitutional Heritage

Agree The Supreme Court regulates interstate commerce and therefore has the authority to end segregation.

Disagree The Supreme Court ruled in *Plessy* v. *Ferguson* that separate-but-equal facilities were legal.

Economics

Agree Booker T. Washington urged African Americans to concentrate on gaining economic stability and strength within the larger economic system.

Disagree Certain reformers urged minority groups to withdraw from the larger economic system and organize their own economies.

Cheryl A. Brown

American college students held antiapartheid demonstrations in the United States

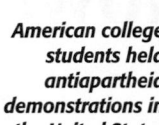

1970
Daily Life
Cheryl A. Brown of Iowa becomes the first African American contestant in the Miss America Beauty Pageant.

1972
Politics
Barbara Jordan of Texas is elected to the U.S. House of Representatives.

1974
World Events
Drought in Africa leads to widespread famine.

1976
World Events
Antiapartheid riots erupt in several major cities in South Africa.

| 1970 | 1972 | 1974 | 1976 | 1978 |

1970
The Arts
Charles Gordone wins a Pulitzer Prize for his play *No Place to Be Somebody.*

1974
Daily Life
Baseball player Hank Aaron breaks Babe Ruth's career home-run record.

1975
Business and Finance
Wally Amos founds Famous Amos Chocolate Chip Cookies, which achieves sales of more than $5 million by 1980.

1978
Politics
The Supreme Court outlaws racial quotas in education in the case *University of California* v. *Bakke.*

Hank Aaron

Famous Amos cookies

What's Your Opinion?

Themes Journal *Do you* **agree** *or* **disagree** *with the following statements? Support your point of view in your journal.*

Citizenship Methods of social protest that prove effective in one part of the country can be used successfully in all regions of the nation.

Constitutional Heritage
The Supreme Court is responsible for ending segregation.

Economics Integration within the larger economic system is the best way for minority groups to improve their standard of living.

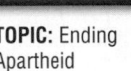

OBJECTIVE 1 Explain how civil rights demonstrators used nonviolence to achieve their goals, and note what the effect was.

OBJECTIVE 2 Discuss why civil rights leaders used nonviolent tactics, and explain how protests in Albany, Georgia, and Birmingham, Alabama, differed.

OBJECTIVE 3 Analyze why supporters pushed for a civil rights bill, and discuss what factors influenced the bill's passage.

LET'S GET STARTED!

Write the term *nonviolence* on the chalkboard. As students enter the classroom, ask them to write what they know about the term on a sheet of paper. Ask volunteers for their responses, then write the responses on the chalkboard. Tell students that in Section 1 they will learn how activists used nonviolent protest to achieve social change.

SECTION **1** RESOURCES

REPRODUCIBLE

▸ Guided Reading Strategy 22.1
▸ Primary Source Reading 22: James Baldwin: Wordsmith and Social Critic
▸ Literature Reading 22: Harper Lee's Masterpiece
▸ Biography Reading 22: Ralph Abernathy

TECHNOLOGY

▸ One-Stop Planner, Lesson 22.1
▸ American Music Selection 23: "He's Got the Whole World in His Hands"
▸ Holt Researcher: American History CD–ROM
▸ Homework Practice Online
▸ HRW Go site

REINFORCEMENT, REVIEW, AND ASSESSMENT

▸ Section 1 Review, p. 655
▸ Daily Quiz 22.1
▸ Main Idea Activity 22.1
▸ English Audio Summary 22.1
▸ Spanish Audio Summary 22.1

SECTION **1**

READ TO DISCOVER

1. How was nonviolence used in the civil rights movement, and how effective was it?
2. How did protests in Albany, Georgia, and Birmingham, Alabama, differ?
3. Why did supporters push for a civil rights bill, and what led to its passage?

DEFINE

nonviolent resistance
sit-ins

IDENTIFY

Southern Christian Leadership Conference
Martin Luther King Jr.
Student Nonviolent Coordinating Committee
Congress of Racial Equality
Freedom Riders
T. Eugene Connor
Diane Nash
James Meredith
Medgar Evers
Laurie Pritchett
Civil Rights Act of 1964

▶ WHY IT MATTERS TODAY

Young people continue to be actively involved in reform movements today. Use **CNNfyi.com** or other **current events** sources to find out about a reform effort taking place in the United States today. Record your findings in your journal.

Freedom Now!

EYEWITNESSES TO History

"What do we do and to whom do we do it against?"

—Joseph McNeil, quoted in *Voices of Freedom*, by Henry Hampton and Steve Fayer

Joseph McNeil, an African American student at North Carolina Agricultural and Technical College in Greensboro, pondered such questions as he and three friends discussed ways to protest racial segregation. They were impressed by the courage of the African American students who had integrated the schools in Little Rock, Arkansas, in 1957. They "wanted to make a contribution and be a part of something like that," recalled McNeil. On February 1, 1960, the four students went to a nearby dime store and "sat at a lunch counter where blacks never sat before. And people started to look at us." McNeil recalled that "the help, many of whom were black, looked at us in disbelief too. They were concerned about our safety." The management refused to serve them, but the students returned the following day, vowing to continue their protest until they received service. In this way, McNeil and thousands of other young people across the South worked to bring an end to racial segregation.

The lunch counter where McNeil and his friends protested

Nonviolence in Action

Following the success of the Montgomery Bus Boycott, civil rights leaders met in 1957 in Atlanta to discuss future strategy. They expanded the Montgomery Improvement Association (MIA) into the **Southern Christian Leadership Conference** (SCLC), an alliance of church-based African American organizations dedicated to ending discrimination. **Martin Luther King Jr.** led the new organization. The SCLC pledged to use **nonviolent resistance** in its protests. Nonviolent resistance required that protesters not resort to violence, even when others attacked them. King called it confronting "the forces of hate with the power of love."

Student protests. Many non-SCLC members soon launched nonviolent protests of their own. In 1958, African American protesters in Oklahoma and Kansas conducted protests at segregated lunch counters. At **sit-ins**, demonstrators protest by sitting down in a location and refusing to leave. By April 1960 some 50,000 students, both African American and white, were involved in sit-in protests. That month, the leaders of these demonstrations founded the **Student Nonviolent Coordinating Committee** (SNCC), a loose association of student activists from throughout the South.

White response to the sit-ins tested the students' commitment to nonviolence. White onlookers taunted the demonstrators and dumped food and drinks on them. When the harassment turned into physical attacks, demonstrators received

---

TEACH OBJECTIVE 1

LEVEL 1: Pair students and have each pair create T-shirts to commemorate famous nonviolent protests conducted by civil rights demonstrators. Tell students that the front of each T-shirt should mention the nonviolent action taken. For the back, students should create a slogan to describe the effect of the action. *(Students should note that examples of successful nonviolent resistance include sit-ins, which led to the desegregation of lunch counters and restaurants; the march through Birmingham, which led to increased public support for the civil rights movement; the Freedom Rides, which led the Interstate Commerce Commission to strengthen its desegregation regulations; and the Montgomery Bus Boycott, which led to*

the desegregation of buses in Montgomery, Alabama.) Have students present their T-shirt designs to the class.
English Language Learners, Cooperative Learning

LEVELS 2 AND 3: Tell students to imagine that they are television newscasters during the civil rights struggles of the 1960s. Pair students and have each pair prepare an on-location newscast from a civil rights demonstration mentioned in Section 1. Newscasts should describe the nonviolent actions taken by protesters. Newscasts should conclude with a summary of the reasons for the protest and an assessment of the protest's effect. *(See the Level 1 lesson for examples of nonviolent protests and the effects of these protests.)* Have each pair "broadcast" its newscast to the class. **Cooperative Learning**

---

little assistance from local authorities. After an angry mob beat nonviolent protesters in Nashville, Tennessee, the police ended the confrontation by arresting the protesters. Despite such incidents, the protesters remained committed to nonviolence. The tactic proved effective. Soon many restaurants and other eating establishments across the South had been integrated.

The Freedom Rides. The success of the student sit-ins inspired the **Congress of Racial Equality** (CORE). This northern-based civil rights group hoped to launch new nonviolent protests against racial discrimination. In December 1960 the Supreme Court ruled that segregation in facilities such as bus stations that served interstate travelers was illegal. CORE leaders planned to send an integrated group of **Freedom Riders** on bus trips through the South. They hoped to draw attention to violations of the Supreme Court ruling.

Violence erupted when they crossed the Alabama state line. Outside the town of Anniston, Alabama, a white mob firebombed one of the two buses carrying the activists. They also beat the riders as they tried to escape. The mob then followed the riders to the local hospital to prevent them from receiving medical care.

The Freedom Riders on the other bus were attacked in Birmingham, Alabama. Freedom Rider Walter Bergman, a white man, was beaten so badly that he suffered permanent brain damage. The local police sent no officers to the bus terminal. Birmingham's city commissioner of public safety, **T. Eugene "Bull" Connor,** blamed the Freedom Riders for the violence. He declared, "I have said for the last 20 years that these out-of-town meddlers were going to cause bloodshed if they kept meddling in the South's business." SNCC leaders moved quickly to find replacement riders for those from CORE.

President John F. Kennedy supported the constitutional rights of the riders to continue. However, he did not want the violence to become an issue in an upcoming meeting with Soviet leader Nikita Khrushchev. Kennedy told his aides to contact civil rights leaders and urge them to end the rides. SNCC refused to comply with the president's request. SNCC leader **Diane Nash** explained why.

History Makers Speak

❝I strongly felt that the future of the movement was going to be cut short if the Freedom Ride had been stopped as a result of violence. The impression would have been given that whenever a movement starts, all you have to do is attack it with massive violence and the blacks will stop.**❞**

—Diane Nash, quoted in *Eyes on the Prize,* by Juan Williams

SNCC sent the Freedom Riders to Birmingham. There, they were quickly arrested and transported to the state line. The students made their way back to Birmingham. Anxious to prevent further conflict, U.S. Attorney General Robert Kennedy reached an agreement with Alabama's governor, John Patterson. They agreed that the riders would receive protection. The Freedom Riders soon departed from Birmingham. However,

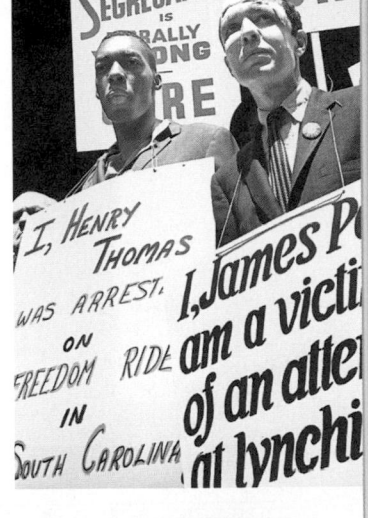

INTERPRETING THE VISUAL RECORD

Violence. Demonstrators like these at a CORE rally often suffered harassment and violence. **What actions are these two men protesting?**

Freedom Riders regroup outside their bus after it was firebombed in Alabama.

CITIZENSHIP

Freedom Rides. The Freedom Riders who were arrested in Jackson, Mississippi, were sent to a maximum-security prison. There they tried to keep their spirits up by singing freedom songs. The guards threatened to take their mattresses away if the prisoners kept singing. Freedom Rider Jim Bevel said, "What they're trying to do is take your soul away. It's not the mattress, it's your soul." Another called the guards and said, "Come get my mattress. I'll keep my soul."

CRITICAL THINKING What might Bevel have meant when he said that by taking the mattresses the guards were trying to take the riders' souls?

ANSWER: Students might suggest that Bevel meant that the guards were trying to break the riders' spirits and make them feel demoralized and defeated.

VISUAL RECORD ANSWER

Students might note that the men are protesting a lynching.

LEVEL 1: Pair students and have each pair create two cause-and-effect diagrams to illustrate why civil rights leaders used nonviolent tactics. *(Pairs should mention that nonviolent tactics have the potential to draw attention to a protest by eliciting a violent response from those in power. Nonviolent protest can cause a crisis that forces an otherwise unresponsive opponent to negotiate.)* Have volunteers present and explain their diagrams to the class. Then copy the graphic organizer at right on the chalkboard, omitting the italicized answers. Have students fill in information to compare and contrast the protests in Albany and Birmingham.

English Language Learners, Cooperative Learning

Protest in Albany, Georgia / **Protest in Birmingham, Alabama**

The police did not resort to violence. The Albany protest was not a success.

Protesters were arrested.

The police attacked protesters. Protesters gained support. The Birmingham protest was a success.

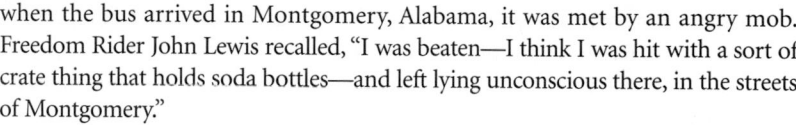

James Meredith. James Meredith had served nine years in the air force and nearly completed a degree at the historically black Jackson State College in Jackson, Mississippi, when he decided to apply to the University of Mississippi. Knowing that his application would be rejected, Meredith enlisted the help of civil rights activist Medgar Evers and attorney Thurgood Marshall. Meredith wrote to Marshall, "I am familiar with the probable difficulties involved in such a move as I am undertaking and I am fully prepared to pursue it all the way to a degree from the University of Mississippi." Meredith's subsequent enrollment in the university, with the protection of armed guards, symbolized the commitment of civil rights activists to end segregation.

CRITICAL THINKING What might have convinced Meredith that his application would be rejected?

ANSWER: Students might suggest that Meredith would have known about the tendency of many government officials to disregard federal orders to desegregate.

VISUAL RECORD ANSWER

Students might suggest that James Meredith encountered shock and anger from the white community.

INTERPRETING THE VISUAL RECORD

Integrating universities. The NAACP obtained a court order requiring the University of Mississippi to admit black student James Meredith. *What type of reaction do you think Meredith encountered?*

when the bus arrived in Montgomery, Alabama, it was met by an angry mob. Freedom Rider John Lewis recalled, "I was beaten—I think I was hit with a sort of crate thing that holds soda bottles—and left lying unconscious there, in the streets of Montgomery."

President Kennedy finally sent federal marshals to protect the riders. In Jackson, Mississippi, however, state officials arrested the protesters. Hundreds of other activists carried on the protest. In response, Robert Kennedy pressured the Interstate Commerce Commission into strengthening its desegregation regulations. By early 1963 he was able to claim that "in the past year, segregation in interstate commerce has ceased to exist."

✔ **READING CHECK: Summarizing** Why did civil rights demonstrators participate in sit-ins and the Freedom Rides? **They wanted to help achieve integration at public facilities in a nonviolent manner.**

Continued Struggles

The Freedom Riders' courage and commitment to nonviolence helped advance their effort to end racial discrimination. However, segregation remained in many areas of southern life, including the South's schools and public facilities.

University of Mississippi. Civil rights activists who worked to open colleges and universities to African American students met with strong opposition. In 1962 the National Association for the Advancement of Colored People (NAACP) obtained a court order. It required the University of Mississippi to admit **James Meredith**, an African American applicant. Mississippi governor Ross Barnett was defiant. He declared, "No school will be integrated in Mississippi while I am your Governor." Accompanied by two federal officials, Meredith arrived at the campus in September 1962. Barnett personally prevented Meredith from registering.

When word got out on the evening of September 30 that Meredith was on the campus, a riot broke out. President Kennedy ordered army troops to restore order. The outbreak quickly died out, but two people had been killed and 375 injured. Meredith registered the next day and attended classes the rest of the year with the protection of armed guards. He graduated from the university in 1963.

Civil rights activists viewed Meredith's enrollment as a great success. Myrlie Evers recalled, "It was a major breakthrough. It said, indeed, that there is hope, and that we are moving forward and that perhaps the sacrifices that had been made had been worth it." Yet events elsewhere revealed that the movement for civil rights still faced strong opposition. In 1963 Myrlie Evers's husband, NAACP field secretary **Medgar Evers**, was killed by a white assassin.

Albany and Birmingham. Nonviolent protests were not always successful. In Albany, Georgia, for example, civil rights organizations held a number of nonviolent protests in 1961. Police Chief **Laurie Pritchett** was prepared for the demonstrations. He arranged to fill all the jails in the surrounding areas with protesters. Pritchett called his method of law enforcement meeting "nonviolence with nonviolence." He quietly arrested all the protesters.

Tell students to imagine that they are participants in a roundtable conference entitled The Effectiveness of Nonviolent Protest: Case Studies in Albany, Georgia; and Birmingham, Alabama. Organize the class into two groups. Have one group act as questioners and the other group act as civil rights leaders. Have members of both groups prepare by discussing why civil rights leaders used nonviolent tactics and by contrasting the protests in Albany and Birmingham. (See the Level 1 lesson for the tactical goals of nonviolent protest and the outcomes of the Albany and Birmingham protests.) Then conduct the conference. **Cooperative Learning**

TEACH OBJECTIVE 3

LEVEL 1: Tell students to imagine that they are newspaper reporters assigned to cover the passage of the Civil Rights Act of 1964. Pair students and have each pair write headlines explaining why supporters pushed for a civil rights bill and what circumstances were factors in the bill's passage. (Pairs should mention that supporters believed that federal civil rights legislation—enforced by the federal government—was necessary to give all Americans equal access to educational facilities, public services, and employment. Events in Birmingham, the success of the March on Washington, and the support of Presidents Kennedy and Johnson were factors in the bill's passage.) **English Language Learners, Cooperative Learning**

Hoping to revive the Albany protests, Martin Luther King Jr. allowed himself to be arrested and jailed. However, Pritchett simply released him. Without a violent incident to draw the attention of the news media, the Albany movement stalled.

This experience taught SCLC leaders that progress would come only when racists responded to peaceful demonstrations with violence. As the SCLC's Bayard Rustin later noted, "Protest becomes an effective tactic to the degree that it elicits [brings forth] brutality and oppression from the power structure."

After the events in Albany, the SCLC focused its attention on Birmingham. Protesting in Birmingham meant danger and possibly even death. Ralph Abernathy later explained the civil rights activists' strategy.

> "As for [police chief] Bull Connor and the City of Birmingham, it was true that they constituted the hardest and most mean-spirited establishment in the South. Yet if we beat them on their own home grounds, we might be able to prove to the entire region that it was useless to resist desegregation, that Its time had finally come. To win in Birmingham might well be to win in the rest of the nation. So in the long run the gamble [of confronting violence in Birmingham] might actually save time and lives in our struggle for equality."
>
> —Ralph Abernathy,
> *And the Walls Came Tumbling Down*

In April 1963 the SCLC began a series of boycotts, marches, and sit-ins to protest the city's segregation laws. The protests initially drew hundreds of participants. Many were jailed after violating a judge's order banning further demonstrations. As weeks passed, the number of demonstrators willing to go to jail declined. By the end of April the Birmingham protests seemed likely to end in failure.

To save the protest, James Bevel and other SCLC leaders suggested using schoolchildren in the demonstrations. Bevel later recalled, "A boy from high school, he can get the same effect in terms of being in jail, in terms of putting pressure on the city, as his father—and yet there is no economic threat on the family because the father is still on the job." King

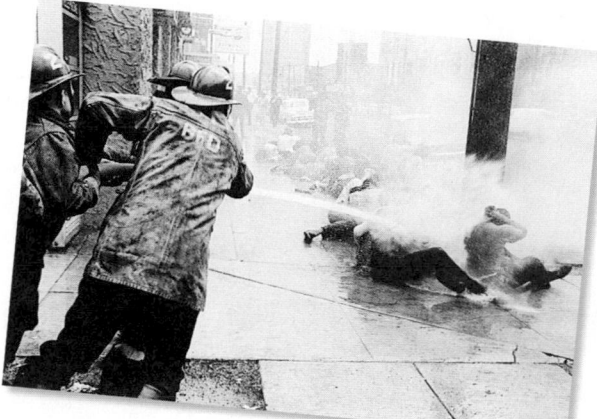

To break up the nonviolent civil rights rally in Birmingham, city firefighters turned their water hoses on protesters.

★ HISTORICAL DOCUMENTS ★

MARTIN LUTHER KING JR.
Letter from Birmingham Jail

While confined in a Birmingham jail in 1963, Martin Luther King Jr. wrote to local religious leaders who had urged him to slow down his protests. Widely published in newspapers, the letter offered a response to critics who questioned the need for protests. **According to King, what did the local religious leaders really mean when they asked him to wait?**

You may well ask: "Why direct action? Why sit-ins, marches, and so forth? Isn't negotiation a better path?" You are quite right in calling for negotiation. Indeed, this is the very purpose of direct action. Nonviolent direct action seeks to create such a crisis and foster such a tension that a community which has constantly refused to negotiate is forced to confront the issue. . . . I have earnestly opposed violent tension, but there is a type of constructive, nonviolent tension which is necessary for growth. . . .

We know through painful experience that freedom is never voluntarily given by the oppressor; it must be demanded by the oppressed. Frankly, I have yet to engage in a direct-action campaign that was "well timed" in the view of those who have not suffered unduly from the disease of segregation. For years now I have heard the word "Wait!" It rings in the ear of every Negro with piercing familiarity. This "Wait" has almost always meant "Never." We must come to see, with one of our distinguished jurists, that "justice too long delayed is justice denied."

The Governors. Governor George Wallace of Alabama and Governor Ross Barnett of Mississippi became well known for defending segregation. In speeches and writings, Wallace and Barnett challenged northern politicians by referring to segregation in northern cities. Barnett argued, "The big difference is that we are honest about segregation in Mississippi and we intend to remain honest, law abiding and segregated." In his 1963 inaugural address in Alabama, Wallace characterized the federal government's actions as "tyranny." Wallace said, "In the name of thc greatest people that ever trod the earth, I draw the line in the dust and toss the gauntlet before the feet of tyranny . . . and I say . . . segregation now . . . segregation tomorrow . . . segregation forever."

CRITICAL THINKING Why might Wallace have used the word *tyranny* in his speech?

ANSWER: Students might mention that Wallace's words would have evoked powerful memories of the Civil War and Revolutionary War ideals of freedom from tyranny.

HISTORICAL DOCUMENTS ANSWER
Students might suggest that they meant "never."

INTERPRETING THE VISUAL RECORD

March on Washington. During the 1963 March on Washington, African American leaders met with President John F. Kennedy. *Based on this photograph, would you conclude that the march leaders were successful in bringing civil rights issues to the forefront of U.S. politics in 1963? Explain your answer.*

was initially reluctant to place young people in danger. In the end, he supported Bevel's plan.

On May 2 more than 1,000 youths marched in Birmingham's streets. Police arrested some 600 students that day. When protests continued the next day, Bull Connor ordered police to attack the marchers. The police used dogs, fire hoses, and nightsticks against protesters. Public support for the civil rights movement increased when scenes of these attacks appeared in newspapers and on television.

✔ **READING CHECK: Comparing** Compare the protests in Albany, Georgia, and Birmingham, Alabama. Albany— quiet, without violence protest stalled; Birmingham— children protested, police attacked; great public support

The Civil Rights Act of 1964

Events in Birmingham forced President Kennedy to take a stand on civil rights. In the summer of 1963, Kennedy asked Congress "to enact legislation giving all Americans the right to be served in facilities which are open to the public."

The March on Washington. To build support for the civil rights movement, African American leaders organized a march on Washington, D.C. More than 200,000 people gathered at the Lincoln Memorial on August 28, 1963. Many musicians and speakers from diverse backgrounds participated. The march director, 74-year-old A. Philip Randolph, testified to the long struggle for civil rights. Other speakers included SNCC's John Lewis and Rabbi Joachim Prinz of the American Jewish Congress.

BIOGRAPHY
Martin Luther King Jr.

Martin Luther King Jr. gave the final speech—a highlight of his civil rights career. Born on January 15, 1929, in Atlanta, King was the son of a Baptist minister. He received a degree from Morehouse College in 1948. King then attended the integrated Crozer Theological Seminary in Pennsylvania. He became familiar with the Social Gospel movement, which encouraged Christians to become involved in social reform. He was also exposed to the thinking of Mohandas K. Gandhi, the nonviolent leader of India's independence movement.

King then pursued a doctorate at Boston University. There, he met and married Coretta Scott. In 1954 King accepted a position at Dexter Avenue Baptist Church in Montgomery. He soon became involved in the civil rights movement and helped to organize the Montgomery bus boycott.

King often faced violence and abuse. In January 1956 his home was bombed, and his wife and young child narrowly escaped injury. His personal courage and commitment to nonviolence soon made him the leading civil rights activist in the eyes of most white Americans.

King's "I Have a Dream" speech at the March on Washington rally in 1963 has become one of the most famous addresses in U.S. history. King spoke of his vision of what the United States could and should be.

REVIEW

Have students complete the **Section 1 Review** on p. 655.

ASSESS

Have students complete **Daily Quiz 22.1**. As **Alternative Assessment**, you may want to use the T-shirts or the dialogue in this section's lessons.

RETEACH

Have students complete **Main Idea Activity for English Language Learners and Special-Needs Students 22.1**. Have students work in groups, with each student in the group outlining a subsection. Have members of the group exchange outlines and use the outlines to quiz each other.
English Language Learners, Cooperative Learning

EXTEND

Organize the class into four groups and have each group conduct research on one of the following people: Medgar Evers, Martin Luther King Jr., John Lewis, or James Meredith. After completing the research, members of each group should present an oral report about their subject's activities and contributions to the civil rights movement.
Block Scheduling, Cooperative Learning

History Makers Speak

❝I have a dream that one day this nation will rise up and live out the true meaning of its creed: 'We hold these truths to be self-evident; that all men are created equal.' . . . When we let freedom ring, when we let it ring from every village and every hamlet [small town], from every state and every city, we will be able to speed up that day when all of God's children, black men and white men, Jews and Gentiles, Protestants and Catholics, will be able to join hands and sing in the words of the old Negro spiritual, 'Free at last! Free at last! Thank God Almighty, we are free at last!'❞

—Martin Luther King Jr., speech on August 28, 1963, at the Lincoln Memorial in Washington, D.C.

The act passes. The success of the March on Washington raised the hopes of civil rights workers. However, their joy was short-lived. In September a bomb exploded in a Birmingham church and killed four young African American girls. Then, in November 1963, President Kennedy was assassinated. The future of civil rights legislation, which had stalled in Congress, was unclear.

The new president, Lyndon B. Johnson, strongly supported passage of a civil rights bill. Several southern members of Congress worked hard to kill the legislation. The House of Representatives approved the bill in February 1964. The Senate debated the measure for 75 days before passing it. Johnson signed the bill into law on July 2. The **Civil Rights Act of 1964** banned discrimination in employment on the basis of race, color, religion, sex, or national origin. The act also outlawed discrimination in public accommodations and gave the Justice Department the authority to bring lawsuits to enforce school desegregation. To allow for equal voting rights, the act also removed some registration restrictions.

President Johnson signed the Civil Rights Act into law in 1964 in the presence of civil rights leaders, including Martin Luther King Jr.

✔ **READING CHECK: Drawing Conclusions** How does Martin Luther King Jr.'s speech at the March on Washington reflect our national identity? It reflects a desire for all Americans to be equal and free.

SECTION 1 REVIEW

1. Define and explain:
nonviolent resistance
sit-ins

2. Identify and explain:
Southern Christian Leadership Conference
Martin Luther King Jr.
Student Nonviolent Coordinating Committee
Congress of Racial Equality
Freedom Riders
T. Eugene Connor
Diane Nash
James Meredith
Medgar Evers
Laurie Pritchett
Civil Rights Act of 1964

3. Comparing Copy the chart below. Use it to explain different civil rights initiatives in the early 1960s.

Protest	Goal	Outcome
Student Sit-Ins		
Freedom Rides		
Birmingham Protest		
March on Washington		

4. **Finding the Main Idea**

a. Why did Martin Luther King Jr. and other leaders support nonviolence as a strategy for civil rights demonstrations?

b. How did the federal government's response to the civil rights movement change from 1957 to 1964?

c. In what ways were Bull Connor and Laurie Pritchett similar? How did they differ in their responses to demonstrators?

5. **Writing and Critical Thinking**

Supporting a Point of View Write a letter to President Kennedy urging him to introduce civil rights legislation in 1963.
Consider:
• the constitutional issues involved
• King's strategy in Birmingham
• the media's role in Birmingham

Homework Practice Online
keyword: SE3 HP22

• Student Nonviolent Coordinating Committee, p. 650
• Congress of Racial Equality, p. 651
• Freedom Riders, p. 651
• T. Eugene Connor, p. 651
• Diane Nash, p. 651
• James Meredith, p. 652
• Medgar Evers, p. 652
• Laurie Pritchett, p. 652
• Civil Rights Act of 1964, p. 655

3. sit-ins—to integrate lunch counters, some were integrated; Freedom Rides—to integrate traveling facilities in the South, the ICC strengthened desegregation regulations; Birmingham—to protest segregation, increased support for the movement; March—to demonstrate the movement's support, raised spirits of activists

4a. The protests contrasted love and compassion with the anger of the social structure they were protesting.

b. In 1957 the federal government left it to local authorities to protect protesters. During the Freedom Rides and James Meredith incident the federal government offered support and protection. In 1964 Congress passed the Civil Rights Act.

c. They shared a determination to defeat the protesters; Connor reacted in anger, while Pritchett was calculated.

5. Letters will vary but might mention the constitutional guarantee of freedom, as well as the media coverage of Birmingham.

SECTION ②

OBJECTIVE 1 *Explain why early efforts to register voters in Mississippi failed.*

OBJECTIVE 2 *Relate why the Freedom Summer project met with limited success.*

OBJECTIVE 3 *Discuss how the Mississippi Freedom Democratic Party affected relations between civil rights activists and the federal government.*

OBJECTIVE 4 *Describe how the Selma protest led to the passage of the Voting Rights Act.*

🔊 *LET'S GET STARTED!*

Copy a voter registration card and place it on an overhead transparency. Project the voter registration card for students and ask them to identify the various parts. (*Students might mention the federal congressional district, state district, township, and so on.*) Discuss each political district with students and explain that being registered to vote is a fundamental right for citizens of a democracy. Tell students that in Section 2 they will learn about efforts to register African American voters in the South.

SECTION ② RESOURCES

REPRODUCIBLE

▶ Guided Reading Strategy 22.2

▶ Geography Activity 22: The Civil Rights Movement

▶ Graphic Organizer Activity 22: In the Words of the Leaders

▶ American History Outline Map 21: Desegregation

TECHNOLOGY

▶ One-Stop Planner, Lesson 22.2

▶ Holt Researcher: American History CD–ROM

▶ Homework Practice Online

REINFORCEMENT, REVIEW, AND ASSESSMENT

▶ Section 2 Review, p. 660

▶ Daily Quiz 22.2

▶ Main Idea Activity 22.2

▶ English Audio Summary 22.2

▶ Spanish Audio Summary 22.2

SECTION ②

READ TO DISCOVER

1. Why did early efforts to register voters in Mississippi fail?
2. Why did the Freedom Summer project meet with limited success?
3. How did the Mississippi Freedom Democratic Party affect relations between the civil rights activists and the federal government?
4. How did the Selma protest lead to the passage of the Voting Rights Act?

IDENTIFY

Robert Moses
Council of Federated Organizations
Twenty-fourth Amendment
Freedom Summer
Andrew Goodman
James Chaney
Michael Schwerner
Mississippi Freedom Democratic Party
Fannie Lou Hamer
Voting Rights Act

WHY IT MATTERS TODAY

Many Americans today conduct voter-registration drives designed to help increase voter turnout on election day. Use **CNNfyi.com** or other **current events** sources to find out about recent drives to increase the number of registered voters. Record your findings in your journal.

CNNfyi.com

Voting Rights

Volunteers help black Mississippians register to vote.

EYEWITNESSES TO History **"*I just didn't see how the Negroes in Madison County could be so badly off.*"**

—Anne Moody, *Coming of Age in Mississippi*

Anne Moody was a young African American woman who lived in Mississippi during the 1950s. She recalled her reaction to the economic and political status of African American farmers in Madison County, Mississippi. African Americans outnumbered the county's white residents three to one. However, only about 200 of the some 29,000 African Americans in the county were registered to vote. Moody hoped to change that by working in a voter registration drive sponsored by CORE. She quickly learned why life in Madison County was so hard for African Americans. She remembered that after a month, "we had only been able to send a handful of Negroes to the courthouse to attempt to register and those few who went began to get fired from their jobs." Moody also explained that the CORE workers "were constantly being threatened." Moody's experiences revealed the difficulties that civil rights workers faced as they organized voter registration drives in the South.

Registering Voters

While civil rights demonstrators used nonviolent protests to bring an end to racial segregation, other activists focused their attention on voter registration. The Kennedy administration had been troubled by the Freedom Rides and other protests that resulted in violence. However, it supported the voter registration efforts. As Robert Kennedy later recalled, "I felt nobody could really oppose voting. It was not like school desegregation with people saying, 'We don't want our little blond daughter going to school with a Negro.'" However, Kennedy underestimated the extent of opposition to African American suffrage in the South.

Mississippi. Civil rights activists focused their efforts on promoting voter registration in Mississippi, where African Americans were often denied their voting rights. African Americans made up some 40 percent of the state's population, but just 5 percent of eligible black adults were registered to vote. Many counties did not have a single registered African American voter. Literacy tests, which included interpreting portions of the state constitution, were one means used to prevent African Americans from registering.

Mississippi had a history of racial violence—at least 33 lynchings occurred between 1939 and 1950. Still, civil rights organizers believed that it was the best place to carry out their plans. As SNCC organizer John Lewis later argued, "If we can crack Mississippi, we will likely be able to crack the system in the rest of the country."

SNCC's **Robert Moses** selected McComb, Mississippi, a town of some 12,000 citizens. With just 250 registered African Americans, it would be the site of his first effort

TEACH OBJECTIVES 1 AND 2

ALL LEVELS: To help students understand the failure of early efforts to register voters in Mississippi and the limited success of the Freedom Summer project, copy the graphic organizer at right on the chalkboard, omitting the italicized answers. Pair students and have each pair complete the chart. When students have completed their charts, tell them to imagine that it is the fall of 1964 and that they are SNCC volunteers who have been involved in voter registration drives in Mississippi for the past four years. Ask each student to write a letter to a friend or family member explaining the failure of early efforts to register voters in Mississippi and the limited success of the Freedom Summer project. Ask volunteers to read their letters to the class.

English Language Learners, Cooperative Learning

💻 **REASONS FOR THE FAILURE OF VOTER REGISTRATION EFFORTS IN MISSISSIPPI AND THE LIMITED SUCCESS OF FREEDOM SUMMER**

Voter Registration in Mississippi	Freedom Summer
1. *murder of Herbert Lee/violence against African Americans* 2. *violence against SNCC volunteers* 3. *arrest of student demonstrators in McComb, Mississippi* 4. *arson at SNCC office*	1. *murders of James Chaney, Andrew Goodman, and Michael Schwerner* 2. *fear of violence against African Americans*

to register black voters. He arrived in July 1961. By mid-August he had helped six African Americans to register to vote. However, this modest success drew the attention of white officials who were determined to stop him. In less than a month's time, Moses was jailed, released, beaten by the sheriff's cousin, and chased by an angry mob.

The violence increased in September. Herbert Lee, a farmer who had driven Moses around the area, was murdered by a member of the Mississippi state legislature. Despite evidence to the contrary, a jury ruled that the killing had been committed in self-defense. Less than two weeks after Lee's death, local high school students held a protest march. Demonstrator Hollis Watkins later recalled the risks associated with civil rights activities.

History Makers Speak

❝One thing I risked—and did face—was being ostracized [banished] by my family.... My relatives would see me walking down the street and then they would pass over on to the other side rather than meet me on the street. Because they was afraid of what white people might do to them because they were my relatives.... In addition to that, I put on the line the whole thing of being able to ever get a job in Mississippi.... Or whether that mark would go through onto my children and their children—or onto my mother and father.❞

—Hollis Watkins, quoted in *Voices of Freedom*, by Henry Hampton and Steve Fayer

Moses and other SNCC workers accompanied the protesters. Police officers arrested the students. Meanwhile, a mob attacked the SNCC workers, who were then also arrested. The voter registration drive in McComb came to an end with fewer than 24 new voters on the rolls.

Renewed efforts. The difficulties in McComb did not stop efforts to register African American voters. Several civil rights organizations, including SNCC and SCLC, established the **Council of Federated Organizations** (COFO) to coordinate voter registration drives. The Voter Education Project provided money from private foundations to fund registration projects.

The abuse from state and local officials and mob violence continued as activists helped African Americans in Mississippi and other southern states to register to vote. SNCC's Ivanhoe Donaldson recalled, "Fear was always a major reality that you had to live with.... Almost every organizer in the Deep South was constantly faced with harassment. They'd been beaten, they'd been shot at." The SNCC office in Greenwood, Mississippi, was burned to the ground. Despite the bloodshed, few officials from the Kennedy administration offered assistance.

The ongoing violence frightened many African Americans. Many refused to attempt to register. A year-long registration drive in Leflore County resulted in just 50 new voters. Nonetheless, many African Americans in Mississippi still hoped to become voters one day. In 1963 COFO conducted two mock elections in which anyone could vote, even if they were not registered. Some 27,000 African Americans voted in the first mock election, and some 80,000—four times the number of registered black voters in the state—voted in the second election. The "freedom

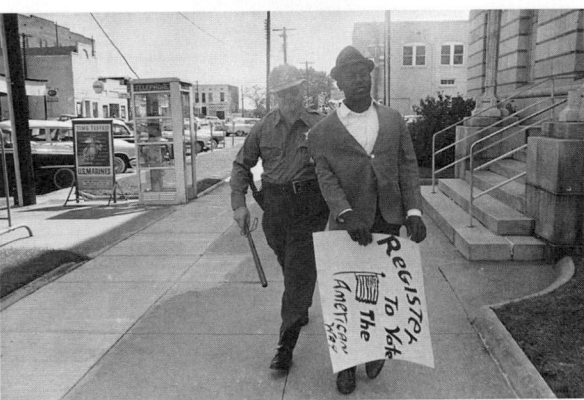

INTERPRETING THE VISUAL RECORD

Voting. Many activists who tried to register African Americans to vote faced harassment. *How does the message on this activist's sign contrast with the way he is being treated?*

Voter registration was an important weapon in the fight for civil rights.

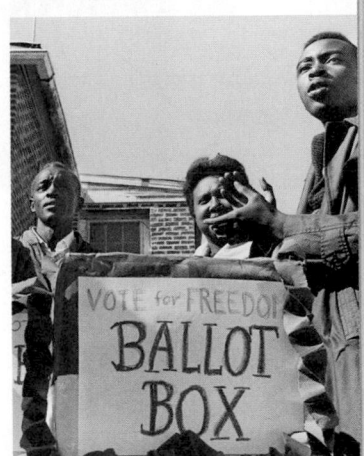

VOTE for FREEDOM
BALLOT BOX

Robert Moses. Robert Moses was working at a New York private school when he first heard of the sit-ins in the South. He instantly felt a connection with the demonstrators. Moses went to Mississippi, where he became the SNCC field secretary and began a drive to register African American voters. Moses was a good leader for the Mississippi movement, maintaining calm in the face of frightening circumstances. One of the white students working with Moses during Freedom Summer remembered, "Bob Moses stood out for everybody. He was an incredibly strong figure. He was calm. He was effective. What he said made sense, and you wanted to do what he said should be done."

CRITICAL THINKING Why might the Mississippi movement have needed a calm leader?

ANSWER: Students might suggest that because of the constant harassment and danger, the movement needed a leader who would not react in anger or desperation and who could inspire the other workers.

VISUAL RECORD ANSWER

Students might suggest that the activist has gotten in trouble for attempting to exercise his right to free speech and the vote.

HOMEWORK *Referring to the recruitment of white volunteers to help register black voters, Robert Moses said, "It changes the whole complexion of what you're doing, so it isn't any longer a question of Negro fighting white. It's a question of rational people fighting against irrational people." Ask students to write a short essay explaining what Moses might have meant. Ask volunteers to read their essays to the class.*

TEACH OBJECTIVE 3

LEVEL 1: Pair students and have each pair write a paragraph based on the following questions: Who helped create the Mississippi Freedom Democratic Party? *(Pairs should note that the Council of Federated Organizations helped to create the MFDP.)* Why was the MFDP

created? *(Pairs should indicate that the party was created after Mississippi's 1964 Democratic convention rejected all African American candidates.)* What was the goal of the MFDP delegation to the Democratic National Convention, and what happened to the delegation at the convention? *(Pairs' responses should mention that the MFDP delegates wanted to be recognized instead of the regular state delegation. Instead, the delegates were offered two token seats.)* How did civil rights activists' views of the Democratic Party change after the MFDP's experience at the Democratic National Convention? *(Students should note that activists concluded that the Democratic Party could no longer be trusted to advance their interests.)* Have volunteers read their paragraphs to the class.
English Language Learners, Cooperative Learning

GEOGRAPHY

Freedom Summer and Its Lessons. Many Freedom Summer volunteers wrote about the hard lessons they learned about race, poverty, and the law. Realizing they were in constant danger, the volunteers learned "to live with fear as a condition, like heat or night." For students who had always trusted the police and the government, it was disheartening to learn, as one volunteer put it, that "the instruments of the law and the institutions of the law are your enemy." Aside from their new attention to safety, the volunteers learned about poverty. "I've been to hundreds of houses I could kick down with my feet and a small hammer," wrote one volunteer. Another realized "how much it took to be a Negro in Mississippi twelve months a year for a lifetime."

ACTIVITY: Have students imagine that they are Freedom Summer volunteers risking danger in order to help African Americans register to vote. Have them write diary entries about what they witness or how their work makes them feel.

Freedom Summer Workers

teen Life

Peter Orris was a white teenager in his freshman year at Harvard University when he decided to volunteer for the Freedom Summer project. He later recalled, "At eighteen years old, to be able to be involved in this kind of a struggle was very important to me."

Orris attended volunteer training sessions in Ohio, where "we playacted situations where angry groups of people, mobs, would be attacking us and how we would handle ourselves in that situation." Orris was assigned to a voter registration drive in Mileston, Mississippi. He recalled, "We were much younger than many of the people we were speaking to, and it was necessary to establish a relationship or an understanding of the respect that we paid to them for their age and their situation." Despite such efforts, African Americans were often reluctant to talk to volunteers. "We knew we were not getting [our message] across, we knew they were just waiting for us to go away because we were a danger to them, and in many ways we were." Orris remembered, "We had much less to risk than they did. This was their lives, their land, their family, and they were going to be here when we were gone."

Freedom Summer volunteers

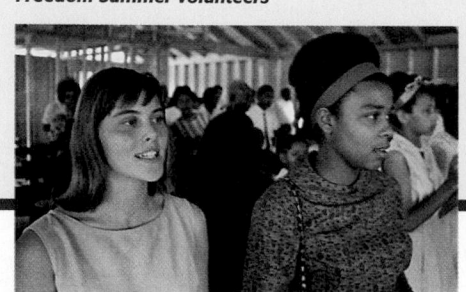

elections" introduced many African Americans to voting procedures and revealed the deep interest that many unregistered voters had in exercising their rights.

✔ **READING CHECK: Summarizing** What steps were taken to register African Americans to vote? **SNCC and COFO sponsored voter registration drives.**

A New Approach

After learning that the Voter Education Project was unable to fund registration drives in Mississippi, SNCC leaders met in November 1963. They debated a new strategy. SNCC leader Robert Moses suggested bringing white volunteers into the voter registration efforts. Moses noted, "It changes the whole complexion of what you're doing, so it isn't any longer Negro fighting white. It's a question of rational people fighting against irrational people." Several SNCC members opposed the new strategy.

Freedom Summer. The **Twenty-fourth Amendment**, which banned the payment of poll taxes as a condition for voting in federal elections, was ratified in January 1964. The amendment did not apply to state elections but offered some hope to civil rights activists. That spring, SNCC decided to implement Moses's plan, known as **Freedom Summer**. SNCC recruited volunteers on university campuses in northern states. The volunteers attended training classes in Ohio before heading to Mississippi. Lawyers and health-care professionals also took part in the project, offering legal and medical assistance to the civil rights workers.

Andrew Goodman, a college student from New York, arrived in Mississippi on June 20. The following day Goodman and two CORE workers, **James Chaney** and **Michael Schwerner**, disappeared. Their bodies were discovered six weeks later, buried in an earthen dam. The murders of Goodman and Schwerner, both of whom were white, shocked Americans in a way that the murders of African Americans had not. President Johnson ordered the Federal Bureau of Investigation (FBI) to investigate the killings. Stunned volunteers carried on. Fearing that they would also become victims of violence, however, many African Americans refused to register. By the end of the summer, just 1,600 African Americans had been added to the voting rolls.

Despite limited gains, Freedom Summer changed the lives of many African Americans in Mississippi. Unita Blackwell recalled her experiences.

History Makers Speak

❝For black people in Mississippi, Freedom Summer was the beginning of a whole new era. People began to feel that they wasn't just helpless anymore, that they had come together.... Students came and we wasn't a closed society anymore. They came to talk about that we had a right to register to vote, we had a right to stand up for our rights. . . . I mean, hadn't anybody said that to us, in that open way, like what happened in 1964.**"**

—Unita Blackwell, quoted in *Voices of Freedom*, by Henry Hampton and Steve Fayer

✔ **READING CHECK: Evaluating** How effective were Freedom Summer efforts to register voters? limited; just 1,600 voters were added to the voting rolls by summer's end

Political organization. COFO leaders also worked to place African Americans on Mississippi's delegation to the Democratic National Convention. The convention was to be held in Atlantic City, New Jersey, in August 1964. When a state party convention rejected all African American candidates, COFO helped create the **Mississippi Freedom Democratic Party** (MFDP). The MFDP formed its own delegation. **Fannie Lou Hamer**, an African American who had lost her job and her house when she registered to vote in 1962, was among the MFDP delegates.

In Atlantic City the MFDP delegation requested that the national convention recognize it rather than the regular state delegation. The MFDP delegates believed that they should be recognized because so many black Mississippians had been prevented from voting. President Johnson, who wanted the convention to proceed smoothly, worked behind the scenes to grant the MFDP recognition without making it the official delegation. In the end, the MFDP delegates were offered two token seats. The MFDP rejected this compromise as an insult. MFDP delegate Victoria Gray later explained the decision.

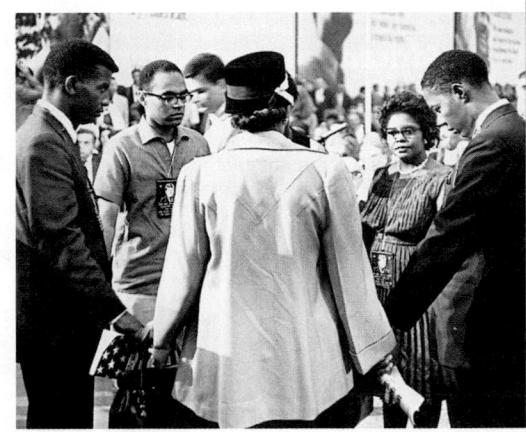

Facing the disappointment of not being recognized by the Democratic National Convention, Mississippi Freedom Democratic Party members join hands in prayer.

"Those who are unable to understand why we were unable to accept that compromise did not realize that we would have been betraying the many people back there in Mississippi whom we represented. They had not only laid their lives on the line, but many had given their lives in order for this particular event to happen.**"**

—Victoria Gray, quoted in *Voices of Freedom*, by Henry Hampton and Steve Fayer

Johnson's actions led many activists to conclude that he and the Democratic Party could no longer be trusted to advance their interests.

✔ **READING CHECK: Analyzing Information** What were the goals of the Mississippi Freedom Democratic Party? The MFDP wanted to be recognized as Mississippi's delegation to the Democratic National Convention.

Selma and the Voting Rights Act

In early 1965, civil rights workers launched a registration drive in Selma, Alabama. Of Selma's 15,000 eligible African Americans, just 383 were registered voters. The activists invited Martin Luther King Jr., who had won the Nobel Peace Prize the previous year, to lead them. African Americans who attempted to register at election commission offices in the Selma area were beaten and arrested. Civil rights leaders responded by calling for a protest march from Selma to Montgomery. Governor George Wallace immediately banned the protest.

Despite the governor's opposition, some 600 people began the 54-mile trek on Sunday, March 7. Just outside Selma, police attacked the marchers. An eight-year-old girl taking part in the march recalled that "some of them had clubs, others had

INTERPRETING THE VISUAL RECORD

Selma. This issue of *Life* magazine reached newsstands the week after the civil rights march outside Selma turned violent. *Based on this cover, what group do you think the article favored, the civil rights marchers or the Selma police? Explain your answer.*

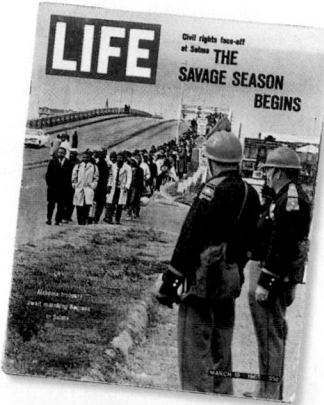

REVIEW

Have students complete the **Section 2 Review** on p. 660.

ASSESS

Have students complete **Daily Quiz 22.2.** As **Alternative Assessment,** you may want to use the memoir or the position paper entry in this section's lessons.

RETEACH

Have students complete **Main Idea Activity for English Language Learners and Special-Needs Students 22.2.** Organize students into small groups. Each group should create a poster summarizing the information in a subsection. Have each group present its poster to the class.
English Language Learners, Cooperative Learning

EXTEND

Provide students with excerpts from the Voting Rights Act of 1965. Pair students and ask each pair to study the excerpts and create a chart that outlines the provisions of the act, the circumstances (*e.g., Jim Crow laws*) that the provision is addressing, and how the provisions are to be implemented. Ask students to present and discuss their work with the class.
Block Scheduling, Cooperative Learning

- James Chaney, p. 658
- Michael Schwerner, p. 658
- Mississippi Freedom Democratic Party, p. 659
- Fannie Lou Hamer, p. 659
- Voting Rights Act, p. 660

2. Freedom Summer—to register African Americans in Mississippi to vote, resulted in deaths but few registrations; MFDP—to give African American voters a voice at the Democratic National Convention, resulted in no official recognition and distrust of President Johnson; Selma March—to protest attempts to prevent African Americans from registering to vote, resulted in public support of the Voting Rights Act

3a. threats, beatings, murder, loss of jobs for African American voters, difficulty gaining people's trust

b. If officials recognized the MFDP at the convention, they risked losing the support of most white Democrats.

c. They established COFO, implemented Freedom Summer, organized the Mississippi Freedom Democratic Party, and they marched from Selma to Montgomery, which led to the Voting Rights Act.

4. Answers will vary. Students might write that they faced angry mobs and violence; that the number of black voters registered was very small, and that fear kept many from registering.

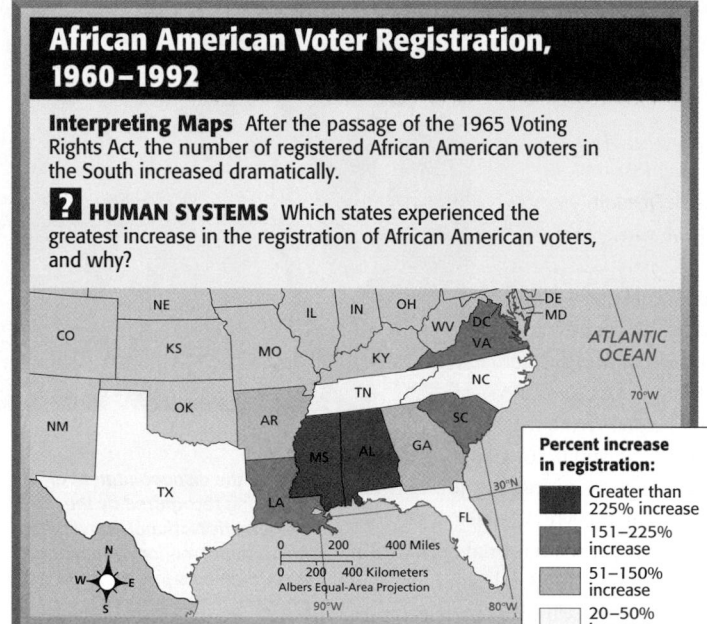

African American Voter Registration, 1960–1992

Interpreting Maps After the passage of the 1965 Voting Rights Act, the number of registered African American voters in the South increased dramatically.

? HUMAN SYSTEMS Which states experienced the greatest increase in the registration of African American voters, and why?

Percent increase in registration:
- Greater than 225% increase
- 151–225% increase
- 51–150% increase
- 20–50% increase

ropes, or whips, which they swung around them like they were driving cattle."

Outraged by the attack, thousands of Americans poured into Montgomery to show support for the marchers. President Johnson was also shocked by Selma's "Bloody Sunday." On March 15, before a joint session of Congress, he asked for speedy passage of a voting rights bill. He also declared that all Americans ought to take up the struggle for civil rights: "All of us . . . must overcome the crippling legacy [history] of bigotry [racism] and injustice. And we *shall . . .* overcome."

About one week later, under the protection of federal marshals and the National Guard, the marchers successfully completed their march. Five months later, Congress passed the **Voting Rights Act** of 1965, which put the entire registration process under federal control. Within days, federal examiners descended upon the South to sign up new African American voters. By 1968 the number of eligible African Americans in Alabama registered to vote jumped to 57 percent. Mississippi experienced the greatest percentage increase, from less than 7 percent in 1964 to some 59 percent in 1968.

✔ **READING CHECK: Drawing Conclusions** How did the Voting Rights Act affect the relationship between the federal government and state and local governments?
It transferred control over voter registration from the states to the federal government.

SECTION 2 REVIEW

1. Identify and explain:
Robert Moses
Council of Federated Organizations
Twenty-fourth Amendment
Freedom Summer
Andrew Goodman
James Chaney
Michael Schwerner
Mississippi Freedom Democratic Party
Fannie Lou Hamer
Voting Rights Act

2. Evaluating Copy the chart below. Use it to explain the impact of efforts including Freedom Summer, the Mississippi Freedom Democratic Party (MFDP), and the Selma march.

Freedom Summer	MFDP	Selma March
Stated Goal	Stated Goal	Stated Goal
___	___	___
___	___	___
Effect	Effect	Effect

3. Finding the Main Idea

a. What obstacles did civil rights workers encounter in their attempts to register voters?

b. Why did officials in the Democratic Party regard the MFDP as a potential source of conflict?

c. What actions did African Americans take in the 1960s to expand their political rights?

4. Writing and Critical Thinking

Drawing Conclusions Imagine that you are a Freedom Summer volunteer. Write a letter to a friend back home describing your experience.
Consider:
- the violence that people encountered
- the total number of African American voters registered
- the interaction between black Mississippians and civil rights workers

Homework Practice Online
keyword: SE3 HP22

SECTION 3

After completing Section 3, students should be able to:

OBJECTIVE 1 Describe how Malcolm X's message differed from that of other leaders of the civil rights movement in the early 1960s.

OBJECTIVE 2 Explain why nonviolent protest and the goal of racial integration lost support.

OBJECTIVE 3 Discuss how northern racial discrimination and urban riots changed the civil rights movement.

🔔 LET'S GET STARTED!

Write the name *Malcolm X* on the chalkboard. As students enter the classroom, tell them to write down what they know about him. Ask volunteers to share their responses, then compile a list of responses on the chalkboard. Tell students that in Section 3 they will learn about alternative means of achieving civil rights that were proposed by civil rights leaders.

SECTION 3

READ TO DISCOVER

1. What role did Malcolm X play in the civil rights movement during the early 1960s?
2. Why did nonviolent protest and the goal of racial integration lose support?
3. How did northern racial discrimination and urban riots change the civil rights movement?

IDENTIFY

James Farmer
Nation of Islam
Elijah Muhammad
Malcolm X
Stokely Carmichael
Black Power
Bobby Seale
Huey Newton
Black Panther Party
Kerner Commission
Poor People's Campaign

▶ WHY IT MATTERS TODAY

People from various racial groups today also strive to expand their economic opportunities. Use **CNNfyi.com** or other **current events** sources to find out about a recent example of such activity. Record your findings in your journal.

CNNfyi.com

Challenges for the Movement

 EYEWITNESSES TO History "*We wanted control of the communities where we were most numerous, and the institutions therein. At the same time, we felt that we were due, because of taxpaying, free access to and equal treatment in public facilities.*"

—Huey Newton, quoted in *Voices of Freedom,* by Henry Hampton and Steve Fayer

A Black Panther pin

Huey Newton recalled his decision to form a new, more confrontational civil rights organization with his friend Bobby Seale. The appearance of this new movement and the prominence of Black Muslim leader Malcolm X signaled a new phase in the struggle for civil rights in the mid-1960s. Many activists were dissatisfied with the direction the civil rights movement had taken and were frustrated with the slow pace of change. In reaction, many African American leaders rejected nonviolence as a strategy. Seale and Newton chose the black panther to symbolize their new group. Seale explained, "If you drive a panther into a corner, if he can't go left and he can't go right, then he will tend to come out of that corner to wipe out or stop its aggressor."

New Directions

As the civil rights movement continued, some African Americans questioned the effectiveness of nonviolence and the goals of the movement. In 1962 CORE director **James Farmer** explained, "We no longer are a tight fellowship of a few dedicated advocates [supporters] of a brilliant new method of social change. We are now a large family spawned [created] by the union of the method-oriented pioneers and the righteously indignant [angry] ends-oriented militants." The "militants" of whom Farmer spoke were people who were attracted to the views of African American organizations such as the **Nation of Islam.**

Black Muslims. Little is known about Wallace D. Fard, the founder of the Nation of Islam. Fard started the group, also known as the Black Muslims, in Detroit, Michigan, in 1930. The organization was based on the Islamic religion founded by the prophet Muhammad. However, the Black Muslims emphasized the supremacy of black people over all other races. By the early 1930s, when **Elijah Muhammad** became its leader, the Nation of Islam claimed some 8,000 members. Muhammad preached a message of black nationalism. He declared that African Americans should create their own republic within the United States. Many Black Muslims rejected their last names as relics of slavery and used "X" to symbolize lost African names.

Muhammad stressed self-discipline as the way to achieve the dream of a separate African American nation. Black Muslims were not allowed to drink alcohol or smoke and were expected to maintain a strict diet. Muhammad also encouraged self-reliance. During the Great Depression, Black Muslims were not permitted to

SECTION 3 RESOURCES

REPRODUCIBLE
▶ Guided Reading Strategy 22.3

TECHNOLOGY
▶ One-Stop Planner, Lesson 22.3
▶ The American Nation Video Program Segment: Malcolm X; Teacher's Guide, pp. 135–40
▶ **CNN** Presents America: Yesterday and Today Segment: "I Have a Dream"
▶ Holt Researcher: American History CD–ROM
▶ Homework Practice Online

REINFORCEMENT, REVIEW, AND ASSESSMENT
▶ Section 3 Review, p. 666
▶ Daily Quiz 22.3
▶ Main Idea Activity 22.3
▶ English Audio Summary 22.3
▶ Spanish Audio Summary 22.3

TEACH OBJECTIVE 1

LEVEL 1: To help students understand how Malcolm X's views differed from those of mainstream civil rights leaders, copy the graphic organizer in the next column on the chalkboard, omitting the italicized answers. Have each student complete the organizer. Ask volunteers to share their answers with the class. Conclude by leading a discussion about the differences of opinion that existed within the civil rights movement about the most effective means of obtaining civil rights for African Americans. **English Language Learners**

LEVELS 2 AND 3: Pair students and tell one student in each pair to imagine that he or she supports the views of mainstream civil rights leaders regarding the strategy for the civil rights movement. Tell the other student to imagine that he or she supports Malcolm X's message. Have students write a brief dialogue discussing their views. *(See the graphic organizer from the Level 1 lesson for major points of difference.)* Ask students to read their dialogues for the class. **Cooperative Learning**

Views of Mainstream Civil Rights Leaders	Views of Malcolm X
Civil rights will be obtained through 1. *nonviolence* and 2. *integration.*	Civil rights will be obtained through 1. *"any means necessary"* and 2. *African American separatism.*

HISTORY MAKERS SPEAK

Ossie Davis in *Voices of Freedom*

Remembering Malcolm X.

Many African Americans were uncomfortable with Malcolm X's ideas. Ossie Davis, an African American actor and playwright, described his reaction to Malcolm X. At first, Davis said, "I was amazed at his capacity to communicate and at the naked honesty with which he expressed his feelings about black people, about white people. He scared me. I'm sure he intended to."

ACTIVITY: Have students compare and contrast the opinions Davis and Sanchez had of Malcolm X.

The American Nation
VIDEO PROGRAM

Malcolm X; Teacher's Guide; pp. 135–40

Search 28273, Play to 35398
Videodisc 2, Side B

Play   Pause

See *Teacher's Guide* for Spanish barcode.

PRIMARY SOURCE ANSWER

Students might note that Sanchez believes Malcolm X said what many African Americans felt.

PRIMARY SOURCE

A Civil Rights Worker's View of Malcolm X

Many white Americans found Malcolm X's views threatening. However, many African Americans embraced them. New York civil rights activist Sonia Sanchez described the effect that Malcolm X had on some African Americans. **What opinion is Sanchez expressing about Malcolm X?**

❝I've never seen anyone appeal to such a broad audience.... And he understood the bottom line is that if you tell people the truth then it will appeal to everyone. If you tell them all about their oppression, in a fashion they ain't never heard before, then they will all gravitate towards you.... You see, what he said out loud is what African-American people had been saying ... forever behind closed doors.... He said it out loud. Not behind closed doors. He took on America for us.❞

Research on the ROM

Free Find: Malcolm X
After reading about Malcolm X on the **Holt Researcher CD–ROM**, explain how his experiences as a youth influenced his civil rights efforts.

---

accept any assistance from the federal government. Black Muslims were also discouraged by their leaders from serving in the U.S. military. As a result, Muhammad and many of his followers were sentenced to prison for draft evasion during World War II.

While in prison, Muhammad realized that African American prisoners were largely ignored by most African American organizations. Muhammad actively recruited convicts, calling on them to change their lives through the strict discipline required by the Nation of Islam. He also brought his message to many lower-income African Americans. These recruitment efforts proved effective. By the early 1970s there were an estimated 100,000 Black Muslims spread throughout the United States.

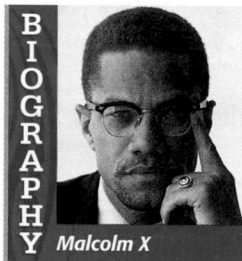

Malcolm X

Malcolm X. The growth of the Nation of Islam during the 1950s was in part the work of **Malcolm X**, a charismatic young minister. Malcolm X was born Malcolm Little in 1925. He grew up in Michigan. His father was a Baptist minister and organizer for Marcus Garvey. Malcolm's father was killed in what many people considered a racially motivated murder.

Despite his father's death, Malcolm Little tried to ignore the racism he encountered. This changed when Little, who was an excellent student, told his white English teacher that he wanted to become an attorney. The teacher replied that this was an unrealistic goal for an African American. Malcolm X later recalled, "The more I thought afterwards about what he said, the more uneasy it made me.... It was then that I began to change—inside." He remembered that he "drew away from white people" after the conversation with his teacher.

Little dropped out of school and drifted into a life of crime. He was eventually sentenced to 10 years in prison. While in prison he embraced the teachings of Elijah Muhammad. Released in 1952, he changed his name to Malcolm X and soon became a leading minister for the Nation of Islam. A powerful speaker, Malcolm X championed African American separatism and called for freedom to be brought about "by any means necessary." The time for nonviolence had passed, he argued.

History Makers Speak

❝You're getting a new generation that has been growing right now, and they're beginning to think with their own minds and see that you can't negotiate up on freedom nowadays. If something is yours by right, then fight for it or shut up. If you can't fight for it, then forget it.❞

—Malcolm X, speech to the London School of Economics, February 1965

Malcolm X criticized the goals and the strategies of civil rights organizations that worked for racial integration. He argued that "it is not integration that Negroes

Have students conduct research on James Farmer. Tell students to focus on Farmer's role in the Congress on Racial Equality (CORE), sit-ins in Chicago, the Freedom Rides, the Nixon administration, and Farmer's life in the 1970s, 1980s, and 1990s. Then ask each student to use this information to create a Coming Attractions poster for a documentary film on Farmer's life. **Block Scheduling**

NOTE: To help students make meaningful connections between events in U.S. history and those in their own hometown, use the Chapter 22 **Hands-On History Activity**, Voters and Voting Rights in Your Community.

TEACH OBJECTIVE 2

LEVEL 1: Pair students and tell them to imagine that they are civil rights activists who have grown frustrated with the strategy of nonviolent protest and the goal of racial integration. Have each pair write a letter to Stokely Carmichael explaining its views. *(Pairs should note that activists who had endured violence and jail questioned nonviolence as a strategy. Many African American volunteers on the Freedom Summer project believed that white students were taking over the project. Also, activists were angered that the deaths of white civil rights supporters generated more concern than the deaths of African American activists.)* Have volunteers read their letters to the class. **English Language Learners, Cooperative Learning**

---

in America want, it is human dignity." Criticizing Martin Luther King Jr., Malcolm X claimed, "Any Negro who teaches other Negroes to turn the other cheek is disarming that Negro . . . [of] his natural right to defend himself."

Many white Americans found Malcolm X's tone frightening. During the mid-1960s, however, Malcolm X began undergoing a transformation in his beliefs. In 1964 he made a pilgrimage to the Islamic holy city of Mecca. In Mecca he was exposed to more traditional Islamic beliefs. He also gained a greater acceptance of the universal humanity of people of all races. That same year he broke with the Black Muslims. Turning away from separatism, Malcolm X converted to orthodox Islam and began calling for unity among all people. His new outlook was reflected in a 1964 speech. He declared, "We will work with anyone, with any group, no matter what their color is, as long as they are genuinely interested in taking the type of steps necessary to bring an end to the injustices that black people in this country are afflicted by." However, Malcolm X had little time to act on his new ideas. In February 1965 he was gunned down by three Black Muslim assassins.

✔ **READING CHECK: Contrasting** How did Malcolm X's message differ from that of Martin Luther King Jr.? He championed African American separatism and endorsed the use of physical violence in self-defense.

The Movement Fractures

Most white Americans perceived the civil rights movement as a unified effort led by Martin Luther King Jr. In fact, the movement was made up of diverse groups united by the common goal of ending racial segregation. By the mid-1960s many conflicts had surfaced among these organizations.

Black Power. Civil rights activists who had endured violence and jailings in their efforts to register voters in Mississippi began to question the strategy of nonviolent protest. CORE's David Dennis summed up the growing frustration with nonviolence in June 1964. Dennis declared, "I'm sick and tired of going to funerals of black men who have been murdered by white men. . . . I've got vengeance in my heart tonight."

Some African American activists also began to question the goal of integration, in part because of their experiences in Mississippi. The presence of white volunteers for the Freedom Summer project had created tensions within SNCC. African American workers believed that white students were taking over the project. "Suddenly, in an instant, in our town are five or six brightly scrubbed white kids from the North," SNCC's Bob Zellner recalled. "Here's Jesse (Negro) laboriously doing the stencil. Sally (white) . . . comes along and says, 'Here, I type 120 words a minute, let me do it.'" These frustrations led many African American activists, particularly those involved with SNCC and CORE, to express a growing interest in black nationalism.

Many African Americans were also angry that the death of white volunteers such as Andrew Goodman and Michael Schwerner generated widespread public

Martin Luther King Jr. and Malcolm X met only once, at the U.S. Capitol during a Senate filibuster of a civil rights bill in March 1964.

INTERPRETING THE VISUAL RECORD

Black nationalism. Frustrated by their experiences in the civil rights movement, some African Americans began to embrace black nationalism. *How does this button symbolize the new direction of some civil rights activists?*

HISTORY MAKERS SPEAK

Stokely Carmichael in "What We Want"

Carmichael's Definition of Black Power. After Stokely Carmichael's phrase "Black Power" was broadcast all over the nation, people demanded to know what he meant. In the *New York Review of Books.* Carmichael wrote, "Politically, black power means . . . the coming-together of black people to elect representatives and to *force those representatives to speak to their needs."* Carmichael also argued against integration. "As a goal, [integration] has been based on complete acceptance of the fact that *in order to have* a decent house or education, blacks must move into a white neighborhood or send their children to a white school."

CRITICAL THINKING What might Carmichael have suggested that African Americans do to improve their situation other than integrate?

ANSWER: Students might suggest that Carmichael would have wanted African Americans to attain economic equality and improve their own neighborhoods and schools.

VISUAL RECORD ANSWER

Students might suggest that the clenched fist symbolizes a more aggressive method of achieving equality.

LEVEL 2: Have each student create a collage that expresses the discontent that many civil rights activists felt with the strategy of nonviolent protest and the goal of racial integration. *(See the Level 1 lesson for the correct reasons.)* Have students display and explain their collages to the class.

LEVEL 3: Tell students to imagine that they are editors of a major daily newspaper in 1966. Have each student write a one-page editorial that explains why many civil rights activists were frustrated with the strategy of nonviolent protest and the goal of integration. *(See the Level 1 lesson for the correct reasons.)*

HOMEWORK *Write on the chalkboard the following statement made by Martin Luther King Jr. in reference to the Black Power movement: "If you really have power you don't need a slogan." Ask each student to write one to two paragraphs in agreement or disagreement with King's statement. Students should provide specific reasons for their positions.*

CONSTITUTIONAL HERITAGE

Interracial Marriage. In the midst of the breakup of the civil rights movement, one Virginia couple was becoming a civil rights success story. Mildred Jeter, an African American woman, and Richard Loving, a white man, had been married in Washington, D.C., where interracial marriages were legal. When they returned to their Virginia home, they were charged and indicted for their marriage, which was illegal in Virginia. The couple's sentence was to spend one year in jail or leave the state for 25 years. They chose to move to Washington, D.C., and began a series of appeals of the Virginia court's decision. Their case made it to the Supreme Court as *Loving* v. *Virginia.* In 1967 the Court decided that the ban on interracial marriages violated the Fourteenth Amendment.

ACTIVITY: Have students assume the roles of either the Lovings, representatives of Virginia, or members of the Supreme Court and write a defense of their position.

VISUAL RECORD ANSWER

Students might suggest that the pin represents the Black Panthers' desire for total participation in their movement and attempt to improve African American life.

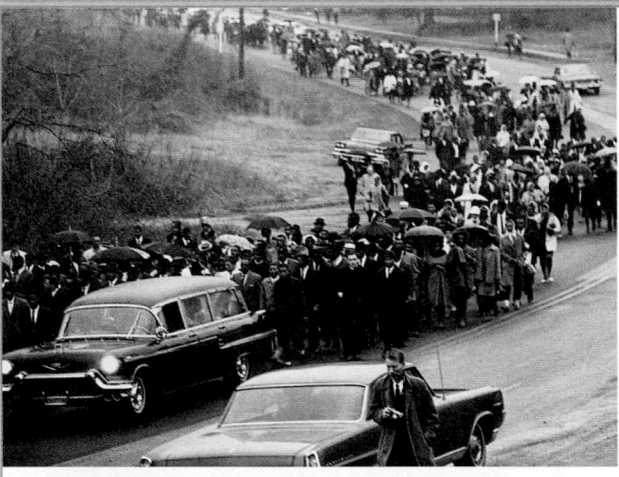

The deaths of civil rights activists such as Jimmie Lee Jackson, whose 1965 funeral is shown here, led to growing frustration among African American leaders who began to embrace the Black Power movement.

INTERPRETING THE VISUAL RECORD

Black Panthers. Members of the Black Panther Party drew public attention by carrying guns and supporting the Black Power movement. *How do you think the message of the pin reflects the values of the Black Panther Party?*

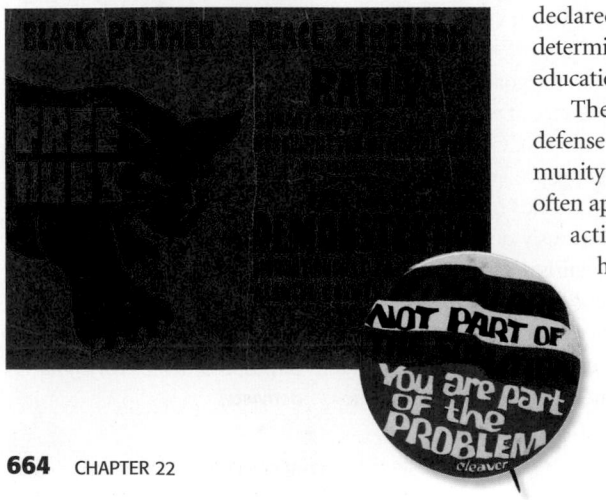

concern. However, African American victims of violence did not receive similar attention. SNCC's **Stokely Carmichael** noted, "What you want is the nation to be upset when anybody is killed. . . . It's almost like, for this to be recognized, a white person must be killed. Well, what does that say?"

The split in the civil rights movement became public in 1966. That year James Meredith, the first African American to graduate from the University of Mississippi, decided to make a "journey against fear" by marching across Mississippi. After he was shot and wounded on the second day of the march, several civil rights organizations vowed to continue his journey. Determined to turn the march into an expression of black nationalism, Stokely Carmichael convinced the NAACP and the Urban League, two more conservative organizations, to abandon the event.

At a march rally on June 16, Carmichael told the crowd, "This is the 27th time I've been arrested. I ain't gonna be arrested no more." In the days that followed, Carmichael and others asked the crowd, "What do you want?" and received the chanted reply, "Black power!"

King asked Carmichael to stop using the slogan, but Carmichael admitted, "I deliberately decided to raise this issue on the march in order to give it a national forum." The **Black Power** movement called for black separatism. It had many positive aspects, including an emphasis on racial pride and an interest in African culture and heritage. However, many moderate leaders such as King feared that the movement would create hostility toward civil rights among the nation's white population. King confided to one adviser, "If you go around claiming power, the whole society turns on you and crushes you. If you really have power you don't need a slogan."

The Black Panthers. Despite King's misgivings, many African Americans were attracted to Carmichael's Black Power message. **Bobby Seale** worked with **Huey Newton** at an antipoverty center in Oakland, California. He later recalled, "Huey and I began to try to figure out how could we organize youthful black folks into some kind of political, electoral *power* movement." The two created a political organization called the **Black Panther Party.** The party platform declared, "Black people will not be free until we are free to determine our own destiny." It called for "land, bread, housing, education, clothing, justice, and peace" for African Americans.

The platform also called for the creation of "black self-defense groups that are dedicated to defending our black community from racist police oppression." Black Panther members often appeared in public carrying firearms—at the time a legal activity in California. They participated in a number of highly publicized gun battles with police. Huey Newton was convicted of manslaughter in the death of an Oakland police officer. Elaine Brown, who joined the organization in 1967, offered one reason why African Americans joined the Black Panthers:

TEACH OBJECTIVE 3

LEVEL 1: Pair students and have each pair create bumper stickers that describe the changing goals of the civil rights movement after it encountered northern racial discrimination and after the urban riots. *(Bumper stickers might include that economic power became emphasized. Martin Luther King Jr. believed that the Vietnam War diverted spending from social programs. King planned to lead a Poor People's Campaign to protest what he saw as a misuse of government spending.)* Have each pair present and explain its bumper stickers to the class.
English Language Learners, Cooperative Learning

LEVEL 2: Tell students to imagine that they are trying to rally support for the changing goals of the civil rights movement in the late 1960s in response to northern racial discrimination and urban riots. Have each student write a short speech advocating these new goals. *(See the Level 1 lesson for the correct goals.)* Have students deliver their speeches to the class.

LEVEL 3: Have each student create a mobile with objects that symbolize the changing goals of the civil rights movement after the urban riots and incidents of northern racial discrimination. *(See the Level 1 lesson for the correct goals.)* Ask each student to display his or her mobile in the classroom and to explain the meaning of each symbol.

History Makers Speak

❝The party reached out mostly to men, to young, black urban men who were on the streets, who knew that there were no options somewhere in their lives. . . . We offered them the opportunity to make their lives meaningful. . . . And a lot of brothers did make their commitment with that conscious understanding that coming away from the gang was something that they were ultimately building for themselves and for the community.**❞**

—Elaine Brown, quoted in *Voices of Freedom*, edited by Henry Hampton and Steve Fayer

✔ **READING CHECK: Making Generalizations** Why did some African Americans embrace the Black Power movement? **They began to question the goal of integration.**

Tragic Events

The Black Power movement was not the only challenge that Martin Luther King Jr. and other civil rights leaders faced during the mid-1960s. White Americans had mixed reactions to efforts to extend the civil rights struggle beyond desegregation and into areas such as housing and economic justice. Many opposed the movement's expanded focus.

Chicago. By 1966 the SCLC was virtually the only major civil rights organization still primarily focused on nonviolent protest. That year King decided to battle racial discrimination in Chicago. In January he and his family moved into a slum apartment. He hoped to draw attention to the housing problems that African Americans faced in the urban North. Throughout that spring, amid periodic journeys to the South, King provided leadership and support for the movement in Chicago.

At a rally on July 10, 1966, King announced his continued determination to end housing discrimination in Chicago. Less than a month later, he was struck in the head by a rock while leading a peaceful march through a Chicago neighborhood. Some 4,000 white people threatened the marchers. The marchers were protected by local police. Next, King announced that he would lead a march in Cicero, Illinois, a town with a history of violence against African Americans. Chicago city leaders pledged to meet King's demands.

King claimed victory in Chicago, but the experience showed that significant obstacles to full equality remained. The fight against racial discrimination in the North did not draw support from white Americans in the way that demonstrations against segregation in the South had a few years earlier.

Analyzing Primary Sources

Drawing Conclusions What did the Black Power movement offer young, urban African Americans?

an opportunity to make their lives meaningful

Urban Unrest, 1965–1968

Interpreting Maps Hundreds of race-related riots rocked U.S. cities in the mid-1960s.

? **PLACES AND REGIONS** Which section of the country experienced the most incidents of urban unrest between 1965 and 1968? Explain your answer.

• Site of urban unrest

Homecoming at Howard.
In 1966 Robin Gregory—a student at Howard University, a historically black university—ran a unique campaign for homecoming queen. She wore her hair in an Afro, which was a statement of Black Power. Her campaign speeches focused on politics. One student described the presentation of the new queen. "As the stage revolved and turned around toward the audience, the lights began to come up at the same time. Well, before you saw Robin, you saw the way the lights cast a silhouette on the curtains, and you saw the silhouette of her Afro before you saw her. Well, the auditorium exploded. It was a wonderful moment."

CRITICAL THINKING How might Gregory's homecoming victory have been seen as a victory for Black Power?

ANSWER: Students might note Gregory's hair style and political speeches.

MAP ANSWER
the Northeast and the Midwest; those areas have urban areas with great numbers of African Americans

REVIEW

Have students complete the **Section 3 Review** on p. 666.

ASSESS

Have students complete **Daily Quiz 22.3.** As **Alternative Assessment**, you may want to use the speech or the bumper stickers in this section's lessons.

RETEACH

Have students complete **Main Idea Activity for English Language Learners and Special-Needs Students 22.3.** Then pair students and have each pair summarize the subsections in Section 3. Have pairs create at least four questions and answers for each subsection. Collect pairs' questions and use them to quiz the class as a whole.
English Language Learners, Cooperative Learning

EXTEND

Ask each student to conduct research on and write a report about one of the following: Stokely Carmichael, Elijah Muhammad, Huey Newton, Bobby Seale, or Malcolm X.
Block Scheduling

REVIEW SECTION 3 ANSWERS

1. Identify
- James Farmer, p. 661
- Nation of Islam, p. 661
- Elijah Muhammad, p. 661
- Malcolm X, p. 662
- Stokely Carmichael, p. 664
- Black Power, p. 664
- Bobby Seale, p. 664
- Huey Newton, p. 664
- Black Panther Party, p. 664
- Kerner Commission, p. 666
- Poor People's Campaign, p. 666

2. 1.—Some activists believed that nonviolent protests were not working fast enough. 2.—Some began to question the move for integration. 3.—Many were angered when people were outraged over the deaths of white civil rights activists but not those of African Americans.

3a. Malcolm X believed in violent action and African American independence within the movement.

b. discrimination—failed to draw as much public support as in the South; violence—weakened support for the movement

c. King fought housing discrimination, organized the Poor People's Campaign, and supported a sanitation worker's strike.

4. Essays will vary but might suggest that discrimination still existed and African American groups disagreed on solutions.

666

Urban violence. In the mid-1960s a white backlash against the civil rights movement emerged, and the Johnson administration became reluctant to press for further gains. The Black Power movement and a series of urban riots turned many white Americans away from the civil rights movement. Despite the successes of the civil rights movement, discrimination still affected the lives of most African Americans. In August 1965 frustration turned to violence. A routine arrest by Los Angeles police in the African American neighborhood of Watts triggered a riot that raged for six days. When the National Guard finally restored order, 34 people had been killed, hundreds injured, and almost 4,000 had been arrested.

Over the next two years, more than 100 riots broke out in cities across the country. The worst came in Detroit, where 43 people died. President Johnson appointed the **Kerner Commission** to investigate the violence. Its report charged that white racism was largely responsible for the tensions that led to the riots. "Our nation," the report warned, "is moving toward two societies, one black, one white—separate and unequal."

Seeking to address the frustration of the late 1960s, King embraced some of the Black Power movement's ideas, such as the need for African Americans to gain economic power. He became increasingly upset that funding for social programs was being diverted to the war in Vietnam. In March 1968 King called for a **Poor People's Campaign** that would include a march on Washington, D.C., to protest what he saw as a misuse of government spending.

Before the march, King went to Memphis, Tennessee, to show his support for a sanitation workers' strike. On the evening of April 4, 1968, the man who was the symbol of nonviolence met a violent end when he was shot by a sniper. Within hours of King's death, African American neighborhoods across the country exploded in outrage. A week of rioting left 45 dead and thousands injured.

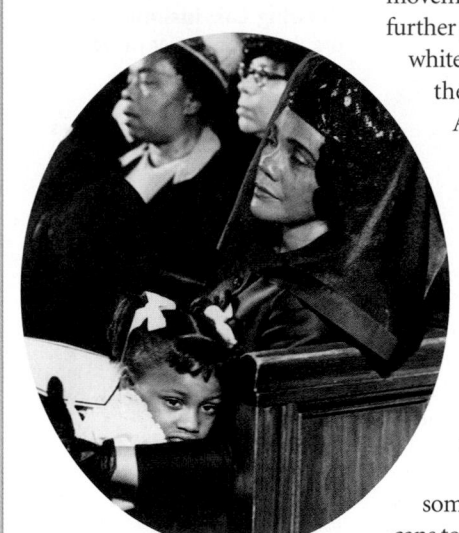
Most Americans joined Coretta Scott King in mourning after the assassination of Martin Luther King Jr.

✔ **READING CHECK: Making Generalizations** Why did the civil rights movement begin to falter as it turned its focus to economic problems? Many white Americans in the North did not support the fight against racial discrimination; race riots also hurt the civil rights movement.

SECTION 3 REVIEW

1. Identify and explain:
James Farmer
Nation of Islam
Elijah Muhammad
Malcolm X
Stokely Carmichael
Black Power
Bobby Seale
Huey Newton
Black Panther Party
Kerner Commission
Poor People's Campaign

2. Sequencing Copy the graphic organizer below. Use it to explain the factors that led activists to move from nonviolence to Black Power.

Non-violence → 1. → 2. → 3. → Black Power

3. **Finding the Main Idea**
a. How did Malcolm X's attitudes differ from those of other civil rights leaders?
b. How did northern discrimination and urban violence affect the civil rights movement?
c. How did civil rights leaders try to improve economic opportunities for African Americans?

4. **Writing and Critical Thinking**
Identifying Points of View Write a brief essay explaining how the nation remained divided in the 1960s.
Consider:
- conflicts within the civil rights movement
- economic issues

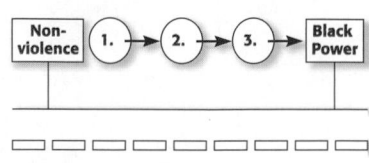
Homework Practice Online
keyword: SE3 HP22

After completing Section 4, students should be able to:

OBJECTIVE 1 Describe the problems many leading African American organizations encountered in the early 1970s.

OBJECTIVE 2 Explain effects of Supreme Court decisions on busing and affirmative action programs.

OBJECTIVE 3 Identify the gains African Americans made during the early 1970s.

LET'S GET STARTED!

Write the italicized statements below on the chalkboard. As students enter the classroom, tell them to copy the statements into their notebooks and note whether each statement is true or false. Students should correct false statements.

During the late 1960s civil rights leaders placed new emphasis on increasing the economic power of African Americans. (true)

Civil rights gains during the 1960s resulted almost exclusively from private efforts. (false—through a combination of public and private efforts)

Tell students that in Section 4 they will learn about the civil rights struggle in the 1970s.

SECTION 4

READ TO DISCOVER

1. What problems did many leading African American organizations encounter in the early 1970s?
2. How did the Supreme Court limit busing and affirmative action programs?
3. What gains did African Americans make during the early 1970s?

DEFINE

busing
affirmative action
quotas

IDENTIFY

Ralph Abernathy
University of California v. Bakke
Allan Bakke
Carl Stokes
National Black Political Convention

WHY IT MATTERS TODAY

Affirmative action remains a controversial topic. Use **CNNfyi.com** or other **current events** sources to find recent Supreme Court or other federal court rulings on affirmative action. Record your findings in your journal.

CNNfyi.com

The Movement Continues

EYEWITNESSES TO History

"When I took over from Martin, I did so after the civil rights movement had peaked and the SCLC had already begun to decline in influence.... Through our efforts and those of others, legal segregation in most areas of public life had been eliminated.... When we tried to change our focus and attack economic injustice, we lost many of our former supporters.... After a decade of fighting for racial justice, many people, black and white, were weary of the struggle and were ready to give up, to lay down their swords and shields.**"**

—Ralph Abernathy, *And the Walls Came Tumbling Down*

This SCLC poster was created to encourage support for the Poor People's Campaign.

Ralph Abernathy assumed leadership of the SCLC after the assassination of Martin Luther King Jr. His recollections reveal the frustration that many African Americans felt as the struggle for civil rights moved into the 1970s.

A Crisis in Direction

The assassination of Martin Luther King Jr. marked a turning point in the struggle for civil rights. With King's death, the movement lost its most visible figure and the leading supporter of nonviolent protest. At the same time, Black Power groups also began to decline. During the 1970s African American civil rights leaders addressed new problems.

SCLC. Determined to continue King's work, SCLC leaders went ahead with the Poor People's Campaign. **Ralph Abernathy** told the marchers on their way to Capitol Hill, "We have business on the road to freedom.... We must prove to white America that you can kill the leader but you cannot kill the dream." Once they had reached Washington, D.C., protesters constructed Resurrection City. Completed in mid-May 1968, the city was a settlement of tents and shacks on public land designed to draw attention to poverty. William Rutherford explained, "The technique, the tactic being used, was to gather the poorest of the poor in the nation's capitol in the heart of the wealthiest country in the world ... [and] take the plea and the complaint of the poor to each of the government agencies."

Resurrection City was a disaster. Constant rain turned the shantytown into a sea of mud. SCLC leaders also had to deal with violence. In June of 1968, police evicted demonstrators from the site and tore down Resurrection City.

The failure of the Poor People's Campaign left many civil rights activists in a state of despair. "It dawned on me that this was the end of an entire period in my life," Michael Harrington recalled. "One of the most marvelous political movements in America in the form which it took under Martin Luther King ... had come to an end." During the 1970s financial contributions to SCLC shrank. The organization no longer played a leading role in civil rights issues.

SECTION 4 RESOURCES

REPRODUCIBLE

▶ Guided Reading Strategy 22.4

TECHNOLOGY

▶ One-Stop Planner, Lesson 22.4
▶ Holt Researcher: American History CD–ROM
▶ Homework Practice Online

REINFORCEMENT, REVIEW, AND ASSESSMENT

▶ Section 4 Review, p. 671
▶ Daily Quiz 22.4
▶ Main Idea Activity 22.4
▶ English Audio Summary 22.4
▶ Spanish Audio Summary 22.4

LEVEL 1: Pair students and have each pair create a chart showing the problems faced by civil rights organizations in the 1970s. *(Pairs' answers should include some of the following: the SCLC's new focus on economic justice led to a loss of support for the organization; the SCLC's Resurrection City project was a failure; financial contributions to the SCLC shrank; the FBI investigated black nationalist organizations; internal conflicts plagued many organizations; financial contributions to the SNCC declined; the SNCC disbanded in the early 1970s; the Black Panthers lost influence as many Black Panther leaders were imprisoned or died.)*

English Language Learners, Cooperative Learning

LEVELS 2 AND 3: Tell students to imagine that they must design a Web site about the problems many African American political organizations faced in the early 1970s. Have each student complete a design for a Web site that includes an explanation of how the information is organized as well as suggestions for links. *(See the Level 1 lesson for the correct problems.)* Have volunteers present their designs to the class.

NOTE: For an additional teaching idea, see the Chapter 22 ranking lesson in the **Creative Teaching Strategies** handbook.

The Southern Manifesto.

The busing controversy brought the issue of desegregation to the entire nation, but many southern politicians had been working since 1956 to reverse the Supreme Court's *Brown* v. *Board of Education* decision. After the decision, 96 southern members of Congress signed the Southern Manifesto. Part of it read, "The original Constitution does not mention education. Neither does the 14th Amendment nor any other amendment. . . . This unwarranted exercise of power by the Court . . . is destroying the amicable relations between the white and Negro races. . . . It has planted hatred and suspicion where there had been heretofore friendship and understanding."

CRITICAL THINKING Why might the manifesto have claimed that the races had lived in friendship and understanding prior to *Brown* v. *Board of Education?*

ANSWER: Students might suggest that the absence of civil rights protests prior to the decision was interpreted to be salutary rather than an indicator of oppression.

VISUAL RECORD ANSWER

Students might note that the cover shows a white child going to an inner-city area, while an African American child is going to a suburban area.

Pictured here leaving a Senate subcommittee hearing, FBI director J. Edgar Hoover organized counterintelligence programs to block the activities of black nationalist and civil rights groups.

INTERPRETING THE VISUAL RECORD

Busing. Many Americans opposed the integration of public schools by busing children. *How does this* **Time** *magazine cover from 1971 portray the differences in the neighborhoods to which students would be bused?*

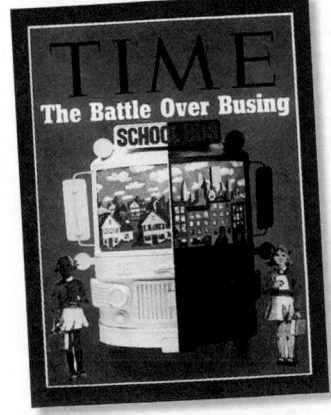

Black nationalism. Like the SCLC, organizations that supported black nationalism faced growing problems. These problems included scrutiny by the U.S. government. In 1967 FBI director J. Edgar Hoover launched a program designed to "expose, disrupt, misdirect, discredit, or otherwise neutralize the activities of black nationalist, hate-type organizations and groupings, their leadership, spokesmen, membership, and supporters." Numerous operations were begun against various civil rights organizations.

Many organizations also suffered from internal conflicts. Under Stokely Carmichael's leadership, SNCC began controversial protests against the Vietnam War. Financial contributions to SNCC declined dramatically.

In February 1968, SNCC and Black Panther leaders announced plans to unite. However, many SNCC members were reluctant to join a group that openly supported violence. The union lasted only until July. The following month SNCC expelled Stokely Carmichael. The crises in direction and leadership proved to be too much. SNCC disbanded in the early 1970s. The Black Panthers also lost influence. Many of the group's leaders were imprisoned or dead.

Unlike SNCC and the Black Panthers, the Black Muslims survived the early 1970s, despite losing some support following Malcolm X's departure. Elijah Muhammad continued to lead the Nation of Islam. After Muhammad's death in 1975, his son Wallace took over as leader.

✔ **READING CHECK: Identifying Cause and Effect** How did Martin Luther King Jr.'s death and organizational problems harm the civil rights movement? **The Poor People's Campaign was a disaster without King, and the SCLC no longer played a leading role. SNCC and Black Panthers split over the issue of violence.**

Backlash

Civil rights organizations faced growing opposition from white Americans. Some claimed that civil rights reform was depriving them of their own rights. One of the first targets of white anger was court-ordered busing to desegregate the nation's public schools.

Busing. The Supreme Court had banned racial segregation in public schools in the 1954 case *Brown* v. *Board of Education.* However, because residential neighborhoods in most U.S. cities remained segregated, many schools in both the South and the North were also segregated. Some school officials decided to use **busing,** or sending children to schools outside of their neighborhoods, to integrate schools.

In 1971 the Supreme Court approved a busing plan in Charlotte, North Carolina. The plan worked, and Charlotte's schools were quickly desegregated. Polls, however, revealed that white Americans opposed court-ordered busing by a 3-to-1 margin. Many African Americans also had doubts about such plans. Court-ordered busing met with strong opposition in a number of cities, most notably Boston. One angry white Bostonian warned: "You heard of the Hundred Years War? This will be the eternal war. It will be passed down from father to son."

TEACH OBJECTIVE 2

ALL LEVELS: Pair students and have each pair summarize decisions the Supreme Court made in the 1970s that limited the impact of busing and affirmative action. *(Pairs should note that in* Milliken *v.* Bradley *in 1974, the Court struck down a lower court's order that would have merged inner-city and suburban school districts in Detroit. In* University of California *v.* Bakke *in 1978, the Court ruled that affirmative action plans using quota systems are unconstitutional.)* Then have each student write dissenting opinions in the cases. Have volunteers read their opinions to the class.

English Language Learners, Cooperative Learning

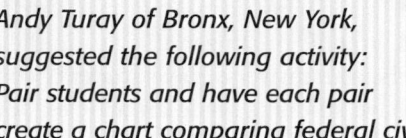 Teacher to Teacher

Andy Turay of Bronx, New York, suggested the following activity: Pair students and have each pair create a chart comparing federal civil rights policy during the Kennedy, Johnson, and Nixon administrations. Then have each pair write two paragraphs that assess the impact of federal policy. Have students present their charts and paragraphs to the class.

By the fall of 1974, violent protests against busing had erupted in Boston. Yet despite the risks, many African American parents believed that busing was necessary to achieve equal education opportunities. One African American woman told her two children that busing would make school difficult.

History Makers Speak

❝I'm afraid this isn't going to be an easy year for either of you. You're going to be called a lot of ugly names. You're going to be spat at, maybe pushed around some. But it's not the first time this has happened and it won't be the last. It's something we have to go through—something you have to go through—if this city is ever going to be integrated.❞

—Rachel Twymon, quoted in *Common Ground*, by J. Anthony Lukas

The busing controversy quieted down after the Supreme Court limited the use of busing as a means to achieve racial integration. In 1974 the Court ruled in *Milliken* v. *Bradley* to end a plan that promoted desegregation in Detroit by merging inner-city school districts with the city's suburban districts. The ruling was a severe blow to activists hoping to continue the process of desegregation in neighborhood schools. Justice Thurgood Marshall dissented from the Court ruling. He declared, "Unless our children begin to learn together, there is little hope that our people will ever learn to live together."

Affirmative action. Civil rights gains during the 1970s resulted from both public and private efforts. In order to uphold federal antidiscrimination laws and to end unfair labor practices, the Civil Rights Division of the Justice Department brought suits against corporations and labor unions. Many schools and businesses instituted **affirmative action** programs to compensate for previous discrimination. These programs gave preference to ethnic minorities and women in admission and hiring.

Many elected politicians did not support affirmative action. The Supreme Court nevertheless upheld the constitutionality of such programs in the 1971 case *Griggs* v. *Duke Power Co.* The Court ruled that tests given by the power company to decide on promotions had the effect of limiting the advancement of its African American workers. In the future, companies would have to explain why such tests were necessary. The case encouraged companies to create affirmative action programs.

Many white critics of affirmative action argued that it led to "reverse discrimination." In 1978 the Supreme Court handed down an important ruling affecting affirmative action. In **University of California v. Bakke**, it ruled that a white man, **Allan Bakke**, had been unfairly denied admission to medical school on the basis of **quotas**. This system reserved a fixed number of openings for certain groups of people. Although not ruling out all forms of affirmative action, the Court did strike down the quota system in regard to university admissions. Again, Justice Thurgood Marshall dissented from the Court's majority ruling. Marshall explained, "The dream of America as the great melting pot has not been realized for the Negro; because of his skin color he never even made it into the pot."

✔ **READING CHECK: Categorizing** What decisions did the Supreme Court make on busing and affirmative action? The Court approved a busing plan in Charlotte, North Carolina; *Griggs* v. *Duke Power Co.* upheld affirmative action, but *University of California* v. *Bakke* struck down a school quota system.

INTERPRETING THE VISUAL RECORD

Reaction to busing. In Boston, the court order to bus students outraged many white residents. *What clues can you gather from this image of an anti-busing rally in Boston in 1974 that support the argument that the busing issue was an emotional one for many Americans?*

VISUAL RECORD ANSWER

Students might suggest that the flag waving, signs calling for impeachment, and the woman's expression show that busing was an emotional issue.

SKILL-BUILDING STRATEGIES ANSWERS

(for p. 670)

Practicing the Skill

1. Answers will vary. Students should include the title and appropriate production information.

2. Answers will vary. Students should provide the main idea of the documentary as well as supporting evidence.

3. Answers will vary. Students should note the point of view of the documentary and identify any biases.

4. Answers will vary. Students should note the relation between their topic and the civil rights movement.

GRAPH ANSWER

(for p. 671)

high school increase: more than doubled; college increase: doubled

SECTION
REVIEW 4 ANSWERS

1. Define
- busing, p. 668
- affirmative action, p. 669
- quotas, p. 669

TEACH OBJECTIVE 3

ALL LEVELS: To help students understand the gains made by African Americans during the 1970s, copy the graphic organizer at right on the chalkboard, omitting the italicized answers. Have students complete the organizer. Also, have students write an article about African American successes during the 1970s. Ask volunteers to present their articles to the class. **English Language Learners**

Carl Stokes became the first African American to be elected mayor of Cleveland.

African Americans formed strong alliances and effective lobbies.

The number of African Americans enrolled in colleges and universities increased.

By the end of the 1970s more than 4,500 African Americans held elected office.

Gains Made by African Americans During the 1970s

African Americans played a crucial role in the 1976 presidential election.

The number of African American businesses rose.

The income gap between whites and African Americans narrowed.

2. Identify
- Ralph Abernathy, p. 667
- *University of California* v. *Bakke*, p. 668
- Allan Bakke, p. 669
- Carl Stokes, p. 670
- National Black Political Convention, p. 671

3. goals—integrating schools with busing, integrating universities and workplaces with affirmative action; white reactions—angry about busing, some initiated violent protests, some whites challenged affirmative action; outcomes—Supreme Court limited busing and prohibited the use of quotas to achieve racial equality. More African Americans went to college and found better jobs.

4a. They suffered from the loss of Martin Luther King Jr. Many white Americans began to work against some gains of the civil rights movement.

b. limited busing—by ending merging of Detroit's school districts; affirmative action—by outlawing the use of quotas.

c. Students should support their hypotheses with specific details.

5. Answers will vary. The movement integrated some schools, universities, and workplaces. More African Americans were getting college educations, finding better jobs, voting, and holding elected offices. However, 31 percent still lived below the poverty line.

Skill-Building Strategies

Using Multimedia Resources

Multimedia resources are sources of information such as television documentaries and CD–ROMs that incorporate words, sounds, and images in a single package. They are among the newest and most interesting research tools available to students. Multimedia resources often include ideas and data on historical topics from a variety of primary and secondary sources. The audiovisual formats they use to present this information can be very interesting.

Multimedia resources must be studied and analyzed carefully. The materials that make up multimedia resources—databases, motion pictures, photographs, recordings, and written documents, for example—are distinct types of historical sources that should always be examined for accuracy and bias. It is also important to evaluate the manner in which a multimedia resource selects, presents, and discusses these materials.

How to Use a Multimedia Resource

1. **Find an appropriate resource.** Use your school or local public library to find a multimedia resource on the topic you wish to research. Once you have located an appropriate resource, take note of its title, publication date, and the people or organization that produced it.
2. **Study the resource carefully.** Study the resource carefully, identifying any main ideas and the specific means it uses to convey information. If you are using a CD–ROM, make sure to explore a variety of the materials it offers.
3. **Evaluate the resource.** Once you have examined the resource thoroughly, identify any factual inaccuracies and assess the manner in which it explains any differing points of view. Then evaluate any general biases that the resource displays in its selection, presentation, and discussion of historical evidence.
4. **Put the information to use.** Compare the resource with other materials that you find while researching your topic. Then use the results of your analysis to form generalizations and draw conclusions.

Applying the Skill

Use your school or local public library to find a videotape of a film or television documentary about the civil rights movement. Then view the documentary and write a report that summarizes its main ideas and evaluates it.

Practicing the Skill

Answer the following questions.
1. What is the title of the documentary you found? Who produced it? When was it produced?
2. What main ideas does the documentary convey? What types of evidence does it provide to convey these ideas?
3. How does the documentary handle any differing points of view about the civil rights movement? What biases, if any, does the documentary display?
4. How does the documentary contribute to your understanding of the civil rights movement?

Successes of the Movement

The civil rights movement suffered setbacks during the 1970s. African Americans, however, did make some advances during this period. For example, **Carl Stokes** was elected mayor of Cleveland. He became the first African American to be elected mayor of a major U.S. city. Geraldine Williams, the campaign secretary who helped Stokes win his bid for office, remembered the election.

History Makers Speak

❝Definitely there was a connection with the civil rights movement. We got blacks to register, to vote, to take part in government. We convinced them that if you don't speak out and ask for things, you're never going to get them. You can't just sit there. We taught them that their vote does mean something, that it counts.❞

—Geraldine Williams, quoted in *Voices of Freedom*, by Henry Hampton and Steve Fayer

REVIEW

Have students complete the **Section 4 Review** on p. 671.

ASSESS

Have students complete **Daily Quiz 22.4**. As **Alternative Assessment**, you may want to use the chart or the dissenting opinions in this section's lessons.

RETEACH

Have students complete **Main Idea Activity for English Language Learners and Special-Needs Students 22.4**. Then ask each student to list the key terms and key people in Section 4. Create a comprehensive list on the chalkboard and have each

student use the list to create an annotated time line that includes the events and people discussed in the section. Display students' time lines around the classroom. **English Language Learners**

EXTEND

Ask students to conduct research on an African American mayor of a large city who was elected during the 1970s or 1980s. *(Examples include Tom Bradley, Carl Stokes, and Harold Washington.)* Have each student write a report about the mayor's platform, term of office, whether the mayor received political support from a coalition of white and black Americans, and the mayor's major achievements while in office. **Block Scheduling**

To ensure that African Americans would continue to gain political influence, activists met in Gary, Indiana, in 1972 for the **National Black Political Convention**. Some 2,700 delegates and another 4,000 people attended the convention.

African American leaders also worked hard to get out the vote. Although just 58.5 percent of eligible black voters were registered in 1976, African Americans played a crucial role in the presidential election that year. Their more than 6.5 million votes for Democrat Jimmy Carter helped him win the popular vote by fewer than 2 million votes. By the end of the 1970s, more than 4,500 African Americans held elected office—three times the number in 1969. The roster of elected black officials in 1978 included 16 members of the House of Representatives.

African Americans also experienced some economic gains. The number of African American–owned businesses rose from 163,073 in 1969 to 231,195 in 1977. However, some 31 percent of African Americans still lived below the poverty line. Increased enrollment in colleges and universities ensured that more African Americans would gain better-paying jobs. By 1976 the number of African American college students stood at more than 800,000—four times higher than it had been in 1964.

African American Education, 1960–1975

Sources: *Historical Statistics of the United States; Statistical Abstract of the United States: 1997*

Interpreting Graphs As the civil rights movement progressed, the number of African Americans who finished high school and went on to college increased dramatically.

? Skills Assessment By how much did the percentage of the African American population with a high school diploma increase from 1960 to 1975? By how much did the percentage of those with a college degree increase?

✔ **READING CHECK: Summarizing** How did the increased participation of African American voters affect the United States? helped elect Carter in 1976 and brought more diversity to Congress

---

SECTION 4 REVIEW

1. Define and explain:
busing
affirmative action
quotas

2. Identify and explain:
Ralph Abernathy
University of California v. Bakke
Allan Bakke
Carl Stokes
National Black Political Convention

3. Sequencing Copy the flowchart below. Use it to explain changing strategies and goals within the post-1968 civil rights movement, white reactions to those goals, and outcomes.

Goals after 1968

White Reactions

Outcomes

4. Finding the Main Idea
a. Why did many African American organizations experience difficulties during the 1970s?
b. How and why did the Supreme Court limit busing and affirmative action?
c. How might the civil rights movement have evolved differently in the 1970s if Martin Luther King Jr. had lived?

5. Writing and Critical Thinking
Evaluating Create a report card for the civil rights movement by the mid-1970s.
Consider:
• the political successes of the movement
• economic and educational advances for African Americans
• civil rights goals left unfinished

Homework Practice Online
keyword: SE3 HP22

THE CIVIL RIGHTS MOVEMENT **671**

Creating a Time Line
Each event should have an explanation and the correct date.

Writing a Summary
See the Reading Checks in each section for main ideas.

Identifying People and Ideas
1. civil rights leader who advocated nonviolent protest

2. people who rode buses through the South to force integration of public facilities on the interstates

3. prohibited discrimination in employment and public facilities

4. summer of 1964, during which civil rights workers tried to register African Americans in Mississippi to vote

5. MFDP delegate who lost her job and house when she registered to vote

6. African American religious sect based on some aspects of Islam

7. African American activist who originated the Black Power movement

8. reported that white racism was causing tensions that led to riots

9. giving preference to ethnic minorities and women in hiring and school admission

TECHNOLOGY

▶ Chapter 22 Test Generator (on the One-Stop Planner)
▶ Global Skill Builder CD–ROM
▶ HRW Go site

REINFORCEMENT, REVIEW, AND ASSESSMENT

▶ Chapter 22 Review, pp. 672–73
▶ Chapter 22 Tutorial for Students, Parents, Mentors, and Peers

▶ Chapter 22 Test (Form A or B)
▶ Portfolio Activities and Alternative Assessment Handbook, Chapter 22
▶ Chapter 22 Test for English Language Learners and Special-Needs Students

REVIEW

Have students complete the **Chapter 22 Review** on pp. 672–73.

ASSESS

Use one of the chapter tests to assess students' understanding of the content. For **Alternative Assessment**, see the **Portfolio Activities and Alternative Assessment Handbook.**

10. Supreme Court decision making quotas for college admission unconstitutional

Understanding Main Ideas

1. Sit-ins, Freedom Rides, protests in Albany and Birmingham, and the March on Washington

2. White activists were involved in the drive.

3. It gave the federal government the power to enforce voting rights for African Americans.

4. black separatism; encourage self-reliance

5. Black separatism caused a lack of unity, and the SCLC turned its attention to economic and educational discrimination.

Reviewing Themes

1. It faced the same threats and violence as in the South but also a reluctance by the federal government to support civil rights in large northern cities.

2. It supported school desegregation but struck down racial quotas in university admissions.

3. They favored the growth of African American businesses and political power.

Thinking Critically

1. integrating public areas, because it interfered with business and because the federal government eventually took steps to protect protesters from violence

CHAPTER 22 Review

Creating a Time Line

Copy the time line below onto a sheet of paper. Complete the time line by filling in the events and dates from the chapter that you think were most significant. Pick three events and explain why you think they were significant.

| 1960 | 1965 | 1970 | 1975 |

Writing a Summary

Using standard grammar, spelling, sentence structure, and punctuation, write an overview of events in the chapter.

Identifying People and Ideas

Identify the following terms or individuals and explain their significance.

1. Martin Luther King Jr.
2. Freedom Riders
3. Civil Rights Act of 1964
4. Freedom Summer
5. Fannie Lou Hamer
6. Nation of Islam
7. Stokely Carmichael
8. Kerner Commission
9. affirmative action
10. *University of California* v. *Bakke*

Understanding Main Ideas

SECTION 1 *(pp. 650–655)*
1. What events led to the passage of the Civil Rights Act of 1964?

SECTION 2 *(pp. 656–660)*
2. How did Freedom Summer differ from earlier voter registration drives?
3. Why did the Voting Rights Act mark a major turning point in the civil rights struggle?

SECTION 3 *(pp. 661–666)*
4. What were the goals of the black nationalists?

SECTION 4 *(pp. 667–671)*
5. How did the civil rights movement change in the late 1960s and early 1970s?

Reviewing Themes

1. **Citizenship** What difficulties did the SCLC face when it attempted to bring the civil rights struggle to northern cities?
2. **Constitutional Heritage** What effect did Supreme Court rulings have on the civil rights movement?
3. **Economics** What type of economic growth did black nationalists favor?

Thinking Critically

1. **Evaluating** In what circumstances was nonviolent protest most effective? Why?
2. **Analyzing Information** What contributions did Martin Luther King Jr. and Malcom X make to the civil rights movement?
3. **Identifying Points of View** Why did SNCC workers such as Stokely Carmichael abandon nonviolent protest?
4. **Summarizing** What actions did African Americans take in the 1960s and early 1970s to expand economic opportunities and political rights?
5. **Supporting a Point of View** Would you have supported the goal of black nationalism at the 1972 National Black Political Convention? Why or why not?

Writing About History

Analyzing Information Copy the following chart and use it to write an essay that explains the benefits and drawbacks of Black Power for the civil rights movement.

Benefits	Drawbacks

RETEACH

Organize students into triads. Have each triad create an annotated time line of important events or developments in the civil rights struggle from the Montgomery Bus Boycott in 1958 through the end of the 1970s. Display students' time lines around the classroom.

English Language Learners, Cooperative Learning

EXTEND

Have each student conduct research on major businesses in the United States owned or controlled by African Americans. Have students represent their findings in a collage.

Block Scheduling

Building Social Studies Skills

Interpreting Maps

Study the map below. Then use it to help answer the questions that follow.

The Freedom Rides in 1961

→ CORE route
→ SNCC route
☆ Arrests
✦ Violence

PA
OH
IN
MD
DE
Washington, D.C.
May 4
WV
Richmond
75°W
KY
VA
Greensboro
MO
Nashville
Charlotte NC
May 8
35°N
TN
Rock Hill
May 9
AR
Memphis
SC
Winnsboro
May 10
Atlanta
AL
Augusta
Birmingham
May 14
Anniston
May 14
GA
May 17
Meridian Selma
ATLANTIC
OCEAN
Montgomery
May 20
Jackson
May 24
Albany
30°N
LA
New
Orleans
Intended
destination
FL
80°W
90°W
0 100 200 Miles
Gulf of Mexico
0 100 200 Kilometers
Albers Equal-Area Projection
85°W

1. What is the longest period of time Freedom Riders experienced between arrests or acts of violence?
   a. 2 days
   b. 3 days
   c. 4 days
   d. 5 days

2. How were the Freedom Rides an extension of earlier civil rights efforts?

Interpreting the Visual Record

Study the photograph below of workers dismantling Resurrection City after the failure of the Poor People's Campaign in 1968. Then answer the questions that follow.

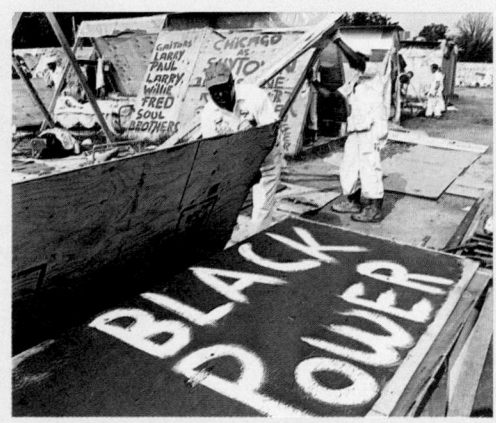

3. Which of these captions would make the most fitting title for the photograph?
   a. Black Power Resurrected
   b. African Americans in Chicago
   c. Dismantling a Movement
   d. African Americans Oppose Black Power

4. Explain the main reasons for a decline in effectiveness of the civil rights movement after 1968.

Alternative Assessment

Building Your Portfolio

U.S. HISTORY

Culture

Imagine that you are a museum curator creating an exhibit on the civil rights movement from the 1700s to the present. As part of your exhibit, create an illustrated time line that displays important civil rights events from the 1700s to 1975. Write captions for the images and then create five questions for museum visitors (other students) to answer about the time line.

⬛ internet connect

Internet Activity: go.hrw.com
KEYWORD: SE3 AN22

Choose a topic on the civil rights movement to:
- create a poster comparing the beliefs and goals of Malcolm X and Martin Luther King Jr.
- learn about the movement to end apartheid in South Africa.
- create a newspaper reporting on the main events of the movement in 1963.

go.hrw.com

2. King—nonviolent protests led to desegregation and the Civil Rights Act; Malcom X—encouraged African Americans to take pride in their racial identity and heritage

3. Some activists believed that nonviolent protests were not working fast enough. Others questioned the move for integration. Many were angered that the deaths of white activists provoked more outrage than did those of African Americans.

4. political—protests and voter registration drives in the South, the March on Washington, Black Power movement; economic—protests against housing discrimination, Poor People's Campaign, affirmative action and school desegregation

5. Students should explain their choices.

Writing
Answers will vary. Students should clearly identify the reasons for their positions.

Building Social Studies Skills
1. c

2. Answers will vary. Students might suggest that they were an extension of the Montgomery bus boycott, as well as sit-ins.

3. c

4. Answers will vary. Students might suggest that the death of Martin Luther King Jr. and the fragmentation of the movement led to its decline.

Struggles for Change

CHAPTER RESOURCE MANAGER

Objectives	Pacing Guide	Reproducible Resources
SECTION 1 **Women's Rights** pp. 676–81 ★ Describe what *The Feminine Mystique* revealed about women, and discuss how readers responded to it. ★ Explain how the federal government tried to assist working women in the early 1960s. ★ Relate what tactics the leaders of the women's movement used. ★ Identify the gains and setbacks the women's movement experienced during the 1970s.	**Regular** 2 days **Block Scheduling** 1 day *Block Scheduling Handbook with Team Teaching Strategies, pp. 133–38*	**RS** Guided Reading Strategy 23.1 **RS** Graphic Organizer Activity 23: Protesting the Status Quo
SECTION 2 **The Chicano Movement** pp. 682–88 ★ Discuss why La Huelga was important to Mexican Americans throughout the country. ★ Explain how conflicts over land rights and education motivated Mexican Americans to protest. ★ Describe how aggressive activists shaped the Chicano movement. ★ Analyze how the Chicano movement changed the lives of Mexican Americans.	**Regular** 2 days **Block Scheduling** 1 day *Block Scheduling Handbook with Team Teaching Strategies, pp. 133–38*	**RS** Guided Reading Strategy 23.2 **E** Creative Teaching Strategy: Choosing and Acting Lesson **E** Hands-On History Activity: Write a Biography
SECTION 3 **More Groups Mobilize** pp. 689–93 ★ Describe what Red Power movement activists demanded, and discuss how successful they were. ★ Explain how Americans with disabilities gained public support for their causes. ★ Identify the issues that activists for senior citizens and children addressed.	**Regular** 1 day **Block Scheduling** .5 day *Block Scheduling Handbook with Team Teaching Strategies, pp. 133–38*	**RS** Guided Reading Strategy 23.3 **PS** Primary Source Reading 23: American Indian Activism Begins **PS** Biography Reading 23: Marian Wright Edelman
SECTION 4 **A Cultural Revolution** pp. 694–99 ★ Explain why protests developed on American college campuses. ★ Describe the problems that weakened the counterculture. ★ Explain how doubts about American society led to new movements in religion and the arts. ★ Analyze how musical styles reflected the social changes of the era.	**Regular** 1 day **Block Scheduling** .5 day *Block Scheduling Handbook with Team Teaching Strategies, pp. 133–38*	**RS** Guided Reading Strategy 23.4 **IC** Literature Reading 23: High Style **SM** Geography Activity 23: The Environment Under Assault

Chapter Resource Key

PS	Primary Sources	**REV** Review	Video
RS	Reading Support	**ELL** Reinforcement and English Language Learners	Internet
IC	Interdisciplinary Connections		Holt Presentation Maker Using Microsoft® PowerPoint®
E	Enrichment	Transparencies	
SM	Skills Mastery	CD-ROM	
A	Assessment	Music	

One-Stop Planner CD-ROM

See the *One-Stop Planner* for a complete list of additional resources for students and teachers.

One-Stop Planner CD–ROM

It's easy to plan lessons, select resources, and print out materials for your students when you use the **One-Stop Planner CD–ROM with Test Generator.**

Technology Resources

 One-Stop Planner, Lesson 23.1

 The American Nation Video Program Segment: The Women's Rights Movement; Teacher's Guide, pp. 209–10

 Holt Researcher: American History CD–ROM

 Homework Practice Online

 One-Stop Planner, Lesson 23.2

 The American Nation Video Program Segment: César Chávez; Teacher's Guide, pp. 167–68

 CNN Presents America: Yesterday and Today, Modern Times Segment: Women and Sports

 Holt Researcher: American History CD–ROM

 Homework Practice Online

 HRW Go site

 One-Stop Planner, Lesson 23.3

 Holt Researcher: American History CD–ROM

Homework Practice Online

 One-Stop Planner, Lesson 23.4

 American Music Selection 25: "Blowin' in the Wind"

 Holt Researcher: American History CD–ROM

Homework Practice Online

Reinforcement, Review, and Assessment

REV Section 1 Review, p. 681
A Daily Quiz 23.1
ELL Main Idea Activity 23.1
ELL English Audio Summary 23.1
ELL Spanish Audio Summary 23.1

REV Section 2 Review, p. 688
A Daily Quiz 23.2
ELL Main Idea Activity 23.2
ELL English Audio Summary 23.2
ELL Spanish Audio Summary 23.2

REV Section 3 Review, p. 693
A Daily Quiz 23.3
ELL Main Idea Activity 23.3
ELL English Audio Summary 23.3
ELL Spanish Audio Summary 23.3

REV Section 4 Review, p. 699
A Daily Quiz 23.4
ELL Main Idea Activity 23.4
ELL English Audio Summary 23.4
ELL Spanish Audio Summary 23.4

⧉ internet connect

HRW ONLINE RESOURCES
GO TO: go.hrw.com
Then type in a keyword.

TEACHER HOME PAGE
KEYWORD: SE3 Teacher

CHAPTER INTERNET ACTIVITIES
KEYWORD: SE3 AN23
Choose an activity to:
• learn about issues in the women's rights movement.
• create a brochure on César Chávez and the United Farm Workers.
• explore the cultural revolution in the arts and music.

CHAPTER ENRICHMENT LINKS
KEYWORD: SE3 CH23

ONLINE ASSESSMENT
Homework Practice
KEYWORD: SE3 HP23

Standardized Test Prep
KEYWORD: SE3 STP23

Rubrics
KEYWORD: SS Rubrics

ONLINE MAPS, CHARTS, AND GRAPHS
KEYWORD: SE3 MCG
• Women in the Professions

CONTENT UPDATES
KEYWORD: SS Content Updates

HOLT PRESENTATION MAKER
KEYWORD: SE3 PPT23

ONLINE READING SUPPORT
KEYWORD: SS Strategies

CURRENT EVENTS
KEYWORD: S3 Current Events

Meeting Individual Needs

Ability Levels

Level 1 Basic-level activities designed for all students encountering new material

Level 2 Intermediate-level activities designed for average students

Level 3 Challenging activities designed for honors and gifted-and-talented students

English Language Learners Activities that address the needs of students with Limited English Proficiency

Chapter Review and Assessment

 Global Skill Builder CD–ROM

HRW Go site

REV **Chapter 23 Tutorial for Students, Parents, Mentors, and Peers**

REV **Chapter 23 Review, pp. 700–01**

Chapter 23 Test Generator (on the One-Stop Planner)

A **Chapter 23 Test (Form A or B)**

A **Alternative Assessment Handbook**

A **Chapter 23 Test for English Language Learners and Special-Needs Students**

Build on What You Know

Ask students to answer the following questions.

Why might the African American civil rights movement have inspired other groups to work for civil rights?

Consider:

• the significance of a successful example

• the discrimination that other groups faced

How might women, Mexican Americans, American Indians, and others have begun to demand fair treatment?

Consider:

• the methods used by the African American civil rights movement

• the importance of government action and support

---

exploring the time line

AMERICAN EVENTS

internet connect

TOPIC: Women's Rights Movement
GO TO: go.hrw.com
KEYWORD: SE3 AN23

Have students access the Internet through the HRW Go site to conduct research on the history of the women's rights movement. Ask each student to make a graphic organizer comparing and contrasting issues from the women's rights movement in 1848 and in the 1960s. Then ask students to write summary statements about the evolution of the women's rights movement.

CHAPTER 23

1963–1975

Struggles for Change

Valentina V. Tereshkova

Mexican American migrant workers

1963
Science and Technology
Soviet cosmonaut Valentina V. Tereshkova becomes the first woman in space.

1963
Politics
Congress passes the Equal Pay Act.

1965
Business and Finance
Migrant farmworkers in California begin a strike against grape growers.

1963 — **1965** — **1967**

1964
The Arts
The Beatles perform on *The Ed Sullivan Show* to a record television audience.

1964
Daily Life
The Ford Motor Company introduces the Mustang, which immediately becomes one of the nation's most popular car models.

1966
Politics
The National Organization for Women (NOW) is founded.

A Ford Mustang

The Beatles

Build on What You Know

The prosperity that followed World War II brought many changes to American society. A youth rebellion began in the 1950s with the beats and rock 'n' roll. African Americans continued to fight for equal rights. In this chapter you will learn how women, Mexican Americans, American Indians, and others began to demand fair treatment. You will also learn that during the 1960s some Americans challenged the beliefs and traditions of older generations. The result was a cultural revolution that eventually affected the entire nation.

What's Your Opinion?

To help students create their Themes Journal entries, provide the following examples of appropriate agree/disagree statements.

Constitutional Heritage

Agree Temperance advocates perceived drinking as a national crisis, although many modern-day historians disagree with that assessment.

Disagree Many groups have attempted to amend the Constitution; some were inspired by a national crisis and some were inspired by a political goal.

Economics

Agree As a whole, the prosperous 1920s were not marked by political protest.

Disagree The struggle for African American civil rights intensified during a period of relative economic prosperity.

Culture

Agree During the Great Depression, Americans watched motion pictures to forget their problems.

Disagree Harriet Beecher Stowe's novel *Uncle Tom's Cabin* helped galvanize the antislavery movement in the North during the 1850s.

THE MOTION PICTURE CODE AND RATING PROGRAM
a system of self-regulation

MOTION PICTURE ASSOCIATION OF AMERICA

Symbol for the MPAA rating system

**1968
The Arts**
The Motion Picture Association of America adopts a film rating system.

**1968
Daily Life**
Some 100 people protest the Miss America Pageant in Atlantic City, New Jersey.

**1968
Politics**
The American Indian Movement is organized.

**1970
Science and Technology**
Marine biologist Sylvia Earle Mead and five other female scientists spend two weeks underwater without surfacing.

The first issue of Ms. magazine

**1972
Business and Finance**
The first issue of *Ms.* magazine sells 250,000 copies.

**1972
Politics**
The Equal Rights Amendment is sent to the states for ratification after its approval by Congress.

**1974
Daily Life**
Engineer Art Fry invents Post-It Notes.

1969	1971	1973	1975

**1969
World Events**
Golda Meir becomes the prime minister of Israel.

**1971
Business and Finance**
Community organizers in East Los Angeles work with the United Auto Workers to create the East Los Angeles Community Union.

**1975
Politics**
Congress passes the Education for All Handicapped Children Act.

Golda Meir

An instructor assists a child learning to walk with leg braces.

What's Your Opinion?

Themes Journal *Do you agree or disagree with the following statements? Support your point of view in your journal.*

Constitutional Heritage Amending the Constitution is a serious matter that should only be undertaken in the face of a national crisis.

Economics A rising standard of living makes young people so satisfied that political protests decrease.

Culture Music, fashion, and art are merely for pleasure and entertainment and have little social or political significance.

GLOBAL EVENTS

PEOPLE IN HISTORY

1963 ■ Valentina V. Tereshkova. Valentina V. Tereshkova was born in the Soviet Union in 1937, the daughter of a laborer on a collective farm. As an adult, Tereshkova worked in a factory. In her free time she learned to parachute with a local aviation club. This experience eventually led to her selection for the cosmonaut training program. In 1963 she became the first woman in space. However, after her flight she never ventured into space again, but spent much of her time on Communist Party political activities.

ACTIVITY: Tell students to imagine that they are American journalists who have a strong interest in women's achievements and in the space race between the United States and the Soviet Union. Have each student write a short article about Valentina V. Tereshkova's spaceflight and the event's larger significance. Alternately, have each student write several newspaper headlines announcing the flight and its significance.

📻 LET'S GET STARTED!

Have students read the quotation by Betty Friedan on this page. Then ask them to respond to the quotation in writing, explaining how the feelings expressed in the quotation might have sparked the modern-day women's movement. Have volunteers share their responses. Then tell students that in Section 1 they will learn about how women pursued equal rights in the 1960s and 1970s.

SECTION ① RESOURCES

REPRODUCIBLE
- Guided Reading Strategy 23.1
- Graphic Organizer Activity 23: Protesting the Status Quo

TECHNOLOGY
- One-Stop Planner, Lesson 23.1
- The American Nation Video Program Segment: The Women's Rights Movement; Teacher's Guide, pp. 209–10
- Holt Researcher: American History CD–ROM
- Homework Practice Online

REINFORCEMENT, REVIEW, AND ASSESSMENT
- Section 1 Review, p. 681
- Daily Quiz 23.1
- Main Idea Activity 23.1
- English Audio Summary 23.1
- Spanish Audio Summary 23.1

SECTION ①

READ TO DISCOVER

1. What influence did *The Feminine Mystique* have on the women's movement?
2. How did the federal government try to assist working women in the early 1960s?
3. What tactics did leaders of the women's movement use?
4. What gains and setbacks did the women's movement experience during the 1970s?

IDENTIFY

Betty Friedan
Equal Pay Act
National Organization for Women
Gloria Steinem
National Women's Political Caucus
Education Amendments Act
Phyllis Schlafly
Bella Abzug
Shirley Chisholm

WHY IT MATTERS TODAY

Women continue to play important roles in the U.S. economy. Use **CNNfyi.com** or other **current events** sources to research jobs where more women have begun working in recent years. Record your findings in your journal.

CNNfyi.com

Women's Rights

EYEWITNESSES TO History

"*I guess I've been pretty much influenced by the Women's Movement because of the people I work with. . . . A lot of them were in that movement, so I've become more aware of it that way. I've just become much more aware of being a woman and the rights a woman should have. . . . Before, what I knew about the movement was really limited to just what I saw—people in demonstrations and the type of women who were professionals and their side of things.*"

—Cathy Tuley, quoted in *Nobody Speaks for Me!*, by Nancy Seifer

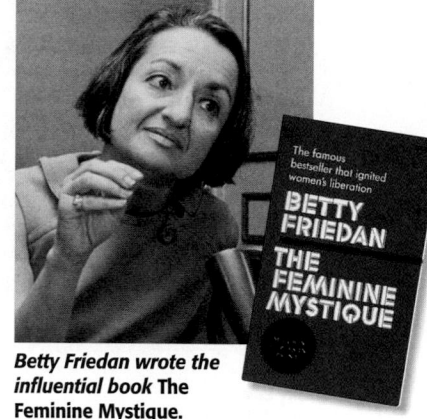
Betty Friedan wrote the influential book **The Feminine Mystique.**

Cathy Tuley, a hospital clerical worker, discussed her perceptions of the women's movement. Tuley's experiences mirrored those of many other women who entered the workforce during the 1960s and 1970s.

A Revived Women's Movement

One of the lasting effects of the 1960s was a change in the traditional roles of women. After years of inaction, the women's movement experienced a widespread revival, sparked in part by the work of author **Betty Friedan**.

In 1957 Friedan conducted a survey of women who, like herself, had graduated from Smith College 15 years earlier. She hoped to dispute the popular notion that higher education was harmful to women. To Friedan's surprise, the women who responded to her questionnaire expressed dissatisfaction with their lives. Almost all the women whom Friedan surveyed were full-time homemakers. Many found their lives unfulfilling. In her 1963 book, *The Feminine Mystique*, Friedan concluded that many women felt trapped by the "comfortable concentration camp" of domestic life.

History Makers Speak

"*The problem lay buried, unspoken, for many years in the minds of American women. It was a strange stirring, a sense of dissatisfaction, a yearning that women suffered in the middle of the twentieth century in the United States. Each suburban wife struggled with it alone. As she made the beds, shopped for groceries, matched slipcover material, ate peanut butter sandwiches with her children, chauffeured Cub Scouts and Brownies . . . she was afraid to ask even of herself the silent question—'Is this all?'*"

—Betty Friedan, *The Feminine Mystique*

By the end of the decade *The Feminine Mystique* had sold more than 1 million copies. Inspired by its message, many women began to examine their lives. Seeking change, they demanded increased opportunities and fair treatment in the workplace.

✔ **READING CHECK: Summarizing** What did *The Feminine Mystique* reveal about women, and how did readers respond to it? Women felt dissatisfied with their lives. Some who read the book were inspired to seek career opportunities and fair treatment in the workplace.

Teacher to Teacher

Jenifer Rowray of Runnells, Iowa, suggested the following activity: Organize students into small groups and have them pick one year between 1963 and 1975. Ask each group to conduct research on events that took place during its chosen year. Tell students to determine the short- and long-term effects of these events. Then have each group prepare a short oral report on the year. To create a living time line, ask students to deliver their reports in chronological order.

TEACH OBJECTIVE 1

ALL LEVELS: Conduct a brief discussion on what *The Feminine Mystique* revealed about women and how readers responded to it. *(Students might answer that many women, particularly homemakers, felt dissatisfied with their lives. Inspired by the book, many women began to demand increased opportunities and fair treatment in the workplace.)* Then pair students and ask each pair to write a paragraph summarizing why many American women were dissatisfied. Have volunteers share their paragraphs with the class.
English Language Learners, Cooperative Learning

Helping Women at Work

Most of the women polled by Betty Friedan were homemakers. However, the number of women in the workplace had grown dramatically in the years before her book was published. The number of working women rose from 25 percent in 1940 to 35 percent in 1960. By 1963 almost 25 million working women made up more than one third of the American labor force. Yet female workers received lower wages than men did. In 1960, for example, women who worked full-time earned 40 percent less than working men. Women typically held service jobs that paid poorly, but in many cases they received lower wages even when they did the same work as men. As one business executive confessed, "We pay [women] less because we can get them for less."

Kennedy responds. The Kennedy administration hired few women but did not ignore the problems that working women faced. President Kennedy issued an executive order requiring that civil-service hiring occur "solely on the basis of ability to meet the requirements of the position, and without regard to sex." His administration also backed a new bill that would make it illegal for employers to pay female workers less than male workers for the same job. Congress approved this **Equal Pay Act**, which Kennedy signed in June 1963. The act had a limited impact, however. Its provisions did not cover women in agricultural, professional, or service industries—about two thirds of working women. Nevertheless, the law served as an important first step toward equality in the workplace. In the decade following its passage, 171,000 workers used the law to win $84 million in back pay.

Kennedy also created the President's Commission on the Status of Women (PCSW) and appointed former first lady Eleanor Roosevelt as its chairperson. Kennedy authorized the PCSW to investigate the lives of American women. Completed in October 1963, the commission's report noted that female workers continued to experience discrimination in the workplace despite their increasing numbers. The report set new goals for the treatment of working women and called for "equal opportunity in hiring, training, and promotion."

Title VII. Female workers received additional and unexpected assistance from the federal government in 1964. That year Congress debated legislation intended to protect the civil rights of African Americans. Representative Howard Smith of Virginia proposed adding a clause to the bill that would protect women from discrimination. Smith opposed the civil rights bill and actually hoped that his amendment would weaken its chances of passing.

In June 1963 President John F. Kennedy signed the Equal Pay Act, which required that women receive equal pay for equal work.

Occupations of Women, 1960–1970

Source: *Historical Statistics of the United States*

Legend:
- Manual labor, service
- Farming
- White collar
- Unknown

1960 — Total 22.3 (1.3, 0.4, 8.9, 11.7)
1970 — Total 30.3 (0.06, 0.2, 11.6, 18.4)

Interpreting Graphs The number of working women increased from 1960 to 1970.

? Skills Assessment By how much did the number of women working in white-collar professions increase?

GOVERNMENT

The President's Commission on the Status of Women.
President Kennedy gained a significant political advantage when he created the President's Commission on the Status of Women. The creation of the group pleased female voters—citizens who might support Kennedy in future elections. In addition, forming the commission allowed Kennedy to appear to support women's rights without taking a stand on any specific issues. Kennedy's motivations were not purely political, however. He understood that women often experienced discrimination in the workplace. A 1957 study had recommended that the Department of Labor study the underuse of female workers.

CRITICAL THINKING Why might women have been an underused source of labor?

ANSWER: Students might suggest that the limited conception of women's roles barred women from certain occupations.

GRAPH ANSWER
by 6.7 million

LEVEL 1: Pair students and ask each pair to list the ways that the federal government tried to assist work-ing women in the early 1960s. *(Pairs should list the Equal Pay Act, the President's Commission on the Status of Women, Title VII, and the Equal Employment Opportunity Commission.)* Then have each pair rank these efforts from most important to least important, writing paragraphs to present and justify its selections. Ask students to share their rankings with the class. Conduct a discussion on their selections.
English Language Learners, Cooperative Learning

LEVEL 2: Tell students to imagine that it is 1966 and that they are presidential advisers. Have each student write a short memo to the president describing the government's efforts to assist working women in the early 1960s and suggesting a future course of action. *(See the Level 1 lesson for the correct efforts.)* Have volunteers read their memos to the class.

LEVEL 3: Conduct a brief discussion on the ways that the fed-eral government tried to assist working women in the early 1960s. *(See the Level 1 lesson for the correct efforts.)* Then orga-nize students into two large groups—one that supports further government action on women's rights and one that opposes it. Give students time to prepare their arguments and then conduct a debate on the topic. Remind students that their arguments should be grounded in fact and analysis rather than personal opinion. **Cooperative Learning**

The EEOC works to prevent discrimination in employment.

Analyzing Primary Sources

Identifying Bias What reason does this speaker give for the EEOC's failure to respond to women's needs? Most Americans were not aware of discrimination against women.

Buttons and patches like these served as outward signs of women's determination to win equality with men.

Female members of Congress seized the opportunity. Representative Martha Griffiths of Michigan declared, "A vote against this amendment today by a . . . man is a vote against his wife, or his widow, or his daughter, or his sister." Congress approved the Smith amendment, and the bill passed. As a result, Title VII of the Civil Rights Act of 1964 outlawed sexual discrimi-nation in employment. The act also created the Equal Employment Opportunity Commission (EEOC). This federal agency is charged with ensuring that employers followed the provisions of Title VII.

✔ **READING CHECK: Identifying Cause and Effect** How did Smith's opposition to a civil rights bill lead to an opportunity for women's rights? He added a clause to protect women, hoping that it would weaken the bill's chances.

Heightened Activism

Women quickly discovered that many government officials were not interested in fighting gender discrimination. Herman Edelsberg, director of the EEOC, called Title VII "a fluke." Sonia Pressman, an attorney for the EEOC, later explained why the agency did not respond to women's needs.

 "We had an agency with a mandate [order] to prohibit sex discrimination . . . in a country that was not conscious of the fact that women were the victims of discrimination. After all, while the creation of the EEOC was in direct response to the movement for black rights in this country, there had been no similar movement immediately prior to 1965 for women's rights."

—Sonia Pressman, quoted in *Faces of Feminism*, by Sheila Tobias

NOW. In June 1966 a group of women attending a conference on women's status met in Betty Friedan's hotel room to discuss their frustration. Some wanted to create an organization to lobby for women's rights. Instead, the group decided to present a resolution condemning the EEOC. Participant Pauli Murray recalled, "I left Betty Friedan's room that night thoroughly discouraged; it seemed to me that we had fumbled a major opportunity to begin mobilizing [organizing] women nationally to press for their civil rights."

The next day, the conference rejected the resolution. During lunch these women decided to form a women's rights group. The **National Organization for Women** (NOW) was the result. NOW claimed some 1,000 members within its first year in existence. The organization lobbied, or tried to influence, elected officials to ensure social and economic equality for women.

A new generation. Some women rejected NOW's moderate approach to polit-ical change. Critic Marlene Dixon maintained that NOW would secure "limited and elitist [exclusive] day-care programs . . . [and] an effective end to job discrimination at least on the elite level." Dixon argued that "these programs give the illusion of suc-cess, while in fact assuring the destruction of any hope for women's liberation."

Dixon voiced the opinion of a new generation of female activists. Many of these women had participated in other social movements, such as the struggle for civil rights. They realized that they faced just as much gender discrimination in these movements as they did in mainstream society. Mary King and Casey Hayden were volunteers for the Student Nonviolent Coordinating Committee (SNCC).

TEACH OBJECTIVE 3

LEVEL 1: Ask students to relate what tactics the leaders of the women's movement used. *(Students should indicate that Betty Friedan and others founded the National Organization for Women (NOW), which pushed for equal rights for women. In addition, other groups encouraged women to run for political office.)* Then pair students and tell them to imagine that it is 1967 and that they are women preparing to form an organization supporting women's rights. Have each pair develop a list of goals and methods for its organization. Ask volunteers to share their lists with the class. Conduct a discussion on the goals and methods.
English Language Learners, Cooperative Learning

LEVELS 2 AND 3: Organize students into triads. Tell them to imagine that it is 1967 and that they are women preparing to form an organization supporting women's rights. Have each triad develop a mission statement that describes the organization and its goals. Have volunteers read their statements to the class. To conclude, conduct a brief discussion on the tactics used by leaders of the women's rights movement. *(See the Level 1 lesson for the correct tactics.)* Post students' mission statements around the classroom. **Cooperative Learning**

 HOMEWORK *Ask each student to write a short poem about the tactics used by the leaders of the women's rights movement.*

In 1964 they noted that SNCC's "assumption of male superiority" was "as widespread and deep rooted and . . . as crippling to . . . women as the assumptions of white supremacy are to the Negro."

During the late 1960s many female social activists began standing up for their own rights. Numerous small women's groups sprang up nationwide. Some held discussion sessions to improve their self-image. Others took direct, and often controversial, action. In 1968, feminists disrupted the Miss America Pageant, charging that beauty contests degraded women.

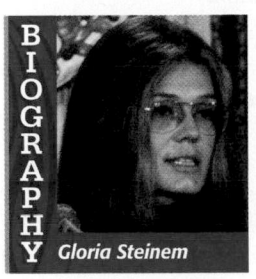
Gloria Steinem

Journalist **Gloria Steinem** was one of the women inspired to activism during the late 1960s. Steinem was born on March 25, 1934, in Toledo, Ohio. She spent most of her teenage years caring for her invalid mother. In 1952 Steinem entered Smith College, where she graduated with honors. "I loved Smith," she recalled. "They gave you three meals a day to eat, and all the books you wanted to read—what more could you want?" Her love of reading and writing led her to become a journalist.

In 1968 Steinem started writing a political column for *New York* magazine. Her work brought her into contact with many activists. Steinem did not initially consider herself a feminist. She later recalled, "Though I was old enough to be part of the *Feminine Mystique* generation, I wasn't living in the suburbs, wondering why I wasn't using my college degree. I'd ended up in the workforce many of these other women were trying to enter."

Steinem's interest in civil rights and political activism eventually led her to consider the status of women in American society. She began writing openly feminist articles. In one article Steinem stated that cooperation by radical feminists, middle-class reformers, and poor women could create a powerful movement for women's causes. In 1971 she helped found the **National Women's Political Caucus** to encourage women to run for political office. The next year, she became editor of a new magazine for women entitled *Ms.*

"There is nothing outside of [the movement]," Steinem said. "I once thought I would do this for two or three years and go home to my real life." Steinem remains a leader in the women's movement. She has written several books and helped found numerous organizations for women, including the Coalition of Labor Union Women and Women Against Pornography.

INTERPRETING THE VISUAL RECORD

Women's rights. These women are marching through the streets of Washington, D.C., to demand equal rights. ***Based on this march, how well did the women's movement appeal to women of all ages? Explain your answer.***

✔ **READING CHECK: Categorizing** In what different ways did female activists participate in the women's movement? Some established women's rights groups such as NOW and the National Women's Political Caucus. Others took more direct action.

ALL LEVELS: Ask students to identify common sources of opposition to the women's rights movement in the 1970s. *(Students should identify internal conflict within the movement, debate over the Equal Rights Amendment and* Roe *v.* Wade, *and opposition from conservative female activists.)* To help students understand the gains and setbacks that the women's movement made during the decade despite this opposition, copy the graphic organizer at right on the chalkboard, omitting the italicized answers. Then have each student complete the organizer. **English Language Learners**

> **WOMEN'S RIGHTS MOVEMENT DURING THE 1970s**
>
> **Gains**
> - *Educational Amendments Act*
> - *Roe v. Wade*
> - *Increase in the number of female politicians*
>
> **Setbacks**
> - *ERA*
> - *opposition from conservative female activists*

The ERA and Congress.

When Congress approved the Equal Rights Amendment in 1972, it included a provision limiting the ratification period to seven years. In 1979 Congress extended the period by an additional three years without the approval of a two-thirds majority. In the 1981 case *Idaho* v. *Freeman*, a federal judge ruled that Congress did not have the power to extend the deadline without the two-thirds majority. The judge also declared that the states that had already approved the amendment could rescind, or withdraw, their approval. The deadline for ratification passed before the U.S. Supreme Court could hear the case.

CRITICAL THINKING Why might Congress have extended the ERA's ratification deadline?

ANSWER: Students might suggest that many congressmembers wanted the ERA to be ratified.

The American Nation VIDEO PROGRAM

The Women's Rights Movement; Teacher's Guide, pp. 209–10

Search 48258, Play to 49209
Videodisc 1, Side B

Play   Pause

See *Teacher's Guide* for Spanish barcode.

★ Then and Now

Women and Sports

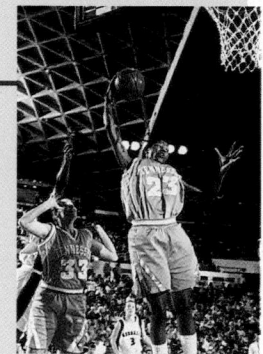

Basketball player Chamique Holdsclaw

The women's movement supported increased opportunities for women in all areas of life, including sports. Before 1972 just 1 percent of the money spent on athletic programs at institutions of higher education was spent on women's sports. As a result, only some 16,000 women attending colleges and universities participated in sports programs.

Title IX of the 1972 Education Amendments Act declared that "no person in the United States shall, on the basis of sex, be excluded from participation in, be denied the benefits of, or be subjected to discrimination under any education program or activity receiving federal financial assistance." The law did not mean that all college sports had to become coeducational. Rather, it required universities to fund women's sports programs fairly. By 1984 spending on women's athletics had improved. That year, women's sports received 16 percent of all athletic funds, and some 150,000 women participated in college sports activities. By the 1990s more than 160,000 women were involved in college athletics. The increase in girls' participation in high school sports programs was even more impressive. The number of female high school athletes rose from 294,105 in 1972 to some 2.6 million in 1999.

The Women's Movement Gains Momentum

The women's movement made progress in the 1970s. Leaders worked to elect more women to public office. Many all-male colleges allowed female students to enroll for the first time. Other universities instituted courses in women's studies. In 1972 Congress passed the **Education Amendments Act**, which outlawed sexual discrimination in higher education.

Mixed success. In 1973 the Supreme Court handed down a landmark decision affecting women. In the case *Roe* v. *Wade*, the Court overturned a state law limiting women's access to abortion during the first three months of pregnancy. The Court ruled that a woman and her doctor, not the state, should make such decisions. While most feminists hailed *Roe* v. *Wade* as a victory, opponents protested that the ruling violated the right to life of the unborn.

During the 1970s controversy also followed the Equal Rights Amendment (ERA). A proposed constitutional amendment, the ERA sought to bar discrimination on the basis of sex. Activists had first proposed such an amendment during the 1920s, but it did not pass. The ERA received strong support from NOW and other women's groups. Gloria Steinem testified before Congress on behalf of the amendment.

> **History Makers Speak**
>
> "Women suffer second-class treatment from the moment they are born. They are expected to *be* rather than to achieve, to function biologically rather than learn. A brother, whatever his intellect, is more likely to get the family's encouragement and education money, while girls are pressured to conceal ambition and intelligence."
>
> —Gloria Steinem, testimony before Congress, 1970

Congress passed the ERA in 1972, but the amendment required the approval of at least 38 states. Ratification initially seemed certain. However, conservative groups that regarded the ERA as a threat to traditional women's roles launched a campaign to prevent ratification. By the 1982 deadline set by Congress, the ERA was still three states short of ratification. As a result, the amendment failed to become law.

Opposition. The fight over the ERA revealed that many women believed that the women's movement primarily served wealthy white women. Many nonwhite women and working-class white women felt left out. These women felt that the leaders of NOW and other feminist groups simply did not understand the problems they faced every day. Referring to Gloria Steinem, Cathy Tuley stated, "I feel she's fighting for women like herself, professional women, and that she's not thinking of women in the whole sense, just part of them."

REVIEW

Have students complete the **Section 1 Review** on p. 681.

ASSESS

Have students complete **Daily Quiz 23.1**. As **Alternative Assessment**, you may want to use the government action debate or the women's rights organization mission statement in this section's lessons.

RETEACH

Have students complete **Main Idea Activity for English Language Learners and Special-Needs Students 23.1**. Then organize students into triads. Have each triad create a detailed outline of Section 1. Then ask each triad to exchange its work with another triad. Have triads study each others' outlines and use them to develop and answer between 5 and 10 possible quiz questions. **English Language Learners, Cooperative Learning**

EXTEND

Ask students to select a prominent women's rights activist mentioned in Section 1, such as Bella Abzug, Shirley Chisholm, Betty Friedan, or Gloria Steinem. Have students conduct research on their chosen figures. Then tell each student to write a short "Who Am I?" monologue in the role of his or her chosen activist, omitting the person's name. Have volunteers deliver their monologues to the class and ask students to identify the activist. **Block Scheduling**

The movement also offended many middle-class women. These women viewed *Roe* v. *Wade* and the ERA as threats to traditional family life. Critics warned that the ERA would "nullify [cancel] any laws that make any distinction between men and women." Eventually, they argued, men and women would even be forced to share public restrooms. Conservative critic **Phyllis Schlafly** was pleased when the ERA failed to win ratification. She claimed, "The defeat of the Equal Rights Amendment is the greatest victory for women's rights since the woman's suffrage movement of 1920."

Despite such disagreements over the role of women in American society, women had made some gains by the end of the 1970s. More female politicians took office in the U.S. Congress, although they made up less than 5 percent of its members. New York representatives **Bella Abzug** and **Shirley Chisholm** received national attention. Abzug became an outspoken supporter of women's issues in Congress. In 1972 Shirley Chisholm—the first African American woman elected to Congress—also became the first African American woman to run for president. Although she did not receive the Democratic Party's nomination, her campaign illustrated how far some women had come. Most women still held low-paying jobs, but the number of women holding professional jobs had increased. In 1970 just 5 percent of the nation's lawyers and 25 percent of all accountants were women. Ten years later, 12 percent of lawyers and 33 percent of accountants were women.

✔ **READING CHECK: Making Generalizations** How did *Roe* v. *Wade* and the ERA define the women's movement during the 1970s? Both revealed controversy and division in the women's movement.

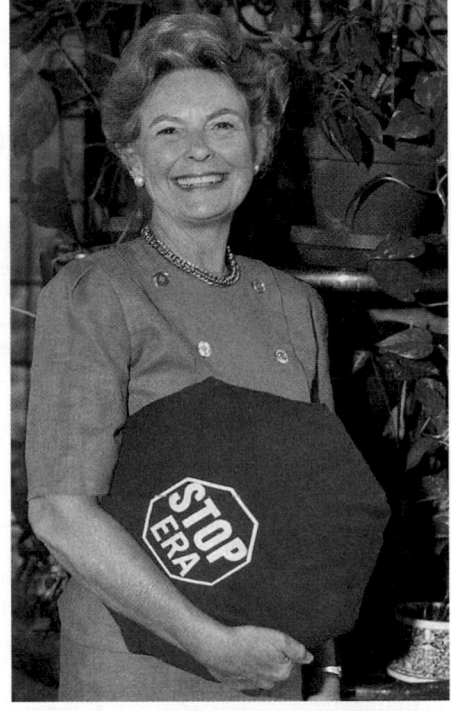

Phyllis Schlafly was a vocal opponent of the Equal Rights Amendment.

SECTION 1 REVIEW ANSWERS

1. Identify
- Betty Friedan, p. 676
- Equal Pay Act, p. 677
- National Organization for Women, p. 678
- Gloria Steinem, p. 679
- National Women's Political Caucus, p. 679
- Educational Amendments Act, p. 680
- Phyllis Schlafly, p. 681
- Bella Abzug, p. 681
- Shirley Chisholm, p. 681

2. dissatisfaction—felt stifled by domestic life and workplace discrimination; responses—Equal Pay Act, presidential commission, Title VII; NOW—pressured elected officials; new generation—direct action; successes—Educational Amendments Act; *Roe* v. *Wade*; setbacks—ERA

3a. limited roles and opportunities available to women; led to increased demands for new opportunities and fair treatment

b. Answers will vary. Some students might note that the government passed the Equal Pay Act and Title VII.

c. For—it would give women legal equality; against—it would benefit only upper-class professional women and was a threat to traditional family life

4. Answers will vary. Students should explain what NOW hoped to achieve and what it actually achieved. Students should also discuss whether it was fair to all women.

SECTION 1 REVIEW

1. Identify and explain:
Betty Friedan
Equal Pay Act
National Organization for Women
Gloria Steinem
National Women's Political Caucus
Education Amendments Act
Phyllis Schlafly
Bella Abzug
Shirley Chisholm

2. Sequencing Copy the graphic organizer below. Use it to explain the development of the women's movement.

1. Sources of Dissatisfaction Among Women
2. Federal Government Responses
3. Goals and Tactics of NOW
4. Goals and Tactics of New Generation
5. Successes and Setbacks

3. **Finding the Main Idea**

a. What was the source of the frustration that Betty Friedan identified in *The Feminine Mystique*? How did the book affect its readers?

b. How did the federal government support the women's movement?

c. What were the arguments for and against the ERA?

4. **Writing and Critical Thinking**

Supporting a Point of View Write a position paper explaining whether you support the goals of NOW.

Consider:
- the reforms that NOW hoped to achieve
- the strategies it used to achieve these reforms
- the difference in background between NOW members and their critics

Homework Practice Online
keyword: SE3 HP23

After completing Section 2, students should be able to:

OBJECTIVE 1 Discuss why La Huelga was important to Mexican Americans throughout the country.

OBJECTIVE 2 Explain how conflicts over land rights and education motivated Mexican Americans to protest.

OBJECTIVE 3 Describe how aggressive activists shaped the Chicano movement.

OBJECTIVE 4 Analyze how the Chicano movement changed the lives of Mexican Americans.

LET'S GET STARTED!

Write the following terms on the chalkboard: *boycott*, *strike*, and *urban activism*. Ask students to define the terms and to write a brief statement describing how these actions might have been used in a civil rights movement. Have volunteers share their responses. Then tell students that in Section 2 they will learn how the Mexican American civil rights movement and the Chicano movement utilized boycotts, strikes, and urban activism.

SECTION 2 RESOURCES

REPRODUCIBLE
▶ Guided Reading Strategy 23.2

TECHNOLOGY
▶ One-Stop Planner, Lesson 23.2
▶ The American Nation Video Program Segment: César Chávez; Teacher's Guide, pp. 167–68
▶ CNN Presents America: Yesterday and Today Segment: Women and Sports
▶ Holt Researcher: American History CD–ROM
▶ Homework Practice Online
▶ HRW Go site

REINFORCEMENT, REVIEW, AND ASSESSMENT
▶ Section 2 Review, p. 688
▶ Daily Quiz 23.2
▶ Main Idea Activity 23.2
▶ English Audio Summary 23.2
▶ Spanish Audio Summary 23.2

SECTION 2

READ TO DISCOVER
1. Why was La Huelga important to Mexican Americans throughout the country?
2. How did conflicts over land rights and education motivate Mexican Americans to protest?
3. How did aggressive activists shape the Chicano movement?
4. How did the Chicano movement change the lives of Mexican Americans?

IDENTIFY
César Chávez
Dolores Huerta
La Huelga
United Farm Workers
Reies López Tijerina
Alianza Federal de Mercedes
Brown Berets
Rodolfo Gonzales
Crusade for Justice
Mexican American Youth Organization
José Angel Gutiérrez
La Raza Unida Party

WHY IT MATTERS TODAY
Hispanics make up a larger portion of the U.S. population than ever before. Use CNNfyi.com or other **current events** sources to learn about ways Hispanics take part in U.S. politics today. Record your findings in your journal.

CNNfyi.com

The Chicano Movement

EYEWITNESSES TO History

"One night I went to a dance. I didn't know that it was a place with mostly Anglo girls. An Anglo policeman told me to leave the premises. At that point I questioned him, and he arrested me. I asked him why he was arresting me, and he uttered some very racist sentiments. At the station, they let me go. Nevertheless, I spent a very embarrassing and uncomfortable few hours in jail."

—Cesar Caballero, quoted in *New Americans*, by Al Santoli

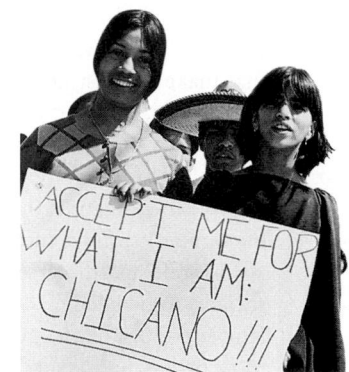
Chicano protesters

Cesar Caballero recalled his years as a high school student in El Paso, Texas, during the early 1960s. Caballero and many other Mexican Americans reacted to the discrimination they experienced by demanding their civil rights and greater opportunities in American life.

Stirrings of Protest

Like the African American civil rights movement and the women's movement, the Mexican American struggle to secure equal rights became a powerful political force during the 1960s. Almost 4 million Mexican Americans lived in the United States in 1960, with more than 3.4 million living in southwestern states. They were among the poorest and least-educated people in the country. Although 80 percent of Mexican Americans lived in cities, it was the actions of California farmworkers that initially inspired many Mexican Americans to activism.

A model for the movement. Migrant agricultural workers, many of them Mexican Americans, received low wages for backbreaking labor. In September 1965 a group of Filipino workers went on strike in Delano, California, in the San Joaquin Valley. They refused to harvest grapes until they received a pay increase. Other migrant workers, including Mexican Americans, soon joined the strike.

When the Filipino workers struck, leaders of a union called the National Farm Workers Association (NFWA) were faced with a dilemma. A few months earlier they had won a labor dispute with rose growers, but this strike promised to be much more difficult to win. Led by **César Chávez**, NFWA leaders decided to join the strike.

BIOGRAPHY
César Chávez

Born in Yuma, Arizona, in 1927, César Chávez was the son of Mexican American farmers. After losing their land during the Great Depression, Chávez's family became migrant workers. During his childhood Chávez attended nearly 30 different schools. The Chávez family repeatedly experienced discrimination in their travels searching for work. Looking back on his childhood, Chávez recalled, "There were lots of racist remarks that still hurt my ears when I think of them."

LEVEL 1: Conduct a brief discussion on the importance of La Huelga to Mexican Americans throughout the country. *(Students might mention that it resulted in important advances for workers, elevated César Chávez as a movement leader, and encouraged Mexican Americans to fight discrimination.)* Then tell students to imagine that they are Mexican American farmworkers who participated in the strike. Have each student write a paragraph explaining why the strike was important to him or her. **English Language Learners**

LEVEL 2: Tell students to imagine that they are farmworkers who participated in La Huelga. Have each student write a brief speech explaining why the strike was important to Mexican Americans. *(See the Level 1 lesson for the correct reasons.)* Ask volunteers to deliver their speeches to the class. Students may wish to include the scripts for their speeches in their portfolios.

NOTE: For an additional teaching idea, see the Chapter 23 choosing and acting lesson in the **Creative Teaching Strategies** handbook.

Chávez was strongly influenced by his parents, particularly his mother, who often assisted fellow migrant workers. He remembered, "We were migrants but we were a service center. We did all kinds of work for people." After serving in the navy during World War II, Chávez moved to San Jose, California. He became involved in the Community Service Organization (CSO), where he learned community-organizing techniques. Father Donald McDonnell, a Catholic priest, taught Chávez that labor unions could be a powerful force for social change.

Chávez wanted to organize migrant agricultural workers. When this project did not receive support from the CSO, he left the organization. With help from former CSO workers **Dolores Huerta** and Gil Padilla, Chávez founded the NFWA. His wife, Helen, ran the credit union they had created to assist the workers. By 1965 the NFWA claimed some 1,700 members.

Strike and boycott. On September 16, 1965, Mexican Independence Day, Chávez asked a gathering of NFWA members to join the Filipino strikers. Eliseo Medina was then a 19-year-old worker. He later recalled the union meeting.

> **"People started talking about how unfair . . . the growers were . . . and why we needed to fight back. . . . And then, so César gets up and he's this little guy . . . very soft spoken. I say, 'That's César?' You know, I wasn't very impressed . . . but the more he talked, the more I thought that not only could we fight, but we could win."**
>
> —Eliseo Medina, quoted in *Chicano!*, by F. Arturo Rosales

After NFWA members voted to strike, Chávez and other leaders collected donations of money and food to support the striking workers. The union also constructed a medical clinic and operated a gas station for its members. As Chávez explained, "We are a union of have-nots. So we must satisfy basic needs before other things."

Chávez realized that a strike alone would not win the union any concessions. He therefore adopted other strategies used in the civil rights movement to gain support. In 1966, to encourage public sympathy for the strike, Chávez conducted a 300-mile march to Sacramento, the capital of California. When Chávez called for a nationwide boycott of grapes, consumers responded enthusiastically. An estimated 17 million Americans refused to buy grapes. The resulting economic pressure forced grape growers to negotiate a settlement.

Known as **La Huelga**, the Delano grape strike lasted until 1970, when the last of the grape growers signed new contracts with the union. During that time the NFWA merged with another union, eventually forming the **United Farm Workers** (UFW). The UFW was not exclusively a Mexican American organization and included many non-Hispanic members. However, its accomplishments and Chávez's leadership inspired many Mexican Americans to fight discrimination

The Religious Spirit

THE IDEAL OF NONVIOLENCE

Most religions consider life to be sacred and have strict standards against the use of violence. During the early 1900s Mohandas K. Gandhi used the idea of nonviolence taken from Hinduism to oppose British rule in India. Martin Luther King Jr. and other African American civil rights activists followed Gandhi's example. They were also influenced by Christian teachings to use nonviolent tactics in their struggle for equal rights.

Many religions use the dove as a symbol of peace.

César Chávez also believed that nonviolence was the best way to bring about social change. Chávez was a deeply religious man. He once declared, "For me, Christianity happens to be a natural source of faith." He maintained that Jesus Christ "was extremely radical, and he was for social change." Chávez drew strength from his Catholic faith. He also studied Gandhi, whom he called "the most perfect man, not including Christ." Chávez noted, "Gandhi's philosophy of nonviolence, it really forces us to think, really forces us to work hard. But it has power. It attracts the support of the people." ■

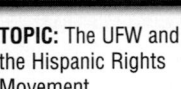

TOPIC: The UFW and the Hispanic Rights Movement
GO TO: go.hrw.com
KEYWORD: SE3 AN23

Have students access the Internet through the HRW Go site to conduct research on César Chávez and the United Farm Workers. Then have each student create a brochure outlining the history of the UFW and the Hispanic Rights Movement.

The American Nation
VIDEO PROGRAM

César Chávez; Teacher's Guide, pp. 167–68

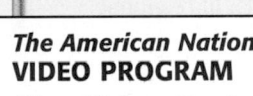

Search 38963, Play to 39584
Videodisc 2, Side B

Play

Pause

See *Teacher's Guide* for Spanish barcode.

INTERPRETING THE VISUAL RECORD

The UFW. The UFW fought poor working conditions with boycotts like the one against lettuce growers that the flag above announces. *What are the workers in this picture doing? Do you think it is hard work? Why?*

Reies López Tijerina fought to help Mexican Americans regain lands that had been taken from them.

in their lives. The union's symbol, a black Aztec eagle, came to represent the Mexican American civil rights movement that developed during the late 1960s. César Chávez led many similar strikes before his death in 1993.

✔ **READING CHECK: Analyzing Information**
What was César Chávez's role in La Huelga?
He asked NFWA members to join the strike; he collected money and food and organized a grape boycott.

Mexican American Activism

César Chávez became nationally known during the late 1960s. He was respected for his tireless efforts and his commitment to nonviolent protest. Senator Robert Kennedy of New York hailed Chávez as "one of the heroic figures of our time." Other Mexican American activists during the 1960s used tactics different from those of Chávez and the UFW.

Land rights. In northern New Mexico, **Reies López Tijerina** led the **Alianza Federal de Mercedes**, or "Federal Alliance of Land Grants." This organization worked to regain land that had been taken from Mexican Americans—often through fraud or deception—over the years. Tijerina spoke to Mexican American farmers.

History Makers Speak
❝You have been robbed of your lands by Anglo-Americans with some Spanish-American accomplices. . . . The federal and state governments are not interested in you. Join the Alianza. Together we will get your lands back . . . preferably through court action. If the courts do not respond, then we will have to resort to other methods.❞

—Reies López Tijerina, quoted in *The Mexican-Americans*, by Manuel P. Servín

Although New Mexico governor David Cargo showed sympathy for the Alianza cause, many other state officials were determined to stop the *aliancistas*, as Tijerina's followers were known. Several *aliancistas* were arrested for unlawful assembly in June 1967 when they tried to attend a meeting in Coyote, New Mexico. Outraged, other *aliancistas* stormed the courthouse in Tierra Amarilla, New Mexico, in an attempt to free their friends. A gun battle broke out, and two police officers were wounded. Governor Cargo was in Michigan at the time of the courthouse incident. He later recalled being told, "You've got a civil war going on in New Mexico."

The Tierra Amarilla incident marked a turning point in the conflict between the *aliancistas* and their opponents. The group became entangled in lawsuits, and Tijerina eventually spent two years in prison for an assault conviction. Although Tijerina did not achieve his goals, he did inspire a generation of young Mexican American activists.

TEACH OBJECTIVE 2

ALL LEVELS: To help students understand how conflicts over land rights and education motivated Mexican Americans to protest, copy the chart at right on the chalkboard, omitting the italicized answers. Have each student complete it. Then pair students and have each pair write either newspaper headlines or newspaper articles describing the attack on the courthouse in Tierra Amarilla, New Mexico; or the school walkouts in East Los Angeles, California. Have volunteers share their work with the class.
English Language Learners, Cooperative Learning

MEXICAN AMERICAN PROTESTS		
Issue	**Conflict**	**Protests**
land rights	*loss of land; theft of land; attempt to regain land*	*Alianza protests*
education	*the poor quality of local schools*	*school walkouts; Brown Beret activism*

Student action. While Tijerina fought his battles in New Mexico, students in California also took to active protest. Many Mexican Americans in East Los Angeles resented the poor quality of the local schools. Some students began planning a mass demonstration. On March 1, 1968, about 300 students at Wilson High School walked out of their classes to protest the cancellation of a school play. The walkout, called a blowout by the students, quickly spread. Within one week some 15,000 students had joined the protest. Police responded by arresting students and, in some cases, beating them.

The Educational Issues Coordinating Committee (EICC) tried to use the walkouts to bring about change in the school system. The school reform movement met with opposition in June 1968. That month, 13 people—including many EICC members—were indicted for conspiracy to create riots and disturbing the peace.

Known as the L.A. Thirteen, the individuals indicted included several members of the **Brown Berets**. Inspired by the Black Panthers, the Brown Berets was an activist group formed in 1967 in response to police brutality against Mexican Americans in Los Angeles. Recalling his arrest after being indicted, Carlos Munoz, a Brown Beret leader and L.A. Thirteen member, declared, "They put the cuffs on me. I'll never forget this as long as I live." Charges against Munoz and the other L.A. Thirteen were later dropped.

The East Los Angeles school walkouts brought national attention to Mexican American concerns and drew many students into militant activism. John Ortiz was a college student who took part in the protests. He later recalled, "As the strike intensified and people were getting arrested, the students became politically aware. The events politicized the students. And that's why they walked out of their classes!"

✔ **READING CHECK: Finding the Main Idea** What issues did Mexican American activists address? They worked to regain land taken from them and protested the poor quality of schools.

Nationalism and Politics

During the late 1960s some Mexican Americans began embracing a form of cultural nationalism similar to that supported by black nationalists. They called themselves Chicanos, a shortened form of *mexicanos*. These leaders worked to create a national movement by uniting regional efforts in many southwestern states.

INTERPRETING THE VISUAL RECORD

The Chicano movement. This Los Angeles mural celebrates the Chicano movement's fight for equal rights. *What do you think the various elements of the mural represent?*

IN THE NEWS

Land Rights in New Mexico. The conflict over land ownership in New Mexico continued into the 1990s. The 150th anniversary of the signing of the Treaty of Guadalupe Hidalgo was in February 1998. The treaty had forced Mexico to cede some of its land in the Southwest to the United States. Many holders of Spanish land grants from the 1700s lost their land. In 1998, Mexican American descendants of the original grantees demanded the return of some 1.5 million acres of land controlled by the U.S. Forest Service.

CRITICAL THINKING How might the government resolve conflicts over land claims?

ANSWER: Answers will vary. Some students might argue that the government should honor all previous treaties.

THAT'S INTERESTING!

In 1972 the Brown Berets occupied Santa Catalina, an island off the California coast, for about 24 hours. The Berets hoped that their protest would draw attention to the issue of land rights.

VISUAL RECORD ANSWER

Students might suggest that the fist represents Chicano power and that the eagle symbolizes triumph.

TEACH OBJECTIVE 3

LEVEL 1: Ask students to identify aggressive Chicano activists. *(Students should identify Rodolfo Gonzales and José Angel Gutiérrez.)* Have each student write a paragraph explaining how these activists helped shape the Chicano movement. *(Students should note that Gonzales concentrated on urban residents and promoted Mexican American nationalism. Gutiérrez organized student protests and formed a political party.)* Ask volunteers to read their paragraphs to the class. Students may wish to include their paragraphs in their portfolios. **English Language Learners**

LEVELS 2 AND 3: Tell students to imagine that they are aggressive Chicano activists who participated in the Chicano movement. Have each student write a short memoir explaining his or her efforts to shape the movement. *(See the Level 1 lesson for the correct effects.)* Ask volunteers to read their memoirs to the class. Students may wish to include their memoirs in their portfolios.

CITIZENSHIP

School Walkouts. The Crusade for Justice conducted a number of school walkouts to achieve its goals. One of the most violent walkouts took place in a Denver high school in 1969 after a teacher made racist remarks. The strike lasted for three days. During that period, a riot took place, with heavily armed police officers battling protesters. Many demonstrators, including Rodolfo Gonzales, were arrested and jailed.

CRITICAL THINKING Do you think that school walkouts were an effective protest technique?

ANSWER: Some students might suggest that some observers might have viewed school walkouts as a way for students to skip classes. Other students might suggest that the walkouts drew attention to the protesters' grievances.

MAP ANSWER

in the Southwest; because most Chicanos in America settled in Texas, New Mexico, and California, all of which are near Mexico

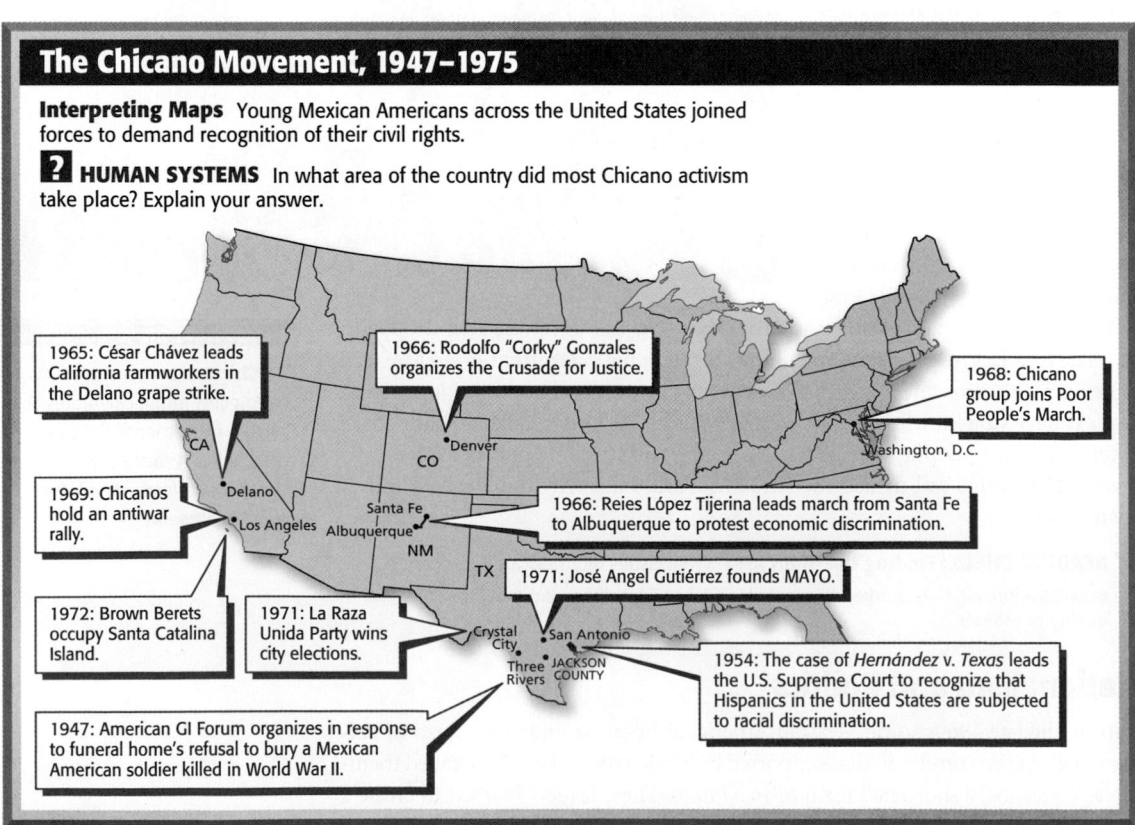

Rodolfo Gonzales testifies before the U.S. Department of Education on discrimination in American schools.

Urban activism. Rodolfo "Corky" **Gonzales** became one of the leading figures in the Chicano movement. Gonzales was interested in issues other than farmworkers' rights, land grants, and educational reform. He expressed a vision that appealed to a large number of Mexican Americans, particularly those living in cities.

A former boxer, Gonzales became involved with Democratic Party politics and antipoverty programs in Denver during the late 1950s and early 1960s. Over time Gonzales grew dissatisfied with politics, which he believed did little to help Mexican Americans. He later recalled, "I became disenchanted with the electoral system and disenchanted with the two political parties."

In 1966 Gonzales founded the **Crusade for Justice**, a group that promoted Mexican American nationalism. Operating out of an old church, the group offered legal aid, a theater for promoting cultural awareness, a newspaper, and other community services. It also ran a school. Gonzales praised the Crusade as "the embodiment [representation] of nationalism that now exists here in the Southwest. It has been a dream of the past, but we're now creating a reality out of it."

Gonzales popularized the use of the nationalist term Chicano to refer to Mexican Americans. He also composed an epic poem, *I Am Joaquín*, which served as an anthem for the *movimiento*, or "Chicano movement." In March 1969 Gonzales and the Crusade for Justice sponsored the National Chicano Liberation Youth Conference. María Varela attended the conference:

The Chicano Movement, 1947–1975

Interpreting Maps Young Mexican Americans across the United States joined forces to demand recognition of their civil rights.

❓ HUMAN SYSTEMS In what area of the country did most Chicano activism take place? Explain your answer.

1965: César Chávez leads California farmworkers in the Delano grape strike.

1966: Rodolfo "Corky" Gonzales organizes the Crusade for Justice.

1968: Chicano group joins Poor People's March.

1969: Chicanos hold an antiwar rally.

1966: Reies López Tijerina leads march from Santa Fe to Albuquerque to protest economic discrimination.

1971: José Angel Gutiérrez founds MAYO.

1972: Brown Berets occupy Santa Catalina Island.

1971: La Raza Unida Party wins city elections.

1954: The case of *Hernández* v. *Texas* leads the U.S. Supreme Court to recognize that Hispanics in the United States are subjected to racial discrimination.

1947: American GI Forum organizes in response to funeral home's refusal to bury a Mexican American soldier killed in World War II.

LEVEL 1: Organize the students into small groups. Tell each group to write several sentences explaining how the Chicano movement changed the lives of Mexican Americans. *(Groups should indicate that the movement encouraged universities to establish Chicano Studies programs, helped spark a Chicano Renaissance, and encouraged activists to enter politics.)* As each group reads its sentences, compile a comprehensive list on the chalkboard. When the list is complete, discuss the items with the class. Ask students to analyze each item's short-term and long-term impact on Mexican Americans' lives.
English Language Learners, Cooperative Learning

LEVELS 2 AND 3: Tell students to imagine that they are Mexican Americans who witnessed key events in the Chicano movement. Have each student write a letter to a friend in Mexico detailing those events and explaining how the Chicano movement changed the lives of Mexican Americans. *(See the Level 1 lesson for the correct changes.)* Letters should describe the activities of both conservative and aggressive groups. Ask volunteers to read their letters to the class.

HOMEWORK *Have students study the mural in this section. Then ask each student to design a mural celebrating the achievements of the Chicano movement and its effects on Mexican Americans.*

History Makers Speak

"It was in reality a fiesta: days of celebrating what sings in the blood of a people taught to believe that they are ugly, discovering the true beauty in their souls during the years of occupation and intimidation. . . . This affirmation grew into a *grito*, a roar, among the people gathered in the auditorium of the Crusade's Center."

—María Varela, quoted in *Chicano!*, by F. Arturo Rosales

Conference delegates produced *El Plan Espiritual de Aztlán*, or "The Spiritual Plan of Aztlán," a document calling for Chicano separatism. *El Plan* declared, "We are a bronze people with a bronze culture. Before all the world, before all of North America, before all our brothers in the Bronze Continent, we are a Nation."

The Texas movement. Mexican Americans in Texas also turned to protest during the 1960s. In 1967 a group of students at St. Mary's University in San Antonio formed the **Mexican American Youth Organization** (MAYO). One of MAYO's founders, **José Angel Gutiérrez**, had been inspired by a 1966 farmworkers' protest march.

Under Gutiérrez's leadership, MAYO took radical positions on issues affecting Mexican Americans. Gutiérrez declared, "We have to be revolutionary in our demands and make every sacrifice necessary, even if it means death, to achieve our goals." Moderate opponents of MAYO's radical stance included Henry B. González, the first Mexican American from Texas to be elected to the U.S. Congress.

Gutiérrez and MAYO had some success in the fight for civil rights in Texas. In 1969 Gutiérrez helped organize a protest in his hometown, Crystal City. Mexican American students at Crystal City High School were angry about discrimination in extracurricular activities, including cheerleading. The school board initially agreed to allow three Mexican Americans on the cheerleading squad but backed out of the deal in June.

In November about 100 Mexican American students and their parents took a list of complaints to the school board. After the school board denied any charges of discrimination, the students walked out. The walkout extended to middle and elementary schools. The federal Justice Department helped resolve the crisis. The settlement required the school board to meet most of the students' demands, including bilingual and bicultural education.

Political power. Mexican American leaders had begun discussing the possibility of creating a Chicano political party in 1967. After his success in Crystal City, Gutiérrez formed **La Raza Unida Party** (RUP). In elections held in 1970, the RUP gained control of the Crystal City city council and positions in some other Texas cities. That same year Rodolfo Gonzales organized a Colorado branch of the RUP. The Colorado party did not have many electoral victories, but it did draw attention to Chicano causes. The RUP also expanded into California, where it registered some 10,000 new voters and ran several candidates for state offices. The RUP soon appeared in other states, including Arizona, Nebraska, and New Mexico.

RUP leaders hoped to transform the party from a collection of regional parties into a strong national organization. In 1972 the RUP held its first national convention in El Paso, Texas. About half of the some 1,500 participants were women.

INTERPRETING THE VISUAL RECORD

La Raza. José Gutiérrez (left) and Rodolfo Gonzales (center) appear before the national convention of La Raza Unida Party in 1972. **What do you think Gonzales' raised fist symbolizes?**

RAMSEY **MUNIZ** FOR GOVERNOR RAZA UNIDA PARTY

Aztlán. The ancient Aztec identified Aztlán as their homeland. Modern-day scholars do not know whether Aztlán was a real or mythological place. Regardless, the idea of Aztlán united Mexican American activists in their struggle for economic power and civil rights during the 1960s and 1970s. Many of them believed that Aztlán had been located in the American Southwest. The activists worked for the day when the Mexican Americans living there would have political and economic power.

CRITICAL THINKING Why might people be inspired by mythology?

ANSWER: Students might suggest that myths can serve to unite people.

VISUAL RECORD ANSWER

Students might suggest that the raised fist symbolizes strength and struggle.

VISUAL RECORD ANSWER

(for p. 688)

Students might suggest that many of the workers addressed by the poster are Hispanics.

REVIEW SECTION **2** ANSWERS

1. Identify
- César Chávez, p. 682
- Dolores Huerta, p. 683

REVIEW

Have students complete the **Section 2 Review** on p. 688.

ASSESS

Have students complete **Daily Quiz 23.2**. As **Alternative Assessment**, you may want to use the La Huelga script or the activist paragraph in this section's lessons.

RETEACH

Have students complete **Main Idea Activity for English Language Learners and Special-Needs Students 23.2**. Organize students into small groups. Have each group summarize the information in a subsection by designing a poster. Have volunteers present their posters to the class.
English Language Learners, Cooperative Learning

EXTEND

Ask students to conduct research on a Chicano Renaissance artist. Have each student write a brief biography of the artist, discussing his or her background and work. Ask volunteers to read their biographies to the class. **Block Scheduling**

- La Huelga, p. 683
- United Farm Workers, p. 683
- Reies López Tijerina, p. 684
- Alianza Federal de Mercedes, p. 684
- Brown Berets, p. 685
- Rodolfo Gonzales, p. 686
- Crusade for Justice, p. 686
- Mexican American Youth Organization, p. 687
- José Angel Gutiérrez, p. 687
- La Raza Unida Party, p. 687

2. Chávez—rights for farm-workers; Tijerina—regain lost land; Gonzales—nationalism; Gutiérrez—protect and promote civil rights

3a. Chávez led a successful strike and helped launch the Chicano movement. La Huelga encouraged Mexican Americans to fight discrimination.

b. economic—low wages and poor working conditions for migrant farmers, land rights; social—equality in school programs and extracurricular activities, increased political power

c. electoral victories in some Texas cities and Muniz's 6 percent of the vote for governor in 1972; organizations in Colorado, California, New Mexico, Arizona, and Nebraska drew attention to Chicano causes

4. Brochures will vary but might suggest that internal conflict needs to be avoided and that the convention will emphasize movement goals.

INTERPRETING THE VISUAL RECORD

1974 rally. This poster calls for immigrants from Latin America and South Africa to rally for better working conditions. **Why might Hispanics support this cause?**

Gutiérrez was elected the party's first national president. In the 1970s the RUP supported candidates in numerous states. Its greatest success came in Texas, where it won several seats in local and statewide elections. In 1972 the RUP candidate Ramsey Muníz received 6 percent of the total vote for governor in Texas.

✔ **READING CHECK: Categorizing** What responses to discrimination did the Chicano movement offer? It fought discrimination against Hispanic students and created a new political party.

The Movement Weakens

The Chicano movement lost some of its political power during the 1970s. The Brown Berets dissolved in 1972, and the RUP did not offer any candidates after the late 1970s. Some activists later claimed that the ethnic nationalism embraced by many of the movement's members was politically impractical and had caused many moderate Mexican Americans to lose interest.

Despite its shortcomings, the Chicano movement had a positive impact on the lives of many Mexican Americans. During the 1960s and 1970s several universities established Chicano Studies programs. The Chicano movement also inspired Mexican American artists, novelists, and playwrights to create new works. This led one critic to declare a Chicano Renaissance. Some activists entered mainstream politics, inspiring others to maintain their efforts to change American society. One participant, Rosalio Muñoz, later stated that the Chicano movement "helped crystallize for people making a commitment, just like in my own life, a commitment from there to go on."

✔ **READING CHECK: Evaluating** How effective was the Chicano movement? It lost some power during the 1970s but inspired the Chicano Renaissance and the creation of a political party and Chicano Studies programs.

SECTION 2 REVIEW

1. Identify and explain:
César Chávez
Dolores Huerta
La Huelga
United Farm Workers
Reies López Tijerina
Alianza Federal de Mercedes
Brown Berets
Rodolfo Gonzales
Crusade for Justice
Mexican American Youth Organization
José Angel Gutiérrez
La Raza Unida Party

2. Categorizing Copy the chart below. Use it to list the goals of the Mexican American leaders.

Leader	Goals
César Chávez	
Reies López Tijerina	
Rodolfo Gonzales	
José Angel Gutiérrez	

3. **Finding the Main Idea**
a. Why did César Chávez and La Huelga become leading symbols of Mexican American activism?
b. What economic and social conditions motivated Mexican American activists to protest?
c. What impact did La Raza Unida Party have as a third political party?

4. **Writing and Critical Thinking**
Summarizing Write a brochure for a Chicano movement convention.
Consider:
- the different goals within the movement
- the conflicts between movement leaders
- the movement's effects on Mexican Americans

Homework Practice Online
keyword: SE3 HP23

LET'S GET STARTED!

Write the following terms on the chalkboard: *American Indian Movement, American Association of Retired Persons,* and *Children's Defense Fund.* As students enter the classroom, ask them to write a few sentences explaining what these terms have in common. Ask volunteers to share their responses. Then tell students that in Section 3 they will learn about other groups that sought to expand their rights during the 1970s.

SECTION 3

READ TO DISCOVER

1. What did Red Power movement activists demand, and how successful were they?
2. How did Americans with disabilities gain public support for their causes?
3. What issues did activists for senior citizens and children address?

IDENTIFY

American Indian Movement
Russell Means
Ed Roberts
Rehabilitation Act
Education for All Handicapped Children Act
American Association of Retired Persons
Gray Panthers
Maggie Kuhn
Older Americans Act
Children's Defense Fund
Marian Wright Edelman

▶ WHY IT MATTERS TODAY

The children's rights movement continues to help protect the rights of American youths. Use **CNNfyi.com** or other **current events** sources to learn about a recent children's rights issue. Record your findings in your journal.

More Groups Mobilize

EYEWITNESSES TO History

❝*Let me tell you first of all that you can take credit for us being on Alcatraz because you and your government forced our backs against the wall. We're out there to create a starting point for basic changes in Indian-white relations. We reject the alternatives of the federal Indian policy. We reject either extermination of our cultures, which we refuse to have end up on museum walls for the pleasure of non-Indians. We reject the chronic and cyclical [repeating] poverty of reservations and the relocation transfer of that poverty into Red Ghettoes in the cities. We reject these alternatives. . . . We're creating our own alternatives!*❞

—Shirley Keith, quoted in *Like a Hurricane,*
by Paul Chaat Smith and Robert Allen Warrior

American Indians dance during the Alcatraz occupation.

Shirley Keith explained to a California audience in 1969 why a group of American Indians had occupied Alcatraz Island in San Francisco Bay. American Indians were among the many groups that demanded change in American society during the 1960s and 1970s.

American Indian Activism

Many Americans did not benefit from the nation's widespread prosperity in the 1950s and 1960s. American Indians were particularly affected by poverty. Mary Crow Dog grew up on a Rosebud Sioux reservation in South Dakota. She later recalled, "We had no shoes and went barefoot most of the time. I never had a new dress." In 1960 the average income of American Indian men was less than half that of white men.

Spurred by extreme poverty and inspired by other groups' civil rights gains, American Indians formed the Red Power movement during the 1960s. Participants in the movement called for self-determination, or the right to govern their own communities. They also continued to demand that the U.S. government pay tribes for lands that had been taken from them illegally. Although these issues had long concerned supporters of American Indians' rights, Red Power gained more attention and participation among Indians than any previous movement.

The Alcatraz occupation. In November 1969 a group of Red Power activists called the Indians of All Tribes occupied the abandoned federal prison on Alcatraz Island in San Francisco Bay. The protest received national news coverage. Some 150 American Indians eventually traveled to the island to join the protest. The protesters offered to buy the island from the government with beads and cloth—the same price Dutch colonists had paid for Manhattan Island in 1626. Protest leaders urged other American Indians to support their cause:

SECTION 3 RESOURCES

REPRODUCIBLE
▶ Guided Reading Strategy 23.3
▶ Primary Source Reading 23: American Indian Activism Begins
▶ Biography Reading 23: Marian Wright Edelman

TECHNOLOGY
▶ One-Stop Planner, Lesson 23.3
▶ Holt Researcher: American History CD–ROM
▶ HRW Go site
▶ Homework Practice Online

REINFORCEMENT, REVIEW, AND ASSESSMENT
▶ Section 3 Review, p. 693
▶ Daily Quiz 23.3
▶ Main Idea Activity 23.3
▶ English Audio Summary 23.3
▶ Spanish Audio Summary 23.3

LEVEL 1: Pair students and have each pair identify the demands of Red Power activists. *(Pairs should indicate that Red Power activists called for self-determination, repayment for illegally seized land, and a renewal of American Indian culture.)* Then ask pairs to write paragraphs assessing the success of Red Power efforts. *(Paragraphs should indicate that although the Red Power activists attracted public attention, they achieved few of their goals.)* Have volunteers read their paragraphs to the class.

English Language Learners, Cooperative Learning

LEVELS 2 AND 3: Write the following statement on the chalkboard: *Although Red Power activists succeeded in attracting public attention, they achieved few of their goals.* Have each student write an essay in response to the statement. Have volunteers read their essays to the class.

HOMEWORK *Tell students to imagine that it is 1975 and that they are television reporters preparing for an interview with a Red Power activist. Have each student develop several questions to ask the activist. Then ask students to write answers to their questions.*

HISTORY MAKERS SPEAK

Richard Nixon in *Red Power: The American Indians' Fight for Freedom*

President Nixon on American Indian Issues.
In a 1970 message to Congress, President Nixon committed his administration to assisting American Indians: "Both as a matter of justice and as a matter of enlightened social policy, we must begin to act on the basis of what the Indians have long been telling us. The time has come to break decisively with the past and to create the conditions for a new era in which the Indian future is determined by Indian acts and Indian decisions."

CRITICAL THINKING What important American Indian activist goal might Nixon have affirmed in his speech when he called for a future "determined by Indian acts and Indian decisions"?

ANSWER: Students might suggest that Nixon affirmed the goal of self-determination.

VISUAL RECORD ANSWER

Students might suggest that changes needed to be made in order for him to have a better future.

INTERPRETING THE VISUAL RECORD

Protest. These American Indians in New Mexico are participating in a civil rights protest. *What do you think is the message of this child's sign?*

Research on the R🔵M

Free Find: Russell Means
After reading about AIM leader Russell Means on the **Holt Researcher CD–ROM**, imagine that you are a writer for a newsmagazine. Write a short profile of Means for an article about AIM.

History Makers Speak

"We are issuing this call in an attempt to unify all our Indian Brothers behind a common cause.... If we can gather together as brothers and sisters and come to a common agreement, we feel that we can be much more effective, doing things for ourselves, instead of having someone else do it, telling us what is good for us."

—Anonymous American Indians, quoted in *Native Americans,* by James S. Olson and Raymond Wilson

Not all American Indians approved of the Alcatraz occupation. John Knifechief complained that the protesters "have no reason whatsoever to be militant or be demanding of anything.... I can't see what these young people are demanding." Interest in the Alcatraz protest gradually declined, and in 1971 federal authorities removed the few remaining protesters from the island.

Wounded Knee. Organized in Minnesota in 1968, the **American Indian Movement** (AIM) became the major force behind the Red Power movement. AIM called for a renewal of American Indian culture and recognition of American Indians' rights. **Russell Means**, a Sioux who was born on the Pine Ridge Reservation of South Dakota, became a prominent figure in AIM. In 1970 Means and other AIM members occupied the *Mayflower II*—a replica of the Pilgrim ship—during Thanksgiving Day celebrations in Plymouth, Massachusetts. Means justified AIM's aggressive tactics in a 1971 interview. "In all our demonstrations we have yet to hurt anybody or destroy any property," he said. "However, ... we have found that the only way the white man will listen is by us creating a disturbance in his world."

In 1972, AIM members and other American Indians conducted a protest they called the Trail of Broken Treaties. The group occupied the Bureau of Indian Affairs (BIA) headquarters in Washington, D.C. The following year AIM took its most dramatic action—the seizure of the trading post at Wounded Knee, South Dakota. U.S. cavalry units had killed more than 300 Sioux there in 1890. Means declared that the government had two choices: "Either they attack and wipe us out like they did in 1890, or they negotiate our reasonable demands." AIM wanted the government to initiate hearings on past broken treaties and investigate alleged BIA misconduct.

For 71 days AIM members and U.S. marshals engaged in a grim standoff. Finally, after two AIM activists had been killed and a federal marshal wounded, the government agreed to consider AIM's grievances. The siege came to an end. The following year Means and other AIM leaders were put on trial for the Wounded Knee incident. When defense lawyers presented evidence of government misconduct against AIM, however, the case was dismissed.

Gaining ground. AIM's confrontational tactics captured headlines and media attention. Other American Indian leaders worked to renew tribal life through other methods, including lawsuits and political lobbying. The Taos Pueblo of New Mexico had struggled for decades to recover 48,000 acres of land that included Blue Lake, which was sacred to them. The tribe rejected a $10 million settlement because they would have had to give up their rights to the land. Their efforts were rewarded in 1970. That year Congress approved legislation returning the land to the Taos Pueblo. American Indians in Maine who claimed that more than half that state had been illegally taken from them also scored a victory. Congress awarded them $81.5 million and the right to buy up to 300,000 acres of land.

TEACH OBJECTIVE 2

LEVEL 1: Ask students to identify the ways in which Americans with disabilities gained public support for their causes. *(Students should indicate that Americans with disabilities appealed for equal access, used the media to attract public attention, and lobbied Congress for various laws.)* Have volunteers list these methods on the chalkboard. Then ask students to write a sentence explaining the rationale and effectiveness of each method. **English Language Learners**

LEVELS 2 AND 3: Conduct a brief discussion on the ways that Americans with disabilities gained public support for their goals. *(See the Level 1 lesson for the correct methods.)* Then have each student write a short essay comparing and contrasting the methods of the disability rights movement with those of the African American or Mexican American civil rights movement. Ask volunteers to read their essays to the class.

HOMEWORK *Have each student create a detailed outline of the subsection entitled Others Struggle for Their Rights.*

American Indians continued to face many problems. Unemployment rates remained high in the 1970s, averaging 40 percent and reaching as high as 90 percent on some reservations. The high school dropout rate among Indians was the highest in the nation. Nonetheless, the Red Power movement succeeded in drawing public attention to the concerns of American Indians. It also instilled a sense of pride in American Indians nationwide.

✔ **READING CHECK: Analyzing Information** What actions did American Indians take to expand their political and economic rights? They formed the Red Power Movement, occupied Alcatraz and Wounded Knee, and brought lawsuits for the return of land.

Others Struggle for Their Rights

Several other groups of Americans sought recognition and protection of their civil rights during the 1960s and 1970s. Activists fought on behalf of people with disabilities, elderly Americans, and children.

Disability rights. Many Americans with disabilities wondered why their tax dollars helped pay for the construction of public facilities that they could not easily use. **Ed Roberts**, a young Californian who had become a quadriplegic after having polio, was among them. Roberts, who wanted to attend the University of California at Berkeley, insisted that people with disabilities deserved equal access to public facilities. Officials at the university argued that the campus did not have facilities that could accommodate Roberts. Supporters of Roberts used the media to raise public awareness of his cause. The university eventually admitted Roberts and he enrolled in 1962.

When other students with disabilities joined Roberts at Berkeley, they formed a support group called the Rolling Quads. In 1969 the group convinced the Berkeley city council to change the design of street curbs so that people in wheelchairs could move easily through the city. Other state and local governments also passed laws requiring wheelchair ramps and special parking spaces at public facilities. Many buildings began to include signs in braille to help the visually impaired.

In 1973 Congress added to these efforts to expand opportunity when it passed the **Rehabilitation Act**. This act forbade discrimination in jobs, education, or housing because of physical disabilities. Two years later Congress passed the **Education for All Handicapped Children Act**, which required public schools to provide education for children with physical or mental disabilities.

✔ **READING CHECK: Drawing Conclusions** How did Americans with disabilities organize their campaign for equal access to public facilities? They used the media and appealed to local and state governments.

★ **Then and Now**

Education and Deaf Americans

Thomas Hopkins Gallaudet founded the nation's first school for the deaf in Hartford, Connecticut, in 1817. By 1835 most institutions relied upon a sign language developed by deaf people, which eventually became known as American Sign Language. During the 1880s supporters of "oralism" opposed signing. They claimed that the hard of hearing should be taught to speak English and to read lips. Although most deaf Americans preferred signing, many schools compromised by teaching both signing and oral language. During the 1970s some schools adopted a method of teaching called Total Communication, which combined signed and spoken language.

During the 1980s deaf Americans demanded that society accept them as citizens capable of living their lives without unwanted assistance. A 1988 protest at Gallaudet University, a school for deaf and hard-of-hearing students in Washington, D.C., symbolized this new activism. Gallaudet students responded with anger to the news that the university's new president was not deaf and could not even sign. They demanded a "Deaf President Now." After a week of protests, university officials backed down and announced that I. King Jordan, a university employee, would become Gallaudet's first deaf president.

Students at Gallaudet University protested the appointment of Elisabeth Zinser (left) as president because she was not deaf.

IN THE NEWS

American Indian Poverty. Poverty has remained a persistent problem on many American Indian reservations throughout the 1900s. In 1999 President Clinton visited the Pine Ridge reservation in South Dakota. At the time of his visit, the unemployment rate on the reservation was between 75 and 85 percent—much higher than that during the Great Depression. The reservation, which covers some 3,100 square miles, had just 62 miles of paved road.

CRITICAL THINKING How might geographical location affect poverty on certain American Indian reservations?

ANSWER: Students might note that many reservations are in remote rural areas that have not experienced much economic development.

THAT'S INTERESTING!

In 1995 some 4.4 million Americans between the ages of 6 and 14 had some sort of disability. Some 659,000 had a severe disability.

TEACH OBJECTIVE 3

ALL LEVELS: To help students understand the issues that activists for senior citizens and children addressed, copy the graphic organizer at right on the chalkboard, omitting the italicized answers. Have each student complete it. Then ask students to imagine that it is 1975. Have each student write a short letter to the editor of a local newspaper, discussing an issue that either group addressed. Ask volunteers to read their letters to the class. **English Language Learners**

Senior Citizens' Issues
forced retirement, medical care

Groups and Tactics
American Association of Retired Persons and Gray Panthers; formed organizations and lobbied for improvements

MOTIVATIONS FOR THE SENIOR CITIZENS' AND THE CHILDREN'S RIGHTS MOVEMENTS

Children's Issues
poverty, lack of medical insurance, discrimination

Groups and Tactics
Children's Defense Fund; pursued lawsuits and lobbied for improvements

SKILL-BUILDING STRATEGIES ANSWERS

Applying the Skill
Reports will vary but should clearly summarize the Web site's main ideas and evaluate its content.

Practicing the Skill
1. Answers will vary but should include the name of the Web site and its authors or producers.

2. Answers will vary but students should summarize the site's main ideas and historical materials it offers.

VISUAL RECORD ANSWER

(for p. 693)

Students might suggest that the poster reveals democracy to be our national identity if we practice it.

SECTION REVIEW 3 ANSWERS

1. Identify
• American Indian Movement, p. 690
• Russell Means, p. 690
• Ed Roberts, p. 691
• Rehabilitation Act, p. 691
• Education for All Handicapped Children Act, p. 691
• American Association of Retired Persons, p. 692

Skill-Building Strategies

Evaluating Web Sites on the Internet

Of all the resources that you can use to conduct historical research, the Internet is one of the largest and most promising. While the Internet is an extremely valuable research tool, it is important that you learn to evaluate the quality of the Web sites you find.

How to Evaluate Web Sites

1. **Determine what topics are covered in the Web site, in how much depth they are covered, and how unique the coverage is.** First you must decide whether a site offers enough of the type of information you are looking for. Would you be better off finding the same information in a reference book? If so, it is probably better to use an already trusted resource. However, the site may contain additional and unique information.

2. **Determine if the information in the Web site is accurate.** The saying that you cannot believe everything you read is more relevant than ever on the Internet, where anyone can be a publisher. Conduct a preliminary review of the site. If there are spelling errors, grammatical errors, or profanity, avoid the site. Compare the information in the site to other reference sources. Examine claims made in the source to see that they are backed up with reasoned arguments and verifiable evidence. Sites full of unsupported claims and undocumented facts should be avoided.

3. **Establish who the author is and what his or her qualifications are.** You need to determine the credentials of the person or group who created and published a Web page. Look to see if the Web site is

published by a reputable firm, institution, or government agency. In the case of individuals, try to find out if the author has credentials in the field or a list of printed publications.

4. **Evaluate how objective the information is.** The objectivity of a site should not be taken for granted. It is important that you identify the purpose of a Web site. Some sites may be created to provide information, to sell things, or to promote a cause. Their facts may be correct, but you should understand the writer's point of view. If the purpose of a Web site is to persuade, then ask yourself what the other side of the issue is.

Applying the Skill

Use the computer system at your school or local public library to find a Web site on one of the following topics:
a. the history of the American Indian Movement
b. the history of the disability rights movement
c. the history of the Gray Panthers or the American Association of Retired Persons

Then explore the Web site and write a one-page report that summarizes its main ideas and evaluates its content.

Practicing the Skill

Answer the following questions.
1. What was the name of the Web site you found? Who produced it?
2. What main ideas does the Web site attempt to convey? What historical materials does it offer?

Older Americans organize. During the late 1950s, retired Americans who joined social clubs often discussed political and legal issues affecting older adults. These concerns led to the formation of organizations dedicated to lobbying for the needs of older citizens. Founded in 1958, the **American Association of Retired Persons** (AARP) became the largest such group. AARP sought to eliminate mandatory retirement. The National Council of Senior Citizens (NCSC) represented the interests of lower-income older Americans. In 1965 some 1,400 NCSC members traveled to Washington, D.C., to support Medicare legislation.

Smaller than AARP or NCSC but much more visible to the public eye was a group called the **Gray Panthers**, founded by **Maggie Kuhn**. She recalled that when she was forced to retire, "I was hurt and then, as time passed, outraged." The Gray Panthers fought for greater rights for older Americans. Kuhn explained the goals of the senior movement when she testified before Congress in 1977:

History Makers Speak

"The Gray Panthers are a national coalition of old, young, and middle-aged activists . . . working to eradicate ageism and all forms of age discrimination in our society. We define ageism as the arbitrary [irrational] discrimination against persons and groups on the basis of chronological age."

—Maggie Kuhn, quoted in *The Senior Rights Movement*, by Lawrence Alfred Powell, Kenneth J. Branco, and John B. Williamson

The federal government's responses included holding several White House Conferences on Aging. In 1965 Congress passed the **Older Americans Act**, which committed the government to providing elderly Americans with adequate income and medical care.

Children's issues. Activists also organized for children's rights. In 1967 the Supreme Court ruled in the case *In Re Gault* that minors accused of a crime possessed nearly the same rights as adults. The case sparked interest in children's rights.

The 1970 White House Conference on Children, which was attended by some 3,700 people, issued the Children's Bill of Rights. This document declared that children had the "right to grow in a society which respects the dignity of life and is free of poverty, discrimination, and other forms of degradation." The Children's Bill of Rights also maintained that children had the right to receive an education, "to be healthy," and "to grow up nurtured by affectionate parents."

Founded in 1973, the **Children's Defense Fund** (CDF) quickly became the leading children's rights organization. Director **Marian Wright Edelman** explained the group's purpose as "identifying, publicizing, and correcting selected serious problems faced by large numbers of American children." The CDF has focused on helping poor and minority children. The group has also sought health insurance for children and federally funded child care.

✔ **READING CHECK: Evaluating** How well did the federal government respond to activists for senior citizens and children? senior citizens—Congress passed the Older Americans Act; children—the White House Conference on Children issued the Children's Bill of Rights

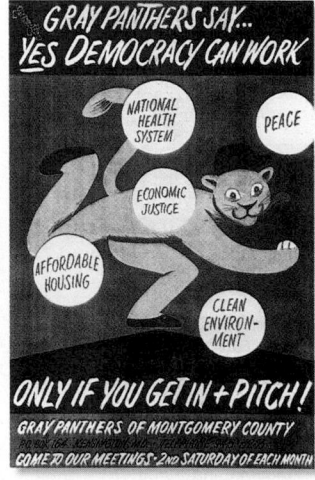

INTERPRETING THE VISUAL RECORD

Senior citizens. The Gray Panthers fought to protect older Americans against discrimination. *What does this poster reveal about democracy and our national identity?*

SECTION 3 REVIEW

1. Identify and explain:
American Indian Movement
Russell Means
Ed Roberts
Rehabilitation Act
Education for All Handicapped Children Act
American Association of Retired Persons
Gray Panthers
Maggie Kuhn
Older Americans Act
Children's Defense Fund
Marian Wright Edelman

2. Comparing Copy the graphic organizer below. Use it to compare tactics used by activists seeking to expand the rights of the groups listed.

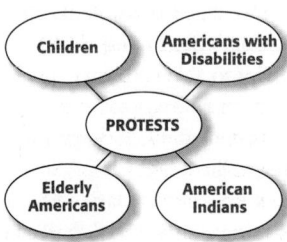

3. ▓ **Finding the Main Idea**
a. How did the demands of American Indians differ from those of other minorities who struggled for their civil rights during this era?
b. What issues would you address if you were a lobbyist for senior citizens? for a children's rights organization?
c. How did the federal government respond to different reform groups?

4. ▓ **Writing and Critical Thinking**
Supporting a Point of View Imagine that you are a member of the Red Power movement in 1972. Write a newsletter article detailing the group's goals and achievements.
Consider:
• the outcome of the Alcatraz occupation
• the response to the occupation at Wounded Knee
• the efforts of other American Indian activists

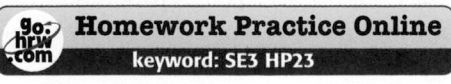
Homework Practice Online
keyword: SE3 HP23

After completing Section 4, students should be able to:

OBJECTIVE 1 *Explain why protests developed on American college campuses.*

OBJECTIVE 2 *Describe the problems that weakened the counterculture.*

OBJECTIVE 3 *Explain how doubts about American society led to new movements in religion and the arts.*

OBJECTIVE 4 *Analyze how musical styles reflected the social changes of the era.*

💿 LET'S GET STARTED!

As students enter the classroom, play Selection 25, "Blowin' in the Wind," from the **American Music Audio CD Program**. Have students respond to the song in writing. Ask volunteers to share their responses. Then tell students that in Section 4 they will learn more about the counterculture and its music.

SECTION ④

READ TO DISCOVER

1. Why did protests develop on American college campuses?
2. What problems weakened the counterculture?
3. How did doubts about American society lead to new movements in religion and the arts?
4. How did musical styles reflect social changes of the era?

DEFINE

generation gap
counterculture
pop art

IDENTIFY

Mario Savio
Timothy Leary
British invasion
Joan Baez
Bob Dylan
James Brown
Aretha Franklin
Woodstock

▶ WHY IT MATTERS TODAY

Music continues to influence people's lives today. Use **CNNfyi.com** or other **current events** sources to learn about music of social importance today. Record your findings in your journal.

CNNfyi.com

A Cultural Revolution

EYEWITNESSES TO History

"Everything on the tube tearing us apart was almost perfectly balanced by the remarkable unity [we heard] on the radio. It was the only place in the history of the United States where, for a fleeting [brief] moment, we created a world of seemingly genuine racial and sexual equality, embraced by everyone under thirty—and millions more who fell in love with the beat. . . . The composers, performers, managers, and producers . . . filled the airwaves with the most eclectic-electric-wrathful-revolutionary-romantic-soulful-psychedelic music ever played, simultaneously, on every rock-and-roll radio station in the world."

—Charles Kaiser, *1968 in America*

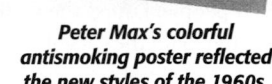

Peter Max's colorful antismoking poster reflected the new styles of the 1960s.

Charles Kaiser was a teenager during the 1960s who later became a writer. He reflected on the contrast between violent events—such as assassinations, riots, and the Vietnam War—that he witnessed on television with the sense of peace of the 1960s youth culture.

The Student Movement

Cold War fears, massive civil rights protests, and the Vietnam War led many young Americans to question the values of American society. They began to blame their parents for creating the problems that the country faced. This **generation gap** between the baby boomers and their elders grew wider as the decade wore on. Many children of the baby boom began entering young adulthood in the 1960s. Between 1960 and 1970 the number of Americans aged 15 through 24 increased almost 50 percent. In 1964 the first wave of the baby-boom generation entered college.

The 1960s youth movement began on college campuses among white middle-class students. In 1964 officials at the University of California at Berkeley announced a new policy restricting space available to student groups for organizing and making speeches. To many students, this was a violation of their right to free speech and assembly. Their discontent quickly exploded into protest.

Student activist **Mario Savio** and others helped organize the protests. Savio compared the university to a machine. He declared, "You've got to indicate to the people who run it, to the people who own it, that unless you're free, the machine will be prevented from working at all." A large number of Berkeley students stopped attending classes. They rallied, held sit-ins, and picketed university administration buildings. Their intention, they declared, was to "Shut This Factory Down." The protests quieted when university officials agreed to many of the students' demands.

In 1965 similar protests took place on college campuses nationwide. One woman who participated in the student movement at Columbia University in New York recalled the mood of the students:

TEACH OBJECTIVE 1

ALL LEVELS: Write the following question on the chalkboard: *How might the existence of a generation gap have created protests on college campuses?* Have students respond to the question in writing. *(Students might suggest that the existence of a generation gap might have led students to rebel against their parents and other authority figures.)* To help students understand why protests developed on American college campuses, copy the graphic organizer at right on the chalkboard, omitting the italicized answers. Have each student complete it. Then, for each cell of the graphic organizer, have students write a sentence that explains why the element sparked protests on campuses. **English Language Learners**

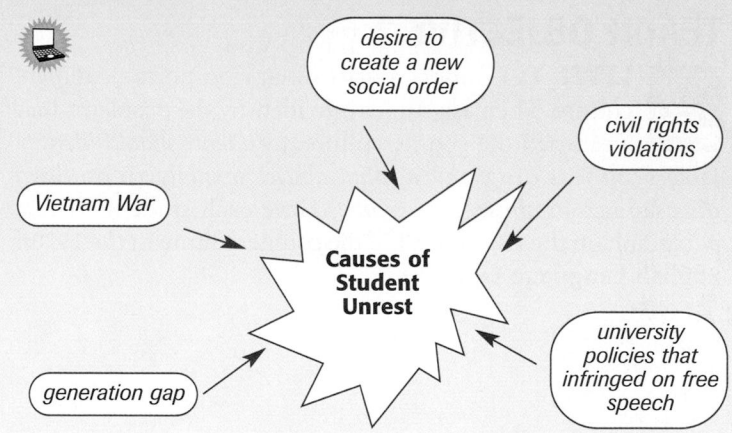

desire to create a new social order

Vietnam War

civil rights violations

Causes of Student Unrest

generation gap

university policies that infringed on free speech

History Makers Speak

❝There was an incredible exhilaration, that here we were making history, changing the world. . . . Everybody believed that this university would never be the same, that society would be . . . changed, that there'd be a revolution in the United States within five years, and a whole new social order.❞

—Nancy Biberman, quoted in *From Camelot to Kent State*, by Joan Morrison and Robert K. Morrison

✔ **READING CHECK: Identifying Cause and Effect** How did the baby boom contribute to the youth movement? **There were 50 percent more young people aged 15 to 24; many of whom entered college in the 1960s.**

The Counterculture

Some Americans hoped to create a new order by rejecting everything connected with mainstream America, which they called the Establishment. Known as hippies, these Americans sought to create a **counterculture**, or alternative lifestyle.

Dropping out. Like the beats before them, hippies rejected the materialism and work ethic of past generations in favor of simplicity and "doing your own thing." Many hippies tried to shock older Americans, whom they dismissed as "squares," with behavior that included public displays of nudity and the use of profanity. Some hippies formed communities in run-down urban neighborhoods, such as the Haight-Ashbury district of San Francisco. Others "dropped out" of society by joining rural communes, where they attempted to live collectively in harmony with nature. Residents of communes typically rejected most modern conveniences, grew their own food, and shared all property. Between 1965 and 1975 some 10,000 such communes were established.

Many hippies searched for new physical experiences by experimenting with harmful mind-altering drugs such as LSD (lysergic acid diethylamide), commonly known as acid. Harvard University instructor **Timothy Leary** became the drug's leading supporter. He used LSD on his students. Leary was fired from his job in 1963 for violating rules governing experiments on human subjects. Leary invited people to "turn on to the scene, tune in to what is happening, and drop out—of high school, college, grad school, junior executive—and follow me, the hard way."

Fashion. Hippies also often adopted a casual and colorful style of dress. Shirts that had been tie-dyed—dipped in colorful dyes while knotted to produce vibrant patterns—grew in popularity. People increasingly wore blue jeans, which traditionally had been considered work clothing. Men began wearing their hair longer, and beards became commonplace. Beads, which on men represented a rejection of the necktie, became a standard accessory. Some African Americans sported Afros, a natural hairstyle that came to symbolize racial pride. Many African Americans adopted the dashiki, an African shirt usually decorated with bright colors.

INTERPRETING THE VISUAL RECORD

Hippies. Some young Americans rejected traditional values and customs. Other activists embraced other cultures and wore clothing such as this African dashiki. *What do the clothing styles seen here reveal about the counterculture?*

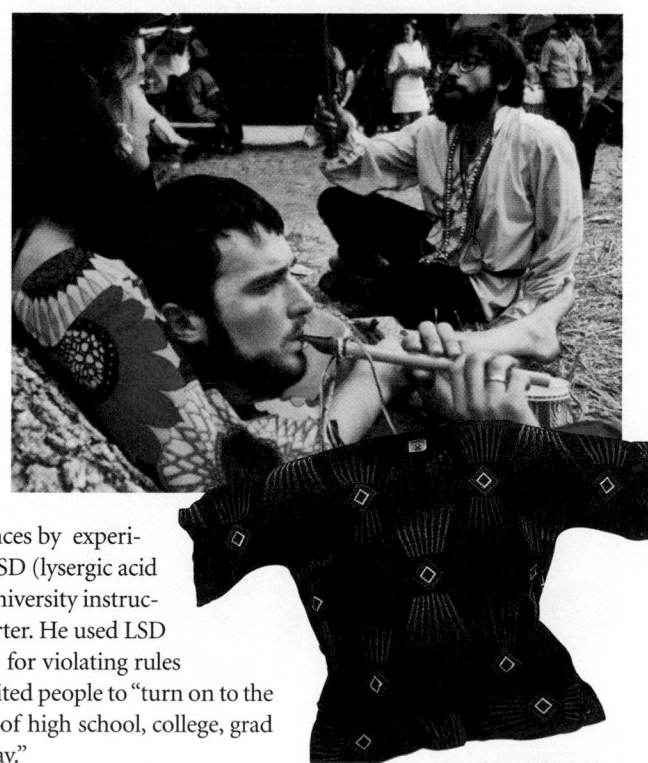

An African dashiki

PEOPLE IN HISTORY

Timothy Leary. Born in 1920, Timothy Leary studied psychotherapy at the University of California at Berkeley. He was a respected scholar before he became well known for his liberal attitudes toward drug use. In the 1960s Leary was convicted of drug possession. He escaped from a California prison in 1970, was recaptured in 1973, and was finally released in 1976. Leary later worked as a lecturer. After his death in 1996, Leary's ashes were shot into space.

ACTIVITY: Tell students to reread the quotation by Timothy Leary on this page. Then have each student write several paragraphs explaining why Leary and his ideas appealed to some Americans during the 1960s.

THAT'S INTERESTING!

During the California Gold Rush, Levi Strauss designed the first blue jeans, which quickly became popular with the working class. Political activists of the 1960s frequently wore blue jeans to capitalize on this heritage.

VISUAL RECORD ANSWER

Students might mention that they reveal an alternative to "mainstream" clothing.

LEVEL 1: Conduct a brief discussion on the counterculture. Then ask students to identify the problems that weakened the counterculture. *(Students should identify factors such as drug and alcohol abuse, sexually transmitted diseases, sexual abuse, and crime.)* Have each student write a paragraph on the rise and fall of the counterculture in the 1970s.
English Language Learners

LEVELS 2 AND 3: Conduct a brief discussion on the counterculture. Then ask students to reread the subsection on the pitfalls of the counterculture. Tell students to imagine that they are anticounterculture leaders in Haight-Ashbury. Have each student develop a leaflet similar to the one mentioned in the subsection. Students' leaflets should identify the problems that weakened the counterculture and urge runaways to return home. *(See the Level 1 lesson for the correct problems.)* Have volunteers discuss their leaflets with the class.

Haight-Ashbury. Over time, Haight-Ashbury became so well known that a local bus company operated a tour through the neighborhood called the Hippie Hop. In response to the increased media attention and commercialism, some hippies conducted a Death of Hippie ceremony in October 1967, holding a mock funeral procession.

CRITICAL THINKING Why might tourists have wanted to go on the Hippie Hop tour?

ANSWER: Students might suggest that tourists were intrigued by the hippies and their alternative lifestyle.

THAT'S INTERESTING!

Zen Buddhism teaches that an individual can unite with the universe through contemplation and meditation. The mystical aspects of Zen Buddhism appealed to some young people as an alternative to the materialism of American life.

VISUAL RECORD ANSWER

Answers will vary. Students might suggest that its comic-book appearance makes them think that it is not art.

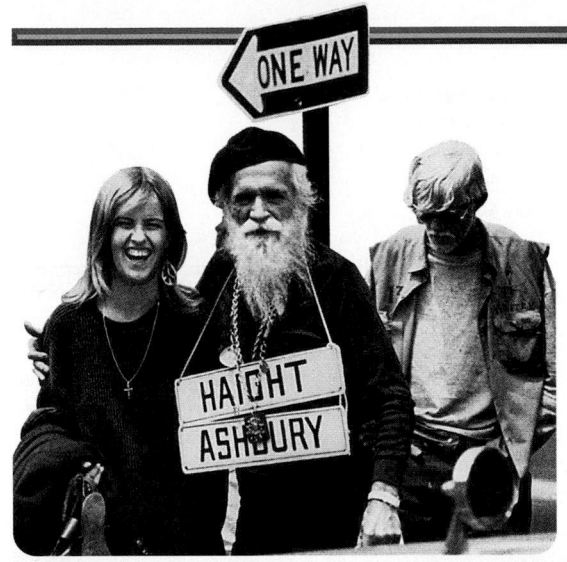

San Francisco's Haight-Ashbury district attracted a wide variety of people.

INTERPRETING THE VISUAL RECORD

Pop art. Roy Lichtenstein used bright colors and a comic-strip style in his artwork. *What elements of this painting make you think it is, or is not, art?*

Pitfalls of the counterculture. For some hippies, the experimentation of the era came at a high price. Reported cases of drug addiction and sexually transmitted diseases increased. In addition, some women perceived the era's new sexual freedom as yet another way for men to take advantage of women. Feminist Robin Morgan charged that "the so-called Sexual Revolution has . . . reinstituted [re-created] oppression by another name."

Young Americans who moved to Haight-Ashbury in search of cultural freedom found a harsh urban neighborhood troubled by crime. One leaflet handed out during the era declared, "Kids are starving on the Street. Minds and bodies are being maimed as we watch. . . . Are you aware that Haight Street is as bad as the squares say it is?" The counterculture also attracted sinister characters such as Charles Manson, who moved to Haight-Ashbury in 1967. Two years later Manson and a handful of his followers were responsible for a mass murder in California that horrified the nation.

✔ **READING CHECK: Categorizing** Give four examples of ways the counterculture expressed itself. dropping out of society; experimenting with mind-altering drugs; adopting colorful dress and different hairstyles; adopting a new sexual freedom

Changing American Society

The rise of the counterculture reflected the doubts that many citizens—particularly the young—held about the direction of American society. Americans increasingly questioned cultural traditions on a variety of issues from religion to the arts.

Religion. In a 1957 poll more than 80 percent of Americans claimed that religion could answer all or most of society's problems. By 1969, however, 70 percent said that religion was losing its influence on American life.

Americans did not necessarily lack spiritual faith. However, many lost confidence in the ability of established churches to provide spiritual direction. Some believed that the challenges of the nuclear age had made traditional religious answers irrelevant. Reflecting the search for alternative answers, the number of college courses in religion—and enrollment in them—grew dramatically. Interest in Eastern religions such as Zen Buddhism also rose.

The arts. The questioning of tradition extended into the art world. Many new visual artists argued that the art world had become a slave to upper-class tastes and customs. They claimed that established artists created works only to please a few cultural critics, not to appeal to the majority of nonartists. These new artists created a style called **pop art** because it was intended to appeal to

TEACH OBJECTIVE 3

ALL LEVELS: Write the following statement on the chalkboard: *Both religion and the arts are influenced by doubts about American society, as in the 1960s.* Have each student write a short response to the statement. *(Students should indicate that doubts about American society in the 1960s resulted in expanded interest in Eastern religions and helped give rise to pop art.)* Ask volunteers to read their responses to the class.
English Language Learners

SPOTLIGHT on Pop Art

Have students conduct research on pop art of the 1960s and 1970s. Ask students to bring examples of pop art to class. Display these examples around the classroom and have students study them. Then organize the class into two groups— one that supports pop art and views it as art, and one that opposes pop art and views it as nonart. Give each group time to prepare its arguments and then conduct a debate about the meaning and worth of pop art.
Cooperative Learning, Block Scheduling

---

popular tastes. Artists took inspiration from elements of popular culture including advertising, celebrities, comic books, and movies.

Film also underwent a broadening of subject matter as censorship rules were increasingly ignored. Rather than continuing to allow the Catholic Legion of Decency to make recommendations regarding motion pictures, the film industry adopted its own ratings system. The system informed audiences about the content of movies. The ratings system ranged from G, which meant that the film was intended for general audiences, to X, which meant that people under the age of 17 would not be admitted. The rating system was adopted to gain favor with the viewing public, who wanted more information about the content of films. However, some artists argued that the new standards allowed box-office receipts, rather than artistic concerns, to determine content. Movies rated for adult audiences increasingly drew larger crowds than more family-oriented films.

✔ **READING CHECK: Making Generalizations** How did new movements in religion and the arts reflect American society in the 1960s? They reflected the search for alternative answers in religion and the questioning of tradition in the art world.

AMERICAN ARTS
Pop Art

In the early 1960s a number of New York painters and sculptors emerged who wanted to make art more accessible to the general public. They accomplished their goals by using "found objects"—cardboard packaging, cartoon strips, furniture, tin cans, and other everyday articles—as the subjects of their works. The leading supporters of this method, called pop art, included Roy Lichtenstein and Claes Oldenburg. Lichtenstein's huge paintings were done in comic-strip style. Oldenberg used a variety of materials to make giant sculptures of such things as clothespins, hamburgers, and toothpaste tubes.

The best-known pop artist was Andy Warhol. His most notable paintings include depictions of Campbell's soup cans, rows of Coca-Cola bottles, and a brightly colored photograph of Marilyn Monroe reproduced multiple times. Initially, Warhol painted his own works by hand, but he switched to a stencil-printing process called silk screen. Eventually, he simply created designs for his team of assistants to reproduce. Warhol's message—that everything, even art, can be mass-produced—both glorified and mocked American consumerism.

Andy Warhol painted these oversized soup cans in 1962.

Understanding the Arts

1. What did pop artists use as subjects?
2. How did pop art reflect the changing times of the 1960s?
3. What do you think Andy Warhol was trying to communicate in the painting shown above?

INTERDISCIPLINARY CONNECTIONS

►ART◄

Protesting Commercialism. During the 1960s and 1970s some artists worried that works of art had been reduced to mere commodities. These artists attempted to create art that had no monetary value and that would not be bought and sold by collectors. One such artist, Robert Smithson, used a bulldozer to create *Spiral Jetty,* a long spiral of land in the Great Salt Lake.

ACTIVITY: Conduct a brief discussion on noncommercial art. Then have each student design or create a piece of noncommercial art.

AMERICAN ARTS ANSWERS

1. found objects

2. Like many things in the 1960s, pop art was for everyone to understand and appreciate.

3. Students might suggest that Warhol was trying to convey a sense of beauty or wonder in everyday objects.

LEVEL 1: Pair students and tell them to imagine that they are young people during the 1960s. Direct each pair to create a message for a time capsule that will be opened in 2020. Messages should describe 1960s music and explain how it was influenced by the social changes of the era. *(Pairs should note that the music of the 1960s reflected the era's emphasis on civil rights, diversity, experimentation, and political protest.)* Have volunteers read their messages to the class. Then conduct a discussion comparing and contrasting 1960s music and 1990s music.

English Language Learners, Cooperative Learning

LEVELS 2 AND 3: Tell students to imagine that they are rock critics at Woodstock. Have each student write a brief review discussing the event, the music, and the performers. Reviews should also discuss how the musical styles reflect the social changes of the era. *(See the Level 1 lesson for the correct answers.)* Have volunteers read their reviews to the class.

HOMEWORK *Ask each student to write a press release for a rock star of the 1960s. The release should contain information about the artist's goals, influence, and music. In their releases, students should explain how the artist's musical style reflects the social changes of the era. Remind students that the purpose of a press release is to advertise the artist while providing information for the fans.*

SECTION 4 REVIEW ANSWERS

1. Define
- generation gap, p. 694
- counterculture, p. 695
- pop art, p. 696

2. Identify
- Mario Savio, p. 694
- Timothy Leary, p. 695
- British invasion, p. 698
- Joan Baez, p. 698
- Bob Dylan, p. 698
- James Brown, p. 699
- Aretha Franklin, p. 699
- Woodstock, p. 699

3. conflicts—generation gap and social problems such as Cold War fears, civil rights protests, and the Vietnam War; complaints—universities limited free speech and creativity; tactics—launched sit-ins and rallies

4a. Answers will vary. Students might suggest that drugs are more prevalent; religion is less important; fashion, art, and movies reflect independent spirit; and rock 'n' roll is here to stay.

b. the influence of the counterculture and internal doubts; led artists to challenge conventions

c. It was bright, vivacious, and joyful, but it also protested against the rules of society at large, and these were both signatures of the counterculture movement.

5. Answers will vary. The event proved that a peaceful culture united by music could overcome serious obstacles and change the world.

Sounds of the 1960s

Changes in the visual arts were matched by developments in popular music. The social and political movements of the 1960s marched to new forms of music that ranged from rock to folk to soul.

Rock music. A major influence on the youth rebellion of the 1950s, rock 'n' roll continued to reflect social change in the 1960s. The year 1964 marked the musical **British invasion**—the introduction of new British bands to an American audience. Groups such as the Beatles and the Rolling Stones drew on 1950s rock 'n' roll and African American blues, thrilling American teenagers. Jane Berentson was a high school student in 1964. She later recalled of the Beatles, "The girls all decided right away which one they were in love with. And the boys all decided which one they looked like."

The use of electrically amplified instruments such as the electric guitar inspired musicians to try out innovative—and very loud—sounds on their audiences. Seattle native Jimi Hendrix was the master of the electric guitar in the 1960s. This new music served as a soundtrack for the counterculture. As one observer noted, the counterculture "is bright, vivacious [full of life], ecstatic, crowd-loving, joyful—and its music is rock."

The music of the 1960s reflected the many changes that were occurring in American society.

Folk's rebirth. During the 1930s artists such as Woody Guthrie had used folk music to point out flaws in American society. By the 1950s this tradition had lost influence. During the 1960s, however, folk music gained popularity once again. Folk artists such as **Joan Baez** and **Bob Dylan** wrote lyrics that sent a political message to listeners. Dylan's 1962 hit, "Blowin' in the Wind," was one of these.

History Makers Speak **"How many years can a mountain exist before it's washed to the sea?**
Yes, 'n' How many years can some people exist before they're allowed to be free?
Yes, 'n' How many times can a man turn his head pretending he just doesn't see?
The answer, my friend, is blowin' in the wind
The answer is blowin' in the wind."

—Bob Dylan, "Blowin' in the Wind"

Dylan linked folk and rock music in 1965. He appeared on stage with an electric guitar instead of an acoustic guitar, the instrument traditionally used in folk music. Many fans of folk music felt that Dylan had betrayed them. Charles Kaiser attended a 1966 Dylan concert. He noted that the audience "screamed, shouted, walked out . . . even threw things at the stage"—but Dylan had brought folk music firmly into the rock realm.

Motown and soul. Despite rock's roots in African American blues, the British invasion pushed many African American performers off the record charts. Berry Gordy brought African Americans back into the forefront of popular music with Motown Records, his record company based in Detroit. By 1975 Motown was earning over $50 million annually. This made it one of the country's most successful

REVIEW

Have students complete the **Section 4 Review** on p. 699.

ASSESS

Have students complete **Daily Quiz 23.4**. As **Alternative Assessment**, you may want to use the anticounterculture leaflet or the music review in this section's lessons.

RETEACH

Have students complete **Main Idea Activity for English Language Learners and Special-Needs Students 23.4**. Then have each student write a paragraph that summarizes Section 4

and defines all the key terms and identifies people listed in this section. **English Language Learners**

EXTEND

Organize the class into small groups. Have each group select a musician from the 1960s or 1970s. Ask each group to design a music video for one of the performer's songs. Students should create detailed storyboards that display the sequence and look of their music videos. Have volunteers present their storyboards to the class. **Cooperative Learning, Block Scheduling**

African American–owned businesses. Successful Motown artists included the Supremes and the Temptations.

Perhaps the most dynamic artist of the era was **James Brown**. Performing a form of rhythm-and-blues music known as soul, Brown captivated audiences with his athletic, emotionally charged shows. Nicknamed the Godfather of Soul, Brown had started performing at the age of 12. He had his first hit record in 1956, with the song "Please Please Please."

Matching Brown in popularity and career length was **Aretha Franklin**, known as the Queen of Soul. In the late 1960s she scored a string of hits that included "Respect," "Chain of Fools," and "Think."

Woodstock

Rock music was the focal point of the Woodstock Music and Art Fair. The event marked both the height and the beginning of the end for the counterculture movement. In August 1969 some 400,000 young people descended on rural upstate New York for the three-day festival, closing the New York State Thruway in the process. Despite driving rain, knee-deep mud, and severe shortages of food and water, the concert remained a peaceful gathering. Listeners reveled in the music of rock's top performers, including Jimi Hendrix, Joan Baez, and Janis Joplin.

Woodstock was more than just a rock concert. It was the celebration of an era and marked the high point of the counterculture movement. However, the excitement of the Woodstock experience was short-lived. Four months later, the Rolling Stones held a free concert at Altamont Raceway near San Francisco. At the concert a security team made up of members of a motorcycle gang stabbed a young African American to death in full view of the stage. The event raised doubts about the idealistic spirit of the youth movement.

INTERPRETING THE VISUAL RECORD

Woodstock. The 1969 Woodstock Music and Art Fair attracted hundreds of thousands of young Americans. *What do you think the picture on this poster symbolizes?*

✔ **READING CHECK: Summarizing** How did musical styles change in the 1960s?
the British invasion, electrically amplified instruments, political folk music, and development of soul music

SECTION 4 REVIEW

1. **Define and explain:**
   generation gap
   counterculture
   pop art

2. **Identify and explain:**
   Mario Savio
   Timothy Leary
   British invasion
   Joan Baez
   Bob Dylan
   James Brown
   Aretha Franklin
   Woodstock

3. **Analyzing Information** Copy the graphic organizer below. Use it to explain how other conflicts in society influenced protests on college campuses.

   Social Conflicts → Student Complaints → Student Protest Tactics

4. **Finding the Main Idea**
   a. What lasting changes did the counterculture have on American society?
   b. Why did a growing number of Americans question religion and traditional social values during the 1960s? How did this affect the arts?
   c. Why was rock 'n' roll music so influential in the counterculture?

5. **Writing and Critical Thinking**
   Evaluating Imagine that you attended Woodstock. Write a letter to a grandchild explaining how the event illustrated the ideals of the counterculture.
   Consider:
   • the beliefs of the counterculture's followers
   • the role of rock music
   • the audience's behavior at Woodstock

go.hrw.com **Homework Practice Online**
keyword: SE3 HP23

★★
CHAPTER
23
REVIEW AND ASSESSMENT RESOURCES

TECHNOLOGY

▶ Chapter 23 Test Generator (on the One-Stop Planner)
▶ Global Skill Builder CD–ROM
▶ HRW Go site

REINFORCEMENT, REVIEW, AND ASSESSMENT

▶ Chapter 23 Review, pp. 700–01
▶ Chapter 23 Tutorial for Students, Parents, Mentors, and Peers

▶ Chapter 23 Test (Form A or B)
▶ Portfolio Activities and Alternative Assessment Handbook, Chapter 23
▶ Chapter 23 Test for English Language Learners and Special-Needs Students

REVIEW

Have students complete the **Chapter 23 Review** on pp. 700–01.

ASSESS

Use one of the chapter tests to assess students' understanding of the content. For **Alternative Assessment**, see the **Portfolio Activities and Alternative Assessment Handbook**.

Understanding Main Ideas

1. to pressure elected officials to work for women's equality

2. Steinem—helped found the National Women's Political Caucus, wrote books on the women's movement, and was a strong supporter of the ERA; Chisholm—became the first African-American woman elected to Congress, and ran for the Democratic nomination for president

3. Chávez founded the NFWA and helped striking migrant workers with food and support; he also encouraged public sympathy for Chicano causes; and he inspired other Mexican Americans to fight discrimination.

4. to protest the poor quality of the schools they attended

5. Students might suggest that AIM gained media attention but achieved few of its goals.

6. Musicians such as Bob Dylan used their lyrics to express political criticism.

Reviewing Themes

1. Answers will vary but should refer to the ERA.

2. They objected to various university policies and social problems. In addition, they had the time and money to pursue protests.

3. art—questioned materialism and capitalism; fashion—expressed rejection of traditional beliefs; music—spread political messages and offered an innovative sound and a new way of thinking

★
★★
CHAPTER
23

Review

Creating a Time Line

Copy the time line below onto a sheet of paper. Complete the time line by filling in the events and dates from the chapter that you think were most significant. Pick three events and explain why you think they were significant.

| 1960 | 1965 | 1970 | 1975 |

Writing a Summary

Using standard grammar, spelling, sentence structure, and punctuation, write an overview of events in the chapter.

Identifying People and Ideas

Identify the following terms or individuals and explain their significance.

1. Betty Friedan
2. Equal Pay Act
3. César Chávez
4. Brown Berets
5. La Raza Unida Party
6. American Indian Movement
7. Maggie Kuhn
8. counterculture
9. Mario Savio
10. Woodstock

Understanding Main Ideas

SECTION 1 *(pp. 676–681)*

1. Why was the National Organization for Women founded?
2. What contributions did leaders like Gloria Steinem and Shirley Chisholm make?

SECTION 2 *(pp. 682–688)*

3. Explain the role and significance of César Chávez in the Chicano movement.
4. Why did high school students in Los Angeles hold walkouts?

SECTION 3 *(pp. 689–693)*

5. Did the American Indian Movement achieve its goals? Explain your answer.

SECTION 4 *(pp. 694–699)*

6. What was the relationship between music and political protest?

Reviewing Themes

1. **Constitutional Heritage** When should the Constitution be amended? Explain your answer.
2. **Economics** Why did middle-class university students turn to political protest?
3. **Culture** How did Americans use art, fashion, and music to question American values?

Thinking Critically

1. **Analyzing Information** How did women's roles change in the 1960s, and how did these changes affect American society?
2. **Identifying Cause and Effect** In what ways did the African American civil rights movement influence the protest methods of other groups in American society?
3. **Summarizing** What problems did Mexican American activists encounter as they tried to create national organizations?
4. **Drawing Conclusions** In what ways did the increased participation of minority groups in the political process change American society?
5. **Evaluating** What forms of protest proved most effective during the 1960s and 1970s?

Writing About History

Supporting a Point of View Write a speech intended to persuade an audience to either support or oppose ratification of the Equal Rights Amendment. Use the graphic below to organize your thoughts.

| Reasons to Support | ERA | Reasons to Oppose |

RETEACH

Pair students and assign each pair one of the sections in this chapter. Have each pair create detailed graphic organizers for the material in its assigned section. Ask students to present their graphic organizers to the class. To provide a review tool for students, display the graphic organizers around the classroom.
English Language Learners, Cooperative Learning

EXTEND

Have students conduct research on a social issue of the late 1990s, such as drug abuse or violence. Ask each student to write a short report discussing experts' analysis of its causes and presenting experts' recommendations for addressing the problem. Then have students compare and contrast their chosen issues with those studied in this chapter. Conduct a discussion on students' responses. **Block Scheduling**

Building Social Studies Skills

Interpreting Maps
Study the map below. Then use it to help answer the questions that follow.

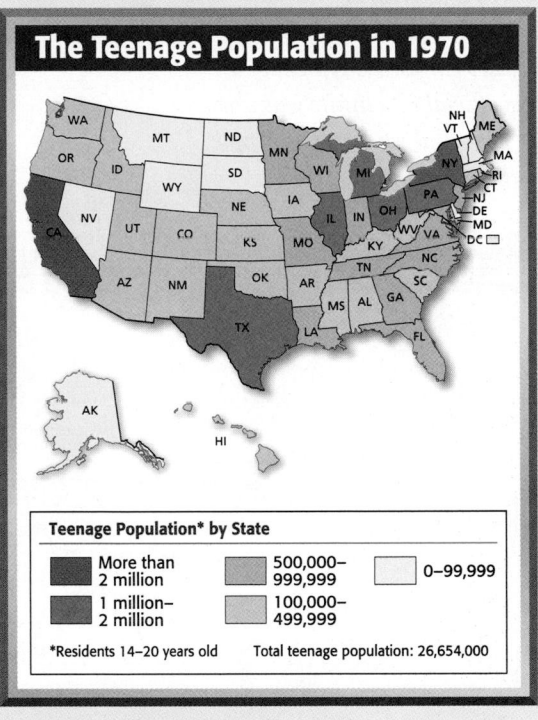

The Teenage Population in 1970

Teenage Population* by State

- More than 2 million
- 1 million– 2 million
- 500,000– 999,999
- 100,000– 499,999
- 0–99,999

*Residents 14–20 years old   Total teenage population: 26,654,000

1. Which states had the highest teenage population?
  a. New York and California
  b. Illinois, Michigan, Ohio, Pennsylvania, and Texas
  c. Montana, North Dakota, and South Dakota
  d. Florida, Georgia, and Tennessee

2. What were some important influences of the student movement on American society in the 1960s?

Analyzing Primary Sources
Analyze the following remarks made by Dorothy Height, president of the National Council of Negro Women, in 1970. Then answer the questions that follow.

❝To be black and a woman is to labor under the double handicap of racism and sexism. Historically, the black woman has carried this dual burden. She has had to work alongside the black man in a struggle unlike that of any other group in the United States. . . .

Today, when black women have entered every field of work that women have entered and the earnings of black women have increased, the black woman is still to be found largely in the lowest paid jobs. And it is true that her earnings are today 78 percent of those of white women. . . .

Many who are the heads of families still live below the poverty line. In 1968, 16 percent of the white families headed by a woman and 45 percent of the black families headed by a woman who worked during the year were still below the poverty line.❞

3. What kind of evidence does Height provide to support her claims?
  a. No evidence provided
  b. Statistical evidence
  c. Opinion
  d. Personal narratives

4. From your study of U.S. history, what evidence supports Height's claims?

Alternative Assessment

Building Your Portfolio

Culture
Imagine that you are a radio reporter in 1969. You have been allowed on Alcatraz Island during its occupation by Red Power activists. Conduct interviews with some of the participants and include them in your report on why the activists took over the island. Be sure to include the location of the island and its history.

internet connect

Internet Activity: go.hrw.com
KEYWORD: SE3 AN23
Choose a topic on the struggles for change to:
- fill in an interactive organizer comparing issues in the women's rights movement.
- create a pamphlet on César Chávez and the United Farm Workers.
- explore the cultural revolution in the arts and music.

Thinking Critically
1. Women began to examine their lives and many left the home to get jobs. This led to the Equal Pay Act. With the fight over the ERA, America became more equal.

2. It inspired the idea of nonviolent protest and demonstrated the effectiveness of public demonstrations.

3. They faced violent resistance and internal conflicts.

4. With the increased participation of women, African Americans, Native Americans, disabled Americans, older Americans, and children, America became a place where everyone was free.

5. Answers will vary. Some students might note that political lobbying proved effective for many groups.

Writing
support—possibility of better jobs and wages for women and protection against discrimination; oppose—possibility of negative consequences for traditional gender roles

Building Social Studies Skills
1. a

2. Answers will vary. Students might suggest that they demonstrated that questioning and rebelling have their places in a democracy.

3. b

4. Answers will vary. Students might suggest that women were paid less than men, even after the Equal Pay Act, and that all minorities were treated worse than whites in the workplace.

LET'S GET STARTED!

Write the name of the following city on the chalkboard: *Los Angeles.* Have students list all the words that they associate with the city. *(Students might list words such as Hollywood, movies, traffic, and so on.)* Ask volunteers to share their lists with the class. Then tell students that they will learn more about the urban United States, concentrating on Los Angeles as a case study, in the Unit 6 America's Geography.

TEACH AMERICA'S GEOGRAPHY— URBAN AMERICA

Pair students and have them study the America's Geography feature. Then have each pair translate the maps and the graph into written form. *(Pairs should note that the 1920s map shows the importance of electric trolleys and stream trains in the Los Angeles area, that the 1980s map displays the enormous growth of the city and its highway system, and that the graph shows the population boom in the city.)* Ask volunteers to read their summaries to the class.

English Language Learners, Cooperative Learning

Population Distribution. As urban Los Angeles grew, so did the diversity of its population. According to a 1990 census, nonwhite ethnic and racial groups made up more than half of the population. South Central Los Angeles had a primarily African American population while East Los Angeles had a high concentration of Hispanic residents.

CRITICAL THINKING How might residential segregation work against the ideals of a democratic society?

ANSWER: Answers will vary. Some students might suggest that democratic ideals involve social integration.

AMERICA'S GEOGRAPHY ANSWERS

1. steam train

2. approximately 45 miles

AMERICA'S Geography

Urban America

As more people moved to the cities and suburbs after World War II, metropolitan areas—large cities or groups of cities and their surrounding areas—were created. The city of Los Angeles is typical of a metroplex. In the 1920s most of the land inside the official city limits was not developed. As the city grew, it engulfed numerous surrounding areas as people increasingly moved outside the city and commuted to work.

Suburban growth.

Los Angeles was at the forefront of the creation of the suburban housing system. By the 1920s, Los Angeles had built the nation's most extensive electric railway-car system in an effort to encourage people to live outside the city and commute. City boosters used this system and the area's geography to encourage migration. Boosters noted the sunny climate and pleasant beaches nearby.

Land Use in the Los Angeles Area, 1920s to 1980s

	Official city limits		Industrial centers		Built-up areas	**Transportation**		Electric trolleys

Ethnic Neighborhoods

10% or more African American and 20% or more foreign-born Mexican American — 10% or more African American — Steam trains

Filming an early Hollywood western

Hollywood. Early filmmakers were attracted to Los Angeles because of its geography. The city's dry climate and nearness to many different types of landscapes, including the beaches, mountains, and desert, made filming easy.

GEOGRAPHY AND HISTORY Skills

THE WORLD IN SPATIAL TERMS

1. If you had lived in Anaheim, California, in the 1920s and wanted to commute to downtown Los Angeles, what kind of transportation would you have taken?

2. What is the distance between the northernmost and the southernmost points of the official city limits?

AMERICA'S Geography

Los Angeles Area, 1980s

Los Angeles River · Burbank · San Gabriel River · Hollywood · San Bernardino · Beverly Hills · LOS ANGELES · Santa Monica · Watts · Santa Ana River · PACIFIC OCEAN · Anaheim · Long Beach · Santa Ana

0 10 20 Miles
0 10 20 Kilometers
Lambert Conformal Conic Projection

Average Traffic Flow per Day
- 200,000 or more vehicles
- 100,000–199,999 vehicles
- 50,000–99,999 vehicles
- 49,999 or fewer vehicles
- Other major road

Ethnic Neighborhoods
- 40% or more African American
- 40% or more Hispanic
- 30% or more Asian
- Mixed ethnic population

Changes. By the 1940s automobiles had replaced the railway system as the preferred means of transportation in Los Angeles. Wartime employment caused the city to grow rapidly. The creation of a huge new freeway system encouraged this growth.

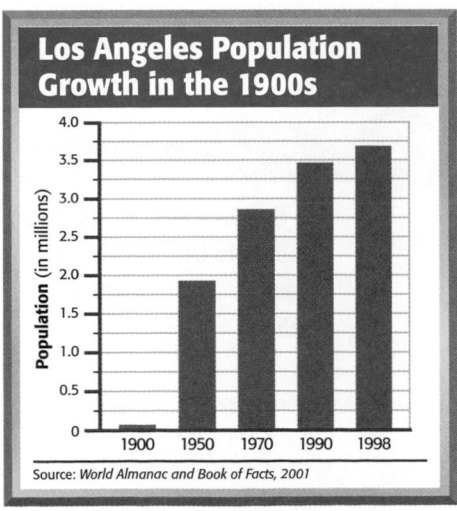

Los Angeles Population Growth in the 1900s

Population (in millions): 4.0, 3.5, 3.0, 2.5, 2.0, 1.5, 1.0, 0.5, 0
Years: 1900, 1950, 1970, 1990, 1998

Source: *World Almanac and Book of Facts, 2001*

GEOGRAPHY AND HISTORY Skills

HUMAN SYSTEMS

1. By how much did the population of Los Angeles increase between 1900 and 1950?
2. How many miles of freeways had an average traffic flow of at least 200,000 vehicles per day?

INTERDISCIPLINARY CONNECTIONS

▶GEOGRAPHY◀

Los Angeles. The city of Los Angeles covers some 464 square miles. Not surprisingly, cars are crucial in this sprawling environment. One commentator, invoking the scholarly practice of studying Italian to read Dante, said that he learned to drive so that he could "read Los Angeles in the original."

ACTIVITY: Ask students to conduct research to identify the 10 largest cities—in terms of square miles—in the United States. Have each student create a visual display presenting the results of his or her research. Ask students to inspect the visual displays. To conclude, conduct a brief discussion on the advantages and disadvantages of so-called "mega cities."

THAT'S INTERESTING!

According to the 1990 census, California had more automobiles than any other state. It also had the highest number of vehicle miles of travel.

AMERICA'S GEOGRAPHY ANSWERS

1. by about 1.75 million people
2. about 115 miles

CHAPTER 24

War in Vietnam

CHAPTER RESOURCE MANAGER

Objectives	Pacing Guide	Reproducible Resources
SECTION 1 **Background to Conflict** pp. 706–11	★ Analyze why China and France wanted to control Vietnam. ★ Explain why the United States refused to support Vietnamese independence in the 1940s and 1950s. ★ Discuss why President Kennedy increased U.S. involvement in Vietnam.	**Regular** 2 days **Block Scheduling** 1 day *Block Scheduling Handbook with Team Teaching Strategies, pp. 139–44*	**RS** Guided Reading Strategy 24.1 **SM** American History Outline Map 22: The Vietnam War **SM** Geography Activity 24: Geography and the Vietnam War
SECTION 2 **The War Escalates** pp. 712–19	★ Identify the constitutional issue the Tonkin Gulf Resolution raised. ★ Describe the strategies U.S. forces used in the Vietnam War. ★ List factors that frustrated U.S. military efforts in Vietnam. ★ Explain why some Americans opposed the war, and describe how the government responded.	**Regular** 2 days **Block Scheduling** 1 day *Block Scheduling Handbook with Team Teaching Strategies, pp. 139–44*	**RS** Guided Reading Strategy 24.2 **IC** Literature Reading 24: Jungle Warfare **RS** Graphic Organizer Activity 24: A Divided Nation **PS** Biography Reading 24: Muhammad Ali
SECTION 3 **A Turning Point** pp. 720–25	★ Explain why the Tet Offensive weakened many Americans' confidence in their government. ★ List the key events of the 1968 presidential campaign. ★ Summarize how President Nixon attempted to end the war. ★ Describe how Americans reacted to President Nixon's plan to end the war.	**Regular** 2 days **Block Scheduling** 1 day *Block Scheduling Handbook with Team Teaching Strategies, pp. 139–44*	**RS** Guided Reading Strategy 24.3 **E** Hands-On History Activity: The Vietnam Era and the Armed Forces **E** Creative Teaching Strategy: Dialogue Debate Lesson
SECTION 4 **The War Ends** pp. 726–31	★ Explain why the United States agreed to a cease-fire in January 1973. ★ Describe the war's long-term effects on Vietnam and the Vietnamese people. ★ Evaluate the war's long-term effects on the American people.	**Regular** 2 days **Block Scheduling** 1 day *Block Scheduling Handbook with Team Teaching Strategies, pp. 139–44*	**RS** Guided Reading Strategy 24.4 **PS** Primary Source Reading 24: The Return of Vietnam Veterans

Chapter Resource Key

PS	Primary Sources	**REV** Review	Video
RS	Reading Support	**ELL** Reinforcement and English Language Learners	Internet
IC	Interdisciplinary Connections		Holt Presentation Maker Using Microsoft® PowerPoint®
E	Enrichment	Transparencies	
SM	Skills Mastery	CD–ROM	
A	Assessment	Music	

One-Stop Planner CD–ROM

See the *One-Stop Planner* for a complete list of additional resources for students and teachers.

One-Stop Planner CD–ROM

It's easy to plan lessons, select resources, and print out materials for your students when you use the **One-Stop Planner CD–ROM with Test Generator.**

Technology Resources

 One-Stop Planner, Lesson 24.1
 Holt Researcher: American History CD–ROM
 Homework Practice Online

 One-Stop Planner, Lesson 24.2
 Everyday Life in America Transparency 30: Protest During the Vietnam War
The American Nation Video Program Segment: Vietnam and the Media; Teacher's Guide, pp. 141–46
 Holt Researcher: American History CD–ROM
 Homework Practice Online

 One-Stop Planner, Lesson 24.3
 CNN Presents America: Yesterday and Today, 1850 to the Present Segment: America Honors the Vets
 Holt Researcher: American History CD–ROM
 Homework Practice Online

 One-Stop Planner, Lesson 24.4
 Holt Researcher: American History CD–ROM
 Homework Practice Online
HRW Go site

Reinforcement, Review, and Assessment

REV Section 1 Review, p. 711
A Daily Quiz 24.1
ELL Main Idea Activity 24.1
ELL English Audio Summary 24.1
ELL Spanish Audio Summary 24.1

REV Section 2 Review, p. 719
A Daily Quiz 24.2
ELL Main Idea Activity 24.2
ELL English Audio Summary 24.2
ELL Spanish Audio Summary 24.2

REV Section 3 Review, p. 725
A Daily Quiz 24.3
ELL Main Idea Activity 24.3
ELL English Audio Summary 24.3
ELL Spanish Audio Summary 24.3

REV Section 4 Review, p. 731
A Daily Quiz 24.4
ELL Main Idea Activity 24.4
ELL English Audio Summary 24.4
ELL Spanish Audio Summary 24.4

☑ internet connect

HRW ONLINE RESOURCES
GO TO: go.hrw.com
Then type in a keyword.

TEACHER HOME PAGE
KEYWORD: SE3 Teacher

CHAPTER INTERNET ACTIVITIES
KEYWORD: SE3 AN24
Choose an activity to:
• create a newspaper on the last phases of the Vietnam War.
• research the changes in Southeast Asia since the end of the Vietnam War.
• learn about the history and meaning of the Vietnam Veterans Memorial.

CHAPTER ENRICHMENT LINKS
KEYWORD: SE3 CH24

ONLINE ASSESSMENT
Homework Practice
KEYWORD: SE3 HP24

Standardized Test Prep
KEYWORD: SE3 STP24

Rubrics
KEYWORD: SS Rubrics

ONLINE MAPS, CHARTS, AND GRAPHS
KEYWORD: SE3 MCG
• Landscape of Indochina
• Election of 1968

CONTENT UPDATES
KEYWORD: SS Content Updates

HOLT PRESENTATION MAKER
KEYWORD: SE3 PPT24

ONLINE READING SUPPORT
KEYWORD: SS Strategies

CURRENT EVENTS
KEYWORD: S3 Current Events

Meeting Individual Needs

Ability Levels

Level 1 Basic-level activities designed for all students encountering new material

Level 2 Intermediate-level activities designed for average students

Level 3 Challenging activities designed for honors and gifted-and-talented students

English Language Learners Activities that address the needs of students with Limited English Proficiency

Chapter Review and Assessment

Global Skill Builder CD–ROM

HRW Go site

REV Chapter 24 Tutorial for Students, Parents, Mentors, and Peers

REV Chapter 24 Review, pp. 732–33

Chapter 24 Test Generator (on the One-Stop Planner)

A Chapter 24 Test (Form A or B)

A Alternative Assessment Handbook

A Chapter 24 Test for English Language Learners and Special-Needs Students

Build on What You Know

Ask students to answer the following questions.

**How might the Vietnam War
have been similar to the
Korean War?**
Consider:

• U.S. goals in Korea

• public attitudes toward
both wars

**Why might the Vietnam War
have inspired protests?**
Consider:

• the ways in which the United
States became involved in the
Vietnam War

• the length of the war

• other conflicts in American
society during the 1960s

---

exploring the time line

AMERICAN EVENTS

**PEOPLE
IN HISTORY**

**1960 ■ *To Kill a
Mockingbird.*** Author Harper
Lee grew up in the town of
Monroeville, Alabama. Her
childhood there inspired the
setting and some of the characters of *To Kill A Mockingbird.*
Her father, Amasa Lee, was a
lawyer and the model for the
novel's hero Atticus Finch.
Harper Lee herself studied to
be a lawyer at the University
of Alabama and at Oxford
University. However, she moved
to New York City six months
short of a law degree. Lee won
a Pulitzer Prize for her novel in
1961. While she continues to
write, she has never published
another novel.

ACTIVITY: Have students write
a brief outline for a novel using
their hometown as a model
for the setting. Students should
provide a historical context
for their novel.

CHAPTER

24

1954–1975

War in Vietnam

An early
microchip

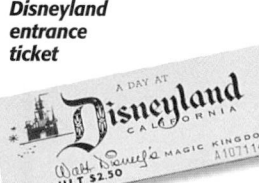

Disneyland
entrance
ticket

**1955
Daily Life**
The Disneyland
amusement park
opens in Anaheim,
California.

**1959
Science and Technology**
Working independently,
Jack Kilby and Robert
Noyce revolutionize elec-
tronic technology with the
invention of the microchip.

**1960
The Arts**
Alabama writer
Harper Lee
publishes *To Kill
a Mockingbird.*

**1963
World Events**
Military officers
overthrow the
South Vietnamese
government.

**1963
The Arts**
The Beatles have a
hit song, "I Want to
Hold Your Hand."

1954

1957

1960

1963

**1954
Science and Technology**
The first nuclear-powered
submarine, the *Nautilus*, is
launched at Groton, Connecticut.

**1957
Business
and Finance**
The Treaty of Rome
establishes the
European Economic
Community, removing
trade barriers among
Belgium, France, Italy,
Luxembourg, the
Netherlands, and
West Germany.

**1959
World Events**
Rebel leader Fidel Castro
seizes power from Cuban
dictator Fulgencio Batista.

*The USS
Nautilus*

*Fulgencio
Batista*

Build on What You Know

After World War II the United States took a stand opposing the spread of
communism anywhere in the world. In the early 1950s U.S. troops
fought against communist forces in Korea. In this chapter you will learn
how the United States became involved in a similar war in Vietnam, which had
won its independence from the French in 1954. Eventually more than 2 million
Americans served in the Vietnam War. The conflict, which lasted more than a
decade, left deep scars on both Vietnam and the United States.

What's Your Opinion?

Global Relations

Agree U.S. involvement in World War II helped the Allies win the conflict and defeat Nazi Germany, thus saving many lives.

Disagree Every nation has the right to self-determination.

Constitutional Heritage

Agree The framers of the Constitution created a checks-and-balances system to guard against tyranny.

Disagree In the interest of national security, the president often must take action without consulting Congress.

Citizenship

Agree In a democracy, people have the unlimited right to protest government actions.

Disagree The U.S. government limited civil rights and protests during the Civil War to promote the war effort.

U.S. Army helicopters remove infantry troops from a search-and-destroy mission in southern Vietnam.

The Kent State shooting

1966 World Events U.S. military strategy in Vietnam focuses on search-and-destroy missions.

1970 Daily Life At an antiwar rally at Kent State University in Ohio, National Guardsmen open fire, killing four people and wounding nine.

1975 World Events North Vietnamese forces capture the South Vietnamese capital of Saigon.

1966   **1969**   **1972**   **1975**

1967 Daily Life Boxer Muhammad Ali is sentenced to five years in prison for refusing to report for military duty.

Muhammad Ali

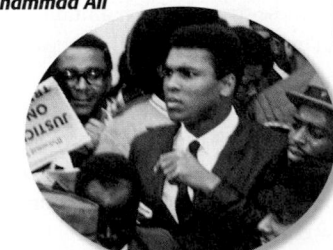

1968 World Events Soviet troops invade Czechoslovakia to crush a reform movement.

1968 Politics Richard M. Nixon is elected president.

1971 World Events General Idi Amin seizes power in Uganda.

Nixon campaign bolo tie

1975 Science and Technology President Gerald Ford signs the Metric Conversion Act to move the United States to the metric system.

What's Your Opinion?

Themes Journal *Do you agree or disagree with the following statements? Support your point of view in your journal.*

Global Relations Under certain circumstances one nation has the right to intervene in the affairs of another.

Constitutional Heritage The system of checks and balances will be damaged if one branch of government becomes too strong.

Citizenship In a democracy there should be no limits to a person's right to protest government actions.

exploring the time line

GLOBAL EVENTS

internet connect

TOPIC: The Last Phases of the Vietnam War
GO TO: go.hrw.com
KEYWORD: SE3 AN24

Have students access the Internet through the HRW Go site to conduct research on the last phases of the Vietnam War. Then ask students to assume one of the following roles: a U.S. Marine, a Vietcong soldier, a South Vietnamese civilian, or a Vietnamese citizen who was evacuated out of Saigon. Tell each student to create a newspaper from the perspective of his or her chosen role. Have volunteers read their newspapers to the class.

After completing Section 1, students should be able to:

OBJECTIVE 1 Analyze why China and France wanted to control Vietnam.

OBJECTIVE 2 Explain why the United States refused to support Vietnamese independence in the 1940s and 1950s.

OBJECTIVE 3 Discuss why President Kennedy increased U.S. involvement in Vietnam.

🎙️ LET'S GET STARTED!

As students enter the classroom, ask them to list 10 words that they associate with the Vietnam War. Have volunteers share their word lists. (*Students might list words such as violent, unjust, mistake, and so on.*) Tell students that in Section 1 they will learn more about the background of the conflict in Vietnam.

SECTION ① RESOURCES

REPRODUCIBLE
▶ Guided Reading Strategy 24.1
▶ American History Outline Map 22: The Vietnam War
▶ Geography Activity 24: Geography and the Vietnam War

TECHNOLOGY
▶ One-Stop Planner, Lesson 24.1
▶ Holt Researcher: American History CD–ROM
▶ Homework Practice Online

REINFORCEMENT, REVIEW, AND ASSESSMENT
▶ Section 1 Review, p. 711
▶ Daily Quiz 24.1
▶ Main Idea Activity 24.1
▶ English Audio Summary 24.1
▶ Spanish Audio Summary 24.1

SECTION ①

READ TO DISCOVER

1. Why did China and France want to control Vietnam?
2. Why did the United States refuse to support Vietnamese independence in the 1940s and 1950s?
3. Why did President Kennedy increase U.S. involvement in Vietnam?

DEFINE

domino theory

IDENTIFY

Le Loi
Ho Chi Minh
Vietminh
Ngo Dinh Diem
Vietcong

WHY IT MATTERS TODAY

The United States still sends military troops to areas around the world even when war has not been declared. Use **CNNfyi.com** or other **current events** sources to learn about places where U.S. troops have played an important role. Record your findings in your journal.

CNNfyi.com

Background to Conflict

 EYEWITNESSES TO History

❝*I want to rail against the wind and the tide, kill the whales in the sea, sweep the whole country to save the people from slavery, and I refuse to be abused.*❞

—Trieu Au, quoted in *Vietnam*, by Stanley Karnow

A Vietnamese print showing Trieu Au

Trieu Au's defiant words inspired the Vietnamese people to revolt against China in A.D. 248. Although the rebellion she led was defeated, the cause Trieu Au fought for was not. For centuries invaders desired the fertile river deltas and coastal lowlands of Vietnam. The people of Vietnam were not easily conquered, however. For more than 1,000 years they fought for their freedom and independence.

Vietnam

The easternmost country of Southeast Asia, Vietnam covers about 130,000 square miles of mostly hills and dense forests. It is bordered on the north by China and on the west by Laos and Cambodia. Vietnam's population is centered around the Red River Delta in the far north and the Mekong (MAY-kawng) Delta in the south.

Chinese occupation. The moist, tropical climate of the deltas and coastal lowlands allows Vietnamese farmers to grow at least two crops of rice a year. It was this agricultural abundance that tempted China to invade the Red River Delta about 200 B.C. For more than a thousand years, the Chinese struggled to maintain control over northern and central Vietnam. The Vietnamese resisted and finally won limited independence from China in A.D. 939.

In the 1400s China tried to reassert control over Vietnam. A Vietnamese military leader named **Le Loi** used guerrilla warfare to defeat the Chinese invaders. Le Loi's rebels worked as peasants by day and took up arms to attack the Chinese by night. By 1428 the rebels had driven the Chinese from the country and won independence for Vietnam. Le Loi became the new emperor.

French colonization. Vietnam again lost its independence during a surge of European imperialism in the mid-1800s. This time the invaders were French. Despite the stubborn resistance of the Vietnamese, French military power ultimately won out. In 1883 the Vietnamese were forced to grant France complete control of the country. France later combined Vietnam with Laos and Cambodia to form French Indochina, one of its richest colonial possessions.

✔ **READING CHECK: Making Predictions** How might Vietnam's history of invasions have affected its citizens? After Chinese and French invasions, the Vietnamese people were wary of any foreign army occupying their country.

LEVEL 1: Ask students why China wanted to control Vietnam. *(Students should indicate that China wanted to benefit from Vietnam's agricultural abundance.)* Then ask them why France wanted to control Vietnam. *(Students should indicate that France was gripped by the general surge of European imperialism and wanted to gain colonial possessions.)* Pair students and have each pair draw a political cartoon commenting on the tug-of-war over Vietnam. Display pairs' cartoons around the classroom.
English Language Learners, Cooperative Learning

LEVEL 2: Distribute Outline Map 22, The Vietnam War, from **American History Outline Maps.** Have each student label Vietnam's major rivers, mountain ranges, highlands, ports, cities, and delta regions. *(See the map on this page for the correct names and locations.)* Then ask students to write accompanying paragraphs explaining why both China and France wanted to control Vietnam. *(See the Level 1 lesson for the correct reasons.)* Display students' maps around the classroom.

Vietnamese Independence

Like the Chinese, the French gained control of the land but not the hearts of the Vietnamese. Nationalist feelings remained strong. Foremost among the nationalists was Nguyen That Thanh (NY-uhn TAHT TAHN). A world wanderer and man of many names, he is best known as **Ho Chi Minh** (HOH CHEE MIN)—"He Who Enlightens."

During the 1920s and 1930s Ho lived in China and the Soviet Union while working for Vietnamese independence. He became committed to the ideals of communism. In 1940 the Japanese army occupied all of French Indochina, the Philippines, Malaya, and Indonesia. Ho's chance had come.

France and the Vietminh go to war. After 30 years away from home, Ho secretly returned to Vietnam in early 1941. He organized a resistance movement called the League for the Independence of Vietnam, or **Vietminh** (vee-ET-MIN). When the Japanese withdrew from Indochina after surrendering to the Allied Powers in August 1945, the Vietminh declared independence. In Hanoi on September 2, 1945, more than 500,000 people gathered at an independence celebration to hear Ho speak. In an effort to gain U.S. support, Ho echoed the language of the U.S. Declaration of Independence in his speech.

U.S. policy toward Vietnam was soon put to the test. By 1946 the French and the Vietnamese were once again locked in battle. President Truman ignored Ho's pleas for assistance and threw U.S. support behind France. Truman viewed France as a vital ally in the struggle against the spread of communism in postwar Europe. He also was unwilling to back the Vietminh because of Ho's Communist Party connections.

Presidential advisers feared that communism would engulf Asia. This fear was reinforced in 1949 when Mao Zedong's Communists took over China—Asia's most populous country and a former U.S. ally. By 1950 the United States was caught up in a bloody ground war, trying to turn back communist North Korea's invasion of South Korea. Meanwhile, Communist-led nationalist revolts rocked Indonesia, the Philippines, and Malaya.

These developments led U.S. policy-makers to vow to hold the line against communism in East Asia. Truman's successor, Dwight D. Eisenhower, continued this policy. Eisenhower warned that if

Ho Chi Minh led the Vietnamese fight for independence.

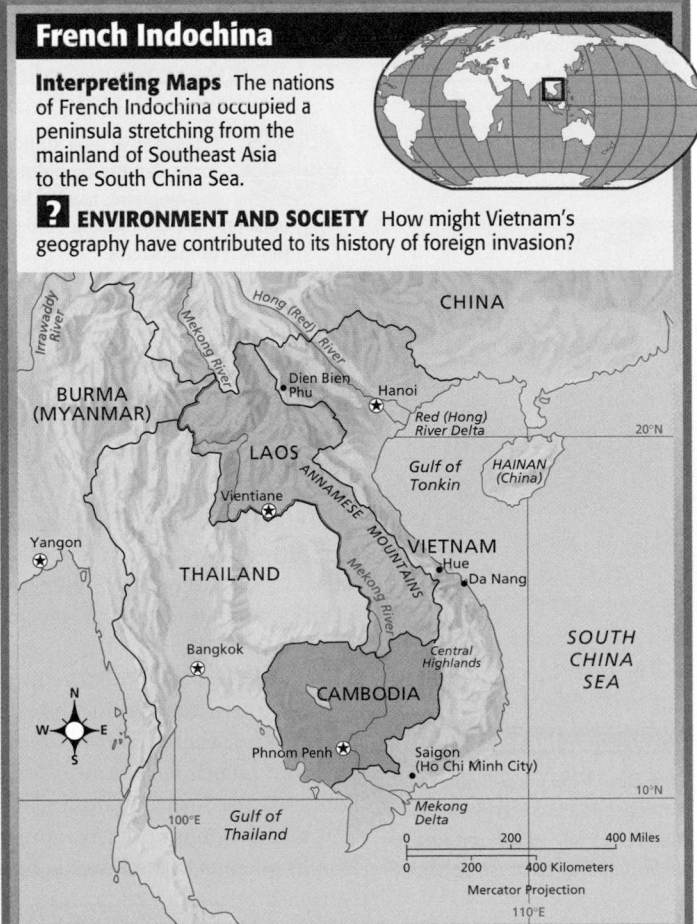

French Indochina

Interpreting Maps The nations of French Indochina occupied a peninsula stretching from the mainland of Southeast Asia to the South China Sea.

2 ENVIRONMENT AND SOCIETY How might Vietnam's geography have contributed to its history of foreign invasion?

CHINA

Irrawaddy River

Mekong River

Hong (Red) River

Dien Bien Phu

Hanoi

Red (Hong) River Delta

20°N

BURMA (MYANMAR)

LAOS

ANNAMESE MOUNTAINS

Vientiane

Gulf of Tonkin

HAINAN (China)

Yangon

VIETNAM

Hue

Da Nang

THAILAND

Mekong River

Bangkok

Central Highlands

SOUTH CHINA SEA

CAMBODIA

Phnom Penh

Saigon (Ho Chi Minh City)

10°N

100°E

Gulf of Thailand

Mekong Delta

0   200   400 Miles

0   200   400 Kilometers
Mercator Projection

110°E

ECONOMICS

Southeast Asia. A desire for natural resources was one reason for the long-standing U.S. interest in many Southeast Asian nations. Between the two world wars, the United States imported some 90 percent of its rubber and some 75 percent of its tin from Southeast Asia.

CRITICAL THINKING Why might rubber be a crucial resource in both peacetime and wartime?

ANSWER: Students should note that many peacetime products—such as shoes—and many wartime products—such as tires—are made of rubber.

THAT'S INTERESTING!

During his travels as a young man, Ho Chi Minh stopped in many countries, including the United States. After visiting Boston and San Francisco he worked in Brooklyn, New York. He lived in the United States for about one year.

LEVEL 3: Ask students why both China and France wanted to control Vietnam. *(See the Level 1 lesson for the correct reasons.)* Then have each student write a poem about Vietnam's early history and struggle for independence. Tell students to write their poems from the point of view of the country itself—in other words, from the perspective of Vietnam. Ask volunteers to read their poems to the class. Students may wish to include their poems in their portfolios.

SPOTLIGHT
on Dien Bien Phu

Pair students and tell them to conduct research on Dien Bien Phu. Have each pair create a detailed map of the battle that took place at Dien Bien Phu. Each pair should write a short military brief describing the battle to accompany its map. Have volunteers present their maps and briefs to the class.
Cooperative Learning, Block Scheduling

SCIENCE, TECHNOLOGY, AND SOCIETY

Nuclear Weapons. During the siege at Dien Bien Phu, some U.S. military advisers recommended the use of nuclear weapons to help the French defeat the Vietminh. President Eisenhower immediately rejected the idea, in part because he could not envision the United States using nuclear weapons against an Asian population for the second time in less than a decade.

ACTIVITY: Tell students to imagine that they are presidential advisers. Have each student write a memo to President Eisenhower commenting on the potential use of nuclear weapons at Dien Bien Phu.

PRIMARY SOURCE ANSWER

Students might answer that the French display their contempt in all forms of written and verbal communication.

VISUAL RECORD ANSWER

Students might suggest that the soldiers appear to be fleeing an attack.

PRIMARY SOURCE

Asian View of French Colonization

In the 1880s the Vietnamese fought the French, who wanted to colonize Vietnam. Ham Nghi, the 13-year-old emperor of Vietnam, had joined the rebellion against the French. In 1885, while fleeing from French forces, Ham Nghi issued a royal order to the Vietnamese people. He called upon "the rich to give their wealth, the mighty their strength, and the poor their limbs so that the country might be rescued from the invader." Several years later Phan Chu Trinh, a supporter of Ham Nghi, returned to Vietnam. In an open letter to the French government, Phan Chu attacked France's colonial practices in Vietnam. **According to Phan Chu, how do the French display their contempt for the Vietnamese?**

❝In your papers, in your books, in your plans, in your private conversations, there is displayed in all its intensity the profound contempt with which you overwhelm us. In your eyes, we are savages, dumb brutes, incapable of distinguishing between good and evil. Some of us, employed by you, still preserve a certain dignity . . . and it is sadness and shame that fills our hearts when we contemplate our humiliation.❞

INTERPRETING THE VISUAL RECORD

Dien Bien Phu. The Vietminh overwhelmed the French base at Dien Bien Phu. **What appears to be happening to these soldiers?**

Vietnam fell to communism the rest of Southeast Asia would soon follow. "You have a row of dominoes set up. You knock over the first one, and what will happen to the last one is a certainty that it will go over very quickly." This idea came to be called the **domino theory.** By 1954 the United States was paying much of the cost of France's war effort. Even with massive aid, however, the French suffered defeat after defeat.

Money and military equipment were of limited use against Vietminh guerrilla tactics. The Vietminh chose when and where to attack, struck without warning, and then disappeared into the jungle. In 1946 Ho Chi Minh had expressed to an American journalist his people's determination to succeed. Ho characterized the fight as "a war between an elephant"—the French—"and a tiger"—the Vietnamese.

History Makers Speak

❝If the tiger ever stands still, the elephant will crush him with his mighty tusks. But the tiger does not stand still. . . . He will leap upon the back of the elephant, tearing huge chunks from his hide, and then the tiger will leap back into the dark jungle. And slowly the elephant will bleed to death. That will be the war of Indochina.❞

—Ho Chi Minh, quoted in *America Inside Out*, by David Schoenbrun.
© 1994 by **McGraw-Hill Companies, Inc.** Reprinted by permission of the publisher.

Frustrated, the French tried to lure the Vietminh into a conventional battle at Dien Bien Phu (DYEN BYEN FOO), deep within Vietminh-held northern Vietnam. The plan backfired. Some 13,000 French soldiers soon found themselves encircled by more than 50,000 Vietminh troops. The French commander urged his war-weary soldiers to hold out—offering them the hope of a rescue. "The Americans will not let us down; the free world will not let us down."

Help did not come. Although willing to commit money, Eisenhower was reluctant to become directly involved in another Asian war so soon after the Korean War. The Vietminh defeated the French and on May 7, 1954, forced their surrender.

The Geneva Conference. Just one day after the French surrender at Dien Bien Phu, an international conference to settle the Indochina conflict began in Geneva, Switzerland. There, representatives of the French and the Vietminh attempted to map out Indochina's future. Cambodia, Great Britain, Laos, the People's Republic of China, the Soviet Union, and the United States joined the discussions.

China's communist government had been aiding the Vietminh since 1950 and hoped to limit U.S. influence in the region. The Chinese also wished to prevent the establishment of a strong, unified Vietnam. The Americans, meanwhile, did not want to see Vietnam handed over completely to the Communists.

ALL LEVELS: To help students understand why the United States refused to support Vietnamese independence during the 1940s and 1950s, copy the graphic organizer at right on the chalkboard, omitting the italicized answers. Have each student complete it. To conclude the lesson, have students write short letters explaining the U.S. refusal to support Vietnamese independence. Ask volunteers to read their letters to the class. **English Language Learners**

valued France as a world ally against communism

Why the United States Did Not Support Vietnamese Independence in the 1940s and 1950s

feared the domino effect in Southeast Asia

disliked Ho Chi Minh's affiliation with the Communist Party

HOMEWORK *Have each student use the information in his or her completed graphic organizer to write a few sentences agreeing or disagreeing with the U.S. refusal to support Vietnamese independence.*

A cease-fire was agreed to, but no definite political settlement was achieved. Vietnam was temporarily divided at the 17th parallel. Vietminh forces withdrew to the north, where they held undisputed power. South of the line, the French regained control. General elections to reunify the country were scheduled for July 1956. Fearing that the Communists would win a nationwide election, the United States refused to support the agreement.

✔ **READING CHECK: Drawing Conclusions**
What role did Ho Chi Minh play in Vietnamese independence? organized the Vietminh and tried to gain U.S. support for Vietnamese independence

The Rule of Ngo Dinh Diem

President Eisenhower hoped that southern Vietnam, at least, might be kept noncommunist. He pinned his hopes on **Ngo Dinh Diem** (NGOH DIN de-EM), a former government official under the French. U.S. officials hoped that Diem's nationalist beliefs would make him an acceptable leader to the people of South Vietnam.

Diem takes power in the south. Ngo Dinh Diem was strongly anticommunist. He had spent several years in the United States, where his political views attracted powerful backers. In 1955 Diem became president of the newly established Republic of Vietnam, or South Vietnam, in an election that was obviously rigged. In Saigon, for example, Diem received more than 605,000 votes from just 450,000 registered voters. Diem knew that he had no chance of winning a nationwide election against Ho Chi Minh. Therefore, when the July 1956 date set by the Geneva Conference rolled around, Diem refused to call an election in the south.

Diem, a Roman Catholic, was unpopular from the start. The large Buddhist population resented the favoritism he showed toward Catholics. Peasants disliked his land policies, which favored wealthy landholders. Almost everyone objected to power being kept solely in the grip of Diem's family. Above all, people feared his ruthless efforts to root out his political enemies. Diem's hated security forces routinely tortured and imprisoned opponents.

By the late 1950s armed revolution had erupted in the south. In 1959 military assistance began flowing from the north to the Vietminh who had stayed in the south. In 1960 the southern Vietminh formed the National Liberation Front (NLF). The NLF's main goal was the overthrow of Diem's government. Members of this rebel force were called **Vietcong**, for Vietnamese Communists, by their opponents. Not all NLF supporters, however, were Communists.

Many peasants joined the ranks of the NLF. Some did so because of government cruelty. Others joined out of fear of the NLF. Like Diem's forces, the NLF used terrorist tactics, assassinating hundreds of government officials. Soon much of the countryside was under Vietcong control.

INTERPRETING THE VISUAL RECORD
Victory. Vietminh soldiers march in a parade in Hanoi to celebrate their victory over the French. *Do these women look like combat troops? Explain your answer.*

This North Vietnamese poster reads "Imperial America is the enemy with whom we cannot live under the same sky."

GOVERNMENT

The 1956 Election in Vietnam. As Vietnam's 1956 national election approached, the Communists seemed likely to win because the population in North Vietnam was larger than that in South Vietnam. The U.S. government had been supporting efforts to prevent a communist victory. The Central Intelligence Agency (CIA) had conducted a campaign to destroy communist credibility in the South, distributing leaflets that promised violence if northerners gained control of the country. In addition, the CIA had carried out secret operations in the North. They had destroyed printing presses, put acid in bus oil, and placed explosives in railroad coal.

CRITICAL THINKING Do you think that the United States should have engaged in a campaign to prevent a communist victory?

ANSWER: Answers will vary. Some students might argue that the communist threat justified any action, while others might suggest that many of these methods violated the democratic ideal of a fair election.

VISUAL RECORD ANSWER
Students might answer yes and note the women's clothing and weapons.

TEACH OBJECTIVE 3

LEVEL 1: Pair students and have each pair write a series of newspaper headlines that explain why President Kennedy increased U.S. involvement in Vietnam. *(Pairs' headlines should indicate that President Kennedy subscribed to the domino theory and wanted to bolster the global image of the United States.)* Have volunteers read their headlines to the class.
English Language Learners, Cooperative Learning

LEVEL 2: Have students complete the Level 1 lesson. Then have each student choose one headline and write a short article to accompany it. Have volunteers read their articles to the class.

LEVEL 3: Organize students into small groups and tell them to imagine that they are foreign-policy advisers to President Kennedy. Have each group develop an oral presentation supporting increased involvement in Vietnam. *(See the Level 1 lesson for the correct motivations.)* Ask volunteers to deliver their presentations to the class. **Cooperative Learning**

Ngo Dinh Diem. Ngo Dinh Diem was born in 1901. His ancestors had converted to Christianity during the 1600s. As a child, Diem attended a French Catholic school. He even considered becoming a priest. Diem was a dedicated nationalist who bitterly opposed communism and the Vietminh, who had murdered one of his brothers. During the 1950s Diem spent time in the United States, where he met a number of important politicians, including then-Senator John F. Kennedy.

CRITICAL THINKING How might Ngo Dinh Diem have differed from Ho Chi Minh?

ANSWER: Students might suggest that Diem and Ho advocated different means for achieving independence. In addition, Diem followed a religion that many Vietnamese regarded as foreign.

SKILL-BUILDING STRATEGIES ANSWERS

Practicing the Skill
1. Students should list the title of each source and note who produced each source.

2. Students should assess the accuracy of each source and identify possible biases.

3. Students should indicate how they would use each source in a research paper.

Skill-Building Strategies

Evaluating Sources

Interpreting and evaluating historical sources are essential skills for learning about the past. This is particularly true when selecting sources for a research paper or project. To determine whether to use a source, one must assess its reliability and usefulness on a variety of levels. The quality of its reasoning, the accuracy of its information, the biases it displays, and its relevance to the topic at hand are all important factors to consider.

How to Evaluate a Source

1. **Identify the type, title, and creator of the source.** First, identify the type of source you will be evaluating and determine whether its title displays any obvious biases toward its subject. Then, if possible, find out about the historical background of the source's creator and the intended audience of the source.
2. **Examine the source carefully.** Study the source carefully, taking note of its main ideas and supporting details.
3. **Evaluate the source's reasoning.** Once you have examined the source thoroughly, assess the quality of its reasoning. Ask yourself the following questions: Are the arguments in this source logical? Are the cause-and-effect relationships fully proven? Do the conclusions follow from the information provided?
4. **Assess the accuracy and fairness of the source.** As you evaluate the source's reasoning, identify any factual inaccuracies that it contains and assess any biases that it displays in its selection, presentation,

and discussion of historical evidence. Make sure to note any instances in which the source presents a one-sided view of a person, event, or topic.
5. **Determine the relevance and usefulness of the source.** After you have evaluated the source's soundness, determine the extent to which it relates to your research topic. Then decide if and how the source should contribute to your project, and use it accordingly.

Applying the Skill

After you have read this chapter, use your school or local public library to conduct research on the Vietnam War. Use the following sources:
  a. an encyclopedia article
  b. two or more books
  c. a videotape of a film or television documentary
  d. a CD–ROM
  e. a database
Then evaluate each source and decide if and how you would use it in a research paper that focuses on the early role of the United States in Vietnam.

Practicing the Skill

Use your sources to answer the following questions.
1. What is the title of each source? Who produced each source, and when?
2. Is the information in each source accurate? What biases does each source display?
3. How would you use each source in a research paper?

U.S. troops arrive in Vietnam.

U.S. involvement deepens. John F. Kennedy, who became president in 1961, fully agreed with the domino theory. He was also eager to improve the U.S. image in the world. This image had been tarnished early in his presidency by the failed Bay of Pigs invasion and the building of the Berlin Wall. Aiding South Vietnam provided the United States with a chance to assert its power.

In December 1960 there were some 900 U.S. military advisers in South Vietnam training Diem's Army of the Republic of Vietnam (ARVN). During the next few years, Kennedy increased that number to more than 16,000. As Vietcong attacks mounted, Kennedy authorized U.S. forces to engage in direct combat. As a result, the number of Americans killed or wounded climbed from 14 in 1961 to nearly 500 in 1963.

Diem's overthrow. Political conflict also increased. South Vietnam's Buddhist leaders had begun to openly oppose Diem's rule. Diem was waging a brutal

REVIEW

Have students complete the **Section 1 Review** on p. 711.

ASSESS

Have students complete **Daily Quiz 24.1.** As **Alternative Assessment**, you may want to use the map activity or the newspaper headlines in this section's lessons.

RETEACH

Have students complete **Main Idea Activity for English Language Learners and Special-Needs Students 24.1.** Then organize students into triads. Ask each member of the triads to

select one of the section objectives, avoiding duplication. Direct students to write at least five questions on the material related to their selected objectives. Then have students take turns quizzing each other within their groups.
English Language Learners, Cooperative Learning

EXTEND

Have students conduct research on Trieu Au, a Vietnamese woman who fought for independence. Have each student write a short report on Trieu Au and her fight. Ask volunteers to read their reports to the class. **Block Scheduling**

campaign to control the Buddhists. Hundreds of Buddhists were arrested, and many were killed in the crackdown. In response, several Buddhist monks publicly set themselves on fire. These gruesome protests shocked Americans. U.S. officials in Saigon threatened to withdraw support for Diem unless he ended the campaign.

Henry Cabot Lodge, U.S. ambassador to South Vietnam, met with Diem in August 1963. Lodge later recalled that Diem "absolutely refused to discuss any of the topics that President Kennedy had instructed me to raise." U.S. leaders began to quietly encourage a group of South Vietnamese army officers plotting Diem's overthrow. On August 29, Lodge described the situation.

> **"We are launched on a course from which there is no respectable turning back: the overthrow of the Diem government. There is no turning back because U.S. prestige is already publicly committed to this end in large measure, and will become more so as the facts leak out. In a more fundamental sense, there is no turning back because there is no possibility, in my view, that the war can be won under a Diem administration."**
>
> —Henry Cabot Lodge, quoted in *Vietnam*, by Stanley Karnow

The plotters struck in early November 1963, murdering both Diem and his brother. Diem's assassination upset U.S. advisers, who had been prepared to fly Diem out of the country.

Diem's overthrow did nothing to ease Kennedy's growing concern over U.S. involvement in Vietnam. In an interview shortly before Diem's fall, Kennedy had said of the South Vietnamese: "In the final analysis it is their war. They are the ones who have to win or lose it." It is unknown how Kennedy might have handled the situation. Three weeks after Diem's murder, Kennedy himself was assassinated in Dallas.

✔ **READING CHECK: Identifying Cause and Effect** How did U.S. involvement in Vietnam increase internal conflict there? The United States backed Diem, and many South Vietnamese resented his rule. When Diem cracked down on Buddhists, U.S. leaders encouraged Diem's overthrow.

Henry Cabot Lodge meets with Ngo Dinh Diem in Saigon.

SECTION 1 REVIEW

1. Define and explain:
domino theory

2. Identify and explain:
Le Loi
Ho Chi Minh
Vietminh
Ngo Dinh Diem
Vietcong

3. Sequencing Copy the graphic organizer below. Use it to list the steps that led to U.S. troops being sent to Vietnam.

1428: Vietnam gains its independence.

1962: U.S. troops arrive in Vietnam.

4. ■ **Finding the Main Idea**
a. Why did President Truman refuse Ho Chi Minh's requests for help against the French?
b. What attracted the Chinese and the French to Vietnam?
c. Imagine that you are an adviser to President Eisenhower in 1959. On the basis of what you would know at the time, prepare a statement outlining the benefits and drawbacks of U.S. involvement in Vietnam. Then write a one-paragraph policy recommendation.

5. ■ **Writing and Critical Thinking**
Summarizing Write a press release that explains President Kennedy's decision to increase U.S. involvement in Vietnam.
Consider:
• U.S. foreign policy during the early 1960s
• the goals and actions of the North Vietnamese
• the strength of the Diem government

Homework Practice Online
keyword: SE3 HP24

SECTION 1 ANSWERS

1. Define
• domino theory, p. 708

2. Identify
• Le Loi, p. 706
• Ho Chi Minh, p. 707
• Vietminh, p. 707
• Ngo Dinh Diem, p. 709
• Vietcong, p. 709

3. 1883—France gains control of Vietnam; 1945—Vietnam proclaims its independence; 1954—French forces withdraw from Vietnam

4a. He wanted to keep France as an ally against the spread of communism and disliked Ho's communist connections.

b. Chinese—agricultural abundance; French—imperialism and the desire for colonial possessions

c. Policy recommendations will vary but lists should include: pro—the necessity of opposing communism; con—the possibility of another land war in Asia.

5. Answers will vary. Students should note the Cold War atmosphere, the desire to increase U.S. prestige and to defeat communism, the relative success of the North Vietnamese, and the relative unpopularity of Diem in South Vietnam.

SECTION ②

After completing Section 2, students should be able to:

OBJECTIVE 1 *Identify the constitutional issue the Tonkin Gulf Resolution raised.*

OBJECTIVE 2 *Describe the strategies U.S. forces used in the Vietnam War.*

OBJECTIVE 3 *List factors that frustrated U.S. military efforts in Vietnam.*

OBJECTIVE 4 *Explain why some Americans opposed the war, and describe how the government responded.*

LET'S GET STARTED!

As students enter the classroom, display Everyday Life in America Transparency 30, Protest During the Vietnam War, from **American History Visual Resources**. Ask students to complete the accompanying worksheet. Then ask students to share their responses with the class.

SECTION ②

READ TO DISCOVER

1. What constitutional issue did the Tonkin Gulf Resolution raise?
2. What strategies did U.S. forces use in the Vietnam War?
3. What role did the media play in the Vietnam War?
4. Why did some Americans oppose the war, and how did the government respond?

DEFINE

escalation
defoliants
search-and-destroy missions
pacification
doves
hawks

IDENTIFY

Robert S. McNamara
Tonkin Gulf Resolution
Operation Rolling Thunder
Ho Chi Minh Trail
Students for a Democratic Society
J. William Fulbright

▶ WHY IT MATTERS TODAY

Civilians who live in war-torn regions are often affected by the fighting. Use CNNfyi.com or other **current events** sources to identify a country or region that is suffering or has suffered under the violent conditions of war. Record your findings in your journal.

CNNfyi.com

The War Escalates

EYEWITNESSES TO History

"*Renewed hostile actions against United States ships on the high seas in the Gulf of Tonkin have today required me to order the military forces of the United States to take action in reply. The initial attack on the destroyer Maddox, on August 2, was repeated today by a number of hostile vessels attacking two U.S. destroyers with torpedoes. . . . We believe at least two of the attacking boats were sunk. There were no U.S. losses. . . . But repeated acts of violence against the Armed Forces of the United States must be met not only with alert defense, but with positive reply. That reply is being given as I speak to you tonight. Air action is now in execution against gunboats and certain supporting facilities in North Vietnam which have been used in these hostile operations.*"

—Lyndon B. Johnson, nationally televised speech, August 4, 1964

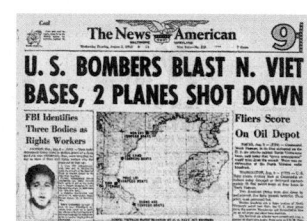

The Gulf of Tonkin incident drew the United States deeper into the Vietnam War.

Near midnight on August 4, 1964, President Lyndon B. Johnson appeared on national television. His announcement to the American people that night marked a new stage in U.S. involvement in the war in Vietnam.

The Tonkin Gulf Resolution

In 1963 Secretary of Defense **Robert S. McNamara** had advised President Johnson that he would have to increase the U.S. military commitment to South Vietnam to prevent a Communist victory. Before increasing the U.S. commitment, Johnson needed to get congressional backing. The events in the Gulf of Tonkin gave him the opportunity. Johnson asked Congress to authorize the use of military force "to prevent further aggression." In response, both houses of Congress overwhelmingly passed the **Tonkin Gulf Resolution**. This gave the president authority to take "all necessary measures to repel any armed attack against forces of the United States."

Johnson claimed that the attacks in the Gulf of Tonkin were unprovoked. In reality, however, the U.S. destroyer *Maddox* had been spying in support of South Vietnamese raids against North Vietnam and had fired first. The second attack, moreover, probably never occurred. Some U.S. sailors apparently misinterpreted interference on their radar and sonar as enemy ships and torpedoes. Nonetheless, Johnson and his advisers got what they wanted: authority to expand the war.

Wayne Morse of Oregon was one of just two senators who voted against the Tonkin Gulf Resolution. He warned, "I believe that history will record we have made a great mistake. . . . We are in effect giving the President war-making powers in the absence of a declaration of war." In other words, by passing the resolution, Congress had essentially given up its constitutional power to declare war.

✔ **READING CHECK: Analyzing Information** How did President Johnson mislead the American public? *Johnson claimed that attacks in the Gulf of Tonkin were unprovoked, when actually the United States had fired first.*

LEVEL 1: Conduct a brief discussion on the constitutional issue raised by the Tonkin Gulf Resolution. *(The Tonkin Gulf Resolution allowed the president to respond to military aggression without further congressional approval.)* Then pair students and ask each pair to write a few sentences or a paragraph summarizing the discussion. Have volunteers read their sentences or paragraphs to the class.
English Language Learners, Cooperative Learning

LEVELS 2 AND 3: Pair students and tell them to imagine that they are members of Congress debating the wisdom of passing the Tonkin Gulf Resolution. Have each pair develop a short dialogue explaining the constitutional issue raised by the Tonkin Gulf Resolution. *(See the Level 1 lesson for the correct issue.)* Ask volunteers to conduct their dialogues for the class.
Cooperative Learning

U.S. Forces in Vietnam

President Johnson soon called for an **escalation**, or buildup, of U.S. military forces in Vietnam. He ordered the Selective Service, the agency charged with carrying out the military draft, to begin calling up young men to serve in the armed forces. In April 1965 the Selective Service notified 13,700 draftees.

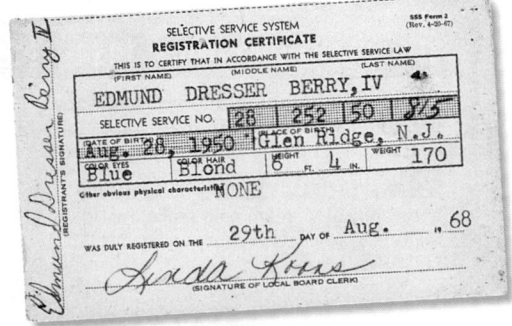

During the Vietnam War millions of American men received draft registration certificates like this one.

The troops. During the war more than 2 million Americans served in Vietnam. In the beginning most were professional soldiers who were already enlisted in the armed forces. As the demand for troops grew, however, more and more draftees were shipped to Vietnam. The average U.S. soldier in Vietnam was younger, poorer, and less educated than those who had served in World War II or in the Korean War.

One out of four young men who registered for the draft was excused from service for health reasons. Another 30 percent received non-health-related exemptions or deferments—postponements of service. Most of these were for college enrollment. Mainly because of college deferments, young men from higher-income families were the least likely to be drafted. As a result, poor Americans served in numbers far greater than their proportion in the general population.

African Americans and Hispanics served in combat in very high numbers, particularly during the early years of the war. Many served in the most dangerous ground units. As a result, they experienced very high casualty rates. In 1965, for example, African Americans accounted for almost 24 percent of all battle deaths, even though they made up just 11 percent of the U.S. population.

The most vivid images of the war show soldiers facing the hardships and terrors of battle. Some confronted the enemy in well-defined battles in the highlands. Others cut their way through the jungle, where they heard but seldom saw the enemy. Still others waded through rice paddies and searched rural villages for guerrillas. Most Americans who went to Vietnam, however, served in support positions such as administration, communications, engineering, medical care, and supply and transportation. They were rarely safe. Enemy rockets and mortars could—and did—strike anywhere.

Some 10,000 servicewomen filled noncombat positions in Vietnam, mostly as nurses. Although they did not carry guns into battle, nurses faced the horrors of combat on a daily basis. Edie Meeks described the experience of working as a nurse at a field hospital.

History Makers Speak

> **"We really saw the worst of it, because the nurses never saw any of the victories. If the Army took a hill, we saw what was left over. I remember one boy who was brought in missing two legs and an arm, and his eyes were bandaged. A general came in later and pinned a Purple Heart on the boy's hospital gown, and the horror of it all was so amazing that it just took my breath away. You thought, was this supposed to be an even trade?"**
>
> —Edie Meeks, quoted in *Newsweek*, March 8, 1999

Another 20,000 to 45,000 women worked in civilian capacities, many as volunteers for humanitarian organizations such as the Red Cross.

INTERPRETING THE VISUAL RECORD

Nurses. First Lieutenant Elaine Niggemann served at the 24th EVAC Hospital. *What is the lieutenant doing?*

HISTORY MAKERS SPEAK

Lyndon B. Johnson in *The Triumph and Tragedy of Lyndon Johnson*

President Johnson on the Draft. The Selective Service System was administered by local draft boards, many of which had only white people as members. In 1966 President Johnson dedicated himself to improving the equality of the draft and diversifying draft boards, saying, "We must continue to ask one form of service—military duty—of our young men. . . . The Nation's requirement that men must serve, however, imposes this obligation: that in this land of equals, men are selected as equals to serve. . . . A just nation must have the fairest system that can be devised for making that selection."

ACTIVITY: Conduct a brief discussion on the draft. Then ask each student to write an editorial commenting on the draft during the Vietnam War.

Tell students that Vietnam was a grueling environment for U.S. soldiers. Ask students to conduct research on soldiers' experiences in Vietnam. Then tell students to imagine that they are soldiers fighting in Vietnam. Have each student write a series of diary entries about life during the war. Have volunteers read their diary entries to the class.
Block Scheduling

TEACH OBJECTIVE 2

LEVEL 1: Ask students to list the strategies U.S. forces used in the Vietnam War. (*Students should list escalation, the air war, and the ground war.*) Note students' responses on the chalkboard. Then pair students and ask each pair to write sentences describing and analyzing each of the items on the chalkboard list. (*Pairs should note that escalation increased the number of troops in Vietnam, that the air war attempted to secure a quick victory, and that the ground war began when the air war failed.*) Have volunteers read their sentences to the class.

English Language Learners, Cooperative Learning

SCIENCE, TECHNOLOGY, AND SOCIETY

The U.S. Air Campaign in Southeast Asia. Between 1962 and 1973 the United States dropped some 8 million tons of bombs on Vietnam, Laos, and Cambodia. More than half of the total tonnage was dropped in South Vietnam. South Vietnam, a U.S. ally, thus became the most bombed country in the history of aerial warfare.

CRITICAL THINKING What might the heavy U.S. aerial bombardment of South Vietnam, presumably an ally, indicate about the nature of the U.S. campaign in Vietnam?

ANSWER: Answers will vary. Some students might suggest that the bombardment of South Vietnam indicated that many enemy strong points were located in South Vietnam.

MAP ANSWER
The Ho Chi Minh Trail stretched through Laos and Cambodia before veering into South Vietnam.

The Vietnam Conflict, 1954–1975

Interpreting Maps U.S. efforts to destroy the Ho Chi Minh trail caused the war to spill over into neighboring Laos and Cambodia.

? PHYSICAL SYSTEMS How did the geography of Vietnam help make the Ho Chi Minh Trail an effective weapon against U.S. and ARVN forces?

Map labels: CHINA; Hong (Red) River; NORTH VIETNAM; MYANMAR (BURMA); Dien Bien Phu; Hanoi; Hon Gai; Haiphong; Xam Nua; North Vietnam bombed, 1965–1968 (Operation Rolling Thunder), 1972; 20°N; Final French defeat by Vietminh, 1954; LAOS; Muang Ngat; Vinh; Gulf of Tonkin; Gulf of Tonkin Incident, 1964; Vientiane; Mekong River; Quang Tri; Demilitarized Zone (DMZ); U.S. Seventh Fleet; 17th Parallel; Demarcation Line of 1954; Khe Sanh; Hue; Laos invaded, 1971; HO CHI MINH TRAIL; Da Nang; THAILAND; 15°N; My Lai; Kon Tum; Pleiku; CAMBODIA; SOUTH VIETNAM; South China Sea; Nha Trang; Cam Rahn; Vinh; Da Lat; U.S. Seventh Fleet; Cambodia bombed, 1969–1973; invaded, 1970; Phnom Penh; Bien Hoa; Saigon; Tan Son Nhut; Gulf of Thailand; Can Tho; Vung Tau; Mekong Delta; Surrender of South Vietnam, 1975; 10°N; 100°E; 105°E; 110°E

Legend:
- Major U.S. air strikes
- Areas of prolonged conflict
- Major U.S. bases
- Major areas of Tet offensive, 1968
- Areas under Vietcong control, 1968

Scale: 0 100 200 Miles; 0 100 200 Kilometers; Mercator Projection

The defoliant Agent Orange proved harmful to humans as well as plants.

The air war. President Johnson hoped that air power could secure a quick victory. In March 1965 he launched **Operation Rolling Thunder**, a bombing campaign against military targets in the North. The goal was to weaken the enemy's will to fight. Johnson also wanted to assure the South Vietnamese of the U.S. commitment to them.

A key target of the bombing was the **Ho Chi Minh Trail**—a network of jungle paths. The North Vietnamese used the Ho Chi Minh Trail to bring weapons and supplies into South Vietnam. Roads and bridges along the trail, parts of which snaked through neighboring Cambodia and Laos, were bombed repeatedly. The Vietcong, however, quickly repaired them or managed without them. They also built many facilities underground to protect against bombing. Some 300,000 people worked full-time to maintain the Ho Chi Minh Trail.

When the bombing did not bring about North Vietnam's collapse, Johnson increased its intensity. By 1967, U.S. aircraft were dropping a daily average of 800 tons of bombs on North Vietnam. Repeated increases in bombing failed to produce the desired results. Frustrated, President Johnson broadened the air war to include strikes against areas of bordering Laos and much of South Vietnam.

U.S. forces used a variety of deadly weapons. Napalm, a jellied gasoline mixture, was used in firebombs. "Cluster bombs" sprayed razor-sharp metal fragments when they exploded. U.S. planes sprayed **defoliants**—chemicals that strip the land of vegetation—over thousands of acres. The goal of the spraying was to expose jungle supply routes and enemy hiding places. They also wanted to destroy the Vietcong food supply. The most widely used of these chemicals was Agent Orange.

The ground war. Physician Ton That Tung recalled that the North Vietnamese clearly understood the goal of the air war. "The Americans thought that the more bombs they dropped, the quicker we would fall to our knees and surrender." Rather than surrender, North Vietnam sent more troops and supplies south.

The bombing led many South Vietnamese to join the Vietcong. Soon the opposition forces included more South Vietnamese than North Vietnamese. The United States countered by launching a ground war. Between 1965 and the end of 1967 the number of U.S. troops in Vietnam grew from about 185,000 to some 486,000.

Sheer numbers were not enough to defeat an enemy who seemed to be everywhere. Aided by regulars of the North Vietnamese Army, the Vietcong struck at U.S. patrols or government-held villages and then melted back into the jungle. Vietnamese peasants who appeared peaceful by day sided with the Vietcong at night. U.S. forces conducted thousands of **search-and-destroy missions** that attempted to drive the Vietcong from their hideouts. Ground patrols first located the enemy and then called in air support to kill them. Once an area was "cleared," the patrols moved on in search of more Vietcong. Snipers and booby traps made these missions extremely dangerous and frustrating. Making matters worse, villages seldom remained cleared of the Vietcong.

To provide security in rural areas, U.S. forces began a program of **pacification**. When security forces were not enough they moved the residents to secure locations and then burned the villages. In such warfare, progress could not be shown on a map. Instead, the daily body count of enemy dead became the sole measure of success—and a questionable measure at that. The U.S. military regularly guessed at or inflated the numbers by counting all Vietnamese dead as the enemy. Said one officer responsible for body-count statistics: "If it's dead and Vietnamese, it's VC [Vietcong]."

U.S. morale declines. The first U.S. troops had arrived in Vietnam in a hopeful mood. As marine lieutenant Philip Caputo explained, "When we marched into the rice paddies on that damp March afternoon, we carried, along with our packs and rifles, the implicit [unquestioned] convictions that the Vietcong could be quickly beaten." This optimism began to fade as the hazards of fighting a nearly invisible foe in an alien landscape became apparent. "We kept the packs and rifles," Caputo wrote; "the convictions, we lost."

Equally frustrating was the enemy's will to continue fighting, despite mounting casualties. U.S. war planners believed that superior U.S. technology would win the war. Yet at the end of 1967, victory seemed no closer than in 1963. Ho Chi Minh's earlier warning to the French now seemed applicable to Americans. "You can kill ten of my men for every one I kill of yours, but even at those odds, you will lose and I will win."

INTERPRETING THE VISUAL RECORD

Infantry patrol. During Operation Hawthorne in 1966, U.S. infantry troops attacked Vietcong forces around central Vietnam. *How does this photograph show the difficulties U.S. soldiers faced in Vietnam?*

✔ **READING CHECK: Evaluating** How effective were U.S. strategies in the Vietnam War?
somewhat effective—the United States conducted bombing missions; Vietnamese snipers and booby traps made ground missions difficult; the Vietnamese sent more supplies south; and more South Vietnamese joined the Vietcong

Pair students and ask one student in each pair to summarize U.S. military strategies and tactics and the other to summarize Vietnamese strategies and tactics. *(Students summarizing U.S. strategies should note intensive bombing, defoliation, pacification of villages, and so on. Students summarizing Vietnamese strategies should note guerrilla warfare, booby traps, and so on.)* Then have pairs compare and contrast these two approaches in a Venn diagram. Ask volunteers to present their summaries and diagrams to the class.
Block Scheduling, Cooperative Learning

TEACH OBJECTIVE 3

LEVEL 1: Pair students and ask each pair to create a bulleted list of the factors that frustrated U.S. military efforts in Vietnam. *(Pairs should note the failure of bombing and technological assaults, guerrilla tactics, and declining morale.)* Have volunteers call out factors as you record them on the chalkboard. Tell students to write in their notes any factors that they missed for future reference.
English Language Learners, Cooperative Learning

AMERICAN LETTERS ANSWERS

1. Ehrhart indicates that the Vietcong dress like civilians and speak the same language as civilians. He also notes that the Vietcong included women and children, not typical enemies.

2. Students might suggest that Trinh Cong Son saw the war as a means of exacting revenge on enemies.

3. Ehrhart's poem views Vietnam and its people as outsiders; for Trinh Cong Son, the Vietnamese are his people.

The American Nation
VIDEO PROGRAM

Vietnam and the Media;
Teacher's Guide, pp. 141–46

Search 13498, Play to 23297
Videodisc 2, Side B

Play   Pause

See *Teacher's Guide* for Spanish barcode.

AMERICAN *Letters*

Views of Vietnam

U.S. soldiers and the Vietnamese saw the war from very different perspectives. Some people who were there later expressed their feelings through writing. The following poem by William D. Ehrhart, a marine who served in Vietnam, describes his experiences fighting against the Vietcong guerrillas. Trinh Cong Son, a Vietnamese poet, captured the horror of battle in the poem below.

"Guerrilla War"
by William D. Ehrhart

It's practically impossible
to tell the civilians
from the Vietcong.

Nobody wears uniforms.
They all talk
the same language
(and you couldn't under-
    stand them
even if they didn't).

They tape grenades
inside their clothes,
and carry satchel charges
in their market baskets.

Even their women fight;
and young boys,
and girls.

It's practically impossible
to tell civilians
from the Vietcong;

after awhile
you quit trying.

William D. Ehrhart

Trinh Cong Son

[Title Unknown]
by Trinh Cong Son

I saw, I saw, I saw holes and trenches
full of the corpses of my brothers and sisters.
Mothers, clap for joy over war.
Sisters, clap and cheer for peace.
Everyone clap for vengeance.
Everyone clap instead of repentance.

UNDERSTANDING LITERATURE

1. What examples does Ehrhart give of the difficulty identifying the enemy in Vietnam?
2. Do you think Trinh Cong Son believed any good came out of the war?
3. How do these poems differ in their portrayal of the Vietnam War?

The Media and the War

By the end of 1967 more than 16,000 Americans had been killed in Vietnam. Thousands more had been injured or disabled. Despite the government's optimistic forecasts, a U.S. victory seemed increasingly distant. American television news programs showed gruesome images of terrified Vietnamese civilians and dead or injured soldiers. Some Americans demanded that the military be allowed to do whatever it took to win. Others wanted the United States to pull out of Vietnam.

The Vietnam War invaded American homes in a way that no previous conflict had. During previous wars the military had imposed tight press restrictions. In this war, reporters, photographers, and TV camera crews accompanied soldiers on patrol and interviewed people throughout South Vietnam. Television beamed footage and reports of the war into people's homes on a nightly basis. As a result, Americans saw images that seemed to contradict the government's reports.

Reporters such as David Halberstam of the *New York Times* and Neil Sheehan of United Press International criticized the government's optimism. As early as 1962 they argued that the war could not be won as long as the United States supported the unpopular and corrupt regime of Ngo Dinh Diem. Journalists also reported on the ineffectiveness of South Vietnam's troops and accused the U.S. government of inflating enemy body counts to give the appearance of progress.

As the gap between official government reports and media accounts grew wider, doubts at home increased. The administration found itself criticized by both **doves**—people who opposed the war—and **hawks**—people who supported the war's goals. Hawks criticized the way the war was being fought. They argued for more U.S. troops and heavier bombing. Air force general Curtis LeMay expressed the frustration of many hawks. "Here we are at the height of our power. The most powerful nation in the world. And yet we're afraid to use that power."

Doves opposed the war for many reasons. Pacifists such as Martin Luther King Jr. believed that all war was wrong. Some doves, such as diplomat George Kennan, were convinced that Vietnam was not crucial to national security. Others feared that the United States might use nuclear weapons. Pediatrician and author Dr. Benjamin Spock and others argued that the United States was fighting against the wishes of a majority of Vietnamese.

INTERPRETING THE VISUAL RECORD

The media. Television coverage brought the horrors of the Vietnam War into Americans' living rooms. *What do you think this journalist is doing?*

✔ **READING CHECK: Drawing Conclusions** How did the media shape Americans' perceptions of the war? **News programs showed gruesome images and suggested that U.S. troops could not win the war. This prompted many Americans to have doubts.**

The Antiwar Movement

A variety of civil rights, pacifist, religious, and student groups shaped the antiwar movement. The pacifist groups included Women Strike for Peace and the National Committee for a Sane Nuclear Policy as well as radical student groups like **Students for a Democratic Society** (SDS). The movement attracted a broad range of people. Doctors, ministers, teachers, and other professionals joined homemakers, retired citizens, and students in protest against the war.

ALL LEVELS: To help students understand who supported and who opposed the war, copy the graphic organizer at right on the chalkboard, omitting the italicized answers. Have each student complete it. Then have students write a few sentences describing the government's response to such opposition. *(Students should note that the U.S. government justified its actions on the grounds of support for an ally.)* Then conduct a brief discussion on the antiwar movement in the 1960s and 1970s. **English Language Learners**

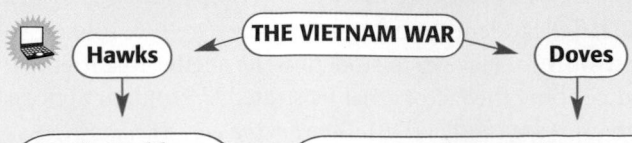

THE VIETNAM WAR

Hawks

Basic Positions
- *generally supported the war's goals*
- *wanted more troops and heavier bombing*

Doves

Basic Positions
- *generally opposed the war*
- *thought it drew money from social programs*
- *opposed all wars*
- *believed that Vietnam was not crucial to U.S. national security*
- *feared that the United States would use nuclear weapons in the conflict*

Attitudes Toward the War. The debate over the Vietnam War highlighted racial and gender differences in American society. In a 1966 poll, 65 percent of white men supported the war; 53 percent of African American men did. Among white women, 54 percent approved of the conflict, but just 43 percent of African American women did. A 1970 poll revealed that overall support for the war was diminishing while race and gender differences remained. Some 41 percent of white men and 27 percent of black men supported the war. However, just 30 percent of white women and 19 percent of black women still approved of it.

ACTIVITY: Have each student use the information above to prepare a bar graph demonstrating attitudes toward the war in 1966 and 1970.

VISUAL RECORD ANSWER

(for p. 719)

Students might suggest that the protester is wearing a uniform to show that even military forces opposed the draft.

HISTORICAL DOCUMENTS ANSWER

Students might suggest freedom and equality for all and government of, by, and for the people.

★ HISTORICAL DOCUMENTS ★

STUDENTS FOR A DEMOCRATIC SOCIETY
The Port Huron Statement

The Students for a Democratic Society (SDS) national convention met in Port Huron, Michigan, the week of June 11–15, 1962. Members of the SDS released the Port Huron Statement, which outlined the organization's goals for change in American society. **What values do SDS members identify as part of the national identity?**

We are people of this generation, bred in at least modest comfort, housed now in universities, looking uncomfortably to the world we inherit.

When we were kids the United States was the wealthiest and strongest country in the world: the only one with the atom bomb, the least scarred by modern war, an initiator of the United Nations that we thought would distribute Western influence throughout the world. Freedom and equality for each individual, government of, by, and for the people—these American values we found good, principles by which we could live as men. Many of us began maturing in complacency [self-satisfaction].

As we grew, however, our comfort was penetrated by events too troubling to dismiss. . . .

While two-thirds of mankind suffers undernourishment, our own upper classes revel [celebrate] amidst superfluous abundance. . . . Uncontrolled exploitation [usage] governs the sapping [draining] of the earth's physical resources. . . .

Major social institutions—cultural, educational, rehabilitative, and others—should be generally organized with the well-being and dignity of man as the essential measure of success. . . . As students for a democratic society, we are committed to stimulating this kind of social movement, this kind of vision and program in campus and community across the country. If we appear to seek the unattainable, [as] it has been said, then let it be known that we do so to avoid the unimaginable.

By the end of 1965 the SDS had members on 124 college campuses. Although it was just one of many groups opposing the war, to many Americans the SDS *was* the antiwar movement. At colleges across the United States, the SDS and other student groups and faculty members held antiwar rallies and debates. These groups particularly criticized the involvement of universities in research and development for the military. They also protested the draft, the presence of the Reserve Officers' Training Corps (ROTC) on campus, and the recruitment efforts by the armed services, the Central Intelligence Agency (CIA), and defense contractors.

The SDS organized the first national antiwar demonstration. It was held in Washington, D.C., on April 17, 1965. More than 20,000 people participated. After an afternoon of speeches, the crowd marched to the Capitol and delivered to Congress a petition demanding that lawmakers "act immediately to end the war." Countless demonstrations followed during the next decade. Demonstrators protested U.S. involvement in Southeast Asia with tactics borrowed from the civil rights movement.

Civil rights activists were among the most outspoken critics of the war. In 1967 Martin Luther King Jr. complained that the war was stealing resources from poverty programs.

> *History Makers Speak*
>
> **"I watched the [antipoverty] program broken and eviscerated [gutted] as if it were some idle political plaything of a society gone mad on war, and I knew that America would never invest the necessary funds or energies in rehabilitation of its poor so long as Vietnam continued to draw men and skills and money like some demonic, destructive suction tube."**
>
> —Martin Luther King Jr., sermon opposing the Vietnam War, 1967

Many civil rights activists criticized the U.S. government. They said it was sending great numbers of young African Americans off to war yet doing little to end discrimination at home. The Student Nonviolent Coordinating Committee (SNCC) expressed the views of growing numbers of African Americans. SNCC officials noted that "16 percent of the draftees from this country are Negro, called on to stifle [block] the liberation of Vietnam, to preserve a 'democracy' which does not exist

ASSESS

Have students complete **Daily Quiz 24.2**. As **Alternative Assessment**, you may want to use the U.S. strategy telegram or the Tonkin Gulf dialogue in this section's lessons.

RETEACH

Have students complete **Main Idea Activity for English Language Learners and Special-Needs Students 24.2**. Then organize students into small groups. Assign each group member a subsection of Section 2. Direct students to write a few sentences or paragraphs summarizing their assigned subsections. Have group members circulate their summaries to other group members to read. Then have students take turns quizzing each other within their groups about the information contained in the summaries.
English Language Learners, Cooperative Learning

EXTEND

Have students locate either a Vietnam War veteran or a former war protester in their community. Ask each student to interview that person and write a short biography. Students' biographies should focus on their subjects' involvement with the Vietnam War but can also include other information. Have volunteers read their biographies to the class. **Block Scheduling**

---

for them at home." Polls showed that African Americans were much more likely than whites to consider the war a mistake.

Despite their high visibility, antiwar protesters made up a small percentage of the U.S. population. Many Americans opposed the antiwar movement, particularly the extreme groups. Some believed that fighting for one's country was a patriotic duty. Others objected to the antiwar movement's tactics. These people found certain acts of protest—such as burning the American flag, occupying buildings, and burning draft cards—particularly upsetting. Many veterans of past wars were angered by young men who tried to avoid the draft.

Most Americans who disagreed with the antiwar movement expressed their opposition in private. However, some organized rallies in support of the war. Demonstrators at these rallies often carried signs proclaiming "America, Love It or Leave It" or "My Country, Right or Wrong."

Government in Conflict

President Johnson and his advisers responded to antiwar protesters by insisting that the United States was helping to defend an ally against aggression. If the United States failed to support South Vietnam, asked Secretary of State Dean Rusk, what U.S. ally would ever trust the country again?

The administration also faced criticism in Congress. Doves such as Senator **J. William Fulbright** of Arkansas, head of the Foreign Relations Committee, sharply criticized the Johnson administration's policies as too extreme. Fulbright held congressional hearings in 1966 to give the war's critics a forum. These televised hearings made the antiwar position more acceptable to mainstream Americans.

✔ **READING CHECK: Categorizing** What were the main arguments of antiwar protesters? The SDS and civil rights protesters complained that too many resources were being taken from poverty programs and used for the war.

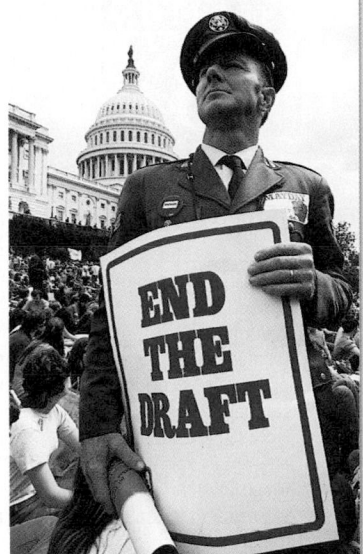

INTERPRETING THE VISUAL RECORD

Protest. This man joined other Americans at a rally in front of the U.S. Capitol Building. *Why do you think he is wearing a uniform?*

SECTION 2 REVIEW

1. Define and explain:
escalation
defoliants
search-and-destroy missions
pacification
doves
hawks

2. Identify and explain:
Robert S. McNamara
Tonkin Gulf Resolution
Operation Rolling Thunder
Ho Chi Minh Trail
Students for a Democratic Society
J. William Fulbright

3. Comparing Copy the chart below. Use it to outline U.S. tactics in the air war and on the ground in Vietnam.

Air War	Ground War

4. Finding the Main Idea

a. Why did some members of Congress believe that the Tonkin Gulf Resolution was unconstitutional?

b. Why did minority and poor Americans serve in Vietnam in large numbers?

c. What role did college students play in the antiwar movement, and how did the government respond?

5. Writing and Critical Thinking

Evaluating Write a paragraph explaining what factor you think played the biggest role in shaping American views toward the Vietnam War.

Consider:
• television coverage of the war
• economic effects of the war
• social conditions in the United States

Homework Practice Online
keyword: SE3 HP24

REVIEW 2 ANSWERS

1. Define
• escalation, p. 713
• defoliants, p. 714
• search-and-destroy missions, p. 715
• pacification, p. 715
• doves, p. 717
• hawks, p. 717

2. Identify
• Robert S. McNamara, p. 712
• Tonkin Gulf Resolution, p. 712
• Operation Rolling Thunder, p. 714
• Ho Chi Minh Trail, p. 714
• Students for a Democratic Society, p. 717
• J. William Fulbright, p. 718

3. air war—bombed supply routes and personnel, and dispersed defoliants; ground war—used search-and-destroy missions and pacification

4a. because it gave the president war-making powers without a congressional declaration of war

b. Most young men who were excused from service received educational deferments. Many minorities at the time could not afford college.

c. To many, SDS was the antiwar movement; they held rallies and organized the first national antiwar demonstration in Washington, D.C. The government defended its actions by saying it was helping an ally fight an aggressor.

5. Answers will vary. Students should select one factor and support it.

SECTION ③

After completing Section 3, students should be able to:

OBJECTIVE 1 Explain why the Tet Offensive weakened many Americans' confidence in their government.

OBJECTIVE 2 List the key events of the 1968 presidential campaign.

OBJECTIVE 3 Summarize how President Nixon attempted to end the war.

OBJECTIVE 4 Describe how Americans reacted to President Nixon's plan to end the war.

SECTION ③

A Turning Point

EYEWITNESSES TO History

"After a while, survival was the name of the game as you sat there in semidarkness, with the firing going on constantly, like at a rifle range. And the horrible smell. You tasted it as you ate your rations, as if you were eating death. It permeated [seeped into] your clothes, which you couldn't wash because water was very scarce. You couldn't bathe or shave either. My strategy was to keep as many of my marines alive as possible, yet accomplish our mission. You went through the full range of emotions, seeing your buddies being hit, but you couldn't feel sorry for them because you had the others to think about."

—Myron Harrington, quoted in *Vietnam*, by Stanley Karnow

U.S. Marines on patrol in Vietnam

Myron Harrington described the fighting through which he led his company of 100 marines. The grim determination Harrington and others felt about the war in Vietnam began to weaken in 1968. That year a massive attack by the Vietcong shattered the illusion that the United States would soon win the war. Soon many Americans were wondering why the country was fighting.

The Tet Offensive

January 30, 1968, marked the start of Tet, the Vietnamese New Year. In past years the holiday had been honored by a lull in fighting. However, late that night, as most South Vietnamese and their U.S. allies slept, Vietcong guerrillas and North Vietnamese troops struck. They crept from their jungle camps and city hideouts to execute a carefully planned strike. Within hours countless villages, more than 100 cities, and 12 U.S. military bases came under attack from nearly 84,000 communist soldiers. Heavy fighting raged in such U.S. strongholds as Saigon and Da Nang. At one point the Vietcong even occupied the courtyard of the U.S. Embassy.

North Vietnam expected the **Tet Offensive** to bring down South Vietnam's government as the people rallied behind their "liberators." North Vietnam's leaders were disappointed, however. When the assault ended, more than a month later, some 40,000 communist soldiers lay dead.

General **William Westmoreland**, the commander of U.S. forces in Vietnam, described the offensive as a Vietcong defeat. In a military sense, the general had a point. At a cost of 1,100 American and 2,300 ARVN lives, most of the attackers had been repelled. Despite suffering heavy losses, however, the Vietcong remained strong in many places. They had faced overwhelming U.S. firepower and were still standing—more determined than ever to continue fighting.

Tran Do, the deputy commander of communist forces in South Vietnam, had played a major role in the Tet Offensive. He explained the goals and effects of the offensive:

TEACH OBJECTIVE 1

LEVEL 1: Write the following question on the chalkboard: *The Tet Offensive was in fact a military failure for North Vietnamese forces. Why did it weaken many Americans' confidence in their government?* Then pair students and have each pair write a paragraph responding to the question. *(Pairs should note that the Tet Offensive revealed that no part of South Vietnam was secure, exposed how few South Vietnamese supported their own government, and revealed how determined the North Vietnamese were.)* Have volunteers read their paragraphs to the class.
English Language Learners, Cooperative Learning

LEVELS 2 AND 3: Have students complete the Level 1 activity. Then tell students to imagine that it is February 1968 and that they are watching a television news story on the Tet Offensive. Have each student write a letter to President Johnson explaining why the Tet Offensive has weakened his or her confidence in the U.S. government. Have volunteers read their letters to the class. Students may wish to include their letters in their portfolios.

NOTE: To help students make meaningful connections between events in U.S. history and those in their own hometown, use the Chapter 24 **Hands-On History Activity,** The Vietnam Era and the Armed Forces.

History Makers Speak

"In all honesty we didn't achieve our main objective, which was to spur uprisings throughout the south. Still, we inflicted heavy casualties on the Americans and their puppets, and that was a big gain for us. As for making an impact in the United States, it had not been our intention—but it turned out to be a fortunate result."

—Tran Do, quoted in *Vietnam*, by Stanley Karnow

The political effect of the offensive was stunning. It shook U.S. confidence by revealing that no part of South Vietnam was secure—not even downtown Saigon. Respected journalist Walter Cronkite, anchor of the *CBS Evening News*, expressed Americans' bewildered mood: "I thought we were winning the war! What the hell is going on?" To one of his aides, President Lyndon B. Johnson groaned, "If I've lost Cronkite I've lost middle America."

After the Tet Offensive, public criticism of the war rose dramatically. Influential magazines such as *Time* and *Newsweek* expressed doubts about the war and began calling for its end. Largely because of the shift in public opinion, Johnson denied General Westmoreland's urgent request for 206,000 more troops. President Johnson granted a small increase in the number of troops but made it clear that he would not increase the number any further.

✔ **READING CHECK: Drawing Conclusions** Why did the North Vietnamese launch the Tet Offensive? to bring down the South Vietnamese government by having the South Vietnamese people support their "liberators"

The Election of 1968

After the Tet Offensive three out of four Americans disapproved of President Johnson's conduct of the war. With the presidential election nearing, Johnson was under attack from all sides.

Democratic challengers. Early in 1968 Senator **Eugene McCarthy** of Minnesota, a critic of the war, challenged Johnson for the Democratic presidential nomination. In the New Hampshire primary held that March, McCarthy won almost as many votes as Johnson. McCarthy's impressive showing drew another leading critic of the war into the race. Senator **Robert F. Kennedy** of New York was the brother of the slain President Kennedy and a former U.S. attorney general. His large national following—particularly among African Americans, Hispanics, the poor, and the young—made Robert F. Kennedy a strong contender for the Democratic nomination.

Shaken by the division within his party, President Johnson made a shocking announcement to the nation on March 31. Physically and emotionally exhausted, Johnson declared that he would not seek re-election. He explained that he wanted to spend his last months in office trying to end the war. Johnson's withdrawal from the race left it wide open. Senators McCarthy and Kennedy and Vice President Hubert Humphrey went head-to-head in several state primaries. Kennedy won most of them, including the crucial California primary in June. To many he seemed destined to receive the Democratic nomination.

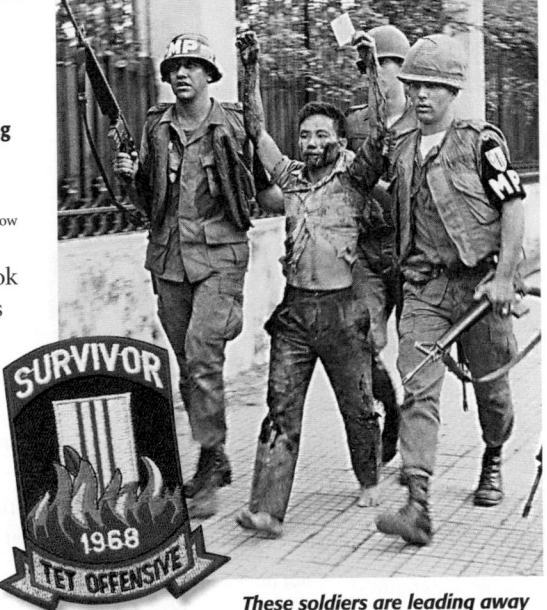

These soldiers are leading away one of the Vietcong guerrillas who attacked the U.S. Embassy in Saigon during the Tet Offensive.

Senator Robert F. Kennedy was so popular that supporters often tore off his cuff links while scrambling to shake his hand.

GEOGRAPHY

The Secret Offensive. In order to draw attention away from their preparations for the Tet Offensive, the North Vietnamese created a diversion by attacking a distant U.S. Marine outpost called Khe Sanh. The diversion worked—President Johnson feared that Khe Sanh would become an American Dien Bien Phu. One U.S. commander, however, suspected that the North Vietnamese were coordinating a large-scale offensive. He noticed that his troops were meeting fewer communist soldiers in distant parts of Vietnam, while communist radio communications in the Saigon area were increasing. The U.S. commander requested additional combat battalions for Saigon, which made its later defense easier.

ACTIVITY: Ask students to consider the evidence presented in the annotation above. Then ask each student to write a short military brief evaluating that evidence and either recommending or opposing additional combat battalions for Saigon.

THAT'S INTERESTING!

Eugene McCarthy was particularly popular with young students, many of whom decided to "go clean for Gene" and volunteered to help his presidential campaign.

TEACH OBJECTIVE 2

 ALL LEVELS: To help students understand the key events of the 1968 presidential campaign, copy the following time line on the chalkboard, omitting the italicized answers. Have each student complete it. Then pair students and have each pair write a newspaper headline and a topic sentence for each event. Ask volunteers to share their headlines and sentences with the class.

English Language Learners, Cooperative Learning

 HOMEWORK *Tell students to imagine that they were delegates at the Democratic National Convention in Chicago. Have each student write a short recollection of the events there.*

March—*Senator Eugene McCarthy wins almost as many votes as President Johnson in the New Hampshire primary.*

March 31—*President Johnson announces his withdrawal from the race.*

June—*Senator Robert F. Kennedy wins the California primary and is assassinated.*

August—*Police violently disperse antiwar protesters at the Democratic convention in Chicago.*

November—*Richard Nixon wins the election.*

1968

HISTORY MAKERS SPEAK

Theodore White in *The Making of the President, 1968*

Conflict in Chicago. Writer Theodore White described the clash between protesters and police in Chicago: "Slam! Like a fist jolting, like a piston exploding from its chamber, comes a hurtling column of police from off Balbo [Avenue] into the intersection, and all things happen too fast: first the charge as the police wedge cleaves through the mob; then screams, whistles, confusion, people running off into Grant Park, across the bridges, into hotel lobbies. And as the scene clears, there are little knots in the open clearing—police clubbing youngsters, police dragging youngsters, police rushing them by the elbows, their heels dragging, to patrol wagons, prodding recalcitrants [resisters] who refuse to enter quietly."

CRITICAL THINKING How might the violence in Chicago have affected voters?

ANSWER: Students might suggest that voters probably linked the violence to the Democrats and consequently considered voting for the Republicans.

The Generation Gap

I n the 1960s many young people began to feel that something had gone wrong with the United States. Prosperity had followed World War II, but peace had not. Fascism had been defeated, and the prewar years of depression were all but forgotten. Younger Americans— members of the baby-boom generation—increasingly found themselves at odds with their parents, who had grown up during the Great Depression and World War II. A wide generation gap developed.

The faith and optimism of American youth were shaken by seemingly senseless violence and death. Many young people demanded change. They accused the previous generation of valuing conformity and material comfort over equality and fairness. Younger Americans also increasingly distrusted their government and questioned the reasons for U.S. involvement in Vietnam. Many older Americans remembered past struggles and urged young people to have faith in their government. An inability to communicate contributed to the violent clash at the Democratic Party's 1968 convention in Chicago.

Many parents of the World War II era did not understand their Vietnam-era children, like this teenager.

On the night of his California victory, however, Kennedy was shot by Sirhan Sirhan, a young Jordanian immigrant. Kennedy died the next day. A nation already in shock over the murder of Martin Luther King Jr. just two months earlier was now faced with yet another assassination.

The convention in Chicago. Amid the turmoil, the Democrats met in Chicago to settle on a candidate for the November election. The convention was a cheerless affair. Despite his close identification with the unpopular President Johnson, Vice President Humphrey received the nomination. He chose Senator Edmund Muskie of Maine as his running mate.

The Democrats' difficulties were underscored by the chaos on the streets outside the convention. Some 10,000 antiwar protesters had massed in the city and rallied in Grant Park, across from the hotel where many delegates were staying. They held rallies, chanted antiwar slogans, and called police insulting names.

Outraged to see his city overrun by people he viewed as dangerous revolutionaries, Chicago mayor **Richard J. Daley** ordered helmeted police to clear out the protesters. Attacking on the night of August 28, the police clubbed protesters and used tear gas to disperse the crowd. Hundreds of protesters were injured; hundreds more were hauled to jail. Reporters, passersby, and police were also injured in the struggle.

The Republicans capitalize. The violent spectacle at the Chicago convention raised Republicans' hopes of capturing the White House. **Richard Nixon** dominated the Republican National Convention in Miami Beach, Florida. Appealing to the patriotism of mainstream America, he won the nomination easily. He chose Maryland governor Spiro Agnew as his running mate. Promising a "law-and-order" crackdown on urban crime, Nixon sought support from those Americans who neither approved of the disorderly antiwar protests nor wanted a U.S. defeat in Vietnam. Nixon told voters he had a secret plan to end the Vietnam War, although he revealed no details.

As election day neared, Humphrey's campaign picked up steam, boosted somewhat by Johnson's announcement in late October of a bombing halt. Time ran out for the Democrats, however. The election results were close. Of the 73 million votes cast, Richard Nixon received just 510,314 more than Hubert Humphrey. Nixon's margin in the electoral college was much wider. He won 32 states to Humphrey's 13. Former Alabama governor **George Wallace** ran as a candidate of the newly formed American Independent Party. He appealed to Democrats opposed to liberal policies. Most of his supporters were white southerners and laborers. Wallace was an important factor in the close contest, as he received some 10 million votes and won five states in the South.

✔ **READING CHECK: Analyzing Information** What role did George Wallace play as a third-party candidate in the 1968 presidential campaign? He won votes of white southern Democrats and carried five states in the 1968 election.

TEACH OBJECTIVE 3

 LEVELS 1 AND 2: Pair students and tell them to imagine that they are Vietnam veterans who have recently returned home. Have each pair develop a short dialogue explaining how President Nixon attempted to end the war. *(Pairs should indicate that President Nixon followed a plan called Vietnamization and ordered the widespread bombing of Cambodia.)* Have volunteers perform their dialogues for the class. **English Language Learners, Cooperative Learning**

LEVEL 3: Tell students to imagine that they are either hawks or doves. Have each student write a short newspaper editorial describing President Nixon's plan to end the war. *(See the Levels 1 and 2 lesson for the correct features.)* Remind students that their editorials should reflect their personal opinions toward that plan as either a hawk or a dove. Ask volunteers to read their editorials to the class. Students may wish to include their editorials in their portfolios.

NOTE: For an additional teaching idea, see the Chapter 24 dialogue debate lesson in the **Creative Teaching Strategies** handbook.

Nixon, Vietnamization, and Cambodia

President Richard Nixon made foreign affairs his top priority. Nixon's key foreign-policy adviser was **Henry Kissinger**. Born in 1923 in Fürth, Germany, Henry Kissinger fled the country as a teenager with his parents to escape the Nazis. He arrived in New York City in 1938 and became a U.S. citizen in 1943. That same year, Kissinger joined the U.S. Army Counter-Intelligence Corps and served for three years. From 1946 to 1949, Kissinger was a captain in the Military Intelligence Reserve while attending Harvard University, where he graduated with honors. He received his Ph.D. from Harvard in 1954 and joined its faculty as a professor of government.

Henry Kissinger

Kissinger occasionally advised Presidents Eisenhower, Kennedy, and Johnson. He was particularly influential during the Nixon presidency. Kissinger served as national security adviser before becoming secretary of state. In both positions he worked closely with President Nixon to improve relations with communist China and the Soviet Union. Kissinger won the Nobel Peace Prize in 1973 for his role in the negotiations that eventually ended the Vietnam War. He later served as a foreign-affairs adviser to Presidents Ronald Reagan and George Bush.

Kissinger and Nixon devised a plan to fulfill the president's campaign pledge to end the war. Part of this plan was called **Vietnamization**, which involved turning over the fighting to the South Vietnamese while gradually pulling out U.S. troops. This strategy, said Nixon, would bring "peace with honor." At best, Nixon hoped that Vietnamization might produce a stable anticommunist South Vietnam. At worst, it would delay a collapse long enough to spare the United States the humiliation of outright defeat.

Nixon also hoped that Vietnamization would remove a major obstacle that had been blocking a peace agreement with North Vietnam. The North Vietnamese had first warned President Johnson and then Nixon that the United States would have to set a date for troop removals if peace talks were to continue. In August 1969, as U.S. troop withdrawals began, Henry Kissinger met secretly in Paris with longtime revolutionary **Le Duc Tho** (LAY DUHK TOH) of North Vietnam.

The process of troop withdrawal was slow. When Nixon took office in 1969, U.S. troops in Vietnam numbered about 540,000. At the end of 1972 about 24,200 Americans still remained in Vietnam.

Secretly, Nixon planned to expand the war into neutral Cambodia to cut off the North Vietnamese supply lines along the Ho Chi Minh Trail. Early in 1969 Nixon ordered the widespread bombing of Cambodia. He wanted to show Hanoi that the United States was still willing to use force, and even expand the war, in pursuit of his goal of "peace with honor." Nixon and Kissinger concealed the Cambodian air strikes from the American people, Congress, and key military leaders—even the secretary of the air force.

Research on the ROM

Free Find: Henry Kissinger
After reading about Henry Kissinger on the **Holt Researcher CD–ROM**, write an editorial for your local newspaper. Describe Kissinger's accomplishments and explain why you think he helped or hurt the United States.

Soldiers of the 25th Infantry Division withdraw from a Cambodian village as an attack helicopter strikes the village.

TEACH OBJECTIVE 4

LEVEL 1: Ask students to describe how Americans responded to President Nixon's plan to end the war. *(Students should note that the bombing and invasion of Cambodia provoked outrage in the United States and that Congress repealed the Tonkin Gulf Resolution.)* Then tell students that many doves wore buttons to declare their feelings about the war and other issues. Have each student design a button expressing Americans' reactions to President Nixon's plan to end the war. Students' buttons might express a simple slogan or present a visual image. Have volunteers present their designs to the class. **English Language Learners**

LEVELS 2 AND 3: Pair students and tell one member of each pair to imagine that he or she supports President Nixon's plan to end the war. Tell the other member to imagine that he or she opposes the plan. Have each pair develop a short dialogue expressing its reactions to the plan. *(See the Level 1 lesson for the correct reactions.)* Ask volunteers to present their dialogues to the class. Then have each student write a few paragraphs summarizing the material presented in the dialogues.
Cooperative Learning

HISTORY MAKERS SPEAK

Richard Nixon in *Grand Expectations*

Bombing Cambodia.
President Nixon defended his decision to bomb Cambodia in a nationally televised speech: "If, when the chips are down, the world's most powerful nation, the United States of America, acts like a pitiful, helpless giant, the forces of totalitarianism and anarchy will threaten free nations and institutions around the world. I would rather be a one-term president and do what I believe was right than to be a two-term president at the cost of seeing America become a second-rate power."

CRITICAL THINKING Do you agree with President Nixon's defense of the bombing? Why or why not?

ANSWER: Answers will vary. Some students might argue that the United States had to defend its international prestige and power.

THAT'S INTERESTING!

The parking spaces in which the Kent State victims died remained open to cars until 1999, when the spaces were dedicated as memorials, with markers bearing the students' names.

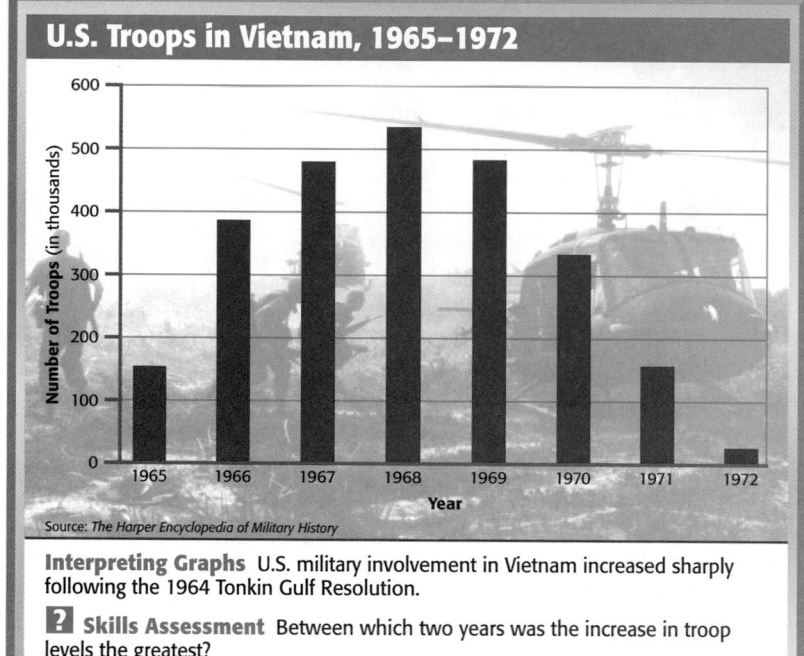

U.S. Troops in Vietnam, 1965–1972

Number of Troops (in thousands) / Year

Source: *The Harper Encyclopedia of Military History*

Interpreting Graphs U.S. military involvement in Vietnam increased sharply following the 1964 Tonkin Gulf Resolution.

? Skills Assessment Between which two years was the increase in troop levels the greatest?

Because of Cambodia's neutrality, Nixon feared an international uproar. When a revolt ousted Cambodia's ruler in March 1970, however, Nixon's strategy changed. Since the new Cambodian government was pro-American, Nixon made his strategy public. He justified the air strikes as defense of a friendly nation. Nixon then sent some 80,000 U.S. and ARVN troops into Cambodia.

This invasion destroyed the delicate balance that had kept Cambodia out of the war. North Vietnamese Army (NVA) troops were forced into the interior of Cambodia, where the bombing destroyed much of the countryside.

✔ **READING CHECK: Comparing** How did President Nixon's stated goal of ending the war compare to his actions? He began Vietnamization and gradually pulled U.S. troops out of Vietnam, but he also started a secret bombing campaign in Cambodia and sent troops there.

Antiwar Protest Increases

News of the bombing and invasion of Cambodia provoked outrage in the United States, particularly on college campuses. After someone at Kent State University in Ohio set fire to the campus ROTC building, Ohio's governor vowed to "eradicate" the protesters. On May 4, 1970, National Guard troops that had been sent to control demonstrators shot randomly into a large group of students. They killed four and injured nine others. Some of the students were merely walking across campus. The **Kent State shootings** shocked the nation.

Just 10 days later, state police in Jackson, Mississippi, fired at protesters in a dormitory at Jackson State College, killing two students and wounding nine others. Enraged, students and faculty on hundreds of college campuses went on strike.

Members of Congress were also upset by the Cambodian invasion. In response, Congress repealed the Tonkin Gulf Resolution in December 1970. Nixon insisted, however, that this action did not affect his authority to carry on the war. Congressional leaders soon developed plans to stop the war by cutting off funding once U.S. troops were withdrawn.

In 1971 another incident boosted the antiwar movement. The *New York Times* began publishing a collection of secret government documents relating to the war. Known as the

A young woman cries over the body of a student shot by National Guard troops at Kent State.

REVIEW

Have students complete the **Section 3 Review** on p. 725.

ASSESS

Have students complete **Daily Quiz 24.3**. As **Alternative Assessment**, you may want to use the campaign time line or the newspaper editorial in this section's lessons.

RETEACH

Have students complete **Main Idea Activity for English Language Learners and Special-Needs Students 24.3**. Then have each student write a brief summary of one of the subsections in Section 3. Have volunteers read their summaries to the class. Have students vote to choose the best summary of each subsection. **English Language Learners**

EXTEND

Have students conduct research on the bombing campaign in Vietnam. Then have each student write a short analysis of the campaign, explaining why it failed to achieve its objectives. In order to make their analyses, students might compare and contrast the bombing campaign in the Vietnam War with those of previous wars. **Block Scheduling**

Pentagon Papers, these documents revealed that the government had frequently misled the American people about the course of the war. The documents had been leaked to the press by Daniel Ellsberg, a former Department of Defense official. Ellsberg had strongly supported the war until he spent time in Vietnam studying the war's effects. While there, he found that few South Vietnamese supported their government.

The War Continues

As commander in chief, President Nixon not only ordered the invasion of Cambodia but also renewed the bombing of North Vietnam. Nixon explained his plan to his chief of staff, H. R. "Bob" Haldeman.

History Makers Speak

❝I call it the Madman Theory, Bob. I want the North Vietnamese to believe that I've reached the point where I might do anything to stop the war. We'll just slip the word to them that, 'for God's sake, you know Nixon is obsessed about Communists. We can't restrain him when he's angry—and he has his hand on the nuclear button'—and Ho Chi Minh himself will be in Paris in two days begging for peace.❞

—Richard Nixon, quoted in *Vietnam*, by Stanley Karnow

Nixon miscalculated the opposition's endurance. Rather than ending, the war suddenly grew more fierce. Hoping to reveal the weaknesses of Nixon's Vietnamization strategy, North Vietnam staged a major invasion of South Vietnam in March 1972. NVA troops drove deep into South Vietnam. In response, Nixon ordered heavy bombing of North Vietnam. Despite these steps, the opposition now held more territory in South Vietnam than ever.

✔ **READING CHECK: Sequencing** In what order of events did Americans' opposition to the war increase? College protests increased; students were shot at two colleges; some campuses went on strike; the Pentagon Papers were released; and many citizens were further outraged at being misled by the government.

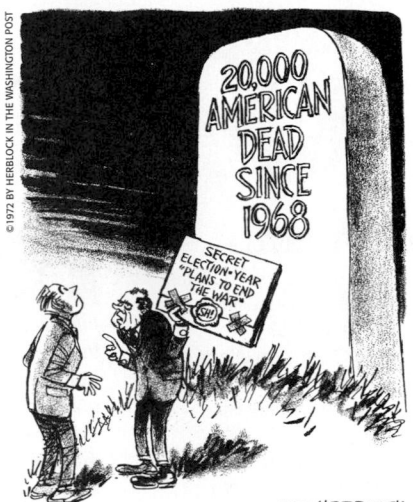

"NOW, AS I WAS SAYING, FOUR YEARS AGO"

INTERPRETING POLITICAL CARTOONS

Nixon's plan. This 1972 cartoon criticizes President Nixon's efforts to end the war. *What do you think the cartoonist was suggesting about Nixon's secret plan to end the war?*

POLITICAL CARTOON ANSWER

Students might suggest that the cartoon indicates that Nixon's plan was going to be ineffective.

SECTION
REVIEW ③ ANSWERS

1. Identify
- Tet Offensive, p. 720
- William Westmoreland, p. 720
- Eugene McCarthy, p. 721
- Robert F. Kennedy, p. 721
- Richard J. Daley, p. 722
- Richard Nixon, p. 722
- George Wallace, p. 722
- Henry Kissinger, p. 723
- Vietnamization, p. 723
- Le Duc Tho, p. 723
- Kent State shootings, p. 724
- Pentagon Papers, p. 725

2. efforts—Vietnamization and troop withdrawals backed by bombing; outcome—bombing widened and intensified the war

3a. 40,000 communist soldiers dead, 1,100 American soldiers and 2,300 ARVN lives lost; increased public criticism of the war and fewer U.S. troops sent to Vietnam

b. The Democrats and Republicans were split over the war; the election was close because the country was divided over the war.

c. wider bombings and expansion into Cambodia

4. Editorials will vary. Some students might argue that without public oversight the government could violate the law.

SECTION ③ REVIEW

1. Identify and explain:
Tet Offensive
William Westmoreland
Eugene McCarthy
Robert F. Kennedy
Richard J. Daley
Richard Nixon
George Wallace
Henry Kissinger
Vietnamization
Le Duc Tho
Kent State shootings
Pentagon Papers

2. Evaluating Copy the chart below. Use it to describe Nixon's efforts to end the war and how well they succeeded.

Nixon's Efforts to End the War

↓

Outcome

3. **Finding the Main Idea**
a. What were the costs of the Tet Offensive?
b. How did the 1968 presidential election reflect Americans' feelings about the war?
c. Which of President Nixon's policies led to renewed antiwar protests?

4. **Writing and Critical Thinking**
Supporting a Point of View Imagine that you are the publisher who decided to print the Pentagon Papers. Write an editorial explaining your position.
Consider:
- the importance of security to military operations
- the public's right to know what the government is doing
- the constitutional protection of free press

Homework Practice Online
keyword: SE3 HP24

LET'S GET STARTED!

As students enter the classroom, tell them to reread the quotation by presidential candidate George McGovern on this page and to write a few sentences in response to it. Have volunteers read their responses to the class and conduct a brief discussion on them. Then tell students that in Section 4 they will learn about the end of the Vietnam War and its long-term effects.

SECTION 4

READ TO DISCOVER
1. Why did the United States agree to a cease-fire in January 1973?
2. What long-term effects did the war have on Vietnam and the Vietnamese people?
3. What long-term effects did the war have on Americans?

IDENTIFY
George McGovern
Twenty-sixth Amendment
Le Ly Hayslip
War Powers Act
Vietnam Veterans Memorial
Maya Ying Lin

WHY IT MATTERS TODAY
Although the Vietnam War ended more than 25 years ago, many Americans and Vietnamese still remember the war very well. Use **CNNfyi.com** or other **current events** sources to identify ways Americans view the effects of the Vietnam War today. Record your findings in your journal.

CNNfyi.com

The War Ends

EYEWITNESSES TO History

"*We have heard many times that Vietnam will no longer be an issue by the time the fall election approaches. . . . For the sake of the thousands of Vietnamese peasants still dying from American bombing raids, the GIs still dying . . . the American POWs rotting in the jails of Hanoi, I sincerely hope it will not be an issue. But Vietnam thinking surely will be an issue, regardless of what happens in Indochina in the next four months. By 'Vietnam thinking' I mean wasting our strength on paranoiac [irrational] defense policies while neglecting the needs of our own people.*"

—George McGovern, "Where I Stand," *The Progressive*, July 1972

George McGovern

In July 1972 Senator George McGovern made clear his opposition to the war. He hoped that the American people's frustration with Vietnam would carry him into the White House.

Nixon's Re-election

Senator **George McGovern** of South Dakota campaigned in the 1972 Democratic presidential primaries as an antiwar candidate. An air force pilot in World War II, McGovern had been a history professor before entering politics. His opposition to the war ran deep. In one emotional Senate speech he declared in a trembling voice, "This chamber reeks [smells] of blood." George Wallace opposed McGovern for the Democratic nomination. In May, however, Wallace was shot at a political rally in Maryland. The injury paralyzed him from the waist down, and he withdrew from the race.

After the disastrous 1968 convention, the Democrats adopted new rules to increase the representation of ethnic minorities, women, and young people in party organizations. Passed in 1971, the **Twenty-sixth Amendment** had lowered the voting age from 21 to 18. Thus, it gave many men drafted to serve in Vietnam the right to vote. McGovern drew much of his support from these groups. He easily captured the nomination at the Democratic convention.

The Republicans renominated Richard Nixon and Spiro Agnew. Nixon again stressed his strong commitment to law and order within the United States and assured voters that the war would soon be over. Indeed, a few weeks before the election, Henry Kissinger announced a breakthrough in the negotiations to end the war. "Peace is at hand," he declared.

Nixon won the election by a landslide. He received 47 million votes to McGovern's 29 million. In the electoral college, McGovern carried just Massachusetts and the District of Columbia.

ALL LEVELS: To help students understand the key events that led to the 1973 cease-fire, copy the graphic organizer at right on the chalkboard, omitting the italicized answers. Have each student complete it. Then ask students how things might have been different if, for example, the South Vietnamese president had not rejected the first agreement or if President Nixon had not bombed Hanoi and Haiphong. Have each student write a few sentences or paragraphs speculating on the possible outcomes. Ask volunteers to read their sentences or paragraphs to the class.
English Language Learners

STEPS LEADING TO THE 1973 CEASE-FIRE

Henry Kissinger meets with Le Duc Tho.

South Vietnam's president rejects the agreement and the United States supports him.

North Vietnam demands reinstatement.

President Nixon bombs Hanoi and Haiphong.

Nixon ends the talks, and bombing resumes.

The parties make minor changes and declare a cease-fire.

A Cease-fire at Last

In August 1969 Henry Kissinger and North Vietnam's Le Duc Tho met secretly in Paris to begin negotiations aimed at finding a way to end the war. For nearly three years the two men engaged in a series of difficult peace negotiations. "I don't look back on our meetings with any great joy," Kissinger recalled. "Yet he was a person of substance and discipline who defended the position he represented with dedication."

Finally, in October 1972 North Vietnam offered a peace plan that Kissinger and President Nixon found acceptable. The plan called for a cease-fire, the pullout of all foreign troops from Vietnam, and an end to U.S. military aid. The agreement also planned for the creation of a new government in South Vietnam. This government would include the country's current president, Nguyen Van Thieu, as well as representatives of the National Liberation Front. Thieu, who had not been included in the negotiations, objected to the proposed government. He believed it would reduce his power. Rather than abandon Thieu, the United States rejected the agreement.

When North Vietnam demanded that the agreement be reinstated, Nixon responded by ordering round-the-clock bombing of Hanoi and Haiphong. A furious Nixon declared to the chairman of the Joint Chiefs of Staff: "This is your chance to use military power to win this war, and if you don't, I'll consider you responsible." Some 40,000 tons of bombs rained on the two cities for nearly two weeks, with the barrage only halting for Christmas Day. The intensive bombing did not sway the North Vietnamese, however. At the end of December 1972 Nixon called off the bombing and agreed to resume talks.

On January 27, 1973, the negotiators in Paris announced a cease-fire. The plan differed little from the one agreed to in October, but minor changes allowed each side to claim a victory. The United States pledged to withdraw its remaining forces from South Vietnam and to help rebuild Vietnam. The peace settlement also included a prisoner-exchange agreement. It did not, however, address the major issue behind the war—the political future of South Vietnam. While urging Thieu to accept the cease-fire, Nixon secretly pledged that the United States would come to South Vietnam's aid if fighting resumed.

Two years after U.S. forces withdrew, South Vietnam's military government collapsed. In January 1975, North Vietnamese troops overran the northern part of South Vietnam. As South Vietnamese troops retreated in panic, new waves of refugees poured into Saigon.

In early April the noose around Saigon tightened. The U.S. military rushed to evacuate the several thousand Americans still in the city. Some escaped from the U.S. Embassy roof by helicopter as North Vietnamese troops stormed the compound. Some 120,000 Vietnamese who had worked for the U.S. government were flown to the United States. On April 30, 1975, South Vietnam surrendered unconditionally.

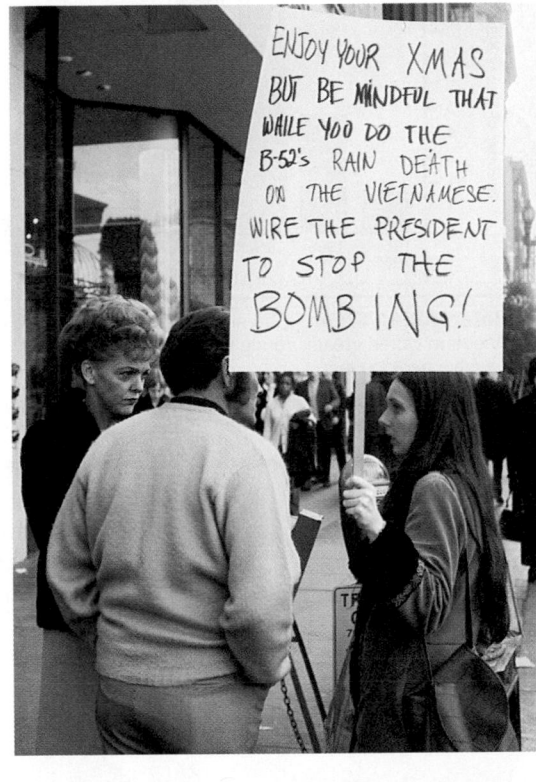

ENJOY YOUR XMAS BUT BE MINDFUL THAT WHILE YOU DO THE B-52's RAIN DEATH ON THE VIETNAMESE. WIRE THE PRESIDENT TO STOP THE BOMBING!

INTERPRETING THE VISUAL RECORD

Protest. This woman is protesting the "Christmas bombing" campaign ordered by President Nixon. *What does the woman's sign ask Americans to do?*

The Christmas Bombing.
The so-called Christmas bombing resulted in a storm of criticism. As a result of the bombing, the United States lost 26 aircraft and 93 airmen. President Nixon's public approval rating dropped to 39 percent, and many members of Congress indicated that they would take action against the president when the next session began.

CRITICAL THINKING Why might the Christmas bombing have received so much criticism?

ANSWER: Students might suggest that it was a brutal attack at a time of year when many Americans want to celebrate peace and goodwill.

THAT'S INTERESTING!
As the peace talks dragged on, U.S. troops in Vietnam became increasingly disillusioned. The desertion rate reached 7 percent, and twice as many soldiers went absent without leave. Some troops even attacked their own officers instead of following orders.

VISUAL RECORD ANSWER
Students might suggest that the sign asks Americans to consider the Vietnamese and the war against them during the Christmas season.

LEVEL 1: Pair students and tell them to imagine that they are Vietnamese citizens who lived through the war. Have each pair create a list of words describing the war's long-term effects. *(Pairs might list words such as death, violence, destruction, and so on.)* Ask volunteers to write their words on the chalkboard. Then have pairs use the words on the chalkboard to write topic sentences describing the effects of the war. *(Pairs' sentences should note that the war resulted in enormous casualties and destroyed the Vietnamese economy.)* Ask volunteers to read their sentences to the class.

English Language Learners, Cooperative Learning

LEVEL 2: Tell students to imagine that they are Vietnamese citizens who lived through the war. Have each student write a poem or a song about the war's long-term effects on Vietnam and the Vietnamese people. *(See the Level 1 lesson for the correct effects.)* Have volunteers read their poems or songs to the class. Students may wish to include their poems or songs in their portfolios.

LEVEL 3: Tell students to imagine that they are reporters leaving Vietnam after the cease-fire. Have each student write a short article on the war's long-term effects on Vietnam and the Vietnamese people. *(See the Level 1 lesson for the correct effects.)* Have volunteers read their articles to the class.

GLOBAL RELATIONS

Cambodia. In April 1975, Cambodian Communists gained control of Phnom Penh, the country's capital. Pol Pot and other Communist leaders soon declared their intention to purify Cambodian society of outside influences. They proclaimed their victory to be the beginning of a new era and designated the year as "Year Zero." Over the next few years, they tortured and murdered their own people. It is estimated that some 2 million Cambodians died under Pol Pot's rule, which ended in 1978 when Vietnam invaded Cambodia.

CRITICAL THINKING What might the events in Cambodia reveal about the legacy of war in Southeast Asia?

ANSWER: Students might suggest that the events reveal that the war disrupted society and made violence a commonplace occurrence.

THAT'S INTERESTING!

The war devastated the Vietnamese economy, leaving the nation one of the poorest in the world. At the war's end, per capita income averaged only $100. By the 1990s, per capita income had reached only $200.

GRAPH ANSWER

1968

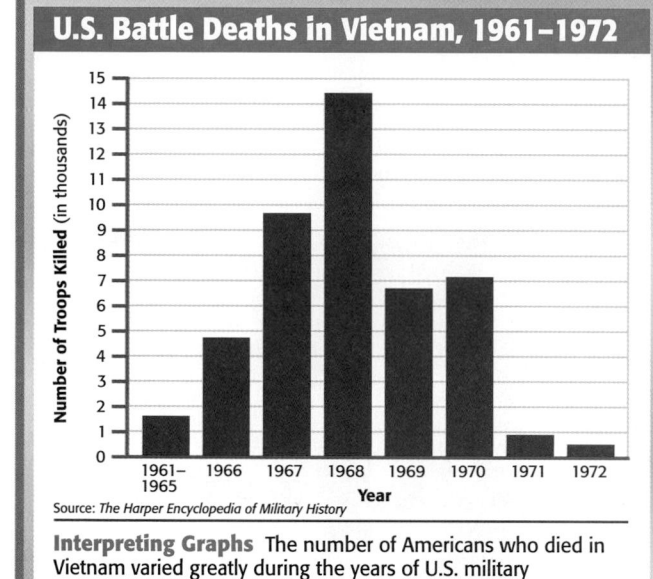

U.S. Battle Deaths in Vietnam, 1961–1972

Source: *The Harper Encyclopedia of Military History*

Interpreting Graphs The number of Americans who died in Vietnam varied greatly during the years of U.S. military involvement there.

❓ **Skills Assessment** During which year did the United States suffer the greatest number of battle deaths in Vietnam?

Analyzing Primary Sources

Identifying Bias How does Hayslip's view of the Vietnamese differ from that of U.S. troops?

She is Vietnamese and saw them as her people, not as the enemy.

For Americans the Vietnam War was over. The long, costly effort to prevent the creation of a united, independent Vietnam under Communist rule had failed. The war had spread to Cambodia and Laos, which had been heavily damaged. However, the predicted collapse of all Southeast Asia—the so-called domino theory—never occurred. Quarrels soon broke out between the Communist leaders of Vietnam and those of China and Cambodia. International communism was not as unified a world force as U.S. policy makers had feared.

✔ **READING CHECK: Sequencing** What events led to the end of U.S. involvement in Vietnam?
1969—Paris peace talks; 1972—renewed bombing; 1973—peace agreement reached and U.S. troops withdraw

Effects of the War

The war devastated the Vietnamese people. According to Saigon government figures, some 185,000 South Vietnamese soldiers died in combat. Estimates put the number of South Vietnamese civilian dead at nearly 500,000. The exact number of Vietcong and North Vietnamese Army war dead is unknown but may have been near 1 million. In addition, about 800,000 Vietnamese were orphaned, and 181,000 were disabled. Among the disabled were those exposed to chemicals such as Agent Orange. These people have been plagued by high rates of liver cancer and other illnesses.

BIOGRAPHY

Le Ly Hayslip

Vietnamese refugees. Le Ly Hayslip was one survivor of the Vietnam War. Hayslip was born in a village near Da Nang in 1949 and experienced constant warfare as a child. By the time she was 14, she had been imprisoned by the South Vietnamese government. Suspected of being a revolutionary, Hayslip was tortured and sentenced to death. She escaped, however, and returned home. Surviving as best she could, Hayslip worked in a hospital, as a waitress, and as a black-market vendor.

Hayslip's brothers fought on both sides of the war. In 1970 she married a U.S. civilian worker. Soon they fled to the United States. Although she escaped the fighting, she was unable to escape its effects. Hayslip described watching television coverage of Vietnam with her family.

History Makers Speak

❝Where the Munros [Hayslip's in-laws] saw faceless Orientals fleeing burning villages, tied up as prisoners, or as rag dolls in a roadside trench (even innocent villagers were "VC" or "Charlie"), I saw my brother Bon Nghe, who fought twenty-five years for the North; my mother's nephew, who was lieutenant for the South; my sister Lan, who hustled drinks to the Americans in Danang; and my

sister Hai, who shared sleepless nights with my mother in our family bunker at Ky La. I saw floating on the smoke of battle the soul of my dead brother, Sau Ban, victim of an American land mine, and the spirit of my father, who drank acid to avoid involving me again with the Viet Cong terrorists. I saw in those tiny electronic lines, as I saw in my dreams, the ghosts of a hundred relatives, family friends, and playmates who died fighting for this side or that, or merely to survive. 〞

—Le Ly Hayslip, *Child of War, Woman of Peace*

Shortly after arriving in the United States, Hayslip began writing her memoirs. Published in 1989, her highly acclaimed book, *When Heaven and Earth Changed Places,* describes growing up in a constant state of war. In 1987 Hayslip created a charitable organization, the East Meets West Foundation, to provide comfort to all victims of the war. The foundation provides assistance to Vietnamese people trying to rebuild their lives. It also helps U.S. veterans cope with the effects of the war.

More than 1.5 million Vietnamese like Hayslip fled Vietnam after the fall of Saigon. Desperate to escape economic and social hardships, many braved the rough South China Sea and Gulf of Thailand in tiny, crowded boats. They were joined by thousands of other refugees from Southeast Asia—such as the Hmong (MUHNG) of Laos—also fleeing grave postwar conditions. More than 730,000 of these refugees have settled in the United States since the war.

✔ **READING CHECK: Finding the Main Idea** How did the war affect Vietnam and
its people? 500,000 South Vietnamese civilians died, 800,000 orphaned; 1.5 million
refugees fled Vietnam; more than 730,000 settled in the United States.

Vietnam veterans. More than 2 million Americans were involved in the Vietnam War. More than 58,000 of them died, and more than 300,000 were wounded. About 2,500 were missing in action. Improved emergency medical services saved the lives of many U.S. soldiers who had severe wounds that would have been fatal in previous wars. As a result, there were a large number of paralyzed and otherwise severely disabled Vietnam veterans.

More than 600 Americans were held as prisoners of war (POWs). Some POWs spent more than six years in North Vietnamese jails, where they endured long periods of solitary confinement and torture.

One of the most visible tragedies of the war was the fate of its veterans. No ticker-tape parades celebrated the return of soldiers from the Vietnam conflict. On the contrary, veterans often became targets for the anger, guilt, or shame of fellow citizens frustrated by the war. Many other Americans met the veterans with stony silence.

The public's negative reaction enraged and demoralized many veterans. They had faced a life-and-death struggle, obeying orders that they trusted were in their country's best interests. Vietnam veteran Ron Kovic recalled the pain of this lack of support in his 1976 book, *Born on the Fourth of July:*

INTERPRETING THE VISUAL RECORD

Destruction. The effects of a B-52 bombing raid are clearly visible in this part of the Vietnamese countryside. *What long-term effects do you think the bombing might have had?*

Ron Kovic (holding flag) led this 1972 protest against the Vietnam War.

TEACH OBJECTIVE 3

LEVEL 1: Write the following headings on the chalkboard: *Vietnam Veterans, Public Policy,* and *Healing the Wounds of the War.* Organize students into three groups and assign each group one of the headings. Have each group create a short lesson plan on the content of its assigned subsection. *(The veterans group should discuss social attitudes and social problems that affected veterans. The public policy group should discuss the War Powers Act and public opinion. The wounds group should discuss the Vietnam Veterans Memorial and other efforts to honor veterans.)* Then have volunteers teach their lessons to the class. Encourage students to take notes on groups' presentations.

English Language Learners, Cooperative Learning

LEVELS 2 AND 3: Tell students to imagine that they work for a national weekly newsmagazine that will be publishing a feature section called The Legacy of Vietnam in the United States. Have each student write an article on a topic of his or her choice. *(See the Level 1 lesson for the correct effects.)* Encourage students to include images or graphic organizers to complement the information in their articles. Display students' completed articles around the classroom.

HOMEWORK *Have each student create a detailed outline of the subsection entitled Effects of the War.*

VISUAL RECORD ANSWER

(for p. 731)

Students might suggest that the soldiers experienced a feeling of painful cleansing.

SECTION 4 REVIEW ANSWERS

1. Identify
- George McGovern, p. 726
- Twenty-sixth Amendment, p. 726
- Le Ly Hayslip, p. 728
- War Powers Act, p. 730
- Vietnam Veterans Memorial, p. 730
- Maya Ying Lin, p. 730

2. economic—expensive, less money for domestic programs; lives lost—high casualty rates; other costs—veterans' problems and public tensions and divisions

3a. Answers will vary. Students should clearly state and support their positions.

b. It led Congress to pass the War Powers Act and attempt to have a greater role in directing U.S. military forces.

c. Letters will vary. Some students might call for expanded social services to help veterans with physical and mental illnesses.

4. Essays will vary. Some students will note the human and economic costs. Other students might suggest that the war made the United States more careful about using its military power. With increased media attention, secret bombings, like Cambodia, are not likely to occur.

★ Then and Now

No More Vietnams

During a military crisis in 1990, President George Bush assured the nation, "This will not be another Vietnam." The memories of Vietnam have haunted every U.S. leader who has considered committing U.S. troops to foreign conflicts. To avoid long, drawn-out conflicts, recent presidents have committed U.S. troops only to operations in which the fighting was likely to be over very quickly.

The memory of the Vietnam War has also affected media coverage. To keep the flow of war-zone information from eroding public support, the U.S. military has put tight restrictions on media access to the front lines. It has also closely screened what has been broadcast. The military does not want to expose Americans to the kind of gruesome images and grim statistics that fueled the Vietnam antiwar movement.

The men and women returning from recent armed conflicts have received a very different welcome than their Vietnam-era counterparts. Even many Americans who oppose armed conflicts have emphasized their support for the troops and the sacrifices that they have made.

These high school students are protesting a military operation in the 1990s.

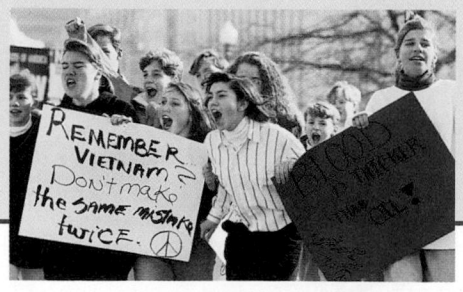

> *History Makers Speak*
>
> **"I didn't want to believe it at first—people protesting against us when we were putting our lives on the line for our country. . . . How could they do this to us? Many of us would not be coming back and many others would be wounded or maimed [disabled]."**
>
> —Ron Kovic, *Born on the Fourth of July*

In their despair, thousands of Vietnam veterans turned to drugs. Many others had trouble finding jobs or adjusting to life as civilians. Some ended up homeless.

Soldiers affected by the spraying of defoliants later developed certain forms of cancer at an unusually high rate. Their children had a very high rate of birth defects. Research in the 1970s linked their medical problems to Agent Orange. In 1984 the manufacturers of the chemical created a relief fund for the veterans and their families. In the early 1990s the government extended permanent disability benefits to these veterans.

Public policy. The war shook Americans' confidence in their government. Many were shocked to discover that their leaders had misled them during the war. The actions of both Presidents Johnson and Nixon raised a crucial constitutional question: under what authority can presidents wage an undeclared war? In 1973, seeking to prevent "another Vietnam," Congress passed the **War Powers Act.** This act reaffirms Congress's constitutional right to declare war by setting a 60-day limit on the presidential commitment of U.S. troops to foreign conflicts.

The Vietnam War also left a dismal economic legacy. It cost American taxpayers directly more than $150 billion, adding greatly to the national debt and fueling inflation. The war also diverted funding that might have gone to domestic programs, such as those that help the poor.

The Vietnam War taught U.S. policy makers that hostile public opinion and deep national divisions can impose severe restraints on the use of military force. Since Vietnam, leaders have been hesitant to commit U.S. troops in far-off regions without being certain of the consent of the American people and the nation's political allies.

✔ **READING CHECK: Analyzing Information** What were the economic effects of the war in Vietnam? It cost $150 billion, contributed to the national debt and inflation, and diverted funds from domestic programs.

Healing the Wounds of the War

Long after the war's end, Americans tried to come to terms with the conflict. The **Vietnam Veterans Memorial** in Washington, D.C., designed by **Maya Ying Lin,** became an attempt to heal divisions. Lin, a Chinese American, was an architecture student at Yale University when her design was chosen. Of the memorial, she said, "An honest memorial makes you accept what happened before you overcome it."

Have students complete the **Section 4 Review** on p. 731.

ASSESS

Have students complete **Daily Quiz 24.4**. As **Alternative Assessment**, you may want to use the graphic organizer activity or the newsmagazine "Legacy of Vietnam" activity in this section's lessons.

RETEACH

Have students complete **Main Idea Activity for English Language Learners and Special-Needs Students 24.4**. Then have each student summarize the entire section in one page or less. Have students trade summaries with a partner and read each other's work, discussing any differences in content or emphasis. **English Language Learners**

EXTEND

Have students conduct research on modern-day Vietnam and the current relationship between the United States and Vietnam. Encourage students to focus their research on a particular topic: growing business contacts, for example, or growing travel contacts. Have each student create an oral presentation on his or her research. Ask volunteers to deliver their presentations to the class. **Block Scheduling**

Inscribed on a huge wall of black granite are the names of the more than 58,000 Americans who died in Vietnam. Some names have been added since it was first built. Lin insisted that the names be listed in chronological order, not in alphabetical order or by rank. She explained that this way "if you were in the war, you could find your time and a few people you knew." Veteran Bruce Weigl attended the dedication ceremony on Veterans Day 1982. Weigl later reflected on the reasons he and other veterans attended.

History Makers Speak ❝I think we came, without really knowing it, to make the memorial our wailing wall. We came to find the names of those we lost in the war, as if by tracing the letters cut into the granite we could find what was left of ourselves.... No veteran could turn his back on the terrible grace of Maya Lin's wall and the names of the 57,939 who died or disappeared in Vietnam from July 1959 to May 1975.❞

—Bruce Weigl, quoted in *The Vietnam Years*, by Marilyn B. Young

Hundreds of people visit the memorial daily. Many leave flowers, personal mementos, or written messages. Others simply ponder the meaning of the memorial.

✔ **READING CHECK: Categorizing** How did the Vietnam War affect veterans? Some turned to drugs, had difficulty adjusting to civilian life, suffered medical problems linked to Agent Orange, or felt rejected. The Vietnam Memorial helped heal divisions.

INTERPRETING THE VISUAL RECORD

The wall. Reminders of the war like the Vietnam Veterans Memorial and the hat at left bring back strong emotions. *How did visiting the memorial affect these soldiers?*

SECTION 4 REVIEW

1. Identify and explain:
George McGovern
Twenty-sixth Amendment
Le Ly Hayslip
War Powers Act
Vietnam Veterans Memorial
Maya Ying Lin

2. Drawing Conclusions Copy the diagram below. Use it to list what you think were the costs of the Vietnam War.

WAR

Economic Costs

Lives Lost

Other Costs

3. Finding the Main Idea
a. Do you think the terms of the 1973 cease-fire represented a victory or a defeat for the United States? Explain your answer.
b. What impact did the Vietnam War have on the president's ability to direct U.S. military forces?
c. Imagine that you are a veteran of the Vietnam War. Write a letter to the president explaining how you think Vietnam veterans should be honored.

4. Writing and Critical Thinking
Evaluating Write a short essay evaluating the domestic and international effects the Vietnam War has had on the United States.
Consider:
• the lives lost on both sides of the war
• the changes in the way the United States uses its military
• the increased media attention to government actions

Homework Practice Online
keyword: SE3 HP24

REVIEW AND ASSESSMENT RESOURCES

TECHNOLOGY

▶ Chapter 24 Test Generator (on the One-Stop Planner)
▶ Global Skill Builder CD–ROM
▶ HRW Go site

REINFORCEMENT, REVIEW, AND ASSESSMENT

▶ Chapter 24 Review, pp. 732–33
▶ Chapter 24 Tutorial for Students, Parents, Mentors, and Peers

▶ Chapter 24 Test (Form A or B)
▶ Portfolio Activities and Alternative Assessment Handbook, Chapter 24
▶ Chapter 24 Test for English Language Learners and Special-Needs Students

REVIEW

Have students complete the **Chapter 24 Review** on pp. 732–33.

ASSESS

Use one of the chapter tests to assess students' understanding of the content. For **Alternative Assessment**, see the **Portfolio Activities and Alternative Assessment Handbook**.

Understanding Main Ideas

1. to keep France as an ally against communism and to stop the spread of communism in Asia

2. The jungle terrain mde the fighting more difficult.

3. Some believed that all war was wrong. Others feared that the United States might use nuclear weapons. Others saw Vietnam as relatively unimportant and thought the war took resources from poverty programs and worked against the wishes of the Vietnamese.

4. It turned American public opinion against the war.

5. It resulted in the deaths and injuries of many Americans, caused problems for veterans, cost an enormous amount of money, introduced social divisions, and made many people distrust the government.

6. It created diplomatic problems between the United States and certain Southeast Asian countries and made U.S. officials more hesitant about committing troops in distant conflicts.

Reviewing Themes

1. The United States became involved in the war to stop the advance of communism.

2. Some members of Congress feared that Congress was losing some of its constitutional war-making authority.

3. by demonstrating that Americans had the freedom to openly criticize their government's actions

---

CHAPTER 24

Review

Creating a Time Line

Copy the time line below onto a sheet of paper. Complete the time line by filling in the events and dates from the chapter that you think were most significant. Pick three events and explain why you think they were significant.

| 1954 | 1965 | 1975 |

Writing a Summary

Using standard grammar, spelling, sentence structure, and punctuation, write an overview of events in the chapter.

Identifying People and Ideas

Identify the following terms or individuals and explain their significance.

1. Ho Chi Minh
2. domino theory
3. Vietcong
4. Tonkin Gulf Resolution
5. doves

6. Tet Offensive
7. Henry Kissinger
8. George Wallace
9. Vietnamization
10. Le Ly Hayslip

Understanding Main Ideas

SECTION 1 *(pp. 706–711)*
1. What were the main reasons the United States first became involved in Vietnam?

SECTION 2 *(pp. 712–719)*
2. How did the geography of Vietnam affect the fighting there?
3. What were the main reasons for Americans' opposition to the war?

SECTION 3 *(pp. 720–725)*
4. How did the Tet Offensive change the war?

SECTION 4 *(pp. 726–731)*
5. How has the Vietnam War influenced Americans?
6. What effect did the Vietnam War have on U.S. foreign policy?

Reviewing Themes

1. Global Relations How did the U.S. stance on communism lead to involvement in Vietnam?
2. Constitutional Heritage During the Vietnam War the president assumed increasing amounts of power. Why did this alarm Congress?
3. Citizenship How did antiwar protests illustrate American democratic values?

Thinking Critically

1. Supporting a Point of View Imagine that you are an adviser to President Kennedy. Suggest at least two ways the United States might support South Vietnam without committing U.S. troops.
2. Evaluating Do you think President Johnson had good reasons to escalate the U.S. war effort? Explain your answer.
3. Analyzing Information How did the Tonkin Gulf Resolution and the War Powers Act affect the relationship between the legislative and executive branches of the federal government?
4. Drawing Conclusions How did the Twenty-sixth Amendment help both U.S. troops in Vietnam and college antiwar protesters gain greater influence upon the course of the war?
5. Identifying Cause and Effect A major goal of U.S. involvement in Vietnam was to stop the spread of communism. What effect did U.S. actions have on the spread of communism?

Writing About History

Supporting a Point of View Imagine that it is 1968 and you have just been drafted. Write a poem or song that expresses your feelings. Use the following graphic to organize your thoughts.

| State of the War | + | Public Opinion of the War | = | Your Feelings About Being Drafted |

RETEACH

Organize the class into four groups. Assign each group one of the sections of the chapter. Have each group create visual displays to convey the information in its assigned section. Groups might draw graphic organizers, posters, and so on. Have students present their visual displays to the class.
English Language Learners, Cooperative Learning

EXTEND

Organize students into small groups. Have each group prepare a short multimedia presentation about some aspect of the Vietnam War. Encourage students to cover the major events of the war in creative ways: by interviewing veterans about their experiences; by presenting a slide show of images that tell a story by themselves; by playing music of the time period that comments on the war and the feelings of those opposed to it; and so on. Have students deliver their presentations to the class.
Cooperative Learning, Block Scheduling

Building Social Studies Skills

Interpreting Charts

Study the cause-and-effect chart below. Then use it to help answer the questions that follow.

Causes and Effects of Vietnam War

Long-Term Causes
• Fear of communist expansion
• U.S. support of South Vietnam's government

Immediate Causes
• Gulf of Tonkin incident
• Communist attacks against South Vietnam

Vietnam War

Effects
• Many thousands of Americans and Vietnamese killed and injured
• Vietnam united as a communist nation
• Political divisions created in the United States
• Ailments suffered by U.S. veterans

1. Which immediate cause led President Johnson to mislead the American public?
   a. fear of communist expansion
   b. U.S. support of North Vietnam
   c. Gulf of Tonkin incident
   d. Communist attacks against South Vietnam

2. How did Cold War tensions contribute to the Vietnam War?

Analyzing Primary Sources

Read the excerpt from an African American soldier's account of his experiences in Vietnam. Then answer the questions that follow.

66When I got back everything was changed. The way I feel about life now . . . it's just a bum trip. I have flashbacks and people can't understand me sometimes. I sit by myself and I just think. You try to talk to somebody about it, they think you're out of your mind or you're freaked out. . . . That's why I go to these veteran rap [discussion] groups that they have now every Wednesday. I just blow off the heat that I have built up inside.99

3. Which statement best summarizes the passage?
   a. It was wrong for the United States to have been involved in the Vietnam War.
   b. The United States did not provide sufficient support for returning soldiers.
   c. Civilians understand the long-term effects of combat.
   d. Some veterans suffered from long-lasting personality changes and other challenges.

4. In what way does the passage indicate the long-lasting effects of the Vietnam War?

Alternative Assessment

Building Your Portfolio

U.S. HISTORY

Global Relations

Imagine that you are a U.S. delegate to the Geneva Conference in 1954. Create a visual presentation that shows your proposal for Indochina's future. Then write a short statement indicating how your plan could lessen the risk of U.S. military involvement in Vietnam.

✓ **internet** connect

go.hrw.com

Internet Activity: go.hrw.com
KEYWORD: SE3 AN24

Choose a topic on the war in Vietnam to:
• research the changes in Southeast Asia since the end of the Vietnam War.
• create a poster of U.S. involvement in the Vietnam War.
• learn about the Vietnam Veterans Memorial.

REVIEW AND ASSESSMENT RESOURCES

TECHNOLOGY

▶ Global Skill Builder CD–ROM
▶ Holt Researcher: American History CD–ROM
▶ HRW Go site

REINFORCEMENT, REVIEW, AND ASSESSMENT

▶ Unit 6 Review, pp. 706–07
▶ Unit 6 Test (Form A or B)
▶ Portfolio Activities and Alternative Assessment Handbook, Unit 6
▶ Unit 6 Test for English Language Learners and Special-Needs Students

To review elements of Unit 6 in a single class period, assign one of the following activities or graphic organizers, omitting the italicized answers, to individuals or groups.

1 Decision Making

Ask students to imagine they are members of Congress in August 1964. President Johnson has just asked Congress to authorize the use of military force in Vietnam. Divide students into two groups, one favoring and one opposing the president's request. Have the two groups debate their respective positions. Students should use information about the Vietnam War as

---

A Selection from Further Reading

Black Veterans and the Civil Rights Movement.
In *Voices of Freedom*, Henry Hampton and Steve Fayer present an oral history of the civil rights movement from the 1950s to the 1980s. In the following excerpt, activist Bayard Rustin discusses the origins of the modern civil rights movement. "I think the beginning of this period from 1954 has its roots in the returning soldiers after 1945. There was a great feeling on the part of many of these youngsters that they . . . had fought in the war—they were not getting what they should have. . . . There was a building up of militancy, not so much by going into the streets as by a feeling of 'We are not going to put up with this anymore.' What was lacking was that they did not have the Supreme Court backing them. But when the Supreme Court came out with the *Brown* [v. *Board of Education*] decision in '54, things began rapidly to move."

COMPREHENSION According to Rustin, why was the *Brown* v. *Board of Education* decision so important?

ANSWER: Students might answer that the *Brown* decision represented a fundamental first step toward African American equality. Once the Supreme Court codified that principle, activists began to work in earnest.

UNIT
6

Review

BUILDING YOUR PORTFOLIO

Outlined below are three projects. Independently or cooperatively, complete one and use the products to demonstrate your mastery of the historical concepts involved.

1 Decision Making

You are a member of Congress in August 1964. President Johnson has just announced that the U.S. destroyer *Maddox* has been attacked in the Gulf of Tonkin by North Vietnamese forces. He has asked Congress to authorize the use of military force to "prevent further aggression." Follow these steps to make a decision on whether to support his request.

Use your textbook and other resources to *gather information* that might influence your decision whether to move. Be sure to use what you learned about the Vietnam War and the constitutional authority of the executive and legislative branches to help you make an effective decision. You may want to divide up different parts of the research among group members.

Anti-Vietnam protest in New York City

United Farm Workers marching

Once you have gathered information, *identify options*. Based on the information you have gathered, consider the options you might recommend for supporting or denying the president's request. Be sure to record your possible options for your presentation.

Once you have identified these options, *predict the consequences* for each option. For example, what might happen if you pass a Tonkin Gulf Resolution? How will a resolution affect the relationship between the executive and legislative branches? Once you have predicted the consequences, record them as notes for your presentation.

Take action to implement your decision. Once you have considered your options, you should create a presentation about your decision. You will need to support your decision by including information you gathered and by explaining why you rejected other options. You may want to create maps or a sequencing diagram to help you explain your decision. Have one person present the decision to the class.

well as about the relations between the different branches of government in preparing their arguments. Each side should explain why they did not choose another option. For concluding arguments, have each side predict the consequences of the opposing side's decision.

2 Culture

Have each student write a brief introduction and a table of contents for a book entitled *Advancements in the U.S. Civil Rights Movement: 1945–1975*. The book should focus on how the civil rights movement has led to increased participation of minorities in the political process. Students' tables of content should include both chapter and section titles.

3 Science, Technology, and Society

2 Culture

For many Americans the greatest strides in civil rights came in the 30 years following World War II. African Americans, Hispanics, American Indians, Americans with disabilities, women, and other groups took action to secure rights that had long been guaranteed to others. *Rehearse and present a 15-minute news program* to the class discussing how these groups expanded their economic opportunities and political rights. Your program should also discuss how these groups have helped to shape our national identity. You may wish to use portfolio materials you designed in the unit chapters to help you.

3 Science, Technology, and Society

In the 1960s advances in science and technology, population growth and shifts, and a rising standard of living helped transform the daily lives of Americans. *Develop a slide show* that documents some of the changes in everyday life during the 1960s. You may want to create slides that show how these changes were connected. For example, you may want to show how technological innovations changed the standard of living.

You may wish to use portfolio materials you designed in the unit chapters to help you.

Cereal advertisement

Further Reading

DuPlessis, Rachel Blau, and Ann Sitnow, eds. *The Feminist Memoir Project.* Crown, 1998. Accounts from the new generation of female activists in the 1960s and 1970s.

Evans, Sara M. *Personal Politics.* Knopf, 1980. A discussion of the women's rights movement and its relationship to the civil rights movement.

Gitlin, Todd. *The Sixties.* Bantam Books, 1993. A history of the decade with personal accounts from a former SDS president.

Hampton, Henry, and Steve Fayer. *Voices of Freedom.* Bantam Books, 1991. An oral history of the civil rights movement.

May, Ernest R., and Philip D. Zelikow, eds. *The Kennedy Tapes.* Belknap Press, 1998. Transcripts of tapes made in the Kennedy White House during the Cuban missile crisis.

O'Brien, Tim. *The Things They Carried.* Random House, 1998. A war veteran's fictional account of the experiences in the Vietnam War.

Young, Marilyn B. *The Vietnam Wars, 1945–1990.* HarperCollins, 1991. History of the Vietnam War and its aftermath.

Internet Connect & Review on the ROM

In assigned groups, develop a multimedia presentation about the United States between 1960 and 1978. Choose information from the chapter Internet Connect activities and from the **Holt Researcher CD–ROM** that best reflects the major topics of the period. Write an outline and a script for your presentation, which may be shown to the class.

A Selection from Further Reading

The Experience of War.
In *The Things They Carried,* Tim O'Brien provides a fictional account of the experiences of U.S. soldiers in the Vietnam War. In the following excerpt, the novel's narrator explores the thoughts and emotions of the men in his platoon.
"They carried all the emotional baggage of men who might die. . . . They carried shameful memories. They carried the common secret of cowardice barely restrained, the instinct to run or freeze or hide, and in many respects this was the heaviest burden of all, for it could never be put down, it required perfect balance and perfect posture. They carried their reputations. They carried the soldier's greatest fear, which was the fear of blushing. Men killed, and died, because they were embarrassed not to. . . [,] to avoid the blush of dishonor. They died so as not to die of embarrassment."

EVALUATING SOURCES
According to O'Brien, why did U.S. soldiers in Vietnam take part in the grave risks and responsibilities of war?

ANSWER: Students might indicate that they took part because they did not want to appear weak and unreliable to their fellow soldiers.

Modern Times

CHAPTER 25 From Nixon to Carter

When President Richard M. Nixon took office in 1968, the United States was experiencing social and economic turmoil. Nixon worked for an era of détente in foreign relations, establishing a new relationship with China. The Nixon administration faced serious trouble when the Watergate scandal erupted. Nixon resigned from the presidency in August 1974. Gerald Ford succeeded Richard Nixon as president but lost the 1976 election to Jimmy Carter.

CHAPTER 26 The Republican Revolution

With Ronald Reagan's election as president in 1980, many observers hailed the beginning of a "Republican Revolution." President Reagan tried to decrease the size of the federal government, and he reduced taxes and eliminated regulations on certain industries. Reagan pursued a strong anticommunist foreign policy, greatly increasing the defense budget and increasing U.S.

U·N·I·T

7

Modern Times

1968–Present

Many Americans celebrated the nation's bicentennial in 1976 with fireworks.

involvement in Latin America. During Reagan's last years in office, the Soviet sphere of influence began to dissolve.

Launching the New Millennium

CHAPTER 27

In 1992 Democrat Bill Clinton won the presidency. In part due to the failure of a national health care plan, the Republicans made stunning gains in House and Senate representation. Although the U.S. economy prospered during President Clinton's second term, his term was dominated by political scandals. Clinton also faced many international challenges as post–Cold War ethnic tensions flared up in several former Communist countries. In the hotly contested presidential election of 2000, Republican George W. Bush defeated Democrat Al Gore. Responding to the terrorist attacks of September 11, 2001, dominated Bush's presidency.

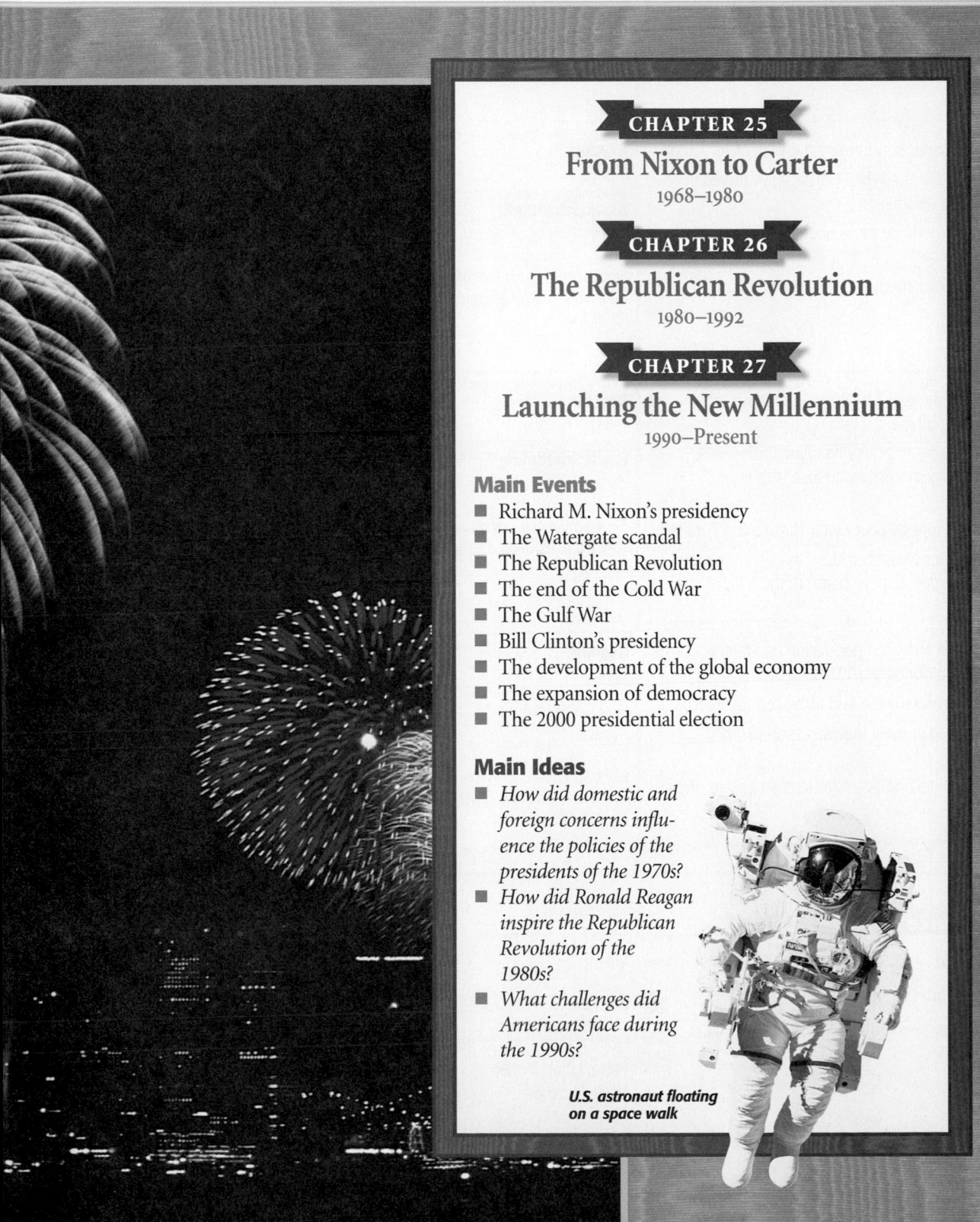

CHAPTER 25

From Nixon to Carter
1968–1980

CHAPTER 26

The Republican Revolution
1980–1992

CHAPTER 27

Launching the New Millennium
1990–Present

Main Events
- Richard M. Nixon's presidency
- The Watergate scandal
- The Republican Revolution
- The end of the Cold War
- The Gulf War
- Bill Clinton's presidency
- The development of the global economy
- The expansion of democracy
- The 2000 presidential election

Main Ideas
- *How did domestic and foreign concerns influence the policies of the presidents of the 1970s?*
- *How did Ronald Reagan inspire the Republican Revolution of the 1980s?*
- *What challenges did Americans face during the 1990s?*

U.S. astronaut floating on a space walk

From Nixon to Carter

CHAPTER RESOURCE MANAGER

Objectives	Pacing Guide	Reproducible Resources
SECTION 1 **The Nixon Years** pp. 740–46 ★ Discuss how President Nixon's domestic policies differed from those of Presidents Johnson and Kennedy. ★ Describe how Nixon responded to economic problems. ★ Identify the causes and effects of the energy crisis. ★ Summarize Americans' efforts to help clean up the environment. ★ Explain how Nixon made foreign-policy decisions.	**Regular** 2 days **Block Scheduling** 1 day *Block Scheduling Handbook with Team Teaching Strategies, pp. 145–50*	**RS** Guided Reading Strategy 25.1 **PS** Biography Reading 25: Ralph Nader **IC** Literature Reading 25: Nixon's Visit to China
SECTION 2 **From Watergate to Ford** pp. 747–53 ★ Summarize the issues surrounding the Watergate scandal. ★ Discuss the role that the White House tapes played in President Nixon's resignation. ★ Explain why President Ford was unable to achieve his domestic-policy goals. ★ Report on how Ford attempted to continue Nixon's foreign policies.	**Regular** 2 days **Block Scheduling** 1 day *Block Scheduling Handbook with Team Teaching Strategies, pp. 145–50*	**RS** Guided Reading Strategy 25.2 **PS** Primary Source Reading 25: A President Resigns **RS** Graphic Organizer Activity 25: The Nixon Administration
SECTION 3 **Carter: The Outsider as President** pp. 754–59 ★ State why voters thought that Jimmy Carter was a different kind of politician. ★ Explain how President Carter's handling of domestic issues caused some Americans to lose faith in his administration. ★ Contrast Carter's foreign policy with Nixon's and Ford's. ★ Analyze how Carter weakened U.S.-Soviet relations, and relate how he helped achieve peace in the Middle East.	**Regular** 1 day **Block Scheduling** .5 day *Block Scheduling Handbook with Team Teaching Strategies, pp. 145–50*	**RS** Guided Reading Strategy 25.3 **SM** Geography Activity 25: Southern Africa in the 1970s **E** Hands-On History Activity: The Future of Energy
SECTION 4 **Life in the 1970s** pp. 760–65 ★ Describe how the American population and family structure changed during the 1970s. ★ Explain why Americans were said to be self-absorbed. ★ List forms of entertainment that were popular in the 1970s. ★ Analyze how new technologies affected Americans' lives.	**Regular** 1 day **Block Scheduling** .5 day *Block Scheduling Handbook with Team Teaching Strategies, pp. 145–50*	**RS** Guided Reading Strategy 25.4 **E** Creative Teaching Strategy: Inner-Outer Circle Lesson

Chapter Resource Key

PS	Primary Sources	**REV**	Review
RS	Reading Support	**ELL**	Reinforcement and English Language Learners
IC	Interdisciplinary Connections		
E	Enrichment		Transparencies
SM	Skills Mastery		CD–ROM
A	Assessment		Music

 Video

Internet

Holt Presentation Maker Using Microsoft® PowerPoint®

One-Stop Planner CD–ROM

See the *One-Stop Planner* for a complete list of additional resources for students and teachers.

One-Stop Planner CD–ROM

It's easy to plan lessons, select resources, and print out materials for your students when you use the **One-Stop Planner CD–ROM with Test Generator.**

Technology Resources

- One-Stop Planner, Lesson 25.1
- The American Nation Video Program Segment: Nixon in China; Teacher's Guide, pp. 197–98
- Holt Researcher: American History CD–ROM
- Homework Practice Online

- One-Stop Planner, Lesson 25.2
- The American Nation Video Program Segment: Richard Nixon Resigns; Teacher's Guide, pp. 215–16
- Holt Researcher: American History CD–ROM
- Homework Practice Online
- HRW Go site

- One-Stop Planner, Lesson 25.3
- **CNN** Presents America: Yesterday and Today, 1850 to the Present Segment: Congresswoman Barbara Jordan
- Holt Researcher: American History CD–ROM
- Homework Practice Online

- One-Stop Planner, Lesson 25.4
- Everyday Life in America Transparency 31: *Star Wars*: Sign of the Seventies
- Holt Researcher: American History CD–ROM
- Homework Practice Online

Reinforcement, Review, and Assessment

REV	Section 1 Review, p. 746
A	Daily Quiz 25.1
ELL	Main Idea Activity 25.1
ELL	English Audio Summary 25.1
ELL	Spanish Audio Summary 25.1

REV	Section 2 Review, p. 753
A	Daily Quiz 25.2
ELL	Main Idea Activity 25.2
ELL	English Audio Summary 25.2
ELL	Spanish Audio Summary 25.2

REV	Section 3 Review, p. 759
A	Daily Quiz 25.3
ELL	Main Idea Activity 25.3
ELL	English Audio Summary 25.3
ELL	Spanish Audio Summary 25.3

REV	Section 4 Review, p. 765
A	Daily Quiz 25.4
ELL	Main Idea Activity 25.4
ELL	English Audio Summary 25.4
ELL	Spanish Audio Summary 25.4

internet connect

HRW ONLINE RESOURCES
GO TO: go.hrw.com
Then type in a keyword.

TEACHER HOME PAGE
KEYWORD: SE3 Teacher

CHAPTER INTERNET ACTIVITIES
KEYWORD: SE3 AN25
Choose an activity to:
- research popular culture of the 1970s.
- create a brochure on President Nixon's trip to China.
- learn about the Watergate scandal.

CHAPTER ENRICHMENT LINKS
KEYWORD: SE3 CH25

ONLINE ASSESSMENT
Homework Practice
KEYWORD: SE3 HP25

Standardized Test Prep
KEYWORD: SE3 STP25

Rubrics
KEYWORD: SS Rubrics

ONLINE MAPS, CHARTS, AND GRAPHS
KEYWORD: SE3 MCG
- The Impeachment Process

CONTENT UPDATES
KEYWORD: SS Content Updates

HOLT PRESENTATION MAKER
KEYWORD: SE3 PPT25

ONLINE READING SUPPORT
KEYWORD: SS Strategies

CURRENT EVENTS
KEYWORD: S3 Current Events

Meeting Individual Needs

Ability Levels

Level 1 Basic-level activities designed for all students encountering new material

Level 2 Intermediate-level activities designed for average students

Level 3 Challenging activities designed for honors and gifted-and-talented students

English Language Learners Activities that address the needs of students with Limited English Proficiency

Chapter Review and Assessment

- **Global Skill Builder CD–ROM**
- **HRW Go site**
- **REV Chapter 25 Tutorial for Students, Parents, Mentors, and Peers**
- **REV Chapter 25 Review, pp. 766–67**
- **Chapter 25 Test Generator (on the One-Stop Planner)**
- **A Chapter 25 Test (Form A or B)**
- **A Alternative Assessment Handbook**
- **A Chapter 25 Test for English Language Learners and Special-Needs Students**

Build on What You Know

Ask students to answer the following questions.

Why were many Americans concerned about law and order?

Consider:

- the protests against the Vietnam War
- the increasing militancy of civil rights protesters during the late 1960s

How might a presidential scandal affect the office of the president?

Consider:

- the symbolic importance of the office
- how a scandal might affect Americans' attitudes toward the president

---

exploring the time line

AMERICAN EVENTS

CONSTITUTIONAL HERITAGE

1972 ■ Cigarette Ads. Broadcasters objecting to the law banning cigarette advertisements from radio and television maintained that if cigarettes were a harmful product, Congress should have banned all advertising. In the case of *Capital Broadcasting Company* v. *U.S.*, however, a federal court ruled that Congress had the power to single out broadcasters while allowing cigarette ads in print media. The court ruled that the Constitution did not require Congress to "prohibit all like evils, or none."

ACTIVITY: Ask students to write a brief essay explaining both sides of the court case, as well as predicting future consequences for other types of products and media.

CHAPTER
25

1968–1980

From Nixon to Carter

Neil Armstrong walks on the Moon.

1968

1969 Science and Technology Astronaut Neil Armstrong becomes the first person to walk on the Moon.

The cast of All in the Family

1970

1971 The Arts The television situation comedy *All in the Family*, which examines controversial issues such as racial conflict, debuts.

1972 Daily Life A federal law banning cigarette advertisements on radio and television goes into effect.

1972 World Events Chinese leaders welcome Richard Nixon, the first U.S. president to visit China.

President Nixon at the Great Wall of China

1972

1973 Politics Vice President Spiro Agnew resigns from office.

1973 World Events War breaks out in the Middle East when several Arab states attack Israel.

Build on What You Know

Throughout the 1960s the United States increased its involvement in the Vietnam War. Criticism of the role the United States played in the conflict also escalated. Republican Richard Nixon won the presidential election of 1968, promising to end the war and to restore law and order to society. In this chapter you will learn how scandal ruined Nixon's presidency and how Presidents Gerald Ford and Jimmy Carter struggled to lead the nation. You will also learn how the tensions of the era transformed American culture.

Think About Themes

To help students create their Themes Journal entries, share the following examples of appropriate **agree**/**disagree** *statements.*

Government

Agree It was necessary to keep the development of the atomic bomb secret from the American public in order to protect the national security of the United States.

Disagree The Pentagon Papers revealed that the U.S. government had frequently misled Americans about U.S. progress in the Vietnam War.

Economics

Agree Innovations in technology and production techniques after World War I helped end the economic recession and create prosperity.

Disagree Franklin D. Roosevelt's New Deal helped many Americans who were in a desperate situation during the Great Depression.

Global Relations

Agree Woodrow Wilson's call to make the world save for democracy after World War I was a failure.

Disagree While the United States and European countries tried to avoid involvement in another costly war, Adolf Hitler invaded Austria and the Sudetenland.

President Ford's inauguration

Apple I computer

1974
Politics
Gerald Ford becomes the first U.S. president to hold office by appointment.

1975
The Arts
Steven Spielberg's *Jaws* becomes the highest-earning motion picture released to date.

1975
Daily Life
Americans are able to purchase video games that can be played on television sets.

1976
Business and Finance
Steven Jobs and Stephen Wozniak found the Apple Computer company.

1978
Politics
The U.S. Senate ratifies the Panama Canal Treaties by very close votes.

1979
World Events
Soviet troops invade Afghanistan and install a pro-Soviet government.

1979
Daily Life
Radiation is released from the Three Mile Island nuclear power plant after a cooling system fails.

1974   **1976**   **1978**   **1980**

1976
Daily Life
Americans celebrate the nation's bicentennial, the 200th anniversary of the signing of the Declaration of Independence.

1977
The Arts
The Bee Gees, a disco group, begin their record string of six straight number-one hit singles.

1980
Business and Finance
The Rollerblade company begins production of in-line roller skates.

1980
World Events
The United States and 64 other nations boycott the Summer Olympics held in Moscow.

Bicentennial fireworks in New York City

Misha the Bear, official mascot of the 1980 Olympics

exploring the time line

GLOBAL EVENTS

internet connect

go.hrw.com

TOPIC: Nixon's Foreign Policy
GO TO: go.hrw.com
KEYWORD: SE3 AN25

Have students access the Internet through the HRW Go site to conduct research on President Richard Nixon's foreign policy, including the trip to China and the establishment of closer ties between the United States and China. Then ask each student to create a brochure in which to document their research.

What's Your Opinion?

Themes Journal *Do you* **agree** *or* **disagree** *with the following statements? Support your point of view in your journal.*

Government The president has the right to keep certain information secret from the American public.

Economics Government should not intervene during an economic recession because the business cycle will always correct itself.

Global Relations A nation's foreign policy should be based on practical national-security interests, not on moral or ethical ideals.

LET'S GET STARTED!

As students enter the classroom, tell them to read the quotation from Richard Nixon on this page. Ask each student to summarize the quotation and to briefly explain what Nixon was saying. Ask volunteers to share their summaries with the class. Tell students that in Section 1 they will learn about Richard Nixon's domestic policies and his foreign-policy decisions.

SECTION 1

READ TO DISCOVER
1. How did President Nixon's policies differ from those of Presidents Johnson and Kennedy?
2. How did President Nixon respond to economic problems?
3. What were the causes and effects of the energy crisis?
4. What did Americans and the government do to help clean up the environment?
5. What beliefs guided Nixon's foreign-policy decisions?

DEFINE
southern strategy
stagflation
realpolitik
détente

IDENTIFY
Silent Majority
Family Assistance Plan
Warren Burger
Organization of Petroleum Exporting Countries
Environmental Protection Agency
Endangered Species Act
Henry Kissinger
Leonid Brezhnev
Strategic Arms Limitation Talks
Salvador Allende
Golda Meir

▶ WHY IT MATTERS TODAY

Energy resources in the United States remain a topic of concern. Use CNNfyi.com or other **current events** sources to learn about U.S. dependence on resources such as oil, gas, or nuclear energy. Record your findings in your journal.

CNNfyi.com

The Nixon Years

Richard Nixon

EYEWITNESSES TO History

"As I saw it, America in the 1960s had undergone a misguided crash program aimed at using the power of the presidency and the federal government to right past wrongs by trying to legislate social progress. This was the idea behind Kennedy's New Frontier and Johnson's Great Society. The problems were real and the intention worthy, but the method was foredoomed [bound to fail]. By the end of the decade its costs had become almost prohibitively high in terms of the way it undermined [weakened] fundamental relationships within our federal system, created confusions about our national values, and corroded American belief in ourselves as a people and as a nation.**"**

—Richard Nixon, *The Memoirs of Richard Nixon*

After he won the 1968 presidential election, Richard Nixon recalled his attitude toward the policies of Presidents Johnson and Kennedy. Nixon attempted to redefine the relationship between the federal government and the states during the early 1970s. However, he encountered domestic and foreign-policy crises.

Courting the Silent Majority

Much of President Nixon's support came from middle-class voters weary of the social unrest of the 1960s. Nixon called these people the **Silent Majority**—"the forgotten Americans, the non-shouters, the non-demonstrators." He won their votes by pledging to restore law and order and to cut back Democratic programs.

Reforming welfare. Nixon wanted to cut Great Society programs that had failed to significantly decrease poverty in the United States. He believed that liberal policies had created a complex, inefficient system that made people dependent on the federal government. The welfare system, which had grown from some 5.9 million recipients in 1960 to some 12.8 million in 1970, came under particular attack. "From the first days of my administration I wanted to get rid of the costly failures of the Great Society," Nixon later recalled. "Welfare reform was my highest domestic priority."

Under the existing welfare system, much of the aid for poor families was in the form of services such as Medicaid and nutrition programs. Nixon proposed replacing this system with the **Family Assistance Plan** (FAP), which would guarantee families a minimum income. Under the plan, adults able to work would have to accept job training or work assignments. The federal government would assume most of the welfare costs then borne by the states. Supporters of the FAP argued that giving money directly to families would reduce welfare programs and the waste that went with them. Some critics charged that such direct aid would make poor families even more dependent on the federal government.

TEACH OBJECTIVE 1

ALL LEVELS: Tell students that President Nixon pledged to implement domestic policies that were different from those of Presidents Johnson and Kennedy. Ask students to describe the domestic agendas of Kennedy and Johnson. *(Students should mention civil rights legislation and Great Society programs such as the War on Poverty.)* To help students understand how Nixon's domestic policies differed from those of Presidents Kennedy and Johnson, copy the Venn Diagram at right on the chalkboard, omitting the italicized answers. Have each student complete it. Ask volunteers to share their answers with the class. **English Language Learners**

Kennedy's and Johnson's Policies
- *Great Society programs expanded the welfare system and provided services to poor Americans.*
- *proposed and supported civil rights legislation*
- *increased government spending on social programs*

- *believed that some form of government assistance was necessary to combat poverty*

Nixon's Policies
- *wanted to reform welfare system by replacing the government provision of services with the Family Assistance Plan*
- *no new civil rights legislation*
- *pledged to cut back Democratic programs*

The Senate ultimately voted down the FAP. Nixon also proposed a system of revenue sharing called New Federalism. Under this system, the federal government gave block grants to the states. Local leaders then decided how to use this money.

Seeking southern support. Nixon also planned not to ask for any new civil rights legislation. This decision was part of his **southern strategy**—a plan to woo conservative southern white voters away from the Democratic Party. As part of this approach, Nixon delayed pressuring southern schools to desegregate. When the Supreme Court ruled in 1971 that busing could be used to integrate schools, Nixon opposed the ruling.

When Chief Justice Earl Warren retired in 1969, Nixon appointed a conservative justice, **Warren Burger**, to head the Court. The Senate rejected two other Nixon nominees, both from southern states. Nixon used these rejections to win southern support. He complained, "The real reason for their rejection was their legal philosophy . . . and also the accident of their birth, the fact that they were born in the South." The president eventually appointed three conservative justices: Harry Blackmun, Lewis Powell, and William Rehnquist.

✔ **READING CHECK: Contrasting** Contrast the policies of President Nixon with those of Presidents Johnson and Kennedy. Nixon proposed an alternative to welfare and appointed a conservative to lead the Supreme Court.

Tackling the Economy

Reversing the liberal policies of the 1960s was not the only challenge President Nixon faced. He also had to manage a faltering economy. The United States had enjoyed an economic boom during the 1960s, but the economy had begun to show signs of trouble by the time Nixon took office. Heavy government spending on social programs and on the Vietnam War had contributed to a recession and growing unemployment. Normally, when unemployment is high, inflation is low. Yet when Nixon took office, both inflation and unemployment rose. This combination of rising unemployment and inflation is called **stagflation**.

Chief Justice Warren Burger (center) poses with the other members of the Supreme Court.

PRESIDENTIAL *Lives*

Richard M. Nixon

1913–1994
In Office 1969–1974

Richard Milhous Nixon's hard work and intense ambition helped him rise to the top ranks of the Republican Party. Having grown up in a poor family in California, Nixon was determined to succeed.

One of the most famous examples of Nixon's ability to bounce back from political challenges came during the 1952 presidential election. Nixon, who was Dwight Eisenhower's vice presidential running mate, had been accused of accepting personal gifts from wealthy businessmen. He appeared on national television to deny the charges. In what came to be called the Checkers speech, Nixon admitted to accepting one personal gift. "You know what it was?" the candidate asked. "It was a little cocker spaniel dog . . . black, white, and spotted, and our little girl Tricia, the six-year-old, named it Checkers. . . . And I just want to say this, right now, that regardless of what they say about it, we're going to keep it." The Checkers speech was well received and may have saved Nixon from being dropped from the Republican ticket.

Richard Nixon

USA 32

Harry Blackmun. Nixon's first appointee to the U.S. Supreme Court, Harry Blackmun, was from Minnesota, as was Chief Justice Warren Burger. At first, Blackmun voted like Burger, so much so that they were dubbed the "Minnesota Twins." However, Blackmun became increasingly liberal, voting in favor of abortion rights, opposing the death penalty, and supporting the expansion of civil liberties.

CRITICAL THINKING What might Blackmun's career reveal about the practice of labeling people as conservative or liberal?

ANSWER: Students might point out that an individual's views can sometimes change a great deal over time and that such labels must be applied with caution.

THAT'S INTERESTING!

First Lady Pat Nixon urged her husband to appoint the first woman to the U.S. Supreme Court. Richard Nixon considered nominating Judge Mildred Lillie, but did not because Lillie did not have the support of the American Bar Association, the nation's leading legal organization.

LEVEL 1: Ask students to identify the major economic problems that President Nixon faced. *(Students should mention rising unemployment and inflation.)* Then ask students how Nixon dealt with these problems. *(Students should mention that Nixon temporarily froze prices, rents, and wages.)* Pair students and have each pair brainstorm at least two other ways that Nixon might have dealt with stagflation. *(Students might suggest government jobs programs, raising interest rates to curb spending, or ending the Vietnam War.)* Ask volunteers to share their ideas and encourage the class to evaluate and briefly discuss each idea.

English Language Learners, Cooperative Learning

LEVELS 2 AND 3: Ask students to identify the major economic problems that President Nixon faced and what caused these problems. *(See the level 1 lesson for the correct problems; causes included heavy spending on social programs and the Vietnam War).* Then tell students to imagine that they are President Nixon's press secretary. Have each student write a short press release describing and explaining Nixon's response to stagflation. Ask volunteers to read their press releases to the class.

ECONOMICS

Unemployment.

Demographic changes and changing attitudes toward the role of women in American society contributed to the unemployment problem of the 1970s. The baby boom generation was entering the job market, as were an increasing number of women. As a result, some 10.1 million new workers entered the labor force between 1964 and 1970.

ACTIVITY: Have students write a paragraph explaining what changes in the 1960s contributed to the increased number of female workers.

THAT'S INTERESTING!

Nixon administration officials were intent on enforcing the freeze on wages and prices. Treasury agents stopped a Detroit hotel from replacing 10-cent locks on stalls in the men's bathrooms with 25-cent locks.

POLITICAL CARTOON ANSWER

Students might suggest that the cartoon's title and picture do not show support for Nixon.

MAP ANSWER

Algeria, Iran, Iraq, Kuwait, Libya, Nigeria, Qatar, Saudi Arabia, United Arab Emirates

INTERPRETING POLITICAL CARTOONS

Inflation. President Nixon used price and wage freezes to fight inflation. ***Does this cartoon dollar bill support Nixon's actions? Explain your answer.***

In August 1971 Nixon took a drastic step to curb inflation by imposing temporary freezes on prices, rents, and wages. This action surprised many people, since Republicans typically opposed such action. Labor leaders feared that wage freezes would hurt those earning the least. AFL–CIO president George Meany called it "Robin Hood in reverse, because it robs from the poor and gives to the rich." Nixon, however, was bowing to political reality. Democratic Party leaders had started referring to the nation's economic troubles as the result of "Nixonomics." Nixon hoped that taking action on the economy would help him win the upcoming presidential election. The strategy worked. Inflation slowed, and Nixon was re-elected in 1972. However, when he eased controls, inflation shot up again. In 1974 the inflation rate topped 12 percent.

✔ **READING CHECK: Identifying Cause and Effect** How did the Vietnam War contribute to stagflation? by plunging the government into debt and contributing to a recession and growing unemployment

The Energy Crisis

During the 1970s rising oil costs became a major cause of inflation and consumer worry. Since World War II, the U.S. economy had grown increasingly dependent on foreign oil. By 1973 Americans consumed twice as much oil as they produced.

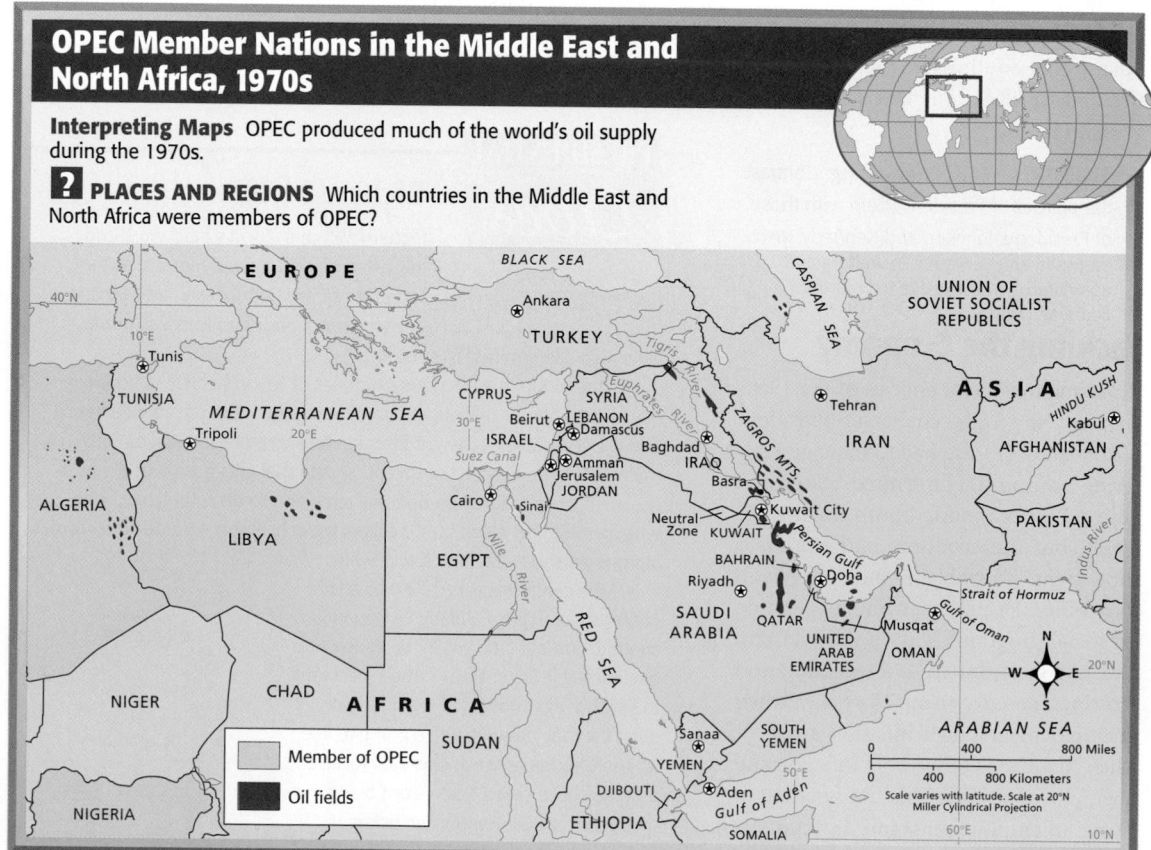

OPEC Member Nations in the Middle East and North Africa, 1970s

Interpreting Maps OPEC produced much of the world's oil supply during the 1970s.

? PLACES AND REGIONS Which countries in the Middle East and North Africa were members of OPEC?

TEACH OBJECTIVE 3

LEVEL 1: Pair students and have each pair create a comic strip that identifies the causes of the energy crisis of 1973–74. *(Comic strips should show U.S. dependence on foreign oil, U.S. support of Israel, the oil embargo, and OPEC price hikes.)* Then ask students how Nixon responded to this crisis. Record responses on the chalkboard and encourage students to copy the information into their notes. *(Students should mention that Nixon called for energy conservation, signed a bill to reduce the speed limit to 55 MPH, approved the construction of an oil pipeline from Alaska, and supported the development of nuclear energy.)* Tell students that U.S. dependence on foreign oil is still a national concern.
English Language Learners, Cooperative Learning

LEVELS 2 AND 3: Have each student create an annotated time line of the events that led to the energy crisis of 1973–74. *(See the Level 1 lesson for the correct causes.)* Then have each student write a few paragraphs identifying and explaining what he or she believes was the primary cause of the crisis. Ask volunteers to share their paragraphs with the class. Students may wish to include their time lines and paragraphs in their portfolios.

★ Changing Ways   Gasoline Consumption

■ **Understanding Change** The energy crisis of the 1970s led to increased calls for vehicles that were more fuel-efficient and for an overall decrease in gasoline consumption. *Since then, how much has the average gas mileage per car changed? Given the changes in average gas consumption per car, what might account for the increase in total gasoline consumption?*

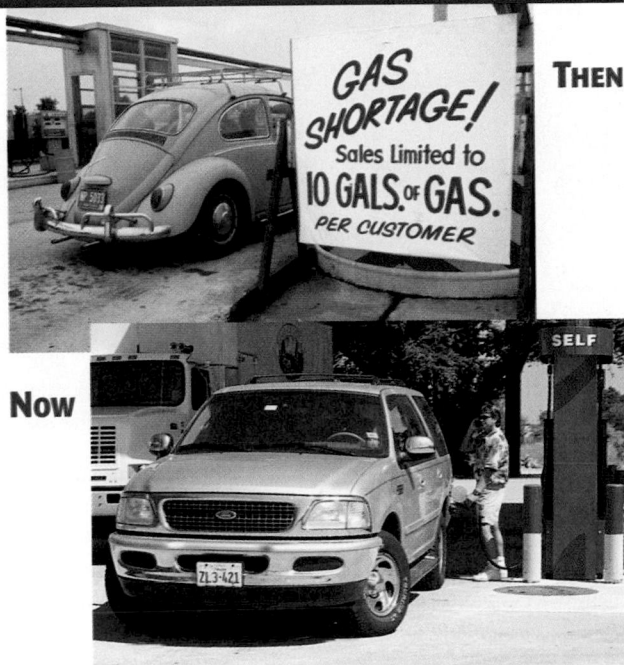

THEN

Now

Gasoline Consumption

		THEN	Now
Total gas consumption		92.3 billion gallons	154.9 billion gallons
Average annual consumption per car		688 gallons	548 gallons
Average gas mileage	cars	13.5 miles per gallon	21.4 miles per gallon
	trucks	5.5 miles per gallon	6.4 miles per gallon

Source: *Statistical Abstract of the United States: 2000.* Data reflect 1970 and 1998.

Price hikes. In June 1973 President Nixon warned the nation that the "supply of domestic energy resources available to us is not keeping pace with our ever growing demand." Americans soon learned the costs of this problem. That October several Arab nations cut off oil shipments to the United States as punishment for the U.S. support of Israel in a new Arab-Israeli war. In December the **Organization of Petroleum Exporting Countries** (OPEC)—a group founded in 1960 by five oil-producing countries that wanted to increase oil prices—announced a price hike. A barrel of oil that had sold for about $3.00 in the summer of 1973 cost $11.65 in December 1973, an increase of almost 400 percent.

The oil embargo and price hike triggered an energy crisis in the United States during the winter of 1973–74. The cost of electricity, gasoline, and heating oil soared, causing severe hardship in some parts of the country. One Detroit hospital told its patients to stay in bed to keep warm. "We had so little oil left that we just had to cut back the thermostats," noted one hospital official. "In storage rooms and areas with no patients, it got as low as 40 degrees."

The energy crisis also created a great deal of anxiety. Public-opinion analyst Daniel Yankelovich noted "signs of panic" among Americans who were "growing fearful that the country has run out of energy." Across the nation motorists lined up at gas stations to buy a few extra gallons. Lines in New Jersey sometimes stretched four miles long. The Arab nations lifted their embargo in March 1974, but the price of oil remained high.

✔ **READING CHECK: Sequencing** Create a time line showing the developments of the energy crisis. 1960—OPEC established; 1973—Nixon warns Americans that energy resources are not keeping pace with demand; October 1973—oil embargo imposed; December 1973—OPEC raises oil prices; March 1974—embargo lifted

---

TEACH OBJECTIVE 4

LEVEL 1: Tell students to imagine that it is 1974 and that they are organizing a display for Earth Day. Organize students into triads and have each triad prepare a two-panel visual display entitled Protecting Our Environment. The first panel should identify citizen and government initiatives to clean up and protect the environment. *(Students' displays should mention Earth Day activities, the creation of the EPA, and passage of the Clean Air Act, the Water Quality Improvement Act, and the Endangered Species Act.)* The second panel of the display should set goals for the future. Display completed projects around the classroom.
English Language Learners, Cooperative Learning

LEVELS 2 AND 3: Tell students to imagine that they are the officers of an environmentalist group in 1975. Pair students and have each pair prepare an informational brochure for prospective members. The brochure should identify important environmental issues, explain citizen and government initiatives that have cleaned up or protected the environment during the early 1970s, and outline the current goals of the organization. *(See the Level 1 lesson for the correct citizen and government initiatives.)* Display students' completed brochures on the classroom walls. **Cooperative Learning**

INTERPRETING THE VISUAL RECORD

The energy crisis. Rising prices and fuel shortages made gasoline difficult to find and contributed to many other economic problems. ***How do you think lines such as this one could have been prevented?***

Energy policy. In response to the crisis, Nixon announced a program designed to make the United States less dependent on foreign oil. He called for energy conservation and signed a bill that reduced the highway speed limit to 55 miles per hour, thereby saving some 3.4 billion gallons of gas per year. He also signed a bill authorizing construction of a pipeline to transport oil south from Alaska.

The government also supported replacing the use of fossil fuels with nuclear energy. Nuclear power was regarded as a cleaner and more economical source of energy because it did not burn fossil fuels. The Atomic Energy Commission predicted that nuclear power plants would generate half the nation's electrical power by the end of the century. By January 1974 there were 42 nuclear power plants in operation, and more than 160 new plants were under construction or in the planning stages. Yet many critics worried that the risks of a nuclear accident outweighed the benefits of nuclear power.

Cleaning up the environment. President Nixon took office at a time when Americans were becoming increasingly worried about the environment. Two events helped raise awareness of environmental issues. The first was a massive oil spill off the coast of Santa Barbara, California, in 1969. The second was the first Earth Day celebration in April 1970. Some 20 million Americans across the nation took part in Earth Day activities. At an event in New York City's Central Park, Episcopal priest Paul Moore spoke to a group of schoolchildren. "Unless we stop stealing, exploiting [taking advantage of] and ruining nature for our own gain, we will lose everything."

In 1970 Congress responded to growing public concern by creating the **Environmental Protection Agency** (EPA), which had the power to enforce environmental laws. That same year, Congress passed two laws intended to limit pollution. The Clean Air Act set air-quality standards and tough emissions guidelines for automakers. The Water Quality Improvement Act required oil companies to pay some of the cleanup costs of oil spills. A 1972 act set limits on the discharge of industrial pollutants into water. To protect wildlife in danger of extinction, Congress passed the **Endangered Species Act** in 1973.

✔ **READING CHECK: Categorizing** What legislative measures did the government take to protect the environment? created EPA, approved the Clean Air Act, Water Quality Improvement Act, and Endangered Species Act

Foreign Affairs Under Nixon

Although domestic issues demanded much of President Nixon's attention, his main interest was foreign affairs. Working closely with his national security adviser, **Henry Kissinger**, Nixon sought to reshape U.S. foreign policy.

TEACH OBJECTIVE 5

 LEVELS 1 AND 2: Ask students how Nixon made foreign-policy decisions. *(Students should mention that Nixon and his secretary of state believed in realpolitik— the idea that national interests should take precedence over ideals such as democracy or human rights.)* Organize students into groups of four and have each group evaluate the effectiveness of realpolitik in U.S. relations with China, the Soviet Union, Chile, and the Middle East. Have each group present its evaluations to the class. Encourage students to discuss briefly each group's assessment of Nixon's foreign policy.
English Language Learners, Cooperative Learning

LEVEL 3: Tell students to imagine that they are Henry Kissinger and that they are writing a memoir. Have each student write an excerpt from the memoir describing how Nixon made foreign-policy decisions. Excerpts should also assess the effects of his foreign policy in various parts of the world. *(See the Level 1 lesson for the correct foreign-policy strategy.)* Ask volunteers to share their memoirs with the class. Students may wish to include their memoirs in their portfolios.

 HOMEWORK *Tell students to imagine that they are Chinese reporters covering President Nixon's visit to China. Have them write an article describing his visit including why he came.*

The Nixon-Kissinger approach. Nixon and Kissinger shared a belief in **realpolitik**, or practical politics. According to this theory, national interests—rather than ideals such as democracy and human rights—should guide U.S. foreign policy. Nixon believed that governments allied with the United States should receive U.S. support even if they sometimes violated human rights.

The chief goal of the Nixon-Kissinger foreign policy was to establish a balance of power among the world's five major powers. These powers were China, Japan, the Soviet Union, the United States, and Western Europe. Nixon explained his reasoning in 1972.

 History Makers Speak "The only time in the history of the world that we have had any extended period of peace is when there has been a balance of power. It is when one nation becomes infinitely more powerful in relation to its potential competitors that the danger of war arises."

—Richard Nixon, quoted in *Years of Discord*, by John Morton Blum

The China visit. In keeping with his belief in realpolitik, President Nixon sought to improve relations with the People's Republic of China. By the 1970s China and the Soviet Union had become bitter enemies. Nixon followed the ancient military strategy that "the enemy of my enemy is my friend." He hoped that closer U.S. ties with China would further divide the communist world.

In 1972 Nixon visited China. The two nations agreed to work together to promote peace in the Pacific region and to develop trade relations and cultural and scientific ties. Furthermore, Nixon promised the eventual withdrawal of U.S. forces from Taiwan in order to lessen Chinese support for the North Vietnamese. Although many conservative Americans were stunned by this move, it gave the president leverage to promote a new policy with the Soviet Union.

The Moscow summit. In May 1972, just three months after visiting China, Nixon flew to Moscow for talks with Soviet leader **Leonid Brezhnev**. The two agreed to promote trade and to cooperate on other issues of mutual concern.

Nixon and Brezhnev also signed a treaty limiting nuclear weapons. This treaty was the product of the **Strategic Arms Limitation Talks** (SALT). It limited the number of intercontinental nuclear missiles—those capable of traveling long distances to other continents— each nation could have. Although the SALT treaty did not end the arms race, it was a small first step toward reducing the nuclear threat. As a result of the arms talks, the United States and the Soviet Union entered into a period of **détente**—a lessening of military and diplomatic tensions between the countries.

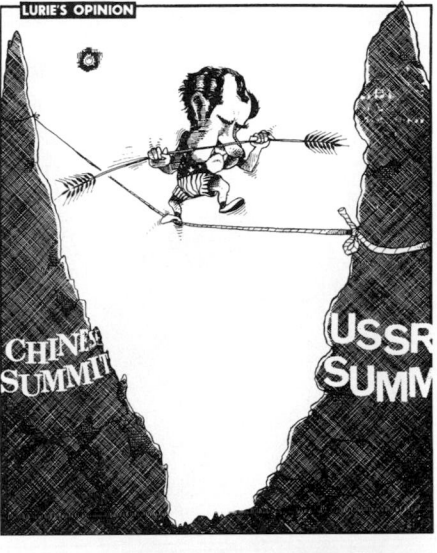

LURIE'S OPINION

CHINESE SUMMIT

USSR SUMMIT

INTERPRETING POLITICAL CARTOONS

Foreign policy. President Nixon tried to improve relations with China without increasing U.S.-Soviet tensions. *What does this cartoon suggest about the difficulties Nixon faced?*

PRIMARY SOURCE

Chinese Views of Nixon's Visit

At a dinner banquet in President Nixon's honor, Premier Jou En-lai explained some of the Chinese government's goals for its meeting with Nixon. **What terms does Premier Jou En-lai request for normalization of relations between the United States and China?**

"The peoples of our two countries have always been friendly to each other. But owing to reasons known to all, contacts between the two peoples were suspended for over twenty years. . . . At the present time it has become a strong desire of the Chinese and American peoples to promote the normalization of relations between the two countries and work for the relaxation of tension. . . . Differences should not hinder China and the United States from establishing normal state relations on the basis of the Five Principles of mutual respect for sovereignty [political authority] and territorial integrity, mutual nonaggression, noninterference in each other's internal affairs, equality and mutual benefit, and peaceful coexistence."

REVIEW

Have students complete the **Section 1 Review** on p. 746.

ASSESS

Have students complete **Daily Quiz 25.1.** As **Alternative Assessment**, you may want to use the energy crisis comic strips or the realpolitik evaluation activity in this section's lessons.

RETEACH

Have students complete **Main Idea Activity for English Language Learners and Special-Needs Students 25.1.** Then organize students into groups and assign one subsection to each group member. Have each group member summarize his

or her assigned subsection. Members should then pass the completed summary to every other group member to read. Finally, have students within their groups take turns quizzing each other about the information in Section 1.
English Language Learners, Cooperative Learning

EXTEND

Have each student write a position paper responding to the following statement: *As president, Richard Nixon achieved greater success in foreign affairs than he did with domestic programs.* Tell students to justify their responses with facts and examples. Have volunteers read their papers to the class. Encourage the class to discuss the differing opinions. **Block Scheduling**

- détente, p. 745

2. Identify
- Silent Majority, p. 740
- Family Assistance Plan, p. 740
- Warren Burger, p. 741
- Organization of Petroleum Exporting Countries, p. 743
- Environmental Protection Agency, p. 744
- Endangered Species Act, p. 744
- Henry Kissinger, p. 744
- Leonid Brezhnev, p. 745
- Strategic Arms Limitation Talks, p. 745
- Salvador Allende, p. 746
- Golda Meir, p. 746

3. causes—dependence on foreign oil, high energy consumption, conflicts with Arab nations over U.S. support for Israel; effects—55 MPH speed limit, the Alaskan pipeline, support for nuclear energy

4a. Johnson and Kennedy—supported antipoverty programs and civil rights legislation; Nixon—reduced government welfare, offered no new civil rights bills and opposed busing

b. imposed freezes on prices, rents, and wages; reduced speed limit, called for conservation; authorized construction of Alaskan pipeline

c. the 1969 oil spill near Santa Barbara and the 1970 Earth Day celebration; created the EPA and passed environmental legislation

5. Some students might note Nixon's achievements in China and the SALT treaty as successes. Others might claim that the overthrow of Allende was inappropriate.

Israeli prime minister Golda Meir

Trouble spots. In general, Nixon and Kissinger ignored countries that were not of direct strategic importance to the United States. One exception was the South American nation of Chile. In 1970 Chile elected **Salvador Allende**, a Socialist, as president. Fearing that Allende planned to turn Chile into "another Cuba" allied with the Soviet Union, Nixon tried to topple his government. Nixon cut off aid to Chile and provided funds to Allende's opponents in the Chilean military. He also instructed the Central Intelligence Agency (CIA) to disrupt economic and political life in the country. In September 1973 the Chilean army killed Allende and set up a pro-American military dictatorship.

Shortly after the Chilean revolt, conflict erupted in the Middle East. Six years earlier, in 1967, Israel had defeated its Arab neighbors—Egypt, Jordan, and Syria—in the Six-Day War. However, the Arab states continued to harass Israel, and Israel continued to strike back. Israeli prime minister **Golda Meir** later recalled that "the only time that Arab states were prepared to recognize the existence of . . . Israel was when they attacked it in order to wipe it out."

In October 1973 Egypt and Syria invaded Israel hoping to recover land lost in the Six-Day War. The attack, which came on the Jewish holiday of Yom Kippur, surprised the Israelis. They launched a counterattack, however, that threatened Egypt's capital, Cairo. When the Soviets threatened to intervene by sending troops into the region, President Nixon put all U.S. forces on alert. A major military confrontation seemed possible. Within days, however, the superpowers persuaded the Arabs and Israelis to accept a cease-fire. Détente had survived a critical test, but prospects for a lasting peace in the Middle East remained in doubt.

✔ **READING CHECK: Analyzing Information** In what ways was realpolitik a new foreign policy theory? It focused on national interests, rather than ideals such as human rights.

SECTION REVIEW

1. Define and explain:
southern strategy
stagflation
realpolitik
détente

2. Identify and explain:
Silent Majority
Family Assistance Plan
Warren Burger
Organization of Petroleum
    Exporting Countries
Environmental Protection Agency
Endangered Species Act
Henry Kissinger
Leonid Brezhnev
Strategic Arms Limitation Talks
Salvador Allende
Golda Meir

3. Identifying Cause and Effect Copy the chart below. Use it to explain the causes and effects of the energy crisis.

| Causes |
| Energy Crisis |
| Effects |

4. **Finding the Main Idea**

a. How did President Nixon's policies differ from those followed by Lyndon B. Johnson and John F. Kennedy?

b. How did President Nixon respond to the nation's economic crisis?

c. Why did Americans take an increased interest in the environment during the 1970s? How did the government respond?

5. **Writing and Critical Thinking**

Supporting a Point of View Do you agree with President Nixon's belief that realpolitik was an appropriate approach to foreign policy? Write a short paragraph explaining why or why not.
Consider:
- the effect of Nixon's visit to China
- the SALT treaty
- events in Chile

 Homework Practice Online
 keyword: SE3 HP25

After completing Section 2, students should be able to:

OBJECTIVE 1 Summarize the issues surrounding the Watergate scandal.

OBJECTIVE 2 Discuss the role that the White House tapes played in President Nixon's resignation.

OBJECTIVE 3 Explain why President Ford was unable to achieve his domestic-policy goals.

OBJECTIVE 4 Report on how Ford attempted to continue Nixon's foreign policies.

⦾ LET'S GET STARTED!

Write the following statement on the chalkboard: *What actions might cause you to question the integrity of an elected official?* As students enter the classroom, tell them to respond to the statement in writing. Tell students that they may use examples of recent controversies surrounding elected officials to support their responses. Ask volunteers to share their responses with the class. Tell students that in Section 2 they will learn how the actions of President Nixon led to his resignation and shook the nation's ideals about integrity in government.

SECTION ②

READ TO DISCOVER

1. What were the issues surrounding the Watergate scandal?
2. What role did the White House tapes play in President Nixon's resignation?
3. Why was President Ford unable to achieve his domestic-policy goals?
4. How did Ford attempt to continue Nixon's foreign policies?

IDENTIFY

Committee to Re-elect the President
Bob Woodward
Carl Bernstein
Sam Ervin
Watergate
James McCord
John Dean
Archibald Cox
Spiro Agnew
Gerald Ford
Saturday Night Massacre
Barbara Jordan
Whip Inflation Now
Mayaguez

▶ WHY IT MATTERS TODAY

The balance of power among the three branches of the U.S. federal government remains an important issue. Use CNNfyi.com or other **current events** sources to learn more about how the United States or another country distributes power within its government. Record your findings in your journal.

CNNfyi.com

From Watergate to Ford

EYEWITNESSES TO *History*

"Nixon had three goals: to win by the biggest electoral landslide in history; to be remembered as a peacemaker; and to be accepted by the 'Establishment' as an equal. He achieved all these objectives by the end of 1972 and the beginning of 1973. And he lost them all two months later—partly because he turned a dream into an obsession."

—Henry Kissinger, *Years of Upheaval*

Henry Kissinger reflected on the presidency of his former boss years after Richard Nixon left the White House in disgrace. Nixon's personality flaws led him to destroy his presidency. His behavior caused a constitutional crisis that shook the nation and caused many Americans to lose faith in their leaders.

Richard Nixon (left) and Henry Kissinger

Crisis in the Presidency

During his first term in the White House, President Nixon increasingly behaved as though there should be no limits on his power. He shifted much of the authority of the cabinet, whose appointments required Senate approval, to his personal White House staff. He also hid vital information from Congress and the public.

Dark secrets. In 1971 Nixon ordered his staff to compile an "enemies list" of critics who opposed his policies. After Daniel Ellsberg's leak of the Pentagon Papers, Nixon told aide Charles Colson, "Do whatever has to be done to stop these leaks. . . . I want it done, whatever the cost." The White House organized a secret unit called the plumbers that included former agents of the CIA and Federal Bureau of Investigation (FBI). The group was ordered to stop leaks and to carry out a variety of illegal actions in the name of "national security."

By 1972 these secret activities had grown into a full-scale effort to ensure Nixon's re-election. In June five men were caught breaking into the offices of the Democratic National Committee in the Watergate office and apartment complex in Washington, D.C. They were carrying wiretap equipment and other spying devices. It was soon discovered that these men were being paid with funds from Nixon's campaign organization, the **Committee to Re-elect the President** (CRP).

The White House denied any link to the break-in, calling it a "third-rate burglary." However, *Washington Post* reporters **Bob Woodward** and **Carl Bernstein** kept digging for the truth. A high-level source known as Deep Throat informed them that White House officials and the CRP had hired 50 agents to sabotage the Democrats' chances in the 1972 election.

SECTION ② RESOURCES

REPRODUCIBLE

▶ Guided Reading Strategy 25.2
▶ American History Political Cartoon 29: Watergate
▶ Primary Source Reading 25: A President Resigns
▶ Graphic Organizer Activity 25: The Nixon Administration

TECHNOLOGY

▶ One-Stop Planner, Lesson 25.2
▶ The American Nation Video Program Segment: Richard Nixon Resigns; Teacher's Guide, pp. 215–16
▶ Holt Researcher: American History CD–ROM
▶ Homework Practice Online
▶ HRW Go site

REINFORCEMENT, REVIEW, AND ASSESSMENT

▶ Section 2 Review, p. 753
▶ Daily Quiz 25.2
▶ Main Idea Activity 25.2
▶ English Audio Summary 25.2
▶ Spanish Audio Summary 25.2

TEACH OBJECTIVE 1

LEVEL 1: Pair students and have each pair list in chronological order the events related to the Watergate scandal. *(Students should mention that Nixon shifted authority from the cabinet to his personal staff, hid information from Congress and the public, ordered his staff to compile an "enemies list" of critics, the Watergate break-in occurred, reporters connected the break-in to CRP and the White House, the government investigated White House activities and cover-up attempts, and witnesses implicated Nixon in the cover-up.)* Ask each pair to read its list to the class. Then ask students to summarize the issues surrounding the Watergate scandal. *(Students should mention that Nixon tried to circumvent the democratic process and constitutional limitations on his power when he broke the law and covered up his activities.)* Tell students that the name "Watergate" has become synonymous with scandal.
English Language Learners, Cooperative Learning

LEVELS 2 AND 3: Tell students to imagine that they are Americans upset by the Watergate scandal. Have each student write a letter to President Nixon that summarizes the issues surrounding the Watergate scandal and describes why Nixon's behavior is of public concern. *(See the Level 1 lesson for the correct issues.)* Ask volunteers to read their letters to the class. Students may wish to include their letters in their portfolios.

---

internet connect

go.hrw.com

TOPIC: The Watergate Scandal
GO TO: go.hrw.com
KEYWORD: SE3 AN25

Have students access the Internet through the HRW Go site to conduct research on the Watergate scandal. Then have each student create a "most wanted" poster that presents information about the break-in, its investigation and evidence, the people involved, and Nixon's resignation.

SKILL-BUILDING STRATEGIES ANSWERS
Practicing the Skill

1. evidence that showed that the illegal actions made the difference in Nixon's victory

2. Nixon's popularity with voters, as evidenced by his margin of victory

3. Students might suggest that Nixon's large margin of victory supports an alternative hypothesis.

The American Nation
VIDEO PROGRAM

Richard Nixon Resigns;
Teacher's Guide, pp. 215–16

Search 47518, Play to 49620
Videodisc 2, Side B

Play	Pause

See *Teacher's Guide* for Spanish barcode.

748

Skill-Building Strategies

To write a successful history research paper, one must first formulate a hypothesis around which to organize the paper. A *hypothesis* is a statement that tries to explain why a situation existed or an event took place. It must be formed from and tested against the historical evidence that one gathers while conducting research. The hypothesis provides a central point for analyzing and discussing this evidence in one's paper.

How to Formulate a Hypothesis

1. **Conduct research.** Identify the topic that you wish to research and develop one or more questions that you hope to answer in your paper. Then conduct research at your school or local public library.
2. **Analyze the evidence.** Study the information in your sources carefully, keeping in mind your questions about the topic. Look for cause-and-effect relationships and long-term developments that emerge from the facts you examine.
3. **Develop an idea that is based on the evidence.** Use your analysis of the evidence to formulate an idea that answers your questions about the topic. Make sure that this idea, or initial *hypothesis*, is supported by specific information in your sources.
4. **Consider other possibilities.** Once you have formed your initial hypothesis, think about other ways to answer your questions about the topic. Then adjust your idea if necessary to include one or more of these different explanations.
5. **State your hypothesis.** After you have settled on a final hypothesis, write it out in a short, declarative statement. This statement should express clearly the central idea that you plan to present in your paper.

Formulating a Hypothesis

Applying the Skill

Read and evaluate the following hypothesis statement, which tries to explain why Richard Nixon won a landslide victory in the 1972 presidential election.

> Richard Nixon was re-elected to the presidency because of the secret activities and electoral "dirty tricks" of the CRP.

Practicing the Skill

Answer the following questions.
1. What historical evidence could be used to support the hypothesis presented above?
2. What are some other ways to explain Nixon's landslide victory in 1972? What evidence could be used to support these explanations?
3. In your opinion, what hypothesis best explains Nixon's landslide victory in 1972?

The investigation. Despite the Watergate break-in, Nixon won re-election in 1972 by a landslide. By the spring of 1973 both the executive and the legislative branches of government were investigating the charges of criminal activities and the attempted cover-up. Senator **Sam Ervin** of North Carolina led the Senate investigation into the scandal known as **Watergate.** One of the witnesses was **James McCord,** a former CIA agent who had taken part in the Watergate break-in. McCord admitted that top White House officials had helped plan the break-in. He linked the cover-up to "the very highest levels of the White House." McCord's admissions broke the case wide open.

The biggest bombshells were yet to come, however. In May 1973 live television coverage of the Senate hearings began. Across the nation millions of Americans watched as senators grilled witnesses and compiled evidence of official misconduct. Several top White House officials were eventually convicted in criminal trials and sent to jail. However, Nixon's role in Watergate remained unclear. Time and again, Howard Baker of Tennessee, a key member of the Senate committee, asked, "What did the president know and when did he know it?"

Microphones used during the Watergate break-in

SPOTLIGHT
on Woodward and Bernstein

Have students find and read Woodward and Bernstein's *Washington Post* articles that exposed the White House/CRP plot. Have each student write an essay in response to the articles. Encourage students to think about the following questions as they write: How might citizens have reacted to the articles? Were the reporters justified in writing the articles? How might things have been different for the United States if Woodward and Bernstein had not written the articles? Ask volunteers to read their essays to the class. **Block Scheduling**

TEACH OBJECTIVE 2

LEVEL 1: Ask students to list the events surrounding the release of the White House tapes and Nixon's resignation. Compile a list of students' responses on the chalkboard. *(Students should mention that Nixon claimed executive privilege, refused to release the tapes, had the special prosecutor fired, released some tapes, was forced by the Supreme Court to turn over all the tapes, and finally resigned. Students should note that the tapes were the key to proving Nixon's involvement in the cover-up.)* Then have each student write a series of newspaper headlines covering the events listed on the chalkboard.
English Language Learners

In June 1973 Nixon's former White House attorney **John Dean** provided the stunning answer. The president had been directly involved in the cover-up.

✔ **READING CHECK: Finding the Main Idea** What were the results of the Senate investigation into the Watergate burglary? the conviction of several of the Watergate burglars and the discovery that Nixon was involved in the cover-up

The Nixon Resignation

President Nixon denied Dean's charges. There seemed to be no way to prove that Dean was telling the truth. Then, in a surprising revelation, another witness testified that Nixon had secretly tape-recorded his conversations in the White House.

The White House tapes. Investigators believed that the tapes would reveal the truth about Watergate. A battle for control of the tapes followed. The Justice Department's special prosecutor, **Archibald Cox**, demanded that the president turn over the tapes. Nixon refused. Citing executive privilege, he claimed that releasing the tapes would endanger national security.

In the midst of the controversy over the tapes, in October 1973 Vice President **Spiro Agnew** was charged with income tax evasion. Agnew pleaded no contest and resigned on October 10 in exchange for reduced punishment. Nixon then nominated **Gerald Ford**, the Republican leader in the House of Representatives, for vice president.

Shortly before Agnew's resignation, a federal judge ordered Nixon to release the White House tapes. The president refused. On October 20, after Special Prosecutor Cox demanded that he obey the judge's order, Nixon ordered Attorney General Elliot Richardson to fire Cox. Both the attorney general and Deputy Attorney General William Ruckelshaus resigned rather than obey the president. The task of firing Cox fell to Solicitor General Robert Bork, who complied. This series of events, known as the **Saturday Night Massacre**, outraged the public and led to calls to impeach Nixon. In his own defense, Nixon declared, "People have the right to know whether or not their President is a crook. Well, I am not a crook." Partly as a result of these events, in 1978 Congress authorized the appointment of investigators called independent counsels to conduct investigations into high crimes by top government officials.

Archibald Cox (center) is sworn in as special prosecutor.

Final days. Nixon eventually agreed to release some of the White House tapes, but he resisted turning over the entire set. Not until July 1974, when the Supreme Court rejected Nixon's argument of executive privilege, did Nixon abandon his efforts to keep the tapes. About the same time that the Court announced its ruling, the House Judiciary Committee held nationally televised debates on whether to impeach Nixon. Among the members who favored impeachment was Representative **Barbara Jordan**, a first-term Democrat from Texas.

LEVEL 2: Tell students to imagine that they are reporters and that President Nixon has just resigned. Have each student write a newspaper article summarizing the role that the White House tapes played in Nixon's resignation. *(See the Level 1 activity for the correct role.)* Have volunteers read their articles to the class.

LEVEL 3: Tell students to imagine that they are radio journalists and that President Nixon has just resigned. Pair students and have each pair write a script for a discussion about the role that the White House tapes played in President Nixon's resignation. *(See the Level 1 lesson for the correct role.)* Ask students to conduct their discussion for the class. **Cooperative Learning**

HOMEWORK *Have each student write a paper analyzing the public's perceptions of government after Watergate. Tell students to trace public sentiment immediately following Watergate through the present. Tell students to pay particular attention to what the Clinton impeachment seemed to indicate about the public's changing attitude toward government officials.*

HISTORY MAKERS SPEAK

Richard Nixon in *Public Papers of the Presidents of the United States*

Nixon's Farewell. Nixon made a farewell speech to the White House staff on the morning of August 9, 1974. "Sure, we have done some things wrong in this Administration, and the top man always takes the responsibility, and I have never ducked it. But I want to say one thing: We can be proud of it—5 1/2 years. No man or no woman came into this Administration and left it with more of this world's goods than when he came in. No man or no woman ever profited at the public expense or the public till. That tells something about you. Mistakes, yes. But for personal gain, never."

CRITICAL THINKING How does Nixon seem to define wrongdoing in this speech?

ANSWER: Students might point out that Nixon describes wrongdoing as involving personal financial gain at public expense—a definition that excludes his Watergate actions.

VISUAL RECORD ANSWER

Students might suggest that Nixon's expression was inappropriate for the occasion because he was being forced to resign but he looks happy.

Research on the ROM

Free Find: Barbara Jordan
After reading about Barbara Jordan on the **Holt Researcher CD–ROM,** write a script for a short play that illustrates Jordan's accomplishments and the obstacles she overcame.

BIOGRAPHY

Barbara Jordan

Barbara Jordan brought a strong sense of moral authority to the Democratic Party. Born in 1936, she grew up in Houston. She excelled in school and eventually received a law degree from Boston University. In 1966 Jordan became the first African American woman elected to the Texas state senate. Her tireless efforts on behalf of social reform won praise from President Lyndon B. Johnson. He noted, "She proved that black is beautiful before we knew what it meant."

In 1972 Jordan was elected to the U.S. House of Representatives. She soon gained a reputation as a skilled legislator and brilliant public speaker. On July 25, 1974, she explained why she supported impeachment.

History Makers Speak

❝'We the people'—it is a very eloquent beginning. But when the Constitution of the United States was completed on the seventeenth of September in 1787, I was not included in that 'We the People.' . . . But through the process of amendment, interpretation and court decision, I have finally been included in 'We the People.' . . . My faith in the Constitution is whole. It is complete. . . . I am not going to sit here and be an idle spectator to the . . . destruction of the Constitution.❞

—Barbara Jordan, *Barbara Jordan*

Despite her outstanding record in Congress, Jordan announced in 1977 that she would not run for a fourth term. She accepted a teaching position at the University of Texas at Austin. Jordan became one of the most popular instructors at the university's Lyndon B. Johnson School of Public Affairs. She was inducted into the National Women's Hall of Fame in 1990. Jordan died in 1996.

With the release of the Nixon tapes, Americans discovered the truth. Nixon had directed the Watergate cover-up and had authorized illegal activities. The House Judiciary Committee recommended that impeachment charges be brought against him. Facing almost certain impeachment by the full House, Nixon finally accepted his fate. On August 8, 1974, he told the nation: "I shall resign the presidency effective at noon tomorrow."

The Washington Post

Nixon Resigns

Ford Assumes Presidency Today

INTERPRETING THE VISUAL RECORD

Nixon. As President Nixon boarded a helicopter to leave the White House, the *Washington Post* announced his resignation. ***Does Nixon's expression seem appropriate for the occasion? Explain your answer.***

On August 9, 1974, Vice President Gerald Ford was sworn in as the 38th president. He then nominated Governor Nelson Rockefeller of New York for vice president, and Congress confirmed his choice. For the first time in U.S. history, both the president and vice president held office by appointment, not election.

✔ **READING CHECK: Drawing Conclusions** What evidence would have been used to justify impeachment of President Nixon? the White House tapes and witnesses agreeing to testify against Nixon

ALL LEVELS: To help students understand why President Ford was unable to achieve his domestic-policy goals, copy the following graphic organizer on the chalkboard, omitting the italicized answers. Have each student complete it.

When students have completed the diagram, organize the class into groups of four. Tell them to imagine that they are advisers to President Ford. Instruct each group to propose at least three suggestions for overcoming these roadblocks. Ask one member of each group to summarize his or her group's ideas for the class. **English Language Learners, Cooperative Learning**

Roadblocks to Ford's Domestic Policy
→ *Ford's approval rating drops after he pardons Nixon.*
→ *The Democratic majority in Congress blocks presidential legislation, while Ford vetoes Democrats' legislation.*
→ *Congress does not approve Ford's budget cuts.*

Ford Tries to Reunite the Nation

As leader of the Republicans in the House, Gerald Ford had won the respect of colleagues for his honesty and modesty. "I'm a Ford, not a Lincoln," he once joked. The new president, however, lost much of the nation's goodwill just one month after taking office.

Pardon and clemency. In September 1974 Ford granted President Nixon a full pardon. He explained that if Nixon were put on trial, "ugly passions would again be aroused. . . . And the credibility [believ-ability] of our free institutions of government would again be challenged at home and abroad." Many people found Ford's explanation unconvincing. They suspected that the pardon had been agreed upon in advance in exchange for Nixon's resignation—a charge that Ford denied. Critics of the pardon argued that the full truth of Watergate would never emerge. They pointed to the double standard that allowed Nixon to go free while his co-conspirators were punished. As a result of the pardon, Ford's popularity fell. His approval rating dropped from 71 percent to 50 percent.

Ford took another controversial step one week later. He offered clemency, or official forgiveness, to Vietnam draft evaders. In exchange, they had to reaffirm their allegiance to the United States and spend up to two years performing public service. Supporters of the Vietnam War believed that the offer was unfair to soldiers who had served their country. Meanwhile, just 19 percent of those eligible responded to the offer. Some war resisters, like Dee Knight, contrasted it with the full pardon that Nixon had been granted.

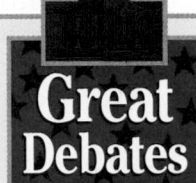

Great Debates

Watergate

On the day he took office, President Ford declared, "Our constitution works. Our great republic is a government of laws and not of men. Here the people rule." After Richard Nixon resigned from office, many journalists and average citizens agreed with Ford's observation that the system had worked. Through the application of the rule of law found in the Constitution, Richard Nixon, the most powerful official in the government, had been forced to resign from office for his misdeeds.

Some observers have not been as optimistic about the effect of Watergate on American political life. They argue that Nixon was only forced from office because he made the error of secretly taping evidence that was used against him. Had the tapes never existed, or been destroyed, he probably would have remained in office. Moreover, these critics point out that congressional reforms intended to prevent future scandals have had little effect. In the years after Watergate, political scandals reaching all the way to the White House continued to trouble the American public.

History Makers Speak **"We knew the clemency was proclaimed just to offset [make up for] the Nixon pardon, which was an insult. We weren't criminals, and Nixon was, but Ford proposed to pardon Nixon unconditionally while offering 'alternative punishment' to us."**

—Dee Knight, quoted in *From Camelot to Kent State*, by Joan Morrison and Robert K. Morrison

Troubles continue. Ford soon ran into other problems. In the November 1974 congressional elections, Democrats gained 43 seats in the House and three in the Senate. Ford quickly encountered conflicts with the Democratic majority that controlled Congress. He vetoed a number of social-welfare bills sponsored by Democrats. In all, Ford vetoed 66 bills during his brief term in office, more than any other president had in such a short time.

This political cartoon suggests that Richard Nixon controlled President Ford's policies.

GOVERNMENT

Amnesty and Clemency. President Ford did not offer unconditional amnesty to the Vietnam draft evaders. Unconditional amnesty would have meant that they would have been absolved of their offense. Instead, Ford offered the draft evaders clemency, which meant that their crimes would be recognized, but that the punishment would be merciful. Many antiwar activists had hoped that the president would grant the draft evaders amnesty. They called his offer of clemency "shamnesty."

CRITICAL THINKING Why might antiwar activists have been so opposed to the clemency offer?

ANSWER: Some students might suggest that antiwar activists viewed the Vietnam War as an illegitimate undertaking for a democratic nation; therefore, they did not view draft evasion as a crime.

VISUAL RECORD ANSWER
(for p. 752)
Students might suggest that the button was intended to encourage public support for the program.

LEVEL 1: Tell students to imagine that they are editors of a presidential encyclopedia. Pair students and have each pair write a brief entry describing how Ford attempted to continue Nixon's foreign policies. *(Paragraphs should mention that Ford retained Henry Kissinger as secretary of state, tried to maintain U.S. influence in Southeast Asia, supported anticommunist forces in Angola, and tried to continue the policy of détente toward the Soviet Union.)* Ask students to read their paragraphs to the class.
English Language Learners, Cooperative Learning

LEVELS 2 AND 3: Ask each student to write an essay analyzing how Ford tried to continue Nixon's foreign policies. *(See the Level 1 lesson for the correct policy decisions.)* Students may wish to include their essays in their portfolios.

The *Mayaguez*. Vessels from the United States had been seized by other nations prior to the *Mayaguez* incident. Over a period of 23 years, Ecuador had seized 23 American commercial ships. In those instances, the U.S. government had chosen to pay fines rather than use force in exchange for the return of the ships.

CRITICAL THINKING What international event might have led Ford and his advisers to decide to use force to recapture the *Mayaguez*?

ANSWER: Students might suggest that after the fall of South Vietnam to communism in April 1975, Ford wanted to show the world that the United States would still respond to threats.

POLITICAL CARTOON ANSWER
(for p. 753)

Students might note that the cartoon suggests that U.S. involvement in Angola could prove, like Vietnam, to be difficult.

1. Identify
- Committee to Re-elect the President, p. 747
- Bob Woodward, p. 747
- Carl Bernstein, p. 747
- Sam Ervin, p. 748
- Watergate, p. 748
- James McCord, p. 748

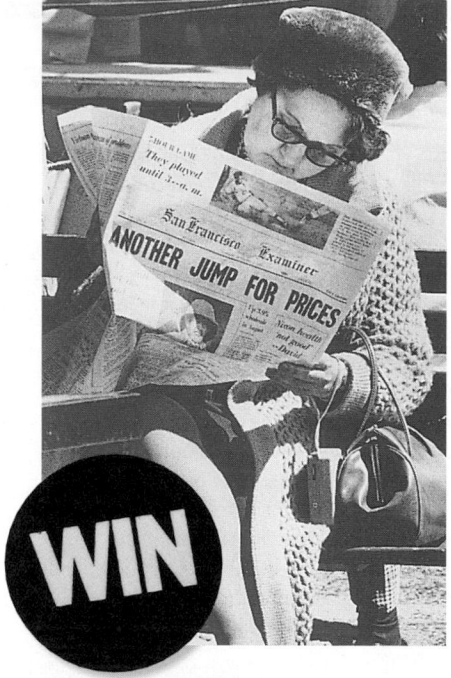

INTERPRETING THE VISUAL RECORD

Inflation. Widespread price increases led President Ford to create his Whip Inflation Now program. *What do you think the purpose of the button was?*

The cargo ship Mayaguez was seized by Cambodian Communists in 1975.

As Ford's relations with Congress worsened, he found it increasingly difficult to enact his policies. One of his main goals was to combat inflation, which was being fueled by the soaring cost of oil. Like Nixon, Ford hoped to curb inflation by cutting federal spending. In October 1974 Ford asked Congress to cut some $4 billion from Nixon's proposed budget for the coming year and to increase corporate taxes. During his speech the president sported a button that read WIN. He explained that it stood for **Whip Inflation Now**. Although some 100,000 Americans joined a voluntary organization supporting the president's battle against inflation, Congress rejected Ford's plan.

One year later, in October 1975, President Ford told the nation, "Much of our inflation should bear a label, 'Made in Washington, D.C.'" He recommended a combination of tax cuts and budget cuts. Congress approved the tax cut but rejected a spending cap. While the White House and Congress battled over economic policy, the nation experienced an economic recession.

✔ **READING CHECK: Analyzing Information** How did President Ford's relationship with Congress affect his domestic-policy record?
Congress rejected his tax-cut and budget-reduction proposals.

Ford's Foreign Policy

In foreign affairs, President Ford continued many of President Nixon's policies. The continuity between the administrations was reflected in Ford's decision to retain Nixon's chief foreign-policy adviser, Henry Kissinger, as secretary of state.

Asia. Ford tried to maintain U.S. influence in Southeast Asia. Toward that end, he requested $722 million in military aid for Cambodia and South Vietnam. Opposed to additional military ventures in Southeast Asia, Congress rejected any military aid but did approve $300 million in humanitarian assistance. Then, in May 1975, Cambodian Communists seized the *Mayaguez*, an unarmed U.S. cargo ship. The Ford administration saw the seizure as an opportunity to prove that the president could exercise leadership in a crisis. Henry Kissinger urged, "Let's look ferocious." In response, Ford launched a military action intended to free the vessel and its crew. Forty-one Americans were killed in the effort to release about 40 crew members.

The president later claimed that the *Mayaguez* incident "had an electrifying reaction as far as the American people were concerned." Ford's job approval rating climbed 11 points after the rescue attempt. While some applauded the president's action, others criticized it as hasty and ill-timed. It was later discovered that the *Mayaguez* crew had already been released before the U.S. attack began.

REVIEW

Have students complete the **Section 2 Review** on p. 753.

ASSESS

Have students complete **Daily Quiz 25.2**. As **Alternative Assessment**, you may want to use the radio script or letter to the president in this section's lessons.

RETEACH

Have students complete **Main Idea Activity for English Language Learners and Special-Needs Students 25.2**. Then have each student write one or two sentences summarizing the main idea of each subsection in the section. Have volunteers read their sentences to the class. Have the class choose the best summary sentences for each subsection. Compile a list of these sentences on the chalkboard, and tell students to copy them into their notes. **English Language Learners**

EXTEND

Have students conduct research on the passage of the 1978 law authorizing the creation of independent counsels and Congress's decision to let the independent counsel statute expire in 1999. Students should focus on the reasons that the law was passed and why Congress decided to let it expire. Have each student present his or her findings in an essay. **Block Scheduling**

The Cold War continues. During the mid-1970s Africa became a scene of Cold War conflict. Both Nixon and Ford had largely ignored Africa, but the outbreak of a civil war in Angola attracted U.S. attention. The Soviet Union supported the Popular Front for the Liberation of Angola. The Ford administration secretly provided millions in aid to an opposing group, the National Front. When the Popular Front seized control of Angola, Ford authorized further secret funding. However, Congress learned about the secret payments and ordered the president to halt the operation. Ford complained, "This abdication [giving up] of responsibility by the majority of the Senate will have the greatest consequences for the long-term position of the United States and for international order."

Despite the conflict in Africa, Ford tried to continue the policy of détente toward the Soviet Union. U.S.-Soviet relations grew increasingly strained, however. Former secretary of defense Melvin Laird wrote in 1975, "Clearly, we must shed any lingering illusions we have that détente means the Russians have abandoned their determination to undermine [weaken] Western democracy."

One source of conflict was the Soviet emigration policy, which did not allow Jews and opponents of the government to leave the country. When members of Congress criticized this policy, the Soviets canceled a proposed U.S.-Soviet trade pact. Although Ford successfully negotiated an arms-limitation treaty during a summit meeting in the Soviet Union, the Senate failed to ratify it.

✔ **READING CHECK: Comparing** How was Ford's foreign policy similar to Nixon's?

Ford retained Kissinger as secretary of state and tried to continue the policy of détente toward the Soviet Union.

INTERPRETING POLITICAL CARTOONS

Angola. President Ford supported the anticommunist National Front in Angola's civil war. *What does this cartoon suggest about U.S. involvement in the war?*

SECTION 2 REVIEW

1. Identify and explain:
Committee to Re-elect the President
Bob Woodward
Carl Bernstein
Sam Ervin
Watergate
James McCord
John Dean
Archibald Cox
Spiro Agnew
Gerald Ford
Saturday Night Massacre
Barbara Jordan
Whip Inflation Now
Mayaguez

2. Sequencing Copy the graphic below. Use it to explain the major events of the Watergate scandal.

1. Crime
2. Cover-Up
3. Investigation
4. Nixon's Response
5. The Court Ruling
6. The Resignation

3. **Finding the Main Idea**

a. Do you agree with the Supreme Court ruling that required President Nixon to turn over the White House tapes? Why or why not?
b. Did responsibility for the failure to manage the economy lie with President Ford or with Congress? Explain your answer.
c. Imagine that you are a State Department official. How would you have advised President Ford to respond to the seizure of the *Mayaguez*?

4. **Writing and Critical Thinking**

Evaluating Write a review of Gerald Ford's performance as president.
Consider:
• Watergate's effect on public attitudes toward government
• Ford's relations with Congress
• Ford's handling of foreign-policy problems

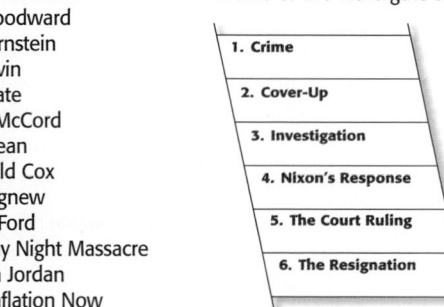

Homework Practice Online
keyword: SE3 HP25

• John Dean, p. 749
• Archibald Cox, p. 749
• Spiro Agnew, p. 749
• Gerald Ford, p. 749
• Saturday Night Massacre, p. 749
• Barbara Jordan, p. 749
• Whip Inflation Now, p. 752
• *Mayaguez*, p. 752

2. crime—Watergate break-in, dirty campaign tricks; cover-up—Nixon's denial of involvement; investigation—reporters Woodward and Bernstein, congressional committees; Nixon's response—executive privilege to prevent release of the White House tapes; Court ruling—Nixon could not claim executive privilege; resignation—facing impeachment, Nixon resigned

3a. Answers will vary. Some students might agree with the Supreme Court, on the grounds that Nixon invoked executive privilege in an attempt to hide his wrongdoing—not in the interests of national security, as he had claimed.

b. Answers will vary. Some students might note that Congress refused to support Ford's efforts to curb inflation.

c. Answers will vary. Some students might advise the president not to take military action because of its potential cost in human lives.

4. Answers will vary. Students should take into consideration the difficulties Ford faced.

SECTION 3

After completing Section 3, students should be able to:

OBJECTIVE 1 State why voters thought that Jimmy Carter was a different kind of politician.

OBJECTIVE 2 Explain how President Carter's handling of domestic issues caused some Americans to lose faith in his administration.

OBJECTIVE 3 Contrast Carter's foreign policy with Nixon's and Ford's.

OBJECTIVE 4 Analyze how Carter weakened U.S.-Soviet relations, and relate how he helped achieve peace in the Middle East.

SECTION 3

READ TO DISCOVER

1. Why did voters think that Jimmy Carter was a different kind of politician?
2. How did President Carter's handling of domestic issues cause some Americans to lose faith in his administration?
3. How did Carter's foreign policy differ from that of Nixon and Ford?
4. How did Carter weaken U.S.-Soviet relations, and how did he help achieve peace in the Middle East?

DEFINE

apartheid

IDENTIFY

Jimmy Carter
National Energy Act
Department of Energy
Three Mile Island accident
Panama Canal Treaties
Anwar Sadat
Menachem Begin
Camp David Accords

WHY IT MATTERS TODAY

Humanitarian concerns still play a role in foreign-policy decisions. Use **CNNfyi.com** or other **current events** sources to research issues being raised by humanitarian groups and others about some country in the world today. Record your findings in your journal.

CNNfyi.com

Carter: The Outsider as President

EYEWITNESSES TO History

"Carter has figured out a couple of very important things. What national leaders and other candidates perceive as a political crisis is actually a spiritual crisis, and that more symbolic communication is the best way to reach Americans drifting in an atmosphere saturated with instant communication."

—Richard Reeves, *New York* magazine, March 1976

Journalist Richard Reeves evaluated Jimmy Carter, a candidate for the Democratic Party's nomination for president, in a March 1976 magazine article. Frustrated by Watergate, Americans sought a different kind of leader, one who emphasized the values of honesty and openness.

CHALLENGING LEADERSHIP FOR CHALLENGING TIMES

CARTER ★ MONDALE
FOR PRESIDENT ★ FOR VICE PRESIDENT

1976 campaign poster

The Election of 1976

At the 1976 Republican National Convention, Gerald Ford narrowly won the party's nomination for president over his more conservative challenger, Ronald Reagan of California. Ford chose Republican senator Bob Dole of Kansas as his running mate.

At the Democratic convention, former Georgia governor **Jimmy Carter** won his party's nomination. Senator Walter Mondale of Minnesota was his running mate. Little known outside the South, Carter ran as a Washington outsider untouched by Watergate. Central to his campaign was the idea of a new approach to government. Carter promised, "I will never lie to you; I will never mislead you." He noted that he was a born-again Christian whose religious beliefs strongly shaped his politics. During the campaign Carter pledged to make the government decent, honest, and trustworthy. The election was close, however. Carter won by capturing 297 electoral votes to Ford's 240.

On Inauguration Day the new president and his family walked down Pennsylvania Avenue to the White House instead of riding in a limousine. Carter's decision to walk symbolized his desire to keep his administration open to public view. During his presidency, he held several town meetings and radio and television call-in sessions to keep in touch with the people.

✔ **READING CHECK: Identifying Cause and Effect** How did Watergate help Jimmy Carter get elected president? He promised Americans that he would not lie to them or mislead them, as Nixon had done.

Carter's Domestic Agenda

On his first full day in office, President Carter announced an unconditional pardon for most Vietnam-era draft evaders. This pardon went further than the clemency that had been offered by President Ford. Although this gesture helped

LEVEL 1: Tell students that many Americans became skeptical about politicians' integrity after the Watergate scandal. Ask students why voters thought that Jimmy Carter was a different kind of politician. *(Students should mention that Carter ran as a Washington outsider, held strong religious beliefs, walked to the White House on Inauguration Day instead of riding in a limousine, and held regular town meeting and call-in sessions to keep in touch with Americans.)* Ask students whether they would be more or less likely to vote for a candidate on the basis of a label such as "outsider." Discuss students' responses as a class. **English Language Learners**

LEVELS 2 AND 3: Have each student create a collage that symbolizes why voters thought that Jimmy Carter was a different kind of politician. *(See the Level 1 answer for the correct reasons.)* Ask volunteers to display and explain their collages to the class. Students may wish to include their collages in their portfolios.

NOTE: To help students make meaningful connections between events in U.S. history and those in their own hometown, use the Chapter 25 **Hands-On History Activity**, The Future of Energy.

heal lingering divisions caused by the war, many Americans disagreed with it. Nonetheless, Carter's approval rating rose, reaching 75 percent after his first 100 days in office. Carter's popularity fell, however, when he tried to tackle other problems facing the nation.

Economic policy. One of Carter's first tasks as president was to stimulate the economy, which was just beginning to emerge from a recession. To revive the economy and create jobs, Carter enacted a series of economic measures, including a tax cut. The Carter administration's policies helped reduce unemployment slightly, but they also fueled inflation, which reached 13.3 percent by 1979. To curb inflation, Carter called for voluntary wage and price controls, along with cuts in federal spending. "Hard choices are necessary if we want to avoid consequences that are even worse," he told the nation. Carter's anti-inflation program, however, did not slow inflation and produced more unemployment. By the summer of 1980 the economy was once again in recession. In a report to Congress, Carter admitted, "There are no economic miracles waiting to be performed."

Facing the energy crisis. The high price of oil was a major cause of the nation's economic woes. In April 1977 Carter introduced a complex energy proposal that won approval from the public. However, it did not do well in Congress, where significant changes were made to the bill. By the time the **National Energy Act** passed in 1978, few of Carter's original proposals remained intact.

Congress did create the **Department of Energy** in 1977 to oversee energy issues. Despite the efforts of the White House and Congress, however, world events continued to threaten the nation's energy supply. In January 1979 a revolution in Iran disrupted world oil shipments. A few months later, OPEC raised the price of oil 50 percent, leading to another U.S. energy crisis. As gasoline supplies dwindled, many gas stations closed or reduced their hours. Tempers flared as frustrated drivers had to wait hours to fill their gas tanks. To promote energy conservation, Carter asked Americans to "honor the 55-m.p.h. speed limit, set thermostats no higher than 65 degrees and limit discretionary [nonessential] driving." Some people responded by driving less and by adopting other energy-saving measures such as installing solar heaters in their homes.

In the midst of the energy crisis another event dramatized the energy problems facing the United States. In late March 1979 a nuclear reactor failed at the Three Mile Island power plant in Pennsylvania. The accident nearly caused a catastrophic meltdown—the melting of the reactor's core. Some 100,000 people fled or were evacuated from the area. Despite grave public doubts about nuclear power after the **Three Mile Island accident**, Carter argued that the nation needed nuclear energy. "We cannot simply shut down our nuclear power plants," he declared.

Lower speed limits were established to conserve gasoline.

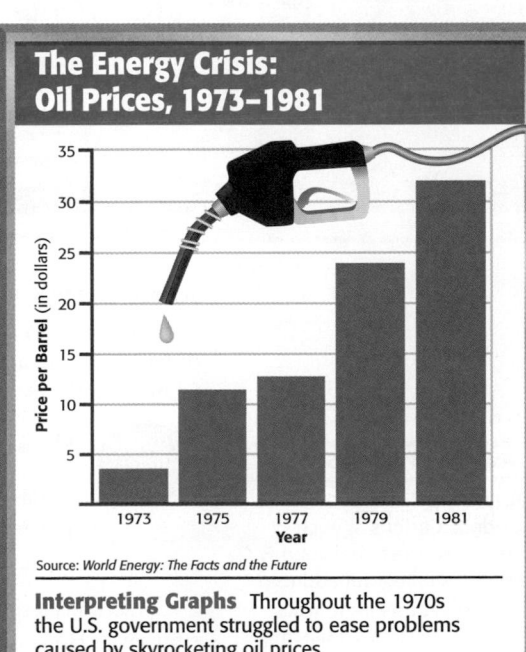

**The Energy Crisis:
Oil Prices, 1973–1981**

Price per Barrel (in dollars) / Year

Source: *World Energy: The Facts and the Future*

Interpreting Graphs Throughout the 1970s the U.S. government struggled to ease problems caused by skyrocketing oil prices.

? **Skills Assessment** Approximately how much did oil prices rise from 1977 to 1981? What led to this price increase?

Pardons. The Constitution gives the president the power to grant pardons. The framers of the Constitution regarded the power to grant pardons as a useful tool to end domestic unrest or rebellions. By offering pardons to rebel leaders, the president might effectively end violent conflict. The pardon power often has been used to heal the wounds of war. Pardons were granted to former Confederates after the Civil War, and following World War II President Truman pardoned some 1,500 people who had violated the nation's draft laws.

CRITICAL THINKING Do you agree with President Carter's decision to pardon most Vietnam-era draft evaders?

ANSWER: Answers will vary. Students should take into account Carter's wish to end social conflict over the Vietnam War.

GRAPH ANSWER
about $20.00 per barrel; a decline in the oil supply

LEVEL 1: Pair students and have each pair create a graphic organizer depicting how President Carter's handling of domestic problems caused some Americans to lose faith in his administration. *(Organizers should mention that Carter's economic policies did not revive the economy, that his energy proposals underwent significant changes in Congress, and that his response to the Three Mile Island accident ignored grave public doubts about nuclear power.)* Ask students to present and explain their graphic organizers to the class.

English Language Learners, Cooperative Learning

LEVEL 2: Tell students to imagine that they are editors who must write a dust jacket summary for a book about the Carter presidency. Have each student write a brief summary describing how President Carter's handling of domestic issues caused some Americans to lose faith in his administration. *(See the Level 1 lesson for the correct issues.)* Students may wish to include their summaries in their portfolios.

LEVEL 3: Tell students to imagine that it is 1979 and that they are political advisers to Carter who have received poll data indicating that some Americans have lost faith in the Carter administration. Have each student write a memo to the president explaining why people have lost faith. *(See the Level 1 lesson for the correct issues.)* Ask volunteers to read their letters to the class.

Carter's Popularity. After reaching a high of 75 percent in March 1977, President Carter's job approval ratings slowly sank. They dropped to 28 percent in June 1979 when Americans experienced severe gasoline shortages. By early January 1980, his approval ratings had climbed to 58 percent. By December of that year, however, they had again slipped, falling to 34 percent by the middle of the month.

CRITICAL THINKING Do you believe that job approval ratings accurately reflect a president's job performance?

ANSWER: Some students might note that job approval ratings might reflect positive attitudes among the public toward economic trends or other events that have little to do with the president's performance.

SCIENCE & TECHNOLOGY ANSWERS

1. by using flat black plates that are exposed to the sun and by using special cells that convert solar energy into electricity

2. Water is pumped through solar collectors, where it is heated and then released through the heater.

Science & Technology

Solar Power

The energy crisis of the 1970s prompted Americans to look for new energy sources. Potential energy sources included synthetic fuels, geothermal energy, and even burning garbage. One alternative source that received much attention was solar power. In 1978, supporters of solar energy held Sun Day in order to draw attention to their cause. President Carter also supported the use of solar energy.

Solar energy has several benefits. It is abundant, clean, and renewable.

Scientists have estimated that covering 1 percent of the surface of the lower 48 states with solar collectors could supply most of the nation's energy needs. Solar energy can be collected by two different methods. The first method uses flat black plates that are exposed to sunlight. The plates grow hot and can then be used to heat air or water. This air or water can heat a house or building. The second method involves using special cells that convert solar energy into electricity. The cells are still very expensive. Moreover, both systems require the development of better means of storing energy for those times when clouds block sunlight.

solar collector

cold water

hot water

water tank

heater

Understanding Science and History

1. What are the two methods by which solar energy can be collected?
2. How does the solar heating system shown at left work?

A loss of faith. While Carter struggled with the nation's problems, Americans lost confidence in his leadership. By March 1979 Carter's job approval rating had dropped considerably. He recognized that his presidency was in trouble. On July 15 he spoke to the nation.

History Makers Speak

❝I want to talk to you right now about a fundamental threat to American democracy. . . . In a nation that was once proud of hard work, strong families, close-knit communities, and our faith in God, too many of us now tend to worship self-indulgence [pampering] and consumption.❞

—Jimmy Carter, speech, July 15, 1979

Americans responded favorably to Carter's discussion of the nation's spiritual emptiness. However, within days Carter asked some of his cabinet members to resign from office. This gave the American people the impression that the White House lacked leadership and was in disorder.

✔ **READING CHECK: Summarizing** How did the energy crisis affect the Carter administration? **Many Americans lost confidence in the Carter administration.**

LEVEL 1: In a classroom discussion, ask students how Carter's foreign policy differed from that of Nixon and Ford. *(Students should mention that Carter rejected realpolitik and tried to inject moral principles into foreign policy, particularly in the area of human rights, and that he tried to improve the U.S. image in the developing world, as exemplified by the Panama Canal Treaties.)* Then ask students whether national self-interest or concern for human rights should guide U.S. foreign policy today. Give students a few minutes to think about the question and to jot down some thoughts and ideas. Then call on students to express and justify their opinions. **English Language Learners**

LEVELS 2 AND 3: Organize students into triads. Have each triad write an imaginary dialogue among Presidents Carter, Nixon, and Ford in which they discuss their approaches to foreign policy. *(See the Level 1 lesson for how Carter's approach differed from that of Nixon and Ford.)* Each student should explain his or her president's approach to foreign policy and state why it is the best approach. Ask volunteers to conduct their dialogues for the class. **Cooperative Learning**

HOMEWORK *Have students conduct research on the status of the Panama Canal today. Students should report their findings in a brief essay.*

A New Foreign Policy

While struggling with domestic issues, President Carter charted a new course in foreign affairs. Rejecting the realpolitik of the Nixon presidency, he tried to inject moral principles into U.S. foreign policy.

 "We are deeply concerned . . . by the . . . subtle erosion in the focus and morality of our foreign policy. Under the Nixon-Ford administration, there has evolved a kind of secretive 'Lone Ranger' foreign policy—a one-man policy of international adventure. This is not an appropriate policy for America."

—Jimmy Carter, speech, June 1976

Carter's new approach to foreign policy was most evident in the area of human rights. He particularly supported the universal right to freedom from torture and unlawful detention. Declaring that "our commitment to human rights must be absolute," Carter called for strong diplomatic and economic pressure on countries whose leaders violated human rights. Not surprisingly, many dictatorships that limited the rights of their people strongly opposed Carter's policy. Some U.S. diplomats also had their doubts. They warned that meddling in the domestic affairs of other countries might increase world tensions.

The Panama Canal. Carter's position on the Panama Canal added to the controversy over his human rights policy. Carter pushed for Senate ratification of the **Panama Canal Treaties**, which granted control of canal operations to Panama by the year 2000. Critics charged that Carter was giving away the canal. Ronald Reagan condemned the treaties. He charged, "The fatal flaw is the risk they contain for our national security. . . . We're turning one of the world's most important waterways over to a country no one can believe." Gradually, however, public opinion shifted in Carter's favor. After a long and bitter political battle the Senate narrowly ratified the treaties in 1978. In Latin America, where U.S. control of the canal had long been a sore point, the treaties met with general approval.

President Carter's stance on the Panama Canal issue signaled a more flexible approach to relations

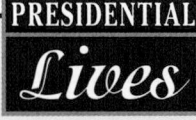

PRESIDENTIAL Lives

Jimmy Carter

1924–
In Office 1977–1981

Historian John Whiteclay Chambers II has called Jimmy Carter "one of America's greatest ex-presidents." In the years immediately following his presidency, Carter focused on teaching in Atlanta and helping to found the Carter Presidential Center, which includes the Jimmy Carter Museum and Library. During the mid-1980s, he committed himself to the humanitarian causes he had championed as president. For example, he lent his support to Habitat for Humanity, a nonprofit organization whose volunteers help build houses for people with low incomes. Carter spent one week each year helping volunteers build houses. In 1991 he announced the creation of The Atlanta Project, which uses corporate contributions and volunteer efforts to aid disadvantaged Atlanta residents.

Carter also became involved in international affairs. He showed special interest in the democratic process, monitoring elections in nations such as Panama and Nicaragua to prevent voter fraud. During the 1990s he acted as an elder statesman for the United States. Carter conducted diplomatic negotiations with governments in Haiti, North Korea, and Somalia. In 1994 he helped bring about a cease-fire in Bosnia that contributed to the peace agreement signed the following year.

Good Luck From Kentucky

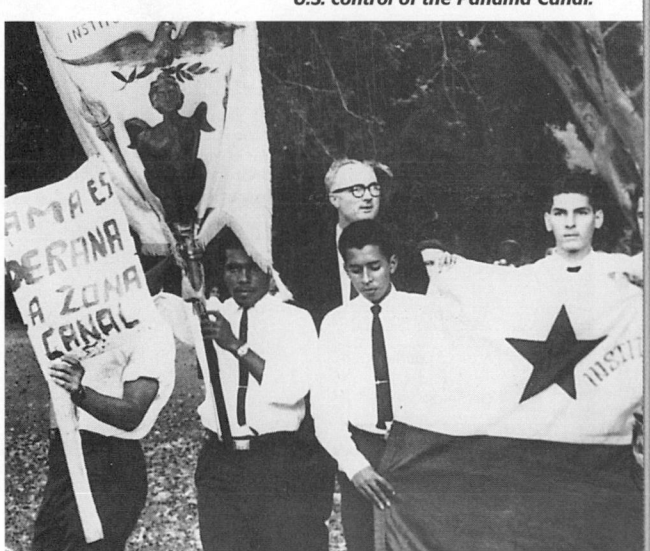

Panamanian students protest U.S. control of the Panama Canal.

CONSTITUTIONAL HERITAGE

Presidents and Treaties. In 1978, while Congress was not in session, President Carter announced the termination of the Mutual Defense Treaty of 1954 between the United States and Taiwan. Senator Barry Goldwater argued that the president could not terminate a treaty without first obtaining the agreement of the Senate. In the 1979 case of *Goldwater* v. *Carter,* the Supreme Court ruled that the conflict was a political question between two equal branches of government and that the Court did not have the authority to resolve the dispute.

CRITICAL THINKING What do you think was the result of the Court's ruling?

ANSWER: Students might suggest that Carter's termination of the treaty would stand unless Congress found some way to force the president to act otherwise.

ALL LEVELS: Tell students that Jimmy Carter's foreign policies had mixed success. To help students understand how Carter weakened U.S.-Soviet relations and how he helped to achieve peace in the Middle East, copy the graphic organizer at right on the chalkboard, omitting the italicized answers. Have each student complete it. Ask volunteers to share their answers with the class. Then have each student write several paragraphs evaluating President Carter's policies toward the Soviet Union and the Middle East. Tell students to justify their evaluations with facts and examples. Ask volunteers to share their evaluations with the class.

English Language Learners

WEAKENED RELATIONS WITH THE SOVIET UNION	PEACE IN THE MIDDLE EAST
Event	**Events**
The Soviet Union invades Afghanistan in December 1979.	*In September 1978 Carter hosts meetings between Israel's Menachem Begin and Egypt's Anwar Sadat at Camp David.*
Result	**Result**
President Carter cut grain sales to the Soviets and announced the U.S. boycott of the Moscow Olympics.	*Israel and Egypt sign the Camp David Accords, ending a 30-year state of war between the two countries.*

PEOPLE IN HISTORY

Andrew Young. Jimmy Carter's ambassador to the United Nations, Andrew Young, had a long career in the civil rights movement and in public service. The son of a dentist and schoolteacher, Young graduated from Howard University and the Hartford Theological Seminary and was ordained as a minister. He served as a pastor and then joined the Southern Christian Leadership Conference (SCLC), to which he was appointed executive director in 1964. In 1972 Young became the first African American from Georgia to be elected to the U.S. House of Representatives since the Reconstruction era. As UN ambassador, Young was an outspoken and often controversial figure. He resigned from the UN ambassadorship in 1979 and later served two terms as mayor of Atlanta.

CRITICAL THINKING Why might Jimmy Carter have appointed Andrew Young as UN ambassador?

ANSWER: Students might suggest that the president valued Young's experience with the civil rights movement because of his own interest in human rights.

MAP ANSWER

the Iran hostage crisis and the Soviet invasion of Afghanistan

with developing countries. Carter hoped the approach would improve the image of the United States and diminish the appeal of communism.

✔ **READING CHECK: Categorizing** How did Carter try to inject morality into foreign policy? He called for strong diplomatic and economic pressure on countries whose leaders violated human rights.

Africa. In Africa, the United States and the Soviet Union competed for influence among the continent's newly independent states. Carter tried to win allies among African nations by helping them resolve problems in their own way. One Carter official noted, "It is not a sign of weakness to recognize that we alone cannot dictate events elsewhere. It is rather a sign of maturity in a complex world."

Former civil rights activist Andrew Young was Carter's ambassador to the United Nations. He criticized imperialism in Africa. Young also condemned South Africa's policy of **apartheid**, in which the white minority ruled and the black majority had few rights. Young supported black majority rule in Rhodesia—present-day Zimbabwe. Conservative members of Congress attacked Carter's Africa policy. African leaders such as Kenneth Kaunda of Zambia, however, asserted that Carter had "brought a breath of fresh air to our troubled world."

Conflicts in the Middle East, 1948–1981

Interpreting Maps Growing U.S. dependence on foreign oil required good relations with oil-producing Arab states, a situation complicated by hostility between the Arabs and Israelis.

❓ **HUMAN SYSTEMS** Not all conflicts in the Middle East were between Arabs and Israelis. According to the map, what other conflicts began in 1979?

U.S.-Soviet relations. The decline of détente that had taken place during the Ford administration continued during Carter's presidency. The U.S.-Soviet relationship reached its low point in December 1979. That month Soviet troops invaded the country of Afghanistan to install a pro-Soviet leader. This invasion put Soviet troops within striking distance of major oil routes. Carter warned the Soviets to withdraw from Afghanistan. When they refused, he cut grain sales to the Soviet Union and announced a boycott of the 1980 Summer Olympics in Moscow. Many Americans did not support the decision to boycott the Olympics. Congress also postponed the signing of a key U.S.-Soviet arms-control treaty.

Anwar Sadat (left), President Carter, and Menachem Begin (right) sign the Camp David Accords.

Carter and the Middle East. President Carter's chief foreign-policy triumph was a Middle East peace accord. Carter had taken office amid fears of more Egyptian-Israeli armed conflict. Egyptian president **Anwar Sadat** and Israeli prime minister **Menachem Begin** met for peace talks, but those talks deadlocked.

In September 1978 Carter met with Begin and Sadat at Camp David, a retreat in northern Maryland for U.S. presidents. After several days of negotiations, the three leaders agreed on a framework for achieving peace in the Middle East. Their agreement became known as the **Camp David Accords**. As a result of their efforts, Sadat and Begin shared the Nobel Peace Prize for 1978. The following year, they signed a formal peace treaty that ended a 30-year state of war between Egypt and Israel. Carter later regarded his work at Camp David as "one of the most gratifying achievements" of his life.

✔ **READING CHECK: Evaluating** What were the positive and negative aspects of President Carter's foreign policy? positive—a peace treaty between Israel and Egypt and greater freedom in Africa; negative—decline in détente and a return to more hostile relations between the United States and the Soviet Union

---

SECTION 3 REVIEW

1. Define and explain:
apartheid

2. Identify and explain:
Jimmy Carter
National Energy Act
Department of Energy
Three Mile Island accident
Panama Canal Treaties
Anwar Sadat
Menachem Begin
Camp David Accords

3. Evaluating Copy the chart below. Use it to evaluate why Americans lost faith in President Carter's attempts to solve the nation's problems.

Carter's Policies	
Economic	**Energy**

4. **Finding the Main Idea**

a. How did Watergate and Jimmy Carter's image affect the 1976 election?

b. Do you agree with President Carter's decision to make human rights an important issue in U.S. foreign policy? Why or why not?

c. What were President Carter's contributions to the Middle East peace effort?

5. **Writing and Critical Thinking**

Drawing Conclusions Imagine that you are participating in a debate on whether President Carter could have had more success in improving relations with the Soviet Union. Write notes on your position.

Consider:
• his commitment to human rights
• the decline of détente during the 1970s
• the invasion of Afghanistan

Homework Practice Online
keyword: SE3 HP25

After completing Section 4, students should be able to:

OBJECTIVE 1 Describe how the American population and family structure changed during the 1970s.

OBJECTIVE 2 Explain why Americans were said to be self-absorbed.

OBJECTIVE 3 List forms of entertainment that were popular in the 1970s.

OBJECTIVE 4 Analyze how new technologies affected Americans' lives.

🎙️ *LET'S GET STARTED!*

As students enter the classroom, tell them to compile a list of clothing styles, movies, music, slang words, and other elements of popular culture that they believe originated during the 1970s. Ask students which, if any, of these items are still popular today. Tell students that in Section 4 they will learn about popular culture, family life, population changes, and technological developments during the 1970s.

SECTION 4 RESOURCES

REPRODUCIBLE
▶ Guided Reading Strategy 25.4

TECHNOLOGY
▶ One-Stop Planner, Lesson 25.4
▶ Everyday Life in America Transparency 31: *Star Wars:* Sign of the Seventies
▶ Holt Researcher: American History CD–ROM
▶ Homework Practice Online

REINFORCEMENT, REVIEW, AND ASSESSMENT
▶ Section 4 Review, p. 765
▶ Daily Quiz 25.4
▶ Main Idea Activity 25.4
▶ English Audio Summary 25.4
▶ Spanish Audio Summary 25.4

SECTION 4

READ TO DISCOVER
1. How did the American population and family structure change during the 1970s?
2. Why did some observers argue that Americans were self-absorbed?
3. What forms of entertainment were popular during the 1970s?
4. How did new technologies affect the lives of many Americans?

DEFINE
personal computer

IDENTIFY
Voting Rights Act of 1975
Bilingual Education Act
Sunbelt
Steven Spielberg
Neil Armstrong
Edwin "Buzz" Aldrin
Apollo 11
Skylab
Steven Jobs
Stephen Wozniak

WHY IT MATTERS TODAY
Population movement is still changing the United States. Use **CNNfyi.com** or other **current events** sources to learn about current immigration and migration trends in the United States. Record your findings in your journal.

CNNfyi.com

Life in the 1970s

This serving dish was decorated to celebrate the bicentennial.

EYEWITNESSES TO History ❝*Did the way in which Americans commemorated the nation's 200th birthday contribute to the American dream embodied in the Declaration of Independence, the Constitution, and the Bill of Rights? Having witnessed, along with all other Americans, the renewed spirit of dedication, patriotism and friendship that flowed across the land on the Bicentennial weekend, it seems to me that the answer is an unqualified [without reservation] yes. Americans used the Bicentennial to renew their faith in themselves, to gain knowledge and understanding of their neighbors, and to begin again the quest for liberty, justice, and equality for all.*❞

—Edward W. Brooke, quoted in *The Bicentennial of the United States of America*

Senator Edward W. Brooke of Massachusetts praised the celebrations that took place throughout the nation on July 4, 1976. For many Americans, the bicentennial celebration provided a welcome break from the anxiety and stress of the decade.

A Changing Population

American society evolved during the 1970s, both on the national level and within people's homes. Immigration from abroad and migration within the nation's borders changed the makeup and distribution of the population. Americans also experimented with new ways to raise families.

Immigration. During the 1970s the U.S. population was greatly affected by continued immigration, mostly from Asia and Latin America. Most Latin American immigrants came from Mexico, but many others came from the Caribbean. In 1980, for example, nearly 120,000 Cubans fled their communist nation for the United States, settling mainly in the Miami area.

Having opened the way for emigration after President Nixon's visit, China supplied some of the new Asian population in the United States. Many of these Chinese immigrants were highly skilled and well-educated professionals fleeing political persecution. Despite their backgrounds, many found that discrimination and their difficulty speaking English prevented them from getting jobs that paid well. The experiences of Wei-Chi Poon, a biology professor from China, and her husband, a skilled architect, were typical. Neither knew any English when they immigrated to the United States. As a result, she had to work in a laundry factory for $1.85 per hour, while he took on two low-paying jobs. "We were so busy working and so tired," she recalled. "We had no time and energy to study English."

Congress passed two new laws designed to aid such immigrants. The **Voting Rights Act of 1975** required states and communities with a large number of

LEVEL 1: Organize students into triads. Have each triad create a collage of images that shows how the American population and family structure changed during the 1970s. *(Collages should depict immigration from Asia and Latin America, people moving to the Sunbelt, the rise in single-person households, the rise in divorce, fewer children per family, and the rise in single-parent households.)* Display students' collages in the classroom.
English Language Learners, Cooperative Learning

LEVELS 2 AND 3: Have each student write a short essay that discusses the changes in the American population and family structure during the 1970s. Essays should compare those trends to current trends in population and family structure. *(See the Level 1 lesson for the correct changes.)* Tell students to evaluate or speculate on whether the trends of the 1970s continue today or whether they have changed. Ask volunteers to read their essays to the class.

NOTE: For an additional teaching idea, see the Chapter 25 inner-outer circle lesson in the **Creative Teaching Strategies** handbook.

non-English-speaking residents to print voting materials in various foreign languages. The **Bilingual Education Act** of 1974 increased funding for public schools to provide instruction to students in their primary languages while they learned English. Some critics opposed bilingual education, which they claimed slowed the adjustment of immigrants to American life. Yet there was little question that the United States was becoming an increasingly multicultural society. Coping with new immigrants remained an important challenge for the country.

Rise of the Sunbelt. Americans moved more often in the 1970s than in previous decades. A growing number of Americans migrated from the North and the East, which some people mocked as the Frostbelt. They moved to the **Sunbelt** states of the South and the West. The Sunbelt states became increasingly important in national politics. This was particularly true of California, Florida, and Texas, where migration caused population growth to outpace that of the rest of the nation.

Americans moved to the Sunbelt for a number of reasons. The successes of the civil rights movement of the 1960s made the South a more attractive region in which to live. Some 7 million people moved there between 1970 and 1978. Economic growth spurred by increased defense spending after World War II had created more job opportunities in the region. Some migrants merely sought a warmer climate and a suburban lifestyle. Suburbs were more common and more spacious in the Sunbelt than in the Northeast because of the greater availability of land.

Improved technology also encouraged population growth in the Sunbelt. Air conditioning had become widely available, allowing people to tolerate the region's heat. However, not everyone welcomed this development. One Florida woman complained, "I hate air conditioning; it's a[n] . . . invention of the Yankees. If they don't like it hot, they can move back up North where they belong."

Family life. During the 1970s an increasing number of Americans chose to live alone. By the end of the decade some 22.5 percent of American households included just one person. Men and women waited longer to marry, driving up the average age at marriage. They were also more willing to leave unhappy marriages. This was in part because most states instituted laws that made divorces easier to obtain. The divorce rate continued to rise during the 1970s. There were 5.2 divorces per 1,000 Americans in 1980, up from 2.2 in 1960 and 3.5 in 1970. However, the increase in the divorce rate did not mean that Americans rejected the institution of marriage. In fact, remarriage rates also increased during this period.

Attitudes regarding family size also changed. In 1967 some 34 percent of women polled hoped to have four or more children. Four years later, just 15 percent of women polled expressed that desire. Not surprisingly, birthrates dropped sharply, averaging two births per woman. At the peak of the baby boom, the average family had three children. By 1980 that number had dropped to about 1.6 children per family.

By the end of the 1970s the idea of the "average family" had to be revised. Just 15 percent of American families matched the traditional image of a working father and a mother who stayed home to raise the children. During the 1970s the number

Because of funding for bilingual education, students can receive instruction in their primary language while they learn English.

TEACH OBJECTIVE 2

 ALL LEVELS: Have each student compile a list of American attitudes and trends in the 1970s that might suggest why some observers argued that Americans were self-absorbed. (*Lists should mention the rising divorce rate, self-improvement fads—including new spiritual movements that focused on the self—and the fitness craze*). Call on students to read items from their lists to the class; record these items on the chalkboard. Then ask students to discuss other trends or habits associated with American lifestyles in the 1970s. (*Students might mention the ideal of simple living as well as poor health habits such as alcohol and fast-food consumption.*) Ask students what these trends might indicate about society during the 1970s. (*Students might suggest that Americans had little free time*

or were disenchanted with modern life.) To conclude, lead a discussion about whether any of 1970s trends, fads, or ideals still exist, then ask students to interpret the meaning of these trends. **English Language Learners**

TEACH OBJECTIVE 3

LEVEL 1: Pair students and have each pair create a poster depicting forms of entertainment that were popular in the 1970s. (*Posters should depict movies, particularly blockbuster movies; and music, particularly big-business rock music, disco, and punk.*) Display students' posters around the classroom. **English Language Learners, Cooperative Learning**

CULTURE

New Age Beliefs. During the 1970s many Americans became interested in the various spiritual beliefs known as the New Age movement. Influenced by Asian religions, a desire to improve the self, and health practices such as massage therapy and acupuncture, New Agers held a wide variety of beliefs. Some were interested in health and environmental issues, while others pursued spiritual advancement through practices such as the use of crystals.

CRITICAL THINKING How might changes in U.S. immigration laws have contributed to some New Age practices?

ANSWER: Students might suggest that the increasing number of Asian immigrants contributed to a greater acquaintance with Asian religions.

THAT'S INTERESTING!

In 1965 some 42 percent of American adults smoked. By 1970 that number had dropped to about 37 percent. A decade later it had fallen to some 33 percent. In 1995 just some 25 percent of American adults smoked.

VISUAL RECORD ANSWER

Students might answer that it reflects an emphasis on self.

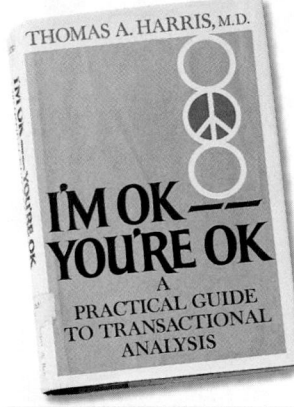

INTERPRETING THE VISUAL RECORD

Changing attitudes. To some observers, Americans seemed increasingly concerned about themselves during the 1970s. *How does this book cover represent the focus of the 1970s?*

In the 1970s running became popular among Americans, in part because of Jim Fixx's book.

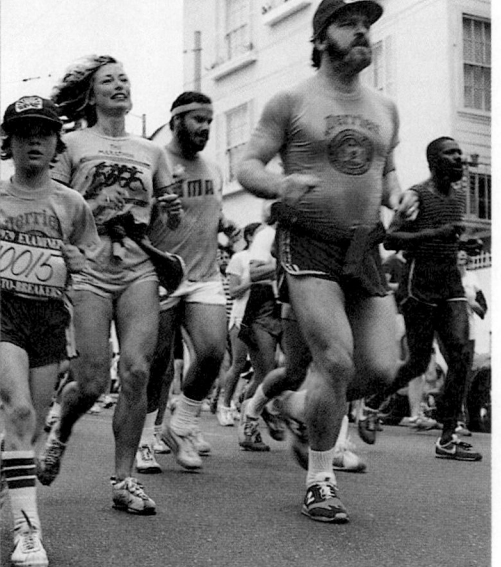

of households with single women raising children rose to 8 million—an increase of 50 percent from the beginning of the decade. Single men raised children in some 1.5 million households.

✔ **READING CHECK: Analyzing Information** How did immigration and migration change American society in the 1970s? Immigration increased the population, added new non-English speaking cultures, and led to the creation of programs like bilingual education. Sunbelt states gained political influence.

American Attitudes

Some observers cited the rising divorce rate as proof that Americans had become selfish and self-absorbed. Journalist Tom Wolfe characterized the 1970s as the "Me Decade." In reality, American attitudes were varied and complex.

Improving the self. One popular response to the political and economic turmoil of the 1970s was the human potential or self-actualization movement. Millions of Americans turned to activities such as yoga in an effort to improve their inner selves. Self-help books such as *Looking Out for Number One* and *I'm OK— You're OK* topped the best-seller lists. Former used-car salesman Werner Erhard made about $9 million per year sponsoring seminars that helped people "get in touch with themselves."

Nontraditional religious groups also enjoyed increased popularity. The Maharishi Mahesh Yogi, teacher of a technique called Transcendental Meditation, claimed some 350,000 followers, including some well-known entertainers. The interest in new spiritual movements also had a dark side. In 1978 some 900 members of the People's Temple religious cult either killed themselves or were murdered at their compound in Jonestown, Guyana. Most of the victims were Americans. The incident shocked the world and heightened concern about alternative religions.

Some Americans embraced the ideal of simple living. Seeking to escape the tensions of modern life, many moved to rural areas where they could live closer to nature. Others turned to home gardening, an increasingly popular hobby. Writer Tom Bender explained in a 1975 article the reasons for living simply.

> *History Makers Speak* **"We are learning that too much of a good thing is not a good thing, and that we would often be wiser to determine what is enough rather than how much is possible. . . . Our major goal is to be happy with the least . . . services necessary. . . . The fewer our wants, the greater our freedom from having to serve them."**
>
> —Tom Bender, *Sharing Smaller Pies*

Fitness and food. The interest in self-improvement extended into the area of physical fitness. Americans flocked to health spas and tennis clubs. Sales of running shoes boomed as millions of Americans took up running or jogging to stay fit. Jim Fixx's *The Complete Book of Running* sold some 620,000 copies in 1978. The number of smokers also began to decline.

The interest in fitness may have been sparked by concerns over health habits, particularly alcohol consumption and diet. Liquor consumption rose significantly during the 1970s. The American diet also posed health risks. In 1977 a Senate report on nutrition

Lead a discussion about the forms of popular entertainment that were popular in the 1970s. *(See the Level 1 lesson for the correct forms.)* Then ask students to explain why movies and disco music grew increasingly popular during the 1970s. *(Students might mention new technologies and the fading of counterculture values.)* Then tell students to imagine that they are high school students in the 1970s. Have each student write a brief personal statement describing whether he or she is a disco fan or a punk fan and why. Ask volunteers to read their statements to the class.

Teacher to Teacher

Deanna Spring of Cincinnati, Ohio, suggested the following activity: Organize students into triads. Have each triad identify forms of music that were popular in the 1970s and that are still part of current musical culture. Then have each triad prepare a report that explains how the forms of music that were popular in the 1970s have changed in meaning today.

---

concluded that an improved diet would reduce deaths from heart disease by 25 percent. The popularity of fast food contributed to Americans' poor eating habits. In 1972 the fast-food chain McDonald's passed the U.S. Army to become the single largest provider of meals in the United States. By 1977 some 35 percent of the money Americans spent on food went to pay for meals prepared outside the home.

✔ **READING CHECK: Making Generalizations** Why did some observers call the 1970s the "Me Decade"? the rise in divorce rates, self-help interests, and the desire to obtain better mental and physical fitness

Entertainment

During the 1970s Americans spent more money than ever before on music and motion pictures. The entertainment industry underwent significant changes in its attempt to respond to consumer demands.

Movies. The 1970s brought a boom to the motion picture industry, which had grown slowly after the introduction of television. Blockbusters—movies with heavy advance promotion that opened on hundreds or thousands of screens across the country—accounted for much of the increased interest in movies. One of the most popular movies of the decade was *Jaws*, a film directed by 28-year-old **Steven Spielberg**.

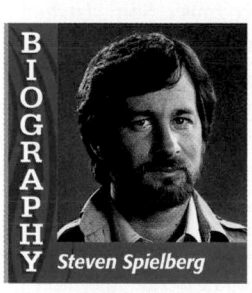

BIOGRAPHY

Steven Spielberg

Born in 1947 in Cincinnati, Ohio, Steven Spielberg was a regular television watcher as a child. He later admitted, "I was, and still am, a TV junkie." He was also interested in filmmaking. In 1958 his father loaned him a small movie camera so that he could earn a Boy Scout merit badge in photography. Four years later, the teenager's 40-minute film *Escape to Nowhere* won an amateur film contest.

Spielberg remained interested in films while studying at California State University. He dropped out during his junior year in order to direct television programs. His first major motion picture, *Sugarland Express*, received positive reviews but had little success at the box office. His next film, *Jaws*, was based on a novel about a shark that terrorizes a resort town. Released in 1975, *Jaws* became the top-grossing motion picture of all time within just 78 days of its release. Spielberg later explained how he was able to create such a suspenseful movie.

History Makers Speak

"Fear is a very real thing for me. One of the best ways to cope with it is to turn it around and put it out to others. I mean, if you are afraid of the dark, you put the audience in a dark theater. I had a great fear of the ocean."

—Steven Spielberg, quoted in *Steven Spielberg*, by Joseph McBride

Spielberg continued to make movies that people around the world enjoyed. His *Close Encounters of the Third Kind* (1977) and *E.T. the Extra-Terrestrial* (1982) portrayed aliens as kind and well intentioned. The 1981 movie *Raiders of the Lost Ark* was influenced by the adventure films that Spielberg had enjoyed as a child. *Jurassic Park*, his 1993 movie about modern-day dinosaurs, was a tremendous commercial success. That same year he released *Schindler's List*, a movie about the Holocaust.

HIS ADVENTURE ON EARTH

A STEVEN SPIELBERG FILM

E.T.
THE EXTRA-TERRESTRIAL

Poster advertising E.T.

MORE ON THE MAP

Entertainment. In 1975 Americans spent some $70 billion on recreational and entertainment activities. These expenditures represented 6.9 percent of the total amount of money spent on personal consumption. In 1996 Americans spent some $431 billion on recreation and entertainment. This figure represented 8.3 percent of total personal consumption. Americans spent some $6.3 billion on motion pictures and about $23 billion on books and maps.

ACTIVITY: Have students calculate the total amount of money spent by Americans on personal consumption in 1975 and in 1996. *(1975—$1.0145 trillion; 1996—$5.1928 trillion)*

THAT'S INTERESTING!

As of 1998, Steven Spielberg's films included 6 of the top 25 top-grossing movies of all time, with revenues totaling some $1.7 billion.

Research on the R✺M

Free Find: Steven Spielberg

After reading about Steven Spielberg on the **Holt Researcher CD–ROM**, write a screenplay for a short film about your favorite historical event.

ALL LEVELS: To help students understand how technological developments affected the lives of many Americans, copy the chart at right on the chalkboard, omitting the italicized answers. Have each student complete it.

English Language Learners

HOMEWORK *Have students choose a technological development from the graphic organizer. Have each student write a brief essay discussing the short- and long-term impact of the 1970s technology and how it has affected Americans' perceptions and attitudes. Tell students to include a few sentences about the ways that technology has affected their lives.*

Technological Development	Short-Term Impact	Long-Term Impact
the space program (Apollo missions and Skylab)	*boosted national pride, improved relations with Soviet Union, changed view of universe*	*development of sophisticated space equipment, advancement of a global point of view*
personal computers	*success of Apple Computer, increased availability of computers*	*revolutionized computer industry, made information revolution and Internet possible*
video games, VCRs, telephone answering machines	*added convenience, changed habits and leisure activities*	*potential negative impact of video games on children's social skills and health*

VISUAL RECORD ANSWER

(for p. 765)

Students should answer Earth.

REVIEW SECTION 4 ANSWERS

1. Define
- personal computer, p. 765

2. Identify
- Voting Rights Act of 1975, p. 760
- Bilingual Education Act, p. 761
- Sunbelt, p. 761
- Steven Spielberg, p. 763
- Neil Armstrong, p. 764
- Edwin "Buzz" Aldrin, p. 764
- *Apollo 11,* p. 764
- *Skylab,* p. 765
- Steven Jobs, p. 765
- Stephen Wozniak, p. 765

3. more single-person households, increasing divorce rate, declining birthrate, more single-parent households

4a. The Sunbelt grew increasingly important in national politics.

b. Answers will vary. Students should discuss the idea of self-improvement versus social improvement, or the ideal of simple living.

c. Answers will vary. Students should consider the impact that personal computers and other technologies introduced in the 1970s have had on the lives of many Americans.

5. Students might suggest that businesses targeted audiences and shaped products to appeal to a large number of people.

The Disco Generation

Many of the discotheques that appeared during the 1970s offered a wild sensory experience. Discos were equipped with fog and bubble machines, strobe lights, and enormous sound systems that pumped out loud dance music. The disco crowd also presented a sight to see, as everyone was well dressed. Blue jeans and sandals were out; fancy dresses, tight pants, jewelry, and blow-dried hair were in. New Yorker Johnny Boy Musto, 18, explained his disco fashion code. "It's very important that you don't wear the same thing for at least four weeks."

Disco dancers

The young adults who flocked to the clubs offered many reasons for their love of disco. Anibal Campa, a 19-year-old who claimed to go discoing six nights a week, declared, "I'll get tired eventually, but not for another ten to fifteen years. . . . I'd rather disco. If it wasn't for this music, I think I wouldn't want to be in this world." Yolanda Cimino explained, "What I like about dancing here is that you don't have to talk to the guy." A young beautician told a reporter, "I came here to get out of the house. . . . I think kids come here to escape the problems of growing up. When you dance, there's no one to give you a dirty look if you're doing something wrong."

Schindler's List won Spielberg an Academy Award for best director. He received the honor again five years later for *Saving Private Ryan,* a film about men who fought in World War II. In 1994 he founded the Survivors of Shoah Visual History Foundation, a project that films the testimony of Holocaust survivors.

Music. For some music critics, the beginning of the 1970s represented the end of an era. The most important rock band of the 1960s, the Beatles, officially broke up. During the 1970s much of rock music changed from being the music of the counterculture to becoming big business. Record company executives and radio stations marketed rock music by packaging it and targeting consumers.

The most popular musical style was disco, a type of dance music. Discotheques, or clubs where patrons danced to recorded music instead of live bands, had gone out of fashion during the 1960s. Their popularity returned in the 1970s. At the height of the disco phenomenon, there were thousands of discotheques in the United States.

Not all Americans enjoyed disco music. Some latched on to a new sound called punk rock. Artists such as Lou Reed, Patti Smith, and a New York band called the Ramones rejected technical precision in favor of energy and expressive lyrics. Although punk rock received media attention and influenced a new generation of performers, it never matched the commercial success or popularity of disco.

✔ **READING CHECK: Drawing Inferences** How did Steven Spielberg's movies have an impact on the rest of the world? They were blockbusters popular around the world.

Technological Advances

Sophisticated technological developments changed the way that Americans viewed the universe. Other innovations of the 1970s would eventually change the ways that Americans worked, played, and communicated.

The space program. On July 20, 1969, Americans cheered as astronauts **Neil Armstrong** and **Edwin "Buzz" Aldrin** landed their *Apollo 11* lunar module on the Moon. Stepping onto the lunar surface, Armstrong declared, "That's one small step for [a] man, one giant leap for mankind." Between 1969 and 1972 the United States sent six more Apollo missions into space. Only *Apollo 13,* which experienced technical problems so severe that the lives of the astronauts were in danger, did not reach the Moon.

Skylab, the first U.S. space station, was placed in orbit in 1973. Over the course of a year, three astronaut teams visited *Skylab,* logging some 171 days aboard the station. In 1975, U.S. astronauts and Soviet cosmonauts met and worked together

REVIEW

Have students complete the **Section 4 Review** on p. 765.

ASSESS

Have students complete **Daily Quiz 25.4**. As **Alternative Assessment**, you may want to use the collage or the personal statement in this section's lessons.

RETEACH

Have students complete **Main Idea Activity for English Language Learners and Special-Needs Students 25.4**. Then pair students and have each pair summarize Section 4 in one page. Have each pair trade its summary with another pair.

Students should read each other's work and discuss any differences in content or emphasis.
English Language Learners, Cooperative Learning

EXTEND

Have each student select one of the following people: Steven Spielberg, Neil Armstrong, Edwin "Buzz" Aldrin, Steven Jobs, or Stephen Wozniak. Tell each student to write a short biographical profile of his or her chosen individual for inclusion in a book titled *Who's Who of the 1970s*. Students' profiles should focus on their subjects' activities and achievements during the 1970s. **Block Scheduling**

in space on the Apollo-Soyuz mission. The space program also led to many inventions that were adapted for use in daily life. For example, smoke detectors were first used on *Skylab* to help detect toxic vapors. Portable, self-contained tools were originally developed to help Apollo astronauts drill on the Moon. This technology has led to the development of items such as cordless vacuum cleaners and power tools. Other "spin-off" technologies include television satellite dishes, automobile designs, medical imaging, and high-tech construction materials.

Innovations. In 1976 **Steven Jobs** and **Stephen Wozniak**, two college dropouts who worked for computer companies, founded Apple Computer company. The two had built a small **personal computer** (PC) in the garage of Jobs's parents' house. Unlike earlier computers, which were very large and very expensive, PCs were affordable and small enough to sit on a desk. In 1977 Jobs and Wozniak introduced the Apple II, a 12-pound computer that revolutionized the computer industry. By 1980 stock in Apple was valued at $1.3 billion, and major corporations such as IBM were preparing to market their own personal computers. PCs also changed the nature of business.

Other technological innovations of the 1970s affected entertainment and communications. In 1975 Atari introduced a video-game system that was played on television sets. Within a year Americans had spent some $250 million on such games. Low-cost videocassette recorders (VCRs) changed television viewing habits. The telephone answering machine also became commonplace after improvements made the devices more affordable.

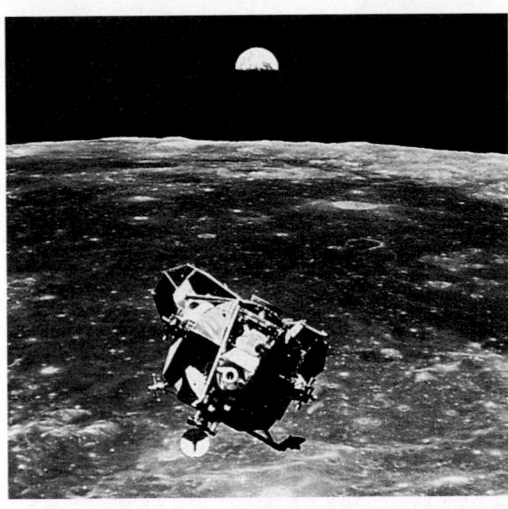

INTERPRETING THE VISUAL RECORD

Technology. The space program used advanced technology to successfully land astronauts on the Moon. *Which planet is shown at the top of this photograph?*

✔ **READING CHECK: Categorizing** How did space technologies lead to innovations that affect daily life in the United States? Many space technologies were adapted for use in daily life.

SECTION 4 REVIEW

1. Define and explain:
personal computer

2. Identify and explain:
Voting Rights Act of 1975
Bilingual Education Act
Sunbelt
Steven Spielberg
Neil Armstrong
Edwin "Buzz" Aldrin
Apollo 11
Skylab
Steven Jobs
Stephen Wozniak

3. Summarizing Copy the diagram below. Use it to illustrate changes in American families during the 1970s.

AMERICAN FAMILY

4. ▸ **Finding the Main Idea**
a. What effects did migration to the Sunbelt have on American life?
b. Do you agree that Americans were self-absorbed during the 1970s? Why or why not?
c. What would life in the United States today be like without the technological innovations developed in the 1970s?

5. ▸ **Writing and Critical Thinking**
Analyzing Information Write a brief report on how the entertainment industry changed in the 1970s.
Consider:
• the rise of blockbuster movies
• changes in the music industry
• technology in entertainment

Homework Practice Online
keyword: SE3 HP25

CHAPTER 25

REVIEW AND ASSESSMENT RESOURCES

TECHNOLOGY

► Chapter 25 Test Generator (on the One-Stop Planner)
► Global Skill Builder CD–ROM
► HRW Go site

REINFORCEMENT, REVIEW, AND ASSESSMENT

► Chapter 25 Review, pp. 766–67
► Chapter 25 Tutorial for Students, Parents, Mentors, and Peers

► Chapter 25 Test (Form A or B)
► Portfolio Activities and Alternative Assessment Handbook, Chapter 25
► Chapter 25 Test for English Language Learners and Special-Needs Students

REVIEW

Have students complete the **Chapter 25 Review** on pp. 766–67.

ASSESS

Use one of the chapter tests to assess students' understanding of the content. For **Alternative Assessment,** see the **Portfolio Activities and Alternative Assessment Handbook.**

Understanding Main Ideas

1. High prices led to economic hardship, long lines at the gas station, and anxiety that the country had run out of energy.

2. He acted as if there were no limitations on his power, leading him to abuse his powers.

3. because of the Soviet invasion of Afghanistan and the U.S. embargo on grain sales to the Soviets

4. interest in escapist entertainment and the human-potential movement

5. personal computers, video-cassette recorders, video games, telephone answering machines

Reviewing Themes

1. Officials claimed that the tapes contained proof of Nixon's efforts to cover up the Watergate scandal.

2. Answers will vary. Some students might suggest that the U.S. government should encourage alternative sources of fuel.

3. Answers will vary. Some students might argue that Carter's support for human rights hurt relations with repressive dictatorships but improved relations with some African nations.

Thinking Critically

1. The policy of détente focused on reduction of arms and increased peace between nations.

766

CHAPTER 25 Review

Creating a Time Line

Copy the time line below onto a sheet of paper. Complete the time line by filling in the events and dates from the chapter that you think were most significant. Pick three events and explain why you think they were significant.

1968   1972   1976   1980

Writing a Summary

Using standard grammar, spelling, sentence structure, and punctuation, write an overview of events in the chapter.

Identifying People and Ideas

Identify the following terms or individuals and explain their significance.

1. Silent Majority
2. stagflation
3. Henry Kissinger
4. Watergate
5. Barbara Jordan
6. Jimmy Carter
7. National Energy Act
8. apartheid
9. Sunbelt
10. Steven Spielberg

Understanding Main Ideas

SECTION 1 *(pp. 740–746)*
1. How did the energy crisis affect life in the United States?

SECTION 2 *(pp. 747–753)*
2. How did President Nixon's management of the presidency contribute to his eventual resignation from office?

SECTION 3 *(pp. 754–759)*
3. Why did U.S.-Soviet relations worsen during President Carter's administration?

SECTION 4 *(pp. 760–765)*
4. What cultural trends indicate that the 1970s were an anxious time for many Americans?
5. What new technologies appeared during the 1970s?

Reviewing Themes

1. **Government** Why did the Justice Department and Supreme Court demand that Nixon turn over the White House tapes?
2. **Economics** Was the U.S. government right to try to end the country's dependence on imported oil in the 1970s? Explain your answer.
3. **Global Relations** Did President Carter's support for human rights serve the international interests of the United States? Explain your answer.

Thinking Critically

1. **Comparing and Contrasting** How was the Cold War fought during the Nixon, Ford, and Carter administrations?
2. **Evaluating** How did Watergate affect the relationship between the executive and legislative branches of government?
3. **Making Generalizations** In what ways did Presidents Nixon, Ford, and Carter contribute to Americans' declining trust in the government?
4. **Analyzing Information** How did some technological innovations lead to other innovations that affect daily life?
5. **Making Predictions** Why did popular music change from the protest songs that had appeared during the 1960s and become more dance-oriented?

Writing About History

Comparing Write an essay that compares Nixon's policy toward Chile, Ford's response to the *Mayaguez* incident, and Carter's position on the Panama Canal Treaties. Use the following graphic to organize your thoughts.

Nixon and Chile	Ford and the *Mayaguez*	Carter and the Panama Canal

RETEACH

Organize the class into four groups and assign each group one of the sections of this chapter. Have each group put together and present a short multimedia presentation that covers the important points of its assigned section. Tell students to be sure to cover all of the sections' objectives in their presentations.
English Language Learners, Cooperative Learning

EXTEND

Have your classes organize a '70s Day celebration. Tell students to work individually, in small groups, or as a class to create an authentic 1970s atmosphere for a day. Help students plan and create costumes, props, food, activities, entertainment, visual displays, and so on. Invite other classes to participate.
Cooperative Learning, Block Scheduling

Building Social Studies Skills

Interpreting Maps

Study the map below. Then use it to help answer the questions that follow.

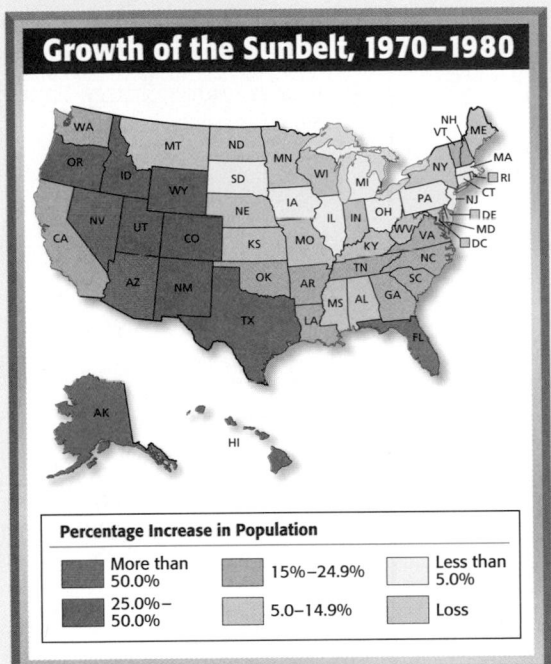

Growth of the Sunbelt, 1970–1980

Percentage Increase in Population

- More than 50.0%
- 25.0%– 50.0%
- 15%–24.9%
- 5.0–14.9%
- Less than 5.0%
- Loss

1. What reasons besides climate might have accounted for the population movement indicated by the map?

2. Which statement best summarizes the population movement indicated by the map?

a. People moved from northern and eastern states to southern and western states.
b. People moved from northern and western states to southern and eastern states.
c. People moved from southern and eastern states to northern and western states.
d. People moved from southern and western states to northern and eastern states.

Analyzing Primary Sources

Read the following comments by Hugh Sloan, a Nixon administration staff member. Then answer the questions that follow.

"The night Nixon resigned I felt truly sad for the country. This was the first president ever driven from office. And I always thought that it didn't have to happen that way. If Nixon had acted early and asked his entire campaign staff to resign, a lot of the mess could have been avoided. But he was an individual who obviously had some flaws, and he really brought this thing on himself. I felt a personal disappointment in what happened. I had had the opportunity to work for the government and to serve the White House and it all came to a tragic end."

3. Whom does Hugh Sloan blame for President Nixon's resignation?
a. President Nixon
b. First Lady Pat Nixon
c. The news media
d. Nixon's campaign director

4. Based on the excerpt, what conclusions can you draw about the effect of the Watergate scandal on many Americans?

Alternative Assessment

Building Your Portfolio

U.S. HISTORY

Constitutional Heritage

Imagine that you are an adviser to a member of Congress in 1974. Write a brief report on how the Watergate affair and President Nixon's resignation have changed Americans' views on the role of the federal government. Be sure to discuss whether those events altered the relationship between the executive and legislative branches and between the executive and judicial branches.

internet connect

Internet Activity: go.hrw.com
KEYWORD: SE3 AN25

Choose a topic on the 1970s to:
- research popular culture.
- create a brochure on the political and diplomatic legacy of President Nixon.
- learn about the Watergate scandal.

---

2. The legislative branch became untrusting and hostile toward the executive branch due to Nixon's illegal actions; the executive branch felt betrayed by Congress.

3. Nixon's Watergate cover-up, Ford's pardon of Nixon, Carter's failure to accomplish his campaign promises; all three failed to solve the energy crisis

4. Answers will vary. Students might suggest that innovations in the space program led to the use of smoke detectors, cordless tools, satellite dishes, and medical imaging; computer advances led to desktop computers and video games.

5. Students might suggest that the counterculture had diminished in social importance.

Writing

Essays will vary but should compare the motivations of each president and the outcomes of each foreign-policy initiative.

Building Social Studies Skills

1. Answers will vary. Students might suggest job growth and plentiful land at cheaper prices.

2. a

3. a

4. Answers will vary. Students might suggest that many Americans were disappointed in Nixon and the federal government.

CHAPTER 26

The Republican Revolution

CHAPTER RESOURCE MANAGER

	Objectives	Pacing Guide	Reproducible Resources
SECTION 1 **Reagan Comes to Power** pp. 770–75	★ Discuss the factors that helped Ronald Reagan win the presidency in 1980. ★ Explain President Reagan's main economic program, and evaluate how successful it was. ★ Describe the significant developments in the Cold War during the early 1980s. ★ Recount how the Reagan administration became involved in events in El Salvador and Nicaragua.	**Regular** 2 days **Block Scheduling** 1 day *Block Scheduling Handbook with Team Teaching Strategies, pp. 151–56*	**RS** Guided Reading Strategy 26.1 **IC** Literature Reading 26: Corridos: Songs of Exodus **SM** Geography Activity 26: The Arms Race **PS** Primary Source Reading 26: Cutting Government Down to Size
SECTION 2 **Reagan's Second Term** pp. 776–82	★ Analyze how the Republicans won the 1984 election, and discuss how the makeup of the Supreme Court changed in the 1980s. ★ Describe what events began to shake public confidence in the economy. ★ Explain how the Iran-Contra affair developed. ★ Identify the developments that eased tensions between the United States and the Soviet Union in the late 1980s.	**Regular** 1 day **Block Scheduling** .5 day *Block Scheduling Handbook with Team Teaching Strategies, pp. 151–56*	**RS** Guided Reading Strategy 26.2 **RS** Graphic Organizer Activity 26: Economics in the 1980s **E** Creative Teaching Strategy: Unfinished Story Alternatives Lesson
SECTION 3 **Bush and Life in the 1980s** pp. 783–91	★ Summarize how American society changed in the 1980s. ★ Explain how the Cold War ended. ★ Describe what led to the Persian Gulf War, and analyze how it differed from previous U.S. military conflicts. ★ Discuss the domestic problems the Bush administration faced.	**Regular** 1 day **Block Scheduling** .5 day *Block Scheduling Handbook with Team Teaching Strategies, pp. 151–56*	**RS** Guided Reading Strategy 26.3 **PS** Biography Reading 26: Sally Ride **E** Hands-On History Activity: The Americans with Disabilities Act and Your Community

Chapter Resource Key

PS	Primary Sources	**REV**	Review		Video
RS	Reading Support	**ELL**	Reinforcement and English Language Learners	Internet	Internet
IC	Interdisciplinary Connections				Holt Presentation Maker Using Microsoft® PowerPoint®
E	Enrichment		Transparencies		
SM	Skills Mastery		CD–ROM		
A	Assessment		Music		

One-Stop Planner CD–ROM

See the *One-Stop Planner* for a complete list of additional resources for students and teachers.

One-Stop Planner CD-ROM

It's easy to plan lessons, select resources, and print out materials for your students when you use the **One-Stop Planner CD-ROM with Test Generator.**

 One-Stop Planner, Lesson 26.1

 Linking Geography and History Transparency 22: Central America and the Caribbean

 Holt Researcher: American History CD–ROM

 Homework Practice Online

REV Section 1 Review, p. 775

A Daily Quiz 26.1

ELL Main Idea Activity 26.1

ELL English Audio Summary 26.1

ELL Spanish Audio Summary 26.1

 One-Stop Planner, Lesson 26.2

 CNN Presents America: Yesterday and Today, 1850 to the Present Segment: The Wall Comes Down

 Holt Researcher: American History CD–ROM

 Homework Practice Online

REV Section 2 Review, p. 782

A Daily Quiz 26.2

ELL Main Idea Activity 26.2

ELL English Audio Summary 26.2

ELL Spanish Audio Summary 26.2

 One-Stop Planner, Lesson 26.3

 Everyday Life in America Transparency 32: The AIDS Quilt Project, 1980s

 The American Nation Video Program Segment: U.S. Troops in the Persian Gulf; Teacher's Guide, pp. 199–200

 Holt Researcher: American History CD–ROM

 Homework Practice Online

 HRW Go site

REV Section 3 Review, p. 791

A Daily Quiz 26.3

ELL Main Idea Activity 26.3

ELL English Audio Summary 26.3

ELL Spanish Audio Summary 26.3

internet connect

HRW ONLINE RESOURCES
GO TO: go.hrw.com
Then type in a keyword.

TEACHER HOME PAGE
KEYWORD: SE3 Teacher

CHAPTER INTERNET ACTIVITIES
KEYWORD: SE3 AN26
Choose an activity to:
• research the Persian Gulf War.
• learn about Sandra Day O'Connor.
• understand the causes and effects of the collapse of the Soviet Union.

CHAPTER ENRICHMENT LINKS
KEYWORD: SE3 CH26

ONLINE ASSESSMENT
Homework Practice
KEYWORD: SE3 HP26

Standardized Test Prep
KEYWORD: SE3 STP26

Rubrics
KEYWORD: SS Rubrics

ONLINE MAPS, CHARTS, AND GRAPHS
KEYWORD: SE3 MCG
• Breakup of the Soviet Sphere
• Conflicts in the Middle East
• Living Below the Poverty Level
• U.S. Crime Rate, 1980–1992

CONTENT UPDATES
KEYWORD: SS Content Updates

HOLT PRESENTATION MAKER
KEYWORD: SE3 PPT26

ONLINE READING SUPPORT
KEYWORD: SS Strategies

CURRENT EVENTS
KEYWORD: S3 Current Events

Meeting Individual Needs

Ability Levels

Level 1 Basic-level activities designed for all students encountering new material

Level 2 Intermediate-level activities designed for average students

Level 3 Challenging activities designed for honors and gifted-and-talented students

English Language Learners Activities that address the needs of students with Limited English Proficiency

Chapter Review and Assessment

 Global Skill Builder CD–ROM

 HRW Go site

REV **Chapter 26 Tutorial for Students, Parents, Mentors, and Peers**

REV **Chapter 26 Review, pp. 792–93**

 Chapter 26 Test Generator (on the One-Stop Planner)

A **Chapter 26 Test (Form A or B)**

A **Alternative Assessment Handbook**

A **Chapter 26 Test for English Language Learners and Special-Needs Students**

Build on What You Know

Ask students to answer the following questions.

Why might domestic problems have hampered Jimmy Carter's presidency?

Consider:

• the energy crisis, inflation, and unemployment

• the public frustration with government after the Watergate scandal

What reforms might Reagan have suggested during his presidential campaign?

Consider:

• the economic problems facing the nation

• the perceptions of U.S. power and prestige abroad

---

exploring the time line

AMERICAN EVENTS

internet connect

TOPIC: Sandra Day O'Connor
GO TO: go.hrw.com
KEYWORD: SE3 AN26

Have students access the Internet through the HRW Go site to conduct research on the life and career of Sandra Day O'Connor. Then tell each student to imagine that it is 1981 and that he or she is President Ronald Reagan. Have each student write a letter to the U.S. Senate explaining why O'Connor has been nominated and urging the Senate to confirm her nomination.

CHAPTER 26

1980–1992

The Republican Revolution

Ronald and Nancy Reagan

A compact disc

1983
Science and Technology
CD–ROM technology is introduced.

Geraldine Ferraro campaign button

1984
Politics
Democratic vice presidential candidate Geraldine Ferraro becomes the first woman to run on a major-party presidential ticket.

1986
Daily Life
Six million Americans form a human chain in Hands Across America, an effort to raise money for the homeless.

| **1980** | | **1982** | | **1984** | | **1986** |

1980
Politics
Ronald Reagan is elected president.

1980
World Events
Labor strikes in Poland threaten Soviet control over the nation.

1981
Politics
Sandra Day O'Connor becomes the first woman to serve on the U.S. Supreme Court.

1983
Business and Finance
Inflation falls to 4 percent, signaling recovery from the economic recession.

1986
Science and Technology
The space shuttle *Challenger* explodes, killing all on board.

A space shuttle being transported by airplane

Build on What You Know

Public frustration with the federal government grew in the 1970s as the Watergate scandal broke, the energy crisis emerged, and the economy continued to weaken. Democrat Jimmy Carter was elected president with a promise to reform government. Numerous obstacles, including a worsening economic situation, hampered his presidency. In this chapter you will learn how Ronald Reagan was elected president in 1980 and set out to reform the economy and foreign relations.

What's Your Opinion?

 To help students create their Themes Journal entries, provide the following examples of appropriate agree/disagree statements.

Economics

Agree Working-class Americans did not benefit from the Republican tax cuts during the 1920s.

Disagree Tax cuts during the Harding and Coolidge administrations helped contribute to U.S. economic prosperity in the 1920s.

Global Relations

Agree The competition among European nations to build larger armies was a major factor in World War I.

Disagree The development of atomic weapons motivated the United States and the Soviet Union to work to avoid a war.

Science, Technology, and Society

Agree The printing press and its impact on European society occurred independently from modern economic cycles.

Disagree The widespread availability of automobiles and household electricity transformed Americans' lives during the economic boom of the 1920s.

Amy Tan's The Joy Luck Club

After Iraq invaded Kuwait, international forces gathered for Operation Desert Storm.

1987
Business and Finance
Investors lose almost $1 trillion when the stock market crashes.

1989
The Arts
Amy Tan publishes *The Joy Luck Club*.

1990
Science and Technology
The Hubble Space Telescope is launched.

1991
World Events
The Persian Gulf War begins.

1992
Daily Life
The 78-acre Mall of America, the country's largest shopping center, opens in Minnesota.

1988   **1990**   **1992**

1987
World Events
U.S. and Soviet leaders sign the INF Treaty, eliminating medium-range nuclear weapons in Europe.

1988
Politics
George Bush is elected president.

1989
World Events
The Berlin Wall falls, signaling the end of the Cold War.

A piece of the Berlin Wall

George Bush

What's Your Opinion?

Themes Journal *Do you agree or disagree with the following statements? Support your point of view in your journal.*

Economics Cutting corporate taxes will not boost the economy because it has no effect on ordinary Americans.

Global Relations Building stronger defense systems and weapons will only lead to war, never to peace.

Science, Technology, and Society An economic boom will have little effect on how technology shapes society.

GLOBAL EVENTS

GLOBAL RELATIONS

The INF Treaty. The Intermediate-Range Nuclear Forces (INF) Treaty came about in part because Americans and Europeans protested the buildup of nuclear weapons in Western Europe. After several years of negotiations, the United States and the Soviet Union agreed to eliminate all ground-based missiles with a range of 320–3,400 miles. Some U.S. politicians, including former president Richard Nixon, expressed doubts about the wisdom of the treaty, in part because the Soviets had more intermediate-range missiles. However, the U.S. Senate ratified it with a 93-to-5 vote. The treaty was the first to result in the elimination of nuclear weapons systems. Historians regard the INF Treaty as one of the first signs that the Cold War was coming to an end.

CRITICAL THINKING Why might historians regard the INF Treaty as evidence that U.S.-Soviet relations were improving?

ANSWER: Students might suggest that the ability to reach an agreement to limit nuclear weapons revealed a willingness to cooperate on important issues.

After completing Section 1, students should be able to:

OBJECTIVE 1 Discuss the factors that helped Ronald Reagan win the presidency in 1980.

OBJECTIVE 2 Explain President Reagan's main economic program, and evaluate how successful it was.

OBJECTIVE 3 Describe the significant developments in the Cold War during the early 1980s.

OBJECTIVE 4 Recount how the Reagan administration became involved in events in El Salvador and Nicaragua.

⏰ *LET'S GET STARTED!*

Write the term *conservative* on the chalkboard. As students enter the classroom, tell them to describe, in writing, what this term means to them in terms of politics. Ask students to explain why measures such as reducing federal regulations and cutting taxes might be considered "conservative." Tell students that in Section 1 they will learn about the conservative policies of Ronald Reagan.

SECTION ① 1

READ TO DISCOVER

1. What factors helped Ronald Reagan win the presidency in 1980?
2. What was President Reagan's main economic program, and how successful was it?
3. What were the significant developments in the Cold War during the early 1980s?
4. How did the Reagan administration become involved in events in El Salvador and Nicaragua?

DEFINE

supply-side economics

IDENTIFY

Iran hostage crisis
Ayatollah Khomeini
Ronald Reagan
New Right
Moral Majority
Jerry Falwell
Reaganomics
Strategic Defense Initiative
Solidarity
Lech Walesa
José Napoleón Duarte
Sandinistas
Contras

▶ WHY IT MATTERS TODAY

Terrorism overseas continues to pose a challenge to U.S. national security interests. Use **CNNfyi.com** or other **current events** sources to learn about recent incidents of terrorism abroad. Record your findings in your journal.

CNNfyi.com

Reagan Comes to Power

EYEWITNESSES TO History

❝You always used to think in this country that there would be bad times followed by good times. Now, maybe it's bad times followed by hard times followed by harder times.❞

—Chicago homemaker, quoted in *It Seemed Like Nothing Happened*, by Peter N. Carroll

This unnamed Chicago homemaker expressed a sentiment that became increasingly common toward the end of the 1970s. Even Jimmy Carter noted that Americans were suffering from a loss of faith in the future. Reporters labeled the condition he described the national malaise, or illness. The president urged Americans to pull themselves up out of this despair. However, many Americans considered the president to be part of the country's problems.

The cheerful smiley face popular in the 1970s seemed out of place by the end of the decade.

The Election of 1980

Although Jimmy Carter had achieved some notable successes as president, by July 1980 just 31 percent of Americans approved of his job performance. Richard Nixon's approval rating had only fallen to 24 percent when he resigned. Many Americans were frustrated with President Carter's inability to find solutions to the nation's domestic problems, such as the energy crisis, inflation, and unemployment.

Iran hostage crisis. Of all the difficulties Carter faced, none was more damaging than the **Iran hostage crisis**. Iran had long been regarded as critical to U.S. interests in the Middle East. In the 1950s the United States had helped overthrow Iran's premier and return sole power to Shah Mohammad Reza Pahlavi. Although the shah's rule was very harsh, the United States maintained its support of him. In 1979, followers of the **Ayatollah Khomeini** (eye-uh-TOH-luh koh-MAY-nee), a militant Islamic leader, forced the shah to flee Iran. Khomeini established an Islamic republic. The new Iranian government was outraged when President Carter allowed the shah into the United States for medical treatment. On November 4, 1979, Iranian militants seized more than 50 Americans at the U.S. Embassy in Tehran, Iran's capital. The Iranian militants hoped that taking these hostages would force the United States to return the shah to Iran for trial.

Fifty-two Americans remained hostages as the crisis continued. In April 1980 a rescue mission failed. U.S. military helicopters crashed in the Iranian desert, killing eight Americans. As frustration over the crisis mounted, the American public became angry at Carter. Many felt that his failure to free the hostages signaled America's decline as a world power. Even a former member of Carter's cabinet admitted, "Khomeini would not have touched the Soviet Embassy."

LEVEL 1: Tell students to imagine that they are foreign exchange students living in the United States during 1980. Pair students and have each pair write a letter to a friend or family member back home that analyzes the factors that helped Ronald Reagan win the presidency. *(Students' letters should include the frustration with the Iran hostage crisis, Carter's inability to solve domestic problems, Americans' insecurity about the future, and Reagan's appeal across party lines.)* Have volunteers read their letters to the class.
English Language Learners, Cooperative Learning

LEVEL 2: Tell students to imagine that it is 1980 and that they are television news analysts. Inform students that Ronald Reagan has just been elected president. Have each student write a brief analysis of the factors that helped Reagan win the presidency in 1980. *(See the Level 1 lesson for the correct factors.)* Ask volunteers to read their analyses to the class.

LEVEL 3: Tell students to imagine that it is 1980 and that Ronald Reagan has just been elected president. Pair students and have each pair write a short breakfast-table dialogue discussing the factors that helped Reagan win the election. *(See the Level 1 lesson for the correct factors.)* Ask students to perform their dialogues for the class. **Cooperative Learning**

The campaign. Republican candidate **Ronald Reagan** echoed these opinions during the 1980 presidential campaign. The former California governor attacked Carter as a weak leader who had presided over a decline in U.S. power. Reagan's promise to "make America strong again" appealed to voters, many of whom crossed party lines to support him. These so-called Reagan Democrats reflected the widespread dissatisfaction with Carter's presidency.

Reagan and his running mate, George Bush of Texas, easily won the election. Reagan captured 489 electoral votes to 49 for Carter and his running mate, Walter Mondale of Minnesota. John Anderson, an independent candidate, failed to capture any electoral votes but did win almost 7 percent of the popular vote. This strong showing further reflected public frustration with the Carter administration. The Democrats' majority in the House declined, and for the first time since 1952, the Republicans won control of the Senate.

Despite his defeat, Carter continued to negotiate for the release of the hostages. On January 20, 1981, after 444 days in captivity, the hostages were finally freed—just moments after Reagan was sworn in as president.

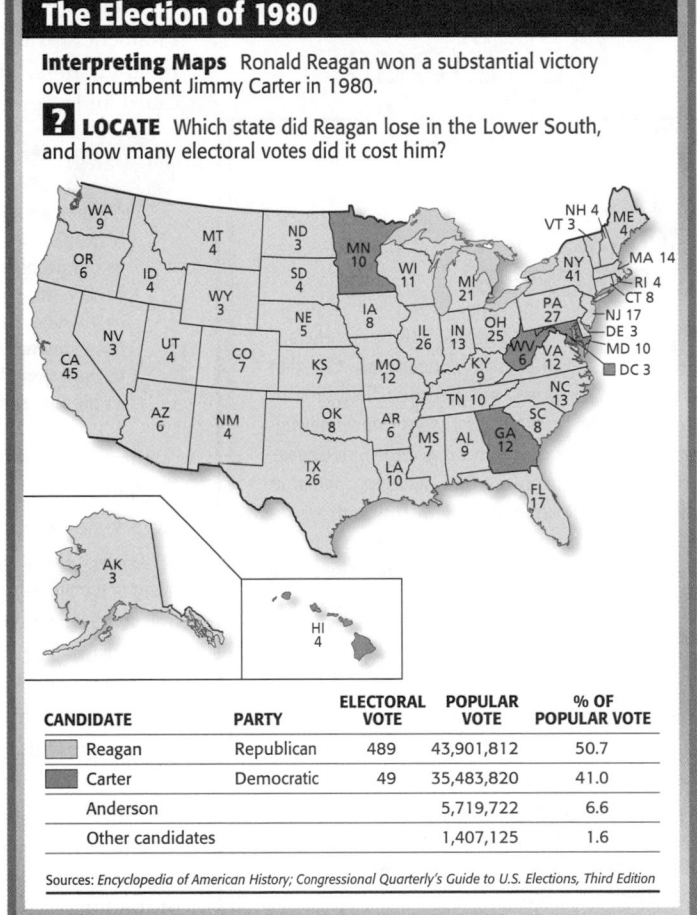

The Election of 1980

Interpreting Maps Ronald Reagan won a substantial victory over incumbent Jimmy Carter in 1980.

? LOCATE Which state did Reagan lose in the Lower South, and how many electoral votes did it cost him?

CANDIDATE	PARTY	ELECTORAL VOTE	POPULAR VOTE	% OF POPULAR VOTE
Reagan	Republican	489	43,901,812	50.7
Carter	Democratic	49	35,483,820	41.0
Anderson			5,719,722	6.6
Other candidates			1,407,125	1.6

Sources: *Encyclopedia of American History; Congressional Quarterly's Guide to U.S. Elections, Third Edition*

Role of the New Right. Ronald Reagan was a former New Deal Democrat turned conservative Republican. He appealed to a wide range of voters who were unhappy with liberal politics. Reagan's strongest support, however, came from a growing movement of political conservatives known as the **New Right**. At the fore-front of the New Right was the **Moral Majority**—a fundamentalist Christian organization founded in 1979. Reverend **Jerry Falwell** was the group's leader.

Reagan and the New Right shared many of the same political goals. Both supported school prayer, a strong defense, and free-market economic policies. Both opposed abortion, the Equal Rights Amendment, gun control, and busing to achieve racial balance in schools.

Members of the New Right were largely responsible for the Republicans gaining control of the Senate in 1980. This powerful political force played a significant role in shaping Republican policy throughout the 1980s.

✔ **READING CHECK: Drawing Inferences** Why does John Anderson's 6.6 percent of the popular vote represent a "strong showing"? An independent candidate rarely gets more than a few percentage points in the election.

The Anderson Campaign. A long-time Republican, John Anderson ran as an independent candidate in what he called the National Unity Campaign. His running mate was Patrick Lucey, a Democrat who had once been governor of Wisconsin. Anderson opposed income tax cuts for individuals and proposed a 50-cent-per-gallon tax on gasoline. The tax revenues would be used to reduce Social Security taxes. Anderson also wanted to reduce U.S. dependence on foreign oil.

CRITICAL THINKING Why did Anderson, a Republican, choose a Democrat for his running mate?

ANSWER: Students might suggest that he wanted to attract voters from both major parties.

THAT'S INTERESTING!

Ronald Reagan had supported Democrats Franklin D. Roosevelt and Harry Truman, but in the 1952, 1956, and 1960 elections he voted for the Republican candidates. It was not until 1962, however, that Reagan registered as a Republican.

MAP ANSWER
Georgia; 12 votes

ALL LEVELS: Tell students that President Reagan's economic program was considered a radical departure from the programs of all the previous administrations since the New Deal. To help students understand President Reagan's economic program and how successful it was, copy the graphic organizer at right on the chalkboard, omitting the italicized answers. Have each student complete the organizer. Ask volunteers to share their answers with the class.

English Language Learners

REAGAN'S ECONOMIC PROGRAM	
supply-side economics—lowered top income tax rates as a way to increase investment in businesses	*reductions in the size and influence of government— cuts in government regulation of industries and cuts in social programs*
Successes	**Failures**
economic recovery—drop in the inflation rate, increased consumer spending, business recovery, soaring stock market	*some citizens excluded from recovery—cuts in social programs hurt the poorest Americans, high unemployment among African Americans, Hispanics, and factory workers, increased homelessness*

ECONOMICS

Tax Rates. Despite the Reagan tax cuts, the U.S. government receives a higher percentage of its revenues from income tax than most other developed nations. For example, some 36 percent of the government's revenues came from income taxes. Only Canada, with about 39 percent, and Sweden, with about 37 percent, received higher percentages of revenue from income tax. The Netherlands received 20 percent of its revenues from income tax; and France, about 13 percent.

CRITICAL THINKING Do the figures above indicate that people in France pay less in taxes than Americans?

ANSWER: Students might suggest that the French may pay more in other types of taxes.

THAT'S INTERESTING!

The economic recovery that Reagan promised the nation did not occur immediately. In 1982 a severe recession caused the highest U.S. unemployment levels since the Great Depression.

Technology Resources

Linking Geography and History Transparency 22: Central America and the Caribbean

The Religious Spirit

A RETURN TO CONSERVATIVE CHURCHES

The New Right benefited from Americans' increased interest in conservative Christian churches after the spiritual experimentation of the 1960s and 1970s. Christian Fundamentalism in particular experienced a surge in followers. This spiritual movement had become popular in the 1920s and continued to grow throughout the 1900s. Many members of the movement found that Fundamentalism's focus on strictly following the Bible gave them clear spiritual direction in a society that seemed to have lost its values.

Led by several prominent and politically active ministers, Fundamentalism became a major force for political and social change in the country in the 1980s. Baptist minister Jerry Falwell started the trend during the U.S. bicentennial in 1976. Falwell warned that the nation was facing numerous problems because its political leaders and institutions had turned away from the Christian values upon which the nation was founded. The solution to this problem, he argued, was for conservative Christians to become more involved in politics. As a political movement, Fundamentalism became the driving force behind the antiabortion campaign and efforts to restore prayer in public schools. ■

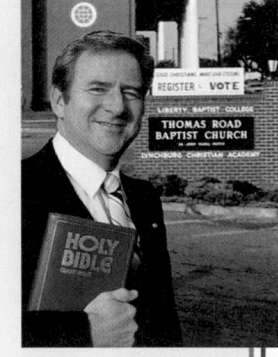

Reverend Jerry Falwell was the head pastor at a Fundamentalist Baptist church.

Reagan's Economic Program

President Reagan entered office with a comprehensive economic program. In his inaugural address he explained the plan, which called for less government involvement in the economy.

History Makers Speak

❝These United States are confronted with an economic affliction of great proportions. We suffer from the longest and one of the worst sustained inflations in our national history.... In this present crisis, government is not the solution to our problem; government is the problem.... It is my intention to curb the size and influence of the Federal establishment.... In the days ahead I will propose removing the roadblocks that have slowed our economy and reduced productivity.... It is time to reawaken this industrial giant, to get government back within its means, and to lighten our punitive tax burden.❞

—Ronald Reagan, "Inaugural Address," January 20, 1981

This plan, called **Reaganomics**, was based on the theory of **supply-side economics**. This "trickle down" theory argued that lowering the top income tax rates would spur economic growth. Supporters of supply-side economics claimed that people would invest their tax savings in businesses, thereby creating jobs, increasing consumer spending, and eventually generating increased tax revenues. Congress responded to Reagan's program by passing a three-year plan to cut federal income taxes by 25 percent.

Congress also supported another part of Reagan's economic plan—drastic cuts in government regulation of industries such as airlines, banking, television, and trucking. The Reagan administration's pro-business, antiregulation stance was evident in the Department of the Interior's handling of public lands. Secretary of the Interior James Watt leased huge areas of the seafloor to private companies searching for off-shore oil and gas. He also leased federal lands to coal companies.

Critics charged that Reagan's tax cuts favored wealthy Americans while spending cuts and deregulation weakened programs to protect consumers, poor Americans, and the environment. Critics also warned that big tax cuts combined with increased military spending—another important element of Reaganomics—would produce enormous shortages in the federal budget.

By 1983 supply-side economics had begun to help the economy. The inflation rate had dropped to a manageable 4 percent. Responding to this development, Americans increased their spending during the mid-1980s. This boosted the economy even further. Businesses revived, and the stock market soared.

Critics continued to note that not all Americans benefited from the recovery. Deep cuts in federal funding for social programs hurt poor citizens. Although employment rose overall, joblessness remained high among African Americans and Hispanics, particularly for unskilled workers living in the inner cities. Unemployment among factory workers in the Midwest, once America's industrial heartland, also remained high.

✔ **READING CHECK: Finding the Main Idea** What was the theory behind President Reagan's main economic program? Reaganomics was based on supply-side economics. This "trickle down" theory argued that lowering the top income tax rates would spur economic growth.

Reagan and the Cold War

The Reagan administration's emphasis on increased military spending was in part a reflection of Ronald Reagan's strong anticommunist views. He took a hard line against the Soviet Union, even branding it an "evil empire" in one speech. To counter the Soviet threat, Reagan called for new weapons systems and an increased U.S. military presence in such areas as the Indian Ocean and the Persian Gulf.

New weapons. Between 1981 and 1985 the Pentagon's budget grew from some $150 billion to about $250 billion. Much of the money was spent on nuclear weapons. Secretary of State Alexander Haig suggested that "nuclear warning shots" might be useful in a conventional war.

The talk of nuclear war stirred public fears. In town meetings and a few state referendums, voters urged a freeze on the testing and deployment of nuclear weapons. Many Americans marched in rallies to show their support for the proposals.

In response, Reagan proposed the **Strategic Defense Initiative** (SDI), a space-based missile-defense system, in March 1983. SDI quickly became controversial. Many critics labeled it "Star Wars" after the popular 1977 movie and said it was based on untested technological theories and was probably unworkable. They also warned that SDI research would intensify the arms race. President Reagan countered that SDI would be a weapon for peace—one that killed weapons, not people. He explained this in a national address.

> **History Makers Speak** "I call upon the scientific community in our country, those who gave us nuclear weapons, to turn their great talents now to the cause of mankind and world peace: to give us the means of rendering these nuclear weapons impotent [powerless] and obsolete."
>
> —Ronald Reagan, speech, March 23, 1983

U.S.–Soviet relations. Even before Reagan took office, U.S.-Soviet relations had cooled because of the Soviet Union's 1979 invasion of Afghanistan. Relations deteriorated further in August 1980, when Polish workers in Gdańsk and Szczecin (SHCHET-sheen) staged a series of massive strikes. They protested high prices and demanded the right to form trade unions free from government or Communist Party control. At first, things went well for the strikers. Faced with the threat of a nationwide general strike, the Soviet-backed Polish government legalized independent union activity in late August. On September 17, labor activists voted to form **Solidarity**, an independent trade union. **Lech Walesa** (vah-LEN-suh), an electrician at a Gdańsk shipyard who had helped launch the initial strikes, became the union's leader.

ANOTHER "GIANT LEAP FOR MANKIND"—BACKWARDS—

RUSSKIES! RUSSKIES! BLAST 'EM WITH TH' PHASERS, SCOTTY!

AYE AYE, MR. PRESIDENT—

STARSHIP RON

BEN SARGENT

INTERPRETING POLITICAL CARTOONS

SDI. President Reagan's plan for a space-based missile defense system was very controversial. *Do you think this cartoon supported SDI? Explain your answer.*

LEVELS 2 AND 3: Tell students to imagine that they are editors of an encyclopedia of the Cold War. Have each student write an entry on the significant developments in the Cold War during the early 1980s. *(See the Level 1 lesson for the correct developments.)* Ask volunteers to read their entries to the class.

TEACH OBJECTIVE 4

 ALL LEVELS: Pair students and have each pair create a graphic organizer depicting how the Reagan administration became involved in events in El Salvador and Nicaragua. *(Organizers should show that Reagan feared that Latin American countries would fall under Soviet influence.*

In El Salvador, the administration offered aid to the Duarte government, which was fighting rebels in a civil war. In Nicaragua, the administration used the CIA to support Contras in their war with the leftist Sandinista government.) Have students use their organizers to write an article describing the Reagan administration's actions in Central America. Ask volunteers to read their articles to the class.

English Language Learners, Cooperative Learning

HOMEWORK *Tell students to imagine that it is the 1980s and that they are international TV reporters covering Central America. Have each student write a script describing how the Reagan administration became involved in El Salvador and Nicaragua.*

GLOBAL RELATIONS

Aiding the Contras. The term *Contras* comes from the Spanish term *contrarevolucionarios*, which means "counterrevolutionaries" in English. In the late 1970s Argentine government advisers began working with some former members of Nicaraguan dictator Anastasio Somoza's National Guard. These men became the first Contras. The CIA also played an important role in developing the Contras. In 1979 the CIA helped evacuate some Contras from Nicaragua to Miami in a plane disguised with Red Cross symbols. President Reagan approved some $20 million in assistance to the Contras during his first year in office.

CRITICAL THINKING Why might the fact that the United States supported the Contras seem surprising?

ANSWER: Some students might suggest that it is surprising that the United States would support people with anti-democratic views.

VISUAL RECORD ANSWER

Students might suggest that the demonstrators have anti-communist sentiments.

INTERPRETING THE VISUAL RECORD

Solidarity. These Boston residents are demonstrating to show their support for Solidarity. *What do the people's signs reveal about their motives for demonstrating?*

PRESIDENTIAL Lives

Ronald Reagan

1911–
In Office 1981–1989

Ronald Reagan was nicknamed the Great Communicator because of his speaking abilities. One of Reagan's gifts was a sharp wit. After a debate with Jimmy Carter during the 1980 campaign, a reporter asked if he had been nervous appearing on stage with the president. "No, not at all," Reagan replied. Then, referring to his career in Hollywood, he added, "I've been on the same stage with John Wayne."

Reagan's wit helped reassure the nation after a lone gunman shot him on March 30, 1981. As the wounded president was wheeled into the operating room, he looked around at the surgeons and joked, "Please assure me that you are all Republicans!" While he was recuperating in intensive care, Reagan sent several humorous notes to his staff members. One read, "If I had had this much attention in Hollywood, I'd have stayed there!"

In December 1981 Poland's government changed its stand and instituted martial law. Government troops shut down Solidarity centers and arrested union leaders. Expecting resistance, Soviet troops prepared to brutally "restore order." This move was similar to Soviet actions in Hungary in 1956 and in Czechoslovakia in 1968. Reagan warned the Soviets not to invade Poland and called for new trade restrictions against the Soviet Union. Moscow heeded the warning and stayed out of Poland.

Tensions between the United States and the Soviet Union flared again in 1983. On September 1, the Soviets shot down a Korean commercial airliner over Soviet airspace. All 269 passengers, including many Americans, were killed. Despite an international outcry, the Soviets defended their action, claiming the plane had been spying. Later that year, when the United States placed nuclear missiles in Great Britain and Germany, the Soviets walked out of arms-control talks. The Soviets boycotted the 1984 Summer Olympics in Los Angeles, and relations between the two superpowers sank to their lowest point in years.

✔ **READING CHECK: Sequencing** In what order of events did U.S.-Soviet relations worsen? **1979—Soviet invasion of Afghanistan; 1980–81—strikes in Poland, Soviets threaten to intervene; 1983—Korean airliner shot down; 1984—Soviet Union boycotts Olympics**

Reagan and Latin America

Fearing that developing nations in Latin America would fall under Soviet influence, President Reagan increased U.S. involvement in the region. He focused in particular on the countries of El Salvador and Nicaragua.

The Reagan administration soon found itself pulled into events in El Salvador. In 1979 a group of young military officers had seized power and instituted a brutal government. The army and so-called death squads killed and tortured opposition leaders. Fighting intensified between government forces and rebels who demanded radical reform.

In 1984 **José Napoleón Duarte,** a moderate, won election by promising reforms and an end to the civil war. Eager to prevent a rebel victory that might allow El Salvador to fall under Soviet influence, the Reagan administration offered Duarte military and economic aid and sent military advisers to train government troops. The civil war raged on, however, until intense international pressure forced both sides to sign a peace treaty in 1992.

REVIEW

Have students complete the **Section 1 Review** on p. 775.

ASSESS

Have students complete **Daily Quiz 25.1.** As **Alternative Assessment,** you may want to use the headlines or the dialogue in this section's lessons.

RETEACH

Have students complete **Main Idea Activity for English Language Learners and Special-Needs Students 26.1.** Then organize students into small groups. Have each group prepare an outline of one of the subsections of Section 1. Ask each group to present its outline to the class, and ask the class to supply any information missing from groups' outlines.
English Language Learners, Cooperative Learning

EXTEND

Organize the class into four groups. Assign each group one of the following topics: the New Right movement, the Solidarity movement, the Islamic Revolution in Iran, or the Sandinista revolution. Have each group conduct research on its assigned movement, with a focus on the movement's guiding principles, key figures in the movement, and important events in the movement's history. Then have each group create a multimedia presentation on its topic. Have students give their presentations to the class. **Block Scheduling, Cooperative Learning**

Reagan also focused U.S. attention on the political situation in Nicaragua. In 1979, Nicaraguan rebels known as **Sandinistas** had overthrown the dictatorship of Anastasio Somoza. The Somoza family had controlled Nicaragua since the 1930s. Soon after he took office, Reagan cut all U.S. aid to Nicaragua. He argued that the Sandinistas were backed by the Soviet Union. He also charged that the Sandinistas were "exporting revolution" by shipping Cuban and Soviet weapons to the rebels in El Salvador.

The Sandinistas reacted to U.S. pressure by strengthening their ties to Soviet bloc countries. Reagan then decided to support the Nicaraguan **Contras,** a rebel army recruited, financed, and armed by the CIA. Reagan hoped the group would overthrow the Sandinista government. He called the Contras "freedom fighters" and even compared them to the founders of the United States.

Many Americans opposed the CIA-sponsored war against the Sandinistas. They feared that it would end up as devastating as the Vietnam War had been. In response, Congress passed laws that banned U.S. action against the Sandinista government. The Boland Amendment of 1984 stopped any U.S. government agency, including the CIA, from giving military aid to the Contras. Americans would soon learn that the White House continued to finance the Contras despite the congressional ban.

With funds provided by the CIA, Contras were equipped with a variety of weapons.

✔ **READING CHECK: Drawing Conclusions** How was U.S. involvement in El Salvador and Nicaragua related to the Cold War? Reagan feared that the Soviet Union would gain power in Central and South America, bringing Latin America into the Cold War.

SECTION 1 REVIEW

1. **Define and explain:**
   supply-side economics

2. **Identify and explain:**
   Iran hostage crisis
   Ayatollah Khomeini
   Ronald Reagan
   New Right
   Moral Majority
   Jerry Falwell
   Reaganomics
   Strategic Defense Initiative
   Solidarity
   Lech Walesa
   José Napoleón Duarte
   Sandinistas
   Contras

3. **Categorizing** Copy the graphic organizer below. Use it to list the factors that led to Ronald Reagan's victory over Jimmy Carter in 1980.

VICTORY

4. **Finding the Main Idea**
   a. Describe President Reagan's economic program, and evaluate its level of success.
   b. What effect did the Cold War have on defense spending?
   c. Imagine that you are a citizen of El Salvador or Nicaragua in the early 1980s. Describe the political situation in your country and explain why you think the United States is intervening in your country's affairs.

5. **Writing and Critical Thinking**
   Summarizing Write an opening statement for President Reagan to give in a 1984 presidential debate.
   Consider:
   • Reagan's opinion of the role of government
   • the administration's approach to the economy
   • the administration's approach to the Cold War

Homework Practice Online
keyword: SE3 HP26

OBJECTIVE 1 Analyze how the Republicans won the 1984 election, and discuss how the makeup of the Supreme Court changed in the 1980s.

OBJECTIVE 2 Describe what events began to shake public confidence in the economy.

OBJECTIVE 3 Explain how the Iran-Contra affair developed.

OBJECTIVE 4 Identify the developments that eased tensions between the United States and the Soviet Union in the late 1980s.

 LET'S GET STARTED!

As students enter the classroom, tell them to read the Reagan campaign poster on this page. Ask students to respond to the poster in writing. Have them identify the ideas that the poster is trying to convey and to characterize its mood. Ask volunteers to share their answers with the class. Tell students that in Section 2 they will learn about how confidence in the economy wavered during Ronald Reagan's second term in office.

SECTION 2

READ TO DISCOVER

1. How did the Republicans win the 1984 election, and how did the makeup of the Supreme Court change in the 1980s?
2. What events began to shake public confidence in the economy?
3. How did the Iran-Contra affair develop?
4. What developments eased tensions between the United States and the Soviet Union in the late 1980s?

DEFINE

insider trading
glasnost
perestroika

IDENTIFY

Walter Mondale
Geraldine Ferraro
Sandra Day O'Connor
Gramm-Rudman-Hollings Act
S&L crisis
Iran-Contra affair
Oliver North
Mikhail Gorbachev
Intermediate-Range Nuclear Forces Treaty

WHY IT MATTERS TODAY

The U.S. government continues to strive for a balanced federal budget. Use **CNNfyi.com** or other **current events** sources to find out recent federal budget proposals. Record your findings in your journal.

Reagan's Second Term

EYEWITNESSES TO History *"It's morning again in America. . . . In a town not too far from where you live, a young family has just moved into a new home. Three years ago, even the smallest house seemed completely out of reach. Right down the street, one of the neighbors has just bought himself a new car with all the options. The factory down the river is working again. Not long ago, people were saying it probably would be closed forever. . . . Life is better. America is back."*

—Ronald Reagan campaign ad, 1984

Reagan-Bush campaign poster

This advertising campaign promoted the economic achievements of Ronald Reagan's first term in office. By 1984 the economy was booming, consumerism was growing, and the malaise of the 1970s was fading. Reagan's supporters asked voters, "Now that our country is turning around, why turn back?"

The Election of 1984

A small-scale military action in 1983 added to President Reagan's popularity heading into his 1984 re-election campaign. On the tiny Caribbean island of Grenada, a rebel group overthrew the government and killed the prime minister. Several Caribbean nations requested U.S. intervention. Beginning October 25, 1983, several thousand U.S. Marines and Army Rangers went ashore on Grenada. They unseated the coup leaders and set up a government favorable to the United States. The successful operation boosted Americans' confidence in the military.

Soon after the Grenada invasion, Reagan announced that he and Vice President George Bush would seek a second term. Former vice president **Walter Mondale** won the Democratic nomination. He picked Representative **Geraldine Ferraro** of New York as his running mate. Ferraro became the first woman to run on a major-party presidential ticket. Some predicted Ferraro's presence would increase support for the Democratic Party among women. Ferraro commented on the situation.

 History Makers Speak *"By choosing an American woman to run for our nation's second-highest office, you send a powerful signal to all Americans. . . . There are no doors we cannot unlock. We will place no limits on achievement. If we can do this, we can do anything."*

—Geraldine Ferraro, *Ferraro: My Story*

Republicans had also been taking steps to expand the role of women in their party. President Reagan had appointed several women to high public offices, including Elizabeth Dole as secretary of transportation and Margaret Heckler as secretary of health and human services. He also appointed Jeane Kirkpatrick as head of the U.S. delegation to the United Nations. She was the first woman to hold the post.

TEACH OBJECTIVE 1

LEVEL 1: Pair students and ask each pair to draw two political cartoons depicting how the Republicans won the 1984 election and how the makeup of the Supreme Court changed in the 1980s. *(Pairs' cartoons should depict the Republicans' efforts to expand the role of women in their party, the appointment of the first woman to the Supreme Court, and the Court's more conservative membership.)* Display pairs' cartoons around the classroom.
English Language Learners, Cooperative Learning

LEVEL 2: Tell students to imagine that they are editors who must write a summary for the dust jacket of a book about the Supreme Court during the 1980s. Have each student write a summary about how the Republicans won the 1984 election and how the makeup of the Supreme Court changed during the 1980s. *(See the Level 1 lesson for the correct changes.)* Ask volunteers to read their dust-jacket summaries to the class.

LEVEL 3: Tell each student to write a short poem about how the Republicans won the 1984 election and how the makeup of the Supreme Court changed during the 1980s. *(See the Level 1 lesson for the correct changes.)* Ask volunteers to recite their poems to the class. Students may wish to include their poems in their portfolios.

Republicans also sought—and received—the support of women who did not identify with the feminist movement. Female opponents of the Equal Rights Amendment and abortion embraced the Republican Party. As a result, the percentage of female delegates to the Republican National Convention increased from 24 percent in 1980 to 44 percent in 1984.

Ferraro's presence did not ultimately win many votes for the Democrats. On election day, Reagan received 54.5 million popular votes to Mondale's 37.6 million. The Republicans swept the electoral vote 525 to 13.

The Supreme Court

One issue during the 1984 presidential campaign was the growing conservative emphasis of the Supreme Court. President Reagan vowed to appoint justices who would uphold his conservative agenda. In 1981 he had appointed conservative justice **Sandra Day O'Connor**, the first woman ever to serve on the Supreme Court.

Sandra Day O'Connor

Sandra Day O'Connor was born in El Paso, Texas, in 1930. She grew up working on her family's cattle ranch. "The whole family had to get out and help on the ranch," she recalled. "We learned to be pretty independent that way." She attended Stanford University and graduated from Stanford Law School in 1952. At Stanford, she met and married fellow law student John O'Connor.

O'Connor began her law career in California but later moved to Arizona. There she served as Arizona's assistant attorney general from 1965 to 1969. From 1974 to 1981, she served in several different judicial positions before being appointed to the Supreme Court. O'Connor was once asked whether she would vote differently than a male justice. She responded to the question.

History Makers Speak
"Judges are supposed to be objective; they're supposed to study and look at the law and apply the law to the particular case in an objective way, not from any particular point of view. So does being a woman make a difference in what answer is given? I tend to think that probably at the end of the day, a wise old woman and a wise old man are going to reach the same answer."

—Sandra Day O'Connor

INTERPRETING THE VISUAL RECORD
1984. Democratic candidates Water Mondale and Geraldine Ferraro received strong support at this 1984 parade in New York. The poster at left shows Ferraro as Liberty. *What point do you think the poster was making about Ferraro's candidacy?*

Research on the ROM
Free Find:
Sandra Day O'Connor
After reading about Sandra Day O'Connor on the **Holt Researcher CD–ROM**, write a biography about one of your favorite people. Describe the choices he or she made and the obstacles he or she overcame.

CULTURE

Professional Women. Sandra Day O'Connor experienced firsthand the problem of gender discrimination. After graduating third in her law school class in 1952—future chief justice William Rehnquist was ranked first—O'Connor could not find a job as an attorney with a private law firm because she was a woman. One law firm offered her a job as a legal secretary. Instead, O'Connor chose to practice law as a county deputy attorney. That position marked the beginning of O'Connor's long career in public service.

CRITICAL THINKING How might women respond to such discrimination today?
ANSWER: Students might mention that the 1964 Civil Rights Act made sex discrimination illegal. Women today also have legal recourse to address discrimination.

THAT'S INTERESTING!
In the 1984 election, Ronald Reagan won the electoral votes of 49 states. Walter Mondale only won the votes of the District of Columbia and Minnesota, his home state.

VISUAL RECORD ANSWER
Students might suggest that the poster is making the point that Ferraro was a standard-bearer for women

ALL LEVELS: Tell students that developments during President Reagan's second term began to shake the public's confidence in the economy. To help students understand the factors that led to this, copy the graphic organizer at right on the chalkboard, omitting the italicized answers. Have each student complete it. Ask volunteers to share their answers with the class. To conclude, ask students to name some ways in which the nation's economic health is measured. *(Students might mention the Dow Jones average, inflation, unemployment, and so on.)* Tell students that falling public confidence in the economy can exacerbate an economic downturn as consumers reduce spending. **English Language Learners**

Falling Confidence in the Economy

1. *huge federal deficits lead to the passage of the Gramm-Rudman-Hollings Act*
2. *illegal insider trading—the use of personal confidential information for personal gain—is revealed*
3. *stock market crash leads to a sharp drop in stock values*
4. *the S&L crisis forces the federal government to pay billions of dollars to cover losses*

HOMEWORK *Ask students to write summaries of the following terms: insider trading, stock market crash of 1987, the S&L crisis, the Gramm-Rudman-Hollings Act.*

The Bork Nomination.
Reagan's nomination of Robert Bork to the Supreme Court led to an unprecedented public debate over the nominee's fitness to serve on the Court. Opponents and supporters mounted public relations campaigns that included radio and television advertisements. Some observers complained that the media coverage was unfair because it favored those who were opposed to Bork's confirmation.

CRITICAL THINKING Should conflicts over appointments to the Supreme Court be waged like other political battles?

ANSWER: Answers will vary. Some students might argue that the Supreme Court should be separate from politics because it is responsible for interpreting the Constitution. Other students might argue that Supreme Court decisions can have a huge impact on U.S. politics and that Court nominations should therefore be debated.

POLITICAL CARTOON ANSWER
Students might suggest that the cartoonist had a favorable opinion, as indicated by the caption and the pleased look on the statue's face.

GRAPH ANSWERS
about $1.5 trillion; almost $3 trillion

"WELL, IT'S ABOUT TIME"

© 1981 BY HERBLOCK IN THE WASHINGTON POST

INTERPRETING POLITICAL CARTOONS

The Supreme Court. In this 1981 cartoon the spirit of Justice comments on Sandra Day O'Connor's appointment to the Supreme Court. *What do you think was the cartoonist's opinion of the appointment?*

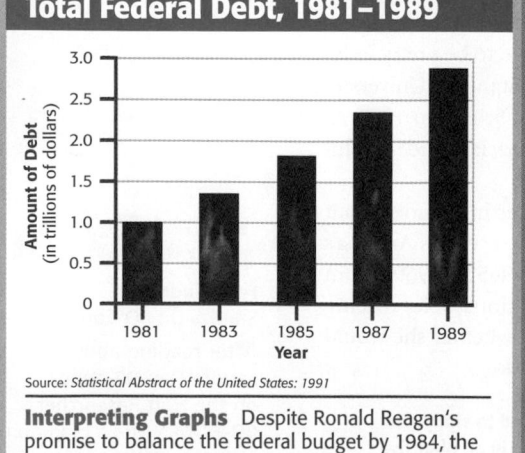

Total Federal Debt, 1981–1989

Amount of Debt (in trillions of dollars)

Year: 1981, 1983, 1985, 1987, 1989

Source: Statistical Abstract of the United States: 1991

Interpreting Graphs Despite Ronald Reagan's promise to balance the federal budget by 1984, the total federal debt continued to grow dramatically throughout the 1980s.

? Skills Assessment Approximately how much was the federal debt in 1984? in 1989?

As a Supreme Court justice, O'Connor has proven to be less conservative than many supporters originally thought she would be. She has often delivered the deciding vote when the Court has been split on certain issues.

When Chief Justice Warren Burger retired in 1986, Reagan elevated Associate Justice William Rehnquist to chief justice. To fill Rehnquist's position, Reagan nominated Antonin Scalia, a conservative. When another justice retired in 1987, Reagan nominated Robert Bork, a federal judge and law professor who held a much narrower interpretation of the Bill of Rights than the Court had upheld in recent years. He believed, for example, that civil rights laws restricted individual freedoms. Bork's views concerned many people, including a number of senators. The Senate rejected Bork's nomination. Reagan's next choice, Douglas Ginsberg, withdrew after press reports emerged that he had smoked marijuana as a law professor. Conservative judge Anthony Kennedy of California won Senate confirmation and joined the Supreme Court in 1988.

✔ **READING CHECK: Drawing Conclusions** How can the executive and legislative branches exert influence over the Supreme Court? **The executive branch exerts influence on the Supreme Court through its appointments. The legislative branch confirms appointments.**

Concerns over the Economy

In addition to the failure of the Bork nomination, the growing federal deficit was a sign that the so-called Reagan Revolution was weakening. The deficit had topped $200 billion in 1985. Seeking to balance the budget with forced spending cuts, Congress passed the Balanced Budget and Emergency Control Act in 1985. It was called the **Gramm-Rudman-Hollings Act** after its Senate sponsors. The law required automatic across-the-board cuts in government spending when the deficit exceeded a certain amount. Other legislation focused on specific issues. The Tax Reform Law of 1986, for example, eliminated special tax breaks that certain groups had been receiving.

The stock market also showed signs of trouble. President Reagan's tax cuts and business deregulation had stimulated a stock market boom. With this boom came a wave of illegal **insider trading**—the use of confidential financial information for personal gain. Stockbroker Chris Burke described the culture of the times.

 History Makers Speak

"**Wall Street in the 1980s was like nowhere else on this planet. It was a culture of greed and back-stabbing and partying. Your best buddy is the one who's gonna stab you in the back tomorrow if it means some more greenbacks in his pocket. It wasn't a good way to live.**"

—Chris Burke, quoted in *The Century*, by Peter Jennings and Todd Brewster

Several large brokerage firms pleaded guilty to illegal activities and faced severe penalties. These scandals eroded investors' trust in stockbrokers.

LEVEL 1: Pair students and have each pair create an annotated time line of the events leading up to the congressional investigation of the Iran-Contra affair. (*Time lines should include the following: Congress cuts off funds to the Contras; the Reagan administration sells arms to Iran to obtain the release of hostages in Lebanon; the administration uses profits from the arms sales to illegally fund the Contras; the illegal arms sales are discovered.*) Ask volunteers to share their time lines with the class. To conclude, lead the class in a discussion about why the Iran-Contra affair was considered a serious crisis in government.

English Language Learners, Cooperative Learning

LEVELS 2 AND 3: Ask students why the Iran-Contra affair was considered a serious government crisis. (*Students might point out that the Reagan administration circumvented congressional oversight of the government's conduct of foreign policy by using third-party funds to pay for the operation.*) Have each student write a short analytical essay about how the Iran-Contra affair developed and the constitutional implications of the administration's actions. (*See the Level 1 lesson for the correct events.*) Ask volunteers to read their essays to the class.

Then, on October 19, 1987, after several years of a bull market, the stock market crashed. On paper, stock losses totaled half a $1 trillion. The value of Eastman Kodak stock, for example, fell by more than 30 percent. Other major corporations experienced similar sharp drops in their stock values.

A crisis also hit the nation's savings and loan (S&L) associations and banking industry. Freed of federal regulation, banks and S&Ls, particularly in the Southwest, had made risky loans to developers to build office towers, shopping malls, and other projects. In the late 1980s the real-estate market collapsed. Hundreds of S&Ls and banks that had loaned money to developers failed. Since the federal government insures S&L and bank depositors, it had to pay billions of dollars to cover these losses, further straining the federal budget. The **S&L crisis** weakened many people's confidence in the health of the economy.

✔ **READING CHECK: Analyzing Information** How did the deregulation of some businesses and financial institutions affect the economy?
It allowed some businesses to involve themselves in risky deals, which meant they often could not repay loans to S&Ls.

The Iran-Contra Affair

The Reagan administration also faced continued problems in the Middle East and Latin America. These frustrations led to the most serious crisis to hit the Reagan White House—the **Iran-Contra affair**.

After Congress cut off funds for the Contras' war against Nicaragua's Sandinista government, the Reagan administration sought other sources of funding. At the same time, the White House was secretly bargaining with Iran for the release of U.S. hostages held by pro-Iranian groups in Lebanon. As part of the bargain, the administration shipped more than 500 antitank missiles to Iran by way of Israel. Without informing Congress, the administration used the profits from these arms sales to pay for weapons and supplies for the Contras.

When knowledge of the arms sales became public in 1986, President Reagan appointed a commission to investigate. The commission cleared Reagan of any direct involvement. However, it heavily criticized other White House officials, some of whom resigned. The secret funding of the Contra war soon leaked out as well. The American public learned that Lieutenant Colonel **Oliver North**, a White House aide, had funneled millions of dollars from the Iranian arms sales to the Contras after Congress had forbidden direct U.S. government aid.

In 1987, House and Senate committees investigated the affair. North admitted that he and his secretary, Fawn Hall, had destroyed key documents. However, North insisted that they had acted out of loyalty and patriotism. North testified: "I am not in the habit of questioning my superiors. . . . I don't believe that what we did even under those circumstances is wrong or illegal."

In its report, the Senate committee denounced North's activities and criticized the loose White House management style that had allowed North to operate as he did. The chair of the Senate committee, Senator Daniel Inouye (in-oh-e)

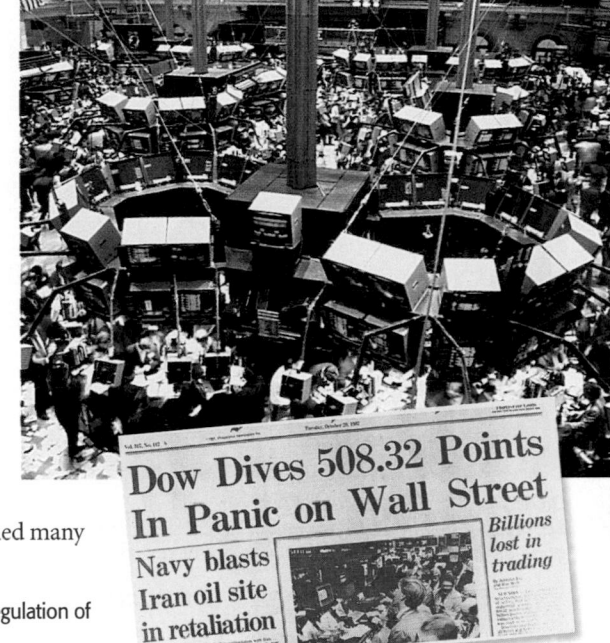

Dow Dives 508.32 Points In Panic on Wall Street

Navy blasts Iran oil site in retaliation

Billions lost in trading

INTERPRETING THE VISUAL RECORD

Wall Street. The 1987 stock market crash brought back memories of the Great Depression. **Does this picture of the New York Stock Exchange reflect the headline shown? Explain your answer.**

HISTORY MAKERS SPEAK

George Shultz in *Reagan: The Man and His Presidency*

The Iran-Contra Affair. Former secretary of state George Shultz reflected on the effect of the Iran-Contra affair on President Reagan. "The revelations weighed on him, and I think the thing that bothered Ronald Reagan more than anything else was that before, he had always felt that if he believed something was in the U.S. interest, he could go to the American people and explain it, and they would support him. He tried to do that in this case, and it was obvious that they didn't support him."

CRITICAL THINKING What might Shultz's remarks reveal about Reagan's attitude toward the Iran-Contra affair?

ANSWER: Students might suggest that Reagan believed he was acting in the nation's best interest.

THAT'S INTERESTING!

In 1980 a total of 11 S&Ls failed. Over the next eight years another 552 S&Ls failed, with 190 failing in 1988 alone.

VISUAL RECORD ANSWER
Answers will vary but students might suggest that the photograph shows panic.

LEVEL 1: Tell students that when Mikhail Gorbachev became leader of the Soviet Union in 1985, he initiated several measures that eased tensions between the United States and the Soviet Union. Ask students to name these measures and other developments that eased Cold War tensions. Compile a list of responses on the chalkboard. (*Students should mention glasnost, perestroika, the INF Treaty, Gorbachev's policy of détente with the United States, and the withdrawal of Soviet troops from Afghanistan.*) Then have each student write a paragraph about the developments that eased tensions between the United States and the Soviet Union in the late 1980s.

English Language Learners

LEVEL 2: Tell students to imagine that they are writing a book about the easing of Cold War tensions. Have each student prepare a brief summary of a chapter about the developments that eased tensions between the United States and the Soviet Union in the late 1980s. (*See the Level 1 lesson for the correct developments.*) Ask volunteers to share their summaries with the class.

CONSTITUTIONAL HERITAGE

The Power to Make Foreign Policy. An important issue at stake in the Iran-Contra affair was whether Congress and the president should share the power to make U.S. foreign policy. Oliver North and others responsible for diverting funds to the Contras acted in violation of the Boland Amendment, which forbade the U.S. government from providing any military or paramilitary support to the Contras. Moreover, the Constitution gives Congress the exclusive power to appropriate funds to carry out the business of the United States. As historian Theodore Draper put it, the use of foreign or private funds to carry out U.S. foreign-policy goals would put "wealthy donors or foreign countries in a position to conduct, determine, or make American foreign policy."

CRITICAL THINKING Why might the constitutional power to make foreign policy have been given to two branches of government?

ANSWER: Students might suggest that the framers had been guided by the principle of checks and balances.

MAP ANSWER

El Salvador, Grenada, Guatemala, Haiti, and Nicaragua

Oliver North testified before the Senate that he had acted for the good of the country.

of Hawaii, countered North's claim that he was just following orders.

> *History Makers Speak*
>
> **"[The] colonel was well aware that he was subject to the Uniform Code of Military Justice. . . . And that code makes it abundantly clear that orders of a superior officer must be obeyed by subordinate [lower in rank] members—but it is lawful orders. . . . In fact, it says members of the military have an obligation to disobey unlawful orders."**
>
> —Daniel Inouye, quoted in *Guts and Glory*, by Ben Bradlee, Jr.

In 1988 a court-appointed special prosecutor filed criminal charges against North and against Reagan's national security adviser, Admiral John Poindexter. North was convicted on various charges, including the destruction of government documents and lying to Congress. The conviction was later reversed on a legal technicality.

✔ **READING CHECK: Making Predictions** How did the Iran-Contra affair affect the Reagan administration? It made the administration appear unorganized, allowing illegal actions to take place without the knowledge of the president and other top officials.

Central America and the Caribbean, 1980s

Interpreting Maps The United States intervened in Central America and the Caribbean several times during the 1980s.

? HUMAN SYSTEMS Which Caribbean and Central American nations saw guerrilla activity or civil war during the 1980s?

⚜ Guerrilla activity or civil war

🧍 U.S. military presence or intervention

UNITED STATES

Gulf of Mexico

Miami

ATLANTIC OCEAN

Havana

BAHAMAS

CUBA

Guantánamo Bay (U.S. base)

1986: Duvalier ousted; political instability followed

MEXICO

Mexico City

CAYMAN IS. (Br.)

JAMAICA

Kingston

HAITI

Port-au-Prince

DOMINICAN REPUBLIC

Santo Domingo

PUERTO RICO (U.S.)

GUATEMALA 1982

Belmopan

BELIZE

HONDURAS

1983, 1988

CARIBBEAN SEA

PACIFIC OCEAN

Guatemala City

EL SALVADOR 1981

San Salvador

Tegucigalpa

NICARAGUA

Managua

COSTA RICA

San José

Panama Canal

PANAMA

GRENADA 1983

Caracas

1981–1992: Civil war between U.S.-backed Salvadoran government and leftist guerrillas supported by Cuba and Nicaragua

1989

VENEZUELA

Georgetown

Scale at 20°N:
0   250   500 Miles
0   250   500 Kilometers
Scale varies with latitude.
Miller Cylindrical Projection

1981–1987: United States aided the anti-Sandinista Contras in Nicaragua; civil war ended in 1990

Bogotá

COLOMBIA

GUYANA

SURINAME

BRAZIL

LEVEL 3: Tell students to imagine that they are Mikhail Gorbachev. Have each student write an excerpt from an imaginary memoir in which he or she describes the developments that eased tensions between the United States and the Soviet Union in the late 1980s. *(See the Level 1 lesson for the correct developments.)* Ask volunteers to read their memoirs to the class. Students may wish to include their memoirs in their portfolios.

NOTE: For an additional teaching idea, see the Chapter 26 unfinished story alternatives lesson in the **Creative Teaching Strategies** handbook.

SPOTLIGHT
on the INF Treaty

Have students conduct research on the INF Treaty and why it was considered an important measure. Students should focus their research on antinuclear protests in Europe prior to the treaty negotiations, the strategic importance of medium-range missiles, and the provisions of the treaty. Have each student write a report about his or her findings.
Block Scheduling

Skill-Building Strategies

Creating an Outline

Along with formulating a hypothesis, creating an outline is an indispensable part of preparing to write a history research paper. An *outline* is an organizational tool that summarizes the ideas and evidence that one plans to discuss in a speech or piece of writing. By presenting this information concisely and in a logical order, an outline serves as a kind of "road map" that can make the actual process of writing a paper much easier.

How to Create an Outline

1. **Write your thesis statement.** First, formulate the hypothesis that you plan to focus on in your paper and write it out in a short, declarative statement. This thesis statement should make up the first major heading of your outline and be included in your paper's introduction.
2. **Organize your material.** Once you have settled on a thesis statement, organize logically the material that you wish to present in the paper. Determine what information belongs in the introduction, what should make up the body of the paper, and what to put in the conclusion.
3. **Summarize the main ideas.** Identify and briefly summarize the main ideas that you plan to use to support your thesis statement. Each of these main ideas should serve as a major heading in your outline and be labeled with a Roman numeral.
4. **List the supporting details.** As you summarize each main idea, identify the details or facts that support it and list them as subheadings in your outline. Make sure to order the subheadings logically and label them with descending levels of letters and numbers.

5. **Put your outline to use.** When you write your paper, structure it according to your outline. Each major heading, for instance, might form the basis of a topic sentence that begins a paragraph. Corresponding subheadings would then indicate the content of each paragraph. In a more lengthy paper, each subheading might constitute the basis of an entire paragraph.

Applying the Skill

Read the following thesis statement, which presents a hypothesis about the causes of the Iran-Contra affair and President Reagan's responsibility for the crisis. Then create an outline for the portion of this chapter that discusses the Iran-Contra affair and use it to evaluate the statement.

> A desire to free U.S. hostages held in Lebanon and fight communism in Nicaragua led to the Iran-Contra affair. White House officials sold weapons to Iran and used the profits to supply the Contras. As president of the United States Ronald Reagan was responsible for the actions of people serving in his administration.

Practicing the Skill

Use your outline to answer the following questions.
1. What main ideas serve as major headings in your outline?
2. What supporting details are listed as subheadings in your outline?
3. How did you order the headings and subheadings in your outline?
4. How does your outline support your thesis statement?

Cold War Tensions Ease

The most significant achievement of President Reagan's second term was a dramatic easing of Cold War hostilities. When **Mikhail Gorbachev** became leader of the Soviet Union in 1985, a new era of Soviet history began.

By the 1980s the Soviet Union was burdened by a failing economy, a repressive political system, and heavy military costs. Gorbachev's initiatives included **glasnost** (GLAZ-nohst), his policy of openness that promised more freedom for the Soviet people. Equally dramatic was **perestroika** (per-uh-STROY-kuh)— Gorbachev's plan to restructure the Soviet economy and government. On the economic front, he called for increased foreign trade and reduced military spending.

REVIEW

Have students complete the **Section 2 Review** on p. 782.

ASSESS

Have students complete **Daily Quiz 26.2**. As **Alternative Assessment**, you may want to use the memoir or the time line in this section's lessons.

RETEACH

Have students complete **Main Idea Activity for English Language Learners and Special-Needs Students 26.2**. Organize students into small groups and assign each group a subsection. Have each group prepare a brief summary of the material in its subsection. Ask students to read their summaries to the class. **English Language Learners, Cooperative Learning**

EXTEND

Have students conduct research on one of the key people listed in this chapter. Then have each student prepare a short "Who Am I?" monologue in the role of his or her chosen person, omitting the person's name. Have students deliver their monologues to the class, then ask students to identify the person. **Block Scheduling**

INTERPRETING THE VISUAL RECORD

The Reagan style. President Reagan and his wife, Nancy, hosted Mikhail and Raisa Gorbachev at the Reagans' ranch in California. **How does the setting for this photograph reflect Reagan's style?**

The revenues from these changes were to be used to modernize Soviet factories. These reforms marked the first time since before the Bolshevik Revolution that a Soviet leader had seemed open to some ideas of capitalist democratic government. These reforms began to dramatically change life in the Soviet Union. Glasnost encouraged people to criticize the government. Many complained about the economy, which some felt had been weakened by the heightened arms race of the 1980s.

To further his domestic goals and defuse the costly Cold War conflict, Gorbachev pursued détente with the United States. In 1987, after a series of meetings, Gorbachev and President Reagan signed the **Intermediate-Range Nuclear Forces (INF) Treaty**. This treaty eliminated all medium-range nuclear weapons from Europe. Gorbachev also agreed to withdraw Soviet troops from Afghanistan. Gorbachev addressed these issues in a speech to the United Nations in 1988.

 History Makers Speak

❝The use or threat of force no longer can or must be an instrument of foreign policy. . . . All of us, and primarily the stronger of us, must exercise self-restraint and totally rule out any outward-oriented use of force.❞

—Mikhail Gorbachev, speech, December 9, 1988

In May 1988, as the Senate prepared to ratify the INF Treaty, Reagan flew to Moscow. In front of television cameras, the U.S. president and the Soviet leader embraced like old friends.

✔ **READING CHECK: Evaluating** How did changes made by Soviet leader Mikhail Gorbachev affect the United States? *Glasnost and perestroika led to more friendly relations with the United States.*

SECTION 2 REVIEW

1. Define and explain:
insider trading   perestroika
glasnost

2. Identify and explain:
Walter Mondale
Geraldine Ferraro
Sandra Day O'Connor
Gramm-Rudman-Hollings Act
S&L crisis
Iran-Contra affair
Oliver North
Mikhail Gorbachev
Intermediate-Range
   Nuclear Forces Treaty

3. Summarizing Copy the graphic organizer below. Use it to show how each political party tried to appeal to voters in the 1984 presidential election.

Voters

Republicans   Democrats

4. **Finding the Main Idea**

a. How did President Reagan change the makeup of the Supreme Court?

b. Imagine that you are a member of a congressional committee appointed to investigate the Iran-Contra affair. Write a short report that summarizes the results of the investigation.

c. What led to an easing of Cold War tensions in the late 1980s? What were some outcomes of this change?

5. **Writing and Critical Thinking**

Analyzing Information Write a letter to a friend in Europe explaining why public confidence in the economy was shaken in the late 1980s.
Consider:
• the federal deficit
• the stock market crash
• the S&L crisis

Homework Practice Online
keyword: SE3 HP26

After completing Section 3, students should be able to:

OBJECTIVE 1 Summarize how American society changed in the 1980s.

OBJECTIVE 2 Explain how the Cold War ended.

OBJECTIVE 3 Describe what led to the Persian Gulf War, and analyze how it differed from previous U.S. military conflicts.

OBJECTIVE 4 Discuss the domestic problems the Bush administration faced.

📀 LET'S GET STARTED!

Write the following statement on the chalkboard: *Presidential popularity usually increases during a war just as it decreases during economic hard times.* As students enter the classroom, have them respond to the statement in writing. Ask students to share their responses with the class. Tell students that in Section 3, they will learn more about the presidency of George Bush, whose term in office could be described by the statement above.

SECTION ③

Bush and Life in the 1980s

EYEWITNESSES to History ❝*What the president and Mrs. Reagan have done is extraordinary at a time in our history when there was a depressed mood in this country. They came and made it positive. How can you put a value on that? . . . If we have all these negative feelings, I don't think we can function as well as an individual or as a family or as a nation. Didn't it make you feel better? That the nation itself was having a better feeling about itself?*❞

—Sugar Rautbord, quoted in *Ordinary Americans*, edited by Linda R. Monk

Sugar Rautbord of Chicago was just one of many Americans who felt the optimism generated by President Reagan in the 1980s. Many people hoped that this feeling would continue even after Reagan left office.

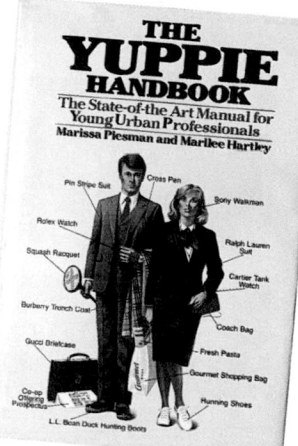

The Yuppie Handbook reflected the prosperity of the 1980s.

READ TO DISCOVER

1. How did American society change in the 1980s?
2. How did the Cold War end?
3. What led to the Persian Gulf War, and how did it differ from previous U.S. military conflicts?
4. What domestic problems did the Bush administration face?

IDENTIFY

Christa McAuliffe
Challenger
AIDS
Jesse Jackson
Michael Dukakis
Lloyd Bentsen
George Bush
Dan Quayle
Commonwealth of Independent States
Operation Desert Storm
Norman Schwarzkopf
Colin Powell
Americans with Disabilities Act
War on Drugs

WHY IT MATTERS TODAY

The Middle East is still an important focus of U.S. foreign policy. Use **CNNfyi.com** or other **current events** sources to find out about U.S. relations with one nation in the Middle East. Record your findings in your journal.

CNNfyi.com

America in the 1980s

Overall, the 1980s were much more positive years than the 1970s. Singer Bobby McFerrin summed up the mood of the times with his humorous 1988 tune, "Don't Worry, Be Happy." Other popular singers reflected the spirit of consumerism that characterized the era.

Economics. Most families benefited from the economic boom of the 1980s. Some did extremely well. Many young urban professionals—so-called yuppies—took advantage of the increased number of financial services jobs. Newly wealthy yuppies set many style trends during the decade.

However, not all families prospered, particularly single-parent families. From 1970 to 1991 the number of children living in single-parent households more than doubled. In 1991 some 20 percent of white children, 60 percent of African American children, and 30 percent of Hispanic children lived with one parent, usually their mothers. Most single parents faced serious financial burdens. "Let's see the beginning of the end of this business where if you're born poor, you gotta die in the slums," said Frank Lumpkin, an unemployed steelworker. "All these kids [around here today] can do is sell hubcaps and tires to the junkman. And steal. The answer to crime is full employment. We gotta start figurin' a way to get it. It's no mystery."

Science and technology. During the 1980s Americans spent more and more money on a vast new array of electronic goods. One of the most popular items was the personal computer (PC). The PC explosion began in 1981, when IBM introduced its first model for consumers. By 1984 IBM was selling 3 million PCs per year. Computer experts began to experiment with the possibilities of the new technology. In 1984 Jaron Lanier, a 24-year-old inventor, developed "virtual reality." This system allowed viewers to experience and interact with three-dimensional

SECTION ③ RESOURCES

REPRODUCIBLE
▶ Guided Reading Strategy 26.3
▶ Biography Reading 26: Sally Ride

TECHNOLOGY
▶ One-Stop Planner, Lesson 26.3
▶ Everyday Life in America Transparency 32: The AIDS Quilt Project, 1980s
▶ The American Nation Video Program Segment: U.S. Troops in the Persian Gulf; Teacher's Guide, pp. 199–200
▶ Holt Researcher: American History CD–ROM
▶ Homework Practice Online
▶ HRW Go site

REINFORCEMENT, REVIEW, AND ASSESSMENT
▶ Section 3 Review, p. 791
▶ Daily Quiz 26.3
▶ Main Idea Activity 26.3
▶ English Audio Summary 26.3
▶ Spanish Audio Summary 26.3

LEVEL 1: Tell students that economic growth during the 1980s and the availability of new technology contributed to cultural and social changes in the United States. Pair students and have each pair create a bulleted list of the changes in American society during the 1980s. *(Lists should include the growth of the yuppie lifestyle, a doubling of the number of single-parent households, the PC explosion and rise of techno-culture, and the emergence of AIDS.)* Have students share their lists with the class.
Cooperative Learning, English Language Learners

LEVEL 2: Tell students to imagine that they are sociologists writing a journal article about the 1980s. Have each student write an article about the ways American society changed during the 1980s. *(See the Level 1 lesson for the correct changes.)* Ask volunteers to read their articles to the class.

LEVEL 3: Tell students to imagine that they are cultural historians who must analyze the cultural and social changes that occurred during the 1980s for a television talk show. Pair students and have each pair create a dialogue about how American society changed in the 1980s. *(See the Level 1 lesson for the correct changes.)* Have students perform their dialogues for the class. **Cooperative Learning**

PEOPLE IN HISTORY

Christa McAuliffe. In many ways Christa McAuliffe was an average American. Born in Boston in 1948, she watched with excitement when astronauts from *Apollo 11* walked on the Moon in 1969. The following year she graduated from college and got married. She and her husband had two children. McAuliffe taught history and social sciences in secondary schools while her husband worked on a law degree. When she learned that NASA wanted to send an educator into space, she applied. McAuliffe was chosen from some 11,000 applicants for the position.

CRITICAL THINKING Why would NASA want to send a schoolteacher into space?

ANSWER: Students might suggest that the mission would generate interest in the space program because many Americans could identify with a person who was not a professional scientist.

Technology Resources

Everyday Life in America Transparency 32: The AIDS Quilt Project, 1980s

VISUAL RECORD ANSWER

Students might suggest that women, African Americans, and Asian Americans were represented in the crew.

A personal computer from the early 1980s

Analyzing Primary Sources

Drawing Inferences Why do you think a teacher was chosen to be the first civilian aboard the space shuttle?
to inspire students and get them interested in science

INTERPRETING THE VISUAL RECORD

Challenger. The seven members of the *Challenger* crew posed for this picture shortly before their tragic flight. *How did the crew represent the diversity of American society?*

images created solely through computer technology. Through virtual reality, people could actually experience an imaginary world.

Also in 1984, writer William Gibson published the science-fiction book *Neuromancer*. Gibson warned of a future in which technology takes over the world. In this new world, "The sky above the port was the color of television, turned to a dead channel." Gibson's work spawned a new generation of computer-oriented science fiction called cyberpunk.

As the cyberpunk writers noted, technology offered hopes as well as challenges. The U.S. space program also experienced these ups and downs. Plagued by rising costs and falling interest in missions, the space program had declined somewhat since the 1970s. To cut costs of future flights, scientists began working on a reusable space shuttle. In 1981 the launch and successful landing of the space shuttle *Columbia* marked a new age in space technology.

Five years later, NASA announced that a civilian would be allowed to travel aboard a space shuttle. Social studies teacher **Christa McAuliffe** was chosen for a flight aboard the space shuttle *Challenger*. McAuliffe exhibited an enormous enthusiasm for space exploration.

History Makers Speak

❝I remember the excitement in my home when the first satellites were launched. My parents were amazed and I was caught up with their wonder. . . . John Kennedy inspired me with his words about placing a man on the moon. . . . I watched the Space Age being born and I would like to participate.❞

—Christa McAuliffe, quoted in *No Downlink,* by Claus Jensen

About 70 seconds after takeoff in January 1986, *Challenger* exploded, killing all seven people on board. In part because of McAuliffe's participation, the takeoff was being watched live by a huge television audience. A horrified nation witnessed the worst disaster in NASA's history. Shuttle flights were suspended for two years until corrections could be made to the shuttle systems.

LEVEL 1: Tell students that economic problems in the Soviet Union led to the rapid political changes that marked the end of the Cold War. Pair students and have each pair create an annotated time line of the events that led to the Cold War's end. *(Time lines should include the Soviet policy of nonintervention, the free elections in Poland and Hungary, the fall of communist governments in Czechoslovakia and Romania, pro-democracy demonstrations in East Germany, the opening of the Berlin Wall and the reunification of Germany, and Gorbachev's loss of power and the dissolution of the Soviet Union.)* Have volunteers share their time lines with the class.
English Language Learners, Cooperative Learning

LEVEL 2: Tell students to imagine that they are citizens of East Germany who are experiencing the rapid political changes of the late 1980s and early 1990s. Have each student write a series of diary entries in which he or she describes the events that are leading to the end of the Cold War. *(See the Level 1 lesson for the correct events.)* Ask volunteers to read their diary entries to the class.

Health. In the 1980s many Americans became concerned by the emergence of a new, deadly disease called acquired immune deficiency syndrome, or **AIDS**. This syndrome represents the final deadly stage of an illness caused by the human immunodeficiency virus, or HIV. Doctors first reported cases of AIDS in 1981. By the end of the decade, hundreds of thousands of people worldwide had died from the disease.

AIDS cases appeared around the world. In the African nation of Zambia, the president's son died of AIDS. In 1991 basketball star Earvin "Magic" Johnson announced that he had tested positive for HIV. Other celebrities struck by the disease included movie star Rock Hudson and tennis legend Arthur Ashe.

✔ **READING CHECK: Making Generalizations** How did new technology affect American society in the 1980s? Technology led to increased use of personal computers, and an increased interest in science fiction and cyberpunk.

The 1988 Election

Domestic concerns were among the issues that worried voters as the 1988 presidential election approached. With President Reagan prohibited from running for a third term, Democrats hoped to regain the White House. African American leader **Jesse Jackson**, who had run in 1984, was one of many candidates seeking the Democratic nomination. Jackson hoped to attract a "Rainbow Coalition"—a diverse group of voters representing all races, classes, and creeds. As a candidate in 1984, Jackson had helped generate the largest turnout of African American voters ever for a Democratic primary.

In 1988 Jackson appealed to an even wider range of voters. On "Super Tuesday," the largest single day of primary voting, Jackson won more votes than any other Democratic candidate. Governor **Michael Dukakis** of Massachusetts won the most delegates, however, and eventually gained the nomination. Dukakis, the son of Greek immigrants, selected Senator **Lloyd Bentsen** of Texas as his running mate. Vice President **George Bush** won the Republican presidential nomination and chose **Dan Quayle**, a U.S. Senator from Indiana, as his running mate.

The 1988 presidential campaign proved to be one of the harshest in recent years. Initially, Bush tried to appeal to voters' sense of optimism by promising "a kinder and gentler nation." By the final weeks of the campaign, however, most of the Republican ads had a negative focus. For instance, one commercial attacked Dukakis's environmental record by showing scenes of Massachusetts's heavily polluted Boston Harbor.

The most controversial Republican advertising campaign, however, was intended to attract voters troubled by the nation's rising crime rate. Crime had increased by more than 12.5 percent between 1984 and 1988. A series of television and print ads portrayed Dukakis as weak on crime by associating him with convicted killer Willie Horton. While out on a weekend pass under a Massachusetts prisoner-release program, Horton had attacked a Maryland couple.

The Democrats were slow to respond to the Republicans' attacks. When they did, their efforts were poorly organized and ineffective. Dukakis tried to convince voters of his skills as a manager, arguing that the election should be about competence. This approach failed. In the November election, Bush won 426 electoral

These campaign buttons are from the 1988 election.

LEVEL 3: Have each student create a collage that represents the political events that led to the end of the Cold War. *(See the Level 1 lesson for the correct events.)* Ask volunteers to present and explain their collages to the class.

HOMEWORK *Have each student write an essay that analyzes the events leading to the end of the Cold War. Students may wish to include their essays in their portfolios.*

SPOTLIGHT
on the Reunification of Germany

Have students conduct research on the events leading to the reunification of Germany and the celebrations that took place afterward. Students should focus on political events as well as events that were symbolic of the Cold War's end. Have each student create a multimedia presentation based on his or her research. Then have students give their presentations to the class. **Block Scheduling**

votes to Dukakis's 111. The Democrats did increase their majorities in both houses of Congress, however, and kept control of most state legislatures.

The End of the Cold War

When President Bush entered office, he faced a rapidly changing world. As part of Mikhail Gorbachev's reform efforts, the Soviet Union held its first democratic elections since 1917. Gorbachev's economic reforms were not as successful. Some Soviets began to demand greater change. Many scholars argue that President Reagan's plan to increase U.S. defense systems contributed to the Soviet economy's instability. As the Soviets spent more money on defense systems to keep up with the United States, they neglected serious economic issues at home.

These economic problems forced the Soviet Union to change its relationship with its satellite nations. In July 1989 Gorbachev announced that the Soviet Union was adopting a policy of nonintervention in Eastern and Central Europe. The former superpower was no longer willing or able to bear the costs of supporting other communist governments. Sticking to this policy, the Soviet government did not try to stop free elections in Poland and Hungary. It also did not respond when communist governments in Czechoslovakia and Romania fell.

The Soviets also did not intervene when pro-democracy demonstrations broke out in East Germany in the fall of 1989. During the fall, tens of thousands of East Germans fled to the West through Hungary. In October demonstrators forced Communist leader Erich Honecker to resign. Hoping to restore calm, the East German government opened the Berlin Wall on November 9 and lifted restrictions on travel to the West. It was too late. The pressure for German reunification—the reuniting of East and West Germany as one nation—was too great. After free elections, the two nations were united as the Federal Republic of Germany on October 3, 1990, without opposition from the Soviet Union.

In 1991 Gorbachev faced more problems in the Soviet Union. Alarmed by the pace of reforms, Communist hard-liners attempted to oust him. Their attempt collapsed quickly, but Gorbachev's days in power were numbered. On December 1 the Ukrainians voted for independence. On December 25 Gorbachev resigned as president of the Soviet Union. He turned over control of the armed forces to Boris Yeltsin, the president of Russia. The next day, the presidents of Belarus, Russia, and Ukraine declared that the Soviet Union was "ceasing its existence." They formed a loose confederation called the

INTERPRETING THE VISUAL RECORD

The Berlin Wall. Protesters climbed the Berlin Wall in 1989. *How does this scene symbolize the end of the Cold War?*

LEVEL 1: Tell students to imagine that the Persian Gulf War has ended and that they are newspaper reporters who must write a synopsis of the war. Pair students and have each pair prepare an outline of a newspaper article that includes what led to the war as well as an analysis of how the war was different from previous U.S. military conflicts. (*Outlines should mention that Iraq invaded Kuwait and ignored the deadline for withdrawal set by the United Nations; and that the war was different because it was won with high-tech weapons, featured an unprecedented level of television coverage, and had female troops playing a significant role.*) Have volunteers share their outlines with the class.
English Language Learners, Cooperative Learning

LEVEL 2: Pair students and tell one student in each pair to imagine that he or she is a newspaper reporter, then tell the second student to imagine that he or she is General Norman Schwarzkopf. Have each pair prepare a transcript of an interview in which General Schwarzkopf explains what led to the Persian Gulf War and analyzes how the war was different from previous U.S. military conflicts. (*See the Level 1 lesson for the correct cause and differences.*) Have students conduct their interviews for the class. **Cooperative Learning**

Commonwealth of Independent States (CIS). Eventually, the former Soviet republics of Armenia, Azerbaijan, Georgia, Kazakhstan, Kyrgyzstan, Moldova, Tajikistan, Turkmenistan, and Uzbekistan joined the CIS.

In early 1991 President Bush reflected on the promise of a new era free from Cold War pressures. "Now we can see . . . the very real prospect of a new world order," he declared, "a world in which freedom and respect for human rights find a home among all nations."

Communism still posed a threat to freedom, however. Pro-democracy reformers in China met a different fate from those in Europe. In May 1989, students and others took to Beijing's streets to protest Communist Party policies. On June 4 the government sent soldiers and tanks to remove the peaceful protesters gathered in Tiananmen Square. Estimates of the number of protesters killed range from a few hundred to more than a thousand.

✔ **READING CHECK: Sequencing** What events led to the end of the Cold War? Gorbachev makes reforms; 1989—free elections take place in Europe; 1991—Gorbachev resigns, Yeltsin becomes president, and CIS is formed

The Persian Gulf War

With the end of the Cold War, President Bush was determined to reassert U.S. leadership in world affairs. Before being elected president, Bush had served as U.S. ambassador to the United Nations, representative to China, and director of the CIA. His strong interest in foreign affairs was reflected in his presidency.

Operation Desert Storm. Bush assumed a strong leadership role in August 1990 when Iraq's ruler, Saddam Hussein, invaded neighboring Kuwait, a major oil producer. The United Nations condemned the attack. It also imposed economic sanctions on Iraq and set a deadline for Iraqi withdrawal from Kuwait. As the January 15, 1991, deadline neared, military forces representing the United States, Great Britain, France, Egypt, and Saudi Arabia prepared for war. Some 690,000 troops—including about 540,000 Americans—assembled in Saudi Arabia and on ships in the Persian Gulf. On January 16, bombing attacks began against Iraqi forces and military and industrial targets.

A ground assault began on February 23. Within days, the Iraqis had been driven back, and Kuwait's ruling al-Sabah family returned to power. American casualties included some 150 killed and 450 wounded, while an estimated 100,000 Iraqis died. U.S. air attacks also severely damaged Baghdad, the Iraqi capital, and other cities. Many hailed the success of this offensive, named **Operation Desert Storm**. The commander of U.S. forces, General **Norman Schwarzkopf** (SHWAWRTS-kawf), received a hero's welcome in New York City. Bush's approval rating soared following the war. The president praised the leadership of Secretary of Defense Richard Cheney and General **Colin Powell**, chairman of the Joint Chiefs of Staff.

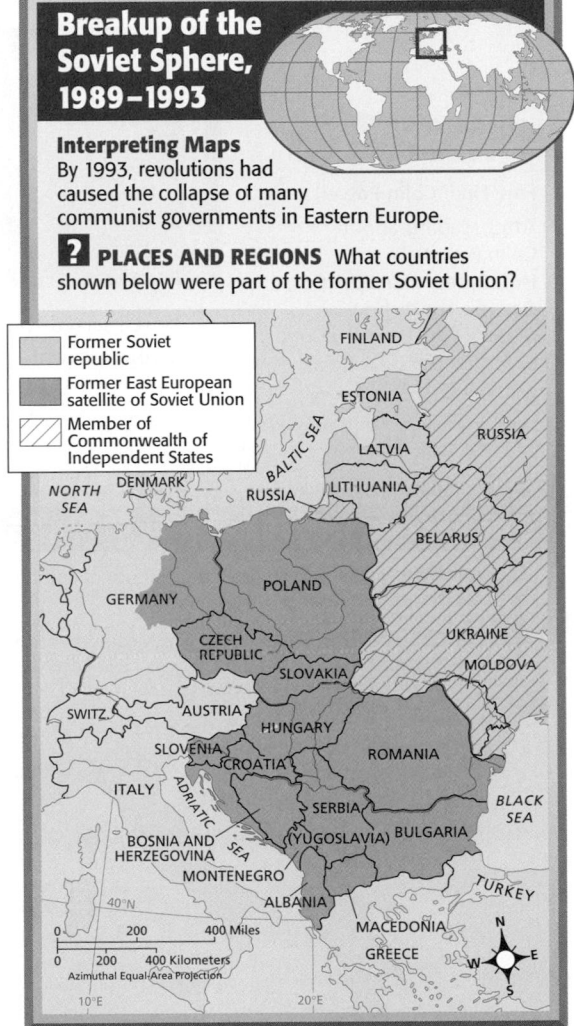

Breakup of the Soviet Sphere, 1989–1993

Interpreting Maps
By 1993, revolutions had caused the collapse of many communist governments in Eastern Europe.

❓ **PLACES AND REGIONS** What countries shown below were part of the former Soviet Union?

Legend:
- Former Soviet republic
- Former East European satellite of Soviet Union
- Member of Commonwealth of Independent States

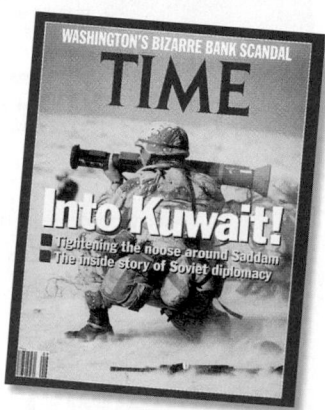

The Persian Gulf War received extensive media coverage.

THAT'S INTERESTING!

President Bush's job approval rating reached nearly 90 percent during the Persian Gulf War. Political analysts note, however, that presidents often receive high approval ratings during times of national crisis, and that such ratings often prove to be short-lived.

MAP ANSWER

Belarus, Estonia, Latvia, Lithuania, Moldova, Russia, and Ukraine

MAP ANSWER
(for p. 788)

Saudi Arabia; Syria

LEVEL 3: Organize students into groups of four. Have each group write a skit depicting what led to the Persian Gulf War and how the war was different from previous U.S. military conflicts. *(See the Level 1 lesson for the correct cause and differences.)* Have each group perform its skit for the class.
Cooperative Learning

SPOTLIGHT
on Civilian Life During the Persian Gulf War

Have students conduct research on civilian life in Iraq, Israel, or Kuwait during the Persian Gulf War. Students should focus on the dangers and hardships faced by civilians. Have each student

write a series of diary entries from the perspective of a civilian in one of the three countries mentioned. Have volunteers read their diary entries to the class. **Block Scheduling**

SPOTLIGHT
on Female Soldiers in the Persian Gulf War

Have students conduct research on the various roles played by female soldiers during the Persian Gulf War. Students should attempt to find firsthand accounts from women who served in the U.S. military during the war. Have each student present his or her research in a short report.
Block Scheduling

Iraq Invades Kuwait.
Facing a national debt of $80–100 billion, Iraq claimed that Kuwait was hurting its economy by overproducing oil. This drove down international oil prices. Saddam Hussein began sending Iraqi troops to the Kuwaiti border. The United States and most other nations did not believe, however, that Saddam intended to go to war. They thought he would use the military threat to force Kuwait to negotiate an economic settlement. Saddam interpreted the lack of U.S. concern to mean that the United States would not intervene militarily.

ACTIVITY: Have students write a memo outlining plans for immediate action against Iraq shortly after troops built up along the Kuwaiti border.

***The American Nation*
VIDEO PROGRAM**

U.S. Troops in the Persian Gulf; Teacher's Guide, pp. 199–200

Search 49621, Play to 51970
Videodisc 2, Side B

Play   Pause

See *Teacher's Guide* for Spanish barcode.

Research on the ROM

Free Find: Colin Powell
After reading about Colin Powell on the **Holt Researcher CD–ROM,** create a chart showing reasons why Powell would or would not be a good president.

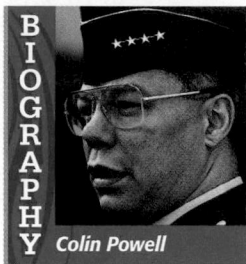

BIOGRAPHY

Colin Powell

Colin Powell was born in 1937 to Jamaican immigrants living in New York City. Powell's parents always stressed the importance of education and hard work. While attending City College of New York, Powell joined the Reserve Officers' Training Corps (ROTC). This experience led him to a career in the military. He graduated at the top of his ROTC class in 1958 and immediately received a commission in the United States Army. "The Army was my life," he recalled.

Powell served several tours of duty in Vietnam, where he was wounded twice. During one incident, an injured Powell rescued several comrades from a burning helicopter. After the war, he received an advanced degree from George Washington University and worked in both the Nixon and Carter administrations. During the

The Persian Gulf War, 1991

Interpreting Maps After more than a month of bombing, UN allied forces ended the Gulf War with a short ground offensive.

? PLACES AND REGIONS From which country did most UN allied troops advance during the ground war? Could these troops have advanced from any other country?

1 Jan. 16: Operation Desert Storm began with massive bombing of strategic targets in Iraq and Kuwait.

2 Deployment of U.S. Marines off the coast made the Iraqis expect a landing there.

3 Iraqis set oil fields and storage tanks ablaze and pumped oil into the Persian Gulf in an effort to foul a Saudi water plant.

4 Feb. 23: The four-day ground war began.

5 Feb. 25: Iraqi SCUD missile killed 28 U.S. service personnel in their barracks.

6 Feb. 26: Helicopters brought in the 101st Air Assault Division to block the escape of Iraqi forces.

7 Feb. 26: Bush announced that the allied forces had liberated Kuwait City and would cease fire.

Legend:
- UN allied forces
- Neutral countries
- U.S. base
- UN bombing
- SCUD missile attack
- Iraqi nuclear site
- UN advance
- Iraqi forces
- U.S. naval vessels
- Oil field

TEACH OBJECTIVE 4

ALL LEVELS: Tell students that many Americans perceived George Bush as being unconcerned with the nation's domestic problems. To help students understand the domestic problems faced by the Bush administration, copy the graphic organizer at right on the chalkboard, omitting the italicized answers. Have students work in pairs to complete the organizer. Ask volunteers to share their answers with the class. Then ask students why many women might have been angered by the Thomas-Hill hearings. *(Students might suggest that the Senate Judiciary Committee appeared to be insensitive to women or that many women have experienced sexual harassment in the workplace.)* Tell students that the Thomas-Hill hearings publicized the issue of sexual harassment of women in the workplace. **English Language Learners, Cooperative Learning**

DOMESTIC PROBLEMS FACED BY THE BUSH ADMINISTRATION

The Thomas-Hill hearings—law professor Anita Hill alleged that Bush Supreme Court nominee Clarence Thomas sexually harassed her when both of them were working at the EEOC. The bullying tactics used by some members of the Senate Judiciary Committee, which investigated Hill's allegations, outraged many women.	*Economic troubles—the federal deficit surged, partly as a result of the costs of the Persian Gulf War and the S&L bailout. The U.S. trade deficit with Japan persisted, and an economic recession occurred and persisted through the 1992 election year. The number of people living in poverty also grew.*

Persian Gulf War, Powell expressed great faith in the U.S. troops.

History Makers Speak

❝I had no doubt that we would be successful. We had the troops, the weapons, and the plan. What I did not know was how long it would take, and how many of our troops would not be coming home.❞

—Colin Powell, *My American Journey*

In the early 1990s Powell retired from the military. He continued to serve national and international interests. He focused on increasing volunteerism in the United States. In 2001 President George W. Bush selected Powell as Secretary of State, making him the first African American to hold the post.

A unique war. Unlike previous U.S. engagements, the Persian Gulf War was won almost entirely by using high-tech weapons. These weapons included Tomahawk cruise missiles, which are extremely accurate long-range missiles, and Stealth fighter aircraft. Virtually undetectable by radar, the Stealth aircraft flew deep into Iraqi territory to release missiles and laser-guided bombs. Soldiers in the Persian Gulf relied on handheld Global Positioning System (GPS) receivers to help them navigate in the desert landscape. Developed by the U.S. Department of Defense, GPS is a satellite-based system that provides precise positioning information. Television reporters also provided unprecedented coverage of the war, including live coverage of the air assaults. News correspondent Bernard Shaw reported the first allied bombings on Iraq. "Something is happening outside. . . . The skies over Baghdad have been illuminated. We're seeing bright flashes going off all over the sky."

The technological nature of the war highlighted another unique aspect of Operation Desert Storm—the significant role played by women. More than 35,000 American women served in the Persian Gulf conflict—some 6 percent of all U.S. troops involved. Eleven American female soldiers were killed, and two were taken prisoner. Although the U.S. military banned women from serving as combat pilots, they served in almost every other capacity—including flying support planes and working on missile crews.

The role of women in Desert Storm and the nature of the war caused many people to question the policy of banning women from combat. With technology playing an increasingly significant role in modern warfare, critics charged, physical differences between men and women would become less important than technological skills. In December 1991 the Senate removed the ban against women serving as combat pilots but continued to limit female soldiers' role in ground battles.

✔ **READING CHECK: Contrasting** How did the Persian Gulf War differ from previous U.S. military conflicts? through the use of high-tech weapons, unprecedented war coverage by television reporters, and an increased female involvement in the war

PRIMARY SOURCE

A View of the Persian Gulf War

The Persian Gulf War affected many people, including residents of Israel. To get revenge against UN forces, Iraq launched a missile attack on Israel. Palestinian philosopher Sari Nusseibeh, living in Israel at the time, recalled his impressions. **How did the Persian Gulf War affect people living in Israel?**

❝It was January 29, 13 days since the aerial bombardment in the Gulf War had started. For fully two weeks we had been placed under a total 24-hour curfew, interspersed [interrupted] only by three two-hour intervals in which we were allowed to do our shopping. All of us—my wife, my three children, and myself—had taken to sleeping together on the floor of the sitting-dining area of our apartment. This way we kept each other company through the SCUD [missile] scares (. . . we wondered each time where the rockets would fall, and what deadly poison they might be carrying). . . .

For almost two weeks we lived in a state of suspension between TV scenes of missiles hitting Iraqi targets and footage of missiles flying over our heads.❞

This soldier is one of many women who served in the Persian Gulf War.

The Missile War. When the Iraqis used SCUD missiles to attack Saudi Arabia and Israel, the United States provided those nations with Patriot air defense missiles. Although there were many technical problems surrounding the use of Patriots to defend against SCUD attacks, the new technology reassured Israelis and contributed to their decision not to declare war on Iraq.

CRITICAL THINKING What might have been the Patriot missiles' most important contribution made during the Gulf War?

ANSWER: Students might indicate that the Patriot missiles provided psychological reassurance if not excellent military performance.

PRIMARY SOURCE ANSWER

They were forced to remain indoors, in constant fear of a missile attack from Iraq

VISUAL RECORD ANSWER

(for p. 790)

Students might answer that the act increased her access to all public facilities and buildings.

SECTION

REVIEW 3 ANSWERS

2. Identify
• Christa McAuliffe, p. 784

789

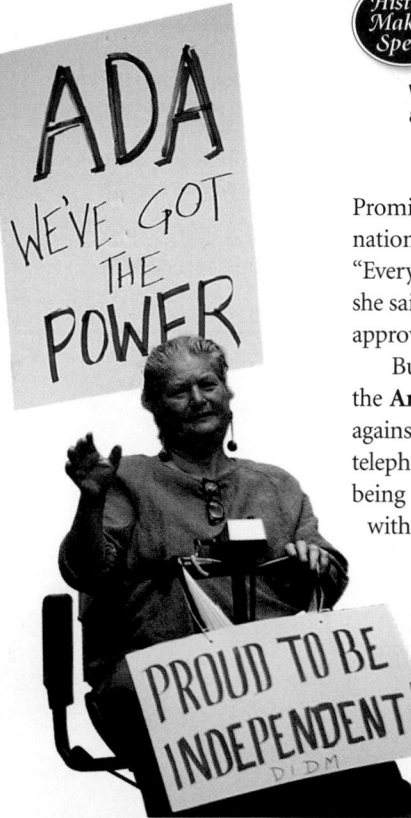

INTERPRETING THE VISUAL RECORD

Americans with disabilities. This woman supports the Americans with Disabilities Act. *In what ways might the ADA promote independence for this woman?*

Domestic Concerns

President Bush's successes in foreign affairs won him popularity and international praise, but some critics charged that he was neglecting problems at home. As the 1992 presidential campaign approached, domestic issues—particularly the economy and a growing political controversy—weakened support for the president.

Bush's domestic policies. Bush had entered office telling the public, "We don't need radical new directions." However, he did propose a domestic agenda that differed from that of President Reagan. Bush explained his program.

> *History Makers Speak*
>
> **"America is never wholly herself unless she is engaged in high moral principle. We as a people have such a purpose today. It is to make kinder the face of the Nation and gentler the face of the world. My friends, we have work to do.... I am speaking of a new engagement in the lives of others, a new activism, hands-on and involved, that gets the job done."**
>
> —George Bush, "Inaugural Address," January 20, 1989

Promising to be the "education president," he proposed reforms to improve the nation's schools. First Lady Barbara Bush launched a campaign to end illiteracy. "Everything would be better if people could learn to read, write, and understand," she said. Congress rejected many of Bush's proposed education reforms, but it did approve increased funding for college loans and the Head Start program.

Bush ushered in a new era for citizens with disabilities. In July 1990 he signed the **Americans with Disabilities Act** into law. The act prohibits discrimination against people with physical or mental disabilities in employment, transportation, telephone services, and public buildings. The disabilities subject to the law included being afflicted with diseases such as AIDS. The act also requires that companies with 15 or more employees remove structural barriers from offices.

The president addressed growing concerns over crime and drug use by launching the **War on Drugs**. This initiative provided more money to stop drug smuggling and illegal drug use. As a first step in this attack, Bush ordered the arrest of Panamanian dictator and drug smuggler General Manuel Noriega. In December 1989, U.S. Marines invaded Panama to bring Noriega back to the United States to face drug charges. Guillermo Endara, the democratically elected president, took control of the Panamanian government. In 1992 a federal court convicted Noriega of drug smuggling and sentenced him to 40 years in prison.

The Thomas-Hill hearings. Bush continued Reagan's efforts to move the Supreme Court in a conservative direction. In 1990 he filled a vacancy on the Court with David Souter, a conservative New Hampshire judge. In 1991 Justice Thurgood Marshall announced his retirement. Bush nominated Clarence Thomas, a conservative African American judge and former head of the federal Equal Employment Opportunity Commission (EEOC), to take his place.

During the confirmation hearings, law professor Anita Hill, who had worked with Thomas at the EEOC, accused the nominee of sexual harassment. This is the use of unwelcome sexual language or behavior that creates a hostile working environment. In televised hearings, the Senate Judiciary Committee investigated

REVIEW

Have students complete the **Section 3 Review** on p. 791.

ASSESS

Have students complete **Daily Quiz 26.3**. As **Alternative Assessment**, you may want to use the interview transcript or the skit in this section's lessons.

RETEACH

Have students complete **Main Idea Activity for English Language Learners and Special-Needs Students 26.3**. Organize students into triads. Have each triad write two or three sentences that identify and explain the significance of six of the key people, places, or terms in Section 3. Collect triads' identifications and use them to quiz the class.
English Language Learners, Cooperative Learning

EXTEND

Have students conduct research on three of the key people mentioned in this section. Have each student write brief biographical capsules summarizing the pertinent information about each person. **Block Scheduling**

Hill's charges. The bullying tactics used by some members of the committee in their questioning of Hill outraged many women. After the Senate narrowly approved Thomas's Supreme Court nomination, female activists vowed to show their disapproval in the next election. The hearings stirred debate across the country about sexual harassment.

The economy. President Bush's main domestic concern quickly became the U.S. economy. In August 1989 he authorized $166 billion to bail out many S&Ls and banks. In late 1990 a sharp recession hit. These events, along with the need to balance the federal budget, forced Bush to abandon his 1988 campaign pledge of "no new taxes." He asked for a significant tax increase, which did little to reduce the federal deficit. In 1991 the deficit surged to some $270 billion. It reached $291 billion in 1992.

The U.S. economy also suffered from an international trade deficit. In 1990 it reached a high of almost $102 billion. The massive annual sales of Japanese automobiles and electronic goods to American consumers accounted for a large part of the deficit. On a 1992 trade mission to Japan, President Bush and American business leaders met with little success as they tried to persuade the Japanese to increase imports from the United States.

As the U.S. economy faltered, unemployment rose. States facing budget deficits cut their welfare programs. The number of Americans living below the poverty line grew by more than 2 million in 1990. The recession continued through 1992, hurting Bush's re-election hopes.

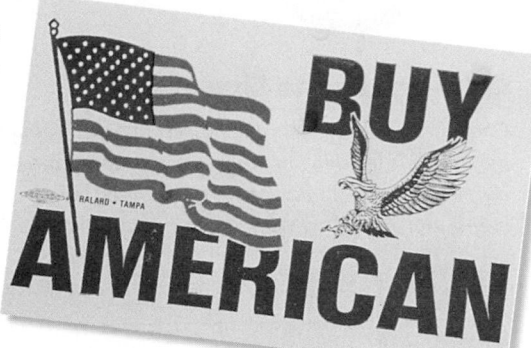

Some Americans favored buying only goods produced in the United States as a way to strengthen the economy and reduce the trade deficit.

✔ **READING CHECK: Summarizing** What economic problems did the Bush administration face? sharp recession, an unbalanced budget, an international trade deficit, and a rise in unemployment

---

SECTION 3 REVIEW

1. Identify and explain:
Christa McAuliffe
Challenger
AIDS
Jesse Jackson
Michael Dukakis
Lloyd Bentsen
George Bush
Dan Quayle
Commonwealth of
   Independent States
Operation Desert Storm
Norman Schwarzkopf
Colin Powell
Americans with
   Disabilities Act
War on Drugs

2. Sequencing Copy the graphic organizer below. Use it to describe the events that marked the end of the Cold War.

| 1. Soviets adopt non-intervention policy |
| 2. |
| 3. |
| 4. |
| 5. |
| 6. |
| 7. Gorbachev resigns |

3. Finding the Main Idea
a. Why did the United States participate in the Persian Gulf War? What were the outcomes of the war?
b. How did new technologies used in the Persian Gulf War meet specific needs?
c. How did the U.S. trade deficit with Japan make economic problems worse for the U.S. free-enterprise system?

4. Writing and Critical Thinking
Evaluating Imagine that you are a campaign adviser to President Bush in 1992. Write a briefing on how domestic issues are affecting public support for Bush.
Consider:
• Bush's domestic policies and their effects
• reactions to the Thomas-Hill hearings
• the state of the economy by the early 1990s

Homework Practice Online
keyword: SE3 HP26

REVIEW CHAPTER 26 ANSWERS

Creating a Time Line
Each event should have an explanation and the correct date.

Writing a Summary
See the Reading Checks in each section for main ideas.

Identifying People and Ideas
1. incident in which Iranian militants held 52 American hostages for 444 days

2. U.S. president from 1981 to 1989

3. Reagan's vice president who was elected president in 1988

4. theory that lowering top income tax rates will spur economic growth

5. space-based missile-defense system

6. Nicaraguan faction supported by the CIA that opposed the Sandinistas

7. first woman appointed to the U.S. Supreme Court

8. space shuttle that exploded in 1986

9. allied military operation against Iraq in 1991

10. chairman of the Joint Chiefs of Staff who became a hero during the Persian Gulf War

CHAPTER 26
REVIEW AND ASSESSMENT RESOURCES

TECHNOLOGY
▶ Chapter 26 Test Generator (on the One-Stop Planner)
▶ Global Skill Builder CD–ROM
▶ HRW Go site

REINFORCEMENT, REVIEW, AND ASSESSMENT
▶ Chapter 26 Review, pp. 792–93
▶ Chapter 26 Tutorial for Students, Parents, Mentors, and Peers

▶ Chapter 26 Test (Form A or B)
▶ Portfolio Activities and Alternative Assessment Handbook, Chapter 26
▶ Chapter 26 Test for English Language Learners and Special-Needs Students

REVIEW
Have students complete the **Chapter 26 Review** on pp. 792–93.

ASSESS
Use one of the chapter tests to assess students' understanding of the content. For **Alternative Assessment**, see the **Portfolio Activities and Alternative Assessment Handbook.**

Understanding Main Ideas

1. Reagan promised solutions to problems that Carter seemed unable to solve.

2. increased military spending, a tougher stance toward the Soviet Union

3. rising deficit, 1987 stock market crash, and S&L crisis

4. sale of weapons to Iran, illegal funding of the Contras, Reagan's role in the scandal

5. economic boom, new computer technology, AIDS

6. Iraq's invasion of Kuwait

Reviewing Themes

1. increased the wealth of many Americans but also led to cuts in social programs and decreased government regulation

2. Reagan's hard-line stance and emphasis on buildup of nuclear weapons led to increased tensions.

3. Personal computers became widely available, and virtual reality was invented.

Thinking Critically

1. More and more people were tired of liberal policies, and the increased participation of conservative Republican voters led to the election of conservative politicians.

2. Both involved the misuse of government power and

CHAPTER 26 Review

Creating a Time Line

Copy the time line below onto a sheet of paper. Complete the time line by filling in the events and dates from the chapter that you think were most significant. Pick three events and explain why you think they were significant.

| 1980 | 1984 | 1988 | 1992 |

Writing a Summary

Using standard grammar, spelling, sentence structure, and punctuation, write an overview of events in the chapter.

Identifying People and Ideas

Identify the following terms or individuals and explain their significance.

1. Iran hostage crisis
2. Ronald Reagan
3. George Bush
4. supply-side economics
5. Strategic Defense Initiative
6. Contras
7. Sandra Day O'Connor
8. *Challenger*
9. Operation Desert Storm
10. Colin Powell

Understanding Main Ideas

SECTION 1 *(pp. 770–775)*

1. Why did voters choose Ronald Reagan over Jimmy Carter in the 1980 presidential election?
2. How did the Reagan administration fight the Cold War in the early 1980s?

SECTION 2 *(pp. 776–782)*

3. Why did public confidence in the economy begin to weaken in the late 1980s?
4. What were the main issues in the Iran-Contra affair?

SECTION 3 *(pp. 783–791)*

5. What changes occurred in American society in the 1980s?
6. What led to the Persian Gulf War?

Reviewing Themes

1. **Economics** What effects did President Reagan's economic policies have on the country?
2. **Global Relations** How did President Reagan's approach to defense change the Cold War?
3. **Science, Technology, and Society** How did computer technology change in the 1980s?

Thinking Critically

1. **Summarizing** In what ways did participation in the democratic process in the 1980s reflect our national identity?
2. **Comparing and Contrasting** How was the Iran-Contra affair both similar to and different from the Watergate scandal?
3. **Evaluating** What contributions did George Bush make as president?
4. **Analyzing Information** What role did the United States play in ending the Cold War?
5. **Making Predictions** How did the breakup of the Soviet Union present new challenges to the United States?

Writing About History

Analyzing Information Write an essay that explains the significance of the passage of the Americans with Disabilities Act and how it increased economic opportunities for some Americans. Use the following graphic to organize your thoughts.

Challenges for people with disabilities	Benefits of Americans with Disabilities Act

RETEACH

Organize students into small groups. Have each group use at least 20 of the Define and Identify terms in this chapter to create a crossword puzzle with clues. Have students in each group exchange their crossword puzzles with another group and then solve them. **English Language Learners, Cooperative Learning**

EXTEND

Have each student conduct research on the so-called Republican Revolution. Why has Ronald Reagan's agenda for the United States been described as revolutionary? What lasting effects has the Republican Revolution had on the U.S. government and U.S. politics? Have each student write an analytical essay presenting his or her research. **Block Scheduling**

Building Social Studies Skills

Interpreting Maps
Study the map below. Then use it to help answer the questions that follow.

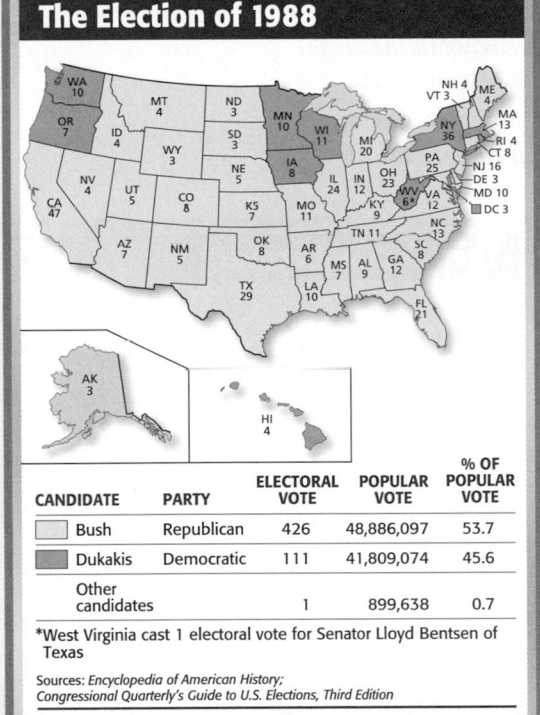

The Election of 1988

CANDIDATE	PARTY	ELECTORAL VOTE	POPULAR VOTE	% OF POPULAR VOTE
Bush	Republican	426	48,886,097	53.7
Dukakis	Democratic	111	41,809,074	45.6
Other candidates		1	899,638	0.7

*West Virginia cast 1 electoral vote for Senator Lloyd Bentsen of Texas

Sources: *Encyclopedia of American History*; *Congressional Quarterly's Guide to U.S. Elections, Third Edition*

1. About 50 percent of registered voters participated in the 1988 election. What are some possible reasons for the low voter turnout?

2. Which statement represents the election results?
   a. Dukakis received 45.6 percent of the popular vote and about 20 percent of the electoral vote.
   b. Bush received 53.7 percent of the popular vote but lost the election.
   c. Dukakis won the election.
   d. Bush carried the electoral vote in 11 states.

Analyzing Primary Sources
Read the following excerpt from political researcher David M. Mason's book, *Mandate for Leadership IV.* Then answer the questions that follow.

“The Reagan Administration excelled at the overall policy management process, with every element in place. The President himself consistently enunciated [stated] a compelling vision. . . .
   In short, Reagan and his team knew what they wanted, knew how to get as much of it as the political circumstances allowed, and knew how to sell the program to the public to maximize their political leverage [power] and to ensure public support (and credit) for the resulting laws and policies. The Reagan program was a success because the most important elements as defined and explained to the public (tax cuts, budget restraint, and the defense buildup) were approved.”

3. Which of the following is not a factor in the success of President Reagan's agenda?
   a. Republican insistence on achievement of the entire program without compromise
   b. a powerful vision
   c. a staff that knew how to get what it wanted
   d. skillful marketing of the Reagan agenda

4. How might this statement reveal the author's bias?

Alternative Assessment

Building Your Portfolio

Global Relations
Imagine that you are a reporter for a television news show in 1999. Provide a brief review of the events of the Iran-Contra affair. Your report should also discuss how the political scandal affected the Reagan administration and Americans' views of the role of the federal government.

internet connect

Internet Activity: go.hrw.com
KEYWORD: SE3 AN26

Choose a topic on the Republican revolution to:
• research the Persian Gulf War.
• write a biography of Sandra Day O'Connor.
• understand the causes and effects of the collapse of the Soviet Union.

money; Nixon was forced out of office, whereas Reagan was never implicated.

3. He presided over the U.S. victory in the Cold War and the Persian Gulf War and made a positive impact on the war on drugs.

4. The United States slowed the arms race and participated through the INF Treaty in peace talks with Gorbachev.

5. Conflicts between former Soviet-controlled countries began to break out.

Writing
challenges—employment discrimination, access to buildings; benefits—banned employment discrimination, made employers remove structural barriers

Building Social Studies Skills
1. Answers will vary. Students might suggest that neither candidate excited voters; many voters might have believed Bush would win easily, so their votes did not matter.

2. a

3. a

4. Answers will vary. Students should suggest that opinions dominate the statement, and the opinions show that the author was biased toward the Reagan administration.

Ask students to identify recent examples of natural disasters or industrial accidents in their local area or region. Have students share their examples with the class. Then ask students to explain how these disasters or accidents affected the natural environment. Tell students that they will study the *Exxon Valdez* spill, the Yellowstone fires, air pollution, and recycling efforts in the Unit 7 America's Geography.

TEACH AMERICA'S GEOGRAPHY— THE NATURAL ENVIRONMENT

Have students study the America's Geography feature. Then ask each student to write a caption for each of the maps and charts and graphs in the feature. *(Students' captions will vary. Students should accurately and fully represent the information in the given map, chart, or graph in their captions.)* Ask volunteers to read their captions to the class. **English Language Learners**

The Oil Pollution Act. In response to the *Exxon Valdez* disaster, Congress passed the Oil Pollution Act of 1990. This act enabled various federal agencies to respond more quickly to large oil catastrophes. The act established guidelines for future oil storage, provided for the purchase of damaged land, and set up a trust fund—financed by an oil tax—to aid in future clean-up efforts.

CRITICAL THINKING Why might Congress have failed to consider an oil pollution act prior to 1989?

ANSWER: Answers will vary. Students might suggest that the United States had not expected or conceived of a large oil disaster prior to the *Exxon Valdez* spill.

AMERICA'S GEOGRAPHY ANSWERS

1. the Becharof National Wildlife Refuge, the Chugach National Forest, the Katmai National Park, the Kenai Fjords National Park, and the Kodiak National Wildlife Refuge and Preserve

2. about 475 miles

3. lands in the Chugach National Forest, the Kenai Fjords National Park, the Kenai National Wildlife Refuge, and the Kodiak National Wildlife Refuge

---

AMERICA'S Geography

The Natural Environment

The increasing population and rapid development of land in the United States has led to greater concerns about the future of the natural environment. In the late 1900s, however, much progress was made toward protecting the environment and decreasing pollution. The creation of national parks and wildlife refuges helps preserve the natural landscape and save endangered animals from possible extinction.

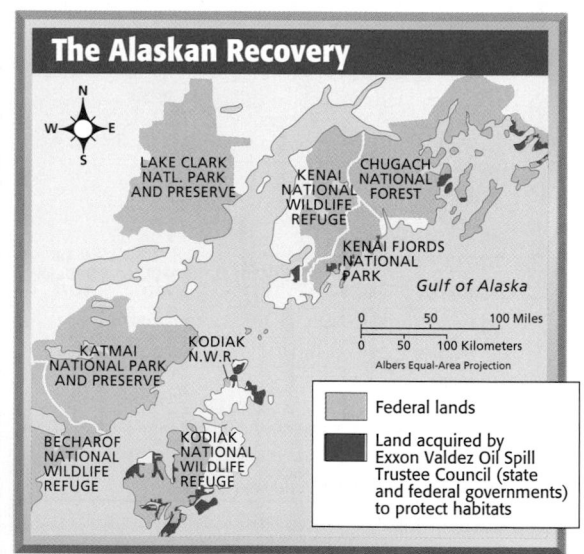

The Alaskan Recovery

Federal lands

Land acquired by Exxon Valdez Oil Spill Trustee Council (state and federal governments) to protect habitats

The Alaskan Oil Spill of 1989

Federal lands

Spilled oil

Alaskan oil spill. Industrial accidents can have devastating effects on the environment. In 1989 the *Exxon Valdez* oil tanker spilled about 11 million gallons of oil when it ran aground near the Alaskan coastline. The cleanup for the oil spill was long and expensive. To help preserve the coastal areas, the U.S. government purchased some of the affected lands. Ten years later, some parts of Alaska still had not fully recovered.

GEOGRAPHY AND HISTORY *Skills*

ENVIRONMENT AND SOCIETY

1. Which federal lands were affected by the Alaskan oil spill of 1989?
2. According to the map of the Alaskan oil spill, how many miles did the spilled oil spread?
3. Which lands were purchased by the government after the oil spill?

SPOTLIGHT
on the *Exxon Valdez* Spill

Have students locate and use a variety of primary and secondary sources to learn more about the *Exxon Valdez* spill. Then tell students to imagine that they are radio reporters at the scene. Have each student write a three-minute broadcast describing the spill and discussing its implications. Remind students that they will need to synthesize and summarize their research in order to present a full broadcast in just three minutes. Ask volunteers to read their broadcasts to the class.
Block Scheduling

SPOTLIGHT
on Air Pollution Control

Pair students and ask them to conduct research on recent efforts to control air pollution. Have each pair develop a visual presentation on these efforts. Pairs' presentations should include both images and text. Tell each pair to set up its presentations around the classroom and ask students to visit their classmates' stations. To conclude, conduct a discussion on air pollution control measures.
Block Scheduling, Cooperative Learning

AMERICA'S Geography

The Yellowstone Fires of 1988

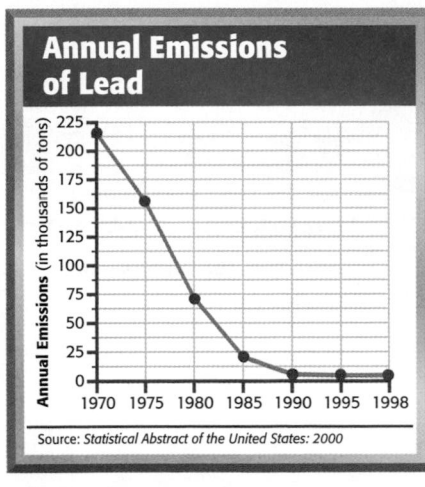

Annual Emissions of Lead

Source: *Statistical Abstract of the United States: 2000*

Yellowstone Recovery

Albers Equal-Area Projection

Legend		
Fully developed Engleman Spruce and Subalpine Fir	Pygmy Lodgepole Pine	Whitebark Pine after 1988 fires
Lodgepole Pine after 1988 fires	Aspen	Developing Whitebark Pine
Developing Lodgepole Pine	Douglas Fir after 1988 fires	Fully developed Whitebark Pine
Fully developed Lodgepole Pine	Developing Douglas Fir	Nonforested
	Fully developed Douglas Fir	

Pollution control. Air pollution had become a serious problem by the 1970s. New laws helped decrease air pollutants, particularly lead and carbon monoxide. Americans also fought pollution by recycling more waste items.

Yellowstone fires. In 1988 a natural disaster struck Yellowstone National Park. Lightning started forest fires that eventually burned some 45 percent of the park. The lands recovered quickly from the fires. Within just a few years much of the park had experienced a significant regrowth of its vegetation.

Percentage of Waste Recycled

1980 9.6%
90.4%

1998 28.2%
71.8%

Percent recycled
Percent not recycled

Source: *Statistical Abstract of the United States: 2000*

GEOGRAPHY AND HISTORY Skills

ENVIRONMENT AND SOCIETY

1. Use both maps to write a paragraph about the Yellowstone fires and recovery.
2. By how much did the level of lead in the air drop between 1970 and 1995?
3. How much did the percentage of waste recycled increase between 1980 and 1996?

Launching the New Millennium

CHAPTER RESOURCE MANAGER

Objectives	Pacing Guide	Reproducible Resources
SECTION 1 **Clinton's First Term** pp. 798–803 ★ Discuss how the 1992 presidential election differed from other recent elections. ★ Explain what led to the Republican comeback in the 1994 congressional elections. ★ Analyze how regional conflicts and terrorism affected the world. ★ Assess how successful the United Nations was in maintaining world peace after the Cold War ended.	**Regular** 1 day **Block Scheduling** .5 day *Block Scheduling Handbook with Team Teaching Strategies, pp. 157–62*	RS Guided Reading Strategy 27.1 SM Geography Activity 27: The Republicans Take the House
SECTION 2 **Clinton's Second Term** pp. 804–09 ★ Discuss the issues that affected the 1996 presidential election. ★ Describe the domestic issues that shaped President Clinton's second term. ★ Relate what led to the impeachment of President Clinton, and describe what the outcome was. ★ Analyze why NATO launched air strikes against Yugoslavia in 1999.	**Regular** 1 day **Block Scheduling** .5 day *Block Scheduling Handbook with Team Teaching Strategies, pp. 157–62*	RS Guided Reading Strategy 27.2 RS Graphic Organizer Activity 27: The Serbian Conflict PS Biography Reading 27: Madeleine Albright
SECTION 3 **Society in the 1990s** pp. 810–14 ★ Discuss the events that shaped the space program in the 1990s. ★ Explain the issues surrounding technology in the 1990s. ★ Analyze how U.S. popular culture affected the rest of the world. ★ Describe how immigration changed in the 1990s. ★ Identify the issues that affected family life in the 1990s.	**Regular** 1 day **Block Scheduling** .5 day *Block Scheduling Handbook with Team Teaching Strategies, pp. 157–62*	RS Guided Reading Strategy 27.3 IC Literature Reading 27: Caught Between Two Cultures E Creative Teaching Strategy: Open-Ended Statements Lesson
SECTION 4 **George W. Bush's Presidency** pp. 815–19 ★ Identify the factors that shaped the global economy. ★ Describe how the environment and population growth issues concerned people in the 1990s. ★ Explain how the 2000 presidential election was unusual. ★ Discuss the domestic and international issues that George W. Bush faced.	**Regular** 1 day **Block Scheduling** .5 day *Block Scheduling Handbook with Team Teaching Strategies, pp. 157–62*	RS Guided Reading Strategy 27.4 PS Primary Source Reading 27: Antarctica: A New View
SECTION 5 **September 11, 2001: A Day That Changed the World** pp. 820–25 ★ Describe how the United States was attacked on September 11, 2001, and identify how Americans responded. ★ Explain how the events of September 11 affected the economy. ★ Evaluate the steps American leaders took to find those responsible and to bring them to justice.		

Chapter Resource Key

PS Primary Sources	**REV** Review	Video
RS Reading Support	**ELL** Reinforcement and English Language Learners	Internet
IC Interdisciplinary Connections		Holt Presentation Maker Using Microsoft® PowerPoint®
E Enrichment	Transparencies	
SM Skills Mastery	CD-ROM	
A Assessment	Music	

One-Stop Planner CD-ROM

See the *One-Stop Planner* for a complete list of additional resources for students and teachers.

One-Stop Planner CD–ROM

It's easy to plan lessons, select resources, and print out materials for your students when you use the **One-Stop Planner CD–ROM with Test Generator.**

internet connect

HRW ONLINE RESOURCES
GO TO: go.hrw.com
Then type in a keyword.

TEACHER HOME PAGE
KEYWORD: SE3 Teacher

CHAPTER INTERNET ACTIVITIES
KEYWORD: SE3 AN27
Choose an activity to:
- create a brochure on the contemporary space program.
- create a database and chart on the impact of NAFTA.
- create a multimedia presentation about the history of personal computers and the Internet.

CHAPTER ENRICHMENT LINKS
KEYWORD: SE3 CH27

ONLINE ASSESSMENT
Homework Practice
KEYWORD: SE3 HP27

Standardized Test Prep
KEYWORD: SE3 STP27

Rubrics
KEYWORD: SS Rubrics

ONLINE MAPS, CHARTS, AND GRAPHS
KEYWORD: SE3 MCG
- Wetlands
- U.S. Trade Balance

CONTENT UPDATES
KEYWORD: SS Content Updates

HOLT PRESENTATION MAKER
KEYWORD: SE3 PPT27

ONLINE READING SUPPORT
KEYWORD: SS Strategies

CURRENT EVENTS
KEYWORD: S3 Current Events

Technology Resources

 One-Stop Planner, Lesson 27.1
 Holt Researcher: American History CD–ROM
 Homework Practice Online

 One-Stop Planner, Lesson 27.2
 Holt Researcher: American History CD–ROM
 Homework Practice Online

 One-Stop Planner, Lesson 27.3
 Holt Researcher: American History CD–ROM
 Homework Practice Online
 HRW Go site

 One-Stop Planner, Lesson 27.4
 Linking Geography and History Transparency 23: The Global Environment
Holt Researcher: American History CD–ROM
Homework Practice Online

 CNN Presents: September 11, 2001: A Turning Point in History
 HRW Go site

Reinforcement, Review, and Assessment

REV Section 1 Review, p. 803
A Daily Quiz 27.1
ELL Main Idea Activity 27.1
ELL English Audio Summary 27.1
ELL Spanish Audio Summary 27.1

REV Section 2 Review, p. 809
A Daily Quiz 27.2
ELL Main Idea Activity 27.2
ELL English Audio Summary 27.2
ELL Spanish Audio Summary 27.2

REV Section 3 Review, p. 814
A Daily Quiz 27.3
ELL Main Idea Activity 27.3
ELL English Audio Summary 27.3
ELL Spanish Audio Summary 27.3

REV Section 4 Review, p. 819
A Daily Quiz 27.4
ELL Main Idea Activity 27.4
ELL English Audio Summary 27.4
ELL Spanish Audio Summary 27.4

REV Section 5 Review, p. 825

Meeting Individual Needs

Ability Levels

Level 1 Basic-level activities designed for all students encountering new material

Level 2 Intermediate-level activities designed for average students

Level 3 Challenging activities designed for honors and gifted-and-talented students

English Language Learners Activities that address the needs of students with Limited English Proficiency

Chapter Review and Assessment

 Global Skill Builder CD–ROM
 HRW Go site
REV Chapter 27 Tutorial for Students, Parents, Mentors, and Peers
REV Chapter 27 Review, pp. 826–27
 Chapter 27 Test Generator (on the One-Stop Planner)

A Chapter 27 Test (Form A or B)
A Alternative Assessment Handbook
A Chapter 27 Test for English Language Learners and Special-Needs Students

Build on What You Know

Ask students to answer the following questions.

How might economic problems damage a president's political standing?

Consider:

• the importance of the economy in everyday American life

• the president's role in economic matters

How might globalization and new advances in technology change American society?

Consider:

• the effect of new technologies on communications

• the ways that an international market for goods might affect the U.S. economy

---

exploring the time line

AMERICAN EVENTS

CITIZENSHIP

1995 ■ The Oklahoma City Bombing. The terrorist responsible for the Oklahoma City bombing was Timothy McVeigh, a U.S. citizen and veteran who had been decorated for his service in the Persian Gulf War. McVeigh was involved in paramilitary groups that believed the U.S. government had become a threat to Americans' liberty. He was convicted of the crime and executed in 2001.

ACTIVITY: Have students conduct research on the Oklahoma City bombing, focusing on efforts the city made to rebuild and to remember the victims.

CHAPTER 27

1990–Present

Launching the New Millennium

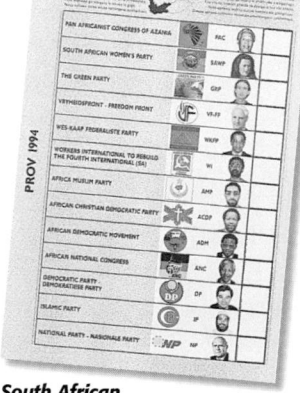

South African election ballot

**1990
The Arts**
Mark Strand serves as poet laureate of the United States.

**1991
World Events**
The Persian Gulf War ends as a United Nations force pushes Iraqi troops out of Kuwait.

**1992
Daily Life**
Riots erupt in Los Angeles.

**1992
The Arts**
Gish Jen publishes her novel *Typical American.*

**1993
Business and Finance**
Congress ratifies the North American Free Trade Agreement (NAFTA).

**1993
Politics**
Bill Clinton is sworn in as the 42nd president of the United States.

**1994
World Events**
South Africa holds its first all-race national elections.

**1994
Politics**
Republican candidates for Congress present the Contract with America.

`1990`   `1992`   `1994`

President Clinton giving his first inaugural address

Build on What You Know

During the 1980s Republican presidents Ronald Reagan and George Bush won wide support for their efforts to reduce federal regulation. Despite the success of the Persian Gulf War, Bush's bid for re-election was harmed by an economic recession and an ongoing budget-deficit problem. In this chapter you will learn about Bill Clinton's presidency and the campaign to elect his successor. You will also learn how American society changed as a result of increasing globalization, new advances in technology, and the expansion of democracy abroad.

What's Your Opinion?

To help students create their Themes Journal entries, provide the following examples of appropriate agree/disagree statements.

Economics

Agree Although the Soviet Union was still a military power, its economic troubles led to its political disintegration.

Global Relations

Agree The U.S. foreign policy of isolationism allowed the country to avoid geopolitical entanglements during most of the 1800s.

Disagree Despite the wishes of many Americans to maintain U.S. neutrality, the United States was unable to avoid involvement in World Wars I and II.

Disagree The United States and its European allies resorted to military means to force Iraqi forces to retreat from Kuwait.

Science, Technology, and Society

Agree The invention of the telephone allowed Americans to communicate with people in distant locations.

Disagree By leading to the creation of many monotonous jobs, the development of the assembly line had a negative impact on many Americans' daily lives.

exploring the time line

GLOBAL EVENTS

John Glenn (waving) and the space shuttle crew

Firefighters raise an American flag at the site of the collapse of the World Trade Center towers.

1995
Daily Life
A terrorist truck bomb destroys the Murrah Federal Building in Oklahoma City, killing 168 people.

1996
The Arts
Rent, a Broadway rock musical, wins the Pulitzer Prize for best American drama.

1998
Science and Technology
At age 77, John Glenn becomes the oldest person ever to travel in space.

1999
Business and Finance
The Dow Jones industrial average surpasses 10,000 points as the stock market booms in the wake of mergers and record profits.

1999
World Events
NATO launches air attacks on Yugoslavia.

2001
World Events
On September 11, terrorists attack the World Trade Center and the Pentagon.

1996   **1998**   **2000**   **2002**

1995
Daily Life
Louis Farrakhan leads the Million Man March in Washington, D.C.

1996
Politics
President Clinton is re-elected as the U.S. economy prospers.

1996
Daily Life
The Summer Olympics in Atlanta are interrupted when a bomb explodes during a concert.

1997
Science and Technology
Scottish scientists successfully clone a mammal, a sheep named Dolly.

1997
The Arts
The Getty Museum in Los Angeles opens to the public.

2000
Politics
Five weeks after Americans voted, they learn that George W. Bush will be their next president.

Such A Ticket!
GORE LIEBERMAN 2000

Our Next First Family **Laura and G.W. Bush 2000**

Campaign buttons from the 2000 election

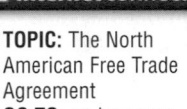
internet connect

TOPIC: The North American Free Trade Agreement
GO TO: go.hrw.com
KEYWORD: SE3 AN27

Have students access the Internet through the HRW Go site to conduct research on the North American Free Trade Agreement (NAFTA) and the controversy surrounding the treaty's goals. Then have each student use the Holt Grapher to create a database and chart that shows benefits and consequences of the trade treaty. Students should cite the sources of the information they include in their charts.

What's Your Opinion?

Themes Journal

Do you agree or disagree with the following statements? Support your point of view in your journal.

Economics Economic influence is more important than military strength in determining the political power of nations.

Global Relations Americans' experiences are disconnected from events around the world.

Science, Technology, and Society New advances in technology will improve American society by expanding communication and easing the struggles of daily existence.

After completing Section 1, students should be able to:

OBJECTIVE 1 *Discuss how the 1992 presidential election differed from other recent elections.*

OBJECTIVE 2 *Explain what led to the Republican comeback in the 1994 congressional elections.*

OBJECTIVE 3 *Analyze how regional conflicts and terrorism affected the world.*

OBJECTIVE 4 *Assess how successful the United Nations was in maintaining world peace after the Cold War ended.*

SECTION 1 RESOURCES

REPRODUCIBLE

▶ Guided Reading Strategy 27.1
▶ Geography Activity 27: The Republicans Take the House

TECHNOLOGY

▶ One-Stop Planner, Lesson 27.1
▶ Holt Researcher: American History CD–ROM
▶ Homework Practice Online

REINFORCEMENT, REVIEW, AND ASSESSMENT

▶ Section 1 Review, p. 803
▶ Daily Quiz 27.1
▶ Main Idea Activity 27.1
▶ English Audio Summary 27.1
▶ Spanish Audio Summary 27.1

LET'S GET STARTED!

Write the following sentence on the chalkboard: *It's the economy, stupid.* As students enter the classroom, tell them that one of then-candidate Bill Clinton's political strategists coined the sentence during the 1992 presidential election. Tell students to explain in writing what the sentence might mean. Ask volunteers to share their responses with the class. Tell students that in Section 1 they will learn about the role of the economy in the 1992 election and in Clinton's continued political success.

SECTION 1

READ TO DISCOVER

1. How did the 1992 presidential election differ from other recent elections?
2. What led to the Republican comeback in the 1994 congressional elections?
3. How did regional conflicts and terrorism affect the world?
4. How successful was the United Nations in maintaining world peace after the Cold War ended?

IDENTIFY

Bill Clinton
Hillary Rodham Clinton
Ross Perot
Contract with America
Newt Gingrich
Nelson Mandela
Operation Restore Hope
Yasir Arafat
Yitzhak Rabin
Mu'ammar Gadhafi

WHY IT MATTERS TODAY

The president must work with Congress to get legislation passed. Use **CNNfyi.com** or other **current events** sources to learn more about the current president's legislative successes and failures. Predict how one legislative success will affect you. Record your findings in your journal.

CNNfyi.com

Clinton's First Term

 EYEWITNESSES TO History "*Today, a generation raised in the shadows of the Cold War assumes new responsibilities in a world warmed by the sunshine of freedom but threatened still by ancient hatreds and new plagues. . . . Though our challenges are fearsome, so are our strengths. . . . Our democracy must be not only the envy of the world but the engine of our own renewal. There is nothing wrong with America that cannot be cured by what is right with America.*"

—Bill Clinton, "Inaugural Address," January 21, 1993

1992 Democratic Party campaign button

After successfully campaigning on the issue of governmental renewal, Bill Clinton was elected president in November 1992. He continued his message of renewal for the nation in his inaugural address in 1993. With the Cold War over, many Americans optimistically expected solutions to political gridlock, continued violence overseas, and tensions within the United States. This confidence was shaken, however, by new challenges and dangers at home and abroad.

The Election of 1992

Despite the nation's economic woes, President Bush's popularity remained high, particularly after the Persian Gulf War in 1991. One of the few Democrats willing to challenge him in the 1992 election was Governor **Bill Clinton** of Arkansas.

The Democratic challenger. Bill Clinton was born William Jefferson Blythe in 1946 in Hope, Arkansas, shortly after his father's death. His mother, Virginia, later married Roger Clinton. Bill Clinton's childhood experiences of dealing with poverty and a troubled home life—including an alcoholic adoptive father—shaped his outlook on the world. After meeting President John F. Kennedy as a teenage delegate to Boys' Nation in 1963, Clinton decided on a political career.

While studying law at Yale University he met Hillary Rodham, a fellow law student. Rodham later served as a staff member with the House Judiciary Committee as it considered the impeachment of President Nixon. The couple married in 1975 and settled in Fayetteville, Arkansas. Three years later, Clinton became the nation's youngest governor. As a baby boomer, Clinton reflected many traits of his generation. He opposed the war in Vietnam and for a time tried to avoid being drafted. Influenced by the idealism of the 1960s, he believed strongly in diversity and equality.

As first lady of Arkansas, **Hillary Rodham Clinton** served on several influential committees, including one that developed a ground-breaking education-reform program. Bill Clinton acknowledged his wife's key role in advising him. During the 1992 campaign he said that voters would be getting "two for the price of one" if he were elected president. Some Americans, however, were uncomfortable with the idea of a president's wife in a policy-making role.

TEACH OBJECTIVE 1

LEVEL 1: Tell students to imagine that they are foreign exchange students living in the United States during the 1992 elections. Have each student write a postcard to a friend or family member back home to describe how the 1992 election has been different from other recent U.S. elections. *(Students should mention high voter turnout, the success of independent candidate Ross Perot, and the record number of female candidates who ran for public office.)* Ask volunteers to read their postcards to the class. **English Language Learners**

LEVEL 2: Tell students to imagine that the 1992 elections have just ended and that they are journalists who must write an article about the elections. Have each student write a short article in which he or she analyzes how the 1992 elections differed from other recent elections. *(See the Level 1 lesson for the correct differences.)* Ask volunteers to share their articles with the class.

The campaign.

After years of low voter participation, citizens turned out in large numbers in 1992 to make their voices heard. Candidates used public forums such as television talk shows and radio call-in programs to answer questions directly from the public. A master of this sort of publicity was **Ross Perot**.

Perot, a billionaire from Texas, ran as an independent candidate for president. He promised to reform the federal government by decreasing the influence of political lobbyists and by giving the public a greater voice. He also promised to use his business skills to cut government spending and balance the budget. Perot's message appealed to many voters who were concerned about the economy and the federal deficit.

President Bush said little about the economy in his campaign. He focused largely on the personal character of the candidates. Some people questioned Bill Clinton's integrity. Some of his political enemies in Arkansas referred to him as "Slick Willie," comparing him to old-time con artists selling snake oil as a cure-all.

Comments about Clinton's character had little effect at the polls. He and his running mate, Senator Al Gore of Tennessee, won 43 percent of the popular vote and 370 electoral votes. Bush won 37 percent of the popular vote and 168 electoral votes. Although Perot failed to pick up any electoral votes, he captured 19 percent of the popular vote. This was more than any third-party presidential ticket since that of Theodore Roosevelt, the Progressive Party candidate, in 1912. Many of Perot's supporters were dissatisfied Republicans. Their votes ultimately helped Clinton.

Voter frustration.

Perot's popularity and the Democratic victory reflected the belief of many voters that politicians were out of touch. Female voters—particularly those outraged by the Clarence Thomas–Anita Hill hearings—were active in the 1992 election. Shortly after the hearings, feminist Eleanor Smeal spoke out. "The Senate did more in one week to underscore the critical need for more women in the Senate than feminists have been able to do in 25 years." Women responded by running for public office in record numbers.

The increase in female candidates led the press to dub 1992 "the year of the woman." Many of these candidates won election. Four prominent female Democrats gained U.S. Senate seats, including Patty Murray of Washington and African American Carol Moseley-Braun of Illinois. California filled both of its Senate seats with women—Barbara Boxer and Dianne Feinstein.

✔ **READING CHECK: Drawing Conclusions** How did Ross Perot's candidacy affect the 1992 election? His candidacy led to record voter turnout and helped Clinton win.

Clinton Takes Office

At President Clinton's inauguration, poet Maya Angelou read her poem that celebrated the diversity of Americans and expressed hope for the future:

INTERPRETING THE VISUAL RECORD

The 1992 election. Ross Perot ran a strong third-party campaign for president. *What type of image does this button suggest?*

Incumbent senator Barbara Mikulski (far right) welcomes newly elected senators Carol Moseley-Braun, Patty Murray, and Barbara Boxer (left to right).

TEACH OBJECTIVE 2

 LEVEL 1: Tell students that Democrats won a majority in both houses of Congress in 1992, the year Bill Clinton was elected president. Pair students and have each pair compile a list of factors leading to the Republican comeback in the 1994 congressional elections. *(Students should mention the slow economic recovery; the early failures of the Clinton administration, including health care reform and the Whitewater investigation; and Republicans' Contract with America.)* Ask each pair to share its list of factors with the class, then compile a list on the chalkboard. To conclude, lead a class discussion about the role that each factor might have had in the Republicans' success.
English Language Learners, Cooperative Learning

 Primary Source

> **"Lift up your eyes upon
> This day breaking for you.
> Give birth again
> To the dream. . . .**
>
> **Here on the pulse of this new day
> You may have the grace to look up and out
> And into your sister's eyes and into
> Your brother's face, your country
> And say simply
> Very simply
> With hope
> Good morning."**

—"On the Pulse of Morning"

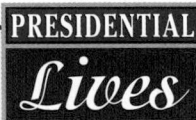 **PRESIDENTIAL *Lives***

**1946–
In Office 1993–2000**

Bill Clinton

Bill Clinton's presidency marked many firsts in the White House. He was the first president born in the post–World War II era and the first president from Arkansas. Clinton was also the first president to play the saxophone at his own inaugural celebration.

Clinton's career goal as a youngster was to become a jazz musician. He was heavily influenced by African American jazz artists and early rock 'n' roll stars such as Elvis Presley. He excelled at playing the saxophone and was offered numerous music scholarships to college after he graduated from high school. Although Clinton went on to make a career in politics, he frequently used his musical talents in campaigns. During the 1992 presidential election, he put on a pair of sunglasses and played the saxophone on a popular late-night talk show. Despite his love of music, Clinton believes that he made the right career choice. "I would have been a very good musician," he once noted, "but not a great one."

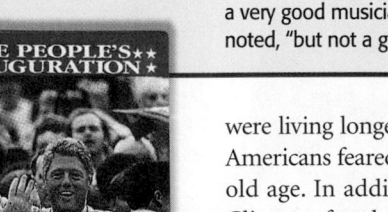

**★★THE PEOPLE'S★★
★INAUGURATION★**

**Bill Clinton · President
★★★ Jan. 20, 1993 ★★★**

Once in office, Clinton put these ideas into practice by creating a diverse cabinet. His appointees included Mexican American Henry Cisneros as secretary of housing and urban development. He also appointed African Americans Ron Brown and Joycelyn Elders as secretary of commerce and surgeon general, respectively. Other female appointees included Press Secretary Dee Dee Myers, Attorney General Janet Reno, and Secretary of Health and Human Services Donna Shalala. Clinton also nominated Ruth Bader Ginsburg to fill a vacancy on the Supreme Court.

Clinton suffered a series of setbacks early in his presidency. An elaborate plan to reform the nation's health care system, drafted by a task force headed by Hillary Rodham Clinton, died in Congress. Clinton had hoped the reform plan would address voters' concerns about the rising costs of medical care. More Americans were living longer, and the baby boom generation was passing middle age. Many Americans feared that they would not be able to afford quality health care in their old age. In addition to being unable to move health care reform forward, the Clintons faced questions of possible past improper financial dealings. Most involved a failed Arkansas real-estate development called Whitewater.

On the economic front, however, President Clinton had some success. In August 1993 Congress narrowly passed a budget act that combined tax increases and spending cuts to reduce the national debt. Over time, the act worked. By 1996 the deficit dropped to about $107 billion, less than half that of 1992. Unemployment dropped to 5.4 percent, the lowest since 1989, and inflation hovered at about 3 percent. As investors gained confidence, the stock market boomed.

A Republican Comeback

As the 1994 congressional elections approached, voter frustration with the slow recovery began to build. Encouraged by President Clinton's early setbacks,

LEVELS 2 AND 3: Have each student create a collage representing the factors that led to the Republican comeback in the 1994 congressional elections. *(See the Level 1 lesson for the correct factors.)* Ask volunteers to present and explain their collages to the class. To conclude, lead a class discussion about the role that each factor might have had in the Republicans' success.

TEACH OBJECTIVE 3

 LEVEL 1: Tell students to imagine that they are journalists living through the late 1980s and 1990s. Pair students and have each pair write several headlines describing how regional conflicts and terrorism affected the world. *(Headlines should mention conflicts in Eastern Europe,* *Operation Restore Hope, the Israeli-Palestinian peace accord, U.S. retaliation against Libya and Iraq, and the deaths of Americans in various international and domestic terrorist incidents.)* Ask students to read their headlines to the class.

English Language Learners, Cooperative Learning

LEVELS 2 AND 3: Tell students to imagine that they are journalists who are writing about the effect of regional conflicts and terrorism on the world between 1986 and 1996. Have each student write a magazine article on this topic. *(See the Level 1 lesson for the correct incidents and effects.)* Ask volunteers to read their articles to the class. Students may wish to include their articles in their portfolios.

Republicans prepared for the election. Many Republican candidates signed the **Contract with America**, which pledged a balanced-budget amendment and other reforms.

Voters gave Republicans control of both the House and Senate for the first time since the 1952 elections. **Newt Gingrich** of Georgia, who became Speaker of the House, commented on the election.

 66This election was actually about some fairly big ideas: which direction do you want to go in? . . . Those who argued for counter-culture values, bigger government, redistributionist economics, and bureaucracies deciding how you should spend your money, were on the losing end in virtually every part of the country.**99**

–Newt Gingrich, speech, November 11, 1994

✔ **READING CHECK: Drawing Conclusions**
Why did many Americans vote for Republicans in the 1994 congressional elections?
frustration with economic recovery and the Contract with America

Foreign and Domestic Dangers

Amid these domestic and political challenges, the Clinton administration confronted a range of global crises. It also wrestled with an increase in terrorism.

Regional conflicts. As the Cold War faded, regional conflicts intensified. The end of Communist rule in Eastern Europe unleashed bitter ethnic and local disputes. Bosnia and Herzegovina, a region that once was part of Yugoslavia, was torn apart by fighting among Serbs, Croats, and Slovenes.

The 15 newly independent republics of the former Soviet Union experienced conflict as various groups struggled for power and self-rule. Russia and Ukraine argued over control of the Black Sea fleet, while Christians in Armenia battled with Muslims in neighboring Azerbaijan (a-zuhr-by-JAHN).

On a brighter note, a new era dawned in South Africa when decades of apartheid came to an end. In 1994 South Africa held its first elections allowing all races to vote. Black civil rights activist **Nelson Mandela**, who had spent years as a political prisoner in South Africa, won the presidency. Despite conflict between rival political and ethnic groups, South Africa's future looked hopeful.

Elsewhere in Africa, however, turmoil reigned, worsened by famine and poverty. Civil war raged in Liberia, Mali, Somalia, and Zambia. In December 1992 a UN force, including many Americans, launched **Operation Restore Hope** to provide relief to famine-stricken Somalia. Fighting among rival clans in that country had previously

---

★ HISTORICAL DOCUMENTS ★

Contract with America

Drawn up by members of the Republican Party, the Contract with America offered a list of reforms and 10 pieces of legislation that Republicans promised to propose. In 1994 some 300 candidates for public office pledged their support to the positions outlined in the document, stating, "If we break this contract, throw us out." **In what specific ways does the contract promise to "restore the bonds of trust between the people and their elected representatives"?**

As Republican members of the House of Representatives and as citizens seeking to join that body we propose not just to change its policies, but even more important, to restore the bonds of trust between the people and their elected representatives. . . .

On the first day of the 104th Congress, the new Republican majority will immediately pass the following major reforms:

First, require all laws that apply to the rest of the country also apply equally to the Congress;

Second, select a major independent auditing firm to conduct a comprehensive audit [complete study] of Congress for waste, fraud, or abuse;

Third, cut the number of House committees, and cut committee staff by one-third;

Fourth, limit the terms of all committee chairs;

Fifth, ban the casting of proxy votes in committee;

Sixth, require committee meetings to be open to the public;

Seventh, require a three-fifths majority vote to pass a tax increase;

Eighth, guarantee honest accounting of our federal budget by implementing [putting into effect] zero baseline budgeting.

Nelson Mandela. Nelson Mandela was imprisoned for 27 years because of his political opposition to the apartheid regime in South Africa. He belonged to the then-outlawed African National Congress (ANC), which had been founded in 1912 with the goal of creating a state where all races would share political power. During his early years in prison, Mandela–a lawyer by profession–was forced to do hard labor, including crushing rocks. Released from prison in 1990, Mandela was elected president four years later in the first national elections in which black South Africans were allowed to vote.

CRITICAL THINKING Why might Mandela's long prison term have given him moral authority?

ANSWER: Students might suggest that Mandela's long prison term indicated a willingness to suffer for his political beliefs.

HISTORICAL DOCUMENTS ANSWER

Students might note that it requires Congress to abide by the same laws as the people, calls for an independent financial audit, and for committee meetings to be open to the public.

TEACH OBJECTIVE 4

ALL LEVELS: Tell students that when the Cold War ended, many people hoped that the United Nations would be able to maintain world peace. To help students assess the success of the United Nations in maintaining world peace after the Cold War, copy the graphic organizer at right on the chalkboard, omitting the italicized answers. Have each student complete the organizer by describing various UN actions around the world and their results. Ask volunteers to share their answers with the class. To conclude, ask students why UN efforts met with mixed results. *(Students might point out that peacekeepers had difficulty in complicated political situations such as the Somalian civil war and the ethnic fighting in Bosnia.)* Tell students that the end of the Cold War led to the rise of ethnic conflicts that had been previously suppressed by communist governments. **English Language Learners**

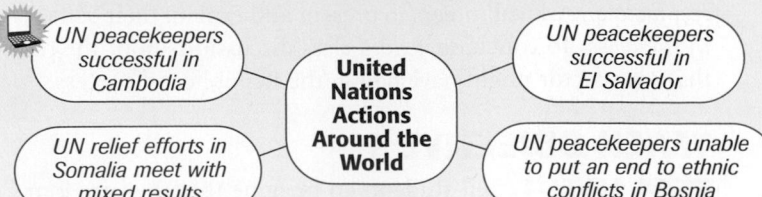

HOMEWORK *Tell students to imagine that they are editors writing an encyclopedia entry. Have each student write an entry about the success of the United Nations in maintaining world peace after the Cold War.*

President Clinton looks on as Yitzhak Rabin (left) and Yasir Arafat shake hands to seal their 1993 peace accord.

INTERPRETING THE VISUAL RECORD

Terrorism at home. Mourners attached mementos to a fence surrounding the destroyed Murrah Federal Building in Oklahoma City. *How does this memorial reflect many people's emotions after the attack?*

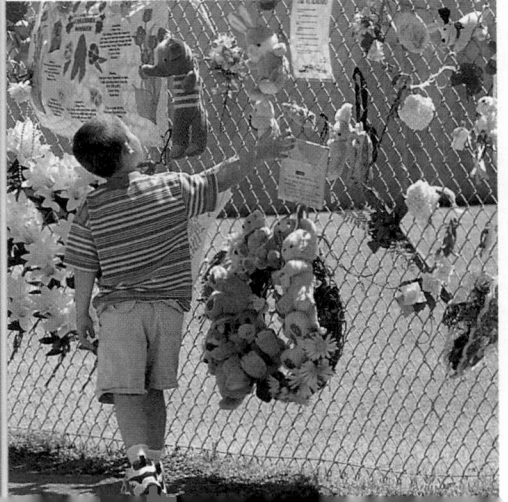

prevented relief workers from getting food and other supplies to starving Somalis. Despite the UN effort, Somalia's suffering continued.

The Middle East. In the Middle East some peace efforts were made. Palestinian leader **Yasir Arafat** and Israeli prime minister **Yitzhak Rabin** signed a peace accord, in which Israel and the PLO officially recognized each other. The 1993 agreement also set guidelines for Palestinian self-rule in occupied areas of Israel. Overseeing the signing at the White House, President Clinton described it as a "historic and honorable compromise."

The peace process suffered a setback in 1995, when a young Israeli with extreme nationalist views assassinated Rabin. In 1996 Benjamin Netanyahu was elected prime minister of Israel. He pledged to be less willing to compromise in peace negotiations. New outbreaks of violence followed.

President Clinton tried to move the peace process forward at Camp David in July 2000. In September longtime Israeli government official Ariel Sharon visited a contested religious site in east Jerusalem. His visit sparked violence that continued into 2001. In February Sharon was elected as Israel's new prime minister. Violence continued in the area.

Terrorism. An increase in international terrorist activity accompanied the end of the Cold War. Some experts estimate that the number of terrorist acts rose by 11 percent from 1991 to 1992.

U.S. leaders usually responded quickly to international terrorism linked directly to a particular nation. In 1986 President Reagan had ordered a bombing attack on Libya. Evidence had linked that country's leader, **Mu'ammar Gadhafi** (guh-DAH-fee), to an attack at a West Berlin nightclub. The attack killed one U.S. soldier and injured many others. In the summer of 1993, Clinton ordered the bombing of the Iraqi intelligence service headquarters. The Federal Bureau of Investigation (FBI) had uncovered an Iraqi plot to assassinate former president George Bush.

Terrorism also occurred in the air. In 1988 a bomb destroyed a Pan American airliner flying over Lockerbie, Scotland. All 259 aboard were killed, including many Americans. The bomb was traced to two Libyans, but Gadhafi refused to send them to the United States for trial. In 1998 bombs exploded at U.S. embassies in Kenya and Tanzania, killing more than 200 people.

Domestic terrorism proved particularly chilling. On February 26, 1993, a bomb blast rocked the World Trade Center in New York City, killing six people and injuring more than 1,000. The suspects arrested had ties to an Egyptian fundamentalist leader who was linked to several other terrorist acts. In April 1995 a truck bomb destroyed a federal building in Oklahoma City, killing 168 people. Two American men with ties to antigovernment militia groups were convicted. A year later, the FBI arrested the so-called Unabomber, a loner with a grievance against modern technology, who had carried out a series of mail-bombings. Then, during the 1996 Summer Olympics in Atlanta, a bomb killed one person and injured more than 100 others.

✔ **READING CHECK: Sequencing** Place in chronological order the major conflicts and acts of terrorism in the 1990s. 1993—World Trade Center bombing; 1995—Oklahoma City bombing; 1996—Olympics bomb blast in Atlanta; 1998—attacks on U.S. embassies

REVIEW

Have students complete the **Section 1 Review** on p. 803.

ASSESS

Have students complete **Daily Quiz 27.1**. As **Alternative Assessment**, you may want to use the postcards or the dinner-table conversation in this section's lessons.

RETEACH

Have students complete **Main Idea Activity for English Language Learners and Special-Needs Students 27.1**. Then pair students and have each pair create flash cards for all of the Define and Identify terms in this section's lessons. Students should write the name of the Define or Identify term on one side of the card and a brief description of the term on the reverse side of the card. Ask each pair to use the flash cards to quiz each other.
English Language Learners, Cooperative Learning

EXTEND

Ask students to conduct research on one of the following individuals: Yasir Arafat, Ruth Bader Ginsburg, Nelson Mandela, Yitzhak Rabin, or Donna Shalala. Have each student write a biographical report about his or her chosen individual.
Block Scheduling

The Role of the United Nations

With the end of the Cold War, many foreign-policy observers hoped that the United Nations would become the international force for peace that its founders had envisioned. By 1992 there were thousands of UN forces serving on peacekeeping missions in locations throughout the world. In countries such as Cambodia and El Salvador, UN peacekeepers played a successful role.

The United Nations had mixed results, however, in its dealings with complex situations such as in Somalia. In Bosnia and Herzegovina, ethnic fighting among Croats, Serbs, and Slovenes left some 150,000 people dead or missing by the end of 1993. The United Nations and the North Atlantic Treaty Organization (NATO) sent peacekeeping forces to the area and launched an investigation into war crimes, but the fighting continued.

As the Bosnian Serbs seized land, bombed cities, and killed or expelled Bosnian Muslims, the Clinton administration at first did little. By 1995, however, as the Bosnian Serbs continued their aggression, President Clinton took a stronger stance. The United States and NATO cooperated in bombing Bosnian Serb positions. In November 1995 the United States brought the leaders of the warring groups to Dayton, Ohio, to hammer out a peace accord. The resulting agreement provided for a multiethnic Bosnian federation. It also required war crimes trials and elections, which were held in the fall of 1996. In addition, Clinton sent some 20,000 Americans to Bosnia to help the NATO troops enforce the Dayton accords. Ethnic hatreds in Bosnia ran deep, however, and the fate of the U.S. peace initiative remained uncertain.

INTERPRETING THE VISUAL RECORD

United Nations. British troops participating in a UN operation travel past a destroyed mosque in Bosnia. *What type of protection do you think the UN force provided for the people of Bosnia?*

✔ **READING CHECK: Summarizing** How did the United Nations and NATO respond to conflicts after the Cold War? UN—peacekeeping missions and war crimes investigation; NATO—bombed Bosnia and enforced peace accords

SECTION 1 REVIEW

1. **Identify and explain:**
   Bill Clinton
   Hillary Rodham Clinton
   Ross Perot
   Contract with America
   Newt Gingrich
   Nelson Mandela
   Operation Restore Hope
   Yasir Arafat
   Yitzhak Rabin
   Mu'ammar Gadhafi

2. **Summarizing** Copy the graphic organizer below. Use it to describe the regional conflicts and events that shaped the world in the early 1990s.

   - Middle East
   - REGIONAL CRISES & EVENTS
   - Former Soviet Union
   - Africa

3. **Finding the Main Idea**
   a. How was the 1992 presidential election different from other recent elections?
   b. How did the Republicans gain control of the House and the Senate just two years after Democrat Bill Clinton was elected president?
   c. What factors led to an increase in regional conflicts and terrorist activity? How did these conflicts affect the United States and the world?

4. **Writing and Critical Thinking**
   Evaluating Write a brief article explaining how the role of the United Nations in major conflicts revealed the organization's limits.
   Consider:
   • successes of the UN in the 1990s
   • the outcome of the UN missions in Somalia and Bosnia
   • why the UN missions had mixed results

Homework Practice Online
keyword: SE3 HP27

SECTION REVIEW 1 ANSWERS

1. **Identify**
• Bill Clinton, p. 798
• Hillary Rodham Clinton, p. 798
• Ross Perot, p. 799
• Contract with America, p. 800
• Newt Gingrich, p. 801
• Nelson Mandela, p. 801
• Operation Restore Hope, p. 801
• Yasir Arafat, p. 802
• Yitzhak Rabin, p. 802
• Mu'ammar Gadhafi, p. 802

2. Middle East—violence between Israelis and Palestinians continued; former Soviet Union—conflict between Armenian Christians and Muslims in Azerbaijan, and between Ukraine and Russia over the Black Sea fleet; Africa—civil war in Liberia, Mali, Somalia, and Zambia

3a. increased voter turnout; strong independent candidate

b. by capitalizing on voter frustration over economic issues

c. The collapse of the Soviet Union unleashed ethnic and religious tensions in Eastern Europe and the former Soviet Union. The United States became embroiled in conflicts between various ethnic groups. Terrorism led to the deaths of Americans.

4. Answers will vary. Students may suggest that although it claimed successes in El Salvador and Cambodia, UN forces could not stop the violence in Somalia and Bosnia.

SECTION 2

After completing Section 2, students should be able to:

OBJECTIVE 1 Discuss the issues that affected the 1996 presidential election.

OBJECTIVE 2 Describe the domestic issues that shaped President Clinton's second term.

OBJECTIVE 3 Relate what led to the impeachment of President Clinton, and describe what the outcome was.

OBJECTIVE 4 Analyze why NATO launched air strikes against Yugoslavia in 1999.

LET'S GET STARTED!

Copy the following statement on the chalkboard: *In 1996, Americans cast a vote for divided government—a situation in which one major party controls the White House and the other party controls one or both houses of Congress. Voters have been unable to trust either party enough to give it a clear mandate to run government.* As students enter the classroom, tell them to respond in writing to the statement. Tell students that in Section 2 they will learn about the issues that affected the outcome of the 1996 election and about President Clinton's second term.

READ TO DISCOVER

1. What issues affected the 1996 presidential election?
2. What domestic issues shaped President Clinton's second term?
3. What led to the impeachment of President Clinton, and what was the outcome?
4. Why did NATO launch air strikes against Yugoslavia in 1999?

IDENTIFY

Bob Dole
Reform Party
Alan Greenspan
Rodney King
Los Angeles riots
Initiative on Race
James Byrd Jr.
Kenneth Starr
Slobodan Milosevic
Kosovo crisis
Madeleine Albright

▶ **WHY IT MATTERS TODAY**

The United States continues to play an active role in world affairs. Use CNNfyi.com or other **current events** sources to learn more about U.S. involvement in a particular country or U.S. views on an international issue today. Record your findings in your journal.

Clinton's Second Term

 EYEWITNESSES TO History **"***Let me be the bridge to a time of tranquillity, faith and confidence in action. And to those who say it was never so, that America's not been better, I say you're wrong. And I know because I was there. And I have seen it. And I remember.***"**

–Bob Dole, quoted in *Time*, November 4, 1996

Bob Dole campaigning in 1996

Campaigning in the months before the presidential election of 1996, Republican Bob Dole of Kansas reminisced about an earlier era of prosperity, morality, and tranquillity in America. Democratic critics viewed the senator's memories as misleading. Nonetheless, Dole attempted to present himself as a mature and dignified candidate in contrast to the emerging accounts of scandals and dishonesty in President Clinton's administration. Many Americans, however, believed that Dole was out of touch with their concerns and problems.

The Election of 1996

Despite Republicans' large gains in the 1994 congressional elections, President Clinton's popularity improved as the economy boomed. Economist David Wyss described the nation's healthy financial conditions.

History Makers Speak **"***If you look at the economy during the Clinton administration, you have to say that it's been a success. We have low inflation, full employment, and steady growth. This is really just about the best of all [economic] worlds.***"**

—David Wyss, quoted in *The New Yorker*, June 10, 1996

Americans' approval of the president climbed as the Republican-led Congress failed to enact key measures in the Contract with America. They also tried to cut popular social and environmental programs. When Clinton and Congress battled over a budget bill in 1995, the federal government was briefly shut down. Voters largely blamed the Republicans. Clinton also benefited from divisions among Republicans, who split over such issues as budget cuts, government regulations, social issues, and taxes. These divisions sharpened as the 1996 presidential campaign began. From a large field of Republican candidates, **Bob Dole** emerged victorious from the primaries and tried to unite his party's competing groups.

The race. A disabled World War II veteran, Dole was also a senator with 34 years of experience in Congress. Yet as a 73-year-old, he would be the oldest person ever elected president if he won. His age concerned voters. Dole also proved to be an ineffective campaigner. "He never . . . offered the sustained and layered argument that precedes the applause line," concluded political analyst Peggy Noonan. "He just declared things—And there'll be no more crime in a Dole Administration—and waited for people to clap as he cleared his throat."

LEVEL 1: Tell students that in 1996 voters sent a mixed message to President Clinton and Congress about which issues were important to them. Ask students to identify the issues that affected the 1996 presidential election. *(Students should mention economic prosperity, divisions within the Republican Party, Republicans' failure to enact Contract with America measures and their attempt to cut social and environmental programs, the fact that voters held the Republicans responsible for the government shutdown, Clinton's ability to seize the middle ground, and Dole's lackluster presidential campaign.)*

Discuss these issues with students. Then have each student write headlines discussing the issues that affected the 1996 presidential election. Ask volunteers to read their headlines to the class. **English Language Learners**

LEVELS 2 AND 3: Have each student write a poem about the issues that affected the 1996 presidential election. *(See the Level 1 lesson for the correct issues.)* Ask volunteers to read their poems to the class. To conclude, lead a class discussion about what message voters might have been trying to send the president and Congress.

Meanwhile, Clinton seized the middle ground on many issues. The president echoed the Republicans' call for economic growth, smaller government, anticrime programs, and middle-class tax relief. Clinton also agreed with the Republican criticism of the nation's welfare system. The president and Republican leaders cooperated to design welfare reforms that would limit benefits, introduce work requirements, and shift programs from federal to state control. Clinton signed a welfare-reform bill in August 1996 that resulted in the most extensive overhaul of the welfare system since the New Deal. It replaced the federally funded Aid to Dependent Children with block grants to states. Each state became responsible for designing and operating its own welfare program.

Clinton and Dole differed on issues such as environmental protection and gun control. Clinton favored these efforts while Dole opposed them. Clinton also called for stricter measures to discourage smoking, particularly among young Americans.

President Clinton celebrates his 1996 re-election.

The result. Clinton's strategy proved successful. He became the first Democrat since Franklin D. Roosevelt to win a second term. He won 49 percent of the popular vote and 379 electoral votes. Dole won 41 percent of the popular vote and 159 electoral votes. Ross Perot won 8.4 percent of the vote as a candidate of the **Reform Party**. The Reform Party promised to change politics in the nation's capital.

Although several Republicans elected in 1994 failed to win re-election, the party maintained its majorities in Congress. Clinton's victory marked the first time that a Democrat had been elected president while the Republicans won both the House and the Senate. As he approached his second term, President Clinton insisted that "the vital American center is alive and well." He pledged to provide health insurance for children and people with disabilities, revise parts of the welfare bill, and connect classrooms to the Internet.

✔ **READING CHECK: Making Generalizations**
What did the 1996 presidential election reveal about American society? Americans worried that Dole's age made him out of touch with their needs. Clinton's middle-of-the-road style appealed to many.

Domestic Prosperity and Concerns

The continued booming economy helped President Clinton achieve some of his second-term goals. The first step was to maintain the nation's economic health.

The economy. During the 1990s the U.S. economy experienced the longest and largest boom in its history. While almost everyone benefited from the prosperity, the number of people who were very wealthy grew at an amazing rate. A booming stock market contributed to much of this wealth.

INTERPRETING POLITICAL CARTOONS

Prosperity. The Dow represents the Dow Jones industrial average of some stocks. As it rose, so did the stock market and the personal wealth of many Americans. *What is the reaction of the people in the cartoon to the rising Dow?*

THEY HAD TO ELONGATE THE BUSINESS SECTION AGAIN TODAY.

DOW AT 10,000

Daily Inkwire

Bob Dole. Bob Dole was a pre-med student at the University of Kansas when World War II began. He enlisted in the army and was sent to Italy, where he was wounded by German machine-gun fire. Dole was so badly wounded that he spent more than three years in hospitals. At one point he nearly died. As a result of his injuries, Dole lost the use of his right arm and had to learn to write with his left hand. He decided that his disability would make a medical career difficult, so he switched to the study of law. Dole was elected to the Kansas legislature while still a law student at Washburn University.

CRITICAL THINKING How might Dole's wartime service have served him well in his political career?

ANSWER: Students might point out that Dole could rightfully claim that he had made important sacrifices while serving his country, a fact that appealed to many voters.

POLITICAL CARTOON ANSWER
Students might suggest that the people in the cartoon expect the Dow to continue its rise.

TEACH OBJECTIVE 2

LEVEL 1: Pair students and have each pair prepare an outline for a report about the domestic issues that shaped President Clinton's second term. *(Outlines should mention the economic boom, which was characterized by a soaring stock market, low unemployment, and low inflation; and race relations, which came to the nation's attention through the Los Angeles Riots, Clinton's Initiative on Race, and the murder of James Byrd Jr.)* Ask volunteers to present their outlines to the class. **English Language Learners, Cooperative Learning**

LEVELS 2 AND 3: Tell students to imagine that they are journalists who work for a newsmagazine and who must produce a lead article and magazine cover for the next issue. Organize the class into small groups. Have each group write an article about the domestic issues that shaped President Clinton's second term and create a magazine cover to accompany the article. *(See the Level 1 lesson for the correct issues.)* Ask students to present their magazine articles and covers to the class.
Cooperative Learning

HOMEWORK *Have each student select one domestic policy initiative from President Clinton's second term and evaluate its success in a short essay.*

Poverty in the 1990s.
The percentage of Americans who lived below the poverty line remained fairly constant through the 1990s, despite the decade's prosperity. In 1990 some 13.5 percent of all American families lived in poverty. Six years later, 13.7 percent of American families lived in poverty.

CRITICAL THINKING What do you think the levels of poverty reveal about the economic boom of the 1990s?

ANSWER: Students might point out that the benefits of the boom were not distributed evenly throughout American society.

THAT'S INTERESTING!

When adjusted for inflation, investments in stocks, on average, made no profits for investors during the 1970s. That poor performance turned around during the 1980s, when the total return earned on stocks reached almost 12 percent. From 1990 to 1997, the total return climbed above 13 percent, making stocks a sound investment for many Americans.

CHART ANSWER
Yahoo

Selected Technology Stock Prices, June 1, 1998, to June 1, 1999

Stock	Lowest price per share	Highest price per share
Amazon.com	$13.75	$221.25
Dell	$19.93	$55.00
IBM	$53.00	$123.00
Microsoft	$41.81	$95.62
Yahoo	$25.12	$244.00

Source: New York Stock Exchange

Interpreting Charts The boom in computer technology in the 1990s led to enormous investment in technology stocks.

 Skills Assessment Which stock experienced the greatest increase in price between June 1, 1998, and June 1, 1999?

The value of technology stocks in particular soared. Some companies that did not even make a profit in the 1990s still saw the value of their stock rise enormously. In 2000 many of these stock prices fell just as quickly as they had risen.

The economic boom led to the lowest unemployment rates in years. Low unemployment usually leads to inflation, which the Federal Reserve tries to halt by raising interest rates. During the 1990s, however, unemployment, the rate of inflation, and interest rates remained low. Many economists credited Federal Reserve Chairman **Alan Greenspan** with this reversal of stagflation. He raised and lowered interest rates to help fuel the boom.

This economic expansion also created a huge amount of extra money, or a surplus, in the government's budget. The surplus in 1999 alone was $124 billion. Clinton wanted to use the extra money to strengthen domestic programs such as Social Security, Medicare, and education. He also proposed a plan to pay off all of the federal debt by 2015 and give tax cuts to some groups.

The Republican Congress argued that most of the surplus should be returned to the American people in the form of tax cuts. As a result of their differences, the president and Congress failed to agree on a budget in the fall of 2000. Clinton vetoed the Republicans' budget plan that included a congressional pay raise. He explained, "I cannot in good conscience sign a bill that funds the operation of the Congress . . . before funding our classrooms, fixing our schools and protecting our workers."

Race relations. During his second term Clinton also focused on race relations. In the 1990s racial conflicts continued to plague the country. The South Central section of Los Angeles exploded in violence in April 1992 after four white police officers were acquitted of beating African American motorist **Rodney King**. The verdict and the **Los Angeles riots** disheartened many people. Even Rodney King appeared on television during the riots, urging people to "try to work it out" peacefully. He asked, "Can we all get along?"

In 1997 Clinton launched an **Initiative on Race** to encourage people to discuss racial issues and concerns. Critics argued that the program produced little meaningful action. Meanwhile, racial violence continued. In June 1998 white racists in Jasper, Texas, killed **James Byrd Jr.**, an African American. The killers had tied Byrd to a pickup truck and dragged him to death. Some people reacted to this modern-day lynching by calling for tougher federal laws against hate crimes.

✔ **READING CHECK: Categorizing** How did the economy and race relations shape President Clinton's second term? economy—a boom and low unemployment drew support; race—he launched an Initiative on Race, but racial violence continued

TEACH OBJECTIVE 3

ALL LEVELS: To help students understand what led to President Clinton's impeachment, and what the major outcomes of the trial were, copy the graphic organizer at right on the chalkboard, omitting the italicized answers. Pair students and have each pair complete the organizer. Ask volunteers to share their answers with the class. To conclude, lead a class discussion about why a president might be impeached. *(Students might mention "high crimes and misdemeanors" or suggest that impeachment is a politically driven process.)* Ask students whether the House should have proceeded with impeachment even though a majority of Americans supported the president. **English Language Learners, Cooperative Learning**

 What Led to President Clinton's Impeachment

- *Independent Counsel Kenneth Starr expands his investigation to include a civil sexual harassment lawsuit against President Clinton.*
- *Clinton gives a video-taped testimony in the civil trial.*
- *Starr investigates whether Clinton had conducted an improper relationship with a White House intern and lied about it during the civil trial.*
- *The president testifies before a grand jury in the Starr investigation. He acknowledges the affair with the intern but insists he did not commit perjury.*
- *The House Judiciary Committee investigates, disagrees with Clinton, and recommends impeachment.*
- *The House of Representatives votes to impeach the president.*

Senate Trial's Outcome

- *The Senate votes to acquit Clinton.*
- *Many Americans say they distrust the president.*
- *Congress lets the independent counsel law expire.*

AMERICAN Letters

Reflecting America in Literature

The national dialogue on race highlighted the growing racial and ethnic diversity of the U.S. population. Many popular writers in the 1990s reflected this diversity in their works. Jimmy Santiago Baca's poem tells the story of a boy growing up in a modern Mexican American community. Gish Jen's novel centers around a Chinese American couple who see the path to success in becoming as "Americanized" as possible.

from "Martín IV"
by Jimmy Santiago Baca

On visiting days with aunts
  and uncles,
I was shuttled back and
  forth—
between Chavez bourgeois
  in the city
and rural Lucero sheepherders,
new cars and gleaming furniture
and leather saddles and burlap
  sacks,
noon football games and six packs of cokes
and hoes, welfare cards and bottles of goat milk.

I was caught in the middle—
between white skinned, English speaking altar boy
at the communion railing,
and brown skinned, Spanish speaking plains nomadic child
with buffalo heart groaning underworld earth powers. . . .

Caught between Indio-Mejicano rural uncles
who stacked hundred pound sacks of pinto beans
on boxcars all day, . . . and Chavez uncles and aunts
who vacationed and followed the Hollywood model
of My Three Sons* for their own families.

* a popular television show of the 1960s
** Italics indicate words spoken in Chinese.

Jimmy Santiago Baca

from *Typical American*
by Gish Jen

Ralph advocated buying a car.
  "Seems like someone's becoming one-hundred-percent Americanized,"** Theresa kidded.
  "What's so American? We had a car, growing up. Don't you remember?" Ralph argued that in fact this way they could avoid getting too Americanized. *"Everywhere we go, we can keep the children inside. Also they won't catch cold."*
  "I thought we agreed the children are going to be American," puzzled Helen.
  Ralph furrowed his brow. When Callie turned three they had decided that Mona and Callie would learn English first, and then Chinese. This was what Janis and Old Chao were planning on doing with Alexander; Janis didn't want him to have an accent.
  Now Ralph drummed his fingers. He stopped and smiled. *"And what better way to Americanize the children than to buy a car!"*

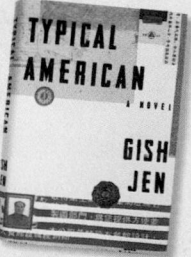
Gish Jen's novel

UNDERSTANDING LITERATURE

1. In Baca's poem, what two different ways of life do the two sides of the speaker's family represent?
2. How do Jen's characters become "Americanized"? What aspects of Chinese culture do they retain?
3. How do you think these works reflect life in the United States in the late 1900s?

HISTORY MAKERS SPEAK

Bill Clinton in *Public Papers of the Presidents of the United States*

Race in America. President Clinton addressed the troubled state of American race relations in a 1997 speech. "Can we be one America respecting, even celebrating, our differences, but embracing even more what we have in common? . . . Our hearts long to answer yes, but our history reminds us that it will be hard. The ideals that bind us together are as old as our Nation, but so are the forces that pull us apart."

CRITICAL THINKING What ideals and forces might Clinton have been referring to?

ANSWER: Students might suggest that Clinton was referring to the ideals of equality and liberty and the forces of bigotry and racism.

AMERICAN LETTERS ANSWERS

1. an urban life of affluence and a rural life of poverty

2. learning English, buying American products; the Chinese language

3. They reveal the tensions between traditional cultures and the process of Americanization that minority groups face in the United States.

LEVEL 1: Ask students whether they can name the two ethnic groups involved in the Kosovo crisis. (*Students should mention the Serbians and ethnic Albanians.*) Tell students that many ethnic groups inhabit the Balkan region and that the Balkans have had a troubled history. Explain that Yugoslav president Slobodan Milosevic wanted to drive ethnic Albanians out of Kosovo province, which is part of Serbia. Discuss with students why NATO launched air strikes against Yugoslavia in 1999. (*Students should mention that Serbians were carrying out mass murders and other atrocities against ethnic Albanians in Kosovo and that NATO air strikes were designed to end the violence.*) Then have each student synthesize information from the class discussion to write two headlines for a newspaper article related to why NATO launched air strikes against Yugoslavia in 1999. Ask volunteers to read their headlines to the class. **English Language Learners**

LEVELS 2 AND 3: Pair students and tell one student to imagine that he or she is Secretary of State Madeleine Albright, then tell the other student to imagine that he or she is a journalist. Have each pair create a transcript for an interview about why NATO launched air strikes against Yugoslavia in 1999. (*See the Level 1 lesson for the correct reasons.*) Ask students to conduct their interviews for the class. **Cooperative Learning**

Independent Counsel Kenneth Starr conducted an investigation into Bill Clinton's alleged misconduct.

INTERPRETING THE VISUAL RECORD

Kosovo crisis. Fleeing violent Serbian attacks, Kosovar Albanian refugees resettled in camps in Albania and Macedonia. *What do you think these refugees might have carried with them as they fled?*

A Presidential Scandal

Although President Clinton maintained high job-approval ratings in public polls, his second term was marred by scandal. In 1994 a former Arkansas state employee had sued Clinton, claiming that he had sexually harassed her while he was governor of Arkansas. As the civil case proceeded, the woman's lawyers began to investigate other alleged misconduct by Clinton.

During this same time, Independent Counsel **Kenneth Starr** was investigating Bill and Hillary Clinton's past financial dealings. In January 1998 Starr received permission from a panel of three federal judges to expand his investigation. He included the possibility that Clinton was trying to tamper with witnesses in the civil lawsuit. Although a federal judge later dismissed the civil lawsuit, Clinton's videotaped testimony in the case almost brought down his presidency.

Starr began to investigate whether Clinton had conducted an improper relationship with a young White House intern and lied about it during the civil trial. After the president repeated his testimony to a grand jury, the House Judiciary Committee launched its own investigation. Although Clinton finally acknowledged the affair with the intern and apologized, he insisted he had not committed perjury. The Republican-led Judiciary Committee disagreed and recommended impeachment. On December 20, 1998, the House of Representatives voted to impeach Clinton on the grounds that his actions had violated his constitutional oath of office.

For just the second time, a U.S. president underwent a trial by the Senate. Some Republicans called for conviction. Most Democrats claimed that Clinton's behavior, while offensive, did not meet the constitutional test of "high crimes and misdemeanors." In public opinion polls, most Americans agreed. In February 1999 the Senate acquitted Clinton of the charges against him by a significant margin.

The scandal had lingering effects. Many Americans said that they distrusted the president personally. Others worried that the scandal had weakened the office of the president. Critics of Starr's investigation noted that it had cost more than $40 million but had yielded few convictions. A few months after the impeachment trial, Congress let the law providing for independent counsels expire.

✔ **READING CHECK: Summarizing** Why was President Clinton impeached?
He allegedly perjured himself in testimony to a grand jury; House Republicans said Clinton violated his constitutional oath of office.

War in Kosovo

As the impeachment trial ended, U.S. officials became concerned about events overseas. The mainly Serbian nation of Yugoslavia, led by President **Slobodan Milosevic** (sloh-buh-DAHN mi-LOH-suh-vitch), had begun a crackdown on the province of Kosovo. About 90 percent of Kosovo's residents were of Albanian heritage. Some Kosovars, or residents of Kosovo, began to demand independence. In response, Milosevic's troops killed thousands of Kosovar Albanians and forced thousands more to leave their homes. Western nations initially paid little attention to the developing **Kosovo crisis**. Serbian military forces increased their attacks on the Kosovars in March 1999. NATO responded by launching air strikes on Serbia.

REVIEW

Have students complete the **Section 2 Review** on p. 809.

ASSESS

Have students complete **Daily Quiz 27.2**. As **Alternative Assessment**, you may want to use the poem or the interview in this section's lessons.

RETEACH

Have students complete **Main Idea Activity for English Language Learners and Special-Needs Students 27.2.** Organize students into small groups and have each group create an outline of the information in one of Section 2's subsections. Have volunteers present their outlines to the class.
English Language Learners, Cooperative Learning

EXTEND

Have students conduct research on the process of impeachment and the independent counsel statute. Students should focus their research on the legal basis for impeachment and the independent counsel statute as well as historical information about both. Have each student write one or two paragraphs about each issue. **Block Scheduling**

BIOGRAPHY
Madeleine Albright

U.S. Secretary of State **Madeleine Albright** played a central role in the Kosovo crisis. Albright was born in Prague, Czechoslovakia, in 1937. Her father was a Czech diplomat. When Albright was a child, her family fled religious and ethnic oppression from Adolf Hitler's Nazi regime and then from communist forces in Eastern Europe. Eventually, her family moved to Colorado. She studied political science at Wellesley College, graduating in 1959, and later received a Ph.D. from Columbia University.

Albright worked for the National Security Council, the White House, the Center for National Policy, and numerous schools and institutes for foreign affairs. In 1993 Clinton appointed her U.S. representative to the United Nations. Four years later, she was sworn in as the first female secretary of state.

Albright was highly critical of governments that mistreated people because of their religious or ethnic backgrounds. She warned that if NATO delayed in taking action the Kosovo crisis could get worse. After nearly three months, the air strikes paid off. Milosevic agreed to withdraw his troops from Kosovo and to allow NATO forces into the area to enforce a peace agreement. In September 2000 voters in Yugoslavia elected a new president. Milosevic initially refused to accept defeat. In response, thousands of Serbians demonstrated in the streets of Belgrade on October 6. Later that day, Milosevic made a televised statement congratulating the president-elect. World leaders quickly recognized the new government. A few days later the European Union lifted economic sanctions and promised to help rebuild Yugoslavia. In July 2001 Milosevic appeared before the International War Crimes Tribunal in The Hague. He was charged with committing crimes against humanity in connection with the Kosovo crisis.

✔ **READING CHECK: Analyzing Information** How did NATO respond to events in Yugoslavia in 1999? NATO launched air strikes against Serbia; after three months, NATO ground forces moved into Kosovo to enforce the peace agreement.

Research on the R•O•M

Free Find:
Madeleine Albright
After reading about Madeleine Albright on the **Holt Researcher CD–ROM**, create a script for a television news show that focuses on Albright's life and work.

SECTION ② REVIEW

1. Identify and explain:
Bob Dole
Reform Party
Alan Greenspan
Rodney King
Los Angeles riots
Initiative on Race
James Byrd Jr.
Kenneth Starr
Slobodan Milosevic
Kosovo crisis
Madeleine Albright

2. Contrasting Copy the graphic organizer below. Use it to outline how the candidates in the 1996 presidential election differed on the issues.

Bill Clinton	Bob Dole

 Homework Practice Online
keyword: SE3 HP27

3. Finding the Main Idea
a. What factors caused the economic growth of the 1990s?
b. What were the major causes of President Clinton's impeachment trial?
c. How did events in Yugoslavia represent new, post–Cold War challenges for the United States?

4. Writing and Critical Thinking
Evaluating Write a newspaper editorial evaluating the Initiative on Race as a solution to the problem of strained race relations.
Consider:
• what events revealed strained race relations
• how talking about the issue might help
• what other approaches might have worked

SECTION ② REVIEW ANSWERS

1. Identify
• Bob Dole, p. 804
• Reform Party, p. 805
• Alan Greenspan, p. 806
• Rodney King, p. 806
• Los Angeles riots, p. 806
• Initiative on Race, p. 806
• James Byrd Jr., p. 806
• Kenneth Starr, p. 808
• Slobodan Milosevic, p. 808
• Kosovo crisis, p. 808
• Madeleine Albright, p. 809

2. Clinton—middle ground on economic issues, called for environmental protection and gun control; Dole—opposed environmental protection and gun control, failed to clarify his position on many issues

3a. booming stock market, and low unemployment, inflation, and interest rates

b. Starr's investigation expands; Clinton gives testimony in a civil trial; Starr claims Clinton lied about a relationship with an intern; the House investigates and impeaches

c. During the Cold War, the United States worried about the spread of communism; in Yugoslavia, it was human rights violations that concerned the United States and NATO.

4. Students' articles might question the effectiveness of the Initiative on Race and offer other solutions that are more effective than mere discussion of the problem of race relations.

After completing Section 3, students should be able to:

OBJECTIVE 1 Discuss the events that shaped the space program in the 1990s.

OBJECTIVE 2 Explain the issues surrounding technology in the 1990s.

OBJECTIVE 3 Analyze how U.S. popular culture affected the rest of the world.

OBJECTIVE 4 Describe how immigration changed in the 1990s.

OBJECTIVE 5 Identify the issues that affected family life in the 1990s.

🔊 LET'S GET STARTED!

Write the following names and terms on the chalkboard: *Mir, Dolly, Y2K bug, John Glenn.* Have students write sentences identifying each item. *(Students should identify: the Russian space station, the first successfully cloned mammal, the fear that computer systems would crash on January 1, 2000, and the oldest American to fly in space.)* Ask volunteers to share their responses with the class. Tell students that in Section 3 they will learn more about how Americans reacted to technological developments during the 1990s.

SECTION ③ RESOURCES

REPRODUCIBLE
▶ Guided Reading Strategy 27.3
▶ Literature Reading 27: Caught Between Two Cultures

TECHNOLOGY
▶ One-Stop Planner, Lesson 27.3
▶ Holt Researcher: American History CD–ROM
▶ Homework Practice Online
▶ HRW Go site

REINFORCEMENT, REVIEW, AND ASSESSMENT
▶ Section 3 Review, p. 814
▶ Daily Quiz 27.3
▶ Main Idea Activity 27.3
▶ English Audio Summary 27.3
▶ Spanish Audio Summary 27.3

SECTION ③

READ TO DISCOVER
1. What events shaped the space program in the 1990s?
2. What issues arose surrounding technology in the 1990s?
3. How did U.S. popular culture affect the rest of the world?
4. How did immigration change in the 1990s?
5. What issues affected family life in the 1990s?

IDENTIFY
Mir
Shannon Lucid
John Glenn
Bill Gates
Internet
World Wide Web
Telecommunications Act
Y2K bug
Immigration Act of 1990
Family and Medical Leave Act

▶ WHY IT MATTERS TODAY
Popular culture activities such as sports give historians clues about daily life in a particular country or community. Use CNNfyi.com or other **current events** sources to learn more about the sports heroes you believe historians will recognize 50 years from now. Record your findings in your journal.

CNNfyi.com

Society in the 1990s

EYEWITNESSES TO History
"**Multiple networks . . . will carry a broad range of services and information technology applications into homes, businesses, schools and hospitals. These networks will form the basis of evolving national and global information infrastructures, in turn creating a seamless web uniting the world in the emergent Information Age. The result will be a new information marketplace, providing opportunities and challenges for individuals, industry and governments.**"

—Al Gore, *Global Information Infrastructure: Agenda for Cooperation*

A teenager uses the Internet.

In 1994 Vice President Al Gore described the future of information technology and its coming effects on American life. New technologies such as computers, the Internet, and the World Wide Web changed the way Americans communicated, conducted business, and related to the rest of the world.

Technology and Society

Many incredible achievements in science and technology were made during the 1990s. Public fascination with technology encouraged innovation.

Space. After suffering a terrible setback with the space shuttle *Challenger* explosion in 1986, the U.S. space program found renewed energy. With the Cold War over, the National Aeronautics and Space Administration (NASA) focused on commercial and scientific projects more than military efforts. The Hubble space telescope, launched in 1990 and repaired in 1993, transmitted vital information and breathtaking photos from deep space. In 1995 the United States joined with Russia for a project aboard the space station **Mir**. Astronaut **Shannon Lucid** broke the U.S. record for the most consecutive days in space. She spent 188 days aboard the *Mir*.

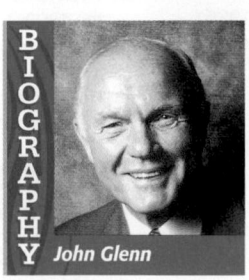
BIOGRAPHY
John Glenn

U.S. astronaut **John Glenn** came out of retirement to break space records in the 1990s. Glenn had been the first American to orbit Earth. He also became the oldest American to fly in space. Born on July 18, 1921, in Cambridge, Ohio, Glenn enrolled in Muskingum College in 1939 in New Concord, Ohio, his hometown. He studied engineering and began flying at the nearby New Philadelphia airfield. In 1942 he enrolled in the Naval Aviation Cadet Program.

Glenn joined the U.S. Marine Corps in 1943 and flew 59 missions during World War II. During the Korean War he flew 90 more. In 1957, as an officer on the project F8U-1 Crusader, Glenn set the transcontinental speed record. He flew from Los Angeles to New York in three hours and

LEVEL 1: Tell students that Americans found renewed interest in space exploration and the space program in the 1990s. Pair students and have each pair draw a cartoon depicting the events that shaped the space program in the 1990s. *(Cartoons should depict the end of the Cold War, photos taken using the Hubble Telescope, the joint U.S.-Russian project aboard the space station* Mir *and Shannon Lucid's 188 days aboard* Mir, *and John Glenn's flight as the oldest American in space.)* Discuss with students some of the issues involving technology in the 1990s. *(Students should mention free-speech rights involving the Internet, the fear that a fully computerized society will make human workers obsolete, the concern that social divisions will deepen because the poor do not have access to com-* puter technology, the Y2K bug, and the ethical issues surrounding the possible cloning of humans.) Have each pair create a series of bumper stickers that identify the issues surrounding technology in the 1990s. Display students' cartoons and bumper stickers around the classroom.
English Language Learners, Cooperative Learning

NOTE: For an additional teaching idea, see the Chapter 27 open-ended statements lesson in the **Creative Teaching Strategies** handbook.

---

23 minutes. In 1959 he was selected as one of seven astronauts for the Project Mercury space-flight training program. In 1962 Glenn orbited Earth in the space capsule *Friendship 7.*

Glenn retired from the space program in 1964. In 1974 he was elected as a Democratic senator from Ohio. He served in the U.S. Senate until 1992. In 1998 Glenn returned to the space program. At age 77 he served as a payload specialist on the space shuttle mission STS-95. NASA scientists studied Glenn's reaction to space travel to learn more about the relationship between the process of aging and the body's ability to adapt to weightlessness.

✔ **READING CHECK: Summarizing** What contributions did Shannon Lucid and John Glenn make to the space program in the 1990s?
Lucid broke the U.S. record for most consecutive days spent in space; Glenn became the oldest American to fly in space.

The computer age. During the 1990s personal computer (PC) technology evolved rapidly. **Bill Gates,** head of Microsoft Corporation, was a leader in the computer revolution. By the mid-1990s most business offices and public institutions were computerized, and nearly 40 percent of American homes had PCs.

The **Internet,** an enormous computer-based communications and information system, enabled users to communicate worldwide, join discussion groups, and gather information from countless databases. It had its roots in a 1960s Defense Department communications project. Internet use exploded in the early 1990s after a group of scientists based in Switzerland developed the **World Wide Web.** It linked Internet sites offering text, animation, and graphics covering a seemingly endless range of topics. Some observers hoped that this so-called information highway would bring together people from different social classes, cultures, and countries.

Internet expansion also contributed to the U.S. economic boom. The high-tech industry was responsible for nearly one third of real U.S. economic growth in the late 1990s. There were about 1.25 million Internet-related jobs in 1998. That number doubled in 1999. As more Americans began using the Internet in their daily lives, some people began to worry about a "digital divide" in the United States. This divide was between people who used technology and those who did not. The worry was that those who did not have access to or use of technology would be hurt in the new economy. During his last year in office, President Clinton promised to help make the Internet "as universal as the telephone is today."

Concerns about technology. In addition to creating new opportunities, new technologies created new concerns. In response, Congress passed the **Telecommunications Act** of 1996, which attempted to regulate indecency on the Internet. A federal court quickly struck down key parts of this law, however, as a violation of the First Amendment right to free speech.

DNA Testing
BY MARY CARROLL JOHANSEN

Modern scientific techniques like DNA testing are enabling scientists and historians to resolve controversial questions that have puzzled people for centuries. For example, in 1802 a journalist published rumors that President Thomas Jefferson had fathered children by his slave Sally Hemings. For years Jefferson's supporters strongly denied it. Recently, scholars such as Joseph Ellis and Annette Gordon-Reed have debated the historical evidence of the Jefferson-Hemings affair without reaching a definitive conclusion. In 1998 the use of DNA analysis brought historians and scientists closer to an answer.

Scientists have found that most of the Y chromosomes in DNA pass intact from father to son, allowing them to trace paternal lineage. Since Jefferson had no sons, scientists compared DNA from male-line descendants of Jefferson's paternal grandfather with DNA from descendants of Eston Hemings, Sally Hemings's youngest son. They found a match. Since the chances of a match were less than one percent, Jefferson very likely was Eston Hemings's father.

DNA has helped settle other historical mysteries. In 1995, scientists announced that Anna Anderson had not been Anastasia, the daughter of murdered czar Nicholas II of Russia, as she had claimed. Pathologists have also used DNA to determine that President Zachary Taylor died of natural causes, not arsenic poisoning as some suspected.

PEOPLE IN HISTORY

Bill Gates. When Bill Gates was 12 years old, he became so interested in computers that he and his friends dug through trash bins at a local computer company to find notes that the company's programmers had discarded. While a senior in high school, Gates was offered a job as a computer programmer. Three years later he cofounded Microsoft. His interest in computers took him far in the business world—Gates became a billionaire at age 31.

CRITICAL THINKING What personal attributes might have contributed to Gates's success?

ANSWER: Students might suggest that Gates's natural aptitude, curiosity, and drive have contributed to his success.

□ internet connect

TOPIC: The History of PCs and the Internet
GO TO: go.hrw.com
KEYWORD: SE3 AN27

Have students access the Internet through the HRW Go site to conduct research on the development of the personal computer and the Internet. Then have each student create a multimedia presentation about the history of the PC and the Internet.

LEVELS 2 AND 3: Pair students and tell one student in each pair to imagine that he or she is John Glenn, then tell the other student to imagine that he or she is a journalist assigned to interview Glenn. Have each pair create a transcript of an interview about the events that shaped the space program in the 1990s. *(See the Level 1 lesson for the correct events.)* Ask each pair to conduct its interview for the class. Tell students that many Americans have been concerned about the consequences of technology on society. Have each student write an essay that analyzes the issues surrounding technology in the 1990s. *(See the Level 1 lesson for the correct issues.)* Ask volunteers to read their essays to the class. **Cooperative Learning**

TEACH OBJECTIVES 3 AND 4

ALL LEVELS: Ask students why the response to the export of U.S. popular culture might not always be positive. *(Students might suggest that people in other countries want to maintain their own cultures and traditions.)* Then discuss where the majority of new and often well-schooled immigrants to the United States are coming from. *(Students should mention Asia, Latin America, and the Caribbean.)* Discuss why these immigrants might be important to the economy. *(Students might answer that many new immigrants tend to be highly skilled and important to high-tech industries.)* Tell students that Congress has hotly debated immigration issues in recent years. **English Language Learners**

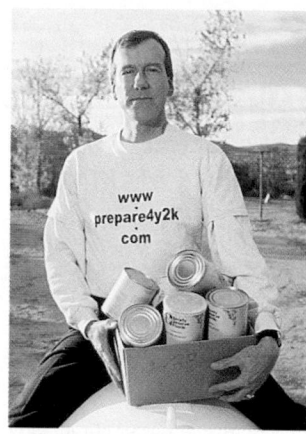

Worried about computer systems failures, some Americans began to store food and other necessities as the year 2000 approached.

INTERPRETING THE VISUAL RECORD

Exporting mass culture. Many American businesses have spread overseas. *How do these employees of an American-style fast-food restaurant in Jakarta, Indonesia, maintain their Islamic culture?*

Some observers worried about the uses of technology. In 1997 Scottish scientists announced the first successful cloning of a mammal, an adult sheep named Dolly. People debated the wisdom of using this technology to eventually clone humans. Other people worried that scientific advances would deepen social divisions. Wealthy, well-educated Americans would master new technologies, as poorer citizens lagged behind.

As the year 2000 approached, programmers warned that many computer systems would fail, because they would read the year 2000, or '00, as 1900. In order to save space when developing computer programs, some programmers had abbreviated references to years, leaving out the digits 1 and 9. The problem came to be known as the **Y2K bug**. Businesses and governments worldwide spent millions of dollars hiring experts to reprogram their computers before the end of 1999. Few computers experienced problems and many viewed the Y2K bug as hype.

In May 1998 the U.S. Justice Department filed an antitrust suit against Microsoft, claiming that the company had used its monopoly position to restrict competition and harm consumers. In particular, the Justice Department accused Microsoft of trying to dominate the market for software used to browse, or surf, the Internet. Microsoft had combined its Internet browser with Windows, its popular operating system. In April 2000 a federal judge ruled that Microsoft had violated some sections of the Sherman Antitrust Act by using its monopoly power to restrain free trade. The judge ordered Microsoft to break up its operations. A federal appeals court upheld the finding that Microsoft had violated federal antitrust laws but overturned the order to break up the company.

✔ **READING CHECK: Analyzing Information** How did the Sherman Antitrust Act affect Microsoft? Microsoft was found to have violated antitrust laws, but an order to break up the company was overturned.

Exporting Mass Culture

The Internet aided in the exportation of American popular culture. By 1990 popular culture had become one of the most profitable U.S. exports, with annual revenues topping $5 billion. The sales of American TV shows in Europe alone totaled some $600 million a year. Similarly, the music industry earned about 70 percent of its revenues from overseas sales. Reported a British economics journal: "America is to entertainment what . . . Saudi Arabia is to oil."

American consumer products, from hamburgers and soda to blue jeans, were also popular. The overseas division of the McDonald's Corporation, for instance, grew enormously during the 1990s. In 1992 McDonald's opened more restaurants overseas—including one in Beijing, China—than it did in the United States. Of McDonald's $12.4 billion sales in 1995, approximately 60 percent was generated by its some 12,500 restaurants in foreign nations.

Some critics expressed concern that this American popular culture would suffocate other cultures. They also worried that Hollywood movies and television shows gave the world a distorted impression of life in the United States. A Jamaican journalist wrote about the effects of American television on his fellow citizens:

ALL LEVELS: Tell students that many social changes have affected families in the United States during the past two decades. To help students understand the issues that affected family life in the 1990s, copy the graphic organizer at right on the chalkboard, omitting the italicized answers. Have each student complete the organizer. Ask volunteers to share their answers with the class. To conclude, lead a discussion about what the passage of the Family and Medical Leave Act might reveal about the changing priorities of American society. **English Language Learners**

rising number of single-parent households

Issues Affecting Family Life in the 1990s

working parents' need for affordable day care

rising number of families in which both parents work

passage of the Family and Medical Leave Act

HOMEWORK *Tell students to imagine that it is January 1993 and that they are working parents. Have each student write a letter to his or her congressional representative that describes the issues affecting family life in the 1990s and urges the representative to vote for the Family and Medical Leave Act.*

History Makers Speak

❝Because of what they see on television, everyone in Jamaica thinks . . . that everything in America is wonderful. . . . It makes people think that money and material wealth are the only ways to be rich in this world.❞

—Jamaican journalist, quoted in *Sleepwalking Through History,* by Haynes Johnson

The shared global culture also had advantages, however. Through orbiting communications satellites, television linked the entire world. Events in one nation were instantly transmitted around the globe. Thus, events like natural disasters often quickly produced a global outpouring of sympathy and help.

✔ **READING CHECK: Drawing Conclusions** How has American popular culture affected the rest of the world? Some foreigners feared their native culture would be suffocated; others received aid.

A New Wave of Immigration

Many people in other countries continued to see the United States as a land of opportunity. The 1990 census revealed that more immigrants had come to the United States in the 1980s than in any decade since 1910. More than 80 percent of these immigrants came from Asia, the Caribbean, and Latin America. By the 1990s many native-born Americans had grown alarmed by the wave of immigrants. Many blamed immigrants for taking jobs from native-born residents.

Supporters of immigration argued that immigrants created new businesses that revitalized urban areas and helped the economy. They also noted that many recent immigrants, in particular those from China, India, Korea, and the Philippines, had on average more schooling than native-born Americans or European immigrants. Asian immigrants, they pointed out, made up about one third of the engineers in Silicon Valley, California's center of computer technology, located near San Jose.

President George Bush had recognized these benefits when he signed the **Immigration Act of 1990**. The new law set a permanent limit of 675,000 immigrants per year after 1994. It also doubled the number of skilled workers allowed into the United States each year. The act authorized special visas for overseas investors interested in establishing businesses in economically depressed areas of the country.

In the mid-1990s, however, Congress acted to curb new immigration. In 1996 Congress passed an immigration law that strengthened control of U.S. borders in an effort to halt illegal immigration. The law attempted to keep new immigrants off welfare. For example, sponsors of immigrants were required to have incomes at least 125 percent above the poverty level. It also prevented legal immigrants who were not U.S. citizens from receiving most forms of welfare benefits.

✔ **READING CHECK: Contrasting** How was immigration in the 1990s different than earlier immigration? The number of skilled workers allowed into this nation doubled; also, foreign investors were allowed to come here and open a business.

The Religious Spirit

GROWING RELIGIOUS DIVERSITY

The Masjid Omar Al-Khattab mosque in Los Angeles

The increase in the number of Asian immigrants led to a growing religious diversity in the United States. By the end of the 1990s Christianity was still by far the most common religion, representing about 84 percent of the U.S. population. However, membership in traditionally Eastern religions such as Buddhism, Hinduism, and Islam was growing. In 1998 Islam had some 5 to 6 million followers in the United States. By 2010 it is expected to overtake Judaism as the nation's second-most-practiced religion.

As these religions grew in prominence, so did the number of non-Asian converts. By 1998 more than 80,000 American Muslims were of Western European descent. Buddhism also attracted many non-Asian converts. In many places, American Buddhism evolved into a distinct faith. It moved away from Asian Buddhism's traditional focus on the intense spiritual training of monks and nuns. American Buddhism tends to emphasize the personal spiritual growth of lay members. Some followers argue that such an approach is in keeping with the American democratic traditions. "What [American Buddhists] are doing," noted one observer in 1997, "is taking a path of enlightenment in a lay culture without priests and temples and structures, and moving it right into daily practice in everyday life."

GLOBAL RELATIONS

American Culture. Some critics have noted that the global market for films has shaped the choices that film production companies make when they invest in a film. Because movies comprehensible only to American audiences have little chance of making profits overseas, many filmmakers choose to de-emphasize dialogue in their films and to make action and adventure movies that people from a wide variety of cultures can enjoy.

CRITICAL THINKING What consequences might filmmakers' choices have for American movie audiences?

ANSWER: Students might suggest that American audiences might have fewer opportunities to see films that have meaningful or complex dialogue.

THAT'S INTERESTING!

In 1996 the United States received more immigrants from Mexico than from any other nation. Some 163,600 Mexicans arrived in the United States that year.

VISUAL RECORD ANSWER

(for p. 814)

Students might note the sign in the background, which points to a child care center, as well as her business attire.

REVIEW

Have students complete the **Section 3 Review** on p. 814.

ASSESS

Have students complete **Daily Quiz 27.3**. As **Alternative Assessment**, you may want to use the cartoons or the interview in this section's lessons.

RETEACH

Have students complete **Main Idea Activity for English Language Learners and Special-Needs Students 27.3**. Pair students and assign each pair one subsection from Section 3.

Have each pair write three questions about the material in its assigned subsection. Collect pairs' questions and use them to quiz the class.
English Language Learners, Cooperative Learning

EXTEND

Ask each student to conduct research on one of the following people or topics: Shannon Lucid, John Glenn, Bill Gates, *Mir*, or the Y2K bug. Have each student create a collage depicting pertinent facts about his or her chosen subject. Display students' collages around the classroom. **Block Scheduling**

SECTION 3 REVIEW ANSWERS

1. Identify
- *Mir*, p. 810
- Shannon Lucid, p. 810
- John Glenn, p. 810
- Bill Gates, p. 811
- Internet, p. 811
- World Wide Web, p. 811
- Telecommunications Act, p. 811
- Y2K bug, p. 812
- Immigration Act of 1990, p. 813
- Family and Medical Leave Act, p. 814

2. pros—computers and the Internet allow instant access to information, assistance for the disabled, and worldwide communication; cons—indecency not regulated on the Internet, job losses to computers, deepening social divisions, the Y2K bug

3a. focus on commercial and scientific projects, joint U.S.-Russian project on the *Mir* space station, John Glenn's successful return to space

b. because of fears that American culture would overwhelm their own

c. Most immigrants came from Asia, the Caribbean, and Latin America; increased quota of immigrants and skilled workers in 1990, immigration restrictions in 1996.

4. The increase in the number of single-parent households made child care an important issue for employers and for working parents trying to balance work and family.

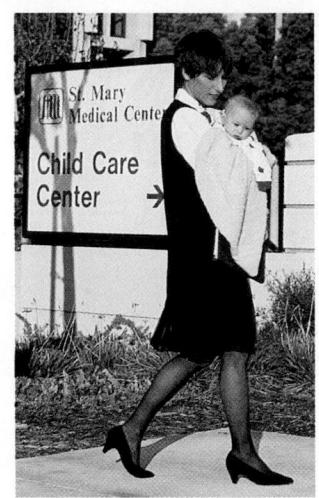

INTERPRETING THE VISUAL RECORD

Children. The number of single-parent households and households with both parents working outside the home is rising. *What clues in this photograph might lead you to assume that this mother works outside the home?*

Work and Family

Some observers expressed concern about the state of the American family in the 1990s. By 1998 only 26 percent of American households were made up of married couples with children. Most single parents had a difficult time financially. Patricia Mull, a Los Angeles seamstress who stretched her income to send her daughter to private school, described the stress she faced. "I worry about the rent. I worry if I can make the payment in time. I worry if I have enough money left for other things. I worry about money every day, every night."

Many two-parent families shared Mull's concerns as they struggled to balance job and family responsibilities. Nearly 60 percent of married women worked outside the home in 1995, up from about 30 percent in 1960. The increase of single-parent families and families with both parents in the workforce created the need for affordable day care. Employers increasingly realized that family concerns affected their employees' jobs. To help employees balance work and family, a group of businesses in 1992 announced a program to build more day-care and elder-care centers across the country.

The U.S. government also recognized the need to help working families. In February 1993, just two weeks after his inauguration, President Clinton signed into law the **Family and Medical Leave Act**. The legislation requires large companies to provide workers up to 12 weeks of unpaid leave. Workers can use this time for family and medical emergencies without losing their medical insurance or their jobs.

This legislation reflected the significant changes in attitudes toward work and family that have occurred in the United States in the 1990s. As businessperson Florence Skelly noted in 1993, "Rather than trying to climb the economic ladder, people are becoming more concerned with relationships and family and community involvement."

✔ **READING CHECK: Making Predictions** How did government efforts help families in the 1990s? A new law required large companies to give workers unpaid leave for emergencies, without losing health insurance or their job.

SECTION 3 REVIEW

1. Identify and explain:
- *Mir*
- Shannon Lucid
- John Glenn
- Bill Gates
- Internet
- World Wide Web
- Telecommunications Act
- Y2K bug
- Immigration Act of 1990
- Family and Medical Leave Act

2. Evaluating Copy the graphic organizer below. Use it to describe the pros and cons of increasing dependence on technology in the 1990s.

Technology

Pros   Cons

3. **Finding the Main Idea**
a. How did the U.S. space program rebound from its setbacks of the 1980s?
b. Why might people in other countries oppose the spread of American popular culture?
c. How had immigration changed by the 1990s? How did this affect the 1990 and 1996 immigration bills?

4. **Writing and Critical Thinking**
Identifying Points of View Write a brief report identifying why family issues became a political concern in the 1990s.
Consider:
- the increase in single-parent households
- concerns over child care
- what influenced the passage of the Family and Medical Leave Act

Homework Practice Online
keyword: SE3 HP27

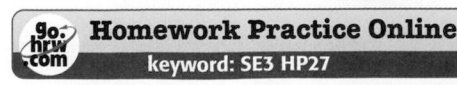

SECTION 4

After completing Section 4, students should be able to:

OBJECTIVE 1 *Identify the factors that shaped the global economy.*

OBJECTIVE 2 *Describe how the environment and population growth issues concerned people in the 1990s.*

OBJECTIVE 3 *Explain how the 2000 presidential election was unusual.*

OBJECTIVE 4 *Discuss the domestic and international issues that George W. Bush faced.*

LET'S GET STARTED!

As students enter the classroom, tell them to compile a written list of the major challenges facing the United States and the world today. Ask volunteers to share their lists with the class, and compile a comprehensive list on the chalkboard. Tell students that in Section 4 they will learn about major challenges and developments in the world today.

SECTION 4

READ TO DISCOVER

1. What factors shaped the development of the global economy?
2. How did the environment and population growth concern people in the 1990s?
3. How was the 2000 presidential election unusual?
4. What domestic and international issues did George W. Bush face?

DEFINE

multinational corporations
recycling

IDENTIFY

European Union
North American Free
 Trade Agreement
Chernobyl disaster
Al Gore
George W. Bush
Bush v. Gore

WHY IT MATTERS TODAY

What do you think is the most important issue facing the world today? Use **CNNfyi.com** or other **current events** sources to learn more about an issue you believe is critical to the world's future. Record your findings in your journal.

CNNfyi.com

George W. Bush's Presidency

 EYEWITNESSES TO History *"How, then, shall we live? How must we live to preserve free societies and to be worthy of the blood and pain? This is the unfinished business of our century."*

—Michael Novak, *New York Times*, May 24, 1998

Young Americans perform community service.

In an editorial for the *New York Times,* social critic Michael Novak reflected on the future. At the start of a new millennium, his questions represent a growing reassessment of America's future. What role will Americans play in determining the fate of the world and its inhabitants? What historic trends can we foresee in the future? What challenges do we face in the coming years? While these questions cannot be answered with certainty, we can consider the recent past and offer valuable speculations about the possible future of our country.

A Global Economy

The world's major industrial nations are linked by billions of dollars' worth of trade. In 1992 journalist Bruce W. Nelan predicted the growing importance of global economics.

 History Makers Speak *"Just as wars—two World Wars and, equally important, the Cold War—dominated the geopolitical map of the 20th century, economics will rule over the 21st. All the big questions confronting the world in the century ahead are basically economic."*

—Bruce W. Nelan, quoted in *Time*, Fall 1992

International trade. International trading blocs may provide stiff economic competition for the United States in coming years. The **European Union** (EU), a Western European trading bloc, was formed in 1993. The EU is designed to allow capital, goods, and labor to move freely among member nations. It also encourages cooperation on matters such as crime, culture, education, foreign policy, and health. Some predict that a full political union—the "United States of Europe," which could include as many as 20 member states—will eventually form.

By 1993 concern over such economic competition led to growing support for U.S. ratification of the **North American Free Trade Agreement** (NAFTA). The agreement provides for a lowering of tariffs and other trade barriers among Canada, Mexico, and the United States. Supporters hoped that NAFTA would increase trade. Many also hoped that NAFTA would help the U.S. free-enterprise system compete more effectively in the global economy. By 2000 U.S. exports to Canada and Mexico had increased more than $111 billion since NAFTA was signed. Imports from Canada and Mexico increased by some $150 billion. Yet some economists estimate that between 1993 and 2000 the United States lost more than 750,000 job opportunities under NAFTA. Most of these jobs were in the manufacturing sector.

SECTION 4 RESOURCES

REPRODUCIBLE

▶ Guided Reading Strategy 27.4
▶ Primary Source Reading 27: Antarctica: A New View

TECHNOLOGY

▶ One-Stop Planner, Lesson 27.4
▶ Linking Geography and History Transparency 23: The Global Environment
▶ Holt Researcher: American History CD–ROM
▶ Homework Practice Online

REINFORCEMENT, REVIEW, AND ASSESSMENT

▶ Section 4 Review, p. 819
▶ Daily Quiz 27.4
▶ Main Idea Activity 27.4
▶ English Audio Summary 27.4
▶ Spanish Audio Summary 27.4

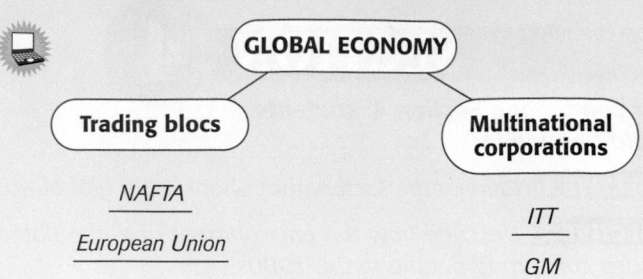

GLOBAL ECONOMY

Trading blocs

NAFTA

European Union

Multinational corporations

ITT

GM

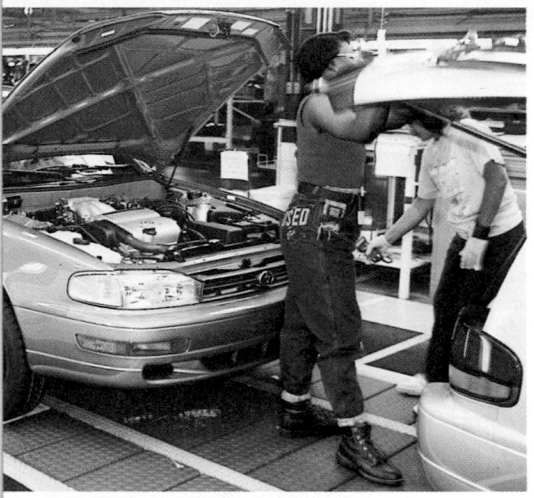

INTERPRETING THE VISUAL RECORD

Global business. Workers assemble Toyota cars in a Kentucky factory. *What do you think the workers shown are doing?*

Multinational corporations. The global economy is increasingly dominated by **multinational corporations**. These companies invest money in a variety of business ventures around the world. Multinational corporations sometimes benefit the United States economically. Leading Japanese corporations, for example, have opened factories in the United States. Such plants boost the U.S. economy, although most of the profits go to the parent corporations in Japan.

Many American businesses are also expanding their investments in other countries. For example, the New York–based ITT Corporation began as a communications company. By the 1990s, however, ITT held major interests worldwide in such diverse businesses as finance, food processing, hotels, insurance, and real estate. Other corporations, such as General Motors, IBM, and Texaco, also operate worldwide.

✔ **READING CHECK: Summarizing** How has the growth of the global economy affected the United States? *The United States ratified NAFTA; the growing role of multinational corporations has sometimes benefited the United States.*

The Environment and Population

The future of energy resources and the environment concerns many experts. In 1998 the world consumed an amount of energy equivalent to that of about 65 billion barrels of oil. The United States is home to less than 5 percent of the world's population yet accounted for nearly 25 percent of the world's energy consumption that year. Some 38 percent of U.S. energy came from oil, 24 percent from natural gas, and 22 percent from coal. Just 8 percent came from alternative sources such as solar or hydroelectric power and 8 percent from nuclear power.

A 1986 accident at the Chernobyl nuclear power plant in the Soviet Union near Kiev, Ukraine, sent a dangerous radioactive cloud drifting across Europe. The **Chernobyl disaster** released 50 times more radioactive material into the environment than the two atomic bombs dropped on Japan in 1945 combined.

The Chernobyl disaster heightened anxiety over nuclear power. People began calling for increased research on other energy sources. These include solar power, geothermal power (geysers and hot springs), and wind power. They also include biomass (materials such as wood or waste products that can be burned or used to make fuel) and hydrogen. Renewed calls for alternative energy sources came in 2001 as the state of California experienced rolling blackouts, or losses of electrical power.

As scientists search for energy sources, many environmentalists focus on protecting the world's remaining forests and wildlife. Private nonprofit conservation organizations have worked to help preserve some of these areas. For example, in

This car uses fuel-cell technology and produces no harmful emissions.

TEACH OBJECTIVE 2

 ALL LEVELS: Tell students to imagine that they are editors of an environmental magazine. Organize students into small groups. Have each group prepare a table of contents for a special section on environmental issues, including population growth, concerning people in the 1990s. Each group should also prepare a short summary of each article. *(Students should mention nuclear power, the consumption of fossil fuels, the need for alternative energy sources, and how population growth affects the environment.)* Ask volunteers to present their tables of contents and summaries to the class. **English Language Learners, Cooperative Learning**

Deanna Spring of Cincinnati, Ohio, suggested the following activity: Pair students and have each pair write a dinner-table conversation about the environmental issues that concerned people in the 1990s. Ask each pair to perform its conversation for the class.

2000 President Clinton created the Giant Sequoia National Monument in California to protect more than 30 groves of ancient sequoia trees. The monument was the result of conservation efforts started some 100 years earlier. In 1892 naturalist John Muir founded the Sierra Club to protect ancient forests as unspoiled parts of nature. The Sierra Club, along with other conservation groups, lobby for the protection of natural areas under the authority of the Antiquities Act of 1906. Other nonprofit conservation groups support projects in the United States and around the world to protect sensitive natural areas. At times, conservation efforts can come into conflict with economic growth. One of society's greatest challenges is to balance the need for protecting the environment with the careful management of natural resources.

As environmental awareness has increased, **recycling**—the collection and processing of waste items for reuse—has gained support. Recycling reuses scarce natural resources and reduces the amount of solid waste that must be buried, burned, dumped, or shipped elsewhere. By 1991 some 4,000 curbside recycling programs were under way in the United States, a 250 percent increase from 1989.

An increase in the worldwide population also poses challenges. By 2000 the world's population stood at 6 billion, and it was growing by a rate of nearly three people per second. Population growth is most rapid in poorer countries. Experts predict that India's population will jump from 984 million in 1998 to 1.4 billion by 2025. They also predict that Mexico's will rise from 98.6 million to 141.6 million, and Bangladesh's from 127.6 million to 180.7 million.

✔ **READING CHECK: Making Generalizations**
What effects might population growth have on the environment? It might lead to more energy shortages and worsen environmental and waste-disposal programs.

History on Hold: The 2000 Election

In 2000 the Democrats nominated Vice President **Al Gore** as their presidential candidate. Gore chose Senator Joseph Lieberman of Connecticut as his running mate. Lieberman became the first Orthodox Jew to run on a major party ticket in the United States. Gore and Lieberman campaigned on a promise to use the federal government surplus to help pay the national debt. They also wanted to increase funding of domestic programs such as education and health care.

Republicans nominated **George W. Bush**, the son of former president George Bush and governor of Texas, as their candidate. Bush selected former Defense Secretary Dick Cheney as his running mate. Bush ran as what he called a "compassionate conservative." He pledged to return most of the government surplus to voters in the form of tax cuts.

Consumer advocate Ralph Nader ran as the presidential candidate for the Green Party. His campaign focused on winning the 5 percent of the popular vote necessary to qualify for federal campaign funding in 2004.

Research on the ROM

Free Find: Hunger in Africa
After studying the digital map on hunger in Africa on the **Holt Researcher CD–ROM**, write a short essay explaining how future environmental problems might worsen conditions in Africa.

INTERPRETING THE VISUAL RECORD

Population growth. The continued growth of urban populations presents environmental challenges. *Looking at this photograph of Mexico City, what might some of these challenges be?*

VISUAL RECORD ANSWER
Students might suggest smog and housing.

SKILL-BUILDING STRATEGIES ANSWERS
(for p. 818)
Practicing the Skill
Answers will vary depending on the student's topic.

TEACH OBJECTIVE 3

 ALL LEVELS: Ask students why the 2000 presidential election was unusual. (*Students might note the length of time for a winner to be announced, the court cases, that the winner did not receive a majority of popular votes, and that George W. Bush's father had been president.*) Have students list suggestions on how to prevent problems in future presidential elections. **English Language Learners**

TEACH OBJECTIVE 4

 ALL LEVELS: Have students make a chart of the domestic and international problems that President George W. Bush faced. (*Charts should include under domestic—bringing the nation together after the election, education and tax reform, and the Democrats' gaining a majority in the Senate; international—missile defense system and responding to changing relationships among nations.*) Have students use their charts to write a brief summary of the issues.
English Language Learners

CONSTITUTIONAL HERITAGE

The Electoral College.
In the 2000 presidential election Al Gore won the popular vote but lost the election to George W. Bush, winner of the electoral vote. It was difficult for many Americans to understand how one candidate could win the a majority of the votes cast but lose the election. This happened because of the way the electoral college works. The electoral college consists of each state's electors, which are equal to its total number of senators and representatives. Thus, each state has two more votes than its proportionate population. In most states, the electoral college votes are awarded in a "winner-take-all" fashion, meaning that even though Bush won Florida by fewer than 600 votes, he won all 25 electoral votes. The number of states won, and not the overall popular vote count, decides the outcome of the election.

ACTIVITY: Have students conduct research on other close presidential elections in U.S. history. Then ask them to create a chart that identifies the candidates, the parties, and the eventual outcome.

The presidential election of 2000 was unlike any political contest before it. A winner was not announced promptly. The vote was so close that several states could not declare a winner. Florida's 25 electoral votes became the key to the White House. Bush led by fewer than 2,000 votes out of more than 6 million votes cast. With such a small margin, Florida law required an automatic recount. Disputes soon arose and citizens and officials from both parties took their cases to the courts. In the five weeks following the election, state and federal courts debated the merits of machine counts, hand recounts, and absentee ballots.

On December 12, the U.S. Supreme Court ruled in *Bush v. Gore* that hand recounts in several Florida counties were not valid. As a result, with a lead of 537 popular votes, Bush was awarded Florida's 25 electoral votes. These votes gave him 271 electoral votes—one more than needed for victory. Gore, however, had won the national popular vote, with more than 48 percent. Thus, Bush became the first president in over 100 years to win the electoral vote but not the popular vote.

✔ **READING CHECK: Summarizing** What events or outcomes made the 2000 presidential election so unusual? The vote was not decided until five weeks after election day; Bush received a majority of the electoral vote but not the popular vote.

Skill-Building Strategies

Writing a Research Paper

Writing a history research paper can be both a challenging and a rewarding experience. Many of the steps that go into preparing for a paper require one to use a variety of important critical thinking skills.

How to Write a Research Paper

1. **Identify the topic, develop questions, conduct research, and evaluate your sources.** First, identify the topic that you wish to research and develop one or more questions that you hope to answer in your paper. Then conduct research at your school or local public library and evaluate the sources that you find.
2. **Formulate a hypothesis.** Analyze the information in your sources and develop a hypothesis that answers your questions about the topic. This hypothesis should serve as the focus of your paper and be presented in a thesis statement.
3. **Create an outline.** Organize the ideas and evidence that you plan to discuss into an outline. This step will make the actual process of writing much easier.
4. **Write a first draft.** Compose a first draft of your paper, using your outline as a guide. It should have an introduction with a clear thesis statement, a body of material that supports the thesis statement, and

a conclusion that provides a summary of what has been said.
5. **Review and edit the first draft.** After you have completed a draft of your paper, read it over and make corrections as needed.
6. **Write a final draft.** Once you have settled on a final version of your paper, prepare a neat, clean copy for submission to your teacher or classmates.

Applying the Skill

Write a five-page research paper on a topic of recent historical importance. You may select your own topic or use one of the following suggestions:
1. global environmental problems during the 1990s
2. the Internet's effect on international commerce
3. the 2000 presidential election

Practicing the Skill

Before writing your paper, answer the following questions.
1. What questions do you hope to answer in your paper?
2. What is your thesis statement?
3. What ideas and evidence will you use in the paper to support your thesis statement?

Bush as President

In his inauguration speech, Bush called on Americans to help one another.

History Makers Speak

❝I ask you to seek a common good beyond your comfort; . . . I ask you to be citizens—citizens, not subjects; responsible citizens, building communities of service and a nation of character.❞

—George W. Bush, "Inaugural Address," January 20, 2001

In his first weeks in office, President Bush sent an education reform package and a plan for tax cuts to Congress. The newly-seated Congress was almost equally divided between Republicans and Democrats. In the House of Representatives, the Republicans kept a small majority. The Senate was split 50-50, with Vice President Cheney holding the tie-breaking vote. In late May Congress approved Bush's tax cut plan, the first major tax cut in 20 years. Over ten years taxes would be cut by $1.35 trillion.

Less than one week later, the balance of power shifted again when Jim Jeffords, a senator from Vermont, left the Republican Party to become an independent. With one less Republican in the Senate, the Democratic Party gained control of the Senate for the first time since 1994.

In foreign affairs, Bush has proposed a missile defense system similar to one proposed by President Reagan. Some of Bush's other challenges include responding to the changing relationships among nations. The United States continues to encourage democracy worldwide as it also tries to expand political rights, economic opportunities, and individual freedoms to all Americans.

✔ **READING CHECK: Analyzing Information** What domestic and international challenges did President Bush face? tax reform, education reform, Republican minority in the Senate, missile defense system

Analyzing Primary Sources

Identifying Points of View
What does this Bush mean by "citizens, not subjects"?

He wants Americans to take an active role in government.

Former Texas governor George W. Bush is sworn in as president.

SECTION 4 REVIEW

1. Define and explain:
multinational corporations
recycling

2. Identify and explain:
European Union
North American Free Trade Agreement
Chernobyl disaster
Al Gore
George W. Bush
Bush v. *Gore*

3. Summarizing Copy the graphic organizer below. Use it to describe the factors that supported the development of the global economy.

4. ▸ Finding the Main Idea ◂
a. Why do you think that many Americans were interested in environmental and population issues during the 1990s? What issues received public attention?
b. What issues did the 2000 presidential election raise?
c. What contributions did President Bush make?

5. ▸ Writing and Critical Thinking ◂
Categorizing Write a report for President George W. Bush describing the global issues that might create problems for Americans in the future.
Consider:
• the role of American businesses in the global economy
• future environmental challenges
• the role of the United States in international affairs

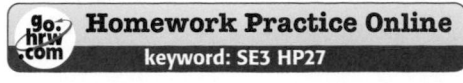
Homework Practice Online
keyword: SE3 HP27

After completing Section 5, students should be able to:

OBJECTIVE 1 Describe how the United States was attacked on September 11, 2001, and identify how Americans responded.

OBJECTIVE 2 Explain how the events of September 11 affected the economy.

OBJECTIVE 3 Evaluate the steps American leaders took to find those responsible and to bring them to justice.

LET'S GET STARTED!

Write *September 11, 2001* on the chalkboard. As students enter the classroom, ask them to write down where they were when they first heard about the terrorist attacks of September 11, 2001, and their reaction to the events. Ask volunteers to share what they wrote with the class. Tell students that in this section they will learn about the attacks of September 11, 2001, their economic and social consequences, and the response by Americans and the U.S. government.

SECTION
5 RESOURCES

TECHNOLOGY

▶ **CNN** Presents: September 11, 2001: A Turning Point in History

REINFORCEMENT, REVIEW, AND ASSESSMENT

▶ Section 5 Review, p. 825

SECTION **5**

READ TO DISCOVER

1. How was the United States attacked on September 11, 2001, and how did Americans respond?
2. How did the events of September 11 affect the economy?
3. What immediate steps did U.S. leaders take to find those responsible and bring them to justice?

IDENTIFY

World Trade Center
Pentagon
Rudolph Giuliani
George W. Bush
Tom Ridge
Donald Rumsfeld
Colin Powell

▶ WHY IT MATTERS TODAY

The terrorist attacks of September 11, 2001, continue to affect American life and U.S. foreign policy. Use **CNNfyi.com** or other **current events** sources to learn about the latest issues and events stemming from this national tragedy. Record your findings in your journal.

CNNfyi.com

September 11, 2001: A Day That Changed the World

EYEWITNESSES TO History On Tuesday morning, September 11, 2001, it was business as usual in the downtown financial district of New York City. In the World Trade Center complex, an estimated 10,000 employees were starting their workday, most of them within the Twin Towers that dominated the Manhattan skyline. Others were still on their way to work. On Fifth Avenue a group of pedestrians noticed a large airplane pass overhead. "We all looked up," recalled one man. "We all thought it would be unusual for a plane to be flying so low over the city." Moments later they witnessed a terrible disaster unfold.

Fire department of New York uniform patch

The Attack

At 8:48 A.M., the routine of a city and a nation was shattered when an American Airlines passenger jet crashed into the north tower of the **World Trade Center**. The impact was devastating, as though a bomb had struck the 110-story building. Lynn Simpson, who was working on the 89th floor, recalled, "I heard an enormous crash. The ceiling fell in, the lights went out and the sprinklers went on. . . . I told everyone to get out." People began evacuating the building as emergency crews rushed to the scene. Then at 9:03 A.M. a second plane—United Airlines Flight 175—slammed into the south tower and exploded.

Many Americans saw the second crash broadcast live on television. Shocked observers began to realize that this was not an accident but a deliberate terrorist attack. Moreover, it was soon clear that New York was not the only target. At approximately 9:40 A.M. a third plane, American Airlines Flight 77, hit the west side of the **Pentagon**. Located just outside Washington, D.C., the Pentagon is the headquarters of the U.S. military. The impact of the crash caused massive damage and started fires deep within the huge, five-sided building.

At the World Trade Center complex, rescue workers struggled to aid victims while firefighters tried to control the raging fires. In the midst of their efforts, further disaster struck. At 9:59 A.M. the south tower suddenly collapsed, followed half an hour later by the fall of the north tower. "It [the south tower] just fell down in perfect symmetry, one floor, then another floor, then another," said a stunned witness. The collapse of the massive buildings killed or trapped thousands of people still inside or near the towers, including hundreds of firefighters, police officers, and other rescuers.

LEVEL 1: To help students understand how the United States was attacked on September 11, 2001, ask students to create a time line of the events of that day. (*8:48 A.M.—north tower struck; 9:03 A.M.—south tower struck; 9:40 A.M.—Pentagon struck; 9:59 A.M.—south tower collapses; 10:10 A.M.—United Airlines Flight 93 crashes; 10:30 A.M.—north tower collapses.*) Ask students to include a section on how Americans responded to the attacks in the following days. (*Rescue workers from across the nation came to New York to aid in the rescue effort, Congress approved a relief package, and the American public donated blood and money.*)
English Language Learners

LEVELS 2 AND 3: Ask students to imagine that they are newspaper reporters covering the events of September 11, 2001. Tell students to write newspaper articles describing the events of September 11, 2001, including how Americans responded. (*Descriptions will vary. See the Level 1 lesson for the events and responses.*) Ask volunteers to read their articles to the class.

A fourth plane—United Airlines Flight 93—was also hijacked and still in the air over southern Pennsylvania. Cell phone calls from passengers aboard the plane indicate that they learned of the other attacks and decided to stop the terrorists on board from hitting their next target. Flight 93 crashed southeast of Pittsburgh at 10:10, between the times of the collapse of the World Trade Center's Twin Towers.

In downtown New York City, clouds of smoke, dust, and ash drifted through the streets along with thousands of battered and dazed survivors. Thousands more people were unaccounted for in the wreckage. Meanwhile, emergency teams battling fires in the Pentagon were unable to search for survivors. All 265 passengers and crew aboard the four hijacked flights had been killed. Americans everywhere were shocked, wondering what was to come.

✔ **READING CHECK: Sequencing** In what order did the events on the morning of September 11, 2001, take place? A hijacked plane crashes into the north tower; another hits the south tower. A plane crashes into the Pentagon. The south tower collapses, a plane crashes in Pennsylvania, and then the north tower collapses.

The Nation Responds

Government officials raced to mount rescue efforts and placed the U.S. military on full alert. The Federal Aviation Administration grounded air traffic nationwide and closed airports. Key government centers, such as the White House and the Capitol, were briefly evacuated.

Rescue and relief. Firefighters and other rescue workers from across the nation came to New York. There they joined state and city emergency personnel searching the rubble for survivors. Their efforts were blocked by the intense heat from underground fires. New York hospitals mobilized hundreds of doctors but found that there were relatively few survivors to treat. New York mayor **Rudolph Giuliani** said of the final death toll, "It will be more than we can bear." About 2,500 people were killed by the attack on the World Trade Center. This number included more than 300 firefighters and many other rescue workers who were on the scene. At the Pentagon, 184 military and civilian personnel, including those on the hijacked plane, had been killed.

Congress swiftly approved a $40 billion relief package to help the nation recover from the attacks. The money would fund emergency assistance and national security measures. The government also passed legislation that provided compensation to the families of victims. Democrats and Republicans displayed an unusual degree of cooperation in pushing through these measures. "I think the message is very simply we are united . . . when it comes to a national threat as great as this," said Senate Majority Leader Tom Daschle of South Dakota.

George Howard

Port Authority police officer George Howard was honored for rescuing an elevator full of children during the 1993 World Trade Center bombing. He died at the World Trade Center while helping others on September 11. President Bush showed Americans Howard's badge as a symbol of courage.

As seen from New York Harbor, downtown Manhattan is obscured by smoke, ash, and debris after the attacks.

SCIENCE, TECHNOLOGY, AND SOCIETY

World Trade Center. Each a little more than 1,360 feet high and consisting of 110 floors, the Twin Towers were designed to withstand significant structural damage. Completed in the early 1970s, the towers were built from 200,000 tons of steel and 425,000 cubic yards of concrete. The building's construction featured two sets of steel columns. The outer perimeter was composed of closely spaced steel columns in the form of a rectangle, which formed a load-bearing exterior wall. The inner core of steel columns connected to concrete floors over ceiling trusses. On September 11, 2001, the buildings collapsed from the heat of burning jet fuel, which weakened the steel columns, resulting in the collapse of both towers.

CRITICAL THINKING Why might the terrorists have hijacked a transcontinental flight instead of a local flight?

ANSWER: Students might suggest that a jet involved in a transcontinental flight would carry a much larger load of fuel, necessary for the destruction of the terrorists' targets.

LEVEL 1: To help students understand how the terrorist attacks of September 11, 2001, affected the economy, copy the following graphic organizer onto the chalkboard, omitting the italicized answers. Have each student complete it. **English Language Learners**

Terrorist Attacks of September 11, 2001		
Financial Industry	**Airline Industry**	**General Public**
• *NYSE closed for four days.* • *NYSE suffered one of its worst weeks ever.*	• *Airlines suffered heavy financial losses.* • *Thousands of airline workers were laid off.*	• *$25 billion in physical damage* • *decline in tourism* • *fall in consumer confidence*

Peter Ganci. The New York City Fire Department's highest ranking uniformed officer, Peter Ganci died in the collapse of the World Trade Center as he commanded the rescue efforts on the front lines. A 33-year department veteran, Ganci joined "New York's bravest" in the 1960s. He worked his way to managing all uniformed personnel, as well as being responsible for the Bureau of Emergency Medical Services. He died just minutes after talking on his radio to New York City mayor Rudolph Giuliani. Fire commissioner Howard Safir, Ganci's direct superior, said Ganci "would never ask anyone to do something he didn't do himself. . . . You would never see Pete five miles away, in some command center."

ACTIVITY: Have students conduct research on other individuals, such as passengers on United Airlines Flight 93, who risked their lives to save others during the attacks on September 11.

President Bush visited the World Trade Center site to express his appreciation for the efforts of the rescue workers.

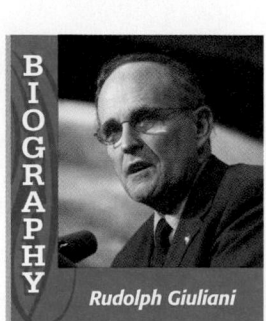

BIOGRAPHY

Rudolph Giuliani

As mayor of New York City, Rudy Giuliani played a key role during the early weeks of the crisis. Coordinating relief efforts, consoling victims, and calling for resolve and renewed confidence, he served as an important symbol of strength to the city and to the nation.

A nation united. Political leaders also tried to rally Americans' spirit on the day of the attack. Mayor Giuliani assured fellow New Yorkers, "We're going to rebuild and rebuild stronger." President **George W. Bush**, who had been in Florida visiting an elementary school, was moved to a safer location. From there, he gave a brief speech to the nation and told Americans, "We [the United States] will do whatever necessary to protect America and Americans." Republican and Democratic members of Congress issued a joint declaration from the Capitol steps. They said that the United States would not be intimidated by terrorism. The members then sang a chorus of "God Bless America."

Perhaps the greatest show of unity came from the American public. Many were inspired to displays of charity and patriotism. Within two days Wal-Mart, the nation's largest retail chain, had sold its entire stock of half a million American flags. Charitable groups moved swiftly to raise funds for relief efforts. Thousands of people went to Red Cross centers to donate blood. "It's just amazing," said one nurse in New York. "There'll be a three- or four-hour wait, and just look at all of these people standing here." Actors and musicians held a special telethon, "America: A Tribute to Heroes," on September 21. The effort raised some $150 million to benefit the families who had lost loved ones in the attacks.

People also came together to heal their wounds and show their strength. When professional sports leagues resumed their schedules, stadiums were filled with patriotic tributes and fans waving flags. Actor James Earl Jones drew cheers as he opened a mass prayer service held in New York City's Yankee Stadium.

History Makers Speak ❝Our spirit is unbroken. In fact, it is stronger than ever. Today we reaffirm our faith in the essential dignity of every individual. What we share as Americans and as human beings is far greater than what divides us.❞

—James Earl Jones, prayer service, September 23, 2001

Religious leaders representing many faiths led prayers for the victims and called for unity as a nation. The Boys and Girls Choir of Harlem sang a stirring rendition of "We Shall Overcome," with its refrain, "We are not afraid. . . . We shall live in peace."

✔ **READING CHECK: Summarizing** In what ways did Americans respond to the terrorist attacks? with rescue efforts, government aid, displays of patriotism, and charitable donations

The Investigation

Immediately after the attacks, the largest criminal investigation in U.S. history began. Within 48 hours the Federal Bureau of Investigation (FBI) placed more than 4,000 special agents on the case. The FBI soon released the names of

LEVEL 2: Have each student write a journal entry from the perspective of either a New York City stockbroker, an airline worker, or an average citizen in which they reflect on how the September 11, 2001, terrorist attacks affected the economy. *(Entries from the stockbroker perspective should mention that the New York Stock Exchange closed for four days and then suffered one of its worst weeks ever. Airline worker entries should mention that airlines suffered heavy financial losses and thousands of workers were laid off. Average citizen entries should mention the $25 billion in physical damage, the decline in tourism, and the fall in consumer confidence.)* Ask volunteers to read their entries to the class.

LEVEL 3: Tell students to imagine that they are economic advisers to President George W. Bush. Have each student write a memo for the president detailing the economic effects of the September 11, 2001, terrorist attacks. Have students include a section advising the president on actions the government should take to help the economy. *(See the Level 2 lesson for the economic effects. Sections on government actions will vary but might mention the bail-out of the airline industry.)* Ask volunteers to read their memos to the class.

19 suspected hijackers from several Middle Eastern nations. Investigators gathered evidence suggesting that each group of hijackers included trained pilots and that some of these men had been living and training in the United States for months. Even more crucial was the identity of those who had planned these acts of terror.

A prime suspect surfaced almost immediately—Osama bin Laden. This wealthy Saudi Arabian exile was already wanted for his suspected role in earlier terrorist attacks against U.S. forces overseas. A supporter of an extreme form of Islamic fundamentalism, bin Laden had publicly called for attacks on the United States, which he claimed had corrupted and oppressed Muslims. U.S. officials believed that bin Laden's global terrorism network, known as al Qaeda, or "the Base" in Arabic, was one of the few terrorist groups with the resources and organizational structure to have carried out the attacks.

Experts also agreed that the attacks of September 11 likely involved the cooperation of more than one terrorist group. Investigators from a broad range of federal agencies, with assistance from other nations, began a worldwide search for anyone with knowledge of the attacks. Agents sifted through debris at the crash sites to find physical evidence and tracked financial records to trace terrorists' movements. Several hundred suspects were detained at home and abroad for questioning. Although the complexity of the task and the need to provide security forced officials to be cautious, the Bush administration pledged to release conclusive evidence about who carried out the attacks as soon as it was feasible to do so.

✔ **READING CHECK: Summarizing** What early conclusions did investigators draw about the source of the attacks, and how did they investigate them? There were 19 suspected hijackers, some of whom had trained in the United States as pilots. Agents believed that Osama bin Laden was responsible. They investigated the crash sites and financial records.

The Economic Impact

The terrorist attacks on the World Trade Center had a high cost in economic terms as well as in lives. The costs related to the immediate physical damage were estimated at $25 billion. In addition, the New York Stock Exchange (NYSE) had to shut down operations for four days following the attack. This was the NYSE's longest shutdown since World War I in 1914. When it reopened, the NYSE had one of the worst weeks in its history. The Federal Reserve quickly cut interest rates in an effort to help the economy.

One area of particular concern was the airline industry. Forced to shut down operations for days and facing greatly increased security expenses and a public reluctance to fly, major airlines took heavy financial losses. They laid off thousands of workers, and at least one smaller carrier went out of business. The air-travel crisis caused wider problems as well. Tourism declined severely around the nation, and companies relying on supplies shipped by air endured shortages. The president and Congress rushed to pass a $15 billion bail-out package to help keep the nation's airlines operating.

One of the most difficult economic problems for the government to address was falling consumer confidence. Many Americans had been concerned by the weakness of the economy before the terrorist attacks. Uncertainty and fear raised by the events of September 11 worsened the situation. As one economist stated,

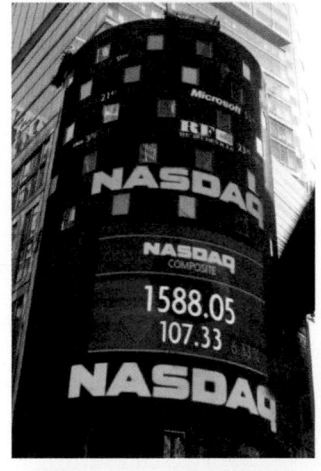

INTERPRETING THE VISUAL RECORD
The stock market. Prices on the NYSE and the NASDAQ stock exchange fell dramatically after they reopened following the terrorist attacks. ***How does this photograph reflect that decline?***

VISUAL RECORD ANSWER
Students might mention the red arrow indicating a fall in stock prices.

HISTORICAL DOCUMENTS ANSWER
(for p. 824)
Students might suggest that President Bush calls on other nations to decide whether they will support or oppose terrorism.

LEVEL 1: Ask students to list the steps U.S. leaders took to find those responsible for the September 11, 2001, attacks and bring them to justice. *(Lists should mention the war against terrorism, the freezing of assets of groups tied to terrorism, the international coalition against terrorism, and the missile and bomb attacks aimed at Taliban and al Qaeda camps.)* Have students write newspaper headlines announcing each of these efforts. **English Language Learners**

LEVELS 2 AND 3: Have students use the library or the Internet to find the headlines for September 12, 2001, the day after the terrorist attacks. Ask students to write two or three paragraphs outlining what steps they might have taken to find those responsible for the attacks. Then have students use the textbook or the library to conduct research on the steps U.S. leaders took to find those responsible and bring them to justice. Have students write two or three paragraphs summarizing their research. *(See the Level 1 activity for the correct steps.)* Have students write one more paragraph in which they compare their own ideas with how the U.S. government responded. Ask volunteers to read their final paragraphs to the class.

SECTION 5 REVIEW ANSWERS

1. Identify
- World Trade Center, p. 820
- Pentagon, p. 820
- Rudolph Giuliani, p. 821
- George W. Bush, p. 822
- Tom Ridge, p. 824
- Donald Rumsfeld, p. 824
- Colin Powell, p. 825

2. security—organized Office of Homeland Security; economic—$40 billion relief package, $15 billion airline bail-out, and reduced interest rates; diplomatic—organized a coalition of nations; military—mobilized forces

3a. The FBI initially identified 19 hijackers. Further evidence pointed to Osama bin Laden.

b. Federal investigators examined evidence from the airline crashes, airline records, and financial records to trace the movement of the terrorists.

c. The immediate physical damage was about $25 billion. The stock market suffered one of its worst weeks ever, the airline industry suffered heavy losses causing thousands of airline workers to lose their jobs, and consumer confidence was damaged.

4. Paragraphs will vary. Students might mention giving blood or money to the Red Cross. Students might also suggest that the attacks brought Americans closer together.

★ HISTORICAL DOCUMENTS ★

PRESIDENT GEORGE W. BUSH
Bush's Address to the Nation

On September 20, 2001, President Bush addressed the joint houses of Congress and the American people. The following is an excerpt from his speech responding to the September 11 attacks. **What did President Bush call on other nations to do?**

Tonight we are a country awakened to danger and called to defend freedom. Our grief has turned to anger, and anger to resolution. Whether we bring our enemies to justice, or bring justice to our enemies, justice will be done....

Every nation, in every region, now has a decision to make. Either you are with us, or you are with the terrorists. From this day forward, any nation that continues to harbor or support terrorism will be regarded by the United States as a hostile regime....

Great harm has been done to us. We have suffered great loss. And in our grief and anger we have found our mission and our moment. Freedom and fear are at war. The advance of human freedom—the great achievement of our time, and the great hope of every time—now depends on us. Our nation—this generation—will lift a dark threat of violence from our people and our future. We will rally the world to this cause by our efforts, by our courage. We will not tire, we will not falter, and we will not fail.

"We do have to fear fear itself, it matters, it affects consumer spending." Government officials responded to such concerns by emphasizing that the long-term health of the economy was strong, even if difficult times lay ahead.

✔ **READING CHECK: Finding the Main Idea**
What immediate effects did the terrorist attacks have on the U.S. economy?
The stock market fell; airline workers were laid off; and consumer confidence fell.

A Call to Action

In a national address on September 20, President George W. Bush called the attacks on the World Trade Center and the Pentagon "an act of war." He promised that the United States would bring those responsible to justice.

A war on terrorism. The president also declared that the United States would wage war on terrorism itself. Bush emphasized that U.S. efforts would be aimed not only against terrorist organizations but also against national governments that supported and protected terrorists.

In his speech Bush singled out one government—the Taliban regime of Afghanistan—as a key sponsor of terror. The Taliban emerged in the mid-1990s as a splinter group of fundamentalist Muslims. Many members had fought against the Soviets during their occupation of Afghanistan. Taliban leaders had developed ties to Osama bin Laden, whom they later sheltered.

Domestic security. The campaign against terrorism involved defensive and offensive measures. Bush appointed Pennsylvania governor **Tom Ridge** to head the Office of Homeland Security, a new cabinet-level position. This office was created to coordinate the domestic national security efforts of various government agencies.

Key goals included improving airport security and protecting from attack vital systems such as transportation and power networks. Political leaders, including U.S. Attorney General John Ashcroft, called for expanded law-enforcement powers to combat terrorism. This led to debate over how best to protect Americans' civil liberties while increasing domestic security.

A difficult mission. Administration officials, including Secretary of Defense **Donald Rumsfeld**, agreed that locating and striking at terrorists outside the United States would be difficult. "This is a worldwide problem of terrorist networks," Rumsfeld emphasized. The Bush administration used economic, diplomatic, and

REVIEW

Have students complete the **Section 5 Review** on p. 825.

ASSESS

As **Alternative Assessment**, you may want to use the New York journal entries or economy graphic organizers in this section's lessons.

RETEACH

Have students complete create a packet of notecards that can be sequenced describing the events of September 11, 2001, and the days following. Divide students into groups of 2 or 3 and give each group a packet to correctly sequence.
English Language Learners, Cooperative Learning

EXTEND

Organize students into groups of 2 to 3. Briefly review the subjects of this section, and then write the following question on the board: *How have the terrorist attacks changed the United States?* Have each group write one way in which the terrorist attacks have changed the United States. Then conduct a class discussion in which students explain their choices.
Cooperative Learning, Block Scheduling

military means to fight terrorism. The president froze the assets of individuals, groups, and companies with suspected terrorist ties. Secretary of State **Colin Powell** led U.S. efforts to build an international coalition against terrorism and to isolate the Taliban regime.

The United States also began mobilizing military forces. Aircraft-carrier groups and ground troops were assembled. On October 7, the United States and Great Britain began air strikes against Afghanistan. These strikes targeted al Qaeda and Taliban training camps, air-defense systems, and airfields, as well Kabul, the country's capital. The Northern Alliance, an Afghan group that had fought against the Taliban since the early 1990s, provided ground support. The United States and Great Britian also sent ground troops. The troops slowly drove out the Taliban and captured members of al Qaeda. On December 17, the American flag was raised at the U.S. embassy in Kabul for the first time since 1989. Four days later, a new Afghan government was established.

Meanwhile, Americans and the military remained on alert for other possible terrorist actions. Several letters containing dried anthrax spores were sent to locations in Florida, New York City, and Washington, D.C., including Senator Tom Daschle's office. Some who handled these letters, including postal workers, became infected and died. Anthrax is a potentially deadly disease caused by spore-forming bacterium.

As U.S. leaders planned strategies, it was clear that a new era in global relations had begun. The world had changed since September 11, but where the changes would lead was still unclear. The vulnerability of the United States had been exposed but so had its strength.

Americans nationwide joined together to remember victims of the September 11 attacks.

internet connect

GO TO: go.hrw.com
KEYWORD: SS Attack
FOR: Web sites about the events of September 11, 2001, and the aftermath.

✔ **READING CHECK: Summarizing** What early steps did U.S. leaders take to respond to the terrorist attacks on the United States? Bush called for a war on terrorism, appointed Tom Ridge as head of homeland security, and launched air strikes on Afghanistan.

SECTION 5 REVIEW

1. Identify and explain:
World Trade Center
Pentagon
Rudolph Giuliani
George W. Bush
Tom Ridge
Donald Rumsfeld
Colin Powell

2. Analyzing Information
Copy the graphic organizer below. Use it to explain some of the ways in which the U.S. government responded to protect Americans and bring terrorists to justice.

Security — Government Actions — Diplomatic
Economic — Government Actions — Military

3. Finding the Main Idea
a. Whom did investigators suspect of carrying out and supporting the terrorist attacks of September 11, 2001?
b. What methods did the federal government use to pursue the suspected terrorists?
c. How did the September 11 attacks affect the economy?

4. Writing and Critical Thinking
Evaluating Imagine that you are first learning of the attacks on September 11, 2001, and want to help however you can. Write a paragraph describing possible actions you could take to assist those in need.
Consider:
• the efforts of relief agencies to help victims
• the need for national unity
• the importance of tolerance

Homework Practice Online
keyword: SE3 HP27

REVIEW 27 ANSWERS

Creating a Time Line
Each event should have an explanation and the correct date.

Writing a Summary
See the Reading Checks in each section for main ideas.

Identifying People and Ideas
1. Democrat elected president in 1992 and 1996

2. 1994 Republican campaign pledge that promised a balanced-budget amendment and other reforms

3. Republican presidential candidate in 1996

4. revealed the persistence of racial tensions in the United States

5. first female secretary of state for the United States

6. astronaut and senator who returned to space in 1998 at age 77

7. computer-based communications and information system

8. required large companies to provide workers with time off for family and medical emergencies without losing their insurance or jobs

9. Western European trading bloc

10. Republican president elected in 2000

CHAPTER 27 REVIEW AND ASSESSMENT RESOURCES

TECHNOLOGY

▶ Chapter 27 Test Generator (on the One-Stop Planner)
▶ Global Skill Builder CD–ROM
▶ HRW Go site

REINFORCEMENT, REVIEW, AND ASSESSMENT

▶ Chapter 27 Review, pp. 826–27
▶ Chapter 27 Tutorial for Students, Parents, Mentors, and Peers

▶ Chapter 27 Test (Form A or B)
▶ Portfolio Activities and Alternative Assessment Handbook, Chapter 27
▶ Chapter 27 Test for English Language Learners and Special-Needs Students

REVIEW

Have students complete the **Chapter 27 Review** on pp. 826–27.

ASSESS

Use one of the chapter tests to assess students' understanding of the content. For **Alternative Assessment**, see the **Portfolio Activities and Alternative Assessment Handbook.**

Understanding Main Ideas

1. the participation and election of a record number of women and the strong showing of independent candidate Ross Perot

2. It became involved militarily and suffered some human losses.

3. He was impeached for perjury in a civil trial and for violating his oath of office.

4. It provided new services and access to information but threatened to deepen social divisions between those with and without access to technology.

5. Growing economic competition contributed to international trading blocs and growth of multinational corporations.

6. by helping with rescue efforts, providing economic aid, and supporting the government's efforts

Reviewing Themes

1. Economic power, like military power, can be used to promote political goals.

2. The exportation of American popular culture creates an impression about American life, leads other countries to fear for the survival of their own cultures, and creates a cultural link between nations.

3. provided new ways to communicate information and created worries about indecency on the Internet, loss of jobs, and the Y2K bug

CHAPTER 27 Review

Creating a Time Line

Copy the time line below onto a sheet of paper. Complete the time line by filling in the events and dates from the chapter that you think were most significant. Pick three events and explain why you think they were significant.

1990   1996   2002

Writing a Summary

Using standard grammar, spelling, sentence structure, and punctuation, write an overview of events in the chapter.

Identifying People and Ideas

Identify the following terms or individuals and explain their significance.

1. Bill Clinton
2. Contract with America
3. Bob Dole
4. Los Angeles Riots
5. Madeleine Albright
6. John Glenn
7. Internet
8. Family and Medical Leave Act
9. European Union
10. George W. Bush

Understanding Main Ideas

SECTION 1 *(pp. 798–803)*

1. What made the elections of 1992 unique?
2. How was the United States affected by conflicts in other countries and by terrorism in the 1990s?

SECTION 2 *(pp. 804–809)*

3. Why was President Clinton impeached?

SECTION 3 *(pp. 810–814)*

4. Why was computer technology both helpful and controversial in the 1990s?

SECTION 4 *(pp. 815–819)*

5. How did the global economy develop?

SECTION 5 *(pp. 820–825)*

6. How did Americans respond to the terrorist attacks of September 11, 2001?

Reviewing Themes

1. Economics How has a nation's economic strength become as important as its military power in foreign policy?
2. Global Relations How does American culture affect the rest of the world?
3. Science, Technology, and Society How have new technologies changed American society and the world?

Thinking Critically

1. Identifying Points of View How did the Contract with America reflect the ideals of Republican congressional candidates in 1994?
2. Making Generalizations What were the origins of the domestic and foreign policy issues President Bush faced as he entered office in 2001?
3. Evaluating How did President Clinton's impeachment affect U.S. citizens' views of the federal government?
4. Analyzing Information How did the government and private organizations try to conserve natural resources in the 1990s?
5. Making Predictions How might a reform of the electoral college system affect state and local governments?

Writing About History

Summarizing Imagine that you are a reporter covering John Glenn's 1998 space shuttle flight. Write a short description of the significance of Glenn's flight. Use this graphic to organize your thoughts.

Impact of Glenn's Shuttle Flight

| Glenn's History with the Space Program | Setbacks for the Space Program |

RETEACH

Organize students into small groups. Have each group use at least 20 of the Define and Identify terms in this chapter to create a crossword puzzle with clues. Have each group exchange its crossword puzzle with another group and then solve them.
English Language Learners, Cooperative Learning

EXTEND

Have each student conduct research on the growth of the world's population during the past 100 years. Students should focus their research on the size of the world's population, changing birthrates, and the projected world population in 2025. Have each student create a chart presenting his or her research. Ask volunteers to present their charts to the class.
Block Scheduling

Building Social Studies Skills

Interpreting Political Cartoons

Study the political cartoon below. Then use it to help answer the questions that follow.

1. What does this cartoon suggest about the effect of rising oil prices on the U.S. economy?
   a. Increased oil prices would lead to a more stable economy.
   b. The economy might suffer if oil prices keep increasing.
   c. OPEC will lower oil prices in response to U.S. government efforts.
   d. More Americans should ride trains.
2. How might Americans and the U.S. government respond to rising oil prices?

Analyzing Primary Sources

Analyze the following quotation by Justice Sandra Day O'Connor, the first woman ever to serve on the Supreme Court. In 1993 Ruth Bader Ginsburg joined her on the Supreme Court. Then answer the questions that follow.

❝Judges are supposed to be objective; they're supposed to study and look at the law and apply the law to the particular case in an objective way, not from any particular point of view. So does being a woman make a difference in what answer is given? I tend to think that probably at the end of the day, a wise old woman and a wise old man are going to reach the same answer.❞

3. What point of view does Justice O'Connor express?
   a. Men make better judgments than women do on legal issues.
   b. Women make better judgments than men do on legal issues.
   c. Men and women make the same types of objective judgments on legal issues.
   d. Men and women come to different conclusions on legal issues in most cases.

4. Do you agree or disagree with Justice O'Connor's statement? Explain your answer.

Alternative Assessment

Building Your Portfolio

Government

Imagine that you are a member of a Congressional committee charged with revising federal presidential election procedures. Write a press release on the committee's final recommendations. Your press release should include reasons why this revision is occurring and how this revision will affect the relationship between state and federal governments.

U.S. HISTORY

🖸 internet connect

Internet Activity: go.hrw.com
KEYWORD: SE3 AN27

Choose a topic on life in the contemporary United States to:

- create a database on the impact of NAFTA and then create a graph to represent your data.
- make a mind map or three-dimensional model of the social impact of the invention of personal computers and the Internet.
- create a brochure on the contemporary space program.

go. hrw .com

Thinking Critically

1. Answers will vary. Students might suggest that the Contract aimed at restoring trust between voters and elected officials.

2. European Union and multi-national corporations–international trade; population explosion–environmental challenges; close election–left Bush without support of the majority

3. Many Americans began to distrust Clinton personally, which led many to lose faith in the office of the president itself.

4. by using alternative sources of energy; by protecting sensitive natural areas; by recycling

5. Because states determine electors, changes to the electoral college will put added responsibility on state and local governments.

Writing

Reports should discuss the *Challenger* explosion, Glenn's first flight in 1962, and the excitement generated by his 1998 trip into space.

Building Social Studies Skills

1. b

2. Answers will vary. Students might suggest that Americans conserve energy and that the government explore new energy sources.

3. c

4. Answers will vary. Students should provide evidence to support their answer.

TECHNOLOGY

▶ Global Skill Builder CD–ROM

▶ Holt Researcher: American History CD–ROM

▶ HRW Go site

REINFORCEMENT, REVIEW, AND ASSESSMENT

▶ Unit 7 Review, pp. 822–23

▶ Unit 7 Test (Form A or B)

▶ Portfolio Activities and Alternative Assessment Handbook, Unit 7

▶ Unit 7 Test for English Language Learners and Special-Needs Students

To review elements of Unit 7 in a single class period, assign one of the following activities or graphic organizers, omitting the italicized answers, to individuals or groups.

1 Problem Solving

Ask students to imagine that it is 1990 and they are U.S. diplomats concerned with ethnic and religious conflict in the new nations of Europe. Have students compose reports on the challenges that new nations face, as well as different options that might solve these problems. Students should discuss the role the United States should play in the development of these new nations. After considering the advantages and disadvantages of each option, students should select their best option. Have students imagine the consequences of their plan of action, and ask

---

A Selection from **Further Reading**

Richard Nixon's Decision to Resign. In *The Final Days*, Bob Woodward and Carl Bernstein describe the last days of Richard Nixon's presidency. In the following excerpt, they relate an encounter between Nixon and his Secretary of State, Henry Kissinger, on the evening that the president decided to resign from office: "Nixon summoned Kissinger. . . . They sat for a time and reminisced about events, travels, shared decisions. . . . Then Nixon said that he wasn't sure he would be able to resign. Could he be the first President to quit office? Kissinger responded by listing the President's contributions, especially in diplomacy. 'Will history treat me more kindly than my contemporaries?' Nixon asked, tears flooding his eyes. Certainly, definitely, Kissinger said. . . . But he was certain that Nixon would never escape the verdict of Watergate."

ANALYZING SOURCES

According to Bernstein and Woodward, what aspect of the resignation did Nixon find particularly troubling?

ANSWER: Students might suggest that Nixon was concerned by the possibility that history would judge him harshly for the Watergate scandal and his decision to resign.

U·N·I·T 7

Review

BUILDING YOUR PORTFOLIO

Outlined below are three projects. Independently or cooperatively, complete one and use the products to demonstrate your mastery of the historical concepts involved.

1 Problem Solving

The year is 1990. During the past 20 years the United States has opened negotiations with China, improved relations with the Soviet Union, helped win the Cold War, and witnessed the breakup of the Soviet Union. Regional and local conflicts emerged, however, as newly formed nations were torn apart by ethnic and religious struggles. Your assignment is to identify the challenges of changing relationships among nations and create a solution.

Use your textbook and other resources to ***gather information*** that might influence your solution. Remember that your solution must include a plan of

Nixon aide John Dean testifying before Congress

action. The information you might need to solve the problem includes major foreign policy issues currently facing the United States and the historical background of the Cold War.

Once you have gathered information, ***list and consider options***. These options might include laws, amendments, government changes, or actions taken by private citizens. Once you have identified these options, ***consider the advantages and disadvantages*** of each option. Which option do you think has the best chance for success?

Choose and implement a solution. Complete the plan of action. ***Evaluate the effectiveness*** of your solution. Was it the best option? Would one of your earlier options have been effective? How could you modify your plan to make it more effective?

Destruction of the Berlin Wall

them to write a brief report evaluating the effectiveness of their solution. Ask volunteers to read their reports to the class.

2 Constitutional Heritage

Ask students to imagine that they have just heard the President Nixon has resigned because of the Watergate scandal. Have students write down their reactions, including what concerns they have about the presidency. Next, have students imagine they have just witnessed the Iran-Contra hearings. Have students again write down their reactions, including what concerns they have about the federal government. Students should focus on what the two events have in common. Ask volunteers to share their reactions with the class.

3 Culture

allows people to communicate with others who share interests around the world

gives anyone with a personal computer access to virtually many different kinds of information

DAILY LIFE

EFFECTS OF COMPUTERS AND THE INTERNET ON AMERICAN SOCIETY

BUSINESS

has increased the multinational nature of business

allows individuals and businesses to sell products and services globally through Web sites

---

2 Constitutional Heritage

The Watergate scandal and the Iran-Contra affair challenged the foundation of constitutional government. *Write an editorial* that examines the ways in which the Watergate scandal was both similar to and different from the Iran-Contra affair. Be sure to discuss how these political incidents affected the views of U.S. citizens concerning the role of the federal government. You may wish to use portfolio materials you designed in the unit chapters to help you.

3 Culture

In the past several decades, new advances in computers have made communications and the transfer of information around the world quicker and easier. These changes have brought Americans into increasing contact with citizens worldwide as well as introducing American popular culture to millions of people around the world. *Write an editorial* that examines the impact that American popular culture has had on the rest of the world. Your editorial should also address the impact the entertainment industry has had on the U.S. and international economies. You may wish to use portfolio materials you designed in the unit chapters to help you.

American fast-food restaurant in Thailand

Further Reading

Johnson, Haynes. *Sleepwalking Through History: America in the Reagan Years.* Anchor, 1992. An overview and critical analysis of the Reagan years.

Lewis, Michael. *Liar's Poker: Rising Through the Wreckage on Wall Street.* Norton, 1989. An insider account of Wall Street and the savings and loan industry of the 1980s.

Maraniss, David. *First in His Class: The Biography of Bill Clinton.* Simon & Schuster, 1996. A biography of the 42nd president of the United States.

Schulman, Bruce J. *The Seventies.* Free Press, 2001. A cultural, political, and social history of the 1970s.

Time Life Editors. *Pride and Prosperity: The 80s.* Time-Life, 2000. A photographic look at life in the United States during the 1980s.

Woodward, Bob, and Carl Bernstein. *The Final Days.* Simon & Schuster, 1989. A chronicle of the last days of Richard Nixon's presidency.

Internet Connect & Review on the R◉M

In assigned groups, develop a multimedia presentation about the United States between 1968 and the present. Choose information from the chapter Internet Connect activities and from the **Holt Researcher CD–ROM** that best reflects the major topics of the period. Write an outline and a script for your presentation, which may be shown to the class.

A Selection from Further Reading

Bill Clinton's Use of Public Opinion Polls. In *First in His Class: A Biography of Bill Clinton,* David Maraniss provides an in-depth account of Bill Clinton's life and career. In the following excerpt, he describes how Clinton used public opinion polls as political tools while serving as governor of Arkansas. "[Clinton used] voter surveys in . . . perpetual fashion, taking poll results to shape the substance and rhetoric of policy debates. The goal was to discover more than whether voters supported or opposed an initiative. Word by word, line by line, phrase by phrase, paragraph by paragraph, rhetorical options would be tested to see which ones were most effective in moving the public a certain direction. It was polling as a form of copy writing, as a way for Clinton to organize his thoughts."

ANALYZING SOURCES

According to Maraniss, what role did poll results play in Bill Clinton's political strategy?

ANSWER: Students might indicate that Clinton used poll results to shape both his political positions and the manner in which he discussed these positions.

Reference

Facts About the States

State	Year of Statehood	2000 Population	Reps. in the House	Area (sq. mi.)	Population Density (sq. mi.)	Capital
Alabama	1819	4,461,130	7	51,705	86.3	Montgomery
Alaska	1959	628,933	1	591,004	1.1	Juneau
Arizona	1912	5,140,683	8	114,000	45.1	Phoenix
Arkansas	1836	2,679,733	4	53,187	50.4	Little Rock
California	1850	33,930,798	53	158,706	213.8	Sacramento
Colorado	1876	4,311,882	7	104,247	41.4	Denver
Connecticut	1788	3,409,535	5	5,018	679.5	Hartford
Delaware	1787	785,068	1	2,057	381.7	Dover
District of Columbia	–	572,059	–	69	8,290.7	–
Florida	1845	16,028,890	25	58,664	273.2	Tallahassee
Georgia	1788	8,206,975	13	58,910	139.3	Atlanta
Hawaii	1959	1,216,642	2	6,471	188.0	Honolulu
Idaho	1890	1,297,274	2	83,557	15.5	Boise
Illinois	1818	12,439,042	19	56,400	220.6	Springfield
Indiana	1816	6,090,782	9	36,291	167.8	Indianapolis
Iowa	1846	2,931,923	5	56,275	52.1	Des Moines
Kansas	1861	2,693,824	4	82,277	32.7	Topeka
Kentucky	1792	4,049,431	6	40,395	100.2	Frankfort
Louisiana	1812	4,480,271	7	48,523	92.3	Baton Rouge
Maine	1820	1,277,731	2	33,265	38.4	Augusta
Maryland	1788	5,307,886	8	10,460	507.4	Annapolis
Massachusetts	1788	6,355,568	10	8,284	767.2	Boston
Michigan	1837	9,955,829	15	58,527	170.1	Lansing
Minnesota	1858	4,925,670	8	84,068	58.6	St. Paul
Mississippi	1817	2,852,927	4	47,689	59.8	Jackson
Missouri	1821	5,606,260	9	69,697	80.4	Jefferson City
Montana	1889	905,316	1	147,046	6.2	Helena
Nebraska	1867	1,715,369	3	77,355	22.2	Lincoln
Nevada	1864	2,002,032	3	110,561	18.1	Carson City
New Hampshire	1788	1,238,415	2	9,279	133.5	Concord
New Jersey	1787	8,424,354	13	7,787	1,081.8	Trenton
New Mexico	1912	1,823,821	3	121,593	15.0	Santa Fe
New York	1788	19,004,973	29	49,576	383.4	Albany
North Carolina	1789	8,067,673	13	52,669	153.2	Raleigh
North Dakota	1889	643,756	1	70,655	9.1	Bismarck
Ohio	1803	11,374,540	18	41,222	275.9	Columbus
Oklahoma	1907	3,458,819	5	69,956	49.4	Oklahoma City
Oregon	1859	3,428,543	5	97,073	35.3	Salem
Pennsylvania	1787	12,300,670	19	45,333	271.3	Harrisburg
Rhode Island	1790	1,049,662	2	1,212	866.1	Providence
South Carolina	1788	4,025,061	6	31,113	129.4	Columbia
South Dakota	1889	756,874	1	77,116	9.8	Pierre
Tennessee	1796	5,700,037	9	42,144	135.3	Nashville
Texas	1845	20,903,994	32	266,807	78.3	Austin
Utah	1896	2,236,714	3	84,899	26.3	Salt Lake City
Vermont	1791	609,890	1	9,609	63.5	Montpelier
Virginia	1788	7,100,702	11	40,767	174.2	Richmond
Washington	1889	5,908,684	9	68,192	86.6	Olympia
West Virginia	1863	1,813,077	3	24,181	75.0	Charleston
Wisconsin	1848	5,371,210	8	56,154	95.7	Madison
Wyoming	1890	495,304	1	97,914	5.1	Cheyenne

PRESIDENTS OF THE UNITED STATES

The Official Portraits

1 George Washington

Born: 1732 **Died:** 1799
Years in Office: 1789–97
Political Party: None
Home State: Virginia
Vice President: John Adams

2 John Adams

Born: 1735 **Died:** 1826
Years in Office: 1797–1801
Political Party: Federalist
Home State: Massachusetts
Vice President: Thomas Jefferson

3 Thomas Jefferson

Born: 1743 **Died:** 1826
Years in Office: 1801–09
Political Party: Republican*
Home State: Virginia
Vice Presidents: Aaron Burr, George Clinton

4 James Madison

Born: 1751 **Died:** 1836
Years in Office: 1809–17
Political Party: Republican
Home State: Virginia
Vice Presidents: George Clinton, Elbridge Gerry

5 James Monroe

Born: 1758 **Died:** 1831
Years in Office: 1817–25
Political Party: Republican
Home State: Virginia
Vice President: Daniel D. Tompkins

6 John Quincy Adams

Born: 1767 **Died:** 1848
Years in Office: 1825–29
Political Party: Republican
Home State: Massachusetts
Vice President: John C. Calhoun

7 Andrew Jackson

Born: 1767 **Died:** 1845
Years in Office: 1829–37
Political Party: Democratic
Home State: Tennessee
Vice Presidents: John C. Calhoun, Martin Van Buren

8 Martin Van Buren

Born: 1782 **Died:** 1862
Years in Office: 1837–41
Political Party: Democratic
Home State: New York
Vice President: Richard M. Johnson

* The Republican Party of the third through sixth presidents is not the Republican Party of Abraham Lincoln, which was founded in 1854.

9 William Henry Harrison
Born: 1773   **Died:** 1841
Years in Office: 1841
Political Party: Whig
Home State: Ohio
Vice President: John Tyler

10 John Tyler
Born: 1790   **Died:** 1862
Years in Office: 1841–45
Political Party: Whig
Home State: Virginia
Vice President: None

11 James K. Polk
Born: 1795   **Died:** 1849
Years in Office: 1845–49
Political Party: Democratic
Home State: Tennessee
Vice President: George M. Dallas

12 Zachary Taylor
Born: 1784   **Died:** 1850
Years in Office: 1849–50
Political Party: Whig
Home State: Louisiana
Vice President: Millard Fillmore

13 Millard Fillmore
Born: 1800   **Died:** 1874
Years in Office: 1850–53
Political Party: Whig
Home State: New York
Vice President: None

14 Franklin Pierce
Born: 1804   **Died:** 1869
Years in Office: 1853–57
Political Party: Democratic
Home State: New Hampshire
Vice President: William R. King

15 James Buchanan
Born: 1791   **Died:** 1868
Years in Office: 1857–61
Political Party: Democratic
Home State: Pennsylvania
Vice President: John C. Breckinridge

16 Abraham Lincoln
Born: 1809   **Died:** 1865
Years in Office: 1861–65
Political Party: Republican
Home State: Illinois
Vice President: Hannibal Hamlin,
Andrew Johnson

17 Andrew Johnson
Born: 1808   **Died:** 1875
Years in Office: 1865-69
Political Party: Republican
Home State: Tennessee
Vice President: None

18 Ulysses S. Grant

Born: 1822 **Died:** 1885
Years in Office: 1869–77
Political Party: Republican
Home State: Illinois
Vice President: Schuyler Colfax,
Henry Wilson

19 Rutherford B. Hayes

Born: 1822 **Died:** 1893
Years in Office: 1877–81
Political Party: Republican
Home State: Ohio
Vice President: William A. Wheeler

20 James A. Garfield

Born: 1831 **Died:** 1881
Years in Office: 1881
Political Party: Republican
Home State: Ohio
Vice President: Chester A. Arthur

21 Chester A. Arthur

Born: 1829 **Died:** 1886
Years in Office: 1881–85
Political Party: Republican
Home State: New York
Vice President: None

22 Grover Cleveland

Born: 1837 **Died:** 1908
Years in Office: 1885–89
Political Party: Democratic
Home State: New York
Vice President: Thomas A.
Hendricks

23 Benjamin Harrison

Born: 1833 **Died:** 1901
Years in Office: 1889–93
Political Party: Republican
Home State: Indiana
Vice President: Levi P. Morton

24 Grover Cleveland

Born: 1837 **Died:** 1908
Years in Office: 1893–97
Political Party: Democratic
Home State: New York
Vice President: Adlai E. Stevenson

25 William McKinley

Born: 1843 **Died:** 1901
Years in Office: 1897–1901
Political Party: Republican
Home State: Ohio
Vice President: Garret A. Hobart,
Theodore Roosevelt

26 Theodore Roosevelt

Born: 1858 **Died:** 1919
Years in Office: 1901-09
Political Party: Republican
Home State: New York
Vice President: Charles W. Fairbanks

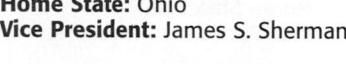

27 William Howard Taft

Born: 1857   **Died:** 1930
Years in Office: 1909–13
Political Party: Republican
Home State: Ohio
Vice President: James S. Sherman

28 Woodrow Wilson

Born: 1856   **Died:** 1924
Years in Office: 1913–21
Political Party: Democratic
Home State: New Jersey
Vice President: Thomas R. Marshall

29 Warren G. Harding

Born: 1865   **Died:** 1923
Years in Office: 1921–23
Political Party: Republican
Home State: Ohio
Vice President: Calvin Coolidge

30 Calvin Coolidge

Born: 1872   **Died:** 1933
Years in Office: 1923–29
Political Party: Republican
Home State: Massachusetts
Vice President: Charles G. Dawes

31 Herbert Hoover

Born: 1874   **Died:** 1964
Years in Office: 1929–33
Political Party: Republican
Home State: California
Vice President: Charles Curtis

32 Franklin D. Roosevelt

Born: 1882   **Died:** 1945
Years in Office: 1933–45
Political Party: Democratic
Home State: New York
Vice President: John Nance Garner,
Henry Wallace, Harry S Truman

33 Harry S Truman

Born: 1884   **Died:** 1972
Years in Office: 1945–53
Political Party: Democratic
Home State: Missouri
Vice President: Alben W. Barkley

34 Dwight D. Eisenhower

Born: 1890   **Died:** 1969
Years in Office: 1953–61
Political Party: Republican
Home State: Kansas
Vice President: Richard M. Nixon

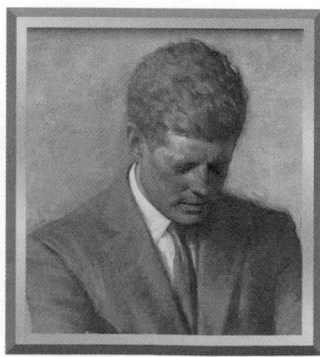

35 John F. Kennedy

Born: 1917   **Died:** 1963
Years in Office: 1961–63
Political Party: Democratic
Home State: Massachusetts
Vice President: Lyndon B. Johnson

36 Lyndon B. Johnson

Born: 1908　　**Died:** 1973
Years in Office: 1963–69
Political Party: Democratic
Home State: Texas
Vice President: Hubert H. Humphrey

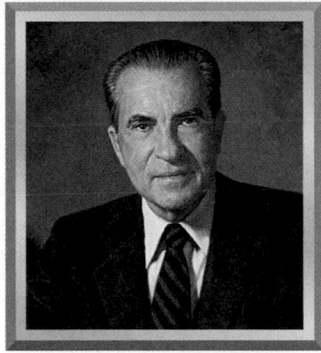

37 Richard M. Nixon

Born: 1913　　**Died:** 1994
Years in Office: 1969–74
Political Party: Republican
Home State: California
Vice President: Spiro T. Agnew,
Gerald R. Ford

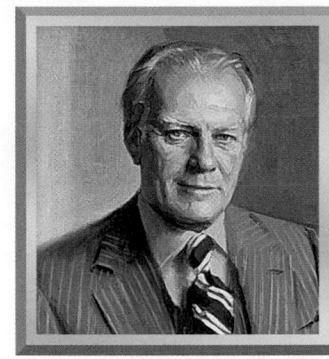

38 Gerald R. Ford

Born: 1913
Years in Office: 1974–77
Political Party: Republican
Home State: Michigan
Vice President: Nelson A.
Rockefeller

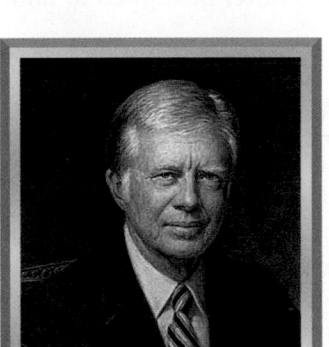

39 Jimmy Carter

Born: 1924
Years in Office: 1977–81
Political Party: Democratic
Home State: Georgia
Vice President: Walter F. Mondale

40 Ronald Reagan

Born: 1911
Years in Office: 1981–89
Political Party: Republican
Home State: California
Vice President: George Bush

41 George Bush

Born: 1924
Years in Office: 1989–93
Political Party: Republican
Home State: Texas
Vice President: Dan Quayle

42 Bill Clinton

Born: 1946
Years in Office: 1993–2001
Political Party: Democratic
Home State: Arkansas
Vice President: Al Gore

43 George W. Bush

Born: 1946
Years in Office: 2001–
Political Party: Republican
Home State: Texas
Vice President: Richard B. Cheney

THE AMERICAN FLAG

The American flag is a symbol of the nation. It is recognized instantly, whether as a big banner waving in the wind or a tiny emblem worn on a lapel. The flag is so important that it is a major theme of the national anthem, "The Star-Spangled Banner." One of the most popular names for the flag is the Stars and Stripes. It is also known as Old Glory.

THE MEANING OF THE FLAG

The American flag has 13 stripes—7 red and 6 white. In the upper-left corner of the flag is the Union—50 white five-pointed stars against a blue background.

The 13 stripes stand for the original 13 American states, and the 50 stars represent the states of the nation today. According to the U.S. Department of State, the colors of the flag also are symbolic:

Red stands for courage.

White symbolizes purity.

Blue is the color of vigilance, perseverance, and justice.

DISPLAYING THE FLAG

It is customary not to display the American flag in bad weather. It is also customary for the flag to be displayed outdoors only from sunrise to sunset, except on certain occasions. In a few special places, however, the flag is always flown day and night. When flown at night, the flag should be illuminated.

Near a speaker's platform, the flag should occupy the place of honor at the speaker's right. When carried in a parade with other flags, the American flag should be on the marching right or in front at the center. When flying with the flags of the 50 states, the national flag must be at the center and the highest point. In a group of national flags, all should be of equal size and all should be flown from staffs, or flagpoles, of equal height.

The flag should never touch the ground or the floor. It should not be marked with any insignia, pictures, or words. Nor should it be used in any disrespectful way—as an advertising decoration, for instance. The flag should never be dipped to honor any person or thing.

SALUTING THE FLAG

The United States, like other countries, has a flag code, or rules for displaying and honoring the flag. For example, all those present should stand at attention facing the flag and salute it when it is being raised or lowered or when it is carried past them in a parade or procession. A man wearing a hat should take it off and hold it with his right hand over his heart. All women and hatless men should stand with their right hands over their hearts to show respect. The flag should also receive these honors during the playing of the national anthem and the reciting of the Pledge of Allegiance.

THE PLEDGE OF ALLEGIANCE

The Pledge of Allegiance was written in 1892 by Massachusetts magazine (*Youth's Companion*) editor Francis Bellamy. (Congress added the words "under God" in 1954.)

I pledge allegiance to the flag of the United States of America and to the republic for which it stands, one nation under God, indivisible, with liberty and justice for all.

Civilians should say the Pledge of Allegiance with their right hands over their hearts. People in the armed forces give the military salute. By saying the Pledge of Allegiance, we promise loyalty ("pledge allegiance") to the United States and its ideals.

"THE STAR-SPANGLED BANNER"

"The Star-Spangled Banner" is the national anthem of the United States. It was written by Francis Scott Key during the War of 1812. While being detained by the British aboard a ship on September 13–14, 1814, Key watched the British bombardment of Fort McHenry near Baltimore. The attack lasted 25 hours. The smoke was so thick that Key could not tell who had won. When the air cleared, Key saw the American flag that was still flying over the fort. "The Star-Spangled Banner" is sung to music written by British composer John Stafford Smith. In 1931 Congress designated "The Star-Spangled Banner" as the national anthem.

I

Oh, say, can you see, by the dawn's early light,
What so proudly we hailed at the twilight's last gleaming,
Whose broad stripes and bright stars through the perilous fight,
O'er the ramparts we watched were so gallantly streaming?
And the rockets' red glare, the bombs bursting in air,
Gave proof through the night that our flag was still there.
Oh, say, does that star-spangled banner yet wave
O'er the land of the free, and the home of the brave?

II

On the shore, dimly seen through the mists of the deep,
Where the foe's haughty host in dread silence reposes,
What is that which the breeze, o'er the towering steep,
As it fitfully blows, half conceals, half discloses?
Now it catches the gleam of the morning's first beam,
In full glory reflected, now shines on the stream.
'Tis the star-spangled banner; oh, long may it wave
O'er the land of the free, and the home of the brave!

III

And where is that band who so vauntingly swore
That the havoc of war and the battle's confusion
A home and a country should leave us no more?
Their blood has washed out their foul footsteps' pollution.
No refuge could save the hireling and slave
From the terror of flight, or the gloom of the grave:
And the star-spangled banner in triumph doth wave
O'er the land of the free, and the home of the brave!

IV

Oh! thus be it ever when freemen shall stand
Between their loved homes and the war's desolation!
Blest with victory and peace, may the heaven-rescued land
Praise the Power that hath made and preserved us a nation!
Then conquer we must, for our cause it is just,
And this be our motto: "In God is our trust!"
And the star-spangled banner in triumph shall wave,
O'er the land of the free, and the home of the brave!

Sheet music for the national anthem

"AMERICA, THE BEAUTIFUL"

One of the most beloved songs celebrating our nation is "America, the Beautiful." Katharine Lee Bates first wrote the lyrics to the song in 1893 after visiting Colorado. The version of the song we know today is set to music by Samuel A. Ward. The first and last stanzas of "America, the Beautiful" are shown below.

O beautiful for spacious skies,
For amber waves of grain,
For purple mountain majesties
Above the fruited plain!
America! America!
God shed his grace on thee
And crown thy good with brotherhood
From sea to shining sea!

• •

O beautiful for patriot dream
That sees beyond the years
Thine alabaster cities gleam
Undimmed by human tears!
America! America!
God shed his grace on thee
And crown thy good with brotherhood
From sea to shining sea!

SUPREME COURT CASES

LEADING SUPREME COURT CASES

1 *Marbury* v. *Madison*
1 Cranch (5 U.S.) 137 (1803)

What was this case about?

The story. The Federalist Party had been defeated in the election of 1800. However, President-elect Thomas Jefferson was not scheduled to take office until March 4, 1801. In the meantime, the outgoing president, John Adams, chose a number of Federalist supporters as justices of the peace in the District of Columbia. These justices received their appointments in the final hours of the Adams administration. However, they were unable to take office until their commissions were delivered. After the new president took over, he found that the previous secretary of state, John Marshall, had not had time to deliver all of the commissions. Jefferson immediately ordered his new secretary of state, James Madison, not to deliver the remaining commissions.

As one of the people whose commission was not delivered, William Marbury sued Madison. Marbury took advantage of a law passed by Congress that allowed him to make this kind of complaint directly to the Supreme Court. He asked the Court to order Madison to deliver the commission even though this request meant disobeying the president. Marbury probably expected the Court to do as he asked because John Marshall had been appointed Chief Justice of the United States.

The question. As Chief Justice Marshall saw it, the question before the Court had three parts. First, did Marbury have a right to receive the commission? Second, if he did have a right to the commission, was the government required to ensure that he received the commission? Finally, if the government was required to do so, would it have to order Madison to deliver Marbury's commission, as Marbury requested?

The issues. Chief Justice Marshall wanted the Court to be able to decide if laws passed by Congress were constitutional. Whether the Court had this power of judicial review—the power to decide if laws made by Congress are allowed by the Constitution—had not yet been decided. Marshall posed the question before the Court in three parts in order to discuss judicial review.

How was the case decided?

In 1803 the Court ruled against ordering Madison to deliver Marbury's commission.

What did the Court say about governmental powers?

The Court's reasoning passed through three stages:

Step 1. Pointing to a federal law that outlined the appointment process for District of Columbia justices of the peace, the Court said that Marbury had a right to the commission.

Step 2. The Court said that when government officials hurt people by neglecting legal duties, our laws require a remedy.

Step 3. Marbury had asked that the Supreme Court order Madison to deliver the commission. Here Chief Justice Marshall did something surprising. He declared that a court could issue such an order, but that the Supreme Court was not the right court to issue it.

Marbury had taken advantage of a federal law that allowed complaints such as his to be taken straight to the Supreme Court. However, Chief Justice Marshall declared this law unconstitutional. The Constitution mentions several kinds of cases that can be brought straight to the Supreme Court. All other kinds of cases must go through lower courts first. The chief justice explained that Marbury's lawsuit was one of the kinds of cases that must go through lower courts first. It did not matter that Congress had passed a law saying something different, because the Constitution is a higher law.

Marshall's cleverly written opinion excused the Supreme Court from hearing lawsuits such as the Marbury case before lower courts had heard them. Marshall accomplished this by claiming for the Court an even greater power—the power of judicial review.

What implications did this case have for the future?

If the Supreme Court did not have judicial review, Congress would decide for itself on the constitutionality of the laws it passed. Marshall's opinion in *Marbury* v. *Madison* removed that power from Congress. By deciding on the constitutionality of the other two branches' actions, the Supreme Court is the nation's final authority on the meaning of the Constitution.

2 *Martin* v. *Hunter's Lessee*
1 Wheaton (14 U.S.) 304 (1816)

What was this case about?

The story. In 1777, during the Revolutionary War, Virginia passed a law declaring that land owned by people who were still loyal to Great Britain no longer belonged to them. When Thomas Lord Fairfax died in

England in 1782, his Virginia lands passed first to his American relative Denny Martin and then to Thomas Martin, Denny's nephew. However, Virginia gave Fairfax's land to David Hunter.

Thomas Martin considered himself the true owner of the land. Hunter disagreed and rented it to someone else. The renter (called the "lessee") tried to have Martin evicted. Virginia's highest court ruled that Hunter owned the land.

Martin appealed his case to the U.S. Supreme Court. He reminded the Court of the treaties between the United States and Britain. These treaties promised to protect the rights of British subjects who had owned property in America before the Revolution. Because of these treaties, he said, Virginia's 1777 law was not valid. The Supreme Court agreed. It sent the case back to the Virginia court with orders to change its decision.

However, the Virginia court denied that the Supreme Court had the authority to tell a state court what to do. Therefore, Martin asked the Supreme Court to reverse the Virginia court's judgment.

The question. In cases that involve the federal Constitution, laws, and treaties, does the Constitution give federal courts the power to reverse state court judgments?

The issues. In *Marbury* v. *Madison* the Supreme Court asserted the power of judicial review, but that did not settle the issue of how far the power of judicial review extends. In *Marbury* v. *Madison* one of the other branches of the federal government had been overruled, but in this case Martin was asking the Supreme Court to overrule one of the branches of a state government.

How was the case decided?
In 1816, in an opinion written by Justice Joseph Story, the Supreme Court did what Martin asked. It reversed the judgment of the Virginia court.

What did the Court say about governmental powers?
Justice Story thought that the Constitution gave the Supreme Court the power to reverse state courts in cases involving the federal Constitution, laws, and treaties. To explain his decision, he first tried to show why various objections to his view were mistaken. One such objection was that the Constitution does not affect state governments, but rather the people living in those states. Justice Story pointed out that the Constitution is "crowded" with conditions that affect the state governments. Another objection was that federal judges might abuse the power they had to decide the meaning of the federal Constitution, laws,

and treaties. Justice Story explained that the power of final decision has to be put somewhere and that it was placed with the Supreme Court.

Finally, Justice Story asserted the need for uniformity. If federal judges were not allowed to reverse state court judgments, then state courts all over the country might interpret the federal Constitution, laws, and treaties in different ways.

What implications did this case have for the future?
Under the Constitution, power is divided between two levels: state and national. U.S. history is full of various kinds of conflicts between the states and the national government. Usually, as in *Martin* v. *Hunter's Lessee*, the national government has won these conflicts. Thus, there has been a slow drift of power from the states to the national government. Justice Story, however, did not claim that federal courts could overrule state courts in all cases. He said only that they could overrule state courts in cases involving the U.S. Constitution, laws, and treaties.

3 *McCulloch* v. *Maryland*
4 Wheaton (17 U.S.) 316 (1819)

What was this case about?
The story. In 1791 Congress passed a law that set up the Bank of the United States. An attempt to renew the Bank's charter in 1811 failed. A number of states took advantage of this situation to charter their own banks.

After the War of 1812, the federal government needed money to pay for the war. Instead of being able to borrow money from one central bank, it had to deal with many state banks. Thus, Congress set up the Second Bank of the United States in 1816. The states generally opposed the National Bank, and several states passed laws that hindered it. For instance, they taxed branches of the Bank within their borders. When the Maryland branch of the Bank refused to pay the tax, Maryland sued the bank's cashier, James McCulloch. In 1819 the legal battle reached the Supreme Court.

The question. As Chief Justice John Marshall saw it, the question before the Court had two parts. Does the Constitution give Congress the power to establish a national bank? If so, does the Constitution allow a state to tax that bank?

The issues. The question of whether Congress had the power to establish a bank was not new. In 1791, after Congress had passed the bill that established the First Bank of the United States, President George Washington had asked his cabinet for advice. He noted that although Article I, Section 8, of the Constitution lists the powers of Congress, it does not mention the power to charter a bank. Yet the article does state that in addition to the listed powers, Congress may also make all laws that are "necessary and proper" for carrying out the listed powers.

Alexander Hamilton and Thomas Jefferson presented Washington with sharply opposing views. Hamilton considered the power to charter a bank constitutional because it had "a natural relation" to the powers of collecting taxes and regulating trade. By contrast, Jefferson said that while the power to charter a bank may be "convenient" for carrying out this power, it was not "necessary," and thus was unconstitutional. Finding Hamilton's argument more convincing, Washington signed the bill. Maryland, however, wanted the Supreme Court to interpret the Constitution as Jefferson had done.

How was the case decided?

Led by Chief Justice Marshall, the Supreme Court ruled that the Constitution allowed Congress to establish the National Bank. The Court also asserted that the Constitution did not allow a state to tax the Bank.

What did the Court say about governmental powers?

Jefferson's argument against the First Bank of the United States had rested on a strict interpretation of the word "necessary" in the necessary and proper clause. The state of Maryland used the same argument. In deciding the first question, Marshall said that Maryland's interpretation of the Constitution was not broad enough. He explained that when the Constitution says that certain means are "necessary" to an end, it usually does not mean that the end cannot be achieved without them. Rather, it means that they are "calculated to produce" the end. The power to charter a bank is calculated to help carry out the other constitutional powers, so the Constitution permits it.

The second question before the Court was whether the Constitution allows a state to tax the National Bank. If the states could tax one of the federal government's activities, they could tax any of them. Marshall said that because "the power to tax involves the power to destroy," this could not be permitted. The supremacy clause in Article VI states that the Constitution and laws of the federal government come before state constitutions and laws.

What implications did this case have for the future?

As new cases arise, members of the Supreme Court try to settle them by using principles that have been established in earlier cases. This case involves the principles of implied powers and national supremacy. Some powers given to the federal government by the Constitution are listed. These are called enumerated powers. Others, called implied powers, are understood as given because they are needed to help carry out the enumerated powers. The federal government has only those powers that are enumerated and implied in the Constitution. However, when the federal government is using powers that do belong to it, the states must give way.

4 Scott v. Sandford
19 Howard (60 U.S.) 393 (1857)

What was this case about?

The story. In 1833 a slave named Dred Scott was purchased by John Emerson, an army doctor. As the army transferred Emerson from post to post, Scott went with him. First they went to Illinois; later they moved to Wisconsin Territory. When Emerson was transferred yet again, he sent Scott to Missouri, a slave state, to live with his wife, Eliza Irene Sanford Emerson. She inherited Scott when her husband died in 1843.

At this time, slavery was illegal in Illinois and in Wisconsin Territory. Scott believed that because he had lived on free soil for five years, he should be free.

In 1846 Emerson moved to New England and left Scott with sons of Scott's original owner. One son opposed the spread of slavery. He helped Scott file a lawsuit. In 1850 a Missouri court declared Scott free.

In 1852 the Missouri Supreme Court reversed the lower court's ruling. In 1854 lawyers who wanted the issue of slavery in the territories to be resolved filed Scott's lawsuit in federal court. Scott's case worked its way to the Supreme Court.

The question. As Chief Justice Roger B. Taney saw it, the case raised two questions. First, does the Constitution give an African American the right to file a suit in federal court? Second, does the Constitution allow Congress to pass a law that frees slaves who are brought into a free territory?

The issues. If African Americans were U.S. citizens, then they must have all of the rights of other citizens, including the right to sue in a federal court. Therefore, the first question before the court involved the Constitution's definition of a citizen.

The second question before the Court involved the kinds of limits the Constitution puts on laws about property. If slaves were property, then Congress faced the same limits when it made a law about slavery as when it made a law about property.

How was the case decided?

The Court ruled that the Constitution denied African Americans the right to sue in federal court and denied Congress the power to make a law abolishing or prohibiting slavery in the territories.

What did the Court say about constitutional rights?

The first theme of the Court's opinion was the relationship between race and citizenship. The opinion reflected the prejudices of the day. Taney said that African Americans had "none of the rights and privileges" of citizens. This statement was particularly startling because it applied to free African Americans as well as to slaves. Taney ignored the important fact that many states considered free African Americans to be state citizens. In addition, Article III, Section 2, of the Constitution gives the federal courts jurisdiction over various kinds of suits involving state citizens.

The other theme of the Court's opinion concerned slavery. The Fifth Amendment states that no one may be "deprived of life, liberty, or property, without due process of law." First, the chief justice reasoned that because slaves are "property," they could not be taken away without due process of law. Second, he reasoned that a law taking away citizens' property just because they entered a free territory cheated them of their due process of law. In addition, Taney ruled that the Missouri Compromise was unconstitutional.

What implications did this case have for the future?

By the time the Court made its decision, the Kansas-Nebraska Act had already canceled the Missouri Compromise's ban on slavery in certain federal territories. Therefore, it might seem that the Court's judgment did not matter. However, the Kansas-Nebraska Act was unpopular with people who opposed the spread of slavery. Many of them would have liked to have seen a return to something like the Missouri Compromise. The decision made such a return impossible and worsened the controversy over slavery in the territories.

Furthermore, this case established that merely freeing slaves was not enough to guarantee their U.S. citizenship. Not until 1868, when the Fourteenth Amendment was passed, did the Constitution guarantee that African Americans were U.S. citizens.

5 *Lochner* v. *New York*
198 U.S. 45 (1905)

What was this case about?

The story. In 1895 the New York legislature passed a law regulating the number of hours that bakery employees could be required or allowed to work. This law was necessary to prevent workers from having to agree to work long hours out of fear of losing their jobs. The legislature claimed that workers should not be allowed to work long hours because of potential harm to their health.

Joseph Lochner, a bakery owner convicted of violating the law, appealed. He said that the law was unconstitutional because it took away his liberty to make a contract. Lochner said that liberty of contract is promised by a clause in the Fourteenth Amendment that says that no state may "deprive any person of life, liberty, or property, without due process of law."

The question. Do limits on the number of hours an employee may work violate the Fourteenth Amendment?

The issues. State governments have a general power—called the police power—to make regulations that support the safety, health, morals, and general welfare of their citizens. The basic issue in this case is whether the Constitution can limit state governments' police power in some cases.

Various amendments set limits on the power of state governments, but the most general is the due process clause of the Fourteenth Amendment. To apply this clause to the New York bakery law, the Supreme Court had to decide what freedoms are meant by the word *liberty* and what is promised by the guarantee of due process of law.

How was the case decided?

The Court ruled that the law limiting the hours of labor in bakeries was unconstitutional.

What did the Court say about governmental powers?

Justice Rufus Wheeler Peckham argued that the New York legislature's interference with liberty of contract was improper. Peckham did not mean that the Constitution forbids all interference with liberty of contract. In fact, he stressed that the Court had approved a similar Utah law that said that no one could work more than eight hours a day in an underground mine except in cases of emergency. Such uses of the police power, he said, were "fair, reasonable, and appropriate." They regulate liberty without taking it away. By contrast, he argued, the New York law had nothing to do with safety, morals, or general welfare and was not necessary to protect health.

What implications did this case have for the future?

Even though the Court tries to rely on the same principles over and over, sometimes its members change their minds about controversial issues. Four justices dissented, or disagreed with the *Lochner* ruling. As the membership of the Supreme Court has changed, so have the attitudes of the justices. In 1937 the Court began to reverse the precedent it had set in *Lochner*.

6 *Plessy* v. *Ferguson*
163 U.S. 537 (1896)
Brown v. *Board of Education*
347 U.S. 483 (1954)

What were these cases about?

The stories. These two cases illustrate a major change in the legality of racial segregation. *Plessy* v. *Ferguson* began with an 1890 Louisiana law that required all railway companies to provide "equal but separate" accommodations for white and African American passengers. A group of people who thought the law was unfair recruited Homer Plessy to get arrested in order to test the law. Plessy entered a train and took an empty seat in an all-white area. When he refused to move to an all-black section, he was arrested and jailed. In his defense, he said that the 1890 law was unconstitutional. The case eventually worked its way up to the Supreme Court.

More than 50 years later, an African American man named Oliver Brown and his family moved into a white neighborhood in Topeka, Kansas. The Browns assumed that their daughter Linda would attend the neighborhood school. Instead, the Board of Education ordered her to attend a distant all-black school that was supposedly "separate but equal." Charging that school segregation violated the Fourteenth Amendment to the Constitution, Mr. Brown sued the Board.

The question. The question raised by the Court was the same in both cases. Do racially segregated facilities violate the equal protection clause of the Fourteenth Amendment?

The issues. The state of Louisiana argued that separate railway carriages could be equal. For instance, they could be equally clean and equally safe. The state of Kansas said much the same thing, claiming that its all-black and all-white schools were equal in such features as teachers' skills and buildings' quality.

In the days of racial segregation, the claim that segregated facilities were equal in tangible, or measurable, features was almost always a terrible lie. The issue facing the Court, however, went deeper. Even if things were made equal in racially segregated facilities, was there something fundamentally unequal about segregation?

How were the cases decided?

In *Plessy* v. *Ferguson,* the Court ruled that the Fourteenth Amendment's equal protection clause allows racial segregation. In *Brown* v. *Board of Education,* however, the Court unanimously ruled that the clause does not allow racial segregation.

What did the Court say about constitutional rights?

Justice Henry Billings Brown wrote the Court's opinion in *Plessy.* He admitted that the purpose of the Fourteenth Amendment was "to enforce the absolute equality of the two races before the law." However, he said that this statement meant political equality, not social equality. Brown declared that there was no truth to the argument that separate facilities implied that African Americans were inferior.

In *Brown* the Court's opinion was written by Chief Justice Earl Warren. He said that separation of black schoolchildren from white schoolchildren of the same age and ability "generates a feeling of inferiority ... that may affect their hearts and minds in a way unlikely ever to be undone." He said that when racial segregation is required by law, the harm is even greater. It makes no difference that "the physical facilities and other 'tangible' factors may be equal."

What implications did these cases have for the future?

In *Brown* v. *Board of Education,* the Court did not say that the "separate but equal" doctrine was completely invalid. It ruled that the doctrine had no place in public education. This statement, although limited, influenced future cases that eventually abolished all segregation. Taken together, *Plessy* and *Brown* show that interpretation of the Constitution's legal principles may change as society changes.

7 *Gideon* v. *Wainwright*
372 U.S. 335 (1963)

What was this case about?

The story. Clarence Earl Gideon was accused of breaking and entering a Florida poolroom. When Gideon's case came to trial, he could not afford a lawyer, so he asked that the court pay for one. The judge refused, the case proceeded, and Gideon was found guilty. While in prison, Gideon appealed to the U.S. Supreme Court. He claimed that by refusing to appoint him a lawyer, Florida had violated rights promised him by the Sixth and Fourteenth Amendments.

The question. Do the Sixth and the Fourteenth Amendments require that a poor person accused of a crime have access to an attorney free of charge?

The issues. The Sixth Amendment ensures certain rights to people accused of crimes. For example, "The accused shall enjoy the right . . . to have the Assistance of Counsel [a lawyer] for his defense." By itself, this amendment requires that poor people be provided with free lawyers in federal trials. Yet Gideon had been accused of breaking state laws and was tried in a state court. Still, the Fourteenth Amendment ensures that states cannot deprive people of life, liberty, or property without due process of law. Jailed, Gideon had been deprived of liberty. Had this liberty been taken away without due process of law?

How was the case decided?
In a unanimous opinion written by Justice Hugo Black, the Court ruled in Gideon's favor.

What did the Court say about constitutional rights?
Members of the Court based their decision on two different views of the Fourteenth Amendment. One is the incorporation view, which holds that the purpose of the due process clause is to incorporate most of the Bill of Rights into state court procedures. The second is the fundamental liberties view, which holds that "due process of law" means "whatever is necessary for justice." What is necessary for justice may not include every assurance in the Bill of Rights, but it may include assurances that go beyond anything in the Bill of Rights. In *Gideon* v. *Wainwright* the justices came to the same conclusion by different means.

In the Court's decision Justice Black accommodated both the incorporation view and the fundamental liberties view. The opinion was a compromise. It said that the Sixth Amendment's assurance of the "assistance of counsel" is necessary for a fair trial in any court, but it did not say that due process covers every other assurance in the first eight amendments.

What implications did this case have for the future?
Gideon v. *Wainwright* was one of several Supreme Court cases guaranteeing government payment to lawyers defending poor people accused of crimes. The Criminal Justice Act of 1964 established the defender services program.

8 *Miranda* v. *Arizona*
384 U.S. 436 (1966)

What was this case about?
The story. On March 13, 1963, a woman was kidnapped near Phoenix. Ernesto Miranda was arrested for the crime, and the victim identified him in a police lineup. Two officers then questioned him. Although at first Miranda denied the crime, after a short time he wrote out and signed a confession.

At the trial the officers testified that they had warned Miranda that anything he might say could be used against him in court and that Miranda had understood. The officers also said that he had confessed without any threats or force. They admitted, however, that they had not told Miranda about his right to silence or legal assistance. Miranda was found guilty. Eventually, he appealed to the U.S. Supreme Court.

The question. Is it a violation of the Fifth, Sixth, or Fourteenth Amendment to use a confession to convict someone who has not been informed of the constitutional rights to silence and legal assistance?

The issues. The Fifth Amendment ensures a person the right to remain silent: "No person . . . shall be compelled [forced] in any criminal case to be a witness against himself." Without such a right, innocent people could be tortured into confessing to a crime they did not commit. The Sixth Amendment ensures the assistance of a lawyer to defendants in criminal trials in federal courts. The Fourteenth Amendment does the same for defendants in state courts.

One issue is the point at which Fifth and Sixth Amendment rights begin. Do they begin only at the trial? Or do these rights begin earlier?

A deeper issue concerns the meaning of being forced to be a witness against oneself. Perhaps keeping a person ignorant of his or her rights is a kind of force. If so, then it violates the Fifth Amendment.

How was the case decided?
By a 5-to-4 majority, the Supreme Court ruled that taking Miranda's confession without informing him of his rights to silence and legal assistance had violated his constitutional rights.

What did the Court say about constitutional rights?
The Court ruled that the Fifth and Sixth Amendment rights exist as soon as a person is in custody. The Court also ruled that failing to inform the accused of his or her rights is a violation of the right not to testify against oneself.

Today if prisoners are not informed of their rights, judges may rule that what the accused tells the police cannot be used as evidence in court. Furthermore, the court must disregard any evidence that is based on what the accused said.

What implications did this case have for the future?
The *Miranda* ruling has been controversial because it deals with the delicate balance between protecting the

accused and protecting society. A hotly debated aspect of the decision has been the ruling that confessions given by accused people who have not been informed of their rights may not be used as evidence. The Court did this to prevent innocent people from being found guilty. Some people argue, however, that it prevents the guilty from being convicted.

9 Roe v. Wade
410 U.S. 113 (1973)

What was this case about?

The story. In 1970 Norma McCorvey, an unmarried pregnant woman living in Texas, sought to obtain a legal abortion in a medical facility. Because of Texas's antiabortion statute, no licensed physician would agree to perform the procedure. McCorvey was financially unable to travel to another state with a less-restrictive abortion law. She faced either continuing an unwanted pregnancy or having the procedure performed in a nonmedical facility, which she believed would endanger her life.

McCorvey claimed that the Texas antiabortion law was unconstitutional because it interfered with her right of personal privacy that is protected by the Ninth and Fourteenth Amendments. She took legal action, naming the Dallas County district attorney, Henry Wade, in her lawsuit. Throughout the case, McCorvey used the pseudonym Jane Roe.

The question. Is it a violation of a person's right to privacy for a state to prevent a woman from terminating a pregnancy through an abortion?

The issues. The Fourteenth Amendment states that "no state shall make or enforce any law which shall abridge [diminish] the privileges . . . of citizens of the United States . . . nor deny to any person . . . the equal protection of the laws." The Ninth Amendment states that "the enumeration [naming] in the Constitution of certain rights shall not be construed [interpreted] to deny or disparage [reduce] others retained by the people." Do these amendments include and protect a woman's right to a legal abortion?

How was the case decided?

In an opinion written by Justice Harry Blackmun, the Court ruled that the Fourteenth Amendment's due process guarantee of personal liberty ensures the right to personal privacy. This guarantee protects a woman's decision about abortion and assures that a state's laws do not abridge this right. The vote was seven to two.

What did the Court say about constitutional rights?

In ruling that a state cannot prevent a woman from terminating a pregnancy during the first three months, the Court relied on the citizens' right to privacy. Justice Blackmun stated in his opinion that "[t]his right of privacy, whether it be founded in the Fourteenth Amendment's concept of personal liberty and restrictions upon state action, as we feel it is, or . . . in the Ninth Amendment's reservation of rights to the people, is broad enough to encompass [include] a woman's decision whether or not to terminate her pregnancy." In its ruling, however, the Court recognized the right of a state to regulate abortions as a pregnancy progressed. During the first three months of a pregnancy, a woman has a virtually unrestricted right to an abortion.

During the second trimester, a state can regulate abortions to protect a woman's health. Only in the final three months of a pregnancy can a state forbid an abortion, unless the procedure is necessary to protect a woman's life.

The ruling also said that a state cannot adopt a theory of when life begins. This prevents a state from giving a fetus the same rights as a newborn.

What implications did this case have for the future?

Since the 1973 ruling, related cases have been decided that some people claim weaken the legislative impact of *Roe* v. *Wade*. In *Harris* v. *McRae* (1980), the Court upheld a law that blocked the use of federal funds to pay for abortions for women on welfare. Critics of the ruling claimed that women who could not afford the procedure would, like Jane Roe, be faced with either continuing an unwanted pregnancy or resorting to dangerous measures to terminate it. The ruling in *Webster* v. *Reproductive Health Services* (1989) added more restrictions to the availability of abortions.

10 Regents of the University of California v. Bakke
438 U.S. 265 (1978)

What was this case about?

The story. A white man named Allan Bakke twice applied to the medical school at the University of California, Davis, during the years in which the medical school operated two different admissions programs. After the Civil Rights Act of 1964, schools and other institutions were under pressure to provide special admissions programs for minority students. There were, however, no specific guidelines on how to accomplish this.

At the University of California, Davis, medical school 84 of the 100 places in the incoming class were filled from the regular program. The remaining 16 spots were set aside for a special program that used a quota system. The regular program was for students of all races, as long as they met admission requirements, including a minimum grade point average. Only members of racial minorities could apply through the special program, and their grades did not have to meet the minimum.

Bakke applied through the regular program and was turned down. He thought he had been treated unfairly because in both years, students had been admitted through the special program whose grades and test scores were much lower than his. He sued the state university system. Bakke said the special program, established to fulfill the racial quota, violated his Fourteenth Amendment right to equal protection of the law.

The California Supreme Court made two rulings. One said that Davis's admission system was illegal and ordered Bakke admitted. The other ordered that in the future, admissions decisions must not take race into consideration. The California university system appealed to the U.S. Supreme Court.

The questions. First, does the use of a racial quota in admissions violate the Fourteenth Amendment's equal protection clause? Second, does this clause require that race be completely ignored in admissions?

The issues. Historically, most racial discrimination in our country has hurt members of racial minorities. Bakke complained of reverse discrimination, a type of discrimination that supposedly hurt members of the racial majority in order to help members of racial minorities.

The Fourteenth Amendment was primarily written because African Americans who had recently been freed from slavery needed protection from discrimination by the white majority. This fact suggests that the equal protection clause protects racial minorities more than the racial majority. On the other hand, what the amendment actually says is that no state may deny to any person the equal protection of the laws. This fact suggests that the equal protection clause gives the same protection to people of all races. The intent of the amendment seems to have been to protect minorities, but its wording does not specify this intent.

How was the case decided?

The U.S. Supreme Court agreed that racial quotas in admissions was unconstitutional and ordered that Bakke be admitted. It rejected the idea that an admissions system may never pay any attention to race.

What did the Court say about constitutional rights?

Justice Lewis Powell wrote the Court's opinion. He said that the equal protection clause does not completely prohibit states from taking race into account when they are making laws and official policies. However, it does make the consideration of race "suspect," or suspicious. When such a law or policy is challenged in court, judges must apply a two-part test. First, are the purposes of the law or policy legitimate? Second, is the consideration given to race necessary to achieve these purposes? California told the Court that its racial quota had four purposes.

Purpose 1. To correct the shortage of racial minorities in medical schools and among doctors. Justice Powell said that this purpose was not acceptable. "Preferring members of any one group for no reason other than race or ethnic origin is discrimination for its own sake."

Purpose 2. To counteract the effects of racial discrimination in society. Justice Powell said that this was an acceptable purpose. He approved of helping people who belong to groups that have been hurt by past discrimination. However, he said that helping them by hurting others is right only when it makes up for hurts caused by those other people. Bakke was not responsible for past discrimination against people of racial minorities.

Purpose 3: To increase the number of doctors who will be willing to practice medicine in communities where there are not enough doctors. This purpose was also acceptable. However, California had not shown that racial quotas were needed to accomplish this purpose.

Purpose 4. To improve education by making the student body more diverse. This purpose, too, was acceptable. However, Justice Powell pointed out that racial diversity is only one aspect of overall diversity and that racial quotas are not the only way to increase racial diversity.

What implications did this case have for the future?

This decision revealed that the members of the Court disagreed sharply about reverse discrimination. Furthermore, Powell stressed that the Court's decision concerned only reverse racial discrimination. He warned that reverse sexual discrimination may or may not have to be treated the same way as reverse racial discrimination. In the 1982 case *Mississippi University for Women* v. *Hogan,* however, the Court ruled that it was unconstitutional for a state-run school of nursing to refuse admission to men.

GLOSSARY

This glossary contains terms you need to understand as you study American history. After each key term there is a brief definition or explanation of the meaning of the term as it is used in *The American Nation*. The page number refers to the page on which the term is introduced in the textbook.

Phonetic Respelling and Pronunciation Guide

Many of the key terms in this textbook have been respelled to help you pronounce them. The letter combinations used in the respellings throughout the narrative are explained in the following phonetic respelling and pronunciation guide. The guide is adapted from *Merriam-Webster's Collegiate Dictionary, Merriam-Webster's Geographical Dictionary,* and *Merriam-Webster's Biographical Dictionary.*

MARK	AS IN	RESPELLING	EXAMPLE
a	alphabet	a	*AL-fuh-bet
ā	Asia	ay	AY-zhuh
ä	cart, top	ah	KAHRT, TAHP
e	let, ten	e	LET, TEN
ē	even, leaf	ee	EE-vuhn, LEEF
i	it, tip, British	i	IT, TIP, BRIT-ish
ī	site, buy, Ohio	y	SYT, BY, oh-HY-oh
	iris	eye	EYE-ris
k	card	k	KAHRD
ō	over, rainbow	oh	OH-vuhr, RAYN-boh
ů	book, wood	ooh	BOOHK, WOOHD
ö	all, orchid	aw	AWL, AWR-kid
öi	foil, coin	oy	FOYL, KOYN
aů	out	ow	OWT
ə	cup, butter	uh	KUHP, BUHT-uhr
ü	rule, food	oo	ROOL, FOOD
yü	few	yoo	FYOO
zh	vision	zh	VIZH-uhn

*A syllable printed in small capital letters receives heavier emphasis than the other syllable(s) in a word.

A

Adamson Act (1916) Federal law reducing the workday for railroad workers from 10 to 8 hours with no cut in pay. **317**

affirmative action Practice by some government agencies, businesses, and schools of giving preference to ethnic minorities and women in admissions and hiring. **669**

Agricultural Adjustment Administration (AAA) Federal agency created by the Agricultural Adjustment Act in 1933 to reduce farmers' output and increase crop prices. **471**

Agricultural Revolution Ancient shift from hunting and gathering to the domestication of plants. **4**

AIDS (acquired immune deficiency syndrome) Often-fatal disease that forces the body's immune system to shut down, making it easier for a person to contract other illnesses. **785**

Alianza Federal de Mercedes Federal Alliance of Land Grants; group led by Reies López Tijerina to try to regain land taken from Mexican Americans. **684**

Alien and Sedition Acts (1798) Laws passed by a Federalist-dominated Congress making it easier to deport foreigners and illegal to print or speak words hostile to the government. **75**

Alliance for Progress President John F. Kennedy's program of economic aid to Latin America; designed to encourage democratic reforms and to promote capitalism. **626**

Allied Powers World War I alliance that included Britain, France, Russia, and later the United States, and that fought against the Central Powers. **357**; World War II alliance between Britain and France, and later the United States and other countries, that fought against the Axis Powers. **519**

American Association of Retired Persons (AARP) Largest lobbying group on behalf of senior citizens; founded in 1958. **692**

American Federation of Labor (AFL) Union founded in 1886 by Samuel Gompers for skilled workers. **214**

American Gothic One of the most famous regionalist paintings, by Grant Wood. **491**

American Indian Movement (AIM) Organization formed in 1968 to fight for the rights of American Indians. **690**

Americanization The process of preparing foreign-born residents for full U.S. citizenship. **292**

American Plan Policy promoted by business leaders during the 1920s that called for open shops. **399**

Americans with Disabilities Act (ADA) (1990) Law that prohibits discrimination against people with disabilities in employment, transportation, telephone services, and public buildings. **790**

American System Plan developed by Henry Clay for raising tariffs to pay for internal improvements such as roads and canals. **79**

amnesty An official pardon issued by the government. **131**

Anaconda Plan Union plan during the Civil War for a naval blockade of the South; compared to an Anaconda snake. **103**

anarchists People who oppose all forms of government. **213**

Antifederalists People who feared a powerful national government and opposed the Constitution as written. **33**

anti-Semitism Hatred of Jews. **514**

apartheid South African political system in which the white minority ruled and the black majority had few rights. **758**

Apollo 11 U.S. space mission that resulted in the first man on the Moon on July 20, 1969. **764**

appeasement Giving in to an aggressor to avoid conflict. **518**

arbitration Process by which two opposing sides allow a third party to settle a dispute. **304**

Area Redevelopment Act (ARA) Law passed in 1961 that provided financial assistance to economically distressed regions. **635**

Articles of Confederation (1777) Document that created an association of states while guaranteeing each state its "sovereignty, freedom, and independence." **29**

assembly line Production system created by Henry Ford to make goods faster by moving parts on a conveyor belt past workers. **415**

Atlantic Charter (1941) Pledge signed by U.S. president Franklin D. Roosevelt and British prime minister Winston Churchill not to acquire new territory as a result of World War II and to work for peace after the war. **522**

Atomic Energy Act (1946) Federal law that created the Atomic Energy Commission to oversee nuclear weapons research and to promote peacetime uses of atomic energy. **568**

automation Use of machines to replace humans in production. **599**

auto-touring Craze that encouraged Americans to take long sightseeing trips in their automobiles. **418**

Axis Powers Military alliance formed by Italy and Germany in 1936; later joined by Japan. **518**

Aztec Mexica; warrior empire that dominated what is now Mexico during the Middle Ages. **5**

B

baby boom Soaring birthrate in the United States following World War II. **601**

Ballinger-Pinchot affair Incident in which President William Howard Taft fired Gifford Pinchot as head of the U.S. Forestry Service for criticizing Secretary of the Interior Richard Ballinger's approval of the sale of Alaskan land; weakened support for Taft. **311**

bank holiday (1933) New Deal proclamation that temporarily closed every U.S. bank to stop massive withdrawals. **468**

barbed wire Inexpensive fencing material invented by Joseph Glidden in 1874. **181**

Baruch Plan (1946) Bernard Baruch's proposal to create an international agency that would impose penalties on countries that violated international controls on nuclear weapons. **568**

Bataan Death March (1942) Brutal forced march of American and Filipino prisoners during World War II up the Bataan Peninsula; more than 10,000 died. **532**

Battle of Antietam (1862) Union victory in Maryland during the Civil War; marked the bloodiest single-day battle in U.S. military history. **114**

Battle of Bunker Hill (1775) Revolutionary War battle in Boston that resulted in more than 1,000 British casualties and fewer than 450 Patriot casualties. **18**

Battle of Gettysburg (1863) Union victory at Gettysburg, Pennsylvania, during the Civil War that turned the tide against the Confederates; more than 40,000 soldiers died or were wounded. **118**

Battle of Iwo Jima (1945) Six-week struggle for control of a key Pacific island that resulted in an Allied victory. **552**

Battle of Leyte Gulf (1944) Last, largest, and most decisive naval engagement in the Pacific during World War II; afterward, the Japanese fleet no longer seriously threatened the Allies. **550**

Battle of Midway (1942) World War II battle in which the Allied forces crippled Japan's navy. **532**

Battle of Okinawa (1945) Bloody battle in the Pacific during World War II; resulted in an Allied victory. **552**

Battle of Shiloh (1862) Civil War battle; resulted in greater Union control over the Mississippi River valley. **110**

Battle of the Argonne Forest (1918) Successful Allied effort to push back German troops from a rail center in Sedan, France. **377**

Battle of the Atlantic World War II naval campaign fought between German U-boats and Allied naval and air forces. **543**

Battle of the Bulge (1944) World War II battle in which the Allies defeated the final German offensive. **546**

Battle of the Coral Sea (1942) World War II battle in which the Allies stopped the Japanese advance on Australia. **532**

Battle of the Little Bighorn (1876) Battle between U.S. soldiers, led by George Armstrong Custer, and Sioux warriors; worst U.S. Army defeat in the West. **165**

Battle of the Somme (1916) World War I battle in which the British lost some 60,000 troops in a single day. **359**

Battle of Yorktown (1781) Last major battle of the Revolutionary War; site of British general Charles Cornwallis's surrender to the Patriots in Virginia. **23**

bear market Downward trend in stock prices. **443**

beats Small but influential group of writers who challenged literary conventions and the lifestyle of the middle-class in the 1950s. **613**

benevolent societies Organizations that helped immigrants in cases of sickness, unemployment, and death. **223**

Berlin Airlift (1948–49) Operation in which British and U.S. planes carried food and supplies to West Berlin, which had been cut off by a Soviet blockade. **570**

Berlin Wall Barrier built between East and West Berlin; widely recognized symbol of the Cold War. **628**

Bessemer process Efficient method of making steel; developed by British inventor Henry Bessemer and American inventor William Kelly in the 1850s. **192**

Big Four Collective name given to U.S. president Woodrow Wilson, British prime minister David Lloyd George, French premier Georges Clemenceau, and Italian prime minister Vittorio Orlando during the 1919 peace conference at Versailles. **378**

Bilingual Education Act (1974) Law that encouraged public schools to provide instruction to students in their primary language while they learned English. **761**

Bill of Rights First 10 amendments to the U.S. Constitution; ratified in 1791. **70**

Black Codes Laws passed in the southern states during Reconstruction that greatly limited the freedom of former slaves. **133**

black nationalism Movement to create a new political state for African Americans in Africa. **406**

Black Panther Party–Compromise of 1877

Black Panther Party Political organization formed in the 1960s that called for empowerment of and defense for African Americans. **664**

Black Power Black separatist movement founded due to frustration with the slow pace of the civil rights movement. **664**

Blackshirts Followers of Benito Mussolini who gained power in Italy in the early 1920s. **512**

Black Thursday October 24, 1929; the day investors caused a panic on Wall Street by selling their stocks. **443**

Black Tuesday October 29, 1929; day the stock market crashed; contributed to the Great Depression. **444**

Bland-Allison Act (1878) Federal law that required the government to buy and mint silver each month. **263**

Blitzkrieg "Lightning war"; type of fast-moving warfare used by German forces in 1939. **521**

blues Music that grew out of slave music and religious spirituals; featured heartfelt lyrics and altered or slurred notes that echoed the mood of the lyrics. **430**

Bolsheviks Group of radical Russian socialists who seized power in 1917 following the overthrow of the czar. **375**

bonanza farm Large-scale farm usually owned by a large company and run like a factory. **173**

Bonus Army Group of World War I veterans who marched on Washington, D.C., in 1932 to demand the immediate payment of their pension bonuses. **461**

Boston police strike (1919) Failed police strike that led to public disorder and the firing of all striking officers. **391**

Boxer Rebellion (1900) Revolt in which Chinese nationalists known as Boxers attacked foreigners in order to end foreign involvement in China's affairs; put down by an international force after two months. **330**

braceros Mexican farm and railroad workers who came to the United States during World War II as a result of a U.S.-Mexican agreement. **539**

breadlines Lines formed by people waiting for free food, such as those that occurred during the Great Depression. **450**

brinkmanship Policy in the 1950s that called for threatening all-out war in order to confront Communist aggression. **576**

British invasion Introduction of new British bands to Americans in the 1960s. **698**

Brotherhood of Sleeping Car Porters Union founded by A. Philip Randolph in 1925 to help African Americans who worked for the Pullman Company. **406**

Brown Berets Activist group formed in 1967 in response to police treatment of Mexican Americans. **685**

Brownshirts Nazi storm troopers. **513**

Brown* v. *Board of Education (1954) Supreme Court case that declared segregated public schools unconstitutional. **607**

bull market Upward trend in stock prices. **443**

Bureau of Indian Affairs Government agency responsible for managing American Indian issues. **162**

Bursum Bill Bill proposed in 1922 to legalize non-American Indian claims to Pueblo lands in the Southwest; failed to pass. **409**

Bush* v. *Gore Supreme Court ruling that hand recounts of the 2000 presidential election votes in several Florida counties were not valid. **818**

business cycle Regular ups and downs of business in a free-enterprise economy. **447**

busing Sending children to schools outside of their neighborhoods, usually to promote integration. **668**

C

cabinet Group that advises the U.S. president, made up of the heads of the executive departments. **70**

Camp David Accords (1978) Peace agreement between Israel and Egypt, negotiated by President Jimmy Carter. **759**

capitalism Economic system in which private business runs most industries, and competition determines how much goods cost and workers are paid. **201**

carpetbaggers Northern Republicans who moved to the South during Reconstruction. **144**

caudillos Latin American military leaders during the 1930s who used force to maintain order. **511**

Central Intelligence Agency (CIA) Federal agency created in the late 1940s to conduct covert operations. **576**

Central Powers World War I alliance that included Austria-Hungary, Germany, the Ottoman Empire, and Bulgaria. **357**

Challenger U.S. space shuttle that exploded in 1986 after takeoff, killing all seven crew members. **784**

Chernobyl disaster (1986) Nuclear accident near Kiev, Ukraine, that released massive amounts of radiation into the air. **816**

Children's Defense Fund (CDF) Children's rights organization founded in 1973. **693**

Chinese Exclusion Act (1882) Law that denied U.S. citizenship to people born in China and prohibited Chinese immigration of laborers. **225**

City Beautiful movement Movement that stressed the importance of including public parks and attractive boulevards in the designs of cities. **236**

Civilian Conservation Corps (CCC) New Deal agency established in 1933; employed young men on conservation projects. **470**

Civil Rights Act of 1866 First U.S. civil rights law; declared everyone born in the United States a citizen with full civil rights. **138**

Civil Rights Act of 1875 Law that prohibited businesses that served the public from discriminating against African Americans. **146**

Civil Rights Act of 1957 Law that made it a federal crime to prevent qualified persons from voting. **610**

Civil Rights Act of 1964 Law banning racial discrimination in the use of public facilities and in employment practices. **655**

Clayton Antitrust Act (1914) Law that clarified and strengthened the Sherman Antitrust Act by clearly defining what a monopoly or trust was. **316**

closed shop Workplace in which all the employees must belong to a union. **283**

Cold War (1945–91) Long power struggle between the United States and the Soviet Union; waged mostly on economic and political fronts, rather than on the battlefield. **566**

Committee on Civil Rights Committee appointed by President Harry S Truman in 1946 to examine racial issues. **595**

Committee on Public Information (CPI) Agency created in 1917 to increase public support for World War I. **373**

Committee to Re-elect the President (CRP) Organization that ran President Richard Nixon's 1972 re-election campaign; used "dirty tricks" to undermine the Democrats. **747**

Common Sense (1776) Pamphlet written by Thomas Paine that stirred up public support for the American Revolution and called for the end of British rule in the colonies. **18**

Commonwealth of Independent States (CIS) An alliance formed by many of the former Soviet republics in December 1991. **787**

communism Political theory that proposes that all people should collectively own property and the means of production and that individual ownership should not be allowed. **202**

Compromise of 1850 Agreement proposed by Henry Clay; allowed California to enter the Union as a free state and divided the rest of the Mexican Cession into two territories where slavery would be decided by popular sovereignty; also settled land claims between Texas and New Mexico, abolished the slave trade in the District of Columbia, and toughened fugitive slave laws. **89**

Compromise of 1877 Agreement to settle the disputed presidential election of 1876; Democrats agreed to accept Republican Rutherford B. Hayes as president in return for the removal of federal troops from the South. **147**

compulsory education laws Laws requiring parents to send their children to school. **233**

Comstock Lode One of the world's richest silver mines, discovered in Nevada in the mid-1800s. **183**

Confederate States of America The Confederacy; nation formed by seceding southern states in 1861. **91**

Congress of Industrial Organizations (CIO) Labor group formed in 1938 that organized all workers in a particular industry into one union. **480**

Congress of Racial Equality (CORE) Northern-based civil rights group that organized nonviolent protests. **651**

conscription Compulsory draft into military service. **108**

conspicuous consumption Spending money just to display one's wealth. **228**

Constitutional Convention (1787) Meeting in Philadelphia at which state delegates wrote the U.S. Constitution. **31**

containment U.S. foreign policy during the Cold War that sought to prevent the expansion of Soviet communism. **567**

Contract with America 1994 Republican reform plan. **801**

Contras Anti-Sandinista rebel army in Nicaragua that was supported by the Reagan administration. **775**

convoy system Use of armed vessels to escort unarmed merchant vessels transporting troops, supplies, or volunteers through the North Atlantic during World War I. **367**

cooperatives Groups that pool members' resources to sell products directly to markets and to buy goods at wholesale prices. **260**

Copperheads Northern Democrats who sympathized with the South during the Civil War. **109**

corporation Company that sells shares of ownership called stock to investors in order to raise money. **202**

Corporation for Public Broadcasting Nonprofit organization created during the Johnson administration; offers educational television programming. **642**

cotton gin Device developed by Eli Whitney in 1793 to separate short-staple cotton seeds from the bolls. **82**

Council of Economic Advisers Federal agency created by the Employment Act of 1946 to counsel the president on economic policy. **592**

Council of Federated Organizations (COFO) Group created by several civil rights organizations to coordinate voter registration drives in the 1960s. **657**

counterculture Alternative lifestyle; for example, the culture of the hippies in the 1960s. **695**

Crittenden Compromise (1860) Senator John Crittenden's plan to resolve conflict between North and South by extending the Missouri Compromise line westward through the remaining territories; rejected by President Lincoln. **96**

crop-lien system Arrangement in which sharecroppers promised their crops to merchants in exchange for supplies on credit. **148**

Crusade for Justice Group founded in 1966 by Rodolfo "Corky" Gonzales to promote Mexican American nationalism. **686**

Crusades (1096–1221) Series of five wars fought between Christians and Muslims for control of Palestine. **6**

Cuban missile crisis (1962) Standoff between the United States and the Soviet Union in which the Soviets agreed to remove missiles from Cuba if the United States promised not to invade the island; followed by an easing of Cold War tensions. **630**

D

Dawes General Allotment Act (1887) Legislation that required that American Indian lands be surveyed and Indian families be given allotments of 160 acres, with the remaining land sold; resulted in the loss of two thirds of American Indian land. **168**

D-Day (1944) June 6; World War II Allied invasion of France. **544**

Declaration of Independence (1776) Statement of the Second Continental Congress that officially declared the new United States of America to be independent of Great Britain. **20**

defoliants Chemicals that strip land of vegetation. **714**

demobilization Transition from wartime to peacetime production and employment levels. **390**

Democratic Party Political party formed by supporters of Andrew Jackson after the presidential election of 1824. **80**

Department of Energy Executive department created in 1977 to oversee energy issues. **755**

depression A sharp drop in business activity, accompanied by rising unemployment. **30**

détente Period in the 1970s when tensions between the United States and the Soviet Union lessened. **745**

direct primary Nominating election in which voters choose the candidates who later run in a general election. **298**

disarmament Reduction of the size of a country's military. **503**

Dixiecrats States' Rights Party; formed in 1946 by southern Democrats who were dissatisfied with President Harry S Truman's support for civil rights issues. **596**

dollar diplomacy President William Howard Taft's policy of influencing Latin American affairs through economic influence rather than military force. **344**

domino theory Cold War–era belief that if one nation in Southeast Asia fell to communism, the rest of Southeast Asia would also fall. **708**

doves Americans who opposed the Vietnam War. **717**

***Dred Scott* decision** (1857) Supreme Court ruling that African Americans were not U.S. citizens, that the Missouri Compromise's restriction on slavery was unconstitutional, and that Congress did not have the right to ban slavery in any federal territory. **91**

Dust Bowl Name given to parts of the Great Plains in the 1930s after a severe drought struck the region. **482**

E

Education Amendments Act (1972) Federal law prohibiting sexual discrimination in higher education. **680**

Education for All Handicapped Children Act (1975) Federal law requiring public schools to provide education for children with physical and mental disabilities. **691**

Eighteenth Amendment (1919) Constitutional amendment that barred the manufacture, sale, and distribution of alcoholic beverages in the United States; repealed in 1933. **289**

elastic clause "Necessary and proper clause"; clause of the U.S. Constitution that allows Congress to exert its powers in ways not specifically outlined in the Constitution. **35**

electors Delegates selected by state legislatures to represent the popular vote in federal elections. **33**

Elementary and Secondary Education Act (1965) Federal law that provided $1.3 billion to aid schools in poor areas. **642**

Elkins Act (1903) Federal law that prohibited shippers from accepting rebates. **305**

Emancipation Proclamation (1863) Order announced by President Abraham Lincoln in 1862 that freed the slaves in areas rebelling against the Union; took effect January 1, 1863. **114**

Employment Act (1946) Law that established the Council of Economic Advisers and pledged that the government would promote full employment and production. **592**

Endangered Species Act (1973) Law to protect wildlife in danger of extinction. **744**

Enforcement Acts (1870–71) Three acts passed by Congress allowing the government to use military force to stop violence against southern African Americans. **145**

Enola Gay U.S. B-29 bomber that dropped the first atomic bomb on Hiroshima, Japan, on August 6, 1945. **553**

Environmental Protection Agency–*Grapes of Wrath, The*

Environmental Protection Agency (EPA) Federal agency established in 1970 to enforce environmental laws. **744**

Equal Pay Act (1963) Federal law that made it illegal for employers to pay female workers less than male workers for the same job. **677**

Equal Rights Amendment (ERA) Proposed constitutional amendment that would guarantee women's rights by outlawing discrimination based on gender. **399**

escalation President Lyndon B. Johnson's policy of building up U.S. military forces in the Vietnam War. **713**

Espionage Act (1917) Federal law that outlawed acts of treason during World War I. **374**

European Union (EU) Western European trading bloc formed in 1993. **815**

Exodusters Southern African Americans who settled western lands in the late 1800s. **172**

F

Fair Deal Series of reform programs proposed by President Harry S Truman after the 1948 election; achieved mixed results. **597**

Fair Employment Practices Committee (FEPC) Group created in 1941 to prevent discrimination in war industries and government jobs. **539**

Family and Medical Leave Act (1993) Federal law requiring large companies to provide workers up to 12 weeks of unpaid leave for family and medical emergencies without losing their medical insurance or jobs. **814**

Family Assistance Plan (FAP) President Richard M. Nixon's proposed replacement for the welfare system; would guarantee families a minimum income; voted down by the Senate. **740**

Fascist Party Political party founded in Italy in the 1920s; followers believed a military-dominated government should control all aspects of society. **512**

Federal Deposit Insurance Corporation (FDIC) New Deal agency created in 1933 to insure bank savings deposits. **469**

federalism System of governing in which power is divided between a strong central government and state governments. **34**

Federalists People who supported a strong national government and ratification of the Constitution. **32**

Federal Project Number One New Deal program that encouraged pride in American culture by employing artists and writers. **487**

Federal Reserve Act (1913) Act that created a national banking system to help the government control the economy. **316**

Federal Trade Commission (FTC) Commission established in 1914 to investigate corporations and to try to keep them from conducting unfair trade practices. **317**

feminists Women's rights activists. **399**

feudalism System in the Middle Ages in which nobles pledged loyalty and military aid to rulers in return for land and protection. **5**

Fifteenth Amendment (1870) Constitutional amendment that gave African American men the right to vote. **142**

54th Massachusetts Infantry African American Union regiment that helped capture Fort Wagner in South Carolina during the Civil War. **115**

First Battle of Bull Run (1861) Battle of Manassas; first major battle of the Civil War; resulted in a Confederate victory. **101**

First Battle of the Marne (1914) World War I battle in which the Allies stopped a German advance near the Marne River. **358**

flappers Young women in the 1920s who challenged social traditions with their dress and behavior. **423**

flexible response Strategy adopted by the Kennedy administration of keeping a range of options open for dealing with international crises. **626**

Food Administration World War I agency headed by Herbert Hoover; encouraged increased agricultural production and the conservation of existing food supplies. **369**

Foraker Act (1900) U.S. law establishing that Puerto Rico's governor and upper house be appointed by the United States and lower house be elected by Puerto Ricans. **340**

Fordney-McCumber Tariff Act (1922) Federal law that raised tariff rates on manufactured goods and levied high duties on imported agricultural goods. **398**

Fourteen Points (1918) President Woodrow Wilson's plan for organizing post–World War I Europe and for avoiding future wars. **378**

Fourteenth Amendment (1868) Constitutional amendment giving full rights of citizenship to all people born or naturalized in the United States, except for American Indians. **138**

Freedmen's Bureau Agency established by Congress in 1865 to help southerners left homeless and hungry by the Civil War. **137**

freedom of contract Freedom of workers to negotiate the terms of their employment. **283**

Freedom Riders Group of civil rights workers who took bus trips through southern states in 1961 to protest illegal bus segregation. **651**

Freedom Summer Campaign to register African American voters in Mississippi during the summer of 1964. **658**

free enterprise Belief that the economy will prosper if businesses are left free from government regulation and allowed to compete in a free market. **72, 201**

Fundamentalism Protestant religious movement that teaches that the Bible is literally true. **428**

Fundamental Orders of Connecticut (1639) Colonial document that is widely considered to be the first written constitution in the world. **12**

G

generation gap Difference in years, attitudes, and cultural beliefs between generations; applied to baby boomers and their elders during the 1960s. **694**

genocide Deliberate annihilation of an entire people. **545**

Gettysburg Address (1863) Speech given by President Abraham Lincoln to dedicate a cemetery at the Gettysburg, Virginia, battlefield; a classic statement of democratic ideals. **119**

GI Bill of Rights (1944) Servicemen's Readjustment Act; law that established pensions and government loans to veterans for education, businesses, or to buy houses or farms. **592**

Gilded Age Name applied by Mark Twain and Charles Dudley Warner to late 1800s America to describe the corruption and greed that lurked below the surface of society. **255**

glasnost Soviet policy established in the 1980s that promoted political openness and freedom of expression. **781**

gold standard Type of monetary system in which money is worth a specific amount in gold. **262**

Gone With the Wind (1936) The best-selling novel of the 1930s, by Margaret Mitchell; made into one of the most popular films of all time in 1939. **488**

Good Neighbor policy President Franklin D. Roosevelt's foreign policy of promoting better relations with Latin America through mutual respect. **508**

graduated income tax System in which the rate of taxation varies according to income. **260**

graft Acquisition of money or political power through illegal or dishonest methods. **249**

Gramm-Rudman-Hollings Act (1985) Law that required the government to cut spending when the deficit grows above a certain level. **778**

Grapes of Wrath, The (1939) John Steinbeck's classic novel about Dust Bowl migrants who move to California during the Great Depression. **488**

Gray Panthers Activist group for senior citizens' rights; founded by Maggie Kuhn in 1970. **692**

Great Depression Serious global economic decline that began with the crash of the U.S. stock market in 1929. **445**

Great Migration Mass migration of African Americans to the northern United States during and after World War I. **372**

Great Society President Lyndon B. Johnson's program to improve American society. **640**

Great Upheaval (1886) Year of intense worker strikes and violent labor confrontations in the United States. **213**

gross national product Total value of all goods and services produced by a country in a given year. **445**

habeas corpus Constitutional protection against unlawful imprisonment. **109**

hard-rock mining Mining technique that involves sinking deep mine shafts to get at ore in veins of rock. **187**

Harlem Renaissance Period of great African American artistic accomplishment that began in the 1920s in the Harlem neighborhood of New York City. **432**

hawks Americans who supported the Vietnam War. **717**

Hay–Bunau-Varilla Treaty (1903) Agreement that gave the United States sovereignty over a 10-mile-wide canal zone across the Isthmus of Panama. **341**

Haymarket Riot (1886) Incident in which a bomb exploded during a labor protest held in Haymarket Square in Chicago, killing several police officers. **213**

Hepburn Act (1906) Law that authorized the Interstate Commerce Commission to set railroad rates and to regulate other companies engaged in interstate commerce. **305**

Highway Act (1956) Law that provided money to create a national highway system. **600**

Ho Chi Minh Trail Network of jungle paths from North Vietnam through Laos and Cambodia and into South Vietnam; served as the major supply route of the Vietcong. **714**

Hollywood Ten Group of film directors and writers who went to jail rather than answer questions from the House Un-American Activities Committee. **579**

Holocaust Nazi Germany's slaughter of European Jews. **545**

Homestead Act (1862) Law that encouraged settlement in the West by giving government-owned land to small farmers. **170**

horizontal integration Ownership of several companies that make the same product. **205**

hot line Teletype connection between the United States and the Soviet Union that allowed leaders to communicate directly. **630**

House of Burgesses Colonial Virginia's elected assembly. **10**

House Un-American Activities Committee (HUAC) Congressional committee originally created in 1938 to investigate fascists; became known for investigating U.S. citizens accused of communist ties in the late 1940s. **579**

hydraulic mining Mining technique that uses water pressure to remove gravel and dirt, exposing the minerals underneath. **187**

hydrogen bomb H-bomb; a type of nuclear bomb. **583**

Immigration Act of 1924 Federal law reducing the annual immigration quota for each nationality to 2 percent of the 1890 census figures. **408**

Immigration Act of 1990 Federal law that increased the number of immigrants allowed into the United States each year. **813**

Immigration Restriction League Organization formed in 1894 that sought to impose a literacy test on all U.S. immigrants. **225**

imperialism Quest for colonial empires. **326**

Inca South American civilization that controlled the Andes. **5**

Industrial Workers of the World (IWW) Union formed in 1905 that opposed capitalism. **284**

initiative Policy allowing voters to introduce new legislation. **299**

Initiative on Race Initiative launched by President Bill Clinton in 1997 to encourage discussion of racial issues and concerns. **806**

insider trading Use of confidential financial information by stockbrokers for personal gain. **778**

installment plan A way of purchasing goods in which the consumer pays for goods in small increments over time. **420**

Intermediate-Range Nuclear Forces Treaty (INF) (1987) Treaty signed by President Ronald Reagan and Soviet leader Mikhail Gorbachev; eliminated all medium-range nuclear weapons from Europe. **782**

Internal Security Act (1950) Law that required suspected communist groups to register with the government and imposed controls on immigrants suspected of being communist sympathizers. **580**

International Ladies' Garment Workers Union (ILGWU) Influential union established in New York City in 1900 to organize workers in sewing shops. **284**

Internet Worldwide system of computer networks. **811**

internment Forced relocation and imprisonment of people. **540**

Interstate Commerce Act (1887) Law that regulated railroad shipping between states. **260**

Intolerable Acts (1774) Coercive Acts; four laws passed by Parliament to punish colonists for the Boston Tea Party and to tighten government control of the colonies. **16**

Iran-Contra affair Name given to the 1980s scandal in which the Reagan administration secretly sold weapons to Iran in exchange for the release of American hostages in Lebanon and then used the profits from the sale to fund the Contras in Nicaragua. **779**

Iran hostage crisis (1979–81) Situation in which 52 Americans were held hostage in the U.S. Embassy in Tehran, Iran. **770**

island-hopping U.S. World War II strategy of conquering only the Pacific islands that were important to the Allied advance toward Japan. **549**

isolationism National policy of avoiding involvement in the affairs of other nations. **502**

jazz Music combining a variety of musical styles; originated with African American musicians in New Orleans and gained national popularity in the 1920s. **430**

Jim Crow laws Laws that enforced segregation in the South. **150**

Jones Act of 1916 U.S. law that gave Filipinos the right to elect both houses of their legislature. **339**

judicial review Power of the courts to declare an act of Congress unconstitutional. **76**

Judiciary Act of 1789 Law that created a federal court system. **70**

juvenile delinquency Antisocial behavior by young people. **604**

K

kamikaze Japanese suicide planes during World War II. **552**

Kansas-Nebraska Act (1854) Law that created the territories of Kansas and Nebraska and allowed voters there to choose whether to allow slavery. **90**

Keating-Owen Child Labor Act (1916) Law that outlawed the interstate sale of products produced by child labor; declared unconstitutional by the Supreme Court in 1918. **318**

Kellogg-Briand Pact (1928) Pact signed by the United States and 14 other nations that outlawed war, except for self-defense. **505**

Kent State shootings (1970) Incident in which National Guard troops fired at a group of students during an antiwar protest at Kent State University in Ohio, killing four people. **724**

Kentucky and Virginia Resolutions–Montgomery Improvement Association

Kentucky and Virginia Resolutions Statements passed in 1798 and 1799 that denounced the Alien and Sedition Acts. **75**

Kerner Commission Federal commission that investigated the 1960s riots and blamed them on white racism. **666**

kickbacks Payments of part of the earnings from a job. **249**

Knights of Labor One of the first national labor unions in the United States, organized in 1869; after 1879 it included workers of different races, genders, and skills. **212**

Kosovo crisis Result of a violent campaign launched by Serbian forces against Albanians in Kosovo; stopped by UN bombing strikes in 1999. **808**

Kristallnacht (1938) "Night of Broken Glass"; November 9; night when Nazis destroyed many Jewish buildings. **514**

Ku Klux Klan Secret society created by former Confederates in 1866 that used terror and violence to keep African Americans from obtaining their civil rights. **144**

La Huelga (1965–70) Successful strike by migrant farmworkers in California against grape growers; led by César Chávez. **683**

La Raza Unida Party (RUP) Mexican American political party formed by José Angel Gutiérrez in the late 1960s. **687**

League of Nations International body of nations formed in 1919 to prevent wars. **378**

League of United Latin American Citizens (LULAC) Group formed in 1929 to lobby for Hispanic concerns and issues. **611**

Lend-Lease Act (1941) Law that allowed the United States to offer weapons and other war supplies to the Allied Powers to fight against the Axis Powers in World War II. **521**

Limited Nuclear Test Ban Treaty (1963) Agreement signed by U.S. president John F. Kennedy and Soviet leader Nikita Khrushchev; ended aboveground testing of new nuclear weapons. **630**

literacy tests Tests used to prevent people who could not read from voting. **149**

Little Rock Nine Nine African American students who first integrated Central High School in Little Rock, Arkansas, in 1957. **608**

long drives Long overland treks on which cowboys herded cattle from ranches to rail lines. **178**

loose construction Philosophy of constitutional interpretation; holds that within broad limits the government can do anything the Constitution does not specifically forbid. **72**

Los Angeles riots (1992) Riots that erupted after four white police officers were acquitted of using excessive force against an African American motorist. **806**

Lost Generation A group of writers whose works reflected the horrors of the death and destruction of World War I and criticized consumerism and superficiality in postwar society. **435**

Louisiana Purchase (1803) U.S. purchase of French land between the Mississippi River and the Rocky Mountains. **76**

M

Maginot Line Line of defenses built by France along its border with Germany after World War I. **521**

Manhattan Project Secret U.S. project begun in 1942 to develop an atomic bomb. **553**

manifest destiny Belief of many Americans in the mid-1800s that God intended the United States to expand westward. **86**

Mann-Elkins Act (1910) Federal law that extended the regulatory powers of the Interstate Commerce Commission to telephone and telegraph companies. **310**

Marbury v. *Madison* (1803) Supreme Court case that established the principle of judicial review. **76**

margin buying Purchasing stock with borrowed money. **443**

Marshall Plan European Recovery Program; U.S. program of giving money to European countries to help them rebuild their economies after World War II. **569**

Massacre at Wounded Knee (1890) U.S. Army's killing of about 300 Sioux at Wounded Knee Creek in South Dakota; ended U.S.–American Indian wars on the Great Plains. **166**

mass transit Public transportation systems, such as commuter trains and subways. **226**

Maya Mesoamerican civilization that rose to prominence about A.D. 300. **5**

Mayaguez Unarmed U.S. cargo ship seized by Cambodian Communists in 1975; 41 Americans died in the effort to save about 40 crew members. **752**

Mayflower Compact (1620) Document written by Pilgrim settlers that established a self-governing colony based on majority rule of the male church members. **10**

McClure's Magazine Progressive magazine that explored corruption in politics and business. **277**

Meat Inspection Act (1906) Federal law that required government inspection of meat shipped across state lines. **306**

Medicaid Federal program created in 1965 to provide free health care to the needy. **641**

Medicare Federal health insurance program for people over the age of 65; created in 1965. **641**

mergers The combining of two or more companies to achieve greater efficiency and higher profits. **398**

Mexican American Youth Organization (MAYO) Mexican American activist group formed in 1967 by college students in San Antonio, Texas. **687**

Mexican Cession Land that Mexico gave to the United States after the Mexican War through the Treaty of Guadalupe Hidalgo; includes present-day California, Nevada, and Utah, as well as parts of Arizona, Colorado, New Mexico, Texas, and Wyoming. **87**

Mexican Revolution Struggle to end dictatorship that led to years of instability in Mexico in the early 1900s. **346**

Middle Passage Voyage that brought enslaved Africans across the Atlantic Ocean to North America and the West Indies. **13**

Migrant Mother Dorothea Lange's most famous photograph from the Great Depression, showing an exhausted mother and her children; led to increased support for migrant workers in California. **484**

militarism Glorification of military strength. **357**

Mir Russian space station; site of joint U.S.-Soviet space projects in the 1990s. **810**

Mississippi Freedom Democratic Party (MFDP) Group that sent its own delegates to the Democratic National Convention in 1964 to protest discrimination against black voters in Mississippi. **659**

Missouri Compromise (1820) Agreement proposed by Henry Clay that allowed Missouri to enter the Union as a slave state, Maine to enter as a free state, and banned slavery in the Louisiana Purchase north of the 36°30′ line. **80**

Model T Popular low-cost automobile developed by Henry Ford in 1908. **415**

Modern Republicanism Name given to President Dwight D. Eisenhower's attempt to balance liberal domestic reforms with conservative spending during the 1950s. **598**

monopoly Exclusive economic control of an industry. **203**

Monroe Doctrine (1823) President James Monroe's statement that the United States would not interfere in European colonies in Latin America but would consider any new attempt to colonize in the Western Hemisphere an act of hostility. **79**

Montgomery Improvement Association (MIA) Organization formed by African Americans in Montgomery, Alabama, in 1956 to strengthen the bus boycott and to coordinate protest efforts of African Americans; led by Martin Luther King Jr. **610**

Moral Majority–Organization of Petroleum Exporting Countries

Moral Majority Conservative religious political organization; founded in 1979. **771**

Morrill Act (1862) Federal law that gave land to western states to build agricultural and engineering colleges. **170**

muckrakers Investigative journalists who wrote about corruption in business and politics, hoping to bring about reform. **277**

mugwumps "Big chiefs"; referred to Republican reformers who supported Democrat Grover Cleveland in the presidential election of 1884. **257**

Muller v. *Oregon* (1908) Supreme Court case that upheld protective legislation for female workers in Oregon. **283**

multinational corporations Companies that invest money in a variety of international business ventures. **816**

Munich Conference (1938) Meeting between British, French, German, and Italian leaders in which Germany was given control of the Sudetenland in exchange for German leader Adolf Hitler's promise to make no more claims on European territory. **518**

mutualistas Mutual-aid societies formed by Mexican American communities to help local residents. **450**

N

National Aeronautics and Space Administration (NASA) Agency established by Congress in 1958 to promote space technology. **585**

National American Woman Suffrage Association (NAWSA) Group formed in 1890 to win the vote for women. **319**

National Association for the Advancement of Colored People (NAACP) Group founded by W. E. B. Du Bois and others in 1909 to end racial discrimination. **291**

National Black Political Convention (1972) Meeting of civil rights activists to ensure that African Americans would continue to gain political influence. **671**

National Defense Act (1916) Military preparedness program established prior to U.S. entry into World War I that increased the size of the National Guard and the regular U.S. army. **363**

National Defense Education Act (1958) Federal law that appropriated money to improve education in science, math, and foreign languages. **585**

National Energy Act (1978) Law passed to ease the energy crisis. **755**

National Grange National Grange of the Patrons of Husbandry; organization founded by Oliver Hudson Kelley in 1867; addressed economic and political issues concerning farmers. **260**

National Industrial Recovery Act (NIRA) (1933) Federal law designed to encourage economic growth by suspending antitrust laws and eliminating unfair competition between employers; declared unconstitutional in 1935. **470**

nationalism National pride or loyalty. **79**

nationalize To assert government control over a business. **509**

National Organization for Women (NOW) Women's rights group; formed in 1966 to pressure elected officials to ensure social and political equality for women. **678**

National Park Service A federal agency established in 1916 to help supervise national parks and monuments. **309**

National Security Council (NSC) Organization created in 1947 by Congress to advise the president on strategic matters. **579**

National Urban League Group founded in 1911 to fight for racial equality. **291**

National War Labor Board (NWLB) Agency created during World War I to settle disputes between workers and employers. **370**

National Women's Political Caucus Group founded by Gloria Steinem and others in 1971 to encourage women to run for political office. **679**

National Youth Administration (NYA) New Deal agency that provided part-time jobs to people between the ages of 16 and 25. **476**

Nation of Islam Black Muslims; black nationalist religious group founded by Wallace D. Fard in 1930. **661**

nativism Favoring native-born Americans over foreign-born. **82**

NATO North Atlantic Treaty Organization; alliance formed in 1949 by the United States, Western European nations, and other countries to help defend each other in case of attack. **571**

Nazi Party National Socialist Party; political group led by Adolf Hitler that rose to power in Germany in the 1930s. **513**

New Deal President Franklin D. Roosevelt's programs for helping the U.S. economy during the Great Depression. **468**

New Freedom President Woodrow Wilson's progressive reform program; proposed during the 1912 presidential election. **313**

New Frontier President John F. Kennedy's domestic agenda. **634**

new immigrants Immigrants who came to the United States between the 1880s and 1910s, mostly from southern and eastern Europe. **220**

New Right Various conservative voters' groups that grew in strength in the 1980s. **771**

Nineteenth Amendment (1920) Constitutional amendment that granted women the right to vote. **321**

no-man's-land Strip of bombed-out territory that separated the trenches of opposing armies along the Western Front during World War I. **358**

nonaggression pact (1939) Agreement between German leader Adolf Hitler and Soviet leader Joseph Stalin not to attack one another and to divide Poland. **519**

nonviolent resistance Protest strategy that calls for peaceful demonstrations and the rejection of violence. **650**

North American Free Trade Agreement (NAFTA) (1993) Trade agreement among the United States, Canada, and Mexico. **815**

Northwest Ordinance (1787) Legislation that established a system for governing the Northwest Territory. **30**

nouveau riche "Newly rich"; new class of American city-dwellers that arose in the late 1800s; most made their fortunes from business during the Second Industrial Revolution. **228**

Nuremberg Trials War crimes trials of high-ranking Nazi officials held by an international military tribunal in Nuremberg, Germany; began in 1945. **562**

O

Office of Economic Opportunity (OEO) Government agency formed in 1964 to coordinate antipoverty programs. **639**

Office of War Information U.S. agency that controlled the flow of war news at home during World War II. **535**

Office of War Mobilization (OWM) Federal agency that coordinated all government agencies involved in the war effort during World War II. **530**

Older Americans Act (1965) Law committing the government to provide the elderly with adequate income and medical care. **693**

old immigrants Immigrants who came to the United States before the 1880s, mostly Protestants from northwestern Europe. **220**

Open Door Policy (1899) Declaration made by Secretary of State John Hay that all nations should have equal access to trade and investment in China. **330**

open range Public land used by cattle ranchers. **180**

open shop Nonunion workplace. **284**

Operation Desert Storm (1991) UN invasion led by the United States to make Iraq withdraw from Kuwait. **787**

Operation Restore Hope (1992) UN attempt to ensure that relief efforts reached famine-stricken Somalia. **801**

Operation Rolling Thunder U.S. bombing campaign during the Vietnam War. **714**

Organization of Petroleum Exporting Countries (OPEC) Alliance formed in 1960 by major oil-producing nations to maintain high prices by controlling the production and sale of oil. **743**

pacification–republicanism

P

pacification U.S. and South Vietnamese policy of moving villagers to refugee camps and then burning their villages. **715**

Pacific Railway Act (1862) Law that provided land grants to railroad companies to help them build a rail line linking the East and West Coasts. **170**

Paleo-Indians The first Americans; crossed from Asia into North America sometime between 12,000 and 40,000 years ago. **4**

Palmer raids (1919–20) Raids ordered by U.S. attorney general A. Mitchell Palmer on suspected radicals. **394**

Pan-Africanism Movement to unite people of African descent worldwide. **406**

Panama Canal Treaties Agreements by U.S. and Panamanian leaders in the 1970s to transfer control of the Panama Canal to Panama by the year 2000. **757**

Panic of 1873 U.S. economic depression that distracted the Republicans from Reconstruction efforts. **145**

patent Exclusive right to manufacture or sell an invention. **193**

patio process Mining technique developed in Mexico and South America during the 1700s that used mercury to extract silver from ore; used in the western United States. **184**

Payne-Aldrich Tariff (1909) High-tariff measure signed by President William Howard Taft; angered progressives. **311**

Peace Corps Program begun by President John F. Kennedy to send volunteers to work in developing nations for two years. **626**

Pendleton Civil Service Act (1883) Act that established the Civil Service Commission to administer competitive examinations to people seeking government jobs. **257**

Pentagon Papers Secret government documents published in 1971; revealed that the U.S. government had misled Americans about the Vietnam War. **725**

perestroika Soviet policy established in the 1980s that initiated political and economic reforms. **781**

personal computer (PC) Small computer for individual use. **765**

Philippine Government Act (1902) Organic Act; federal law that established a governor and a two-house legislature for the Philippines, with the governor and members of the legislature's upper house appointed by the United States. **339**

Pickett's Charge (1863) Failed Confederate attack during the Battle of Gettysburg. **119**

Pilgrims First English settlers in Massachusetts; left England because of religious conflicts. **10**

planned obsolescence Practice of manufacturing products that are designed to go out of style. **420**

Platt Amendment (1902) Amendment to the Cuban constitution; limited Cuba's right to make treaties and authorized the United States to intervene in Cuban affairs as it saw necessary. **340**

Plessy v. *Ferguson* (1896) Supreme Court ruling that established the "separate-but-equal" doctrine for public facilities. **150**

political bosses Leaders of political machines. **246**

political machines Well-organized political parties that dominated local and state governments in the late 1800s. **246**

poll taxes Taxes that a person had to pay in order to vote. **149**

Poor People's Campaign Martin Luther King Jr.'s movement to protest the perceived misuse of government spending away from antipoverty programs. **666**

pop art Movement that challenged the values of traditional art by taking inspiration from popular culture. **696**

Popular Front International alliance united against fascism; term used by Soviet leader Joseph Stalin in a 1935 speech. **514**

popular sovereignty Practice of allowing voters in a territory to decide whether to permit slavery there. **89**

Populist Party People's Party; national political party formed in 1892 that supported a graduated income tax, bank regulation, government ownership of some companies, restrictions on immigration, shorter workdays, and voting reform. **263**

Potsdam Conference (1945) Meeting of U.S. president Harry S Truman, British prime minister Winston Churchill, and Soviet leader Joseph Stalin after Germany's surrender in World War II; resulted in the division of Germany into four zones of occupation. **560**

Progressive Party Bull Moose Party; reform party that ran Theodore Roosevelt for president in 1912. **313**

progressivism Reform movement of the early 1900s concerned with curing problems of urbanization and industrialization. **274**

prohibition Complete ban on the manufacture, sale, and distribution of alcohol. **288**

protectorate Country dependent on another for protection. **340**

Pure Food and Drug Act (1906) Law that prohibited the manufacture, sale, or transportation of food and patented medicine containing harmful ingredients; also required food and medicine containers to carry ingredient labels. **306**

Q

quotas System of reserving a fixed number of openings in schools or jobs for certain groups of people. **669**

R

ragtime Style of music created in the 1890s by African American pianists who played a driving rhythm with one hand and an improvised melody with the other. **238**

railhead Town located along a railroad; long cattle drives usually ended there. **178**

Reaganomics President Ronald Reagan's economic program; based on large tax cuts to encourage business investment. **772**

realpolitik "Practical politics"; President Richard M. Nixon's policy that national interests rather than moral principles should be the guiding force in U.S. foreign policy. **745**

recall Procedure enabling voters to remove an official from office by calling for a special election. **299**

reclamation Process of making damaged land productive. **309**

Reconstruction (1865–77) Period following the Civil War during which the U.S. government worked to rebuild the former Confederate states and reunite the nation. **131**

Reconstruction Acts (1867) Laws that divided the former Confederate states, except Tennessee, into military zones and required them to draft new constitutions upholding the Fourteenth Amendment. **140**

Reconstruction Finance Corporation (RFC) Agency created in 1932 to stimulate the economy by lending money to railroads, insurance companies, and banks and other financial institutions. **460**

recycling Collection and processing of waste items for reuse. **817**

Redeemers Democratic supporters of white-controlled governments in the South during the 1870s. **146**

Red Scare Period of anticommunist hysteria; swept the United States after World War I. **393**

referendum Procedure allowing citizens to force the legislature to place a recently passed law on the ballot for public approval. **299**

Reform Party Political party created in the 1990s promising to reform national politics. **805**

regionalists Midwestern artists popular in the 1930s who emphasized local folk themes and customs in their work. **491**

Rehabilitation Act (1973) Federal law forbidding discrimination in education, jobs, or housing because of physical disabilities. **691**

Renaissance Rebirth of European learning and artistic creativity that began in the late Middle Ages. **6**

reparations Payments for damages and expenses in war. **378**

republicanism A system of government in which citizens select representatives and give them the authority to make and enforce laws. **28**

Republican Party Political party formed in 1854 by antislavery Whigs and Democrats, along with some Free-Soilers. **90**

Reynolds **v.** *Sims* (1964) Supreme Court case that further extended equality in the voting booth by affirming the "one person, one vote" principle. **644**

rock 'n' roll Popular music introduced in the 1950s; influenced by African American rhythm and blues. **605**

Roosevelt Corollary (1904) President Theodore Roosevelt's addition to the Monroe Doctrine; stated that the United States would police affairs in the Western Hemisphere to keep Europeans from intervening in the region. **343**

Rosie the Riveter Symbol of patriotic female defense workers during World War II. **538**

Rough Riders U.S. cavalry unit in the Spanish-American War led by Theodore Roosevelt. **336**

rugged individualism Belief that success comes through individual effort and private enterprise. **457**

S

Sand Creek Massacre (1864) Attack by U.S. Army troops in which some 200 peaceful Cheyenne were killed in Colorado. **163**

Sandinistas Revolutionary political party in Nicaragua that overthrew a pro-U.S. dictator in 1979. **775**

S&L crisis Economic collapse in the savings and loan and banking industries caused by risky loans in the 1980s. **779**

satellite nations Countries controlled by the Soviet Union. **566**

Saturday Night Massacre Name given to the series of events in 1973 that included the firing of a special prosecutor investigating Watergate and the resignations of the U.S. attorney general and his next in command for refusing to fire the prosecutor. **749**

scalawags "Scoundrels"; name that former Confederates gave to southern Republicans during Reconstruction. **144**

scientific management Theory promoted by Frederick W. Taylor; held that every kind of work could be broken into a series of smaller tasks and that rates of production could be set for each individual task. **414**

Scopes trial (1925) Trial of John Scopes, a high school science teacher who was prosecuted for teaching evolution. **428**

search-and-destroy missions U.S. strategy in Vietnam in which ground patrols searched for hidden enemy camps and supplies and destroyed them with massive firepower and air raids. **715**

Seattle general strike (1919) Large-scale strike that opponents blamed on Bolsheviks and foreigners; weakened support for organized labor. **391**

Second Great Awakening Evangelical religious movement that spread through the United States beginning in the early 1800s. **83**

Securities and Exchange Commission Federal agency that regulates companies that sell stocks and bonds. **470**

Sedition Act (1918) Federal law enacted during World War I that made written criticism of the government a crime. **374**

segregation Separation of people by category, usually race. **150**

Selective Service Act (1917) Law that initially required men between the ages of 21 and 30 to register for the draft. **364**

Selective Training and Service Act (1940) Law providing for the first peacetime draft in U.S. history. **530**

Seneca Falls Convention (1848) First national women's rights convention; site where the Declaration of Sentiments was written. **85**

settlement houses Community-service centers that were founded in the late 1800s to offer educational opportunities, skills training, and cultural events to impoverished neighborhoods. **231**

Seventeenth Amendment (1913) Constitutional amendment that gives voters the power to directly elect U.S. senators. **299**

shantytowns Collections of makeshift shelters built by homeless people. **450**

sharecropping System used on southern farms after the Civil War in which farmers worked land owned by someone else in return for supplies and a small share of the crops. **148**

Share-Our-Wealth Radical relief program proposed by Senator Huey Long in the 1930s; sought to empower the government to seize wealth from the rich through taxes and to provide a guaranteed minimum income and home to every American family. **475**

Sherman Antitrust Act (1890) Law prohibiting monopolies and trusts that restrained trade. **209**

Sherman Silver Purchase Act (1890) Federal law that required the government to buy and mint silver each month. **263**

Siege of Vicksburg (1863) Union army's blockade of Vicksburg, Mississippi, that led the city to surrender during the Civil War. **119**

Silent Majority Middle-class voters weary of the social upheaval of the 1960s; sought after by Richard Nixon during his presidential campaigns. **740**

sit-down strike Method used by striking workers of preventing owners from replacing them by refusing to leave the factories. **480**

sit-ins Demonstrations in which protesters sit down in a location and refuse to leave. **650**

Sixteenth Amendment (1913) Constitutional amendment that permitted Congress to levy income taxes. **311**

Skylab First U.S. space station; placed in orbit in 1973. **764**

skyscrapers Large, multistory buildings. **226**

Smoot-Hawley Tariff (1930) High-tariff law that contributed to a global economic downturn in the 1930s. **446**

social Darwinism Theory adapted by philosopher Herbert Spencer from Charles Darwin's theory of evolution; argued that society progresses through competition, with the fittest rising to positions of wealth and power. **202**

Social Gospel Movement begun by Protestant ministers in the late 1800s; applied Christian principles to social problems. **232**

socialism Economic system in which the government or the workers own most of the factories, utilities, and transportation and communications systems. **283**

Social Security Act (1935) Law that provides retirement pensions, unemployment insurance, and payments to people with disabilities and to widows and children of male workers who have died. **477**

Society of American Indians Organization formed in 1911 by middle-class American Indians to address Indian problems. **292**

sod houses Buildings made from chunks cut from heavy topsoil that were stacked like bricks. **173**

Solidarity Polish independent trade union and social movement that was formed in 1980. **773**

sonar Equipment that uses sound waves to detect underwater objects. **543**

Southern Christian Leadership Conference (SCLC) Alliance of church-based African American organizations formed in 1957 and dedicated to ending discrimination. **650**

southern strategy President Richard M. Nixon's attempt to woo conservative white voters from the Democratic Party by promising not to support new civil rights legislation. **741**

spheres of influence Regions where a particular country has exclusive rights over mines, railroads, and trade. **330**

Sputnik The world's first artificial satellite; launched by the Soviet Union in 1957. **585**

Square Deal Theodore Roosevelt's 1904 presidential campaign slogan pledging to balance the interests of business, consumers, and labor. **304**

stagflation Economic condition characterized by rising inflation and unemployment. **741**

Stalwarts Republicans in the late 1800s who opposed reform. **255**

Stamp Act (1765) Law passed by Parliament that placed a tax on printed matter. **15**

steerage Poor accommodations in a ship's lower levels; many immigrants to the United States traveled in this space. **221**

Strategic Arms Limitation Talks–U.S. Department of Agriculture

Strategic Arms Limitation Talks (SALT) (1972) Talks between U.S. president Richard M. Nixon and Soviet leader Leonid Brezhnev that led to a treaty limiting the number of ICBM missiles each country could have. **745**

Strategic Defense Initiative (SDI) Plan for a defense system in space to protect the United States from Soviet missiles; never actually implemented. **773**

strict construction Philosophy of narrowly interpreting the Constitution; holds that the government can do only what the Constitution specifically allows. **72**

strike Refusal of workers to perform their job until employers meet union demands. **82**

Student Nonviolent Coordinating Committee (SNCC) Student organization formed in 1960 to coordinate civil rights demonstrations and to provide training for protesters. **650**

Students for a Democratic Society (SDS) Student group that actively protested the Vietnam War. **717**

subsidy Government payment made to farmers. **328**

suburbs Residential neighborhoods on the outskirts of a city. **227**

Sunbelt States in the South and the West that attracted many new residents and businesses in the 1970s. **761**

supply-side economics Economic theory stating that tax cuts would lead to increased economic activity and tax revenues, and therefore to a balanced budget. **772**

supremacy clause Clause in the U.S. Constitution; states that the Constitution and all federal laws outrank state constitutions and state laws. **34**

Sussex **pledge** (1916) Promise issued by German officials during World War I not to sink merchant vessels without warning or without assuring the passengers' safety. **363**

T

Taft-Hartley Act (1947) Law that gave judges the power to end some strikes, outlawed closed-shop agreements, restricted unions' political contributions, and required union leaders to swear they were not Communists. **594**

Teapot Dome scandal Scandal during President Warren Harding's administration; involved Secretary of the Interior Albert Fall's leasing of oil reserves in return for personal gifts and loans. **400**

Telecommunications Act (1996) Law that attempted to regulate indecency on the Internet; parts of it were later struck down by a federal court. **811**

telegraph Machine patented by Samuel Morse in 1837; sent messages over long distances by using electric current to transmit a system of dots and dashes over wire. **196**

Teller Amendment (1898) Resolution stating that the United States did not intend to take over and annex Cuba. **335**

tenements Poorly built apartment buildings that housed many impoverished city-dwellers in the late 1800s and early 1900s. **230**

Tennessee Valley Authority (TVA) New Deal program established in 1933; built dams and power stations to provide hydroelectric power and flood control to the Tennessee River valley. **472**

Tet Offensive (1968) Attack by North Vietnamese and Vietcong troops against South Vietnam during the Vietnam War; came during Tet, the Vietnamese New Year; demonstrated that the North Vietnamese were still militarily strong. **720**

Texas longhorn Hardy breed of cattle created by interbreeding English and Spanish cattle. **177**

Texas Revolution (1835–36) Revolt against Mexico by American settlers and Tejanos in Texas. **86**

Thirteenth Amendment (1865) Constitutional amendment that abolished slavery. **133**

Three Mile Island accident (1979) Incident in which a nuclear reactor in Pennsylvania nearly had a catastrophic meltdown. **755**

Tonkin Gulf Resolution (1964) Congressional measure that gave President Lyndon B. Johnson the authority to wage war in Vietnam. **712**

totalitarian state Political system in which the government controls every aspect of citizens' lives. **513**

total war Strategy of fighting in which an army destroys its opponent's ability to fight by attacking civilian and economic, as well as military, targets. **122**

Trail of Tears (1838–39) An 800-mile forced march the Cherokee made from their homeland in the Southeast to Indian Territory in present-day Oklahoma; resulted in the deaths of almost one quarter of the tribe's members. **81**

transcontinental railroad Railroad that crossed the continental United States; completed in 1869. **194**

Treaty of Paris (1783) Peace agreement that officially ended the Revolutionary War and established Britain's formal recognition of the United States. **23**

Treaty of Versailles (1919) Treaty ending World War I that required Germany to pay huge war reparations and that established the League of Nations. **379**

trench warfare World War I military strategy of defending a position by fighting from the protection of deep ditches. **358**

Triangle Shirtwaist Fire (1911) Incident that resulted in the deaths of some 140 garment workers; led to increased safety regulations for businesses. **282**

Truman Doctrine (1947) President Harry S Truman's policy stating that the United States would help any country fighting against communism. **569**

trunk lines Major railroads connected to outlying areas by feeder or branch lines. **194**

trust Arrangement grouping several companies under a single board of directors to eliminate competition and to regulate production. **203**

Twenty-first Amendment (1933) Constitutional amendment that ended prohibition by repealing the Eighteenth Amendment. **423**

Twenty-fourth Amendment (1964) Constitutional amendment that banned the payment of poll taxes as a condition for voting in federal elections. **658**

Twenty-sixth Amendment (1971) Constitutional amendment that lowered the federal voting age from 21 to 18. **726**

U

Underground Railroad Network of abolitionists who helped slaves escape to the North and Canada. **83**

United Farm Workers (UFW) Group formed in the 1960s to improve working conditions for migrant farmworkers. **683**

United Mine Workers strike (1919) Strike for pay increases and better working hours that further weakened public support for unions; first UMW strike led by John L. Lewis. **392**

United Nations (UN) International organization chartered in 1945; created to settle problems between nations. **563**

Universal Negro Improvement Association (UNIA) Association founded by Marcus Garvey in 1914 to foster African American economic independence and establish an independent black homeland in Africa. **406**

University of California v. Bakke (1978) Supreme Court decision that established that while some forms of affirmative action were legal, quota systems were not. **669**

Untouchables Nickname given to a group of detectives led by Eliot Ness who targeted gangsters during Prohibition. **423**

urban renewal Program launched by the federal government in the 1950s to replace old, run-down inner-city buildings. **615**

U.S. Department of Agriculture Executive department created in 1862 to help farmers. **173**

U.S. Sanitary Commission Federal agency headed in part by Dr. Elizabeth Blackwell; battled disease and infection among Union soldiers during the Civil War. **107**

USS *Maine* U.S. battleship that exploded in Havana Harbor in 1898; although cause was never determined, the incident was a catalyst for the Spanish-American War. **335**

U-2 incident Incident in which U.S. pilot Francis Gary Powers was captured while spying on the Soviet Union; damaged relations between the United States and the Soviet Union. **578**

V

vaudeville "Light play"; type of variety show featuring a wide selection of short performances. **238**

vertical integration Ownership of businesses involved in each step of a manufacturing process. **204**

Vietcong National Liberation Front; communist guerrilla force that began fighting against Ngo Dinh Diem's government in South Vietnam in the 1950s. **709**

Vietminh League for the Independence of Vietnam; group of Vietnamese nationalists organized in the 1940s by Ho Chi Minh to drive the Japanese out of Vietnam. **707**

Vietnamization Policy followed by the Nixon administration of gradually turning over all the fighting in the Vietnam War to the South Vietnamese Army. **723**

Vietnam Veterans Memorial Memorial dedicated in Washington, D.C., in 1982 to honor those people who died in or are missing from the Vietnam War. **730**

Virginia Statute for Religious Freedom (1786) Statute stating in part that the human mind was created free and that government control over religious beliefs or worship is tyrannical. **29**

Volstead Act (1919) Federal law that enforced the Eighteenth Amendment (prohibition). **422**

Volunteers in Service to America (VISTA) Domestic version of the Peace Corps; established in 1964. **640**

Voting Rights Act (1965) Law that put voter registration under federal government control. **660**

Voting Rights Act of 1975 Federal law requiring states and communities with large non-English speaking populations to print voting materials in various foreign languages. **760**

W

Wagner-Connery Act (1935) National Labor Relations Act; law that guaranteed labor's right to organize unions and to bargain for better wages and working conditions. **480**

War Industries Board (WIB) Agency led by Bernard Baruch during World War I; allocated scarce goods, established production priorities, and set prices on goods. **369**

war of attrition Union general Grant's Civil War strategy of fighting until the South ran out of men, supplies, and will. **120**

War on Drugs President George Bush's organized effort to end drug smuggling and illegal drug use. **790**

War on Poverty President Lyndon B. Johnson's programs to help poor Americans; announced in 1964. **639**

War Powers Act (1973) Legislation that reaffirmed Congress's constitutional power to declare war; set a 60-day limit on the president's authority to commit U.S. troops to serve in a foreign conflict. **730**

War Production Board (WPB) World War II agency that was in charge of converting factories to war production. **529**

Warren Commission Special group led by Chief Justice Earl Warren to investigate the assassination of President John F. Kennedy. **637**

Warsaw Pact Military alliance formed in 1955 by the Soviet Union and other Eastern European communist countries. **571**

Washington Conference (1921) International conference held in Washington, D.C., that focused on naval disarmament and security in the Pacific. **503**

Watergate Scandal in which President Richard M. Nixon authorized the cover-up of a break-in at the Democratic National Committee headquarters; led to Nixon's resignation in 1974. **748**

Whip Inflation Now (WIN) President Gerald Ford's slogan to garner support for his anti-inflation program. **752**

Wisconsin Idea Robert M. La Follette's reform program for Wisconsin in the early 1900s; became a model for other state governments. **302**

Woman's Christian Temperance Union (WCTU) Reform organization that led the fight against alcohol in the late 1800s. **289**

Woodstock (1969) Rock concert near Woodstock, New York, that marked the highpoint of the counterculture era. **699**

Works Progress Administration (WPA) New Deal agency created in 1934 to put American men and women to work. **476**

World Wide Web System developed by Swiss scientists in the early 1980s that links Internet sites. **811**

Y

Yalta Conference (1945) Meeting of U.S. president Franklin D. Roosevelt, British prime minister Winston Churchill, and Soviet leader Joseph Stalin to plan for the postwar world. **546**

yellow journalism Style of sensational reporting used by newspapers to attract readers. **235**

Y2K bug Widespread computer progamming problem created by date abbreviations that threatened to shut down computer systems on January 1, 2000. **812**

Z

zaibatsu Huge corporations run by single families that monopolized the Japanese economy before World War II. **561**

Zimmermann Note Cable sent to the German minister in Mexico by Germany's foreign secretary during World War I; proposed an alliance between the two countries. **364**

Zionism Movement pushing for the formation of a Jewish homeland in Palestine. **564**

zoot-suit riots (1943) Series of attacks by U.S. sailors against Mexican Americans in Los Angeles. **540**

GLOSSARY/GLOSARIO

Este glosario contiene términos que necesitarás conocer para estudiar la historia de Estados Unidos. Después de cada término se presenta una breve explicación de su significado tal como se usa en *The American Nation*. El número incluido es el número de página en la que aparece el término en el libro de texto.

A

Adamson Act/Ley Adamson (1916) Decreto federal que redujo de 10 a 8 horas las jornadas laborales de los trabajadores de las compañías ferrocarrileras, sin disminuir su salario. **317**

affirmative action/acción afirmativa Práctica de algunos departamentos del gobierno, comercios y escuelas en la que otorgan preferencia a los grupos minoritarios y a las mujeres en sus procesos de admisión y selección. **669**

Agricultural Adjustment Administration/Administración para el Ajuste Agrícola (AAA) Agencia federal creada por la Ley de Ajuste Agrícola en 1933 con la finalidad de reducir la producción agrícola y permitir el aumento de los precios de las cosechas. **471**

Agricultural Revolution/revolución agrícola Proceso de modernización en el que se pasa de los antiguos métodos de caza y recolección de frutos a la siembra de cultivos. **4**

AIDS/SIDA (Síndrome de Inmunodeficiencia Adquirida) Enfermedad que suele tener consecuencias mortales al anular la acción del sistema inmunológico del cuerpo y facilitar el acceso de agentes infecciosos que producen enfermedades. **785**

Alianza Federal de Mercedes/Alianza Federal de Mercedes Departamento Federal de Concesión de la Tierra; organización encabezada por Reies López Tijerina que busca recuperar las tierras expropiadas a personas de origen mexicano-estadounidense. **684**

Alien and Sedition Acts/Leyes de extranjería y sedición (1798) Leyes aprobadas por un congreso de mayoría federalista que facilitan la deportación de extranjeros y hacen ilegal la publicación de cualquier mensaje verbal o escrito en contra del gobierno. **75**

Alliance for Progress/Alianza para el Progreso Programa de ayuda económica para América Latina creado por el presidente John F. Kennedy para favorecer las reformas democráticas y promover el capitalismo. **626**

Allied Powers/potencias aliadas Alianza creada durante la Primera Guerra Mundial por Gran Bretaña, Francia, Rusia y más tarde Estados Unidos para combatir a las potencias centrales. **357**; Alianza creada durante la Segunda Guerra Mundial por Gran Bretaña, Francia y más tarde Estados Unidos para combatir al Eje. **519**

American Association of Retired Persons/Asociación Estadounidense de Personas Retiradas (AARP, por sus siglas en inglés) Grupo creado en 1958 para proteger los derechos de las personas retiradas. **692**

American Federation of Labor/Federación Estadounidense del Trabajo (AFL, por sus siglas en inglés) Sindicato fundado en 1886 por Samuel Gompers para proteger los derechos de los trabajadores especializados. **214**

American Gothic/American Gothic Una de las obras regionalistas más famosas del pintor Grant Wood. **491**

American Indian Movement/Movimiento Indígena Estadounidense (AIM, por sus siglas en inglés) Organización creada en 1968 para luchar por los derechos de los indígenas de Estados Unidos. **690**

Americanization/americanización Proceso de preparación de los residentes en E. U. nacidos en el extranjero para adquirir la ciudadanía estadounidense. **292**

American Plan/Plan estadounidense Política promovida por los líderes comerciales en los años veinte con la finalidad de permitir la libre apertura de tiendas. **399**

Americans with Disabilities Act/Ley de estadounidenses con discapacidad (ADA, por sus siglas en inglés) (1990) Ley que prohíbe la discriminación de personas con discapacidad en empleos, transportes, servicios telefónicos y edificios públicos. **790**

American System/Sistema estadounidense Plan creado por Henry Clay para elevar los aranceles con el propósito de financiar mejoras internas como la construcción de carreteras y acueductos. **79**

amnesty/amnistía Perdón oficial emitido por el gobierno. **131**

Anaconda Plan/Plan Anaconda Plan desarrollado por los sindicatos durante la Guerra Civil para realizar un bloqueo naval en el sur del país; llamado así por su parecido con la serpiente anaconda. **103**

anarchists/anarquistas Personas que se oponen a cualquier forma de gobierno. **213**

Antifederalists/Antifederalistas Personas que temían la creación de un poderoso gobierno nacional, por lo que se oponían a la redacción de la Constitución. **33**

anti-Semitism/antisemitismo Odio hacia los judíos. **514**

apartheid/apartheid Sistema político sudafricano controlado por la minoría blanca que reprimía los derechos de las personas de raza negra. **758**

Apollo 11/Apollo 11 Misión espacial que llevó al primer hombre a la Luna el 20 de julio de 1969. **764**

appeasement/pacificación Acción de ceder ante el ataque de un enemigo para evitar conflictos. **518**

arbitration/arbitraje Proceso en el que dos partes permiten que una tercera resuelva una disputa. **304**

Area Redevelopment Act/Ley de reconstrucción regional (ARA, por sus siglas en inglés) Ley aprobada en 1961 que ofrecía apoyo económico a regiones con problemas. **635**

Articles of Confederation/Artículos de la Confederación (1777) Documento que creó una asociación de estados que garantizaba en cada uno "soberanía, libertad e independencia." **29**

assembly line/línea de ensamblado Sistema de producción creado por Henry Ford para fabricar productos con mayor rapidez usando una banda transportadora en la que cada trabajador ensamblaba una parte. **415**

Atlantic Charter/Carta del Atlántico (1941) Documento firmado por el presidente de Estados Unidos Franklin D. Roosevelt y el primer ministro de Inglaterra Winston Churchill en la que se comprometían a no adquirir nuevos territorios después de la Segunda Guerra Mundial y a trabajar juntos por la paz mundial. **522**

Atomic Energy Act/Ley de energía atómica (1946) Decreto federal que creó la Comisión de Energía Atómica para supervisar el desarrollo de armas nucleares y promover el uso pacífico de la energía atómica. **568**

automation/automatización Uso de máquinas para reemplazar al ser humano en las líneas de producción. **599**

auto-touring/auto-excursiones Movimiento que cobró gran popularidad cuando miles de estadounidenses empezaron a usar sus propios automóviles para realizar largos viajes de placer. **418**

Axis Powers/potencias del Eje Alianza militar formada por Italia y Alemania en 1936 a la que más tarde se unió Japón. **518**

Aztec/azteca Mexica; imperio guerrero que dominó el territorio actualmente ocupado por México durante los últimos siglos de la Edad Media. **5**

B

baby boom/auge de los bebés Aumento importante de la tasa de natalidad en Estados Unidos en los años posteriores a la Segunda Guerra Mundial. **601**

Ballinger-Pinchot affair/asunto Ballinger-Pinchot Incidente que debilitó la popularidad del presidente de Estados Unidos William Howard Taft por despedir al jefe de relaciones exteriores Gifford Pinchot, quien había criticado al secretario de asuntos internos Richard Ballinger al aprobar la venta de parte del territorio de Alaska. **311**

bank holiday/cierre de los bancos (1933) Proclama que cerró de manera temporal todos los bancos para evitar el retiro masivo de capitales invertidos en ellos. **468**

barbed wire/alambre de púas Material económico inventado por Joseph Glidden en 1874. **181**

Baruch Plan/Plan Baruch (1946) Propuesta de Bernard Baruch para crear una organización internacional que impusiera castigos a los países que violaran las leyes mundiales de control de armas nucleares. **568**

Bataan Death March/marcha de la muerte de Bataan (1942) Brutal marcha obligada en la península de Bataan, donde más de 10,000 prisioneros estadounidenses y filipinos murieron durante la Segunda Guerra Mundial. **532**

Battle of Antietam/Batalla de Antietam (1862) Victoria del ejército de la Unión en Maryland, durante la Guerra Civil, que se recuerda como la batalla de un solo día más sangrienta de la historia de Estados Unidos. **114**

Battle of Bunker Hill/Batalla de Bunker Hill (1775) Batalla realizada en Boston durante la Guerra Revolucionaria en la que perdieron la vida más de 1,000 soldados británicos y aproximadamente 450 elementos patriotas. **18**

Battle of Gettysburg/Batalla de Gettysburg (1863) Victoria del ejército de la Unión en Gettysburg, Pennsylvanna, durante la Guerra Civil que inclinó la balanza en contra de los confederados y en la que más de 40,000 soldados de ambos bandos resultaron heridos o muertos. **118**

Battle of Iwo Jima/Batalla de Iwo Jima (1945) Disputa de seis semanas por el control de una isla del Pacífico de la que finalmente el ejército aliado salió victorioso. **552**

Battle of Leyte Gulf/Batalla del golfo de Leyte (1944) La batalla naval más larga e importante en la costa del Pacífico durante la Segunda Guerra Mundial, después de la cual los ataques japoneses no lograron amenazar seriamente a los aliados. **550**

Battle of Midway/Batalla del Midway (1942) Batalla de la Segunda Guerra Mundial en la que las fuerzas aliadas diezmaron severamente la flota naval de Japón. **532**

Battle of Okinawa/Batalla de Okinawa (1945) Sangrienta batalla del Pacífico durante la Segunda Guerra Mundial en la que el ejército aliado obtuvo la victoria. **552**

Battle of Shiloh/Batalla de Shiloh (1862) Batalla de la Guerra Civil en la que el ejército de la Unión obtuvo mayor control del valle del río Mississippi. **110**

Battle of the Argonne Forest/Batalla del bosque de Argonne (1918) Esfuerzo exitoso de las tropas aliadas por alejar al ejército alemán de un centro ferrocarrilero localizado en Sedan, Francia. **377**

Battle of the Atlantic/Batalla del Atlántico Lucha de la Segunda Guerra Mundial entre las fuerzas navales alemanas y las tropas navales y aéreas de los aliados. **543**

Battle of the Bulge/Batalla del Bulge (1944) Batalla de la Segunda Guerra Mundial en la que los aliados derrotaron a la última ofensiva alemana. **546**

Battle of the Coral Sea/Batalla del Mar de Coral (1942) Batalla de la Segunda Guerra Mundial en la que las tropas aliadas lograron detener el avance del ejército japonés en Australia. **532**

Battle of the Little Bighorn/Batalla de Little Bighorn (1876) Batalla librada entre las tropas de George Arsmtrong Custer y los guerreros sioux que marcó la peor derrota del ejército estadounidense en territorio del oeste. **165**

Battle of the Somme/Batalla del Somme (1916) Batalla de la Primera Guerra Mundial en la que el ejército británico perdió a más de 60,000 soldados en un solo día. **359**

Battle of Yorktown/Batalla de Yorktown (1781) Última batalla importante de la Guerra Revolucionaria y sitio en que las tropas del general británico Charles Cornwallis se rindieron ante los patriotas en Virginia. **23**

bear market/tendencia a la baja Tendencia a la baja del mercado de valores. **443**

beats/beats Reducido grupo de escritores de gran influencia que desafiaron los convencionalismos literarios y el estilo de vida de la clase media en la década de los cincuenta. **613**

benevolent societies/sociedades de beneficencia Organizaciones que brindaron ayuda a los inmigrantes en caso de enfermedad, desempleo y muerte. **223**

Berlin Airlift/Ayuda aérea de Berlín (1948–49) Operación en la que aviones británicos y estadounidenses transportaron alimentos y otros suministros a Berlín occidental, ciudad que había sido sitiada por las tropas soviéticas. **570**

Berlin Wall/Muro de Berlín Enorme muro construido para separar las partes oriental y occidental de Berlín; símbolo bien conocido de la guerra fría. **628**

Bessemer process/proceso Bessemer Método eficaz de fabricación de acero desarrollado en conjunto por el inventor británico Henry Bessemer y el inventor estadounidense William Kelly, en la década de 1850. **192**

Big Four/Los Cuatro Grandes Nombre colectivo dado al grupo formado por el presidente de Estados Unidos Woodrow Wilson, el primer ministro británico David Lloyd George, el primer ministro francés Georges Clemenceau y el primer ministro italiano Vittorio Orlando durante la conferencia de paz de 1919 en Versalles. **378**

Bilingual Education Act/Ley de educación bilingüe (1974) Ley que fomentó el uso del idioma materno de los estudiantes inmigrantes en las escuelas públicas mientras aprendían inglés como segundo idioma. **761**

Bill of Rights/Carta de Derechos Primeras diez enmiendas de la Constitución, ratificadas en 1791. **70**

Black Codes/códigos negros Leyes aprobadas en los estados del sur durante el periodo de Reconstrucción para restringir la libertad recién otorgada a los esclavos. **133**

black nationalism/nacionalismo negro Movimiento creado con la finalidad de desarrollar un nuevo estado de derecho para los afroestadounidenses en Estados Unidos. **406**

Black Panther Party/Partido de las Panteras Negras Organización política formada en la década de 1960 para obtener poder y defender los derechos de los afroestadounidenses. **664**

Black Power/Poder Negro Movimiento separatista originado por la frustración de los afroestadounidenses al ver el lento avance del movimiento en favor de sus derechos civiles. **664**

Blackshirts/camisas negras Seguidores de Benito Mussolini, líder que ascendió al poder en Italia en la década de 1920. **512**

Black Thursday/jueves negro 24 de octubre de 1929; día en que los inversionistas causaron una oleada de pánico en Wall Street al vender apresuradamente sus acciones. **443**

Black Tuesday/martes negro 29 de octubre de 1929; día del colapso del mercado de valores que originó la Gran Depresión. **444**

Bland-Allison Act/Ley Bland-Allison (1878) Ley federal que obligaba al gobierno a comprar cierta cantidad de plata cada mes para acuñar monedas. **263**

Blitzkrieg/Blitzkrieg "Guerra relámpago"; rápido avance militar usado por las tropas alemanas en 1939. **521**

blues/blues Tipo de música desarrollado por los esclavos con la influencia de la música espiritual que se caracterizaba por sus dramáticas letras y el uso de notas musicales alteradas para armonizar perfectamente con la emotividad de la letra. **430**

Bolsheviks/bolcheviques Grupo radical socialista que ascendió al poder en 1917 después de derrocar al zar de Rusia. **375**

bonanza farm/granja de bonanza Granjas de grandes dimensiones usadas como fábricas por grandes empresas productoras de alimentos. **173**

Bonus Army/Ejército de Bonificación Grupo de veteranos de la Primera Guerra Mundial que en 1932 realizaron una marcha a Washington, D.C., para exigir el pago inmediato de sus bonos de pensión. **461**

Boston police strike/Huelga de la Policía de Boston (1919) Huelga fallida de los grupos policiacos que generó disturbios en la ciudad y el despido de los oficiales participantes. **391**

Boxer Rebellion/Rebelión de los Bóxers (1900) Revuelta en la que un grupo de chinos nacionalistas conocidos como Bóxers atacaron a un grupo de extranjeros para acabar con la intervención de otras naciones en los asuntos internos de China; este movimiento fue controlado después de dos meses por fuerzas internacionales. **330**

braceros/braceros Grupo de trabajadores agrícolas y ferrocarrileros que llegaron a Estados Unidos en la Segunda Guerra Mundial por un acuerdo laboral entre Estados Unidos y México. **539**

breadlines/filas del pan Filas de personas que esperaban una ración de alimentos durante la Gran Depresión. **450**

brinkmanship/brinkmanship "Llegar al límite"; política común en la década de 1950 que llegaba al punto de declarar la guerra a toda agresión comunista. **576**

British invasion/invasión británica Ingreso de diversas grupos británicos de rock al mercado estadounidense en la década de 1960. **698**

Brotherhood of Sleeping Car Porters/Hermandad de Porteros de los Vagones Dormitorio Unión formada por A. Philip Randolph en 1925 para luchar por los derechos de los afroestadounidenses que trabajaban en las compañías de ferrocarriles. **406**

Brown Berets/Boinas Pardas Grupo de activistas formado en 1967 como respuesta al trato que daba la policía a los mexicano–estadounidenses. **685**

Brownshirts/camisas pardas Tropas nazis de ataque relámpago. **513**

Brown* v. *Board of Education/Brown* versus *Consejo de educación Caso en que la Suprema Corte declaró anticonstitucional la segregación racial en las escuelas públicas. **607**

bull market/mercado a la alza Alza en el precio de las acciones del mercado de valores. **443**

Bureau of Indian Affairs/Departamento de Asuntos Indígenas Agencia creada por el gobierno para administrar los asuntos relacionados con los grupos indígenas. **162**

Bursum Bill/Carta Bursum Propuesta hecha en 1922 para legalizar las tierras no reclamadas del sudoeste como territorio indígena; esta propuesta fue rechazada por el Congreso. **409**

Bush* v. *Gore/Bush* versus *Gore Caso de la Suprema Corte que invalidó el recuento manual de los votos en varios condados de Florida durante las elecciones presidenciales del año 2000. **818**

business cycle/ciclo comercial Periodos de alza y baja en las ganancias de un negocio bajo el sistema de la libre empresa. **447**

busing–Crittenden Compromise

busing/escuela en autobús Uso de autobuses para transportar a los estudiantes a escuelas foráneas con el propósito de promover la integración social. **668**

C

cabinet/gabinete Grupo de consejeros que encabezan los departamentos ejecutivos para ofrecer asesoría al presidente. **70**

Camp David Accords/Acuerdos de Campo David (1978) Acuerdo de paz entre los gobiernos de Israel y Egipto negociado por el presidente de Estados Unidos Jimmy Carter. **759**

capitalism/capitalismo Sistema económico en el que capitales privados son propietarios de las industrias y la competencia determina el precio de los bienes y el salario de los trabajadores que los fabrican. **201**

carpetbaggers/*carpetbaggers* Republicanos del norte que emigraron al sur en la época de la Reconstrucción. **144**

caudillos/caudillos Líderes militares de América Latina que en la década de 1930 usaron la fuerza para mantener el orden. **511**

Central Intelligence Agency/Agencia Central de Inteligencia (CIA, por sus siglas en inglés) Agencia federal creada a finales de la década de 1940 para realizar investigaciones secretas. **576**

Central Powers/potencias centrales Alianza formada en la Primera Guerra Mundial que acabó con el pacto del imperio Austro Húngaro, Alemania, el Imperio Otomano y Bulgaria. **357**

Challenger*/*Challenger Transbordador espacial estadounidense que en 1986 explotó en el aire poco después de su despegue, produciendo la muerte de sus siete tripulantes. **784**

Chernobyl disaster/Catástrofe de Chernobyl (1986) Accidente ocurrido en una planta nuclear cerca de Kiev, Ucrania, que liberó cantidades masivas de radiación al aire. **816**

Children's Defense Fund/Fondo de Defensa para la Infancia (CDF, por sus siglas en inglés) Organización fundada en 1973 para proteger los derechos de los niños. **693**

Chinese Exclusion Act/Ley de exclusión de China (1882) Ley que negaba la ciudadanía estadounidense a toda persona nacida en China y prohibía la inmigración de trabajadores chinos a Estados Unidos. **225**

City Beautiful movement/movimiento de embellecimiento de la ciudad Campaña que destacó la importancia de incluir los parques y calles más importantes en el diseño conjunto de una ciudad. **236**

Civilian Conservation Corps/Corporación de Conservación Civil (CCC) Agencia establecida por el *New Deal* en 1933 para emplear a hombres jóvenes en proyectos de conservación. **470**

Civil Rights Act of 1866/Ley de derechos civiles de 1866 Primera ley estadounidense de derechos civiles; en ella se declaraba ciudadano estadounidense a cualquier persona nacida dentro de Estados Unidos. **138**

Civil Rights Act of 1875/Ley de derechos civiles de 1875 Ley que prohibía a los negocios de atención al público la discriminación de las personas de origen afroestadounidense. **146**

Civil Rights Act of 1957/Ley de derechos civiles de 1957 Ley que calificaba como crimen la prohibición del voto a cualquier persona que tuviera derecho a éste. **610**

Civil Rights Act of 1964/Ley de derechos civiles de 1964 Ley que prohibía la discriminación racial en los edificios públicos y en los empleos. **655**

Clayton Antitrust Act/Ley Clayton antimonopolio (1914) Ley que especificaba y apoyaba la Ley Sherman antimonopolio y definía con claridad el significado del término monopolio. **316**

closed shop/taller agremiado Comercio cuyos empleados deben pertenecer a un gremio. **283**

Cold War/guerra fría (1945–91) Larga lucha de poder entre Estados Unidos y la Unión Soviética, caracterizada por ataques políticos y económicos no militares. **566**

Committee on Civil Rights/Comité de Derechos Civiles Comité creado en 1946 por el presidente Harry S Truman para el análisis de los asuntos raciales. **595**

Committee on Public Information/Comité de Información Pública (CPI, por sus iniciales en inglés) Agencia creada en 1917 para promover el apoyo de la población durante la Primera Guerra Mundial. **373**

Committee to Re-elect the President/Comité Pro Reelección Presidencial (CRP, por sus iniciales en inglés) Comisión que manejó la campaña de reelección del presidente Richard Nixon en 1972 usando "trucos sucios" para minar el poder de los demócratas. **747**

Common Sense*/*Common Sense (1776) Folleto redactado por Thomas Paine para solicitar el apoyo de la población a la Revolución Estadounidense, con el propósito de terminar con el reinado británico en las colonias. **18**

Commonwealth of Independent States/Comunidad de Estados Independientes (CIS, por sus iniciales en inglés) Alianza formada en diciembre de 1991 por varias repúblicas que habían formado parte de la ex Unión Soviética. **787**

communism/comunismo Teoría política que declara que los medios de producción deben ser propiedad de la población y que no debe permitirse la propiedad privada. **202**

Compromise of 1850/Compromiso de 1850 Acuerdo propuesto por Henry Clay para permitir la integración de California como estado libre en la Unión, dividir el resto de la cesión mexicana en dos territorios donde la abolición o la legalidad de la esclavitud sea decidida por la población, determinar la propiedad de las tierras localizadas entre Texas y Nuevo México, abolir la esclavitud en el distrito de Columbia y reformar las leyes de esclavos fugitivos. **89**

Compromise of 1877/Compromiso de 1877 Acuerdo creado para resolver las disputas en las elecciones presidenciales de 1876; con este acuerdo, los Republicanos aceptaron a Rutherford B. Hayes como presidente a cambio del retiro de las tropas federales del sur. **147**

compulsory education laws/leyes obligatorias de educación Leyes que obligaban a los padres de familia a enviar a sus hijos a la escuela. **233**

Comstock Lode/veta de Comstock Una de las minas de plata más ricas del mundo, descubierta en Nevada a mediados del siglo XIX. **183**

Confederate States of America/Estados Confederados Confederación; nación formada en 1861 por los estados separados del sur. **91**

Congress of Industrial Organizations/Congreso de Organizaciones Industriales (CIO, por sus siglas en inglés) Grupo laboral fundado en 1938 para organizar en sindicatos a los trabajadores de cada industria. **480**

Congress of Racial Equality/Congreso de Igualdad Racial (CORE, por sus siglas en inglés) Grupo defensor de los derechos civiles creado para organizar protestas no violentas en el norte del país. **651**

conscription/conscripción Selección obligatoria de estadounidenses para el servicio militar. **108**

conspicuous consumption/consumismo ostentoso Gasto hecho para demostrar la riqueza que se posee. **228**

Constitutional Convention/Convención Constitucional de Filadelfia (1787) Reunión realizada en Filadelfia en la que los delegados de los estados redactaron la Constitución. **31**

containment/contención Política adoptada por el gobierno estadounidense en la guerra fría con el propósito de evitar la expansión del comunismo soviético en el mundo. **567**

Contract with America/Contrato con Estados Unidos Planes de reforma presentados en 1994 por los Republicanos. **800**

Contras/Contras Ejército rebelde antisandinista de Nicaragua patrocinado por la administración de Ronald Reagan. **801**

convoy system/sistema de convoy Uso de vehículos armados para proteger a vehículos no armados que transportaban tropas, suministros o voluntarios al Atlántico Norte durante la Primera Guerra Mundial. **367**

cooperatives/cooperativas Grupos que reúnen los recursos de sus integrantes para vender sus productos de manera directa y comprar productos a precios de mayoreo. **260**

Copperheads/*copperheads* Demócratas del norte que simpatizaban con los gobiernos del sur durante la Guerra Civil. **109**

corporation/corporación Compañía que vende parte de sus posesiones en forma de acciones del mercado de valores con la finalidad de reunir fondos. **202**

Corporation for Public Broadcasting/Corporación de Transmisiones Públicas Organización no lucrativa creada por el presidente Lyndon B. Johnson para transmitir programas educativos por televisión. **642**

cotton gin/clesmotadora de algodón Dispositivo creado por Eli Whitney en 1793 para separar con facilidad las semillas del algodón de las plantas. **82**

Council of Economic Advisers/Grupo de Consejeros Económicos Agencia federal creada con la ley del empleo de 1946 para brindar asesoría a la presidencia en materia de economía. **592**

Council of Federated Organizations/Consejo de Organizaciones de la Federación (COFO, por sus siglas en inglés) Grupo creado por varias asociaciones de defensa de los derechos civiles para coordinar las campañas de registro de votantes en la década de 1960. **657**

counterculture/contracultura Estilo alternativo de vida que generó la cultura de los hippies en la década de 1960. **695**

Crittenden Compromise/Compromiso de Crittenden (1860) Plan del senador John Crittenden para resolver el conflicto entre los estados del norte y el sur mediante la extensión al oeste del límite definido en el Compromiso de Missouri; esta propuesta fue rechazada por el presidente Lincoln. **96**

crop-lien system/cultivo de intercambio Acuerdo en el que se ofrece una cosecha como garantía por el ofrecimiento de créditos para la compra de suministros. **148**

Crusade for Justice/Cruzada por la Justicia Grupos fundados en 1966 por Adolfo "Corky" González para promover el nacionalismo entre los mexicano estadounidenses. **686**

Crusades/cruzadas (1096–1221) Serie de cinco guerras entre cristianos y musulmanes por el dominio de Palestina. **6**

Cuban missile crisis/Crisis de los misiles de Cuba (1962) Situación en que la Unión Soviética acordó retirar sus misiles de Cuba a cambio de que Estados Unidos no invadiera la isla, lo cual alivió la tensión de la guerra fría. **630**

D

Dawes General Allotment Act/Ley Dawes de lotificación (1887) Ley que hacía un conteo de las familias indígenas para asignarles una porción de tierra de sólo 160 acres y vender el resto de su territorio; esta medida provocó que los indígenas perdieran una tercera parte de sus tierras. **168**

D-Day/día D (1944) 6 de junio; invasión de territorio francés por las tropas aliadas durante la Segunda Guerra Mundial. **544**

Declaration of Independence/Declaración de Independencia (1776) Presentación del Segundo Congreso Continental que oficialmente declaraba la independencia de Estados Unidos de la Gran Bretaña. **20**

defoliants/defoliantes Sustancias químicas que acaban con la vegetación de una zona. **714**

demobilization/desmovilización Transición de la guerra a la paz mediante la recuperación de los niveles de productividad y empleo. **390**

Democratic Party/Partido Demócrata Partido político formado por simpatizantes de Andrew Jackson después de las elecciones presidenciales de 1824. **80**

Department of Energy/Departamento de Energía Departamento ejecutivo creado en 1977 para supervisar los asuntos de la nación en materia de energía. **755**

depression/depresión Fuerte disminución de las actividades comerciales de un país, acompañada por el aumento del desempleo. **30**

détente/détente Periodo de la década de 1970 en el que se redujeron las tensiones entre Estados Unidos y la Unión Soviética. **745**

direct primary/elecciones primarias Elección nominal en la que los votantes eligen a sus candidatos para las elecciones generales. **298**

disarmament/desarme Reducción de las fuerzas militares de un país. **503**

Dixiecrats/Dixiecrats Partido de los Derechos de los Estados creado en 1946 por demócratas del sur insatisfechos con la política del presidente Harry S Truman en materia de derechos civiles. **596**

dollar diplomacy/diplomacia del dólar Política adoptada por el presidente William Howard Taft para influir en los países de América Latina mediante el poder económico en lugar del poder militar. **344**

domino theory/teoría del dominó Creencia común en la época de la guerra fría que explicaba que si una nación del sudeste de Asia caía víctima del comunismo, las demás naciones de la zona también caerían. **708**

doves/palomas Estadounidenses que se oponían a la intervención de Estados Unidos en la guerra de Vietnam. **717**

Dred Scott* decision/decisión *Dred Scott (1857) Decisión de la Suprema Corte que negaba a los afroestadounidenses el derecho de ser ciudadanos, prohibía la restricción de la esclavitud en Missouri y establecía que el Congreso no tenía autoridad para abolir la esclavitud en territorio federal. **91**

Dust Bowl/Cuenca del Polvo Nombre dado en la década de 1930 a una región de las Grandes Planicies debido a la severa sequía que la había afectado. **482**

E

Education Amendments Act/Ley de enmiendas educativas (1972) Ley federal que prohibía la discriminación sexual en las universidades. **680**

Education for All Handicapped Children Act/Ley de educación para los niños discapacitados (1975) Ley federal que obligaba a las escuelas públicas a ofrecer educación a los niños con discapacidad física o mental. **691**

Eighteenth Amendment/Decimoctava enmienda (1919) Enmienda constitucional que prohibió la fabricación, venta y transporte de bebidas alcohólicas durante la prohibición; esta ley fue anulada en 1933. **289**

elastic clause/cláusula elástica "Cláusula propia y necesaria"; cláusula de la constitución de Estados Unidos que permite al Congreso ejercer cualquier acción no prohibida de manera específica por la Constitución. **35**

electors/electores Delegados elegidos por los legisladores estatales para representar el voto popular en las elecciones federales. **33**

Elementary and Secondary Education Act/Ley de educación primaria y secundaria (1965) Ley federal que otorgó 1,300 millones de dólares para construir escuelas rurales en áreas marginadas. **642**

Elkins Act/Ley de Elkins (1903) Ley federal que prohibió realizar rebajas de precio en los embarques. **305**

Emancipation Proclamation/Proclamación de Emancipación (1863) Decreto anunciado por el presidente Abraham Lincoln en 1862 para abolir la esclavitud en los territorios que se rebelaran contra la Unión; este decreto entró en vigor el 1 de enero de 1863. **114**

Employment Act/Ley de empleos (1946) Ley que creó el Consejo de Consultores de Economía y declaró que el gobierno era capaz de promover el empleo y la producción sin ayuda externa. **592**

Endangered Species Act/Ley de especies en peligro de extinción (1973) Decreto que protege a la vida silvestre en peligro de desaparecer. **744**

Enforcement Acts/leyes de ejecución (1870–1871) Conjunto de tres leyes aprobadas por el Congreso con la finalidad de permitir al gobierno el uso de las fuerza militar para detener la violencia en contra de los afroestadounidenses del sur. **145**

Enola Gay/Enola Gay Nombre del bombardero B-29 que lanzó la primera bomba atómica en Hiroshima el 6 de agosto de 1945. **553**

Environmental Protection Agency/Departamento de protección al medio ambiente (EPA, por sus siglas en inglés) Agencia federal establecida en 1970 para supervisar la aplicación de las leyes de protección del ambiente. **744**

Equal Pay Act/Ley de pago igualitario (1963) Ley federal que prohibía a los empleadores pagar menores salarios a las mujeres que a los hombres por desempeñar el mismo trabajo. **677**

Equal Rights Amendment/Enmienda de Derechos Igualitarios (ERA, por sus siglas en inglés) Propuesta de enmienda constitucional que garantizaba los derechos de la mujer al prohibir la discriminación por género. **399**

escalation/intensificación Política del presidente Lyndon B. Johnson para aumentar de manera gradual el número de tropas estadounidenses en la guerra de Vietnam. **713**

Espionage Act/Ley de espionaje (1917) Ley federal que prohibió cualquier acto de traición al país durante la Primera Guerra Mundial. **374**

European Union/Unión Europea de Naciones (EU, por sus siglas en inglés) Agrupación formada por las naciones de Europa Occidental en 1993. **815**

Exodusters/Éxodo Afroestadounidenses que emigraron al oeste a finales del siglo XIX. **172**

F

Fair Deal/*Fair Deal* Programas de reforma propuestos por el presidente Harry S Truman en las elecciones de 1948 que produjeron buenos y malos resultados. **597**

Fair Employment Practices Committee/Comité de Prácticas Justas en el Empleo (FEPC, por sus siglas en inglés) Grupo creado en 1941 para evitar la discriminación en las industrias de guerra y en los empleos ofrecidos por el gobierno. **539**

Family and Medical Leave Act/Ley de ausencia por motivos familiares y médicos (1993) Ley federal que permite a los empleados recibir permisos hasta por 12 semanas sin goce de sueldo por razones personales o de salud, sin perder sus prestaciones ni su empleo. **814**

Family Assistance Plan/Plan de Apoyo Familiar (FAP, por sus siglas en inglés) Propuesta del presidente Richard M. Nixon y rechazada por el Congreso para reemplazar el sistema de ayuda social con la finalidad de garantizar a las familias un ingreso mínimo específico. **740**

Fascist Party/Partido Fascista Partido político fundado en Italia en la década de 1920 con la creencia de que un gobierno militarizado tendría mayor control en todos los aspectos de la sociedad. **512**

Federal Deposit Insurance Corporation/Corporación de Seguros para Depósitos Federales (FDIC, por sus siglas en inglés) Agencia creada en 1933 por el *New Deal* con el propósito de asegurar los depósitos en los bancos. **469**

federalism/federalismo Sistema de gobierno en el que el poder se divide en una administración central y varias administraciones estatales. **34**

Federalists/federalistas Personas que apoyan un gobierno fuerte y la ratificación de la Constitución. **32**

Federal Project Number One/Proyecto Federal Número Uno Programa del *New Deal* que fomentaba el orgullo de la cultura estadounidense mediante obras de artistas y escritores reconocidos. **487**

Federal Reserve Act/Ley de la reserva federal Ley que creó un sistema bancario nacional para ayudar al gobierno a regular la economía. **316**

Federal Trade Commission/Comisión Federal de Comercio (FTC, por sus siglas en inglés) Comisión establecida en 1914 para investigar a las corporaciones y evitar que realizaran prácticas ilegales de comercio. **317**

feminists–House of Burgesses

feminists/feministas Activistas que luchan por los derechos de la mujer. **399**

feudalism/feudalismo Sistema común en la Edad Media en el que los comunes juraban lealtad y ayuda militar a los gobernantes a cambio de tierras y protección. **5**

Fifteenth Amendment/Decimoquinta enmienda (1870) Enmienda constitucional que otorgó el derecho al voto a los afroestadounidenses. **142**

54th Massachusetts Infantry/54ava Infantería de Massachusetts Regimiento de la Unión formado por afroestadounidenses que participó en la toma del Fuerte Wagner en Carolina del Sur durante la Guerra Civil. **115**

First Battle of Bull Run/Primera Batalla de Bull Run (1861) Batalla de Manassas; victoria del Ejército Confederado en la primera batalla importante de la Guerra Civil. **101**

flappers/*flappers* Mujeres jóvenes que en la década de 1920 desafiaron las tradiciones sociales con su vestimenta y conducta. **423**

flexible response/respuesta flexible Estrategia del presidente John F. Kennedy para ofrecer mayor variedad de opciones en las negociaciones de los conflictos internacionales. **626**

Food Administration/Administración de Alimentos Agencia creada durante la Primera Guerra Mundial y encabezada por Herbert Hoover para fomentar el desarrollo agrícola y la conservación de los suministros alimentarios existentes. **369**

Foraker Act/Ley Foraker (1900) Ley federal que permitía a Estados Unidos designar un gobernador y la cámara alta de Puerto Rico; los ciudadanos de ese país sólo podían elegir a sus representantes en la cámara baja. **340**

Fordney-McCumber Tariff Act/Ley de aranceles Fordney-McCumber (1922) Ley federal que aumentó los aranceles de los productos manufacturados y redujo los de los productos agrícolas importados. **398**

Fourteen Points/Los catorce puntos (1918) Plan del presidente Woodrow Wilson para reorganizar a la naciones europeas después de la Primera Guerra Mundial y evitar futuras guerras. **378**

Fourteenth Amendment/Decimocuarta enmienda (1868) Enmienda constitucional que otorgaba derechos de ciudadano a toda persona nacida dentro de Estados Unidos, excepto a los indígenas. **138**

Freedmen's Bureau/Oficina de liberados Agencia creada por el Congreso en 1865 para ayudar a las personas sin hogar ni recursos en los estados del sur durante la Guerra Civil. **137**

freedom of contract/libertad de contrato Libertad de los trabajadores para negociar los términos de sus contratos. **283**

Freedom Riders/Jinetes por la libertad Grupo de defensores de los derechos civiles que en 1961 recorrieron los estados del sur en autobús para protestar por la segregación racial en los autobuses públicos. **651**

Freedom Summer/Verano de la libertad Campaña de registro de votantes afroestadounidenses en Mississippi en el verano de 1964. **658**

free enterprise/libre empresa Creencia de que la economía sólo prosperaría mediante la negociación comercial sin restricciones del gobierno, en un mercado libre. **72, 201**

Fundamentalism/fundamentalismo Movimiento religioso que declara que el contenido de la Biblia es cierto por naturaleza. **428**

Fundamental Orders of Connecticut/Decretos Fundamentales de Connecticut (1639) Documento redactado en la época colonial que se considera como la primera Constitución del mundo. **12**

G

generation gap/brecha generacional Diferencia en edad, actitud y tendencias culturales de diferentes generaciones, especialmente entre las personas nacidas en el auge de los bebés y sus familiares mayores. **694**

genocide/genocidio Asesinato deliberado de una gran cantidad de personas. **545**

Gettysburg Address/Discurso de Gettysburg (1863) Discurso del presidente Abraham Lincoln al dedicar un cementerio a la Batalla de Gettysburg Virginia que se convirtió en una declaración clásica de los ideales democráticos. **119**

GI Bill of Rights/Carta GI de derechos (1944) Ley de reajuste para los hombres en servicio; esta ley ofreció pensiones y préstamos a los veteranos de guerra para ayudarlos en sus necesidades educativas, de vivienda o para emprender negocios. **592**

Gilded Age/Época de la codicia Nombre dado por Mark Twain y Charles Dudley Warner a la época de finales del siglo XIX para referirse a la corrupción y avaricia que se ocultaba detrás de la máscara de la sociedad. **255**

glasnost/Glasnost Política soviética desarrollada en la década de 1980 para promover la apertura política y la libertad de expresión. **781**

---

gold standard/estándar del oro Sistema monetario en el que una reserva de oro determina el valor de la moneda. **262**

Gone With the Wind/Lo que el viento se llevó (1936) Novela de Margaret Mitchell que se convirtió en la obra más vendida en la década de 1930 y en una de las películas más importantes de todos los tiempos desde su presentación en 1939. **488**

Good Neighbor policy/política del buen vecino Política del presidente Franklin D. Roosevelt para promover las buenas relaciones de Estados Unidos con América Latina basándose en el respeto mutuo. **508**

graduated income tax/impuesto acorde al ingreso Sistema en el que el impuesto pagado por una persona depende de sus ingresos. **260**

graft/soborno Adquisición de poder económico o político mediante el uso de prácticas deshonestas o ilegales. **249**

Gramm-Rudman-Hollings Act/Ley de Gramm-Rudman-Hollings (1985) ley que obliga al gobierno a reducir sus gastos cuando sobrepasa cierto límite en su déficit. **778**

Grapes of Wrath, The/Las uvas de la ira (1939) Novela clásica de John Steinbeck acerca de los migrantes de la Cuenca del Polvo durante la Gran Depresión. **488**

Gray Panthers/Panteras grises Grupo de activistas fundado en 1970 por Maggie Kuhn para luchar por los derechos de las personas de edad avanzada. **692**

Great Depression/Gran Depresión Seria disminución del desarrollo económico que inició con el colapso del mercado de valores en 1929. **445**

Great Migration/Gran Migración Migración masiva de afroestadounidenses a los estados del norte durante y después de la Primera Guerra Mundial. **372**

Great Society/Gran Sociedad Programa de mejoramiento de la sociedad estadounidense implantado por el presidente Lyndon B. Johnson. **640**

Great Upheaval/Gran Levantamiento (1886) Año de constantes huelgas y violentos enfrentamientos laborales en Estados Unidos. **213**

gross national product/Producto Interno Bruto Valor total de los bienes y servicios producidos por un país en un año. **445**

H

habeas corpus/habeas corpus Protección constitucional contra la aprehensión ilegal de una persona. **109**

hard-rock mining/minería de suelo duro Técnica minera en la que es necesario cavar profundos túneles para llegar a los yacimientos minerales. **187**

Harlem Renaissance/Renacimiento de Harlem Periodo de desarrollo artístico afroestadounidense iniciado en la década de 1920 en el vecindario de Harlem, Nueva York. **432**

hawks/Halcones Estadounidenses que apoyaron la intervención de Estados Unidos en la guerra de Vietnam. **717**

Hay–Bunau-Varilla Treaty/Tratado Hay–Bunau-Varilla (1903) Acuerdo que daba a Estados Unidos soberanía en el canal y un rango de 10 millas a ambos lados del istmo de Panamá. **341**

Haymarket Riot/revuelta de Haymarket (1886) Explosión de una bomba durante una protesta realizada en la plaza Haymarket de Chicago que dio como resultado varios oficiales de policía muertos. **213**

Hepburn Act/Ley de Hepburn (1906) Ley que autorizaba a la Comisión Interestatal de Comercio a definir las tarifas ferroviarias y regular las compañías que participaban en el comercio interestatal. **305**

Highway Act/Ley de carreteras (1956) Ley que designó una cantidad de dinero para la creación de un sistema nacional de carreteras. **600**

Ho Chi Minh Trail/Sendero Ho Chi Min Red de senderos y caminos que comunicaba a Vietnam del Norte desde Laos y Camboya con Vietnam del Sur; ésta fue la principal ruta de envío de suministros para el Vietcong. **714**

Hollywood Ten/Los Diez de Hollywood Grupo de directores y escritores de cine que fueron enviados a la cárcel sin ser sometidos a un interrogatorio del Comité de Actividades Antiestadounidenses. **579**

Holocaust/Holocausto Asesinato de millares de judíos europeos a manos de los nazis. **545**

Homestead Act/Ley de colonización (1862) Ley que fomentaba la migración al oeste mediante la cesión de tierras a quien lo solicitara. **170**

horizontal integration/integración horizontal Propiedad de las compañías que intervienen en la elaboración de un mismo producto. **205**

hot line/línea caliente Conexión vía teletipo entre Estados Unidos y la Unión Soviética que permitía a los líderes de estas naciones comunicarse de manera directa. **630**

House of Burgesses/Casa de los Burgueses Asamblea de representantes de Virginia en la época de la colonia. **10**

House Un-American Activities Committee/Comité de Actividades Antiestadounidenses (HUAC, por sus siglas en inglés) Comité establecido originalmente en 1938 para investigar actividades fascistas; más tarde conocido por investigar brotes de comunismo entre los ciudadanos a finales de la década de 1940. **579**

hydraulic mining/minería hidráulica Técnica minera que usa chorros de agua a presión para remover la grava y la tierra de los yacimientos minerales. **187**

hydrogen bomb/bomba de hidrógeno Bomba H; tipo de bomba nuclear. **583**

I

Immigration Act of 1924/Ley de inmigración de 1924 Ley federal que redujo la cantidad de inmigrantes permitidos a cada nación al 2 por ciento de las cifras del censo de 1890. **408**

Immigration Act of 1990/Ley de inmigración de 1990 Ley federal que aumentó la cantidad de inmigrantes permitidos en Estados Unidos. **813**

Immigration Restriction League/Liga de Restricción de Inmigración Organización formada en 1894 para imponer un examen de alfabetización a los inmigrantes llegados a Estados Unidos. **225**

imperialism/imperialismo Lucha por la expansión colonial. **326**

Inca/Inca Civilización establecida en la región de los Andes en América del Sur. **5**

Industrial Workers of the World/Trabajadores Industriales del Mundo (IWW, por sus siglas en inglés) Unión formada en 1905 como medida de oposición contra el capitalismo. **284**

initiative/iniciativa Política que permite a los votantes proponer nuevas leyes. **299**

Initiative on Race/Iniciativa racial Iniciativa lanzada en 1997 por el presidente Bill Clinton para fomentar el análisis de los asuntos y problemas raciales. **806**

insider trading/intercambio interno Uso de información financiera por parte de los corredores de bolsa para obtener ganancias personales. **778**

installment plan/plan de pagos Método de compra en el que el consumidor liquida el valor de un producto mediante una serie de pagos. **420**

Intermediate-Range Nuclear Forces Treaty/Tratado de Fuerzas Nucleares de Alcance Medio (INF, por sus siglas en inglés) (1987) Tratado firmado por el presidente de Estados Unidos Ronald Reagan y el líder soviético Mikhail Gorvachev para eliminar el armamento nuclear de alcance medio en Europa. **782**

Internal Security Act/Ley de seguridad interna (1950) Ley que obligaba a supuestos grupos comunistas a registrarse ante el gobierno, además de imponer un control de inmigración más estricto hacia los posibles simpatizantes del comunismo. **580**

International Ladies' Garment Workers Union/Unión Internacional de Trabajadoras de la Industria Textil (ILGWU, por sus siglas en inglés) Influyente unión creada en Nueva York en 1900 con el propósito de organizar a las trabajadoras del ramo textil. **284**

Internet/Internet Sistema mundial de redes de computadoras. **811**

internment/internamiento Reubicación obligatoria de prisioneros. **540**

Interstate Commerce Act/Ley de comercio interestatal (1887) Ley que regulaba el envío de productos por ferrocarril entre estados. **260**

Intolerable Acts/Leyes intolerables (1774) Leyes de coerción; conjunto de cuatro leyes aprobadas por el Parlamento para castigar a los colonos que habían participado en el Motín del té y reforzar el control de las colonias. **16**

Iran-Contra affair/Asunto Irán-Contras Nombre con el que se conoció el escándalo en que participó la administración Reagan en la década de 1980 al vender en secreto armas a Irán a cambio de la liberación de un grupo de rehenes estadounidenses en Líbano, y después usar las ganancias para patrocinar al grupo de los Contras en Nicaragua. **779**

Iran hostage crisis/Crisis de rehenes en Irán (1979–81) Situación de los 52 estadounidenses que fueron mantenidos como rehenes en la embajada de Estados Unidos en Teherán. **770**

island-hopping/islas importantes Estrategia de las tropas estadounidenses para invadir sólo aquellas islas del Pacífico que favorecieran el avance de los aliados contra Japón en la Segunda Guerra Mundial. **549**

isolationism/aislamiento Política que prohíbe a un país participar en los asuntos internos de otros. **502**

J

jazz/jazz Música que combina varios estilos musicales afroestadounidenses y que surgió en Nueva Orleáns y cobró popularidad a nivel nacional en la década de 1920. **430**

Jim Crow laws/Leyes de Jim Crow Leyes que favorecían la segregación en los estados del sur. **150**

Jones Act of 1916/Ley Jones de 1916 Ley estadounidense que dio a los filipinos el derecho de elegir a sus representantes en ambas cámaras del Congreso. **339**

judicial review/revisión judicial Poder que tiene la corte para declarar anticonstitucional una decisión del Congreso. **76**

Judiciary Act of 1789/Ley judicial de 1789 Ley que creó el Sistema Federal de Justicia. **70**

juvenile delinquency/delincuencia juvenil Conducta antisocial de algunos jóvenes. **604**

K

kamikaze/kamikaze Aviones japoneses suicidas de la Segunda Guerra Mundial. **552**

Kansas-Nebraska Act/Ley Kansas-Nebraska (1854) Ley que estableció los territorios de Kansas y Nebraska, además de permitir a los votantes decidir si la esclavitud debía ser abolida o permitida. **90**

Keating-Owen Child Labor Act/Ley Keating-Owen del trabajo de menores (1916) Ley que prohibió la venta interestatal de productos fabricados con mano de obra infantil; esta ley fue declarada anticonstitucional por la Suprema Corte en 1918. **318**

Kellogg-Briand Pact/Pacto Kellogg-Briand (1928) Pacto firmado por Estados Unidos y otras 14 naciones para hacer ilegal la guerra, excepto en los casos de autodefensa. **505**

Kent State shootings/matanza de Kent (1970) Incidente en el que la Guardia Nacional disparó contra un grupo de estudiantes durante una manifestación contra la guerra de Vietnam en la universidad de Kent, Ohio, matando a cuatro personas. **724**

Kentucky and Virginia Resolutions/Resoluciones de Kentucky y Virginia Declaraciones aprobadas en 1798 y 1799 para enunciar las leyes de extranjerismo y sedición. **75**

Kerner Commission/Comisión Kerner Comisión federal que al investigar las revueltas de la década de los 60 llegó a la conclusión de que fueron ocasionados por el racismo de los blancos. **666**

kickbacks/retribuciones Pago de una parte de las ganancias por un trabajo. **249**

Knights of Labor/Caballeros del Trabajo Fundado en 1869, fue uno de los primeros sindicatos laborales de Estados Unidos; en 1879 empezó a aceptar personas de diferentes razas, géneros y habilidades. **212**

Kosovo crisis/Crisis de Kosovo Resultado de una violenta campaña lanzada por las fuerzas serbias contra los albaneses de Kosovo; fue controlada por escuadrones de bombarderos de la ONU en 1999. **808**

Kristallnacht/Kristallnacht (1938) "La noche de los vidrios rotos"; 9 de noviembre; noche en que los alemanes destruyeron una gran cantidad de edificios judíos. **514**

Ku Klux Klan/Ku Klux Klan Sociedad secreta formada en 1866 por antiguos partidarios de la confederación que usa el terror y la violencia para reprimir los derechos civiles de los afroestadounidenses. **144**

L

La Huelga/La Huelga (1965–70) Huelga exitosa realizada en California por trabajadores del campo encabezados por César Chávez en contra de los productores de uvas. **683**

La Raza Unida Party/Partido de La Raza Unida (RUP, por sus iniciales en inglés) Partido político méxico-estadounidense formado por José Ángel Gutiérrez a finales de la década de 1960. **687**

League of Nations/Liga de las Naciones Organismo internacional de naciones formado en 1919 con la finalidad de prevenir guerras. **378**

League of United Latin American Citizens/Liga de Ciudadanos Latinoamericanos Unidos (LULAC, por sus iniciales en inglés) Grupo formado en 1929 para apoyar las causas y resolver los problemas de las personas de origen hispano. **611**

Lend-Lease Act/Ley de préstamos (1941) Ley que permitía a Estados Unidos ofrecer armas y otros suministros de guerra a las Potencias Aliadas para combatir a las potencias del Eje durante la Segunda Guerra Mundial. **521**

Limited Nuclear Test Ban Treaty/Tratado de Prohibición Parcial de Armas Nucleares (1963) Acuerdo firmado entre el presidente de Estados Unidos John F. Kennedy y el líder soviético Nikita Khrushchev para prohibir las pruebas de armas nucleares no subterráneas. **630**

literacy tests/pruebas de alfabetismo Pruebas usadas para evitar que las personas que no supieran leer pudieran votar. **149**

Little Rock Nine–National American Woman Suffrage Association

Little Rock Nine/Los Nueve de LittleRock Los nueve estudiantes afroestadounidenses que se inscribieron por primera vez en la secundaria central de Little Rock, Arkansas en 1957. **608**

long drives/arreo de ganado Largos recorridos en que los arrieros llevaban al ganado de los ranchos a las estaciones de ferrocarril para ser transportados. **178**

loose construction/libre interpretación Filosofía de interpretación constitucional; explica que dentro de los límites de la nación el gobierno puede adoptar cualquier medida que la constitución no prohíba directamente. **72**

Los Angeles riots/disturbios de Los Ángeles (1992) Disturbios ocasionados cuando cuatro policías de raza blanca fueron acusados de utilizar la fuerza bruta en contra de un conductor afroestadounidense. **806**

Lost Generation/generación perdida Grupo de escritores cuya obra refleja los horrores de muerte y destrucción ocurridos durante la Primera Guerra Mundial además de criticar severamente el consumismo y la superficialidad de la época de la posguerra. **435**

Louisiana Purchase/Compra de Louisiana (1803) Proceso mediante el cual Estados Unidos compró el territorio francés localizado entre el río Mississippi y las Montañas Rocosas. **76**

M

Maginot Line/Línea Maginot Línea de defensa construida por los franceses a lo largo de su frontera con Alemania después de la Primera Guerra Mundial. **521**

Manhattan Project/Proyecto Manhattan Proyecto secreto creado en 1942 por el gobierno de Estados Unidos para desarrollar la bomba atómica. **553**

manifest destiny/destino manifiesto Creencia de muchos estadounidenses de mediados del siglo XIX de que Dios había destinado la expansión de Estados Unidos hacia el oeste. **86**

Mann-Elkins Act/Ley de Mann-Elkins (1910) Ley federal que otorgaba a las compañías de telégrafos y teléfonos los mismos poderes regulatorios de la Comisión Interestatal de Comercio. **310**

Marbury v. Madison/Marbury versus Madison (1803) Caso en que la Suprema Corte estableció el principio de la revisión judicial. **76**

margin buying/compras al margen Compra de bienes con dinero de otras personas. **443**

Marshall Plan/Plan Marshall Programa de recuperación en que Estados Unidos ofrecía apoyo económico a los países europeos para ayudarlos a recuperar su economía después de la Segunda Guerra Mundial. **569**

Massacre at Wounded Knee/Matanza de Wounded Knee (1890) Suceso en que el ejército de Estados Unidos asesinó a alrededor de 300 indios Sioux en el arroyo Wounded Knee al sur de Dakota; este suceso dio por terminada la guerra por las Grandes Planicies. **166**

mass transit/tránsito masivo Sistemas de transporte público como los trolebuses y el tren subterráneo **226**

Maya/maya Civilización mesoamericana que tuvo su auge alrededor del año 300 después de Cristo. **5**

Mayaguez /Mayaguez Barco de carga estadounidense sin armamento secuestrado por comunistas camboyanos en 1975; 41 estadounidenses murieron en su intento por rescatar a los 40 integrantes de la tripulación. **752**

Mayflower Compact/Síntesis del Mayflower (1620) Documento redactado por los colonos en el que se establecía una forma de autogobierno basada en las decisiones de los ancianos de la iglesia. **10**

McClure's Magazine /McClure's Magazine Publicación de tipo progresista que analizaba la corrupción en la política y el comercio. **277**

Meat Inspection Act/Ley de inspección de la carne (1906) Ley federal que hacía obligatoria la inspección de la carne que cruzara los límites estatales. **306**

Medicaid /Medicaid Programa federal creado en 1965 para brindar asistencia médica gratuita a las personas de bajos recursos. **641**

Medicare /Medicare Programa federal de seguro médico para personas mayores de 65 años; fue creado en 1965. **641**

mergers/fusión Combinación de dos o más compañías con la finalidad de aumentar su eficiencia y ganancias. **398**

Mexican American Youth Organization/Organización Juvenil México-estadounidense (MAYO, por sus siglas en inglés) Grupo activista mexicano–estadounidense fundado en 1967 por estudiantes universitarios en San Antonio, Texas. **687**

Mexican Cession/cesión mexicana Tierras que México cedió a Estados Unidos mediante la firma del Tratado de Guadalupe Hidalgo después de la guerra entre Estados Unidos y México; el territorio cedido incluyó a California, Nevada y Utah, así como parte de Arizona, Colorado, Nuevo México, Texas y Wyoming. **87**

Mexican Revolution/Revolución Mexicana Lucha contra la dictadura que condujo a México a muchos años de inestabilidad a principios del siglo XX. **346**

Middle Passage/Travesía media Viaje que hacían los barcos que transportaban esclavos africanos a través del océano Atlántico para llegar a Estados Unidos y las Indias Occidentales. **13**

Migrant Mother/Madre en migración La imagen más famosa de la fotógrafa Dorothea Lange durante la época de la Gran Depresión en la que muestra a una madre exhausta y su hijo; esta imagen logró que los trabajadores migratorios de California recibieran mayor apoyo. **484**

militarism/militarismo Glorificación del poder militar. **357**

Mir /Mir Estación espacial rusa; sitio de reunión de estadounidenses y rusos en convenios espaciales en la década de 1990. **810**

Mississippi Freedom Democratic Party/Partido Demócrata de Liberación del Mississippi (MFDP, por sus siglas en inglés) Grupo que envió a sus propios delegados a la Convención Nacional Demócrata de 1964 para protestar por la discriminación racial contra los votantes de raza negra. **659**

Missouri Compromise/Compromiso de Missouri (1820) Acuerdo propuesto por Henry Clay para permitir que Missouri se incorporara a la Unión sin abolir la esclavitud en su territorio y a Maine como estado libre, además de prohibir la esclavitud al norte del meridiano 36°30' a partir de la Compra de Louisiana. **80**

Model T/Modelo T Automóvil popular de bajo costo creado por Henry Ford en 1908. **415**

Modern Republicanism/republicanismo moderno Nombre dado al intento del presidente Dwight D. Eisenhower por equilibrar las reformas liberales del país con un presupuesto conservador en la década de 1950. **598**

monopoly/monopolio Control económico exclusivo de una industria. **203**

Monroe Doctrine/Doctrina Monroe (1823) Declaración en la que el presidente James Monroe expresaba su decisión de no interferir en la relación de los países europeos con sus colonias en América, aunque consideraba un acto de hostilidad cualquier intento por crear nuevas colonias en el hemisferio occidental. **79**

Montgomery Improvement Association/Asociación de Mejoras Montgomery (MIA, por sus siglas en inglés) Organización formada en 1956 por afroestadounidenses de Montgomery, Alabama, y encabezada por Martin Luther King Jr. para apoyar el boicot a los autobuses y coordinar las protestas de los afroestadounidenses. **610**

Moral Majority/Mayoría Moral Organización conservadora político religiosa que se fundó en 1979. **771**

Morrill Act/Ley de Morrill (1862) Ley federal que otorgó territorio a los estados del oeste para que construyeran escuelas de agricultura e ingeniería. **170**

muckrakers/muckrakers Periodistas investigadores que escribían sobre la corrupción en las empresas y la política, con la esperanza de propiciar la reforma. **277**

mugwumps/mugwumps "Grandes jefes"; la manera de referirse a los reformadores republicanos que apoyaban al demócrata Grover Cleveland en la elección presidencial de 1884. **257**

Muller v. Oregon/Muller versus Oregón (1908) Caso de la Suprema Corte que sostuvo la legislación que protegía a las trabajadoras en Oregón. **283**

multinational corporations/corporaciones multinacionales Compañías que invierten dinero en nuevos negocios diversos a escala internacional. **816**

Munich Conference/Conferencia de Munich (1938) Reunión de líderes ingleses, franceses, alemanes e italianos donde Alemania recibió el control de Sudetenland a cambio de la promesa del líder alemán Adolf Hitler de no reclamar más territorio europeo. **518**

mutualistas/mutualistas Sociedades de apoyo mutuo que formaron las comunidades mexicano-estadounidenses para ayudar a los residentes locales. **450**

N

National Aeronautics and Space Administration/Administración Nacional de Aeronáutica y el Espacio (NASA, por sus siglas en inglés) Agencia fundada por el Congreso en 1958 para promover la tecnología espacial. **585**

National American Woman Suffrage Association/Asociación Nacional por el Sufragio de la Mujer Estadounidense (NAWSA, por sus siglas en inglés) Grupo formado en 1890 para lograr que las mujeres tuvieran derecho al voto. **319**

National Association for the Advancement of Colored People/Asociación Nacional por el Progreso de las Personas de Color (NAACP, por sus siglas en inglés) Grupo fundado por W. E. B. Du Bois y otros más en 1909 para dar fin a la discriminación racial. **291**

National Black Political Convention/Convención Nacional de Política para Personas de Color (1972) Reunión de activistas de derechos civiles que se celebró con el fin de asegurar que los afroestadounidenses continuaran ganando influencia política. **671**

National Defense Act/Ley de defensa nacional (1916) Programa de preparación militar establecido antes de la entrada de Estados Unidos a la Primera Guerra Mundial, y que incrementó la dimensión de la Guardia Nacional y del ejército regular de Estados Unidos. **363**

National Defense Education Act/Ley de educación de la eefensa nacional (1958) Ley federal que asignó dinero para mejorar la educación en ciencias, matemáticas e idiomas extranjeros. **585**

National Energy Act/Ley nacional de energía (1978) Ley aprobada para aligerar la crisis de energía. **755**

National Grange/Agricultura Nacional (*Natio nal Grange of the Patrons of Husbandry*) Protectores de la Agricultura; organización fundada por Oliver Hudson Kelley en 1867; abordaba asuntos económicos y políticos relacionados con los agricultores. **260**

National Industrial Recovery Act/Ley de recuperación de la industria nacional (NIRA, por sus siglas en inglés) (1933) Ley federal elaborada para alentar el crecimiento económico mediante la suspensión de las leyes antimonopolio y la eliminación de la competencia desleal entre patronos; se declaró como constitucional en 1935. **470**

nationalism/nacionalismo Orgullo o lealtad nacional. **79**

nationalize/nacionalizar Ejercer el control del gobierno sobre un negocio. **509**

National Organization for Women/Organización Nacional para la Mujer (NOW, por sus siglas en inglés) Grupo en favor de los derechos de la mujer; se formó en 1966 para presionar a los funcionarios electos con el objeto de asegurar la igualdad social y política de la mujer. **678**

National Park Service/Servicio Nacional de Parques Instancia federal que se fundó en 1916 para ayudar a supervisar los parques y monumentos nacionales. **309**

National Security Council/Consejo Nacional de Seguridad (NSC, por sus siglas en inglés) Organización que el Congreso creó en 1947 para dar asesoría al presidente en cuestiones estratégicas. **579**

National Urban League/Liga Nacional Urbana Grupo fundado en 1911 para luchar a favor de la igualdad racial. **291**

National War Labor Board/Consejo Nacional de Trabajos de Guerra (NWLB, por sus siglas en inglés) Oficina creada durante la Primera Guerra Mundial para resolver las disputas entre trabajadores y patronos. **370**

National Women's Political Caucus/Junta Nacional de Mujeres Políticas Grupo fundado por Gloria Steinem y otros más en 1971 para promover que las mujeres se postularan para puestos políticos. **679**

National Youth Administration/Administración Juvenil Nacional Agencia del *New Deal* que ofreció trabajos de medio tiempo a personas entre los 16 y los 25 años de edad. **476**

Nation of Islam/Nación del Islam Musulmanes negros; grupo religioso nacionalista fundado por Wallace D. Fard en 1930. **661**

nativism/nativismo Preferencia para los nacidos en Estados Unidos por encima de quienes no eran originarios. **82**

NATO/NATO (por sus siglas en inglés) Organización del Tratado del Atlántico Norte (OTAN); alianza conformada en 1949 entre Estados Unidos, los países de Europa Occidental y otras naciones con el objeto de defenderse entre sí en caso de algún ataque. **571**

Nazi Party/Partido Nazi Partido Nacional Socialista; grupo político presidido por Adolf Hitler que en la década de 1930 llegó al poder en Alemania. **513**

New Deal/*New Deal*** Programas del presidente Franklin D. Roosevelt para ayudar la economía de Estados Unidos durante la Gran Depresión. **468**

New Freedom/Nueva Libertad Reforma progresiva del presidente Woodrow Wilson; se propuso durante las elecciones presidenciales de 1912. **313**

New Frontier/Nuevas Fronteras Agenda doméstica del presidente John F. Kennedy. **634**

new immigrants/nuevos inmigrantes Inmigrantes que llegaron a Estados Unidos entre la década de 1880 y la de 1910, en su mayoría provenientes del sur y el este de Europa. **220**

New Right/Nuevos Derechos Grupos diversos de votantes conservadores cuyo poder político creció en la década de 1980. **771**

Nineteenth Amendment/Decimonovena enmienda (1920) Enmienda constitucional que garantizaba a las mujeres el derecho al voto. **321**

no-man's-land/Tierra de nadie Franja de territorio de bombardeo que separaba las trincheras de posiciones enemigas en el frente occidental durante la Primera Guerra Mundial. **358**

nonaggression pact/pacto de no agresión (1939) Acuerdo entre el líder alemán Adolf Hitler y el líder soviético Joseph Stalin para no atacarse mutuamente y repartirse el territorio de Polonia. **519**

nonviolent resistance/resistencia de no violencia Estrategia de protesta que hace un llamado a las manifestaciones pacíficas y rechaza a la violencia. **650**

North American Free Trade Agreement/Tratado de Libre Comercio de América del Norte (NAFTA, por sus siglas en inglés; TLC, en español) (1993) Acuerdo comercial entre Estados Unidos, México y Canadá. **815**

Northwest Ordinance/Ordenanza del Noroeste (1787) Ley creada para establecer un sistema de gobierno en el territorio del noroeste. **30**

nouveau riche/nouveau rice "Nuevo rico"; nueva clase social de comerciantes surgida a finales del siglo XIX, la mayoría de los cuales había obtenido su fortuna mediante la venta de productos durante la Revolución Industrial. **228**

Nuremberg Trials/Juicios de Nuremberg Enjuiciamiento de funcionarios nazis de alto rango acusados de crímenes de guerra que llevó a cabo un tribunal militar internacional en la ciudad de Nuremberg, Alemania, a partir de 1945. **562**

Office of Economic Opportunity/Departamento de Oportunidades Económicas (OEO, por sus siglas en inglés) Agencia creada por el gobierno en 1964 para coordinar los programas de lucha contra la pobreza. **639**

Office of War Information/Departamento de Información de Guerra Agencia que controlaba el flujo de noticias provenientes de los sitios en conflicto durante la Segunda Guerra Mundial. **535**

Office of War Mobilization/Departamento de Movilización de Guerra (OWM, por sus siglas en inglés) Agencia federal que coordinaba a todos los departamentos del gobierno que participaban en la Segunda Guerra Mundial. **530**

Older Americans Act/Ley de ciudadanos de edad avanzada (1965) Ley mediante la cual el gobierno se comprometió a ofrecer ayuda médica y económica a las personas de edad avanzada. **693**

old immigrants/primeros inmigrantes Inmigrantes que llegaron a Estados Unidos antes de la década de 1880, la mayoría de ellos protestantes provenientes del noroeste de Europa. **220**

Open Door Policy/política de puertas abiertas (1899) Declaración en la que el secretario de estado John Hay demandaba iguales privilegios para todas las naciones que tuvieran relaciones comerciales y de inversión con China. **330**

open range/campo abierto Tierras comunes usadas por todos los ganaderos. **180**

open shop/taller franco Lugar de trabajo no sindicalizado. **284**

Operation Desert Storm/Operación Tormenta del Desierto (1991) Ataque de las tropas de las Naciones Unidas encabezadas por Estados Unidos al ejército iraquí para obligarlo a retirarse de Kuwait. **787**

Operation Restore Hope/Operación de Restauración de la Esperanza (1992) Cruzada de las Naciones Unidas para aliviar los efectos de la hambruna en Somalia. **801**

Operation Rolling Thunder/Operación Trueno Rodante Ataques estadounidenses de bombardeo durante la guerra de Vietnam. **714**

Organization of Petroleum Exporting Countries/Organización de Países Exportadores de Petróleo (OPEC, por sus iniciales en inglés; OPEP, en español) Alianza formada en 1960 por las principales naciones productoras de petróleo para manejar el precio de este recurso mediante el control de la producción. **743**

pacification/pacificación Campaña en la que los aldeanos de Vietnam del Sur eran trasladados a campos de refugiados y después se destruían sus viviendas. **715**

Pacific Railway Act/Ley de ferrocarriles del pacífico (1862) Ley que cedía tierras a las compañías de ferrocarriles para motivarlos a construir una red ferroviaria que uniera las ciudades del este y el oeste. **170**

Paleo-Indians/paleoindígenas Las primeras personas que llegaron a América del Norte provenientes de Asia entre el año 40,000 y el 12,000 a.C. **4**

Palmer raids/Redadas de Palmer (1919–20) Redadas ordenadas por el fiscal general A. Mitchell Palmer para atrapar a supuestos radicales. **394**

Pan-Africanism/panafricanismo Movimiento creado para unir a las personas de origen africano en todo el mundo. **406**

Panama Canal Treaties/Tratados del Canal de Panamá Acuerdos realizados en la década de 1970 por líderes de Estados Unidos y Panamá para ceder el control del Canal de Panamá a este país a partir del año 2000. **757**

Panic of 1873/Pánico de 1873 Depresión económica que restringió los esfuerzos de los republicanos en la época de la Reconstrucción. **145**

patent/patente Derecho/ho de exclusividad para la fabricación y venta de nuevo producto. **193**

patio process/proceso de patio Técnica minera desarrollada en México y América del Sur en el siglo XVIII y más tarde aplicada en Estados Unidos para extraer plata de otros minerales utilizando mercurio. **184**

Payne-Aldrich Tariff/arancel Payne-Aldrich (1909) Medida de aumento de aranceles autorizado por el presidente William Howard Taft que causó el enojo de los progresistas. **311**

Peace Corps/Corporaciones de Paz Programa de dos años de duración en el que el presidente John F. Kennedy enviaba voluntarios a otras naciones para brindar asistencia de desarrollo. **626**

Pendleton Civil Service Act/Ley de servicio civil Pendleton (1883) Ley que estableció una comisión para realizar pruebas competitivas a las personas que solicitaban empleos en el gobierno. **257**

Pentagon Papers/documentos del Pentágono Documentos secretos presentados en 1971 que revelaron que el gobierno de Estados Unidos había proporcionado información falsa a los habitantes durante la guerra de Vietnam. **725**

perestroika/perestroika Política soviética creada en la década de 1980 para iniciar una serie de reformas políticas y económicas. **781**

personal computer/computadora personal (PC, por sus siglas en inglés) Computadora pequeña de uso individual. **765**

Philippine Government Act/Ley del gobierno de Filipinas (1902) Ley orgánica federal que estableció la necesidad de que el gobierno de Estados Unidos nombrara un gobernador y un congreso de dos cámaras para gobernar Filipinas. **339**

Pickett's Charge/Ataque de Pickett Ataque fallido del ejército confederado durante la Batalla de Gettysburg. **119**

Pilgrims/peregrinos Primeros habitantes de Massachusetts que emigraron de Inglaterra debido a conflictos religiosos. **10**

planned obsolescence/obsolescencia planeada Fabricación de productos diseñados para pasar de moda rápidamente. **420**

Platt Amendment/Enmienda de Platt (1902) Enmienda de la constitución cubana que limitaba los derechos de este país para realizar acuerdos y autorizaba a Estados Unidos a intervenir en sus asuntos externos si lo consideraba necesario. **340**

Plessy v. Ferguson/Plessy versus Ferguson (1896) Dictamen de la Suprema Corte que estableció la doctrina de igualdad con separación racial en los edificios públicos. **150**

political bosses/caciques políticos Líderes de la maquinaria política. **246**

political machines/maquinaria política Partidos políticos bien organizados que acapararon el poder en los gobiernos estatales y federal a finales del siglo XIX. **246**

poll taxes/impuesto de voto Impuesto pagado por una persona para tener derecho al voto. **149**

Poor People's Campaign/Campaña por los Pobres Movimiento iniciado por Martin Luther King Jr. para protestar por el aparente mal uso de los fondos destinados a los programas de lucha contra la pobreza. **666**

pop art/arte pop Movimiento que desafiaba los valores tradicionales mediante la creación de obras inspiradas en la cultura popular. **696**

Popular Front/Frente Popular Alianza internacional en contra del fascismo; término usado por el líder soviético Joseph Stalin en uno de sus discursos en 1935. **514**

popular sovereignty/soberanía popular Práctica en la que los votantes decidían si la esclavitud se abolía o continuaba. **89**

Populist Party/Partido Popular Partido del pueblo; partido político formado en 1892 con la finalidad de apoyar el aumento gradual de impuestos, la reglamentación de los bancos, la propiedad de las compañías por parte del gobierno, las restricciones de inmigración, la reducción de las jornadas laborales y las reformas electorales. **263**

Potsdam Conference/Conferencia Postdam (1945) Reunión del presidente de Estados Unidos Harry S Truman, el primer ministro de la Gran Bretaña Winston Churchill y el líder soviético Joseph Stalin después de la rendición alemana en la Segunda Guerra Mundial, que dio como resultado la división de Alemania en cuatro zonas de ocupación. **560**

Progressive Party/Partido Progresista Partido reformista que desarrolló la campaña presidencial de Theodore Roosevelt en 1912. **313**

progressivism/progresivismo Movimiento de reforma iniciado a principios del siglo XX para resolver problemas relacionados con la urbanización y la industrialización. **274**

prohibition/prohibición Prohibición absoluta de la fabricación, venta y distribución de bebidas alcohólicas. **288**

protectorate/protectorado País que depende de la protección de otro. **340**

Pure Food and Drug Act/Ley de alimentos y medicamentos puros (1906) Ley que prohibía la fabricación, venta y transporte de alimentos o medicamentos elaborados con ingredientes peligrosos, además de exigir que estos productos mostraran una lista de ingredientes en sus etiquetas. **306**

Q

quotas/cuotas Sistema mediante el cual se reservaba una cantidad fija de lugares en las escuelas o empleos para ciertos grupos de personas. **669**

R

ragtime/ragtime Estilo musical creado en la década de 1890 por un pianista afroestadounidense que ejecutaba el compás principal con una mano e improvisaba una melodía con la otra. **238**

railhead/poblado ferroviario Poblado ubicado en una vía ferroviaria; por lo general, éste era el punto final de las travesías de ganado. **178**

Reaganomics/Reaganomics Programa económico del presidente Ronald Reagan basado en grandes reducciones de impuestos para fomentar la inversión privada. **772**

realpolitik/política real "Política práctica"; política adoptada por Richard Nixon que anteponía los intereses de la nación a cualquier principio moral en el manejo de asuntos externos. **745**

recall/revocación Proceso mediante el cual los votantes podían solicitar la remoción de un funcionario público antes de completar su periodo en caso necesario. **299**

reclamation/recuperación Proceso por el que un terreno dañado se vuelve productivo. **309**

Reconstruction/Reconstrucción (1865–77) Periodo posterior a la Guerra Civil en que el gobierno de Estados Unidos enfocó sus acciones en restablecer a los estados confederados y reunificar a la nación. **131**

Reconstruction Acts/Leyes de reconstrucción (1867) Leyes que convirtieron los antiguos territorios confederados, con excepción de Tennessee, en zonas militares en las que debía redactarse nuevas constituciones conforme a la decimocuarta enmienda. **140**

Reconstruction Finance Corporation/Corporación de Finanzas de Reconstrucción (RFC, por sus siglas en inglés) Agencia creada en 1932 para estimular la economía mediante el ofrecimiento de préstamos a las compañías de ferrocarriles, bancos y otras instituciones financieras. **460**

recycling/reciclaje Recolección y procesamiento de productos de desecho para volver a usarlos. **817**

Redeemers/redentores Simpatizantes demócratas de los gobiernos dominados por funcionarios de raza blanca en los estados del sur en la década de 1870. **146**

Red Scare/Temor rojo Periodo de histeria anticomunista que se extendió a todo Estados Unidos después de la Primera Guerra Mundial. **393**

referendum/referéndum Proceso que permite a los ciudadanos obligar al Congreso a presentar al juicio popular las leyes recién aprobadas. **299**

Reform Party/Partido de Reforma Partido político creado en la década de 1990 cuya campaña se basó en promesas de reformas a las políticas nacionales. **805**

regionalists/regionalistas Artistas del medio oeste que cobraron popularidad en la década de 1930 enfocando su obra en costumbres y tradiciones populares locales. **491**

Rehabilitation Act/Ley de rehabilitación (1973) Ley federal que prohibía la discriminación educativa, laboral o habitacional a personas con discapacidad. **691**

Renaissance/Renacimiento Reencuentro con el aprendizaje y la creatividad artística iniciado a finales de la Edad Media. **6**

reparations/compensaciones Pago de daños y gastos de guerra. **378**

republicanism/republicanismo Sistema de gobierno en el que los ciudadanos eligen a sus representantes y les dan autoridad para proponer y aplicar las leyes que los rigen. **28**

Republican Party/Partido Republicano Partido político formado en 1854 por demócratas y whigs abolicionistas, junto con algunos simpatizantes de los territorios libres. **90**

Reynolds v. Sims/Reynolds versus Sims (1964) Caso en que la Suprema Corte reafirmó la igualdad en las votaciones con el principio "una persona es un voto". **644**

rock 'n' roll/rock 'n' roll Estilo de música creado con influencias del rhythm and blues de origen afroestadounidense, popularizado en la década de 1950. **605**

Roosevelt Corollary/corolario Roosevelt (1904) Adición del presidente Theodore Roosevelt a la Doctrina Monroe en la que ofrecía la participación de Estados Unidos en los asuntos del hemisferio occidental para evitar la intervención europea. **343**

Rosie the Riveter/Rosie la Riveteadora Símbolo de la mujer defensora de los derechos de las trabajadoras durante la Segunda Guerra Mundial. **538**

Rough Riders/Jinetes rudos Unidad de caballería estadounidense que participó en la guerra contra los españoles mandada por Theodore Roosevelt. **336**

rugged individualism/individualismo duro Creencia de que el éxito es fruto del esfuerzo personal y la libre empresa. **457**

S

Sand Creek Massacre/Masacre de Sand Creek (1864) Ataque de las tropas estadounidenses a la tribu Cheyenne de Colorado en el que más de 200 indígenas resultaron muertos. **163**

Sandinistas/sandinistas Partido político revolucionario de Nicaragua que en 1979 derrocó a un dictador que favorecía los intereses de Estados Unidos. **775**

S&L crisis/crisis S&L Colapso económico de las empresas bancarias ocasionado por inversiones riesgosas en la década de 1980. **779**

satellite nations/países satélite Naciones controladas por la Unión Soviética. **566**

Saturday Night Massacre/Masacre de sábado por la noche Serie de sucesos ocurridos en 1973 que ocasionaron el despido de un investigador especial del caso Watergate, así como la renuncia del fiscal encargado del caso y sus asistentes por negarse a despedir al investigador mencionado. **749**

scalawags/scalawags "Sinverguenzas"; nombre dado a los republicanos del sur por los exconfederados en la época de la Reconstrucción. **144**

scientific management/administración científica Teoría promovida por Frederick W. Taylor en la que explica que cualquier trabajo puede dividirse en varias tareas menores, y que a cada tarea se le puede asignar una tasa de producción específica. **414**

Scopes trial/juicio de Scopes (1925) Juicio de John Scopes, un profesor de secundaria acusado de enseñar la teoría de la evolución en su clase de ciencias. **428**

search-and-destroy missions/misiones de búsqueda y destrucción Estrategia estadounidense en la que patrullas especiales buscaban campamentos y depósitos de suministros ocultos para destruirlos mediante grandes ataques aéreos sorpresa. **715**

Seattle general strike/huelga general de Seattle (1919) Huelga de gran escala cuyos detractores atribuyen a los bolcheviques y otros extranjeros; debilitó el apoyo a los sindicatos del trabajo. **391**

Second Great Awakening/segundo Gran Despertar Movimiento religioso evangélico extendido a todo Estados Unidos a principios del siglo XIX. **83**

Securities and Exchange Commission/Comisión de Seguridad e Intercambio Agencia federal creada para regular a las compañías que venden bonos y acciones en el mercado de valores. **470**

Sedition Act/Ley de sedición (1918) Ley federal creada durante la Primera Guerra Mundial que elevó a rango de crimen la publicación de críticas a la nación. **374**

segregation/segregación Separación de las personas, por lo general basada en criterios raciales. **150**

Selective Service Act/Ley de servicio selectivo (1917) Ley que pedía a todos los hombres entre 21 y 30 años que se registraran para la selección del servicio militar. **364**

Selective Training and Service Act/Ley de entrenamiento y servicio selectivo (1940) Ley que creó la primera selección del servicio militar en tiempos de paz. **530**

Seneca Falls Convention/Convención de Seneca Falls (1848) Primera convención de mujeres en favor de los derechos civiles y lugar en el que se redactó la primera Declaración de sentimientos. **85**

settlement houses/casas de recreo Centros de servicio a la comunidad creados a finales del siglo XIX para ofrecer capacitación laboral y actividades recreativas y culturales a personas de bajos recursos. **231**

Seventeenth Amendment/Decimoséptima enmienda (1913) Enmienda constitucional que dio a los votantes el derecho de elegir a sus representantes en el senado. **299**

shantytowns/ciudades perdidas Grupos de viviendas hechas por indigentes con materiales de desperdicio. **450**

sharecropping/agricultura compartida Sistema agrícola usado durante la Guerra Civil en el que los campesinos sembraban en tierras ajenas a cambio de una pequeña parte de la cosecha. **148**

Share-Our-Wealth/Bienestar compartido Programa radical de ayuda propuesto por el senador Huey Long en la década de 1930 para aumentar los impuestos de los ricos y así garantizar un ingreso mínimo a las familias de bajos recursos. **475**

Sherman Antitrust Act/Ley Sherman antimonopolios (1890) Ley que prohibía los monopolios que restringieran el libre comercio. **209**

Sherman Silver Purchase Act/Ley Sherman de adquisición de plata (1890) Ley federal que obligaba al gobierno a comprar cierta cantidad de plata cada mes para la acuñación de monedas. **263**

Siege of Vicksburg/Sitio de Vicksburg (1863) Bloqueo por el ejército de la Unión en Vicksburg, Mississippi, que condujo a la rendición de esta ciudad durante la Guerra Civil. **119**

Silent Majority/mayoría silenciosa Votantes de clase media que se percataron de los levantamientos sociales en la década de 1960, objetivo de Richard M. Nixon en su campaña presidencial. **740**

sit-down strike/huelga de brazos caídos Método en el que los trabajadores permanecen en sus instalaciones de trabajo para evitar que los administradores los reemplacen. **480**

sit-ins/plantones Manifestaciones en las que las personas se niegan a abandonar el lugar de protesta. **650**

Sixteenth Amendment/Decimosexta enmienda (1913) Enmienda constitucional que permitió al Congreso aumentar los impuestos recaudados. **311**

Skylab/Skylab Primera estación de investigación espacial, colocada en órbita en 1973. **764**

skyscrapers/rascacielos Enormes edificios de muchos pisos. **226**

Smoot-Hawley Tariff/arancel Smoot-Hawley (1930) Arancel demasiado elevado que contribuyó al debilitamiento de la economía en la década de 1930. **446**

social Darwinism/darwinismo social Teoría del filósofo Herbert Spencer, creada a partir de la teoría de la evolución de Charles Darwin en la que se explica que la sociedad progresa mediante la competencia y que sólo los más aptos son los que llegan a las posiciones de riqueza y poder. **202**

Social Gospel/*Gospel* social Movimiento iniciado por ministros protestantes a finales del siglo XIX aplicando los principios cristianos a la resolución de los problemas sociales. **232**

socialism/socialismo Sistema económico en el que el gobierno o los trabajadores son propietarios de las fábricas e instalaciones, así como los sistemas de transporte y comunicación **283**

Social Security Act/Ley de seguridad social (1935) Ley que ofrece pensiones de retiro, seguros de desempleo y ayuda a personas con discapacidad, viudas e hijos de empleados fallecidos. **477**

Society of American Indians/Sociedad de Indígenas Estadounidenses Organización formada en 1911 por estadounidense de origen indígena para tratar de resolver los problemas de sus hermanos de raza. **292**

sod houses/casas de adobe Edificios construidos con bloques de tierra extraídos de zonas de suelo firme. **173**

Solidarity/Solidaridad Sindicato polaco independiente creado en Polonia que originó el movimiento social del mismo nombre en la década de 1980. **773**

sonar/sonar Dispositivo que usa onda sonoras para detectar objetos bajo el agua. **543**

Southern Christian Leadership Conference/Conferencia de Líderes Cristianos del Sur (SCLC, por sus siglas en inglés) Alianza de organizaciones religiosas afroestadounidenses formada en 1957 para luchar contra la discriminación racial. **650**

southern strategy/estrategia del sur Intento del presidente Richard M. Nixon por ganar la confianza de los blancos conservadores simpatizantes con el partido demócrata con la promesa de no apoyar nuevas reformas a la ley de derechos civiles. **741**

spheres of influence/esferas de influencia Regiones en las que un país tiene derechos exclusivos sobre las minas, líneas ferroviarias y el comercio. **330**

Sputnik/Sputnik Primer satélite artificial del mundo, lanzado por la Unión Soviética en 1957. **585**

Square Deal/Trato justo Campaña presidencial de Theodore Roosevelt lanzada en 1904 para equilibrar los intereses de los comerciantes, consumidores y la fuerza laboral. **304**

stagflation/*stagflation* Condición económica caracterizada por una gran inflación y desempleo. **741**

Stalwarts/*Stalwarts* Republicanos de finales del siglo XIX que se oponían a la reforma. **255**

Stamp Act–*University of California* v. *Bakke*

Stamp Act/Ley del timbre (1765) Ley aprobada por el Parlamento para cobrar un impuesto a toda compra de material impreso. **15**

steerage/tercera clase Parte inferior del casco de un barco en la que viajaban de manera incómoda muchos inmigrantes que llegaban a Estados Unidos. **221**

Strategic Arms Limitation Talks/Pláticas de Reducción de Armamento Estratégico (SALT, por sus siglas en inglés) (1972) Pláticas entre el presidente de Estados Unidos Richard M. Nixon y el líder soviético Leonid Brezhev que condujeron a la firma de un tratado que limitaba el número de misiles ICBM que podía tener cada país. **745**

Strategic Defense Initiative/Iniciativa de Defensa Estratégica (SDI, por sus siglas en inglés) Plan de creación de un sistema espacial de defensa como medida de protección contra los misiles soviéticos; nunca se llevó a la práctica. **773**

strict construction/interpretación estricta Interpretación especial de la Constitución que permite al gobierno federal adoptar solamente aquellas medidas que la carta magna permite de manera expresa. **72**

strike/huelga Negativa de los trabajadores a realizar su trabajo hasta que los patronos satisfagan las demandas de su sindicato. **82**

Student Nonviolent Coordinating Committee/Comité de Coordinación Estudiantil por la No Violencia (SNCC, por sus siglas en inglés) Organización estudiantil formada en 1960 para coordinar las protestas en favor de los derechos civiles y ofrecer capacitación a los protestantes. **650**

Students for a Democratic Society/Sociedad de Estudiantes por una Sociedad Democrática (SDS, por sus siglas en inglés) Grupo estudiantil que protestó activamente contra la guerra de Vietnam. **717**

subsidy/subsidio Pago de una bonificación del gobierno a los granjeros. **328**

suburbs/suburbios Vecindarios residenciales en las afueras de una ciudad. **227**

Sunbelt/Sunbelt Estados del sur y del oeste que atrajeron a muchas personas y comercios en la década de 1970. **761**

supply-side economics/supply-side economics Teoría económica según la cual la disminución de impuestos permiten aumentar la actividad económica, la recaudación y la adopción de un presupuesto equilibrado. **772**

supremacy clause/cláusula de supremacía Cláusula de la Constitución de E. U.; estados en los que la Constitución y las leyes federales están por encima de las constituciones y leyes estatales. **34**

Sussex* pledge/promesa de *Sussex (1916) Promesa de los líderes alemanes en la Primera Guerra Mundial de no atacar a barcos mercantes sin previa advertencia o sin respetar la seguridad de los pasajeros. **363**

T

Taft-Hartley Act/Ley Taft-Hartley (1947) Ley que otorgaba a los jueces autoridad para terminar con algunas huelgas, declarar ilegales los acuerdos para cerrar tiendas, restringir la participación política de los sindicatos y exigir a los líderes de los sindicatos que realizaran juramentos en contra del comunismo. **594**

Teapot Dome scandal/escándalo Teapot Dome Escándalo que afectó a la administración del presidente Warren G. Harding cuando el secretario de asuntos internos Albert Fall fue acusado de la venta ilegal de reservas petroleras a cambio de favores y préstamos personales. **400**

Telecommuncations Act/Ley de telecomunicaciones (1996) Ley que intentó regular la indecencia en la Internet; algunas de sus partes fueron derogadas más tarde por una corte federal. **811**

telegraph/telégrafo Aparato patentado por Samuel Morse en 1837; envía mensajes a través de largas distancias al transmitir un sistema de puntos y rayas por un cable de corriente eléctrica. **196**

Teller Amendment/Enmienda Teller (1898) Resolución que establece que Estados Unidos no intentaría invadir y apropiarse de Cuba. **335**

tenements/barracas Bloques de viviendas muy modestas que habitaban los citadinos empobrecidos durante finales del siglo XIX y principios del XX. **230**

Tennessee Valley Authority/Autoridad del Valle de Tennessee (TVA, por sus siglas en inglés) Programa del *New Deal* establecido en 1933; proponía la construcción de presas para suministrar energía hidroeléctrica y contar con un medio de control de inundaciones en el valle del río Tennessee. **472**

Tet Offensive/Ofensiva del Tet (1968) Ataque de las tropas de Vietnam del Norte y del Vietcong al ejército de Vietnam del Sur en la guerra de Vietnam; ocurrió durante el Tet, celebración de año nuevo en Vietnam, y demostró que Vietnam del Norte aún tenía suficiente poder militar. **720**

Texas longhorn/cuernos largos Raza vacuna de gran tamaño creada por la mezcla de ganado inglés y español. **177**

Texas Revolution/Revolución de Texas (1835–36) Rebelión contra México de los colonos estadounidenses y tejanos en Texas. **86**

Thirteenth Amendment/Decimotercera enmienda (1865) Enmienda constitucional que abolió la esclavitud. **133**

Three Mile Island accident/accidente de Three Mile Island (1979) Suceso en el que un reactor nuclear de Pennsylvania estuvo cerca de sufrir una catastrófica sobrecarga. **755**

Tonkin Gulf Resolution/Resolución del Golfo de Tonkin (1964) Medida constitucional que dio al presidente Lyndon B. Johnson autoridad para declarar la guerra a Vietnam. **712**

totalitarian state/totalitarismo Sistema político en el que el gobierno controla todos los aspectos de la vida de los habitantes. **513**

total war/guerra total Estrategia de lucha en la que un ejército destruye la capacidad de combate de su oponente atacando objetivos civiles, económicos y militares. **122**

Trail of Tears/Sendero de las lágrimas (1838–39) Marcha forzada que a lo largo de 800 millas realizaron los cheroquis desde su tierra natal hasta territorio indio en la actual Oklahoma y tuvo como resultado el fallecimiento de casi un cuarto de los integrantes de esa tribu. **81**

transcontinental railroad/ferrocarril transcontinental Ferrocarril que cruzaba la parte continental de Estados Unidos y que fue concluido en 1869. **194**

Treaty of Paris/Tratado de París (1783) Acuerdo de paz que oficialmente da por terminada la Revolución y en el que la Gran Bretaña reconoce legalmente a Estados Unidos. **23**

Treaty of Versailles/Tratado de Versalles (1919) Tratado con el que finaliza la Primera Guerra Mundial y en el que se exige a Alemania el pago de varios miles de millones de dólares como gastos de guerra, además de establecer la Liga de las Naciones. **379**

trench warfare/guerra de trinchera Estrategia militar de la Primera Guerra Mundial con la que se defendía una posición peleando desde la protección de hondas trincheras. **358**

Triangle Shirtwaist Fire/Incendio de la fábrica de camisas Triángulo (1911) Incidente que causó la muerte de 146 trabajadores de la industria del vestido, suceso que obligó a establecer nuevas medidas de seguridad en las fábricas. **282**

Truman Doctrine/Doctrina Truman (1947) Política con la que el presidente Harry S Truman estableció que Estados Unidos debía ofrecer ayuda económica a cualquier país que combatiera al comunismo. **569**

trunk lines/líneas principales Vías principales de ferrocarril que conectan con regiones lejanas a través de líneas ramales o secundarias. **194**

trust/monopolio Acuerdo legal que agrupa a varias compañías bajo el mando de un solo consejo directivo para eliminar la competencia y reglamentar la producción. **203**

Twenty-first Amendment/Vigesimoprimera enmienda (1933) Enmienda constitucional que dio por terminada la prohibición mediante la anulación de la decimoctava enmienda. **423**

Twenty-fourth Amendment/Vigesimocuarta enmienda (1964) Enmienda constitucional que prohibió el pago de impuestos de votación como condición para votar en elecciones federales. **658**

Twenty-sixth Amendment/Vigesimosexta enmienda (1971) Enmienda constitucional que redujo la edad mínima de los electores en las votaciones federales de 21 a 18 años. **726**

U

Underground Railroad/ferrocarril clandestino Red de los abolicionistas que ayudaban a los esclavos a huir hacia el norte y a Canadá. **83**

United Farm Workers/Unión de Trabajadores Agrícolas (UFW, por sus siglas en inglés) Grupo formado en la década de 1960 para mejorar el salario y las condiciones de trabajo de los campesinos inmigrantes. **683**

United Mine Workers strike/huelga de la Unión de Trabajadores Mineros (UMW, por sus siglas en inglés) (1919) Huelga por aumento salarial y mejor horario de trabajo que más tarde debilitó el apoyo del gobierno a los sindicatos; fue la primera huelga de la UMW encabezada por John L. Lewis. **392**

United Nations/Organización de las Naciones Unidas (UN, por sus siglas en inglés; ONU, en español) Organismo internacional creado en 1945 para resolver conflictos entre las naciones. **563**

Universal Negro Improvement Association/Asociación Universal por el Mejoramiento de la Raza Negra (UNIA, por sus siglas en inglés) Asociación fundada por Marcus Garvey en 1914 con el propósito de promover la independencia económica de los afroestado unidenses y establecer una madre patria de raza negra e independiente en África. **387**

University of California* v. *Bakke*/Universidad de California versus *Bakke (1978) Decisión con la que la Suprema Corte estableció que mientras algunas formas de acción afirmativa eran legales, los sistemas de cupo no lo eran. **669**

Untouchables/Intocables Apodo dado a un grupo de detectives dirigidos por Eliot Ness, quien combatió a los gángsters durante la prohibición. **423**

urban renewal/renovación urbana Programa lanzado por el gobierno federal en la década de 1950 para sustituir las viejas construcciones del interior de la ciudad. **615**

U.S. Department of Agriculture/Departamento de Agricultura de Estados Unidos Departamento ejecutivo creado en 1862 para ayudar a los granjeros. **173**

U.S. Sanitary Commission/Comisión Sanitaria de Estados Unidos Agencia federal encabezada en parte por la Dra. Elizabeth Blackwell; combatió las enfermedades e infecciones entre los soldados de la Unión durante la Guerra Civil. **107**

USS *Maine*/USS Maine Nave de guerra de E. U. que estalló en el Puerto de La Habana en 1898; aunque las causas de la explosión nunca fueron determinadas, el incidente desató la guerra entre Estados Unidos y España. **335**

U-2 incident/incidente U-2 Incidente en el que el piloto Francis Gary Powers fue capturado mientras espiaba en territorio de la Unión Soviética, lo que deterioró las relaciones entre Estados Unidos y la Unión Soviética. **578**

V

vaudeville/vaudeville "Teatro de variedades"; tipo de espectáculo de variedades en el que se presenta una amplia selección de actos breves. **238**

vertical integration/integración vertical Propiedad de los medios implícita en cada paso de un proceso de manufactura. **204**

Vietcong/Vietcong Frente de Liberación Nacional; fuerza guerrillera comunista que inició su lucha contra el gobierno de Ngo Dinh Diem en la guerra de Vietnam, en Vietnam del Sur, durante la década de 1950. **709**

Vietminh/Vietminh Liga para la Independencia de Vietnam; grupo de vietnamitas nacionalistas organizado en la década de 1940 por Ho Chi Minh para expulsar a los japoneses de Vietnam. **707**

Vietnamization/vietnamización Política adoptada por la administración Nixon para delegar gradualmente la lucha de la guerra de Vietnam al ejército de Vietnam del Sur. **723**

Vietnam Veterans Memorial/Monumento a los veteranos de vietnam Monumento construido en Washington, D.C., en 1982; para honrar a quienes murieron o desaparecieron en la guerra de Vietnam. **730**

Virginia Statute for Religious Freedom/Estatuto de Virginia para la libertad religiosa (1786) Estatuto que en parte establecía que la mente humana fue creada libre y que el control del gobierno sobre las creencias y las actividades religiosas es una tiranía. **29**

Volstead Act/Ley Volstead (1919) Ley federal que reforzó la decimoctava enmienda (prohibición). **422**

Volunteers in Service to America/Voluntarios para el Servicio a Estados Unidos (VISTA, por sus siglas en inglés) Versión local de los organismos de paz; fue establecida en 1964. **640**

Voting Rights Act/Ley de derecho al voto (1965) Ley que puso el registro del voto bajo el control del gobierno federal. **660**

Voting Rights Act of 1975/Ley de derecho al voto de 1975 Ley federal que requería a los estados y a las comunidades con grandes poblaciones que no hablaran inglés que imprimieran el material de votación en varios idiomas. **760**

W

Wagner-Connery Act/Ley Wagner-Connery (1935) Ley nacional de relaciones laborales; garantizaba los derechos laborales para organizar gremios y obtener mejores condiciones de trabajo y salarios. **480**

War Industries Board/Consejo de Industrias de Guerra (WIB, por sus siglas en inglés) Agencia dirigida por Bernard Baruch durante la Primera Guerra Mundial, la cual reunía productos escasos, establecía prioridades de producción y los precios de los productos. **369**

war of attrition/guerra de desgaste Estrategia del general Grant durante la Guerra Civil para combatir al sur del país hasta que se quedara sin hombres ni provisiones y se sometiera. **120**

War on Drugs/guerra contra las drogas Esfuerzo del gobierno del presidente George Bush para terminar con la venta y consumo ilegal de drogas. **790**

War on Poverty/guerra contra la pobreza Nombre dado por el presidente Lyndon B. Johnson a la serie de programas de ayuda a los necesitados; se promulgó en 1964. **639**

War Powers Act/Ley de poderes de guerra (1973) Ley que exige la aprobación del congreso para declarar la guerra; da un límite de 60 días a la autoridad presidencial para comprometer a las tropas a actuar en un conflicto armado. **730**

War Production Board/Consejo de Producción de Guerra (WPB, por sus siglas en inglés) Agencia creada durante la Segunda Guerra Mundial para supervisar la producción de las industrias de guerra. **529**

Warren Commission/Comisión Warren Grupo especial dirigido por el fiscal Earl Warren para investigar el asesinato del presidente John F. Kennedy. **637**

Warsaw Pact/Pacto de Varsovia Alianza militar formada en 1955 por la Unión Soviética y otros países comunistas de Europa del este. **571**

Washington Conference/Conferencia de Washington (1921) Conferencia internacional efectuada en Washington, D.C., enfocada en el desarme naval y la seguridad en el Pacífico. **503**

Watergate/Watergate Escándalo en el que se vio involucrado el presidente Richard M. Nixon al autorizar el acceso de un grupo secreto al cuartel general del Partido Demócrata; este suceso provocó la renuncia del presidente Nixon en 1974. **748**

Whip Inflation Now/Whip Inflation Now (WIN) "Acabemos ya con la inflación"; eslógan del presidente Gerald Ford para obtener apoyo a su programa antiinflacionario. **752**

Wisconsin Idea/Idea de Wisconsin Programa de reformas creado por el gobernador de Wisconsin Robert M. La Follette a principios del siglo XX que se convirtió en modelo a seguir para otros estados. **302**

Woman's Christian Temperance Union/Unión de Mujeres Cristianas por la Abstinencia (WCTV por sus siglas en inglés) Organización reformista que luchaba contra el consumo del alcohol a finales del siglo XIX. **289**

Woodstock/Woodstock (1969) Concierto de rock realizado cerca de Woodstock, Nueva York, que se convirtió en símbolo del espíritu idealista de la contracultura. **699**

Works Progress Administration/Administración del Progreso Laboral (WPA, por sus siglas en inglés) Agencia del *New Deal* creada en 1934 para poner a trabajar a hombres y mujeres estadounidenses. **476**

World Wide Web/World Wide Web "Red mundial"; sistema desarrollado por científicos suizos a principios de la década de 1980 que une sitios de Internet. **811**

Y

Yalta Conference/Conferencia de Yalta (1945) Encuentro del presidente de Estados Unidos Franklin D. Roosevelt, el primer ministro de la Gran Bretaña Winston Churchill y el líder soviético Joseph Stalin para planear la situación del mundo en la postguerra. **546**

yellow journalism/amarillismo Estilo de reportaje sensacionalista usado en los periódicos para atraer lectores. **235**

Y2K bug/defecto Y2K Problema de programación de computadoras creado por la abreviatura de la fecha que amenazaba con apagar los sistemas de cómputo el 1 de enero del año 2000. **812**

Z

zaibatsu/zaibatsu Grandes corporaciones a cargo de familias únicas que monopolizaron la economía japonesa después de la Segunda Guerra Mundial. **561**

Zimmermann Note/Nota Zimmermann Cable enviado al ministro alemán en México por la secretaría del exterior de Alemania durante la Primera Guerra Mundial para que propusiera una alianza entre ambos países. **364**

Zionism/sionismo Movimiento judío que pugna por la formación de un territorio patrio en Palestina. **564**

zoot-suit riots/revueltas zoot-suit (1943) Ataques de marinos estadounidenses a mexicano-estadounidenses que residían en Los Ángeles. **540**

INDEX

Key: c = chart   m = map
f = feature   p = picture

A

American Red Cross, 107, 367
American Revolution. *See* Revolutionary War
American Sign Language, *f691, p691*
Americans with Disabilities Act (ADA), 790, *p790*
American System, 79–80
amnesty: after Civil War, 131
Amos 'n' Andy (television show), 604
amusement parks, *f236, p236*
Anaconda Plan, 103
anarchists: definition of, 213
Anderson, Marian, 473, *p473*
Anderson, Mary, 399–400
Angel Island (San Francisco), 221–22
Angelou, Maya, 799–800
Angola, *A5;* civil war in, 753, *p753*
Anthony, Susan B., 85, 319
anthrax, 825
Antifederalists, 33
Anti-Saloon League (ASL), 289
anti-Semitism, 514
antislavery movement. *See* abolition
Anzio, Italy: World War II and, 543, *p543, m547*
Apache, 162, *m164,* 167
apartheid, 758, 801
Apollo 11 (spacecraft), *f628, p628,* 764
appeasement, 518
Appomattox Courthouse, Virginia, 122–123, *p123*
Arafat, Yasir, 802, *p802*
Arapaho, 163–64, *m164*
arbitration, 304
architecture: in the 1920s, 437, *p437*
Area Redevelopment Act (ARA), 635
Arizona, *A1, R9;* Mexican Cession and, 87; military campaigns against Navajo in, 169; sheep ranching in, 177; silver mining in, 183–84
Arizona, USS, 523
Arkansas, *A1, R9;* desegregation in, 608–09; secession of, 98
armed forces: McCarthyism and, 582–83; military bases overseas, c. 1965, *m589;* women in, 530–31, *p531,* 789, *p789.* *See also* specific battles and wars
Armstrong, Louis, 431, *p431*
Armstrong, Neil, 764–65
Army-McCarthy hearings, 583
Arnaz, Desi, 604, *p604*
art: Armory Show, *f318;* evaluating, *f490;* influence of progressive reforms on, *f318;* in the 1920s, 436, *p436;* in the 1930s, 491, *p491;* in the 1960s, 696–97, *f697;* photography, *f105, p105;* political cartoons, *f250, p250;* pop, 696–97, *p696, f697, p697;* western frontier artists, *f179, p179;* in World War II, *f537, p537. See also* specific artists and works
Arthur, Chester A., 256–57, R5
Articles of Confederation, 29, *p29*
Asia, *A5, f242;* Cold War and, 572–74, 706–31, 745; early world trade and, 5, 6; Ford and, 752; imperialism in, 326–32, *p326;* missionaries in, *f327, p327;* in the 1920s and 1930s, 517, *p517,* 523; U.S. trade and, *c331;* in World War II, 528, 531–33, 549–55,

p549, m551, p552. See also specific Asian countries
Asian Americans: discrimination and, 234, 611–12; during Great Depression, 450; immigration and, 222, *c222, f222,* 224–25, *p224, f242, m242, m243,* 408, 611, *p611,* 729, 760–61, 813, *f813;* labor unions and, 285; new working class and, 211; in the 1950s, 611–12, *p611;* public schools and, 234; in the West, 172, *p172;* in World War II, 540–41, *m540*
As I Lay Dying (Faulkner), 455
Asimov, Isaac, *f581*
assembly line, 415, *p415*
Association of American Painters and Sculptors, *f318*
astronauts, 764–65, *p765,* 784, *p784,* 810–11
Atlanta, Georgia: capture of, in Civil War, 121–22, *p121*
Atlantic Charter, 522
Atlantic Ocean, *A5;* World War II and, 521–22, 543
Atomic Energy Act, 568
Atomic Energy Commission (AEC), 568
atomic weapons. *See* nuclear weapons
Auschwitz, Poland, 545
Australia, *A5;* development of secret ballot in, 299, *p299;* World War II and, 550
Austria, *A5;* German invasion of, 514
Austria-Hungary: World War I and, 356–57, *m359, m379, c380*
Autobiography of an Ex-Colored Man, The (Johnson), 434
automation, 599, *p599*
automobile industry: assembly line and, 415, *p415;* growth of, 415; horseless carriage, forerunner to, 195; impact on culture, 418, *p418;* impact on factory work, 416–17, *p416;* impact on family life, 418–19, *p418;* Model T and, 415–16, *p415, f416, p416;* revolution of transportation and, 418, *p418*
auto-touring, 418
aviation: in the 1920s, 427; World War I and, 360, *p360;* World War II and, 543–44; Wright brothers and, 195–96, *p196*
Axis Powers, 518, 528
Aztec, 5, 7–8

B

Babbitt (Lewis), 435
baby boom, 601
baby-boom generation, 601–02, *f722*
Baca, Jimmy Santiago, 807, *p807*
back-to-Africa movement, 407, *f407*
Baez, Joan, 698, 699
Bahamas, 7
Baker, Ray Stannard, 278
Baker v. Carr, 644
Bakke, Allan, 669
Balch, Emily Greene, 503
Balfour Declaration, 381
Balkans, 356, *p356. See also* Bosnia; Kosovo; Yugoslavia
Ball, Lucille, 604, *p604*
Ballinger, Richard, 311–12

Ballinger-Pinchot affair, 311–12
bank holiday, 468
banking: Andrew Jackson and, 81; New Deal programs and, 468–69; progressive reform and, 316; savings and loan crisis, 779; stock market crash of 1929 and, 444
Bank of the United States, 72–73
barbed wire, 181–82, *p182*
Barchus, Eliza, *f179*
Barrett, Janie Porter, 232
Bartlett, Caroline, 232
Barton, Clara, 107
Baruch, Bernard, 369, 568
Baruch Plan, 568
baseball, 237, *p237,* 426–27, *p426, f454, p454*
basketball, 238, *p238*
Bataan Death March, 532
Batista, Fulgencio, 627
Battle of Antietam, 114, *p114*
Battle of Bunker Hill, 17–18, *p18*
Battle of El Alamein, 533
Battle of Gettysburg, *m112,* 118–19
Battle of Iwo Jima, *m551,* 552, *p552*
Battle of Lexington, 17
Battle of Leyte Gulf, 550, *m551*
Battle of Manassas. *See* First Battle of Bull Run
Battle of Midway, 532–33, *p533, m551*
Battle of Okinawa, *m551,* 552
Battle of Seven Pines, 112, *m112*
Battle of Shiloh, 110–11, *m111*
Battle of Stalingrad, 534, *p534*
Battle of the Argonne Forest, 377
Battle of the Atlantic, 543–44
Battle of the Bulge, 546, *m547*
Battle of the Coral Sea, 532, *m551*
Battle of the Little Bighorn, 165–66, *p165*
Battle of the Somme, 359–60, *m359*
Battle of Yorktown, 23
Baumfree, Isabella. *See* Sojourner Truth
Bay of Pigs, 627, *p627*
Bayonet Constitution, 328
Beadle, Erastus, 235
bear market, 443
Beatles, 698
beats, 613, *p613*
Beauregard, P. G. T., 97, 110
Begin, Menachem, 759, *p759*
Beiderbecke, Bix, 431
Beijing, China, 787
Belgian Congo. *See* Congo
Belgium, *A5;* German occupation of, 521; World War I and, 358, *m359*
Bell, Alexander Graham, 197, *p197*
benevolent societies, 223
Ben-Gurion, David, 564–65
Benton, Thomas Hart, 491
Bentsen, Lloyd, 785, *p785*
Berlin, Germany: after World War II, 560–61, *m561,* 570–71, *p571;* World War II and, 548
Berlin Airlift, 570–71
Berlin Wall, 628, 786, *p786*
Bernadotte, Folke, 565
Bernstein, Carl, 747
Berry, Chuck, 606
Bessemer, Henry, 192
Bessemer process, 192

capitalism; free market
Free France, 521
free market, *f398. See also* global economy; trade
French and Indian War, 15
French Indochina, *m707;* French occupation of, 706–07; Geneva Conference and, 708–09; Japanese occupation of, 523, 707
Friedan, Betty, 676–77, *p676*
frontier novels, 235
Fuel Administration, 369
Fugitive Slave Act, 89, *p89*
Fulbright, J. William, 719
Fuller, Henry Blake, 226
Fuller, Ida May, *f477, p477*
Fundamentalism, 428; in the 1980s, 771, *f772;* the Scopes trial and, 428–29
Fundamental Orders of Connecticut (1639), 12

G

Gadhafi, Mu'ammar, 802
Gage, Thomas, 17
Galbraith, John Kenneth, 612
Gallaudet, Thomas Hopkins, *f691*
Gallaudet University: student protest at, *f691*
Gama, Vasco da, 6
Garbo, Greta, 427, 454
Garfield, James A., R5; assassination of, 256–57, *p256;* election of 1880 and, 256
Garland, Hamlin, *f174, p174*
Garner, John Nance, 463
Garnet, Henry Highland, 84
Garvey, Marcus, 406–07, *p406*
gasoline consumption, *c743, f743*
Gates, Bill, 811
Gaza Strip, 565
Gehrig, Lou, 426
General Federation of Women's Clubs, 409
General Motors Company, 420
generation gap, 694, *f722*
Geneva Conference, 708–09
genocide, 545
geography: agriculture, 494–495, *m494–495;* environment, 794–95, *m794–95;* growth of Los Angeles, 702–03, *m702–03;* immigrant migration, 242–43, *m242–43;* national defense, 588–89, *m588–89;* regionalism, 126–27, *m126–27;* world trade, 352–53, *m352–53*
George, David Lloyd, 378, *p378,* 505, *p505*
George, Henry, 209, *p209*
Georgia, A1, R9
German immigrants, 82, 172
Germany, A5; anti-Semitism in, 514; Axis Powers and, 518; Berlin Airlift, 571; Blitzkrieg, 521; Brownshirts in, 513; expansion of; 1935–1941, *m520;* Holocaust in, 545–46, *p545, p546;* impact of World War I debt and reparations, 505–06; inflation in, 505–06, *p506;* invasion of Soviet Union, 522; involvement with China, 330; Maginot Line, 521; Munich Conference and, 518; Nazi Party

in, 513, *p514;* nonagression pact with Soviet Union, 519; post–World War II occupation of, 560–61, *m561;* pre–World War II aggressions, 514; rise of Hitler in, 513–14, Third Reich in, 513; unification of, 786; World War I and, 357–60, *m359,* 362–63, *p363,* 375–77, 379, *m379,* 381; World War II and, 528, 533–34, 542–43, *m547,* 548
Geronimo, 167
Gershwin, George, 431
Gettysburg Address, 119, *f119*
Ghost Dance, 166, *f167, p167*
GI Bill of Rights, 592
Gibson, William, 784
Gideon v. Wainwright, 644
Gilded Age: definition of, 255; political machines in, 246–51; political scandals during, 252–55, *p252, p253;* Populist movement in, 259–65; reforming corruption in, 255–58
Gilded Age, The (Twain and Warner), *f254,* 255, *p255*
Gingrich, Newt, 801
Ginsberg, Allen, 612
Ginsburg, Ruth Bader, 800
Girl Scouts of America, 371, *f371*
Giuliani, Rudolph, 821, *p822*
Gladden, Washington, 232, 259, 304
glasnost, 781
Glenn, John, 810–11, *p810*
global economy: 815–16; Great Depression and, 445–47, *f445, m446*
global warming, 816
gold: in Alaska, 184; Black Hills, South Dakota, and, 165; California and, 87–88; Klondike Gold Rush, 184; mining boom and, 183–87
Gold-Diggers of 1933 (film), 488, *p488*
Goldman, Emma, 394
Goldmark, Josephine, 283
gold standard, 262–63
Goldwater, Barry, 640–41, *p641*
Gompers, Samuel, 280, *p280, p281,* 284, 317
Gone With the Wind (film), 488
Gone With the Wind (Mitchell), 488
Gonzales, Rodolfo "Corky," 686–87, *p686*
González, Henry B., 687
Goodman, Andrew, 658
Goodman, Benny, 491
Good Neighbor Policy, 508
Goodwin, Richard, 634
Gorbachev, Mikhail, *p782;* end of Cold War and, 786–87; perestroika and, 781–82; resignation of, 786
Gordy, Berry, 698
Gore, Al, *p798,* 799, 810, R7; election of 2000 and, 817–18
Gorgas, William, 340, 342
"Gospel of Wealth" (Carnegie), 204, *f204*
gospel music, 490
Gould, Jay, 203, 213, 252
government: progressive reform of, 298–302. *See also* Congress; Constitution; elections; Senate; Supreme Court
graduated income tax, 260
graft: definition of, 249; political machines and, 248–51
Graham, Billy, 583

Gramm-Rudman-Hollings Act, 778
Grand Ole Opry (radio show), 490
Grant, Madison, 292
Grant, Ulysses S., 141, R5; in Civil War, 110, 119–20, *p120,* 121–23; Crédit Mobilier scandal, 253; election of 1868 and, 141; scandal in the White House and, 252–53, *p253;* second term of, 253; Whiskey Ring and, 253
Grapes of Wrath, The (Steinbeck), 488, *p488, f489*
Gray Panthers, 692–93, *p693*
Great Britain: air strikes on Afghanistan and, 825; Atlantic Charter and, 522; Balfour Declaration and, 381; Geneva Conference and, 708; involvement with China, 330; Lend-Lease Act and, 521; limited test ban on nuclear weapons, 630; Munich Conference and, 518; in Persian Gulf War, 787; Suez crisis and, 577; U.S. foreign policy and, 21; War of 1812 and, 78; Washington Conference and, 504; World War I and, 357–60, *m359,* 362, 378, *m379;* World War II and, 533, 544, *m547*
Great Depression: African Americans during, 449; banking crisis during, 444; business failures during, 445; causes of, 445–47; Dust Bowl and, 482–84; end of, 529; family life in, 452–53, *p452;* farm crisis, 459–60; farmers during, 450–52, *p451;* global depression, 445–46, *f445, m446;* Hoover's philosophy on, 456–58; Mexican Americans during, 451–52; migrant farmers and, 451–52; photographing, *p452,* 484–85, *p485;* popular culture during, 454–55; psychological impact of, 454; radical protests during, 461–62, *p461, p462;* rural life in, 450–52, *p451;* shantytowns, 450; stock market crash, 443–44, *c443, p444;* unemployment during, 448–49, *p448, p449;* urban life during, 449–50
Great Gatsby, The (Fitzgerald), 435, *p435*
Great Migration: of African Americans, 372–73, *p372*
Great Plains: American Indian land rights and, 162–69, *m164;* Dust Bowl in, 482–84, *p482;* farm life on, 175; settlement of, 170; storytellers of the, *f174,* 176
Great Society, 640–44, *p645;* decline of, 644–45
Great Train Robbery (film), 289
Great Upheaval, 213
Greece, A5; civil war in, 568; German occupation during World War II, 533
Greek Orthodox Church, *f223*
Greeley, Horace, 253, *p253*
Green Berets, 626, *p626*
Grenada, A5; U.S. invasion of, 776, *m780*
Griggs v. Duke Power Co., 669
Grimké, Angelina, 84–85
Grimké, Sarah, 84–85
grocery chains, 421
gross national product, 445
Groves, Leslie R., 553
Guadalcanal: in World War II, 533, *m551*
Guam, A5; as U.S. territory, 336
Guantánamo Bay, Cuba, 340
Guatemala, A5; caudillos and, 511; Cold

Kansas Fever–Los Alamos

migrant farmworkers–Ness

Panama Canal Treaties–Qur'an

Taft–United Nations

Wimar–zoot-suit riots

For permission to reprint copyrighted material, grateful acknowledgment is made to the following sources:

Beacon Press, Boston: From *Man's Search for Meaning* by Viktor E. Frankl. Copyright © 1959, 1962, 1984, 1992 by Viktor E. Frankl.

Donadio & Olson, Inc.: From *The Good War: An Oral History of World War Two* by Studs Terkel. Copyright © 1984 by Studs Terkel.

Greenwood Publishing Group, Inc., Westport, CT: Quote by George Robinson from *Listening to Radio, 1920–1950* by Ray Barfield. Copyright © 1996 by Ray Barfield.

Harcourt, Inc.: Quote by Leonard Korgie from *The Korean War: Pusan to Chosin, An Oral History* by Donald Knox. Copyright © 1985 by Donald Knox.

Henry Holt and Company, LLC: From "U.S. 1946 King's X" from *Complete Poems of Robert Frost, 1949*. Copyright © 1949 by Robert Frost.

Houghton Mifflin Company: From *Turbulent Era: A Diplomatic Record of Forty Years, 1904–1945* by Joseph C. Grew, edited by Walter Johnson. Copyright 1952 by Joseph C. Grew; copyright renewed © 1980 by Elizabeth Lyon, Anita J. English, and Lilla Levitt. All rights reserved.

ACKNOWLEDGMENTS

For permission to reprint copyrighted material, grateful acknowledgment is made to the following sources:

Victor Alba: From *Alliance Without Allies: The Mythology of Progress in Latin America* by Victor Alba. Copyright © 1965 by Victor Alba.

Bantam Books, a division of Random House, Inc.: From *Voices of Freedom: An Oral History of the Civil Rights Movement from the 1950s Through the 1980s* by Henry Hampton and Steve Fayer with Sarah Flynn. Copyright © 1990 by Blackside, Inc.

Bentley Historical Library, University of Michigan: From a poem on *Sputnik* by Governor G. Mennen Williams of Michigan on October 4, 1957. Copyright © 1957 by G. Mennen Williams. Papers are located in G. Mennen Williams Gubernatorial Papers, Box 213, at the Bentley Historical Library.

Bethune-Cookman College Archives: Quotation by Mary McLeod Bethune.

Robert Bly: From "The United Fruit Co." by Pablo Neruda from *Neruda and Vallejo: Selected Poems*, chosen and translated by Robert Bly. Copyright © 1974 by Robert Bly. Published by Beacon Press, 1974.

Peter N. Carroll: Quote by a Chicago housewife from "The Loss of Connection" from *It Seemed Like Nothing Happened: America in the 1970s* by Peter N. Carroll. Copyright © 1982 by Peter Carroll.

Sheyann Webb Christburg: Quote by eight-year-old Sheyann Webb from "The Turbulent Sixties" from *The Enduring Vision: A History of the American People* by Paul S. Boyer et al.

Don Congdon Associates, Inc.: From "The Watchers" from *Weird Tales* by Ray Bradbury. Copyright © 1945 by Street & Smith Publications; copyright renewed © 1972 by Ray Bradbury.

Crisis Publishing Co., Inc.: From "The Bronx Slave Market" by Ella Baker and Marvel Cooke from *The Crisis*, vol. 42, November 1935. Copyright 1935 by Crisis Publishing Co., Inc.

Donadio & Olson, Inc.: From *The Good War: An Oral History of World War Two* by Studs Terkel. Copyright © 1984 by Studs Terkel.

Doubleday, a division of Random House Inc.: From *The Martian Way and Other Stories* by Isaac Asimov. Copyright © 1955 by Isaac Asimov. *The Century* by Todd Brewster and Peter Jennings. Copyright © 1998 by ABC Television Network Group, a division of Capitol Cities, Inc. From "Can Wars Be Just?" by Sari Nusseibeh from *But Was It Just?: Reflections on the Morality of the Persian Gulf War* by Jean Bethke Elshtain et al., translated by Peter Heinegg, edited by David E. Decosse. Copyright © 1992 by Jean Bethke Elshtain, Stanley Hauerwas, Sari Nusseibeh, and George Weigel. From *The Blue Eagle from Egg to Earth* by Hugh S. Johnson. Copyright 1935 by Hugh S. Johnson.

Dutton, a division of Penguin Putnam Inc., electronic format by permission of Evan McLeod Wylie: From *Movin' On Up* by Mahalia Jackson and Evan McLeod Wylie. Copyright © 1966 by Mahalia Jackson and Evan McLeod Wylie.

W. D. Ehrhart: "Guerrilla War" from *Beautiful Wreckage: New & Selected Poems* by W. D. Ehrhart. Copyright © 1999 by Adastra Press.

Facts On File, Inc.: From "Carla Martinelli" from *Ellis Island Interviews: In Their Own Words* by Peter Morton Coan. Copyright © 1997 by Peter Morton Coan.

The Gale Group: Adaptation of map from *We the People* by James Paul Allen and Eugene James Turner. Copyright © 1988 by Macmillan Publishing Company.

GRM Associates, Inc., Agents for the Estate of Ida M. Cullen: From "Yet Do I Marvel" from *Color* by Countee Cullen. Copyright © 1925 by Harper & Brothers; copyright renewed 1953 by Ida M. Cullen.

Grove/Atlantic, Inc.: From *1968 in America: Music, Politics, Chaos, Counterculture, and the Shaping of a Generation* by Charles Kaiser. Copyright © 1988 by Charles Kaiser.

James A. Henretta: Quotation by a coal miner's daughter from "Herbert Hoover and the Great Depression" and from quote by a Chicago schoolteacher from "Family Values" from *America's History* by James A. Henretta et al. Copyright © 1987 by The Dorsey Press.

The Heritage Foundation: From "Moving an Agenda Through Congress" by David M. Mason from *Mandate for Leadership IV, Turning Ideas Into Action* by Stuart M. Butler and Kim R. Holmes accessed June 20, 2001, at: www.heritage.org/mandate/1996/ch1/chapt1.html.

Hill and Wang, a division of Farrar, Straus and Giroux, LLC.: From *Night* by Elie Wiesel, translated by Stella Rodway. Copyright © 1960 by MacGibbon & Kee; copyright renewed © 1988 by The Colling Publishing Group.

Roy Hoopes: From *Americans Remember the Home Front: An Oral Narrative of the World War II Years in America* by Roy Hoopes. Copyright © 1977, 1992 by Roy Hoopes.

Houghton Mifflin Company: From *Typical American* by Gish Jen. Copyright © 1991 by Gish Jen. All rights reserved.

Howe Brothers Publishers: Excerpt by Gerald One Feather from *Indian Self-Rule: First-Hand Accounts of Indian-White Relations from Roosevelt to Reagan*, edited by Kenneth R. Philp. Published by Howe Brothers Publishers, 1986.

Independent Woman: From a quote by female aircraft worker from "Comments on 'Womanpower 4F'" from *Independent Woman*, November 1943; and quote by a shipyard manager from "Anchors Aweigh!" by Beatrice Oppenheim from *Independent Woman*, March 1943. Published by the Washington National Federation of Business and Professional Women's Clubs, Inc.

Charles H. Kerr & Company, Chicago: From "The March of the Mill Children" from *The Autobiography of Mother Jones*, edited by Mary Field Parton. Copyright 1925, © 1972 by Charles H. Kerr & Company.

The Heirs to the Estate of Martin Luther King, Jr., c/o Writers House, Inc. as agent for the proprietor: From "I Have a Dream" by Martin Luther King, Jr. Copyright © 1963 by Martin Luther King, Jr.; copyright renewed © 1991 by Coretta Scott King. From "Sermon Against the War in Vietnam" by Martin Luther King, Jr. Copyright © 1963 by Martin Luther King, Jr.; copyright renewed © 1991 by The Estate of Martin Luther King, Jr. From "Letter from Birmingham Jail" from *Why We Can't Wait* by Martin Luther King, Jr. Copyright © 1963 by Martin Luther King, Jr.; copyright renewed © 1991 by Coretta Scott King.

Alfred A. Knopf, Inc., a division of Random House, Inc.: "I, Too" from *Collected Poems of Langston Hughes*. Copyright © 1994 by the Estate of Langston Hughes.

Kodansha Ltd.: From *War Wasted Asia: Letters, 1945–46*, edited by Otis Cary. Copyright © 1975 by Kodansha International Ltd. All rights reserved.

Leiber & Stotter: Lyrics from "Yakety Yak" by the Coasters. Copyright © 1958 by Jerry Leiber Music and Mike Stoller Music.

Maya Ying Lin: Quote about the Vietnam Veterans Memorial.

Ludlow Music, Inc.: From lyrics from "Talking Dust Bowl." Words and music composed by Woody Guthrie. TRO—© Copyright 1960, copyright renewed © 1963 by Ludlow Music, Inc., New York, NY.

Macmillan Ltd.: From "Economy (1931)" from *The Collected Writings of John Maynard Keynes: Volume IX, Essays in Persuasion*. Originally published as "The Problem of Unemployment–II" in the *Listener*, January 4, 1931.

Naomi Long Madgett: "Midway" from *Star* by Naomi Long Madgett. Copyright © 1965 by Naomi Long Madgett. Published by Harlo Press in 1965, Evenill in 1970, and Lotus in 1972.

Patricia Mull: Quote by Patricia Mull from "What $152 a Week Buys" by Nancy Gibbs from *Time*, September 10, 1990. Copyright © 1990 by Patricia Mull.

Multimedia Product Development, Chicago, IL, agent for Jeane Westin: From "Erma's Story" from *Making Do: How Women Survived the '30s* by Jeane Westin. Copyright © 1976 by Jeane Westin. All rights reserved.

NAACP: From advertisement "Let 'Em Walk" by the NAACP.

New Directions Publishing Corporation: From "Martin IV" from *Martin and Meditations on the South Valley* by Jimmy Santiago Baca. Copyright © 1987 by Jimmy Santiago Baca. From "I Am Waiting" from *A Coney Island of the Mind* by Lawrence Ferlinghetti. Copyright © 1958 by Lawrence Ferlinghetti.

The New York Times Company: Quote by Michael Novak from the Op—Ed page of *The New York Times*, May 24, 1998. Copyright © 1998 by The New York Times Company.

The New Republic: From "The De Luxe Picture Palace" by Lloyd Lewis from *The New Republic*, vol. 58, March 27, 1929. Copyright 1929 by The New Republic.

Newsweek, Inc.: Quote by Hugh Austin from "Business and Finance" from *Newsweek*, November 19, 1973. Copyright © 1973 by Newsweek, Inc. All rights reserved. From "Nursing the Dying" by Edie Meeks from *Newsweek*, March 8, 1999, p. 61. Copyright © 1999 by Newsweek, Inc. All rights reserved.

W. W. Norton & Company, Inc.: From *Sleepwalking Through History: America in the Reagan Years* by Haynes Johnson. Copyright © 1991 by Haynes Johnson.

Harold Ober Associates Incorporated: From "...I Could Not Eat The Poems I Wrote" by Langston Hughes. Copyright © 1963 by Langston Hughes. Published by Freedomways.

Pathfinder Press: From "OAAU Founding Rally" and from "Short Statements: Fight or Forget It" from *By Any Means Necessary: Speeches, Interviews, and a Letter* by Malcolm X. Copyright © 1970, 1992 by Betty Shabazz and Pathfinder Press.

Penguin Putnam Inc.: "I saw, I saw, I saw holes and trenches" by Trinh Cong Son from *Vietnam: A History* by Stanley Karnow. Copyright © 1983 by WGBH Educational Foundation and Stanley Karnow.

Publishers Weekly: From interview with Gloria Steinem from *Publishers Weekly*, August 12, 1983. Copyright © 1983 by R. R. Bowker Company.

G. P. Putnams Sons, a division of Penguin Putnam Inc. From "Their Finest Hours," a speech delivered to the House of Commons, June 18, 1940, by Winston Churchill from *Blood, Sweat, and Tears* by The Right Honorable Winston S. Churchill. Copyright © 1941 by Winston S. Churchill. From "The Yom Kippur War" from *MyLife* by Golda Meir. Copyright © 1975 by Golda Meir.

Random House, Inc.: From "On the Pulse of Morning" from *On the Pulse of Morning* by Maya Angelou. Copyright © 1993 by Maya Angelou.

The Reader's Digest Association, Inc.: From "The Spread of Grass-Roots Capitalism" by Edward Maher from *Reader's Digest*, June 1955. Copyright © 1955 by The Reader's Digest Association, Inc.

Estate of Erich Maria Remarque: From *All Quiet on the Western Front* by Erich Maria Remarque. Copyright 1929, 1930 by Little, Brown and Company; copyright renewed © 1957, 1958 by Erich Maria Remarque. All rights reserved. "Im Westen Nichts Neues" copyright 1928 by Ullstein A. G.; copyright renewed © 1956 by Erich Maria Remarque.

Roosevelt University, Labor Education Division: From "Automation" by Joe Glazer from *Songs of Work and Freedom*, edited by Edith Fowke and Joe Glazer. Published by Roosevelt University, Labor Education Division, 1960.

Karen Schwarz and her agent, Robin Straus Agency, Inc. New York: Quote by Donna Shalala from *What You Can Do for Your Country: An Oral History of the Peace Corps* by Karen Schwarz. Copyright © 1991 by Karen Schwarz. Published by William Morrow & Co., Inc.

Scribner, a division of Simon & Schuster, Inc.: From *A Farewell to Arms* by Ernest Hemingway. Copyright 1929 by Charles Scribner's Sons; copyright renewed © 1957 by Ernest Hemingway. From "German Inflation" from *By-line: Ernest Hemingway*, edited by William White. Copyright © 1967 by Mary Hemingway. From *The Sun Also Rises* by Ernest Hemingway. Copyright 1926 by Charles Scribner's Sons; copyright renewed 1954 by Ernest Hemingway. From *For Whom the Bell Tolls* by Ernest Hemingway. Copyright 1940 by Ernest Hemingway; copyright renewed © 1968 by Mary Hemingway. From "Special Problems of the Depression" from *Interpretations, 1931–1932* by Walter Lippmann. Copyright © 1932 by Walter Lippmann. From "We Lived on Relief" by Ann Rivington from *Scribner's Magazine*, vol. 95, 1934, pp. 282–5. Copyright 1934 by Charles Scribner's Sons; copyright renewed © 1962 by Charles Scribner's Sons.

Scripps Howard Foundation: From *Ernie's War: The Best of Ernie Pyle's World War II Dispatches*, edited by David Nichols. Copyright © 1986 by Simon and Schuster.

SIGI Productions, Inc.: Quotes by Arthur Komori and Francis Tsuzuki from "I Can Never Forget": Men of the 100th/442nd by Thelma Chang. Copyright © 1991 by SIGI Productions, Inc.

Simon & Schuster: From "Special Problems of the Depression" from *Interpretations, 1931–1932* by Walter Lippmann. Copyright © 1932 by Walter Lippmann. From *Nobody Speaks for Me! Self-Portraits of American Working-Class Women* by Nancy Seifer. Copyright © 1976 by Nancy Seifer.

Small Planet Communications: From "Expansion in the Pacific" from *An On-Line History of the United States: The Age of Imperialism*, on-line, September 22,1999. Copyright © 1996 by Small Planet Communications. Available http://www.smplanet.com/imperialism/hawaii.html.

Special Rider Music: From lyrics from "Blowin' in the Wind" by Bob Dylan. Copyright © 1962 by Warner Bros. Music; copyright renewed 1990 by Special Rider Music. All rights reserved. International copyright secured.

Gloria Steinem: Quotations by Gloria Steinem about the women's movement.

Time Inc.: From "The Men Who Fought" from *Time*, vol. 143, no. 23, June 6, 1994. Copyright © 1994 by Time Inc. From "The Century Ahead: How The World Will Look in 50 Years" by Bruce W. Nelan from *Time*, October 15, 1992. Copyright © 1992 by Time Inc.

Sheila Tobias: From *Faces of Feminism: An Activist's Reflections on the Women's Movement* by Sheila Tobias. Copyright © 1997 by Westview Press, a division of HarperCollins Publishers, Inc. Published by Perseus Books Group.

Margaret Truman and SCG, Inc., 381 Park Ave., So., NYC, NY 10016: From *Memoirs by Harry S. Truman: Years of Trial and Hope*. Copyright © 1956 by Time Inc. Published by Doubleday and Company.

The University of North Carolina Press: From "Tore Up and a-Movin'" from *These Are Our Lives* by the Federal Writers' Project. Copyright © 1939 by The University of North Carolina Press.

Warner Brothers Music Corporation: From "We're In the Money." Music and lyrics by Harry Warren and Al Dubin. Copyright 1933 by Remick Music, Inc.

Warner Bros. Publications U.S. Inc., Miami, FL., 33014: From lyrics from "Get a Job" by Earl Beal, Richard Lewis, Raymond Edwards, and William Horton. Copyright © 1957 by EMI Longitude Music. All rights reserved.

Wieser & Wieser, Inc., Literary Agency: From *Japan's War: The Great Pacific Conflict, 1853 to 1952* by Edwin P. Hoyt. Copyright © 1986 by Edwin P. Hoyt.

Estate of G. Mennen Williams: From poem on Sputnik by Governor G. Mennen Williams of Michigan on October 4, 1957. Copyright © 1957 by G. Mennen Williams.

Women's International League for Peace and Freedom: From "Freedom of Thought and Speech" statement at 1949 annual meeting of the Women's International League for Peace and Freedom in Peace as a Women's Issue: A History of the U.S. Movement for World Peace and Women's Rights by Harriet Hyman Alonso. Copyright © 1993 by Syracuse University Press.

SOURCES CITED:

From "Driving Cattle from Texas to Iowa, 1866" by George Crawford Duffield from *Annals of Iowa*, vol. XIV, 1924.

Quotes by Donna Shalala from "Shalala Remembers Kennedy's Call to Peace; Cabinet Secretary Comes to Austin for Peace Corps Reunion" by Ben Wear from *Austin American-Statesman*, August 4, 1995.

From "Women's Role in American Society: Retrospect and Prospect, To Be Black and a Woman" by Dorothy Height from *Women's Role in Contemporary Society: The Report of The New York City Commission on Human Rights*, September 21–25, 1970. Published by Avon Books, New York, 1972.

Quote by Martha Ann Morrison Minto from "Female Pioneering in Oregon, 1844" from a Manuscript Diary, Bancroft Library, University of California, Berkeley, CA.

Quotes by Reverend Harold Toliver and Nelson Poynter from *Americans Remember the Home Front: An Oral Narrative of the World War II Years in America* by Roy Hoopes. Published by Berkley Books, New York, 1992.

From a quote by Deputy Reyes to the Honduran Congress from *Boletin Legislativ* (Legislative Record), series iv, no. 31, January 23, 1933.

Quotes from a Boxer handbill and from a British officer from "Missionary Martyrs of the Boxer Rebellion," from *Christian History Magazine*, issue 52, vol.XV, no. 4.

Quote by Elisha Stockwell from *The Boys' War: Confederate and Union Soldiers Talk About the Civil War* by Jim Murphy. Published by Clarion Books, New York, 1990.

Quote by Captain José Fernandez, translated by Valeska Bari from *The Course of Empire: First Hand Accounts of California in the Days of he Gold Rush of '49* compiled by Valeska Bari. Published by Coward-McCann, Inc., New York, 1931.

Quote by Mary Mackey and from *Great Expectations: America and the Baby Boom Generation* by Landon Y. Jones. Published by Coward, McCann & Geoghegan, New York, 1980.

From "The First Tanks in Action, 15 September 1916" by Bert Chaney from *People at War, 1914—1918* by Michael Moynihan. Published by David and Charles, 1973.

Quote by Clara Hancox, quote by a German officer describing the fighting at Stalingrad, 1942, and quote by Albert Sindlinger from "Tinkering with the Wireless: Can Anyone Hear Me West of Steubenville?" from *The Century* by Peter Jennings and Todd Brewster. Published by Doubleday, a division of Random House, Inc., New York, 1998.

From *Edison's Open Door: The Life Story of Thomas A. Edison* by Alfred O. Tate. Published by E. P. Dutton, New York, 1938.

Quote about Lyndon B. Johnson from *With No Apologies: The Personal and Political Memoirs of United States Senator Barry Goldwater* by Barry Goldwater. Published by Greenwillow Books, a division of William Morrow & Company, New York, 1996.

Quote by an African American woman from *The American Slave: Georgia Narratives*, Part 1, vol. 12, edited by George P. Rawick. Published by Greenwood Publishing Group.

From *Their Eyes Were Watching God* by Zora Neale Hurston. Published by Harper & Row Publishers, New York, 1937.

Ellen Levine Literary Agency: From "Goodbye to Our Boy" by Garrison Keillor from *Time*, August 2, 1999, p.1. Copyright © 1999 by Garrison Keillor.

The Nation: From "U.S. Cultural Invasion: Hungary for American Pop" by Miklos Vamos from *The Nation*, March 25, 1991. Copyright © 1991 by The Nation.

Sierra Club Books: From *Nature's Economy: The Roots of Ecology* by Donald Worster. Copyright © 1977 by Donald Worster.

University of Minnesota Press: From *Uncertain Dimensions: Western Overseas Empires in the Twentieth Century* by Raymond F. Betts. Copyright © 1985 by the University of Minnesota.

Sources Cited:

Quote by Roger Ailes from "Ailes: What He Wants Next: Bush Adman Aims Attack at Madison Ave." by Steven W. Colford from *Advertising Age*, November 14, 1988, p. 67. Published by Crain Communications, Inc., New York, 1988.

Quotes by Oscar Ameringer, Len De Caux, CIO organizer Sidney Lens, William Allen White, and from a union song from *Redeeming the Time: A People's History of the 1920s and the New Deal* by Page Smith. Published by Penguin Books, New York, 1991.

Quotes by Lisa Anderson, Sally Belfrage, and Marshall Ganz from *Like a Holy Crusade: Mississippi 1964—The Turning of the Civil Rights Movement in America* by Nicolaus Mills. Published by Ivan R. Dee, Inc., Chicago, IL, 1992.

From *And the Walls Came Tumbling Down* by Ralph David Abernathy. Published by HarperCollins Publishers, Inc., New York, 1989.

Quote by Bruce Weigl from *The Vietnam Wars: 1945–1990* by Marilyn B. Young. Published by HarperCollins Publishers, New York, 1991.

From a quotation by Eleanor Roosevelt's cousin, Corinne, from *Without Precedent: The Life and Career of Eleanor Roosevelt*, edited by Joan Hoff-Wilson and Marjorie Lightman. Published by Indiana University Press, Bloomington, IN, 1984.

From "Something Should Be Done" from *The Great Crash 1929* by John K. Galbraith. Published by Houghton Mifflin Company. Boston, 1988.

From ". . . The hawk had come" by Gordon Parks from *Brother Can You Spare a Dime? The Great Depression, 1929–1933* by Milton Meltzer. Published by Alfred A. Knopf, Inc., New York, 1969.

Quote by Mrs. Townsend from "Young Mother" from *Ladies' Home Journal*, 1956.

Quote by Helen Farmer, Thomas Minehan, and by an anonymous teenager from *The Great Depression: America in the 1930s* by T. H. Watkins. Published by Little, Brown and Company, New York, 1993.

From *Red Power: The American Indians' Fight for Freedom* by Alvin M. Josephy, Jr. Published by McGraw-Hill, New York, 1971.

From "No Men Wanted" by Karl Monroe from *The Nation*, August 6, 1930. Published by The Nation, New York, 1930.

Quotes by José Angel Gutiérrez from interview by Hector Galán, December 12, 1994. Transcripts from National Latino Communications Center, Los Angeles, CA, and Galán Productions, Rodulfo Acuña, Austin, TX.

Quotes by Eliseo Medina from interview by Sylvia Morales, November 18, 1995. Transcripts from National Latino Communications Center, Los Angeles, CA, and Galán Productions, Austin, TX.

Excerpt about the Bay of Pigs from *The New York Times*.

From "The Stock Market Crash" by Elliott V. Bell from *The New York Times*, October 24, 1929.

From "Still 'A Little Left of Center'" by Anne O'Hare McCormick from *The New York Times*, June 21, 1936.

Quote by David Wyss from "Ace in the Hole" by John Cassidy from *The New Yorker*, June 10, 1996.

Quote by Robert Reich from "They're Rich (and You're Not)" by Adam Bryant from *Newsweek*, July 5, 1999. Published by Newsweek, Inc., New York, 1999.

Quotes by New Yorker Johnny Boy Musto, Anibal Campa, and a 21-year-old beautician from "Get Up and Boogie" by Maureen Orth et al, from *Newsweek*, November 8, 1976. Published by Newsweek, Inc., New York, 1976.

Quote by Harley Shaiken from "Big Brown's Union Blues" by Daniel Pedersen from *Newsweek*, August 18, 1997. Published by Newsweek, Inc., New York, 1997.

From quote by Christa McAuliffe from *The New York Times*, January 29, 1986. Published by the New York Times Company, New York, 1986.

From *Cesar Chavez: Autobiography of La Causa* by Jacques E. Levy. Published by W. W. Norton & Company, Inc., New York, 1975.

Quote by Shirley Keith in concert, "Benefit for Alcatraz," at Stanford, CA, December 18, 1969. Recording at Pacifica Radio Archives, North Hollywood, CA .

Quote by Sugar Rautbord from *The Great Divide* by Studs Terkel. Published by Pantheon Books, New York, 1988.

Quote by Dr. Alfred Crosby from *The American Experience: Influenza 1918*, on-line, June 28, 1991. Available at http://www.pbs.org/wgbh/pages/amex/influenza/filmmore/transcript/.

From *The Road Ahead* by Bill Gates with Nathan Myhrvold and Peter Rinearson. Published by Penguin Books, New York, 1996.

Quote by Tran Do, Myron Harrington, Ton That Tung, and excerpt from *Vietnam: A History* by Stanley Karnow. Published by Penguin Books, New York, 1983.

Quotes by Bernice Johnson and Charles Houston from *Eyes on the Prize* by Juan Williams. Published by Penguin Books, New York, 1988.

A quotation regarding Charles E. Hughes from Unknown Observer from *Toward a New Order of Sea Power: American Naval Policy and the World Scene, 1918–1922* by Harold and Margaret Sprout. Published by Princeton University Price

From *The Presidential Papers* by Norman Mailer. Published by G. P. Putnam's Sons, New York, 1963.

From *Sharing Smaller Pies* by Tom Bender. First published in Rain, Portland, OR, 1975.

From "A Black GI" from *Everything We Had: An Oral History of the Vietnam War* by Al Santoli. Published by Random House, Inc., New York, 1981.

From *Steven Spielberg: A Biography* by Joseph McBride. Published by Simon & Schuster, New York, 1997.

From a quote by Anne O'Hare McCormick from *Truman* by David McCullough. Published by Simon & Schuster, New York, 1992.

Quotes by MacArthur Cotton and Mendy Samstein from *Notes on Mississippi Staff Meeting*, November 1963, State Historical Society of Wisconsin: Howard Zinn Papers.

Quote by Mary Margaret Funk from "Buddhism in America" by Jeanne McDowell and Richard N. Ostling from *Time*, on-line, Oct. 13, 1997, vol. 150, New York, 1997.

Quotes by J. García and M. A. Zumbado R. from *Sociedad Económica de Amigos del País*, Estudio relativo a los Contratos Bananeros celebrados entre el Gobierno de Costa Rica y Mr. M. M. Marsh y la United Fruit Company, San Jose, CA, 1929.

Quote by D. Clayton Brown of Texas Christian University, from *Encyclopedia of Southern Culture, vol. 1, Agriculture–Environment*, edited by Charles Reagan Wilson et al. Published by the University of North Carolina Press, Chapel Hill, NC, 1989.

From John Ortiz from *Social Protest in an Urban Barrio: A Study of the Chicano Movement, 1966–1974* by Marguerite V. Marin. Published by University Press of America, Lanham, MD, 1991.

Quote by Maria Valera about the National Chicano Liberation Youth Conference, 1969, from *Youth, Identity, Power: The Chicano Movement* by Carlos Muñoz. Published by Verso, London, England, 1989.

Quote by Cesar Caballero from "Chuppies" from *New Americans: An Oral History: Immigrants and Refugees in the U.S. Today* by Al Santoli. Published by Viking Press, New York, 1988.

From *The Grapes of Wrath* by John Steinbeck. Published by the Viking Press, New York, 1939.

From a quotation by Indira Gandhi from "The India of My Dreams" from *My Truth* by Indira Gandhi, presented by Emmanuel Pouchpadass. First published in English in 1981 by Vision Books Pvt. Ltd., New Delhi, in collaboration with Editions Stock, Paris.

Quote by Jane Berentson from interview with Charles Kaiser, July 7, 1986, from *1968 in America: Music, Politics, Chaos, Counterculture, and the Shaping of a Generation* by Charles Kaiser. Published by Weidenfeld & Nicolson, New York, 1988.

Photo Credits

Abbreviations used: (t) top, (c) center, (b) bottom, (l) left, (bckgd) background, (bdr) border

FRONT MATTER: Page iii (t), courtesy Paul Boyer; iii (cl), courtesy Yasuhide Kawashima; iii (tr), courtesy Nan Woodruff; iii (cr), courtesy Alfred Young; iii (tl), courtesy Ronald Foore; iii (b), courtesy Lucinda Lucero Sachs; iii, Courtesy Dr. Sterling Stuckey; v, Rick Vargas/ Smithsonian Institution; vi (t), Museum of the City of New York, Gift of Mary and Charles Odgen.; vi (bl), The Granger Collection, New York; vi (br), Smithsonian Institution, neg no. 91-6501; vii (b), Frank Driggs Collection; ix, CORBIS-Bettmann; x (l), HRW Photo by Sam Dudgeon; x (r), Sylvia Johnson/Woodfin Camp & Associates; xi (t), David Hume Kennerly / CORBIS Sygma; xi (b), Richard B. Levine; xii (t), Selwyn Tait / Newsmakers; xii (b), George Hall/Check Six; xiii (t), NASA; (b), Printed by permission of the Norman Rockwell Family Trust (c)1943 / Photo courtesy of the Curtis Publishing Company; xiv (r), U.S. Postal Service / Harcourt ; xv (t), Library of Congress/ PRC Archive; xv (b), Bob Daemmrich Photo, Inc.; xvi, HRW Photo by Victoria Smith; xviii (l), Courtesy of the Museum of the American Numismatic Association; xviii (r), Cook Collection, Valentine Museum, Richmond, Virginia; xviii–xx (flags) Image Copyright (c) 1997 PhotoDisc, Inc.; xix, NASA; xx, Photo by Byron, The Byron Collection, Museum of the City of New York; xxi (t), Library of Congress; xxi (b), Richard B. Levine; xiv (l), U.S. Postal Service / Harcourt; viii (t), The Granger Collection, New York;

UNIT 1: Pages 0–1, Kirby Collection of Historical Paintings, Lafayette College, Easton, Pennsylvania ; 1, Colorado Historical Society.

CHAPTER 1: Page 2 (t), Runk/ Schoenberger from Grant Heilman Photography; (tr) AKG Photo; (b), The Granger Collection, New York; 3 (tl), (c) Bettmann/ CORBIS; 3 (bl), Stock Montage, Inc.; 3 (tr), Peter Newark's American Pictures; 3 (br), National Museum of American Numismatic Collection, New York Numismatic Collection; 4 (b), AKG Photo, London; 5 (t), Mireille Vautier / Woodfin Camp & Associates, Inc.; 6, (c) Allan Eaton / Ancient Art & Architecture Collection Ltd.; 7 (t), (c) Marilyn "Angel" Wynn/ Sun Valley Video; 7 (b), The Granger Collection, New York; 8, Art Resource, NY; 9, Peter Newark's American Pictures; 10, Peabody Essex Museum, Salem, Massachusetts; 11, The Granger Collection, New York; 12 (t), Courtesy of the Pilgrim Society, Plymouth,

Massachusetts; 12 (b), Boltin Picture Library; 13 (t), Royal Albert Memorial Museum, Exeter, Devon, UK/Bridgeman Art Library, New York/London; 13 (b), The Granger Collection, New York; 14, Fitzwilliam Museum, University of Cambridge, UK/Bridgeman Art Library, New York/London; 15, Colonial Williamsburg Foundation; 16 (b), Peter Newark's American Pictures; 16 (t), The Granger Collection, New York; 17, The Granger Collection, New York; 18, The Granger Collection, New York; 20 (t), The Granger Collection, New York; 20 (b), The Granger Collection, New York; 21, Carroll Reece Museum, Center for Appalachian Studies, East Tennessee University; 23, Free Library of Philadelphia/Scala/Art Resource, NY; 24 (l), The Granger Collection, New York; 24 (r), Stock Editions/HRW Photo Research Library; 26, The Historical Society of Pennsylvania (HSP), "The Congress Voting Independence" by Robert Edge Pine and/or Edward Savage, acc. # 1904.1; 28, SuperStock; 30, The Granger Collection, New York; 31, CORBIS-Bettmann; 32, The Granger Collection, New York; 33, The Granger Collection, New York.

CONSTITUTION HANDBOOK: Page 38, Library of Congress; 39, Independence National Historical Park Collection; 40 (c), U.S. Postal Service/ Harcourt; 40 (b), U.S. Postal Service/ Harcourt ; 40 (t), The Granger Collection, New York; 41 (t), Independence National Historical Park Collection; 41 (b), David Young-Wolff/ PhotoEdit; 42, Nebraska State Historical Society; 44 (b), CORBIS-Bettmann; 44 (t), The Granger Collection, New York; 45 (t), Independence National Historical Park Collection; 45 (t), National Archives, photos no. 2363.249, 2361.2498, 2362.2429; 50, Independence National Historical Park Collection; 53, Collection, The Supreme Court Historical Society; 57 (b), Jeffrey Brown/Liaison Agency; 57 (t), Joe Marquette/AP/Wide World Photos; 58, Bob Daemmrich Photo, Inc., 59, Louis Psihoyos /Contact Press Images / Woodfin Camp & Associates ; 60, Library of Congress; 62 (t), HRW Photo by Sam Dudgeon; 62 (b), Underwood & Underwood/ CORBIS-Bettmann; 63, Sophia Smith Collection, Smith College; 64, R. Foulds / Washington Stock Photo; 65, AP/Wide World Photos, x.; 66, Jeff Greenberg/PhotoEdit; 67 (t), The Granger Collection, New York; 67 (cr), Chicago Historical Society, #X.1354; 67 (cl), HRW Photo by Sam Dudgeon; 67 (b), Tom Pantages; 68 (tr), North Wind Picture Archives, 68 (bl), Superstock ; 68 (br), Missouri Historical Society.

CHAPTER 2: Page 68, (b) Bettmann / CORBIS; 69 (t), Colorado Historical Society; (c) D. Donne Bryant/DDB Stock Photo; 69 (tl), The Granger Collection, New York; 69 (bc), Library of Congress; 69 (br), The Museum of American Political Life, University of Hartford, West Hartford, CT; 70, Sally Andersen-Bruce Photography; 71, Stock Montage, Inc.; 72 (t), Larry Stevens / Nawrocki Stock Photo; 72 (b), United States Postal Service / Harcourt; 73, Ohio Historical Society; 75, The Granger Collection, New York; 76, Nawrocki Stock Photo; 77, Peter Newark's Western Americana; 78, Archive Photos; 79, The Granger Collection, New York; 80 (b), The Granger Collection, New York; 80 (t), Archive Photos; 81, WOOLAROC MUSEUM, BARTLESVILLE, OKLAHOMA; 82, Slater Mill Historic Site; 83 (t), Collection of the New-York Historical Society, neg. no. 50473; 83 (b), Courtesy of the Illinois State Historical Library; 84 (b), The Metropolitan Museum of Art, Gift of I.N. Phelps Stokes, Edward S. Hawes, Alice Mary Hawes, Marion Augusta Hawes, 1937. [37.14.22]; 84 (t), Library of Congress / PRC Archive; 85, The Granger Collection, New York; 86, Carl Socolon/The Landis Valley Museum; 87 (t), Texas State Library and Archives Commission; 87 (b), courtesy of the California History Room, California State Library, Sacramento, California; 89 (b), The Granger Collection, New York; 89 (t), Print Collection, Miriam and Ira D. Wallach Division of Art, Prints and Photographs, The New York Public Library, Astor, Lenox and Tilden Foundations; 90, The Granger Collection, New York; 91, Library of Congress.

CHAPTER 3: Page 94 (tl), Library of Congress/ PRC Archive; 94 (tr), COURTESY GEORGE EASTMAN HOUSE; 94 (bl), The Granger Collection, New York; 94 (bc), Library of Congress/photo by Ken Cobb; 94 (br), (c) Bettmann/CORBIS; 95 (tl), Tom Lovell / National Geographic Image Collection; 95 (tr), Courtesy of the Museum of the American Numismatic Association; 95 (b), The Museum of the Confederacy, Richmond, Virginia; 96 (t), Chicago Historical Society, neg. no. IChi-22144; 97 (t), Library of Congress; 97 (b), U.S. Postal Service / Harcourt; 98, PRC Archive; 99, 100, The Museum of the Confederacy, Richmond, Virginia. Photography by Katherine Wetzel; 101, From *The Civil War: Forward to Richmond*. Photograph by Al Freni, (c) 1983 Time-Life Books, Inc. Courtesy, Troiani Collection; 102, The Granger Collection, New York; 103 (l), (c) Collection of Kean Wilcox. All rights reserved / PRC Archive; 103 (r), Private Collection/ PRC Archive; 104, Library of Congress; 105, Library of Congress /PRC Archive; 106 (b), Courtesy Mulberry Plantation, Camden, SC/Photo by Alt Lee, Columbia, SC; 106 (t), National Portrait Gallery, Smithsonian Institution, Washington DC/Art Resource, NY; 107, Library of Congress / PRC Archive; 108 (t), Chicago Historical Society;108 (b), The Museum of the Confederacy, Richmond, Virginia. From ECHOES OF GLORY: Arms and Equipment of the Confederacy (c) 1991, Time Life, Inc. Photo High Impact/Larry Sherer 109, The Granger Collection, New York; 110 (t), Collection of Michael J. McAfee / PRC Archive; 110 (b), Library of Congress; 111, Chicago Historical Society, no. P&S 1932.0027; 113 (t), Collection of The Mercer Museum of The Bucks County Historical Society; (b), Library of Congress; 114, CORBIS / Bettmann; 114 (t), Library of Congress; 115, Library Company of Philadelphia; 116, West Point Museum Collections, United States Military Academy; 117, Anne S. Brown Military Collection, Brown University; 118 (t), Library of Congress / PRC Archive; 120 (t), Laurie Platt Winfrey/ Woodfin Camp & Associates; (b), Library of Congress; 121, Atlanta History Center; 122, Library of Congress; 123, Tom Lovell / National Geographic Image Collection (detail).

CHAPTER 4: Page 128 (tl), Library of Congress; 128 (t), The Granger Collection, New York; 128 (b), Jubilee Singers, Courtesy of Fisk University Library Special Collections; 129 (tr), The Western Reserve Historical Society, Cleveland, Ohio; 129 (tl), Atlanta History Center; 129 (b), LEGISLATIVE DEPARTMENT LE Series 1 Petitions (National Archives of New Zealand Head Office); 130, Hulton Getty / Newsmakers; 131, Bob Daemmrich Photography; 132, Library of Congress; 133, Print Collection, Miriam and Ira D. Wallach Division of Art, Prints and Photographs, The New York Public Library, Astor, Lenox and Tilden Foundations; 134, The Western Reserve Historical Society, Cleveland, Ohio; 135 (t), National Archives (NARA)/ PRC Archive; 135 (b), CORBIS-Bettmann; 136, Library of Congress; 137 (t), Library of Congress/PRC Archive; 137 (b), The Granger Collection, New York; 138 (b), Louisiana Collection, Howard Tilton Memorial Library, New Orleans, LA 70118; 139 (t), U.S. Postal Service / Harcourt; 140 (b), The Granger Collection, New York; 140 (t), The Granger Collection, New York; 140 (t), Keystone-Mast Collection, neg.# 24039, UCR / California Museum of Photography, University of California, Riverside; 141 (t), U.S. Postal Service / Harcourt; 141 (b), Frank & Marie-Therese Wood Print Collection, The Picture Bank, Alexandria, VA; 143 (t), North Wind Picture Archives; 144 (t), Library of Congress / PRC Archive; 144 (tr), Collection of Nancy Gewirz, Antique Textile Resource/ PRC Archive; 144 (b), Tennessee State Museum Collection/ Photo by June Dorman; 146 (b), Frank & Marie-Therese Wood Print Collection, The Picture Bank, Alexandria, VA ; 148 (t), The Metropolitan Museum of Art , Morris K. Jesup Fund, 1940. (40.40). Photograph by Malcolm Varon. Photograph (c) 1984 The Metropolitan Museum of Art; 149 (b), The Granger Collection, New York; 149 (tl), Brown Brothers; 149 (tr), (c) Joe Sohm / The Image Works; 150 (t), The Granger Collection, New York; 150 (b), South Carolina Historical Society; 151 (l), The Western Reserve Historical Society, Cleveland, Ohio; (r), Ohio Historical Society; 152 (t), Underwood Photo Archives; 152 (b), Photographs and Prints Division, Schomburg Center for Research in Black Culture, The New York Public Library. Astor, Lenox and Tilden Foundations; 153, CORBIS-Bettmann; 156 (t), Peter Newark's American Pictures; 156 (b), PRC Archive; 157 (t), Private Collection/ PRC Archive; 157 (b), Peter Newark's American Pictures.

UNIT 2: Page 158–159, Peter Newark's American Pictures; 159, National Park Service Collection / Gift of Angelo Forgione, c. 1991.

CHAPTER 5: page 160 (tl), Courtesy Wells Fargo Bank; (tc), Courtesy of the Seward House, Auburn, NY; (tr), FORBES Magazine Collection, New York/The Bridgeman Art Library, New York/London; 160 (br), Boston Public Library/Rare Books Department. Courtesy of the Trustees; 160 (br), Boltin Picture Library; 161 (tl), Nawrocki Stock Photo; 161 (t), Library of Congress; 161 (b), (c) Bettmann/CORBIS; 161 (tr), FORBES Magazine Collection, New York, USA / The Bridgeman Art Library, New York/London; 162, The Granger Collection, New York; 164 (t), Courtesy of Colorado Historical Society; 164 (b), Photo by Blair Clark, courtesy Museum of New Mexico, Neg. no. 155365; 165 (t), COURTESY OF THE SOUTHWEST MUSEUM, LOS ANGELES; 165 (t), Photo by D.F. Barry, the Denver Public Library, Western History Collection; 165, From Pennsylvania Historical & Museum Commission. Drake Well Museum Collection, Titusville, PA; 166, The Field Museum, #A111822-2c; 167, National Anthropological Archives, Smithsonian Institution, Washington, D.C., neg. #81-9626; 168 (t), Boston Public Library/Rare Books Department. Courtesy of the Trustees; 168 (b), The Granger Collection, New York; 169 (t), National Anthropological Archives, Smithsonian Institution, Washington, DC, neg no. 57489; 169 (b), National Anthropological Archives, Smithsonian Institution, Washington, DC, neg no. 57490; 170, Collection of the New-York Historical Society, neg. no. 41800; 171 (tr), Peter Newark's Western Americana; 171 (tl), Kansas Collection, Kenneth Spencer Research Library, University of Kansas Libraries; 171 (b), Chicago Historical Society, neg. no. IChi 29620; 172 (t), Nebraska State Historical Society; 172, Library of Congress; 173 (t), Batavia Depot Museum, Batavia, Illinois/Courtesy, Chicago Historical Society; 174 (t), California Historical Society, FN-16661; 174 (t), State Historical Society of Wisconsin, negative (X3)1804; 175 (t), The Kansas State Historical Society, Topeka, Kansas; 175 (t), Fred Hultstrand History in Pictures Collection, NDSU, Fargo, ND; 176 (b), Boston Public Library/Rare Books Department. Courtesy of the Trustees; 176 (t), Photography Collection, Miriam and Ira D. Wallach Division of Art, Prints and Photographs, The New York Public Library, Astor, Lenox and Tilden Foundations; 177 (t), The Kansas State Historical Society, Topeka, Kansas; 178, Peter Newark's Western Americana; 179 (t), The Granger Collection, New York; 179 (b), The Museum of Fine Arts, Houston, The Hogg Brothers Collection, Gift of Miss Ima Hogg; 180, (c) John Eastcott/Yva Momatiuk/The Image Works; 181, Peter Newark's Western Americana; 182, The Granger Collection, New York; 182 (t), Courtesy of the Oakland Museum of California; 184, The Granger Collection, New York; 183 (t), Colorado Historical Society; 186, Montana Historical Society, Helena; 187, Colorado Historical Society; 189, HRW Photo by Victoria Smith; 189, HRW Photo by Victoria Smith.

CHAPTER 6: Page 190 (tl), Colorado Historical Society, # IChi-30421; 190 (bl), Library of Congress; 190 (tc), Property of AT&T Archives. Printed with permission of AT&T; 190 (br), Los Angeles County Museum of Art, Acquisition made possible through Museum Trustees: Robert O. Anderson, R. Stanton Avery, B. Gerald Cantor, Edward W. Carter, Justin Dart, Charles E. Ducommun, Mrs. F. Daniel Frost, Julian Ganz, Jr.,

Quotes by Jim Bevel, Ossie Davis, and Paula Giddings from *Voices of Freedom: An Oral History of the Civil Rights Movement from the 1950s Through the 1980s* by Henry Hampton, Steve Fayer, with Sarah Flynn. Published by Bantam Books, New York, 1990.

From *A Very Different Age: Americans of the Progressive Era* by Steven J. Diner. Published by Hill and Wang, a division of Farrar, Straus and Giroux, LLC, New York, 1998.

Quote by Miss Egan ("Hello Girls") from *American Women in World War I: They Also Served* by Lettie Gavin. Published by University Press of Colorado, Niwot, CO, 1997.

Quotes by Jeff Greenfield, Harriet Osborn, and Jack Trachsel from *The Century* by Peter Jennings and Todd Brewster. Published by Doubleday, a division of Random House, Inc., New York, 1998.

From "Women on the Breadlines" by Meridel Le Sueur, *New Masses 7*, January 1932.

From "The Meaning of the Kellogg Treaty" by Henry Cabot Lodge, Jr., from *Harper's Magazine*, New York, December 1928.

From *Three Years in Mississippi* by James H. Meredith. Published by Indiana University Press, Bloomington, IN, 1966.

Quote by George Washington Plunkitt from *Plunkitt of Tammany Hall* by William L. Riordon. Published by E. P. Dutton, New York, 1963.

Dr. Armand Hammer, Hart Lenart, Dr. Franklin D. Murphy, Mrs. Joan Palevsky, Richard E. Sherwood, Maynard J. Toll and Hal B. Wallis. Photography (c) 2000 Museum Associates/LACMA, M.77.68; 190 (tr), Private Collection/PRC Archive; 191 (tr), Carnegie Library of Pittsburgh; 191 (bl), CORBIS-Bettmann; 191 (br), CORBIS-Bettmann; 191 (tl), Ann Ronan / Image Select, Inc.; 192, Property of AT&T Archives. Reprinted with permission of AT&T ; 194 (l), Union Pacific Railroad Museum ; 194 (r), Chicago Historical Society, no. 1920.53ab; 194 (b), The California Department of Parks and Recreation; 195, Library of Congress; 196 (t), National Air & Space Museum, Smithsonian Institution, Washington, D.C., neg. no. A26767B-2 ; 196 (b), Division of Political History, Smithsonian Institution, Washington DC / Charles Phillips / PRC Archive; 196 (bl), Smithsonian Institution, neg no. 91-6501 ; 197 (b), The Granger Collection, New York; 197 (c), The Granger Collection, New York; 197 (tl), The Granger Collection, New York; 197 (tr), David Young-Wolff/PhotoEdit; 198, Division of Political History, Smithsonian Institution, Washington, D.C., neg. # 91-6449; 199 (b), The Granger Collection, New York; 199 (t), National Portrait Gallery, Smithsonian Institution, Washington, DC / Art Resource, NY; 200, Harcourt Photo Library; 201, Collection of Dennis Kurlander; 202, Downe House, Downe, Kent, UK/The Bridgeman Art Library; 203 (t), Culver Pictures, Inc.; 203 (b), National Portrait Gallery, Smithsonian Institution, Washington DC/ Art Resource, NY ; 204, Carnegie Library, Pittsburgh; 205, Archive Photos; 206, The Granger Collection, New York; 207 (t), Illinois State Historical Library; 207 (b), PRC Archive; 208 (b), Chicago Historical Society, Neg no. IChi 01622 ; 208 (t), Sears, Roebuck and Co.; 209 (t), Culver Pictures, Inc. ; 210, Chicago Historical Society, DN #954; 211, CORBIS-Bettmann; 212 (b), The Granger Collection, New York; 212 (t), 213,214, CORBIS-Bettmann; 215, The Granger Collection, New York.

CHAPTER 7: Page 218 (tl), Library of Congress; 218 (bl), Library of Congress/ PRC Archive; 218 (br), (c) Collection of The New-York Historical Society, neg. no. 51392; 218 (tr), HRW Photo Research Library; 219 (tl), PRC Archive; 219 (b), Collection of Sandy Marrone; 219 (tr), Courtesy of the Rockefeller University Archives; 220, Photography by Karen Yamauchi for Chermayeff & Geismar Inc./ MetaForm Inc.; 220, Library of Congress/PRC Archive; 221, Library of Congress; 222 (t), Brown Brothers; 222 (tr), Uniphoto Picture Agency; 223 (b), "Children's Playground on Ellis Island (Roof Garden)," c. 1890. Photographed by Augustus Sherman, The Jacob A. Riis Collection #476, Museum of the City of New York; 223 (t), Mark Gallery, London, Bridgeman Art Library, New York/London ; 224, Culver Pictures, Inc ; 225, Library of Congress; 226 (t), Detroit Publishing Company Collection, Library of Congress; 227, Photo by Byron, The Byron Collection, Museum of the City of New York; 228 (t), Culver Pictures, Inc.; 228 (bl), Museum of the City of New York, Gift of Mary and Charles Odgen; 228 (br), Courtesy of the Oakland Museum of California; 229, Whitford & Hughes, London, UK / Bridgeman Art Library, New York/London; 230 (b), Courtesy the Museum of the City of New York; 230 (t), Costume Division, Smithsonian Institution, Washington DC, neg. no. 74-9637; 231 (t), Brown Brothers; 231 (br), Jane Addams Memorial Collection (JAMC neg 227), Special Collections, University Library, University of Illinois at Chicago; 231 (bl), The Newberry Library; 232, Caroline Bartlett Crane Collection, Archives and Regional History Collections, Western Michigan University; 232, The Granger Collection, New York; 233 (t), Curt Teich Postcard Archives, Lake County (IL) Museum; 234, Library of Congress; 235 (t), HRW Photo Research Library; 235 (b), HRW Photo Research Library; 236 (b), The Granger Collection, New York; 236 (t), Brooklyn Historical Society, # V1974.39.5; 237 (tl), Cincinnati Museum Center Image Archives; 237 (tr), Division of Political History, Smithsonian Institution, Washington, D.C. ; 237 (b), CORBIS-Bettmann; 238 (t), The Granger Collection, New York; 239 (r), Division of American Political History, Smithsonian Institution, neg no. 91-10334; 239 (l), Library of Congress / PRC Archive.

CHAPTER 8: Page 244 (tl), Courtesy of the Museum of the American Numismatic Association; 244 (tr), Musee d'Orsay, Paris, France / Peter Willi / Bridgeman Art Library, New York/London; 244 (bl), The Granger Collection, New York; 244 (br), CORBIS-Bettmann; 245 (br), W. K. KELLOGG is a trademark of Kellogg Company. All rights reserved. Used with permission; 245 (tl), Replica Courtesy Deere & Company ; 245 (tr), COURTESY GEORGE EASTMAN HOUSE; 245 (bl), National Museum of American History, Smithsonian Institution, Washington, D.C., neg.#89-13226; 245, (detail) (c) Collection of the New-York Historical Society, neg. no. 40908; 246 (t), Collection of Janice L. and David J. Frent/PRC Archive; 246 (b), From Political History of Jackson County; Kansas City: Marshall & Morrison, 1902; KC27, N4, Western Historical Manuscript Collection - Kansas City; 246, CORBIS-Bettmann; 249, (c) Collection of The New-York Historical Society, neg. no. 49183; 250, Library of Congress / PRC Archive; 251, Library of Congress; 252 (t), The Granger Collection, New York; 253 (t), Museum of American Political Life, Sally Andersen-Bruce ; 253 (r), Collection of Janice L. and David J. Frent/PRC Archive; 253 (b), The Granger Collection, New York; 254 (l), University of California at Berkeley, Bancroft Library; 254 (r), The Newberry Library; 255 (t), The Newberry Library; 255 (b), National Postal Museum, Smithsonian Institution, Washington, DC; 256 (t), Paul Conklin / PhotoEdit; 256 (b), The Granger Collection, New York ; 257 (t), United States Postal Service / Harcourt; 257 (b), Collection of Janice L. and David J. Frent/PRC Archive; 259 (b), Randy Leffingwell; 261, The Granger Collection, New York; 262 (t), The Burns Archive; 262 (bl), State Historical Society of Wisconsin, negative (IHAA) 633; 262 (br), Grant Heilman Photography; 263 (tr), Courtesy of the Museum of the American Numismatic Association ; 263 (tl), Courtesy of the Museum of the American Numismatic Association; 263 (b), Nebraska State Historical Society ; 264 (t), CORBIS-Bettmann; 264 (b), Library of Congress / PRC Archive; 265, United States Postal Service / Harcourt; 268 (t), CORBIS-Bettmann; (b), Sally Fox Collection / PRC Archive; 268 (br), United States Postal Service, Inc.; (c) Rube Goldberg, Inc.; 269 (b), The Granger Collection, New York; 269 (t), The Granger Collection, New York.

UNIT 3: Pages 270–271, Gift of Dwight Franklin, Museum of the City of New York; 271, Collection of David J. and Janice L. Frent / PRC Archive.

CHAPTER 9: Page 272 (t), Archive Photos; 272 (tr), Library of Congress; 272 (b), Edison National Historic Site, National Park Service/ U.S. Department of the Interior; 272 (br), Benjamin K. Edwards Collection, Library of Congress; 272 (b), Toledo-Lucas County Public Library; 273 (tl), The George Meany Memorial Archives; 273 (bl), CORBIS-Bettmann; 273 (br), (c) Bettmann/CORBIS; 273 (tr), Detroit Publishing Company Photograph Collection, Library of Congress; 273 (tc), Eben Comins / Collection of the Supreme Court of the United States; 273 (bc), HRW Photo by Sam Dudgeon; 274, The Newberry Library 275 (t), Image Copyright (c) 1998 PhotoDisc, Inc.; (b), (c) Bettmann/CORBIS;276 (t), The Granger Collection, New York ; 276 (t), Brown Brothers; 277 (r), Culver Pictures, Inc.; 277 (l), CORBIS-Bettmann; 278 (t), Library of Congress /PRC Archive; 278 (b), COURTESY GEORGE EASTMAN HOUSE; 279 (b), Rare Book and Manuscript Library, University of Pennsylvania, Philadelphia, PA; 279 (c), The Newberry Library ; 279 (t), The Newberry Library; 280, The George Meany Memorial Archives ; 281 (t), Culver Pictures; 281 (b), The George Meany Memorial Archives; 282 (b), UPI/CORBIS-Bettmann; 282 (t), The Granger Collection, New York; 283 (t), Archive Photos; 283 (b), HRW Photo by Victoria Smith; 284 (t), UNITE Archives, Kheel Center, Cornell University; 284 (b), The Granger Collection, New York; 285, CORBIS-Bettmann; 286 (t), Library of Congress / PRC Archive; 286 (b), Brown Brothers; 287 (t), Daniel H. Burnham in a flowered tie, signed. Photograph c 1996, The Art Institute of Chicago.; 287 (b), View of the City from Jackson Park to Grant Park, plate 49 from Plan of Chicago, 1907, 104x477 cm delineated by Jules Guerin, watercolor and pencil on paper, 1907, on permanent loan to the Art Institute of Chicago from the City of Chicago, 2.148.1966, detail. Photograph (c) 1996, The Art Institute of Chicago. All rights reserved; 288 (b), Culver Pictures; 288 (t), Uniphoto; 289 (c), HRW Photo Research Library; 289 (b), CORBIS-Bettmann; 289 (t), John Hay Library, Brown University ; 290 (b), The Newberry Library; 290 (t), Library of Congress 291, The Newberry Library; 291, ; 292, CORBIS-Bettmann, 293, Photography by Karen Yamauchi for Chermayeff & Geismar inc./ MetaForm Inc.

CHAPTER 10: Page 296 (tl), Archives Division - Texas State Library; (bl), Courtesy of the Rosenberg Library, Galveston, Texas; 296 (tr), CORBIS-Bettmann; 296 (tl), (c) Michael Freeman / CORBIS; 296, HRW Photo by Sam Dudgeon; 296, HRW Photo by Sam Dudgeon; 297 (bl), Collection of Janice L. and David J. Frent/PRC Archive; 297 (t), The Granger Collection, New York; 297 (b), Library of Congress; 298 (t), Brown Brothers; 299, The Granger Collection, New York; 300 (t), Library Legacy Foundation, Toledo-Lucas County Public Library; 301, The Granger Collection, New York; 302, Library of Congress ; 303 (t), Collection of Janice L. and David J. Frent/ PRC Archive; 304 (c), Sagamore Hill National Historic Site; 304 (t), United States Postal Service / Harcourt; 304 (b), George Meany Memorial Archives; 304, Department of Anthropology, Smithsonian Institution, Washington, DC. Neg. no. 2000-10647, Smithsonian photo.; 305, Library of Congress / PRC Archive; 306 (t), Culver Pictures; 306 (b), Chicago Historical Society, neg # ICHI1978.154.4 ; 307 (l), The Newberry Library; 307 (r), Laurie Platt Winfrey / Woodfin Camp & Associates; 308, National Museum of American Art, Smithsonian Institution, lent by the U.S. Department of the Interior/ Art Resource, NY; 309, Andre Jenny/New England Stock Photos; 310 (t), (c) Bettmann / CORBIS; 312, The Granger Collection, New York; 313, Theodore Roosevelt Collection, Harvard College Library; 314, CORBIS-Bettmann; 315 (t), City of Edinburgh Museum and Art Galleries / The Bridgeman Art Library, New York/London; 316 (t), United States Postal Service / Harcourt; 316 (b), Stock Montage, Inc.; 317 (t), PRC Archive 317 (b), Walter P. Reuther Library, Wayne State University; 318, "Nude Descending a Staircase, No. 2" (c) 2001Artists Rights Society (ARS), New York/ADAGP, Paris/Estate of Marcel Duchamp/ Bridgeman Art Library, New York/London; 319 (t), Culver Pictures; 319 (b), CORBIS-Bettmann; 320 (l), PRC Archive; 320 (r), Library of Congress / PRC Archive 323 (b), Collection of Janice L and David J. Frent/ PRC Archive; 323 (t), CORBIS-Bettmann.

CHAPTER 11: Page 324 (t), The Granger Collection, New York; 324 (bl), Knudsens Fotosenter, Oslo; 324 (br), Superstock; 325 (tl), Courtesy of The Mariners' Museum, Newport News, VA; 325 (tc), Photo Deutsches Museum, Munich; 325 (tr), Library of Congress/PRC Archive; 325 (b), The Lester S. Levy Sheet Music Collection, The Milton S. Eisenhower Library of The Johns Hopkins Library; 326 (t), The Granger Collection, New York; 327, By permission of the Houghton Library, Harvard University; 328 (t), (c) Hawaiian Legacy Archive/Pacific Stock; 328 (b), Culver Pictures; 329 (t), Hawaiian Legacy Archive / Pacific Stock; 329 (t), Hawaii State Archive; 330 (t), (c) A Dawson Gallery Image - Annapolis, MD; 330 (b), Trustees of the British Museum; 331, Library of Congress; 333 (t), The Granger Collection, New York; 333 (b), Brown Brothers; 334 (b), Nawrocki Stock Photo; 334 (t), Hulton Getty / Newsmakers ; 335 (t), Laurie Platt Winfrey / Woodfin Camp &

Associates; 335 (b), Library of Congress; 336 (t), Courtesy LIFE Magazine, (c) Time, Inc. Watercolor by C.J. Post, photo by Herb Orth.; 336 (b), National Archives / PRC Archive; 337, The Granger Collection, New York; 338, CORBIS; 339, CORBIS-Bettmann; 340 (b), Underwood & Underwood/CORBIS-Bettmann ; 342, The Granger Collection, New York; 344, CORBIS-Bettmann; 345 (t), CORBIS-Bettmann-UPI; 346 (t), CORBIS-Bettmann-UPI; 346 (bl), Latin Focus (c) All rights reserved; 346 (br), Keith Dannemiller/ SABA; 347 (b), (c) Bettmann/CORBIS ; 348, CORBIS-Bettmann; 349. The Granger Collection, New York.

CHAPTER 12: Page 354 (tl), PRC Archive; 354 (tc), Collection of Colonel Stuart S. Corning, Jr. (c) Rob Huntley/Lightstream/PRC Archive; 354 (bl), The Granger Collection, New York; 354 (tr), CORBIS-Bettmann; 354 (br), UPI/ CORBIS-Bettmann; 355 (tl), HRW Photo by Sam Dudgeon; 355 (b), The Trustees of the Imperial War Museum, London; 355 (tr), Willard Clay/ FPG International Corp.; 356, Nawrocki Stock Photo; 357, Laurent Van Der Stock / Newsmakers; 358, Trustees of the Imperial War Museum, London; 360, Photo by Dane Penland, National Air and Space Museum, Smithsonian Institution, Washington, DC (SI Neg. No. 80-2086); 361 (t), HRW Photo; 361 (b), UPI/Bettmann Newsphotos; 362, Mary Evans Picture Library; 364, National Archives, photo no. 86220212(82A); 365, HRW Photo by Eric Beggs; 366 (b), Archive Photos; 366 (t), The Granger Collection, New York; 367, American Stock Photography; 368, The Granger Collection, New York; 369, Herbert Hoover Presidential Library/ PRC Archive; 370 (t), CORBIS-Bettmann; 370 (b), National Archives, photo no. NWDNS-4-P176; 371 (l), Courtesy Archives of the Girl Scouts of the U.S.A./PRC Archive; 371 (r), CORBIS-Bettmann; 372, Brown Brothers; 373 (t), The Granger Collection, New York; 373 (b), The Granger Collection, New York; 374, HRW Photo by Lance Schriner; 375, The Granger Collection, New York; 376, HRW Photo by Victoria Smith; 377 (tr), Archive Photos; 377 (tl), (c)Dorling Kindersley Ltd./Courtesy of Spink & Son Ltd., London; 377 (b), UPI/CORBIS-Bettmann ; 378, The Granger Collection, New York; 380, Property HRW Photo Research Library; 381, Culver Pictures, Inc.; 383, The Granger Collection, New York; 384 (t), The Granger Collection, New York; 384 (b), PRC Archive; 385, Curt Teich Postcard Archives, Lake County Museum, Illinois; 385 (t), Snark International / Art Resource, NY.

UNIT 4: Pages 386–387, © Collection of The New-York Historical Society, neg. no. 1963.150; 387 (r), Christie's Images.

CHAPTER 13: Page 388 388 (tl), Collection of Janice L. and David J. Frent/PRC Archive388 (tr), The Granger Collection, New York; (bl), CORBIS-Bettmann; (br), *Babbit* by Sinclair Lewis; Newberry Library; 389 (bl), Chicago Historical Society, ICHI-22640; 389 (tl), Private Collection / PRC Archive; 389 (tr), Shahn, Ben. *Bartolomeo Vanzetti and Nicola Sacco* from the Sacco-Vanzetti series of twenty-three paintings (1931–32). Tempera on paper over composition board 10 1/2 x 14 1/2" (26.7 x 36.8 cm). The Museum of Modern Art, New York. Gift of Abby Aldrich Rockefeller, Photograph (c)2003 The Museum of Modern Art, New York. (c) Estate of Ben Shahn/Licensed by VAGA, New York, NY; 389 (r), Brown Brothers; 390, Library of Congress / PRC Archive; 391 (l), Leslie's Illustrated Newspaper September 20, 1920/ PRC Archive; 391 (b), Museum of History and Industry, Seattle, WA; 392 (t), UPI/Bettmann-CORBIS; 392 (bl), Walter P. Reuther Library, Wayne State University; 392 (br), AP / Wide World Photos; 393, The Granger Collection, New York; 394 (t), Collection of Janice L. and David J. Frent/PRC Archive; 394 (c), Brown Brothers; 394 (b), *The Anaconda Standard*, Jan. 4, 1920 / PRC Archive; 396, AP / Wide World Photos; 397, Collection of Janice L. and David J. Frent/PRC Archive; 398, Bob Daemmrich Photo, Inc.; 399, The Hagley Museum and Library; 400 (t), COURTESY GEORGE EASTMAN HOUSE; 400 (b), The Granger Collection, New York; 401 (t), Collection of Janice L. and David J. Frent/PRC Archive; 401 (br), Museum of American Political Life, University of Hartford, Photo by Steven Laschever; 401 (br), Coolidge Collection at Forbes Library; 402 (r), Collection of Janice L. and David J. Frent/ PRC Archive; 402 (l), Collection of Janice L. and David J. Frent/ PRC Archive; 403 (t), The Chicago Defender, April 7, 1917; 404, Brown Brothers; 405 (t), Archive Photos; 405 (b), Collection of Janice L. and David J. Frent/ PRC Archive; 406 (tl), Chicago Historical Society, Photo # IChi-12255; 406 (tr), The Messenger magazine Sep 1926 (Vol VIII, no. 9); Newberry Library; 406 (b), James Van Der Zee photo; 408 (t), Frank Driggs Collection; 408 (b), "Juan Salvador and Lupe's Wedding, 1929", from *Rain of Gold* by Victor Villasenor is reprinted with permission of the publisher (Arte Publico Press, University of Houston, 1991); 409, Underwood Photo Archives.

CHAPTER 14: Page 412 (bl), Library of American Broadcasting/ University of Maryland; 412 (tl), Archive Photos; 412 (tr), Brown Brothers; 412, Christie's Images; 413 (bl), (c) 2001 The Georgia O'Keeffe Foundation / Artists Rights Society (ARS), New York. The Metropolitan Museum of Art, Alfred Stieglitz Collection, 1969. (69.278.1) Photograph (c) 1987 The Metropolitan Museum of Art.; 413 (tc), Culver Pictures; 413 (br), Brown Brothers; 413 (tr), The Granger Collection, New York; 413 (tl), Gift of John P. Axelrod. Courtesy Museum of Fine Arts, Boston. Reproduced with Permission © 2000 Museum of Fine Arts, Boston. All Rights Reserved; 414 (t), CORBIS-Bettmann; 415 (t), Archive Photos; 415 (b), From the Collections of Henry Ford Museum and Greenfield Village; 416, PRC Archive; 417 (b), From the Collections of Henry Ford Museum and Greenfield Village; 417 (t), From the Collections of the Henry Ford Museum and Greenfield Village; 418 (t), Brown Brothers; 418, Arnold Genthe Collection, Library of Congress; 419, November 1927 Ladies Home Journal, The Newberry Library; 420 (t), Christie's Images; 420 (b), Rare Book, Manuscript and Special Collections Department, Perkins Library, Duke University ; 421, Brown Brothers; 423 (t), Chicago Historical Society, Photo no. IChi 14414, 423 (t), The Granger Collection, New York; 424 (t), Private Collection / PRC Archive; 424 (t), CIRCA / PRC Archive; 424 (b), The Granger Collection, New York; 425, Robin Nelson/Black Star; 426 (t), Henry Groskinsky; 426 (b), National Baseball Hall of Fame Library & Archive, Cooperstown, NY; 426 (c), HRW Photo Research Library; 427 (t), PRC Archive; 428, CORBIS-Bettmann; 428, Flower Pentecostal Heritage Center; 429, Brown Brothers; 430, Frank Driggs Collection; 431 (t), Frank Driggs Collection 431 (b), Historic New Orleans Collection; 433 (r), Archive Photos; 433 (l), *Color* by Countee Cullen, poetry 1926 reprint of author's first (1925) book, Harper and Brothers, NY; 434 (t), Photo by Carl Van Vechten, courtesy Van Vechten Trust. Yale Collection of American Literature, Beinecke Rare Book and Manuscript Library, Yale University.; 434 (b), Library of Congress / PRC Archive; 435 (t), The Granger Collection, New York; 435 (l), The Granger Collection, New York; 436 (t), (c) Addison Gallery of American Art, Phillips Academy, Andover, Massachusetts. All Rights Reserved; 436 (b), Mural: Detroit Industry, North Wall, 1932–33. Diego M. Rivera, Gift of Edsel B. Ford, Photograph (c) 1991 The Detroit Institute of the Arts; 437, Ezra Stoller (c) ESTO.

CHAPTER 15: Page 440 (b), Private Collection / The Bridgeman Art Library, New York / London; 440 (tr), UPI/Bettmann-CORBIS; 440 (tl), CPIO Classic Partners; 441 (tl), Culver Pictures, Inc.; 441 (tr), AP / Wide World Photos, Inc. ; 441 (bl), Franklin D. Roosevelt Library; 441, Christie's Images; 442, © 1945 Gordon Parks; 443 (t), Archive Photos; 443 (b), (c) CORBIS Images; 444, The Granger Collection, New York; 445, (c) Tribune Media Services, Inc. All Rights Reserved. Reprinted with permission; 447, PRC Archive; 448, Minnesota Historical Society; 449, Culver Pictures; 450 (t), National Museum of American Art, Smithsonian Institution, Washington, DC / Art Resource, NY; 450 (b), CORBIS-Bettmann; 451, National Archives / PRC Archive; 453, Cindy Lewis Photography; 454 (b), Library of Congress; 454 (t), Courtesy of Bert Corona and Mario T. Garcia; 455 (r), CORBIS-Bettmann; 455 (l), Lost Horizon by James Hilton, Newberry Library; 456 (t), CORBIS-Bettmann; 456 (b), The Granger Collection, New York; 457, The Salvation Army National Archives; 458, Herbert Hoover Presidential Library; 459 (t), Department of the Interior, National Park Service, 1937. National Museum of American Art, Washington, DC; Art Resource, NY; 459 (b), U.S. Postal Service / Harcourt; 460, National Archives, photo no. 111-G-CAL-4; 461 (t), CORBIS-Bettmann; 461 (b), Culver Pictures, Inc.; 462 (t), Culver Pictures; 462 (b), CORBIS-Bettmann; 463, Franklin D. Roosevelt Library.

CHAPTER 16: Page 466 (tl), CORBIS-Bettmann; 466 (bl), AP/Wide World Photos, Inc.; 466 (br), Library of Congress/PRC Archive; 466 (tr), HRW Photo by Sam Dudgeon; 467 (t), National Archives/ PRC Archive; 467 (bl), From *The Incredible Ball Point Pen* by Stuart Schneider and Henry Gostony, Schiffer Publishing Ltd., Atglen, PA; 467 (tc), *Superman* is a trademark of DC Comics (c) 2000. All rights reserved. Used with permission / The Michael Barson Collection/ Past Perfect/PRC Archive; 467 (tr), Margaret Bourke-White/Life Magazine (c) 1937 Time Inc.; 467 (br), Shooting Star International; 468, Franklin D. Roosevelt Library; 469, Franklin D. Roosevelt Library; 470, National Archives, photo no. NRIS-95-REG6LANTERN-1; 471 (b), Louise Boyle/Southern Historical Collection, University of North Carolina at Chapel Hill; 471, HRW Photo by Victoria Smith; 473, United States Department of the Interior/ PRC Archive; 474, Library of Congress; 475, Russell Billiu Long Papers, Mss. 3700, Louisiana and Lower Mississippi Valley Collections, LSU Libraries, Louisiana State University, Baton Rouge, LA; 476 (bl), Franklin D. Roosevelt Library; 476 (br), The Granger Collection, New York; 476 (t), U.S. Postal Service/Harcourt ; 477 (l), Franklin D. Roosevelt Library / PRC Archive 477 (r), Social Security Administration; 478 (t), Stock Montage, Inc.; 478 (b), The Granger Collection, New York; 479, CORBIS-Bettmann-UPI; 480 (l), Library of Congress/ PRC Archive; 480 (r), Walter P. Reuther Library, Wayne State University; 481, FSA/OWI Collection, Library of Congress; 482, John E. Allen, Inc./Franklin D. Roosevelt Presidential Library / PRC Archive; 483, Frank Driggs Collection/ CORBIS-Bettmann; 484 (t), Library of Congress; 484 (b), The Granger Collection, New York; 485 (t), Library of Congress; 486, The Granger Collection, New York; 487, National Archives; 488 (t), "Cover 1939 Edition" From THE GRAPES OF WRATH by John Steinbeck. Copyright 1939 renewed (c) 1967 by John Steinbeck. Used by permission of Viking Penguin, a division of Penguin Putnam, Inc. The Granger Collection, New York; 488 (b), Photofest; 489 (l), CORBIS-Bettmann-UPI; 489 (r), Photo by Carl Van Vechten, courtesy Van Vechten Trust. Yale Collection of American Literature, Beinecke Rare Book and Manuscript Library, Yale University; 490, Grant Wood, American, 1891–1942, American Gothic, oil on beaverboard, 1930, 74.3 x 62.4 cm. Friends of American Art Collection, All rights reserved by the Art Institute of Chicago and VAGA, New York, NY; 491, (c) 2001 The Georgia O'Keeffe Foundation/ Artists Rights Society (ARS), New York. The Metropolitan Museum of Art, Alfred Stieglitz Collection, 1952. (52.203) Photograph (c) 1994 The Metropolitan Museum of Art.; 496 (t), Missouri Historical Society, St. Louis; 496 (b), CORBIS /Underwood & Underwood; 497 (t), The Granger Collection, New York; 497 (b), CORBIS-Bettmann.

UNIT 5: Pages 498–499, Naval Historical Foundation; 499, Library of Congress.

CHAPTER 17: Page 500 (tl), Poseidon Pictures; (tr), AP/Wide World Photos, Inc.; 500 (bl), Boltin Picture Library; (br), FPG International Corp.; 501 (tr), *The Des Moines Register*, October 31, 1938.; 501 (bl), Hershenson-Allen Archives/ PRC Archive; 501 (b), HRW Photo by Victoria Smith; 501 (tl), (c) Hulton-Deutsch Collection /

From letter by pregnant housewife to Eleanor Roosevelt, January 2, 1935, from *Down and Out in the Great Depression: Letters from the "Forgotten Man,"* edited by Robert S. McElvaine. Published by University of North Carolina Press, Chapel Hill, NC, 1983.

From *Development as Freedom* by Amartya Sen. Published by Alfred A. Knopf, Inc., a division of Random House, Inc., New York, 1999.

From *Combed Out* by F. A. Voigt. Published by Dial Press, New York, 1929.

Quotes by volunteers from *Letters from Mississippi*, edited by Elizabeth Sutherland. Published by McGraw-Hill, Inc., New York, 1965.

ACKNOWLEDGMENTS

CORBIS; 502, CORBIS/BETTMANN-UPI; 503 (l), CORBIS-Bettmann; 503 (r), Jean Louis Atlan / CORBIS Sygma; 505 (t), Nawrocki Stock Photo; 505 (b), CORBIS-Bettmann; 506, AKG London; 508, Franklin D. Roosevelt Library; 508 (t), HRW Photo by Sam Dudgeon; 509, Curt Teich Postcard Archives; 510 (t), Everett/ CSU Archives; 510 (c), Curt Teich Postcard Archives/ Lake County, IL Museum; 510 (b), Rob Schoenbaum/ Black Star; 511, Library of Congress; 512, UPI/CORBIS-Bettmann; 513 (t), UPI/CORBIS-Bettmann; 513 (b), The Granger Collection, New York; 514 (t), The Granger Collection, New York; 514 (b), CORBIS-Bettmann; 515, Brown Brothers; 516 (t), Brown Brothers; 516 (r), Jacket cover from First edition of FOR WHOM THE BELL TOLLS by Ernest Hemingway. Copyright 1940 by Ernest Hemingway. Copyright renewed (c) 1968 by Mary Hemingway. Reprinted by permission of Scribner, a division of Simon and Schuster; 517, Library of Congress; 518, CBS Radio ; 519, (c) Tribune Media Services, Inc. All Rights Reserved. Reprinted with permission; 521 (r), CORBIS-Bettmann; 521 (l), (c) Bettmann / CORBIS; 522, Archive Photos; 523, The Granger Collection, New York; 525, The Granger Collection, New York; 525, Digital Image © 2003 PhotoDisc, Inc.

CHAPTER 18: Page 526 (br), Nawrocki Stock Photo; 526 (tl), Hershenson-Allen Archives/ PRC Archive; 526 (tr), Used Courtesy of The RCA Records Label, A Unit of BMG Entertainment. Private Collection/ PRC Archive; 526 (bl), Cindy Lewis Photography; 526 (c), Courtesy of the Museum of the American Numismatic Association; 527 (bl), FSA/OWI Collection, Library of Congress; 527 (t), Schalwijk / Art Resource, NY; 527 (br), HRW Photo by Sam Dudgeon, stamps courtesy Kristen Darby; 528, Courtesy of Joseph Rygiel / PRC Archive; 529, FSA-OWI Collection, Library of Congress, 530, CORBIS-Bettmann; 531 (r), U.S. Government Photo; 531 (l), General Douglas MacArthur Foundation; 532, United States Marine Corps; 533 (t), Division of Political History, Smithsonian Institution, Washington, D.C.; 533 (b), Trustees of the Imperial War Museum; 534, Ria-Novosti/ Sovfoto; 535 (t), National Archives; 536 (r), Collection of Chester Scott/ PRC Archive; 536 (l), PRC Archive; 537, Printed by permission of the Norman Rockwell Family Trust (c)1943 / Photo courtesy of the Curtis Publishing Company; 538 (t), National Archives/ PRC Archive; 538 (b), FSA-OWI Collection, Library of Congress; 539 (t), UPI/CORBIS-Bettmann; 539 (br), National Archives; 539 (bl), FSA-OWI Collection, Library of Congress; 541, AP / Wide World Photos; 542, National Archives; 543, United States Naval Institute; 514, CORBIS; 545, National Archives; 546 (t), AP / Wide World Photos; 546 (b), United States Naval Institute; 548, Yevgeni Khaldei - Sovfoto / Eastfoto; 549, Christie's Images; 550 (l), National Archives; 550 (r), Photri; 552, PRC Archive; 553 (b), CORBIS; 553 (t), United States Postal Service / Harcourt ; 554 (l), U.S. Air Force/ National Geographic Image Collection; 554 (r), Philip Jones-Griffiths/ Magnum Photos, Inc.; 557, Digital Image © 2003 PhotoDisc, Inc.

CHAPTER 19: Page 558 (tl), Collection of Colonel Stuart P. Corning, Jr. Courtesy PRC Archive; 558 (tr), The Granger Collection, New York; 558 (bl), Collection of Michael Barson/Past Perfect/ PRC Archive; 558 (br), Hulton Deutsch Collection / Woodfin Camp & Associates 559 (tl), RAUSCHENBERG, Robert. Bed. (1955) Combine painting: oil and pencil on pillow, quilt, and sheet on wood supports, 6' 3 3/4" x 31 1/2" x 8" (191.1 x 80 x 20.3 cm). The Museum of Modern Art, New York. Gift of Leo Castelli in honor of Alfred H. Barr, Jr. Photograph (c) 2003 The Museum of Modern Art, New York. (c) Untitled Press, Inc./ Licensed by VAGA, New York, NY; 559 (tc), Sovfoto/Eastfoto; 559 (br), AP/Wide World Photos, Inc.; 559 (r), UPI/CORBIS-Bettmann; ; 559 (bl), The Viking Press, New York City; 560, U.S. Army Photo/Harry S. Truman Presidential Library; 561, HRW Photo by Victoria Smith; 562, CORBIS-Bettmann; 562 (br), American Stock Photography; 563, Franklin D. Roosevelt Presidential Library; 564, The Jewish Museum, NY / Art Resource, NY; 565, National Archives; 566 (t), Archive Photos; 567 (b), National Portrait Gallery, Smithsonian Institution, Washington, DC, Gift of TIME Magazine/ Art Resource, NY; 568, (c) CORBIS; 569 (l), The National Portrait Gallery, Smithsonian Institution, Washington, D.C. / Art Resource, NY; 569 (r), (c) Bryan McBurney/Newsmakers; 570 (r), Courtesy of the German Marshall Fund of the United States; 571 (r), FPG International; 571 (r), HRW Photo by Sam Dudgeon; 572, CORBIS-Bettmann-UPI; 573 (r), Photri; 573 (l), PRC Archive; 575, CORBIS-Bettmann; 576 (b), AP/Wide World Photos; 576 (t), U.S. Postal Service/Harcourt ; 578, (c) Jerry Cook; 579, Captain America appears courtesy Marvel Entertainment Group. The Michael Barson Collection / Past Perfect/ PRC Archive; 580 (t), Photofest; 580 (b), Archive Photos; 581 (l), From THE MARTIAN CHRONICLES (BANTAM ED: JACKET COVER) by Ray Bradbury, copyright 1946, 1948, 1950, 1958 by Ray Bradbury. Copyright renewed 1977 by Ray Bradbury. Used by permission of Bantam Books, a division of Random House, Inc. The Michael Barson Collection / Past Perfect/ PRC Archive. Photo by Rob Huntley/ Lightstream; 581 (r) "cover" from THE MARTIAN WAY by Isaac Asimov, copyright (c) 1955 by Isaac Asimov. Used by permission of Dutton Signet, a division of Penguin Putnam, Inc.; 582, UPI/CORBIS-Bettmann; 583, Archive Photos; 584 (t), Loomis Dean / Life Magazine (c) Time, Inc.; 584 (b), The Michael Barson Collection/Past Perfect/ PRC Archive; 585, Herblock (c) 1957 The Washington Post. From HERBLOCK's SPECIAL FOR TODAY (Simon & Schuster, 1958); 587, The Michael Barson Collection / Past Perfect/ PRC Archive.

CHAPTER 20: Page 590 (tl), Archive Photos; 590 (tl), U.S. Postal Service; 590 (tr), CORBIS-Bettmann; 590 (tl), CORBIS-Bettmann; 590 (tr), (c) www.corbis.co./CORBIS; 590 (b), National Air & Space Museum, Smithsonian Institution, Washington, DC. neg. no. 79-756, photo by Dane Penland; 590 (bl), HRW Photo by Victoria Smith; 592, Library of Congress; 593 (t), Lambert/Archive Photos; 593 (b), (c) 1994 Tom & Dee Ann McCarthy/ The Stock Market; 594, CORBIS-Bettmann; 594, Courtesy Chalet Suzanne Foods, HRW Photo by Sam Dudgeon; 595 (l), Collection of Janice L. and David J. Frent/PRC Archive; 595 (r), Harry S Truman Library; 596, Collection of David J. and Janice L. Frent/ PRC Archive; 597, National Archives (NARA), # NWDNS 44 PA 997; 598 (r), HRW Photo by Sam Dudgeon; 598 (l), Collection of Janice L. and David J. Frent/PRC Archive; 599, Ewing Galloway; 600, American Stock Photography; 602, (c) Bettmann/CORBIS; 603 (r), PRC Archive; 603 (l), Used with Permission of Vlasic Foods International, Campbell Soup Company; 604 (t), AP /Wide World Photos, Inc.; 604 (b), By permission of TV Guide, courtesy Lenore's TV Guides. HRW Photo by Sam Dudgeon; 605 (b), The Michael Barson Collection/Past Perfect / PRC Archive; 605 (t), Library of Congress/ PRC Archive; 606 (l), SuperStock; 607, CORBIS-Bettmann; 608 (t), UPI/CORBIS-Bettmann; 609 (t), CORBIS-Bettmann-UPI; 609 (b), AP/ Wide World Photos, Inc.; 610, Charles Moore / Black Star; 611 (tr), Dr. Hector P. Garcia Papers, Special Collections & Archives, Texas A&M University, Corpus Christi Bell Library; 611 (l), Dr. Hector P. Garcia Papers, Special Collections and Archives, Texas A&M University-Corpus Christi Bell Library; 611 (b), Francis L.K. Hsu and Family from his 1971 book, The Challenge of the American Family: The Chinese in the United States; 612, AP /Wide World Photos, Inc.; 613 (tr), CORBIS-Bettmann; 613 (tl), From ON THE ROAD by Jack Kerouac, copyright (c) 1955, 1957 by Jack Kerouac; renewed (c) 1983 by Stella Kerouac, renewed (c) 1985 by Stellan Kerouac and Jan Kerouac. Used by permission of Viking Penguin, a division of Penguin Putnam, Inc. ; 613 (b), (c) Joe Sohm/Chromosohm/Stock Connection; 614 (l), Harry Redl/ Time Magazine; 614 (r), Courtesy Naomi Long Madgett; 615, Courtesy of the Ford Foundation; 617, Digital Image © 2003 PhotoDisc, Inc. ; 618 (r), U.S. Army Photograph; 618 (l), Moorland-Spingarn Research Center, Howard University; 619 (t), Photri, Inc.; 619 (b), National Archives (NARA), photo no. NWDNS 44 PA 997.

UNIT 6: Pages 620–621, ©1976 Matt Herron/Take Stock; 621 (r), Bill Eppridge / Life Magazine © Time, Inc.

CHAPTER 21: Page 622 (bc), Sally Andersen-Bruce, Museum of American Political Life; 622 (bl), HRW Photo by Sam Dudgeon ; 622 (r), UPI/CORBIS-Bettmann; 622 (tl), Topham Picture Service; 622 (tr), National Archives (NARA), photo no. NWCTF-JFKCO-WC-FBIEXHIBITS-K051; 623 (t), CORBIS-Bettmann; 623 (b), UPI/CORBIS-Bettmann; 623 (c), Collection of Janice L. and David J. Frent/PRC Archive; 625 (l), CORBIS-Bettmann; 625 (r), CORBIS-Bettmann; 626 (tl), West Point Museum, U.S. Military Academy, West Point, NY. Photo by Josh Nefsky; 626 (b), Colorfax / PRC Archive; 627 (b), Sanford Kossin/ LIFE Magazine (c) Time, Inc.; 627 (t), Les Immel / Peoria Journal Star; 627 (tl), Paul Conklin / Peace Corps Photograph; 627 (b), Michael Dwyer/ Stock, Boston; 629, (c) Rolando Pujol/Woodfin Camp & Associates; 631 (t), John F. Kennedy Presidential Library; 632 (r), AP / Wide World Photos; 632 (l), United States Postal Service / Harcourt ; 633, Arthur Rickerby / Black Star; 634, Sarge O'Neill/John F. Kennedy Presidential Library; 635 (l), Reprinted with the permission of Scribner, a division of Simon & Schuster from The Other America: Poverty in the United States by Michael Harrington (New York: MacMillan, 1962).; 635 (br), AP / Wide World Photos, Inc.; 636, Chicago Daily News; 637, Library of Congress, Prints & Photographs Division, Look Magazine Photograph Collection/ Stanley Tretick (LC-L901-63-1625, #1); 638, AP / Wide World Photos, Inc.; 639 (b), Elizabeth Hamlin / Stock, Boston; 639 (t), United States Postal Service / Harcourt ; 640 (t), Paul Conklin; 640 (b), Collection of Janice L. and David J. Frent/PRC Archive; 641 (t), Michelle Bridwell / Frontera Fotos; 641 (b), AP/ Wide World Photos; 642 (t), Children's Television Workshop; 642 (b), Alfred Eisenstaedt/ LIFE Magazine (c) Time, Inc.; 643, SILENT SPRING courtesy Houghton Mifflin Company; 644, Paul Conklin; 645, Lyndon B. Johnson Presidential Library, reprinted through the courtesy of Edward Germano and the Brockton Enterprise.

CHAPTER 22: Page 648 (tl), UPI/Bettmann-CORBIS; 648 (br), (c) 1964 Time Inc.; 648 (tr), CORBIS-Bettmann; 648 (bl), Lyndon Baines Johnson Presidential Library, Photo No. MUS46.40.3; 649 (bl), CORBIS-Bettmann; 649 (br), Courtesy Famous Amos Cookies, Keebler Company; 650 (b), Smithsonian Institution / photo courtesy of Salamander Books. Ltd.; 651 (t), UPI/Bettmann-CORBIS; 652, AP / Wide World Photos, Inc.; 653, Charles Moore/ Black Star ; 654 (t), PRC Archive; 654 (tl), John F. Kennedy Library, Photo No. ST-C277-1-63; 654 (b), UPI / CORBIS-Bettmann; 655, Cecil Stoughton / Lyndon Baines Johnson Presidential Library ; 656, Charles Moore / Black Star; 656 (t), (c) Danny Lyon / Magnum Photos ; 657 (b), (c) 1978 Matt Herron / Take Stock; 658, Matt Herron / TAKE STOCK; 659 (t), CORBIS-Bettmann ; 659 (b), Charles Moore/ LIFE Magazine (c) Time, Inc.; 660, Carlos Chavez/AP/Wide World Photos; 661, Collection of Janice L. and David J. Frent/PRC Archive; 662, (c) 1998 John Launois / Black Star; 663 (t), AP / Wide World Photos, Inc. ; 663 (r), Collection of Janice L. and David J. Frent/PRC Archive; 664 (t), UPI/CORBIS-Bettmanx 664 (br), HRW Photo by Victoria Smith; 666, AP / Wide World Photos, Inc. ; 666 (t), Fred Kaplan/Black Star/PNI; 667, Collection of Janice L. and David J. Frent/ PRC Archive; 668 (t), UPI/CORBIS-Bettmann; 668 (b), (c)1971 Time, Inc. Reprinted by Permission.; 669, Stock, Boston; 673 (b), AP/Wide World Photos, Inc.; 673, Gene Anthony / Black Star.

CHAPTER 23: Page 674, (bl), CORBIS- Bettmann; 674 (br), (c) 1988 Cindy Lewis All Rights Reserved; 674 (tr), (c) 1973 Bob Fitch / Take Stock; 674 (l), SOVFOTO/ EASTFOTO; 674 (t), William Hamilton/Superstock;

674 (b), Everett Collection; 675 (t), PRC Archive; 675 (br), CORBIS-Bettmann/UPI; 675 (tl), Motion Picture Corporation; 675 (tr), Courtesy of Lang Communications; 675 (bl), (c) 1969 Time, Inc.; 676 (bl), UPI / CORBIS- Bettmann; 676 (br), From THE FEMININE MYSTIQUE (JACKET COVER) by Betty Friedan, copyright. Used by permission of Dell Publishing, a division of Random House, Inc. Collection of Bettye Lane/ PRC Archive; 676, UPI/CORBIS-Bettmann; 677 (br), HRW Photo by Johanna Fellhauer; 677 (tc), National Archives (NARA), photo no. NWDNS-111-34613; 678 (t), U.S. Equal Employment Opportunity Commission; 678 (bl), Al Freni / LIFE Magazine (c) Time, Inc. ; 678 (br), PRC Archive; 679 (b), Sylvia Johnson/Woodfin Camp & Associates; 679 (t), (c) Bettmann / CORBIS; 680, Bob Rosato / Sports Illustrated (c) Time Inc. ; 681, CORBIS-Bettmann; 682 (t), (c) 1978 George Ballis/TAKE STOCK; 682 (b), Archive Photos; 683, Jack Weinhold, courtesy PRC ; 684 (t), Collection of Janice L. and David J. Frent/PRC Archive; 684 (c), Archive Photos; 684 (b), (c) 1976 George Ballis / Take Stock; 685, C. Aurness / Woodfin Camp & Associates; 686, Maria Varela / Take Stock; 687, AP / Wide World Photos, Inc.; 688, Library of Congress; 689 (t), Ralph Crane / LIFE Magazine (c) Time, Inc.; 689 (b), Collection of David J. and Janice L. Frent/ PRC Archive; 690, Paul Fusco / Magnum Photos, Inc.; 691, CORBIS-Bettmann/UPI; 693, PRC Archive; 694 (t), "Life is So Beautiful" Vintage Poster, 16" x10.75", 1968 (c) Peter Max 2000. Courtesy The American Cancer Society/ PRC Archive; 695 (b), HRW Photo by Chris Casselli; 696 (l), UPI/CORBIS-Bettmann; 696 (b), (c) Burstein Collection/ CORBIS; 697, (c) 2001 The Andy Warhol Foundation for the Visual Arts / ARS, New York. Photo (c) Bettmann/CORBIS; 698 (b), (c) Courtesy of Atlantic Recording Corporation /Archive Photos; 698 (b), (c) Experience Hendrix, L.L.C./ Archive Photos; 698 (t), Courtesy of Columbia/Epic Records/ Archive Photos; 699, Library of Congress.

CHAPTER 24: Page 704 (tl), (c) Disney Enterprises, Inc.; 704 (bl), National Archives; 704 (br), AP / Wide World Photos, Inc.; 704 (tr), Courtesy Texas Instruments, Inc.; 705 (bl), AP / Wide World Photos; 705 (tr), Howard Ruffner / Life Magazine (c) Time, Inc.; 706 (t), Maurice Durand Collection of Vietnamese Art, Yale University; 707, Archive Photos; 708, Archive Photos; 709 (t), (c) Roger Viollet / The Newsmakers; 709 (b), (c) Lee Lockwood/ Life/ TimePix; 710, AP / Wide World Photos, Inc.; 711, Larry Burrows / LIFE Magazine (c) Time, Inc.; 712, The News American; 713 (t), PRC Archive; 713 (b), National Archives, photo no. NWDNS-111-C-CC78122; 714, Collection of Janice L and David J. Frent/PRC Archive; 715, National Archives, photo no. NWDNS-111-C-CC35682; 716 (l), Courtesy William Ehrhart; 716 (r), Ho Thanh Duc / Vietnam Art Gallery / Kicon; 717, CBS News; 719, Shelly Rusten / Black Star; 720 (t), Larry Burrows / LIFE Magazine (c)Time Inc. ; 721 (b), Steve Schapiro / Black Star; 721 (tl), HRW Photo by Sam Dudgeon; 722, CORBIS/Henry Diltz; 723 (b), (c) Larry Burrows Collection; 723 (t), AP / Wide World Photos; 724 (b), John Filo; 724 (t), National Archives (NARA), photo no. NWDNS 111 C 34613; 725, (c) 1972 by Herblock in The Washington Post; 726, Dennis Brack / Black Star; 727, Roger Lubin / Jeroboam; 728, Courtesy Le Ly Hayslip ; 729 (t), Charles Bonnay / Black Star; 729 (b), Eddie Adams / Time Magazine (c) 1972 Time, Inc.; 730, AP / Wide World Photos, Inc.; 731 (r), Christopher Morris / Black Star; 731 (l), PRC Archive; 734 (b), (c) Mark Stewart / Jeroboam; 734 (t), AP / Wide World Photos, Inc.; 735 (t), PRC Archive; 735 (r), Hulton Getty / Newsmakers.

UNIT 7: Page 736–737, Ralph Krubner / H. Armstrong Roberts. 737, NASA.

CHAPTER 25: Page (c) CBS, Inc. 1991/The Kobal Collection; 738 (t), NASA; 738 (br), AP / Wide World Photos, Inc.; 739 (bl), R. Krubner / H. Armstrong Roberts; 739 (tl), Hershenson-Allen Archives / PRC Archive; 739 (tr), Martin A. Levick; 739, AP/Wide World Photos, Inc.; 739 (br), Bear (c) Organizing Committee of the 1980 Olympic Games in Moscow / HRW Photo by Victoria Smith; 739 (c), National Museum of American History, Division of Information Technology & Society Smithsonian Institution, Washington, DC. neg. no. 92-13442, Photo by Eric Long; 740, Erich Hartmann/ Magnum Photos; 741 (b), HRW Photo by Sam Dudgeon; 741 (t), Photographer: Robert S. Oakes, National Geographic, Courtesy of the Supreme Court of the United States; 742, Archive Photos; 743 (t), CORBIS; 743 (b), Bob Daemmrich Photo, Inc.; 744 (t), UPI / CORBIS-Bettmann; 745, (c) R.R. Lurie; 746, UPI/CORBIS-Bettmann; 747, CORBIS-Bettmann-UPI; 748, National Archives (NARA) photo no. NWDDA-21-USDISTCTDC-CR-USLIDDV-GOVEX133; 749, CORBIS-Bettmann; 750 (bl), CORBIS-Bettmann; 750 (br), Photri; 750 (l), Bob Daemmrich Photo, Inc.; 751, Jos. A. Smith as printed in Newsweek, September 23, 1974. Collection of the Artist; 752 (tl), CORBIS-Bettmann; 752 (tr), Rose Skytta / Jeroboam; 752 (b), UPI/CORBIS-Bettmann ; 753, Copyright Paul Conrad, Distributed by Los Angeles Times Syndicate. Reprinted by permission; 754 (t), Collection of Janice L. and David J. Frent/ PRC Archive; 755, Bob Daemmrich Photo, Inc.; 757 (b), UPI/CORBIS-Bettmann; 757 (t), Collection of Janice L. and David J. Frent/ PRC Archive; 759, D.B. Owen / Black Star; 760, Gerald R. Ford Presidential Library; 761 (t), Bohdan Hrynewych / Stock, Boston; 761 (b), Mike Yamashita / Woodfin Camp & Associates; 762 (t), I'm O.K.—You're O.K. by Thomas Harris. Courtesy Harper and Row Publishers, (c)1967; 762 (br), From THE COMPLETE BOOK OF RUNNING by James Fixx, (c) 1977 Random House, Inc. cover photo: Neal Slavin. Reprinted courtesy of Random House, Inc.; 762 (bl), Kent Reno/Jeroboam; 763 (t), Collection of Hershenson-Allen Archives/ PRC Archive; 763 (l), (c) 1982 Universal City Studios. All rights reserved / The Kobal Collection; 764, CORBIS/James L. Amos; 767, NASA; 767 (l), CORBIS-Bettmann; 767 (r), (c) 1973 Newsweek, Inc. All rights reserved. Reprinted by permission.

CHAPTER 26: Page 768 (tl), Lester Sloan/ Woodfin Camp & Associates; 768 (tc), PRC Archive; 768 (tr), HRW Photo by Sam Dudgeon; 768 (br), NASA; 768 (t), Copyright (c)1989 by Gretchen Shields. Reprinted by permission of the author and the Sandra Dijkstra Literary Agency; 768 (tr), (c) John Ficara / Woodfin Camp & Associates, Inc.; 769 (br), Courtesy of The Patton Museum of Cavalry & Armor, Fort Knox, KY; 769 (tr), George Bush Presidential Library; 770 (t), Image Copyright (c) 1998 PhotoDisc, Inc.; 772, Wally McNamee / Woodfin Camp & Associates; 773, Ben Sargent; 774 (t), Mike Cullen / The Picture Cube / Index Stock Photography; 774 (b), Richard B. Levine; 775, (c) James Nachtwey / Magnum Photos, Inc.; 776 (t), Collection of Janice L. and David J. Frent /PRC Archive; 777 (c), Collection of Janice L. and David J. Frent/PRC Archive; 777 (t), UPI / CORBIS-Bettmann; 777 (b), Collection, the Supreme Court of the United States, courtesy the Supreme Court Historical Society; 778 (t), (c) 1981 by Herblock in The Washington Post; 779 (b), Ed Carlin/ Index Stock Photography; 779 (t), Alex Quesada / Woodfin Camp & Associates; 780, CORBIS-Bettmann; 782, Reuters / CORBIS-Bettmann; 783, Reprinted with the permission of Pocket Books, a division of Simon & Schuster from The Yuppie Handbook by Marissa Piesman and Marilee Hartley. Copyright (c) 1983. HRW Photo by Sam Dudgeon; 784 (t), National Museum of American History, Division of Information Technology & Society, Smithsonian Institution, Washington, D.C., neg. no. 1986.0683.01 & 1986.0683.02; 784 (b), NASA; 785 (t), HRW Photo by Sam Dudgeon; 785 (br), Bob Daemmrich Photo; 785 (bl), HRW Photo by Sam Dudgeon; 786, A. Avakian / Woodfin Camp & Associates; 787, (c) 1991 Time Inc.; 788, AP / Wide World Photos, Inc.; 789, Bill Gentile/SIPA Press Photos/Woodfin Camp & Associates; 790, Richard B. Levine; 791, Michael J. Okonlewski / Newsmakers; 793, Neuromancer by William Gibson (c) 1984, Ace Science Books, Berkeley Group. ; 793 (t), CORBIS-Bettmann.

CHAPTER 27: Page 796 (tl), Tannenbaum/CORBIS Sygma; 796 (b), Ron Edmonds/AP /Wide World Photos; 796 (tr), HRW Photo by Victoria Smith; 797 (tl), Bob Daemmrich Photo, Inc.; 797 (tc), courtesy RENT; 797 (tr), David Hume Kennerly / CORBIS Sygma; 797 (b), Tannenbaum /CORBIS Sygma; 798 (t), Collection of Janice L. and David J. Frent/PRC Archive; 799 (b), Mike Theiler / CORBIS-Bettmann; 799 (t), Collection of Janice L. and David J. Frent / PRC Archive; 800, Bob Daemmrich Photo, Inc.; 802 (t), The White House; 802 (b), Gail Oskin, AP / Wide World Photos; 803, Corinne Dufka/ CORBIS-Bettmann; 804 (t), CORBIS-Bettmann; 805 (t), Cynthia Johnson/ Newsmakers; 805 (b), Jim Borgman / Cincinnati Inquirer (c)1999; 806 (t), Image Copyright (c) 1998 PhotoDisc, Inc.; 807 (r), Cover, from TYPICAL AMERICAN. Copyright (c) 1991 by Gish Jen. Reprinted by permission of Houghton Mifflin Co. All rights reserved.; 807 (l), (c) 1998 David Huang; 808 (t), Haviv / SABA Press Photos; 808 (b), Bill Greene / Boston Globe; 809, Timothy Greenfield-Sanders / CORBIS Outline; 810 (t), Bob Daemmrich Photo, Inc.; 810 (bl), NASA; 810 (br), William Coupon's Gallery of Politicians, Newsmakers/ Getty Images; 812 (t), Lara Jo Regan / Newsmakers/ Getty Images; 812 (b), AP / Wide World Photos, Inc. ; 813, Michael Newman/ PhotoEdit; 814, Jonathan Nourok / PhotoEdit; 815 (t), Robert Baker/ Habitat for Humanity; 815 (bl), (c) European Communities; 815 (br), (c) European Communities; 816 (t), Renato Rotolo/Newsmakers/ Getty Images; 816 (b), Robert Trippett/ SIPA Press Photos; 817, Uniphoto; 819, Paula Bronstein / Newsmakers; 821 (tr), CORBIS-Bettmann; 822 (t), Gjon Mili / LIFE Magazine, (c) Time, Inc.; 822 (b), (c) Bruce Kliewe / Jeroboam; 823 (b), Guans/SIPA Press/Woodfin Camp & Associates; 823 (b), Lisa Quinones / Black Star.

BACK MATTER: Page R1, HRW Photo by Sam Dudgeon; R3–R7, (all) White House Collection, copyright White House Historical Association, R7(last) Courtesy The White House, photo by Eric Draper.

Illustrations

Abbreviations used: (t) top, (c) center, (b) bottom, (l) left, (r) right
All maps created by MapQuest.com, Inc. All other illustrations, unless noted below, created by Holt, Rinehart and Winston.
TABLE OF CONTENTS: Page xiv/(vr), Craig Attebery/Jeff Lavaty Artist Agent
UNIT 1: Page 41 (b), Saul Rosenbaum/Deborah Wolfe Ltd.; 65 (l), DECODE, Inc.; 88 (bl), Craig Attebery/Jeff Lavaty Artist Agent; 99 (l), 121 (t), DECODE, Inc.
UNIT 2: Page 169 (tl), DECODE, Inc.; 170 (b), Uhl Studio Inc.; 194 (t), 214 (cl, cr), 215 (bl), 234 (bl), DECODE, Inc.
UNIT 3: Page 314 (t), Uhl Studio Inc.; 318 (bl), 324 (bl), DECODE, Inc.
UNIT 4: Page 371 (br), DECODE, Inc.; 388 (tl), Craig Attebery/Jeff Lavaty Artist Agent; 466 (bl), DECODE, Inc.
UNIT 5: 482 (bl), DECODE, Inc.; 502 (l), Leslie Kell; 549 (t), Saul Rosenbaum/Deborah Wolfe Ltd.; 560 (t), 565 (tl), DECODE, Inc.; 575 (t), Christy Krames
UNIT 6: 599, DECODE, Inc.; 600, Craig Attebery/Jeff Lavaty Artist Agent; 675 (bl), DECODE, Inc.
UNIT 7: 715 (bl), DECODE, Inc.; 727 (br), Saul Rosenbaum/Deborah Wolfe Ltd.; 728, Uhl Studio Inc.; 750 (bl), Saul Rosenbaum/Deborah Wolfe Ltd.; 767 (bl, bc), DECODE, Inc.
UNIT 8: 802 (b), 852 (bl), 853 (tr), 883 (br), DECODE, Inc.